WORLD WAR II DAY *by* DAY

Notes about the consultants

These notes describe the positions occupied by the consultants during the period when they were preparing this book for its first publication, which took place in 1990.

•

Air Chief Marshal Sir Michael Armitage
was Chief of Defence Intelligence and Commandant of the Royal College of Defence Studies;

Admiral of the Fleet Lord Lewin
was First Sea Lord and Chief of the Naval Staff of the Royal Navy and Chief of the Defence Staff, United Kingdom;

Field Marshal Sir John Stanier
was Chief of the General Staff of the British Army and chairman of the Royal United Services Institute for Defence Studies.

•

Terry Charman
was Research Assistant, Department of Printed Books, Imperial War Museum, London;

Dr Peter Kornicki
was lecturer in Japanese history, University of Cambridge;

Dr John Pimlott
was Deputy Head, Department of War Studies, Royal Military Academy, Sandhurst;

Dr G. T. Tiedeman
was lecturer in Chinese History, School of Oriental and African Studies, University of London.

WORLD
WAR II DAY *by* DAY

A Dorling Kindersley Book

LONDON, NEW YORK, DELHI, PARIS,
MUNICH and JOHANNESBURG

This edition first published in Great Britain in 2001
by Dorling Kindersley Limited,
80 Strand, London WC2R 0RL

First published in 1990 as *Chronicle of the Second World War*
by Longman Group and Chronicle Communications Ltd

2 4 6 8 10 9 7 5 3 1

ISBN (UK) 0-7513-3399-9
ISBN (US) 0-7894-7997-4

Library of Congress Cataloging-in-Publication Data

World War II.-- 1st American ed.
    p. cm.
  ISBN 0-7894-7997-4 (alk. paper)
    1. World War, 1939-1945--Chronology.   I. Title: World War Two.
II. Title: World War 2. III. Dorling Kindersley Publishing, Inc.
  D743.5 .W68 2001
  940.53'02'02--dc21

2001028294

Photographs inside front and back covers: **Front cover:** Polish cavalrymen on manoeuvres
at Konaski, 1939 **Back cover:** Searching for loved ones at Kerch, 1942

Editorial and design updated in 2001 by
AMBER BOOKS LIMITED
Bradleys Close, 74–77 White Lion Street
London N1 9PF, UK

Senior Editor • *Edward Bunting*

Senior Art Editor • *Anna Benjamin*

Managing Editor • *Sharon Lucas*

Senior Managing Art Editor • *Derek Coombes*

DTP Designer • *Sonia Charbonnier*

Production Controller • *Mel Alsopp*

Editorial Consultants • *Reg Grant, Ian Paton*

Picture Research for Jacket and pages 3–15, 662–687 • *Franziska Marking and Richard Gilbert*

Colour reproduction by Colourscan, Singapore
Printed and bound in Belgium by Brepol

See our complete catalog at

www.dk.com

Contents

Introduction..........*6*

Countdown to War
Late 1920s to August 1939..........*12*

Chronicle
September 1939–August 1945..........*16*

Aftermath of War
September–December 1945..........*662*

Timelines
Each year's major events displayed in chart form..........*666*

Who's Who
Biographies of key personnel..........*680*

Index..........*688*

Acknowledgments..........*726*

Introduction

World War II was the most destructive conflict in human history. It is estimated that the war caused the deaths of 50 million people. Roughly two-thirds of those who lost their lives were civilians, victims of cold-blooded massacre, strategic bombing, or general hardship and starvation. Yet, unlike the Great War that preceded it, World War II has rarely been regarded as a senseless slaughter. The future of the world was at stake and a different military outcome would have radically altered the face of human society.

On one side in the war were regimes with an outspoken contempt for humanitarianism, the rule of law, and individual freedom. Adolf Hitler's Nazi Germany, imperial Japan with its military-dominated government, and Italy under the Fascist dictator Benito Mussolini celebrated the warrior virtues of ruthlessness, obedience, and devotion to the state. They envisaged a world based on the permanent subjection of "inferior" to "superior" races.

Ranged against these militarist states, by the end of 1941, was the "Grand Alliance" – principally the United States, Britain and its dominions, and the Soviet Union (China was also recognized as a major ally, but this was a purely honorary status, while France started the war as an ally of Britain but only won reacceptance as a major ally towards the end of the conflict). Even if their practice fell short of their ideals, the United States and Britain were in principle committed to freedom, democracy, and humane values. In the Soviet Union, however, dictator Joseph Stalin rivalled Hitler in his brutality and in his contempt for "bourgeois" freedom and parliamentary democracy.

Causes of war

There is no great dispute about the causes of World War II. Germany, Japan and, to a lesser extent, Italy were clearly the aggressors – although this is not to say that they planned for war to happen as or when it did. They were all eager to use force to change the world in their favour. Hitler wanted to reverse the verdict of World War I and make Germany a major world power, exercising uncontested domination over Europe. His ultimate dream was to create an empire in the Slav lands that stretched eastward to the Urals, where German colonists would exploit the local population as slave labour. Mussolini also had a vision of his country as an imperial power, although on a more modest scale.

Japan's quest for an empire was driven by a desire to achieve economic security and equal standing with the white imperial powers. The initial aim of the Japanese military leadership was to subjugate China, but they later became determined to seize British, French, American, and Dutch colonies in southeast Asia.

The Western Allies

The United States, Britain, and France were, by contrast, contented powers with no desire to change the shape of the world. The British government of Neville Chamberlain and its French counterpart were so keen to avoid conflict that they not only made disastrous concessions to Hitler in the run-up to war, but were also reluctant to begin actual fighting even after war had been declared. Yet this does not mean that the Western Allies were passive victims of aggression. The war in Europe was precipitated by the decision of Britain and France to resist Hitler's assertion of German power, and was kept going after June 1940 by Britain's heroic refusal to make peace when, to all appearances, Hitler had won. Similarly, the Japanese had no desire to fight the United States. It was the Americans' refusal to countenance Japanese ambitions that precipitated the attack on Pearl Harbor.

For the first two years of the war in Europe, Stalin behaved as a loyal ally of Hitler in return for the right to take control of former

areas of the old Russian Empire lost at the time of the revolution. He did not seek the war with Germany that came in 1941, but at the end of the conflict exploited military victory to extend Soviet control into the heart of central Europe.

The start of World War II is traditionally dated to 1 September 1939, when Nazi Germany invaded Poland. By then, however, China had already been at war with Japanese invaders for two years. This Sino-Japanese War was one of a number of regional conflicts that, overlapping and interacting, eventually built up into global war at the end of 1941.

The German invasion of Poland seemed for a time likely to prove an isolated successful act of aggression. Within four weeks the Poles were defeated and their country was partitioned between Germany and the Soviet Union. Although France and Britain declared war on Germany on 3 September, it was an ineffectual gesture. French troops along the border with Germany stayed inside the defensive fortifications of the Maginot Line, while Britain put in place a naval blockade which, it was optimistically hoped, would bring the German economy to its knees.

In fact, Germany was amply supplied with essential materials by the Soviet Union, which concentrated on its own expansion. In 1940 Latvia, Lithuania, and Estonia came under Soviet rule without a fight. Finland proved a tougher proposition, inflicting heavy losses on a Soviet invasion force in the winter of 1939–40. There was a momentary possibility that, in defiance of all strategic logic, Britain and France might come to the defence of the Finns. In the event Finland, like Poland, was defeated before the British and French could organize a military intervention.

War between Germany and the Western Allies finally broke out in earnest in April 1940, when Germany invaded neutral Denmark and Norway to secure essential mineral supplies. Attempting to resist the takeover of Norway, the Allies were swept aside. This was the last straw for the British House of Commons, where discontent with Neville Chamberlain's leadership had been building up since before the war. Winston Churchill, a maverick Conservative, became prime minister at the head of a coalition government.

Nazi rally in Germany, c. 1935
A different military outcome to the war would have radically altered the face of human society.

German invasion
Machine-gun crew of Germany's 10th Army at the outskirts of Warsaw, 15 September 1939

On the same day that Churchill took office, Germany launched an offensive in Belgium and the Netherlands. Whereas Britain and France deployed their armoured vehicles in support of infantry, the German army employed tanks in massed formations to punch holes through enemy lines and drive deep into the rear, threatening strategic objectives. The Germans also used aircraft as a sort of long-range artillery in support of these fast-moving armoured formations. Their "Blitzkrieg" was an astonishing success. Advancing through the Ardennes and breaking through the French line at Sedan, they thrust north to the Channel, cutting off the British Expeditionary Force and a large part of the French army. Seventeen days after the start of the German offensive, the British began evacuating their forces from Dunkirk.

The defeat of France took another four weeks. The German army occupied the north and west of France, while a pro-German government under Marshal Petain was set up in Vichy to govern the rest of the country.

British cities blitzed

The war on the European mainland was over, but Churchill would not sue for peace, and opinion rallied around him. In the summer of 1940 the *Luftwaffe* attempted to win command of the skies over Britain as a prelude to a possible invasion, but British air defences were the best organized in the world and the attempt failed. With all thought of an invasion abandoned, the *Luftwaffe* was instead used to bomb London and other British cities by night. This Blitz caused death and destruction on a large scale, but came no closer to persuading Britain to quit the war. A more serious threat to Britain's survival was posed by German U-boats, which took a heavy toll of merchant shipping.

It is often said that at this period Britain "stood alone", but this is not strictly true. The Dominions all came to Britain's aid, and European governments-in-exile were set up in London, some, including the Czechs, Poles, Free French, Dutch, and Belgians, providing armed forces. Most importantly, Britain began to benefit from the support of the United States. President Roosevelt won the 1940 presidential election on a promise to keep America out of the war, but he was able to express his hostility to Naziism in increasingly concrete

form. From March 1941, under the "lend-lease" scheme, the United States started supplying arms to Britain without immediate payment. By the following autumn, American destroyers operating in defence of Britain-bound merchant convoys in the western Atlantic were sinking, and being sunk by, German U-boats.

Mussolini entered the conflict in June 1940. Although he had well-founded fears about his forces, the Italian dictator invaded Greece, as well as fighting the British in north

and east Africa. Germany was forced to intervene in both theatres to save the Italians. In the spring of 1941, overrunning Yugoslavia on the way, the Germans swiftly conquered Greece, including the island of Crete seized by airborne troops. In the North African desert, Rommel's *Afrika Korps* went on the offensive and soon threatened the Suez Canal.

For Hitler, the war in the Mediterranean and North Africa was a distracting side issue. He had already decided to embark on the

Warsaw Ghetto
*In the summer of 1942 around
300,000 Warsaw Jews lost their
lives under the Nazi regime.*

conquest of the Soviet Union, despite the failure to pacify the British. Operation *Barbarossa* was launched in June 1941. It was intended as another short war – troops were not issued with winter equipment. But the last of Hitler's Blitzkrieg failed. Moscow escaped his grasp as winter weather closed in and the Germans found themselves committed to a long and ultimately disastrous war.

Hitler's triumph

Still, the scale of Hitler's triumph by December 1941 was astounding; he exercised direct or indirect control over Europe from Moscow to the Atlantic. Italy, Romania, Hungary, Bulgaria, Croatia, Slovakia, and Finland were Germany's willing allies. Spain was ideologically aligned with the Nazis, although it kept out of the war except for sending some troops to fight on the eastern front. Neutral Sweden and Switzerland only kept their independence because they were useful to and cooperative with the Germans. Collaborators in Norway, the Netherlands, Belgium, and Vichy France ran their countries for Germany's benefit, under more or less tight German supervision. But Hitler was unable to consolidate his "New Order" in Europe because in practice, it was nothing but

a system of ruthless German domination and exploitation, maintained by terror. Massacres and mistreatment turned goodwill to hatred.

In many parts of Europe, the exploitative and oppressive nature of German rule bred resistance movements, in which communists often played the leading role. At first resistance was largely ineffectual, but by 1944 some partisan groups, especially in the western Soviet Union, Yugoslavia, and northern Italy, had become substantial military

forces. The Polish resistance, one of the few in which communists played little part, had the most tragic fate, crushed by the Nazis and later finished off by Stalin.

The crimes committed by the Nazis in Occupied Europe were many and various. They included the imprisonment of political opponents and other people of whom the Nazis disapproved in concentration camps; the deaths of millions of Soviet prisoners of war through hardship or neglect; and the use of indiscriminate reprisals, sometimes involving the eradication of entire villages, as a response to acts of resistance. But the vilest crime was undoubtedly genocide. From 1941 the Nazis began the deliberate extermination of all European Jews. The killings began with mass shootings in German-occupied areas of the Soviet Union and gassings in the backs of vans, then purpose-built extermination facilities were created in German-occupied Poland. The Jews were far from being the only victims of Nazi massacre – homosexuals and Gypsies were among other groups to suffer grievously. But the extermination of the Jews obsessed Hitler above every other goal. Some six million died in the Holocaust.

While the Nazis were entering the moral abyss of genocide, events in Europe had a knock-on effect in Asia. The defeat of France and the Netherlands, and Britain's perilous

Italian partisans
*Fighters who helped the South African
Army into Pistoia by ferreting out
German snipers, 9 December 1944.*

8

circumstances, left the European colonies in southeast Asia vulnerable to attack. In pursuit of its war in China, Japan wanted to cut off supplies to Chiang Kai-shek's Chinese government forces, which were arriving through French Indochina and the British colony of Burma. The Japanese military leadership was also tempted by a wider scheme of conquest, involving a takeover of all of southeast Asia as well as China. The United States was backing Chiang Kai-shek and its relations with Japan were already critical by the summer of 1940.

Trade embargo against Japan

The major block to military adventure, in the eyes of the Japanese leadership, was the threat of war with the Soviet Union. In 1938 and 1939 there had been serious fighting on the Manchuria-Siberia border, but in April 1941 the Japanese signed a non-aggression pact with Stalin. The German invasion the following June made it most unlikely that the Soviet Union would want to renege on this agreement. The Japanese felt free to pursue their "Southward Advance". In September 1941 Japanese forces occupied French Indochina. The United States, drawing Britain and Dutch Indonesia in its wake, responded with a trade embargo against Japan.

At a stroke this cut off three-quarters of Japan's imports, including 90 percent of the country's oil supplies. America's terms for lifting the embargo were not only a Japanese withdrawal from Indochina, but also the withdrawal of Japanese forces from China. The Japanese had the choice either of abandoning all their imperial ambitions or of rapid action to seize control of the sources of oil and other raw materials in the southeast Asian colonies.

Fearing the naval power of the United States, the Japanese gambled on winning an overwhelming advantage in their initial offensive. The brilliantly executed attack on Pearl Harbor by Japanese naval aircraft on 7 December 1941 was the prelude to an astonishing string of victories that gave Japan control of the Philippines, Malaysia, Singapore, Indonesia, Burma, and part of New Guinea by February 1942.

There might have been no connection between the Pacific and European wars but for Hitler's quixotically loyal declaration of war on the United States in support of Japan. The Japanese did not reciprocate by declaring war on the Soviet Union; Japan and the Soviets were not at war until August 1945. Hitler's declaration of war enabled President Roosevelt to impose on the American people his vision of a worldwide struggle for freedom, in which precedence had to be given to victory in Europe.

Declaration of the United Nations

Attempting to define their war aims, the United States and Britain had already produced the ringing declaration of the Atlantic Charter in August 1941, calling for self-determination, democracy, and free speech, the peaceful settlement of international disputes, and a more equitable economic world order. These principles were endorsed in the Declaration of the United Nations, signed by 26 countries in January 1942. Since one of these countries was the Soviet Union, however, the declaration's shining idealism was tarnished by hypocrisy from the start.

From the entry of the United States into the war, the potential preponderance of force lay with the "United Nations" or "Grand Alliance". However, both Germany and Japan had established positions of great strength and it was some time before the Allied superiority could be brought to bear. The Germans continued to advance deeper into the Soviet Union through 1942, threatening to seize the

Baku oilfields. In the Atlantic, German U-boats inflicted such losses on merchant shipping that Britain's survival was still in doubt. In the Pacific, the Japanese planned a new offensive and plotted to destroy the US fleet.

The turning of the tide came with a series of decisive Allied victories in 1942–43. At the Battle of Midway in June 1942, the destruction of four Japanese aircraft carriers abruptly ended the brief period of Japanese naval superiority in the Pacific. The British-led victory at El Alamein in October, and the Allied landings in French North Africa in November, were followed by the surrender of Axis forces in the desert war. The military catastrophe at Stalingrad in January 1943 ended Germany's hopes of conquering the Soviet Union. And in May 1943 the U-boat menace was finally mastered, heavy losses leading Donitz to withdraw his "wolfpacks" from the Atlantic.

By the summer of 1943 there was no doubt which side was going to win the war. Italy had been invaded and Mussolini deposed; German forces had suffered another devastating defeat in the Soviet Union at the great tank battle of Kursk; German cities were being laid waste by Allied bombing raids; and Japan, although still holding most of its conquests, was suffering unsustainable losses of aircraft and merchant shipping. The rest of the war was a long, massively destructive end-game. German and Japanese strategy was, in essence, to try to make victory so costly for

the Allies that they would agree to some form of negotiated settlement. Many Germans – including both Hitler and some of those who sought his overthrow – believed that the Western Allies might be induced to make a pact with Germany to fight the Soviet Union.

In the event, the Western allies and the Soviet Union held together for the duration of the war. At a conference in Tehran in 1943, Roosevelt, Churchill, and Stalin established an adequate working agreement for the prosecution of the war and the organization of the postwar world. Ultimately, the Grand Alliance was cemented by the commitment to obtaining Germany's unconditional surrender; any hint of negotiations with the Germans might well have raised mutual suspicions to an unsustainable level. Nonetheless, the policy of unconditional surrender has been criticized by many commentators for unnecessarily prolonging the war and undermining Hitler's opponents in Germany.

Even without any encouragement from the Allies, German plotters narrowly failed to assassinate Hitler in July 1944. By then, the Red Army was advancing into Poland and the Western Allies had consolidated their position in Normandy after the June D-Day landings. Paris was liberated in the last week of August and Brussels in the first week of September.

The defeat of Germany seemed imminent. But on both fronts the Allied advance then ran out of momentum. The Red Army stopped outside Warsaw, where a rising by the Polish resistance was crushed by the German occupiers. In the west, a bold British-led airborne assault at Arnhem in the Netherlands failed. In December, the Germans launched an offensive in the Ardennes that put Allied troops under severe pressure.

Race for Berlin

During the Cold War years, the final period of the war in Europe was often presented as a "race for Berlin" between the Western Allies and the Red Army. But this was a retrospective distortion. In reality, the Soviet Union had urged the Western Allies to launch an invasion of western Europe at the earliest possible date, to create a "second front" that would take the pressure off Soviet forces. And by the start of 1945, the Western Allies were begging Stalin to bring forward the date of the final Soviet offensive as their own troops suffered heavy casualties. Stalin duly obliged. German forces were soon being driven back into their homeland from the east and west.

Stalin, Churchill, and Roosevelt met for the last time at Yalta in February 1945. They agreed on the setting up of the United Nations Organization, the division of Germany into zones of occupation, and changes to Poland's borders. An atmosphere of trust and confidence reigned. Two months later Roosevelt died. The new president, Harry S. Truman, was deeply suspicious of Stalin. Whether the Grand Alliance could have successfully continued after the war had Roosevelt lived must be questionable. With Truman in office it was improbable.

At the end of April Soviet troops fought their way into Berlin. Hitler committed suicide in his bunker, raving to the last about "international Jewry and its accomplices", which he blamed for the downfall of Germany. An orderly German surrender proceeded in stages, and by 9 May the war in Europe was over.

The war against Japan, however, still seemed far from finished. As the Americans had followed their strategy of "island-hopping" across the Pacific toward Japan, losses had mounted sharply. In February 1945, US Marines suffered 26,000 casualties, a third of their force, in taking the island of Iwo Jima. The battle for Okinawa the following April cost 49,000 American dead and wounded. The Japanese soldiers mostly fought to the death – only 1,000 of the 25,000 Japanese defending Iwo Jima surrendered – although this was partly because American troops had a policy of taking no prisoners.

Kamikaze tactics

Japanese air forces had adopted "kamikaze" tactics, using aircraft as manned flying bombs to crash-dive on the decks of enemy warships. At the battles of the Philippine Sea and Leyte Gulf in 1944 Japanese aircraft and warships had suffered massive losses without inflicting any significant damage on American forces. At least kamikaze tactics allowed inexperienced pilots to hit their targets.

The aim of the Japanese leadership, facing certain defeat, was to find a way of avoiding unconditional surrender. They sought a ceasefire on terms that would allow them to maintain their own government and manoeuvre for advantage against the victors. The disagreement inside the Japanese government was between those who thought that most was to be gained by a stance of total resistance and those who believed negotiations should begin.

The Americans meanwhile followed every possible avenue to military victory: a total naval blockade that threatened the Japanese with imminent starvation; massive air attacks that devastated Japan's cities; a possible invasion of the Japanese mainland; the involvement of the Soviet Union in the war against Japan, agreed at the Potsdam conference in July–August 1945; and the use of a secret weapon that had been under development since 1942 – the atomic bomb.

Making parachutes

In Britain and America, women made a telling contribution to the successful pursuit of the war.

The US administration, having spent a fortune building the most powerful weapon in the world, gave no serious consideration to the possibility of refraining from using it. President Truman later said: "The atom bomb was no 'great decision'. That was not any decision that you had to worry about." On 6 and 9 August respectively, the populations of the cities of Hiroshima and Nagasaki became the first, and so far only, victims of nuclear attack. In the meantime, the Soviet Union declared war on Japan and invaded Manchuria. The combination of these events convinced the Japanese leadership that further resistance was hopeless. Emperor Hirohito broadcast to his people on 15 August announcing Japan's surrender.

Victory for industry and technology

The outcome of the war was, in a sense, a victory for industrial productive power and technological efficiency over sheer fighting spirit. Both the Germans and the Japanese often depended on remarkably primitive technologies: much of the Japanese invasion of southeast Asia was carried out by bicycle, and horsedrawn vehicles were still the backbone of the German army when it invaded the Soviet Union in 1941.

Germany geared up very slowly for the demands of total war – its economy was not really on a war footing until 1942. Whereas Britain conscripted women for work in the armed forces, factories, and farms, Hitler never abandoned his view that a woman's place was in the home. Even the ruthless exploitation of slave labour was undermined by the irrational drive to extermination. Not only the United States but also the Soviet Union proved capable of outproducing the Germans, let alone the Japanese. And Hitler's obsessive quest for a secret weapon that would turn the tide of the war only resulted in the relatively ineffectual V2 rocket, a mere squib alongside America's A-bomb.

Necessary war in a just cause

The war demonstrated the extraordinary ability of modern states to command allegiance. Total war demanded the mobilization of the whole population for the war effort. Yet, except for Italy, none of the major combatant countries had difficulty in maintaining the support of the vast majority of their people even, in the case of Germany and Japan, when facing certain defeat. Nor did they have much problem winning approval, or at least compliance, for acts that trampled on normally accepted moral values.

Although they may not have been aware of the full extent of the Holocaust, Germans could have questioned the flagrant ill-treatment of Jews or the widespread use of slave labour, but they did not; nor, on the whole, did Britons or Americans oppose the terror bombing of civilians, up to and including the devastation of Hiroshima and Nagasaki.

This is not meant, however, to suggest a moral equivalence between the two sides in the conflict. Every country occupied by Germany or Japan felt "liberated" by the Allied victory, even when, as in French Indochina or Poland, they bitterly resented the postwar settlement. Those Allied troops who uncovered the horrors of Belsen or of the Japanese prisoner of war camps could rightly feel that they had fought a necessary war in a just cause.

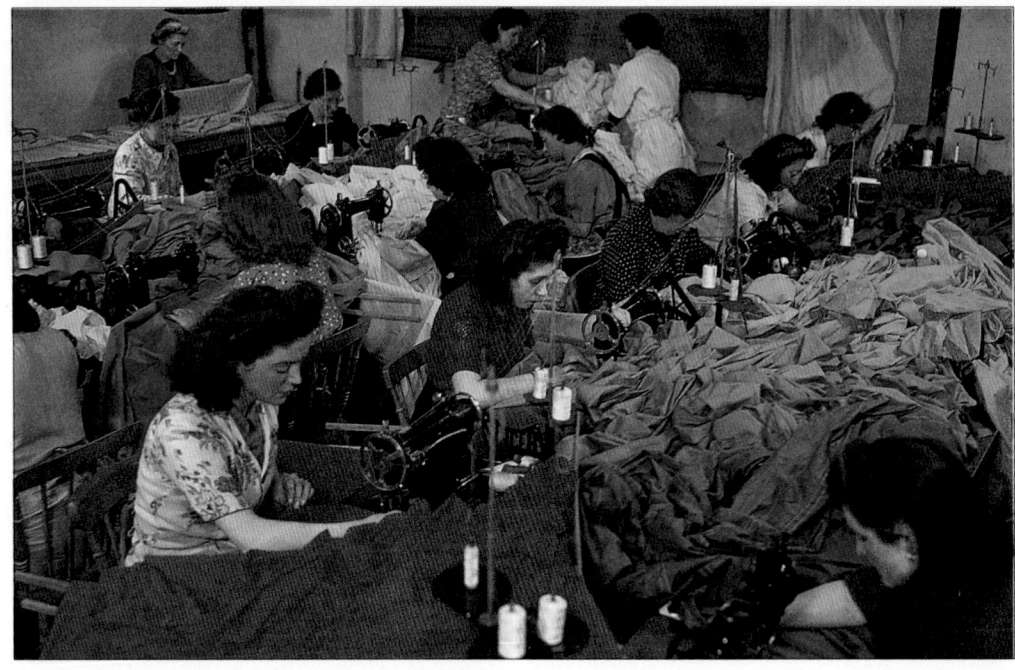

Countdown to War

On 27 August 1928, representatives of 15 countries, including Germany, Britain, France, Japan, Italy, and the United States, solemnly signed an agreement outlawing war and providing for the peaceful settlement of all international disputes. Known as the Kellogg-Briand Pact, this agreement was soon accepted by every major country in the world.

The vision of world peace might not have proved such a momentary illusion but for the economic crisis of the Great Depression, which from 1929 onward brought unemployment and poverty to millions. Germany was one of the countries worst hit, and extreme nationalist movements suddenly drew a mass following. Most prominent of these was Adolf Hitler's Nazi Party, which by 1932 was the largest single party in the German Reichstag.

An outstanding political campaigner and propagandist, Hitler won popular support above all by blaming Germany's economic misfortunes directly on the terms of the Versailles Treaty. His nationalism and his anti-communism won him the support not only of more than a third of German voters, but also of many of Germany's traditional ruling class – army officers, landowners, and businessmen. On 30 January 1933, German president Paul von Hindenburg appointed Hitler chancellor, at the head of a coalition government.

Japanese incursion into Manchuria

In Japan, the impact of the Depression strengthened the hand of those who argued for an expansionist policy of military conquest. In 1931, Japanese army officers launched an incursion into Manchuria, the northernmost area of China. The incursion soon developed into a full-scale occupation. In 1932 Manchuria became the Japanese puppet state of Manzhuguo.

The military occupation of Manchuria was a clear breach of the Kellogg-Briand Pact and of the principles of the League of Nations, of which Japan was a founder-member. The forerunner of the United Nations, the League had been set up after World War I to guarantee peace and security. But no action was taken against Japan, beyond the publication of a critical report.

Before launching into an aggressive foreign policy, Hitler needed to consolidate his hold on power in Germany. This he did with startling rapidity and ruthlessness. Within six months of his becoming chancellor, all

opposition to the Nazis had been crushed and Germany had become a single-party state. On the Night of the Long Knives, in June 1934, potential rivals to Hitler within the Nazi ranks were butchered. The following August, after Hindenburg's death, the army swore a personal oath of allegiance to Hitler as Führer.

Terms of the Versailles Treaty

Under the terms of the Versailles Treaty, the size and equipment of Germany's armed forces had been severely restricted. If Britain and France took resolute action to maintain this limitation then Germany would not have the means to threaten their security. But in March 1935 Hitler announced that he would no longer respect the limit on armed forces imposed at Versailles, and that the peacetime strength of the German army would be set at 600,000. Britain, France, and Italy condemned Germany's action, but did nothing.

Emboldened, Hitler prepared for another gamble. The Rhineland, a substantial area of Germany bordering on France and the Low Countries, had been declared a demilitarized zone. This meant that, in effect, any time the Germans stepped out of line, France could occupy the area unopposed. On 3 March 1936, Hitler marched his troops into the Rhineland. This was in breach not only of the Versailles Treaty but also of the 1925 Locarno Pact, which had committed Britain and Italy to come to France's aid in just such an event. But Hitler encountered nothing but the frail impotence of British and French disapproval.

Meanwhile, Italy's bombastic Fascist dictator Benito Mussolini was making another test of the wavering commitment to "collective security" within the League of Nations. In October 1935 Italian forces invaded Abyssinia (Ethiopia). The League promptly denounced Italy as an aggressor and imposed economic sanctions. Britain and France, however, hesitated to enforce sanctions rigorously. While they prevaricated, Italy completed its conquest of Abyssinia, seizing the capital, Addis Ababa, in May 1936. The farce of denunciation and sanctions stung Mussolini into aligning himself with Hitler. In November 1936 he announced the "Rome-Berlin Axis", around which Europe was supposed to revolve.

Communism and nationalism

The "Axis" was part of a wider reorganization of international relations on ideological lines. The Bolshevik Revolution of 1917 and the subsequent formation of the Soviet Union as the world's first communist state had created a radical alternative to capitalism. Through the Comintern (Communist International), founded in 1919, the Soviets sought to export their revolution abroad. It was partly this communist challenge that stimulated the creation of new radical nationalist movements such as the Italian Fascists and the Nazis. By the mid-1930s, many countries were ruled by anti-communist authoritarian right-wing governments – in Europe, only Britain, France, Czechoslovakia, the Low Countries, Spain, Switzerland, and Scandinavia were still liberal democracies.

Both the communists and the "fascists" were dismissive of "bourgeois democracy", but in the 1930s, confronted in particular by Hitler's rise to power, the Soviet Union adopted a policy of cooperation with any group in the democracies that it considered "anti-fascist". In France and Spain, "Popular Front" alliances between the communists and other parties of the left and centre won election victories in 1936. The Soviet Union also sought to escape from diplomatic isolation, belatedly joining the League of Nations in 1934 and signing a defensive pact with France in 1935. Hitler's riposte was the

Portrait of Adolf Hitler
This portrait was painted by B. Jacobs in 1933, the year in which Hitler became Chancellor of Germany.

Crossing the Rhine
Crowds watch a military band in a
triumphal march across one of the
Rhine bridges, 3 March 1936.

Anti-Comintern Pact, a statement of shared attitudes and aims agreed with Japan's military-dominated government in 1936, and to which Italy acceded in the following year.

It was in this ideologically charged atmosphere that the Spanish Civil War broke out in July 1936. The war began when a group of army officers in Spanish Morocco, including General Francisco Franco, attempted to overthrow Spain's recently elected Popular Front government. The government armed socialist and anarchist militias in its defence and the coup failed. It took three years of warfare for the right-wing Nationalists to finally crush the Republic, at a cost of 700,000 lives.

This victory was achieved largely thanks to military support from Mussolini and Hitler. On the other side, thousands of idealists from Britain, France, and other countries went to Spain to fight for the Republic in the International Brigades. But the British and French governments followed a policy of "non-intervention" and tried to impose an arms embargo, which in practice meant a blockade on arms for the Republic while Italy and Germany poured in support for Franco.

Aversion to war

The failure of Europe's leading democracies to intervene in Spain reflected a confusion and weakness that Hitler was to exploit mercilessly. In France, the Third Republic was ruled by a succession of governments that failed to provide strong national leadership. Many officers in the French armed forces admired Hitler and despised the Republic. In Britain, too, many members of the predominantly Conservative National Government welcomed a revived Germany as a bulwark against the Soviet Union. The opposition Labour Party was confusedly in favour of resisting Hitler but opposed to rearmament. In both Britain and France, most of the population and their leaders shared a strong desire to avoid a repetition of the slaughter of the Great War.

An aversion to war was also powerfully expressed by the people of the United States. A series of Neutrality Acts passed by Congress in the mid-1930s banned the supply of arms or financial backing to combatant countries in a foreign war. The United States was, on balance, more concerned by the rise

of Japanese power in Asia than by events in Europe. By 1933, after the takeover of Manchuria and the fighting that occurred in its wake, Japan had taken possession of northern China as far south as Peking. There matters rested until July 1937 when a clash between Japanese and Chinese soldiers outside Peking was followed by a full-scale Japanese offensive. This could arguably be described as the start of World War II, for the Sino-Japanese War was the first of the regional conflicts that were eventually to coalesce into a single global conflict. After the Japanese occupied Nanking, the Chinese Nationalist capital, in December 1937, an estimated 250,000 of the city's inhabitants were massacred by its conquerors. President Roosevelt denounced the Japanese as aggressors and looked for ways of applying economic pressure to force them to withdraw from China. Meanwhile, Chinese government forces retreated to a remote area of the interior and waited in hope of securing American military aid.

In Europe, there seemed to be no stopping Germany's rise to dominance. By 1938 a buoyant Hitler was prepared to embark on a new phase in his challenge to the Versailles Treaty. It had long been a goal of German nationalists to incorporate all ethnic Germans within a single Greater German state. At Versailles the victorious powers had specifically forbidden the absorption of Austria – overwhelmingly German in

population – into Germany. The borders agreed by the peacemakers had also left substantial minorities of ethnic Germans in states on Germany's borders, most notably in the Sudetenland area of Czechoslovakia.

Austrian Nazi movement

Austria had its own powerful Nazi movement. Austrian Nazis had murdered Chancellor Engelbert Dollfuss in an attempted coup in 1934, and Dollfuss's successor, Kurt von Schuschnigg, had been forced by pressure from Germany to include Nazis in the Austrian government from 1936. Schuschnigg was thus in a weak position to resist Hitler's thrust for Anschluss (unification) of the two countries. In February 1938 the unfortunate Austrian chancellor was summoned to Hitler's mountain villa at Berchtesgaden and browbeaten into handing over control of the Austrian ministry of the interior to the Nazis. When Schuschnigg showed signs of trying to resist a Nazi takeover of power, German troops crossed the border into Austria on 12 March 1938. They encountered no resistance.

The incorporation of Austria added eight million to the population of the German Reich, as well as valuable economic assets. It might have been expected that Britain and France would at least protest strongly at the armed takeover of an independent country, but their response was muted. After all, the population of Austria was German, and one of the basic principles espoused by the Versailles peacemakers had been national self-determination – that all people of the same nationality should, if they wished, be united under their own government. This principle had patently not been applied to Germans. Neville Chamberlain, who had become British Prime Minister in 1937, believed that lasting peace might be secured if the "just demands" of German nationalism were met.

Sudeten Germans in Czechoslovakia

Czechoslovakia, Hitler's next target, was a multinational state, with a population of Czechs, Slovaks, Poles, Magyars, and Ruthenes, as well as about three million Germans. By 1938, with encouragement from Berlin, the Sudeten Germans were campaigning for autonomy and agitating against alleged mistreatment by the Czechs. After the Anschluss, Hitler told the Sudeten German leader Konrad Henlein to enter into negotiations with the Czech government.

In theory, Czechoslovakia was in a strong position. It was a stable democracy with efficient armed forces and a modern industrial economy, and its border was impressively fortified. It was guaranteed against aggression by an alliance with France dating from 1924 and a more recent treaty with the Soviet Union. Unfortunately, Chamberlain decided that the peace of Europe would not be secure until the Sudeten question had been settled to Hitler's satisfaction.

Taking the initiative, Chamberlain twice flew to Germany to negotiate with Hitler. At the first meeting on 15 September 1938, Hitler demanded the secession of the Sudetenland from Czechoslovakia. At the second, a week later, he delivered an ultimatum requiring the annexation of the Sudetenland by Germany within five days. This was unacceptable even to the British cabinet and Europe began preparing for war. In a last ditch attempt to preserve peace, a conference was hastily assembled at Munich on 29–30 September. There Hitler, Chamberlain, Mussolini, and French Prime Minister Edouard Daladier agreed on the rape of Czechoslovakia. Czech representatives were informed that they must allow German forces to occupy the Sudetenland or fight Germany alone. Unsurprisingly, the Czechs capitulated. Chamberlain arrived back at Croydon airport waving a peace of paper bearing Hitler's signature and claiming to gave secured "peace in our time".

Kristallnacht atrocities

On 9–10 November the Nazis carried out brutal attacks on Jews across Germany in retaliation for the murder of a German diplomat in Paris. These "Kristallnacht" atrocities bore especially heavily upon the substantial Jewish population of newly annexed Austria. An uncomfortable awareness spread that it might in the end be necessary to go to war with Hitler anyway – in which case having sacrificed a large part of Czechoslovakia, including its border defences, without a fight had been an act of monumental folly.

The transformation of British opinion was completed in March 1939, when Hitler recognized the independence of Slovakia and sent his army into Prague to establish a "protectorate" over Bohemia and Moravia.

The Czech army did not attempt to resist the German takeover. Hungary stepped in to seize Ruthenia as Czechoslovakia ceased to exist. None of this surprised the Czechs. They knew that the Munich agreement had handed Czechoslovakia to Germany bound hand and foot. But the British were shocked and outraged. As far as they were concerned, Hitler was now unmasked as an insatiable aggressor. The predominant British attitude swung from the pursuit of peace at any price to stopping Hitler at any cost.

Six days after the occupation of Prague, Germany annexed Memel (now Klajpeda), a port city in Lithuania with a predominantly German population. Hitler's obvious next target was another Baltic port, Danzig (Gdansk). In the Versailles Treaty, newly independent Poland had been handed a strip of formerly German territory to provide it with an outlet to the sea. This "Polish corridor" cut off East Prussia from the rest of Germany. Danzig, the main port within the corridor, had been declared a Free City. In the winter of 1938, Hitler proposed to the Polish government that Germany should take control of Danzig, which had a largely German population, and that an autobahn should be built across the Polish corridor to link Germany with East Prussia. Once the occupation of Prague had been accomplished, Hitler took up this issue again in earnest. He berated the Poles for their failure to accept Germany's proposals and set in motion a by-now familiar propaganda campaign in favour of the "oppressed" Germans of Danzig.

Chamberlain was still determined to avoid war, but he now believed that peace could only be preserved by displaying a resolute commitment to the use of force if necessary. On 30 March he gave the Poles an unconditional guarantee that, in the event of a German attack, Britain and France would come to their defence. Overflowing with confidence, Hitler responded to Britain's guarantee by telling his generals to prepare for a war with Poland in September.

Poland was a very different country from Czechoslovakia. Its anti-semitic, anti-communist, authoritarian military government had seemed likely to fit comfortably into a Nazi-dominated "new order" in Europe. On the other hand, its leaders were temperamentally averse to the art of survival

Sino-Japanese War
Japanese soldiers parading through the Jessfield area of Shanghai, China, in 1937 during the Sino-Japanese War.

Sudeten Militia
*A rally of Sudeten German militiamen
in Germany in early 1938, inspected
by their leader Konrad Henlein.*

by submission. Bolstered by the British guarantee, the Polish government responded to mounting German pressure with an uncompromising refusal to make concessions.

At the same time that Britain was tying the future of peace in Europe to the fate of Poland, the long agony of the Spanish Civil War came to an end with the victory of General Franco's Nationalists. One of Franco's first acts as dictator of Spain was to join the Anti-Comintern Pact. In April another Pact member, Benito Mussolini, made his own contribution to the mounting international tension by invading and annexing Albania. The following month Germany and Italy signed an offensive alliance, melodramatically publicized as the Pact of Steel.

Military assistance for Poland

With war looking increasingly likely, Britain and France had to turn their attention to the tricky question of what, in military terms, they would actually do in the case of a German invasion of Poland. British and French military chiefs told the Poles that their role was to hold out against the invaders while Britain and France prepared a swift counter-offensive in the west. But in reality the French army was not prepared to depart from its established defensive strategy, which placed unshakeable faith in the impregnability of its frontier fortifications, the Maginot Line.

Britain had carried through a substantial rearmament programme since 1936, but this had concentrated on the air force and the navy, rather than the army. In fact, the only serious chance of effective military assistance for Poland lay in an alliance with the Soviet Union. In August 1939 an Anglo-French military mission set off for Moscow.

The Soviet dictator, Joseph Stalin, was in principle Hitler's most dedicated ideological rival. The Soviet Union and the international communist movement it headed were the specific enemies targeted by the Anti-Comintern Pact. Stalin was already in conflict with one Pact member, Japan, as Soviet and Japanese troops clashed on the border between Manchuria and Siberia in the summer of 1938 and again in 1939. He undoubtably viewed Hitler's growing strength with intense alarm.

But Stalin also distrusted Britain and France, suspecting them of intending to save their own skins by deflecting Hitler's

aggression against the Soviet Union. And he was definitely no friend of Poland. The population of eastern Poland was predominantly Belorussian and Ukrainian. Stalin wanted to absorb this area into the Soviet Union, a fact well known to the Poles, who flatly refused to agree that Soviet troops should enter Polish territory to help resist a German invasion.

The Ribbentrop-Molotov Pact

Hostile to Stalin's communist dictatorship and dismissive of the military potential of the Red Army, the French and British governments pursued a Soviet alliance with a marked lack of urgency. Their military mission proceeded to Russia in leisurely fashion by sea. The Nazis sensed an opportunity. On 23 August, a week after the Anglo-French mission arrived in Moscow, German Foreign Minister Joachim von Ribbentrop flew in from Berlin and clinched a dramatic deal with his Soviet opposite number, Molotov. The Ribbentrop-Molotov Pact publicly pledged the two countries to non-aggression, but privately went much further. A secret protocol provided for the partition of Poland between Germany and the Soviet Union, and allowed the Soviets a free hand to take over Latvia, Estonia, and Finland should they so wish.

When a stunned world learned of the non-aggression pact between those supposedly mortal enemies, Nazi Germany and Soviet

Russia, few doubted that war was imminent. Hitler hoped, however, that it could be restricted to a conflict between Germany and Poland. The Nazis employed a Swedish businessman, Birger Dahlerus, as go-between for secret negotiations with the British, seeking to induce them to withdraw support from the Poles. The British and French governments did their best to persuade the Poles to make concessions to Germany – Chamberlain privately considered Hitler's demands reasonable – but Poland held firm and British public opinion would not allow the government to renege on its guarantee. On 25 August, Britain signed a formal alliance with Poland.

Hitler first ordered the invasion of Poland to take place on 26 August. This order was countermanded at the last moment, either because of the signature of the Anglo-Polish alliance, or because Mussolini momentarily deflated Hitler's exultant mood by announcing that, despite the Pact of Steel, he intended to remain neutral. On 31 August the Italian dictator proposed an international conference in a last effort to preserve peace. This proposal was welcomed with enthusiasm by the French, but ignored by Hitler. The invasion of Poland began on 1 September. Two days later, facing a revolt in the House of Commons, Chamberlain reluctantly declared war on Germany.

1939

September

Su	Mo	Tu	We	Th	Fr	Sa
					1	2
3	4	5	6	7	8	9
10	11	12	13	14	15	16
17	18	19	20	21	22	23
24	25	26	27	28	29	30

1. Europe: Norway, Finland and Switzerland declare their neutrality, while Italy affirms its "non-belligerency" (→ 5).

2. Gibraltar: The first British convoy of the war leaves for Cape Town.

3. Europe: France and Britain give Germany an ultimatum to withdraw from Poland, despite Italian efforts to convene a peace conference.→

3. London: A French civilian plane near Croydon airport sparks off the first air-raid warning of the war.

3. Poland: Polish civilians and rearguard massacre hundreds of German residents as they flee the city of Bydgoszcz (→ 8).

4. Japan: The new prime minister, Nobuyuki Abe, promises to keep out of the war in Europe.

4. Kiel Canal: Seven RAF aircraft are lost – the first of the war – in near-disastrous raids on Wilhelmshaven and Brunsbuttel. Only eight out of the 27 RAF bombers on the raid manage to locate German naval bases (→ 6).

5. Poland: Germans enter Piotrkow and set fire to the Jewish district (→ 16).

5. Washington: US neutrality, announced by Roosevelt in a broadcast on 3 September, becomes official.→

5. Warsaw: The government leaves for Lublin (→ 8).

6. South Africa: The prime minister, Jan Christian Smuts, declares war on Germany.→

7. Germany: The death penalty is decreed for anyone "endangering the defensive power of the German people".

9. Poland: The German 4th *Panzer* Division reaches the outskirts of Warsaw, but Polish units counter-attack on the river Bzura (→ 9).

9. Berlin: Field Marshal Goering boasts: "The Polish Army will never emerge again from the German embrace."→

9. Britain: The last of 13 RAF squadrons flies to France in moves begun on 4 September to strengthen the British Expeditionary Force.

Germans invade Poland at daybreak

German soldiers take down the Polish eagle and cross the border from the Polish corridor into the free state of Danzig.

Poland, 1 September

German tanks thundered across the Polish border at precisely 0445 hours today. Supported by Junkers Ju87 ("Stuka") dive-bombers, which are being used as airborne artillery, they are making rapid progress in penetrating Poland's forward defences. The assault is fast and violent, with units racing ahead to envelop and destroy the Polish defenders.

Warsaw has been bombed. Heinkel and Dornier bombers are pounding Polish airfields and strategic targets while Messerschmitt fighters hunt down those Polish planes which have managed to get airborne. First reports speak of the German Army Group South striking north-east from Silesia while the Fourth Army is advancing from Pomerania to link up with the Third Army pushing south-west from East Prussia.

The pattern that is emerging is of the Germans using their traditional technique of the double pincer movement against Polish forces which are largely concentrated near the frontier to protect the industrial areas. It seems that the Polish commander-in-chief, Marshal Smigly-Rydz, hopes to hold the line until Britain and France come to his rescue. The force of the attack mounted by General Walter von Brauchitsch must cast doubts upon the Poles' ability to resist until their allies attack in the west.

The Poles are undoubtedly brave, but they have only a handful of light tanks and a dozen cavalry brigades to face nine highly-trained armoured divisions and are outnumbered in artillery and infantry and in the air. The old German battleship *Schleswig-Holstein* has also joined in the fight. Sent to Danzig as part of the war of nerves, she is using her big guns against Polish fortifications.

It is already evident that modern war involves everyone. The bombing raids on Warsaw are designed to terrorize, while refugees clogging the roads are being mercilessly machine-gunned by the Stukas. Tanks crush everything under their steel treads. There are no non-combatants in this war (→ 5).

Secret peace envoys fail to avert attack

Britain, 1 September

As Europe races towards war, anti-Hitler emissaries have been holding secret talks with Neville Chamberlain, the British prime minister, and his foreign secretary, Lord Halifax. Contact was made early this summer. Some envoys talked of overthrowing Hitler while others brought proposals for a deal over Danzig. Even today the two British leaders and foreign office officials have kept the talks going. However, they have never been fully convinced that the emissaries represent a genuine peace movement. There appear to be two separate groups.

One is largely representative of Germany's aristocratic and conservative upper classes. The other, much more mysterious, is represented by a Swedish businessman, Birger Dahlerus, who claims to be a close friend of Goering and says the German field marshal wants peace. Today Dahlerus telephoned London, urging British leaders to persuade the Poles to be reasonable. He was told to tell his German friends to get out of Poland (→ 29/9).

War engulfs Europe for second time in 25 years

One last minute of peace time.

London and Paris, 3 September
Britain and France are once again at war with Germany. For most Britons the news came this sunny Sunday morning through the wireless and the sombre voice of Neville Chamberlain, the prime minister, who had sought to appease Herr Hitler's territorial demands. Berlin had been warned, he said, that if Germany did not stop all aggressive action against Poland and begin to withdraw from Polish territory by 11am, Britain and Germany would be at war. At 11.15am Mr Chamberlain announced in his radio broadcast that "no such undertaking has been received and that consequently this country is at war with Germany".

Almost immediately a siren sounded in London, its haunting monotone sending people hurrying to shelters; but it turned out to be a false alarm.

The French ultimatum expired at 5pm, after two days of increasingly fraught consultations between London and Paris. Anger spilt over in an emergency Saturday session of the House of Commons when Chamberlain failed to set a deadline for declaring war against Germany after the attack on Poland.

Georges Bonnet, France's foreign minister, was hoping Musso-lini would come to the rescue with a big power conference, while the French premier, Edouard Daladier, pleaded that the French generals were fearful of German air attacks. By late yesterday the British were in the position of issuing an ultimatum not only to Germany but also to France: if the French did not act, Britain would go it alone.

Twenty-five years ago what was then called the Great War was the "war to end all wars". Today another generation of Europeans finds itself with more powerful weaponry than ever with civilians threatened as never before by the threat of aerial bombardment (→ 5).

Children evacuated from major cities

London, 3 September
The mass evacuation of children from cities to the reception areas considered safe from air attack has been proceeding for three days. By tonight nearly 1,500,000 evacuees will have been moved – 827,000 being schoolchildren travelling with their teachers. Another 535,000 are women expecting babies or with children under school age.

Each child was labelled with name, address and school number and carried a gas mask, night clothing, toothbrush, comb, soap and towel, spare underwear, handkerchief and overcoat if available. The children were marshalled at railway stations and issued with blank tickets – no destinations were given. Parents will be informed where they are as soon as possible. Distribution centres were organized in towns like Oxford, Cambridge, Reading, Brighton, Gloucester, Scarborough and Ilkley, and in North Wales and the Scottish Highlands. In Bedford the cattle market was used as a reception centre for onward dispersal to the country; Dagenham children went by pleasure steamer to Yarmouth. Those taking evacuees will be paid 10/6 (52¹/₂p/$2.34) a week for one child and 8/6 for each extra child (→ 31/1).

Britain mobilizes to meet war challenge

Britain, 3 September
The British armed forces have already mobilized for war. All members of the reserve forces received call-up notices at the beginning of this month, ordering them to report to their depots. Since March the Territorial Army (TA) has been doubled. In July the first TA conscripts were called up – 20- and 21-year-olds. Their training now complete, they will join the new TA divisions. Today Parliament passed the National Service (Armed Forces) Act making all men aged between 18 and 41, other than those in reserved occupations, liable for conscription. It will be some days yet before the first of these receive call-up papers.

The Royal Navy has meanwhile deployed to its war stations. The Home Fleet has returned to its 1914-18 anchorage at Scapa Flow in the Orkneys, and elements are preparing to escort the British Expeditionary Force (BEF) across to France. The BEF itself will initially consist of four regular divisions under General Lord Gort, VC, but will be joined by other divisions as they are made ready. The RAF yesterday sent ten Fairey Battle light bomber squadrons to France, and more fighter and bomber squadrons will follow (→ 11).

Tired and a little puzzled, city children arrive at their billet in Eastbourne.

He's back: Churchill joins war cabinet

London, 3 September
From the admiralty an exhilarating message was flashed to the Royal Navy: "Winston is back." After years in the political wilderness as he warned Britain about what he saw as the growing Nazi menace, Winston Churchill tonight joined the new war cabinet as first lord of the admiralty. He was in that job from 1911 to 1915.

Mr Chamberlain also appointed Anthony Eden as dominions secretary. This was the prime minister's recognition that he must bow to public clamour for the return to office of two leading Tories vociferously opposed to the policy of appeasing Hitler (→ 1/10).

Churchill arrives at the Admiralty: the wilderness years are now over.

German U-boats attack Allied ships

North Atlantic, 4 September
One hundred and twelve passengers and crew of the liner SS *Athenia* perished last night, the first victims of German submarine warfare. The 13,581-ton liner was sailing from Glasgow to Montreal. She was hit by a torpedo at 7.45pm last night, but thanks to a massive rescue operation during the night most of the 1,418 people on board were saved.

Captain James Cook said: "The torpedo went right through the ship to the engine room. It completely wrecked the galley." One Czech passenger said: "There was a column of water near the ship, and a black thing like a cigar shot over the sea towards us. There was a bang, and then I saw men on the submarine turn a gun and fire it."

They were firing at the radio mast, but they missed. At 8.59pm the SOS call was heard by Malin Head radio station in Ireland. A Norwegian ship, *Knut Nelson*, was first on the scene, soon joined by a Swedish yacht, the *Southern Cross*. They picked up about 500 survivors and three destroyers then raced up and rescued the rest. Germany's submarines had been preparing for

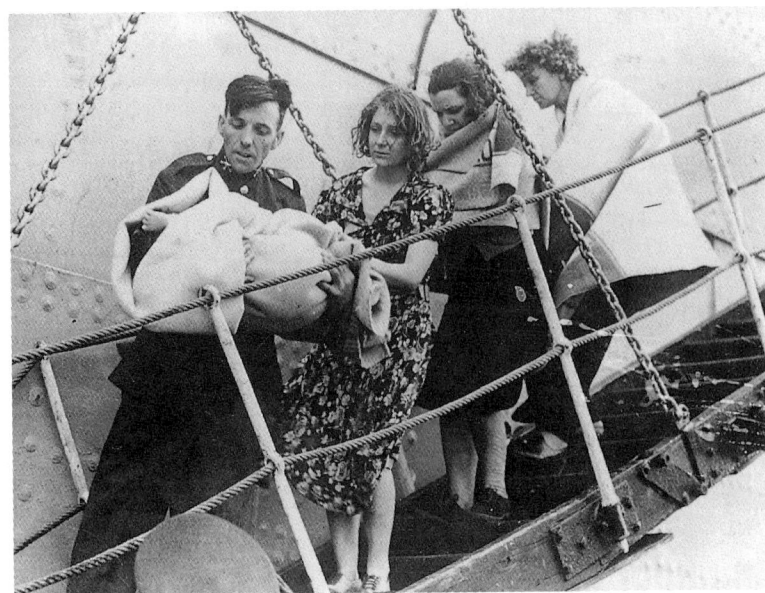
Stunned and bedraggled, survivors of the torpedoed "Athenia" come ashore.

war. On 19 August a "submarine officers' reunion" was scheduled – the code telling the U-boats to take up war stations around Britain. However, it is unlikely that the High Command wanted to sink a liner, especially one with 300 Americans on board. The sinking of passenger ships, such as the

Lusitania in 1915, partly led to the US entry into the last war.

Tonight desperate efforts were being made by the Germans to reduce the propaganda value of an attack on a civilian liner. Hitler himself has sent out a signal that in future passenger ships should not be attacked (→ 14).

RAF rains twelve million propaganda sheets on Germany

London, 9 September
Whitley bombers of the RAF have been engaged in dangerous but successful raids over Germany since the first night of the war. They have dropped their "loads" on Hamburg, Bremen and the Ruhr, but have not caused a single civilian casualty for they have dropped leaflets, not bombs.

Twelve million of these leaflets, pointing out Hitler's responsibility for plunging the world into war, have been scattered over wide areas and it is hoped that their appeal to reason will make the German people "insist on peace".

Some of the RAF crews are not too keen on these propaganda

Join the RAF and drop "bumph".

raids; they call them "bumph drops" and would rather be dropping the real thing on the enemy, a sentiment echoed by the more warlike members of the government such as Winston Churchill.

However, the raids, quite apart from their effect on German morale, are providing the bomber crews with useful training for the day when their loads become lethal.

The crews are also under orders to report activity at enemy airfields and the position and accuracy of searchlights and anti-aircraft guns. So far, their main enemies have been cold and fatigue on their long, arduous flights (→ 20).

French advance troops cross German frontier at Saarbrucken

Western Front, 7 September
Units of the French Fourth and Fifth Armies have advanced into Germany, captured two villages and are poised to cut off the industrial city of Saarbrucken. The Germans have pulled back towards their Siegfried Line fortifications. Though heavy artillery fire and

some aerial reconnaissance has been reported, nothing like a general offensive is under way. The Germans are puzzled. France has deployed 85 fully armed divisions against the Germans' 34 divisions, 20 of them reserve units. The German *Panzers* are all in Poland.

The Poles, reeling under the

German hammer blows, have sent desperate appeals for action. In reply, General Maurice Gamelin, France's C-in-C, says he is doing everything he can; though he admitted to the British the Saar operation is only "a little test". The Germans think Gamelin has no intention of waging real war (→ 12).

Volunteers queue to enlist all over France. Here, Czechs and Slovaks wait to join their armies in Paris.

Polish cavalry crumples under tank "Blitzkrieg"

In the first war pictures to reach London, German tanks roll into Poland.

The Polish artillery sets off on horseback to do battle with German tanks.

Warsaw, 9 September

A new word, *Blitzkrieg*, the lightning war, is being used to describe Germany's invasion of Poland, and the utmost bravery is no proof against lightning, as the Polish Pomorska Cavalry Brigade discovered to its cost.

The story goes that these fine horsemen, full of *elan*, charged a German tank force with swords and lances. The tanks simply hosed them out of their saddles with machine-gun fire.

In another incident a Polish artillery regiment on the march was caught by the *Panzers* and flattened. Hitler, who arrived in his special train, *Amerika*, to gloat over

the triumphs of his army, was astonished when he saw the remains of the guns and was told they had been destroyed by tanks. He thought they had been bombed by Stukas.

The tank expert General Heinz Guderian, who has set up headquarters in a castle at Finkenstein and is sleeping in a room once occupied by Napoleon, has even had time to go hunting, bagging a 12-point stag in the castle's deer park.

The pace of the German advance is largely attributable to the *Luftwaffe's* complete command of the air. The Polish pilots, outnumbered and flying obsolete aircraft, have fought gallantly, but they have been shot out of the sky by the German

aces who learnt their trade in the Spanish Civil War and are flying the brilliant Bf109. The plight of the Polish soldiers is not enviable. Encircled by tanks, hammered from the air and with communications and supply systems cut by marauding Panzers, many units are losing cohesion and can offer no proper resistance.

There are, however, signs today that General Tadeusz Kutrzeba's Poznan Army is about to launch an attack across the Bzura river against the flank of the German Eighth Army which is protecting the mechanized column racing across open country to Warsaw.

It is possible that the Germans

have become over-confident and have left themselves open to a damaging blow from the Poles. But while the German advance may be checked, the overall situation is unlikely to change and the danger is that the Poles will be sucked into a trap and destroyed.

The situation in Warsaw is becoming desperate. Units of the XVI Panzer Corps are already probing the south-east suburbs of the city but, having lost 60 tanks, are waiting for reinforcements before attacking the city's main defences. Bombing has caused great damage and four days ago the government fled to Lublin to carry on a struggle which now seems hopeless.

Germans adopt new tactics of warfare

Warsaw, 9 September

Military analysts studying the German *Blitzkrieg* tactics have concluded that the Poles are fighting with 1918 methods and equipment while the Germans have adopted completely new rules of warfare.

General Guderian's revolutionary tactics allow his tanks to break through linear defences and bypass pockets of resistance, ignoring the risk to their open flanks.

Opposition is crushed by dive-bombers called up by *Luftwaffe* radio vans travelling with the tanks. Speed, violence and radio are at the heart of this new warfare.

THE GERMAN ONSLAUGHT

Danzig — EAST PRUSSIA

Warsaw

Lodz — Brest-Litovsk

GERMANY — POLAND

Cracow — Lwow

CZECHOSLOVAKIA

German advances

100 miles
160 km

© Chronicle Communications Ltd

RUSSIA

Victors purge politicians, intelligentsia

Warsaw, 9 September

A dreadful truth is emerging from the bloody chaos of Poland: the Germans are systematically destroying the Polish leadership. The aristocracy, politicians, the intelligentsia and the officer corps are being rounded up by special SS units and taken away. Their fate is not yet known, but it is feared that they are being put to death on a massive scale.

It is known that 19 Polish officers who had surrendered after fighting bravely were murdered outside the village of Mrocza three days ago. The Germans are also

using terror to cow the populace. Five days ago they rounded up a thousand civilians at Bydgoszcz and shot them against a wall in the market place with the spurious excuse that "brutal guerrilla war has broken out everywhere".

The Jews are the special targets of the SS *Einsatzgruppen*, the Action Squads which follow front-line troops into Jewish areas. These units have been ordered by their commander, Theodor Eicke, to "incarcerate or annihilate" every enemy of Nazism. Fears grow that the Jewish community is being massacred (→10).

How the world reacted

Empire rallies to the British cause

London, 9 September
All over the world the British Empire has rallied to Britain's side. Australia and New Zealand are already at war, Canada will be at war tomorrow. In Palestine Arabs and Jews have put aside their differences. All over Africa governors, councils and petty monarchs have committed themselves to the Allies.

There are only three places where support is uncertain. In Egypt neutral Italy is marginally more disliked than Britain, but there is no animosity towards Germany. In South Africa the pro-Axis premier, Hertzog, had to be replaced by Smuts. India's millions remain unenthusiastic (→ 10).

Mussolini: keeping out of the war.

"We're staying out," says US president

Washington, 9 September
In a "fireside chat" radio talk, President Roosevelt said that he hoped fervently that the country could stay out of the war. He said: "I have seen war and I hate war"; he hoped that the United States could remain neutral. Asked today at a press conference whether the United States would be able to "keep clear", he said he would make every effort to do so. Roosevelt faces opposition from isolationists in Congress as he tries to revise the Neutrality Law to allow the Allies to buy US arms (→ 15).

Italy: Mussolini to keep out of the war

Rome, 9 September
Italians learnt with relief today that their country will not join its German ally in war – despite its traditional rivalry with France. Many will not be surprised if Italy's Fascist dictator, Mussolini, uses the conflict further north as a pretext for invading the Balkans from Albania, which he overran in April.

Fiercely anti-Bolshevik Fascists have taken to the streets to demonstrate against the Hitler-Stalin pact. The Nazi and Soviet rape of Poland, another Catholic country, has also shocked Italians (→ 31/10).

Mixed feelings from the rest of the world

3 September
Germany's Scandinavian neighbours were swift to make their positions clear. The Danish government, anxious to keep vital trade links with Germany open, has promised to observe strict neutrality. Sweden, a prime supplier of iron ore to the Germans, and Norway followed, the latter ordering its shipping to head for neutral or Norwegian ports without delay. General Franco, the dictator of

Spain, has meanwhile appealed to world leaders not to let the war escalate beyond Poland itself, urging them to "save the peoples the sufferings and tragedy which the Spaniards experienced".

President Smetona of Lithuania called for national unity. Soldiers of belligerent nations entering Belgium will be disarmed and interned, and Switzerland has banned the export of arms and services to any country at war.

Civvy Street goes to war with sandbags, gas masks, rattles, blackouts and records

Britain, 9 September
Despite continual appeals to the public to take care of their gas masks, they are piling up in lost property offices in hundreds every day. London Passenger Transport Board now has nearly 2,000, inscribed only with such names as "Mum" or "Aunt Ethel". "The extraordinary thing is that their owners do not seem in any hurry to claim them," said an official.

Some 38 million gas masks were distributed last year and school children have been given practice in wearing them in class. Many cinemas refuse admission to people without gas masks; they are even carried by prisoners in the dock at the Old Bailey. Leaflets advise householders on how to gas-proof a room or know a gas by its smell – of pear drops, geraniums or musty hay. Attacks will be announced by wardens with hand rattles.

The tops of pillar boxes have been painted with chemical paint that will change colour in the presence of gas. Shoulder bags for the cardboard boxes in which gas masks are supplied are very popular, although it is suspected that perhaps a third of them do not contain gas masks but packed lunches. Sandbags, piled round the doors and windows of shops and public buildings to deflect blast, are increasing in price. The government supplied 400 million to local au-

Even the moon has to be blacked out.

thorities at 3d each (1¼p/5¢), but private purchasers are being charged from 6d to 9d because speculators have bought up large stocks. Blackout material is scarce, as are brown paper and black paint. Drawing pins and number eight size torch batteries have disappeared. London Zoo has destroyed all of its poisonous and many of its non-poisonous reptiles in case they escape during a bomb attack. On 3 September the BBC merged regional broadcasting into one "Home Service" of hourly news bulletins, announcements and gramophone records. The BBC's television service to 20,000 viewers was suspended (→ 12).

Fun and games at the Fuhrer's expense for Territorial anti-aircraft men.

1939
September

Su	Mo	Tu	We	Th	Fr	Sa
					1	2
3	4	5	6	7	8	9
10	11	12	13	14	15	16
17	18	19	20	21	22	23
24	25	26	27	28	29	30

10. Ottawa: Canada declares war on Germany.→

10. Poland: The army attacks the Germans along the river Bzura near Poznan (→ 12).

11. Berlin: Germany responds to a threatened British naval blockade by announcing a counter-blockade (→ 29/11).

11. Germany: Cipher experts crack the British merchant ship code, identifying convoy meeting points.

11. India: Plans for federation are postponed indefinitely.

12. Abbeville, France: The Anglo-French Supreme War Council meets for the first time.→

12. Poland: Polish troops push the Germans south of Kutno and recapture Lowicz (→ 14).

12. Britain: The home office opens an inquiry into blackout rules (→ 22).

13. Paris: The stained glass windows are removed from Notre-Dame for safety.

14. Russia: *Pravda* launches an anti-Polish propaganda campaign (→ 15).

14. Atlantic: The U-boat U39 attacks the aircraft carrier HMS *Ark Royal*, but is sunk by accompanying destroyers; 43 crewmen are captured (→ 17).

14. Budapest: Hungary refrains from declaring its neutrality on the grounds that it is not threatened by Hitler.

14. Poland: The Germans enter Gdynia, west of Danzig (→ 16).

15. Moscow: Russia concludes a cease-fire treaty with Japan, enabling it to pull forces away from Mongolia and look west.→

15. Canada: The first British transatlantic convoy sets sail.→

15. Britain: Motorists besiege petrol stations, although no date for rationing has been fixed yet (→ 22).

16. Britain: The Duke of Windsor is appointed a liaison officer with the French army.

16. Warsaw: On the eve of the Jewish New Year, *Luftwaffe* planes dive-bomb the Jewish quarter (→ 21).

Britain sends troops over to France

Western Front, 11 September
Four British army divisions, 158,000 men with 25,000 vehicles, have crossed the Channel to France without a hitch. The operation, carried out in great secrecy, brought men from all parts of Britain to ports in the south of England, where transports waited. An escort of destroyers picked them up as they set sail. If there were German U-boats in the area, they kept well away from the convoys.

Once ashore in France the men were taken to temporary barracks before being deployed at the front alongside their French allies.

The British soldier of today carries a good deal of extra equipment unknown to the men of 1914. Regular issue today includes gas mask, gas cape and two pouches each containing 60 rounds of ammunition. When wearing full marching gear, the infantryman carries a large pack on his back holding a greatcoat, a cardigan and a few personal belongings. In all, the equipment, with uniform, steel

Members of the British Expeditionary Force land "somewhere in France".

helmet and ankle-boots, comes to a weighty 70 pounds (32 kilograms).

But the British Expeditionary Force is still seriously short of equipment. A secret report by the British Chiefs of Staff reveals that of the 352 anti-aircraft guns assigned to the BEF only 152 have been delivered. And the British Advanced Air Striking Force, which requires a minimum of 48 light anti-aircraft guns, has received none at all. The number of aircraft is also well below strength (→ 12).

Western Front sees first skirmishes

Western Front, 12 September
General Gamelin's forces, advancing in battalion strength, have driven five miles (eight km) into Germany on a 15-mile (24-km) front in the Saarland. The French claim that their pressure on the Western Front has forced the Germans to transfer six divisions from Poland, a claim received with scepticism by British observers. The most likely explanation for German divisions moving to the west is the virtual collapse of Polish resistance. French talk of an offensive is also not being taken seriously. The advance into the Saar has brought the French to within half a mile of the Siegfried Line, and a frontal assault on such a formidable system of fortifications is judged to be out of the question (→ 24).

A French tank takes cover in a clump of trees while waiting to attack.

France creates new war departments

Paris, 13 September
Edouard Daladier, the French prime minister, sent the president of the republic, Albert Lebrun, the long-awaited details of his war cabinet today. The prime minister will retain the portfolios of war and national defence and in addition will take over foreign affairs. The former foreign minister, Georges Bonnet, goes to the ministry of justice.

There are two new portfolios, those of Raoul Dautry as minister of armaments and Georges Pernot as minister of blockade, each with responsibilities specifically related to the war effort. Daladier has taken such trouble over putting his team together because he is keen to have a war cabinet that will enable France to put recent divisions behind it and fight the war in a spirit of national unity. The task may prove difficult; several members of the new cabinet were until recently convinced that France must at all costs stay out of the war (→ 22).

September

Su	Mo	Tu	We	Th	Fr	Sa
					1	2
3	4	5	6	7	8	9
10	11	12	13	14	15	16
17	18	19	20	21	22	23
24	25	26	27	28	29	30

British ships stick together for safety

Halifax, Nova Scotia, 15 September
The first Atlantic convoy from Canada to Britain left today. From now on all ships carrying vital supplies of Canadian wheat and US munitions are to travel in convoys scheduled and protected by the Brittish and Canadian navies. It seems that the Royal Navy has learnt the lesson of the Great War when British merchant shipping suffered devastating losses from the U-boats. The first convoy sailed from Gibraltar the day before war broke out. The vital Glasgow-Thames coastal trade is now moving in convoys. Last week the first convoy from Liverpool set sail for the US.

Russia signs peace treaty with Japan

Moscow, 15 September
Russia and Japan have agreed an armistice in their four-month-old conflict along the Mongolia-Manchukuo [*Manchuria*] border. Both sides have been under pressure from Germany to settle the dispute since the signing of the German-Soviet non-aggression pact. Peace talks were initiated by Japan's new cabinet, appointed two weeks ago after Japan lost 17,000 men in one battle (→ 1/10).

Britons deprived of weather and school

London, 15 September
Britain has now been living for almost a fortnight without a weather forecast, the first deprivation of war. Another, not so badly missed, is schooling. Some 2,000 city schools have been requisitioned for use in Civil Defence, and a million unevacuated children have no classes to go to.

A National Register of the civilian population will be made on 29 September for the issue of identity cards and ration books. Petrol ration cards are already issued, but rationing, due to begin tomorrow, was postponed last night after motorists drained the pumps dry of "Pool" petrol at 1/6 (7$^{1}/_{2}$p/33¢) a gallon.

Air hero urges America to stay out of war

Washington, 15 September
The isolationist campaign against American involvement in the war is reaching a crescendo. In three days alone, a total of more than a million pieces of mail reached Capitol Hill, urging senators and congressmen to vote against selling arms to the Allies.

The isolationists have taken to the air waves. Several of their leading broadcasters are themselves members of Congress, many of them from the Middle West like Senators Borah Nye and Vandenberg. But their most effective advocate is Colonel Charles Lindbergh, who captured the imagination of America when, at the age of 25, he flew his monoplane, *The Spirit of St Louis*, non-stop to Paris.

Lindbergh married the poet Anne Morrow, the daughter of the banker Dwight Morrow of the House of Morgan. In 1932 their child was kidnapped and later found dead. Deeply embittered by their loss and by ghoulish publicity, the Lindberghs moved to Europe. Charles Lindbergh became close to the "Cliveden set" in Britain, who advocated appeasing Germany, and to the pro-German US ambassador Joseph Kennedy.

Lindbergh praised Nazi Germany's "sense of decency", called Hitler "undoubtedly a great man" and accepted a Nazi decoration.

Colonel Lindbergh makes his plea for continued American neutrality.

The isolationists generally are an outlandish mixture. They include conservative bankers who hate Roosevelt, and farm-state radicals who hate bankers; Irish-Americans who do not want the United States to be allied with Britain, and German-Americans who do not want to be enemies of Germany.

One of their leaders is Father Coughlin, the anti-Semitic broadcaster. Another is Fritz Kuhn, who founded the anti-Semitic "Friends of the New Germany" organization in 1933 (→ 14/10).

Canada adds weight to Empire and Allies

Ottawa, 14 September
Canada, the last of the great Dominions to declare war, will become the arsenal of the Allies, providing food, industries, convoy escorts and air training facilities, according to the prime minister, Mr Mackenzie King. He said: "Canada's liberties came down from those men in England and France who never hesitated to lay down their lives when their freedom was threatened."

Mr King will not bring in conscription, though, particularly not during an election campaign. Like most Canadians he abhors the idea of Canadians being fed into the Western Front as happened in 1914-18, and prefers the more profitable role of supplier of raw materials rather than men (→ 20/10).

Mackenzie King: boost for Allies.

17. Moscow: Russia promises to respect Finnish neutrality.

17. Warsaw: St John's Cathedral is bombed during mass; the dead are being buried in public parks as the cemeteries are full (→ 18).

18. Poland: The Battle of the Bzura ends. The Germans take 170,000 prisoners of war (→ 19).

18. Poland: Members of the Polish cipher bureau, with vital knowledge of the German *Enigma* code, flee the country and head for Paris (→ 1/10).

18. Berlin: A week after making his first broadcast to Britain, the Irish ex-Mosleyite William Joyce is given a contract with German radio.

19. Danzig: Hitler swears that Danzig will be German forever and Germany will fight to the bitter end (→ 20).

19. London: The first wartime episode of *It's That Man Again* (ITMA), starring Tommy Handley, is broadcast.

19. Poland: The Russian and German armies join up at Brest-Litovsk.→

20. Aachen: RAF planes clash with the *Luftwaffe*; two RAF Fairey Battles and one Messerschmitt are downed (→ 2/10).

20. London: The Allies reply to Hitler: they will fight on.

21. USA: Newspapers allege that senior Nazis, including Goebbels and Hess, have foreign investments worth over $12 million (£3 million).

21. Berlin: Reinhart Heydrich orders Polish Jews to be concentrated in a few urban areas as the first stage of a plan to exterminate them (→ 23).

21. Britain: The government publishes its "Blue Book" of pre-war diplomatic documents.

22. Britain: Petrol rationing is introduced (→ 29).

22. Poland: Russian troops take Bialystok and Lwow.→

23. Panama: American nations agree to a 300-mile (480-km) neutral zone off the American coast (→ 2/10).

23. Germany: Wireless sets are confiscated from all Jews.

Poland squeezed on all sides as Russians attack

German infantrymen advance on a deserted street in the suburbs of Warsaw.

One of the many Russian contingents crossing the border into Poland.

Besieged capital resists Nazi demands

Warsaw, 16 September

The besieged defenders of Warsaw today spurned a German demand for their surrender. Well positioned in powerful fortifications, Major-General Czuma's men have already fought off one determined attack by General Reinhardt's tanks.

In a battle lasting three hours the Poles inflicted heavy casualties on the Germans, knocking out 60 tanks and forcing Reinhardt to report that if ordered to continue the attack his 4th *Panzer* Division would not remain operational.

He then withdrew to his original positions, and when he was ordered to attack again replied that this was impossible. Since then the defenders have been subjected to constant artillery bombardments, but the attention of the German High Command has been centred on the Battle of the Bzura. This battle came about when General Tadeusz Kutrzeba struck at the flank of the armoured forces racing towards Warsaw on the night of 9 September and considerably disrupted the German advance.

The Poles enjoyed a gallant but all too brief moment of success. The Germans, belatedly realizing the seriousness of the situation, turned on them with the full force of their armour and Stukas, putting all the troops in the battle under the command of General von Rundstedt. The battle is now coming to an end. It will be remembered as a most gallant episode in Polish history, but only a few of the troops engaged in it have managed to fight their way through to Warsaw. Now it is that city's turn to face the invader's might (→ 17).

After the invasion: a Messerschmitt on patrol over Polish countryside.

Russia sends Red Army across the border

Warsaw, 17 September

Stalin has stabbed the Poles in the back. Just before dawn this morning the Red Army invaded Poland along the 800-mile (1300-kilometre) length of the border. The Polish High Command, desperately engaged with Hitler's *Panzers*, has been taken by surprise and the Russians have brushed aside the border guards. The Red Army is advancing virtually unopposed and this must surely signal the end of Polish resistance. The government, harried from the air, is fleeing towards the safety of the Roumanian border. The Russians set the scene for their attack with complaints that Polish aircraft had violated the Soviet frontier, and two days ago *Pravda* attributed what it called Poland's "military debacle" to its "brutal treatment" of its national minorities, especially the Polish Ukrainians and White Russians.

"The ruling circles of Poland," said the newspaper, "boasting their love of freedom, have done everything possible to transform the Western Ukraine and Western White Russia into colonies deprived of rights and delivered up to looting by Polish colonists." Now, in a move carefully coordinated with the Germans, Stalin has sent in his army, claiming that the aim of Germany and Russia is to "restore peace and order in Poland, which has been destroyed by the disintegration of the Polish state". His proclamation pledges that Russia and Germany will help the "Polish people establish new conditions for its political life". The Poles, with long experience of Russian rule, know better (→ 18).

▷

Aggressors divide their Polish spoils

Poland, 23 September

The victors are quarrelling over the carcass of their prey. There have been clashes between Russian and German forces as the Germans, in hot pursuit of the fleeing Poles, cross the demarcation line agreed in the secret clauses of the pact signed by Molotov and von Ribbentrop.

In one clash the Germans opened fire on a Cossack unit, killing two men, and the Russians retaliated with a sabre charge in which 15 Germans were killed before the local commanders put a stop to the fighting.

According to the agreed division of the spoils, the Russians are to occupy all the territory east of the Narew-Vistula-San River Line, an arrangement which does not please the Germans who have fought a number of sharp engagements with the Poles east of that line.

They have had to hand over the city of Lwow to the Russians, and there is much grumbling among the German soldiers who accuse the Russians of leaving them to do all the fighting and then walking in to take possession.

It is also understood that there are political as well as military problems with the division of spoils, and there is much haggling going on between Hitler and Stalin, which could lead to revisions in the demarcation line even while the fighting continues.

Hitler is demanding that the province of Lublin be added to his share of Poland, which would effectively move the demarcation eastwards to the river Bug. Stalin, unwilling to clash with the rampaging *Panzers*, is likely to give in to these demands. This would mean Germany getting the whole of Warsaw, due to be divided under the original agreement. The Germans also have their eyes on Gdynia, the largest port on the Baltic, and the manufacturing towns of Lodz and Katowice, the centre of the Silesian coalfields. Nearly all Poland's heavy industry could be put to churning out war material for the Nazis.

There may be rich pickings for the Russians though, such as the communications centre of Brest-Litovsk, rich agricultural lands, and, most important of all, the oilfields of Galicia (→ 23).

Red Army soldiers distributing Moscow newspapers to Polish peasants.

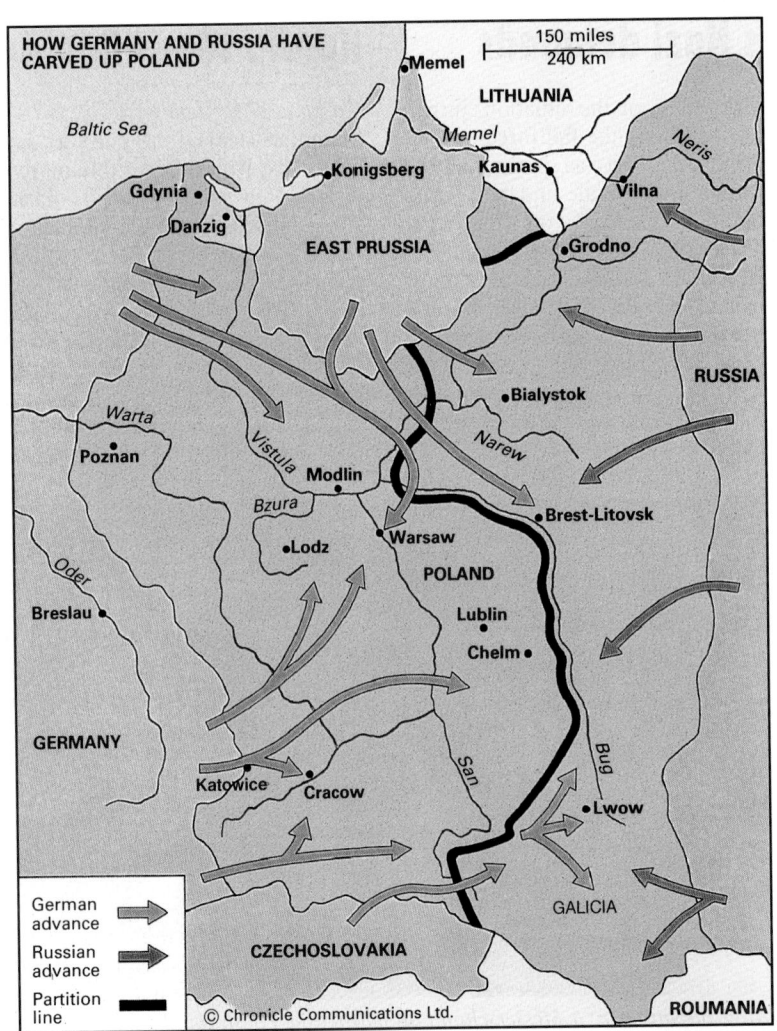

HOW GERMANY AND RUSSIA HAVE CARVED UP POLAND

150 miles / 240 km

Baltic Sea

LITHUANIA

Memel

Memel

Konigsberg

Kaunas

Neris

Gdynia

Vilna

Danzig

EAST PRUSSIA

Grodno

RUSSIA

Warta

Bialystok

Poznan

Vistula

Narew

Modlin

Bzura

Brest-Litovsk

Oder

Lodz

Warsaw

POLAND

Breslau

Lublin

Chelm

GERMANY

Bug

Katowice

Cracow

San

Lwow

GALICIA

German advance →
Russian advance →
Partition line

CZECHOSLOVAKIA

© Chronicle Communications Ltd.

ROUMANIA

Help for Poland is too little, too late, say British MPs

Westminster, 20 September

The British government was denounced by the Labour opposition in parliament this afternoon for failing to help Poland enough against the German and Russian invaders. The strong criticism came after the prime minister, Neville Chamberlain, had given one of his periodic reviews of the war. Arthur Greenwood, the deputy opposition leader, told MPs: "It is a matter of very deep regret that once an understanding was reached with Poland she was not provided far more generously with sorely needed assistance." He warned that the nation's now active allies might become merely passive friends unless Poland gets more help.

Tory, Labour and Liberal MPs all rejected what they deemed a spurious peace offer by Hitler in a recent speech in which the German leader said that he harbours no ill-will towards Britain and France. Parliament's view was that Britain must not be deflected.

Secret meeting for Allied war leaders

Britain, 22 September

Members of the Allied Supreme War Council, including the British and French premiers, met today at a secret rendezvous in Hove, Sussex. Chamberlain, with Lord Halifax, the foreign secretary, and Lord Chatfield, the minister for co-ordination of defence, travelled to the meeting by train. M Daladier, with General Gamelin, the C-in-C on the Western Front, Admiral Darlan, the Chief of the French Naval Staff, and M Dautry, arrived by air.

A communique afterwards said that the Allied leaders discussed supplies of munitions and reached "complete agreement" on plans for the future conduct of the war. Though the meeting was supposed to be secret a large crowd gathered outside the building and when Mr Chamberlain left he was loudly cheered. A woman broke through the police cordon and threw a bunch of flowers at him (→ 29).

U-boat sinks British aircraft carrier

The enemy view of the sinking British aircraft carrier "Courageous".

Hebrides, 17 September
HMS *Courageous*, one of the navy's oldest aircraft carriers, was torpedoed by a U-boat west of here today. It is the navy's first serious loss of the war. *Courageous* was leading a submarine hunt when U29, which had sunk three British tankers, scored two direct hits.

Although the *Courageous* sank in 15 minutes, just over half of the 1,000-strong crew were rescued. Marine M Reidy, a printer in civilian life, said: "The only boat they could get out was the cutter, and directly they got down to the water,

she sank." The survivors jumped overboard, and many were in the water for over an hour, keeping up their spirits by singing "Roll out the Barrel" and "Show Me the Way To Go Home". Another survivor said the sea "was so thick with oil we might have been swimming in treacle". Three days ago U39 got near enough to fire several torpedoes at *Ark Royal*, the navy's most modern carrier. She was not hit, and her destroyers sank U39. Today, although destroyers escorting the sinking *Courageous* dropped depth charges, U29 got away (→ 24).

Blackout blamed for road carnage and crime wave – but sweethearts benefit

Britain, 22 September
Road accidents after dark have trebled in the three weeks since the blackout began, according to the Metropolitan Police Commissioner. Figures are not being issued, but there have been many fatalities and injuries because of the total lack of street lighting and the extinguishing of car headlights. Coroners have commented that motorists who hug the white lines in the middle of roads are bound to have accidents and have called for kerbs to be painted white. "Only cross the street where there are traffic lights," advised the Birmingham city coroner today.

Magistrates' courts have been packed with cases of blackout infringement by flashing torches and striking matches. Small fines are usual, but some offenders have turned aggressive when ordered to "put that light out!". A London chambermaid who attacked a policeman with a poker, saying "Who are you ordering about?", got six months' hard labour from Clerkenwell court. A girl who flashed her torch in policemen's faces, saying "It's better than bumping into people", was given a month by Wisbech magistrates. Pedestrians are injuring themselves by walking into lampposts and other obstructions; several have fallen

Don't step out after blackout.

into canals and drowned. They are now to be allowed to carry torches provided that these are obscured by two thicknesses of tissue paper and pointed downwards. Posters urge them to "wear something white".

"Pinpoint" street lighting is to be introduced at road junctions, and masks for car headlamps with louvred slits are being designed. Railway carriages, hitherto pitch black, are being fitted with dim blue bulbs. The only beneficiaries of the blackout have been burglars and courting couples (→ 13/10).

Roumanian prime minister shot down

Bucharest, 22 September
Armand Calinescu, the prime minister of Roumania, was assassinated yesterday by members of the pro-Nazi Iron Guard who blocked the path of his car with a wooden cart and then pumped pistol shots into him and his bodyguards.

The assassins then shot their way into the radio station where they broadcast a proclamation claiming that "the death sentence on Calinescu has been executed".

They were then overpowered and last night taken to the spot where they had killed the prime minister. There, watched by a great crowd, they were shot. Their bodies will lie there for 24 hours (→ 12/11).

Roosevelt wants to end arms embargo

Washington, 21 September
President Roosevelt today faced a joint session of Congress in person and urged the repeal of the Neutrality Act's embargo on arms sales to belligerent countries. "Our acts must be guided by one single hard-headed thought – keeping America out of this war," the president said. Allowing arms to be sold on a cash-and-carry basis would be "better calculated than any other means to keep us out of war".

The coming of war in Europe has weakened isolationist sentiment, and the president asked to speak to Congress because he thought that the battle over the arms embargo could be won (→ 7/10).

The Duke of Windsor raises his hat to an enthusiastic crowd awaiting his arrival at the War Office on the morning of Monday 18 September. He is expected to discuss taking up a war appointment shortly.

1939
September

Su	Mo	Tu	We	Th	Fr	Sa
					1	2
3	4	5	6	7	8	9
10	11	12	13	14	15	16
17	18	19	20	21	22	23
24	25	26	27	28	29	30

Cruel jackboot stamps on Poland

The bodies of Polish troops taken in battle and shot by the Germans.

Warsaw, 23 September
The Nazi jackboot is crushing Poland with a brutality which is even drawing protests from German army officers, horrified at the conduct of the SS and *Gestapo* in the occupied territories.

A catalogue of horror is being built up of the German treatment of the Jewish community. It tells of rabbis being burnt with their holy books, of families being herded into synagogues and burnt alive, of a girl trying to say goodbye to her doomed father but herself being shot for her "impudence".

At the village of Pilica all the Jewish men were rounded up and taken to the marketplace where they were forced to shout in German: "We are traitors of the people." They were then shot.

While especially degrading treatment is being meted out to the Jews, all Poles are feeling the weight of German oppression. Any display of dissent brings instant, cruel retaliation from the conquerors.

The Gestapo operates at night, and in the morning posters give the names of those executed for carrying arms, for having insulted the Fuhrer or spoken ill of the *Reich*. This is the other side of the *Blitzkrieg*. It is called *Schrecklichkeit*, meaning frightfulness (→ 7/10).

German general dies mysteriously

Berlin, 22 September
Mystery surrounds the death of Baron Werner von Fritsch, the former army commander sacked by Hitler in 1938 after being framed by the *Gestapo*. An official statement says von Fritsch died today after being hit by machine-gun fire near Warsaw, while visiting the regiment of which he was honorary colonel. But there are no other reports of serious fighting on that front.

Von Fritsch, who created the modern German army, fell out with Hitler when the Fuhrer revealed plans for war. Himmler then said he was a homosexual. He was exonerated, but never reinstated.

The disgraced Baron von Fritsch.

24. Germany: France fires guns on the eastern border and bombs the German Zeppelin base at Friedrichshafen.→

24. Atlantic: U-boats sink a Swedish steamer and a British cargo ship (→ 26).

24. Roumania: Poland's President Moscicki and its armed forces chief, Marshal Smigly-Rydz, are interned (→ 26).

25. Germany: Bread and flour rationing is introduced (→ 1/10).

25. Germany: Hitler issues his fourth war directive, ordering increased attacks on Allied shipping and a swift conclusion to the Polish war (→ 27).

26. Atlantic: A German claim to have sunk *Ark Royal* is not denied by the admiralty (→ 30).

26. France: The Communist Party is dissolved and its leaders interned.→

26. London: Winston Churchill claims that Britain is winning the U-boat war.

26. Poland: The German Eighth Army, under the German army's C-in-C, von Brauchitsch, joins the attack on Warsaw.→

27. Germany: Hitler tells his commanders that he intends to attack France in November.

27. Germany: Hitler formally establishes the *Reichssicherheitshauptamt* [Reich Chief Security Office] (RSHA) under Reinhart Heydrich, who now heads the *Gestapo*, the Criminal Police (*Kripo*) and the Security Service (SD) (→ 7/10).

28. Poland: Modlin garrison surrenders after 18 days' siege.→

29. Moscow: Russia and Estonia sign a ten-year assistance and trade agreement, giving Russia important naval bases on the Baltic (→ 5/10).

29. New York: Fritz Kuhn, the leader of the pro-Nazi German-American *Bund*, is jailed.

29. Britain: A national census is taken to obtain information on rationing and mobilization.

30. Berlin: Germany warns Britain that armed ships may be sunk without warning.→

"Graf Spee" sinks British cargo ship

South Atlantic, 30 September
A British cargo ship, SS *Clement*, was sunk this afternoon by a German pocket battleship off Pernambuco, Brazil. The fast, heavily-armed 10,000-ton *Admiral Graf Spee* was scouring the South Atlantic to disrupt the cargo traffic to Britain. Captain F Harris spotted the *Graf Spee* at 1am. She sent a sea plane which without warning machine-gunned the bridge. The chief officer was slightly hurt, but the 50-strong crew took to the boats before the *Graf Spee's* shells sank the *Clement*.

RAF loses planes in raid on naval base

London, 29 September
The RAF lost five Hampden bombers today in a daylight raid on the Heligoland area. The raid was in two waves. In the first, six Hampdens attacked two German destroyers but did no damage; the second wave of five planes was wiped out. These raids began on 4 September; one of the 29 aircraft engaged in the raid on that day, a Blenheim flown by Flt-Lt K C Doran, came out of the cloud over the Kiel Canal so low that Doran could see washing on the deck of the pocket battleship *Admiral Scheer* (→ 2/11).

Income tax raised to meet cost of war

Westminster, 27 September
Income tax has risen to 7/6 in the pound (37.5%) – the highest level in the nation's history. Sir John Simon, the chancellor of the exchequer, announced this and other huge tax increases in his special war budget presented to parliament this afternoon. Surtax rates will range from 1/3 (6.25%) on incomes of £2,000 ($9,000) to 9/6 (47.5%) for incomes of over £30,000 ($134,000).

Duties on tobacco, beer and spirits are also raised. The price of a bottle of whisky will be 13/9 (69p/$3.07) in future. The chancellor said: "I am confident taxpayers will want to fight hard to win the war."

Hitler batters Warsaw into surrender

Germany and USSR sign treaty which seals Poland's fate

Eyes to the sky in Warsaw as German planes continue to bombard the city.

Hitler watches his troops march.

Moscow, 29 September
At five o'clock this morning, after much haggling interrupted by a state banquet in the Kremlin and a visit to the Bolshoi to see *Swan Lake*, Molotov and von Ribbentrop signed a new pact on behalf of their masters. It is officially called the "German-Soviet Boundary and Friendship Treaty". In effect, it carves up eastern Europe into zones of influence between the Nazi and Communist states.

The public clauses settle their boundaries in the "former Polish state" and with a deep cynicism assure "the people living there a peaceful life in keeping with their national character". Yet it is the secret clauses which hold the truth of the treaty. Under them Russia is to be allowed a free hand with the Baltic states while Germany gets the whole of Warsaw and the province of Lublin. Ominously, under another secret clause both countries pledge that they "will tolerate in their territories no Polish agitation" and "will suppress ... all such agitation" (→ 30).

Warsaw, 27 September
The gallant defenders of Warsaw capitulated today after enduring three days and nights of constant bombardment by guns and bombers. The once beautiful city is a burning wreck. There is not a building still intact and 40,000 people are thought to have died or been injured. So complete is the German command of the air that they have even been using Ju52 transport aircraft to tip more bombs on the city.

The people, fighting alongside the army, have suffered terribly. There is no water, no power, no gas, no food. The fires burn out of control because the water mains have been smashed.

German communiques have insisted that their bombardments have been directed at military targets. In fact, the whole of Warsaw was one huge target. The Church of the Saviour and the Ujazden Red Cross Hospital, with the red cross clearly marked on its roof, are among the buildings hit by bombs and shells.

Typhoid has broken out in the city and there is a desperate shortage of medicine and bandages to treat the wounded. Many people are buried under the rubble. Others risked death from shrapnel as they clawed at the ruins of their homes trying to rescue their entombed families.

Right to the end the Germans had little success in penetrating the city. Their tanks, which had roared across the open plains to surround it, were stopped by the permanent fortifications and the anti-tank traps dug by the citizens.

Polish soldiers using bayonets kept the German infantry at bay, and it became obvious to the Germans that they would suffer severe casualties in street fighting against determined opposition. The decision was then taken to blast Warsaw into submission, which has been done with the utmost ruthlessness. The speed of its success does no discredit to the defenders. It simply confirms the terrible consequences of modern warfare.

General von Blaskowitz, who received the Polish surrender, has recognised the Poles' gallantry by allowing their officers to keep their swords and promising that their men would go into captivity for only as long as it takes to "dispose of the necessary formalities". The terms of the capitulation provide for the immediate succour of the civilian population and the wounded. But von Blaskowitz is known to be an officer of the old school. It remains to be seen if the SS and the *Gestapo* will honour his word.

Fighting continues at the fortress of Modlin some 20 miles (36 km) from Warsaw, where the garrison is holding out under intense bombardment. It is expected, however, that with the surrender of the capital, Modlin will also give up the struggle. This spells the end for Poland. Further resistance is impossible. But, as one surrendering officer told the victors: "A wheel always turns. This one will" (→ 29).

Exiled government finds French home

France, 30 September
General Wladyslaw Sikorski, who has been both prime minister and defence minister of Poland, has set up a Polish government in exile in Paris and is taking command of those forces which succeed in escaping from occupied Poland.

General Sikorski, who was in Paris when his country was overrun, has escaped the fate of the commander-in-chief, Marshal Smigly-Rydz, and the government who fled to Roumania and, after being sympathetically received, were interned when the Germans brought pressure to bear on the Roumanians.

Sikorski is a fervent Polish patriot who should be able to rely on moral support from France. Some – although by no means all – of the French leaders are embarrassed at letting Poland down in its hour of need (→ 7/10).

Driven by starvation, desperate citizens in the streets of one of Warsaw's most exclusive residential districts carve up the carcass of a dead horse.

1939
October

Su	Mo	Tu	We	Th	Fr	Sa
1	2	3	4	5	6	7
8	9	10	11	12	13	14
15	16	17	18	19	20	21
22	23	24	25	26	27	28
29	30	31				

Allies reject Hitler plan

London, 29 September
Neville Chamberlain, the British prime minister, today dismissed the German "peace offensive". This public rejection follows a series of private contacts leading from Hitler and Goering to Queen Wilhelmina of the Netherlands, a British diplomat in Oslo – and the omnipresent Birger Dahlerus, the Swedish businessman who was commuting between London and Berlin in the last days of peace.

In the House of Commons today Chamberlain said that Britain and France went to war to stop Nazi aggression and nothing had changed that position. This is taken as a reference to a conversation between Dahlerus and Ogilvie Forbes, a counsellor at the British legation in Oslo. Dahlerus claimed that Hitler and Goering had suggested Wilhelmina should issue a call for peace, which could be followed by a secret Anglo-German armistice meeting in Holland. At such a meeting Hitler would guarantee the security of Britain, France and the Low Countries.

But Chamberlain said Hitler's assurances and promises were worthless. He is equally dismissive of the Molotov-Ribbentrop call for the liquidation of the war and the promise of "consultations on necessary measures" if the Nazi peace effort failed (→ 3/10).

VC heads British Army on Western Front

Lord Gort in Whitehall with two members of the Sharpshooters Yeomanry.

Somewhere in France, 30 September
The Guards officer who has been appointed commander-in-chief of the British Expeditionary Force was skiing in Switzerland before the war. Coming down a mountain he collided with another skier. "Who the hell are you?" the victim demanded. "Gort," said the other. Thus the future C-in-C met the British secretary for war, Leslie Hore-Belisha, who soon afterwards appointed him military secretary.

John Standish Surtees Prendergast Vereker, Viscount Gort, is a soldier's soldier. He won the Victoria Cross in the closing weeks of the last war. In September 1918 he took the Grenadier Guards across the Canal du Nord, coming under heavy artillery and machine-gun fire. Though wounded, he crossed open ground to bring a tank into action. Wounded for a second time, he continued to direct the attack until the enemy position was taken and 200 prisoners captured. Gort became Chief of the Imperial General Staff in 1937, ahead of 90 more senior generals (→ 3/10).

Communists in the west are rocked by pact with Fascists

London, 30 September
Stalin's pact with Hitler and the carve-up of Poland between the two dictators has sent communists in the west reeling into confusion and demoralisation.

In London, Harry Pollitt, the British party's general secretary, had just published a pamphlet, *How to Win the War,* when Stalin gave orders that the war against fascism had to be attacked as an imperialist war. At the central committee meeting Pollitt protested violently, but the committee overwhelmingly voted to do as Stalin ordered. Pollitt has been sacked.

The French Communist Party's foreign affairs expert, Gabriel Peri, sits slumped over his desk in the offices of *Humanite* while juniors cobble up some sort of explanation for readers. With the party's leaders, Maurice Thorez and Jacques Duclos, maintaining a stunned silence, the party seemed to be heading for a break-up when the premier, Edouard Daladier, banned it, thus allowing it to stay silent and hide its humiliation.

Big business moves out to the country

London, 30 September
The great exodus from London goes on, with institutions, businesses and civil servants moving to country houses, colleges, spa hotels and large schools all over "safe" areas.

Much of the BBC has been removed to the west country: the drama department to Wood Norton, a country house near Evesham, the variety department to Bristol. The banks' central clearing house is at Trentham Park, near Stoke-on-Trent. The Prudential has gone to Torquay. Sections of the admiralty are at Bath, the war office at Droitwich and the air ministry in Worcester's former workhouse.

Some 3,000 country houses are now hospitals, stately homes like Blenheim and Longleat are housing public schools, and the Great Western Railway has moved its HQ to its Reading waiting room.

1. Poland: The last Polish soldiers in action, at the Hel naval base, surrender.→

1. Paris: Polish cryptologists arrive with a cargo of two *Enigma* machines (→ 31/10).

1. Britain: Winston Churchill makes his first broadcast of the war, saying Russia will stop Hitler's plans for the east (→ 18/11).

2. France: The government agrees to the formation of a Czech National Army in exile.

2. Germany: The RAF makes its first night leaflet raid on Berlin.

2. Panama: The Pan-American Conference sets up the 300-mile (480-kilometre) security and neutrality zone around the American coast agreed on 23 September.

3. London: Chamberlain dismisses German peace proposals outright (→ 18).

3. Poland: The German Tenth Army pulls out and heads for the Western Front.

3. France: The 1 Corps of the BEF moves into position on the border with Belgium (→ 11).

4. Lwow: Nikita Khrushchev announces the communisation of eastern Poland (→ 5).

5. Warsaw: Hitler makes a tour of the conquered capital before returning to Berlin (→ 7).

5. Moscow: Latvia and the USSR sign a mutual assistance pact, giving the Soviets sea and air bases on the Baltic.→

5. Germany: The Nazi anti-Semitic weekly, *Der Sturmer*, publishes a "Hymn of Hate" calling England the "curse of the world".→

6. China: Chinese forces repel Japan to win the First Battle of Changsha.→

7. Germany: To mark Himmler's birthday, Hitler appoints him Commissioner for Consolidation of the German Race; his task is to eliminate "inferior" peoples from the *Reich.*

7. Germany: Hitler issues a decree ordering Poles to be evicted from western Poland or killed (→ 12/10).

Germans get taste of food rationing

Berlin, 1 October

Despite their military triumphs Germans are facing restrictions on the home front. Food ration cards were introduced on 28 August and now cover meat (16 ounces a week, for instance), dairy products, sugar, eggs, bread, cereals and fruit. There are multi-coloured cards for the different types of food.

Farmers are exempt from rationing while miners are allowed larger amounts as "extra heavy workers". Petrol has also been rationed since the beginning of the war, reflecting Germany's concern about its vulnerability to an Allied naval blockade of its trade routes.

Japan purges anti-Soviet army chiefs

Japan, 1 October

Senior officers of the *Kwantung* army, the Japanese troops stationed in Japan's puppet state of Manchukuo [*Manchuria*], have been dismissed in the wake of the agreement which was signed in Moscow last month settling the border war with Russia.

Soviet forces had inflicted heavy casualties on the Japanese, and now the leaders of the vanquished army are paying the price. The failure of the anti-Soviet offensive has bolstered the cause of those in Japan favouring confrontation with US interests in the Pacific rather than with Russia.

Off-duty Japanese soldiers in China trying to wash off the grime of war.

Chinese ambush lures Japan to a defeat

Changsha, 6 October

Over 40,000 Japanese troops died here after an 11-day battle in which the Japanese expeditionary force suffered its first major setback against Chinese Nationalists since the outbreak of war two years ago. As well as heavy troop losses, the 120,000-strong Japanese force lost huge quantities of arms as it was ambushed by troops defending Changsha, the capital of Hunan.

For the Chinese the morale-boosting victory is being seen as vindication for the tactical switch to more mobile guerrilla warfare and proof that the retraining of troops is paying off. The Nationalists, led by Generalissimo Chiang Kai-shek, have been claiming for some time that Japanese supply lines were becoming over-stretched and that the enemy had been weakened by the Japanese-Soviet conflict. Ironically, it was the recent signing of the non-aggresssion pact with Russia which persuaded Japan that it could now safely resume the war against the Nationalists.

It was after years of Japanese imperialist activity in China that war finally broke out in July 1937. Japan occupied Manchuria in 1931, the province of Rehe in 1933, and was making plans for an autonomous state in the north. Since 1937 the Chinese Nationalists have lost Peking, Tianjin, Shanghai, and even the capital, Nanking, to the Japanese (→ 19/11).

Russia builds up influence over its Baltic neighbours

Moscow, 5 October

Stalin, given a free hand with the Baltic states by the German-Soviet Boundary and Friendship Treaty, has wasted no time in bringing pressure to bear on their fearful governments.

Even as von Ribbentrop, the German foreign minister, flew back to Berlin in Hitler's personal four-engined Condor on 29 September, the Soviet Union signed a Treaty of Mutual Assistance with Estonia, giving the Russians the right to occupy the naval bases of Narva, Baltiski, Haapsalu and Parnu. Today it is the turn of the Latvians to be forced into signing a "treaty of mutual assistance". Under this treaty the Russians have the right to establish military bases in Latvia.

Lithuania is next on Stalin's list. Specifically named in the German-Soviet pact, it has no chance of escaping the grip of the Red bear. "Talks" have started, but they can only have one conclusion: another "treaty of mutual assistance".

This means that the three Baltic states which escaped from the ruins of czarist Russia after the last war will once again be controlled by Russia. What remains to be seen is what action Stalin will take about his northern neighbour, Finland, which once also owed allegiance to the czars (→ 10).

Thousands of civilians are killed in bomb-shattered Warsaw

Warsaw, 6 October

The human cost of the *Blitzkrieg* that struck Poland is still being counted, but it is already known that as many as 25,000 Polish civilians lost their lives in the aerial and artillery bombardments. Most Poles died in Warsaw itself.

More than 60,000 servicemen died fighting the Germans, with many more wounded. It is the plight of the wounded, both soldiers and civilians, which is so horrific. The Germans refused to bring help to shattered Warsaw for three days after its surrender and many of the wounded died. It is not known how many Poles have been executed by the SS and *Gestapo*.

Victors and victims: while transporting their wounded away from the battle zone, Polish troops pass a column of advancing German soldiers.

Hitler triumphantly offers a fresh peace and a new order in eastern Europe

Berlin, 6 October
At noon today Hitler appeared in the *Reichstag* and spoke eloquently of his desire for peace. He said that he had no quarrel with France and had given his best efforts to fostering Anglo-German friendship. War in the west, he went on, would be a senseless waste of lives and wealth. He proposed a conference of leading European powers to prepare a statute giving peace and security for all. He also suggested that a set of rules should be prepared to make war less terrible.

Within hours of Hitler ending his speech, the British government dismissed his so-called peace proposals as "vague and obscure". The speech "abounded in perversions of the truth" and made no suggestions for reparations for the wrongs done by Germany to other peoples. In Berlin, neutral observers who listened to the Hitler speech described it as the same old tune the dictator has played after every act of aggression. Did he really believe that the British and French could be taken in? It seems that he had reason to believe that they could.

Diplomatic sources in Berlin say the Italian and Spanish envoys have been telling the Germans that a mood of defeatism prevails in France. According to one source, most of the French cabinet are pleading for a peace conference. However, Daladier, the premier, is resolutely opposed. He told the Senate foreign affairs commission that France and Britain are "fighting the war to put an end to the reign of aggression" and "will only lay down arms when peace is effectively assured" (→9).

US backs Poland's exiled government

Washington, 7 October
The United States will continue to recognize the exiled Polish government, the state department said today. Most of the 1939 Polish government is interned in Roumania, but General Sikorski has set up a government-in-exile at Angers, in France. Berlin will see the decision to treat this as a legal government as more evidence of anti-German feeling in America (→24).

Curfew set to save Land Girls' virtue

Wales, 4 October
Members of the Glamorgan Agricultural Committee met today to voice their anxieties about "gossip and goings-on" between Land Army girls and soldiers billeted around the farms in the area. A strict 9 o'clock curfew was urged to keep the girls, aged from 17 to 40, out of mischief during blackout hours. Only Alderman David Davis rose to their defence: "They are good-looking English girls, with the right spirit. Good girls do not need looking after" (→10).

What the British Tommy is wearing

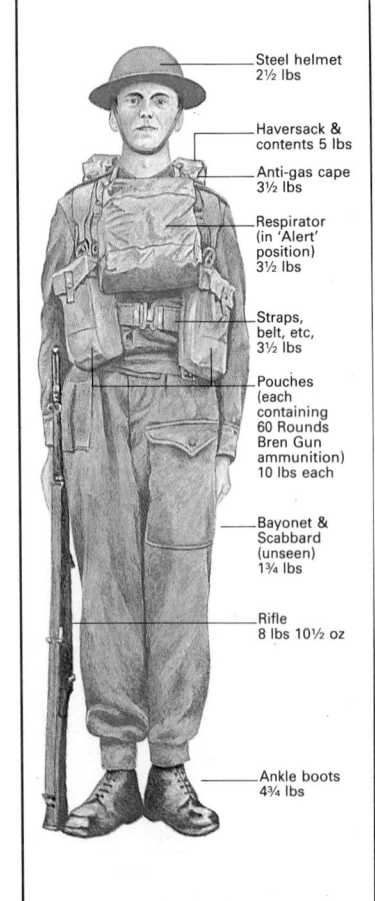

Steel helmet 2½ lbs

Haversack & contents 5 lbs

Anti-gas cape 3½ lbs

Respirator (in 'Alert' position) 3½ lbs

Straps, belt, etc, 3½ lbs

Pouches (each containing 60 Rounds Bren Gun ammunition) 10 lbs each

Bayonet & Scabbard (unseen) 1¾ lbs

Rifle 8 lbs 10½ oz

Ankle boots 4¾ lbs

1939
October

Su	Mo	Tu	We	Th	Fr	Sa
1	2	3	4	5	6	7
8	9	10	11	12	13	14
15	16	17	18	19	20	21
22	23	24	25	26	27	28
29	30	31				

8. Germany: Hitler formally incorporates the Polish border areas into the German *Reich*.

9. Germany: Hitler issues war directive number six, ordering preparations for "Plan Yellow" – an attack on Holland, Belgium and France (→19).

9. Britain: War conditions have allegedly brought food profiteering, with tenpenny steaks quadrupled in price.

9. Helsinki: Finland calls up its military reserves in response to Russian pressure for border changes (→12).

10. Moscow: Russia signs a 15-year mutual assistance pact with Lithuania, completing its military presence in all three of the Baltic states (→15).

10. Britain: Recruitment into the Women's Land Army is suspended after 25,000 have enrolled.

11. Scotland: A Pacifist candidate draws 1,060 votes at the Clackmannan and East Stirling by-election.

11. Westminster: The war secretary, Leslie Hore-Belisha, says 158,000 BEF troops are now in France (→28).

11. Berlin: A false radio report of the British government's fall and declaration of an armistice leads to open rejoicing.

12. Helsinki: Russia presents its official demands for an exchange of territory (→14).

12. Cracow: Hitler appoints the Nazi lawyer Hans Frank to head the new administration for German-occupied Poland, now renamed the "General Government" (→26).

12. Europe: Eichmann begins deporting Jews from Austria and Czechoslovakia into Poland.→

13. Bletchley: Three people die when two express trains collide in the blackout (→3/11).

14. Britain: The 1940 edition of *Who's Who*, published today, gives Hitler four more lines than Chamberlain.

14. Moscow: Russia refuses to consider Finnish counter-proposals for a land exchange on their borders (→15).

Einstein alerts US president to power of "atomic bomb"

Washington, 11 October
President Roosevelt today ordered American scientists to investigate the feasibility of building an "atomic bomb".

A group of refugee European scientists is concerned that its German colleagues might use atomic energy to provide Hitler with a weapon with unimagined destructive power. It was Albert Einstein who persuaded a banker friend of Roosevelt, Alexander Sachs, to warn the US president of the possibility of an atomic bomb.

"What you're after", the president said, "is to see the Nazis don't blow us up." Then he called an aide and said: "This requires action."

Einstein: warning America.

Germans capture the "City of Flint"

North Atlantic, 9 October
A US cargo ship, the *City of Flint*, has been captured by the German pocket battleship *Deutschland* as part of efforts to damage British trade. The Germans searched the ship and seized her when they found supplies for Britain which they said were "contraband" under the Prize Rules for war at sea.

Now the *City of Flint* is heading for the Russian port of Murmansk with a German prize crew, which is hoping eventually to bring her to a German port (→23/10).

U-boat ace sinks British battleship

The great battleship "Royal Oak".

The hero of the day, Gunther Prien.

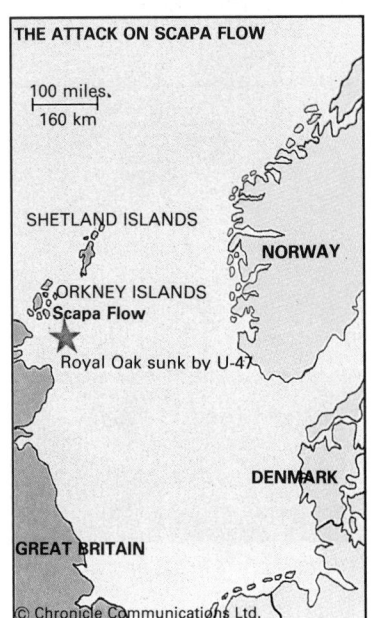

THE ATTACK ON SCAPA FLOW

100 miles.
160 km

SHETLAND ISLANDS

NORWAY

ORKNEY ISLANDS
Scapa Flow

Royal Oak sunk by U-47

DENMARK

GREAT BRITAIN

© Chronicle Communications Ltd.

Scapa Flow, 14 October

In a daring raid last night a German U-boat struck into the heart of Britain's navy – the anchorage at Scapa Flow, the base of Britain's Home Fleet. Luckily, most of the fleet were at sea. But the *Royal Oak*, a 29,150-ton battleship veteran of the Battle of Jutland, was sunk at anchor at 1am.

German aerial reconnaissance photographs had revealed a gap in the Scapa Flow defences. The entrance to Kirk Sound was only half blocked by cables and wires, leaving a 50-foot gap, quite big enough for a U-boat. Lieutenant-Commander Gunther Prien in U47 was immediately dispatched to strike before the defences were finished.

He spent the whole of yesterday on the seabed, and surfaced at 7pm. There was no moon but the *aurora borealis* made it seem like daylight to the Germans. There was a strong current against them so the U-boat had to stay on the surface. Boldly, the Germans just sailed right into the harbour.

Three of the seven torpedoes fired hit, and in 13 minutes the ship rolled over and capsized. Altogether 414 of the crew were saved, but the other 810 perished as the blazing ship sank in minutes (→ 16).

Gestapo wages reign of terror as Jews are herded into ghettoes

Germans burn Jewish religious equipment in Myslenice market square.

Warsaw, 13 October

Diplomats of neutral nations fear that the Germans are committing the most appalling, degrading cruelties against Polish Jewry. In one incident, on the Day of Atonement, the holiest day in the Jewish calendar, several thousand were imprisoned in the synagogue at Bydgoszcz and, refused permission to use the lavatories, were forced to use their prayer shawls to clean up the resulting mess.

Hundreds are shot every day with casual brutality, but there are signs that the *Gestapo's* campaign of terror is becoming more organized. Jews, even farmers, are being herded into ghettoes in the cities and allowed no contact with the rest of the city. They are thus under the complete control of the Gestapo and there must be fears for their ultimate fate (→ 19).

Rumours feed on war's uncertainty

London, 14 October

The news blackout by censors has left people eager to listen to rumour. And on the propaganda front the ministry of information is being beaten by Germany. The ministry's posters are disliked. One says: "YOUR Courage, YOUR Cheerfulness, YOUR Resolution will bring US Victory", making people ask whom they mean by "us"? The government and its friends? People are fed up with the leaflets carrying patronizing slogans such as "Kill that Rumour – It's Helping Hitler!". "Fred Karno's Army has nothing on the Ministry of Information," says the *Daily Mirror*.

Meanwhile, an estimated one million people are tuning in to "Lord Haw-Haw", broadcasting from Hamburg. He was nicknamed this by the *Daily Express* because of his upper-class drawl which announces "Jairmany Calling!". He presents amusing skits of old buffers in a London club grousing about the war or the "blasted socialists". Sir Jasper Murgatroyd and Bumbleby Mannering (a clergyman) are two more of his characters. Posing as a well-meaning adviser to the British, Haw-Haw needles them about food prices, war profiteers and censors who keep them in the dark. "Where is the *Ark Royal*? Britons, ask your government!" He says working men should "demand social justice and call for peace" (→ 22).

TITTLE TATTLE
LOST THE BATTLE

1939

October

Su	Mo	Tu	We	Th	Fr	Sa
1	2	3	4	5	6	7
8	9	10	11	12	13	14
15	16	17	18	19	20	21
22	23	24	25	26	27	28
29	30	31				

The wartime hero who now leads France

Paris, 11 October
Edouard Daladier today formally rejected Hitler's peace proposals. Thus a man who won the *Croix de Guerre* and the *Legion d'Honneur* in the Great War becomes his country's leader in what is now being called the Second World War.

Short and broad, Daladier exudes determination and courage. He has been called a *Jacobin*, with a passion for national defence. He was born in Carpentras in 1884, and entered national politics after the war when he was elected to the Chamber of Deputies as a Radical Socialist. He later became a minister in six different governments before becoming prime minister for the first time on the same day that Hitler became chancellor (→ 16).

Daladier speaks to the French people.

Senators attack Lindbergh neutrality talk

Washington, 14 October
Colonel Charles Lindbergh has caused deep anger both in Canada and in many circles in the United States by his radio broadcast last night in which he questioned the right of Canada "to draw this hemisphere into a European war because they prefer the Crown of England to American independence".

Senator Key Pittman of Nevada, the chairman of the Senate foreign relations committee, attacked Colonel Lindbergh's speech. The New York *Herald Tribune* called it "as fantastic in logic as it is bad in taste". Many Canadian leaders have already wired their fury to Washington, and Canadian ex-servicemen's groups have protested.

Lindbergh appeared to try to meet the charge that he is pro-German by calling for both Nazi and Communist influence in America to be "stamped out". He also said that British and French colonies in the Caribbean should be handed to the US to pay war debts.

Land Army girls in practical, loose-fitting dungarees prove to themselves and to their critics that they are as useful in the fields as any man.

15. Estonia: The government signs a treaty to return Estonians of German origin to the *Reich*.

15. Finland: Compulsory national service is introduced (→ 18).

16. Saarbrucken: The German army pushes French troops back to the Maginot Line.→

16. Germany: Warships are ordered to torpedo Allied merchant shipping without warning.

17. Ankara: Turkey breaks off talks for a defence treaty with Russia (→ 19).

17. Scapa Flow: German aircraft attack, damaging the depot ship HMS *Iron Duke*, which has to be beached (→ 20).

18. London: Chamberlain announces that eight Nazi planes have been shot down, and Churchill claims that one in three of the German submarine force have been sunk.

18. Stockholm: The Scandinavian kings meet Finland's president to discuss the Russian threat (→ 22).

19. Poland: A Jewish ghetto is established at Lublin, the centre of a Jewish "reserve" in eastern Poland (→ 30).

19. Berlin: The army High Command issues *Fall Gelb* [Plan Yellow], the strategy for a western offensive.→

19. Ankara: The Allied commanders Maxime Weygand and Archibald Wavell sign a mutual assistance pact with Turkey.

20. Australia: The prime minister, Robert Menzies, announces compulsory military training.

20. Britain: The war office recommends that soldiers at the front read both *Mein Kampf* and the *Communist Manifesto*.

21. Western Front: Opposing forces exchange artillery fire in heavy rain.→

21. North Sea: *Luftwaffe* raiders are repelled by a British convoy; four planes are shot down.

Firth of Forth is first UK target for "Luftwaffe" planes

Firth of Forth, 16 October
RAF Spitfires harried Junkers Ju88 bombers across the Edinburgh rooftops this afternoon after a dozen of the Junkers attempted to bomb warships in the Firth of Forth. Passengers on a train crossing the Forth Bridge were amazed to see great waterspouts springing up alongside the bridge.

The bombs inflicted casualties on the crew of the destroyer *Mohawk* which was one of four ships hit. Spitfires manned by the "part-time" pilots of the Glasgow and Edinburgh Auxiliary Air Force squadrons took off after the Junkers, and their cartridge cases fell like rain into the streets. They shot down two of the raiders (→ 17).

Knitting for victory is new British craze

Britain, 16 October
Women across the country are taking up their knitting needles in accordance with instructions from the admiralty.

Basic specifications for every shape of garment, from the seaboot stocking to the Balaclava helmet, have been issued and unending supplies are needed. A firm of wool experts is currently advising the admiralty on the production of detailed patterns, but in the meantime British knitters of all ages are being urged to get clicking.

Grandad does his bit with the needles.

Phoney war makes all quiet on the Western Front

French drink in an improvised bar underneath the Maginot Line.

Hitler inspects the Siegfried Line, in which Germany has put its trust.

Half a million soldiers waiting for a fight

Somewhere in France, 21 October
To the French it is *La Drole de Guerre*, and to the British the Phoney War. With 110 French and British divisions in the Allied front line, the almost complete lack of action to help the battered Polish forces has left public opinion in the west confused and – in France – increasingly demoralized.

Although the western Allies were not to know it, the Germans had awaited an attack with apprehension. In the critical first ten days of the war, during the Polish campaign, General Alfred Jodl, the *Wehrmacht's* Chief of Operations,

could spare only 23 active German divisions for the Western Front. Nine more divisions were then added, but there was apparently not one German tank in the front line during September, and the stock of ammunition would not have lasted for more than three days. And the *Luftwaffe* was in the east.

As Polish resistance began to collapse, General Gamelin told a meeting of the Supreme War Council at Abbeville on 13 September that he was calling off any further military action on the Western Front. He says his report "brought a sense of relief to everyone".

France puts its trust in the Maginot Line

Allied HQ, France, 21 October
The official Allied communiques referring to offensive action against German forces in the Saar sector of the front are phoney, like the war itself. Small French units last month advanced into territory evacuated by the enemy, and when a few weeks later, after the Polish campaign, the Germans advanced, the French pulled back.

On 21 September General Gamelin, the Allied C-in-C, said that he had no intention of attacking the Germans. He issued orders that if the enemy attacked in strength the French should retreat behind the

Maginot Line. This is a a series of elaborate fortifications built largely underground parallel to the German border [*see map below*].

The main forts are linked by a labyrinth of tunnels and protected by a battery of tank traps and gunposts. It is a formidable barrier, but one that has left the French army more intent on defence than attack. It also exists only along the border with Germany, leaving a long unprotected border with Belgium.

Behind Gamelin's attitude is a profound distrust of the British. He believes that the British intend France to fight the war alone.

British ideas for alternative uses of the German Siegfried Line.

British troops plug the Maginot gap

Western Front, 21 October
Since they arrived in France last month the British have spent their time digging defence works along the Belgian border to fill in the gap between the end of the Maginot Line and the Channel coast. The lucky ones are behind the lines, in billets or temporary barracks. The food, generally, is the traditional bacon and eggs, meat and two veg, bread and jam, washed down with a mug of strong tea (→ 28).

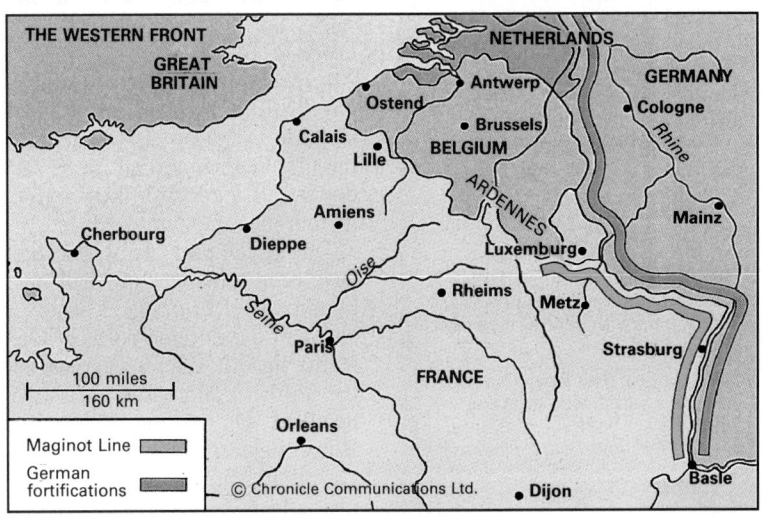

1939

October

Su	Mo	Tu	We	Th	Fr	Sa
1	2	3	4	5	6	7
8	9	10	11	12	13	14
15	16	17	18	19	20	21
22	23	24	25	26	27	28
29	30	31				

22. Berlin: The propaganda minister, Josef Goebbels, calls Churchill a liar in a radio broadcast.

22. Helsinki: Finnish envoys leave for new talks in Moscow (→ 3/11).

23. Murmansk: A German crew steers the US ship *City of Flint* into Kola Bay (→ 4/11).

24. Paris: Poland's gold reserves arrive, having travelled from Warsaw via Roumania and Syria.

25. Mexico City: Leon Trotsky is reported to have said: "Stalin is afraid of Hitler, and is right to be so."

25. Britain: The Handley Page Halifax bomber makes its maiden flight.→

26. Cracow: Hans Frank takes up his post as governor-general of Poland.→

26. Britain: The Auxiliary Military Pioneer Corps is formed.

27. Vatican: Pope Pius XII issues his first encyclical, condemning racism, dictators and treaty violations.

28. Bratislava: Joseph Tiso becomes the first president of Slovakia.

28. Berlin: Himmler issues his *Lebensborn* decree, urging single German women to dispense with the "bourgeois custom" of marriage to bear racially pure children (→ 19/11).

28. France: The BEF is reported to have enough food to feed its nearly 200,000 troops for 46 days (→ 10/11).

30. London: A government white paper exposes Nazi brutality towards dissidents and Jews, including the concentration camp system (→ 2/11).

30. Britain: *The Lion Has Wings,* the first war film of the conflict, is shown.

31. Italy: Mussolini reshuffles his cabinet, replacing pro-Nazi members with neutral members (→ 8/12).

31. At Sea: The Royal Navy starts a world-wide hunt for the pocket battleships *Admiral Graf Spee* and *Deutschland*.→

Allied ships search the ocean for U-boats

North Atlantic, 31 October
The Royal Navy is stepping up its offensive action against German submarines. Since the *Royal Oak* was sunk at anchor in Scapa Flow a fortnight ago the fleet has stayed at sea. German battleships have seized at least six merchant ships in the last month, but most damage has been effected by the U-boats.

The submarines have been laying mines on all the routes out of the Scottish supply bases and prowling close to shore. Only yesterday the U56 got in amongst the biggest ships of the fleet, including HMS *Hood*. Two torpedoes actually hit HMS *Nelson*, the flagship of the Home Fleet, but did not explode.

British destroyers, frigates and corvettes are in constant action against U-boats, relying mainly on an echo-sounding device from the last war, ASDIC (from its inventors, the Allied Submarine Detection Investigation Committee).

The pocket battleship "Deutschland".

Patches of oil can give rise to a "kill" claim, but these are often deceptive. The navy's claim of 18 U-boat sinkings since the war began is almost certainly too high (→ 13/11).

Wireless booms as families stay at home

London, 24 October
A boom in sales of wireless sets and gramophones is a sign of the way the blackout has transformed home life in Britain. Sales have leapt by about 30 per cent. The misery of travelling in the blackout (and the closing of theatres and cinemas after 6pm) disrupted social life. Entertaining has virtually ceased, so people stay at home and listen to records or radio shows such as *Band Waggon* or *ITMA*. Families whose children are not evacuated are being drawn closer together. "There are many firesides where the family groups itself as it has not done since Victorian days," says the *Daily Telegraph*. "Some of us have begun to ponder what our ancestors did in the dark winter evenings to while away the hours before bedtime."

The answer is that they sang their songs themselves, instead of playing records.

Polish cryptologists work on an Enigma

France, 31 October
Colonel Gwido Langer, the leader of the brilliant Polish cryptologists who have been working with their French and British counterparts to solve the mysteries of the German *Enigma* enciphering machine, arrived in France this month with his team and two Enigma machines. The Poles have thus fulfilled the orders of their General Staff that "In the case of a threat of war the Enigma secret must be used as our Polish contribution to the common cause of defence and divulged to our future allies".

It is hoped that the Poles, helped on their journey by the British Secret Service, will carry on with their work to enable the Allies to read the Germans' secret codes.

"Enigma": the top-secret machine.

Heinkel He111 is first German plane shot down over Britain

Scotland, 28 October
An He111 was brought down today by RAF fighters east of Dalkeith in south-eastern Scotland – the first German aircraft to be shot down over the British Isles. Two of its four-man crew survived.

During the past two weeks there have been a number of small raids by aircraft of *Luftflotte* 2, which is based in the extreme north of Germany, against shipping targets off the northern and eastern coasts of Scotland. On 16 and 17 October British fighters of the RAF's No 13 Group fought off attempted German attacks (→ 13/11).

Locals and soldiers inspect the wreck of the Heinkel He111 bomber.

Frank starts annihilation of Polish Jewry

Warsaw, 26 October

Hans Frank, the Nazi lawyer who was made governor of the General Government region of Poland a fortnight ago, has issued his first proclamation. It bodes ill for Polish Jewry and all those Jews from Germany, Austria and Czechoslovakia who are being transported in sealed cattle trucks without food or water to "Jewish reservations" in Poland. The officer in charge of this mass movement of people is said to be called Adolf Eichmann, described as an efficient bureaucrat.

Under Frank's orders all Jewish men aged between 14 and 60 are to be "obliged to work" on official labour projects. Some, organised into "work brigades", will travel each day to work in projects near the cities. Others are to be sent to special labour camps. As none of these camps exist the Jews will have to build themselves shelter in the harshest of conditions.

It is not only the Jews who are suffering under the Nazi occupation. All Polish citizens of Torun have been told that they must "leave the pavement free" for Germans because "the street belongs to the conquerors, not the conquered". They were also warned: "Whoever annoys or speaks to German women and girls will receive exemplary punishment. Polish women who speak to or annoy German nationals will be sent to brothels." Frank has set

Dr Frank: arch-enemy of the Jews.

out his policy: "The Poles will become the slaves of the greater German *Reich.*"

It is, however, the threat to the Jews which appears the more dangerous. The moves against them are so calculated that it is obvious that a long-term plan has been put into operation; there are now real fears for their future. This plan is believed to have been discussed at a meeting in Berlin, called by Reinhart Heydrich, of all SS commanders in Poland. Heydrich, rabidly anti-Semitic (possibly because he is falsely rumoured to be part-Jewish), spoke chillingly of "the final solution of the Jewish question" (→ 30).

Nazis clamp down on Czech parades

Prague, 28 October

Czech students felt the full ferocity of Nazi occupation today – the 20th anniversary of their country's birth. Students parading through the city were charged by armoured cars and prisoners are reported to have been tortured by the *Gestapo*.

Street fighting broke out later in the city centre with Sudeten Germans using pistols, whips and rifle-butts against Czech patriots. One student is reported to have been killed by revolver shots, and more than 3,500 people are packing the city prisons. It is six months since the German army marched into Prague – on the pretext of "restoring order" (→ 15/11).

The front cover of a magazine previews the film "The Lion Has Wings", featuring newsreel of an air attack on a German fleet.

Su	Mo	Tu	We	Th	Fr	Sa
			1	2	3	4
5	6	7	8	9	10	11
12	13	14	15	16	17	18
19	20	21	22	23	24	25
26	27	28	29	30		

1. Poland: Germany formally annexes western Poland, Danzig and the Polish Corridor. This adds the new districts of Posen, Greater East Prussia and Danzig West Prussia to the *Reich.*

1. Poland: The western Ukraine is incorporated into the Ukrainian Soviet Socialist Republic (→ 2).

1. Netherlands: The government proclaims a state of siege in frontier areas and flood zones (→ 5).

1. Switzerland: Contingency plans are laid in case of an invasion.

2. Europe: Western White Russia is incorporated into Byelorussia (→ 6).

2. Britain: King George decorates five RAF pilots, leaders of a raid on the Kiel Canal.

2. Berlin: Hitler recalls his ambassadors from Moscow and Rome for consultation.

3. Britain: After complaints from employers and trades unions, the blackout is reduced by an hour. It now runs from half an hour after sunset to half an hour before sunrise (→ 20).

3. Moscow: Russia and Finland continue talks on an exchange of territory; the Finns refuse to give Russia a military base in Finland (→ 13).

3. South Africa: The prime minister, General Smuts, promises to defend British colonies in Africa if required (→ 9).

4. Oslo: A "German scientist who wishes you well" leaves a prototype proximity mine fuse and a report with details of German weapons research on a British consulate windowsill.

4. Britain: Rear Admiral Hugh Sinclair, the head of MI6, dies and is succeeded by Colonel Stewart Menzies.

4. Norway: The Norwegian admiralty reports that it has interned the German crew of the captured US freighter *City of Flint* after she docked at Haugesund, en route from Murmansk to Germany (→ 6).

"Cash and carry" law ends American arms embargo

Washington, 4 November

President Roosevelt today signed the new Neutrality Act repealing the embargo on the export of arms to belligerent countries. His signature releases at least £44 million of arms ordered by Britain and France before the embargo came into effect with the declaration of war.

Between 300 and 400 aircraft are said to be waiting in crates in American ports for shipment to Britain or France, and orders for at least another 2,500 have been held up.

Congress passed the Neutrality Act in 1935 and renewed it in 1936 and 1937. It was backed by isolationists who believed that America was pressured into war against its interests in 1917 and who insist that it must remain neutral and keep out of any European conflict.

On 21 September the president went before Congress and asked it to repeal the law. The Senate responded on 28 October and the House of Representatives followed.

The vote reflects a perceptible shift in American public opinion towards the Allies, due mainly to stories of Nazi atrocities.

In theory, the embargo affected all belligerents, so its lifting could allow Germany, as well as the Allies, to buy arms from American factories. In practice, Britain and France control the seas, so the lifting of the embargo is being hailed as a great victory for the Allies.

A warlike spirit stirs in America, despite isolationism, as news of Nazi atrocities reaches more people.

Su	Mo	Tu	We	Th	Fr	Sa
			1	2	3	4
5	6	7	8	9	10	11
12	13	14	15	16	17	18
19	20	21	22	23	24	25
26	27	28	29	30		

British told of Dachau concentration camp

London, 2 November
Fresh news of Nazi brutality at the Dachau concentration camp, set up near Munich in 1933, has reached the British public. A Jewish refugee from Vienna told readers of the *Daily Telegraph* today how he was arrested without reason last year.

Crammed into a small railway compartment for 14 hours, the transportees were forced to look upwards at the electric light for the whole journey; those who complained were shot or stabbed to death by the guards. Three were executed immediately on arrival at the camp. The refugee writes: "I was one of 18,000 prisoners. We slept 200 in a hut built to accommo-

date, perhaps, 50. There was a single washbasin for every two huts." He tells how inmates who had not been able to reach the basin had buckets of ice-cold water thrown over them at 4.30am. Prisoners were made to stand in the square of the camp for up to ten hours in all weather, including sleet and snow.

Frequent executions were part of the brutal regime. Thus the Nazis hope to keep "undesirables" like Jews, homosexuals, communists, religious fundamentalists and gypsies under control. Camps operate at Ravensbruck, Sachsenhausen and Buchenwald. The signs are that the system is being extended into occupied Poland (→ 4).

Inmates of Dachau, described in Nazi propaganda as "political repeat offenders" – "persons who would not stop their agitation and subversive activity".

Jews told to form ghetto in Warsaw

Poland, 4 November
Today the *Gestapo* ordered Warsaw's Jews to move into an area of the city which will be designated as a ghetto. They have taken 24 hostages whom they will shoot if the Jews do not comply. The area will eventually be surrounded by barbed wire and placed under guard.

With the conquest of Poland, some two million Jews have come under Nazi rule. The victorious German soldiers have been taught since their schooldays to hate the Jews as the age-old "enemies of the German people".

It is no surprise, then, that 5,000 Jews have already been killed and countless numbers terrorized in random attacks. More than a million live in, or have fled eastwards into, the Soviet-occupied zone, but there is little hope for those trapped in the General Government area governed by Hans Frank.

Just three weeks after the invasion a senior SS official, Reinhart Heydrich, outlined plans to clear western Poland of Jews. They are to be moved east and "resettled" in labour camps and ghettoes.

Adolf Eichmann, a former emigration officer, has been put in charge of resettlement and the movement of Jews to Poland. He sent a transport of Czech Jews to Lublin last month; many fear that the Nazis intend to move all Jews under their control into the General Government area's cramped conditions (→ 7).

How wives and children coped when the men were called up

London, 4 November
Nearly a million British men have been called up to join the services, and the wives and families they have left behind are in many cases experiencing financial hardship. The average pay of a private soldier, naval rating or aircraftman is 2/- (10p/45¢) a day, of which married men allot half to their families. The wife of a private therefore receives 7/- a week stopped from her husband's pay, and a government allowance of 17/-, plus 5/- for the first child and 3/- for the second. The money is paid weekly at the post office.

Average wages on the eve of the war were £3/9/- (£3.45/$15.39) for men, £1/1/2/6 (£1.62¹/₂p/$7.25) for women. Many service wives with young children have to find part-time work or home work such as sewing to make ends meet. Meanwhile the cost of living is rising by over ten per cent.

There is a wedding boom, many couples marrying before the man is called up. The number has increased by 100,000 over 1938, reaching 459,000. But despite the call-up there are still 1,270,000 unemployed. Family life for many re-

volves round visiting their evacuated children. For those who cannot afford to travel, cheap tickets at single fare are allowed once a month on Sundays. There are widespread complaints that the billeting allowances are inadequate. The 8/6 (42¹/₂p/$1.90) a week has been increased to 10/6 for boys over 15, but hosts say that they often have to feed boys of 11 and upwards out of their own pockets. The government has brought in compulsory contributions from parents of 6/- a week. In the absence of air raids, many evacuees are heading home.

5. Germany: Hitler sets 12 November as the date for the attack on the Low Countries and France.→

5. Paris: Churchill visits the French Marine Headquarters.

6. London: A tramp is found dead inside a wall of sandbags.

6. Moscow: Molotov says Russia's aim is peace, and blames the war on the forces of world capitalism.

7. London: A double agent, Paul Thummel, passes details of the planned German western offensive to the Czech government in exile.

7. Germany: The western attack planned for 12 November is postponed due to bad weather (→ 8).

7. Warsaw: The edict ordering the city's Jews into a ghetto is withdrawn (→ 19).

8. Britain: One in three listeners tunes in to the first episode of the BBC's drama-documentary *Shadow of the Swastika*, featuring Marius Goring as Adolf Hitler.

8. Netherlands: Reports of German movements on the Dutch border cause the government to widen the defensive flooding zone (→ 10).

9. Berlin: The press and radio accuse Britain of organising the Munich beercellar bomb.

9. South Africa: An alleged Nazi plot by armed blackshirts to sabotage vital industries in Johannesburg and Pretoria is revealed.

10. London: Chamberlain is suffering from gout.

10. Western Front: Germany sends reinforcements to the Siegfried Line (→ 20/11).

10. Amsterdam: The US consulate advises Americans to quit the Netherlands (→ 11).

10. Netherlands: The main defensive area is flooded.

11. Europe: The Allies exchange friendship messages to mark Armistice Day.

11. Berlin: The foreign office repeats earlier assurances that the neutrality of Holland and Belgium will be respected (→ 14).

Hitler escapes beercellar bomb blast

Munich, 8 November

Hitler's speech in the *Burgerbraukeller* on the anniversary of his 1923 *putsch* was shorter than usual and afterwards he hurried off to catch the Berlin train. Minutes later a powerful explosion wrecked the place, killing eight people and injuring 60. Hitler, told of the bomb, cried: "Providence intends me to reach my goal!"

The bomb had been hidden in a pillar immediately behind the spot where Hitler had been speaking. Hours after the explosion no official statement was forthcoming; then Freemasons and Jews or disgruntled Nazi party members were blamed.

According to the much-delayed final version, Georg Elser, a cabinet maker with communist sympathies, had been picked up on the Swiss border and found to possess plans of the beercellar. Interrogated by the *Gestapo*, he confessed.

Another version, however, is that Himmler pulled Elser out of a concentration camp and made him plant the bomb as a means of boosting the Fuhrer's popularity.

Himmler then had a brainwave. He ordered his Gestapo agents, who had been duping the British with a yarn about a big anti-Hitler conspiracy, to kidnap two British intelligence officers on the Dutch border so that he could blame the British for the bomb plot *[see story below]*. German radio reports "stupendous" demonstrations of support for Hitler (→ 9).

Unaware of the threat to his life, the Fuhrer addresses Nazis in Munich.

The Munich beercellar in ruins after the bomb blast: but Hitler gets away.

Churchill predicts victory in sea war

Westminster, 8 November

Winston Churchill, the first lord of the admiralty, stirred the House of Commons today with a rousing speech about the Royal Navy. He openly admitted that it had suffered greater loss of life than all the other forces, British and French, on land, sea and air. But "we are gaining a definite mastery over the U-boat attack ... and in the end we shall break their hearts," he said.

He poured ridicule on German claims to have sunk the aircraft carrier *Ark Royal* several times, and said: "We should be quite content to engage the entire German navy, using only the vessels which at one time or another they declared they have destroyed" (→ 19).

"City of Flint" is back in US hands

Bergen, 6 November

Captain Joseph H Gainard told today how his US cargo ship, *City of Flint*, was taken by the German battleship *Deutschland*. A party from the *Deutschland* came aboard on 9 October and declared the ship a prize of war. The Germans painted out all US insignia and headed for Murmansk in Russia, and then for Germany. But they were stopped by the Norwegian navy, and another German ship ordered them to Haugesund where the US ship was returned to her captain (→ 27/1).

Gestapo arrests British bomb suspects

Venlo, Holland, 9 November

Two British agents in Holland who believed that they were in contact with army officers plotting to overthrow Hitler were today kidnapped and carried off into Germany. For the past month Captain S Payne Best and Major Richard Stevens had been meeting a Major Schaemmle at Venlo, five miles (eight km) from the German border.

To prove his *bona fides* Captain Best arranged for a special news item to be broadcast on the BBC German Service. Major Schaemmle then promised to produce the general who was leading the plotters.

When Best and Stevens turned up at Venlo this afternoon, they were told the Germans were afraid of venturing too far inside Holland. The British agreed to rendezvous at a cafe a few yards from the German border. There they noticed that the German barrier had been lifted. The next moment their car was hit by machine-gun fire and they were seized by a posse of Germans.

"Major Schaemmle", it turned out, was in fact a *Gestapo* officer, Walther Schellenberg. Immediately after the Munich bomb, Himmler had ordered Schellenberg to kidnap the Britons (→ 12).

Dutch tipped off on Nazi invasion plan

Brussels, 5 November

King Leopold of the Belgians and Queen Wilhelmina of the Netherlands have been alarmed by confidential messages warning them that Hitler plans to invade their countries within a matter of days. The messages came, via the Dutch military attache in Berlin, Colonel Jacobus Sas, from a Colonel Hans Oster of German military intelligence. The two sovereigns are holding urgent talks at The Hague to decide what to do to save their countries from catastrophe (→ 12).

The crew of the "City of Flint", happy to be back in control.

1939
November

Su	Mo	Tu	We	Th	Fr	Sa
			1	2	3	4
5	6	7	8	9	10	11
12	13	14	15	16	17	18
19	20	21	22	23	24	25
26	27	28	29	30		

Queen wants women to keep up their "vital work" at home

London, 11 November

Queen Elizabeth broadcast an Armistice Day message to the women of the Empire from Buckingham Palace tonight, while the king listened on a wireless in another room. "War has at all times called for the fortitude of women," she said, "but now we, no less than men, have real and vital work to do. To us also is given the proud privilege of serving our country in her hour of need.

"The tasks you have undertaken cover every field of national service." But these tasks are not for every woman. It is the worries and irritations of carrying on wartime life in ordinary homes which are often so hard to bear. Many of you have had to see your family life broken up, your husband going off to his allotted task, your children evacuated to places of greater safety.

"The king and I know what it means to be parted from our children and we can sympathize with you." (The two princesses have remained at Balmoral since the outbreak of war.) "All this has meant sacrifice and I would say to those who are feeling the strain: You are taking your part in keeping the Home Front, which will have dangers of its own, stable and strong."

So far 45,000 women have been recruited as volunteers for the women's services – the WRNS (3,400), the ATS (24,000), the WAAF (8,800) and the nursing services (8,000). Recruiting for the WRNS (Women's Royal Naval Service) has been halted because the waiting lists are already so long. The ATS (Auxiliary Territorial Service) takes women from the ages of 18 to 43. The age limit for the WAAF (Women's Auxiliary Air Force) has been raised to 50 for those with experience. Women pilots are being accepted in the Air Transport Auxiliary which flies planes from the factories to their squadrons.

Recruiting has also been suspended for the Women's Land Army, for which 25,000 women have registered. Only a proportion of those who have completed training have yet been found work. The Marchioness of Reading, who founded the Women's Voluntary Service for Civil Defence (the WVS) last year, says that nearly 500,000 women have volunteered for it (→ 7/12).

Queen Elizabeth prepares for her Armistice Day broadcast to the Empire.

A woman warden at work in London.

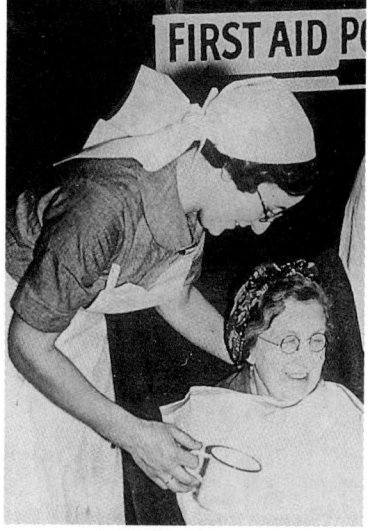
Nurses of the Order of St John.

Women members of the ATS practise their new skills on a Harrods van.

12. Germany: Hundreds of dissidents and Jews have been arrested in the search for the Munich bombers.

12. Germany: Clothes rationing cards are issued (→ 23).

12. Roumania: King Carol offers his services as a mediator between the belligerents (→ 16).

13. Moscow: Finnish delegates leave for Helsinki after peace talks break down; Stalin orders preparations for war against Finland.→

13. Britain: HMS *Blanche* is mined and sunk off the Thames Estuary, the first destroyer lost by the Royal Navy (→ 20).

13. London: General Henry Crerar sets up the Canadian military headquarters (→ 17/12).

14. Berlin: Hitler rejects Queen Wilhelmina's and King Leopold's offer of mediation.

14. Europe: The Allies agree to draw up defensive lines on the river Dyle in Belgium if Germany attacks (→ 17).

14. London: General Sikorski, the head of the exiled Polish government, arrives.

15. Prague: The *Gestapo* arrests and summarily executes nationalist protesters at the funeral of Jan Opletal, a student leader wounded in protests on 28 October (→ 17).

15. France: Three hours are added to the working week, making it 43 hours long.

16. Roumania: King Carol's offer of mediation is rejected by both sides (→ 22/12).

16. Britain: The cost of living rose by 2.5 per cent in October.

17. London: The Allied Supreme War Council endorses the plan to defend the river Dyle against Nazi attack.

17. Paris: The ex-president of Czechoslovakia, Eduard Benes, sets up the "Czech National Committee" (→ 18).

18. Czechoslovakia: Martial law is declared in Prague (→ 19).

18. London: The IRA is blamed for four bombs in Piccadilly (→ 23/12).

Allies turn deaf ear to royal peace plea

London, 12 November
In his Sunday evening broadcast Mr Churchill told his listeners that the first ten weeks of the war had gone well for the Allies. But no one supposed it was going to be a short or easy war. "It may be that at any time violent and dire events will open," said the first lord of the admiralty. "If so, we shall confront them with fortitude." He disregarded the peace appeal issued last week by King Leopold of the Belgians and Queen Wilhelmina of the Netherlands. The two sovereigns offered "in a spirit of friendly understanding" to assist in seeking "the elements of an agreement" before war begins in western Europe. The appeal is seen as a forlorn attempt to avert a German invasion (→ 14).

King Leopold: advocate of peace.

ENSA gives its first concerts of the war

France, 12 November
The first concert given by ENSA (Entertainment National Service Association) took place "somewhere in France" with the British Expeditionary Force (BEF) behind the Front today. ENSA – which has been organized by Basil Dean, the theatre director – is a union of professional organisations of actors and musicians. The veteran actor-manager Sir Seymour Hicks was master of ceremonies and appeared in a sketch with Claire Luce. Gracie Fields was the star. There were also songs from Dennis Noble, conjuring by Duveen and tap dancing by the Three Astors.

Dutch liner sunk by German mine: 86 die

North Sea, 18 November
A Dutch passenger liner today became the latest civilian ship to fall victim to German mines. The *Simon Bolivar* sank with about 400 passengers and crew aboard. It is estimated that 86 people, many of them women and children, have lost their lives.

People were playing games on deck when a terrific explosion hit the *Simon Bolivar* under the bridge. Captain Voorspuiy was killed instantly. The liner's oil pipes burst and the ship listed heavily, making it difficult to lower the boats. Many passengers swarmed down the ropes or jumped over the side.

A Sister of Charity nun was rescued clinging to a piece of driftwood. One British passenger, Sydney Preece of Maidenhead, put his three-year-old daughter in a wooden box and swam with it through the oil-covered icy water for nearly an hour.

Many of the survivors were landed at an east coast port. An air raid warning immediately after sent them hurrying for the air raid shelter. There were heartrending stories of children whose parents had drowned, and one West Indian lost his own wife and two children but managed to rescue a white child aged three.

Dutch public opinion is outraged because the mine was in a major traffic lane. International law, as well as common humanity, requires

A U-boat crew takes its last meal in the open before putting to sea.

that any such mine-laying must be notified. The Dutch believe that the mines are a deadly new magnetic type. This view was supported today by a Danish skipper, Captain Knudsen, giving evidence in Copenhagen about the sinking of his ship, *Canada*, off the Humber on 4 November. The Germans, who claim that their U-boats sank 115 ships in the first two months of the war, are clearly putting a further massive effort into the war at sea. The total British tonnage lost so far is small – only around 300,000 out of nearly 18 million tons. No one knows how many mines are already laid (→ 21).

Finland mobilizes as peace talks fail

Helsinki, 16 November
Finland mobilized its forces today as the talks over Russia's demands for an exchange of territory broke down in acrimony. Russia, seeking to protect its naval bases at Leningrad and Murmansk, from possible attack by Germany is demanding the cession of strategic Finnish territory and the lease of Finnish ports in exchange for land in the desolate swamps and forests of Karelia.

The Finns, fearful that this would merely be the prelude to a Soviet takeover of their country, are refusing. It is now obvious that they are prepared to go to war against their giant neighbour to defend their nation (→ 26).

"Luftwaffe" bombs Shetland Islands

Shetland Islands, 13 November
German bombers appeared out of the mist today and dropped bombs on British soil for the first time in this war. Damage was confined to a deserted crofter's cottage and a rabbit. The bombers – which had flown nearly 600 miles (960 kms) – missed naval vessels and anchored flying boats. The Germans claimed hits on a cruiser and two aircraft. "This is only the beginning," said their spokesman (→ 20).

Spy fever grips Britain as censors check the mail for clues

London, 16 November
Britain is in the grip of spy fever, although more than 6,000 suspected men and women have already been detained. In the first few days of the war, the entire detective force of Scotland Yard was employed in rounding up suspected enemy agents and sympathizers who had already been identified by the intelligence services. They have been detained for the duration of the war.

Hundreds of thousands of items which leave Britain by post every week for neutral countries are being examined and censored, mainly at Liverpool. A staff of 1,700 linguistic experts examines letters not only for what they say but also for messages in invisible ink.

Workers in a postal censorship department in the north of England.

1939

November

Su	Mo	Tu	We	Th	Fr	Sa
			1	2	3	4
5	6	7	8	9	10	11
12	13	14	15	16	17	18
19	20	21	22	23	24	25
26	27	28	29	30		

19. Warsaw: The first barricades are erected around the Jewish ghetto (→ 23).

19. Czechoslovakia: Fifty thousand people are reportedly under arrest; the Nazis execute three more dissidents (→ 2/1).

19. London: Churchill proposes mining the river Rhine by air (→ 20).

19. China: The Nationalist government at Chungking orders a winter offensive against the Japanese.→

20. Britain: *Luftwaffe* planes start parachuting mines into the Thames Estuary, having dropped the first magnetic mines into coastal waters on 18 November.→

20. Germany: Hitler issues a second directive for the attack on the west.

20. Britain: The minesweeper HMS *Mastiff* is blown up by a mine (→ 21).

21. Britain: German mines damage the cruiser HMS *Belfast* and sink the Japanese liner *Terukuni Maru*.→

21. Westminster: Chamberlain says that German merchant shipping will be seized in retaliation for mine attacks.

22. Britain: A national savings scheme is launched under the slogan "*Lend to Defend the Right to be Free.*"

22. Britain: Navicerts, warrants first issued in 1915 to neutral ships carrying cargoes not harmful to the Allies, are reintroduced.

23. Cracow: Dr Frank orders all Jews over the age of ten in the General Government area to wear armbands marked with the Star of David (→ 27).

23. North Atlantic: In a brief battle, the German warships *Scharnhorst* and *Gneisenau* sink the armed merchant cruiser HMS *Rawalpindi*, killing 265.

23. Germany: Food rationing for pets is announced.

25. Britain: After attempts to save New Forest ponies in the blackout by painting them like zebras, they are removed to safe pastures.

Germans unleash the magnetic mine

An awesome new weapon: the king inspects Ouvry and Baldwin's mine.

A last view of the destroyer "Gypsy", blown up by a German mine.

Portsmouth, 25 November

The Royal Navy's Mine and Torpedo School at HMS *Vernon*, Portsmouth, may soon have an antidote to the German magnetic mine, which on 21 November sank the destroyer HMS *Gypsy* and put the new cruiser HMS *Belfast* out of action. Since the war began magnetic mines have also been responsible for sinking 29 merchant vessels.

Conventional contact mines are buoyant and easy to sweep. Magnetic mines, which the Germans have been laying in British coastal waters, harbours and estuaries, especially the Thames Estuary, have proved more complicated. They lie on the seabed and are activated by the magnetic fields which all steel-hulled ships have. They have been laid by U-boats, E-boats, destroyers and, since 18 November, by aircraft dropping them by parachute.

Because of the growing number of sinkings the admiralty has placed top priority on recovering an intact mine. On 20 November the minesweeper HMS *Mastiff* was blown up when she attempted to recover a magnetic mine in a fishing net. In the evening of 21 November a soldier on duty at the artillery range at Shoeburyness saw a low-flying Heinkel He111 drop an object by parachute in the nearby Thames Estuary. The admiralty was immediately informed and two mine experts, Lieutenant Commanders R C Lewis and J G D Ouvry, were dispatched to the scene.

By now the tide in the Thames Estuary was on the ebb and, stepping out across the mudflats, they were able to locate the mine. Noting that it had two brass fittings, which clearly had to be removed to make it safe, they made a rubbing so that a nearby army workshop could make a non-magnetic brass tool.

At dawn Lewis and Ouvry were joined by Chief Petty Officer Baldwin and Able Seaman Vearncombe, who brought with them non-magnetic tools.

Ouvry and Baldwin now made their way out to the mine, realising that they had to make it safe before the tide covered it once more.

There was also the fear that the mine might be acoustic, and so they had to approach it very gingerly. One detonator and then another were identified and carefully removed, the second ticking loudly. Luckily for them the clock had jammed. It had been designed to activate the mine hydrostatically when it settled on the seabed.

Now made safe and towed ashore by tractor, the mine was taken to HMS *Vernon*. During the next 18 hours, having steamed out the 60 pounds of explosive, the scientists were able to establish exactly how it worked (→ 26/11).

Survivors of the mined "Simon Bolivar": a father holds his motherless son.

Japan takes Chinese city of Nanning

Nanning, S China, 24 November

The Japanese claimed today to have occupied the strategically important city of Nanning, despite fierce resistance by 100,000 Chinese Nationalist troops.

The capture of Nanning would be Japan's first major victory since its forces advanced west into Kwangsi province in a bid to deprive the Chinese of their last remaining links with Indochina.

The loss of Nanning has effectively diverted the Chinese from their winter offensive, which the *Kuomintang* leader Chiang Kai-shek had declared would drive the Japanese back to the lower Yangtze river and the pre-1937 borders. Instead, the Chinese have now lost a key supply route and face a new threat on their southern flank. The Japanese claim that they now control the road which hitherto had been the route for 70 per cent of China's supplies from Indochina.

Last night Chiang Kai-shek ordered his remaining reservists into Kweichow and Yunnan to reinforce security on the Yunnan-Hanoi railway – now China's only link with Indochina.

The Japanese High Command, however, is now intent on continuing its advance, aiming to sever China's connection not only with Indochina but also with Burma. This would leave Soviet Russia as the only source from which the Chinese could obtain war materials.

The Japanese occupation of Nanning was preceded by a heavy aerial bombardment. Civilian casualties were slight (→ 30/12).

If it's teatime, it must be the rush hour

London, 20 November

For the first time since war began, London's workers travelled home in blackout conditions this evening. On the first business day after the change from British Summer Time the blackout began at 4.30pm.

Many offices in the city closed at 4pm to give employees a chance to get home before the lights went out. Staff had started early and cut short their lunch hours to make up the time. Shops in the West End closed early, too, with only a few still serving customers after 5pm.

The change has brought the rush hour forward by an hour, and London Transport is considering adjusting services. This evening's bright moonlight made journeys in the darkened city more romantic than perilous (→ 2/1).

Himmler emerges as Hitler's henchman

Heinrich Himmler with the Fuhrer.

Berlin, 19 November

The most feared man in Germany and occupied Poland is a mild-mannered former poultry farmer with a yen for astrology and violence. Heinrich Himmler has been at Hitler's side from the earliest days of the Nazi Party. The son of a Bavarian schoolmaster, Himmler was present at the failed Munich *putsch* of 1923 and took over the SS in 1928. In the 1934 "Night of the Long Knives" he provided the firing squads for the killing of Ernst Rohm and other Brownshirts who were becoming a nuisance to Hitler. He organized the concentration camps and planned massacres of Jews and Poles in eastern Europe.

Himmler controls the *Gestapo* and the Security Service as well as the regular criminal police. As *Reichsfuhrer-SS* he commands the regime's notorious *Schutzstaffel*, or SS, for which he has drawn up a rigid code of conduct. A member can marry only after the Gestapo has investigated a would-be bride. Himmler plans to send the SS to Britain after the German invasion. If this happened, British Jews and socialists, first among the many targets for Nazi brutality, would have no illusions about their fate: the SS has been responsible for carrying out most of the Nazis' atrocities in occupied western Poland.

Nazis seize assets of their richest friend

Berlin, 24 November

Fritz Thyssen, the multi-millionaire steel magnate who fled from Germany at the beginning of the war, has had all his property seized by the Nazis because he refuses to return. Thyssen, who gave millions of *marks* to the Nazis to help them win power, says that he fears for his life because he opposed the war and the persecution of the Jews.

Along with other Ruhr industrialists, Thyssen believed the Nazis would discipline labour and allow businesses to prosper; instead, they got state control and forced levies. "What a fool I was," says Thyssen, in hiding in Locarno.

Hitler insults army generals in speech

Berlin, 23 November

Hitler today gave his senior generals a dressing-down for their opposition to his plans for launching an offensive against Britain and France. Summoning them to the chancellery, he told them that he had led the German people to great heights, while they had only shown lack of faith in him. "I am irreplaceable," he stormed at the unhappy brass-hats. "I shall attack France and England at the earliest moment. My decision is unchangeable."

1939

November

Su	Mo	Tu	We	Th	Fr	Sa
			1	2	3	4
5	6	7	8	9	10	11
12	13	14	15	16	17	18
19	20	21	22	23	24	25
26	27	28	29	30		

26. Britain: The prime minister, Neville Chamberlain, makes his first broadcast of the war, saying that Britain knows the secret of the magnetic mine (→ 12/12).

26. North Sea: Ten die when the Polish liner *Pilsudski*, on charter to the Royal Navy, is torpedoed and sunk.

26. Moscow: Russia claims that Finland has fired artillery into Soviet territory, and demands the withdrawal of Finnish troops from the Karelian isthmus, near Leningrad (→ 27).

27. Helsinki: Finland denies the Russian charges, saying the artillery fire was from the Russian side of the border (→ 28).

27. Norway: No Nobel peace prize is to be awarded this year.

27. Germany: "Aryans" are given 12 months to divorce Jewish spouses.→

28. London: The king signs orders in council for the seizure of German exports on the high seas.

28. Friesian Islands: RAF fighters attack *Luftwaffe* mine-laying seaplanes at Borkum.

28. Moscow: Russia renounces the 1932 Russo-Finnish non-aggression pact (→ 29).

28. Poland: Dr Frank orders the setting up of a *Judenrat* [Jewish council] in each ghetto, to carry out Nazi orders (→ 11/12).

29. USA: Fritz Kuhn, the leader of the German-American *Bund* [Association], is found guilty of grand larceny and forgery.

29. Britain: It is reported that the chancellor has received family jewels, gold and gifts from foreigners to help finance the war effort.

29. Moscow: Russia breaks off diplomatic relations with Finland.→

29. Madrid: Spain ratifies its friendship pact with Germany, adding secret clauses allowing Germany to use Spanish ports and promising cooperation on police and propaganda.

Russo-Finnish negotiations are over: Russian artillery fires its opening shot against the front line of the Finnish army.

Red Army launches attack on Finland

Helsinki, 30 November
Stalin, impatient at the Finns' refusal of his territorial demands, sent the Red Army crashing into Finland this morning. The main Soviet attacks are directed against the fortified Mannerheim Line on either side of Lake Ladoga and, in the far north, against Petsamo, west of the naval base of Murmansk.

Soviet warships are bombarding Finnish ports and Helsinki has suffered several severe bombing raids. There is no question of these raids being directed at military targets. Stalin is trying to do what Hitler did to Warsaw and bludgeon the capital into surrender with indiscriminate attacks on civilians.

The hospitals are filling with casualties, but, rather than destroying Finnish morale, the raids have aroused great anger and the Finns are determined to fight on.

On paper they would seem to have little chance, with only nine divisions totalling 130,000 men to face the 500,000 men in 26 divisions that the Soviets have unleashed. In the air, too, the Finns are hopelessly outnumbered, with only 145 planes against the Soviets' 1,000. It is not just a question of numbers, however. The Red Army's officer corps has been seriously weakened by Stalin's purges which led to the execution or imprisonment of many of the USSR's best officers.

It was noted during the little fighting that the Soviets undertook when they seized their Polish spoils that they were poorly led and that

Finnish soldiers ready for Stalin.

both their tactics and equipment were out of date. The Finns are hardy and well trained, especially in winter warfare, and if they can hold the Soviets until the snow comes they could give the Red Army a lesson in how to fight a winter war.

They are also led by the redoubtable Field Marshal Baron Carl Mannerheim, aged 72, a veteran fighter for Finnish nationhood against the Soviets, who has been appointed "Defender of Finland" and commander-in-chief. It is he who organized the fortifications which bear his name and on which the Finns are basing their defence in the south.

This line, although not as sophisticated as France's Maginot Line, consists of anti-tank "dragons' teeth", pill-boxes sited to cover the few tracks through the forest, and well-camouflaged weapon pits. What the Finns lack in numbers and heavy weapons they make up in mobility and individual skills.

It is doubtful, however, if their martial skill and ardour will enable them to resist the might of the Soviet Union for long (→ 1/12).

Hitler plans to put England under siege

Berlin, 29 November

Hitler has told his military commanders that England is the "leading enemy power" and "animator of the fighting spirit of the enemy". Defeat of England (as he calls Britain) is essential to final victory, he says, and in a secret directive he has ordered his navy and air force to carry the war to English industry, by mining and blocking ports, attacking shipping and bombing factories, oil tanks and food stores.

London, Liverpool and Manchester are identified as the most important ports which, Hitler says, handle 95 per cent of foreign trade. He says French ports should not be attacked unless they are used to break what he calls "the siege of England" (→8/12).

BRITAIN'S SEA POWER

Maintain it with your SAVINGS

The power that Hitler would destroy.

Germans tell Jews to wear armbands

Germany, 27 November

Anti-Semitic measures were stepped up today when "Aryan" Germans were warned to divorce their Jewish spouses or face the consequences. In the General Government area of Poland, where Jews are ordered to wear identifying armbands, typhus is reported to be sweeping the Jewish labour camp near Lublin, which houses some 45,000 deportees from Austria, Czechoslovakia and western Poland (→ 28).

Spiders weave web to help war effort

Britain, 30 November

Spiders are doing their patriotic best to help the war effort. Vice-Admiral Sir Harold Brown of the ministry of supply has revealed the existence of special web factories, where spiders are kept in comfortable conditions and fed the choicest rations. Their mission is to weave webs which are used in the making of lens sights. What next – squadrons of mosquitoes trained to bite Germans?

...and Hovis and butter for tea

The simple pleasures of life are unaffected by wartime rationing.

1939
December

Su	Mo	Tu	We	Th	Fr	Sa
					1	2
3	4	5	6	7	8	9
10	11	12	13	14	15	16
17	18	19	20	21	22	23
24	25	26	27	28	29	30
31						

1. Finland: Russia sets up the puppet "Democratic Republic of Finland", under Otto Kuusinen, at Terijoki (→4).

2. South Africa: The German liner *Watussi* is scuttled.

2. Britain: Conscription is extended to all men between the ages of 19 and 41 (→1/1/40).

3. South Africa: The Royal Navy battlecruiser *Renown* and aircraft carrier *Ark Royal* arrive at Cape Town.

4. Moscow: Russia rejects a Swedish offer to mediate in the war with Finland (→5).

5. Moscow: Russia rejects a League of Nations proposal to end the war with Finland.

5. Finland: Russian troops reach the Mannerheim Line, Finland's main defensive position (→7).

5. Washington: Roosevelt asks for $1,319 million out of his $9,000 million budget to be spent on defence (→10).

6. Germany and Poland: The SS has shot dead the inmates of Stralsund and Chelm mental asylums (→9/1).

7. Finland: A Russian division breaks through to the town of Suomussalmi.

7. Europe: Denmark, Sweden and Norway declare their strict neutrality in the Russo-Finnish war.→

7. Paris: George VI lunches with President Lebrun and the prime minister, Edouard Daladier.→

8. Washington: The USA protests at the British blockade of Germany, saying it interferes with the right of neutral nations to trade freely.

8. Rome: The Fascist Grand Council confirms the Axis alliance, but votes to remain out of the conflict (→9).

9. France: Corporal Thomas Priday, of the King's Shropshire Light Infantry, is killed, the first British fatal casualty on the Western Front.

9. Moscow: Russia discovers that Italy is sending military supplies to Finland via Germany (→16).

First RAF bomb drops on Germany

London, 3 December

RAF Wellingtons today dropped the first Allied bomb on German soil – by accident. Twenty-four aircraft, flying in sections of three at 20,000 feet (6,282 metres), attacked German shipping and scored, according to the RAF, a hit on a cruiser. However, one Wellington of 115 Squadron suffered a "hang up" when one of its bombs failed to drop. It later fell off on the island of Heligoland, the first bomb of the war to land on Germany. The planes were engaged by antiaircraft fire and Messerschmitt Bf109 and Bf110 fighters. One Bf109 may have been shot down; all the Wellingtons got home safely (→18).

Jews murdered on Nazi death march

Poland, 9 December

Two hundred Polish Jews, exhausted and starving, tonight crossed the river Bug into Soviet-occupied Poland. The Jews, mainly middleaged men from the cities of Hrubieszow and Chelm, have been "deported" – brutally forcemarched – from their homes by the Germans. The march took a week, in which time 1,400 of the original 1,800 Jews were murdered, often by soldiers competing to see how many could be killed in a given time. A further 200 died from exhaustion and maltreatment.

Queen, evacuee for a day, eats stew

Chichester, Sussex, 7 December

Two hundred South London children far from home today had the pleasure of sitting down to lunch with Queen Elizabeth. They shared a 3d (1¼p/5¢) menu of stewed steak, potatoes and jam tart with their royal visitor, who pronounced it all "very good".

The queen was visiting evacuees during a surprise tour of the area. It was a gesture of appreciation for the invaluable work of the Women's Voluntary Service during the evacuation programme.

Russia bombs Helsinki

Helsinki, 9 December
"General Winter", normally Russia's wartime ally, has come to the aid of the Finns. Bad weather has prevented the Red bombers from resuming the attacks on Helsinki which so badly damaged the Finnish capital in the first two days of the war.

The respite has given the Finns a chance to organize their defences. The fires caused by incendiary bombs have been put out, the rubble has been cleared, and the women and children who fled to the safety of the snow-covered forest have been properly evacuated.

The Finns are in no doubt that the Red bombers will return to their capital as soon as the weather clears, but now they are ready for them. Shelters have been prepared, fire-fighting teams set up, patients evacuated from hospitals and, with the women and children out of harm's way, Helsinki's defenders are confident they can now defy the bombers.

Eighty people died in the first raids, but their deaths and the photographs of the devastation, far from sapping the Finns' morale, have served only to strengthen their determination to carry on the fight.

Nowhere is this determination more evident than in the Finnish air force. With only 36 Dutch Fokker DXXI fighters backed up by obsolete Bristol Bulldogs, the Finnish pilots have torn into the swarms of Russian aircraft wherever they have appeared over the battle front.

It is true that the Russians, confident of overwhelming the Finns, have not sent in their most modern fighters, but the *elan* and skill of the

Helsinki lies in smouldering ruins after the first Russian air attack.

Finnish pilots in attacking large formations virtually single-handed have proved to the Russians that this war will not be a walkover.

The Finns' tactics are simple, brave and effective. They charge into the middle of the Russian formations, causing them to scatter like a flock of starlings, and then pick off their individual "birds".

These were the tactics used by Lieutenant Eino Luukkanen when he intercepted and shot down an SB-2 bomber on its way to Helsinki on the second day of the war. The four machine-guns of his Fokker riddled the twin-engined Russian and sent it crashing into the snow.

Help is on its way to the hard-pressed Finns. Britain is sending 30 Gloster Gladiators, and a volunteer squadron of Swedish pilots is being formed (→ 11).

Citizens leave Helsinki in a lull between Soviet bombing raids on the city.

King inspects army in the trenches

Western Front, 9 December
King George VI has completed a five-day visit to British and French troops defending the Western Front, which he began on 4 December. He has talked with men who had clashed with Germans during night patrols and with pilots who had shot down enemy aircraft. He also ate chicken pie and cheese in a French *estaminet* and was awarded the Maginot Medal, given to men who serve in the "impregnable" fortifications system. The king crossed the Channel in bad weather and was met by the British C-in-C, Lord Gort.

He made a 100-mile (160-km) tour of the British lines, inspecting trench systems built along the Belgian border to close the gap between the Maginot Line and the Channel coast. He frequently left his car to walk down lines of cheering troops paraded in his honour. On 7 December, visiting the French lines, he was met by President Albert Lebrun. General Gamelin took the king on one of the underground ammunition and troop trains. From a fortified observation post he looked across three miles of no-man's-land to the German defences and was shown the Order of the Day: "Be vigilant, keep cool and fire low – to the last round and the last man and a bit more ... your proud watchwords will be: '*On ne passe pas, on les aura*' [They will not pass, we will win]."

On his return to London the king sent Lord Gort this message: "I am satisfied from all you have shown me that the British soldier of today is at least the equal of his predecessor, both in efficiency and spirit."

King George VI on his tour of the trenches on the Western Front.

Churchill attacks German naval tactics

Westminster, 5 December
Germany has descended to "the lowest form of warfare that can be imagined", Winston Churchill told the House of Commons today. The first lord of the admiralty said that the Germans had first abandoned the gun for the torpedo and had now dropped that for the mine.

He claimed great success for Britain's policy of moving ships in convoys. There were always 2,000 ships at sea, and losses in convoy were down to one in 750. Two-thirds of the ships now being sunk by the mines belonged to neutrals. As far as the war at sea was concerned, "German friendship has proved far more poisonous than German enmity", Mr Churchill said. He did not mention the capture off Brazil yesterday of the liner *Ussukuma*, which had been attempting to take supplies to German pocket battleships in the South Atlantic.

1939

December

Su	Mo	Tu	We	Th	Fr	Sa
					1	2
3	4	5	6	7	8	9
10	11	12	13	14	15	16
17	18	19	20	21	22	23
24	25	26	27	28	29	30
31						

10. Washington: The USA loans Finland $10 million (→ 18).

10. France: The sale of meat is forbidden on Mondays, Tuesdays and Fridays.→

11. Suomussalmi: Finnish soldiers cut off the Russian 163rd Division.

11. Geneva: The League of Nations demands that Russia cease hostilities against Finland (→ 12).

11. Poland: A forced labour programme is instituted for all Jews in the General Government area (→ 14/1).

11. Germany: Hitler meets Vidkun Quisling, the head of the pro-Nazi Norwegian National Unity Party (→ 14).

12. Moscow: Russia rejects the League of Nations' demands for peace with Finland.→

12. Germany: The German liner *Bremen* arrives at Bremerhaven from Murmansk, having evaded the British blockade (→ 13).

12. Germany: Hitler orders the production of sea mines and ammunition to be almost doubled (→ 19).

13. Heligoland Bight: The British submarine *Salmon* damages the German cruisers *Leipzig* and *Nurnberg*.

14. Germany: Hitler orders his Supreme Command to prepare plans for *Weserubung* [Exercise Weber], the invasion of Norway (→ 18).

14. Mexico: The German liner *Columbus* leaves Vera Cruz in an attempt to run home (→ 19).

14. China: Nationalist forces occupy the town of Ningxian after a bitter clash with the Communists.

15. France: Chamberlain visits the British Expeditionary Force on the Western Front.

15. Germany: Hundreds of factories are said to be producing *ersatz* (artificial) coffee from barley, figs, berries and other substitutes.

16. Rome: Count Galeazzo Ciano, Mussolini's foreign minister, attacks Russia in a speech to the Fascist assembly.

Royal Navy corners the "Graf Spee"

Montevideo, 13 December

Just before sunset tonight one of Germany's finest modern ships, the *Admiral Graf Spee*, steamed into sight heading for the harbour here. Two British cruisers, the *Ajax* and the *Achilles*, stood off in the mouth of the estuary. The Battle of the River Plate had lasted for less than two hours. The biggest British ship, the *Exeter*, had limped off to the Falklands for repairs. And although the *Graf Spee* still had her engines and armaments intact, she had been hit 20 times and needed a respite.

The *Graf Spee* is one of three pocket battleships, built small so that they appeared to fit in with the 10,000-ton limit imposed on Germany by the Versailles Treaty, but in fact armed more heavily than much bigger vessels. Today she weighs in at 16,000 tons with her full load of wartime guns, stores and ammunition. She has six 11-inch guns, eight 5.9 inch guns and six 4.1 inch guns.

Today only the *Exeter* with 8-inch guns could get near enough to

The German pocket battleship "Graf Spee" limps into Montevideo harbour.

inflict any serious damage. However, by the time the action was over she had only two guns left intact and was listing heavily to starboard.

Under Captain Hans Langsdorff the *Graf Spee* has spearheaded the German campaign to harass ships in the South Atlantic supplying vital goods to Britain. To date she has claimed ten ships totalling over 50,000 tons. However, Captain Langsdorff has been scrupulous in avoiding loss of life. He stops and boards his prey and takes off crew and passengers before sinking their ships (→ 17).

Barrage balloons float above British cities to deter air attacks

Britain, 11 December

Britons who live in and around cities and large towns, or close to strategic targets, will have now become used to that new sight in the sky, the barrage balloon. This seemingly innocuous object provides a vital part of Britain's air defences.

The barrage balloon's weapon against the German bomber is its tough steel cable which keeps it tethered to the ground – and threatens amputation of the wings of any He111 or Ju88 which tries to bomb by flying low. Balloons force the Germans to fly higher, which puts them in the sights of General Frederick "Tim" Pile's Anti-Aircraft Command, now made up of five Territorial divisions.

The barrage balloons are manned by the men of RAF Balloon Command. Some 40,000 members of the Royal Auxiliary Air Force make up the command. Their balloons are filled with hydrogen and can be winched to the required height in just a few minutes. In high winds, however, the balloons have to be lowered. One person who knows

Balloons rise to Britain's defence: their steel cables amputate aircraft wings.

what it is like to fly into their cables is a Canadian fighter pilot, Flight Lieutenant John Kent. A Farnborough test pilot, he deliberately flew aircraft into cables to see what

would happen. On one occasion he lost three feet of wing but still managed to land safely. Whether the balloons will effectively deter the *Luftwaffe* remains to be seen. ▷

Skiing Finns stem Russian advances

Helsinki, 16 December

The Finns have stopped the Russian "steamroller" in its tracks. Fighting skilfully on skis and camouflaged in white to blend in with the snow, they are inflicting terrible casualties on the Russians, who were so confident of an easy victory that they had not even been issued with winter clothing.

The Russian soldiers, many of whom have frozen to death, call their white-shrouded tormentors *Bielaja Smert* – the White Death. The Russians know that if they are wounded death is almost inevitable from frostbite. The Finns have developed a tactic they call *motti*, their name for a stack of wood ready for chopping. They move like ghosts round the Russian columns strung out along the forest roads, sniping, then disappearing on their skis. They lay mines on the tracks, booby-trap farm animals, burn down their own farms to deny the invaders shelter, and have become expert at using "Molotov cocktails", bottles filled with petrol with burning rags round the necks, to knock out the Red Army's tanks. Sometimes they attack in force at several points, chopping the Russian columns into several disorganized pieces, then surrounding the pieces and wiping them out as they flounder in the snow.

The situation along the 800-mile (1,280-km) length of the Russo-Finnish border is that in the south, along the Gulf of Finland, the Finns have repulsed a number of amphibious attacks and are holding the main thrust of the Red Army at the Mannerheim Line on both sides of Lake Ladoga.

North of Lake Ladoga the Russians have made more progress because the Finns do not have enough men to guard the long frontier. But the Russians do not seem to have the mobility to exploit their successes. They have been thrown out of Suomussalmi, which they took on 9 December. In the far north, on the Arctic Ocean, they have succeeded in capturing Petsamo and advancing southwest down the Arctic Highway, but are being held at Nautsi. Nowhere have they scored the simple victory which they had expected. The Finns are proving very tough nuts to crack (→ 17).

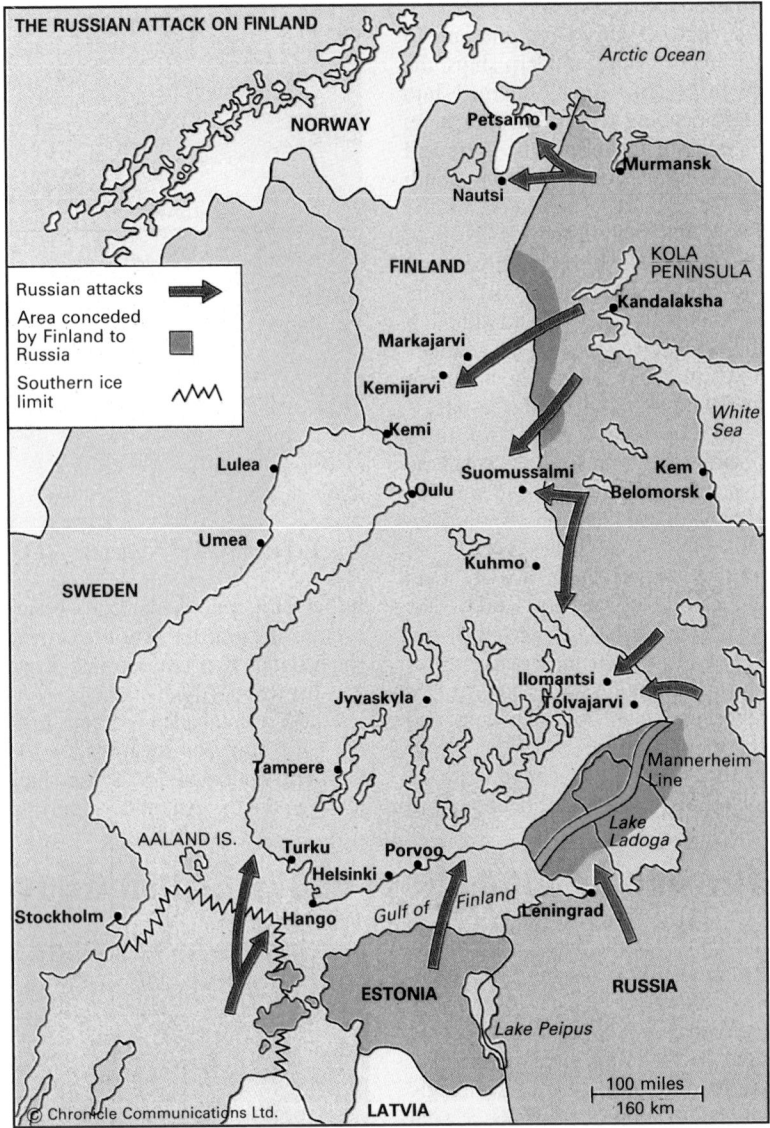

THE RUSSIAN ATTACK ON FINLAND

Russian attacks

Area conceded by Finland to Russia

Southern ice limit

Arctic Ocean
NORWAY
Petsamo
Murmansk
Nautsi
FINLAND
KOLA PENINSULA
Kandalaksha
Markajarvi
Kemijarvi
White Sea
Kemi
Lulea
Oulu
Suomussalmi
Kem
Belomorsk
Umea
Kuhmo
SWEDEN
Ilomantsi
Jyvaskyla
Tolvajarvi
Tampere
Mannerheim Line
Lake Ladoga
AALAND IS.
Turku
Porvoo
Stockholm
Helsinki
Hango
Gulf of Finland
Leningrad
ESTONIA
RUSSIA
Lake Peipus
100 miles
160 km
© Chronicle Communications Ltd.
LATVIA

Finnish soldiers on the Northern Front preparing for a night in the cold.

Chic fashions but fewer patisseries in wartime France

France, December

"War? What war?" is the question being asked in French cities as life carries on much unchanged. Although the army has been called up, France appears still to be playing at war rather than actually fighting it.

Elegant Parisiennes are trying to make war *chic*. The latest evening wear is a tailored suit bearing the crest of the RAF. Society hostesses have joined the war effort as only they know how, giving glittering charity balls for the Red Cross or the army. In the same spirit, the top *couturier* Coco Chanel has closed her Rue Cambon salon and put her seamstresses to work making gloves and knitwear for the army – all bearing her exclusive designer label. They are much appreciated; this winter is turning out to be a chilly one and, with coal in short supply, the nation's humbler knitters are also keeping busy. Many families are living in single, draughtproof rooms to save fuel. Although there is no shortage of food or of *Saint-Raphael*, the vital warming tonic wine, *patisseries* are becoming hard to find as bakers turn their attention to bread rather than cakes – and rough wholemeal flour has not proved popular.

Perhaps the most striking change in the last few months has been the sudden dearth of men. Millions of women have been left on their own to cope with the worry and uncertainty of war. Many of them also have to adjust to working outside the home, doing the jobs the men left behind or helping in the munitions industry. In rural areas the strain is heaviest as farmers' wives struggle in relative isolation to keep farms and smallholdings running while their men are away at the front. The troops manning the forts of the Maginot Line are kept happy by entertainers such as Maurice Chevalier and Josephine Baker.

1939

League of Nations expels the USSR

Geneva, 14 December

The League of Nations, meeting in emergency debate, expelled the Soviet Union today because of its unprovoked invasion of its small, peaceful neighbour, Finland. The League also called on its members to give all possible help to the Finns. Although the League has little power in this war-torn world its plea will fall on receptive ears.

France has announced a substantial programme of military aid, Britain has promised 30 fighter aircraft, and a number of foreign volunteers have travelled to Helsinki to join the Finnish forces. The USA, not a member of the League, has made a strong protest to Moscow (→16).

MPs discuss arms in secret session

Westminster, 13 December

The House of Commons met in secret session today for the first time since 1918, in what were then the dire days of the last world war.

Following ancient usage, the prime minister "spied strangers". This was the signal for the public, minor officials and members of the press gallery to be ordered out. The doors were locked.

According to a tense statement issued after seven and a half hours of debate, MPs discussed "the organization of supplies for the prosecution of the war". It would be a grave breach of privilege for anyone to report what was said.

December

Su	Mo	Tu	We	Th	Fr	Sa
					1	2
3	4	5	6	7	8	9
10	11	12	13	14	15	16
17	18	19	20	21	22	23
24	25	26	27	28	29	30
31						

17. Finland: The army claims that it has smashed two Russian divisions, taken 36,000 men prisoner and has a further 20,000 surrounded (→18).

17. Western Front: An increase in German reconnaissance flights is reported.

17. Britain: The admiralty announces that 61 men of HMS *Exeter*'s crew died during the Battle of the River Plate.→

18. Washington: The US Navy agrees to send 40 planes to Finland (→21).

18. Berlin: Hitler promises Quisling money in return for helping a German invasion of Norway.

19. Atlantic: The German liner *Columbus*, closely trailed by the US cruiser *Tuscaloosa*, is scuttled; 577 survivors are taken to Ellis Island in New York harbour (→20).

19. Germany: The surface raider *Atlantis* is launched.

20. Atlantic: The RDF system of the *Graf Spee* is hurried to Britain for examination (→20).

20. Buenos Aires: Hans Langsdorff, the commander of the *Graf Spee*, commits suicide in his hotel room (→23).

20. Britain: *O Thou whose righteous judgements stand*, a new wartime hymn with music composed by Ralph Vaughan Williams, is published.

20. Washington: The USA forbids the export of technical data for producing aviation fuel to belligerent countries.

21. Finland: The army stages a successful counter-attack at Kemijarvi.→

22. Bucharest: Roumania signs a trade convention with Germany.

22. Britain: The government states that it has seized 870,000 tons of goods destined for Germany since the war began.

23. South America: Several countries protest to Germany and the Allies about the Battle of the River Plate, which breached the Pan-American security zone (→31).

"Graf Spee" is scuttled

The burning wreck of the "Graf Spee" rests on the bed of the river Plate.

Montevideo, 17 December

Thousands of people lined the riverbank tonight as the German pocket battleship *Admiral Graf Spee* left harbour just before sunset. In the river mouth three British cruisers waited for their prey – the *Ajax* and *Achilles*, which had fought in the battle four days ago, and the much more powerful *Cumberland*, which had just arrived to give support.

All of Montevideo, and much of the world by their wireless sets, waited to see how Captain Hans Langsdorff would end the drama of the last four days. International law permits a warship to remain for 24 hours for emergency repairs, and the Germans had won a 72-hour extension. Langsdorff thought that a substantial Royal Navy force was waiting to pounce on him. He had been misled by rumours in Montevideo, by a mistaken "sighting" by one of his own officers, and by BBC reports suggesting that the main British reinforcements had actually arrived when they were really still several days away.

Langsdorff had asked for instructions and Hitler himself had said that he only had two – scuttle, or fight it out on the open sea. Just before the three-mile limit the ship stopped and the crowd saw the crew taking to the boats. Minutes later came a series of shattering explosions and flames lit up the approaching dusk. The ship settled on the river bed, her upper decks above the water and still burning.

For the Royal Navy the news should be as much of a tonic as was the defeat of Admiral Graf Spee's squadron at the Falklands in the early stages of the last war (→19).

Captain Langsdorff, having brought his crew safely into Montevideo harbour.

Scientists defeat magnetic mines

London, 19 December
Admiralty scientists led by Dr C F Goodeve and Dr E C Bullard have now found a way to defeat the magnetic mine threat. Since the mines are detonated by a ship's magnetic field, a system of cancelling this out has been developed. Ships will be fitted with electric cables passed round the hulls and connected to the generators. Known as "degaussing", this will create a magnetic field exactly opposite to the ship's.

Methods have also been found for sweeping these mines. Experiments using wooden trawlers towing sweeps made up of energized electrical cables have proved successful in safely detonating them. A Wellington bomber has also been fitted with energized coils and a petrol generator, although it has to fly as low as 60 feet to explode the mines (→ 8/1).

IRA steals Irish small-arms ammo

Dublin, 23 December
Troops and police cordoned off the Irish capital tonight in a search for a huge IRA arms haul. The theft of more than a million rounds of rifle, revolver and machine-gun ammunition stolen from the magazine fort in Phoenix Park has led to the biggest round-up of IRA suspects since the civil war. Sixteen men have been arrested. All have refused to make statements or apply for bail. Three have been charged with possession of firearms.

Roadblocks have been set up on major roads throughout Eire and troops have searched hundreds of cars, lorries and buses. Pedestrians are being stopped for random checks and women are being compelled to open their shopping bags and allow prams to be searched. Two large hauls of bullets – weighing half a ton – have been recovered in County Kildare.

Maximum security has been imposed on the Ulster border. The IRA continues to regard itself as being "in a state of war" with Great Britain, and many Irish politicians fear a diplomatic backlash from an angry British government.

Outnumbered Finns stun mighty USSR

A Russian transport column overrun by the Finns yields a portrait of Stalin.

Helsinki, 23 December
The Finns continue to astonish the world with the defeats which they are inflicting on the immensely more powerful Red Army. Yesterday they caught the Russian 44th Motorised Division as it approached Suomussalmi to attempt the relief of the trapped 163rd Division.

The Finns blocked the road in front of and behind the Russians and then began their log-cutting tactics, using Suomi sub-machine guns, very effective weapons for close range forest work, then going in with grenades and knives. They have inflicted enormous casualties and tonight both Russian divisions are fighting for their lives in temperatures as low as minus 40 degrees Fahrenheit (also minus 40 degrees Celsius). Russian losses also include tanks and artillery.

At the same time the Finns entrenched near Taipale, at the eastern end of the Mannerheim Line, have cut down whole Russian battalions attempting to storm their positions. Few Finns are under any illusions. They know they cannot hold out forever, but they are putting up a magnificent fight (→ 25).

Air forces battle over Heligoland

London, 18 December
Twenty-two Wellington bombers fought a tremendous battle in a cloudless sky over the North Sea today. As they approached the Heligoland Bight, off north-western Germany, on their mission to bomb German warships, they could see a swarm of Bf109 and Bf110 fighters waiting for them. Soon the sky was full of bullets and cannon shells as the German pilots, working in co-ordination with the *Flak* [anti-aircraft guns] tore into the Wellingtons. They attacked from the beam, trying to avoid the fire of the nose and rear gun turrets.

The stoutly-built Wellingtons took a tremendous amount of punishment. One had both turrets smashed, lost most of the fabric from its wings and had its petrol tank holed. It was forced to ditch. Wing Commander R Kellett, who led the raid, said afterwards that it was "the biggest aerial battle ever fought". He insisted that his crews had "returned confident that on the next occasion the enemy will suffer a far heavier blow. The occasion they hope will not be too distant." Brave words, but, although his men have shot down four Germans, 12 Wellingtons were lost and three more made forced landings. These sort of losses cannot be sustained by a relatively small air force.

First Canadian troops land in Britain to join war against Hitler

Liverpool, 17 December
Beneath battleship grey clouds, the first Canadian troops to reach Britain – 7,400 men of the First Division – docked in Liverpool. For a country with a permanent army of 4,500 men, five mortars and 16 tanks to create a division in three months is some achievement.

The Canadians, under the command of Major-General McNaughton, arrived in five liners. Officers slept in suites and men in first class cabins. It was a better trip than McNaughton made in the last war, cramped in a hammock for 28 days. Otherwise things have hardly changed since 1914-18. There are the same infantry manuals, same weapons, and probably the same stretch of front in France (→ 26).

Hundreds of Canadian troops come ashore at a British port.

Stalin at 60: half beast, half giant, but Russian master

Joseph Stalin, a dictator and warlord.

Moscow, 21 December
As the son of a cobbler from a primitive village in Georgia was celebrating his 60th birthday amid the czarist splendours of the Kremlin in Moscow, a telegram was handed to him:

"To Joseph Stalin: Best wishes for your personal well-being as well as for the prosperous future of the peoples of the friendly Soviet Union. Adolf Hitler." A delighted Stalin replied: "To the Chancellor of the German Reich, A Hitler. The friendship of the peoples of Germany and the Soviet Union, cemented by blood, has every reason to be lasting and firm."

There was more than a hint of unease in Stalin's reference to a lasting friendship cemented in blood. The blood is that of the Polish people, victims of the unholy Nazi-Soviet alliance, and neither of the dictators trusts the other. Stalin, whose Red Army is at this moment being mauled by the Finns, observed with mounting apprehension the German *Blitzkrieg* in Poland. Hitler, who speaks of Stalin as "half beast, half giant", believes that war with Russia is less than a year away.

December

Su	Mo	Tu	We	Th	Fr	Sa
					1	2
3	4	5	6	7	8	9
10	11	12	13	14	15	16
17	18	19	20	21	22	23
24	25	26	27	28	29	30
31						

25. Finland: Finnish troops enter Russian territory for the first time in the war (→ 27).

25. Western Front: Hitler spends Christmas Day visiting his forces.

26. Britain: The Royal Navy starts laying a mine barrier from the Moray Firth to the Thames Estuary.

27. Turkey: A powerful earthquake is estimated to have killed 8,000 people.→

27. Poland: After two German officers are killed in a scuffle in a bar at Wawer, the authorities round up and shoot dead 107 men and boys selected at random.

27. Cambridge: A verdict of accidental death is given in the case of a couple who cycled into a river during the blackout and drowned.

27. Europe: The Allies lobby Sweden for permission to ship unofficial aid to Finland through Sweden (→ 31).

28. At Sea: The British battleship HMS *Barham* is torpedoed by a U-boat but suffers only minor damage.

28. France: The first Indian troops arrive to join the British Expeditionary Force.

28. Switzerland: The exiled industrialist and erstwhile Nazi fund-raiser Fritz Thyssen protests to Hitler: "I have not sacrificed my millions for Bolshevism but against it" (→ 29).

29. Turkey: The estimated death toll has risen to 20,000 as earth tremors continue (→ 31).

29. Germany: Police issue a warrant for the arrest of the tycoon Fritz Thyssen, who once funded but now opposes the Nazis. He is believed to be in Portugal.

31. Turkey: Floods and further earthquakes push the death toll up to 30,000.

31. Finland: The Finns claim to have pushed the Red Army back across the frontier on the Suomussalmi-Kemijarvi front.→

31. London: Police arrest New Year revellers shining torches in the blackout onto Eros to see in 1940.

Pope makes Christmas Eve peace appeal

Rome, 24 December
In a delicately phrased Christmas address to his College of Cardinals today, Pope Pius XII spoke of the right of all nations – strong and weak – to life and independence. "When this equality of rights has been destroyed or damaged or imperilled, the juridical order calls for reparation and justice," he added.

Peace, he said, must be founded on disarmament. "The nations must be freed from the burden of armament races and from the danger that material forces may become not the defender but the tyrannical violator of right." The pope appealed for a peace conference at which "lessons could be drawn from past experience".

Pius XII: appealing for peace.

King makes poetic broadcast to Empire

London, 25 December
King George VI thanked the Empire in his Christmas Day broadcast for its sacrifices in coming to Britain's aid in the war. "The Mother Country can never be sufficiently grateful to you," he said. "We are all members of the great family of nations which is prepared to sacrifice everything that freedom of spirit may be saved." He movingly quoted from *God Knows*, by Minnie Louise Haskins): "And I said to the man who stood at the gate of the year: 'Give me a light that I may tread safely into the unknown'. And he replied: 'Go out into the darkness and put your hand into the hand of God.'"

Evacuated children in Essex put a brave face on Christmas away from home.

Thousands die in Turkish earthquake

Anatolia, 28 December
More details are coming in of the havoc wreaked by yesterday's earthquake in eastern and northern Anatolia, the central province of Turkey. It is feared that up to 20,000 may have died, with many thousands more now homeless in the bitter winter weather. There were seven violent shocks between 2am and 5am yesterday. The regions of Tokat and the Black Sea tobacco-growing centres of Samsun and Ordu are among the worst hit. An emergency relief operation is under way (→ 29).

No peace on earth as armies realize that the war won't be all over by Christmas

Somewhere in France, 25 December
This is the day in the British Army when officers serve Christmas dinner to the other ranks. It is a tradition that belongs to the peacetime professional army of volunteers with a strong sense of regimental loyalty. In spite of the neither-war-nor-peace situation, the tradition has been preserved as far as possible. The mood is at once relaxed and uneasy. To the big question – why hasn't the real fighting started? – nobody, it seems, has an answer.

On the other side, behind the fortifications of the Siegfried Line, Hitler is visiting the troops and joining in the Christmas celebrations. He is reported to have said that he will force Britain to its knees in eight months with his magnetic mines.

Home for Christmas – gun in hand.

No grumbles at Christmas on the rations

London, 25 December
Britons made the most of their traditional turkey and plum pudding Christmas dinner today. There may have been less on the plates, but most families had hoarded sufficient quantities of luxuries like sweets and sugar to ensure a normal belt-loosening feast. If rationing is introduced, Christmas may become a much more spartan affair.

Preparation for the wartime feeding of 45,000,000 people has been under way for several months – with the ministry of food drawing on the last war's experience to ensure fair distribution.

There have been several snags – the decentralization of London's meat, fish and vegetable markets, for instance, due to the threat of bombing, has caused chaos; and the government has found it difficult to cope with the large numbers of evacuees. Some areas have enjoyed a glut of bacon, others a shortage of butter; but real hardship is no worse than in peacetime.

The fruit market in Covent Garden before it was moved to a safer place.

Australians fly in to join Britain

Pembroke, Wales, 26 December
The main body of No 10 Squadron, Royal Australian Air Force, arrived here today from Australia to join Coastal Command. The squadron, equipped with Short Sunderland flying boats, is the first Dominion air force unit to be committed to active service in the European war. Australia's air minister, J V Fairbairn, told them: "Australia is confident that you will play your part in whatever spheres you may be called upon to serve."

Elements of all three Australian services were committed to war roles after Australia declared it would stand by Britain. All vessels of the Royal Australian Navy have been put under British orders, and in October five Australian destroyers were sent to the Mediterranean to replace RN ships needed for home waters. But there are those who believe Australia must keep a wary eye on Japan, run by an aggressive military hierarchy and Germany's ally through the anti-Comintern pact.

In September the Australian government decided that a 20,000-strong force, later designated the 6th Division, 2nd Australian Imperial Force, was to be created for service either at home or abroad. Earlier this month an advance party was sent to Palestine under the command of Lieutenant-General Thomas Blamey, a veteran of Gallipoli in the Great War.

The first contingent of Australian airmen arrives on British soil.

Honours are equal in the battle at sea

London, 31 December
Despite the recent destruction of the *Graf Spee*, the year-end balance sheet of the war at sea is little better than even. Britain has lost 422,232 tons of shipping, compared with around 224,322 tons for the Germans. The British figure amounts to only two per cent of the fleet, but the smaller German loss is five per cent of their fleet. Britain's blockade has resulted in the confiscation of around one million tons bound for Germany. But German naval activity may lead to the rationing of essential foodstuffs in Britain.

Japan and China sign secret treaty

Hanoi, 30 December
A breakaway group of Chinese Nationalists led by the *Kuomintang's* ex foreign minister, Wang Chingwei, appears to have finalized agreement with Japan to set up a rival Nationalist government under Japanese protection. The Tokyo-educated Wang Chingwei, once Chiang Kai-shek's main rival for the Kuomintang leadership, fled to Hanoi a year ago to start a peace movement in response to Japan's call for a "new order in Asia". Since the loss of Wuhan he had become convinced that the war against Japan was unwinnable (→ 8/1).

Hitler declares his "new order" in Europe

Berlin, 31 December
In his New Year message to the German people, Hitler said: "We shall only talk of peace when we have won the war. The Jewish-capitalistic world will not survive the twentieth century." He looked forward to the creation of a new Europe under German leadership, a Europe liberated from "British tyranny".

His message, with its emphasis on the "capitalistic enemy", seemed to be partly aimed at offering reassurance to Stalin. One of the most significant events of the past year, he said, was "the conclusion of the non-aggression and consultative pact with Soviet Russia".

In a separate Order of the Day to the armed forces, Hitler was in a more sombre mood. He told them that in the effort to create a new order in Europe "the hardest struggle for the existence or non-existence of the German people lies before us".

Goering, for his part, struck a bombastic note. He told his *Luftwaffe* crews that, when Hitler gave the order, they would unleash against Britain "such an onslaught as has never before been known in the history of the world".

Russians pushed back on 150-mile front

Finnish soldiers examine a trophy of their counter-attacks: a Soviet tank.

Helsinki, 31 December
The battle which has been raging outside Suomussalmi for the past week has ended in the destruction of two Russian divisions. Some 27,000 Russian soldiers have died and their frozen bodies are stacked like cordwood in the forests. The Finns, who lost only 900 men in this classic battle of ambush and destroy, have now pushed the Russians back over their own border and General Wallenius, the commander of the Finnish Northern Army, has revealed that his men are now operating on Soviet territory. "We don't let them rest," he said, "we don't let them sleep. This is a war of numbers against brains.

We train our men to fight individually and they can do it, whereas the Russian can never rid himself of his natural gregarious instincts."

Colonel Hjalmar Siilasvuo, who planned and led the destruction of the Russian divisions, has been promoted to general and sent south with the objective of inflicting a similar fate on another Russian division trapped by the "White Death" Finns in the forest at Kuhmo. The Russians have also been driven back over their frontier further south after their defeat at Tolvajarvi where they lost 2,000 dead and 600 prisoners. "There were," said a Finn, "more Russians than we had bullets" (→ 2/1).

Arts: comic radio and escapist cinema

Radio is now the foremost medium of entertainment in Britain. For several days the BBC seemed to have nothing to offer but gramophone records and **Sandy Macpherson** at the theatre organ – he made 45 broadcasts in the first fortnight of war while other entertainers were being evacuated. But on 16 September *Band Waggon* was back with **Arthur Askey** and **Richard Murdoch** still in their flat on top of Broadcasting House (in fact in a Bristol parish hall).

Three days later the familiar voice of the Liverpool comedian **Tommy Handley** came on talking faster than ever as "that man" of *It's That Man Again*, whose title is taken from a *Daily Express* headline accompanying Hitler's doings. It was soon referred to by its initials as *ITMA*. Handley takes the part of the minister of aggravation and mysteries, housed at the office of twerps – a dig at ubiquitous wartime officialdom.

"Good evening, Great Britain," he began, "I have several hundred irritating restrictions to impose on you. I have the power to seize anything on sight." The chief sound effects of this surrealist fantasy by **Ted Kavanagh** are the *ITMA* door, which opens to admit a stream of unlikely characters, and the telephone down which the incompetent

"Run, Rabbit, Run" was a hit song for the Crazy Gang.

German spy Funf announces his presence. The voice is supplied by **Jack Train** (via a glass).

The first war film, **Alexander Korda's** *The Lion Has Wings*, tells of an RAF raid on a German battle fleet with what the *Daily Telegraph* calls "a welcome restraint – only once does an officer show emotion". Films have otherwise been escapist: *Goodbye Mr Chips* and Hollywood's *Wuthering Heights*, *Stagecoach*, and *The Wizard of Oz* starring **Judy Garland**.

On stage in Britain the **Crazy Gang** scored a hit with the song "Run, Rabbit, Run". **Flanagan and Allen** have also recorded "We're Gonna Hang Out the Washing on the Siegfried Line".

Judy Garland and friends in "The Wizard of Oz", one of this year's films.

"Battle of Britain" by Paul Nash.

Paul Nash

January

Su	Mo	Tu	We	Th	Fr	Sa
	1	2	3	4	5	6
7	8	9	10	11	12	13
14	15	16	17	18	19	20
21	22	23	24	25	26	27
28	29	30	31			

1. Britain: A royal proclamation extends the liability of men for military service to the age of 27.→

1. France: Rail links with Spain are reopened, having been closed three and a half years ago during the Spanish Civil War.

1. Britain: Fifty women resign from the Auxiliary Fire Service in protest at being told to scrub floors (→13).

1. Rome: Russia recalls its ambassador to Italy following anti-Soviet demonstrations in Rome.

2. Finland: Russian forces launch a major offensive in the Karelian isthmus (→3).

2. Britain: The blackout is said to have established the importance of Vitamin A for good eyesight in the dark.→

2. Prague: Journalists and ex-army officers are rounded up in a new wave of arrests by the Nazis.

3. Finland: The government claims to have destroyed 400 Russian tanks and brought down 150 planes since the fighting began (→5).

3. Leningrad: Finnish planes drop three million pamphlets over the city.

4. Washington: Roosevelt asks Congress for a defence budget of $1.8 billion (→9/2).

4. Germany: Goering takes control of the national war economy and all German war industries (→24).

4. Britain: The bacon ration to be introduced on 8 January is fixed at four ounces per person per week (→8).

5. Finland: The Soviet 18th Division is encircled north of Lake Ladoga.→

5. London: Vivien Leigh is sued for divorce on the grounds of her adultery with Laurence Olivier.

6. Britain: Dogs are reportedly wearing bicycle reflectors on their collars to boost their visibility in the blackout.

6. Finland: Two Finnish Fokker fighters destroy seven Ilyushin bombers over Utti, 60 miles north-east of Helsinki (→7).

Russia forced to go on the defensive

Winter war: Finnish soldiers stand proudly round a captured Russian tank.

Helsinki, 6 January
The Finns have succeeded in doing what the world thought was impossible: they have not only stopped the Russians, they have thrown them back on the defensive.

The Russians have been forced to abandon their purely offensive tactics and are now digging in opposite the entire middle of the Mannerheim Line which they have tried so strenuously and at such great cost to break.

They are barricading themselves behind tank traps and barbed wire, building pillboxes, using dynamite to blow trenches in the frozen ground and siting their guns in defensive positions.

However, what is not certain is whether these positions are purely defensive or form a screen behind which a massive new offensive is being prepared.

The Russians have learnt quickly how to fight a winter war; they have brought in their most modern aircraft, and now that the sea has frozen solid they have moved big guns over the ice to bombard the Finnish positions.

It is also understood here that General Timoshenko is to replace the failed Voroshilov and Meretskov as leader of the invaders. This shaven-headed, granite-faced soldier would exercise the iron control over the Russian forces which has been missing until now.

With his determination allied to rigorous training and new equipment, the Red Army could emerge from its defensive positions with renewed power (→6).

Unity Mitford comes home on a stretcher

England, 3 January
Unity Mitford went to Germany when Hitler's brand of fascism attracted many English admirers. She returned today by stretcher, nursing a self-inflicted bullet-wound.

Miss Mitford, aged 24, is a member of the large and remarkable family of Lord Redesdale; her sisters are renowned for their politics, writing and socialite connections. Unity became known as the Storm Trooper Maiden in the *Osteria Bavaria* restaurant in Munich after Hitler invited her to his table; but when war broke out she went to the *Englischer Garten* and put a gun to her head.

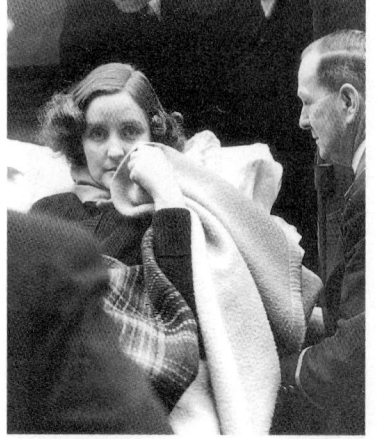

Unity Mitford returning home after attempting suicide in Munich.

Your country needs two million of you

London, 1 January
A total of two million men aged between 20 and 27 are now liable for call-up into the armed forces following a royal proclamation this evening.

Since war was declared men have queued to enlist voluntarily, although in nothing like the numbers of 1914. The new move is intended to structure the supply of men to the services, boosting Britain's military potential to three million men.

Call-up groups are based on year of birth. Men aged 19 will register, but will not be liable for service until they are 20. First to be summoned for service (on 1 March) are those aged 23, and other groups will soon follow. All those eligible will be in uniform by the end of the year.

Minister quits after rows with generals

Hore-Belisha leaves the War Office.

London, 5 January
Leslie Hore-Belisha, the secretary of state for war, has resigned from the cabinet. Mr Chamberlain told him that he could have another senior post, but must be moved from the war office. Mr Hore-Belisha, who had quarrelled with the army generals over strategy and his own insistence on better welfare services for the troops, retorted that he preferred to leave the government.

1940
January

Su	Mo	Tu	We	Th	Fr	Sa
	1	2	3	4	5	6
7	8	9	10	11	12	13
14	15	16	17	18	19	20
21	22	23	24	25	26	27
28	29	30	31			

BBC chief to be nation's morale booster

London, 6 January
Sir John Reith, the founder of the BBC and its first director-general, is to take over as minister of information. He inherits a troubled ministry whose 999 civil servants, based in the Senate House of London University, have been criticized in press and parliament for their ineptitude at raising morale against the constant sniping of Germany's "Lord Haw-Haw".

Many functions of the ministry of information (MoI) have been taken away. The press and censorship bureau is independent under Sir Walter Monckton, British propaganda to enemy countries is a joint effort of the MoI, the foreign office and the ministry of economic warfare, and postal censorship is a war office function. The resulting muddle has left the MoI open to the charge that it has no information and no use (→ 22).

Haw-Haw: sniping from Germany.

Irish premier takes emergency powers

De Valera: leading a crackdown.

Dublin, 6 January
Eamon de Valera, the prime minister of Eire, is calling for new emergency powers to aid a nationwide crackdown on the IRA. The move came swiftly following an Irish High Court ruling which set free 53 men detained under the Emergency Powers Act. An amended and draconian version of the act has been proposed in the *Dail*, the Irish parliament.

The amended act would allow the government the right to arrest and detain suspects without trial. Most of the freed men – who include several IRA leaders – are almost certainly "on the run".

Cod-liver oil cures blackout blindness

Britain, 2 January
People are being advised that they will see better in the blackout if they ensure that there are adequate amounts of Vitamin A in their diets. Recent experiments show that it improves the ability of the eyes to adjust quickly in going from light to dark – as happens on going outdoors in the blackout. Cod-liver oil capsules are recommended.

A survey shows that one person in five has had an accident in the blackout. Deaths in road accidents in the blackout exceed 2,000 in the four months since it began, 1,700 more than the average for the period in peacetime. Most of them are pedestrians.

The figures should improve. Cars are getting fewer and motorists have to paint the bumpers and running boards white. Kerbs and tree trunks are being whitened. Cycle rear lights are compulsory. Next month a 20mph speed limit applies after dark and "summer" time begins on 25 February (→ 6).

7. Finland: General Semyon Konstantinovich Timoshenko takes command of the Soviet forces.→

7. Finland: 50,000 Russian soldiers are believed to have perished in the last five weeks.

7. North Sea: The British submarines *Seahorse* and *Undine* are scuttled after depth charge attacks by a German minesweeper in the Heligoland Bight (→ 9).

8. China: Japan claims to have killed 25,000 Chinese in battle north of Canton (→ 16).

8. Germany: A new army headquarters is reported to have been established at Recklingshausen, ten miles from the Dutch border.

8. North Sea: A converted Wellington bomber fitted with an energized metal hoop to explode magnetic mines does its first successful trials (→ 18).

9. Berlin: The West Prussian SS chief reports the successful "elimination" of 4,000 incurable mental patients in Poland.

9. North Sea: The British submarine *Starfish* is scuttled after a depth charge attack by a German minesweeper in the Heligoland Bight (→ 19).

9. France: The first colonial contingent, of Cypriot troops, arrives to reinforce the BEF.

10. Germany: Hitler tells his generals that he has set 17 January as the date for attack on the Western Front (→ 13).

12. France: The government bans the sale of meat (except pork, goat and horseflesh) on Mondays and Tuesdays; Fridays have been meat-free since 10 December 1939.

12. Germany: General Albert Kesselring is given command of the *Luftwaffe's* 2nd Air Fleet.

13. Germany: Bad weather forecasts force Hitler to postpone the western offensive to 20 January (→ 16).

13. Europe: Belgium mobilizes and Netherlands cancels all army leave; both countries are put on a state of alert for invasion from Germany.

Women play their part with vital role in the war effort

Britain, 13 January
Two days ago the Women's Section of the Air Transport Auxiliary delivered its first aeroplane from factory to depot. This is one more indication of women's increasing usefulness in the war effort, but not everybody likes it. There has been considerable public protest against the use of women pilots while men are kept idle on the waiting list for the RAF.

Women's place in the Land Army has been more easily accepted, though fears have been voiced about "the wisdom of casting on one side, even temporarily, the whole elaborate system of agricultural education built up during the last 25 years, for the purpose of training a few hundred land girls".

Not everyone shares this view. A course was held this week in London to advise headmistresses on the changing face of women's work during the war.

No one need fear that the pilots of the Women's Section of the Air Transport Auxiliary are underqualified. The nine women – one first officer, Pauline Gower, with eight second officers in her command – have over 7,500 hours' flying time between them. The youngest of them, Joan Hughes, is 22 and learnt to fly at 17 before she left school. She is also qualified as an instructor (→ 6/2).

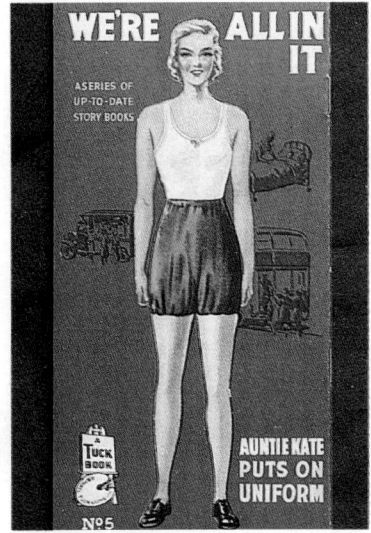
Teaching children the ways of the war: paper dolls in uniform.

Finns celebrate victory

White war: Finnish soldiers keep their skis ready for a quick escape.

Helsinki, 8 January
The Finnish victory over two Soviet divisions at Suomussalmi was even greater than at first reported. Details of the battle released by Finland's General Staff today show that it ended with the utter annihilation of the 44th Division, trapped while going to the support of the defeated 163rd Division. Among the booty captured by the victorious Finns were 102 field guns, 43 tanks, over 300 vehicles and 1,170 horses.

Helsinki is celebrating this crushing victory tonight. Church bells are ringing, flags fly from the houses and strangers are embracing each other in the streets.

Eye-witness reports emphasize the ferocity of the fighting, with white-shrouded Finns hiding in pits dug alongside the forest tracks, waiting to engage the Soviet tanks with "Molotov cocktails" [*see page 67*] at close range. The effect of these weapons can be seen inside the burnt-out tanks whose four-man crews met horrifying deaths by fire. Other Soviet troops froze to death, with nothing to protect them from the bitter cold except crude shelters of spruce branches.

The Finns, far better trained for winter warfare, allowed cold and hunger to do much of their work for them. They cut the Soviet supply lines and then waited for ten days while the bitter cold and dwindling food supplies sapped the Soviet Army's resistance. When the Finns attacked, some of the opposing troops were too weak to stand, too cold to fight (→ 17).

Armoured cars, tanks and trucks abandoned by the defeated Russians.

Hungry? A smear of butter, a spoonful of sugar and a slice of bacon is your ration

Britain, 8 January
Four months after the war began, rationing was introduced today when housewives had to take their ration books to buy butter, sugar and bacon from the retailers with whom they have registered. The most keenly felt sacrifice will be of butter at only four ounces a week. Adults are allowed 12 ounces of sugar and four of bacon or uncooked ham – less of cooked ham.

Hotels are allowed to serve one-sixth of an ounce of butter – a circular pat the thickness of three pennies – with each meal, including afternoon tea. Some have installed special weighing machines.

They can serve one-seventh of an ounce of sugar, or two lumps.

Rationing began in Germany last August and includes bread, meat, milk, margarine, cheese and jam. The weekly ration is smaller than in Britain – approximately three ounces of butter and eight ounces of sugar per person.

British housewives will be allowed extra sugar for making marmalade by the ministry of food, providing that the treasury and board of trade permit the import of Seville oranges. Obtaining rationed food from Eire is punishable by six months' imprisonment, unless it is sent as small gifts.

Watched closely, a shop assistant cuts out the customer's ration coupons.

Labour shortfalls worry Nazi government

Germany, 13 January
Falls in the size of the German male workforce are giving the regime in Berlin cause for concern and could lead to a relaxation of the Nazi doctrine, fostered since 1933, that a woman's place is firmly at home.

The Nazis foresaw the potential problem as early as February 1939, when a new regulation allowed employers to recruit any skilled worker not yet called-up for military service for compulsory work in any industrial sector important to a war economy. This measure has led to a partial redistribution of the German workforce to agriculture and armaments, but it may still prove inadequate to make up expected shortfalls. In 1939 1.5 million men were called up for the armed services, but four times that number could get their papers this year.

The idea of employing more women is opposed by senior Nazi leaders on the grounds that it contravenes the Nazi belief that women are fit mainly to be housewives and mothers. But the *Reich* may yet find it has little choice.

1940

January

Su	Mo	Tu	We	Th	Fr	Sa
	1	2	3	4	5	6
7	8	9	10	11	12	13
14	15	16	17	18	19	20
21	22	23	24	25	26	27
28	29	30	31			

Invasion plans found in German plane

Berlin, 10 January
The *Luftwaffe* HQ was in turmoil here today after news from the German embassy in Brussels told of the crash-landing of a German military plane near the Belgian town of Mechelen-sur-Meuse.

The plane, on a flight from Munster to Cologne, became lost in thick cloud. After it came down, one of the passengers jumped out and raced for a clump of bushes, where he set fire to papers he had taken from his briefcase. Belgian soldiers closed in and retrieved the partly-burnt papers.

The man was identified as Major Helmut Reinberger, a Luftwaffe staff officer, and the papers were operational plans, complete with maps, for a German airborne attack on the west, to begin on 14 January with saturation bombing attacks on French airfields.

When distraught aides gave news of the lost plans to Hitler, he said: "It's things like this that can lose us the war." (→ 16).

Jobless total rises despite war footing

Britain, 9 January
People are shocked that, after only four months of war, the British unemployment figure for January stands at 1,603,000. Despite the call-up of over 1,500,000 men, the unemployed have increased by 120,000 over the average for last year.

The harsh winter weather is partly responsible, by reducing outdoor employment, together with a slump in the building trade. Because of government restrictions on civil building and the shortage of timber, 250,000 building workers have been laid off. Germany states that it has only 18,000 unemployed.

Rail buckles under blackout pressure

Britain, 10 January
Widespread complaints about train delays have been excused by the Railway Executive on the grounds of the blackout, which prolongs the loading of goods vans and makes for late starting. It also blames unexpected arrivals at ports of shipments of fresh food, which have to be distributed hurriedly by commandeering trains. Troop movements are also a factor.

Passengers point out that this does not explain why so many trains run late in the daytime. Even daily commuter journeys habitually take half an hour longer than advertised, if not more.

The half-submerged wreck of the 10,000-ton liner "Dunbar Castle" after her back was broken by a German mine on 9 January off the south-east coast of England; 152 people are feared dead, including many children.

14. Europe: Leave is cancelled for all Dutch, Belgian and BEF troops (→ 16).

14. USA: Eighteen members of the pro-Nazi *Bund* organization are arrested for conspiracy.

14. Warsaw: Deaths, mainly from starvation, in the Jewish ghetto are running at 70 a day.→

15. Belgium: The government refuses to grant transit rights to enable Allied troops to cross Belgian territory.

15. Finland: Russia starts bombing the Finnish lines at Summa (→ 17).

16. Germany: Following the loss to the Allies of invasion plans, and with the weather worsening, Hitler cancels the attack on the west and orders preparations for an assault on Scandinavia (→ 20).

17. Europe: Seventy-nine degrees of frost are reported in Moscow, and the sound between Denmark and Sweden freezes over.

17. Finland: Russians on the Salla front are driven back 12 miles (19 km) (→ 19).

17. Europe: RAF Whitley bombers make night leaflet raids on Prague and Vienna.

18. Essex: Nazi saboteurs are blamed for an explosion at an arms factory which killed five people.

18. Warsaw: The *Gestapo* shoots dead 250 Jews in woods outside the city following the arrest of the Jewish-born Catholic resistance leader Andrzej Kott (→ 26).

19. Finland: The Finnish army stages an unsuccessful attack on Russian positions at Salla.→

19. North Sea: The destroyer HMS *Grenville* is sunk by a mine; 81 men are feared to have died (→ 21).

20. London: Churchill asks the uncommitted nations of Europe to join the Allies, and condemns Russia's invasion of Finland.

20. Washington: The USA protests to Britain over the detention of its ships in Gibraltar.

Poetic general is Middle East leader

Wavell: an intellectual warrior.

Cairo, 15 January
As Italy looks at Britain with growing hostility from its African colonies, the man in the front line is General Sir Archibald Wavell, Britain's C-in-C Middle East.

An officer in the Boer War at the age of 18, he lost an eye at Ypres and later became an advocate of mobile warfare. As GSO (General Staff Officer) 1 of 3 Division he was closely involved in the training of the Experimental Armoured Force when it was formed as part of the division in 1927, and from 1930 he commanded the 6th Infantry Brigade. A poet and an intellectual, Wavell is both an outstanding staff officer and a formidable leader of men; his book *Generals and Generalship* (1939) is a classic.

New ways to tackle magnetic mines

London, 18 January
A British company has today delivered the first of a very large admiralty order for buoyant electrical cable. It is to be used in the fight to remove the threat of the magnetic mine to British ships. When the cable is towed behind a wooden trawler, a current generated by the ship will produce a magnetic field around it sufficient to detonate a mine. In the meantime ships continue to be sunk by mines – over 260,000 tons between September and December 1939 (→ 10/2).

Record snowfalls and plunging temperatures freeze war plans

Europe, 20 January
All Europe is held in the icy grip of one of the severest frosts on record. Switzerland has recorded 34 degrees of frost, the lowest since 1920. Heavy snow has fallen in Oporto, Portugal, for the first time for 40 years and in Corunna, Spain, for the first time since 1800.

On the borders of Norway and Sweden the mercury froze in the thermometers. The Danube is frozen in Hungary and 1,200 ships are held by the ice. In the Baltic islands ships can only move preceded by ice-breakers, and German mines off Heligoland are being exploded by ice-floes. A German ship was sunk by an iceberg off Iceland.

On the Finnish front a temperature of 100 degrees of frost was recorded. Nearly 1,000 Russian troops are believed to have died of exposure. In China 20,000 have died and the war has been halted.

The expected German attack on the Western Front has not material-

French machine-gunners take cover in a snow-covered no-man's-land.

ized, presumably at least partly because of the weather. Both Holland and Belgium are expecting an onslaught at any moment. The Germans have evacuated civilians from the area adjoining the Dutch border and trains passing through have to draw their blinds. Captured plans show that the invasion should have taken place on 14 January (→ 31).

Poles tell of death and forced labour

Angers, France, 16 January
A report which vividly describes Nazi atrocities in Poland was presented today to the exiled Polish government here. It contains graphic accounts of public executions, forced labour, looting and hostage-taking on a vast scale.

In Poznan, for example, the invaders are said to have shot 5,000 Poles. Thousands more are being held in makeshift concentration camps. Mass arrests of prominent Poles are commonplace. Germans take precedence over Poles for food, clothes and housing.

The two million Jews and gypsies in Nazi-occupied Poland suffer the most brutal persecution and indignities (→ 18).

The Chinese Communist leader, Mao Tse-tung, with peasants of Yangchialing in Yenan, his base. Mao's "united front" with his old Nationalist foe General Chiang Kai-shek against the Japanese is already crumbling.

Admiral heads new Japan government

Tokyo, 16 January
The emperor of Japan today appointed Admiral Mitsumasa Yonai, aged 60, to form a new cabinet after General Abe and his ministers resigned after an urgent session early on 14 January.

The resignation of General Abe's government is a set-back for the pro-war hawks in the army. It has come under mounting criticism for the way the war in China has been allowed to drag on. The army's plans to reduce the China Expeditionary Army and deploy troops to strengthen Japanese positions along the border with the Soviet Union have been thwarted by the Chinese Nationalists' winter offensive. Instead Japan has had to send additional troops to China.

Anti-war elements in the *Diet* [parliament] have become increasingly reluctant to float yet more loans, which are crippling government finances, to support the war. It is not known whether the new premier, who was a compromise choice after the army failed to get its own candidate appointed, is a hawk or a dove (→ 22).

Russian bombers hit back at Finnish strength on ground

Helsinki, 20 January
There is a lull in the ground fighting as the Russians prepare for the expected "big push", but the war goes on as fiercely as ever in the air with the Russian bombers trying to make up for the superior skill of the Finns on the ground.

They attack the Finnish positions every day, not only in the front line but ranging over most of the country. The news has been released that the historic castle at Aabo on the Baltic coast has been destroyed by incendiary bombs.

The port of Viipuri, only 70 miles (112 km) from Leningrad, is under constant attack. A hospital has been hit and many patients have been killed. But the Russians are not having it all their own way.

The Finns, flying British-built Blenheim bombers, have carried out raids on the Soviet island bases of Oesel and Dagoe and scattered three million leaflets over Leningrad, giving the true facts of the situation in Finland.

The Finnish fighters have also been in furious action, hurling themselves at the Red bombers whenever they appear.

One of the fighter pilots, Jorma Sarvanto, has scored a most spectacular success, knocking down six out of a formation of seven Ilyushin bombers while he was on a lone patrol over the devastated town of Mikkeli (→ 27).

The French cartoonist Henri Monnier shows Finnish resistance bouncing back harder than expected.

1940

January

Su	Mo	Tu	We	Th	Fr	Sa
	1	2	3	4	5	6
7	8	9	10	11	12	13
14	15	16	17	18	19	20
21	22	23	24	25	26	27
28	29	30	31			

21. Japan: The British cruiser HMS *Gloucester* stops the Japanese liner *Asanu Maru* off Honshu, and removes 21 German technicians on board (→ 29/2).

21. Atlantic: All 175 crew are lost when a U-boat sinks the British destroyer *Exmouth* (→ 30).

21. Vatican: The pope condemns Nazi rule in Poland (→ 29).

22. Helsinki: The Finns announce the formation of a foreign legion.

23. London: Britain and France warn that they will attack German shipping encountered by their navies in the PanAmerican neutral zone.

24. Berlin: Field Marshal Goering appoints the *Gestapo* chief Reinhart Heydrich to "solve the Jewish question by emigration and evacuation" (→ 30).

24. Madrid: The Spanish council of ministers passes a law banning Freemasonry throughout Spain.

25. Canada: Controversy over the state of preparedness for war forces the dissolution of parliament.

26. Poland: Jews are forbidden by the German authorities to travel on the public railways (→ 30).

27. Baltimore: The *City of Flint* arrives back at her home port following her adventures in the Baltic.

28. Finland: The Finnish army drives a wedge into the Soviet 54th Division at Kuhmo (→ 1/2).

29. Paris: The Polish government in exile says that the Nazis have killed 18,000 prominent Poles.

30. Berlin: Heydrich orders more expulsions of Jews from the *Reich* to Lublin in eastern Poland; Himmler authorizes the deportation of 30,000 gypsies (→ 10/2).

30. Atlantic: The sloop HMS *Fowey*, the destroyer HMS *Whitshed* and an RAF Sunderland flying boat sink a U-boat off Ushant, Brittany (→ 4/2).

Ministry news vetting "not censorship"

London, 22 January
From today newsreels have to be submitted to the ministry of information before they are exhibited. Newsreels have been exempt from scrutiny by the British Board of Film Censors because they are produced to tight deadlines twice weekly. Now this loophole is closed. The ministry's film division has appointed a liaison officer to convey "do's and don'ts" of film propaganda. An "editor" from the ministry will view all newsreels before release. The word "censor" is not used in the announcement.

The Control of Photography Order already makes it an offence to film or photograph any object of war interest without a permit. But the ban on the representation of living persons in feature films has been lifted in regard to enemy aliens such as Nazi leaders.

Sir John Reith (right), the minister of information, with Lord Trenchard.

South African MPs reject peace move

Cape Town, 27 January
In an extraordinary spectacle, with the former prime minister, General Hertzog, openly supporting Hitler, South Africa's all-white parliament has rejected the call for a separate peace with Germany.

The pro-British premier, General Jan Smuts, likened the speech of Hertzog, his former Boer comrade-in-arms, to a chapter from *Mein Kampf*. "Goebbels could not have done it better," he said.

The division in the lobby was clear-cut, reflecting the division in the country – the English-speakers and liberal Afrikaners in one camp, the irreconcilable Boers, with their own theories of racial supremacy, in the other.

Finns await new onslaught by Red Army

Helsinki, 27 January
There is an expectant air about the Mannerheim Line today as the Finns prepare for the massive attack that they know is being prepared by General Timoshenko, who has been whipping the Red Army into shape behind his defensive lines on the Karelian isthmus. This does not mean that there is no action. Soviet guns have kept up a steady pounding of the Finnish positions and small groups of soldiers, now well trained in winter tactics, have launched a series of attacks to wear down the Finns (→ 30).

Captured by the Finns, two Russian soldiers stand to attention in the cold.

Homesick evacuees return to cities

Britain, 31 January
A survey of evacuees by local authorities reveals that out of 734,883 unaccompanied children evacuated from the cities since 1 September 1939, 316,192 have returned home. In addition 145,681 mothers with 233,381 young children have gone back, about 90 per cent of accompanied evacuees. About 500,000, mainly schoolchildren, remain in the "safe areas".

A third of London's schoolchildren and more than a third of Liverpool's are still evacuated, but in most cities only ten per cent are still away and the number is falling. Only two of the hutted camps built for evacuees at a cost of over £1 million ($4 million) are in use. One in six firms that evacuated are back in London. Apart from the absence of air raids, the reason for the failure of the evacuation scheme has been the homesickness of the children, their parents' anxieties and the attempt to collect a charge of 6/- (30p/$1.21) a week per child from parents.

Waste not wasted, but wanted for war

Britain, 30 January
A national campaign was launched today to utilize almost all of the 120 million tons of household waste that are disposed of every year. Scrap iron and steel are urgently needed for conversion into armour plate for guns, ships and tanks. "Old bedsteads, bicycles, fire-irons – we want them all," said the chairman of the scrap merchants' federation. The National Farmers' Union is to arrange collection from farms of the many discarded ploughs, harrows, scythes, drills, milk pails and other rusting implements.

Waste paper is urgently needed for pulping to save imports. The paper controller is appealing for people to bundle their newspapers, wrapping paper, cardboard and old letters beside the dustbin. There is also an appeal for kitchen waste to be kept separately from tins and bottles, because it is wanted for pigswill. Even bones are wanted for grinding up as fertilizer.

1940
February

Su	Mo	Tu	We	Th	Fr	Sa
				1	2	3
4	5	6	7	8	9	10
11	12	13	14	15	16	17
18	19	20	21	22	23	24
25	26	27	28	29		

It's been the worst winter this century, but don't tell anyone – it's a secret

Working to free a train from a snow drift in Scotland during the secret winter.

Britain, 31 January

It can now be revealed that, like the rest of Europe, Britain has been shivering since Christmas in the coldest spell since 1895. All reference to the weather is censored until 15 days after the event.

Temperatures of 20 or 25 degrees Fahrenheit below freezing (-12 degrees Celsius) have been common, and a remarkable 35 degrees of frost were recorded at Edgbaston observatory. The Thames was frozen for eight miles (13 km) between Teddington and Sunbury, and ice covered stretches of the Humber, Mersey and Severn. The sea froze along the shoreline at Felpham, near Bognor Regis. Folkestone harbour and Southampton docks iced over. The Grand Union Canal was at a standstill from London to Birmingham. Even central London was below freezing for a week, and Londoners have been skating on ice six inches thick on the Serpentine. Skating has been possible on Rydal Water in the Lake District, and skiing has been in full swing on the South Downs. Main roads have been blocked in Kent with snowdrifts up to 12 feet deep. A foot of snow fell in an hour at Folkestone and covered some villages up to the rooftops, marooning occupants unless they could dig themselves out.

Some people have been cut off for a fortnight. Last weekend only seven games of League soccer could be played. The west coast rail route to Scotland was cut. The number of deaths is unknown (→ 11/2).

Germans migrate into Reich's new lands

Western Poland, 26 January

The resettlement of ethnic Germans from Wohlhynien (western Ukraine) and eastern Galicia into the territories of the *Reich*, agreed during negotiations with the USSR, has been completed. The "migrants" come from what used to be eastern Poland, which has been under Soviet occupation since September. The resettlement has been pushed on with all haste since 20 December, with ethnic German groups covering 40 miles (64km) a day in temperatures as low as -40 degrees Fahrenheit (-40C). German-Soviet agreements late last year mean that some 205,000 ethnic Germans can leave the Soviet "sphere of interest" for the Reich. Many are earmarked by the Reich's Agency for the Organization of Space to displace Poles in the General Government area (occupied western Poland), regarded by the Nazis as part of the Reich's new *Lebensraum* [living space]. Just over 100,000 families from southern Germany are also expected to resettle in the occupied zone.

ENSA troupes learn lesson from their first night failures

London, 23 January

Following allegations by troop entertainers that ENSA's organization in France is in a "chaotic muddle", its officials are to report to the war office.

Jack Payne, who has just completed a three-week tour of France with his dance band, says that they missed four concerts completely owing to bad organization, including their Christmas Day concert with Gracie Fields. "When we arrived in France there was no transport and no-one at the port had heard of us," he said in a press interview headlined "Sack the Lot!". Billy Cotton and his band missed their engagements because a

Gracie Fields: the troops' favourite

bridge collapsed, leaving the lorry carrying their instruments on one side and the coachload of players on the other.

There have been many complaints about the standard of entertainment offered, and Lord Haw-Haw has sneered on German radio that the troops have to be paid to attend ENSA shows. Basil Dean, who runs ENSA from the Theatre Royal, Drury Lane, does not deny that mistakes had been made, but said that time was needed to perfect the service overseas. Since ENSA went to France, 383 live shows have been given, led by Gracie Fields, Leslie Henson, Will Hay and other stars.

1. Japan: Expenditure on defence is to account for half of the national budget.

1. Finland: The USSR is reported to have lost 200,000 men in the campaign (→ 4).

1. Yenan, China: Mao Tse-tung calls for the US to stand firm against Japan (→ 28).

1. Britain: A veteran of the Great War commits suicide because he is too old to participate in this one.

3. Whitby: A Heinkel He111 bomber is the first German plane shot down over England.

4. North Sea: The minesweeper HMS *Sphinx* sinks a day after being bombed by German aircraft (→ 5).

4. Helsinki: Fourteen are killed and 179 injured in heavy Russian air raids.→

5. Netherlands: General Reynders, the Dutch commander-in-chief, resigns over Holland's lack of military preparedness.

5. Atlantic: The destroyer HMS *Antelope* sinks a U-boat in the south-western approaches to Britain.→

6. London: An IRA bomb explodes at Euston station, injuring four people (→ 7).

7. Birmingham: Two IRA men are hanged for the Coventry bomb murders of 25 August 1939 (→ 14).

8. Paris: Police raid the Soviet Press Agency and discover that it is being used as a front for pro-German propaganda.

9. Washington: The undersecretary of state, Sumner Welles, is to be sent to Europe to try to negotiate a peace settlement (→ 26).

10. Europe: The USSR agrees to sign a trade treaty tomorrow to supply Germany with grain, oil and raw materials.

10. Washington: President Roosevelt condemns the USSR, saying that the US backs Finland.

10. Britain: The first magnetic mine is swept, by HMS *Salve* and HMS *Servitor*, off a sunken lightship.

Russia launches fresh Finland attack

Air attacks back Karelian offensive

Helsinki, 9 February

Fierce fighting continued today as General Timoshenko pressed his massive and well-organized attack on the Mannerheim Line. The offensive opened with a barrage so concentrated that 300,000 shells fell on Finnish positions near Summa in the first day.

The Russian guns are virtually wheel to wheel as they pour their shells onto the Finns. At the same time bombers are attacking the Finnish lines of communication and reserve bases.

It is estimated that the Russians have assembled some 1,500 aircraft of all types, including the modern Ilyushin I16/17 fighter, for this fresh offensive. Joseph Stalin does not mean to fail this time.

The Russians are also using a new weapon, troop-carrying armoured cars mounted on sledges and armed with machine guns. These are dashing forward, laying smoke screens, dropping off their troops and then moving on.

Tanks, each accompanied by a group of soldiers, are then sent forward through the smoke to attack the Finnish positions. In this way the Russians are avoiding the terrible casualties they suffered in the first round of fighting when they drove forward in massed ranks and were mown down (→ 11).

American and Swedish volunteers in the Finnish army on the Northern Front.

Allies pledge aid, but it may be too late

Paris, 5 February

The Supreme War Council, meeting in Paris, decided today to send an Anglo-French expedition of three or four divisions to the aid of Finland. The plan is to land the force either through Petsamo (in northern Finland), which is under attack from the Russians, or through Narvik (in northern Norway). The route to Finland from Narvik passes through Sweden, but the War Council favours it because holding Narvik would allow the Allies to cut off Germany's supply of Swedish iron ore, which has to be carried by rail to Narvik for shipment to Germany. It is not clear what action would be taken if Norway or Sweden refuses to cooperate.

Meanwhile, all possible aid has been promised to the Finns, and some equipment and a few thousand volunteers, mainly Scandinavians, have already arrived. It may be, however, that too little will arrive too late (→ 14).

Nazis order Czech Jews to close shops

Prague, 10 February

The Nazis today ordered the closing down of all Jewish-owned textile, clothing and leather goods stores, and warned that Baron von Neurath, the "*Reich* Protector" of Bohemia-Moravia, may order all other Jewish businesses to shut.

The baron has also ordered the sale of all jewellery, gold, platinum, silver and works of art owned by Jews. The measures are seen here as part of a plan to eliminate the Jews from the economic life of what used to be Czechoslovakia (→ 12/3).

Entertainment goes on: the US hit "Pinocchio" is heading for Britain.

Britain covers up shipping losses

Westminster, 6 February

Pressure from the admiralty led to new guidelines for BBC war reporting being agreed at Broadcasting House today. From now on the sinking of a small ship may be mentioned only once on a BBC news bulletin. Sinkings of larger ships, like the Canadian Pacific freighter *Beaverburn*, sunk today, may still be mentioned in consecutive bulletins. The government is worried by the rising effectiveness of German U-boats, and fears that zealous reporting by the BBC will give the impression that British losses are even greater than they are (→ 12).

Rabbits hop to the top of the menu

Britain, 2 February

The popularity of rabbit meat has increased by leaps and bounds as part of the menu in British households since meat rationing began.

Recipes for enhancing – or disguising – its taste fill the cookery columns. Rabbit, they point out, can be stewed, blanched, fricasseed, jugged or, of course, put in a pie. It is also plentiful and cheap, at 2/- (10p/40¢) for one rabbit. Fish is also unrationed but always seems to be scarce and is getting expensive. Cod is now 1/4 (6½p/27¢) a pound. Herring, the price of which is controlled, costs 6d (2½p/10¢) a pound.

Recipes for making the most of it.

1940

February

Su	Mo	Tu	We	Th	Fr	Sa
				1	2	3
4	5	6	7	8	9	10
11	12	13	14	15	16	17
18	19	20	21	22	23	24
25	26	27	28	29		

Britons warned: watch your tongues

London, 6 February

A nationwide campaign to stamp out war gossip has been launched under the slogan "Careless Talk Costs Lives". The ministry of information is distributing two and a half million posters to offices, hotels, shops, banks and public houses about the dangers of giving information to enemy sympathizers.

Some are amusing, such as the drawing of two women chattering on an underground train, with Hitler and Goering sitting on a seat behind them. The caption is "You never know *who's* listening!". Drawn by the *Punch* cartoonist "Fougasse" (Kenneth Bird), it is in a series that shows Hitler eavesdropping from train luggage racks or telephone kiosks, or concealed in the framed portraits on the walls.

The artist Norman Wilkinson has painted a torpedoed ship plunging to the bottom with the reminder "A few careless words may end in this". Other posters show a man telling his wife at breakfast "Of course, there's no harm in *your* knowing", or a seductive siren listening in at an officers' club with the caption "Keep mum, she's not so dumb". The posters are snappier than an earlier ministry effort which read: "Do not discuss any-

Teaching the British to keep mum even over intimate dinners and in the club.

thing which might be of national importance. The consequence of any such indiscretion may be the loss of many lives."

The ministry's film division, directed by Kenneth Clark, is financing three short films to be made by Michael Balcon at Ealing Studios on the same theme. In *All Hands* a sailor tells his girl-friend in a cafe that his ship is sailing at 9 o'clock that night from Portsmouth. The

waitress who serves them tells the manageress, who is an informer. An agent signals from the shore and a waiting U-boat torpedoes the ship. "Such a nice couple, I wish I could have done something for them," sighs the waitress. "We don't want people to think there is a spy in every public house," said Kenneth Clark, "but our job is to show the danger of careless chatter."

Women work in munitions factories and take to the lifeboats

Britain, 6 February

Women who turned out of their beds at dawn yesterday to help drag a north-east coast lifeboat a mile across land before it could be launched showed the determination and energy which is there to be tapped by the war industry.

Talks between Ernest Brown, the minister of labour and national service, and the national executive committee of the Amalgamated Engineering Union began yesterday to hammer out, among other things, possible ways of speeding up the supply of women workers to the munitions factories. As the idea of women taking over men's work becomes more generally accepted, pressure is also growing for equal pay to be given to the new recruits. Negotiations are under way between engineering employers and the unions.

A woman worker in a munitions factory pauses for the camera.

11. Europe: Intense cold still grips the continent, with 58 degrees of frost in Stockholm.

11. Finland: The Red Army breaches the Mannerheim Line at Summa (→15).

11. Montreal: Canada's governor-general, Lord Tweedsmuir (well-known as the author John Buchan) dies after surgery for a head injury.

12. Egypt: The first echelon (4th Brigade) of the New Zealand Division arrives.

12. North Sea: The sloop HMS *Gleaner* sinks a U-boat in the Firth of Clyde.

12. Atlantic: As part of an operation to intercept six German merchant vessels, the destroyer HMS *Hasty* captures the *Morea* in the Atlantic and the cruiser HMS *Glasgow* captures a trawler off Tromso, Norway.

12. Britain: Paper rationing is introduced, with supplies cut by 40 per cent.

14. Britain: British citizens are given permission to join the Finnish Foreign Legion (→27).

14. Birmingham: Five IRA bombs explode (→22).

14. North Sea: A Hudson of Coastal Command locates the German supply ship *Altmark* in Norwegian waters.

14. Vatican: Rationing is introduced.

14. Britain: The government says that North Sea merchant shipping will be armed (→15).

15. Germany: In reply to the British, the government says that it will regard all merchant shipping as warships.→

15. Finland: Summa falls to the Soviet Army, and the Finns are forced to retreat to the second line of Mannerheim Line defences (→17).

17. Finland: The USSR has completed its conquest of the Mannerheim Line, with Timoshenko's 54 Red Army divisions facing 15 depleted Finnish divisions.→

17. Stockholm: The Swedish government rejects Finnish requests for assistance (→19).

Hitler orders unlimited U-boat war

Copenhagen, 15 February

U-boat commanders have been ordered by Hitler himself to take the gloves off in the battle to stop essential supplies of food and war material reaching Britain. Any ship which is likely to come under British control can now be torpedoed without warning.

This directive means that any neutral ship which is sailing towards a British-controlled war zone – and one such is the English Channel, the world's busiest shipping lane – can be attacked without warning. Any ship which is following a zig-zag course is also liable to be sunk without warning.

The policy is already in effect, as is evidenced by the sinking of Danish, Dutch, Norwegian and Swedish ships in the last few days. Danish newspapers today are full of protests against the sinking of the 5,177-ton *Chastine Maersk* by a U-boat.

Danish, Norwegian and Swedish shipowners have been meeting here and have decided to press for urgent action by their governments;

A convoy of British merchant ships sails under escort by the Royal Navy.

one possibility is that neutral ships should henceforth travel in convoys protected by naval vessels.

Last night the British admiralty announced the sinking of two more U-boats, including the one which

sank a 12,000-ton meat ship in the Bay of Biscay. Any joy at the sinkings needs to be countered by the news that German shipyards are now building U-boats faster than Britain can sink them (→ 19).

Russia breaches Mannerheim Line to force Finnish withdrawal

Helsinki, 17 February

Marshal Mannerheim has ordered his weary, battered men to abandon the first line of the Mannerheim Line defences and fall back to a second line of defences up to ten miles away. The Finns have performed bravely, fighting off attack after attack for 16 days under a storm of cannon fire and bombs.

Yet now, tied to their defences, there is little they can do except hope to survive. Casualties are severe. Some regiments have lost two-thirds of their strength. Untrained recruits and veterans of the National Civil Guard have been thrown into the line where men have literally disappeared, blown away by the force of the bombardment.

General Timoshenko has cleverly chosen to concentrate his attack on the Summa area where the forest opens out into fields and there is room for his tanks to manoeuvre. The Russians soldiers, now welled and well-trained, are showing themselves to be hardy and brave – and there are many more of

them than of the Finns. A spokesman for the Finnish General Staff said last night that there were enormous heaps of Russian dead in front of the Finnish positions. He added: "Yet in spite of these losses we always feel that there are tens of thousands of Russians to be sent in. We need men and material, especially planes. So far the Finnish army has been able to hold its own, but we need the civilized nations to aid us to the utmost."

Meanwhile the fighting continues with the Finns, still resolute, making the Russians pay in blood for every yard they gain of Finnish territory (→ 20).

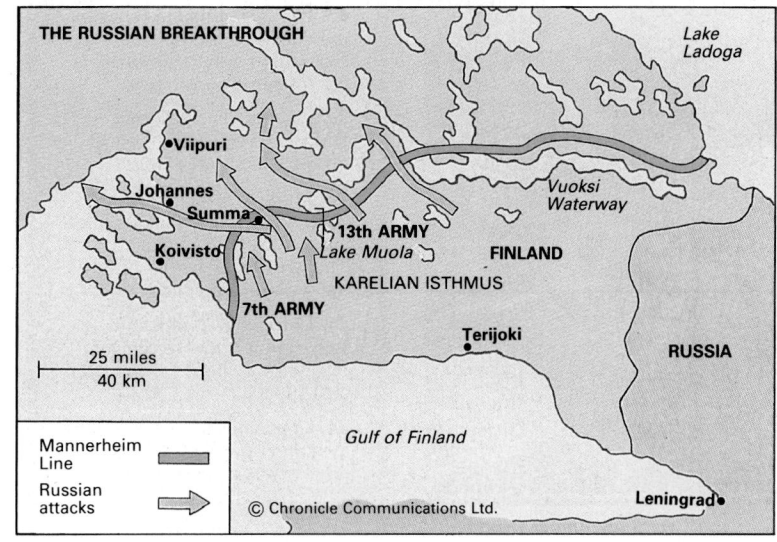

THE RUSSIAN BREAKTHROUGH

Lake Ladoga

Viipuri

Johannes

Summa

Koivisto

13th ARMY

Lake Muola

7th ARMY

Vuoksi Waterway

FINLAND

KARELIAN ISTHMUS

Terijoki

RUSSIA

25 miles
40 km

Mannerheim Line

Russian attacks

Gulf of Finland

Leningrad

© Chronicle Communications Ltd.

BBC to play dance music on Sundays

London, 15 February

The BBC's Forces Programme, which takes the air on 18 February, will broadcast dance music on Sundays, removing a ban which has been in force since the BBC was set up in 1922. The service has been brought in because troops in France were bored with the Home Service. They tuned in to *Radio Fecamp*, the French commercial station, before it closed down on 4 January. Home listeners can also hear the new service, from 11am to 11pm.

Army wives receive better allowances

London, 12 February

Women living in the London postal area whose husbands are away in the services are to receive increased allowances, payable immediately. The rise brings the separation allowance to 3/6 (17½p/70¢) a day and will date back to 4 December. Oliver Stanley, the new secretary of state for war, promised a full review of the army pay system when he took office last month. This increase follows widespread complaints about hardships experienced by service wives while their husbands are away.

Government to run railway network

Britain, 13 February

The present owners of Britain's railways will continue to run them during the war – but under strict government control. MPs were assured tonight that the private interests of the various companies which have been unprofitable in recent years will not be allowed to impede the war effort.

A proposal by the Labour Party for the nationalization of all forms of inland and coastal transport was then defeated in a Commons vote. While controlling railway fares and charges, the government will now guarantee the companies against financial losses. Railway company shares have risen sharply in the past few weeks.

Su	Mo	Tu	We	Th	Fr	Sa
				1	2	3
4	5	6	7	8	9	10
11	12	13	14	15	16	17
18	19	20	21	22	23	24
25	26	27	28	29		

Navy rescues seamen held by Germans

Bergen, 16 February

Some 299 British seamen held prisoner on the *Altmark* were rescued tonight by the destroyer HMS *Cossack*. The *Altmark* was the supply ship for the German pocket battleship *Admiral Graf Spee*, and the prisoners had been taken from merchant ships captured by her.

After the sinking of the *Graf Spee*, the *Altmark* sailed for Europe taking a route near the Arctic to avoid detection. Incredibly, the Norwegians who stopped and searched her found neither her concealed guns nor the prisoners. Two British destroyers then chased her into Jossingfjord. The *Cossack* lowered two boats, but they could not move through the ice.

The *Altmark* then made two attempts to ram the *Cossack*. As the two ships scraped together several members of a boarding party leapt aboard the German ship. The *Altmark* then ran aground and the rest of the Royal Navy party scrambled over the side, opening fire with their rifles and charging with fixed bayonets. Four German crewmen were killed. One prisoner said: 'It was a hit and run affair along the decks and round corners, ... more of a rathunt than anything. You can imagine our joy when we heard an English voice shouting down "The Navy's here!".'

The captain of the *Altmark* had denied the existence of prisoners right up to the end. One prisoner told how they had shouted, hammered and blown SOS whistles to

The "Altmark" in Jossingfjord after the prisoners had been released.

attract the attention of the Norwegian search party at Bergen. The Germans turned a fire hose on them to stop them, and to drown the noise they turned on a winch. Even so the prisoners found it difficult to understand why the Norwegians had not noticed something of their presence. Afterwards the Germans told them that their behaviour was mutiny and put out a notice saying: "On account of today's behaviour of the prisoners, they will get bread and water tomorrow instead of the regular meals."

To mount the rescue the *Cossack* had to violate Norwegian territorial waters, but since the Norwegians had failed to find guns or prisoners most Britons will feel that this was justified (→ 18).

Jubilation for the prisoners the Norwegians missed, on board the "Cossack".

18. London: The British government presses Norway to intern the *Altmark*.

18. USA: The secretary of state, Cordell Hull, applies the American "moral embargo" to Russia.

18. Paris: The French government agrees to allow the reconstitution of the Polish air force on French soil.

18. Off Duncansby Head, Scotland: The British destroyer HMS *Daring* is torpedoed, with the loss of 157 lives (→ 21).

19. Sweden: King Gustav announces his support for his government's decision to refuse Finland military aid (→ 23).

20. Moscow: Russia offers fresh peace talks to Finland.→

20. Germany: General Nikolaus von Falkenhorst, who commanded XXI Corps in the invasion of Poland, is given command of the invasion force for Norway.

21. North Sea: British trawlers fire back at *Luftwaffe* bombers with their new machine guns.

21. North Atlantic: The cruiser HMS *Manchester* and the destroyer HMS *Kimberley* capture another of the six German merchant vessels which the Royal Navy is hunting (→ 23).

23. Turkey: A state of emergency is declared following the alleged crossing of the Caucasian border by a Soviet detachment.

23. Helsinki: Finland repeats its request to Sweden and Norway to grant transit rights for foreign troops (→ 24).

23. Faeroes: The destroyer HMS *Gurkha* sinks a U-boat off the islands (→ 25).

24. Munich: Hitler warns: "We cannot be defeated either economically or militarily ... The world may be full of devils but we will succeed."

24. Europe: Germany and Italy sign a trade agreement giving the Italians an increased coal supply.

24. Copenhagen: The Scandinavian foreign ministers meet to discuss war problems (→ 27).

Ardennes invasion strategy gets Hitler seal of approval

Berlin, 24 February

Hitler is considering a radical new plan for attacking western Europe by mounting a massive *Panzer* drive through the wooded Ardennes of Belgium into France near Sedan. If successful the German forces would sweep towards Paris and the Channel coast, cutting off British forces from their French allies and by-passing the Maginot Line.

Details of an earlier plan fell into Allied hands when a *Luftwaffe* staff officer crash-landed in Belgium; the Belgian government called the plan "most extraordinary and serious" and protested to Germany. The Belgian protest did not worry Hitler, but the security leak did. He ordered a rethink and General Erich von Manstein suggested an assault through the Ardennes.

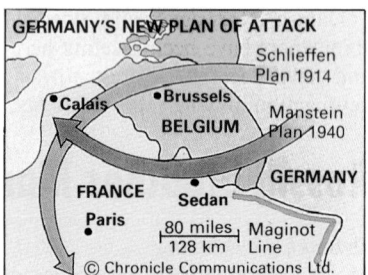

War work schemes "fail to hit target"

Britain, 24 February

The government is launching a big recruiting and training drive for the engineering and metal industries. At the same time it acknowledges that it will still fail to meet the vast demand for skilled labour.

Unemployed men aged between 17 and 45 will be given up to six months' training at 22 ministry of labour centres. Within a year 40,000 should be ready for work in the arms factories.

Unemployed men over 45 will be accepted "if fit and handy". Men between 20 and 25 are excluded from the scheme. They will soon all be conscripted into the armed forces. All men in training will get free midday meals on each day of attendance at the centres.

Russia lays down Finnish surrender terms

Finns continue their winter war with the Russians despite Stalin's final terms.

Moscow, 23 February
The Soviet government today sent its "final" peace terms to Finland, with Sweden acting as intermediary. The terms are even harsher than the demands whose refusal led to the war. The USSR wants the whole of the Karelian isthmus including Viipuri, Finland's second largest city; the naval base at Hango, which the Finns regard as the key to their country; and all the land round Lake Ladoga. The Russians will evacuate the territory they have seized around Petsamo in the far north if the Finns agree to a treaty guaranteeing the security of the Gulf of Finland against external threats. It is still not certain if the Finns will accept these demands, but there is one more card they can play: they can invite the Allies to intervene. But Sweden seemed to rule that out today by banning Allied troops from moving across its territory (→ 5/3).

Feb 23. Londoners cheer the men of the "Exeter" and the "Ajax" for their part in the sinking of the "Admiral Graf Spee". They are on their way to the Guildhall for lunch with the Mayor.

Five-year-old boy is new Dalai Lama

Lhasa, 22 February
Buddhists all over the Far East touched the floor with their foreheads at 4pm today as they bowed in the direction of the almost inaccessible Potala Palace above Lhasa, the capital of Tibet. In monasteries and temples across the Buddhist world they were celebrating the enthronement of the new Dalai Lama – the spiritual leader of the Tibetan Buddhists.

The new representative of this holy line is a five-year-old peasant boy called Lhamo Dhondup, born in the village of Taktser north-east of Lhasa.

Lhamo, who was selected from three boys in his region, is the 14th in the line of Dalai Lamas which began in the 14th century.

Calendar February 1940

Su	Mo	Tu	We	Th	Fr	Sa
				1	2	3
4	5	6	7	8	9	10
11	12	13	14	15	16	17
18	19	20	21	22	23	24
25	26	27	28	29		

25. Copenhagen: The Scandinavian foreign ministers reaffirm their countries' neutrality (→ 28).

25. Rome: The American envoy Sumner Welles arrives at the start of his European peace mission (→ 26).

25. Atlantic: The Royal Navy ships *Escort*, *Imogen* and *Inglefield* and the submarine *Narwhal* sink a U-boat off north-west Scotland (→ 29).

26. Finland: The army evacuates Koivisto fort, and prepares for a prolonged siege at Viipuri.

26. Britain: The war office announces that northern Scotland is to become out of bounds for unauthorized people from 11 March.

26. Paris: Anti-aircraft guns drive *Luftwaffe* reconnaissance planes away from the city.

26. Rome: Sumner Welles meets Mussolini and his son-in-law Count Galeazzo Ciano, the foreign minister (→ 1/3).

27. Scandinavia: Sweden and Norway again refuse Finland's request for transit rights for foreign troops.

27. Britain: The first volunteers leave to aid the Finnish forces.

28. Berlin: The propaganda minister, Dr Goebbels, tells neutral countries to "curb their public opinion" and warns Sweden against aiding Finland.

28. Britain: The first of a new class of battleship, HMS *King George V*, is launched.

28. China: Communist troops retake Anding, near Yenan, from the Japanese (→ 14/3).

29. West Indies: The destroyer HMS *Despatch* intercepts the German merchant ship *Troja* off Aruba; she is scuttled by her German crew (→ 2/3).

29. Japan: Britain hands back to Japan nine of the 21 Germans taken off the *Asama Maru*.

29. Uruguay: The wreck of the scuttled German pocket battleship *Admiral Graf Spee* is sold to a local company for scrap.

Rationing and price freeze in France

Paris, 29 February
Faced with a serious drop in industrial production, continual class conflict and war apathy, Paul Reynaud, the finance minister, has ordered a price freeze and petrol and food rationing. The aim is to create some sort of national unity and to win the support of the working class for the war by halting inflation and ensuring fair shares for all. But the Communists remain anti-war and the non-Communist Left remains unenthusiastic – almost as unenthusiastic as the Right, which fears the Left more than it fears Hitler.

Germans told to be good housekeepers

Germany, 29 February
Good housekeeping with what is available is the message from the *Reich* ministry of food and agriculture to the German consumer. The Nazis are keen to avoid the food shortages of the last war; since the introduction of rationing in August 1939 propaganda has focused on self-sufficiency, with farmers told to make the best use of land and livestock, and householders urged to plant vegetables rather than flowers. Rations (about 16 ounces of meat and ten ounces of fat a week per person) have led to black marketeering, for which stiff penalties were introduced last September.

Divers capture key to U-boat secrets

Scotland, 28 February
Divers have recovered three rotors from the top-secret *Enigma* enciphering machine on board U-33. The U-boat, caught minelaying off Scotland, scuttled herself after being forced to surface by depth charges from the sloop HMS *Gleaner*, which marked the spot and sent for the divers.

The rotors have been rushed to Bletchley Park in Buckinghamshire where code-breaking scientists are working furiously to solve the secrets of Enigma. The rotors could help break the vital U-boat code.

Canadian forces arrive to back the Allies

From across the ocean they come: Canadian soldiers disembark to fight Hitler.

Liverpool, 25 February
The first battle squadron of the Royal Canadian Air Force arrived in Britain today to join the RAF in the Allied cause against Hitler. They follow their fellow-countrymen from the army, who are already in Britain.

"The men come from coast to coast, from Nova Scotia to Vancouver. No fewer than 146 cities, town and villages in every province of the Dominion are represented," said Squadron-Leader W D van Vliet, a first-class rugby player and ice hockey champion. "About 20 per cent of them are French-speaking Canadians, and they are all especially anxious to get to France."

They were welcomed at the dockside by the Earl of Derby, who said to them: "It is not for me to wish you a good time. What I will do, if I may be pardoned the language, is to wish you as good a time as you can have, and I will wish the *Boche* [German] what I know he will get – and that is a hell of a time."

The Canadians lined up on the quayside – pilots, crewmen, gunners, fitters, riggers and cooks – were urged by their officers to cheer the earl, though few appeared to have any idea who the elderly gentleman was (→ 5/3).

Clark Gable as Rhett Butler and Vivien Leigh as Scarlett O'Hara in the film of the American Civil War novel "Gone with the Wind". The film, which has broken box office records in America, opens soon in Europe.

1940

March

Su	Mo	Tu	We	Th	Fr	Sa
					1	2
3	4	5	6	7	8	9
10	11	12	13	14	15	16
17	18	19	20	21	22	23
24	25	26	27	28	29	30
31						

1. Berlin: Hitler issues a war directive ordering the invasion of Denmark and Norway. He also meets Sumner Welles, to whom he says that "there is no other solution than a life-and-death struggle" (→ 3).

1. Britain: Women are urged to wear light clothes in order to save darker dyes for forces uniforms (→ 16/3).

2. Denmark and West Indies: The cruiser HMS *Berwick* intercepts the German SS *Wolfsburg* in the Denmark Strait and the cruiser HMS *Dunedin* intercepts the *Heidelberg* in the Caribbean, but both German ships are scuttled (→ 3).

2. Henley: Cambridge wins an unofficial wartime boat race.

2. France: Army intelligence reveals German preparations for an attack on Scandinavia.

3. Berlin: Goering meets Sumner Welles, and evades his questions about cruelty to Polish Jews; he prefers to show Welles his vast art collection (→ 7).

3. Atlantic: The cruiser HMS *York* intercepts the German SS *Arucas* off Iceland, but the German crew scuttles her.

3. Britain: The public have invested £100 million in National Savings since war broke out.

5. Finland: The government accepts Russia's offer to reopen negotiations for a truce and for the cession of border areas (→ 8).

5. Toronto: Canada promises to send 1,000 volunteers to fight with the Finns.

6. North Sea: German aircraft bomb and machine-gun two lightships.

7. Paris: The prime minister, Edouard Daladier, meets the US envoy Sumner Welles (→ 11).

7. Poland: The RAF flies from bases in France to drop leaflets over western Poland.

8. Finland: After the fall of part of Viipuri, Russia rejects Finland's request for an immediate armistice.→

9. Europe: Britain and France promise troops and planes to Finland to fight the Russians.

Finns edge towards reluctant surrender to Russian demand

Helsinki, 9 March
The Finns, in danger of being overwhelmed by a Russian offensive all along the front, have today sued for peace despite the harshness of the Russian terms.

Events took on a certain inevitability after the Russian ultimatum for the acceptance of the final peace terms ran out on 1 March. Two days later Marshal Timoshenko launched another crushing attack and the town of Viipuri, shattered by Russian bombs and shells, came under direct attack; it became obvious that the Finns could not hold out for much longer.

On 6 March a delegation headed by the prime minister, Mr Ryti,

Paasikivi: championing Finland.

travelled to Moscow. Mr Paasikivi, the minister in charge of the negotiations, hoped to force concessions from the Russians.

Coldly received by the foreign minister, Vyacheslav Molotov, and denigrated in scornful language by the Soviet press, the delegation continued to negotiate until the shattering news came that Viipuri had fallen. The Finns asked for an armistice. Molotov said "*niet*" and Ryti was forced to capitulate.

There are still many details to be settled and Ryti is in constant touch with his government in Helsinki. Meanwhile the fighting continues on all fronts and men are still dying, but it is all over now. Finland has been defeated (→ 12).

Luxury liner in secret dash to New York

The world's biggest liner, the "Queen Elizabeth", pulls into New York harbour.

New York, 7 March
The Cunard Line's newest ship, the *Queen Elizabeth*, was given a heroine's welcome when she docked here at 5pm today. The 83,673-ton liner, the biggest in the world, braved the menace of the U-boat war in the Atlantic in what must have been one of the most hazardous maiden voyages ever.

The liner's dash across the Atlantic was kept a firm secret – until today, that is, when her immense bulk, shrouded in wartime grey, appeared over the horizon moving towards Nantucket. Special planes carrying newspaper reporters, photographers and broadcasters flew out in the small hours. One radio man gave his listeners an eyewitness report from above the liner at 7.45 this morning.

The liner crossed the Atlantic at an average of 24.5 knots. She relied on her speed to evade the submarines, and dropped her escort destroyer after one day out. "It is unique to leave without trials and find yourself in New York," said Captain Townley. His chief engineer was now confident that the *Queen Elizabeth* would prove the fastest as well as the biggest liner afloat. Today she passed her sister ship, the *Queen Mary*, already docked here, and the two dipped ensigns to each other. All the other ships in port sounded their sirens in greeting. On the quayside a crowd of 10,000 had been waiting for most of the afternoon, and in the city office workers showered the streets with ticker tape in welcome.

Strict security is still being maintained, with no visitors allowed on board. The ship is fitted with a new magnetic mine protector device. How much of the final fitting-out work has been done is not yet clear, but what is certain is that she will be prepared for war work, not luxury passengers (→ 21).

Sneering Haw-Haw has big following

Britain, 1 March
Two-thirds of the adult population tunes in to Lord Haw-Haw's broadcasts from Hamburg, according to BBC audience research just completed. One person in six is a regular listener to his propaganda. Some 16 million listeners hear the BBC nine o'clock news every night, and about six million of them switch straight over to Lord Haw-Haw afterwards.

Speculation continues about the identity behind his superior drawl, which has been compared with Bertie Wooster's. Norman Baillie-Stewart, the officer imprisoned in the Tower for passing information to Germany before the war, and William Joyce, a former member of Sir Oswald Mosley's British Union of Fascists, have been suggested.

After much debate the BBC decided not to answer his broadcasts with direct refutation, but it has begun weekly broadcasts at the same hour by a commentator with the pseudonym "Onlooker", believed to be Norman Birkett, the eminent QC.

Italian coal ships seized in Channel

Dover, 5 March
Six Italian ships carrying cargoes of German coal were arrested in mid-Channel by British warships today after a warning that Britain will seize all German coal found at sea. The ships are anchored off the Kent coast while the government decides whether their cargoes should be unloaded.

Four more Italian colliers sailed from Rotterdam today, and a further six are loading with Rhineland coal destined for Italian ports. All are likely to be seized following an announcement by the ministry of economic warfare that German coal exported to any foreign port would be regarded as contraband.

Severe weather in Germany has reduced normal supplies of coal to Italy, where rationing is now in force. Many Italians believe that the seizure of their ships is a deliberate attempt to force them to buy British coal on British terms.

British sources are insisting that the blockade of German produce applies to all neutral ships, and deny discrimination against Italy.

Fiery Finnish cocktails harry Soviet forces

Finland, 9 March
One legacy of Finland's brave yet unavailing fight against the USSR is a simple but deadly projectile. It consists of a bottle – empty vodka bottles are preferred – filled with petrol, or paraffin, and tar. Strips of rag are used as a stopper for the bottle. The rag is lit, causing the contents of the bottle to ignite on impact with the engine compartment of a tank, the usual target; the flaming tar seeps into the engine. In this way countless Soviet tanks were wrecked, and the Finns sardonically dubbed their new weapon the "Molotov cocktail".

Molotov: immortalised in flames.

The war delivers blow to French stomachs

Paris, 1 March
The Frenchman's love affair with gastronomy took a knock today with the publication of new restrictions on what can be eaten – and drunk. Meals in hotels and restaurants will be restricted to two, only one of which can be meat, and the sale of spirits will be limited to four days a week. Eating at home offers no escape: ration cards are to be distributed, with bread, pastries and chocolates among foods either restricted or even banned (→ 11/3).

1940

March

Su	Mo	Tu	We	Th	Fr	Sa
					1	2
3	4	5	6	7	8	9
10	11	12	13	14	15	16
17	18	19	20	21	22	23
24	25	26	27	28	29	30
31						

11. London: Sumner Welles meets the king, and discusses possible peace and mediation condition terms with Chamberlain and Halifax.→

11. USA: The government lifts its arms embargo to allow Britain and France to buy some P40 fighter planes.

11. Toulon, France: The French battleship *Bretagne* and cruiser *Algerie* sail for Canada with 2,379 gold bullion bars, part of the national reserves.

11. North Sea: An RAF Blenheim sinks the U-boat U-31 off Borkum (→ 20).

12. Lublin: Seventy-two German Jews, out of 1,000 deported in sealed freight cars from Stettin, die of exposure after an 18-hour march in a blizzard (→ 23).

12. Moscow: Finnish envoys initial a peace treaty with Russia (→ 13).

13. Finland: Hostilities cease at 11am (→ 14).

13. London: Sir Michael O'Dwyer, the former governor of the Punjab, is assassinated by an Indian nationalist.

14. Finland: 470,000 Finns evacuate the area ceded to Russia.→

14. Paris: The exiled Polish government publishes documents revealing German plans to invade Russia.→

14. Germany: Goering decrees that all articles made of copper, bronze, nickel and other useful metals must be given up for the war effort.

14. China: Twenty-seven out of 30 Chinese fighter planes are shot down by the Japanese over Chengtu (→ 30).

14. Australia: The prime minister, Robert Menzies, forms a coalition cabinet.

15. Roumania: Imprisoned members of the pro-Nazi Iron Guard are given an amnesty after swearing an oath of allegiance to King Carol.

15. Poland: RAF planes drop over six million leaflets on Warsaw. One returning RAF Whitley lands in a German field before realizing its mistake and taking off again.

Finns ratify Russia pact

Helsinki, 15 March

The Finnish *Diet*, meeting in secret session, tonight ratified the Moscow peace agreement by 145 votes to three. Speaking before the vote was taken, the prime minister, Mr Ryti, said: "Finland, as well as as the whole of Western civilization, is still in the greatest danger, and no one can say what tomorrow may bring. We believe that by choosing peace we have acted in the best way for the moment."

There is some bitterness here towards those countries, especially Sweden, thought by the Finns to have let them down. Sweden refused to allow Allied troops to cross its territory, although by then it might already have been too late.

Finland's immediate thoughts, however, are concentrated on the evacuation of people from those areas which are being occupied by the Russians. Many refugees are already trudging along the icy roads with their livestock. All transport in the south-east has been mobilized to cope with the migration of the 470,000 people, one-eighth of the population, who will lose their land and homes (→ 19).

Finnish infantry retreats from Viipuri after the successful Russian attack.

Britons face limit on meat spending

MEAT RATION PLANS
LATE EXTRA EVENING NEWS

News that is no shock to the nation.

Britain, 11 March

Meat rationing began today with no sign of queues at butchers' counters. Most people had stocked up in advance. Meat is rationed by price, the allowance being 1/10-worth (9p/37¢) per week. Children under six get half as much.

At current prices a family with two children over six could buy a six-pound joint of lamb at 1/4 a pound. Poultry, game, offal, sausages and meat pies remain off the ration. Restaurants are allowed to serve meat without asking customers for their coupons (→ 19).

Doing the Blackout Stroll with girls in taffeta gowns

England, 16 March

Long evening dresses are making a come-back in London, particularly in the restaurants and clubs frequented by young soldiers on their way to France. In contrast to the utilitarian wear of the early war months, luxury fabrics such as chiffon, lace, tulle and taffeta are now favoured for a night on the town. Far from their wives and girlfriends, the soldiers are happy to find places where partners are provided. The latest new dance, a great favourite among the soldiers and their dancing partners, is "The Blackout Stroll" during which the lights go out and everyone changes partners.

Elegant evening wear and army boots: waiting for the dancing to start.

First civilian killed in Scapa Flow raid

Scotland, 16 March
The first civilian to be killed in an air raid during the present war died today during a German raid on the naval base at Scapa Flow.

James Isbister, aged 27, who lived in the village of Bridge of Waithe on Loch Stenness, was standing in the doorway of his home. An enemy aircraft that had turned tail dropped 19 bombs wounding seven civilians and killing Mr Isbister. Apparently he had been about to run across the road to help a neighbour, Mrs McLeod, whose cottage had been hit. He leaves a widow and an infant son. According to an admiralty communique, the raid on Scapa Flow began at 7.50pm. "About 14 enemy aircraft reached the objective. A considerable number of bombs was dropped, one hitting a warship [HMS *Norfolk*] which sustained only minor damage." Six crew were killed in the raid and seven injured. The raid was the first on Scapa Flow since 17 October when the old battleship *Iron Duke* was hit.

None of the enemy aircraft was shot down, although several were claimed to have been damaged in fights with RAF machines. It was reported, but not confirmed, that the raiders also tried to reach the Forth Bridge, but failed (→ 19).

After the air raid: Mrs McLeod stands at the door of her shattered house.

Mussolini has talks with peace envoy

Rome, 16 March
Sumner Welles, the American under-secretary of state, today had talks with Mussolini, Count Ciano, the foreign minister, and King Victor Emmanuel III on the last leg of his mission to discuss conditions for mediation or peace talks in Europe. He received a cordial but non-committal welcome from the Italians which contrasted with the cool response he got from Goering and Hess in Berlin on 3 March, at the start of his trip. He left Germany via Switzerland for talks with French and exiled Polish leaders in Paris, and was in London from 10 to 13 March before leaving for Rome, via Paris again (→ 20).

Poles reveal Nazi designs on Russia

Angers, 14 March
The Polish government in exile published a white paper today giving a general view of Poland's relations with Germany between May 1933 and October 1939. One of its most interesting revelations – which will not please Stalin – is that Hitler tried to involve Poland in a plot to attack the Soviet Union.

It was proposed by Goering during a visit to Warsaw in February 1935. In a discussion with the Polish leader, Marshal Pilsudski, he suggested that Poland and Germany should mount a joint invasion of the Ukraine. The Poles insist that they gave the Germans no encouragement whatsoever.

1940
March

Su	Mo	Tu	We	Th	Fr	Sa
					1	2
3	4	5	6	7	8	9
10	11	12	13	14	15	16
17	18	19	20	21	22	23
24	25	26	27	28	29	30
31						

17. Berlin: Dr Fritz Todt is appointed *Reich* minister for armaments and munitions.→

17. Britain: Nottinghamshire miners vote to forgo part of their holidays to boost the war effort.

18. London: Walt Disney's new film *Pinocchio* opens to a warm reception from the critics.

18. London: A new organization is formed to liaise between the British and French colonial authorities.

19. Helsinki: Official figures are released showing that 25,000 Finns were killed in the war with Russia.

19. Westminster: Chamberlain defends the lack of Allied aid to Finland, saying that Mannerheim only requested it once, in January.

19. London: A woman is fined £75 for buying enough sugar for 140 weekly rations; she drove away from the shop in a Rolls-Royce.

20. Moscow: Russia warns of its opposition to an alliance of Scandinavian countries in the belief that it would be hostile.

20. North Sea: German bombers attack a neutral convoy, damaging three ships.

20. North Sea: The destroyer HMS *Fortune* sinks the U-boat U-44 off Narvik in Norway.→

20. Italy: President Roosevelt's envoy, Sumner Welles, sails from Genoa, ending his efforts on behalf of the US to end the war.

21. Syria: British and Turkish delegations hold a secret meeting in Aleppo.

21. New York: The *Queen Mary* sails for a secret destination.

22. Ankara: All large Turkish steamers in foreign waters are ordered to return home as soon as possible.

23. Devon: IRA prisoners stage a riot at Dartmoor prison.

23. Germany: Field Marshal Goering orders a halt to transports of Jews in eastern Europe, but is ignored.

The small man with a big task as new French premier

Reynaud: chosen to fight for France.

Paris, 21 March
Paul Reynaud, who has succeeded Edouard Daladier as the prime minister of France, can be expected to do what he has been chosen by parliament to do: to fight the war with more vigour.

The fall of Daladier took place in a strange, unintended fashion. He went to the Chamber for a vote of confidence, and the Chamber gave it to him by 245 votes to only one – but with no fewer than 294 deputies abstaining. The abstainers did not want him to go; they wanted him to get on with things. They were infuriated by his insistence on retaining the portfolios of national defence and foreign affairs as well as the prime ministership. But he chose to take their abstentions as so many votes of no confidence.

Reynaud is a tiny man with hunched shoulders, a deeply lined face and a nasal, tinny voice; in spite of this he is one of the three or four most respected speakers in the Chamber. Before becoming a minister he was a leading Paris lawyer. He is also an expert on finance, and was minister of finance until last night. He has taken a keen interest in defence, and is one of the backers of those officers, like Colonel Charles de Gaulle, who urge that France must rely less on the defensive Maginot Line and more on attack (→ 26).

▷

Scientists hint at atomic super bomb

London, 21 March
Ever since the atom was split in 1919 by Ernest Rutherford there has been a growing belief among scientists that vast amounts of energy can be produced from nuclear fission. Two days ago two *emigre* German scientists, Otto Frisch and Rudolf Peierls, presented a paper to Sir Henry Tizard, the government scientific adviser, arguing that it would be possible to produce a super bomb through nuclear chain reaction. This would need just a few pounds of the uranium isotope U235. The government is taking the matter seriously.

RAF raids Sylt to avenge Scapa Flow

Westminster, 19 March
Fifty RAF bombers – 30 Whitleys and 20 Hampdens – tonight attacked a German seaplane base at Hornum, at the southern end of the North Sea island of Sylt. The crews reported many hits, but the extent of any damage is not known. The raid, publicly disclosed in the Commons by the prime minister as it was happening, is a reprisal for the German bombing of Scapa Flow three days ago, in which six sailors and a civilian were killed.

Hitler appoints Todt his minister of arms

Dr Fritz Todt: a likeable Nazi.

Berlin, 20 March
An amiable civil engineer who built Germany's motorways has been given the job of mobilizing all available manpower, including the conquered Poles and Czechs, to work in the munitions factories of the *Reich*. Dr Fritz Todt, said by foreigners who have met him to be the most likeable of the leading Nazis, becomes minister for armaments and munitions; he will be the biggest employer of labour in Germany, and will also control the allocation of scarce raw materials.

Todt's labour battalions built the massive Siegfried Line opposite the Maginot Line and have recently been working on the construction of an *Ostwall* opposite the Stalin Line in the east.

Mussolini and Hitler: after the fanfares, an Italian pledge to join the war.

Hitler and Mussolini meet at Brennero

Brennero, Italy, 18 March
Under a leaden sky, with a snow-storm whipping down from the Alps, Europe's two most prominent dictators shook hands on the railway station at the Austrian border here today – and set the world speculating on the possibility of a peace plan. Nothing could be further from the truth. In two hours of discussion, Hitler extracted a promise from his Italian counterpart that Italy would – eventually – come into the war.

Mussolini was the first to arrive, in his armoured train. Thirty minutes later Hitler's train steamed in to a fanfare of trumpets and two national anthems, the *Deutschlandlied* and the *Horst Wessel* song. The two men exchanged fascist-style salutes and walked the length of the platform to Mussolini's saloon car for talks over a small table behind drawn blinds. They were joined later by their foreign ministers, Count Ciano – Mussolini's son-in-law, who, it is understood, is strongly opposed to Italian intervention – and von Ribbentrop. The atmosphere at the talks was described as "cordial" (→ 31).

Britain steps up its Norwegian patrols

Copenhagen, 21 March
The 4,947-ton German steamer *Heddernheim* was torpedoed this evening eight miles off the Danish coast by the British submarine *Ursula*. Though the steamer is not large, her sinking represents the first *coup* in a major step-up in British efforts to cripple Germany's vital iron ore supplies.

Germany's armaments depend on imported iron ore. No less than nine million tons come from Sweden, much of it brought through Narvik, a Norwegian port which is ice-free all year round. The Royal Navy is now moving in destroyers and submarines to make the route dangerous if not impossible (→ 28).

Yum yum, popsies and sprogs are talk of wartime

Britain, 1940
It might be news to many of you that London streets are now regularly filled with body-snatchers in a flap. Or that, if they were body-snatchers from north of the border, they might cool off afterwards with some bottled sunshine.

These are just a couple of the phrases coined by the men in Britain's armed services. The body-snatchers are first-aid workers, and when in a flap they are working in an air raid. The bottled sunshine is, of course, beer.

Parachuting is an activity that has fired the men's imaginations. The 'chute itself is known as a bag by some, and is used for a brolly hop by pilots, or bus drivers, as bomber pilots are called. Unlucky pilots ditch in the herring pond or the gravy (the Atlantic) or in the drink (the Channel).

Amorous activities have provided one of the richest sources of servicemen's slang. Girlfriends are known as charmers, lush bints, popsies or pushers. Those who are seeing a girl regularly are said to be nibbling.

On an evening off men get into their swanks (civilian clothes) and take the liberty bus into town to pitch a woo. Those separated from their lovers receive yum yum by post if they're lucky. An amorous couple may be described as kittens in a basket.

Friends, too, are described in a variety of inventive ways. A sailor's chum is his brassy or sprog. When they have a disagreement they part brassrags, each taking his cleaning rags back to his own quarters.

During time off, bottled sunshine (alternatively known as brown food) gets you horizontal, stitched, shot up or shot to ribbons. Char (tea) the next morning can be accompanied by gunfire – biscuits so-called because they crackle loudly when bitten.

1940

March

Su	Mo	Tu	We	Th	Fr	Sa
					1	2
3	4	5	6	7	8	9
10	11	12	13	14	15	16
17	18	19	20	21	22	23
24	25	26	27	28	29	30
31						

24. North Sea: A British submarine sinks the German cargo ship *Hugo Stinnes IV* off the Danish coast (→ 28).

25. London: Easter crowds flock to the West End, ignoring the blackout.→

25. Rome: The Hungarian premier, Count Paul Teleki, has lengthy talks with the Italian foreign minister, Count Galeazzo Ciano.

26. New Zealand: Michael Savage, the Labour prime minister, dies aged 68.

26. Moscow: Stalin refuses to meet Hitler for talks on the Polish border question (→ 29).

26. France: Reynaud appeals to his people to carry on the total war against Germany.→

27. France: The government asks the USSR to recall its ambassador in Paris.

28. Britain: New blue £1 and mauve ten shilling (50p) notes are announced.

28. Denmark Strait: HM Armed Merchant Cruiser *Transylvania* intercepts the German merchant ship *Mimi Horn*, but she is scuttled by her crew (→ 31).

29. Moscow: Molotov declares that the USSR will stay neutral in the war (→ 30).

30. Washington: The US refuses to recognize the Japanese regime in Nanking.→

30. Germany: Hitler publicly orders that priority be given to transporting arms to Russia, while privately planning to attack the USSR next year.

30. Britain: In a broadcast, Churchill says that Britain has no quarrel with the Russians but vows to "follow this war wherever it leads".

31. Atlantic: Since the war began, Germany has sunk 1.13 million tons of Allied shipping; U-boat actions alone account for 753,000 tons.

31. Italy: Mussolini warns King Victor Emmanuel III that Italy will join the war.

31. Germany: The surface raider *Atlantis* sets sail for operations against Allied shipping.

Allied leaders hold London summit

No separate peace deal with Germany

London, 28 March
The new French premier, Paul Reynaud, arrived in London today with General Gamelin, the Allied C-in-C, for a meeting of the Supreme War Council. In a "solemn declaration" issued after the meeting, Reynaud and Britain's Neville Chamberlain pledged their governments never to agree to "an armistice or treaty of peace except by mutual agreement".

Reynaud, a close friend of Winston Churchill, is believed to favour a more vigorous prosecution of the war, and he put to the council a number of ideas, some of which were backed by Chamberlain.

Reynaud's weakness, however, is his lack of parliamentary support. His predecessor, Daladier, fell after being denounced in the French parliament for inaction, not against

Churchill: backing a tough line.

Germany, but against the Soviet Union over Finland. Reynaud, elected by a majority of one in the Chamber of Deputies, came to London with a plan for bombing Soviet oilfields in the Caucasus, aimed at stopping oil deliveries to Germany and crippling the Soviet Union. The British were unenthusiastic.

Neutral Norway's waters to be mined

London, 28 March
A bold plan for stopping Swedish iron ore deliveries to Germany is being worked out by British chiefs of staff after the Supreme War Council discussed a joint Anglo-French operation to lay mines in Norwegian territorial waters.

Most of Germany's iron ore from Sweden comes through ice-free Narvik in northern Norway. The Allies had hoped to use the Finnish war to persuade Norway and Sweden to allow them to land forces in the northern regions of those two countries, ostensibly to aid Finland but mainly to interrupt Germany's iron ore supplies. Norway and Sweden firmly rejected this infringement of their neutrality. Now the Allies are preparing to go ahead with their plan, irrespective of the pleas of neutrality (→ 3/4).

Japan sets up puppet leader in Nanking

Nanking, March 30
A breakaway group of Chinese Nationalists led by the former foreign minister, Wang Chingwei, today established a rival *Kuomintang* in Japanese-occupied Nanking.

The Reformed Kuomintang gained immediate recognition from Japan, Germany and Italy, but none from the Allies. The new government has agreed to Japanese troops remaining in China. Persuading a politician of Wang Ching-wei's stature to lead the new government is a propaganda *coup* for Japan, which has now dissolved its two muchridiculed puppet governments in China and placed them under his control (→ 2/4).

Wang Ching-wei: puppet leader.

Mackenzie King wins Canadian poll

Ottawa, 29 March
In a record poll Canadians have given the prime minister, William Mackenzie King, and his Liberal Party the biggest electoral victory in Canadian history – 179 seats in the 245-seat federal legislature.

Bearing in mind Mr Mackenzie King's strategy of limiting the number of Canadian troops sent to Europe while building war industries on the safe side of the Atlantic, it is a resounding vote for war with moderation. The Conservatives retained most of their seats, with the Liberal victory being gained at the expense of the radical parties.

Easter crowds pack London's West End and defy the blackout

London, 25 March
People treated themselves to a pre-war-style night out in the West End to celebrate the Easter holiday. Until late this evening, Easter Monday, there were crowds besieging restaurants and bars and filling the streets with torchlight, despite the blackout. Piccadilly, Shaftesbury Avenue and the Strand felt like Boat Race night.

By 5pm it was impossible to get a seat for any West End show. Some queues outside the cinemas were 100 yards (91 metres) long. "In 35 years I have never known such a rush for seats," said a theatre manager. Impromptu sing-songs began at main line railway stations, where troops and evacuees were flocking back from leave or from their weekend in town. A special train took civil servants back to their exiled ministries in Blackpool.

April

Su	Mo	Tu	We	Th	Fr	Sa
	1	2	3	4	5	6
7	8	9	10	11	12	13
14	15	16	17	18	19	20
21	22	23	24	25	26	27
28	29	30				

1. Britain: The government says that it will intervene to keep food prices down.

1. South Africa: Parliament passes General Smuts' War Measures Bill.

1. Germany: Hitler fixes the date of Operation *Weserubung* [Exercise Weser], the invasion of Norway and Denmark, at 9 April and orders preparations to start (→ 3).

2. Netherlands: Border garrisons are put on full alert.

3. Baltic: The first German supply ships leave for Narvik, disguised as cargo ships (→ 6).

3. Britain: A Heinkel shoots down a Spitfire of 41 Squadron, RAF Fighter Command, over the Yorkshire coast; the Heinkel is also lost.

3. Britain: Churchill is made chairman of the Ministerial Defence Committee, following Lord Chatfield's resignation as minister for the coordination of defence; Berlin radio says that Churchill has been promoted from "warmonger" to "grand warmonger".→

3. Britain: Lord Woolton, the director of the supply ministry, is made food minister.

4. London: Churchill leaves for Paris to attempt to get more French cooperation in mining Norwegian waters (→ 5).

5. Katyn, USSR: Secret police remove a group of Polish officers from Kozelsk prisoner-of-war camp and shoot them dead in a wood. It is feared that this could be the first of a series of killings.

5. Oslo: The Allies tell Norway that they reserve the right to cut off Norwegian supplies to Germany.

5. Scapa Flow: British mine-laying ships leave for Norwegian waters (→ 7).

6. Britain: After dropping 65 million leaflets, RAF Bomber Command suspends leaflet raids over Germany.

6. Kiel: RAF photo reconnaissance reveals heavy naval activity at German ports in the area, believed to be in preparation for invasions of Norway and Denmark (→ 9).

Chamberlain: Adolf has missed the bus

Britain, 5 April
The prime minister told a Conservative Party meeting today that after seven months of war he feels ten times as confident of victory as he did at the start. In this unusually buoyant mood Mr Chamberlain said: "One thing is certain. Hitler has missed the bus."

The speech appeared to be aimed at dispelling some signs of public impatience about the conduct of the war. Mr Chamberlain recalled that Germany was turned into an armed camp in the years before the war while Britain postponed rapid re-armament so long as any hope of peace remained.

He went on: "It was natural then to expect that the enemy would take advantage of his initial superiority to make an endeavour to overwhelm us and France before we had time to make good our deficiencies. Is it not extraordinary that no such attempt was made?"

Having made his point, he declared: "Whatever the reason, Hitler has very little margin of strength still to call upon."

Portal is new chief of Bomber Command

London, 3 April
Air Marshal Charles Portal has been appointed C-in-C of Bomber Command in succession to the much-respected Air Chief Marshal Sir Edgar Ludlow-Hewitt, who becomes inspector general of the RAF. Portal is a brilliant staff officer with an analytical brain who sometimes loses sight of the sensibilities of his colleagues.

He is the favourite disciple of Lord Trenchard, the "Father of the RAF", and faithfully follows his mentor's advocacy of all-out attack by bombers. Despite the success of the Stuka dive-bombers supporting land forces, Portal is an opponent of co-operation between Bomber Command and the army.

Cold but brilliant: Charles Portal, the new C-in-C of Bomber Command.

Chinese push back Japan at Wuyuan

Wuyuan, 2 April
Chinese Nationalist troops have recaptured the north-western city of Wuyuan for the second time after ambushing a column of 3,000 Japanese troops.

The city, which first fell under Japanese control in February, was recaptured by the Nationalists two weeks ago. However, the Japanese sent in reinforcements a week ago as a result of which they once more took the city. Its successful retaking by the Nationalists will give heart to beleaguered Chinese forces in the south of the country (→ 1/5).

Churchill gets mine plan past cabinet

London, 3 April
Winston Churchill, who today became chairman of the Ministerial Defence Committee, has persuaded the cabinet to adopt his plan for mining Norwegian territorial waters – six months after he first made the proposal. Churchill raised it soon after the outbreak of war as a means of exploiting Britain's superiority at sea. Then, Chamberlain rejected it; now, influenced by reports of planned German moves against Norway, he has changed his mind (→ 4).

Douglas Bader, the legless air hero, is back in the RAF cockpit

London, 1 April
Douglas Bader, the brilliant pilot and rugby footballer who lost both his legs when he crashed his Bristol Bulldog fighter in December 1931, is back in the cockpit, flying fighters again with the RAF.

He left the RAF because he was no longer allowed to fly despite his mastery of his "tin legs". But immediately war was declared he started to pull strings until he was given a test on a trainer. All his old skill came flooding back – flying was still "a piece of cake".

Now he can be seen stumping towards his Hurricane, as aggressive as ever, to fly patrols over Channel convoys, and when he takes off he flies like all the other pilots – only better than most.

Douglas Bader, the legless fighter ace, with his Hawker Hurricane.

April

Su	Mo	Tu	We	Th	Fr	Sa
	1	2	3	4	5	6
7	8	9	10	11	12	13
14	15	16	17	18	19	20
21	22	23	24	25	26	27
28	29	30				

7. North Sea: The British Home Fleet and German troop carriers both set sail for Norwegian waters (→ 8).

8. North Sea: The Royal Navy starts mine-laying operations off the Norwegian coast.

8. North Sea: German ships blow up the destroyer HMS *Glowworm* after it rams the heavy cruiser *Admiral Hipper*.

8. North Sea: The Polish submarine *Orzel* sinks the German troopship *Rio de Janeiro*.

9. Norway: The Nazis set up a regime in Oslo under the ex-war minister Vidkun Quisling (→ 15).

9. Norway: The destroyer HMS *Gurkha* is sunk and the battleship HMS *Rodney* is damaged by a German air attack off Bergen.

9. Norway: The battle cruiser HMS *Renown* forces the withdrawal of the *Gneisenau* and the *Scharnhorst*.

10. Narvik: In the first major naval engagement of the war outside the Atlantic, a British flotilla sinks two German ships, eight merchant ships and an ammunition ship, but loses two of its own ships. →

10. Norway: The submarine HMS *Truant* sinks the German cruiser *Karlsruhe* in the Skagerrak.

10. Shetlands: The destroyer HMS *Hero* sinks U-boat U50.

10. Norway: The U-boat U4 sinks the submarine HMS *Thistle* off Stavanger.

10. Norway: Fleet Air Arm Blackburn Skua bombers sink the cruiser *Konigsberg* at Bergen; it is the first major warship to be sunk by air attack in the war.

10. Iceland: Parliament severs its constitutional links with Denmark (→ 16).

11. Norway: The British submarine *Spearfish* sinks the German cruiser *Lutzow*.

13. Narvik: The Royal Navy sinks eight German ships (→ 14).

13. Denmark: The first mines dropped by the RAF are laid in Danish waters.

Germany opens Scandinavian assault

Oslo, 9 April

German troops moved into Denmark and Norway in the early hours of this morning. The attack took the Allies by surprise – which is something of a surprise itself, since the Allies themselves had just mined Norwegian territorial waters against German shipping, had been warned of the invasion by Colonel-General Beck (of the anti-Hitler opposition) and, until the Finnish-Soviet armistice of 13 March, had themselves been planning to occupy northern Norway. Germany's aim is to secure safe passage for its iron ore imports from Sweden and build naval bases beyond the blockaded North Sea. The Allies' aim for their projected invasion was to disrupt ore shipments and open a second front away from France – though cynics say it was to open a second front away from Whitehall.

HMS *Cossack*'s daring release of 299 British seamen on the *Altmark* in Norwegian waters – threatening by implication both Germany's iron ore supply and the ribbon of neutral Norwegian water giving German ships access to the Atlantic – concentrated German minds.

While the Allies fumbled, Germany moved. Using mostly second-rate reservists, with Major-General Eduard Dietl's Mountain Division and the *Luftwaffe*'s First Parachute Regiment as the spearhead, the German army under General Kaupitsch has occupied Denmark with hardly a shot fired [*see below*]. Simultaneously, the German navy has landed troops under General Nikolaus von Falkenhorst in every major Norwegian port as far north as Narvik, in a daring amphibious operation that took the Royal Navy entirely by surprise (→ 10).

Nazi storm troopers march into defenceless Denmark, meeting no resistance.   *Nazi arms in occupied Copenhagen.*

After 24 hours, Danish king orders a ceasefire and surrender

Copenhagen, 10 April

German troops are in occupation of all Denmark. The occupation, as a German General Staff paper confidently predicted, took a mere 24 hours. Denmark's airfields, ports, islands and inlets are now available to the Germans as forward bases for their attack on Norway, now in its second day.

The invasion began at 5am yesterday when three troopships sailed silently into Copenhagen harbour. A lone policeman who resisted the invaders with a pistol fell, and the city was taken without further fighting. Simultaneously, trawlers escorted by E-boats brought German troops into all Denmark's ports and major islands, giving them control of the vital sea passages, the Skagerrak and the Kattegat, between Denmark and Norway. At the same time, airborne troops landed at the airfield at Aalborg and motorized troops crossed Denmark's land frontier at Flensburg and Tondern. At Gjedser a ferry came in carrying troops and an armoured train.

After 12 Danish deaths King Christian X ordered a ceasefire at about 6am. The Danish C-in-C, General Pryor, recalling an earlier battle at Copenhagen, applied the Nelson touch and ignored the order. Then, at 6.45am, the king sent his personal adjutant to ensure that it was obeyed. The occupation puts Germany in an unprecedented legal position. Since Denmark did not resist, Denmark is not at war with Germany. It is still neutral. The Germans are faced with a coalition government embracing most Danish democratic parties which they cannot depose without undermining their claims, however tenuous, of not threatening other neutral nations.

German justification for the occupation is that it had to act to prevent the Allies from occupying northern Norway and depriving Germany of its iron ore supply from neutral Sweden. The most important gain for Germany is control of the airfields at Aalborg, at the northern tip of the Jutland peninsula – a key strategic location in the air battle for Norway and also for patrolling the sea passages to Germany's Baltic ports (→ 14).

Allies look to Norway after the fall of Denmark

British cause heavy German naval loss despite fleet delays

Narvik, 10 April

With battle-ensigns straining from their mainmasts and all guns blazing, six British destroyers raced through a snowstorm today to surprise a larger flotilla of German ships at the end of a Norwegian *fjord*. In the short and furious battle that followed, two German destroyers were sunk and two more crippled. Two British destroyers, *Hardy* and *Hunter*, were sunk and their flotilla commander, Captain Warburton-Lee, was killed in the engagement.

The naval action off Norway began with a mine-laying operation aimed at forcing ships carrying iron ore to Germany out of neutral Norwegian waters. The operation was set to begin on 8 April, and on 5 April a force left Scapa Flow under Vice-Admiral Whitworth.

The destroyer *Glowworm* was separated from the force when one of her seamen was washed overboard in heavy seas. The last heard from her was that she was sinking after taking on the heavy cruiser *Admiral Hipper*. Whitworth's force was joined by four minelayers and Warburton-Lee's destroyers.

As early as 4 April the admiralty had intelligence of a German move on Norway, and signs of naval activity in the Baltic grew stronger on 6 April. The admiralty concentrated on the possibility of a break-out of German warships via the North Sea to the North Atlantic, rather than the invasion of Norway. Thus, when major German naval groups were known to be heading north-west into the North Sea, and the Home Fleet finally sailed, it steered north-east, leaving the central North Sea uncovered.

By 8 April the Germans' invasion intentions were clearer and Admiral Forbes, the C-in-C, adjusted course and sent more destroyers to the mine-laying force to the north.

Next day the Germans lost two cruisers, one sunk by a submarine, the other by torpedoes fired by the Norwegians in Oslo fjord (→13).

German paratroopers wait for airborne reinforcements in the attack on Norway.

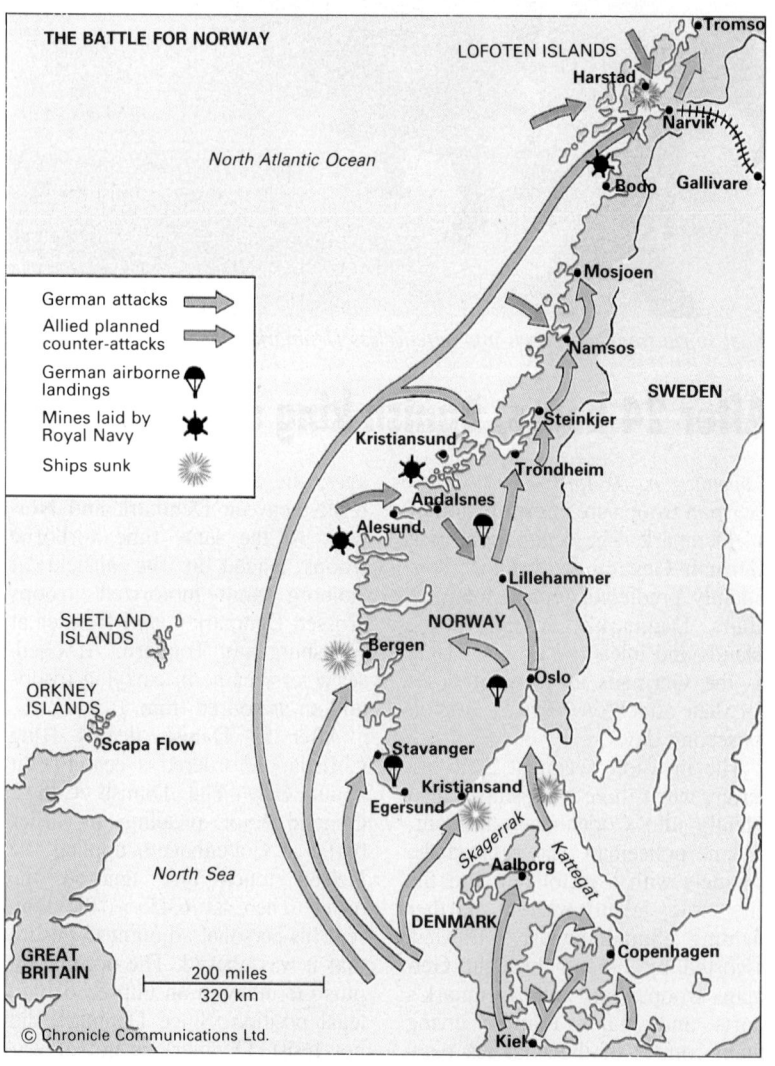

THE BATTLE FOR NORWAY

LOFOTEN ISLANDS

North Atlantic Ocean

Tromso
Harstad
Narvik
Bodo
Gallivare
Mosjoen
Namsos
SWEDEN
Steinkjer
Kristiansund
Trondheim
Andalsnes
Alesund
Lillehammer
SHETLAND ISLANDS
NORWAY
Bergen
ORKNEY ISLANDS
Oslo
Scapa Flow
Stavanger
Kristiansand
Egersund
Skagerrak
Aalborg
Kattegat
North Sea
DENMARK
GREAT BRITAIN
Copenhagen
Kiel

German attacks ➡
Allied planned counter-attacks ➡
German airborne landings
Mines laid by Royal Navy
Ships sunk

200 miles
320 km

© Chronicle Communications Ltd.

Swastikas fly over Oslo, but battles begin in mountains

Oslo, Norway, 13 April

In the early hours of 9 April the German cruiser *Blucher* led a troop convoy into Oslo harbour. The assault was a failure, although there were only a few hundred guardsmen on ceremonial duties defending the capital. The *Blucher* was sunk by torpedoes from Fort Oscarsborg and the attack abandoned.

It was left to a battalion of paratroopers to take the capital from the rear. However, King Haakon, the Labour government, the *Storting* [parliament] and Norway's gold reserves had left for Hamar, 70 miles (112 km) inland, to organize resistance. At the same time as the *Blucher* was sinking, the German fleet was carrying troops to six Norwegian ports, as far north as the Arctic Circle: Kristiansand, Egersund, Stavanger, Bergen, Trondheim and Narvik.

Norway's army, a few hundred guardsmen and a part-time militia, was no match for the German army. The only effective unit was far away guarding the Finnish frontier when the invasion started. Still, the unit was raced to the south and, together with what is left of Norway's reservists, is now under Norway's new C-in-C, General Otto Ruge, an intellectual reputed to work well under pressure.

Ruge's strategy is to prevent the main German force now landed at Oslo from linking up with the coastal foothold, by blocking the valleys. Thus the German advance has been punctuated by bloody localized assaults, sending back a steady stream of casualties amongst General von Falkenhorst's reservists. Falkenhorst's tactics have been to use his elite 169th Mountain Division to outflank the Norwegian blocks and to apply "aerial artillery" (dive-bombers) against them.

In spite of the Stukas, General Ruge is unlikely to surrender. "The defeat or captivity of her forces is better for the nation than their voluntary capitulation," he said (→14).

1940

April

Su	Mo	Tu	We	Th	Fr	Sa
		1	2	3	4	5	6
7	8	9	10	11	12	13
14	15	16	17	18	19	20
21	22	23	24	25	26	27
28	29	30				

14. New York: *Lights Out In Europe*, a film showing how war broke out, opens.

14. Norway: The Allies land troops at Namsos and Harstad (→ 16).

14. Norway: The submarine HMS *Tarpon* is sunk by a German trawler (→ 15).

15. Tokyo: The foreign minister, Mr Arita, warns that if hostilities spread to the Netherlands and thus to the Dutch East Indies, peaceful coexistence in the Pacific will be damaged (→ 17).

15. Norway: The destroyer HMS *Fearless* sinks the U-boat U49 (→ 16).

15. Bletchley Park: British Intelligence deciphers the German *Enigma* code used in Norway (→ 22/5).

15. Oslo: The Germans remove Quisling from the government, replacing him with the puppet Ingolf Christensen (→ 19).

16. Norway: The submarine HMS *Porpoise* sinks the U-boat U1 (→ 17).

16. Norway: British troops land at Narvik (→ 18).

16. Iceland: The government appeals to the US for aid and recognition.

17. Norway: The cruiser HMS *Suffolk* shells Sola airfield, near Stavanger, and is then damaged in an air attack (→ 18).

17. Washington: The secretary of state, Cordell Hull, says that any threat to the *status quo* in the Dutch East Indies would imperil peace in the Pacific.

18. Norway: Allied troops disembark at Andalsnes and Trondheim, and occupy the Faeroe Islands. →

18. Norway: The submarine HMS *Sterlet* is sunk by German anti-submarine vessels in the Skagerrak channel (→ 30).

19. Norway: The country becomes a *Reichskommissariat*, led by Josef Terboven under the control of the German foreign office.

20. Germany: On his 51st birthday, Hitler orders a new SS regiment to be set up containing Norwegians and Danes as well as Germans.

Neutrality of Italy and Hungary looks ever more unsure

Rome and Budapest, 13 April

Italy and Hungary seem to be sliding ever nearer involvement in the war. In Italy's case it is only the dictator Mussolini's fear of the consequences which has kept him out. He has so far not fulfilled his obligation to Hitler under the "Pact of Steel" which committed Italy to go to Germany's aid with "all its military forces" in time of war.

"I must emphasize to you," he wrote to Hitler, "that I cannot assume the initiative of warlike operations, given the actual conditions of Italian military preparations." However, with Germany's continued military success there are indications that the Duce is preparing himself to go to war in case he misses any of the spoils.

Hungary's case is different. It is caught between Russia and Germany and, although its army is reputed to be the best in the Danube basin, its central plain makes ideal tank country.

Every time its giant neighbours move, Hungary trembles. Admiral Horthy, the regent of this kingless kingdom, tries to placate both of them. Soon he may be forced to choose between Nazi Germany and Communist Russia.

The actress Beatrice Tanner, Mrs Patrick Campbell, the heroine of Shaw's "Pygmalion" in 1914. She died on 9 April aged 75.

Danes ignore their German "protectors"

Copenhagen, 14 April

The German occupation of Denmark is now five days old, and the Germans are finding it unexpectedly embarrassing. Since the Danes did not resist they have not been defeated. Germany is obliged to keep to its word, that German troops went in to "protect" Scandinavia from the Allies. Thus it is faced with a king, a constitution and recognized democratic government.

Outside Denmark, the Danes are flocking to the Allies, 5,000 Danish seamen bringing 90 per cent of Denmark's tonnage into friendly ports. Inside Denmark, Danes continue to live as if the Germans do not exist, ignoring them, as King Christian ignores the salutes of the German sentries.

For Germany to disband the government and rule directly would be a great blow to its prestige among neutrals. But to continue is exasperating. These Nordic people, who should be welcoming Germans, are responding with a policy once favoured by illiterate Irish peasants: the "boycott".

Londoners still wait for war to arrive

Goodbye Piccadilly: Eros has been evacuated, just in case of war damage.

London, 20 April

Everywhere in London there are signs of preparation against air attack but ten million Londoners – the biggest bombing target in Europe – are still waiting for the action to begin.

It is a city of sandbags, piled high round the windows and doorways of public buildings, shopfronts and underground shelters. They are beginning to turn green as they weather and to leak at the corners.

Estate agents' boards blossom in Belgravia and Mayfair, where the rich and titled have flown to safer nests in the shires. In Eaton Square only six houses out of 120 are occupied. There are no takers.

But in the City, which was so quiet six months ago when 3,500 firms fled to the provinces, daily life has returned to near-normal. At least 700 firms are back again, and thousands of office workers pour along almost traffic-free streets. Hardly one carries a gas mask.

The city's public monuments and statues have mostly disappeared under sandbag protection. Eros has been removed from Piccadilly Circus to a place of safe storage and his plinth covered with hoardings advertising National Savings.

There are no paintings on view at the National Gallery – they are stored in a slate quarry in Wales – but it is filled every day with music lovers who come to Myra Hess's lunch-time concerts. The middle of Hyde Park is wired off as a military area, and sandbagged shelters disfigure all the parks. But the barrage balloons shining in the evening sun look almost romantic – like pearls strung from the clouds.

75

1940
April

Su	Mo	Tu	We	Th	Fr	Sa
	1	2	3	4	5	6
7	8	9	10	11	12	13
14	15	16	17	18	19	20
21	22	23	24	25	26	27
28	29	30				

Allied troops land on Norway coast

Lofoten Islands, 19 April

British and French troops have landed in Norway at Namsos and Andalsnes and in the Lofoten Islands. A force left Scapa Flow and the Scottish mainland in three convoys. Some units, originally earmarked for a pre-emptive Allied occupation of key ports in Norway (a plan overtaken by events), had been embarked, disembarked and then re-embarked, losing their artillery in the process. Naval and army staffs were so mentally and strategically separate that they travelled in separate ships.

The aim of the Lofoten Islands force, under Major-General Mackesy, is to take Narvik, while the Namsos and Andalsnes forces, under Major-General Carton de Wiart, are aiming to take Trondheim. So far, however, there is scant evidence that the aims will be carried out. Mackesy's force dithers off Narvik, so fearful of the memories of Gallipoli, that it cannot make a sea-borne assault. De Wiart's Namsos force, as yet without artillery, anti-aircraft guns or transport, is being constantly harassed by Stukas; yesterday the Andalsnes force was diverted south to Lillehammer to give support to the hardpressed Norwegian army.

But what help these troops – who, with the exception of the French *Chasseurs Alpins*, are untrained in mountain warfare – will be against General Eduard Dietl's crack 169th Mountain Division is uncertain (→ 21).

A pall of smoke hangs over the harbour of war-torn Narvik in Norway.

The rise of a canny classroom warrior

London, 18 April

General Sir John Dill, the commander of 1 Corps of the British Expeditionary Force in France, has been brought back to England to become the vice-chief of the Imperial General Staff.

Aged 59, Dill is a former director of military operations. Before the war he commanded the army's Staff College. In France he has earned a considerable reputation as commander of one of three army corps holding ground between two French army groups, an allied wall of men which has the impregnable fortress of the Maginot Line on its right. Dill is a man of mature judgement whom friends describe as "canny" and opponents as irresolute. However, among his admirers is Winston Churchill, the first lord of the admiralty, who is not known for his dithering.

Dill, like some French military leaders, has risen to prominence as a classroom warrior who prefers to make his move only after all information is to hand. The German High Command is reputed to have a low opinion of British officers who are averse to taking decisions; but Dill is probably of tougher mettle than his detractors think.

People queue to Go With The Wind

London, 18 April

Gone With the Wind, the film colossus famed for costing $4 million (£1 million) to make, taking three hours and 40 minutes to see and winning Oscars galore, including one for Vivien Leigh as best actress, had its premiere at no fewer than three West End cinemas tonight. It has broken box office records in America. The critics' reception in Britain has been warm, but not ecstatic. "Very good indeed but no masterpiece," declares Campbell Dixon in the *Daily Telegraph*.

21. Norway: German troops push Norwegian and British forces out of Lillehammer (→ 22).

22. Norway: The Allies clash with the Germans north of Trondheim (→ 26).

23. Norway: RAF bombers raid Nazi-occupied airfields near Oslo, the latest raid in a series since 15 April.

24. France: The premier, Paul Reynaud, urges Mussolini not to enter the war (→ 29).

25. Dublin: An IRA landmine kills six people.

26. Norway: Allied units in northern Norway begin retreating (→ 28).

27. Berlin: Germany officially declares war on Norway.

28. Norway: Major-General Bernard Paget, the commander of British land forces at Andalsnes, stages an unsuccessful attempt to break out of Trondheim (→ 30).

29. Auschwitz: The camp's new commander, Rudolf Hoess, takes up office and drafts 30 violent convicts from Sachsenhausen to be senior camp guards (*kapos*) (→ 14/6).

29. Washington: Roosevelt sends Mussolini a message asking him to use his influence to bring peace (→ 1/5).

30. USA: A group of Pittsburgh residents offers a million-dollar reward for the capture of Hitler alive.

30. Norway: The cruiser HMS *Glasgow* evacuates King Haakon and his government from Molde to Tromso, as German forces from Oslo and Trondheim link up.→

30. Britain: Two civilians are killed and 150 injured when a mine-laying Heinkel crashes at Clacton and explodes, the first civilian deaths of the war on mainland Britain.

30. Norway: British troops start to pull out of their foothold at Andalsnes.→

30. Germany: Believing the Scandinavian campaign to be over, Hitler orders his generals to make their final preparations for an attack on the west.→

Germans push back Allies in Norway

German heavy tanks in the streets of Oslo, bringing war to a neutral city.

Heavy aerial bombardment forces retreat

Namsos, Norway, 30 April

The Allied adventure in Norway has failed to prevent the Germans from advancing, and singularly failed to achieve its main objectives – the ejection of the Germans from Narvik and Trondheim.

Instead, the ill-prepared force is subject to continual dive-bombing by Stukas and, with neither anti-aircraft guns nor artillery (they were left behind on embarkation), is steadily retreating in front of General von Falkenhorst's troops which are pushing up from Oslo to link up with General Eduard Dietl's 169th Mountain Division in Narvik and Trondheim.

The British generals face a formidable opponent in Dietl, a superb commander, and their troops are no match for his tough Alpine companies which, though outnumbered, are easily holding off halfhearted and poorly organised Allied attempts to dislodge them (→ 1/5).

Members of the navy's "Rendering Safe of Mines Squad" on the east coast of England, rolling a German mine into position for a "blow up".

Fleet Air Arm has key role for Allies

Norwegian Sea, 30 April

As the German advance into Norway continues, Allied resistance depends increasingly for air cover and reconnaissance on the Royal Navy Fleet Air Arm. Mountainous terrain ashore and German occupation of the populated south have made this an air-sea campaign, and Norway is beyond the range of RAF fighters in Scotland. The Fleet Air Arm's Blackburn Skua dive-bombers and Roc fighters are the answer. The Skua carries its 500-pound bomb in a nose-down power dive from 11,000 feet to 2,000 feet in 25 seconds before releasing the bomb onto the target, usually an enemy ship. On 11 April Skuas hit German vessels in Trondheim *fjord* and then sank a cruiser offshore. The Roc, with a rear gunner, is a slow but reliable fighter useful for aerial reconnaissance.

Despite its successes on land, Germany has suffered setbacks at sea. Before Oslo was taken the shore battery helped to destroy one cruiser, the *Blucher*. At Narvik ten destroyers were lost for two British ships. The loss of vessels on this scale greatly reduces Hitler's scope for a seaborne assault on Britain.

New tax puts up the cost of beer and cigarettes

London, 23 April

Taxpayers were called up in a big way for the war effort today. In Parliament Sir John Simon, the chancellor of the exchequer, announced Budget proposals for higher income tax and surtax. He also increased duties on tobacco, beer, spirits and matches as well as announcing dearer postal and telephone charges.

On top of all that there will be a novel new "Purchase Tax" on the sale of most goods not already heavily taxed. Exactly how it will work has still to be decided. The standard tax rate will be 7/6 in the £ (37.5%), and surtax starts on incomes of over £1,500 ($6,000) a year instead of £2,000. Cigarettes will now cost 1/5 (7p/28¢) for 20, and beer is up a penny a pint while whisky will cost 16/- (80p/$3.22) a bottle.

The rate for a three-minute telephone trunk call will be 1/2 (6p/24¢) above 50 miles. There will be a basic charge of 9d (4p/15¢) for nine words instead of 6d, and greetings telegrams will cost 1/- instead of 9d. Sir John explained that this War Budget is intended to curb spending. He warned that when peace returns the government will take effective action against those making "colossal war fortunes".

Hitler plans his attack on western Europe

Berlin, 30 April

Confident that he will soon be able to see off the Allied forces in Norway, Hitler today turned his attention to the planned offensive in western Europe. He told General Alfred Jodl, the chief of staff to Field Marshal Keitel, and other military commanders to be prepared to launch operations on 5 May or within 24 hours of any later day.

Intelligence reports of an imminent German attack have been received by the Dutch and Belgian governments through the Vatican, which was alerted by German officers opposed to Hitler's plans. Intercepts of the Vatican messages, decoded by the Germans, have been shown to Hitler. He intends to go ahead notwithstanding (→ 11/5).

General Alfred Jodl: converting Hitler's orders into effective actions.

Nazi thugs herd Jews into ghetto

Lodz, Poland, 30 April
SS thugs have established a total reign of terror over Jews in this city. Women have been forced to dance naked at gunpoint, and all Jews are forced to wear armbands with the Star of David. The SS set fire to the synagogue and summoned the fire brigade – to stop the fire spreading to other buildings. Jews have been herded into a ghetto which at midnight tonight will be sealed off.

The ghetto is one of the most run-down areas of the city, comprising 32,000 mainly one-room apartments, only 700 of which have running water. Into these cramped and insanitary conditions the Nazis have kicked, beaten and prodded 160,000 people (→ 25/5).

More women to do German war work

Berlin, 27 April
The German employment ministry today drafted a confidential programme to make registration compulsory for all women aged from 15 to 40, as a result of which many women never before employed and thus not registered with an employment office will become available to work in industry.

How women will react to the measure is uncertain, since a woman's pay for any given job is on average only 80 per cent of what a man would get. And the idea of general compulsory employment for women is opposed by some senior Nazis, such as Goering, because it runs counter to the Nazi doctrine of women as domestic creatures.

Empire's air training scheme takes off

Off-duty RAF pilots attend a lecture on enemy aircraft and discuss tactics.

Ottawa, 29 April
A plan to train 20,000 aircrew in Canada as part of the Empire's war effort is set to take off. The deal with Britain is said to impose a "staggering responsibility" on Canada where 40,000 experts are needed to teach flying at 58 centres. The first of these opens next month at Camp Borden, where the first qualified pilots will be kept as instructors. Observers and air gunners will also be trained under the deal signed by the prime minister, William Mackenzie King, and Lord River-

dale. Australia hopes to provide some 10,000 aircrew each year for the RAF; although some RAAF squadrons are joining the fight as complete units it seems that the Australian role will be as a training service for the RAF. Other significant help is coming from Rhodesia and individual Americans.

Britain's air ministry first proposed a Commonwealth Air Training Scheme before 1939, but, ironically, the Canadians were unenthusiastic. The outbreak of war has rapidly changed people's minds.

1940

May

Su	Mo	Tu	We	Th	Fr	Sa
			1	2	3	4
5	6	7	8	9	10	11
12	13	14	15	16	17	18
19	20	21	22	23	24	25
26	27	28	29	30	31	

1. Rome: Roosevelt sends a personal message to Mussolini urging him to stay out of the war; the Duce tells the US ambassador, William Phillips, that Germany cannot be defeated in Europe (→ 2).

1. Berlin: Germany announces the surrender of 4,000 Norwegian soldiers in the Lillehammer sector.

1. Norway: As the Germans close in on Andalsnes, the Allies evacuate over 4,000 men from the port but are forced to leave behind their equipment (→ 2).

1. China: Japanese troops advance from Xinyang, thrusting towards the Yangtze river (→ 31).

1. Washington: The US government announces that the USA and Greenland, a Danish territory, have agreed to the mutual establishment of consulates "in view of the German occupation of Denmark".

2. Norway: Under heavy *Luftwaffe* bombardment, Allied forces start to evacuate Namsos; 5,400 soldiers embark today (→ 3).

2. Rome: Mussolini proposes a bargain with Roosevelt: he will refrain from invading the USA if the president keeps America out of the war in Europe (→ 11).

3. Norway: The French destroyer *Bison* and the British destroyer *Afridi* are sunk at Namsos by German bombing while evacuating troops.→

3. Norway: After the evacuation of the last Allied troops from the area at the end of April, the remaining Norwegian troops in southern Norway surrender.

3. Greenland: The government appeals to the USA for military protection.

3. Norway and Denmark: The RAF continues bombing of strategic German airfields.

4. Netherlands: Twenty-one suspected saboteurs and Nazi fifth-columnists are arrested in a crackdown on anti-government elements.

4. Narvik: The *Grom*, a Polish destroyer, is sunk with the loss of 56 lives.

Eire seeks US aid in maintaining its war neutrality

Dublin, 1 May
In a desperate move to remain out of the war, the Irish government appealed today to the United States to guarantee its neutrality. Eire – the only Commonwealth nation which has not rallied to the Allied cause – chose neutrality when it considered its position shortly before the outbreak of war.

The cool attitude of the prime minister, Eamon de Valera, to the British cause and his refusal to allow British convoy escorts to be based in Irish ports have infuriated many British politicians, so much so that there is genuine fear of a British invasion in Dublin. Equally, the possibility of a German invasion is not being ruled out.

Although Washington is unlikely to offer a formal guarantee, the Irish-American lobby is a powerful political force in a country whose support is vital to Britain.

Britain has appealed to de Valera to join a defence union with Northern Ireland. The former British detainee is unlikely to cooperate. The Irish government is being markedly active against the IRA, however, with Irish *garda* cooperating with British police in the hunt for terrorists. Despite de Valera's views, thousands of his countrymen are crossing the Northern Ireland border to volunteer for the British forces, so Britain is likely to refrain from any hostile moves (→ 16/6).

The new glamour of the forces.

Britain and France withdraw from Norway

Namsos lies in ruins: a French sailor watches a British destroyer on patrol.

Namsos, Norway, 3 May
After only a fortnight's fighting, British and French forces are to evacuate central Norway. Four days ago King Haakon and his government were evacuated to Tromso in the north to continue the fight. Three days ago the last of Major-General Carton de Wiart's forces, sent to take Trondheim, were shipped out of Norway. Yesterday the rearguard of the Namsos force boarded evacuation ships.

Allied support for Norway has so far been less than successful, despite heavy German naval losses at the two Battles of Narvik. The Royal Navy was initially caught off guard; it had begun to lay mines to divert ships carrying iron ore to Germany out of neutral Norwegian waters, and planned to take control of key ports if the Germans retaliated. But a full-scale invasion was not expected, and the British believed that the Germans were attempting a breakout into the North Atlantic before it became clear that German naval movements were aimed at Norway's key ports.

This gave the Germans vital time to establish themselves. The Norwegians under General Ruge are still fighting in central Norway, but Ruge's coastal front is now open to the Germans (→ 7).

French destroyer sunk in North Sea

North Sea, 3 May
German aircraft today claimed their first victim amongst French warships. The destroyer *Bison*, along with the British destroyer, *Afridi*, was sunk by bombs while protecting a convoy transporting troops withdrawing from Namsos. None of the troop transports was hit and two German planes were shot down. A large number of both crews were rescued, including Captain P L Vian of the *Afridi*. Previously he was captain of her sister ship, HMS *Cossack*. He won the DSO for the daring boarding of the German supply ship *Altmark* in a Norwegian fjord in February.

Return our jewels, pleads Sweden

Stockholm, 3 May
Intensive and highly secret diplomatic talks are taking place between Sweden and Germany for the safe return of Sweden's crown jewels and gold reserves, which were taken by train for safe-keeping in Oslo six months ago. Sweden believed that it was under threat from its old antagonist Russia, or from Germany which coveted its iron ore reserves.

Many believe that the principal bargaining lever is permission for German troops to cross neutral Sweden into Norway and an assurance that ore supplies to Germany will not be cut.

1940
May

Su	Mo	Tu	We	Th	Fr	Sa
			1	2	3	4
5	6	7	8	9	10	11
12	13	14	15	16	17	18
19	20	21	22	23	24	25
26	27	28	29	30	31	

5. London: The Norwegian defence and foreign ministers arrive for talks.

5. Denmark: The British submarine *Seal*, damaged by a mine in the Kattegat channel, surrenders.

5. Norway: French Foreign Legion troops land at Tromso.

5. Paris: The newspaper of the exiled German Social Democratic Party, *Neuer Vorwarts* [New Way Forward], closes down after key members flee to London.

6. Britain: The Norwegian gold reserve, worth £33 million ($133 million), arrives safely.

7. Westminster: Chamberlain is unable to explain why time was wasted landing troops at Namsos and Andalsnes rather than attacking Trondheim (→ 9).

7. Netherlands: The mobilization programme is completed (→ 10).

8. Russia: Marshal Semyon K Timoshenko is appointed commissar for defence.

8. China: Japanese forces seize Tsaoyang, in Hupeh province.

9. Belgium: The government declares a state of emergency and puts the army on alert.

9. Westminster: Chamberlain asks the Labour Party to join him in a coalition government.→

9. France: The prime minister, Paul Reynaud, threatens to resign in order to secure the removal of Maurice Gamelin, the forces' supreme commander, who is backed by Daladier.

10. Netherlands: Allied naval demolition parties land at Dutch ports, evacuate ships, tugs and barges and destroy oil stores.→

10. Netherlands: Queen Wilhelmina makes "a flaming protest against this unprecedented violation of good faith".→

10. Switzerland: The country is placed on military alert.

11. Belgium: German soldiers reach the Albert Canal (→ 12).

11. West Indies: A British force lands on the Dutch islands of Curacao and Aruba.

British troops land to occupy Iceland

Reykjavik, 10 May
Following the German invasion of Denmark, British troops have made an unopposed landing to occupy the Danish colony of Iceland, which declared itself independent of the Danes last month. The occupation of this strategically important island, which has no defence force, pre-empts German hopes of using it as a submarine or air base from which to attack Allied convoys.

At the moment there is a mood of calm in Iceland, but there is some covert sympathy for Germany. The "Tommies" believe that they can break the ice.

George Lansbury, Labour leader, dies

Britain, 7 May
The pacifist George Lansbury, Labour Party leader from 1931 to 1935, died today aged 81. Lansbury had many critics but no enemies. He was the "Cockneys' MP" for Bow and Bromley for 30 years and a former mayor of the East End borough of Poplar. As first commissioner for works in the first Labour government in 1924 he introduced swings and sandpits for children in London parks. He resigned the leadership in 1935 after Ernest Bevin, the union leader, attacked him for "hawking his conscience" around the land when preaching against war and rearmament.

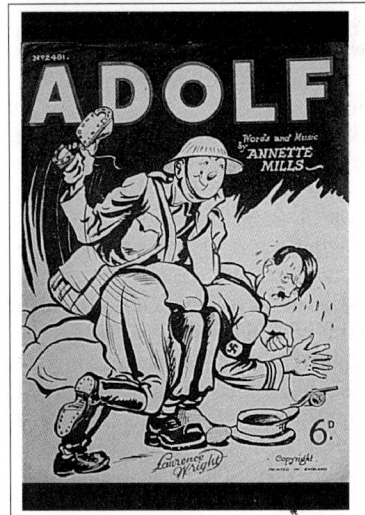

Giving the Fuhrer a spanking.

Germany's Blitzkrieg comes to the Low Countries

Low Countries, 10 May
It was war such as had never been imagined. These invaders from the east were no foot-slogging infantrymen with rifles and bayonets. Instead, bombing planes came out of the pale dawn sky, striking at airfields and crippling the tiny Dutch and Belgian air fleets. Parachutists came down to seize bridges and destroy river defences. Airborne troops in gliders struck at Rotterdam, The Hague and the supposedly impregnable Belgian fortress of Eben Emael *[see below]*. Stuka dive-bombers spread panic as they came screaming down to soften up the defenders. When the ground forces appeared they were heavy *Panzers* with 37mm guns. Hitler's *Blitzkrieg* has come to the Low Countries.

Brussels and The Hague had long known that the Fuhrer intended to attack but, fearful of provoking him, they had refused all cooperation with the British and French armies manning defences on the border to the west. Now desperate appeals for help have gone to London and Paris. But in the pocket state of Luxemburg, tucked between Belgium and Germany, there are no illusions; the Grand Duchess Charlotte is in headlong flight.

In spite of detailed contingency plans, the British and French response has been indecisive. The British are laying mines in the Rhine and, to halt the Germans, are demolishing Dutch and Belgian port installations at the mouth of the Scheldt. But some 15 per cent

Footage from a German weekly news film: German troops advance into battle in the invasion of the Low Countries.

of France's front line troops are on leave. The commander of the First Army Cavalry Corps, General Rene Prioux, who should have been leading the advance into Belgium, is some 50 miles (80 kilometres) away on target practice; the first he knew of hostilities was when German bombs began falling near his lodgings at St Quentin.

By noon the Dutch had fallen back to their Fortress Holland positions screening Amsterdam, Rotterdam and The Hague; but the Germans are already holding Rotterdam airfield. The Belgians are no better off: paratroops have landed between the first and second echelons of the Belgian 7th Division holding the Albert Canal. Hitler's 200,000-strong force, backed by 3,000 aircraft, is annihilating the Dutch and Belgians, who lack armour and air power (→ 11).

German glider team captures Belgian fort

Brussels, 10 May
The Germans have captured the supposedly impregnable Belgian fortress of Eben Emael in a daring *coup de main* operation. The guns of this fort, situated between Maastricht and Liege, threatened the advance of the German Sixth Army into Belgium, so it had to be captured; but its massive concrete walls and other defences presented a problem. The Germans built a replica and, after months of study, came up with the perfect solution.

At dawn 42 gliders, towed by Ju52 transports, flew over the Belgian border. The bulk of the force seized nearby bridges, but ten gliders landed on top of the fort of Eben Emael itself. Seventy-eight parachute engineers jumped out and immediately attacked the gun emplacements from above, whereas its defenders were prepared for assaults from below. To overcome the thick concrete they used specially designed hollow charges. The guns were quickly destroyed. The totally surprised 1,100 man garrison has withdrawn to the complex network of passages and chambers under the fort, and efforts continue to winkle it out; but the way ahead for the German army is now clear.

Roadblocks delay Allied reinforcements

On the Belgian border, 10 May
Allied troops began crossing into Belgium soon after 7am today, but the deployment has been erratic. When French troops arrived by rail at the Belgian border there were no Belgian locomotives to haul them. Also, the Belgians had failed to remove the frontier roadblocks and the French were held up for an hour or more on demolition work. The British 3rd Division, commanded by Major-General Bernard Montgomery, was held up by a Belgian officer who demanded to see a permit for the British to enter. Finally, the British rammed their way through with heavy trucks. Still, by midnight Allied cavalry and light armoured divisions had reached the planned defensive line running east of Brussels down to Namur in the south.

With 30 French divisions, nine British and the bulk of the 22 Belgian, the Allies are greatly superior to the 30 German divisions on this front, though the *Luftwaffe* is poised to seize air supremacy. The Germans believe, however, that the Allies have walked into a trap without realizing it. "I could weep for joy," Hitler cried when he heard of the Allied advance (→ 11).

Allies reel under assault

Dutch foil Nazi plan to seize their queen

The Hague, 11 May

A daring plan to occupy the airfields around The Hague, seize the capital and kidnap Queen Wilhelmina has been foiled by Dutch forces. Recovering from their early disarray when parachutists landed, Dutch infantry, backed by artillery, have driven the Germans from the three airfields.

This has saved the queen and the government, but it has tied down substantial Dutch reserves, which are badly needed on the Amsterdam and Rotterdam sectors. The German Eighteenth Army, under General Georg von Kuchler, has taken intact vital bridges over the Meuse; one company actually splashed down on the river at Rotterdam in ancient seaplanes.

At 1300 hours the Germans, having penetrated the Dutch defences, made contact with General Henri Giraud's Seventh French Army at Tilburg near the Belgian border. The French, who were to have linked up with the Dutch, found they had already retreated. Left to fend for himself and lacking air support and anti-aircraft and anti-tank guns, Giraud has been forced to pull back to Antwerp. This has opened the way for the 9th *Panzer* division to thrust towards Rotterdam and relieve airborne troops holding the bridges across the river there. But the Dutch are holding firm and Hitler has ordered forces from the Belgian front to move against the Dutch. "Resistance must be broken speedily," he says.

The exiled German *kaiser*, Wilhelm II, who lives at Doorn, was offered asylum in Britain by Churchill. He rejected the offer, and a few hours later Hitler's *Panzers* overran his home (→ 13).

Allies form new line – but in right place ?

Mons, Belgium, 11 May

In a desperate attempt to create an effective command structure, Edouard Daladier, the French war minister, Gaston Billotte, the C-in-C of the 1 Army Group, and Sir Henry Pownall, the BEF Chief of Staff, are meeting King Leopold at the Belgian GHQ near Mons.

Yesterday evening two divisions, one British and one Belgian, were both ordered to occupy the Louvain sector, and 24 hours later the confusion has still not been sorted out. And General Prioux, advancing to the Gembloux Gap between the Dyle and Meuse rivers, reports: "There are no real trenches, no barbed wire, practically nothing." He ends dismally: "The enemy won't give us time to dig in."

In spite of the command confusion and the disarray produced by the enemy's bewildering speed of manoeuvre, the Allies are confident that, within the next 48 hours, they will have established a continuous defence line.

This will extend from the mouth of the Scheldt, north of Antwerp, south-east to Louvain, where the nine British divisions are taking up positions, then to Wavre and Namur on the Meuse, where two Belgian divisions with fortress artillery are in place.

This line offers good defence positions. But south of the Meuse the situation suddenly looks alarming. General Heinz Guderian has debouched from the woods of the Ardennes with a big force of *Panzers*. Are the Allies massing on the wrong front? (→ 14).

Refugees from the Low Countries.

They came from the air, they came by land: the day the "phoney war" ended

War from the air: German paratroops rain down on the Netherlands.

War on land: a German anti-tank gun crew in position north of Ghent.

The price of war: dead Dutch soldiers lie among abandoned bicycles.

France braces itself for Nazi attack

French HQ, Vincennes, 11 May
General Gamelin has set up his command post here on the outskirts of Paris, because – as he says – he wants to be close to the government while escaping the atmosphere of the capital. He has delegated to General Alphonse Georges responsibility for field operations. Georges has his GHQ at La Ferte-sous-Jouarre, 35 miles (56 km) east of Paris, but remains for much of the time at his residence 12 miles (19 km) away. The general staff officers are at a third HQ at Montry, between Vincennes and La Ferte. The French air force HQ is at Coulommiers, some ten miles (16 km) from La Ferte.

Gamelin remains quietly confident. Of the 104 divisions at his disposal he has put 31, including nine British, on the northern, left, flank, and these have advanced into Belgium. On the right flank, behind the Maginot Line, he has 44 divisions. In reserve he has 22 divisions. The general says: "I feel sure we can stop the Germans."

Others, however, are less certain. Colonel Charles de Gaulle, who has just been given command of an armoured division which, he says, does not yet exist, found Gamelin's HQ as hushed and peaceful as a convent. There is no teletype link with the field armies and no radio. Gamelin keeps in touch by driving from Vincennes to the other HQs, and is content that 48 hours is all that is needed for orders to reach his commanders.

Gamelin's confidence rests on the Maginot Line, superiority over the Germans in artillery (11,200 guns against the Germans' 6,000) and equality, at least, with the Germans in tanks. But the tanks are dispersed as small infantry support groups, unlike the *Panzers* which are deployed in strength for lightning blows. French artillery, mostly horse-drawn, lacks mobility.

For Gamelin the only cloud on the horizon is a message, just received, telling him that Belgian forces, under heavy German pressure, are pulling back behind the line of the Meuse between Liege and Namur. In fact, the Belgians are carrying out a secret decision, made last January, not to risk even a delaying action in the Ardennes.

Rescue workers clear the rubble in the garrison town of Nancy in eastern France – one of many towns bombed by the Germans in the opening onslaught.

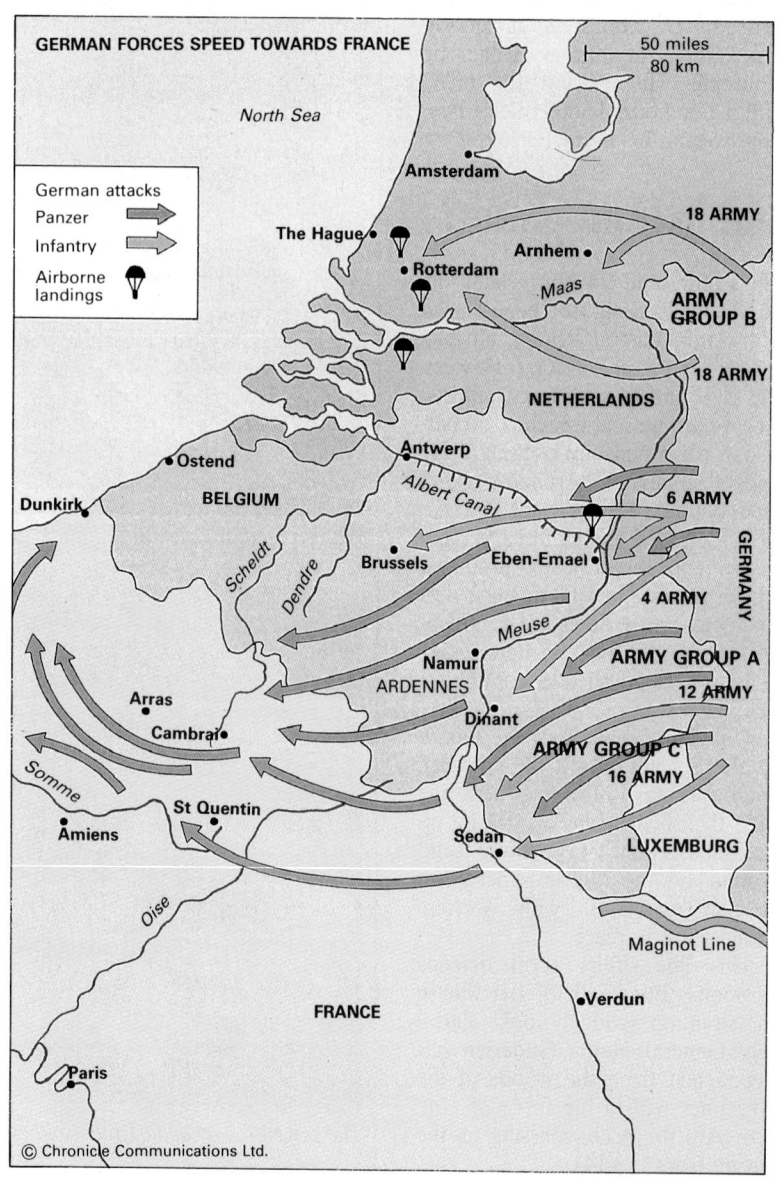

German advances threaten the US, warns Roosevelt

Washington, 11 May
President Franklin D Roosevelt plans to warn a special joint session of the US Congress next week that the German advances in western Europe mean that even the Atlantic Ocean is no longer a protection for the United States. He believes that aviation, parachute troops and the "Fifth Column" now make the United States vulnerable to attack.

The president wants a mobile expeditionary force to be created as well as a programme to expand and modernize the US armed forces. At present the American army is not one of the 12 largest in the world. Mr Roosevelt would like the rate of production of military aircraft in US factories to be increased to 50,000 a year – and he will tell Congress not to interfere, as it did until recently by the terms of the Neutrality Acts, with arms deliveries to the Allies.

Italy still keeps out of encroaching war

Rome, 11 May
Despite constant urging by Hitler, Italy continues to pursue a course of neutrality – although many observers believe that, sooner or later, Mussolini will take advantage of Allied setbacks to enter the war. The Duce has never dropped his ambition to turn the Mediterranean into an "Italian lake".

The bulk of the Italian press has become increasingly vociferous and pro-Nazi, with glowing accounts of German victories in France and Norway. Mussolini's propaganda machine is claiming that Britain's Royal Navy is largely obsolete and no match for his impressive array of battleships which are taking part in well-publicized exercises in the Adriatic.

For all his bombast, Mussolini is aware that his country – with a coastline as long as Britain's – is vulnerable to invasion and that British domination of the Straits of Gibraltar in the west and Suez in the east could effectively blockade imports to Italy.

Prime minister is toppled by House of Commons debate

Westminster, 8 May

"You have sat too long for any good you have been doing. Depart, I say, and let us have done with you. In the name of God, go!" With devastating effect Leo Amery, one of the most senior Tory MPs, tonight quoted in the House of Commons those angry words used by Oliver Cromwell to the Long Parliament in the 17th century.

Mr Amery pointed at the prime minister as he uttered them. It was the most dramatic moment in the tumultuous two-day debate on the disastrous Norway campaign.

In the vote at the end the government's majority was reduced to 81 from a normal figure of over 200. Some 40 Tories, including former cabinet members, voted with the opposition parties against Mr Chamberlain. A large number of other Tories deliberately abstained from voting.

Most MPs now feel that a change in premiership must be imminent. Ahead of the critical vote, Chamberlain petulantly snapped: "I have got my friends in the House." He soon discovered how many of them deserted him when he faced what was in effect a vote of no-confidence.

As the shaken prime minister left the House, Harold Macmillan and a few other Tory rebels sang the opening bars of *Rule Britannia* while others chanted: "Go, Go, Go!"

There were startling moments before that. Admiral of the Fleet Sir Roger Keyes, a Tory MP and hero of the last war, arrived in the House in full uniform with six rows of medal ribbons on his chest. He denounced Mr Chamberlain and volunteered personally to lead another naval assault on the enemy in Norway.

As first lord of the admiralty Mr Churchill stoutly declared that he took the fullest share of responsibility for the Norwegian campaign. David Lloyd George, prime minister in the last war, told him: "Don't allow yourself to be converted into an air-raid shelter to keep the splinters from your colleagues" (→9).

Churchill heads coalition government

Ecstatic crowds greet Churchill, Britain's new prime minister following Chamberlain's resignation.

London, 10 May

Neville Chamberlain, who resigned as prime minister two days ago, tonight advised the king to send for Winston Churchill to form a new government. Mr Churchill, who has emerged as the most credible candidate to lead the war effort, was immediately summoned to the Palace. He told the king that he will build an all-party team to achieve ultimate war victory. In addition to being prime minister, Mr Churchill will act as minister of defence. He will have a small war cabinet. Mr Attlee and Mr Arthur Greenwood, the leader and deputy leader of the Labour Party, were at Admiralty House late tonight. It is understood that the new premier discussed the allocation of posts with them. Some trade union leaders will be brought into the government.

Mr Chamberlain had hoped to remain in office in spite of his huge humiliation in the House of Commons the night before last. His decision to quit came only after Mr Attlee told him that Labour's national executive had decided that the party should join a coalition only if there were a new prime minister. On getting this daunting news Chamberlain called a special cabinet meeting and said that he must resign immediately in view of the swift deterioration of the war situation with Germany's invasion of Holland, Belgium and Luxemburg.

Mr Chamberlain broadcast to the nation this evening. He disclosed that Mr Churchill has asked him to be a member of the new war cabinet; he has agreed. Mr Chamberlain also said with a tremor in his voice: "As long as I believed there was a chance of preserving peace honourably I strove equally hard to wage it with all my might."

However, the probable verdict of the nation now is that he never looked like a great war leader. Tonight Britain is praying that it now has one in the pugnacious Winston Churchill (→22).

Labour men who backed Churchill

Westminster, 10 May

It was the Labour leader, Clement Attlee, and his deputy, Arthur Greenwood, who effectively put Winston Churchill in Downing Street. They made it clear that Labour would join a coalition government only if it was led by Churchill – and not if Lord Halifax, the foreign secretary, became prime minister.

Attlee and Greenwood.

1940

May

Su	Mo	Tu	We	Th	Fr	Sa
			1	2	3	4
5	6	7	8	9	10	11
12	13	14	15	16	17	18
19	20	21	22	23	24	25
26	27	28	29	30	31	

Aliens are interned or put under curfew in eastern Britain

Britain, 12 May

Three thousand enemy aliens were rounded up for internment today throughout the eastern counties of England and Scotland, from the Isle of Wight to Inverness. The home secretary, Sir John Anderson, applied the order to all German and Austrian men between 16 and 60, excluding invalids. No German or Austrian may enter the restricted area without permission.

All other aliens, of whatever nationality, living in the eastern counties must report daily to the police and are forbidden to use cars or bicycles or to go out between 8pm and 6am. The restrictions apply to about 11,000 aliens.

On the outbreak of war many aliens were rounded up, but only 486, or fewer than one per cent, were detained by the Aliens' Tribunals. A further 8,000 had their movements restricted. Over 50,000 stayed at liberty. Most of them are refugees from the Nazi regime.

There is no evidence of the existence in Britain of a "fifth column" of Nazi sympathizers. Some were sent to establish a network here in the two years before the war, but the police Special Branch kept them under observation and arrested them as war was declared.

"WE HAD AN ESCAPED GERMAN PRISONER HIDING IN OUR HOUSE LAST NIGHT!"
"HOW DID YOU KNOW?"
"I HEARD MUM TELL DAD THERE WAS A JERRY UNDER THE BED!"

Current misinterpretations of the monsters under the bed.

12. Belgium: Five RAF Fairey Battle bombers attack bridges over the Albert Canal but are shot down; the Belgians blow up all the bridges over the River Meuse to stop the German advance (→ 13).

13. Belgium: German *Panzer* Divisions under Guderian, Reinhardt and Rommel cross the Meuse at Sedan.

13. Belgium: German troops throw back a French force at Sedan and at Dinant in Belgium.→

13. Norway: Allied troops advance on Narvik from Harstad.

13. London: Queen Wilhelmina of the Netherlands arrives in exile.→

14. Netherlands: Rotterdam falls to the Germans after heavy bombing from the air kills 980 people and destroys 20,000 buildings. There are 78,000 homeless after the raids.→

14. Belgium and France: The RAF loses 70 aircraft and the French air force 40 in attacks on bridges across the Meuse.

14. London: Churchill, signing himself "Former naval person", writes to Roosevelt asking for aid (→ 16).

15. Netherlands: The Dutch army surrenders to the Germans.

15. Netherlands: The destroyer HMS *Valentine* is bombed off Walcheren and beached.

16. Washington: Roosevelt asks Congress for a sharp increase in military spending to fund the building of 50,000 planes a year.

16. Paris: Churchill is shaken when Gamelin and Reynaud tell him that they have no military reserves left.

17. Norway: The British cruiser *Effingham* runs aground south of Narvik and sinks.

17. Belgium: Germany occupies Brussels, Louvain, Malines and Namur (→ 18).

18. Belgium: Antwerp capitulates, while in France St Quentin and Cambrai fall.→

Germany takes Holland

The city of Rotterdam, shattered and charred by the German air attack.

Hilversum, 14 May

At dawn today the Dutch were still hoping to hold on. German airborne troops at The Hague had been captured or driven off, and Rotterdam, the key to the defence of Fortress Holland, still held out. During the morning, however, a German officer under a white flag warned the Dutch that unless the city surrendered it would be destroyed. While negotiations were going on, bombers diverted from the Belgian front appeared and in 90 minutes pulverized the city.

Wild rumour and, some say, Allied propaganda have spread the story that up to 30,000 civilians died in the raid. In fact, about 980 died, but nearly 80,000 have been made homeless and two-thirds of the city has been destroyed.

With the loss of Rotterdam, General Henri G Winkelman, the Dutch C-in-C, decided further resistance would lead only to the complete destruction of the country. He broadcast his surrender on Hilversum radio this evening. "By vast superiority of the most modern arms, the enemy has been able to break our resistance," he said. "But ultimately the Netherlands will rise again as a free nation. Long live our queen!"

So the fight goes on. Queen Wilhelmina and her cabinet, brought to England by the Royal Navy, have proclaimed London to be the seat of the Netherlands government. Wilhelmina, in a navy blue coat and skirt and with a gas mask slung from her shoulder, arrived at Liverpool Street station with officers of the royal guard and was met by King George, who kissed her on both cheeks. She told him that the Dutch people in the colonies overseas would continue to fight alongside the Allies (→ 15).

RAF steps up continental bombing raids

London, 16 May

Bomber Command was unleashed against the Germans last night with 99 aircraft, the largest force yet employed in one operation, attacking military installations in the Ruhr, and another 12 striking at German communications in Belgium.

A communique issued by the Air Ministry today says: "Each crew was given specific military objectives and instructions that bombs were not to be dropped indiscriminately. A few aircraft failed to locate their objectives and did not drop their bombs, but the majority found and bombed their targets with great effect causing widespread damage and many explosions." The pilots claim that they hit important road and rail communications and mechanized columns heading for the front. One Wellington was lost. This raid will please Bomber Command, which believes it can bring Germany to its knees by concentrated bombing of strategic targets within Germany.

Panzers break through at Sedan

Sedan, 14 May

"Impenetrable" was the word French strategists used for the Ardennes, with its narrow roads winding through wooded hills; so they left the area to be defended by a light screen of cavalry. Now Lieutenant-General Heinz Guderian, known as "Father of the *Panzers*", has come tearing out of the hills with seven armoured divisions, totalling over 2,000 tanks, to give the French cavalry a severe mauling.

Less than three days after his force was spotted by French scouts, he has reached the Meuse on an 80-mile (128-kilometre) front. The French General Andre Corap, on the left bank, has two divisions there; the rest of his Ninth Army is some 60 miles (96 km) distant. "So the Germans have reached the Meuse," he remarked, for he was confident that the decisive battle was being fought elsewhere, in Belgium; the Meuse was impassable.

But this morning Guderian had three bridgeheads, backed by an armoured brigade, across the Meuse. At last the French counter-attacked, to be ripped apart by German tanks swarming across the river. So this afternoon Guderian has smashed a mighty hole in the French defences. Corap's Ninth Army, its artillery paralysed, its horses slaughtered by low-flying fighters, its HQ bombed and its communications in ruins, is in full retreat.

German troops set off to cross the supposedly impassable river Meuse.

The streets of Sedan lined with burnt-out cars after the German attack.

How Germany's crack "Panzer" divisions outstrip the enemy

France, 18 May

Now that the German *Panzers* have broken out of their bridgeheads over the river Meuse and are advancing rapidly west, the Allied command and control system is becoming increasingly numbed. The *Blitzkrieg* which overcame the Poles is in danger of doing the same to the British and French. What is the secret of their success?

The idea that mechanized armies can radically increase the pace of battle is nothing new. The eminent British military theorists Major-General J F C Fuller and Captain Basil Liddell Hart have preached this for the past 20 years. The Germans have recognised that victories are won by thinking and acting

more quickly than your enemy. The tank, by virtue of its mobility, firepower, protection and radio communications, provides this ability.

General Heinz Guderian, who had much to do with the creation of the Panzer force and whose Panzer corps broke through the French defences at Sedan, believes that once the momentum of an advance has been built up it must not be allowed to die. To ensure this he insists that commanders at all levels must be well forward so that they can react quickly to rapidly changing situations. Mention must be made too of the highly responsive fire support provided by the Ju87 Stuka dive-bombers and controlled by ground-to-air radio.

Guderian: Father of the Panzers.

Belgian forces are retreating as Nazis conquer Brussels

Bruges, 18 May

King Leopold has set up an improvised HQ in a remote *chateau* at Bruges, a few miles from the coast at Ostend. The atmosphere is sombre. The Germans are in Brussels; Antwerp is about to fall; the French, in near panic over the Sedan breakthrough, have begun withdrawing their forces from the Belgian front without informing the British or the Belgians; and the roads of Belgium and northern France are choked with refugees.

Lord Gort, the BEF commander, learned of the French decision by chance when a British officer visiting General Gaston Billotte's 1 Army Group HQ noticed a message awaiting dispatch. The Belgians were told the following day. "It came like a shout out of the blue," says General Olivier Derousseaux, Leopold's deputy chief of staff. "We had to shake ourselves back into action."

The British and Belgian armies began withdrawing along a 50-mile (80-kilometre) front without interference from the enemy, most of the *Panzers* having been taken south to the Sedan sector. But the French Seventh Army, pulling back from the mouth of the Scheldt, cut through the British and Belgian lines, causing chaos (→ 20).

British plan attack, but is it too late?

Arras, 18 May

British forces in Belgium and northern France, threatened by the sweep of German *Panzers* towards the Channel and by the disintegration of the French First Army, are planning a counter-attack against the 7th Panzer and the motorized SS *Totenkopf* divisions near Arras.

Major-General Erwin Rommel has been surprised by the ease of his troops' passage into France, which has meant that their reserves are virtually untapped. The British commanders are confident that they will give Rommel a tough battle, but some worry that their attack may be too late.

▷

France recalls war hero

Paris, 18 May
Paul Reynaud, the French prime minister, has recalled to his cabinet Marshal Philippe Petain, the defender of Verdun and, with Marshal Foch, one of France's two greatest military heroes of the Great War. Marshal Petain comes into the government as vice-premier.

M Reynaud has taken over the ministry of war from Edouard Daladier, his predecessor as premier, and Daladier now becomes minister of foreign affairs. Another veteran of 1914-18, Georges Mandel, becomes the minister of the interior, with responsiblity for defeating the "Fifth Column". Mandel was "right-hand man" of the French leader Georges Clemenceau in 1917-1918.

The choice of Marshal Petain has been well received, in spite of his advanced age – he is 84. Petain was something more than one of the toughest and most successful of France's generals in the Great War. As the successful organizer of the defence of Verdun he became a symbol of French courage and patriotism. "*Ils ne passeront pas!* [They shall not pass]" he said of the Germans, and pass they did not, even

Marshal Petain: now vice-premier.

though the flower of a nation's manhood marched up the "sacred way" into the worst "mincing-machine" of the Great War.

Then, as the German artillery intensified its bombardments and the casualty lists lengthened, Petain came out with a second slogan that again put fresh heart into his men: "*On les aura*! [We'll get them!]"

In 1917, after the casualties of Verdun had led to widespread mutinies, Petain, as the new commander-in-chief, restored morale by his firm but restrained authority.

Churchill rallies nation: "I have nothing to offer but blood, toil, tears and sweat"

Westminster, 13 May
Today Winston Churchill made his first speech to the House of Commons following his appointment as prime minister three days ago. He told MPs that he was forming an administration "on the broadest possible basis" in accordance with "the evident wish and will of parliament and the nation". He said that he had formed "a war cabinet ... of five members, representing, with the Opposition Liberals, the unity of the nation". Further appointments will be made tomorrow.

The prime minister went on to remind the House that: "we are in the preliminary stage of one of the greatest battles in history, that we are in action in many points in Norway and in Holland, that we have to be prepared in the Mediterranean, that the air battle is continuous and that many preparations have to be made here at home ... I would say to the House, as I said to those who have joined this Government: "I have nothing to offer but blood, toil, tears and sweat."

"We have before us an ordeal of the most grievous kind. We have

before us many, many long months of struggle and of suffering. You ask what is our policy?

"I will say: It is to wage war, by sea, land and air, with all our might and with all the strength that God can give us: to wage war against a monstrous tyranny, never surpassed in the dark, lamentable catalogue of human crime. That is our policy.

"You ask, What is our aim? I can answer in one word: Victory – victory at all costs, victory in spite of all terror, victory, however long and hard the road may be; for without victory there is no survival.

"Let that be realised; no survival for the British Empire; no survival for all that the British Empire has stood for, no survival for the urge and impulse of the ages, that mankind will move forward towards its goal.

"But I take up my task with buoyancy and hope. I feel sure that our cause will not be suffered to fail among men. At this time I feel entitled to claim the aid of all, and I say, 'Come, then, let us go forward together with our united strength'."

Erstwhile political foes work together in Churchill's war cabinet

Britain, 14 May
Winston Churchill has now filled most of the major posts in the new coalition government. Political foes – Tory, Labour and Liberal – are sitting shoulder-to-shoulder at the cabinet table. "A crowd of able men" he is calling them. First the prime minister announced his inner war cabinet – himself as minister of defence, the ex-premier Chamberlain as lord president of the council, Lord Halifax staying as foreign secretary, Clement Attlee, who will be lord privy seal and deputy prime minister, and Arthur Greenwood as minister without portfolio. The former foreign secretary, Anthony Eden, Dominions secretary since war broke out, becomes secretary for war. Labour's A V Alexander is first lord of the admiralty, and the Liberal leader Sir Archibald Sinclair is Secretary for Air. Other important appointments go to two of Labour's senior

Bevin: working-class champion.

Beaverbrook: buccaneer publisher.

men – Herbert Morrison as minister of supply and Hugh Dalton as minister for economic warfare. The trade union leader Ernest Bevin becomes minister of labour and national service in charge of the na-

tion's manpower. A new ministry for aircraft production has been created, which goes to the fiery newspaper proprietor Lord Beaverbrook, a friend of Mr Churchill (→ 19).

Britons flock to the local defence force

Britain, 15 May
"We are going to ask you to help us in a manner which I know will be welcome to thousands of you. We want large numbers of men of 17 to 65 to come forward and offer their services. The name of the new force will be the Local Defence Volunteers ..." This was the appeal of Anthony Eden, the war secretary, on the radio at 9.15pm yesterday. By the same time tonight, 250,000 men had rushed to their local police stations to volunteer. They have been promised uniforms and arms but for the present there are neither – 250,000 armbands inscribed LDV have been ordered. The LDV force was called for primarily to deal with Germans parachuted behind the lines, as they were during the invasion of Holland, some disguised reportedly as peasants or clergymen.

1940

May

Su	Mo	Tu	We	Th	Fr	Sa
				1	2	3	4
5	6	7	8	9	10	11
12	13	14	15	16	17	18
19	20	21	22	23	24	25
26	27	28	29	30	31	

19. Britain: Churchill makes his first broadcast as prime minister, calling Nazism "the foulest and most soul-destroying tyranny that has ever darkened and stained the pages of history" (→ 4/6).

20. France: Amiens falls to the Germans, and a force under Rommel surrounds Arras.

20. France: German forces reach the English Channel at Noyelles (→ 28).

20. London: Tyler Kent, a clerk at the US embassy, has been arrested on suspicion of sending copies of secret documents to Axis sympathizers.

20. Netherlands: Artur Seyss-Inquart, the Austrian who played a key role in Germany's 1938 takeover of Austria, is appointed *Reich* Commissioner for the occupied Netherlands.

22. Britain: The price of petrol is more than doubled, increasing from 11d (4$\frac{1}{2}$p/18¢) a gallon to 1/11$\frac{1}{2}$p/39¢).

23. France: The Allies start to evacuate Boulogne as the Germans press on to the Channel ports (→ 24).

23. Britain: R V Jones, a scientist with Air Intelligence, tells the government that intersecting radio beams could guide *Luftwaffe* bombers to their targets (→ 22/6).

24. London: The British government decides to withdraw all forces from Norway.

24. Mexico City: The exiled former Russian leader Leon Trotsky is injured when gunmen attack his home.

24. Germany: Hitler issues his war directive number 13, ordering the annihilation of the Allies in Artois and Flanders and an aerial attack on Britain (→ 25).

25. France: Germany captures Boulogne; the Allies fall back to Dunkirk.→

25. Germany: Himmler tells Hitler that through large-scale emigration "the concept of Jew will have completely disappeared from Europe".

Allied troops forced back to Channel

Flanders, 25 May

The Germans are closing in on the Belgian army, the remnants of the French 1st and 7th Armies and the bulk of the British Expeditionary Force (BEF). Calais is still in Allied hands, being defended desperately by a small British force in the hope that the Germans will be obliged to use up their armour there instead of turning it on Dunkirk, where Lord Gort is concentrating his strength.

Gort was alerted to the danger of a rupture of the Franco-Belgian front after a British patrol captured German plans which showed that the main enemy thrust was to be directed at Menin. He threw in his last reserves in a bid to keep open his lines of communication to the coast. Lieutenant-General Alan Brooke, commanding BEF's 2 Corps, noted: "Nothing but a miracle can save the BEF." Churchill, while urging Gort to fight on, has told the Royal Navy to assemble as many small ships as it can (→ 26).

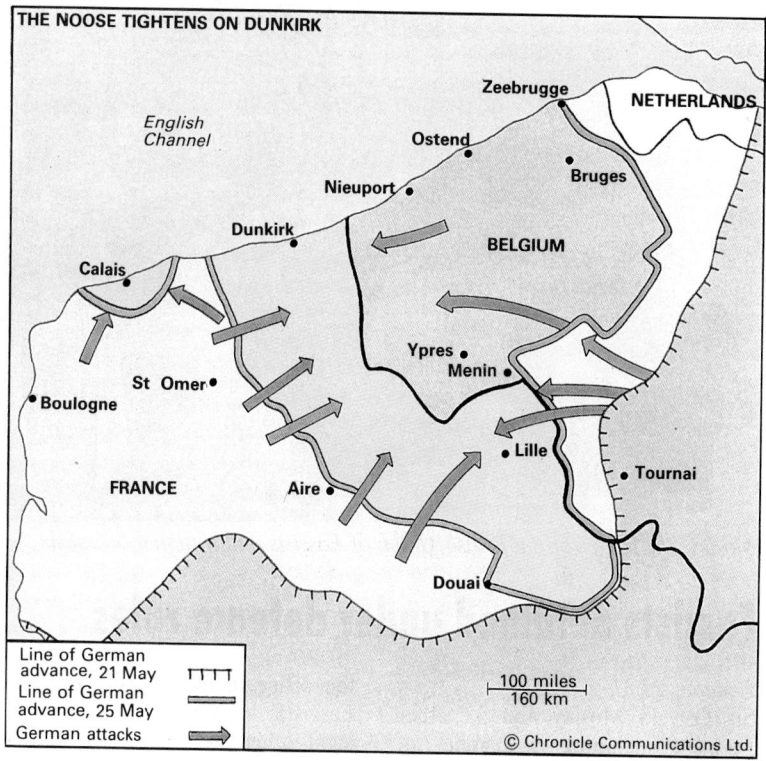

THE NOOSE TIGHTENS ON DUNKIRK

Line of German advance, 21 May
Line of German advance, 25 May
German attacks
100 miles / 160 km
© Chronicle Communications Ltd.

Hitler orders Panzers to hold back on the brink of victory

Dunkirk, 25 May

With the British Expeditionary Force and remnants of French and Belgian units trapped in the Dunkirk pocket, and Guderian's *Panzers* closing in for the knockout blow, Hitler has suddenly and inexplicably ordered a halt.

The stunning victories of the German forces have delighted and worried Hitler. He is afraid that the Panzers are being over-extended, and when General von Rundstedt suggested that the armour should be halted until infantry support could be brought up, Hitler agreed. General Franz Halder, Hitler's chief of staff, protested. "The

Fuhrer is terribly nervous," he wrote in his diary. "Afraid to take any chances." While Hitler hesitated, Goering barged in with the boast that he could take care of things. An enraged Halder wrote: "Finishing off the encircled enemy army is to be left to the air force! "

Hitler's controversial order has given Lord Gort a vital reprieve, which he and the Royal Navy and Air Force are exploiting to the full. General Wilhelm Keitel, the chief of the OKW (*Wehrmacht* High Command), says that every war sees missed opportunities and sooner or later one of them proves fatal. This could be the one (→ 26).

A German tank awaiting support.

Bletchley Park breaks Luftwaffe cipher

Britain, 22 May

The code-breakers of Hut Six at Bletchley Park in the English countryside 40 miles (64 km) north of London, where scientists, mathematicians and chess-masters are working against time to solve the secrets of the German *Enigma* enciphering machine, have made a great breakthrough. Using their

first British-built *Bombe*, an electro-mechanical device which can do hundreds of computations every minute, they have broken the *Luftwaffe's* "Red" key. This means that all the Luftwaffe's operational and administrative traffic can be read despite the added security devices built into the Enigmas in preparation for the assault on the west.

Raids on England

Britain, 25 May

Although the war in the air is confined mainly to targets in the south of England and the Channel, sporadic *Luftwaffe* raids continue elsewhere – apparently testing out air defences. The North Riding of Yorkshire, and rural parts of East Anglia, were the latest victims. Eight civilians are reported hurt. ▷

Britain gets ready for war in earnest

Mosley, the leader of the British Union of Fascists and National Socialists.

Fascists detained under defence rules

London, 23 May
Sir Oswald Mosley and 33 other Fascists, including a member of Parliament, were arrested today on the orders of Britain's home secretary. Under Defence Regulation 18B he has powers to detain members of organizations which may be used for purposes prejudicial to national security.

Mosley was arrested on returning to his flat in Dolphin Square in London. After a lightning raid on the office of the British Union of Fascists in Great Smith Street, eight other leading members were arrested. The MP arrested is Captain A M Ramsay, the member for Peebles and president of the anti-Semitic Right Club.

The male detainees were taken to Brixton Prison. Six women detainees were in Holloway Prison last night. An official of the ministry of health, a secret Fascist, was also arrested.

Government takes emergency powers

Westminster, 22 May
Parliament took less than three hours today to rush into law the most drastic legislation known in British history. It gives the government almost unlimited power over the life, liberty and property of everyone in the land.

Under the Emergency Powers Act banks, the munitions industry, profits, wages and working conditions are all now subject to rigorous state control. There is also an unprecedented mobilization of manpower.

In his first speech as lord privy seal and deputy premier in the new government, Clement Attlee urged the nation to keep calm. "Everyone should continue at their jobs until ordered otherwise," he said.

At the same time Ernest Bevin is being given dictatorial power, as minister of labour and national service, to direct anyone to do anything needed in the struggle for national survival.

With the emergency powers settled, MPs then quickly passed a Treachery Act redefining the scope of traitorous acts punishable by death (→ 5/6).

Embattled Allied forces find a new army commander

General Weygand: taking control.

Paris, 20 May
Paul Reynaud, the French premier, has at last got rid of Gamelin, the general whom he disliked and distrusted as an incompetent defeatist. Maxime Weygand, aged 73, who served with Marshal Foch in the Great War, has been given the task of rescuing the Allied fortunes on a battlefield dominated by *Panzers* and Stuka dive-bombers.

Until now the self-assured General Weygand, a devout Catholic and a royalist contemptuous of republican politicians, has been in virtual exile in Syria. Now his appointment as supreme commander is hailed in the press; but he is a staff officer who has never commanded armies in battle.

He has disregarded plans already made for the Allied armies in north and south to attack and cut off the exposed German armoured columns, still unprotected by the infantry. He spent his first day making ceremonial visits to the French president and cabinet ministers. Then he said he would visit the front, as his hero Foch had always done. He set off by air for Ypres to talk to French, British and Belgian commanders. During the meeting King Leopold decided that Weygand was completely ignorant of the desperate plight of the Allied armies. What Leopold did not know was that Weygand has decided the war is already lost (→ 28).

Railings grubbed up, bandstands melted down for war effort

London, 26 May
Old bandstands from the parks as well as the railings around them are being scrapped to help the war effort. Mrs Hugh Dalton, the wife of the minister for economic warfare, is leading a drive to uproot railings as chairman of the London County Council parks committee. One bandstand to be demolished is in Temple Gardens beside the Embankment. Streets, squares and crescents of Victorian and Regency houses are having the railings chopped from their garden walls. Some people claim that London looks better without them. Victorian churchyards are also yielding up their railings, but so far Buckingham Palace railings are sacrosanct. There is a proposal to take up disused tramlines for scrap.

Any old iron goes into the melting pot in the search for scrap metal.

1940

May

Su	Mo	Tu	We	Th	Fr	Sa
				1	2	3	4
5	6	7	8	9	10	11
12	13	14	15	16	17	18
19	20	21	22	23	24	25
26	27	28	29	30	31	

26. Dunkirk: The evacuation of Allied troops begins (→ 27).

26. Germany: Hitler belatedly orders his armies to attack Dunkirk (→ 27).

26. Norway: A German aerial attack sinks the British cruiser *Curlew*.

27. France: Calais falls to the German army, which now surrounds the Allies at Dunkirk; only 8,000 men are evacuated today.→

27. London: Dill takes over from Ironside as Chief of the Imperial General Staff.

27. Britain: The butter ration is cut back to four ounces per person per week.

28. Norway: Allied forces, under French command, occupy Narvik (→ 9/6).

28. Dunkirk: 17,800 men are taken off (→ 29).

29. Europe: The Germans take Ostend and Ypres in Belgium and Lille in France.

29. Dunkirk: Three allied destroyers are sunk and seven are damaged; 47,300 men are taken off (→ 30).

30. Rome: Mussolini decides that Italy will enter the war on 5 June, and forewarns Hitler (→ 10/6).

30. Dunkirk: 53,820 men are taken off, amongst them Lieutenant-General Alan Brooke whose 2 Corps has played a large part in the successful withdrawal to the Channel (→ 31).

31. Dunkirk: Lord Gort hands over the command of British troops still in France to Major-General Harold Alexander, and departs for Dover; 68,000 troops also leave today (→ 1/6).

31. Tokyo: Launching a bombing campaign against south-east China, Japan says that it will bomb Chungking until the Nationalist spirit breaks.

31. Washington: Roosevelt asks Congress to authorize an extra $1,300 million in defence spending (→ 11/6).

31. Britain: Signposts are removed from crossroads to confuse any invasion force.

BEF starts big retreat from Dunkirk

Dunkirk, 27 May

In his underground bunker deep within the cliffs of Dover – a room which held electrical plant in the last war and was known as the Dynamo Room – Vice-Admiral Bertram Ramsay gave the order for the emergency evacuation of troops from the beaches of Dunkirk, some 70 miles (112 kilometres) away across the Channel: "Operation Dynamo must begin."

British and French forces hold a 30-mile (48-km) stretch of coastline running from Gravelines through Dunkirk to Nieuport. Inland, the front reaches almost to Lille, where six French divisions are surrounded by seven German ones. Hitler, who has realized his mistake in halting land attacks to await reinforcements, has ordered a full-scale air and land assault on the Dunkirk pocket. In the meantime Lord Gort's BEF has made good use of Hitler's error, and the attackers are suffering heavy losses. One German officer, asking for air and artillery help, said that he would not wish to face these men if they were fully armed and rested.

At Dover, Ramsay has put together a vast fleet of small ships, including pleasure steamers and London Fire Brigade boats, as well as 40 Dutch coasters, now manned by the Royal Navy. He has to keep the Channel clear of mines, provide the bombardment of German batteries at Calais, drive off U-boats and depend on the RAF to hold back Goering's *Luftwaffe*. Ramsay believes he has two days before the Germans overrun the beachhead, and reckons that he might succeed in lifting up to 45,000 men.

Frustrated Germans report that the British are retreating into the Dunkirk pocket, abandoning their vehicles as they go. Running along breakwaters, the British clamber aboard ships moored side by side and so escape in spite of the continuous air raids. Many ships have been hit, including the Isle of Man steamer *Mona's Isle* which was mined and sank in two minutes.

A grim fate may await those who fall into German, especially SS, hands. Ninety men of the Royal Norfolk Regiment were today brutally slaughtered [*see report overleaf*].

Queuing for rescue: soldiers of the British Expeditionary Force wade out to boats waiting off the beaches of Dunkirk. Operation Dynamo is in action.

Looking back on Dunkirk as smoke rises from the bombed-out town; despite constant air attacks by German planes, the rescue operation goes ahead.

Belgian king tells army to surrender

Bruges, 28 May

On orders from King Leopold, Belgian forces laid down their arms at 1100 hours today. At Ypres, a few units without communications continued fighting for two hours.

Leopold's action has been denounced as "illegal and unconstitutional" by his cabinet ministers, who have fled to Paris. Britain's liaison officer to the Belgian king, Admiral Sir Roger Keyes, passed on a message from King George VI appealing to Leopold to escape and lead resistance from England. Leopold brushed this aside, saying that it was a repetition of what his ministers had been saying. "The cause of the Allies is lost," he said.

Leopold has been little liked by the British and French. In peacetime he pulled Belgium out of its alliance with them, and when war came he failed to rejoin it although the German threat was manifest. His troops have fought valiantly. Not once, under relentless bombing and repeated tank assaults, did they break during the 18 days of fighting against overwhelming odds.

It has been learnt that Leopold decided to surrender several days ago after an all-night row with his ministers, during which he refused to allow them to be seated. Then, two days ago, the king sent this message to the Allies: "The Belgian command intends to continue the fight to the very end. But the limits of resistance have now practically been reached."

Yesterday he sent General Derousseaux, his deputy chief of staff, to ask the Germans for an armistice. Almost six hours later, after having been fired on by German troops, Derousseaux returned with the answer: the Fuhrer was demanding unconditional surrender. Leopold capitulated.

This morning the German High Command made a further demand, requiring Leopold to give unhindered passage through the Belgian lines to the sea. Half an hour later German columns were moving on Ostend and Dixmude and encountering resistance from British forces led by Lieutenant-General Alan Brooke (→ 1/6).

Exiled: van Cauwelaert, the president of Belgium's chamber of representatives, addresses ministers who had opposed King Leopold's order to surrender.

Britons massacred by SS infantrymen

Le Paradis, France, 27 May

A farm outside this sleepy village was a scene of horror this afternoon when the SS 33rd Infantry Regiment wiped out a company of the Royal Norfolk Regiment left behind in the rush for Dunkirk.

Surrounded by Germans and cut off in a cowshed, Major Lisle Ryder opted to surrender with his 80 men. The SS marched them to a barn. Machine guns set up opposite the long, low wall opened fire on the column of soldiers; many were killed instantly. At a signal, the firing stopped and the Germans moved in on the pile of bodies, finishing the job with bayonets and pistols. Incredibly, Albert Pooley and William O'Callaghan survived, though seriously injured.

German economy geared to a short war

Germany, 31 May

Germany's economy is being reshaped to bolster its military campaigns. The ministry of armaments and munitions was set up under Fritz Todt in March to improve the flow of arms to the front line.

Unlike the other warring powers, Germany was preparing for war as early as 1936, when a four-year economic plan was introduced which included large-scale investment in armaments. Despite this, Germany's reserves are not geared to cope with a protracted war; this is one reason behind Hitler's *Blitzkrieg* strategy. With other heavy industries, armaments have been hit by shortages of labour and raw materials, although the latter should be eased by the occupation of areas rich in iron ore, such as Norway and Luxemburg.

Fritz Todt: the man in charge of organizing Germany's arms output.

Churchill thwarts cabinet appeasers with Labour help

Westminster, 30 May

Winston Churchill is determined that the grim news from France, as the battered British Expeditionary Force retreats towards Dunkirk, should not deflect Britain from its absolute opposition to Germany, whatever the cost. But he needed the support of the two Labour Party members of his five-man war cabinet to sustain his position.

At a secret meeting in the prime minister's room at the House of Commons last night the war cabinet is understood to have debated Italy's offer to mediate towards a negotiated peace. Lord Halifax, the foreign secretary, believes that Britain might secure better terms now, before, as seems likely, France is forced to surrender.

Chamberlain, ousted as premier earlier this month, was sympathetic to the Halifax line; Churchill, predictably, was hostile. He turned to the Labour men, for so long his political opponents. Clement Attlee said that if negotiations ever began the morale of the people would suffer a disastrous blow. His deputy, Arthur Greenwood, agreed – and the two-hour meeting ended with Britain still defiantly at war.

King leads prayers for Allied victory

Britain, 26 May

Large congregations gathered in churches of all denominations this Sunday for the National Day of Prayer "on behalf of the nation and Empire, of their allies and of the cause in which they are united", as German armies poured into France and the British reached Dunkirk.

The king and queen were at Westminster Abbey, accompanied by the refugee queen of the Netherlands, Queen Wilhelmina, and Mr Churchill. In his sermon the archbishop of Canterbury, Dr Lang, called the war "a mighty conflict against the powers of evil". At Westminster Cathedral Cardinal Hinsley spoke of a "just crusade for deliverance from the evil which rests on force alone".

1940

June

1. Norway: A week after deciding to withdraw from Norway, the Allies announce the evacuation of all troops.

1. China: Hsiangyang falls to the Japanese (→ 3).

1. Paris: Leopold III, the king of the Belgians, is struck off the Order of the Legion of Honour.

1. Dunkirk: 64,420 men are evacuated despite very heavy air attacks which sink four British ships (→ 2).

2. Dunkirk: A further 26,250 men are taken off.→

3. Paris: 254 civilians are killed when 200 *Luftwaffe* bombers bombard the city (→ 7).

3. China: Chinese forces counter-attack, retaking Hsiangyang and capturing Tsaoyang (→ 6).

4. Dunkirk: The last ship, the destroyer HMS *Shikari*, leaves at 3.40am; 26,175 men have been taken off in 24 hours, leaving 40,000 behind.

4. Norway: The evacuation of Allied forces from Harstad begins.

5. France: Three German *Panzer* corps launch *Fall Rot* [Plan Red], the attack on the Somme.

5. France: Edouard Daladier, the foreign minister, leaves the government. Charles de Gaulle is appointed under-secretary to the ministry of national defence.→

5. France: Captain Werner Molders, the leading German air ace, is shot down and taken prisoner by the French.

6. France: XV *Panzer* Corps breaks through the Somme defences near Amiens.→

6. China: Japanese troops take Chingmen, in Hupeh province (→ 10).

7. Germany: The French naval aircraft *Jules Verne* makes the first bombing raid of the war on Berlin.

8. Tromso: King Haakon and his government leave Norway with the last of the Allied troops; 24,500 troops have been evacuated from Harstad since 4 June.

British government bans strike action

Britain, 5 June

Strikes and lock-outs are now banned in Britain. Arbitration in industrial disputes is compulsory. Machinery in arms factories will run seven days a week, but workers can have one day's rest in seven. It will be a criminal offence for an employer in certain vital industries – especially engineering – to engage a worker without government permission. Miners and farm workers will have to stay in their jobs. Plans are being prepared for possible large-scale transfers of population and communal feeding.

These decrees and emergency measures were announced today by Ernest Bevin, the minister of labour and national service. He is rapidly becoming the most powerful member of the cabinet after Mr Churchill himself.

In summing up the drastic changes in industrial relations and work practices Mr Bevin said: "I cannot have a peacetime economy in wartime. I do not want one soldier to come back and say: 'You sent me there ill-equipped'."

He advised people not to have holidays. When asked what workers were to spend any higher pay on when there were shortages of goods in the shops, the labour minister said: "They should save part of their wages which might be useful when they have a week or two off after the war."

Mr Bevin gave an assurance that all the new controls and restrictions are for wartime only.

Wealthy send their children to Canada

London, 5 June

Many middle-class parents are planning to send their children abroad because of the invasion danger. They are making private arrangements with relatives and friends in Canada, other Dominions and the United States. The government is also planning an evacuation scheme of five to 16-year-olds through the Children's Overseas Reception Board. Offers to take British children are pouring in.

Nazi cruisers sink three British ships

North Sea, 8 June

Two German battlecruisers, the *Scharnhorst* and the *Gneisenau*, this evening sank the British aircraft carrier *Glorious* and her two escorting destroyers, which were returning from the failed expedition to Narvik. The destroyer *Acasta* took on the *Scharnhorst* and managed to hit her in the stern with a torpedo before going down herself. As a result the cruisers were forced back to Trondheim for repairs.

Priestley gives BBC a northern voice

J B Priestley: new voice on the BBC.

Britain, 5 June

A new voice was heard giving the postscript to the BBC News tonight – the novelist J B Priestley, who talked of the Dunkirk evacuation in tones as downright and northern as Yorkshire pudding. "What was characteristically English about it was the part played by the little pleasure steamers. These *Brighton Belles* left that innocent world of theirs to sail into the inferno to rescue our soldiers. Some of them will never return." He singled out the ferryboat *Gracie Fields*: "Now this little steamer, like all her brave and battered sisters, is immortal."

Navy captain wins first VC of the war

London, 7 June

The first Victoria Cross – the British Empire's highest award for heroism – of the war has been awarded posthumously to Captain Bernard Warburton-Lee of the destroyer HMS *Hardy*. He led the raid on Narvik in Norway in April in a blinding blizzard, knowing that the Germans held Narvik in greater force than was at first thought. Nevertheless he made three successful attacks on warships and merchant vessels in the harbour; as he withdrew he engaged five German destroyers. Captain Warburton-Lee was fatally wounded when a shell landed on *Hardy's* bridge.

On a Sunday visit to a small-arms factory, to see the seven-day-a-week munitions drive, King George fires a Bren gun on the practice ranges.

Operation Dynamo succeeds: 338,226 men saved

Rearguard troops in burnt-out streets; they hold Dunkirk while others escape.

The wreck of a bombed British warship towers over German soldiers at Dunkirk.

Dunkirk, 4 June
In the early hours of this morning Major-General Harold Alexander toured the shore line in a fast motor boat to make sure that no soldiers remained to be lifted off; then he went back to the quayside and took ship to Dover, the last Allied soldier to leave Dunkirk. Behind him, Dunkirk was a lurid backcloth of flames and thick oily smoke rising from burning vehicles and stores.

In seven days no fewer than 338,226 men have been evacuated under relentless enemy attack. The killed, wounded or missing number 68,000. All told, 222 naval vessels and some 800 civilian craft joined in the operation; six destroyers and 243 other ships have been sunk. Churchill speaks of the operation as "a miracle of deliverance".

Goering had boasted that his *Luftwaffe* would annihilate the BEF. But his aircraft were often grounded by bad weather and could not operate at night. "Dense fog over the Channel is giving cover to the British in their headlong flight," the German news agency reported. General Halder fumed: "We must now stand and watch countless thousands of the enemy get away to England right under our noses." Goering lost 150 of his planes in seven days and RAF Fighter Command lost 106. Not all those brought to safety have been military personnel. Among the last to come ashore at Dover were seven French telephone operators, a party of railway engineers and a girl aged five, rescued from a Belgian farm.

French commanders accused the British of saving their own men and abandoning the French; Weygand said that the English were playing their usual double game. This is not quite true, as Churchill pointed out yesterday afternoon in an urgent message to Reynaud: "We are coming back for your men tonight. Please ensure that all facilities are used promptly. For three hours last night many ships waited idly at great risk and danger."

British and French estimates put the number awaiting rescue at 30,000. But when the ships began taking men on board a swarm of men appeared out of cellars and wrecked buildings and raced towards the mole. About 118,000 mainly French, but also Belgian and Dutch, troops were brought back. The Dunkirk survivors, a weary, defeated army, were put aboard trains and taken to barracks. The British welcomed them, as heroes who will fight another day and plied them with tea, food and cigarettes (→8).

Three faces of war: captured, rescued and injured

Misery: one more prisoner of war.

Joy: BEF troops evacuated from Flanders are given a heroes' welcome.

Exhaustion: the wounded limp away.

Eye-witnesses tell of the great escape

Churchill vows: "We shall fight on the beaches"

Huge lines wind across the sands: the waiting seems interminable for the thousands of men still stranded on the beach.

The soldier: "men were screaming"

England, 2 June
Sergeant Leonard Howard left Dunkirk yesterday. He describes the hours he spent waiting to be rescued: "I lay in the sand, in the dunes at Dunkirk, and I slept because I was really completely exhausted. And the next morning I went into the water in the hope of getting a boat, being picked up. And there was no hope. They tried to organise queues but it was very difficult; there was a great deal of panic. I saw British troops shoot British troops ... a small boat came in, and they piled aboard it to such a degree that it was in danger of capsizing. And the chap in charge of this boat decided that unless he took some action ... and he shot a hanger-on. I saw chaps run into the water screaming because mentally it had got too much for them."

Yesterday morning Howard and another man found a canoe in which they paddled out towards the rescue boats. "As the rope from this ship that finally picked us up hit the canoe, it literally sank the canoe and we held onto the rope and were pulled onto the ship."

The sailor: "ships seemed endless"

England, 2 June
Leading Seaman Ernest Frederick Eldred was on the destroyer HMS *Harvester* during the evacuation from Dunkirk. The crew members thought that they were simply on patrol; then they saw the boats steaming across the Channel.

"I suppose you would call it more of a holiday scene with every type of boat and craft, an endless line across the Channel; some being towed by larger boats. It was a fantastic sight." As a destroyer, the *Harvester* was responsible for fighting off German air attacks as well as picking up as many men as possible from the beach. "I don't think the destroyers have ever carried so many men as we did, there must have been hundreds, literally hundreds, crammed in every space you could think of; you could hardly have got a cat aboard each time."

He recalls that they just "set them down anywhere we possibly could ... down the stokehole, engine room, mess decks were full, upper deck was crowded, everywhere. The only place we couldn't have them was by the guns."

The nurse: "bombs hit ambulances"

England, 2 June
Nursing Sister Catherine Mary Butland, who was evacuated from Dunkirk after two weeks at a clearing station in Belgium, has accused the Germans of ignoring the universal Red Cross sign and bombing ambulance trains. She and seven other nurses were driven to Dunkirk in a truck by a colonel.

"We were being attacked from the air all the way down," she said later. "The towns were being bombed constantly and the fact that we were an ambulance train made no difference. If they wanted to bomb it they'd bomb it. If they wanted to come down and machine-gun while you were getting your patients off the ambulances they came down and machine-gunned." Sister Butland and her companions were taken aboard the converted hospital ship *Worthing*. "We put our bedding rolls down and we went to work because there were casualties being brought in in all states of injury, wanting treatment" she added. "The whole way through the atmosphere was one of: I want to get back to the unit."

Britain, 4 June
Mr Churchill today reviewed the war situation. In parliament he said: "We shall go on to the end ... we shall fight on the beaches, we shall fight on the landing grounds, we shall fight in the fields and in the streets, we shall fight in the hills; we shall never surrender ..."

Rousing MPs' patriotic fervour, he continued: "Even if – which I do not for a moment believe – this land or a large part of it were subjugated and starving, then our Empire beyond the seas, armed and guarded by the British Fleet, would carry out the struggle until in God's good time the New World, with all its power and might, steps forth to the rescue and the liberation of the Old."

Earlier in his sombre report the prime minister described the Dunkirk evacuation of the bulk of the British Expeditionary Force as "a miracle of deliverance" even though there had been "a colossal military disaster". Now, he said, Britain faced an imminent threat of invasion. But Napoleon had failed and so, too, would Hitler (→18).

Military triumph or disastrous fiasco?

Britain, 4 June
People are already talking about the Dunkirk evacuation as a miracle, and the British troops have been welcomed home as heroes rather than as members of a defeated army. This hides the extreme seriousness of the situation.

For a start, the BEF left behind almost all its weapons and there is little available in Britain to replace them. The Royal Navy has suffered severe warship losses, and three squadrons' worth of fighters are now missing from the RAF's order of battle. Now that the victorious German armies are turning south the question is: can France resist them? There is little optimism in Whitehall that it will be able to for long. If so, Britain, its defences now weakened, will be left very much on its own.

Germans push on into the heart of France

Paris, 8 June
The tide of battle on the Somme has turned decisively in favour of the Germans. General Rommel's 7th *Panzer* Division has broken through the French front between Abbeville and Amiens and in a lightning thrust has reached the outskirts of Rouen. Rommel has sliced the French Tenth Army in two, leaving the British 51st Highland Division with its back to the sea and facing destruction.

The French are fighting with desperate tenacity, but they are outnumbered two to one and able to manoeuvre their armour only slowly, while the Germans are shifting their Panzers from one sector of the front to another with bewildering speed (→ 10).

"Somewhere in France" in ruins.

Parisians prepare for German onslaught

Parisians inspect bomb damage.

Paris, 7 June
A dull rumble can be heard north and east of Paris, the rumble of heavy guns. The broken glass from Paris's first air raid four days ago still tinkles under the feet of the refugees moving east along the *boulevards*. The restaurants are empty, the Ritz deserted. For the third time in a lifetime, Paris prepares for a siege.

The air raid on 3 June came at lunchtime. Leaflets giving warnings, dropped by German planes the night before, caused near-hysteria, but when the raid came it was an anti-climax – though 254 are reported dead. Paris's anti-aircraft guns were "well-nourished", as the French say, and the 200 planes kept too high to be accurate. There was no panic; the city seemed to accept its fate.

Only the cafes remain open, and it is there, amongst the clientele, that you can see some Parisians face change, the jaws taking on prominence, the cheekbones becoming defined, the eyes staring out. It is not hunger. There is lots of food in Paris. It is fear (→ 10).

De Gaulle joins the French government

Paris, 5 June
Paul Reynaud, the French prime minister, has brought into his government, as under-secretary for national defence, General Charles de Gaulle, who distinguished himself in last week's fighting as the commander of a tank division and has long been known as the advocate of more aggressive military tactics. De Gaulle's rise has been rapid. He only received his first divisional command, as a colonel, less than a month ago. His career was long held back by opponents of his ideas. In his book *Towards a Professional Army* he advocated a war of movement similar to that proposed by the German tank expert General Guderian (→ 18).

1940
June

Su	Mo	Tu	We	Th	Fr	Sa
						1
2	3	4	5	6	7	8
9	10	11	12	13	14	15
16	17	18	19	20	21	22
23	24	25	26	27	28	29
30						

9. Narvik: Germany formally reoccupies the port, and Norway's High Command orders the army to stop fighting at midnight.→

10. France: With the Germans just 50 miles (80 km) away, the government leaves Paris and heads southwest for Tours.

10. Joinville, France: After fighting for two hours, French reserves fail to stop the Germans crossing the Aisne (→ 11).

10. China: Japanese forces attack Ichang on the Yangtze river.→

11. Washington: Congress passes the Naval Supply Act, giving $1,500 million to the US Navy (→ 13).

11. Soissons, France: The French army pulls back across the Aisne river.

11. Paris: General Hering, the military governor, declares Paris an open city.

11. Malta: The island suffers its first air raids of the war; in seven attacks Italian planes kill 11 civilians and six soldiers, with 130 civilians and some soldiers injured.

12. France: Germany has occupied Rheims and Rouen.

12. Italy: RAF bombers attack Milan and the port of Genoa from airfields in the south of France.

12. France: General Weygand orders a general retreat (→ 13).

12. North Africa: British troops capture 62 Italians in the first skirmish along the Egypt-Libya border.

13. Washington: Congress votes to give $1,800 million to the army.

14. Auschwitz, Poland: The concentration camp opens officially with the arrival of 728 Poles from Tarnow.

14. Tangier, Morocco: Spain occupies the international zone, to preempt Italian occupation.

15. Verdun, France: Germany captures the city, bitterly fought over in the last war.

15. Cherbourg, France: The evacuation of British and Canadian troops begins (→ 19).

Heavy losses as Japan advances into heart of China

Ichang, 12 June
Japanese forces are within 400 miles (640 km) of the Chinese Nationalist capital, Chungking, after capturing the gateway city of Ichang today. The taking of Ichang – the westernmost city to fall to the Japanese – is the culmination of a three-month campaign by Japan's China Expeditionary Army to put the Nationalists back on the defensive after their success at Wuyuan and their continuing guerrilla attacks on Japanese units.

Japan's response has been to hit back with a massive invasion of the Nationalist-held provinces in south and west central China. So far the price has been high. In the see-saw battle for Tsaoyang in May the Japanese suffered 45,000 wounded or killed, and they had to pull in reinforcements from Manchukuo before taking Ichang (→ 17).

Allied soldiers and king leave Norway

Narvik, Norway, 9 June
The Norwegian campaign is over, two months after the German invasion – a remarkable display of British military incompetence. For six weeks 24,000 men besieged a few thousand Alpine troops here. Only at the end, when French and Polish forces under the command of General Bethovart seized Narvik, did the Allies display any effective generalship. Even then General Dietl's troops broke out into the mountains to fight another day.

Now, with France facing defeat, Norway has become a side-show and the troops are needed in Britain. One of the last to be evacuated was King Haakon, taken aboard HMS *Devonshire* yesterday. Even in the evacuation Britain suffered casualties: the aircraft carrier *Glorious* was sunk by the battlecruiser *Gneisenau*, with 1,500 drowned.

General Ruge and his Norwegian rearguard stay. So strong is Dietl's admiration of their courage that he is allowing them to return to their homes – an act of chivalry rare in this age.

Mussolini takes Italy into the war

Rome, 10 June

After months of bombastic indecision, Benito Mussolini, Italy's Fascist dictator, tagged his forces on to Hitler's victorious *Panzers* today and declared war on the Allies. Informed sources here believe that the Duce's great fear is peace, which will prevent him winning glory.

British and French ambassadors here were informed of the Italian decision today by Count Galeazzo Ciano, Mussolini's son-in-law and foreign minister. Asked why Italy should enter the war, he replied: "Mussolini is only carrying out the plans he has made with Hitler."

Mussolini was not even able to choose his own date for the declaration. Five days ago he pleaded with Hitler to be allowed to join the fight against France. The Fuhrer prevailed on him to hold back until the French air force was completely destroyed. Hitler is insistent on a complete *German* victory. Nor, should France fall, will Mussolini be allowed to join Germany in armistice talks. More than 250,000 cheering and flag-waving people heard the Duce declare war from the balcony of his official residence, the Palazzo Venezia. "We will conquer," he roared. "People of Italy, to arms! Show your tenacity, your courage, your worth."

Images of war: how an Italian magazine saw Mussolini's declaration of war.

US isolationists feel anti-Italian backlash

New York, 12 June

Italy's sudden entry into the war may well have provoked a pro-Allied, anti-isolationist backlash in the United States with serious long-term consequences for the Axis.

Tomorrow's *New York Times* sums up the opinions of many Americans about Italy's sudden entry into the war. "With the courage of a jackal at the heels of a bolder beast of prey Mussolini has left his ambush," says an editorial. It was not the decision of the Italian people, it adds. It was the decision of one man "which now takes Italy into the darkness of night and makes her the moral enemy of every democratic people".

The *Baltimore Sun* describes Italy's action as a "long and dangerous gamble ... inevitably it is

a losing one". As other influential American newspapers joined in a chorus of disgust at Mussolini's action, the official American view came from President Roosevelt, bringing more cheer to the Allies, anxious for America's support.

Italy, said the president, has "scorned the rights of security of other nations", and he added that the United States would extend to the opponents of force the material resources of his nation.

"Some still hold to the obvious delusions that the United States can become a lone island – in a world dominated by the philosophy of force," added the president. "Such an island represents to the overwhelming majority of Americans a helpless nightmare – of a people without friends."

RAF bombers strike first Italian targets

Cairo, 12 June

Britain replied swiftly to Italy's declaration of war today with bombing raids on Milan and Genoa, while RAF and South African bombers struck at Italian aircraft on the ground, petrol depots and ammunition dumps in Libya and East Africa. The Italians were caught by surprise, according to official sources, and only light anti-aircraft fire was met. The RAF claimed that the raids had crippled Italy's striking power in the Middle East. The first Italian bombs of the war fell on the British island of Malta in a series of seven raids which hit civilian targets, including a hospital. Seventeen people died and two bombers were destroyed, it is reported.

Carve-up continues as Russian troops invade Lithuania

Kaunas, 15 June

The Red Army marched into Lithuania today. There was no resistance as the Soviet troops crossed the frontier in great strength and President Smetona fled by plane from the capital with his family and other leading Lithuanians.

Two hundred Soviet tanks led the occupation of Kaunas. Russian soldiers have taken up positions at all the public buildings. Planeloads of Soviet officials, including NKVD agents, are pouring into the airport. One of the first acts of the secret policemen was to arrest General Skucas, the minister of the interior, and Mr Povilaitus, the chief of the state police. Martial law has been declared and there is a night-long curfew.

The Lithuanians, who realize that there is nothing they can do to resist the Russians, are resigned to the occupation of their country, but there is considerable excitement among the local German population, which besieged its legation today demanding to go home.

The occupation is seen here as another move by Stalin to build a barrier of occupied countries between the Soviet Union and Germany. He has the eastern part of Poland, he has forced Finland to give up strategic territory, now he has Lithuania, and the other Baltic states tremble. Where will the Russian bear strike next? (→ 17).

RUSSIA'S BALTIC NEIGHBOURS

Helsinki
Tallinn • Leningrad
ESTONIA

Riga
LATVIA

Baltic Sea

LITHUANIA

• Danzig • Kaunas

Warsaw •

RUSSIA

GERMANY   POLAND

Occupied by Russia
Occupied by Germany

100 miles
160 km

© Chronicle Communications Ltd.

Germans move towards Paris as France crumbles

Nazi darkness falls on "City of Light"

Paris, 14 June
"The German Army are inside the gates of Paris!" These were the dramatic words with which the US ambassador to France, William Bullitt, announced to another US diplomat in Tours that the French capital was on the verge of falling to Hitler's armies.

That was at 7pm yesterday. All day the Germans had been closing in on the great city. To the west, spearheads of motorized and *Panzer* columns had crossed the river Seine at various points between Paris and Rouen. North of the capital, at least 12 divisions had begun a fierce attack along the river Oise. To the east, Panzer divisions had crossed the river Marne and were believed to be in Meaux.

It is four days since Reynaud's government fled westwards to Tours, leaving Paris in the hands of a military governor, General Hering. The Battle of France was reaching its violent climax, and as the Germans swept all before them General Hering declared Paris an open city to save it from enemy bombardment. That was on 11 June, and since then a great exodus of Parisian citizens has been under-

German troops assemble for a victory parade through the streets of Paris.

way, organized by Georges Mandel, the minister of the interior, who stayed behind to meet the invaders. He has ordered the police to hand over their arms to their superiors.

An air of deep gloom descended on those who remained in Paris, and the normally bustling *boulevards* and cafes were silent and deserted. The silence was occasionally broken by distant explosions as the French blew up munitions factories.

It was at 10am today that the Germans goose-stepped into the centre of the "City of Light". The only resistance came from some

workers near the *Porte d'Aubervilliers*, who punched passing soldiers, who ignored them. The Germans posted machine-gunners in key positions as they marched through near-empty streets, and a senior officer drove to M Laingeron, the chief of the Paris police, to tell him to remain in office until further notice and to be responsible for keeping public order. The *swastika* now flies from the Eiffel Tower and from German headquarters, established in one of the city's most luxurious hotels. The French army is still fighting south of the city, but the loss of Paris seems a fatal blow.

Refugees stream from battle zones

France, 15 June
Twelve million people – fleeing soldiers and terrified civilian refugees – are crowding roads out of every city in the north as *Panzers* race across France and panic grips the country. In Nancy, students working in bomb-proofed cellars at the university are being snatched from their end of term examinations by worried parents to join the chaotic stream heading west and south – in any direction away from the Germans. The town council has ordered the evacuation of the city, unaware that the enemy is relying on confusion and blocked roads to prevent the French army from regrouping. With barely time to gather a few belongings, families turn anything from prams – the quintessential image of this exodus – to wheelbarrows into makeshift vehicles. Even hearses can be seen, people desperately crowding onto the running boards. Their rooftops protected from bullets by mattresses, the few cars passing jangle with the pots and pans hanging from their doors.

This fleeing crowd is an easy target for the Germans, and the roads are soon strewn with bodies. Entire families are torn apart, children aimlessly wandering the roads. Many have no idea where they are headed. They have only one goal: to get away from the Germans. The German forces, meanwhile, advanced towards Paris, which began to resemble a ghost town. On 10 June, French government officials left the capital and headed south for Tours and, later, Bordeaux. The statement declaring Paris an open city on 11 June accelerated the departure of its population. A handful of frightened passers-by who still occupy the streets of the capital have been faced with drawn windows and closed shutters. Yesterday, when Paris was occupied, the Parisians were reassured by the apparent kindness of German soldiers, who responded willingly to questions from braver inhabitants. Not everyone is convinced that this will last (→ 17).

Allied leaders meet for council of war, but defeatism grows

Briare, near Orleans, 11 June
Churchill arrived here this afternoon with senior figures including Mr Anthony Eden and Sir John Dill, Chief of the Imperial General Staff, to find out what the French are planning to do. Weygand, established in a railway carriage, greeted the British with the news that "the last line of defence has been pierced ... We are going to have to ask how France can continue the war".

This evening, after dinner, Reynaud told Churchill that Marshal Petain had already written down an appeal to the Germans for an armistice, but, Reynaud said: "He is ashamed to show it to me." Churchill told the gloomy French leaders that no matter what they did "we shall fight on forever".

Left to right: Churchill, Dill, Attlee and Reynaud at an earlier summit.

1940

June

Su	Mo	Tu	We	Th	Fr	Sa
						1
2	3	4	5	6	7	8
9	10	11	12	13	14	15
16	17	18	19	20	21	22
23	24	25	26	27	28	29
30						

16. Mediterranean: Naval war in the Mediterranean begins: the British submarines *Grampus* and *Orpheus* are sunk by the Italians.

16. Dublin: The premier, Eamon de Valera, recognizes the potential German threat and mobilizes Eire's armed forces.

16. France: Allied evacuations from Brest and St Malo start, as Germany pushes to Pontarlier on the Swiss border.

17. Indochina: Japan starts a blockade to cut off military supplies to China.→

17. France: With German forces pouring through the Maginot Line, Petain's government sues for peace.→

17. Mediterranean: The French sink an Italian submarine off Oran in Algeria.

17. Moscow: Stalin sends troops to occupy Estonia and Latvia in order to "pre-empt joint defence measures against the USSR" (→ 26).

18. London: De Gaulle broadcasts, calling France to carry on resistance.→

19. Aden: An Italian submarine is captured off the British territory.

19. Cherbourg: The Allies complete their withdrawal by blowing up the docks.

19. France: The Polish and Belgian governments in exile move to London (→ 22).

20. France: The government asks Italy for armistice terms (→ 21).

21. Roumania: King Carol tries to unite the country by assuming dictatorial powers at the head of a new "National Party".

21. France: Italian soldiers push into France on a wide front.

21. Britain: Impressed with German paratroop tactics, Churchill orders a corps of at least 5,000 soldiers to be trained in parachuting.

22. St-Jean-de-Luz, France: The remnant of the Polish army sails for England on the liner *Batory*.

Churchill proclaims the "finest hour"

Britain, 17 June

"Let us brace ourselves to our duty and so bear ourselves that if the British Commonwealth and Empire lasts for a thousand years men will still say, 'This was their finest hour'." With this inspirational peroration Winston Churchill today ended a speech in the House of Commons. It was later repeated in a broadcast to the nation. The prime minister faced up squarely to the chance that Britain might now have to fight alone and he told MPs: "Our professional advisers of the three services unitedly advise that we should continue the war and that there are good and reasonable hopes of final victory."

The prime minister said that it was not yet certain that France's military resistance to the Germans was over. Britain had not felt able to release the French from their treaty obligation not to make a separate peace. But whatever happens, he continued: "We will fight on, if necessary for years." The Battle of Britain was about to begin and Hitler knew that he "will have to break us in these islands or lose the war".

Mr Churchill said that 1,250,000 men are now under arms in Britain. Behind them are 500,000 Local Defence Volunteers, and soldiers from the Dominions have also arrived. These forces include seven out of every eight soldiers originally sent to France, while many of the re-

Churchill promises the nation: "We will fight on, if necessary for years."

mainder are still operating alongside French forces with considerable success. As for the immediate future, the prime minister reminded the House of Commons that Britain has home defence forces which are now expanding rapidly, with "very large additions" to their weaponry expected soon. He then said that the survival of Christian civilization as well as the continuity of British life must depend on the outcome of the Battle of Britain. He warned the United States that, if Germany wins, then the whole world, including America, "will sink into the abyss of a new dark age". The Commons decided to go into secret session before the end of the week for further discussion of the dire military situation. Churchill told MPs that the scope of the debate would not be too restricted. He was insistent that the service chiefs are prepared for enemy parachute landings and other ingenious invasion tricks, including, he said, help from a "fifth column".

Mussolini and Hitler meet in Munich to plan a fascist future

Munich, 18 June

In the *Fuhrerhaus*, where Neville Chamberlain signed away Czechoslovakia two years ago, Mussolini and Hitler met today to discuss the armistice terms to be imposed on France. Mussolini has been surprised at the German insistence on moderate terms for the defeated enemy.

The Fuhrer's aim is to encourage the French to break with the English and to discourage them from continuing the war in North Africa. Petain and the peace lobby must be encouraged, Hitler said. So Mussolini has been told he will not be allowed to seize huge areas of southern France (→ 20).

Hitler and Mussolini at their meeting in Munich to carve up France.

French surrender is signed in a railway carriage

Compiegne, 22 June

Shortly after 6.30 this evening, General Wilhelm Keitel lost patience with the French. He told them to sign the armistice terms within the next hour or they would be sent packing and the war would go on. In less than ten minutes the French capitulated.

In a voice choked with emotion General Charles Huntziger, the leader of the French delegation, said: "Forced by the fortunes of war to give up the struggle in which she was engaged on the side of her Allies, France sees very hard demands imposed on her under conditions which underline their severity." He expressed the hope that Germany "will be guided by a spirit which will permit the two great neighbouring peoples to live and work in peace".

Seated at a table in the railway carriage in which the Germans had been forced to sign the surrender at the end of the First World War, Huntziger signed the armistice terms. They are less harsh than had been expected. The Germans will occupy three-fifths of metropolitan France, but a French government will be responsible for the unoccupied zone and will be permit-

General Huntziger signs away France's freedom in the historic carriage.

ted to raise a small force for the preservation of order. However, all warships are to be recalled to France and laid up under German or Italian supervision.

France has found it difficult to swallow other German demands. All anti-Nazi German refugees are to be handed over to the German authorities; any French nationals caught fighting for Britain are to be shot at once; all French prisoners

of war will remain in German camps. The armistice takes effect as soon as France has signed a similar agreement with Italy tomorrow.

The armistice teams met for the first time yesterday afternoon, with a triumphant Hitler, Goering and von Ribbentrop present. A preamble to the terms, read by Keitel, consisted of a tirade against the 1918 armistice terms imposed on Germany "although the enemy had

not defeated the German army, navy or air force in any decisive action". This ceremony in the coach at Compiegne would "blot out once and for all ... the greatest German humiliation of all time".

After listening to this polemic, the Fuhrer gave the Nazi salute and left the carriage. Outside, he read, with a grim expression, the inscription on the granite memorial to the 1918 Armistice and then ordered the stone to be blown up.

Since the beginning of the month Weygand and Petain have been resigned to defeat. When de Gaulle urged them to continue the war from North Africa, Weygand responded contemptuously: "Nonsense. In a week Britain will have her neck wrung like a chicken."

As the armistice was being signed, French troops were surrendering *en masse*. In Alsace-Lorraine 500,000 have laid down their arms; in Brittany and the west 200,000; over 1,500,000 French soldiers are now in German hands. *Panzers* are roaming at will in central France; General Rommel, in a letter to his wife, cheerfully likens his advance to a holiday excursion. The charade of French military press conferences has been abandoned (→ 24).

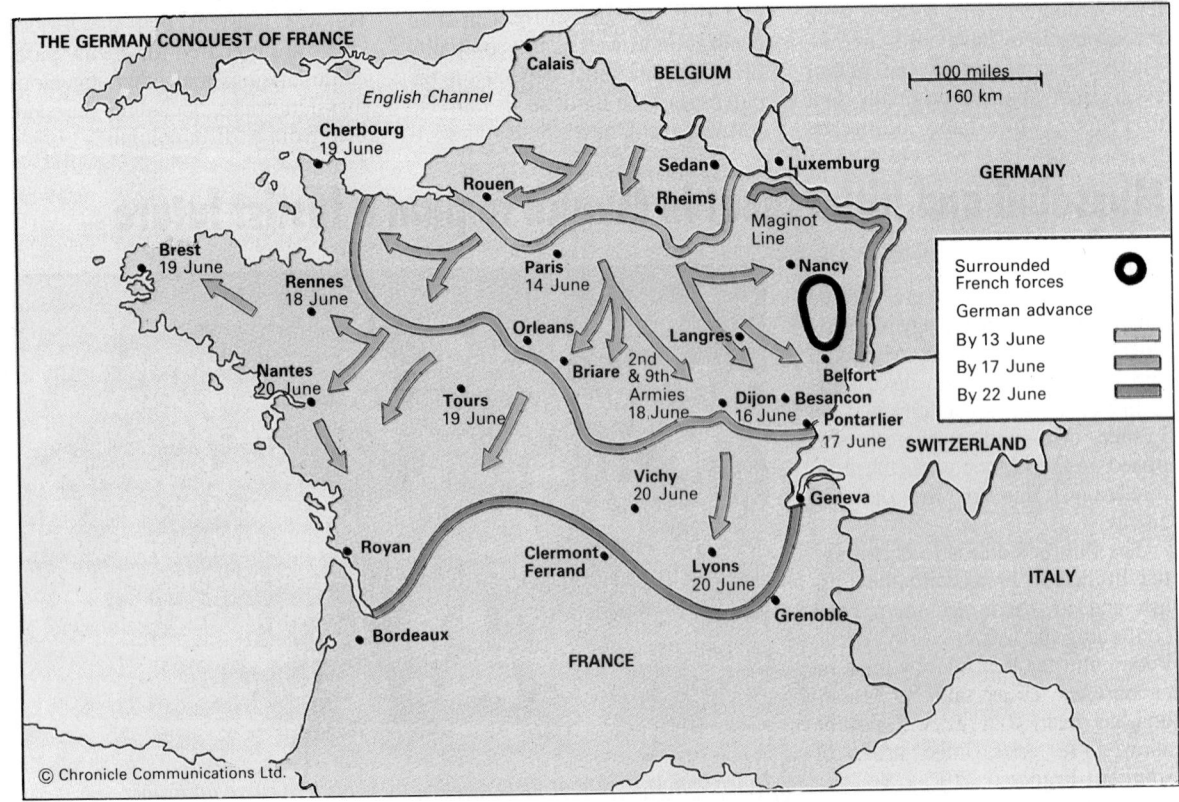

THE GERMAN CONQUEST OF FRANCE

Calais
English Channel
BELGIUM
100 miles
160 km
Cherbourg 19 June
Sedan
Luxemburg
GERMANY
Rouen
Rheims
Brest 19 June
Maginot Line
Paris 14 June
Nancy
Rennes 18 June
Orleans
Langres
Surrounded French forces
German advance
By 13 June
By 17 June
By 22 June
Nantes 20 June
Briare
2nd & 9th Armies 18 June
Belfort
Dijon Besancon 16 June
Pontarlier 17 June
SWITZERLAND
Tours 19 June
Vichy 20 June
Geneva
Royan
Clermont Ferrand
Lyons 20 June
ITALY
Bordeaux
Grenoble
FRANCE
© Chronicle Communications Ltd.

A triumphant Hitler shows his joy as France capitulates at Compiegne.

De Gaulle rallies the "Free French"

Defiant: Charles de Gaulle seeks to keep the flame of resistance alive.

London, 18 June
General Charles de Gaulle, little known even in France outside military circles until he became undersecretary for national defence in the last days of the Reynaud government, has flown to England and broadcast this appeal:

"Speaking in full knowledge of the facts," he said, "I ask you to believe me when I say that the cause of France is not lost." He called on French officers and men, including civilians, to get in touch with him. "Whatever happens," declared the general, "the flame of French resistance must not and shall not die."

Before this month de Gaulle, a career officer who fought both in the Great War and against the Bolshevik invasion of Poland in 1919, was scarcely known even in France, except as a tank expert who derided the defensive theories current in French military thought.

However, he commanded an armoured division with determination during the battles of early June and was chosen by Paul Reynaud as his military deputy in the closing days of his government. De Gaulle emerged as the strong man in Bordeaux, and was flown to Cornwall by the RAF last Sunday (→ 22).

Troopship is sunk by German bombers

As the bombed "Lancastria" finally sinks, thousands swim for safety.

St Nazaire, 17 June
More than half the 5,000 people on board the Cunard White Star liner *Lancastria* died today in an attack by five German aircraft. They dive-bombed and machine-gunned the liner as she lay at anchor in the harbour here. Survivors claimed later that the Germans had continued to fire after the ship had sunk and men were struggling in the water.

One man said: "I was flung into the sea which can only be described as one almost solid mass of men clinging together like flies and covered with thick black oil. Some of them were horribly burnt by the explosion, others were hanging on to debris, others were swimming until they finally sank; it was every man for himself."

The famous cruising liner had been converted into a troopship. Most of the passengers today were troops from the British Expeditionary Force and the RAF returning to England from France. In addition there were Church Army workers and a number of French people fleeing the German occupation.

Anglo-French union offered by Churchill

London, 22 June
It was revealed here last night that last Sunday His Majesty's Government offered to France a solemn union with Great Britain. The offer was conveyed to the Reynaud government by the British ambassador, Sir Ronald Campbell, who proposed that France and Britain should no longer be two nations but one Franco-British Union.

The union's constitution would set up joint institutions for defence, finance and foreign and economic policy, and every citizen of each country would become a citizen of the other – but France declined.

Mr Churchill commented, on the news of the fall of the French government, that "nothing will alter our feelings towards [the French people] or our faith that the genius of France will rise again" (→ 28).

Japan gets its way on French colonies

Tokyo, 20 June
Japan today took advantage of the fall of France by warning the French administration in Indochina that it must stop helping the Chinese Nationalist government in Chungking immediately.

The protest was delivered by Japan's foreign minister, Mr Tani, to the French ambassador. He was warned that France's governor in Indochina must stop the transit of war materials across the Chinese border or face severe repercussions. At the same time Japan has formally asked Germany and Italy to preserve the *status quo* in Indochina.

Reports that Japanese forces are massing on Hainan island have increased fears that Japan is about to invade the French colony. French and British ships have been told not to call at Indochinese ports (→ 24).

Empire stands loyally by mother country

London, 20 June
In spite of Britain's defeats, most of its Empire remains loyal to the motherland. Canada, Australia and New Zealand are sending it troops. In East Africa, a key test of the Empire's loyalty, Sudanese, Somalis, Kenyans and South Africans are fighting the Italians in Ethiopia. Ironically, the highest proportion, in terms of population, of new volunteers comes from Eire, part of the Commonwealth although no longer part of the Empire, with a neutral and apparently anti-British government. In India, however, the Hindus and the Congress Party seem "above" the war. In Egypt, some nationalists see Britain's difficulty as Egypt's opportunity.

RAF detects bent beam guidance system

Britain, 22 June
The suspicion held for some time by the air ministry scientific intelligence expert Dr R V Jones and others that the *Luftwaffe* has a system of radio beams for guiding its bombers onto targets in England was finally confirmed last night.

An Avro Anson from the RAF's Boscombe Down-based Blind Flying Development Unit located one such beam. Using a powerful US Hallicrafter receiver the crew identified a beam transmitted from Germany passing over the Rolls-Royce aeroplane engine factory at Derby. It was tracked down to a transmitter in Schleswig-Holstein.

Urgent research is under way to counter the deadly system that the Germans call *Knickebein* [crooked leg].

June

Su	Mo	Tu	We	Th	Fr	Sa
						1
2	3	4	5	6	7	8
9	10	11	12	13	14	15
16	17	18	19	20	21	22
23	24	25	26	27	28	29
30						

23. London: General Charles de Gaulle announces the formation of a French national committee.→

23. Paris: Pierre Laval is appointed vice-premier of France.

23. France: The first British commando raid fails to capture German guards and defence information at Boulogne.

24. Tokyo: Pu Yi, the puppet emperor of Manchukuo and last emperor of China, arrives on an official visit.

24. France: Twenty-two thousand soldiers who had been holding out in the Vosges mountains surrender.

24. Tokyo: Japan formally requests Britain to close the Burma Road, stop the flow of war materials through Hong Kong and withdraw its garrison at Shanghai (→ 29).

24. London: The Allies discuss how to prevent the French navy falling to the Germans.

25. Europe: As Germany starts ten days of official celebrations, France observes a day of national mourning.

26. Moscow: Russia demands that Roumania give up Bessarabia [*Moldavia*] and northern Bukovina.→

27. France: German troops reach the border with Spain.

27. Moscow: All factories in the USSR are put on a seven-day working week.

28. Channel Islands: Germany bombs Jersey and Guernsey.→

28. Libya: The Italian governor-general, Italo Balbo, is killed by his own anti-aircraft guns while flying over Tobruk.

29. Tokyo: Japan announces its interest in controlling the South China Sea, which it sees as part of its sphere of influence.

29. Germany: Radio propaganda interprets British moves to block landing strips as popular sabotage of the wealthy classes' cricket pitches.→

30. Berlin: Hermann Goering orders an aerial blockade of Britain.

De Gaulle recognized as leader of France

London, 28 June
The British government today gave its formal recognition to General Charles de Gaulle as leader, in exile, of the French nation.

The move follows the formation by de Gaulle of a French National Committee in London on 23 June. Two days ago the general, who was under-secretary for national defence in the Reynaud administration which handed over to Petain, also announced the creation of a French volunteer legion in Britain and of a French centre for armament and scientific research. It is de Gaulle's belief that the Petain government gave in too easily to the Germans, "before all means of resistance had been exhausted", as he said in a broadcast on 23 June.

He went on: "The French National Committee will take under its jurisdiction all French citizens at present on British territory, and will assume the direction of all military and administrative bodies who are now, or may be in the future, in this country."

De Gaulle, who two months ago was a little-known colonel, ended on a defiant note: "The war is not lost, the country is not dead, hope is not extinct. Vive la France!"

France signs peace deal with Italy

Rome, 24 June
France faced its final humiliation today when the terms of the armistice with Italy were published. Although Italian troops made little headway against fierce French resistance during the few weeks of campaigning, demilitarized zones are to be established in France, Tunisia and Algeria – with Italian troops remaining on their advanced lines. The French are required to clear the battlefields of mines. France will allow Italy "full and constant right" to the port of Jibuti [*Djibouti*] in Somaliland.

French colonies vow to fight on

London, 25 June
Despite a call by the Petain government in Bordeaux to cease hostilities, French colonies show no sign of giving up the battle against Germany. At least one commander, General Nogues in North Africa, has refused orders from Marshal Petain to return to France. French generals in Somaliland have cabled their support for the Allies; calls have come from Syria and Lebanon for France to continue the fight; and the French governor-general in Indochina has refused to lower the *tricouleur*.

Anzac reinforcements arrive in Britain

London, 30 June
The first convoy bringing in Australian and New Zealand troops for the defence of Britain has landed in England. The Anzac arrivals, who include a battalion of Maoris from New Zealand, were congratulated on their safe arrival by a Mr Shakespeare, the under-secretary for the Dominions, who spoke of "a thrill in every heart and every home in this country".

Already Australian and New Zealand troops are stationed in Palestine. "It has fallen to your lot to come to the United Kingdom itself," King George told the new arrivals in a message of welcome, "and as you take your place beside us, you find us in the forefront of the battle."

Newly-arrived New Zealand soldiers on leave in London embark on a trip up the Thames in high spirits.

Hitler tours the sights of Paris

The Fuhrer sees the sights of Paris.

Paris, 23 June
Adolf Hitler, the artist turned conqueror, fulfilled a long-held ambition today and toured the great monuments of Paris, accompanied by the three intellectuals he likes best: two architects, Albert Speer and Hermann Giesler, and a sculptor, Arno Breker.

Hitler flew to Le Bourget airport at 4am, and entered the city which he said he had ordered his troops to spare "because it was important to preserve this culture for generations to come". His visit was recorded by a photographer and a cine-cameraman.

At *Les Invalides* he gave orders for the remains of the son of the Emperor Napoleon I to be brought from Vienna to lie next to his father. "That," said the one-time Viennese painter later, "was the greatest and finest moment of my life." At the *Opera* he asked the usher, who refused a 50-*mark* tip, to show him near-forgotten rooms which he knew of from architectural plans. Hitler boasted of his knowledge. A newsboy offered him a French newspaper, *Le Matin*, but ran away when he saw who his customer was. Two million other Parisians have already fled.

"Swastika" flies over Channel Island

St Peter Port, Guernsey, 30 June
The first that Major John Sherwill, the attorney-general of Guernsey, knew of German occupation was a telephone call telling him that a Junkers aircraft had landed at the small airport. A little while later there was a knock on his door. Two German officers were admiring his early roses. Sherwill invited them in.

"Please use the side door," he requested them. "The children are asleep in the hall." The Germans were happy to oblige.

It has been a most orderly surrender as white flags fly over British soil and German troops begin to land in numbers on the Channel Islands. No shots have been fired, and the only reported resistance has come from an Irish worker who punched a German soldier on the nose in a pub brawl.

The decision to demilitarize the islands – which lie only a few miles from the French coast – was taken by the Churchill government earlier this month when it became obvious that there was no way in which they could be defended without huge loss of civilian life. Panic ensued as British-born nationals crowded on to the few available boats and drained the local banks of funds. Thousands of dogs and cats were shot on the quayside before

Good propaganda: the swastika is hoisted on the Channel Islands.

the last boat left five days ago. The widely-predicted German move came in the form of orders dropped in canvas bags with red streamers attached.

White crosses were to be painted on the airport runway, the main square and a car park. Every building was to fly a white flag. "If these signs of a peaceful surrender are not observed ... heavy bombardment will take place," threatened the Germans. A white sheet was being flown from every house as the Islanders awaited the Germans' ar-

rival. First reports suggest that German behaviour is "correct" and that the civil population is obeying instructions to offer no resistance.

A Guernsey shop is advertising cycles ("your best friend in months to come") and the Regal cinema in St Peter Port is showing Tommy Trinder in "Laugh it Off".

Across the water, the larger island of Jersey awaits its turn as German aircraft circle. Alderney has been completely evacuated; but the Germans have yet to meet the formidable Dame of Sark.

Red Army occupies Bessarabia, part of Roumania

Bucharest, 28 June
The Soviet Union has forced the Roumanians to give up the rich provinces of Bessarabia and Northern Bukovina. Throughout the day motorized units and tanks of the Red Army have been entering the areas. King Carol has ordered general mobilization. This, however, is a move aimed not at Russia but at Roumania's smaller neighbours. The fear here is that Bulgaria and Hungary will take advantage of Roumania's weakness. Hungary has claims on Transylvania, and Bulgaria has already demanded the return of its former Black Sea territory, Dobruja (→ 13/8).

Churchill's mimic broadcasts speech

London, 30 June
On 4 June Britons were moved to hear on the wireless Mr Churchill's magnificent "We shall fight on the beaches" speech which had been delivered earlier that day in the House of Commons. It can now be revealed that the broadcast was in fact made by an actor, one of the BBC's repertory staff, Norman Shelley, because Churchill was too busy. Churchill approved his stand-in's reading in advance.

Britain prepares to resist invasion, expected any day now

The cartoonist David Low shows a British soldier happy to go it alone.

Britain, 30 June
An island fortress is preparing to repel invaders expected at any moment. Sea-fronts and sands on the south and east coasts are bare of visitors and children, while gun emplacements, barbed wire and pill-boxes, disguised as chalets, teastalls, even haystacks, spring up everywhere. Scaffolding and concrete blocks cover beaches, and piers have been cut off from the shore. To prevent troop gliders from landing, open spaces, downs and golf courses are strewn with obstacles – old cars and buses, carts, even iron bedsteads. All signposts have been removed and station names painted out. Motorists must lock and immobilize parked cars. Church bells are silent – to be rung if the invasion should come.

German troops seen here with carrier pigeons, still used in occupied France for communications.

July

Su	Mo	Tu	We	Th	Fr	Sa
	1	2	3	4	5	6
7	8	9	10	11	12	13
14	15	16	17	18	19	20
21	22	23	24	25	26	27
28	29	30	31			

1. France: The government moves to the spa town of Vichy, where the empty hotels are suitable new homes for government departments (→ 10).

1. Libya: Marshal Rodolfo Graziani succeeds the late Italo Balbo as commander-in-chief of Italian forces (→ 17/8).

1. Japan: Rationing of sugar, matches and other goods is introduced.

1. Atlantic: The U-boat U26 is sunk off Ireland by the corvette HMS *Gladiolus* and a Sunderland plane of the RAAF (→ 2).

2. Germany: Hitler orders a study into a possible invasion of Britain.→

2. Atlantic: A U-boat torpedoes and sinks the ship *Arandora Star,* killing 613 of 1,500 German and Italian internees en route to Canada.→

3. Britain: British forces seize 59 French warships in British ports.→

3. Netherlands: Henri Winkelman, the former Dutch commander-in-chief, is arrested and taken to Germany.

4. New York: A bomb in the British hall of the World's Fair goes off, killing two people.

4. Lisbon: The Duke of Windsor is appointed governor of the Bahamas.

4. East Africa: Italian forces advance into Sudan, occupying Kassala and Gallabat.

5. Roumania: The new pro-Iron Guard government decides to align its policy with that of the Axis (→ 9).

5. Stockholm: The government signs an agreement allowing Germany to use Swedish railways to move troops and supplies to and from Norway.

5. Washington: Roosevelt bans the export of minerals, chemicals and aircraft parts to Japan.

6. Berlin: Hitler's return from the Western Front is greeted by vast enthusiastic crowds.

6. Norway: The submarine HMS *Shark* is sunk by German anti-submarine forces.

Britain destroys French navy at Oran

Mers-el-Kebir, North Africa, 3 July
British sailors wept unashamedly as their 15-inch guns pounded the near-helpless French fleet today, sinking three battleships with the loss of 1,297 men – their allies until a few days ago. A battle cruiser, the *Strasbourg,* and five destroyers managed to escape under a pall of smoke.

The decision to open fire was a distressing one for senior officers. It came after six hours of tense negotiation with Vice-Admiral Sir James Somerville on his flagship, HMS *Hood,* who offered the French four choices: join the British; sail to British ports with reduced crews; sail to French West Indies ports with reduced crews; or scuttle within six hours. A fifth, unstated, option was for the French ships to demilitarize in their present berths.

Operation Catapult took five minutes. The battleship *Bretagne* became a sheet of flames in a matter of seconds with the loss of 977 men. The British fire was returned by ships and shore batteries, but they scored no hits.

With Britain facing invasion – and heavily dependent on naval superiority – the tough decision was made by Churchill, despite a pledge by Admiral Darlan, the Vichy naval minister, that French ships would not fall into German hands.

French ships already in British ports were seized by the Royal Navy today (→ 5).

Mers-el-Kebir: the French battleship "Provence" opens fire on the Royal Navy.

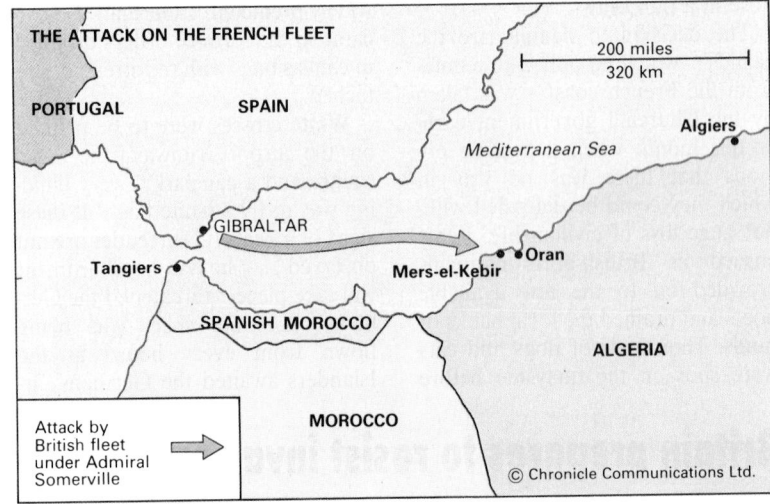

THE ATTACK ON THE FRENCH FLEET
200 miles / 320 km
PORTUGAL · SPAIN · Algiers · Mediterranean Sea · GIBRALTAR · Tangiers · Mers-el-Kebir · Oran · SPANISH MOROCCO · ALGERIA · MOROCCO
Attack by British fleet under Admiral Somerville
© Chronicle Communications Ltd.

Petain cuts diplomatic links with Britain

Vichy, 5 July
France has severed diplomatic relations with Britain as a result of the British attack on the French fleet at Mers-el-Kebir, the naval base in Algeria, it was officially announced last night.

The French statement spoke of an "unjustifiable attack by a powerful English fleet". M Baudouin, the foreign minister in the Petain government, called the British attack "an indelible blot on British honour", and the German government has declared that it will suspend Article 8 of the armistice with France, in effect serving notice that it will use those French warships still in German control against Britain, as expressly forbidden by the terms of the armistice.

In London, however, the Royal Navy's action at Oran, carried out with much reluctance, is being hailed as a major strategic success. Adding the powerful French fleet to the German and Italian navies would have roughly doubled Axis naval forces, made the blockade of a lengthened Nazi-controlled border harder, and raised doubts about the protection of the vital Atlantic convoys. With the French fleet now in British hands or at the bottom of the sea, the admiralty can breathe more easily (→ 7).

French court orders jail for de Gaulle

Toulouse, 4 July
General Charles de Gaulle, the leader of the Free French, has been sentenced in his absence to a four-year term of imprisonment by a military court in Toulouse.

De Gaulle, who was the under-secretary for national defence in the French government when he flew to London in June, was also fined 100 *francs,* or about 11/6 (57p/ $2.32). He had already been reduced in rank to colonel. Vice-Admiral Muselier, commanding Free French air and naval forces, is also to be prosecuted (→ 14).

Roosevelt: five freedoms of democracy

New York, 5 July

President Roosevelt today warned the American people to entertain no thoughts of compromise with what he called "the new corporate governments" of the world – Germany, Italy and the USSR.

Speaking at a press conference, the president said that the many Americans who were evidently impressed with the efficiency of the "corporate" or totalitarian states should not be deluded into compromising with them. They were indeed more efficient than the democracies, but only because they swept aside the democratic system of checks and balances in the legislature, executive and judiciary: "The new governments generally destroy the legislative and judicial branches and delegate all powers to an executive or a dictator, thus striking at the heart of fundamental liberties by which men should and must live." He outlined "Five Freedoms" as conditions for a permanent peace:

1. Freedom from fear.
2. Freedom of information.
3. Freedom of religion.
4. Freedom of expression.
5. Freedom from want.

Mr Roosevelt said that it was an important issue whether the USA should encourage, by lack of opposition, countries which removed these "freedoms". Such sentiments should give heart to Mr Churchill and his embattled nation (→ 10).

Roumania backs the Axis powers

Bucharest, 1 July

Oil-rich Roumania, the chief source of Hitler's oil supplies, today renounced the Anglo-French guarantee of its frontiers and sent "important emissaries" to Berlin.

These moves confirm the Allied fears that King Carol would look to the Nazis for protection following Russia's occupation of the provinces of Northern Bukovina and Bessarabia.

For the moment all is quiet in the capital, although there are reports of clashes between troops and workers at the port of Galatz (→ 5).

Writers included in Nazi "black book"

Berlin, 6 July

The Nazis have decided that when they have conquered Britain all men aged between 17 and 45 will be deported to Germany. Himmler's SS has also prepared a Black Book with the names of 2,820 people who are to be rounded up as dangerous adversaries. They include Noel Coward, Virginia Woolf, Aldous Huxley, E M Forster, J B Priestley, H G Wells, Bertrand Russell and Beatrice Webb. Bernard Shaw is not on the list, which has Sigmund Freud, who died last year, and "Lady Carter-Bonham" (→ 13).

The "Arandora Star", sunk by a U-boat off Ireland on 2 July while carrying 1,500 German and Italian internees to Canada. Hundreds died.

1940
July

Su	Mo	Tu	We	Th	Fr	Sa
	1	2	3	4	5	6
7	8	9	10	11	12	13
14	15	16	17	18	19	20
21	22	23	24	25	26	27
28	29	30	31			

7. Alexandria: Under pressure from the British Mediterranean commander, Admiral Sir Andrew Cunningham, Admiral Godfroy agrees to demilitarize the French fleet of one battleship, three destroyers, four cruisers and a submarine.

7. French West Africa: British forces disable the French battleship *Richelieu* at Dakar; this follows a second attack at Oran yesterday.

9. Bucharest: Roumania is declared to be under German military protection (→ 11).

10. Washington: Roosevelt asks Congress for a $4,848 million defence budget to fund a 1.2 million-man army and 15,000 new planes (→ 17).

10. Britain: German bombers raid Swansea, Falmouth and convoys in the Bristol and English Channels.→

11. London: Lord Beaverbrook appeals for housewives to hand over aluminium artefacts for the war effort; Lady Reading, the head of the Women's Voluntary Service, will handle the collection of donations.→

11. Europe: The RAF raids enemy airstrips in the Netherlands and munitions factories in Germany.

11. Mediterranean: The destroyer HMS *Escort* is sunk by an Italian submarine (→ 13).

11. Paris: The first issue of *La Gerbe*, a collaborationist weekly paper, appears.

11. Roumania: The government withdraws from the League of Nations (→ 24).

12. Britain: *Luftwaffe* raiders bomb Wales, Scotland and the south-west of England.

13. Britain: The first Free Polish fighter squadron of the RAF is formed (→ 21/9).

13. Mediterranean and Arabia: Italian aircraft raid the British possessions of Malta and Aden (→ 25).

13. Berlin: Hitler's directive no 15 orders the *Luftwaffe* to destroy the RAF in preparation for Operation Sealion – the invasion of Britain.→

Petain and Laval at France's new helm

Pierre Laval: France's vice-premier.

Vichy, 10 July

The Third Republic, which has governed France since 1875, is no more. It has been replaced by the *Etat Francais* [French State], based at the southern spa town of Vichy. The "Head of the French State" and prime minister will be Marshal Philippe Petain.

The National Assembly today voted by 569 to 80, with 17 abstentions, to grant Petain the power to promulgate a new constitution. Petain will be aided by Pierre Laval, the vice-premier (→ 28).

Nazi: "Put Jews on Madagascar"

Berlin, 10 July

Franz Rademacher, the official in charge of Jewish affairs at the foreign office, has proposed moving the estimated four million Jews expected to be living under German rule after the war to the French Indian Ocean island of Madagascar. In the document *The Jewish Question after the Peace Treaty* he says that putting the Jews on Madagascar – which France will hand over to the *Reich* – rather than in the Lublin area of Poland, as planned at present, will make them easier to control (→ 16).

▷

Tense Britons prepare for imminent Nazi invasion

Convoys threatened from the air and sea: depth charges for a detected U-boat.

Local Defence Volunteers: a motley crew, but handy with Molotov cocktails.

"Luftwaffe" steps up convoy offensive

Dover, 10 July
The *Luftwaffe* mounted its biggest attack yet on a convoy off the south-east coast today. Spitfires and Hurricanes, warned by RDF of a build-up of raiders, found the sky full of German bombers and fighters.

Although heavily outnumbered, the British fighter pilots tore into the Germans and a tremendous dogfight started. Machine-gun fire could be clearly heard in coastal towns as the planes whirled over-head. The fury of the RAF attack drove off the attackers who succeeded in hitting only one ship in the convoy. Two German fighters were destroyed for the loss of six British aircraft, including a Hurricane which crashed into the Channel after colliding with a Dornier Do17 which also crashed. The German raids on coastal shipping are becoming so intense that this part of the country is now known as "Hellfire Corner" (→ 29).

Over a million men join the Home Guard

Britain, 8 July
In the eight weeks since Anthony Eden's appeal, 1,060,000 men have signed on with the Local Defence Volunteers. However, they still have no uniforms, no ranks, and few weapons apart from rifles borrowed from museums and even from London's Drury Lane theatre.

The LDV average age is high, and some units include several generals of the last war now in the ranks. In two days' time the first course begins at the LDV training school set up at Osterley Park, near London. It is run by Tom Wintringham, the former commander of the British volunteers in Spain, whose articles in *Picture Post* on guerrilla fighting inspired its publisher, Edward Hulton, to set up the "guerrilla" school.

The LDV may soon see a change of name. Churchill recently suggested to Eden that they be given the shorter title "Home Guard" (→ 23).

Psst ... paratrooping Nazi nuns wield death rays in Scotland!

Britain, 10 July
Britain is alive with reports of parachute landings, which were officially denied today. In the invasion of Holland, some parachutists were disguised as clergymen. Some rumours say that they have been disguised as nuns in Scotland. Other rumours of "fifth column" activity include secret rays in operation, which stop car engines dead, and spy messages concealed in the personal column of *The Times*. It is now an offence to spread rumours – a man was fined £25 yesterday for saying that 20 parachutists had landed in Kent. The ministry of information has asked people to join the "Silent Column" and to report defeatist talk.

The Nazi rumour is that London docks are destroyed: they bustle with trade.

Germans decide plan for invasion

Berlin, 13 July
While Hitler still hopes that Britain will make peace, he has already set in train preparations for invasion. On 2 July he ordered a study of the idea, and today he has issued a military directive to the effect that Germany must gain air superiority over the RAF before an invasion can take place. Today Grand Admiral Erich Raeder, the German naval commander, stated that invasion should be regarded as a last resort to make Britain sue for peace. He believes, however, that Britain can be brought to its knees more effectively by throttling its maritime trade and bombing its cities (→ 16).

1940

July

JULY 1940

Su	Mo	Tu	We	Th	Fr	Sa
	1	2	3	4	5	6
7	8	9	10	11	12	13
14	15	16	17	18	19	20
21	22	23	24	25	26	27
28	29	30	31			

British and Italian navies clash in Med

Malta, 9 July

The British propaganda machine is making much of a brief clash today off Punta Stilo in Calabria, Italy, between equally-matched units of Italian and British ships. After battleships of "Force H", the Gibraltar-based British squadron, had opened fire, the Italian ships retreated behind a smoke screen. One Italian ship, the *Bolzano*, was hit, as was HMS *Gloucester*. Italian planes attacked both sides – but scored no hits.

The encounter has helped to quell fears of a strong Italian navy in the Mediterranean and is a good boost to British morale. Bewilderingly, though, Mussolini has told his fleet: "You have obtained our first naval victory!" (→ 11).

Home secretary to ban British Fascists

Britain, 10 July

The pro-German Fascist organization now calling itself the British Union was effectively outlawed tonight. Sir John Anderson, the home secretary, signed an order under Regulation 18A of the new Defence Regulations. This makes it an offence to call or attend a meeting of the Union, distribute leaflets about any such meeting, or otherwise invite support.

Sir Oswald Mosley, the leader of the organization, which dropped the word "Fascists" from its title last year, was interned last month along with more than 700 others who had been in the BUF. His wife Diana, a sister of Hitler's doting admirer the Honourable Unity Mitford, was detained a fortnight ago.

Beaverbrook demands pans for Spitfires

One boy's way of turning old aluminium pots and pans into a Spitfire.

London, 13 July

Lord Beaverbrook's appeal to the women of Britain to "Give us your aluminium and we will turn your pots and pans into Spitfires and Hurricanes, Blenheims and Wellingtons" has brought an amazing response. Women, keen to help the RAF pilots who are defending them, have rushed to the depots set up by the Women's Voluntary Service to hand over some of their cooking utensils. A typical response to the minister of aircraft production's appeal was that of a woman aged about 80 who walked a mile and a half to donate a saucepan. "It is very useful," she said, "but I give it gladly to the country."

Hundreds of tons have already been collected although the appeal is only a couple of days old. In one town so much was collected that a steam roller was used to flatten the utensils in order to make more room. As well as pots and pans, tennis racket presses and cigarette cases, an artificial leg and a racing car with an aluminium body are among the possessions that their owners hope will be turned into fighters and bombers (→ 2/8).

---

15. Baltic States: Plebiscites held yesterday are said to show unanimous support for union with the USSR (→ 21).

16. London: The Labour MP Hugh Dalton is appointed political head of the Special Operations Executive (→ 22).

16. Berlin: Hitler issues his directive no 16, "On the Preparation of a Landing Operation against England (Sealion)".→

16. France: The Vichy government deprives naturalized Jews of their French citizenship (→ 27/8).

16. Palestine: Italian bombers attack the British base at Haifa (→ 24).

16. France: Germany expels 22,000 French citizens from Alsace-Lorraine, which it claims as part of the *Reich* (→ 9/11).

16. Tokyo: Military pressure forces the resignation of the premier, Admiral Mitsumasa Yonai (→ 22).

17. USA: Roosevelt wins the Democratic nomination for the presidential elections.→

18. Germany: "Radio Caledonia" starts broadcasting to Britain, urging Scottish separatism.

19. Britain: General Alan Brooke is appointed C-in-C Home Forces, replacing Field Marshal Sir Edmund Ironside who retires.

19. Germany: Hitler issues a "Last Appeal to Reason", urging Britain to make peace; he also promotes 12 generals to field marshal, including von Brauchitsch, Keitel, von Rundstedt and Kesselring; he gives Field Marshal Goering the new and unique title of *Reichsmarschall* (→ 29).

19. Crete: The Australian cruiser *Sydney* and five RN destroyers sink the Italian cruiser *Bartolomeo Colleoni* and damage another off Cape Spada.

19. Denmark: The government withdraws from the League of Nations.

20. Britain: The buying and selling of new cars is banned.

Burma Road closed to stop arms flow

London, 18 July

In a bid to reduce tension in the Far East, Britain has bowed to Japanese demands and agreed to close the 726-mile (1160-km) Burma Road to China for a three-month period. The decision stops the flow of arms, ammunition, petrol, lorries and railway materials.

Mr Churchill told the Commons that Britain would not agree to a permanent closure as this would be to default on obligations to China. Observers say that the closure will have little real effect on the Chinese war effort as traffic is slight because of the monsoon (→ 26).

Chiang Kai-shek: Chinese leader.

Roosevelt approves "two-ocean" navy

Washington, 19 July

Congress today passed the bill asked for by President Roosevelt to pay for a "two-ocean" navy. The House of Representatives approved a bill appropriating an additional $4 billion to build enough warships to enable the US to confront the danger of war with Germany and its allies in the Atlantic, and simultaneously with the Japanese in the Pacific.

It will take six years for the first new ships to be ready. But by 1947 the US Navy will have 701 ships, as against 369 today. The number of battleships will rise from 15 today to 35 in the future (→ 23).

Farcical commando raid on Guernsey

Plymouth, 15 July
Britain's latest commando raid (the first was last month) has ended in farce. A team of untrained men designated as special forces of No 3 Commando was to raid Guernsey airport. Compass failure sent it in error to tiny Sark. Other men hit undefended points on Guernsey to no purpose. As they withdrew, their commanding officer slipped and fired his revolver, alerting the enemy. Three men said that they could not swim to the pick-up boat.

Bell-ringing rector is sent to prison

Spilsby, Lincolnshire, 15 July
The rector of Old Bolingbroke, Lincolnshire, was sentenced to four weeks' jail today for ringing his church bell. He claimed that he did not know of the order prohibiting the ringing of church bells except as warning of an airborne invasion. It came into force a month ago, on 14 June. PC Peck said that he found the rector in his belfry pulling the bell rope on 16 June.

The rector, the Rev Robert Grant Colvin Graham, insisted that he was a loyal citizen. He had not then read the letter from his bishop banning bell-ringing.

Hitler issues battle orders for invasion

Berlin, 16 July
Hitler is talking about invading England with 20 divisions, to be put ashore on the south coast between Ramsgate and Lyme Regis. In a directive to the armed forces, he says that the aim is "to eliminate the English mother country as a base from which the war against Germany can be continued".

General Alfred Jodl says that the invasion should be seen as a river crossing on a broad front, and in place of bridging operations the navy would keep the sea lanes secure against British attacks. The Luftwaffe would, of course, knock out the RAF. Operation Sealion, as it is called, will be ready in nine weeks.

But the admirals in the *Kriegsmarine* are unhappy. In the absence of purpose-built landing craft, they say that they cannot guarantee to protect hundreds of river barges being towed slowly across the Channel. Among other things, Hitler's famed mechanized army uses several thousand horses to pull its guns. How, ask the admirals, do you propose to get horses across the Channel under fire?

Being prepared: a London family in one of the "Anderson Shelters", named after the home secretary, which are being built in many English gardens.

Women called up to aid war effort

Britain, 20 July
Now that the so-called "phoney" war is over, women all over Britain are expecting to be asked to play a larger part in the war effort – whether they want to or not.

For many, work in a munitions factory, even on a part-time basis, seems out of the question. Caring for children and elderly relatives, just keeping a home together, takes even more time and energy now than it did in peacetime. There are long queues for essential provisions; little economies around the home to make things last longer and go further all take time. Many are also taking the full responsibility of raising families alone with their husbands away.

The reluctance felt by many women about taking jobs outside the home is reinforced by their menfolk's disapproval. There have been public outcries over nearly every new opening, however small, for women that the war has created. The Land Girls have been seen as a threat to agricultural training programmes and moral standards, the women pilots of the Air Transport Auxiliary have been accused of taking the jobs not "for the sake of doing something for their country but for the sake of publicity".

Add these popular beliefs to the very real burdens of caring for a family in war time, and it's no wonder that many women prefer to remain at home (→9/11).

De Gaulle lays wreath to mark Bastille Day in London

De Gaulle inspects Foreign Legionnaires in the Free French forces.

London, 14 July
General de Gaulle's Free French volunteers celebrated Bastille Day on foreign soil in London today.

In the morning General de Gaulle, accompanied by Vice-Admiral Muselier, the head of his naval force, and M Labarth, the director of technical services, laid a wreath at the Cenotaph. He shouted *"Vive l'Angleterre!"* and then *"Vive la France!"* and the crowd took up his cry. Later, units of the Free French forces marched to the statue of Marshal Foch at Victoria, and 2,000 of de Gaulle's men attended a film show. Mr Churchill sent a message saying he looked forward to the time, "not far distant", when they would celebrate 14 July in France (→ 25).

Braving criticism from family and strangers: a woman bus conductor.

July

Su	Mo	Tu	We	Th	Fr	Sa
	1	2	3	4	5	6
7	8	9	10	11	12	13
14	15	16	17	18	19	20
21	22	23	24	25	26	27
28	29	30	31			

22. Tokyo: Prince Fumimaro Konoye is appointed prime minister.→

23. USA: A British mission is given permission to buy 40 per cent of the USA's production of aircraft.→

23. Britain: The Local Defence Volunteer force is renamed the "Home Guard" (→ 19/8).

24. Palestine: Italian planes bomb Jerusalem, killing 46 (→ 9/9).

24. Roumania: The government seizes British oil interests (→ 27).

25. Mediterranean: Italian bombers attack British naval bases at Haifa and Alexandria (→ 15).

25. London: Charles de Gaulle appoints Captain Jacques Philippe, Vicomte de Hauteclocque [*alias Philippe Leclerc*] to command Free French forces in Equatorial Africa (→ 2/8).

26. Japan: The government agrees to block supplies to China through Indochina while securing its own via the Dutch East Indies.→

27. Bavaria: Bulgaria's prime minister confers with Hitler at Berchtesgaden; yesterday Roumania's premier did the same (→ 30/8).

27. North Sea: The British destroyers *Codrington* and *Wren* are sunk by air attack.

28. France: Germany bans all movement between the Vichy and occupied zones (→ 31).

29. Belgium: Germany annexes Eupen, Malmedy and Moresnet.

29. Germany: The German navy reports that landings on the British coast cannot take place until mid-September (→ 1/8).

31. Vichy France: The government decrees the death penalty for French servicemen who join a foreign army.

31. Vichy France: *Chantiers de Jeunesse* [Youth Workshops], a youth organization service run by the state, is founded.

"Luftwaffe" bombards "Hellfire Corner"

German bombs rain down on Dover harbour while the pilots fight it out.

Dover, 29 July
"Hellfire Corner" was attacked by the *Luftwaffe* again today as Junkers Ju87 ("Stuka") dive-bombers, protected by Messerschmitt fighters, screamed down on shipping at Dover. The concussion of bursting bombs shook buildings and broke windows all along the seafront, while waterspouts dropped tons of water onto ships bobbing like corks among the bombs in the harbour.

RAF Hurricanes and Spitfires tore into the enemy formations, already heavily engaged by the anti-aircraft defences. Twelve out of 80 German planes engaged were downed to three RAF machines.

While it is difficult to make specific claims in the heat of battle, it is becoming clear that the Stukas, which were so effective in France, are sitting ducks for fighters like the Spitfires.

Britain sets up secret operations team

London, 22 July
The war cabinet today approved a draft document signed on 19 July by Neville Chamberlain, now the lord president of the council, creating a new secret organization, the Special Operations Executive (SOE). Its aim, in Churchill's words, is to "set Europe alight".

It will come under the Labour MP Hugh Dalton, the minister for economic warfare in the coalition government, who was asked to

head the planned SOE on 16 July. Both MI6, which has its own sabotage department, and the army have expressed opposition to the formation of SOE because it intrudes into their territory, but Dalton is determined it will succeed.

"Regular soldiers," he argues, "are not the men to stir up revolution, to create social chaos or to use all those ungentlemanly means of winning the war which come so easily to the Nazis."

Baltic states vote to join Soviet Union

Helsinki, 21 July
The Baltic states of Estonia, Latvia and Lithuania today succumbed to Russian pressure and "unanimously" decided to become Soviet Republics and join the Soviet Union.

The newly-elected parliaments of the three countries met to announce their decision, but the Soviet influence was easy to see under the facade of democracy. Estonia's parliamentary session was attended by Stalin's representative, Mr Zhdanov, and the hall was decorated with Soviet flags. The Baltic peoples are bitter at losing their hard-won freedom from Russia, but there is nothing they can do in face of Soviet might (→ 25/8).

Benes forms exiled Czech government

London, 23 July
Dr Eduard Benes, the Czech leader, has formed a provisional Czechoslovak government in London with the approval of the British government. It is probable that a British minister will be accredited to Dr Benes's government.

Dr Benes, who becomes president, said today: "Our main effort will be the organization of our forces on land and in the air so that our share in the defence of Britain and the defeat of Nazism will be as effective as possible."

Dr Benes, who has become Czech president in exile in London.

Emergency budget puts tax on luxuries

Furs become a wartime casualty.

Britain, 23 July
An emergency budget today ushered in tough new taxes, including 24 per cent on luxuries such as furs, real silk stockings and cosmetics. "In the hard circumstances of the times we can do without them," said Sir Kingsley Wood, the chancellor of the exchequer. He also announced all-round tax increases, including an extra shilling on income tax. This will be 8/6 in the pound (42.5%) from next January.

In future, income tax will also be compulsorily deducted at source. People will "pay as they earn" instead of the present system with lump sums paid twice a year.

French sailors die in torpedo tragedy

English Channel, 24 July
Some 383 Frenchmen lost their lives tonight when their ship was sunk by a German motor torpedo boat off the coast of Brittany. The *Meknes* left Southampton early today carrying 1,277 French naval officers and ratings who were being repatriated to France.

She was showing all lights and had a searchlight trained on the French ensign when she was attacked at 10.30pm. One officer said: "Why should they torpedo us when the war was over as far as we were concerned?"

Britain to embargo Africa and Europe

Westminster, 30 July
Britain is to extend the naval blockade of ships which may be carrying supplies to Germany to take in virtually all ships crossing the North Atlantic. The minister for economic warfare, Hugh Dalton, told the Commons today that the steps were necessary now that Germany controlled the European coast from the North Cape to the Pyrenees. Neutral countries will be granted "Navicerts" to cover domestic needs, but not for re-export. France and all French Africa are to be designated enemy territory.

While Europe wars, Japan may expand

Tokyo, 26 July
Japan intends to take advantage of the war in Europe to expand its empire in Asia, according to a new military-inspired national plan to prepare Japan for war.

Unveiled by Prince Konoye four days after becoming premier, Japan's "new order" for Greater East Asia envisages Japan leading a strong union combining Japan, Manchukuo and China, the Chinese Nationalists defeated and the Japanese armed forces ready to go to war with Britain and the US within 12 months if talks fail to stop arms reaching China through British and French territories (→ 3/8).

Flowers go as Britain digs hard for victory

They even dig for victory in a royal park: now the harvest is gathered in.

Britain, 31 July
The face of Britain is being transformed by the war as a massive effort gets under way to ensure that the country is not starved into submission. From rural hills to suburban gardens, "digging for victory" has become a patriotic duty.

Barely one-third of the nation's food was produced at home when the war began – and Hitler knows it, boasting that his U-boat blockade will bring Britain to its knees. Rationing should mean that less food is consumed, but equally important is the campaign to produce more food at home. Land traditionally used for grazing, such as the Downs in southern England, is now being ploughed up to produce cereal crops such as wheat or potatoes. Arable land is expected to increase by 14 per cent this year.

Government money is being pumped into agriculture in order to guarantee prices and because the rural depression of the 1930s left most farmers with too little money to finance the tractors, milking machines and fertilizers required to boost output quickly. Although farms form the frontline of this campaign, flowers are being replaced by vegetables in gardens, and allotments are appearing on commons and in parks.

Oil: the fuel which shapes war strategy

Washington, 31 July
As this conflict develops, it has become increasingly clear that not only has oil become crucial to the waging of modern war but that it is also shaping much of the underlying strategy. Starved of it a country will very quickly succumb. Germany, Italy and Britain all lack oilfields and so have to obtain oil from other countries. Successive British governments have ensured that adequate supplies are available from the Middle East and Southeast Asia, and if necessary from the US, but U-boats are posing an increasing threat to Britain's oil imports.

In March 1939 Hitler reached an agreement with King Carol of Roumania for Germany to be supplied from the rich Ploesti oilfields, and on 27 May 1940 Carol agreed to even closer cooperation. Germany's position is further secured by the pact made with Stalin in August 1939, under which it receives oil from the Russian Caucasus. Germany also produces synthetic oil in large amounts.

Although Allied plans to bomb the Caucasus oilfields were abandoned for fear of the political complications, and attacking Roumania is not an option while that country remains a non-belligerent, the naval blockade of Germany is preventing oil from being imported from elsewhere (→ 3/8).

Winston Churchill tries out a Tommy gun during a tour of the fortifications in eastern Britain.

1940

August

Su	Mo	Tu	We	Th	Fr	Sa
				1	2	3
4	5	6	7	8	9	10
11	12	13	14	15	16	17
18	19	20	21	22	23	24
25	26	27	28	29	30	31

1. Germany: Hitler sets the date for the invasion of Britain at 15 September, and issues his directive no 17 ordering intensification of the air war from 5 August (→ 5).

1. North Sea: The submarine HMS *Spearfish* is sunk.

1. The Hague: A *Luftwaffe* conference is held to plan the invasion of Britain (→ 5).

2. Vichy France: The government sentences General de Gaulle to death in his absence (→ 10).

2. Southern England: German bombers drop leaflets detailing Hitler's August peace proposals.

3. Tokyo: Japan protests at the US embargo on aviation fuel exports.

5. Germany: Bad weather conditions force the postponement of the air offensive against Britain.→

6. USA: The secretary of state, Cordell Hull, calls for a massive build-up of arms to dissuade enemy attacks.

8. India: To boost India's contribution to the war viceroy, Lord Linlithgow, offers "immediate, but limited" constitutional reform and a full inquiry into independence "after the war".

9. London: Britain promises Japan that it will pull out of Shanghai and northern China; its manpower is needed elsewhere (→ 27).

10. Roumania: Anti-Semitic legislation is passed.

10. Vienna: Baldur von Schirach becomes *Gauleiter* of Vienna; Artur Axmann will take over as *Reich* youth leader.

10. Vichy France: Laval offers Germany 200 pilots to help fight the Battle of Britain (→ 13).

10. Britain: Despite the threat of invasion, Churchill decides to send three regiments of tanks (about 150) to North Africa.

10. Atlantic: A U-boat sinks the British armed merchant cruiser *Transylvania* off Ireland.

"Luftwaffe" steps up air war over Britain

London, 8 August
It is now a week since the *Luftwaffe* began its latest attempt to destroy the RAF in preparation for Hitler's planned invasion of Britain. In spite of relentless intensive fighting in the air over the Channel and along the south coast, on the evidence of today's battles it is still a long way from succeeding in that aim.

As the bomber formations with fighter escorts in close attendance roared in over the coast to attack harbours, naval bases and airfields, the Hurricanes and Spitfires of Fighter Command, carefully fed into the battle, took a terrible toll of the Germans. They lost 31 planes to the RAF's 17.

The main battles developed between 9am and 5pm when gaggles of dive-bombers attacked a convoy in a three-phase attack. In the last phase no less than 150 Stukas and Messerschmitt fighters were thrown into the dangerous skies over "Hellfire Corner".

The British pilots, guided to their targets by a controller watching the movements of the enemy as they were plotted by RDF, were able to meet each wave of enemy aircraft as the attack developed.

Among the most successful of the RAF pilots are Poles who have fought the Germans in their own skies, over France and now over Britain. They burn with hatred for the Nazis and roar into the battle with reckless courage. One British

German bomber team set for action.

pilot told tonight how he shot down two Ju87s: "I was forced to retire owing to engine failure, but dived on a Ju87. After a three-second burst it went into an inverted dive straight into the sea.

"My engine started again so I went after another Ju87 and attacked him before he was able to dive-bomb the convoy. He dived into the sea at high speed. After this my engine packed up for good and I only just got back to England."

He managed to land the stricken aircraft at a coastal airfield. Tomorrow he will fly again, determined that the Luftwaffe will not win this battle (→ 11).

Duke of Windsor spurns Nazi plot

Lisbon, 1 August
The Duke and Duchess of Windsor left here today aboard the US liner *Excalibur* after the collapse of a Nazi plot to pressure them into leading peace moves against the duke's brother, King George, and Churchill. The couple, who were living in France, fled to Spain when the Germans invaded and went on to Lisbon. At von Ribbentrop's request, the Falangist Miguel Primo de Rivera contacted the duke and was gratified to be told Churchill was a warmonger. Rivera suggested the duke might again be king. "Oh, no," the duke said. "That would be unconstitutional."

Japanese nationals arrested in colonies

London, 5 August
Britain today responded to the recent arrests of seven British subjects in Tokyo by detaining leading Japanese businessmen in London, Rangoon, Hong Kong and Singapore.

Japan has protested at the arrests and the British ambassador, Sir Robert Craigie, has been summoned by Mr Matsuoka, the Japanese foreign minister, who described the arrests as "unwarrantable". Among the detainees is the manager of the London branch of Mitsubishi Trading. Seven officials of the Salvation Army in Japan have been arrested on espionage charges (→ 9).

Ruthless press lord joins war cabinet

London, 2 August
Lord Beaverbrook, the dynamic newspaper proprietor and close crony of Mr Churchill, joined the war cabinet tonight.

The prime minister brought Beaverbrook into the government when it was reconstructed under his own leadership in May, and he has been one of its outstanding successes. Since he became minister of aircraft production – a new post – in May, he has boosted the improved output of fighters for the RAF which had already begun that month. In February there was a shortfall: 141 planes produced against a planned 171. In May, however, this had been turned around, with 261 planes planned and 325 built. Under Beaverbrook, this month's planned output of 282 is expected to be exceeded by up to 200 machines.

Churchill is known to consider that his friend has rendered signal service to the nation during this critical summer. Beaverbrook will continue with his aircraft supply job "for the time being".

The Canadian-born press baron's success has been achieved through force of personality. He has been aggressively cutting through Whitehall red tape and treading on other ministerial toes in purloining all accessible supplies for aircraft factories.

Beaverbrook: no time for red tape.

Italy marches into British Somaliland

British Somaliland, 5 August

The Somali town of Hargeisa fell to the Italian army this afternoon, assaulted by infantry and tanks after a three-hour bombardment. It was defended by two battalions of Indian and East African troops plus some of the Somali Camel Corps – most of whom got away.

Two days ago General de Simone crossed the Ethiopian frontier into British Somaliland, with twelve Eritrean battalions to do the hard work and four Blackshirt battalions to take the credit. Just in case anything went wrong, he had another six battalions in reserve.

On the morning of the invasion he spoke to his motor cycle troops, "as only a valorous soldier can speak", according to one present. "Your task is to be the vanguard, an arduous and difficult work which I know you will carry out to your uttermost. Our end is to reach Berbera and reach it we will."

From the episode at Hargeisa a certain ponderousness can be detected, and it might take de Simone, valorous as he may be, some time.

But the British force of five battalions and a camel corps cannot hold out for ever – something of an understatement considering Somaliland's defence budget of just £900 ($3,600). Any serious defence of So-

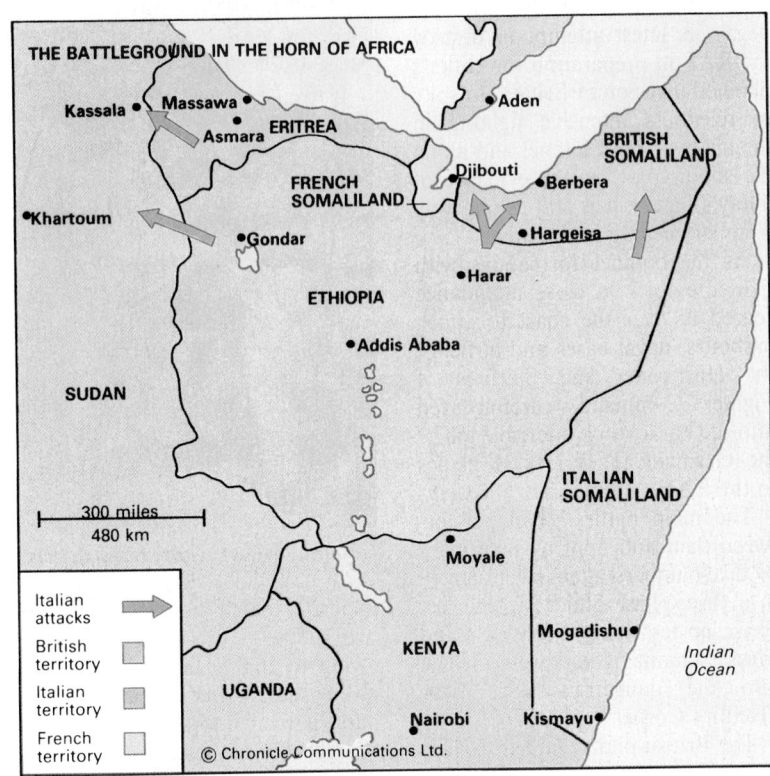

THE BATTLEGROUND IN THE HORN OF AFRICA

300 miles
480 km

Italian attacks
British territory
Italian territory
French territory

© Chronicle Communications Ltd.

maliland lost all chance of success last week when the pro-Allied governor of neighbouring French Somaliland, General Legentilhomme, was replaced by General Germain.

Elsewhere on the borders of Ethiopia, Italy's 300,000-man army seems reluctant to act aggressively, content with the symbolic occupation of a few border towns, such as Moyale in Kenya and Kassala in the Sudan, and in harassing the British in northern Kenya with some remarkably effective guerrilla columns. It is so short of petrol that it can do nothing else (→ 11).

Colonies and dominions send airmen to boost "mother country"

London, 6 August

The first contingent of airmen from Southern Rhodesia arrived in Britain today to add its strength to the increasingly international air force which is waging war on Germany. The men join not only British and Polish pilots but also airmen from Canada, Australia and New Zealand – not to mention volunteers from Ireland and the USA.

Throughout the Empire, towns, islands, colonies and even tribes are donating money for individual planes to the mother country. Soon more airmen will arrive from the colonies to pilot the planes that the colonies have donated. Already Canada is training hundreds of fighter pilots. More generally, India has 500,000 men under arms; Australasia, 225,000; Canada 200,000, and South Africa 80,000 (→ 2/10).

A contingent of the Royal Canadian Air Force arrives in the mother country.

1940

August

Su	Mo	Tu	We	Th	Fr	Sa
				1	2	3
4	5	6	7	8	9	10
11	12	13	14	15	16	17
18	19	20	21	22	23	24
25	26	27	28	29	30	31

11. Somaliland: Italian troops attack British forces at Tug Argan (→ 16).

11. Washington: The government is to supply Britain with 4,000 tanks.

11. Britain: 35 *Luftwaffe* and 82 RAF planes are downed in air battles today (→ 13).

12. Dover: The first German shell to fall on British soil destroys four houses (→ 13).

12. Britain: Germany loses 45 planes and Britain 13 (→ 15).

13. Germany: The *Luftwaffe* makes 1,485 sorties to mark *Adlertag* [Eagle Day] – the start of full-scale bombing of Britain.

13. Vichy France: In a move aimed against the Freemasons, all secret societies are banned.

14. Luxemburg: Germany suspends the constitution; henceforth the duchy will be ruled by the German civil service (→ 5/9).

14. London: Sir Henry Tizard leaves for the USA with various British scientific items and ideas for development, including the magnetron.

15. Britain: Germany loses 76 planes and Britain 35. The Royal Canadian Air Force gets its first "kill" when Ernest McNab shoots down a Dornier bomber (→ 17).

15. Belgium: The first issue of the underground newspaper *La Libre Belgique* [Free Belgium] is published.

15. Mediterranean: The Greek cruiser *Helle* is sunk by an Italian submarine (→ 17).

16. Europe: 150 RAF bombers attack targets in Germany and Holland.

16. Somaliland: British forces pull out of Tug Argan (→ 19).

17. Germany: The *Luftwaffe* removes Stukas from its attacking force, as they have proved too vulnerable.→

17. Libya: The Royal Navy Mediterranean Fleet bombards Italian positions at Bardia and Fort Capuzzo (→ 20).

17. Greece: Armed forces are mobilized (→ 22).

"Luftwaffe" and RAF join battle for air supremacy

London, 17 August
The air battles over Britain are continuing with unabated ferocity as the *Luftwaffe* maintains its attempt to overwhelm Fighter Command. Goering, convinced that the RAF is at its last gasp after the hard fighting of the *Kanalkampf* [the Channel War], named last Tuesday, 13 August, as *Adlertag*, Eagle Day, when the RAF would be swept from the sky and the invasion of Britain would be made possible. Airfields and RDF stations [*see below*] were hammered, but the RAF's pilots, fed frugally into the battle by Air Vice-Marshal Keith Park, not only stayed in the air but had the best of the fighting, knocking down 46 Germans for the loss of 13.

So furious was the fighting that both sides took advantage of bad weather the next day to lick their wounds. Even so the Luftwaffe lost 27 planes and the RAF 11.

Then, on Thursday 15 August, German aircraft took off from airfields ranging from Norway to Brittany. Soon the battle raged along the east coast from Tyneside down to the Channel and along the south coast to Devon. Newspaper billboards displayed the day's score like a Test Match. Close of play showed that the RAF had shot down 90 for the loss of 42. These casualty figures do not take account of those German bombers which limped home with dead and dying crew members in their bullet-riddled aircraft. They came again yesterday, attacking RDF stations and airfields, losing 44 to the RAF's 24.

Mr Churchill spent the afternoon watching the progress of the battle in the "ops room" of No 11 Group at Uxbridge, near London. He could hardly contain his excitement as he followed the progress of the battles. The gallantry of the RAF against constant attack from the Luftwaffe made a deep impression on him. Later, driving home, he said: "Don't speak to me; I have never been so moved" (→ 18).

Aerial fireworks: the night is lit up as pilots battle for control of European skies, fighting not only each other but "flak" and gunfire from the ground.

The planes: how the fighters compare

London, 17 August
One of the crucial factors in the battle being fought in the skies over southern England is the relative quality of the fighters taking part. The backbone of the *Luftwaffe* is the Messerschmitt Bf109E, which has more powerful firepower than its two main RAF adversaries, the Spitfire and the Hurricane. The Bf109E has three 20mm cannon and two 7.9mm machine guns, and with a top speed of 350mph and an operating ceiling of 35,000ft it is compact and highly manoeuvrable, with a fast climb and dive. It does have a major drawback, however:

its lack of range. It can only remain airborne for one hour, which means no more than 20 minutes over England. While the twin-engine Bf110 does have the range, its lack of manoeuvrability makes it easy meat for the Spitfires and Hurricanes.

Sidney Camm's Hurricane IIA is not as fast as the Bf109E, nor as manoeuvrable, but its good sights and excellent cone of fire make it an ideal bomber destroyer. It has eight machine guns, as does the late R J Mitchell's Spitfire, which, although slightly slower than the Bf109E, has a better rate of climb and turning performance.

The technology: Britain's secret weapon

London, 17 August
In 1932, the then prime minister, Stanley Baldwin declared that "the bomber will always get through". At the time this was accepted by everyone, including the air ministry. The problem was that if a bomber stream was spotted there was not enough time to scramble the biplane fighters of the day in order to intercept the bombers before they had dropped their deadly loads. Today, as we are witnessing, the situation is different. This is thanks to the high speed monoplane and Radio Direction Finding, or RDF. Known by the US Navy as "Radar"

(radio detection and ranging), RDF was pioneered in Britain by Professor Robert Watson-Watt, the head of the National Physical Laboratory Radio Department.

He set up an experimental station on the east coast in 1935. A year later work began on the Chain Home system of RDF stations along the east and south coasts. RDF stations detect enemy aircraft up to 100 miles (160km) from the British coast, giving enough warning for RAF fighters to intercept them in time. No wonder Goering has been trying – so far in vain – to knock out the RDF stations. ▷

Britain swaps bases for 50 US ships

Washington, 16 August

The United States is to "swap" 50 ageing destroyers for 99-year, rent-free leases on British naval and air bases in the western hemisphere.

The draft agreement was made public two days ago, and was re-affirmed by President Roosevelt in a press conference today stressing the advantages of the deal to the USA. The destroyers in question are obsolescent, but still service-able, "four-stackers" dating from the Great War, which the British prime minister, Winston Churchill, has told President Roosevelt are desperately needed to escort con-voys under attack from the German U-boat "wolf-packs".

The bases involved stretch all the way from Newfoundland off the Canadian coast and, by way of Ber-muda, to the Bahamas and across the Caribbean to British Guiana.

It is understood that the deal had its origins in a personal appeal from Mr Churchill to the president on 15 May. He explained that the Ger-mans' overrunning of the whole coastline of western Europe from the north of Norway to the Pyr-enees, the entry of the Italian fleet, with 100 new submarines, into the war, and the loss of almost half Britain's submarines in actions to protect convoys had seriously weakened Britain's ability to defeat an invasion and keep the Atlantic sea lanes open for imports of wheat,

Philadelphia navy yard, where old destroyers are reconditioned for Britain.

oil and munitions from the United States and elsewhere. It was, Mr Churchill said, "a matter of life and death", and King George added a personal message saying that the need for the destroyers was "great-er every day".

It is known that the president first felt that the legal and political difficulties of helping Britain were insuperable. On 1 August, how-ever, the Century Group – which lobbies for US aid to Britain – came up with the idea of exchang-ing the ships for British bases.

The president was still concerned about potential reactions from the

isolationists in Congress, many of them Republicans. Mr Churchill was reluctant to let the exchange seem too hard a bargain, and pre-ferred it to be seen as "two friends in danger helping each other".

Still the president persevered; hence today's press conference. One senator who supports the deal reminded his colleagues: "If you jump on the destroyer transfer, you're jumping on the acquisition of defence bases."

Mr Roosevelt has said he believes the swap will be the "most import-ant action in national defence since the Louisiana Purchase" (→ 2/9).

The comedian George Formby takes time off from the filming of "Spare a Copper" to help with collection of scrap metal from women in Ealing.

Half-blinded pilot downs German foe

London, 16 August

The many acts of heroism of the RAF's fighter pilots were epito-mized today by Flt-Lt James Nicol-son of 249 Squadron. Shot in the head and half-blinded when he was "bounced" by a Messerschmitt Bf110, he was baling out when another enemy plane flew past his burning Hurricane. Ignoring the flames searing his hands, he chased the German and shot him down. Only then did he bale out, playing dead when a third German plane flew towards him. Even then he was shot at by the Home Guard as he drifted to earth. Nicolson is being recommended for the VC.

1940

August

Su	Mo	Tu	We	Th	Fr	Sa
				1	2	3
4	5	6	7	8	9	10
11	12	13	14	15	16	17
18	19	20	21	22	23	24
25	26	27	28	29	30	31

18. Britain: In the heaviest day of fighting so far, the *Luftwaffe* loses 67 planes to the RAF's 33; another 29 RAF machines are wrecked on airfields.

18. Berlin: Goering rebukes *Luftwaffe* generals dor their disappointing campaign. Fighter ace Adolf Galland's sarcastic riposte is to ask him for a supply of Spitfires!

18. North America: Canada and the USA set up a joint defence board to coordinate military decisions.

19. Britain: The admiralty oil depot at Pembroke Dock is bombed, and burns fiercely.

19. Britain: The Home Guard is preparing stocks of Molotov cocktails.

20. Europe: One hundred and twenty RAF bombers attack targets in Germany and airfields in France, Belgium and the Netherlands.

20. Mediterranean: Italian planes bomb Gibraltar (→ 22).

20. Rome: Mussolini announces a blockade of British ports in the Mediterranean.

22. Athens: Britain promises to send sea and air forces to aid Greece is she is attacked by the Axis.

22. Mediterranean: Swordfish aircraft from the carrier HMS *Eagle* sink an Italian destroyer, depot ship and submarine on their way to launch a human torpedo raid on the British fleet in Alexandria (→ 2/9).

22. London: MPs condemn the internment of aliens.

22. Germany: British raiders bomb industrial targets at Frankfurt and Cologne.

23. Berlin: The propaganda minister, Josef Goebbels, worried by recent British successes, orders that ridicule of the English way of life must stop and the enemy's fighting spirit be stressed instead.

24. London: The city has its first bombing raid when ten German planes returning home jettison their loads by mistake. Germany loses 38 planes today and Britain 22 (→ 26).

"Luftwaffe" targets Britain's airfields

London, 24 August

The *Luftwaffe* today concentrated its attacks on Fighter Command's airfields. The first raid appeared at 8.30am when 40 Dornier Do17s and Junkers Ju88s, escorted by 66 Messerschmitt Bf109s, approached the coast. Twelve squadrons of Spitfires and Hurricanes went up to intercept. But the raid was a feint, and the real attack was timed to catch the British fighters on the ground as they refueled.

Hornchurch and North Weald took heavy punishment, with the fighters scrambling to get into the air as the bombs dropped. Hornchurch was saved from severe damage largely by its anti-aircraft guns, while Hurricanes from neighbouring Romford came to the rescue at North Weald.

Manston, in its exposed position on top of the Kentish cliffs, took a terrible hammering, although stories about a "mutiny" among ground staff – allegedly refusing to come out of underground shelters despite threats and entreaties from their superior officers – appear to have arisen from a series of misunderstandings, as have tales of civilian workers refusing to fill in bomb craters under enemy fire. Tonight Manston has ceased to exist as a front line fighter base, and is being used only as an emergency field. This is not the only weakness which today's attacks have shown

British crews race to get airborne before the Germans bomb the airfield.

up. Five of 264 Squadron's lumbering Defiants have been shot down. It is obvious that, like the Stukas, they cannot live in the fury of this battle.

There is also something wrong with the cooperation between Air Vice-Marshal Keith Park's hard-pressed 11 Group and Air Vice-Marshal Trafford Leigh-Mallory's 12 Group.

When Park asked for help today, 12 Group's squadrons took so long in forming their "big wing" that the raiders had bombed and gone before 12 Group appeared on the

scene. The Germans also got through to Portsmouth where, attempting to bomb the dockyard, they were heavily engaged by anti-aircraft fire. Many of their bombs fell into the town and caused heavy civilian casualties. Ramsgate was also hit. As the result of the day's fighting the Germans lost 41 aircraft and the RAF 20. But the day is not yet over.

Goering has ordered a round-the-clock offensive, and there are reports tonight of raids on Cardiff, Swansea, South Shields and many areas around London (→ 26).

Churchill: "Never ... was so much owed by so many to so few"

London, 20 August

Winston Churchill addressed the House of Commons today and praised the RAF for its heroic struggle against the *Luftwaffe*.

"The gratitude of every home in our island, in our Empire, and indeed throughout the world ... goes out to the British airmen who, undaunted by odds, unwearied in their constant challenge and mortal danger, are turning the tide of the world war", he said. "Never in the field of human conflict was so much owed by so many to so few. All hearts go out to the fighter pilots, whose brilliant actions we see with our own eyes day after day." Comparing this war with the last, the prime minister found many dif-

ferences: "The slaughter is only a small fraction, but the consequences to the belligerents have been even more deadly. We have seen great countries with powerful armies dashed out of coherent existence in a few weeks ... Moves are made upon the scientific and strategic boards, advantages gained by mechanical means."

He continued: "There is another more obvious difference from 1914. The whole of the warring nations are engaged, not only soldiers, but the entire population, men, women and children ... Our people are united and resolved, as they have never been before. Death and ruin have become small things compared with the shame of defeat" (→9/10).

A Hurricane pilot: one of the "few".

Trotsky, Stalin's greatest enemy, is killed by ice-pick

Mexico City, 22 August

Leon Trotsky, the exiled Bolshevik leader, died in hospital today of a fractured skull. He was attacked in his home here yesterday by a man with an ice-pick.

His assassin is reported variously to be a Canadian, the son of a Belgian diplomat or an American journalist. In the ambulance after the attack Trotsky spoke of the man as "either a member of the *Ogpu* or a fascist". Trotsky was deprived of his Russian citizenship in 1932, though he had been a leading ally of Lenin in founding the Soviet Union. Stalin had come to regard him as the USSR's greatest enemy.

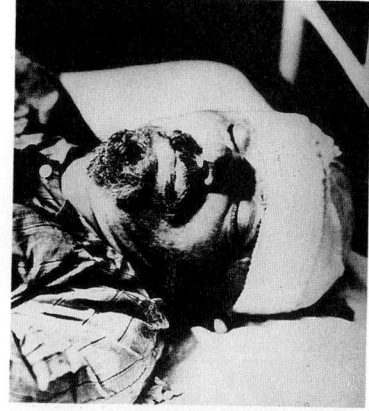

Trotsky: assassinated in exile.

Bulgaria to nibble away at Roumania

Bucharest, 21 August

Bulgarian troops are tonight poised to enter Roumanian territory after talks here ended with an agreement to revert to pre-1912 borders. Southern Dobruja, containing the two provinces Durastor and Caliacra bordering the Black Sea, will be ceded to Bulgaria, and up to 100,000 Roumanians moved to their diminishing homeland. Roumania has already lost control of Bessarabia to Russia. And Roumania's troubles are not over yet: Hungary is eyeing eagerly the province of Transylvania, in western Roumania, and Germany would like access to Roumanian oil.

▷

1940

August

Su	Mo	Tu	We	Th	Fr	Sa
				1	2	3
4	5	6	7	8	9	10
11	12	13	14	15	16	17
18	19	20	21	22	23	24
25	26	27	28	29	30	31

Italy ousts Britain from Somaliland

Berbera, Somaliland, 19 August
A line of African troops clambered from the jetty onto *dhows*, as the Australian warship *Hobart* stood on the horizon. The British were evacuating Somaliland, the capital of which, Berbera, fell today. For 16 days 6,000 Imperial troops fought nearly 30,000 Italians. Now mathematics has asserted itself over tactics and Mussolini has tasted his first victory. While the last of the rearguard, the Black Watch, embarked, Indian army engineers blew up the port's installations. Only the Somali Camel Corps stayed behind, some to go home, others to go into the bush to fight another day (→ 29).

Communist cadres attack Japanese

Shansi Province, China, 20 August
The Japanese army's strategic security network of garrisons in northern China was suddenly cut off from the world today as 40,000 men of the Chinese Communist Eighth Route Army launched a series of well-coordinated surprise attacks on road and rail installations, severing communications in the region.

The success of the attacks by the army's 115 regiments provides a much-needed morale boost for the Chinese forces, and will help to silence critics in the *Kuomintang* who claim that the Communists are more intent on attacking them than the Japanese (→ 6/9).

French outposts swing to de Gaulle

Abeche, Chad, 26 August
French Equatorial Africa is the latest French colony to support General de Gaulle's Free French. Governor Eboue of Chad, France's first black governor in Africa, said today that he refused to accept capitulation. The other Equatorial territories will make similar statements in the coming days. Elsewhere in French Africa, recent weeks have seen the replacement of pro-Allied officials with Vichy supporters, although the Ivory Coast rallied to de Gaulle on 26 July. The first colony to back de Gaulle was the New Hebrides, in the Pacific, on 22 July.

25. Baltic: Latvia, Lithuania and Estonia are formally incorporated into the Soviet Union.

26. Europe: The RAF last night made its first bombing raid on Berlin, as the *Luftwaffe* bombed London again (→ 27).

26. Britain: Portsmouth is heavily bombed.

26. Africa: Chad declares its allegiance to Free France and General de Gaulle.→

27. China: Britain completes the withdrawal of troops from Shanghai.

27. Iceland: RAF Coastal Command sets up an air base to help protect Atlantic convoys.

27. London: An air raid stops play at Lord's cricket ground.→

27. Vichy France: Laws forbidding anti-Semitism in the press are repealed (→ 28).

27. Atlantic: The sloop HMS *Dunvegan Castle* is sunk by a U-boat off Northern Ireland.

28. Vichy France: The government breaks off relations with European governments in exile (→ 27/9).

28. Britain: Liverpool is raided for the first time.

29. Africa: The South African Air Force bombs Italian bases in Somaliland.

30. Bucharest: Under pressure from Germany, Roumania cedes 20,000 square miles of territory – half of Transylvania – to Hungary (→ 31).

30. Britain: German raiders target Biggin Hill in Kent and important industries in Luton; incendiaries are dropped on London (→ 31).

31. Britain: Vital airfields in the south-east, including Biggin Hill, Lympne, Manston and Hawkinge, are bombed out of action; Fighter Command loses 38 planes, its greatest daily loss so far.→

31. Moscow: Russia protests that it was not consulted on the award of Transylvania, territory it has long coveted, to Hungary.

Air raid kills three in neutral Wexford

Dublin, 26 August
Ireland's neutrality, assiduously preserved by the premier, Eamon de Valera, has not won immunity from German air raids. *Luftwaffe* bombs hit four places in County Wexford today, 130 miles (208km) from the border. Two of the three young women killed while working at a creamery were sisters. The third, a blast victim, was found sitting at a dining table, knife and fork in hand. The motive for the attack is not clear, for Ireland, like neutral Spain and Turkey, is an intelligence goldmine for the Germans. Dublin's representative in Berlin has protested.

Channel echoes boom of heavy shellfire

A German gun blasts a shell across the Channel to the English coast.

Dover, 22 August
German batteries shelled Dover tonight during a cross-Channel duel which had lasted all day. Their first target was a convoy of cargo ships edging up the English side of the Channel under Royal Navy escort. Then the guns turned on Dover. In the air, RAF fighters broke up waves of *Luftwaffe* bombers. Other British aircraft hit back until long after nightfall. By then the convoy, with its 50,000 tons of food and war material, was snug at anchor.

The Germans have installed 14-inch batteries with a 20-mile (32-km) range along the coast from Boulogne to Calais as part of the plan to invade England. Those guns were used for the first time today when shells sent water spouts 100 feet above the convoy. RN escorts laid smoke to conceal the convoy.

With dusk, the guns turned on civilian targets in Dover. During a 45-minute barrage a shell burst through the stained glass of a church and exploded near the altar. By midnight, refugees carrying bedding were seeking shelter as their homes were demolished. Across the Channel, the RAF lit up the gun pits with parachute flares, then bombed them.

Desperate fighting in aerial struggle over Britain

Capitals bombed by rival air forces

London, 31 August

Berlin and London both came under attack from the air yesterday. This war of the capitals started when more than one Heinkel 111 flew too far up the Thames and bombed the City of London by mistake on the night of 24 August.

Churchill immediately ordered the bombing of Berlin, and the next night 81 British bombers attacked the German capital – much to the dismay of the Berliners and the fury of Hitler, who had promised that Berlin would never feel the weight of British bombs.

Hitler, who had dreamed of a triumphal procession through an undamaged London like the one through Paris, was incensed. He will doubtless be pondering further reprisals on the British capital, which will please his new *Reichsmarschall*, Hermann Goering, who is of the view that London is the only target which British air power will have to defend at all costs; in doing so, he believes, the RAF will almost certainly be destroyed.

So far most attacks on London have been over the southern suburban fringes, because that is where the prime targets are – airfields such as Biggin Hill and Kenley.

The *Luftwaffe* also comes by night, dropping high explosive and incendiary bombs on these outskirts. These night raids have not caused very much damage; likewise, RAF damage to Berlin has also been fairly insignificant so far.

One of the RAF bomber pilots reported: "When we arrived we found the target well on fire. We could see it when we were 25 minutes flying time away. We put our stick of bombs down just to the left of this big fire. Then four more fires started. Altogether we were cruising around over Berlin for about half an hour."

It seems certain that the bombing of both London and Berlin will intensify. It remains to be seen which of the capitals will best be able to sustain its morale; this depends on the people's will as well as the pilots' skill.

Churchill watches a dogfight from Dover, as the Germans home in on Britain.

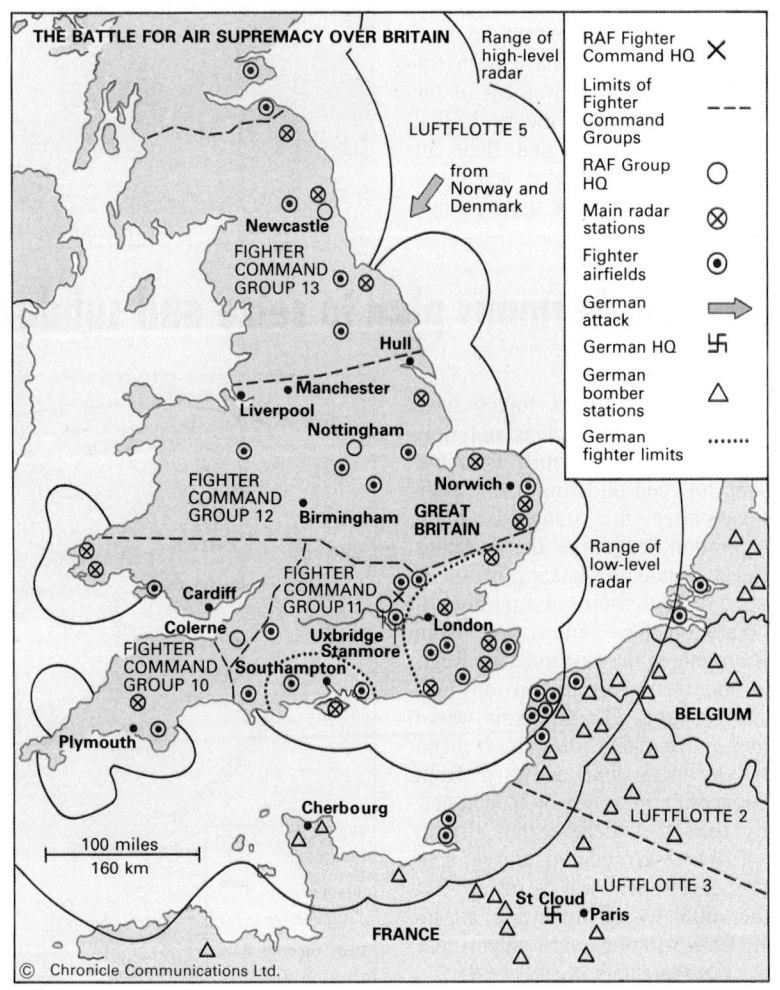

Invaders are ready to sail for England

Berlin, 31 August

Brushing aside the misgivings of his generals and admirals, Hitler has given orders for Operation Sealion, the invasion of England, to go ahead. Goering has promised to destroy the fighter defences in the south of England in four days and the rest of the RAF in two or three weeks. So the Fuhrer says that he will decide on the invasion date in the next fortnight.

The transfer of shipping to the Channel ports is beginning, and plans for a feint attack against the east coast of Britain have been made. But Hitler has still not resolved a bitter dispute between the army and the navy over the deployment of the invasion force.

The army has planned a landing on a 200-mile (320-km) front from Ramsgate to Lyme Regis, throwing into action 1,722 barges, 1,161 motor boats, 470 tugs and 155 transports. Grand Admiral Erich Raeder says that it is quite impossible for his navy to protect such a vast and widely dispersed force. He has told Hitler that the navy would risk having all its ships sunk by the British.

Raeder, who was made a grand admiral by Hitler on 1 April 1939, says that the army should concentrate on a narrow front, between Folkestone and Eastbourne. "Complete suicide," General Halder, the chief of staff, responded furiously. The British would hit them with overwhelming force. "I might just as well put the troops through a sausage machine."

During a strategy meeting at Hitler's Obersalzberg retreat, Hitler asked Raeder to give his opinion. "All things considered," Raeder said, "the best time for the operation would be May 1941." This certainly was not the answer the Fuhrer wanted. By next year the British would have had even longer to prepare plans to counter an invasion, the British Army would have recovered from its Dunkirk defeat, and the German *Kriegsmarine* would still not be able to challenge the Royal Navy (→ 3/9).

115

September

Su	Mo	Tu	We	Th	Fr	Sa
1	2	3	4	5	6	7
8	9	10	11	12	13	14
15	16	17	18	19	20	21
22	23	24	25	26	27	28
29	30					

1. Kovno, Lithuania: the Japanese consul Sempo Sugihara, who has been issuing exit visas to Jews, is expelled.

2. Mediterranean: The battleship HMS *Valiant* and carrier HMS *Illustrious* arrive from Gibraltar to reinforce Admiral Cunningham's Royal Navy fleet (→ 2/10).

2. Washington: Britain and the US sign the deal giving Britain 50 aged destroyers in exchange for permission for the US to make use of British naval bases in the West Indies (→ 28).

3. Europe: Since yesterday a total of 84 RAF bombers have attacked a U-boat base at Lorient in France and tried to set forests alight in South Germany.

3. Britain: The cabinet approves compensation of up to £2,000 for each house destroyed by *Luftwaffe* air raids.

3. Berlin: Hitler postpones the invasion of Britain, scheduled for 15 September, to 21 September (→ 4).

3. Bucharest: King Carol of Roumania survives an assassination attempt (→ 5).

4. Berlin: "I have tried to spare the British ... they have replied by murdering German women and children," says Hitler, threatening savage reprisals on British cities (→ 6).

5. North Sea: Four thousands German troops are believed drowned when a British submarine torpedoes the transport ship *Marion*.

5. Roumania: Parliament is dissolved and the constitution is suspended.→

5. Luxemburg: The authorities adopt Germany's anti-Semitic Nuremberg Laws, and seize all Jewish-owned businesses (→ 29).

6. Britain: Heavy *Luftwaffe* raids put armed forces on yellow alert, meaning invasion is expected within three days.→

6. China: The Nationalist government designates Chungking as its wartime capital (→ 13).

British forces put on invasion alert

London, 7 September
Today 350 German bombers protected by as many fighters appeared over London's docks. They were followed by another 247 tonight. A few hours later, with 2,000 Londoners dead or injured and the whole area engulfed by flames, all railway links south were blocked, and the decision was taken at GHQ Home Forces to send out the code-word "Cromwell": invasion imminent. Home Guard and regular troops were called out, church bells rung and some bridges blown.

Churchill has been warning the chiefs of staff that if an invasion is to be tried it cannot be long delayed, because the weather may break at any time. For the past few weeks hundreds of self-propelled barges have been observed moving down from German and Dutch harbours to ports of northern France. They have come under heavy bombardment from the RAF and the Royal Navy. But the massive bombing attack on London docks, which British forces interpreted as a prelude to an attempted German landing, does not appear to have been followed up by any movement of the invasion fleet. One theory is that the Germans hope that their air raids on civilian targets will cause such panic and chaos that invasion will be unnecessary.

Aerial view of the port of Boulogne, showing lines of invasion barges.

How the Germans plan to seize and subdue southern England

Berlin, 7 September
The German armed forces have drawn up detailed plans not only for invading the British Isles but also for consolidating their positions after the initial landings. Operation Sealion, as the Germans call it, entails the landing of a first wave of 13 divisions at a number of points on the south coast, from Ramsgate in the east to Lyme Regis in the west. Airborne troops will also be used. The Germans would then move inland to establish themselves on a line eastward from Gloucester to south of Colchester. By then they believe that Britain will have surrendered and a military government will be set up. But the difficulty of mounting an invasion without air superiority worries the chiefs of staff (→ 9).

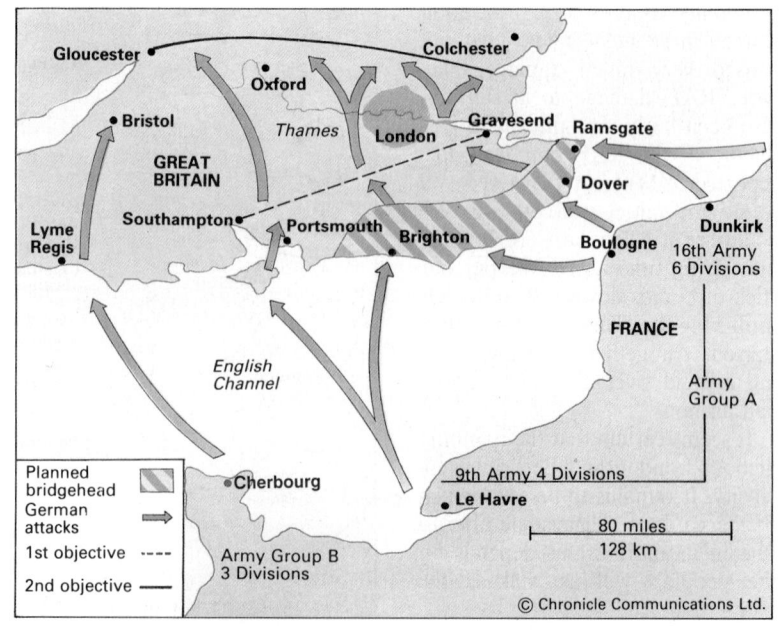

Hitler unleashes "Blitz" terror on Britain's cities

Goering brings RAF to breaking point

London, 7 September

Fighter Command has reached crisis point as it faces increasingly ferocious attacks on its airfields and RDF stations and mounting losses in the air. Goering, desperate to finish off the RAF fighters, is using large numbers of fighters, which RDF cannot distinguish from bombers, to tempt them into battle.

Air Chief Marshal Sir Hugh Dowding's tactics are to refuse battle with the fighters and concentrate on the bombers, and he is feeding in his planes in miserly fashion in order to preserve his command. But while he has enough planes, he does not have enough men. Newly-trained pilots with only 20 hours' flying time in Spitfires are thrown into battle and too often shot down on their first *sortie*. Dowding has lost 11 of his 46 squadron commanders and 39 of his 97 flight commanders, and those who survive are physically exhausted.

But what the RAF does not yet know is that Goering has chosen this very moment, when the fortunes of Fighter Command are at such a low ebb, to switch his main attack from British airfields to the cities. What *he* does not know is that he is handing the RAF a breathing space on a plate (→ 14).

Dowding: concentrates on bombers.

Vast clouds of smoke rise from London's blazing docks: "The whole bloody world's on fire," one of the fire officers said.

Bomber attack brings widespread devastation and 450 deaths

London, 7 September

London's dockland is on fire tonight after a massive daylight raid in which more than 300 tons of high explosive and incendiary bombs rained on the capital, with the RAF seemingly unable to stop the death and destruction which fell from a stately procession of bombers onto the streets of East London. It is feared that up to 450 people have died, with about 1,600 injured.

Goering directed the attack from a cliff top in France, whence he watched 350 bombers escorted by 650 fighters stream across the Channel. Broadcasting from his HQ, he said that he could see waves of planes heading for England.

It seems that this time the RAF was wrong-footed despite *Enigma* warnings of an attack on London. There had been raids on Hawkinge airfield that morning and, thinking that the new wave of raiders was heading for airfields north of London, the 11 Group controller kept his squadrons north of the capital

not realizing that London was the real target until it was too late. Eventually 21 out of 23 squadrons airborne managed to get into action and shot down 41 German planes for the loss of 25, but by then the damage had been done.

The first bombs set fire to bonded warehouses. Blazing rum, paint and sugar floated on the Thames. Many people had to be evacuated by boat. "Send all the pumps you've

got," pleaded one fire officer, "the whole bloody world's on fire." One of the problems facing the firefighters was that the level of the Thames had fallen in the dry summer and they had difficulty in getting their pumps to work. Later the sirens sounded again, and in the night 247 German aircraft attacked the capital, dropping 352 tons of high explosive and 440 canisters of incendiary bombs (→ 14).

"Ack-ack" guns lift spirits in shelters

London, 7 September

As the capital experienced its first big air raid today, Londoners began to learn the sounds of battle. The sound that pleases them most is that of anti-aircraft guns, but only 97 guns are on site in the London area, compared with the 2,232 heavy guns and one-third of the 1,860 light guns sought when war began. "Ack-ack" guns, as they are called, range from small calibre

Lewis machine guns to big Royal Navy weapons mounted on railway bogeys. They throw up a storm of hot metal, forcing the raiders higher, but one drawback is the shower of shell splinters raining down on the streets, where a helmet is essential during a raid. Yet civilians in shelters such as church crypts and coal cellars like the sound of the guns; it makes them feel less like passive targets (→ 8).

1940
September

Su	Mo	Tu	We	Th	Fr	Sa
1	2	3	4	5	6	7
8	9	10	11	12	13	14
15	16	17	18	19	20	21
22	23	24	25	26	27	28
29	30					

Carol toppled from Roumanian throne

Bucharest, 6 September
King Carol of Roumania today surrendered to the dictator General Ion Antonescu and abdicated in favour of his son, Prince Michael.

The king, who will seek asylum in Switzerland, declared: "I have decided to abdicate in face of the misfortunes which have come to this country. I hope by this sacrifice to save my country." This is the second time that Carol has given up his throne. He renounced his right of succession in 1925 for love of his mistress, Magda Lupescu, before returning to turn his son off the throne in 1930 (→ 7/10).

Well-dressed spies swiftly arrested

Lydd, Kent, 3 September
Mabel Cole, the wife of the publican of the *Rising Sun*, had every reason to be suspicious when a well-dressed young man knocked on the door at nine o'clock in the morning and asked for a glass of cider. He spoke with a foreign accent in a prohibited area – and he was plainly ignorant of English licensing laws. Mrs Cole sent him across the road to Tilbey's stores to buy some cigarettes while she summoned help.

The young man, a Dutchman, was one of four well-dressed spies – two of them German – who landed on the beach here today before being arrested.

LEND TO DEFEND HIS RIGHT TO BE FREE
BUY NATIONAL SAVINGS CERTIFICATES

8. London: Air attacks kill 412 people and injure 747.

9. Palestine: Italian planes bomb Tel Aviv.

9. Britain: Germany loses 27 planes and Britain 20 in air battles.

9. Germany: The RAF bombs Hamburg, Bremen, Emden, Ostend and Boulogne.

9. Berlin: Hitler postpones the invasion of England until 24 September (→ 11).

10. London: Buckingham Palace is slightly damaged by a German bomb.→

10. Albania: Italian troops pour in, reinforcing the army in preparation for an attack on Greece.

11. Westminster: Churchill tells the Commons that he expects Germany will try to invade in the next week (→ 14).

11. London: The lord mayor opens the Air Raid Relief Fund (→ 5/10).

12. Helsinki: Finland signs an agreement giving German troops transit rights to Norway (→ 1/10).

12. France: French schoolboys discover ancient wall paintings in caves at Lascaux, in the Dordogne.

13. North Africa: An Italian offensive starts at Sollum, on the border of Libya and Egypt.→

13. Britain: The battleships HMS *Rodney* and HMS *Nelson* at Rosyth, in Scotland, and HMS *Revenge* at Plymouth move to likely invasion sites.

13. China: The Japanese "Zero" fighter plane sees action for the first time over Chungking (→ 20).

13. East Africa: Italian troops from Ethiopia advance 20 miles into the British colony of Kenya.

14. Britain: The work of the London docks is transferred to the Clyde in Scotland.

14. Berlin: Hitler brings the invasion of Britain forward to 17 September on advice from Goering that the *Luftwaffe* is close to success.→

Why Germans changed their air tactics

In the sights of an enemy gun: a Spitfire dives through a bomber formation.

London, 14 September
The *Luftwaffe's* change of tactics, bombing London and Liverpool instead of continuing its attacks on Fighter Command's airfields, has brought death and destruction to the cities but blessed relief to the fighter pilots. While they are still fighting as hard as ever in the sky, they can relax on the ground.

The bomb holes are being filled in, communications restored and equipment repaired. The pilots have safe havens to return to from the dangerous skies. It is as if a boxer who had his opponent on the ropes had backed away and allowed him to recover. The RAF has Hitler himself to thank for this respite. He was so enraged when the RAF mounted its retaliatory raid on Berlin on 25 August that he threatened that, if the attacks continued, "we will raze their cities to the ground".

Now he is carrying out that threat by day and night, but the *Luftwaffe*, already strained by the losses in men and aircraft inflicted on it by the British fighters, is becoming tired of and cynical about the claims that the RAF is finished. The Germans appear to have made a fundamental blunder (→ 15).

Italy invades Egypt and takes Sollum

Sollum, Egypt, 13 September
After months of prodding by a Mussolini hungry for victory, Marshal Graziani's army is making a ponderous advance in North Africa and has finally crossed the barbed-wire fence that marks the Egyptian border with Libya. Bells are being rung in Rome to celebrate the capture of Sollum, a tiny settlement of mud-huts.

Graziani has insisted on "digging in" at frequent points along the coastal road, harassed continually by British defenders (→ 17).

France pays for army of occupation

Paris, 14 September
The financial penalties imposed by Germany on France for the privilege of paying the costs of the army of occupation are far steeper than reparations imposed on Germany after the Great War.

Under the armistice signed at Compiegne in June France must pay 20 million *Reichsmark* a day, or RM7.3 billion a year, almost three times what Germany had to pay under the Dawes plan of 1924 – one billion a year rising after four years to 2.5 billion.

British cities "blitzed"

London, 14 September

Britain's cities and their people are now in the front line of the war. German bombers, while claiming to attack military targets, are showering their deadly cargoes over homes and public buildings in an attempt to terrorize the British people into submission.

The Nazi rulers would rather that Britain surrendered, as the Dutch did after the bombing of Rotterdam, than risk their army in a crossing of the Channel.

The RAF's nightly bombing of their invasion fleet has convinced them of the dangers of this enterprise. The French coastline is so well lit up by burning barges that it has become known as the "Blackpool Front" to the RAF bomber pilots.

In return the Germans are "blitzing" South Wales, Merseyside and London. Following its first devastating daylight attack on the capital's dockland, on 7 September, the *Luftwaffe* mounted a "rolling" night raid by 247 bombers which kept Londoners in their shelters for nine hours.

A daylight raid on 9 September was beaten off with heavy losses, but the bombers were back that night, killing an estimated 370 people. And so it goes on. The feeling is that the battle is building up to a climax (→ 18).

Six bombs fall on Buckingham Palace

London, 13 September

Buckingham Palace has been hit by bombs for the second time. A stick of six bombs fell in the Palace grounds today about 80 yards from where King George and the queen were sitting in a small room overlooking the quadrangle. The blast showered them with broken glass.

Two of the bombs fell in the quadrangle, two in the forecourt. One wrecked the royal chapel and one exploded harmlessly in the garden. This incident has caused Mr Churchill to fear for their safety, but the king and queen refuse to be driven from London.

Germans set docks ablaze in London

London, 14 September

The *Luftwaffe* broke through London's defences today and again set fire to the docks. They are an easy target, a sprawling mass of warehouses packed with combustibles, found easily by the Germans who simply flew up the Thames.

The RAF's response to the raid was weaker than usual, and the German pilots thought that at last they detected signs of the promised collapse of Fighter Command.

This feeling was reinforced by the tally sheet for the day's fighting. The score was eight German losses to 13 British.

How Londoners coped with the bombers

London, 14 September

A week ago today the Nazis turned the full force of the *Luftwaffe* against London. The Blitz had begun. To the people of London, waiting for months for the inevitable onslaught, the earliest raids have come almost as a relief.

An air raid warden, Celia Fremlin, said of the first nights: "When it began and you got the measure of what it was like, terrifying though it was, it wasn't quite as bad as most of us envisaged."

Others, however, could probably not imagine it being any worse. Sixteen-year-old Kitty Murphy, from North Woolwich, described the night her house was bombed: "As I lay there looking through where the windows had been blown out, I heard the air-raid warden shouting my mother's name: 'Nance, come on, you've copped it girl, come out of there, you've got five incendiary bombs! ' ... all this time my mum's shouting, come out, come out you silly ... Then she grabbed me ... let it burn, she said. And I just went to get away from her when the whole of the house caved in. She saved my life. I would have been in there, picking up the clock and the ornaments off the mantelpiece."

From Belgravia to Mile End, Londoners wake up to a city they hardly recognize

London sprawls beneath a Heinkel He111 bomber with its deadly cargo.

Inspecting the damaged Palace.

Putting out the fires in the City.

A London bus thrown over like a toy: rescue workers search for survivors.

1940

September

Su	Mo	Tu	We	Th	Fr	Sa
1	2	3	4	5	6	7
8	9	10	11	12	13	14
15	16	17	18	19	20	21
22	23	24	25	26	27	28
29	30					

15. France: The Pas-de-Calais and surrounding region are put under the control of German military command in Belgium.

15. Canada: Single men aged between 21 and 24 are called up.

15. London: A survey shows that two-thirds of the capital's population are getting under four hours' sleep.→

15. Britain: The RAF destroys 61 German planes, losing 29 aircraft itself.→

17. Mediterranean: Aircraft from the carrier HMS *Illustrious* attack Benghazi; destroyers bombard Sidi Barrani and Sollum (→ 18).

17. Atlantic: A U-boat torpedo sinks the SS *City of Benares,* killing 77 British children and 248 crew en route for Canada.

17. Berlin: Artur Axmann, the new German youth leader, decrees that all Hitler Youth aged between 14 and 18 in areas vulnerable to air raids must attend air-raid practice on Sunday mornings – thus keeping them out of church.

17. Paris: The Nazis set up a task force, based at the *Musee du Jeu de Paume,* to acquire art treasures for the *Reich.*

18. North Africa: Italian forces come to a halt and start fortifying their position (→ 15/11).

19. Pacific: The French colony of New Caledonia declares its allegiance to de Gaulle.

19. France: The German invasion fleet starts to pull out of the Channel ports.

20. China: The Chinese Eighth Route Army attacks Japanese lines, launching the second phase of a Communist "Hundred Regiments Offensive" against the Japanese which began on 20 August.

21. London: To Churchill's suggestion that one Pole is worth three Frenchmen, General Lord Gort replies that it is nearer ten.→

21. London: Official permission is given for the Underground to be used as a bomb shelter (→ 3/10).

Despite bombs, London stays defiant

London, 18 September
The *Luftwaffe* returned to London in daylight today but, even after two days' rest following its defeat last Sunday, it could only put 70 heavily-escorted bombers into the air, in three waves, and they achieved little.

However, the bombs continue to rain down on the capital at night, with the drone of some 230 bombers making every night hideous. Unable to pinpoint their targets, they drop their bombs at random, causing terrible damage and casualties in the streets and among civilians.

Some of London's most famous landmarks have been destroyed or damaged. Eight City churches have been hit. One bomb, weighing a ton, lies, unexploded, outside the west door of St Paul's Cathedral, where Royal Engineers bomb disposal experts are working on it.

The West End, Downing Street, the Law Courts and the House of Lords have all been hit by either high explosives or incendiaries. But it is the ordinary people who are taking the brunt of the attack. Sheltering in the Underground, they still raise the Union Jack over the rubble of their homes or declare "Business as usual" on handwritten signs nailed to the wreckage of their shops and businesses.

The king and queen, who have been bombed twice in Buckingham Palace, have made several visits to the East End where they have been greeted sympathetically as fellow-sufferers from German barbarism. When Churchill, cigar clenched in his teeth, visited the bombed-out areas he got a clear message from the people: "Give it 'em back."

At work on a 1200-lb time bomb dropped at the German hospital in London.

The burnt-out John Lewis's in Oxford Street, blackened but not flattened.

Bomb disposal teams: brave new heroes of the Home Front

Britain, 21 September
"Suicide Squad" reads a cheerful handwritten sign on the back of one of the vans driven by men of the Bomb Disposals Section of the Royal Engineers. Typically they make light of the mortally dangerous tasks that are all in a day's work.

On 17 September it was announced that four members of the section were to be given the Medal of the Military Division of the Most Excellent Order of the British Empire in recognition of their bravery. One of the awards went to Lieutenant E W Reynolds for his work in defusing time bombs. Twice in a fortnight he dealt with fuses in delayed-action bombs which were still ticking, despite the imminent likelihood of explosion. Lieutenant Talbot received the award for having carried a live time bomb on his shoulder for 200 yards to a safe place while keeping his men under cover.

Lance-Sergeant W J Button has been decorated for a story with a less happy ending. He and his team were ordered to continue excavating an unexploded bomb which was likely to explode at any minute. He persevered with great coolness. Finally, it did explode, killing five members of the team.

RAF claims victory in air war's "Battle of Britain"

London, 15 September
RAF Fighter Command has today won a stinging victory over the *Luftwaffe*. This was going to be the day that the Germans wiped the RAF out of the sky and cleared the way for Operation Sealion, the invasion of Britain, which Hitler plans to put into operation on 17 September. Instead, it is the Germans who have been scurrying back to their bases leaving southern England littered with the smoking wrecks of their aircraft. The tally at the end of the day is 61 Germans lost to 29 British. Everything went right for the RAF today. The pilots had enjoyed a comparatively easy week and they were ready for the fray. RDF, unbothered by the newly-introduced jamming by the Germans, picked up the hostile formations over northern France. There were no feints.

The first enemy formation of about 100 bombers escorted by 400 fighters came boring in over the coast heading straight for London and Air Vice-Marshal Park was able to put up 11 squadrons to harry them all the way to London where they were met by fighters of 12 Group.

The mere sight of so many fighters demoralized the Germans, who had once again been told that the RAF had only a few fighters left. Many of the bombers simply jettisoned their loads and headed for home. They did not leave in peace. Spitfires and Hurricanes slashed at them all the way back.

Goering mounted a second attack in the afternoon. The result was the same. Air Chief Marshal Sir Hugh Dowding, warned by an immediate *Enigma* message, was waiting for them. The day was not without its anxieties, however. Churchill, visiting Park's headquarters at Uxbridge, west of London, asked at one stage: "What other reserves have we?" Park replied: "There are none." But the RAF's response to raids such as this and the one exactly a month ago, when the Germans lost 76 planes to the RAF's 35, belie Goering's boast that British air power is finished (→ 17).

Pilots recall their battles in the sky

Britain, 21 September
As the battle rages in the skies over Britain, RAF pilots have described harrowing experiences.

One young officer flew for several weeks without coming into contact with any German planes: "I was fairly frightened when it finally happened. I felt a nasty chill when I saw that black cross on the aircraft and thought 'My God, it's going round the back of me'."

"I wasn't going to let it get on my tail. I worked very hard to make sure it didn't, doing a high-speed stall getting around to follow it ... I chased it, fired at it ... it went on its back and went down through the cloud."

Eighteen-year-old Sergeant Jim Hannah, who has been recommended for a VC, miraculously survived a mid-air fire during an attack on enemy barges at Antwerp: "We got caught in a terrific 'ack-ack' barrage. Our plane went on fire ... I realised that we were liable to blow up at any minute, so I made for my parachute only to discover that it was on fire, too. By this time the navigator and gunner had baled out, and the plane was a blazing mass and a terrific target for the 'ack-ack' guns.

"Still, I did some quick thinking and started throwing all the blazing mass overboard. During this, ammunition on the kite was going off ten a penny with the heat. Finally I got the fire out and the pilot and I limped home. They rushed me to hospital right away."

How technology thwarted the "Luftwaffe"

The Hurricane and Spitfire: aircraft that will go down in British history.

London, 17 September
Today's decision by Hitler for an indefinite postponement of his invasion of Britain means that Goering's *Luftwaffe* has failed in its bid to establish air supremacy over southern England. This was an essential precondition for a successful cross-Channel invasion. Two months ago, at the outset of what has become known as the Battle of Britain, just 600 RAF fighters faced 2,500 German aircraft. Given this overwhelming numerical superiority, why did the Luftwaffe fail?

While there is little to choose between the fighter pilots and their aircraft on both sides, the British Home Chain RDF [radar] system has played a vital role in giving timely warning of impending Luftwaffe attacks. Communications have also played their part. The ability of the RDF stations and the Observer Corps posts, responsible for tracking the bombers once they cross the coast, to send messages to RAF Fighter Command's sector HQs and from there to Dowding's HQ at Bentley Priory has enabled the Spitfires and Hurricanes to take off and intercept the German aircraft. Credit must be given too to the Government Code and Cipher School at Bletchley Park for its ability to crack the Luftwaffe's top-secret *Enigma* code, and to the men and women of the RAF's Y Service for their monitoring of the Luftwaffe's wireless frequencies.

Tactically, Goering's worst error was his decision to switch from attacks on airfields and RDF stations to London itself. Ultimately, by allowing the RAF time to regroup, this proved decisive.

Hitler postpones invasion of Britain

London, 17 September
The results of the RAF's gallant and successful fight to deny the *Luftwaffe* air supremacy over the south of England and the Channel became clear today: Hitler has put off Operation Sealion, his plan to invade Britain, scheduled for today.

The news came in an *Enigma* decoding of a message from the German General Staff to the officer responsible for loading the transport aircraft earmarked for the invasion. The message orders him to dismantle his air-loading equipment; without that equipment there can be no invasion.

This is a triumph for the RAF in general and for Air Chief Marshal Sir Hugh Dowding and Air Vice-Marshal Keith Park in particular.

Air Vice-Marshal Keith Park: high flyer in the Battle of Britain.

Roosevelt brings conscription to the US

In serious mood: Roosevelt signs.

Washington, 16 September
The United States Senate today passed the Selective Service Bill under which all Americans between the ages of 21 and 35 will be liable to be drafted for military service.

The bill now goes to the House of Representatives for debate, starting at the beginning of next week. The Senate amended the bill to limit the number of men under training at any one time to 900,000.

Yesterday Mr Roosevelt also signed a bill giving him authority to call the 238,000 members of the National Guard, controlled by individual states, and the Officers' Reserve, roughly equivalent to the British Officer Training Corps, into the army for a year (→ 15/10).

Italian invaders advance to Sidi Barrani

Sidi Barrani, Egypt, 16 September
Italian troops have managed to fight their way to this Egyptian coastal outpost as Lieutenant-General Maitland Wilson, GOC Egypt, and his heavily-outnumbered force of British and Indian troops are withdrawing to a prepared defence line at Mersa Matruh.

Although the next battle could be decisive – with an Italian victory leaving Egypt open to Marshal Graziani's army – the Italians are fortifying Sidi Barrani, with the marshal ignoring furious orders from the Duce to attack, preferring to put up monuments to his "victorious advance". While Mussolini fumes, Churchill in beleaguered Britain has taken the "awful and right" decision to dispatch over 150 tanks and other desperately-needed weapons to General Wavell, Britain's C-in-C Middle East.

Although small in number – with fewer than 30,000 men facing 250,000 Italians – the hard core of Wavell's army is professional, tough and confident. The question now is whether the British line can hold until the tanks are unloaded in Alexandria (→ 17).

American military personnel put the prototype of the new General Purpose army vehicle through its paces. Known as the Jeep for short, it will replace a large variety of specialized vehicles and will be usable in most terrains.

Pilots who came from occupied Europe to help fight Nazi menace in the air

Czech fighter crews flying for Britain race out to their waiting machines.

London, 21 September
Miroslav Liskutin is a young Czech pilot who escaped to France when the Germans invaded his country. The French put him and 50 other aviators into their Foreign Legion until April, when he transferred to an air squadron near Bordeaux, where aircraft were sabotaged.

Liskutin now flies with the RAF whose Czech airmen (in three squadrons, 310-312) fought their first action in the big battle of 26 August, shooting down a Dornier bomber and a Messerschmitt Bf110 fighter. His story can be repeated many times. Poles, Yugoslavs, Norwegians, Danes – even, it is rumoured, some Germans – have joined the RAF Volunteer Reserve in the battle to stop Hitler.

The Polish air force, with its own London HQ, will now retain its separate identity under general RAF command. Its 300 pilots, with two years' training, an average of 500 flying hours and burning hatred of Germans, are a huge asset. The first two Polish squadrons, 302 and 303, flying from Northolt, Middlesex, are already claiming a high number of kills.

Some volunteers have a talent for flying, but still need training. About 700 Norwegians are at an air school near Toronto. Another small European country represented in the air war is neutral Eire. The RAF is delighted to have Paddy Finucane as an emerging ace. Regardless of nationality, volunteers are desperately needed.

The aircraft industry can produce more than 200 aircraft a week, making good most of the airframe losses, but pilot attrition is a different matter. Such casualties, killed and disabled, are running at 120 a week. Survivors are exhausted, premature veterans of more than one crash who (like Ginger Lacey) often conceal burns and other injuries. Total fighter pilot strength is 840 pilots and the trainers are producing only 260 a month. Some squadrons needing 26 pilots have only 16.

Learning by watching others fly: Poles on a Wellington bomber.

1940
September

Su	Mo	Tu	We	Th	Fr	Sa
1	2	3	4	5	6	7
8	9	10	11	12	13	14
15	16	17	18	19	20	21
22	23	24	25	26	27	28
29	30					

22. Adriatic: The submarine HMS *Osiris* sinks an Italian destroyer off Durazzo in Albania.

22. Atlantic: The British convoy HX-72 has lost 12 ships in two days of U-boat attacks.→

23. Germany: Himmler orders that all gold teeth are to be removed from dead camp inmates, the proceeds to go into an SS account in the *Reichsbank* under the name of Max Heiliger.

24. Germany: Last night Berlin was heavily bombed by 129 RAF aircraft (→ 25).

24. Germany: The *Luftwaffe* ace Adolf Galland receives the Oak Leaves to his Knight's Cross; Hitler agrees with his admiration for the RAF.

25. USA: Military intelligence reads the Japanese "Purple" code for the first time.

25. Europe: The RAF bombs Berlin and the Channel coast.

26. Washington: Roosevelt announces a ban on scrap iron and steel exports except to the western hemisphere and to Britain. The ban's target is Japan.

27. France: All Jews are forced to carry special identity cards.→

27. Berlin: Professor Franz Six, an SS colonel, is appointed to head the German secret police in Britain in the event of an invasion.

28. Germany: Hitler secretly orders the economy to be mobilized towards the invasion of Russia (→ 12/11).

28. Britain: The first of 50 old destroyers arrives from the USA (→ 20/11).

28. Norway: The Nazi commissioner Josef Terboven formally deposes the king and nominates Vidkun Quisling "sole political leader".

29. Luxemburg: The grand duchy is incorporated into the German *Reich* on the grounds that it "derives from the German race" (→ 10/10).

30. Britain: Civilian casualties of the Blitz this month are 6,954 killed and 10,615 hurt.

De Gaulle abandons attack on Dakar

Dakar, Senegal, 25 September

The fleet of British and Free French warships that had been shelling Dakar for two days has sailed away into the Atlantic mist. In the city's street the pro-Vichy police are rounding-up the usual suspects. The Allied invasion of Dakar has failed, and Senegal's black middle class, which demonstrated in support of General de Gaulle, is paying the price.

It was the pro-Allied street demonstrations and an unsuccessful naval mutiny that persuaded the Allies that Senegal was fertile ground for the Free French. And so it was. Then the pro-Allied governor was replaced by the present Governor Boisson, and the colony was purged of Free French sympathizers. Worse, the amphibious force arrived two days after three French cruisers had docked, bringing reliable Vichy reinforcements – although the Royal Navy did prevent several more French warships from sailing further south to overawe the Free French supporters in French Equatorial Africa. For the Royal Navy failure is bad news, since it fears that Dakar may become a German U-boat base.

A landing at Dakar and an air attack by planes from HMS *Ark Royal* were both resisted and failed. Throughout both days shore batteries and the immobilized battleship *Richelieu* engaged in shelling with the battleship HMS *Barham*. Finally, de Gaulle was forced to admit defeat – this time.

Calling off the invasion of Dakar: General de Gaulle and his officers.

The port of Dakar under fire from British and Free French warships.

Vichy France hits back: Gibraltar bombed

Gibraltar, 24 September

The Rock of Gibraltar has been hit by bombs for the first time in the war – dropped by a former ally. It was inevitable, after the British operation in Dakar, that the Vichy government would have to make some reprisal. The 100-bomber raid should have wrecked the port, but a large number of the French pilots appeared to have deliberately dropped their loads into the sea, and a larger number of the fuses of the bombs that did land had apparently been tampered with so that they would not explode. The authorities are now strenuously applying themselves to retrieving the unexploded bombs, but these are the least of their problems. It is the diplomatic efforts of Hitler to bring Spain into the Axis, and of President Roosevelt to browbeat Spain back into neutrality, that are most concentrating their minds. If Spain does come in, then Gibraltar's anti-aircraft gun toll of three planes last night is not a good sign. Gibraltar remains Britain's most vital strategic outpost; a key base for convoy escorts. Now, with Mussolini's fleet menacing the Mediterranean, any threat to the Rock must be viewed very seriously (→ 25).

French Indochina in Japanese air deal

Hanoi, 22 September

With just two hours to go before its ultimatum expired, Japan has gained a strategic foothold in French Indochina, allowing it to station troops and aircraft in Tongking so that it can prevent supplies reaching China from the south.

The decision by the governor-general, Admiral Decoux, to capitulate to Japanese demands led to an immediate protest from China. Under the deal Japan can use three airbases in Indochina and station 62,000 troops there (→ 27).

Japan joins the Axis

Saburo Kurusu reads Japan's declaration of alliance with the Axis powers.

Berlin, 27 September
Today, in the Berlin chancellery, the Japanese ambassador, Saburo Kurusu, put his signature to a tripartite pact which extends the Rome-Berlin Axis to the Far East. In a move clearly directed at the United States, the three countries pledge themselves to aid one another with "all political, economic and military means" should one of them be attacked by "a power not involved in the European war".

Japan accepts the hegemony of Germany and Italy in Europe, and they in turn recognize Japan's right to organize "the Greater East-Asia Co-prosperity Sphere". The pact contains a clause promising to preserve the *status quo* in relations with the Soviet Union.

In Washington, Roosevelt called his defence advisers to the White House to review the implications of the pact. Asked if he had expected Japan to join the Axis, the president said: "Yes and No."

A navy department spokesman said that the pact would not mean any change of policy. The navy, he said, would continue to be based at Pearl Harbor (→ 29).

Britain to re-open China's road to Burma

London, 29 September
Britain has served notice on Japan that it intends to re-open the Burma Road to China when the current three-month agreement expires on 17 October. The move, announced by the prime minister, Winston Churchill, is the first direct result of the Japan-Axis pact. Mr Churchill told the House of Commons that Britain had originally agreed to ban the transit of war materials from Burma to China while the two sides tried to reach a settlement. Japan had not taken the opportunity and had signed a ten-year pact with the Axis. To cheers from the House the prime minister said that in the circumstances Britain could not see its way to re-newing the agreement (→ 18/10).

CHINA'S LIFELINE TO THE ALLIES

Burma Road
BURMA — Kunming CHINA
Lashio
Mandalay — Hanoi
Paklai
Rangoon — HAINAN
THAILAND
Bangkok
Phnom Penh — INDO-CHINA
Saigon
250 miles / 156 km
MALAYA

British territory ☐
Japanese territory ☐

© Chronicle Communications Ltd.

King gives George Cross to civilian heroes

London, 23 September
King George has instituted a new decoration, to be called the George Cross, for "deeds of valour by civilian men and women in all walks of life". It will rank with the Victoria Cross and be worn in front of all other decorations.

The king himself announced the award in a broadcast from Buckingham Palace during an air raid last night. "It is London that is for the time being bearing the brunt of the enemy's spite," he told the nation. "I am speaking to you now from Buckingham Palace, with its honourable scars, to Londoners first of all. The queen and I have seen many of the places which have been most heavily bombed."

He thanked the ARP workers [*see below*] of the capital "who work on regardless of danger, though the sirens have sounded, and all who night after night uncomplainingly endure discomfort, hardship and peril in their homes and shelters.

Home heroics: later propaganda.

The walls of London may be battered but the spirit of the Londoner stands resolute and undismayed." The George Medal is also being instituted for civilians, to rank with decorations for gallantry. Bomb disposal men are expected to be among those to receive the GC.

How rescuers save lives during air raids

London, 30 September
When a high-explosive bomb falls, the first person on the scene is the local air raid precaution (ARP) warden, patrolling the sector on foot or bicycle – one in six are women. Wardens fix the location of the "incident", and report to their posts their assessment of casualties and likely survivors. They keep lists of who sleeps where in their sector. The post calls out the rescue services.

The scene is a chaos of brick and plaster dust, filling the lungs and shrouding everything in a reddish-brown pall. In the fog, gas mains are often ablaze, water mains gushing and broken glass littering the area and people who cannot recognize each other under the dust are stumbling around in the dark, screaming or numb with shock. There is a raw smell of explosive, brick-dust and escaping gas.

Heavy Rescue Squads are based at depots in each borough, mainly made up of building workers and led by surveyors or engineers, who know the pockets in collapsed buildings where people are likely to survive. Tunnelling into the debris, they keep silence every few minutes while they call, tap and listen for answering sounds. Digging out a wrecked house is done mostly by hand and basket, so as not to injure buried bodies. Often rescuers have to drop through crevices, risking a collapse on top of them, followed by a nurse or doctor with morphine for the trapped. Many will not end their shift until they reach their quarry, especially if it is a child.

Stretcher party and rescue teams work to clear the rubble of a bombed house in the search for survivors.

1940
October

Su	Mo	Tu	We	Th	Fr	Sa
		1	2	3	4	5
6	7	8	9	10	11	12
13	14	15	16	17	18	19
20	21	22	23	24	25	26
27	28	29	30	31		

U-boat fears grow in North Atlantic

North Atlantic, 22 September
The Royal Navy is anxious about the growing U-boat menace in the Atlantic. Merchant convoys carrying essential supplies from the USA are obvious, and vulnerable, targets: convoy HX-72, for instance, has lost 12 ships in the last two days. The U-boat threat is not confined to merchant shipping; last month an evacuee ship, the *Volendam*, was torpedoed. All lives were saved, but on 17 September 77 children sailing to Canada were among 325 who died when a U-boat sank the *City of Benares*.

Edinburgh station's German spy drama

Edinburgh, 30 September
A dramatic arrest was made at the left-luggage office at Waverley station here tonight of a German agent who had earlier landed by seaplane on a remote beach in North-East Scotland. He was travelling under the name of Werner Walti, with two accomplices, Karl Drucke and Vera Erikson, who were arrested at another station.

The suitcase Walti had deposited was water-stained and proved to contain a transmitter. When he returned to claim it, a detective superintendent disguised as a porter grabbed his wrist as he reached for his pistol.

France's Jews face harsh Nazi laws

France, 30 September
The Nazi noose is starting to tighten around the neck of the Jewish community here. Last month, Marshal Petain repealed France's law forbidding the incitement of racial hatred. This month, Jews were ordered to carry special identity cards and their shopkeepers have to put up notices in their windows saying "Jewish business". Today, the *Reich* Chief Security Office set up a special section in Paris under orders from Adolf Eichmann in Berlin. It will register France's entire Jewish population (→ 3).

1. China: The Nationalist 89th Army attacks Chen Yi's Communist New Fourth Army at Taixing on the Yangtse.

1. China: Weihaiwei is occupied by the Japanese (→ 29).

1. Finland: The government agrees to give Germany sole rights to Finnish nickel exports in exchange for arms.

1. Poland: Germany starts Operation *Otto* to improve road and rail links to the USSR using slave labour.

2. Mediterranean: The Royal Navy completes a sweep of the eastern Mediterranean, during which additional forces were landed on Malta; today the British destroyers *Hasty* and *Havock* sank an Italian submarine (→ 11).

3. Warsaw: All Jews are ordered to move into the Jewish district (→ 16).

3. Britain: Chamberlain resigns on grounds of ill health; Kingsley Wood and Ernest Bevin join the war cabinet (→ 19/11).

3. Vichy France: Not under German pressure, the regime bans Jews from public employment and the army (→ 7).

3. Europe: Seven RAF bombers make daylight raids on Rotterdam, Dunkirk and Cherbourg; last night 81 bombed targets in Germany, Eindhoven airfield and the Channel ports.

4. Britain: Sir Charles Portal is chosen to be Chief of the Air Staff, with effect from 24 October, to replace Sir Cyril Newall, who has been appointed governor of New Zealand. Air Marshal Sir Richard Peirse is named Portal's successor as C-in-C Bomber Command.

4. London: Churchill asks Roosevelt to send US ships to help to defend Singapore, a British colony (→ 14/11).

5. Britain: The lord mayor of London's Air Raid Relief Fund has raised £5 million.

5. Tokyo: Japan's prime minister, Prince Konoye, warns that war with the US is inevitable if the US goes on seeing the Axis as hostile (→ 7).

Italy doubts Fuhrer's boasts of victory

Fascist summit: Mussolini, Hitler and Ciano confer in an armoured train.

Brenner Pass, 4 October
"The war is won," Hitler told Mussolini today when the two dictators met for a three-hour exchange of views in an armoured train – a gift from the Fuhrer to the Duce – at the Brenner Pass. The British people were under an "inhuman strain" and, the Fuhrer claimed, it was only a question of time before they cracked. Hitler failed to mention that he had lost over 400 aircraft over Britain in seven weeks and had decided to abandon daylight raids.

In Berlin, a foreign office spokesman told neutral correspondents that the principal subject discussed by the two leaders and their foreign ministers may have been an appeal to the British to call off the war. However, the Italians were quick to note that Hitler no longer talks about invading Britain.

Count Ciano, the Italian foreign minister, noted in his diary that this obvious setback for their Axis partner put Mussolini in an exceptionally good mood. "Rarely have I seen the Duce in such good humour," Ciano comments. Back in Rome, Ciano seems to have organized a briefing for the press. *Il Popolo di Roma*, commenting on the Brenner talks, speaks of a long war in prospect and says Hitler's plans for invading Britain have failed at least for this year (→ 12).

Advertising and the war: an armoured car boosts Dunlop.

Another commercial break: this time for the heroes of the RAF.

Londoners go down Tube

Cheek by jowl but sound asleep: Londoners bed down on Piccadilly station.

Imperial strength adds to British muscle in East African battles against Italians

United by a common cause: a poster celebrates Commonwealth troops.

London, 2 October

There are New Zealand troops in Palestine, Australians in Egypt, South Africans in Kenya, Canadians in Britain and the Caribbean, and Indian troops in Singapore; Malta is raising its own regiment, and there is even a "Bikaner Camel Corps", the private army of an Indian prince, in the Middle East.

But nowhere are the benefits of Britain's Empire more apparent than in East Africa, where – save for a mere half a dozen battalions – the entire theatre of war is manned by Imperial troops. To the indigenous Sudan Defence Force, Somali Camel Corps and Kenyan King's African Rifles have been added troops from India, South Africa, Uganda, Tanganyika, Rhodesia and West Africa. Virtually all the logistical support for the war effort in Sudan comes from India, and that for the war effort in Kenya from South Africa, whose prime minister, General Jan Christian Smuts, is the effective continental warlord, playing the same role in Africa as his friend and former Boer War adversary, Winston Churchill, plays in Britain.

London, 3 October

Nobody invited Londoners to use the Tube stations as shelters – they took them over for themselves. On the fifth night of the Blitz, the East Enders invaded Liverpool Street and other stations to get away from the ruin and the racket. They had no Anderson shelters because they had no gardens to put them in. They mistrusted the brick street shelters as dank death-traps. Many of them huddled in warehouses under railway arches, in church crypts or cellars. Underground stations offered deep protection and – almost as important – comparative peace after sleepless weeks.

They bought the cheapest penny-ha'penny tickets and rode from station to station, looking for spaces to camp on the platforms. The authorities gave way and now there are queues outside the stations from early afternoon to be first for the best pitches at the back of the platforms. Along the front edges spaces two yards deep are left for passengers until 7.30pm. After that, one yard is left clear. When the trains stop at 10.30pm the current is switched off and people bed down between the rails. The Aldwych branch line and a tunnel at Liverpool Street are now permanent shelters for over 10,000 people. Altogether some 177,000 people spend the night at 79 different stations. Piccadilly Circus station attracts 5,000, many latecomers having to sleep on the escalators.

Herbert Morrison, who becomes home secretary and minister of home security today, is urged to "Go to it, Herbert" by the *Daily Herald*, which talks of Londoners "seething with resentment" at the inadequate provision for them. He plans to instal a million bunks and sanitation in shelters and Tubes.

A New Zealand soldier doing his bit for the Middle East Allied forces in Egypt finds squatting Arab-style presents just a few problems.

1940
October

Su	Mo	Tu	We	Th	Fr	Sa
		1	2	3	4	5
6	7	8	9	10	11	12
13	14	15	16	17	18	19
20	21	22	23	24	25	26
27	28	29	30	31		

7. South-East England: After small-scale raids yesterday, the region has suffered only scattered attacks during the night.

7. Vichy France: Algerian Jews are deprived of their French citizenship (→ 14).

7. Washington: The Japanese ambassador, Kensuke Horinouchi, warns the USA that the embargo on scrap metal exports "cannot fail to be regarded as directed against Japan and, as such, an unfriendly act" (→ 8).

8. Westminster: Churchill reports that civilian deaths from air raids, at one time reaching 6,000 a week, have halved.

8. USA: The government advises US citizens in the Far East to leave (→ 14).

9. Germany: One hundred and eight RAF bombers raid targets including the battleship *Tirpitz* in dry dock at the port of Wilhelmshaven.

9. London: A bomb falls on St Paul's Cathedral in the early morning, exploding inside the roof and severely damaging the High Altar.→

10. Luxemburg: A German-run plebiscite shows that 97 per cent of the population opposes Nazi occupation of the country.

10. France: The Royal Navy bombards German shipping at Cherbourg.

11. Australia: General election results, giving Robert Menzies another term as prime minister, are announced.

11. Britain: German raiders bomb Liverpool, sinking four ships in the port.

11. Vichy France: Petain tells Frenchmen that they must abandon traditional ideas of who is their ally and who their foe.

12. Dayton, Ohio: President Roosevelt rejects appeasement, and promises to defend America and its seas against enemy aggression (→ 30).

12. Germany: Hitler postpones the invasion of Britain to April 1941.

German army occupies oil-rich Roumania

Bucharest, 7 October

The Axis Powers have marched into Roumania. Two divisions of German troops, totalling 30,000 men, along with token Italian units today passed through Hungary to take control of the oilfields and the harbours from which the oil is shipped. The Germans claim that their soldiers have been sent to Roumania "in accordance with an agreement with the Roumanian government for training and reorganizing the Roumanian army with all the equipment essential for modern warfare". In another announcement, however, the Germans claim that their action was taken to protect Roumania from British plans to sabotage the oilfields. Certainly the oilfields, developed largely by British capital, are the prime reason for the invasion.

Last week the government of the dictator Ion Antonescu arrested British officials on allegations that they were plotting to set fire to the oilfields. Some of these officials have been subjected to ill-treatment. It is apparent that the entry of the Germans has been made with

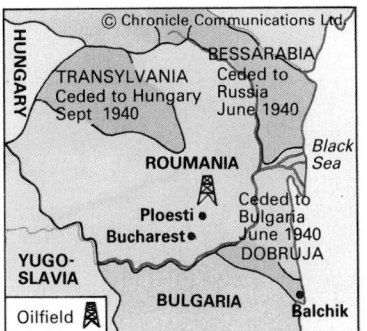

the consent and co-operation of the Antonescu regime. Barracks in the capital have been evacuated by the Roumanian army to make way for the Germans. An expeditionary force GHQ has been set up and contact established with the Roumanian General Staff.

The invasion is seen as one of the first-fruits of the meeting between Hitler and Mussolini at the Brenner Pass last Friday. There is no doubt that it was undertaken to ensure the supply of Roumanian oil to the Axis, which is cut off from Middle Eastern sources. At this stage there is little Britain can do against this latest example of Nazi expansion.

HMS "Ajax" sinks three Italian warships

Mediterranean, 11 October

The Mediterranean may be "Italy's boating lake" to a boastful Mussolini – but the Duce has not reckoned with the Royal Navy. In a short and brutal confrontation 80 miles (128 km) south of Sicily, HMS *Ajax*, the veteran of last year's *Graf Spee* encounter, sank three Italian naval vessels.

Ajax was taking part in a massive 3,000-mile sweep of the eastern and central Mediterranean when contact was made. Her six-inch guns made short work of two torpedo boats which sank immediately, a third making off at speed.

In a later engagement with an Italian squadron, *Ajax* crippled a destroyer, the 1,620-ton *Artigliere*, which was found the following morning and sunk by shellfire from HMS *York* after her crew had abandoned ship. Radio signals were transmitted on Italian frequencies giving the position of survivors, and a Sunderland flying boat guided an Italian hospital ship to the scene (→ 20).

The "York" sinks the "Artigliere".

Nationalist fervour ends party politics

Tokyo, 7 October

Japan is to become a one-party state with the inauguration next week of the ultra-nationalistic Imperial Rule Assistance Association, which will replace all existing political parties. The two leading mainstream parties, *Rikken Seiyukai* and *Rikken Minseito*, which dominate Japan's parliament, will be voluntarily dissolved.

The new organization, the brain-child of the premier, Prince Konoye, is intended to capitalize on the growing patriotic fervour among the Japanese and mobilize mass political support for land-hungry Japan's plans to expand its territorial borders in China and south-east Asia.

The IRAA, with offices in every prefecture, will mirror precisely Japan's current legislative structure. Discussions on the IRAA began in July, with moderates and nationalists battling over how closely it would imitate the totalitarian aspects of Europe's Nazi and Communist parties.

Churchill elected Tory Party leader

Britain, 9 October

Winston Churchill was this afternoon elected as Tory Party leader in succession to Neville Chamberlain who retired from the government last week for health reasons. The decision – taken at a private party meeting – was reported to have been unanimous.

Mr Chamberlain had continued as Tory leader after relinquishing the premiership. Mr Churchill had many enemies in the party before the outbreak of war, and there was an abortive attempt by party establishment figures this morning to appoint formally a deputy leader "to keep an eye on the boss".

After his election Mr Churchill, who knew what had been going on, referred obliquely to his past differences with the party – sometimes while a member of it and sometimes not. "Varying opinions are entertained about my career," he said with a grin. "But I think I can call myself a Tory."

1940

October

Su	Mo	Tu	We	Th	Fr	Sa
		1	2	3	4	5
6	7	8	9	10	11	12
13	14	15	16	17	18	19
20	21	22	23	24	25	26
27	28	29	30	31		

US pilots join RAF "Eagle Squadron"

London, 9 October
The accents of Ohio, New York and Texas are to be heard in an RAF mess these days as American citizens learn to fly for freedom. Although their homeland is neutral, these US idealists argue that they are defending America as well as Britain by joining a unique, all-American team known as the Eagle Squadron. Its leader, Squadron-Leader W E Taylor, left the Marine Corps Reserve to join.

There is a good historical precedent for the Eagles. During the Great War, 180 Americans switched from the French Foreign Legion, after service in the trenches, to fly with the Lafayette Squadron. They shot down 199 enemy aircraft.

Myra Hess plays on at National Gallery

Myra Hess plays on undaunted.

London, 12 October
The National Gallery was hit by a bomb today, but Myra Hess carried on with her Gallery Concerts as she has been doing for the past year. Against the bare walls of the central galleries (the pictures are safe in a Welsh slate quarry), lunch-time chamber music concerts are given to 1,500 people, who pay a shilling (5p/20¢) a head to hear pianists like Solomon and Denis Matthews as well as Myra Hess's Bach and Beethoven. Much of the music – like the bomb damage – is German.

It's business as usual for blitzed London

A milkman does his rounds in shattered London: milk is still not rationed.

London, 12 October
With a hole through the roof and its altar shattered, St Paul's carries on with its services. Parliament and the Law Courts, both damaged, are still sitting. St Thomas's, badly smashed, goes on operating. So does the Stock Exchange. In the early days everything stopped with the "Alert" – now ministries, post offices, banks and offices employ roof spotters and only take shelter when a raid is imminent. At night only 40 per cent of London's population take shelter; the rest take their chance at home. West End shops sweep up their broken plate glass windows and try to stay open.

Swan and Edgar and other stores and offices have made their basements into shelters, for which the public queues at night. West End hotels such as the Dorchester and the Savoy offer their dinner-dance guests basement beds for the night and are always crowded. Some cinemas stay open until the "All Clear". Many people take blankets and see the programme round again, or stand-by films, before settling down beneath the circle.

There are few absentees. Office workers pick their way over the rubble and work by candlelight. Shops bear defiant signs – "More Open Than Usual".

Homeless but not downhearted: three generations on the move in London.

Donitz steps up U-boat convoy war

North Atlantic, 19 October

Royal Navy commanders were to-night counting the cost of Admiral Donitz's escalation of the U-boat war in the Atlantic. German submarines are now ordered to hunt in "wolfpacks" of up to a dozen boats. One pack has sunk over 30 ships from two convoys and damaged another in the last two days.

The slaughter began when Lieutenant Heinrich Bleichrodt in U48 spotted a slow convoy, SC-7, escorted by two sloops and a corvette. Without waiting for the rest of the pack to catch up, Bleichrodt attacked and sank two merchant ships. He was then chased by a Sunderland flying boat and a sloop.

After dark last night he was joined by five other pack members. They struck together with devastating effectiveness, sinking 15 ships in six hours. Tragically, the escorts could do little to help as they floundered around picking up survivors.

By this time U48 and two others had used up all their torpedoes and headed for home. The others stayed to pick off some of the stragglers and to look for new prey. The pack leader was Gunther Prien, called the "Bull of Scapa Flow" in recognition of his daring *sortie* into the home of the British fleet. He homed in on the 49-ship convoy HX-79.

Cautiously Prien waited for three other submarines to join him, by which time the convoy had an escort of two destroyers, four corvettes, three trawlers and a Dutch submarine. Again Prien waited and then after nightfall struck suddenly with his full force. Within hours he had hit six ships and his colleagues had hit seven – 12 sank. In the chaos the defending forces mistook the Dutch boat 014 for a German submarine and attacked it twice.

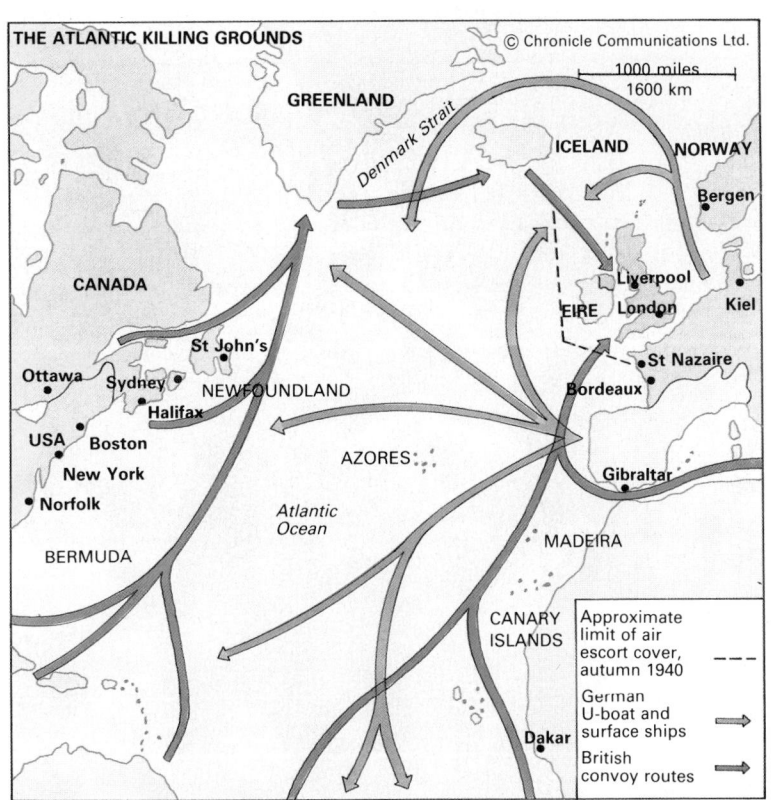

THE ATLANTIC KILLING GROUNDS © Chronicle Communications Ltd.

Approximate limit of air escort cover, autumn 1940 – – –

German U-boat and surface ships →

British convoy routes →

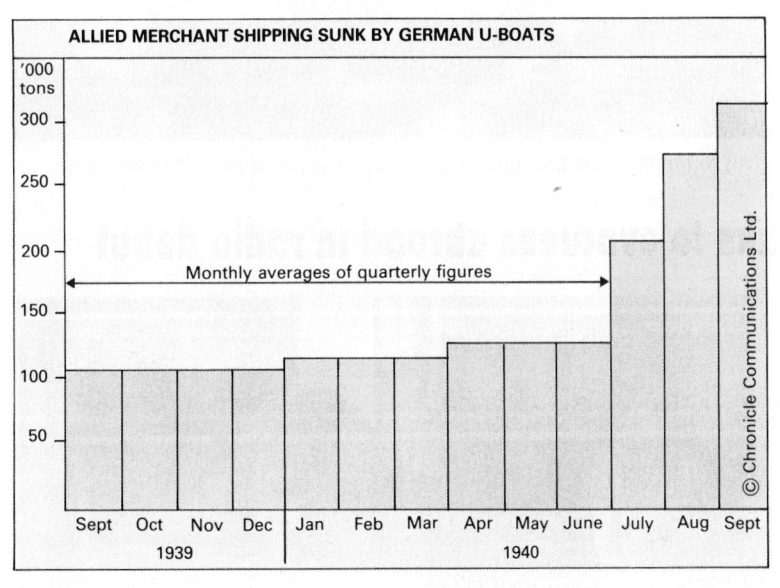

ALLIED MERCHANT SHIPPING SUNK BY GERMAN U-BOATS

Monthly averages of quarterly figures

© Chronicle Communications Ltd.

Britain opens route to China, defying Japanese threats

Kunming, China, 18 October

The first lorries to bring war supplies along the re-opened Burma Road – closed three months ago by agreement between Japan and Britain – arrived here this evening from Lashio. Drivers reported an uneventful journey free from the air attacks threatened by Japan against the Chinese section of the road.

Sixty lorries arrived in the first convoy and another 2,000 – given a banquet send-off in Burma – are expected tomorrow. Waiting at Rangoon are another 500,000 tons of war supplies, including planes and munitions. On the return leg the lorries will carry tungsten, wood, tin, oil and pig bristles for export to the US (→ 29).

"Posthumous" VC is alive and well

London, 15 October

Lieutenant (Acting Captain) Eric Charles Twelves Wilson of the East Surrey Regiment, reported killed and awarded a VC posthumously last Saturday, is alive and a prisoner of war. The war office has informed his parents, the Reverend Cyril and Mrs Wilson of Hunsdon Rectory near Ware, Hertfordshire.

Wilson was awarded his VC, the 12th of the war, for outstanding bravery while attached to the Somaliland Camel Corps. Between 11 and 15 August he kept a machine-gun post on Observation Hill in action despite being wounded and suffering from malaria. His mother said tonight that she had never given up hope.

Rumours of the invasion that never was

Britain, 16 October

Despite official denials, rumours persist that the Germans attempted an invasion in the late summer and perished disastrously. Large numbers of dead Germans are believed to have been washed ashore on the south coast between the Isle of Wight (where the "invasion" was aimed) and Cornwall. One story is that the corpses were charred, because the sea was set on fire.

A further theory is that the Germans held an ill-fated rehearsal of the invasion and that the barges were sunk in storms. No-one has seen the bodies, but that is explained by the authorities concealing them. In fact, any bodies washed up are of German airmen shot down.

Italian air raiders go far, but miss target

Rome, 19 October

Four Italian aircraft have made an audacious long-range attack on the British oil refinery at Bahrain, in the Gulf. The SM82 bombers were in the air for more than 15 hours, flying 3,000 miles (4,800 kilometres) from Rhodes in the Mediterranean to Massawa, in Eritrea, on a triangular route whose most easterly point was Bahrain island. Each aircraft dropped 66 30-pound bombs on the complex. Pilots say: "We saw fires for hundreds of miles as we left the area."

This does not match British claims that there was no damage. A refinery engineer asserted that safety flares were turned up to simulate uncontrolled fires.

Su	Mo	Tu	We	Th	Fr	Sa
		1	2	3	4	5
6	7	8	9	10	11	12
13	14	15	16	17	18	19
20	21	22	23	24	25	26
27	28	29	30	31		

City children flee the Blitz once again

London, 18 October

A second evacuation of the half a million children in the London area is under way. They are leaving at the rate of 2,000 a day in small parties under a "trickle" evacuation scheme. Over 20,000 left in September. A further 89,000 mothers and young children are being assisted to leave this month.

When the heavy bombing began on 7 September, thousands of East Enders fled from the devastation. Some 5,000 trekked to Epping Forest and camped there. Others took lorries to the Kent hopfields where they bedded down on straw in the hop-pickers' huts. About 10,000 Londoners and local people are now living in the Chislehurst caves in Kent. They are equipped with electric light and a canteen and sick bay. Families have taken over individual caves and installed beds and furniture.

Some 25,000 went to Paddington and took trains to places such as Reading, Basingstoke and Oxford, which alone billeted 15,000 refugees. Most of these "trekkers" have now returned. East Enders clearly hate leaving their familiar neighbourhoods or being placed in West End billets – even when they are bombed out.

Eyes to the sky: London children are being evacuated for the second time.

Princess Elizabeth speaks to evacuees abroad in radio debut

London, 13 October

The 13,000 children evacuated overseas to the Dominions and the United States heard a message from home tonight delivered by Princess Elizabeth. In her first broadcast, at the age of 14, her coolness and resemblance in voice to her mother, the queen, was striking.

"My sister, Margaret Rose, and I feel so much for you as we know from experience what it means to be away from those we love most of all," said the princess. "We children at home are full of cheerfulness and courage and are trying to bear our own share of the danger and sadness of war ... My sister is by my side and we are going to say goodnight to you – come on, Margaret. Good night and good luck to you."

The queen has decided that the princesses should not go to Canada.

Princess Elizabeth speaks to the children of Britain, Margaret at her side.

20. Egypt: Italian planes bomb Cairo for the first time.

20. Germany: Helmuth James, Count von Moltke, writes a manifesto for the liberal resistance group known as "The Kreisau Circle" after his estate; it envisages a democratic post-Nazi Germany.

20. Gibraltar: Royal Navy destroyers sink Italian submarines off the colony.

21. London: Churchill broadcasts to the French people, calling for their help against "Hitler and Hitlerism".

21. Red Sea: A British convoy repels an Italian attack, sinking the destroyer *Francesco Nullo*.

21. Liverpool: The city suffers its 200th air raid.

21. Britain: Eggs go up in price to 4/- (20p/80¢) a dozen, and purchase tax on all goods except food and children's clothes comes into operation.

22. Montoire, France: Hitler discusses France's role in Europe's "new order" with the vice-premier, Pierre Laval (→ 26).

22. Rhineland: Five thousand German Jews are deported to camps in France.

23. Hendaye, France: Hitler fails to persuade Spain's General Franco to join the Axis or to let Germany attack Gibraltar through Spain.→

25. Britain: The Italian expeditionary air corps, based in Belgium, mounts its first attack on the port of Harwich.

25. Germany: RAF bombers raid Berlin and heavily attack Hamburg.

26. Rome: With 162,000 Italian troops massed on the Albanian border, Italy accuses Greece of attacking Albania (→ 28).

26. Atlantic: The liner *Empress of Britain*, the flagship of the Canadian Pacific fleet, is damaged by bombs off Ireland.→

26. Vichy France: It is announced that Petain and Hitler have agreed on principles of cooperation (→ 30).

No trains today: St Pancras station after the German bombing raid.

Britain frees Belgian leaders from Spain

London, 25 October
The Belgian prime minister, Hubert Pierlot, and his foreign minister, Paul-Henri Spaak, have arrived in London after fleeing from Vichy France and escaping from arrest in Spain.

After the armistice, Pierlot and Spaak stayed on in France to maintain diplomatic links with the Vichy regime. But Vichy, under German orders, broke off relations. The two Belgians spent three nights in a field between the French and Spanish borders before being admitted to Spain, there to find themselves placed under arrest.

Their chance for freedom came on 18 October. Spanish guards, who had been ordered to keep the Belgians under strict surveillance in a Barcelona hotel, slipped up when they left their prisoners – who had promised faithfully not to try to escape – in order to watch an important football match. As soon as the game started, Spaak and Pierlot sneaked out of the hotel in a van supplied by the Belgian consulate. For 24 hours they hid underneath the driver's seat; finally, exhausted but relieved, they arrived at Lisbon. Yesterday a British seaplane took them to Bournemouth. They will now start to coordinate Belgian efforts to resist the Nazi occupation and, more importantly, to help the British war machine.

Railways next target for bombardment

London, 26 October
Transport in London has taken a hammering as the *Luftwaffe* keeps up its nightly attacks on the capital. Railways in particular have been hard hit, not just at the docks but with main-line stations regularly bombed. This week it was the turn of St Pancras station, but the forecourt of Victoria station has also been badly damaged.

For travellers train services, especially on the Southern Railway, often terminate in the suburbs, and commuters face new puzzles every day in finding "passable" routes to the office. Unexploded bombs closing many streets add to the frustration by diverting bus routes. So many buses and tramcars have been bombed that Londoners see the unfamiliar colours of buses borrowed from as far away as Aberdeen and Exeter on their streets.

The Underground has also been interrupted by bombs. Four stations have been hit, the worst being Balham, where 600 people sheltering were deluged with a river of sludge when the road and water mains above caved in, suffocating 64 of them.

The Belgians Hubert Pierlot and Paul-Henri Spaak, safe in London.

Britain signs secret arms deal with USA

London, 26 October
Britain and the USA have concluded a secret arms deal which should boost the British effort to turn the tide against Hitler, probably in 1942. Under the deal, signed two days ago and described by Churchill as "splendid", the USA promises to equip and maintain ten British divisions with weapons currently under production. Churchill received more good news today when he was told that US military supplies destined for Britain include 250 aircraft engines, 2.5 million tons of explosives, 78 million cartridges for the Thompson machine gun and 78 million rounds of rifle ammunition (→ 20/11).

German bombers cripple Atlantic liner

North Atlantic, 26 October
The 42,348-ton *Empress of Britain*, Canadian Pacific's flagship which brought the king and queen back from their Canadian tour, was crippled today by German bombers 150 miles off the Irish coast. She is the latest, and the largest, victim of the Germans' stepped-up campaign against British shipping in the Atlantic. The vessel is now limping back to port under the constant threat of renewed German attack, especially from U-boats (→ 28).

"Empress of Britain" after being bombed: the threat of attack still exists.

MPs slam Wells's unpatriotic speech

London, 23 October
MPs protested today at critical comments by the author H G Wells, now lecturing in America, about British politicians and generals, whom he has also criticized in the *Sunday Pictorial* magazine. The government was asked why he had been allowed to go abroad to denigrate his country at its hour of peril. Emanuel Shinwell, a Labour MP, deplored Wells's speech but said that we were fighting for the right of free expression. Mr Peake, the parliamentary under-secretary at the home office, said that Britain needed all the dollars it could earn; an American senator has said that Wells is harming Britain's cause. ▷

Petain and Franco rebuff Hitler's pleas

All smiles as Franco greets Hitler: no hint of the rejections to come.

Berlin, 24 October

A frustrated and furious Hitler has returned to Germany after journeying across France aboard his armoured train *Amerika* in a bid to persuade Franco and Petain to help him against Britain.

At Montoire in German-occupied territory, he told Petain that he wanted "closer collaboration" from him in the fight against Britain. But though compliance could have secured the release of 1.5 million French prisoners, Petain said he could not go to war against Britain. Hitler had to be satisfied with a piece of paper which said that France wished to see England defeated "as soon as possible".

The slippery customer, however, was Franco, whom Hitler had met at Hendaye on the Spanish border the previous day. Hitler and Mussolini had helped him win the Spanish Civil War, but now, when Hitler asked him to attack Gibraltar with the help of German experts, Franco responded loftily that Spanish honour required Gibraltar to be taken by Spaniards alone. The two dictators argued in vain for nine hours. "Rather than go through that again," Hitler said afterwards, "I'd have my teeth pulled out" (→ 26).

Serenaded amid a sea of "swastikas", Berlin children set off for safer parts until the RAF turns its fury on a target other than their city.

1940
October

Su	Mo	Tu	We	Th	Fr	Sa
		1	2	3	4	5
6	7	8	9	10	11	12
13	14	15	16	17	18	19
20	21	22	23	24	25	26
27	28	29	30	31		

27. Africa: Free French forces under General de Larminat occupy Lambarene in Gabon (French Equatorial Africa).→

27. Europe: In a night of widespread bombing, the RAF successfully targets the key Skoda arms plant at Plzen [*Pilsen*] in Czechoslovakia.

28. Atlantic: The German submarine U32 torpedoes and sinks the damaged Canadian liner *Empress of Britain*.

28. Vichy France: Laval is appointed foreign minister.

28. Florence: Hitler conceals his fury at news of the Italian invasion of Greece and pledges military support if Mussolini requires it.→

28. Khartoum: The British secretary of state for war, Anthony Eden, the C-in-C Middle East, General Sir Archibald Wavell, the South African premier, General Jan Smuts, and the Ethiopian Emperor Haile Selassie meet to try to reconcile their different war aims in Africa.

29. Mediterranean: The Royal Navy attacks the Dodecanese island of Stampalia (→ 31).

29. Britain: A new type of German mine, set off by the noise of a ship, is discovered near Porthcawl.

30. North Atlantic: Royal Navy destroyers sink a U-boat in the north-western approaches.

30. Gibraltar: An Italian attempt to attack British shipping in the harbour with "human torpedoes" is a failure.

30. Greece: Italy bombs Patras five times (→ 1/11).

31. Mediterranean: British troop reinforcements land on Crete (→ 11/11).

31. Britain: This month, 6,350 civilians have been killed and 8,700 injured by enemy action.

31. Germany: The Protestant cleric Dietrich Bonhoeffer, who is banned from preaching and teaching, this month issued a "confession" that the church has been "silent when it should have screamed, because the blood of the innocent cries to heaven".

French to cooperate with the Germans

Vichy, 30 October

Marshal Petain has called upon the French people to collaborate with Germany. This represents a major change from the originally announced purpose of Petain's government, which sought peace with Germany, not alliance, and results from a number of diplomatic moves. On 22 October Pierre Laval, the Vichy vice-premier, saw Hitler at Montoire, in occupied France. Later, Marshal Petain also met Hitler on his train at Montoire and agreed on collaboration (→ 11/11).

Vichy propaganda poster of Petain: "Do you know more than him about the problems of the hour?"

French colonies are wooed by de Gaulle

Brazzaville, 27 October

General de Gaulle has arrived in Brazzaville, the capital of French Equatorial Africa, and proclaimed the creation of a Council of Defence of the French Empire. He was welcomed by the governor, Felix Eboue, and huge crowds.

Most of French Equatorial Africa, with 12 million inhabitants, rallied to de Gaulle in late July after the arrival of emissaries sent from London led by General Leclerc. Attempts to rally French West Africa suffered a setback with de Gaulle's failure to capture Senegal from Vichy in September (→ 7/11).

Mussolini orders troops into Greece

Athens, 28 October

To the fury of Adolf Hitler, his Axis partner, Mussolini's army invaded Greece today. In the firm belief that they would meet little opposition from the dictator General Metaxas's forces, Italian tanks and infantry crossed from occupied Albania into the mountains of Epirus before dawn. Hitler heard the news on his train *Amerika* between Munich and Florence. When he arrived, the Italian leader was delighted to tell him, in German: "Fuhrer, we are on the march!"

Hitler was rather less enthusiastic, to say the least. Five days ago he failed to persuade General Franco to lead Spain into the war, and now, in his opinion, the Duce is making a critical strategic mistake. Hitler was convinced that the capture of Gibraltar, with assistance from Franco, and Italy's conquest of Egypt, especially the great British naval base at Alexandria, would ensure Britain's collapse.

Mussolini in his turn was convinced that the pro-German Metaxas – who has based his *Asfalia* secret police on Hitler's *Gestapo* and abolished most democratic institutions in his country – would succumb quickly and offer little resistance. The Duce did not reckon with Hellenic national integrity, however. Metaxas rejected the Itali-

Mounted Italian troops advancing on Greece from the Albanian borderlands.

an ultimatum – which he received in his bed from an Italian envoy at six o'clock this morning – an hour after Italian troops crossed the border.

Visconti Prasca, the Italian commander, has made what appears to be a serious mistake in not blocking the road to the north, thus allowing three newly-mobilizing Greek divisions to move quickly to the front. He is moving slowly, clearly not having learned from the *Blitzkrieg* tactics of German *Panzers*. And Greece is mobilizing quickly (→ 30).

China forces Japan to withdraw troops

Nanning, 29 October

Japan's strategy for seizing control of southern China suffered a major setback today as its troops were forced to withdraw south into Indochina after losing Nanning, the capital of Kwangsi, China's southern border province. The loss of Nanning, a key city on the Hanoi-Peking line, counterbalances Japan's recent gain in being allowed to station troops in French Indochina. During seven months of bitter fighting for Nanning both sides suffered heavy losses (→30/11).

Roosevelt promises "no foreign wars"

Washington, 30 October

President Roosevelt, fighting off a surge by his Republican opponent in the presidential election, promised in Boston last night: "I shall say it again and again and again: your boys are not going to be sent into any foreign wars."

As polls showed Wendell Willkie, the Republican candidate, cutting into his lead, the president has stressed his reluctance to lead America into war. A week ago in Philadelphia he attacked "the fantastic misstatement" that he had made secret alliances. Willkie has cut Roosevelt's lead in the polls to four points (→5/11).

Builders recalled from army to repair London's shattered homes

London, 31 October

The government is to release 5,000 building workers from the army to try to catch up with the urgent task of repairing bomb damage. In London 60,000 houses are uninhabitable, 130,000 less badly damaged, and 16,000 totally destroyed. Three-quarters of the houses in the East End area of Stepney are estimated to be wrecked.

So far only 7,000 people have been rehoused by local authorities, out of 250,000 who have been made homeless, at least temporarily. No more repair workers are to be called up until further notice. In the meantime, 5,000 men of the Pioneer Corps are clearing debris. London's "Rest Centres" are badly overcrowded, with 25,000 homeless people seeking shelter each night.

East London: the homeless gather their possessions, but where do they go now?

Worst week at sea since war started

North Atlantic, 29 October

Allied shipping losses this week totalled a massive 88,000 tons. This is eight times greater than the weekly average loss in the spring. Mines and bombings have played their part, but U-boats made the change.

German use of French ports, with direct access to the Atlantic, enables even the smaller boats to reach the trade routes, and the new policy of hunting in packs is taking a heavy toll. There are also more U-boats now that the Norwegian campaign is over, and numbers are being boosted still further by a crash building programme.

1940

November

Su	Mo	Tu	We	Th	Fr	Sa
					1	2
3	4	5	6	7	8	9
10	11	12	13	14	15	16
17	18	19	20	21	22	23
24	25	26	27	28	29	30

1. Greece: Italian forces reach the river Kalamas, near Epirus (→ 2).

1. France: General Karl-Heinrich von Stulpnagel is appointed head of the military regime in the occupied zone.

2. Greece: Italian raiders bomb Salonika, killing 200 civilians, but fail to reach the Corinth canal (→ 3).

2. Atlantic: The destroyer HMS *Antelope* sinks the U-boat U31 in the north-western approaches.

3. Greece: An RAF bomber squadron arrives to help to fight the Italians (→ 5).

3. Albania: Greek forces surround the Italian base at Koritsa (→ 4).

3. Atlantic: The U-boat U99 sinks British armed merchant cruisers *Laurentic* and *Patroclus* in the north-western approaches.

4. Albania: The Greek counter-attack starts, and reaches the Koritsa-Peratia road (→ 4).

5. Greece: Italian bombers raid Piraeus.→

6. Britain: A *Luftwaffe* bomber is brought down by a British radio beacon sending signals which convince the pilot that he is over France.

6. East Africa: Lieutenant-General William Slim leads an unsuccessful attack on the Italians at Gallabat.

7. Gabon, French Equatorial Africa: General Leclerc's Free French forces land near Libreville.

8. Munich: The RAF bombs the city, forcing Hitler to delay his traditional speech marking the anniversary of his attempted coup in 1923.

8. Roumania: 1,000 people are feared dead in an earthquake which has damaged oilfields.

8. Bass Strait: The *City of Rayville* is sunk by a mine, the first US merchant ship to be lost in the war.

9. France: The Germans start to expel 180,000 Frenchmen from Alsace-Lorraine, which they have annexed.

Landslide for Roosevelt

Washington, 5 November
Early this morning it became plain that President Roosevelt had won a third term in the White House. He was leading in states with a total of 427 electoral college votes, while the Republican, Wendell Willkie was ahead in states with a total of only 87 votes.

Shrugging off a strong late run by his Republican rival, Roosevelt is the first man in history to be elected president of the United States for a third time, and once again he has won by a landslide. The new vice-president is Henry A Wallace, the publisher of a farm newspaper.

With Roosevelt already carrying Ohio, which has 26 electoral votes, it is plain that in New York – the largest state, with 47 votes – Pennsylvania, the second (36), and Illinois, the third (29), the president's lead among big city voters in New York City, Philadelphia, Pittsburg and Chicago will outweigh the vote for Willkie in rural areas. And the consequences of Mr Roosevelt's electoral victory for the course of the war in Europe are incalculably great.

For the past year, while attempting to warn the American people about the dangers of fascism and the impossibility of isolationism, Mr Roosevelt has had to take very great care not to alienate potentially isolationist sentiment by seeming too eager to involve the United States in the war. Now he can be expected to move decisively to increase help for Britain.

No blackout in New York: crowds pack Times Square for the election results.

Chamberlain dies, dogged by failure of Munich mission

Chamberlain: misunderstood?

Britain, 9 November
Neville Chamberlain died tonight at the age of 71. It is now stated that he was already suffering from cancer of the stomach when he was forced out of the premiership six months ago during the political crisis over how to fight the war.

Mr Chamberlain's distinguished earlier career as an austere and clear-minded administrator is inevitably forgotten now in the controversy over his policy of appeasement of the European dictators – and in particular the 1938 "peace for our time" Munich agreement with Hitler. His friends insist that he bought precious time for rearmament and has been the most misunderstood statesman of the century. Mr Churchill said: "He acted in perfect sincerity according to his lights" (→ 14).

RAF bombs German armaments factory

Germany, 7 November
The RAF struck at the heart of the Geman war machine tonight in a bombing raid which put a torch to the Krupp armaments factory in the Ruhr. The complex was hit for four hours by successive waves of aircraft. After the first assault, flames 100 feet (91 metres) high were a beacon for follow-up bombers. Claims that these were decoy fires are rejected by aircrews.

Eire refuses to lend Britain naval bases

Dublin, 7 November
Despite Winston Churchill's anger, Eire will remain neutral and continue to refuse to allow the use of its ports as British bases, the prime minister, Eamon de Valera, told the *Dail* [parliament] today. He denied rumours that German submarines were being refuelled and re-provisioned in Eire.

"I say it is a lie," he said. "And I say further that is known to be a falsehood by the British government itself." In a speech last week, the British prime minister spoke of the handicap under which Britain was suffering as a result of being denied naval and air facilities in Eire. He described it as a "grievous burden which should never have been placed on our shoulders".

The use of Irish ports could extend the range of convoy escorts by several hundred miles, and the fact that Irish ships themselves are protected is being stressed in a major British propaganda campaign in the United States.

Greeks force Italian HQ to order retreat

Northern Greece, 9 November
Less than two weeks after crossing the Greek border in great strength, the Italian army is retreating in total disarray. The Italian commander, General Visconti Prasca, has been sacked and Mussolini's crack *Julia* alpine division routed with huge losses in men and equipment. The Italians have been taken completely by surprise by the speed and ferocity of the Greeks.

Six days after the Italian invasion, Greece's General Papagos ordered the first counter-attack. A small Greek force crossed the Albanian frontier and took Pissoderi, a mountain near the captured town of Koritsa. The main road out of Koritsa was cut by another Greek force. With their superior knowledge of the terrain, the tough and well-trained Greeks have abandoned the valleys and taken to the mountains from whence they can infiltrate enemy positions.

Fighting at an altitude of over 5,000 feet (1,524 metres) – in the most severe winter for years – Papagos's single division has proved more than a match for the numerically superior Italians whose armour is confined to the lower ground. Italian tanks are being knocked out by anti-tank weapons dropped by the RAF.

The Italians have paid the penalty for having allowed the Greeks to hold the mountainous centre of the front. The Julia division found itself trapped. Five thousand men have surrendered, and the Greeks are claiming a further 25,000 dead and seriously wounded (→ 10).

German attack sinks the "Jervis Bay"

The battleship "Admiral Scheer".

North Atlantic, 5 November
The armed merchant cruiser HMS *Jervis Bay*, a converted liner of the Aberdeen Commonwealth Line, sank today after a heroic battle. She was the sole escort of convoy HX-84, and the 37 ships were half way out from Canada when the German pocket battleship *Admiral Scheer* attacked. Captain Fogarty Fegen realised that his ship had no chance against the battleship's firepower, but told the convoy to scatter under a smokescreen. He took on the *Admiral Scheer* head on. His guns could not even reach the German ship, but he fought on with decks ablaze. Enough time was gained to save all the convoy except five small ships.

First quiet night in London for months

London, 4 November
Last night, Sunday, the sirens failed to sound in London. It was the first night without a raid since the Blitz began on 7 September, and it was an unnaturally quiet weekend; the All Clear went before midnight on Saturday. As a result, Londoners found it hard to sleep. They miss the noise. When the sirens have not gone by 6.30pm, people ask: "What's happened to Jerry?"

Woman jailed for helping Haw-Haw

London, 7 November
Anna Wolkoff, the daughter of a former Russian naval attache in London, has been jailed for ten years for offences under the Official Secrets Act and the Defence Regulations. Mr Justice Tucker said that she had tried to send a coded letter to Lord Haw-Haw, "a traitor who broadcasts from Germany for the purpose of weakening the war effort of this country".

Women in the services: tracking enemy targets, but men still fire the bullets

Jaunty propaganda leaves a lot of Britain's women out in the cold.

The lucky ones? ATS women aim "ack-ack" guns: men fire them.

Britain, 9 November
Despite gallant propaganda about plucky Land Girls and "Miss England" being "busier than ever", more British women are now out of work than before the war. Some women are finding work with the services, but even here their contribution to the war effort is less dramatic than recruiting posters imply.

Each of the three services has a branch or an organization for women – the Auxiliary Territorial Service (ATS) is the women's branch of the army, the Wrens work alongside the Royal Navy, and the WAAFs are linked to the currently glamorous RAF. Many of their number do indeed play crucial roles. In RDF [radar] stations they help to plot enemy aircraft movements, for instance, and women can also be found in anti-aircraft batteries and naval command centres. But they are always in noncombatant roles; women may track the targets, but men fire the guns.

Lack of direct involvement is by no means the only complaint amongst women who answered the patriotic call to duty – and who overcame parental fears about presumed moral dangers. Many of those who have signed up have been dismayed by the menial tasks which they are asked to perform. Though women can be trained to do anything which does not make them into combatants, in practice cooking and cleaning are the commonest assignments.

Outside the services there are still vast numbers of women who were made redundant last autumn by non-essential industries who are still without jobs. Earlier this year a protest was made to parliament by the Federation of Business and Professional Women. More than half of the nearly 7,000 women registered with them were unemployed. The government has so far resisted any coordinated redirection of redundant women into war work. But pressure is growing for some form of intervention, possibly even compulsory female mobilization, an unprecedented step.

Women in control of searchlights and sound locators in the Blitz.

1940

November

Su	Mo	Tu	We	Th	Fr	Sa
					1	2
3	4	5	6	7	8	9
10	11	12	13	14	15	16
17	18	19	20	21	22	23
24	25	26	27	28	29	30

10. Albania: General Soddu replaces General Prasca as the head of the Italian attack on Greece (→ 16).

11. Dachau: Fifty-five Polish intellectuals are executed in the camp's first official mass execution.

11. Paris: German guards violently break up a patriotic demonstration by students at the *Arc de Triomphe*.

11. Britain: Six out of 50 Italian planes are shot down in an abortive raid on the Thames Estuary.

11. Vichy France: Jean Moulin, the uncooperative prefect of the Eure-et-Loire district, is sacked by the authorities (→ 23).

12. Berlin: A displeased Hitler evades Molotov's questions about the role of Russia in the future of Europe (→ 13).

12. Berlin: Hitler issues his 18th war directive, ordering political measures to bring Spain into the war and death by slow strangulation for Britain.

13. Berlin: Hitler orders Goering to prepare the *Luftwaffe* for an invasion of Russia next May (→ 29).

13. Pacific: The Dutch East Indies agrees to supply Japan with nearly two million tons of oil a year.

14. Singapore: Air Marshal Sir Robert Brooke-Popham arrives as C-in-C Allied Forces in the Far East.

14. London: Neville Chamberlain's funeral is held at Westminster Abbey.

15. Warsaw: The Jewish ghetto, with 400,000 inhabitants, is sealed off from the rest of the city (→ 19).

16. Greece: 3,500 British military personnel have been ferried from Alexandria to Piraeus (→ 18).

16. Coventry: The home secretary, Herbert Morrison, escorts King George VI through the ruins of the city.

16. Atlantic: The British submarine *Swordfish* is sunk off Ushant, off the Brittany coast.

Coventry is razed to the ground

Coventry, 15 November

German bombers tore the heart out of Coventry last night. The cathedral was turned into a mound of smoking rubble, and many factories making munitions, engines for tanks and aircraft and other supplies for the war effort were badly damaged. In all, 568 people died and 863 were seriously hurt. "Coventry is finished," said one survivor.

The citizens are in a daze. Many have fled from the shattered remains of this once-beautiful mediaeval city. The army wants to impose martial law until essential services are restored. There is no water supply or transport. There are no telephones. Pubs and shops which survived remain shut. The air is still warm from the fire which raged through the city centre. Daylight is obscured by a pall of sooty fog.

The raid shows the terrible power of a concentrated attack on a small, densely-populated area. There were 449 bombers, led by the specialized pathfinders of KG100 Squadron, which arrived in three streams over Lincolnshire, Portland and Dungeness. The first bombs, 10,224 incendiaries and 48 small high-explosive devices, were dropped by 13 He111 planes of KG100 at 7.20pm. They started fires which acted as beacons for the main force. Land mines, high explosive and incendiary bombs came crashing down. Groups of bombers were assigned to particular factories, but the factories are situated in residential areas and ordinary homes took the brunt of the bombing. It is estimated that 60,000 out of the city's 75,000 buildings have been damaged, among them 111 factories, 600 shops, 28 hotels, 121 offices and all the city's railway lines.

The city's defences were ineffectual. Coventry had 40 anti-aircraft guns, reinforced by light guns and mobile batteries, and 120 *sorties* were flown by night fighters ranging from obsolete Gladiator biplanes to Beaufighters carrying experimental airborne RDF. But the Germans lost only one of the 450 bombers that set out for Coventry, and that probably by accident. The tragedy of the Coventry raid is that it was known that the Germans were planning just such a raid against an industrial city.

The interrogation of prisoners and decoding of *Enigma* messages had even revealed its codename: "Moonlight Sonata". What were not known were the precise target and date of the raid. Even if they had been known, Churchill could have done nothing without revealing one of Britain's greatest secrets: that it has cracked Enigma.

The target was still unclear until 3pm, barely four hours before the first bombs fell, when the British Radio Counter-measures Organisation reported that the German *Knickebein* targeting beams were intersecting over Coventry.

Various counter-measures under the code name "Cold Water" were immediately put into operation. They included attacks on the airfields occupied by KG100, a precision attack on the *Knickebein* transmitters, an attack on a German city and maximum use of night fighters and anti-aircraft guns. But none of the measures could prevent the tragedy that befell Coventry.

The morning after the "Moonlight Sonata" sounded the death knell for Coventry, citizens walk through the rubble.

136

Coventry cathedral reduced to mounds of rubble

The morning after: bemused citizens eth their shattered cathedral. One small consolation is that its stained-glass windows had been removed.

⊳

British attack Italian fleet in Taranto

1940
November

Su	Mo	Tu	We	Th	Fr	Sa
					1	2
3	4	5	6	7	8	9
10	11	12	13	14	15	16
17	18	19	20	21	22	23
24	25	26	27	28	29	30

Malta, 11 November

Mussolini, whose forces are taking a humiliating battering in Greece, has a new worry tonight. The balance of maritime power in the Mediterranean has been changed at a stroke by a British air attack which disabled three Italian battleships in a few minutes. The target was the core of Mussolini's fleet tucked away in Taranto harbour, in southern Italy, surrounded by anti-aircraft batteries.

The attack, codenamed Operation Judgement, took place in bright moonlight. Twenty-one Swordfish of the Royal Navy's Fleet Air Arm flew from the carrier HMS *Illustrious*, after the carrier HMS *Eagle* was pulled out at the last moment.

The pathfinders were Swordfish which dropped flares. Immediately behind them came the torpedo carriers, swooping from 8,000 to 5,000 feet (2,438 to 1,524 metres) before making a perilous, gliding approach to only 20 feet (six metres) above water before releasing their torpedoes as cannon fire erupted around them. In the confined space of the harbour the torpedoes had a devastating impact. At least nine torpedoes struck their targets. In all, seven ships were severely damaged, including the battleships *Littorio*, *Conte di Cavour* and *Caio Duilio*. As this attack ended, a bomber which had been delayed on

A later painting: the view from a Fairey Swordfish torpedo bomber in the thick of the Fleet Air Arm's attack on the Italian battleships in Taranto harbour.

take-off arrived to attack a pair of cruisers tucked away in the inner harbour, and soon they too were sinking.

British sources point out that earlier this year the Italian fleet of six battleships and numerous cruisers, destroyers and submarines was stronger than the Royal Navy in the Mediterranean. Now, however, after suffering earlier losses (two cruisers, nine destroyers and 25 submarines) Italy is no longer the region's dominant sea power.

The cost of the latest exploit is two Fleet Air Arm aircraft missing. The crew of one of these is in captivity. The first lord of the admiralty, A V Alexander, is fond of pointing out that the Fleet Air Arm has destroyed at least 55 enemy aircraft off Norway and the British Isles and in the Mediterranean. A hard-pressed RAF has been augmented by 68 Royal Navy pilots.

In such an attack as Operation Judgement the stability of the aircraft must be matched by the pilot's nerve as he flies into enemy gunfire. Confirmation of the raid's results by photo-reconnaissance is now awaited. The prime minister is expected to underline the significance of what he already calls "a determined, successful attack" with a statement in parliament (→ 26).

Biggest mass raid by RAF on Europe

High Wycombe, 10 November

The RAF is hitting many targets in Germany tonight, according to its headquarters here in Buckinghamshire. The raid has set a new record by the RAF for attacks on distant enemy locations. A total of 111 aircraft of Bomber Command were dispatched to many targets, the largest – to which 25 Wellingtons were sent – being the German town of Gelsenkirchen. Bad weather over Europe made the raid a hazardous business. Ice, thunder and cloud in some cases from near ground level to 18,000 feet (5,500 metres) would have made this a difficult flight in peacetime.

Libya: British troops prepare for battle

Sidi Barrani, 15 November

As Italian troops work to fortify this remote coastal village, the limit of their advance towards the Nile Delta, British troops are carrying out clandestine preparations for a major counter-offensive. Moving only by night, and lying low under camouflage netting by day, they are burying large quantities of fuel and water in secret dumps along the 75-mile "no-man's-land" from Mersa Matruh westwards. Marshal Graziani shows no sign of advancing further. An Italian observer reports a "holiday atmosphere" in their ranks as more British tanks arrive in Egypt (→ 9/12).

Elsie and Doris Waters, sisters of the actor Jack Warner, star as radio's "Gert and Daisy".

17. Somaliland: British naval forces bombard Mogadishu.

18. Rome: Mussolini says that he had to invade Greece because it had given the Allies use of important air and sea bases (→ 19).

18. East Africa: The cruiser HMS *Dorsetshire* bombards Zante in Italian Somaliland.

19. Warsaw: The German authorities execute a Pole for throwing bread over the wall of the Jewish ghetto (→ 26).

19. Switzerland: The government bans the pro-Nazi Swiss National Movement (→ 21/12).

19. Atlantic: A Sunderland flying boat uses air-to-surface-vessel (ASV) radio-location gear for the first time to detect a U-boat nearing a convoy.

19. Greece: The Italians are driven back behind the river Kalamas (→ 21).

20. Birmingham: *Luftwaffe* raiders bombarded the city last night in a nine-hour raid.

21. Australia: The government presents a budget calling for increased taxation to finance a boost in defence spending.

21. North Africa: RAF raiders attack Italian bases at Benghazi, Benina and Berka.

21. Greece: The Italians retreat to Elbasan as the Greeks advance on the Epirus front (→ 22).

21. Atlantic: The British corvette *Rhododendron* sinks the U-boat U104 in the north-western approaches.

22. Italy: RAF bombers attack Bari.

22. Greece: Italian planes bomb Cephalonia, Corfu and Samos.→

23. Southampton: The city suffers a heavy night raid (→ 30).

23. Vichy France: Admiral William Leahy is appointed US ambassador to the French government (→ 10/12).

23. Berlin: The Roumanian premier, Ion Antonescu, agrees to join the Tripartite Pact, paving the way for German intervention in Greece (→ 13/12).

"Battle of Britain" chiefs are replaced

London, 17 November
The commander-in-chief of Fighter Command since 1936, Air Chief Marshal Sir Hugh Dowding, and Air Vice-Marshal Keith Park, the commander of 11 Group, the two men who planned and controlled the strategy which won the Battle of Britain, have been deprived of their jobs.

It may be argued that the austere Dowding – nicknamed "Stuffy" – was overdue for retirement, and that the New Zealander Park is worn out and deserves a rest, but the manner of their dismissal has enraged their young pilots. Dowding, a brilliant organizer whose uncompromising manner has never made him popular with the Air Staff, was told, albeit courteously, that he had to go in a personal interview on 13 November. The official letter informing him of his retirement says that the Air Council has "no other work to offer you", although this may not exclude a non-operational role. Park will take over No 23 Training Group.

Air Vice-Marshal Trafford Leigh-Mallory, the commander of 12 Group, is known to have opposed the tactics of Dowding and Park. Leigh-Mallory is a believer in the "big wing" rather than in Dowding's "penny packet" tactics. He seems to have won his point; he is to take over Park's group.

Heroes of the Battle of Britain: now their leaders are to be sidelined.

Last Italian stronghold falls in Greece

Defeated Italians near Koritsa show their Greek captors their ammunition.

Koritsa, Albania, 21 November
With bands playing and their blue and white flags held high, kilted Greek troops marched in triumph through the streets of Koritsa today as the last Italian invaders fled from Greek soil. Mussolini's boast that "we will break Greece's back" had not taken into account the speed of Greek counter-attacks.

Koritsa had been surrounded for several days before the Greeks finally stormed the Italians' shallow trenches with bayonets and trench-knives. The invaders surrendered in their hundreds, with retreat becoming a rout as they abandoned a complete arsenal of heavy guns, anti-tank weapons, food and a huge stock of petrol. Some reports speak of rape and other atrocities as blackshirt divisions retreat through Albanian villages.

As news of the fall of Italy's biggest base in occupied Albania was flashed to an electrified world, Winston Churchill cabled to General Metaxas: "We are all inspired by this feat of Greek valour ... long live Greece!" (→ 23).

Bomber penetrates US neutrality laws

Washington, 20 November
An American bomber fresh off the drawing board has penetrated not only German defences but also the complex web of US law prohibiting the supply of war material to belligerents.

Two years ago a British defence team, shopping in the US, asked Lockheed for a long range reconnaissance bomber. None existed, but the Lockheed Super-Electra airliner was adapted in 24 hours. This became the Hudson. When war began, some legal way had to be found of avoiding the infringement of US neutrality. President Roosevelt revived an 1892 law permitting the lease of army property "not required for public use" for periods up to five years (→ 3/12).

Hungary signs pact with Axis powers

Vienna, 20 November
Hungary today signed a protocol linking itself to Germany, Italy and Japan. After the ceremony, held in the Belvedere Palace, the former home of Emperor Franz Josef, the Hungarian foreign minister, Count Csaky, emphasized that this did not mean that Hungary would change its attitude towards Russia. In fact, the protocol merely regularizes the existing situation in which Hungary accedes to all of Germany's demands (→ 24).

Breakfast without marmalade for UK

London, 20 November
There may be no marmalade for British breakfasts unless the ministry of food stops haggling over the price it is prepared to pay for the current crop of Seville oranges. Any further delay means that the fruit will start going bad. The dispute is over £77,000, which could make the difference of a farthing to a two-pound jar of marmalade. Housewives who are waiting to make their own marmalade are getting frustrated. Extra sugar is available – but no oranges.

Indian troops reinforce Allies in Africa

The Indians arrive in Egypt: a bugler sounds a call at a desert camp.

Port Suez, 20 November
On the dust-swept docks of Suez and Port Sudan, Hindu, Moslem, Sikh, Untouchable and British cooks prepare meals for their separate company messes. Egyptians and Sudanese sniff the conflicting *cuisines* with amazement. The British Indian Army and its baggage have arrived in Africa.

The role of these soldiers is not popular with the Hindu majority back home in India where the Congress Party remains aloof from the war. Moslems, on the other hand, support the war effort, a situation which can only widen the gap between the two communities when India's future is discussed after the war. However, few reinforcements have been more welcome. Britain has only 8,000 troops in the Sudan against 92,000 Italians in Ethiopia.

1940

November

Su	Mo	Tu	We	Th	Fr	Sa
					1	2
3	4	5	6	7	8	9
10	11	12	13	14	15	16
17	18	19	20	21	22	23
24	25	26	27	28	29	30

24. Europe: The German puppet government of Slovakia signs the Tripartite Pact (→ 25).

25. Europe: Bulgaria responds to Soviet pressure and refuses to join the Axis pact (→ 20/12).

25. Haifa, Palestine: Jewish refugees from Germany, Czechoslovakia and Austria blow up their ship, the *Patria*, to try to avoid being deported to Mauritius by the British authorities.

25. At Sea: The first success of mine sweepers against German acoustic mines; three are exploded.

25. Britain: The De Havilland Mosquito, a wooden-framed light bomber, makes its maiden flight.

25. Britain: Arthur Harris is appointed deputy chief of the Air Staff.

26. Africa: The Belgian Congo [*Zaire*] declares war on Italy.

26. Libya: The British Fleet Air Arm raids Tripoli.

26. Mediterranean: Planes from the aircraft carrier HMS *Illustrious* attack Italian targets on Rhodes (→ 27).

27. Bucharest: Pro-Nazi Iron Guards massacre 64 former aides of the exiled king (→ 28).

27. Mediterranean: Italian ships attack a British fleet protecting a Gibraltar-Alexandria convoy in the Battle of Cape Sportivo off Sardinia; the Italian force retreats after damaging the cruiser HMS *Berwick*.

28. Berlin: *Der ewige Jude* [The Eternal Jew], a film purporting to prove the Jews' evil influence, opens.

28. Bucharest: The Roumanian government declares a state of emergency.→

28-29. Britain: Liverpool suffers a devastating overnight raid by the *Luftwaffe* (→ 30).

29. Berlin: The German High Command completes its planning for Operation *Barbarossa*, the invasion of Russia (→ 18/12).

30. Britain: 4,588 civilians have been killed and 6,202 injured in air raids this month.→

Southampton hit by Coventry-style raid

Southampton, 30 November
After a week in which *Luftwaffe* bombers have struck at several British cities, notably Liverpool and Bristol, it was the turn of Southampton to experience tonight the terror of sustained bombardment from the air. Some 137 people are feared to have died and nearly 500 to have been injured in an attack lasting for more than seven hours.

The style of the attack – using thousands of small incendiary devices to start fires, followed by heavy high-explosive bombs – followed the pattern of the raid on Coventry earlier this month. In Southampton, hundreds of flares were dropped as successive waves of bombers hit churches, offices, shops and homes. At one time burning buildings included convents, theatres, cinemas and hotels. A theatre and a newspaper office were burnt out. As a hospital's patients were evacuated, a porter threw an incendiary bomb from the hospital roof. Sixty people left a pub just before it was blown up by high-

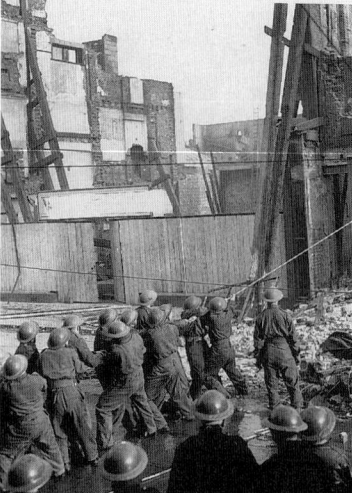

After the raid: soldiers demolish unsafe buildings in Southampton.

explosive bombs. Inside, a voice cried: "Find me! I'm near the dartboard." Other customers returned and dug him free.

Pressure is growing to evacuate all women and children, although some of the bravest ambulance drivers here are female (→ 1/12).

Firemen: front-line heroes of the Blitz

Britain, 30 November
The ferocious raid on Southampton tonight illustrates the problems that firemen have to face night after night. After lighting the sky with flares, the Germans rained incendiaries on the centre of the city, creating an inferno, followed by high-explosive bombs which fractured 74 water mains. Water pressure fell sharply. Many fires had to be left to burn while what water there was was concentrated on the town centre and the docks.

The local fire brigades were reinforced by 200 men from other authorities, which sent 160 pumps from London, Newbury, even Newport, Monmouthshire, and Nottingham. But many of them could not be used because their hose couplings did not fit Southampton's hydrants. Standardization is badly needed.

Lack of water pressure meant that many pumps stood idle while the glow of the fire could be seen from Staines. German radio claims that it could be seen from France.

Like raids on Coventry, Birmingham and Bristol earlier this month,

Southampton demonstrated the heroism and devotion to duty of the regular firemen and the 60,000 men of the Auxiliary Fire Service. Their tours of duty (48 hours on, 24 off) often keep them fire-fighting for as long as 40 hours non-stop while the bombs fall round them. Hundreds have been killed, thousands injured and many blinded.

Battling with a city in flames: firemen emerge as front-line fighters.

Civil war breaks out in Roumania

Bucharest, 29 November
Roumania is in a state of anarchy today following the massacre of 64 political prisoners by the extremist Iron Guard movement. There is shooting in the streets as the Guards clash with the army and rival factions of the Guards fight among themselves.

The young King Michael, who has just succeeded to the throne abdicated by his father, is reported to have fled from the capital and to be seeking refuge in Yugoslavia.

Among the victims of the anarchy are the former premier, Professor Jorga, and Dr Madgearu, a former minister of finance. German involvement is suspected, but so far unproven (→ 4/12).

Craigavon, premier for 19 years, dies

Northern Ireland, 24 November
Viscount Craigavon, the prime minister of Northern Ireland since 1921, died tonight. He was 69. Formerly James Craig, a typical Ulsterman of Scottish descent, he was a rugged man with no claim to intellectual attainment. He had fiercely resisted Home Rule – the establishment of the Irish Free State and two separate parliaments in Ireland. After *Sinn Fein* outrages in 1922 he was responsible for a law instituting the punishment of the lash for carrying guns or bombs.

Japanese recognize Chinese "puppets"

Nanking, 30 November
Japan has formally recognized China's breakaway Reformed *Kuomintang* government and its premier, Wang Ching-wei, after last minute secret peace talks with Marshal Chiang Kai-shek's Kuomintang in Chungking broke down.

Chungking is now expected to go on a diplomatic offensive against what its calls Wang Ching-wei's puppet government and warn foreign governments that it will break off relations with any power that recognizes the new regime (→ 5/12).

Warsaw Jews to be blockaded into ghetto

Warsaw Jews enter the ghetto through a hole in the wall now being built.

Warsaw, 26 November

Work began today on sealing Warsaw's Jewish ghetto, the aim being to cut off its 400,000 inhabitants, living six to a room, from the outside world. Jewish workmen are being forced to build a nine-foot (2.7-metre)-high wall around the streets that have become their prison. They are whipped and beaten if they slow down.

Last month, the Nazis deported the 113,000 Poles who used to live in this dilapidated part of the city in order to make room for the 138,000 Jews from other parts of the city. Then, the ghetto was sealed: there are just 28 exit points, all guarded by German and Polish militia assisted by the ghetto's own Jewish police

force. Only 53,000 people have permits to leave the ghetto: the rest must stay inside on pain of death.

Over 150,000 people, unable to leave the ghetto's confines in order to go to work, roam the streets begging for a new job. All wireless sets have been confiscated; telephone lines have been cut.

The Nazis have appointed a *Judenrat* [Jewish Council] to run the ghetto's affairs, including supervizing its economy and providing a Jewish police force. Its leader, Adam Czerniakow, tries to cushion his people from the constant German demands for enormous bribes and slave labour, but finds himself cast in the role of collaborator and hated by his people (→ 31/1).

Bananas banned: buy now for Xmas

Britain, 26 November

Yes, we will have no bananas after Christmas. After present stocks run out the government will allow no further imports, to save shipping space for essentials. Lemons and onions are also very scarce. People are asking why, as soon as unrationed foods are price-controlled, they disappear from the shops. The reason is that supplies are diverted to the Black Market for people who are prepared to pay more. Lord Woolton promises a little extra tea and sugar for Christmas (→ 3/12).

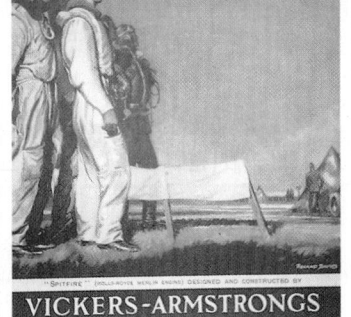

Advertising the Spitfire, the spearhead of Britain's air defence.

1940
December

Su	Mo	Tu	We	Th	Fr	Sa
1	2	3	4	5	6	7
8	9	10	11	12	13	14
15	16	17	18	19	20	21
22	23	24	25	26	27	28
29	30	31				

1. Southampton: The city has a second successive night of heavy bombing.

1. Italy: Flour, spaghetti, macaroni and rice are rationed.

2. Atlantic: The armed merchant cruiser HMS *Forfar* sinks the U-boat U99 in the western approaches.

2. Britain: Bristol tonight suffers a heavy night raid by 121 German bombers.

3. London: The food ministry announces extra rations of four ounces of sugar and two ounces of tea per person for Christmas.

3. Britain: The government orders 60 merchant ships from the USA to replace losses in the Atlantic (→ 17).

3. Africa: The RAF bombards the Italian base at Kassala in the Sudan.

3. Britain: The *Luftwaffe* bombs the Midlands tonight, targeting Birmingham in particular (→ 11).

4. Roumania: The army manages to contain the civil unrest which has been going on for a week (→ 14/1).

4. Albania: Greek forces occupy Premeti.→

5. Germany: Hitler meets his generals to discuss his initial plans for the invasion of the USSR.

5. Europe: The RAF last night carried out raids on Dusseldorf and Turin.

6. Albania: Greek forces occupy the Santi Quaranta naval base and Sarande on the Adriatic, pushing north along the coast.→

6. Italy: Marshal Pietro Badoglio resigns as Chief of the Italian General Staff – a post he has held since 1925. He is succeeded by Ugo Cavallero.

6. Far East: Japan and Thailand sign a treaty of friendship.

6. Mediterranean: The submarine HMS *Regulus* is sunk.

7. Germany: The RAF tonight bombs the industrial city of Dusseldorf.

US ambassador to Britain goes home

Washington, 1 December

Joseph P Kennedy, the pessimistic US ambassador in London, has resigned. For many months there have been reports that President Roosevelt was displeased with his ambassador, who made no secret of his belief that Hitler should be appeased, or of his conviction that Britain would lose the war. He has great influence on Wall Street, however, and Roosevelt needed his endorsement.

There are reports that his resignation followed a painful scene at the president's home at Hyde Park in New York state.

The ex-ambassador has not gone home empty-handed. He has taken a London air-raid siren to instal in his Cape Cod home.

Kennedy: unwelcome in London.

Franco promises to keep out of the war

Madrid, 2 December

In a significant act of defiance, the Spanish dictator, General Franco, today ignored pressure from Nazi Germany and signed a financial pact with Britain. At the same time Franco gave a categorical assurance to Britain and the US that in no circumstances will Spain join the war against Britain or allow Spain to be used for military operations. The pact with Britain will release Spanish funds in London which have been frozen since the start of the Spanish Civil War.

▷

141

1940

December

Su	Mo	Tu	We	Th	Fr	Sa
1	2	3	4	5	6	7
8	9	10	11	12	13	14
15	16	17	18	19	20	21
22	23	24	25	26	27	28
29	30	31				

Chinese batter Japanese in north China

Troops from China's Eighth Route Army show off loot captured in a raid.

China, 5 December

Japan appears to have lost control of large areas of northern China following a three-month offensive by Chinese Communist troops of the Eighth Route Army to disrupt Japanese installations in the region.

Within the last few days there have been signs that the exhausted Communists are winding down the operation, known as the Hundred Regiments campaign, in the belief it has achieved its political aim of disrupting talks between Chiang Kai-shek's nationalists and Japan.

According to Communist claims, the campaign, which has seen Chinese troops abandon hit-and-run tactics for outright confrontation, has achieved all its military aims; attacks on Japanese outposts have forced the enemy to retreat into large enclaves; and those positions still held by the Japanese have been so severely damaged that it will be at least six months before most major installations are operative again. Among the most heavily damaged are the Peking-Hankow railway, cut in 86 places, and the Anshan steel mills in Manchukuo. According to Communist estimates, Japan's North China Army has lost at least five battalions.

However, internal critics fear that the extravagant use of manpower – with the Chinese outnumbering the enemy by ten to one – is too expensive with Communist casualties of 22,000.

Italians retreat in southern Albania

Albania, 6 December

Mussolini today sacked Marshal Pietro Badoglio as Chief of the General Staff – a scapegoat for Italy's humiliating reverse at the hands of Greece. The leader may have gone, but there is no end to the misery of his erstwhile troops. Not content with driving the Italian army from their homeland, Greek troops have now fought their way deep into Albania and are forcing the Italians back along a wide front.

With the RAF harrying the Italians from the air and the Royal Navy attacking supply convoys in the Aegean, the Italians are in full retreat before the cock-a-hoop Greek army (→8).

Cavallero: Badoglio's successor.

How the RAF cares for physical and mental health of airmen

London, 1 December

Among the many lessons learnt by the RAF during the Battle of Britain was how to care for the mental and physical health of its young but exhausted, and often dreadfully burnt, pilots.

The RAF got off to a slow start. One serious problem for the pilots was the lack of proper air-sea rescue arrangements at the start of the battle. Many young men who survived in the air drowned in the sea because nobody came to pick them up. This was a need which was soon rectified. There was another need, however, which had been recognized. When aircraft are hit they burn and their pilots burn with them. The RAF organized a Burns Unit at the Queen Victoria hospital at East Grinstead and put a dapper little plastic surgeon in charge of it.

He is Archibald McIndoe, and he is already rightly famous for the way in which he is rebuilding the faces and restoring the confidence of his "guinea-pigs". McIndoe has to treat the minds of his young men as well as their bodies. "Imagine how they feel," he says. "On Friday night they are dancing in a nightclub with a beautiful girl and by Saturday afternoon they are a burnt cinder."

There are other pilots who carry no physical marks but whose minds are wounded. These are the men who can no longer fly through fear. Some are stripped of their rank and labelled "LMF" – Lack of Moral Fibre. Officially, their numbers are small – only 0.4 per cent of Bomber Command pilots were classed as "LMF" at the height of the *Luftwaffe* offensive.

8. London: The House of Commons and the Tower of London are hit in a heavy *Luftwaffe* raid tonight.

8. Albania: Greek forces capture Argyrocastro and Delvino as Italy pulls back towards Himara (→9).

8. Madrid: Franco refuses to cooperate with Hitler's plan to invade Gibraltar, forcing the operation to be cancelled.

9. Libya: Allied troops of the Western Desert Force launch a surprise attack, taking 1,000 Italian prisoners in the first thrust of Operation Compass (→11).

9. Albania: The Greeks capture Pogradec, over 40 miles inside Albanian territory (→20).

10. Berlin: Hitler issues a directive for the seizure of French military resources and the future occupation of Vichy France (Operation *Attila*), and cancels plans to invade Gibraltar via Spain (Operation *Felix*) (→12).

10. Washington: Roosevelt announces that the export licence system will be extended to iron and steel.

11. Libya: Ships of the British Mediterranean fleet shell Sollum (→13).

11. Birmingham: German raiders devastate a wide area in attacks tonight.

12. Washington: Lord Lothian (Philip Kerr), Britain's ambassador to the US, dies.

12. Sheffield: The city suffers heavy *Luftwaffe* raids tonight.

12. Belgrade: In order to improve relations with Germany, Yugoslavia signs a friendship pact with Hungary.

13. Libya: RAF bombers damage Italian bases at Derna and Bardia (→3/1).

14. Mediterranean: The destroyers HMS *Hereward* and HMS *Hyperion* sink an Italian submarine off Bardia; Royal Navy Swordfish aircraft based on Malta bomb Tripoli.

14. Britain: Churchill enjoys a private screening of Charlie Chaplin's film *The Great Dictator*.→

African desert victory for British

Sidi Barrani, 11 December

As the blood-red sun rose over the western desert today, Scottish soldiers appeared from a ridge overlooking the town of Sidi Barrani and charged into the ruins. After an hour of fierce hand-to-hand fighting, the Italian blackshirts began to hold up white flags. The first phase of the assault planned by Major-General Richard O'Connor was complete – and now the main British problem is the handling of over 15,000 Italian prisoners.

The key victory was won – by guile and surprise – two days ago at Nibeiwa when British tanks stormed its advanced Italian fort. Tanks and men had spent two days advancing slowly under the cover of darkness with hurricane lamps – shaded from the Italians – to guide them over the rough desert tracks. Windscreens were removed from vehicles to avoid the sun reflecting on them. By day, 30,000 men and machines lay entirely still in the burning sun.

The Italian defensive positions faced the east. The defenders were preparing breakfast of coffee and rolls when the British barrage began. They looked up to see British and Indian troops advancing towards them supported by tanks. The attack was from the west. Two more forts surrendered later (→ 17).

A newly-captured Italian PoW has his pockets turned out by a British soldier.

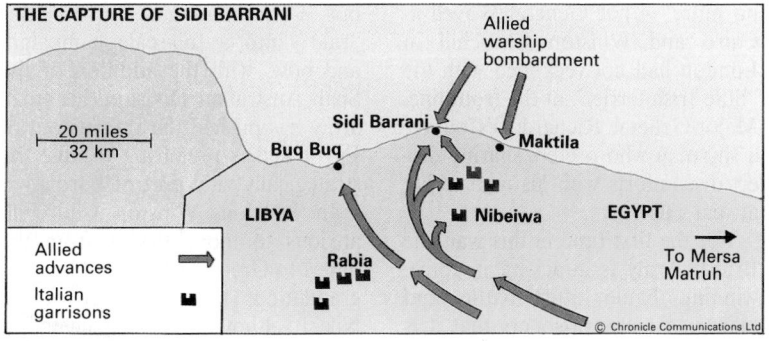

THE CAPTURE OF SIDI BARRANI

Allied warship bombardment

20 miles / 32 km

Sidi Barrani

Buq Buq

Maktila

LIBYA

Nibeiwa

EGYPT

Rabia

To Mersa Matruh

Allied advances

Italian garrisons

© Chronicle Communications Ltd

Hitler orders more divisions to move into the Balkans

Berlin, 13 December

Hitler has today ordered a build-up of forces in southern Roumania in order to take on operation *Marita*, the occupation of Salonika and, if necessary, the entire mainland of Greece.

Twenty-four divisions – including the 16th *Panzer* Division – will be earmarked for this enterprise. They will move through Bulgaria on the arrival of favourable weather. Hitler has told his generals: "We can rely on Bulgarian support." It seems that he is alarmed by Mussolini's failure to complete his conquest of Albania and fears that Britain will establish an air base in the Balkans to attack Italy and the Roumanian oilfields.

The build-up is being carefully planned to take place under Hitler's usual cloak of deception. The arrival of the invasion force in Roumania will be explained away as "reinforcements for the military mission".

Nothing is said about Russia in these orders, but when *Marita* takes place the Soviet generals cannot fail to notice that its effect will be to safeguard Germany's southern flank in the event of a war with Russia.

Petain dismisses his vice-premier

Vichy, 13 December

Pierre Laval, the vice-premier of France, has been dismissed by Marshal Petain and there are reports that he is under arrest.

He has been replaced as foreign minister by Pierre-Etienne Flandin, and the post of vice-premier has been abolished. The National Assembly is to be abolished and replaced by a new puppet consultative assembly.

The son of an innkeeper, Laval became a schoolteacher, a lawyer and a member of parliament. He started life as a socialist, but became a vehement anti-communist. Twice prime minister in the 1930s, he organized the situation that brought Petain to power (→ 17).

First German spies executed in Britain

London, 10 December

Two Nazi spies, Jose Waldberg and Carl Meier, are the first people to be executed since the start of the war. They were hanged today at Pentonville jail in London.

The pair landed in this country several weeks ago with a radio transmitter, English money and some iron rations. They planned to spend their nights hiding in the woods, and their days collecting information – from the unwary public in trains, pubs and buffets, and by observation of military bases.

An anti-espionage officer reported that, though Waldberg had been motivated by patriotism, his companion, Meier, was only interested in the money.

Chaplin stars as "The Great Dictator"

Charlie Chaplin takes the world in his hands in "The Great Dictator".

London, 13 December

Charlie Chaplin's one-man offensive against Hitler, his film *The Great Dictator*, won admiring reviews from the London critics today, except for its ending. Chaplin impersonates a humble barber who looks exactly like the moustached dictator "Adenoid Hynkel". His dictator is a devastating parody, screaming gibberish through the microphone to his ecstatic followers. The train bearing his fellow-dictator "Benzino Napoloni" fails to stop at the red carpet. The resulting shunting scene is a comic set-piece.

Finally, Chaplin as the little barber addresses the audience with a long, passionate appeal against hatred and war. Like his satire, his message is too late.

1940

December

Su	Mo	Tu	We	Th	Fr	Sa
1	2	3	4	5	6	7
8	9	10	11	12	13	14
15	16	17	18	19	20	21
22	23	24	25	26	27	28
29	30	31				

15. Paris: The Germans ceremonially return the ashes of Napoleon II to the city.

16. Germany: RAF planes attempt the area bombing of Mannheim as revenge for recent German raids on Coventry and other cities, but very little damage is done.

17. Vichy France: Otto Abetz, the German ambassador, is believed to have warned Petain that German cooperation would be withdrawn if Laval were not freed from arrest.→

17. Washington: Roosevelt outlines the Lend-Lease scheme to supply Britain with arms and equipment, telling pressmen: "We should do everything to help the British Empire defend itself."→

18. Harrow: Churchill visits his bomb-damaged old school.

18. London: Churchill writes to Wavell "ask and it shall be given" (Matthew VII, 7) (→ 19).

18. Adriatic: The submarine HMS *Triton* is sunk by an Italian destroyer.

19. North Africa: Wavell writes back to Churchill asking for more planes, commenting "every good gift and every perfect gift is from above" (James I, 17) (→ 22).

19. Finland: Risto Ryti takes over as president from Dr Kallio.

20. Albania: Greece starts a bombardment of Klisura (→ 23).

20-21. Liverpool: *Luftwaffe* bombers stage another damaging night-time raid.

20. Bulgaria: Laws to crack down on Jews and Freemasons are introduced (→ 13/1).

21. Geneva: The Swiss government cuts off diplomatic relations with the USSR.

21. Berlin: Germany says the US's pro-British stance is one of "insult, challenge and moral aggression".

21. Norway: The chief justice resigns rather than administer the Nazi system of justice.

21. Mediterranean: Aircraft from the British carrier *Illustrious* sink two Italian ships off Tunisia (→ 22).

British take Italian bases in North Africa

Members of the Egyptian Camel Corps doing their bit in the Western Desert.

Bardia, North Africa, 17 December
The British desert offensive had been planned as a "five-day raid, no more" – but General Wavell in Cairo and Winston Churchill in London had not reckoned with the "little Irish terrier" at the front line, Major-General Richard O'Connor, a shy man who prefers sharing desert discomforts with his men to life at rear HQ.

For the first time in this war, the British Army is attacking in force, winning battle after battle and taking so many prisoners that it is embarrassed by numbers. O'Connor is living up to his nickname in tenacity. Headquarters expected him to stop at Sidi Barrani or Buq Buq, 30 miles (48 km) further west, but O'Connor has turned this "raid" into a full-scale campaign; and now, with the addition of the Sixth Australian Division, his small army has pushed the Italians out of Egypt and is preparing to take the strategically vital port of Bardia.

In London, Winston Churchill, anxious to move troops from the desert to Greece, has cabled his congratulations to the "Army of the Nile", although he neglected to mention the name of General Richard O'Connor (→ 19).

The poetic general waging the desert war

Cairo, 17 December
Correspondents were summoned to headquarters today to find General Archibald Percival Wavell reading Ovid as he waited for them to assemble and hear of British victories at Sidi Barrani and beyond. Poetry is Wavell's hobby and delight; he is rarely without a classic in his briefcase. Among Churchill's generals, Wavell, a markedly taciturn man, is well suited for the Middle East command. After fighting on the Western Front in the Great War – he lost an eye at Ypres – he was on Allenby's staff in Cairo in 1918. Churchill is among those who admire his intellect, but for Wavell the greatest challenge is still to come.

General Wavell: a lover of poetry and a hardened desert fighter.

Hitler gives orders for Russian attack

Berlin, 18 December
Hitler has ordered the German General Staff to prepare for the invasion of Russia under the codename "Operation *Barbarossa*". In his war directive 21, issued today, he says: "The German Armed Forces must be prepared, even before the conclusion of the war against England, to crush Soviet Russia in a rapid campaign." It is to be an all-out war aimed at destroying the Russian army by "daring operations led by deeply penetrating armoured spearheads".

Dutch ships escape to join the Allies

Hull, 20 December
On the lines of Dunkirk, a more modest but still impressive escape has been made by the entire Dutch navy. Not only are there cruisers, destroyers, torpedo boats, minesweepers and submarines but also passenger vessels, cargo ships, pilot cutters and trawlers. All came overloaded with volunteers. A Dutch liner is now a depot ship for naval trainees. A cargo ship brought 1,500 German prisoners. When the *Luftwaffe* flew over, the captain opened the hatches, but gave a Jew a machine-gun to forestall escape attempts.

Planes top Britain's US shopping spree

Washington, 19 December
At five o'clock this morning, the British Purchasing Commission in Washington finished a $750 million (£186 million) shopping list of war orders. The list has been prepared at President Roosevelt's request, but contracts will not be signed until Congress has been consulted. The first contract, the US treasury secretary, Henry Morgenthau, said today, will be for 60 merchant ships, to be completed within 12 months. The biggest single item will be 12,000 aircraft, costing about $300 million. Guns, tanks and other war supplies for Britain will total $450 million (→ 30).

1940

December

Su	Mo	Tu	We	Th	Fr	Sa
1	2	3	4	5	6	7
8	9	10	11	12	13	14
15	16	17	18	19	20	21
22	23	24	25	26	27	28
29	30	31				

Admiral Darlan is the victor in battle for power in Vichy

Vichy, 17 December

The political situation in Vichy France is confused. Pierre Laval, who was arrested in what is being called a "palace revolution" on 13 December, has been released, but is still out of political favour.

The new minister of foreign affairs, Pierre Flandin, holds similar views to those of Laval, and it is hard to discover any significant differences of policy achieved by the fall of Laval. In power terms, however, the winner is Admiral Darlan.

Darlan is interested in collaborating with Germany, not so much because of ideological affinity for Nazism, but because he hopes to negotiate German protection for the French fleet and the French colonial empire.

Admiral Darlan is to meet Hitler next week, and hopes to persuade Hitler that France will be a more powerful ally in the Mediterranean than either Italy or Spain.

Hitler has just met General Franco and failed to persuade him to join in the war. He knows that Mussolini is in difficulties both in Africa and in Greece. Yet he still refuses to make any political concessions to Vichy. The crucial test for Hitler will be whether Petain will be willing to fight against Britain, his ally in 1914-18 (→ 3/1).

"CALLING ALL WORKERS"

"UP AND AT 'EM!"

A humorous incentive to the British work force, though the clock says it's only 4.45am.

22. North Africa: Fifteen aircraft from the carrier HMS *Illustrious* bomb Tripoli.

23. London: Churchill assures the Australian prime minister, Robert Menzies, that Australia has a higher defence priority than the Mediterranean.

23. France: Jacques Bonsergent, a 28-year-old engineer who had a fight with a German sergeant, is the first Frenchman to be executed by the Nazis in Paris.

23. Albania: The advancing Greeks capture the town of Himara (→ 26).

24. Abbeville, France: In an address to his fighter pilots, Hitler tells them that German U-boat successes and the neutralization of the USSR make victory certain.

25. London: Churchill gives King George a one-piece "siren suit" as a Christmas present.

25. Atlantic: The British cruisers *Berwick* and *Bonaventure* drive off and slightly damage the German cruiser *Admiral Hipper*.

26. Albania: Greek troops launch a fresh offensive north of Pogradets, but start to find that Italian resistance is stronger (→ 3/1).

27. Pacific: The disguised German raider *Komet*, flying the Japanese flag, bombards phosphate plants on the Australian protectorate of Nauru.

27. London: There is a major night attack by over 100 bombers (→ 29).

29. London: Another major attack on the City starts huge fires.→

31. Germany: Hitler writes to Franco, telling him that he is sorry that Franco decided not to join the Axis.

31. Britain: With German incendiary bombs causing ever more damage, firewatching at night is to be made compulsory.

31. Britain: Civilian casualties this month are 3,793 people killed and 5,244 injured.

Anthony Eden becomes foreign secretary

Anthony Eden greets Newfoundland and Canadian troops at a west coast port.

Britain, 23 December

Anthony Eden is back as foreign secretary – the post from which he resigned in 1938 in protest against the pre-war Chamberlain government's readiness to recognize Italy's annexation of Ethiopia. His appointment is part of a cabinet reshuffle. Viscount Halifax leaves the foreign office to become ambassador in Washington.

Mr Eden, who moves from the war office, has been a close ally of Mr Churchill for the past few years. As Tory rebels at the time of Munich they were under the same pressures to toe the party line.

Captain David Margesson, chief whip in the Baldwin and Chamberlain governments, becomes war minister. Thus the prime minister has balanced promotion of an old friend with the advancement of an old foe who had a hand in attempts to get Churchill and Eden dislodged from their constituencies.

Canadian corps to be formed in Britain

Ottawa, 24 December

A full Canadian corps will be formed in Britain, it was announced here today by Colonel J Saul, the Canadian defence minister. The Canadians will join an impressive array of troops now mustered under the Imperial banner.

The land forces currently in action are those in East and North Africa. Sudanese, South Africans, Indians and Cypriots are embroiled in East Africa while, under General Wavell in North Africa, there are Australians, New Zealanders and Indians all fighting for a "mother country" which hardly any of them has ever visited.

Bethlehem blacked out for Christmas

Bethlehem, 25 December

For the first time in history Bethlehem is celebrating a darkened Christmas. While Mussolini's air menace hangs over the city even the windows of the Church of the Nativity have been obscured by blue. At Jerusalem the Stations of the Cross are dark and silent.

Despite the blackout, members of the church are determined to make it a Christmas to remember for the hundreds of Empire troops in the city. The Church of the Nativity has been lit from within by a myriad candles, and the traditional sheep are being roasted in the fields near the manger.

City of London devastated by fire-bomb raid

London, 30 December

Many of the City of London's most cherished buildings were gutted this weekend in a series of incendiary raids on the capital. The event is becoming enshrined in Cockney folklore as "the night they tried to set the City on fire".

London has been the target of Coventry-style "fire raids" before, but this latest attack is the most devastating yet. It was learnt afterwards that 22,068 fire bombs were dropped by 136 planes. The ensuing blaze left eight Wren churches burnt, along with three hospitals and the Old Bailey. The Guildhall, the seat of local government for the City of London, was wrecked. The Daily Telegraph headquarters in Fleet Street was among buildings severely damaged.

In addition to the incendiaries some 127 tons of high explosive were dropped by *Luftflottes* 2 and 3. The aircraft attacked between 6pm and 9.30pm so that they could be back at their bases before the predicted bad weather set in. Even without successive waves of attackers this was a night when this new fire of London was greater in scale than its 17th-century predecessor.

It is easier to identify buildings still intact than those seriously damaged. St Paul's stands proudly above blocks of charred neighbours. (Inside the cathedral, Christmas candles are still burning.) The Mansion House and the Bank of England are undamaged in spite of German claims that they are gone. But there are grievous losses: St Bride's gutted, its bells (one of 28cwt) shattered; the statues of Gog and Magog, the Guildhall sentinels, charred; the 16th-century Girdlers' Hall reduced to rubble, as is St Lawrence Jewry where Grinling Gibbons's carvings were kept. The rector of St Andrew by the Wardrobe, the Rev J R Sankey, rescued vestments and a church register started in 1566.

A total of 20,000 firemen, regular and part-time auxiliaries, fought the fires. Some travelled 20 miles across London to do so. Many died. British civilian casualties for December are so far feared to be over 3,700 people dead, with over 5,000 seriously injured.

The dome of St Paul's towers above the smoke and fire on the night that the Germans tried to set the City alight.

In a view from St Paul's, devastated buildings lie all around: but the statue of Justice still stands with her sword defiant.

US will be the "arsenal of democracy"

Washington, 30 December
President Roosevelt, in a "fireside chat" on radio, yesterday called for the United States to become "the arsenal of democracy". The president made "the direct statement to the American people that there is a far less chance of the United States getting into war if we do all we can now to to support the nations defending themselves against attack by the Axis than if we acquiesce in their defeat".

At a press conference nine days ago, Mr Roosevelt used a homely metaphor to explain his idea of Lend-Lease. If your neighbour's house is on fire, he said, and he wants to borrow your garden hose, you don't ask to be paid, you just want your hose back.

There are signs that the president's campaign to alert the American people to the danger of war is succeeding. His fireside chat is the most successful he has ever given. According to polls today, more than three-quarters of the population were aware of it, and more than 60 per cent agreed with what he said.

Other polls and informal soundings by journalists alike confirm that the American public's attitude to the war has changed dramatically in the course of the year that is now ending. A poll for *Fortune* magazine, for example, showed that where a year ago American businessmen looked unsympathetically on the predicament of Britain and France, now the majority are

Roosevelt: supporting the British.

determined to do whatever needs to be done to help Britain defeat Hitler, even though they still hope they will not need to fight themselves.

The president has recently received a telegram from 150 leaders calling on him to make it "the settled policy of this country to do everything that may be necessary to ensure the defeat of the Axis powers". One of the signers is Hamilton Fish, a conservative Republican congressman who was until recently chairman of the Isolationist Group; another is Mrs Dwight Morrow, the mother-in-law of isolationist Charles Lindbergh.

Not even the Boston Irish want an Axis victory, nor do Mid-Westerners of German descent or Italian-Americans.

Black market boom in Christmas fare

Germany, 24 December
A Christmas bonus is being distributed within the German *Reich* – an additional 26 ounces (750 grams) of rice and vegetables, plus just over a pound (500 grams) of sugar, jam and coffee. But the bonus has not prevented a rash of black-market deals for food and presents. A confidential report by the SS in Dortmund this month reported that "the tracking down of game and poultry began some time ago and exorbitant prices are being demanded". Goose is costing ten *Reichsmark* per pound.

Ethnic Germans are resettled at home

Germany, 31 December
At least 200,000 ethnic Germans now living in countries outside Greater Germany are to be resettled within the *Reich* under agreements signed this year. Most will come from Roumania and Bulgaria, but there are also 50,000 Germans in Lithuania, Latvia and Estonia whose transfer has been agreed with Russia. So far, however, it has been easier to reach international agreements than to cope with the physical upheaval of so many people, and few have yet to arrive in their notional Fatherland.

Arts: the newsreaders make headlines

The BBC's new stars this year, with audiences bigger than any known before, are the newsreaders. After years of anonymity, they began to announce their own names: "Here is the news and this is **Alvar Lidell** reading it" – or **Stuart Hibberd, Frank Phillips, Joseph MacLeod, Bruce Belfrage** – all of them now household names and voices. They are on the air six times a day. There was a perceptible pause in Bruce Belfrage's delivery after he had given the nine o'clock news headlines on 15 October. A muffled bang was heard and a voice asked: "Are you all right?" A delayed-action bomb had entered Broadcasting House on the fifth floor and had just gone off, killing seven people. Belfrage carried on without fluffing.

A land mine on 8 December badly damaged the heavily-sandbagged building, causing the evacuation of the European Service, which is now broadcasting to occupied Norway, Denmark, Holland and Belgium. Churchill's "Finest Hour" broadcast and "Postscripts" by **J B Priestley** were the highlights of a year in which the wireless helped to keep the nation together. It also saw the start of "Kitchen Front", often manned by **Elsie and Doris Waters**, and of "Music While You Work" for those in factories.

Early in the year the BEF

Vera Lynn: forces' sweetheart.

voted on its favourite singer: it was not **Judy Garland** but a plumber's daughter from East Ham – **Vera Lynn**, who sang with the **Ambrose** dance band. Among her songs are "Faithful for Ever" and "We'll Meet Again", which came out last year. Surprisingly, the favourite song of the Blitz is the sophisticated "A Nightingale Sang in Berkeley Square".

Films have been mainly escapist. *The Wizard of Oz* arrived, closely followed by Disney's *Pinocchio*, then Hollywood's Sherlock Holmes in the lean, sinewy shape of **Basil Rathbone**. **Daphne du Maurier's** *Rebecca* was heavy with Hitchcockian brooding.

Arrival at Manderley: Laurence Olivier and Joan Fontaine in "Rebecca".

Detail from "Devastation, 1941: an East end street" by Graham Sutherland.

1941

January

Su	Mo	Tu	We	Th	Fr	Sa
			1	2	3	4
5	6	7	8	9	10	11
12	13	14	15	16	17	18
19	20	21	22	23	24	25
26	27	28	29	30	31	

1. Belgium: Leon Degrelle, the head of the fascist Rexist movement, calls for greater collaboration with Germany.

1. Germany: 141 RAF bombing targets tonight include Bremen, where 95 planes attack shipyards and, especially, the city's Focke-Wulf aircraft factory.→

1. Britain: The BBC broadcasts its first "Brains Trust", in which a panel of experts discusses topical questions of the day.

1. Mediterranean: The *Luftwaffe* has around 150 bombers and fighters in Sicily, compared with the RAF's 15 Hurricanes in Malta (→ 10).

2. France: The bread ration is cut to ten ounces (300 grammes) a day.

2. Britain: The "Twenty Committee", formed to co-ordinate the activities of double agents based in Britain, meets for the first time.

2. Mediterranean: HMS *Terror*, HMS *Aphis* and HMS *Ladybird* bombard Bardia in preparation for an assault on it (→ 3).

3. Vichy: Paul Baudouin resigns as secretary of state in the Petain government (→ 9).

3. Mediterranean: Midshipman Prince Philip of Greece joins the battleship HMS *Valiant*, which, with the battleships HMS *Barham* and HMS *Warspite*, later bombards Bardia.

3. Bardia: About 30,000 Italian prisoners are taken in the first day of the attack by Australian troops.→

3. Albania: The first *Luftwaffe* units arrive to back up the Italian forces (→ 4).

3. Dublin: The prime minister, Eamon de Valera, lodges a protest to Germany after the third air raid on Eire in 24 hours.

4. USA: The German-born actress Marlene Dietrich becomes a naturalized US citizen.→

4. Albania: Greek forces launch a drive westwards, towards Valona (→ 13).

Australians take 45,000 Italian prisoners

Australian troops advance towards the strategic African port of Bardia.

Cairo, 4 January
In their first action of the war, Australian troops are tonight poised to take the heavily-defended North African port of Bardia.

The troops, members of the 6th Australian Division, began their assault at dawn yesterday, taking the Italians by surprise. It was preceded by heavy raids by the RAF and bombardment from British ships of the Royal Navy's Mediterranean fleet offshore. Under fire, Australian engineers blew gaps in the Italian barbed wire and broke down the sides of anti-tank ditches. Tanks penetrated deeply into the zone of fortifications.

Singing and shouting, the Australian infantry then attacked Italian defensive posts. By 7am the Italian line had been breached and British tanks moved in. At some points the defenders fought hard and the Australians suffered severe casualties. In other positions large numbers surrendered after little resistance.

By this evening the fortress had been cut in two, and it is now estimated that around 45,000 prisoners will be captured – almost double the original estimate of the garrison's strength.

Australian casualties to date are over 100 killed and at least 300 wounded. One Australian battalion suffered heavy casualties when it launched a diversionary attack. After the Australians penetrated the wire, the Italians met one of the companies with machine guns, rifles and grenades (→ 5).

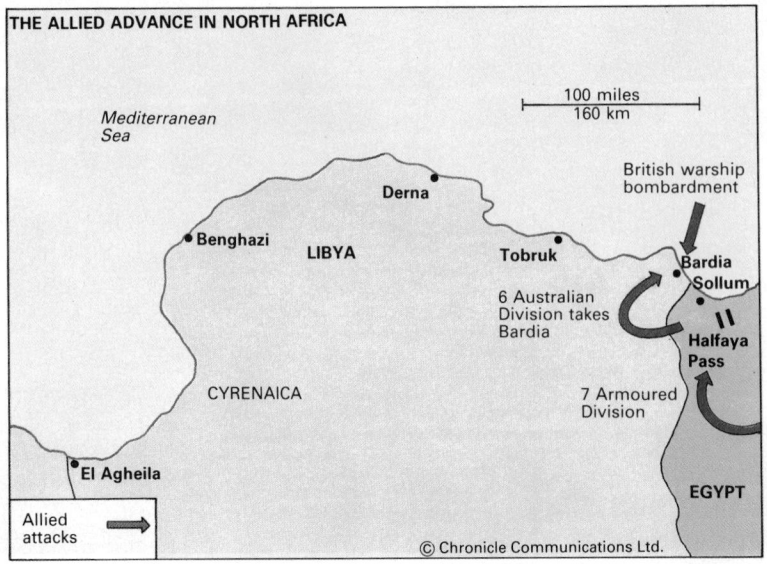

THE ALLIED ADVANCE IN NORTH AFRICA

Mediterranean Sea

100 miles / 160 km

Derna

British warship bombardment

Benghazi • LIBYA

Tobruk

Bardia / Sollum

6 Australian Division takes Bardia

Halfaya Pass

CYRENAICA

7 Armoured Division

El Agheila •

EGYPT

Allied attacks

© Chronicle Communications Ltd.

Neutral Eire hit by the "Luftwaffe"

Dublin, 2 January
A 100-mile (160-km) swathe of neutral Irish territory was bombed by German aircraft today for the second time in 48 hours. At Knockroe, Co Carlow, a house containing five members of the Shannon family was hit and a woman aged 50, a 16-year-old girl and a man aged 40 were killed. Two men were injured.

Six counties bordering the Irish Sea were attacked. The first raid hit Drogheda, north of Dublin. On Curragh racecourse an incendiary bomb was identified as a German device. The attacks may not have been accidental. It is thought that they might be intended to intimidate the Irish into remaining neutral in spite of Anglo-American pressure for the use of Irish bases to help to protect convoys.

There are reports, too, of efforts by the Germans to augment their already large diplomatic team in Dublin with agents parachuted into the country to spy on British fleet activities in Northern Ireland. It would be no surprise if these were to contact the IRA (→ 3).

Fire becomes main weapon of air war

London, 3 January
More than 20,000 incendiaries as well as tons of high explosive were dropped on the German industrial arsenal of Bremen on the night of 1 to 2 January, starting a fire which could be seen by later waves of RAF bombers 120 miles (192 km) away. In spite of 50 earlier raids against Bremen, there seem to have been a remarkable number and variety of targets still available. These included warships under construction in docks extending over 126 acres, the Focke-Wulf aircraft factory, oil refineries and food warehouses. The latest attack, by 95 aircraft, lasted over three hours and was pressed home through intense *flak*. After Bremen, 100 *Luftwaffe* machines last night made a reprisal raid on Cardiff. The tactic of using incendiaries to create a fire after the initial bombing was again the principal weapon. Both sides use it and both strike by night (→ 10).

1941

January

Su	Mo	Tu	We	Th	Fr	Sa
			1	2	3	4
5	6	7	8	9	10	11
12	13	14	15	16	17	18
19	20	21	22	23	24	25
26	27	28	29	30	31	

US plans a fleet of 200 merchant ships

Washington, 3 January
President Roosevelt announced at a press conference here today a programme for building about 200 new merchant ships in one year to take the place of shipping sunk in the war.

The plan, which will cost $350 million (£87.5 million), is based on the assumption that when the war ends there will be a world shipping shortage.

Mr Roosevelt said that the ships would look "ugly", but they could be quickly and cheaply built.

The president also announced that he is sending his close confidant, Harry Hopkins, to London as his personal representative until a new ambassador can be sent to replace Joseph Kennedy.

A social worker before he became US secretary of commerce, Harry Hopkins loves to play poker. He is 50, and so close a friend of Mr Roosevelt that he has lived in the White House for the past year. His mission to London is evidence of the extreme importance the president attaches to maintaining close relations with Britain (→6).

January 4: The German-born actress Marlene Dietrich – one of Hollywood's most glamorous stars – who became a naturalized American citizen today.

5. Maolin, China: A large *Kuomintang* force attacks troops of the Communist New Fourth Army (→17/1).

5. Bardia: The Italian garrison surrenders to the British, who take 45,000 prisoners, 462 guns, 130 tanks and over 700 trucks (→7).

6. Gibraltar: A convoy protected by "Force H" leaves for Malta, carrying vital supplies.

7. Libya: British forces capture Tobruk airport.→

7. Faeroe Islands: The corvette HMS *Anemone* sinks the Italian submarine *Nani*.

8. Washington: The defence budget for 1942 is announced as $17,486 million.

9. Mediterranean: Three squadrons of Hurricanes and two of Blenheims are sent to Greece to boost air cover (→10).

9. London: Roosevelt's Lend-Lease programme envoy, Harry Hopkins, starts negotiations with the government.→

10. Netherlands: All Jews are ordered to register with the authorities (→22).

10. Mediterranean: Yesterday and today *Luftwaffe* planes have assisted Italian attacks on British warships off Sicily; off the island of Pantellaria the destroyer HMS *Gallant* is badly damaged by a mine, while the destroyer HMS *Hereward* sinks the Italian torpedo boat *Vega* off Malta.→

10. London: Churchill insists that assistance to Greece must be top priority after the capture of Tobruk (→13).

11. Britain: Portsmouth was attacked last night by 155 *Luftwaffe* planes which dropped 140 tons of high explosive and over 40,000 incendiaries.→

11. Germany: Hitler issues his 22nd war directive, ordering preparations for reinforcements to be sent to aid Italian armies in North Africa and Albania.

11. Mediterranean: The cruiser HMS *Southampton*, damaged by a Stuka attack, sinks (→12).

Crash kills air ace Amy

Pilot Amy Johnson: feared dead.

London, 5 January
Amy Johnson, the airwoman who made flying history with her 10,000-mile solo flight to Australia ten years ago, is feared to have died today when the aircraft she was ferrying for the Air Transport Auxiliary (ATA) crashed into the Thames Estuary. There was no enemy air activity at the time, and it is thought that 38-year-old Miss Johnson lost her way in bad weather conditions and ran out of fuel. The crew of the naval trawler *Haslemere* saw her bale out of the plane and the trawler's captain, Lieutenant-Commander W E Fletcher, dived into the sea despite the heavy swell and reached her, but was unable to support her. He was so exhausted by his valiant efforts and so frozen by the bitter sea that he died in hospital.

Miss Johnson's family heard of the accident when they were telephoned by Miss Pauline Gower, the head of the ATA which ferries aircraft from the factories to the front line squadrons.

"Amy has been flying as a ferry pilot for six months," her mother said tonight. "She was intensely happy in the knowledge that she was working for her country in this way; in fact, I have never known her as light-hearted as she has been during recent months."

Jim Mollison, Amy Johnson's former husband, is also serving with the ATA.

Coal shortage hits freezing Germans

Germany, 11 January
The bitterly cold winter weather across many parts of Europe is also affecting the ordinary Germans, who are finding that their meagre coal rations are insufficient to heat their flats and houses.

The situation seems unlikely to improve. Next week the Security Service of the SS is to produce one of its regular reports for the Berlin government on the conditions and mood of the country, which is expected to reveal acute shortages of coal for households and small businesses throughout the *Reich*.

This shortage is in spite of current record coal production, and can be blamed mainly on the Nazi government's policy of giving priority to the armaments industry. But in some areas the weather has dealt a double blow: it has boosted demand for coal, but has frozen many of the canals and rivers on which new supplies would be carried.

Pact seals Russo-German friendship

Moscow, 10 January
Germany and Russia signed a new, enlarged, economic agreement in Moscow today. The agreement is of special value to the Nazi war machine, for the Russians are sending the Germans industrial raw materials, oil products and foodstuffs, particularly grain.

It is believed that among the raw materials are rubber, manganese and chromium. Vital in the production of weapons, these materials are in short supply in Germany because of the British blockade. The Germans will also get petroleum products and trainloads of wheat from the Ukraine, the "bread-basket of Europe".

In return the Russians will receive German machine tools to re-equip the Soviet Union's out-of-date factories. According to the official Soviet communique: "This new economic agreement marks a great step forward" (→31).

▷

Roosevelt proclaims the "four freedoms" which underpin support for Allied cause

Washington, 6 January
President Roosevelt today promised that the United States would serve as an arsenal for the democracies, and would support all those who struggle on behalf of the four freedoms: freedom of speech and of religion, freedom from want and from fear. He also proposed that the United States should not lend money to Britain, but should supply weapons to be paid for after the war was over.

The president said that Britain and its allies did not need American manpower. They did need billions of dollars' worth of weapons. The time was near, the president went on, when the Allies would not be able to pay for those weapons in ready cash: "We cannot and we will not tell them they must surrender because of their present inability to pay for weapons which we know they must have." The president therefore did not recommend to Congress that the United States should grant Britain and the Allies loans which would have to be repaid in dollars.

"I recommend," he said, "that we make it possible for those nations to continue to obtain war materials in the United States, fitting their orders into our own programme." Mr Roosevelt said that he spoke at a moment of unprecedented danger in American history. "The democratic way of life," he said, "is at this moment being directly assailed either by arms or by the secret spreading of poisonous propaganda." Recalling the example of Norway, he said that German agents might seize strategic points in America (→ 9).

Freedom of Speech

Freedom of Worship

Freedom from Want

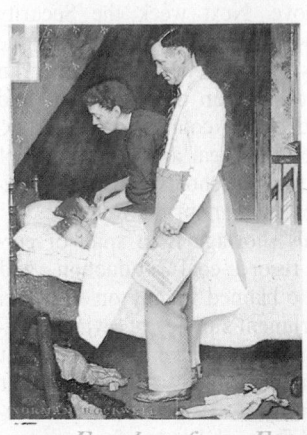
Freedom from Fear

OURS...to fight for

The four freedoms sacrosanct to Americans, as seen by Norman Rockwell.

Dive-bombers cripple HMS "Illustrious"

Smoke and steam rise from the deck of the stricken carrier "Illustrious".

Mediterranean Sea, 10 January
In a brilliantly-orchestrated attack, 30 Stuka dive-bombers took no more than six and a half minutes today to cripple HMS *Illustrious* – leaving the British carrier burning furiously and wallowing helplessly, her steering gear smashed. The *Luftwaffe*, in the form of the elite X *Fliegerkorps*, a unit specially trained to dive-bomb surface ships, has arrived in the Mediterranean.

On the bridge of his flagship, HMS *Warspite*, Vice-Admiral Sir Andrew Cunningham was supervising the transfer of a Malta-bound convoy when two Italian torpedo bombers attacked *Illustrious*. They were decoys. Fighters took off from the carrier in pursuit, leaving her without air protection.

Almost immediately, Stukas appeared in immaculate formation at 12,000 feet (3,658m). *Illustrious* was hit six times, one bomb hitting her bows, peeling back her flight-deck like a sardine can. Burning badly and gushing clouds of smoke, *Illustrious* is making her way slowly to Malta (→ 11).

Churchill promises aid for the Greeks

London, 6 January
Winston Churchill promised today that Britain would go to the help of Greece in the event of a German advance in the Balkans. In a letter to the Chiefs of Staff Committee the prime minister says: "It is quite clear to me that supporting Greece must have priority after the western flank of Egypt has been made secure."

He says that more Hurricane squadrons should be sent from the Middle East along with some artillery regiments and "some or all of the tanks of the 2nd Armoured Division, now arrived and working up in leisurely fashion in Egypt" (→ 7).

RAF gives backing to Ethiopia advance

Gubba, Ethiopia, 9 January
From the hills surrounding this Italian fort, just 25 miles (40 km) from the Sudanese frontier, Tigrean and Amharic guerrillas today watched three antiquated RAF planes bomb the fort. As it happened, the bombs all missed, but what matters to the guerrillas is that the Italian air force no longer has a monopoly of the air. Allied air support means that the guerrillas can move out of their caves, and march in daylight. Already mule trains are making their way up the Ethiopian escarpment with arms, and a British military mission is now establishing itself in Ethiopia (→ 15).

US Congress to consider Lend-Lease Bill

Washington, 10 January
The administration's leading supporters in Congress asked their colleagues today to give President Roosevelt what amounts to a blank cheque to arm Britain. The bill authorizing massive deliveries of arms to Britain is popularly known as the "Lease-and-Lend" Bill. It empowers the president to send weapons, munitions, aircraft, ships, machinery and blueprints to any country whose defence he deems vital to that of the United States. Estimates of the eventual cost of the bill have reached $2.5 billion. The bill also gives the president sweeping powers to:

* Test, inspect, fit out or otherwise place in good working order any defence article for any government whose defence it deems vital;

* Sell, transfer, exchange, lease, lend, or otherwise dispose of any defence article;

* Communicate to any such government any defence information.

At the same time the president took special powers to prevent six essential raw materials from reaching the Axis powers – copper, brass, bronze, zinc, nickel and potash. Mr Roosevelt refused to say how much Lease-and-Lend would cost. If it was US policy to help the democracies to survive, he told a press conference, speedy methods must be used which were strictly legal (→ 17).

Allies race to capture Tobruk stronghold

Italian troops surrender at Bardia: O'Connor pushes on towards Tobruk.

North Africa, 7 January
Little, it seems, can stop the British 7th Armoured Division and the 16th Australian Infantry Brigade from taking the vital seaport of Tobruk in the next few days and clearing North Africa of Italians. The Italian retreat has become a rout, with obviously disillusioned Italian soldiers lining the roads leading to Tobruk and asking to join the thousands taken at Bardia.

Using captured Italian buses and lorries carrying freshly-painted names like "Benito's Bus" and "Rome next Stop", Major-General O'Connor's desert infantry is almost racing the tanks along the coastal road – guided by some-what unconventional military signs such as: "If you lika the spaghetti, *keep going!* Next stop, TOBRUK – 27 kms."

What the victorious Allied "Desert Army" does not know is that Winston Churchill is pleading with the Greek dictator, General Metaxas, to accept his offer of British troops. Despite Wavell's doubts about the success of such a move, Churchill has sent a cable to his C-in-C. "Nothing must hamper capture of Tobruk," said the premier, "but thereafter all operations in Libya are subordinated to aiding Greece. We expect and require prompt and active compliance with our decisions" (→ 10).

Petain cultivates order and virtue

Vichy, 9 January
Vichy France plans to order all men aged 20 to do eight months' service in the *Chantiers de Jeunesse* [Youth Workshops] which were created last July. Run on military lines, the Chantiers are a tool in Marshal Petain's "National Revolution", a euphemism for autocratic government, discipline and "traditional" moral values under his guardianship. To this end Petain last month reintroduced religious instruction in state schools (→ 27).

Naval Portsmouth hit by "Luftwaffe"

Portsmouth, 11 January
Last night the historic maritime city of Portsmouth – "Pompey" to locals and the navy – was devastated by the *Luftwaffe*. Around 140 tons of high explosive and oil bombs and 50,000 incendiaries turned many streets into infernos, and there was not enough water to fight the fires; the principal water main was hit when the tide was out. Casualty figures would have been higher had not many people left town for the night.

Long-range Lancaster bomber makes its short maiden flight

The new British bomber, the Avro Lancaster, given its test flight today.

Manchester, 9 January
Britain's latest heavy bomber made its first flight at Ringway Airport here today. The Avro Lancaster is a four-engined development of the Avro Manchester, which is just entering RAF service. It has a longer range and heavier bomb-load than any other British bomber. The aircraft that flew today, however, is only a prototype, and it will be some months yet before the Lancaster begins to roll off the production lines. Even so, as the Avro chief test pilot, Bill Thorne, took her into the air, the managing director Sir Roy Dobson turned to the designer Roy Chadwick and said: "Oh boy, oh boy ... what an aeroplane! What a piece of aeroplane!"

The British keep their festive spirits up in an Anderson shelter.

1941

January

Su	Mo	Tu	We	Th	Fr	Sa
			1	2	3	4
5	6	7	8	9	10	11
12	13	14	15	16	17	18
19	20	21	22	23	24	25
26	27	28	29	30	31	

12. Sicily: RAF Hurricanes based in Malta strafe Catania airfield to try to delay further air attacks on the island.

13. Athens: Greek generals ask Britain's Mediterranean commander, General Wavell, for nine divisions to enable them to repel an expected German offensive; he can offer only a small force.

13. Albania: General Ugo Cavallero, the Chief of the Italian General Staff, relieves General Soddu of the Italian command as Greek troops consolidate their advance on the Klisura front.→

13-14. Britain: Plymouth suffers a heavy night air raid by 50 bombers.

14. Germany: The government presses Roumania to enter the war on the Axis side (→ 24).

14. Libya: RAF bombers continue their frequent attacks on shipping in Benghazi harbour (→ 21).

15. Luxemburg: German soldiers loot the ancient monastery of Clairvaux.

15. London: The admiralty announces the promotion of Vice-Admiral Sir Andrew Cunningham, C-in-C of the Mediterranean Fleet, to admiral.

16. Britain: Incendiaries and high explosive are dropped on Bristol in a prolonged severe air raid tonight.

16. Britain: The former US presidential candidate, Wendell Willkie, arrives on a morale-boosting visit (→ 5/2).

17. China: The Nationalist government disbands the Communist New Fourth Army as rebellious (→ 18).

17. Britain: Swansea is badly hit by incendiaries and high explosives in a heavy German air raid tonight.

18. China: The Communist Party describes the New Fourth Army incident as "planned by pro-Japanese conspirators and anti-Communist diehards" (→ 29).

18. Malta: *Luftwaffe* planes attack the island's airfields (→ 23).

Malta comes under sustained air attack

An Allied merchant ship ablaze in Valetta's Grand Harbour after an air raid.

Malta, 16 January
Now it is Malta's turn to withstand the full onslaught of Hitler's *Luftwaffe*. The Fuhrer has ordered the "neutralizing" of this strategically vital island south of Sicily. His Stukas have wasted no time in obeying. In successive waves, 80 of them of them hit Valetta harbour, causing major damage to port installations and several nearby churches. The casualty figures are said to be high – and soldiers and sailors were called in to unload ships when stevedores refused to work under fire.

The Luftwaffe's principal target was the aircraft carrier HMS *Illus-* trious, which had managed to limp to Malta after being severely damaged by the same Stuka unit that attacked her today. Only one bomb hit the carrier, which is undergoing emergency repairs, but more damage was caused to her hull by underwater explosions. HMAS *Perth* was also damaged in the raid.

The Maltese population failed to take adequate shelter in today's raids. Tonight, they are digging deep into Malta's limestone strata, suddenly aware that, despite the defending British aircraft – which shot down five Stukas today – the Luftwaffe will not let up (→ 18).

Hitler may come to help his Italian ally

Mediterranean, 14 January
German intervention in the Mediterranean theatre of war – always regarded by Hitler as something of a sideshow – is now more likely after a string of humiliating reverses for his Italian ally which have surprised even the Allies.

Few Allied leaders believed that General Wavell's small army would be doing so well against an overwhelming Italian force in the Western Desert, Eritrea or Ethiopia; the Royal Navy had been equally convinced that the powerfully-armed Italian fleet would present a potent opposition, even to the world's biggest battle fleet. But the Italians had not reckoned with Allied air power, vividly demonstrated by the Fleet Air Arm at Taranto.

Then the small Greek army took on the might of Mussolini's invading legions and drove them out of its country. Now the *Luftwaffe*'s attack on HMS *Illustrious* has provided a display of German power which, if supported by German troops in the Balkans and North Africa, would dramatically change the balance of power in the Mediterranean.

Key Albanian town taken from Italians

Athens, 13 January
The Greeks have captured the key town of Klissura as they push the invading Italians back through Albania. The crack "Wolves of Tuscany" division has been badly cut up and over 1,000 of its men have surrendered.

When this latest victory was announced shortly after noon today the church bells were rung and it seemed that the whole population of Athens was celebrating in the streets. King George and General Metaxas, the premier, appeared on a balcony and received a tumultuous reception.

The Greek army is now advancing on Valona, the Italian base port on the Adriatic, harrying the Italians through the frozen Albanian mountains. Valona is reported to be crowded with 30,000 wounded and frost-bitten soldiers waiting to be shipped home (→ 20).

Plea for help: an American poster.

James Joyce dies in a Swiss hospital

Zurich, 13 January
James Joyce died in hospital here today after an emergency intestinal operation. Educated for the priesthood, he studied medicine and singing and ran a cinema in Dublin before becoming a full-time author, living mainly in Paris, where he published *Ulysses* in 1922. It was banned in England and America. The "Molly Bloom" of the novel is based on Norah Barnacle, who left Dublin with him in 1904 and whom he married in 1931.

154

Britain moves to beat food racketeers

BETTER POT-LUCK with Churchill today

THAN HUMBLE PIE under Hitler tomorrow

DON'T WASTE FOOD!

No market for Nazi pies in Britain.

Britain, 14 January

Lord Woolton, the minister of food, spiked the guns of speculators when the prices of 21 foodstuffs were pegged today at the level at which they stood at the beginning of last December. Prices of many of them will fall, but retailers welcomed his action. They say that they have been forced to buy supplies at inflated prices. Chickens, which come under the order, have risen since December from 2/3 (11p/45¢) a pound to 3/3. Price controls also apply to coffee, cocoa, honey, tinned food, meat paste, rice and pasta, pickles and sauces, jellies and custard, biscuits, nuts and processed cheese.

"I am always glad to catch the speculator," said Lord Woolton. Further price controls are expected soon on jam, syrup, treacle and tinned soup.

A survey of the cost of living just completed by the ministry of labour shows that families earning less than £250 ($1,000) a year spend £1/14/1 (£1.70/$6.85) per week on food, out of an average family budget of £4/6/3 (£4.31/$17.37). The survey was begun in 1937 and presumably does not take account of recent wartime price rises as goods become scarce.

Internal tensions dent Chinese war effort

Kiangsi, Central China, 15 January

The growing tension between rival Nationalist and Communist factions, which flared into open violence last week when the 10,000-strong New Fourth Army of the Communists was surrounded and disarmed, is likely to be made worse by the Nationalist *Kuomintang* ruling that the New Fourth must now be disbanded.

The incident is feared to have severely damaged the Chinese war effort and removed any prospect of further military collaboration between the two rivals against Japan.

Communists are denouncing the disarming as part of a Nationalist-Japanese plot. The Communists fear that 25,000 comrades who are still in Kiangsi, which is Nationalist-dominated, face a similar danger. They claim that the original Nationalist order to the New Fourth to cross the Yellow River was always intended to trap it (→ 17).

Chinese soldiers seen listening to a speech "somewhere in China".

Selassie returns home

Emperor Haile Selassie returns to Ethiopia to take command of his troops.

Ethiopia, 15 January

Five years after he was forced into exile Haile Selassie, the emperor of Ethiopia (or Abyssinia), is home. He was flown over the frontier from Sudan shortly after 11am by the RAF and was greeted by a welcoming party of British officers, native chiefs and troops from the Ethiopian regular army.

The emperor had been forced into exile by the Italian invasion, pleading in vain for aid at the League of Nations. Today he issued a proclamation urging his people to rebel themselves against the Italian invaders: "Italy is cornered by the grip of Great Britain by sea, air and land power. The Italians will not escape my trusted warriors."

Haile Selassie, who was accompanied by his two sons, thanked the government and people of Britain for their support in his "bitter trials". So the man who had lived in Bath as plain Mr Smith was once more "His Imperial Majesty – Lion of Judah, king of the kings of Ethiopia". His return is expected to boost even further the momentum of British attacks on Mussolini's faltering empire (→ 18/2).

Churchill wants US weapons for Europe

Glasgow, 17 January

Winston Churchill today ended his tour of the civil defence organization here with a speech made in the presence of President Roosevelt's personal envoy, Harry Hopkins. The prime minister told his American visitor: "We don't require in 1941 large armies from overseas. What we do require are weapons, ships and aeroplanes. All that we can pay for we will pay for, but we require far more than we shall be able to pay for ..." (→ 8/2).

Bulgaria pressured to join Axis effort

Sofia, 13 January

King Boris of Bulgaria, "invited" to Germany by Hitler, has been been given a series of demands by the Fuhrer which would bring Bulgaria into the war on Germany's side. Hitler wants Bulgaria to join Germany, Italy and Japan in the Tripartite Pact; to allow German troops to pass through its territory in order to attack Greece; and to take an active part in Axis military operations. Boris would like the benefits without going to war (→ 23).

1941

January

Su	Mo	Tu	We	Th	Fr	Sa
			1	2	3	4
5	6	7	8	9	10	11
12	13	14	15	16	17	18
19	20	21	22	23	24	25
26	27	28	29	30	31	

19. Sudan: Major-General William Platt opens an offensive against the Italians in Eritrea with the 4th and 5th Indian Divisions; Kassala is retaken.

19. Mediterranean: The British destroyer *Greyhound* sinks the Italian submarine *Neghelli* off Phalconera.

20. Far East: Japan offers to mediate in the conflict between French Indochina and Thailand (→ 7/2).

20. Washington: Roosevelt is sworn in for his unprecedented third term as president.

20. Albania: The RAF heavily raids Valona (→ 26).

21. Tokyo: Yosuke Matsuoka, the foreign minister, warns the US against meddling in Asian affairs (→ 27).

21. Mediterranean: HMS *Gnat*, HMS *Ladybird* and HMS *Terror* bombard Tobruk.→

22. Lublin, Poland: Governor Hans Frank tells a meeting of Nazi officials: "We who for 20 years have been fighting beside the Fuhrer cannot be asked to have any consideration left for the Jews" (→ 24).

23. Sofia: General Boydev, the Bulgarian army chief of staff, has agreed terms for cooperation with German military officials (→ 8/2).

23. Malta: The damaged British aircraft carrier *Illustrious* limps out of Valetta harbour for full repairs at Alexandria.

24. Australia: The prime minister, Robert Menzies, leaves Melbourne, bound for Britain.

24. Libya: In one of the first tank battles in this arena, the British 4th Armoured Brigade pushes back Italian forces at Mechili (→ 26).

24. Bucharest: Roumania's leader, Ion Antonescu, finally puts down the revolt of the pro-Nazi Iron Guard (→ 10/2).

25. Washington: Viscount Halifax, the new British ambassador, asks the secretary of state, Cordell Hull, for swift American aid.

Roumania's Iron Guard slaughters Jews

Sofia, 21 January
The story is gradually emerging here of a terrible slaughter of Jews by the pro-Nazi Iron Guard in Bucharest. Some were burnt to death in buildings set on fire by the rioting guards. Others were beaten senseless, robbed, and then doused in petrol and set on fire.

In the most horrific incident some 50 Jews had their throats cut in a barbarous parody of *kosher* butchering in the municipal slaughter house. Tiring of this sport, the berserk guards beheaded scores more. In another incident 160 Jewish leaders who had been imprisoned at Jilava were taken into a field and shot down (→ 23).

Agents of terror: the Iron Guard.

USA turns down Vichy plea to take Jews

Washington, 24 January
The United States has rejected an appeal from the Vichy government to admit Jewish refugees from Germany, of whom there are now many thousands in unoccupied France.

The Vichy government argued that Jewish refugees added to its food and relief difficulties, and asked the United States, either alone or in conjunction with Latin-American countries, to open its doors to German Jewish refugees. However, the United States declined to pass this request on to Latin-American governments for

fear of seeming to put pressure on them. The United States has two reasons for declining to admit these refugees: firstly, it believes that refugees should not be distinguished on racial and religious grounds; secondly, no change could be made in the existing immigration laws with their system of quotas.

A US spokesman added that his government did not want to be a party to forced migration which might have "serious and unhappy consequences to the economic and social equilibrium" in the receiving states.

Britons must enrol for Civil Defence

Britain, 20 January
Fire-watching becomes compulsory today as part of Britain's new Defence Regulations, under which men and women aged between 16 and 60 are to register for part-time Civil Defence service.

For the time being, the powers of Herbert Morrison, as minister of home security, will only be exercised to require 48 hours of firewatching a month by men during the blackout hours. All factories, offices, shops, cinemas and theatres, churches, blocks of flats and private houses in the danger areas are to arrange fire-watching rotas. Empty properties will be the responsibility of local authorities.

In commercial premises management have the same obligation as employees to take turns of duty in watching for incendiaries and dealing with them, unless the outbreak is so big that the fire brigade must be called.

Mr Morrison explained: "Big buildings will draw their parties from within their own walls. Small ones will combine together." In residential districts, fire-watching parties will be made up, some on patrol with stirrup pumps and sandbags at hand, some within call for when they are needed. No-one who is unfit or would suffer exceptional hardship has to enrol (→ 15/2).

Chum, an Airedale with a brave pedigree, wins the "Dogs' VC"

London, 25 January
The first medal of the war awarded to an animal has gone to Chum the Airedale. He has been awarded the "Dogs' VC" – the Bravery Medal of Our Dumb Friends' League – for saving the life of Mrs Marjorie French of Purley.

Mrs French was trapped in her air-raid shelter after her home had been destroyed by a bomb. The first signs of rescue were two large paws digging fast and furiously. When he had cleared a large enough opening, Chum seized Mrs French by the hair and dragged her to safety. He did not wait around for rewards and it has taken Our Dumb Friends' League a while to trace him. He is owned by Mr and Mrs Chant of Whyteleaf Road, Purley.

Mrs Marjorie French and her gallant rescuer, Chum the Airedale "VC".

British advances loosen Mussolini's grip on Africa

British and Empire troops push forward to take Tobruk town from the Italians.

Under cover of a Bren gun carrier, Indian troops clear an Eritrean village.

Allies capture vital supply port of Tobruk

Tobruk, 22 January
For several days there was only one enemy: a fierce, howling sandstorm that struck at attackers and defenders alike with total impartiality. It clogged air-intakes on aircraft, tanks and gun breeches, and filled the eyes, ears, mouths and noses of men who sought shelter anywhere from this merciless sandblasting.

And there was to be no respite for the Italian defenders. Throughout the following days, British gunners hurled thousands of tons of high explosive into Fortress Tobruk – augmented by constant bombing from the air.

The barrage was intensified two nights ago until it matched that of Ypres in 1917, and stopped only at dawn. Australian sappers went forward to cut the barbed wire on the outer perimeter, clearing the way for infantrymen who had moved to within 1,000 yards (910 metres) of the Italian trenches during the night.

Backed by British armour, the Australians faced stiff resistance at first with many Italians firing until the very end and dying at their guns. Before long, however, white flags were flying from the trenches and thousands of prisoners were being taken. The outer ring of

Tobruk's defences had been breached; and now the tanks roared in to attack the remaining defenders in the rear.

Three forts remained to be taken before the town itself could be reached. The first of these was stormed by the infantry and taken after fierce hand-to-hand fighting. The other two surrendered quickly. As dusk fell last night, Tobruk was in full view of the attackers. It took just a few bursts of machine-gun fire to force the town's surrender. No Union Jack could be found, so an Australian "Digger's" hat flies from the flagpole over Tobruk this morning (→ 24).

British push towards Italian Somaliland

Tana River, Kenya, 24 January
With the fall today of the frontier post of Liboi, Lieutenant-General Alan Cunningham is poised to advance from Kenya into Italian Somaliland.

At the same time, South African troops are moving across Kenya's northern frontier districts to Moyale for an advance northwards. Cunningham's 12th African Division, made up of East, West and South Africans, has been pushing further south, heading for Jubaland (southern Italian Somaliland). This is arid country, where thorn thickets stretch to the horizon, and tactics are reduced to tiny groups am-

bushing other tiny groups. Everywhere there are flies. "Hit them, hit them hard and hit them again!" Cunningham said when his action against the Italians began last month. Some soldiers assume that he meant the flies.

Six months ago, when Italy declared war, Britain had one battalion and a brigade of King's African Rifles in Kenya. Now it has 75,000 men, mostly from African colonies, South Africa and India. Cunningham aims to cross into Italian Somaliland as far as the river Juba and the port of Kismayu, before a major advance further into the territory and into Ethiopia after the rains next June.

Facing him is an army on paper of 100,000 Italian and 200,000 Black African troops. In reality it is less formidable. One-third is tied down by Ethiopian guerrillas, and another third is defending Eritrea against the British in Sudan. In addition, the Italians are so short of petrol that they cannot concentrate large numbers in any key spot.

General de Simone, the Italian commander who seized British Somaliland last August, is aware of this, and is forming a line on the river Juba to try to force the British into linear warfare where their mobility would be useless (→ 14/2).

Hitler and Mussolini hold crisis talks

Berchtesgaden, 19 January
A chastened Mussolini arrived here today to plead with Hitler for military aid. The location is significant – until now, the two dictators have met on "equal terms" on their borders. The Duce was "frowning and nervous" on his special train – clearly worried that Hitler would use this opportunity to condescend to him after Italy's string of defeats in North Africa,

Greece and Albania. Much to his surprise – and obvious relief – Mussolini found Hitler cordial and welcoming. The Fuhrer has already agreed to bolster the Italian army in Libya with anti-tank formations and squadrons of the *Luftwaffe*, and to send an army corps of two and a half divisions to Albania. The price to the Duce is total subordination to Hitler in all military matters (→ 6/2).

January

Su	Mo	Tu	We	Th	Fr	Sa
				1	2	3	4
5	6	7	8	9	10	11
12	13	14	15	16	17	18
19	20	21	22	23	24	25
26	27	28	29	30	31	

26. Albania: Italy mounts an unsuccessful counter-attack on the town of Klisura, captured by the Greeks two weeks ago (→ 27).

26. Libya: Italian forces withdraw from Mechili, south of Derna, in Cyrenaica.→

27. Tokyo: The Peruvian ambassador to Japan warns his American counterpart, Joseph Grew, that the Japanese plan to destroy the US fleet; Grew passes the information on to Washington.→

27. Vichy: All civil servants and state officials are ordered to swear an oath of allegiance to Marshal Petain (→ 8/2).

27. Albania: Italy's foreign minister, Count Galeazzo Ciano, takes command of a bomber squadron (→ 9/3).

29. Singapore: On his way to Britain, the Australian prime minister, Robert Menzies, is appalled at the neglect of the island's defences, which he considers an easy target for Japan (→ 16/2).

29. China: Nationalist soldiers and *Kuomintang* guerrillas recover Zhenyang from the Japanese (→ 3/2).

29. Washington: Top British and American officials hold a secret meeting (ABC1) to hammer out a joint strategy in the event of the USA joining the war against the Axis powers (→ 27/3).

30. Berlin: Convinced that 1941 will be "the crucial year of the great New Order in Europe", Hitler threatens to blow up US aid ships bound for Britain.

31. Britain: Josef Jakob, a German spy, parachutes into the village of Ramsey in Huntingdonshire. He breaks his leg on landing and is immediately arrested.

31. China: Eighty thousand square kilometres are flooded and a million people are made homeless when the Yellow River bursts its banks.

31. Germany: The *Wehrmacht* completes the initial plans for Operation *Barbarossa* – the proposed invasion of the USSR (→ 12/2).

Italians counter-attack in battle for Derna

A British machine-gun battalion looks towards the town of "sweet" water.

Derna, Libya, 30 January
For the first time in this desert war, British and Australian troops found themselves facing a major counter-attack as Italian troops covered the evacuation of civilians – most of them Italian settlers – and the bulk of the garrison from this once-thriving seaport town.

Eight days after their successful attack on Tobruk, armour and infantry found the defenders making the best use of the rugged, hilly countryside, their artillery directing heavy and accurate fire with 20mm guns mounted on lorries. The Italian air force, which has not been seen for several days, joined in the attack, dive-bombing and machine-gunning British positions.

As they forced the Italians back to an escarpment, the British faced two more desert foes – blinding sandstorms and thirst as water supplies, carried over 100 miles (160 km) of desert, began to run out.

Derna has an ample supply of good "sweet" water – and perhaps that was one major incentive for infantry and tanks to make the final assault on the escarpment and literally run down the other side into the town where the few remaining Italian troops waited with their hands up in surrender.

As the bulk of the Allied forces moves westward across Cyrenaica, the strength of the resistance here suggests a tough fight at Benghazi, the ultimate objective (→ 7/2).

Morrison closes down the "Daily Worker"

Westminster, 28 January
In the House of Commons tonight, Herbert Morrison, the home secretary and minister of home security, was given the overwhelming backing of MPs for his decision to shut down the *Daily Worker,* the newspaper of the Communist Party of Great Britain, because its anti-war stance was subversive and calculated to help the enemy.

Morrison, whose war responsibilities include censorship and the detention of potential enemies of the state, said that the paper had conducted a sustained campaign of vilification, telling people that they were being killed and injured in enemy air raids because the government wanted to make big profits for capitalists and imperialists. It was "cruel and cynical, sheer snivelling hypocrisy" to preach defeatism to people who were enduring great hardship.

Aneurin Bevan, the left-wing Labour MP, said that although he detested the *Daily Worker*'s propaganda, he believed the ban did a disservice to the cause of freedom. Despite this plea, MPs voted 297 to 11 to back the home secretary.

General Metaxas, Greek leader, dies

Athens, 29 January
General Joannis Metaxas, the premier of Greece and hero of his country's resistance to the Italian aggressors, has died at the age of 70. A soldier who was exiled for being too pro-German in the Great War, he was a fervent royalist and nationalist. He was the "father" of the modern Greek army. As chief of staff on three occasions, he reorganized the army, built a northern defensive line, and established a military academy.

Above all he imbued the Greeks with his own fighting spirit, and when he contemptuously rejected Mussolini's ultimatum the country united behind him. His monument will be Greece's string of victories over the Italians.

Greek hero: Joannis Metaxas.

Shipborne "radar" boosts Royal Navy

Britain, 31 January
New types of on-board radio direction finding equipment (RDF, or "radar") are now being fitted to all major British warships. The Royal Navy's ships have had the ability to detect aircraft and enemy ships with on-board RDF since the beginning of the war. Now types 282 and 283 are for controlling anti-aircraft fire, while type 284 is used for surface gunnery. These will radically increase the navy's ability to detect, track and destroy (→ 28/3).

Setback for British Eritrean advance

Barentu, Eritrea, 27 January
For eight days the British have been advancing from Sudan into Italian-held Eritrea. They have now been stopped at the mountain fortress of Barentu and the bridge across the river Baraka at Agordat.

The 4th and 5th Indian Divisions and the Sudan Defence Force began by retaking the border town of Kassala. Next day they crossed the frontier, into "a tormented landscape," according to one Italian officer, "like a stormy sea moved by the wrath of God".

The 5th Indian Division found Tessanai deserted, its garrison in retreat, and went on to Barentu. Forty miles north a flying column under Colonel Frank Messervy, "Gazelle Force", penetrated as far as Keru Gorge before being stopped. There the British suffered their only set-back so far.

The 10th Indian Brigade, trying to outflank the Keru defences, got lost, was strafed by planes, and its commander, Major General Bill Slim, retired with a bullet in his backside. It was two days before Messervy was through the gorge, his artillery fighting off a frontal cavalry charge on open sights. Now Messervy is outside Agordat and the 5th Indian is outside Barentu – their first major obstacles (→ 4/2).

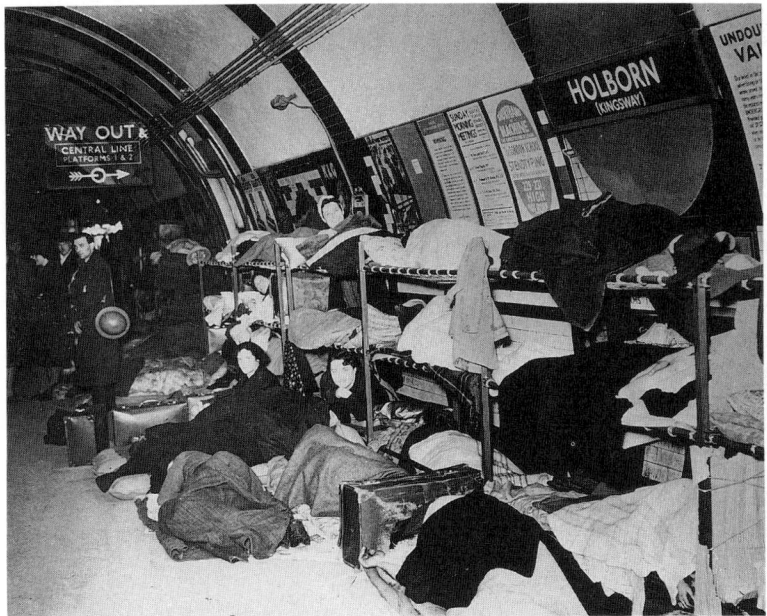
Waiting for the last train while those with bunks get their beauty sleep.

London's deep sleepers get used to Tube

London, 29 January
Londoners are beginning to enjoy a modicum of comfort when using public shelters or the Underground. The government has started installing 600,000 bunks in the shelters, 22,000 of them in the Tube stations. Regular shelterers are now given a ticket for a specific bunk. Sanitary facilities are being provided and the larger shelters supply snacks. There are food trains which run from station to station each evening and early in the morning. Some shelters are run by marshals or voluntary committees, which expel undesirables (down-and-outs have their own shelter under the rail arches at Charing Cross).

One Tube shelter even has its own newspaper, *The Swiss Cottager*. Some have regular concerts and many hold card parties. There have been reports of plagues of mosquitoes and lice, but no epidemics. The number of people sheltering in Tube stations has fallen from a peak of 177,000 to 96,000.

Washington told of Japan's naval plan

Tokyo, 27 January
The United States ambassador here, Joseph C Grew, is understood to have cabled Washington a report today that the Japanese navy secretly plans to attack the US naval base at Pearl Harbor in Hawaii. The report is said to have been passed to Mr Grew by the Peruvian ambassador here.

Japan's foreign minister, Yosuke Matsuoka, talks of peace, but last year the navy minister, Yoshida Zengo, approved a policy towards America which envisaged the possibility of war. The essential Japanese strategy since 1936 has been to "strike south" to secure oil from Borneo. An attack on the US fleet at Pearl Harbor would protect Japan's eastern flank (→ 19/2).

Matsuoka: Japan's foreign minister.

Military chiefs hold secret war meeting

Washington, 27 January
This week, for the first time in history, senior US and British military staff officers will meet here in secret to hammer out a common strategy in case the United States finds itself at war with Germany or Japan (or both) in alliance with Britain. The talks, known as "ABC1", illustrate how quickly Washington is changing its view of the danger of war. On 12 November Admiral Stark, the chief of US naval operations, sent "Plan Dog" to the navy secretary, Frank Knox, giving priority to war in the Atlantic and urging closer links with Britain (→ 27/3).

Thousands of Jews starve to death in horror of Warsaw Ghetto

Warsaw, 31 January
The Nazis are throttling food supplies to the Jewish ghetto. "Almost daily," writes one chronicler, Emanuel Ringelblum, "people are falling dead or unconscious in the street." Starvation and disease kill 65 people a day out of the ghetto population of 377,000.

The governor, Hans Frank, has a calculated policy allowing the Jews about half the food they need. Teetering on the edge of famine, they can be cajoled into submission by the promise of more food or the threat of even less. Starvation saps their physical and mental strength, undermining their will to resist. Best of all, says Frank, killing a Jew by hunger saves a valuable bullet, needed for the master race's inevitable conquest of the world (→ 18).

Bodies of Jews that have starved to death in the ghetto are taken for disposal.

February

Su	Mo	Tu	We	Th	Fr	Sa
						1
2	3	4	5	6	7	8
9	10	11	12	13	14	15
16	17	18	19	20	21	22
23	24	25	26	27	28	

1. US: Admiral Husband Kimmel becomes C-in-C of the Pacific Fleet based at Pearl Harbor.

3. China: Japanese forces occupy Tamshin, east of Canton.→

3. At Sea: The German battlecruisers *Scharnhorst* and *Gneisenau* break out of the North Sea into the Atlantic.

4. US: The United Services Organization is formed to serve the welfare, social and educational needs of the armed forces and defence industries.

4. Eritrea: British troops begin a battle to wrest Keren, in the north of the country, from the Italians (→ 12).

5. Britain: The US politician Wendell Willkie's morale-boosting visit to Britain ends.

6. Washington: John Gilbert Winant is appointed the new US ambassador to Britain.

6. Germany: Hitler appoints General Erwin Rommel to command the *Afrika Korps* [Africa Corps], formed to support Italy in Libya (→ 12).

7. Tokyo: Peace talks between Vichy French Indochina and Thailand open, under Japanese auspices, a week after an armistice was signed.

7. Britain: Command headquarters for the western approaches of the Atlantic is moved from Plymouth to Liverpool.

7. Libya: Free French troops under General Leclerc besiege the Italian garrison at Koufra.

7. Libya: After a two-day battle, Italian forces surrender at Beda Fomm, the first important British victory of the war; 250,000 Italians are taken prisoner.

8. Vichy: Admiral Darlan succeeds Pierre-Etienne Flandin as foreign minister (→ 10).

8. Berlin: The German and Bulgarian military staffs agree arrangements for German troops to enter Bulgaria (→ 22).

8. Washington: The House of Representatives passes the Lend-Lease Bill (→ 17).

Benghazi seized by British Empire force

British and Empire infantrymen in North Africa take on an enemy tank.

Benghazi, 7 February
Benghazi fell today in a brilliantly-orchestrated attack, which took the Italian defenders entirely by surprise, when British armour – traversing barren and waterless desert tracks from Tobruk – suddenly appeared at Beda Fomm, south of Benghazi, cutting off any chance of Italian retreat.

It was then that Australian tanks and infantry swept in from the north to join the British from the south and west in a combined assault on the town. Italian tanks fought hard, but stopped after 60 of them had been destroyed.

Benghazi has fallen – and the victors claim the spoils as huge quantities of ammunition and fuel

fall into Allied hands. The Italian commander, General Tellera, was found badly wounded, bleeding to death in a tent; and his Thirteenth Army commander, General "Electric Whiskers" Bergonzoli, whose monumental moustache aroused much mirth among the Australians, stood miserably with his staff, waiting, with thousands of his troops, to be taken into captivity.

As Major-General Richard O'Connor's men continue westwards – advanced units have arrived at Sirte, with Tripoli itself under threat – the battle has moved to Whitehall. Churchill's Defence Committee is insisting that Greece, even Turkey, are now Wavell's priorities (→ 9).

China drives Japan back in Henan

Sinyang, 7 February
After 13 days of bitter fighting, Chinese forces have crushed a major Japanese offensive in central China intended to make Japan's garrison at Wuhan safer. By this morning Chinese troops had re-occupied Sinyang and all points north. The strategically crucial city along the Wuhan-Peking railway had fallen on 25 January when three Japanese divisions broke through Chinese lines before advancing and taking Wuyang.

The turning-point in the battle for southern Henan came when Japanese forces suffered heavy losses as they attempted to take Fangcheng to the north-west of Sinyang and were forced to retreat (→ 6/3).

War costs Britain £11 million a day

Britain, 4 February
The cost of the war for Britain is now soaring rapidly. Last July it was about £7.5 million a day. Now it is above £11 million ($44 million).

Sir Kingsley Wood, the chancellor, gave this grim news today. Higher war output and other military preparations have far exceeded Treasury calculations. The current budget deficit is twice the size estimated eight months ago. MPs are now braced for drastic tax increases. Tax is meeting only one-quarter of all expenditure.

Red Cross reports conditions satisfactory for Allied PoWs

Europe, 1 February
It is estimated that some two and half million prisoners of war are currently being held in camps across Germany and German-occupied territory. The vast majority, nearly two million, are French; hundreds of thousands are Polish; tens of thousands are Belgian, Dutch and Norwegian, and about 44,000 are British.

Red Cross delegates are allowed into the camps to report on conditions. Although these vary considerably, they are generally

found to be satisfactory. Inmates in *oflags*, camps in which officers are held, are usually better-fed and more comfortable than those in *stalags*, where privates and NCOs are confined. *Dulags* are transfer camps where the prisoners are sent first. A Red Cross delegate, Dr Marti, wrote in his report on Dulag *Luft*: "Rooms with one to three beds; tables, easy chairs; exceptional comfort; dining-room; whisky every evening; papers; various games; walks outside camp ..."

The prisoners' main com-

plaint is boredom, brought on by the routine and, perhaps most of all, by the diet of soup and potatoes that is standard camp fare. In several camps visited recently by the Red Cross the lack of winter clothing was also a problem. The situation was not helped by the Germans selling extra garments at vastly inflated prices.

But compared with the treatment of "dissidents" and, in particular, Jews, in Nazi camps, conditions for prisoners of war seem positively humane.

1941

February

Su	Mo	Tu	We	Th	Fr	Sa
						1
2	3	4	5	6	7	8
9	10	11	12	13	14	15
16	17	18	19	20	21	22
23	24	25	26	27	28	

Terror bombing has failed, says Hitler

Berlin, 6 February
Hitler as good as admitted today that the *Luftwaffe* assault on Britain has not achieved the "knock-out blow" it aimed at. His war directive no 23 – *Directions for Operations against the English War Economy* – says that the bombing campaign has had "least effect of all, so far as we can see, on the morale and the will to resist of the English people. No decisive success can be expected from terror attacks on residential areas."

However, bombing is to be intensified on shipping and the ports to inflict the greatest possible damage on the British economy "and also to give the impression that an invasion is planned for this year".

Eating wisely and waiting for Hitler.

Pro-Nazi party is formed in France

Paris, 1 February
A French version of the Nazi Party was formed in Occupied France today. It is called the *Rassemblement National Populaire* (RNP) [Popular National Assembly], and its aims include "cooperation with Germany" and "protection of the race", that is, anti-Semitism.

Based near the Gare St Lazare, the German-sponsored RNP is led by Marcel Deat, and members include a veterans' leader, Jean Goy. So far, however, the French seem reluctant to join the new party (→ 8).

9. Libya: British troops occupy El Agheila (→ 18).

10. Berlin: Spain signs a secret treaty with Germany, undertaking to resist any Allied attack (→ 13).

10. Italy: In Britain's first parachute operation of the war, paratroopers destroy the Tragino aqueduct in Apulia.

11. Netherlands: The Stirling bomber made its operational debut last night in a raid on oil storage tanks at Rotterdam.

12. Britain: Anthony Eden, the foreign secretary, and Sir John Dill, Chief of the Imperial General Staff, leave for a tour of Egypt, Turkey and Greece (→ 19).

12. Moscow: General Georgi Zhukov is appointed Soviet Chief of the General Staff and deputy commissar for defence.

12. Libya: Rommel arrives in Tripoli to head the German *Afrika Korps.*→

12. Eritrea: Italian alpine troops recapture positions at Keren, forcing British forces to retreat (→ 13).

13. Eritrea: Aircraft from the carrier HMS *Formidable* attack Massawa (→ 21).

13. Spain: King Alfonso XIII, who left Spain in 1931, renounces the throne in favour of his son Juan.

13. Merano, Italy: Admirals Arturo Riccardi of Italy and Erich Raeder of Germany meet to discuss naval cooperation.

14. Libya: The first units of the German *Afrika Korps* arrive.→

14. Germany: The heavy cruiser *Admiral Hipper* ends a 14-day cruise in which it has sunk 64 Allied vessels.

14. Vichy: Admiral Darlan is appointed interior minister; he keeps his other posts (→ 24).

14. Berchtesgaden: Hitler presses the Yugoslav premier, Dragisa Cvetkovich, to join the Tripartite Pact (→ 4/3).

15. Austria: The deportation of Jews to ghettoes in Lublin and Kielce, in Poland, begins at the rate of 1,000 a month (→ 25).

African Imperial troops capture Kismayu

Ethiopian guerrillas who have joined the Imperial fight against the Italians.

Italian Somaliland, 14 February
The Italians are on the run in East Africa. Their latest loss is the port of Kismayu, on the Indian Ocean, which was occupied at two o'clock this afternoon by West, East and South African troops under the command of Lieutenant-General Alan Cunningham.

The port is the first major prize in what he plans will become a two-pronged drive, up the coast to Mogadishu, the colonial capital, and northwards up the river Juba to Ethiopia. His offensive into Italian territory began in earnest only three days ago, after an eight-week preliminary operation to recapture first parts of Kenya occupied by the Italians and then frontier posts on the Kenya-Somaliland border. On 12 February the town of Afmadu, about 100 miles (160 km) east of the border and 100 miles north of Kismayu, was taken, an action in which the King's African Rifles were prominent.

The little resistance Cunningham has since met on the road to Kismayu has been dealt with by the Gold Coast Regiment and an Indian mountain battery, while South African planes have pounded the port. Next stop: Mogadishu (→ 16).

Royal Navy bombs Italian home ports

Genoa, 9 February
British battleships appeared off the coast of northern Italy today and began the systematic shelling of this historic port.

HMS *Renown* and HMS *Malaya* fired 300 tons of shells from their 16-inch guns onto dock installations, warehouses and the Ansaldo Electric works, while Fleet Air Arm Swordfish aircraft from the carrier HMS *Ark Royal* bombed oil refineries at Leghorn [*Livorno*], a major railway junction at Pisa and other rail connections.

161

Hitler sends troops to trouble spots

"Afrika Korps" to boost Italian army

Tripoli, Libya, 14 February
The first troops of Hitler's new *Afrika Korps* disembarked today, two days after their commander, General Erwin Rommel, arrived with orders to rescue the wretched Italian army, which in two months has lost 130,000 prisoners of war, 380 tanks and 845 guns to Britain.

Rommel has been promised two divisions, one armoured, but these will not arrive until late April. For the time being, then, he has to face the British with only a reconnaissance battalion and an anti-tank battalion. He plans to hoax the enemy with dummy tanks mounted on *Volkswagen* motor cars.

Despite orders that he should not attempt an offensive until his two divisions arrive, Rommel is already planning a probe into the British defences. He could be luckier than he expects. The British are strung out along the coast of Libya for over 500 miles (800 km) from the Egyptian border to El Agheila.

General Wavell's battle-weary 7th Armoured Division has been pulled back to Egypt for rest and refitting. Its place has been taken by

German troops unload equipment.

the new and inexperienced 2nd Armoured Division. Other British forces have been diverted to Greece, greatly weakening Wavell's strength in the Western Desert. The key to North Africa is the Mediterranean supply route. German aircraft are bombing Malta from Sicily, so the RAF can no longer strike at Axis shipping sailing for Tripoli. And the British, unable to use the Mediterranean, must take supplies round the Cape of Good Hope.

Army penetrates deep into Balkans

Bucharest, 12 February
With at least 40 troop trains a day crossing Hungary to Roumania, Hitler is set to build up a formidable 600,000-strong army on the border with the Ukraine. Much of the equipment carried by the German forces is of French make, having been seized after the French collapse last year.

The Germans' next move, now the ice has broken on the Danube, is to float pontoon bridges in the river to enable troops to enter Bulgaria, under a secret agreement reached with the Bulgarian government four days ago. The Germans have promised the Bulgarians a slice of Greek territory to give them access to the Aegean Sea – but only after the war.

The massive German move into the Balkans has set off a wave of speculation that Hitler may be about to go to the rescue of his Italian ally, who has been badly mauled by the Greeks. Some observers, however, believe that Hitler, despite his treaty of friendship with Stalin, is planning to invade the Soviet Union (→ 22).

"Give us the tools" pleads Churchill

Churchill: keen to "finish the job".

Britain, 9 February
Churchill broke five months of radio silence today. He explained his absence from the airwaves by talking of "deeds, not words".

It was a speech of praise and encouragement for both the forces and the civilians. "We have stood our ground and faced the two dictators in the hour of what seemed their overwhelming triumph, and we have shown ourselves capable, so far, of standing up against them alone." The prime minister reserved particular praise for the victory two months ago over the Italians in Libya: "In barely eight weeks, by a campaign which will long be studied as a model of the military art, an advance of over 400 miles has been made."

He went on to speak of the vital importance of American aid, concluding: "We shall not fail or falter; we shall not weaken or tire. Neither the sudden shock of battle, nor the longdrawn trials of vigilance and exertion will wear us down. Give us the tools, and we will finish the job."

Darlan is to be France's new vice-premier

Vichy, 10 February
Marshal Philippe Petain today announced that he had appointed Admiral Francois Darlan as not only vice-premier but also minister for foreign affairs. And to underline Darlan's triumph in the backstairs conflict with the former vice-premier, Pierre Laval, the marshal designated the admiral as his successor.

A year ago Darlan seemed the cheerful ally of the Royal Navy. Born into a family that has held commissions in the French navy since Trafalgar, Darlan was head of the naval officers' training school, and in the 1930s helped to re-equip the fleet with new ships, including *Strasbourg* and *Dunkerque*. However, he was embittered by the British sinking of "his" ships at Mers-el-Kebir last July (→ 14).

Marshal Petain's newly-appointed number two: Admiral Darlan.

Britain cuts links with Roumania

London, 10 February
General Ion Antonescu's decision to allow Roumania to be used as a base for a massive German expeditionary force today led to a diplomatic rupture with Britain. After a half-hour meeting with Antonescu, later described as "extremely painful", the British envoy, Sir Reginald Hoare, returned to the legation to pack his bags.

Most of Germany's oil supplies come from Roumania, and German engineers have for some time been running the country's oil wells. When German troops began arriving, Antonescu said that they were to train the Roumanian army. The British told him that a full expeditionary force was not needed to train a few Roumanians.

1941

February

Su	Mo	Tu	We	Th	Fr	Sa
						1
2	3	4	5	6	7	8
9	10	11	12	13	14	15
16	17	18	19	20	21	22
23	24	25	26	27	28	

16. Italian Somaliland: South African troops begin to cross the river Juba (→ 22).

16. Singapore: Britain mines the waters round the colony.→

17. Washington: The Senate starts debating the Lend-Lease Bill (→ 11/3).

18. Benghazi: Italian planes bomb the port so badly that Britain has to abandon it for supply purposes (→ 20).

18. USSR: Commander Pavlov asks for road-building operations in the western USSR to be speeded up.

18. Ethiopia: The South Africans take Mega (→ 23).

19. Cairo: Anthony Eden sends a telegram to Churchill saying that the British commanders Dill, Wavell and Cunningham agree that "we should do everything in our power" to help Greece "at the earliest possible moment".

19. Washington: The Japanese ambassador, Admiral Kochisaburo Nomura, says there will be war with the US only if the US wants it (→ 25).

20. Libya: British and German troops have their first clash in the desert, at El Agheila.

20. Libya: Free French troops under Leclerc attack the Italian-held El Raj fort (→ 26).

21. Italy: Olive oil, cooking fat and butter rations are halved.

21. Eritrea: Planes from the carrier *Formidable* attack Massawa (→ 28).

22. Bulgaria: German military staff arrive in Sofia as 17 divisions, eight of which are heading for Greece, cross the border (→ 23).

22. Warsaw Ghetto: The daily bread ration is set at three ounces (85 grammes), as deaths from starvation reach 400 a week.

22. Amsterdam: SS troops arrest 400 Jews after a German officer is accidentally hurt in a Jewish-owned bar.

22. Italian Somaliland: The cruiser HMS *Shropshire* bombards Brava, on the coast between Kismayu and Mogadishu (→ 25).

Australians reinforce Singapore garrison

Army trucks gather, but two Australian soldiers try an older form of travel.

Singapore, 18 February
Australian troops, 12,000 strong, arrived in Singapore today to reinforce the British garrison. Already the 11th Indian Division has arrived in the theatre, and the III Indian Corps headquarters under Lieutenant-General Sir Lewis Heath is due to be set up in May.

The build-up of British strength is in response to the growing menace of Japanese military expansion to the south. Nazi Germany has been urging the Japanese to attack Singapore at once.

The southward advance of Japan continues to cause anxiety in Australia at a time when the greater part of the Australian forces are engaged in the Middle East. The Singapore base is regarded by Australians as the keystone of defence against Japan, and Britain has assured Australia that if a Japanese attack appeared imminent, a British battlefleet would be sent at once to Singapore.

However, the clear need exists for an army and air force strong enough to hold out in Singapore and Malaya until the fleet arrived. Australia decided therefore to contribute a brigade of infantry to the garrison (→ 24).

During a practice gas alert in Brighton the warden sounds the rattle warning and women put on their masks. During the half-hour alert gas masks were worn by everyone, and those without were kept out of the area.

U-boats hold the key to Battle of the Atlantic

North Atlantic, 22 February
The commander of the German fleet was himself in the front line today some 650 miles (1,040 km) off the Newfoundland coast.

Vice-Admiral Lutjens commanded an action which sank five British merchant ships. It could hardly be called a battle, however. Lutjens, on board the heavily armed *Gneisenau*, accompanied by her sister battle cruiser *Scharnhorst*, came across a convoy of Allied ships. Due to a shortage of destroyers the convoy had no escorts and no firepower capable of answering the German guns. The battle cruisers are only one of the worries for the British in what promises to be one of the worst months for the war at sea.

Mines continue to take a heavy toll of merchant and navy ships, particularly the new acoustic mines which are detonated by the noise of a ship. German aircraft have been playing an increasing role since last October when a new base was opened up at Stavanger, in Norway. Now the *Kondor* long-range aircraft can take off in Germany and land at Stavanger, flying deep out into the Atlantic on the way. The biggest threat, however, remains the U-boats.

In January bad weather hampered the submarine commanders and they sank only 127,000 tons of Allied shipping out of a total of 320,000. This month, however, they are already sinking at nearly twice that rate. Worse still, British efforts to sink the U-boats have so far failed dismally. The last U-boat sunk was the U104 sunk by the corvette *Rhododendron* before Christmas; the Germans have only lost 32 submarines since the war began. The appalling Allied losses have been effected by a force which has never exceeded more than about 30 U-boats active at any one time; but Germany is now building submarines faster than the Allies are sinking them.

British desert troops to move into Greece

A distinguished line-up: Eden, Dill, Cunningham, Longmore and Wavell.

Athens, 22 February
The foreign secretary, Anthony Eden, arrived in Athens today with a senior military mission including General Sir John Dill, the Chief of the Imperial General Staff (CIGS), General Sir Archibald Wavell, the Middle East commander, Admiral Sir Andrew Cunningham, C-in-C Mediterranean Fleet, and Air Marshal Sir Arthur Longmore, the chief of the RAF in North Africa. The main item for discussion with King George and his government is the question of British military aid to Greece.

There is some reluctance on the part of the Greeks to accept the help offered by Eden, on the grounds that insufficient British help might serve only to precipitate an attack by the Germans.

Eden's task is to reassure the Greeks that, although the forces being offered, which would have to be withdrawn from the army fighting the Italians in North Africa, are all that Britain can spare at the moment, they are well-equipped and trained and will acquit themselves well.

Talks are well under way this evening, and look like lasting well into the night, with the Greeks insisting that they will fight with or without British help. (→ 23)

Turks sign treaty with Bulgarians

Ankara, 17 February
The heavy emphasis on mutual goodwill and warm and friendly relations in the treaty signed here this afternoon is a reflection of the deep mistrust Turkey and Bulgaria have long felt for each other.

Bulgaria has never ceased to fear that one day Turkey will seek to regain territory lost after the Great war and in the Balkan Wars before it, while the build-up of German troops in Bulgaria in recent weeks has alarmed the Turks, who are worried that the Germans' next blow will be delivered in the Balkans and threaten Turkey (→ 22).

Women answer call for military duty

Britain, 22 February
Not many young women dream of a life in uniform, but increasing numbers are volunteering for the services. Most of them go into the Auxiliary Territorial Service – the ATS – though the Wrens, who work with the Royal Navy, are seen as the *elite*, and the WAAFs have a certain glamour by association with pilots.

In the ATS, women are trained to do almost anything that does not involve them directly in combat. Many are learning to operate the aiming mechanisms of anti-aircraft guns, though they are not allowed to fire them; large numbers are also trained as drivers and mechanics. Cooking, cleaning and clerical work are the commonest jobs.

The most novel, and the physically hardest, job in the Women's Auxiliary Air Force (WAAF) is crewing the barrage-balloon operations. The balloons are so heavy that teams of ten men are being replaced by 16 women. WAAFs also train as mechanics, photographers, bombplotters and radio-operators. But not everyone believes that the women are doing a good job. One woman told a mass-observation survey: "Those ATS girls are a disgrace. They come in this pub at night and line up against that wall. Soldiers give them drinks and when they're blind drunk they carry them out into the street."

Jewish Litvinov is dropped by Stalin

Moscow, 21 February
Maxim Litvinov, the former Soviet commissar for foreign affairs, has been further downgraded by Stalin by being expelled from the central committee. Litvinov, a Jew married to an Englishwoman and bitterly opposed to Hitler, is an embarrassment to Stalin in his dealings with the Fuhrer.

Polina Molotova, the wife of the current, hardline foreign affairs commissar, Vyacheslav Molotov, has also been sacked. She was appointed commissar for the fishing industries in 1939. She, too, is Jewish.

The ATS glamour girl: used to draw in the young women volunteers.

1941
February

Su	Mo	Tu	We	Th	Fr	Sa
						1
2	3	4	5	6	7	8
9	10	11	12	13	14	15
16	17	18	19	20	21	22
23	24	25	26	27	28	

23. Rome: While admitting the loss of 200,000 troops in Ethiopia, Mussolini says victory is assured, and that Italy will fight "to the last drop of blood" (→ 6/3).

23. Athens: After talks lasting all night and much of today, the Greek premier, Alexander Korizis, agrees to Eden's proposal for British aid.→

24. Mediterranean: Italian forces repel a British attempt to capture the island of Castelrosso, in the Dodecanese.

24. Mediterranean: The monitor HMS *Terror*, which has been of valuable aid to the army in North Africa, sinks off Derna, in Libya, after three days of air attacks; the destroyer HMS *Dainty* is sunk off Tobruk.

24. Vichy: Admiral Darlan is appointed head of the government (→ 10/3).

25. Netherlands: The SS clamps down on a wave of popular demonstrations and strikes protesting against the persecution of the Jews (→ 27).

25. Mediterranean: The British submarine *Upright* attacks an Italian convoy, sinking the cruiser *Armando Diaz*.

25. Tokyo: Yosuke Matsuoka, the foreign minister, demands that Oceania should become part of the Japanese "new order" in the Pacific.→

26. Koufra, Libya: Leclerc's Free French force blows up the Italian ammunition dump of 250 cases of bombs.

27. Amsterdam: Martial law is declared as 389 Jews, arrested last week, are deported to Buchenwald camp.

27. London: Robert Menzies agrees to send Australian troops to Greece.

27. Maldive Islands: The New Zealand cruiser *Leander* sinks the Italian armed merchant raider *Ramb I*.

28. Eritrea: RAF planes bomb the town of Asmara (→ 15).

28. Britain: 2,289 people have been killed and 3,080 injured in air raids in the last two months.

Italians lose Mogadishu

Mogadishu, 25 February

Italy's rout in East Africa at the hands of Lieutenant-General Alan Cunningham and his African soldiers is almost complete. Yesterday Cunningham took Brava, 120 miles (192 km) from Mogadishu, the capital of Italian Somaliland; this evening his forces have begun to occupy Mogadishu itself, after a day's lightning advance under the heat of the East African sun.

The British offensive in Italian Somaliland began a fortnight ago after an operation to secure the Kenya-Somaliland frontier region. East, West and South African troops took Afmadu on 12 February, followed by the important port of Kismayu on 14 February, and

encountered no serious resistance until the river Juba, where the Italians under General de Simone established a line.

But by 23 February the South Africans in the south and the Gold Coast Regiment in the north had both crossed the river, winding up the Italian front between them. From then on Italian resistance collapsed. The main Italian force surrendered at Jelib, leaving the capital almost defenceless. With the Royal Navy shelling the retreating Italians on the coastal road, the way was open for Cunningham and, in the swiftest British advance of the war so far, he pressed on to take Mogadishu and become master of Italian Somaliland (→ 16/3).

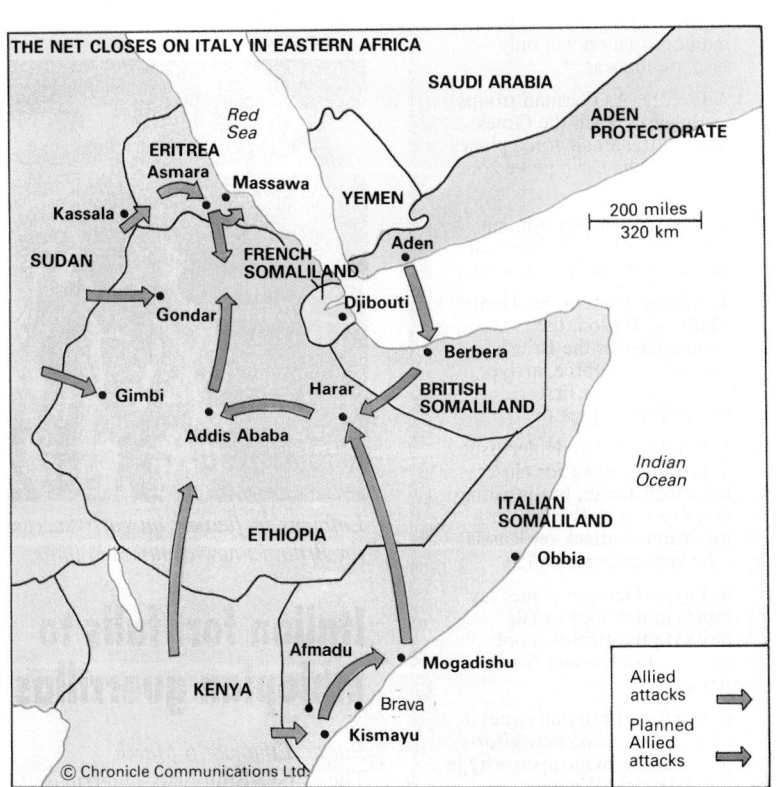

First German tanks roll into Bulgaria

Germans enter Bulgaria on 2 March, after Bulgaria joined the Axis Pact.

Sofia, 23 February

German tanks and motorized columns have been infiltrating Bulgaria from their bases in Roumania over a remote crossing of the Danube at Cernavoda in Dobruja. At the same time they have ostentatiously made no attempt to cross the main bridges over the river.

This piecemeal invasion seems to indicate that Hitler means to increase his pressure by degrees and

wait for Britain to serve an ultimatum on Bulgaria before moving into the country openly to "save it from the British".

The secrecy surrounding these moves is helped by the rigid censorship of the Bulgarian press. All military news is banned and domestic news is replaced by foreign despatches. Ordinary Bulgarians have no idea that German *Panzers* are rolling through their land (→ 1/3).

Turkey and Britain agree on Balkan issue

Ankara, 27 February

Britain and Turkey today reached full agreement on Balkan and eastern Mediterranean problems. A delegation led by Anthony Eden, the foreign secretary, flew here from Cairo for discussions with the Turkish prime minister, Dr Saydam, and Mr Sarajoglu, the foreign minister. General Sir John Dill, the CIGS, and Marshal Chakmak, the

Turkish chief of general staff, also took part. The talks were so successful that there is no need for a further conference and, according to the official spokesman, both sides "expressed deep gratification at the tenor of the conversations".

Ankara Radio said tonight that Mr Eden "is the champion of civilization and humanity against the Axis powers" (→ 2/3).

Hitler threatens increased U-boat war

Munich, 24 February

"Now our sea warfare can begin in earnest," Hitler told a hand-picked audience here today. He was speaking in a charged atmosphere at the beercellar where what became the Nazi Party was founded in 1919. He pulled no punches. "Our Nazi methods were unattractive to many," he said. "But I was a soldier and had come from the front, where

I had got used to a rough tongue." Hitler reported on the progress of the intensive training of U-boat crews to man the new boats streaming out of his shipyards.

His claim that U-boats have sunk 190,000 tons of Allied shipping in the last two days may be an exaggeration; that is more like the month's total. Nevertheless it is far more than the Allies can afford.

Japanese demands met by the French

Vichy, 28 February

France has capitulated to Japan's ultimatum to accept its proposals for settlement of the border dispute between its colony in Indochina and Thailand.

The Vichy cabinet's decision in the early hours of this morning came only hours after the Japanese ultimatum expired. Throughout yesterday Japan made it clear that

it was ready to implement its proposals by force if necessary.

When the agreement is signed Indochina will cede to Thailand all of Laos west of the Mekong and an important part of north-western Cambodia. Japan wants military bases in southern Indochina and Thailand, and expects to capitalize on its intervention by making a military pact with Thailand (→ 11/3).

Nazi persecution sparks protests in Amsterdam

Hundreds of Jews are rounded up

Many die, many more disappear

The people of Amsterdam suffer the consequences of protesting against the Nazi regime. They staged a mass demonstration following the seizure of Jewish men and youths on 22 February. Many of the protesters were themselves shot or arrested.

Japan wants white races to give way

Tokyo, 24 February

In the clearest statement yet on Japan's expansionist policy and the ideology behind it, the foreign minister, Yosuke Matsuoka, today declared Japan's belief in its "natural right" to Oceania – the western Pacific, including Australia.

Speaking to the Japanese parliament he said: "I believe the white race must cede Oceania to the Asiatics." Mr Matsuoka said that the region has sufficient natural resources to support 600-800 million people. "I believe we have a natural right to migrate there," he said.

The name Oceania usually refers to the islands of the Pacific, but an Oceania for 600 million would also have to include Australasia (→ 28).

US refuses to send ships to Singapore

Washington, 24 February

The United States has ruled out the possibility of the dispatch of US Navy capital ships to Singapore. The US view is that the loss of Singapore, while it would be unfortunate, would not have a decisive effect on the outcome of the war but could imperil the US Pacific fleet. The United States announced its decision at the Anglo-American staff conversations which opened here last month (→ 28/4).

New heavy bomber joins raid on Brest

London, 25 February

Last night 57 RAF bombers attacked the heavy cruiser *Admiral Hipper*, currently in dry dock at Brest, but caused no damage to her. Among their number were six Avro Manchester twin-engined bombers of 207 Squadron.

This marks the operational debut of this heavy bomber, and follows that of the Short Stirling on the night 10-11 February. No aircraft were lost to enemy action during the raid, but one Manchester crashed with engine trouble – the cause of frequent complaints by the men who have to fly it.

1941

March

Su	Mo	Tu	We	Th	Fr	Sa
						1
2	3	4	5	6	7	8
9	10	11	12	13	14	15
16	17	18	19	20	21	22
23	24	25	26	27	28	29
30	31					

1. Libya: The Italian stronghold at Koufra surrenders to the Free French army under Colonel Leclerc (→ 21).

1. Sofia: Bulgaria joins the Axis Pact.→

1. Greece: An earthquake leaves 10,000 people homeless in the area of Larissa (→ 3).

2. Turkey: The authorities close the Dardanelles to shipping without a permit (→ 4).

3. Moscow: The USSR warns Bulgaria that it does not approve of its pro-Axis regime, saying that the German occupation will only escalate the war.→

3. Greece: As German troops in Bulgaria reach the Greek border, Italian air force planes bombard the earthquake zone at Larissa.

4. Turkey: The government turns down Hitler's personal plea to join the Axis powers.

4. Athens: General Sir Henry Maitland Wilson, the commander of the British expeditionary force, arrives in Greece as the first troops leave Egypt (→ 7).

5. Berchtesgaden: Hitler issues a directive calling for closer links with Japan, but insisting that Operation *Barbarossa* – the planned attack on Russia – be kept a secret (→ 19).

6. Egypt: German planes lay mines in the Suez canal, blocking the British supply route to Greece and North Africa.

6. London: Churchill issues a directive ordering new efforts to break German superiority in the Atlantic: "We must assume the Battle of the Atlantic has begun."

7. Greece: The first troops of the British expeditionary force land at Piraeus and Volos.

7. Atlantic: The British destroyer *Wolverine* sinks the submarine ace Gunther Prien's U-boat U47.

8. Britain: In *Luftwaffe* air raids of renewed vigour, 34 people are killed and 80 injured tonight when London's Cafe de Paris nightspot is bombed (→ 15).

Commandos stage raid on Lofotens

Lofoten Islands, 4 March

Britain's new raiding force, the Commandos, has destroyed 18 factories producing fish oil – a commodity which is made into glycerine, a basic ingredient of high explosive – on the Norwegian Lofoten Islands. About 800,000 gallons of oil and petrol were burnt, 11 ships sunk and 225 Germans and Norwegian collaborators (dubbed "Quislings" after Norway's Nazi puppet leader) taken prisoner. The Germans will need to be especially vigilant from now on.

Led by Brigadier Charles Haydon of the Irish Guards, 500 commandos with 100 other specialists went in escorted by five destroyers and a submarine.

Lofotens in flames: an early success for Britain's new commando units.

Italian fort falls to Ethiopian guerrillas

Burye, Ethiopia, 6 March

The first Ethiopian guerrillas to enter Burye wore a hybrid mixture of captured Italian uniforms and tribal robes. There was no resistance. Bombed by the RAF and besieged by the Sudanese and Ethiopians, the 6,000-man garrison slipped out in the night; Ethiopia's "Patriots" have won their first victory. The Italians had resisted for a week, but an attack on their communications by the guerrilla leader Haile Yusuf forced them to withdraw. However, they did destroy one Ethiopian battalion blocking the retreat (→ 10).

German push raises Balkan tensions

Russia and Britain criticise Bulgaria

Sofia, 5 March

Britain has broken off diplomatic relations with Bulgaria. George Rendel, the British minister, today handed the Bulgarian government a strongly-worded note protesting against Bulgaria's active cooperation with Germany which, it declared, constituted a grave threat to Britain's ally, Greece, and was "incompatible with the maintenance of British diplomatic representation in Bulgaria".

Mr Rendel added a verbal note in even more scathing terms. Alluding to the disappearance of one Mr Grenovich, a Bulgarian official at the British legation, he said: "It has poisoned affairs and put Bulgaria's civilization back 100 years. I tried for years to deal with Bulgarians as a civilized western people. Now that appears to be impossible."

The USSR has also condemned the entry of German troops into Bulgaria. "It cannot be regarded", said the Kremlin, "as furthering peace possibilities in the Balkans." But, as German tanks and troops continue to cross the Danube in great force, there is little that the Russians can do about it.

German transport troops ride into Bulgaria in the shadow of the Shipka Pass.

Nazis cross the Danube into Bulgaria

Sofia, 2 March

Germany officially admitted today that its troops had entered Bulgaria. According to a High Command communique: "The German army, in agreement with the Royal Bulgarian government, has been marching into Bulgaria since Saturday." In the Bulgarian parliament the prime minister, Professor Filov, said that Germany had asked permission to send in the troops on a temporary basis in order to "safeguard peace in the Balkans".

All day today the Germans have been pouring into Bulgaria by way of pontoon bridges across the Danube. Meanwhile there are reports that the vanguard of the German forces is already approaching the Greek frontier at four points. With the *Luftwaffe* present in strength, the German attack on Greece seems imminent (→ 3).

Yugoslavia's Prince Paul agrees to meet Hitler's demands

Munich, 4 March

Prince Paul, the regent of Yugoslavia, was summoned to the Berghof, the Fuhrer's mountain retreat, this evening and given the usual treatment accorded to small powers. After listening to Hitler's threats and ranting into the early hours, Prince Paul buckled and agreed to follow Roumania and Bulgaria into the German camp and sign the Axis Pact.

Hitler, in high spirits at having got his way, offered the prince a consolation prize – the Greek port of Salonika, which would give Yugoslavia access to the Aegean. Paul, aware that joining the Axis will be unpopular at home, has arranged for the signing of the treaty to take place in great secrecy in ten days' time (→ 11).

An earlier, happier meeting between Hitler and the prince regent, Paul.

Admiralty takes control of Britain's shipyard labour

London, 7 March

Ernest Bevin, the minister of labour and former leader of the Transport and General Workers' Union, has been given powers to schedule any factory or firm as being engaged on essential work of national importance. Once scheduled, no employee can either leave or be dismissed without the consent of the local national service officer of the ministry. The object is to prevent labour turnover damaging the war effort. As a condition of being rated "essential", employers must guarantee weekly wage rates and welfare arrangements that satisfy the ministry, and workers may be disciplined for lateness or absenteeism.

The first "Essential Work Orders" will apply to the engineering, aircraft, building and shipbuilding industries, the railways, the docks and the mines. The 221,000 workers in the five royal dockyards and in 52 private yards are now put under the control of the admiralty, which will decide priorities.

Shipyards have been plagued by stoppages at a time when nearly a million tons of shipping have been sunk in the current quarter. This week John Brown's on Clydeside is on strike (→ 9).

Japan launches an attack on Chinese

Ichang, 6 March

Fierce fighting has broken out on the western bank of the Yangtze river in western Hupeh, as Japanese troops today launched a new offensive aimed at driving the Chinese back into the mountains, west towards the *Kuomintang* capital at Chungking.

The offensive – the first in the region since November – began at 0530 hours as Japanese artillery shelled Chinese positions to provide cover for three regiments which advanced and took the Chinese stronghold at Chang-kang-ling. At the same time, on another flank, between 600 and 700 Japanese infantry, with aerial and artillery support, took Fan-chia-hu (→ 13).

Auschwitz to grow on Himmler's order

Auschwitz, 1 March

Himmler, the former poultry farmer who has dedicated himself to ridding Europe of Jews and Bolsheviks, visited the Auschwitz concentration camp today to announce a big programme of expansion.

He told Rudolf Hoess, the camp commandant, to get the camp ready to accommodate 130,000 prisoners, some 10,000 of whom must be put to work in the I G Farben synthetic rubber factory. Hoess, an ex-convict once found guilty of murdering a political opponent, is delighted with his new assignment; he promises to go to work with great zeal.

BOAC starts secret flights to Sweden

London, 2 March

Civilian pilots of the British Overseas Airways Corporation (BOAC) in a slow, unarmed aircraft are running the gauntlet of German fighters and anti-aircraft guns to maintain communications with Sweden.

They take in news of Britain and important passengers and bring back ball-bearings vital to the defence industry. Their only aircraft so far is a Lockheed flown out of Poland by its crew when the Germans overran their country. With the identification letters of BG, it is known as "Bashful Gertie, the Terror of the Skagerrak".

LET'S GO-

WINGS FOR VICTORY

1941
March

Su	Mo	Tu	We	Th	Fr	Sa
						1
2	3	4	5	6	7	8
9	10	11	12	13	14	15
16	17	18	19	20	21	22
23	24	25	26	27	28	29
30	31					

9. Albania: Greek forces hold firm against a strong Italian offensive, led by Mussolini himself, between the Devoli and Vijose rivers (→ 13).

9. Britain: Portsmouth is heavily bombed by the *Luftwaffe* tonight.→

9. Atlantic: The British destroyers *Southdown* and *Worcester* repel a German attack on convoy FS-429A.

10. Poland: Germans shoot 17 civilians after resistance fighters kill an actor who announced he was not Polish but German.

10. Ethiopia: British troops who have just marched 600 miles from Mogadishu clash with Italians at Dagabur (→ 17).

11. French Indo-China: France cedes part of Laos and part of Cambodia to Thailand. Japan is given full use of Saigon airport and a monopoly of the colony's entire rice production.

11. Belgrade: Demonstrators hold a protest rally against growing Axis influence (→ 13).

11. Europe: The Handley-Page Halifax bomber made its operational debut last night in an RAF raid on Le Havre.

13. Berlin: Germany repeats its demand that Yugoslavia join the Axis (→ 21).

13. Britain: Glasgow and Clydeside suffer their first major *Luftwaffe* raid tonight; 236 aircraft drop 272 tons of high explosive and 59,400 incendiaries.→

13. Germany: Hitler appoints Alfred Rosenberg minister of the eastern occupied territories; he gives control of future eastern conquests to Himmler; Goering is to exploit the Soviet economy to serve Germany (→ 20).

15. Eritrea: Indian divisions launch a series of attacks towards Keren (→ 27).

15. Liege: Belgian politicians of all parties form the "Independent Front" resistance movement.

15. China: Japanese forces take Fengxin, in Kiangsi province, in a major new assault on Shanggao (→ 2/4).

Lend-Lease Bill signed

In sombre mood: Roosevelt signs.

Washington, 11 March

President Roosevelt this afternoon signed into law the Lend-Lease Bill which in effect makes the United States a partner of Britain in the war.

The bill passed both the House of Representatives and the Senate with large majorities. It seeks, as its congressional sponsors put it, to give "legislative form to the policy of making this country an Arsenal for the Democracies and seeks to carry out President Roosevelt's pledge to send to these countries in ever-increasing numbers, ships, aeroplanes, tanks and guns". The bill empowers the president to lease to Britain munitions owned and paid for by the US government.

Debate on the bill was fierce, and its isolationist opponents in the Senate filibustered against it. On 6 March, however, Senator Walter George, the influential chairman of the Senate foreign relations committee, made a powerful speech in favour of its passage, arguing that "the collapse of the British Empire would mean chaos in this world". Two days later the bill was finally passed by the Senate – by 60 votes to 31.

Immediately after the bill was signed the US Army and Navy approved the export of the first material to be released under the terms of the act. Though what is involved is being kept secret for military reasons, it is believed that the first shipments will include 24 motor torpedo boats already ordered to British design which have been held up by the US attorney-general and will help to defend Britain against invasion.

Most of the material released today will go to Britain. Some will go to Greece, and some to China. The president's assistant, Laughlin Currie, has been sent to determine what the Chinese need.

A few hours after the vote the president sent Congress a request for $7,000 million for munitions. The *New York Times* predicted that if American convoys are needed to deliver the products from the arsenal to the democracies, they will be sent (→ 12).

Counter-attack by Nationalist Chinese

Ichang, 13 March

Chinese Nationalist forces have successfully repulsed Japan's latest offensive in western Hupeh after a week of heavy fighting in which the Japanese are thought to have suffered at least 4,000 casualties.

The Nationalist counter-attack, which has driven the Japanese back to their old positions at Ichang, has been a mix of guerrilla attacks and conventional flanking movements by the River Defence Force, which has managed to penetrate behind enemy lines (→ 15).

Lisbon is gateway from European hell

Lisbon, 15 March

The Portuguese capital has become a haven for refugees from all over Europe fleeing from Nazi persecution. Many spend weeks in miserable accommodation here waiting in terror for a passage on a ship to Australia or the Americas, as far as possible from the Third *Reich*. There are now so many refugees in the Atlantic port that the American Export Line, the only US shipping line with a regular European service, has stopped taking bookings until existing ones are cleared.

Bevin tells women: factories need you

Britain, 9 March

In a speech in Newcastle the minister of labour, Ernest Bevin, today asked 100,000 women to sign up for munitions work within the next fortnight. He said the women were needed desperately – primarily in shellfilling factories – and he asked them not to wait for instructions or registration but simply to come forward. "I cannot offer them a delightful life," he said. "I want them to come forward in the spirit that they are going to suffer some inconvenience, but with a determination to help us through.

"We are anxious that the children shall be looked after properly and to assist them we are subsidizing the cost of minding. We have left the woman to pay only what she would have paid before the war, which is about sixpence a day, and we are paying an additional sixpence."

Instructions for management in companies which are not used to employing women are to be issued, and new terms of employment and wages for women employed in war work will also be announced soon.

Both the British and the German war economies are both becoming more reliant on women workers. In Germany, the Nazis have been forced by circumstances to relax their ideological standpoint that women are good only for housework and maternity (→ 17).

Women's work is in the factories: 100,000 volunteers are needed now.

"Luftwaffe" launches its spring offensive

Bomb damage at Buckingham Palace: workers begin to clear the rubble.

Britain, 15 March

The *Luftwaffe* has begun its spring offensive against British cities in the past week. The new night bombing assault began on 8-9 March when London was attacked. Buckingham Palace was hit: after it was showered with incendiaries, a stick of high explosive fell across the front courtyard. A lodge disappeared and a policeman was killed, but most bombs fell in Green Park.

Later that evening the Cafe de Paris in London's West End was crowded with fashionable women in evening dress and officers on leave when at 9.30pm two bombs crashed through the building above the basement nightspot. The first exploded in the gallery above the band, killing them outright, including their leader "Snakehips" Johnson. The second bomb hit the crowded dance floor causing horrific scenes and 100 casualties, although it did not explode. Some of the patrons stumbled out of the wreckage calling for help. Women tore up their dresses to bind up wounds. Ambulances were swamped and many injured were removed by taxi. Of 34 people killed, some were unidentified for days.

For the next two nights Portsmouth suffered heavy raids, the second (10-11 March) by 244 bombers, the heaviest raid yet this year. By night much of the city's population shelters in the tunnels of Portsdown Hill or the surrounding countryside. Despite this 750 citizens have been killed.

Birmingham was hit on 11-12 March. Prolonged raids on Merseyside on 12-13 and 13-14 March hit Birkenhead and Wallasey, sank two ships in dock, damaged others and killed 630 people. In Cardiff the Royal Infirmary was hit. Worst of all was the damage to Clydeside on 13-14 March. In the shipbuilding town of Clydebank only seven houses were undamaged, and three-quarters of its population were made homeless. The raid left 1,100 dead and 1,000 injured, in Scotland's worst air raid to date (→ 22).

Clydebank: tenements wrecked in Scotland's worst raid of the war.

Priceless Parisian art treasures are stolen by Goering

Paris, 15 March

The city's art collectors have had the recent honour of receiving a most distinguished visitor – *Reichsmarschall* Hermann Goering. He is here to pick for himself the best of the privately-owned works of art which Hitler has ordered to be considered as war booty – to be used as a bargaining weapon in future peace negotiations with France.

He has already chosen works by Rembrandt, Rubens and Goya from the stock of stolen art work stored at the *Louvre* and the *Jeu de Paume*. They will be taken to Carinhall, his mansion near Berlin, and added to the collection which he proudly shows off to all visitors.

Soon after the German occupation Alfred Rosenberg, the Nazi *Reichsleiter* for home affairs, set up a special organization to bring works back to Germany. Its task was to sort out works of art that were valuable enough to be of interest to the Fuhrer, important enough to go to Goering's personal collection, or "Aryan" enough for public display.

By the autumn of last year, Rosenberg estimated that some 22,000 objects of value had been collected, including 5,281 paintings and 2,477 pieces of furniture. Special care has been taken to seize Jewish-owned works of art. The assets of the fabulously wealthy Rothschild banking family, whose members fled the country when the Nazis came, have been rushed to Germany in special trains. Rosenberg took a personal interest in the Rothschild library of 30,000 Polish works, now in the hands of German scholars in Berlin.

The looting of art is prohibited under the Hague Convention. But that makes no difference to the greedy Goering. "Let me worry about that," he told a German official. "I am the highest jurist in the land. My orders are decisive and you will act accordingly."

Italian attack is bogged down in Albania

Greek troops inspect an Italian Pavesi truck abandoned in the Albanian snow.

Tirana, Albania, 13 March
Leading splendidly and noisily from the rear – but rarely out of his armoured car and constantly surrounded by his bodyguards – the Duce himself arrived in Albania today to take temporary charge of his flagging legions, ordering them to attack at all costs. The costs were brutally high, despite the courage of Mussolini's blackshirts who fought furiously to regain vital heights in the Tempeleni region.

Whether or not they were inspired by their dictator's presence in Albania is not known, but Mussolini's crack divisions battled today as never before. They attacked the heights in close-packed waves, but suddenly tonight their offensive stopped, leaving thousands of dead on the mountainside.

A Greek statement insisted that no ground had been taken. The Italians had been forced to drop leaflets among their own men, stressing the presence of the Duce to maintain flagging morale.

Mussolini, perhaps inured to failure, is returning to Rome – where government-controlled newspapers are making much of his brief visit to the front line, but little of his losses.

Vichy warns Britain over food convoys

Vichy, 10 March
Admiral Darlan, the French navy minister, today threatened to use the French navy to protect convoy foodships bound for France if the Royal Navy continues to seize them. Darlan was speaking in the presence of Marshal Petain to a press conference for American journalists here.

"I am responsible for feeding 40 million people, plus millions more in Africa," Darlan said. "I will feed them even if I have to use force." Petain added that before the war the French ate about a pound of bread (454 grammes) each a day; now the ration is half that amount.

Roosevelt promises aid for democracies

Washington, 15 March
President Roosevelt said here to-night that there is no longer the slightest doubt that the American people have demanded a policy of all-out, unqualified aid for Britain, Greece, China and the governments of the democracies in exile.

Prussian autocracy was bad enough, the president told the White House correspondents' dinner in a key address, but "Nazism is far worse".

Mr Roosevelt spoke of the "vital bridge across the ocean, the bridge of ships" carrying goods and arms to "those who are fighting the good fight".

1941
March

Su	Mo	Tu	We	Th	Fr	Sa
						1
2	3	4	5	6	7	8
9	10	11	12	13	14	15
16	17	18	19	20	21	22
23	24	25	26	27	28	29
30	31					

16. Berlin: Hitler predicts that Britain will fall by 1942, no matter how much aid it gets from the US.

16. Ethiopia: The British are back and wreaking havoc among the Italians after last August evacuation (→ 20).

17. Ethiopia: Lieutenant-General Cunningham captures Jijiga, 1,000 miles (1,600 km) from the Kenyan border (→ 22).

17. Britain: Jam and marmalade are rationed to eight ounces (240 grammes) per person per month (→ 19).

17. Morocco: Spain hands the residence of the *mendoub* of Tangiers, the representative of the *sultan* of Morocco ejected by Franco yesterday, to the German consul.

19. London: Free French officials set up their own central banking system.

19. Britain: Mass-produced vegetable rissoles are to be sold at 8d (3p/13¢) a pound.

19. London: Exiled German socialist groups join together to form the Union of German Socialists, pledged to work for a "democratic and socialist future for Germany".

19-20. London: A massive German raid by 479 bombers leaves 750 people dead.→

20. Berlin: Hitler appoints Alfred Rosenberg "Delegate for Central Planning for Questions of the Eastern European Area".

20. Moscow: General F I Golikov, chief of army - intelligence, assures Stalin that while Britain remains undefeated, Hitler will never attack the USSR.

20. Somaliland: British forces take Hargeisa.→

22. Ethiopia: Italy declares Harar an open city, and Belgian colonial troops seize Gambelo (→ 4/5).

22. Atlantic: The German battle-cruisers *Scharnhorst* and *Gneisenau* end a 20-day cruise in which they sank 22 ships.

22. Britain: The government agrees to let US grain ships deliver an emergency cargo of flour to Vichy France.

Desert outpost falls after Allied siege

Jarabub, Libya, 21 March
The longest siege so far in this desert war came to a quiet, though abrupt, end at this tiny outpost in the very heart of the Libyan desert today. For political reasons – Jarabub is sacred to the the Senussi sect – neither the Italian garrison nor British besiegers were anxious to upset the Arab people by desecrating the shrine. After 15 weeks of observation by a small detachment of British and Australian troops, the Allies moved in and took Jarabub with little or no resistance. No damage was done to either the shrine or the sacred relics, according to Allied sources (→ 24).

Allied troops push on with the attack.

Canada and US in joint defence pact

Ottawa, Canada, 19 March
In an agreement signed by Adolf Berle, the assistant US secretary of state, and William Mackenzie King, the prime minister of Canada, the Great Lakes will soon become the biggest shipbuilding area in the world – the ships to be built on the Canadian side, with power and finance from the US side.

"The extent to which intensified submarine and air attacks on convoys necessitate an expansion in the programme is still unknown," said President Roosevelt, but he estimated that the number of ships needed would be "several times" those now available.

Bombers bring Blitz back to Britain

London, 22 March
The *Luftwaffe* is stepping up its night bombing of British cities. London suffered its worst raid of the year on 19-20 March with the Germans dropping 122,292 incendiaries on the capital in an attack by "several hundred planes".

Bristol was also attacked severely on 16-17 March. Fire-watchers dealt with the incendiaries, but there were heavy casualties, many of them caused by a bomb which hit a crowded public shelter.

Last night it was Plymouth's turn. So many incendiaries were dropped during the city's fiercest raid of the war that they sounded like hail bouncing off the roofs. The bombers arrived shortly after the king and queen had completed their visit to the shipyards.

The bombs wreaked havoc in residential areas and shopping streets. Many fires were started, and Plymouth is still burning today. Fire appliances have been sent from all over the south-west to relieve the city's exhausted firemen. Remarkable work is being done by the rescue services in bombed areas. In

In a wrecked street in Bristol: "We shall give it to them back," vowed Churchill.

Clydeside yesterday two men were rescued after being buried for a week in a wrecked tenement.

During these raids a number of German bombers have been shot down by the increasingly effective anti-aircraft and night-fighter defences. Many of the German losses are accounted for by Bristol Beau-

fighters equipped with RDF and flown by a new breed of ace pilots such as Flight-Lieutenant "Cat's Eyes" Cunningham. Although intelligence sources believe that the increased Luftwaffe activity could be a blind to distract attention from Nazi moves in the east, their bombs remain only too real.

Royal Navy dispatches Germany's three great U-boat heroes

North Atlantic, 17 March
Today, off the coast of Iceland, the Royal Navy has just completed its most cheering week since the war at sea began. The destroyer HMS *Vanoc*, one of seven ships escorting Convoy HX-112, accepted the surrender of U99, crippled by repeated depth charge attacks from the destroyer HMS *Walker*, which picked up survivors. The last man swimming was the captain, Otto Kretschmer.

Kretschmer was the top U-boat ace in terms of volume of Allied tonnage sunk. His capture tops a run of successes in the war against the U-boats. Yesterday, *Vanoc* rammed and sank U100 with its ace skipper, Joachim Schepke.

All this comes ten days after the sinking of U47, when all 47 men on board perished, including the captain, Gunther Prien. Prien was the legendary ace who inspired the whole fleet. He was the hero of the raid on Scapa Flow, the navy's main home base, where he sank the

Kretschmer: ashore as a captive.

Prien: the "Bull of Scapa Flow".

battleship *Royal Oak*. He sent 161,000 tons of shipping to the bottom, all, except *Royal Oak*, in the Atlantic. Shortly after midnight a week ago U47 was stalking convoy OB-293 200 miles south-east of Iceland. Escort destroyers dropped depth charges and U-47 surfaced

yards away from the destroyer HMS *Wolverine*. It immediately dived again. The *Wolverine* dropped another batch of depth charges and her sailors saw an orange glow under the water. The man they called the "Bull of Scapa Flow" was dead at the age of 31.

Bevin puts women in men's shoes

Britain, 17 March
The minister of labour, Ernest Bevin, gave more details today of his plans to mobilize the women of Britain. His basic rule is that no man will do any job in the services or in industry which could be done by a woman.

Next month all women aged 20 and 21 will be registered. Thousands of women will then take jobs in new munitions factories, fill positions vacated by men who will soon be de-reserved under new regulations, and provide enough labour to work continuous three-shift systems in shell-filling factories.

Yugoslav ministers resign on Axis Pact

Belgrade, 21 March
Prince Paul's decision to sign up with the Axis powers led to a major cabinet crisis tonight, when three ministers resigned and a fourth threatened to do so.

Paul, the regent of Yugoslavia, tried to refuse the resignations; but the ministers were adamant that in no circumstances would they accept Germany as an ally or agree to German military rail transports crossing Yugoslavia.

The cabinet crisis threatens to delay the signing of the pact. Ministers who were due in Vienna today to meet Hitler have postponed the visit (→ 23).

Coal cartel to boost German production

Germany, 19 March
The entire coal-mining industry and the coal trade in Germany have been amalgamated into a giant cartel known as the *Reich* Coal Union. It is hoped that, with centralized control, this vital industry will be able to increase its production beyond the massive 246 million tons achieved this year. A significant boost is necessary if the increase in arms production demanded by the government is to be possible and the hard-pressed German people are to be able to buy fuel.

1941

March

Su	Mo	Tu	We	Th	Fr	Sa
						1
2	3	4	5	6	7	8
9	10	11	12	13	14	15
16	17	18	19	20	21	22
23	24	25	26	27	28	29
30	31					

23. Belgrade: Anti-Nazi demonstrations sweep Yugoslavia as Hitler presses the government to join the Axis.→

24. Libya: The *Afrika Korps* reoccupies El Agheila (→1/4).

26. Suda Bay, Crete: An Italian explosive motor boat raid sinks a Norwegian tanker and cripples the cruiser HMS *York*.→

27. Washington: Congress approves spending $7,000 million in Lend-Lease aid.

27. Balkans: Germany sends about 500 *Luftwaffe* planes to Bulgaria and Roumania.

28. Britain: The RAF declares its "Eagle" Squadron, crewed by US volunteers, to be operational.

28. USA: A team of physicists reports the discovery of a new isotope of uranium which it calls *plutonium-239* (→30/6).

29. Vichy: Xavier Vallat is appointed to the new position of "commissioner for Jewish questions" (→3/4).

30. Western Desert: Air Marshal Arthur Tedder crash-lands, but is not seriously injured.

30. Berlin: Hitler privately addresses 250 officers on the inevitability of war in the east and on the necessity of destroying Bolshevism.

31. USA: 875 German and Italian sailors are arrested and charged with sabotage.

31. Off Crete: The Italian submarine *Ambra* sinks the cruiser HMS *Bonaventure*.

31. Switzerland: Private Coe of the British Army Dental Corps arrives on neutral soil, the first escapee from a German PoW camp since war broke out.

31. Britain: Civilian casualties in the Blitz this month are 4,259 people killed (including 598 children) and 5,557 injured.

31. France: The RAF sent 109 bombers to attack the German battle cruisers *Scharnhorst* and *Gneisenau* in the port of Brest last night; no hits were scored (→5/4).

Cape Matapan: Italian fleet crushed

Mediterranean Greece, 29 March
A Royal Navy task force under Admiral Sir Andrew Cunningham is heading for Alexandria today after a major naval victory over the Italians off Cape Matapan in Greece.

The admiral knew from *Enigma* that an Italian fleet had sailed to attack British convoys – and was determined to lure them to his three battleships, *Warspite*, *Barham* and *Valiant*. The battleships slipped quietly from their moorings at Alexandria at night on 27 March and sailed at full speed towards Crete. In the meantime, an advance squadron of four Allied cruisers – *Ajax*, *Orion*, *Gloucester* and the Australian *Perth* – left Piraeus in Greece and allowed themselves to be pursued by heavy Italian cruisers towards the battleships.

Then the British fleet's prime target – the new 35,000-ton *Vittorio Veneto* – joined the action and began shelling the British cruisers, which were now in grave danger of being trapped between two superior forces. At this moment Swordfish aircraft from the carrier HMS *Formidable* began to attack the Italian battleship with torpedoes while RAF bombers attacked her from 10,000 feet (3,048 metres). A torpedo struck *Vittorio Veneto* close to her bows. Escorted by cruisers, she limped towards Taranto. But with radio-location playing a key role for the first time at sea, Cunningham sank three cruisers (*Pola*, *Zara* and *Fiume*) and two destroyers – but not the *Vittorio Veneto*.

Cunningham's fleet wreaks havoc amongst the Italians at Cape Matapan.

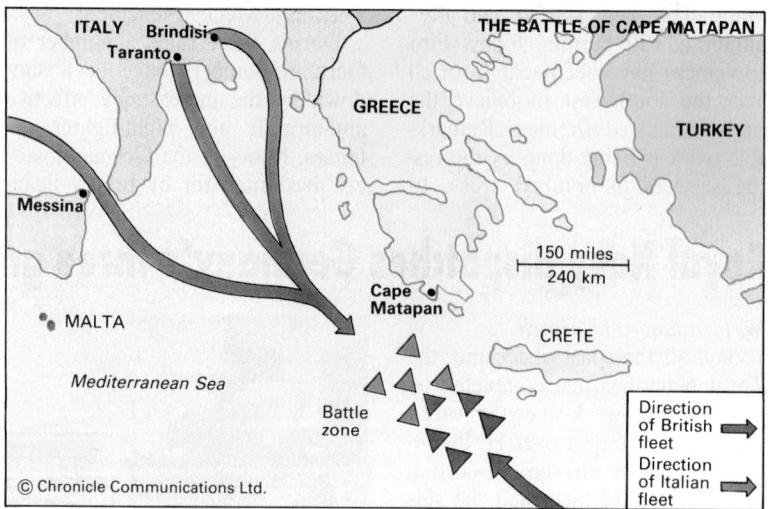

SS uses snooper network to report on mood of German people

Germany, March
Secret reports on the mood of the German population are being produced twice weekly by the *Sicherheitsdienst* (Security Service) of the SS.

These *Reports from the Reich* are put together from information gleaned across the country by a comprehensive network of spies under the leadership of Otto Ohlendorf.

More than 550 field agencies are involved, and over 30,000 individual employees and contacts. Their task is to "take every opportunity to conduct unobtrusive conversations aimed at discovering the real effect on the popular mood of all important external and internal policies and measures".

As well as recording the public response to recent events, special attention is paid to anti-Nazi feeling, especially ideas spread by the church.

On 17 March a report noted: "Even a foreign-language prophecy which admits of no ambiguity has been used in church circles, saying that the time has come for Germany to be called the most warlike nation of the world ... the most dreadful warrior will rise from her ranks to spread war throughout the world and the peoples of the world will bear weapons and call him the Antichrist."

On 10 March the report dealt with the sale of "Pictures of the Fuhrer at Annual Fairs", noting: "At present popular feeling ... does not approve of the sale of pictures of the Fuhrer alongside images of saints, rosaries and devotional objects."

Secret talks give Britain backing of US military chiefs

Washington, 27 March

The secret Anglo-US staff talks (ABC1) which began in January ended today with broad agreement on plans for strategic cooperation in the event of US entry into the war against Germany or Japan or both.

In 14 meetings since 29 January the two sides have discussed the American plan, put forward by Captain Turner of the US Navy and Colonel Mcnarney of the US Army, carefully reviewed by President Roosevelt. The result is Plan ABC1. Its main thrust is that Germany must be defeated first. The US would give strategic priority to the Atlantic and to Europe, although the US Navy would be used offensively in the Pacific as British staff officers have drawn attention to the vulnerability of Singapore. One US general said: "If we lose in the Atlantic we lose everywhere."

Ethnic Germans are resettled in Reich

Baltic States, 25 March

The resettlement within the *Reich* of 60,000 Germans from Latvia, Lithuania and Estonia has been completed. The migrations were carried out in accordance with a German-Soviet agreement signed on 10 January, and in return Germany has sent 20,000 Lithuanians, Russians and White Russians into the USSR.

Since 1936 the Nazis have planned ways of encouraging – or forcing – ethnic Germans outside the *Reich* to immigrate. In 1938 a resettlement agency was set up, under the direct authority of Hitler until 1939 when Himmler took over. So far over 400,000 ethnic Germans have been "repatriated", the largest number – 100,000 – in 1939 from the South Tyrol, a part of Austria given to Italy after the last war.

Many of the Reich's new citizens live in poor conditions in camps in Nazi-occupied eastern Europe, and they have been promised farms and other possessions of deported Jews and Poles.

Hitler orders smashing of Yugoslavia

Berlin, 27 March

Hitler flew into a blind rage when he heard that the Yugoslavs had overthrown their pro-Axis government. He ordered military leaders to come to the chancellery in Berlin at once, and for several hours harangued them about the terrible punishment that would be visited on the Yugoslavs.

Demanding an immediate invasion, he said that Yugoslavia must be destroyed with "merciless harshness". Von Ribbentrop, the foreign minister, was sent off to tell Italy, Hungary and Roumania that they would be given pieces of Yugoslav territory. Only the pro-German Croats would be allowed to survive with a puppet state. Hitler then dashed off a midnight letter to Mussolini:

"Today's reports leave no doubts as to the imminent turn in foreign policy in Yugoslavia. Therefore I have arranged for all necessary measures ... I consider it necessary, Duce, that you should reinforce your forces on the Italian-Yugoslav front with all available means and with utmost speed."

As Germany's military chiefs set about implementing the Fuhrer's new orders, their misgivings increased. Hitler had closed his stormy session by revealing a potentially significant decision. Because of the Yugoslav campaign, the launching of Operation *Barbarossa* – the long-planned attack on the Soviet Union – would have to be postponed by four weeks.

How the crisis arose: on Tuesday, Yugoslavs back the Germans

Vienna, 25 March

In Vienna's ornate Belvedere Palace today, the Yugoslav premier, Dragisa Cvetkovich, put his signature to the pact which binds his country to Germany and the Axis. He had left behind in Belgrade a government and country deeply divided, with the Serbs passionately pro-British and the Croats equally pro-German.

After the signing, the premier said that his chief aim was peace and security for the Yugoslav people. Von Ribbentrop welcomed Yugoslavia as a "new partner", and promised that Germany would respect the country's territorial integrity and not make military demands. Nobody believes him, least of all the Yugoslav premier.

The Yugoslav premier signs the Axis Pact in a grim ceremony in Vienna.

The Yugoslav crisis, two days later: riots topple Hitler's allies

Belgrade, 27 March

At 2.30 this morning the Yugoslav regency council, headed by Prince Paul, resigned; his nephew, King Peter, who is 17, took over and appointed as his prime minister General Dusan Simovic, the chief of staff. Simovic organized the coup after two days of anti-Axis and anti-Nazi demonstrations. Soon after a radio announcement of the successful *coup*, King Peter was wildly cheered as he drove through Belgrade. A seething mass of people surged along the streets chanting "Now we are free". Outside the Soviet legation, the crowd were shouting "Long live Britain!", "Long live Russia!" and "Down with Hitler!" (→1/4).

Yugoslavs take to the streets in celebration following King Peter's "coup".

1941

April

Su	Mo	Tu	We	Th	Fr	Sa
		1	2	3	4	5
6	7	8	9	10	11	12
13	14	15	16	17	18	19
20	21	22	23	24	25	26
27	28	29	30			

Allies make good progress in Eritrea

British troops in Eritrea: pushing on to win a strategic, if not a moral battle.

Keren, Eritrea, 27 March
The Battle of Keren is over. The strategic victory has gone to Britain, after a 52-day struggle against Italian Bersaglieri, Alpini and Caribinieri and Eritrean colonials.

It has been no easy task for the British and their Free French allies and for once the Italians have won themselves much respect from those who have defeated them. Swiss Radio spoke of the Italians' "gallant resistance".

For the 4th and 5th Indian Divisions and the Sudan Defence Force, the advance into Eritrea from Sudan seemed easy. Two battles brought them to Keren: one at Agordat, the other at Barentu, where two companies of the Highland Light Infantry were sent up a coverless conical hill and slaughtered by 300 Italian Eritrean troops, which should have been a warning.

Then they reached Keren, the northern gateway to the Ethiopian Highlands. At first the Italians were outnumbered. Even after General Nicolangelo Carmineo brought in reinforcements, their numbers were only equal to their enemy's, and they were far worse armed, but the Italian positions were rarely surrendered, and were usually only taken at great cost.

Today the British broke through, leaving a route covered with the bodies of Cameron Highlanders and Savoia Grenadiers. It has cost 536 British lives and 3,229 wounded, and around 3,000 Italian lives and 4,500 wounded (→ 1/4).

The cruiser "York" riding heavy seas. On 26 March she was crippled in Suda Bay, Crete, in a daring raid by the Italians. The men steered the explosive motor boats by riding them until the last minute.

Conscripts can opt for Civil Defence

Britain, 26 March
As a result of the call-up, there is a shortage of full-time firemen in the Auxiliary Fire Service, and of workers in the first-aid and rescue services. As a result of the National Service Bill introduced today, men called up will be able to state a preference to serve in Civil Defence instead of the armed forces. At present 90 per cent of Civil Defence workers are volunteers.

Compulsory Civil Defence service will apply equally to those registered "conditionally" as Conscientious Objectors – those required to continue their present jobs or work on the land, in hospitals or with the ambulance service. They can now be directed into Civil Defence but not into the Police War Reserve, which sometimes carries arms. Some have refused to take up the work imposed upon them by the tribunals. Michael Tippett was sentenced to three months in jail for refusing to do full-time work in Civil Defence whereas Benjamin Britten, his fellow composer, was granted unconditional exemption from service. Since the call-up began, 31,000 men out of two million have registered as objectors.

Axis ships in US ports impounded

New York, 30 March
Twenty-seven Italian ships in various US ports were boarded today by the US coastguard service after reports that the crews of five of them were starting to sabotage their craft in Newark, New Jersey. The most valuable ship, the *Brennero*, is loaded with diesel and aircraft fuel.

The order was given by the secretary of the treasury, Mr Morgenthau. Rumours abound as to motives for the action. Some say that the Italians were acting on orders to destroy ships which might be used to transport arms for the Allied cause. Others say that the sailors are trying to get themselves held in the US to avoid going home to face possible conscription into the Italian armed forces. The US has also placed guards on two German ships in US ports (→ 31).

1. Westminster: The Commons rejects government proposals to allow theatres to open on Sundays.

1. Libya: The British retreat from El Agheila is hampered by the breakdown of most of their tanks (→ 2).

2. Germany: The He280V-1 jet makes its maiden flight. →

2. Libya: Rommel retakes Agedabia and Zuetania (→ 3).

2. China: The battle of Shanggao ends (→ 20).

3. Paris: The Jewish affairs commissioner, Xavier Vallat, meets the German ambassador, Otto Abetz, to agree measures to speed Jewish "emigration".

3. London: Churchill sends the British ambassador in Moscow, Sir Stafford Cripps, a warning to be passed to Stalin of a German attack on Soviet Russia.

3. Libya: British troops evacuate Benghazi.→

3. Britain: Bristol suffers a heavy night raid.

4. Atlantic: German U-boats sink ten vessels of a 22-ship US convoy, and the merchant raider *Thor* sinks the British armed merchant cruiser *Voltaire*; one U-boat is sunk.

4. Berlin: Hitler meets Matsuoka again, and promises to join Japan in fighting the US if it should declare war.

4. Germany: The anti-British propaganda film *Ohm Kruger* [Uncle Kruger], which depicts British atrocities against the South Africans in the Boer War, is released.

4. Ethiopia: Italian forces quit Addis Ababa (→ 6).

4. Washington: Roosevelt permits damaged British warships to be repaired in US shipyards.

5. Moscow: Yugoslavia and the USSR sign a treaty of friendship and non-aggression, which the Germans condemn.

5. France: An RAF Beaufort torpedoes and badly damages the *Gneisenau* at Brest; the plane is shot down (→ 6).

5. USSR: The Russian MiG-3 fighter plane has its first flight.

Rommel launches African offensive

Hungarian premier takes his own life

Budapest, 3 April

Count Teleki, the Hungarian prime minister, shot himself at dawn today. Not prepared to give in to Hitler, but unable to stand out against his demands without plunging Hungary into war, Count Teleki decided that death was preferable to dishonourable capitulation.

It is reported that he left a letter addressed to Admiral Horthy, the regent, in which he wrote: "You will understand that I am unable to carry on in face of the spectre of war." It is unlikely that his death will have any effect on Hitler's determination to conquer the Balkans. German troops are reported to be crossing the Hungarian frontier already, but Teleki has absolved his name from guilt.

Emden: RAF drops 4,000-pounders

London, 1 April

The RAF unleashed a new weapon on Germany last night. Six Wellingtons from 9 and 149 Squadrons attacked the German North Sea port of Emden. One specially-modified aircraft from each squadron dropped a 4,000-pound bomb on the target. Like the 2,000-pounder, which was first used last July, this new bomb has a thin, blunt-nosed case packed with high explosive. Already nicknamed the "cookie" or "blockbuster" by air and ground crews, this weapon marks a dramatic escalation of the bombing war.

North Africa, 5 April

From the air, the Libyan desert is a mass of swirling clouds of sand – but this is no natural sandstorm. General Erwin Rommel's tanks are on the move eastwards, driving a depleted British force back along the desert roads that it fought over so recently. In the two months since the Fuhrer ordered him to Africa with a small tank force – one light division, one *Panzer* division and a number of anti-tank weapons – Rommel's *Afrika Korps* has transformed the war map of Africa.

Eleven days ago, Rommel – renowned for the swiftness of his Panzers in the invasion of France – took El Agheila on the Tripolitanian border. Moving at an unbelievable speed, with their commander urging them on at every point from his staff car or an aircraft, German tanks recaptured Benghazi yesterday, and today advance units are poised to take the town of Barce; this puts them 200 miles (320 km) from El Agheila.

The main reason why Rommel is meeting so little resistance is that so many men have been withdrawn from Wavell's army to join the British expeditionary force to Greece. The 2nd Armoured Division is new in the desert; its men are untrained in this unique form of mobile warfare, and many of its tanks have broken down.

German armoured cars roll into Benghazi watched by bewildered inhabitants.

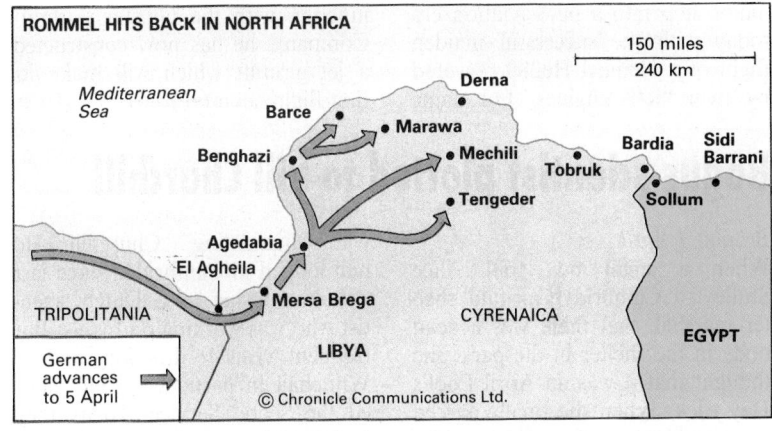

The schoolmaster's son who is giving Britain a lesson in Africa

North Africa, 5 April

His men worship him and already, just a few weeks since he arrived in Libya, General Erwin Rommel, a schoolmaster's son from Wurttemberg, is seen as a major threat by British staff officers reeling at the speed of his offensive. What none of them know is that, before Rommel flew here, Hitler handed him a number of illustrated English and American papers showing the way in which Wavell's armies had beaten the Italians so successfully.

"Of particular interest was the masterly coordination these showed between armoured land forces, air force and navy," he wrote. Rommel also studied closely the unconventional tank tactics – invariably involving shock and surprise –

used by Major General Richard O'Connor with devastating results.

Rommel was commander of the 7th *Panzer* ("Ghost") Division which swept into France from the Ardennes – always hitting the enemy at his weakest points. This former commander of Hitler's HQ in the Polish campaign is ever such an opportunist. He was disgusted when Germany failed to follow up Dunkirk with a swift invasion when British troops were still numb with shock. Rommel's orders were to hold the British back – and to be subordinate to an Italian. Knowing that the British were withdrawing so many of their men, he chose to ignore Hitler's brief and to move quickly to the offensive. The result is one more German victory (→ 6).

Rommel: the "Desert Fox".

Heinkel experimental jet plane takes off

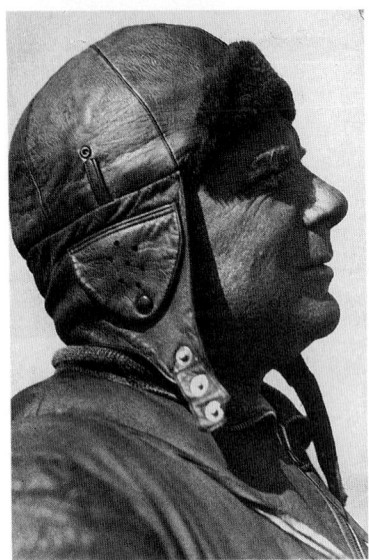

Udet: not yet convinced by the jet.

Marienehe, Germany, 2 April
German aircraft engineers took a major step into a new aviation era today with the successful maiden flight of a Heinkel He280 powered by twin "jet" engines. For some years now a few aeronautical engineers have believed that the limits for propeller aircraft will shortly be reached at high altitude, so teams in both Britain and Germany have been developing a revolutionary new aircraft engine – the turbojet.

At present it seems that the German Heinkel aircraft company is leading the way. On 27 August 1939 its He178 became the first aircraft to be powered by a jet engine. General Ernst Udet, who is responsible for the *Luftwaffe's* technical development, was unimpressed by the He178, and Heinkel has received little backing for its jet programme. However, Udet will now see the He280 in action.

Meanwhile in Britain a company called Power Jets Ltd has been leading the way under the driving force of a serving RAF officer, Wing Commander Frank Whittle. In conjunction with the Gloster Aircraft Company, he has now constructed a jet aircraft which will make its first flight soon (→ 15/5).

Bogus scientist plotted to kill Churchill

Britain, 1 April
When a small boy told Alice Stutley, a Cambridge air-raid shelter marshal, that there was a dead body in the shelter in the park, she thought that it was an April Fool's Day trick. When she finally agreed to go and look she found a man who had shot himself through the head.

The body was that of Jan Willen Ter Braak, a German spy charged with "liquidating" Churchill. He had lodged in Cambridge since last autumn, posing as a Dutch scientist who was working on fossils. But frequent visits to London, and to Whitehall in particular, soon alerted the Secret Service. Today they had found a transmitter, a Luger pistol and a file on Churchill's movements in Ter Braak's rooms and were waiting for him to return.

Hitler steps up pressure on Yugoslavia

Belgrade, 1 April
Still seething at the neutralist stance of the new Yugoslav government, Hitler today made demands that he knew must be rejected. He called for demobilization of the Yugoslav army and ratification of the Axis Pact. A third demand – that Yugoslavia apologize for the anti-Nazi demonstrations – is less of a problem for Belgrade. It was the signing of the pact that led to the overthrow of Prince Paul, the regent, and his replacement by his nephew King Peter.

Meanwhile the German military chiefs are making their plans to attack Yugoslavia, in line with the Fuhrer's 25th war directive. Belgrade faces the initial onslaught.

Yugoslav officials, fearing the worst, are planning to sign a non-aggression pact with the Soviet Union, Germany's ally. A treaty now being drawn up promises no enmity between the two nations and that each country will come to the aid of the other, should one be attacked by a third party. What aid Russia could offer Yugoslavia if – or when – Germany attacks is uncertain. Hitler's troops are on their borders, while Russia's are hundreds of miles away (→ 8).

Pro-Axis Rashid Ali takes power in Iraq

Baghdad, 3 April
In a German-backed *coup* which began two days ago, Rashid Ali, the pro-Axis former premier of Iraq, has seized power and established a new regent to govern the country in the name of six-year-old King Faisal II. Ali claimed that "the army has entrusted me with the responsibility for peace and order". The deposed regent, Emir Abdul Ilah, has accused Rashid of "instigating rebellious elements who have adopted falsehood as a weapon". British intervention is almost certain. Iraq is treatybound to offer Britain "all facilities and assistance in the event of war – including aerodromes" (→ 10).

Iraq's new premier, Rashid Ali.

Eritrean capital captured by British

Asmara, Eritrea, 1 April
Asmara, the capital of Eritrea, has surrendered to the advancing 5th Indian Division. Its fall was inevitable after Italy's last reserves in Eritrea had been lost at the battle of Keren. The gallant General Carmineo, though wounded in the leg, tried with scraps of his defeated army to hold up the Indian advance at Ad Tecesan, 35 miles from Asmara. He failed. With nothing left, the Italians sent out two policemen with a white flag, and declared Asmara an open city (→ 5).

1941
April

Su	Mo	Tu	We	Th	Fr	Sa
		1	2	3	4	5
6	7	8	9	10	11	12
13	14	15	16	17	18	19
20	21	22	23	24	25	26
27	28	29	30			

6. Libya: Axis troops reoccupy Mechili and Msus (→ 7).

6-7. Greece: *Luftwaffe* bombers blow up an ammunition ship in Piraeus harbour, putting the Allies' only supply port out of action.

7. Bulgaria: RAF planes bomb Sofia in retaliation for enemy raids on Belgrade.

7. Atlantic: The US Navy opens a base in Bermuda.

7. North Africa: Derna is overrun by the *Afrika Korps*; General O'Connor is among those captured (→ 10).

7. Kiel: The heaviest RAF attack on a single target yet, involving 229 aircraft, takes place.→

8. Belgrade: Two nights of German air raids wreak havoc; estimates of dead range from 15,000 to 30,000 people (→ 12).

8. Eritrea: The last centre of Italian resistance, at Massawa, falls to the Allies (→ 10/6).

8. Red Sea: The British cruiser *Capetown* is torpedoed by an Italian submarine off Mersa Kuba.

9. Britain: Birmingham is attacked by the *Luftwaffe* with 237 bombers.

10. Libya: Rommel lays siege to the Australian 9th Division, which has retreated to Tobruk (→ 14).

10. Britain: The war cabinet agrees to send troops serving in India under General Auchinleck to Iraq (→ 19).

10. Atlantic: Germany and the US have their first military encounter when the US destroyer *Niblack* engages a U-boat.

11. Colditz, Germany: A French officer, Lieutenant Alain le Ray, is the first PoW to escape from the castle now serving as a prison camp.

12. Balkans: Croatia is proclaimed a sovereign state, with Ante Pavelich as head of the puppet Axis state (→ 18/5).

12. Hammerfest, Norway: A British raiding party on a Norwegian destroyer attacks a fish-oil factory.

Hitler unleashes German assaults in the Balkans

Belgrade flattened by heavy bombers

Belgrade, 8 April

The first of Goering's heavy bombers, escorted by fighters, appeared over Belgrade at dawn on Sunday morning. Successive waves followed during the next two days and into evening, leaving the city a mass of smoking ruins tonight. Nobody knows how many have died; some estimates say as many as 30,000. All communications with the city have been disrupted.

Berlin radio broadcast a gloating account of how within minutes the city was covered with a pall of smoke from the many fires. "There are no demonstrations any longer," the reporter said. "No British flags. Serbian anti-aircraft guns are in action, but are unable to cope with the mass attack. The planes turn and leave burning Belgrade behind. All the planes are back."

The Yugoslav authorities had declared Belgrade an open city, but Hitler brushed this aside with the order to Goering: "Destroy Belgrade in attacks by waves." The Fuhrer is determined to make the Yugoslav people pay dearly for their refusal to become allies of the Nazi and Fascist dictators.

The destruction was backed by an invasion of Yugoslavia and Greece by the German Twelfth Army, with the Second Army expected to add support shortly. In Berlin, von Ribbentrop told the Yugoslav envoy that "a clique of conspirators" had prevented Yugoslavia from joining the Axis, which would have ensured "a happy future for the Yugoslav people" (→ 8).

The invasion of Greece: German paratroops take cover from heavy shelling.

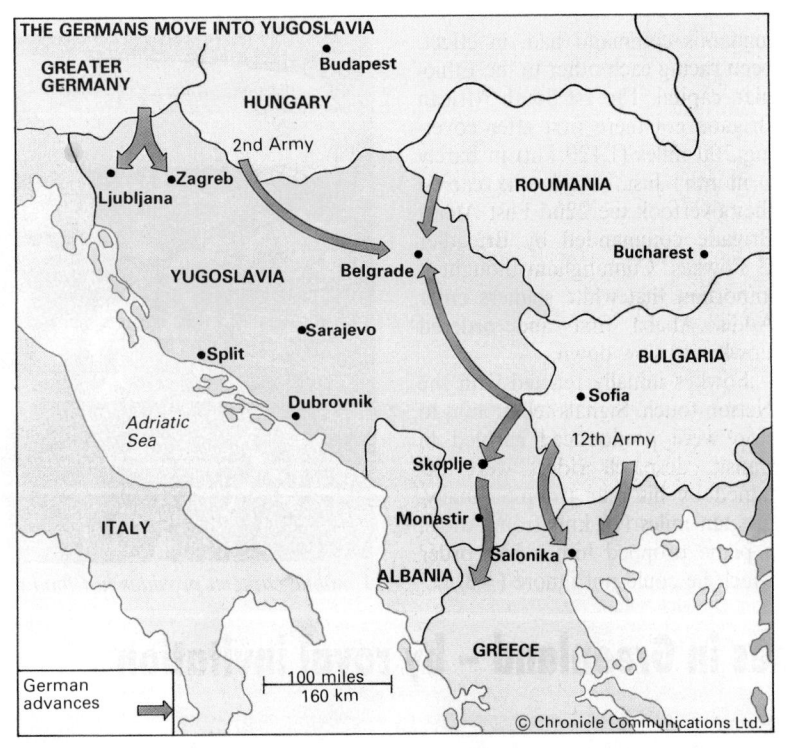

THE GERMANS MOVE INTO YUGOSLAVIA

GREATER GERMANY

Budapest

HUNGARY

2nd Army

Ljubljana · Zagreb

ROUMANIA

YUGOSLAVIA · Belgrade

Bucharest ·

· Sarajevo

· Split

BULGARIA

Dubrovnik

· Sofia

Adriatic Sea

12th Army

Skoplje ·

ITALY

Monastir ·

Salonika ·

ALBANIA

GREECE

German advances

100 miles
160 km

© Chronicle Communications Ltd.

Nazi forces capture crucial Greek port

Salonika, 9 April

Within three days of crossing into Greece from Bulgaria, German forces have captured the key port of Salonika. This brings them within striking distance of the main defence line, which is manned by British, Australian and New Zealand troops who began landing in Greece at the beginning of the week. The Germans made strenuous attempts to disrupt the landings with heavy air raids on the port of Piraeus. Six Allied ships with military supplies were sunk, and then the port itself was shattered when a British ammunition ship, SS *Clan Fraser*, with 200 tons of explosives, blew up and sank ten other ships.

The strongest resistance to the Germans has been in the Struma valley, where the frontiers of Yugoslavia, Greece and Bulgaria meet. German military spokesmen admitted that the Greeks were putting up a tough fight. But then the weight of German armour forced the Yugoslavs to withdraw, leaving the Greek flank exposed. The Greeks were brushed aside and the *Panzers* raced on to Salonika.

In a message to his people, King George of the Hellenes says: "We shall win with the help of God and the benediction of the Holy Virgin. Yes, we shall win! The historians will once again have to write that the country renowned for Marathon and Salamis does not waver, does not submit, does not surrender. Forward, Children of Hellas, for the supreme struggle, for your altars and your hearths." (→ 10)

British soldiers retreat to Mount Olympus

Northern Greece, 12 April

The British and Imperial forces, deployed along rugged terrain from the Gulf of Salonika to Edhessa in the Vermion mountains, have been pulled back to Mount Olympus, the next defensible line, some hundred miles to the south. The Allied C-in-C, General Sir Henry Maitland Wilson, decided he had no other choice when he learnt that the Germans were pouring into Greece through the Monastir Gap and Yugoslav resistance was crumbling.

The 53,000-strong British and Imperial forces have had little or no time to prepare their defences, and their strength is insufficient to organize a defence in depth. If the Germans are not stopped at Monastir they will soon be turning the British left flank (→ 13).

Stalin wary of Germany's Balkan invasion

Moscow, 12 April

When he joined Hitler in the non-aggression pact with its secret protocols, Stalin believed that he had secured his western border. Now he has been observing with mounting concern Hitler's occupation of the Balkans – in flagrant violation of the pledges made in the pact. Seeking allies, Stalin turned to Yugoslavia and signed a treaty of friendship in the early hours of 6 April. On that day Belgrade was obliterated by German bombers, which instantly rendered the treaty worthless. Stalin has now issued a secret directive for the strengthening of the western frontier fortified zones. Some 150,000 construction workers have been drafted in, but work is held up by shortages of such materials as timber and cement (→ 17).

Allies take Addis Ababa

White South African troops pile up captured Italian rifles in Addis Ababa.

Addis Ababa, Ethiopia, 6 April
The capital of Ethiopia is in the hands of the Allies. This was announced tonight by the British GHQ in Cairo, which said that "leading detachments of our Imperial Forces" reached Addis Ababa in the evening.

South African troops were first into the capital, which had been abandoned by its Italian defenders who are believed to be heading north-east to re-group with other units of Mussolini's beleaguered East African army. Many Italian women and children are still in Addis Ababa, suggesting that the Italian army's evacuation was a last-minute affair. Two brigades under Lieutenant-General Cunn-

ingham's command had, in effect, been racing each other to the Ethiopian capital. The 1st South African Brigade got there first after covering 700 miles (1,120 km) in barely a month. Just outside the capital they overtook the 22nd East Africa Brigade commanded by Brigadier C Fowkes. Cunningham thought it important that white soldiers enter Addis Ababa first and ordered Fowkes to slow down.

Fowkes initially reacted with the Nelson touch. Signals telling him to stop were pronounced garbled in transit; despatch riders were detained by his rear troops. Finally, just ten miles (16 km) from Addis, a plane dropped him a halt order which he could not ignore (→ 3/5).

Heavy casualties in raids across Britain

Britain, 12 April
Countrywide night raids by the *Luftwaffe* are making April a month of heavy casualties, like March, in which 4,259 people were killed in air raids. This is the highest number for four months, bringing the total since last September to just under 24,000 killed and nearly 34,000 seriously injured.

Coventry has again been made a target this week. This time some 230 aircraft dropped 330 tons of bombs, but the fires started by the incendiaries did not get out of control, thanks to prompt action by fire-watchers and the Auxiliary Fire Service (AFS). A hospital was hit repeatedly by high explosive over several hours. The staff struggled to save 160 patients by moving them to the basement as ward after ward was hit. At one point oxygen

cylinders were used to provide air in the packed conditions. Several doctors and nurses were killed.

Birmingham has also been badly bombed for two nights running. Many of those made homeless the first night were bombed out again on the second. Newcastle and Bristol have also been attacked.

Mobile canteen convoys known as "Queen's Messengers" were in action in the raids helping to feed the bombed-out. They consist of tankers and lorries carrying 6,000 meals apiece, with mobile kitchens and canteens manned by the Women's Voluntary Service (WVS) and the Society of Friends. Most of the 144 vehicles have been provided by Americans through the British War Relief Society. Queen Elizabeth gave her name to the convoys on condition that she paid for one.

A mobile canteen provides hot food and drink for Coventry's bombed citizens.

Americans to build bases in Greenland – by royal invitation

Washington, 12 April
The United States has decided to establish naval and air bases in Greenland, under an agreement concluded here yesterday between Henrik Kauffman, the Danish minister, and the US secretary of state, Cordell Hull. Kauffman has been disowned by Danish leaders in Nazi-occupied Copenhagen, but he said that he was acting in the name of the Danish king. In terms of war, if not law, it will ease the ferrying of aircraft to Britain and enable the US Navy to patrol further eastwards to protect Allied convoys.

US personnel in Greenland celebrate the first Mass here for five centuries.

Britons face record bill for income tax

Britain, 7 April
The standard rate of income tax was today hoisted from 8/6 in the pound (42.5%) to 10/- in the pound (50%) – a record level. Personal allowances and tax exemption limits are also drastically reduced. Money raised by the cuts in allowances will be treated as compulsory savings, to be repaid through Post Office savings accounts sometime after the war. Steps to peg the cost of living have been promised.

RAF bombers pound Kiel in record attack

A view of Kiel showing the devastation RAF raids have brought to the city.

High Wycombe, 8 April
Bomber Command has disclosed that it hit the naval base of Kiel for the 36th time in a five-hour raid which began last night. A total of 229 Whitley, Wellington and Hampden bombers using 40,000 incendiaries spread fire across the whole of the urban area in the RAF's heaviest attack yet on a single target.

Both sides now combine "area bombing" with incendiaries. RAF chiefs concluded after studying the Coventry effect that incendiaries are ten times more effective than high explosive. Churchill said re-cently: "Bombers alone provide the means of victory," while Hitler orders the *Luftwaffe* to "erase" UK cities. Critics behind the scenes in Britain argue: "The only target Bomber Command can be trusted to hit by night is a large German town." To improve its accuracy the RAF is considering some sort of marker bomb as a target designator. Such a bomb might combine flares with a high-explosive bomb.

What has yet to be demonstrated is that the RAF view prior to 1939, that strategic bombing would be a decisive war-winner without other weapons, really holds good.

Douglas Fairbanks Jr joins the US Navy

United States, 10 April
The actor Douglas Fairbanks Jr has been commissioned as a junior-grade lieutenant in the US Navy. Fairbanks has been campaigning for continued and increased Ameri-can support of the Allies since the war began. As a well-connected international figure he has seen fascism for himself, meeting von Ribbentrop, when the latter was German ambassador to London, and Count Ciano.

Attacked recently by the press for being a passionate advocate of American involvement but having never been in uniform, Fairbanks has every reason to be pleased with his appointment.

Lieutenant Fairbanks in uniform.

1941
April

Su	Mo	Tu	We	Th	Fr	Sa
		1	2	3	4	5
6	7	8	9	10	11	12
13	14	15	16	17	18	19
20	21	22	23	24	25	26
27	28	29	30			

13. Germany: Hitler orders swift mopping-up operations in Yugoslavia and Greece (→ 14).

13. Malta: The island is heavily bombed by the *Luftwaffe* (→ 27).

14. Yugoslavia: The Germans smash the southern army and pour through the Monastir Gap, cutting off the Greek army in Albania (→ 16).

14. London: Convinced that his troops have borne an unfair share of the fighting, the Australian prime minister, Robert Menzies, moves to end Churchill's "dictatorship" of the war.

14. Egypt: King Farouk sends a secret message to Hitler expressing the hope that Egypt will soon be liberated from the "British yoke" (→ 26).

14. London: Churchill tells the information ministry to stop publishing the demoralizing weekly figures for shipping losses.

15. Belfast: A heavy air raid kills 758 people and seriously injures 454.

16. Yugoslavia: German forces enter Sarajevo and demolish the main synagogue.→

16. London: The last remaining tower of the Crystal Palace is demolished because it makes too clear a landmark.

16-17. London: Al Bowlly, a top dance-band singer, is killed in the heaviest air raid of the war so far, involving 685 enemy aircraft.

17. London: Churchill agrees to evacuate mainland Greece, but insists that Crete must be held with force (→ 19).

17. South Atlantic: The German raider *Atlantis* sinks the Egyptian liner *Zamjam* and takes 220 passengers prisoner.

18. Athens: The Greek prime minister, Alexander Korizis, commits suicide.

19. Greece: The Germans take Olympus and Larissa, the SS *Adolf Hitler* Division cutting off the Greek retreat (→ 20).

19. Iraq: The first Indian troops land at Basra (→ 25).

British gunners put Rommel on the run

Rommel's men: forced to turn back.

Tobruk, 14 April
In the fiercest battle he has faced so far in this campaign, Rommel saw his tanks withdraw from Tobruk's hastily prepared defences under a withering hail of fire from British anti-tank guns and heavy artillery; and then watched them literally chased back into the desert in con-fusion by tank attacks on his flanks. Although his *Afrika Korps* had managed deep penetration into what earlier reconnaissance had selected as a "weak spot", their light tanks were no match for Brit-ish gunnery. Seventeen were knock-ed out before General Olbrich, the *Panzer* commander, ordered the withdrawal.

The indications are that Rommel is coming to the limit of his spec-tacular charge across Libya. His supply lines are seriously stretched, his men are tired and his tanks are badly in need of servicing. And he faces the prospect of a long siege here at Tobruk which can be sup-plied by sea so long as the Royal Navy controls the Mediterranean.

There is one important change, however. Rommel was sent to North Africa to bolster up the Ita-lian garrison and to hold the Allies back from Tripolitania. Hitler is so delighted with his *protege*'s pro-gress that he is sending massive rein-forcements. He believes that Malta can be neutralized by bombing to block the Royal Navy and defend German convoys; U-boats would then roam free in the Mediterra-nean against British convoys (→ 21).

Yugoslavia surrenders to Nazi army

Russia recognizes Manchukuo by pact with Japanese

Moscow, 13 April

In a treaty designed to safeguard both parties' borders, the Soviet Union and Japan today signed a neutrality pact, valid for five years.

By acknowledging existing borders the pact, negotiated by Vyacheslav Molotov, the Soviet foreign minister, gives Russian recognition to Japanese Manchuria (now know as Manchukuo) for the first time. Under the pact, should either the Soviet Union or Japan become the object of military action, then the other party will observe neutrality.

The impetus came from Russia, increasingly concerned by the deterioration of its relationship with Germany. In Tokyo the pact was welcomed as guaranteeing Japan's "back door".

Brandishing anything white that they can find, Yugoslav troops come forward to surrender to the Germans.

Molotov, the Soviet foreign minister.

Belgrade, 17 April

After 12 days of resistance against overwhelming odds the Yugoslav government signed the act of surrender to the triumphant Germans in Belgrade today. In Sarajevo, south-west of the capital, remnants of the army gave themselves up to the enemy; around 6,000 officers and 335,000 men were marched off to PoW camps. King Peter and his prime minister, General Simovic, have escaped to Greece.

From the outset, the Yugoslav General Staff was committed to fighting an unwinnable campaign. The bitter divisions between the country's many nationalities – especially between Croats and Serbs – meant that an attempt had to be made to defend the whole country; no parts could be sacrificed for a flexible defence strategy.

The Yugoslav forces were thus strung out along the frontier without depth or necessary reserves. The Germans, jumping off from Hungary, Roumania and Bulgaria, plunged into Yugoslavia along the mountain passes, accompanied by the now all-too-familiar scream of the Stuka dive-bombers. A week later, German forces were entering Belgrade.

So swift was the German advance that many Yugoslav units never saw battle, and even after today's surrender they remain in remote areas, still with their weapons. Field Marshal Wilhelm List, the German commander-in-chief, repeated methods successfully used in France of smashing through the enemy defences, certain that after the surrender all the defeated soldiers would give up their arms. That has not yet happened in Yugoslavia, where some have retreated to rugged mountains and thick forests to fight as partisans or guerrillas (→ 3/7).

Attack on Russia is likely to be delayed

Berlin, 17 April

Yugoslavia's surrender today and the worsening situation in Greece can be added to Hitler's growing list of *Blitzkrieg* victories. They also put Britain's position in the eastern Mediterranean under growing threat. Hitler's decision, taken towards the end of last month, to invade the Balkans may, however, affect his plan to invade Russia.

German planning for the invasion, codenamed *Barbarossa*, has always been based on the need to complete the invasion by mid-October, before the onset of the Russian winter. Accordingly, Hitler had ordered all preparations to be completed by mid-May. Now that he has diverted troops earmarked for Barbarossa to the Balkans, he may well be forced to put back its launch date. This makes the time available to achieve the final objectives very tight. Even so, the army's high command remains confident that it can break the back of Russian resistance in six weeks (→ 6/5).

Belfast is blitzed

Belfast, 16 April

Belfast has suffered a major air-raid overnight, with over 700 dead and over 400 injured. Another 15 people were killed in Londonderry and 5 in Bangor. Among the targets hit were the Harland and Wolffs shipyard and York Road railway station. Parachute mines devastated working-class areas of north and west Belfast. The government is being criticised for leaving the city defenceless: there were only 16 heavy anti-aircraft guns in Belfast.

1941

April

Su	Mo	Tu	We	Th	Fr	Sa
		1	2	3	4	5
6	7	8	9	10	11	12
13	14	15	16	17	18	19
20	21	22	23	24	25	26
27	28	29	30			

Royal Navy breaks convoy to Africa

Malta, 16 April

In its most successful attack to date on a German convoy, the Royal Navy today sank five ships which were carrying 20,000 tons of supplies from Sicily to Tripoli off Cape Bon in Tunisia. The three escorting destroyers were also sunk. One ship which was carrying ammunition blew up; another was heavily laden with lorries. HMS *Mohawk*, a destroyer, was also sunk, although most of her crew were rescued. Meanwhile, Rommel's tanks and supply wagons in North Africa, forced to use the coastal road, are constantly harassed by navy guns.

Allies to evacuate mainland of Greece

Athens, 16 April

After six months of fighting, first against the Italians and then the Germans, Churchill has agreed to a secret appeal from General Alexander Papagos, the Greek C-in-C, for British and Empire forces to withdraw from mainland Greece in order to save the country from further destruction. But Churchill is insisting that Allied forces must try to hold Crete. Greek, British, Australian and New Zealand troops counted on support from the Yugoslav army, now facing defeat by the Germans (→ 17).

Women sign on for war work register

Britain, 19 April

Labour exchanges across Britain were filled today with women of 20 and 21 signing up for war work under the new Employment Order.

Under the order, brought in by the minister of labour, Ernest Bevin, women with young children will not be compelled to work for the war effort, but they must all register so that their cases can be considered. Subsidized childcare is being made available.

The government has also issued an Essential Work Order compelling reluctant companies to employ women bound to do war work.

20. Greece: Allied forces pull back to Kalamata, Nauplia and Monemvasia (→ 23).

20. China: Japan captures Ningbo (→ 22).

21. Libya: The Royal Navy shells Benghazi harbour (→ 22).

21. Melbourne: Politicians move to oust the prime minister, Robert Menzies, whom they blame for high Australian casualties in Greece.

22. Libya: British warships shell Tripoli (→ 25).

22. China: Japanese forces occupy Fuzhou.

23. Greece: The government flees to Crete (→ 24).

24. Greece: As German paratroopers capture the islands of Samothrace, Limnos and Thasos, the Allies start to evacuate their troops from the mainland (→ 26).

25. Baghdad: Germany and Italy undertake to give financial and military aid to Rashid Ali (→ 30).

25. Atlantic: The US Navy enforces a new security zone 2,000 miles off the east coast.

25. Germany: Hitler orders Operation Mercury, the invasion of Crete (→ 30).

25. North Africa: The *Afrika Korps* attacks the Halfaya Pass and drives the British back to Buq Buq (→ 15/5).

26. Greece: German paratroopers capture the Corinth Canal bridge.→

27. Britain: Churchill warns that if Egypt is not held, blood will flow and he will "shoot the generals" (→ 15).

27. Malta: The carrier *Ark Royal* delivers 23 Hurricane fighters to the island (→ 1/5).

28. London: Churchill orders an end to the reinforcement of Singapore and Malaya.

30. Iraq: Rashid Ali lays siege to 2,000 British troops and 9,000 civilians sheltering at the Habbaniya RAF base (→ 2/5).

30. Crete: Major-General Bernard Freyberg takes command of British and Imperial forces (→ 15).

Parachute mines are new Blitz terror

The north transept of St Paul's Cathedral: hit by the latest bombing raid.

Britain, 20 April

In what German radio described as a reprisal for the RAF's attacks on Berlin, London last night experienced its heaviest air raids since the "Great Fire" of 29 December last year. Birmingham has been among other cities hit as the *Luftwaffe* returned to the offensive with a new weapon – land mines which fall to their targets by parachute.

The attack on London began last night and continued into the early hours. It involved 712 aircraft dropping 153,096 incendiaries, which started a record 1,500 fires, followed by a rain of 1,026 tons of high explosive and parachute mines. These are as large as pillar-boxes, weighing over two tons (2,000 kg), and drift down on the wind, exploding on impact on the surface with the maximum blast effect. Two can completely obliterate a street, as happened in Pimlico on Wednesday. "It looked like Flanders," said a rescue worker. One mine failed to explode and lodged on the railway bridge leading to Charing Cross, where it was disarmed on the spot by a naval squad.

Other places were not so lucky. Eight London hospitals, including Guy's, were hit. Christie's auction rooms, Maples' furniture store and the Shaftesbury theatre were destroyed, parts of Selfridge's set on fire, the Speaker's House at Westminster, the Royal Hospital, Chelsea, the Law Courts and Wellington Barracks badly damaged.

St Paul's is closed after a 500-pound bomb crashed through the north transept, strewing the crypt below with wreckage. Fortunately the St Paul's Watch, whose rest room is beneath, were all on the roof dealing with incendiaries. All the remaining windows were shattered, but the dome was not shaken by the blast.

Other churches destroyed or burnt out included St Andrew's, Holborn – Wren's largest after St Paul's – the City Temple, St Clement Danes and Chelsea Old Church. Tonight the raiders returned in force to the docks and the East End (→ 23).

A street in Birmingham devastated by the "Luftwaffe"'s latest attack.

Allies evacuate Greece as Panzers roll into Athens

"Swastika" flies over the Acropolis

Athens, 27 April

German *Panzers* rolled into the Greek capital early today, and this Sunday afternoon the *Swastika* is flying from the Acropolis, the city's ancient citadel. The final phases of the Greek war began on Hitler's birthday, 20 April, when Allied forces retreated southwards through Thermopylae, with some detachments remaining to slow the German advance.

The Greek army surrendered to the Germans and Italians on 23 April, and the main evacuation of Allied forces began from Kalamata, Nauplia and Monemvasia on the Peloponnese on 24 April. The troops at Thermopylae were withdrawn and themselves evacuated from Megara, Rafina and Porto Rafti, near Athens, the following day, before yesterday's seizure of the Corinth Canal by paratroopers and the German advance into the Peloponnese.

The final retreat of the Greek forces from Thebes was a macabre mix of the barbaric and the idyllic within sight of the cloud-capped majesty of Mount Parnassus. Greek soldiers, many bare-footed, limped along the road, throwing themselves to the ground when a distant roar told of approaching dive-bombers. Alongside them, sheep continued grazing, their bells tinkling as they moved along with their grizzled shepherds. Wild flowers swayed in a light breeze and then suddenly vanished in a shower of earth as the German shells struck.

Greek officers ordered their surrendering troops to smash their rifles. Perhaps the most painful humiliation for the Greeks was having to surrender to the Italians as well as to the Germans; the Germans they recognized as victors, but the Italians they had thrashed again and again in six months of fighting.

For some the humiliation of defeat was too much. One officer, Artillery-Major Versis, was ordered by the Germans to surrender. He assembled his guns, saluted them and, as his men sang the Greek national hymn, shot himself (→ 30).

A German armoured vehicle patrols in the shadow of the Parthenon.

Some who did not get away: British soldiers become German prisoners.

"Second Dunkirk": 50,000 Allies leave

Peloponnese, 30 April

The last British, Australian, New Zealand and Polish troops were taken on board ship today from Kalamata in the Peloponnese after a fighting ten-day retreat from Thermopylae. About 7,000 men were captured at Kalamata by a German *Panzer* force before they could be evacuated.

However, 50,732 men were taken from harbours and beaches in this "second Dunkirk", called Operation Demon, and many have been transported to Crete for the island's defence. There was too little time however, to take off all their heavy weapons, trucks and aircraft. As the Allies left the Germans began occupying islands in the Aegean.

The Germans attempted to cut off the Allied retreat by dropping paratroops on the bridge over the Corinth Canal. Though the paratroopers seized the bridge undamaged, two British officers opened fire on pre-set demolition charges. When these exploded the bridge collapsed into the canal.

In the Greek campaign, British and Empire forces lost 900 men in battle, 1,200 wounded and 9,000 taken prisoner. The Germans suffered 1,518 dead and 3,360 wounded in Greece, in addition to the 151 dead, 15 missing and 392 wounded in the Yugoslav campaign. In terms of strategy, the Greek campaign was a mistake for the Allies. Inferior in numbers and weaponry, they lost men and material that were badly needed in the Western Desert to face Rommel's *Afrika Korps*. But, as Churchill put it, to have refused the Greek appeal for help "would have been fatal to the honour of the British Empire".

The Royal Navy has also come out of the evacuation with honour. As at Dunkirk, British warships ensured that the transportation of the Imperial expeditionary force to Crete was accomplished so successfully, although the navy has suffered losses. Two troop transports were sunk on 25 April and the destroyers HMS *Diamond* and HMS *Wryneck* on 27 April.

Lindbergh resigns from US Reserves

Washington, 28 April
Colonel Charles Lindbergh, the air hero and leader of the isolationist "America First" group, has resigned from the US Army Air Force Reserve after President Roosevelt questioned his loyalty. Lindbergh recently said that the US was being "led towards war by a minority", after which Roosevelt compared him to Northerners in the civil war who favoured peace with the South. Roosevelt's press secretary wondered if Lindbergh, who received a Nazi order in 1938, would be "returning his decoration to Hitler".

US and Canada join up to aid Britain

Hyde Park, New York, 21 April
President Roosevelt and the Canadian prime minister, William Mackenzie King, today agreed at the president's family home here on an unprecedented measure of collaboration ultimately aimed at helping the British war effort.

Canada and the US will provide each other with whatever war materiel each is best able to produce. The US may also be prepared to take a role in the defence of Canada to release more Canadian troops for service overseas.

British army gets its own "Panzers"

Bovington, Dorset, 22 April
British tank regiments armed with Cruiser-type tanks have been re-organized as more effective fighting units. In future they will have their own support arms in the front line, including motorized infantry, combat engineers, artillery, anti-aircraft and anti-tank units. It is the sort of mixture which has given such strength to the German *Panzer* divisions.

The government believes that Cruisers – Matildas, Crusaders, Cavaliers or Cromwells – are as good as anything that the Germans or Italians can put into the field. But victims of the Panzer MkIV are not so sure.

Plymouth devastated: 30,000 homeless

The dog gets a lift as children in Plymouth salvage some of their furniture.

Plymouth, 24 April
For the last three nights Plymouth has been the *Luftwaffe*'s objective again. Much of the city centre, already devastated by raids on 20 and 21 March, has once more been subjected to a hammering. The first raids on Plymouth wiped out an area of 600 yards' radius around the Guildhall; mediaeval buildings that Sir Francis Drake would have known simply vanished.

But as ever in these raids – both German and British – it has been civilians who have suffered the most. After the March raids one highly experienced mass observer remarked: "The civic and domestic devastation exceeds anything we have seen elsewhere." In all, 1,000 people have died, with 30,000 made homeless as 18,000 houses have been destroyed.

However, Devonport dockyard – the bombers' target – is still working. The Royal Navy is clearing the wreckage, and the lord mayor and lady mayoress, Lord and Lady Astor, have been raising morale. A band is playing on Plymouth Hoe for open-air dancing. At night 50,000 people leave Plymouth to shelter on the moors, in barns, churches, even cow-sheds.

Crucifix is banned in Bavarian schools

Munich, 30 April
Bavarians are outraged by a ban on crucifixes in their schools. The state culture minister, Adolf Wagner, has declared that crucifixes, church decorations and religious pictures "have no place in our schools" and ordered their gradual removal. Bavaria was the breeding ground of Nazism, but it is also intensely Catholic. Farmers have refused to deliver milk in protest, and parents have blocked school entrances or withdrawn their children. Michael von Faulhaber, the cardinal of Munich and Freising, has protested about the Nazis' continued "destruction of Christianity in public life".

Rommel pushes the Allies back across Egyptian frontier

Cairo, 26 April
Rommel's forces crossed the Egyptian border today, with three motorized columns of Italian troops breaking through to the thinly defended "Hellfire Pass" at Halfaya – opening the way to Egypt itself.

Meanwhile, 300 miles (480 km) to the west, the garrison at Tobruk has withstood two more assaults by Rommel's tanks and taken over 2,000 prisoners. That is about the only good news for a country whose army was close to throwing Italy out of Africa four months ago.

The British withdrawal is leading to increasingly icy communications between Winston Churchill and the C-in-C, Sir Archibald Wavell. The prime minister wants a decisive Allied success.

Wavell has complained about the quality of British tanks against *Panzers* and German anti-tank weapons. Mechanically, also, they are not reliable and break down too frequently.

Rommel, too, is facing problems with his masters. General Paulus is on his way here with orders from OKH to bring Rommel under control and stop him from making further attacks on Tobruk. But will the maverick – and successful – general listen? (→ 27)

Chief Ras Seyoum addresses a group of Ethiopian patriots: these fighters are proving powerful allies for Britain against Italy in East Africa.

1941
May

Su	Mo	Tu	We	Th	Fr	Sa
					1	2	3
4	5	6	7	8	9	10
11	12	13	14	15	16	17
18	19	20	21	22	23	24
25	26	27	28	29	30	31

1. Malta: In one of their almost daily attacks, Axis aircraft raid Valetta; the destroyer HMS *Jersey* sinks after hitting a mine in Valetta harbour entrance (→ 21).

2. Iraq: Allied troops occupy Basra and oil installations, and start to evacuate women and children from the Habbaniyah air base (→ 4).

3. Ethiopia: Heavy fighting between the Allies and the Italians breaks out at Amba Alagi.→

3. Belfast: The city suffers a heavy night bombing raid.

4. Iraq: Allied forces make bombing raids on Baghdad.

4. Libya: Rommel's attacks on Tobruk stall.

5. Vichy France: In response to appeals by Petain's government, the US delivers 14,000 tons of flour.

6. USSR: Stalin succeeds Molotov as chairman of the council of people's commissars, adding to his authority.

6. Vichy: The vice-premier, Admiral Darlan, agrees to let Hitler send German troops to Iraq via Syria.

6. Moscow: The Soviet military attache in Berlin warns Soviet High Command that Germany is preparing to invade the USSR (→ 15).

7. Mediterranean: Operation Tiger, an attempt to get a British convoy to North Africa, begins.

7. Britain: Liverpool and Hull are bombed.→

7. Off Iceland: The German weather ship *Munchen* yields an *Enigma* cipher machine and codebook when captured by the British destroyer *Somali*.→

7. China: Japanese troops assault Shansi in an attempt to occupy the Chungtiao mountains.

8. Indian Ocean: The cruiser HMS *Cornwall* sinks the disguised German merchant raider *Pinguin*.

10. Germany: A rocket engine for the Messerschmitt Me163 reaches a test speed of 623mph (1,002kmph) (→ 2/10).

Casualties mount in Atlantic battles

North Atlantic, 9 May
Convoy OB-318 has lost five of its 38 ships here in the last two days, thanks to daring U-boat attacks. Although the convoy has a strong escort group of ten, U94 and U110 risked depth charges to fire their torpedoes. But U94 was severely damaged and U110 captured with its valuable code machines [*see report on opposite page*].

Today's sinkings coincide with the publication of the April figures which show Allied shipping losses up 50 per cent from March at a staggering 488,124 tons. The U-boats accounted for 58 ships and 249,375 tons of this total. More than half the sinkings were made by the new long-range Type IX boats which, with planes based in Norway, have vastly extended the danger zone for Allied ships.

There are hopeful signs, however. Last month the U-boats were able to strike at convoys before the escorts arrived. In this way, convoy SC-26 lost ten of its 22 ships. Now a radical new strategy developed by the new Battle of the Atlantic Committee is in action.

This committee was formed by the prime minister in March to co-ordinate strategy at the highest level. It involves a combined HQ in Iceland sending out the RAF's flying boats and patrol planes and the navy's destroyers. It also arranges cover by the Royal Canadian Navy in the western Atlantic.

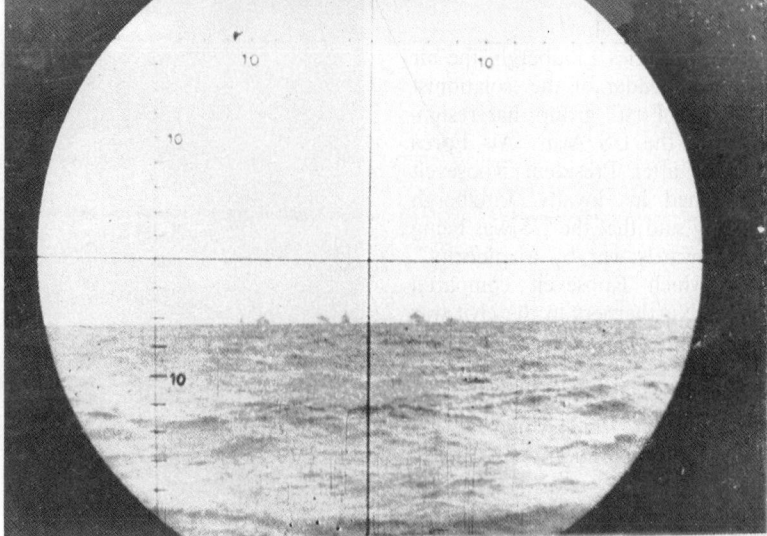
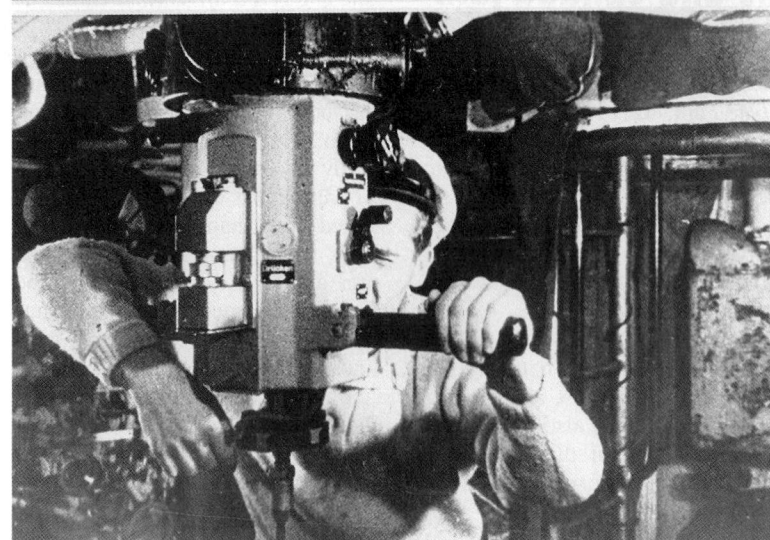

The killer in the deep blue sea: a U-boat captain locates his next target.

Germans expand concentration camps

Germany, 1 May
The Nazis have used concentration camps to imprison their political opponents ever since they came to power, but the number – and severity – of such camps has increased dramatically since the war began. Originally, communists and trade unionists were the main victims to be despatched to camps; today such political dissidents have been joined by activists from occupied countries, "social outcasts" such as homosexuals and gypsies, and, above all, Jews.

Another change is that in the early days, after the *Reichstag* fire, no secret was made of the existence of the camps; there were even visits by reporters. Now, no information is officially released about the numbers imprisoned. It is known, however, that many inmates are forced to perform strenuous physical work for industrial companies who are, in effect, using slave labourers. A combination of underfeeding, overworking and disease kills off many of them.

The Germans are expanding existing camps, including Dachau, Sachsenhausen and Gross-Rosen. In occupied Poland, the closely guarded ghettoes, filled with Jewish deportees put to work for German-owned factories, are effectively giant concentration camps where death is never very far away.

Pro-Axis coup fuels tension in Iraq

Baghdad, 8 May
Tension has been mounting in Iraq's capital since 2 May, when Iraqi troops ringed the British air base at Habbaniyah. The Iraqi move came after the pro-Axis premier, Rashid Ali, seized power a month ago. Sir Kinahan Cornwallis, the British ambassador in Baghdad, has sent notes to Ali demanding the withdrawal of his troops, although he is really playing for time, knowing that British reinforcements are on their way. Ali is equally confident that Germany will come to his aid. At stake is control of the Iraqi oilfields (→ 13).

Liverpool is "cut off" by seven nights of bombing

Queen Victoria stands unscathed in the centre of Liverpool: around her is the devastation caused by a week's solid bombing by the Germans.

Liverpool, 7 May
For the seventh successive night Liverpool and Merseyside are ablaze, devastated by *Luftwaffe* bombers. The raids began on 1 May under cloudless moonlit skies and since then the fires, especially in the docks, have never gone out. On the worst night, last Saturday, the city centre was reduced to a field of brick and rubble, killing over 400.

An ammunition ship, the *Malakand*, loaded with 1,000 tons of bombs and shells intended for the Middle East, was set on fire by a blazing barrage balloon which fell onto her decks. The resulting explosion blew Huskisson Dock to pieces and sank six other ships. Parts of the ship's plates were found over two miles away. An ammunition train also caught fire and was shunted to a siding by railwaymen as the ammunition was exploding.

In the city proper the Custom House, Corn Exchange, Museum and Central Station were destroyed, Lewis's department store was gutted and a wing of Walton jail was demolished, killing 22 prisoners. A Mersey ferry, the *Royal Daffodil*, was sunk and a school shelter was hit, killing 160. Sixty patients and staff of a hospital died in a direct hit. One of the worst fires occurred at the Bryant and May match factory.

Troops have been brought in to help to clear the streets of wreckage. Cars have been banned from entering the centre, and so many telephone cables and exchanges are out of action that people have been unable to get through to get news of their families. During the period that the city was cut off, rumours proliferated that there were "50,000 dead", mass cremations, peace demonstrations and martial law in Liverpool. The actual number killed in this "May Week" is 1,450, bringing the total killed in Liverpool, Bootle, Birkenhead and Wallasey in 68 raids to nearly 4,000 people, the most outside London. Over 70,000 are homeless.

Haile Selassie returns to Addis Ababa after five years' exile

Addis Ababa, Ethiopia, 5 May
Haile Selassie, the emperor of Ethiopia, King of Kings, and "Mr Smith", as he was known to Allied signallers, has returned to his capital in triumph. The long journey home began in Bath, in Somerset, England and continued on muleback with Major Orde Wingate's Gideon Force and Ethiopian "Patriots". The streets of the city from which he fled in the face of Mussolini's invading army in 1936 were lined with black and white African troops. After being welcomed with a 21-gun salute he spoke of his gratitude "to Almighty God that I stand in my palace from which the Fascist forces have fled" (→ 16).

General Cunningham, C-in-C of the East African force, greets Haile Selassie.

Captured U-boat yields codebook

Atlantic, 9 May
The Royal Navy pulled off a *coup* today when HMS *Bulldog* forced U110 to surrender south of Greenland. The U-boat's captain, Lieutenant-Commander Lemp, tried to destroy U110 – already depth-charged by HMS *Aubretia* – but a navy party was able to board her and seize her *Enigma* cipher machine and codebooks.

These should enable British codebreakers at Bletchley Park to decipher signals sent between the U-boats and their HQ near Paris so that convoys can avoid U-boat concentrations.

Hitler's deputy lands on Scottish soil

Glasgow, 10 May
The beetle-browed German who parachuted from a crashing Messerschmitt fighter near Glasgow tonight has been identified as Rudolf Hess, Hitler's trusted deputy and devoted Nazi Party comrade. Hess says that he decided on his flight after astrologers told him he was destined to bring about peace between Germany and Britain.

Hess was greeted by a ploughman armed with a pitchfork, who took him home. "My old mother got out of bed and made tea," David Maclean said. "But the German said he did not drink tea at night." After treatment for a broken ankle, the Deputy Fuhrer was taken to a secret hideout near London to be questioned by Ivone Kirkpatrick, a former first secretary at the British embassy in Berlin. Hess said that Hitler would give Britain a free hand in running the Empire in return for Germany being given a free hand in Europe. Kirkpatrick

Rudolf Hess: the stars foretold he was destined to bring about peace.

declined the offer. Hess says that he flew to Scotland to see the Duke of Hamilton, who he believes leads the anti-war party in Britain. Hess claims that they met at the 1936 Berlin Olympics, but the duke has

Inspecting the damage to the aircraft that brought Hess to Scotland.

no recollection of this. Meanwhile, a distracted Hitler has ordered that Hess, who only last week was sitting beside him in the *Reichstag*, is to be described as having hallucinations (→ 13).

The bombers return to hit London and the port of Hull

London, 10 May
Late tonight, under a brilliant full "bombers' moon", the heaviest air raid of the Blitz is in progress. Over 2,000 fires are raging, nine of them classed as "conflagrations" requiring 100 pumps, but there is little water. Countless mains have been broken and the ebb tide of the Thames is very low.

The House of Commons, the roof of Westminster Hall and the top of the Victoria Tower are alight. In the City of London, the Mint and the Tower are both ablaze. The latest major port to be "coventrated" is Hull. For two nights it has been mercilessly pounded, leaving 40,000 people homeless and 1,000 dead out of a population of 330,000. Dock warehouses burst open and thousands of tons of burning grain slid into the river Humber (→ 11).

Hitler boasts that Nazi "Reich" will last a thousand years

Berlin, 4 May
Flanked by Goering and Hess, the Fuhrer today strode into the Kroll Opera House – where *Reichstag* deputies have met since the fire of 1933 – to deliver a speech marking German victories in the Balkans.

"In this Jewish-capitalist age", Hitler declared, "the National Socialist state stands out as a solid monument to common sense. It

will last for a thousand years." The greater part of the speech consisted of a sustained attack on Churchill, who was portrayed as a bloodthirsty warmonger lacking the qualities needed to fight a war.

"The gift Mr Churchill possesses is the gift to lie with a pious expression on his face and to distort the truth until finally glorious victories are made of the most terrible de-

feats," Hitler declared. Meanwhile Grand Admiral Raeder is urging Hitler to exploit the victories in Greece and Yugoslavia and launch a major offensive to capture Egypt and Suez. "This stroke", Raeder says, "would be more deadly to the British Empire than the capture of London." But Hitler is obsessed with Operation *Barbarossa* – the conquest of the Soviet Union (→ 6).

Churchill shuffles cabinet ministers

Westminster, 1 May
Frederick Leathers, an industrialist who started work as an office boy in the coal trade, was tonight appointed head of a new ministry of wartime communications by Mr Churchill. He will amalgamate the ministries of shipping and transport, and gets a peerage on joining the government. Another change is the move of Lord Beaverbrook to be minister of state – a rank without precedent. Lord Brabazon now takes over as minister of aircraft production.

Australian salute for "weaker sex"

Menzies: admirer of British women.

Britain, 4 May
The prime minister of Australia, Mr Robert Menzies, paid a glowing tribute to British womanhood in a speech broadcast today. He praised "the courage, the action, the endurance of Britain's women. Wherever I go I see them and I marvel at them. Is it possible to believe that not long ago we called them 'the weaker sex'?"

May 10. A crowd of 60,000, including many soldiers, watches Preston North End and Arsenal draw, 1-1, in a thrilling Cup Final at Wembley (→ 31).

1941

May

Su	Mo	Tu	We	Th	Fr	Sa
				1	2	3
4	5	6	7	8	9	10
11	12	13	14	15	16	17
18	19	20	21	22	23	24
25	26	27	28	29	30	31

11. Libya: Five Royal Navy destroyers bombard the harbour (→ 16).

11. USA: Herbert Hoover, the former president, says that America must stay out of the war in order to help Britain.

12. Alexandria: The Allied *Tiger* convoy arrives bearing 238 tanks and 43 Hurricane fighters, desperately needed supplies for the Allied desert army.

13. Germany: The media depict Hess as a true idealist wanting to further the Fuhrer's sincere desire for peace.→

13. Baghdad: The exiled *mufti* of Jerusalem urges Islamic nations to rise up against Britain (→ 16).

14. New Zealand: A Royal New Zealand Navy minesweeper is lost sweeping mines laid by the German raider *Orion*.

14. Vichy: Darlan tells Petain that he will collaborate with Hitler to prevent France's "Polandization".

14. Britain: Karl Richter, a German spy, is arrested in East Anglia shortly after parachuting in.

14. Paris: French police arrest 1,000 foreign Jews and hand them over to the Germans, who deport them (→ 20).

15. Crete: The *Luftwaffe* starts bombing the island (→ 19).

15. Tokyo: Richard Sorge, a Soviet spy, warns Moscow that Germany plans to invade during the third week in June (→ 25).

15. Egypt: General Wavell launches Operation Brevity, to capture the Halfaya Pass from Rommel.→

15. Germany: Dr Sigmund Rascher asks Himmler for permission to carry out medical experiments on prisoners at Dachau concentration camp (→ 31).

16. Iraq: Heinkel He111s carry out minor raids on the RAF base at Habbaniyah (→ 19).

16. Libya: Rommel is ordered to attack Sollum and leave Tobruk to the Italian army (→ 27).

Italian force surrenders

Defeated Italians at Fort Toseli are accorded the honours of war by the victors.

Amba Alagi, Ethiopia, 16 May
The Italian and Allied guns at Amba Alagi are silent, after 13 days. The largest Italian army in East Africa still in the field is seeking terms of surrender.

Here in the arid mountains of Tigre, with the defeated remnants of the Italian divisions ejected from Eritrea and Ethiopia, the Duke of Aosta, Italy's viceroy in East Africa, made his last stand.

His defences seemed unscaleable, but his 18,000 troops fought with ever-decreasing hope. Even their tough Eritrean levies deserted them when they learnt of Britain's promise to give self-determination to Eritrea.

With over-stretched defences, and believing that the main attack would come through the Falaga Pass in the east, the Italian western defences crumbled against an attack by Indian and British troops. Now the guns have stopped – and Italian staff officers are trying to negotiate terms (→ 19).

Stretched supplies slow down Rommel

Western Desert, 15 May
As spring turns to summer, the desert has turned into a broiling cauldron by day, the heat and frequent sandstorms slowing Rommel's tank advance to little more than a crawl. His lines of communication are severely stretched; his tanks are short of petrol; and his men are tired.

That was the intelligence assessment which led to the first real British counter-attack today. Tanks and infantry succeeded in retaking Sollum. Within hours, however, the British were forced to withdraw, leaving garrisons on the escarpment at Halfaya (→ 16).

RAF bombers raid European cities

London, 12 May
The RAF's attack on targets in northern Europe continued last night for the second night running. There have been raids on Hamburg, Bremen, Berlin, Emden and Rotterdam, and, although not terribly effective, they have had some spectacular and deadly results. One airman described the explosion of a heavy bomb on Hamburg: "The flash was like a great flaming red ball, half a mile across ... we felt a kick from the blast."

British jet prototype, the Gloster Pioneer, makes maiden flight

Cranwell, Lincolnshire, 15 May
Hard on the heels of the maiden flight of the first twin-engined German jet [*see page 176*] comes that of the Gloster Pioneer. At 7.40pm today the first British jet, piloted by Gloster Aircraft Company's chief test pilot, Gerry Sayer, took off from RAF Cranwell and successfully flew for 17 minutes.

Afterwards Wing-Commander Frank Whittle, Britain's jet engine pioneer, said: "I was very tense, not so much because of any fears about the engine, but because this was a machine making its first flight." Afterwards there was an impromptu celebration in the officers' mess. Further test flights will now be made.

The Gloster E28/39, powered by a single Whittle W1 turbojet.

187

London in flames: the Blitz reaches new peaks

The shattered skeleton of a city: a view of London from St Paul's dome.

Churchill stands amidst the ruins of parliament; but government goes on.

The worst yet: fires gut impassable city

London, 11 May

The scale of last night's all-out attack on London by over 500 German bombers has left people almost stunned. When dawn broke, the sky above London was a dark pall of brown smoke which continued to blot out the sun, turning a spring day into a winter one. The air smells acrid. An electricity supply station in St Martin's Lane is belching smoke from its burning diesel tanks. Charred pieces of rag are floating in the wind from a burning dump in South London, and shreds of burnt paper have drifted 20 miles (32 km) into the countryside.

So many streets are impassable – estimated at a third – that people can hardly struggle to work. Every main line railway terminus is out of action. Some, like Victoria,

have been hit repeatedly. Over 150,000 people are without gas, water or electricity. Pavements are littered with burnt-out incendiaries.

At least 5,000 houses have been destroyed. Provisional figures for casualties are a record: over 1,400 people dead and 1,800 badly injured. Rescue parties are still digging them out. Among the dead are the mayors of Westminster and Bermondsey. Many of the record number of fires – 2,200 classified as "serious" – are still burning underneath the wreckage. There is a huge gin fire in City Road, and in the west the burning Palmolive soap factory is perfuming the air as the water directed on it turns into hot froth. Everyone is awaiting the raiders' return (→ 13).

Westminster hit: new home for Commons

London, 13 May

Homeless members of the House of Commons met today in Church House, Westminster, normally the assembly hall of the Church of England. Their own chamber is a heap of rubble open to the sky after last Saturday night's raid. Only the scorched walls remain – the Speaker's chair, the table and its despatch boxes all perished. A small bomb struck Big Ben, denting and blackening the clock face, but it is still chiming the hours. The hammerbeam roof of Westminster Hall (built c.1100) was saved, but the members' lobby lost its roof.

"Parliamentary business will not be interrupted by enemy action," Mr Churchill declared at Question Time in the substitute chamber. The House had already been sitting there since last November, and had just moved back to the Palace of Westminster in time for the raid. The House of Lords, though damaged, is useable, but Mr Churchill could not say whether it would be

made available to the Commons. Other London landmarks that are casualties of the great raid include Westminster Abbey, whose lantern roof collapsed in streams of molten lead – lack of water made the Abbey firewatch powerless. The Deanery was destroyed. Lambeth Palace, Scotland Yard, the War Office, St James's Palace, Victoria Station, the Law Courts, Gray's Inn and Lincoln's Inn were damaged. At the Royal College of Surgeons, pickled bodies were rescued from the debris. Fire destroyed 250,000 books at the British Museum. The Tower of London was hit by 100 incendiaries and Tower Pier was demolished, taking a naval vessel with it.

The luckiest escape was at the London Palladium theatre, where a parachute mine fell through the roof and dangled from the ropes of the flies above the stage until it could be removed and exploded safely. St Thomas's and Charing Cross were among 15 hospitals hit.

Britons learn to cope with the air raids
1: Looking after bombed-out homeless

London, 13 May

There have been no more raids since the big one on 10 May, and Londoners can hardly believe the lull that they are enjoying. Since the Blitz began eight months ago, 39,678 people have died in air raids in Britain (20,000 of them in the London region) while 46,119 have been badly injured. Pre-war estimates were for 600,000 dead, so the wrong preparations were made: millions of cardboard coffins and 750,000 empty hospital beds were not needed, but nothing had been planned for 2,250,000 homeless.

London alone had only 129 ill-furnished "Rest Centres" to cope with 1,400,000 bombed-out survivors – one person in six. They were overwhelmed.

Sanitary facilities, feeding, blankets and first aid were all hopelessly inadequate at first. Shocked people who had lost everything were given a floor to sleep on, bread and tea to live on, and no information on how to get clothes, housing, ration books or compensation. Now there are rest centres for 100,000, a Londoners' Meals Service and mobile canteens. Better late than never.

2: Organizing a national fire service

London, 13 May

The home secretary, Herbert Morrison, announced the nationalization of the country's fire services today. The 1,450 local fire authorities in England and Wales will be replaced by a central command divided into 12 Civil Defence regions. The Blitz has shown up the weakness of having a multiplicity of fire brigades, many of them very small, which refuse to amalgamate or cooperate. Some would not go to the help of others until payment was agreed. Their equipment, ranks and words of command all differ, causing confusion when two brigades are fighting the same fire side by side (→ 18/8).

Firemen at work in the blitzed City.

3: Bending the German radio beams

Britain, 13 May

To ordinary citizens the visible weapons in the battle against the *Luftwaffe* during the past eight months of the Blitz have been the anti-aircraft (AA or "Ack-Ack") gun and barrage balloon. The latter has discouraged low-flying aircraft, but AA guns are still very inaccurate. It is also only recently that the RAF's night fighters have begun to enjoy some success against the German bombers, thanks to airborne RDF (Radio Detection Finding).

More significant has been the highly secret "Battle of the Beams" waged by British and German scientists, the "Backroom Boys". In June last year [*see page 99*] the

existence of the *Knickebein* system for guiding German bombers to their targets was confirmed. A counter – powerful radio transmitters known as "Aspirins" – was developed to confuse the bombers.

The Germans then introduced the more sophisticated "*X-Gerat*" beam system. One Luftwaffe squadron was equipped with this, and marked targets with incendiaries for other bombers to hit. The British answer was the Bromide jammer, while decoy fires ("Starfish") were lit. On 8 May the Germans raided what they thought were Nottingham and Derby; thanks to beam-bending and Starfish, most of the bombs fell in fields.

US seizes French ships in its home ports

Washington, 15 May

Relations between Vichy France and the United States degenerated sharply today as the Senate passed a bill empowering the government to seize foreign shipping in US harbours.

Under the Ship Seizure Bill the US can take over vessels "by purchase, charter, requisition" or may take them "into protective custody". Although not specifically aimed at Vichy, the measure is a response to Petain's decision to collaborate more closely with Germany. Armed guards have already been placed on board all French ships in US ports, including the 83,423-ton liner *Normandie*. A score of French merchant ships will be put in "protective custody" as they arrive.

Meanwhile, it was announced officially in London that the RAF had bombed *Luftwaffe* aircraft on the ground at three airfields in Vichy-French Syria: Damascus, Rayak, east of Beirut, and Palmyra. General Dentz, Petain's high commissioner in Syria, protested last

A French peacetime poster: now the US is to seize Vichy-French ships.

night at the raids, which were a response to German efforts to ship aircraft, tanks and other arms to Iraq to bolster Rashid Ali, the anti-British politician who seized power in Iraq last month (→ 7/6).

Hess arrives at the Tower of London

London, 17 May

The prisoner in the Tower today is Rudolf Hess, brought by train from Scotland after his "peace flight" from Germany. He is kept in a room near the White Tower and spends much of his time watching guardsmen drilling. He will remain in the Tower until a Hampshire country house has been fortified for his detention.

Hess has been examined by army psychiatrists who say that they believe that he is sane, but his condition is deteriorating. He claims that attempts are being made to poison him. He dresses in his *Luftwaffe* uniform and insists that he should be given diplomatic status.

In Germany, Hitler has ordered the arrest of Willi Messerschmitt; Hess took off from the company airfield at Augsburg, but the aircraft chief knew nothing of his plan. Hess's aides have also been arrested. Everybody, British and German alike, remains baffled by Hess's flight to Scotland (→ 16/6).

Happy birthday to the Home Guard

Britain, 14 May

The Home Guard mounted guard at Buckingham Palace today in honour of its first birthday and was congratulated on its keenness by the king in an order of the day. Its strength is now 1,500,000 men, organized in 1,200 battalions. Their makeshift weapons have changed to regulation rifles and American Tommy guns.

The Home Guard takes up positions.

May

Su	Mo	Tu	We	Th	Fr	Sa
				1	2	3
4	5	6	7	8	9	10
11	12	13	14	15	16	17
18	19	20	21	22	23	24
25	26	27	28	29	30	31

18. Rome: The Duke of Spoleto accepts the crown of Croatia from a Croatian delegation; he will be King Tomislav I.

18. Gdynia: The German battleship *Bismarck*, the largest ship in the German fleet, sets sail on her first Atlantic raid, escorted by the cruiser *Prinz Eugen.*→

19. Crete: The last RAF fighters leave for Egypt.→

19. Germany: In exchange for greater collaboration from the Vichy regime, 100,000 French PoWs are released.

19. Iraq: British forces based at Habbaniyah capture Fallujah (→ 23).

20. Paris: The *Gestapo* arrest the Communist and Resistance leader Gabriel Peri.

21. Off Crete: German aircraft sink the destroyer HMS *Juno* (→ 22).

21. Atlantic: A U-boat sinks the US merchant ship *Robin Moor* inside the security zone.

22. Off Crete: German aircraft sink the British destroyer *Greyhound* and the cruisers *Gloucester* and *Fiji*, and cripple the cruiser *York*.→

23. Crete: King George of the Hellenes flees to Egypt (→ 24).

23. Germany: Hitler orders military support for Rashid Ali's rebels in Iraq (→ 28).

23. Germany: Goering issues a directive for the economic exploitation of the USSR, in which he says that famine and the deaths of millions of Russians are inevitable.

23. Britain: The "black propaganda" station GS1 (purporting to be based in Europe and to be anti-British *and* anti-Hitler) makes its first broadcast to Germany, calling Churchill a "flat-footed bastard of a drunken old Jew".

24. Crete: The Allies are pushed back to Galatas as German forces build up around Maleme (→ 27).

24. Mediterranean: The British submarine *Upholder* sinks the Italian troopship *Conte Rosso*.

24. Ethiopia: Soddu falls to the Allies (→ 21/6).

Biggest cruiser is sunk

HMS "Hood" in calm waters at Scapa Flow before her last fateful journey.

Greenland, 24 May
Britain was stunned today by the loss of a great symbol of its naval might. HMS *Hood*, the world's biggest battle cruiser, blew up and sank within four minutes, hit by a shell from the biggest vessel in the German fleet, the battleship *Bismarck*. Only three of the *Hood*'s crew of 1,416 survived.

The *Hood*, with her sister ship the *Prince of Wales*, had been stalking the *Bismarck* off the coast of Greenland. The *Hood* fired first on the heavy cruiser *Prinz Eugen*, but the *Bismarck* was close enough to use her guns with devastating effect. Commander Jasper on the *Prinz Eugen* described the scene: "There was an explosion of quite incredible violence ... Through huge holes which opened up in the hull, enormous flames leapt up from the depths of the ship ... and blazed for several seconds through an ashcoloured pall of smoke." It was the *Hood*'s only battle; completed in 1920, her armour could not withstand the single shell that set fire to her main magazine (→ 25).

South African PM is field marshal

Cape Town, 21 May
Jan Smuts, South Africa's prime minister and war overlord, was today given a present for his 71st birthday: a field marshal's baton.

"Your promotion to the highest military rank will be warmly welcomed," King George cabled, "not only for your great and devoted services, but as a leader of a people whose fighting men have been playing a most brilliant part in the victorious campaign in East Africa."

The esteem in which Smuts is now held by Britain is not without its ironies; in the Boer War at the turn of the century he had been the leader of a Boer *kommando* group against the British forces. Later, after the peace negotiations, he was widely regarded as the architect of South Africa's dominion status.

His links with Britain became closer in 1916 when he commanded Empire forces in East Africa and joined the British war cabinet, and he was a strong supporter of the need to create a single air force, which happened in 1918. He became premier of South Africa in 1919, but was rejected by the voters for his anti-trades union policy. He opposed the 1926 Colour Bar Bill (which failed) and in 1939 the new call to arms brought him, like his friend Winston Churchill, back to government.

Thousands more Italian troops surrender at Amba Alagi

Amba Alagi, Ethiopia, 19 May
The largest Italian army still fighting in Ethiopia formally surrendered today at Amba Alagi. Eighteen thousand Italian and colonial troops have marched out of the fortifications into prison camps. Few Italian troops now remain to be "mopped up" in Ethiopia.

It is Italy's East African viceroy, the liberal Duke of Aosta, who has abandoned this last Italian stand in Ethiopia, to avoid further bloodshed. As befits a man admired by his enemies, the British gave him a guard of honour. Aosta was not ideally cast to do Mussolini's work. He was too honourable to fight for a fascist victory, but also too honourable to betray his country or become Italy's de Gaulle (→ 24).

Italian colonial troops march into captivity after being taken in Ethiopia.

German paratroopers land on Crete

Crete, 22 May
Two days ago, for two long hours, wave after wave of German bombers pounded the airports of Maleme and Heraklion with thousands of tons of high explosive until most of the defending aircraft and anti-aircraft guns were destroyed. The few remaining RAF aircraft had flown off to Egypt, and now the defenders, who had been forced to leave most of their heavy weapons in Greece, had only Bren guns and rifles to face the airborne invasion which they knew – from *Enigma* code signals – was coming.

The last wave of bombers had only just disappeared over the horizon on 20 May when the air was filled with an ominous new sound: the roar of 493 Junkers Ju52 transport aircraft, heavily escorted by fighters. The biggest airborne invasion in history had begun, and swarms of German paratroopers landed at Maleme, Heraklion, Canea and Rethymnon. Australians and New Zealanders watched the parachutes – "like thousands of soap bubbles from a child's pipe", according to one New Zealander – and began firing at men swaying in their harnesses.

At Maleme – the principal target – the paratroops were followed by glider-borne troops who found themselves under heavy fire as they scrambled out of their frail craft

and ran to take their pre-arranged objectives. Some were successful – a vital bridge was quickly captured – others less so as they were pinned to the ground in open country and picked off easily.

An entire battalion of paratroops landed unopposed west of Maleme and were able to form up without disturbance before going to the glider force's assistance. Hampered by lack of communications – telephone lines had been cut by bombing and his wireless was virtually useless – Colonel George Andrews, the New Zealand battalion commander, was not aware that the battle was going relatively well for his men. He ordered his reserves into the battle, his infantry coming under withering fire that killed all but nine. When a German troop reinforcement convoy of small ships was severely mauled at sea by British cruisers – many of them were simply cut in half by ramming – it seemed for a few hours that the invasion had failed.

In a fiercely-fought battle in the evening, however, German airborne troops managed to take Maleme airport, and despite a night counter-attack German transport aircraft were landing thousands of troops yesterday. German air power is winning the battle of Crete. Stukas sank two British cruisers today (→ 23).

More fighters are delivered to Malta

Malta, 21 May
Malta is meeting the full savagery of the *Luftwaffe*. Bombed daily, this tiny island, just 66 miles (106 km) from Sicily, is under siege. Malta is essential if the Royal Navy is to harass Rommel's supply convoys. Small wonder, then, that its people turned out to cheer the 48 Hurricanes which flew in today – during a raid – from HMS *Ark Royal* and HMS *Furious*. The *Ark Royal* had delivered 23 Hurricanes in April when 47 Spitfires also arrived on the US carrier *Wasp*.

Goering mentions a "final solution"

Berlin, 20 May
Have the Nazis decided what to do with the millions of Jews whom they now rule in Europe? A circular issued by the central office of emigration today hints that they have. It tells German consulates that Goering has banned all emigration of Jews from France and Belgium because of the "doubtless imminence of the final solution".

What that "final solution" could be remains unclear, but Hitler appears to have given up his earlier scheme to solve the "Jewish problem" by emigration (→ 31/7).

Dive-bombers sink Mountbatten's ship

Crete, 23 May
Soon after sinking two German supply ships close to the Cretan shore, the British destroyers *Kelly* and *Kashmir* were today sunk themselves after continuous attacks by high-level bombers and Stukas. The *Kashmir* was broken in two and sank immediately. Shortly afterwards, the *Kelly*, hit by a 1,000-pound bomb just above the engine room and sinking, continued firing with her men refusing to abandon ship until ordered to do so by their captain, Lord Louis Mountbatten.

Many of the survivors were rescued by HMS *Kipling* after being machine-gunned in the water.

Germans coming in to land on Crete.

The Germans wreak havoc on Allied shipping in Suda Bay, north Crete.

May

Su	Mo	Tu	We	Th	Fr	Sa
				1	2	3
4	5	6	7	8	9	10
11	12	13	14	15	16	17
18	19	20	21	22	23	24
25	26	27	28	29	30	31

25. Atlantic: The *Bismarck* evades a British force sent to engage her (→ 26).

25. Haiphong, Indochina: Japanese soldiers remove $10 million worth of American goods from two warehouses.

25. Europe: One hundred troop trains are moved every 24 hours as the German High Command builds up its attacking forces on the Russian border (→ 6/6).

26. Atlantic: Swordfish planes from the *Ark Royal* locate and attack the *Bismarck*, firing a torpedo that wrecks the German ship's steering gear.→

26. Dodecanese: The British carrier *Formidable* and destroyer *Nubian* are badly damaged by Stuka bombers from Scarpanto.

26. US: America's first experimental blackout takes place at Newark, New Jersey.

27. Crete: Freyberg orders his troops withdrawn as Canea and Suda fall to the Germans; the battleship *Barham* is damaged by an air attack.→

27. Egypt: Rommel recaptures the Halfaya Pass from British troops (→ 7/6).

27. Paris: The Vichy vice-premier, Admiral Darlan, signs the "Paris Protocols", giving Germany access to Syrian and Lebanese military facilities and naval bases at Tunis and Dakar (→ 2/6).

28. Iraq: The Allies capture Ur.→

29. Crete: The British destroyers *Hereward* and *Imperial* are sunk (→ 31).

29. Washington: The US agrees to train RAF pilots to fly American planes supplied under Lend-Lease.

31. Crete: The last British contingent is evacuated from Sphakia (→ 1/6).

31. Germany: Himmler has approved Sigmund Rascher's request to subject prisoners at Dachau to pressure-chamber experiments.

31. Blackburn: Preston North End win the Cup Final replay 2-1 against Arsenal.

Britain rejoices as "Bismarck" sinks

North Atlantic, 27 May

The Royal Navy avenged the loss of HMS *Hood* today, sinking the much-feared battleship *Bismarck* after a thrilling chase across the Atlantic by more than 100 ships. Unlike the *Hood*, the *Bismarck* was modern, fast, well-armoured and a serious threat to Britain's convoys.

Nonetheless, she sank at 10.36am today only a few hundred miles from the safety of Brest in Brittany, and a tantalisingly short distance outside the range of U-boats and planes based in Brest that might have saved her. Her pursuers included Britain's most modern battleships, but it was 14 Swordfish "stringbags" from the *Ark Royal* which struck the crucial blow just before 9pm yesterday.

One of two hits struck beneath the stern and put the steering-gear out of action. Already trailing oil, the *Bismarck* began to turn helplessly in circles.

The German commander, Admiral Lutjens, sent a message just before midnight: "Ship incapable of manoeuvring. Will fight to the last shell. Long live the Fuhrer."

The *Bismarck* floundered helplessly in the heavy seas as the full force of the Royal Navy closed in: first the 4th Flotilla destroyers, then the battleships *King George V* and *Rodney*. They pounded the helpless giant with 16-inch and 14-inch guns from ever-decreasing range. Hundreds of shells turned the ship into a blazing hulk, but still she remained afloat thanks to her honeycomb pattern of watertight compartments which her designers claimed made her unsinkable.

The big ships were running out of fuel and were ordered home. It fell to the cruiser *Dorsetshire* to make the kill with torpedoes. Over two hours after the final action had begun, the *Bismarck*'s bows reared up and she turned on her side. The 2,200 men who died included Admiral Lutjens, whose 52nd birthday it was, and her captain, Ernst Lindemann.

The *Dorsetshire* and other British ships stood by to pick up survivors – but made off when told that a U-boat was believed to be in their vicinity. Only 110 of the *Bismarck*'s crew were saved (→ 4/6).

The "Bismarck" firing at HMS "Hood" on 24 May.

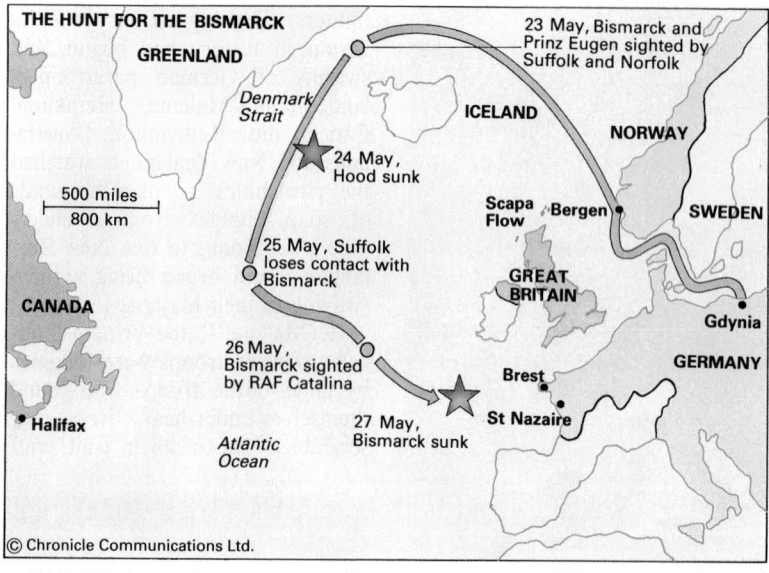

THE HUNT FOR THE BISMARCK

GREENLAND · Denmark Strait · ICELAND · 23 May, Bismarck and Prinz Eugen sighted by Suffolk and Norfolk · NORWAY · 24 May, Hood sunk · Scapa Flow · Bergen · SWEDEN · 500 miles / 800 km · 25 May, Suffolk loses contact with Bismarck · GREAT BRITAIN · CANADA · Gdynia · GERMANY · 26 May, Bismarck sighted by RAF Catalina · Brest · St Nazaire · Halifax · Atlantic Ocean · 27 May, Bismarck sunk

© Chronicle Communications Ltd.

Admiral Lutjens: died with his ship.   *Captain Martin of the "Dorsetshire".*

MAY 1941

Roosevelt damns the Nazi menace

Washington, 27 May
In his radio "fireside chat" President Roosevelt today warned Americans of Nazi designs on the Americas, promised to extend US patrols in the Atlantic to protect the sea-lanes to Britain, and announced that he had proclaimed an "unlimited national emergency". The US was rearming only for self-defence, he said, but modern warfare meant that a new Bunker Hill [a famous battle in the American War of Independence] "might be thousands of miles from Boston".

Church is against children's camps

Germany, 31 May
The German government has urged parents in areas most affected by the war to send their children to country camps where they will be cared for by specially-trained teachers. But the church is unhappy about this evacuation and says that the camps are being used to separate children from their parents and institute "education by the state". Artur Axmann, the *Reich* youth leader, recently visited camps in Slovakia in an attempt to reassure parents.

Allies evacuate Crete after a week of hell

A convoy of evacuated Allied troops sets sail from Suda Bay for Alexandria.

Heraklion, Crete, 28 May
To the constant, mind-numbing scream of Stuka dive-bombers, British soldiers, exhausted and beaten after a week of unrelenting battle, fought their way to the sea last night. Under cover of darkness they are being evacuated by the Royal Navy. More troops are being taken off in the south.

Anzac, British, Greek and Cretan irregulars have fought hard since General Kurt Student's airborne forces succeeded in establishing a bridgehead a week ago. Hampered by inadequate equipment – steel helmets had to be used to dig slit trenches – poor communications and an almost complete lack of air cover, they counter-attacked continually, always harassed by *Luftwaffe* fighters.

German losses have been high, with more than 40 per cent of the airborne troops killed by the end of the first day. "I never expected such bitter fighting," wrote one German officer. "We began to despair of ever gaining our objectives or indeed of surviving at all."

British commandos under Brigadier Robert Laycock landed at Suda Bay two days ago to cover the evacuation (→ 29).

"Dunera" trip fans controversy over internees

Britain, 31 May
The voyage of the SS *Dunera*, a troopship which sailed to Australia last July with 2,700 internees aboard, has led to the court martial of three of their British Army escort, including the commanding officer, after repeated questions in parliament.

After the ship reached Australia in September, it was reported that the internees, most of them Jews who had fled from Hitler, had been brutally searched; their luggage had been confiscated and ripped open with bayonets, their valuables removed and never returned by their army guards. They themselves were confined below deck during the two-month journey in squalid conditions. Some were physically assaulted. One jumped overboard.

The court martial found three men guilty, including Major William Patrick Scott, the CO, who was severely reprimanded. His regimental sergeant major was jailed for 12 months.

The voyage was the worst incident of several which followed a series of decisions between 12 May and 26 June 1940 to intern anyone from Germany, Austria and Italy who was in Britain, although the great majority were eager to help the war with Hitler. All were put into transit camps – on racecourses, at holiday camps, in a derelict mill – until transferred to camps and boarding houses on the Isle of Man. At the peak there were 27,000 in custody.

Four ships left for Canada, including the SS *Arandora Star* which was sunk by a U-boat with the loss of 175 Germans and 486 Italians. Soon afterwards the tide of opinion turned in favour of the internees. In a Commons debate wholesale internment was denounced as callous and called a "bespattered page in our history". Over 15,000 internees have been released and more will be, including many from the *Dunera*.

British forces quash Rashid Ali's Nazi-backed rebellion in Iraq

Baghdad, 30 May
With no sign of promised German assistance against an advancing British force – and no sign of gold promised to him personally – Rashid Ali, the pro-Axis prime minister of Iraq, lost his nerve here and fled to Iran accompanied by the German and Italian ministers. The British "Habforce", which included 300 men of Major Glubb's Arab Legion, was met by the mayor of Baghdad bearing a flag of truce and asking for an armistice.

Fighting began here when Iraqi troops ringed the British base at Habbaniyah only to find themselves bombed by obsolete British aircraft. Under the armistice, Britain will keep the base and use of Iraqi ports. Six-year old King Faisal is known to be safe (→ 1/6).

RAF armoured car crews round up Bedouin Arabs inside Fort Rutbah, Iraq.

193

Viruses spread as doctors go to war

Germany, 31 May
As more and more doctors are called up for service with the *Wehrmacht*, ordinary German citizens are finding themselves at the bottom of the list for medical care. The Westphalian town of Hagen, for instance, has one newly-qualified doctor for 33,000 people. The privations of the war and the conditions in which thousands of resettled people live are leading to the rapid spread of viruses. Trachoma, previously confined to Africa, now affects 200,000 in occupied Poland and 100,000 in the *Reich*.

Guerrilla tactics thwart Japanese

Chungtiao Shan, 25 May
Chinese Nationalist forces have beaten off a major Japanese offensive to gain control of the north bank of the Yellow River and establish a foothold in western Hunan.

The turning-point in the three-week battle, to which Japan committed six divisions and three brigades, came when the Chinese switched to guerrilla tactics after being forced to retreat to the Chungtiao mountains. While guerrillas kept the Japanese pinned down, a Chinese main force was to attack the enemy's rear.

A recruitment poster shows a helmeted ATS girl astride her motorbike as Nazi planes fly overhead.

Many die in "Luftwaffe" raid on Dublin

Rescue workers in Dublin clear the rubble after the worst German raid so far.

Dublin, 31 May
In its heaviest raid yet on neutral Eire, the *Luftwaffe* killed at least 28 people and injured 87 early today. Twenty of the dead were asleep in the early hours of the morning in the working-class Dublin suburb of North Strand when the bombs struck without any warning. Apart from no air-raid siren, other scenes were reminiscent of blitzed London and Rotterdam as rescue workers dug into the debris in a race against time to save life.

A vigorous protest about the latest outrage is expected from Dublin through its *charge d'affaires* in Berlin. This is the latest in a series of bombings by the German air force against Eire. In January, six counties were attacked, though casualties were fewer. The main victim was a family in Carlow which suffered three fatal and two non-fatal casualties.

Such episodes damage the credibility of anti-British Irish and Irish-American politicians. These range from IRA representatives thought to be in Germany to Joseph Kennedy, US ambassador to Britain until December.

Eire protest halts Ulster conscription plan

Westminster, 27 May
Northern Ireland will not be affected by obligatory military service, the prime minister, Winston Churchill, told the Commons yesterday. The decision follows protests from the Dublin premier, Eamon de Valera.

American diplomats in Dublin and London have been influential in swaying Churchill against conscription in Ulster. They suggested that it was not worth giving de Valera an excuse to reunify his country by force on a popular issue (conscription of unwilling northern Catholics to fight for Britain). Conscription could also disaffect the 80,000 southern Irishmen who are serving Britain as volunteers. Brit-

ain argued that those wanting to avoid service would simply cross into Eire, but the pro-British American ambassador in Dublin, David Gray, described the conscription plan as a "madness" which would provoke "holy war". Finally, after talks with the US envoy in London, Churchill wrote: "It would be more trouble than it is worth to go through with conscription [in Northern Ireland]."

The Stormont government in Belfast will not be pleased at the plan to halt conscription, and accuses Dublin of "unwarrantable interference". But is also true that the number of men available from such conscription would be a mere 60,000.

Allies send agents behind enemy lines

London, 26 May
The Special Operations Executive (SOE), ordered by Churchill to "set Europe ablaze", has dropped a team of General de Gaulle's men into France by parachute to attack KG100, the German pathfinder force, at Vannes, in south Brittany.

SOE had some difficulty in getting aircraft for the job because Air Marshal Sir Charles Portal believes that "the dropping of men in civilian clothes to kill members of the opposing forces is not an operation with which the RAF should be associated".

Air cover holds key to convoy safety

Westminster, 31 May
Continuous escort for convoys over the whole of the North Atlantic route is now a reality, according to Winston Churchill, the prime minister. Yet, even with the strengthening of the Iceland bases and the increased Canadian navy effort, that is still not quite true. Last month only ten ships of the 43 sunk by U-boats were in convoy. But less than two weeks ago one convoy lost nine ships at longitude 40 degrees west. That is too far out for aircraft and it is these, rather than the naval escorts, which are the U-boats' main fear. A "black gap" remains in mid-Atlantic where Allied air cover does not yet exist.

A survivor of a U-boat torpedoing.

1941
June

Su	Mo	Tu	We	Th	Fr	Sa
1	2	3	4	5	6	7
8	9	10	11	12	13	14
15	16	17	18	19	20	21
22	23	24	25	26	27	28
29	30					

1. Iraq: British forces enter Baghdad and the regent is returned to power (→ 3).

1. London: Air Vice-Marshal Arthur Tedder is appointed C-in-C air forces in the Middle East.

1. Mediterranean: The British AA (anti-aircraft) cruiser *Calcutta* is sunk returning from Crete to Alexandria.

2. Vichy: The government grants the use of Bizerta port in Tunis to the Axis.

2. North Atlantic: The escorts *Wanderer* and *Periwinkle* sink a U-boat.

3. Iraq: British Gurkha troops occupy Mosul.

3. Baghdad: Arab supporters of Rashid Ali riot, killing hundreds of Jews and looting Jewish shops (→ 4).

4. Iraq: A new, pro-British cabinet is formed.

4. Holland: Wilhelm II, Germany's exiled *kaiser*, who was born in 1859 and abdicated in 1918, dies.→

4. Atlantic: British ships sink four of the *Bismarck*'s support vessels.

5. Washington: The Roosevelt administration asks Congress for $10,400 million for defence spending in 1942.

6. London: British Intelligence receives reliable information that Germany will attack Russia on 22 June (→ 11).

6. Hitler orders the *Wehrmacht* to eliminate all commissars – Communist Party officials – in the planned assault on the USSR; he says: "Any German soldier who breaks international law will be pardoned. Russia did not take part in the Hague Convention and thus has no rights under it." →

6. Mediterranean: The British carriers *Furious* and *Ark Royal* deliver more Hurricanes to Malta.

7. North Africa: The RAF bombards Benghazi and Derna (→ 15).

7. France: RAF bombers attack the *Prinz Eugen* at Brest, but fail to hit her.

Allies abandon bloody fight in Crete

Sphakia, Crete, 1 June

It is midnight and an eerie silence reigns on this bay where, earlier, bombs poured down on British troops as they waited patiently for the Royal Navy to take them off the beaches of Crete. It is exactly one year since Dunkirk.

Many men were wounded; many more have slept in the sun, exhausted after days of bitter retreat across rough mountainous terrain, harried by bombing and machinegunning from the air. A shuttle service of flat-bottomed boats is taking them, 50 at a time, to waiting ships. There is no sense of humiliation among these men. They know that they have fought well and hard; they believe that they could have beaten off the Germans, given support from the air. As it is, the Germans have lost 220 planes to the RAF's 46.

British Commonwealth losses amount to 1,742 dead and 1,737 wounded, while the Germans have lost 3,985 dead and missing and 2,131 wounded. The Royal Navy has taken a severe pounding – three cruisers and six destroyers sunk and 17 ships crippled, with the loss of 2,011 lives. But by the time the last soldiers leave the beaches tonight, the navy will have rescued about 18,000 men. Even so, nearly 12,000 will have to be left behind to be taken prisoner.

Left behind in Nazi-occupied Crete: British soldiers captured by paratroopers.

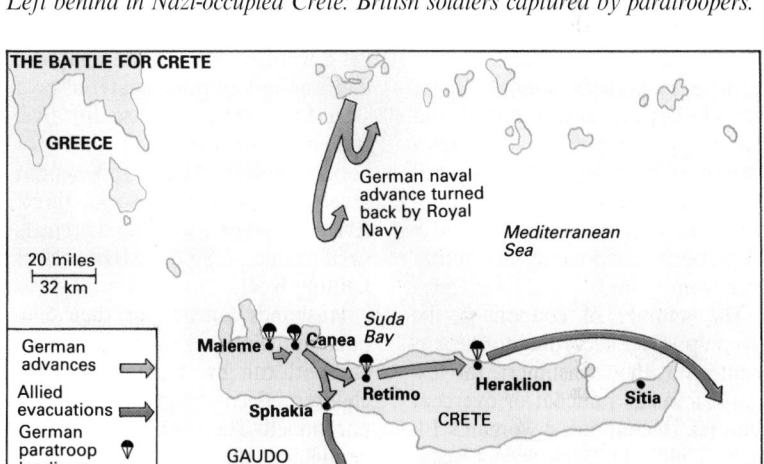

Hitler tells Duce of his war plans

Brenner Pass, 2 June

The Fuhrer called Mussolini to a summit meeting at the Brenner Pass today, supposedly to review the war situation. For two hours the two dictators were alone, and Hitler did most of the talking, dropping hints about German plans for action "if the shipping losses do not suffice" to knock Britain out of the war. At the end Mussolini departed for Rome no wiser than when he had arrived. Not so the Japanese ambassador in Berlin, Hiroshi Oshima, who was given the same "hint-hint" treatment by Hitler. Oshima told his foreign ministry in Tokyo that Hitler was about to attack Russia.

Cyprus feared new target for Hitler

Nicosia, Cyprus, 2 June

Under a top-secret order from Winston Churchill, Cyprus is being prepared for long-term guerrilla warfare. After a string of disasters in the Middle East, few believe that the island could hold out for more than a few weeks against the kind of assault that took Crete.

Engineers are building a series of "hides" in the Troodos mountains – filling them with weapons, ammunition and medical supplies – to act as "mini-bases" for clandestine British hill fighters. Churchill believes that several German divisions could be pinned down by a "ghost army" should Cyprus be invaded.

"Luftwaffe" moves to eastern airfields

Berlin, 7 June

Behind the screen of the continuing raids on Britain, the *Luftwaffe* is being switched to the east. The powerful air fleet which destroyed Belgrade and blasted the way clear for the *Wehrmacht* to march through the Balkans is being transferred to Poland, where it is being joined by more squadrons taken from France. There are now 2,770 German aircraft, formed into three fleets, facing the Soviet Union.

These moves support the belief that Hitler will soon attack the USSR, with which he has a non-aggression pact. He may find himself short of aircraft, however, for many were lost in the Balkans.

Rush for cast-offs as clothes are rationed

A non-woollen dress in Selfridge's goes for the regulation seven coupons.

Britain, 1 June
People were taken completely by surprise by today's announcement that clothes are now rationed and that they must give up their margarine coupons to buy them until special ration cards have been printed. Each man, woman or child will be given 66 coupons to last until a year from today.

The number of coupons to be given up varies according to the garment and the consumer; for example a man's raincoat or overcoat requires 16 coupons, a woman's 14, and a child's 11. Men need 13 coupons for a jacket, eight for trousers and five for a waistcoat, so a three-piece suit takes 26. A woman can get a woollen dress for 11 coupons, and one in any other material or a skirt for seven, a blouse for five, stockings for two, and shoes or boots for five. Men's shoes need seven, and a pair of socks three. Even a tie or two handkerchiefs need a coupon. So do two ounces of knitting wool.

Husbands can give up their coupons to their wives (and vice versa), and both can give them up for their children. Second-hand clothes are unrationed. There was a run on second-hand shops today. None of the traders in Petticoat Lane street market were taking coupons.

US begins to seize foreign shipping

Washington, 7 June
President Roosevelt has signed the bill authorizing the seizure of all foreign merchant ships arriving at US ports which was, passed by the Senate on 15 May [*see page 189*].

The marine commission has begun to commandeer foreign vessels and allocate them to whatever service may be most useful for national defence. They include 39 Danish, 28 Italian and two German ships as well as others in Lithuanian, Estonian, and Roumanian registry. The pride of the catch is the 83,423-ton French liner *Normandie*, the former holder of the Blue Riband for the fastest crossing of the Atlantic.

June 4. Kaiser Wilhelm II, who abdicated after his imperialist ambitions had contributed to the Great War, died today.

1941
June

Su	Mo	Tu	We	Th	Fr	Sa
1	2	3	4	5	6	7
8	9	10	11	12	13	14
15	16	17	18	19	20	21
22	23	24	25	26	27	28
29	30					

8. Middle East: Allied and Free French forces enter Lebanon and Syria (→ 9).

8. Beirut: Captain Moshe Dayan, leading a section of the Allied attack, receives an eye injury when a stray bullet hits his binoculars.

9. Syria: The Allies capture Tyre.→

10. France: The German authorities expel most of the foreign diplomatic staff from Paris.

11. Germany: Hitler starts to prepare for the period after *Barbarossa*, ordering his generals to plan for an assault on Gibraltar and operations in Turkey and Iran (→ 12).

11. Washington: Roosevelt frees a British division by agreeing to replace the British garrison in Iceland with American troops (→ 7/7).

11. Russia: Red Army units from the Transbaikal are transferred westwards, but are not put on alert (→ 12).

11. Germany: The RAF starts a series of raids on the Ruhr and Rhineland industrial areas.

11. Eritrea: The port of Assab is captured by Indian troops landed by the Royal Navy yesterday (Operation Chronometer).

12. Germany: One hundred and thirty army divisions are reported massed on the Russian border (→ 13).

12. Malta: RAF and Italian fighters engage in fierce battles (→ 15).

12. Norway: The pocket battleship *Lutzow* is severely damaged by RAF Beaufort torpedo bombers.

13. Moscow: The official news agency TASS says "rumours of a German intention to attack the USSR are without foundation" (→ 14).

14. Germany: Commander Theodore Eicke of the SS Death's Head division informs his officers of Hitler's "Commissar" order to kill all Communist officials on sight.

14. Moscow: The foreign minister, Vyacheslav Molotov, says that "only a fool would attack Russia" (→ 15).

Bolsheviks must be killed, says Hitler

Berlin, 12 June
German soldiers have been told to eliminate any Russian commissars they capture. This order, known as the *Kommissarbefehl* [commissar order] was issued by Hitler six days ago under the title *Guidelines for the Conduct of the Troops in Russia*. Other key points are:

1. Bolshevism is the mortal enemy of the National Socialist German people; Germany's struggle is directed against this destructive ideology and its carriers.

2. This struggle demands ruthless and energetic measures against Bolshevik agitators, guerrillas, saboteurs and Jews, and the elimination of all resistance (→ 13).

Keitel: co-signed the new decree.

Allies free Red Sea for US shipping

Massawa, Eritrea, 10 June
Here in the dockyard sappers are already preparing for the arrival of US-registered ships in the Red Sea. This is the prize for the Allied victory in Eritrea. Last year, when Italy declared war, the US Congress declared the Red Sea a combat zone. Neutral US ships must stay out. For 11 months supplies were unloaded at the Cape, reloaded onto British ships and brought to Egypt. Now, with all the East African coast in Allied hands, and Italy's naval squadron at the bottom of the Red Sea, Congress will reverse its position, and US ships may sail to Suez (→ 11).

French fight French in battle for Syria

Free France's desert cavalry, the "Spahis", in their native terrain in Syria.

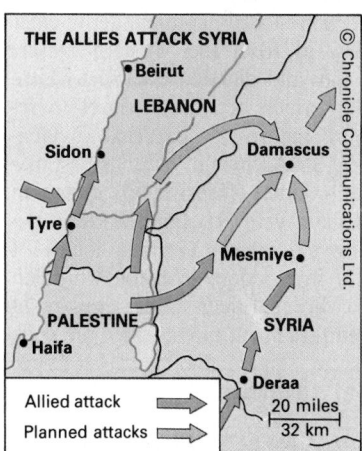

The map above shows the two stages planned by the Allies in their moves – by land and sea – against Syria. Their ultimate target: Damascus.

Damascus, Syria, 13 June
The Free French and British have invaded Vichy Syria. So stretched are General Wavell's men and materials that half the invading army are riding to war on horseback.

German penetration of Syria has been going on for months. The German consul, von Hentig, is Germany's finest Orientalist, and organized anti-British revolts in the Middle East in the 1914-18 War. Lately a steady stream of *Luftwaffe* aircraft have used Syrian aerodromes as staging posts while flying supplies to Rashid Ali in Iraq.

Bowing to political pressure from Churchill and de Gaulle, Britain's long-suffering commander in the Middle East scraped together what forces he could spare from the pressures of Libya, Crete, Iraq, Palestine, Egypt and East Africa. As well as two Free French brigades under General Legentilhomme, there were bits of the 6th and 7th Australian Divisions, 4th Indian Division and the 1st Cavalry Division, some dragoons, a commando from Cyprus, Glubb Pasha's Arab Legion, and several thousand Druze tribesmen under the gay and flamboyant Colonel Gerald de Guary – one of the Lawrence generation. On 8 June, while the 21st Australian Brigade crossed the Litani on the coast road heading for Beirut, two columns advanced from Jordan, aiming for Damascus.

All three columns encountered bitter resistance, but none more so than the Free French – at times this campaign is beginning to resemble a civil war between Frenchmen with every olive grove being fought over.

Against them – and inflicting heavy casualties on them – are 45,000 men under General Dentz, the majority colonial troops and Foreign Legionnaires, unlikely to listen to appeals from loud-speaker vans to "wash out the shame of Vichy's capitulation" (→ 15).

Roosevelt freezes Axis assets in US

Washington, 14 June
The sinking of the American freighter *Robin Moor* by a German U-boat decided President Roosevelt to freeze Axis assets in the United States. Naval activity here is hectic. Two destroyers were launched yesterday in Boston. Large cargo ships are being converted into escort carriers capable of launching 15 aircraft, and Congressmen believe that the next step will be to arm merchantmen.

Germany and Italy have taken measures with a view to freezing US assets, said to be worth $420 million (£105 million) in Germany and $144 million (£36 million) in Italy.

Forcing the US to wake up to Nazism.

Resistance grows in France one year after the fall of Paris

France, 14 June
A year ago today the Germans occupied Paris. A humiliating surrender was only days away. Twelve months later, despite the acquiescence of the pro-Nazi regime in Vichy, there are signs that resistance is beginning to stir in occupied France.

A coal-miners' strike has just ended in the Pas-de-Calais region, which cost the Germans 500,000 tons of coal. One hundred thousand miners downed tools on 26 May, shouting "No coal for the enemy" and paralysing two entire regions.

This show of strength, along with the student demonstration in Paris on 11 November, is the most spectacular resistance action France has yet seen. But so far the Resistance lacks both finances and organization within France. Most would-be resistants prefer to work alone or in small groups.

The circles of intellectuals, like the famous group *Musee de l'Homme*, which suffered severe losses in February, prefer to hand out pamphlets or clandestine newspapers. Others have opted for concrete action, like sabotaging some military installations, storing weapons, helping Jewish prisoners to escape and organizing uprisings.

Paul Koepfler managed to help 120 people escape to the south on Christmas Eve; soon after, he was arrested by the Germans. The risks are extremely high, regardless of the type of resistance chosen – especially since informing on one's neighbours is encouraged by the Vichy rulers.

Many French citizens oppose the enemy by means of individual gestures, like placing flowers at the *Arc de Triomphe* or tearing up German posters. Despite the arrests, the torture and the deportation awaiting the resistant, the number of people joining the resistance movement continues to grow.

Churchill defends his record to MPs

Westminster, 10 June
Winston Churchilll told MPs today: "I have not heard that Herr Hitler had to attend the *Reichstag* and say why he sent the *Bismarck* on her disastrous cruise. I have not heard that Signor Mussolini has made a statement about losing the greater part of his African empire." He was annoyed that the Commons forced a debate about the loss of Crete, and said that it would be better for the government to decide the timing of discussions about the conduct of the war. He fiercely defended the government, but insisted that as parliament's "lifelong servant" he will do as it says.

1941

June

Su	Mo	Tu	We	Th	Fr	Sa
1	2	3	4	5	6	7
8	9	10	11	12	13	14
15	16	17	18	19	20	21
22	23	24	25	26	27	28
29	30					

15. Lebanon: Allied troops capture Sidon (→ 16).

15. Libya: British forces suffer setbacks during Operation Battleaxe, launched yesterday to relieve Tobruk.→

15. Berlin: German warships are ordered to annihilate Soviet submarines (→ 18).

16. Aldershot, Hampshire: In military custody, Rudolf Hess tries to commit suicide by throwing himself off a staircase, but only breaks a leg.

16. Syria: Royal Navy planes sink the Vichy destroyer *Chevalier Paul* (→ 21).

17-18. Germany: The RAF bombs Cologne, Duisburg and Dusseldorf.

18. Ankara: Germany and Turkey sign a ten-year treaty of friendship.

18. Ukraine: A German defector to Russian territory says the attack will be made at 4am on 22 June.

18. USSR: Stalin leaves Moscow for his holiday (→ 21).

19. Europe: In tit-for-tat reprisals, Germany and Italy expel the US consuls.

20. Washington: Roosevelt accuses the Nazi government of being international outlaws, engaging in piracy with the aim of world conquest.

20. USA: Major-General H "Hap" Arnold is appointed C-in-C of the US Army Air Force.

21. Syria: Australian and Free French troops occupy Damascus, and the "Habforce" Commonwealth army advances from Syria into Iraq.→

21. Ethiopia: The Italian garrison at Jimma surrenders to Ethiopian troops under British command (→ 3/7).

21. Rastenburg, East Prussia: Hitler and his staff arrive at the *Wolfsschanze* [Wolf's Lair], Hitler's eastern headquarters.

21. USSR: Fighter pilots are ordered not to fire on a German plane which flies over Soviet airspace. The border guard is put on alert, but is forbidden to take any "provocative" action (→ 22).

Germans smash British desert tanks

Cairo, 17 June
A grim-faced commander-in-chief flew in from the Western Desert today and dictated a cable to London which began: "I regret to report failure of 'Battleaxe'." General Sir Archibald Wavell's first major counter-offensive has ended in defeat, with 91 British tanks destroyed against German losses of 25. In London, Winston Churchill – who had sent a fast convoy of reinforcement tanks under the code name "Tiger" and had high hopes for "Battleaxe" – took the news calmly. He has already decided to replace Wavell.

Wavell, too, had been optimistic, although he had grave doubts about the mechanical capacity of many of his tanks. He had not allowed for Rommel's intelligence which forewarned of the attack; or the devastating use by the *Afrika Korps* of the 88mm "ack ack" gun as an anti-tank weapon. With armoured support, Indian troops fought hard to take the Halfaya Pass; but a hastily improvised *Panzer* counter-attack was the decisive factor (→ 20).

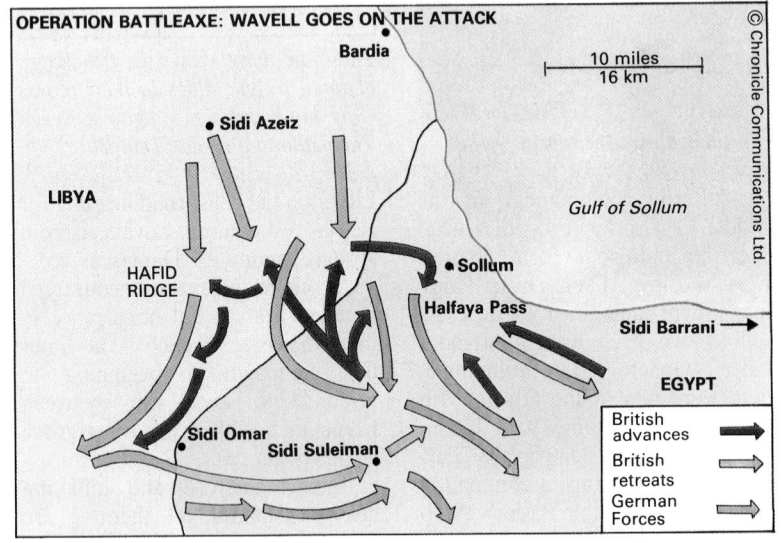

Auchinleck to take over African campaign

London, 20 June
In view of the failure of Operation Battleaxe, the British attack against Rommel to relieve Tobruk, Churchill has decided to replace Sir Archibald Wavell as C-in-C Middle East. He believes that the defeat, coming so soon after Rommel's succesful offensive and his rebuff of the Allied attack last month, shows that fresh blood is needed to restore British fortunes.

Wavell will be told shortly that his successor is to be General Sir Claude Auchinleck, C-in-C India. Although the latter's only combat experience so far in this war has been command of the Anglo-French forces at Narvik, he saw much action in Mesopotamia in 1914-18 and later on the North-West Frontier of India. Known as "The Auk", he is highly regarded and has a keen brain, although he is not as intellectual as Wavell.

Wavell (right) with his successor.

"Radio-location" secrets revealed

London, 17 June
This evening the British public was let into the secret of radio-location (also known as RDF, or radar) for the first time. Air Chief Marshal Sir Philip Joubert, who last week took over RAF Coastal Command, paid tribute to Robert Watson-Watt, the scientist who pioneered the system which did much to help win the Battle of Britain. He gave no technical details, but he did say that it was a system of rays "which are unaffected by fog or darkness. Any aircraft or ship in the path of this ray immediately sends back a signal to the detecting station." Watson-Watt himself, who has been made a CB and Fellow of the Royal Society, insists: "I am just an ordinary man."

Free French troops occupy Damascus

Damascus, Syria, 21 June
General Legentilhomme's Free French forces have taken Damascus, 15 days after Allied troops invaded Vichy Syria. The city, which Vichy troops evacuated yesterday, surrendered to Colonel Cateau. It has been a bloody triumph; the bodies of 200 Punjabis in the Damascus suburb of Mezze – not to mention French, Australian and British ones on the line of advance – are testament of that (→ 3/7).

A "Spahi" sergeant, one of the desert cavalry fighting for Free France.

Finns mobilized as Russian tension grows

Hurricane fighters boost Allies in Malta

Finnish soldiers on the march again – driven by hatred of the Russians.

Malta, the tiny island that is so vital to both the Allies and the Axis powers.

Helsinki, 17 June

Finland today ordered general mobilization of its armed forces, effective in three days' time. Notices on street corners order all reservists up to the age of 44 to report for duty.

Tension is running high here as rumours that Hitler is preparing to march on the Soviet Union sweep the city. There is no doubt that if the Germans do attack Russia the Finns will fight alongside them. The bitter memories of the "Winter War" in which the Russians crushed Finland despite its gallant defence run too deep for any other

course; there are reports that the 10,000 German troops who arrived in Finland recently, ostensibly on their way to northern Norway, are still in Finland preparing for a joint thrust with the Finns at Leningrad.

The Finnish army, with its knowledge of the country and ability to use the terrain, would also be able to hold the Russian army in the north while the Germans launched a *Blitzkrieg* towards Moscow. Many in Britain will be sad to see the Finns allying with Hitler, but hatred of the Russians outweighs all other considerations (→ 28).

Valetta, 15 June

Forty-three Hurricane fighters were delivered to the beleaguered island of Malta yesterday, greatly strengthening the RAF's air defences in what has become a key battle in the struggle for control of the Mediterranean and, indirectly, the battlefields of North Africa.

Both Britain and the Axis powers recognize the prime strategic importance of Malta. On the day of Italy's entry into the war it made eight air attacks on the island, and since the *Luftwaffe* moved into Sicily and southern Italy last Jan-

uary these attacks have shown a marked increase. The Royal Navy has devoted much effort to keeping Malta supplied so that Malta-based forces can continue to operate against Axis targets.

Malta sits astride the main Axis supply route to North Africa, especially to the Libyan port of Tripoli. If the overall Axis aim of securing the Suez Canal is to be achieved, this supply route must be made secure. On the other hand, in order to prevent an Axis build-up in North Africa the British must hang on to the island (→ 17/7).

US state department kicks out German consular staff

Ho Chi Minh calls for a free Vietnam

Washington, 17 June

President Roosevelt has ordered all 24 German consulates in the USA to shut by 15 July and all consular staff to be expelled. Diplomats in the embassy here are not affected.

Although US-German relations are deteriorating generally, the administration maintains that the consulates are not being shut down for that reason but because they were being used for espionage and fifth-column activities "wholly outside the scope of their legitimate duties". The reason why the administration did not take this step sooner is that it is bound to lead the Germans to close US consulates, which are useful listening posts inside Europe (→ 19).

US postal workers burn sacks of propaganda taken from a German consulate.

Saigon, 15 June

A Vietnam Independence League (*Viet Minh*) has been formed to be an army of liberation aimed at eliminating not only Japanese but also French control of Indochina. The League held its first meeting last month under the auspices of the Communist Party at Pao Bo. Although led by the Communists, the Viet Minh aims to provide a united front for all parties who want to end foreign domination of Vietnam. Its driving force is the founder of the Vietnamese Communist Party, Nguyen Van Thanh – better known as Ho Chi Minh, meaning "He Who Enlightens".

June

Su	Mo	Tu	We	Th	Fr	Sa
1	2	3	4	5	6	7
8	9	10	11	12	13	14
15	16	17	18	19	20	21
22	23	24	25	26	27	28
29	30					

22. London: In a broadcast speech, Churchill promises to give all possible help to the USSR.→

23. Libya: The Italian and German air forces bombard Tobruk (→9/7).

24. Westminster: The foreign secretary, Anthony Eden, announces an Anglo-Soviet mutual aid agreement.→

24. Europe: Recruitment of volunteers willing to fight with Germany on the eastern front begins in Spain and Denmark.

25. Helsinki: Finland considers itself at war with the USSR after Soviet planes bomb the Finnish capital (→28).

26. Germany: The meat ration is cut to 14 ounces per week (double for labourers); the artificial honey ration is raised in an attempt to compensate.

27. Budapest: Hungary declares war on the USSR.

27. Bialystok: Over 2,000 Jews are killed when German troops rampage through the city (→28).

27. USSR: Members of the Communist Party and of the *Komsomol* [League of Communist Youth] are mobilized as "political soldiers".

28. USSR: Finnish troops push towards Murmansk (→16/7).

28. Kovno, Lithuania: Local police and freed convicts beat hundreds of Jews to death (→29).

28. Europe: Albania declares war on the USSR.

29. USSR: The new Committee of Defence, headed by Stalin, takes complete control of the country.→

29. Britain: A cabinet reshuffle brings Beaverbrook to the ministry of supply.

29. Jassy, Roumania: Local police and militiamen kill 260 Jews in their homes, rounding up 5,000 for deportation in sealed cattle trucks (→4/7).

30. USSR: The western front commander, General Dmitri Pavlov, and his leading officers are executed for incompetence on Stalin's orders.

Germany attacks former Russian ally

Moscow, 22 June
At 3.15 this morning Germany attacked the Soviet Union along an 1,800-mile (2,880 km) front from the Baltic to the Black Sea. The Germans have thrown 151 divisions – just over three million men – into the battle, accompanied by an armoured fist of tanks, guns and aeroplanes.

Stalin, despite the warnings given to him by Churchill and his own spies, seems to have been taken completely by surprise. The first that the Russians knew of the invasion was when the guns began to speak. At four o'clock this morning Vladimir Dekanozov, the Soviet ambassador in Berlin, was called to the *Wilhelmstrasse* to be told that Germany had entered Russia in response to "border violations".

In fact, the invasion is the culmination of months of planning by the German general staff, acting on Hitler's orders. Operation *Barbarossa* is designed to destroy the Soviet Union and Bolshevism. Hitler is certain of success. He has told General Alfred Jodl: "We have only to kick in the door and the whole rotten structure will come crashing down." In a proclamation broadcast this morning Hitler boasted that the German army's movements were "the greatest the world has ever seen". First reports indicate that the Finns and the Roumanians are fighting alongside the Germans. Britain's first official reaction came tonight in a broadcast speech by Winston Churchill in which he promised the Russians "any technical or economic assistance in our power".

Russian soldiers in training: now the German army has invaded for real.

How the military machines compare as "Barbarossa" begins

Europe, 23 June
The Germans have unleashed a massive war machine on the unsuspecting USSR. The three million troops (including those held in reserve) have the support of 3,350 tanks, 7,184 guns and 2,815 aircraft. In addition, eight divisions have been deployed in Finland.

This leaves Hitler just 61 divisions (amounting to 600,000 men) to cover the remainder of Europe and North Africa, but divisions from Finland, Roumania, Slovakia and Hungary, plus some Italian forces, should head for the USSR in a few days or weeks if, as seems likely, those countries declare war on the USSR.

The USSR has about 132 divisions including 34 armoured divisions (2,500,000 men) in the border districts of the west, a further 20 facing Finland, and 133 divisions in the interior and Far East. This will more than double once mobilization is complete. The Russian tank armoury has some 20,000 machines, although many are obsolete, with new, more powerful, types only just being introduced. First line fuel, ammunition and tank radios are in short supply. The Red Air Force has 18,000 aircraft, of which well over half are in the west. Most are obsolete, and over 3,500 have already been lost. Even more serious are Stalin's refusal to prepare for an invasion, his unfinished reorganization of the Red Army, and his purge of many of his best commanders before the war.

Churchill promises alliance with Russia

London, 27 June

Stalin has accepted Churchill's offer of an alliance to fight Hitler. It has been agreed that military collaboration between the two nations will be on a "mutual and reciprocal basis". Military and economic missions are to be sent to Moscow to coordinate the joint war effort.

In his broadcast last Sunday after receiving the expected news of the German invasion, Churchill, who has often been outspoken in his opinions of the USSR, said that no one had been a more consistent opponent of communism than he. "I will unsay not a word that I have spoken about it," he said. "But all this fades away before the spectacle which is now unfolding."

He insisted that "any man or state who fights against Nazidom will have our aid. Any man or state who marches with Hitler is our foe ... We have but one aim and one irrevocable purpose. We are resolved to destroy Hitler and every vestige of the Nazi regime."

He forecast an even greater alliance: "The Russian danger is therefore our danger and the danger of the United States, just as the cause of any Russian fighting for his hearth and home is the cause of free men and free peoples in every quarter of the globe" (→ 12/7).

Stalin is supremo: Red Army hits back

Moscow, 29 June

Stalin, recovering from the shock of being attacked by his former ally, has put himself at the head of a committee of defence in which the whole power of the state will be concentrated to fight the Nazis. The Red Army, too, is recovering from its initial unpreparedness and its well-armoured, fast T34 tank has given the Germans a nasty surprise. What has really surprised the Germans, however, is the resistance being put up by the ordinary Russian soldiers fighting in defence of their homeland (→ 30).

Nazi allies in war against Bolsheviks

Helsinki, 27 June

Roumania, Hungary and Finland have now joined what Baron Mannerheim has described as a "holy war" against Russian Bolsheviks. The Roumanians have fought with the Germans since the first day of *Barbarossa*. Hungary, a base for the German invasion, declared war today. The Finns have not declared war, but considered a Soviet air raid on Helsinki two days ago to be the start of new hostilities with their old foe, their resentment of whom has overridden all qualms about fighting with Hitler (→ 28).

The atrocities begin as SS killers move in

Moscow, 30 June

Hitler's hangmen are pouring into the USSR behind his tanks. As the Germans advance they festoon the landscape with multiple gallows, each with its full quota of Soviet officials and political commissars.

This policy of terror is being carried out by the front-line troops as well as by the special task forces of the *Gestapo*. Hitler has ordered that every officer has the right and duty to shoot any person suspected of "criminal action".

Russians, like all Slavs, are regarded as *Untermenschen*, subhumans, by the Germans and are killed with casual brutality. No preparations have been made to deal with the thousands of prisoners that the Germans are taking, and they are being left to rot without food or medical attention. There is no doubt that the Nazis intend to follow the extermination policy which they inflicted on the Poles and wipe out all those Russians capable of mounting any form of resistance. They intend to rule by terror.

In an even more sinister move Himmler has been delegated to act independently of the army to carry out "special tasks". His SS *Einsatzgruppen*, the special killing squads, have moved into the war zone and are carrying out a massacre of the Jews, who are being forced to dig their own graves and are mown down by machine guns. A terrible slaughter is taking place.

The German invaders came by land ...

A Nazi officer leads his men up an open road over the frontier into Russia.

They swarmed across Russian rivers ...

Nazi soldiers crowd into a makeshift boat to cross a river into Russia.

And their bombs devastated the cities

Russian women in Kiev, horror-struck by the ferocity of the German attack.

Massive German attack forces Red Army retreat

Speed of "Panzer" attacks catches the Soviets by surprise

Moscow, 30 June

The Red Army, with its officer corps decimated by Stalin's purges, and totally unprepared for war because of Stalin's blind insistence that Hitler would not attack, has taken a terrible hammering in the first week of Operation *Barbarossa*.

The fast-moving German armoured columns have pierced the Soviet defences wherever they have attacked, and have pushed on, deep into Russia, leaving behind thousands of disorganized, demoralized Russian soldiers to be dealt with by the infantry following the *Panzers*.

General "Fast Heinz" Guderian is covering 25 miles a day with his panzer group, crossing rivers with tanks fitted with *schnorkel* air tubes and extended exhausts. Yesterday he linked up near Minsk with another Panzer group under General Hermann Hoth, creating a huge Soviet pocket. The Germans estimate that they have already taken 150,000 prisoners, and destroyed 1,200 tanks and 600 guns.

As the campaign develops it can be seen that the German plan is based on three army groups:

1. Field Marshal Wilhelm von Leeb, commanding Army Group North, is driving through the Baltic states towards Leningrad, which is also being threatened by the Finns.

2. Field Marshal Fedor von Bock's Army Group Centre has the strongest tank forces and has been ordered to encircle and destroy the Soviet forces in Byelorussia, thus opening the road to Moscow.

3. Army Group South, under Field Marshal Gerd von Rundstedt, is preparing for a holding attack from Roumania into Bessarabia, while a tank force thrusts deep into the Ukraine towards Kiev to cut off the defenders.

There are signs, however, that the Soviet defence is beginning to stiffen, with counter-attacks being launched against all three groups. They have not succeeded in holding the Germans, but the Soviet soldiers are fighting furiously.

Blazing a trail for Operation "Barbarossa": Germans burn a farmhouse.

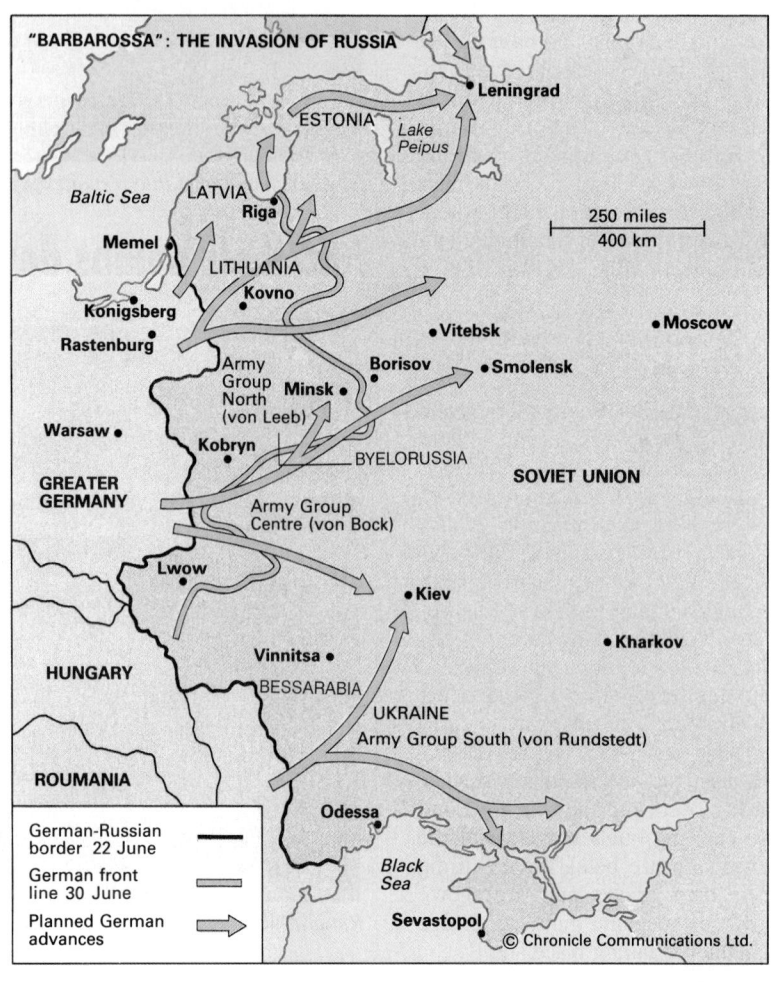

"BARBAROSSA": THE INVASION OF RUSSIA

German-Russian border 22 June

German front line 30 June

Planned German advances

© Chronicle Communications Ltd.

Germans win first round in battle for air supremacy

Moscow, 30 June

The *Luftwaffe* scored a shattering victory over the Red Air Force in the first minutes of Operation *Barbarossa*. Aircrews flying Heinkel He111, Junkers Ju88 and Dornier Do17 bombers in flights of three at great height to avoid detection swooped on 66 Russian airfields.

The Russians did not stand a chance. Their aircraft, parked wingtip to wingtip, were blasted by small fragmentation bombs, and then the bombers wheeled over the airfields to machine-gun the burning wreckage. Hardly a shot was fired back.

The Russians have not yet recovered from those first devastating minutes. The surprise attack was followed up by Stukas and Messerschmitts systematically working their way round the airfields which, along with HQs, barracks and artillery positions, had been pinpointed by high-flying reconnaissance aircraft in the weeks before the invasion. Those aircraft that did get into the air, mostly obsolete Polikarpov I-15 and I-16 fighters, were slaughtered by the Messerschmitt Bf109s which had proved their superiority over the stubby Russian fighters during the Spanish Civil War.

Now the Germans are ranging the battlefield virtually unhindered in support of the *Panzers*. Stukas are being used as tank-busters while the heavier bombers are raiding the cities, softening them up for the army. The fortress of Brest-Litovsk, which held out for a week, fell yesterday after it was wrecked by Ju88s.

After a day's fighting the Soviets had lost 1,811 aircraft – 1,489 on the ground and 322 in the air – for the loss of only 35 German machines. Russian fighter pilots are flying valiantly, sometimes ramming their opponents, while the Tupolev SB-2 and Ilyushin-4 (or DB-3) bombers, often unescorted by fighters, take terrible casualties in attacks on airfields and armoured columns. They are buying time with their lives (→ 2/7).

1941

July

Su	Mo	Tu	We	Th	Fr	Sa
		1	2	3	4	5
6	7	8	9	10	11	12
13	14	15	16	17	18	19
20	21	22	23	24	25	26
27	28	29	30	31		

M.A.U.D. Committee reports on A-bomb

London, 30 June
The M.A.U.D. Committee, set up last year to study the feasibility of producing a bomb based on nuclear fission, has concluded that making such a bomb is practicable, that a bomb containing 25 pounds of active material would produce an effect equivalent to 1,800 tons of TNT, and that the construction of an atomic bomb is "likely to lead to decisive results in the war". The material for a first bomb could be ready by 1944, but the plant to produce it would cost £1.25 million ($5 million).

U-boat "wolfpack" hits British convoy

Greenland, 29 June
Another U-boat has been sunk by the escort of convoy HX-133, which has been harried by German submarines for most of the past week.

The "wolfpack", originally of ten U-boats, has sunk five ships of the convoy despite a strong escort including the Canadian destroyer *Ottawa*. The pack struck first on 23 June, sinking one merchantman. Four more ships have been lost since, although the Canadians with their Asdic equipment and depth charges have so far replied by sinking three U-boats.

British writer gives radio talk in Berlin

Berlin, 26 June
P G Wodehouse, the creator of Jeeves and Bertie Wooster, broadcast a talk to the United States from Berlin tonight. He described how he was interned after the Germans overran Le Touquet, where he had a villa: "Wodehouse, old sport, I said to myself, this begins to look like a sticky day." Aged nearly 60, he has been released four months early from camp and brought to Berlin, where he agreed to do a series of talks. He said that internment was "quite an agreeable experience". He is staying at the Adlon, Berlin's best hotel (→8/7).

1. Cairo: General Sir Claude Auchinleck officially takes over as C-in-C Middle East from General Wavell, who has been appointed C-in-C India (→11).

1. USA: All men aged 21 or over have to register for the draft today, and US Navy planes start patrolling the North Atlantic for U-boats.

1. Latvia: German troops occupy the capital, Riga (→2).

1. China: Germany and Italy officially recognize the Japanese puppet government of Wang Chingwei.→

2. Moscow: Marshal Semyon Konstantinovich Timoshenko is appointed western front commander.→

2. Canada: The Canadian Women's Auxiliary Air force is set up.

2. Latvia: German forces break through Russian border defences on the Dvina river (→5).

2. France: RAF bombers damage the cruiser *Prinz Eugen* at Brest.

3. Syria: Allied troops capture Palmyra and Deir el-Zor from French troops loyal to the Vichy regime (→12).

3. Ethiopia: "Mopping up" of the Italian forces in East Africa continues as the Italian garrison at Debra Tabor surrenders to the British; General Gazzera's army in the south surrenders to a Belgian force.→

4. US: Roosevelt urges Americans to pledge their lives as well as their work to the defence of human freedom.

4. Kovno: Lithuanian militiamen kill 463 Jews (→5).

5. USSR: The German Sixth Army breaks through the Stalin line near Lwow (→6).

5. Aegean Sea: The British submarine *Torbay* sinks the Italian submarine *Jantina*.

5. Rastenburg: Hitler's adjutant says that the murder of thousands of Russian Jews by SS *Einsatzgruppen* [action squads] or by local militia is part of a "necessary mopping-up operation" (→6).

Chiang Kai-shek cuts links with Axis

Chungking, 1 July
The Chinese Nationalist *Kuomintang* government has broken off diplomatic relations with Germany and Italy in retaliation for the decision by the Axis powers to recognize its new rival, the Reformed Kuomintang, the puppet regime set up by the Japanese in Nanking under Wang Chingwei.

The Kuomintang leader, General Chiang Kai-shek, has reluctantly ordered the recall of the Kuomintang's ambassador in Berlin and its *charge d'affaires* in Rome.

The Axis decision to support the Nanking regime is the result of diplomatic pressure from Tokyo, overriding the views of German officials in China who oppose recognition for Nanking. They argue that, following the outbreak of war with the Soviet Union, Germany and China – the latter at war with the Communists in the north – should unite against communism (→18).

Chiang Kai-shek: new Axis enemy.

Japan calls up a million fighting men

Tokyo, 2 July
Japan is preparing for war against Britain and the US over Indochina by conscripting one million men and recalling all its merchant ships from the Atlantic. While 400,000 conscripts will reinforce the *Kwantung* army in China, the rest will be committed to south-east Asia. The decision to open up the southern front – known as the Greater East Asia Co-Prosperity Sphere – has been spurred by the speed of the German successes in Europe. At an imperial conference at which the emperor made a rare appearance the war minister, Hideki Tojo, urged the cabinet that now is the time to secure more empire or risk missing the bus.

July 1. Mackenzie King, the Canadian leader, at Downing Street where he presented Winston Churchill with the Canadian "Torch of Victory".

203

Stalin orders scorched-earth tactics

Victors' spoils: smouldering ruins.

On Stalin's orders: Russians burn their towns and villages to the ground.

Moscow, 3 July

Stalin broke his silence today and, calling his people "brothers" and "sisters" rather than "comrades", called on them to fight a total war against the invading Germans not only in the modern sense but also in the grim "old Russian" way.

In a speech broadcast throughout the Soviet Union, he called on the people to lay the land waste before the invader. Everything possible must be removed, he said, and that which cannot be moved must be destroyed.

It was a speech designed to stir the people's ancient love of Russia: "We must not leave a single pound of grain or a single gallon of petrol to the enemy." He called on the people whose ancestors had helped to defeat Napoleon by "scorching the earth" to follow their example and deny Hitler's invaders food and shelter. Crops and villages are to be burnt, livestock killed, dams destroyed. Partisan bands are to be formed "with the launching of guerrilla warfare everywhere, with blowing up bridges and roads, with wrecking telephone and telegraph communications, and with setting forests, depots and trains on fire. It is necessary to create in invaded areas unbearable conditions for the enemy."

Fuel is of special importance in this scorched-earth policy, for the German supply lines are becoming over-stretched and the thirsty tanks and aircraft must rely to a large extent on captured fuel.

The burning of houses is not important at the moment, for the weather is hot and fine, but if this campaign extends into the bitter Russian winter then the lack of shelter could hit the Germans as cruelly as it did Napoleon's men.

Stalin has demanded a great deal from the people of the Soviet Union. Some of them will not obey him – in some areas the invading Germans have been welcomed with bread and salt – but others will do anything for Holy Mother Russia, if not for communism (→ 5).

Tito leads Yugoslav resistance fighters

Belgrade, 5 July

A 49-year-old Communist who organized groups of his fellow Yugoslavs to fight Franco in the Spanish Civil War today issued a call to his country "to rise like one man in the battle against the invaders and hirelings".

Josip Broz, alias "Tito", has recruited many partisans from the Yugoslavs who have fled to the mountains to escape forced labour under the Germans. Another resistance group has sprung up in western Serbia, led by Colonel Draza Mihailovich; but this royalist detests the Communist Tito more than the Nazis (→ 8).

Tito: the Yugoslav resistance leader.

First American dies as Eagle Squadron duels over France

Britain, 2 July

The American Eagle Squadron of the RAF has suffered its first fatalities. During a raid by Blenheim bombers on a German aerodrome in northern France, the American escorts encountered stiff resistance from about 60 Messerschmitt Bf109 fighters.

In a confused close-quarter dogfight two RAF fighters were destroyed in a mid-air collision. One or both are thought to be Eagles. But the RAF fighters in turn shot down three Messerschmitts. Two were shot down by young US pilot officers. A third fell to the British flight leader. In the same action a British sergeant pilot shot down two planes with a single fusillade.

Some of the RAF's American Eagles seen beside a Hawker Hurricane.

"Blithe Spirit" is a London smash hit

London, 3 July

Noel Coward brought a pre-war touch back to the West End with last night's opening of his latest play, *Blithe Spirit*, at the Piccadilly Theatre. Described by its author as "an improbable farce", it contains no references to the war whatsoever. In the play a *seance* conjures up the mischievous spirit of a husband's first wife – Elvira, the "blithe spirit" of the title, ethereally played by Kay Hammond in ghost-grey make-up. Cecil Parker is her suffering spouse and Margaret Rutherford at her dottiest is the medium, Madame Arcati. The curtain came down to cheers.

1941

July

Su	Mo	Tu	We	Th	Fr	Sa
		1	2	3	4	5
6	7	8	9	10	11	12
13	14	15	16	17	18	19
20	21	22	23	24	25	26
27	28	29	30	31		

Italian forces in Ethiopia give up

Addis Ababa, 4 July

With the Italian surrender at Amba Alagi, all that remains for the Allies in East Africa is clearing up. Yesterday General Gazzera surrendered his divisions in Sidamo to a Free Belgian force. The alternative to the Belgians was the Ethiopian "Patriots", led by Major Orde Wingate, who reputedly wears a purse made from the scrotum of a dead Italian. A few Italians divisions remain around Gondar in the north-west, and in the far west, and the rains – which make all roads impassable – will give them a few months' life, but they present no strategic threat to anyone.

One lump or two? Coal is rationed

Britain, 4 July

From today only one ton a month of coal, coke or any other type of solid fuel can be supplied for domestic use. Even that amount is not guaranteed to be available. Coal production is falling because of the call-up of young miners. Ernest Bevin, the minister of labour, has appealed for 50,000 ex-miners to return to the pits, without success; he is now ordering ex-miners to register for recall. The new restriction of supply affects all households, hotels, flats, clubs and offices, and is intended to save fuel for industry.

GUINNESS IS GOOD FOR YOU

Quenching the censor's thirst.

6. USSR: Roumanian troops occupy Chernovsky (→ 7).

6. Kovno: Lithuanian militiamen, on German orders, kill 2,514 Jews (→ 10).

6. Britain: London has its sunniest day this century, 15 hours and 48 minutes of sunshine.

6. South America: A border dispute between Peru and Ecuador flares up into war (→ 26).

7. USSR: Russian and German tanks clash at Ostrov, a key point on the road to Leningrad (→ 9).

7. Europe: Nazi-inspired anti-Bolshevik campaigns start in France and Belgium.

7-8. Cologne: The city is attacked overnight by 114 RAF Wellingtons.

8. Belgrade: Germany and Italy announce plans to dismember Yugoslavia.

8. Baltic States: Jews are ordered to wear a yellow badge of identification.

9. USSR: Vitebsk and Pskov fall to the Germans; 300,000 Soviet prisoners have now been taken (→ 11).

9. Tobruk: British positions are bombarded by Axis aircraft and artillery (→ 18/8).

10. Lithuania: SS troops drive the entire Jewish population of Jedwabne (1,600 people) into the market place, torture them for several hours, and finally burn them alive in a barn.→

10. Lebanon: Australian units occupy Damur, leaving Beirut as the only Vichy stronghold.

11. Washington: Roosevelt asks for appropriations of $3,300 million (£800 million) for the US Navy, in addition to the $4,700 million (£1,175 million) requested yesterday for the US Army.

11. USSR: The Germans, who have taken 600,000 Russians prisoners, are ten miles from Kiev (→ 12).

11. Simla: Wavell takes up his post as C-in-C India.

12. USSR: Moscow is raided by the *Luftwaffe* for the first time (→ 13).

US relieves British garrison in Iceland

Reykjavik, Iceland: US soldiers arrive to relieve the island's British garrison.

Washington, 7 July

President Roosevelt today informed Congress that United States forces have landed in Iceland.

The immediate occasion for the decision for the US to join British and Canadian troops in defending Iceland was the report that Germany has assembled an expeditionary force in northern Norway to invade Iceland. It would clearly have been a strategic disaster for Britain to allow the Germans to seize a bastion in the middle of the vital western shipping lanes from North America to the Western Approaches. However, the significance of the US move goes beyond Iceland itself.

It signals the administration's willingness to relieve Britain of any burdens which a non-belligerent can undertake, so as to free British manpower for operations elsewhere.

The White House released copies of three-cornered negotiations between Washington, London and the prime minister of Iceland, Herman Jonasson, in which the US recognized the sovereignty of Iceland and promised to withdraw all military forces as soon as the war came to an end.

RAF keeps up the pressure in Europe

High Wycombe, 9 July

Bomber Command headquarters here has received a new directive instructing it to concentrate attacks on German transport and to aim at breaking the morale of the German population. Recent attacks include two daylight bombing raids in northern France and night-time raids on Bremen, Cologne, Duisburg, Cherbourg and Rotterdam. Key transportation targets are the railways, and air war planners have faith in the crippling effect of such strikes. At the same time the RAF has carried out some raids on U-boat bases and warships in Brest harbour, France.

Merchant sailor is hanged for treason

Britain, 9 July

The first British citizen to die under the 1940 Treachery Act was hanged today at Wandsworth jail. He was sentenced to death at the Old Bailey on 8 May. George Johnson Armstrong, a ship's engineer, was arrested on his return to Britain from America. While in the US he had met a German consul and offered his services as a spy for the Nazis.

Three foreigners have been executed for treachery, having landed on a wild piece of the British coast with radio sets. The other Briton to be sentenced to death, Dorothy O'Grady, has had her sentence commuted to 14 years in jail.

Anglo-USSR pact signed

Moscow, 12 July

Britain and Russia are allies again after nearly 25 hostile years. Sir Stafford Cripps (British ambassador to Moscow) and Vyacheslav Mol-Molotov, the Soviet foreign minister, today signed a pact which promised that both countries would "render each other assistance and support of all kinds in the present war against Hitlerite Germany".

Stalin looked on, smiling, as the two men signed the documents and the official blue ribbons and red wax seals were applied at a ceremony in the Kremlin. Then chocolates and glasses of Georgian champagne were handed round and Stalin, raising his glass, toasted Anglo-Russian cooperation for victory.

The pact, proposed by Churchill, goes further than an agreement to wage war against Hitler; it also commits both countries to an undertaking that "during this war they will neither negotiate nor conclude an armistice or treaty of peace except by mutual agreement".

Churchill has a long memory. It was Lenin's decision to make peace with Germany in 1918 that enabled the Germans to mount their last great and nearly successful offensive on the Western Front (→ 19).

A Jewess is abused by Nazi murderers: one of millions praying for their lives

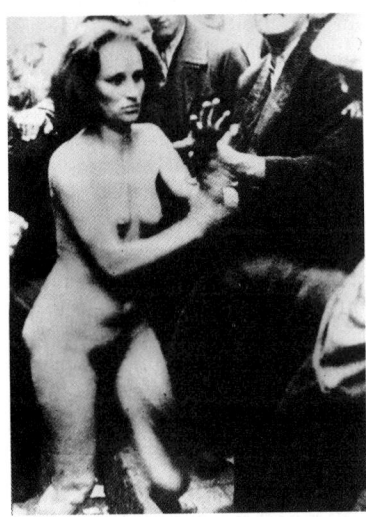

The utter humiliation of a Jewess.

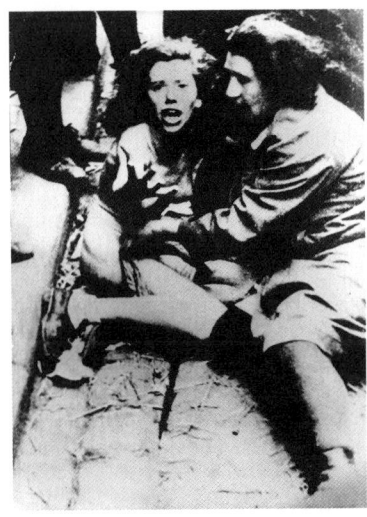

Naked and abused, but still defiant.

Lwow, 12 July

Her crime is simply to be Jewish. Since the Germans entered the city a fortnight ago, she has known no peace. And now it is her turn to be stripped, humiliated, punched and kicked. Maybe they will rape and torture her in jail. Maybe they will just kill her in the street.

The Nazis have exploited a local tradition of nationalism and anti-Semitism to suit their evil purposes. Photographs of Ukrainian nationalist prisoners slaughtered by the retreating Russians were posted up in the town and captioned "Jewish killings". The Germans recruited a local militia. Just two days after the Germans arrived, local people were massacring Jews in *Aktion Petlura*,

a symbolic revenge for the killing of a Ukrainian by a Jew in Paris 15 years ago. A coolly-worded report that 7,000 Jews have been rounded up and shot has gone to Berlin.

The eastward progess of the Germans has activated a wave of *pogroms*. In Kovno, Lithuanian police have murdered over 3,000 Jews under German supervision. In Jassy, Roumanian troops killed over 200 Jews and crammed 5,000 into sealed cattle trucks. In Bialystok, the Nazi soldiers spent their first day of occupation herding the city's Jews into their own blazing synagogue, where they died. Tarnopol, Dvinsk, Zolochew, Luck, Lubieszow and Lutsk: they all run red with Jewish blood (→ 17).

Minsk falls to the Panzers' advance

Smolensk, 10 July

Hitler's tanks are thundering into the heart of Russia. The city of Minsk finally fell yesterday. General Guderian has crossed the Beresina, where Napoleon was crushed on his retreat from Moscow, and tonight the German *Panzer* leader is preparing to cross the Dnieper with his sights fixed on Smolensk, the ancient gateway to Moscow.

While Guderian takes the direct route, General Hoth is sweeping north to by-pass Smolensk and cut the road to Moscow. The advance of the Panzers is marked by a pall of yellow dust, stirred up from the plain baked dry by the summer sun, and smoke from burning villages.

The Russians are taking desperate measures to stop the Nazis. Pavlov, the failed commander of the Bialystok sector, has been shot on Stalin's orders, and a new line of defence has been established under the command of the defence minister, Marshal Timoshenko (→ 13).

Wodehouse could face prosecution

London, 8 July

P G Wodehouse could be prosecuted after the war for making his broadcasts from Berlin, which are being recorded as evidence. Mr Eden told the Commons yesterday that "the government has seen with regret the report that he has lent his services to the German propaganda machine".

Armistice brings peace to Syria

Acre, Palestine, 12 July

The first armistice between British and French forces since the Battle of Waterloo was initialled today in the light of a motor cycle headlight. The armistice, ending the fighting in Syria and Lebanon between the Vichy French and the Allies, comes as Allied forces tighten their grip on Beirut. For Vichy's commander, General Dentz, it is virtually a surrender. The first burst of French fratricide since 1871 is over (→ 15).

1941

July

Su	Mo	Tu	We	Th	Fr	Sa
		1	2	3	4	5
6	7	8	9	10	11	12
13	14	15	16	17	18	19
20	21	22	23	24	25	26
27	28	29	30	31		

13. USSR: German troops push on from Pskov (→ 14).

14. USSR: German forces reach the river Luga and now threaten Leningrad directly.

14. Smolensk: The Katyusha mobile rocket-launcher is used in action for the first time.

15. USSR: The Red Army launches a counter-offensive near Leningrad.

15. Newfoundland: The US sets up an air base at Argentia Bay.

16. USSR: The Germans reach the outskirts of Smolensk, and take Stalin's son, Lieutenant Jacob Djugashvili, prisoner (→ 19).

16. USSR: Finnish troops take up positions at the northern end of Lake Ladoga (→ 29).

17. Malta: Axis aircraft bomb Allied bases (→ 25).

17. USSR: Field Marshal Keitel's son Hans-Georg dies from battle wounds.

17. Germany: Hitler appoints Alfred Rosenberg to the post of *Reich* minister of the occupied territories following a conference at Angersburg; he will be responsible for the exploitation of subject Soviet peoples and the elimination of Jews and Communists.→

18. Japan: Prince Konoye reshuffles his government, excluding the pro-Axis foreign minister, Yosuke Matsuoka (→ 22).

18. China: Over 35,000 pro-Japanese soldiers attack the New Fourth Army's stronghold in Kiangsu (→ 1/8).

18. Moscow: The USSR signs a friendship treaty with the Czech government in exile.

19. Britain: The Home Fleet patrol ship HMS *Umpire* is rammed and sunk by the German destroyer *Peter Hendricks* off the Wash.

19. Rastenburg: Hitler orders Guderian's 2nd Panzer Group to move south (→ 22).

19. Lithuania: In small groups, 5,000 Jews have been been shot dead and thrown into pits at Ponar, outside Vilna (→ 21).

German troops head for Leningrad

Moscow, 19 July

The Germans are continuing their thrust towards Leningrad in the face of increasing Russian resistance. There was heavy fighting yesterday near Lake Peipus where the German infantry has still not been able to break through in support of its advance tank units. A Soviet communique claims that Red Army troops surrounded and destroyed enemy mechanized units between Pskov and Porkov, 180 miles south-west of Leningrad.

The former czarist city is now under attack from three directions: the Finns are approaching from the north and north-east, on both sides of Lake Ladoga, while the Germans are attacking through Estonia and the *Luftwaffe* is mounting heavy raids on the city and the rail link with Moscow. But Leningrad is a hard nut to crack (→ 22).

German soldiers smash their way into a Bolshevik snipers' hideout in Russia.

V for Victory: BBC urges Europeans to resist German rule

London, 20 July

A "V for Victory" campaign was launched by the BBC at midnight last night. It began with a message from Churchill to occupied Europe: "The V sign is the symbol of the unconquerable will of the people of the occupied territories and a portent of the fate awaiting the Nazi tyranny."

The broadcaster in charge of the campaign, "Colonel Britton", said: "Tomorrow the V army, Europe's invisible army of many millions, will come into being. You are asked to do two things. Take a vow to continue this fight for your country's independence. Second, to demonstrate to the Germans by putting Vs on the wall, and everywhere you can put them, and beating out

Nazi murder squads set loose in Russia

Russia, 17 July

The *Einsatzgruppen* are coming. Reinhart Heydrich today issued his orders for the four SS action squads which are attached to the regular German army as it pushes eastwards. Their task is not military but ideological; they are to exterminate all Jewish and gypsy communities and terrorize the populace. Heydrich has given them the authority to slaughter other "politically intolerable elements", such as Communist Party and Soviet state officials, and "inferior Asiatic peoples". They are tackling their task with gusto (→ 19).

Heydrich: authorizing slaughter.

Russia gets British "Enigma" decodes

London, 19 July

Mr Churchill, determined to help the Russians in their fight against Hitler, has decided to send them high-level secret intelligence based on *Enigma* decoding. The Russians will not, however, be told that Britain has cracked the Enigma secret, for the Soviet Union's own codes are being read by the Germans.

Instead, the "sanitized" messages are being disguised under the cover of "a well-placed source in Berlin" and passed on through the military mission in Moscow (→ 20/9).

The sign to be chalked on every wall.

the V sound whenever you get the chance." The "V"-sign began to appear in Europe last January after a BBC broadcast to Belgium in which Victor de Laveleye suggested that Belgians who were chalking up the letters RAF should add a V for *vrijheid* (Flemish for freedom). V also stands for *victoire*, the French for victory.

"Colonel Britton" (a pseudonym for Douglas Ritchie of the BBC European Service) suggested an audible V, using the morse code rhythm – three dots and a dash. This is the rhythm of the opening bars of Beethoven's Fifth Symphony, which is now used as a station call-sign by the BBC in its broadcasts to Europe.

Syria comes under Allied umbrella

Beirut, 15 July

The Allies have entered Beirut in triumph, and will hand over Syria and Lebanon to their inhabitants. When they invaded a month ago General de Gaulle said in a broadcast: "I come to end the mandatory regime and to proclaim you free and independent." Thus Syria and Lebanon – to strong Vichy protests – join Eritrea in being offered self-determination.

Information ministry given new powers

London, 20 July

Tighter centralized control of British news and propaganda services was announced today when Brendan Bracken, the swashbuckling Tory MP who has been Mr Churchill's parliamentary private secretary, took over as minister of information.

It is expected that there will be more systematic and rigorous censorship in future. This follows calls from politicians in all parties for greater and more ruthless use of propaganda as a main war weapon. That goes particularly for the BBC's overseas services.

Lord Moyne, the colonial secretary, said in the House of Lords last week: "We must remember that we alone in the Old World have a free press, and that no other country now enjoys our advantage of quick information and well-informed comment which the British Press provides." In Fleet Street, journalists smiled. What they print is already vetted by the MoI.

1941

July

Su	Mo	Tu	We	Th	Fr	Sa
		1	2	3	4	5
6	7	8	9	10	11	12
13	14	15	16	17	18	19
20	21	22	23	24	25	26
27	28	29	30	31		

21. Minsk: SS troops rope 45 Jews together and order 30 White Russians to bury them alive in a pit; when the White Russians refuse, all 75 victims are machine-gunned to death (→ 24).

21. Britain: Hugh Dalton, the minister for economic warfare and head of the Special Operations Executive, tells Churchill that he can now "set in motion ... schemes for full-scale revolution in Europe".

21. Gibraltar: Convoy "Substance" leaves for Malta (→ 27).

22. Tokyo: The new foreign minister, Teijiro Toyoda, reaffirms Japan's alliance with Germany and Italy (→ 27/8).

22. USSR: The Axis armies pause in their advance, having conquered 700,000 square miles of Russian territory (→ 24).

23. Mediterranean: Italian planes damage the destroyer HMS *Fearless*, which has to be sunk by the British, and the cruiser HMS *Manchester*.

24. USSR: After a long siege, the Soviet defenders of Brest-Litovsk are forced to surrender (→ 28).

24. La Pallice, France: RAF bombers badly damage the German battle cruiser *Scharnhorst*.

24. Poland: An *Einsatzgruppe* [action squad] commander reports back to Berlin that 4,435 Jews have been liquidated in the town of Lachowicze.→

25. South Atlantic: The British cruiser *Newcastle* intercepts the German ship *Erlangen*, which scuttles herself.

26. US: Roosevelt incorporates the armed forces of the Philippines into the US Army and sends General Douglas MacArthur to take up the command of US forces in the Far East.→

26. South America: Peru and Ecuador declare a truce in the border war.

26. France: The British ships *Cattistock*, *Mendip* and *Quorn* bombard Dieppe.

US and Britain freeze Japan's assets

Washington, 26 July
Japan's seizure of French military bases in Indochina [*see below*] has brought economic sanctions intended to deal the most drastic blow possible short of actual war. By freezing Japanese assets worth at least £33 million, Britain and the United States have put an end to appeasement in Asia.

In an executive order issued last night, President Roosevelt brought all financial transactions involving Japanese interests under the control of the US government. Today the British treasury announced similar restrictions on all orders affecting Japanese holdings in Britain and the Dominions. By request of the Chinese government, the freeze is also applied to Chinese assets in order to thwart Japanese attempts to abuse its position as the occupier of key Chinese financial centres.

At a stroke, Japan has lost 80 per cent of its oil imports and most of its supply of wheat, cotton, zinc, iron ore, bauxite and manganese – vital war materials; it must now eat into its stocks. Its two biggest export markets, for £55 million worth of silk a year to the US and £40 million worth of cotton cloth to Britain, have disappeared.

Japan hit back today by freezing all British and American assets in Japan. These are believed to be relatively small (→ 28).

Konoye: Japan's prime minister.

Vichy France agrees to Japanese occupation of Indochina

A unit of Japanese troops arrives in newly-surrendered French Indochina.

Vichy, 25 July
The risk of war in the Far East escalated today with the surrender by the Petain regime of its military bases in Indochina to Japan. Britain and America have both denounced the French surrender and will implement a contingency plan to freeze all Japanese assets in their territories from midnight tonight.

By gaining access to airfields in western Indochina, Japan can now launch more frequent bombing missions against the Burma Road, the vital highway for the transport of arms to China. Occupation of Indochina's east coast ports constitutes a potential threat to the Philippines, 800 miles (1,280 km) away, and Singapore, 750 miles (1,200 km) away (→ 26).

Stalin promoted to chief of defence

Moscow, 20 July
Stalin, the "man of steel", has taken over the position of commissar of defence from Marshal Timoshenko and is now in supreme command of the Soviet Union's armed forces, a post traditionally occupied by a soldier. Stalin has thus gathered all military and civilian power into his own hands. It will be a heavy burden, but there is no doubt that the ruthless Georgian leader will bear it with his customary resilience (→ 29).

Britons expelled from unoccupied France

Paris, 25 July
The German-controlled radio here announced that the Vichy government had decided to deport all British subjects from its territory.

Members of the sizeable British expatriate community on the *Cote d'Azur* were told to leave a month ago. Many of them are elderly and cut off from their incomes by the speed of the French collapse last year.

Now Vichy has decided to deport British subjects from France and "to regulate the position of Britons in France". In part, the decision reflects increasing German pressure on the Vichy rulers. "After getting rid of the Free French parasites and the enemies of France as well as of the communists and the Jews," Paris radio said, "it is now the turn of the British."

The decision also reflects the bitter anti-British resentment of Admiral Darlan, the Vichy vice-premier, over what the radio called "the numberless British aggressions" against Dakar, Syria and the French fleet.

"Luftwaffe" takes battle to Moscow

Fighting off the Luftwaffe: anti-aircraft gun emplacements in Gorky Park.

Maltese gunners repel Italian attack

An oil-covered officer rescued from one of the ships that did not make it.

Moscow, 21 July
The London "Blitz" has come to Moscow. German bombers raided the city again last night, dropping incendiary and high explosive bombs on the Russian capital. The official German news agency said that the raid equalled "the heaviest blows dealt by the *Luftwaffe* on targets of military importance in Britain".

As in Britain, however, most of the bombs fell on ordinary homes, and, as in Britain, the ordinary people reacted to the danger with courage and humour.

The first raiders dropped flares and incendiaries, hoping to light the way for the main force of bombers, but the well-organized Muscovites dealt swiftly with the fire-bombs, smothering them with sand before they could take hold.

The city's anti-aircraft guns put up a tremendous barrage, with a fiery display of tracers and "flaming onions". The searchlights "coned" a number of the raiders which were immediately surrounded by shell-bursts. One raider was seen to stagger and fall away as the tracers struck. The Russians claim to have shot down 22 of the raiding force of some 200 bombers (→ 22).

Malta, 25 July
With the Grand Harbour at Malta unusually filled with merchant ships from a newly-arrived convoy – Operation Substance – high-speed Italian motor boats, their bows packed with high explosive, made a daredevil attack here tonight. Only one freighter had been damaged in this successful attempt to beat the Axis in "bomb alley" – although the cruiser HMS *Manchester* was damaged and the destroyer *Fearless* sunk. Fifteen brave young Italians died when their MTLs (literally "tourist motor boats") came under fire from harbour defences manned by the Royal Malta Artillery. The attack had been planned for months.

One group of "frogmen" would blow up a hindrance net suspended from a bridge to allow the MTLs access to the harbour. The MTL pilots would race down the huge harbour and aim their exploding boats at ships before ejecting themselves over their sterns.

The plan almost worked, except that one of the Italians, Major Tesei, blew up the bridge and himself, blocking access to the MTLs, which found themselves helpless, floodlit by harbour searchlights.

Nazis hold Vilna Jews to ransom

Vilna, Lithuania, 26 July
This morning the Germans arrested members of the ghetto's *Judenrat* [Jewish council]. They demanded five million *roubles* for their release, of which two million must be found by tomorrow morning. Failure to pay will mean their execution.

As the news spreads through the ghetto, the Jewish community is trying desperately to raise the money to save their lives. Men are donating watches and women jewellery. But it looks as though they will fall short of the sum required and that the Nazi executioners will carry out their threat.

"Target for Tonight" is cinema sensation

London, 26 July
People are flocking to *Target for Tonight*, a new, authentic kind of war film made by Harry Watt and the film-makers of the Crown Film Unit (formed from the pre-war GPO film unit). The film is an understated, unemotional account of an RAF bombing mission over Germany by a Wellington bomber code-named "F for Freddie".

The "actors" are real aircrew from Mildenhall airfield, in Suffolk, performing their real-life roles. After bombing the target in heavy *flak*, the plane is hit and has to limp home to England to land in dense fog. It is piloted by Squadron-Leader Pickard.

Targeting the potential high-flyers.

Roosevelt recalls MacArthur to arms

Washington, 26 July
Amid the tensions created in the Far East by the Japanese occupation of southern Indochina, and the freezing of all Japanese assets in the United States as a result, President Roosevelt has recalled a distinguished American soldier to the active list and appointed him to command the US Army Forces in the Far East.

The soldier is General Douglas MacArthur, who says that he is confident that the Philippines – an obvious Japanese objective – can be defended if war should spread to the Far East.

1941

July

Su	Mo	Tu	We	Th	Fr	Sa
		1	2	3	4	5
6	7	8	9	10	11	12
13	14	15	16	17	18	19
20	21	22	23	24	25	26
27	28	29	30	31		

27. Gibraltar: The ships that escorted Convoy Substance to Malta arrive safely back in Gibraltar.

27. Britain: After ten weeks of peace, German bombers attack London tonight.

27. Vilna: The Germans murder two members of the *Judenrat* [Jewish council] when the community fails to pay an enormous bribe (→ 31).

28. USSR: German forces start to liquidate Soviet troops trapped near the town of Smolensk (→ 30).

29. Far East: Vichy France signs a treaty giving Japan control of its colonies in Indochina in the event of enemy attack (→ 7/8).

29. Moscow: Stalin sacks General Georgi Zhukov for advising a tactical surrender at Kiev, replacing him with Marshal Boris Shaposhnikov (→ 7/8).

30. Scandinavia: German shipping and military facilities at Kirkenes in Norway and Petsamo in Finland are attacked by planes from the British carriers *Victorious* and *Furious* respectively. Of 29 planes from *Victorious*, 13 are shot down.

30. Moscow: Roosevelt's adviser, Harry Hopkins, arrives to discuss ways to help the Soviet war effort.

30. Rastenburg: Hitler orders assaults towards Leningrad and the Caucasus rather than a frontal attack on Moscow (→ 31).

31. USSR: At the end of 14 days of continuous slaughter, *Einsatzkommando* groups have killed 10,000 Jews at Kishinev and 2,500 at Zhitomir.→

31. USSR: The German army reaches Lake Ilmen and the Finnish army starts an attack aimed at Viipuri (→ 31/8).

31. North Africa: Axis forces are reorganized; General Ludwig Cruwell takes over command of the *Afrika Korps* while Rommel commands the new *Panzerarmee Afrika*.

31. Britain: Civilian air raid casualties this month were 900 people killed and 908 injured.

"Final Solution" ordered for Jews

Reichsmarschall Hermann Goering.

Berlin, 31 July
Nazi plans to rid Europe of Jews took a step forward today, when Reinhart Heydrich, the head of the RSHA (*Reichssicherheitshauptamt* [Reich Chief Security Office], which controls the police and *Gestapo*) received the following directive from Goering:

"I commission you to carry out all organizational, material and financial preparations for a total solution of the Jewish question in the German sphere of influence in Europe. If the competency of other organizations is affected by this, these organizations are to participate.

"I further order you to submit to me as soon as possible a report showing the ... measures already taken for the execution of the final solution of the Jewish question."

This order gives Heydrich full administrative power to set up a pan-European programme, operated by Himmler's SS, to dispose of the Jews. The nature of the programme is still unfinalized, but some things are becoming clear.

First, the thoroughness of *Einsatzkommando* massacres in occupied Russia in the last six weeks suggests that murder on a massive scale, rather than emigration, has become the "solution" to the "problem". Secondly, recent discussions between Himmler and Rudolf Hoess, the Auschwitz commandant, show that the order for that solution comes from Hitler himself.

It looks as though the Auschwitz camp and one to be built at Majdanek, near Lublin, are to become the main centres for the operation.

How violence against Jews has grown

Daubed with large Stars of David, Russian Jews are forced to clean the streets.

Germany, 31 July
The Nazis have devoted more energy to stirring up hatred of the Jews than to any other single issue.

In 1933 Hitler opened the first concentration camp (at Dachau, initially for political opponents) and ordered a boycott of Jewish businesses. In 1935 the Jews were excluded from public life. Physical attacks on Jews and their businesses became everyday events, culminating in *Kristallnacht* (Crystal Night, because of the broken glass) in 1938. The SS and the army incited *pogroms* in Poland. In October the first transports of Jews from Vienna arrived in the ghettoes of Warsaw, Vilna and other cities, already packed with refugees from German-occupied Poland. All Jews were made to wear a blue Star of David on a white armband; the ghettoes were then sealed.

Anti-Semitic laws and attacks came to Jews in western Europe soon after invasion. The invasion of Russia brought with it pogroms and the specialist murder groups called *Einsatzgruppen* or *Einsatzkommandos* [action squads] [*see report alongside*].

Nazi death squads in mass slaughter

Moscow, 31 July
The SS *Einsatzgruppen* [action squads] – 3,000 men trained at a special school by the *Gestapo* and sworn to carry out "special duties in the name of the Fuhrer" – are sowing horror and death behind the German lines with the cooperation of the regular army. At Kishinev they have just slaughtered 10,000 Jews and 2,000 other "undesirables" in mass executions.

Immediately a region is occupied by German troops the *Einsatzgruppen* move in, gather together the local Jews, strip them of clothing and valuables and shoot them dead in a remote part of the countryside. The corpses are thrown into a shallow ditch.

Local people, especially in the Ukraine and Lithuania, join in the sport, mounting their own *pogroms* against the Jews. Nobody is spared, from oldest to new-born.

It is not only the extent of the massacres which is so horrifying but the way in which the Germans, the lovers of *kultur*, are carrying them out. Hose-pipes are forced into the mouths of Jews and turned on until the victims burst; children have their brains dashed out; soldiers watch mass executions as if they are at a football match (→ 1/8).

Japanese troops advance southwards into French Indochina

Saigon, 28 July

The crisis in the Far East worsened today when 30,000 Japanese troops entered French Indochina. The build-up includes elements of the Japanese navy, which have sailed into Camranh Bay, and aircraft which are flying into Saigon. Japanese troops have also begun disembarking in Cambodia where 8,000 men will be within striking range of Thailand.

The Japanese thrust has come soon after a conference in Tokyo on 2 July decided on a southward advance rather than the attack on Russia which the Germans wanted.

Malaya is now seriously threatened from Indochina, which is providing the Japanese with a naval base within 750 miles (1,200 km) of Singapore and airfields within 300 miles (480 km) of northern Malaya. The Japanese move has isolated the Philippines and menaces the oil-rich Dutch East Indies.

The Vichy regime has given the Japanese a free hand in Indochina

The streets of Saigon come to a halt as Japanese forces of occupation arrive.

on the pretext that it was threatened by British and Gaullist plots.

The US and Britain have reacted quickly. All Japanese assets in the United States have been frozen, with an embargo on the supply of

oil, steel and other strategic materials to Japan. Britain and the Dutch East Indies followed suit and Japan, faced with economic strangulation, has either to yield to western demands or go to war.

Estonian capital surrounded as Germans push deep into Russia

Moscow, 31 July

The German army is pushing ever deeper into the great land mass of Russia. The Red Army, despite the inspired courage of its soldiers, has so far been unable to cope with the German *Blitzkrieg* tactics, and city after city falls to the *Wehrmacht*.

Tallinn, the Estonian capital, has been surrounded by von Leeb's Army Group North as he strikes for Leningrad. "Fast Heinz" Guderian's tanks are approaching Smolensk, only 200 miles from Moscow. Kiev is threatened by von Kleist and, on the Black Sea, the Roumanian 4th Army is advancing on Odessa. The triumphal progress of the Wehrmacht is shown by the scale of Russian casualties – over a million in little more than a month of fighting.

It has been an astonishing achievement, although Germany too has had its losses. In six weeks of fighting it has lost more men than in all its other campaigns, with over 100,000 casualties to date. Weaknesses are also beginning to show in the German war machine. Some tanks are breaking down because their air filters cannot cope

with the dust of the Russian steppes. More ominously, the supply lines are stretched to breaking point; for instance, General Hopner, leading the *Panzer* thrust to Leningrad has been forced to delay his attempt to seize the city because he is short of shells.

The sheer size of Russia is also intimidating. The Germans drive on

and on, but Russia never ends. The Russians are also learning how to fight them. New T-34 tanks and MiG fighters are taking part in the battle and, even more important, men like Koniev and Rokossovsky have emerged to lead them. The scorched-earth policy is also denying the invaders the opportunity to live off the conquered lands (→ 5).

German troops advance into the Estonian city of Narva on the Leningrad road.

Russo-Polish pact signed in London

London, 30 July

Russia and the Polish government in exile signed a treaty of friendship in London today which Mr Churchill described as "proof of the fact that hundreds of millions of men all over the world are coming together on the march against the filthy gangster power which must be effectively and finally destroyed".

The first result of the treaty will be the formation of a Polish army from prisoners of war held in Russia. General Sikorski, the exiled Polish prime minister, said after the signing that, while not all questions had been settled between Russia and Poland, the treaty provided a basis for useful collaboration.

Escort system is extended by Allies

North Atlantic, 31 July

Navy hopes are high as this month ends that they are over the worst in their battle with the U-boats. Losses to Allied shipping are now running at under one-fifth of the peak rate of 688,000 tons suffered in April.

There has been a steady improvement, thanks to more escorts and better support at the Iceland base, with the US now helping out as well as Canada. And the Germans have had less air support since the Russian front opened.

Japan is sorry, but bombs US gunboat

Chungking, China, 30 July

Within hours of damaging the US gunboat *Tutuila* in a bombing raid here, Japan has formally apologized to the USA. It is unlikely, however, that the latter will be reassured. The state department is certain now that Japan, having moved into Indochina, has its eyes on the Dutch East Indies and is testing United States resolve. Four days ago the USA and Britain froze all Japanese assets, and two days ago they cut off almost all its oil. If Japan is to go to war, it must do so before very long.

1941

August

Su	Mo	Tu	We	Th	Fr	Sa
					1	2
3	4	5	6	7	8	9
10	11	12	13	14	15	16
17	18	19	20	21	22	23
24	25	26	27	28	29	30
31						

1. Washington: Roosevelt bans the export of oil and aviation fuel except to the western hemisphere, Britain and the British Empire. Japan will be badly hit.

1. China: Japan attacks Communist troops in the Shansi-Chahar-Hopeh border area, launching the "Three All" campaign (→ 13).

1. Kishinev, USSR: Germans shoot dead over a thousand Jews and communists (→ 3).

2. US: Roosevelt sends the first aid to the USSR under Lend-Lease provisions (→ 4).

2. USSR: The Italian "Pasubio" and "Torino" divisions join the German armies in the southern sector.

3. Mediterranean: HMS *Maplin*, a fighter catapult ship, scores her first success when a Hurricane launched from her deck shoots down a Focke-Wulf Condor.

3. Jelgava, Latvia: SS *Einsatzkommandos* under Lieutenant Hamann murder 1,550 Jews (→ 12).

4. Washington: The US makes a formal commitment to send military supplies to the USSR.→

6. Tokyo: Japan proposes concessions to the US in south-east Asia if its assets are unfrozen (→ 27).

6. USSR: General Wladyslaw Anders is appointed C-in-C of the new Polish army to be formed in Russia.

7. Moscow: Stalin appoints himself Commander-in-Chief of the army.

7. Gibraltar: The British destroyer *Severn* sinks the Italian submarine *Michele Bianchi*.

8. Brussels: The pro-Nazi Rexist (Belgian fascist) leader, Leon Degrelle, leads his volunteer "Walloon Legion" to fight with the Nazis on the Eastern Front.

8. USSR: German troops smash Russian defenders at Kazaki, taking 38,000 PoWs.

9. Newfoundland: Churchill and Roosevelt arrive for a conference to discuss what help the United States can give in the conflict.

US Flying Tigers help Chiang Kai-shek

Chinese pilots train in Curtiss Hawks: now they are joined by Flying Tigers.

Chungking, 1 August
American mercenary pilots hired to fly fighter and bombing missions for the Chinese Nationalists are to become official members of the Chinese armed forces on the orders of General Chiang Kai-shek.

The 101 volunteers, nicknamed the Flying Tigers but officially designated the American Volunteer Group, are due here next month.

All the pilots are retired officers of the US Army and Navy Air Forces' or serving officers who have been granted leave on "inactive status" and guaranteed no loss of seniority after their one-year con-

tracts expire. They are being paid $750 a month each, plus a $500 bonus for every Japanese plane they shoot down.

The Tigers will fly P-40 fighters, rejected as obsolete by Britain, financed by the US under the recent $50 million lend-lease agreement between China and the USA. Their commander is Captain Claire L Chennault, a 51-year-old Texan maverick compulsorily retired from the US Army Air Corps in 1937 because of deafness. He came here shortly after to retrain Chinese pilots at the direct request of Madame Chiang Kai-shek.

State of emergency declared in Norway

Norway, 1 August
The German authorites have imposed a state of emergency in Norway to try and clamp down on native resistance to the occupation. Strikes have virtually crippled some regions and acts of sabotage by partisans aimed at *Wehrmacht* installations and railways have also had a devastating effect. The Germans regard British radio propaganda as responsible for the resistance and they have confiscated 90 per cent of the population's radios.

Bishop denounces murder of invalids

Germany, 3 August
In his Sunday sermon today the bishop of Munster, Clemens August Graf, courageously spoke out against the Nazi murders of the sick and the old. He said: "It is a terrible doctrine which seeks to justify the murder of innocent people and which allows the violent killing of invalids, cripples, the incurably ill, the old and weak who are no longer able to work ... once the principle that it is permissible to kill "unproductive" humans has been admitted and applied then we must all pity ourselves when we, too, grow old and weak" (→ 24/8).

Australian unease grows over Japanese expansion in Indochina

Canberra, 9 August
Australia now feels increasingly vulnerable to the menace of Japan. Notwithstanding all the crippling trade embargoes imposed on Japan following the Japanese move into Indochina, the Australian government is pressing for a definite joint declaration by Britain and the United States which might halt any further Japanese encroachment in south-east Asia.

As another Australian brigade, the 27th, is committed to the Far Eastern garrisons, Robert Menzies, the Australian prime minister, is urging Britain to warn Japan that war will result if it attacks Thailand, with the consequent threat to Singapore. He believes that the war is taking an ominous turn.

Striking fear into the Far East: Japanese soldiers emerge from cover to attack.

Germans destroy "Smolensk pocket"

Moscow, 5 August

The Germans have wiped out the "Smolensk pocket", destroying the Russian Sixteenth and Twentieth Armies and capturing 300,000 Russian soldiers, 3,200 tanks and 3,100 guns. It is a shattering defeat for the Red Army.

The pocket was created by General Hoth's *Panzer* Group 3 and General Guderian's Panzer Group 2 sweeping on from their victory at Minsk and then splitting north and south to encircle Smolensk.

Smolensk itself, the "gateway to Moscow", fell on 16 July and the Russian forces east of the city were surrounded. At first they were contained only by the tanks, which had to wait for the infantry to arrive before attacking the pocket.

Last night the German High Command claimed: "The mass of Soviet forces surrounded east of Smolensk is now annihilated. The remainder faces disbandment."

Marshal Timoshenko, commanding several newly-raised armies, tried to rescue the trapped armies, but his attacks were poorly prepared and, although some units broke through, the rescue attempt failed.

Fighting continues around Roslavl where the Russian Twenty-Eighth Army had also been hastily assembled to try to break the ring. Guderian launched his tanks against Roslavl on 1 August, captured it three days ago and badly mauled the Twenty-Eighth Army in the process.

So total is this victory that many of the German soldiers think that there is little left between them and Moscow; they are putting up signposts pointing the way to the Russian capital. However, Hitler has already decided to switch Hoth to the north to reinforce the attack on Leningrad and Guderian to Kiev in the south, leaving Moscow to the infantry.

German communiques continue to insist that territorial gains are not the main object of warfare – "what matters is that battles of extermination are proceeding".

In the meantime, reserve Soviet units are being hurried into a new defensive line 20 miles (32 km) to the east of Smolensk. It is a thin line, but it could hold the German infantry deprived of tanks (→ 8).

Conquering ashes and rubble: Germans watch as Smolensk goes up in flames.

Tiny figures caught in the vast machine of war: children outside Smolensk.

Russians hit back at Berlin itself

Moscow, 8 August

The Russians, seeking revenge for the bombing of Moscow, raided Berlin last night. Five Soviet Ilyushin-4 bombers took off from airfields on the Estonian islands of Dago and Oesel for the hazardous 1,500-mile round trip.

Two of the twin-engined aircraft were shot down before they got to Berlin, and two more failed to find the target. But the last one got through and dropped its bombs on a suburb of Berlin. It was a small raid, but it was an indication of Russian determination to strike back at the Germans (→ 12).

US promises Russia arms and supplies

Washington, 4 August

The United States last night promised to speed up aid to the Soviet Union. The Soviet ambassador, Mr Oumansky, has welcomed the acceleration of US supplies as "an expression of confidence" that US aid would correspond to Soviet needs.

The US decision reveals a shift in policy by President Roosevelt. In the first days after the Nazi invasion of Russia on 22 June, he was reluctant to commit supplies to Russia, as he was advised that the Red Army would only hold out for a few weeks.

German commuters are left standing

Germany, 1 August

Making even a short journey as a civilian in war-torn Germany is now fraught with every imaginable difficulty. Since the outbreak of war the entire transport system of the *Reich* has been geared towards the *Wehrmacht* and the armaments industry.

Now shortages of spare parts and fuel have made cars a largely forgotten luxury, so that there are more commuters seeking fewer trains. In Breslau in June passenger demand is reported to have exceeded train capacity by 200 per cent.

1941

August

Su	Mo	Tu	We	Th	Fr	Sa
					1	2
3	4	5	6	7	8	9
10	11	12	13	14	15	16
17	18	19	20	21	22	23
24	25	26	27	28	29	30
31						

10. South America: Plots to stage pro-Nazi coups are uncovered in Argentina, Cuba and Chile.

10. London: Britain and the USSR promise to go to the assistance of Turkey in the event of an attack by the Axis powers.→

12. Roumania: All Jews are ordered to register for forced labour (→ 15).

12. Atlantic: A U-boat sinks the Royal Canadian Navy ship *Picotee*.

12. USSR: In a supplement to his war directive no 34, Hitler orders increased efforts in the north to capture Leningrad and a new offensive to take Kharkov and the Crimea in the south, suspending military activity in the central front around Moscow (→ 16).

12. Britain: Two squadrons (40 aircraft) leave Britain on HMS *Argus* bound for the Soviet ports of Murmansk and Archangel to boost the Russian war effort.

13. China: After seven days of heavy Japanese bombing, the city of Chungking is devastated (→ 17).

13. Germany: A Wellington bomber carrying prototype "Gee" navigation equipment is lost after a raid on Hamburg.

14. London: The German spy Josef Jakobs is executed by firing squad at the Tower of London.

15. Tokyo: The Japanese government confirms that it will not invade Russia from the east.

15. USSR: The Germans estimate that they have lost 30,000 lives in the Russian campaign so far.

15. USSR: Jews in the German-occupied zone are ordered to wear the yellow star and live in designated ghettoes. The Nazi administration bans them from public places and transport and forbids the ownership of wireless sets or motor cars (→ 18).

16. USSR: German forces cross the Volkhov river near Novgorod (→ 17).

Petain imposes fascist rule on France

Vichy France, 12 August
Marshal Petain, responding to what he called an "evil wind" of discontent, has introduced what is, in effect, a fascist constitution for France. All political activity has been suspended, and political meetings are banned through the length and breadth of Vichy France.

The powers of the police and of the departmental prefects have been increased, and a council for political justice will be set up to punish those responsible for the collapse of France last year. Commissioners will be appointed to root out secret societies, and action will be taken immediately against Freemasons in particular. All ministers and high officials will be required to take an oath of allegiance to Marshal Petain.

The marshal acknowledged that his "national revolution" was proving more difficult than he had expected, and that the collaboration "offered with great courtesy" by Hitler was slow. Minds were falling prey to anxiety, he conceded; he even admitted that this unease was in part caused by "insidious propaganda", an apparent admission of the widespread popularity of BBC news broadcasts from London.

In effect, the marshal proposes to replace "Petainism by persuasion" with "Petainism by discipline" – thus imposing on the French people a conservative revolution which they have refused to adopt of their own free will (→ 22).

British guidance system has first outing

A Wellington loads up with its deadly cargo: now more will reach their target.

Europe, 12 August
Last night 24 Wellington bombers attacked a railway target at Munchen-Gladbach, on the edge of the Ruhr. All the bombers returned safely. Although cloud covered the target, the raid was noteworthy in that two aircraft, from 115 Squadron, were equipped with a new navigation device codenamed "Gee".

Until now British bombers have had to rely on dead reckoning and astro-navigation to find their way to targets by night. The result has been that up to 90 per cent of bombs have missed their target. Robert Dippy, a scientist working at the Telecommunications Research Establishment (TRE) at Worth Matravers, in Dorset, has produced a radio navigation system known as TR 1335. This is based on three radio transmitters, situated on a 200-mile (320 km) baseline, sending signals to the aircraft. These are observed by the navigator on a cathode-ray tube and can tell him his position to within a mile.

The initial results are very encouraging. The only drawbacks are that the system is line-of-sight and limited to a range of 400 miles, and that it can be jammed. As yet there are only 12 sets available, and it is planned to carry out further operational trials with these this month before TR 1335 is cleared for production.

RAF bombs Cologne in broad daylight

Germany, 12 August
In one of the biggest daylight raids of the war Cologne has been hit by 54 Blenheims and four US-made Flying Fortresses, setting fire to two power stations. Thirteen planes were lost.

The attack follows a bombing directive by Air Vice-Marshal Norman Bottomley, the deputy chief of the air staff, claiming that strikes on industrial towns undermine civilian morale. Last month he wrote: "Destroy the morale of the civilian population as a whole and the industrial workers in particular."

The air ministry says that the raiders had a fighter escort to Antwerp. Then "the bombers went on alone, ... on their 150-mile penetration of the German defence system. The power stations were attacked at point blank range."

BOMBER COMMAND

Hitting the heart of enemy territory.

Britain and US sign 'Atlantic Charter'

Washington, 14 August
It is now known that, in one of the best-kept secrets of the war, President Roosevelt had meetings with the British prime minister, Winston Churchill, on board the American cruiser *Augusta* and the British battleship *Prince of Wales* at Placentia Bay, in Newfoundland, over the last five days.

The British deputy prime minister, Clement Attlee, has broadcast the terms of a joint Anglo-American declaration of common principles. It is already being called "the Atlantic Charter".

The United States and Britain declare that they seek no territorial gains from the war. They say that they hope that all nations will cooperate economically after the war, and they look forward to a lasting peace and the end of the use of force. Mr Roosevelt feels that the entry of the Soviet Union into the war makes it desirable that the western democracies should spell out their creeds. To British relief, he did not insist on denouncing protectionism or empires (→17).

A hymn of hope: Roosevelt and Churchill on board the "Prince of Wales".

Anglo-Soviet trade agreement signed

Moscow, 16 August
An Anglo-Soviet trade pact signed here today was hailed as a landmark in financial relations between the two countries. Britain is granting Russia a £10 million credit at three per cent interest. Whitehall stressed that this low rate shows that Russia is seen as a dependable customer. Considerable two-way trade is promised. The credit covers only the balance by which British exports to Russia exceed Soviet ones to Britain, and there will be similar credits when these are needed. Russia expects to pay cash for some imports.

Aid promised for Turkey if attacked

Ankara, 12 August
Britain and Russia have assured neutral Turkey that they will come to its aid in the event of an attack by any European power. In identically-worded statements presented to the Turkish foreign office by their ambassadors, the two Allies have also pledged themselves to "observe the territorial integrity of the Turkish republic".

The statements are seen as counters to German propaganda claiming that Russia would take advantage of Turkey and invade should the latter enter the war.

Russian prisoners treated savagely as Germans race eastwards

Moscow, 16 August
The many thousands of Russian prisoners of war swept up in the great German encircling movements are being abominably treated. To some extent this is because the *Panzer* forces simply do not have the resources to cope with large numbers of prisoners.

They are often left to their own devices, without food, water or shelter. Many of them, having been forced to surrender, disappear into the woods and join the partisans.

Like the Jews, however, the Russians are regarded as *Untermenschen* [sub-humans] by the Germans and are treated as such. As far as the Germans are concerned, the Geneva Convention's rules on the treatment of PoWs does not apply to the Russians.

Reports from the occupied territories speak of them being brutally beaten and shot if they show any sign of resisting their tormentors. Anyone thought to be a commissar or even a member of the Communist Party is shot out of hand.

Partisans are hanged without trial whether they are in uniform or not. The ordinary German soldier has been given a dispensation from normal military law to deal with prisoners as he wishes. Disciplinary action for ill-treating or killing prisoners is only taken by unit commanders "for the preservation of discipline". This reign of terror is not, however, having its intended effect. Even some Russians who greeted the Germans as liberators have turned against them.

From rags to fake silk in Germany

Germany, 16 August
An appeal to housewives to donate unwanted rags and cloth for recycling is to end next week. They have been asked to bring their "textile scrap" to collection points so that it can be used to make reprocessed wool and cotton wool – both of which are used in the production of synthetic fibre and artificial silk.

Nazi propaganda explains that the money saved by the recycling will be used for the armaments industry. But the people have been unenthusiastic, many fearing that a bottleneck in textile supplies will result in more rationing.

Russians surrender to the Germans: but what fate awaits them as prisoners?

1941

August

Su	Mo	Tu	We	Th	Fr	Sa
					1	2
3	4	5	6	7	8	9
10	11	12	13	14	15	16
17	18	19	20	21	22	23
24	25	26	27	28	29	30
31						

17. London: Britain and the USSR protest to Iran about the large number of German "tourists" in Iran (→ 25).

17. China: The Nationalist government endorses the Anglo-US Atlantic Charter (→ 24/9).

17. USSR: German troops capture the Black Sea naval port of Nikolayev and the city of Novgorod (→ 18).

18. Rastenburg: Hitler rejects proposals from General Franz Halder, the chief of staff, and Field Marshal Walter von Brauchitsch, the army C-in-C, for an attack on Moscow (→ 23).

18. Rastenburg: Hitler orders the deportation of Berlin's remaining 76,000 Jews to ghettoes in Poland (→ 20).

18. Mediterranean: The patrol boat P32 is sunk by a mine while attacking a convoy.

18. USSR: In the south, Soviet troops start to withdraw behind the Dnieper river.→

19. Norway: A joint Anglo-Canadian-Norwegian expedition lands on Spitzbergen to sabotage the coal mines and bring the miners back to Britain (→ 3/9).

19. Atlantic: The British liner *Aquilla* is sunk by a U-boat.

20. Paris: Five thousand foreign-born Jews are arrested and sent to a deportation camp at Drancy (→ 28).

21. Atlantic: The first Arctic convoy sets sail from Iceland to northern Russia.

21. USSR: The Red Army pulls out of Gomel one day after Marshal Voroshilov orders the defenders of Leningrad to fight to the death.→

23. Rastenburg: Hitler is unimpressed by the argument of the *Panzer* commander, General Heinz Guderian, that Moscow should be the next target for attack; Guderian's 2nd Panzer Group begins an attack to the south (→ 25).

23. France: The German merchant raider *Orion* returns to port after a 510-day cruise in which she sank nine Allied ships.

Red Army blows up Dnieper dam

Stalin's sacrifice: the Dnieper dam.

Moscow, 20 August
The Red Army, pursuing to the utmost its scorched-earth policy, has blown up one of the great construction achievements of the Soviet Union: the Lenin-Dnieproges dam at Zaporoje, on the Dnieper.

The dam, a monument to communism, was the world's greatest hydro-electric power complex. Completed in 1932, it was proudly shown to foreign visitors as an example of Communist efficiency, although American engineers designed and built most of it.

It consisted of nearly half a mile of ferro-concrete, and contained huge sluices and docks which enabled cargo ships to pass along the river. The importance of the dam to Soviet industry cannot be over-estimated. The industries of the Dnieper valley, including the iron mines at Krivoi Rog, captured by the Germans, depended on the power it produced. Kharkov, a vital part of the Soviet defence industry, with its tractor works and machine-tool factories, was heavily dependent on the dam's power. The Russians claim that new factories now coming into operation east of the Urals will compensate for the loss.

Certainly this colossal piece of destructive self-sacrifice – yet to be officially announced – will deprive the Germans of much of the riches of the Ukraine. Nothing could better illustrate Stalin's determination to defeat Hitler (→ 21).

Deadly battle rages as German forces close in on Leningrad

The women of Leningrad erect wooden posts to impede the enemy's advance.

Moscow, 22 August
A great battle is raging at the approaches to Leningrad as Field Marshal von Leeb throws in all his forces to capture the city, Russia's "window to the west", before the autumn rains set in and bog down his tanks.

Both sides recognize the importance of the battle. Marshal Voroshilov has issued a call to arms to the people of the city to defend it to the end, side by side with the Red Army: "The enemy will never set foot in our beautiful city. Leningrad never has and never will be in the hands of the enemy."

In reply, Goebbels' propaganda machine threatens the destruction of the city which, he says, "will be ground to rubble" (→ 30).

Slumbering America musters its reserves

Washington, 22 August
The slumbering giant of America is gathering its strength with an impressive growth in its military manpower.

Just over a year ago the regular US Army numbered 265,000, plus 243,000 National Guard reservists. By April this year there were 487,000 regulars, 286,000 National Guard, 38,000 reserve officers called to the colours, and 374,000 selective service trainees: a total of 1,185,000 men. It is also almost 12 months since President Roosevelt signed a bill imposing call-up liability on 16.5 million men aged between 21 and 35. Congress passed the measure reluctantly after a three-month debate. Important strings were attached to it. Conscripts are to serve within the western hemisphere and US possessions, including the Philippines. They will serve for a year (possibly to be extended to 30 months) and be paid the same as regulars. Roosevelt wants two million men.

British fire services are amalgamated

Britain, 18 August
The National Fire Service was inaugurated today, 118,000 strong, with 180,000 part-time auxiliaries and 60,000 women, under Sir Aylmer Firebrace, a former London fire chief. Some 1,450 previous commands have been merged into 37 fire forces and 200 divisions. Fire drills have been standardized and emergency water tanks are now installed on bomb sites.

"Rats of Tobruk" keep Rommel at bay

The "rats" dug in at Tobruk: Luftwaffe raids are all part of a night's work.

Tobruk, 18 August
The eyes of the world have focused since April on this dusty, sand-blown seaport, much of it lying in ruins after four months of bombardment. In Berlin, the Goebbels propaganda machine has delighted in calling the Australian garrison "rats caught in a trap". It was not long before the Aussies themselves took up the title and were calling themselves "the Rats of Tobruk".

They beat off one massive German assault, and have remained a major thorn in the flesh for Rommel, who desperately needs Tobruk's port facilities to ease his heavily-stretched supply lines. Despite the *Luftwaffe's* nightly bombings – the record so far is 21 raids between dusk and dawn – the real hazards for the garrison are boredom and the monotony of a diet of bully beef, tinned stew and canned fruit supplemented by vitamin tablets. The local water, rationed to six pints a day per man, tastes foul.

For all the air raids and frequent long-range bombardments, morale is good in Tobruk. The Aussies make their own bawdy stage entertainments, and their local paper, *Tobruk Truth*, is printed each morning using BBC news.

Although the siege continues, night-time ferries have nonetheless brought in some supplies, and the Australians were delighted last night when Polish, British, South African and Indian troops broke through to join them after a daring naval operation in darkness.

French prisoners are now hostages of war

Paris, 22 August
A German naval officer cadet was shot dead in the Paris *metro* yesterday. Today the Germans announced that all Frenchmen imprisoned in occupied France for any cause will be considered hostages:

"In the event of another such act, a number of the hostages, corresponding to the gravity of the crime, will be shot." One hundred have been selected on Hitler's orders, and 50 will be shot should there be more outrages and their corpses displayed in the *Place de la Concorde*.

The shooting took place at Barbes-Rochechouart, the Communist Party's working-class citadel in Paris, and reflects the growing resistance to the occupation authorities by the Communists and their various stalking horses in the trades unions. So far this resistance has been most marked on the railways, where the railwaymen's union is co-ordinating sabotage. The metro shooting is their first act of assassination (→ 24).

1941

August

Su	Mo	Tu	We	Th	Fr	Sa
					1	2
3	4	5	6	7	8	9
10	11	12	13	14	15	16
17	18	19	20	21	22	23
24	25	26	27	28	29	30
31						

24. Vichy: Anti-terrorist laws, aimed at crushing the Resistance, are passed giving "terrorists" the death penalty.→

24. USSR: German forces attack in the Ukraine, meeting stiff resistance (→ 26).

25. Tehran: An Anglo-Russian occupation begins.→

25. Rastenburg: In talks with Mussolini, Hitler rails against Spain's refusal to join the war.→

25. USSR: The Bryansk front commander, General Eremenko, tells Stalin, "I will smash this scoundrel Guderian, no doubt about it."

26. Ukraine: German forces capture Dnepropetrovsk (→ 31).

27. Tokyo: Japan protests to the US that aid ships sailing to Vladivostok are violating Japanese waters.

27. Off Ireland: The Royal Navy captures U-boat U570 with her *Enigma* cipher gear intact after an RAF Hudson bomber brings her to a halt.

28. Tehran: Ali Furughi leads a new government into office and orders a cease-fire (→ 9/9).

28. Australia: The PM, Robert Menzies, resigns and is replaced by Arthur Fadden.

28. Paris: Three Resistance members are guillotined under the new anti-terrorist laws (→ 3/9).

28. Sicily: A landing party from HMS *Triumph* demolishes an important railway bridge near Carsonia.

28. Kedainiai, Lithuania: Over 2,000 Jews are driven into a ditch and shot dead (→ 29).

29. Kamenets-Podolski, Ukraine: After a two-day "special action", SS troops have massacred 11,000 Jewish Hungarian forced labourers (→ 1/9).

30. Serbia: General Milan Nedic is made head of a Nazi puppet government (→ 15/9).

30. USSR: German troops capture Mga, cutting off Leningrad's last rail link.→

31. Ukraine: German forces, starting to run short of supplies and manpower, face a renewed Red Army offensive.

Churchill accuses Nazis of "merciless butchery" in East

Hitler's most determined enemy.

London, 25 August
In his broadcast last evening, Churchill accused the Germans of perpetrating the wholesale massacre of civilians in occupied Soviet territories. "Whole districts are being exterminated," Churchill said. "Since the Mongol invasions of Europe in the 16th century there has never been methodical, merciless butchery on such a scale. We are in the presence of a crime without a name."

Churchill made no mention of Jews being the main victims; to have done so would have let the Germans know that British Intelligence is intercepting secret reports to Berlin from the Nazi extermination squads in the field. These conscientiously list the locations and numbers of those shot and thrown into ditches, often several thousand at a time.

Cover girl gets a wartime face.

217

Anglo-Russian force invades Iran

Tehran, Iran, 25 August
Iran has been invaded, its prime minister, Ali Mansur, told the *Mejlis* [parliament] this afternoon, by Soviet columns from the north and British ones from the south. There are condemnations from all over the Middle East. The neutral world – or that part of it that is not yet totally cynical – is shocked.

The attack began in the early hours of this morning. While Soviet columns under General Novikov headed for Tabriz and Kazvin, Indian troops, crowded onto steamers and motor boats, silently approached the port of Abadan in an operation similar to the 1940 German landing at Copenhagen. Another force, under Major-General Slim, crossed the border near Kermanshah. Iranian troops have resisted, but – apart from the gallant Admiral Bay Endor, who died at his post – not much.

Since Britain and Russia divided Iran (then Persia) into two spheres of influence in 1908, Iranians have looked to Germany to escape the Anglo-Russian vice. There are many Germans in Iran, running posts, telegraphs and railways, as the Allies claim; but most have been there for years.

As Iran is neutral the Allies have compromised that neutrality. Britain justifies its action by its need for oil from Abadan, while the USSR needed a supply line from the Persian Gulf. And neither country wanted Germany to commandeer any Middle East oil (→ 28).

Allied troops take up possession of one of Iran's valuable oil refineries.

Dictators meet on the eastern front

Moscow, 29 August
Mussolini has met Hitler at the Fuhrer's military headquarters at Rastenburg, in East Prussia. After talks about military and political strategy, the dictators toured the recently-conquered territory in the Ukraine and visited the Italian units serving alongside the Germans. This, the seventh meeting between the two men since the start of the war, was a full-scale affair with Mussolini, resplendent in uniform, striding past knocked-out tanks and blasted buildings.

Accuracy of RAF bombing is questioned

London, 31 August
Grave doubts about Bomber Command's claims of damage done to enemy targets are prompted by a new analysis of photographs of the targets. This is made by D M D Butt, a civil servant member of the war cabinet secretariat.

Butt examined 633 flash photographs taken from aircraft at the moment of bomb release, on 100 separate raids against 28 targets on 48 nights during June and July. He allowed as a hit any bomb falling within five miles of the target area: a zone of 75 square miles. He found that on average only one bomber in three got its hit within the zone. In the industrial Ruhr, the ratio lengthened to one in ten. Aided by a full moon, two out of five scored, but so did the enemy, for the better light-aided night fighters. Since these figures excluded aircraft which did not find or attack the target area (and many did not), the proportion of hits to total *sorties* was well under one in three. The prime minister has said that the report demands urgent attention. Air Vice Marshal Robert Saundby, a senior air staff officer, accepted the report, but said that Butt's figures "might be wide of the mark".

French patriot tries to kill Pierre Laval and Marcel Deat

Versailles, 27 August
Pierre Laval, the vice-premier of Vichy's council of state until last December, has been almost killed in an assassination attempt. The shooting took place today while Laval was seeing off the first members of the *Legion des Volontaires Francais contre le Bolshevisme* on their way to the Russian front. Marcel Deat, the editor of the fascist *L'Oeuvre*, was also wounded. Paul Colette, aged 21, has been arrested.

Laval was close to death when a German officer told him: "Your assassin has been arrested; we are about to shoot him." Always a politician, he replied: "Don't do that. You do not know the French reaction as I do." He had a bullet just half a centimetre from his heart when he said this and his teeth were discoloured by blood.

Few are upset by the shooting. Laval – who rose from peasant to prime minister, and favours strong collaboration with Germany – is not popular in France as Marshal Petain is. "An *audouillette* is like a government," Laval once said of black pudding, "you need some dung in it, but not too much."

This is not the first act of violence by the French Resistance. Last week a German naval officer cadet called Moser was shot in the Paris *metro*. Six Communists have been executed in reprisal (→ 28).

Hitler orders end to euthanasia

Germany, 24 August
Hitler has ordered the termination of the "T4" action, under which 70,273 mentally-ill people have been liquidated since September 1939.

Although the murders were supposed to be carried out in strict secrecy, rumours about the specially-designed "euthanasia" centres have been spreading. On 28 July the bishop of Munster denounced the killings in a sermon. Hitler now appears to have bowed to public pressure.

Russia buckles as Germany steps up pressure

Leningrad in peril, but Reds fight back

Leningrad, 31 August
Field Marshal von Leeb is tightening his grip on Leningrad. The Red Army has abandoned Novgorod, 100 miles south of the city, after a savage week-long battle, and tonight Moscow Radio admits "the enemy is at the approaches of Leningrad". In the city posters proclaim: "The enemy is at the gates."

The Russians are receiving help from a source they did not expect for the autumn rains have started early and the battlefield has been turned into a quagmire, halting the *Panzers* and grounding the *Luftwaffe*. The respite granted by the weather is being used by the Russians to turn the city into a fortress. Shop windows are full of sandbags, militia units march through the streets, and every gate is guarded.

Everyone is expected to fight. Andrei Zhdanov, the city's Communist Party secretary, says: "We must dig fascism a grave in front of Leningrad" (→ 2/9).

Finns seize their chance to attack

Stockholm, 31 August
The Finns, learning of the withdrawal of eight Russian divisions from the Karelian Isthmus to bolster the defences of Leningrad, have made a rapid advance to the village of Kivennapa, on the Leningrad to Viipuri road.

They have thus recovered almost all the territory that they lost to the Russians in the "Winter War" last year. The Russians have abandoned, or been forced out of, their fortifications based on the former Finnish defences of the Mannerheim Line, and have taken up new positions in the Stalin Line across the isthmus north of Leningrad.

Despite the Finnish advance, there are constant rumours here that the Finns would like to make peace with Russia but that Hitler will not allow them to do so. The basis of these rumours is Finland's desperate shortage of food (→ 4/9).

Russians manning the defences of Leningrad with the enemy at the gates.

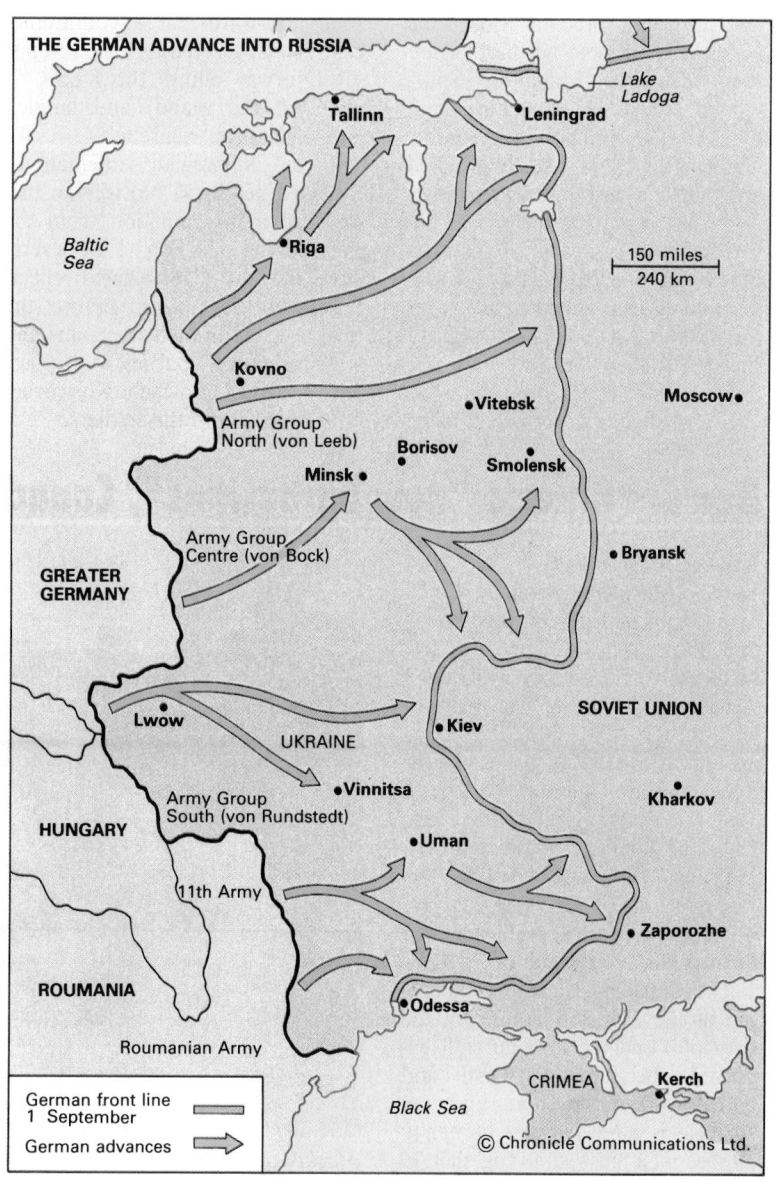

Life gets tougher on the home front

Moscow, 31 August
When the *Luftwaffe* mounted three heavy raids on successive nights against Moscow in July it was feared that the Russian capital was about to suffer the same nightly dose of death and destruction as London. The raids faded away, however, and now the Germans can only scrape together a dozen or so aircraft to attack the city.

There are a number of reasons for this. Firstly, the original raids were ordered by Goering only because Hitler said that his pilots did not have the guts to fly over 300 miles (480 km) of enemy territory to attack Moscow.

Now the Luftwaffe needs all the planes that it can put in the air to support the army in its increasingly severe battles rather than indulge in "city busting". Moreover, the fuel and ammunition supply system is so precarious that the airmen are being forced to limit their missions.

Nevertheless, the Muscovites are taking the threat from the air seriously. Just like the Londoners, they are using the underground as a shelter and are efficiently organized in teams like the ARP which go into action when "Fritz" comes over.

The situation is different in Leningrad, now almost completely surrounded. It will soon be under siege and in range of not only the medium bombers but also the Stukas and long-range artillery.

Large fires have already been started in the city by General Wolfram von Richthofen's *Fliegerkorps* VIII. These are being fought by action groups organized by Leningrad's boss, the ruthlessly efficient Andrei Zhdanov.

Special teams have also been organized to guard Leningrad's treasures. Fire units are based on the city's beautiful czarist palaces and churches, now kept as museums, ready to deal with the incendiary bombs. The priceless paintings of the Hermitage are already safe. An armoured train took 500,000 of the finest works to safety as the threat to the city developed (→ 3/9).

September

Su	Mo	Tu	We	Th	Fr	Sa
	1	2	3	4	5	6
7	8	9	10	11	12	13
14	15	16	17	18	19	20
21	22	23	24	25	26	27
28	29	30				

1. USSR: Marshal Timoshenko leads a counter-attack at Gomel (→ 3).

1. Berlin: All Jews over the age of six are ordered to wear, from 19 September, a yellow star of David with the word *Jude* [Jew] written on it.→

1. Atlantic: The US Navy undertakes convoy protection between Newfoundland and Iceland (→ 16).

1. Vladivostok: A Russian mine sinks a Japanese fishing boat.

2. Tokyo: The government sets up the Air Defence Bureau, which will organize air-raid precautions throughout Japan (→ 6).

3. China: Chinese forces recapture Foochow from Japan (→ 7).

3. Moscow: All Russian men aged 18 or over are called up for military service (→ 5).

4. Rastenburg: Hitler, infuriated by the slow progress of the German advance, starts looking for a scapegoat.

4. USSR: Finnish troops capture Belostrov (→ 1/10).

4. Paris: The first detachment of the *Legion des Volontaires Francais* [Legion of French Volunteers] sets off to join the German army on the eastern front.

5. Moscow: As the Germans approach, all children under the age of 12 are evacuated from the city (→ 6).

5. Baltic: German forces complete the occupation of Estonia, occupied by the USSR in 1940.

6. Paris: A German non-commissioned officer, Hoffman, is shot in the *Gare de l'Est* (→ 8).

6. Lithuania: The Nazis establish a "large" and a "small" ghetto at Vilna (→ 12).

6. Tokyo: The government decides that preparations for war should be completed in six weeks (→ 16/10).

6. USSR: Soviet troops recapture Yelna, near Smolensk, on the Moscow front (→ 20).

Allied taskforce wrecks Norwegian mines

Allied troops taking control of the northernmost point of Nazi territory.

Spitzbergen, 3 September
An Allied task force has robbed the Nazis of their most northerly asset: the Norwegian island of Spitzbergen, 500 miles (800 km) from the North Pole. The civilian population of 700 has been evacuated and valuable coal mines wrecked.

It was a piquant operation. No Germans were present as an invading force of Norwegians, Canadians and British landed to take over the radio station. When it was clear that the soldiers were welcome the force commander, from Saskatchewan, made a formal landing from a small commando craft and soon afterwards, at a community centre, was greeted by the commissar (Norway allows the USSR to mine on the island) and handed gifts of Russian cigarettes.

At the Norwegian settlement of Svalbard nearby, a Norwegian major read a proclamation from the exiled King Haakon. For several days the invaders billeted cheerfully with the locals. Before the final evacuation of Norwegians and Russian miners, parties took place and a dance at which Norwegian girls danced with the soldiers.

U-boat attack fans American hostility

Reykjavik, 4 September
A US destroyer, *Greer*, just managed to avoid two torpedoes fired by a U-boat off the south-west coast of Iceland today. The *Greer* in her turn dropped depth charges, but U652 escaped unharmed. The destroyer was bringing mail for the rapidly growing US forces at the base here.

The bloodless incident reflects the growing involvement of the US as a result of the meeting between President Roosevelt and Winston Churchill at Placentia Bay last month. At that meeting Roosevelt publicly made "the final destruction of the Nazi tyranny" a part of US policy. Privately, he assured Churchill that the US Navy would progressively take over the policing of the western Atlantic.

In practice this means that, although the US is not at war with Germany, armed conflict cannot be long delayed. The hard-pressed Royal Navy is handing over convoy escort duties to the Americans. This is expected to release 50 destroyers and corvettes for duties elsewhere. The *Greer*, like all the US ships supplying the Iceland bases, was sailing under wartime conditions with all lights blacked out. She is equipped with the latest submarine detectors (→ 11).

Beware Hitler's "new barbarians", Canadian leader warns US

London, 4 September
William Mackenzie King, the Canadian prime minister, warned today that Britain is now the only obstacle in the way of an attack by Hitler's "enslaving hordes of new barbarians" on the New World. He made an impassioned plea to the US for a declaration of support for Britain similar to that promised by Mr Churchill for the Americans in the Far East. Otherwise, he said, "the war may drag on for years, carrying in its train famine, pestilence and horrors still undreamed of".

The Canadian leader was speaking at the Mansion House, in the City of London. Mr Churchill endorsed the Canadian call and added: "Time is short and the struggle is dire. To save humanity all free men must stand together."

Mackenzie King visits Aldershot and inspects a Canadian guard of honour.

Battle rages just 20 miles from Leningrad

Leningrad, 2 September

A desperate battle is raging at Gatchina, some 20 miles (32 km) southwest of Leningrad, as the defenders try to halt the German advance. The guns of the naval squadron on the river Neva have joined in the battle, pounding the German positions with heavy shells.

To the south-west the railway town of Mga has fallen to the Germans after a see-saw battle lasting three days. This means that Leningrad's rail links with the rest of Russia have been severed and the German ring round the city is almost complete. There is, however, little left here except people. While the Red Army has been holding up the Germans nearly 300 trains have carried the machine tools of 90 factories, including two heavy tank works, to safety behind the Urals where they are being reassembled.

The major problem which is emerging is food. Leningrad's population of 2,500,000, with 100,000 refugees and the armed forces, must all be fed if a siege is mounted. Lack of bread, not bombs, may bring about Leningrad's capitulation (→ 8).

Two of Russia's starving millions scavenge among potato peelings for food.

Poison gas used to kill Auschwitz inmates

Auschwitz, 3 September

Since the autumn of 1939 the Germans have used carbon monoxide to kill their incurable mental patients and other "undesirables". Today Rudolf Hoess, the commandant here, tried out a new method.

He chose 600 Russian prisoners of war and 250 Jews from the infirmary to be his guinea pigs. Crammed into a cellar, they noticed that the windows had been blocked up. Suddenly the door opened and guards threw in a powder. Fumes filled the room and soon all the prisoners were dead. The experiment was later judged a success.

The powder, *Zyklon B*, is crystalline hydrogen cyanide, supplied by a Hamburg firm under licence from the chemical giant IG Farben. It is usually used for killing rats (→ 6).

A German Jew: branded by Nazis.

1941
September

Su	Mo	Tu	We	Th	Fr	Sa
	1	2	3	4	5	6
7	8	9	10	11	12	13
14	15	16	17	18	19	20
21	22	23	24	25	26	27
28	29	30				

7. Paris: The Germans execute Pierre Roche, a member of the Resistance who sabotaged German military telephone lines.

7. Suez: German aircraft sink the US merchant ship *Steel Seafarer*.

7. China: Japanese forces attack Chinese positions near Yuezhou at the beginning of the Second Battle of Changsha (→ 26).

7. USSR: Two squadrons of RAF Hurricanes arrive at Archangel, in the north of Russia (→ 14).

8. Paris: The German authorities arrest 120 leaders of the city's Jewish community as hostages for the murder last week of a German officer (→ 12).

8. USSR: The ethnic German community in the Volga region (about 600,000 people) is exiled to Siberia because of Kremlin fears that it might become a fifth column of Nazi sympathizers.

8. Germany: RAF bombers inflicted heavy damage on Berlin last night in the heaviest raid yet on the German capital.

9. Tehran: Iran expels German and Italian "tourists" and diplomats (→ 16).

10. USSR: German Army Groups Centre and South launch a joint offensive on Kiev (→ 12).

11. Britain: The RAF takes delivery of its first Hawker Typhoon fighter.

12. Atlantic: A U-boat torpedoes the US cargo ship *Montana*.

12. Paris: The Germans shoot 12 of the Jewish hostages taken on 8 September (→ 16).

12. USSR: As the first snows of winter begin to fall, the 2nd and 3rd Panzer Armies join up at Lokhvitsa, near Rovno, completing the encirclement of Kiev (→ 17).

12. Lithuania: An SS *Einsatzkommando* [action squad] murders 3,434 Jews at Ponary, outside Vilna.

13. USSR: Chernigov falls to the Germans.

Two-way bomber strikes hit Italy

Italy, 12 September

Flying from bases in Britain and North Africa, British bombers struck at Italy's industrial north and at targets in Sicily, in the south, tonight. The British-based Stirlings took advantage of the longer nights to fly 1,200 miles (1,920 km) across France and the Alps and bomb the royal arsenal at Turin, where at least nine large fires were started.

More fires were started at Messina and Palermo – both major supply ports for the Italian army in Libya – with crews reporting hits on merchant ships, oil tanks and a power station.

Eat potato skins, Germans are told

Berlin, 13 September

The food shortage is beginning to bite in the Third *Reich*. In a report soon to be issued by the ministry for food and nutrition, Germans will be urged to be more economical in the way that they eat potatoes.

"In every household in Germany, potatoes should now only be served in their skins," it says. "It is most important that in restaurants and canteens, potato peelers are not used" (→ 17).

Chaplin under fire from isolationists

Washington, 10 September

Charlie Chaplin was accused today of using the cinema to "poison the minds of the American people to go to war". Senator Bennett Champ Clark, a leading isolationist, told a Senate sub-committee investigating propaganda charges against Hollywood that United Artists was dominated by Chaplin and Alexander Korda, two British subjects, who were using it to make pro-war propaganda. United Artists made *The Great Dictator*.

Chaplin, he said, had made his fortune in America, but never thought well enough of it to become a US citizen. He claimed that British propaganda had dragged America into the last war.

Germans surround Leningrad: the siege begins

Members of the Russian home guard who are fighting to defend Leningrad.

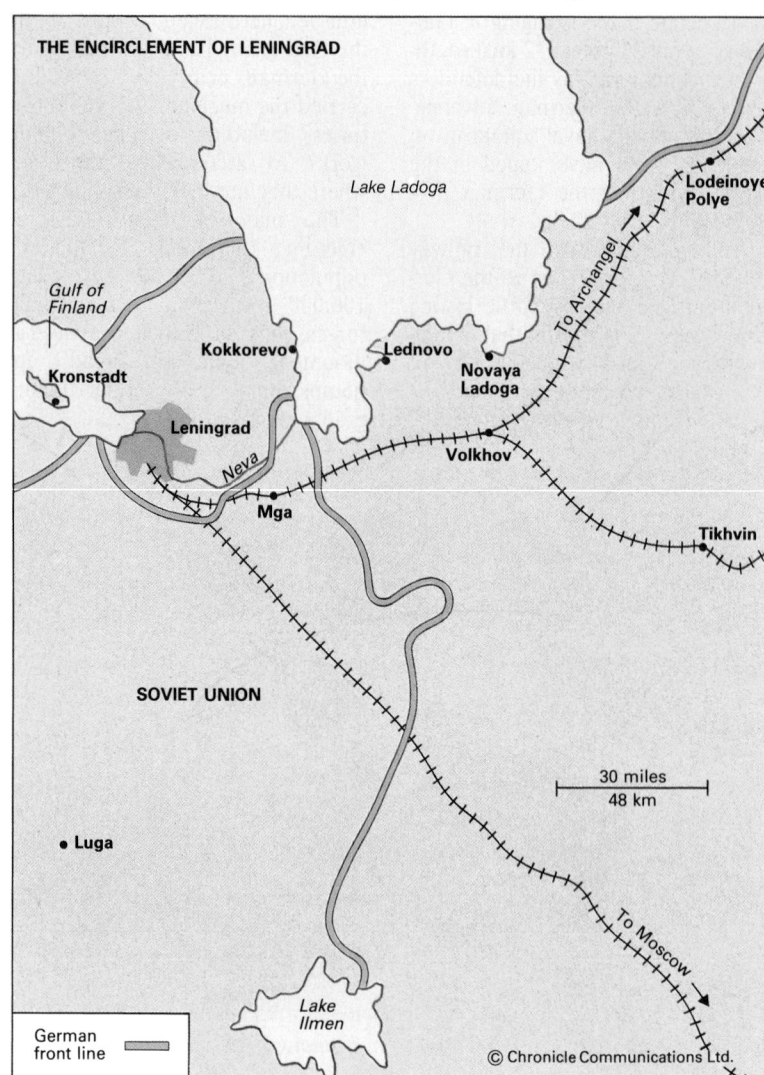

THE ENCIRCLEMENT OF LENINGRAD

Lake Ladoga

Gulf of Finland

Kronstadt

Kokkorevo

Leningrad

Lednovo

Novaya Ladoga

Volkhov

Neva

Mga

To Archangel

Lodeinoye Polye

Tikhvin

SOVIET UNION

30 miles
48 km

Luga

To Moscow

Lake Ilmen

German front line

© Chronicle Communications Ltd.

Leningrad, 8 September
The city of Leningrad is now completely encircled by German and Finnish troops. The Germans reached Schlusselburg on Lake Ladoga today, breaking the last land route, while the Finns cut the Stalin Canal which leads from Lake Ladoga to Lake Onega.

Field Marshal von Leeb's *Panzers* are within ten miles (16 km) of the city, which is being pounded by long-range artillery and the *Luftwaffe*. More than 6,000 incendiaries have been dropped today and, in a terrible blow for the defenders, the huge Badayev food warehouse has been destroyed along with hundred of tons of irreplaceable supplies.

The Russians are heavily outnumbered in the air, but their pilots are fighting ferociously against the swarms of Stukas which are attacking the heavy Russian ships in the

harbours of Kronstadt and Leningrad. They are carrying specially-developed 2,000-pound bombs; their particular targets are the battleships *Marat* and *October Revolution*, whose 12-inch guns are pounding the German rear echelons.

The land attack on the city is being mounted by the 1st *Panzer*

Division thrusting along the left bank of the Neva and the 6th Panzer Division following the Moscow-Leningrad railway line. It is not going to be a walkover for them. They have been held up for three weeks by suicidal Russian counter-attacks. Their men and machines are worn out by fighting both the

Russians and the mud caused by incessant rain. If they had made their assault a month ago they would be in the Romanovs' palaces today. Instead, they are caught up in hastily-built defences manned by *Opolchenye* – militia units armed with rifles, Molotov cocktails and grenades. This is not the sort of fighting the Panzers enjoy. In fact, von Leeb's attempt to capture the city may not last. Hitler wants to switch his tanks to the forthcoming attack on Moscow, leaving Leningrad to "wither on the vine".

He would rather subject the city to a long siege by gun and bomber and so relieve the German army of the necessity of feeding the population during the winter. Von Leeb, however, can almost taste the glory of capturing the old czarist capital and will carry on his assault until told to stop (→ 29).

Hitler's allies join in war on USSR

Berlin, 9 September
The *Wehrmacht* is getting help from a motley group of allies in its assault on Russia. Mussolini has sent an expeditionary corps, the Roumanian army is engaged in the drive on Odessa, the Hungarians are supporting the thrust through the Ukraine and Franco has sent a contingent of Spanish

"volunteers". The Slovaks, too, have soldiers fighting for the Germans, and volunteers from Holland, Denmark, Belgium and Norway have been formed into legions of the Wehrmacht. The Finns are a disappointment to the Germans, doing no more than holding the northern line round besieged Leningrad.

Shoot first at intruders, US Navy ordered

Washington, 11 September
President Roosevelt took the USA one step nearer to war today. In a broadcast to the nation at 9pm he termed the attack last week on the *USS Greer* as "piracy, legally and morally". He said the outposts the USA has established in Iceland, Greenland, Labrador and Newfoundland would protect Atlantic shipping of all nations; but he stressed that the US Navy only provided "invincible protection" if Britain's Royal Navy survived.

The president emphasized the difficulty of defending ships from torpedoes fired from submarines: "When you see a rattlesnake poised to strike, you do not wait until he has struck before you crush him." America would henceforth have a shoot-first policy because "these Nazi submarines and raiders are the rattlesnakes of the Atlantic – they are a menace to the free pathways of the high seas". The talk was delivered in the style he has made

A U-boat boasts of its successes.

his own – that of the informal fireside chat to each American in his home – but Roosevelt took care to ensure political support. He showed a draft to key Congressional leaders before the broadcast (→16).

Nazis declare martial law in restless Oslo

Oslo, 10 September
Guards with Tommy guns are patrolling the streets of Oslo tonight after a savage crackdown by Josef Terboven, Hitler's commissioner for Norway. Two trade union leaders have been executed after a summary court martial and four others have been sent to gaol.

An 8pm to 5am curfew is in force. Dance halls are closed and the sale of alcohol is forbidden. Newspaper editors have been sacked and all meetings, indoors and

outdoors, have been banned. Terboven declared martial law after reports that the Norwegian unions were calling a general strike in opposition to the Nazi regime. Terboven accused "communist elements" in the unions of "disturbing the industrial peace in a criminal manner".

The underground anti-Nazi newspaper *Fri Ragbevegelse* has called on the people to remain calm, but to fight "with all secret means" for their rights.

Keitel tells troops to kill Russian Jews

Rastenburg, 12 September
Field Marshal Wilhelm Keitel, the chief of the German army's High Command, today issued an explicit directive to his troops on how they should treat Jews in the USSR. Headed "Jews in the newly occupied eastern territories", Keitel's directive says: "The struggle against Bolshevism demands ruthless and energetic measures, above all against the Jews, the main carriers of Bolshevism" (→16).

1941
September

Su	Mo	Tu	We	Th	Fr	Sa
	1	2	3	4	5	6
7	8	9	10	11	12	13
14	15	16	17	18	19	20
21	22	23	24	25	26	27
28	29	30				

14. Germany: Hitler's order of 1 September, that all Jews under German rule must wear a yellow Star of David, comes into effect (→22).

15. Yugoslavia: Widespread unrest causes martial law to be imposed in Serbia and Croatia. →

15. Moscow: Stalin asks for 25 to 30 British divisions to be sent to aid the Soviet struggle against invasion.

16. Hamburg: The city suffered a heavy RAF attack last night.

16. Paris: The authorities execute ten French hostages in reprisal for attacks on German military property (→20).

16. Damascus: Free French forces, with British backing, terminate the French mandate and agree to guarantee Syria's independence.

16. USSR: Field Marshal Wilhelm Keitel orders 100 Russians to be executed for every German soldier killed by partisans.

16. Nova Scotia: Convoy HX-150, the first to be escorted by the US Navy, leaves for Europe.→

17. USSR: The *Stavka* [Soviet High Command] belatedly orders a withdrawal from Kiev in the Ukraine, as German forces pierce the outer defences of the city.→

18. Washington: Roosevelt asks Congress for $5,985 million to fund extra Lend-Lease supplies (→27).

18. Mediterranean: The British submarine *Upholder* sinks the Italian troop ships *Neptunia* and *Oceania*; 384 people are drowned.

19. Atlantic: The Canadian escort ship *Levis* is sunk by a U-boat.

19. Yugoslavia: The resistance leaders Mihailovich and Tito meet to discuss joint strategy, but fail to agree (→21/10).

20. Paris: A curfew is imposed between 9pm and 5am (→23).

20. UK: *Enigma* decodings give Britain and the USSR advance warning of an all-out German assault on Moscow.

Shah of Iran quits the peacock throne

The new shah: chosen by the Allies.

Tehran, 16 September
Reza Shah Pahlevi, the *shah* of Iran, has abdicated. With Soviet and British armies threatening Tehran, he had little choice. His pliable 22-year-old son, Mohammad Reza, has replaced him at Allied insistence. For two weeks, since the armistice following the Anglo-Russian invasion, the shah had refused Allied demands to expel Germany's legation, to hand over Iran's German community for internment, and to facilitate Allied rail links from the Persian Gulf to the USSR. Now he pays the price for neutrality. So ends the career of a man who started as a private in the Persian Cossacks and rose to shah – crushing liberals and clerics – to drag Iran into the 20th century. For 20 years he played Britain and Russia against each other; now he has finally lost (→19).

British troops enter the capital of Iran

Tehran, 19 September
They are changing the guard today at the Peacock Palace. Soviet troops who have occupied the city for several days are leaving and British troops are replacing them, with much saluting. This is the first time that British and Russian troops have seen each other. The British troops are impressed by the Russian soldiers' armour. The Russian troops seem surprised by the British soldiers' short trousers.

German armies seize shattered Kiev

Rastenburg, 19 September
Hitler's headquarters claimed the capture of Kiev, the capital of the Ukraine, today as the result of a huge pincer movement carried out by the *Panzer* armies of Generals Guderian and von Kleist.

In a series of communiques the Nazis boasted: "The attack on Kiev was begun in the course of encircling operations. After a bold thrust through the strong fortifications on the banks of the Dnieper our troops have penetrated into the town. The *Reich* flag has been flying from the citadel since this morning." The communiques claim that the jaws of the pincer snapped shut at Lokhvitsa, 125 miles (200 km) east of Kiev: "The ring has thus been closed round four Soviet armies. Their annihilation is now in progress."

It is feared that at least 500,000 Russians have been caught in the trap because of Stalin's obstinacy. His orders were: "Stand fast, hold out, and if need be die." When Marshal Budenny, the Soviet commander in the south, requested permission to retreat, Stalin sacked him.

General Kirponos, commanding in Kiev, eventually got Stalin's permission to withdraw. But it has come too late. Kirponos has been killed in an ambush along with most of his 1,000-strong command

German soldiers pick their way into the smouldering ruins of the city of Kiev.

column; the Red Army is facing its greatest disaster of this war.

Trapped in the open, the Russian infantrymen are fighting with their customary stubbornness as the German tanks hunt them down and Stukas blast their strongpoints. But they are running out of ammunition and food. The end cannot long be delayed. Kiev itself is a shattered shell of a once beautiful city, littered with the debris of war and stripped bare of anything of use to the invader. Power stations and waterworks have been put out of

action, and thousands of time-bombs have been left to complete the destruction. The executions of party officials and Jews, to "liquidate the Bolshevik menace", have already started in the city as the SS murder squads move in on the heels of the Panzers.

This victory, great as it is, has not been accomplished without cost to the Germans. They have lost many men, guns, tanks and aircraft. It was announced in Berlin today that Germany has suffered an estimated 400,000 casualties so far in Russia.

RAF sends fighter planes to aid Stalin

Archangel, 14 September
British forces are operating from Russian soil for the first time since Lord Ironside's expedition to help the White Russians in 1919. In a changed world, the "Reds" are now Britain's allies against Germans, so RAF pilots are flying Hurricanes from Vaenga. Two squadrons – 81 and 134 – began operations three days ago after arriving at Archangel on 7 September on the carrier *Argus*. Their chief target is a force of Stuka dive-bombers, the main German tool against Soviet defences, whether tanks or cities. The RAF will not stay here for the rest of the war. It will teach Soviet pilots to fly the Hurricanes and hand them over (→ 15).

Shipping is crippled in Bay of Gibraltar

Gibraltar, 20 September
Led by a prince, six determined Italian frogmen penetrated the Bay of Gibraltar last night and succeeded in crippling 20,000 tons of British shipping. With Prince Giunio Borghese leading, three two-man submarines left their mother ship – a converted submarine – off the Spanish coast and attached explosive warheads to two tankers and an armed freighter. All six crewmen returned safely.

Belgrade is placed under martial law

Belgrade, 17 September
Following attacks on German soldiers in the city, indefinite martial law has been proclaimed by the Serbian puppet regime set up by the Nazis. The regime is planning a punitive expedition into the mountains to round up rebels.

At dawn today, a Royal Navy submarine landed a British agent, Colonel D T Hudson, on the Dalmatian coast for a rendezvous with Tito and the other resistance leader, Mihailovich. Hudson's orders are to find out which of the two is putting up the tougher fight against the Nazi occupation (→ 19).

"Potato Pete" called up to urge Britons to eat more vegetables

Britain, 17 September
The British are being cajoled into eating more potatoes, one of the few staple foods of which there is no shortage. The ministry of food has fixed their retail price at a penny a pound throughout the year.

Ministry advertisements featuring a cartoon character called "Potato Pete" suggest serving a pound per person per day. "Use potatoes in pastry," he recommends, even going so far as to recommend mashed potato sandwiches. The ministry also sings the praises of carrots and swedes in all guises.

Plans are now being made to apply "points" rationing to tinned foods, beginning in November. Each person will get 16 points to spend on what he or she chooses every four weeks.

Having listened to "Potato Pete", housewives queue for their spuds in Sutton.

The struggle to secure Britain's Atlantic lifeline

US to protect west Atlantic convoys

Halifax, Canada, 16 September
Convoy HX-150, which sailed from here today, will be the first to benefit from the increased US support for the Allied cause. It will be escorted by the Canadian navy up to a point south of Newfoundland, where US Navy destroyers will take over, giving formal protection for Allied convoys for the first time. They will take the convoy to the mid-ocean meeting point where the escort will be handed over to the British Western Approaches Command. This is intended to be the pattern for all fast convoys of the HX type in future. The Canadians will continue to escort the slower SC convoys all the way to the mid-ocean meeting point.

The eastbound convoys are bringing war supplies and many foodstuffs which the British are beginning to accept as their daily diet, such as condensed milk, powdered egg, spam and baked beans.

The escort support from the US will mean that the Royal Navy will be able to divert three escort groups from the North Atlantic to cover Gibraltar and Sierra Leone convoys. US Navy Catalinas, operating from bases in Iceland, and US Army Flying Fortresses, based in Argentina, are also expected to take on convoy escort duties.

An Allied ship battles with a gale.

Watching over a convoy of British vessels from the deck of the escort ship.

Shipping losses cut as code-breakers aid fight against U-boats

North Atlantic, 16 September
Today's announcement that US escort vessels will accompany convoys carrying lend-lease materials as far east as Iceland [*reported alongside*] will greatly strengthen the Allied counter-attack against the menace of the U-boats. July and August have already seen a dramatic decrease in the number of merchant ships sunk in the Atlantic. During the first half of the year monthly losses averaged 400,000 tons; they have now dropped to little over 100,000 tons per month. There are several reasons for this. For a

start, Bletchley Park is now able to read a significant part of the U-boat *Enigma* signal traffic.

The information from this is passed to the admiralty's submarine tracking room which can then identify U-boat concentrations. It passes details of these to HQ Western Approaches in Liverpool, the naval command responsible for the Battle of the Atlantic, which can then re-route convoys.

Located with the Western Approaches HQ, and under its operational control, is No 15 Group RAF Coastal Command. Its air-

craft range far and wide over the north-east Atlantic from their bases in Scotland, Northern Ireland and Iceland. The north-west Atlantic is covered by the Royal Canadian Air Force. Both forces still suffer from a lack of very-long-range aircraft, which means that the mid-Atlantic, south of Greenland, does not have air cover. Known as the "Black Pit" or "Black Gap", it presents the most dangerous area for convoys. Despite this, improved methods of detecting U-boats, with more and better-trained escort vessels, are helping reduce losses.

How Allied shipping has been ravaged

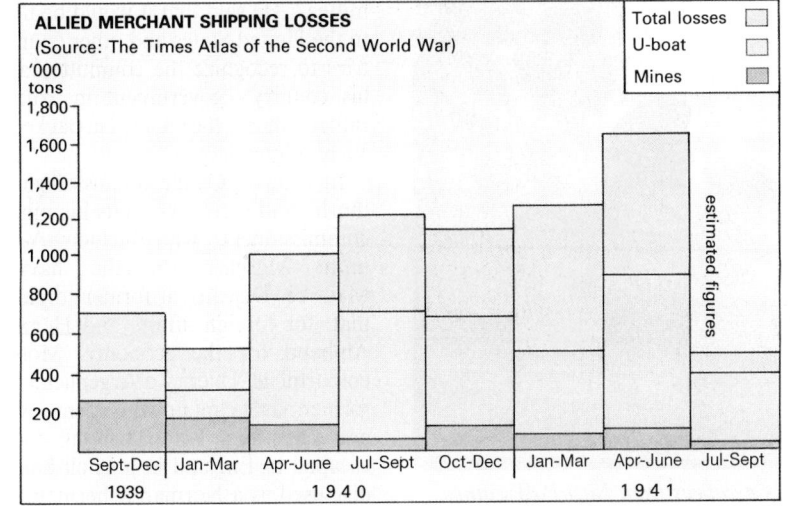

ALLIED MERCHANT SHIPPING LOSSES
(Source: The Times Atlas of the Second World War)

Total losses
U-boat
Mines

'000 tons
1,800
1,600
1,400
1,200
1,000
800
600
400
200

estimated figures

| Sept-Dec | Jan-Mar | Apr-June | Jul-Sept | Oct-Dec | Jan-Mar | Apr-June | Jul-Sept |
| 1939 | | 1940 | | | | 1941 | |

Nineteen days adrift: one seaman's story

Iceland, 16 September
A Danish first officer, Henrik Bjerregaard of the *Sessa*, has recently recovered sufficiently from an ordeal of 19 days adrift in Arctic waters to tell his story.

The *Sessa*, a former Danish ship flying the Panamanian flag, was transporting provisions from New York to the American troops in Iceland when she was torpedoed by a U-boat. She sank in two minutes. Bjerregaard remembers: "I had no lifebelt, but I grabbed a pole as I was thrown into the water. A seaman joined me, and we hung on for two hours. Then we floated to a lifeboat which was upside down ...

we stayed on the lifeboat all night ... Next day a raft from the ship drifted alongside, and as we could not right the boat we jumped on the raft ... After seeing we had a drum of water and tin of biscuits, I cut a sliver off the raft and started to keep a log.

"Every day at sunrise I made a notch to mark another day. After the tenth day one man died, and on the 13th two more died ... On the 17th day all our water went ... on the 19th day, as I lay utterly exhausted, I heard to my joy a ship's siren and raised myself weakly to see the Stars and Stripes of an American destroyer."

1941

September

Su	Mo	Tu	We	Th	Fr	Sa
		1	2	3	4	5	6

(calendar grid)

	1	2	3	4	5	6
7	8	9	10	11	12	13
14	15	16	17	18	19	20
21	22	23	24	25	26	27
28	29	30				

21. Latvia: Soviet forces evacuate the capital, Riga, and the Germans capture the key naval base at Oesel.

21. China: There is a total eclipse of the sun.

22. Britain: King George of the Hellenes and the Greek government arrive in London from Egypt.

22. Vinnitsa, USSR: A squad of SS-trained Ukrainian militia kills 28,000 Jews. →

23. USSR: German soldiers massacre the population of Krasnaya Gora after partisans kill three German sentries.

23. France: German troops are ordered to send their blankets to their eastern front colleagues (→ 13/12).

24. Mediterranean: The first German U-boat enters the Mediterranean through the Straits of Gibraltar.

25. USSR: German forces cut off the Crimea from the rest of the USSR (→ 30).

26. China: Japanese forces encircle Changsha (→ 29).

26. Washington: US Naval Command orders the sinking of all Axis shipping found in home waters.

27. Mediterranean: The British battleship *Nelson* is damaged in an Italian air attack south of Sardinia.

27. USA: The first batch of "Liberty" ships is launched (→ 30/10).

29. Rastenburg: Hitler orders that Leningrad be wiped off the face of the earth and its population exterminated (→ 3/10).

29. China: Relief troops arrive at Changsha, forcing the Japanese to retreat (→ 1/10).

29-30. Germany: RAF bombers raid Stettin and Hamburg overnight.

30. Ankara: Turkey embargoes chrome exports to Germany.

30. USSR: Guderian's 2nd *Panzer* Army, back in the north, attacks towards Orel and Bryansk; von Kleist's 1st Panzer Army heads for Donetsk. →

Maltese cheer as convoy reaches harbour

Running the Mediterranean gauntlet to Malta: a ship goes up in smoke.

Malta, 28 September
The entire population of Malta seemed to have crowded the shoreline to cheer as three cruisers – their bands playing and crews lined up as though they had been on a peacetime cruise – led a vitally needed convoy into the Grand Harbour of Valetta today.

Few convoys have had such a powerful escort: three battleships – *Nelson, Rodney* and *Prince of Wales* – the carrier *Ark Royal*, five cruisers and 18 destroyers. They were shepherding nine fast merchant ships, totalling 81,000 tons, with 2,600 troops divided among the transports and warships.

Three days out from Gibraltar the convoy, codenamed Operation Halberd, came under fierce air attack, with the *Ark Royal's* fighters stretched to the limit. The *Nelson* was slowed down by a torpedo hit.

Despite reports that the Italian fleet had left port, no ship-to-ship encounters took take place, although the convoy came under further torpedo attacks from the air with one transport, *Imperial Star*, hit – but her troops were taken off before she sank.

Fifteen states back the Atlantic Charter

London, 24 September
The Atlantic Charter drawn up by Churchill and Roosevelt last August was today endorsed by the 15 countries at war with or occupied by Germany. With Anthony Eden, the British foreign secretary, in the chair, the meeting began in the ornate Picture Gallery of St James's Palace, with a statement by Ivan Maisky, the Soviet ambassador.

Speaking in English, Maisky denounced the "gang of Hitlerite marauders, armed to the teeth and proclaiming itself to be the master race". By contrast, he spoke of the Soviet Union, "guided by the principle of self-determination of nations" and committed to defending the territorial integrity of every country and the "right to establish such a social order and a form of government as it deems opportune and desirable". He did not mention the Nazi-Soviet pact of 1939, which provided for the occupation and partition of Poland.

The Atlantic Charter commits its signatories to a post-war world of mutual cooperation and of freedom for countries under Nazi occupation, with no annexations or frontier changes without the freely expressed wishes of the people concerned.

De Gaulle forms committee to be French government in exile

De Gaulle inspecting Free French troops - escapees from Nazi PoW camps.

London, 23 September
General Charles de Gaulle, the leader of the Free French, today announced at a press conference here the setting up of a "national committee". He said that it would be up to the United States and other countries to recognize the committee as his country's government in exile, rather than the German-backed Vichy regime.

In fact, de Gaulle retains all authority and merely consults his nine commissioners, who include Admiral Muselier for the navy, Maurice Dejean, a former diplomat, for foreign affairs and Herve Alphand for the economy. Most colourful is Thierry d'Argenlieu, a former naval captain who spent several years as a Trappist monk and escaped to England in a small boat disguised as a Norman fisherman.

Jews thrown down ravine at Babi Yar

Kiev, 30 September
Members of *Einsatzgruppe C*, led by Otto Rasch, are relaxing at the end of a particularly efficient piece of work. In two days they have murdered 33,771 Jews at Babi Yar, a ravine on the outskirts of the city.

Four days ago they put up posters asking Jews to report for resettlement. Rasch is proud to report that none of those who duly reported apparently realized that they were to die. The masses gathered at the prescribed place with their bundles of food and clothing. Divided into groups of 100, they were marched to the edge of the ravine.

The SS men varied their routine. First they machine-gunned the Jews and kicked them off the edge. Then they made them walk a plank and shot them in the neck. Children were simply thrown over.

The dead and half-dead piled up at the bottom, slowly moving as the living struggled to prevent themselves being suffocated by the growing weight of the dead. Moaning and sobbing rose up from the bleeding, bruised mound. When there was a break in the killing at the top of the ravine, the SS moved in at the bottom and used pistols to despatch those who still moved.

Miraculously, a handful of Jews escaped from Babi Yar. Among them was Dina Pronicheva, who pretended to be dead (→ 1/10).

Shells bounce off tough new Russian tank

Germans struggle to get vital supplies through: Russia gets tougher daily.

Moscow, 30 September
Fierce fighting continues along the length of the front from Leningrad to the Crimea. The news from Leningrad is good. The city's defenders have stopped the Germans seven miles (11 km) from the city, within sight of its church spires, and their morale has been boosted by the arrival of the tough General Zhukov to take charge of the battle.

Outside Moscow 15 new armies have been entrenched ready for the German onslaught on the city which is expected at any moment now that Kiev has fallen. With every day that passes the capital's defences grow stronger. Hitler is still preoccupied with the Ukraine, however, and it seems that the attack on Moscow will have to wait until General von Rundstedt has completed the operation which he started five days ago towards Kharkov and the Crimea.

This may take longer than planned, for increasing numbers of the Russians' excellent T34 tank are appearing on the battlefield and proving superior to the German *Panzers*. Normal anti-tank shells just bounce off the T34s' armour, and the Germans have been forced to form special squads to attack them with grenades and satchel-charges (→ 1/10).

Hostages taken to punish Partisans

Paris, 23 September
The three-day curfew imposed on Paris by the military governor, General Karl-Heinrich von Stulpnagel, has now been lifted. He had imposed draconian measures after a spate of attempts by the Resistance to assassinate members of the German occupation forces. Travel has been banned between 9pm and 5am, and places of entertainment have been forced to close at 8pm.

Those arrested for breaking the curfew are treated as hostages to prevent any further resistance. Last week, the Germans murdered 22 hostages in reprisal for crimes which included the attempted assassination of a *Wehrmacht* captain.

Russian aid appeal launched in Britain

London, 29 September
Mr Churchill today told British MPs about an historic meeting which began yesterday in Moscow between the USSR, Britain and the USA. He told them that although Allied aid to Russia has only now been formally agreed, many desperately needed supplies have already been dispatched. Russia's relative inaccessibility, hemmed in on all sides by enemies or freezing weather, is a major obstacle (→ 1/10).

Heydrich to rule Czechs with fist of iron

Prague, 29 September
Himmler's unsavoury deputy, General Reinhart Heydrich, has taken over in Prague as deputy protector of Bohemia and Moravia, with the task of wiping out all opposition to the Nazi occupation. Martial law was declared yesterday and hundreds of Czechs have been rounded up, including, today, the puppet premier, General Alois Elias. He has been sentenced to death.

Hitler intends to turn Bohemia into a German province. Czech universities have been closed, German is taught in preference to Czech, and Czechs are being ejected from their homes to make room for German immigrants from the Baltic states.

Sept 27. "Liberty Ships" lit up for night-time construction: today America launched the first of these general-purpose freighters in Baltimore.

Heydrich: Bohemia's "protector".

1941

October

Su	Mo	Tu	We	Th	Fr	Sa
			1	2	3	4
5	6	7	8	9	10	11
12	13	14	15	16	17	18
19	20	21	22	23	24	25
26	27	28	29	30	31	

1. Odessa: German forces use gliders to land behind Russian lines (→ 6).

1. Vilna: Three thousand Jews are rounded up and shot dead in Ponary woods (→ 2).

1. USSR: Petrozavodsk, west of Lake Onega, falls to the Finns (→ 7).

2. USSR: German armies in the central sector commence Operation Typhoon, the main assault on Moscow; in the south they attack towards the Sea of Azov (→ 4).

2. Zagare, Lithuania: SS *Einsatzkommandos* [action squads] machine-gun 2,146 Jews to death (→ 7).

3. Paris: Nazis sympathisers use dynamite to blow up six synagogues.

3. Berlin: The propaganda minister, Josef Goebbels, announces that 150,000 mothers have been evacuated to safer parts of Germany.→

3. USSR: German troops capture Tsarskoe Selo, outside Leningrad, and the industrial centre of Orel.→

3. India: Mahatma Gandhi calls upon all the subjects of the British Raj to start a campaign of passive resistance (→ 25/12).

3. Berlin: Hitler tells a rally that Russia has been crushed "and will never rise again".

4. Vichy: Petain commutes the death sentence on Paul Colette, who attempted to assassinate Pierre Laval and Marcel Deat, into life imprisonment (→ 16).

4. Oslo: The Nazi regime warns the Norwegian people to co-operate or face starvation, after growing unrest and street riots (→ 30).

4. Vichy: Petain makes a single trade union compulsory for all workers.

4. USSR: General Hopner's *Panzer* Group is attacking near Vyazma, while General Hoth is attacking between Vyazma and Rzhev (→ 5).

4. Washington: Britain and the US confirm agreement to send planes and tanks to the USSR every month (→ 11).

Japanese army is defeated at Changsha

Japanese soldiers cleaning the rifles they are taught to regard as sacred.

Changsha, 1 October
Japanese troops were today on the run in Hunan after the collapse of their two-month-long offensive aimed at seizing the provincial capital, Changsha. First estimates put the Japanese losses for the campaign as high as 40,000.

The failure to take this vital town on the Manchukuo-Canton railway is a setback for the Japanese. Control of Changsha would have made possible the opening of a new route for moving troops and materials to the Burmese and Malayan fronts.

The turning-point came four days ago as the Japanese main force, supported by 100 planes, launched an all-out attack on Changsha. By late afternoon a Japanese detachment in civilian clothes had got inside the city. But its back-up, an airborne unit which it should have linked up with to destroy the city's defences, was dropped too close to the Chinese front line and wiped out.

The Chinese troops, under General Hsueh Yueh, encircled the retreating Japanese between the Lao-tao and Liu-yang rivers, inflicting heavy casualties. A simultaneous offensive was launched in Yichang, tying down the only Japanese force available to relieve the fleeing 11th Corps.

John Curtin is new Australian leader

Canberra, 3 October
The Labour leader, John Curtin, aged 56, is Australia's new prime minister following the fall of the Country Party government. Curtin had refused to join a coalition with Robert Menzies, contending that Australia needed a strong opposition. Two independents combined with Labour to beat the government by 36 votes to 33.

The new prime minister is fully committed to the prosecution of the war against the Axis, but he has in the past given greater weight to the threat from Japanese imperialism and less to the Middle East, where Australian forces are mostly concentrated (→ 26/12).

John Curtin: Australia's new PM.

Anglo-US mission agrees military aid programme for Russia

Beaverbrook brings home this cartoon of the aid programme's effects on Hitler.

Moscow, 1 October
An Anglo-American mission, led by Lord Beaverbrook and Averell Harriman, has agreed to boost its military aid to Stalin next year. The USA will allocate 1,200 tanks a month to Britain and the USSR between July 1942 and January 1943, and a further 2,000 tanks a month for the following six months. This will mean initial US consignments of 400 tanks a month for the Soviets from 1 July.

In addition the USA will send 3,600 aircraft to Russia between 1 July 1942 and 1 July 1943, over and above the planes already being sent by Britain. The Soviets will supply Britain and the USA with urgently needed raw materials (→ 4).

Tanks spearhead new attack on Moscow

Russia, 2 October

Two thousand German tanks today advanced against Russian lines as Hitler launched Operation Typhoon – the renewed attack on Moscow. It is the "last, great decisive battle of the war", the Fuhrer told his troops in a communique broadcast before battle commenced.

Forces have been withdrawn from south and north to boost the German assault, which many generals had wanted to make several weeks ago before Hitler ordered a diversion to capture industrial and coal-mining areas in the south. Today the massive German attack made rapid progress, but the invaders must now race against time to beat not only the dogged resistance of Soviet soldiers but also the

onset of the harsh Russian winter. The attack offers some respite for beleaguered Leningrad. Field Marshal von Leeb has failed in his attempt to take the city by storm, and his *Panzers* have been withdrawn to take part in "Typhoon". Hitler still expects von Leeb to capture Leningrad, but he is to do it by artillery, aerial bombardment and that ancient weapon of siege warfare, starvation. The city, says Hitler, "will fall like a leaf".

The Leningraders are already suffering terribly. Over 4,000 people have died in 200 artillery bombardments and 23 air raids in the past month. The first deaths from starvation have been reported – and the siege will now be tightened remorselessly (→ 10).

Leningrad: first they dug trenches, now they battle with starvation.

Russian partisans fighting behind enemy line slow down the German war machine

German troops round up some of the much-feared Soviet guerrilla fighters.

Moscow, 4 October

The organization of the marauding partisan bands operating against the Germans deep behind the front line is becoming formalized as they are brought under the control of the *Stavka* [Soviet High Command].

The partisans came into being when pockets of Russian soldiers were cut off by the Germans; often frightened of being punished if they returned to their own lines, they took to the forests and lived by raiding German supply lines. Gradually, however, they have become a potent guerrilla force, harassing the

Wehrmacht and sending information back to the regular formations of the Red Army.

Officers, political commissars, radio transmitters and weapons are parachuted to the bands and a rigid discipline imposed. Some of them operate as cavalry, swooping out of the forest onto luckless Germans in the rear echelons. Much feared, they are tying up thousands of German soldiers in protection duties; if they are caught they are killed with great brutality, their bodies left hanging from a gallows as a dire warning to others (→ 26).

Messerschmitt sets new speed record

Peenemunde, 2 October

The Messerschmitt Me163A rocket aircraft has today recorded a staggering top speed of 623.85mph at Germany's top secret rocket development centre. Previous flights showed that the aircraft expended almost all its fuel climbing to altitude. Today the test pilot, Heini Dittmar, was towed to 13,000ft by a Bf110 before casting off. Dittmar himself said that the Me163A suffered severe vibration and loss of control for a moment and he had thought that he had "had it at last". Security will naturally prevent the Germans from claiming it as an official world record.

Crowded classrooms offer lessons of war

Britain, 1 October

The war has dramatically changed the lives of children as well as adults on the home front. After the turmoil and tears of evacuation – often more than once, as the threat of aerial bombing came and went – a major problem has been how to keep an education system alive.

Hundreds of schools have been hit by bombs, forcing children to have lessons in churches or even pubs. Many private schools have moved lock, stock and blackboard to the country. But after the first wave of evacuation many school buildings which escaped unscathed were used as Civil Defence depots. By January 1940 it was estimated that one third of all city children

were receiving no schooling at all. Large numbers of evacuees also swamped village schools, so many were taught in people's homes.

There has also been a desperate shortage of teachers, as many were called up for war duties. Classes have therefore become quite large, often with as many as 50 or 60 pupils in a single classroom. And when the children can get to school, what they learn is also affected by the war. Pencils are shared, and margins have been abolished because of the paper shortage. Geography is taught by following troop movements and gardening has replaced games in many schools, where it is taught as part of the "dig for victory" campaign.

A US propaganda poster brings home the dire consequences of careless talk during wartime: men of the merchant navy look back on their blazing ship.

1941

October

Su	Mo	Tu	We	Th	Fr	Sa
			1	2	3	4
5	6	7	8	9	10	11
12	13	14	15	16	17	18
19	20	21	22	23	24	25
26	27	28	29	30	31	

5. Moscow: The Russians put German losses in the campaign at three million and their own at 1.1 million.

6. Bucharest: Roumanian forces claim to have killed 70,000 Soviet soldiers on the eastern front and taken 60,000 prisoners, at a loss to themselves of 20,000 dead.

6. USSR: On a day when over 100,000 Soviet troops are taken prisoner, the SS Adolf Hitler Division captures most of the Soviet Ninth Army at Berdyansk, on the Sea of Azov (→ 16).

7. Helsinki: Finland refuses to heed Allied pressure to stop fighting the USSR, saying it has no political axe to grind but is grateful it "need not fight alone this time" (→ 4/12).

7. Rovno, Poland: SS men take 17,000 Jews to pits outside the town, ordering them to strip before shooting them dead. Those who refuse to undress have their eyes gouged out.→

8. USSR: Mud and rain start severely to hinder German progress on the Moscow front, where battle rages in the Bryansk and Vyazma sectors. In the south, Mariupol on the Sea of Azov is captured.→

8. China: Chinese troops arrive outside Yuezhou, ending the Second Battle of Changsha (→ 24/12).

8. Rome: Mussolini calls on the Japanese to pull their weight in the Axis by waging war on Britain (→ 28).

9. Europe: Turkey signs a trade treaty with Germany to supply raw materials in exchange for manufactured goods.

9. Washington: Roosevelt asks Congress to arm US Atlantic merchant ships (→ 17).

10. Luxemburg: The Nazi referendum on the annexation of Luxemburg to Germany is a failure, as 97 per cent of the population abstain.

11. USSR: Soviet T34 tanks, powerful and mobile weapons first used last month, go into action for the first time on the Moscow front.

Wall crumbles as "Typhoon" hits Moscow

German motorcyclists commandeer horses to pull them out of the Russian mud.

Moscow, 10 October
Stalin has summoned General Zhukov [*see profile below*] back from Leningrad to take command of the defences before Moscow which are crumbling under the impact of Operation Typhoon, the German assault on the capital.

Moscow is in great danger. Orel has fallen to the Germans; so have Bryansk and Vyazma. The first phase of Typhoon has been completed and another 663,000 Russian soldiers have fallen into German hands. Marshal Timoshenko was cut off and had to be flown to safety. The second phase of the operation has begun, but it is being held up because the tanks and heavy rain in the last few days have turned the ground into a quagmire.

The *Wehrmacht* is feeling the onset of the Russian winter and regretting the time wasted before the assault on Moscow. In the south the Germans have captured Perekop, cutting off the Crimea, and reached the Sea of Azov at Mariupol. In the north Leningrad holds out, hungry but indomitable (→ 11).

Zhukov, the hard man defending Moscow

Moscow, 11 October
The man in charge of the desperate defence of Moscow is Georgi Zhukov, the son of a village shoemaker and a former czarist cavalry NCO. His square, tough features exude confidence, and Stalin relies on him as his trouble-shooter.

It was Zhukov who defeated the Japanese in the battles of Khalkin-Gol which secured Mongolia in 1939, and a grateful Stalin made him a Hero of the Soviet Union.

He also gained for himself a reputation as a harsh disciplinarian. Much-wounded, he does not tolerate lack of courage in others, and in Leningrad he hanged officers who ran away; but he is also a thinking soldier, a leading expert on tank warfare (→ 12).

Zhukov: Stalin's trouble-shooter.

British plan attack to relieve Tobruk

Egypt, 5 October
British military leaders have devised a plan to hit back at Rommel and his *Afrika Korps*. The Allied enclave at Tobruk will be the prime target of Operation Crusader. It was agreed two days ago and despite pressure from Churchill for quick action, General Sir Claude Auchinleck, the C-in-C, wants to build up his supplies before taking the offensive next month.

Lt-Gen Sir Alan Cunningham will lead the British campaign at the head of the Eighth Army, formed last month from XIII and XXX Corps. In addition to the British troops, Sir Alan will have Australian, Indian, New Zealand, Polish and Free French forces under his command.

Grumbly Germans

Berlin, 11 October
Don't listen to foreign broadcasts, the German people are warned today by the Nazi propaganda minister, Josef Goebbels. He is reported by Berlin Radio to have said: "It is not a question of being afraid to hear what they say. It is simply a preventative measure. Germs are treacherous enemies, even of a healthy people." One result, he adds, is too much grumbling.

Von Reichenau tells soldiers to kill Jews

Occupied Russia, 10 October
Field Marshal Walther von Reichenau, the C-in-C of the German Sixth Army, today told his men:

"In the east, the soldier is not merely a fighter according to the rules of the art of war, but also the bearer of an inexorable national idea and the avenger of all bestialities inflicted upon the German people and its racial kin. Therefore the soldier must always have a full understanding for the necessity of a severe but just atonement on Jewish subhumanity."

Hitler likes the wording so much that he is going to have it issued as a model for other generals on the eastern front (→ 15).

1941
October

Su	Mo	Tu	We	Th	Fr	Sa
			1	2	3	4
5	6	7	8	9	10	11
12	13	14	15	16	17	18
19	20	21	22	23	24	25
26	27	28	29	30	31	

First convoy via Arctic route gets through

Archangel, 11 October

PQ-1, the first convoy bringing much-needed supplies to help the Russian war effort here, arrived today. It sailed from Hvalfjord in Iceland on 28 September escorted by the cruiser HMS *Suffolk*, two destroyers and an anti-submarine group. Depending on the ice conditions, convoys using this route may have to travel up to 2,000 miles (3,200 km), frequently on stormy seas and in freezing temperatures.

Convoys on this route have to take an oil tanker with them to fuel the escorts. This means working to a complicated schedule so that the tankers can return safely with the westbound convoys which will be designated QP. Efforts were made to establish a refuelling base for the route on the Norwegian island of Spitzbergen.

Rear-Admiral Philip Vian took two cruisers and two destroyers there on 27 July, but he found it too exposed to German air attack to be safe as a port of call.

The second PQ convoy is due to leave next week. By the time it arrives here the winter freeze will have begun. The Russians are hoping to keep the port open throughout the winter, but the Allies are nervous of risking valuable ships sailing hazardously through narrow channels in the ice. They may divert to Murmansk.

HMS "Suffolk" in calm seas: she braved ice and storms to reach Russia.

Thanks to Haw-Haw, PoW exchange fails

Newhaven, 6 October

An official German statement on Bremen radio by "Lord Haw-Haw" – the renegade William Joyce – tonight led to the abrupt cancellation of plans for the exchange of badly wounded British and German PoWs. Two hospital ships were about to leave Newhaven for Dieppe when the war office telephoned ordering the cancellation. No immediate explanation was forthcoming, but the Haw-Haw broadcast spoke of an exchange of 100 Britons for a corresponding number of Germans. Such a man-for-man exchange is barred by the Geneva Convention of 1929, which provides for the exchange of all seriously wounded, irrespective of numbers.

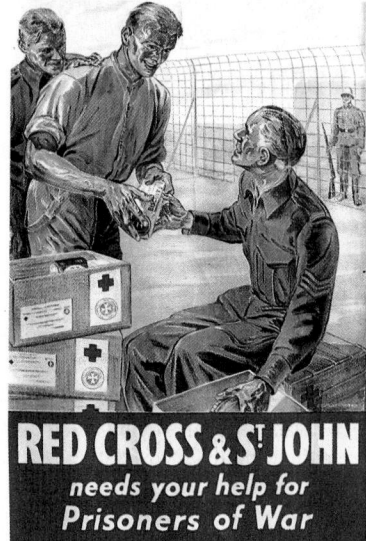

RED CROSS & St JOHN
needs your help for
Prisoners of War

Trying to ease the lot of the PoWs.

12. USSR: Soviet troops quit Bryansk, and civilians start being evacuated from Moscow (→ 13).

12. Libya: Following an earlier operation to relieve the Australian garrison in Tobruk, between 12 and 22 September, another relief operation begins; the Australians are to be replaced by the British 70th Infantry Division (→ 26).

12-13. Germany: RAF bombers make their first large-scale night raid on Nuremberg.

13. USSR: Soviet forces evacuate Vyazma; the Germans occupy Kaluga, 100 miles southwest of Moscow (→ 14).

14. USSR: The German attack reaches Kalinin and Tula on the Moscow front, with advance units just 60 miles from the capital, but meets ever stiffer resistance (→ 16).

15. Mediterranean: The British submarine *Torbay* bombards the Libyan port of Apollonia (→ 14/11).

16. Tokyo: The premier, Prince Fumimaro Konoye, resigns, following Roosevelt's refusal to grant him a summit meeting and division in the Japanese cabinet over negotiation with the USA.→

16. Moscow: Over half a million men, women and children complete building new defences around the city – 5,000 miles of trenches, 60 miles of anti-tank ditches and 177 miles of barbed wire.→

16. Vichy: The pre-war leaders Blum, Daladier, Reynaud and Mandel, together with General Gamelin, are detained on Marshal Petain's orders.

16. Atlantic: A U-boat attacks the British corvette *Gladiolus*.

17. Washington: All US merchant ships in Asian waters are ordered to put in at friendly ports (→ 19).

18. USSR: Mozhaisk, west of Moscow, falls to the 4th Panzer Division; the conquered area east of the Dniester is incorporated into Roumania and renamed Transdniestria (→ 19).

Russian master spy captured in Tokyo

Tokyo, 18 October

Richard Sorge, one of the most successful spies in the history of espionage, has been arrested in Tokyo. The son of a German engineer and a Russian mother, he was brought up in Germany, joined the Communist Party, and became a Soviet agent in 1928, serving in America, China and Japan under journalistic cover. He then got Stalin's permission to go back to Germany and become a member of the Nazi Party. He returned to Tokyo as correspondent for a Frankfurt newspaper. Sorge, a craggy-faced womanizer and drinker, soon charmed his way into the confidence of the German ambassador.

He also set up a highly-placed ring of Japanese agents, and soon he was sending a flood of economic, political and military information back to Moscow. One of his major *coups* was to warn Stalin that Hitler was preparing to attack Russia. He gave the precise date for the invasion – but Stalin ignored him.

Perhaps his greatest service to the Soviet cause was also his last. Just three days ago he was able to tell Moscow that the Japanese have no intention of attacking Russia. This means that Stalin will be able to transfer many divisions from Siberia to defend Moscow.

U-boat torpedoes American destroyer

Reykjavik, 17 October

A US destroyer, the *Kearny*, was torpedoed off the coast here two hours after midnight. She was one of five US destroyers which went to the aid of convoy SC-48, which had come under attack from a U-boat pack after losing half her Canadian escort in a gale.

Last night, despite the reinforcements, the U-boats sank six more merchant ships. The *Kearny* was illuminated by the blazing vessels and suffered a direct hit from U568 on the starboard side. Eleven people have been killed and there are many injured. However, the engines are still working and the *Kearny* is attempting to limp back to the base here.

▷

Russia panics as Nazis push deeper

Moscow threatened by German advance

Moscow, 16 October

The Germans are drawing ever closer to Moscow. Their tanks are only 50 miles (80 km) away. Kalinin, to the north-west of the city, has fallen. The Mozhaisk defences in front of the capital are under severe attack and may soon be abandoned. In the south-west Kaluga has been lost and in the south Tula, defended by worker battalions, is under heavy attack. The 50th Army, caught in the Bryansk pocket, has been destroyed. The only cheering news for the Russians is that the IV Tank Brigade, equipped with T34s, has given Germany's General Guderian a bloody nose outside Mtsensk.

In Moscow itself, Molotov has told the foreign embassies that they are to be evacuated to Kuybishev. The streets are full of charred paper as secret documents are burnt. Party members are tearing up their cards. Pictures of Stalin are being taken down.

There is panic in the air as rumours spread that German tanks are in the suburbs. There is no transport; the buses and taxis have been commandeered to take troops to the front. Some officials and policemen, fearful of what will happen to them if the Germans arrive, are fleeing from the city, and looters are taking advantage of their departure. General Zhukov, recalled from Leningrad, is working fever-

Driven underground by Hitler: the citizens of Moscow take refuge in the tube.

ishly to organize a new line of defence. He has ordered the setting up of artillery and anti-tank strongpoints to ambush the German *Panzers* on their approach routes.

Reinforcements are being rushed to Moscow from other sectors, and almost half a million Muscovites have been set to work digging trenches and setting up roadblocks.

Worker battalions, armed by Moscow's own factories, are taking their places in the front line. In the midst of all this feverish activity, the Associated Press correspondent has been asked to write a story on Lenin's tomb. He had time to send one message – "Tomb closed" – before he joined the exodus to Kuybishev (→ 18).

Odessa falls to Germans, but all they find is a burnt-out shell

Odessa, 16 October

The Roumanians and Germans who have been besieging the Black Sea port of Odessa since August finally marched into the city today, only to find it empty and burning.

Its defenders had sailed for Sevastopol during the night in a secret evacuation involving 30 ships and 35,000 men. The rearguard was taken on board at 4am. The last man to leave was Captain Makarenko, the commander of the port.

Most of the garrison and party officials had already been evacuated, along with several thousand

prisoners. All the material that had to be left behind was burnt. The big guns of the 95th Rifle Division were dumped into the harbour.

The Roumanians are making the most of the Soviet withdrawal: "Troops of our Fourth Army marched into Odessa this afternoon. The last nests of resistance are being cleared up in street fighting. The population greeted German and Roumanian forces with enthusiasm." In fact the Roumanian dictator, Ion Antonescu, is so angry at the Russian escape that he has sacked the army's commander, General

Ciuperdea. It has not been a glorious episode in Roumanian military history. The Russians estimate that the ferocious fighting during the 69-day siege has cost the Roumanians 250,000 casualties. In exchange they have got a burnt-out shell of a city, with all the war installations destroyed and the Red Army gone. The soldiers and sailors who have been evacuated are being used to strengthen the defences of the great fortress of Sevastopol, itself under threat of siege as von Manstein's Eleventh Army advances through the Crimea (→ 22).

General Tojo is appointed prime minister of Japan

Tokyo, 18 October

Japan's deadlocked political crisis has been ended with the appointment of the army strongman General Hideki Tojo, aged 57, as the new prime minister in the wake of the Konoye cabinet's resignation.

One of General Tojo's first moves has been to extend the deadline for diplomacy to prevent war with the United States until 25 November. This overturns the decision of the last imperial conference, calling for a decision on war or peace with the US no later than 15 October, which divided the Konoye cabinet and precipitated its resignation. General Tojo insisted on being given a "clean slate" on this issue before accepting his appointment from Emperor Hirohito.

Tojo's emergence as premier has been sudden. Until last night the favourite was Prince Higashikuni. However Marquis Kido, the emperor's personal adviser, told the seven ex-premiers advising the emperor on a successor that General Tojo was the only candidate capable of controlling the war advocates in the army – blamed by many for this latest crisis.

General Tojo, known as *Kamisori* [the Razor] retains his portfolio as war minister. It is the first time that Japan has had a serving general as prime minister (→ 1/11).

General Tojo: Japan's strongman.

SS barbarity against Jews shocks officers

Warsaw, 15 October
The sufferings of the Jews in the Warsaw Ghetto are growing worse by the day under the brutal rule of the German occupiers of the Polish capital. The governor of the General Government area (German-occupied Poland), Dr Hans Frank, is stepping up the regime of punishment and starvation which is killing hundreds every day. "As for the Jews," he told his colleagues last week, "quite frankly they must be done away with, one way or the other."

As the Germans press on into Russia, eastern Europe is feeling Hitler's furious loathing for "sub-human" people – gypsies, homo-sexuals, communists and, above all, Jews. The architects of the geno-cide of the Jews, Reinhart Heydrich and Heinrich Himmler, refer to the Jews as vermin or lice: degenerate creatures who must be cleansed from the *Reich*.

Einsatzgruppe massacres happen virtually every day, and their barbarity shocks even some of the most hardened regular officers. Major Rosler, the commander of the German garrison at Zhitomir in the USSR, has resolved to write to Berlin about what he witnessed recently. He wonders what bloodstained SS men, filling a ditch with dead Jews, contribute to the war effort. Earlier this week, for instance, at

Nazis line up to watch the cold-blooded murder of a Jewish man.

Stanislawow, German and Ukrainian police staged a "special action". They rounded up the town's Jews – about 8,000 people in all – and kicked them two miles to a deep mass grave in the Jewish cemetery where they were made to hand over their valuables and take off all their clothes. SS machine guns killed them as they leapt naked into the ditch (→ 22).

"Picture Post" becomes British best seller

Britain, 18 October
Picture Post, the magazine founded in 1938 by Edward Hulton, which has reached a circulation of a million in the last two months, is now a national institution under its editor Tom Hopkinson. It has made its name by its brilliant picture treatment and its hardhitting captions attacking Hitler at the time of appeasement. At home it criticizes military commanders, ineffective weapons and bureaucratic delays in helping air-raid victims. It founded a Home Guard training school at Osterley Park and gave tips on resistance fighting to its readers. Now it is running articles on post-war reforms such as full employment, minimum wages and a national health service. The response has been huge.

Tom Hopkinson at work on "Picture Post", Britain's radical magazine.

1941

October

Su	Mo	Tu	We	Th	Fr	Sa
			1	2	3	4
5	6	7	8	9	10	11
12	13	14	15	16	17	18
19	20	21	22	23	24	25
26	27	28	29	30	31	

19. Sea of Azov: Taganrog falls to the advancing German Eleventh Army (→ 27).

19. USSR: Troops from Siberia and the Far East arrive at the Moscow front (→ 20).

19. Atlantic: A U-boat sinks the US merchant ship *Lehigh* off the west coast of Africa.

20. USSR: The government moves from Moscow to Kuybishev, on the Volga river, and in the south Stalino falls to the Germans.→

20. Nantes, France: Resistance fighters assassinate the regional military commander, Lieutenant-Colonel Karl Holz.→

21. Kragujevac, Yugoslavia: Germans and local fascist militiamen massacre 2,300 Serbs in reprisal for recent partisan attacks (→ 26).

22. Bordeaux: One hundred more hostages are taken and a curfew is imposed following the assassination of another German officer (→ 23).

22. Odessa: A delayed-action bomb blows up General Glugoscianu, the commander of the Roumanian corps, and 50 of his staff; 5,000 Jews are slaughtered both in and outside the city in retaliation (→ 24).

23. London: General de Gaulle asks Resistance members to stop murdering German military personnel, to avoid further retaliation against the French populace (→ 24).

23. USSR: The Soviet command system is reorganized: Zhukov takes over the northern sector, Timoshenko the southern.

24. Bordeaux: The Germans execute fifty hostages (→ 25).

24. Berlin: Adolf Eichmann approves a scheme to gas Jews using exhaust fumes in specially adapted vans (→ 27).

25. London: Churchill condemns German reprisal killings in occupied territories.

25. Britain: The battleship *Prince of Wales* leaves for Singapore to be the flagship of Britain's new fleet in the Far East (→ 2/12).

Germans kill fifty to revenge murder of top commander

Nantes, France, 21 October
Fifty hostages were shot here this morning – in reprisal for the killing of Lt-Col Karl Holz, the local German commander. He was shot six times as he walked past the cathedral yesterday morning, two of the bullets hitting his neck.

Now the Vichy authorities have announced that, "considering the gravity of the crime", 50 more hostages will be shot unless the killers are found by tomorrow. The statement coincides with a visit to occupied France by Admiral Darlan, the Vichy vice-premier.

General Karl-Heinrich von Stulpnagel, the commander of the German occupation forces, described the killers as "cowardly criminals, paid for by England and Moscow". So far – after an enthusiastic round-up which netted the prefect of the Loire, the commandant of the Nantes *gendarmerie* and three perfectly innocent policemen – they have not been found.

Since the Germans invaded the USSR and the French Communist Party roused itself from a policy of "masterful inactivity", there has been a steady increase in anti-German terrorism, though the majority of the French have had no strong feelings either way. What are slowly changing their attitudes are the German and Vichy counter-measures. So far 131 Frenchmen have been executed as hostages; no one can tell in which direction opinion will go (→ 22).

KEEP DEATH OFF THE ROAD
CARELESSNESS KILLS

Germans race to beat Russia's old ally: winter

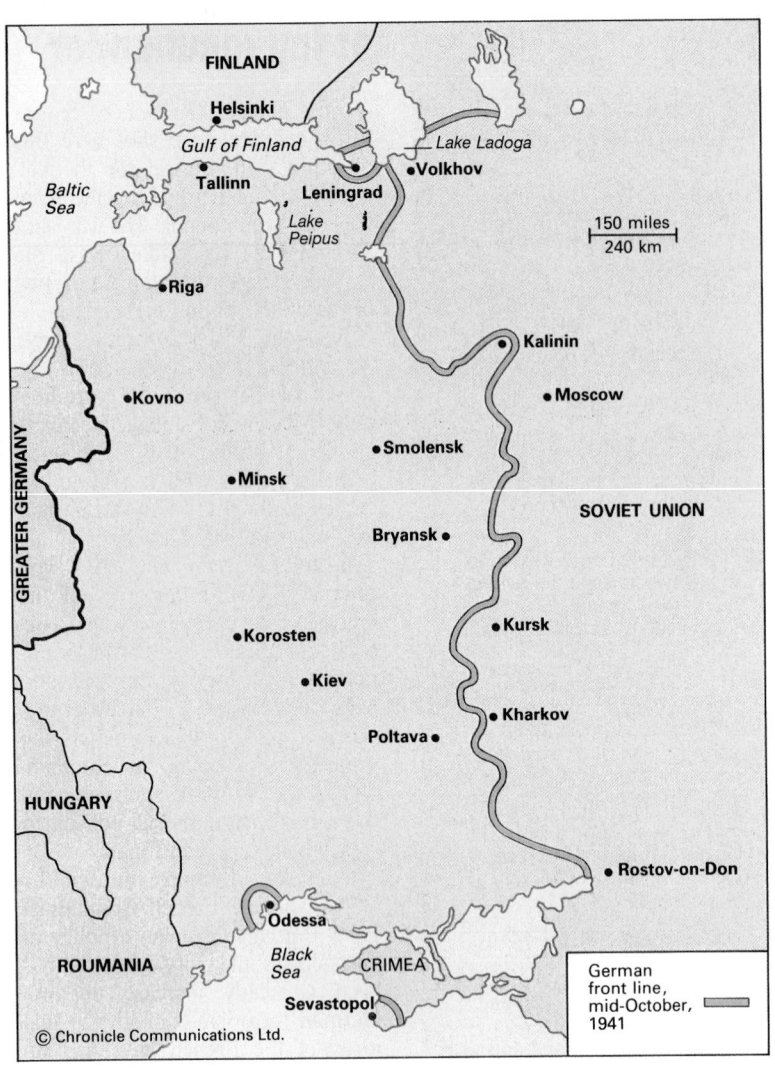

German troops enter the city of Kharkov across a heavily-damaged bridge.

Stalin declares state of siege in Moscow

Moscow, 20 October

Stalin has today declared a state of siege in Moscow. The Soviet leader, who has remained in Moscow despite the threat of the German tanks, has moved swiftly and ruthlessly to quell the growing panic in the Russian capital and stiffen the resolve of the Red Army. His decree appeals to all workers "to keep calm and orderly and to render the Red Army defending Moscow all possible help". It also says that all enemies of public order are to be handed over at once to court martials and that all *provocateurs*, spies and other enemies inciting riot are to be shot on the spot.

Stalin has called on other Russians to support his call to arms. The author Alexei Tolstoy, a kinsman of the great novelist, issued a stirring message to the Red Army today: "Grit your teeth! Squeeze the enemy's throat! Not a step backwards! Smash the German hordes with a storm of bombs and the fiery storm of artillery, with the steel of your bayonets and the fury of your anger!" (→ 24).

Why Hitler needs to secure Russian oil

Moscow, 20 October

The huge military machine of Germany has access to only some three per cent of the world's crude oil assets – a little more than it had before the outbreak of war, but less than it needs. Germany's problems would be solved if it captured the Soviet oilfields centred on Baku, in the Caucasus, which would quadruple its supplies. Meanwhile, the coming winter means that operations in Russia must slow. This will cut oil demand, but also means that the conquest of the Caucasus cannot take place before next spring.

Kharkov falls despite valiant defenders

Moscow, 24 October

Kharkov, the great industrial city in the Donets basin, has fallen to the German Sixth and Seventeenth Armies after days of vicious street fighting in the suburbs. The city has suffered severely from artillery fire and bombing, and many of its fine buildings have been destroyed. The Russians fought hard in its defence, giving ground reluctantly and inflicting heavy casualties on the Germans. Finally, Marshal Timoshenko was ordered to abandon the city to prevent the Germans from surrounding the defenders and inflicting a terrible defeat. This time the Red Army withdrew in good order and is continuing its slow, stubborn retreat, fighting every inch of the way against a tiring enemy in weather conditions which are growing worse as each day passes.

However, there can be no disguising the fact that the German advance into the Donets basin has robbed Russia of much of its coal, pig-iron, steel and grain, all needed to feed the people and make the tanks (→ 28).

1941
October

Su	Mo	Tu	We	Th	Fr	Sa
			1	2	3	4
5	6	7	8	9	10	11
12	13	14	15	16	17	18
19	20	21	22	23	24	25
26	27	28	29	30	31	

26. Tobruk: The operation to relieve the Australian garrison with the British 70th Infantry Division, begun on 12 October, ends; at least one ship, the minelayer HMS *Latona*, has been lost to Stuka dive-bombers (→ 14/11).

26-27. Germany: The RAF attacks Hamburg overnight with 115 bombers.

27. Kalisz, Poland: Germans kill 290 Jews from an old people's home in the first trial of a van specially adapted to suffocate them with engine exhaust fumes.

27. Kovno, Lithuania: Nine thousand Jews, including 4,273 children, are massacred by German *Einsatzkommandos*.→

27. Crimea, USSR: German troops capture Kramatorsk and reach Sevastopol, the last remaining Soviet possession in the area (→ 1/11).

27. Atlantic: The British destroyer *Cossack* sinks after being torpedoed by a U-boat.

28. Rome: Mussolini declares that the "coalition of Bolshevism and its European and American allies" will be destroyed.

28. USSR: Guderian launches a renewed assault on Moscow, but finds that the ground is too soft and muddy to make any real progress (→ 30).

30. Atlantic: The US Navy supply ship *Salinas* is damaged by a U-boat.

30. Washington: Roosevelt gives the USSR a $1,000 million interest-free loan to buy equipment under Lend-Lease (→ 11/11).

30. USSR: The Germans halt their land attack on Moscow in order to give the ground time to harden (→ 31).

31. Estonia: SS Commander Erich von dem Bach-Zalewski reports back to Berlin that there are no Jews left in Estonia (→ 7/11).

31. Moscow: The *Luftwaffe* bombs the city in 45 attacks today (→ 7/11).

31. Britain: 262 civilians have been killed and 361 injured in air raids this month.

U-boat sinks first US warship in action

Reykjavik, 31 October
As dawn was breaking over the sea to the west of Iceland the US Navy lost its first warship to the U-boats. The *Reuben James* was hit by a torpedo from U552 which exploded the magazine. The ship split into two parts. The aft section stayed afloat for five minutes, but as it sank depth charges exploded killing a number of men in the water. The *Reuben James* was escorting con-voy HX-156. Other US destroyers are performing such regular escort duties. This is the first US Navy combat ship to be lost, and 115 of the 160-man crew have perished as well.

At present the US maintains diplomatic relations with Germany. Later today President Roosevelt said that no immediate change was in train; but the loss of US seamen will encourage those who want war.

How the British army feeds the inner man

Britain, 31 October
One of the lessons learnt in the last war was that bully beef and mutton stew, no matter how plentiful, neither satisfied the appetites of the troops nor kept up their morale.

The Army Catering Corps has now been formed, and chefs for all branches of the armed forces go through a sophisticated training programme. Professional caterers have been moved from their hotels and restaurants and put to work analysing the needs of serving men in climates as different as Libya and Iceland. They have developed no fewer than 89 rationing scales.

However, civilians should not feel that they are getting the scraps from the army's table; the ministry of food says it takes their needs just as seriously.

"Is everything all right?" New conscripts get their first taste of army fare.

Louis Mountbatten gives combined ops a dash of glamour

Lord and Lady Louis Mountbatten.

London, 27 October
The dashing 41-year-old Lord Louis Mountbatten has been appointed director of Combined Operations and told to put some zip into hit-and-run attacks on German positions on the Continent.

Lord Louis, who is related to most of Europe's royal families, gained his reputation for courage and audacity when, virtually single-handedly, he brought his destroyer *Kelly* back to port under continuous German air attack after she had been torpedoed in the North Sea.

Lord Louis's father, Prince Louis of Battenberg, who settled in Britain, was forced by anti-German hysteria to resign as first sea lord during the Great War. Lord Louis is determined to erase this slur on his family's reputation; he hopes one day to succeed to his father's old job.

Mystery man of many names organizes Yugoslav resistance

Belgrade, 26 October
They seek him here in the ruined capital of Yugoslavia: they seek him out there in the rugged, mountainous countryside so ideal for guerrilla fighting; the Germans seek him everywhere and bring in more and more troops daily to search for this man whose name they do not know and his partisan bands who grow in numbers daily.

Josip Broz, a former sergeant in the Austro-Hungarian army, became a dedicated communist while a prisoner of the Russians and spent years in Yugoslav prisons for his beliefs. While he organized his partisan bands from a luxury villa here – with an escape hatch behind the wash-basin – he used more than 20 aliases until he settled on "Tito". Until today, Tito's partisans have maintained a guarded alliance against the Germans with the *Chetnik* fighters who are led by an army colonel, Drazha Mihailovich. The two men met today soon after the Germans started killing 100 Yugoslavs for every German soldier killed. Tito wants a joint command, but Mihailovich is opposed to sharing leadership in this way (→ 9/11).

Propaganda war gets snappier, but ducks communist menace

London, 31 October
For years the Nazis have been masters of propaganda, with Goebbels the ringmaster of spectacular rallies and powerful cinema films. But Britain ministry of information is now showing signs of growing sophistication after a shaky start.

Posters have gained in artistic impact; slogans are snappier. So far the focus of propaganda has been directed within Britain, cajoling the citizens into public-spirited behaviour, whether it be avoiding gossip, growing vegetables or mending clothes. As thoughts begin to turn to promoting the Allied cause abroad, the changing line-up of war powers has caused some problems even at home.

For the past four months, for instance, the backroom boys of the ministry of information have been juggling with a tricky question: Now that we have Joe Stalin as an ally, what do we tell the public about communism?

Churchill appointed Brendan Bracken, the journalist and financier, to head the ministry soon after Hitler attacked the Soviet Union. Bracken found the civil servants fearful of a communist takeover. Bracken has now solved the problem: Stalin and his armed forces are to be praised to the skies, but with absolutely no mention of communism. Any attempts by British communists to exploit public admiration for Russia will be forestalled by the ministry organizing Tanks-for-Russia campaigns.

In its early months, the ministry had been ridiculed for its fondness for exhortation: *Your* courage, *your* cheerfulness, *your* resolution will bring us victory. At a policy meeting after the outbreak of war, contingency plans for the ministry were examined; a proposal that cups of tea should be provided to prevent panic after air raids was amended to cups of coffee. It only slowly dawned on the officials that what people wanted was not rallying cries but actual information, particularly as, in its absence, rumours flourish.

The iron-fisted German propaganda machine pulls no punches. The message is clear: "Europe's victory means prosperity for you."

A Red Army rifle butt crushes the life out of the deadly Nazi spider.

Stirring words and a stern face make powerful propaganda.

Ten thousand Jews slain by a finger

Kovno, Lithuania, 28 October
By order of the Nazis, the entire population of the ghetto, some 27,000 Jews, assembled in the main square at daybreak this morning. The SS commander, Rauca, stood on a hillock, his dog by his feet. The Jews passed before him one by one. Eating sandwiches and drinking coffee, he pointed the way for each one with his finger. He sent the younger and healthier people to the left. Young children, the old and the sick went to the right. To the left meant life, albeit in slavery; to the right, death. It is thought that some 10,000 Jews were thus condemned to die (→ 31).

Hitler seeks funds from pay-packets

Berlin, 31 October
German workers are being forced to "volunteer" as much as 25 *Reichsmark* (£2.08/$8.40) a week from their wages to pay for Hitler's war. Those who resist payment are likely to be approached by Nazi Party members in their factories.

An illegal underground newspaper, the *Suddeutsche Volksstimme*, is claiming that this "iron savings" system means that Hitler is "extorting nearly six billion marks from the people to pay for armaments".

RAF raids key Nazi base in Norway

Norway, 30 October
RAF Hudson bombers have struck a body blow at the German Navy's supply system in the northern seas. A raid on the Norwegian port of Aalesund is thought to have left six supply ships irreparably damaged. The Hudsons flew through driving snow over the North Sea to find a target lit by moonlight. One pilot described how he hit his target from 30 feet before flying across the town at rooftop height, firing machine guns. He then put incendiary bombs through a factory roof. Norwegians resent occupation more than the raids (→ 27/12).

1941
November

Su	Mo	Tu	We	Th	Fr	Sa
						1
2	3	4	5	6	7	8
9	10	11	12	13	14	15
16	17	18	19	20	21	22
23	24	25	26	27	28	29
30						

1. Tokyo: Joseph C Grew, the US ambassador, sends a second telegram to President Roosevelt warning that the Japanese may be planning an attack on an American target.→

1. USSR: German forces launch a major offensive aimed at Rostov-on-Don and the Caucasus, and clear up the last remnants of resistance at Simferopol, a vital communications centre in the Crimea (→ 4).

2. Europe: The RAF flies the last in a long series of sweeps against German shipping (→ 7).

2. Yugoslavia: Rival partisan forces – Drazha Mihailovich's *Chetniks* and Tito's fighters – clash at Uzice.

3. Mediterranean: British planes stage a series of attacks on Sicily.

3. USSR: The Germans capture Kursk.

4. Leicester: A woman who refused to sign up for war work with the army ordnance department is fined £2.

4. Crimea, USSR: Feodosia falls to the Germans (→ 8).

5. Tokyo: The Japanese government sends Saburo Kurusu to Washington to help with negotiations with the Americans on a settlement to the question of Japan's role in South-east Asia.→

6. Atlantic: The US cruiser *Omaha* and destroyer *Somers* capture the *Odenwald*, a German armed merchantman.

7. Minsk, USSR: Twelve thousand Jews are slaughtered and buried in mass graves outside the city (→ 1/12).

7-8. Germany: RAF bombers attack Cologne, Berlin and Mannheim in the heaviest bombing effort on a single night so far.→

8. USSR: The Germans occupy Yalta, in the Crimea, and Tikhvin, in the north, completing the encirclement of Leningrad (→ 14).

8. Atlantic: Martlet aeroplanes from HMS *Audacity* shoot down two Focke-Wulf FW200s during an attack on Convoy ON-76.

Japan plans US attack

Tokyo, 5 November

Japan's commanders today ordered the imperial Japanese navy to prepare for a surprise attack on the US fleet at Pearl Harbor in Hawaii.

The secret move follows the Japanese decision this autumn to carry out a simultaneous attack on Malaya and the Philippines to get to the oilfields of the Dutch East Indies. Some commanders were reluctant to attack the Philippines, which are US territory, and bring the USA into the war, and a pre-emptive strike was seen as essential to hamper US defence efforts.

The idea of attacking Pearl Harbor was not new, but it took the determination of the Japanese C-in-C, Admiral Isoroku Yamamoto, to sell it to his colleagues. He studied English at Harvard and was a naval attache in Washington, and knows the potential power of the USA. He believes only a surprise air attack will guarantee success. However, Japan's leaders agree that

Admiral Isoroku Yamamoto.

before any attack there should be one last attempt at a negotiated deal on Japan's role in the Far East. If this fails, Japan and the USA will be at war before Christmas (→ 10).

Oil supplies are reason for going to war

Tokyo, 3 November

Japan has one good reason for further expansion in the Far East: oil. The country has been starved of oil since the USA decided in July, following the Japanese occupation of French Indochina, to extend the licensing of exports for Japan. It was not intended to ban oil exports to Japan, but US officials refused all applications to export oil and gas.

Roosevelt felt that to reverse the refusals would be a sign of weakness; since then the USA has operated a *de facto* embargo. With virtually no oil supplies of its own, Japan's eyes are now firmly set on the oil-rich Dutch East Indies (→ 5).

Envoy pelted with eggs and tomatoes

Detroit, 5 November

The British ambassador in America, Lord Halifax, was pelted with eggs and tomatoes by women protesters last night as he completed a two-day tour of Detroit's arms productions centre.

Only one well-aimed egg actually hit the envoy. One hour later he visited the Henry Ford hospital to have an eye infection treated. The women were protesting against the possible entry of America into the war, though the identity of the group is not known. The American Mothers and The Mothers of the USA both blamed each other.

South Africa takes five Vichy ships

Cape Town, 4 November

British and South African naval ships have intercepted a Vichy French convoy carrying tin and rubber from Indochina to Germany. The convoy of five ships, escorted by a sloop, the *D'Iberville*, was captured by four cruisers. The ships tried to scuttle, but boarding parties took them over and prevented the holds from flooding.

The action has already drawn predictable protest from Vichy which regards it as akin to piracy. The convoy was carrying "supplies for the natives of French West Africa, and for French people in the unoccupied zone", according to a statement from Vichy. "There was no contraband or material that could be used for war." For some time Britain has watched impotently while Germany brings vital war supplies into Europe on French vessels.

On 30 March a convoy of four French merchantmen escorted by the destroyer *Simoun* was seen passing the Straits of Gibraltar. When Royal Navy ships ordered the convoy to halt it took refuge in the Algerian port of Nemours. At the time Vichy said that the ships were bringing food to the native Algerians. Later the convoy reached Marseilles. It was carrying rubber from Thailand. This time the Allies have ensured that the rubber has not got through.

Poised for take-off: a Hawker Hurricane, or "Hurricat", about to be launched from an experimental catapult designed for merchant ships.

The traditional military march past Lenin's mausoleum: the soldiers will go straight from the procession to the battle front.

Stalin urges second front as war rages for Moscow

Moscow, 7 November

In a major speech commemorating the 24th anniversary of the Revolution, Stalin yesterday called on the west to establish a "second front" in Europe against the Nazis. He told a rally of Moscow party workers: "There is no doubt that the absence of a second front is making the enemy's task easier, but we hope that a second front will be established, and in the near future, thus relieving the task of the Russian army."

The delegates, meeting in the ornate marble hall of the Mayakov-sky Underground station because of the *Luftwaffe's* continuous attacks, gave Stalin a thunderous welcome and cheered again when he told them that the Germans, who had been given orders to kill everything Russian, "would get their war of annihilation and would be exterminated without mercy". It was a brave speech to make with the Germans hammering at the gates of Moscow, but Stalin was full of confidence: "Our army must win, and will win. The German army must be defeated, and will be defeated."

There are three basic facts, he said, which will lead to Hitler's army being crushed: "The first of these facts is the instability of German imperialism, and Hitler's New Order. We are assured that Hitler acts like Napoleon in everything. I can tell you that Hitler no more resembles Napoleon than a kitten resembles a lion.

"Secondly, Napoleon fought for liberal forces against reactionary forces. Hitler is fighting for reaction and will perish by the hand of progressive forces. "Thirdly, who doubts that Britain and the United States will give us full support to conquer Hitler? ... Modern war is a war of machines. The war will be won by the one who has an overwhelming superiority on the output of machines. This is one of the fundamental reasons for the inevitable doom of the predatory Nazi imperialism. Our task is now revenge." Today, at the traditional military parade before Lenin's tomb in Red Square, Stalin urged the army to defend "Holy Russia". The soldiers, in full battle kit, marched straight from Red Square to take their place in Moscow's front line (→ 12).

RAF raiders fall to German air defence

Germany, 8 November

The RAF is radically reviewing its bombing strategy after German air defences took a heavy toll of RAF bombers and aircrew tonight. A total of 380 aircraft attacked Berlin, Cologne, Mannheim and the Ruhr; 34 – nearly a tenth – were lost.

Germany's Kammhuber Line, as it is known to the RAF, is responsible. This is a series of ground-controlled interception "boxes" along the most frequently-used routes; in each "box" a night-fighter waits to pounce, so far with great effect.

Priest who prayed for Jews is arrested

Berlin, 8 November

Reliable sources said today that the *Gestapo* has arrested Bernhard Lichtenberg, the dean of St Hedwig's Roman Catholic Cathedral here. Renowned for his opposition to the Nazis, he used to close all his services with a prayer for the Jews and for prisoners in the concentration camps.

This summer the police questioned him after he preached a series of sermons criticizing Nazi policies and the behaviour of the Gestapo in particular. He was released, but continued to challenge Hitler inside and outside church; together with his colleague the Roman Catholic bishop of Munster, he carried on preaching against the Nazi regime.

Most recently, he wrote to the *Reich* chief physician, Leonardo Conti, to protest against the authorities' "euthanasia" campaign of killing mentally defective and incurably ill patients. "As a human being, a Christian, a priest and a German," he wrote, "I demand ... that you answer for the crimes that have been perpetrated with your consent, which will bring the vengeance of the Lord on the heads of the German people." (→ 3/11/43).

1941
November

Su	Mo	Tu	We	Th	Fr	Sa
						1
2	3	4	5	6	7	8
9	10	11	12	13	14	15
16	17	18	19	20	21	22
23	24	25	26	27	28	29
30						

9. Mediterranean: The British cruisers *Aurora* and *Penelope*, with the destroyers *Lance* and *Lively*, attack two Italian convoys; two destroyers, the *Fulmine* and *Libeccio*, and ten merchant ships are sunk.

9. Yugoslavia: Mihailovich's *Chetnik* partisans continue their attack on Tito's communist group, weakening organized resistance to the Nazis.

11. Washington: Lend-Lease aid is extended to General de Gaulle's Free French fighters.

11. Ethiopia: Allied troops attack Chilga and Kulkaber in a new drive to push the last Italians out (→21).

12. Orsha, USSR: General Franz Halder, Hitler's army chief of general staff, holds a conference to agree plans for a final assault on Moscow.→

12. China: The Nationalist government asks Britain to provide air cover on the Burma Road.

12. Mediterranean: The British carriers *Ark Royal* and *Argus* deliver 34 Hurricanes to Malta (Operation Perpetual).→

13. USSR: The temperature on the eastern front has fallen to -4 degrees Fahrenheit (-20 degrees Celsius) (→ 15).

14. Leningrad: Supplies are airlifted in for the first time (→ 20).

14. London: The Burmese premier, U Maung Saw, leaves, having failed to get promises of independence from the British.

14. Libya: British commandos, with a mission to attack Rommel's campaign headquarters, are landed from the submarines *Talisman* and *Torbay* near Apollonia (→ 18).

14. London: Writing to the *Jewish Chronicle* on its centenary, Churchill writes: "None has suffered more cruelly than the Jew the unspeakable evils wrought ... by Hitler and his vile regime."

15. USSR: Mechanical failures due to extreme cold, together with the collapse of logistical support, mean that only 150 of the 2nd *Panzer* Army's 1,150 tanks are operational.→

Congress votes to revise Neutrality Act

Washington, 13 November

The House of Representatives voted here tonight by 212 votes to 194 to revise the Neutrality Act of 1939 to allow US merchant ships to unload munitions in British ports.

The roll was called in tense silence. As soon as it was over, the Speaker, Sam Rayburn of Texas, who immediately before the vote went on to the floor and read a letter from the president urging passage, happily signed it. The president will sign it on Monday.

The bill's history was a notable demonstration not only of the declining, though still formidable, power of the isolationists but also of President Roosevelt's political skill. Realizing that he did not at first have the votes for revising the Neutrality Act so drastically as to allow American ships to enter war zones, he first sent a bill allowing US merchantment to be armed to the House. Polls suggested that most Americans were in favour, and the bill passed the House by almost two votes to one on 17 October. Then, after making a speech in which he claimed to have documents proving that the Nazis planned to subjugate Central and South America, he sent the more ambitious bill allowing ships to go into war zones to the Senate, where it passed by 50 to 37. That was close.

Senator Hiram Johnson, a leading isolationist, told his son that it was a good result, given that "the bundles to Britain crew and all the Anglophiles were pulling and hauling and doing everything they could". But only then did the president send the stronger bill to the House of Representatives.

U-boat sinks "Ark Royal" off Gibraltar

Gibraltar, 14 November

Lord Haw-Haw had claimed the sinking of the *Ark Royal* so many times that it had become a standing joke with the British. It was no joke today, however, when the great carrier sank 25 miles from Gibraltar after a fight to keep her afloat.

In an attack by U81 and U205 yesterday she had been hit amidships by one torpedo from U81. The *Ark Royal* began to list at once, losing all power and light. For a few hours it seemed as if she could reach Gibraltar under tow by two tugs, her list corrected and steam raised in one boiler. In the early hours of this morning, however, fire broke out in her port boiler room and her list increased to 35 degrees. The *Ark Royal* was abandoned and sank at 6.13 this morning with the loss of only one crew member.

With *Illustrious* and *Formidable* both under repair in the USA, the Mediterranean Fleet is left without a carrier – a parlous situation since Hitler, desperate to supply Rommel, is preparing to order one *Fliegerkorps* of bombers from Russia to Sicily – a serious threat to Malta and the Royal Navy.

Crew of the badly-damaged "Ark Royal" wait to be rescued by HMS "Legion".

Canadian soldiers land in Hong Kong

Or should it be: "Let's go home"?

Hong Kong, 15 November

The converted passenger liner *Awatea* arrived here this evening, carrying 2,000 Canadian troops under Brigadier J Lawson.

The Canadians will boost the garrison in Hong Kong, but, as Churchill himself has pointed out, two semi-trained Canadian battalions are unlikely to deter Japan from war, but will merely increase the numbers of prisoners the Japanese can take. The Canadians seem only too aware of this. "Oh God, another Dunkirk," Signalman William Allister said when he heard where he was going. "No, fella," another voice added, "at Dunkirk they had somewhere to go."

Vichy war minister dies in plane crash

Nimes, France, 12 November

General Huntziger, the Vichy war minister, was killed 50 miles north of here today, in a plane accident. He was returning from a mission to North Africa, to consult General Weygand on a possible German bid to use French North Africa.

Though Huntziger signed the armistice with the Germans in June last year, he was a staunch defender of French interests against German encroachment, and the strongest opponent of Laval's efforts to open French ports to Germany.

"XX" agents are hoodwinking Nazi spymasters

London, 9 November
Stories in the British press this morning about sabotage at a food warehouse at Wealdstone will give the *Abwehr*, the German military intelligence, a great deal of satisfaction, for it believes that the fire bomb attack was carried out by two of its secret agents who landed in Scotland from Norway seven months ago.

In fact, the agents, both Norwegian, have been working for British Intelligence from the day they landed, and their sabotage exploit was carefully contrived to establish their credentials with the Germans.

Code-named "Jack" and "OK" by the Germans, but known to the British by the cartoon character names of "Mutt and Jeff", they are being run by the "Twenty Committee", so-called because of the Roman numerals of double-cross. The committee, chaired by an Oxford don, John Masterman, was set up last January. Its purpose is to feed information, a mixture of fact and fiction, to the Germans through their own agents.

Captured agents are given the choice: work for us or be executed as a spy. Two of the first Abwehr agents parachuted into England a year ago were given this choice. They both chose to live and now, code-named "Summer" and "Tate", are employed in sending disinformation to their former bosses.

Other agents, like "Snow", a Welshman, offer their services to the Germans with the intention of becoming double-agents.

Great care is taken to build up a disinformer's "legend". The committee has to decide what genuine information can be sent to the Germans and what actions can be allowed to go ahead in order to maintain the double-agent's credibility.

British Intelligence is also gaining valuable knowledge of the inner workings of the German secret service (→ 18/8/43).

Fresh German attack on Moscow

Moscow, 13 November
The Germans today resumed their attack on Moscow. Taking advantage of the frost-hardened ground, they have launched one of their customary pincer movements in a final attempt to capture the city before the winter strikes the exposed German army with all its severity.

The plan is for Guderian's 2nd *Panzer* Group to take Tula, to the south of the Russian capital, and then sweep up behind Moscow to Kolomna. Hoth's 3rd Panzer Group is to form the northern arm of the pincer with the task of driving eastwards to the Volga Canal and then wheeling towards Moscow while Hopner's 4th Panzer Group attacks in the centre.

This may well be the Germans' last chance to take Moscow before "General Winter" takes an icy hand in this war. The Germans are happy that the frost has made the ground hard enough for their tanks and horses and men to operate, but if they cannot reach the shelter of Moscow within the next few weeks they will be forced to go onto the defensive [*see below*]. The initial reports of the fighting show that it is going to be much harder for them to take Moscow than seemed possible last month when panic gripped the city.

Tula has been turned into a strongpoint, and unless the Germans take this communications centre and its airfield they cannot complete their pincer movement. Stalin has put heart into the people of Moscow, and Zhukov has created an effective defence. With both sides desperately weary and apparently short of men and machines, Moscow's fate now hangs in the balance (→ 27).

How the onset of winter improves Russia's chances of survival

Moscow, 15 November
On the night of 6-7 November the frost which heralds the arrival of the Russian winter gripped the steppes of western Russia. The temperature plummeted, but overnight the mud which had bogged down the German thrust on Moscow for the past month vanished. Today, with light snow on the ground but under clear skies, the Germans were able to resume their offensive. Winter has restored the mobility of the German armies, but it has also brought a host of problems which are bound to grow worse.

The cold, far more intense than in western Europe – with temperatures of -40 degrees Fahrenheit (-40 Celsius) – affects everything. Tank and truck engines can only be started if fires are kept lit under the vehicles. Guns and vehicles become frozen in and can only be freed by chipping away at the ice with pickaxes. Weapons seize up because the oil in them freezes. Worse, only a small proportion of the German troops on the eastern front have been issued with winter clothing – a sign of the dangerous over-optimism with which Hitler and his generals were imbued at the start of the campaign. The result is that frostbite is rapidly increasing the sick list.

Soviet troops, on the other hand, especially the Siberian divisions passing through Moscow to the front, are used to these conditions. "General Winter" is an ally of the USSR, not Germany, and may yet deny Hitler Moscow (→ 13/12).

Crawling through snow: "General Winter" could be Germany's worst enemy.

1941

November

November

Su	Mo	Tu	We	Th	Fr	Sa
						1
2	3	4	5	6	7	8
9	10	11	12	13	14	15
16	17	18	19	20	21	22
23	24	25	26	27	28	29
30						

17. China: The Nationalist leader, Chiang Kai-shek, calls for the western democracies to take action against Japan.

17. Germany: After a series of arguments with *Luftwaffe* Field Marshal Erhard Milch, and disgraced by air failures in the east, the former air ace Ernst Udet commits suicide (→ 22).

18. Strokovo, USSR: In an act of tremendous heroism, 11 Red Army engineers hold up 20 German tanks.

18. Libya: The US M3 Stuart light tank has its first trials in action with the British Eighth Army, at the start of Operation Crusader, a major offensive against Rommel→.

19. Libya: The British army reaches Sidi Rezegh (→ 21).

20. Vichy: General Weygand is relieved of his posts in North Africa as a result of German pressure.

20. USSR: In the south, Rostov-on-Don falls to the Germans (→ 24).

20. Leningrad: Personal food rations in the besieged city are cut for the fifth time in two months (→ 1/12).

21. Ethiopia: Italian forces at Kulkaber surrender (→ 27).

21. Libya: New Zealand forces, crossing the border from Egypt, capture Fort Capuzzo (→ 22).

22. Breslau, Germany: The *Luftwaffe* air ace Werner Molders, flying to Udet's funeral, dies when his plane hits a factory chimney.

22. Washington: The secretary of state, Cordell Hull, says that all differences with Japan could be resolved if he could be convinced that their intentions were peaceful (→ 26).

22. Libya: South African troops clash with the 21st Panzer Division at Sidi Rezegh; the fighting here is some of the toughest of the Desert War so far.→

22. Atlantic: The British cruiser *Devonshire* sinks the German raider *Atlantis*, which has sunk 22 Allied ships totalling 145,697 tons.

Britain "ready for war with Japan"

London, 10 November

In a sombre reference to the Far Eastern danger, Churchill said today that should Japan become involved in war with the United States, a British declaration would follow "within the hour". The prime minister was speaking at the traditional Lord Mayor's Day banquet in the City of London.

He spoke of a powerful force of the Royal Navy ready for service in the Indian and Pacific oceans. It would be "a very hazardous adventure" for Japan to plunge into war with the US and the British Empire, which had three-quarters of the world's population (→ 20).

Paratroopers form an "SAS" Brigade

Cairo, 15 November

A "Special Air Service Brigade" which was formed in the summer has lost 32 out of 55 men in an attempted para-drop in a sandstorm. The targets – Rommel's airfields – are untouched. The leader, Captain David Stirling, who proposed the idea of the SAS Brigade in July, was retrieved by another special force, the Long Range Desert Group. The LRDG, formed 14 months ago, comprises pre-war desert explorers practising deep reconnaissance with special vehicles. Stirling wants a partnership with it after this debacle.

Auchinleck leads British desert offensive

Western Desert, 22 November

Operation Crusader, a bold new assault on Rommel, is now in its fifth day with the heaviest fighting in the Desert War so far at Sidi Rezegh.

Extensively re-equipped and reinforced for the new campaign, the Allied forces now have more than 700 tanks against Rommel's 320 and nearly 700 aircraft against 320 Axis planes. To Churchill's annoyance the new commander-in-chief, General Claude Auchinleck, refused to begin the offensive until all the new supplies had arrived.

The aim of Operation Crusader is to pin down Axis troops on the frontier, outflank them in the desert, and smash through Rommel's forces to link up with the Tobruk garrison 70 miles from the frontier.

At the start of the campaign the Allies had surprise on their side, and caught Rommel unawares planning his own attack on Tobruk. But yesterday British forces setting out from Sidi Rezegh for Tobruk were savagely hit from the south and east by two panzer divisions. At midday today the 21st Panzer Division struck at the western flank of the British position, over-running the airfield and leaving devastation and confusion by nightfall (→ 23).

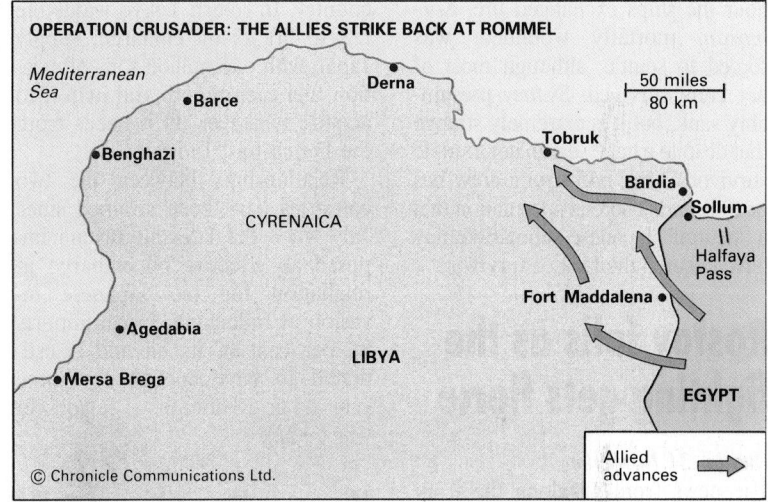

OPERATION CRUSADER: THE ALLIES STRIKE BACK AT ROMMEL

© Chronicle Communications Ltd.

Disastrous raid on Rommel headquarters

North Africa, 18 November

The order was "Get Rommel". In one of the most daring operations of this war, a small commando unit led by Lieut-Colonel Geoffrey Keyes landed by night on beaches behind the enemy lines. Their objective was a villa several miles inland used by the Germans as headquarters. Rommel – the "Desert Fox" – was to be captured or killed as the British launched a major offensive.

Several men were drowned in the heavy swell; the rest came ashore to rough, rainswept terrain.

As they approached the villa, a sentry who tackled the colonel had to be shot. All surprise was lost.

Opening one door, they found 12 Germans preparing for a fight. Keyes opened it again to throw in a grenade. He was shot dead. Most of the survivors were taken prisoner. Colonel Robert Laycock and one companion escaped back to the British lines. There they learnt that Rommel had been in Rome at the time of the raid (→ 19).

The "Desert Fox" with an officer.

German ship sinks Australian cruiser

Australia, 19 November

There was no reason for the cruiser HMAS *Sydney*, sailing off Shark Bay in Western Australia while heading home to Melbourne from escort duty, to suspect the freighter, which was flying the Dutch flag and carried the name *Streat Malakka*. It was not until the ships were within a mile of each other that the freighter hoisted the German ensign and opened fire: she was the *Kormoran*, an armed raider.

Sydney was hit within seconds, and her bridge and gunnery director tower badly damaged. For half an hour the ships exchanged fire. *Kormoran*, mortally wounded, was forced to scuttle, although most of her crew survived. *Sydney* presumably sank, but it is extremely strange that despite a huge search not a single survivor of her 645-strong crew has been found. There is speculation that a "neutral" Japanese submarine may have ensured the lack of survivors.

Rostov falls as the fighting gets fierce

Russia, 21 November

The news from all along the front is of furious German assaults and desperate Russian resistance. In the south Rostov-on-Don has been captured by von Kleist's *Panzers*, although the Red Army is regrouping in an attempt to reclaim the battered city. In the north the siege of Leningrad is biting hard. Despite an airborne evacuation there are still too many mouths to feed, and the Germans have cut the communications centre of Tikhvin, 120 miles (192 km) to the east.

Tula is still holding out, blocking Guderian's way to Moscow. Although the Germans are making some progress north of the city, the Russians are fighting with great tenacity. A Siberian division armed with T34 tanks has also joined the battle near Venev, 60 miles south of Moscow. The fortress of Sevastopol, the last Russian stronghold in the Crimea following the German breakthrough into the peninsula, has also fought off all attempts to penetrate its defences. It is becoming the Russian Tobruk (→24).

Roosevelt rejects Japanese peace terms

Washington, 21 November

The Roosevelt administration has rejected the latest proposals put forward by Saburo Kurusu, Japan's special envoy. The secretary of state, Cordell Hull, says that US acceptance would be tantamount to "aiding and abetting Japan in her efforts to create a Japanese hegemony in and over the western Pacific". Hopes of averting war have been weakened by Japan's warning that time for negotiations is limited.

New proposals from Japan's premier, Hideki Tojo, rule out the use of force by both sides and offer withdrawal from southern Indochina to the northern part of that country. In return Tokyo wants the US to lift its oil embargo, supply Japan with one million tons of aviation fuel each month and help it to acquire whatever oil it needs from the Dutch East Indies.

Relationships between the two countries have been strained since July when the US and Britain imposed an effective oil embargo in retaliation for the Japanese invasion of Indochina. Japan imports 88 per cent of its oil and is estimated to have enough for three years – or 18 months if it goes to war (→22).

Japan's Premier Tojo (bottom).

Young Brooke, at 58, heads British Army

General Sir Alan Brooke, CIGS.

London, 18 November

Winston Churchill has chosen General Sir Alan Brooke as the new Chief of the Imperial General Staff (CIGS). Brooke comes from a well-known Ulster Loyalist family whose home is in County Fermanagh. There is a well-established tradition of having a loyal Irishman as Britain's top soldier. The list includes Sir Henry Wilson, assassinated by the IRA in 1922, as well as Brooke's immediate predecessor, Sir John Dill.

General Brooke has a passion for innovation in military mobility, mechanization and gunnery. He commanded II Corps of the BEF in the Dunkirk withdrawal. On his return he took over from Lord Ironside as chief of the home defence forces, becoming responsible for leading resistance to invasion. Now aged 58, he is described by Dill as "a young man" who should have a chance to get on.

War clouds loom as America marks Thanksgiving Day

United States, 20 November

The spectre of a coming war hangs over America, but even as they listen to the latest news from the Atlantic, Britain, Germany and the Russian front and await the arrival on the west coast of Japan's special envoy, US citizens are buying their Thanksgiving Day turkeys and shopping early for Christmas. Holiday trade will be up five to 15 per cent over last year. But not all the economic news is rosy. Congress and the president are preparing anti-inflationary tax legislation, and Roosevelt is threatening a government takeover of the coal mines.

The president, in announcing that he will delay his planned trip to Georgia, blames the coalminers' strike, but insiders say that he wants to hear what Japan's special envoy, Saburo Kurusu, has to offer. There is not much optimism, given the tenor of recent statements by Japan's leaders in Tokyo.

President Roosevelt did get the Neutrality Act amended and he is hearing less and less from "America Firsters". One restaurant in New York removed a flag belonging to Charles A Lindbergh until, the owner states, "he comes to his senses".

A craven Churchill licks Roosevelt's boots: the German view.

1941
November

Su	Mo	Tu	We	Th	Fr	Sa
						1
2	3	4	5	6	7	8
9	10	11	12	13	14	15
16	17	18	19	20	21	22
23	24	25	26	27	28	29
30						

23. East Indies: By agreement with the Dutch government in exile, US troops occupy Dutch Guiana [*Surinam*] to guard the bauxite mines.

23. Libya: British and German forces clash on a wide front in the area between Sidi Rezegh and Bir el-Gubi (→ 24).

24. Libya: Rommel makes a "dash for the wire", an abortive attempt to outflank British forces attacking towards Tobruk; meanwhile, the British occupy the Axis supply depot at Garbut (→ 26).

24. USSR: The Germans evacuate Rostov-on-Don (→ 27).

24. Central Atlantic: The cruiser HMS *Dunedin* is sunk by the U-boat U124.

26. Libya: Lieutenant-General Ritchie takes over command of the British Eighth Army from Lieutenant-General Cunningham (→ 27).

26. Kurile Islands: The Japanese Pearl Harbor task force sets sail from Tankan Bay.→

27. Mediterranean: A U-boat sinks the Australian sloop *Paramatta* off Tobruk, killing 138 on board.

27. Copenhagen: Two days of riots follow the government's signing of the anti-Comintern pact in Berlin.

27. Libya: New Zealand forces link up with the besieged Tobruk garrison.→

27. Beirut: The Free French General Georges Catroux proclaims Lebanon's independence.

27. USSR: The Soviets reoccupy Rostov-on-Don (→ 30).

28. Ethiopia: The Italian commander, General Guglielmo Nasi, surrenders.

28. Libya: General von Ravenstein, the commander of the 21 *Panzer* division, becomes the first German general to fall into Allied hands (→ 1/12).

30. USSR: Field Marshal Gerd von Rundstedt is sacked as commander of Army Group South after abandoning Rostov-on-Don, in contravention of an order from Hitler never to withdraw.

German guns heard in middle of Moscow

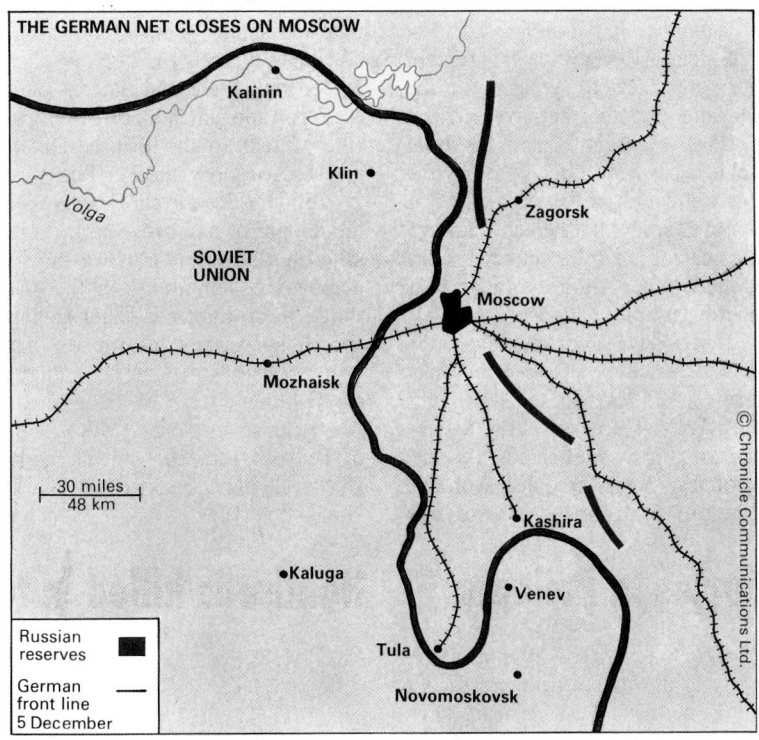

THE GERMAN NET CLOSES ON MOSCOW

Russian reserves ▪
German front line 5 December ▬

Moscow, 27 November
The sound of the guns from the battle raging in front of Moscow can be heard clearly in the capital tonight. The Germans are now only 25 miles (40 km) away. They have broadened the wedge that they have driven into the Russian forces northwest of the city and are claiming to have captured the town of Klin. They are, however, still being held at Tula, south of Moscow.

The seriousness of the situation is reflected in an order of the day broadcast to the Red Army today, urging the soldiers to hold on: "The enemy has advanced nearer to Moscow. The situation is increasingly difficult but we must, and can, stand the strain."

The order went on to say that Hitler is putting everything into his last thrust, which he hopes will bring him to the gates of the city, and, recalling the French at Verdun, it demanded: "You must fight to the last. The enemy shall not pass" (→ 5/12).

Russia protests at maltreatment of PoWs

Moscow, 25 November
Vyacheslav Molotov, the Soviet foreign minister, has sent an impassioned Note to all the non-Axis powers protesting against Germany's barbaric treatment of Russian prisoners of war.

Broadcasting from embattled Moscow, Mr Molotov claimed that "prisoners have been tortured with red-hot irons, their eyes have been poked out, and their ears and noses ripped open. They have been tied to tanks and pulled to pieces."

He went on to accuse the Germans of the systematic extermination of Russian prisoners by shooting, beating and starvation: "The German High Command has order-ed that Soviet prisoners shall be given worse and less food than prisoners of other countries. In the early morning, whatever their state of health, they are roused by blows with sticks and clubs and driven out to work. In one day alone in the Chernukhinsk camp in the Ukraine 95 prisoners were shot."

These appalling revelations are by no means the full story of German cruelty towards Russian prisoners. Many PoWs are being gassed in experiments to find the most efficient method of exterminating the Jews. Over 18,000 Russians have been killed at Sachsenhausen concentration camp alone since the invasion started (→ 21/12).

Rommel fights on in Western Desert

Western Desert, 30 November
As the Allies' Operation Crusader drags on into the 13th day, Rommel has finally succeeded in driving the 6th New Zealand Brigade off the Sidi Rezegh ridge, the scene of the worst fighting yet in the Desert War. He is now in an excellent position to disrupt the effective relief of Tobruk garrison – the principal aim of the operation. New Zealand troops linked up with forces from the garrison on 27 November.

Throughout the latest campaign Rommel has lived up to his reputation, with bold, offensive action in response to the Allied assault. On 24 November the German commander led his forces in a "dash for the wire", attempting to outflank the Allies heading for Tobruk. Having advanced some 60 miles in five hours, Rommel then turned back to rejoin units that were following on. Picked up by one of his senior commanders, General Cruwell, the "Desert Fox" found himself in the bizarre position of spending the night in a vehicle captured from the British, surrounded by enemy forces.

The next day Rommel discovered that further advance was impossible: the Italians bringing up the rear had been stopped by the 1st South African Brigade, and transport columns had not arrived. Delivered from this threat, the British then received a psychological boost with the replacement of Lt-Gen Cunningham, who had been urging retreat, by General Ritchie (→ 1/12).

General Ritchie, the new commander of Operation Crusader.

Far East tension at breaking point

Japan's Kurusu lands in the US.

Washington, 30 November
President Roosevelt is tonight hurrying back to Washington by car and private train from Warm Springs, Georgia, where his brief holiday has been interrupted by the grave situation in the Pacific. It was only yesterday that he left Washington, saying that the policy of the United States towards Japan was one of "infinite patience".

Three days ago Roosevelt delivered a ten-point note of final terms to the Japanese, after talks with Tokyo's special envoy, Saburu Kurusu, had foundered. At the same time a Japanese fleet with five divisions of troops on board was reported sailing south of Formosa. A cabinet meeting on 28 November agreed that these and other Japanese troop movements posted a "terrific" threat to the British, Dutch and Americans in the Far East.

President Roosevelt is aware of the danger of a surprise attack. He asked top advisers "how we should manoeuvre them into firing the first shot". In an informal Thanksgiving speech he warned his friends that by next year American boys might be fighting "for the defence of American institutions". More news of Tokyo's troop movements made Roosevelt hurry back to the White House (→ 1/12).

Location first for Coastal Command

Britain, 30 November
Today RAF Coastal Command has celebrated its first unaided U-boat sinking of the war (it has shared five with the Royal Navy). Bletchley Park intercepted an *Enigma* transmission and was able to locate U206 in the Bay of Biscay, heading for the Mediterranean. A Whitley from 502 Squadron was tasked to hunt for her. Its ASV RDF [radar] located the U-boat at a range of five miles, enabling the aircraft to home in on and destroy the sub with its Mark VIII depth charges. This is a triumph for both Bletchley Park and the ASV RDF.

Britain defeats Italian forces in Ethiopia

Gondar, Ethiopia, 27 November
The last Italian forces in Ethiopia have surrendered. After holding out for nine months, aided by the mountains and the rains, General Nasi's battle-hardened troops were overwhelmed today. The British have taken 11,500 Italian and 12,000 native troops prisoner.

Previous British assaults on Gondar had failed. Remembering only the collapse of Italian armies in mobile warfare in the deserts of Libya and Somalia, the British forgot the Italian infantryman's skill at positional warfare. At times, when the Italians were facing Ethiopian "Patriots" unsupported by air cover, they even advanced. After whittling away at the Italian defences for six days the 12th East African Division, under the redoubtable Major-General C C Fowkes, began its attack on a broad front early this morning, supported by the South African Air Force.

At 7,000 feet (2,134 metres) above sea level – in bitter cold – the King's African Rifles were advancing through clouds. By midday the battle had been decided, but there was almost a massacre when Ethiopian Patriots got into Gondar before the East Africans. Fowkes had to send in armoured cars to rescue the Italian prisoners (→ 28).

Hundreds killed in torpedoed battleship

HMS "Barham" is ripped apart by a salvo of torpedoes fired by U331.

Crete, 25 November
The U-boats claimed their second British battleship – the first was the *Royal Oak* at Scapa Flow in 1939 – at 4.29pm today. Admiral Cunningham had sailed from Alexandria to chase an Italian convoy. He brought up his three battleships to support the destroyers and cruisers in the Ionian Sea in case the enemy fleet attacked.

Baron von Tiesenhausen in U331 dived beneath the destroyer screen and fired a salvo of torpedoes at HMS *Barham* from a range of a few hundred yards. There were three direct hits, producing an explosion so violent that the U-boat was forced to the surface. Four minutes later there was a second explosion and the *Barham*, the flagship of the Fleet's second-in-command, Vice-Admiral Pridham-Wippell, sank. The captain and 858 crew perished. Amazingly, some survived.

HMS *Hotspur* hauled many of them on board. Lieutenant-Commander Hugh Hodgkinson described the scene: "Each man as he came over the side was black with oil. Bales of cotton waste were brought up from the store to clean them. The whole upper deck became layered with oil, so that one could hardly stand." One man, swimming by a raft to give weaker men a chance, was the last hauled up: "He put up an arm ... It seemed to be nothing but gold stripe, and I realized who it was. I never expected to receive an admiral on board in such circumstances."

After the final surrender: Italian prisoners are marched through Gondar.

1941

December

Su	Mo	Tu	We	Th	Fr	Sa
	1	2	3	4	5	6
7	8	9	10	11	12	13
14	15	16	17	18	19	20
21	22	23	24	25	26	27
28	29	30	31			

1. Leningrad: Eleven thousand people died from starvation last month (→ 31).

1. Lithuania: Colonel Karl Jaeger of the SS *Einsatzkommando* reports that his force has killed 230,000 Baltic Jews since June (→ 7).

1. Malta: The island has its 1,000th air raid.

2. Tokyo: The Premier, Hideki Tojo, publicly rejects US proposals for peace, and secretly orders the Pearl Harbor task force to "climb Mount Niitaka" – go into action against the US fleet (→ 4).

2. Libya: Rommel's troops recapture Sidi Rezegh to join the *Panzer* divisions previously cut off by the British (→ 8).

2. Singapore: The battleship HMS *Prince of Wales* and battle cruiser HMS *Repulse* arrive to boost the British colony's defences (→ 9).

3. USSR: General Walther von Reichenau succeeds von Rundstedt as commander of Army Group South.

4. China: A Japanese invasion force sails from Hainan and heads for Malaya (→ 5).

4. USSR: The Finns take Hango, and German Army Group Centre presses hard on the Moscow front (→ 5).

4. Moscow: Poland's exiled premier, General Wladyslaw Sikorski, signs a mutual assistance pact with Stalin.

5. Tokyo: Japan assures the USA that its build-up of troops in Indochina is a purely defensive measure (→ 6).

5. Rastenburg: Hitler halts the Moscow offensive because of bad weather. He also orders *Luftflotte 2* and *Fliegerkorps* II to be shifted from the eastern front to the Mediterranean.

5. USSR: The Soviets launch a major counter-offensive.→

6. Pacific: Japanese forces leave Palau for the Philippines.→

6. Mediterranean: The British submarine *Perseus* is sunk by a mine; one survivor escapes from a depth of 170 feet and swims ten miles to shore.

Women called up for Britain's war drive

Westminster, 4 December
Unmarried women are to be called up to serve in the police, fire services and armed forces under rules announced by the prime minister. Those affected are aged between 20 and 30. Married as well as single women up to the age of 40 are to register as available labour which might be directed to industry.

Mr Churchill describes the new arrangement as "another instalment of toil and sweat". The age of call-up for men is down to 18 years and six months, while those aged between 41 and 50 are also liable for armed service. Boys and girls aged 16 must register their names as a first step toward uniform, and boys aged 16 are being encouraged to join the Home Guard as cadets. As Mr Churchill sees it: "We must be careful that our boys do not run loose."

Single women with illegitimate or adopted children, and other special hardship cases, are exempt. Female conscientious objectors can claim exemption even though women do not serve in most combat units. Among men, lay preachers and farm workers are among those whose "reserved occupations" keep them out of uniform. Yet the potential pool of labour resulting from the new rules will contain nearly 1.7 million single women and 70,000 youths.

Germans fair game for French killers

Paris, 5 December
If Parisians thought December 1940 was bad – a city occupied, relatives in prison camps, meagre rations – this year looks like being worse. In addition there is now another problem – terrorism. The last 24 hours have seen a German officer shot by a cyclist on the Left Bank, a fusillade of shots at Germans at the *Porte d'Issy* and a bomb explosion in *Boulevard Blanqui*. For the Germans this means not sitting in the cafes' glass terraces; for Parisians it means body searches, queues and the continual demand for *papiers* (→ 15).

High-speed tanks dominate desert battle to relieve Tobruk

Western Desert, 1 December
As British, German and Italian tank formations clash from all directions in the brutal fight to relieve Tobruk, any resemblance between this battle and traditional warfare has long since disappeared. "This is sea warfare," said one general. "Our tanks are ships that appear and disappear at such speed that often no one knows where their lines are."

Today, though heavily outnumbered, Rommel cut the link between the Tobruk force and the New Zealanders at Belhamed. A planned counter-attack was foiled before it began, and the survivors retreated to the east and south.

British Cruiser tanks move forward to attack Axis troops in the Libyan desert.

Advertising in tune with the nation's wartime preoccupations.

Curtin cancels all Australian army leave

Canberra, 5 December
The Australian government today cancelled all army leave as the prospect of war with Japan grows more likely. Japanese convoys are on the move in Asia, and the only question now seems to be where, not whether, they will strike.

Allied forces have been brought to the first degree of readiness. Australian service chiefs have been summoned and the Australian war cabinet has issued orders for emergency measures in the Pacific.

However, Australia has the bulk of its army strength – three divisions – in North Africa and the Middle East. So far there is no question of their return, as the war cabinet does not believe that there is an immediate threat to Australia.

Meanwhile John Curtin, the Australian prime minister, is anxiously following the efforts of the United States to negotiate with the Japanese and thereby avert an extension of the European war to the Pacific. The government here wonders whether, if negotiations fail, the United States will take the lead in armed defence against Japanese aggression. Despite the links with Britain and the British base at Singapore, it is the Americans who are seen as potentially the major Allied power in the Pacific.

Soviet forces counter-attack Germans at Moscow

Soviet troops well-equipped for the freezing weather march through Moscow.

Russians go on the attack near Moscow, aiming to cut off the 4th Army.

Moscow, 6 December

The Russians have thrown a new army, secretly gathered behind Moscow, against the German forces attacking the capital, and have won a stunning victory against the exhausted, frozen Germans.

Only four days ago, a German reconnaissance battalion mounted on motor cycles drove into the northern suburbs, only 12 miles (19 km) from the Kremlin. It was pushed out by hastily-armed workers rushed to the spot. Some German tanks in another sector came within sight of Moscow's spires. This was to be the high tide of the Nazi assault.

Tonight the Germans are being driven back all along the front as the Red Army attempts to encircle the whole of the German 4th Army as it stands before Moscow. The Russians, well equipped and well fed, are advancing against an enemy ravaged by continuous fighting, shortage of supplies and the extreme cold.

The Germans do not have the correct oil in their tanks to cope with this weather and are lighting fires under the engines to start them. Their frozen machine guns are refusing to fire on automatic and their men are in full retreat.

They are being hammered by Russian ski troops, T34 tanks and Ilyushin I-62s, the armoured assault planes which are doing to the German army what the Stukas did

to the Poles and the French. In the north, the Germans are retreating along the single road through Klin, abandoning their heavy equipment. In the first day's fighting General Lelyushenko's Thirtieth Army has advanced some 11 miles (18 km) in this sector.

To the south, the defenders of Tula have turned into attackers, emerging from their strong points to strike at Guderian's tanks. A gap has opened between Guderian and von Kluge's 4th Army which General Zhukov is trying to exploit. The story is the same all along the 500-mile (800-km) front from Kalinin in the north to Yelets in the south. The Red Army is inflicting on the *Wehrmacht* its first great defeat. It is not being done without cost. The Russians are too eager to go over to the attack, and many of their assaults are made frontally against German strong points. Their casualties are very high and General Zhukov has issued a directive calling for outflanking tactics.

The counter-assault before Moscow is not the Red Army's only success. It has driven the Germans out of the ruins of Tikhvin, the supply town south-east of Leningrad, and reopened the precarious route to Lake Ladoga where lorries run the gauntlet of the ice.

These gains can be added to last month's great victory in the south, where Timoshenko retook Rostov-on-Don (→13).

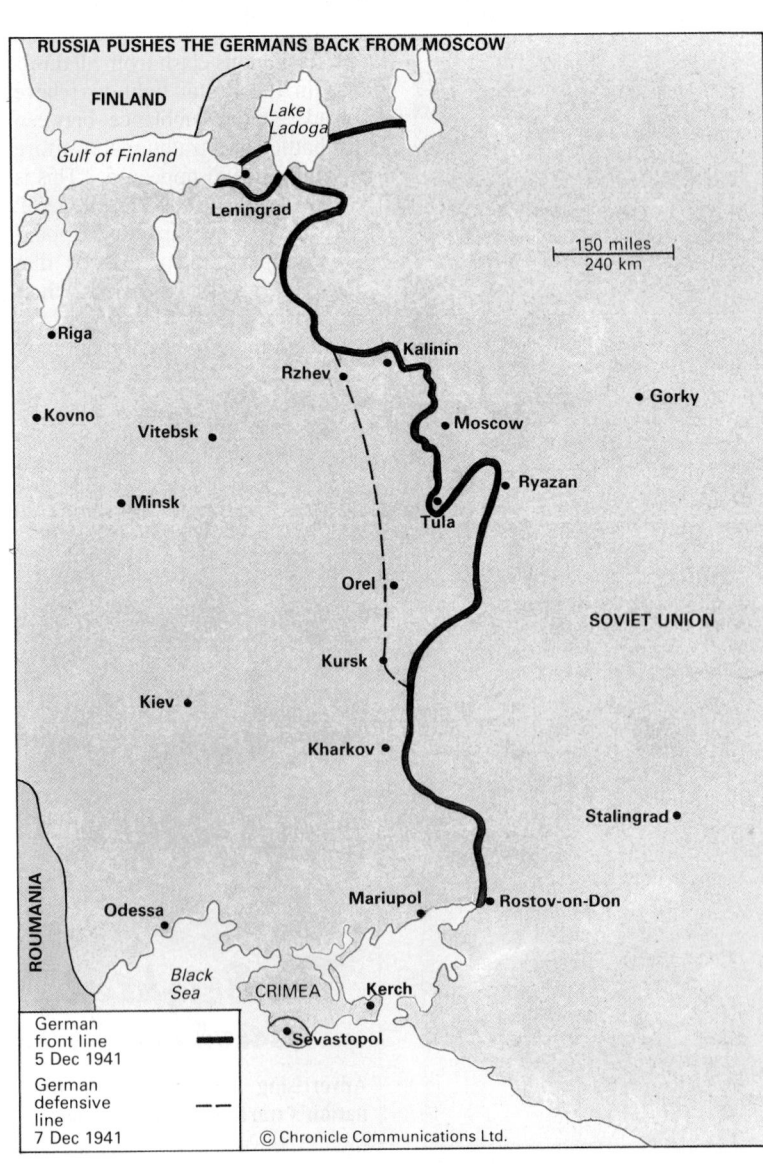

RUSSIA PUSHES THE GERMANS BACK FROM MOSCOW

FINLAND
Lake Ladoga
Gulf of Finland
Leningrad
150 miles
240 km
Riga
Kalinin
Rzhev
Gorky
Kovno
Vitebsk
Moscow
Ryazan
Minsk
Tula
Orel
SOVIET UNION
Kursk
Kiev
Kharkov
Stalingrad
ROUMANIA
Mariupol
Rostov-on-Don
Odessa
Black Sea
CRIMEA
Kerch
German front line 5 Dec 1941
German defensive line 7 Dec 1941
Sevastopol
© Chronicle Communications Ltd.

Roosevelt asks Hirohito to prevent war

Washington, 6 December
President Roosevelt has sent an urgent personal note to the emperor of Japan "because of the deep and far-reaching emergency". The president, who is pessimistic about the danger of war in the Pacific, stressed that it was only because of the extraordinary importance to both countries that he addressed himself to the emperor rather than to his ministers.

A year ago Japan reached an agreement with Vichy by which between 5,000 and 6,000 Japanese soldiers were to be based in French Indochina. In recent weeks, Roosevelt said, Japanese military, naval and air forces have been sent to south-east Asia in such force that it was reasonable for the people of the East Indies, Malaya, Thailand and the Philippines to fear attack.

Mr Roosevelt said that both he and the emperor had "a sacred duty to restore traditional amity and prevent future death and destruction". He expressed the "fervent hope" that the emperor would help to dispel "the dark clouds".

"This son of man has just sent his final message to the Son of God," the president told some guests in

Emperor Hirohito: "Son of God".

the White House. And when tonight he received a Japanese reply to an earlier American proposal, he told his friend and aide Harry Hopkins: "This means war" (→ 7).

Malaya declares a state of emergency

Singapore, 1 December
All British, Indian and Australian forces in Malaya are at battle stations following the declaration of a state of emergency as fear of a Japanese invasion grows. Reservists and volunteers have been called up, forcing many offices to close. The decision was taken by the governor of the Straits Settlements, Sir Shen-ton Thomas, after consultations with the Commander-in-Chief Far East, Air Chief Marshal Sir Robert Brooke-Popham. They emphasize that the state of emergency does not signify a deterioration in the diplomatic situation. Singapore will also be reinforced by the warships *Prince of Wales* and *Repulse* in the next few days (→ 10).

Britain declares war on more countries

London, 6 December
Britain today reluctantly declared war on the country which, only two years ago, she was planning to defend. When the Germans invaded the Soviet Union, Finnish forces joined in; for the past five months Britain has been appealing to the Finns to withdraw.

Stalin recently stepped up the pressure on Britain to declare war on Hitler's three little satellites, Finland, Hungary and Roumania.

They were given a deadline, which expires at midnight.

Though Finland now becomes an enemy, the hundreds of Finnish merchant seamen serving aboard British ships will be offered the option of remaining in service or being interned. Other Finns, along with Hungarian and Roumanian nationals, have been ordered to report to the police. Those regarded as unreliable will be sent to internment camps (→ 7).

1941
December

Su	Mo	Tu	We	Th	Fr	Sa
	1	2	3	4	5	6
7	8	9	10	11	12	13
14	15	16	17	18	19	20
21	22	23	24	25	26	27
28	29	30	31			

7. Hawaii: Japan launches air attacks on Pearl Harbor, Guam and Wake Island; its navy bombards Midway Island.→

7. Kolo, Poland: Seven hundred Jews are deported to nearby Chelmno.→

8. Manila: Japan smashes the US airbase at Clark Field (→ 10).

8. Thailand: Simultaneously with the attack on Pearl Harbor, on the other side of the international dateline, Japan invades. The Thai government surrenders (→ 12).

8. Hong Kong: Japanese aircraft destroy the five planes on the RAF Kowloon airfield.→

8. China: Japan occupies the foreign concessions at Shanghai, Gulang Island and Tianjin (→ 9).

8. Rastenburg: Hitler admits that the eastern *Blitzkrieg* has failed and orders his generals to prepare for a long struggle.

8. Libya: The Allies retake Sidi Rezegh and begin to relieve the garrison at Tobruk and raise the siege of the port.→

9. China: The Nationalist government declares war on Japan, Germany and Italy.

10. Philippines: Japanese forces land in northern Luzon and start to build air bases.→

10. Malaya: Japanese aircraft sink the British battleship *Prince of Wales* and battle cruiser *Repulse*.→

10. Pacific: Japan takes Guam.

11. USA: After receiving declarations of war from Italy and Germany, Roosevelt declares war on them.

12. USSR: The Red Army forces Guderian back from Stalinogorsk.→

12. Thailand: Japanese troops infiltrate Burma.→

13. Borneo: Indian troops destroy oil installations in Sarawak and Brunei (→ 16).

13. Mediterranean: In a brilliant night action, the British ships *Legion*, *Sikh* and *Maori* and the Dutch *Isaac Sweers* sink two Italian cruisers off Cape Bon.

Moscow: Germans blame the winter

Moscow, 13 December
The Germans have admitted that they have been defeated before Moscow, but they are blaming it on the weather rather than the Red Army. "The army", said Berlin tonight, "does not expect to capture Moscow this year. Major campaigning must be suspended until the spring. Then Moscow can be taken ..." "Officers and men trying to take cover freeze to the ground," said a spokesman. "Fighting under these conditions is practically impossible. We have no reason to expose our troops to the terrible rigours of the Russian winter" (→ 19).

Australians holding Tobruk are relieved

Tobruk, 10 December
The Allied garrison at Tobruk has today been finally relieved, some 18 days after the start of Operation Crusader which has been masterminded by Sir Claude Auchinleck.

This vital Mediterranean port was taken from the Italians in January this year by General Wavell's forces. Since April it has been held by the 7th Australian Division, and some 32,667 troops, 34,000 tons of supplies, 7,516 wounded and 7,097 Axis PoWs have been ferried in and out of the harbour (→ 18).

Nazis use gas vans for mass killings

Chelmno, Poland, 8 December
In what could be a new stage in the much-discussed Nazi programme to annihilate the Jews, all the 700 Jews evacuated here from Kolo have been murdered.

In groups of 80, they were loaded into the back of a van. The exhaust pipe led straight into their compartment; the fumes suffocated them all. The van reached a wood where it disgorged its grisly contents. The corpses' gold teeth and fillings were extracted with pliers. Their clothes and jewellery having been removed, the dead Jews were thrown into a mass grave (→ 15).

Japanese planes destroy US fleet at Pearl Harbor

The "Arizona" goes down in a pall of smoke after her magazine exploded: 2,403 American servicemen lost their lives in the devastation at Pearl Harbor.

Honolulu, 8 December
The message was simple and stark: "AIR RAID, PEARL HARBOR. THIS IS NO DRILL."

Japan's devastating opening blow of the Pacific war against the United States came plunging out of a sunny Hawaiian sky yesterday when 184 aircraft from six Japanese aircraft carriers of Vice-Admiral Chuichi Nagumo's Strike Force caught the American defenders completely unawares at Pearl Harbor, Oahu, at 7.55am [*local time*].

Japanese spies had reported that the Pacific Fleet was almost certain to be in Pearl Harbor on a Sunday morning. They were right. Eighty-six warships of the fleet were spread out before the eager eyes of the Japanese pilots. They included seven battleships – the prime targets in the absence of carriers –

moored close to each other in "Battleship Row", and another, the *Pennsylvania*, in dry dock.

This audacious operation, designed to neutralize the Pacific Fleet in one blow, succeeded in sinking four battleships in a total of 19 warships sunk or disabled. It destroyed 188 military aircraft and damaged 159, and killed 2,403 Americans, 1,000 of them in the battleship *Arizona* which blew up and sank at her mooring early in the attack. For the battle force of the US Pacific Fleet it was the hour of doom.

Japanese losses were light. Only 29 Japanese aircraft failed to make it back to the carriers, and one Japanese I-class submarine and five midget submarines were sunk.

Such a spectacular victory on the first day of war has no parallel in the history of warfare. In Washing-

ton today, President Roosevelt described the Japanese action as "a day that will live in infamy".

The six Japanese carriers, *Akagi, Kagi, Hiryu, Soryu, Zuikaku* and *Shokaku*, had met in late November at Tankan Bay in the Kuriles and with naval escort, approached in great secrecy to the flying-off position 275 miles north of Hawaii.

The first attacking wave comprised 50 high-level bombers, 40 planes carrying shallow-running torpedoes, 51 dive-bombers and 43 Zero fighters. Their approach was detected by army radar at a distance of 132 miles, but they were thought to be friendly planes.

By 7.40am the Japanese strike force was over Oahu, and 15 minutes later the attack began with dive-bombers blasting the army, navy and marine airfields to neu-

tralize American air power so that the attack on warships could proceed without interference.

The torpedo planes, high-level and dive-bombers attacked the warships initially without any opposition whatever. Amid the roar of engines and the crash of bombs, they turned Pearl Harbor into a smoke-filled inferno of blazing, exploding warships and installations.

At 8.30am a lull developed, but within 45 minutes a second strike force of 176 planes launched its attack. They withdrew by 10am and the raid was over. The big disappointment for the Japanese was the absence of the aircraft carriers of the Pacific Fleet which were on manoeuvres at the time of the raid. By this action alone, the Japanese have proved the value of big carriers in any naval campaign (→9).

'Day of infamy': Japanese attacks bring global war

Under a sky black as Judgement Day, Americans try to extinguish the fires.

As the fires rage and their ship sinks, men pour off the USS "California".

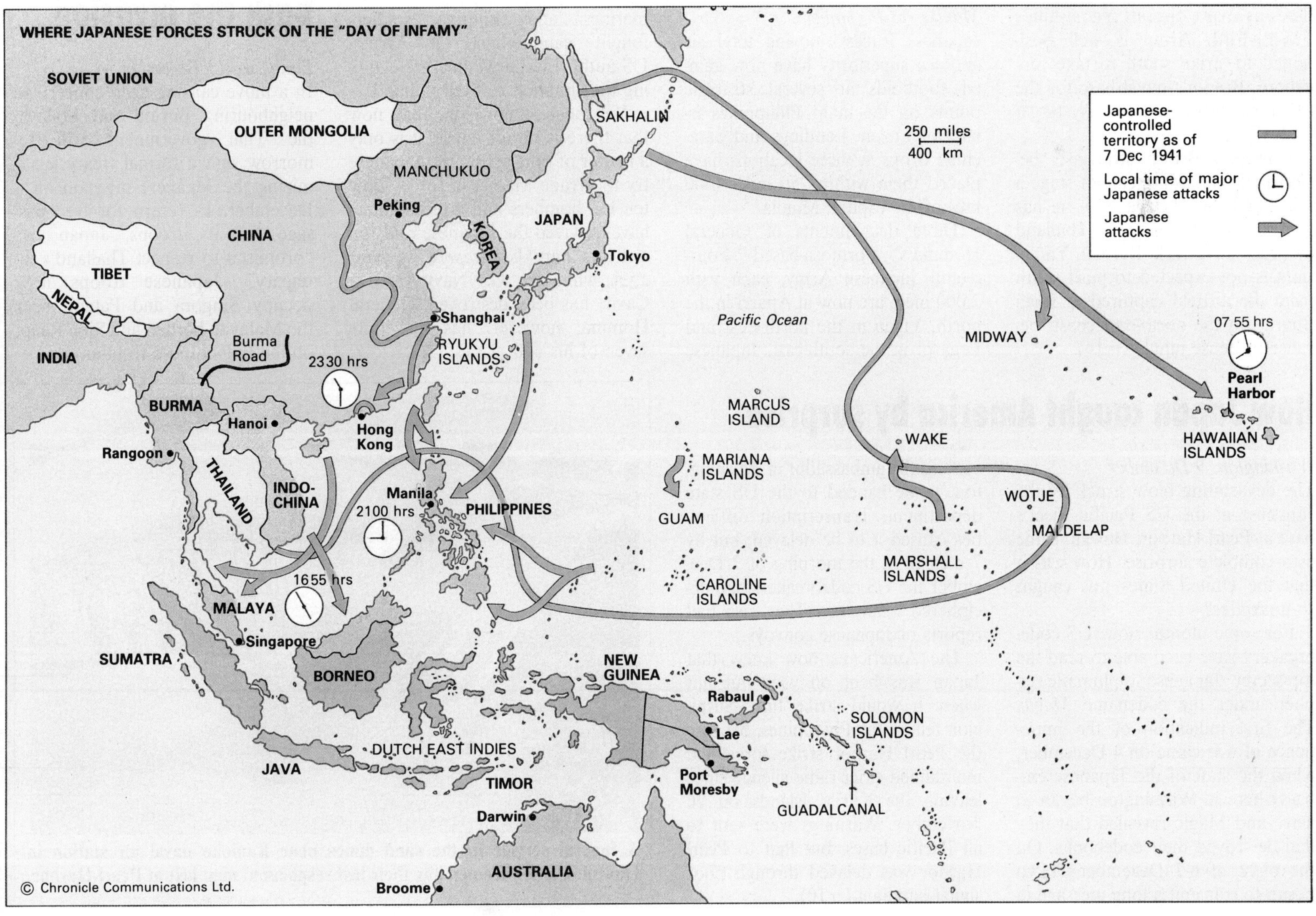

WHERE JAPANESE FORCES STRUCK ON THE "DAY OF INFAMY"

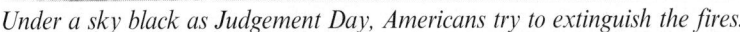

SOVIET UNION

OUTER MONGOLIA

MANCHUKUO

Peking •

CHINA

TIBET

NEPAL

INDIA

Burma
Road

BURMA

Rangoon •

Hanoi •

THAILAND

INDO-
CHINA

KOREA

JAPAN

Tokyo •

• Shanghai

RYUKYU
ISLANDS

2330 hrs

Hong
Kong

Manila

2100 hrs

PHILIPPINES

MALAYA

1655 hrs

• Singapore

SUMATRA

BORNEO

JAVA

DUTCH EAST INDIES

TIMOR

Darwin •

Broome •

AUSTRALIA

NEW
GUINEA

Rabaul •

• Lae

Port
Moresby

SOLOMON
ISLANDS

GUADALCANAL

Pacific Ocean

MARCUS
ISLAND

MARIANA
ISLANDS

GUAM

CAROLINE
ISLANDS

SAKHALIN

MIDWAY

WAKE

WOTJE

MALDELAP

MARSHALL
ISLANDS

07 55 hrs

Pearl
Harbor

HAWAIIAN
ISLANDS

Legend:
Japanese-
controlled
territory as of
7 Dec 1941

Local time of major
Japanese attacks

Japanese
attacks

250 miles
400 km

© Chronicle Communications Ltd.

Japanese forces fan out across the Pacific Ocean

Malaya: invaders push southwards

Malaya, 13 December
Five days after their first suprise landings Japanese forces now control northern Malaya's two key airfields, following the capture today of Alor Star on Malaya's northwest coast. The town was taken by Japanese troops advancing across the Thai isthmus from Singora, in south-east Thailand, the site of major landings five days ago.

Japan's commander, General Yamashita, now has overwhelming air and sea superiority following the sinking of four of the six ships in the British Far East Fleet, including the battle cruiser *Repulse* and the battleship *Prince of Wales* with the loss of 840 lives three days ago [*see report on page 252*]. With four times as many aircraft Yamashita's Twenty-Fifth Army is well positioned to strike south to take Singapore, Britain's naval base for the Far East, inside the 100-day target set by Tokyo.

However, British strategists believe that Yamashita cannot stage a full attack on Malaya until he has consolidated his forces in Thailand in order to attack Burma. Yamashita is not expected to push south from the airfield captured at Kota Bharu, on the north-east coast, because of dense jungle (→ 14).

Japanese marines wade ashore on the island of Luzon in the Philippines.

Philippines: air battles go Japan's way

Manila, 13 December
Japanese forces enjoying total air and sea superiority have now gained footholds at several strategic points on the main Philippines island of Luzon. Landings and parachute drops at three locations have placed them within 250 miles (400 km) of the capital, Manila.

Three detachments of General Homma's Formosa-based Fourteenth Japanese Army, each with 2,000 men, are now at Aparri in the north, Vigan in the north-west and Legaspi in the south-east. Japanese marines and Filipino soldiers fought hand-to-hand at Aparri. US authorities in Manila are claiming the situation is "well in hand".

Yet most acknowledge that, now that there is no air cover, it is only a matter of time before the Japanese try to invade Manila in force. Only ten US bombers and a few fighters have survived the Japanese raids on airfields here [*see report on page 252*], while the US Navy yard at Cavite has been destroyed. General Homma, however, has lost only seven of his 490 planes.

Hong Kong: island comes under siege

Hong Kong, 13 December
Britain's Crown Colony is in a full state of siege following the evacuation today of the last British, Canadian and Indian troops from the mainland across the harbour to Hong Kong Island after five days of fighting. The decision to evacuate came after the Japanese 38th Division broke through the last mainland line of defence, the reinforced redoubt known as the Gindrinkers' Line. Hong Kong lost its limited air force in the first few hours of the conflict and has been hit by incessant air bombardment since (→ 20).

Thailand: leaders back the invasion

Bangkok, 13 December
In a move causing deep concern to neighbouring Burma and Malaya, the Thai government will tomorrow sign a formal treaty legitimizing the Japanese invasion on 8 December. In return for free passage for its troops, Japan has "promised to respect Thailand's integrity". Japanese troops now occupy Singora and Patani, near the Malayan border, and Sien Reap, on the Indochinese frontier.

How Japan caught America by surprise

Washington, 9 December
The devastating blow struck by the Japanese at the US Pacific Fleet's base at Pearl Harbor, Hawaii, came as a complete surprise. How was it that the United States was caught so unawares?

For some months now, US codebreakers have been able to read the top-secret Japanese diplomatic cipher under the codename *Magic*. The first indication of the imminence of war came on 4 December, when the staff of the Japanese embassy here in Washington began to leave and Magic revealed that they had destroyed their codebooks. On the night of 6-7 December Tokyo began to transmit a long message in code to the ambassador in Washington, to be handed to the US state department. Transcription difficulties caused it to be delayed, but by 7 o'clock in the morning of 7 December the US codebreakers had deciphered it anyway. They also had reports of Japanese convoys.

The Americans now knew that Japan was bent on war, but not *where* it would strike first. Suspicion fell on the Philippines, because the Pearl Harbor strike force had maintained strict radio silence since leaving the Kurile Islands on 26 November. Warnings were sent to all Pacific bases, but that to Pearl Harbor was delayed through poor signal handling (→ 10).

A funeral service in the sand dunes near Kanioke naval air station in Hawaii: US servicemen pay their last respects to men lost at Pearl Harbor.

United States declares war on Japan

Washington, 8 December
In just eight minutes President Roosevelt today called on the Congress of the United States to declare war on Japan. It took a further 20 minutes for congressmen to vote America into the world conflict.

The president called yesterday – the day that Japanese carrier-borne aircraft attacked the Pearl Harbor naval base without warning, killing 2,403 people – "a day that will live in infamy".

The Senate passed the war resolution without debate by 82 votes. In the House of Representatives it passed by 388 votes to one. The sole dissenter was Jeanette Rankin of Montana, who also voted against the declaration of war in 1917. The resolution was then signed by Vice-President Henry Wallace as presiding officer of the Senate, and by Sam Rayburn, the speaker of the House, and taken by them to the White House, where the president signed it at 5.10pm Washington time.

The United States as a whole has learnt above all from the radio of the coming of war. Stations kept open all night, and recorded dance music was punctuated with appeals for Red Cross workers to report to headquarters, or for volunteers to contact air-raid wardens. After two years of remote but often angry de-

Wearing a black armband, Roosevelt signs America's declaration of war.

bate about the possibility the United States is united as never before by the prospect of war. Diplomats and members of Congress agree that the Japanese, by attacking the US fleet at Pearl Harbor, have taken the one action, out of many alternatives available to them, that was certain to bring the United States into the war. Isolationism, the dominant philosophy here since 1919, is dead.

The isolationist Republican Congressman Hamilton Fish said today

that he would volunteer for service, as he did in 1917. Herbert Hoover former president, also an isolationist, said: "We must fight with everything we have got." Only the arch-isolationist Senator Gerald Nye of North Dakota continued to say: "The Japanese attack is just what Britain planned for us."

But the isolationist *Chicago Tribune* said that its readers must "strike with all our might to protect and preserve American freedom" (→ 13).

Americans rush to enlist as US prepares to join Allies at war

Washington, 13 December
Shocked by the perfidy of the the attack of Pearl Harbor, Americans are flocking to volunteer for the United States Navy and the Marine Corps, which do not take conscripts. In the meantime the US Army has already grown almost tenfold since the Selective Service Act introduced conscription, known here as the "draft", in 1940.

In September 1939 the US Army's strength was only 174,000 men, less than Portugal. The Burke-Wadsworth Act of June 1940 provided for a year of training for 1.4 million men.

Some concern has been expressed about the poor physical condition of conscripts, especially those from the industrial regions and southern states.

Conscripts swell the ranks of the US Army after the carnage at Pearl Harbor.

Britain throws its hat in the ring to fight the Japanese

London, 8 December
A special session of parliament was held today to hear the prime minister explain Britain's declaration of war against the Japanese empire. Churchill told MPs that he had intended to time Britain's declaration to follow America's, which required the approval of Congress.

But then news reached London of a Japanese landing in Malaya. The cabinet at once approved the declaration, which was delivered to the Japanese envoy at 1pm today. In his broadcast tonight, the prime minister gave a warning that the extension of the war will lead to a shortage of warplanes for the next few months.

The war becomes ever more universal

Chungking, 9 December
After Britain's declaration of war on Finland, Roumania and Hungary earlier this week, and with the seismic events of two days ago bringing the US and the British Empire into direct confrontation with Japan, China's formal declaration of war today on Japan, Germany and Italy serves to emphasise how truly the conflict may be described as a second *world* war.

Churchill says US aid will be decisive

London, 11 December
"We have a very hard period to go through," Winston Churchill told MPs in a report on the new situation created by the Japanese attacks on US and British possessions in the Far East. But within a few months the flow of munitions and aid from the US "will vastly exceed anything that could have been expected on the peacetime basis that has ruled up to the present". Then, he said, Britain, the US and the Soviet Union would teach the "gangs and cliques of wicked men" a lesson that would not be forgotten in a thousand years.

▷

US planes hit in new "surprise" attack

Battles girdle the globe

On board a Japanese carrier, preparing to give the Americans a nasty surprise.

Manila, 10 December
In another disastrous reverse for America, Japanese naval aircraft have destroyed half the US Far East Air Force in the Philippines.

Despite the shock of Pearl Harbor, the Americans were once again taken by surprise. Several warnings had been sent to General Douglas MacArthur, the US commander in the islands, but US headquarters vacillated. For example, it refused the air commander, General Brereton, permission to launch a pre-emptive strike against Japanese air

bases in Formosa – which might have prevented the attack.

The Japanese pilots were delighted to find the American aircraft laid out, as if for inspection, on the runways at Clark, Ibu and Nicholls Fields. It took them under half an hour to ensure that Japan will have the air superiority needed for the invasion of the Philippines. Meanwhile, the Japanese third air division mounted "extermination" raids on RAF airfields in northern Malaya. On the first day, half Britain's air strength was lost (→ 20).

London, 11 December
Hitler was at his Wolf's Lair underground HQ near Rastenburg, in East Prussia, when he was told of the Japanese attack on Pearl Harbor. "Now it is impossible for us to lose the war," he cried in delight. Churchill, dining at Chequers, said when *he* heard the news: "So we have won after all!" The Fuhrer's thoughts were on Japan's formidable armed forces; Churchill was thinking of America's immense economic power, very nearly equal to that of the rest of the world put together.

The Japanese attack turned the fighting in Europe into a world war. But the United States is the only nation capable of fighting a global war, by deploying full-scale land, sea and air forces in two hemispheres according to an overall strategic plan coordinated with Britain, the Empire and the Soviet Union.

British and American agents, busily probing the secrets of the Axis powers, had failed to discover any joint war plans. There are none. The Germans fight one war and the Japanese fight another, and they do nothing to maximize their strength by cooperation. As Churchill said last week, Britain is very fortunate that the Japanese did not attack its Far East possessions "in our period of weakness after Dunkirk". The Japanese High Command evidently

Hitler: sure that victory will be his.

hopes that, with the conquest of South-east Asia and vast areas of the South Pacific, the Americans will be unwilling to pay the price of dislodging them. But since the US is resolved to fight, the Japanese are committed to sitting it out until the Americans are ready to attack.

Similarly, in Europe, with Hitler's armies bogged down in the Soviet Union and no longer able to threaten Britain, Germany, too, must await the moment – and place – when the Anglo-Saxons choose to attack.

Britain loses its two Pacific battleships in Japanese air attack

Warship survivors recall the sinkings

Far East, 10 December
Three days after the shock of Pearl Harbor, Allied naval power has suffered another catastrophic blow with the sinking of the battleship HMS *Prince of Wales* (35,000 tons) and the battle cruiser HMS *Repulse* (26,500 tons) in the South China Sea. It took 88 Japanese aircraft less than two hours to destroy the only two effective Allied warships left in the Pacific; 840 men died.

Without an aircraft carrier to provide air cover, Admiral Sir Tom Phillips was relying on the RAF at Singapore to provide fighter escort. But Japan's assault on Malaya tied up the RAF and denied them two airfields from which they might have operated. Then the ships were seen by a Japanese submarine (→ 11).

Two survivors: "Repulse's" Captain Tennant and chaplain Canon Bezzant.

Off Malaya, 11 December
The *Repulse* and the *Prince of Wales* were heading for Singapore when they were attacked by Japanese aircraft. One of the *Repulse's* survivors describes the end: "The *Prince of Wales* is hardly distinguishable in smoke and flame ... I can see one plane release a torpedo ... It explodes against her bows. A couple of seconds later another explodes amidships and astern." Immediately after this the *Repulse*, too, was hit and the men plunged into oil-filled water. A destroyer later picked up the lucky ones: "We were stripped, bathed and left naked ... to sweat the oil out of the pores in the great heat."

1941

December

Su	Mo	Tu	We	Th	Fr	Sa
	1	2	3	4	5	6
7	8	9	10	11	12	13
14	15	16	17	18	19	20
21	22	23	24	25	26	27
28	29	30	31			

14. Malaya: Japanese forces land in Penang and Gurun.→

14. Mediterranean: The cruiser HMS *Galatea* is sunk by the U-boat U557 off Alexandria.→

15. Paris: The Germans execute the Communist leader, Gabriel Peri, and 100 hostages.

15. USSR: The Russians recapture Klin and push on to Kalinin (→16).

15. Simferopol, Crimea: In three days, *Einsatzkommandos* have killed 14,300 Jews (→16).

15. Libya: The British 8th Army attacks Rommel's position at Gazala.→

15. Atlantic: HMAS *Nestor* sinks the U-boat U127 off Cape St Vincent.

16. USSR: The Red Army captures Kalinin from the German Ninth Army (→20).

16. Borneo: The Japanese land at Miri and Seria; they meet little opposition, but find the oil fields sabotaged (→18).

16. Cracow: Governor Hans Frank says: "We must annihilate the Jews wherever we find them" (→5/1).

17. Mediterranean: Admiral Philip Vian engages the Italian Fleet off Sirte in an inconclusive battle.→

17. USA: Chester Nimitz succeeds Husband Kimmel as Admiral of the Pacific Fleet.

18. Borneo: The Japanese destroyer *Shinomone* is sunk by a mine (→23).

19. USSR: Field Marshal Gunther von Kluge succeeds Fedor von Bock as C-in-C of Hitler's Army Group North.

19. Tripoli: The cruiser HMS *Neptune* and destroyer HMS *Kandahar* are sunk when they sail into a minefield.→

20. Kunming, China: The US Flying Tiger volunteer group of the Chinese air force downs ten Japanese bombers in its first engagement.

20. USSR: The Red Army liberates Volokolamsk (→5/1).

20. Washington: Admiral Ernest King is appointed C-in-C of the US fleet.

British Mediterranean fleet smashed

Mediterranean, 19 December
The Royal Navy is reeling from a series of heavy blows which have left senior admiralty figures contemplating total withdrawal from the Mediterranean.

The sinking by a U-boat torpedo of the cruiser *Galatea*, near Alexandria, was the beginning of the present difficulties. Two days later, Axis aircraft attacked the four cruisers and sixteen destroyers escorting the supply ship *Breconshire* on one of her many trips to Malta.

Yesterday evening the convoy ran straight into an enemy convoy heading for Benghazi. The Italians opened fire, but beat a retreat when the British mounted a counterattack. Tragedy struck early this morning after the *Breconshire* had been delivered to Malta: the escorts sailed into a minefield. The cruiser *Neptune* was sunk, the destroyer *Kandahar*'s stern has been blown off, and the cruisers *Penelope* and *Aurora* have been damaged.

Meanwhile, in Alexandria harbour, Italian frogmen used midget submarines to blow up the battleships *Queen Elizabeth* and *Valiant*, a destroyer and a tanker. Admiral Cunningham's Mediterranean fleet is much the weaker tonight.

A midget submarine used by the Italians to fix mines on Allied shipping.

Rommel is pushed into Libyan retreat

Libya, 19 December
Allied troops of the 4th Indian Division today added Derna to the list of towns captured since the Eighth Army launched Operation Crusader barely a month ago. Rommel signalled the retreat on 16 December after the Allies attacked his defensive line at Gazala.

A counter-attack by *Panzers* had bought time, but only at a price: Rommel was left with fewer than 40 tanks for the *Afrika Korps* against nearly 200 for the Eighth Army. He decided to move a long way back – into Cyrenaica – in order to await reinforcements from a secure position. By the time Britain's 4th Armoured Brigade began the pursuit, Rommel and his Italian allies were well on their way.

The Afrika Korps and the Italian Mobile Corps are heading west by an inland desert route, while the Italian infantry divisions have marched along the coastal road. Like the vanquished, the British are also running short of supplies: a large proportion of their forces is in danger of being stalled for lack of petrol. In fact, both sides are weary after a month of bloody fighting, never more so than at Sidi Rezegh and at Tobruk, the main prize of this campaign to date (→24).

Princesses Elizabeth and Margaret Rose shall go to the ball

Britain, 19 December
Some two hundred troops watched the heir to the throne and her sister perform in a royal pantomime of *Cinderella* today. The show, "somewhere in England", was in aid of the Royal Household wool fund.

Margaret Rose was the star as a pretty little Cinders, while Elizabeth was her dashing Prince Charming. Accompanied by a military orchestra, the princesses sang many of the old favourites, inviting the audience to join in the choruses. The pumpkin-turned-carriage was a sedan chair used by Queen Anne.

The rest of the cast was made up of children from the local village, all of whom had been coached by the local schoolmaster. Buttons, played by the brother of one of Queen Elizabeth's maids, was singled out for special praise.

Cinderella learns to use a fan while Prince Charming banters with a courtier.

German troops need warmer clothes

Teenagers called up as Roosevelt gains war powers

Berlin, 20 December

The propaganda minister, Josef Goebbels, appealed to the German people yesterday to hand over their warm clothing so that it can be sent to the freezing soldiers in Russia.

He made no admission that Hitler had expected Russia to crumble to defeat before the snows came and had therefore not issued winter kit to the army. Instead, he insisted that winter had come early and was more than normally severe.

The authorities had done everything possible to provide ample equipment, he said, "using the last available transport to send enormous quantities of equipment even to the front line. But despite all these preparations the troops still need a lot more things."

He added: "Those at home will not deserve a single peaceful hour if even one soldier is exposed to the rigours of winter without adequate clothing."

Goebbels's appeal is widely discussed in the German press today. One newspaper says: "The strict clothes rationing of the past few years has not made it possible for us to have any clothing to spare. We have no surplus and we must therefore give away what we ourselves need. We must expect to shiver because of the soldiers' needs." The

Grimacing with the cold in Russia.

Nazi Party newspaper *Volkischer Beobachter* argues: "Hitler does not make it easy for us; but we do not ask why you should surrender what you so badly need yourself. Be grateful you are not at Smolensk, Minsk or Vyazma."

All this does little for the German soldier in those places. Propaganda pictures show him healthy and smiling in a steam bath. The reality is that he is infested with lice because it is too cold for him to wash. Sentries who fall asleep

Goebbels: covering up for Hitler.

freeze to death. The roads are littered with frozen horses.

In order to try to correct this shambles brought about by Hitler's overweening confidence, the Germans have placed huge orders for wooden huts, fur-lined overcoats, skis and snow-shoes.

Skis, sweaters and blankets have been seized in Norway and the Baltic states. Soon a soldier somewhere in Russia's frozen wastes will be wearing a fur coat that once belonged to a Berlin *Hausfrau.*

Washington, 19 December

America is rolling up its sleeves. The bill giving President Roosevelt extraordinary war powers passed both Houses of Congress today.

As well as lowering the minimum age for military service from 21 to 19, which will bring an additional 2.4 million men under conscription, Congress gave the president sweeping powers which its predecessors would have jealously guarded even in time of war.

These include the power to censor the press; to control an estimated $7 billion of enemy property in the United States; and to let contracts without competitive tendering.

The president is authorized to reorganize the executive branch of the government in any way that he pleases to prosecute the war more effectively.

The executive news editor of the Associated Press, Byron Price, aged 50, has been appointed "director of censorship". The president has appointed Mr Justice Owen Roberts of the Supreme Court as chairman of the board of inquiry into American unpreparedness for the Pearl Harbor raid.

Britons urged to salvage waste paper

Britain, 20 December

A renewed appeal for salvaged waste paper was made yesterday by Sir Charles Portal, the chief of the air staff, in a broadcast. "You have all got munitions of war in your homes," he told people. Old magazines and newspapers, Christmas cards and decorations, food cartons and cigarette packets are all needed to make parts of shell cases, mines, machine-gun bullets and radio sets for tanks and aircraft.

Scrap metal is also urgently required, although 5,000 tons of iron railings have already been collected. Some people have put up stiff resistance to the removal of their railings. Some have connected them to the mains electricity. One man even drew a revolver and warned that if anyone touched his railings he would fire.

Waste paper is women's work now.

Hitler takes over as commander-in-chief

Berlin, 19 December

With his armies in Russia crippled by heavy snow and sub-zero temperatures, Hitler today abruptly sacked his commander-in-chief and took over the job himself, "following his own intuitions", as the official announcement put it.

Field Marshal von Brauchitsch, appointed C-in-C in 1938, is reported to be deeply dismayed by the army's desperate plight in Russia, caused by the Fuhrer's order that there must be no retreats in any circumstances. Field Marshal von Rundstedt has already been sacked for quitting Rostov-on-Don.

Hitler – failed artist and ex-corporal, Fuhrer and chancellor of the German *Reich*, supreme commander of the armed forces and C-in-C – says that von Brauchitsch is a nincompoop (→ 20).

Field Marshal von Brauchitsch: Hitler reckons he is a nincompoop.

Japanese steamroller crushes Pacific resistance

Philippines: fresh landings in south

Philippines, 20 December
Japanese troops last night landed at Davao on Mindanao, the more southerly of the Philippines' two largest islands. The next stage of Japan's pincer attack on the US territory has begun. The Japanese have moved swiftly since they landed on the islands on 10 December. By 14 December around 6,500 troops had disembarked on the northern island of Luzon, the largest of the Philippines.

But as the imperial army has advanced the beleaguered US defenders have put up a brave fight. On 14 December the Japanese took Tuguegarao in northern Luzon, and US bombers attacked their troop convoys. One pilot, Captain Hewitt T Wheless, was delayed by engine trouble and reached his target only after the other bombers had gone. Suddenly 18 Japanese fighters descended on him like a swarm of wasps, but he dropped his load and headed home, pursued by fighters for 75 miles. His radio operator died and a gunner was wounded, but he made it, downing, so it is said, 11 fighters on the way (→ 22).

Japanese soldiers charge into Penang, Malaya, after arriving on their bikes.

Malaya: provinces fall, pressure grows

Singapore, 20 December
The authorities here have made an urgent request to London for more troops and aircraft to counter the growing threat of a Japanese invasion. In north-west Malaya, British troops yesterday abandoned the island of Penang following the loss days before of the state of Kedah and the province of Wellesley. Penang's mainland neighbour, the tin-mining state of Perak, is under attack as the Japanese move south. In Wellesley the Japanese captured Butterworth airfield, 360 miles (576 km) from Singapore, giving them control of five of Malaya's 11 airfields. British troops are being pulled back to the river Krian, thought to provide better defences. Further south at Port Swettenham, a 6pm curfew has been imposed (→ 27).

Burma: new attack aims for Rangoon

Bangkok, 15 December
Burma has become the latest target of the Japanese onslaught in Southeast Asia. The invasion began this morning with troops of the Japanese Fifteenth Army advancing from Thailand west across the Kra isthmus and capturing the three key southern airfields, Victoria Point, Tavoy and Tennasserim.

Tokyo decided to give permission to the Fifteenth Army's commander, General Shojiro Iida, to launch the attack because it is satisfied that the invasion of Malaya is going to plan and that General Yamashita's Twenty-Fifth Army no longer requires the Fifteenth to secure its rear.

Iida's first objective is to take Rangoon and cut the main Allied supply line to Chiang Kai-shek's Chinese Nationalists. Logistics favour Iida. At his disposal he has 35,000 men, in two divisions, and 100 planes. He also has in place a "Fifth Column" of Japanese army-trained Burmese nationalists ready to help defeat the British, who are as yet ill-organized, with only a few thousand men (→ 24).

Hong Kong: beleaguered governor rejects surrender demand

Hong Kong, 18 December
Hong Kong's days as a British colony appear numbered as 40,000 Japanese troops stand by to storm an island defended by just 8,000. This evening a contingent of Japanese troops succeeded in establishing a bridgehead at Tai Koo, on Hong Kong Island, after crossing the 500-yard wide stretch of water separating the island from the mainland.

Japanese gunners, aided by superb intelligence, have targeted and destroyed pillboxes, fixed defences and air-raid shelters on the island's North Shore. The Hong Kong governor, Sir Mark Young, urged on by messages from Mr Churchill, continues to reject Lt-Gen Takaishi Sakai's offers to surrender "on the grounds of humanity". Today Sir Mark "flatly rejected" the third such offer in five days (→ 25).

The British take steps to keep Chinese war refugees out of Hong Kong.

Islands: Wake is target for attack

Wake Island, Pacific, 20 December
"The Japanese are occupying all the islands," Hitler declared two days ago. "They will get Australia. The white race will disappear from those regions." He has mixed feelings about his ally's success.

One island Japan has so far failed to occupy is Wake, a treeless atoll halfway between Manila and Pearl Harbor, defended by 400 US marines, 1,000 contruction workers, a dozen planes and six 5-inch guns. The Japanese fleet arrived off Wake on 11 December, after three days of bombing. Major Devereux, the marine commander, waited until the ships were in range of his guns, then fired. Two destroyers were sunk and a cruiser damaged. The defenders fight on (→ 23).

1941
December

Su	Mo	Tu	We	Th	Fr	Sa
	1	2	3	4	5	6
7	8	9	10	11	12	13
14	15	16	17	18	19	20
21	22	23	24	25	26	27
28	29	30	31			

21. Minsk, USSR: Thousands of Soviet PoWs are thrown into a mass grave, having been frozen to death in sub-zero temperatures by Nazi guards.

21. Atlantic: The captured German freighter *Hannover*, the first fighter catapult ship, is sunk by a U-boat after a desperate convoy battle.

22. Philippines: Japanese soldiers land at Lingayen, aiming for Manila (→ 23).

22. Washington: Churchill arrives for talks with Roosevelt.→

23. Borneo: Japanese troops land in Sarawak (→ 10/1).

23. Philippines: Manila is declared an open city.→

23. Pacific: Japan takes control of Wake Island, renaming it "Island of Birds".

24. Burma: Japan launches an air offensive on Rangoon (→ 29).

25. India: Mahatma Gandhi resigns the leadership of the Congress Party when it decides to support the British war effort.

26. Washington: The Australian prime minister, John Curtin, warns Churchill and Roosevelt that the Pacific war must not be considered secondary to the European war.→

27. Far East: Lieutenant-General Sir Henry Pownall succeeds Air Marshal Sir Robert Brooke-Popham as British C-in-C Far East.

27. Malaya: Japanese landings threaten Kampar and Kuantan.→

28. Pacific: Japanese paratroopers land on Sumatra.

29. Burma: British attacks push Japanese troops at Bokpyin back into Thailand (→ 18/1).

29. Crimea, USSR: Soviet forces land at Feodosia (→ 30).

30. USSR: The Red Army retakes Kaluga on the Moscow front, and mounts a heavy attack in the Crimea (→ 1/1).

31. Colditz, Germany: At news of German setbacks in the USSR, PoWs break into a chorus of national anthems.

Leningrad suffers under Nazi siege

Struck down by cold and starvation - the people of Leningrad draw water from a nearly frozen well.

Leningrad, 31 December
Leningrad is still holding out after four months of siege, but its people are suffering terribly from hunger and cold. It is commonplace to see a sledge with the swaddled body of a child being dragged to a cemetery by the child's mother. Sometimes she falls down dead beside her infant, exhausted by the effort.

It is estimated that some 3,000 people are dying every day from starvation despite the suicide runs of lorry convoys across the frozen ice of Lake Ladoga. These lorries, running by night along a marked track, come under fire from the German guns, and almost every night one of them slips through the ice to be swallowed up.

There is no fuel for buses and no electric heating for houses. Ancient wood-burning stoves have been recovered from the scrap heap. Many people keep warm only by burning their furniture. The people are also suffering from the diseases of malnutrition.

Scurvy is prevalent. The thick overcoats of the women who queue for hours for the bread which often never arrives hide bellies swollen by hunger.

Flour is mixed with sawdust. The strong brave the long dangerous trek to the frozen fields where they dig for potatoes. And as the long agony of Leningrad goes on there are rumours of cannibalism (→ 1/3).

Imported raw materials keep the Nazi war machine in action

Berlin, 31 December
Despite its setback outside the gates of Moscow, the territory controlled by the Third *Reich* is far greater than it was a year ago. Overall the war still appears to be going well for Germany, but how is the Nazi war economy standing up?

For the first year of the war, the Third Reich – well prepared for war – suffered few real changes in the life style of its people. The country has had to double its arms production. Brit-

ain, on the other hand, faced a sixfold increase, and American arms production has soared by a factor of more than eight. In the early days of the war, Germany was able to draw on adequate supplies. Rapid victories in Poland and France used less material than had been planned for. It was the Battle of Britain, followed by the Russian invasion, that began to cause gaps.

The sinking of the *Bismarck* and other naval losses brought about the mobilization of re-

sources for extra shipbuilding, with workers, factories and raw materials being diverted from civilian goods production.

Germany has become increasingly dependent on imported or confiscated raw materials. In Poland, France and occupied Russia, everything that might be of value is taken. At the beginning of the year, the Nazi regime concluded a trade deal for 9,000 tons of non-ferrous metal with the Soviet Union. Most had been delivered before the invasion.

Weary Eighth Army captures Benghazi

Benghazi, 24 December
Battle-worn and weary after a month of continuous fighting, men of the Eighth Army captured this wrecked town today. Rommel has fought all the way, shielding his few remaining *Panzers* with potent anti-tank fire and fending off British attempts to outflank his retreating *Afrika Korps*. His main threat came from the Desert Air Force, which itself was frequently hampered by bad weather.

With heavy casualties to his men and the loss of 170 fighting vehicles, Rommel's army has been badly hurt by Operation Crusader, and its commander faces a long wait for replacements.

General Auchinleck *could* press on towards Tripoli and complete victory in North Africa. But his men are tired, and his tanks have suffered badly in fierce desert com-.... The replacement crews are "green", and the pattern of desert war is repeating itself in that it is the British turn to suffer from stretched lines of communication.

British troops were in a similar position once before – only to be moved to Greece and disaster. On 12 December, Auchinleck was told that his much-needed reinforcements of two divisions, four light bomber squadrons and a consignment of anti-tank guns were being diverted – to the Far East (→ 2/1).

British combined forces raid islands

The Allies blaze their way into Norway, setting fire to snow-covered houses.

Norway, 27 December
Commandos have combined forces with the RAF and Royal Navy to spread havoc on Vaagso, an island north of Bergen.

Eight hundred commandos took part in the raid on Vaagso, the latest in a series of attacks designed to make the Germans believe that the Allies intend to invade Norway.

It was not all plain sailing for the British force, however. Stiff resistance from the German garrison meant house-to-house fighting for five hours. Navy guns silenced shore batteries while RAF Blen-heims bombed the wooden runways of the nearest *Luftwaffe* base 100 miles away, closing the airfield. Nineteen men were killed, including Captain John Giles, the former heavyweight boxing champion from Bristol. Eight ships and eight aircraft were lost.

Around 100 Germans were killed and about the same number taken prisoner. At the same time, 243 Norwegians have also come away with the force – but voluntarily. They are patriots who will be a welcome addition to the Norwegian Free Forces.

Australians brace themselves for war

Canberra, 31 December
"This is the gravest hour of our history," declared John Curtin, the Australian prime minister, on 8 December after Pearl Harbor.

Nothing has prepared this country for the disasters to come. For two years Australia has been fighting a war mainly in overseas theatres as part of the British war effort. But now Australians see themselves in a direct struggle for survival – with combat taking place on or near Australian territory. After the initial shock, the mood here was confident. It was not conceivable that the mighty United States, could be defeated in the war by Japan.

But the debacle at Pearl Harbor, the destruction of the American Far East air forces in the Philip-

Australia prepares for war: Japan's threat is too close for comfort.

pines and the Japanese landings in Malaya and Thailand, together with the sinking of the *Prince of Wales* and *Repulse* have alarmed the Australian people and their government to a marked degree.

After two weeks of war in Southeast Asia, the situation is grave. Major-General Gordon Bennett, the Australian army commander in Malaya, has asked for at least one Australian division to be transferred from the Middle East. The Australian government has sent a message to Churchill and Roosevelt, meeting in Washington, asking for Singapore to be reinforced. The loss of the base would mean the isolation of this continent.

Convoy HG-76 shaken but sinks U-boats

North Atlantic, 23 December
Convoy HG-76 is finally safe this morning after one of the toughest voyages ever. Trouble had been expected, so departure from Gibraltar was delayed until a powerful escort of two sloops, three destroyers, seven corvettes and *Audacity*, a captured German liner converted to an aircraft carrier, was ready.

In the last six days 14 U-boats have attacked the convoy. Commander "Johnnie" Walker, an anti-submarine expert, used *Audacity's* planes brilliantly and destroyed five U-boats and two long-range reconnaissance aircraft with the loss of only two of his 32 merchant ships. Yesterday U751 sank *Audacity*, but was blown up herself hours later.

A U-boat crew in the conning tower.

Free French occupy islands off Canada

St Pierre, 25 December
Yesterday the 350-strong population of St Pierre was given a Christmas present – the vote.

Free French sailors under Admiral Muselier, the chief of the Free French navy, landed on this cold, windswept left-over from France's North American empire, and on its neighbour, Miquelon. Within an hour the Vichy governor, Baron de Bournat, and the island's only known fascist, Henri Moraze, were arrested. Shortly afterwards, the island's men were herded into the town hall to vote to remain with Vichy or join de Gaulle. The result: 98 per cent for de Gaulle.

Hong Kong surrenders to Japanese

Hong Kong, 25 December
The Japanese flag is tonight flying over Hong Kong. After 18 days of fighting, the last seven marked by continual air and artillery bombardment, the governor, Sir Mark Young, formally surrendered at 7.05pm local time. He had been advised that with the loss of reservoirs there was less than a day's water supplies left. A communique from the colonial office in London said that Sir Mark took the decision to surrender after he had been advised by his commanders that "no further effective resistance can be made".

The garrison of British, Canadian and Indian troops ceased firing in mid-afternoon following a command by radio. An isolated contingent at Stanley in the south-east is fighting on until it receives a written order to surrender.

Sir Mark is being held at the Peninsula Hotel where, in a 15-minute candle-lit ceremony, he told the Japanese C-in-C, Lt-Gen Sakai: "I am here to become a prisoner by ordering the entire British forces to cease all resistance."

British and Japanese losses are estimated at approximately 2,000 each. However, British losses are feared higher following reports of atrocities by troops of the 229th Regiment under Colonel Tanaka,

Sakai leads victorious Japanese troops into Hong Kong after the surrender.

who ordered his men to take no prisoners. After overrunning an anti-aircraft battery three days ago they roped together 20 survivors and bayoneted them to death. Fifteen staff and wounded were also bayoneted in similar circumstances at a medical station captured by the 229th.

The final phase of the Japanese invasion began three days ago when 40,000 infantrymen wrong-footed the British by landing on the island's north-east coast instead of

the north-west. They then thrust south to Deep Water Bay, capturing all the high ground and splitting the defending force which London had expected would hold out for 90 days.

Sakai's victory has been aided by superb intelligence and planning. Spies on the island, including the Peninsula Hotel barber, who now turns out to be a Japanese army colonel, had provided the troops with accurate and up-to-date maps of every British gun emplacement.

Indian division on retreat in Malaya

Singapore, 30 December
Troops of the 11th Indian Division defending central Malaya have surrendered Kampar and retreated from the river Perak. They are now regrouping further south on the river Slim.

Major-General Heath's hopes of making a stand against the Japanese main force as it advanced south on the coast road were crushed when a second Japanese column emerged on his eastern flank from the jungle, hitherto thought impassable, after marching from Thailand. Morale in the Indian Division is good despite the defection of a unit of pro-Indian independence troops a few weeks ago (→4/1).

China's simmering war flares again

Changsha, 24 December
Central China's gateway city of Changsha is in danger of being overrun by Japanese forces for the third time in 12 months as the deadlocked conflict betwen Japan and China flares again. The Japanese have moved on Changsha to head off a Chinese Nationalist force from Hunan that was being moved south to Canton to attack Japanese forces in order to relieve pressure on Hong Kong.

Second Japanese force lands to tighten the noose on Manila

Manila, 24 December
The Japanese noose is beginning to close on the capital of the Philippines. A second support force, numbering 7,000, landed today at Lamon Bay, on Luzon's east coast, and is expected to try to link up with General Homma's 43,000-strong main force which landed two days ago by 85 transports in the Lingayen Gulf and is only 120 miles (192 km) from Manila.

However, because of intelligence overestimates, the US C-in-C, General MacArthur, believes that the Japanese invasion force may be closer to 90,000. Because of this MacArthur, who has only 25,000 US troops and Filipino scouts available to defend Manila, has declared it an open city and started to withdraw his men to the Bataan peninsula where they will regroup (→31).

Ever-advancing across the Pacific: Japanese infantry take cover in a farm.

Bleak new year for Allies in Pacific

South-east Asia, 31 December
It has been a bad Christmas for American commanders in the Pacific as the Japanese juggernaut rolls remorselessly on. Not only are Japan's soldiers on the Philippines [*see report alongside*], but the news is no better elsewhere.

Of the smaller islands, Guam fell on 10 December while Wake Island has just succumbed after a fearsome bombardment by Japanese ships. And today the last British troops crossed from Borneo into the Dutch East Indies. The new year begins with the Allies facing serious threats to their strongholds in the Philippines and Singapore (→2/1).

Churchill gives US Congress a V sign

Washington, 26 December

In a fighting speech to the US Congress today, Winston Churchill said of Japanese and Germans: "What kind of people do they think we are? Is it possible they do not realise we shall never cease to persevere against them until they have been taught a lesson which they and the world will never forget?"

The British prime minister was given round after round of rousing applause. At the end, as he left the rostrum, walking with hunched shoulders, he turned and acknowledged the applause by raising his right hand to give the two-fingered V for victory sign. This brought a renewed storm of cheering.

Churchill's emphasis on the democratic traditions shared by Britain and the US was heard with particular warmth. "The speech was a demonstration of the fine unity that exists between the United States and Great Britain,"

Churchill makes his point in the US.

said Senator Harry F Byrd. The isolationist Senator Burton K Wheeler admitted: "It was a clever speech that under the circumstances would more or less appeal to the average American" (→ 31).

Allied war leaders meet in Washington

Washington, 31 December

Churchill's visit to Washington will be rounded off with a review of the Anglo-American military staff talks – known as the Arcadian conference – which have been taking place during the past week. One outcome of the talks has been the decision, stubbornly opposed by some on the American side, to identify Hitler's Germany as the main enemy, though not, at the moment, the main threat to the Allies.

The immediate danger is presented by the Japanese conquest of

the East Indies, with their vast stores of strategic raw materials. When Japan has been put on the defensive, a full-scale invasion of Europe will be mounted for the decisive battle with Germany.

Soon after Churchill's arrival in Washington, just before Christmas, agreement was reached on the creation of a joint war council and joint supply council. These two bodies will attempt to match the demands of the military planners to the availability of guns, tanks, aircraft and other war materials.

Eden salutes success of talks with Stalin

Moscow, 22 December

After a week of talks between Stalin and Anthony Eden, the British foreign secretary, and their military and diplomatic advisers, the two sides achieved "identity of views" on the conduct of the war against Hitlerite Germany, according to the official communique.

On questions relating to the post-war settlement, however, the communique is evasive. "An exchange of views," it says, "provided much important and useful material which will facilitate the future ela-

boration of concrete proposals." The talks were rounded off with a banquet in the Kremlin given by Stalin. Earlier, Eden was taken to the battlefront. He said the Russian troops were "truly magnificent". He met German PoWs who wore only thin unlined coats and poor boots, and lacked gloves; they were suffering in the bitter cold.

Eden arrived in Moscow by a roundabout route that included a 72-hour train journey. In five sessions he talked with the Russians for some 20 hours.

Arts: Welles is in a class of his own

The film of the year was the virtuoso debut of 26-year-old **Orson Welles** as the author, director and star of *Citizen Kane*. Welles's performance as the loveless megalomaniac and his brilliant use of the camera in evoking the emptiness of his palace of Xanadu put this startling film in a class of its own.

Walt Disney has also been original in his extraordinary animated ballet *Fantasia*. Set to music varying from Bach to Stravinsky, it abounds in felicities and vulgarities. In more usual vein he gave us *Dumbo*, an essay on the pathos of pachyderms with big ears.

British films treated the gulf between dictatorship and freedom in two stories featuring **Leslie Howard**, who is becoming the symbol of understated British ideals. As a visiting archaeologist, snatching victims from Nazi camps in *Pimpernel Smith*, he whimsically outsmarts the Gestapo, amply personified by **Francis L Sullivan**. In *49th Parallel* he is again a deceptively mild intellectual who helps to frustrate a crew of U-boat survivors escaping across Canada. This is the first fiction film made with ministry of information backing.

War took its toll of the mental instability of the novelist **Virginia Woolf**, whose body was found in the river Ouse near her Sussex home, her pockets weight-

Mrs Woolf, who drowned herself.

ed with stones. In *Scum of the Earth* the Hungarian **Arthur Koestler** tells the grim story of his internment in 1939 in the French camp at Vernet, which he compares to Dachau.

Classical concerts are flourishing despite the bombing of the Queen's Hall (the Proms moved to the Albert Hall). This year saw the premiere of **William Walton's** Violin Concerto.

The Brains Trust, a weekly radio debate on listeners' questions between **Julian Huxley**, the biologist, **Dr C E M Joad**, the philosopher, and **Commander A B Campbell**, an old salt with a fund of stories, has huge audiences. *Sincerely Yours* has established **Vera Lynn** as the Forces' favourite.

Mr Kane comes home: Orson Welles as the immaculate megalomaniac.

"The Battle of Egypt, 1942 – Bombing up" by Anthony Gross.

1942

January

Su	Mo	Tu	We	Th	Fr	Sa
				1	2	3
4	5	6	7	8	9	10
11	12	13	14	15	16	17
18	19	20	21	22	23	24
25	26	27	28	29	30	31

1. USSR: The Red Army presses on with the strong counter-offensive launched near Kerch, in the Crimea, on 28 December (→ 19).

1. US: Sales of new cars and trucks are banned, to save steel.→

1. Austria: Fuel rations for factories in Vienna are cut to a sixth of the required amount.

2. Libya: The Allies capture the Axis base at Bardia (→ 6).

2. Philippines: Japanese troops occupy Cavite naval base and Manila as the US withdraws to the Bataan Peninsula (→ 10).

3. Washington: Chiang Kai-shek is appointed C-in-C of Allied forces in China, and General Sir Archibald Wavell is made Supreme Commander of the disparate Allied forces in South-East Asia, ABDACOM (American-British-Dutch-Australian Command).

4. Malaya: Indian forces on the river Slim are bombarded by Japanese aircraft (→ 7).

5. Moscow: Carried away by recent small successes, and against the advice of his chief of general staff, General Georgii Zhukov, Stalin orders a general offensive along the entire eastern front.→

5. Mediterranean: The British submarine *Upholder* sinks an Italian submarine off the Lipari Islands.

6. Libya: As Rommel takes delivery of 55 new tanks, the British advance reaches Mersa Brega and El Agheila (→ 22).

7. Malaya: Japanese troops break the resistance of the Indian 11th Division.→

8. Baghdad, Iraq: A court sentences Rashid Ali, who led an anti-British *coup* last year, to death *in absentia*.

9. Malaya: British forces are ordered to retreat to Johore (→ 12).

10. Philippines: Japanese planes drop leaflets calling on Filipino and US troops to surrender.→

10. Dutch East Indies: General Wavell arrives in Batavia, on Java (→ 3/2).

Allies declare themselves united nations

Washington, 1 January
The United States, Britain, the Soviet Union, China and 22 other countries today signed a solemn agreement to fight to the utmost against the Axis and not to conclude a separate peace.

Besides the four major Allied war powers, the signatory countries included four nations of the British Empire – Australia, Canada, New Zealand and South Africa – the governments in exile of eight European countries overrun by Germany – Belgium, Czechoslovakia, Greece, Luxemburg, the Netherlands, Norway, Poland and Yugoslavia – and nine Latin American republics – Costa Rica, Cuba, the Dominican Republic, El Salvador, Guatemala, Haiti, Honduras, Nicaragua and Panama.

The "united nations", with four-fifths of the world's population, subscribed to the principles of the Atlantic Charter signed by President Roosevelt and Mr Churchill last summer.

Churchill and Roosevelt: united by a determination to fight to the utmost.

More US help for British war effort

Washington, 6 January
President Roosevelt said today that Americans land, sea and air forces would be sent to Britain. He also announced massive increases in war production, including more than doubling the rate of aircraft building. The president was delivering his annual State of the Union message to Congress in person; it was the first time that he had spoken to Congress since the war began.

He announced that US industry would produce 125,000 aircraft in 1943, compared with 60,000 in 1942; 75,000 tanks instead of 45,000; 35,000 anti-aircraft guns as against 30,000; and ten million tons of shipping, rather than eight million.

Mr Roosevelt spoke warmly of Mr Churchill, who recently addressed the same audience, and wished him a safe return.

The enthusiasm with which the members of Congress greeted the name of each ally – Britain, the Soviet Union, the Netherlands and the rest – as the president mentioned them was the clearest sign that, only a month after the Japanese attack on Pearl Harbor, the isolationism which has dominated US politics for years is dead.

Germans forced to retreat as Stalin launches counter-attack

Moscow, 10 January
General Zhukov has launched a powerful offensive against the German "winter line" that runs from Bryansk north through Vyazma to Rzhev. The Germans thought that they would be warm and safe in this line until they chose to resume the campaign in the spring. But the Red Army, unlike the Germans, has no intention of stopping until the warm weather comes. It is forcing Germany into a retreat which, in places, is becoming a rout.

The Russians have taken Mosalsk, on the road to Smolensk, and are threatening to encircle the German base at Mozhaisk. Ilyushin Il-62 "Shturmovik" assault planes are wheeling over the battlefield like starlings before swooping on their targets, and the *Luftwaffe* has moved all available fighters to forward bases to protect the retreating army. The Germans explain the retreat by claiming that they are "allowing the enemy to shed his blood through this defensive action; then, at the right time, we will return to the offensive" (→ 11).

Wartime snowscape: a Russian road lined with vehicles abandoned by the Germans in their chaotic retreat.

Japan tightens Pacific stranglehold

Philippines: battle rages for Bataan

Bataan, 10 January
An endless barrage of artillery shells lights the night sky over the Bataan peninsula, west of Manila, where the 80,000-strong US and Filipino forces under General Douglas MacArthur continue to deny General Homma's Fourteenth Japanese Army outright conquest of the Philippines.

Despite constant strafing by Zero fighter aircraft, the US II Corps gunners, hidden on the jungle-clad slopes of extinct volcanoes from Mount Natib to Abucay, claim to have wiped out 40 Japanese field guns and several Japanese platoons. This success is credited to accurate aerial reconnaisance by the remaining US planes and careful concealment of the guns by Major-General Edward King, who insists that the foliage canopies above them are renewed daily.

Morale among the US troops is high despite a Japanese leaflet drop telling them to surrender. However, few know that Washington has told MacArthur there will be no relief force. The main anxiety is the food shortage. In addition to the troops there are also some 26,000 refugees from Manila to feed. With Manila Bay blockaded there is not enough food to last Bataan a month (→ 23).

Japanese troops on bicycles advance through the Malayan countryside.

Malaya: Allied divisions forced to retreat

Singapore, 9 January
In the fiercest fighting since the Japanese invasion a month ago, Japanese troops supported by tanks and fighter planes have overrun British positions and crossed the Slim river, 200 miles (320 km) north of Singapore.

At the same time Japanese troops are advancing south-eastwards towards Kuala Lumpur, Malaya's largest town. They claim to have broken through the strongly-fortified line at Kuala Kubu, an important junction 25 miles (40 km) north of Kuala Lumpur. The British plan for the defence of

Malaya has been built around the 9th and 11th Indian Divisions and the 8th Australian Division.

Although the British claim that the Japanese suffered heavy casualties in the battle for the Slim, they are pessimistic about holding Kuala Lumpur. Apart from the military its streets are deserted, with most of the civilian population fleeing south to the island of Singapore. After studying the situation in Malaya, General Sir Archibald Wavell, the new Allied Supreme Commander in the Far East, has ordered the immediate fortification of Singapore's north coast (→ 16).

Borneo: Jesselton falls to invaders

British North Borneo, 8 January
Japanese troops have advanced into Jesselton [*Kota Kinabalu*], the capital of British North Borneo, and hauled down the Union Flag. The British had little choice but to quit the town. On 15 December, when the Japanese 124th Infantry Regiment came ashore at the burning oilfields at Miri, all the British Empire had to oppose them was one Indian battalion, the local Sarawak Rangers and the police. From Miri two Japanese battalions sailed west to the airfield at Kuching, where they are still fighting; a third sailed east and took Jesselton (→ 11).

Japanese troops patrol an occupied village as they battle for control.

Australia: troops to move to Malaya

Canberra, 5 January
The Australian war cabinet today agreed to a British request for the transfer of the I Australian Corps, comprising the veteran 6th and 7th Divisions, from the Middle East to South-east Asia. In December Mr Churchill assured the Australian prime minister, John Curtin, that he would do everything possible to strengthen the whole Far Eastern front from Rangoon to Darwin. The British 18th and Indian 17th Divisions were both being moved from the Middle East to Bombay, Ceylon and Singapore with "utmost dispatch".

Dutch churchmen rebuke the Nazis

Amsterdam, 5 January
The Dutch Council of Churches today delivered a public protest against what it described as "the complete lawlessness" of the Nazis in their treatment of Dutch Jews. Despite the protest – the latest of many by the Dutch people – the round-up and deportation of Jews is certain to continue.

A year ago all Dutch Jews were ordered to register with the occupation authorities. Soon afterwards, the deportations to the stone quarries at Mauthausen slave labour camp, near Linz, in Austria began; few deportees survive for more than a few months (→ 13).

British Restaurants go self-service

Britain, 6 January
Self-service cafeterias operated by local authorities as a cheap way of eating out have been named British Restaurants at the suggestion of Mr Churchill. They developed out of emergency services created during the Blitz to feed people who were bombed out of their homes. Their popularity has led to plans to open more of them. The average price of meals is just under a shilling (5p/ 20¢). For that one can get roast meat, two vegetables, pudding, bread and butter and coffee.

Keep mum – she's not so dumb!
CARELESS TALK COSTS LIVES
Reminding the British that fifth columnists come in many guises.

January

Su	Mo	Tu	We	Th	Fr	Sa
					1	2	3
4	5	6	7	8	9	10
11	12	13	14	15	16	17
18	19	20	21	22	23	24
25	26	27	28	29	30	31

11. Borneo: Japanese troops land on Tarakan (→ 17).

11. USSR: Soviet troops cut the Rzhev-Bryansk railway line (→ 14).

11. Dutch East Indies: Japanese paratroopers land on Celebes (→ 24).

12. Malaya: The Japanese take Port Swettenham and Kuala Lumpur.→

12. Tokyo: Japan declares war on the Dutch (→ 3/2).

12. Berlin: Hitler orders the battle cruisers *Gneisenau* and *Scharnhorst* to sail from Brest to Norway (→ 15).

12. Tangiers: A German plan to detect Allied shipping movements in the Mediterranean by sending an infra-red beam across the Straits of Gibraltar is foiled when British agents blow up the transmitter.

13. Atlantic: Six new Type IX U-boats start their second big hunt or "happy time", off the eastern US coast.→

13. Lodz, Poland: Seven hundred Jews are deported to Chelmno death camp, the first of 10,000 down for "resettlement" (→ 20).

14. USSR: Following their seizure of Kirov yesterday, Soviet forces recapture Medya, driving a wedge between two *Panzer* divisions (→ 18).

15. Berlin: Hitler orders the *Tirpitz* to sail north for Norway from France.

15. Moscow: Official Soviet figures claim that Germany lost 55,000 soldiers and 777 tanks in the battle for Moscow.

16. Singapore: Most of the RAF's remaining planes are evacuated to Sumatra.→

17. Borneo: Japanese troops land at Sandakan, in British North Borneo.

17. North Africa: The Axis base of Halfaya is taken, along with 5,500 prisoners (→ 21).

17. Arctic: In the first U-boat attack on an Arctic convoy, the destroyer HMS *Matabele* is sunk by U454 off Murmansk while escorting convoy PQ-8 (→ 1/4).

Bright lights of US shore lure U-boats

An Allied merchantman sinks after being torpedoed off the American coast.

New York, 14 January
Banner headlines in this evening's newspapers have sent tremors all around the island of Manhattan. The news of the torpedoing of the Norwegian tanker *Norness* just 110 miles (176 km) from the piers where liners berth has brought home the realities of war to New Yorkers.

Only two days ago the British merchant ship *Cyclops* was sunk 300 miles off the eastern seaboard. These two attacks are the first signs of what Admiral Donitz called the *Paukenschlag* – roll of drums – to mark America's entry into the war. Donitz has sent his finest long-range U-boats across the Atlantic to prey on America's coastline. They can lie on the seabed by day, and surface at night to pick off ships silhouetted against the bright lights on America's coast.

With orders to "sink as much shipping as possible in the most economical manner", U-boat commanders are relishing the prospect of a second "happy time". The first "happy time" began in 1940, when the U-boats enjoyed a rich crop of sinkings in British home waters.

View from a U-boat conning-tower.

January 16. The actress Carole Lombard, the wife of Clark Gable, died today in an air crash.

South Africans take desert stronghold

Sollum, North Africa, 11 January
With bayonets fixed, South African troops stormed this *Afrika Korps* redoubt today, winkling out snipers from hundreds of caves on the high ground overlooking Sollum. The successful assault means that the 7,000 Axis troops remaining on the Halfaya escarpment are now cut off from seaborne food supplies and their chief source of water. The Halfaya garrison, with its command of the coastal road, is a major hazard to the British Army, which is forced to divert through more than 100 miles of desert to reach the front lines (→ 17).

British PoWs walk free from Colditz

Geneva, 15 January
Two Allied officers, a Briton, Lt Airey Neave and a Dutchman, Tony Lutyen, have arrived safely in Switzerland after escaping from Colditz Castle and walking all the way to the border posing as Dutch labourers. The news of their "home run" will be greeted with cheers at Colditz, where the most persistent escapers are confined. Neave, who was wounded and captured at Calais in 1940, had already made one attempt from a PoW camp in Poland. The two men simply walked out of Colditz wearing fake *Wehrmacht* officers' uniforms, with Lutyen boldly fobbing off a suspicious sentry by demanding a salute.

Hitler purges his "failed" military chiefs

Berlin, 17 January
Hitler is getting rid of the generals who have failed to bring him victory in Russia. He sacked Field Marshal Walter von Brauchitsch on 19 December and took the opportunity to make himself C-in-C of the army. Field Marshal von Leeb, the commander of Army Group North, resigned yesterday after Hitler refused him permission to retreat from Demyansk where 100,000 men are surrounded.

Another field marshal, von Bock of Army Group Centre, was relieved on 20 December at his own request because of stomach trouble brought on by his failure to take Moscow. Field Marshal von Rundstedt of Army Group South was sacked for telling Hitler it was madness not to retreat after the loss of Rostov, making a clean sweep of the commanders in Russia. Today von Reichenau, who took over from von Rundstedt, died of a stroke. The tank genius General Guderian was sacked on Christmas Eve for a withdrawal in defiance of Hitler's orders. Hopner went for the same reason, leaving Hitler now in supreme command.

Kuala Lumpur falls to Japanese army

Exiled governments plan their revenge

Malaya, 12 January

Kuala Lumpur, the Malayan capital, fell last night as elements of the Japanese Twenty-Fifth Army entered the city, thus completing the first phase of Japan's planned conquest of Malaya.

The consequences for Singapore are grave. Despite attempts to burn them, huge quantities of supplies have fallen into Japanese hands, and the possession of airfields in the area will facilitate the intensification of air bombardment against Singapore bases and installations.

The fall of Kuala Lumpur has followed swiftly on the collapse five days ago of the 11th Indian Division on the Slim river. Shortly afterwards, General Wavell visited the III Indian Corps, whose main supply base was at Kuala Lumpur, and ordered its withdrawal to Johore for rest and reorganization.

The exodus from Kuala Lumpur began on 10 January. All day and all night an interminable convoy of every description of vehicle carrying civilians and military rolled south. Little silent groups of Malays, Indians and Chinese gazed in wonder from the roadside as the humbled white *tuans* departed, leaving them to the Japanese.

The Japanese army embarked on the conquest of Malaya when they landed at Kota Bharu, on the northeastern coast. The landing began on 8 December, two hours before the

Government buildings ablaze as Japanese troops charge into Kuala Lumpur.

attack on Pearl Harbor. Shortly after the Kota Bharu landing, elements of the 5th Japanese Division went ashore at Singora and Patani, in southern Thailand. The British defenders in Malaya and Singapore comprised two Indian Divisions in northern Malaya and the 8th Australian Division in the south, together with the Singapore fortress and mobile formations.

The RAF committed to Malaya 476 aircraft, many of which were obsolescent, such as the Wildebeest biplane. However, 64 modern bombers, including Blenheims, and six Catalina flying boats arrived, while

51 Hurricanes are on their way to the region. The RAF planned to deploy 336 first-line planes, but the plan came to nothing owing to the speed of the Japanese advance. In any case, these 336 planes would still have been outnumbered two-to-one by Japanese aircraft.

By 12 December the Japanese had routed the British positions at Jitra, taking 3,000 prisoners. On 26 December a heavy engagement was fought north of Ipoh, and when Japanese tanks succeeded in "hooking" around Indian positions the road to Kuala Lumpur – and beyond it to Singapore – was open (→ 19).

London, 13 January

The perpetrators of atrocities in Nazi-occupied Europe were publicly warned today that they will be called to account after the war and punished. The warning was issued by representatives of nine countries under German occupation, meeting in St James's Palace. This is the first joint Allied decision on trials for war crimes, although the three main Allies have made similiar statements individually. Today's action was initiated by General Sikorski of Poland. Other countries represented were Belgium, Czechoslovakia, France (that is, de Gaulle's French National Committee), Greece, the Netherlands, Luxemburg, Norway and Yugoslavia.

General Sikorski (left) in London.

Japanese advance threatens Singapore

Singapore, 17 January

Time is running out for the hard-pressed defenders of Malaya. With Kuala Lumpur in Japanese hands and its inhabitants in flight, the Japanese 5th and Guards Divisions are pressing southwards to Johore State where the coming battle will decide the fate of Singapore.

In their first clash with the Japanese, at Gemas, the Australians ambushed and slaughtered a large number of bicycle-riding Japanese and withdrew next day in good order. The 45th Indian Brigade was defeated on the Muar river by the Japanese Guards Division. Fierce fighting followed, with Lieutenant-General Percival's army forced to retreat towards Singapore (→ 20).

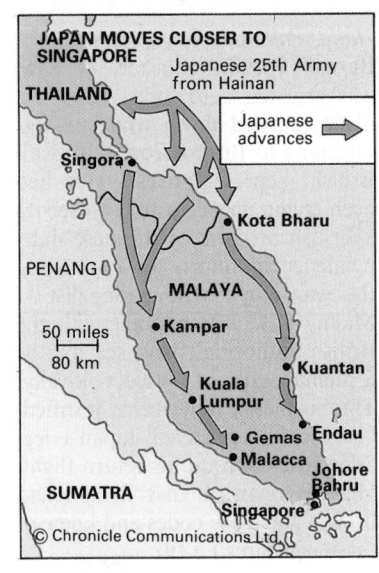

Dutch East Indies invaded by Japan

Singapore, 11 January

The rapid seizure of the oil-rich Dutch East Indies – a critical target for the Japanese war machine – began today when the Japanese used paratroopers for the first time. They landed on Menado, on Celebes, and took Langoan air base. The Dutch garrison fought hard against the Japanese, who landed from 16 transports, but were forced to capitulate after setting fire to their oilfields. Oil is critical to the Japanese who cannot wage war for long without some external means of supply. Rubber is another key need – explaining the urgency in taking the Malayan peninsula (→ 12).

South Americans to break with the Axis

Brazil, 15 January

A united Latin-American front against the Axis powers is now the express aim of a conference which opened in Rio de Janeiro today. Representatives of 21 American republics are attending. In an unprecedented opening address Sumner Welles, the chief US delegate, asked the Latin Americans to break off relations with the Axis. He said that Axis diplomats were informing their capitals of ship movements and continued: "Cast aside the shibboleth of classic neutrality and unite in the common front against the Axis aggressors seeking to conquer the entire world" (→ 28).

1942

January

Su	Mo	Tu	We	Th	Fr	Sa
					1	2	3
4	5	6	7	8	9	10
11	12	13	14	15	16	17
18	19	20	21	22	23	24
25	26	27	28	29	30	31

18. USSR: Soviet paratroopers land behind enemy lines south-west of Vyazma (→ 24).

19. Malaya: After fierce battles to defend road-blocks in the Muar/Yong Peng area, only 850 out of 4,500 Allied troops escape.

19. Burma: Japan takes Tavoy, with a good airstrip (→ 21).

19. USSR: The Red Army recaptures Mozhaisk, 100km west of Moscow (→ 1/3).

20. London: Churchill orders that Singapore "be converted into a citadel and defended to the death".→

21. Darwin, Australia: The US destroyer *Edsall* sinks the Japanese mine-laying submarine I124 (→ 22).

21. Burma: Japanese forces begin a drive on Moulmein (→ 31).

22. Leningrad: Evacuation of nearly 500,000 citizens begins.

22. Libya: Rommel recaptures Agedabia; the Axis forces in North Africa are formally named *Panzerarmee Afrika* from today (→ 26).

22. Tokyo: Tojo warns Australia that "if you continue resistance, we Japanese will show you no mercy".→

23. Manila: Japan sets up a puppet government, in which three-quarters of the pre-war Senate agree to serve (→ 6/2).

23. Novi Sad, Yugoslavia: Hungarian soldiers drive 292 Serbs and 550 Jews onto the frozen Danube river. All 842 are drowned when the ice is then shelled (→ 29).

23. Mediterranean: Four Swordfish naval aircraft based on Malta sink an Italian storeship bound for Tripoli.

24. Pacific: US marines land on the island of Samoa to protect it from the Japanese.

24. East Indies: Japan occupies Kendari, on Celebes; a US-Dutch naval force sinks five Japanese transports off Balikpapan (→ 9/2).

24. USSR: Soviet paratroopers end their series of drops behind German lines south-west of Vyazma.→

Rommel fights back in North Africa

North Africa, 21 January
Within a matter of hours today, the British 1st Armoured Division was in full retreat, racing pell mell across the desert to escape being trapped by German *Panzers*. A German staff officer described the British flight as "one of the most extraordinary routs of the war".

No one – British generals in particular – believed that Rommel could mount a counter-offensive so quickly after being driven back to El Agheila.

The "Desert Fox" had been ordered by Hitler not to attack, and the British were confident that Rommel's Panzers had been so badly bruised by Operation Crusader that it would be months before the Germans could mount any operation of any size – by which time a British offensive would have driven Rommel out of Africa.

They had not reckoned with Rommel's ability to recover from a situation and strike back quickly. Two Italian convoys had brought him tank reinforcements – the Royal Navy, its Force K damaged at Malta, had been unable to stop them – and his Intelligence knew that the British 1st Armoured Division was new to desert warfare.

With Rommel himself commanding one armoured column, the German tanks rolled at dawn in a two-pronged attack towards Agedabia

Though ordered not to attack, the "Desert Fox" (left) has routed the British.

– hitting the British as they breakfasted in the sun. The Panzers are stopping only when they run out of fuel, with Rommel gambling on shock and surprise and his own quick thinking to drive the British eastwards.

Even now, with British tanks fleeing at 25mph and an entire Indian division facing encirclement, Lieu-tenant-General Neil Ritchie, the Eighth Army commander, is apparently convinced that this is no more than a German reconnaissance in force. Ritchie's subordinates are worried about his indecision, and Major-General Frank Messervy of the 4th Indian Division described the commander's attitude as "haywire" (→ 22).

Admiral Kimmel, the US Navy commander at Pearl Harbor, faces accusations of not taking adequate action to defend the Hawaiian navy base last month.

Burmese premier arrested by British

Haifa, Palestine, 18 January
Burma's prime minister, U Saw, was arrested here today when his plane touched down while he was returning to Burma from talks with British representatives. He had been trying unsuccessfully to secure a British promise of Burmese independence in return for supporting the war effort. The nationalist U Maung Saw is unpopular with the British authorities, who see him as a demagogue of suspect loyalty. This suspicion now seems justified, because he contacted Japan's legation in Lisbon on his return flight. He was unaware that Britain had broken Japanese codes and knew of these overtures (→ 19).

Germans to taste front-line meals

Germany, 18 January
German civilians are to get a taste of the fare being eaten by their soldiers at the front – in the form of "field-kitchen meals" to be served in all German restaurants on Mondays and Thursdays. Customers who bring meat, fat or bread vouchers are entitled to change them for the "voucher-free meal of the day" which usually consists of soup or boiled vegetables.

Neither meal – "served from the same pot as our soldiers" – appears to be winning popular approval. They tend to lack calorie-rich foods such as potatoes, peas or noodles, and there is precious little meat in them.

Australian territory comes under attack

Melbourne, 24 January
The Rising Sun flies over Australian territory today after landings by 5,000 Japanese troops on the island chains of New Britain and New Ireland, in Australian New Guinea. A massive assault by aircraft from four carriers preceded the landings in New Ireland and at Rabaul, the capital of New Britain. Thirty warships escorted the invasion fleet, and more than 100 aircraft took part, opposed by a force of eight obsolete RAAF Wirraway fighters which were quickly shot down. Without aircover, and outnumbered, the small defending force had to withdraw (→ 20/2).

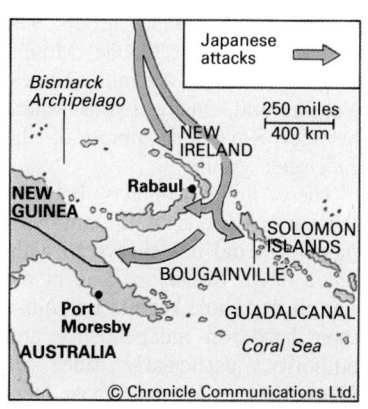

Japanese air force bombards Singapore

Japanese ground troops advance through a rubber plantation in Malaya.

Singapore, 20 January
As Japanese troops threatened the Johore causeway linking Singapore and the mainland, Singapore City had its first taste of war today when 50 people were killed and 150 injured in raids by Japanese bombers. Rumours that the Japanese were using poison gas were quickly denied by military commanders to avoid panic.

The Japanese attempt to drive down the west coast is recognized as a serious threat to Britain's Far East fortress. British aircraft are continuing to bomb and machine-gun invasion barges landing fresh troops at Muar. Fierce fighting is taking place at the mouth of the Muar river and the airfield at Batu Pahat after initial landings at the weekend.

Japanese claims to be less than 18 miles from the Johore causeway have been discounted by the British. So have reports of a large column moving near the main road junction at Yong Peng (→ 28).

Nazis decide how to annihilate Jews at secret meeting

Berlin, 20 January
Over a decent lunch today, followed by brandy and *Kaffee und Kuchen* in the cordial surroundings of the *Villa Am Grossen Wannsee*, the *Reich* security chief, Reinhart Heydrich, outlined his plans for exterminating the Jews. At a secret meeting Germans from the occupied territories, the civil service and security organizations agreed to coordinate efforts to help him.

Heydrich started off by reviewing the development of Nazi policy toward the Jews. Extermination, he said, was now a more realistic option than emigration. He ran through the statistics of how many Jews were alive in the world. National differences notwithstanding, Europe must be "combed through from east to west" for Jews, who will be evacuated to transit ghettoes in the east and finally to death camps where they will be murdered to prevent "a germ cell of a new Jewish development". He assured delegates that these plans, covering 11 million people in Britain, Sweden and Switzerland as well as occupied territory, were approved by the Fuhrer.

The differing degrees of readiness and complaisance in the various countries are to be resolved by giving wide powers to local officials responsible to Heydrich; and it was confirmed that children of mixed marriages are to be eliminated as well (→ 23).

The partisan war: Soviet "irregulars" link up with Red Army

Moscow, 24 January
Russian partisan detachments living and fighting behind the German lines have linked up with the 250th Airborne Regiment and two battalions of the 201st Airborne Brigade dropped south-west of Vyazma, which is now under heavy attack by the advancing Red Army.

The guerrillas and the paratroopers are fighting side by side to cut the German communications with the front. With the partisans acting as guides, the white-shrouded paras are ghosting through the forest to launch swift hit-and-run raids on supply lines and headquarters. This combination of irregular and regular troops is a new tactic on the Russian front. Individual officers and experts have been dropped to the partisans be-

fore, but this is the first time that they have been used in a coordinated campaign by the *Stavka*, the Russian High Command.

With the German defence line breaking up into defended localities, known as "Hedgehogs", there is room for such forces to manoeuvre, and even to hold large areas with established bases and landing strips for light aircraft.

Germans offered bribes – and threats – in productivity drive

Germany, 19 January
Directors of German armament firms were told today that they must increase production by ten per cent this year. The message was delivered by Robert Ley, the leader of the German Work Front. Increasing numbers of foreign workers, as well as PoWs, will be forced to work in German factories during the course

of the year. Armaments remain the main priority and the Nazi authorities intend to offer productivity bonuses in the form of tobacco or brandy for armament workers. Improved conditions for working mothers are also promised, but there is a sterner side to the productivity drive, too: the workforce is also to be motivated by the threat

of various punishments for "slackness", including transfers to concentration camps.

Reports by the Security Service of the SS speak of "idleness" and "insubordination" towards superiors. Certainly Germans do not like the longer working hours – the average working week is up from 47 to 49.2 hours this year.

Reinhart Heydrich (left), seen here with fellow-Nazi Karl Frank.

January

Su	Mo	Tu	We	Th	Fr	Sa
				1	2	3
4	5	6	7	8	9	10
11	12	13	14	15	16	17
18	19	20	21	22	23	24
25	26	27	28	29	30	31

25. Bangkok: Thailand declares war on Britain and the US (→ 5/2).

26. Libya: German troops recapture Msus, crushing the British 2nd Armoured Brigade (→ 7/2).

27. Westminster: Churchill announces the formation of a Pacific war council and a joint Anglo-US chiefs of staff committee, and that an Australian representative is to join the war cabinet (→ 10/2).

27. USSR: In the Ukraine, Soviet troops threaten the main German supply base at Dnepropetrovsk.

28. Pacific: The British carrier *Indomitable* delivers 48 Hurricane fighters, destined for Singapore to Java.→

28. South Africa: Pro-Axis extremists blow up five power stations in an attempt to sabotage supplies to the Rand gold mines (→ 11/3).

28. Rastenburg: Hitler decorates the *Luftwaffe* ace pilot Adolf Galland with the Diamonds to the Knight's Cross. Goering is appalled that the jewels are paste.

28. Brazil: The Brazilian government breaks off relations with the Axis (→ 11/3).

29. Britain: The BBC broadcasts the first edition of *Desert Island Discs*, presented by Roy Plomley.

29. Germany: Hitler orders that all methods should be used to bring forced labourers from occupied territories to work for Germany (→ 21/3).

30. Berlin: In a major speech, Hitler warns: "The result of this war will be the complete annihilation of the Jews ... the most evil universal enemy of all time will be finished" (→ 31).

31. Moluccas: Twenty thousand Japanese troops overcome a tiny Australian garrison defending Amboina.

31. Burma: The Allies have 35 aircraft, against 150 Japanese.→

31. Berlin: SS General Franz Stahlecker, the commander of the *Einsatzgruppe* in the Baltic states, reports that he has killed 229,052 Jews (→ 24/2).

American forces arrive in British Isles

Belfast, 26 January
The first American soldiers have arrived in the British Isles. Air and naval squadrons arrived three weeks ago, but without the fanfares which today greeted the first of many thousand "Doughboys" destined for Europe.

Landfall for today's arrivals – an infantry division from Iowa – was Northern Ireland, where they are to guard war stocks supplied under Lend-Lease. Many of the men are of German or Irish extraction. If some of their cousins are less than happy about their return in uniform, the British are euphoric. The Duke of Abercorn, the governor of the province, John Andrews, the Ulster premier, and Sir Archibald Sinclair, the air minister, welcomed them ashore, as did the Royal Ulster Rifles band with its own version of "The Star-Spangled Banner". Sir Archibald said that their arrival marked a new stage in the world war – "a gloomy portent for Mr Hitler".

Women NAAFI workers give the new arrivals their first British cup of tea.

Stalin to keep Red Army on the attack

Moscow, 31 January
The Red Army's counter-offensive is grinding on against fierce German opposition. A critical battle is being fought for Rzhev, as the Russians thrust south towards Vyazma in an attempt to trap the German Army Group South.

Similar battles are being fought further south as General Zhukov aims for Bryansk to sweep up behind Vyazma and Marshal Timoshenko fights towards Izyum in an attempt to recapture Kharkov.

In yet another Soviet attack General Vlasov has struck across the Volkhov river towards Leningrad. Despite atrocious weather Stalin is relentless in his demands for attack, believing that the Germans will break.

Britain, USSR and Iran sign alliance

Tehran, 29 January
Britain and the USSR, whose forces occupied strategic areas of Iran in a joint operation last August, today signed a treaty of alliance with the young *shah*. Under the terms of the treaty British and Russian troops may remain in Iran until six months after the end of the war.

The Allies undertake to respect Iran's territorial integrity, sovereignty and political independence, and to defend the country from all aggression.

In return, the shah, who succeeded to the "Peacock Throne" after his pro-Nazi father was deposed, promises "not to adopt in his relations with foreign countries an attitude which is inconsistent with the alliance".

Moulin strives to unite Resistance

Paris, 26 January
A simple matchbox can open many a door. The one that Jean Moulin always carries around contains microfilmed orders from General de Gaulle.

Moulin, known as "Max", was formerly mayor of the town of Chartres, and escaped to England nearly five months ago. Ever since he parachuted back into France on 1 January, the top-secret contents of the matchbox have been his letter of introduction to the leaders of the Resistance in the southern sector. De Gaulle has ordered him to unite the Resistance movements under the Free French banner. Despite some qualms, Henri Frenay, the leader of the *Combat* group, was first to rally to de Gaulle. Moulin then travelled to Avignon, Nimes, Valence and, finally, Lyons, where he met Raymond Aibrac of the *Liberation* group.

These initial contacts between the various heads of the anti-Nazi movement did not always go without a hitch. Resistance leaders are not on the whole keen to relinquish their hard-won independence and authority, particularly since de Gaulle has so far only given them a few vague promises in exchange for their support and allegiance.

What they have not seen are the money, arms, ammunition and explosives for which they have been calling so desperately (→ 19/2).

Moulin: forging the Resistance.

"City of the Lion" comes under siege

Japan prepares to attack Singapore

Singapore, 31 January
Now that the remaining British and Imperial troops have withdrawn across the causeway to Singapore all eyes are on this island.

In the past 20 years the naval base at Singapore has been the epi-centre of British military power in the Far East. But the errors that pre-war planners made in believing that Singapore could only be attack-ed from the sea have come home to roost now that Malaya is now in Japanese hands. The great guns which were supposed to have made Singapore impregnable all face south to the open sea – but the Japanese are approaching from the north, with only a narrow strait sep-arating them from the island.

The question now is: should Singa-pore be held or abandoned to its fate? General Wavell, recently ap-pointed overall Allied commander in the region, has advised that the island cannot be defended for any length of time. However, Churchill has ordered that Singapore be held at all costs: not only would sur-render betray the local people but, if Singapore falls, there is no hope for the Dutch East Indies.

On the steady advance through Malaya, Japanese troops ride into Johore.

British forces evacuate the Malayan coast

Singapore, 31 January
A triumphant Japanese army, buoy-ed by the success of its Malayan campaign, is poised to deliver the final blow to this "City of the Lion". A crushing defeat in Johore State forced Lieutenant-General Percival to withdraw all his forces from the coastal strip across the narrow strait from the beleaguered island. A British rearguard crossed into Singapore this morning after a gap was blown in the causeway link-ing the island with the mainland. British and Indian Army forces out-number the invaders, but they are handicapped by Japanese suprem-acy in the air and at sea.

None the less General Wavell, the overall Allied commander, is under strong political pressure to stand firm – from not only Chur-chill but also the Australian prime minister, John Curtin, who says the evacuation of Singapore would be an "inexcusable betrayal" (→4/2).

Kill Rommel myth, says Auchinleck

Benghazi, 29 January
British commanders in the North African war are facing a new threat – a growing myth among British troops that "good old Rommel" is invincible.

In a directive issued to senior of-ficers, General Auchinleck has praised his opponent as "very ener-getic and able". But he continues: "There is a real danger that Rom-mel is becoming a kind of magician or bogeyman to our troops ... I wish you to dispel by all possible means the idea that Rommel represents something more than an ordinary German general".

The ordinary German general's men took Benghazi today (→4/2).

Hitler blames cold for Russian failure

Berlin, 30 January
Hitler turned up at Berlin's Sports Palace today to celebrate the ninth anniversary of his coming to power. There was little to celebrate. He admitted that the offensive on the eastern front was stalled, and blam-ed the extreme cold, with tempera-tures of -40 degrees Fahrenheit (-40 Celsius). He confessed: "I do not know if the war will end this year."

Japan targets Rangoon after conquering Moulmein in Burma

New Delhi, 31 January
The fall of Moulmein, in Burma, to-day threatens the major port of Rangoon which handles the arms and supplies flowing along the Burma Road to Chiang Kai-shek's armies in China. The Japanese as-signed the task to their 15th Army which on 8 December entered Bangkok, in Thailand, and set about the task of seizing British air-fields in southern Burma in prepar-ation for air attacks on Rangoon.

One airfield fell to Japan, and Rangoon itself was attacked con-tinually from 23 December. Allied fighter squadrons – British and American – forced the Japanese to carry out their bombing missions by night. Moulmein fell when the defenders were ordered to with-draw in river boats (→ 13/2).

Having taken the Allied airbase at Moulmein, Japanese troops enter the town: now they are set to take the vital port of Rangoon across the Bay of Martaban.

MPs give Churchill vote of confidence

London, 29 January
By 464 votes to one the House of Commons today promised "sup-port to the utmost in the vigorous prosecution of the war". This vote of confidence in the government came at the end of a debate lasting 19 hours. It was spread over three days because MPs disperse from Westminster before it gets dark.

The only opposition registered was by three Independent Labour Party members – two as tellers and James Maxton as the lone voter. Over 100 MPs were absent – most on military duties. Mr Churchill announced that he will establish a ministry of production. He was grinning broadly as he left the House after the huge vote.

1942

February

Su	Mo	Tu	We	Th	Fr	Sa
						1
2	3	4	5	6	7	8
9	10	11	12	13	14	15
16	17	18	19	20	21	22
23	24	25	26	27	28	

1. Germany: Tobacco rationing starts, with women receiving only half the male allowance.

1. Pacific: Ninety-two planes from the US carriers *Yorktown* and *Lexington* attack Japanese bases on the Gilbert and Marshall Islands.

2. Washington: Lt-General Joseph Stilwell is appointed chief of staff to Chiang Kai-shek and C-in-C of the US forces in the Chinese theatre (→ 11/3).

3. East Indies: Japan attacks Dutch positions on Java, damaging the naval base at Surabaya (→ 20).

3. New Guinea: Japanese aircraft bomb Port Moresby (→ 8/3).

3. Indian Ocean: Port T, a top secret British base on Addu Atoll, becomes operational.

4. Tokyo: Japan demands the surrender of Singapore (→ 5).

4. Cairo: The British ambassador to Egypt, Sir Miles Lampson, presses King Farouk to appoint a pro-Allied government by surrounding his palace with tanks (→ 6).

5. Singapore: The 16,400-ton British liner *Empress of Asia* is the first convoy ship to be sunk delivering supplies to Singapore (→ 9).

6. Cairo: A new *Wafd* (nationalist) government is formed under British pressure.

6. Atlantic: The British ships *Rochester* and *Tamarisk*, escorting convoy OS-18, sink an attacking U-boat.

6. Washington: The Allied Combined Chiefs of Staff hold their first conference.

6. Philippines: Japanese reinforcements arrive on Luzon, but the US mounts a counter-attack (→ 8).

7. Libya: Rommel's advance is halted at the Gazala Line, after he had recaptured the ground which he lost last year (→ 20/3).

7. East Prussia: The Nazi armaments and munitions minister, Fritz Todt, returning to Berlin after talks with Hitler, is killed when his plane crashes on take-off (→ 8/2).

Quisling appointed Norwegian premier

Quisling, back in power in Norway.

Oslo, 1 February
The man whose name has become a synonym for treachery and collaboration with the Nazis has been appointed minister-president of Norway – on Hitler's orders. Vidkun Quisling appointed himself prime minister in 1940 when the Germans invaded; he lasted just six days, the Germans deciding that his conduct was creating more enemies than friends for them.

Now, however, with manpower shortages crippling war production, Hitler cares not whether Norwegians feel friendly; they must be rounded-up for war work, and Quisling is the willing tool for the task. After the installation ceremony in Oslo, he made his acceptance speech in German.

Collaborators fall into line with Hitler

Europe, 1 February
Hitler has been able to count on eager collaborators in the countries of Europe occupied by his armies since 1940. Some, like Anton Mussert of the Netherlands, are mediocrities impressed by talk of the Nazis' New Order; others, like the cynical and devious lawyer and former premier Pierre Laval, are opportunists. Still others, the Great War hero Marshal Petain among them, believe that only by collaborating can they save their people from persecution and privation.

Denmark was occupied in April 1940 and has produced at least six Nazi parties, all proclaiming their admiration for Hitler while wrangling among themselves. In Belgium the old feud between Dutch-speaking Flemings and French-speaking Walloons produced rival Nazi groups, and the Germans have concentrated, with some success, on recruiting Flemings as SS volunteers. King Leopold was reviled for ordering the surrender of his troops in 1940, and in Belgian eyes he has further besmirched his name by paying a visit to Hitler. But he did so in an effort to secure better food rations for his people; he has stubbornly refused to collaborate.

RAF follows bomb ploy of "Luftwaffe"

London, 1 February
RAF Bomber Command, despite being ordered last November to conserve its strength in order to launch a spring campaign, has kept up its attacks on Germany. Emden, Hamburg, Kiel, Cologne and Mannheim were among the cities hit last month. Imitating the *Luftwaffe's* raid on Coventry, Wellingtons loaded with four-pound incendiary bombs are lighting the way for other squadrons with high-explosive bombs. RAF bombers also attacked the *Scharnhorst* and the *Gneisenau* in nine night raids on Brest.

Military discipline for young Germans

Berlin, 5 February
The Hitler Youth leader Artur Axmann has called for camps to teach military discipline for all 17-year-old *Jugend* members soon to be called-up. Youth leaders meeting under the banner "Work in the East and Agriculture" were given descriptions of the numerous war victims and advised that medical training was particularly important in the teaching of military discipline. *Jugend* members are playing a major role in community aid and the care of the dependants of fallen soldiers, it was reported.

New U-boat code baffles the Allies

Atlantic, 1 February
A serious setback to British fortunes in the Battle of the Atlantic has taken place today. The U-boats in the Atlantic have adopted a new cipher, *Triton*, linking them directly to Admiral Donitz's headquarters in Paris. The *Enigma* encoding machines using *Triton* have four rotors rather than the three in the machines using the previous *Hydra* cipher. Bletchley Park's *bombes*, the deciphering machines developed by the mathematician Alan Turing, only have three rotors and hence cannot yet tackle *Triton*. The Germans do not know that the British are reading *Enigma* signal traffic; the change in cipher simply reflects Donitz's wish to control his wolf packs more tightly so that they will sink more ships.

Since the ciphers used by U-boats training in the Baltic (*Tetis*) and in coastal waters (*Hydra*) remain unchanged, the British Admiralty's submarine tracking room can still monitor newly-commissioned U-boats and those entering and leaving the Bay of Biscay and Norwegian waters. However the inability to read *Triton* means that the Admiralty, no longer knowing the intentions of Atlantic U-boats, will find it more difficult to route convoys.

The "Enigma" machine in use: now a new code baffles the British.

1942

February

Su	Mo	Tu	We	Th	Fr	Sa
						1
2	3	4	5	6	7	8
9	10	11	12	13	14	15
16	17	18	19	20	21	22
23	24	25	26	27	28	

FEBRUARY 1942

Rommel's success puts Ritchie under fire

North Africa, 4 February

As the British dig in on the Gazala/ Bir Hakeim line and Rommel contemplates his next move, grave doubts surround the future of the Eighth Army commander, Lt-Gen Neil Ritchie. One popular commander, Lt-Gen A R Godwin-Austen, has resigned and General Auchinleck has ordered Major-Gen Eric Dorman-Smith to sound out senior officers in secret. Auchinleck and Dorman-Smith picnicked today in the desert – where they could talk freely. The major-general said that Ritchie was "not sufficiently quickwitted or imaginative". But Auchinleck – who has already sacked one commander – decided that Ritchie should stay. "To sack another would affect morale," he said.

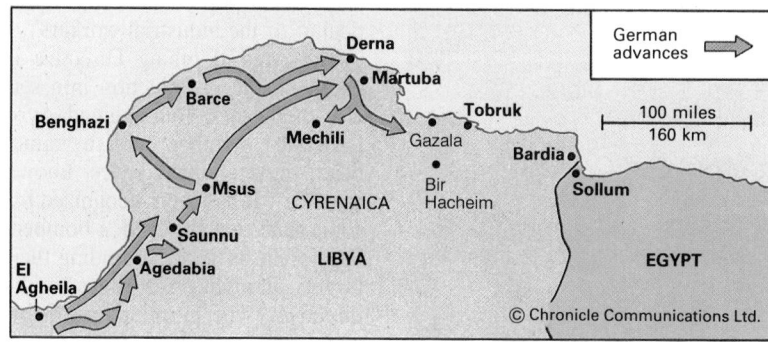

German advances →

Derna, Martuba, Barce, Benghazi, Mechili, Tobruk, Gazala, Bardia, Sollum, Msus, Bir Hacheim, CYRENAICA, Saunnu, LIBYA, El Agheila, Agedabia, EGYPT

100 miles / 160 km

© Chronicle Communications Ltd.

Neutral Eire wants 250,000 more soldiers

Dublin, 3 February

Eire will need 250,000 soldiers, many more than at present, to defend its neutrality, says the prime minister, Eamon de Valera. Speaking at Kildare he predicted that the war would continue for at least four more years.

"The war has only just begun," he asserted. "It will become more fierce. In all probability Ireland will be more and more cut off. We should be able to defend ourselves militarily. If you are attacked by one it is almost certain you will be attacked by the other side."

The arrival of American troops in Northern Ireland has provoked fears in Dublin that the Americans might assist the British in an invasion to secure the Atlantic bases now denied them. The watchful Germans maintain a full diplomatic mission in Dublin.

February 2. A reception committee of workmen at Belfast ship-builders Harland & Wolff stands ready to greet Russian trade union delegates.

---

8. Corregidor: President Quezon asks Roosevelt for immediate independence, so that the Philippines can declare neutrality and the US and Japan can withdraw; Roosevelt rejects the plea (→ 13).

8. Demyansk, USSR: General Kurochkin's troops encircle 90,000 German soldiers (→ 24).

9. Celebes, Dutch East Indies: Japan occupies Makassar.

9. Canada: Anti-conscription candidates are soundly defeated in four by-elections (→ 11).

9. India: Chiang Kai-shek arrives to urge nationalists to join the fight against Japan (→ 21).

10. Singapore: Touring the island's defences, General Wavell falls off a sea wall, injuring his back (→ 11).

10. London: The Pacific War Council meets for the first time (→ 30/3).

10. New York: The impounded French liner *Normandie* capsizes after catching fire; Axis sabotage is suspected.

11. Montreal: A French-Canadian demonstration against conscription flares up into a riot (→ 19).

11. Singapore: British forces start to pull back to their final defensive line (→ 14).

12. Malta: The destroyer HMS *Maori* is sunk while moored in the Grand Harbour (→ 15).

13. Philippines: Japanese dive-bombers raid the Bataan peninsula, killing their own men by mistake (→ 11/3).

13. Pearl Harbor: The superstitious Admiral Halsey refuses to take Task Force 13 out as scheduled; renumbered Task Force 16, it will sail tomorrow.

13. Berlin: Hitler finally cancels the much-postponed Operation Sealion, the planned invasion of Britain.

14. Singapore: Japanese troops, not part of the main force, bayonet 150 patients and staff to death at the Alexandra Military Hospital in Singapore City (→ 15).

Hitler's architect is appointed to head Nazi war industries

Albert Speer with the Fuhrer.

Berlin, 8 February

Hitler has chosen his architect friend, 36-year-old Albert Speer, to succeed Fritz Todt as minister for armaments and war production. Todt was killed yesterday when his plane crashed on take-off after a visit to the Fuhrer. Speer's task is to increase arms production by 50 per cent; he aims to do so by forcing prisoners of war to work in factories. Before his new appointment he was working on plans for a post-war Berlin worthy of the 1,000-year *Reich*.

Britain in a lather over soap rationing

Britain, 9 February

Soap rationing comes into force today as the British government cuts supplies by 20 per cent in order to save imported oils and fats for food rations. Despite elaborate efforts to keep the soap rationing plans secret – government communiques referred to nutmegs – some London chemists reported a run on soap before the official announcement. People will be entitled to four ounces (113 grams) of household soap, or two ounces (56 grams) of toilet soap, soap flakes or chips per person per month. Emergency measures might have to be taken for workers in "dirty" trades (→ 18).

German warships dodge Channel fire

RAF ordered to hit German civilians as well as factories

English Channel, 12 February
To the fury of the British, three of Germany's most powerful ships made a daring dash up the English Channel today. By this evening they were within range of the safety of the German ports.

The battle cruisers *Scharnhorst* and *Gneisenau* and the heavy cruiser *Prinz Eugen* had been sheltering at Brest since last spring. They had been prime targets for the RAF, and no fewer than 110 air raids had been made, damaging but failing to destroy them. The breakout had been ordered by Hitler and planned by Vice-Admiral Ciliax.

The German plan was called Operation Cerberus, but the British had heard about it through the French Resistance and had devised their own plan, Operation Fuller, to thwart it. The Resistance has observed the German preparations over the last few weeks, and last night 18 Wellingtons bombed the ships in Brest. They scored no hits, but they did delay the planned breakout for one hour, until 10.45pm.

This proved a lucky break for the Germans because the watching British submarine decided that the fleet was not going to sail that night and pulled away. British forces were stood off, and it was not until 11.09am today that an RAF Spitfire spotted the German ships, by which time they were in the Straits of Dover. The Dover Castle guns fired, but fell short. The Dover motor torpedo boats sped out, but could not get within range because of the powerful German escort.

Six Swordfish led by Lieutenant-Commander Eugene Esmonde made a brave attack, despite the fact that their Spitfire escort was not ready. Despite their slow speed they managed to get past the Messerschmitt Bf109s and Focke-Wulf FW190s, but they were still all shot down and none of their torpedoes hit the targets. The RAF mustered 242 bombers to attack the ships off the Dutch coast before dark, but it was not until late tonight that mines – dropped by the RAF – succeeded where bombers had failed. The battle cruisers were damaged, *Scharnhorst* seriously, as they neared German waters and ports. The RAF lost 42 aircraft.

The "Gneisenau" seen from "Prinz Eugen" as they dashed up the Channel.

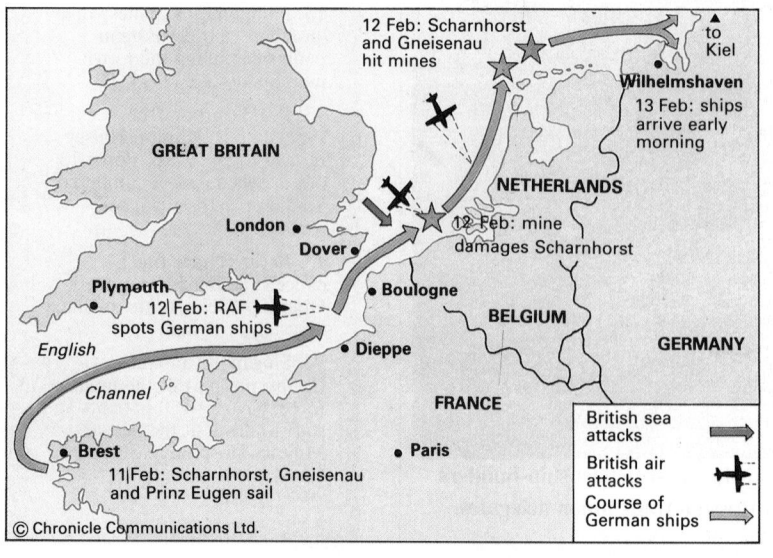

London, 14 February
Bomber Command, after a period of conserving its strength, is being sent back into the attack. It has today been issued with a new directive instructing it to focus its attacks "on the morale of the enemy civil population and, in particular, of the industrial workers".

The Area Bombing Directive is based on the introduction into service of the new four-engined Avro Lancaster bomber and a radio-beam navigational device known as "Gee". It has been recognized for some time that the RAF's bombers have great difficulty in finding their targets at night. According to the directive: "The introduction of this equipment on operations should be regarded as a revolutionary advance in bombing technique which ... will enable results to be obtained of a much more effective nature."

The directive also means that open season has been declared on civilian as well as military targets in Germany (→ 22).

Japan sends paras to attack oilfield

Sumatra, 14 February
More than 700 Japanese paratroops trying to capture Palembang, in Sumatra, the last oilfield in the Dutch East Indies still in Allied hands, are facing stiff resistance.

The paras were dropped early today at three points to capture the airfield at Palembang, codenamed P1, in readiness for sea landings tomorrow by Vice-Admiral Jisaburo Ozawa's western force. Yesterday Ozawa's 25-ship task force was bombed by Australian aircraft from Palembang as it stood off the Anamba Islands.

Palembang, which produces 55 per cent of the Dutch East Indies' oil, has been heavily fortified. The Japanese appear unaware of a second airbase, codenamed P2, where 50 Hurricanes are waiting to attack Ozawa's fleet. If Palembang falls Australia's oil supplies will have to come from the United States or the Persian Gulf (→ 15).

Japanese army invades Singapore Island

Japanese troops repair the Johore causeway leading to Singapore Island.

Singapore, 9 February

After a series of huge artillery barrages, Japanese assault troops succeeded in crossing Johore Strait last night and stormed the mangrove-fringed north-west shore of Singapore Island itself. General Tomoyuki Yamashita concentrated the weight of all three of his divisions on the long, thinly-held line manned by the two brigades of the Australian 8th Division.

Early reports indicate that the Australians have been forced back by the overwhelming weight of the hordes of Japanese who charged their positions with bayonets. By dawn, the Japanese were pouring through a massive gap in the line and Tengan airfield, the initial objective of the Japanese assault, had

fallen to the enemy. Within a few hours, more than 4,000 Japanese troops came ashore in assault craft. Tanks and infantry are being ferried across on rafts. It is estimated that 30,000 Japanese have been successfully landed on Singapore.

The assault by the Japanese 5th and 18th Divisions came after arguments to build stronger defences were resisted by some senior British commanders as damaging to local morale. Also rejected were plans to concentrate defences on the north-west shore; more were sent to the north-east shore and then bypassed by Japan's move. Despite this, some Australian battalions held firm all day. Then, surprised by the speed of enemy attacks, commanders ordered premature retreats (→ 10).

Singaporean women lament one more innocent victim of a world at war.

1942
February

Su	Mo	Tu	We	Th	Fr	Sa
						1
2	3	4	5	6	7	8
9	10	11	12	13	14	15
16	17	18	19	20	21	22
23	24	25	26	27	28	

15. Sumatra: Allied forces head for the west coast as Japanese troops capture the oil refinery at Palembang (→ 28).

15. Mediterranean: Two merchant vessels on a convoy to Malta are sunk (→ 6/3).

16. Singapore: The Japanese flag is hoisted above the former British governor's residence.→

16. Venezuela: German U-boats shell oil refineries on Aruba and Curacao, sinking seven tankers.

17. Tokyo: Singapore is renamed *Shonan* [Light of the South].

18. Atlantic: The French submarine *Surcouf*, the world's largest, sinks in a collision.

18. Westminster: Miners are exempted from soap rationing.

18. Burma: Japanese forces cross the Bilin river, and Britain orders Rangoon to be evacuated (→ 19).

19. Burma: Japan attacks Mandalay (→ 21).

19. Canada: Parliament votes to introduce military conscription (→ 28/4).

19. France: Police arrest several Resistance leaders, including the philosopher Georges Politzer (→ 28/3).

20. Berlin: German casualties in the USSR so far are 199,448 dead, 708,351 wounded, 44,342 missing and 112,627 cases of severe frostbite.

20. Washington: The US supplies the USSR with a $1,000 million loan.

20. New Britain: Japan drives off an attempted attack on Rabaul by the US carrier *Lexington*.

21. Burma: British forces retreat to the Sittang river (→ 22).

21. India: Chiang Kai-shek makes a broadcast asking the people to support China and the Allies in their war against Japan.

21. Berlin: The pocket battleship *Admiral Scheer* and the heavy cruiser *Prinz Eugen* are given orders to head for Norway.

France tries leaders who lost the war

Riom, France, 19 February

Two former premiers of France, Edouard Daladier and Leon Blum, went on trial here today with three of their ministers and the former commander-in-chief of the Allies, General Gamelin, accused of responsibility for defeat.

Both ex-premiers blamed the high command, while Gamelin refused to speak in his own defence. Daladier also blamed Germany.

"I protest against this arbitrary condemnation," he said. "Germany, who is in reality responsible for the war, today by this trial wants to obtain proof of its innocence."

Stafford Cripps to join war cabinet

Cripps: new war cabinet member.

London, 19 February

Winston Churchill reorganized his war cabinet today. It now has seven members instead of nine. Out went Lord Beaverbrook, who ceases to be minister of production. He had often been at loggerheads with Ernest Bevin, the powerful minister of labour. Out also went Sir Kingsley Wood, the chancellor of the exchequer, and Arthur Greenwood, the minister without portfolio. In came Sir Stafford Cripps, the darling of Labour's discontented left-wingers. Clement Attlee, Labour's leader, is now to remain deputy prime minister (→ 25).

Singapore surrenders: Britain's "blackest day"

General Percival (right) on his way to surrender Singapore to General Yamashita after the greatest military defeat in the history of the British Empire.

Singapore, 15 February
Singapore has fallen to the Japanese army. The formal surrender took place this afternoon when Lieutenant-General Arthur Percival, the British commander, met his Japanese counterpart, Lieutenant-General Tomoyuki Yamashita – the "Tiger of Malaya".

This staggering disaster is the greatest military defeat in British history. Tokyo is ecstatic with "victory fever" as the Japanese celebrate their triumph: their army has taken Singapore more than a month ahead of the time table set for it by the Japanese Supreme Command.

The Allied C-in-C, General Wavell, flew to Singapore five days ago to organise attempts to stave off the impending catastrophe. There were angry words at a morning conference at Fort Canning when Wavell showed Percival a melodramatic cable from Churchill.

It read: "Battle must be fought to bitter end. Commander and senior officers should die with their troops. The honour of the British Empire is at stake." Percival issued a provisional plan for a defensive arc around Singapore, with the northern sector to be occupied by the 11th Indian and 18th British Divisions commanded by Major-General Heath. Major-General Bennett was responsible for the western sector, and Major General F K Simmons for the southern sector.

Later that day, Percival, pressed by Wavell, ordered Bennett to mount a counter-attack. It was unsuccessful and led to further losses and confusion. The Japanese did not press their attacks – but the skies were dominated by the enemy and so was the sea. Three Japanese divisions were in invincible positions, and Percival chose not to counter-attack again.

Communications were chaotic. Water supplies were at a critical level and the lives of a million civilians in jeopardy. Despite his earlier cable, Churchill was forced to give Percival discretion to cease resistance. Tonight, 130,000 British and Imperial troops were preparing for a long ordeal as prisoners (→ 16).

Churchill: heavy and far-reaching defeat

London, 16 February
The fall of Singapore was announced to Britain and the world by Mr Churchill on the wireless last night. In a 23-minute broadcast, his first for six months, Mr Churchill said that the loss of Singapore was a "heavy and far-reaching defeat". Invoking Dunkirk, he called for unity and warned that only weakness of purpose "can rob the united nations of victory". The prime minister added: "This is one of those moments when the British race can show its quality and its genius, when it can draw from the heart of misfortune the vital impulse of victory.

"We must remember we are no longer alone. Three-quarters of the human race are now moving with us. The whole future of mankind may depend on our action and on our conduct."

Hirohito: emperor's praise for his troops

Tokyo, 16 February
Amid scenes of almost unbelievable jubilation the Japanese government has announced that it will officially celebrate the fall of Singapore with a national victory day in two days' time. In Singapore the triumphant Twenty-Fifth Army troops are to stage a *banzai* victory march through the city.

On the way to them is a message wrapped in scarlet silk and written in an ancient Japanese script that only the emperor can use. The message simply states: "I praise you all." But the architect of the Japanese victory, Lieutenant-General Yamashita, may find his triumph shortlived. The Japanese premier, General Hideki Tojo, fears that Yamashita may become a candidate for war minister – a portfolio which Tojo holds – and is to transfer him to Manchukuo.

Huge British arsenal falls to Yamashita

The invading army in the city centre.

Singapore, 16 February
The first and sweetest task for General Yamashita, who ordered the assault on Singapore knowing that his men had only a few hours of ammunition left, has been to receive an inventory of the massive array of captured arms and ammunition which could have lasted the defenders for three months.

The haul includes 55,000 rifles with 18 million rounds, 2,300 machine guns with 500,000 rounds and 300 field guns. Half of these are modern 25-pounders with armour-piercing shells – effective weapons against tanks and pillboxes. Also captured in working order are 49 of the 52 fortress guns guarding Singapore's sea approaches – the wrong direction, as it turned out.

Fears grow on Japanese PoW camp policy

Singapore, 16 February
Concern is growing about the fate of the 130,000 Australian, British and Indian prisoners of war who have surrendered here, following reports of Japanese atrocities during the invasion of Malaya and in other parts of the Far East theatre.

The bulk of the Allied prisoners are being moved to Changi, the huge ex-British military base at the south-east corner of the island. With 50,000 men squeezed into four barracks the human density is worse than the Black Hole of Calcutta. Sanitation, water and feeding conditions are so bad that Allied

doctors fear a major epidemic. Japanese attitudes to PoWs are shaped by their belief that it is dishonourable to surrender when it is still possible to fight; but disrespect to PoWs can easily lead to savagery.

One instance of this was reported after Imperial Guard troops beheaded 200 wounded Indians and Australians left behind during the retreat from the Muar river. Similar reports of brutality have also come from Amboina, in the Dutch East Indies, where in three incidents a total of more than 600 Australian PoWs have been bayoneted to death (→ 10/3).

Japanese troops round up more British prisoners to fill the camps.

Japan's conquests continue relentlessly
Australia: naval task force hits Darwin

Surveying the damage after the massive Japanese raid on the port of Darwin.

Canberra, 20 February
A massive aerial onslaught by a Japanese naval task force yesterday shattered the northern Australian port of Darwin. Some of the 188 attacking aircraft were from four of the aircraft carriers that took part in the Pearl Harbor raid, plus land-based bombers operating from Celebes. The raid has temporarily wrecked Darwin's war potential

and has sunk many ships, including the USS *Peary*, and killed 243 people. There was chaos and a little panic when the enemy action was interpreted by some as the prelude to an invasion. But this was clearly not the aim of the Japanese, whose apparent intention was to shatter the morale of Australia, which is fast becoming a rallying point against Japan's expansion (→ 22).

East Indies: the Rising Sun marches on

Jakarta, 20 February
With its latest simultaneous strikes the Japanese Pacific offensive now threatens Java and Australia's northern doorstep. Landings were made yesterday on Timor, and Bali has been invaded today. The Bali landings open the way for an assault on Java, separated from Bali only by two-mile-wide straits.

With the capture by paratroops of the airfield at Kupang, on Dutch Timor, the Japanese now have a base within 500 miles of Australia. The Bali landings were opposed by Allied ships that damaged three enemy warships at the cost of two of their own damaged. In the Philippines, President Quezon has been evacuated (→ 28).

US Japanese to be moved from west coast

Washington, 18 February
Internment camps are being prepared in Arkansas and Texas to house thousands of Japanese-Americans, many of them second- or third-generation citizens, who are to be moved from the west coast as an anti-invasion measure.

The decision was taken at a meeting at the attorney-general's home

between officials of the justice and war departments. The president took no part.

The army is keen to relocate all Japanese. When the assistant secretary of war, John J McCloy, questioned the legality of the move, a senior officer on the coast, General John de Witt, told him: "Out here, Mr Secretary, a Jap's a Jap" (→ 25).

1942

February

Su	Mo	Tu	We	Th	Fr	Sa
						1
2	3	4	5	6	7	8
9	10	11	12	13	14	15
16	17	18	19	20	21	22
23	24	25	26	27	28	

22. Britain: The first USAAF HQ in Europe is formed.

22. London: Hugh Dalton is appointed president of the board of trade.

22. Burma: Civilians flee from Rangoon as British forces retreat to the Sittang river.→

22. Canberra: The Australian prime minister, John Curtin, blocks Churchill's plan to send Australian troops to Burma (→ 3/3).

23. US: The Japanese submarine I-17 bombards an oil refinery in Santa Barbara, California; shells fall on the US mainland for the first time in the war.

24. Black Sea: Some 764 Roumanian Jewish refugees heading for Palestine are killed when a Soviet submarine sinks their steamer *Struma* (→ 28).

25. East Indies: The ABDA Command is abolished, and Wavell returns to India.

25. Westminster: Sir Stafford Cripps makes a speech asking why so many resources are being spent on building up Bomber Command (→ 3/3).

26. Britain: The government outlines a building plan to boost employment and provide cheap housing for all after the war.

26. Burma: The Japanese push west of Sittang to threaten the rail link between Rangoon and Mandalay (→ 4/3).

27. Britain: Anthony Eden, the foreign secretary, speculates in his diary that Churchill has had a stroke.

27. Bay of Bengal: Japan raids the Andaman Islands (→ 12/3).

28. Batavia: HMAS *Ruth* and the US cruiser *Houston*, damaged in the Battle of the Java Sea, are sunk while attempting to escape from Batavia.→

28. Germany: The use of cars other than for war work is banned.

28. Poland: Ten thousand Jews from Lodz were gassed at Chelmno this week, while 4,618 Jews have died of starvation in the Warsaw Ghetto.

Allied disaster off Java

Batavia, 28 February
Two Dutch cruisers, the *De Ruyter* and the *Java*, blew up and sank during a major battle in the Java Sea last night. The Dutch rear-admiral, Karel Doorman, the commander of the combined Allied force, was lost in *De Ruyter*, his flagship, together with 344 of his men. Also lost in the action were the British destroyers *Electra* and *Jupiter* and the Dutch destroyer *Kortenaer*.

On 25 February, General Wavell dissolved his command in Java and handed over operational control to the Dutch. Wavell had advised that efforts to reinforce Java which might compromise the defence of Australia and Burma should not be made. The final battle for the Dutch East Indies was now looming and it would have to be fought with available forces in the area.

Doorman's "Eastern Fleet" was ordered to sea from Surabaya yesterday to seek out and attack the Japanese convoy carrying the invasion force, which was then off Eastern Java. His force included five cruisers and nine destroyers.

The Japanese were quickly aware of the fleet's movements and were able to deploy their forces favourably, exploiting a slight advantage in firepower (→ 1/3).

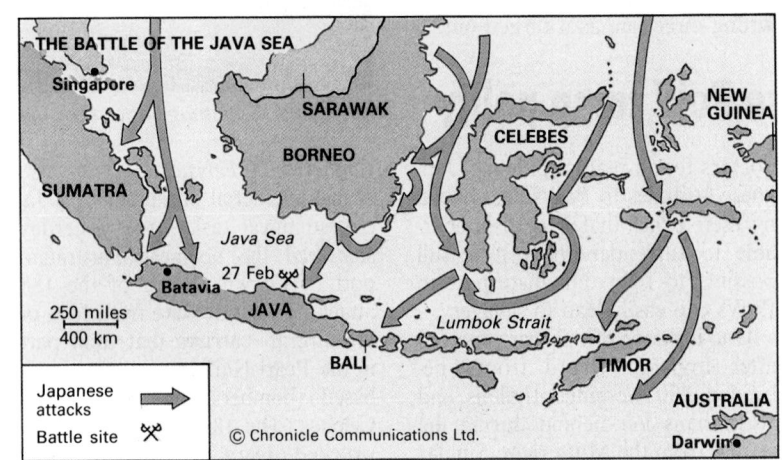

THE BATTLE OF THE JAVA SEA

Singapore · SARAWAK · BORNEO · SUMATRA · CELEBES · NEW GUINEA · Java Sea · 27 Feb · Batavia · 250 miles · 400 km · JAVA · BALI · Lumbok Strait · TIMOR · AUSTRALIA · Darwin

Japanese attacks
Battle site
© Chronicle Communications Ltd.

Australian general's flight stirs up a row

Sumatra, 28 February
Major-General Gordon Bennett, the commander of the 8th Australian Division on Singapore, has sailed from the clutches of the Japanese – and into a bitter controversy.

When the situation on Singapore was desperate, Bennett handed command of his division to his artillery commander, and, without consulting his superior, Lieutenant General Percival, boarded one of the hundreds of small boats leaving the colony. Bennett is being accused of abandoning his troops while other commanders went into captivity with their men. The most senior officer to escape, he is among 3,000 troops and civilians being looked after by locals on Sumatra.

Bomber Command gets a new chief

Veteran airman: Arthur Harris.

London, 22 February
Air Marshal Arthur Harris, who first went to war against the Germans with the 1st Rhodesian Regiment in South-west Africa in 1915, has taken over as commander-in-chief of Bomber Command.

Harris, aged 49, has 20 years' experience of bombing. He learnt the hard way – flying worn-out Bristol Fighters on punitive raids against the tribesmen of the North-West Frontier, and Vickers Vernon transports fitted with bomb racks against Iraqi rebels. He has since commanded No 4 Bomber Group and, for a year of the war, No 5 Bomber Group.

Known to his friends as "Bert", he is a prickly individual and no respecter of authority. It is possibly for this reason that he has caught Winston Churchill's eye. He believes in strategic bombing and can be relied on to carry out Bomber Command's new orders to attack German civilian morale. He faces opposition, however, from those who regard his command as a costly diversion of resources (→ 25).

Retreating Allies stranded after blowing up Sittang Bridge

Rangoon, 23 February
The demolition today of a key bridge across the broad Sittang river in southern Burma has resulted in heavy loss to the 17th Indian Division which was fighting against Japanese troops advancing towards Rangoon.

Unfortunately, Japanese intelligence overheard the radioed order to withdraw and moved swiftly cross-country to the bridge.

The 17th Division held its ground at the bridge as engineers prepared to destroy the only escape route. If the Japanese should capture the bridge, Rangoon would be at their mercy.

The charges were detonated at dawn, cutting off the British and Indian troops on the east side of the river. All who could be spared from fighting off the Japanese began improvising rafts. Amid chaos and confusion, hundreds of men threw away their arms, equipment and clothing and plunged into the river which became a mass of bobbing heads. Many were swept away and drowned (→ 26).

Paratroopers steal Nazi radar equipment

France, 28 February
In a daring raid on France last night Parachute Regiment soldiers seized top-secret German RDF [radar] equipment. The paras had been trained for this operation, jumping at night into snow near the clifftop target at Bruneval, near Le Havre.

The leader, Major John Frost, blew four blasts on his whistle to signal the attack and charged with four men through the front door of the enemy *chateau* overlooking the site, shooting as he went. Royal Engineers, guarded by paratroopers, tore out the aerial and other essential parts of the *Wurzburg* tracking device with crowbars. Enemy bullets hit the equipment as they worked. For a time afterwards it seemed as if the escape route down a cliff to a beach rendezvous was blocked by a clifftop machine-gun post, whose bullets hit Sergeant-Major Strachan in the stomach. Then a team of paras which had landed off the drop zone joined the fight after a forced march. Hit by crossfire – and a Gaelic battle cry as the enemy attacked – the German gunners fled.

On the beach, survivors of the raid waited, but at first no one responded to Frost's signals calling in the boats. As his men prepared to fight to the last round, the word was passed: "The ruddy Navy's here!" The paras embarked with the secret equipment and, as instructed, brought with them a captive RDF operator. They lost three dead and six captured.

Those who made it back after the raid, aboard one of the landing craft.

U-boat "wolfpack" hits US convoy

New York, 25 February
Five U-boats – four of them outward bound from their Biscay bases and fully loaded with torpedoes – have caused havoc with one of the first convoys to leave the United States for Europe. The convoy was sighted 600 miles (960 km) northeast of Cape Race and trailed until the submarines formed a hunting pack and struck.

In the three-day battle that followed, eight ships – six of them large tankers – were sunk. The U-boats escaped unscathed.

Planes are lifeline to 100,000 Germans

Russians inch forward through the snow: but the Germans are clinging on.

Moscow, 24 February
Six German divisions cut off at Demyansk in the northern sector of the Moscow front are defying all the Red Army's efforts to crush them. The Demyansk pocket and other similarly defended localities are frustrating the Soviet offensive.

One remarkable aspect of the Demyansk operation is that the 100,000 men in the pocket are completely cut off and are being supplied with food, fuel and ammunition by air.

All types of aircraft are being used. Junkers Ju52 transports are the main workhorses, but bombers are also carrying in supplies. They are protected by every available Messerschmitt Bf109, but the Russian fighters are having a field day, while other bombers are being shot down by a *flak* corridor set up by the USSR.

Supplies are also being airlifted into another fiercely defended pocket, or "hedgehog", around Kholm. It is even more dangerous here, for the airfield is in range of Russian artillery and the Germans are being forced to drop supplies by parachute or land them by glider.

The effect of the "hedgehogs" is to break up the cohesion of the front. The Russians cannot maintain their offensive and the Germans cannot regroup effectively. Both sides are now showing signs of exhaustion. The Germans lose more men from frostbite than from gunshot, and the Russians are simply running out of steam (→ 19/3).

US citizens interned in invasion scare

Washington, 25 February
Thousands of American residents of Japanese descent are being moved forcibly from the west coast to internment camps in inland states. More than 112,000 people are being ordered into buses and lorries, often at gunpoint – whether or not they are American born or naturalized citizens. Such is the anti-Japanese hysteria in the United States since the attack on Pearl Harbor that most civil rights campaigners are turning blind eyes to the mass evacuation.

All 3,000 Japanese-American residents of Terminal Island, Los Angeles, have been given three days in which to leave.

The decision is a response both to fears on the part of the army and navy that the Japanese might help a Japanese invasion and to pressure from the public and politicians. Since the attack on Pearl Harbor seven Japanese have been murdered by vigilantes.

One senator has called for all Japanese, whether citizens or not, to be placed in "concentration camps". Similar scenes are taking place in western Canada. Men are being parted from their families and placed in labour camps (→ 3/3).

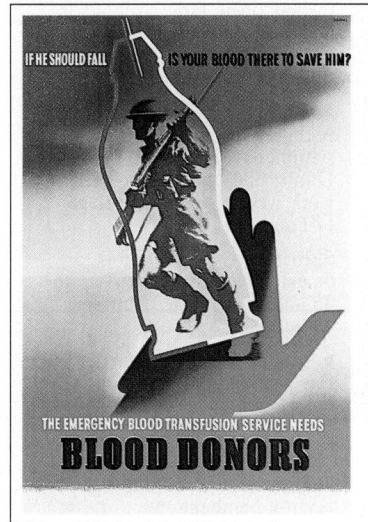

1942

March

Su	Mo	Tu	We	Th	Fr	Sa
1	2	3	4	5	6	7
8	9	10	11	12	13	14
15	16	17	18	19	20	21
22	23	24	25	26	27	28
29	30	31				

1. USSR: Soviet forces launch a Crimea offensive (→ 13).

2. Minsk, USSR: The Germans shoot dead 5,000 Jews (→ 3).

3. Washington: All people of Japanese ancestry, including US citizens, are barred from the Pacific seaboard and are told that they will be deported from the Pacific Coast to inland "Assembly Centres" – internment camps (→ 1/4).

3. Britain: The new Lancaster bomber makes its operational debut, on a mining mission with No 44 Squadron.→

3. Chelmno, Poland: An estimated 3,200 Jews from Zychlin are gassed (→ 4).

4. Pacific: The US carrier *Enterprise* attacks Marcus Island, 1,000 miles from Tokyo, causing much damage.

4. Java Sea: Japanese ships sink the Australian sloop *Yarra*, killing 138 of the crew, and the British destroyer *Stronghold* (→ 7).

4. Burma: General Sir Harold Alexander takes command of the Allied forces (→ 5).

4. Baranowicze, USSR: Three thousand Jews are massacred (→ 13).

4. London: General Alan Brooke replaces Admiral Pound as chairman of the Chiefs of Staff Committee.

5. Rangoon, Burma: The city's prisons and lunatic asylums are thrown open; large-scale arson and looting follow, and a wounded orang-utan escapes from the zoo (→ 8).

5. Kuibyshev, USSR: The premiere of the seventh symphony (*Leningrad*) by Dmitri Shostakovich, a bleak work written during the siege of Leningrad (→ 5/4).

5. Britain: Conscription is to be extended to men aged up to 45 and women aged between 20 and 30.

6. Malta: The British carrier *Eagle* delivers 15 Spitfires to the island, while seven Blenheim bombers fly in from North Africa (→ 26).

7. Java: Japanese troops occupy Lembang.→

Java government flees Japanese forces

Dutch East Indies soldiers struggle to arrest the downhill slide to defeat.

Bandoeng, Java, 7 March
The fight to save Java is over. Displaying white flags, a convoy of cars led by the Dutch C-in-C, Lieutenant-General ter Poorten, is driving this evening to the Japanese-occupied airport at Kalidjati, 25 miles (40 km) to the north, to open negotiations for surrender. Hours earlier the 15 most senior members of the Dutch government and armed forces led by Dr van Mook, the lieutenant-governor of the East Indies, escaped by air to Australia from the last Allied-held airstrip.

At noon the Netherlands News Agency in Bandoeng, the Dutch HQ, transmitted its last bulletin to the outside world, ending with: "Now we shut down. Long live our queen! Goodbye till better times."

Reporting on the last 24 hours it said that the situation in the west part of the island had become critical since the decision to surrender Jakarta by turning it into an open city two days ago. Dutch forces were now outnumbered five to one and the Japanese had absolute air supremacy. Rail links between east and west Java had been severed, and Dutch troops were now blowing up installations to stop them falling into enemy hands (→ 8).

Utility clothing becomes wartime uniform

Britain, 4 March
Clothes made from "utility cloth" will soon be on sale, and the fashion world is trying to assess the likely effect of the new fabrics on styles. Sir Thomas Barlow, the director-general of civilian clothing, has said that although there will be fewer styles available, this will not mean that variety vanishes and civilian clothing becomes like uniform.

Ladies' hemlines are likely to rise as a result of the new measures, and a smaller range of colours will be available. Pleats, and other designs which use a lot of fabric, will also be limited. But Mr Bridgland, the editor of the *Tailor and Cutter*, is of the opinion that men's loss will be the greater with the end of turn-ups and double-breasted coats.

A stitch in time for the war effort.

RAF raids Renault plant at Billancourt

London, 4 March
Air Marshal Arthur Harris, who took charge of RAF Bomber Command on 23 February, has already made an impact. Last night 235 bombers took off to attack the Renault works at Billancourt near Paris, and 224 aircraft claim to have bombed the target.

The raid is unique in a number of respects. The aircraft attacked in three waves. The first, consisting of experienced crews, dropped 1,000-pound bombs and then marked the target with flares while the second attacked, also with 1,000-pounders. Finally, the heavies went in with 4,000-pound bombs.

Since the anti-aircraft defences were known to be light the aircraft were able to attack at under 6,000 feet (1,829 metres) and all were clear of the target in under two hours. German propaganda will make much of the 367 French civilians dead plus 341 badly hurt and 9,250 homeless (→ 9).

British cruiser is sunk off Java coast

Batavia, 1 March
The British cruiser *Exeter* was sunk today in a fight with four Japanese heavy cruisers north of Java. The British destroyer *Encounter* and the US destroyer *Pope* were sunk in the same action.

HMS *Exeter*, hit earlier in the Battle of the Java Sea, faced two enemy cruisers on the port quarter and two on the starboard beam. With all power lost, she sank soon after coming under fire. Her captain and 651 of the crew survived.

The continuing Japanese naval victories are a matter of grave concern to Winston Churchill, who is haunted by the fear that Vichy-controlled Madagascar will fall into Japanese hands. An enemy naval base on the island would menace the western entrance to the Indian Ocean, disrupting vital communications with the Far East and denying the Allies Persian Gulf oil supplies.

The prime minister has told President Roosevelt that Britain intends to take Diego Suarez, Madagascar's main harbour (→ 4).

Japan rips Australian air force at Broome

Perth, 3 March

Japanese Zero fighters swept in over the harbour and RAAF airfield at Broome, in Western Australia, early today in an attack which killed 70 people and destroyed 24 flying boats and land aircraft.

The flying boats had been carrying refugees, including children, from the war in Java, with Broome as a staging post on the evacuation route. Warning of a possible raid was given when a Japanese aircraft appeared yesterday, making three circuits of the port before flying off.

Aircraft captains were warned to take off as soon as possible after daybreak.

In 15 minutes, the raiders – who were not opposed – wrecked every flying boat and destroyed all land planes including two Flying Fortresses and two Liberators, one of which took off only to be shot down over the sea. Only one of the 33 people on board survived. The raid, and smoke sighted at sea, caused the impression among many townspeople that the Japanese were about to invade (→ 20).

Britain turns its mind to plans for peace

A green and pleasant land: many want to reform it radically after the war.

London, 4 March

A minister was appointed today to take charge of planning for post-war reconstruction. He is the Labour MP Sir William Jowitt, KC, the paymaster-general.

Ideas for a better Britain after the war are much in the air and are discussed in *Picture Post*, the *Daily Mirror, Daily Herald, News Chron-*icle and other papers. The archbishop of Canterbury, Dr William Temple, and other church leaders have called for the abolition of "extreme inequality of wealth and possessions" and the introduction of "equal opportunity" after the war. In a new book the archbishop advocates better housing, paid holidays and family allowances.

Germans to be drafted to work on farms

Berlin, 7 March

Hundreds of thousands of Germans and people from Nazi-occupied Europe face being forced to work on German farms. A plan announced today looks first to people from country districts and provincial towns to provide extra labour; as many as 800,000 people could be needed at harvest time. Refusal to undertake such work could lead to what are described as draconian punishments. But attempts to draft women over 55 or those who are pregnant have already encountered strong opposition. Attention is therefore expected to focus on women from more affluent circles as these are thought by Nazi officials to contain the most "shirkers".

Leningrad fears spring thaw may mean the end of its lifeline across icy lakes

Besieged Leningraders read notices of things offered in exchange for food.

Leningrad, 1 March

The people of Leningrad are in a pitiable condition. More than 100,000 died of starvation last month, and there is no sign of the siege being lifted.

There are fears that their rations will be cut even further with the coming of the spring thaw. With great ingenuity the defenders have laid a light railway across the frozen surface of Lake Ladoga.

Supplies are now coming in by the railway and by truck convoys across the ice. This is made possible by the Red Army's recapture on 8 December of Tikhvin, the railway centre which controls access to the southern shore of the lake.

When the ice melts, however, this life-line will disappear and the besieged city will have to rely on small ships running the gauntlet of the Stukas in almost perpetual daylight.

Another worry for the authorities is that when the thaws come thousands of bodies hastily buried in snow drifts – because the ground is frozen too hard to dig graves – will be exposed and bring epidemics to people already suffering from the diseases of malnutrition.

Some 300,000 of the strongest people have been organized into gangs to clean up the city once the ice melts. The Leningraders are determined that their city will come to life again. It must be emphasized that the real heroes of this siege are the ordinary people who, by tremendous courage, are managing to survive an almost impossible ordeal (→ 5).

In the face of untold deprivations, Leningraders keep the Germans at bay.

1942

March

Su	Mo	Tu	We	Th	Fr	Sa
1	2	3	4	5	6	7
8	9	10	11	12	13	14
15	16	17	18	19	20	21
22	23	24	25	26	27	28
29	30	31				

8. New Guinea: Japanese invasion forces land at Lae and Salamaua.→

8. Java: Japan occupies the naval base at Surabaya.→

9. Norway: Albacore aircraft from HMS *Victorious* make an unsuccessful attack on the *Tirpitz* (→ 12).

10. Britain: War spending reaches £9,050 million, exceeding the cost of the entire First World War.

11. Brazil: The government seizes Axis property to avenge merchant ships sunk by German U-boats.→

11. France: The Resistance claims to have killed 250 Germans in Nazi-occupied France by blowing up a troop train.

11. Britain: The maximum sentence for black marketeering is increased to 14 years' penal servitude.

11. Cape Town: General Smuts outrages Afrikaners when he says that he would arm blacks and coloureds to defend "their" country (→ 23/4).

11. Mediterranean: The cruiser HMS *Naiad* is sunk by a U-boat off the Libyan coast.

12. Pacific: US forces land on New Caledonia to build a base at Noumea.→

12. Bay of Bengal: The British garrison on the Andaman Islands is evacuated (→ 2/4).

12. Norway: The *Tirpitz* returns to Trondheim after a six-day *sortie*, during which there was no action, against Convoy PQ-12.

12-13. Germany: RAF Bomber Command sends 251 aircraft to attack Essen (→ 8/4).

13. Crimea, USSR: The Red Army launches a fresh offensive to relieve Sevastopol (→ 20).

13. Belzec, Poland: The second Nazi death camp opens with a transport of 6,000 Jews from Mielec (→ 16).

14. Washington: The US chiefs of staff decide to build up American forces in Britain for an attack on Germany, while fighting a defensive war in the Pacific.

Wave of Japanese conquest rolls on

Naval power forces Java to surrender

New Delhi, 9 March
Java, the greatest prize in the triumphant Japanese campaign of conquest in South-east Asia, has fallen. After bloody engagements in the jungle, the Dutch, British, Australian and US contingents have surrendered.

The Dutch East Indies government has flown out to Australia. Java appeared doomed after Singapore fell three weeks ago. Resistance crumbled rapidly once the three Japanese invasion forces, meeting little resistance on the beaches, came ashore and moved inland. A Japanese column attacked Kalidjati airfield where the defenders, mostly British antiaircraft gunners turned infantrymen, fought bravely until they had been practically wiped out. In the west the Japanese 2nd Division advanced towards Batavia by the coast road and on Buitenzorg by the southern road.

The destruction of the Allied naval forces in the Java Sea last month, the weakness of Allied air power and the blockade imposed by overwhelming Japanese naval dominance made capitulation in Java inevitable. At 9am today Lieutenant-General H ter Poorten, the Allied commander, broadcast that all were to lay down their arms.

Joyous self-congratulation by the Japanese in the fallen city of Rangoon.

Deserted Rangoon falls to the invaders

Rangoon, Burma, 8 March
Only the spire of the *Shwe Dagon Pagoda* rises above the smoke. The city is deserted as Colonel Harada Munaji's 215 Regiment picks its way through the ruined suburbs.

Rangoon has fallen to the Japanese, with much assistance from the Burmese nationalist supporters of the former prime minister, U Maung Saw (interned by the British), who are fighting a guerrilla war against the retreating British forces. For four days the British tried to defend Rangoon, even after most of the population had fled. But after the disaster at Sittang Bridge there was nothing to defend it with, and the British request for the 7th Australian Division was refused by the Australian government. The British were lucky to have got their army out in time. The new commander, General Alexander, and his staff were nearly captured on their way out (→ 19).

General MacArthur quits the Philippines

Bataan, 11 March
Ravaged by hunger and disease, the beleaguered US troops on the Bataan peninsula received a blow to their morale today with the news that Washington considered the Philippines lost and that Roosevelt had ordered the US commander in the islands, General Douglas MacArthur, to go to Australia to lead the Pacific Command from there.

MacArthur, with his wife and three-year-old son, left today by PT boat for Mindanao and will fly on to Darwin. Before leaving he told his successor, Major-General Jonathan Wainwright: "Hold on. I shall return" (→ 15).

Departing commander: MacArthur.

Allied air raids hit New Guinea ports

Papua, New Guinea, 10 March
Allied planes today bombed airports and port installations captured two days ago by the Japanese on New Guinea's north coast to cripple what is feared to be a Japanese attempt to gain control of the 100-mile Torres Straits separating New Guinea and Queensland.

The attacks were against the airports at Salamaua and Lae and shipping at Finschhafen. At the same time the Japanese bombed Port Moresby, the Papuan capital, and there are reports of an invasion fleet heading for the town (→ 1/4).

"Gee" device helps RAF pinpoint Essen

London, 9 March
Bomber Command aircraft fitted with a revolutionary navigational device code-named "Gee" bombed Essen last night in the first large scale use of the new system.

"Gee" works by sending out pulse signals from three different ground stations. These signals are picked up by the bombers and enable their navigators to calculate their positions by observing the time taken for the signals to reach them.

Aircraft equipped with "Gee" illuminated last night's target and were followed by other "Gee" bombers which dropped incendiaries. It is hoped the system will improve night navigation (→ 13).

Stilwell to command Chinese in Burma

New Delhi, 11 March
Lieutenant General "Vinegar Joe" Stilwell, a lanky, thin-lipped American general with a reputation for forcefully speaking his mind, will next week take over command of all Chinese forces in the China-Burma-India war theatre. Stilwell, who served with distinction in the Great War, is a student of Chinese and a former military attache in Peking. He will also be chief-of-staff to Generalissimo Chiang Kaishek – although he prefers to eat and sleep alongside his troops.

Japanese atrocities alleged in Hong Kong

A PoW in the hands of the Japanese.

Westminster, 10 March
Anthony Eden today gave details of alleged Japanese atrocities in Hong Kong to a stunned parliament. MPs and peers heard the chilling facts about the fate of the garrison after its surrender.

Fifty British soldiers were bound hand and foot and then bayoneted to death. Women of all races were raped and abused for the pleasure of the Japanese. More than a week after the surrender, wounded were being brought down from the hills, but the Japanese refused to allow the dead to be buried.

Mr Eden described the Japanese claim that their soldiers are inspired by the chivalric code of the *Samurai*, warriors of feudal Japan, as "nauseating hypocrisy".

Nurses shot down in Japanese outrage

Britain, 10 March
Stories of almost unbelievable horror about atrocities committed by the Japanese are beginning to trickle back. Allied troops, nurses and civilians are being brutalized and murdered in the most callous and inhumane ways. Among the atrocities reported are mass bayonetings of prisoners.

A group of Australian nurses and British soldiers which surrendered to the Japanese in Malaya last month is said to have been summarily executed. The men were bayoneted and shot and the nurses forced to walk into the sea and then machine-gunned down. Two soldiers and one nurse miraculously survived.

The Chinese too have been dealt with mercilessly. Some 5,000 civilians were rounded up in Singapore on 18 February. Two weeks later they were all dead. Many of their bodies were found decapitated with the hands tied behind the backs.

Prisoners who have been taken alive live in fear that every day is their last. Unconfirmed reports tell of the butchering of 120 Australian PoWs on Amboina Island on 20 February. They were executed by the bayonet or sword, kneeling with their eyes covered.

Hitler plans a new Russian offensive

Berlin, 14 March
Adolf Hitler intends to revive German morale, dented after the failure to take Moscow last year, by promising a new offensive against his former Russian ally this summer. He will outline his plans at a ceremony to commemorate Germany's war dead here tomorrow, but the military preparations have been under way for some time.

Where the *Wehrmacht* will strike, however, is by no means clear. Analysis of the situation shows that the Russians are now very strong in front of Moscow. Hitler may well turn again to the Caucasus, its oilfields and the road to the Middle East (→ 15).

Cautious advance by the Germans.

American servicemen arrive in Australia

Melbourne, 14 March
A convoy bringing 30,000 American troops has arrived in Australia. They are to serve in Australia and New Caledonia. After a brief stay in Australia the New Caledonia Task Force of some 14,000 officers and men arrived in Noumea on 12 March.

The first US troops came in an eight-ship convoy which was headed for the Philippines when Japan attacked Pearl Harbor. Two more American divisions are on their way here, and one Australian division is due to arrive back here this month. A concentration of ground forces is now assured (→ 25/4).

Stirring the US spirit of vengeance.

Brazil confiscates all Axis property

Brazil, 11 March
President Vargas has today confiscated up to 30 per cent of the funds of German, Italian and Japanese citizens resident in Brazil, recalled all Brazilian ships to port and confined the Japanese ambassador and his staff to the embassy.

These measures are in response to the torpedoing of a fourth Brazilian vessel by the Germans and the mistreatment of the Brazilian ambassador in Tokyo. They also open the way for a declaration of war against the Axis powers by Brazil (→ 23/5).

Off-white is colour for national bread

London, 11 March
Lord Woolton, the minister of food, announced today that there will be no more white bread on sale after 6 April, in order to save shipping. The "national wheatmeal loaf", which is not brown but off-white in colour, will take its place. It has failed to catch on voluntarily, accounting for only seven per cent of sales. "In spite of advertisements I have issued, the nation has made it quite clear that it prefers white bread," Lord Woolton admitted, "but I don't believe it wants it at the expense of troop movements."

1942

March

Su	Mo	Tu	We	Th	Fr	Sa
1	2	3	4	5	6	7
8	9	10	11	12	13	14
15	16	17	18	19	20	21
22	23	24	25	26	27	28
29	30	31				

15. Philippines: Japan launches an artillery attack on Manila Bay (→ 17).

15. Berlin: With German casualties in the east reaching 250,000 so far this year, Hitler predicts a crushing defeat for the Soviet army this summer.

15. Mediterranean: The British cruisers *Dido* and *Euryalus* bombard Rhodes.

16. Poland: About 1,600 Jews are deported from the Lublin area to Belzec, the second camp – after Chelmno – designed purely for the killing of Jews; it opened on 13 March, when 6,000 Jews from Mielec were murdered (→ 26).

16. London: The Soviet ambassador asks Churchill to open a second front on mainland Europe (→ 23).

17. Darwin, Australia: Three squadrons of US Kittyhawk fighters start operations in the Pacific.

17. Off Sicily: The British submarine *Unbeaten* sinks the Italian submarine *Guglielmotti*.

18. Off Brindisi: The submarine HMS *Upholder* sinks the Italian submarine *Tricheco*.

20. Sevastopol, USSR: A counter-attack by the German 22 *Panzer* Division fails when it marches into a Soviet assembly area and is destroyed (→ 9/4).

20. Tokyo: The navy minister, Admiral Shimada, says that in view of the Allies' "retaliation and hatred", Japan will no longer follow the recognized rules of sea warfare.

20. Libya: Allied soldiers attack Benghazi and Derna to divert Axis attention from a Maltese convoy of four merchant ships, five cruisers and 17 destroyers.

21. Philippines: US forces start a retreat to the heavily-fortified island of Corregidor in Manila Bay (→ 29).

21. Berlin: Severe penalties, including sentences in concentration camps, are announced to deter people from making unnecessary journeys by rail.

Minister threatens to ban "Daily Mirror"

The latest in a stream of "scurrilous misrepresentations" in the "Mirror".

London, 19 March
The *Daily Mirror* was today accused of "a reckless indifference to the national interest" by repeatedly publishing material "calculated to foment opposition to the successful prosecution of the war". The charge was made by Herbert Morrison, the home secretary, although it is understood that Mr Churchill instigated the move.

Mr Morrison summoned the editorial director, Harry Guy Bartholomew, and the editor, Cecil Thomas, and produced a cartoon showing a torpedoed seaman clinging to a raft in a heaving sea; the caption read: "The price of petrol has been increased by one penny – Official." Morrison said that the cartoon was clearly telling people that seamen were risking their lives for the profit of the oil companies. The *Mirror* men, for their part, believed that the cartoon was a warning to the public that the petrol they used cost lives as well as pennies.

Morrison said the cartoon was only the latest example of a stream of "scurrilous misrepresentations, distorted and exaggerated statements and irresponsible generalisations". He quoted a leading article which called the nation's leaders and senior military officers "brass-buttoned boneheads, socially prejudiced, arrogant and fussy ... with a tendency to heart disease, apoplexy, diabetes and high blood pressure". If the paper did not mend its ways, Morrison said, he would shut it down.

How British censors decide what is news

London, 19 March
Churchill has been complaining to the war office about the censors who strike out of news reports the names of famous regiments which have displayed gallantry in battle, even when it is apparent that the enemy is aware of their identities. But the censors are cautious folk: a rule that warships must not be named led one censor to delete HMS *Pinafore* in a theatre review.

The censorship is wide-ranging. Mostly it concerns overseas mail, all of which is censored; all telephone trunk lines are also tapped. Press censorship is theoretically voluntary, but under Emergency regulation 2D the government does have power to ban newspapers (as it did for a time the communist *Daily Worker*). Press censorship affects news only; comment is free. But the pitfalls are many: a report of a football match may be banned if the players are employed by a factory or power station. Deaths and marriages in local papers are censored to remove references to servicemen and merchant seamen.

Malta pounded by German bombs

Malta, 20 March
With its fighter defence force reduced to fewer than 30 Hurricanes, and anti-aircraft ammunition in desperately short supply, Malta is clearly being "softened up" for invasion.

Malta has been under continuous attack since 22 December, with "alerts" lasting as long as 13 hours and as many as 16 alarms in the course of 24 hours. Heavy rains have frequently made the two grass airstrips unserviceable.

The tiny island took the full brunt of the *Luftwaffe* today. Wave after wave of Ju88s with fighter escorts – a total of 143 aircraft – braved the fierce Malta barrage, attacking the three airfields and the harbour area.

General Slim will head Burma Corps

"Bill" Slim with a Soviet general.

Calcutta, 19 March
As Allied forces in Burma retreat before an apparently invincible Japanese army, Lt-Gen William "Bill" Slim has been sent to command the last fighting units there. His corps comprises two ill-equipped divisions (one Indian, one Burmese) commanded by friends from Gurkha Regiment days. He needs friends. One division, swimming a river to elude the enemy, was left with 3,000 men with underpants and no boots, while Allied aircraft are outnumbered tenfold by Japan.

Germany to attack Soviet partisans

Moscow, 19 March
The Germans today launched Operation Munich, a full-scale offensive designed to wipe out the large forces of partisans operating behind the German lines between Vyazma and Smolensk.

A special air detachment set up at Bobruisk has pinpointed the partisan bases in the forests and is now bombing them and harrying the guerrillas as they flee.

Squads of German ski-troops are sweeping through the countryside, burning villages and shooting their inhabitants. The need for the Germans to mount such an operation demonstrates the increasing effect of the partisans on the war.

While the offensive may disperse the units, now stiffened with specially-trained soldiers, there is little doubt that they will regroup and return to raid the supply lines with even greater support from the surviving villagers ($\rightarrow 3/4$).

British rationing to cover fuel supplies

London, 17 March
Rationing of coal, gas and electricity for home heating and lighting was announced in parliament today. Sir William Beveridge, who helped to devise rationing plans in the last war, is now working out details of this new scheme.

Hugh Dalton, the president of the board of trade, told MPs that the situation is now so serious that domestic fuel rationing must be imposed as soon as possible. A cut of at least 25 per cent is likely.

When the scheme starts, everyone will have to watch gas and electricity meters in the knowledge that persistent over-consumption will lead to prosecution and the cutting off of the supply. Meanwhile, in the next three weeks, coal deliveries to households will be limited to six hundredweight at a time.

Cuts in the civilian clothing ration also announced today will release 50,000 more textile workers for war service, and to save petrol all pleasure motor boating is to stop this summer. That includes round-the-bay trips at the seaside.

Able-bodied Europeans to be Nazi slaves

Germany, 21 March
Intent on gearing the German war industry up to the highest possible levels of production, Hitler today appointed Fritz Sauckel as plenipotentiary-general for labour mobilization, to seize forced labourers from occupied Europe. Labour shortages are the greatest impediment to increased production at the moment. Sauckel is to use whatever methods are necessary to obtain sufficient numbers of workers: they may be snatched from the streets or from their homes. They are then to be transported, without food, water or sanitation, to their places of work. Krupp, the manufacturer of guns, tanks and ammunition, is expected to be one of Sauckel's best customers.

Able-bodied men and women from occupied countries are ideal employees from the German point of view. They can be worked unpaid until they drop, and their keep costs almost nothing. Forced labour camps are carefully sited to

Slave labour for the able-bodied.

suit the needs of German industry. There were 2.1 million foreign workers in Germany at the beginning of this year plus 1.5 million PoWs working in German industry or agriculture. Both figures are expected to grow dramatically as a result of today's move.

Cripps raises hopes for independent India

A pro-Japanese propaganda leaflet shows Churchill being driven out.

New Delhi, 21 March
Sir Stafford Cripps, the lord privy seal, arrives here next week armed with new constitutional proposals for India. Although he declined to reveal what these proposals would be before leaving London, there seems little doubt that some sort of independence will be offered. The Labour Party is committed to Indian independence and Churchill, a doughty champion of British rule, has been pressed strongly by President Roosevelt to offer India self-government after the war.

With the possibility of a Japanese threat to India, the millions of Indians who are serving with Allied forces will expect nothing less, whatever the ultimate problems of reconciling the Hindu majority and Moslem minority ($\rightarrow 28$).

Ministry of dirty tricks keeps the Nazis guessing

Woburn, England, 21 March
A story passed to London by British agents in occupied Europe is causing satisfied chuckles among "Leeper's Sleepers" who work at the Duke of Bedford's seat, Woburn Abbey, requisitioned for the duration. Apparently German troops conducted a house-to-house search in Bucharest, looking for a Romanian freedom radio station. They did not find it – in fact the station operates from Woburn Abbey.

It is just one of several clandestine transmitters directed at Hitler's Europe, supposedly operated by anti-Nazis but actually run by a secret government agency, camouflaged as a department of the ministry of economic warfare, which until five days ago was run by Hugh Dalton. Churchill dubbed Dalton "minister of ungentlemanly warfare". Dalton appointed an old hand at the intelligence game, Rex Leeper, and told him that he would back him in any kind of dirty tricks he could work up.

Some are fiendishly simple. As one agent confessed: "It's wonderful the chaos you can cause by switching destination labels on railway wagons."

Subversive slander is another handy and potent weapon, although it can backfire. Rumours of orgies, degeneracy or luxurious living by Nazi leaders while the people suffer have been set off by agents in casual conversations in Europe, only to surface much later as hard intelligence.

Forged ration cards and fake German newspapers with gloomy reports are routine at Woburn Abbey. One of the most successful operations is run by Sefton Delmer, a former *Daily Express* correspondent in Berlin. His *Gustav Siegfried Eins* radio station, supposedly run by disgruntled German soldiers, likes to tell Germans at the front that back home foreign workers are going to bed with their wives and infecting them with VD.

1942

March

Su	Mo	Tu	We	Th	Fr	Sa
1	2	3	4	5	6	7
8	9	10	11	12	13	14
15	16	17	18	19	20	21
22	23	24	25	26	27	28
29	30	31				

22. Prague: Paul Thummel, an important double agent in the *Abwehr* [German military intelligence] is arrested.

22. Burma: British and US airmen abandon Magwe airstrip to the Japanese (→ 31).

23. Germany: Fearing a second front in western Europe, Hitler orders tighter defence of coastal areas (→ 18/4).

24. Egypt: The *Wafd* [nationalist] party wins the general election.

25. Grantham, Britain: The government has its first by-election defeat since September 1939 (→ 29/4).

26. Vichy: Pierre Laval warns Petain that there must be more collaboration if Hitler is not to appoint a *Gauleiter* to run the country (→ 16/4).

26. Malta: The RAF has fought off five big *Luftwaffe* attacks in 48 hours (→ 1/4).

26. Auschwitz: The first deportees, 999 Slovakian Jewesses, arrive at the camp.→

26. Germany: A decree orders that all Jewish homes in the *Reich* must be clearly marked.

27. Atlantic: HF/DF ("Huff Duff"), radio-location by high-frequency direction finding, is used successfully by a British convoy to sink a submarine for the first time.

28. France: The Resistance unit *Francs-tireurs et partisans* is created (→ 15/4).

29. Philippines: Local guerrilla fighters form themselves into the *Hukbalahaps*, the Anti-Japanese People's Army (→ 1/4).

30. Washington: The formation of the Pacific War Council, composed of Australia, Canada, China, the Netherlands, New Zealand, the Philippines, Britain and the US, is announced. Its first meeting was held in London on 10 February.

31. India: The Congress Party demands immediate independence (→ 12/4).

31. Burma: After a fierce ten-day battle, Japan takes Toungoo from the Chinese expeditionary force (→ 2/4).

Royal Navy wins battle of Malta convoy

View of the "Breconshire", one of the casualties of this Malta convoy.

Malta, 24 March
A battered British supply convoy reached harbour in Malta today. On Sunday it was forced to fight a "David and Goliath" operation against a powerful Italian battle fleet, and it won. The five cruisers and 17 destroyers, escorting four merchant ships, were attacked by the battleship *Littorio* – with nine 15-inch guns – which appeared from the north-east with three heavy cruisers and four destroyers in attendance. The odds were very much against the British cruisers (5.25-inch guns) and destroyers (4.7-inch).

Rear-Admiral Philip Vian ordered the convoy to sail at speed to the south-west, and then moved towards the Italians under a smoke-screen. The Italians withdrew, worried by the threat of torpedoes through the smokescreen.

The Italian action delayed the four ships of the convoy, however, and all of them came under heavy air attack. Two of the freighters were sunk and although the other two, the *Talabot* and *Pampas,* succeeded in reaching their destination, the *Luftwaffe* has concentrated on these two survivors in harbour. Some 326 bombers and fighters have been employed in their destruction, and only 5,000 of the 26,000 tons which left Egypt have actually landed in Malta.

Massive RAF raid devastates Lubeck

London, 29 March
RAF bombers devastated the German port of Lubeck last night. Guided towards their target by the new "Gee" navigation system, 234 Wellingtons, Hampdens, Stirlings and Manchesters set it ablaze with over 400 tons of bombs, over half of which were incendiaries.

Lubeck's picturesque old town of close-built wooden houses was, in Air Marshal Harris's words, "built more like a firelighter than a human habitation". Nearly 320 people died in the raid and 784 were injured. This is the heaviest death toll ever in one raid over Germany. Photographs show that 30 per cent of the town has been destroyed.

A number of factories were devastated and dock installations and the railway were heavily damaged. The raid was not, however, aimed at a military target. Its objective was to demonstrate what area bombing by a concentrated force of bombers could achieve.

The chiefs of staff have laid down that the aim of the bombing offensive is "the progressive destruction and dislocation of the enemy's war industrial and economic system, and the undermining of his morale to a point where his capacity for armed resistance is fatally weakened". Lubeck was the first target of that policy. Twelve British aircraft are missing (→ 30).

Goebbels ousts arch-enemy and rehouses the bombed-out

Berlin, 30 March
The heavy RAF bombing raid on the Baltic port of Lubeck on Sunday night gave Goebbels the chance to stage a coup against his detested rival, Wilhelm Frick, the former police official who is now interior minister. When Hitler phoned to ask about the air raid, Goebbels told him that the situation was chaotic and interior ministry officials had even failed to organize proper relief measures for the hundreds of bombed-out families.

The Fuhrer ordered that responsibility for caring for bombed areas should be removed at once from Frick's ministry and handed over to Goebbels. "The Fuhrer conferred sweeping powers on me," observed Goebbels. "By midnight everything was arranged that could possibly be done. I have been given plenary powers to take action without being hindered by the bureaucracy."

The dwarfish, crippled Goebbels longs to be seen as Hitler's deputy. He is a glutton for work. As *Reich* minister for public enlightenment and propaganda he controls all book, magazine and newspaper publishing, broadcasting, film production, theatre productions and artistic exhibitions. Because of his withered leg he did not serve in the Great War; he seeks to impress Hitler with fulsome expressions of loyalty and his large family. His wife Magda is required to produce a baby every year.

Josef Goebbels: a glutton for work.

Allied raiders hit docks at St Nazaire

St Nazaire, France, 28 March
The biggest dry dock in occupied Europe, vital to enemy warships such as the *Tirpitz*, is a flooded ruin after an extraordinary raid last night in which the destroyer HMS *Campbeltown* was converted into a delayed action bomb and rammed onto the dock gates at 20 knots.

Commandos then swarmed on shore to sabotage other key parts of the dock. One demolition party had just 90 seconds' start on its own charges, placed 40 feet below ground. At 11.30 this morning, about 12 hours after the start of the operation, when over half of the Combined Operations raiders were dead or captive, the destroyer blew up, killing more than 380 Germans exploring the ship. The base is now only usable by submarines, whose facilities remain untouched.

The operation was precisely planned and well-executed. But its success was due in a large part to the heroism of the men involved. Some 611 men went into action (345 Royal Navy; 257 Commando; four doctors; three liaison officers and two journalists) of whom 169 were killed – 104 from the navy – and 200 captured.

A flotilla of 17 motor launches and two other small craft joined the trip up the Loire estuary. Only four would return. Surprise was lost and only one launch put its men ashore. Some local residents thinking it was a full-scale invasion, joined in the fighting against the Germans. Admiral Mountbatten, commanding Combined Operations, sought a second destroyer to retrieve the raiders but was overruled (→ 21).

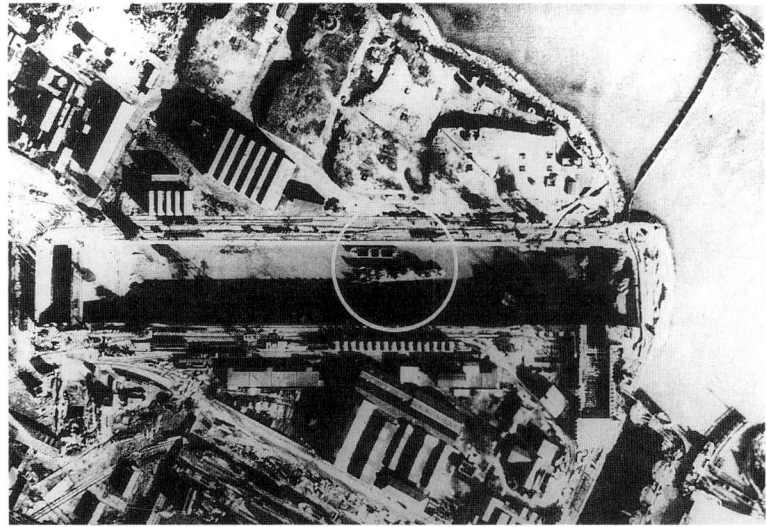
The timebomb "Campbeltown" in position in the dock at St Nazaire.

Nine months later: "Campbeltown's" stern half in the now useless dock.

Special train 767 leaves Paris taking Jews to Auschwitz

Auschwitz, 30 March
At 5.33 this morning, special train 767 steamed into the camp's railway siding with 1,112 Jewish men from Paris on board. The organizer, SS Captain Theodore Dannecker, was annoyed that the goods wagons which he had requested were not available. The deportees had the relative comfort of passenger coaches.

Their journey began three and a half days ago at the Drancy and Compiegne concentration camps. At Compiegne, all the men were ordered to line up in the camp yard. Then the commandant, Kuntze, started to call out names. The prisoners did not know why. Those selected had to stand on one side. The 550 chosen were given 15 minutes to collect their things; they scrambled for their worn blankets and tattered bundles of clothes.

They were put into two heavily guarded huts overnight. The next day the Germans again lined them up, smashing fists and rifle butts into their mouths at random. Then, a haggard, grey, bruised and bloody sight, they were marched through the streets of Compiegne to the railway station. The local townspeople looked on, stunned that such wraiths could truly still be alive.

Now they will have to get used to their new camp. But few of them will last long: gas chambers and crematoria are nearly ready at Birkenau, the annexe to the main camp. Most of them will be dead before autumn (→ 1/4).

India will be first non-white Dominion

New Delhi, India, 28 March
India is to be the first non-white country in the British Empire to have Dominion status – after the war. The announcement was made by Sir Stafford Cripps, the lord privy seal, who is visiting India. He warned that the offer is conditional on "wide acceptance", and, by implication, on support for the war.

Yesterday Cripps spent over two hours with the Congress leader, Mahatma Gandhi, an uncompromising pacifist. The meeting was hardly the dialogue that Cripps expected. The exasperating Gandhi had taken a vow of silence and spoke not a word.

Tomorrow Cripps will talk to Mohammed Jinnah, the pro-Allied leader of the Moslem League. No one wants Cripps to fail more than Winston Churchill, who only sanctioned Cripps' offer under pressure from the US and often states that he is not fighting this war to preside over the dismemberment of the British Empire (→ 31).

Nimitz and MacArthur divide the Pacific

Washington, 30 March
Britain and the US have divided up the world into theatres of war and agreed on their respective areas of responsibility. The US is to assume operational responsibility for the whole of the Pacific theatre including Australia and New Zealand.

The supreme commanders are to be Americans. Parallel to the creation of the Pacific Ocean theatre there will be a middle area stretching from Singapore to the Mediterranean which will be a British responsibility. Australia and New Zealand are to give maximum assistance in this area. The third area will cover the Atlantic and the planning of a second front on the European continent. These are to be the joint responsibility of Britain and the US.

The Pacific Ocean Zone under Admiral Chester Nimitz has been divided into North, Central and South Pacific areas; General Douglas MacArthur is commander of the South-West Pacific Zone.

April

Su	Mo	Tu	We	Th	Fr	Sa
			1	2	3	4
5	6	7	8	9	10	11
12	13	14	15	16	17	18
19	20	21	22	23	24	25
26	27	28	29	30		

1. Mediterranean: The British submarine *Urge* sinks the Italian cruiser *Giovanni delle Bande Nere* off Sicily.

1. Gothenburg, Sweden: Eleven Norwegian merchant ships break out to make a run for England (→ 5).

1. Malta: Two submarines are sunk in harbour by an air attack (→ 16).

1. London: Admiral Sir Andrew Cunningham of the British Mediterranean Fleet joins the Combined Chiefs of Staff Committee in Washington.

1. Bataan: Twenty-four thousand defending troops are reported to be ill from food shortages and tropical diseases (→ 3).

1. New Guinea: The Japanese land at Hollandia, on the north coast, and Sorong, on the west coast.

2. Andaman Islands: US Army Air Force Flying Fortresses bomb the Japanese fleet.

2. Burma: Japan takes the port of Akyab, and the British Burma Corps abandons Prome (→ 11).

3. Philippines: Japan resumes attacks on the remaining Filipino-US units on the Bataan peninsula, opening its assault with a heavy bombardment (→ 4).

4. Bataan: US and Filipino troops retreat (→ 5).

4. Ceylon [*Sri Lanka*]: A Canadian squadron-leader, Leonard Burchill, spots a Japanese fleet heading for Colombo. Admiral Somerville orders all shipping in the port to disperse.→

4. Germany: Hitler orders raids on British historic towns as revenge for the bombing of Lubeck: they are called *Baedeker* raids, after the German tourist guidebooks (→ 29).

4. Germany: Goebbels writes in his diary of his relief that the tough and resilient north Germans have been bombed rather than the softer southerners.

Industrialized liquidation of Jews begins

Auschwitz-Birkenau: roll-call for people whom the Nazis intend to destroy.

Europe, 2 April
For Jews, today is the first day of Passover, the festival of freedom and liberation from slavery. But this year there is nothing to celebrate. The German plan to destroy the Jews is getting into its stride.

The first of a new type of death camp, at Belzec in Poland, has disposed of over 20,000 Jews since it opened on 16 March. Deportees arrive, up to 2,000 at a time, crammed into sealed goods wagons, at a railway siding in the camp. The hardship of the journey itself has already killed the weakest. The guards greet the survivors with dogs and whips. They confiscate the meagre belongings the Jews have brought with them. The healthiest hundred or so are picked out to live in the camp as forced labourers. The rest, including all the women and children, must take a "shower".

Herded into what seems to be a shower block, the Jews strip. They only realize their fate when the "shower-room" door is locked shut and the deadly exhaust fumes fill the air.

The custom-built gas chambers and high-powered crematoria have a kill capacity of 15,000 people a day. Similar installations at Majdanek, Treblinka, Auschwitz and Sobibor are due to be completed later this month with a combined capacity to murder over 100,000 people a day. Efficiency is a watchword of the new system. If everything is working smoothly, the camps can process a human being into a handful of ashes within two hours of arrival (→ 15).

How Nazis process dead Jews' goods

Berlin, 1 April
The Nazis have drawn up a set of rules for disposing of the possessions looted from Jews, down to the last fountain-pen.

They have decreed that German *Mark* are to be paid into the bank account of the SS's administration department, which runs the concentration camps. Foreign currency, precious metals, jewellery and dental gold are to be handed over to the SS for transfer to the *Reichsbank*. Alarm clocks, pocket knives, scissors, wallets and fountain-pens will be sold to troops at the front (→ 2).

Japanese warships arrive off Ceylon

Colombo, Ceylon, 4 April
The Royal Navy's 200 years of supremacy in the Indian Ocean have ended. Its shoe-string fleet of five battleships – all but one of them pre-1918 – and the distinctly middleaged carrier *Hermes* has been scattered by the threat of Admiral Nagumo's fleet of five carriers and four battleships – all veterans of Pearl Harbor. The Japanese fleet cruises the defenceless eastern coasts of Ceylon and India. The British fleet is 600 miles away, and is no match for Nagumo's ships and First Air Fleet (→ 6).

Germans are forced back near Kharkov

Moscow, 3 April
The German and Soviet armies are now sparring for advantage before they launch the major offensives they plan for the spring. Encounters are reported from outside Leningrad, and there is heavy fighting for possession of Novgorod and Staraya Russa in the centre.

Most of the activity is in the south where the spring thaw is releasing the ground. The Russians have pushed the Germans back south-east of Kharkhov. The Germans admitted yesterday that the Russians had penetrated their lines and compelled them to retreat (→ 9).

Recognizing the importance of the eastern front: a British poster.

Women who refuse war work face trial

London, 2 April
The first women to be conscientious objectors since the order directing women into national service came into force have been tried by tribunal. One Salvation Army worker was allowed her appeal after telling the court that she worked in canteens and looked after air-raid shelters. "It would be difficult to find a job in which she would be more useful," said the judge. Several appeals were disallowed. The public gallery applauded when a woman of 21 said she would rather go to prison than do war work.

German U-boats wreak havoc on world shipping

North Atlantic, 1 April
The Allies suffered their worst shipping losses of the war last month. No fewer than 273 merchant ships were sunk, totalling 834,184 tons. The total for the first three months of the year was 1.93 million tons lost, and the vast majority of these – 1.34 million tons – were sunk by the U-boats.

Germany now has 121 operational U-boats, compared with 91 at the beginning of the year. Because of the long distances they have to travel to the main battleground on the eastern seaboard of the US, there are rarely more than a dozen in a position to attack Allied targets at any one time. Nevertheless, their effect has been devastating. In the first quarter of the year U-boats sank 216 ships in the North Atlantic, most of them in the area patrolled by the US Navy [*see report below*].

Admiral Donitz, the German submarine chief, ordered them to go for the easiest targets amongst ships which were strategically important, particularly oil tankers carrying essential fuel for the war in Europe.

More than half of the sinkings have been oil tankers. Moreover, the Germans are stepping up their efforts. The submarine building programme is being accelerated and in six months' time the Allies will be reckoning with the menace of at least another 100 U-boats.

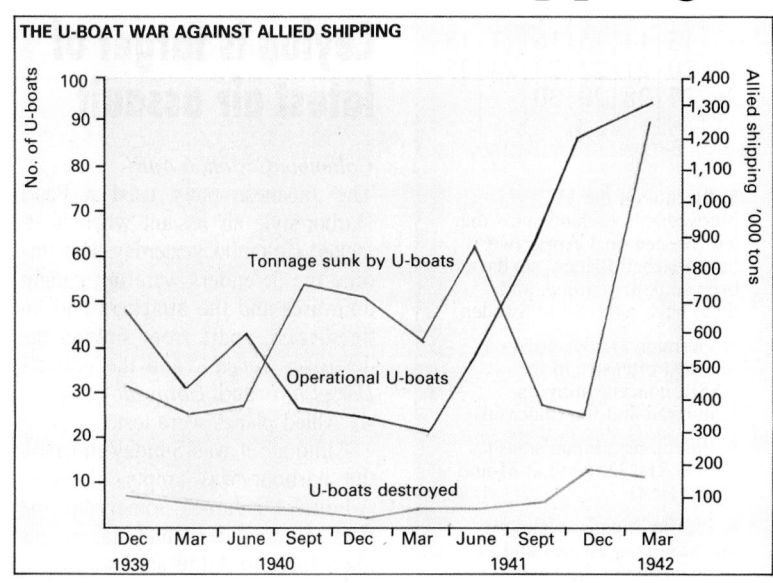

THE U-BOAT WAR AGAINST ALLIED SHIPPING

US introduces convoys on east coast

Another casualty of "the American turkey-shoot" sinks off New Jersey.

New York, 1 April
Admiral Ernest J King, the commander-in-chief of the US Navy, who has his headquarters in downtown Manhattan, has finally accepted the British view on convoys. The devastating successes of the U-boats against merchant ships – most of them in US waters – last month have convinced him that convoys will have to be introduced.

Ironically, the Allies have been doing less well against the U-boats since the US entered the war. Before then the British had established the convoy system with help from Canada and, despite its neutrality, from the US. Once the US joined the war Admiral King took the view that "inadequately escorted convoys are worse than none". Hundreds of ships were allowed to sail unescorted from US ports before joining convoys in midocean. U-boat commanders simply moved closer to the well-lit US shore. So easy did they find it to pick off sitting targets that they called it "the American turkey-shoot".

The US Navy has not got sufficient escort ships to guard all the shipping all the way, however. The new system requires ships to sail in convoy as close to shore as possible during daylight hours, and to anchor at night in harbour.

First Arctic convoy reaches Murmansk

Murmansk, 1 April
The battered convoy PQ-13 arrived here today. Five of the 19 merchant ships which began the voyage had been sunk, two by U-boats, two by aircraft and one by a destroyer. The problems began on 24 March when a violent storm off Bear Island separated them from the escort of a cruiser, HMS *Trinidad*, and two destroyers.

The *Luftwaffe* found the unprotected ships and called in the U-boats and three destroyers from Kirkenes. The escort found its charges too late to save five of them, but it managed to destroy one of the German destroyers, Z26.

The *Trinidad* was crippled by a torpedo but managed to limp into Kola Inlet near here. It was only when her sailors were examining the debris in her boiler rooms that they discovered that the torpedo which had hit her was her own. The severe cold had affected the steering mechanism so that it circled back.

The incident shows the hazards of the Arctic route. Sailors work in icy spray which freezes on the deck. But the improving weather now also means a bigger threat from the Germans. This spring the convoys have to cope with attacks from Germany's most powerful battleship, the *Tirpitz*, sent to these waters a few weeks ago. Yesterday a force of 34 Halifaxes set out to bomb her but failed even to find the target.

Icy conditions where spray freezes on decks add to the perils of the Arctic run.

1942

April

Su	Mo	Tu	We	Th	Fr	Sa
			1	2	3	4
5	6	7	8	9	10	11
12	13	14	15	16	17	18
19	20	21	22	23	24	25
26	27	28	29	30		

5. Britain: Of the 11 Norwegian merchant ships that left Sweden on 1 April, two have reached Britain, six have been sunk or scuttled, and three have returned to Sweden.

5. Germany: Hitler orders a renewed offensive in the USSR, concentrating on Leningrad and the Caucasus.

5. Philippines: Japan smashes the US 21st Division at Mount Samat (→ 8).

6. Pacific: Japanese land on the Admiralty Islands and at Bougainville in the Solomons (→ 3/5).

6. Bay of Bengal: Japan bombs the towns of Vizagapatam [*Vishakhapatnam*] and Cocanada [*Kakinada*] on the east coast of India.

7. Germany: Three Catholic priests and Karl Friedrich Stellbrink, a Protestant theologian, are arrested for anti-Nazi activities.

8. Bataan: US soldiers are ordered to destroy equipment and get ready for surrender.→

8. Germany: Hamburg is raided by 272 RAF bombers in the heaviest raid yet on one target (→ 11).

8. China: The first supplies are flown in over "the Hump" – the Himalayas – from India.

9. Vyazma, USSR: To avoid the dishonour of a surrender to the Germans, General Mikhail Yefremov commits suicide (→ 21).

9. Crimea, USSR: The Red Army launches a new offensive but gains little ground (→ 11).

10. Norway: Bishop Berggrav of Oslo is sent to Bredvedt concentration camp.

10. Philippines: Twelve thousand Japanese troops land on Cebu island (→ 16).

11. Burma: Japan attacks British positions, pushing towards Migyaungye (→ 13).

11. Essen, Germany: An RAF Halifax drops the first 8,000-pound, or four-ton, bomb (→ 17).

11. Crimea, USSR: The German Eleventh Army blocks Soviet attacks at Eupatoriya (→ 8/5).

Japanese raiders cover Indian Ocean

Ceylon is target of latest air assault

Colombo, Ceylon, 6 April
The Japanese navy used a Pearl Harbor-style air assault when it attacked Colombo yesterday. But this time the defenders were not caught unawares and the attackers had little success, apart from sinking the destroyer *Tenedos* and the cruisers *Dorsetshire* and *Cornwall*. Twenty-six Allied planes were lost.

Although it was Sunday morning the harbour was empty of ships. Admiral Sir James Somerville, the fleet commander, had taken his main force to Addu atoll southwest of Ceylon. He sailed from Addu on 4 April to attack the Japanese fleet, but failed to make contact. The Royal Navy had been warned of Japanese intentions in the Indian Ocean by intercepted signals, and ground RDF picked up the air fleet as it approached Ceylon. The aircraft were from the five carriers of Admiral Chuichi Nagumo's First Air Fleet; all had taken part in the Pearl Harbor attack.

They entered the Indian Ocean from Sunda Strait on 3 April and headed for Ceylon, the heart of British naval power in the Far East, with the objective of driving the British Eastern Fleet out of the Indian Ocean. A second Japanese naval force, supported by a light aircraft carrier, at the same time entered the Bay of Bengal through the Straits of Malacca to disrupt British shipping (→ 9).

The aircraft carrier HMS "Hermes" goes down in the Bay of Bengal.

British carrier is sunk in ten minutes

Trincomalee, Ceylon, 9 April
Japanese bombers, with a huge fighter escort, bombed the China Bay airfield and dockyard at Trincomalee today, causing major damage. Warned of the approach, RAF Hurricane fighters and naval Fulmars intercepted, shooting down 15 Japanese aircraft for the loss of eight Hurricanes and three Fulmars. In a gallant attempt at retaliation, nine RAF Blenheims attacked the Japanese carrier fleet.

Five British aircraft were shot down and the remainder damaged. Their bombs scored only near misses, but they destroyed five enemy aircraft. Because of the impending raid shipping had been cleared from Trincomalee, but with the raid over the carrier HMS *Hermes*, with HMAS *Vampire*, turned for home.

A Japanese scout plane had reported their position. Fighters sent to aid the *Hermes* did not arrive in time. Nagumo's carriers flew off 85 bombers and nine fighters which attacked the *Hermes* in waves. Within ten minutes she had been hit by 40 bombs and sunk. Bombers then attacked the *Vampire*, which had 13 direct hits before breaking in two and sinking. A corvette and two tankers were also lost.

Norway's clergy protests against Nazism

Oslo, 7 April
In a mass demonstration of protest 654 of Norway's 699 Lutheran clergymen, resigned today, Easter Sunday, from their positions as civil servants employed by the Quisling ministry for church and education. They will continue to minister to their congregations "so far as this is possible ... in accordance with the Holy Scripture, the Creed and the Altar Book".

In a declaration read from pulpits throughout Norway, the clergy emphasized the supremacy of God rather than of political ideologies. They said they had acted "with a heavy heart" for the sake of the Christian life of the Norwegian people.

The resignations are reported to have shaken the puppet government, which has been trying to force government employees into a Nazi-style Labour Front. Quisling called a hasty meeting of ministers. Afterwards a spokesman said: "It is an act of revolt, a declaration of war." The leaders of the campaign would be punished, he said (→ 10).

Bataan falls: prisoners start long march

Surrendering American troops begin a march that many may never finish.

Bataan, 9 April

After four months' epic resistance the 76,000 emaciated and diseased US and Filipino troops and civilians defending Bataan have surrendered. Major-General King said that he was defying orders not to surrender from Major-General Wainwright, now on Corregidor, in order to avoid a "mass slaughter" by the 50,000-strong Japanese army.

Japan launched the final assault on Bataan on 4 April, with an intensive air and artillery barrage. The strength and vigour of their attack could not be resisted: Mount Samat was swiftly taken and

the 21st Division defending it was massacred. American and Filipino counter-attacks were fruitless in the face of overwhelming Japanese superiority on the ground and in the air. Only 2,000 men out of the 78,000 stationed in Bataan could be evacuated to Corregidor, which is still holding out.

The PoWs pose a logistics problem to their captors who are now turning their attention to the island of Corregidor. The Japanese therefore plan to move the prisoners to Camp O'Donnell, but with the nearest railhead 65 miles (104 km) away they will have to force march them there (→ 10).

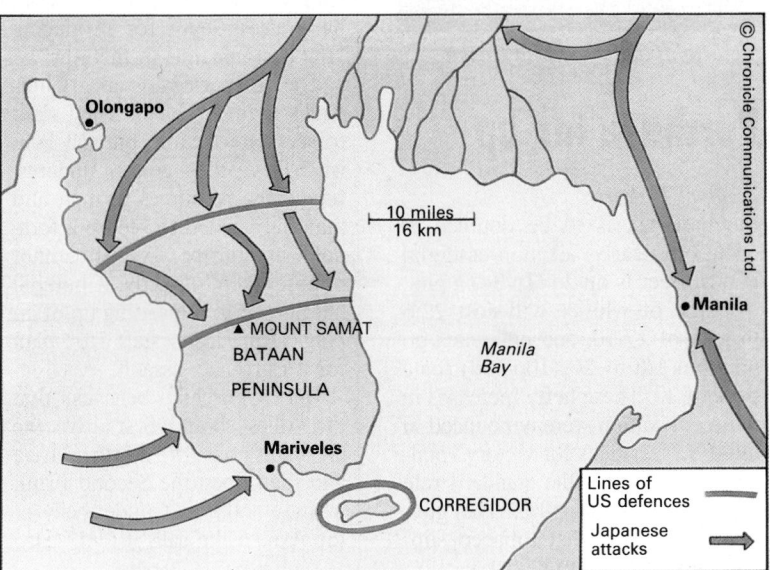

Olongapo

10 miles
16 km

▲ MOUNT SAMAT
BATAAN
PENINSULA

Mariveles

● Manila

Manila Bay

CORREGIDOR

Lines of US defences

Japanese attacks

© Chronicle Communications Ltd.

1942

April

Su	Mo	Tu	We	Th	Fr	Sa
			1	2	3	4
5	6	7	8	9	10	11
12	13	14	15	16	17	18
19	20	21	22	23	24	25
26	27	28	29	30		

12. India: The Congress Party leader, Pandit Nehru, promises no surrender and full resistance to the Axis, despite the rejection of Stafford Cripps's plea for greater Indian military cooperation in exchange for independence after the war.

13. Burma: Allied forces retreat to Magwe, leaving the oilfields of central Burma exposed to the Japanese.→

14. Atlantic: The US destroyer *Roper* sinks the German U 85 in the first US U-boat kill.

14. Mediterranean: The British submarine *Upholder* is sunk by an Italian torpedo boat.

14. USSR: Stalin opens a war loan subscription to raise 10,000 million *roubles*.

16. Philippines: Japan invades the island of Panay with a 4,000-strong force (→ 26).

16. Vichy: Under German pressure, Marshal Petain appoints Pierre Laval head of government and himself becomes a more ceremonial head of state.→

16. Paris: School students stage a demonstration after their history teacher is arrested.

16. Germany: Field Marshal Gerd von Rundstedt, the veteran of the invasions of France and the USSR, is appointed C-in-C of the Atlantic Wall defences.

17. Southampton: Private Nora Caveney becomes the first ATS casualty of the war when she is killed operating a range-finder on an anti-aircraft battery site.

17. Konigstein, Germany: General Henri Giraud, the French commander captured in 1940, escapes from a German PoW camp (→ 22).

17. Dortmund, Germany: The *Gestapo* reports an increase in anti-Nazi graffiti in this city and other industrial areas of the Rhineland.

18. Mauchi, Burma: Japanese soldiers destroy the Chinese 55th division, and the supply road to Lashio is threatened (→ 19).

Laval comes back to power in France

The French Quisling Pierre Laval.

Vichy, 18 April

Pierre Laval, dismissed as vice-premier by Marshal Petain in December 1940, will soon be back in control in Vichy under Petain. Laval is to be named tomorrow as not only head of the government but also minister for foreign affairs, the interior and information.

The Nazis were impatient with Admiral Darlan, whom Laval will replace, not least for his incompetent handling of the Riom war guilt trial. Laval's return to favour has been caused by German pressure. It will leave Marshal Petain as increasingly a figurehead for the Vichy regime (→ 20).

Britain destroys oil fields in Burma

Yenangyaung, Burma, 16 April

Britain's largest oil field in the Far East is a sheet of flame. The 500-foot-high flames silhouette the men of "Burcorps", the remnants of the 17th Indian and 1st Burma Divisions, who have been fighting a delaying action up the Irrawaddy valley and trying to hold on to the oil field.

Three days ago they began to destroy the oil wells to prevent them from falling into Japanese hands; lack of oil is one of the factors behind the Japanese expansion. The oilfields here came under attack after the Japanese forces took Migyaungye on 12 April (→ 18).

▷

289

US planes launch air raid on Tokyo

Washington, 18 April
A totally unexpected air raid today by American bombers on large Japanese cities, including Tokyo, has shocked Japan. The raid, by 16 Mitchell B-25 bombers, was launched from the deck of the American aircraft carrier *Hornet* some 660 miles from Tokyo.

After completing their bombing runs, all 16 aircraft cleared the Japanese home islands and continued westwards towards the coast of China. The raid was planned deliberately as a psychological shock to the Japanese and a much needed boost to sagging Allied morale which has suffered from a cataract of military disasters since the Pacific war began. The US Army Air Force crews volunteered and trained vigorously in secret for this unorthodox and dangerous mission. To take off from the deck of an aircraft carrier with the very heavy fuel load required as well as bombs was a problem never before encountered by army pilots.

Off Pearl Harbor the *Hornet* was joined by an escort force which included the carrier *Enterprise*. The raiding B-25s were unopposed when they crossed the Japanese coast. The raid was led by General James Doolittle. His plane roared over Tokyo at a height of 1,200ft just as an air-raid practice ended and the barrage balloons had been winched down. He dropped his incendiaries before the real alarm was sounded. Over China it was night and the weather was bad. A few pilots force-landed their planes and of 63 crewmen who parachuted, five died and eight were captured (→ 19).

A B-25 bomber lifts off from the carrier "Hornet" for the raid on Tokyo.

In China after the raid: Doolittle (fourth from right) and crew with friends.

Mountbatten joins Chiefs of Staff panel

London, 15 April
Lord Louis Mountbatten's dazzling progress through the military hierarchy continues apace. Less than six months after being appointed chief of the tri-service Combined Operations, he has been made a vice-admiral of the Royal Navy, a lieutenant-general in the army, an air marshal of the RAF and a full member of the Chiefs of Staff Committee. At yesterday's meeting in London of the Anglo-American Combined Commanders' Group it was decided that no major Allied assault on the Nazis in western Europe could be launched this year. The decision puts the onus on Mountbatten at Combined Operations to keep the Germans guessing by delivering a succession of hit-and-run raids. One report, unconfirmed, says that he is planning an assault in strength on one of the French Channel ports. Such an operation, it is said, would provide invaluable experience for a full-scale invasion.

Purchase tax up

London, 14 April
Purchase tax is to be doubled to 66% on nearly all non-essential goods. Beer is up 2d (1p/3¢) a pint. A bottle of whisky will cost 22/6 instead of 17/10, and cigarettes go up from 1/6 to 2/- (10p/40¢) for a pack of 20. These hefty increases in indirect taxation were announced in today's "sacrifices for victory" budget, which keeps the standard rate of income tax at 50%. The government denied that tobacco supplies to shops are to be cut.

Russia pushes for a "second front" in western Europe

London, 18 April
Vyacheslav Molotov, Stalin's foreign minister, is on his way to London to demand an Anglo-American invasion of Europe to relieve the hard-pressed Soviet forces battling with the Germans along a 1,000-mile front. The unsmiling Molotov will be gratified to see the slogan chalked on the walls of the capital, on bombed buildings and on railway bridges everywhere, by the obedient British Communists: SECOND FRONT NOW!

The Communists, who only a few months ago were preaching defeatism, now have curious allies: Lord Beaverbrook, who was in Churchill's cabinet until a few weeks ago, has ordered his *Daily Express* newspapers to call for a second front; and the Americans, led by General George C Marshall, the chief of staff, and Henry Stimson, the secretary for war, are pressing Churchill to agree to a direct onslaught.

There are mixed motives at work. The Communists, as usual, are taking orders from Moscow, but they are also out to embarrass the Labour ministers in the government, by making them appear lukewarm in support of the Soviet Union. Beaverbrook, the Canadian with a liking for baiting Americans, is simply mischief-making when he praises Stalin for producing "the best generals in this war".

The Americans are Churchill's main problem. They want to see some action, but the British believe they greatly underestimate the resources in men and material needed to secure a foothold in Europe. As he cannot oppose them directly, Churchill has agreed to the setting up of an Anglo-American staff to plan for a European assault.

But Churchill believes that the Allies should first drive the Germans out of North Africa and then open the Second Front in Italy – the soft under-belly of the Axis, as he calls it (→ 17/5).

Malta wins George Cross for bravery

Malta, 16 April

In a dramatic and unprecedented gesture King George yesterday awarded the George Cross, the civilian equivalent of the Victoria Cross, to the Mediterranean island of Malta. A message to the island's governor, Lieutenant-General Sir William Dobbie, read: "To honour her brave people I award the George Cross to the Island Fortress of Malta, to bear witness to a heroism and a devotion that will long be famous in history."

No part of the British Empire has taken such a terrible and concentrated series of Axis bombing raids as this small island less than 100 miles (160 km) from Sicilian airfields – and strategically vital to the Allied North African campaign. Malta has been bombed regularly since Italy declared war – but its real ordeal began four months ago when Hitler ordered that it should be "neutralized" in preparation for a German invasion.

Since then the island has suffered 1,000 air raids – an average of seven a day – and the *Luftwaffe* is not letting up. The Maltese people have gone underground, burrowing deep into the soft limestone to build shelters, communications centres and first aid centres, racing for cover when the alert sounds and emerging into the sunlight to carry on a near-normal life – given that many Maltese are on desperately short rations – when they hear the "all clear". The capital, Valetta, is devastated beyond recognition; the Grand Harbour, once the home of the British Mediterranean Fleet, is under such constant bombardment that submarines are forced to remain submerged during daylight.

The submarines are an essential part of the island's lifeline. They bring fuel for the few Spitfires and Hurricanes available to defend Malta from airfields which are bombed daily, with ground crews working round the clock to service the aircraft, often "cannibalizing" wrecked planes for spares.

HMS *Welshman*, one of the fastest ships in the navy, makes regular dashes from Gibraltar, bringing in food and ammunition to help the island resist a bombardment which – the Germans say – has become the "most accurate in the world".

Manning a Bofors gun during yet another air raid on the island of Malta.

Maltese people in an air-raid shelter: they suffer the worst raids in Europe.

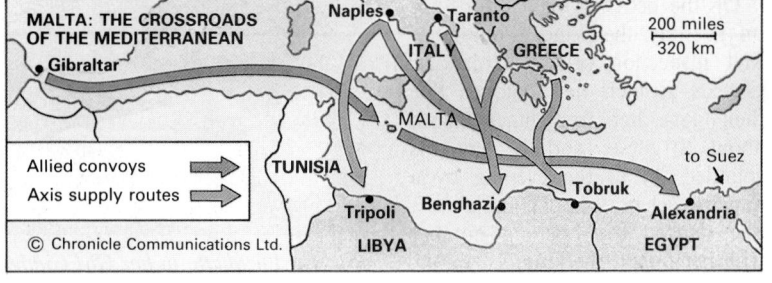

MALTA: THE CROSSROADS OF THE MEDITERRANEAN

200 miles
320 km

Naples • Taranto
ITALY • GREECE
Gibraltar
MALTA

Allied convoys
Axis supply routes

TUNISIA
to Suez
Tripoli • Benghazi • Tobruk
© Chronicle Communications Ltd.   LIBYA   Alexandria
EGYPT

RAF steps up air raids on Germany

Germany, 17 April

The RAF has followed up its devastating fire raid on mediaeval Lubeck with a daring attack from 500 feet on a diesel-engine factory at Augsburg. The object was to "blood" new Lancaster bombers and crews on an industrial target easily identified by vivid landmarks. Seven out of 12 Lancasters, from 44 and 97 Squadrons, were shot down and five damaged. Only eight reached the target and of 17 bombs on target, just 12 exploded. Only four factory workshops were damaged, but the raid has caught public imagination because it was in daylight at low level (→ 25).

New "death camp" opens in Poland

Poland, 15 April

Sobibor, the new camp set deep in the woods near the river Bug, on a former railway siding, is ready to receive its first transports of Polish Jews and gypsies. Like Chelmno and Belzec, it is a death camp: there will be no forced labour here, just immediate extermination in the gas chamber.

SS Staff Sergeant Paul Grot is one of the staff waiting to greet the first arrival. He is especially proud of his enormous dog Barry, trained to rip off the testicles of his master's chosen victim on the command *Jude!* [Jew!] (→ 24).

No lace or frills for wartime underwear

Britain, 15 April

There are to be no more frills and fripperies in Britain as from 1 June. A new order issued by the board of trade bans embroidery, *applique* work and lace on women's and girls' underwear and also introduces stringent rules designed to minimize the work and material put into clothing. Skirts are to have no more than three buttons, six seams, one pocket and two box pleats or four knife pleats. Double-breasted suits are out, and men will also lose pockets on pyjamas.

April

Su	Mo	Tu	We	Th	Fr	Sa
			1	2	3	4
5	6	7	8	9	10	11
12	13	14	15	16	17	18
19	20	21	22	23	24	25
26	27	28	29	30		

19. Washington: Roosevelt tells the White House press corps that the Doolittle raiders came from the mythical land of Shangri-La (→ 15/5).

19. Burma: The Chinese Expeditionary Force holds Twingon, near Yenangyaung, enabling over 7,000 Allied troops to escape the Japanese.→

20. Rennes, France: The Resistance attempts to assassinate the leading French fascist Jacques Doriot.

20. Mediterranean: The US carrier *Wasp* delivers 46 Spitfires to Malta, of which 30 are immediately destroyed by the *Luftwaffe*.→

20. Vichy: Laval broadcasts to the French people, warning that the USSR must not be allowed to win the war and calling for closer cooperation with Germany.→

21. Washington: Roosevelt orders all patents owned or controlled by enemy nations to be seized, in order to forestall German interference in US industry.

21. France: The Germans shoot 20 French hostages "for complicity" during the raid on St Nazaire last month.

21. USSR: Germany relieves the troops who have been trapped in the Demyansk pocket, supplied by airlifts only, for ten weeks.

22. Burma: British troops retreat to Meiktila (→ 23).

23. Cape Town: South Africa breaks off diplomatic relations with Vichy France.

23. Burma: Stilwell leads Chinese soldiers to attack Taunggyi; they only obey orders when promised a cash reward (→ 28).

23. Berlin: A decree issued by Fritz Sauckel, the *Reich* plenipotentiary for labour, orders schoolboys aged 14-16 and schoolgirls aged 16-17 to perform agricultural service.

24. Germany: Jews are barred from using all forms of public transport.

25. Pacific: US troops land on the Free French colony of New Caledonia.

Chinese forces help Britons out of trap

Yenangyaung, Burma, 19 April
The Chinese soldiers who met the Royal Inniskilling Fusiliers here today put their blue caps on their rifle butts and waved them in the air, so that the British would not think they were Japanese. The Japanese saw them do it and did the same. They killed a score of Inniskillings that way.

The Chinese Nationalists, of General Sun Li-jen's division, had been fighting to the east of the British "Burcorps" troops, defending the Burma Road that carries supplies to Chiang Kai-shek's army. When most of "Burcorps" found itself trapped by the Japanese forces, Sun's division fought its way through and enabled the beleaguered Britons to escape (→ 22).

Chinese troops: joining the British.

Australian pro-Nazi plotters are arrested

Sydney, 25 April
Sixteen Sydney people, members of the "Australia First" movement, have been arrested here. Their premises have been searched and documents seized. They were detained because of a suspected relationship between some Sydney members of the movement and four people in Western Australia who had been charged with attending a meeting at which they were told that they would be required to use sabotage to help the Japanese. The prime minister, John Curtin, has told the House of Representatives that the "Australia First" movement has been under constant supervision by military intelligence and that there was a *prima facie* case against 20 individuals.

The movement seeks the recall of Australian forces for the country's defence and aid for Australia before other countries, especially the Soviet Union.

Giraud flees PoW camp in Germany

Paris, 22 April
Paris is exhilarated today by the news that General Henri Giraud, who has been a prisoner of war since he was captured in June 1940, has escaped to unoccupied France.

The 63-year-old general's escape was a romantic adventure, and it has given a much-needed boost to the French morale, which has taken a hammering over the last three years.

He succeeded in freeing himself from the castle at Konigstein, in Saxony, which has been turned into a maximum-security prison, jumped on board a moving train and reached the French border. His plans are not known, but he is unlikely to remain in Europe.

The Petain government has awarded him the *Medaille Militaire*. Hitler, on the other hand, was in such a "black rage" when he heard of Giraud's escape that he ordered the *Gestapo* to find him and assassinate him.

A graduate of the French army officers' school at St Cyr, Giraud is famous for his physical courage. He served for many years in the colonies. Now that he is free, he will inevitably be a rival pole of attraction for French patriots to General de Gaulle, who served under him in 1936.

Princess Elizabeth celebrates birthday by signing war register

Britain, 25 April
Princess Elizabeth has registered for war service today, just four days after her 16th birthday. She was one of about 200,000 sixteen-year-old girls across the country who signed up with the ministry of labour under the youth registration scheme. So far local panels have been reluctant to call such young girls up for interview, so it is unlikely that the princess will be called.

On the occasion of her birthday on Tuesday, the princess made her first inspection of the Grenadier Guards as their new colonel. She then gave her first luncheon to about 30 guests, and the day was rounded off in the evening by a dance to celebrate her "coming out". She danced the opening number with her father, the king.

Princess Elizabeth, in her Girl Guide uniform, signs the war service register.

Rival air forces wage war upon cities

London, 25 April
The RAF hammered the German Baltic port of Rostock for the second night running last night. "An overpowering concentration of bombers was brought over the town," said the air ministry. In last night's attack 125 bombers, including the new four-engined Lancaster, used area bombing tactics against the town and precision bombing by special crews to attack the Heinkel aircraft factory whose bombers did so much damage to British cities.

Some of the precision bombers, Manchesters of No 106 Squadron led by Wing-Commander Guy Gibson, made their bombing runs at under 2,000 feet. However, daylight reconnaissance shows that no damage was done to the Heinkel works during the raid two nights ago, and the centre of the city was barely hit last night.

Despite this, the attacks by the RAF on German cities, though many of the targets escaped direct hits, have enraged Hitler. Following the raid on Lubeck last month he ordered a series of terror raids against British cities with a cultural heritage. He told Goebbels that he would repeat these raids "night after night until the English are sick and tired of terror attacks".

These raids on Britain's historic cities are being called the *Baedeker* raids, after the German travel guides, because after the destruc-

A vicar in Bath inspects the ruins of his church after a "Baedeker" raid.

tion of Lubeck the deputy head of the German foreign office press department said: "Now the *Luftwaffe* will go out for every building marked with three stars in Baedeker". Exeter and Bath have been the first to suffer these travel guide raids. Great damage has been done

to homes and there have been many casualties. It is believed that the Germans are using a new type of electronic beam to guide them to their targets, but they can scrape together only a few aircraft, and RAF fighters are taking a heavy toll of the enemy bombers (→ 27).

Spitfires destroyed on ground in Malta

Malta, 20 April
The handful of Spitfires and Hurricanes defending Malta has continued to dwindle in numbers as wave after wave of German and Italian bombers continue their relentless *Blitzkrieg* on the island. Thus the news that 46 Spitfires were on their way – flown from the American carrier *Wasp* – was enough to electrify Malta's garrison. However, their arrival was also watched on radar screens in Sicily, and Stukas were waiting to destroy almost all of the critically needed aircraft on the ground (→ 28).

German mothers to join the war effort

Berlin, 24 April
For as long as many of them can remember, German women have been told that their true vocation is motherhood. No longer is that the case, it seems. Under a new decree by *Gauleiter* Fritz Sauckel, the plenipotentiary-general for employment, they are obliged to work in industry. This means that many mothers will be working in factories for the first time ... and earning some 20 per cent less than men for doing the same jobs. The women are not happy about that – nor about the extra problems of shopping and bringing up their children.

Laval wants closer links with Germany

Vichy, 20 April
The new head of the Vichy France government, Pierre Laval, today fawned on Hitler and attacked Britain, but sought friendship with the United States. Speaking on the very day that the Nazis shot 30 hostages in Rouen in reprisal for an attack on a German troop train, Laval called Hitler "a conqueror who did not abuse his victory". The gigantic battle that Germany was waging against "Bolshevism", he said, had given a new meaning to the war. But Laval took care not to attack the United States, which he hopes to influence (→ 6/5).

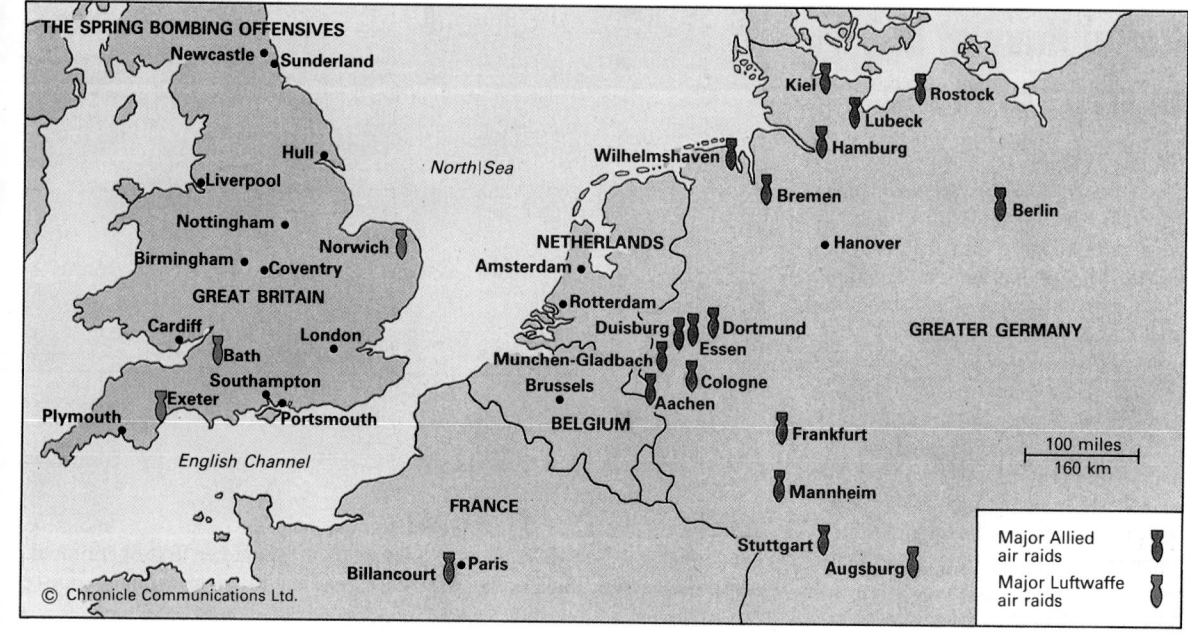

THE SPRING BOMBING OFFENSIVES

Newcastle • Sunderland
Kiel
Rostock
Lubeck
Hamburg
Hull
Wilhelmshaven
North Sea
Liverpool
Bremen
Berlin
Nottingham •
Norwich
NETHERLANDS
Hanover
Birmingham • • Coventry
Amsterdam •
GREAT BRITAIN
Cardiff
Rotterdam
London
Duisburg
Dortmund
GREATER GERMANY
Bath
Munchen-Gladbach
Essen
Southampton
Brussels
Cologne
Exeter
Aachen
Plymouth
Portsmouth
BELGIUM
English Channel
Frankfurt

100 miles
160 km

FRANCE
Mannheim

Stuttgart
Major Allied air raids
Billancourt • Paris
Augsburg
Major Luftwaffe air raids

© Chronicle Communications Ltd.

April

Su	Mo	Tu	We	Th	Fr	Sa
			1	2	3	4
5	6	7	8	9	10	11
12	13	14	15	16	17	18
19	20	21	22	23	24	25
26	27	28	29	30		

26. Berlin: Hitler is made "Supreme Judge" of the *Reich*, and given powers to act independently of the law.

26. Philippines: Japan reinforces its taskforce on Mindanao (→29).

27. Washington: Roosevelt places the US economy on a full war footing.

27. Germany: The RAF bombs Rostock for the fourth night in a row. Seventy per cent of the city has been destroyed and 100,000 are homeless (→20/5).

27. Manchukuo: In the worst mining disaster in history, 1,527 miners have died at the Honkeiko colliery.

27. Theresienstadt, Czechoslovakia: One thousand Jews are deported to their deaths at Belzec and Sobibor (→30).

28. Burma: The Chinese 28th Division, based at Mandalay, is ordered to move to defend Lashio (→30).

29. Belgium: An explosion in a chemical factory, believed to be sabotage, kills 250 people.

29. China: Japanese troops lay siege to the Nationalist 39th Army at Buxian, in south-west Shantung (→5/5).

29. Philippines: Japan applies steady pressure to force the defenders of Mindanao to retreat, and shells Corregidor heavily (→4/5).

30. Barents Sea: The cruiser HMS *Edinburgh*, with a cargo of Soviet gold, is torpedoed and badly damaged by a U-boat (→2/5).

30. Pacific: The Japanese carriers *Shoho*, *Shokaku* and *Zuikaku* set sail for an amphibious attack on Port Moresby in New Guinea.

30. Warsaw: This month, 4,432 Jews have died in the ghetto of starvation and typhoid (→9/5).

30. Burma: General Stilwell is given permission to withdraw his men to India.→

30. Britain: With renewed bombing attacks, civilian casualties this month went up to 938 killed and 998 injured.

"Baedeker" raids on Norwich and York

Terraced houses took the brunt of the damage in the latest raid on Norwich.

London, 29 April
The *Luftwaffe*'s bombers have added Norwich and York to their list of historic towns visited in revenge for the RAF's attacks on Lubeck and Rostock. They bombed and machine-gunned Norwich for over an hour two nights ago, and last night, by the light of a brilliant moon, they struck at the heart of York.

These *Baedeker* raids follow the attacks on Exeter and Bath; in each case the bombers delivered about half of their loads on target and, despite their small numbers, caused considerable damage and killed 400

people. British experts are sure that the bombers' accuracy is due to a new electronic target beam and are working on a way of confusing the pilots so that they drop their bombs in open country.

The Germans are also suffering heavy casualties on these raids. Seventeen bombers have been shot down out of the 150 used, and many of the lost crews were instructors thrown into action to appease Hitler's rage over the RAF attacks.

The Baedeker raids can be seen, therefore, to be doing more harm to the German war effort than to the British in the long run (→4/5).

Royal Navy at bay in siege of Malta

Malta, 28 April
No ships of the Royal Navy ride proudly at anchor in Valetta's Grand Harbour today. The cruiser HMS *Penelope* has been hit so often by German bombs that she was nicknamed "HMS Pepperpot" before she slipped away last night. Two damaged destroyers remain – the last vestige of Britain's shattered naval power in the Mediterranean. The submarines that have supplied Malta with fuel have been forced to leave by the huge number of Axis mines laid outside the harbour. On short rations, Malta is praying for a miracle (→9/5).

Thousands of PoWs in "death march"

Philippines, 28 April
The full horror of a forced march by American and Filipino prisoners – in which as many as 20,000 men are believed to have perished from disease, hunger and the savagery of their Japanese captors – is beginning to emerge. The prisoners, taken after the surrender of the Bataan peninsula earlier this month, died as they were marched 65 miles (105 km) to a captured US barracks near Clark Field air base.

Even before the march began, many of the prisoners were racked by malaria, dysentery, beriberi and other diseases. The Japanese forced the pace with clubs, bayonets and unspeakable cruelty. Dozens of men were bayoneted to death; more were beheaded, shot and beaten at the whim of their captors. Those who could not keep up were clubbed to death or buried alive.

Filipinos bore the brunt of the brutality and, it is believed, the casualties. On 11 April, as the march began, Japanese soldiers massacred some 400 Filipino officers and NCOs – hacking them to pieces with their swords. All the PoWs were looted of personal possessions. One officer who refused to hand over his wedding ring had his finger cut off. The precise number of prisoners who started – and finished – this "death march" is not known, but it is believed that one in three may have died.

The "milch cow" U-459 refuels a submarine at sea on her first operational cruise this month; tankers like this will extend the range of U-boats.

Hitler takes total power in Germany

Berlin, 26 April

In a speech full of foreboding and intimations of catastrophe, Hitler today assumed absolute power of life and death over every German, and abolished all laws that might stand in his way.

A proclamation read to the *Reichstag* and endorsed by the deputies said that the Fuhrer "without being bound by existing legal regulations, in his capacity as Leader of the nation, Supreme Commander of the Armed Forces, Head of the Government, and supreme executive chief, Supreme judge and Leader of the Party, must be in a position to force with all means at his disposal every German, whether common soldier or high official, to fulfil his duties".

In the hour-long speech, the familiar histrionics were almost completely absent. Although the Fuhrer claimed to have mastered "a peril unexampled in history" and averted disaster on the eastern front by ruthless action, he had many references to nerves at breaking point, obedience wavering and sense of duty lacking. His voice rose to a scream when he threatened: "I will ruthlessly eliminate everybody who does not stand up to his task."

He admitted that German forces had been compelled to retreat – he called it "a backward movement".

The Fuhrer who has taken total power and compares himself with Napoleon.

This move, he said, enabled his army to hold the front against "vast masses of new, highly-trained" Soviet troops.

Ominously, Hitler compared the plight of the German forces last winter with the fate of Napoleon's army in 1812. But, he argued: "We have mastered a fate that broke Napoleon." He promised that next winter – an admission that the war would continue for another year - the troops would have better clothing, transport and equipment.

"The Bolshevik colossus will be fought by us until he is smashed," Hitler said. "The loss of this war would be the end of us."

His speech was dutifully applauded, but the usual frenzied acclamations were noticeably absent. Goebbels noted afterwards that the Fuhrer was at times "rather difficult to understand ... the terrific physical and spiritual exertions have taken their toll". After the speech Hitler told Goebbels that he felt numb.

Japanese advance captures Burma Road

Ava Bridge, Burma, 30 April

The Ava Bridge across the Irrawaddy is set to blow up at one minute to midnight tonight. The British retreat to India across rivers, jungles and mountains has begun – and Mandalay is doomed.

Overseeing it is Lt-Gen Slim, serene and stable, "like a friend of the family", according to one soldier. "Bill" Slim is a rarity amongst commanders. His men actually love him. Though they have lost every battle so far, and their Chinese allies have lost the Burma Road, vital to supply China's Nationalists, his very presence raises their morale.

Burmese, Sikhs, Punjabis, Yorkshiremen, Gurkhas and Marines trudge by, carrying each others' wounded, with 900 miles (1,440km) of jungle ahead of them (→ 1/5).

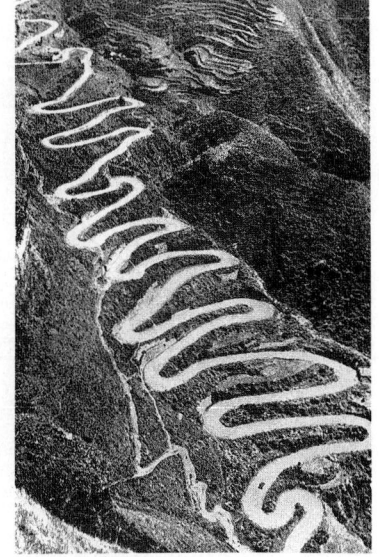
The vital Burma Road which supplies Chinese forces is now lost.

French Canadians vote against draft

Ottawa, 28 April

Canada has voted on conscription in a record turn-out and the country is divided on linguistic grounds. English speakers, the minority, are in favour of a draft for service overseas. The French-speaking minority, is against.

In both 1939 and 1940, the Prime Minister, Mr Mackenzie King, made a solemn pledge to French-Canadians that there would be no such conscription. His fear was that Canada would be split and that a pro-Vichy city council might emerge in Quebec.

Events in the Pacific, including the Hong Kong debacle which netted 1,689 Canadian prisoners have forced the prime minister's hand.

Pay to be curbed as war exerts its hold on America

Washington, 28 April

Following a statement by President Roosevelt that the American "standard of living will have to come down", the prices of all essential items have been frozen and a host of commodities is now rationed. In a message to Congress, the president set a limit on wages of $25,000 after taxes, called for stabilizing all incomes, fixed ceilings for prices on almost all goods and announced that such items as gasoline and sugar will be rationed.

The president will address the nation tonight. His message is the culmination of a series of actions which put America on a war footing. The US Navy has taken over four plants of Brewster Aeronautical Corporation because the management could not assure delivery of aircraft. The government told civilians that little space will be available for them after "air mail, passengers and express goods essential to the war effort" get priority.

The war production board is seeking laws giving it the power to draft executives from private industry for military posts, and it has been announced that 5.5 million new workers are needed to produce war materials. One sign of tougher – or leaner? – times is this advice to women: use less elastic in your girdles.

President Roosevelt, who is taking stringent measures to put America onto a full war footing.

1942
May

Su	Mo	Tu	We	Th	Fr	Sa
					1	2
3	4	5	6	7	8	9
10	11	12	13	14	15	16
17	18	19	20	21	22	23
24	25	26	27	28	29	30
31						

1. Burma: The Japanese take Mandalay.→

1. Moscow: Stalin promises that he has no territorial ambitions abroad.

1. Atlantic: The destroyer HMS *Punjabi* is rammed and sunk by the battleship HMS *King George V* in fog.

2. Arctic: The cruiser HMS *Edinburgh* is sunk by the Royal Navy after being hit by a U-boat on 30 April and by two German destroyers today.→

2. Washington: Roosevelt extends lend-lease aid to Iran and Iraq (→ 2/6).

3. Solomon Islands: Japanese forces land on Tulagi (→ 31/7).

4. Pacific: The Battle of the Coral Sea begins.→

4. Philippines: In 24 hours, Japanese artillery fires 16,000 shells at US positions on Corregidor.→

5. China: Japan enters Yunnan province via the Burma Road, as Chiang Kai-shek launches a surprise attack on Nanking (→ 28).

5. Madagascar: British forces launch Operation Ironclad, to capture the island from Vichy.→

5. Britain: The RAF begins radio jamming, which reduces the success of German *Baedeker* air raids from 50 per cent of bombs on target to 13 per cent.

6. Melbourne: General MacArthur, the C-in-C of Allied Forces in the south-west Pacific, is given wide powers of press censorship.

6. Paris: The *Reich* security chief, Reinhart Heydrich, arrives and places SS Major-General Karl Oberg in charge of police forces in France (→ 19/7).

8. Crimea, USSR: German forces launch Operation Bustard to try to recapture the Kerch peninsula (→ 12).

8. London: The war cabinet orders a new offensive in the Libyan desert (→ 26).

9. Poland: 30,000 Jews from Lublin have been murdered at Belzec death camp since it opened in March (→ 18).

Americans triumph in the Coral Sea

The 3,000 crew members of the USS "Lexington" abandon ship, sliding down ropes hung over the side of the carrier.

Pacific, 9 May

An American naval task force has won the first victory of the war against the Japanese navy in a desperate battle in the Coral Sea, in the south-west Pacific.

Losses on both sides in the Coral Sea Battle were about even, but for the Allies it was undoubtedly a morale-boosting strategic victory with far-reaching consequences. For the first time in the Pacific War a Japanese invasion force was forced to turn back empty-handed. The combat action came from carrier-launched or land-based aircraft attacking surface ships or in combat with enemy aircraft.

The battle was triggered when the Japanese set out from their Rabaul bastion with an amphibious task force to make a two-pronged assault on Port Moresby. A second Japanese amphibious force, also from Rabaul, was to seize Tulagi, in the southern Solomons. The Japanese succeeded at Tulagi, but fell well short of Port Moresby.

Flushed with all their all-conquering early successes, some Japanese military leaders had been urging that Australia should be invaded and knocked out of the war. But this idea died in the discussion stages when army leaders opposed it as "reckless". Because of Allied successes in code breaking, Japanese naval intentions were no secret to the Allies; to defeat the enemy plan, Admiral Nimitz sent into the Coral Sea a task force under Rear-Admiral Frank Fletcher which included two aircraft carriers, the *Lexington* and the *Yorktown*.

Supporting the Japanese operation were the carriers *Shokaku* and *Zuikaku* together with the light carrier *Shoho* which, with four cruisers, was covering the 11 transports carrying the Japanese invasion force. On 7 May in the Coral Sea, Japanese reconnaissance aircraft found and crippled an oiler and sank the destroyer *Sims*.

Fletcher detached the Anzac Naval Squadron and sent it to bar the way of the enemy ships which aimed to sail through Jombard Passage to Port Moresby. In the ensuing actions, the *Shoho* was sunk, the *Shokaku* suffered heavy damage and the *Zuikaku* lost many aircraft. The Japanese damaged the *Yorktown* and sank the *Lexington*, most of whose 3,000 crew were rescued.

Strategic victory for the Americans, but the "Lexington" goes up in smoke.

Japan gains control of Burmese ports

New Delhi, 4 May
The collapse of the bid to establish a firm Allied defensive line in central Burma has led to the final phase of the military campaign. Today the Japanese took Akyab; the last port in Burma is now in enemy hands.

The Japanese capture of Lashio on 29 April has cut the Burma Road to China. There remains now only an air transport link across the Himalayan "hump" from Dinjan to Kunming. Elements of the Chinese armies operating in Burma have reached Ledo from Myitkyina. The bulk of their formations have crossed into China (→ 12).

Japanese on the advance in Burma.

Golden cruiser sunk after U-boat attack

Arctic, 2 May
The Royal Navy was forced to sink one of its cruisers today some 250 miles (400 km) from Murmansk. HMS *Edinburgh* took to the bottom a large cargo of Russian gold.

The *Edinburgh* was escorting convoy QP-11 to Britain when U-boats blew off her stern and wrecked her steering gear three days ago. She turned back for Murmansk, managing to cripple a destroyer, the *Hermann Schoemann*, before being almost blown in two by a torpedo from another German destroyer. British minesweepers took off her crew before a British torpedo sank the doomed cruiser.

US garrison surrenders at Corregidor

Corregidor, 6 May
The island fortress of Corregidor, the last stronghold in the Philippines, surrendered today with more than 12,000 Allied personnel taken prisoner after its defences, weakened by a 27-day artillery barrage, were breached last night by Japanese commandos.

Lieutenant-General Jonathan Wainwright, the US commander, decided to surrender this morning after radioing President Roosevelt and General MacArthur. He told them he feared that his whole garrison might be killed. As he spoke, several hundred Japanese were machine-gunning the eastern entrance of the Manilta Tunnel, Corregidor's underground gallery which was sheltering 6,000 administrative staff untrained for combat and 1,000 sick and wounded. The president told Wainwright: "You have given the world a shining example of patriotic fortitude and self-sacrifice."

The fall of Corregidor has been anticipated since Bataan surrendered 27 days ago. Since then the island, only two miles away, has had 300 air raids and been hit by 300 shells a day, its green hills turning into a bleak moonscape. Yesterday's landings followed a day of 13 air attacks. Coming ashore under a bright moon the enemy was hit by two concealed 75mm guns which inflicted hundreds of casualties – but not enough to halt the attack.

US PoWs in the bayonet's shadow.

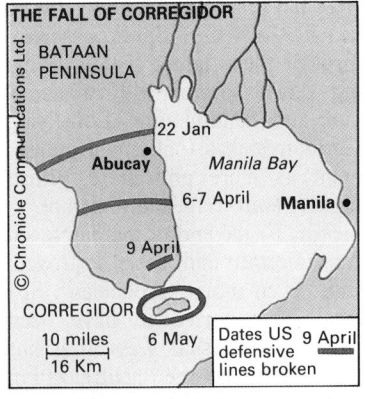

Exeter hit again by "Baedeker" raids

Exeter, 4 May
Exeter was bombed again last night in the latest of a series of raids in reprisal for the RAF's bombing of the historic cities of Lubeck and Rostock at the end of March. Exeter was first to suffer, on 24 April, followed by Bath, Norwich and York.

Many people died in last night's raid, which wrecked the old centre of Exeter. One German official has said these attacks are "*Baedeker* raids", aimed at British towns designated of great cultural interest in the Baedeker guides. But his nickname seems to confirm the Nazis as vandals; Goebbels is furious at this propaganda own-goal (→ 5).

Dutch resistance leaders executed

Amsterdam, 4 May
In a nationwide crackdown on the growing anti-Nazi resistance movement in Holland, the Germans today executed 72 members of the Dutch underground by firing squad. Seven others were sentenced to life imprisonment. Army officers were among the victims.

A German statement broadcast on Hilversum radio said that the men were found guilty of making contact with Germany's enemies and possessing arms and explosives. The executions are seen as evidence that the Nazis have given up hope of persuading the Dutch to support Hitler's New Order.

Partisans the key to Yugoslavia's anti-Nazi battle

Belgrade, 9 May
A two-mile-long army of partisans is on the move in the mountainous north of Yugoslavia – fighting its way out of an Axis trap and heading northwest to challenge the *Ustachi*, the pro-German army of the Croatian fascist Ante Pavelic. The odds are heavily against the mysterious leader of the 6,000 partisans, known only as "Tito".

Many of his men and women have spent months in a barren region of Bosnia, living mainly on a diet of boiled unsalted mutton, and chewing young beech leaves to ward off scurvy. They are desperately short of ammunition; Pavelic's Ustachi jeer at them as "the five bulleteers".

Vengeance is their ally. All of these partisans have seen the results of Ustachi bestiality in Serbian towns and villages where entire populations have been found with throats slashed. Most have lost relatives in an orgy of rape and murder which has taken 750,000 Serbian lives and disgusted even Pavelic's German allies.

The partisans' strength lies in the rigid discipline imposed by Tito. These are communist partisans – they march with mules carrying 5,000 unbound copies of Stalin's *History of the Communist Party* translated into Serbo-Croat by Tito himself. No matter how hard the battles of the day, they assemble each night for indoctrination. Sexual relations are banned (although Tito, it is rumoured, has several mistresses) on pain of death for persistent offenders. And any partisan stealing from local peasants is shot.

Tito has begged for arms from Russia. Stalin has refused, anxious not to upset the west, which is backing the anti-communist partisans (*Chetniks*) of Drazha Mihailovich, a royalist colonel. As far as London is concerned, Tito's partisan army is no more than a rumour; the Nazis know otherwise (→ 3/7).

Spitfires surprise Axis fighters at Malta

The US aircraft carrier "Wasp" bringing in Spitfires to reinforce Malta.

Malta, 9 May
For German and Italian bomber crews, today's raid on Malta should have been a matter of routine. They risked the devastatingly accurate anti-aircraft fire, certainly, but none of them expected fighter opposition. Three weeks ago they succeeded in destroying 17 Spitfires on the ground and damaging 29 within three days of the planes' arrival. It was a very different story today. The RAF had learned from that very bitter lesson.

Every available man was standing by on Malta's airfields. Fuel bowsers waited with engines running as more than 60 Spitfires appeared over the horizon. The pilots had been briefed on the carriers HMS *Eagle* and USS *Wasp*. This time

they knew exactly where to park their aircraft in safety. So fast was the turnaround that some Spitfires were airborne again in a matter of 35 minutes.

High-altitude Italian bombers were the first to be hit and suffered heavily as the Spitfires broke through their fighter screen, bringing down several with machine-gun and cannon fire. Low-flying German Stukas took equal punishment as more and more British fighters were refuelled and took to the air. By the end of the day seven Axis aircraft had been destroyed, with seven more "probables". Sixteen are reported to have been damaged. Marshal Kesselring has told Hitler that the "neutralization of Malta is complete" (→18).

Saboteurs blow up Paris radio mast

Paris, 9 May
The streets are not the only battleground for the *Franc-tireurs* fighting the German and Vichy authorities in France. The battle has spread to the air waves.

Last week the pro-Fascist radio station *Rennes-Bretagne* was suddenly silenced. Yesterday bombers blew up the mast of *Radio Paris*, the German propaganda station, sited almost on the border between the two Frances.

The Germans know the importance of the air waves. Their radio-direction vans search out illegal stations every night.

China raids cities held by Japanese

China, 6 May
Attacks on seven cities yesterday signalled the start of an offensive along a 400-mile (640-km) front by Chinese forces, led by General Chiang Kai-shek, against the Japanese occupation forces.

Shanghai and Nanking were among the cities raided, with Japanese communications and munitions supplies among the principal targets. Nanking, captured by Japan more than four years ago, is the seat of Wang Chingwei's puppet government set up with Japanese support.

British capture Madagascar port to prevent Japanese invasion

Diego Suarez, Madagascar, 7 May
The destroyer HMS *Anthony* ran through the Vichy-French batteries at full speed and came to a halt at the quay. Fifty Marines leapt ashore. Behind the port were flashes from guns supporting the Royal Welch Fusiliers, Royal Scots Fusiliers and East Lancashires. The Marines pushed through into the European town, where they met up with the Royal Welch. Diego Suarez surrendered today. The Allies believed that if Japan had taken the port first, it could control the Indian Ocean. In fact, Japan seems surprised by the invasion which is still being resisted by Vichy Forces elsewhere on the island (→14).

The British race up Madagascan beaches to secure their Suez convoy route.

Su	Mo	Tu	We	Th	Fr	Sa
					1	2
3	4	5	6	7	8	9
10	11	12	13	14	15	16
17	18	19	20	21	22	23
24	25	26	27	28	29	30
31						

10. London: Churchill warns Germany that the British will hit it hard if it introduces poison gas in the USSR.

11. Mediterranean: The British destroyers *Lively, Kipling* and *Jackal* are sunk by a German squadron of 31 Junkers Ju87 dive-bombers.

11. Solomon Islands: A US submarine sinks the Japanese minelayer *Okinoshima*.

11. Canada: A U-boat torpedoes a transport ship on the St Lawrence Seaway.

12. USSR: As Germany launches an assault on the Kerch peninsula, Marshal Timoshenko launches a two-pronged attack on Kharkov (→16).

12. Mediterranean: The RAF shoots down 13 German troop-carrying aircraft off the North African coast.

12. Burma: The monsoon begins, and devastating mud holds up Allied and Japanese operations alike.→

13. USSR: An estimated 3,400 Jews are killed in Radun after the Germans sealed the ghetto there five days ago.

14. London: Despite British assurances that Madagascar will be returned to France after the war, General de Gaulle sends Free French troops to claim the island (→31).

14. Rastenburg: Hitler, obsessed with winning the Russian war, refuses Admiral Donitz's plea for all-out war on Allied merchant shipping.

14. Newfoundland: An area off St John's is mined by a U-boat.

15. China: The Japanese murder 100 Chinese families in reprisal for the Doolittle raid.

15. Arctic Sea: The cruiser HMS *Trinidad* is scuttled after being hit by enemy bombs.

15. Washington: The chief of naval operations, Admiral Ernest King, demands another 1,670,000 tons of warships in the next year.

16. Crimea, USSR: German forces have captured Kerch from the Russians (→18).

Russians break through German line

Moscow, 12 May

The Red Army has taken the offensive with a two-pronged attack on Kharkov, and tonight the Soviet high command is claiming that the Red Army has broken the German line after one of the biggest tank battles of the war.

Torrential rain continues to hamper operations, but the Russians are pressing westwards after the fleeing Germans. They have captured a great quantity of munitions assembled immediately behind the front in readiness for Hitler's long-threatened summer campaign.

Marshal Timoshenko, conducting the Kharkov offensive, issued a rousing order to his soldiers before sending them into battle: "We have entered a new period of the war, the period of liberation of Soviet lands from the Hitlerite rabble.

"I hereby order the troops to begin the decisive offensive against our vilest enemy, the German fas-

German troops come forward in surrender to Russians on the Kharkov front.

cist army; to exterminate its manpower and war materials and to hoist our glorious Soviet banner over the liberated cities and villages." The Russian soldiers, fight-

ing with their usual dogged courage, have obeyed him to the letter. But some of his staff feel that they are advancing too quickly and fear a German trap (→ 17).

Burmese refugees flee to India as Japanese advance

Imphal, India, 15 May

It was days after the first pathetic Burmese refugee arrived here before the first sign of a disciplined body emerged. A column of men wearing what appeared to be eccentrically-shaped pith helmets and gumboots came over the horizon. It was a native fire brigade. The men had no fire engines, but they marched in step all the same.

They were followed by miscellaneous civil servants, public works gangs, clerks without desks – and all the time the refugees, the small change of modern war, rolled by.

Only after they had passed did the army appear, its wounded in the van. For five months it has retreated before the Japanese advance into Burma, attacked by dive-bombers, Japanese infantry and Japan's Burmese nationalist allies all the way. Some units had trudged 900 miles (1,440 km) on foot.

Many soldiers were wrecks; others, bootless and shirtless, still shouldered their rifles. Every man has his own horror story. For Lt-Gen Bill Slim, who commands the corps, it was the sight of a four-year-old trying to spoon-feed her dead mother from a tin of evaporated milk. He watched his troops march by. "They look like scarecrows," he noted. "But they look like soldiers, too" (→ 18).

America has a home front now: 17 states begin to ration fuel

United States, 15 May

Petrol rationing went into effect in 17 eastern states at midnight today, but not without considerable grumbling as well as some severe shortages of the suddenly precious fuel. The basic allotment is three gallons a week, although special cases are allowed more. But even as many motorists complained that three gal-

lons is an unreasonable amount, a number of drivers initially granted extra allotments returned their X and B-3 cards for lesser rations. Even Mrs Roosevelt has an A card, for three gallons a week, saying that she will learn to use her new English bicycle to get around. One US citizen, Bernard Baruch, who is often asked to travel to Washington

for conferences, gave up his special card for an A card. "I came to New York 62 years ago and hoofed it then. I can hoof it now," he said.

Shortages at stations occurred as pre-midnight consumption resulted in many dealers running out of fuel. Some station owners say that they will close on Saturday and Sunday to avoid irate motorists.

Bare legs given modest coat of varnish

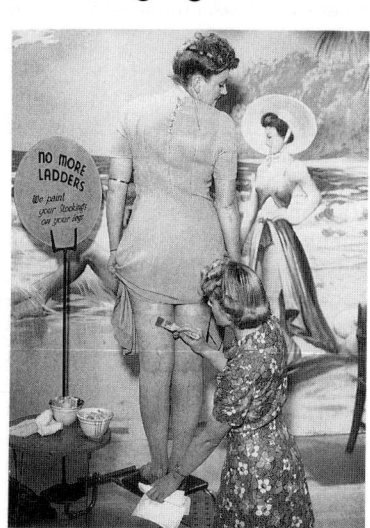

Stockings that need no suspenders.

Britain, 14 May

Stockings have hit the headlines with a request from the board of trade that women should go without in the summer so that there are enough stockings for winter. And parents are being asked not to be concerned about their daughters going bare-legged to work.

While their younger sisters are being urged back into the ankle-socks of their childhood, some women are opting for the "liquid stocking" in preference to revealing their legs to the world. They colour them with anything from suntan lotion to onion skins, and then draw in seams down the back with eyebrow pencil.

The House of Commons Home Guard lines up for inspection by Churchill.

May

17. USSR: The Russian advance on Kharkov grinds to a halt as German resistance stiffens.→

18. Mediterranean: The British carriers *Eagle* and *Argus* deliver 17 Spitfires to Malta (→ 21).

18. USSR: At the end of the Battle of Kerch, two entire Soviet armies have been annihilated by six German and Roumanian *Panzer* and infantry divisions (→ 2/6).

18. Burma: Chiang Kai-shek sends the Chinese Fifth Army to take up defensive positions at Myitkyina.→

18. North Sea: For the second day running the Fleet Air Arm attacks the *Prinz Eugen* off Norway, but she reaches Kiel.

18. Berlin: 27 Jews are shot for organizing a display of anti-Nazi posters (→ 20).

20. Britain: The Singleton report recommends that the RAF adopt the intensive bombing programme proposed by Air Marshal Arthur Harris as a means of prosecuting the war (→ 31).

20. Washington: US naval forces are sent to Midway Island and the Aleutians after intercepted secret messages reveal Japanese preparations for an attack (→ 25).

20. Lodz: Three hundred train-coachloads of underwear belonging to Jews gassed at Chelmno arrive for cleaning and sorting at the ghetto workshops (→ 28).

21. Rastenburg: Hitler postpones the planned invasion of Malta until after Egypt has been conquered by the Axis (→ 6).

22. Mexico City: Mexico declares war on the Axis from 1 June.

23. India: Lieutenant-General Joseph Stilwell and his men arrive at Dimapur, having retreated 150 miles (240 km) through the Burmese jungle. "We took a hell of a beating," he says (→ 11/9).

23. Kharkov, USSR: Germany cuts off Red Army troops in the Izyum salient (→ 31).

Armies locked in fierce fight for Kharkov

Kharkov, 22 May
A titanic struggle is going on south of Kharkov where the Russians and Germans have launched offensives at the same time. Marshal Timoshenko was quicker off the mark and his men, breaking the German line, have advanced 30 miles (48 km) in three days.

The Germans have retaliated by striking at Izyum, at the south-eastern base of the bulge created by the Russian advance. Timoshenko's forces are in danger of being cut off, with the Sixth Army of von Bock's Army Group South coming down from the north to meet von Kleist's group (Seventeenth Army and 1st *Panzer* Army), thus tying the neck of the sack south of Balakleya. There are signs that Timoshenko has realized he is in danger and is trying to reinforce the shoulders of the bulge while pulling his vanguard back to safety. His problem is to persuade the reluctant Stalin to allow him to retreat. The battle grows fiercer every day, with tanks, guns, aircraft and men locked in combat while smoke rises from tanks burning on the Ukrainian steppes (→ 23).

GERMANY OPENS ITS SOUTHERN OFFENSIVE

Kursk • — Voronezh •

Kharkov • — Balakleya — Don

Izyum — SOVIET UNION — Stalingrad

German plan for Caucasus offensive

Front line Dec 1941–May 1942

Dnepropetrovsk •

100 miles / 160 km

• Rostov-on-Don

Sea of Azov

CRIMEA — Kerch

• Stavropol

Sevastopol •

© Chronicle Communications Ltd.

Jews attack anti-Soviet exhibition

Berlin, 18 May
Members of a resistance group which consists largely of Jewish youths tonight attacked an anti-Soviet exhibition being staged in the Berlin pleasure gardens. Eleven people were injured in the attack during which the protesters sought to set alight some of the exhibits assembled under the ironic title "The Soviet Paradise" by the Nazi authorities in the city.

Members of the resistance group, believed to be led by an electrician called Herbert Baum, left leaflets attacking "*Gestapo* lies" during their raid on the exhibition. The Gestapo is now leading the hunt for Baum and his colleagues.

Allies hammer out air policy for the war

Recruiting for the battle of the skies.

Ottawa, 19 May
Canada is becoming the "aerodrome of democracy", President Roosevelt announced today as Allied representatives met to coordinate air strategy. Roosevelt's words were conveyed by his assistant war secretary, Robert A Lovett. The Russians sent no one.

Since the Empire Training Scheme began in Canada in December 1939, almost 50 flying schools have been opened. An enlarged scheme was signed on 5 May, and soon 4,000 aircraft will be in constant use. The scheme, operating in Australia and Rhodesia as well as Canada, will be able to train 20,000 pilots annually. The first 2,200 have already graduated. Volunteers include thousands of Americans.

Burma withdrawal dogged by disease

New Delhi, 20 May
All Burma is now in the hands of the Japanese. China is isolated, and India exposed to the danger of invasion. The Allied defeat in Burma is a military disaster that has brought in its train an unparalleled death toll totalling three-quarters of a million refugees who died from starvation, disease, injury and exhaustion. Some 400,000 have reached India in a mass exodus from the war zone. Many of them are continuing to die from the effects of their terrible ordeal.

Allied losses were high; 13,463 British, Indian, Burmese and Gurkha soldiers lost their lives in the 900-mile fighting retreat, compared with 4,597 Japanese casualties. But not once did the British military formations in Burma lose their cohesion in the longest retreat ever attempted by a British army.

They fought stubborn rearguard actions for hundreds of miles while harassed by constant air attack. Although the troops were ragged and emaciated, more than half still have their weapons and their fighting spirit remains undiminished.

In the Kabow valley, the scenes of collapse were unrelieved. In the burnt-out shambles of Mandalay, where the water became polluted, the death toll from smallpox reached 600 a day (→ 23).

Ulster receives largest GI contingent yet

Belfast: the latest contingent of GIs arrives after a safe journey in convoy.

Belfast, 18 May

Led by Private Marvin O'Neal from South Dakota, the largest contingent of American fighting men yet to arrive in the United Kingdom today disembarked after a convoy voyage hidden by fog. They include artillery and armoured units; soon after landing, 14-ton tanks rumbled from the docks.

Many of the men have Irish forefathers, as did some of the nurses from Harvard university, who arrived wearing trousers to the dismay of Irishmen waiting to whistle them ashore. A new US army helmet resembling the German "coal scuttle" also attracted interest. Some British authorities question the wisdom of the US Army publicizing links between emigrants and the old country, particularly as controversy still rages over the IRA's murder of Constable Patrick Murphy in Belfast a month ago. Six teenage gunmen face hanging as a result, but 207,000 people have signed a reprieve petition.

Cordell Hull, the American secretary of state, is pressuring the British foreign secretary, Anthony Eden, not to hang the killers because "hanging six for one would shock public opinion".

Brazil-US pact for defence of America

Washington, 23 May

The USA today signed an accord with Brazil aimed at boosting the defence of the American continent. The possibility of an Axis attempt to gain a toehold in the Americas has worried the Americans ever since the attack on Pearl Harbor. The long Atlantic seaboard of Brazil, which broke off relations with the Axis powers on 28 January this year, could be a prime target.

Under the pact Brazilian air and naval forces in the north-east of the country will be under the command of the US South Atlantic Force, responsible for sea defence. Land operations will come under the aegis of the Brazilian army (→ 22/8).

Minister backs calls for a second front

Bristol, 17 May

Sir Stafford Cripps, formerly British ambassador in Moscow and now a member of the war cabinet, told his constituents in Bristol today that the government, like the public generally, wanted to see a second front in western Europe.

"The only difference between us is that the public can talk freely about it, whereas we cannot, because we have two responsibilities – to organise it at the proper time and place, and secondly not to give the enemy any information of our intentions. Already the Germans are getting uneasy at the militant offensive spirit of the British and Americans in this matter" (→ 24).

1942

May

Su	Mo	Tu	We	Th	Fr	Sa
					1	2
3	4	5	6	7	8	9
10	11	12	13	14	15	16
17	18	19	20	21	22	23
24	25	26	27	28	29	30
31						

24. London: De Gaulle promises the Soviet foreign minister, Vyacheslav Molotov, that he will press Churchill to open a second front in Europe (→ 26).

25. Japan: Four ships leave Hokkaido to stage a diversionary raid on the Aleutian Islands (→ 3/6).

26. London: Britain and the USSR sign a 20-year mutual assistance treaty (→ 8/9).

27. Pearl Harbor: The damaged US carrier *Yorktown* limps into harbour trailing a ten-mile long oilslick (→ 30).

27. Libya: The American Grant M3 tank makes its operational debut with the British Eighth Army.

28. Norway: two hundred and fifty-eight Jews are executed by the SS to avenge an alleged plot to blow up a Nazi anti-Bolshevist exhibition (→ 29).

28. Berlin: Goebbels writes that "10 Jews in a concentration camp or 6 feet under are preferable to one roaming at large" (→ 31).

29. France: All Jews are ordered to wear the yellow Star of David (→ 31).

29. Rastenburg: Hitler revives plans to occupy Spain and Vichy France.

29. Australia: The Commonwealth Boomerang, Australia's first home-designed and -built aircraft of the war, has its first flight.

30. Libya: Rommel pulls his forces back to the "Cauldron", a small area between Sidra and Aslagh (→ 31).

30. Pearl Harbor: The USS *Yorktown* sets sail for Midway Island after hurried repairs.

31. Europe: Death camps and "special actions" have killed 130,000 Jews in Nazi-occupied territory this month, including 36,000 at Sobibor (→ 1/6).

31. Libya: The whole RAF strength attacks Axis armoured transport for the third day running (→ 1/6).

31. Europe: The RAF's Mosquito aircraft makes its first operational flight, over Cologne.

Chinese provincial capital is overcome

Kinhwa, China, 29 May

More than 40,000 Japanese troops supported by aircraft have overrun Kinhwa, the capital of Chekiang province, 200 miles south-west of Shanghai, as a new Japanese offensive in eastern China gathers pace.

During the fighting 1,500 Japanese were killed crossing a minefield. At Lanch'i, 20 miles (32 km) northwest of Kinhwa, Chinese troops claim to have repulsed ten enemy attempts to cross the Lan river. Poison gas was used in one attack, disabling, but proved too weak to be fatal. The Japanese advance in Chekiang began five days ago with the capture of Chu-chi followed by the fall of Lungyu two days ago (→ 3/6).

Churchmen explore peace conditions

Stockholm, 26 May

Two German churchmen, Hans Schoenfeld and Dietrich Bonhoeffer, today met Britain's bishop of Chichester, George Bell, in neutral Sweden to discuss possible conditions for peace between their two countries if the Nazis were overthrown. The German pastors believe there is growing opposition to Hitler's regime within Germany, particularly among army officers.

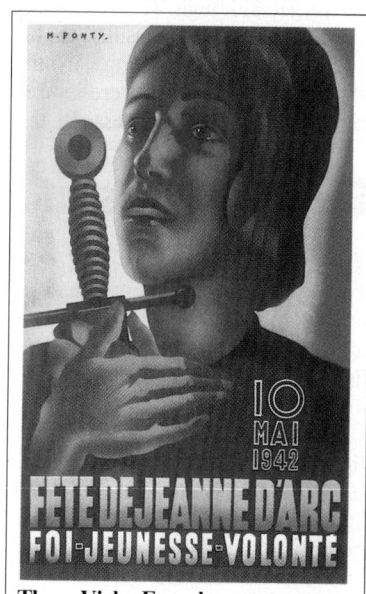

The Vichy-French government puts an old national heroine to a new use in the propaganda war.

RAF sends 1,000 bombers to Cologne

London, 31 May

The RAF filled a brilliant moonlit sky with bombers last night, sending 1,047 aircraft to shatter Cologne in the largest raid in the history of aerial warfare. The planes, crewed by 6,500 young men, jostled for position over the city to drop 1,455 tons of bombs. Two-thirds of them were incendiaries, and the fires could be seen from 150 miles (240 km) away.

The raid, codenamed Operation Millennium, was designed by Air Marshal Arthur Harris not only to saturate the defences of an important industrial city but also as a *coup de theatre* to demonstrate the power of his bombers.

He gathered every possible aircraft, from modern Lancasters to obsolete Whitleys. His five first-line bombing groups put every serviceable bomber into the air.

The raid was planned to take 90 minutes from start to finish, and the crews were ordered to set course for home at zero hour + 90 whether they had bombed or not to avoid having stragglers caught over Germany in daylight. In the event, 868 aircraft actually bombed Cologne.

The danger of collision in a sky filled with *flak* and aircraft taking violent evasive action was obvious. One pilot said it was like being at Piccadilly Circus. In the event only two of the bombers collided over the target although 41 are missing from the raid. The results of the raid have been devastating. Around 480 people died, 5,027 were injured and 45,132 made homeless. In this

The historic city of Cologne: now little more than a shattered skeleton.

historic city 2,500 separate fires were started and 3,330 buildings destroyed, with 2,090 seriously damaged and a further 7,420 partly damaged. The great cathedral is among the victims. With dense smoke still rising from the shattered ruins, reconnaissance planes have been unable to take photographs today. However, the city's chemical works are believed to have been crippled.→

Germany traps five Russian armies in a pincer movement

Kharkov, 31 May

The fighting south of Kharkov which started so brightly for the Red Army has ended in disaster. The Germans, who launched their counter-thrust, Operation *Fridericus*, at the base of the Soviet breakthrough, have destroyed the five Russian armies caught in their pincer movement.

They claim to have captured 241,000 Russian soldiers plus 1,250 tanks and 2,000 guns. Only 23,000 of the trapped Russians were able to break out and cross the Don river to safety. Their commander, General Kostenko, and three other generals were killed. The encircled men fought bravely, and Marshal Timoshenko launched three major assaults to try to break them out, but he could not pierce the Germans' "ring of iron".

An analysis of the battle shows a number of basic faults in the Russian conduct of the battle. Their tanks were not deployed to exploit the initial breakthrough; they did not widen and strengthen the shoulders of the breakthrough; and the control of the counter-attacks was badly coordinated.

Throughout the battle the Russians were poorly supported by their air force, and the Germans had complete supremacy over the battlefield. They now hold a line along the Donets and are preparing to launch further offensives against their badly-mauled enemies (→9/6).

German planes hit Arctic convoy PQ-16

Arctic Ocean, 30 May

Three Russian destroyers joined up today with convoy PQ-16 to help to escort it on the last stage of what has been the most hazardous Arctic journey so far.

The convoy – with 35 ships – the biggest yet on this run, set sail on 21 May for Murmansk and Archangel. For the last three days it has been hammered by no fewer than 260 German aircraft.

The convoy was joined on 25 May by a force of four British cruisers, *Norfolk*, *Nigeria*, *Kent* and *Liverpool*, for the earlier part of its journey. The cruisers left early on 27 May, before the main attacks, led by Heinkel He111 torpedo-bombers and Junkers Ju87 dive-bombers, began. Only one ship has been sunk by U-boat, but six have succumbed to air attack.

At this time of year there is virtually 24-hour daylight in the Arctic, and there has been no respite from the devastating air attack for 72 hours. Nevertheless, 93,000 tons of new war materiel have been delivered to the USSR, including 320 tanks, 125 aircraft and 2,500 military vehicles.

Jews rejoice as bombs rain on Germany

Berlin, 31 May

Hitler told a group of newly-commissioned German officers that he had no doubt of ultimate victory. "Fate has not led me this far for nothing," he said. "She has not done this simply to mock at me and snatch away what had to be gained after so bitter a struggle."

Yet as he was speaking the signs of stiffening resolve against the Nazi tyranny were mounting. In the Soviet Union a central staff for the partisan movement has been set up to direct operations behind the German lines. In the west, the RAF has launched its first 1,000-bomber raid, hitting Cologne with 1,455 tons of bombs which have devastated a wide area of this great cathedral city.

The Cologne raid caused rejoicing in the Warsaw Ghetto. "Cologne is an advance payment", Emanuel Ringelblum wrote in his diary, "on the vengeance that must and shall be taken on Hitler's Germany for the millions of Jews they have killed. After Cologne I walked around in a good mood, feeling that even if I should perish at their hands, my death is prepaid" (→2/6).

Rommel launches attack

An armoured car of the "Afrika Korps": on the move in the Western Desert.

Cairo, 31 May
Rommel has launched his long-awaited offensive in the Western Desert, but is tonight apparently trapped. His tanks, supported by Stuka dive-bombers, began the offensive by attacking British positions in the north with the aim of cutting the coast road at Gazala and driving on to Tobruk.

Another large armoured force swung southwards to attack Bir Hakeim. This desert post is held by the Free French, including Foreign Legion units. A fierce battle developed in front of the French positions between tanks of the Eighth Army and Rommel's *Panzers*.

The offensive began on 26 May and initially surprised the British. But more than a third of the Ger-man tanks were lost on that first day, many to the powerful American Grant tank newly-delivered to the Eighth Army. After two days Rommel, still more than 20 miles (32 km) from the sea, ordered his forces to adopt a defensive position beyond the fortified Gazala line and cut off from the rest of his army.

Allied air forces are now bombing Rommel's beleaguered men in an area nicknamed the "Cauldron". However, German and Italian airmen are joining an air battle every bit as fierce as that raging on the ground, with supply columns and communications the prime targets for bombing attacks. Although the German attempt to reach Cairo appears to have backfired, this desert battle is far from over.

Partisans injure the "butcher of Prague"

Prague, 27 May
The dark-green Mercedes failed to appear at the usual time, and the four men waiting at the tram stop at the bottom of *Kirchmayerstrasse* began to worry. Trams came and went, collecting and setting down passengers. Time dragged by. At last the look-outs, Josef Valcik and Adolf Opalka, gave the signal.

Jan Kubis and Josef Gabcik were at the corner, where the road made a sharp U-turn, when the Mercedes appeared. Gabcik whipped a Sten gun from beneath his raincoat and aimed at the man in the front passenger seat: Reinhart Heydrich, the deputy *Reich* "protector" of Bohemia and Moravia, also known as the "butcher of Prague". The gun jammed; as the car went past, Kubis hurled a grenade.

It blew a huge hole in the bodywork. Heydrich and the driver climbed out. The four Czech resistance fighters, parachuted in from Britain for the assassination attempt, fled. Heydrich was now hold-

Heydrich, now seriously wounded.

ing his back and staggering, clearly in great pain. Taken to hospital, he was found to have a bomb splinter in his spleen, a broken rib and pierced diaphragm (→4/6).

Heydrich's Mercedes after the attempt on his life by Czech resistance fighters.

Japan's midget subs attack Madagascar

Colombo, 31 May
Japanese midget submarines last night sank the tanker *British Loyalty* and damaged the battleship HMS *Ramillies* in Diego Suarez harbour, Madagascar. A Japanese reconnaissance aircraft had prepared the way for the attack; the two submarines were launched ten miles (16 km) from the harbour en-trance. At 8.25pm a torpedo hit the *Ramillies*, causing some damage. An hour later another torpedo sank the *British Loyalty*. The British have been concerned about the danger of the Japanese taking over Madagascar from Vichy France. On 5 May a British force invaded Diego Suarez, which surrendered on 7 May (→10/9).

1942

June

Su	Mo	Tu	We	Th	Fr	Sa
	1	2	3	4	5	6
7	8	9	10	11	12	13
14	15	16	17	18	19	20
21	22	23	24	25	26	27
28	29	30				

1. Sydney: Three Japanese midget submarines attack the harbour; all are lost.→

1. Poland: A third camp is set up at Auschwitz, to supply forced labour to build a factory producing Buna (synthetic rubber).

1. Libya: German tanks virtually wipe out the 150th Northumbrian Infantry Brigade after heavy fighting at Got es Scarab (→4).

2. Washington: China and the US sign a lend-lease agreement (→11).

2. USSR: Germany launches an artillery barrage to soften Sevastopol's defences (→12).

3. Britain: The government announces that it will take over the running of all coal mines.

3. China: Chinese troops abandon Chuchow air base (→11).

3. France: British commandos raid Le Touquet.

4. Pacific: The Japanese attack Midway Island.→

4. Libya: The British Eighth Army launches a counter-attack on Rommel's forces in the area known as the "Cauldron" (→6).

5. USSR: German troops start a major operation to flush out partisans (→30).

5. Washington: The US declares war on Roumania, Hungary and Bulgaria.

5. Bletchley Park: A new type of *Bombe* deciphering machine, nicknamed the "Robinson", is installed to process data using paper-tape loops.

6. Aleutian Islands: The Japanese occupy Kiska (→7).

6. Libya: Following the disastrous collapse of the Allied attack on Rommel's positions around the "Cauldron", the Germans press hard on the Free French and Palestinian defenders of Bir Hakeim (→10).

6. London: Twenty people are killed and 59 injured when a previously undetected German bomb explodes at the Elephant and Castle.

6. Malta: Axis planes mount a heavy attack (→9).

More 1,000-bomber raids over Germany

Before Krupp's became a prime Allied target: work in a steel-casting plant.

London, 2 June
RAF Bomber Command has made its second 1,000-bomber raid in three nights, following up the smashing raid on Cologne with another on Essen last night. Essen, the home of the Krupp arms works, is the industrial centre of the Ruhr and the heart of a great network of railways linking the Westphalian iron and coal fields. Thick cloud and industrial haze over the target hampered the bombers and few crews could pinpoint their targets, but Mr Churchill told the House of Commons today that they had caus-ed "numerous and widespread con-flagrations". The captain of a Lan-caster said of the raid: "To those of us who had often been over the Ruhr before it seemed a pretty good smack at the place. Not a great blaze like Cologne, but in the indus-trial region of Essen there were real-ly large fires when I left for home."

Diversionary attacks were mount-ed by Blenheims of Army Coopera-tion Command while Beaufighters flew intruder missions against Ger-man night fighters. Out of the 956 aircraft which took part in the raids, 31 are missing (→4).

Mass evacuation under way from Cologne

Cologne, 4 June
All inhabitants, except key indus-trial workers, are being evacuated – or have fled – from the devas-tated city of Cologne following the 1,000-bomber raid by the RAF at the end of last month.

The evacuation is announced in Cologne's largest newspaper, *Kol-nische Zeitung*, along with a mes-sage from Hitler asking about the extent of the damage. The paper also reveals that troops have been called in to deal with widespread looting. But across Germany as a whole the extent of the destruction in Cologne is being minimized by the press. People living outside the zones attacked by the RAF have no way of knowing the extent of the damage. Court martial verdicts show that people spreading "ridicu-lous rumours" purporting to be the truth are sentenced to death.

One significant effect of the latest RAF raid is the closing down of many big stores in the target areas because of the destruction of large quantities of supplies and the dangers of looting (→26).

Heydrich dies of infected wounds

Prague, 4 June
Heydrich lived for eight days. The Germans took over the whole sec-ond storey of the Prague hospital, barred it to Czechs and set up SS machine-gun posts. While German doctors fought to save Heydrich's life, SS and *Gestapo* agents and re-gular troops swarmed through the city. Arrests and shootings were widespread, but the hunted men were being sheltered by resistance families and the Germans were still without a lead when Heydrich died, aged 38, of blood poisoning caused by infection from bomb splinters in his back (→8).

Gas is used to kill Jews, claims paper

Warsaw, 1 June
"Bloodcurdling news has reached us about the slaughter of the Jew," says *Liberty Barricade*, the under-ground magazine published by the illegal Socialist Party today. The re-port publishes details of grisly kill-ings by gas and mass burials in open graves at Chelmno, based on the account of Yakow Grobanowski, a man who miraculously escaped from the slaughter and has now reached Warsaw.

Meanwhile, in France and the Netherlands, the Nazis have order-ed all Jews to identify themselves by wearing yellow stars (→11).

An Italian propaganda-artist's view of the Jewish threat to the world.

US sinks four Japanese carriers off Midway Island

The aircraft carrier USS "Yorktown" lists heavily after a savage battering by Japanese bombers and torpedo planes: but her guns still point skywards.

Central Pacific, 6 June
A handful of US Navy dive-bomber pilots devastated the Japanese combined fleet when their bombs tore through the decks of four Japanese aircraft carriers laden with planes, bombs and torpedoes.

The clash took place off Midway Island, north-west of Hawaii. Ironically, the opposing fleets never saw each other in what was one of the biggest – and most crucial – naval encounters in history.

The battle began on 4 June. The Japanese combined fleet, escorting 5,000 crack troops in 15 transports, set out from Japan to seize Midway Island. The Japanese navy planners hoped that the threat to Midway would be the bait that would lure the US fleet to sail out and suffer annihilation. Japan's Midway force included 11 battleships, 14 cruisers, two light cruisers and four aircraft carriers. The Americans deployed their heavy carriers *Enterprise, Hornet* and *Yorktown* and seven cruisers.

The Japanese were seeking to bring the Americans to "a decisive fleet action". But the decision has gone against them. Four of Japan's six great carriers have been sunk, taking some 3,500 Japanese sailors and airmen with them, together with 275 planes. The Americans

lost 307 men and 132 planes. At 2.55pm yesterday Admiral Yamamoto, the commander-in-chief, stunned by the loss of four carriers in 24 hours, ordered the retirement of the combined fleet.

The battle was won and lost by naval intelligence. US codebreakers had allowed the Americans to read Japanese plans, and it was no surprise to them when aircraft from the Japanese carriers *Kaga, Akagi, Soryu* and *Hiryu* attacked Midway. The island's defenders were ready; they suffered heavily, but the Japanese failed to knock out the defences. Admiral Nagumo, the Japanese commander, was now caught between his attempt to bomb Midway for a second time and the need to attack the approaching US fleet, coming to the island's aid. Owing to faulty Japanese intelligence, he was astonished to find that the US ships included three aircraft carriers. Torpedo-bombers from the *Enterprise, Hornet* and *Yorktown* now attacked, but of the 41 attackers only six returned and not a single torpedo found a target. But their attacks caused radical manoeuvring of the Japanese carriers and drew the enemy fighters down to near water level. As a result, when American dive-bombers, flying at 19,000 feet, arrived, they were pre-

dictably unopposed and quickly scored bomb hits. The *Akagi* became an inferno and was torpedoed and sunk the next day. A few minutes later the dive-bombers scored four direct hits on the *Kaga*, again with fatal results. The *Soryu* took three direct hits and was then torpedoed by a US submarine. Aircraft from the *Hiryu* hit the *Yorktown*, but the *Hiryu* was attacked in turn by dive-bombers from the *Enterprise* and was later sunk by Japanese destroyers. The *Yorktown*, badly damaged, was today sunk by a Japanese submarine (→ 7).

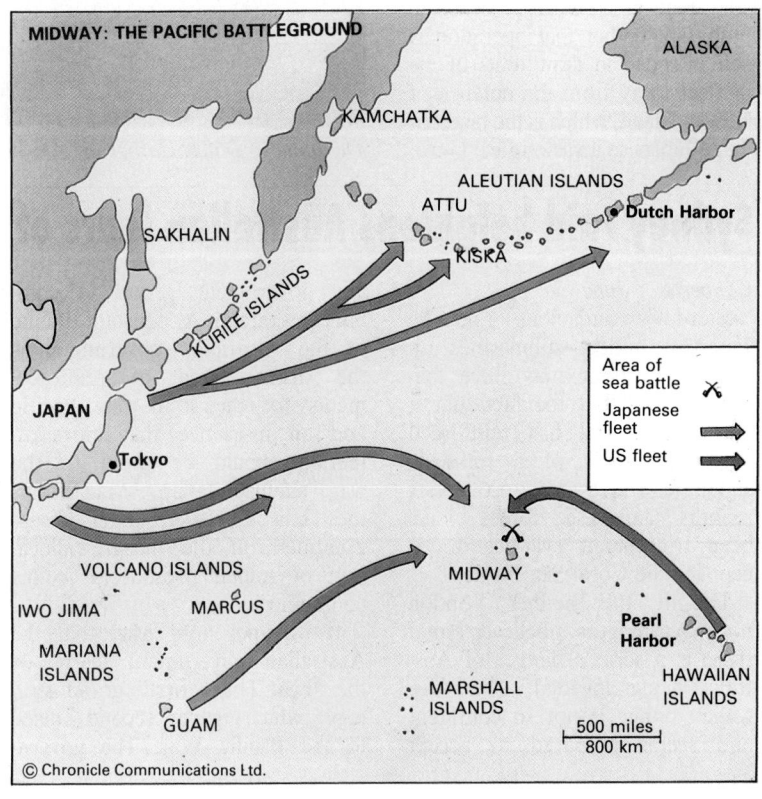

MIDWAY: THE PACIFIC BATTLEGROUND

ALASKA

KAMCHATKA

ALEUTIAN ISLANDS

ATTU

SAKHALIN

Dutch Harbor

KISKA

KURILE ISLANDS

Area of sea battle

Japanese fleet

US fleet

JAPAN

Tokyo

MIDWAY

VOLCANO ISLANDS

IWO JIMA

MARCUS

Pearl Harbor

MARIANA ISLANDS

MARSHALL ISLANDS

HAWAIIAN ISLANDS

GUAM

500 miles
800 km

© Chronicle Communications Ltd.

1942
June

Su	Mo	Tu	We	Th	Fr	Sa
	1	2	3	4	5	6
7	8	9	10	11	12	13
14	15	16	17	18	19	20
21	22	23	24	25	26	27
28	29	30				

Japanese submarines sink Sydney ship

Sydney, 1 June
Japanese midget submarines raided Sydney Harbour last night, firing torpedoes, one of which sank the depot ship *Kuttabull*, killing at least 19 sailors. The midget subs were launched from a flotilla of Japanese submarines now operating off the Australian coast.

On 30 May a float plane was launched from one of the submarines. It carried out a reconnaissance of Sydney Harbour. Burning navigation lights, the float plane twice circled the American cruiser *Chicago*, but no special defence measures were ordered.

The full moon was obscured by mist when the Japanese sent three midget submarines into the harbour the next night. A maritime services board watchman reported "a suspicious object" in the antitorpedo net. Before the submarine could be attacked the crew blew her up.

The *Chicago* sighted a submarine periscope at 500 yards and opened fire with red tracer pom pom. A torpedo passed under a Dutch submarine and struck the harbour bed beneath the *Kuttabull*, where it exploded. Concussion blew out the bottom of the *Kuttabull* and she sank at once. A third submarine was attacked in Taylor Bay. Her crew shot themselves before they could be captured. All three submarines were lost (→ 8).

Allied troop convoy arrives in India

India, 5 June
The largest military convoy ever to leave Britain has reached India safely. It has reinforced that country's defences with thousands of soldiers, airmen, scientists and medical staff as well as vast quantities of military equipment.

Many big liners with famous names sailed in the giant convoy which was escorted by a battleship and a strong force of destroyers. It was dispersed to different ports in the sub-continent when it arrived about a month ago. For security reasons news about it was delayed until today.

Japanese planes raid Alaskan island to divert US from Midway

Aleutian Islands, 3 June
Japanese bombers made a hit-and-run raid at dawn today on secret US air and submarine installations at Dutch Harbor, in the Aleutian Islands, off Alaska. The US Navy said that the raiders, four bombers with 15 fighters, struck for 15 minutes, setting fire to warehouses, but injuries and damage were light.

The raid is part of a Japanese operation to occupy at least some of the Aleutians (to prevent the US from using them as bases from which to bomb Japan), but that operation is itself intended to draw units of the US fleet away from the defence of Midway Island, which is the target of a large Japanese invasion fleet (→ 6).

The quiet of Dutch Harbor off Alaska is shattered by a Japanese attack.

Sydney raid heightens Australian fears of Japanese invasion

Canberra, 1 June
Yesterday's audacious raid by Japanese midget submarines on Sydney Harbour may have failed militarily, but the fact that it happened at all has reinforced Australian fears of a full-scale Japanese invasion. For six months Japanese forces have been triumphant everywhere except for the Coral Sea Battle.

Despite this neither London nor Washington believes that there is a serious danger of Australia being invaded. The Australian public is not so confident and seems prepared to accept any government action to combat the threat. A constant theme of the Australian government is the urgent need of reinforcements for the south-west Pacific and an insistence that more attention should be given to the war against Japan. MacArthur, too, has expressed bitter disappointment at the meagre allocation of military resources to his command.

It was not until May that the Australian government learnt of the "beat Hitler first" grand strategy which gave second place to the Pacific War. The government found it "surprising" that it had not been told of this strategic decision by Britain and the US. After the Battle of the Coral Sea General Mac-Arthur, commanding the Pacific forces, sent John Curtin, the Australian prime minister, an appreciation in which he urged haste in the development of the Australian "defensive bastion".

He told Curtin that there were "most dangerous possibilities" because Japan could now call on troops from the Philippines, Malaya and the Dutch East Indies to strike anywhere (→ 8).

7. Aleutian Islands: Japanese forces occupy Attu (→ 15).

7. US: The *Chicago Tribune* imperils codebreaking operations by printing a report of the Battle of Midway under the headline "Navy had word of Jap plan to strike".

8. Berlin: Hitler lays a laurel wreath, and the Berlin Philharmonic Orchestra plays the funeral march from Wagner's opera *Gotterdammerung*, at the state funeral of Reinhart Heydrich. →

9. Malta: A consignment of 32 Spitfires is delivered by the carrier HMS *Eagle* (→ 11).

9. USSR: Germany launches a new offensive on the Kharkov front (→ 28).

10. Bir Hakeim, Libya: Free French troops retreat to El Gobi on the third day of a heavy German attack.→

11. Berlin: Himmler demands the deportation of 100,000 Jews from Vichy and occupied France to the *Reich* (→ 23).

11. China: Japanese forces attack the Taihang mountain area (→ 12).

11. Mediterranean: Two convoys head for Malta: Operation Harpoon passes Gibraltar and Operation Vigorous sails west from Alexandria (→ 16).

12. Sevastopol: The Soviet army claims to have killed 15,000 Germans in the last three days (→ 14).

12. China: Kiangshan falls to the Japanese (→ 30).

12. Germany: Himmler approves a long-term plan for moving 30 million Slavs from occupied eastern Europe to Siberia.

13. Peenemunde, Germany: A prototype rocket-propelled bomb, the A4, is fired for the first time; it is a failure (→ 19).

13. US: A U-boat lands four German saboteurs on Long Island (→ 17).

13. Libya: The Guards abandon the area known as "Knightsbridge" under pressure from Rommel, who has destroyed over 100 British tanks (→ 15).

Germans annihilate Czech village

Lidice, 10 June
German security police surrounded the mining village of Lidice, outside Prague, early today and rounded up the whole population, more than 400 people. The 173 men and boys over 15 were shot and the 198 women and 98 children have been driven off to concentration camps. Houses and all other buildings have been razed to the ground and the name of the village erased from official records. Another village, Lezaky, suffered a similar fate later today; 17 men and 16 women were shot and 14 children gassed.

An official German statement said the action had been taken "to teach the Czechs a final lesson of subservience and humility" after the assassination of Reinhart Heydrich, the deputy *Reich* protector of Bohemia and Moravia. Thirteen children of Lidice have been allowed to survive – because they have blond hair. They will be raised as good "Aryan" Nazis in Germany.

The Nazis have offered a reward of ten million Czech crowns for information leading to the capture of the assassins. A raincoat, two briefcases and a lady's bicycle which were found at the scene of the attack are on display in a city shoe shop. So far the perpetrators have eluded efforts to find them (→ 18).

Reinhart Heydrich lies in state

US planes target Roumanian oilfield

Cairo, 12 June
Twelve B-24 Liberator bombers of the USAAF, flying from RAF Fayid, in the Suez Canal Zone, today attacked the Roumanian oilfields at Ploesti, Hitler's main source of fuel. These aircraft are the first long-range bombers to appear in the Middle East. Five squadrons of them and one squadron of flying Fortresses form two Heavy Bombardment Groups, and their presence is indicative of the growing strength of American air power in this theatre of war. They pose a threat to targets in southern Europe, previously out of range.

Rommel takes charge as Free French stiffen Allied resistance

North Africa, 13 June
After days in which Rommel's army has withstood constant attacks from the air and from British armour in a series of piecemeal assaults, his tanks have broken out from their defensive Gazala positions. The Desert Fox had deliberately allowed the British – in his words – to "use up their strength in the process".

A German battle group with Italian support is now seeking to outflank the British at Bir Hakeim. Resistance by the Free French garrison is tougher than the Germans had anticipated and Rommel has flown in to take charge, seeking to encircle two British divisions (→ 13).

Hot on Rommel's tail: British Crusader tanks on the move in Libya.

US and Russia sign a lend-lease deal

Washington, 11 June
The White House announced today that Maxim Litvinov, the Soviet ambassador to the United States, has signed a new US-Soviet lend-lease deal. The agreement was worked out by the Soviet foreign minister, Vyacheslav Molotov, who, travelling under the alias of "Mr Brown", secretly visited Washington between 29 May and 4 June.

The deal promises continued US lend-lease aid and provides for post-war economic cooperation. In the talks Molotov stressed, and the USA accepted, the need for a second front in Europe (→ 1/7).

Soviet Captain Savchenko (r) and her first mate Grishina on board their vessel which is crewed entirely by women and operates on the Amur river.

Newcastle and Sydney shelled by Japan

Sydney, 8 June
A week after the spectacular raid in Sydney Harbour, Japanese submarines shelled the major cities of Sydney and Newcastle today. However, little damage was caused and there were no casualties.

The attack on Sydney is believed to have been made by the submarine I24 which launched one of the midget submarines in the Sydney Harbour raid. At 2.15 this morning, a Sydney patrol boat spotted gunfire flashes south east of the MacQuarrie light. Within five minutes the submarine had fired ten shells, only four of which exploded. All fell in residential districts. Five minutes later, air-raid sirens were sounded when an unidentified aircraft was sighted over the city.

At about the same time – after a similar incursion by an aircraft – a submarine opened fire on the seaport of Newcastle. Twenty-four shells landed near the power station and customs house, causing some damage but no casualties. The bombardment stopped when shore batteries opened up on the submarine.

A convoy system has been adopted following the shelling of two merchant ships off the Australian coast. One of the ships blew up and sank.

June

Su	Mo	Tu	We	Th	Fr	Sa
	1	2	3	4	5	6
7	8	9	10	11	12	13
14	15	16	17	18	19	20
21	22	23	24	25	26	27
28	29	30				

14. Washington: Mexico and the Philippines sign treaties agreeing to join the "United Nations".

14. Wellington: US Marines arrive in New Zealand.

15. Aleutian Islands: US Army Air Force planes attack Japanese positions (→ 7/8).

15. Libya: Rommel's *Panzers* block the Tobruk road and reach Sidi Rezegh (→ 18).

15. Atlantic: The US tanker *Robert C Tuttle* sinks after hitting a German mine off Virginia.

16. London: Churchill nominates Anthony Eden, the foreign secretary, to succeed him if he dies.

17. US: A U-boat lands four German saboteurs at Ponte Vedra, Florida, as part of Operation *Pastorius* (→ 26).

17. Atlantic: The British sloop *Wild Swan* is sunk by German aircraft off Bantry Bay.

17. Atlantic: A German mine sinks the US merchant ship *Santore* off Virginia, killing three of the crew.

18. Sevastopol: Only one of the 12 fortifications still holds firm against the German attack as bitter fighting continues for the Crimea port (→ 20).

18. Moscow: The Supreme Soviet ratifies the mutual assistance treaty with Britain.

18. Libya: German forces lay siege to Tobruk.→

19. USSR: A German light aircraft containing Field Marshal von Bock's plans for the summer offensive crashes in the Soviet-held Ukraine (→ 28).

19. Peenemunde: German rocket scientists are ordered to concentrate on developing the flying bomb, which is cheap to produce but must be launched by ramp.

20. Canada: The Japanese submarine I26 shells the Government Telegraph Station on Vancouver Island but misses the target.

20. Crimea, USSR: German troops penetrate to Sevastopol harbour (→ 24).

Battle for Sevastopol causes heavy losses

A German assault in Sevastopol.

Moscow, 14 June
A cruel hand-to-hand battle with many casualties on both sides is being waged for possession of the fortress city of Sevastopol in the Crimea. The assault by von Manstein's Eleventh Army opened six days ago with a massive bombardment by the *Luftwaffe* and the heaviest guns in the *Wehrmacht's* armoury, including the 31.5-inch "Big Dora", the largest gun ever built.

This bombardment crushed Sevastopol's own big guns, but the defenders are fighting in the rubble and the Germans are using flamethrowers to burn them out. Fort Stalin fell to the Germans yesterday, but the fight goes on (→ 18).

Churchill returns to Washington for talks

Washington, 18 June
Churchill has arrived in the United States for his third meeting in ten months with President Roosevelt. They will discuss plans for new offensive action against Germany and the shipping resources necessary to take men and materials into action. A White House spokesman said it would be "perfectly justifiable" to assume that Churchill came to the US to talk about a second front in Europe.

Most of Churchill's ministerial colleagues, except those in the war cabinet, were not told about the visit. The Labour leader, Clement Attlee, as deputy prime minister, is chairing cabinet meetings (→ 23).

Churchill: now visiting Roosevelt.

Rommel heads for Egyptian border

North Africa, 19 June
There appears to be no stopping Rommel now. With the collapse of the Free French garrison at Bir Hakeim – with most of the defenders vanishing into the desert night – his reinforced *Panzers* are roaring non-stop across the desert with the British in flight again. The British commander, Lieutenant-General Neil Ritchie, has ordered the main body of his army to retreat to a line on the Egyptian frontier – ignoring an order by General Auchinleck to defend the port of Tobruk at all costs. Tobruk is isolated, a fat prize for Rommel (→ 21).

Czechs cheat SS by killing themselves

Prague, 18 June
Heydrich's assassins died today after a six-hour battle in the church of St Cyril, on Resslova Street. Three men on look-out above the altar fell to a grenade and machine-gun attack after two hours; the four hiding in the crypt held out for another four hours. They used their last four bullets on themselves. The Germans lost 14 dead and 21 wounded. The seven were betrayed by one of their comrades, Karel Curda, who had arrived with them from Britain to carry out the assassination. His reward: a new name and a German wife (→ 29/9).

Nazis force "Red Orchestra" spy network to play new tunes

Brussels, 20 June
Disaster has overtaken the "Red Orchestra", the Soviet spy network in Belgium. Johann Wenzel, the network's radio operator, has been caught by the *Abwehr*. If forced to reveal secrets under the threat of torture or death, Wenzel could jeopardize several hundred Russian agents throughout Europe, including some working for government departments in Berlin.

Some German spymasters also favour using the system to feed disinformation to Wenzel's former controllers, who are so far unaware of his capture. Wenzel's arrest followed the destruction of the original "Red Orchestra" which was led by Leon Trepper, a skilled Soviet spy, in the suburbs of Brussels, traced by the *Abwehr* radio detection units in December 1941. The fault was Moscow's, for the network was bombarded with so many requests for information that it had to use its radios for long periods, thus enabling the Germans to track transmissions.

Trepper talked his way out of arrest by pretending to be a door-to-door salesman. He fled from Belgium, but the remnants of his organization were revived by a Finn named Yefremoff. His first need was for a radio operator, and he brought in Wenzel who had been operating in Holland. But Wenzel had been compromised by Rita Arnould, who was captured in the raid.

Arnould was sucked dry of information by the *Abwehr* and then shot. Wenzel was now on the wanted list, and when the "Red Orchestra" started to broadcast again from Brussels the Germans knew whom to look for.

Convoy battles highlight Mediterranean sea war

HMS "Malaya", one of the escort of the ill-fated Operation Harpoon.

A peaceful scene in Valetta's harbour before the Axis stepped up the air war.

Allies' two-convoy ruse sails into trouble

Malta, 16 June

The full fury of the Mediterranean sea war has fallen upon two convoys heading for Malta. The idea was to dissipate the increasingly powerful German air strength [*see report alongside*] by sending two convoys simultaneously to Malta: one from Gibraltar (Operation Harpoon) and the other from Alexandria (Operation Vigorous). But both convoys have hit trouble.

Although British ships and aircraft succeeded in sinking a heavy Italian cruiser, the *Trento*, and damaging the battleship *Littorio*, the escorts have suffered badly. The cruiser *Hermione* was sunk by a U-boat soon after the second convoy, Operation Vigorous, was forced to turn back to Alexandria, and three destroyers, *Hasty, Airedale* and *Nestor*, were sunk in bombing attacks. This convoy sailed without carriers or capital ships, relying on a small RAF force for air cover.

Operation Harpoon had a covering force of a battleship, the *Malaya*, two carriers, *Eagle* and *Argus*, three cruisers, *Liverpool, Charybdis* and *Kenya*, and eight destroyers, plus a close escort of another nine destroyers and the anti-aircraft cruiser *Cairo*. Yet of the 17 merchant ships in the two convoys, only two reached Malta.

German planes intensify battle for Malta

Malta, 16 June

The battle for control of the Mediterranean is no longer one between rival navies alone. Air power is playing an increasing role, notably through Stuka dive-bombers. The ability of the Axis powers to launch attacks from bases in North Africa, Italy and Greece has intensified the pressure on the solitary Allied base in the Mediterranean – Malta.

This tiny island is crucial for the Allies, lying as it does at a crossroads in the Mediterranean [*see map below*]. Germany has now sent some Stukas to this battleground from the Russian front in order to reinforce what was initially a largely Italian operation. If Malta falls, then the Allies will be unable to harass Rommel's supply convoys.

From dawn until dusk men on convoy escort ships are therefore at action stations, sweating under anti-flash clothing, their steel helmets getting heavier and hotter under the Mediterranean sun. Throughout the day, Stukas attack in waves, diving directly out of that sun, making nerve-wracking howls until they loose off their bombs and fly off at wave-top height to pick up another load. Nearby will be a tanker carrying aviation fuel; any one of those bombs could turn her into a fireball (→ 19/7).

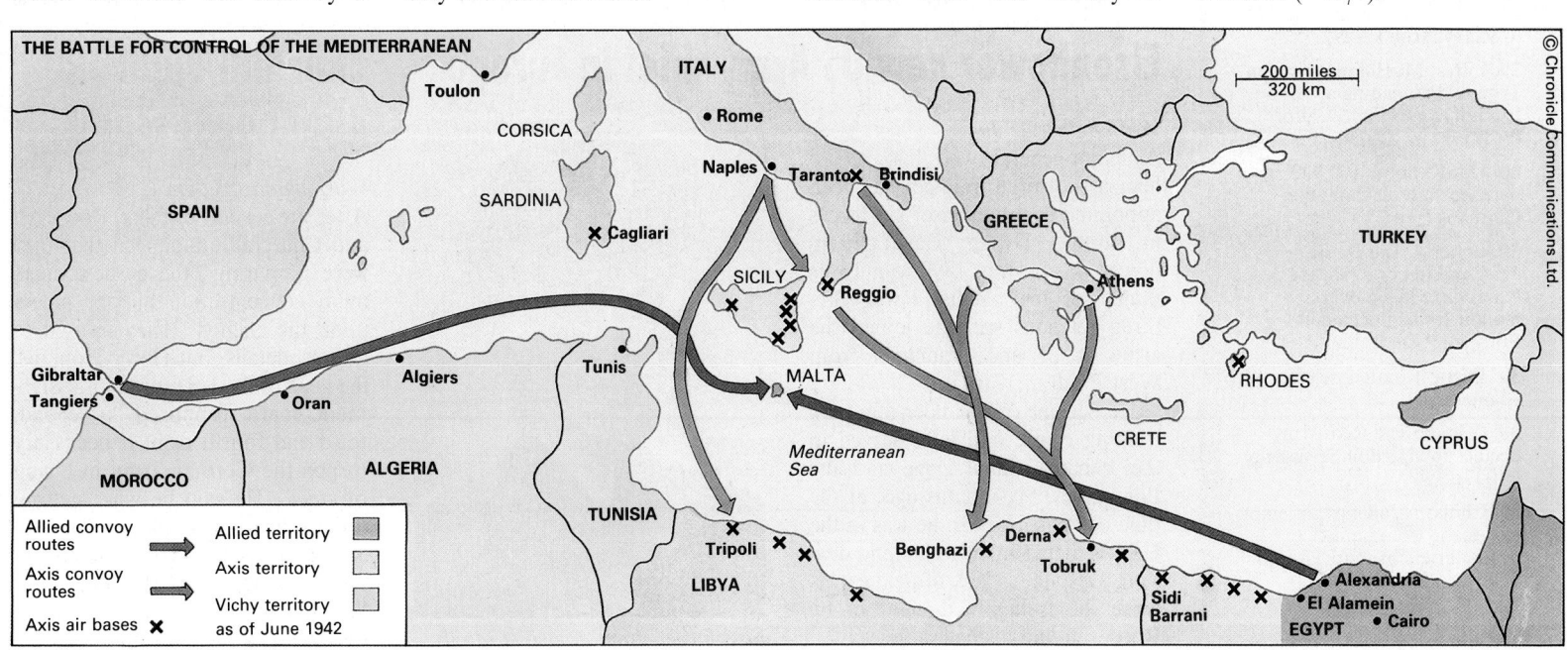

THE BATTLE FOR CONTROL OF THE MEDITERRANEAN

Allied convoy routes	Allied territory	
Axis convoy routes	Axis territory	
Axis air bases ✕	Vichy territory as of June 1942	

© Chronicle Communications Ltd.

1942

June

Su	Mo	Tu	We	Th	Fr	Sa
	1	2	3	4	5	6
7	8	9	10	11	12	13
14	15	16	17	18	19	20
21	22	23	24	25	26	27
28	29	30				

21. US: A Japanese submarine shells Fort Stevens, on the Oregon coast.

22. North Africa: Rommel is promoted to field marshal (→ 28).

23. Auschwitz: The first selections for the gas chamber take place, on a trainload of Jews from Paris (→ 30).

23. Britain: Germany's latest fighter, a Focke-Wulf FW190, is captured intact when it mistakenly lands in Wales.

23. Rastenburg: Hitler is fascinated by the report of Albert Speer, the arms minister, on the latest atomic weapons research.

24. USSR: Soviet marines land in the Crimea to aid Sevastopol (→ 30).

26. US: The FBI arrests eight German saboteurs who landed in Florida and Long Island last week (→ 1/7).

26. Britain: An Independent candidate, Tom Driberg, wins the Maldon by-election following a drop in public esteem for Churchill after the fall of Tobruk (→ 2/7).

27. Pacific: US forces bomb Japanese air bases on Wake Island.

27. Reykjavik: Convoy PQ-17 leaves for Murmansk (→ 1/7).

28. Libya: Axis troops capture Mersa Matruh (→ 29).

29. Libya: Mussolini arrives in Tripoli, anticipating a triumphal entry into Cairo (→ 30).

30. USSR: Some 100,000 partisans are plaguing the Germans (→ 6/7).

30. London: The *Daily Telegraph* reports that the Nazis have killed over a million Jews in occupied Europe (→ 4).

30. Egypt: Rommel reaches El Alamein.→

30. Crimea: The Red Army decides to abandon Sevastopol (→ 1/7).

30. China: A Japanese attempt to destroy Communist headquarters in south-eastern Shansi is defeated (→ 1/7).

Britain's 1,000-bomber fist hits Bremen

Bremen aflame after the latest RAF bombing of this key submarine base.

Germany, 26 June
The RAF's third 1,000-bomber raid caused widespread devastation in Bremen last night. The Focke-Wulf aircraft works were badly hit and 27 acres of the business district were destroyed.

It was also the most costly of these raids so far for the RAF. A total of 48 aircraft out of 1,067 despatched failed to return. This five-per-cent loss, combined with damage to many other machines, leads some observers to conclude that the price of saturation bombing is too high. That view is not shared by Bomber Command's freshly-knighted boss, Air Marshal Arthur Harris. On earlier raids (Cologne 1,047 aircraft and Essen 956) training and conversion units were needed to make up numbers, while Coastal Command was absent, thanks to naval opposition. Tonight, because Bremen is a submarine base, Coastal Command gave 102 bombers.

Dense cloud over the target area hindered accurate identification after a 500-mile flight, although the "Gee" blind-bombing equipment had its first major success and lead crews started accurate guiding fires. Moonlight reflecting off the clouds offered ideal conditions for enemy fighters, however (→ 9/7).

Eisenhower new US Army chief in Europe

Washington, 25 June
A major-general who has yet to hear a shot fired in anger has been appointed commander of US forces in Europe. Dwight David Eisenhower was born in 1890 to a Texas family of the pacifist River Brethren religious sect; he joined the army at 21 and graduated from West Point in 1915.

He became commander of a tank training centre and later served in the Panama Canal Zone and the Philippines. Six months ago, at the time of Pearl Harbor, he was in the US war department's planning division. Despite his lack of field experience, he is highly thought of by Roosevelt and his colleagues.

Eisenhower: from a pacifist family.

PoWs start building railway in Thailand

Ban Pong, 24 June
Work begins today on the first phase of an ambitious plan by Japan to improve its lines of supply by extending the Singapore-to-Bangkok railway 294 miles (470 km) north-west through the jungle to Rangoon. It proposes to build the line using the vast pool of Allied PoW labour now at its disposal.

Six hundred British PoWs led by Major R S Sykes arrived here yesterday from Singapore after a four-day rail journey to begin building the Thai base camp. The first 34 miles of line are on the flat, but at Tha Makham, where the line crosses the fast-flowing Kwae Noi, the PoWs will have to build a 240-yard long wooden trestle bridge.

Ministry calls for home fuel savings

Britain, 30 June
A campaign to save fuel in the home has been launched by the new ministry of fuel and power. It urges householders to turn off all unnecessary lights, use less water – five inches of bathwater is suggested as a maximum – and stop taps dripping. Coal supplies will be restricted, but not rationed. Housewives are urged to sift the ashes of fires for burnable lumps and share their fires with neighbours.

Churchill and FDR plan new assaults

Washington, 23 June
After a weekend of talks, Roosevelt and Churchill announced that they were preparing "the earliest maximum concentration of war power upon the enemy". They refused to go into details, but Harry Hopkins, the head of the US munitions assignment board, promised "a second, third and fourth front if necessary to pen the German army in a ring of steel". He said he was "getting tired of hearing people say the British cannot fight". They had fought against "almost unbelievable odds. We owe Britain a great debt which we intend to repay in full."

Rommel captures Tobruk, taking 35,000 prisoners

Egypt under threat as key fort falls

Cairo, 21 June

Tobruk has fallen. The vital port on the North Africa coast has been taken by Rommel's *Afrika Korps* barely three weeks after the German general was being reported by British newspapers as trapped in the area known as the "Cauldron". Today he has captured 35,000 Allied soldiers, 70 tanks and an immense store of supplies, while dealing British morale its heaviest blow since the loss of Singapore. Winston Churchill was told of Tobruk's fall while meeting President Roosevelt in Washington.

The Eighth Army, confident of success in North Africa after driving the Axis forces so far westwards last year, had allowed Tobruk's defences to deteriorate. The British also lost their numerical advantage in tanks through a series of piecemeal attacks on the Cauldron.

With Rommel's tanks racing in pursuit of a shattered Eighth Army, no one expected him to turn back to attack Tobruk. But then, with incredible speed, Rommel captured two airfields at Gambut and turned back towards Tobruk.

He struck at dawn yesterday with a heavy bombardment by air and artillery before an infantry assault followed by *Panzers* which he himself led. By the afternoon it was all over (→ 22).

Tobruk, a battle-scarred wasteland that has fallen to Rommel's "Panzers".

British prisoners rounded-up by the victorious Germans in the Western Desert.

"Auk" steps in to lead Desert Army

Derna, North Africa, 30 June

Resting *Afrika Korps* soldiers watched with amazement today as two Italian aircraft landed at the airport here. One disgorged the immaculate, bemedalled Benito Mussolini, Il Duce himself. The other carried a white Arab charger upon which the Italian leader proposes to lead his victorious army through the streets of Cairo in the next few days. Such is the confidence of the Axis as Rommel's army nears the fleshpots of Egypt.

Five days ago, on 25 June, a major drama took place further to the east with General Sir Claude Auchinleck, the C-in-C of British forces in the Middle East, taking direct command in the desert, relieving a "tired" Lt-Gen Ritchie. Ritchie had proposed to hold a defensive line at Mersa Matruh. "The Auk" decided against this and is withdrawing further into Egypt, preparing to fight a mobile war in the desert near an obscure railhead called El Alamein.

Rommel captured the Mersa Matruh position two days ago with relative ease, launching his depleted armour, now down to 60 tanks, against a British force of 160 tanks, relying on surprise. Today he wrote to his wife: "Only 100 more miles to Alexandria!" By nightfall, such was the speed of the German advance, the distance was down to 60 miles (96 km) (→ 1/7).

Desert Fox's incredible progress across Libya towards Egypt

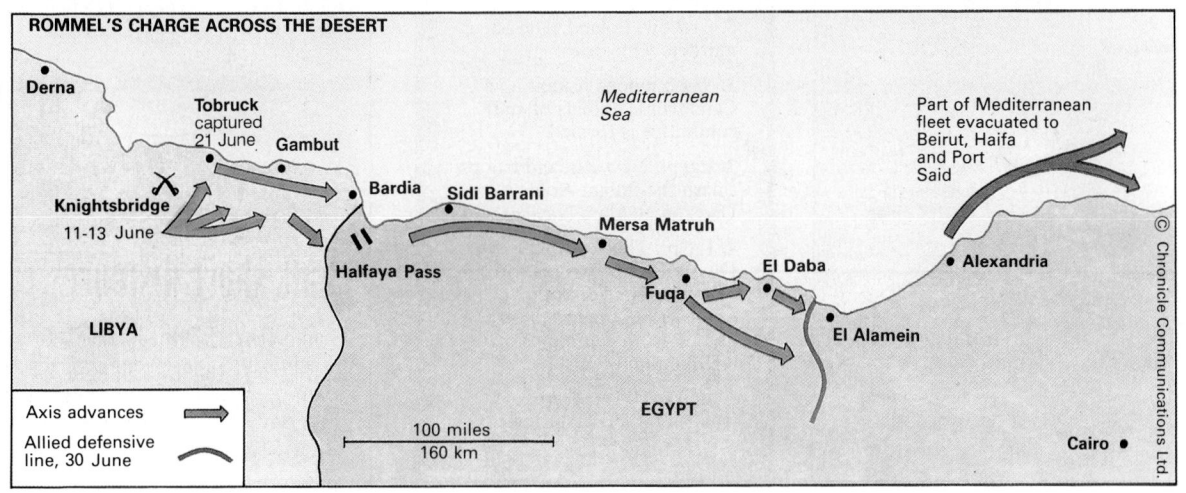

ROMMEL'S CHARGE ACROSS THE DESERT

Derna

Tobruck captured 21 June

Gambut

Knightsbridge 11-13 June

Bardia

Sidi Barrani

Halfaya Pass

Mersa Matruh

Fuqa

El Daba

El Alamein

Mediterranean Sea

Part of Mediterranean fleet evacuated to Beirut, Haifa and Port Said

Alexandria

LIBYA

EGYPT

Cairo

Axis advances

Allied defensive line, 30 June

100 miles
160 km

© Chronicle Communications Ltd.

Auchinleck visits his desert forces.

Germans set their sights on the Caucasus as their tanks advance across Ukraine

Moscow, 28 June

The Germans have unleashed their *Blitzkrieg* again, attacking on both sides of Kursk in the ideal tank country of the rolling Ukrainian plain. The assault, codenamed *Fall Blau* [Plan Blue], was opened by a storm of fire from guns and Stukas hurried north from the siege of Sevastopol. Then the tanks struck.

General Hermann Hoth's 4th *Panzer* Army has already shattered the Russian Fortieth Army, and the Germans are heading for their first objective, the city of Voronezh which controls crossings of the Don and is a vital communications link.

The plan of Fall Blau, one of Hitler's military visions, is extremely ambitious. It calls for an advance along the whole of the German front in south Russia, from the coast near Taganrog along the river Donets towards Kharkov and Kursk.

The units around Kursk are to make the first move, taking Voronezh and then heading down the river Don towards the city of Sta-lingrad. The second phase is then to come into operation with an advance into the Caucasus. The next stage envisages another double drive, one to take the oilfields of Baku and the other to reach the Turkish border at Batumi; lack of oil is a major strategic worry for the German chiefs of staff.

To accomplish this grand vision of conquest reinforcements have been poured into Army Group South (now divided into Army Groups A and B), and it now contains almost half of the *Wehrmacht's* strength in the east. Those troops are now driving forward, raising clouds of dust and leaving behind them burning villages and dead Russians. Yet it could all have ended in disaster.

Nine days ago, on 19 June, a German light aircraft carrying Major Reichel, a staff officer, was forced down over the lines. He had with him detailed orders for Fall Blau. They were rushed to Stalin. But the Soviet premier brushed them aside, dismissing them as "planted evidence" (→ 5).

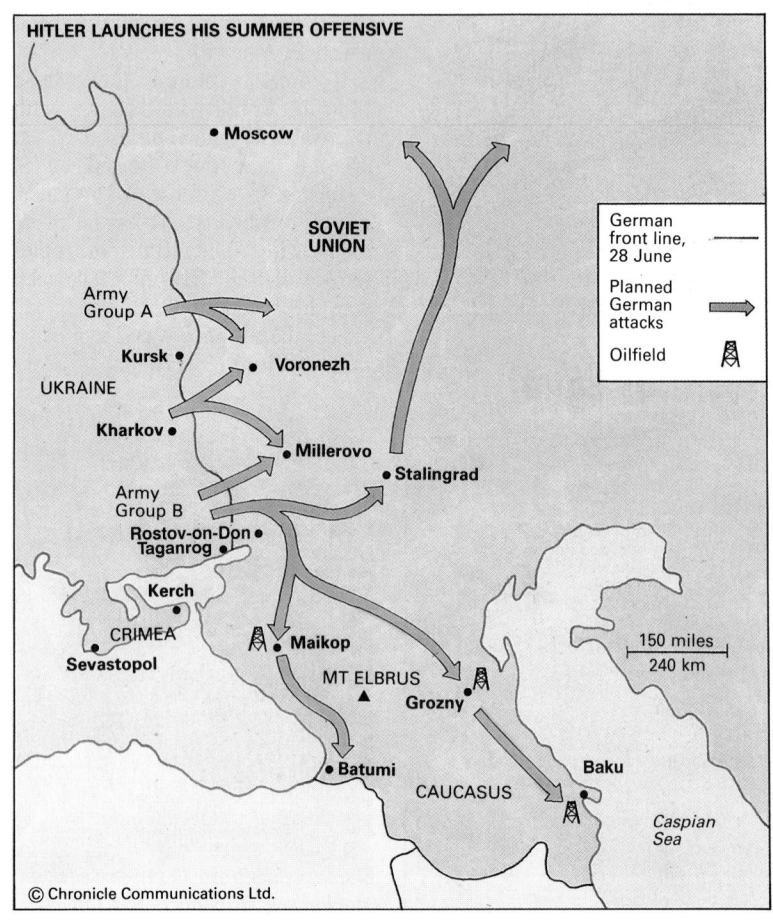

HITLER LAUNCHES HIS SUMMER OFFENSIVE

Moscow • • SOVIET UNION • Army Group A • Kursk • Voronezh • UKRAINE • Kharkov • Millerovo • Stalingrad • Army Group B • Rostov-on-Don • Taganrog • Kerch • CRIMEA • Sevastopol • Maikop • MT ELBRUS ▲ • Grozny • Batumi • Baku • CAUCASUS • Caspian Sea

German front line, 28 June —
Planned German attacks →
Oilfield

150 miles / 240 km

© Chronicle Communications Ltd.

Su	Mo	Tu	We	Th	Fr	Sa
			1	2	3	4
5	6	7	8	9	10	11
12	13	14	15	16	17	18
19	20	21	22	23	24	25
26	27	28	29	30	31	

1. Cairo: *Ash Wednesday* – staff at the British embassy and military headquarters frantically burn papers, expecting the Germans to arrive at any moment.→

1. US: IBM perfects the Vacuum Tube Digital Multiplier, which calculates 1,000 times faster than existing mechanical devices.

1. Washington: The US-Polish lend-lease agreement is signed.

1. US: The FBI arrests 250 aliens who allegedly plotted to blow up the Pennsylvania railroad (→ 11).

1. Palestine: Axis planes raid the port of Haifa.

1. Arctic: Convoy PQ-17 is sighted by two U-boats, confirming German intelligence reports of Allied ships heading for Murmansk (→ 7).

2. France: Tony Brooks, an agent of the British Special Operations Executive, parachutes down to set up a resistance movement among railway workers.

2. East Africa: British forces occupy Mayotte, an island off the north-east coast of Mozambique.

3. Atlantic: The Free French destroyer *Le Tigre* sinks a German U-boat off New York.

3. Yugoslavia: The German army launches an attack on partisans and on peasants thought to be sheltering them (→ 14).

3. Cracow, Poland: The SS murders 93 gypsies.

3. Washington: A joint Canadian-US chiefs of staff committee is formed.

3. Egypt: New Zealand troops smash the Italian Ariete Division at Alam Nayil.→

4. Egypt: The Australian 9th Division arrives to reinforce Allied resistance, as the exhausted German *Panzer* units start to run out of ammunition (→ 9).

4. Lutsk, USSR: German troops murder 4,000 Jews (→ 7).

Churchill beats off vote of censure

Britain, 2 July

With uplifted fingers Mr Churchill gave the V sign as he left the House of Commons tonight. The first formal vote of censure of his conduct of the war had just been beaten off by 476 votes to 25 with 30 abstentions. Yet last month's fall of Tobruk had raised serious doubts about the outcome of the vote. Opinion polls show less than half of the public satisfied with the conduct of the war, and press criticism was strong, too. But in the end the critics were unable to come up with any alternative and Mr Churchill survived.

Japan issues a new threat to guerrillas

Lake Tai, 1 July

Japan's Thirteenth Army is to extend its rural pacification programme in the Lower Yangtze to eliminate Chinese guerrilla activity.

The Thirteenth, working with Wang Chingwei's puppet regime, is setting up a second model peace zone on the Chekiang/Kiangsu border south of Lake Tai, where 5,000 Chinese communist guerrillas are operating. It will be modelled on the successful, militarily-protected peace zone set up last year in the Yangtze Delta. By this April, 600,000 war refugees had returned to live there behind its palisades controlled by collaborators (→ 7).

Go by SHANKS' PONY

Walk short distances

AND LEAVE ROOM FOR THOSE WHO HAVE LONGER JOURNEYS

German advance halts at El Alamein

El Alamein, 3 July

Three nights ago, the *Afrika Korps* radio played romantic music and warned the ladies of Cairo to "make ready for us tonight".

After days of fighting, always advancing – sometimes even chasing the retreating British – victory seemed assured as Rommel formed his tanks and infantry for a final push towards the Nile Delta and the longed-for ladies.

Throughout the night, Allied troops in their desert defensive "boxes" watched as German multi-coloured *Very* lights lit up the sky in an impromptu firework display.

Rommel was banking on bypassing the weak and disorganized remains of the British X Corps at Alamein, leaving Italian infantry to clean up the garrison, and making a direct dash to Alexandria. His army began well, but was slowed by fierce sandstorms, constant air attacks and carefully placed British artillery.

The British commander, General Auchinleck, guessed well and ordered his tanks to counter-attack in the south. He aimed to hit the Germans' flank, but the battle became a head-on confrontation with British armour held back by the lethal 88mm guns which have caused so much havoc to the thinly-armoured British tanks in the past.

By tonight, Rommel's advance had been halted. Auchinleck's tactics are paying off. Axis troops are digging in, no nearer to the ladies of Cairo.

Tin-hatted Allied troops construct trenches under the blazing desert sun.

Auchinleck's men attack: the Germans have been stopped in their tracks.

Allies fear loss of Middle East oil supply

Egypt, 1 July

Rommel's assault on the El Alamein Line, which began today, does not just threaten the British position in Egypt and the Suez Canal. If it is successful its effect could be very much greater.

Hitler believes that he is now in a position to overrun the whole of the Middle East by double envelopment. Field Marshal Sigmund List's Army Group A began a major offensive in the Ukraine on 28 June aimed at the Caucasus. With this secured, von Bock could drive on into Turkey, whose ill-equipped armed forces would offer little resistance, enter the Middle East by the "back door" and join hands with Rommel.

The loss of the Middle East would not only make British communications with India tenuous in the extreme but also deny Britain its main source of oil. This would put even greater pressure on the US oilfields and, in all probability, produce a major fuel crisis for the Allies. This in turn would severely affect strategy, not just against Germany and Italy but in the Pacific as well. It is thus even more crucial that the Eighth Army stops Rommel in his tracks (→ 3).

Axis pledges Egypt "full sovereignty"

Cairo, 3 July

With desert gunfire heard daily in the streets of Alexandria, and Mussolini promising the Egyptian government full sovereignty should the British be defeated, a mass run on the banks is taking place here.

Two days ago the staff at the British embassy burnt thousands of documents, expecting the Germans to roll in at any moment. British warships are leaving for Beirut and other safe harbours as fears grow that Egypt may fall to Rommel's warriors (→ 4).

U-boats take the sea war deep into American waters

Caribbean Sea, 1 July

June was the worst month of the war so far for Allied shipping losses. The total was 173 ships, amounting to 834,196 tons. Of this no less than 144 ships were sunk by U-boats.

The figures are a triumph for the German strategy of taking the U-boat offensive into the heart of American waters. Some 60 per cent of the huge total of sinkings were in the Caribbean and the Gulf of Mexico.

It was already clear by the middle of last month that the situation was grave. The American chief of staff, General George C Marshall, then wrote to Admiral King urging him to introduce convoys. He pointed out that 20 per cent of the Puerto Rican fleet, 22 per cent of the bauxite fleet and 3.5 per cent of all tanker tonnage in use had been lost. "The losses by submarines off our Atlantic seaboard and in the Caribbean now threaten our entire war effort," wrote General Marshall.

Two days later Admiral King himself wrote that "escort is not just *one* way of handling the submarine menace; it is the *only* way that gives any promise of success". He complains, however, that the US still has very little in the form of anti-submarine forces.

SALVAGE SAVES SHIPPING

A stark reminder to the home front.

Germans wear down Sevastopol defences

Some of the last defenders left alive walk out of Sevastopol in surrender.

Rastenburg, 1 July
Hitler's headquarters claimed today that Sevastopol has fallen to the *Wehrmacht* after 25 days of vicious hand-to-hand fighting. To celebrate the capture of the Crimean fortress General von Manstein has been promoted to field marshal.

However, little but ruins has fallen into the Germans' hands. The city has been pounded to pieces by Stuka dive-bombers and the heaviest collection of guns yet used in the war. In the end the defenders, without air cover, could only be supplied by submarine.

The Russians fought from house to house, room to room, and had to be burnt out with flame throwers. The Germans also used toxic gas to force them out. When it became inevitable on 30 June that the city would fall every available boat was used to evacuate the defenders. Many did not get away. Some are fighting on, defiant to the end (→ 5).

US flyers increase their role in air war

London, 4 July
The USAAF marked Independence Day today with its own firework display, piloting six aircrafts in a British daylight raid on German airfields in the Netherlands. They joined six other aircrafts of the RAF. Two of the six planes flown by Americans are missing and a third had a remarkable escape. Damaged by flak, it scraped along the ground but its pilot, Captain Charles "Chuck" Kegelman, hauled it back into the air, put a *flak* tower out of action and flew home on one engine; he is to be recommended for the Distinguished Service Cross. This is a small beginning to American participation in the war in the air over in Europe, but it is an indication of things to come.

American Heavy Bombardment Groups are building up strength in the Middle East in preparation for attacks on Italy and the Rou-manian oilfields. And in China the "Flying Tiger" volunteers, now known as the "China Air Task Force", have officially become part of the USAAF. The RAF's Bomber Command is now looking forward to American Flying Fortresses joining them in the attack on Germany itself (→ 17/8).

The fearsome Flying Tigers' badge.

1942
July

Su	Mo	Tu	We	Th	Fr	Sa
			1	2	3	4
5	6	7	8	9	10	11
12	13	14	15	16	17	18
19	20	21	22	23	24	25
26	27	28	29	30	31	

5. Atlantic: The Leigh Light, an airborne RDF-operated searchlight, scores its first success when an RAF Wellington sinks a U-boat.

5. USSR: German troops enter the suburbs of Voronezh (→ 9).

5. USSR: The last Soviet resistance in the Crimea ends.

6. Buenos Aires: President Castillo announces that Argentina will remain neutral in the war.

6. USSR: The Germans launch Operation Swamp Flower, a massive sweep of partisan fighters in Dorogobuzh.→

7. Britain: Middlesbrough is raided by German bombers.

7. London: Alphonse Timmerman and Jose Keys, Nazi spies, are hanged in a double execution (→ 31).

7. Italy: The RAF bombs Reggio Calabria and Messina.

9. Germany: RAF bombers raid the U-boat base at Wilhelmshaven.→

9. Amsterdam: The Jewish Frank family, including 13-year-old Anne, who keeps a diary, go into hiding from the Nazis (→ 10).

9. Mediterranean: The Italian submarine *Perla* is captured by the corvette HMS *Hyacinth* off Beirut.

9. USSR: Hitler divides Army Group South into two groups with separate attacks on the Caucasus and Stalingrad (→ 10).

10. USSR: The Germans capture Rossosh on the Kharkov front, cutting the rail link between Moscow and Rostov-on-Don and crossing the river Don (→ 11).

10. Egypt: The Australian 9th Division attacks Italian positions at Tel el Eisa, near El Alamein (→ 15).

10. Auschwitz: A hundred Jewish women are taken to the camp hospital for medical experiments (→ 15).

11. China: Japanese troops occupy Futou Island.

11. USSR: The Germans take Lisichansk, on the river Donets (→ 12).

Lancaster bombers smash U-boat yard

A proud pilot in "Admiral Prune".

Britain, 11 July
After Bremen, the RAF offensive against the U-boat menace has continued with an attack against Danzig. Flying 1,500 miles in bad weather without fighter cover, a force of 44 Lancasters took the enemy by surprise tonight with a hazardous run-in over the Baltic. Some dropped time-bombs from rooftop height during a thunderstorm. One machine scraped a roof and brought enemy house bricks home in the cockpit. Others hit submarine pens with high explosive and incendiaries. Remarkably, only two aircraft were lost. Some Coastal Command experts argue, however, that submarines are easier targets at sea rather than when locked in concrete pens (→ 16).

FBI arrests Nazis active in America

New York, 11 July
The FBI has today announced the arrest of 158 German nationals resident in the US on charges of endangering state security. Among those arrested are 30 women. This is the largest group of a single nationality arrested since the US entered the war, and is the latest step in a determined drive against spies and enemy aliens. Those arrested are all members of the German American Vocational League, based on East 86th Street. Five are members of the Nazi Party (→ 8/8).

Arctic convoy shattered

Arctic Ocean, 7 July
Some two-thirds of convoy PQ-17 have been sunk in the worst convoy disaster of the war so far. Twenty-three merchant ships and one rescue ship have been sunk of the 36 merchant ships and three rescue ships which sailed for Russia on 27 June. Nearly 100,000 tons of cargo were lost, including 430 tanks, 2,500 aircraft and 3,350 vehicles, all urgently needed by the Russians.

Controversy over the devastation seems destined to continue for years to come – because it happened without the Germans making the move which the Allies had feared for so long. Operation *Rosselsprung* – meaning knight's move, from chess – had been planned by Grand Admiral Raeder himself. Germany's biggest battleship, the *Tirpitz*, based at Trondheim, was to move out, supported by the heavy cruiser *Admiral Hipper*, the pocket battleships *Admiral Scheer* and *Lutzow*, and six destroyers, to attack an Arctic convoy.

The admiralty had long feared such an attack and knew that by 4 July the support team had joined the *Tirpitz* in Altenfjord ready for Rosselsprung. What it did not know was whether the operation

had actually begun. Sir Dudley Pound, the first sea lord and chief of naval staff, chaired the meeting which began at 8.30pm that day. Pound asked for confirmation that the enemy strike team was still in port. When he could not get this, he closed the meeting at 9.30pm and decided to assume that it was already at sea.

He gave the order for the convoy to scatter, with each ship trying to reach a Russian port as best she could. In fact, at the time of the order the *Tirpitz* was still at anchor. However, there were ample other German forces nearby. During the night the U-boats and the dive-bombers started to pick off the ships. Thirteen were sunk on 5 July, then more yesterday and today.

Meanwhile *Tirpitz* and her supporting armada had sailed. Once the news of the massacre reached Raeder, however, he decided that there was no longer any need to risk his prize ships, so he cancelled Rosselsprung. His knight had won the game without making a move. Admiral Pound's defenders argue that the outcome could have been even worse if he had not given the order to scatter. The *Tirpitz* might have sunk the whole convoy (→ 17).

Partisans carry torch of Soviet resistance

Russian partisans lay an explosive beneath a railway line in German territory.

Moscow, 11 July
Partisans, supported by paratroops, are continuing to make life behind the lines extremely dangerous for the Germans, despite anti-partisan sweeps involving thousands of front-line troops which Hitler needs elsewhere. Five days ago Operation Swamp Flower, against the large partisan units around Dorogobuzh, was launched.

Two major offensives were carried out in June. The first, Operation *Kottbus*, involved more than 16,000 German troops who attacked the partisans' "Republic of Palik" in a large area around Borisov.

The second, Operation Birdsong, sent 5,000 troops into action against 2,500 partisans based in the area between Roslavl and Bryansk.

The Germans claim to have killed 1,193 partisans for the loss of 58 soldiers, but it is likely that most of the partisan dead were in fact peasants, shot out of hand.

The partisans are adept at slipping away into the forests when major operations are mounted against them. Then, when the danger has passed, they return to terrorize German units.

They have become folk heroes to the Russians and, after an initial hesitancy, the government is using their exploits to bolster low morale. They are seen to be carrying the torch of resistance. Their effectiveness may be judged by the savagery with which they are treated by the Germans who festoon the countryside with loaded gallows (→ 17/8).

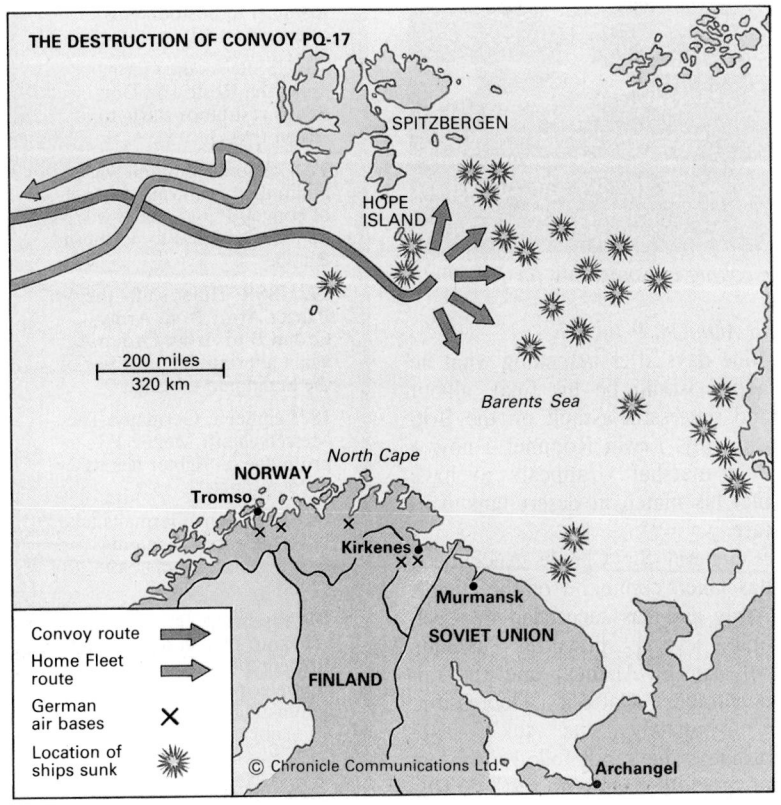

THE DESTRUCTION OF CONVOY PQ-17

SPITZBERGEN

HOPE ISLAND

200 miles
320 km

Barents Sea

North Cape

NORWAY
Tromso

Kirkenes

Murmansk

SOVIET UNION

FINLAND

Convoy route
Home Fleet route
German air bases ✕
Location of ships sunk ✳

© Chronicle Communications Ltd.

Archangel

A group of partisans brings a wounded man back from a mission.

1942

July

Su	Mo	Tu	We	Th	Fr	Sa
			1	2	3	4
5	6	7	8	9	10	11
12	13	14	15	16	17	18
19	20	21	22	23	24	25
26	27	28	29	30	31	

China enters sixth year of war with Japan

Chiang Kai-Shek says the end is in sight; but the wounded keep pouring in.

Chungking, 7 July
Hard on the heels of its successes in the air and on the ground, Generalissimo Chiang Kai-shek's *Kuomintang* enters the sixth year since the Japanese invasion more optimistically than ever, but with a warning to the rest of the Allies that China's fate now hinges on being provided with at least 500 more planes.

The warning was made by Chungking's military *attache* in Washington, General Chu Shih-ming, who said that with 500 bombers, plus the fighters to support them, China would be able to launch an offensive against Japan. But if the planes were not provided there was the danger that Japan, which has now launched an all-out attack against China, might be more successful than the west realized. His remarks were supported by Chinese successes in the last 24 hours.

These include the destruction of six Japanese fighters and the bombing of three Japanese air bases without the loss of a single plane by the United States China Air Task Force.

On the ground the Kuomintang forces have turned back Japanese attacks in Kiangsi province in eastern China and on the Hunan-Kiangsi border, inflicting 1,700 Japanese casualties.

In a speech to mark the fifth anniversary General Chiang had predicted: "We may face worse reverses in the next few months, but these will be short and the final collapse is near" (→ 11).

Keeping up the offensive: Japanese pilots prepare for a raid on China.

Auschwitz doctors become torturers

Berlin, 7 July
At a meeting with senior doctors and SS officials, Heinrich Himmler has ordered that Jewish and gypsy women at Auschwitz should be the subjects of a series of medical experiments. Professor Clauberg, the gynaecologist, is to supervise three sterilization experiments:

1. Burning up the ovaries by electromagnetic rays
2. Transplanting foreign cells into the uterus
3. Injecting radioactive fluid into the uterus.

As at Dachau, where men were subjected to freezing cold and simulated high altitudes to test their endurance, the victims will not be asked for their consent (→ 9).

Auchinleck thwarts Rommel in desert

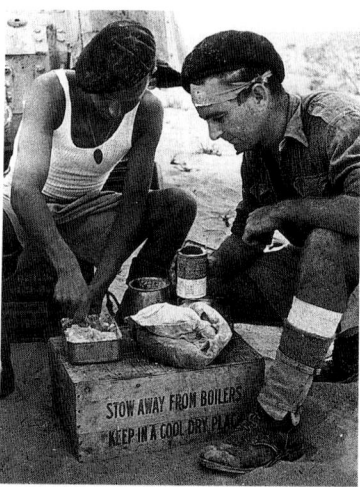

Cooking up something for Rommel?

El Alamein, 9 July
Nine days after launching what he hoped would be his final, all-out and successful assault on the British army, Erwin Rommel – now a field marshal – appears to have met his match in desert tank warfare.

General Sir Claude Auchinleck has taken command of the Eighth Army and has succeeded in repelling several powerful assaults between El Alamein and the impenetrable Qattara Depression. Unfortunately, "the Auk's" subordinates have not followed orders to "give the enemy no rest" (→ 10).

12. USSR: Stalin reorganizes the defence of Stalingrad, putting Marshal Semyon K Timoshenko in charge (→ 13).

12. New Guinea: After a five-day march across the Owen Stanley mountains, Australian troops arrive to defend Kokoda (→ 21).

13. Germany: Hitler decides to make Stalingrad the major objective of Army Group B.

13. China: Japanese marines capture Juian (→ 3/8).

13. USSR: Von Bock is dismissed from the command of Army Group B and replaced by von Weichs (→ 16).

14. Zagreb: The Nazis murder 700 people in reprisal for the murder of the local *Gestapo* chief, SS Major Helm.→

14. London: The Free French are officially renamed the "Fighting French" today at General de Gaulle's request.

15. Amsterdam: Two thousand Jews are deported to Auschwitz, told they are going to labour camps in Germany.→

15. El Alamein: The Allies hit two Italian divisions, forcing Rommel to postpone his offensive (→ 19).

16. USSR: As the Germans approach Rostov-on-Don, Soviet resistance starts to stiffen (→ 17).

17. London: Churchill warns Stalin that, following the fate of convoy PQ-17, there will be no more convoys to northern Russia.

17. USSR: Hitler shifts the 4th Panzer Army from Army Group B to Army Group A, again altering the priorities of the Stalingrad advance.→

18. Leipheim, Germany: The Messerschmitt Me262 V3 prototype jet fighter has its maiden flight.

18. USSR: The Germans take Voroshilovgrad, a mining centre in the Donets basin (→ 23).

18. Auschwitz: Impressed by the camp's harsh regime and efficient gas chamber, Heinrich Himmler promotes its commandant, Rudolf Hoess, to SS major (→ 19).

French track down Jews for Auschwitz

Paris, 16 July
Nine thousand French police combed the city today, snatching every foreign-born Jew they could find. They have arrested nearly half of the 28,000 registered "stateless" Jews in Paris. About 6,000 have been sent to Drancy, the first stop in the long journey to Auschwitz; Three thousand children are among nearly 7,000 Jews gathered in the huge sports stadium called the *Velodrome d'Hiver*, waiting for their turn to go.

The weather is very hot. They have a single water tap and ten latrines between them. Some of those arrested last night have no clothes at all. The guards are brutal, the squalor unimaginable (→ 18).

Kammhuber Line prevents bombers

Germany, 16 July
RAF bombers swooped through cloud to bomb the Ruhr and other targets in north-west Europe at dusk tonight. They were relatively minor raids, using cloud cover as a new tactic to thwart the Kammhuber Line of ground-controlled interception "boxes" in which *Luftwaffe* fighters patrol. First introduced in 1940, the system now has no fewer than 250 fighters. The RAF has been attempting to detour the boxes, but they are being extended to stretch from northern Denmark to south of Paris (→ 27).

Key towns on Stalingrad line evacuated

Germans advance towards Stalingrad, but the Red Army is not defeated.

Moscow, 17 July
The Germans are making further gains in their thrust towards Stalingrad, forcing the Russians to evacuate the towns of Boguchar and Millerovo yesterday. The *Panzers* are rolling through the ripening corn of the steppe, faced, in many cases, only by suicide squads with grenades and Molotov cocktails.

War correspondents with the advancing Panzers are writing about the *Mot Pulk* [motorized square] of trucks and guns guarded by an armoured skin of tanks crushing its way forward like an "irresistible mastodon". But a fierce struggle is still going on for Voronezh, the vital communications centre which was one of the first objectives. When the Germans crossed the Don, Hitler gave permission for the city to be bypassed in order to pursue Marshal Timoshenko's escaping forces, but the commander, at that time Field Marshal von Bock, decided to take it by storm. On 13 July von Bock was replaced by General von Weichs, but resistance at Voronezh has still not been wiped out; tanks which ought to be driving to Stalingrad are still fighting in the suburbs.

On 13 July Hitler made Stalingrad – not the Caucasus – the main objective for Army Group B, and today he switched the 4th Panzer Army to reinforce that attack. Despite the delays, he believes that Timoshenko and the Red Army are finished. This is not the view of his army chiefs of staff (→ 18/8).

Yugoslavia rises up against Nazi rulers

Croatia, 16 July
In a western world beset by gloom, at least one anti-Nazi army is winning victory after victory – but few know about it. Gathering strength every day as it fights its way into Croatia, Tito's partisan army has succeeded in capturing several major towns and hundreds of villages in this country ruled by the pro-German *Ustachi* under their leader Ante Pavelich.

The fighting has been savage, with countless atrocities – particularly by the fanatical, long-haired, bearded Ustachi as they retreat before Tito's disciplined partisans. Captured Ustachi and their collaborators can expect no mercy from Tito's People's Courts. Mass executions are commonplace.

Tito is wasting no time in turning "liberated" Croatia into a soviet state with its own newspaper, postal service, schools and health services. Volunteers are cleaning up and repairing desecrated Orthodox churches.

A courier service – mostly of young girls on cycles or horseback – is playing a vital role in partisan communications (→ 3/11).

RAF ace shot down over the Channel

Britain, 15 July
Brendan ("Paddy") Finucane, at 21 the RAF's youngest wing-commander, was shot down over the English Channel and drowned today. He joins the other 122 fighter pilots said to be "missing" since 1 June. A quiet Dubliner, Finucane had been awarded several decorations after 32 kills.

His end was freakishly unlucky. Finucane was flying just above ground level when his engine was hit by a light-calibre *Wehrmacht* machine gun set up temporarily on dunes near Le Touquet. As he approached the sea he told his comrades, by radio: "This is it, chaps." His Spitfire plunged underwater, taking him down.

"Paddy": Dubliner and RAF ace.

Roosevelt sets up US secret service

Washington, 13 July
Roosevelt has today approved the formation of a central intelligence agency for America. Called the Office of Strategic Services, it has grown out of an organization called the Office of the Coordinator of Information and is headed by "Wild Bill" Donovan, a millionaire lawyer from Wall Street. Donovan, a forceful "can do" man, has close ties with Britain's Special Operations Executive (SOE) and has carried out missions for Mr Churchill.

July

Su	Mo	Tu	We	Th	Fr	Sa
				1	2	3	4
5	6	7	8	9	10	11
12	13	14	15	16	17	18
19	20	21	22	23	24	25
26	27	28	29	30	31	

19. Berlin: Himmler orders the "total cleansing" of Jews from the General Government area of Poland by the end of the year (→ 22).

19. US: U-boats are withdrawn from the east coast because the convoy system has robbed them of targets.

19. Paris: SS Lieutenant-General Kurt Oberg decrees that if any identified resistant does not surrender within 12 days of his crime, his male relatives will be executed and female relatives sent to hard labour camps.

19. Malta: Over the past five days Malta has been resupplied by submarine and fast transport: the carrier HMS *Eagle* has ferried in 31 Spitfires.

19. Egypt: The British cruisers *Dido* and *Euryalus* and four destroyers bombard Mersa Matruh (→ 21).

20. Rome: Mussolini returns, having given up the idea of a victory march in Cairo.

21. El Alamein: Auchinleck attacks but is held on Ruweisat Ridge (→ 30).

22. Germany: Goebbels tells judges that the justice of a sentence is irrelevant: its *utility* is what matters.

22. Washington: Roosevelt accepts that Operation Sledgehammer, the invasion of north-west Europe planned for this summer, is not possible yet (→ 25).

22. New Guinea: The Japanese force that landed at Gona yesterday begins to advance along the Kokoda Trail, heading for Port Moresby (→ 29).

23. USSR: The Germans reach the Don, occupying Rostov (→ 25).

23. Warsaw: The *Judenrat* [Jewish council] leader, Adam Czerniakow, commits suicide (→ 28).

25. USSR: German troops occupy Novocherkassk (→ 27).

25. London: The Allies agree to invade North Africa (Operation Torch) rather than open a second front in Europe.

Japanese troops push on in New Guinea

In the Japanese attack on Port Moresby a bomb narrowly misses a US ship.

Papua, New Guinea, 21 July
The Japanese renewed their offensive in the south-west Pacific last night by seizing Gona, in Papua, New Guinea. The Japanese invaders belong to Major-General Tomitaro Horii's "South Seas force" which is pushing hard along the Kokoda Trail. The Japanese are now endeavouring to take Port Moresby by advancing along the tortuous trail which crosses the Owen Stanley mountains and descends on the other side to the town itself. Young militiamen and the Papuan infantry battalion have been forced to retreat by the well-equipped Japanese troops whose steel helmets are garnished with leaves (→ 22).

Warsaw Jews face death in Treblinka

Warsaw, 22 July
Tonight the Jewish ghetto is in a state of shock after a brutal round-up of children, signalling the start of an operation to "deport" them all "to the east". Their true destination will be the gas chambers at Treblinka.

Trigger-happy SS guards have surrounded the ghetto walls; others roamed the streets, snatching wailing children from their mothers' arms. Whole orphanages have been emptied and their inmates, kicking and yelling, carried off in high-sided carts to the ghetto's railway siding where they were loaded into covered goods wagons. All day long the shrieks of "Mama, mama!" and "Save us!" have tormented the adults who stayed behind.

SS Major Hermann Hofle is in charge of the deportation. He has ordered Adam Czerniakow, the leader of the Jewish council, to deliver 6,000 Jews to the railway siding by 4pm each day, seven days a week. If this is not done, the Nazis' 60 hostages – among them Czerniakow's wife – will die (→ 23).

Disillusioned Russian officers give up the fight for communism

Moscow, 25 July
Soon after the 32,000-strong Second Soviet Assault Army surrendered to the Germans east of Leningrad, a Russian peasant came to German intelligence officers with an intriguing piece of information. The commander-in-chief of the Assault Army, General Andrei Vlasov, awarded the Order of the Red Banner by Stalin as one of the saviours of Moscow, wished to join the fight against communism.

Vlasov, quietly efficient and unassuming, has impressed his interrogators. He is, however, only the latest of thousands of Red Army men, many of them senior officers, who have given up the fight for the Red Army. The 436th Infantry Regiment, commanded by Major I N Kononov, a Cossack, has offered its services to the Germans.

Hitler's orders are that no Slav *Untermensch* [subhuman] can be allowed to carry arms. But German generals in the field have other ideas. They have been using ex-Red

A charge by Cossack cavalry, some of whom have joined the Germans.

Army men as auxiliaries, and many have been in action against their former comrades.

Now it is being put about that Cossacks are not, after all, Slavs, but a Germanic people. Hitler has enthusiastically accepted this fable. The mass defections are a direct consequence of Stalin's liquidation of thousands of senior Red Army officers in the years of the great purges.

1942

July

Su	Mo	Tu	We	Th	Fr	Sa
			1	2	3	4
5	6	7	8	9	10	11
12	13	14	15	16	17	18
19	20	21	22	23	24	25
26	27	28	29	30	31	

27. Germany: RAF bombers raid Hamburg.→

28. Berlin: Heinrich Himmler tells leaders of the SS: "The occupied eastern territories are to become free of Jews. The execution of this very grave order has been placed on my shoulders by the Fuhrer" (→ 31).

28. US: Four million Americans are now doing military service.

29. Westminster: The minister of labour, Ernest Bevin, announces a scheme for universal state pensions.

29. London: The US Lend-Lease representative, Averell Harriman, and the British production minister, Oliver Lyttleton, form a combined production and resources board to control war industry.

30. USSR: Proletarska and Bataisk, south of the river Don, fall to the German troops.→

30. Egypt: Having prevented Rommel's advance, Auchinleck pauses to await reinforcements, thus ending the First Battle of Alamein (→ 3/8).

31. Solomon Islands: US bombers attack Japanese airfields on Tulagi and Guadalcanal (→ 7/8).

31. Atlantic: British convoy escorts are boosted by the introduction of high-frequency direction-finding (HF/DF or "Huff Duff") radio-location equipment.

31. Britain: Franciscus Winter, a German spy working as a steward in the Merchant Navy, is arrested.

31. Germany: The Institute for Practical Research in Military Science has started a collection of Jewish skeletons, obtaining gassed corpses from Oranienburg concentration camp (→ 2).

31. Atlantic: A U-boat mines waters off South Carolina.

31. Britain: Seven hundred and eleven civilians have been killed and 1,208 injured in air raids since 1 June.

31. Atlantic: Three U-boats are sunk in separate actions in the Atlantic.

Bomber Command steps up German raids

Driven to ground: German children while away the time in an air-raid shelter.

Germany, 31 July
"You have no chance," Air Marshal Sir Arthur Harris, the chief of Bomber Command, told the German people tonight as the RAF savaged the key industrial city of Dusseldorf. Broadcasting in German, Sir Arthur said that RAF bomber losses of less than five per cent were more than covered by US output. He said: "We shall be coming every night, every day, rain, blow or snow, we and the Americans."

In the past ten days, Harris's crews have given grim proof of his threat. In the Ruhr, Duisburg was hit three times. At Hamburg four nights ago, 175,000 incendiaries were dropped (the largest number in a single attack) in 35 minutes as the prelude to a storm of two-ton high-explosive bombs.

The raid cost the RAF 29 aircraft, but prompted a public message of congratulation from Sir Arthur on "one of the outstanding attacks of the whole war".

Tonight's Dusseldorf operation followed the high pressure style of Hamburg, but over a wider area, with losses of 29 aircraft out of 630. More than 150 two-ton bombs fell at a rate of three per minute. Heavier bomb loads delivered by the new Lancaster are the key to such intensive attacks (→ 10/8).

Kokoda falls to Japanese invaders

Papua, New Guinea, 29 July
After a rapid advance through rugged mountainous terrain, the Japanese "South Seas force" yesterday seized Kokoda, the halfway point in its drive across the mountains to Port Moresby on the Coral Sea.

Undeterred by the climate on the Papuan coast where disease is a greater enemy than the bullet, the fresh Japanese force has taken only a week to reach Kokoda village which is flanked by 7,000-foot peaks in the Owen Stanley mountains. On the night of 28-29 July the Japanese attacked and, in a confused battle, drove the defenders off and took the village (→ 8/8).

Canada assembly backs conscription

Ottawa, Canada, 29 July
Canada's parliament has amended the National Resources Mobilization Act to permit the introduction of conscription for overseas service. This follows last April's referendum in which the English-speaking majority voted for conscription "if necessary", and the French-Canadian liberals voted against it.

Few leaders have overseen the passage of a bill more reluctantly. The prime minister, Mr Mackenzie King, is convinced of "the wisdom of not attempting any conscription through coercion or in violation of pledges". His hand was forced by pressure from both the US and English-speaking Canadians.

US action urged on German barbarism

Washington, 31 July
President Roosevelt has been asked to issue a final warning to Germany and the rest of the Axis powers against the "barbaric and inhuman crimes committed daily" in the occupied countries. The request came in a note, signed by the Belgian, Czechoslovak, Dutch, Greek, Norwegian, Polish, Luxemburg, Yugoslav and Free French governments, delivered to the secretary of state, Cordell Hull, today (→ 7/10).

Woolton puts wrappers on sweet eaters

A clear plate means A clear conscience

Don't take more than you can eat

Learning to lick the platter clean.

Britain, 26 July
Sweets and chocolate are rationed from today. Adults and children get the same allowance – half a pound must last them for the next four-week period. The ministry of food will announce the ration for subsequent periods.

"Personal Points" must be cut out and given to shopkeepers for each purchase of sweets. Chocolate is rated at 16 points a pound. Penny bars or tubes of sweets will be counted at one point, twopenny bars at two points.

If children want more, it is up to parents or grandparents to give up some of their own rations to them, said Lord Woolton, the minister of food.

319

Russia pulls back to Don

German soldiers push ahead through the crops on the Russian steppes.

Moscow, 27 July

The Red Army is pulling back to the river Don where Marshal Timoshenko, who has withdrawn his main forces in good order, is setting up a new defence line.

The Germans have already claimed the recapture of Rostov-on-Don from which they were driven last December. But many Russian soldiers remain in the shattered city, and, holed up in the ruins of big blocks of apartments, are causing the Germans heavy casualties as they work their way house by house through the city.

North of Rostov, the Germans are pushing on to Stalingrad. Formerly called Tsaritsyn, it has a special affection for Stalin who was active in its defence during the civil war. Today it is a vital industrial and communications centre, guarding the approaches to the Caucasus. There can be no doubt that the Russians will fight for it (→ 30).

Fuhrer's indecision confuses own army

Moscow, 31 July

Hitler is throwing the *Wehrmacht's* advance in southern Russia into confusion as he continually changes his mind. His insistence on splitting von Bock's Army Group South to attack Stalingrad and advance into the Caucasus simultaneously led to protests from von Bock and his dismissal 18 days ago.

The Fuhrer has given orders which have led Hoth and von Kleist to arrive with their *Panzer* armies at the Don crossings at the same time and become dreadfully entangled.

He is, moreover, convinced that the Red Army is finished and is actually removing units from the battlefield. He has sent von Manstein's Eleventh Army from the Crimea to mount another assault on Leningrad, and he has ordered two crack divisions to France to prepare for an Allied invasion.

Stalin orders Red Army: no retreats

Moscow, 31 July

Stalin has ordered the Red Army, retreating before the German double thrust to Stalingrad and the Caucasus, to stand and fight: "We will win or die but never retreat."

Nobody is to be allowed to take another step backwards without orders: "Not one step backwards. Commanders, commissars and political workers who abandon a position without an order from higher headquarters are traitors to the Fatherland and must be treated accordingly."

Stalin's order has been published throughout the country and the army newspaper, *Red Star*, adds: "Any man quailing on the battlefield instead of standing to the death will be condemned as a traitor selling his country into German slavery." Massive reinforcements are being hurried to the southern front (→ 1/8).

Tycoon goes into high gear as America beefs up output of ships and aircraft

United States, 30 July

The man who built the Grand Coulee and Hoover dams has been "drafted" to mass-produce weapons for the American war machine as the country strives to become the "arsenal of democracy". The industrialist Henry J Kaiser has promised Senate committees that he will adopt the same techniques for building cargo planes as he has for manufacturing "Liberty" ships – a ship can be built in 80 hours using assembly-line methods.

A week ago, the House of Representatives' naval committee was told of a 360-per-cent increase in naval ship production. The time required to build an aircraft carrier has been reduced from 45 to 17.3 months. And yesterday a combined British and United States production and resources board was created in London to control the allocation of war materials to industry in both countries. Averell Harriman, the Lend-Lease representative in Britain, and Oliver Lyttleton, the British minister of production, are to be its senior members.

US labour leaders have assured President Roosevelt that "any sacrifice" will be made to meet his quotas of 60,000 planes, 45,000 tanks, 500,000 machine-guns, 20,000 anti-aircraft guns and eight million tons of merchant shipping by the end of the year.

POUR IT ON!

The pace hots up in the American war industry under Henry J Kaiser.

1942

August

Su	Mo	Tu	We	Th	Fr	Sa
						1
2	3	4	5	6	7	8
9	10	11	12	13	14	15
16	17	18	19	20	21	22
23	24	25	26	27	28	29
30	31					

1. USSR: The Germans cut the railway line between Krasnodar and Stalingrad at Salsk (→ 3).

1. USA: Roosevelt urges citizens in the eastern states to use coal rather than oil as a household fuel.

3. USSR: The 4th *Panzer* Army crosses the Don at Tsimlyansky, as Kletskaya comes under heavy attack (→ 5).

4. Belgium: The first trainload of Jews is deported to Auschwitz (→ 7).

4. Mediterranean: The U-boat U372 is sunk off Jaffa by destroyers.

5. USSR: Voroshilovsk [*Stavropol*] falls to German *Panzers* moving south towards the Maikop oilfields; on the Stalingrad front, Panzers capture Kotelnikovo (→ 9).

6. London: Britain renounces the 1938 Munich agreement.

6. Atlantic: The Canadian destroyer *Assiniboine*, escorting convoy SC-94, rams and sinks a U-boat (→ 8).

6. Cairo: General Harold Alexander is appointed C-in-C Middle East; Lieutenant-General William "Strafer" Gott succeeds Ritchie as commander of the Eighth Army.→

7. Palestine: Britain creates a Palestine regiment, with separate Jewish and Arab battalions.

7. Aleutians: The US Navy bombards Kiska (→ 16/9).

7. Netherlands: Nine hundred and eighty-seven Jews are deported to Auschwitz (→ 9).

8. Solomon Islands: Tulagi and Gavutu fall to the US invaders.→

8. Atlantic: Five ships of convoy SC-94 are sunk: one of the escort, the corvette *Dianthus*, sinks U379.

8. US: Six German saboteurs out of eight who landed in Long Island and Florida are executed by electric chair (→ 9).

8. New Guinea: The joint Australian-Papuan Maroubra Force recaptures Kokoda but is unable to hold on to it (→ 11).

US marines take Guadalcanal base

Guadalcanal, 7 August

The first American offensive of the Pacific War began spectacularly today when the 1st Marine Division, preceded by heavy air and naval bombardments, landed on remote Guadalcanal and Tulagi, in the southern Solomon Islands.

The 19,000 marines who landed here were not opposed on the beach-head. It is the first capture of territory from Japan so far in the war, and only token resistance was offered when the marines went on to seize a partially-completed airfield.

But at the second landing on nearby Tulagi island, they ran into a stiff fight to subdue some 1,500 Japanese who resisted fiercely before they were annihilated against American losses of 150 men.

Thus, for the first time in the war American troops have wrested territory from the all-conquering Japanese. The Midway victory had altered the naval balance, and the American Joint Chiefs of Staff moved at once to plan the seizure of the southern Solomons where Japanese activity threatened to cut vital communications between Australia and

Japanese prisoners in Guadalcanal wait to be moved to detention centres.

the United States. Their directive of 2 July called for a two-pronged offensive towards northern New Guinea and the Solomon Islands chain. The ultimate objective of both offensives was to recapture Rabaul and break the barrier of the

Bismarck Islands. Japanese reaction to the Guadalcanal challenge is not expected to be long in coming.

Japan has a strong striking force of bombers and fighters based at Rabaul and will be determined to thwart the US offensive (→ 8).

Japan strikes back in Solomons, killing 1,000 Allied sailors

Solomon Islands, 8 August

The United States Navy suffered a sharp reverse off Guadalcanal today when a Japanese night attack overwhelmed Allied naval units near Savo Island, sinking three American cruisers. An Australian cruiser was also lost. Over 1,000 Allied sailors are feared to have died. However, a vital target, the transports supporting the US invasion of Guadalcanal, was untouched.

The Japanese attacking force of seven cruisers and one destroyer escaped detection in its high-speed dash from Rabaul and suffered very little damage. The US cruisers lost were the *Vincennes*, *Astoria* and *Quincy*, together with the *Canberra* of the Royal Australian Navy. They were all caught by surprise when two radar-equipped American destroyers patrolling off Savo Island failed to detect the approach of the Japanese.

Suddenly today the destroyer *Patterson* saw the Japanese force ap-

proaching and signalled: "Warning, Warning, strange ships entering harbour." But it was too late. The Japanese commander had given the order "every ship attack": torpedoes were on their way to the unsuspecting Allied ships.

Brilliant flares dropped by Japanese float planes silhouetted the US cruiser *Chicago* and the *Canberra*

as the Japanese cruisers opened fire. Within minutes the *Canberra* was mortally wounded and listing, and her captain was dying. The *Chicago* took a torpedo hit, but she stayed afloat.

The Japanese warships swung around Savo Island to catch the American cruisers in a devastating crossfire (→ 10).

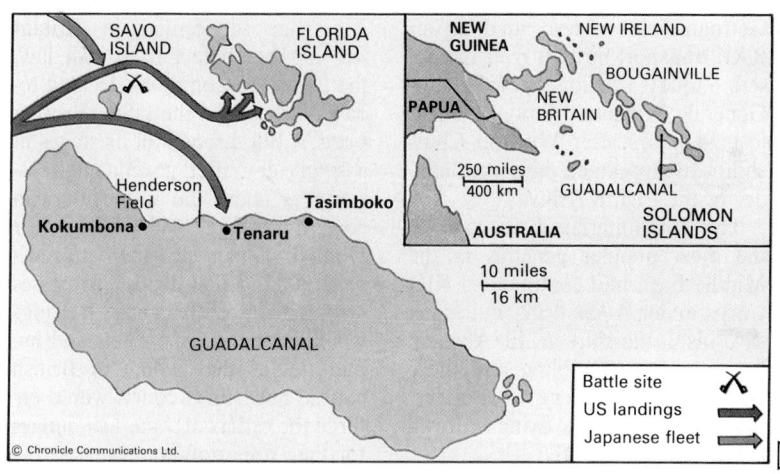

Battle site ✗
US landings ⇒
Japanese fleet ⇒

Churchill decides to replace Auchinleck

Cairo, 4 August
Winston Churchill has decided to shake up the command of British forces in North Africa. The prime minister, who arrived in Cairo yesterday to see for himself, wants a new commander-in-chief. Churchill acknowledges General Auchinleck's success in stopping Rommel at El Alamein last month, but is impatient to take the offensive against the Germans, who are still only 60 miles (96 km) from Alexandria. Auchinleck wants to build up his reinforcements first. The Eighth Army is likely to have a new commander, too (→6).

General killed day after his promotion

Lt-Gen William "Strafer" Gott.

Cairo, 7 August
German fighters descended on an RAF transport aircraft over the desert today, killing Lieutenant-General William "Strafer" Gott just 24 hours after Winston Churchill had appointed him commander of the Eighth Army.

The humanitarian Gott, one of the most popular generals in the Middle East, had commanded XIII Corps under Auchinleck. But many saw his leadership at El Alamein last month as fumbling and tired. Bernard Montgomery, a relatively unknown general, is flying in to fill the vacancy (→12).

Warsaw: more deportations to Treblinka

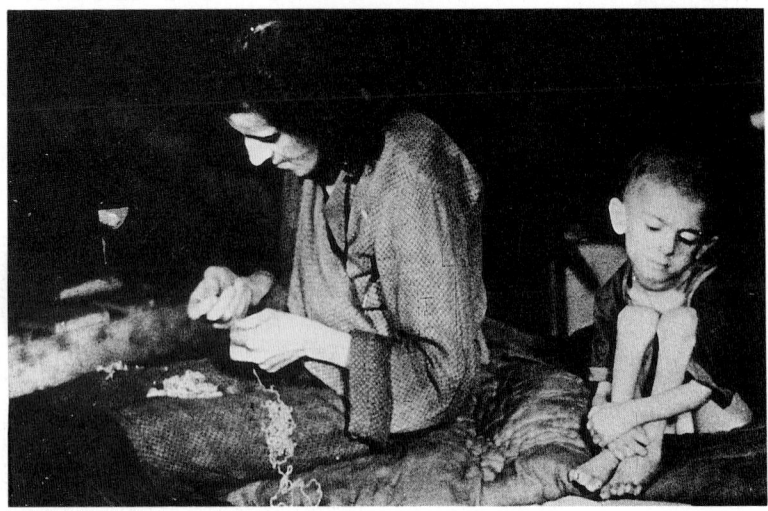

A mother and her child before leaving the Warsaw Ghetto for Treblinka.

Poland, 2 August
Unaware of their destiny, lured by German promises of extra bread and jam, many Jewish families are volunteering for deportation "to the east" from the Warsaw Ghetto rail terminus. Others are rounded up by brutal Ukrainian and German SS guards. Resistance is punished by death. Only those working for German factories in the ghetto are spared the transports.

Crammed 200 to a goods van, 60 wagons to each train, many suffocate in the airless heat as the train trundles the 50 miles to Treblinka station. There it waits for Polish rail workers to uncouple the wagons. Franciszek Zabecki, a railman, alleges some appalling atrocities: "One mother threw a small child wrapped up in a pillow from the wagon, shouting "Take it, there's some money to look after it". An SS man ran up, unwrapped the pillow, seized the child by its feet and smashed its head against a wagon wheel. This took place in full view of the mother, who howled with pain ..."

The wagons are shunted into the death camp 20 at a time. Whip-wielding Nazi guards sort the human cargo into men, women and children. Forced to strip, the deportees walk naked down a lane to the camp's three gas chambers. Twenty minutes later, they are all dead. The empty wagons go back to Warsaw to pick up another load. It is estimated that the Treblinka camp is murdering 40,000 Jews a week (→4).

US servicemen are above British law

Westminster, 4 August
American servicemen in Britain will not be subject to British law, the House of Commons decided today. MPs passed the USA (Visiting Forces) Bill through all its stages in a single day after government reassurances about the way American courts martial will work. Sir Donald Somervell, the attorney-general, said that British witnesses summoned before such hearings would have the same rights and immunities as they would in British courts, but British courts would enforce the orders of American judges for their appearance.

Chinese troops war among themselves

Shantung, 3 August
Internecine warfare has broken out among Chinese troops in the Shantung/Kiangsu district. Early this evening the pro-Nationalist commander of the North-east Army, Yu Hsueh-chung, fled after an uprising by 3,000 Communist troops of its 111th Division. The Communist *coup* was engineered by high-ranking officers, including one who had been under arrest for a similar coup bid two years ago. The 111th, which wants a merger with the Eighth Route Army, accuses Yu of not being prepared to fight the Japanese (→12).

August

Su	Mo	Tu	We	Th	Fr	Sa
						1
2	3	4	5	6	7	8
9	10	11	12	13	14	15
16	17	18	19	20	21	22
23	24	25	26	27	28	29
30	31					

9. US: Nazi saboteurs plough arrows into a field in Long Island indicating the whereabouts of Mitchell Field air base.

9. USSR: In the Caucasus, German *Panzer* armies capture Krasnodar and Maikop only to find that the retreating Red Army has destroyed the oil refineries.→

9. Auschwitz: Edith Stein, a Catholic nun of Jewish parentage, is murdered in the gas chamber.

10. Solomon Islands: On the way back to Rabaul after the Battle of Savo Island, the Japanese heavy cruiser *Kako* is sunk by a US submarine (→20).

10. Britain: *Luftwaffe* bombers raid Colchester.

10. Mediterranean: The British trawler *Islay* sinks the Italian submarine *Scire* off Haifa.

10. Europe: The RAF's area-bombing offensive is threatened as the Germans start jamming the Gee navigation system (→11).

11. Britain: Orders are issued for the establishment by RAF Bomber Command of a pathfinder force, to locate and illuminate targets for subsequent bombardment (→31).

11. Mediterranean: The carrier HMS *Eagle*, escorting the Operation Pedestal convoy, is sunk by the U-boat U73 north of Algiers: 260 men are killed.→

11. New Guinea: Japanese attacks have pushed the Australian-Papuan defenders five miles back up the Kokoda Trail (→18).

12. New Hebrides: US forces start building a base on Espiritu Santu.

12. Moscow: Churchill arrives for a conference with Stalin and informs his colleagues: "I can handle this peasant."→

13. Japan: US planes bomb Formosa [*Taiwan*].

15. Europe: Five thousand Jews from Vichy France are rounded up for deportation to Auschwitz; in Zagrodski, in Poland, German troops shoot dead 500 Jewish families (→28).

New Desert Army chiefs

Cairo, 12 August
Lieutenant-General Bernard Law Montgomery has today taken over command of the British Eighth Army in North Africa. The arrival of this relatively unknown general [*see below*] is the culmination of a week of turmoil in the army hierarchy, as first Winston Churchill pressed for changes and then the newly-chosen commander for the Eighth Army was shot down by German fighters, leaving the way open for Montgomery. The major internal battle has been waged over

the new C-in-C, with Auchinleck now replaced by General Sir Harold Alexander [*see below*].

Auchinleck finally sealed his own fate when he told the PM that there was no chance of a major offensive until his exhausted army was reinforced and retrained, and complained about the inadequacy of his tanks and anti-tank weapons, prompting the premier to storm: "Rommel, Rommel, Rommel! What else matters except beating him?" How quickly the offensive will begin is another matter (→ 15).

Alexander: turning retreat into attack

Gen Alexander with King George.

Cairo, 15 August
Until now the name of General Sir Harold Alexander, the new Commander-in-Chief Middle East, has been associated with the two great retreats of this war – at Dunkirk and in Burma. No one can deny, however, that he conducted them both brilliantly.

At Dunkirk, Alexander was the last to leave the beaches and toured them at dusk to ensure that no one was left behind. In Burma, he succeeded in bringing four-fifths of his men safely across the mountains into India – having fought all the way against the better equipped Japanese. Politically, he will make an excellent foil to Montgomery; but now the challenge is to attack.

Montgomery: insisting on being captain

North Africa, 15 August
At school, they say, he was good at games, but refused to play unless he was the captain. He is arrogant, brusque and so far little known. Bernard Law Montgomery, the new commander of the British Eighth Army in North Africa, is a diminutive professional soldier with sharp features, bird-like eyes, and the total certainty that God is on his side. He won the DSO and was seriously wounded during the First World War. Twenty years later, in much the same part of France and Belgium, he commanded the 3rd Division before the retreat from Dunkirk. Now "Monty" faces his greatest challenge: defeating the "Desert Fox" (→ 31).

Monty: believes God is on his side.

Churchill meets Stalin for first summit

The Moscow summit: Churchill, the US envoy Harriman, Stalin and Molotov.

Moscow, 15 August
In four days of talks with Stalin in the Kremlin, Churchill gave the Soviet leader a detailed explanation of the Anglo-American plans for driving the Germans and Italians out of North Africa and then mounting an attack on the European mainland, in southern Italy.

Stalin was not well pleased; with the Germans at the gates of Stalingrad, on the Volga river and striking deep into the Caucasus, he wanted an Allied second front in western Europe. Churchill argued that a thrust into Italy would put pressure on Hitler to draw off forces from the Soviet front.

Before leaving Moscow to return to London, Churchill sent a mes-

sage to Stalin thanking him for his "comradely attitude" and adding: "I am very glad to have visited Moscow, firstly because it was my duty to speak my mind, and secondly because I am certain that our contact will play a useful part in furthering our cause."

Churchill flew to Moscow in an American Liberator four-engined bomber with a US Ferry Command pilot. His aircraft and two others carrying military and diplomatic advisers were escorted on the final stage of their journey by Red Air Force fighters. The British prime minister broke his journey to Moscow with a stop in Cairo for talks with British military leaders [*see report, page 322*] (→ 22).

Germans arrive at gates of Stalingrad

Stalingrad, 13 August
Fierce fighting is raging in the approaches to Stalingrad, the great city on the Volga. The German Sixth Army, led by General Friedrich Paulus, has forced the Soviet Sixty-Second Army out of the large bend in the Don some 50 miles from the city, but the Russians' stubborn resistance has so far prevented the Germans from crossing the river. Paulus is also being held up at Kletskaya. It seems that he is short of men and is waiting for Hoth's 4th *Panzer* Army from its abortive *sortie* to the south. Meanwhile, the defences of Stalingrad grow stronger every day (→ 17).

A Scottish poster reminds people when to harvest the fruits of the "Dig for Victory" campaign.

French workers to go to Germany in swap for PoWs

France, 11 August

At Compiegne station today the first train carrying freed prisoners crossed with a train loaded with workers en route to factories in the *Reich*. On 22 June, Laval had announced the policy of *La Releve*, introduced by the Germans and aimed at obtaining manpower at all costs. Since not enough "volunteers" had been seduced by the promise of high wages, Hitler asked the *Gauleiter* Fritz Sauckel, who doubles as Reich plenipotentiary for the allocation of labour, to recruit workers in the conquered countries. Sauckel, known as the "slaver of Europe", demanded 250,000 men, of whom 150,000 had to be qualified workers.

To get the French to accept this bitter news, Laval asked Hitler to release French prisoners in exchange for the workers. The Fuhrer was willing to agree to this deal on the condition that each prisoner be replaced by three workers. Despite all the best efforts of the Vichy government, French citizens did not respond: there was still a lack of volunteers.

Hitler thought he had given the French plenty of time to organize a flow of "volunteers". But the threat of compulsion was never far away. Even before Laval's speech Sauckel had issued a directive on 7 May permitting the use of force in recruiting workers in occupied countries. Factories were shut down and round-ups were organized to get together a sufficient number of workers. Despite all this, there was little despair at Compiegne station today, as families were reunited with their soldiers after a long absence. The soldiers permitted to return home for what was called a "holiday from captivity" had been chosen from among the oldest; priority was also given to doctors, and to fathers with more than four children. Laval presided over the welcoming ceremony (→ 30).

Malta saved by Operation Pedestal

Malta, 15 August

Today is the feast of Santa Marijia in Malta, and tonight the churches of Valetta are filled with worshippers celebrating both the saint and the miracle of the battered tanker *Ohio* and four other ships unloading their cargoes in the harbour. If these ships had not managed to reach Malta, the island would certainly have been forced by hunger to surrender. The date – 6 September – had already been broadcast by the governor.

No convoy has been so powerfully escorted. Four aircraft carriers, *Victorious, Indomitable, Eagle* and *Furious* – which carried Spitfire reinforcements – joined the battleships *Nelson* and *Rodney*, together with the cruisers *Nigeria, Kenya* and *Manchester*, the anti-aircraft cruiser *Cairo* and a host of destroyers. Eight submarines were stationed to combat any surface attackers. The convoy sailed through Gibraltar on 10 August. A major setback came on the following day. At 1.30pm HMS *Eagle* was hit by four torpedoes and sank quickly; 900 of her 1,160 crew were rescued. Later, 36 German bombers struck at the convoy but scored no hits.

At noon on 12 August 80 aircraft appeared from the direction of Sicily but were driven off. The *Victorious* was hit by a bomb that failed to explode and the merchant

HMS "Indomitable", escorting the convoy WS-21S, suffers a direct hit.

ship *Deucalion* was damaged by a near miss; later in the day she was sunk by torpedo-bombers.

Ordeal by submarine was to follow, but no ship was hit and an Italian U-boat was rammed and sunk by HMS *Ithuriel*. In the early evening more air attacks began, and four bombs put the carrier *Indomitable's* flight deck out of action. Then the Italian submarine *Axum* succeeded in torpedoing the *Nigeria*, the *Cairo* and the *Ohio*.

At dusk another carefully synchronized air attack sank two merchant ships and slightly damaged the *Kenya*. E-boats were the next menace as the convoy rounded

Cape Bon at midnight. Five more merchantmen were sunk, and the *Manchester* was scuttled later.

Dawn brought continuous air attacks from enemy airfields less than 100 miles away. The *Waimarama*, carrying ammunition and petrol, blew up. The MV *Dorset* was overwhelmed by a hail of bombs but, under protection of RAF fighters from Malta, three ships limped into the Grand Harbour. Next day the damaged mv *Brisbane Star* arrived. This left the *Ohio* with her important cargo of fuel, hit five times and under tow for the last 40 miles. At two knots she arrived to cheers today – Malta was saved.

Japanese mount fresh attack in China

A Chinese Communist soldier.

Shantung, 12 August

Japanese troops today took advantage of the disarray among the divided Chinese forces by launching new operations in central Shantung against the troops of the Nationalist General Yu Hsueh-chung, on the run for the last nine days since Communist troops overran his headquarters before they defected to the Eighth Route Army.

Yu managed to escape by disguising himself as a shepherd as the Communists moved into his old base area to begin mopping up operations against Nationalist diehards. Among those cornered was the militant anti-Communist Ch'in Chijung, who, when surrounded by the Eighth, committed suicide rather than be captured (→ 28).

August 9. The Indian leader Mahatma Gandhi, who was arrested today after riots across the country for independence.

August

Su	Mo	Tu	We	Th	Fr	Sa
						1
2	3	4	5	6	7	8
9	10	11	12	13	14	15
16	17	18	19	20	21	22
23	24	25	26	27	28	29
30	31					

16. Egypt: US Army Air Force planes go into action for the first time, attacking German positions (→ 20).

17. Gilbert Islands: US marines raid Makin, damaging Japanese military installations; but nine are captured and beheaded.

17. USSR: German forces cross the Kuban river in the Caucasus, and capture vital power stations at Yessentuki and Pyatigorsk (→ 21).

18. Rastenburg: Hitler orders greater efforts to crush Soviet partisans.

18. New Guinea: Japanese reinforcements land unopposed at Basabua (→ 19).

19. New Guinea: Troops of the Australian 7th Division start a series of landings at Port Moresby (→ 26).

19. Britain: Duncan Scott-Ford, a Royal Navy sailor, is arrested for passing information to the enemy.

19. Lancashire: Tommy, a racing pigeon who strayed into the Netherlands during a race, arrives home bearing valuable military information attached to his leg by a Dutch resistant.

20. USSR: Squadron-Leader Stephan Horthy, the vice-regent of Hungary, dies fighting with the Germans on the eastern front.

20. France: USAAF bombers raid Amiens (→ 9/10).

20. Guadalcanal: The first American planes – 31 fighters – land at Henderson Field air base.→

21. USSR: German soldiers plant the *swastika* on top of Mount Elbruz, at 18,000 feet (5,500 metres) the highest in the Caucasus (→ 22).

21. France: Marshal Petain congratulates the Germans on their defence of French soil during the Allied raid on Dieppe (→ 27).

22. Stalingrad: German paratroopers landing behind Soviet lines are massacred (→ 23).

22. Lwow, Poland: 75,000 Jews have been deported to Belzec since 10 August.

Europe hit by all-American bombing raid

The cathedral at Rouen surrounded by a wasteland of rubble after the raid.

London, 17 August
Flying Fortresses of the USAAF made their first raid on Europe today with an attack on the marshalling yards at Rouen. Flying at high altitude in daylight, the 12 heavily-armed "Forts" were escorted by RAF, Dominion and Allied fighters. Despite being attacked by Messerschmitt Me109s they all returned safely and one gunner shot down a German fighter.

Brigadier-General Ira C Eaker, the commander of USAAF Bomber Command, led the attack which followed hard on the pledge by Major-General Carl Spaatz, the commander of the USAAF in Europe, to inflict "very powerful Anglo-American air blows on the enemy".

Major-General Spaatz was at the airfield to greet the crews on their return. "They behaved like veterans," he said. "this is the real start of our bombing effort and we are going to keep it up." The Flying Fortress crews were jubilant about their raid. One pilot said: "We have broken the ice at last. This is what we had been waiting for. The big moment came when, at great altitude, we saw the targets, an important marshalling yard and railway terminus with roundhouses to accommodate 250 locomotives. To see all the bombs making dead hits was like all the Fourths of July I have ever known."

This attack not only marked the entry of the USAAF heavy bombers into the war over Europe; it gave the American aviators the opportunity to test their theories of daytime precision bombing under war conditions. They believe that their Fortresses, bristling with half-inch machine guns, can beat off fighters by the defensive fire of their high altitude formations. The RAF, having suffered heavy daytime bombing losses, is sceptical (→ 20).

Brazil declares war on the Axis powers

Rio de Janeiro, 22 August
After a week of anti-Nazi rioting following the recent sinking of six Brazilian ships by Axis submarines, Brazil has today declared war on Germany and Italy. The declaration was made after a meeting between President Getulio Vargas and his cabinet this afternoon, and the country's armed forces were ordered to prepare for "sacrifices until death". Though no explanation has been given as to why Japan was not included in the declaration, it is unofficially pointed out that Japan has not committed any acts of aggression towards Brazil (→ 7/9).

Japanese attack US at Guadalcanal

Guadalcanal, 22 August
Led by a colonel wrapped in a Rising Sun flag, an elite Japanese army combat unit was virtually massacred last night when it attacked a strongly dug-in American Marine force near the mouth of the Ilu in northern Guadalcanal.

The *Ichiki* detachment of some 916 men was rushed from Truk on six destroyers and was expected to retake Guadalcanal in three days. Meanwhile at Tenaru river the first contingent of Japanese reinforcements on Guadalcanal was also annihilated by US Marines (→ 24).

Private rail travel comes under attack

Germany, 16 August
German railways have been running a large-scale campaign this summer designed to restrict private travel. "Will your journey help us to victory?" ask posters pasted up at railway stations. "Must you steal carriage space from the front?" demand newspaper advertisements in which soldiers in full kit glare menacingly at their compatriots. The campaign began in June and is continuing through the holiday season. Leisure or holiday trips, however, are the prime target of the "Wheels must roll for victory" campaign.

▷

Germans massacre Canadian infantry at Dieppe

Before the raid: Canadian troops approach the cliffs of Dieppe.

German troops investigate one of the 27 tanks lost in the abortive raid.

Combined Ops HQ, 20 August
A badly-mauled Allied commando force is returning to England this afternoon after a fruitless nine-hour attempt yesterday to seize the French port of Dieppe and destroy its German defences.

Of the 6,100-strong force of Canadians, British, Americans and Free French, around 4,100 officers and men are reported killed, wounded or missing. The 4,963 Canadians, the bulk of the force, bore the brunt of the casualties: 907 dead and 1,496 taken prisoner. Operation Jubilee, as it was code-named, was planned last April as a reconnaissance in force to test enemy defences on a well-defended sector of the coast, and to cause enough damage to persuade the Germans to withdraw men from the eastern front. A fleet of 252 ships sailed from four south-coast ports and arrived off France at 0330 hours. H-hour was 0450 hours. Five thousand men were ready to go ashore in assault craft. Then the mishaps began.

At 3.47am the commando force in the east ran into an escorted German convoy. In the exchange of fire that followed two German ships were sunk and the eastern flank landing party considerably disordered. Most importantly, the sound of the battle alerted the German land forces and the advantage of tactical surprise was lost.

The force went ashore on an 11-mile (18-km) stretch of coast centred on the port. The task was to destroy a series of shore batteries and a radio-location station and capture the German divisional HQ. One battery was silenced with brisk efficiency and another sniped at; but the others poured a hail of shells on the Canadians trapped against barbed wire on the beaches. Against these heavy guns the Royal Navy destroyers were impotent.

Of 24 tank-landing craft, ten managed to land 27 tanks, all of which were lost. One destroyer and 33 landing craft were sunk. The navy's 550 casualties include 75 dead and 269 missing or captured.

The RAF gave air cover, but lost 106 machines to the Germans' 170. The Germans lost 314 killed and 294 injured in the day's battles; 37 Germans were taken prisoner and brought back to England (→ 21).

The men who gave their lives and the loss of vital weapons

Dieppe, 19 August
Along an 11-mile (18-km) stretch of the French coast, burning tanks, destroyed landing craft and the crumpled bodies of at least 1,000 soldiers remain as a grim memorial to today's disaster. Lieutenant Edwin Loustalot, of the 1st Ranger Battalion, became the first American to be killed in land fighting in Europe in this war. A Canadian chaplain, John Foote, tended wounded on the beach and carried them to the boats to be taken off. He refused to embark with them, preferring to become a PoW and help wounded captives. Lieutenant-Colonel J P Phillips, RM, died almost instantly as he stood to signal rear landing craft to turn back, but saved 200 of his men.

Now in the hands of the Germans: Canadian PoWs rest by the roadside.

Lessons have to be learned, say Allies

Combined Ops HQ, 20 August
The Allied reconquest of Europe must begin with a soldier wading ashore out of the sea. The question to be answered after the Dieppe raid is: How do you get him ashore and ready for battle when the enemy is sitting up there with a battery of guns trained on him? Lord Mountbatten, the chief of Combined Operations, believes that Dieppe shows the need for overwhelming fire support, including close support, during the initial stages of an attack. Dieppe has convinced Allied planners that the massive force needed to open a second front cannot be assembled before 1944 at the earliest.

1942

August

Su	Mo	Tu	We	Th	Fr	Sa
						1
2	3	4	5	6	7	8
9	10	11	12	13	14	15
16	17	18	19	20	21	22
23	24	25	26	27	28	29
30	31					

23. Stalingrad: Six hundred *Luftwaffe* bombers attack the city as its outer defences start to crumble.→

24. Guadalcanal: Japan loses 21 planes, the US just three.→

25. France: German military service is made compulsory in Alsace-Lorraine.

26. USSR: The Red Army launches diversionary attacks on Vyazma and Rzhev to try to take some pressure off Stalingrad (→ 27).

27. USSR: Stalin appoints his deputy supreme commander, Marshal Zhukov, to oversee the defence of Stalingrad (→ 1/9).

27. Rastenburg: Hitler orders the release of 800 French PoWs as a reward for the "exemplary conduct" of the people of Dieppe during the Allied raid (→ 29).

28. Britain: A Junkers Ju86P bomber drops a bomb from a high altitude on Bristol, leaving 48 dead and 26 injured.

28. USA: A Japanese sea-plane launched from the submarine I-25 drops incendiaries on a forest in Oregon.

28. Caribbean: The U-boat U94 is sunk by the Canadian ship *Oakville* and US aircraft.

28. Vichy France: The authorities complete the rounding-up of 7,000 Jews for deportation to Auschwitz.→

29. Britain: The CIGS, Sir Alan Brooke, complains bitterly to Churchill about the dreadful casualties and lack of planning of the Dieppe raid.

30. Luxemburg: Germany introduces conscription.

30. Paris: The *Reich* plenipotentiary for the allocation of labour, Fritz Sauckel, decrees that all men and women in German–occupied lands are liable for forced labour.

30. Pacific: The US carrier *Saratoga* is damaged by a Japanese submarine.

31. Europe: An estimated 400,000 Jews have been slaughtered in occupied Europe this month (→ 2/9).

Japan halted by US in Solomon Islands

American carrier bombers raid the hotly-contested island of Guadalcanal.

Guadalcanal, 25 August
Like a giant magnet, Guadalcanal continues to attract powerful Japanese combat forces whose aim is now to clear the island of the invading Americans.

Yesterday the Japanese lost an aircraft carrier and a large number of aircraft in the Battle of the Eastern Solomons.

The Japanese were attempting to land reinforcements on Guadalcanal, where their situation is critical, but the convoy carrying 1,500 troops was forced to withdraw to the Shortland Islands after a transport was hit and caught fire.

The Americans drew first blood when they sank the light carrier *Ryujo*. The American carrier *Enterprise* suffered serious damage and was withdrawn from the battle. The Japanese lost 90 carrier planes, the Americans 20 (→ 8/9).

"Daily Worker" is back on the streets

London, 26 August
The government ban on the British Communist Party's newspaper, *The Daily Worker*, was lifted last night after 19 months and the paper reappeared today – but only just. At the last minute the printers went on strike.

William Rust, the editor, refused to hire a printer who had worked on the paper before the ban. This was the man who had welcomed police who came to shut down the paper. "I have been expecting you," he had said. "I do not agree with the policies of those bastards upstairs."

Natsopa, the printers' and paper-workers' union, told Rust that it would not agree to selective re-hiring. Rust called the man a trouble-maker. Union officials then ordered their members to stop work. Rust caved in and 120,000 copies were printed, more than double the pre-ban print.

The paper was banned for spreading defeatist propaganda during the period when the Communists were opposed to the war. Party membership fell to 15,000. After the German attack on the Soviet Union, the party switched to support of the war overnight. Membership has risen to 55,000.

British families set to take "utility furniture" into their homes

Britain, 31 August
From now on, all new furniture must conform to the "Utility" specification covering 22 articles, most of them in three alternative designs. The prices are also fixed. A double bed with rails at head and foot costs £3/10/9 (£3.54/$14.27) in oak and £4/11/- (£4.55/$18,34) in mahogany.

There is a convertible bed-chair at £3/19/6 (£3.97/$16.02), an open-arm chair with upholstered seat at £3/12/- (£3.60/$14.50), a spring-upholstered "easy" chair at £6/10/- (£6.50/$26.20) and an adjustable fireside chair at £2/10/6 (£2.52½p/ $10.18). There are no 3-piece suites. designers have chosen the models. Permits to buy Utility furniture will be issued to those who can show that they really need them. People who have lost their furniture in air raids or who are setting up home on marriage get priority.

Simple, practical styles for utility furniture and chinaware in the kitchen.

State of siege declared in Stalingrad

Russian air force bombs cities of Berlin and Danzig

The battle for Stalingrad begins: Russian tanks move towards the front to prepare for a final defiant stand.

Stalingrad, 25 August
The battle for Stalingrad has begun. Paulus's Sixth Army reached the steep banks of the Volga, to the north of the city, two nights ago and it seems that the garrison formed by General Lopatin's army is in danger of being rolled up.

With the bridges over the Volga within artillery and mortar range, the Russians' problems of supply and reinforcement seem insurmountable. Rather than commit the army to costly street fighting, however, the *Luftwaffe* has been called in to deliver the *coup de grace* to the besieged city. For the last two nights von Richthofen's *Luftflotte* 4 has mounted the heaviest strikes since the first day of *Barbarossa*.

Heinkel He111s and even Junkers Ju52 transports have been brought in to add their weight to the Stukas. Stalingrad has been blitzed, with 40,000 people killed by air raids.

Yet Stalingrad refuses to surrender under the hail of bombs. With the enemy at the gates of the city the regional party committee has proclaimed a defiant state of siege today: "We shall never surrender the city of our birth to the depredations of the German invader. Each single one of us must apply himself to the task of defending our beloved town, our homes and our families. Let us barricade every street; transform every district, every block, every house into an impregnable fortress" (→ 26).

Anti-tank action on the outskirts.

Germany, 29 August
Moscow Radio reported today that Soviet aircraft have bombed Berlin for the second time in four nights. Danzig, Konigsberg and Stettin were also hit. In its report the radio says that while over Berlin one of the Russian pilots sent a radio message to Stalin telling him "our task has been carried out".

Berlin has admitted that Russian aircraft reached the city, but says that "only a few stray bombs were dropped". After the previous raid the Germans said that "only single aircraft succeeded in reaching the outskirts".

The Russians insist, however, that 48 fires were started in the German capital and that there were nine big explosions. They give similarly detailed accounts of fires started and damage caused in the other cities. The resumption of raids on Berlin after nearly a year means that the Russians have now succeeded in forming a long-range force capable of flying some 2,000 miles (3,200 km).

Duke of Kent dies in flying accident

London, 26 August
The Duke of Kent, an RAF air commodore and the youngest brother of King George VI, has become the first member of the Royal Family to die on active service and perhaps the first to die in an air disaster. He was killed yesterday when a Sunderland flying boat in which he was travelling crashed in the north of Scotland. An official announcement said that the duke, attached to the staff of the inspector-general of the RAF, was on his way to Iceland, on duty.

A total of 14 people lost their lives when the big aircraft hit a hillside in misty conditions. Shepherds heard the engines cut and the sound of a crash, and saw a spurt of flame. The bodies were recovered at dawn today. One survivor was found wandering in the hills, burnt and shocked. He is Flight-Sergeant Andrew Jack, aged 21, of Grangemouth, the crew's rear gunner. The duke, who was born in 1902, served

in the Royal Navy from 1916 to 1929. He left for medical reasons and started flying as a hobby a year later. He was married to Princess Marina of Greece. Their third child, Prince Michael, was born seven weeks ago.

The duke, who crashed in Scotland.

Japanese wreck airfields and pull back

Chekiang, China, 28 August
The three-month-long Japanese offensive in Chekiang and Kiangsi has ended with Japanese troops completing their two-phase withdrawal eastward as Chinese Nationalists regain control of Chuchow.

The decision to withdraw the nine divisions of Japan's XIII Corps was taken a month ago when the Japanese High Command was

satisfied that the operation had achieved its main retaliatory objective – the destruction of the airfields where long-range US bombers landed after bombing Tokyo.

Chinese tactics throughout the retreat, as well as the offensive, have been to avoid direct confrontations. Instead, to conserve their strength, the Chinese have used guerrilla tactics.

Japanese set up air base in New Guinea

Papua, New Guinea, 26 August
While the fighting in the Solomons continues at full fury, a Japanese naval landing force has invaded Milne Bay in the south-eastern corner of Papua, New Guinea.

The Japanese army desperately wanted to provide air cover for its drive across the Owen Stanley mountains to Port Moresby, to which it had committed 13,500 troops. It also wanted an air base

within reach of northern Australian airfields. Under cover of darkness 1,200 men of the Special Naval Landing Force who sailed from Rabaul entered Milne Bay on 25 August. The invaders soon clashed with Australian troops, and at dawn the next morning Australian aircraft ripped their landing barges with bombs and cannon fire and killed Japanese on the foreshore (→ 3/9).

Rommel stuck in desert

Rommel in victorious mood after Tobruk: now his luck is running out.

Alam el Halfa, 31 August
Rommel's tanks are tonight bogged down in the soft sands to the south of Alam el Halfa ridge, ten miles (16 km) south of El Alamein. The *Afrika Korps* had attacked yesterday, hoping to outflank the British Eighth Army, but progress was slowed by newly-laid Allied minefields. This allowed the 8th and 22nd Armoured Brigades to pound the German forces who were also attacked from the air.

Without the benefit of surprise, Rommel switched the direction of his attack towards the Alam el Halfa ridge, only to encounter not only the sticky sand but also reinforced defences from which the British could pound the German tanks. Rommel's good fortune seems to be running out. He is a sick man, ill with jaundice. One of his generals has been killed; his corps commander, Major-General Walther Nehring, is wounded. The Afrika Korps is also desperately short of fuel, despite the assurance of a petrol airlift by the C-in-C, Field Marshal Kesselring.

Ironically, the British plan to defend the El Alamein position was left for Generals Alexander and Montgomery by their predecessors. Woken to be told about his army's success this morning Monty said: "Excellent – couldn't be better." And went back to sleep (→ 1/9).

RAF "pathfinder" corps is formed

Wyton, Huntingdonshire, 31 August
A perilous form of airmanship – target designation – has been introduced into Bomber Command this month against the wishes of its boss, Arthur Harris. RAF aircrew known as "pathfinders" will fly ahead of the main force and often nearer to the ground to mark the target with parachute flares. Harris has excluded any special training for these crews while increasing their number of continuous operations from the normal 30 to 50. He told the pathfinder leader, Air Vice-Marshal Donald Bennett: "Their chances of survival are small."

Swiss fears mount over fate of Jews

Berne, 29 August
There is growing concern in Switzerland over the neutral republic's attitude towards the Jews and gypsies now being rounded up to be deported from Vichy France to "the east" – in fact, death in the Auschwitz gas chambers. In response to the lively official and press debate on the issue the Swiss government said today that its policy was not to turn back Jewish refugees to Switzerland. In practice, however, Jews trying to flee the brutal mass round-ups in Vichy France are often refused entry by Swiss border guards (→ 31).

Different ways of life for Allied PoWs: Tortured by ruthless Japanese captors

PoWs at a Japanese camp in the Philippines line up for the photographer.

South-east Asia, 31 August
When the Japanese took Hong Kong they were ordered to take no prisoners. Instead they roped together Allied survivors and bayoneted them to death.

There must be times when those who are now captives of the Japanese wonder if that would not have been a better fate.

Some 300 British PoWs and several thousand Australians have been put to work building a rail link between Thailand and Burma. The harshness of their conditions have earned it the name "Railway of Death". Meanwhile in Changi jail, in Singapore, the jailers are preparing a new form of mass torture. Unless each man, in direct conflict with his duties as a PoW, signs a form agreeing not to attempt an escape, all 15,400 prisoners will be confined to the sweltering heat of a barrack square measuring 270 by 135 yards with only two water taps, until they change their minds.

Any prisoner not showing due respect to his captors runs the risk of immediate decapitation or slow and agonizing death.

Concerts and class divisions in Germany

Germany, 31 August
Despite the Red Cross Convention of 1929, which lays down standards of treatment for PoWs, the Nazis are making up the rules as they go along. While most British prisoners in Germany – particularly officers who are confined in *Oflags* – enjoy adequate food and clothing, and even find time to organize entertainments, their Soviet counterparts are brutally exploited as forced labourers and murdered by the thousand. The number of British escapes is high, and this fact also deters their captors from putting them to work outside the camps.

A volley-ball game in Colditz.

1942
September

Su	Mo	Tu	We	Th	Fr	Sa
		1	2	3	4	5
6	7	8	9	10	11	12
13	14	15	16	17	18	19
20	21	22	23	24	25	26
27	28	29	30			

1. USSR: The Germans claim to have captured Kalach, 40 miles (64 km) west of Stalingrad (→ 3).

1. Egypt: The British Eighth Army repels a German attack on the Alam Halfa ridge. →

2. Dzialosyce, Poland: Polish police, Ukrainian militia and German *Gestapo* slaughter 2,000 Jews and deport the remaining 8,000 to Belzec death camp (→ 12).

2. Poland: Soviet aircraft bomb Warsaw.

2. USSR: Germany launches a major drive against partisans in the district of Mogilev (→ 24).

2. Britain: The Hawker Tempest fighter makes its first flight.

3. New Guinea: One thousand Japanese landed last night to reinforce Buna garrison (→ 5).

3. Tokyo: The foreign minister, Shigenori Togo, the only civilian in the cabinet, resigns "for personal reasons"; the war minister and premier, Hideki Tojo, takes over his portfolio for the time being (→ 27).

3. Stalingrad: German troops penetrate the city's western and northern suburbs, and Stalin orders an immediate attack to relieve pressure on the defenders (→ 5).

3. London: A reciprocal lend-lease deal is signed by Britain, the USA, Australia, New Zealand and the Free French.

3. Channel Islands: British commandos captured seven German soldiers and seized codebooks during a raid on a lighthouse last night (→ 4/10).

4. Belfast: Police clash with IRA gunmen in street battles.

5. New Guinea: The Japanese evacuate Milne Bay (→ 7).

5. Stalingrad: Fighting is now taking place in the suburbs; yesterday the Germans reached the Volga, south of the city.→

5. Budapest: The blackout is introduced because of Soviet air raids.

5. USSR: German troops lay siege to the Black Sea naval base of Novorossiisk (→ 6).

Zhukov reinforces defence of Stalingrad

Stalingrad burns as German gunners try to pick off the city's defenders.

Stalingrad, 5 September
General Friedrich Paulus has delayed his attempt to seize Stalingrad quickly in order to mop up the considerable Russian forces which he has bypassed and which he now considers a threat to the northern flank of his salient.

At the same time Russia's Marshal Zhukov, newly arrived to take command, is energetically preparing an attack on the Germans. He is fully aware of the dangers of the situation. In a directive issued two days ago he told his officers: "Stalingrad could be seized today or tomorrow if the northern group of forces is not rendered immediate assistance." His orders are for the "troop commanders north and north-west of Stalingrad to strike the enemy quickly ... No procrastination will be tolerated. Delay now is regarded as criminal."

As he did in Leningrad and Moscow, Zhukov is conscripting the civilian population to prepare and to man last-ditch defences in front of the city. Young boys and old men are marching off to war still in their civilian clothes. There is no doubt that Zhukov intends to impose Stalin's order of "Not a step backwards". Stalingrad is ringing with the slogan: "There is no land beyond the Volga" (→ 9).

Australians to pay for fun and games

Brisbane, 4 September
To strengthen the war effort, the Australian government is moving to cut down on "fun and games" in the domestic scene. In a national broadcast here last night, the prime minister, John Curtin, warned that should Port Moresby and Darwin fall to the Japanese, Australia faced a bloody struggle on its own soil. Austerity measures to be brought in are intended to restrict horse and dog races, raise the tax on all entertainments, reduce the drinking of alcohol, smoking and the eating of expensive meals, check black-marketeering and deglamourize activities described in gossip columns.

Retreating Rommel abandons tanks

Western Desert, 3 September
As Rommel's *Panzers* retreat, badly savaged and harassed all the way by British infantry and the Desert Air Force, it is the turn of the Allies to capture the booty of war. The Germans and Italians were facing a serious fuel shortage when they attacked, and now the desert is littered with abandoned Axis vehicles.

British engineers have been assigned the task of disabling these tanks. One engineer, Sapper Irvine Adam of Paisley, near Glasgow, told how he was ordered to blow up a slightly damaged German tank. "I had just a minute to get away before it blew," he said (→ 6).

Pro-Axis ministers sacked by Franco

Madrid, 3 September
General Franco has fired three key ministers in a rebuff to Spain's fascist party, the *Falange*. The most senior man to go is his own brother-in-law, Ramon Serrano Suner, the foreign minister and Falangist chief. His German sympathies have angered the Spanish army, which is fiercely nationalistic and resents any idea of being a pawn of Hitler. The new foreign minister is a general, Gomez Jordana (→ 8/12).

September 3. On the National Day of Prayer Churchill leaves Westminster Abbey with his wife Clementine, and daughter Mary in ATS uniform.

Women in uniform: how the gentler sex is learning to cope with tougher times

Women NAAFI workers have a uniform too: a sergeant drills them for parade.

Britain, 1 September

Women in the services are not the only ones in uniform these days. Female civilian workers, from nurses to bus conductors and Land Girls, have regulation outfits, too.

The London Passenger Transport Board's women conductors are easily recognizable in their jaunty pale grey jackets and slacks with blue piping. Of the 19,000 transport conductors in the capital – on buses, trams and trolley-buses – 8,000 are now women working under the same conditions as their male colleagues. For their first six months on the road they, just like men, earn the minimum on the scale. Thereafter they work up to the same maximum of £4/19/- (£4.95/$19.95) weekly.

Women who have chosen to work on the land are provided with practical khaki corduroy breeches, green pullovers and smart little khaki felt hats. There are now some 40,000 in the Women's Land Army, working outdoors in all weathers and often living in isolated areas far from home. During their 48-hour week they drive tractors, bring in the harvest, milk the cows and care for the livestock. A minimum wage for a man doing such work is £3 ($12) a week, but for women it is 18/- (90p/$3.63) after paying for board and lodgings. A Cornish farmer recently admitted: "After the land girl is trained she is certainly worth more than we pay for her." The more traditionally female nursing service is crying out

for volunteers. In the spring of this year a call went out for 5,000 new recruits. Women can start as student nurses at £40 ($160) a year with board and lodgings, or join as nursing auxiliaries and receive £55 ($220) yearly.

Though the wages seem low in comparison with the pay packets taken home by men in similar work, for the majority of women their wartime income is considerably bigger than any pre-war earnings. But the satisfaction that many of them derive from their jobs comes from the company as much as the pay. Camaraderie with other working adults can make a welcome change from housework and childcare.

The citizens of Bournemouth watch the local nursing divisions march by.

Su	Mo	Tu	We	Th	Fr	Sa
		1	2	3	4	5
6	7	8	9	10	11	12
13	14	15	16	17	18	19
20	21	22	23	24	25	26
27	28	29	30			

6. Britain: The Messerschmitt Me210 is first used over Britain; two are shot down by Hawker Typhoons over the north Yorkshire coast.

6. Black Sea: The key Soviet base at Novorossiisk falls to the Germans.

6. Egypt: The battle of Alam Halfa ends as German troops, having been forced back to their original positions, start to dig large-scale fortifications and anti-tank defences (→ 14).

7. Rome: Italy declares war on Brazil.

8. Guadalcanal: In the last 24 hours, US marines have landed at Taivu and attacked the Japanese base (→ 12).

8. Washington: Roosevelt broadcasts to the nation, warning that "this is the toughest war of all time" (→ 17).

9. Vinnitsa: Field Marshal List is sacked as commander of Army Group A, currently operating in the Caucasus; General Paul von Kleist succeeds him.→

9. US: A Japanese plane drops incendiaries near Brookings, Oregon, for the second time in ten days, causing very little damage.

10. London: Churchill announces firm measures, including the use of troops, to curb the "revolutionary" activities of the Congress Party in India.

10. US: A U-boat lays 12 mines off the Virginia coast.

10-11. Germany: RAF bombers raid Dusseldorf.→

11. Burma: RAF bombers attack Japanese positions in Prome, Mandalay and Rangoon (→ 21).

12. Guadalcanal: Japan assaults US positions around Bloody Ridge (→ 14).

12. USSR: General Vasili Chuikov is appointed to command the Sixty-Second Army, responsible for the defence of Stalingrad (→ 18).

12. France: Nine out of ten British commandos are killed during a raid on Port-en-Bessin in Normandy.

U-boat sinks ship with 1,500 Italian PoWs and civilians

South Atlantic, 12 September

A double controversy surrounds the sinking today of the former White Star liner *Laconia*, now a troop ship, off Ascension Island. The *Laconia* was carrying 811 British passengers and crew and more than 1,500 Italian PoWs, together with 180 Polish guards, when she was torpedoed. According to the purser, panic among the prisoners hampered the orderly evacuation of the sinking ship. Italian survivors, however, claim that the guards had closed watertight doors, shutting in most of the Italian prisoners.

The other controversy surrounds the consequences of the attempt by U156, which launched the attacks, to rescue survivors. When the U-boat commander, Werner Hartenstein, heard the men in the water talking Italian, he realized that he had hit a PoW ship; he took in as many survivors as he could – 193, including 21 Britons. He then put out a signal in English promising not to attack any ship which came to rescue the others. The question is how Admiral Donitz, Germany's navy chief, will react to the fact that while U156 was helping survivors she was attacked by US aircraft. A planned order that in future no German vessel may pick up survivors would breach an international naval accord of 1936.

French Canadians are urged to buy victory bonds to fend off the claws of Japan and the Nazis.

Warsaw Jews massacred

Bound for the gas chambers: the emaciated faces of children of the ghetto.

Allies push Japanese back in New Guinea

Port Moresby, 7 September
For the first time in the Pacific, a Japanese amphibious invasion force has been defeated and forced to withdraw after establishing a beachhead. The defeat was inflicted by two Australian infantry brigades at Milne Bay, in south-eastern Papua, New Guinea where Japan was denied an air base.

The purpose of the air base was to provide air support for Japan's major thrust across the Owen Stanley Mountains aimed at taking Port Moresby. The Japanese sent 2,400 men of the Special Navy Landing Force to seize the area. But Milne Bay was defended by the 7th Brigade (an Australian militia formation) and the 18th Brigade of the veteran Australian 7th Division, recently returned to the south-west Pacific after service in the Middle East. After landing under cover of darkness on 25 August the Japanese attacked in force on the night of 26-27 August, and after a long and ferocious fight the Australians withdrew to the Gama river.

The Japanese suffered heavy casualties on the night of 31 August when they charged wildly three times in their attempts to seize the airfield. The Australians were firing into groups of Japanese who bunched as they attacked, and many fell in the hail of fire. The operation turned into a Japanese debacle. More Japanese warships were sent to help, but on 5 September Rabaul radioed "try to get them out". By the time the troops had withdrawn they had lost 311 killed with 700 missing (→ 14).

Warsaw, 12 September
The gassing of 2,196 Jews at Treblinka today marks the end of a week of deportations in which about 70,000 Jews have been decanted from the ever-shrinking ghetto here. Since the Nazis started their plan to eliminate the ghetto in July, nearly 255,000 people have been deported to their deaths.

The latest *Aktion*, which the Jews grimly nicknamed the *kesl* [Yiddish for cauldron], started on 5 September when all ghetto dwellers were ordered to report to a new assembly point in Mila Street. Roped off and guarded by armed police, who report shooting 2,648 attempted escapees this week, the Jews have been shipped off to Treblinka at the rate of 10,000 a day. Only around 70,000 remain out of a population of 350,000. There are no families; those who remain are mainly single men in their twenties and thirties, temporarily exempted from death only in order to boost the war effort as labourers in the ghetto's German-owned factories.

Life in the ghetto is worse than ever. Those with the all-important work permits sleep in their workplaces; those without them exist as scavengers on the run, sheltering in burnt-out apartment blocks. Ukrainian militiamen roam the area shooting Jews dead at random. Corpses line the streets (→ 18).

Allied troops and their native bearers stop for a brief rest in New Guinea.

Four-month stalemate in Madagascar broken by British attacks

Madagascar, 10 September
Allied troops have begun an advance to occupy all of the Vichy-French colony of Madagascar. Last May the Allies occupied the port of Diego Suarez, to forestall its use by Japan's navy. Now the Allies claim that Japanese submarines have been using Madagascar as a fuelling base – an accusation which Vichy denies. The British 29 Infantry Brigade has landed at Majunga, on the west coast, followed by the 22nd East African Brigade. They are pushing on to the capital, Tananarive, while the 7th South African Brigade advances from Diego Suarez (→ 18).

Allied troops unload stores on the beach after the capture of Manjunga.

Germans threaten city of Stalingrad

Stalingrad, 11 September
The ruined city of Stalingrad is tonight in immediate danger of falling to the Germans. Paulus has fought off Zhukov's hastily-prepared counter-attack and is working his way towards the heart of the city against stubborn resistance. Russian guns, safe on the eastern bank of the Volga, are pounding the Germans, whose latest communique says that the "fortified belt of steel" around Stalingrad has to be taken "piece by piece" from the Russians, "who resist fiercely and desperately to the end" (→ 12).

1942

September

Su	Mo	Tu	We	Th	Fr	Sa
		1	2	3	4	5
6	7	8	9	10	11	12
13	14	15	16	17	18	19
20	21	22	23	24	25	26
27	28	29	30			

Churchill promises Stalin second front

London, 8 September

In a speech described by MPs as one of "guarded optimism", Churchill told the Commons today that in his talks with Stalin he had promised the Soviet leader that the western Allies would come to his aid "as quickly as possible in the most effective manner without regard to the losses and sacrifices involved". That was as far as the British prime minister felt he could go in meeting Stalin's repeated demands for a second front in western Europe. At the outset of the talks Stalin had made it plain that he did not think the British and Americans were doing enough to take the weight off the Soviet armies facing the Nazi onslaught (→ 26).

The Russians' vision of cooperation.

Dusseldorf one big fire after RAF raid

Germany, 10 September

More than 100,000 incendiaries were dropped on Dusseldorf in less than an hour tonight in an RAF raid which left much of the city on fire. The attackers, 476 bombers including 174 bomber-trainers, flew through a wall of light and *flak* to reach their target, marked by a Pathfinder crew with flares. In what one pilot described as "a nice piece of timing" the first of the bombers reached the city as the flares were burning over it. The RAF, which lost 31 planes, left fires visible 150 miles away (→ 20).

13. Vichy: The authorities have instituted a *Service National du Travail* (STO) [National Work Service] which introduces compulsory labour for all men aged between 18 and 50 and unmarried women between 21 and 35.

14. Guadalcanal: Eleven thousand US defenders repel 60,000 Japanese at the Battle of Bloody Ridge.→

14. New Guinea: The Japanese reach Imita Ridge on the Kokoda Trail, only 30 miles (50 km) from Port Moresby (→ 15).

14. North Atlantic: After four days of attack by a wolfpack of 13 U-boats, convoy ON-127 has lost 12 freighters and one Canadian destroyer; one U-boat has been hit (→ 16/10).

15. New Guinea: US infantry land at Port Moresby (→ 23).

16. Britain: Three Eagle Squadrons, consisting of American volunteers to the RAF, are to be transferred to USAAF command.

16. Aleutian Islands: Japanese forces secretly withdraw from Attu (→ 12/1).

17. Norway: The premier, Vidkun Quisling, reintroduces the death penalty (→ 6/10).

17. US: Roosevelt begins a 15-day, 8,500-mile nationwide inspection of war industries.

17. US: Atomic weapons research is put under military control; Colonel Leslie Groves is appointed to manage the programme (→ 23).

18. Stalingrad: Soviet marines fend off ten German attacks from their positions in the city grain silo.→

18. Paris: One hundred and sixteen people are executed in retaliation for recent attacks on German soldiers (→ 19).

19. Paris: In a further retaliatory measure, all places of entertainment are closed and non-German citizens are curfewed until midnight tonight (→ 21).

19. USSR: Moscow erroneously reports the death of a top German general, Paul von Kleist, in the Ukraine.

Fierce fighting on outskirts of Stalingrad

Stalingrad, 18 September

The Germans, fighting their way yard by bloody yard through the piles of rubble which were once Stalingrad in a war of grenades, bayonets and rifle butts, have been thrown off the *Mamaev Kurgan*, the raised Scythian burial ground which dominates the river crossings of this bridgeless city.

It was General Rodimtsev's 13th Guards Division, ferried across the Volga by night, which stormed the burial ground. Everything now depends on the ferries and other small boats which cross the river at night, lit up by the glow of burning buildings and illuminating shells, with the river erupting in waterspouts as the shells and bombs whistle around them.

They bring in ammunition and reinforcements and carry out the wounded to the safety of the east bank. Many are sunk or riddled with machine-gun fire as they head into the inferno. But they keep on coming, providing the only lifeline to Stalingrad's defenders.

The city is so shattered that the fighting is concentrated around individual buildings. The central station has changed hands four times in three days. General Vasily Chuikov, the abrasive new commander of the battered Sixty-Second Army, has set up his HQ in the *Krasny Oktyabr* factory.

The Germans have command of the air, and some of the bravest people in this battle are the pilots of the flimsy Polikarpov P-2 biplanes which stagger through the shell-rent night sky to bomb the Germans. One squadron is crewed exclusively by women pilots (→ 22).

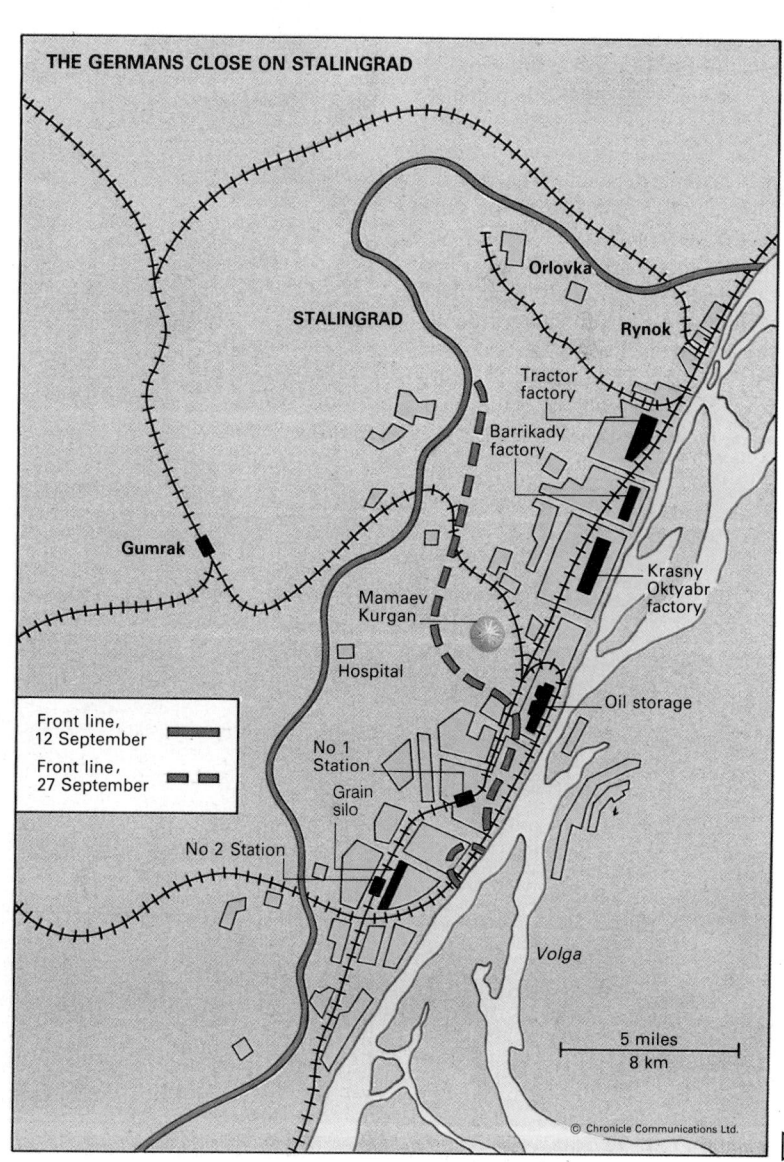

THE GERMANS CLOSE ON STALINGRAD

Orlovka
STALINGRAD
Rynok
Tractor factory
Barrikady factory
Gumrak
Krasny Oktyabr factory
Mamaev Kurgan
Hospital
Oil storage
Front line, 12 September
Front line, 27 September
No 1 Station
Grain silo
No 2 Station
Volga
5 miles
8 km

© Chronicle Communications Ltd.

Biggest convoy yet reaches the USSR

White Sea, 18 September
Convoy PQ-18 reached the safety of the White Sea today with 27 of its original 40 ships intact. Despite the losses, it was the biggest convoy yet to reach Russia. It sailed for Russia on 2 September, after a month in which convoys to the USSR were halted. Following the disastrous July convoy PQ-17, when only 11 out of 36 merchantmen arrived in Russia, Churchill wrote to Stalin suggesting that convoys should be suspended until the longer nights of autumn. Reluctantly, the Soviet leader agreed.

PQ-18 was the most heavily protected convoy so far, with around 50 naval vessels deployed in either the escort or covering forces, including 20 destroyers and the carrier *Avenger*. The German navy had difficulty getting close to the convoy, and air attacks account for most of the 13 convoy ships lost.

The worst day was 13 September. Forty German torpedo-bombers sank eight ships in as many minutes in a stunning assault. The day before, U-boats sank two of the ships in the starboard column. Five torpedo-bombers were shot down and the destroyer *Faulknor* sank U88 with a blitz of depth charges. In all, the Germans lost 20 aircraft and two U-boats. The escort will return with surviving ships of earlier convoys, including PQ-17 (→ 26).

Destroyers of the escort for convoy PQ-18: now they have reached safe waters.

One of PQ-18's oil tankers goes up in flames: despite an ever-vigilant escort, 13 out of 40 ships did not arrive.

British forces win Madagascar port from Vichy French

Madagascar, 18 September
Tamatave, the main port of the French colony of Madagascar, has been taken by the British – a day after the island's Vichy governor, M Annet, rejected General Sir William Platt's surrender terms.

The British fleet arrived off Tamatave at dawn. When the Vichy authorities refused to surrender, it bombarded the port. Three minutes later the white flag was raised. By the time that the 29 Brigade had landed most of the Vichy forces had withdrawn.

With the taking of Tamatave – a week after landing at Majunga, on the west coast – Allied forces are pressing on to the capital Tananarive from east and west, against mainly Malgache and Senegalese troops, through an inhospitable terrain where malaria knocks down more troops than bullets (→ 6/11).

Disastrous raid is launched on Tobruk

Tobruk, 14 September
After a three-hour bombardment and heavy air raids, the British last night launched a raid on this much-fought-over port – aiming to do as much damage as possible to the port and Rommel's supply dumps. But Operation Agreement, as it was called, was a disaster.

The intention was for 350 marines and 150 troops to land on the north and south sides of the harbour respectively and seize coastal defences. The captured defences would then cover a force of destroyers as they entered the harbour, destroyed shipping and port facilities, and took off the marines and soldiers.

A head-on assault by a small force in the face of blistering German counter-fire was risky from the start. Of 21 coastal craft, 19 failed to get troops ashore, and an assault craft with the first wave of marines failed to return. Two destroyers and the anti-aircraft cruiser *Coventry* were also lost, and an MTB was captured; 579 Allied servicemen have been taken prisoner.

SEPTEMBER 1942

Britain's "SAS" fails in Libyan operation

An Allied desert patrol takes a break: the latest raid ended in disaster.

Cairo, 14 September
An ambitious scheme to hit three Libyan targets in a combined operation has blown up in the face of its British planners. At Benghazi, David Stirling's Special Air Service (SAS) found the enemy waiting and ready, so withdrew under heavy fire, losing 18 Jeeps and 25 other vehicles. At Tobruk an assault from

sea and desert using infantry, Marine commandos and the Long Range Desert Group (LRDG) was a failure costing three big ships and many lives [*see previous page*]. At Barce a New Zealand LRDG patrol blew up 24 enemy aircraft, but few of these men are expected to survive the *Luftwaffe* manhunt across the desert (→1/11).

US aircraft carrier sunk by Japanese sub

Guadalcanal, 15 September
The battle for control of Guadalcanal swung in favour of Japan today with the torpedoing of the 14,700-ton aircraft carrier USS *Wasp* south of the island. This will help the Japanese to use their seaborne "Tokyo Express" route to reinforce their defences after failing yesterday to break through the

American marines at Henderson Field airstrip. Japanese forces under General Kawaguchi did breach the US lines on 12 September, along the appropriately named summit of Bloody Ridge; but they were eventually driven back after three days of bitter fighting which left an estimated 600 Japanese and 150 Americans dead (→9/10).

The end for the USS "Wasp" after she was hit by three Japanese torpedoes.

"Social misfits" in Nazi Europe are to wear badges proclaiming "crimes"

Berlin, 18 September
Himmler today agreed that Germany's "asocials" should be handed over to forced labour without proper sustenance or medical help – in effect, worked to death. In the concentration camps, "asocials" wear coloured triangular badges to identify the different categories of outcast: homosexuals (pink), pacifists (purple), political offenders (red), criminals (green), antisocials (black) and Jews (yellow Star of David). Poles, Russians, Czechs and gypsies have been added to the list since 1939.

A policy for dealing with undesirables was introduced soon after Hitler came to power, when it was decided that, in the interests of racial purity, the mentally deficient should be sterilized. Then at a Nuremberg party rally a speaker suggested that Jews should be sterilized also. Hitler promised that, in the event of war, euthanasia not steralization would be introduced; at such a time the church would be unable to speak against it.

In the first two years of the war, up to 80,000 Germans identified as "useless elements" were exterminated. This took place without the publication of a formal decree. When the justice ministry pressed for the text of the Fuhrer's decree, all it received was a photocopy of a handwritten note from Hitler to the head of the *Reich* chancellery. The note ordered chancellery officials to give "duly appointed physicians" powers to "order the mercy killing of incurables". On the basis of this note, euthanasia institutes were set up. These were later to provide the models for the extermination camps for Jews.

Though camp warders initially were ex-soldiers, ex-criminals and the generally unemployable who had joined the SS, intellectuals now serve in the camps, carrying out "scientific" experiments. Prostitutes have been sent to Dachau for tests on reviving frozen human guinea-pigs by the body heat of others.

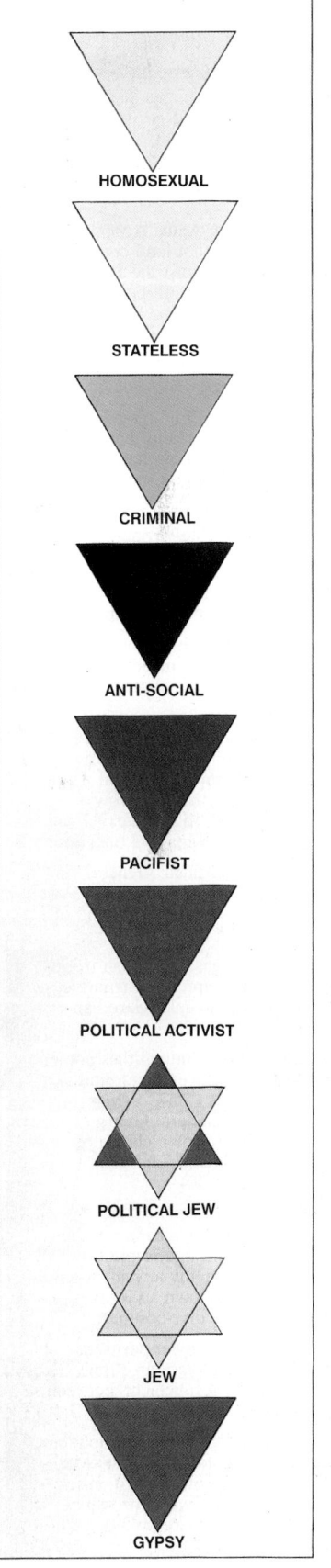

HOMOSEXUAL
STATELESS
CRIMINAL
ANTI-SOCIAL
PACIFIST
POLITICAL ACTIVIST
POLITICAL JEW
JEW
GYPSY

September

Su	Mo	Tu	We	Th	Fr	Sa
		1	2	3	4	5
6	7	8	9	10	11	12
13	14	15	16	17	18	19
20	21	22	23	24	25	26
27	28	29	30			

20. Germany: RAF bombers flew 1,200 miles (1,920 km) to raid Munich last night, killing 65 people; other aircraft hit Saarbrucken (→ 29).

21. Burma: Allied troops mount the first land counter-offensive against the Japanese, in the Arakan on the Bay of Bengal (→ 17/12).

21. US: The Boeing B-29 Superfortress bomber makes its first flight.

21. London: Figures released by the Allies claim that 207,373 non-Jews have been executed by the Germans in occupied Europe.

22. USSR: Hand-to-hand fighting breaks out in the centre of Stalingrad; the Germans take the city's grain silo from Soviet marines.→

22. Vichy: The Nazi execution of 70 hostages in Bordeaux to avenge acts of sabotage is announced.

23. Timor Sea: The Australian destroyer *Voyager* is sunk while attempting to land supplies to the "Sparrow Force" fighting a guerrilla war against the Japanese on Timor.

23. New Guinea: General Sir Thomas Blamey arrives at Port Moresby to take command of Australian land forces.→

23. Madagascar: British troops enter the capital, Tananarive, which has been declared an open city (→ 25).

23. Libya: Rommel flies home for medical treatment, and is replaced as C-in-C *Afrika Korps* by General Georg Stumme; his own choice of General Heinz Guderian is ignored (→ 30).

24. Stalingrad: Olga Yamschchikova becomes the first woman fighter pilot to "kill" an enemy aircraft when she shoots down a German Junkers 88 dive-bomber.

24. USSR: Soviet partisans destroy the German supply station at Ryabchichi, between Bryansk and Smolensk (→ 3/10).

25. London: Britain announces that it has taken Madagascar under its protection to ensure that a friendly regime will be established there (→ 29).

Australians defeat Japan on Kokoda Trail

Australians wade up to their knees as they force the Japanese to retreat.

Papua, New Guinea, 26 September
The Japanese campaign to seize Port Moresby has been defeated, giving the Australian Army its second victory in New Guinea within a month. After weeks of retreat down the horrific Kokoda Trail, the Australians have begun a counter-offensive which is rapidly pushing the Japanese back through the Owen Stanley Mountains.

The Japanese came within 26 miles (42 km) of their objective. At night they could see the searchlights of Port Moresby criss-crossing the sky. That was as far as they got. MacArthur feared that if the Japanese took New Guinea they could use this as a base to attack Australia. The continued retreat from Kokoda had alarmed him and he declared that he no longer had confidence in the Australians. He feared a military reverse. General Blamey, however, was not disturbed. After visiting New Guinea he informed the Australian advisory war council on 17 September of his confidence that the Japanese would not be able to take Port Moresby.

The same day MacArthur telephoned the prime minister, John Curtin, to tell him of his concern. He considered that Blamey should be sent to New Guinea at once to "energize the situation". Curtin agreed. As it happened, on the day that Blamey arrived at Port Moresby the emaciated Japanese received their last rice rations and three days later were ordered to retreat (→ 27).

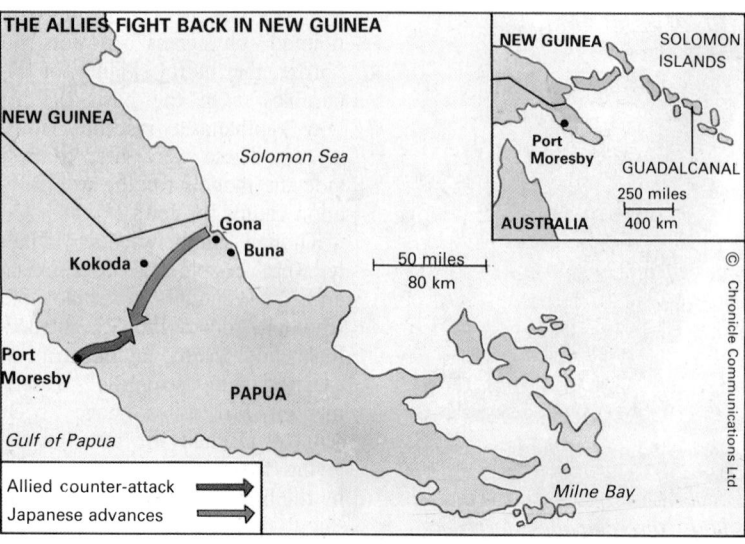

THE ALLIES FIGHT BACK IN NEW GUINEA

NEW GUINEA

Solomon Sea

Gona
Buna
Kokoda

Port Moresby

PAPUA

Gulf of Papua

50 miles
80 km

Milne Bay

NEW GUINEA — SOLOMON ISLANDS
Port Moresby — GUADALCANAL
AUSTRALIA
250 miles
400 km

Allied counter-attack →
Japanese advances →

© Chronicle Communications Ltd.

Hitler sacks his army chief of staff

Berlin, 24 September
Hitler today sacked his army chief of staff, General Franz Halder, who had dared to point out to the Fuhrer that Stalin had a million and a half fresh troops, which were about to be thrown into battle on the Stalingrad front. Germany, said Halder, did not possess the strength to hold the Russians at Stalingrad and also pursue an offensive against the Caucasus oil fields.

Hitler was furious. "We need National Socialist ardour," he told Halder, "not professional ability. I cannot expect it of an officer of the old school like you." Halder told friends later: "So spoke, not a responsible war lord, but a political fanatic."

Halder: lacking "Nazi ardour".

Homebound convoy loses six ships

Scotland, 26 September
Twelve merchant ships reached the safety of Loch Ewe today after a week of battles with U-boats and German aircraft. They are the survivors of convoy QP-14 which left the Russian port of Archangel on 13 September. Three merchant ships were lost as were three escort vessels. Three ships were sunk in a matter of minutes on 22 September after a U-boat penetrated the convoy's defensive screen at a time when it lacked air support (→ 15/12).

Nuclear project given go-ahead in US

Washington, 23 September
At a meeting in the office of Henry Stimson, the secretary of war, today it was decided to put the armed forces in charge of plans for a new secret weapon – the "atomic bomb".

The essence of the decision was that the scientists, who were led by Dr Vannevar Bush, a former vice-president of Massachusetts Institute of Technology, dropped their objections to work on the atomic bomb being carried out by the military. In return, the military agreed to give the bomb top priority.

Colonel Leslie Groves, promoted to brigadier-general today, has been made "managing director" of the project, and left the meeting to go to Tennessee to inspect a site for a gigantic secret atomic "factory".

President Roosevelt was warned in October 1939 by emigre European scientists, led by Albert Einstein, that if the USA did not build an atomic bomb the Nazis might do so first. Earlier this month an American army officer quietly arranged to secure for the US the

Henry L Stimson: secretary of war.

entire output of the Shinkolobwe mine in the Belgian Congo, the world's biggest source of the metal uranium, needed to make the bomb.

Told of his assignment, Colonel Groves said that he would rather go overseas. "If you do the job right," he was told by his superior, "it will win the war" (→ 25/11).

Paramilitary holidays for child evacuees

Germany, 23 September
Thousands of German parents are today marking an unhappy anniversary in the lives of their children: two years ago today a decree by Adolf Hitler increased the power of the authorities to order the evacuation of city children to youth camps in the countryside. Paramilitary exercises form part of the

daily routine in the camps, which are run by the Hitler Youth organization to indoctrinate children in the ways of National Socialism. Thousands of young people are now spending several weeks a year away from home – and from their parents' influence – on "holidays" of this kind in school camps or youth hostels.

Workers' units are key street fighters

Stalingrad, 22 September
What began as a *Blitzkrieg* has become urban warfare, as the Russians defend this city street by street, building by building. Alongside the regular Red Army now are workers' units, determined to make the Germans battle for every factory and exploiting to the full the defensive capabilities of their shattered home town. Today the grain silo was taken by the Germans, but their generals want reinforcements (→ 28).

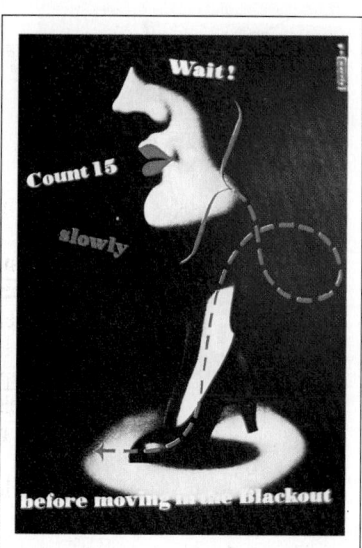

1942

September

Su	Mo	Tu	We	Th	Fr	Sa
		1	2	3	4	5
6	7	8	9	10	11	12
13	14	15	16	17	18	19
20	21	22	23	24	25	26
27	28	29	30			

27. New Guinea: Australian troops force the Japanese to retreat from Ioribaiwa, back down the Kokoda Trail (→ 28).

27. Tokyo: Japan's new foreign minister, Masayuki Tani, says he will continue the policy of non-aggression towards Soviet Russia.

27. Atlantic: The Liberty Ship *Stephen Hopkins*, armed with a single four-inch gun, sinks and is sunk by the German raider *Stier*.

28. Pacific: Japanese reinforcements land on the north coast of Java.

28. New Guinea: The US 32nd Infantry Division arrives at Port Moresby in force, and joins the assault on Wairopi (→ 1/10).

28. USSR: The Stalingrad front is renamed by Soviet commanders as the Don front, and General Eremenko's south-east front becomes the new Stalingrad front (→ 11/10).

29. Tokyo: Richard Sorge, the Soviet spy, is sentenced to death.

29. Madagascar: A South African force lands at Tulearon, in the south-west, to supplement East African troops operating out of Tananarive (→ 19/10).

29. Berlin: Hitler orders five *"flak towers"* to be built in Germany to boost defences against Allied air attacks (→ 17/10).

30. Tobruk: Hans Joachim Marseille, a *Luftwaffe* flying ace and German hero with 151 "kills" to his name, is shot down and killed.

30. Berlin: In a major speech at the *Sportspalast*, Hitler ridicules the Allied leadership as "military idiots ... mentally sick or perpetually drunk".

30. Europe: This month, 14,000 Jews from France, 6,000 from the Netherlands and 5,000 from Belgium have been deported to Auschwitz. Twenty thousand Polish Jews perished at Belzec, and at least 6,000 Jews from Theresienstadt camp, in Czechoslovakia, were slaughtered at Maly Trostenets (→ 3/10).

Czechs to die for sheltering killers

Prague, 29 September
The Germans, pursuing their blood revenge against the Czech people for the assassination of Heydrich, have now condemned 252 people to death for supporting or sheltering Heydrich's assassins. All the relatives of Josef Valcik and Jan Kubis, two of the assassins, have been rounded up from all parts of Czechoslovakia and taken to Mauthausen concentration camp. All the Novak family, including the 14-year-old daughter, Jindriska, are to die; Kubis was sheltered by the Novaks after the attack on Heydrich.

Desert Army probes Rommel's defences

El Alamein, 30 September
While thousands of British troops were undergoing training in desert warfare in the rear lines, watched by their new chief, Lieutenant-General Bernard Montgomery, the Eighth Army set out to probe the defences of the *Afrika Korps*, also – while Rommel is in Germany for medical treatment – under a new chief, General Georg Stumme.

The 44th Division – just two brigades – then mounted a very small action to assess the strength of German positions in the Munassib Depression. Today's battle took place to the south of the Alamein line, with heavy casualties on both sides (→ 20/10).

Schoolchildren die in German raid

Petworth, Sussex, 29 September
A lone German raider dived out of the cloud this morning and dropped its bombs from near-rooftop height on a council school, which was completely demolished with 85 boys inside it. Thirty-one children are dead, with two of their teachers. Parents in this town of 2,500 inhabitants in south-east England came running to the school and began digging in the wreckage with their bare hands. Rescuers dug out 28 boys alive but injured.

American women answer industry's call

A bomber factory: now women are encouraged to take up their tools here.

United States, 30 September
Everyone from the First Lady downwards has made it clear that the American war effort demands that women play dramatically different roles. Not only women themselves are being educated into new ways; so, too, are employers, labour leaders, store owners, men in uniform and legislators.

Mrs Eleanor Roosevelt, for instance, called for easing the burden of housework for those women working to win the war. She suggested that restaurants should prepare meals which working women could pick up and take home for quick service. More child care is needed, she said, as is transportation to and from schools.

Training started this month to teach women such trades as welding, armature winding and burning. Mrs Elinore M Herrick, the newly-appointed director of personnel for Todd Shipyards, which has 12 yards on three coasts, said training for more difficult jobs will start soon, since Selective Service has given semi-skilled males but six months' deferment. At Republic Steel, 1,000 women have been hired in its 27 plants to make and assemble aircraft parts and accessories. They are given uniforms, hairnets and pay equal to men's. But the company says that it will draw the line on women in open-hearth areas because of the 100-degree Fahrenheit (38 Celsius) heat. Ask-

ed if more women would be hired, one Republic vice-president growled: "There are too many women here now." However, he was in the midst of 25 women reporters.

Production jobs are not the only ones open to women. Columbia University has begun a course to train women to be engineering aides for Grumman Aircraft Corporation, and the Red Cross wants more nurses' aides, targeting "leisure-class" women. Women are joining up in record numbers, according to the WAACS and WAVES. The chief of the WAVES (the US equivalent of Wrens), Mildred McAfee, says that she doesn't mind at all being called "the old man".

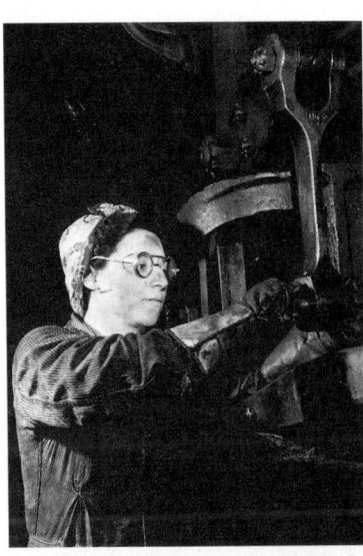

A machinist's helper on the railroad.

1942

October

Su	Mo	Tu	We	Th	Fr	Sa
				1	2	3
4	5	6	7	8	9	10
11	12	13	14	15	16	17
18	19	20	21	22	23	24
25	26	27	28	29	30	31

1. New Guinea: General MacArthur orders the Allies to attack Buna and Gona (→ 17).

2. Pacific: US marines land on Funafuti Atoll to set up a military base.

2. US: The first US jet aeroplane, the Bell XP-59 Airacomet, makes its first flight at Muroc in the Californian desert.

2. Off Ireland: The British liner *Queen Mary* rams her cruiser escort *Curacao*, sinking her with the loss of 338 lives.

3. Poland: The "resettlement" of Warsaw's Jews ends, with 310,332 out of 350,000 shipped to the death camps (→ 21).

3-4. Channel Islands: British commandos launch a raid on Sark.

4. Germany: *Reichsmarschall* Goering says: "This war is not the Second World War: this is the War of the Races. Whether we, the Germanic and Aryan men, or the Jew rule the world – that is the final issue."

5. China: Chiang Kai-shek formally reincorporates Sinkiang province into China and demands that the USSR withdraw its military presence.

6. Norway: Martial law is declared in Trondheim.→

7. South Africa: The British destroyer *Active* sinks the U-boat U179 off Cape Town.

7. Washington: Roosevelt says that a commission will be set up after the war to judge those guilty of atrocities and mass murder (→ 17).

8. Worldwide: Roman Catholics observe a day of prayer for Poland.

9. Solomon Islands: In the last two days US marines have attacked westward from Henderson Field on Guadalcanal and engaged the Japanese on the Matanikau river (→ 10).

9. Moscow: Stalin downgrades political commissars in the army, removing their right to influence military decisions.

10. Solomon Islands: US bombers attack the Japanese supply base at Rabaul on New Britain (→ 12).

Germans add new dimension to war with rocket launch

Peenemunde, 3 October
Today it has been third time lucky here at the German army's top-secret experimental station on the shores of the Baltic. After unsuccessful firings in June and July, the A4 free-flight rocket has made its first successful flight. The brainchild of the brilliant young scientist Wernher von Braun and General Walter Dornberger, the station head, who have been working on rocketry since 1932, the A4 is 46 feet (14 metres) in height and weighs 13 tons (13.2 tonnes). Now Dornberger and von Braun must convince the armaments minister, Albert Speer, that it warrants full-scale production.

PoWs entombed in ship by Japanese

Chekiang, 1 October
A ship carrying Allied prisoners of war became a sealed coffin today when she was torpedoed by the US submarine *Grouper* off China. In all, 840 British and Canadian PoWs from Hong Kong drowned after Japanese guards battened down the hatches before abandoning ship. The 7,152-ton *Lisbon Maru* was carrying 1,816 PoWs. Some managed to force the hatches and dive overboard – only to face machine-gun fire from escorting warships.

Any old iron will have to do.

Nazis crack down on the partisans

Europe, 3 October
Armed opposition to the Nazis is on the increase throughout occupied Europe, and the Germans are retaliating with their customary brutality. Today they launched a massive anti-partisan sweep, Operation Regatta, around the White Russian town of Gorki, near Smolensk. Only yesterday the partisans blew up 50 telegraph poles near Peklina.

Other subject peoples are equally reluctant to allow the occupiers and their sympathizers an easy time. In Denmark, for example, Danes fighting in the German army have been beaten up by angry patriots while on leave from Russia (→ 28/2).

Russian victims of Nazi brutality.

SS add muscle to Nazi winter appeal

Berlin, 1 October
Josef Goebbels, the German minister for propaganda, yesterday launched the country's fourth wartime winter appeal by announcing that last year the population donated some 1.2 billion *Reichsmark* [£100 million/$400 million] for needy families. A growing proportion of the money is now being used to finance official welfare bodies such as the National Socialist People's Welfare (NSV). Money is raised from house-to-house collections made by members of the NSV and other organizations, for example the Hitler Youth, the SA and the SS, who remind reluctant donors of their public "duty".

US planes take war to Germany by day

Crew members of an Eighth USAAF heavy bomber prepare for a raid.

London, 9 October
The US Eighth Army Air Force has recently adopted big daylight bombing operations of a kind virtually abandoned by the RAF in favour of night attacks.

To emphasize the difference of style, the US commander, Brigadier-General Ira Eaker, personally led his men on a precision raid against Rouen's marshalling yards on 17 August. The US approach is to fly heavily-armed bombers in close mass formations by day to destroy the enemy's means of making war, rather than in area attacks by night to undermine the enemy's will.

Today, in the biggest daylight raid from Britain, more than 100 B-17 Flying Fortresses and B-24 Liberators protected by 500 Allied fighters struck at factories in Lille, in northern France. Four bombers were shot down and one crew retrieved. In dogfights, the Poles claim three "kills" and the RAF two. It is not known how many interceptors were shot down by the American bombers.

Oct 4. General Chiang Kai-shek (seen here with his wife, seated) today met Wendell Willkie, now on a 31,000-mile tour as a special US envoy.

Tit-for-tat leaves prisoners in chains

London, 8 October
An unpleasant quarrel between the British and German governments has led to PoWs being handcuffed or put in chains – in defiance of the Geneva Convention of 1921.

Germany first announced that, because of British "brutalities" in the treatment of Germans taken prisoner during a Commando raid on the Channel Island of Sark on 4 October, all 2,190 British prisoners taken in the Dieppe raid would be manacled. Britain promptly retaliated by announcing that an equal number of Germans would also be manacled.

During the raid on Sark five Germans were captured, and their hands were tied while they were being taken to the commandos' escape boat. When the Germans realized how few their captors were they began to struggle. The commandos, fearful of the alarm being raised, shot three of their prisoners and made off.

The Germans, finding the three bodies with their hands tied behind their backs, assumed the men had been shot in cold blood. An enraged Hitler at once ordered reprisals. The Swiss government, which is the protecting power for both British and German PoWs, now has the task of persuading the two powers to see reason (→ 17).

State of emergency declared in Norway

Trondheim, 8 October
Josef Terboven, the *Reich* commissioner for Norway, arrived in the port of Trondheim today, and by mid-afternoon ten people had been shot for sabotage and 700 arrested. The port is used as a German naval base from which attacks on British convoys to Russia are mounted. Norwegian resistance fighters are believed to have sabotaged military communications.

Terboven, acting under a state of emergency, has imposed a dusk-to-dawn curfew, taken over the railways and announced the death penalty for any attempts to interfere with work, supplies or communications.

1942

October

Su	Mo	Tu	We	Th	Fr	Sa
				1	2	3
4	5	6	7	8	9	10
11	12	13	14	15	16	17
18	19	20	21	22	23	24
25	26	27	28	29	30	31

11. USSR: There is no fighting on the Stalingrad front today, marking the end of a month of continuous combat as both sides seek reinforcements (→ 14).

12. Atlantic: An RAF Coastal Command Liberator bomber sinks a U-boat in the first reported "kill" for these long-range aircraft.

12. Washington: Some 600,000 Italian-Americans are taken off the list of "enemy aliens".

13. Solomon Islands: The first US Army unit joins the US Marines at Guadalcanal (→ 14).

13. Baltic: The German authorities declare all Jewish property confiscated.

14. Guadalcanal: The Japanese battleships *Kongo* and *Haruna* bombard and severely damage the US airstrip at Henderson Field (→ 15).

14. Stalingrad: The Dzerzhinsky tractor factory is overrun, but the Red October works still holds out against almost constant attacks.→

14. Vinnitsa: Hitler orders the suspension of all activity on the eastern front except for Stalingrad and the Terek river in the Caucasus.→

14. English Channel: A British motor torpedo boat (MTB326) with destroyer support sinks the German merchant raider *Komet*.

15. Moscow: The Soviet government calls for the immediate trial of Rudolf Hess and all German generals in Allied custody.

16. Thailand: US submarines mine the approaches to Bangkok in Japanese-occupied Thailand (→ 26/11).

16. India: A cyclone kills 40,000 people in Bengal, mainly affecting the area south of Calcutta and badly disrupting supplies to the Burma front.

17. New Guinea: Fighting breaks out at Eora Creek, on the Kokoda Trail (→ 22).

17. Scotland: The Allied invasion fleet for Operation Torch in North Africa next month starts to assemble in the Firth of Clyde (→ 25).

US Navy surprises Japan off Guadalcanal

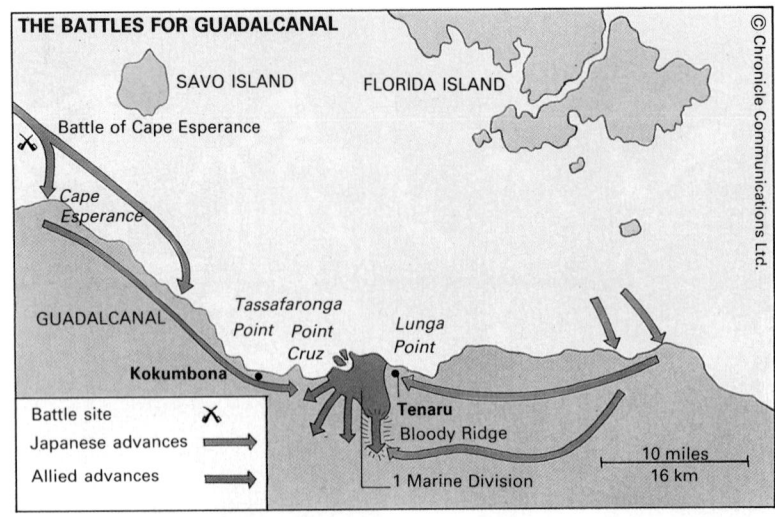

THE BATTLES FOR GUADALCANAL

Guadalcanal, 12 October
In a decisive night encounter off Guadalcanal last night, an American naval task force of cruisers and destroyers caught by surprise and defeated a Japanese naval flotilla. The Japanese lost a cruiser and a destroyer. The Americans lost one destroyer, the USS *Duncan*.

It was a morale-boosting victory for the American navy which disposed of the widely-held belief that the Japanese were superior sailors in night actions. The task of both the Japanese and the American forces was to protect the convoys of soldiers being ferried into Guadalcanal for the coming land battle to control the island.

The Japanese force approaching Guadalcanal from the opposite direction comprised three cruisers, eight destroyers and two sea-plane tenders with 718 members of the Japanese 2nd Division.

Rear-Admiral Norman Scott, who commanded the American force, was ordered to protect the US convoy "by offensive action". Yesterday Scott received an air reconnaissance report of the Japanese force speeding towards Guadalcanal and hastened to intercept it off Cape Esperance.

He caught it by surprise, "crossing the T" of the enemy unaware of his presence. The Americans opened fire, inflicting fatal wounds on the cruiser *Furutaka*. Two more Japanese destroyers were sunk by US aircraft from Henderson Field this morning (→ 13).

US Marines in the Solomons feed themselves up for the forthcoming offensive.

Allies plan to probe German war crimes

London, 17 October
Allied governments are planning to set up a commission to investigate war crimes committed by the Nazis and their collaborators. A list of war criminals will be drawn up and the evidence against them collected by the governments of occupied Europe. Trials after the war are expected to last several years.

Top of the list will be Hitler and Nazi Party leaders and collaborators. Below them will be the names of German agents in occupied countries, nationals of occupied countries but of German origin who have worked with the Nazis, and nationals of the occupied countries who have set themselves up as "quisling" rulers and their henchmen.

Berlin takes stand on chained PoWs

Berlin, 17 October
The enemy's dispute with Britain over the treatment of PoWs was given a new and unpleasant twist today when the German high command declared that "inhumane treatment of prisoners in any theatre of war, for instance on the Soviet front, would have to be paid for by prisoners in our hands without distinction of nationality".

The Germans made no reference to the British offer to unshackle Axis prisoners if the Germans would do the same with the PoWs taken at Dieppe.

Lancasters hit arms factory in France

France, 17 October
A force of 94 RAF Lancaster bombers flew across France at tree-top height today to hit the Schneider gun factory at Le Creusot, 170 miles (272 km) south-east of Paris, at dusk.

One airman, describing this daylight flight without fighter cover, said: "It was like the Grand National, except that no one fell." This was not quite accurate – one of the Lancasters has failed to return.

Stalingrad hit by new German attack

German troops on the move in the blazing streets of Stalingrad: they are even fighting inside the burning buildings.

Stalingrad, 14 October
The *Wehrmacht* launched yet another massive assault on Stalingrad today, with three infantry divisions and two *Panzer* divisions deployed on a three-mile front. The sky has been full of German aircraft bombing and strafing almost constantly.

In the city the Germans' main objectives have been the Dzerzhinsky tractor factory, which fell today and the Barrikady gun factory [*see

map on page 333*]. The ground outside these buildings is littered with German dead, caught by an artillery and *katyusha* barrage as they prepared to attack. Fighting is going on inside the battered, burning buildings. Workshops have become battlefields. The enemies are so close that some can hear each others' breathing. They crawl towards each other. Then in go the grenades. There is a rattle of gun-

fire, the deadly lick of a flame-thrower, screams of agony and another room is cleared.

The slaughter is terrible. Some divisions of the Russian Sixty-Second Army have been wiped out. The 13th Guards exists in name only. Units formed from poorly-trained civilians have taken appalling casualties, but the survivors have become expert street fighters (→ 22).

Convoy SC-104 loses eight ships in fierce battle with U-boats

North Atlantic, 16 October
Convoy SC-104 has fought its way through a fierce running battle with a wolfpack from the *Wotan* U-boat group, despite howling south-west winds and heavy seas which hampered the escort. In total only eight of the convoy's 47 merchant ships have been sunk.

The U-boat pack spotted the convoy on 12 October, and in the next two nights it sank seven vessels, even though the Germans had great difficulty in getting sighting signals in the atmospheric disturbance created by the gales. On 13 October U221 homed-in on the main convoy and sank three ships in 40 minutes. On 14 October she sank two more. And in the small hours of today three other U-boats sank one ship each.

The escort group, according to Commander S Heathcote, "pounced like terriers" on every sign of a U-boat. The rolling of the ships in the raging seas reduced the accuracy of the RDF and Asdic sound-

The high seas of the North Atlantic which conceal wolfpacks of U-boats.

ings, but repeated depth-charge attacks forced some U-boats to the surface, and an RAF Liberator sank U661 yesterday. Last night Lt-Cdr John Waterhouse in the destroyer *Viscount* managed to ram

and sink U619, but the violence of the collision severely damaged the *Viscount*, which has had to pull out of the escort. A third Uboat, U353, was destroyed today by the senior officer's ship, *Fame* (→ 31).

Escape lines set up across France to assist PoWs

Paris, 17 October
Shot-down aircrew and PoWs who have managed to "escape and evade" are returning to England on regular "Underground lines" set up by members of the Resistance and trained agents dropped into France by MI9, the intelligence department in charge of escapes.

MI9 is in experienced hands; one of its leaders is Captain Airey Neave, who escaped from Colditz Castle last January disguised as a German officer and walked to Switzerland.

It is impressed on all servicemen that it is their duty to escape, and they are being provided with the equipment to do so. Unscrew a certain button on a pilot's jacket and it turns into a compass. His silk scarf is a map showing him the way home, and his flying boots convert into walking shoes with a hacksaw blade hidden in a lace and foreign currency in the heels.

All aircrew are taught how to evade capture and live off the country until they can contact the local Resistance. They are never given names and addresses of people to contact, but are told to seek out solid patriotic households and ask the occupants to put them in touch with the Resistance.

If all goes well the escapers are fed, dressed in local clothes, given false papers and passed along the line of "safe houses", either to the Spanish or Swiss borders or to a landing strip to be picked up by a Lysander or a Hudson of the RAF's special duty squadrons.

One of the bravest of those helping the escapers – sometimes known as "conductors" – is a 24-year-old Belgian, Andree de Jongh, who runs the "Comet" line. She specializes in the long trip from Brussels, through Paris and over the Pyrenees to Bilbao where her passengers are taken by fishing boat to Gibraltar (→ 30/11).

1942

October

Su	Mo	Tu	We	Th	Fr	Sa
				1	2	3
4	5	6	7	8	9	10
11	12	13	14	15	16	17
18	19	20	21	22	23	24
25	26	27	28	29	30	31

18. Washington: Vice-Admiral William E Halsey replaces Robert L Ghormley as Commander of the South Pacific theatre.

19. Delhi: General Stilwell presents Chiang Kai-shek with new plans for Chinese forces in Burma, including the arming of 30 more divisions (→3/11).

19. Madagascar: East African troops press southward from Tananarive; the King's African Rifles capture 800 Vichy troops near Ivato (→29).

20. Egypt: The RAF starts a bid to establish air superiority over El Alamein (→23).

21. USSR: The Germans launch an unsuccessful attack on Suho Island on Lake Ladoga to break the Soviet supply route to Leningrad.

21. Poland: After a seven-day action, 20,000 Jews have been sent from the Piotrkow ghetto to Treblinka for gassing (→29).

22. New Guinea: Australian troops land on Goodenough Island (→2/11).

22. Stalingrad: The first snows fall outside the city (→27).

22. Algeria: The US General Mark Clark lands for secret talks with senior pro-Allied French officers and Resistance leaders (→5/11).

23. Burma: The first clashes take place between the British and the Japanese in Arakan.

23. Egypt: Montgomery launches the Second Battle of El Alamein with a heavy artillery barrage.→

23. Morocco: Admiral Darlan arrives in Rabat to rally Vichy colonies (→17/11).

23. Virginia: US forces set sail for North Africa.

24. Guadalcanal: US marines repel Japanese attempts to cross the Matanikau river.→

24. El Alamein: General Stumme dies of a heart attack when his truck is caught in crossfire; Rommel is recalled from his sickbed.→

24. Atlantic: An RAF Liberator sinks U599, the third U-boat sunk by the RAF in four days.

Japanese falter in bid for Guadalcanal

The ruins of a US plane, victim of the fierce fighting for Henderson Field.

Guadalcanal, 24 October
Supported by four battleships and four aircraft carriers, a 20,000-strong Japanese army appears to be losing its struggle to wrest this island in the Solomons from the Americans. The offensive began three days ago when infantry supported by tanks and heavy artillery failed to cross the Matanikau river. The tanks were wiped out.

Two more assaults are under way along the Lunga and Tenaru rivers by the Japanese 2nd Infantry Division under the command of General Maruyama. The Japanese have sustained heavy losses, particularly at the hands of the newly-arrived "Americal" division. The common objective of these attacks is Henderson field which the Japanese commander was confident that he would capture two days ago. The airfield has been wrecked by constant bombardment from air and sea.

In Washington, the president has ordered the chiefs of staff to ensure that Guadalcanal is held at all costs. Roosevelt has taken personal charge of the emergency direction of arms to the island.

Everything depends on the ability of the defenders to withstand the sheer weight of numbers being thrown at them. The normally reliable Japanese intelligence system appears to have failed the commanders this time with miscalculations of US strength (→25).

French workers for German factories

Paris, 20 October
Pierre Laval, the Vichy premier, today called for another 100,000 French workers to join the hundreds of thousands of Frenchmen already working in Germany. On 11 August, at Compiegne, the first train of French PoWs passed the first train taking Frenchmen to work for the Germans. Fritz Sauckel, Hitler's manpower chief, made Laval send three workers to Germany for each PoW freed. In September, Laval mobilized all Frenchmen between 18 and 50 and all unmarried women between 21 and 35 for forced labour (→1/11).

RAF attacks towns in northern Italy

Europe, 24 October
Italian targets have been hit for the first time by British-based RAF Lancaster bombers. Last night 100 Lancasters attacked Genoa, and today a total of 112 machines flew below barrage balloons to hit Milan in day light. Tonight further raids are planned for targets in the Milan/Genoa/Turin triangle.

This prolonged assault is to coincide with the Eighth Army's offensive at El Alamein. A Lancaster pilot said later: "We crossed the Channel at almost zero altitude and over France in one enormous mass at 50 feet. The French waved to us." They flew over the Alps below the summit of Mont Blanc, found Italy under cloud and emerged through this at 4,000 feet (1,219 metres) over Milan railway station. Another crew flew over the football stadium at half-time, the ball clearly visible in the net alongside orange peel. When they released their 4,000-pound "cookies" there was panic below them. One pilot described hitting a factory: "That's a factory, that was." The sun was setting over the Alps as they began the 750-mile (1,200-km) flight home.

Only three of the force were shot down: proof for some that the tactic of flying low, in tight formation, is a recipe for success on daylight missions, despite the lack of firepower on the Lancasters (→25).

October 21: Trafalgar Day. On the anniversary of this famous victory the South African PM, Field Marshal Smuts, addresses members of both Houses and the cabinet wives in an antechamber of the House of Lords.

Monty launches El Alamein offensive

A tank holds back, avoiding the snarl-up and waiting for artillery and infantry units to clear the mines.

El Alamein, 24 October
The months of meticulous planning were over; now, in the desert silence, 195,000 Allied troops braced themselves for the greatest battle yet. Some checked their weapons for the hundredth time that day. Some played cards in the brilliant moonlight. Officers glanced at their watches. Some men prayed.

At 9.40 precisely last night, the desert silence was rent by the crash of 1,000 heavy guns, so powerful that the ground shook under the feet of the engineers who moved forward into the "devil's garden" – Rommel's five-mile-deep minefields – clearing lanes and marking them with white tape.

The first barrage lasted for 15 minutes. For a few seconds before 10pm the skirl of bagpipes could be heard down the lines before an even more intensive bombardment opened up. This was the cue for the infantry to begin its advance with the 51st Highland, 1st South African and New Zealand Divisions, their bayonets fixed, going forward at a steady 75 strides a minute to clear

the way for the waiting armoured divisions. The speed of the Highlanders' advance brought them under fire from their own artillery as well as the Germans'. Casualties were high, but they managed to storm their first objective, the heavily-defended Miteiriya Ridge.

Lieutenant-General Montgomery had no option but to make a direct frontal assault. The impassable Qattara Depression precludes any question of an encircling operation. The 9th Australian Division

is preparing for a tough fight in the north. The Indian 44th Division is fighting a diversionary battle in the south.

Everything depends on the tanks of XXX Corps, new Grants and Shermans, breaking through. But so many tanks are trying to get through that a massive traffic snarl-up is blocking the lanes, a perfect target for German artillery. Sharp words were spoken in "Monty's" caravan later in the day before the tanks moved again (→31).

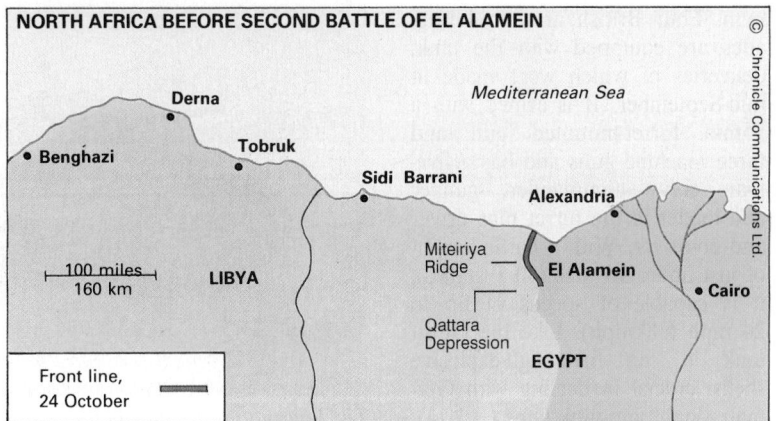

NORTH AFRICA BEFORE SECOND BATTLE OF EL ALAMEIN

Mediterranean Sea

Derna
Benghazi
Tobruk
Sidi Barrani
Alexandria
Miteiriya Ridge
100 miles
160 km
LIBYA
El Alamein
Cairo
Qattara Depression
EGYPT
Front line, 24 October

© Chronicle Communications Ltd.

Germans to shoot commando raiders

Berlin, 18 October
With the tide of war now turning against his armies, Hitler has issued a "Top Secret Commando Order" which says: "From now on, all enemies on so-called commando missions in Europe or Africa ... even if they are in uniform, whether armed or unarmed, in battle or in flight, are to be slaughtered to the last man." Hitler says that he has been compelled to act because of the recent increase – not to mention success – of Allied commando operations. General Jodl, passing on the Fuhrer's order, says that in no circumstances must it fall into enemy hands.

'Luftwaffe' renews assault on Malta

Malta, 20 October
For ten days the *Luftwaffe* has attacked Malta in a desperate attempt to paralyse the tiny island which has defied Axis bombardment ever since Hitler issued his directive on 2 December 1941 concerning air and sea supremacy in the Mediterranean. The fighting in this renewed assault has been fierce, with 100 German bombers claimed to have been shot down by the Allies. But Allied leaders believe that their planned offensive in North Africa will soon force Axis air power to be redeployed (→28).

No Communists at Chinese assembly

Chungking, 22 October
The opening session of the Chinese People's Council today was marked by the absence of any Communist delegates and a warning from Generalissimo Chiang Kai-shek. Speaking obliquely about the continued factional fighting between *Kuomintang* and Communist troops, he pointed out that it was wasting manpower and materials and endangering the Chinese war effort. Success on the war front would not save China if the divisive internal economic and political battles continued, he warned.

October

Su	Mo	Tu	We	Th	Fr	Sa
				1	2	3
4	5	6	7	8	9	10
11	12	13	14	15	16	17
18	19	20	21	22	23	24
25	26	27	28	29	30	31

25. Guadalcanal: Japan assaults US positions on the Lunga and Matanikau rivers (→ 26).

25. Milan: The RAF completes an overnight attack, after a daytime raid yesterday.

25. Bermuda: A squadron of US aircraft carriers sails for North Africa to take part in the "Torch" landings.

26. China: USAAF bombers raid Hong Kong and Canton.

26. Guadalcanal: US forces have only 29 aircraft left in operation.→

26. USSR: Nalchik, south of Pyatigorsk in the Caucasus, falls to the Germans.

27. Stalingrad: German forces push to within firing distance of Soviet landing jetties on the west bank of the Volga. The Soviet-held strip is only 300 yards deep on average (→ 29).

27. Germany: A 17-year-old youth is executed for listening to foreign news broadcasts.

28. Guadalcanal: Japanese reinforcements, nicknamed the "Tokyo Express" by the Americans, start landing on the north-west coast. They meet stiff resistance (→ 1/11).

28. Gibraltar: The British carrier *Furious* sails with Spitfires for Malta (→ 20/11).

29. Madagascar: East African troops capture 440 Vichy troops at Alakamisy, and occupy Fianarantsoa (→ 7/11).

29. Stalingrad: Sixty thousand German troops and two tank divisions launch a new attack, but advance just 50 yards (→ 13/11).

29. Pinsk, USSR: The Germans massacre 16,000 Jews.→

29. Alaska: The Alaska Military Highway is opened.

30. Pacific: US cruisers and destroyers shell Japanese positions on Santa Cruz Island.

31. Atlantic: Convoy SL-125 loses its 13th ship in a week's harrying by U-boats (→ 19/11).

31. Poland: This month, the Nazis have murdered 64,000 Jews and gypsies at Belzec and 82,000 at Treblinka (→ 2/11).

Allies break Axis lines at El Alamein

El Alamein, 31 October
As Allied shells crashed around his headquarters, Rommel wrote his daily letter to his wife, Lu, today. Gone was the confidence that had made him the master of desert warfare. He wrote of "rivers of blood poured out over miserable strips of land that not even the poorest Arab would have bothered about". The blood is not just German and Italian, as the Allies suffered more losses than the Axis forces, but the "miserable strip of land" was a key point in his defences, the "Kidney Ridge", and it is now broken.

Both sides have sustained heavy losses in armour. The Kidney Ridge assaults have cost the 25th *Panzers* all but 31 of their 119 tanks. Further to the north, the British XXX Corps lost 200 tanks driving a two-mile wedge into the German positions to clear the way for the 9th Armoured Brigade and the 7th and 10th Armoured Divisions with New Zealand infantry. The Australians in the north are fighting a relentless battle to take Tel el Eisa and break through to the coastal road.

Fortune has deserted Rommel. He was flown here from a sick-bed in Germany when his stand-in as the head of the *Afrika Korps*, General Stumme, died of a heart attack when his car was caught in crossfire on 24 October. Even the massive "devil's garden" – the five-mile-deep minefield – that Rommel had planted was failing to hold the weight of Allied armour and the determination of the infantry.

Other generals have failed to outmanoeuvre the Desert Fox. His new opponent, Lieutenant-General Bernard Montgomery, is fighting a war of attrition based on superior numbers – he began this battle with 195,000 men to Rommel's 104,000, 1,029 tanks (including 252 Shermans) to 489, 2,311 guns to 1,219 and 750 planes to 675 – and detailed preparations which exploit Allied codebreaking. He knew Rommel's strengths and plans: a secret and possibly vital element in his chances of success.

BREAKTHROUGH AT EL ALAMEIN

Sidi Abd el Rahman •
Mediterranean Sea
Kidney Ridge
• El Alamein
XXX Corps
Gen Leese
PANZER ARMY AFRICA Gen Rommel
Miteiriya Ridge
X Corps Gen Lumsden
Ruweisat Ridge
EIGHTH ARMY Gen Montgomery
20 miles
32 km
XIII Corps Gen Horrocks
Front line, 24 October
Main Allied attacks
Diversionary attacks
Axis minefields
EGYPT
© Chronicle Communications Ltd.

New tank helps British troops race across the baking sands

Cairo, 31 October
Taking part in General Montgomery's attack at El Alamein is a new tank, the American M4 Sherman. Four British armoured brigades are equipped with the tank, deliveries of which were made in mid-September. It is armed with a 75mm turret-mounted gun and three machine guns and has a five-man crew: commander, gunner and loader in the turret plus driver and co-driver. With a battle weight of just under 30 tons (30.5 tonnes), it is capable of speeds of up to 24 mph (38kmph). Like the Grant tank, it can fire high-explosive shells, crucial in dealing with German 88mm anti-tank guns (→ 3/11).

The Sherman tank: now going into battle with Montgomery at El Alamein.

El Alamein: battle rages for control of the desert

A small but symbolic victory for the Allies in the desert: one crew member of a knocked-out German tank surrenders as British infantrymen advance.

A British soldier in the desert remembers what they've suffered back home.

A 4.5 lights up the night sky firing into a concentration of enemy tanks.

US carrier lost in battle of Santa Cruz

Guadalcanal, 27 October

US and Japanese naval forces have suffered severe carrier losses in an indecisive two-day air and sea battle north of Santa Cruz Island, as a major land battle rages further west at Guadalcanal, in the Solomons.

US losses include the sinking of the carrier *Hornet*, with the *Enterprise* severely damaged. This leaves the US without a single carrier operational in its Pacific Fleet. Although no Japanese carrier has been sunk, 1,000-pound bombs dropped on the flight decks of the *Shokaku* and the *Zuiho* have put both out of action for months. The Japanese have also lost over 100 naval aircraft, leaving the *Zuikaku* with virtually no planes. After the losses of the last two days the smaller carriers *Junyo* and *Hiyo* can just muster 100 aircraft between them.

Numerically it is a victory for the Japanese combined fleet commander, Admiral Kondo. But his main objective, to manoeuvre within 30 miles (48 km) of Henderson Field to fly aircraft in, has been thwarted with 23,000 US marines still holding the jungle airstrip. In the last four days they have survived two major attacks, intended to arrive as one. In the first 5,600 Japanese, supported by tanks, attacked the eastern perimeter, but were mown down by artillery fire. The second wave of 7,000, a day late and exhausted by an arduous march, attacked the southern edge but were forced back, losing 3,500 (→ 28).

The beginning of the end for the USS "Hornet" in the Battle of Santa Cruz.

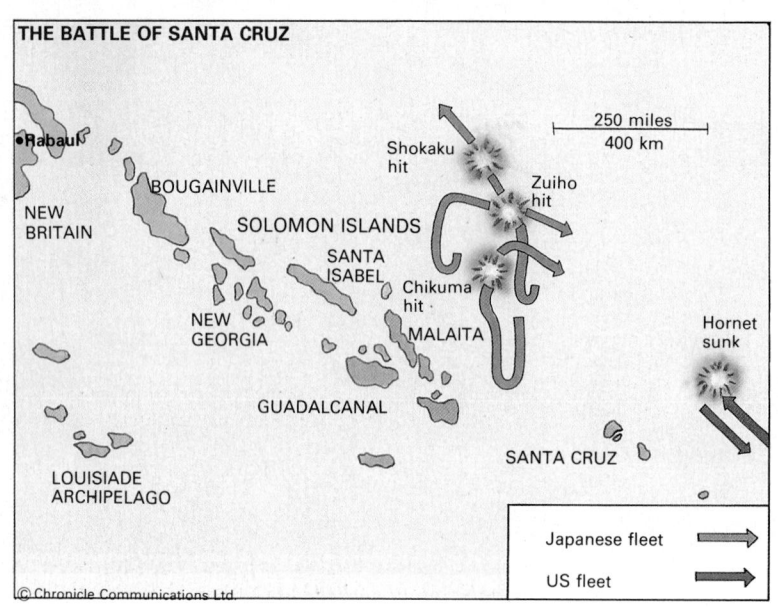

THE BATTLE OF SANTA CRUZ

250 miles / 400 km

Rabaul

BOUGAINVILLE

NEW BRITAIN

SOLOMON ISLANDS

Shokaku hit

Zuiho hit

SANTA ISABEL

Chikuma hit

NEW GEORGIA

MALAITA

Hornet sunk

GUADALCANAL

SANTA CRUZ

LOUISIADE ARCHIPELAGO

Japanese fleet →

US fleet →

© Chronicle Communications Ltd.

Archbishop leads protest on German treatment of Jews

London, 29 October

A demonstration of protest against Nazi atrocities committed against the Jews of occupied Europe was held at the Albert Hall tonight. It was led by the archbishop of Canterbury, Dr William Temple, who described what was being done as "so horrific that the imagination refused to picture it. It is a reversion to barbarism which seems to have the settled purpose of exterminating the Jewish people."

Messages were sent to Jewish victims in ghettoes and camps. The first, from Mr Churchill, read: "The systematic cruelties to which the Jewish people, men, women and children, have been exposed under the Nazi regime are among the most terrible events of history and place an indelible stain upon all who perpetrate and instigate them. When this world struggle ends with the enthronement of human rights, racial persecution will be ended."

Leaders of governments in exile also sent messages. General Sikorski declared: "I assure Polish Jews that they will benefit from victory on equal terms with all Polish citizens." The Czech foreign minister, Jan Masaryk, gave a similar pledge.

There are reports that over a million Jews have been exterminated since the war began. A government white paper with details is expected shortly (→ 31).

"Enigma" ciphers taken from U-boat

Alexandria, 30 October

The Bletchley Park codebreakers who have been unable to read the U-boat *Enigma* cipher for almost a year must thank the self-sacrifice of two men who died today retrieving an Enigma machine and its key settings from a sinking submarine. Lt Tony Fasson and Able-Seaman Colin Grazier boarded U559 as she was being scuttled after an attack by destroyers 70 miles (112 km) off Egypt. They passed their prize to safety, but were unable to escape before the U-boat sank, taking them with her (→ 13/12).

Britons set to lose icing on their cakes

Britain, 25 October

From tomorrow, British cake will become even plainer than it is already. Confectioners will be allowed to add only one layer of jam or chocolate to cakes after baking. White sugar icing has been forbidden since 1940. Cake must now contain no more than 20 per cent fats or 30 per cent sugar. The maximum price will be 1/6 (7½p/30¢) a pound.

The milk allowance is being cut to 2.5 pints a week for adults. A further cut to two pints a week is expected. Pregnant women get an extra pint a day.

Chinese collaborators assemble in Peking

Peking, 27 October

Wang Ching-wei, the leader of the Chinese puppet government in Nanking, today made an official visit to Peking. He attended the third national convention of the *Hsin-min-hui* [New People's Society], north China's central collaborationist political organization.

Though Wang Ching-wei is officially leader of the puppet "central" government of occupied China, in the north the Hsin-min-hui is effectively in control. The organization's purpose is simple: the inculcation of a Japanese philosophy of life, based on Confucian principles, in the people of the region.

Puppet president: Wang Ching-wei.

Caucasus offensive grinds to a halt

USSR, 31 October

The German offensive towards the Caucasus mountains of southern Russia is petering out in the face of strong Soviet resistance and the onset of winter. The 1st *Panzer* Army of General von Kleist is currently stuck five miles (8km) west of Ordzhonikidze with serious supply problems. Ironically, it is lack of oil which has most handicapped what began as a drive through the Caucasus to the oilfields near Baku. At first progress was swift, but neither of the original objectives of the 1942 southern offensives – the oilfields and the capture of Stalingrad – has been secured.

Reprisal air raid blasts Canterbury

Canterbury, 31 October

A week after the RAF bombed the industrial city of Milan the *Luftwaffe* today attacked historic Canterbury, dropping 52 tons of bombs and causing extensive casualties. In a single incident, an attack on a bus, ten people died. The raid followed the tactic masterminded by the RAF: a low-level approach to the target at dusk, the delivery of a short but intensive barrage, and a follow-on raid by night. Sixty-eight fighter-bombers flew in the earlier raid and 68 fighters. Only three were lost (→ 20/11).

Cheering reading for the lonely boys in the front line fighting?

1942

November

Su	Mo	Tu	We	Th	Fr	Sa
1	2	3	4	5	6	7
8	9	10	11	12	13	14
15	16	17	18	19	20	21
22	23	24	25	26	27	28
29	30					

1. Guadalcanal: US marines attack westwards towards the Poha river (→ 3).

1. France: Workers strike in protest against forced labour.

2. New Guinea: Australian troops retake Kokoda, with its vital airstrip (→ 4).

2. Poland: Jews around Bialystok try to resist, but 100,000 of them are taken for deportation to Treblinka.

2. Berlin: Dr Sievers of the "Ancestral Heritage Institute" requisitions 150 dead Jewish Bolshevik commissars for dissection because they exemplify a "revolting but typical subhuman type" (→ 9).

3. Guadalcanal: The Japanese try to divert US attention from Lunga Point by landing 1,500 men at Koli Point, to the east (→ 4).

3. Yugoslavia: Tito's partisans capture Bihac (→ 15/1).

3. Delhi: Chiang Kai-shek puts 15 Chinese divisions under the command of Lieutenant-General Stilwell for the Burmese campaign.

4. Guadalcanal: After wiping out a pocket of Japanese resistance, US forces dig defences near Cruz Point (→ 7).

4. North Africa: The German General von Thoma is captured.→

4. London: Churchill chairs the first meeting of the Anti-U-boat Committee, to co-ordinate scientific and military efforts in the Battle of the Atlantic.

5. Papua: The Australians attack the Japanese at Oivi on the Kokoda Trail.→

6. Madagascar: The Vichy regime formally surrenders the island to the Allies.→

6. Port Moresby: General MacArthur arrives to direct the New Guinea campaign (→ 9).

6. North Africa: Torrential rain turns the desert sand into sludge and cuts radio contact.→

7. Guadalcanal: US troops attack at Koli Point (→ 9).

7. Egypt: Allied troops enter Mersa Matruh, which has been deserted by the Germans.→

Vichy governor "to yield Madagascar"

Madagascar, 6 November

The Madagascar campaign is almost over. A few square miles at Ihosy, in the south of the island, are all that Vichy still controls. Already the South African Pretoria Regiment is within sight of the town. The governor, M Annet, has indicated that he will surrender tomorrow. War casualties have been light in this campaign, which was aimed at forestalling the use of the island as a Japanese naval base. Only 60 Allied troops have been killed in action (mostly East Africans), but some battalions have lost a quarter of their numbers from malaria (→ 14/12).

Stalin looks ahead to "second front"

Moscow, 6 November

Stalin, speaking today at a ceremony to mark the 25th anniversary of the Russian Revolution, blamed the Germans' successes in Russia on Britain and America's failure to open a second front in Europe.

"There is no doubt", he said, "that the Germans would not otherwise have been able to attain a success on our front. The absence of a second front enabled them to carry out this operation without any risk to themselves."

He said he was sure, however, that it will come to pass "because it is no less needed by our Allies than by us".

Fido doggedly clears fog-bound runways

One of the first official photographs of Fido in action released by the RAF.

Britain, 4 November

Now that winter has come the hazards facing airmen are significantly increased. One of the worst is fog, which especially affects RAF bomber crews returning from long flights over Germany. Trying to land a heavy bomber in fog, especially if it has been damaged, is highly dangerous, and many aircraft have been written off and crews killed as a result.

Some months ago Mr Churchill ordered the Petroleum Warfare Department to investigate methods of dispersing fog at airfields. It has now arrived at a solution, Fog Investigation Dispersal Operation (Fido). This consists of petrol burners positioned at intervals at the edges of runways. These are lit shortly before take-off and landing and have proved successful in reducing the fog, as well as providing additional illumination.

The plan is to install Fido at three emergency landing strips, Carnaby (Yorks), Manston (Kent) and Woodbridge (Suffolk). Crippled bombers, using an emergency radio system codenamed "Darkee", will be guided to one of these airstrips, which also have the latest approach-and-landing aids. Later, other airfields will also have Fido fitted. The complexity of the system, which involves laying much underground piping, makes it unlikely that the system will be operational this winter.

Rommel retreats before supercharged offensive

El Alamein, 3 November

The Desert Fox is in retreat. The German general last night ordered his *Afrika Korps* to withdraw in the face of a new offensive launched by General Montgomery's revitalized Eighth Army. Today Hitler sent an order to hold the Alamein position, but it was too late. Rommel did halt his retreat for a while, but this may only reduce his chances of securing a new defensive line.

The decisive breakthrough came after concern had been voiced by Churchill about the slow progress of the initial attack. Montgomery switched to the less well-defended German lines inland. This attack, codenamed "Supercharge", involv-

ed a westward attack by the infantry of XIII Corps under General Leese, with the armoured divisions of X Corps under General Lumsden to resist attacks from Rommel's *Panzers*. The 9th Australian Division maintained diversionary attacks nearer the coast.

The Allied attack began in the early hours yesterday – and the German counter-attack was fierce. More than 200 British tanks were put out of action. But at the end of the day the Allies still had over 600 serviceable tanks against barely 30 for the Germans. With fuel for even these tanks desperately short Rommel ordered a retreat, leaving the way open for the Eighth Army (→ 4).

Rommel's weary men retreat after their commander has granted permission.

Eleven days and nights of desert fighting

Under Monty's orders: troops with fixed bayonets charge an enemy position.

North Africa, 4 November

Many will remember the huge October moon that bathed the desert that night – even more than they will remember the ear-splitting crash of the first artillery salvo. The moon was the last thing of beauty that they would see for 11 terrible days and nights of fighting.

For the soldiers who went out under that barrage with fixed bayonets and experienced the horror of battle at close quarters, the memories will be more vivid.

"Monty's" order was to "hit the enemy for six out of Africa". Lieutenant George Greenfield was serving with the Buffs at Alamein. "It

was not too hard to sit in the pavilion of army headquarters and urge the others out to face the fast bowling." He will always remember holding a fellow soldier's leg while it was amputated: "I was left squatting on the sand, stupidly holding the unattached leg, still in its stocking, webbing gaiter and boot, across my knee. I had never realised before the utter dead weight of a solitary leg." Others will remember the piper, Duncan McIntyre, aged 19, who led the Black Watch to the first ridge. Twice wounded, he continued playing "The Road to the Isles" until a burst of machine-gun fire silenced him for ever (→ 6).

"Monty" is the hero as Rommel retreats

Britain's new hero, Monty, talks to officers of the Highland Division.

London, 7 November

As Britain prepares to ring out the bells for victory, one man's name is on everyone's lips. "Monty" is the general who gave El Alamein to a country desperate for success. "Monty" is the hero.

Until now, Bernard Montgomery has been completely unknown to the British public. Today his picture occupies pride of place on every front page. Future war historians may question many of his decisions at Alamein, but few would dare to do so in Britain today. For the first time since the agonies of Dunkirk, Singapore and Tobruk, the country has a winner. Rommel

is on the run – thanks to "good old Monty". Alamein was won by meticulous planning and Montgomery's insistence on retraining the Eighth Army and ensuring that every man taking part in the battle knew exactly what was expected of him. From the moment that he arrived in Egypt, he was everywhere – planning, bullying, hectoring, cajoling, inspiring his troops and firing any officer whom he regarded as "defensive minded". He woos his troops with care, wearing at least three regimental badges on his array of hats – although he seems now to have settled for the black beret of the Royal Tank Corps (→ 8).

General nearly drowns after secret talks

Gibraltar, 5 November
A senior American general nearly drowned after a clandestine meeting with French leaders in Algeria, it was revealed today. Lieutenant-General Mark Clark, the deputy commander of the Allied Expeditionary Force, was landed by canvas canoe from the British submarine *Seraph* on 22 October.

British commandos stood guard with Tommy guns as he held discussions with the French General Charles Mast, the deputy commander in North Africa. Mast was anxious for details of the coming invasion. Clark gave none, not even the fact that the fleet was on its way. With the local police suspicious, Clark and the commandos prepared to shoot their way out. When they reached the beach, a heavy Atlantic swell was creating huge waves. It was then that a canoe capsized, throwing the general into the water. Clark claims someone shouted: "Never mind the general, get the paddles!" (→ 10)

Crack Special Air Service formed in desert

Major David Stirling, seen here with desert-hardened members of the SAS.

Cairo, 1 November
The enigmatically-named unit known as "L" detachment of the Special Air Service Brigade has been expanded into the 1st Special Air Service Regiment. The handful of survivors of Major David Stirling's 12-month experiment in mayhem behind Rommel's line will be steadily augmented by other veterans of irregular warfare. These include the Middle East Commando (30 officers and 300 rankers, of whom Stirling wants only a third); a Free French SAS squadron (14 officers, 80 others); the Greek "Sacred Squadron" (14 and 100); and the Special Boat Section (15 and 40). Special units still outside Stirling's empire include the Long Range Desert Group; the Special Operations Executive; the Parachute Regiment; Popski's Private Army; and some commandos.

Australians try to outflank Japan at Oivi

Papua, New Guinea, 5 November
Australian troops advancing on the Kokoda Trail today launched a strong attack on the retreating Japanese in a bid to capture the town of Oivi in the foothills of the Owen Stanley Mountains.

After the fall of Kokoda on 2 November, a brigade of Australians encountered strongly-manned Japanese defences some three miles (4.8 km) long near Oivi. The Japanese have dug themselves in and are resisting fiercely. To try and break the impasse another Australian brigade is to move round the southern flank to cut Japanese communications in the rear.

If Oivi can be taken, the road will be open to Gona and Buna on the north coast, although more tough fighting is inevitable (→ 11).

1942
November

Su	Mo	Tu	We	Th	Fr	Sa
1	2	3	4	5	6	7
8	9	10	11	12	13	14
15	16	17	18	19	20	21
22	23	24	25	26	27	28
29	30					

8. Libya: Rommel's army retreats back across the border from Egypt (→ 10).

8. Munich: In his traditional speech on the anniversary of the Beercellar *Putsch*, Hitler says that Stalingrad has fallen "apart from some very small parts" and victory is certain.

8. Vichy France: Ministers announce that the US, by "carrying the war to French territory, had by that very fact broken off diplomatic relations".→

9. New Guinea: US infantry troops are airlifted from Port Moresby to Natunga (→ 11).

9. Poland: A concentration camp opens at Majdanek: 4,000 Jews arrive from Lublin (→ 25).

9. Copenhagen: The Germans force King Christian to appoint the pro-Nazi Erik Scavenius as prime minister.→

10. Egypt: Lieutenant-General Bernard Montgomery is knighted and promoted to general.→

11. Indian Ocean: The Indian minesweeper *Bengal* (with help from the tanker *Ondina*) sinks two Japanese merchant raiders despite being outgunned.

11. Papua: The Australians outflank the Japanese to take the town of Oivi; 600 Japanese died in the battle (→ 13).

11. Libya: The British Eighth Army occupies Bardia without firing a single shot.→

12. France: German troops occupy Marseilles and approach Toulon, where the Vichy fleet is ordered to sail to Africa to evade capture (→ 27).

12. Tunisia: German reinforcements land (→ 14).

13. Solomon Islands: US dive-bombers repeatedly attack the Japanese battleship *Hiei* (→ 15).

13. Papua: The Japanese General Horii pulls back over the Kumusi river, marking the Kokoda campaign's end (→ 17).

14. Tunisia: General Barre, commanding French troops, moves his men in preparation for going over to the Allies.→

Denmark installs pro-Nazi premier

Copenhagen, 9 November
The Nazis have at last forced King Christian to appoint the pro-Nazi Erik Scavenius as prime minister. In September, when the king celebrated his 72nd birthday, Hitler sent him fulsome congratulations. The king, who has no liking for Hitler and his Nazis, responded with a cool acknowledgement of receipt. Hitler, enraged by the "insult", insisted on having a more obedient government installed.

Scavenius, who also retains his post of foreign minister, is disliked heartily by Danes; he has made Denmark a member of the anti-Comintern pact and encouraged Danes to fight against Russia.

Canada breaks off its links with Vichy

Ottawa, 9 November
Within 24 hours of the severance of relations between the United States and Vichy France, Canada has broken off diplomatic relations with the Vichy government. Justifying Canada's two years of diplomatic relations with Vichy France, the prime minister, Mr Mackenzie King, said that they had provided the Allies with vital political information, kept alive the concept of freedom in unoccupied France and helped "pave the way and prepare the background for" the Allied landings in North Africa.

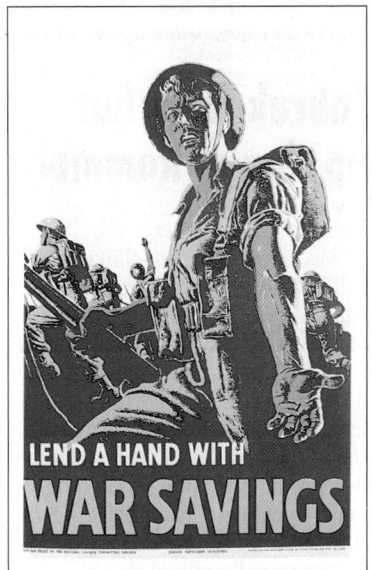

LEND A HAND WITH WAR SAVINGS

Allied Expeditionary Force lands in North Africa

North Africa, 10 November
No heavy gunfire announced the beginning of Operation Torch. As the huge fleet loomed out of the darkness two days ago and waves of landing craft raced across the ocean swell, shipboard loudspeakers broke the silence. "Don't shoot," they blared in French, "we are Americans." The invaders were hoping fervently that French defenders in Morocco and Algeria would welcome them as friends. It was not to be. All three invasion forces faced fierce French resistance. At Algiers, where 33,000 troops were to land, two British destroyers, *Malcolm* and *Broke*, flying American flags, came under shellfire as they tried to land 600 US troops. The *Malcolm* was badly damaged; the *Broke* was sunk. The 250 men who managed to get ashore were made prisoners. The beach parties were more successful.

By early evening, General Juin had surrendered Algiers. Oran, under attack by a landing force of 39,000, fell today, but not without heavy losses. Two Royal Navy sloops, *Walney* and *Hartland*, were destroyed as they tried to enter the harbour, with the loss of 300 troops. Bad weather foiled an airborne attempt to take the town's airports.

The toughest resistance was to come at Casablanca where 34,300 troops were to land. The French battleship *Jean Bart*, still under construction, used her 15-inch guns to challenge the US battleship *Massachusetts* until eight direct hits put the French ship out of action. Major General George S Patton Jnr, the US commander, arrived on the beach to find his army in chaos with landing craft waiting to be unloaded and men, unused to battle, cowering in foxholes as French aircraft roared in from the sea strafing tempting targets. Wearing two pearl-handled Colt revolvers, Patton strode among his men bellowing orders until they moved slowly forward (→11).

American troops wade ashore at Arzeu, near Oran: the French fired on them despite the loudspeakers' plea: "Don't shoot, we are Americans!"

Tobruk falls, but no sign of Rommel

Tobruk, 12 November
It was almost an anti-climax today as Tobruk changed hands once again. Looking around at the ruins of this North African seaport, British troops must have wondered why it had seemed so important when it fell last June. Now the town is a shell, its port installations largely destroyed. And still Montgomery's main quarry – Rommel's fleeing *Afrika Korps* – has eluded him as it continues its retreat (→15).

Ceasefire follows North African bloodshed

North Africa, 11 November
The armies have killed each other. At 2.30 this morning, the guns stopped firing over Algeria as both sides paused in order to lick their wounds. Three days of combat brought heavy losses: at Oran, 17 French warships were sunk, while the entire fleet at Casablanca, in Morocco, has been blasted out of existence.

The human casualties have been great. Over 4,000 men died in the fierce struggle between the Allied invasion force and local French troops under the command of Admiral Jean-Francois Darlan. In the end, it was Darlan who agreed an armistice with the General Mark Clark, the US commander-in-chief, in defiance of Marshal Petain's orders to resist.

The war is not yet won, however. Hitler is not going to relinquish North Africa lightly, and he started to airlift German troops into Tunis today. The *Luftwaffe* remain a potent threat. The allies, now closing in on the Tunisian border, are girding themselves for a stiff fight (→14).

Churchill: "the end of the beginning"

London, 10 November
Buoyant after the desert victory at El Alamein, the Allied landings in North Africa, the relief of the island of Malta and prospects of success in Russia – but still warning of hardships to come for the people of Britain – the prime minister, Winston Churchill, told a Mansion House dinner tonight: "This is not the end. It is not even the beginning of the end. But it is, perhaps, the end of the beginning."

Germans mount final Stalingrad assault

Germans patrol bombed-out streets, but Stalingrad is still unconquered.

Stalingrad, 13 November
General Paulus, desperately anxious to secure Stalingrad before winter sets in, launched yet another offensive against the city's defenders two days ago, with infantry and tanks fighting their way through the rubble behind one of the most intensive barrages of the battle.

The Germans managed to reach the Volga on a 500-yard (460-m) front, thus splitting the defences. They also captured most of the Red October factory, clearing it room by room, floor by floor. Both sides have developed special units for this type of fighting. The Germans call them *Kampfgruppen*, and they fight in cellars and attics and sewers with cruel expertise.

Despite the German successes, the Russians are still holding on, defying Hitler's boast in his Munich Beercellar speech last week that "we've got Stalingrad ... there are only a few more tiny pockets" of resistance.

There are also signs that Paulus may have shot his bolt. His men and machines are exhausted and the Volga has begun to freeze. Meanwhile the Russians have been building up a formidable new army in the east (→ 19).

German troops march into Vichy France

Paris, 11 November
German troops marched into unoccupied France today, allegedly to save Vichy from invasion. Code named Operation *Anton* (the name was changed from Operation *Attila*), the move was ordered by Hitler after Pierre Laval resisted pressure from Berlin to let German forces occupy Tunisia.

A letter from Hitler to Marshal Petain justified the occupation by saying that he wanted to protect the south of France from an Allied invasion.

The occupation was carried out by German and Italian units. Within 24 hours they controlled the whole of the territory formerly ruled by Vichy except for a small enclave round the naval base at Toulon. Field Marshal von Rundstedt, the German commander, said that the "attitude of the population is indifferent", except in Marseilles.

Although the invasion was a defensive response to the Anglo-American "Torch" landings in North Africa, Hitler admitted in his letter to Petain that it was the escape of General Henri Giraud "which chiefly made me behave in this manner". Giraud, who escaped with a home-made rope from the castle of Konigstein, made his way last week to North Africa with the help of British intelligence and a British submarine.

1942

November

Su	Mo	Tu	We	Th	Fr	Sa
1	2	3	4	5	6	7
8	9	10	11	12	13	14
15	16	17	18	19	20	21
22	23	24	25	26	27	28
29	30					

15. New Britain: General Hitoshi Imamura sets up his HQ at Rabaul (→ 25/12).

15. Solomon Islands: Four Japanese transports which survived the Battle of Guadalcanal are sunk off Tassafaronga.→

15. Algeria: The British First Army crosses Tunisia and takes Tabarka (→ 16).

16. Tunisia: Allied forces take Souk el Arba (→ 18).

17. New Guinea: A thousand Japanese reinforcements land at Gona, Buna and Sanananda.→

18. Tunisia: British troops at Djebel Abiod and French troops at Medjez el Bab repel simultaneous German attacks (→ 28).

19. New Guinea: A US attack on Japanese-held Buna is thwarted (→ 30).

19. Libya: Benghazi falls to the Allies.→

19. Norway: Operation Freshman, a British-Norwegian assault on the heavy water plant at Vermork, fails completely after the sabotage team's glider crashes.

19. Stalingrad: At the end of a two-week-long supply operation, 160,000 men, 10,000 horses, 430 tanks, 600 guns, 4,000 vehicles and 7,000 tons of ammunition have been ferried across the Volga (→ 20).

19. Britain: Admiral Sir Max Horton takes over from Admiral Sir Percy Noble as C-in-C Western Approaches, responsible for the safety of Atlantic convoys.

20. USSR: Generals Vatutin, Rokossovsky and Eremenko set out to trap 22 German divisions (270,000 men) between the Volga and Don rivers.→

20. France: Laval makes a broadcast urging Frenchmen to cooperate more with Germany or face rule by "Jews and Communists" (→ 13/12).

20. Italy: Turin is hard hit by an RAF raid (→ 29).

21. Guadalcanal: US forces push the Japanese off Cruz Point (→ 24).

US loses ships, but wins battle to stop Japanese landings

Guadalcanal, 15 November
Three nights of warfare at sea have forced Japan to abandon attempts to reinforce its Guadalcanal garrison. Both the US and Japan lost ships in what were, in effect, two separate naval battles, but for the Japanese the losses were more significant: in future they will supply their besieged garrison by releasing drums from destroyers and hope that they will float ashore.

Round one of the naval battles off Guadalcanal began on the night of 12-13 November when US cruisers spotted a Japanese squadron in "the slot", as the supply route is known. When dawn broke aircraft joined the battle. The US came off worse, with nine warships sunk and eight damaged; Japan lost four ships, with seven transport ships damaged. Round two began two nights later, after Japan had bombarded the US base at Henderson Field during the day.

Again the US suffered heavier losses, with five warships damaged to one lost by Japan, but the effect of the battles was to thwart Japanese attempts to reinforce Guadalcanal. However, the US Navy is to urge that all its ships have night radar to avoid the tragic confusion that led US destroyers to fire on an American ship during the two sea battles (→ 21).

An American poster recalls the village of Lidice which was wiped out in revenge for the assassination of Reinhart Heydrich.

Red Army fights back at Stalingrad

Red Army soldiers defend their position in the suburbs of Stalingrad: the Russians plan a massive pincer movement.

Stalingrad, 21 November
At 7.30am yesterday, on a foggy, dank morning, 3,500 Russian guns thundered out the opening of a massive attack by the Red Army on the German salient before Stalingrad. The attack, codenamed Uranus, was planned in strict secrecy by Zhukov and is aimed initially at the weakest links in the Axis positions – the Roumanian forces north and south of the city.

The first signs are that the Roumanians have been swept away by the onslaught, their officers leaving desks littered with maps and documents. The Germans are desperately trying to stem the tide, but they face ten new Russian armies spearheaded by 900 T34 tanks backed by 13,500 heavy guns.

The offensive, along 250 miles (400 km), involves the forces of three Russian fronts, the southwest under General Vatutin, the Don under General Rokossovsky, and the Stalingrad under General Eremenko. They are supported by 1,100 aircraft, one quarter of all the Red Air Force. Equipped with new Lavochkin La-5 and Yakovlev

Yak-9 fighters, a new version of the Shturmovik battlefield bomber and US-supplied Boston bombers, they are facing a worn-down *Luftwaffe* depleted by the need to reinforce the Middle East.

The Russian plan is a bold one. It involves two concentric pincer attacks with the first striking down from Serafimovich and up from Lake Barmantsak to meet at Kalach, and the second, inner, encirclement to cut off the city itself. Chuikov's Sixty-Second Army and Zhadov's Sixty-Sixth Army, which have defended Stalingrad so valiantly, are also to go over to the offensive. This is the counterstroke which the Germans have feared. They have heard rumours of it from PoWs, but its strength and audacity has astonished them (→ 23).

Zhukov and officers in the dug-out headquarters of the Sixty-Second Army.

Darlan deal gives Allies a headache

Washington, 17 November
President Roosevelt today defended the agreement which the Allied commander in North Africa, Lieutenant-General Eisenhower, has reached with Admiral Darlan, the former Vichy leader, as "a temporary expedient". Four days ago, Darlan announced that he was "assuming responsibility for the government in Africa with the consent of the American authorities". President Roosevelt made it plain, however, that this did not mean that the United States would back Darlan. "We are opposed," he said, "to Frenchmen who support Hitler and the Axis" (→ 1/12).

Australians push Japan into retreat

Port Moresby, 17 November
The steady advance of the Australian army across the Owen Stanley Mountains in Papua continues. Yesterday all seven Australian battalions engaged completed the crossing of the swift-flowing Kumusi river, in the north. In the advance from Port Moresby the Australians found evidence that the enemy had been reduced to eating not only grass but also dead Australians. Approximately 5,000 survivors of Japan's original drive on Port Moresby earlier this year, together with 4,000 reinforcements sent from Rabaul, are now retreating to the north coast (→ 19).

Church bells ring for El Alamein win

Britain, 15 November
Church bells across Britain, silent since June 1940, pealed out this Sunday morning to celebrate victory at El Alamein. The bells of Westminster Abbey were broadcast by the BBC to occupied Europe and Germany. The bells of Coventry Cathedral's only surviving belltower were heard with the 9am news on the second anniversary of the city's great *Luftwaffe* raid. Many bellringers had to be "lent" from the Services (→ 19).

Stone Age convoy breaks siege of Malta

The unloading of Stone Age continues after dark in a floodlit harbour.

Malta, 20 November
The future of Malta was finally assured when British and American merchant ships began unloading at the quayside here today.

The navy was taking no chances with the convoy – Operation Stone Age – that sailed from Port Said three days ago. The four merchantmen were escorted by seven destroyers and the 15th Cruiser Squadron – such was the desperate need of Malta for food and fresh supplies. At 1,500 calories per day, the Maltese population is close to starvation. Despite Allied victories in the desert, Malta remains vulnerable to *Luftwaffe* bombers in Sicily and strategically vital.

Everything depended on Stone Age. Massive air and sea attacks could have been expected, but Axis attention is diverted elsewhere. The four merchantmen were unscathed when they sailed into the Grand Harbour at Valetta today.

Sadly, the cruiser *Arethusa* was hit by an aerial torpedo. Burning fiercely, she is being towed stern-first into Malta by the destroyer *Petard*. One hundred and fifty-five men were lost.

German airlift blocks Allied advance

North Africa, 19 November
The British Eighth Army today recaptured the key Libyan port of Benghazi as Rommel's *Afrika Korps* continued to retreat westwards, but that was the only good news for the Allies in North Africa. Elsewhere their armies are meeting tough resistance from German forces now reinforced by an airlift into Tunis. Already the Germans have forced the British back to Djebel Abiod, although a German assault there two days ago was repelled. Today the French garrison withdrew from Medjez el Bab to Oued Zarga after repulsing German attacks for two days backed by US artillery and British troops. Yesterday General Louis Barre, the C-in-C of the French 19th Corps, rejected a German ultimatum to evacuate, signalling a switch from Vichy to the Allies (→ 23)

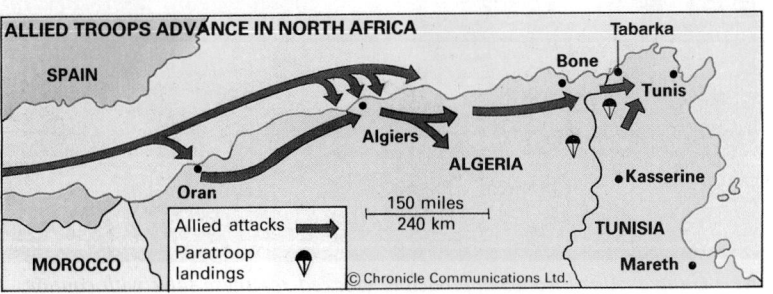

ALLIED TROOPS ADVANCE IN NORTH AFRICA

SPAIN
MOROCCO
Oran
Algiers
ALGERIA
Bone
Tabarka
Tunis
TUNISIA
Kasserine
Mareth

Allied attacks
Paratroop landings

150 miles
240 km

© Chronicle Communications Ltd.

1942
November

Su	Mo	Tu	We	Th	Fr	Sa
1	2	3	4	5	6	7
8	9	10	11	12	13	14
15	16	17	18	19	20	21
22	23	24	25	26	27	28
29	30					

23. USSR: The Russians take Kalach, in the Ukraine, completing their pincer movement.

23. Dakar: The French colony of Senegal joins the Allies under Admiral Darlan.→

23. Rastenburg: Hitler orders Germans at Stalingrad to "dig in and await relief", refusing to yield any ground (→ 24).

23. Libya: Rommel halts at El Agheila to reorganize.→

24. Solomon Islands: Japan lands a team of engineers at Munda, in New Georgia, to build an airfield (→ 3/12).

24. Berlin: Field Marshal von Manstein is appointed to command the newly-created Army Group Don on the Stalingrad front.→

25. Greece: Resistance fighters and British SOE agents blow up Gorgopotamos viaduct, on the Athens-Salonika railway.

25. Norway: Bergen Jews are deported to Auschwitz (→ 30).

26. Thailand: USAAF planes attack Bangkok oil refinery.

28. Rastenburg: Hitler refuses to heed Rommel's plea to evacuate German forces from North Africa (→ 12/12).

28. Tunisia: British and US troops reach Djedeida and meet firm German resistance (→ 29).

29. Tunisia: The Battle of Tebourba begins: the Allied armoured "Blade Force" is beaten off when it tries to storm German hilltop strongholds (→ 2/12).

29. Tunisia: British paratroopers land near Oudna airfield, but are repulsed by the Germans.

30. Yokohama: The German navy supply ship *Uckermark* (previously the *Altmark*) sinks after an accidental explosion, taking the disguised German raider *Thor* with her.

30. Europe: Deportations of Polish Jews approach completion. Since the camps opened, 600,000 Jews have been murdered at Belzec, 360,000 at Chelmno, 250,000 at Sobibor and 840,000 at Treblinka (→ 1/12).

Herbert Morrison joins war cabinet

On the way up: Herbert Morrison.

Britain, 22 November
Herbert Morrison, the ebullient Cockney home secretary, was promoted to the war cabinet tonight. He replaces his fellow socialist Sir Stafford Cripps who is demoted to minister of aircraft production. Mr Churchill will now feel more at ease. Sir Stafford has lately been inclined to tell him how to run the war, and as leader of the Commons he has also rubbed MPs up the wrong way.

Mr Churchill and Sir Stafford, an austere vegetarian lawyer, were uneasy bedfellows. The foreign secretary, urbane Anthony Eden, is the new leader of the house.

Blockbuster bombs dropped on Turin

Italy, 29 November
Lancaster bombers demonstrated their unique lethality tonight by dropping a new 8,000-pound bomb on Italian soil for the first time. The bomber came into service early this year; the bomb was dropped for the first time in April. There have been 11 raids on Turin, the last eight days ago. As well as the new blockbuster, the RAF hit the city with 100,000 incendiaries and other high explosive. Two Stirlings and a Wellington are missing (→ 4/12).

▷

Nazis enter Toulon: fleet is scuttled

A German soldier watches as the scuttled French fleet sinks slowly to rest at the bottom of Toulon harbour.

Toulon, 27 November
French sailors opened seacocks today to scuttle the mighty French fleet and save it from falling into German hands. Two battleships, a battle cruiser, seven cruisers, 29 destroyers and two submarines sank to the bottom of Toulon harbour as frustrated Germans watched.

Admiral Darlan had "advised" that the fleet should join the Allies in North Africa, but its commander, Admiral de Laborde, hesitated

as he awaited confirmation from Petain. An emissary from Darlan carrying firm orders was captured by the Germans. A bewildered de Laborde remained unconvinced that the Germans were preparing to seize his ships – the *Wehrmacht* and the SS had shrewdly left the Toulon base unoccupied when they marched into Vichy France, although they had prepared a plan for capturing the fleet intact. The Germans put their plan into effect

last night. The harbour was mined and E-boats were poised to land troops on the ships. When the sun rose this morning, some 70 craft would fight for neither side.

In London, Winston Churchill had hoped fervently for the fleet to come over. "If I could meet Darlan, much as I hate him, I would crawl on my hands and knees for a mile if I could get him to bring that fleet of his into the circle of Allied forces," he said.

French colonies will support the Allies

Saint Denis, Reunion, 28 November
The *Leopard*, a Free French destroyer, berthed on this Vichy-controlled island in the Indian Ocean this morning to a jubilant, almost operatic, welcome.

After discussions with the destroyer's captain, Commander Jacques Richard, the governor, M Aubert, ended three hours of hostilities with no casualties. This is the second blow to Vichy's colonies in two days. Yesterday troops in Djibouti, in the Horn of Africa, crossed the frontier into British Somaliland and placed themselves at the disposal of the Free French. Meanwhile in Vichy France the Germans are forcibly demobilizing the French Armistice Army.

Rommel's forces halt at El Agheila

Libya, 24 November
Rommel today halted his westward flight from El Alamein 100 miles (160 km) south of Benghazi, at El Agheila. For more than two weeks his battered *Afrika Korps* has kept one step ahead of the pursuit force formed by the 7th Armoured and New Zealand Divisions of the Eighth Army. Rommel would like to withdraw to Europe, but Hitler and Mussolini have vetoed this proposal (→ 28).

New Mexico site for nuclear bomb tests

Santa Fe, 25 November
The decision was taken today to take over a 50,000-acre site at Los Alamos, in the Jemez mountains in New Mexico, 20 miles (32 km) from here, to house a secret laboratory for research into the atomic bomb. The site, formerly a boarding school for boys, is on top of a 7,200-foot plateau.

The site was chosen by the director, Dr J Robert Oppenheimer, appointed in spite of his left-wing politics. Dr Oppenheimer says that his two great loves are physics and desert country; now he can enjoy both at once (→ 2/12).

MacArthur tells general to take Buna or come back in a coffin

Papua, New Guinea, 30 November
Angered by slow progress in the final stages of the Papuan campaign, General MacArthur has told Lt-Gen Robert Eichelberger, the commanding general of US 1 Corps, to take charge of a force no larger than a division at Buna. "I want you to take Buna, or not come back alive," said MacArthur. He offered inducements as well. He said that if Eichelberger captured Buna he would give him a Distinguished Service Cross and "recommend him for a British decoration". Buna was believed to be "easy pickings", but the Japanese survivors of Kokoda are putting up a fanatical last-ditch stand (→ 2/12).

New Guinea: Allied troops approach a wrecked Japanese tank with caution.

Germans trapped by Russian pincers

Stalingrad, 26 November

The Russians have thrown a ring of fire and steel around the German Sixth Army trapped in Stalingrad, the city it had come to capture three months ago. It failed, and now this once proud army faces destruction by the avenging Russians.

Three days ago Lieutenant-Colonel Filippov, the commander of the 14th Motorized Infantry Brigade of the Russian XXVI Tank Corps, led his detachment, with lights full on in the pre-dawn darkness, to the German-held bridge over the Don at Kalach. He was counting on the Germans assuming that his were captured tanks being taken to a nearby German anti-tank warfare training school for practice. The bridge was primed to be blown up, but Filippov's ruse worked. The Germans waved him on and he captured the bridge, holding it with his small force until the rest of the town was captured.

The next day Soviet tanks poured over the bridge and met up with the southern arm of the pincer movement 30 miles to the southeast at Sovetsky. The ring was closed.

Inside it are Paulus's Sixth Army and part of Hoth's 4th *Panzer* Army, 270,000 men comprising 22 divisions. There are also the remains of the Third and Fourth Roumanian Armies, whose men have been surrendering in their thousands. The situation is reminiscent of the Germans' early great encirclement victories, and the Russians' aim is the same as their enemy's was: the destruction of the trapped divisions.

Paulus wants to break out to safety in the west. When he was told of the Russian link-up at Sovetsky he sent a signal to Hitler: "Army heading for disaster. It is essential to withdraw all our divisions from Stalingrad." But Hitler has ordered him to stand firm: "I will do everything in my power to supply the Sixth Army adequately and to disengage it when the time is convenient."

Goering, inspired by the *Luftwaffe's* successful supply of the *Wehrmacht's* "hedgehogs" last winter, has promised Hitler he will be able to airlift sufficient supplies to keep Paulus's army in being until

Russian troops close in on the doomed Sixth Army across snow-covered ruins.

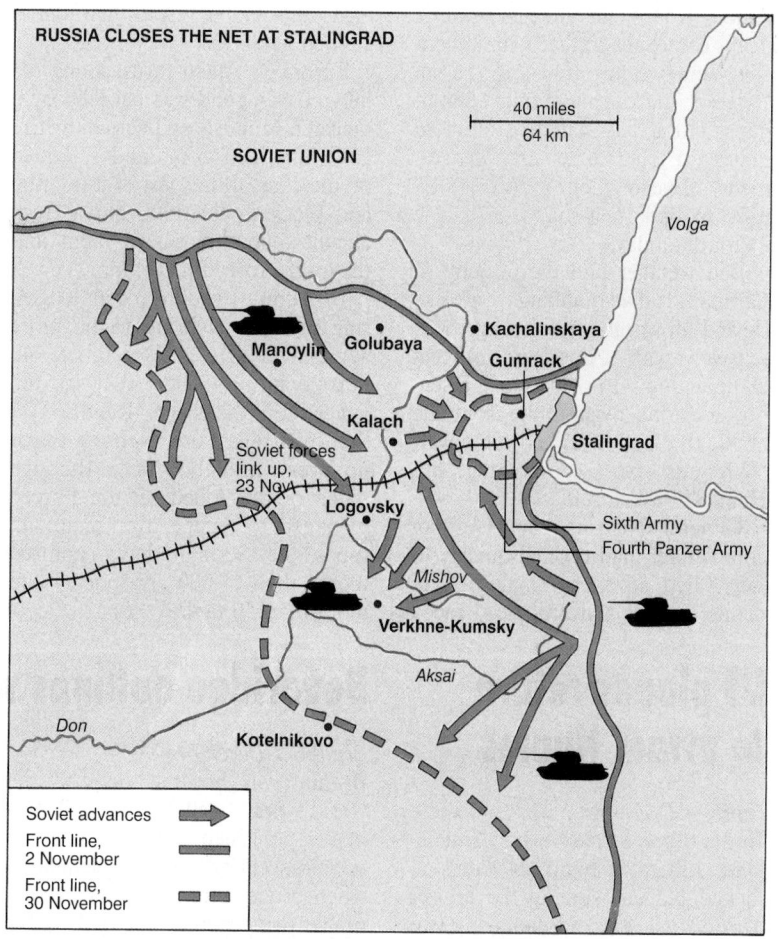

RUSSIA CLOSES THE NET AT STALINGRAD

40 miles
64 km

SOVIET UNION

Volga

Manoylin   Golubaya   • Kachalinskaya
                        Gumrack
        Kalach
Soviet forces   Stalingrad
link up,
23 Nov
Logovsky   Sixth Army
                            Fourth Panzer Army
              Mishov
        Verkhne-Kumsky
              Aksai
Don
        Kotelnikovo

Soviet advances →
Front line,
2 November ——
Front line,
30 November - - -

the Russians are driven off. But the Luftwaffe is going to be hard-pressed. Virtually every transport aircraft in the air force will be needed to carry the daily total of 500 tons of fuel and ammunition necessary to sustain the trapped army. Many of its transport aircraft have been sent to the Middle East; two-thirds of them are unserviceable at any given time. The weather is appalling. The only two airfields still in German hands are in danger of falling to the Russians. As Paulus says, the Sixth Army is heading for disaster (→11/12).

Now resistance is growing in Nazi-occupied Europe

London, 30 November

Rene Duchez, a French housepainter, kept his eyes open when he was set to work redecorating the office of a German officer in the Todt military construction organization in Caen, Normandy. On the desk he spotted a large map. Later he handed it to a friend in the Resistance. When the map eventually reached London, it was found to be a detailed plan of Germany's coastal defences, setting out every strong point, arms dump, booby trap and look-out point.

Duchez is just one of the many thousands of ordinary folk who work for the resistance movements of occupied Europe while carrying on with their regular jobs.

Resistance began almost as soon as the conquering Germans appeared. In the first stunned days and weeks after defeat, it might be no more than a gesture; in Amsterdam, a bar would empty of Dutch customers if a German entered. But then people took to playing tricks, putting sugar in the petrol tank of a German car or throwing tacks on the road. In Belgium, Andree de Jongh, aged 24, the daughter of a schoolmaster, organized an escape route through occupied France and into Spain for crashed aircrew and escaped PoWs.

In July 1940, in Britain, Churchill set up SOE, the Special Operations Executive, with the task of training saboteurs and sending them into Europe to organize and strengthen resistance. Burglary, safebreaking, hand-to-hand combat and silent killing were the skills needed. Savile Row made suits in continental styles and the Science Museum forged papers.

Despite blunders and betrayals – the whole Dutch section of SOE in the Netherlands has been penetrated by the Nazis – the resistance movements continue to flourish in occupied Europe.

December

Su	Mo	Tu	We	Th	Fr	Sa
		1	2	3	4	5
6	7	8	9	10	11	12
13	14	15	16	17	18	19
20	21	22	23	24	25	26
27	28	29	30	31		

1. Addis Ababa: Ethiopia declares war on Germany, Italy and Japan.

1. London: Sydney Silverman, a Labour MP, reports that over two million Polish Jews have been exterminated by the Nazis (→ 13).

1. US: Nationwide petrol rationing starts today.

2. Belgium: Members of the Rexist (fascist) movement are asked to help Germany by spying.

2. Tunisia: Allied troops beat off a German attack on Tebourba but lose forty tanks.→

2. Mediterranean: The British destroyer *Quentin* is sunk by an aircraft torpedo off Bone.

2. New Guinea: Allied air superiority forces Japanese reinforcements trying to land at Buna to land further west (→9).

2. Rome: Mussolini reveals that 40,000 Italians have been killed in action, 86,000 wounded and 231,000 taken prisoner since the war broke out.

3. New Georgia: US bombers start intensive attacks on Munda Point to prevent Japan from building an airfield (→4/1).

3. USSR: Soviet troops break through German positions west of Rzhev.

4. Guadalcanal: US marines complete a month of foraging in which they killed 400 Japanese at the cost of 17 of their own number (→9).

4. Algiers: Admiral Darlan claims the leadership of the imperial council of France on the grounds that Marshal Petain is a prisoner of the Germans (→24).

5. Washington: The US Navy publishes its report on the Japanese raid on Pearl Harbor, revealing how much damage was done.

5. US: Pilots testing the Thunderbolt fighter plane reach 725mph, just short of the speed of sound.

5. Mediterranean: The Allies sink the German hospital ship *Graz* off Libya.

Allied setback in Tunisia

A German Panzer general and his staff walk through Tebourba after their victory.

Algiers, 3 December
Allied troops advancing towards Tunis came face to face with a monster new weapon today – 56-ton "Tiger" tanks mounting 88mm guns. Hitler has sent five of these giants to Tunisia as an "experiment". Two of them played a significant part in a major defeat at Tebourba today.

Bad weather and the ferocity of German dive-bombing attacks slowed down the two-pronged offensive, with American officers complaining to Lt-Gen Eisenhower during a visit to the front line about the lack of Allied air cover. "Why do we see nothing but Heinies?" asked one.

General Nehring, the German commander, had reacted quickly to the Allied advance. Small detachments, mostly paratroopers, raced to take the vital towns of Sousse, Sfax and Gabes from bewildered French garrisons.

The main Allied thrust along the hilly coastal road was checked by a German ambush at Djefna. British and American commandos landed on the coast to the east of this battle and blocked the road, but a fresh assault failed to relieve them and they were forced to withdraw.

In Tunis, Field Marshal Kesselring ordered Nehring to be more aggressive. On 1 December, 40 tanks with anti-tank weapons advanced on the town. Repulsed at first by artillery fire, Nehring called up every available unit. Although much of the Allied "Blade Force" managed to escape over mountain roads, the Germans have captured more than 1,000 prisoners and more than 50 tanks (→ 6).

US planes return to attack Naples

Cairo, 4 December
In the first US raid on Italy's mainland, Liberator bombers today attacked Naples, sinking the cruiser *Muzio Attendolo* and damaging two other cruisers and four destroyers. Some 159 people died and 358 were injured. The raid by long-range Liberators has changed the Mediterranean strategic scene. Naples has been free of raids since Rommel took Allied coastal airfields in North Africa six months ago. Now it is back in range.

Nuclear reaction in a Chicago stadium

Chicago, 2 December
The first controlled nuclear chain reaction took place in a squash court under the university football stadium here today. Scientists led by the Italian physicist Enrico Fermi allowed the "pile" of uranium rods, separated by graphite blocks, to run for four and a half minutes, which produced just one half-watt of power, but proved man can control atomic power.

Scientists waited in awe as the neutron counter clicked faster. Then Fermi raised his hand. "The pile has gone critical," he said. Someone telephoned Dr James Conant, the head of defence science, in Washington. "Jim," he said, "the Italian navigator has just landed in the new world" (→ 28).

Fermi: "Italian navigator".

Beveridge outlines welfare state future

Britain, 1 December
Britain will become one of the world's first "welfare states" if proposals published today for postwar social security are implemented when peace returns. Under a comprehensive scheme prepared by Sir William Beveridge, the Liberal economist, the entire adult population would be brought into a compulsory insurance scheme covering sickness, unemployment, old age and benefit for families.

It was said in Whitehall tonight that the coalition government sees the scheme as a key element in postwar reconstruction and will give it earnest consideration. The Beveridge report envisages state provision from cradle to grave – including free medical care for everybody.

Its proposals are based on the principle of flat-rate weekly contributions: 4/3 (21p/86¢) for men workers and 3/6 (17½p/71¢) for women, with an employer's contribution of 3/3 (16p/65¢) for men and 2/6 (12½p/50¢) for women. Benefits would include a national health service, £2-a-week ($8) retirement pensions and unemployment pay, and £20 ($80) death grants.

1942
December

Su	Mo	Tu	We	Th	Fr	Sa
		1	2	3	4	5
6	7	8	9	10	11	12
13	14	15	16	17	18	19
20	21	22	23	24	25	26
27	28	29	30	31		

DECEMBER 1942

Allied shipping attacked in Indian Ocean

A U-boat service recruiting poster.

Durban, 5 December
At least three Allied ships have been sunk in the Indian Ocean in the past week by enemy submarines. Admiral Donitz, pursuing his policy of hitting at weak points in the Allied defences, has sent some of his long-range U-boats to operate from Japanese bases, sometimes with the help of Japanese boats. They have scored some notable successes. One British steamer, sunk off Zululand, had 1,000 South African troops on board. A British transport was sunk with South African troops and Italian refugees from Eritrea on board. A Greek ship, the *Cleanthis* (formerly the *Framlington Castle*), was sunk on Monday.

Royal Navy sinks Tunisian convoy

Malta, 2 December
A British naval squadron was guided to its target tonight by RAF aircraft dropping flares over a convoy carrying tanks and 2,000 troops from Sicily to North Africa. Once it had made contact, the squadron – three light cruisers, *Aurora*, *Argonaut* and *Sirius*, with the destroyers *Quentin* and HMAS *Quiberon* – attacked from the darkness using RDF [radar]. All four enemy ships and an escorting destroyer were sunk.

The *Quentin* was later sunk by Italian torpedo planes.

US cruiser lost in Solomons battle

Guadalcanal, 1 December
Eight Japanese destroyers on the "Tokyo Express" route – down the "Slot" inside the Solomon Islands to supply the Guadalcanal garrison – have inflicted a stinging defeat on a US Navy task force off Guadalcanal over the last 24 hours. In the Battle of Tassafaronga they sank the cruiser *Northampton* and badly mauled three more US cruisers. The Japanese lost only one destroyer, but the supplies were not delivered so the moral victory at sea does nothing to help their beleaguered forces on land (→4).

Dec 1. American planes on Henderson Field, on Guadalcanal, a vital base around which much fighting is taking place, prepare for a strike.

6. Holland: The RAF makes a heavy raid on Eindhoven, flying at low level by daylight.

6. Tunisia: German troops push back the US 1st Armoured Division in the Eli Guessa heights (→10).

7. Changi, Singapore: A beautiful *shinto* shrine, built by PoWs, is unveiled in the camp.

7. Atlantic: When the U-boat U515 sinks the British liner *Ceramic* only one man a Royal Engineer, survives.

7. Germany: The *Gestapo* arrests over 700 young people, alleged members of a group called "*Edelweiss* Pirates".

7. US: America's biggest battleship, the USS *New Jersey*, is launched.→

8. Madrid: General Franco says that the world has a choice between communism and fascism, and he chooses the latter.

8. Mediterranean: Three Italian midget submarines attempt to attack British shipping in Gibraltar harbour, but fail (→12).

8. Taihu, China: *Kuomintang* forces shoot down a plane carrying top Japanese officers to Wuhan.

9. Guadalcanal: Major-General Alexander Vandegrift of the US Marines hands over command of US land forces to Major-General Alexander C Patch of the US Army XIV Corps (→12).

9. New Guinea: Australian forces capture Gona after a fierce hand-to-hand battle.→

10. Tunisia: British and Free French defenders drive off a strong German attack on Medjez el Bab (→14).

11. Vinnitsa: Hitler refuses to allow the Sixth Army to pull out of Stalingrad (→12).

12. Moscow: Stalin decides to defeat German attempts to supply Stalingrad before crushing Paulus's trapped army.→

12. Berlin: The State Opera House, bombed by the British last year, reopens with a performance of Wagner's *Die Meistersinger*.

Two ships are sunk by Italian frogmen

Algiers, 12 December
Italian frogmen rode into Algiers harbour last night on their two-man underwater chariots, sank two merchantmen and damaged two others.

Despite the clear reluctance of many Italian soldiers to fight alongside the Germans – which led to world contempt in their 1940 desert campaign – the bravery of these frogmen, who have sunk or damaged ships in Gibraltar and Alexandria and during the Crete landings, is much admired by the Royal Navy which has had to take special precautions, including the use of concussion grenades.

Retreating Rommel plagues the Allies

German troops sleep in the sun.

North Africa, 12 December
Beaten but unbowed, the *Afrika Korps* has not lost its ability to sting. The regrouped and replenished Eighth Army has met fierce resistance from the retreating Axis at Mersa Brega, with Rommel ducking a strong right hook by New Zealand tanks. The going has not been easy for the Allies. The road to Tripoli is carpeted with mines and booby traps. In the west, Free French forces and the British 1st Guards Brigade have driven off strong Axis counter-attacks at Medjez el Bab, but German reinforcements are flooding into Tunis. ▷

357

Allies step up air campaign in Europe

US looks back on one year since "day of infamy"

United States, 7 December
One year after the "day of infamy" at Pearl Harbor, the US Navy today launched 15 ships, including the biggest battleship ever built. The huge USS *New Jersey* slid down the ways at the Philadelphia Navy Yard almost on the hour of last December's attack.

Elsewhere in America, an aircraft carrier, two destroyers, a submarine, six minesweepers, two escort craft, a destroyer tender and what the navy called a "special" ship were launched. All this was a tangible demonstration of President Franklin D Roosevelt's message to the people: that the day of surprise was a year ago, the period of defence is over and the offensive is under way. "Coral Sea, Midway, the Solomons, New Guinea and North Africa are shining examples of [our] power," the president said. Admiral Chester W Nimitz, the chief of the Pacific Fleet, said that victory has been assured over the Japanese because the "sea lane across the greatest of oceans" have been made safe. The optimism is tempered by official statistics: 58,307 casualties in the year, a massive 35,822 of which occurred in the Pacific theatre. Many are classified as missing and presumed to be prisoners of war. More than one million US servicemen are now in action.

DECEMBER 7, 1941
The day that will live in infamy.

Bombs rain down from B-17 Flying Fortresses in a daylight raid on Europe.

Seven nations join forces in daylight raid

London, 6 December
Fighter squadrons from seven Allied countries took part yesterday in the biggest series of daylight raids yet mounted on targets in Europe. Among them were two from the Royal Norwegian Air Force, a famous Free French squadron, and three from the USAAF.

Crack Polish squadrons flew alongside others from Canada and New Zealand, and this truly Allied effort was completed by battle-hardened RAF units.

They made independent sweeps to draw off enemy fighters and provided cover for British light bombers to make the main raid, a successful low-level attack on the Philips radio factory at Eindhoven in Holland, and for American Flying Fortresses and Liberators which raided an engineering works at Lille and the Abbeville fighter airfield.

RAF counts cost of mass bomber raids

London, 6 December
The war in the air has reached a stage where German bombers hardly venture into British skies, while Bomber Command pounds German cities almost every night.

It is, however, a time of some concern for the RAF. Bomber losses during the year have been high with 1,453 aircraft lost and 2,724 damaged in action. There are still only 200 Lancasters in service, and the Germans have learnt how to jam Gee, the navigational device.

There is also some confusion about the future role of Bomber Command. Sir Charles Portal, the Chief of the Air Staff, has urged the formation of an Anglo-American force of 4,000-6,000 bombers.

The result, he says, would be "twenty-five million Germans rendered homeless, 900,000 killed and one million seriously injured". The plan has met fierce opposition.

In other areas, Fighter Command continues its often costly offensive sweeps across France; Coastal Command, the "Cinderella" command, is at last getting the aircraft it needs; and in the Middle East the RAF has relearnt how to support an army in the field.

Australians overcome stiff Japanese resistance to take key port

Papua, New Guinea, 10 December
Australian troops yesterday took Gona, a key Japanese defensive position on the north Papuan coast from which the Japanese launched their ill-fated campaign to take Port Moresby. The savagery of the action against the fanatical resistance of the Japanese garrison at Gona is indicated by the 638 bodies found after the battle.

The four Australian battalions of the 21st Brigade assigned to take Gona have suffered dangerously high casualties. Already sharply reduced in numbers by earlier battle casualties and high illness rates from heat exhaustion, malaria and other tropical disease, they suffered a further 530 killed and wounded, more than 40 per cent (→ 15).

Australian troops and tanks go into action against Japan in New Guinea.

Germans launch "Winter Storm" attack

Russian defenders of Stalingrad keep their sights on the advancing enemy.

Stalingrad, 12 December

Field Marshal von Manstein, given the task of rescuing the Sixth Army trapped in Stalingrad, today launched Operation Winter Storm to break the Russian ring.

General Hoth's 4th *Panzer* Army, part of which is trapped in Stalingrad, is spearheading the attack from Kotelnikovo, some 60 miles (96 km) south-west of the city. The Germans are in fact closer to Stalingrad at Niznhe Chirskaye, but to attack from there would involve a crossing of the Don which von Manstein regards as too risky.

The field marshal, ordered to "recapture the positions previously occupied by us", describes his operation as a "race with death", and there is no doubt that the Sixth Army is doomed if he loses. The *Luftwaffe* has failed the impossible task set it by Goering's boast to Hitler that he could keep the trapped army supplied. Heinkel He111 bombers have been pressed into service as transports, but Russian fighters are taking a heavy toll.

The Germans in the Stalingrad pocket are hungry and cold. They are eating their horses; some freeze to death, and it is doubtful if they have enough fuel to break out.

Yet the beleaguered General Paulus is making no effort to link up with Hoth's advancing tanks, which are making good progress. He will not abandon the ruins of Stalingrad until Hitler gives him permission – and Hitler will never do that (→ 14).

Britain's cockleshell heroes canoe into enemy territory and blast German ships

Bordeaux, 12 December

Four merchant ships, one tanker and a naval auxiliary moored in Bordeaux, 60 miles (96 km) from the sea, erupted this morning as limpet mines stuck to their hulls by British canoe commandos blew up. Royal Marine raiders had paddled 81 miles (146 km) through Europe's most dangerous estuary in icy conditions, for five nights, to reach their target. There is no plan to recover survivors. Initially five heavily-laden canoes carrying ten men were left by submarine ten miles south of the Gironde estuary. They had to paddle north, round Pointe de Grave and then south down the Gironde, through tidal races. The first casualties were swept away in heavy seas offshore and taken prisoner. Near the Pointe, five-foot waves capsized a second two-man canoe. The men clung to other cockles, but had to be ordered to let go, a death sentence in such cold water. One whispered: "That's all right sir, I understand." In the river mouth a third canoe was swept off course.

Two cockles and four men survived to attack the fast merchantmen vital to Bordeaux's supply line. The men were Major Hasler, aged 28, his partner, Marine Sparks, and Corporal Laver with Marine Mills. Hidden in riverside reeds by day, they moved with the floodtide by night. In conditions likely to cause hypothermia they slipped alongside their targets, with nine hours to escape. If captured on the way to neutral Spain they will be shot.

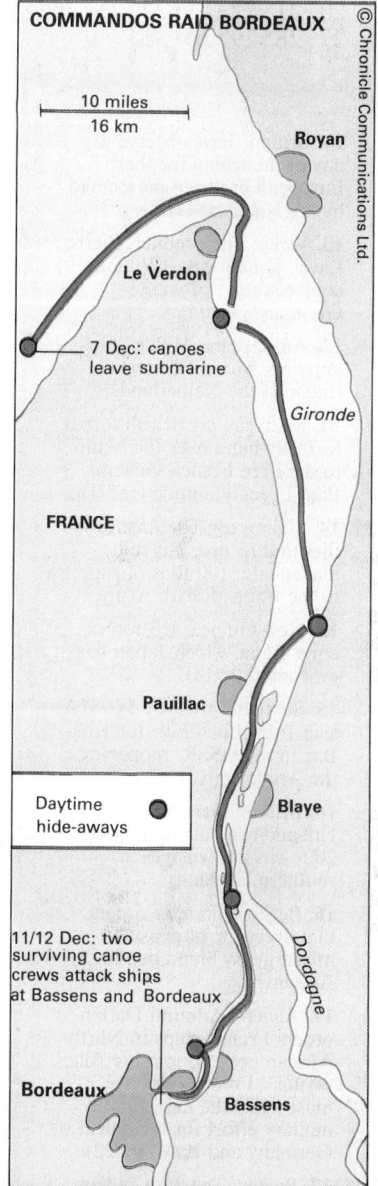

COMMANDOS RAID BORDEAUX

© Chronicle Communications Ltd.

10 miles
16 km

Royan

Le Verdon

7 Dec: canoes leave submarine

Gironde

FRANCE

Pauillac

Daytime hide-aways

Blaye

11/12 Dec: two surviving canoe crews attack ships at Bassens and Bordeaux

Dordogne

Bordeaux

Bassens

In the streets of Stalingrad: Russian troops inch forward in the darkness.

A limpet mine is handed from canoe to frogman in practice for the raid.

1942

December

Su	Mo	Tu	We	Th	Fr	Sa
		1	2	3	4	5
6	7	8	9	10	11	12
13	14	15	16	17	18	19
20	21	22	23	24	25	26
27	28	29	30	31		

13. Britain: Jews observe a day of mourning for their European brethren persecuted by the Nazis (→ 17).

13. Vichy: The premier, Pierre Laval, announces: "Without equivocation ... I want Germany's victory."

13. Amsterdam: Hitler appoints Anton Mussert as leader of the Netherlands.

14. Madagascar: British forces formally hand over the island to the Free French General Paul Legentilhomme (→ 8/1).

14. Stalingrad: The *Luftwaffe* flies in a record, but still inadequate, 100 tons of supplies to the trapped Sixth Army.→

15. New Guinea: US forces enter Buna, which Japan has evacuated (→ 18).

15. Scotland: Convoy JW-51A sails from Loch Ewe for Kola Bay in the USSR, reopening the Arctic convoy route.

16. Britain: German "hit-and-run" air raids strike 20 towns and villages in southern England.

16. Berlin: Himmler orders that everyone of gypsy or mixed gypsy blood be sent to Auschwitz.

17. Algiers: Admiral Darlan orders French ships in North African ports to join the Allies, saying: "French Africa ... must make the maximum military effort for the defeat of Germany and Italy" (→ 22).

17. Burma: The 14th Indian Division occupies Buthidaung.→

17. Mediterranean: The British submarine *Splendid* sinks the Italian destroyer *Aviere* off Bizerta.

18. Guadalcanal: US infantry meet stiff Japanese resistance at Mount Austen (→ 26).

18. New Guinea: The Australians attack Japanese positions at Napapo and Sanananda (→ 27).

18. Mediterranean: The U-boat U565 sinks the British destroyer *Partridge* off Oran.

19. USSR: The Russians retake Kantemirovka, between the Don and Donets rivers (→ 22).

Allies condemn anti-Semitic atrocities

London, 17 December
In the House of Commons today Anthony Eden, the British foreign secretary, read a lengthy declaration by the Allied governments condemning the Nazis' systematic extermination of Europe's Jews and giving warning that those responsible for the atrocities will face retribution after the war. The declaration is being broadcast across Europe by the BBC and other Allied radios.

The declaration speaks of "the appalling horror and brutality" of the Nazis' actions. Poland, it says, "has been made the principal Nazi slaughterhouse", where "the able-bodied are slowly worked to death, the infirm are left to die of exposure and starvation or are deliberately massacred". Sidney Silverman, the Jewish Labour MP for Nelson and Colne, asked whether the Allied governments would consider what measures of immediate relief could be given to Europe's Jews. "We shall do what we can," Eden said, "though I fear that what we can do may inevitably be slight."

In the House of Lords, where Viscount Simon, the lord chancellor, read the declaration, Viscount Samuel, speaking as a Jew, expressed the gratitude of British Jews for the action they were taking. He hoped something could be done, to save at least the children. Other speakers suggested that neutral nations should be offered Allied help for the maintenance of Jews to whom they gave sanctuary (→ 22).

Bound for a concentration camp; Eden said: "We shall do what we can."

VD epidemic hinders British war effort

Britain, 15 December
The government is to launch an all-out campaign to warn people of the dangers of venereal disease, using leaflets, films and broadcasts. The House of Commons today approved a regulation which provides that if two people report a third as a source of infection, that person may be compelled to go for treatment.

The minister of health, Ernest Brown, revealed that the number of new cases of syphilis had risen by 70 per cent since 1939. The rate was now as bad as in 1932. Public education was essential, as well as free treatment available from GPs and an increasing number of clinics. The Labour MP Dr Edith Summerskill said the new regulation did not go far enough. Last year 70,000 cases of VD had been seen by clinics. This meant that the total number was probably 150,000 – more than the casualties of the Blitz.

MPs reported that VD in the factories was seriously affecting the war effort, and that ships were sometimes unable to sail because of it. It was no longer confined to towns. Lady Astor said: "There has been a lowering of the moral tone and the government has done nothing about it."

Rommel slips away from Allied trap

El Agheila, 14 December
The trap was carefully laid for Rommel – but, once again, the wily Desert Fox has succeeded in getting away from Montgomery's Eighth Army. The *Panzerarmee Afrika* (as the *Afrika Korps* is now known) has slipped away from this port where Rommel began his desert campaigns and is heading west for Tripoli and Tunisia. The 2nd New Zealand Division was encircling the town in preparation for a planned frontal assault due to begin today. But under cover of dusk two nights ago Rommel's Panzers began to escape, their commander now hoping to link up with the other Axis forces in Tunisia (→ 17).

U-boats' "Enigma" codes are cracked

London, 13 December
At last Bletchley Park has been able to crack the *Enigma* cipher used by Admiral Donitz to communicate with his U-boats in the Atlantic. *Shark* had baffled the codebreakers from the beginning of this year because of the additional rotor which it uses. Now the admiralty's submarine tracking room will once more be able to route convoys round the wolfpacks. Sadly, Captain Roger Winn, who runs the submarine tracking room, has collapsed and has been ordered to take sick leave.

UNTIL YOUR EYES GET USED TO THE DARKNESS, TAKE IT EASY

LOOK OUT IN THE BLACKOUT

Germans battle to break Stalingrad siege

In the heart of Stalingrad itself the battle goes on in the Red October factory.

Stalingrad, 16 December
One of the fiercest tank battles of the war is raging on the Kalmyk Steppe, south-west of Stalingrad, as Hoth's 4th *Panzer* Army struggles to break through to the Sixth Army, trapped in the city and now fighting a bloody battle for survival, factory by factory, street by street.

In fighting as cruel as the winter the Germans have pushed the Russian Fifth Shock Army back across the Aksai river and almost to the Myshkova river where the Second Guards Army has formed a defence line stretching south-east from the stubbornly-defended Nizhne Chirs-kaye to Kapinsky. Hoth has been stopped there, only 25 miles (40 km) from Stalingrad; his leading tankmen can see the gun-flashes from the perimeter defences. Yet as he struggles to advance Russia has started a new offensive.

Before dawn this morning Zhukov launched Operation Saturn, a stunning blow at the Italian Eighth Army holding the line on von Manstein's flank north-west of Stalingrad. The Italians have crumbled, and a 60-mile (96-km)-wide gap has opened in the German defences – and the Russians are pouring through (→19).

Allies start cautious advance in Burma

Maungdaw, Burma, 19 December
The 14th Indian Division, having advanced 150 miles cross-country from India to the Maungdaw/Buthidaung line between the Burmese coast and the Arakan mountains, is pushing on. Its goal is the Japanese air base on the offshore island of Akyab, 60 miles south.

The campaign is a limited one, to secure an airfield in striking range of Rangoon. Originally General Wavell, the C-in-C in India, had hoped to make a seaborne assault, but there were no landing craft. A land attack was his second choice.

So far there has been little fighting and Japanese forward posts have been withdrawn. Akyab is defended by only one regiment, the 213th, but two divisions, the 55th and the 33rd, are near (→21).

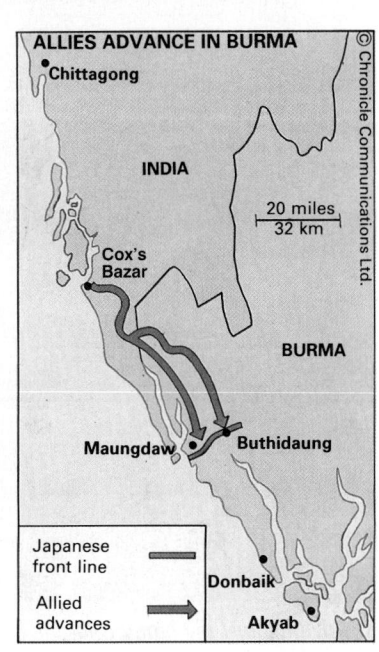

ALLIES ADVANCE IN BURMA
Chittagong
INDIA
20 miles
32 km
Cox's Bazar
BURMA
Maungdaw
Buthidaung
Japanese front line
Allied advances
Donbaik
Akyab

© Chronicle Communications Ltd.

1942
December

Su	Mo	Tu	We	Th	Fr	Sa
		1	2	3	4	5
6	7	8	9	10	11	12
13	14	15	16	17	18	19
20	21	22	23	24	25	26
27	28	29	30	31		

20. India: Japanese aircraft make a night raid on Calcutta.

20. East Indies: Allied planes raid Japanese targets on Sumatra.

20. Cape Inubo, Japan: The first Japanese cargo ship is sunk by a US mine.

21. Burma: Allied forces capture Alethangyaw (→25).

22. Tunisia: British troops launch an offensive to capture Longstop Hill, north of Medjez el Bab (→23).

22. USSR: The Germans start a swift retreat from exposed positions in the Caucasus (→24).

23. Tunisia: Heavy rain stops both sides' operations (→24).

24. USSR: The Russians push Hoth's 4th *Panzer* Army back from the Myshkova river where it was halted in its attempt to rescue German forces trapped in Stalingrad.

24. USSR: Russian forces retake the Red October factory in Stalingrad (→28).

24. Tunisia: A unit of the British Coldstream Guards captures Longstop Hill (→25).

25. New Britain: US bombers from Guadalcanal attack the Japanese headquarters at Rabaul.

25. Burma: Allied troops take Rathedaung (→27).

25. Libya: Axis defenders withdraw from Sirte.

25. Tunisia: The Germans retake Longstop Hill (→30).

26. Norway: Clergy read from the pulpit a message attacking Nazi persecution of the Jews (→31).

26. Algiers: As Bonnier de la Chapelle, Darlan's assassin, is executed by firing squad, General Henri Giraud succeeds Darlan as high commissioner for French North Africa.→

26. French Somaliland: Free French troops enter the colony from British Somaliland and take the railway between Djibouti and Addis Ababa.

26. Atlantic: The British destroyers *Hesperus* and *Vanessa*, escorting convoy HX-219, sink a U-boat.

Jewish resisters kill Germans in Cracow

Cracow, 22 December
Bomb blasts in two of the city's cafes have killed at least 20 German officers. The explosions, the work of a group of young Zionists led by Adolf Liebeskind, mark the climax of a resistance campaign which has included arson attacks on Nazi targets and the theft of weapons from German soldiers and police. Increasing numbers of younger Jews have joined underground resistance movements, often under the umbrella of Soviet and Polish communist partisans. They want to show that the Jewish people will not go to their deaths without putting up a fight (→26).

Germans launch a "bomb" that flies

Peenemunde, 24 December
The German research station here today chalked up a successful test firing of a new type of surface-to-surface weapon system. This is a "flying bomb", known as the FZG 76 or Fi 103. Looking like a small aircraft, with a fuselage length of just over 25 feet (8.5 metres) and wingspan of 18 feet (5.5 metres), it is powered by a pulse jet engine. Today the system was catapulted into the air from a 230-foot ramp and flew some one and a half miles. More test flights are planned to iron out technical bugs in the system.

Japan defies US in Guadalcanal battle

Guadalcanal, 26 December
The US XIV Corps, backed by artillery and air power, is facing fierce resistance on Mount Austen as it advances from Henderson Field. Major-General Alexander Patch, whose XIV Corps relieved the Marines on 9 December, says that possession of Mount Austen is vital to any future offensive. His troops, clearing enemy positions, say that malaria and hunger are rife among captured Japanese, a sure sign that their supplies are running low with few Japanese ships able to outrun the US naval blockade (→31).

▷

Admiral Darlan assassinated in Algiers

Left: Darlan, who was shot today.

Algiers, 24 December
Admiral Jean-Francois Darlan was assassinated here today by a young student, Fernand Bonnier de la Chapelle.

The admiral, the titular high commissioner who was in effect the head of what has been called a Vichy regime with Allied support, left his villa this afternoon to drive to the *Palais d'Ete*. At the door of his office he was shot by his assassin, who is 20 years old.

Bonnier de la Chapelle is apparently an ultra-right-winger, a member of a group called the Free Corps of Africa, and associated with Henri Astier de la Vigerie, a local monarchist leader. Bonnier will go before a court-martial tomorrow (→ 26).

Giraud takes over from Darlan in Africa

Algiers, 26 December
General Henri Giraud has been appointed as high commissioner for French North Africa in succession to Admiral Darlan, who was murdered on Christmas Eve. The appointment was made by the French imperial council here, but the choice was approved by the Allied High Command.

Spokesmen for General Charles de Gaulle, the leader of the Free French in London, commented favourably on Giraud's appointment yesterday, although Giraud is a potential rival to de Gaulle with whom he has a chilly relationship.

A regular officer, graduate of St Cyr, Giraud escaped from a German prison camp in the First World War. In 1940 he commanded the Seventh and then the Ninth Army. Taken prisoner, he spent two years planning his escape.

Last April he lowered himself 130 feet (40 m) down the walls of Konigstein castle by a rope smuggled to him in jam tins by his wife. He travelled to Switzerland by train, and, in November, with the help of British Intelligence, a British submarine and a Canadian flying boat brought him here on the eve of the Allied landings (→ 30).

Giraud with his German captors in 1940: now he heads French North Africa.

While Stalingrad burns, Leningrad faces struggle to survive as starvation worsens

Snow-camouflaged Red Army troops keep up the pressure on the Germans.

Leningrad, 25 December
As this year draws to a close it is the plight of the Germans encircled by the Red Army in Stalingrad that attracts world attention. Yet 1,000 miles (1,600 km) to the north it is the Russians who are besieged in a struggle for survival every bit as desperate: Leningrad has now been under siege for 15 months.

This Christmas Day a rat would be considered a great delicacy in Leningrad. The cats and dogs were eaten a year ago. After the Germans failed to take the city by storm, they settled down to starve it to death; but the food supply, brought in by boat across Lake Ladoga in the summer and across the ice in the winter, has been sta-bilized, and the citizens have learnt how to cope with the intermittent bombing and shelling.

However, nothing can minimize the suffering and the bravery of the people of Leningrad. One million of them have been evacuated by the boats and lorries making the hazardous journey across Lake Ladoga, but for many there has been no escape except by death.

A schoolgirl, Tania Savich, has kept a diary. It records the death of her family from starvation: "Jenia died on 28 December 1941 at 12.30 am. Grandmother died on 25 January 1942. Lena died on 17 March 1942. Uncle Lesha died on 10 May at 4.00pm. 13 May at 7.30am darling Mama died" (→ 11/1).

Muffled against the biting cold, the citizens of Leningrad struggle on.

1942
December

Su	Mo	Tu	We	Th	Fr	Sa
		1	2	3	4	5
6	7	8	9	10	11	12
13	14	15	16	17	18	19
20	21	22	23	24	25	26
27	28	29	30	31		

27. New Guinea: Japanese units at Napopo are ordered to withdraw to Giruwa (→ 28).

27. Burma: Indian troops reach the tip of the Mayu peninsula, meeting no resistance in their drive towards Akyab; but resistance is met at Rathedaung (→ 6/1).

27. Smolensk: Lieutenant-General Andrei Vlasov, under German protection, forms a committee to organize Soviet opposition to Stalin.

27. Atlantic: The U-boat U356 is sunk by the escort of convoy ONS-15.

28. New Guinea: The Japanese at Buna are ordered to retreat to Giruwa (→ 2/1).

28. Tirana: 600 Italian soldiers are reported to have been killed by Albanian freedom fighters.

28. Rastenburg: Hitler orders Greece and Crete to be fortified and Balkan rebellions to be suppressed firmly. He also approves the withdrawal of Army Group A from the Caucasus (→ 29).

28. USA: Roosevelt orders that atomic secrets are not to be shared with the British unless they are working on a particular part of the project.

29. USSR: Soviet troops recapture Kotelnikovo, southwest of Stalingrad (→ 31).

31. Moscow: The USSR claims that 175,000 German troops have been killed in the last six weeks of fighting.→

31. Tokyo: The Japanese high command decides to quit Guadalcanal and pull back its beleaguered garrison to New Georgia.→

31. Libya: French soldiers from Chad, under the command of General Philippe Leclerc, advance into south Fezzan intending to join up with the British Eighth Army.→

31. Rastenburg: Himmler tells Hitler that during August and September 363,211 Jews were "executed" in occupied Europe (→ 20/1).

31. Poniatowa, Poland: 18,000 Soviet PoWs have died this month of starvation.

US plans new offensive on Guadalcanal

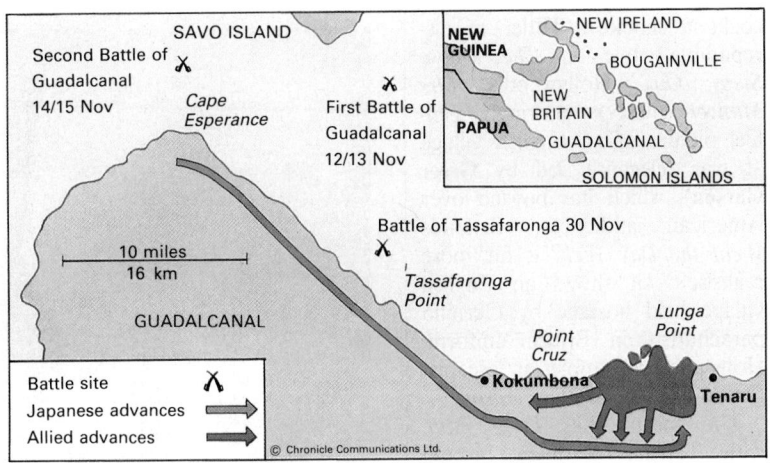

Noumea, 31 December
Guadalcanal, which the Americans have come to know as "the island of death", has become the scene of renewed fighting as fresh US infantry begin a campaign to round up or annihilate the enemy and secure the whole island. Major-General Alexander Patch, the commander of the American XIV Corps, plans to take Mount Austen and begin an enveloping movement. A major offensive is to be mounted in the New Year.

Patch's advance began on 17 December, and by Christmas Eve the Japanese observation post on Mount Austen had fallen. Patch had taken over command of the Guadalcanal garrison on 9 December, relieving Lieutenant-General A Vandergrift, who had command-ed the 1st Marine Division when it landed on Guadalcanal in August 1942. Vandergrift's original intention was to take Mount Austen. Although this had not been achieved, complete victory is in sight at Guadalcanal, so the 1st Marine Division has been sent to Australia for a well-earned rest.

There are now 50,000 US troops on Guadalcanal, while Japanese strength on the island has dwindled to 25,000, many of whom are sick and hungry. The Japanese are virtually isolated and cannot be adequately supplied or reinforced by their navy. In contrast, the Americans, with substantial air force units based on Henderson Field, are able to supply their garrison and relieve and reinforce it with comparative ease.

Henderson, chief appeaser, is dead

London, 30 December
Sir Nevile Henderson, Britain's last envoy to Nazi Germany and the man whose name was firmly joined to the policy of appeasement, has died in London at the age of 60. He went to Berlin in May 1937 and was soon caught up in the diplomatic turmoil of Hitler's repeated territorial demands. During the Sudeten crisis of 1938 Henderson, at a private party, told the Germans there that Britain would not risk even one sailor or airman for Czechoslovakia. On his return to London after the outbreak of war he wrote an account of his work for peace and understanding; he called his book *Failure of a Mission*.

"Oboe" guides RAF bombers to targets

Britain, 31 December
A new navigation device is entering RAF Bomber Command service. This is "Oboe", which has been installed in Mosquitoes of 105 Squadron of the Pathfinder Force. Originally developed from the German 1940 *Lorenz* beams, it first had operational trials against the *Scharnhorst* and *Gneisenau* at Brest in December 1941, but was found to be unreliable. Now refined, it was used by 105 Squadron in an attack on a power station at Lutterade in Holland on the night of 20-21 December. It will be used again tonight against Dusseldorf and a fighter base in Belgium (→ 9/1).

Giraud orders the arrest of 12 VIPs

Algiers, 30 December
General Giraud, the new French high commissioner here since the death of Admiral Darlan, tonight announced that he had ordered the arrest of 12 prominent people, "to prevent further assassinations". Those arrested, he said, were plotting further assassinations, including attempts on the lives of both Giraud himself and President Roosevelt's representative, Robert Murphy (→ 31).

Little Londoners got dressed up to attend a Christmas party given by the US Army Air Force: Sergeant Lewis B Tabor of South Carolina admires one small guest's present, which has come all the way from America.

Arts: imperturbable hero, virile songs

Shostakovich: his Seventh Symphony was begun under siege.

In Which We Serve is being hailed as the best film made so far about the war in either the US or Britain. It is written and directed by **Noel Coward**, who plays the imperturbable captain of the destroyer *Torrin*, sunk in the opening sequence. What the ship means to her captain, petty officer (**Bernard Miles**) and an able-seaman (**John Mills**) is shown in flashback.

Other British films include *The First of the Few*, the struggle of the Spitfire designer R J Mitchell (played by **Leslie Howard**) to get the plane produced in time. The comedian **Will Hay**

cocks a snook at Hitler in disreputable style in *The Goose Steps Out*. Hollywood's *Mrs Miniver* gives a glowingly genteel picture of an English village at war (elegantly led by **Greer Garson**), which has bowled over American audiences. Britain's *Went the Day Well?* is far more realistic – it shows an English village held hostage by German parachutists in British uniform. Hollywood is happier in escapist fiction like *The Maltese Falcon*.

The theatre has *Flare Path*, with **Terence Rattigan** turning the anguish of RAF wives into tense drama. From America comes the sheer hilarity of *Arsenic and Old Lace*: **Lilian Braithwaite** and **Mary Jerrold** play the deadly, ladylike aunts.

The BBC declared its intention to broadcast more "virile" popular songs. Male crooners and "slushy" sentimental numbers are thought to lower the morale of fighting men. But so far there has been no interference with **Vera Lynn's** latest sentimental hit "The White Cliffs of Dover" by an American, **Walter Kent**, who has never seen them. More evocative for some is **Dmitri Shostakovich's** Seventh Symphony, also known as the *Leningrad Symphony* because the composer began work on it while living in the besieged city; it was premiered at the Proms this year.

A bleak moment for Noel Coward as captain of the destroyer "Torrin".

British convoy wins Battle of Barents Sea

In the northern seas the battle is with ice and snow as well as U-boats.

Barents Sea, 31 December
Convoy JW-51B has survived an attack here from a powerful German force comprising the heavy cruiser *Admiral Hipper*, the pocket battleship *Lutzow* and six heavy destroyers. The convoy, the first bound for Murmansk for three months, had been scattered by heavy gales when it was spotted by a U-boat. The German ships sailed to intercept, but Captain Robert Sherbrooke, commanding the escort in the destroyer *Onslow*, had other ideas.

When the enemy was sighted soon after 9am Sherbrooke led four destroyers of the escort out to attack. Mindful of Hitler's orders not to risk losing the big ships, Vice-Admiral Kummetz ordered his force to turn away, but not before

the *Admiral Hipper* had severely damaged the *Onslow* with her 8-inch guns. Sherbrooke was hit in the face by a splinter, leaving his left eye hanging down his cheek. But he continued to direct the battle until Lt-Cdr Kinloch in the *Obedient* took over.

The action then became confused, but the escort behaved like terriers and drove off the much superior force, though not before the destroyer *Achates* and the minesweeper *Bramble* had been sunk. But the *Admiral Hipper* was also damaged and a German destroyer sunk. The convoy, with its cargo of 202 tanks, 2,046 vehicles, 87 fighters, 33 bombers, 11,500 tons of aviation spirit and 54,321 tons of other supplies for Russia, is pressing ahead otherwise unscathed.

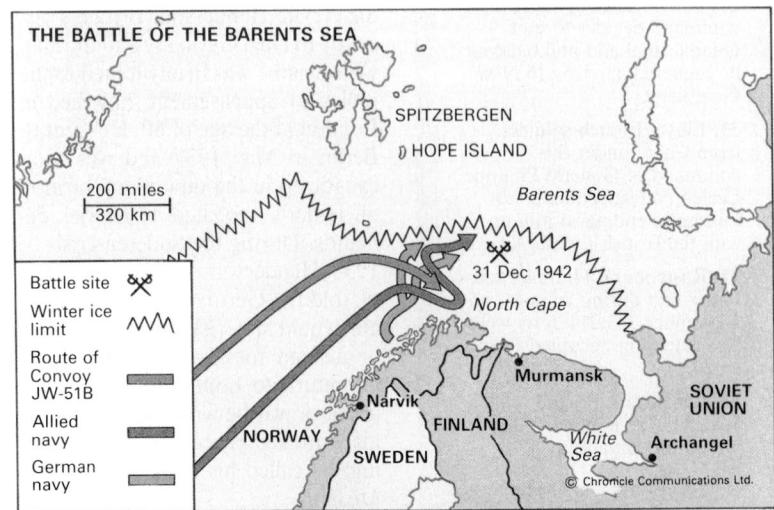

Allies believe tide of war is turning in their favour

London, 31 December
Allied leaders will meet next month to plan the next phase of the war in more confident mood than ever before. As this year comes to an end, they believe the tide is turning in their favour as Axis forces lose ground in Europe and Asia.

However, the borders of Hitler's *Reich* still stretch from the Atlantic to deep inside Russia, from the Arctic to Tunisia. Japan's empire is equally extensive. But its myth of invincibility has been destroyed. Today Japanese forces are in retreat in New Guinea and on Guadal-

canal, in the Solomon Islands. The British have just launched a fresh offensive in Burma where they are backed by Chinese forces hardened by more than five years of war. Yet the tenacity with which Japan has fought demonstrates that the road to Tokyo will be long and bloody.

In Europe, too, it is now the Germans who are forced to tap reserves of fortitude as the Red Army forces them to retreat from the Caucasus. More immediately threatened, though, is the German Sixth Army, encircled and lacking supplies at Stalingrad where Hitler only last

month prematurely proclaimed a "victory". Although a defeat looks more likely, the Germans are redoubtable warriors. They have shown this in Tunisia where reinforcements have halted the Allied advances.

Yet the significance of Tunisia is that it marked the entry of American soldiers into the European theatre of war. The United States is now actively in the war – not only in the Pacific and North Africa and in the air but economically, too, as it produces ever more war supplies. At sea U-boats continue to men-

ace Britain's supply line, particularly in the "black gap" off Greenland where there is no air cover, but there is no longer any real prospect of Britain being invaded. Elsewhere, resistance grows in western Europe while partisans plague Germany in Russia and Yugoslavia. Yet for every brave act of resistance there is bloody retribution, and only this month the Allies drew attention to the massive slaughter of Jews in Nazi-held territories. The tide may be turning, but how many more will die before this Second World War ends?

North Africa: Rommel forced to retreat

North Africa, 31 December
Not since the worst months of the Somme have armies fought in such conditions. For raw Americans, seasoned Britons, reluctant French and the Germans and Italians across the line, the worst enemy is clinging, clawing mud as the rain turns the terrain into a vast quagmire. Operation Torch was to be a fast mobile operation. Instead it has become trench warfare with both sides bogged down.

With Rommel retreating from the east and substantial reinforcements arriving from Europe, Lt-Gen Eisenhower is planning to block Rommel's supply lines with American troops (→ 5/1).

Before the rains: a German crew rests in the shade of its ME110.

Pacific: Japan set to quit Guadalcanal

Pacific, 31 December
Emperor Hirohito is finding Japan's desperate plight on Guadalcanal troublesome. Remarkably, he had to agree today when the imperial general staff sought his concurrence in retreat from the island.

As 1942 came to an end there were abundant signs of a turning of fortunes in the Pacific War. After its strategic triumph in the seas around Guadalcanal, the US Navy felt that it would never be defeated.

Japanese troops are trapped in Papua, and the situation in the Solomons improves daily. The British are pushing laboriously forward through the inhospitable jungles of Burma (→ 1/1).

A US marine armed with a flame-thrower in action against Japan.

Russia: Germans doomed at Stalingrad

Moscow, 31 December
The year is ending on a triumphant note for the Red Army. The great victory at Stalingrad is almost complete, with the survivors of Paulus's army dying of cold, hunger and typhus in the ruins of the city which they sought to capture.

Kotelnikovo, von Manstein's base for the attempt to relieve the city, fell yesterday, and now the whole German position in the Caucusus is threatened as the Russians sweep south. Meanwhile General Zhukov, the architect of the Stalingrad victory, has moved back to Leningrad. Having organized the resistance there a year ago, he has now been ordered by Stalin to break the German siege (→ 1/1).

A Russian view of the "man-eater" whose army they have beaten back.

Germany: forebodings over war setbacks

Berlin, 31 December
Germans end the year in a mood of foreboding, which is reflected in Goebbels's weekly newspaper article. "Wherever we look we see mountains of problems ... Everywhere the path ascends at a steep and dangerous angle and nowhere is there a shady spot where we may stay and rest." A two-day meeting of his propaganda officials has been followed by newspaper articles speaking of setbacks for the Axis forces. Count Galeazzo Ciano, the Italian foreign minister, found the Germans in low spirits when he visited the Fuhrer's HQ. "The atmosphere is heavy," he noted. "No one tries to conceal from me the unhappiness over war news."

"Victory will be ours!" But how many Germans believe this now?

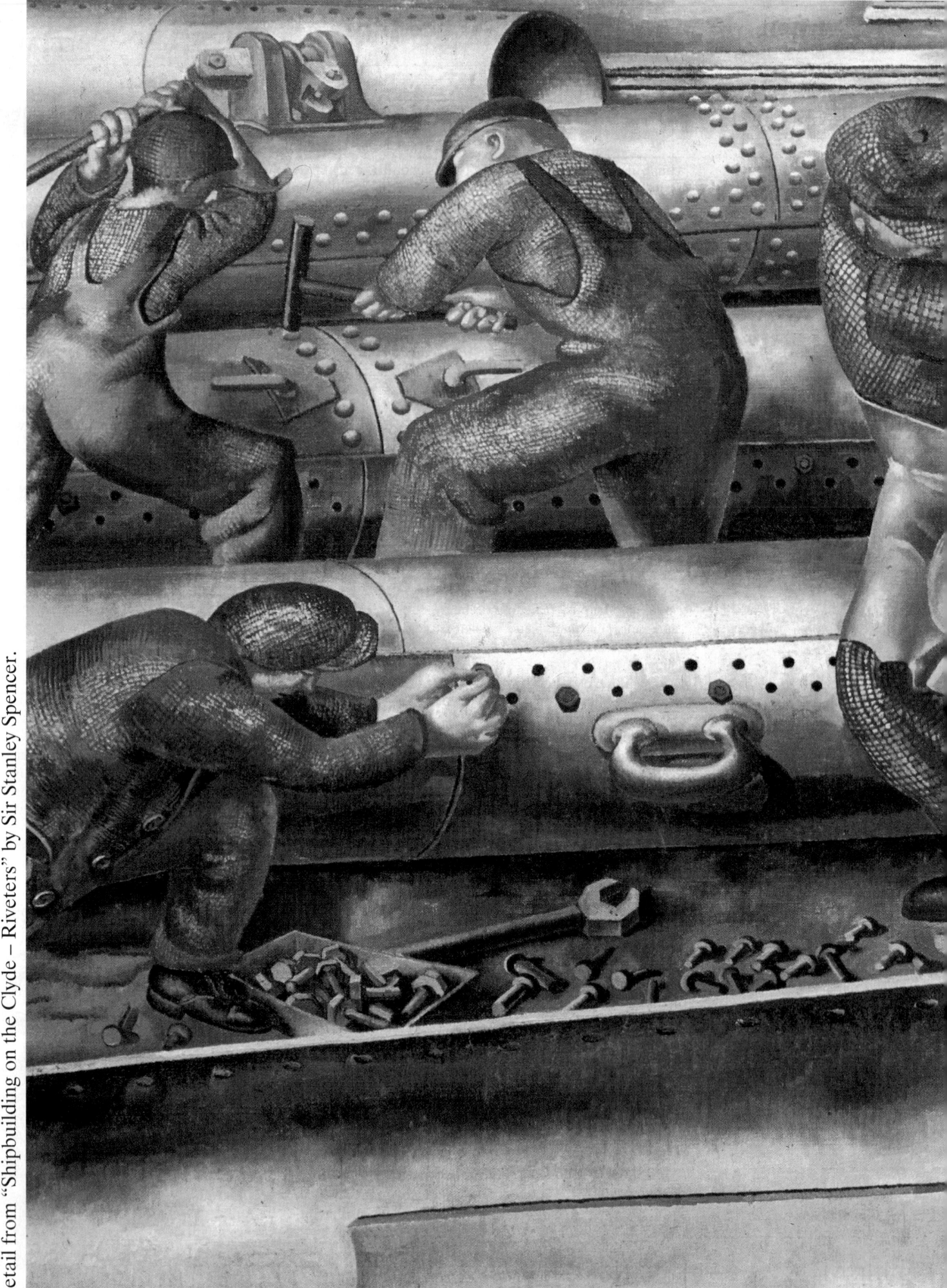

Detail from "Shipbuilding on the Clyde – Riveters" by Sir Stanley Spencer.

January

Su	Mo	Tu	We	Th	Fr	Sa
					1	2
3	4	5	6	7	8	9
10	11	12	13	14	15	16
17	18	19	20	21	22	23
24	25	26	27	28	29	30
31						

1. Tokyo: The Japanese decide to evacuate Guadalcanal (→ 2).

1. Atlantic: The British cruiser *Scylla* sinks the German blockade-runner *Rhakotis* and the Italian transport *Viminale* 200 nautical miles north-west of Cape Finisterre, Brittany.

1. Stalingrad: The Russians squeeze the German army into a pocket of 100 square miles (→ 5).

2. Guadalcanal: US infantry troops attack Gifu on Mount Austen, but fail to overcome Japanese resistance.→

3. Sicily: British "chariots", or human torpedoes, score their first combat success by sinking the Italian light cruiser *Ulpio Traiano* in Palermo harbour.

3. USSR: The Red Army recaptures Mozdok, in the Caucasus (→ 4).

4. USSR: The Russians take Nalchik and Chernyakovsky, the rail centre in the Caucasus.→

4. New Georgia: A US Navy task force bombards the Japanese base at Munda.

5. Tunisia: The Allies make a small advance near Mateur (→ 6).

5. USSR: Soviet forces take Tsimlyansk and Morozovsk, the main airfield used by the *Luftwaffe* to supply Stalingrad.→

6. Libya: The Free French capture the Axis base at Oum el-Araneb (→ 12).

6. Burma: Allied troops meet stiff Japanese resistance at Rathedaung and Donbaik (→ 18).

6. Germany: Grand Admiral Erich Raeder resigns as navy C-in-C following his disastrous handling of the Battle of the Barents Sea.

7. New Guinea: The Japanese land reinforcements at Lae, despite US air attacks (→ 9).

8. Madagascar: General Sir William Platt formally hands over the running of the island to the Free French.

9. New Guinea: The Australian 17th Brigade is airlifted to Wau (→ 13).

Fanatical struggle ends as Buna falls

Papua, New Guinea, 2 January
American troops of the 32nd Division occupied Buna today after a long and intense struggle against fanatical Japanese defenders. The desperate survivors struck out in the surf, clinging to anything that would float. The Japanese had proved themselves great defensive fighters at every point along the Papuan coastal strip, and inflicted sacrificially high casualties on both American and Australian troops.

Buna cost the Allies some 2,870 battle casualties, of whom 913 were Australians. The Japanese are known to have lost 1,390 men killed at Buna. Thus they have inflicted a cost in Allied lives well out of proportion to their numbers. When they saw defeat was inevitable, two of their leaders met solemnly and committed *hara-kiri*.

There were spasmodic flare-ups in the final stages, but at 4.30pm the Government Station, an area of smashed houses, splintered trees and bomb-blasted earth strewn with twisted corpses, was at last in Allied hands. As Buna fell, the Australian 18th Brigade was attacking Japanese positions 1,000 yards, to the east. Lt-Gen Robert Eichelberger ordered a full-scale clearing movement to begin yesterday, to synchronize with the drive by the Australians to clear the Simeni Creek/Giropa Point area. The determined Japanese resistance was a chilling experience for the Allies, who fear that an awful price may have to be paid in time, effort and blood to clear the enemy from the island of New Guinea (→ 7).

The waves wash over Japanese troops who gave their lives in defence of Buna.

Battle for Buna: American troops keep down to avoid Japanese sniper fire.

War declared by puppet Chinese regime

Nanking, 9 January
The Reformed *Kuomintang*, the pro-Tokyo puppet regime which is an offshoot of Chiang Kai-shek's Kuomintang (Nationalists), today gave in to the Japanese and declared war on Britain and America.

In return, Japan has agreed to give up its claims to the international settlement in Shanghai and its territorial concessions in Hankow, Tientsin, Amoy and other major cities. It will also release Wang Ching-wei's client regime from the much-despised Basic Treaty of November 1940 that legitimized Japanese infringements of Chinese sovereignty. Wang's decision to declare war follows a propaganda barrage from Tokyo, culminating two weeks ago in a Japanese decision to adopt a new softer-profile policy towards Wang's China. In place of "supervision" and "guidance", the Wang regime is to receive *koiteki shien* – well-meaning assistance.

Japanese army officers have also been told to be more helpful and respectful to the Chinese, and to avoid harsh, imperious language.

Women want equal rights with men

London, 6 January
A House of Commons select committee today listened to the heads of the women's services and a TUC official putting the case for women to receive war injury compensation on a par with that received by men. The women said that they had heard justifications for differences in pay, but none for the gap in compensation. At present a female officer receives less than a male private for total disablement (→ 7/4).

No surrender, says Stalingrad general

Stalingrad, 9 January
General Paulus, determined to obey Hitler's orders to fight to the end, today ignored a Soviet offer of an honourable surrender for the starving, frozen Germans trapped in the ruins of Stalingrad.

The offer, signed by General Rokossovsky, was carried into the German lines by a Russian captain under the protection of a white flag. The news ran through the weapons-pits and the weary men of the Sixth Army began to think that their ordeal was at last at an end.

This morning they could read the terms of the offer for themselves in leaflets scattered by Soviet aircraft. The Russians promised that everyone who surrendered would be fed and receive medical attention, and that their lives and safety would be guaranteed.

The leaflet also promised that they would "retain their uniforms, badges of rank and decorations, their personal belongings and valuables. Senior officers may retain their swords and bayonets."

Rokossovsky, anxious to free his forces tied down round the city, left no doubt about his intentions if the offer was refused: the Red Army would embark upon the annihilation of the encircled German troops (→ 10).

Russians capture key towns in Caucasus

Driving the Germans south: a Red Army mortar unit loads up in the snow.

Caucasus, 5 January
The Red Army is pushing down from Stalingrad towards Rostov-on-Don with the intention of trapping General von Kleist's Army Group A in the Caucasus. They have only 60 miles (96 km) to go, while von Kleist's nose is stuck into the Caucasus mountains some 400 miles (640 km) away. That nose has been bloodied in the past few days with the Russians recapturing the important towns of Mozdok and Nalchik. Another Soviet drive is developing towards Elista, on the Kalmyk steppe, threatening Armavir, a key link in von Kleist's communi-

cations with Rostov. If the Soviets cut him off they will win a great victory, and Hitler at first seemed to make that possible by refusing to allow von Kleist to withdraw.

He has now changed his mind and von Kleist is conducting a fighting retreat while von Manstein struggles to hold Rostov open for him to escape. It will not be easy. *Der Montag* reports: "Russian tanks come on in solid masses. Between them go units of long-distance ski and snowshoe runners. They carry with them even in the deepest snow, mortar batteries and anti-tank rifles" (→ 11).

Allies give warning about stolen goods

London, 5 January
The Axis powers were given warning today that they will be forced to hand back the vast quantities of loot they have carried off from occupied countries. A foreign office statement claimed that the robberies have "taken every form from open looting to the most cunningly camouflaged financial penetration" and include works of art, bullion, banknotes, shares and commodities. Neutral countries used as hideaways by Axis agents will have to surrender all stolen property. The warning is issued jointly by Britain and its allies.

"Oboe" is no music to citizens of Essen

Germany, 9 January
The RAF is tonight bombing Essen, the home of Krupp's arms factory. Conditions are hazy, but the RAF is using "Oboe", a blind-bombing device that depends on radio pulses transmitted from two stations in England and transmitted back by the aircraft. By measuring the time taken by the pulses to reach the plane and return, its exact position can be calculated, and a short signal is then transmitted to the aircraft to indicate the bomb release point. Errors should normally be of less than 300 yards.

Roumania: mass arrests of plotters

Budapest, 6 January
Conflicting reports received here by telephone from Bucharest speak of arrests and executions following an attempted rising by the disbanded fascists, the Iron Guard, against the pro-Nazi regime of Marshal Ion Antonescu, on the second anniversary of the "civil war" of January 1941. Some say that 80 have been executed; others that 56 leaders of the Iron Guard are in prison. The *coup* was to have coincided with the return of the head of the Iron Guard, Horia Sima, who escaped from Germany but was arrested en route by the Italian police.

Japanese in Guadalcanal fight fiercely despite evacuation plans

Guadalcanal, 4 January
US troops fighting to take Mount Austen, the strategically-located main ridge overlooking the US air base at Henderson Field, have been forced to suspend operations after suffering heavy casualties. The two-week-long attack came to a halt as surprised American troops ran into fire from Japanese pillboxes and foxholes cunningly disguised and cleverly sited to survive the constant US air and artillery bombardment of the last week.

The US suspension provides a breathing space for the 12,000 Japanese under Lt-Gen Hyakutake. With supplies running out he was today ordered to withdraw from the island; but it will be a gradual, fighting retreat, as the US forces discovered on Mount Austen (→ 10).

US marines wading upriver: the battle for Guadalcanal is on temporary hold.

1943

January

Su	Mo	Tu	We	Th	Fr	Sa
					1	2
3	4	5	6	7	8	9
10	11	12	13	14	15	16
17	18	19	20	21	22	23
24	25	26	27	28	29	30
31						

10. Guadalcanal: A US offensive begins (→ 14).

10. USSR: The Russians begin a major offensive all around Stalingrad where the German Sixth Army is trapped (→ 12).

11. USSR: The Red Army launches an offensive against German forces in the Leningrad area. In the Caucasus, the Russians take Pyatigorsk, Georgievsk and Mineralnye Vody (→ 21).

12. Libya: General Leclerc's Fighting (Free) French army captures the Fezzan from the Italians (→ 15).

12. USSR: The attack on Stalingrad is extended with assaults on the Hungarian and German Second Armies (→ 14).

13. Sofia: Thirty-six people are executed and 200 arrested in anti-Nazi protests (→ 5/5).

13. New Guinea: Lieutenant-General Robert Eichelberger takes command of Allied operations (→ 21).

14. Guadalcanal: Japanese troops land at Cape Esperance to prepare evacuation beaches (→ 17).

14. USSR: The Russians take Pitomnik airfield; the German forces at Stalingrad now have only one airfield, Gumrak, connecting them by air with German forces outside the Stalingrad pocket (→ 15).

14. Britain: To counter a "serious increase" in U-boat operations, the RAF switches its bombing campaign from industrial targets to U-boat bases in France, attacking Cherbourg and Lorient.

15. Libya: Allied forces attack Buerat, starting a drive for Tripoli (→ 16).

15. USSR: Soviet troops crush the Hungarian Second Army at Voronezh.

15. Rastenburg: Hitler orders the *Luftwaffe* to fly in 300 tons of supplies a day to the besieged Sixth Army at Stalingrad, an impossible target at this stage.→

16. Baghdad: Iraq declares war on the Axis.

16. Libya: The Allies penetrate the Buerat Line (→ 18).

Summit at Casablanca

The allied leaders, and their chiefs of staff, take a break from the talks.

Casablanca, 14 January
The two men meeting in the heavily-guarded compound at the Hotel Anfa, Casablanca, are known as Admiral Q and Mr P. In fact, they are President Roosevelt and Mr Churchill; with their military advisers, they are planning the next moves against the Axis powers.

The original intention had been to hold a "Big Three" conference, but Stalin said that he could not leave the country; the fighting on the Stalingrad front, he said, demands "my constant presence near our troops". Stalin rounded off his letter to Roosevelt with a reminder that the president and Churchill had promised to open a second front in Europe by spring 1943.

But the US and Britain are keen to exploit the imminent Allied victory in North Africa by striking across the Mediterranean, probably at Sicily although some favour Sardinia, and knocking Italy out of the war. The planned assault on northwest Europe will almost certainly be delayed, as the combined chiefs of staff say that there are as yet too many logistical problems. Italy, however, could be tackled this year and, the British say, would divert German forces from Russia (→ 23).

Total mobilization planned by Hitler

Berlin, 13 January
Adolf Hitler today issued a decree which entitles the authorities to order German men and women to undertake war tasks deemed necessary for the defence of the *Reich*. This first step towards "total mobilization" is intended to release all able-bodied men for military duty or other work at the front.

The decree says it is "necessary to locate all men and women whose efforts towards this goal are not yet fully utilized and to harness their full energies". Large-scale and extended "training and re-orientation" will be introduced. Older men and married women are among the prime targets of this new labour mobilization, which is likely to begin later this month (→ 28).

First RAF raid on Berlin since 1941

Berlin, 16 January
The RAF has returned to Berlin tonight after 14 months away. The city is being hit by 8,000-pound bombs and thousands of incendiaries. The anti-aircraft barrage is surprisingly light; air defences may have been moved, perhaps to the Ruhr. The Germans are relying on camouflage and dummy fires to mislead the bombers; but pilots were told to expect these (→ 17).

Giraud and de Gaulle: two generals speak on behalf of France

Casablanca, 14 January
Two French generals, each claiming to speak for France, have finally met in a villa in a suburb of Casablanca where the Allied leaders are now meeting. Charles de Gaulle, leader of the Fighting (Free) French in London, agreed to talk to Henri Giraud, based in Algiers, only after intense pressure from Churchill.

De Gaulle loftily rejected an invitation from Roosevelt to come to Casablanca; he considered it an insult to be invited by an American to visit French Morocco. At length he gave way, but even then it was some hours before he agreed to meet Giraud, who was lodged in a villa next door. Churchill told him that if he persisted in his obduracy he could find himself abandoned by the British, upon whose goodwill he is entirely dependent.

De Gaulle, who has been the symbol of French resistance since the collapse of 1940, deeply mistrusts the conservative and anti-republican Giraud. For his part, Giraud, who escaped from a German prisoner-of-war camp last year, rejects de Gaulle's claim to be the sole leader of the Fighting French and refuses to cooperate in joint military operations. After a two-hour meeting the two generals agreed on only one point: to keep in touch (→ 23).

Giraud and de Gaulle shake on it.

Red Army intensifies pressure on German forces

Russian troops make their way through the snow-covered ruins of Stalingrad: the city has been almost razed to the ground in the months of fighting and siege.

Assault squeezes the Stalingrad pocket

Stalingrad, 16 January
General Rokossovsky is carrying out his threat to annihilate the Germans trapped in the Stalingrad pocket. Attacking from the west, he is hammering the exhausted, starving Sixth Army against the anvil of the city's Russian defenders.

Pitomnik airfield fell to his tanks two days ago, a grievous blow for the Germans, as it is the only airfield able to take planes at night. Hitler has put Field Marshal Erhard Milch of the *Luftwaffe* in charge of supplying the trapped army, but even that organizing genius can do nothing without air-

fields. Only Gumrak, where Paulus has his headquarters, is still open to the *Luftwaffe*, and that is clogged by the wounded and sick, who lie out on their stretchers, day and night, their blood frozen into red ice, waiting to be flown home.

The Germans are still fighting stubbornly, but they have little left to fight with and the hopelessness of their situation is only too clear to them. One soldier, in a letter home, says: "We're quite alone, with no help from outside. Hitler has left us in the lurch. When Stalingrad falls you will hear about it. Then you will know I shall not return" (→19).

Russians move to break Leningrad siege

Leningrad, 11 January
In the darkness before dawn this morning, with the thermometer at minus nine degrees Fahrenheit (-23 Celsius), the Red Army opened Operation *Iskra* [Spark] to break the German siege of Leningrad.

Two thousand guns and mortars smashed the frozen silence as the white-clad soldiers of the Second Shock Army advanced round the southern shore of Lake Ladoga towards the lakeside town of Schlusselburg. At the same time units of the Sixty-Seventh Army of the Leningrad front, supported by warships of the Baltic fleet, struck at their besiegers across the frozen river Neva. The plan, made by General Zhukov, newly arrived from Stalingrad, calls for the Leningrad army and the relieving force to meet at a workers' housing development south of Schlusselburg. This would enable a supply route to be opened round the lake to bring food to the long-suffering citizens of Leningrad.

One daring part of Zhukov's plan has already succeeded. The 12th Infantry Brigade, all expert skiers, has swooped through the freezing mist

over Lake Ladoga to take the Germans in the rear. The Russian forces are only ten miles (16 km) apart at some points, but they face a well-prepared German army which includes the Spanish Blue Division (*Azul*), "volunteers" sent by General Franco. It will be a bitter struggle (→18).

Timoshenko, who failed to stop the German advance to Stalingrad.

Map labels:
Kharkov
100 miles / 160 km
Russian front line, 31 Dec 1942
SOVIET UNION
Gomrak
Stalingrad
Stalino
Volga
Rostov-on-Don
Astrakhan
© Chronicle Communications Ltd.

1943

January

Su	Mo	Tu	We	Th	Fr	Sa
					1	2
3	4	5	6	7	8	9
10	11	12	13	14	15	16
17	18	19	20	21	22	23
24	25	26	27	28	29	30
31						

US troops brave bitter cold to take island

Aleutian Islands, 12 January

In severe cold and vicious seas, US troops today landed on the island of Amchitka, 90 miles (144 km) from the Japanese-held island of Kiska. Four troop transports ferried the 2,000 men in, but as they were wading ashore through the freezing sea the weather worsened. The destroyer *Worden* sank after she was dashed against the rocks, losing 14 men. The fierce north Pacific gale swept one troop transport aground and smashed most of the landing craft. Nor are their troubles over now that they have landed. Men and jeeps are sinking in the soft ground, and it cannot be long before the Japanese, who moved into the Aleutians last summer, discover them (→ 19).

Ankle-deep on chilly Amchitka.

Germans spearhead fresh assault on Tito

Bihac, Yugoslavia, 15 January

Hitler's fury with Yugoslav partisans boiled over today when 40,000 Germans, Italians and *Ustachi* (Croatian fascists) began the biggest offensive yet against Tito's "ghost army". Tito has already been forced out of his headquarters here on the Croatian border, and his partisans are moving south towards their stronghold on the slopes of Mount Durmitor, in Montenegro.

Organized retreat – with short, sharp counter-attacks, ambushes and demolition before disappearing into the rough terrain – is a technique used by Tito with increasing effect. The frustrated Axis troops can only reply with savagery meted out on any they suspect of collaborating with the partisans. Mass executions are a daily event, with the Ustachi at the forefront in bestiality. Their leader, Ante Pavelich, the Nazis' client ruler of Croatia, has just returned from meeting Hitler in the Ukraine.

Yugoslav partisans are pinning down thousands of Axis troops, but although Stalin is airlifting supplies to Soviet partisans, Tito's pleas for aid have been turned down (→ 15/4).

January 15: US forces pass midstream in Guadalcanal. One boat carries wounded back from the front, while the other is taking supplies upstream.

17. Germany: Raiding Berlin for the second night in a row, the RAF drops 8,000-pound bombs on the city; the BBC broadcaster Richard Dimbleby flies as an observer.

17. London: Anti-aircraft shells and shrapnel kill 23 people and injure 60 during a raid on the city by 118 German planes; six are reported lost.

17. Guadalcanal: The Japanese strongpoint at Gifu is heavily shelled by US forces, who use loudspeakers to broadcast a demand for surrender.→

18. Burma: Indian troops attack Japanese positions at Donbaik (→ 8/2).

18. Moscow: General Zhukov is promoted to marshal of the Soviet Union.→

18. Warsaw: German troops start new deportations from the Jewish ghetto (→ 20).

19. Stalingrad: The siege of the German Sixth Army is holding down 90 of 259 Soviet formations (→ 21).

19. Aleutian Islands: In the past day a US fleet of two cruisers and four destroyers has bombarded Attu Island (→ 26/3).

20. Berlin: Himmler demands more trains to "wind up" the extermination of the Jews quickly, even though they are desperately needed to ferry arms to the eastern front.→

21. New Guinea: US and Australian troops join up at Sanananda.→

21. USSR: Gumrak, the last German airfield inside the Stalingrad pocket, falls. Hitler cables Paulus: "Surrender is out of the question."→

21. USSR: Voroshilovsk, in the Caucasus, falls to the Red Army (→ 22).

22. Rastenburg: Hitler orders that tank production must take priority over shipbuilding.

22. USSR: The *Luftwaffe* air base at Salsk, in the Caucasus, falls (→ 23).

23. USSR: Soviet forces capture Armavir, an important rail junction in the Caucasus oilfields (→ 29).

Allied war leaders put Italian invasion before second front

Casablanca, 23 January

In nine days of talks at Casablanca, in Morocco, Mr Churchill and President Roosevelt have settled their war campaign plans for the year. It was the fourth wartime meeting between the two leaders. The US president told a press conference today that they had agreed on "unconditional surrender" by the Axis powers. There would be no deals; the enemy would be disarmed, and those responsible for atrocities would be put on trial.

The official communique speaks of "war plans and enterprises to be undertaken against Germany, Italy and Japan with the view to drawing the utmost advantage from the favourable turn of events at the close of 1942". No hint was given of where the next blow will fall, but it is believed that the Allies have decided on an invasion of Italy this year. Tribute is paid to "the enormous weight of the war which Russia is successfully bearing"; the "prime object" of the western Allies is "to draw as much weight as possible off the Russian armies by engaging the enemy as heavily as possible at the best selected points". But Stalin's desire for a second front in north-western Europe will have to wait until 1944.

Britain and US give up rights in China

Chungking, 17 January

In a move to strengthen the alliance with China and end a longstanding Chinese grievance, Britain and the US have surrendered their century-old neo-colonial territorial rights to the international settlements. The decision by Britain and America, formally agreed last week, abrogates their citizens' rights to immunity from Chinese law and national rights to station troops under the so-called "unequal treaties", legacies of the Opium Wars and the Boxer Rebellion. The deal was the result of pressure from the Chinese Nationalist leader, Chiang Kai-shek, who said that the humiliation of a century had been wiped away.

Tripoli falls to Monty's Desert Army

Tripoli, 23 January

An hour before dawn today, a lone scout car of the 11th Hussars drove gingerly through the deserted suburbs of Tripoli and into the city centre itself – to find no sign of Axis troops. At first light, a Valentine tank called Dorothy – after the driver's sweetheart in Liverpool – rumbled into the main square with seven Gordon Highlanders clinging to it. Tripoli was in British hands.

Three columns had been poised all night outside the city walls for this moment. Highlanders of the 51st Division had approached from the east along the heavily-mined and booby-trapped coastal road, where every bridge and culvert had been demolished.

Another force had approached from the west; but the most spectacular approach was made by the 7th Armoured Division which had waited on the mountains overlooking Tripoli and charged towards the south of the city.

A delighted Montgomery, who had even predicted the date of Tripoli's fall, accepted surrender from the city's bemedalled mayor, his battledress and beret contrasting markedly with the Italian's full dress uniform. "I have nothing but praise for the men of the Eighth Army," he told his assembled war correspondents (→ 25).

To applause from the citizens of Tripoli an Eighth Army tank rumbles in.

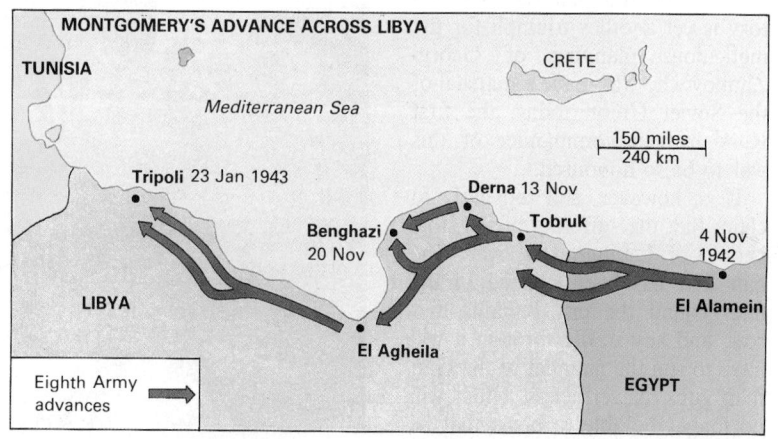

MONTGOMERY'S ADVANCE ACROSS LIBYA

TUNISIA

CRETE

Mediterranean Sea

Tripoli 23 Jan 1943

Derna 13 Nov

Benghazi 20 Nov

Tobruk

150 miles
240 km

4 Nov 1942

LIBYA

El Alamein

El Agheila

Eighth Army advances

EGYPT

Stalingrad defence crumbles as Soviets put on the pressure

Stalingrad, 23 January

The last resistance in Stalingrad is crumbling. The Sixth Army has been been split into two pockets north and south of the city. The last German airfield in the Stalingrad pocket, at Gumrak, fell two days ago to Soviet tanks, which crushed long lines of wounded as they lay on stretchers waiting to be evacuated.

The last men to get out left in a Heinkel He111 bomber. There were 19 of them and seven bags of mail, the last letters from doomed men to their families. Now, the only way in which the defenders can be supplied is by parachute.

With defeat inevitable, some Germans are surrendering or saving their last bullets for themselves. General von Hartmann, the commander of the 71st Infantry Division, stood upright on a railway embankment and fired his carbine at the advancing Russians until he was mown down by a machine gun. Paulus, realising the futility of prolonging his men's agony, has told Hitler: "Further defence senseless. Collapse inevitable." and asked for permission to surrender. Hitler's reply reads: "Surrender is forbidden; Sixth Army will hold their positions to the last man and the last round" (→ 26).

Japanese lose main Guadalcanal base

Guadalcanal, 23 January

Japanese forces beating a clandestine retreat on Guadalcanal suffered two further major losses today with the fall of their main base at Kokumbona and their last outpost on Mount Austen.

Kokumbona's surrender followed a three-day naval barrage as four US destroyers under Rear-Admiral Walden Ainsworth fired 600 shells battering Japanese shore positions. Ainsworth's ships are now heading for Kolombangara, northwest of Guadalcanal, to join an 11-ship squadron shelling the Japanese airfield being built at Vila. On Mount Austen US troops are now in control after 100 Japanese defending Gifu HQ charged into the US lines (→ 24).

Preparing to broadcast a surrender ultimatum to the Japanese.

War work shortens unemployment queue

Britain, 23 January

Britain now has the fullest employment in its history. Nearly 17.5 million men and women are in civilian jobs. Latest unemployment figures from the ministry of labour have dropped below 100,000, less than a tenth of the inter-war figures when there were never fewer than a million unemployed. And the number is still falling.

The figures include 6,769,000 women, an increase of two million on the number working before the war. This includes three million married women. Several hundred thousand more are in part-time jobs. There are 4.7 million men and women in the armed forces, almost equalled by the 4.3 million in munitions industries.

Women employees make light work of their jobs in a brick factory.

Leningrad siege cracks

Russian infantry push forward in the fight to break the blockade of Leningrad.

Leningrad, 18 January
The 16-month-long siege of Leningrad began to crack today when Captain Sabatkin of the Leningrad army exchanged the password with Captain Demidov of the relieving force on a corpse-littered field near Schlusselburg, on the shore of Lake Ladoga. The formalities over, the two men embraced in celebration of their victory.

It has taken five days of fierce fighting for the Russians to break the German ring round the city, for the Germans have spent the last year building their siege fortifications with minefields and a net-

work of concrete pillboxes. The victory is yet another triumph for the meticulous planning of Georgi Zhukov who was made a marshal of the Soviet Union today, the first Russian field commander of this war to be so honoured.

It is, however, still too early to claim that the suffering of the stoic people of Leningrad is over. The gap that has been opened in the lines round the city remains narrow, and any traffic through it will have to run the gauntlet of the German guns. Nevertheless, Hitler will no longer be able to boast that he will destroy this proud city (→ 27).

Starving Japanese end Papuan resistance

Port Moresby, 23 January
The Papuan campaign has ended. After three weeks of bloody fighting in the pestilential swamps of the New Guinea coast, the Allies have occupied Sanananda, eliminating the final enemy pockets in Papua.

The advance on Sanananda began immediately Buna fell, but progress was blocked by mangrove swamps. The Allies used two fresh American battalions to establish road blocks. On 12 January the 18th Australian Brigade was then used to press the encircled enemy, but came under unexpected pressure when its tanks were put out of action. In a disheartening day in which little ground was gained, 100 men were lost.

Next day the Japanese began withdrawing from their forward

positions, and barges were taking them away. It was learned later that the Japanese had no rice left and were dying of starvation. The Japanese commander was ordered to move his forces from Sanananda to the Kumusi or Mambare river mouths and thence to Lae and Salamaua.

Victory has come to the Allies in Papua, but the cost has been high. Australian dead total 2,165, and 3,533 have been wounded. American losses are 671 killed and 2,172 wounded. As against this loss the Allies have won an area vital to the development of airfields and port facilities to support the advance against Rabaul. The Japanese commitment to Papua was about 20,000, of whom 13,000 are estimated to have been killed (→ 1/2).

Sacks of rice that the Japanese were forced to abandon, now in Allied hands.

Brothels may boost SS "performance"

France, 17 January
Brothels should be established at all *Waffen-SS* garrisons in occupied France. This is the view of Heinrich Himmler, the *Reichsfuhrer SS*, who believes that what he calls "this naturalness" will increase the performance of his men, presumably in their military duties.

Himmler's order was conveyed in a letter to Karl Albrecht Oberg, the head of police and the SS in occupied France, on 5 January. He is apparently worried by the increase in sexual diseases amongst the SS soldiers; prostitutes in the brothels, however, would come under regular medical supervision.

Schoolchildren killed in "Luftwaffe" raid on southern England

Rescue workers and anxious relatives at Catford Central School for Girls.

London, 21 January
The first daylight raid on the British capital for six months killed 38 children and six teachers at a girls' junior school at Catford, in southeast London, yesterday. The school was demolished by a bomb from a German raider that dived out of low cloud before a warning had sounded. Most of the children were aged between five and seven.

Rescue work went on all night under flares. Teachers, soldiers and city workers helped to dig for survivors. "The building just fell to pieces," said an eye-witness. "After that it was a pitiful sight, passing the dead and injured children." A Royal Artillery gunner dug with bare hands for his two daughters.

Jews launch armed revolt in Warsaw

Members of the Nazi-controlled Jewish police force in the ghetto: now their own people are fighting for their lives.

Warsaw, 21 January

In an astonishing turn of events, Jews here have staged an armed revolt against their captors. A column of deportees heading down Niska Street to the railway station, and the train to Treblinka, suddenly turned on its Nazi escorts with handguns and grenades.

The Jewish freedom fighters, led by Mordechai Anielewicz, then barricaded themselves into a nearby house, snipers keeping German reinforcements at bay. Eventually the Nazis set the house on fire; the resisters continued shooting to the last bullet. Only one survived the blaze; 12 Germans had been killed.

SS General Jurgen Stroop, ordered by Himmler to liquidate the ghetto by 13 February, is surprised by the strength of Jewish resistance.

He underestimates the bitterness that has been fermenting for the last three years, expressed in the chant: 'Jews will live to settle scores, Jews have lived and will endure" and popular songs with lyrics like:
*When we had nothing to eat
They gave us a turnip, or a beet
Here, take food, take fleas
Have some typhus, die of disease.*

Starvation has killed the weakest, and deportations have sent all the older people and most of the children to their deaths, mostly at Treb-

linka. Those still left behind are mainly stronger, young single men and women who realize that "resettlement" means death. For months the *Zydowska Organizacja Bojowa* [Jewish Fighting Organization] has been smuggling arms into the ghetto; now, the moment for using them has come. As well as fighting the Germans, the Jews are also doing battle with the hated force of Nazi-controlled Jewish police, made up of their own people who have committed atrocities in exchange for meagre privileges.

Today, German grenades hurled through windows were answered by a hail of bullets from every rooftop;

the Germans have withdrawn. With their limited resources, it would be unrealistic to expect the Jews to do more than delay their seemingly inevitable fate.

But pride and hope have returned to the downtrodden, persecuted people of the ghetto. As Tuvia Boryskowski says: "The battle on Niska Street encouraged us. For the first time since the occupation we saw Germans clinging to walls, crawling on the ground, running for cover, hesitating before making a step in the fear of being hit by a Jewish bullet. The cries of the wounded caused us joy, and increased our thirst for battle" (→16/5).

"Respond, at least", Polish Jews beg US

New York, 21 January

Jewish leaders have received a plea from the Warsaw Ghetto-dwellers, who say that they are "poised at the brink of annihilation". It says:

"We notify you of the greatest crime of all times, about the murder of millions of Jews in Poland ...

"Brothers – the remaining Jews in Poland live with the awareness that in the most terrible days of our history you did not come to our aid. Respond, at least, in the last days of our life" (→30).

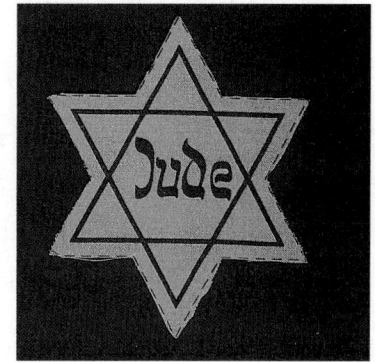

The Nazi brand for Jewish people.

The neutral seven who stay out of European battles

London, 23 January

Though Hitler's tanks have rolled over Europe from the Atlantic to the Urals, seven states have somehow managed to stay out of the fighting war. Yet they are playing a vital role in the deadly struggle between the Allies and the Axis powers.

Switzerland, with its leaky frontier with Germany, is a hive of espionage activity. British agents with top-level contacts in the armed forces, and even in German intelligence, were able to warn Stalin of Hitler's invasion plans. The Russians have built up a major espionage operation in Lucerne; the American Allan Dulles has made Geneva his HQ. The Swiss warned potential invaders in 1939 that at the first sign of attack they would blow up Alpine tunnels.

The Portuguese capital, Lisbon, is another centre for Allied and Axis spies, who are chiefly concerned with shipping movements. British and German agents have an understanding not to use the same cafes. In neighbouring Spain, General Franco was tempted to take his country into the war in 1940, when he thought that Hitler would win; since then the wily *Caudillo* has thought differently, and Spain has become a regular part of the escape route for Allied aircrew and PoWs.

Admiral Canaris and his *Abwehr* undercover agents have tried in vain to use Eire as a back-door into Britain. In the middle of Mussolini's capital the neutral Vatican is being used by anti-Nazi Germans as a contact point with the Allies. Sweden's neutrality is bought by allowing German military trains to cross over to Finland – and by secretly selling ball-bearings to Britain and Germany.

Turkey, strategically placed on the borders of the USSR and the German-occupied Balkans, is another neutral nation humming with the activities of agents and double agents.

1943

January

Su	Mo	Tu	We	Th	Fr	Sa
					1	2
3	4	5	6	7	8	9
10	11	12	13	14	15	16
17	18	19	20	21	22	23
24	25	26	27	28	29	30
31						

24. Guadalcanal: The US Navy shells Japanese positions on the island.→

25. North Africa: General Giovanni Messe of the Italian First Army takes overall command of Axis forces in North Africa (→ 4/2).

26. Stalingrad: The Sixth Army pocket is split as Soviet troops join up to the west of the city (→ 30).

27. USSR: The railway line between Leningrad and Moscow is reopened, enabling supplies to be delivered to the starving population (→ 14/4).

28. Germany: All men between 16 and 65, and women between 17 and 45, are to be mobilized for war work.

29. Berlin: Dr Ernst Kaltenbrunner succeeds the late Reinhart Heydrich as head of the RSHA [*Reich Chief Security Office*], controlling the SS, *Gestapo*, extermination squads and death camps.

29. USSR: Soviet forces liberate Kropotkin, in the Caucasus.

30. Adana, Turkey: Churchill and Alan Brooke promise Turkey direct military help if it is forced into the war.

30. France: Joseph Darnand, a pro-Nazi activist, forms the *Milice Francaise* [French Militia] to help the Germans to round up Resistants and Jews (→ 6/2).

30. Germany: Karl Donitz is promoted to grand admiral and appointed Raeder's successor as C-in-C of the navy.

30. USSR: Soviet forces recapture the Maikop oilfields, in the Caucasus.

30. Stalingrad: On the edge of defeat, Paulus is promoted to field marshal.→

30. Germany: The RAF raids Hamburg tonight, using the H2S radar navigation aid for the first time.

31. General Vittorio Ambrosio succeeds Marshal Ugo Cavallero, whom Mussolini has sacked, as chief of staff of the Italian army.

Stalingrad: first Germans surrender

Stalingrad, 31 January
Field Marshal Friedrich Paulus surrendered to a Russian lieutenant in Stalingrad this evening. Yesterday, knowing that no German field marshal had ever surrendered, Hitler had promoted him to the highest rank in the army. Then the Fuhrer sent one last signal: "Each day the fortress of Stalingrad can continue to hold out is of importance."

The implication was obvious: the new field marshal should die rather than surrender. But Paulus had no more fight left in him. Exhausted, his face twitching, he retreated to the *Univermag*, the department store in the city's Red Square. The Russians captured the square and learnt from a prisoner that Paulus was in the building, which was being pounded by guns and mortars. A German officer waved a white flag at the Russians preparing to rush the store, and Lieutenant Fedor Yelchenko dashed across the square.

The young Russian found Paulus lying, fully dressed, on his camp

The defeated Paulus at Stalingrad.

bed in the cellar. "Well, that finishes it," said the lieutenant. Paulus nodded. Yelchenko sent for a car which took Paulus to Rokossovky's headquarters. Paulus, determined to put an end to his own struggle, but unwilling to sign a formal capitulation, has, in fact, only surrendered himself and his headquarters

staff. Sector commanders are left to make their own arrangements, but as the news of his surrender spreads so the fighting fades away in the southern pocket.

The Germans continue to resist from strongpoints in the northern pocket. Here General Strecker, the commander of XI Corps, is holding out round the tractor works and the Red October ordnance works where so much of the cruel hand-to-hand fighting which has been such a feature of this battle has raged. Hitler has radioed to him: "I expect the northern pocket of Stalingrad to hold out to the finish. Every day, every hour, thus gained decisively benefits the remainder of the front."

Such exhortations mean little to the hollow-eyed, freezing, disease-ridden men fighting to survive in the rubble of Stalingrad. Strecker can hardly hold out for more than a couple of days, and then he and his men will join the columns of prisoners trudging across the icy steppe to captivity.

Stalin's soldiers smash "supermen" myth

Stalingrad, 31 January
The defeat of the *Wehrmacht* at Stalingrad has two immediate strategic effects: colossal losses have been inflicted on the German army, and seven Soviet armies have been released to move against the German forces in the Caucasus. Important as these strategic effects are, the

impact on the morale of the Wehrmacht is even more important. The Fuhrer's Aryan supermen have been humilated by the Russian soldiers whom they despised as *Untermenschen* [subhumans]. German generals have been out-thought, their men outfought, and the legend of the *Blitzkrieg* shattered.

Germany shattered by cost of defeat

Stalingrad, 31 January
The human and material losses of the German army and *Luftwaffe* at Stalingrad are quite staggering. According to the Russians, 120,000 Germans have been killed and 91,000 taken prisoner, including no less than 24 generals. The Roumanian Third and Fourth Armies and the Italian Eighth Army have also been destroyed.

The losses in guns and tanks are enormous, enough to equip 80 divisions. The Russians destroyed or captured 3,500 self-propelled guns and tanks, over 12,000 guns and mortars and 75,000 vehicles.

The Luftwaffe lost 489 transport aircraft in its attempt to supply the trapped army, and 744 bombers and fighters during the battle. Another 542 aircraft, mostly damaged, were captured by the Russians. The Luftwaffe suffered especially from the loss of instructors flying the transports. It is doubtful if either the army or air force will ever fully recover from Stalingrad (→2/2).

HOW THE NET CLOSED ON THE GERMANS

SOVIET UNION

Kotluban
Yerzovka
Tractor factory
Gorodishche
Gumrak
Stalingrad
Volga
Paulus HQ
Alekoeyevka
Karpovka
Krasnaya Sloboda
Staro Dubrovka
Beketovka
Ivanovka

© Chronicle Communications Ltd.

Russian front line, 8 January
Russian front line, 17 January
German pockets 25 January

10 miles
16 km

A German army – and a Russian city – in ruins

The wasteland that is the newly-liberated city of Stalingrad: acres of ruins and bombed-out buildings spread out beneath a covering of snow.

A Stalingrad family returns home.

A Soviet soldier hoists a flag on a building overlooking the central square.

Axis troops finally give up the fight.

1943

February

Su	Mo	Tu	We	Th	Fr	Sa
	1	2	3	4	5	6
7	8	9	10	11	12	13
14	15	16	17	18	19	20
21	22	23	24	25	26	27
28						

Wilhelmshaven hit in first US air raids

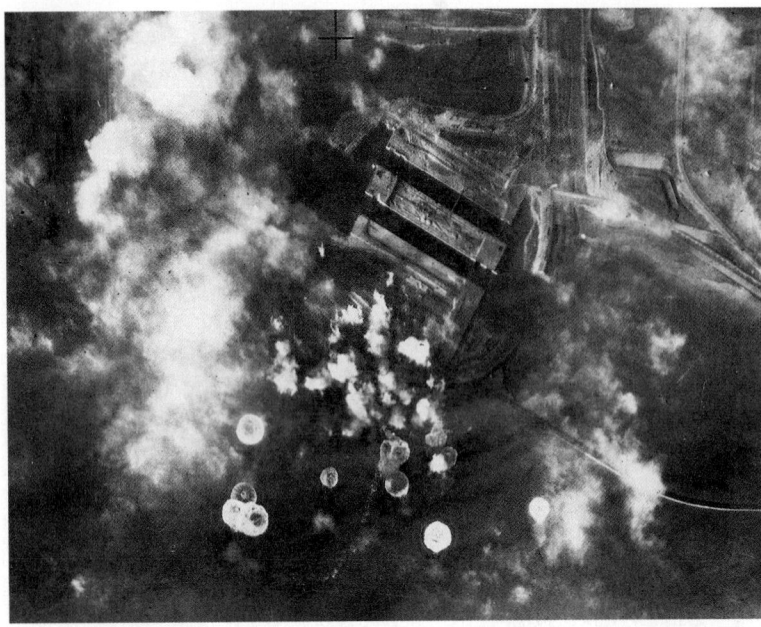

US bombs rain down: some hit their targets, others just make a big splash.

Germany, 27 January

American bombers made their first raids on Germany proper today when 84 Flying Fortresses and seven Liberators made an unescorted daylight raid on the Wilhelmshaven naval base. The Fortresses also hit other targets in north-west Germany.

Wilhelmshaven is considered a tough target by the RAF, but while the 55 bombers which actually carried out the raid were attacked by fighters the crews said it was "not nearly as tough as St Nazaire".

Captain J L Ryan of "Sweetpea" said: "I noticed what might have been a capital ship. I figured we'd get heavy *flak* ... but there wasn't enough to bother us."

Captain Robert Riordan, recently awarded the Distinguished Flying Cross (DFC) for bringing home three crippled "Forts", said that the raid was one of his easiest missions: "We came home on all four engines and that was an agreeable change."

Major E R T Holmes, the Surrey and England batsman, now a flak specialist, flew in the raid and took over a gun when the gunner was injured. He praised the tight formations of the Americans. Three Fortresses failed to return (→ 25/2).

First RAF daylight raids on Berlin

Germany, 30 January

The RAF marked Nazi Germany's tenth anniversary today by twice bombing Berlin. RAF Mosquitoes caught the city by surprise, and the morning raid caused the *Luftwaffe* chief, Hermann Goering, to postpone a radio talk by half an hour. The second raid, in the afternoon, coincided with a speech by the propaganda minister, Dr Goebbels. Three planes flew in each raid, and found Berlin under clear skies. Sgt J Massey of Sheffield said: "The only unusual thing to happen was that we brought a dead gull back on one of our wings" (→ 11/2).

Vichy government hands power to the pro-Nazi "Milice"

Vichy, 31 January

With the three colours of the tricouleur as a backdrop, French leaders met in a hot-springs hotel here today and pledged themselves to help in the fight against Gaullists, Jews, Freemasons and communists – anyone, in fact, who opposes collaboration with Germany.

The newly-founded *Milice Francaise* [French Militia] and its general secretary, Joseph Darnand, was meeting members of the Vichy government, notably Pierre Laval, the head of the government, his junior minister Admiral Platon, Abel Bonnard, the minister of education, and Paul Marion, the junior minister for information.

After the meeting had sung the anthem of the Milice, *Le chant des cohortes,* Darnand and Laval outlined the duties of the future militiamen: to support, by propaganda, the actions of the government, and to help in the fight against the black market and in the maintaining of order. The law creating the Milice was passed yesterday by the Vichy head of state, Marshal Petain. The Milice will be run by the head of the government, assisted by the general secretary, who will be in effective control. Darnand, a man completely loyal to the marshal, Nazism and collaboration, thus becomes a key strongman in the Vichy regime.

Wartime science is hitting the target

London, 31 January

RAF bombers last night used a new navigation device on operations. Called H2S, but already known by the crews as "Home Sweet Home", it is an airborne downward-looking radio-location system. The image of the terrain which the aircraft is overflying is reproduced on a cathode-ray tube, which the navigator can compare with his map. Unlike Gee it is not range-dependent. Aircraft of the newly formed No 8 (Pathfinder) Group used H2S in an attack on Hamburg, chosen because the nearby coast and river Elbe would show up well.

US comes off worst at Rennell Island

Solomon Islands, 30 January

An error by Rear-Admiral Robert Giffen has cost the US a heavy cruiser and damaged a destroyer. Giffen's 15-ship destroyer and cruiser force, TF18, was heading for Guadalcanal. His error was to deploy the cruisers in parallel lines and the destroyers in an arc in front – giving little protection when 31 Japanese G4M bombers struck. Before the raid, which took place 50 miles (80 km) north of Rennell Island, in the Solomons, Giffen allowed two escorting carriers to proceed separately because they were slowing him down (→ 1/2).

1. New Guinea: The Australians repel the Japanese less than 400 yards from Wau airfield (→ 6).

1. Guadalcanal: Twenty Japanese destroyers evacuate 5,000 soldiers from Cape Esperance.→

1. Mediterranean: The fast minelayer HMS *Welshman*, which took urgent stores to Malta during the siege, is sunk by the U-boat U617 off Crete.

1. Rastenburg: Hitler holds a military conference at which he accuses his generals of disloyalty (→ 6).

2. Stalingrad: The last pockets of German resistance surrender (→ 5).

3. USSR: Soviet troops retake Kushchevskaya, south of Rostov-on-Don, and Kupyansk, in the Ukraine (→ 4).

4. North Africa: The first units of the Eighth Army cross from Libya into Tunisia. →

4. USSR: Soviet commandos land behind German lines near Novorossiisk, on the Black Sea (→ 5).

4. Atlantic: Convoy SC-118 comes under concentrated attack from German U-boats.

5. USSR: The Red Army reaches the Sea of Azov at Yeisk, cutting off German troops at Novorossiisk.→

6. New Guinea: Australian reinforcements arrive at Wau; above them, 37 Allied fighters shoot down 26 out of 70 Japanese raiders (→ 10).

6. Algeria: The Canadian corvette *Louisburg* is sunk by enemy aircraft off Oran.

6. Rastenburg: Hitler privately admits blame for the defeat at Stalingrad.→

6. Berlin: Himmler receives an inventory of goods taken from murdered Polish Jews, including 825 rail wagons of clothing for redistribution in Germany and a wagon full of women's hair (→ 12).

6. Washington: The US High Command is restructured, creating a European theatre under General Andrews and leaving General Eisenhower in charge of North Africa.

Stalin keeps up pressure on retreating Germans

Furious Hitler gives order for retreat

Rastenburg, 6 February

Hitler, infuriated by the continual Soviet advance in southern Russia, had Field Marshal von Manstein flown to his "Wolf's Lair" headquarters in East Prussia today. It was his intention to refuse von Manstein permission to make any more withdrawals, but military reality and the shock of Stalingrad have forced him to allow von Manstein to fall back from the Donets to the river Mius, leaving only a rearguard to cover Rostov-on-Don.

The fall of Rostov, which is now imminent, means that the Seventeenth Army, left behind by von Kleist in his retreat from the Caucasus, is now confined to its "Gothic Line" positions around the Taman peninsula between the Black Sea and the Sea of Azov.

Hitler plans to use this army as the springboard for another attack on the Caucasus, but Stalin plans to treat it as he did the Sixth Army in Stalingrad. Two days ago Soviet amphibious forces landed on the peninsula to cut the Germans off from the Crimea. But the Seventeenth Army had been listening to Soviet radio and knew that the assault was coming. They slaughtered the Russians as they came ashore at two of their landing beaches; but another force, put ashore at Novorossiisk, has dug in and is expanding its beach-head.

Meanwhile, General Malinovsky is racing on from the Donets, forcing von Manstein back to Taganrog and the Mius even without Hitler's permission. The Russians now seem poised to take the whole of the Donets basin. It is the same story further north where Hitler has been forced to give General von Kluge, the commander of Army Group Centre, permission to abandon the vulnerable Rzhev salient. Von Kluge now seems likely to lose Kursk in the next few days.

There is one city that Hitler has ordered to be held at all costs: Kharkov, the fourth largest city in the Soviet Union. The newly-formed SS *Panzer Korps* has been ordered to defend it to the death (→ 7).

German prisoners struggle through a fierce Russian blizzard: they can expect little mercy from compatriots of the PoWs whom they cruelly slaughtered.

A Russian night reconnaissance patrol makes its silent way through the forest on the Don front: the liberation of the city of Rostov is now imminent.

A nation mourns Stalingrad defeat

Germany, 6 February

The official three days of mourning for Stalingrad ordered by Hitler are over, but it is doubtful if the German people will ever recover from that terrible defeat. They still cannot come to terms with the crushing of the *Wehrmacht* by the *Untermenschen* [subhumans] of Russia.

Hitler has added to the shock felt in the higher echelons of the Nazi Party by telling a group of *Gauleiters* here at his "Wolf's Lair" "What you are witnessing is a catastrophe of unheard-of magnitude ... If the German people fails then it does not deserve that we should fight for its future; then we can write it off with equanimity."

General Dietmar, Germany's chief military commentator, echoed Hitler's doom-laden message in an extraordinary broadcast from Berlin last night in which he said: "The bitter experience of Stalingrad still weighs heavily on our souls. For the first time we are experiencing the entire tragedy of the reverse. For the first time an entire German army has ceased to exist."

"What we used to inflict on the others has happened to us. We have been encircled, attacked from all directions, compressed into a narrow space, split up into pockets. It is still difficult to realize. We feel it like a sharp physical pain."

Even more painful for hundreds of thousands of German families are the last letters from fathers, sons and brothers killed in the final days of the debacle or marched off across the steppes into captivity by the Russians.

The tale of horror told in these letters and the longing for home which permeate them contrast sadly with the bombastic broadcast of Goering in which he boasted "in spite of everything Germany's ultimate victory was decided there".

In the midst of all the sorrow there is a threat. Goebbels is invoking an old Prussian war decree of 1689 which says: "Whoever, in the midst of a battle, begins to retreat, shall be put to death without mercy."

Ciano sacked in Mussolini purge

Rome, 5 February

The first signs of a major crack in the facade of Mussolini's Fascist Italy began to show today when a tired and bitter *Duce* sacked his son-in-law, Count Galeazzo Ciano, Italy's foreign minister since 1936, and two other senior members of his cabinet. Mussolini himself has taken charge of foreign affairs.

Mussolini today is described as no more than a sad shadow of the bombastic, boastful and vain *Duce* who set out to recreate the grandeur of imperial Rome by engineering excuses to invade soft targets like Albania and Ethiopia – only to see his "empire" snatched from him by Allied troops.

His people are disillusioned. *Il Duce* promised them victories, not lengthy lists of casualties and prisoners. Morale is low throughout the country, and major strikes have taken place in the industrial north for "bread, peace and freedom".

With Anglo-American forces converging on Tunisia, he knows that the invasion of Italy cannot be far away and has pleaded with Hitler to sue for peace in Russia after his defeat at Stalingrad and bolster Italy's shattered army against the Allies.

On the other hand, Count Ciano has been appointed ambassador to the Vatican and many observers believe that the desperate Mussolini has sent him there to negotiate peace with the Allies (→ 12/3).

Ciano in full voice in 1940: now his father-in-law has sacked him.

US claims its first land victory over Japan

A US gun crew prepares to fire: Guadalcanal is now finally in their hands.

Guadalcanal, 4 February

Japan's commander on Guadalcanal, Lt-Gen Haruchi Hyakutake, tonight slipped aboard the destroyer *Hamakaze* and hurried to his cabin, marking the end of Japan's six-month attempt to conquer the island and a first land victory in the Pacific for the Allies.

With Hyakutake are most of his senior staff and 4,000 men, leaving behind a rearguard of 2,000, due to be evacuated in two days' time. During tonight's evacuation a "Tokyo Express", comprising 20 destroyers, raced down to Cape Esperance. During the operation they were harried by airstrikes by 64 US bombers and fighters of the "Cac-

tus Air Force" – named after the codename for the island. US fliers claimed 17 Japanese planes, while Japanese Zero fighters downed ten US planes.

First estimates from this bloody campaign put US total casualties at 6,300 and Japanese casualties at 24,000 dead. Both sides lost 24 ships; tonnage losses are roughly equal. The losses hit harder at Japan, which cannot match America's shipbuilding rate. The US forces also have significant gains, not the least of which is the psychological boost of inflicting a defeat on Japan. The greatest material gain is to deny Japan use of the airstrip at Henderson Field (→ 8).

Allies now rule the waves in the Med

Sicily, 5 February

Operating as a "wolfpack" – in the style of their U-boat counterparts – British submarines have caused havoc to Axis transports off the Sicilian coast, it was learned today. One unnamed submarine even sailed into the Straits of Messina between Sicily and the "toe" of Italy, risking rocks and the legendary whirlpool of Charybdis, to sink a heavy transport under tow by two tugs.

Altogether ten vessels – including an anti-submarine ship – were sunk. The Italian navy was conspicuously absent.

Churchill pays visit to front-line troops

Tripoli, 4 February

Men of the 51st Highland and New Zealand Divisions – all heroes of El Alamein – formed up to march past Winston Churchill today. The prime minister is making a whirlwind tour of the Middle East – with a significant stop in neutral Turkey – and is spending the day with his troops.

The premier toured the harbour – where engineers were clearing blockships and port installations. He leaves for Algiers tomorrow, despite a death threat from a notorious hired assassin (→ 8).

Tanks fail to end Burma stalemate

Burma, 3 February

British forces in Burma have used tanks in a three-day offensive in an attempt to breach Japanese defences at Donbaik and Rathedaung, in the Arakan peninsula. But tonight the attacks ended without a breakthrough. It is now over a month since the 14th Indian Division reached Rathedaung and Donbaik, but successive attacks have failed to take the towns. Strong defences have been built around bunkers, with the Japanese determined to resist the attacks until they are reinforced by General Koga's Japanese 55th Division later this month (→ 8).

Subs to be targets

Britain, 4 February

New guidelines to Allied bomber crews have emerged from the Casablanca summit attended by the prime minister, Mr Churchill, and President Roosevelt last month. An air ministry directive sent to Sir Arthur Harris, the chief of Bomber Command, today says that his primary objective is the "progressive destruction ... of the German military, industrial and economic systems and the undermining of the morale of the German people".

Allied targets range from Bremen to Rabaul, where Japanese warships are hit, but the top priority is the German submarine-building industry.

Exhorting the German people to "save gas for armaments".

1943

February

Su	Mo	Tu	We	Th	Fr	Sa
		1	2	3	4	5	6
7	8	9	10	11	12	13
14	15	16	17	18	19	20
21	22	23	24	25	26	27
28						

7. New Delhi: Chiang Kai-shek agrees to provide manpower to help to reconquer Burma in exchange for US aid.→

7. Rastenburg: Hitler says that if Germany loses the war, the German people rather than the Nazi party will be to blame.

7. USSR: The Russians retake Azov.→

8. Guadalcanal: The last Japanese units are evacuated without US forces noticing; a Japanese rearguard action slows down the US advance towards Cape Esperance (→9).

8. Burma: The first operation of the "Chindit" special force begins.→

8. Berlin: Himmler orders special measures to be taken at concentration camps to prevent mass breakouts during air raids.

9. Guadalcanal: US troops link up at Tenaro to discover that Japan has evacuated the island (→6/3).

9. USSR: The Russians liberate Bielgorod (→12).

10. France: The Lorient district is evacuated after becoming the target of heavy Allied bombings.→

10. New Guinea: US troops reach the Kumusi river mouth, poised for a fresh offensive against Japan (→12).

11. Germany: RAF bombers start a campaign of heavy night raids on Wilhelmshaven naval base tonight.→

12. Dachau: Dr Sigismund Rascher reports that his experiments on prisoners have proved that sexual intercourse can speed the return of warmth to men who have been chilled in ice-cold water (→22).

12. USSR: Soviet troops recapture Krasnodar, in the Kuban (→13).

12. Pacific: Operation Elkton, the Allied plan to push Japan out of New Guinea and New Britain, commences (→9/3).

13. USSR: Soviet troops retake control of the Rostov-on-Don to Voronezh railway line with the recapture of Novocherkassk (→14).

British try new type of warfare in Burma

Japanese troops cross a makeshift bridge in Burma, carrying a covered flag.

Burma, 8 February
Six weeks ago British forces began a frontal attack on Japanese positions in Burma, advancing through malarial and leech-infested jungles between the Arakan and the Bay of Bengal. Today, some 300 miles (480 km) to the north, an assault by stealth is beginning as a specially-trained unit crosses into Burma to fight behind enemy lines.

The northern assault is by men of the 77th Indian Brigade under the leadership of Brigadier Orde Wingate, a passionate disciple of long-range penetration in jungle warfare. Using mule transport and relying on air transport for supplies, this brand of guerrilla warfare within British Army ranks aims to harass Japanese supplies and cut rail links.

Whether or not it succeeds this new initiative will offer no comfort to the 14th Indian Division, which has been brought to a halt by strong Japanese resistance on the Arakan peninsula. For the first time British-Indian troops have come across the Japanese bunker system: well-concealed mutually supporting dug-outs for up to 20 men, reinforced with logs, so resilient to artillery that British gunners thought they were made of concrete (→18).

U-boat base under heavy RAF attack

France, 13 February
The ghost town of Lorient, on the Atlantic coast of France, evacuated by all non-essential personnel last week, was hammered again by the RAF tonight, when 466 planes dropped over 1,000 tons of bombs. The reason for such intense attacks is to deny the port to packs of U-boats using it as a base for attacks on merchant shipping. Around 1,000 *sorties* are made on Lorient each month at present. St Nazaire is also targeted, along with the U-boat engine works at Copenhagen, hit by low-level Mosquitoes 17 days ago.

Tonight's Lorient raid was by Lancaster, Halifax, Wellington and Stirling bombers. Seven are feared lost – three Wellingtons, two Lancasters, a Halifax and a Stirling. Privately, the boss of Bomber Command, Air Chief Marshal Harris, has misgivings about submarine pens as targets: "U-boats using these bases are amply protected by concrete, bomb-proof shelters."

Early intelligence reports suggest that while the port and city adjoining these shelters are being flattened, the submarines survive. Mining the approaches to their bases, convoy escort missions by aircraft, and raids on inland factories building prefabricated U-boats are all more effective (→25).

Roosevelt orders a longer working week to help the war effort

Washington, 9 February
As a step towards a second front in Europe, a minimum working week of 48 hours was decreed today by President Roosevelt, but it will apply only in 32 "labour shortage areas". Wages and prices are also being kept down by government order. The war labour board recently refused a pay increase demanded by the "big four" meat-packing companies because it would violate the wage formula that allows a maximum 15 per cent cost-of-living increase. Those whose hours increase from 40 to 48 hours will receive time and a half for the extra hours. In Britain the ministry of labour advises employers that the hours worked by women should not exceed 56 a week.

A British woman punch operator: no more than 56 hours' work a week.

Kursk falls to advancing Russians

British Eighth Army crosses into Tunisia

Kursk, 8 February
The Russians retook Kursk today with a sudden outflanking movement which took the Germans by surprise. General Golikov's troops also took Korocha, some 70 miles (112 km) to the south, and the Russians now threaten the whole German line from Orel to Kharkov.

Kursk, captured by the Germans in November 1941, became the key to their communications network, the vital link in the shifting of supplies and reinforcements between the southern and central fronts.

It is the first of the three main bases – Kursk, Orel and Kharkov – which the Germans established as their winter line in 1941 to be recaptured.

The Germans used these bases as the starting points for their offensive last summer which led to Stalingrad. Now, it seems that the Russians will use Kursk to launch the northern arm of a pincer attack on Kharkov in order to trap SS General Hausser's *Panzer Korps*. German correspondents reporting the battles at the approaches to Kursk comment with some awe on the numbers of tanks and guns deployed by the Russians.

One writes: "The Russian artillery barrage is like the roll of a giant's drum. It is impossible to hear single explosions. It is an indescribable hurricane of sound. A human feels like an insignificant insect before this gigantic concentration of artillery force" (→9).

A German soldier shows a Soviet a hand bill announcing his surrender.

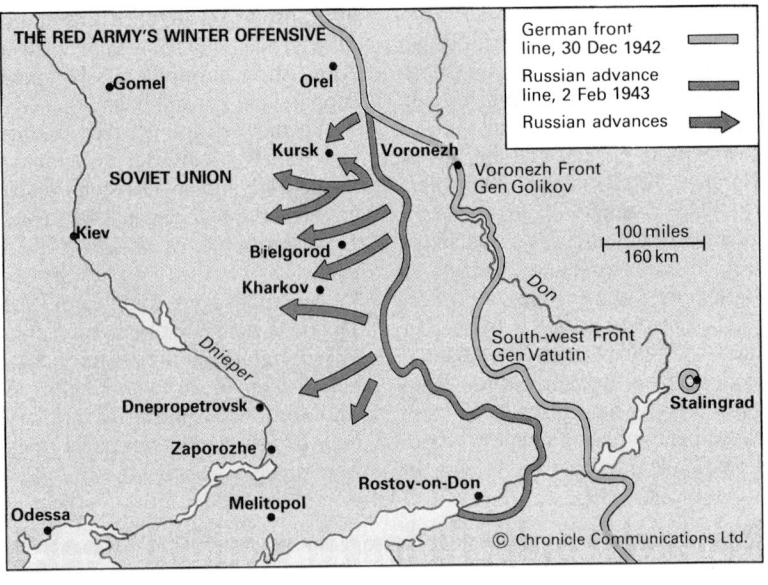

THE RED ARMY'S WINTER OFFENSIVE

German front line, 30 Dec 1942
Russian advance line, 2 Feb 1943
Russian advances

Gomel •   • Orel

Kursk •   • Voronezh

SOVIET UNION   Voronezh Front Gen Golikov

Kiev •

Bielgorod •

Kharkov •

100 miles / 160 km

Dnieper   Don

South-west Front Gen Vatutin

Dnepropetrovsk •

Zaporozhe •

Stalingrad

Odessa •   Melitopol •   Rostov-on-Don •

© Chronicle Communications Ltd.

Tunisia, 12 February
In driving rain, the 7th Armoured Division crossed the Tunisian border in force today, leaving the whole of Libya in Allied hands. With Rommel regrouping his *Panzerarmee Afrika* on the French-built Mareth Line, the next great battles can be expected shortly. General Montgomery is biding his time, re-equipping the Eighth Army with supplies and weapons which are arriving in the newly-cleared harbour at Tripoli by the shipload. His first objectives are Medenine and Ben Gardane – both with valuable airstrips (→14).

Winter nights help U-boats to attack

Atlantic, 9 February
Twenty U-boats have launched a sustained attack on a slow-moving Atlantic convoy, SC-118, over the last five days. Thirteen merchant ships have been sunk from the original 63, despite the presence of ten escort vessels and long-range air cover. Three U-boats were sunk and two more are believed to have been seriously damaged in a battle where the long winter nights helped protect the U-boats from Allied aircraft. Admiral Donitz has concentrated a large force near the "black gap" which Allied aircraft cannot reach, off the coast of Greenland.

Gandhi begins fast to gain his freedom

India, 10 February
The Indian leader Mahatma Gandhi began a 21-day hunger strike today. He is protesting against his imprisonment in the palace of the Aga Khan at Poona and against the British government's policy of interning all members of the All-India Congress Party. He plans to eat nothing and drink only fruit juice mixed with water, but not to fast "unto death". The viceroy, the Marquess of Linlithgow, described Gandhi's action as "political blackmail" for which there is no justification (→21).

Churchill is safely back in London after 10,000-mile journey

London, 8 February
Churchill returned to London today after a four-week, 10,000-mile journey aboard a Liberator bomber with a US pilot, who took him to Casablanca, Cairo, Turkey, Cyprus, Algiers and the front line of the victorious Eighth Army in Tripoli. He completed the journey by rail, arriving at Paddington at 1.01pm, four minutes ahead of schedule. Within hours he was meeting ministers and service chiefs, reviewing the decisions of the Casablanca meeting with President Roosevelt. This evening he plans to watch the new Ingrid Bergman and Humphrey Bogart film, *Casablanca*.

Churchill is applauded by the victorious troops in Tripoli on his recent visit.

1943
February

Su	Mo	Tu	We	Th	Fr	Sa
	1	2	3	4	5	6
7	8	9	10	11	12	13
14	15	16	17	18	19	20
21	22	23	24	25	26	27
28						

14. USSR: Soviet troops reoccupy Voroshilovgrad and Rostov-on-Don (→ 16).

14. Tunisia: Axis forces launch an offensive, taking Sidi Bou Zid and driving a wedge into the Allies (→ 15).

14. Italy: One hundred and forty two RAF bombers attack Milan tonight.

15. Tunisia: Gafsa falls to the *Afrika Korps* (→ 16).

16. USSR: The Red Army reaches Kharkov, Germany's main base in southern Russia (→ 19).

16. Tunisia: The Eighth Army takes Medenine (→ 18).

16. Britain: Anti-Fascist Italian PoWs open Radio *Risorgi* [Resurge], broadcasting for resistance to Mussolini.

16. Vichy: The deeply unpopular *Service Obligatoire du Travail* [Compulsory Labour Service] is introduced; all people aged 20-23 must do it for two years.

17. Burma: The 55th Indian Brigade attacks Donbaik, but fails to penetrate Japanese positions (→ 18).

17. Norway: A special commando group lands near Vermork, aiming to destroy the heavy water plant used by Germany's atomic research programme (→ 28).

18. Burma: The Chindits cut the railway line between Mandalay and Myitkyina, well behind Japanese lines. →

18. Tunisia: Sbeitla falls to the Germans. →

18. Washington: The House of Representatives applauds Madame Chiang Kai-shek when she calls for a Japanese defeat. →

18. Seattle, US: Thirty-one die when a B-29 Superfortress bomber crashes on a test flight.

19. Zaporozhe, USSR: Hitler, on a visit to von Manstein's headquarters, tells German troops that new, top-secret weapons are going to help them win the battle. →

20. USSR: Soviet troops take Pavlograd and engage the enemy at Krasnograd (→ 21).

Rommel seizes North African pass

German guards stand over disconsolate Americans taken prisoner in Tunisia.

ROMMEL COUNTER-ATTACKS
ALGERIA
TUNISIA
Tunis
Thala Sbiba
Tabessa
Fondouk
Kasserine Faid Sidi Bou Zid
Gafsa
Gabes
Mareth Line
Mareth
40 miles
64 km
Front line, 1 Feb
German attacks

Kasserine, Tunisia, 20 February
A shaken American army has come face to face with the military genius of Rommel – and tasted defeat for the first time in the Tunisian campaign. Many vital lessons will be learned from the Battle of the Kasserine Pass.

The command structure itself was a recipe for disaster. Lt-Gen Kenneth Anderson, a Briton, was in command of the British First Army, made up of the British V Corps, led by Lt-Gen C W Alfrey, the American II Corps, under Major-General Lloyd Fredendall, and the XIX French Corps, led by General Louis-Marie Koeltz.

What was not taken into account was that the French, still resentful at the destruction of their fleet at Oran, would refuse to serve under a British commander; Gen Koeltz would "coordinate" – no more. Fredendall dislikes the British, particularly Anderson, and had little time for the poorly-equipped French. Nor did language difficulties help matters.

Rommel believed that a bold move by the Tunisian defenders with his *Panzerarmee Afrika* could avenge the German defeat at Stalingrad. This belief brought about the battle at the Kasserine Pass.

In a typical Rommel *Blitzkrieg* operation, German tanks, supported by Stuka dive-bombers, hit the American sector of the line, taking the village of Sidi Bou Zid and cutting off 2,000 men. In a badly planned counter-attack, tanks of the US 1st Armoured Division were annihilated when they drove directly into German artillery.

With Rommel scenting victory and confusion reigning in the Allied camp, General Alexander, who took command of 18th Army Group, including all these forces, today, ordered that there would be no withdrawal. *Panzers* stormed into the pass yesterday and were stopped by US anti-tank fire. But in a fresh attack today the Americans faced German *Nebelwerfer* rocket-launchers and a huge artillery barrage before Axis tanks and infantry advanced relentlessly. The threat from Rommel is not over (→ 22).

MPs back plans for a "welfare state"

London, 18 February
After a tumultuous debate MPs voted by 335 to 119 today in favour of the Beveridge plan for post-war social security – but in principle only so far. For the first time since the coalition government was formed there was a massive split between the Tories and Labour. The Tories warned against sudden imposition of high taxation on the middle classes in order to finance a welfare state. Labour demanded at least an immediate first instalment to show that after victory Britain really will be a land fit for heroes.

February 18. Madame Chiang Kai-shek arrives on a visit to America.

1943
February

Su	Mo	Tu	We	Th	Fr	Sa
	1	2	3	4	5	6
7	8	9	10	11	12	13
14	15	16	17	18	19	20
21	22	23	24	25	26	27
28						

"Chindits" take war behind enemy lines

Burma, 18 February

British and Gurkha troops operating behind Japanese lines today had their first encounter with the enemy since they crossed into Burma ten days ago to attack railways and other communications in Japanese-held territory. The troops, who detoured south after a skirmish at Mainyaung, are members of the 77th Indian (or Long Range Penetration) Brigade, led by Brigadier Orde Wingate and known as "Chindits" after Wingate misheard an officer use the Burmese word for lion (*Chinthe*). The 3,000-strong Chindits were originally intended to support other major operations. Now they are to act alone as jungle guerrilla fighters (→ 3/3).

Wingate's Chindits: acting alone.

Goebbels calls Germans to "total war"

Berlin, 18 February

In the shadow of the Stalingrad disaster, Goebbels today organized a morale-boosting rally in Berlin's *Sportpalast*, with a well-drilled crowd roaring "Yes! Yes!" as he called for total war and asked them to reaffirm their faith in the Fuhrer. "The British assert that the German people have lost faith in victory," he said. "Are you determined to follow the Fuhrer through thick and thin and shoulder even the heaviest burden?" On cue came the response: "Yes!"

The exact timing of the rally was concealed to prevent an RAF raid.

The German home radio said it would begin at 8.15pm; but two hours before that time the foreign service was broadcasting long extracts from Goebbels's speech.

A significant passage in the speech was later deleted by the official German news agency. This read: "We have always estimated high the danger which threatens us from Russia, but not, unfortunately, high enough. Accordingly, we tried to conduct the war, one might say, with the left hand. The result is unsatisfactory. We must therefore wage the war with the life of the whole people."

Anti-Nazi protests staged in Munich

Munich, 20 February

Anti-Nazi demonstrations without precedent in the Third *Reich* have broken out in Munich. Stunned citizens looked on as students dared to chant anti-Nazi slogans and painted "Down with Hitler" on walls in the centre of the city.

The protests began after the Nazi *Gauleiter* of Bavaria, Paul Giesler, visited the university to investigate the source of anti-Nazi letters circulating in universities. Giesler told women students they would better serve the Fatherland by bearing a child each year. When he offered to provide Nazis to give the women "a thoroughly enjoyable experience", the students bundled the Gauleiter and his guards out of the university.

The anti-Nazi protests were led by Hans Scholl, a 25-year-old medical student, and his sister Sophie, a biology student aged 21. They call their group the "White Rose" and have been circulating the letters with the encouragement of a philosophy professor, Kurt Huber. Yesterday, a caretaker saw Hans and Sophie scattering leaflets from a balcony; he betrayed them to the *Gestapo*. Sophie was said to have been tortured after her arrest, and she appeared in court with a broken leg. She and her brother and Huber were sentenced by Roland Freisler, the bloodthirsty president of the People's Court, to be executed by the guillotine (→ 21).

Red Army captures Kharkov, but Germans plan counter-attack

Kharkov, 19 February

This once-great industrial city, now a ruined ghost town, its inhabitants killed or deported, fell to the triumphant Red Army yesterday. After fighting their way in through the suburbs, street by street, the Russians were astonished to find that the Germans had suddenly fled, despite Hitler's orders that it had to be held to the last man.

The decision to pull out was taken by SS General Paul "Papa" Hausser, the battle-scarred commander of the newly-formed SS *Panzer Korps* composed of the crack *Leibstandarte Adolf Hitler*, *Totenkopf* and *Das Reich* divisions. As the Russian circle around Kharkov drew tighter and tighter, Hausser sent ever more urgent cables to Hitler seeking permission to leave the burning city. Hitler remained adamant, but Hausser, risking execution, has defied the Fuhrer and saved his Panzers from certain destruction. Fighting against odds of seven to one, they stood no chance.

Moscow is delighted: its forces have come 400 miles (640 km) in barely three months. But the Russians are beginning to run out of steam. They have taken heavy losses against stubborn German resistance, and their supply lines have been over-extended. The Germans believe it is time to strike at the Russians' exposed flank (→ 20).

Russians take aim outside Kharkov.

21. Munich: Hans and Sophie Scholl and Christoph Probst, leaders of the "White Rose" rebellion, are guillotined.

21. USSR: German forces launch a big counter-offensive to regain Kharkov (→ 25).

21. Delhi: India observes a day of prayer for Gandhi.

22. Sofia: The government agrees to deport the Jewish population (11,000 people) from Thrace and Macedonia to Treblinka (→ 24).

22. Tunisia: Rommel breaks off the attack on Sbiba and Thala as British reinforcements start to arrive (→ 24).

23. London: De Gaulle asks General Giraud to declare a Free French republic in North Africa.

23. Atlantic: The German *Falke* acoustic torpedo scores its first operational success when a U-boat sinks a tanker from convoy UC-1.

24. Germany: Hermann Esser, the state secretary for tourism, reads a speech by Hitler declaring that the "might of the world Jewish coalition" will soon be smashed (→ 27).

24. Tunisia: Rommel is appointed to command Army Group Africa.→

25. USSR: Stalin orders General Konstantin Rokossovsky to attack towards Gomel and Smolensk, even though only half his troops have arrived in the battle zone (→ 27).

25. Britain: The RAF and USAAF establish a pattern of round-the-clock bombing, hitting Nuremberg today: the RAF makes night raids and the USAAF flies by day (→ 26).

25. New Zealand: Japanese PoWs stage a mass breakout, in which 48 Japanese and one camp guard are killed.

26. Germany: US Flying Fortresses and Liberators bomb the German naval base at Wilhelmshaven (→ 2/3).

27. Berlin: Jewish slave workers in arms factories are deported to Auschwitz.→

27. USSR: German troops regain Lozovaya (→ 1/3).

Britain celebrates "Red Army Day"

Britain, 21 February

A message from Joseph Stalin was read out at meetings held all over Britain today in honour of the 25th anniversary of the founding of the Red Army. Stalin thanked British citizens for their demonstration of "friendly feelings" and expressed confidence in joint victory. Prayers were said for Russia in churches.

At Cardiff, Clement Attlee, the deputy prime minister, said that the battle of Stalingrad was decisive: "Let me pay tribute to the steadfastness of mind of Stalin in holding the Russian reserves until the time for counter-attack." At Sheffield, Sir Stafford Cripps said of Stalin: "For his courage, leadership and consummate skill we and the world owe the deepest gratitude."

Tonight in London 2,000 servicemen and women presented a pageant in honour of the Red Army to an audience of 6,000, including Mrs Churchill, who heads the Aid for Russia fund, and the Soviet ambassador, Mr Maisky. Lieutenant Laurence Olivier, RNVR, gave the call to arms from *Alexander Nevsky* and Lt-Cdr Ralph Richardson narrated. John Gielgud as "the voice of Moscow radio" described the battle for Stalingrad. No mention was made of the Red Army's founder, Leon Trotsky.

Germany repulsed in Tunisia – at a price

A tank abandoned by the retreating Axis troops is checked for booby traps.

Kasserine, 25 February

It was a cavalry charge, with heavy guns this time, almost in the movie tradition of the Seventh Cavalry, that finally saved the day at the Kasserine Pass for the Allies. Brigadier LeRoy's 9th Infantry Division had travelled the 735 miles from western Algeria non-stop, and arrived just as British and French forces were preparing to pull back.

It was a final *sortie* by the 2nd Lothians and Border Horse Regiment that convinced Rommel that he had no chance. British tanks took their objective, but five were lost in the mist and destroyed. Rommel chose to withdraw in the belief, based on this tank assault, that his army would be engulfed by the reinforced Allies. Such was the stealth of his withdrawal that the Allies found themselves attacking empty positions the next morning.

The Battle of the Kasserine Pass is over, and now the Allies count the cost: 10,000 men (6,500 Americans) lost, to the Axis's 2,000. The US II Corps alone has lost 183 tanks and 208 artillery pieces, 500 Jeeps and trucks, and also huge amounts of ammunition (→ 6/3).

Death camps: Nazi kingdom of evil

Occupied Europe, 28 February

In the yard of Block 25 at the Auschwitz-Birkenau camp there is a pile of bodies stacked up like firewood. Occasionally the pile stirs as the dying struggle to free themselves from those already dead. Enormous rats scuttle around gnawing the corpses.

At Treblinka, inmates are made to dig up the buried dead for burning. The stench of rotting flesh fills the air. Female corpses are used as kindling because they burn more quickly; the pregnant women burst open to reveal blackened foetuses.

At Sobibor, the SS guards compete to throw Jewish children the furthest. One of them, Hubert Gomerski, enjoys beating people to death with an iron watering can.

Ten thousand Hungarian Jews have been deported to a Yugoslav copper mine for hard labour that will certainly kill many of them. Four thousand Jews from Marseilles, in France, have been rounded up for deportation, and Bulgaria has agreed to deport 11,000 to Treblinka.

The Nazis are liquidating the Polish ghettoes. The last 5,000 Jews of Bialystok have been dispersed to Treblinka, Majdanek and Auschwitz. All but 300 went straight to the gas chamber (→ 10/3).

Commando raid attacks German atomic research programme

Norway, 28 February

Nine British-trained Norwegian commandos have pulled off one of the most daring and difficult sabotage operations of the war. After parachuting onto a remote frozen lake they covered 50 miles (80 km) of mountain wilderness to attack a heavily-guarded Norwegian laboratory essential to Germany's atomic weapons programme.

They were met by six resistance workers 12 days ago to begin a journey in which they sank up to their armpits in snow. An earlier, abortive attack had alerted the Germans that the plant was at risk. Yet the saboteurs, unseen in freezing darkness, crept past the guards to plant charges which exploded before they escaped, blowing up 286 "heavy water" cells.

An aerial view of the vital German Vermork power plant after the attack.

Women drivers are wanted in Germany

Berlin, 28 February

Women drivers are needed in Germany. An appeal is issued today by the German Women's Association, which plans special courses both to teach women to drive and to help them maintain their vehicles. The courses will be free and the aim, as with other recent measures such as labour mobilization, is to release more men for work at the front; everything is now secondary to war production.

Another sign of this came earlier this month with the decree of 4 February shutting "luxury" businesses – from jewellers to sweet manufacturers – which are not considered essential for the war effort.

▷

Russian partisans take battle honours by their incredible feats of bold defiance

Moscow, 28 February

The bravery and effectiveness of the partisans fighting behind the German lines is now fully recognized by the Soviet government. Fourteen partisans have been made Heroes of the Soviet Union, and a new medal struck to be awarded "To a Partisan of the War for the Fatherland".

The exploits of the partisans make stirring reading, and Stalin has issued a special order urging that the "flame of partisan warfare shall be kindled and spread". Some of the partisan brigades are over 1,000 strong and are supplied from the air with weapons, explosives, radios and even printing presses to spread the word of resistance.

The effect of their activities may be judged from the diary of a German officer killed by partisans in Byelorussia: "We entered a gloomy wilderness in our tanks. There wasn't a single man anywhere. Everywhere the forests and marshes are haunted by the ghosts of the avengers. They would attack us unexpectedly, as if rising from under the earth. They cut us up to disappear like devils into the nether regions. Night is setting in and I feel them stealthily approaching from out of the darkness, they are the ghosts and I am frozen with fear."

Journeys through forested areas are extremely hazardous for the Germans. Bridges are blown, mines laid and ambushes set. Some units

A partisan taken by the Germans.

heading for the front have to fight their way through. These activities have brought a violent reaction from the Germans who mount full-scale operations against the partisans and kill anyone whom they capture. Zoya, a famous 18-year-old girl partisan who was captured near Moscow in 1941, was hanged and mutilated as an example.

Not everyone approves of the partisans. They live off the country and expect the peasants to feed, clothe and shelter them, and the Germans need little excuse to execute those suspected of helping the partisans. The partisans are just as ruthless as the Germans and will kill anyone suspected of collaborating with the enemy.

Vanya Shkelev, an 11-year-old partisan who provides the guerrillas with hay.

1943
March

Su	Mo	Tu	We	Th	Fr	Sa
	1	2	3	4	5	6
7	8	9	10	11	12	13
14	15	16	17	18	19	20
21	22	23	24	25	26	27
28	29	30	31			

1. USSR: Soviet forces recapture Demyansk, Zaluchie and Lychkovo (→ 5).

1. London: Soviet envoys tell the Polish government in exile that the USSR intends to keep eastern Poland, which it invaded in 1939.

2. Rome: Mussolini withdraws his troops from the eastern front.

3. USSR: The Red Army captures the German base of Rzhev, and Lgov, west of Kursk.

3. Burma: The Chindits cross the Mu river, and cut the rail link between Mandalay and Myitkyina for a second time (→ 4).

4. Burma: Operation Cannibal, an Allied drive to recapture Akyab, is stopped by strong Japanese resistance (→ 6).

5. Paris: Fritz Sauckel, the *Reich* plenipotentiary for the allocation of labour, demands 100,000 forced workers from the Vichy regime.

5. USSR: German troops advance to Kharkov and Bielgorod; near Izyum, floating iceblocks prevent German attempts to bridge the Donets river (→ 7).

5. Kiev: Erich Koch, the Nazi commissioner for the Ukraine, says: "We are a master race ... the lowliest German worker is racially and biologically a thousand times more valuable than any one of the population here."

6. Pacific: Japanese aircraft bomb the Russell Islands (→ 31).

6. Tunisia: Lieutenant-General George S Patton Jr is appointed to command the US II Corps.→

6. Moscow: The Supreme Soviet awards Stalin the rank of marshal of the Soviet Union, hailing him as "the greatest strategist of all times and all peoples".

6. Atlantic: U-boats attack the Allied convoy SC-121.

6. Solomon Islands: A US naval task force bombards Japanese airfields at Munda and Vila, sinking two enemy destroyers (→ 7/4).

Americans claim victory in Battle of Bismarck Sea

Port Moresby, 5 March

In the Battle of the Bismarck Sea fought on 3-4 March a joint Allied air attack by 355 planes has disastrously damaged Japanese prospects in New Guinea and the Solomons. The enemy suffered prohibitive losses. Eight troop-laden Japanese military transports and four escorting destroyers were sunk, with the loss of 2,890 Japanese army and navy men killed or wounded. The Japanese tried to send reinforcements to Lae, in New Guinea, despite the danger from growing Allied air power. On the eight transports was the main body of the 51st Division.

Once the convoy left Rabaul, the US Fifth Air Force quickly mustered maximum air strength for a decisive blow. As the convoy entered Huon Gulf on 3 March, the Allies pounced. B-17 bombers struck first. They were immediately attacked by Japanese Zero fighters which, in turn, were intercepted by American Lightnings. Fifteen Zeros were shot down. Quickly following the B-17 strike, Australian Beaufighters swept over at deck level to blast the convoy with cannon and machine-gun fire. Then Mitchell and Boston bombers followed, using a new technique developed in Port Moresby, dropping their 500-pound bombs to "skip" into their targets.

Firing anti-Semitism in Europe.

Allies step up air war on Germany

Ruhr industry the target for bombing

Germany, 6 March
A new combination of RAF bombing aids and techniques has been used to devastating effect on Essen, the home of Krupp's. It was the first raid of Bomber Command's new offensive, the "Battle of the Ruhr".

Out of a force of eight Pathfinder Mosquitoes equipped with Oboe guidance, five made it to drop yellow flares as approach markers 15 miles north of Essen. They then marked the Krupp complex with red target indicators. The next layer of attack comprised 22 Pathfinder heavy bombers which put down green markers on the initial red.

The main force, 157 Lancasters, 94 Halifaxes, 52 Stirlings and 131 Wellingtons, hit the markers with the greatest aerial bomb load yet assembled. A total of 1,070 tons of high explosive and incendiaries was dropped in 38 minutes. At intervals the heavy Pathfinders refreshed the green target markers. Sir Arthur Harris, Bomber Command's chief, believes that an area two miles wide was set alight. Of the 442 aircraft which took off, 362 claim to have attacked Essen, but photographs are expected to confirm that only 153 dropped their bombs within three miles of the target.

Even so this was a vastly more accurate attack than any previous raid. About 160 acres of factory space were destroyed, causing damage which in some cases will take years to repair. Fourteen bombers did not return. Harris is to be promoted soon to Air Chief Marshal (→ 12).

The facade of St Hedwig's cathedral still stands above the smoking rubble.

Berliners suffer their biggest raid so far

Berlin, 2 March
In the heaviest air raid so far of the war against Berlin, RAF heavy bombers dropped 8,000-pound high-explosive bombs and thousands of incendiaries in an attack last night on the city centre. Much damage is concentrated around the *Unter den Linden*, the Opera and cathedral of St Hedwig. One pilot said later: "It was a fearsome sight, but no regrets ... remember what the Nazis did to London." The Germans later said that 191 people were killed and 268 injured. A total of 17 aircraft did not come back. Berlin threatens reprisal raids against New York and Washington, without suggesting how these might be achieved (→ 6).

Allies agree to split defence of Atlantic

Washington, 1 March
The Atlantic Convoy Conference, which opened here today, is deciding the strategy for combating the continuing U-boat menace in the North Atlantic. Losses have mounted because of the increased number of U-boats, the deployment of "milch cow" submarines so that the U-boats can refuel while on patrol, and the shortage of very-long-range patrol aircraft. From 1 April the Royal Navy and the Royal Canadian Navy are to share the escort of convoys on the North Atlantic route, with a dividing line at 47 degrees west, while the US Navy will cover the South Atlantic and Caribbean (→ 20).

Chindits attack key Burmese rail links

Burma, 6 March
The flutterings of 10,000 jungle birds, frightened by the sound of explosions, proclaim the cutting of three key railway bridges in the Bongyaung area of Japanese-held Burma by the Chindits. The 3,000 Gurkhas, Burmese and Liverpudlians are not elite troops, but they have been trained meticulously and ruthlessly by their commander, Brigadier Orde Wingate, as jungle-fighting guerrillas supplied from the air, and are able to beat the Japanese at their own game (→ 15).

Brigadier Orde Wingate plans a move by his specially trained men.

RAF's incredible turbojet fighter, the Gloster Meteor, takes off

Britain, 5 March
Today has witnessed the first flight of Britain's first jet fighter, the Gloster Meteor. It is very different from the first British jet aircraft, the Gloster Pioneer, which made its maiden flight in May 1941, being much larger and powered by two turbojet engines. Surprisingly, these are not designed by the jet engine pioneer Wing-Commander Frank Whittle. He and his company, Power Jets Ltd, have been experiencing problems with their own engine, the W2. Meanwhile, both Rolls-Royce and de Havilland had begun to develop jet engines, but with much direct help from Whittle. The Meteor is powered by the de Havilland Halford H.1, named after the company's chief engineer, Major F B Halford. Rolls-Royce Derwent jet engines will also be tried.

The Meteor was to have been named the Thunderbolt, but the US Republican P-47 piston-engined fighter, now in frontline service as a bomber escort, had already taken the name.

Britons look back on the first year of austere living

Britain, 1 March

A year after "Austerity" was introduced, the population of Britain has reduced its annual consumption to four-fifths of its peacetime level, although incomes are up by over 50 per cent since 1938. Rationing, high taxes and shortages have bitten deep into the average family's way of life. While expenditure on food, clothing and travel has fallen in real terms, that on drink and tobacco has doubled.

"Utility" production applies not only to clothing and furniture but also to many household goods. Only white crockery is being made, and this year's plain white cups are usually without handles, to save material. Licensed manufacture permits only one standard quality of sheets, blankets, pots and pans, kettles and electrical appliances, carpets and linoleum, pens and pencils, lighters and umbrellas. "Fripperies" such as soup spoons and butter knives and ornamental glassware are banned. Toys cannot include rubber, hemp, cork, celluloid or plastic.

Shortages have driven many goods "under the counter" – notoriously cigarettes of all popular brands, razor blades, torch batteries, vacuum flasks, combs, hair grips, needles, safety pins, babies' teats, lipstick and cosmetics, alarm clocks, prams and bicycles. Shortage of newsprint means that national papers are reduced to four pages on several days of the month.

The ministry of food's rhyming exhortations continue – "Don't you know the sight of peelings greatly hurts Lord Woolton's feelings?". Wartime sausages have been dubbed "breadcrumbs in battledress". There are recipes for carrot jam and nettle tea. Unloved dried egg has encouraged people to keep chickens, and two million families are self-sufficient in vegetables thanks to "digging for victory" in gardens and allotments (→ 12/4).

Allies complete new road through Burma

A team of labourers hacks the Burma Road into a steep and barren hillside.

Myitkyina, Burma, 1 March

A new Burma Road, to take material to Chiang Kai-shek's Nationalists, has just been completed. Two Chinese divisions which had retreated into India, the 22nd and 38th, under the command of Chiang Kai-shek's hard-boiled US chief of staff, Lieutenant-General "Vinegar Joe" Stilwell, pushed up from Ledo, 275 miles (440 km) through Hukawng Valley and the Pangsan Pass, to Myitkyina, on the frontier with China.

In three months Stilwell's divisions killed 4,000 Japanese. They were followed by US Army engineers and 15,000 labourers. Since the original Burma Road was cut by the advancing Japanese early in 1942, the Nationalists have not been isolated. For nearly a year US pilots have flown an air bridge from Dinjan, near Ledo, across the Himalayan foothills into Yunnan. It was a dangerous journey, with planes buffeted by turbulent air currents and pilots suffering snow-blindness and crashing. Yet so successful was the air bridge that it carried more supplies than the original Burma Road (→ 3).

Rommel's offensive rebuffed by Allied troops in Tunisia

Tunisia, 6 March

Rommel today sent his tanks into action against the British Eighth Army at Medenine. It was conceived as the second phase of a counter-attack which began with the Battle of the Kasserine Pass last month. But it was delayed by an abortive offensive in northern Tunisia, and this gave Montgomery time to build up his forces.

By the time Rommel had his extra divisions, Monty had even more: Allied strength quadrupled in the last ten days, and tonight this appears to have given the Eighth Army a decisive strength in the battlefield. Rommel had no more than 160 tanks against his enemy's 400, and with three fighter wings operating from forward airfields, the Allies had air superiority, too. The Desert Fox could not even surprise the Allies: they had broken his coded messages and seen his tanks on the move.

When the attack came this morning, Montgomery was waiting in well-sited defensive positions. The Germans were soon pinned down and subjected to withering assault from tanks and the air. Having lost 40 tanks Rommel had no alternative but to withdraw (→ 10).

Tube disaster in London: 178 crushed to death, yet no air raid

London, 3 March

People descending the steps to the shelter at Bethnal Green tube station in East London last night were crushed and suffocated to death in a tragic accident when not a single bomb had fallen. A middle-aged woman carrying a baby tripped near the bottom of the first flight of 20 steps.

Her fall brought down the man behind her, and others hurrying down to the shelter after the air-raid warning fell in their turn. Within minutes dozens of bodies were crushed on top of each other. Unaware, others pressed in from the street building up a wall of death. Out of 400 victims of the disaster, 173 died of suffocation, and 62 were badly injured. The woman lived. Her baby died.

A crowd gathers outside Bethnal Green station, the scene of the disaster.

1943

March

Su	Mo	Tu	We	Th	Fr	Sa
	1	2	3	4	5	6
7	8	9	10	11	12	13
14	15	16	17	18	19	20
21	22	23	24	25	26	27
28	29	30	31			

7. USSR: *Panzer* units attack Soviet-held Krasnograd (→ 9).

8. Germany: The Navy switches from the usual three wheeled *Enigma* cipher machine to a four wheeled one, cutting off UK intelligence just as a U-boat "wolfpack" starts to attack Atlantic convoys.

8. China: Japanese forces cross the Yangtse river (→ 13).

9. New Guinea: Japanese aircraft attack the Allied stronghold at Wau (→ 14).

9. USSR: General Hausser counter-attacks to the north and west of Kharkov.

10. China: The US 14th Army Air Force is created and put under the command of Major General Claire Chennault.

10. Sicily: Allied bombers raid Palermo.

10. Washington: The House of Representatives votes to continue the Lend-Lease scheme.

10. Sicily: The British submarine *Tigris* is sunk by a mine west of Sicilian Channel.

11. Atlantic: Convoy HX-228 comes under attack. The British destroyer *Harvester* sinks one U-boat and is herself sunk by another, which in turn is sunk by the Fighting French corvette *Aconit*.

11. USSR: General Hausser re-enters Kharkov (→ 12).

12. Germany: RAF aircraft drop 1,000 tons of bombs on Essen, severely damaging the Krupps plant (→ 27).

12. Italy: 230,000 workers stage a protest strike against Mussolini's regime, bringing war production to a halt.

12. USSR: Germans and Russians battle at Kharkov (→ 15).

12. Tunisia: New Zealand and British units move south and west of Medenine to prepare to attack the Mareth Line (→ 18).

13. China: The Japanese are pushed back over the Yangtse.

13. Poland: SS troops start to dismantle the ghetto at Cracow, dispersing 14,000 Jews (→ 15.)

Gloomy Rommel ordered on sick leave

Axis tanks go up in smoke in Tunisia – along with Mussolini's ambitions.

Ukraine, 10 March
Hitler has accused his once-favourite soldier, Field Marshal Erwin Rommel, of "pessimism", and ordered him on sick leave until he is ready to lead a hypothetical attack on Casablanca.

Rommel arrived here today from Rome, and was summoned to take tea with the Fuhrer when he did his best to convey the gravity of the situation in Tunisia. He begged Hitler to allow the evacuation of the Axis troops to Italy where they could be re-equipped for the defence of Europe. Hitler refused to listen; Rommel had a similar response from Mussolini yesterday.

Il Duce was worried about the effect on Italian opinion should Tunisia fall, and offered Rommel another division. The offer was refused. Rommel has confided to his diary a "great regard" for the Italian leader, "probably a great actor like most Italians," but the conversation ended on an acrimonious note. "Perhaps I should have spoken to him differently at the end, but I was so heartily sick of all this everlasting false optimism that I just could not do it" (→ 12).

Plot to assassinate Hitler is a failure

Smolensk, 13 March
German army officers plotting the assassination of Hitler planted a bomb made from British plastic explosives aboard his plane when he left Smolensk after a military conference. The bomb should have gone off as the plane passed over Minsk, but two hours later Hitler landed safely at his Rastenburg HQ.

Fabian von Schlabrendorff, a junior officer in the plotters' circle, retrieved the bomb from the plane and discovered that the corrosive chemical had worked, eating away a wire which had then released a striker. The striker had duly hit the detonator – which had proved to be a dud (→ 20).

Germans fight back

Kharkov, 11 March
This city of ruins, liberated only a month ago by the Red Army, is once again threatened by the Germans. SS General Hausser who, against Hitler's orders, extricated his *Panzers* from the then doomed German garrison in the city, has led his men back to crush the Soviet Third Tank Army and establish himself in the approaches to the city. He has sealed off the city and is tonight preparing to attack (→ 12).

Top secret Allied operation sinks three German ships at Goa

Having been moored here since 1939, the German merchant ships are scuttled.

Goa, 10 March
Special Operations Executive (SOE) agents, with volunteers from the Calcutta Light Horse and the Calcutta Scottish, last night raided four Axis merchant ships which had taken refuge in neutral Portuguese Goa when war was declared.

The raiding party, on board a hopper barge which had sailed all the way round India from Calcutta, had hoped to board the German freighter *Ehrenfels* without a fight because her skipper, Captain Rofels, had agreed to be bribed. But when the barge arrived, Rofels opened fire and scuttled his ship. He died along with four of his crew. There were no British casualties, and the German *Braunfels* and *Drachenfels* and the Italian *Anfora*, were also scuttled.

1943

March

Su	Mo	Tu	We	Th	Fr	Sa
	1	2	3	4	5	6
7	8	9	10	11	12	13
14	15	16	17	18	19	20
21	22	23	24	25	26	27
28	29	30	31			

Bulgarian protests save 50,000 Jews

Sofia, 10 March

A popular outcry, backed by the church and King Boris, has saved 50,000 Jews from certain death. Three weeks ago the Jewish affairs commissioner, Alexander Belev, and SS Lieutenant Theodor Dannecker agreed to deport Jews from inside Bulgaria's pre-war borders "to the east". A delegation of parliamentarians and other leading citizens visited the interior minister, Peter Gabrovski, and demanded that the orders be rescinded. Like Italy, Hungary and Finland, Bulgaria has tried to resist German demands for deportations (→ 13).

Back the bombers campaign launched

London, 7 March

The latest National Savings campaign, "Wings for Victory", was launched this weekend with a target of £150 million for building bombers. By last night £30 million had already been collected.

A Stirling bomber stands in front of St Paul's, and a Lancaster in front of the National Gallery in Trafalgar Square. Huge crowds have been attracted; they are urged to buy savings stamps to stick on to 500-pound bombs. The lord mayor of London launched 1,300 pigeons to carry messages to savings groups everywhere.

Sticking saving stamps on bombs.

14. New Guinea: Australian and US troops attack Japanese positions, forcing a slow retreat (→ 31).

14. Mediterranean: The British submarine *Thunderbolt* (accidentally sunk as the *Thetis* in 1939) is sunk again by an Italian submarine.

15. South Atlantic: The Italian submarine *Leonardo da Vinci* sinks the Canadian Pacific liner *Empress of Canada* off Sierra Leone.

15. Berlin: Finland and Germany sign a trade agreement.

15. Britain: The Royal Navy launches its first X-craft, or midget submarine; it is just fifty feet long and five feet nine inches broad.

16. Atlantic: A U-boat pack savages convoy HX-229, sinking eight merchant ships.

16. Moscow: Stalin demands a second front, accusing Churchill and Roosevelt of treachery by failing to open one in Europe (→ 23/4).

17. Burma: Indian troops retreat from Rathedaung to Buthidaung in the face of a renewed Japanese offensive on the Arakan front (→ 18).

18. Tunisia: Gafsa falls to Patton's II Corps, which pushes on to El Guettar.→

18. Burma: Allied soldiers give up the attempt to drive the Japanese from Donbaik (→ 24).

18. South America: French Guiana declares itself on the side of the Free French.

18. Germany: US bombers attack Vegesack.

19. USSR: German troops of the *Gross Deutschland* division reach Bielgorod, but are still battling with Soviet resistance in these northern approaches to Kharkov (→ 22).

20. Berlin: A second attempt by army officers to assassinate Hitler fails. Colonel Rudolf von Gersdorff's plan to blow himself up with the Fuhrer at a show of weapons captured from the Russians is foiled when Hitler leaves the exhibition before the bomb can be detonated.

Allies attack the Mareth Line in Tunisia

An infantry section moves up through a wired position in the Mareth Line.

North Africa, 20 March

True to form, General Montgomery made no attempt to follow up his success at Medenine. The Mareth Line was his objective, and no one doubted that this was going to be a tough nut to crack. The line was built by the French – against the Italians in Libya – and consists of minefields, anti-tank ditches, barbed wire and carefully concealed artillery positions stretching from the sea to the Matmata Hills in the south.

As the American II Corps, now led by the attack-minded Lieutenant-General George Patton Jr, attacks in the north to draw off Axis reserves and 27,000 New Zealanders and 200 tanks make a lengthy outflanking move, Montgomery began his frontal assault today. He is taking a leaf from Alamein, using infantry – three divisions of Lieutenant-General Sir Oliver Leese's XXX Corps – to create a gap for X Corps under Lieutenant-General Brian Horrocks.

Although the infantry has succeeded in getting a foothold in the enemy lines, the tanks have been baulked by mines and the soft going of the Wadi Zigzaou. The infantry, concentrated in a relatively small area, is coming under heavy fire from German artillery. As dusk falls over Mareth, Montgomery is preparing a fresh attack (→ 22).

Vichy anti-Semitic laws are repealed

Algiers, 18 March

General Giraud has issued a series of decrees abolishing Nazi-inspired anti-Semitic laws in Vichy France. In general, says Giraud, all laws passed in France since the armistice was signed on 22 June 1940 are null and void.

Specifically, all discrimination in citizenship against Jews as such is abolished. They are to be reinstated into the public service, and their property is to be returned. European Jews will be treated by law as Frenchmen; North African Jews as Arabs (→ 22).

U-boats fooled by new radio-location

Britain, 20 March

Despite the successes achieved by U-boats in battles now raging in the Atlantic [*see report, page 393*] a new radio-location system has raised Allied hopes of improving their ability to attack enemy submarines. The new system, known as ASV III, cannot be picked up by the *Metox* radio-location detectors which enabled U-boats to avoid aircraft fitted with earlier ASV II systems. ASV III has been fitted to bombers of 172 Squadron, based at Chivenor in Devon, and is being used over the Bay of Biscay (→ 21).

German offensive retakes Kharkov

Rastenburg, 15 March

The Germans have recaptured the city of Kharkov after bitter street fighting. A special communique from Hitler's headquarters last night claimed that three picked divisions of the *Waffen-SS*, the *Leibstandarte Adolf Hitler*, the *Totenkopf* and the *Das Reich*, strongly supported by the *Luft-waffe*, have retaken the city in an encircling attack from the north and west.

The Red Army high command has not yet confirmed the loss of Kharkov, saying only that "heavy fighting continues in the area", but it has uttered Stalingrad-style or-ders to the defenders, and the news-papers have issued a rallying call: "We can and must hurl back the onslaught at Kharkov and on the Donets, no matter what the cost."

North of Kharkov, a new Ger-man attack is developing against Bielgorod, the fortress town on the railway to Kursk, and there is every indication that the Germans intend to try to recapture Kursk.

The German successes stem from the counter-offensive launched by von Manstein on 22 February when he caught the Russians by surprise while they were over-extended in their advance to the west following their great victory at Stalingrad.

One of the first actions of the Germans troops on entering Khar-kov was the murder of 200 people in a hospital. Afterwards they set light to the building (→ 19).

German soldiers keep their gun in operation while under heavy Russian fire.

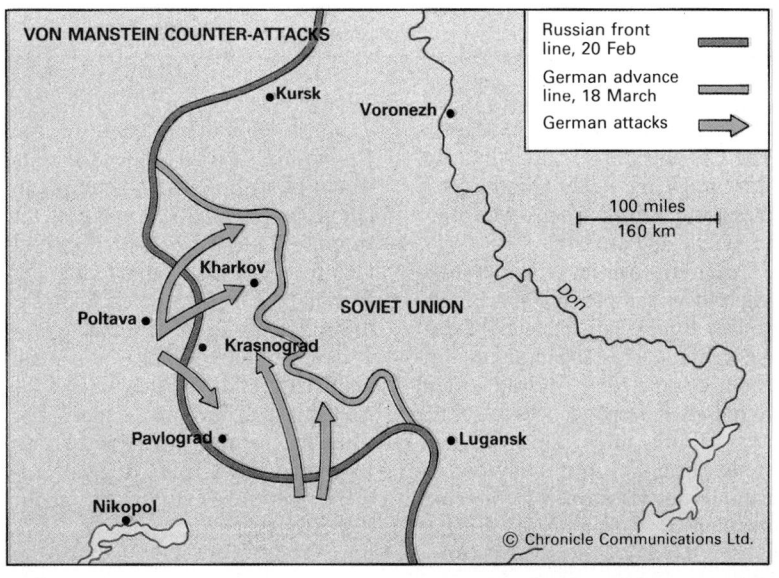

Emergency shelters opened to house homeless Germans

Germany, 17 March

Now more than at any point before in the war the German people live in fear of RAF raids. Thousands have lost their homes in the latest raids, and the industrial heartland of the Ruhr has been devastated.

In the city of Essen alone 80 fac-tory workshops have been hit in two major raids this month, and 54 of them severely damaged. The key armaments factory, Krupp's, has also been hit. Over 3,500 houses were destroyed and at least 650 people killed in the raids on the nights of 5 and 12 March.

No fewer than 33 emergency shel-ters have been opened for people left destitute, but these are simply not enough. Poignant messages are scrawled on the ruins: "Where are you all? Mother is living with the Schmidts." "If you are still alive I am with the Mullers."

Berlin has also been hit. After a night raid on 1 March, the walls of the city were covered with slogans such as "We are obliged to the Fuh-rer for this" and "We want only peace and bread". News of the devastation is no longer censored by the authorities in order to boost morale. Instead they are predicting that "Britain's air offensive" may be expected to go on for a long time. And they are exhorting citizens to follow the British people's example of calm.

Greek Jews rounded up for Auschwitz

Athens, 15 March

The Nazis began by allocating 20 trains for the deportation of Jews from Greece. These carried off only 11,000, and more trains had to be found for the more than 50,000 who remained. They are being rounded up in repeated sweeps that extend to the Aegean Islands. No Jewish community, no matter how small, is safe: the three Jews among the 2,000 people on the island of Samothrace have shared the fate of their brethren on the mainland.

Jews from Salonika arriving at Auschwitz are to be used for exper-iments conducted by Professor Karl Clauberg, a prominent Ger-man gynaecologist, who claims that he can sterilize a thousand woman a day with the use of X-rays. The experiments are backed by Himm-ler, who says that everybody in-volved must be pledged to secrecy. Clauberg's associate, the surgeon Dr Johann Kremer, writing of life at Auschwitz, has noted in his diary: "Excellent food. We had sour duck livers, with stuffed to-matoes, tomato salad etc."

But some Greek Jews are be-lieved to have escaped, fleeing to the hills to join the partisans or being smuggled across the Aegean to Turkey in the hope of reaching Palestine (→ 18).

Chindit fighters cross the Irrawaddy river

Irrawaddy River, Burma, 15 March

Two Chindit columns, under Major Mike Calvert and Major Bernard Fergusson, have crossed the Irra-waddy river and plan to destroy the Gokteik Gorge railway viaduct. Soon they will be joined by the main Chindit force.

Since 13 February, when the Chindit commander, Brigadier Orde Wingate, issued a biblical "we stand on the threshold of battle" order of the day, the 3,000 Chindits have been "stirring a hornet's nest" in Japanese-occupied northern Burma, marching with pack mules and supplied from the air. So far they have been remarkably success-ful, in spite of the well-known diffi-culties of their controversial com-mander, a gunner by training, a guerrilla by experience and a manic-depressive by inclination. Nume-rous vital railway bridges have been destroyed, and thousands of Japan-ese troops have been diverted from moves against India and China to find the Chindits.

But the terrain on the east bank of the Irrawaddy is very different from the jungle on the west bank: treeless hills and coverless lowland, hemmed in on three sides by rivers. It is here that three Japanese divi-sions are now gathering to attack the Chindits (→ 24).

1943

March

Su	Mo	Tu	We	Th	Fr	Sa
	1	2	3	4	5	6
7	8	9	10	11	12	13
14	15	16	17	18	19	20
21	22	23	24	25	26	27
28	29	30	31			

21. Britain: Churchill broadcasts to the nation on his vision for Britain after the war, which strikes some listeners as surprisingly socialist.

22. Auschwitz: Crematorium IV, a modern extermination plant fitted with an underground gas chamber and electric lifts to a custom-built incinerator, is opened (→23).

22. Tunisia: RAF Hurricanes smash a *Panzer* counter-attack near the Germans' Mareth Line (→23).

23. El Guettar, Tunisia: The US 1st Armoured Division avenges its defeat at the Kasserine Pass by beating off the 10th *Panzer* Division, destroying 32 tanks (→25).

23. Denmark: In the first, and so far the only, free elections to be held in Nazi-occupied Europe, the national coalition Government Party wins 143 seats, with the remaining five going to the Danish Nazis and the pro-Nazi Peasant Party.

23. Mediterranean: *Luftwaffe* attackers sink the British troopship *Windsor Castle* off Algeria.

23. Berlin: Himmler's statistician, Dr Richard Korherr, reports that 1,419,467 European Jews have been killed since the outbreak of war (→25).

24. Burma: Wingate is ordered to break up his Chindits and return to India.→

25. Nuremberg: *Der Sturmer*, the Nazi newspaper, announces that "the extermination of the Jews is in progress" (→31).

25. Tunisia: The 4th Indian Division overruns the Mareth Line.→

26. France: Pierre Brossolette sets up a committee to coordinate the five Resistance movements in northern France (→3/6).

26. Germany: Hitler writes to Mussolini that Russia is so weakened by the defence of Stalingrad that it cannot possibly be a serious menace.

27. Clyde Estuary: The escort carrier HMS *Dasher* sinks after an accident in which one of her petrol tanks explodes.

Wingate orders his Chindits to withdraw

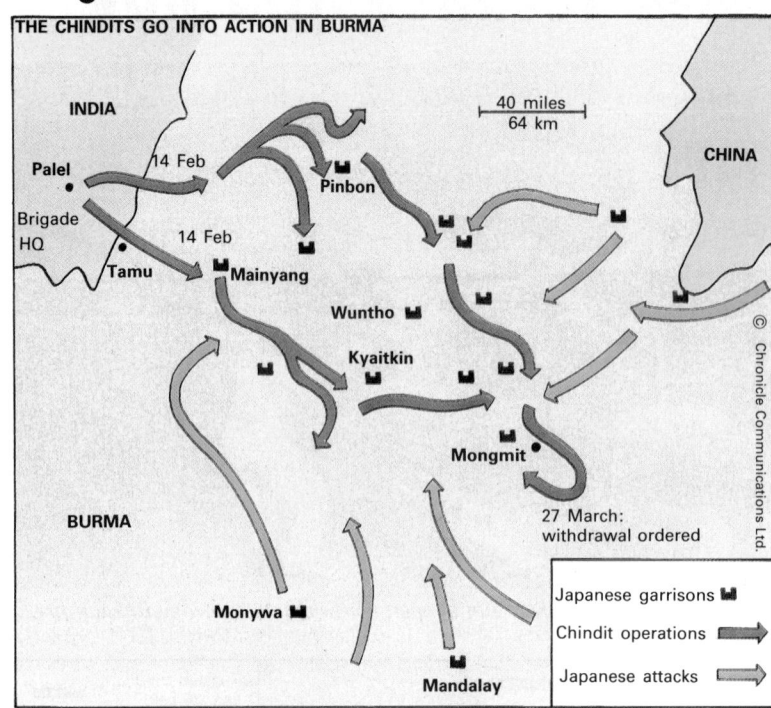

Hehtin Chaung, Burma, 26 March
The Chindits are withdrawing from Burma. Of the 3,000 Gurkha, Burmese and British troops who went in, only 2,200 are left.

After five fruitful weeks destroying bridges and proving that British-Indian troops can fight in the jungle as skilfully as Japanese, the brigade crossed the Irrawaddy and found itself trapped between three rivers, with three Japanese divisions closing in on it. Only two escape routes were open to the commander, Brigadier Orde Wingate – north to India or east to the Keren Hills, where the Chindits would be with a sympathetic population, but beyond the range of air supply. Two days ago General Geoffrey Scoones, commanding the British IV Corps, ordered Wingate to head north towards India.

Despite the withdrawal, some politicians and the proponents of irregular warfare are hailing the Chindits, comparing Wingate to Lawrence of Arabia. Regular soldiers are less enthusiastic about their strategic value (→30/4).

Prison bug reveals German rocket plan

London, 22 March
What might be vital intelligence has today come from a top-secret interrogation centre in Kensington Park Gardens. Two German generals captured in North Africa, Cruwell and von Thoma, were placed in a bugged room and their conversation was monitored. During it they spoke of long-range rockets being developed to strike London and expressed surprise that the capital is not already under attack. This ties in with scraps of information from other sources, and is likely to be treated very seriously by the intelligence world (→30/4).

Nazis destroy the village of Khatyn

Khatyn, 22 March
The SS unit which swept down on the Russian village of Khatyn, near Minsk, was unusual, even by Nazi standards; it had been formed from German criminals released from concentration camps. Commanded by SS Major-General Oskar Dirlewanger, the SS men systematically murdered all but one of the 150 villagers and burned the village to the ground. The atrocity is intended to deter villagers from giving food and shelter to the partisans, about 150,000 of whom are in action behind enemy lines.

US Navy repels Japanese attempt to reinforce Kiska garrison

North Pacific, 26 March
A naval duel fought at long range between US and Japanese forces off the Komandorski Islands today ended in the US force winning against a Japanese force twice as large. The Japanese were escorting two transports and a freighter bringing reinforcements to the lonely garrison on Kiska, in the Aleutians. The Americans were there to prevent this and, since the transports turned back, victory was theirs. The battle – unusual in the Pacific War for being fought in daylight – lasted for nearly four hours, but neither side suffered great damage. The American cruiser *Salt Lake City* was hit (→31).

On the island of Kiska: no reinforcements reached the garrison today.

U-boat menace returns to high seas

North Atlantic, 21 March

In the last three weeks at least 50 Allied merchant ships have been sunk by U-boats in the North Atlantic. Grand Admiral Donitz, who has continued to direct the U-boat campaign since he succeeded Grand Admiral Raeder as the German naval commander-in-chief, has been concentrating on the full eastbound convoys. The U-boats strike in the mid-Atlantic gap which only very-long-range Allied aircraft can reach, and there are simply not enough of them.

In the last few days this policy has led to one of the most devastating U-boat successes of the war. In the stormy seas, with winds up to gale force ten, the fast-moving HX-229 convoy caught up with the slow-moving SC-122. Between them they presented a huge target, a small fleet of 90 merchant ships supported by 16 escorts.

Donitz was given details of the convoys' course by his intelligence service, and designated 38 U-boats to track them down. But the Germans were as hampered as the Allies by the bad weather. They found the convoys more by luck than by judgement, and for much of the time did not know if they were dealing with one convoy or two. By this morning 21 merchant ships had been sunk for the loss of one U-boat. But yesterday Allied Liberators arrived from Northern Ireland and Iceland and began pounding the U-boats. Many are believed to have been damaged, and Donitz has called off his pack (→ 30/4).

An American carrier on convoy duty; but it cannot prevent U-boat attacks.

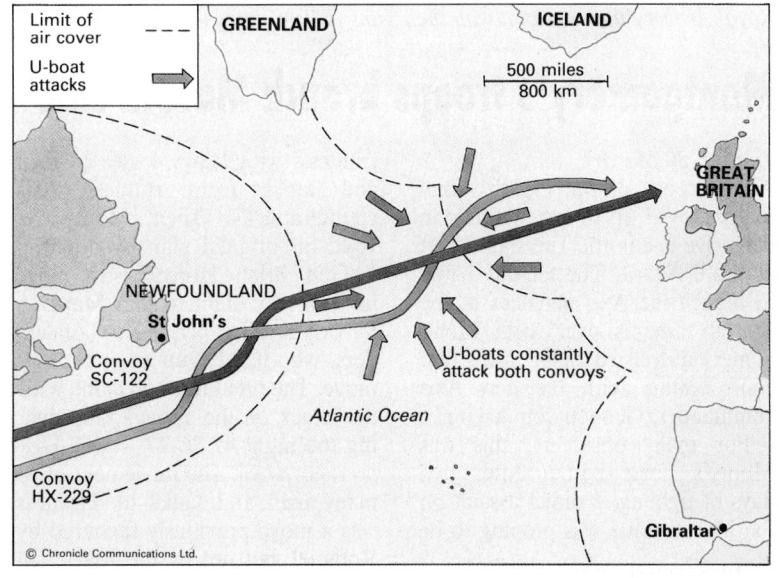

German authorities arrest all Britons

France, 26 March

The Nazis have arrested all the 8,000 remaining British and American men, women and children in the former unoccupied sector of France as part of growing precautions against an Allied invasion. The men are said to have been deported to Germany. All civilians are to be evacuated from Channel and Atlantic coastal areas by 30 March, and demolition has been carried out in ports such as Brest and La Rochelle for defensive purposes.

Thaw brings Russian war to a muddy halt

Moscow, 22 March

Once again the weather has taken a decisive hand in the war in Russia. The thaw has come early this year and both armies are now, literally, bogged down in the morass of mud churned up by the fighting vehicles of both sides.

Where, only a few days ago, tanks could roar at full speed across the hard-frozen steppe, they are now in danger of drowning in a sea of mud, and the runways of airstrips have turned into quagmires which refuse to release aircraft. While the thaw has brought difficulties to both sides, it has hurt the Germans most by bringing Field Marshal von Manstein's successful counter-offensive to a halt.

After recapturing Kharkov he had planned to cut quickly across the Donets behind the Russian armies which were still pushing west. If he had been able to do so, he might well have caught the Red Army in a trap and produced a disaster comparable to Stalingrad. But he had lost too many men and too many machines to achieve the quick result, and now General Thaw has taken command (→ 31).

Overnight assault by New Zealanders breaks Axis lines

Tunisia, 27 March

Soldiers of the New Zealand Corps have broken through the Axis lines after an overnight attack which has outflanked German defences now retreating from the Mareth Line 30 miles (48 km) further east. The New Zealanders – 27,000 men and 200 tanks – attacked a gap in the hills at Tebaga at 4pm yesterday as the sun set over the desert.

The 8th Armoured Brigade and the New Zealand infantry made up the advance wave, followed by the 1st Armoured Division. Their movements were given some cover not only by the encroaching dusk but also by a sandstorm which obscured the vision of the anti-tank guns ranged to defend Tebaga. By daybreak today the Allies had blasted through the gap, ensuring the ultimate breach of the Mareth Line.

Montgomery will push back the Axis forces, now commanded by General Jurgen von Arnim who has replaced Rommel, from two sides: the inland column established through Tebaga, and a direct coastal assault via Gabes. Arnim plans to deploy tanks of the 15th *Panzer* Division to hold off the Allies in order to allow his infantry time to retreat from the doomed Mareth Line to new defensive positions (→ 29).

March 25. King George visited the Home Fleet today and made time to enjoy a show put on by ENSA to mark the occasion.

1943

March

Su	Mo	Tu	We	Th	Fr	Sa
	1	2	3	4	5	6
7	8	9	10	11	12	13
14	15	16	17	18	19	20
21	22	23	24	25	26	27
28	29	30	31			

28. Tunisia: Montgomery telegraphs Churchill: "Eighth Army has inflicted severe defeat on enemy."

29. Rastenburg: Hitler orders the construction of an enormous missile-launch site on the French side of the Channel, to bombard Britain.

29. Tunisia: The British Eighth Army takes Gabes.→

30. Atlantic: Having scuttled their ship, all but six of the crew of the German blockade runner *Regensburg*, from Rangoon, kill themselves when they are intercepted off Iceland by the British cruiser *Glasgow*.

30. Moscow: Stalin is furious to hear that Allied convoys to Murmansk are to be suspended because of heavy losses, suspecting political rather than military motives.

30. Netherlands: RAF Mosquitoes bomb the Philips radio factory at Eindhoven (→ 4/4).

31. Pacific: Japanese aircraft raid the Russell Islands.

31. Washington: The US High Command orders the invasion of Attu, in the Aleutian Islands, on 7 May (→ 24/4).

31. China: The US opens training centres for Chinese infantrymen.

31. Sardinia: A large USAAF bombing force attacks the Axis air base and transit port of Cagliari (→ 15/4).

31. Germany: Major-General Peltz of the *Luftwaffe* is appointed *Angriffsfuhrer England*, in charge of bombing raids on Britain (→ 3/4).

31. Rastenburg: Hitler meets Bulgaria's King Boris III for consultations.

31. Britain: 973 civilians have been killed and 1,191 wounded in air raids since 1 January.

31. New Guinea: US infantrymen under Colonel Archibald MacKechnie land at the mouth of the Waria river.

31. USSR: Soviet troops occupy Anastasyevsk, north of Novorossiisk (→ 2/4).

31. Tunisia: Cap Serrat is occupied by the British (→ 1/4).

Bitter fight ends in Allied breakout

Royal Artillery men push on with their guns in Tunisia: where to now?

Montgomery's troops breach Mareth Line

Tunisia, 30 March
Allied troops of the Eighth Army today moved up to a new German defensive line in the Tunisian desert at Wadi Akarit. The ten-day battle to breach the Axis defences of the Mareth Line is over, with Montgomery a decisive victor in his first confrontation with the new Axis commander, General von Arnim.

For many observers, this was Monty's finest battle. After two days of fighting, a direct assault on the Mareth Line was proving to be fruitless, with heavy losses in men and tanks from ruthless Axis counterattacks. Then Monty revised his original plan by ordering Lt-Gen Brian Horrocks to move his tanks by night to join Maj-Gen Sir Bernard Freyberg's New Zealanders, who had begun an encircling move. The breakthrough came with the attack on the Tebaga Gap during the night of 26-27 March [*see previous page*]. The movement of so many men and tanks in darkness was a move previously favoured by Rommel, but not by the Allies; another tactic deployed to a greater extent than had been customary for the Allies was the use of air power to support attacking land forces.

Forward air controllers were in the front line of the Tebaga attack, using radio to direct pilots in Spitfires and other aircraft to attack tanks and enemy defences. The land forces advanced behind an aerial barrage of cannon fire and bombs from fighter-bombers flying over them in 15-minute relays.

Some 6,000 Axis soldiers, mostly Italian, have been taken prisoner. But although most of the Mareth defenders escaped, they have had little time to prepare new defences against the inevitable next move by Monty's masters of the desert (→ 31).

Map: ALLIED ADVANCES IN NORTH AFRICA

- Enfidaville
- Kasserine Pass
- Sousse
- Kairouan
- TUNISIA
- Kasserine
- Sfax
- Maknassy
- 50 miles / 80 km
- Gafsa
- El Hamma
- Mareth Line
- Front line, 31 March
- US advances
- British advances
- Tebaga Gap
- Medenine

The men who make up the Eighth Army

North Africa, 30 March
Not since the age of Hannibal has such a polyglot army fought over these desolate wastelands. Men from all over the world have shared the dangers and discomfort, the defeats and the triumphs, the intense daytime heat and bitterly cold desert nights. The blood of many races and nationalities has soaked into the North African desert.

Here are *Australians* who fought so stubbornly on the north flank of Alamein, with losses so huge that their government feared the loss of an entire generation; and *New Zealanders* whose tanks have excelled in encirclement operations and whose Maori infantrymen became as feared as the *Indian* Division's Gurkhas in the fighting around Tobruk. The *Free French* stand at Bir Hakeim brought respect even from Rommel; and few have fought more fiercely that the *Palestinian* detachment and the *Poles*.

The *Greek* Brigade has shown the same tenacity as it showed against the Italians and Germans in defence of its homeland.

The *Scots* regiments have distinguished themselves throughout the campaign, often fighting alongside *South Africans* with *English*, *Welsh* and *Irish* county regiments, happy and honoured with the rest to call themselves "Desert Rats".

Monty reads the lesson in Tripoli.

Pacific not the priority, say the leaders

Washington, 28 March

Japan's outer defensive perimeter was crumbling as the Allied leaders met at Casablanca in January to chart the way ahead.

In spite of their warnings of possible disaster, the pleas of the "have nots" of the Pacific war theatre went unheeded. In allotting arms and resources the Allied leaders gave only fifth priority to the Pacific. The agreed "beat Hitler first" grand strategy was not seriously challenged.

Although Pacific commanders were disappointed, the combined chiefs of staff at the Casablanca conference directed that the Allies were to retain the initiative in the Pacific and prepare for a full-scale offensive when Germany had been defeated. At the outset they were to take the Japanese bastion, Rabaul, secure the Aleutians, and then advance east to west across the Pacific through the Gilberts and Marshalls towards Truk and the Marianas.

MacArthur was directed to coordinate two converging drives on Rabaul: one from Guadalcanal, the other from New Guinea.

However, at a conference of Pacific commanders in Washington it was revealed that available reinforcements were not sufficient for an advance all the way to Rabaul. It was therefore agreed that the scope of the tasks would have to be limited to New Guinea, the Solomons and other strategic islands.

Casablanca: Churchill sits down with service chiefs to draw up priorities.

Armaments dominate German economy

Germany, 31 March

With the whole country now geared up for "total war", the armaments industry accounts for a massive 70 per cent of Germany's national product. Since 1939, production of arms and equipment has quadrupled. Overall industrial production has risen by only 12 per cent.

The National Socialist government says that recovery from the appalling losses of the *Wehrmacht* in the USSR will be made on a rising tide of new weaponry, although male armaments workers are being sent to replace their dead countrymen at the front. All businesses that are not essential to the war effort have been closed.

Agricultural production has fallen severely as farmhands are siphoned off to the war industries and fertilizers are increasingly hard to come by. Even production of the much-praised potato has dropped, and it is now illegal to use spuds to feed livestock.

But the economy would be in a far worse state if it were not for the National Socialists' systematic exploitation of the occupied countries' resources and labour. Nearly one-fifth of the food consumed in Germany comes from abroad.

Nazi death factories murder Europe's Jews and gypsies and steal their goods

Auschwitz-Birkenau, 31 March

With the opening of the second of four spanking-new crematoria here today, the camp's capacity to process human beings into ashes has taken another step forward. The extermination of Jews and Gypsies on such a scale brings a new problem: how to dispose of their belongings?

In order to maintain the illusion that they are to be resettled, deportees are allowed to take a bundle of clothes or a small suitcase of belongings each. When they arrive, and undergo the selection that sends most of them straight to the gas chamber, they must drop everything.

A special corner of the camp, called Canada, is full of privileged prisoners whose task is to sort the goods into piles. In the middle of the yard are two enormous mountains: one of blankets, and one of suitcases and knapsacks. Prisoners sort clothing into piles; the yellow stars will be taken off, the bloodstains cleaned up and the old clothes shipped to the *Reich* for distribution to the German needy.

To the right, hundreds of prams; to the left, thousands of pots and pans. All around are huts filled to the rafters with shaving brushes, spectacles, dentures, corsets, wigs, false limbs, shoes, handkerchiefs: the pitiful residue of lives cruelly termi-

A pile of now useless spectacles.

nated in a cloud of poison gas. The children's toys, bottles, dummies and tiny clothes bear mute testimony to the slaughter of the innocents.

Money and valuables – mainly watches, jewellery, and currency – are set aside and sent to the *Reichsbank*. This includes the few diamonds squeezed out of toothpaste tubes where hopeful deportees hid them, and gold teeth and fillings wrenched from the mouths of corpses before cremation (→ 5/4).

An emaciated corpse is shoved into the incinerator by fellow prisoners.

1943

April

Su	Mo	Tu	We	Th	Fr	Sa
				1	2	3
4	5	6	7	8	9	10
11	12	13	14	15	16	17
18	19	20	21	22	23	24
25	26	27	28	29	30	

1. Tunisia: The Allies bomb El Maou airstrip near Sfax.→

2. USSR: Moscow claims that 850,000 Germans have died in the winter campaign (→29/4).

2. Atlantic: The British ships *Black Swan* and *Stonecrop* sink the German submarine U124 off Oporto.

3. Britain: Focke-Wulf FW190 fighter-bombers raid Eastbourne and strafe streets crowded with shoppers.

4. Germany: RAF bombers drop 1,300 tons of bombs on Kiel in a night raid.→

5. Ponar, Lithuania: SS men shoot 4,000 Jews dead (→19).

5. Burma: The Japanese overrun British brigade headquarters on the Mayu peninsula (→7/5).

5. Libya: The crew of the USAAF B-24 Bomber *Lady be Good* bails out over the Western Desert after losing its bearings (→12).

5. Germany: Pastor Dietrich Bonhoeffer is arrested for anti-Nazi activities and sent to Flossenburg concentration camp. Colonel Hans Oster is dismissed as deputy chief of the *Abwehr* [military intelligence].

6. Tunisia: The British Eighth Army resumes offensive operations, attacking the Axis on Wadi Akarit.→

7. Westminster: The government announces that men and women will receive equal war compensation.

7. La Paz: Bolivia declares war on the Axis.

8. Tunisia: Axis forces continue their withdrawal towards Enfidaville (→9).

9. Tunisia: British Eighth Army troops take Mahares, 50 miles north of Gabes (→10).

10. Tunisia: The Allies take Sfax (→12).

10. Germany: Goebbels tours Essen and is shocked by the bomb damage (→12).

10. Sardinia: Eighty-four US Liberator bombers raid La Maddalena, sinking the Italian cruiser *Trieste* and badly damaging the cruiser *Gorizia*.

German armies driven towards coast

Mass air raids hit Mediterranean Axis

Allied tanks continue to push ahead along a dust road in the Tunisian desert.

Axis forces retreat again as Allies attack

Tunisia, 6 April
For Italian Alpine troops high in the hills overlooking the Wadi Akarit, the nightmare came on a starless night. Sentries knew nothing of the assault by the 4th Indian Division until they felt the cold steel of Gurkha *kukris* against their throats. In a few hours more than 4,000 Italians had surrendered. The Indian encirclement – over a wide mountainous area – was an overwhelming success. Below on the plains, the 50th and 51st Infantry Divisions of the Eighth Army began their assault an hour before dawn and succeeded in breaching the German defences. Now was the time for the armour of X Corps to exploit the infantry's success.

The attack has been delayed, however, and German *Panzers* have counter-attacked, forcing the infantry back (→8).

Tunisia, 5 April
As Allied troops prepared for the final push on Tunis and Bizerta, British and American aircraft launched their greatest-ever assault on Axis targets in the Mediterranean today. More than a thousand sorties were flown, a record in the North African campaign.

Allied Fortresses and Mitchells saturated three airfields – Borizza, Boca de Felso and Milo – on the Italian mainland. More than 250 grounded aircraft were destroyed.

Vital Axis supply routes took terrible punishment. Fourteen Junkers Ju52s, loaded with petrol, were shot down by Lightnings off the Tunisian coast, and bombers set fire to three supply ships, blowing up a destroyer escort in the process. Liberators hit the city of Naples in a mass raid at dusk, damaging port facilities and putting an airport out of operation.

As the daylight bombers returned to their bases, RAF Wellingtons hammered targets behind the battle lines, destroying railway stations, barracks and factories near Sfax. Docks and shipping in Sicilian ports were also hit by the night bombers (→6).

Hitler and Mussolini meet to discuss their African misfortunes

Salzburg, 10 April
The appearance of the two great European dictators meeting at the railway station here three days ago has surprised and shocked even their most ardent supporters. Benito Mussolini came for a pep talk from his senior partner; and, although he is only 59, Il Duce looked almost senile in appearance, hunched and greyfaced.

Hitler, too, is showing signs of strain following the successive defeats of his armies on the eastern front and in Africa. He has developed a nervous tic. He, too, looks much older than his 53 years, although his eyes have lost none of their mesmeric fury.

It was the Fuhrer who took command at the meeting here. Il Duce knows that he has lost whatever backing he once had from his own people. Like Hitler's other ally, Antonescu in Roumania, Mussolini is urging peace talks; but Hitler will have none of it.

With growing fervour, he has told the Duce of secret weapons, the *Vergeltungswaffen* – weapons of reprisal – which he is certain will bring the Allies to their knees, and the *Schnorkel* device which will enable U-boats to stay at sea for far longer periods. "By putting every ounce of energy into the effort, I succeeded in pushing Mussolini back on the rails," Hitler told Goebbels later. "When he got out of the train I thought he looked a broken old man; when he left, he was in high fettle, ready for any deed."

Mussolini arrives for his pep talk.

New deal planned for world economy

London, 7 April
An ambitious scheme "for the future economic ordering of the world" was published as a British government white paper today. It was dubbed the Keynes Plan – after its principal author John Maynard Keynes, the treasury's senior adviser and the economist whose theories inspired the "New Deal" policies in the United States of the 1930s. The central aim is post-war establishment of an international bank offering an acceptable means of payment between nations while stimulating trade through greater currency stability. Similar plans for international finance are being developed in Washington by the US secretary of the treasury, Henry Morgenthau.

USAAF error kills Antwerp civilians

Antwerp, 5 April
A US Eighth Army Air Force daylight bombing raid targeted on a *Luftwaffe* repair factory at Antwerp has gone disastrously wrong, and 936 Belgian civilians, including 209 school children, are reported to have been killed. The Germans took over the Minerva motor works when they occupied Belgium in 1940, and 3,000 people are employed there repairing damaged German planes. The Americans sent 200 Flying Fortresses and Liberators across the Channel, initially escorted by RAF Spitfires. When these withdrew at the limit of fighter endurance, the Germans struck, breaking up the US formations. Bombs fell more than a mile from the target (→10).

Yamamoto sinks three ships in Solomons

Guadalcanal, 7 April
In a bid to regain air superiority in the south-west Japan's Pacific commander, Admiral Yamamoto, today put Allied air power in the Solomons to the test as more than 200 Japanese naval aircraft attacked and sank three Allied ships.

The Japanese force of 67 Aichi D3A Val carrier-bombers escorted by 120 Mitsubishi A6M Zero fighters took off from New Britain to attack shipping north of Guadalcanal in Ironbottom Sound, the ocean graveyard of more than 40 warships. During the fighting the US destroyer *Aaron Ward*, a tanker and the New Zealand minesweeper *Moa* were sunk. The Japanese lost 19 aircraft. US losses were seven fighters, but only one pilot missing.

The results show a decline in Japanese pilot quality and are disappointing for Yamamoto. He switched his carrier aircraft to Rabaul a week ago to begin harassing Allied airbases, which have now made the Bismarck Sea a banned area for Japanese shipping after the loss of eight ships there last month (→8/5).

A transport plane silhouetted against the austere beauty of the Aleutians.

1943

April

Su	Mo	Tu	We	Th	Fr	Sa
				1	2	3
4	5	6	7	8	9	10
11	12	13	14	15	16	17
18	19	20	21	22	23	24
25	26	27	28	29	30	

11. Rastenburg: After long delays, Hitler approves Admiral Donitz's request for more U-boats; tank and aircraft manufacture, however, still have priority for scarce steel supplies.

12. Moscow: Stalin writes to Churchill that he is delighted by the damage done to German industrial centres.→

12. Tunisia: Sousse falls to the Allies (→17).

12. Rastenburg: Hitler, perhaps unwittingly, signs an order making Martin Bormann his secretary.

13. Imber, Wiltshire: An RAF pilot, demonstrating new tactics for attacking ground targets, kills 25 when he mistakenly fires on spectators rather than the practice target.

13-14. English Channel: German ships sink the Norwegian destroyer *Eskdale*, which was manned by a joint British/Norwegian crew, in a night attack.

14. Germany: Stalin's son Jacob dies in a PoW camp.

14. Pacific: The Japanese navy completes Operation I, a series of air attacks on New Guinea and the Solomon Islands, with a raid on Milne Bay.

15. Italy: RAF bombers attack La Spezia (→17).

16. Mexico City: Jacques Mornard is sentenced to 20 years' imprisonment for the murder of Leon Trotsky, including six months for carrying an ice-pick.

16. France: The evacuation of all children and non-essential civilians from the Channel ports of Le Havre, Dieppe, Cherbourg, St Malo and Brest is announced.

17. London: The Polish government in exile asks the Red Cross to investigate the Katyn massacre.→

17. Britain: After a raid by 30 Focke-Wulf FW190 fighter bombers on London, one lands by mistake at West Malling aerodrome.

17. Mediterranean: US bombers raid Palermo, Catania and Syracuse.

Germans find Poles buried in Katyn forest mass grave

Katyn, 17 April
Five days ago a devout Russian peasant called on the German Field Security Police at Katyn, near Smolensk, with a grim story. "The Poles are looking for their officers in Siberia, but they lie here, in the forest," he said.

The Germans dug up some 4,100 Polish officers, still in their uniforms, with identity documents, and hands tied behind their backs. All had been shot in the back of the neck. Local Russian peasants told of "Black Ravens", prison coaches driven by Soviet secret police, arriving in spring 1940. Other corpses found nearby are of Soviet civilians who died in Stalin's purges. The

Relatives try to identify the bodies.

discovery has provided a propaganda triumph for Goebbels. "I saw to it that the mass graves were inspected by neutral journalists from Berlin," he noted in his diary.

Professors of forensic medicine from German-occupied countries have been given a free hand at Katyn, but today the exiled Polish government in London has demanded an investigation by the International Red Cross. Moscow has reacted with fury. It says that the Germans carried out the mass killings, and accuses the Poles in London of "aiding and abetting Hitler". The affair is embarrassing Britain, as both Stalin and the Poles are Allies (→18).

Allied air forces step up raids over two continents

Unified command for Mediterranean

North Africa, 15 April
The Allied air forces in the Mediterranean have been completely re-organized in both their functions and their command structure under the overall command of Air Chief Marshal Sir Arthur Tedder.

A North-West Africa Tactical Air Force has been established under the command of Air Marshal Sir Arthur Coningham to use the lessons learnt in the desert to give close support to ground forces in Tunisia. Light bombers and tank-busters protected by fighters will blast the enemy's strongpoints. A Strategic Force has also been set up. Composed of USAAF heavy

The front gunner of a Flying Fortress in an early US raid on Germany.

Air-raid duty for all in Germany

Germany, 11 April
Hermann Goering, the man whose *Luftwaffe* was once going to bring Britain to its knees, has decreed that air-raid patrol duty will be compulsory for every able-bodied German. Women will not be spared their place in the duty rotas which are now being organized in the wake of Goering's decree, issued on 2 April. Factory workers are also being drafted into civil defence or the emergency services as they battle to minimize the effect of the raids on production. The raids have caused particular damage to the rail and road networks, making travel difficult as well as dangerous.

Drawing up plans in North Africa.

and medium bombers and RAF medium bombers, it is responsible for long-range attacks on bases, communications and shipping.

In order to cope with the vast area covered by the Allied air forces they have also been divided into three geographical regions: Middle East Command, stretching from India to Tunis; the North African Air Command in Tunisia under Major-General Carl Spaatz, of the USAAF; and the RAF in Malta. The reorganization is to cope with the vast expansion of Allied air power in the region. The creation of the Tactical Air Force reflects planning for the invasion of Europe.

RAF makes heaviest raid yet on Stuttgart

Germany, 15 April
Bomber Command attacked Stuttgart last night, despatching 462 aircraft to deliver what is officially described as "a very heavy attack" on one of Germany's largest armament and industrial centres.

Halifaxes and Stirlings dropped 4,000-pound and 8,000-pound bombs – "factory-smashers" and "blockbusters" – and thousands of incendiaries. Pilots in the rear of the bomber "stream" were guided to their target by the glow of fierce fires. The raid, the heaviest yet

against Stuttgart, lasted for 45 minutes. Some of the huge four-engined aircraft, filled to capacity with bombs and petrol, flew very low, with gunners shooting up targets in the bright moonlight. One Stirling collided with an electricity pylon and had to jettison part of its load when the incendiaries caught fire. Some 23 of the Allied aircraft are missing.

At the same time, Russian long-range four-engined bombers made individual attacks on Danzig and Konigsberg (→17).

One factory in Stuttgart is now little more than a mass of twisted metal.

US air force wants joint bombing plan

Europe, 17 April
The air war is set to reach a new peak of intensity. RAF Bomber Command is fighting the "Battle of the Ruhr" in which hundreds of bombers go out almost every night to attack armament and industrial factories in what the bomber crews cynically call "happy valley".

At the same time the USAAF, wedded to the doctrine of precison daylight bombing, has carried out its first attacks into the heart of Germany and, despite a loss rate of ten per cent, is determined to carry on.

Major-General Ira Eaker, the commander of the US Eighth Army Air Force, has, in fact, put forward a proposal called "The Combined Bomber Offensive from the United Kingdom" reasserting the belief that a joint Allied bombing campaign could bring Germany to its knees. Major-General Eaker recognises, however, that it will be necessary to "seek the destruction of enemy fighters in the air and on the ground".

The *Luftwaffe* is equally well aware of the dangers posed by the Allied bombers and has decided to concentrate on producing fighters for the defence of the *Reich* by day and night (→21).

Budget tightens the tax screw on austerity Britain

Westminster, 12 April

Sir Kingsley Wood, the chancellor, turned the tax screw more tightly on Britain in a budget which will raise an extra £100 million ($400 million) without altering income tax. Alcohol and tobacco will cost more – beer 1/3 (6p/25¢) a pint, whisky £1/5/6 (£1.27¹/₂p/$5.14) a bottle, wine an extra 1/- (5p/20¢) a bottle, and cigarettes 2/4 (12p/47¢) for 20. Entertainments tax will increase the price of 1/6 cinema seats to 1/9 (9p/35¢) and add 1/- to the cost of a stall in West End theatres.

Purchase tax is removed from all Utility cloth and textiles, including towels, furnishings, linen and handkerchiefs. But on all luxury goods, such as fur coats, silk dresses or fabrics, leather bags and suitcases, gramophone records and musical instruments, gold and silver watches and clocks, cosmetics, perfume and jewellery (real or imitation), the tax is increased to an unprecedented 100 per cent.

The cost of the war is estimated this year at £5,756 million ($23 billion), of which half will be raised in tax. National Savings bring in £30 million ($120 million) a week, making a total of £4,600 million ($18.5 billion) saved by the end of last year.

Yugoslav partisans fight Axis soldiers

A Yugoslav partisan lays a mine: now the Allies are fighting with them.

Montenegro, 15 April

After two years of unaided guerrilla warfare, with huge losses on both sides, Tito's Yugoslav partisans seem to have been recognized by the Allies. Until recently, the misinformed British were dropping weapons to the rival band of partisans, the pro-royalist *Chetniks*.

Today, however, Allied liaison officers, Canadians of Yugoslavian birth, were parachuted into Croatia to find Tito's partisans fighting their way to Montenegro after a major Axis crackdown had failed to destroy them. The fourth major offensive involved five German divisions – including a *Waffen-SS*, a complete infantry regiment, two Italian divisions and their locally-raised *Ustachi* allies.

After savage fighting the outnumbered partisans managed to fight their way out, bringing 4,000 wounded with them. An attempt to trap them failed after a savage series of battles in which no prisoners were taken (→ 15/5).

Red Army rebuffs German attack on Leningrad lifeline

Leningrad, 14 April

The Soviet high command reports today that the Red Army has repulsed a heavy German tank and infantry attack south-east of Leningrad. The attack, says the *Stavka*, was of an "offensive-defensive" nature, and adds laconically that it resulted in "no material change".

It would seem from these reports that, although the Russian corridor to the besieged city is only some 12 miles (19 km) wide in this area, the attack was not a serious attempt to cut the road and railway which the Russians have built to carry supplies to the city's long-suffering people. It is far more likely to have been an attempt to seize a local advantage of terrain before the ground hardens and the Russians renew their attempts to drive the Germans and their allies away from Leningrad for ever.

Following their success in opening a route to the city on 18 January, the Soviets have twice tried to lift the siege completely. In their first attack, on 10 February, they were foiled by the Spanish *Azul* division, and then on 19 March they were driven off again. The situation now is like two boxers sparring, seeking advantage, before unleashing their big punches.

"Lady Be Good" crew lost in desert

Libya, 12 April

An air-sea rescue operation is today being mounted from the US air base at Benghazi to scour the Mediterranean for survivors from a missing Liberator. In reality the eight surviving crew members are making a desperate attempt to walk home in the blazing heat of the Sahara desert. A simple, yet tragic, navigational error seems likely to cost the lives of the crew of *Lady be Good*.

Leaving markers along their trail, the crew are dying off day by day as they head north. Their water has run out. Their captain has written in his diary: "Still praying, eyes bad, lost all our wgt [*sic*], aching all over."

German commanders prepare for last-ditch fight in Africa

Tunisia, 17 April

Despite Rommel's plea to Hitler and Mussolini to evacuate North Africa and prepare for the invasion of Europe, German engineers are working feverishly to prepare new defence lines in Tunisia. The high command in Berlin reasons that if Axis troops can hold out in Tunisia until the autumn, the invasion of mainland Europe will be delayed for another year.

Allied numerical superiority is overwhelming, however. The British and American air forces can muster 3,000 aircraft; the Axis, 500: the Allies have 1,200 tanks; the Axis, 130. Despite this the Germans are skilled improvisers, particularly when it comes to defence (→ 21).

An infantry unit takes some time off from the campaign in North Africa.

April

Su	Mo	Tu	We	Th	Fr	Sa
				1	2	3
4	5	6	7	8	9	10
11	12	13	14	15	16	17
18	19	20	21	22	23	24
25	26	27	28	29	30	

18. Moscow: The USSR accuses the *Gestapo* of concocting the Katyn massacre (→ 30).

18. Mediterranean: In an engagement off Cape Bon lasting just ten minutes, Allied fighters shoot down 59 *Luftwaffe* transports and ten fighter escorts on their way to Tunisia: nine Allied fighters are lost.

19. Warsaw: The Jews rise up and drive 2,000 heavily armed SS troops under Lt-Gen Stroop from the ghetto (→ 23).

20. Mediterranean: One hundred and six German transport aircraft have been shot down in two days.

20. Tokyo: Mamoru Shigemitsu is appointed foreign minister (→ 21).

20. Pacific: USAAF bombers raid the Japanese base on Nauru (→ 21).

21. Pacific: Japanese aircraft bombard US positions on Funafuti in the Ellice Islands, retaliating for yesterday's raid on Nauru.

21. Tokyo: Admiral Mineichi Koga is appointed to succeed Yamamoto as C-in-C of the combined fleet (→ 21/5).

21. Tunisia: New Zealand troops, consisting mainly of Maoris, take Takrouna (→ 22).

21. Washington: President Roosevelt condemns the Japanese execution of US PoWs and warns that the perpetrators will face trial after the war.

22. Tunisia: Allied forces make a series of attacks on Longstop Hill and "Peter's Corner".→

23. Rastenburg: Himmler orders the SS to put down the Warsaw uprising with "the utmost severity".→

23. London: A joint Anglo-US command is set up to plan for a European landing; Lieutenant-General Sir Frederick Morgan is appointed Chief of Staff Supreme Allied Command [COSSAC].

24. San Francisco: A US invasion force sets sail to take Attu, in the Aleutians (→ 26).

SS moves in to crush Warsaw Ghetto

SS men march off a column of captured Jews, but the ghetto's battle goes on.

Stroop (l): still hoping for a medal.

Warsaw, 24 April
SS General Jurgen Stroop told Himmler that he would clear out the Warsaw Ghetto in three days. Now he is having second thoughts. On the eve of the feast of Passover, when the Jews celebrate liberation from their oppressors, he sent in tanks, flame-throwers and dynamite squads; they were met by a barrage of small-arms fire, grenades and home-made bombs. The Germans retreated in confusion.

So it has continued, day after day. Stroop, who refers to the Jews as "trash and subhumans" and "cowards by nature", has had to go for total destruction in order to get at the Jews, who are lodged in cellars, bunkers and sewers, from whence they spring out to take the Germans by surprise. A passing woman produces a pistol from her underclothes and fires point-blank at a German.

When the ghetto was set up in 1940 it held 400,000 Jews. Starved and overcrowded, the Jews died, but not fast enough for Himmler. He ordered them to be sent to extermination camps, but because of the war situation transport was lacking, and with 60,000 still in the ghetto, Stroop was drafted in with 2,090 troops.

The Jews had been preparing for a long time; if they had to die they would die fighting. In factories where they worked under the supervision of German officers they secretly made bombs. When they left the ghetto on burial duties they acquired weapons from Polish resistance fighters.

A pall of black smoke hangs over Warsaw. The Jews stay in the blazing buildings until the last moment, and after they have jumped they strive to crawl into hiding in spite of their broken arms and legs.

Stroop still hopes to get the medal that Himmler promised if the job was done with speed and efficiency. His daily reports to Himmler promise success, in spite of "the cunning fighting methods of the Jews and other bandits" (→ 26).

The joys of English springtime.

British church bells will ring out again

Britain, 20 April
The ban on ringing church bells is to be lifted from next Sunday, Easter Day, said Mr Churchill in the Commons today. The cabinet decided that the ban can be relaxed on Sundays and special occasions "in the light of changing circumstances". Many of the 12,000 parish churches will not be able to ring their bells this Sunday as they have been disused for three years and their bellringers are in the armed forces. No substitute signal of invasion has been announced.

RAF gives Hitler an explosive birthday

Europe, 21 April
The RAF celebrated Hitler's 54th birthday last night with raids against Stettin and Rostock, on the Baltic coast, and Berlin. In the east, the Red Air Force attacked Tilsit. Stettin, a key port supplying Nazi armies in north Russia, was most heavily hit. More than 150 4,000-pound bombs were dropped there in 40 minutes. Simultaneously, other aircraft laid mines off the Brittany coast. Hitler, it is thought, was far from the bombing, in a mountain retreat (→ 27).

1943

April

Su	Mo	Tu	We	Th	Fr	Sa
				1	2	3
4	5	6	7	8	9	10
11	12	13	14	15	16	17
18	19	20	21	22	23	24
25	26	27	28	29	30	

Yamamoto shot down after code broken

Guadalcanal, 18 April

Admiral Isoroku Yamamoto, the supreme symbol of the imperial Japanese navy, is dead. Revered by the Japanese as the architect of the attack on Pearl Harbor, he was ambushed, shot down and killed yesterday by American P-38 Lightning fighter aircraft over southern Bougainville, in the Solomons.

The Americans, tipped off by naval intelligence which had cracked a Japanese coded message, knew of Yamamoto's expected time of arrival over Kahili and sent 17 Lightning fighters from Guadalcanal to intercept. A stickler for punctuality, Yamamoto was right on time, and four Lightnings broke through the Japanese fighter escort and sent the admiral's bomber plummeting into the jungle.

Yamamoto's death will be a significant blow to Japanese military morale, even though the man whose brainchild had been the attack on Pearl Harbor had also been

> "I am looking forward to dictating peace to the United States in the White House at Washington"
> — ADMIRAL YAMAMOTO

What do YOU say, AMERICA?

Yamamoto, one of America's arch-enemies: shot down in the jungle.

the chief proposer of "the decisive battle" which led to the Japanese calamity at the Battle of Midway last summer. He had taken command of all Japan's air forces in the Pacific theatre (→21).

Axis armies face trap in North Africa

Tunisia, 22 April

Slowly but remorselessly, the Allies are advancing on all fronts in Tunisia, driving the Axis into a corner from which escape must be almost impossible. No armies have fought a more savage defensive battle than the poorly-supplied and numerically weaker Axis troops. Their counter-attacks are fierce but always costly in men and tanks. The American

1st Infantry Division is excelling in mountain warfare in the peaks between the Dhjoumine and Tine rivers. Their colleagues of the British 78th Division are locked in brutal combat for a hill called Longstop. The British 6th Armoured Division is fighting an expensive battle – in terms of losses on both sides – with the 10th *Panzer* Division at Sebkret el Kourzia (→26).

Cheerful troops move up for an Allied attack on Longstop Hill.

25. China: Sun Tien-ying, the commander of the Chinese Fifth Army, defects to the Japanese.

25. Atlantic: The British escort carrier *Biter* scores the first "kill" of her class when she and the destroyer *Pathfinder* sink the U-boat U203.

26. Tunisia: Longstop Hill, the gateway to the Tunisian plain, falls to the British V Corps (→1/5).

26. Aleutian Islands: US warships bombard Japanese positions on Attu (→11/5).

26. Off Mauritius: Subhas Chandra Bose, the leader of the Indian National Army, is transferred from a U-boat to a Japanese submarine en route from Berlin to Penang.

26-27. Germany: Duisburg is raided overnight by 561 RAF aircraft.→

27. Britain: The "Ground Grocer" device, based in East Anglia, starts jamming the German early-warning system.

28. Mediterranean: The British submarine *Unshaken* sinks an Italian torpedo boat.

28. Stockholm: Sweden protests against the mining of its territorial waters by Germany.

29. USSR: A series of minor attacks in the Caucasus slowly pushes the Germans back (→5/5).

29. Norway: Six British commandos place limpet mines on German ships, but are caught by a patrol.

29. Atlantic: A U-boat sinks five merchant ships off the West African coast.

30. Tunisia: German *Panzer* units capture Djebel Bou-Aoukaz.

30. London: In an attempt to improve relations with the USSR, the Polish government in exile withdraws its request for a Red Cross inquiry into the Katyn massacre.→

30. Europe: Approximately 1.3 million forced labourers from occupied countries are now working as slaves for Germany.

Katyn claims bring Russo-Polish split

London, 30 April

An International Medical Commission team drawn from German-occupied nations is today spending its third day in Katyn, compiling a report on the 4,143 bodies so far exhumed from a mass grave for murdered Polish officers. The massacre, which seems likely to be the work of Stalin's agents, has caused turmoil amongst Polish exiles. The Union of Polish Patriots in Moscow has accused the London-based Polish government in exile of co-operating in a Hitlerite provocation. On 26 April the Russians ended diplomatic relations with the London Poles (→1/5).

Bomber Command mines Baltic Sea

Britain, 29 April

The RAF has converted key areas of the Baltic into a minefield which paralyses shipping. Known to airmen by the codeword "Gardening" (because areas where mines are laid are named after flowers), mine-laying is a little-publicized form of warfare, yet one which can have deadly results for U-boats on their way to patrol or training areas. Almost 11,400 mines were dropped by Bomber Command last year in spite of heavy *flak* from ships. In all, 23 aircraft were lost in last night's mission (→4/5).

Cars deadlier than the armed services

Britain, 30 April

More people were killed or injured on the roads last year than the total casualties of the UK armed services in the first two years of war. On the battlefields 145,012 people died in those two years, while road casualties last year alone reached 147,500, despite a drop in the number of private cars on the road from two million in 1939 to a mere 718,000 by this year. Leslie Hore-Belisha, who introduced beacon crossings as a road safety measure when he was minister of transport, gave the figures in a speech at Blenheim.

▷

401

Rocket offensive feared by British defence planners

London, 30 April

The potential threat of a German long-range rocket offensive on England is now receiving top priority in government circles. On 11 April the war office submitted a report to the chiefs of staff. It concluded that the Germans were developing a rocket 95 feet in length, carrying a 1.25-ton warhead and having a range of 130 miles (208 km). The prime minister was told and the RAF's photographic interpretation unit at Medmenham, near Henley-on-Thames, ordered to check all air photographs covering areas within 130 miles of London and Southampton.

On 20 April, Duncan Sandys, Churchill's son-in-law and parliamentary secretary to the ministry of supply, was appointed to head a committee to review all evidence of German long-range rocket development. Mr Sandys thinks that the Nazis must have a special base.

A check of air photographs revealed that Peenemunde, on the Baltic, was a likely spot. Medmenham unearthed photographs taken by a bomber pilot on a raid against Kiel in May 1942, which revealed much building and mysterious earthworks. Some photographic *sorties* were immediately launched. On 22 April a Mosquito took photographs of the area. One of these revealed an object projecting from the seaward end of a building. In the next frame, taken four seconds later, the object had vanished and in its place was a small puff of smoke. The British do not realize it, but the photographs show the 21st experimental firing of an A4 rocket. Nevertheless, the Sandys Committee has concluded that Peenemunde is an experimental station dealing with projectiles and explosives. If rockets are being developed there it will be a while before they are operational. Peenemunde is to be kept under observation and every effort made to establish its role.

Chindits complete their Burmese retreat

Uphill all the way for the Chindits, trained to fight the Japanese in the jungle.

India, 30 April

For two weeks they have been arriving, gaunt figures trickling across the Chindwin river to the safety of British India. They are survivors of the first Chindit expedition behind enemy lines in Japanese-occupied Burma. Just over 2,000 of the original 3,000-strong force had made the return trip by yesterday, although 600 are so emaciated by nearly three months' jungle warfare that they may never fight again.

The Chindits are pioneers of what their commander, Brigadier Wingate, calls "long-range penetration". Both the concept and its founder are still controversial within Regular Army ranks. As a plus there have been the Chindits' success in putting the Mandalay/Myitkyina railway out of action for four weeks and the intelligence acquired. Negatively, the Chindits were forced to withdraw and Japan retains control of Burma. Wingate, though, says that the expedition proves that the Allied soldier, given training, can take on the Japanese at jungle warfare with success.

Jews rounded up as the ghetto burns

Warsaw, 26 April

At the close of a busy day, SS General Stroop reported by teletype to SS headquarters from the Warsaw Ghetto: "A further 1,330 Jews pulled out of dug-outs and immediately destroyed; 362 Jews killed in battle." The day before, reporting the capture of 27,464 Jews, he told Himmler that he was ordering a train to take them to Treblinka extermination camp.

Stroop says that he has lost only 16 men in the battles, though the Jews put the figure at several hundred. He claims that the ghetto has been cleared, but there are still Jews hiding in the sewers, while others have escaped to seek refuge in the Christian sector of the city (→ 6/5).

Allies pin invasion hopes on "the man who never was"

Huelva, Spain, 30 April

Excited German intelligence chiefs cannot believe their luck. Top-secret British documents indicating the Allies' next move in the invasion of Europe have been found in a briefcase attached to the body of a British officer washed up on a Spanish beach. A letter from Lord Louis Mountbatten to General Eisenhower indicates that Greece, not Sicily as assumed, is the area selected for the invasion of Europe.

What the Germans do not know is that they are the victims of an elaborate hoax, gruesomely codenamed Operation Mincemeat. The body of "Major Martin" is believed to be that of a down-and-out Londoner who died of pneumonia in an East End hospital. He was carried in an insulated canister and put into the sea by the submarine *Seraph*. The briefcase was handed to the British consul, but not until the *Abwehr* had finished with it.

To add authenticity, "Major Martin" carried a picture of his girlfriend "Pam", a receipt for an engagement ring, a tailor's bill, theatre ticket stubs and a stiff letter from his bank manager. He will be given a military funeral and a death notice in *The Times* (→ 14/5).

Belgian colonial troops from the Congo arrive in British West Africa: they have British equipment and Belgian rifles and wear the traditional fez.

Desperate battle fought for control of the Atlantic

Convoy ONS-5 is top U-boat target

North Atlantic, 30 April
Another major sea battle is about to begin over the slow-moving westward bound convoy ONS-5. The Germans spotted the convoy yesterday 500 miles (800 km) east of the southern tip of Greenland and sank one of the 42 merchant ships. Admiral Donitz is now assembling a pack of 51 U-boats to strike at it before it reaches St John's, Newfoundland. He can afford to: the U-boat fleet is now at a record level of 240 operational submarines.

But British codebreakers have discovered the German plans, and yesterday five destroyers set off from St John's to reinforce the convoy's escort. All available Royal Canadian Air Force Catalinas are also being prepared for air support.

The stage is set for a battle royal, and the outcome may well be decided by the weather. Already the galeforce winds are making it difficult for the convoy to stay together. And the escort leader, the destroyer *Duncan*, has used so much fuel that she has had to sail home (→ 7/5).

Survivors tell tales of hellish journey

North Atlantic, 30 April
Few people in Britain know of the ordeal faced by merchant seamen on Atlantic convoys. In unarmed ships, sometimes miles from their escorting screen of destroyers and frigates, they are constantly subjected to air or torpedo attacks – and yet have to maintain a constant course at a constant speed on the convoy commodore's orders if the convoy is to get through.

Survivors are snatched from the sea – often with hideous burns from fuel oil which can set the sea itself alight. Many spend days in lifeboats or clinging to wreckage until they are rescued. And yet most will sign on for the next voyage – even though they know that 4,500 merchant ships have been sunk so far in this war.

Two U-boats surface in the Atlantic: convoy ONS-5 faces a pack of 51.

A survivor from a sunken U-boat raises his hands and pleads for help.

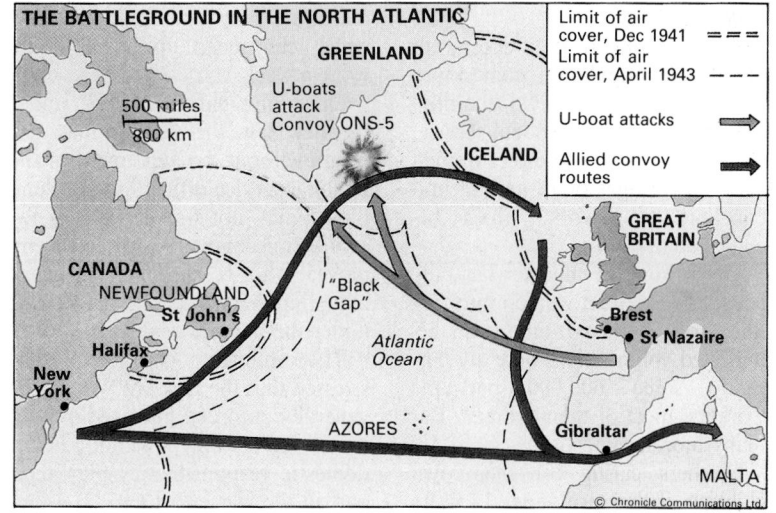

How Allies closed the "Black Gap"

North Atlantic, 30 April
One of the greatest problems which the Allies have had in the battle against the U-boats in the Atlantic has been air cover. This has been especially so in the area south-west of Greenland, the so-called "Black Gap".

The reason that the Black Gap has plagued the Allies for such a long time has been a shortage of very-long-range (VLR) patrol aircraft, because priority of four-engined types has gone to the strategic bomber forces. The British, Canadian and US air forces fighting the Battle of the Atlantic have for some time been demanding more US Consolidated B-24 Liberator aircraft, which have a range of over 2,000 miles (3,200 km).

More Liberators are now available. Equipped with the ASV III centimetric radio-location system, and armed with the Mark IX depth charge, they are formidable aircraft. Liberators are operating from bases in Newfoundland, Iceland and Northern Ireland. No North Atlantic U-boat is safe from them.

Newer technology turns the tables

Britain, 30 April
The naval escorts in the Battle of the Atlantic are now better equipped than ever before for hunting and destroying U-boats. While Asdic will detect a U-boat under water, escorts have two means of locating them on the surface. High-frequency direction-finding – or "Huff Duff" – detects a U-boat's radio transmissions and gives a bearing on it, while the Type 271 radio-location system can pinpoint the submarine up to forty miles. The conventional stern-launched depth charge has now been joined by "Hedgehog", a launcher which throws depth charges forward over the bows. This means that the escort vessel can attack without losing Asdic contact as it does when it runs over the top of a submarine.

May

Su	Mo	Tu	We	Th	Fr	Sa
						1
2	3	4	5	6	7	8
9	10	11	12	13	14	15
16	17	18	19	20	21	22
23	24	25	26	27	28	29
30	31					

1. Tunisia: US forces complete the capture of Hill 609 (→ 3).

1. Britain: German guns shell Dover for 45 minutes.

1. Berlin: The International Medical Commission signs its report on the Katyn massacre, confirming that it took place in 1940 and therefore must have been the work of the Russians.→

2. Australia: Japanese aircraft bomb Darwin (→ 15).

3. Tunisia: US and French troops capture Mateur (→ 5).

4. Mediterranean: British destroyers sink the Italian merchant ship *Campobasso*, taking supplies to Tunisia.

4. Germany: An RAF raid on Dortmund kills 693 people, the highest number of fatalities in a single raid so far (→ 14).

5. Tunisia: The British capture Djebel Bou Aoukaz, securing their left flank (→ 6).

5. USSR: The Russians advance in the Kuban area, taking Krymsk and Neberjaisk (→ 22).

6. Palestine: Haj Amin al-Husseini, the *mufti* of Jerusalem, protests to Bulgaria for allowing Jewish children to sail to Palestine; he says they should be deported to Poland.→

6. Tunisia: Allied forces, heading for Tunis, wipe out the German 15th *Panzer* Division.→

7. Burma: British troops are forced to retreat after the Japanese take Buthidaung (→ 14).

7. Paris: German television starts broadcasting from studios in the old Magic City theatre.

7. Ottawa: Canadian MPs vote an additional $1,000 million towards the war effort (→ 26).

8. China: Japanese forces take Nanhsien (→ 13).

8. Sicilian Narrows: Admiral Cunningham launches Operation Retribution, to prevent Axis armies from evacuating North Africa.

8. Britain: Admiral Sir Bruce Fraser is appointed C-in-C of the Home Fleet, replacing Admiral Sir John Tovey.

Allies capture Tunis and Bizerta

North Africa, 7 May
Thousands of civilians lined the streets of Tunis today to pelt British troops with spring flowers, the women bestowing kisses on embarrassed troops of the Derbyshire Yeomanry as their tanks rolled in. Even then, however, the fighting was not over, as small pockets of fanatical Germans continued to snipe from vantage points on public buildings and mosques.

It was at 3.15am when the order was given to drive into the city. Armoured cars of the 11th Hussars were the first – as they had been in every major town or city captured since Alamein – followed almost immediately by the tanks.

The final assault on the Djebel Bou Aoukaz hills overlooking the city had involved an artillery barrage of an intensity not known since Alamein; the technique was to use a concentration of fire, centrally controlled, on all known enemy positions. Shells landed on every two yards of front, causing total havoc. A huge air attack began at dawn, with the RAF flying more than 200 *sorties*. By 9.30am the 4th Indian Division had cleared a pathway for IX Corps' tanks.

Simultaneously, the US II Corps began its final assault towards Bizerta, in the north. After some tough fighting yesterday, the US 9th Infantry Division drove into the city in the late afternoon; but formal entry is reserved for the French Corps Franc d'Afrique (→ 9).

During the fight for Tunis: Allied soldiers muster behind a Bren gun.

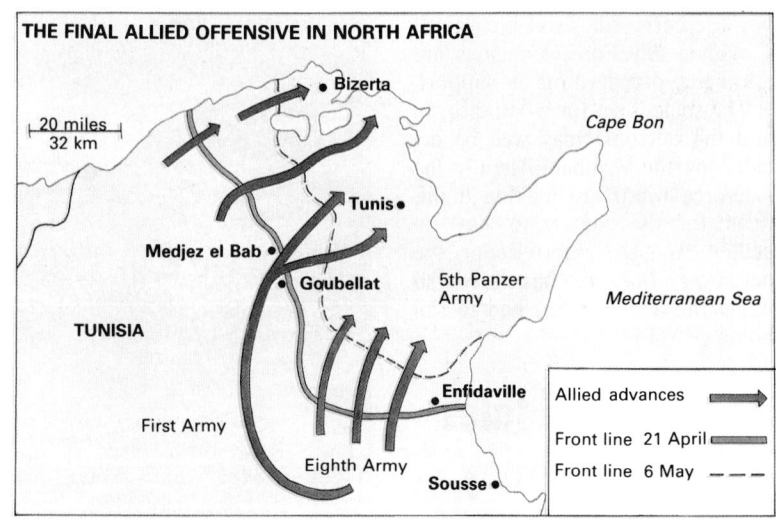

War work compulsory for British women

Britain, 8 May
A new law aimed at "shirkers" in the female population comes into force today. Ernest Bevin, the minister of labour and national service, now has the power to direct women between the ages of 18 and 45 into part-time war work, which becomes compulsory.

Up to now the minister has only been able to direct women into full-time work, with part-time posts being filled voluntarily. There are currently some 600,000 part-time workers, most of them women. But many more are needed.

Mothers caring for their own children, if they are under 14 years old, are exempt from the new law, which can mean up to 30 hours work a week.

Once directed into work under the new law the worker may not resign without the agreement of the national service officer, and her employer may not fire her except for serious misconduct. A directed employee who is absent from work may find herself being prosecuted under the defence regulations.

The ministry of labour has stressed that the new law will not be generally enforced but used only to ensure that women without heavy domestic responsibilities play their part in the war effort (→ 2/7).

Troops seize 1,000 during Sofia curfew

Sofia, 5 May
During a two-day curfew in Sofia, the authorities have seized 1,000 people, including 400 said to be communists. The Bulgarian capital was sealed off while troops conducted a house-to-house search for the killers of Colonel Georgi Pantev, the chief of police, who was shot down as he entered his home two nights ago. Pantev is the third senior official to be assassinated this year. Only relatives, military officers and state officials are to be allowed to attend the police chief's funeral (→ 28/8).

SS captures bunker HQ of ghetto rebels

Warsaw, 8 May
SS Major-General Jurgen Stroop believes that he is at last within sight of clearing the Warsaw Ghetto of Jews. Fewer than 4,000 remain in hiding, he says, after the capture of the bunker which the Jews used as their HQ. To reach it, Stroop's soldiers demolished two machine-tool factories where Jews worked under SS supervision.

Stroop sealed up all entrances to the buildings and pumped in gas. "We won't fall into their hands alive," the fighters inside screamed as they set about killing one another. "All around us", said one survivor, "was the roar of fire, the crash of falling walls. Outside the ghetto it was spring, but here a holocaust reigned."

Poland and Russia pledge friendship

London, 5 May
Just over a week after Stalin broke with the exiled Polish government, he and General Sikorski have patched up their quarrel in the interest of defeating Germany. But Sikorski insists that certain "facts" divide them, probably a reference to the cause of the split: the German discovery at Katyn, in eastern Poland, of a mass grave of Polish officers, allegedly massacred by Soviet troops in 1940 (→ 15).

Japan launches attack in central China

A Nationalist recruitment poster: now they face a new Japanese attack.

Changsha, 5 May
A large force of Japanese troops stormed the beaches on the southern shores of Tungting Lake today as Japan launched a new two-pronged offensive in central China. The landings put the Japanese within 50 miles (80 km) of the war-torn capital of Hunan province, Changsha, where the Chinese Nationalists have managed to repulse three previous attacks.

At the same time as the landings an estimated 7,000-8,000 Japanese troops, heavily supported by air force bombers, struck southward from southern Hupeh, capturing four towns on the Hunan border, north of the lake.

The combination of the two attacks has left Allied strategists unsure as to whether this new offensive is intended to take Changsha, or if the invaders are planning to encircle Chinese forces to the west, enabling the Japanese to ruin or seize the ripening rice crop in one of China's most fertile regions (→ 8).

Noel Coward extols a "happy breed"

London, 1 May
Noel Coward's stage tribute to the ordinary Englishman, *This Happy Breed*, opened last night at the Haymarket. Coward himself played Mr Gibbons, squire of 17 Sycamore Road, Clapham, south London.

The play was first presented in Blackpool on 21 September last year. Nothing could be further removed from the naval captain whom he portrayed in *In Which We Serve*. Yet they are connected by a gritty, undemonstrative patriotism which is not taken in by events – the false hopes of Munich, for instance. The Gibbons family lives through the General Strike, the Depression, the Abdication and the coming of war with phlegmatic common sense and endurance.

Coward as the patriotic Mr Gibbons.

Biggest-ever U-boat wolfpack withdraws from convoy battle

North Atlantic, 7 May
Convoy ONS-5 has just survived more than three days of battering from the biggest U-boat pack assembled in the war so far. The pack, codenamed *"Fink"* [Chaffinch], comprised 51 boats. The 42-ship ONS-5 was hove to in gales when the pack found it. The U-boats sank 13 merchant ships, but the escort hit back using two new devices: Hedgehog, which projects depth charges ahead of the attacking ship, and, in its greatest success so far, Type 271 M radar equipment. Seven U-boats were sunk, two lost in collision and five badly hit. Fink has been called off (→ 13).

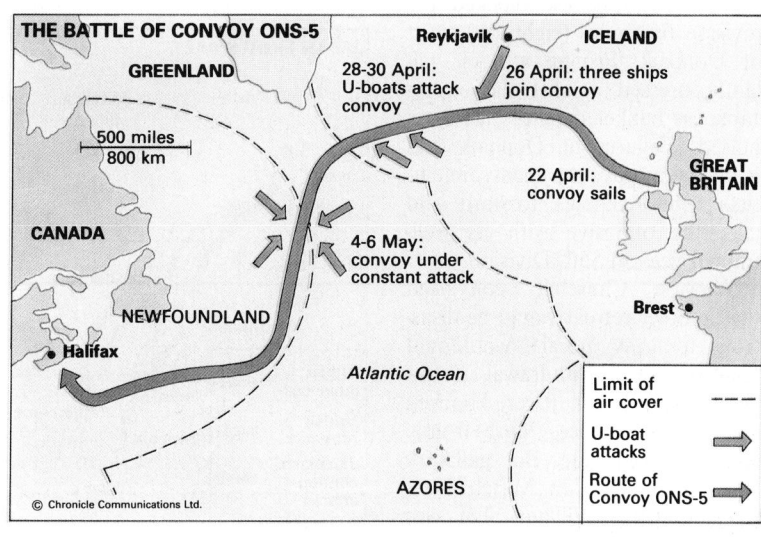

US air raid cripples Japanese destroyer

Solomon Islands, 8 May
US dive-bombers claim to have crippled one Japanese destroyer and damaged two others following multiple bombing raids on shipping and shore installations in the Solomon Islands today. The enemy destroyers were hit as Dauntless dive-bombers surprised Japanese destroyers off Gizo Island. During the raid one destroyer suffered a direct hit from a 1,000-pound bomb. US and New Zealand airmen flying Liberators also strafed and bombed Japanese bases at Kahili, Ballale, Fauro and Munda (→ 12).

1943

May

Su	Mo	Tu	We	Th	Fr	Sa
						1
2	3	4	5	6	7	8
9	10	11	12	13	14	15
16	17	18	19	20	21	22
23	24	25	26	27	28	29
30	31					

9. Tunisia: King George VI tells Eisenhower "the debt of Dunkirk is repaid" as the Allies hold 50,000 Axis prisoners (→ 10).

10. Tunisia: The British 6th Armoured Division ends Axis chances of escape by cutting off the Cape Bon peninsula.→

11. Mediterranean: The Allies end a three-day aerial bombardment of the Italian island of Pantelleria (→ 14).

11. Great Yarmouth: A daylight raid by 20 German bombers kills 26 girls staying at an ATS hostel (→ 30).

11. Washington: Churchill arrives with military staff for "Trident", talks with Roosevelt on Allied strategy after North Africa (→ 19).

11. Aleutian Islands: The US 7th Infantry Division lands on Attu island, helped by dense fog to gain surprise (→ 16).

12. Solomon Islands: US ships shell Japanese positions on Munda and Vila, and lay mines off New Georgia (→ 3/6).

12. Rastenburg: Hitler downgrades the defence of Sicily, giving priority to Sardinia and the Peloponnese.→

12. Rome: Grand Admiral Donitz arrives on a mission to boost Italy's contribution to the Axis effort.

13. Atlantic: The British have sunk three out of seven U-boats hunting convoy HX-237, which has lost three ships.

13. China: Chinese troops, under pressure from Japan, evacuate Kung-an (→ 29).

14. Mediterranean: The Allies' Mediterranean Air Command orders a sea and air blockade of Pantelleria (→ 22).

14. Britain: The intelligence service confirms the success of Operation Mincemeat, in which a corpse was floated ashore off Spain bearing papers aimed at fooling the Germans into thinking that the Allies plan to invade Greece.

15. Tunisia: General Giraud deposes the *bey* of Tunis for collaboration with the Axis (→ 27).

British take stock after Burma retreat

Japanese infantry forge ahead in Burma, having rebuffed the Allied offensive.

New Delhi, 14 May
The first Allied offensive in Burma has ended in total failure. After six months' campaigning, the British Army is back where it started.

The much-heralded offensive from India began last December. The 14th Indian Division advanced down the long narrow Mayu peninsula, on the Bay of Bengal, with the limited objectives of clearing the peninsula and seizing the strategically important Akyab island. Possession of Akyab would put Allied air forces within easy striking distance of Rangoon.

At first all went well. The port of Maungdaw and the town of Buthidaung fell with little opposition. However, early in January, an unfortunate delay occurred when the offensive became bogged down in the inhospitable terrain of the peninsula. The Japanese blocked the division five miles (eight km) short of Donbaik. Frontal attacks, gallantly pressed against the strong Japanese bunker defences, were repulsed. Failures at Donbaik and Rathedaung gave the enemy time to rush reinforcements forward and take the offensive with its well-trained veteran 55th Division.

Winston Churchill, convinced that another retreat would be disastrous to army morale, would not countenance a withdrawal. Tanks were sent in, but they were knocked out almost at once. More frontal attacks were made. But gallantry was not enough. In March Lieutenant-General William Slim was sent to report on the situation. He found that morale was ebbing as a result of repeated failures. Further desperate attempts to dislodge the enemy were met by heavy fire and driven back.

The commander of the 14th Division was replaced by Maj-Gen C Lomax, and Slim was again sent to the front where he found the situation "fantastically" bad. A brigade had disintegrated, and small starving parties were struggling over the hills. Things had gone terribly wrong, and on 8 April Churchill wrote: "We are being completely out-fought and out-manoeuvred by the Japanese."

By early May the Japanese had reoccupied Maungdaw and the fighting stopped with the monsoon. The Allies were back at their starting point (→ 28/6).

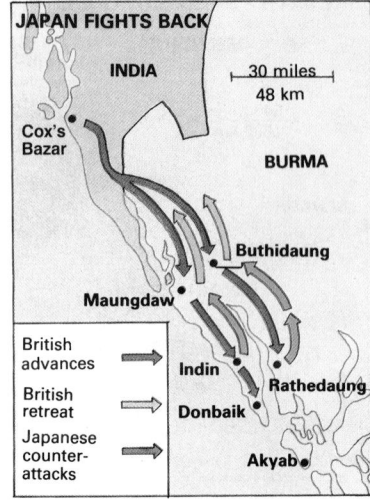

Netherlands placed under martial law

Amsterdam, 9 May
The Germans today proclaimed martial law throughout the Netherlands, imposed an 8pm to 8am curfew, and rounded up several thousand Dutchmen. The action was ordered by *Reich* commissioner, Arthur Seyss-Inquart; it comes in the wake of mounting evidence of resistance to the Germans and increasing economic chaos.

Gatherings of more than five people, the printing and distribution of pamphlets calling for resistance to the Germans, and the sale of spirits in bars, have been forbidden. Strikes and lockouts are illegal. All Dutchmen between 18 and 35 have been ordered to register; they will be sent to work in war factories in Germany (→ 16).

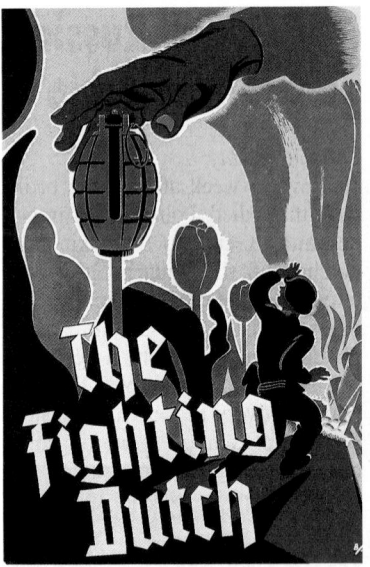

Urging the Dutch to fight occupation.

Hospital ship sunk by a Japanese sub

Brisbane, 15 May
A Japanese submarine, the I-177, sank the Australian hospital ship *Centaur* off Brisbane yesterday with the loss of 268 lives. The *Centaur* was brightly lit and properly marked. Most on board were asleep and had little chance; 11 of the victims were army nurses. An American destroyer picked up 63 survivors, including the only woman found alive, an army nursing sister (→ 18/6).

Allied triumph shatters Axis power in North Africa

Allies hold 250,000 prisoners of war

Tunisia, 13 May

At 2.15pm today, the teleprinter chattered out a message for the British prime minister, who is in Washington. "Sir," said the Allied C-in-C, General Alexander, "it is my duty to report that the Tunisian campaign is over. All enemy resistance has ceased. We are the masters of the North African shores."

The German commander in North Africa, General von Arnim, surrendered yesterday, and the Italian General Messe, the Axis C-in-C, capitulated today. The end came quickly as Axis troops found themselves trapped between two Allied spearheads and began to give themselves up in their thousands. A small 11th Hussar squadron from Montgomery's Eighth Army found itself with 10,000 exhausted men of the once-formidable *Afrika Korps*. Then the deluge began as General von Vaerst, commanding the 5th *Panzer* Army, signalled: "We will fight to the last." – only to watch his beaten troops raise their hands and march into captivity.

On a beach near Bizerta, another Hussar squadron found 9,000 disconsolate Germans awaiting rescue, some trying to build rafts. More Germans had escaped in commandeered small boats, only to be plucked out by the Royal Navy. Altogether, about 125,000 Germans are believed to be in the Allied "bag" – which, including the Italians, could make as many as 250,000 prisoners.

For Hitler, who ordered a defence to "the last bullet", the implications are serious. The defeated *Afrika Korps* would have been invaluable in the defence of Europe.

For the British, American and French, bitter lessons have been learnt. American generals and their troops have seen German armour in action and have learnt how to cope with skilled defensive fighting. The French have learnt to co-operate with the British, despite the sinking of their fleet. And the British, celebrating in the bars of Tunis, have learnt that it is a long way from Alamein (→ 15).

An Arab who was fighting for the Germans: now an Allied prisoner.

General Montgomery receives the formal surrender of Italian and German forces in Tunisia; assembly points for enemy units are fixed on the map.

Italy is next step, but exactly where?

Sardinia, 13 May

After two weeks of constant bombardment from the air, Italian defenders here have been joined by German troops as this island braces itself for an Allied invasion. Few Axis leaders now doubt that Sardinia will be the target, and coastal defences are being rebuilt and the airfields repaired after the Allied raids.

The intensive bombing is an essential part of an Allied deception plan which involved the corpse of a mythical "Major William Martin" of the Royal Marines washed up in Spain last month carrying allegedly secret documents, giving details of the landings from North Africa [*see report, page 402*]. Hitler's *Abwehr* was taken in by the apparent authenticity; hence the reinforcements. Field Marshal Kesselring, the German commander in Italy, is known to be dubious, however, and has kept strong mobile forces in Sicily and Southern Italy which he regards as the more logical area for attack. It was Mussolini who called for reinforcements in Sardinia.

Despite its huge technical ability and industrial capacity, Italy is desperately short of raw materials and cannot supply its army adequately. This was revealed today by Crown Prince Umberto in an Infantry Day statement. He did not mention the strikes which have paralysed the industrial centres of Milan and Turin recently.

However, opposition to the Fascist regime is becoming increasingly vocal. An illegal "freedom" radio, *Milano-Liberta*, has called for Sicilians to revolt. "Chase the Fascists away and open the gates of your island to the democratic powers and freedom!" it said.

In Rome, the extremist Fascist newspaper *Regime Fascista* has unwittingly revealed the level of discontent in the country. The editor, Roberto Farinacci, Mussolini's former second-in-command, has called for blackshirts to take to the streets and "terrorize people into obedience and to redouble their war effort" (→ 14).

Jewish campaigner takes his own life

London, 12 May
The man sent by the Warsaw Jews to tell the free world of Nazi genocide committed suicide today in London. Szmul Zygielboim left a letter in which he wrote: "I cannot live when the remnant of the Jewish people in Poland is being steadily annihilated ... By my death, I wish to express my vigorous protest against the apathy with which the world resigns itself to the slaughter." Zygielboim was a leading member of the Polish Jewish Social Democratic Party. After escaping to England in 1940 he spoke and broadcast frequently on Jewish sufferings under the Nazis (→16).

German radar set acquired by British

Aberdeen, 9 May
A bizarre incident occurred at Dyce airport, near Aberdeen, today. A Junkers Ju88R, based at Kjevik in Norway, landed of its own free will. It was part of a night-fighter unit, and it seems that its crew has gone over to the Allies. The men brought with them a working FuG 202 Lichtenstein air interception radar. This has been enabling the German nightfighters to enjoy much of their recent success against RAF bombers.

The nasty Nazi squander bug jumps up and down in fury at the very idea of War Savings.

Allied air forces step up continental raids

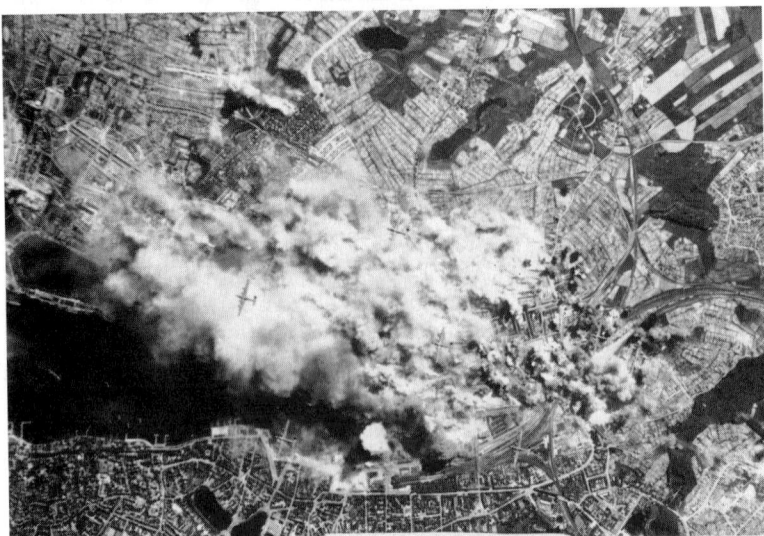

Bombs rain down on a shipyard in Kiel as part of the stepped-up offensive.

Germany, 14 May
The air offensive against Germany's industrial heartland – the Battle of the Ruhr – has reached a new intensity in the past 48 hours. On 12-13 May the inland port of Duisburg was hit for the fifth time in a raid led by ten target-marking "Oboe" Mosquitoes, which were followed by 562 heavy bombers. The total weight of explosive dropped on this one town is now 5,157 tons (5,240 tonnes). On 13-14 May much of Bochum, a coal-rich area near Dortmund, was also reduced to burning rubble. So dense was the coverage that one Stirling returned with three incendiary bombs embedded in its wings.

Yet the raids also extended far beyond the "Happy Valley" of the Ruhr. Targets have included Berlin, Czechoslovakia and Belgium; American Flying Fortresses are tonight attacking the General Motors plant at Antwerp, US-owned before the war. The total bomb tonnage delivered in this 48 hours was 4,000. Seventy-two aircraft have been lost, but Bomber Command reluctantly accepts such losses as inevitable (→24).

Comintern snuffed out to calm Allies

Moscow, 15 May
Stalin has decided to disband the Comintern, the Communist International organization which controls foreign communist parties. The timing of the announcement, which will take effect in a week, is significant. The Grand Alliance against the Axis powers came under strain last month when Moscow broke with the Polish government in London over the Katyn atrocity.

This row still simmers, despite attempts to patch it up ten days ago, and observers believe that Stalin wishes to reassure the west that notions of exporting revolution have been abandoned, and that any countries liberated by the USSR will be allowed to choose their own regimes, undisturbed by Moscow.

Soon after the German invasion in 1941, the Comintern offices were moved from Moscow to Ufa, just west of the Urals, and rumours surfaced in Moscow suggesting that the organization was being disbanded. But it continued its activities under the veteran Bolshevik Dmitry Manuilsky, the Bulgarian Georgi Dimitrov and the Italian Palmiro Togliatti. Many westerners familiar with Stalin's methods doubt whether the Comintern will in fact now be dissolved (→4/7).

Germans launch new offensive against Tito's partisan army

Yugoslavia, 15 May
Axis forces in Yugoslavia today launched their fifth offensive aimed at smashing local resistance. Operation Black, as it is called, is the biggest offensive so far against the partisans, and promises to be the most savage.

Axis troops have been ordered to move "with utmost brutality" against "the hostile population". Four German and Italian divisions are supported by Bulgarian troops and the *Ustachi*, the notorious Croatian irregulars. In all, 120,000 men are lined up against a much smaller force of guerrilla fighters.

The Germans and their allies are using new tactics. Until now they have advanced along main roads; but now they are using Tito's methods, advancing across the countryside, often by night (→27).

Young Yugoslav partisan couriers: now they face a concerted Axis offensive.

1943

May

Su	Mo	Tu	We	Th	Fr	Sa
						1
2	3	4	5	6	7	8
9	10	11	12	13	14	15
16	17	18	19	20	21	22
23	24	25	26	27	28	29
30	31					

16. Netherlands: The Germans confiscate all wireless sets.

16. Aleutian Islands: Japanese forces on Attu retreat to Chichagof Harbour to regroup for a final stand (→ 20).

16. USSR: German troops launch Operation Gypsy Baron, a three-week drive to capture Soviet partisans (→ 3/6).

17. Washington: Britain and the US agree on a free exchange of deciphered signals intelligence, for which the codename "Ultra" is adopted.→

18. London: Montgomery gets more applause than the cast when he attends a performance of *Arsenic and Old Lace*.

18. Hot Springs, Virginia: The United Nations meet to discusss the fairer distribution of food in the post-war world.

19. Atlantic: Grand Admiral Donitz's son Peter is killed when his U-boat is one of four destroyed by British ships escorting convoy SC-130.

19. Berlin: Goebbels announces that the city is free of Jews (→ 24).

20. Attu: US troops are prising fierce Japanese defenders from positions on the Clevesy Pass (→ 22).

21. Tokyo: The Japanese announce the death of Admiral Yamamoto, shot down last month over Bougainville; the US has remained silent until now to avoid revealing that it intercepted a Japanese coded message giving details of his itinerary (→ 5/6).

21. Washington: The Allies agree to stage cross-Channel landings by 1 May 1944 (→ 25).

22. Germany: The *Luftwaffe* ace Adolf Galland test-flies the Messerschmitt Me262 jet fighter at 520mph, and says that it would regain air superiority for Germany. But Hitler wants it to be made into a bomber.

22. Italy: The Allies bomb Sicily and Sardinia (→ 5/6).

22. Aleutian Islands: US troops in south Attu penetrate the valley that leads to Chichagof; those in the north remain in their positions (→ 30).

Final blast destroys Warsaw Ghetto

More Jews are rounded up for extermination: they struggle to keep their hands in the air in the vain hope of mercy.

Warsaw, 16 May

A month after he launched the operation which he reckoned would take a few days only, SS Major-General Stroop has reported to Himmler: "The Warsaw Ghetto is no more." Besides the 14,000 Jews killed in the fighting or sent to the Treblinka death camp, another 42,000 are being deported to labour camps near Lublin.

Stroop rounded off his destruction of the ghetto at 8.15 this evening by blowing up the Thomaebi synagogue. Then he sat down to prepare his report. Only eight buildings have survived: the police lodgings, quarters for factory guards and a hospital. But he says that the ruins contain "a vast amount of stones and scrap metal which could be useful". He is having the report, illustrated with many photographs, typed on top quality paper and bound in fine leather. Stroop has been promised the Iron Cross, first class, for his achievement.

The remnants of the Jewish resistance, driven from their bunkers by poison gas, still refused to give in. One man attacked the Germans with stones; he was beaten with rifle butts, kicked and left soaked in blood. The bodies of two young women lay in the road, and cats and crows appeared to tear pieces of flesh from their faces. Though Stroop says that the ghetto has been destroyed, small groups of Jews are still in hiding there and some others have escaped through the slime of the sewers to seek refuge in the Christian districts of Warsaw.

One of them wrote in his diary: "Though our hearts are still beating, there will never be a joy of life in them" (→ 19).

The end of resistance for men, women and children in the Warsaw Ghetto.

"Dambuster" squadron breaches vital Ruhr dams

Ruhr, Germany, 17 May
Taking off from the grass runways of Scampton in Lincolnshire, 19 Lancasters last night headed for Germany's industrial heartland, the Ruhr, loaded with top-secret bombs being used for the first time.

Flying below 200 feet (60 metres) to evade enemy defences, the aircraft followed a zigzag course across the Netherlands and Germany. The first wave of bombers went for the huge Mohne and Eder dams. On each plane, the radio operator started the motor that set the five-ton, drum-shaped bombs spinning; then the navigator signalled that the aircraft was at the correct altitude – 60 feet (18 metres) – and the bomb-aimer released the bomb.

Travelling along a narrow angle of descent, the bombs rebounded from the surface of the water, bouncing along until they came to the dams and sank. The water pressure set off the fuses. The bombs tore gigantic gaps in first the Mohne dam and then the Eder, releasing millions of gallons of water. Hydroelectric turbines were ruptured, severing power to the Ruhr's industries. A separate wave of bombers approached the Sorpe, Ennepe, Lister and Diemel dams, but only attacked the first two. The Sorpe was hit, but the breach was above water level.

Eight of the specially-adapted Lancasters were lost: four were downed by anti-aircraft fire, one crashed after being damaged by its own bomb, two hit electricity cables, and one crashed into a tree after the pilot was dazzled by a searchlight. Fifty-three of the 133 crew were killed. The operation was planned and led by Wing-Commander Guy Gibson; he is to be recommended for the VC (→ 22).

Thousands of gallons of water pour through the hole blasted in the Mohne dam by the RAF's new "bouncing bombs".

One of the new bombs is dropped by a low-flying Lancaster.

The leader of the raid: Guy Gibson.

How astonishing bouncing bomb evolved

London, 17 May
The amazing "bouncing bombs" used to breach the Mohne and Eder dams last night were designed by Dr Barnes Wallis, already famous for his Wellington bomber. Wallis made his bombs act like a "ducks and drakes" stone, skipping along the surface of the water and then sinking to explode at the base of the dams. The first test was a disaster. The bomb broke up when it hit the water. The "super-boffin" solved that problem by spinning the bomb as it left the aircraft. Wallis is delighted by the success of his bomb, but devastated by 617 Squadron's losses.

Workers drafted in to repair dam havoc

Ruhr, 22 May
As German emergency services deliver bread, milk and coffee to households which have had their power supplies cut, Albert Speer, Hitler's armaments minister, has pulled 7,000 men out of the Atlantic Wall defences in France to repair the breached Ruhr dams. At least 1,294 people died when a nine-foot wave of 100 million cubic metres of water tore through the Mohne valley, wrecking road and rail bridges and flooding towns and villages. Among the dead were 700 slave labourers, including 493 women from the Ukraine. A further 47 died in the Eder area (→ 28).

Allies stage aerial offensive on Italy

Mediterranean, 20 May
The full weight of Allied air power is being thrown at airfields in Italy, Sicily and Sardinia in an attempt to neutralize the *Luftwaffe* and the Italian air force. Over the past 48 hours, at least 186 Axis aircraft have been destroyed in day and night bombing. The most spectacular raid hit Grosseto airfield, 90 miles (144 km) north of Rome. Flying Fortresses saturated the field and installations with fragmentation bombs, leaving 58 Italian bombers wrecked.

Armies prepare to renew eastern war

Moscow, 22 May
There are increasing signs that both sides are about to launch their long-prepared summer offensives on the eastern front. Artillery barrages are rumbling all along the front, and there is intense aerial activity while the ground forces spar for position. The battle will almost certainly centre on the great Soviet salient bulging into the German lines before Kursk. Hitler planned to launch Operation Citadel, a huge attack to cut off the salient, on 9 May, but postponed it on 5 May until mid-June to allow more preparation. He knows that the course of the war depends on it (→ 2/6).

No turn-ups, more materials for war

Britain, 17 May
Nearly two years of clothes rationing has reduced the money spent on clothing by the average family of four by three-quarters, from £30 ($120) per head before the war to only £7/10/- this year. This has saved around £600,000 ($2,400,000) worth of material, with the ban on turn-ups alone saving five million yards of cloth. Coupons for clothes will have to stretch further from next September. Last year men had a quota of 46 coupons and women 50. But the biggest demands for coupons are made by children aged between 14 and 16.

Churchill addresses American Congress

Churchill clasps his lapels in a familiar gesture as he addresses Congress.

Washington, 19 May
In a speech to a joint session of Congress today, Winston Churchill gave a defiant and optimistic account of the progress of the war and the high strategy of the Alliance, and proclaimed that all war plans must be "pervaded and even dominated by the supreme object to get to grips with the enemy".

Mr Churchill, who first addressed a joint session of the Senate and the House of Representatives in December 1941, was greeted by cheering lasting for a minute and a half before he spoke. His 50-minute speech was heard clearly in London by radio. The first cheers during it came when the British prime minister said "our partnership has not done badly". He was cheered again when he promised his government's determination to fight the Japanese in Burma. But he went on to say that in January 1942, when Britain and the United States made a division of labour, the US undertook the main responsibility for fighting Japan while "we took the main burden in the Atlantic". He and President Roosevelt agreed, Mr Churchill said, that "while the defeat of Japan would not mean the defeat of Germany, the defeat of Germany would infallibly mean the defeat of Japan" (→ 25).

The royal family attend a thanksgiving service for victory in North Africa.

Allies to pool all intelligence, and "Ultra" is born

London, 17 May
Britain and America today came to an agreement to share the work and the results of a joint attack on the codes and ciphers of the Axis powers. Britain is to concentrate its efforts on the German and Italian ciphers while the US war department devotes its attention to the Japanese army ciphers.

Experts from both sides will work on each others' cryptanalytic programmes, and there will be a full exchange of information and "decrypts". It was also agreed to adopt the Bletchley Park codename of "Ultra", derived from Ultra-Secret, for all information gleaned from breaking the German *Enigma*, the Japanese "Purple" and the Italian C38M enciphering machines. Bletchley Park in Buckinghamshire, 40 miles (64 km) north of London, is the wartime home of the vastly expanded government code and cipher school whose name gives little hint of the extraordinary work it is doing in allowing Allied commanders to read enemy secrets.

A brilliant collection of men and women is housed there in the mansion and its overflow huts. Dons, mechanical engineers and chess-players are all pitting their sometimes eccentric wits against the Enigma machine which is constantly being upgraded by the Germans. Their work is so secret that people working in one hut do not know what goes on next door; the enemy must get no hint that its codes are being read.

This secrecy extends to the distribution of the material. It is done through liaison units reporting on a "need to know" basis to commanders who have been cleared to receive Ultra intelligence. None may risk capture.

Churchill has no doubts about the war-winning importance of the work being done at Bletchley. Every morning at breakfast he demands "his eggs" from the goose whose eggs are golden.

1943

May

Su	Mo	Tu	We	Th	Fr	Sa
						1
2	3	4	5	6	7	8
9	10	11	12	13	14	15
16	17	18	19	20	21	22
23	24	25	26	27	28	29
30	31					

23. Berlin: Donitz orders all U-boats to be fitted with anti-aircraft guns.→

23-24. Germany: RAF planes dropped 2,000 tons of bombs on Dortmund tonight; 100,000 tons of bombs have been dropped on Germany since the war began (→ 26).

24. Auschwitz: SS Captain Dr Josef Mengele takes up the post of camp doctor (→ 26).

25-26. Germany: RAF planes bomb Dusseldorf in a night raid, but do little damage.→

26. Alexandria: The first through convoy to complete the Mediterranean passage since 1941 arrives without loss; it left Gibraltar on 17 May.

26. Auschwitz: Over 1,000 gypsies are gassed (→ 8/6).

26. Canada: Meat rationing is introduced.

27. Tunisia: Churchill and the US Army Chief of Staff, General George C Marshall, arrive to plan the Italian campaign.

28. London: The award of the Victoria Cross to Wing-Commander Guy Gibson, who planned and led the raid on the Ruhr dams, is announced.

28. Washington: The office of mobilization is established to coordinate war production.

29. China: Chinese troops halt the Japanese advance on Chungking and recapture Yuyangkwan, east of Ichang (→ 1/6).

30. Torquay, England: German raiders bomb a church, killing 20 children and five adults (→ 13/6).

31. Italy: USAAF Flying Fortresses attack Naples (→ 17/6).

31. Algiers: Generals de Gaulle and Giraud begin talks on a provisional government of France; it is also announced that Admiral Rene Godefroy's naval squadron, immobilized at Alexandria, joined Giraud's forces on 7 May (→ 3/6).

31. Germany: Donitz transfers responsibility for naval armaments to Albert Speer's ministry.

Allied leaders agree future war strategy

Washington, 25 May
Churchill and Roosevelt have ended their talks on the next moves against the Axis powers with agreement on the date and place for a cross-Channel invasion of German-occupied north-western Europe next year. They have also agreed to press Turkey to join the Allies.

The invasion should take place by 1 May, with 29 divisions. These details, which must remain a closely-guarded secret, were worked out by British and American staff officers, who studied information gained from high-altitude reconnaissance photographs, hundreds of detailed maps and over ten million holiday snaps and picture postcards assembled after a BBC appeal to the public. During a press conference attended by 151 Allied correspondents, Churchill was asked why senior British officers from India had been brought to Washington. He said that the plan was to increase the intensity of the war against Japan. From now on, the war in both west and east would be waged with equal force.

Allied superiority over the enemy in munitions production was now beginning to tell, Churchill said. Allied air power had become a decisive factor in the war, and the bombing campaign against Germany would be a 24-hours-a-day operation. War would continue until unconditional surrender was obtained "from all those who had molested us". Roosevelt then interrupted Churchill to say that "molested" was the best example of understatement he had heard.

Britain aids trapped Yugoslav partisans

Tito's closely-guarded HQ; at last his pleas for Allied aid have been heard.

Yugoslavia, 28 May
British support for Yugoslavia's partisans arrived today – in the shape of two officers and two wireless operators parachuted onto a mountainside in Serbia in a gale, while a battle raged around them. Their commanding officer, Captain F W Deakin, a former literary assistant to Winston Churchill, will report directly to London.

No visitors could have been more welcome. Tito's hard-pressed army is facing Operation Black, the strongest Axis offensive yet. One of the radio operators, Sergeant Peretz Rosenberg, a Palestinian volunteer, was shown an order to Axis forces to destroy everything, including civilians and animals.

Britain has decided to back Tito, whose requests for help have hitherto been fruitless, rather than the *Chetniks* led by the royalist General Mihailovich. This is largely owing to information on the two groups' merits received from a British Intelligence officer, Major D T "Bill" Hudson, who landed in the country by submarine in 1941 (→ 11/6).

Ernest Bevin adds muscle to Britain's manpower drive

Down to earth: Ernest Bevin.

Britain, 24 May
While Winston Churchill personifies Britain's bulldog spirit to the outside world, it is Ernest Bevin who dominates the war effort at home. As minister of labour he has powers to mobilize and direct labour which are the most far-reaching ever given to a minister in Britain. He can determine the occupation of every adult between 14 and 65, and direct them to any part of the country. So far Bevin has used his powers lightly. There are nearly 23 million people in full-time work or service, and only 400,000 orders directing people to work have been made.

As the former leader of the Transport and General Workers' Union, Mr Bevin's style is always direct and down-to-earth. During a labour dispute in Liverpool he told the dockers: "It is criminal to stop work at this moment. You must not do it. I say to every one of my own people, whom I have worked for all my life, there will be plenty of time – hundreds of years – to go in for strikes after this, but now let us get on with it. You are not doing as well as you ought to be."

This month he warned that coal production will not meet the national requirements this year: "It may be necessary to put entry into the mines on the same footing as service in the forces" (→ 29/7).

Donitz recalls U-boats from Atlantic

German population hit by shortages

North Atlantic, 24 May
Grand Admiral Donitz tonight withdrew his U-boats from the North Atlantic. Earlier in the day he had told U-boat commanders: "Only you can fight the enemy offensively and beat him ... The German nation has long felt that our arm is the sharpest and most decisive and that the outcome of the war depends on the success or failure of the Battle of the Atlantic."

As the day wore on Donitz absorbed yesterday's news that two more U-boats had been sunk while attacking convoy HX-239. That brought the month's losses up to 33, but, worse than that, increasingly they were failing to get through the escorts. Just five days ago a pack of 33 U-boats attacked SC-130 and failed to sink a single ship.

No fewer than five of the pack were sunk. One boat, U954, sunk by a Coastal Command Liberator of 120 Squadron, took all hands to the bottom, including the grand admiral's 21-year-old son, Peter. Although he showed no emotion when told of his personal loss, Donitz could not ignore the growing evidence that the two year battle to rupture the Allies' ocean supply lines was being lost. Radar and the increasing successes in breaking

Recruiting men for the U-boat war.

Sailors braving the Atlantic's perils.

the *Enigma* codes have made the U-boats much more vulnerable to the escorts. Equally, the escorts have been growing in power and effectiveness. Escort carriers, both British and American, have increased the extent of the routes which can be offered air support. And more effective anti-submarine weapons like the Hedgehog and the Squid have been introduced.

The plain fact is that more U-boats have been operating here than at any other time during the war,

but the score of successful sinkings has been rapidly declining. With the month almost over, the Allies have lost less than one-third as much shipping as the 476,000 tons North Atlantic losses in March.

By tonight the U-boats were moving to the South Atlantic to take up positions south of the Azores. A few remain to convince the Allies that the convoys are still in danger. They hope to tie up as many Allied escort ships as possible here for as long as they can (→ 29/6).

Germany, 31 May
Chronic shortages are biting deeper into German civilian morale. Today the government announced a cut in the weekly meat ration from 12 to nine ounces, and the SS, in one of its regular secret reports, noted on 6 May that despite stiff penalties bartering is increasing.

This is not surprising, given the lack of consumer goods. An SS report of 17 May expressed concern at the consequences of a shortage of alarm clocks: arms workers and miners, exhausted from long hours and frequent air raids, have been sleeping through early shifts.

Strikes bite in Italy

Rome, 27 May
For the first time since Italy came into the war, the Italian government admitted to the world today that its people are rebelling against the Mussolini regime and staging strikes. Strikes were forbidden years ago by the Fascist government, and a public decree today ordered all strikers to return to work at once. Fear of an Allied invasion is driving thousands of Italians away from the south of the country (→ 11/6).

Allied bombs pound industrial targets

Ruhr, 30 May
More than 90 per cent of the Barmen district of Wuppertal, the hub of the Ruhr's chemical industry, was obliterated by 1,900 tons of bombs last night. Civilian casualties included 3,400 dead (German figures); 118,000 lost their homes.

The raid was notable both for the accuracy of the Pathfinders, the vanguard of pilots who mark the targets for the main wave, and for the light *flak* over the target. Only 33 of 719 bombers are missing, many shot down during the 20-mile (32-km) run through the guns of the Kammhuber Line, ground-controlled "boxes" patrolled by *Luftwaffe* fighters. The attack is part of an air war of attrition promised at Casablanca (→ 2/6).

American troops recapture Aleutian island of Attu from Japan

North Pacific, 30 May
The American North Pacific island of Attu, seized by the Japanese in June 1942, is back in American hands. American assault troops of the US 7th Infantry Division swept ashore against light resistance on 11 May. The 20-day campaign that followed ended with howling groups of cornered Japanese breaking out of their final positions in a wild charge towards the American lines, where they were mown down by murderous automatic fire.

In a final weak attack yesterday, all the Japanese who were not killed appear to have committed suicide. Total Japanese deaths were 2,622, with just 29 who had been taken prisoner earlier. Of the 15,000 Americans in the campaign, 549 lost their lives and 1,148 were wounded (→ 8/6).

A hot meal for American troops on the newly conquered island of Attu.

June

Su	Mo	Tu	We	Th	Fr	Sa
		1	2	3	4	5
6	7	8	9	10	11	12
13	14	15	16	17	18	19
20	21	22	23	24	25	26
27	28	29	30			

1. USA: Half a million miners go on strike in support of a wage claim (→ 7).

1. Atlantic: The sloop HMS *Starling* and an RAF Liberator E/120 each sink a U-boat in separate actions.

2. USSR: *Luftwaffe* raiders bombard Soviet positions at Kursk; the Russians claim 162 "kills" for the loss of 30 planes.→

2. Rome: In a message aimed at Allied bombing strategists, Pope Pius XII appeals to the warring nations to observe the "laws of humanity" in air warfare (→ 6).

2. Mediterranean: The British destroyer *Jervis* and the Greek ship *Vasilissa Olga* attack an Italian convoy, sinking the torpedo boat *Castore* and two merchant ships.

3. China: Japan seizes all shipping on the Upper Yangtze at the end of its "rice offensive" in western Hupeh (→ 14).

3. USSR: Germany launches Operation *Cottbus*, aiming to destroy Soviet partisans in the area of Borisov.

3. China: Chinese troops recapture Nanhsien, in Hunan province.

3. France: Resistance workers destroy 300 tons of tyres at the Michelin tyre plant at Clermont-Ferrand (→ 26).

3. Solomon Islands: Admiral William Halsey gives orders for Operation Toenails, the invasion of New Georgia, which aims to secure Munda as a base for a series of "hops" through the islands (→ 7).

3. Atlantic: The Panamanian cargo ship *Halma* is sunk by German mines laid by U-boat off Halifax, Nova Scotia.

4. Algiers: General Henri Giraud is appointed C-in-C of the Fighting French Army (→ 6).

4. Atlantic: The British submarine *Truculent* sinks U308 off the Faeroe Islands.

5. Tokyo: Admiral Yamamoto is given a full state funeral.

5. Mediterranean: British ships keep up the heavy shelling of Pantelleria (→ 11).

Free French factions unite for liberation

General Giraud (l) greets General de Gaulle on his arrival in North Africa.

Algiers, 3 June
The French Committee of National Liberation has been reorganized here, after three days of talks including both General Giraud and General de Gaulle. The committee, a communique issued here tonight states, will be the "Central French Power". It will exercise French sovereignty in all territories outside the enemy's power, direct the French war effort and take command of all Fighting French forces.

There will be seven members of the committee in all. Besides Giraud and de Gaulle, they are: Rene Massigli and Andre Philip (appointed by de Gaulle); Jean Monnet and General Georges (for Giraud); and General Catroux, who becomes the new governor-general here, chosen by both sides. The committee is very much a compromise between the two rival factions led by Giraud and de Gaulle. The intention is that their groups should be equal in power. For General de Gaulle, who arrived here on 30 May, this may be counted a success.

In the communique the committee, known as the CFLN, bound itself to overthrow the regime of Marshal Petain and restore French liberties. It called on all Frenchmen to rally to it "so that France should regain through battle and victory her traditional place among the Allied Great Powers" and be represented as such in the post-war peace negotiations and international settlements (→ 4).

Allies raid Japan's forces in China

Ichang, 1 June
Chinese and American airmen flying B-24s claimed a record 20 Japanese fighters yesterday in a 15-minute dogfight as they bombed Japanese forces at Ichang for the second time in 72 hours. In another raid to halt the Japanese advance in Hunan, 24 US fighters and bombers attacked a supply base at Yochow, on the north-east side of Tungting Lake, destroying a train and killing 200 people (→ 3).

Leslie Howard shot down by Germans

London, 3 June
Britain has lost an outstanding actor-director in Leslie Howard, who is presumed dead after the plane in which he was travelling disappeared over the Bay of Biscay two days ago. The British airliner left Lisbon for Eire, and its last radio message was: "Enemy aircraft attacking us."

Leslie Howard had been lecturing in Portugal and Spain on his films *Pimpernel Smith* and *The First of the Few*. As a result, 900 cinemas there are to show British films. He was 50 and was universally popular. After playing Ashley Wilkes in *Gone With The Wind* he returned to Britain, where he was the definitive Professor Higgins in the film of *Pygmalion*.

Leslie Howard: definitive Briton.

"Luftwaffe" bombards Russians at Kursk

Moscow, 5 June
The *Luftwaffe* has launched a series of heavy raids on Kursk, the pivotal point of the Russian salient which bulges dangerously into the German lines between Orel, in the north and Kharkov, in the south.

Despite the withdrawal of fighter squadrons to face the growing threat of the Allied bombers in the west, and the need to reinforce the Mediterranean, the Germans have been able to rebuild Field Marshal von Richthofen's *Luftflotte* 4 into a powerful striking force. His Stukas and Me109s have been joined by Henschel 129 tankbusters and Focke-Wulf FW190 fighters.

However, the Luftwaffe, like the *Wehrmacht*, is devoting a significant part of its strength to containing the threat posed by the Russian partisans who now have their own airstrips behind the German lines. These are used to deliver supplies and evacuate wounded partisans and peasants. A report today on the current anti-partisan Operation *Cottbus* says that these airstrips take twin-engined aircraft (→ 10).

1943

June

Su	Mo	Tu	We	Th	Fr	Sa
		1	2	3	4	5
6	7	8	9	10	11	12
13	14	15	16	17	18	19
20	21	22	23	24	25	26
27	28	29	30			

Concern over morals as illegitimacy soars

Britain, 1 June

The number of illegitimate births in the United Kingdom has risen from 32,000 a year at the beginning of the war to 53,000. They now represent 6.5 per cent of the total and, the trend is still upwards. This was one of the factors discussed at the Convocation of Canterbury which debated present morals.

The bishop of Birmingham, Dr Barnes, said that a widespread decline in truthfulness has coincided with an increase in theft and a growth in sexual licence. Signs of "degeneration" among large sections of the population included "lower standards of personal hygiene and self-discipline".

The war was disrupting families on a scale unparalleled in our history but, he added: "You cannot expect cleanliness, truth and honesty from people brought up in houses which are damp, verminous and without sanitary decency." The bishop of Rochester, Dr Chavasse,

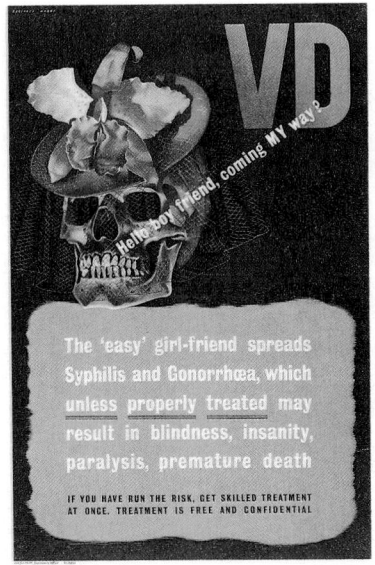

The easy girl – the enemy within?

said: "Decent young women say it is unsafe to go out with 11 out of 12 young men, who tend to look upon young women as potential prostitutes."

Military junta takes power in Argentina

Buenos Aires, 5 June

An almost bloodless *coup* has overthrown the government of Argentina and replaced Dr Ramon Castillo with General Arturo Rawson, who is known to be an Allied sympathizer.

The Castillo government was committed to what it called the "policy of prudence", in reality dictated by fear of the powerful pro-Italian and pro-German forces in Argentine politics.

President Castillo fled from the presidential palace yesterday and sheltered on board the minesweeper *Drummond* as General Rawson's men seized power.

June 1. In the dusty heat of the Roman amphitheatre at Carthage Mr Churchill waves his hat to Allied troops gathered to hear him speak.

6. Madrid: General Franco proposes "no-bombing" zones in Europe; the Allies reject the idea as beneficial to the Axis.→

7. Solomon Islands: Japanese aircraft attack Guadalcanal, destroying nine US planes but losing 23 of their own (→ 12).

7. US: Most of the 500,000 striking miners return to work.

7. Paris: The "Comet" escape line for PoWs and others from occupied Europe is betrayed.

8. Greece: Some 880 Greek Jews from Salonika arrive in Auschwitz (→ 11).

8. Tokyo: The Japanese high command orders the Aleutian island of Kiska to be abandoned (→ 27).

9. Mediterranean: The heavy shelling of Pantelleria continues, and the Allies say that it will go on until the island surrenders.→

10. USSR: Seven hundred Russian night bombers attack German positions at Yaroslavl and airfields west of Kursk; 19 are lost (→ 22).

10. Algiers: De Gaulle threatens to resign over the reorganization of the French army (→ 1/8).

11. Washington: Roosevelt urges the Italian people to overthrow Mussolini.

11. Berlin: Himmler orders all the Polish ghettoes to be liquidated (→ 15).

11. Montevideo: Uruguay is the first country to recognize the French National Liberation Committee (→ 26/8).

11-12. Germany: Nearly 800 RAF aircraft attack Dusseldorf.→

12. Solomon Islands: Allied fighter planes attack Japanese bombers, knocking out 31 aircraft for the loss of six of their own (→ 16).

12. Tripoli: King George arrives in North Africa to meet the victorious Allied servicemen.→

12. Mediterranean: RAF Sergeant Cohen "captures" Lampedusa Island, near Sicily, after making a forced landing (→ 13).

Mengele slots in to Auschwitz routine

Auschwitz-Birkenau, 8 June

With a casual wave of his gloved hand, the new camp doctor, SS Captain Josef Mengele, has just separated 880 Greek Jews from Salonika into two groups: those who will die now, and those who will live a little longer.

He takes a special interest in new arrivals, for they provide human guinea-pigs for his gruesome medical experiments. His interests include the way identical twins react when exposed to disease or torture.

His colleague, Professor Carl Clauberg, has just completed his research into sterilization methods; he reported to Himmler yesterday that, using x-rays, he could sterilize up to a thousand half-Jews and gypsies every day.

Colonel Blimp fuels British controversy

London, 11 June

Winston Churchill last night attended the premiere of a film which he had tried to have banned – *The Life and Death of Colonel Blimp*. He did not like it and it may be banned for export.

The film was intended to show the Americans that the reactionary old-fashioned officer class has been superseded in the British army. "Colonel Blimp", a character invented by the cartoonist David Low to be ridiculed, emerges in the film sympathetically.

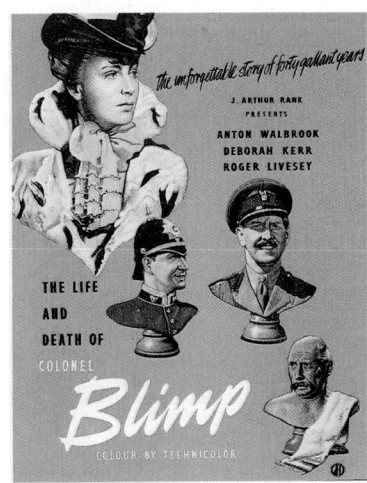

Colonel Blimp, who may be banned from doing service overseas.

Allied directive for bombing campaign

London, 10 June
A modified version of Major-General Ira Eaker's plan for a combined bomber offensive, now renamed the "Pointblank" directive, was issued today to the Allied bomber forces. A highly significant document, it directs the bombers to "seek the destruction of enemy fighters in the air and on the ground", and in so doing concedes that the German fighter force is not only threatening the American day offensive but also the British night offensive.

Both Bomber Command and the USAAF are suffering at the hands of the *Luftwaffe's* fighters which are operating with increasing strength and effectiveness. Eaker's plan is to devote the combined bomber strength to wiping out the German aircraft industry. Pointblank does not commend itself to Sir Arthur Harris, the C-in-C of RAF Bomber Command, who believes that his bombers can knock Germany out of the war with saturation bombing of its cities.

His reaction to the directive is to quote the decision of the combined chiefs of staff at the Casablanca summit that the "primary object" of the bombers should be "the progressive destruction and dislocation of the German military, industrial and economic system, and the undermining of the morale of the German people to a point where their capacity for armed resistance is fatally weakened" (→ 11).

Italian island surrenders to the Allies

British troops advance past a blazing petrol dump on the island of Pantelleria.

Pantelleria, 11 June
This tiny Italian-owned island surrendered today after suffering four days of massive bombing from the air and continual shelling from the sea. For almost 100 hellish hours Pantelleria shook beneath a vast Allied bombardment – with huge formations of Flying Fortresses often bombing for as long as 76 minutes at a time as British cruisers and destroyers poured hundreds of shells on to any available target.

But why such immense force against such an insignificant target? Strategically, Pantelleria offers an airfield which will bring Allied fighters well within reach of Sicily, 65 miles away – assuming that that is the proposed area for the invasion of southern Europe. The shattered harbour cannot be of much use. The real reason, it seems, is the need to bring home the weight of Allied arms to an already nervous and shaky Italian populace. A British destroyer almost emptied its ammunition magazine into one of Pantelleria's two forts yesterday before intercepting a radio signal from the garrison. "Help! Send help," it pleaded.

More than 100,000 leaflets were dropped on the island demanding its unconditional surrender. "The demand was made to save the garrison from unnecessary suffering", said Allied headquarters. "Pantelleria will continue to be subjected to bombing and blockade" (→ 12).

Tito escapes again to thwart Germans

Yugoslavia, 11 June
The partisan leader Josip Broz, better known by his *nom de guerre*, Tito, narrowly escaped capture when his temporary headquarters in a Bosnian farmhouse were surrounded by Axis soldiers, it was revealed today.

Tito heard a warning shout, leapt through a window and spent the next few hours hiding in a ditch listening to the Italian troops in the house. Several of Tito's staff were captured and executed later. The informer can expect little mercy from Tito's men. With a price of 100,000 *Reichsmark* (£8,300/$33,500) on his head, Tito is the most wanted man in Europe and has had several similar escapes (→ 23).

Tito pauses for the camera in Bosnia.

June 12. King George chats with Monty on a visit to troops in Tripoli.

Ruhr city set alight by RAF bomb raid

Dusseldorf, 12 June
The German authorities fear that as many as 140,000 people are homeless today in this industrial city after an overnight raid by 783 RAF bombers. Nearly 2,000 tons of high-explosive and incendiary bombs devastated 130 acres of the city; thousands of separate fires were reported by the authorities, with 1,292 people killed. Munster was also hit by RAF contingents which included Canadian, Australian and Polish squadrons; 38 RAF planes were lost.

De Gaulle calls for "Fourth Republic"

Algiers, 6 June
General de Gaulle, in a controversial speech to the Free (Fighting) French here this morning, called for a fourth republic. His appeal for "national renovation" is being taken by observers here to mean that he does not intend France to return to the pre-war constitution of the Third Republic. De Gaulle also told his audience that "France does not want to be liberated by others, even by her best friends. She does not want gifts. We intend to win our liberty ourselves" (→ 10).

1943
June

Su	Mo	Tu	We	Th	Fr	Sa
		1	2	3	4	5
6	7	8	9	10	11	12
13	14	15	16	17	18	19
20	21	22	23	24	25	26
27	28	29	30			

13. Germany: *Luftwaffe* defenders shoot down 22 out of 60 US bombers attempting to bomb Kiel (→ 14).

13. Britain: German raiders drop "butterfly" anti-personnel bombs for the first time, killing 74 people and injuring 130.

13. Mediterranean: The Italian island of Linosa surrenders to the British.

14. Tokyo: General Tojo meets the pro-Axis Indian leader Subhas Chandra Bose, who has fled from India by submarine (→ 24).

14. Mediterranean: The Italian island of Lampione surrenders to the British.

14. Britain: The creation of the Allied Tactical Air Force in the UK is announced (→ 17).

15. Janowska, Poland: Jewish forced labourers, supervised by SS Colonel Paul Blobel, start digging up the corpses of 1,200 Lwow Jews massacred in March. They extract gold teeth and rings from the bodies before cremating them (→ 21).

15. Munster: The Arado Ar234, the world's first jet bomber aircraft, has its first test flight.

15. Ankara: Turkey confirms its neutrality, reaffirming its separate treaties of friendship with the USSR and Germany.

16. Algeria: King George invests Generals Bernard Montgomery and Henry Maitland Wilson with knighthoods.

16. Guadalcanal: US forces repel a major assault, downing 107 out of 120 Japanese aircraft (→ 21).

17. Italy: The RAF bombs Naples (→ 19).

17. Britain: The BBC warns civilians in occupied Europe to evacuate the vicinity of all factories working for the German war effort (→ 20).

18. Melbourne: The prime minister, John Curtin, says that Australia is no longer in peril of invasion (→ 24).

19. Italy: The people of Naples and of towns in Sicily are told to evacuate their homes.

War leaders exiled to Indian summers

Wavell: now to be viceroy.

New Delhi, 18 June
Field Marshal Sir Archibald Wavell, one of Britain's most senior commanders, has been "shunted aside" by an impatient Winston Churchill. Wavell, the former C-in-C of the Middle East which included the North Africa campaign, was supreme commander in the southwest Pacific. He is now being replaced as C-in-C in India by General Sir Claude Auchinleck and will take up the post of viceroy. Auchinleck has also, in effect, been exiled from the European theatre, but he retains a military role.

Allies start heavy bombardment of Sicily

Sicily, 16 June
Wave after wave of Allied bombers flew unmolested over Sicily today, dropping thousands of tons of high explosive on ports, airfields and other military targets. The island is clearly being "softened up" for an invasion – although Rome radio is still talking of Sardinia as a possible target. An announcer described the country's present situation as "the gravest in the whole of her modern history".

Four British battleships are on station in Gibraltar, and intensive training is under way both in North Africa and in Scotland, where a beach near Troon is being used for commando "rehearsals", although few know the actual destination. Two more Italian islands have surrendered. White flags fluttered over tiny Linosa on 13 June as soon as the British destroyer *Nubian* appeared. Closer to Africa, Lampedusa was pounded heavily from the sea and air before surrendering on 12 June. A British fighter pilot, Sergeant Jack Cohen, force-landed on the island with engine trouble in the middle of the bombardment. Italians came running up to his aircraft waving white flags and shouting: "Can't you stop this?"

Cohen was forced to shelter from Allied bombs and shells for two hours. Italian engineers helped him to mend his aircraft, and he flew off to tell the navy that Lampedusa was surrendering. The capture of Pantelleria and the other islands has virtually closed the Sicilian narrows to German and Italian shipping (→ 28).

Chinese troops restore grip on Hupeh

Kung-an, 14 June
Chinese troops today completed mopping-up operations in western Hupeh, recapturing the last towns lost during the Japanese offensive that had been intended to take Changsha, the rice bin of central China, in readiness for a further advance against Chungking, the Chinese Nationalists' provisional capital. Chinese losses in the six weeks of fighting are estimated at 70,000-80,000, compared with Japanese losses of 3,000-4,000. The tide of battle turned two weeks ago when Japanese troops were forced to retreat, fleeing to Kung-an, one of the towns recaptured today. A week before, the enemy advance had been checked at Shih-pai, as 60,000 Japanese massed on the banks of the Ching river, with the Nationalist leader, Chiang Kai-shek, exhorting his men to defend the town as if it were a Chinese Stalingrad (→ 12/8).

Flying ambulances and floating hospitals care for Med soldiers

Tunisia, 19 June
The British sapper was the victim of a German booby trap. He was bleeding badly. The explosion had almost severed his leg. A razor-sharp piece of shrapnel had penetrated his skull. When medical orderlies reached him, his life was in the balance. Only a miracle or skilled surgery could save him.

The miracle – and the surgery – came in the form of a Dakota aircraft, complete with a surgeon, nursing orderlies and an operating theatre. Within an hour of the explosion, the fight to save Sapper X was taking place in mid-air. The shattered leg was amputated, and the head-wound prepared for more complex surgery in a hospital ship in Algiers. In any previous war, the victim would have stood little chance. But now, the RAF's "flying ambulance" service is playing a vital life-saving role on the battlefield.

Nearly 3,000 lives are known to have been saved by the service in the desert campaigns. Only one-tenth of head-wound cases have failed to survive. Major-General Freyberg, the New Zealand VC, owes his life to a flying ambulance after being picked up from a desert airstrip with severe neck wounds. It is a risky business for the personnel, flying in unarmed planes, often over Axis-occupied territory. One orderly received two bullets in the legs, but continued working until the patient was safely down – then collapsed from lack of blood.

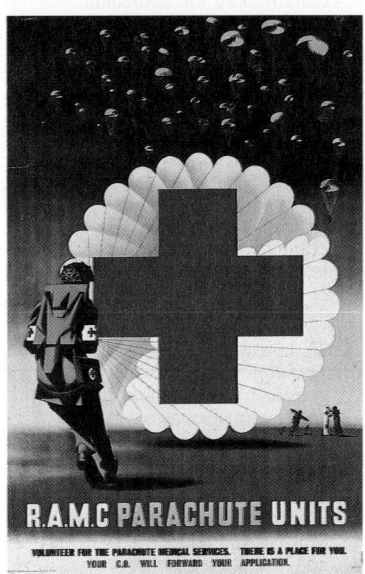

R.A.M.C PARACHUTE UNITS

VOLUNTEER FOR THE PARACHUTE MEDICAL SERVICES. THERE IS A PLACE FOR YOU. YOUR C.O. WILL FORWARD YOUR APPLICATION.

Medical aid comes by parachute too.

June

Su	Mo	Tu	We	Th	Fr	Sa
		1	2	3	4	5
6	7	8	9	10	11	12
13	14	15	16	17	18	19
20	21	22	23	24	25	26
27	28	29	30			

20. Britain: RAF Lancasters take off for the first "shuttle" bombing mission.→

20. New Guinea: The US Sixth Army sets up its headquarters at Milne Bay (→23).

21. Solomon Islands: Men of the 4th (US) Marine Raider Battalion capture Segi Point, the undefended southern tip of New Georgia (→27).

21. Berlin: Himmler orders Jewish ghettoes in occupied Russia to be liquidated (→25).

22. USSR: On the second anniversary of the invasion, Radio Moscow claims that 6.4 million Germans have been killed or taken prisoner (→5/7).

22. Germany: The US Eighth Army Air Force bombs the synthetic rubber plant at Huls, in its first major daylight raid on the Ruhr (→25).

22. Algiers: The Committee of National Liberation decides that Giraud will continue to command the Fighting French in North Africa and that de Gaulle will lead elsewhere.

23. Pacific: US troops land in the Trobriand Islands, southeast of New Guinea, without meeting any opposition (→30).

23. Obersalzberg: Hitler tells an acquaintance who has questioned the deportation of Jews in occupied Europe: "Germany has lost half a million ... on the battlefield. Am I to preserve and minister to these others? ... You must learn how to hate."

24. Tokyo: Subhas Chandra Bose broadcasts an appeal for Indians to rise up against the British (→21/10).

25. Wuppertal, Germany: After a 20-minute RAF bombing raid last night, targeted on the western district of Elberfeld, 870 of the city's 929 acres are in ruins.→

25. Czestochowa, Poland: The Jewish ghetto is annihilated and its inhabitants sent to Auschwitz after an abortive attempt at resistance (→27).

26. Lille: Resistance fighters, led by a British agent, Michael Trotobas, blow up a German locomotive plant (→8/7).

French Resistance leader is arrested

France, 21 June
The *Gestapo* captured one of the most wanted men in France today when it arrested the Resistance leader Jean Moulin.

Moulin, who escaped to England in 1941 in order to meet the Free French leader de Gaulle, agreed to be parachuted back into his native country on 1 January last year, charged with the mission of coordinating the many rival Resistance groups operating there. Today he was to bring his task to fruition at a top-secret meeting in Lyons with Resistance leaders from across France. Instead, he and several others discovered too late that they had been betrayed, when the hated German secret police raided the house and took them all into captivity (→8/7).

The planner supreme prepares for battle

General Marshall at his desk in Washington: a tough-minded strategist.

Washington, 20 June
The most powerful military man in the Allied ranks is this weekend overseeing the final preparations for offensives half a world apart in the Pacific and Mediterranean. Yet General George C Marshall is one of the least known military leaders, lacking the charisma of Montgomery or MacArthur.

It is Marshall, though, to whom President Roosevelt turns first for advice. Born in Pennsylvania in 1880, the young Marshall tasted action in the Philippines and France in 1917. But it was as a master of planning that he began his rise through army ranks, finally leapfrogging many more senior generals to become US Army Chief of Staff in September 1939. It was a surprise, but inspired, appointment by Roosevelt. By the time of the Pearl Harbor attack, Marshall had doubled the size of the US Army. His influence is no longer confined to his own service, however; after

Pearl Harbor he became chairman of the new Joint Chiefs of Staff Committee at a time when increasing numbers of operations involve more than one service.

Marshall has also emerged as a tough-minded strategist on the international stage. Accompanying Roosevelt to Anglo-American conferences, he has resisted British pressure to defer planning for a second front in France while at home countering the US naval chiefs who favour the Pacific theatre.

Marshall is often regarded as remote, even austere, and without close friends. But this is seen by some as an advantage since choosing the best man for a particular command (as he chose Eisenhower from relative obscurity) is as much a part of his job as the renowned mastery of logistics. Whether he can ever be spared to command armies in the field – he has been mooted as an eventual commander in Europe – must be doubtful.

Eire election deals blow to de Valera

Dublin, 25 June
The efforts of Ireland's leader, Eamon de Valera, to keep his country out of a world war have won scant applause at home. In the latest general election he has failed to obtain an overall majority, although his *Fianna Fail* party, with 67 seats, is still the largest in the *Dail*, the Irish parliament. It is four fewer than other parties grouped together and ten below the total he had in 1938. It is uncertain whether he will be ready to serve as a "lame duck" prime minister, saddled with responsibility without power or dependent on a coalition.

GI shot dead after English pub brawl

Bamber Bridge, England, 25 June
Black American troops ran rioting through the streets of this small Lancashire town last night, firing back at American military police who had fired on them. One man was killed and four wounded, including a white American officer.

The trouble began in the local pub, the Old Hob Inn, when American military police attempted to arrest a group of black GIs as it closed. A fight broke out as they walked back to the US Eighth Army Air Force camp. The MPs drew their guns and fired, hitting one man, and later returned in two trucks. The GIs armed themselves and there was a gun battle into the small hours. Local people ran for cover.

The Spirit of 1943

Allied air forces intensify bombardment of Europe

RAF pounds Ruhr in new offensive

London, 25 June

Bomber Command is continuing to pound the German industrial heartland in the "Battle of the Ruhr". The town of Wuppertal was last night's target for 630 aircraft, and heavy damage was reported. This raid follows RAF attacks two nights earlier on Mulheim and Krefeld.

The USAAF joined in the battle on 22 June with a daylight raid on the synthetic rubber factory at Huls. An RAF spokesman says that the attacks will continue until the enemy "haven't enough guns to keep the United Nations out of Europe".

USAAF pilots gather round the operations board to note their assignments.

"Shuttle" raids hit Italy – via Africa

London, 24 June

Lancasters of No 5 Group of Bomber Command have returned to base after a remarkable mission which took them to the shores of Lake Constance to bomb the former Zeppelin factory at Friedrichshafen on the night of 20-21 June, then to Blida, in Algeria from whence, after a day's rest, almost all of the original force of 60 went on to attack the Italian naval base of La Spezia on the way home. Eight remained in Algeria awaiting repair.

The specially-picked crews carried out Operation Bellicose perfectly, doing great damage to the Zeppelin works which now build Wurzburg ground-based radars.

Strangely enough, the German fighters did not put in an appearance, despite a brilliant moon. It can only be assumed that they planned to ambush the bombers on their long flight home. But the Lancasters flew on to Blida without loss.

Among the special tactics developed for the attack on Friedrichshafen is that of "offset" marking, which entails Pathfinder aircraft putting down their guides at a set distance from the target so that they are not obscured by smoke.

This tactic worked well on the German target, but La Spezia had to be bombed blind as its defenders covered the harbour with a dense smokescreen. "Shuttle" bombing is an interesting development and certainly confuses the enemy's defences, but it is unlikely to be used regularly because of the difficulties of servicing Lancasters in North Africa.

Bombing campaign means a million Germans must evacuate

Ruhr, 25 June

The Ruhr and Rhineland areas of western Germany have been declared war zones and Dr Robert Ley, a senior German government official, has ordered the evacuation of over a million women, children, invalids and old people. The action follows the stepping-up of the Allied air offensive against Germany, with the RAF unloading about a thousand bombs a night on the Ruhr alone. The raids are said to have demoralized soldiers whose families are in the bombed areas.

This week's "shuttle" bombing of the Friedrichshafen radar factory in southern Germany [*see report alongside*] has added a new dimension to Allied air power, soon to be further intensified by the US Eighth Army Air Force now based in Brit-

ain. But what the Goebbels-controlled newspapers refer to as "the Battle of the Ruhr" still preoccupies the German authorities, who say that the Rhineland and the Ruhr are "in the front line". A German radio broadcast said that damage caused by the RAF "simply goes beyond human imagination". In his diary, Goebbels has recorded his view that the British aircraft industry and the RAF have wrested air supremacy from the *Luftwaffe*.

At Chequers, Churchill has been watching films taken during RAF raids on Germany. Suddenly, he sat up and said to his guest, the Australian cabinet minister Richard Casey: "Are we beasts? Are we taking this too far?" Casey answered: "We didn't start it. And it was them or us" (→ 28).

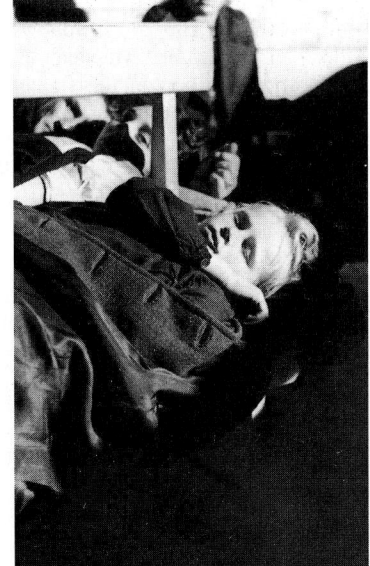

Bombed-out Germans bed down.

Churchill promises aid to Tito's partisans

London, 23 June

Winston Churchill has ordered a military mission, led by a senior British officer, to join Tito in his campaign against the Germans in Yugoslavia. After years of being unable to decide whether to back Tito's partisans or the rival *Chetnik* army led by General Mihailovich, the British now believe that the for-

mer have emerged as the only effective force against the Axis in Yugoslavia.

But although the Chetniks are cooperating with the Italians against Tito's partisans, the British will continue to drop supplies to Mihailovich's men, largely because of pressure by the Yugoslav government in exile (→ 28/8).

Australian leader seeks general election

Canberra, 24 June

The Australian federal parliament is to be dissolved and a general election will take place in August. The decision to go to the people follows a no-confidence motion in the House of Representatives which was defeated by one vote yesterday. Having denounced the government for failing to reach a national agree-

ment, the opposition now faces the task of defeating a government that will stand on its record in a national crisis. Before deciding on the election John Curtin, the prime minister, had said that the defensive phase of the war was over, and that Australia "could be held as a base from which to launch both limited and major offensives" (→ 21/8).

1943

June

Su	Mo	Tu	We	Th	Fr	Sa
		1	2	3	4	5
6	7	8	9	10	11	12
13	14	15	16	17	18	19
20	21	22	23	24	25	26
27	28	29	30			

27. New Georgia: American marines start an overland advance from Segi Point to Viru Harbour (→ 29).

27. Greece: USAAF bombers attack German airfields at Eleusis and Hassani, near Athens.

27. Aleutian Islands: Unaware of Japanese plans for withdrawal, the US bombs Japanese positions on Kiska (→ 22/7).

28. Germany: RAF aircraft bomb Cologne in what the government in Berlin describes as a terror raid.

28. Mediterranean: USAAF bombers attack Livorno, in Italy, and Messina, in Sicily (→ 30).

28. Burma: RAF Wellingtons bomb Akyab (→ 9/7).

29. Warsaw: Five Poles, including a one-year-old infant, are executed for sheltering Jews (→ 2/8).

29. London: Germany is reported to have recalled all U-boats, in anticipation of the Allied invasion of Europe (→ 1/7).

29. Solomon Islands: A US force of four cruisers and four destroyers shells Bougainville and Kolombangara.→

30. Martinique: Admiral Georges Robert, the Vichy high commisioner, for the French West Indies, asks for US military help to avoid bloodshed and organize the colony's transfer to the Fighting French.

30. Mediterranean: US Flying Fortresses attack Palermo and nearby airfields, and bomb Cagliari, in Sardinia.→

30. Washington: The US has spent $71,000 million on defence – 93 per cent of all government expenditure – in the last twelve months. Revenue in the same period was just $21,000 million.

30. London: At the Guildhall ceremony giving him the Freedom of the City of London, Churchill says: "We bear the sword of justice, and we resolve to use that sword with the utmost severity ... to the end."→

Churchill: why it must be unconditional

London, 30 June
The critics of the "Unconditional Surrender" policy adopted at the Casablanca conference were answered by Churchill today when he received the Freedom of the City of London at a Guildhall ceremony. To those who argue that the policy will stiffen the resistance of the enemy he said: "We must take all those far-sighted measures which are necessary to prevent the world from being again convulsed, wrecked and blackened by their calculated plots and ferocious aggressions." Churchill believes that if a set of peace terms were drawn up, as the critics suggest, public opinion would demand conditions that would be more repulsive to the Germans than anything indicated by the general expression "Unconditional Surrender".

Attempts have, in fact, been made to draft a statement of conditions that could be put to Germany. Churchill says that they looked so terrible when written down that they were scrapped at once. He believes that the Allies must completely break the Nazi, Fascist and Japanese tyrannies, but without being moved by "mere lust for vengeance".

Allied raiders bomb Italian mainland

Italy, 30 June
Worried that Italy might defect from the Axis after its defeats in North Africa, the *Luftwaffe* has moved two operational command stations from the Russian front to southern Italy. The move follows Allied air raids on Messina, in Sicily, and Livorno, on the Italian mainland. In London, Winston Churchill talked in a broadcast of Italian speculation about where the coming invasion would land. "It is no part of our business to relieve their anxieties," he said.

Last Jewish ghetto in Poland crushed

Lwow, Poland, 27 June
One of the last great Jewish ghettoes in Poland has now been destroyed. SS Lt-Gen Fritz Katzmann has rounded up the remainder of this city's Jews, an estimated 20,000, and shipped them off to camps, mainly to the extermination centres of Auschwitz and Belzec.

But the SS came up against stiff resistance from those Jews strong enough to fight: they fought back with smuggled Italian handguns, and in the end 500 of them took to the sewers. The Germans are unaware of the Jews' secret weapon: in the last days, they released thousands of lice infected with deadly spotted fever, which they had saved up for the final reckoning (→ 29).

Return of signposts shows victory road

Britain, 30 June
Signposts are to be re-erected in rural areas of Britain, now that the danger of invasion has receded, it was announced today. Tank traps, anti-tank trenches and barbed-wire entanglements will also be removed where they are no longer necessary. Lord Mottistone said that on a windy day at least ten young women had had their frocks ripped on barbed wire within 300 yards (274 metres) of the House of Lords. Anti-tank blockades in the streets were the cause of accidents.

German army plans assault in Ukraine

General Model: preparing to attack.

Ukraine, 30 June
Preparations are being made in the Ukraine for a massive test of strength between the Red Army and the *Wehrmacht*. Hitler has planned Operation Citadel to break the stalemate on the eastern front by pinching out the huge Russian salient around Kursk. He has amassed a vast army with nearly a million men and 2,500 tanks under the command of General Model and General Hoth. But Stalin, alerted by the "Lucy" spy-ring, has built a deep web of defensive positions.

Housewives, elderly men and young boys brave the showers to queue for fish – one of the few foodstuffs which has not been rationed.

American forces draw near to Rabaul

Landing ships, nicknamed "green dragons" by their crews because of their colouring, approach Rendova island.

Music boosts the productivity of British factories

Britain, 30 June
War production in Britain is at its highest since hostilities began. There are now nearly five million men and women employed in the munitions industries, and output of weapons is at its peak. The biggest of all is the aircraft industry, expanded to 1,600,000 workers, 40 per cent of them women, which is turning out 26,000 planes a year, including 7,000 bombers. Fighting vehicles are being produced at the rate of 7,400 tanks and 24,000 armoured cars this year.

Women now make up 57 per cent of the work-force of the Royal Ordnance Factories and 40 per cent of the engineering industry. It is calculated that nine out of ten single women and eight out of ten married women of working age are in industry or the auxiliary forces. The remainder are mostly mothers with young children. Over one million people over 65 are working.

In aircraft factories the average weekly wage is £7/8/7 (£7.43/ $29.94); in engineering it is £6/18/3 (£6.91/ $27.86) for men and £3/9/10 for women. But a highly skilled aero engine fitter can earn £20 ($80) a week.

The employment of women has hastened improvements in industrial welfare. Mr Bevin has recruited factory welfare officers and ordered 5,000 works' canteens to be set up. Tea-breaks, compulsory for women, have been extended to men, and day nurseries for women workers with young children are being opened by local authorities.

Hours worked have been reduced from the 70 or more a week of 1940, as accidents and fatigue lowered productivity. The maximum recommended is 55 hours a week for men, 50 for women, with one day off a week and one week's paid holiday a year. Committees have been set up to increase efficiency. Twice-daily broadcasts of *Music While You Work* raise production by 15 per cent for the next hour.

New Guinea, 30 June
A colossal offensive in the Pacific War theatre has advanced Allied bases in the South and South-west Pacific closer to the major Japanese bastion of Rabaul, in New Britain. MacArthur's forces landed today at Nassau Bay, on the north New Guinea coast, approximately 60 miles (96 kilometres) south of Lae with its substantial Japanese garrison. The move is part of Operation Cartwheel, aimed at giving the Japanese no respite after their defeat at Guadalcanal.

At the same time, Americans went ashore on both Kiriwana and Woodlark Islands, north-east of New Guinea. No Japanese were on either island. Smaller parties had landed on 23 June on both Woodlark and Kiriwana – where there is already an RAAF radar station – to prepare for the arrival of the main bodies of infantry and engineers. Air bases to support later stages of the advance on Rabaul are to be built on these islands by US Seabee engineers.

At Nassau Bay the US and Australian MacKechnie force, which landed soon after midnight, was guided onto the shore by beach lights set up by Australian army patrols. No contact was made with the enemy, sparking speculation that the elusive Japanese are hiding in the hinterland and preparing a counter-offensive.

Meanwhile, 400 miles (640 km) away, Admiral Halsey's forces have begun an offensive, coordinated with the landings in New Guinea, aimed at seizing the island of New Georgia. The first objective is Munda Point airfield. Since Munda cannot be approached by large vessels, "island-hopping" US forces under Admiral Richmond Turner and Maj-Gen John Hester landed at dawn today on Rendova island, within artillery range of Munda, whence they will launch their attack. They also landed on New Georgia itself, at Wickham and Viru (needed as supply points) and Segi Point (needed for an airstrip).

The landings were unopposed, but this afternoon the Japanese launched air attacks on the invasion force, sinking a transport (→ 1/7).

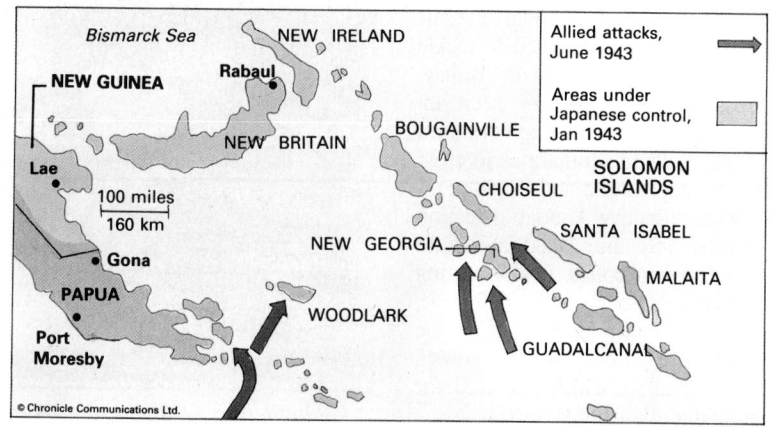

© Chronicle Communications Ltd.

1943

July

Su	Mo	Tu	We	Th	Fr	Sa
					1	2	3
4	5	6	7	8	9	10
11	12	13	14	15	16	17
18	19	20	21	22	23	24
25	26	27	28	29	30	31

1. Rome: Mussolini rejects the suggestion of Marshal Ion Antonescu, the Roumanian premier, that they should both quit the war immediately.

1. New Georgia: US marines capture Viru harbour (→ 3).

2. New Guinea: The MacKechnie force, holding a beach-head at Nassau Bay, makes contact with the Australian 3rd Division (→ 18/8).

3. New Georgia: US forces land unopposed at Zanana, eight miles east of Munda (→ 4).

3-4. Cologne: Night-fighters use "Wild Sow" tactic, a fighter in a *flak*-free zone guided by a ground controller, for the first time in an Allied raid on Germany tonight.

4. New Georgia: US troops advancing on Munda meet stiff Japanese resistance (→ 6).

4. Crete: British commandos stage a successful attack on German military air bases.

5. USSR: Germany attacks on a 170-mile front near Kursk, using *Panzerkampfwagen V* [Panther] tanks for the first time.→

6. Solomon Islands: The US cruiser *Helena* and two Japanese destroyers are sunk in the Battle of Kula Gulf, as Japan supplies Kolombangara; 850 Japanese troops land.→

7. South Africa: General Smuts wins a majority of 67 seats in the general election.

8. Rastenburg: Hitler orders all Russian PoWs to be put to work in arms production, not shot as previously ordered.

9. Solomon Islands: US forces press home their attack, just three miles from Munda (→ 13).

9. Heidelberg: Goebbels vows that Allied bombing will be avenged by a new secret weapon.

9. Atlantic: In the last week eight U-boats have been sunk, from the Bay of Biscay to Brazil, by aircraft patrols (→ 24).

10. Kursk: German forces come to a halt, gaining just five miles at the expense of 25,000 men, 200 aircraft and 200 tanks (→ 12).

Warships sunk in battle for New Georgia

New Georgia, 6 July
Early today US warships tangled with a Japanese navy task force as it attempted to land reinforcements on the island of Kolombangara, just north of New Georgia. Each side lost two warships. On New Georgia itself Japanese resistance to the US landings which began last month appears to be stiffening. But US marines have crossed the five-mile (eight-km) strait between New Georgia and Rendova island to secure a beach-head near Munda where the airstrip is the prime target, and the port of Viru was taken on 1 July. Further US landings have been made at Rice anchorage, in the north of the island (→ 9).

Bringing vital ammunition ashore.

"Gestapo" tortures Moulin to death

France, 8 July
France's most talented Resistance leader, Jean Moulin – known to many as "Max" – has died after being brutally tortured by the *Gestapo*. He betrayed no one. Moulin was arrested on 21 June with Resistance leaders from across the country who were attending a top-secret meeting. He was president of the National Resistance Council and was striving to unite the many Resistance groups fighting in France. His unconscious body was being taken to a concentration camp when he died.

Allied troops seize Japanese-held port

Delhi, 9 July
Anglo-Indian troops in Burma have carried out a lightning raid against the Japanese-occupied port of Maungdaw, on the Bay of Bengal. A communique issued here yesterday says that the Allied troops drove the Japanese out of Maungdaw and occupied the port for some hours. After a fierce exchange the village was surrendered, but Allied sources say that valuable information was gathered and equipment captured before the troops withdrew. Today the RAF bombed Maungdaw (→ 1/8).

General Sikorski is killed in air crash

Gibraltar, 4 July
The man who exemplified the spirit of Polish resistance to the Nazis, General Wladyslaw Sikorski, died today when his Liberator plane crashed on take-off from Gibraltar. Sikorski, the head of the Polish government in London and C-in-C, had been visiting Polish forces in Egypt. Talk of sabotage is being discouraged by the British, but many Poles remain suspicious. Sikorski had angered Stalin by demanding a full inquiry into the thousands of massacred bodies found in the forest at Katyn, many of them Polish officers.

General Sikorski before the war.

Allies step up air and sea attacks on U-boats in Bay of Biscay

Bay of Biscay, 1 July
With only a token force of seven U-boats remaining in the North Atlantic now that the "air gap" has been closed, British naval and air forces are being deployed to tackle the enemy in the Bay of Biscay. Substantial damage has been inflicted, and two weeks ago Admiral Donitz ordered submarines to cross the bay submerged and in pairs.

More effective U-boat detection devices, plus the Allied ability to read German codes, is still putting the German navy on the defensive, however. A particular target for the Allies are the "milch cows", U-boat tankers which are used for refuelling other boats (→ 9).

A kill in the Bay of Biscay: an American plane bombs a surfaced U-boat.

Soviet tanks blunt the German onslaught at Kursk

A line of Soviet T34 tanks moves forward in the battle for Kursk: the sky is full of Shturmovik fighters hammering the stranded German forces.

Kursk, 9 July

Operation Citadel, Hitler's desperate attempt to change the course of the war by destroying the Soviet armies in the Kursk salient, is grinding to a halt as Soviet tanks, cunningly constructed defences, and swarms of *Shturmoviks* blunt the pincer attacks of General Hoth from the south and General Model from the north.

Citadel has been off-balance from the start. Hitler postponed it

three times in order to introduce his new Panther and Tiger tanks and the huge Elephant tank destroyers. But the delays simply gave the Russians time to deploy their own T34s and build formidable anti-tank defences. Surprise, a vital element of the *Blitzkrieg*, was entirely missing. From spies – particularly "Lucy" in Switzerland – from *Enigma* decodings passed on by the western Allies, and from deserters the Russians knew everything

about Citadel. Two and a half hours before German tanks were due to crash over the start line, four days ago, they were hit by a storm of fire from Russian guns.

There were heavy casualties among the Germans caught in the open, and the start of their attack was disrupted. Model's men were hammered by *Katyusha* rockets.

The Elephants, with only one defensive machine gun each, proved themselves useless without infantry

support, and the untried Panthers and Tigers broke down and caught fire. On that first day Model gained only six miles, on the second day only four, and on the third he was fought to a standstill only 12 miles from his starting point. And there he is stuck. Hoth, with a six-to-one advantage in tanks, made better progress, breaking through the first Soviet defence line. But now he is stopped dead by a line of dug-in tanks (→ 10).

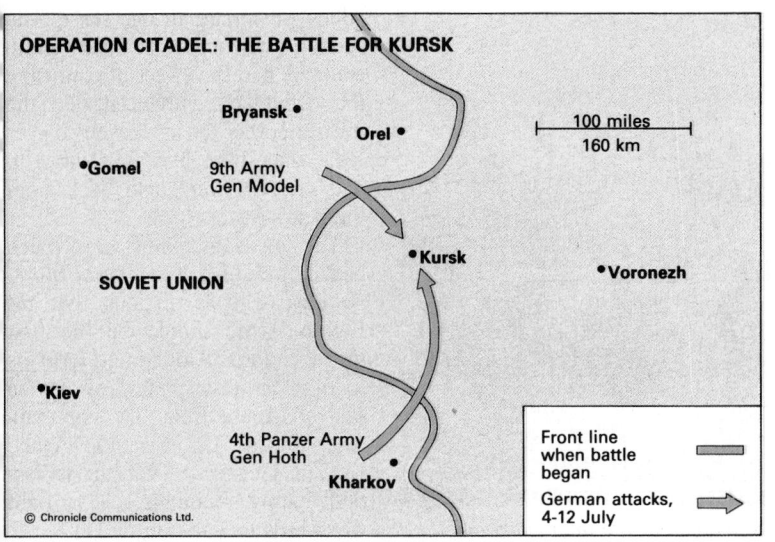

OPERATION CITADEL: THE BATTLE FOR KURSK

Bryansk
Orel
•Gomel
9th Army
Gen Model
100 miles
160 km
•Kursk
SOVIET UNION
•Voronezh
•Kiev
4th Panzer Army
Gen Hoth
Kharkov

Front line when battle began
German attacks, 4-12 July

© Chronicle Communications Ltd.

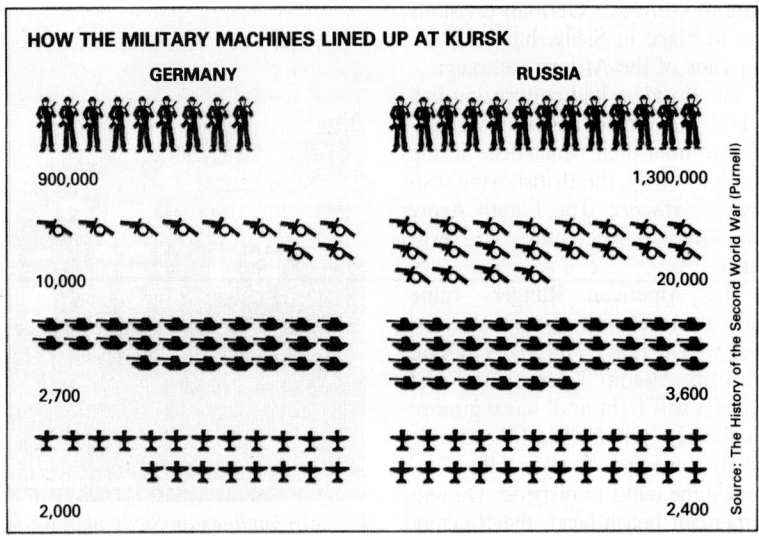

HOW THE MILITARY MACHINES LINED UP AT KURSK

GERMANY	RUSSIA
900,000	1,300,000
10,000	20,000
2,700	3,600
2,000	2,400

Source: The History of the Second World War (Purnell)

Sicily landings take Allies to first Axis homeland

Disaster in the air, success on beaches

Syracuse, Sicily, 10 July

For a few desperate hours, with a sudden storm churning the Mediterranean into a mass of huge white-capped waves, disaster threatened the greatest seaborne invasion of this war. For thousands of troops in small, flat-bottomed landing craft, the battle was against seasickness until, almost unnaturally, the wind dropped, the sea settled and the huge armada of 3,000 ships headed for the Sicilian beaches and entry into Axis-controlled Europe.

The planning for Operation Husky was immaculate. The vast convoy – which had set out from ports in Egypt, North Africa, Malta and the United States – assembled exactly on cue. Only the unseasonal storm delayed H-hour, but by no more than an hour while the convoy sorted itself out.

By dawn this morning more than 150,000 British and American soldiers were safely ashore, with a further 320,000 preparing to join them over the next two days. The storm had convinced the Italian defenders that a landing was impossible: most of them stayed in bed and woke to surrender in their hundreds. Not until the last moment did the defenders really believe that Sicily was the invaders' target. The brilliant deception – involving the use of a corpse with false documents – had convinced Hitler that Sardinia was the convoy's destination. Only two German divisions are in place in Sicily, but both are veterans of the African campaign.

The invaders had contrasting fortunes. As American troops struggled to hold their beach-head in the south of Sicily, the British were resting in Syracuse. The Eighth Army was lucky to meet only light resistance.

The American Rangers came face to face with the crack *Hermann Goering Panzer* Division with its 56-ton Tiger tanks, and faced a stiff fight until naval gunfire – called up from the beach-head with newly invented "walkie-talkies" – forced the tanks to disperse. On one American beach-head, the Rangers

Allied troops struggle up a Sicilian beach, hampered by nothing more than the equipment they are bringing ashore.

captured an Italian command post to find the telephone ringing. A war correspondent who had been stationed in Rome before the war answered in Italian. "Where are the Americans?" asked the voice at headquarters. "Americans? It's all quiet here," he replied. It stayed that way on the beach-head. However, the storm caused chaos in the air for the paratroopers.

Of the 137 British gliders released, 69 came down in the sea, drowning some 200 men. A further 56 landed in the wrong parts of Sicily and only 12 reached the target area – a vital bridge south of Syracuse. US paratroopers fared almost as badly. Their pilots were inexperienced and the navigators were working from daytime photographs in darkness. Dust, anti-aircraft fire and enemy fighters compounded the problems, and most of the 2,781 paratroopers were scattered over a 50-mile (80-km) radius.

The airborne chaos was to the Allies' advantage in one sense. The sudden presence of so many paratroopers had the effect of confusing the defenders, convinced that the invasion was on an even bigger scale than they had first thought, and reserves were held back from the beach-heads.

The invasion plans have been heavily modified by General Montgomery, who is anxious that his Eighth Army should be the first into the port of Messina. He plans to fight his way northwards to the east of Mount Etna. The commander of the US Seventh Army, Lt-Gen George S Patton, is less than happy about his role to fight westwards to Palermo (→11).

In dawn landings on Sicily men wade up to their waists to unload cargo.

1943

July

Su	Mo	Tu	We	Th	Fr	Sa
				1	2	3
4	5	6	7	8	9	10
11	12	13	14	15	16	17
18	19	20	21	22	23	24
25	26	27	28	29	30	31

11. Sicily: British troops take Pozzallo, but US forces are halted by the *Hermann Goering Panzer* Division (→ 12).

12. Krasnogorsk, USSR: Germans in a PoW camp form a "National Committee for a Free Germany".

12. USSR: The Red Army launches a major counter-offensive at Orel (→ 13).

12. Sicily: British and US forces join up at Ragusa, having captured six airfields.

12. Italy: Nearly 300 Lancasters of Bomber Command attack Turin (→ 13).

13. Britain: Discussing the invasion of Italy, Churchill asks "Why should we crawl up the leg like a harvest bug from the ankle up? Let us rather strike at the knee" (→ 14).

13. Kolombangara: In the Battle of Kolombangara a US task force sinks the Japanese cruiser *Jintsu* using radar-directed gunfire, but fails to stop 1,200 Japanese troops landing; the US destroyer *Gwin* is sunk and three cruisers are damaged (→ 15).

13. Rastenburg: Hitler orders German operations around Kursk to end, and starts to redeploy forces to Italy.→

14. Sicily: Allied troops capture the port of Augusta and Biscani airfield, and Messina is heavily bombarded (→ 16).

15. Solomon Islands: US fliers shoot down 45 enemy aircraft over Rendova, for the loss of three of their own (→ 20).

16. Italy: Allied pilots drop leaflets containing a plea by Roosevelt and Churchill urging Italians to depose Mussolini or face Allied attack (→ 17).

16. Germany: The bishop of Wurttemberg, Theophil Wurm, writes a letter of protest against the mass killings in the camps to Hitler.

17. Sicily: AMGOT, the Allied Military Government of Occupied Territories, is set up.→

17. Rastenburg: Hitler orders reinforcements to be sent to the Balkans, believing that the Allies will strike there next.

Russian tanks smash Kursk attack

Kursk, 14 July

The greatest tank battle the world has yet seen has ended in defeat for Hitler's *Panzers*. The open country round the village of Prokhorova, south-east of Kursk, is littered with the smoking hulks of tanks and guns and the wreckage of aircraft.

Hundreds of T34s of General Pavel Rotmistrov's Fifth Guards Army charged the heavier Panthers and Tigers of the SS *Panzer Korps*. In General Guderian's words, "they scurried like rats across the battlefield" and swarmed around the Germans, firing at point-blank range into their flanks.

Soon, according to Rotmistrov, "the earth was black and scorched with tanks like burning torches". The wounded driver of one burning Russian tank deliberately drove it into a Tiger so that both were destroyed in a terrible fireball.

There were nearly 2,000 tanks engaged in the battle and after some eight hours, when darkness fell on the battlefield, both sides had lost half their strength.

The Germans can claim to have inflicted as much damage as they have suffered, but they have shot their bolt. They have lost the Battle of Kursk, and with it they have almost certainly lost the war on the eastern front.

A counter-attack by the Red Army at Orel, to the north of Kursk, on 12 July, contributed to the German downfall.

Hitler is well aware of the importance of this defeat. Throughout the long planning for Citadel he insisted "there must be no failure", and all the offensive power that Germany could assemble was thrown into the battle. In an order of the day read out to troops on 4 July, he said: "You will be taking part in great offensive battles, whose outcome may decide the war." He went on to say: "Your victory will convince the whole world more than ever that all resistance to the German army is, in the end, futile."

Guderian, advising against Citadel, told him that it was a matter of profound indifference to the world whether they held Kursk or not. Hitler, for once, agreed with him: "You are quite right. Whenever I think of this attack my stomach turns over" (→ 19).

View from inside a Soviet tank of the relentless drive against the Germans.

Fire from Russian tanks lights up the night sky during the battle for Kursk.

In the greatest tank battle ever, Soviet infantry advance behind their T34s.

Generals row as Allies "race" north

Messina, 17 July
Resplendent in riding breeches and burnished boots, Lieutenant-General George Patton Jr has arrived back from Algiers to lead the US Seventh Army in an extraordinary race to Messina against General Sir Bernard Montgomery's British Eighth Army.

While the rough terrain and determined German resistance are slowing progress by both armies, a serious rift between the two generals is causing concern in the Allied camp. The fiery Patton had agreed only reluctantly that his army should act as a "shield" to Montgomery, who had planned a fast thrust along the east coast.

When the Eighth Army found itself stalled as it neared Catania, a sudden switch of plans by Montgomery – aiming to attack on the west side of Mount Etna – found his men fighting in the same area as the Americans at Vizzini. It was then that Patton blew up. He flew to protest to General Sir Harold Alexander, the commander-in-chief. The urbane "Alex" was startled at Patton's fury – and gave the American his head.

The row is not just strategic. What worries Alexander is the personal feud between the two men. Patton dislikes Monty's "cocksureness" and his condescension to his less-experienced troops. He does not like the casual dress of Monty's "Desert Rats". Most of all, he does not like playing second fiddle. He wants an *American* victory (→ 18).

While their generals fight a personal battle, troops storm a railway station.

German prisoners taken by the Allies are brought down onto the beach.

Nazi war criminals are tried for mass murder in Russia

Krasnodar, 14 July
The trial has opened here today of 11 Germans accused of the mass murder of Soviet citizens – mainly Jews – while this city in the west Caucasus was occupied by the German army.

Terrible details were revealed of the use of "murder vans" in which victims were locked and then gassed by exhaust fumes fed into an airtight compartment as the van was driven to a huge ditch outside the city. By the time it arrived, all its passengers were dead and were thrown into the ditch.

It was said in evidence that 7,000 people had been killed in this fashion in Krasnodar in addition to indiscriminate shootings and hangings of anyone daring to show disrespect for the Third *Reich*.

In scenes of much emotion, one witness said that "men, women and children were bundled into the van without discrimination". Patients in the local hospital "were brought out on stretchers and the Germans flung them in too".

The Russian authorities have invited western correspondents to cover the trial, and it has something of the trappings of a "show trial". They intend to make it quite clear to those Germans responsible for the appalling crimes committed on Russians that they will not escape justice. This is the first war crimes trial. There will be many more.

Post-war education reform is planned

Britain, 16 July
Free secondary schooling for all children up to the age of 15 – and ultimately 16 – was today foreshadowed for post-war Britain. Mr R A Butler, the president of the board of education, promised that the whole education system will be remodelled. Secondary schools will be divided into grammar, modern and technical ones, with selection at eleven. The provision of school meals is envisaged. Fee-paying, non-state schools – the so-called "public" ones – can continue.

Japan and US fight it out at Bougainville

Solomon Islands, 17 July
The heaviest Allied air raid on the Japanese so far in this war started yesterday evening and lasted for more than 12 hours. Seven enemy ships were sunk and 40 planes damaged or destroyed when more than 200 US and other Allied aircraft attacked the Buin-Faisi area, in south-east Bougainville.

Waves of Liberators and Flying Fortresses hit the airfield of Kahili for nine long hours through the night, preventing enemy opposition from taking off and wrecking scores of aircraft on the ground. This morning Dauntless dive-bombers and Avenger torpedo-bombers took over. While their fighter escorts drew off intercepting Japanese Zeros into savage dog fights, the bombers homed-in on shipping in Buin-Faisi harbour. Seven of the 15 ships in the harbour were sunk – a light cruiser, two destroyers, one submarine chaser, two cargo vessels and a tanker.

Of the swarms of Zeros that rose to the defence of the harbour 44 land planes and five float planes were shot out of the sky in a devastating night for Japan. All but six of the Allied planes returned after a vicious 20-minute battle.

Most men are away but birth rate rises

Britain, 12 July
The birth rate in the United Kingdom reached its highest for 17 years in the first quarter of 1943, despite the fact that so many families have been parted by war service. The rate of 16.8 births per 1,000 of population is equivalent to 684,000 births over the year. In 1940 and 1941 there was a marked drop in the birth rate compared with peacetime. The marriage rate has now sunk to its lowest since the war began. Deaths have also declined to below the 1939 figure.

1943

July

Su	Mo	Tu	We	Th	Fr	Sa
				1	2	3
4	5	6	7	8	9	10
11	12	13	14	15	16	17
18	19	20	21	22	23	24
25	26	27	28	29	30	31

18. Sicily: American troops capture Caltanisetta and Canadian forces take Valguarnerna (→ 19).

19. Italy: US air force bombers attack airfields and rail-marshalling yards near Rome.→

19. London: Churchill unveils a plan to use icebergs as floating air bases.

19. USSR: The Red Army pushes forward, threatening German positions at Bolkhov, in the Orel salient (→ 20).

20. USSR: Soviet forces, under heavy fire from the *Luftwaffe*, push the Germans out of Mtsensk.

20. USSR: The National Committee for a Free Germany broadcasts its manifesto to the German people and army (→ 23).

20. Washington: Roosevelt orders that all atomic weapons research is to be shared with the British (→ 20/8).

20. Solomon Islands: The Allies sink two Japanese destroyers (→ 22).

21. Sicily: The Allies claim 40,000 prisoners, and that they control half the island.

22. Solomon Islands: A US reconnaissance party lands in Vella Lavella (→ 25).

22. Aleutian Islands: A fleet of two US battleships and four cruisers mounts a heavy bombardment on Kiska (→ 30).

23. Mediterranean: The British destroyers *Eclipse* and *Laforey* sink the Italian submarine *Ascianghi* after she torpedoes the cruiser *Newfoundland*.

23. Sicily: Lieutenant-General Patton is ordered to advance on Messina from Palermo.→

23. USSR: The German armies in the Kursk salient are pushed back to their original positions (→ 24).

24. At Sea: In the last week seven U-boats have been sunk in the Atlantic, and one off Trondheim.

24. USSR: German aircraft bomb Leningrad, killing 210 people (→ 26).

Embattled Mussolini under pressure

Hitler urges ally to rally faltering army

Feltre, Northern Italy, 19 July
For five hours today, Adolf Hitler harangued a haggard and listless Mussolini, desperate to rekindle the flame of fanaticism in his partner. Hitler made his surprise visit after hearing reports that the Italian army was "in a state of collapse".

Two days ago, he told his war council that "only barbaric measures" could save Italy. He talked of tribunals and courts-martial to remove "undesirable elements".

Sicily, he insisted to the Duce, could be saved if Mussolini put backbone into his army. Hitler talked of the "voice of history", and told Mussolini that their tasks could not be left to another generation. Hitler promised reinforcements and said that his new U-boats and terror weapons would turn Britain into a "Stalingrad".

His tirade was to no avail. Il Duce said little and picked at his lunch while the Fuhrer stormed; his despair was not helped by a note telling him that Rome was being bombed.

Benito Mussolini, the dictator who once swaggered his way across Europe proclaiming his dream of a new Roman empire, left the meeting a shattered, spent force. He returned to Rome tonight to find the stench of burning buildings and the strong smell of revolt.→

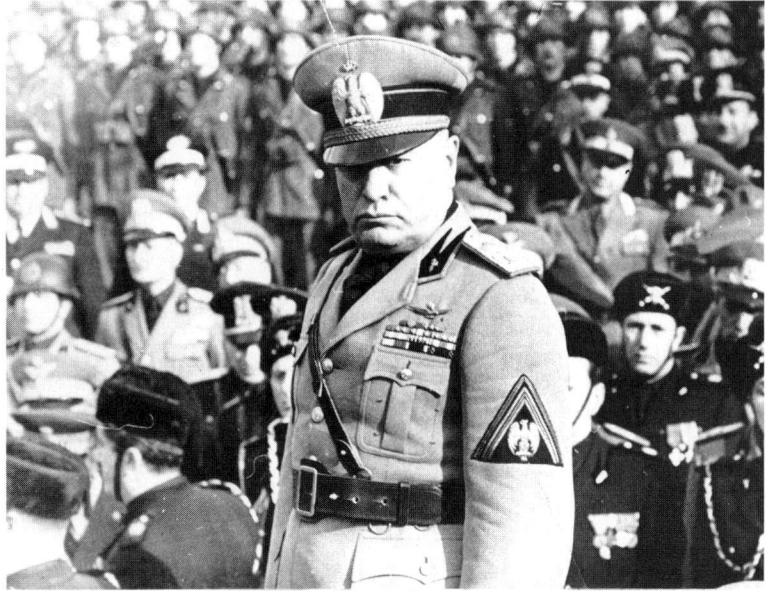

The pugnacious face of Il Duce: now voted against by his former followers.

Fascist assembly votes against Il Duce

Rome, 24 July
Mussolini's toadies turned on their wretched leader today and voted him down at the first meeting of the Fascist grand council since 1939. By 19 votes to eight, a resolution called for Italy's return to a constitutional monarchy and a democratic parliament.

Il Duce, newly returned from a meeting with Hitler, appears to be ignoring the palace revolt. Until now, the council has existed only to rubber-stamp the dictator's decisions. The Fascist rebels are led by Dino Grandi, one of Mussolini's former close friends and admirers, Giuseppe Bottai, and the Duce's son-in-law, Count Galeazzo Ciano. What the Duce does not realize is that he is the target of a far wider plot involving Crown Prince Umberto and leading generals.

Added to the low morale of Italy's constantly-defeated army and recent huge losses by the air force, recent Fascist moves by Carlo Scorza, the virtual dictator of Italy's home front, aimed at tightening the party's grip on all sections of society appear finally to have galvanized the opposition (→ 25).

Anti-Axis protests stir in the Balkans

Sofia, 23 July
Allied military successes in Sicily have set off a wave of unrest in south-eastern Europe. Large-scale rioting is reported from Sofia, the Bulgarian capital. Troops have been called out, and telephone links were severed for a time two days ago. Leaflets scattered by an unidentified plane called on the people to overthrow the government and kick out the Germans. In Roumania all military leave has been cancelled and fresh Axis troops are being brought from Greece.

Russian partisans plan a "rail war"

Moscow, 20 July
The *Stavka*, the Russian high command, has issued an order to all partisan units declaring a "rail war" against the German railway system. From now on every effort will be made to prevent supplies and reinforcements reaching the front. The Germans have already been forced to use armoured trains to fight off partisan attacks and many units have suffered severe casualties on the way up to the front. Now, the railways are going to become even more hazardous.

OUVRIER !

EN TRAVAILLANT POUR L'EUROPE TU PROTÈGES TON PAYS ET TON FOYER

Driving on the Vichy workers.

1943

July

Su	Mo	Tu	We	Th	Fr	Sa
				1	2	3
4	5	6	7	8	9	10
11	12	13	14	15	16	17
18	19	20	21	22	23	24
25	26	27	28	29	30	31

US bombers attack Rome for first time

Rome, 19 July
Panic swept the Italian capital today as Allied bombers dropped more than 500 tons of high-explosive bombs on "military targets" on the outskirts of the Eternal City. The bombing force was made up of 158 B-17s and 112 B-24s, of which only five did not return. As thousands of men, women and children fled the city in vehicles of every description, the pope drove to the scene to comfort victims. He returned, his vestments bloodstained, to announce that Romans could take shelter within the neutral Vatican (→21).

Pope pleads: don't bomb Eternal City

Rome, 24 July
As the stench of burning still hangs over the heavily-bombed suburbs of Rome, the pope has appealed to all combatants to avoid further bombing of the Eternal City. The Vatican has denied that the pope wrote to President Roosevelt condemning the raids – which have badly damaged one church in the city. Vatican radio said: "The pope is impartial. He does not intend to increase the hatred between opposing sides. However, Rome is unique and both sides should recognize this. The pope knows that churches have been destroyed in England, too" (→25).

Massive Allied air attack on Hamburg

London, 24 July
Bomber Command launched Operation Gomorrah against Hamburg tonight with a devastating raid in which 791 heavy bombers set fire to large areas of this important target. Twelve planes did not return. Much of the success of the raid was due to "Window", strips of metallic foil which so confused the radar-controlled defences that the Germans nightfighters were stumbling round the sky and the *flak* was being fired blind. Other attacks on Hamburg are planned (→25).

Axis troops flee as Allies take Palermo

The people of Palermo come out to welcome truckloads of American troops.

Palermo, Sicily, 22 July
As advance units of Lt-Gen Patton's Seventh Army swept down from the mountains and raced along the coastal road towards this city today, the Axis garrison fled in complete disorder.

Patton's advance across Sicily has been spectacular, with opposition weakening daily as the American strength grew. Now the race for Messina, in the east of the island, can really start.

The British Eighth Army, fighting in the shadow of Mount Etna, is facing a much more difficult task against German paratroopers whose 88mm anti-tank guns are again proving a formidable weapon – particularly in hilly terrain.

Canadians of Lord Tweedsmuir's Hastings and Prince Edward Regiment have managed to take the hill town of Assoro using a ruse employed by General Wolfe in his capture of Quebec almost 200 years earlier. The town stands on a precipitous cliff face, and it was this that the Canadian scaled "in 40 sweating, tearing minutes", surprising the German defenders completely. The Canadians began an advance on the main objective, the town of Leonforte, which was cleared today after street fighting which lasted all night (→23).

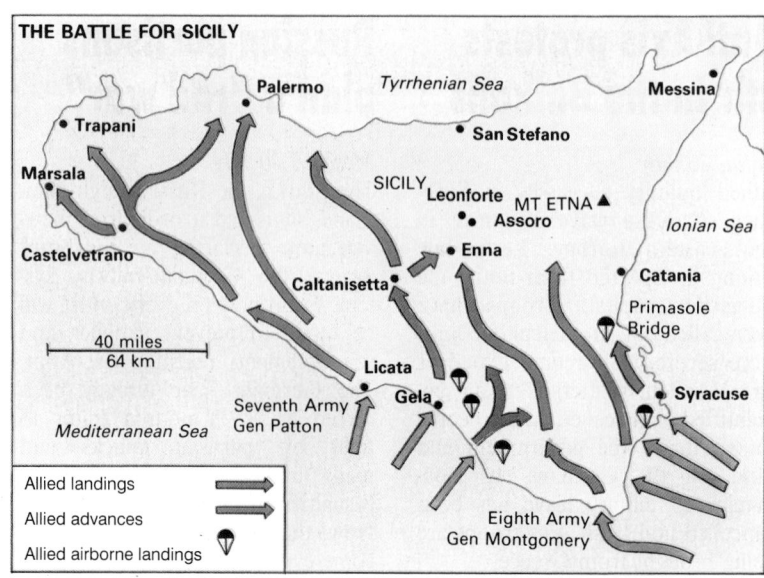

THE BATTLE FOR SICILY

Tyrrhenian Sea — Messina — San Stefano — Palermo — Trapani — Marsala — Castelvetrano — SICILY — Leonforte — Assoro — MT ETNA — Enna — Caltanisetta — Catania — Primasole Bridge — Licata — Gela — Seventh Army Gen Patton — Syracuse — Ionian Sea — Mediterranean Sea — Eighth Army Gen Montgomery

40 miles / 64 km

Allied landings
Allied advances
Allied airborne landings

25. New Georgia: The US 43rd and 37th Divisions launch a major assault on Munda, but make very little progress (→31).

25. Rastenburg: Hitler orders mass production of rockets for attacks on London to avenge today's Hamburg bombing.→

26. Essen: After a heavy raid on the Krupp armaments works last night, Dr Gustav Krupp von Bohlen suffers a stroke when he sees the burning ruins (→31).

26. Rastenburg: Hitler orders defensive preparations in Greece, which he assumes will be the Allies' next landing site.

27. Westminster: Churchill says that if Italy does not surrender, it will be "scarred and blackened from one end to the other" (→28).

27. Rastenburg: Hitler orders Mussolini's liberation and his restoration as puppet leader in a German-occupied Italy (→29).

27. Solomon Islands: US forces assault Horseshoe Hill in New Georgia and sink two Japanese destroyers at Rabaul.

28. Sicily: Allied units capture Nicosia and Agira (→30).

29. Germany: The press celebrates Mussolini's 60th birthday, showing Hitler's continued loyalty to the Duce.

30. Sicily: German forces are trapped in the north-east.→

31. New Georgia: US forces mop up resistance on Bartley Ridge, but are driven off Horseshoe Hill (→7/8).

31. China: Over two million people have died or become refugees because of a severe famine in Hunan province.

31. Europe: Up to 50,000 civilians have been killed and over 800,000 made homeless by the Allied bombing so far.

31. Italy: Hedley Verity, the Yorkshire and England cricket captain, dies in a PoW camp.

31. Moscow: The Supreme Soviet decorates Marshal Georgi K Zhukov with the Order of Suvorov, and General Ivan S Konev with the Order of Kutuzov, for their roles on the eastern front (→5/8).

String of defeats plunges Italy into political chaos

Having overthrown Il Duce, the citizens of Rome break up one of his statues.

Young Italians march through the streets demanding an end to the fighting.

Mussolini sacked by king, then arrested

Rome, 25 July

Benito Mussolini, the Fascist who led this country into a disastrous war, was stripped of his office today by King Victor Emmanuel III after being outvoted by his former supporters on the Fascist grand council. The king has taken command of the armed forces and appointed an anti-Fascist, Marshal Pietro Badoglio, as prime minister.

The heavily-jowled Mussolini arrived back from his meeting with Hitler to find Rome bombed and rebellion in the air. He did not expect a revolt, and he did not expect to be placed under armed guard after making a courtesy visit to the palace. The king was part of a far wider plot to depose the dictator. Mussolini was content to ignore his rubber-stamp council; but he dared not ignore the king.

The latter-day Caesar is under arrest tonight, his whereabouts unknown. Before the palace guard took him away in an ambulance, the king told him: "My dear Duce ... my soldiers don't want to fight any more ... at this moment, you are the most hated man in Italy."

Badoglio has said: "The war continues." However, with anti-war demonstrations sweeping through the industrial north and the Allies storming Sicily in the south, there is little will left for fighting in Italy.

The heavy bombing of Rome and other major cities was the last straw. The people are angry. The Fascists who chanted "*Viva il Duce!*" in their millions are disillusioned. Il Duce promised them victories; only to see his legions defeated in East Africa, Albania, Greece, Egypt, Libya and Tunisia.

Ordinary Italians fear the inevitable invasion of the mainland which will bring war to every town and village. The questions in every mind are: how will Hitler react to the news that he has lost his faithful junior partner? And what will the Allies do? (→ 27)

Army called in as strikes and riots spread

Milan, 30 July

Thousands of workers downed tools here today to march through the streets demanding peace. Soldiers charged with enforcing martial law – which prohibits strikes and demonstrations – refused to open fire. Guards stood back and watched as an angry mob stormed the *Cellari* prison and freed hundreds of anti-Fascist prisoners. Small knots of fanatical Fascists, one of them Mussolini's nephew, Vito, have barricaded themselves in Milan's Fascist headquarters, and there are reports of lynchings from other parts of the country. Events have moved at an extraordinary pace since Mussolini was deposed five days ago.

Not one of Mussolini's ministers remains in Marshal Badoglio's new cabinet. The Fascist insignia are being removed from all public places. Fascist prefects are being removed from their posts. Troops are being recalled from the Adriatic to enforce martial law, and there are reports of fighting between Italian and German soldiers in Trieste and Udine. Hitler has reacted swiftly, closing Alpine passes and ordering Field Marshal Rommel to assemble eight divisions to ensure that bridges and tunnels are not demolished.

As Sicily is poised to fall, the next strategic move must clearly be the invasion of the Italian mainland. After Il Duce's downfall, Allied commanders will be anxious to move quickly before the Germans can establish strong defensive positions in the mountainous centre of the country.

Badoglio is treading a shaky tightrope. General Eisenhower has offered to free Italian prisoners of war if Italy ceases cooperation with the Germans. The new prime minister wants to take his country out of the war; but whether he can take the war out of Italy remains to be seen (→ 2/8).

Badoglio: the man who succeeds Il Duce

Rome, 25 July

Few people in the west have ever heard of Marshal Pietro Badoglio, the man who ousted Mussolini, and yet Hitler hates him and has proposed sending a "hit squad" to murder him. Badoglio was a First World War hero – he took command after the Caporetto disaster in 1917 – and was put in charge when Italy's army was failing in Ethiopia. Although he is not a Fascist, his name has been linked with atrocities in Albania.

Italy's new non-Fascist leader.

RAF firestorm bombs raze Hamburg to the ground

More killed than in the London "Blitz"

Germany, 31 July

Operation Gomorrah has destroyed Hamburg with fire from the air, dropping 8,621 tons of bombs on the city. Protected by "Window" foil which has blinded the German defences, RAF Lancasters have made three raids in five days on this great port, wreaking death and destruction on an unimaginable scale. Flying Fortresses of the US Eighth Army Air Force have joined in the operation, appearing over the burning city by day to add their precision bombing to the RAF's mass attacks. In all, 2,752 planes flew in the raids, and 86 did not return.

During the second attack by the "Lancs", on the night of 27-28 July, the incendiaries whipped up such a firestorm that, within half an hour, the city was transformed into a lake of fire over an area of two square miles. People driven into the shelters by the flames were reduced to ashes as if they were bodies in a crematorium. One army *flak* observer, flying with the bombers, arrived over Hamburg in the last few minutes of the attack. "At that time," he said, "the pall of smoke was five miles high, it was coming out of the target in a spiral and one could see big factory buildings burning. The defences seem to have been completely overwhelmed."

The death-toll is awesome. Some 40,000 people are believed to have been killed – more than during the entire London "Blitz". Refugees, haggard with fear, are fleeing from the smoking ruins. Those that remain are being fed from soup kitchens. The chaos is worsened by the destruction of the telephone exchange.

Enormous damage has been done to war industries: 170,000 tons of shipping and three U-boats have been destroyed, 580 factories wiped out and 37,000 civilians severely wounded. The vital tunnel under the Elbe has been destroyed. One German commentator said: "Terror, terror, terror. Pure, naked bloody terror. Hamburg was heavily hit by this terror raid. It is a fact and we will not deny it."

Daylight raid on terrorized Hamburg: bombs plummet through high cloud.

Charred ruins are all that remain of one of Hamburg's grand theatres.

RAF crews boosted by new technology

London, 31 July

Crucial to the success of the current bombing of Hamburg has been the employment of a new technical aid by RAF Bomber Command. Unlike others in its armoury, this is a very simple one.

"Window", as it is codenamed, consists of bundles of aluminium foil strips, which are dropped from the aircraft over the target. Their object is to confuse the enemy radars. Cut to a particular size they create spurious signals on the radar screen.

When Window was used during the first attack on Hamburg on the night of 24-25 July it threw the German nightfighter controllers into complete confusion. One was overheard exclaiming "The English bombers are propagating themselves!" They could not direct the fighters onto the attacking bombers, which is why so few were lost. During the two subsequent attacks they stopped trying to find individual targets for the fighters, and have merely given a running commentary of the height and position of the bomber stream.

How the firestorm fanned the flames

Hamburg, 31 July

The Hamburg firestorms were made worse by the weather: a long dry spell increased the risk of fire when the RAF bombers dropped their lethal mixture of incendiaries and high-explosive (HE) bombs. The smaller incendiaries set light to roofs, while the heavier penetrated the interiors, starting further fires. The HE bombs, on the other hand, created the blast necessary to fan the flames still further.

At the centre of each major conflagration the available oxygen was quickly used up as the fires grew hotter, and vacuums were created. As the hot air rose, cold air was sucked in, fanning the flames and creating winds strong enough to drag people in with them (→ 3/8).

Germans to retreat as Russians attack

Orel, 26 July

The Germans are pulling out of the great bastion at Orel. Having failed at great cost to cut off the Russian salient at Kursk, the *Wehrmacht* is having to withdraw from its own salient, 200 miles (320 km) south of Moscow, in the face of a massive Soviet counter-offensive.

Hitler reluctantly gave permission for Field Marshal von Kluge to withdraw his armies from the salient two days ago after it became apparent that they were in danger of suffering another defeat on the scale of Stalingrad. The Red Army has broken through the Germans' fortified lines east of Orel on a front 20 miles (32 km) long and has defeated five German divisions.

Both sides are also weighing the lessons, as well as counting the cost, of the great tank battle at Kursk. Each deployed tank-busting aircraft fitted with large-calibre cannon. On the German side the Stuka, fitted with two 37mm *flak* cannon, and the Henschel Hs-129 with its 30mm cannon performed with great effect. The Russians replied with Il-2 Shturmoviks fitted with deadly 37mm cannon which on one occasion reduced 70 tanks of the 9th *Panzer* Division to burning wrecks within 20 minutes (→ 31).

Japanese troops secretly evacuate Kiska

Kiska, 30 July

US B-17s are continuing to bomb Kiska, the last Japanese stronghold in the western Aleutians, unaware that the 5,200-strong Japanese garrison was evacuated two nights ago by two cruisers and twelve destroyers under cover of freezing fog.

Japan's decision to abandon Kiska follows its failure to hold Attu last month and the daily US air and sea bombardment of Kiska from Adak, 200 miles (320 km) and two hours' flying time away. US ignorance about the Japanese departure may be prolonged, as the island is usually shrouded in heavy cloud making reconnaissance difficult and encouraging bombers to climb to high altitudes (→ 5/8).

Japanese troops before evacuation.

Nazi extermination in Poland reported

London, 27 July

The Polish government in exile has received word of a new wave of mass murder in eastern Poland, as German forces clear the area to set up new lines of defence.

According to a report in today's *Daily Telegraph*, the Germans are expelling and murdering Poles from a belt 60 miles wide, settling ethnic Germans there in order to boost defences. Lublin, Cracow and Radom are understood to be the centre of the killings, in which the Germans are accused of massacring the entire population, mainly peasants.

Whole towns and villages have been emptied in the terror, and up to 100,000 people have fled to the forests for sanctuary, abandoning their farms and livestock. It is said that the SS are rounding up Polish civilians by cordoning off areas and using artillery and tanks to flush them out.

Depressed Hitler ponders tactics in the "Wolf's Lair"

Rastenburg, E Prussia, 31 July

Hitler has become very depressed, according to his secretary, Traudl Junge: "He is very serious. He sits and stares into his soup without saying a word."

The mood took hold of him after the catastrophe at Stalingrad and the defeat of the Axis forces in North Africa. Since then, his strategic options have been steadily diminishing. In his Wolf's Lair HQ at Rastenburg he broods on the looming threat of an Anglo-American landing on mainland Europe. German army analyses suggest that the blow will fall in Greece, but Hitler, having seen a transcript of a telephone conversation between Churchill and Roosevelt, knows that King Victor Emmanuel is about to pull Italy out of the war.

Troops and planes have been withdrawn from Russia and sent to Italy to meet the Allied threat, and this at a time when the Russians have shown they can hit back hard. The Germans have had to call off the Kursk battle after losing 3,000 tanks.

Elsewhere, the war news is no less sombre. Allied merchant ship construction has exceeded losses for the first time this month, and Donitz has withdrawn his submarines from the Atlantic after losing 37 in July alone. The RAF has injected an entirely new phenomenon into aerial war: the firestorm. When 2,326 tons of bombs were dropped on Hamburg three nights ago, a shrieking hurricane-style wind was created that dried up canals and uprooted trees; an estimated 40,000 people died.

Even Hitler's closest comrades no longer believe in victory. Himmler has set up a special SS team to go to extermination camps and burial grounds and destroy evidence of the mass murder of Jews. But Hitler still hopes. At Peenemunde, new weapons are being tested: a pilotless plane and a massive rocket bomb.

Manpower shortage means more women needed for war work

London, 29 July

Ernest Bevin, the minister of labour, is stopping recruitment for the women's uniformed services in order to divert more women into aircraft production. He told the House of Commons today that there will be no further volunteers accepted for the ATS, WAAF, WRNS and the Women's Land Army, and no further age groups will be called up.

"We propose to ask those women not required for the services to go into the aircraft factories." He was considering the possibility of using more youths of 16 and 17 in the aircraft industry. Although it had expanded so greatly, the labour force was still insufficient. Bevin announced that women of up to 50 will be registered for war work later this summer.

ATS workers recondition used shells: now aircraft factories are the priority.

1943

August

Su	Mo	Tu	We	Th	Fr	Sa
1	2	3	4	5	6	7
8	9	10	11	12	13	14
15	16	17	18	19	20	21
22	23	24	25	26	27	28
29	30	31				

1. Solomon Islands: The US fast patrol boat PT-109, commanded by Lieutenant John F Kennedy, is rammed and sunk by the Japanese destroyer *Amagiri*; the crew is missing, presumed dead (→ 8).

1. Chungking, China: The National Government breaks off diplomatic relations with Vichy France (→ 2).

1. Algiers: De Gaulle is made president of the National Defence Committee, ceding leadership of the Fighting French to General Giraud only for purely military matters.

2. Chungking, China: Chiang Kai-shek is appointed acting president of the National Government, following the death yesterday of Lin Sen (→ 7).

2. Lisbon: The Italian ambassador to Portugal makes contact with Allied representatives, paving the way for peace talks (→ 4).

3. Hamburg: Seven square miles of the city are reported to be destroyed after the fourth RAF raid in the recent campaign (→ 10).

3. Britain: The Polish cryptanalysts Henryk Zygalski and Marian Rejewski, who first broke the German *Enigma* code, arrive at Hendon aerodrome, ending a long exile in France, Algeria and Spain.

4. Italy: US aircraft attack Naples in what Rome calls "the most barbarous and merciless" raid so far: 150 people are killed.→

5. Aleutian Islands: The US Navy drops over 150 tons of bombs on the deserted island of Kiska (→ 15).

5. Lithuania: The Germans start the final deportation of Jews from the Vilna ghetto with a transport to the Vaivara labour camp in Estonia (→ 16).

5. USSR: Bielgorod falls to General Konev's troops.→

6. Italy: German troops start pouring in to take over the country's defences (→ 8).

7. China: Civil war looms, after clashes between Communist and *Kuomintang* troops at Anch'u and Chuhsien, in Shantung province.

Japan declares Burmese independence

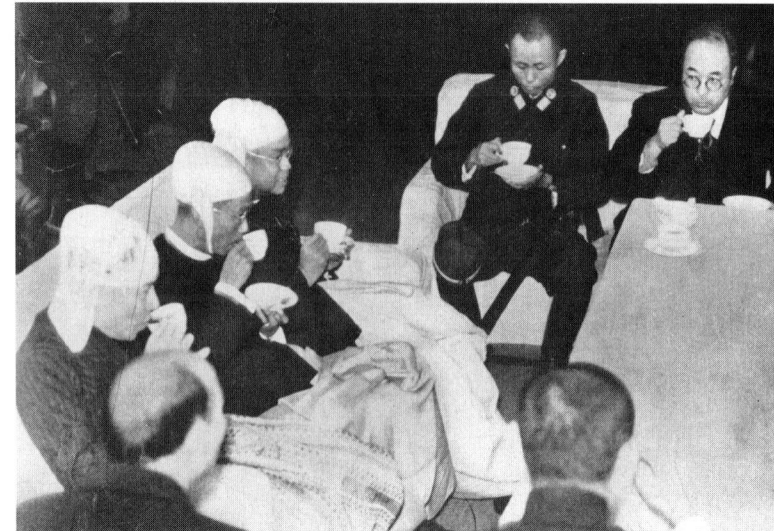

During the run-up towards independence, Burmese envoys take tea in Tokyo.

Rangoon, 1 August
The Japanese government today announced that the British colony of Burma is to be independent. The Japanese military administration now occupying the country under Lt-Gen Mazikazu Kawabe has handed over its powers to the Burmese nationalist leader, Dr Ba Maw, who has been premier under Japan for the last year.

The Burmese people heard of their new status this morning in a broadcast by Radio Tokyo: "Burma has now become the fifth independent country in the Greater East Asia Co-Prosperity Sphere, after Japan, China, Thailand and Manchukuo [*Manchuria*]."

The first act of the new independent state has been to declare war on Britain and the USA. The declaration was read in the Burmese State Assembly by Dr Ba Maw, who on a recent visit to Tokyo spoke of the "sharing of life and death with Japan in the war".

The Japanese move has been expected for some time. Burmese nationalists supporting the Japanese during their 1942 invasion, and now formed into a Burmese National Army, rendered great propaganda benefits to Japan, as has the creation of the Indian National Army, led by the Congress politician Subhas Chandra Bose and recruited from Indian Army prisoners of war. Japan hopes that the granting of Burmese independence will strengthen its claim to be fighting a war against colonialism (→ 13).

Catania and Paterno fall to Allied troops

British troops pass through Catania.

Sicily, 5 August
The race for Messina and victory in Sicily is reaching the final stage. The British have fought their way around Mount Etna on both sides with the Highlanders fighting hard for Biancavilla as the XIII Corps advanced to take Catania and Paterno. The Germans are leaving strong rearguards as they retreat northwards to Messina. The British have been aided by forward landings by airborne forces fighting to save bridges from demolition. The American Seventh Army has used seaborne landings to bypass the Axis defenders along the north coast of the island (→ 6).

German bastion is taken by Red Army

Orel, 5 August
Russia is celebrating the recapture of Orel, which has been in German hands since 1941. In Moscow a 120-gun victory salute was given at midnight. The Russians, who fought hard all the way to the approaches to the city, expected a bloody street battle, but when their patrols moved cautiously in they found the suburbs deserted. The Germans, fearing being cut off, had fled. The fall of this German bastion removes the last threat to Moscow and opens the way for the next stage in the Russian advance. The tide of battle is now rolling towards Bryansk (→ 10).

Goebbels proposes evacuating Berlin

Berlin, 1 August
Berliners at Sunday breakfast were shocked today to hear a radio broadcast by Josef Goebbels calling on all citizens not vital to the war industries to evacuate the city. Up to now propaganda sources have insisted that a major raid on Berlin is very unlikely, and this sudden announcement has fuelled rumours that the capital has been surrendered and this is the beginning of the end. Free travel permits are being issued to women, children, pensioners and the sick, together with ration cards and blankets.

August 1. President Lin Sen (l), who died in Chungking today, is seen here with Chiang Kai-shek.

Ploesti raid threatens Axis oil supply

Cairo, 2 August

B-24 Liberator bombers flying from bases in North Africa carried out a daring long-range raid at tree-top height on the Roumanian oil-fields at Ploesti yesterday afternoon. Brigadier-General U G Ent, the commander of the US Ninth Army Air Force, who led the raid, said on his return: "When we had finished with Ploesti I doubt whether the Axis will be getting anything like its usual 18,000 tons a day out of the place for a long time to come.

"You can't fly a plane without gasoline and this afternoon we went a long way towards cutting the Axis from the source of fuel for their planes and mechanized forces.

"We were first over our target. Our bombs hit what we wanted to get. We found the sky full of A-A fire. They were shooting everything at us, including, I believe, buck shot from shot guns."

The Liberators replied with their heavy machine guns as they roared over the *flak* batteries dropping high explosive, incendiary and de-layed-action bombs which were ex-ploding hours after they had left.

This operation had been minute-ly planned, with single Liberators making dummy runs at low level on targets in Sicily and Italy. On the information gained from these flights it was decided to risk the strong concentration of flak at Ploesti and to try to take out the oilfields in one heavy surprise at-tack at low level.

It was reasoned that such an at-tack could be mounted before the enemy fighters could be brought in-to action. The results have not justi-fied this theory. The oilfields have been hard hit, but at a crippling cost – 56 Liberators lost, including seven that landed in Turkey, out of the 177 which took part.

A US B-24 Liberator bomber in action over the blazing oilfields at Ploesti.

This devastated oilfield still offers important targets to the bombers overhead.

Guards killed when Treblinka inmates stage escape bid

Treblinka, 2 August

Sixteen guards have been killed by inmates in an armed uprising, using weapons stolen from the camp ar-senal. The revolt started at three o'clock this afternoon, when a pris-oner shot at an SS guard whipping one of his co-conspirators. He then gave the signal for the uprising by throwing a hand-grenade.

Earlier today, inmates sprayed petrol instead of the usual disinfec-tant around the huts. At the signal, they set fire to them; soon they were blazing. The fire reached the arsenal, which exploded and spread the fire throughout the camp. In the chaos, prisoners used rifles, handguns and grenades to kill six-teen Germans and Ukrainians, in-cluding SS Sergeant Kittner, the chief guard. One hundred and fifty inmates escaped; the rest, about 550, were murdered in the camp.

Thus the spirit of rebellion has spread from the Polish ghettoes into the extermination camps them-selves. In a hopelessly uneven strug-gle, the Jewish action is little more than a last-ditch protest by men who want to die fighting.

Treblinka, designed to extermin-ate arrivals rather than imprison them, was never meant to hold as many as 700 prisoners. It has been unusually crowded recently be-cause of Himmler's visit this spring, after which he ordered that the hundreds of thousands of corpses buried in huge pits near the camp should be burnt to destroy the evi-dence of mass murder. Extra man-power has been needed to dig up the bodies and burn them on enormous pyres. The men who rose up are forced labourers who have been cremating their own people (→ 5).

Allies capture key airfield on New Georgia

New Georgia, 7 August

Five US warships sank three Ja-panese destroyers early today, 48 hours after capturing the key air-field at Munda. Only the *Shigure* escaped from what is being called the Battle of Vella Gulf. The Japan-ese were surprised trying to run supplies to Kolombangara island, 15 miles (24 km) from Munda, where the remnants of the 5,000-strong Munda garrison have been evacuated; 1,500 of them were burnt in their bunkers. Strategic-ally, Munda brings Allied bombers 200 miles (320 km) closer to the main Japanese naval base at Rabaul, in New Britain.

Swedes cut German supply line to Norway

Stockholm, 5 August

In a move which betrayed Ger-many's weakened position, the Swedish government announced to-night that it would no longer allow the Swedish railways to be used to transport German troops and war material to Norway. The Swedes were forced to concede transit rights to the Germans in 1940 when the Nazi armies were sweeping to victory over most of Europe. Stock-holm newspapers say that the government has acted because a vir-tual state of war exists in Norway today, with British commandos mounting raids and uniformed Allied guerrillas active.

1943

August

Su	Mo	Tu	We	Th	Fr	Sa
1	2	3	4	5	6	7
8	9	10	11	12	13	14
15	16	17	18	19	20	21
22	23	24	25	26	27	28
29	30	31				

8. Sicily: US forces take Sant' Agata and Cesaro, and British troops take Bronte.

8. Mediterranean: Mussolini is imprisoned on Maddalena Island, off Sardinia.

8. Verona: Italy assures the Germans that there will be no separate peace negotiations with the Allies (→ 12).

9. Kreisau, Silesia: Count Helmuth von Moltke convenes a group of German dissidents, which declares its desire to overthrow the Nazi regime. →

9. Ankara: Hungary and Britain reach a secret agreement: Hungary will not fire on Allied aircraft flying to Italy, and the Allies will not bomb Hungarian targets (→ 13).

9. Denmark: Erik Scavenius, the prime minister, refuses to accept German demands that alleged saboteurs should be sent to Germany for trial (→ 24).

10. USSR: Soviet troops take Khotinets, east of Orel.→

10. Germany: In a vast RAF raid on Nuremberg 3,444 tons of bombs are dropped (→ 13).

11. Solomon Islands: Admiral Halsey orders the occupation of Japanese bases on Vella Lavella (→ 15).

12. Italy: 656 RAF bombers devastate Milan, dropping 1,252 tons of incendiary bombs; secret negotiations for an armistice are opened.→

13. India: Auchinleck proposes abandoning all offensive operations in Burma in order to concentrate on supplying China by air (→ 6/10).

13. Morocco: Pierre Pucheu, the former Vichy minister of the interior, is arrested.

13. Europe: The Allies bomb Rome's railyards and, flying over Hungary to make their first raid on Austria, factories at Wiener Neustadt (→ 18).

14. Vichy: The premier, Pierre Laval, refuses to cooperate with German demands to deport all French Jews.

14. Sicily: On orders from General Eisenhower, Lt-Gen Patton apologizes to soldiers whom he had struck in a hospital.

New Italian leader declares Rome "open"

Madrid, 14 August
German agents watched with more than usual suspicion earlier this week as a senior Italian general flew here for secret talks with the British ambassador. The subject was the new Italian government's anxiety to declare Rome an open city after a second day of heavy bombing by Allied aircraft. Simultaneously, another Italian general was meeting Field Marshal Rommel on the Italian frontier, apparently with the same object in mind. Although the new prime minister, Marshal Pietro Badoglio, announced the news to delighted Romans tonight, Allied sources in Algiers said that they had received no official confirmation that Rome would be "open".

A spokesman said that a city could be regarded as "open" only when all ministries, government agencies, military organizations and war industries had gone. "As long as Rome continues to be a German military communications centre, it will constitute a legitimate

War-weary Romans struggle on.

objective of Allied bombings," he said. Many cynical observers believe that Badoglio's declaration should be interpreted as proof that Italy will continue to fight on and has no intention of seeking peace with the Allies (→ 15).

Allied leadership meets in Quebec

Quebec, 13 August
Winston Churchill has arrived here for conferences with Mr Mackenzie King, the Canadian prime minister, and later with President Roosevelt. Mr and Mrs Churchill are staying in the great citadel overlooking the St Lawrence river.

As well as the British chiefs of staff, the prime minister has taken along his daughter Mary, a subaltern in an anti-aircraft unit, Wing-Commander Guy Gibson, the leader of the recent "Dambusters" raid on the Ruhr dams, and Brigadier Orde Wingate, the leader of the Chindits in Burma.

On arrival at Halifax en route for Quebec, Mr Churchill made the reception party sing "The Maple Leaf Forever" – the Canadian national anthem.

It is thought that he and President Roosevelt will discuss a new joint command for South-east Asia and plans for an invasion of western Europe (→ 20).

Top Germans form resistance group and draw up reform list

Germany, 9 August
Some 20 high-ranking individuals have banded together to form a group dedicated to the overthrow of National Socialism in Germany. Calling themselves the Kreisau Circle, after the Kreisau estate belonging to a leading member, Count Helmuth James von Moltke, they have now drawn up a list of principles for post-Nazi reform.

Among the points in this draft document are: "1. Justice, which has been trampled on, must be restored ... 2. Freedom of belief and freedom of conscience will be guaranteed ... 3. Destruction of totalitarian direction of conscience and acknowledgement of the inviolability of human dignity as the foundation for an order of peace and justice ... 4. The basic unit for peaceful coexistence is the family ... 5. Work must be so designed that it arouses the desire for personal responsibility rather than stultifying it ..."

Skilled men may be spared the US draft

Washington, 14 August
The war manpower commission, in a move intended to prevent a national service act, has changed the rules for the draft, the lottery system of conscription. The list of important occupations deferring call-up has been revised to keep men with skills needed by war industry at work. Another change announced by Paul McNutt, the manpower commissioner, is that fatherhood is no longer a reason for deferment. "Fatherhood", said McNutt, "does not excuse any man from making his contribution to victory."

August 12. Captain Clark Gable of the USAAF, seen here with Sergeant-Gunner Phillip Hulse, today flew in a raid on the Ruhr.

Red Army cuts off "Panzers" at Kharkov

A German position under attack in the massive drive against the "Wehrmacht".

Ukraine, 14 August

Russian forces, pushing on in ever increasing strength following the recapture of Bielgorod, have taken the southern outposts of the great Ukrainian city of Kharkov. The Germans defending the city are now in great danger of being cut off as Russian tanks work their way behind their lines.

The continuing Russian offensive, part of their master strategy after the great victory at Kursk, involves 120 Russian divisions. Many of these divisions are absolutely fresh and have been thrown against Field Marshal von Manstein's battered army of only 42 divisions. The Russian commanders, Generals Konev and Vatutin,

thrusting hard at the join in the German line between the 4th *Panzer* Army and the *Kampfgruppe*, have split them apart and are pouring men through the gap.

The apparently inexhaustible supply of Russian divisions is being supported by equally strong aerial armadas. There are now 100 Russian air divisions, with 10,000 aircraft patrolling the battlefield.

Faced by swarms of Russian planes, the *Luftwaffe*, forced to withdraw squadrons to defend Germany from Allied bombers, is finding it increasingly difficult to support the *Wehrmacht*. The question for the German high command now is where to find the reserves to stop the teeming Russians (→ 16).

Ex-ambassador's son helps to save crew after boat is sliced in two by destroyer

Rendova, Solomons, 8 August

A patrol torpedo (PT) boat commander today told how two Solomon Islanders and a coconut shell saved the lives of his crew after they had been stranded for a week and given up for dead.

Lieutenant John F Kennedy, the commander of PT-109, described the ordeal after his PT boat had been sliced in half by the Japanese destroyer *Amagiri* in waters off the Japanese-occupied island of Kolombangara on 1 August. Eleven of the 13 crew survived the impact, although one was injured.

After five hours clinging to the wreckage they managed to reach an island from which Kennedy, the

son of a former US ambassador to Britain, swam out to sea and spent a fruitless night in the water hoping to flag down another PT boat.

Two days later PT-109's crew swam to what the natives know as Plum Pudding Island, 200 yards wide and covered in palm trees, in search of food. But Kennedy and another crew member had to swim to a third island before eventually meeting two natives with a canoe. They gave them a coconut shell inscribed with the message "Nauru Island, Native knows posit. He can pilot. 11 alive, need small boat", and begged them to take it to the US base on Rendova. Within a day help was at hand.

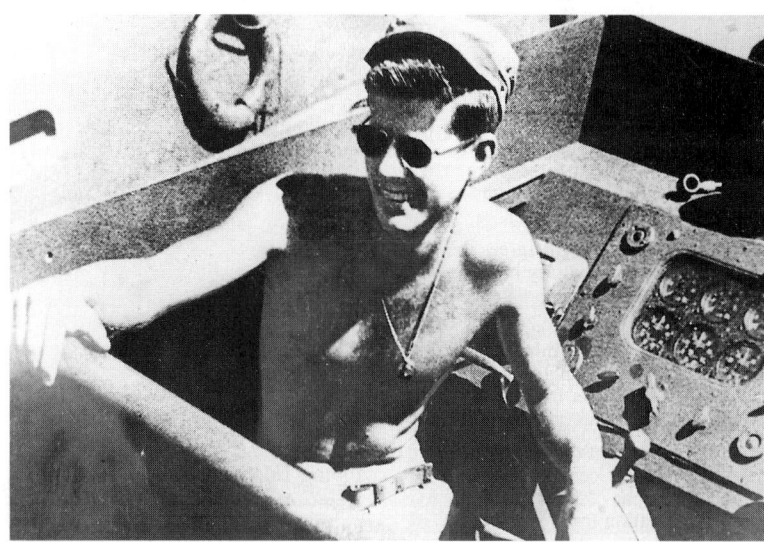

Lieutenant Kennedy, who spent a night in the water trying to flag down help.

Nationalist soldiers face two offensives

Shantung, 12 August

An isolated Chinese Nationalist division in Shantung is in danger of being destroyed as it comes under attack from both Chinese Communists and the Japanese. Members of the *Kuomintang's* 51st Corps, which operates in the Yi-meng Shan area, have been acting as a guerrilla force for the last three months following Japanese attacks. Now the diehard Nationalists have lost their HQ and their commander, following an attack by the rival Chinese Communist Eighth Route Army (→ 15).

Slap-happy Patton shocks doctors and embarrasses his chiefs

Sant' Agata, Sicily, 10 August

Doctors and nurses at a US military hospital looked on in amazement today as a general slapped two soldiers, threatening to shoot one of them. Lieutenant-General George S Patton Jr, the volatile commander of the Seventh Army, was making an unscheduled visit to the 93rd Evacuation Hospital when he saw the soldiers.

The first had malaria. Patton slapped him three times. When Patton asked the second man what the trouble was, he replied: "It's my nerves. I can't stand the shelling any more." Patton slapped the man, shouting: "Shut up that God-

damned crying. I won't have brave men here who have been shot seeing a yellow bastard crying." He struck the soldier again and ordered the medical officer not to admit him.

Patton then turned to the man and said: "You're going back to the front lines and you may get shot and killed, but you're going to fight. If you don't, I'll stand you up against a wall and have a firing squad kill you on purpose." The general reached for his pistol. "I ought to shoot you myself, you Goddamned whimpering coward," he yelled. This was the second such incident in a week and will anger General Eisenhower (→ 14).

Watching from a distance: the general who called a soldier a coward.

August

Su	Mo	Tu	We	Th	Fr	Sa
1	2	3	4	5	6	7
8	9	10	11	12	13	14
15	16	17	18	19	20	21
22	23	24	25	26	27	28
29	30	31				

15. Annecy, France: An RAF Halifax crashes on a secret mission to supply the *Maquis*, killing crew and civilians and damaging property.

15. China: Fighting between Japanese and *Kuomintang* troops in the Shantung region ends, with heavy casualties on both sides.

15. Solomon Islands: US troops occupy Vella Lavella (→ 25/8).

15. Madrid: The Italian General Giuseppe Castellano meets Sir Samuel Hoare, the British ambassador, to ask for Allied assistance to help Italy shake off the German alliance.→

16. Bialystok: Germans enter the Jewish ghetto and start deporting its 25,000 inhabitants (→ 18).

16. USSR: Soviet forces take Zhidra, north-east of Bryansk (→ 21).

17. Lisbon: Portugal agrees to let Britain use military bases in the Azores.

18. China: T V Soong, Chiang Kai-shek's foreign minister, protests to Washington against China's exclusion from high-level Allied conferences.

18. Treblinka, Poland: The death camp receives its final consignment of Jews for extermination (→ 27).

19. Germany: General Hans Jeschonnek, the *Luftwaffe* chief of staff, commits suicide, leaving a note asking that Goering should not attend his funeral.

19. Lisbon: The Allies send official spokesmen to open armistice negotiations with Italy's General Castellano (→ 31).

20. Peenemunde: The head of rocket research is found dead, shot by an unknown assassin.

21. Australia: The Labor Party wins the general election, and John Curtin is returned as prime minister.→

21. USSR: Soviet forces capture Zmiev, south of Kharkov (→ 23).

21. Moscow: Andrei Gromyko is appointed Soviet ambassador to the US.

US raids provoke massive air battle

Flying Fortresses in tight formation over Schweinfurt: but they suffer heavy casualties in daylight raids without escorts.

Germany, 18 August

Flying Fortresses of the US Eighth Army Air Force fought a desperate battle with swarms of German fighters over the heart of Germany yesterday as they flew 800 miles (1,280 km) from the Channel coast to bomb the vital ball-bearing factory at Schweinfurt and the Messerschmitt works at Regensburg.

The *Luftwaffe* harried the bombers all the way to the target and back, but the American crews fought their way through to inflict heavy damage on the factories. Both are high on the "Pointblank" list, which instructs the RAF and USAAF to concentrate raids on German fighter production centres.

The air was full of blazing planes, cannon fire and rockets as the B-17s fought their way through, their formidable half-inch machine guns covering each other, closing up the formation as stricken aircraft staggered and fell out of position. The bombers suffered heavy casualties. Of the 376 Fortresses which set out on the raid, 36 were lost from the Schweinfurt and 24 from the Regensburg formation. Some 25 defending fighters were shot to pieces by the bombers.

The results of the raid are now being assessed by the American commanders. One lesson is already apparent, and it is the same one that RAF Bomber Command learnt early in the war: unescorted bombers cannot make daylight raids on Germany except at a prohibitive cost in men and machines (→ 6/9).

Bomber Command attacks secret German rocket research base

Northern Europe, 18 August

Germany's top-secret rocket and flying bomb centre at Peenemunde, on the Baltic coast, was hit by 597 RAF bombers using new techniques last night. Casualties were heavy on both sides: some 732 of Peenemunde's staff were killed when 1,593 tons of high explosive were dropped on three main targets. The RAF lost 40 bombers. The impact on the German secret weapon programme is harder to assess, but it is likely to be delayed for weeks rather than months.

The new bombing tactics include a "timed run" on a fixed bearing from a known position, the "master bomber" technique used by the Dam Busters, and a red fire marker which burns fiercely for ten minutes some 3,000 feet (914 metres) above ground level.

The Germans were also using a new weapon, the *Schrage Musik* upward-firing cannon, fitted to Me110 night fighters (→ 22).

US retakes Kiska without a struggle

Kiska, Aleutian Islands, 15 August
In a textbook example of the excessive force that has characterized the Aleutians campaign, 34,300 US and Canadian troops today stormed Kiska only to discover that the Japanese had left nearly three weeks ago. Allied HQ is justifying its continued bombardment of the last 18 days by claiming that its attacks had destroyed Japanese radio equipment so there was no way of knowing if anyone was left. The recapture of Kiska, the last Japanese-held island in the Aleutian Chain, ends a 15-month campaign, to which the US has diverted 100,000 men in order to reassure the US public that there is no real Japanese threat to Alaska.

Side by side: two Allied flags.

Nazis losing grip on defiant Norwegians

Oslo, 20 August
A state of siege has been proclaimed throughout Norway. Army officers have been rounded up for deportation to PoW camps in Germany, and the Oslo police commissioner has been shot dead. Gunnar Eilifsen, the police commissioner, repeatedly disobeyed an order to provide men to arrest Norwegian women for compulsory labour in war industries. There is now widespread defiance of German rule. Of the 35,000 new workers demanded by the Germans only 4,000 have been found.

Fall of Messina signals Allied win in Sicily

American troops in Messina comb the smouldering streets for enemy snipers.

Messina, 17 August
Troops of the US 3rd Infantry Division entered this historic city today at 10am, just 50 minutes before the British Eighth Army. The race for Messina was won. The Germans have left in an orderly evacuation. The booty of captured weapons, fuel and ammunition was huge; but nothing could compensate for the sight of the civilian populace emerging from cellars and other hiding places to see their beloved Messina almost flattened by not only Allied bombs and artillery but also, now, shells from the Italian mainland.

There were no flowers or wine or kisses to greet these conquerors. The people of Messina are disorien-tated, dulled and wholly uninterested in the khaki-clad men who roam their city and sit in the few remaining bars and cafes, equally tired and haggard and talking of friends they have buried over the past 39 days of brutal fighting.

The cost in casualties of the Sicilian campaign has been high, though less than anticipated. The British and Canadians have lost 2,721 killed, 2,183 missing and 7,939 wounded – a total of 12,843. The Americans lost a total of 9,968 – 2,811 killed, 686 missing and 6,471 wounded. The British estimate that 164,000 Axis troops were either killed or taken prisoner with 100,000 evacuated to the mainland.

US raiders attack New Guinea base

New Guinea, 18 August
The American Fifth Army Air Force has virtually destroyed the entire Japanese air strength at Wewak, in New Guinea, in concentrated attacks using 166 aircraft over two days. An entire Japanese bombing formation lined up on the runway at Boram with propellers turning was caught just as it was about to take off. Yesterday's losses, which the Japanese described as "The Black Day of 17 August", totalled 150 aircraft. The Americans returned to strike with even greater strength today (→ 23).

Britain and US to share atom secrets

Quebec, 20 August
Britain and the United States have agreed on how they will cooperate on a secret weapon, the atomic bomb, known in code as "Tube Alloys". President Roosevelt and Mr Churchill today signed a simple agreement: never to use "this agency" against each other, and not to use it against third parties without each other's consent.

The agreement caps several months of negotiations between British and American officials. The secret project will be placed under a joint committee in Washington. Mr Roosevelt has also persuaded Mr Churchill to accept the US chief of staff, General Marshall, as the senior Allied commander (→ 23).

Sabotage is bogus

London, 18 August
The Times carries a story today about the sabotaging of an electricity generating station at Bury St Edmunds, in Suffolk. It will no doubt be read with great interest by German intelligence. It was, after all, written especially for them by the "Twenty Committee" – XX – the British Intelligence department which runs double agents reporting false information to the Germans. The "sabotage" was carried out to prove to the Germans the reliability of the two Norwegian double agents nicknamed "Mutt and Jeff".

Soldiers at the New Guinea front vote in the Australian federal elections.

1943

August

Su	Mo	Tu	We	Th	Fr	Sa
1	2	3	4	5	6	7
8	9	10	11	12	13	14
15	16	17	18	19	20	21
22	23	24	25	26	27	28
29	30	31				

22. Baltic: A prototype V1 rocket lands on the Danish island of Bornholm, where an Allied agent photographs it before it is recovered (→ 30/9).

23. New Guinea: Four US destroyers bombard Finschhafen (→ 1/9).

23. China: The Japanese bomb Chungking for the first time since 1941.

24. Denmark: Bomb incidents and strikes mark growing resistance to Nazi rule (→ 29).

24. Germany: Hitler appoints Himmler *Reich* minister of the interior.

26. Canada: Churchill sets off on a four-day fishing holiday in the Laurentian mountains.

26. Washington: Britain, the US and Canada give limited recognition to the French Committee of National Liberation (→ 27).

27. Bay of Biscay: The British sloop *Egret* and the Canadian destroyer *Athabaskan* are hit by German radio-controlled glider bombs, HS293s, nicknamed "chase-me-charlies".

27. Slovenia: German and Croatian troops attack the Italian garrison at Ljubljana.

27. Moscow: The USSR and China give limited recognition to the French Committee of National Liberation.

28. Ellice Islands: US marines land on Nanomea.

29. Denmark: Germany imposes martial law after the government refuses to accept an ultimatum to resign.→

29. Washington: Roosevelt warns Germany that its crimes against civilians in occupied Europe will be brought to account after the war.

30. USSR: Soviets troops take Taganrog and Yelna, moving to cut off the Germans in the Crimea (→ 1/9).

31. Sicily: General Castellano tells the Allies that if they want peace with Italy they must protect the Italians from German reprisals (→ 2/9).

31. France: The Japanese submarine I-8 reaches Brest from Singapore.

Germans lose Kharkov to the Red Army

Moscow, 23 August
A massive 224-gun salute by the Red Army thundered out in Moscow tonight in celebration of the recapture of Kharkov, the principal city of the Ukraine. Troops of General Konev's Steppe front took the city yesterday after Field Marshal von Manstein pulled his XI Corps out in defiance of Hitler's orders that Kharkov had to be held at all costs.

Von Manstein had no alternative. His soldiers were about to be cut off by immensely superior Russian forces sweeping round the city, and he knew that the men of XI Corps were of more value to him than the shattered ruins of Kharkov. In the south, General Tolbukhin has broken the German line at the river Mius and is driving for the Donets basin with the aim of recovering the area's mineral riches and cutting off the German forces still in the Crimea and the Kuban bridgehead. The Germans admit that a "Soviet spring flood" is pouring through the gap smashed in their lines at the Mius (→ 30).

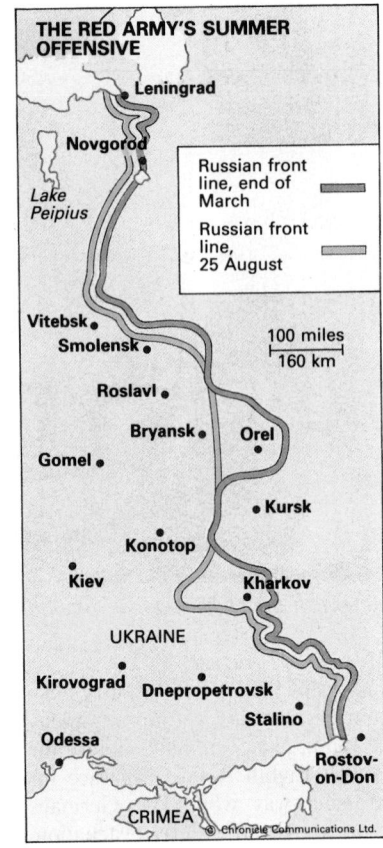

THE RED ARMY'S SUMMER OFFENSIVE

Leningrad
Novgorod
Lake Peipius
Russian front line, end of March
Russian front line, 25 August
Vitebsk
Smolensk
Roslavl
Bryansk
Orel
Gomel
Kursk
Konotop
Kiev
Kharkov
UKRAINE
Kirovograd
Dnepropetrovsk
Stalino
Odessa
Rostov-on-Don
CRIMEA
100 miles
160 km
© Chronicle Communications Ltd.

Anti-Nazi riots follow death of King Boris

Sofia, 28 August
The death of King Boris, often spoken of as "Hitler's pathetic dupe", has been followed by anti-German demonstrations in Sofia and calls for a general strike throughout Bulgaria. Despite an official statement that the king died of heart failure and double pneumonia, many Bulgarians believe that he was murdered on Hitler's orders.

Boris threw in his lot with the Germans after meeting Hitler at Berchtesgaden in November 1940. But most of his subjects remained hostile to the Germans and, in spite of his efforts, the king was unable to raise "volunteers" for service in Russia.

Reports surfacing in Switzerland say that Hitler demanded full mobilization of Bulgaria, the building of extra defences along the Turkish frontier and a free hand for the *Gestapo* in the country. Boris, it is said, decided to abdicate rather than give in. He was then shot by one of his bodyguards. Under Bulgarian law, the king has the right to appoint

King Boris (r): "Hitler's dupe"?

three regents before his death. The fact that Boris did not do so suggests that either he was unconscious for some time before his death, or he died suddenly.

Bialystok ghetto is liquidated by SS

Poland, 27 August
The rising tide of Jewish resistance and the growth of the Jewish Fighting Organization has failed to stop the mass murder of Jews. The 25,000 survivors in the Bialystok ghetto have been deported to the extermination camps at Treblinka and Majdanek.

The entire population was herded into Jurowiecka Square, where an attempted rising was swiftly crushed. A few hundred resisters are defending their hiding places in the city's sewers and makeshift bunkers, but the SS is slowly and surely rooting them out for deportation. Only the Lodz ghetto now remains to face Hitler's "final solution" for Poland's Jews.

Bialystok Jews were the last to arrive at Treblinka, the scene of an armed rebellion earlier this month. A team of Jews whose lives have been extended by a few weeks is busy pulling down the huts. A final trainload of clothes taken from the dead has left for Germany (→ 18/9).

Germans told how to cope with raids

Germany, 28 August
Yet another month of devastating bombing by the Allies is drawing to a close. On 1 August the USAAF wreaked havoc in the Ploesti oilfields in Roumania; on 17 August, the RAF hit the secret rocket-testing centre in Peenemunde; and last night more than 3,000 people died in a raid on Nuremberg.

The German propaganda machine has given up minimizing the damage, and instead newspapers publish instructions and advice to the beleaguered German people. Headlines such as "Protect your property and your life" or "Equipment for air-raid protection and self help" have become commonplace. Citizens in high-risk areas are advised to send valuables to relatives for safe-keeping and to equip their shelters with as much water as possible to extinguish fires. But with some 300,000 people a month now being bombed out of their homes, good advice is simply not enough (→ 11/9).

438

Second front is agreed

Quebec, 23 August

The "Quadrant" conference between Mr Churchill, President Roosevelt and the Canadian prime minister, Mr Mackenzie King, and their staffs has ended with a decision to press for a "second front" against Germany in France. This invasion, to be codenamed "Overlord", would be the top priority.

The communique issued here today said that "the whole field of world operations" had been surveyed, and "the necessary decisions have been taken to provide for the forward action" of Allied forces. Mr Churchill had favoured a number of operations, against Norway and in southern Europe by continuing the offensive in Italy; the

Americans wanted a frontal assault in France. A study is to be made of a landing in southern France.

There were also strategic differences over the conduct of the war in South-east Asia, where the US generals want to invade Burma, while Mr Churchill wants to attack Sumatra. Again the Americans won the argument, although the new South-east Asia Command (SEAC) to direct operations in Burma seems likely to be headed by a Briton. Preparations for a new offensive in Burma will now proceed, along with a second campaign behind Japanese lines by Brigadier Wingate's Chindits. Britain also approved US plans for the next stages of the Pacific War (→ 1/10).

Germans move to crush Danish uprising

Danes lie dead in the street, murdered by the Nazis in reprisal for sabotage.

Copenhagen, 29 August

Confronted by outbreaks of sabotage throughout Denmark, the Germans have moved in 50,000 troops, proclaimed martial law in six provincial towns and disarmed the Danish army. The navy scuttled itself on 29 August.

At noon on 24 August a violent explosion wrecked the capital's Forum Hall, which was capable of holding 16,000 people.

Strikes and sabotage have become more and more frequent as news of Allied victories in Russia and southern Europe has spread.

The Germans demanded the introduction of a curfew, press censorship and the death penalty for sabotage. The Danish government, backed by King Christian, rejected the demands.

In recent weeks, factories have been blown up, trains derailed and a power station in East Jutland wrecked. In the provincial capital of Odense, where strikes have shut factories, crowds have paraded in the streets singing patriotic songs, waving British and American flags and chanting "Long Live the Allies" (→ 1/10).

King, Roosevelt, Churchill and their chiefs of staff line up for the camera.

Allied PoWs flee Stalag 383 in disguise

Stalag 383, Bavaria, 26 August

Two British prisoners made a daring escape from this camp yesterday by walking out of the gate wearing home-made German uniforms and carrying forged passes.

The escapers, Lance-Sergeant Suggit of the 5th (Inniskilling) Dragoon Guards and Sergeant Beeson of the RAOC, had to bring their attempt forward by a day because there is so much activity, masterminded by the escape committee, that their original plan would have clashed with an attempt by others

to "go over the wire". They made their German uniforms from Australian tunics dyed green with dyes acquired from the camp theatre.

Their badges were made of cardboard covered in silver paper, and their medal ribbons cut out of tin coloured with red and black ink. A friendly guard from Alsace lent them his papers so that they could be forged.

At dusk tonight, with sandwiches in their fake holsters, they walked nonchalantly out of the gate.

Mountbatten to be SE Asia commander

Quebec, 25 August

Lord Louis Mountbatten, the 43-year-old head of Combined Operations, has been appointed supreme Allied commander in South-east Asia, it was revealed here today. The dashing Mountbatten, a former destroyer captain – Noel Coward based *In Which We Serve* on him and his ship HMS *Kelly* in Crete – will be responsible for operations based on India and Ceylon. The appointment suggests that commando operations – on land and at sea – will play a major part as Britain strikes back at Japan from its firm bases on the subcontinent and in Ceylon, both of which have been under separate commands until now.

Allies force Japan out of New Georgia

Munda, New Georgia, 25 August

The Allies are now in complete control of New Georgia and its surrounding islands after the move by Japan to evacuate its forces on Kolombangara and Vella Lavella. The decision follows recent Japanese air and surface defeats in the region, crippling Japan's ability to protect supplies to its garrisons.

Most significant has been the loss of Munda airstrip and, five days ago, the destruction of 170 Japanese planes as they stood wing-to-wing on the tarmac at Wewak, in New Guinea. Japanese losses in the New Georgia campaign are estimated at 2,500 dead and 17 warships, compared with Allied losses of 1,000 men and six ships (→ 1/9).

1943

September

Su	Mo	Tu	We	Th	Fr	Sa
			1	2	3	4
5	6	7	8	9	10	11
12	13	14	15	16	17	18
19	20	21	22	23	24	25
26	27	28	29	30		

1. Pacific: Aircraft from the US carriers *Essex*, *Yorktown* and *Independence*, part of the new Fast Carrier Task Force, attack Marcus Island; US troops land on Baker Island to build an airstrip for the forthcoming Gilbert Islands campaign (→ 17).

1. Solomon Islands: US infantrymen who landed at Vella Lavella yesterday reach Orete Cove (→ 3).

1. New Guinea: Air attacks on the Japanese at Lae are increased.→

1. USSR: Dorogobuzh, east of Smolensk, falls to the Russians (→ 2).

1. Washington: Averell Harriman is appointed US ambassador to the USSR.

2. USSR: Soviet troops take Kommunarsk and Lisichansk, in the Donets basin, threatening Stalino (→ 3).

2. Italy: The British battleships *Warspite* and *Valiant* shell the mainland (→ 3).

2. Germany: Hitler appoints Albert Speer, the minister of armaments and munitions, to the new post of *Reich* minister for arms and war production.

3. Solomon Islands: US forces take Arundel Island and consolidate their positions on Vella Lavella (→ 6).

3. USSR: The Red Army pushes forward on a wide front, cutting the Bryansk/Kiev railway line (→ 4).

3. Germany: One million civilians have been evacuated from Berlin in the last month.→

3. Italy: The Allies take the major Calabrian town, Reggio.→

4. USSR: Hitler gives German troops permission to evacuate the Kuban bridgehead.

4. USSR: Soviet troops under Konev and Malinovsky take Merefa, cutting rail access to Kharkov (→ 8).

4. Italy: Allied troops land between Reggio and Catona.

4. Hamburg: "Lord Haw-Haw", the radio propagandist, tells Britain that "the final blow will be struck by Adolf Hitler".

Allied troops land on the toe of Italy

Straits of Messina, 3 September
Following two days of heavy bombardment by four battleships, British troops landed in force on the European mainland today, the fourth anniversary of the declaration of war. General Montgomery took no chances. Every available artillery piece was lined up on the Sicilian coast. Monitors, cruisers and destroyers rained shells ranging from six to 15 inches in size on beaches near Reggio di Calabria.

Eisenhower had planned this invasion – Operation Baytown – to draw German defences away from Salerno, where larger-scale landings are planned. Two *Panzer* divisions had been in the Reggio area, but the Germans had left by the time that the men of XIII Corps – the British 5th and Canadian 1st Divisions of the British Eighth Army – came ashore today. There was little resistance; some Italian soldiers even volunteered to unload the landing craft.

The invaders are fanning out quickly into the hilly countryside of Calabria, and already the lack of roads, the rough terrain and the effects of German demolition work are causing problems in moving men and armour. Meanwhile, convoys are preparing for the second stage of the invasion of Italy. The US Fifth Army, comprising the US VI Corps and the British X Corps, under the command of General Mark Clark, will hit the mainland at Salerno (→ 4).

Officers train their binoculars on the Italian coast as they come in to land.

Unloading equipment at Reggio di Calabria: Italians were eager to help.

Italian general signs secret armistice with Allies in Sicily

Cassibile, Sicily, 3 September
In total secrecy, General Giuseppe Castellano signed his country out of the war today. The US Lt-Gen Walter Bedell Smith signed for the Allies. After weeks of talks in Portugal led by a "freed" British PoW, Lt-Gen Adrian Carton de Wiart, VC, the Allies have agreed an armistice, to be announced "at the right time" – in order not to prejudice the Salerno landings. From the moment that Marshal Badoglio became Italy's premier, he was determined to take his disillusioned country out of the war. But the Germans are unlikely to take kindly to Italy's surrender (→ 8).

General Bedell Smith signs the armistice to take Italy out of the war.

German doctors use human guinea-pigs

Germany, 2 September

German doctors are allegedly turning the Hippocratic Oath on its head, using healthy prisoners as human guinea-pigs for gruesome, often futile, medical experiments.

The experiments are performed at the Ravensbruck concentration camp, near Mecklenburg, according to the Polish interior ministry in exile. Today it published claims of abdominal surgery, the removal of bones and muscle from limbs and the deliberate infection of patients with tetanus and tuberculosis. In this way Professor Julius Gepphard has killed and crippled many.

Meanwhile, at Dachau, a camp near Munich, the Czech surgeon Dr Franz Blaha has become expert at stripping skin from prisoners' corpses; it is then cured and dried until it becomes like leather. In the camp workshops, the skin becomes purses, handbags, gloves, slippers, lampshades and riding breeches. Items of human skin – especially bearing tattoos – are prized by SS men as gifts for their wives.

Should the workshops, manned by prisoners who were previously craftsmen and leatherworkers, run out of material, the senior doctor, Sigismund Rascher, picks out 20 or so healthy-skinned young people and has them shot – in the neck, so as not to spoil their skins.

Ilse Koch, at Buchenwald camp, near Weimar, runs another of Hitler's "tanneries".

Allied troops seize key New Guinea port

Wire mesh is laid down for vehicles to cross soft sands on New Guinea.

New Guinea, 4 September

The reconquest of New Guinea advanced a major step today when battle-hardened Australian veterans of El Alamein and US troops stormed ashore in an amphibious operation aimed at seizing the key New Guinea port of Lae, on the Huon Gulf.

The Australians, of the 9th Division, headed for the beaches as Japanese aircraft attacked their landing craft, killing seven soldiers. Once ashore the Allied troops advanced towards Lae without interruption. The Australians had cloaked their plan to seize Lae by threatening the nearby village of Salamaua without actually attacking it; the Japanese thereupon reinforced Salamaua, thus weakening the defences of Lae. Japanese aircraft from Rabaul have continued making trouble for the Allies during the day, inflicting about 120 casualties. But the attacks failed to interfere with the westward advance of the 9th Division (→ 5).

Twenty million contribute to war effort in Britain

Britain, 1 September

The population of Britain is now more completely mobilized than that of any other country – far more so than Germany's. Ministry of labour figures show that there are 22,750,000 men and women in the services, Civil Defence or essential war work such as munitions and service industries. With another million doing voluntary war work, this accounts for over 70 per cent of the 33 million people aged between 16 and 64. One million people over 65 are also in full-time employment.

Before the war, no expert would have believed this possible, said Ernest Bevin, the minister of labour. "Yet we have had to do it and we have done it." Ten million women up to the age of 45 have already been registered for war work. The recent decision to register those aged between 45 and 50 brought much criticism of Mr Bevin in parliament and the press for "directing grandmothers"; 200 MPs signed a motion of protest. The minister pointed out that 1,500,000 women over 40 are already at work, and 500,000 of them are over 45.

He believes that older women do not resent the part they are being called on to play in the factories; nor do older men. "The average age of the Merseyside docker at the present moment is nearly 51 and he is giving a remarkable turn-round of ships. I saw a man there the other day aged 83, wheeling three-hundredweight bags of Cuban sugar. I do not think I have been hard when these examples are borne in mind."

A third of the women serving in the forces and industry come from the "non-manual, non-industrial classes". Altogether there are 2,250,000 more people working in the munitions industry than in 1914-18. Around 100,000 women have joined the railways, and others are working as welders in the shipyards.

RAF bombers return to Berlin with new tactics and fewer losses

Berlin, 4 September

In the third saturation raid on the city in 11 nights, the RAF last night blasted Berlin with 1,000 tons of bombs within 20 minutes. Only a few days ago the Germans were saying that British losses were so heavy the RAF would not dare to return. Bomber Command adopted new tactics for the raid, concentrating the whole fleet of 316 Lancasters and four Mosquitoes over the city in a short period of time; losses are put at 22 planes, compared with 47 in the raid three nights ago and 56 in the first raid last month. The raid left 422 Berliners dead, and caused widespread devastation (→ 19/11).

What was once a street in Berlin - now a patch of mud strewn with rubble.

1943

September

Su	Mo	Tu	We	Th	Fr	Sa
			1	2	3	4
5	6	7	8	9	10	11
12	13	14	15	16	17	18
19	20	21	22	23	24	25
26	27	28	29	30		

5. New Guinea: Australian and US forces land in the Markham valley and take Nadzab (→ 8).

6. Solomon Islands: Japan counter-attacks on Arundel Island (→ 21).

6. China: Stilwell asks Chiang Kai-shek's Nationalists to join the Communists in order to fight the Japanese more effectively (→ 13).

6. Stuttgart: One hundred and fifty-seven B-17 bombers raid the city, while 181 are despatched to other targets; 45 are lost (→ 16).

7. Corsica: Civilians stage an armed uprising against Italian troops on the island, and occupy Ajaccio (→ 10).

8. New Guinea: US destroyers shell Lae; the Japanese begins a retreat from Salamaua in the face of heavy Australian fire.→

8. USSR: Stalino, the vital industrial centre of the Donets basin, falls to the Red Army.→

9. Germany: A "National Fascist Government" for Italy is formed, in Mussolini's name.

9. Tehran: Iran declares war on Germany.

9. Spitzbergen: German ships bombard the Allied base, and troops of the German 349th Grenadier Regiment land and blow up Allied military installations.→

9. Italy: Marshal Ugo Cavallero, the former Italian chief of general staff, kills himself.→

10. USSR: Soviet troops capture Mariupol, on the Sea of Azov, and land at Novorossiisk, on the Black Sea (→ 14).

10. Mediterranean: The Allies occupy the Dodecanese island of Castelrosso (→ 15).

10. Sardinia: German troops evacuate to Corsica (→ 19).

11. Italy: British forces take Brindisi (→ 12).

11. USSR: German officers imprisoned in a PoW camp at Lunyovo set up the anti-Nazi League of German Officers.

11. Yugoslavia: The partisans occupy Split (→ 17).

Italy "has surrendered"

Italy, 8 September

Italy is out of the war. As a huge invasion convoy sailed towards the beaches of Salerno today, General Eisenhower announced that Germany's former partner has surrendered its forces unconditionally. Two hours later, Marshal Badoglio made a similar announcement on Italian radio. The dramatic announcement was carefully timed to coincide with the major Allied landings – and avoid resistance by Italian troops. It has been a carefully kept secret. Negotiations have been under way for weeks in Lisbon involving the Vatican and Lt-Gen Adrian Carton de Wiart, VC, who had been released from a prisoner-of-war camp. The document of surrender was signed on 3 September in a mess-tent in Sicily by General Giuseppe Castellano for the Italians and General Bedell Smith for the Allies, but kept secret until today (→ 9).

Red Army advances on Ukraine capital

Moscow, 9 September

The Red Army has set out on another stage of its inexorable march to the west with a powerful thrust towards Kiev, the capital of the Ukraine, which the Germans have turned into a major base. This follows the storming of the railway junction of Bakhmach after two days of fighting. *Red Star*, the army's newspaper, says today "we feel the beginning of the end" (→ 10).

New Guinea attack marks Allies' first airborne raids in Pacific

New Guinea, 11 September

Salamaua, made vulnerable by the withdrawal of Japanese troops needed for the defence of Lae further to the north, was attacked and entered today by the Australian 5th Division. The advance on Salamaua was delayed for two weeks while the Australian 7th and 9th Divisions completed preparations for converging attacks on Lae by land and sea.

Six days ago, in the first airborne attack by the Allies in the Pacific War, American paratroopers and Australian artillerymen parachuted into the Markham Valley and took a disused airfield at Nadzab, northwest of Lae, without opposition. By 7 September, the airstrip at Nadzab was serviceable (→ 16).

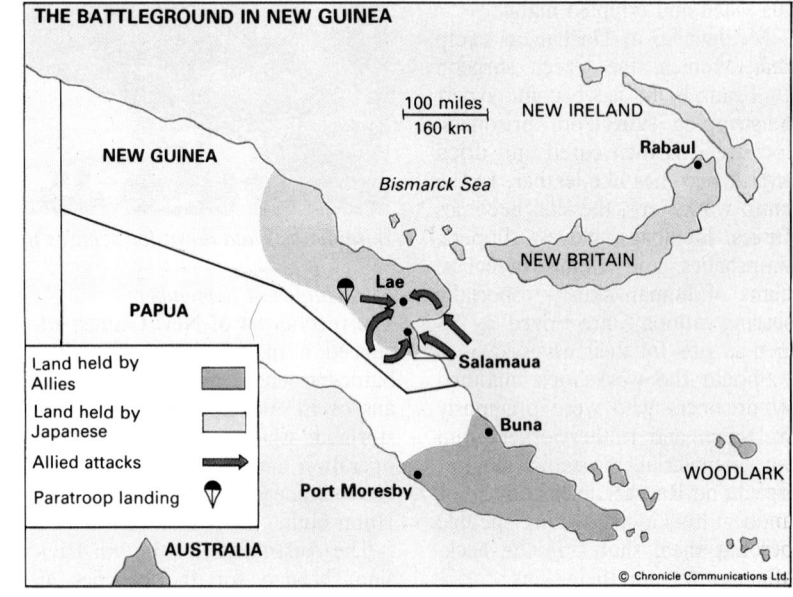

German ships bombard Spitzbergen, destroying installations

The Arctic island of Spitzbergen takes a hammering from the German ships.

Spitzbergen, 9 September

The pride of the German fleet battered the shore installations here today and succeeded in putting the radio station out of action.

The attacking force comprised two battleships, *Tirpitz* and the *Scharnhorst*, and ten destroyers. The *Tirpitz* is Germany's most powerful ship, yet today's action is the first time that her heavy guns have been in action since she was built two years ago.

The modest target chosen is a measure of the Royal Navy's success in keeping this powerful force holed up in Altenfjord, in the north of Norway. The ships will need to race back to Altenfjord to avoid a confrontation with Britain's Home Fleet.

Allied troops land in force on west coast of Italy

Allied troops come ashore in holiday mood near Salerno; but they soon encounter fierce German resistance.

Salerno, 9 September

No invasion has started in such a holiday spirit. Soldiers in this huge convoy were tensed for the start of Operation Avalanche when the voice of their commander-in-chief, General Eisenhower, came over the ships' tannoys announcing the Italian surrender. The announcement was greeted with cheers and whoops and talk of the *signorinas* in Naples tonight. Officers did issue warnings, but the atmosphere was dangerously relaxed as Americans and Britons of the Fifth Army clambered into their landing craft soon after midnight. Some, like the American Rangers and British Commandos, have landed on darkened beaches and have met no resistance until well ashore. Not even the commanders knew that the retreating Germans had shrewdly placed three *Panzer* divisions and the 29th *Panzergrenadier* Division in the Salerno area.

On the right flank of the British X Corps the 56th British Infantry Division met no opposition as it disembarked on empty beaches, but has come under fierce counterattacks from tanks as it advances on the Montecorvino airfield. Others from the division reached the village of Battipaglia, but – despite the aid of naval gunfire – could not dislodge the Germans. Troops from the 46th Division are driving northwards along the coast road to Salerno itself.

To the south of the Sele river – which divides the two Allied beachheads – two regiments of the US 36th "Texas" Division were wading ashore when flares lit the entire scene. The Americans – many facing their first battle – came under withering fire from unseen German defenders and threatened to panic. Weeks of careful planning and rehearsal were forgotten as soldiers dived for cover and landing craft turned back towards the transports out at sea.

While the Texas Division sorted itself out – making its way eventually to its first objective, one-and-a-half miles inland – three battalions of US Rangers succeeded in taking Monte Chiunzi during the night. By dawn today they had taken the twin peaks overlooking the pass and the main highway to Naples.

The huge Allied army is ashore; but the two beach-heads north and south of the Sele remain separated by a seven-mile gap. At sea, General Mark Clark, the US Fifth Army commander, has little idea of what is happening on land. His view of the battle is obscured by smoke, and radio communication is patchy. As German reinforcements race towards Salerno, the holiday is over (→ 10).

Cheers greet paras as naval port falls

Taranto, 9 September

In the hastily-improvised Operation Slapstick, six British warships entered this port today to land 3,600 British paratroopers on Italian soil. No Germans were to be seen, and the Italian garrison cheered as the British came ashore. Taranto was beyond the range of air fighter cover from Sicily, but the Allies wanted to secure a port to supply advances up Italy's eastern flank. They also wanted to ensure that Italian warships did not fall into German hands; but the Italian fleet is already on the way to surrender in Malta (→ 11).

German soldiers occupy Rome as Italian defenders capitulate

Italian troops who had defended the city of Rome surrender to the Germans.

Rome, 10 September

German reaction to Italy's surrender was predictably swift. Within hours of Eisenhower's announcement of the Italian surrender, General von Vietinghoff, the commander of the Tenth Army, today moved paratroopers and a *Panzer* division to occupy Rome.

Five Italian divisions stationed around Rome appeared ready to defend the city, but capitulated quickly as the German commanders put Operation *Achse* [Axis] into force. Ironically, the Americans had been preparing a division-strong airborne landing in the city – but cancelled the operation when Marshal Badoglio protested (→ 11).

Italian fleet hoists black for surrender

Malta, 10 September

"Be pleased to inform Their Lordships that the Italian Fleet lies at anchor under the guns of the Fortress of Malta." With these words Admiral Sir Andrew Cunningham, the commander-in-chief in the Mediterranean, signalled to the admiralty the total surrender of the Italian navy. Flying black flags of surrender and escorted by ships of the Royal Navy, units of the Italian fleet are anchored off Valetta's Grand Harbour. More ships are heading for Gibraltar and other Allied ports, removing the naval threat in the Mediterranean.

"Glider bomb" hits Italian battleship

Malta, 10 September

The Germans have unleashed a new weapon of warfare which claimed as its first victim one of the Italian ships heading here to surrender. The battleship *Roma* was hit by a "glider bomb" off Sardinia and blew up soon after firing her first and last shots in battle.

The Germans have two types of glider bomb – the Ruhrstahl SD-1400 and the Henschel HS-293 – which are released from the air to hit targets on the ground. In effect, they are unmanned missiles which can be used against targets on land as well as at sea (→ 16).

Churchill suggests common citizenship

Cambridge, Mass, 6 September

Winston Churchill, in a speech at Harvard university here today, looked forward to future common citizenship between Britain and the United States. He spoke of a future when British and American people would have "hardly a sense of being foreigners". Mr Churchill has long regarded Anglo-American accord as the linchpin of his policy, but he has never before speculated about so close a relationship. He also warned that the war was now entering "perhaps its most severe and costly phase" (→ 19).

September

Su	Mo	Tu	We	Th	Fr	Sa
				1	2	3	4
5	6	7	8	9	10	11
12	13	14	15	16	17	18
19	20	21	22	23	24	25
26	27	28	29	30		

12. Capri: The Allies take the island without firing a shot.

12. Rastenburg: German *Gauleiters* are appointed for South Tyrol and Venetia, and Speer takes over control of the Italian arms industry (→ 14).

13. Chungking: Chiang Kai-shek is elected chairman and president of the National Government of China (→ 15).

13. Greece: The Italian *Acqui* division resists a German attack in Cephalonia (→ 22).

14. Rastenburg: Hitler orders his armies to withdraw to the Panther Line, between Kiev and Vitebsk.→

14. Italy: British troops take Bari (→ 15).

15. China: Chiang Kai-shek demands the recall of General Stilwell, who asked Chiang to join the Communists against the Japanese, complaining that Stilwell does not understand the realities of China (→ 27).

15. Salo, Italy: Supporters of Mussolini form a Fascist republican rival government to the Badoglio administration.→

16. Aegean Sea: The British take Leros and Samos (→ 18).

17. Italy: Germany starts to withdraw from the west coast, attacking Altavilla and Battipaglia to cover its tracks (→ 20).

17. Pacific: Land-based Liberators raid Tarawa (→ 14/11).

17. Washington: Roosevelt says that Fortress Europe can be broken as "Hitler forgot to put a roof over this fortress".

18. Crowborough, Britain: The Political Warfare Executive takes over Mussolini's National Fascist Radio frequency, to broadcast a false message from an imitation "Mussolini".

18. Mediterranean: The British take Sini, Stamalia and Icaria, completing the Dodecanese attack; the Germans raid airfields on Cos (→ 4/10).

18. Auschwitz-Birkenau: The last "family transport" of women and children from Theresienstadt concentration camp arrives for gassing.

Red Army retakes key German stronghold

Bryansk, 17 September

The Red Army liberated this great industrial centre today, sweeping aside six German infantry divisions before entering the city. They found it devastated. Von Manstein's men have blown up virtually every factory before pulling out. The recapture of Bryansk is, nevertheless, a major strategic victory, for it was the last German stronghold in Russia from which Moscow could be threatened. With six railway lines spreading from it, the city became the junction for the German occupation, feeding men and guns to the battlefields. Now the Russians will use the same tracks to push towards Smolensk, Gomel and Kiev. The Germans are now falling back towards the Dnieper, the next obvious defence line to counter the Russian advance (→ 21).

"Beat the German beasts!" declares a poster aimed at Soviet troops.

British troops land on Greek island

Kos, 15 September

Much to the disapproval of their American allies, British troops have landed on this Dodecanese island only a mile from the Turkish coast. The 5,000-strong Italian garrison is fighting with them. Such is the low priority given to this operation that General Eisenhower refused the use of landing craft, and Britain's Special Boat Squadron was forced to requisition Greek fishing *caiques* to land in Kos.

The SBS was joined by 120 men of the 11th Parachute Battalion, dropped from Dakotas, before the main body of troops, the 1st Battalion Durham Light Infantry, flew in. The British and their Italian allies have been under continual attack from the *Luftwaffe*, and troops from a Dakota have been interned in Turkey after the aircraft was forced down on the sea by a Messerschmitt. Hitler has diverted aircraft from all parts of the Mediterranean to the Dodecanese. Eisenhower, on the other hand, has ruled that the Aegean "campaign" is no more than a British side-show (→ 16).

New Guinea: where the jungle is almost as much of an enemy as the Japanese. An Australian patrol beats its way through near Lae.

Mussolini rescued as the battle rages for Salerno

Rescued on the Fuhrer's orders: Mussolini boards a plane to freedom.

British troops of the Fifth Army advance warily past a knocked-out Nazi tank.

Fallen dictator snatched by paratroopers

Italy, 12 September
Hand-picked paratroopers crash-landed by glider on an Italian mountainside today and snatched Mussolini to freedom. In a brilliant operation involving a hair-raising take-off down a rocky slope in a tiny aircraft, il Duce was delivered safely to an airfield at Pratica di Mare. Tonight he was flown to Vienna en route to Hitler's headquarters in East Prussia.

Hitler's order for the rescue of the former dictator was given to SS Captain Otto Skorzeny. He first had to locate Mussolini, whom the Italians had moved about since his fall to avoid a rescue attempt. Mussolini had been held under guard in a seaside boarding house and later in a villa on a Sardinian island. News of Italy's surrender, including the condition that he would be handed over to the Allies, was kept from him.

Two weeks ago il Duce was moved to the *Campo Imperiale* hotel, 7,000 feet (2,100 metres) up the Gran Sasso mountain in the Apennines, where he was guarded by *carabinieri*. The only access was by cable car. An intercepted message told Skorzeny where Mussolini was being held. But how was he to reach the hotel? Parachute drops were out of the question in the thin air. Skorzeny planned an assault by 12 gliders carrying 108 paratroopers and 26 SS men; not until the

last moment did he realize that what had looked like a landing ground was a steep hill. Only seven gliders made it, but his own aircraft landed less than 35 feet from the hotel.

The SS man saw Mussolini at a window and yelled at him to take cover before bursting into the hotel, kicking a chair from under an Italian wireless operator and smashing the wireless set. He found Mussolini standing against a wall in his room. "Duce!" he said. "The Fuhrer has sent me. You are free!" Mussolini said: "I knew my friend Adolf Hitler would not leave me in the lurch" (→ 15).

SS Captain Otto Skorzeny.

Allies link up to win battle of beach-head

Salerno, 16 September
As advance units of the British Eighth Army linked up with the beleaguered US Fifth Army near the Salerno beach-head today, the German commander of the Tenth Army, General Heinrich von Vietinghoff, ordered his *Panzers* to withdraw northwards. The beach-head is secure, but it has been touch-and-go until the very end.

At one point, the US Fifth Army commander, General Mark Clark, had to order cooks, clerks, drivers and bandsmen to grab the nearest rifles and form a defensive line as German troops threatened to drive the Americans off the beach-head. When German reinforcements arrived from the south, Clark even contemplated withdrawing his armies from Salerno but, instead, pulled back two miles (3.2 km)

while reinforcements were rushed in. The Germans were making effective use of their radio-controlled glider bombs; the British battleship *Warspite* and cruiser *Uganda* were badly damaged.

Clark's main hope was parachute reinforcement by the 82nd Airborne Division. "This is a must," he ordered its commander, General Matthew B Ridgeway, and by midnight on 13 September 1,300 men had landed in Salerno. With a further 2,100 landing on the following day and the arrival of the British 7th Armoured Brigade, evacuation plans were abandoned. German counter-attacks, though fierce, were repelled. A further 600 men of the US 509th Parachute Infantry Brigade were dropped behind the enemy lines to hold off German reinforcements from the north.

Now Mussolini plans a new Fascist state

Munich, 18 September
A new Fascist regime is to be created in German-occupied northern Italy in the name of the ex-dictator Benito Mussolini, with its seat of government at Gargnano, on Lake Garda. The state will be called the "Italian Social Republic" in the absence of the king, who fled with the Badoglio government after the surrender. Similarly, il Duce has changed the name of his party

from the "Fascist National Party" to the "Republican Fascist Party". Broadcasting today on German-controlled radio from Munich for the first time since his escape, Mussolini demanded the restoration of all party posts "to support the Germans and to punish cowards and traitors", and ordered the reinstatement of Fascists ousted by the "capitulation government" and the reconstitution of the Fascist militia.

1943

September

Su	Mo	Tu	We	Th	Fr	Sa
			1	2	3	4
5	6	7	8	9	10	11
12	13	14	15	16	17	18
19	20	21	22	23	24	25
26	27	28	29	30		

19. New Guinea: Australian troops capture Kaiapit after a fierce battle (→ 22).

19. London: Crowds greet Churchill on his return from over six weeks abroad.

20. Italy: The Allies launch an assault on Naples as British and US units link up at Eboli to form a solid line from Salerno to Bari (→ 22).

21. Solomon Islands: US forces capture Arundel, and Japan decides to abandon the fight for the Solomons (→ 24).

21. USSR: Chernigov falls to the Red Army (→ 22).

22. New Guinea: Australian troops land six miles north of Finschhafen (→ 24).

22. USSR: The Red Army retakes the industrial centre of Poltava, in the Ukraine (→ 25).

22. Italy: Allied troops land at Bari and Brindisi (→ 23).

22. Rastenburg: Hitler rejects Goebbels's suggestion that he makes peace with either Churchill or Stalin, in order to avoid war on two fronts.

22. Greece: The Italian *Acqui* division surrenders to the Germans, having lost 1,500 men.

23. Naples: Retreating German troops wreck the port and sink Italian shipping.→

23. Corsica: Free French forces occupy Bonifacio, gaining control of half of the island (→ 4/10).

23. Nantes, France: In USAAF raids on 16 September and today, 1,150 civilians have been killed.

24. New Guinea: Australian troops take Finschhafen airfield (→ 26).

24. Solomon Islands: The Allied airfield at Vella Lavella starts operations (→ 4/10).

25. Atlantic: At the end of the Battle of Convoys ONS-18 and ON-202, 20 U-boats have sunk 36,422 tons of merchant shipping and three escorts; British ships sank three U-boats and damaged a further three.

25. USSR: The Red Army recaptures Smolensk.→

Russians recapture bastion of Smolensk

The unstoppable Red Army: but it reconquers only a devastated landscape.

Smolensk, 25 September
Smolensk, one of the most important bastions still left to the Germans in Russia, was liberated by the men of General Popov's Bryansk front today. Its fall brought yet another order of the day from Stalin commemorating this latest victory by the apparently unstoppable Red Army.

Describing the action which liberated the city after several days of heavy fighting, Moscow says that Popov's men broke into the northern suburbs and drove the Germans back street by street until the city was cleared. The Germans admit that Smolensk has fallen, but claim that it was evacuated by their rearguard in the face of advancing Russian forces "after completing the most important and necessary measures and demolition of important military installations".

Berlin Radio says that bad weather prevented the *Luftwaffe* from intervening in the battle and that "the German formations were faced with the extremely difficult task of holding their positions against the numerically superior enemy".

Roslavl, 37 miles south-east of Smolensk, has also fallen to the Red Army, and fighting is now raging along a 300-mile front on the eastern approaches to the Dnieper.

Stalin has promised to award Russia's highest decoration, the Hero of the Soviet Union, to any soldiers who force crossings of the Dnieper, and there are reports that small bridgeheads have been established in the Rzhintsev/Kanev region, south of Kiev. It is likely that these bridgeheads have been made by Cossack horsemen who specialize in river crossings, swimming their horses across at night, above and below German strongpoints, and then attacking from the rear.

The Russians point out that the Germans have not yet been able to hold a river line, and do not expect them to hold the Dnieper. But the Russians also have their problems. A paratroop drop on the western bank has met with disaster (→ 26).

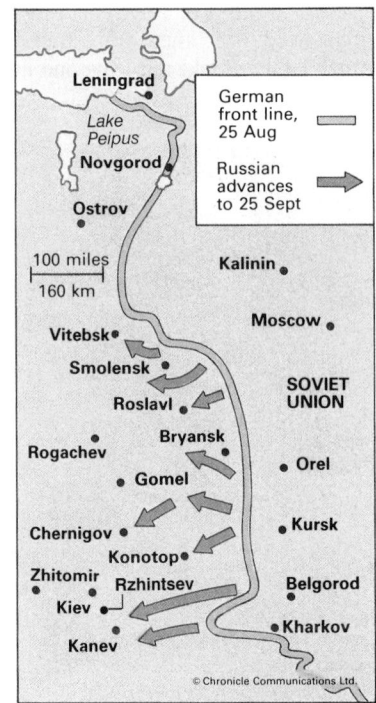

"Special action" is end of Vilna ghetto

Vilna, 24 September
The Nazis have had plenty of practice in destroying Jewish ghettoes. In the second of two "special actions", the Jews here have been robbed, beaten and sent either to Majdanek for gassing or to Estonian labour camps for a slow death. The elderly were simply shot in the nearby Ponary woods. Of Vilna's pre-war population of 60,000 Jews, just two thousand Jews are left, living in prison camps, working for German fur factories (→ 30).

Plans for PAYE tax prepared in Britain

London, 23 September
Ten million of Britain's taxpayers are included in the new pay-as-you-earn plan announced tonight. It will cover weekly wage-earners, and employers will act as tax collectors. There will be no change for salaried employees paid monthly. They will continue to pay twice-yearly lump sums in tax on the income of the previous year. Everyone on PAYE will have a code number telling employers how much tax to deduct. The working classes are now seen as permanently within the income-tax range.

Mutiny sergeants given a reprieve

Italy, 23 September
Three British sergeants were sentenced to death by firing squad, and 189 corporals and other ranks were given long prison sentences, for mutiny after the Salerno landings, it was revealed here today. The men, from the 51st Highland Division and the 50th (Northumbrian) Division, all of whom were wounded in North Africa, had been rushed to the beach-head without proper orders. In the past their divisional commanders had said that they could insist on their right to rejoin their old battalions, so they refused to join the English county regiments. The sentences were suspended when the men agreed to fight with the new units (→ 27).

Subs hit Germany's biggest battleship

Arctic Ocean, 22 September
At 8.12 this morning Germany's biggest battleship, the 46,000-ton *Tirpitz*, was blown up by British midget submarines. The blast lifted the ship, moored in Altenfjord, in northern Norway, several feet out of the water, disabled her three main engines and left her with a 15-degree list. Repairs could take over six months.

Six midget subs were involved in the daring raid. Each has a crew of two, and their only weapons are two detachable charges with clockwork detonators, dropped below the target. The subs were towed by conventional submarines from Loch Cairnbawn in Scotland to a point 150 miles (240 km) from Altenfjord. Two were lost in transit and one had to be scuttled, but three got through the mines and approached the target.

Lt Cameron in X6 lost his periscope and attacked blind. He was sighted, but was too close to the *Tirpitz* to be engaged by other than small-arms, and laid his charges before scuttling his boat. Lt Place in X7 was caught in nets, escaped, laid his charges under the ship, was caught in nets again, and then was blown free by the explosion, but X7 was damaged and had to be abandoned. Both commanders and four of their six men survived and were taken prisoner. Submarine X10, commanded by an Australian, Lt Hudspeth, attacked after X6 but was sunk with all hands.

French troops land on Corsican coast

French troops march up from the port at Ajaccio to join the "maquisards".

Ajaccio, 21 September
French troops, shipped across the Mediterranean from North Africa in the past nine nights, are advancing into the interior of Corsica. So far over 3,000 have come ashore. More are landing from the Free (Fighting) French cruisers *Jeanne d'Arc* and *Montcalm* and the destroyers *Le Fantasque* and *Le Terrible* every night.

The Free French commandos are supporting 20,000 mostly communist resistance fighters, who rose up after the Italian surrender, took to the *Maquis* (the Corsican interior, a traditional hiding place for outlaws), and are now fighting a garrison reinforced to 26,000 men after the German evacuation of Sardinia. This is the first wholly Free French operation on French home territory.

Though the transportation of the troops was a hasty improvisation – the British and Americans, who are committed to the Salerno operation, were unable to provide landing or transport vessels – the actual insurrection, led by the communist guerrilla leaders Vittori and Giovoni, was well-planned. For three months the French submarine *Casabianca* has been bringing in arms, including 20,000 Sten guns. With the Italian surrender the insurrection broke out earlier than expected and Ajaccio was captured, providing General Henri Martin's Free French force with the port it needed to bring its troops ashore (→ 23).

Beaverbrook back in cabinet reshuffle

London, 25 September
After an 18-month absence Lord Beaverbrook has returned to the cabinet. He was named tonight as lord privy seal. Churchill wants his old friend back, after letting him go last year because his feuding with Ernest Bevin, the minister of labour, caused friction in the war cabinet. Since then "the Beaver's" newspapers have been agitating for an early opening of a second front in Europe; his return will thus be welcomed in Moscow. The Labour leader, Clement Attlee, becomes lord president of the council; Sir John Anderson becomes chancellor, following the death of Sir Kingsley Wood two days ago.

Sir John Anderson: new chancellor.

Manpower crisis is looming in Britain

Westminster, 24 September
Britain has run out of manpower. Another 700,000 workers are needed next year, despite the mobilization of 22,750,000 already, said Ernest Bevin, the minister of labour, today. The recruiting of women into the services will virtually stop and they will be diverted into industry. Boys and girls aged 16 and 17 will be placed in aircraft factories. Surface coal workers are being sent below, and cotton operatives of up to 55 will return to work in the mills (→ 30).

British brigadier is sent to boost Tito

Yugoslavia, 19 September
The British Brigadier Fitzroy Maclean has parachuted into Yugoslavia to join Tito as a military adviser. His arrival confirms Britain's recognition of Tito's partisan army as its only reliable ally against the Germans. British arms are to be supplied only to Tito's force. The royalist *Chetnik* organization is disintegrating rapidly with the collapse of General Mihailovich's Italian allies. Widespread drunkenness is reported among officers, and mass defections among the men.

Land Girls near Bury St Edmunds gather in the fruits of their labours.

1943

September

Su	Mo	Tu	We	Th	Fr	Sa
				1	2	3
5	6	7	8	9	10	11
12	13	14	15	16	17	18
19	20	21	22	23	24	25
26	27	28	29	30		

26. New Guinea: Japanese attacks fail to dislodge the Australians from Finschhafen in the east; an air attack on Wewak in the north-east destroys 64 Japanese aircraft and sinks six ships (→ 2/11).

26. USSR: Soviet troops penetrate the suburbs of Kiev.→

26. Germany: Roman Catholic bishops denounce the Nazi programme of euthanasia for the mentally and terminally ill, officially stopped in 1941.

26. Brazil: US forces start using Natal port (→ 22/11).

27. Italy: British forces take Foggia airfield, and Canadian soldiers take Melfi (→ 29).

27. China: Mao Tse-min (Mao Tse-tung's brother) and the Communist Party founder Chen Tan-chi are executed by order of Chiang Kai-shek (→ 16/10).

27. Corfu: The Germans take over the island, wiping out the Italian garrison.

28. Germany: A prototype "Walter" high-speed U-boat, U792, is launched; the turbine, using hydrogen peroxide instead of air for combustion, is designed to reach 25 knots.

29. Malta: General Eisenhower and Marshal Badoglio sign a full armistice treaty on board the British battleship *Nelson* (→ 30).

29. USSR: The Red Army takes control of the Smolensk to Vitebsk railway, in the north-west, and occupies Kremenchug, in the south.

30. France: The underground newspaper *Defense de la France* publishes the first photographs of Nazi concentration camps.

30. France: A French agent, Andre Comps, steals blueprints of a V1 launch site to send to London (→ 28/10).

30. Auschwitz-Birkenau: At least 5,400 Dutch, Belgian and French Jews have been gassed this month.→

30. Italy: An uprising against the Germans by the people of Naples that began on 27 September is put down with considerable losses.→

Australian Special Forces raid Singapore

Singapore, 30 September
A canoe-borne Australian Special Forces group has penetrated the heavily-protected harbour at Singapore and blown up between 37,000 and 38,000 tons of Japanese shipping in Operation Jaywick.

The operation began on the night of 26-27 September. Led by Major Ivan Lyon of the Gordon Highlanders, six "Z" Special men entered the harbour in three canoes and attached limpet mines to seven ships, all of which were sunk or badly damaged. All three canoes were clear of Singapore when the first mines exploded at 5.15am on 27 September.

The "Z" Special group was a mix of army and navy men. Its canoes, limpet mines and equipment were conveyed to a point near Singapore in the 68-ton ketch *Krait*. The ketch left Exmouth Gulf, in Western Australia, on 1 September and on entering enemy waters posed as an Indonesian trading vessel. The *Krait* is a former Japanese fishing vessel, the *Kokufu Maru*, seized from the Japanese in the early part of the Pacific War.

Sailing to Singapore without incident the group sighted the lights of the city on 18 September. While attaching a limpet mine to a tanker two of the canoemen became aware of a sailor watching them intently through a porthole. They froze in their task, but fortunately the sailor did not raise the alarm.

Allies near Naples, but Monty upsets US

Allied troops fight on while their generals worry about Monty's slow progress.

Italy, 30 September
Allied troops have fought their way to the gates of Naples to find that the population has risen against the German garrison. Hundreds have been killed in street fighting. Outside the city, the British V Corps has surrounded Vesuvius; and the US VI Corps has taken Avellino. Naples seems certain to fall, but this anticipated triumph has not stilled the concern voiced by many US (and some British) commanders at the slowness of General Montgomery's Eighth Army in coming to assist the US Fifth Army at Salerno (→ 1/10).

War alters face of British landscape

Harvest from a changed landscape.

Britain, 30 September
This autumn's harvest looks like yielding less than last year's record-breaking crop, but in most areas productivity remains dramatically above pre-war levels. Farmers are "digging for victory" (and guaranteed markets) with such success that profound changes are now under way in the landscape itself.

Four-fifths of Britain is a farmed landscape, so changes in farming change the countryside. When the war began, about 17 million acres were grassland used for grazing livestock, with some 12 million acres as arable land to grow crops. Today the position is reversed.

The reason is simple enough. Before the war 70 per cent of Britain's food was imported. The U-boat blockade threatened that lifeline, so intensive efforts were made to grow more food at home. Crops of potatoes, wheat and barley have virtually doubled, although all but barley will this year dip below the bumper levels of 1942.

This achievement is not without cost. Land such as the chalk downs have been ploughed up, jeopardizing their wildlife. More tractors are being used, encouraging farmers to enlarge fields by removing hedgerows. More fertilizers are also being used to boost yields per acre. The government-appointed Scott committee sees "no antagonism between use and beauty". A minority is dissenting from this view.

Danish Jews are saved from deportation

Stockholm, 30 September
In a bold and hazardous night operation, Danish fishermen are smuggling almost all of Denmark's over 7,000 Jews across the stormy Oresund Strait to the safety of Sweden. The voyage costs £100 for each person; the price of failure is death. Among the refugees are the Nobel prize-winning atomic scientist Niels Bohr and his wife.

About 6,000 Jews and 1,400 half-Jews are at risk, and nearly 700 people married to Jews are expected to leave as well. The roundup of Danish Jews for deportation began a week ago with *Gestapo* agents calling on Jewish homes at night and taking whole families, including the old, the sick and children.

All Jewish private fortunes are being seized. The telephone system in Copenhagen was switched off to prevent Jews from warning one another of the Gestapo's coming.

Bohr came ashore from a Danish fishing boat at Helsingborg; he went straight to Stockholm to beg the Swedish government to help his fellow Jews. The Swedes promised asylum to all who reached their shores and sent a protest note to Germany. Swedish opinion is outraged by the latest persecutions. Even the explorer Sven Hedin, known for his German sympathies, has called them "deplorable". Pastoral letters from bishops condemning the Germans have been read out in Danish churches (→4/10).

Russian forces mass for assault on Kiev

Soviet troops on reconnaissance as the Red Army ploughs on towards Kiev.

Moscow, 30 September
The Red Army continues to steamroller westwards. It has announced the capture of Rudnya, in the northwest and of Kremenchug, the important rail junction on the east bank of the Dnieper, 140 miles (224 km) south of Kiev.

Huge forces are now massing for the final phase of the assault on Kiev, the capital of the Ukraine. Last night's communique says that Russian guns are shelling Gomel, and further north the Red Army has advanced six miles (9.6 km) towards another important German base, Mogilev in White Russia. Un-

official reports from Moscow say that a fierce battle is also going on in the outskirts of Zaporozhe, at the southern end of the Dnieper bend, some 50 miles (80 km) from the town of Dnepropetrovsk.

This means that the Russian forces have now reached every important place along the Dnieper and that the Germans are fighting hard to maintain a toehold on the eastern bank.

More importantly, the Russians have expanded their bridgeheads on the western bank south of Kiev and have begun to link them up to form a solid base (→1/10).

Britain plagued by strikes: discontent spreads in shipyards and Scottish mines

Britain, 30 September
Britain's war effort is being hampered by a wave of unofficial strikes. nine thousand engineers are out at Vickers Armstrong at Barrow-in-Furness. They have been on strike for two weeks in protest at an arbitration award on rates of pay. At a mass meeting today they voted to stay out, despite the urgings of their union, the Amalgamated Engineering Union (AEU). The local strike leaders, critical of AEU officials, demand direct negotiation with Ernest Bevin, the minister of labour, who has refused to intervene. He insists that the honour of the trade union movement is at stake.

Striking is illegal under an Order of 1940, but the impracticality of sending strikers to prison was demonstrated last year at Betteshanger colliery, in Kent. More than 1,000 summonses were taken out against strikers. They were fined, while their union branch officials were sent to prison for a month. When the miners refused to pay the fines, magistrates could not have them arrested because there was not enough room in the prisons. On Mr Bevin's advice, the fines were held in abeyance and the men went back to work.

The same difficulty now applies to a strike of 7,000 miners in the Lanarkshire coalfield in Scotland. It is in protest at the arrest of fellow-miners for non-payment of their fines for joining an earlier unofficial strike. The local miners' president has blamed "outside elements" for extending the stoppage. Mr Bevin recently told the House

If *you* can't go to the factory help the neighbour who *can*

Other concerns of working women.

of Commons that there were three kinds of strike occurring. One was the "last straw" type, by the men. The second type was provoked by the employers. The third type was politically inspired by Trotskyists and others opposed to the war.

"While I will not be a party to anything to weaken the legitimate trade unions in any way – I want to strengthen them – I feel that steps must be taken to see the war effort is not impeded by these activities," he declared. This year has already seen a dock strike at Liverpool, and now a strike of 16,000 workers at the Rolls-Royce aero engine factory at Hillington, Glasgow, is threatened over the unequal rates of pay for women, who now make up two-thirds of the workforce (→5/10).

Women in a factory in Kansas City prepare dried eggs for export to Britain.

1943

October

Su	Mo	Tu	We	Th	Fr	Sa
					1	2
3	4	5	6	7	8	9
10	11	12	13	14	15	16
17	18	19	20	21	22	23
24	25	26	27	28	29	30
31						

1. USSR: Russian forces begin crossing the river Dnieper (→ 7).

1. Denmark: The Germans have been able to round up just 360 out of 7,000 Jews for deportation to Theresienstadt.

1. Britain: Construction work starts in secrecy on floating docks, designed for an Allied invasion of Europe (→ 11).

2. New Guinea: Australian troops take Finschhafen.→

2. Italy: The British 2nd Special Service Brigade seizes the town of Termoli (→ 3).

3. Italy: US VI Corps troops take Benevento (→ 5).

4. Aegean Sea: The Germans take the island of Cos (→ 7).

4. Arctic: In Operation Leader planes from the USS *Ranger*, escorted by HMS *Duke of York* and HMS *Anson*, sink four German freighters.

5. Britain: Shipyard strikers in Barrow return to work (→ 29).

5. Italy: The British X Corps reaches the Volturno river (→ 6).

5-6. Pacific: The US Task Force 14, comprising six carriers, seven cruisers and 25 destroyers, shells Wake Island.

6. Solomon Islands: The 27th Infantry Regiment of the US 25th Infantry Division lands at Kolombangara (→ 12).

6. New Guinea: The Australians take Dumpu as they move into the Ramu valley (→ 15).

6. Burma: General Sir William Slim takes command of the Arakan front and is made C-in-C Eastern Command (→ 2/11).

6. Italy: The US Fifth Army takes Caserta and Capua.→

7. USSR: The Red Army launches a new offensive on a 1,300-mile front (→ 9).

7. Aegean Sea: The British cruisers *Sirius* and *Penelope* and the destroyers *Faulknor* and *Fury* sink a German convoy heading for Cos (→ 26).

9. USSR: Soviet forces complete their occupation of the Kuban, as German forces retreat to the Crimea (→ 13).

Allied tanks roll into city of Naples

Bare-footed girls watch Allied troops drive through the rubble-strewn streets of Resina on their way to Naples.

Naples, 1 October
At the cost of 12,000 British and American casualties in a 21-day campaign, Allied troops entered this wrecked city today. Allied bombs and German engineers have systematically destroyed everything of possible military value in Naples. The port – the Allies' prime target – is a mass of twisted wreckage, the harbour choked by sunken ships and the industrial area almost flattened.

The stench of raw sewage overhangs everything. The retreating Germans blew up the drainage system and the aqueduct that brought fresh water to the city. The population of more than a million people is threatened with mass epidemics and it has to be fed.

British tanks of Lt-Gen Richard McCreery's X Corps were the first to enter the city, but already they are moving on northwards to the Volturno river where the Germans are establishing a defensive line. The American 82nd Airborne Division has moved into Naples to police the city.

Even though the bulk of German forces had retreated north, the fight from Salerno to this city was never easy. To reach the plain of Naples, Allied troops had to cross rugged terrain easily defended by small German demolition detachments – aided by heavy rain that washed away bridges and flooded roads.

With the major ports of Taranto and Bari in Allied hands, Montgomery is preparing a major offensive in the east against Foggia. The Germans are placing much reliance on a new weapon: the radio-controlled glider bomb which crippled HMS *Warspite* at Salerno and sank the Italian flagship *Roma* (→ 2).

German troops loot Rome's art treasures

Rome, 6 October
German troops, some with "shopping lists" from Hermann Goering, are systematically looting the museums and churches of Rome and carrying off priceless works of art to Germany. Manuscripts and old masters are being removed wholesale by the men who came here to "guard" the city against the Allies. And not only works of art are leaving Italy for the *Reich*: thousands of former Italian soldiers are being rounded up and taken to Germany as forced labourers. As Germany intensifies its control over its former Axis partner, Nazi paratroopers have ringed the Vatican, and one report has claimed that the pope has sent a sealed letter to each of his Italian cardinals to be read only in the event of his arrest (→ 10).

Japanese forces evacuate New Georgia

Vila, Solomon Islands, 4 October
Short of food and ammunition, Japanese forces today abandoned Kolombangara, their last stronghold in the New Georgia group of islands in the central Solomons, according to reports from Allied coastwatchers, the undercover observers based on Japanese-held islands who have provided valuable intelligence during this campaign.

For the past 24 hours Japanese ships have struggled to evacuate the remnants of the 10,000-strong garrison which had defended Vila airfield, Japan's last airbase in the central Solomons. During today's fighting Allied aircraft and warships claim to have harassed enemy craft over a wide area, downing 12 Japanese planes and sinking 27 enemy craft. US losses are put at 1,094 killed and 3,873 wounded, against 2,483 Japanese dead.

A communique issued by Allied HQ South-west Pacific claimed that the Japanese evacuation of Kolombangara was the direct result of the Allied decision to bypass the island and let the Japanese there "wither on the vine". A spokesman for Admiral Halsey said that the Allied occupation of Vella Lavella, to the north of Kolombangara, several weeks ago had effectively cut Japanese supply lines into Vila.

With the Allies now firmly in control of the central Solomons the way is now open for the next phase of Operation Cartwheel, an attack on Bougainville, the largest island in the Solomons (→ 6).

Free French take Corsica

American-equipped Free French troops in Corsica – the liberated island.

Ajaccio, Corsica, 4 October
The liberation of Corsica is complete. The losses amongst the communist guerrillas and the Fighting (Free) French regular troops have been light – partly because the Germans were not seriously fighting to hold on to the island.

Fighting between the German garrison, reinforced by troops from Sardinia, and communist guerrillas has been going on since the Italian surrender. Regular Free French troops under General Henri Martin arrived 20 days ago, with only a few hundred landing each night. Furnished with motor and mule transport by the Italian troops on the island, his men seized the island's spine, pushing the Germans back to their bridgehead at Bastia, from which they withdrew today.

The Germans had no intention of holding Corsica; their concern was purely to secure an orderly withdrawal. Under Commander von Liebenstein, who had organized the German evacuation of Sicily, they brought out 26,000 men, 3,200 vehicles, 5,000 tons of stores and 1,200 PoWs, in a movement described by the German News Agency as "an operational and organizational masterpiece".

Himmler speaks of "moral duty" to SS

Poznan, 4 October
In an address to the SS, Heinrich Himmler, the *Reichsfuhrer-SS*, has spoken frankly about the Jews.

"Among ourselves," he said, "this once, it shall be said quite frankly; but in public we will never discuss it. I am talking about the evacuation of the Jews, the annihilation of the Jewish people ..."

"Most of you must know what it means to see a hundred corpses lying side by side, or five hundred, or a thousand. To have stuck this out and – apart from a few cases of human weakness – to have kept our integrity, this is what has made us hard. In our history, this is an unwritten and never-to-be-written page of glory ...

"We had the moral right, we had the duty to our people, to destroy this people which wanted to destroy us ... We do not in the end want to be infected by this germ. I will not see so much as a septic spot appear or gain hold. Wherever it may form, we will cauterize it ..." (→ 14).

Hero of Matapan is new naval supremo

Westminster, 4 October
Sir Andrew Browne Cunningham, the hero of Matapan and Taranto, was appointed first sea lord – chief of the naval staff – tonight. His appointment follows the resignation through illness of Admiral Sir Dudley Pound. Sir Andrew, known throughout the navy as "ABC", has commanded the Mediterranean Fleet for four years, apart from four months as the Royal Navy's representative in Washington last year.

In the Mediterranean, "ABC" had to curtail many of the navy's successful operations when German bombers proved so effective from land bases. "ABC" is a disciplinarian whose voice, allegedly, can be heard "from Pompey to Plymouth Sound".

"ABC": new chief of naval staff.

Poster war: an RAF poster on the bombing campaign in Germany.

British Bombers now attack Germany a thousand at a time!

Australians attack in New Guinea

Port Moresby, 2 October
Australian troops have captured Finschhafen in New Guinea, it was announced here today. Success at Lae came earlier than expected, and the 9th Division was ordered to seize Finschhafen in continuation of the campaign for the conquest of the Huon Peninsula: success would help the Allies to seize objectives in New Britain, thus contributing to the isolation of Rabaul. The 7th Division was also to seize areas in the vicinity of Kaiapit and Dumpu. The first wave of Australians swept ashore near Finschhafen on 22 September. Japanese opposition was fierce, but the beach-heads were soon cleared (→ 6).

1943

October

Su	Mo	Tu	We	Th	Fr	Sa
					1	2
3	4	5	6	7	8	9
10	11	12	13	14	15	16
17	18	19	20	21	22	23
24	25	26	27	28	29	30
31						

10. Mediterranean: US Flying Fortresses attack Greece and the islands of Crete and Rhodes for the first time.

10. Naples: A bomb blast kills 12 people in the cathedral, hours before Lt-Gen Mark Clark and other officers are due to attend Mass (→ 12).

10. Rastenburg: Hitler orders all Russian volunteers fighting in the *Wehrmacht* to move to western Europe.

10. Atlantic: A U-boat mines the entrance to the Panama Canal.

11. Britain: The codename "Mulberry" is adopted for the artificial harbours being built to support proposed landings in Normandy.

12. New Britain: Three hundred and forty-nine US bombers devastate Rabaul in a surprise attack (→ 15).

12. Italy: The US Fifth Army pushes north, attacking the Germans on the Volturno river line.→

14. Berlin: Himmler orders the removal of racial Germans from the USSR and Poland at the age of twelve.

15. New Guinea: Japanese aircraft attack Allied positions in Oro Bay (→ 16).

15. Solomon Islands: Orders are issued for the invasion of the northern Solomons by Task Force 31 (→ 18).

16. New Guinea: Australian troops repel further Japanese attacks on Finschhafen (→ 20).

16. Chungking: Lord Louis Mountbatten, the supreme Allied commander of Southeast Asia Command, arrives for talks with Chinese military leaders (→ 19).

16. Italy: The Germans retreat to the Barbara Line, between the river Trigno and San Pietro (→ 22).

16. Rome: SS troops round up 1,000 of Rome's 7,000 Jews for deportation to Auschwitz (→ 18).

16. Britain: The US Ninth Army Air Force is formed to provide tactical protection for the Eighth air force's bombing raids (→ 23).

US air force steps up attacks on Germany

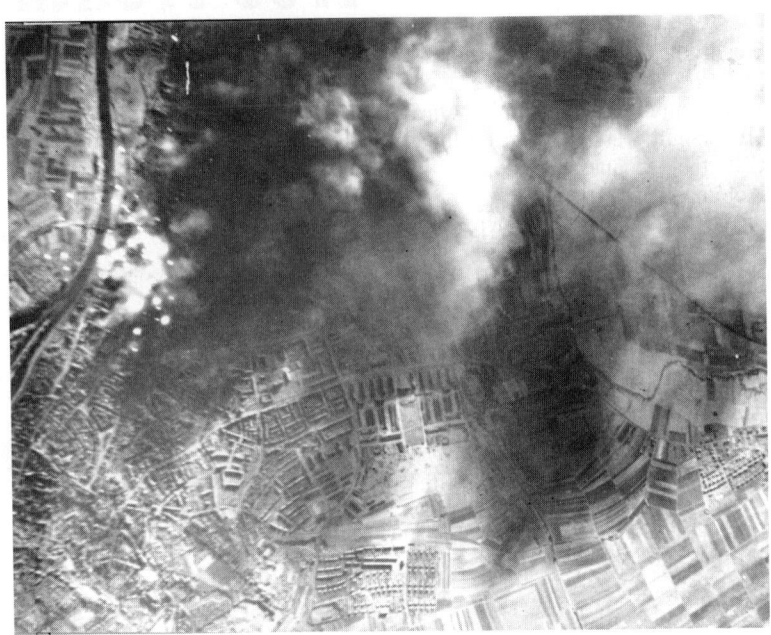

A pall of smoke rises from the bombed ball-bearings factories at Schweinfurt.

London, 14 October
Flying Fortresses of the US Eighth Army Air Force took the dangerous route to the city of Schweinfurt deep inside Germany today to bomb the ballbearings factories vital to Hitler's war industries. The Fortresses' crews claim to have damaged their targets heavily. One said: "When we left the factory was just a mass of smoke and flames. Our bombs were all concentrated right on the target."

However, the bombers have paid a heavy price for their success. Sixty of 291 planes which set out – 228 bombed the target – have failed to return and many more are badly damaged. They were escorted part of the way by Thunderbolt fighters, but when the fighters turned back at the limit of their range, the bombers had to face swarms of German fighters and rely on their own guns and formation flying for protection; it was not enough.

The lesson is that the Fortresses cannot live in the air over Germany without fighters for protection. A ninth air force is therefore to be formed on 16 October to provide escort cover for bombing attacks and, in the longer term, a future invasion of Europe (→ 16).

Portugal lends Azores bases to the Allies

Lisbon, 12 October
The Battle of the Atlantic swung firmly in favour of the Allies tonight when Dr Salazar, the Portuguese leader, revealed that British land, sea and air forces have arrived in the Azores. The islands, strategically placed in mid-Atlantic, will be used for the aerial protection of merchant shipping plying between the United States and Britain.

The move comes after weeks of secret talks between Britain and Portugal. Though the two countries have a treaty relationship that dates from the 14th century, Dr Salazar, in close cooperation with Franco's Spain, has remained cautiously neutral between the Allied and Axis powers. The Azores pact reflects the growing certainty among neutrals that Hitler will eventually lose the war.

The US, though not a signatory to the pact, will use the islands for joint military operations with Britain. Air cover by RAF Catalina and Wellington aircraft based in Britain and Newfoundland left a gap – which will now be closed – of several hundred miles in mid Atlantic, where the U-boats assembled to prey on Allied shipping.

The German consulate in the Azores is being closed and all German citizens are being evacuated. On the Portuguese mainland diplomatic links will continue.

Concentration camp inmates kill guards

Sobibor, 14 October
The six hundred inmates of the extermination camp, mainly women working in the small tailors' workshop, have risen against the camp regime and staged an astonishing escape attempt.

The revolt was spearheaded by a group of White Russian Jewish partisans led by Aleksandr "Sacha" Pieczerski, a 34-year old Russian Jew who had served as a political commissar in the Red Army. The Jews were armed with a few guns and hand-grenades, stolen from the SS barracks, and a handful of knives and hatchets.

The mutiny started this afternoon during the routine inspection of the prisoners' huts. The rebels killed 11 guards, then shouted "Hurrah" to signal a mass breakout. In the chaos that followed, the guards shot 200 inmates dead. Others perished in the minefield that surrounds the camp; estimates of the number who escaped successfully vary from 100 to 300.

Pieczerski and his second-in-command, Leon Feldhandler, are thought to be among those who did escape to join the partisans. A small group of Dutch Jews is apparently trying to get home. In a camp where deportees stand only a one in 40 chance of avoiding immediate death in the gas chambers, today's breakout was a brave attempt to shorten the odds (→ 16).

From blond-haired Vikings to Nazi commandos: a Danish poster urges volunteers to join the fight against Bolshevism.

Marshal Badoglio declares war on Nazis

Madrid, 13 October
Less than five weeks ago, Italy was Hitler's ally. Today it is his enemy. The Italian ambassador here handed Italy's declaration of war to his German counterpart for transmission to Berlin. The declaration, signed by Italy's new leader, Marshal Badoglio, does not make Italy one of the Allies as such. With war crimes charges pending against some Fascist leaders and generals, Italy officially becomes no more than a "co-belligerent". However, Badoglio has called on all Italian soldiers to "fight against the Germans to the last man". In a letter to General Eisenhower, Badoglio said: "By this act, all ties with the dreadful past are broken, and my government will be proud to be able to march with you on to the inevitable victory."

There is debate as to whether Italian forces will be used against the Germans in Italy. However, they are fighting with the British in the Aegean and serve to garrison Sardinia and Corsica. One tricky problem remains to be resolved: the thousands of Italian PoWs in Allied hands (→ 16).

Marshal Badoglio and a US brigadier-general, now on the same side.

US troops battle to cross Italian river

Italy, 13 October
Soldiers of the US Fifth Army today crossed the Volturno river north of Naples after a day of bitter resistance by three German divisions. The attack had begun yesterday, but rain, mud and the swollen river provided sterling assistance to the Germans who had retreated to the river following the Allied capture of Naples on 1 October. The rainy season began a month earlier than usual, slowing the Allied advance and giving the Germans more time to prepare their defences here and further north along the rivers Liri and Rapido (→ 16).

Yugoslav patriots sabotage Krupp's

Zeneca, Yugoslavia, 13 October
Yugoslav partisans struck at the German industrial empire here today, wrecking several of the huge Krupp factories including the biggest steel works in the country. The partisans claim to have destroyed 27 railway engines and 150 wagons. Street fighting is also reported in Zeneca and other towns. German reinforcements are said to be rushing to the district. A partisan communique revealed that the Italian *Venezia* division – which, a few days ago, had been fighting against the partisans – had come over to the Yugoslav side (→ 4/12).

1943
October

Su	Mo	Tu	We	Th	Fr	Sa
					1	2
3	4	5	6	7	8	9
10	11	12	13	14	15	16
17	18	19	20	21	22	23
24	25	26	27	28	29	30
31						

17. Pacific: The US submarine *Tarpon* sinks the *Michel*, the last operational German armed merchantman, off Japan.

17. Goa: Japanese and Allied internees are exchanged.→

18. Britain: General Jean de Lattre de Tassigny, who escaped from a PoW camp six weeks ago, is one of seven Frenchmen flown to Britain from hiding in France.

18. Solomon Islands: The US bombs the Japanese air base at Buin, on Bougainville (→ 27).

18. USSR: Red Army troops reach Melitopol.→

19. Jesselton, North Borneo: Local people rise up against the Japanese, killing 40 but causing savage reprisals.

19. London: Britain and the US pledge the USSR 6,100,000 tons of supplies by June 1944.

20. New Guinea: The Australian 24th Brigade reinforces Finschhafen (→ 22).

20. New Delhi: Field-Marshal Lord Wavell arrives to take up the post of viceroy of India.

21. Manila: The Japanese grant "independence" to the Philippines.

21. Singapore: Subhas Chandra Bose forms a "provisional government of *Azad Hind* [Free India]".

21. London: Vice-Admiral Sir John Cunningham becomes C-in-C Mediterranean Fleet, succeeding his brother, Admiral Sir Andrew Cunningham, who became first sea lord on 4 October following the retirement, due to ill-health, of Admiral Sir Dudley Pound. Pound himself dies today, aged 66.

22. New Britain: Allied aircraft attack Rabaul, destroying 123 Japanese planes (→ 17/11).

22. Italy: British troops cross the river Trigno (→ 24).

23. English Channel: German torpedo boats sink the British cruiser *Charybdis* and destroyer *Limbourne*.

23. Britain: Major-General Robert Laycock is appointed chief of Combined Operations.

Allies to set up war crimes commission

London, 20 October
A meeting of 17 Allied countries at war with the Axis powers agreed today to set up a war crimes commission in London. Its chairman will be Viscount Simon, the British lord chancellor and head of the judiciary in England and Wales. Assisted by a team of lawyers, he will sift evidence provided by Allied governments. The Soviet Union, although not represented at today's meeting, will be asked to cooperate with its enquiries (→ 19/12).

German and British PoWs exchanged

Gothenburg, 19 October
The exchange of thousands of sick and seriously wounded British and German PoWs began at the Swedish port of Gothenburg this afternoon. Most of the British were captured in 1940 at Dunkirk; others, taken in last year's raid on Dieppe, included Canadians. Germans from Rommel's *Afrika Korps* were still in desert uniform.

This is the first PoW exchange between Germany and Britain of the war; negotiations for an earlier exchange in 1941 were broken off by Germany, which this time asked for the exchange: 5,000 Germans and 5,400 British and Imperial forces are now going home (→ 25).

The flags are out for a son's return. ▷

Allies finalize war plans

Eden (l) and Molotov after Eden's arrival at Moscow airport for the talks.

Moscow: plans laid for post-war Europe

Moscow, 19 October
The foreign ministers of the "Big Three" Allied powers – Cordell Hull, Eden and Molotov – sat down together in the Kremlin today to tell one another, in the words of an official spokesman, "frankly and freely what is on each other's minds".

The talks, which are expected to last for ten days, will conclude with a firm pledge that the US, Britain and the Soviet Union will not consider any separate peace negotiations with Germany. Postwar co-operation between the Big Powers to guarantee peace and security will also be discussed. An outline plan for the creation of an international organization, open to all peace-loving states, has been drafted and is expected to be approved.

In a separate meeting in London today the US and Britain promised Stalin big increases in military aid in the next eight months: 2,700,000 tons will arrive via Soviet Pacific ports, 2,400,000 tons via the Persian Gulf and 1,000,000 tons by Arctic convoy (→ 30).

China: strategy for fight against Japan

Chungking, 19 October
The Allies hope to break the dead-locked situation in China by flying more supplies over the "Hump" – the Himalayan route from India – following the loss of the Burma Road. This emerged after talks between Lord Louis Mountbatten, the newly-appointed commander-in-chief for South-east Asia, and the Chinese Nationalist leader, Generalissimo Chiang Kai-shek. Mountbatten also managed to persuade the *Kuomintang* leader not to sack his American chief of staff, General Joseph Stilwell. The two have been at loggerheads since Stilwell urged the Kuomintang to lift its blockade of Chinese Communist forces in the north (→ 4/12).

Madame Chiang between her husband and Stilwell in happier times.

One million Germans "could be encircled"

Moscow, 22 October
The Russians have cut the railway which provides the Germans with their main escape route from their stronghold of Dnepropetrovsk in the Dnieper Bend. General Malinovsky's men are now advancing on Krivoi Rog and are threatening to encircle almost a million Germans in the sweep of the river.

The Germans are well aware of the danger facing them. The Berlin correspondent of the Scandinavian Telegraph Bureau reports that the situation is "extremely serious" and that the Germans would be "compelled to retreat to avoid further encirclement".

German officials quoted by the Stockholm newspaper *Aftonbladet* say that "catastrophe threatens the whole German front in South Russia". But while the Germans appreciate the threat of the Russian advance there seems to be little that they can do about it except retreat and keep on retreating.

They had confidently expected to hold the Dnieper line. They scattered leaflets telling the Russian soldiers: "Germany has clad the west bank of the Dnieper in concrete and shod it with iron.

"We have created an Eastern Rampart there, impregnable as is our Western Rampart on the Atlantic Coast. You are being sent to your deaths. Death awaits you at the Dnieper. Stop before it is too late." But the Russians did not stop. Many of them died, but they crossed the Dnieper (→ 25).

Soldiers of the Red Army press ever onwards: the Germans can only retreat.

Evil of fornication alarms archbishops

Britain, 19 October
The rapid rise in venereal disease in Britain is the occasion of a long statement issued today by the archbishops of Canterbury and York on what they describe as "a moral as well as a medical problem". The chief cause of the spread of the disease is "fornication", which the church condemns as a sin. "Promiscuity threatens to destroy home life ... Moral resistance is of more value than physical precautions," they declare, and they call on Christians to take their stand against it. They also urge that more healthy recreation should be provided in camps and barracks.

Auschwitz women attack SS guards

Auschwitz-Birkenau, 23 October
Jewish women from Warsaw today attacked the SS on the threshold of the gas chamber, killing one and injuring several others. The rebellion started in the undressing room, where a woman seized the revolver of SS Sergeant-Major Josef Schillinger, one of the camp's most sadistic and feared guards, and shot him dead. The other women mauled their oppressors, scalping one and tearing the nose off another. They escaped the gas chamber. But their triumph was brief. Commandant Rudolf Hoess has had the rioters removed from the room one by one, and shot (→ 25).

New bases help 24-hour bomb assault

London, 23 October
Bombs are raining down on enemy targets in Europe from every direction. American heavy bombers used Italian airfields for the first time yesterday to raid Austria, while the air over France and the Low Countries was full of Allied fighters and light bombers, and Bomber Command was out last night, as usual, pounding Germany itself. So intense is the bombing that in the 100 days and nights from 9 July to last Sunday the RAF and the USAAF have dropped 74,000 tons of bombs in round-the-clock raids on Germany and occupied Europe. In the same period the Germans have dropped only 480 tons on Britain in night attacks which have cost them ten per cent of their raiding forces. The Allied loss rate has been under five per cent.

Pounding Germany round the clock.

"Corona" confuses German night fighters

Germany, 23 October
Operation Pointblank, the Anglo-US strategic bombing offensive against Germany, is growing in intensity and technical complexity. RAF Bomber Command now has over 700 operational heavy bombers, compared with just under 300 at the end of 1942, and is pounding German cities by night. Yesterday US chiefs of staff agreed to establish a new bombing force in Italy, the Fifteenth air force, which will strike at targets which the Eighth cannot reach from England.

A growing number of technical aids have been developed to help in the battle against the Germany night fighters. Last night for the first time "Corona" was used: confusing orders, readings from newspapers, even parts of Hitler's speeches were broadcast from England on the fighters' frequency to interfere with the German voice control (→ 3/11).

Nazis send Roman Jews to Auschwitz

Italy, 18 October
Nazi deportations of Italy's Jews to the extermination camps began today when 1,000 Roman Jews were despatched to Auschwitz. The operation against the ghetto in Rome began on 26 September when the German authorities – in control of most of Italy since the surrender – threatened to arrest 200 ghetto inhabitants unless 110 pounds (50 kg) of gold was produced within 36 hours. The whole city gave gold to save them. On Saturday 16 October, the Jewish Sabbath, the arrests began. Today the first transportation left for Auschwitz (→ 23).

'We'll have lots to eat this winter, won't we Mother?'

Grow your own
Can your own

No shortage of food in America where home-grown fruit and vegetables line the larder shelves.

1943
October

Su	Mo	Tu	We	Th	Fr	Sa
					1	2
3	4	5	6	7	8	9
10	11	12	13	14	15	16
17	18	19	20	21	22	23
24	25	26	27	28	29	30
31						

24. Italy: The US Fifth Army captures Sant'Angelo (→ 27).

24. Aegean: The destroyer HMS *Eclipse* is sunk by a mine.

25. Auschwitz-Birkenau: Over two thousand young women from Salonika are murdered in the gas chamber (→ 3/11).

25. USSR: Red Army troops under General Rodion Malinovsky cross the Dnieper, capturing Dnepropetrovsk and Dneprodzerzhinsk (→ 28).

26. Calcutta: A cholera epidemic has killed 2,155 people in the last week.

27. Japan: Emperor Hirohito announces that the war has reached a critical stage.

27. Solomon Islands: Operation Blissful – US marines land on Choiseul as a diversionary tactic.

27. Italy: The Eighth Army captures Montefalcone (→ 29).

27. Sweden: Germany blocks the Skagerrak.

27. Pacific: New Zealand troops land on the Treasury Islands as part of the build-up to the invasion of Bougainville (→ 1/11).

28. Berlin: Goebbels admits that Russia is an "enormous danger", and that the Red Army has broken through the main German defences (→ 31).

28. New Zealand: Butter rationing is introduced.

29. London: Soldiers step in as Thames dockers go on strike.

29. Italy: Cantelupo falls to the Eighth Army (→ 30).

30. Italy: The Fifth Army penetrates the Barbara Line, capturing Mondragone (→ 31).

30. Moscow: The conference of Allied foreign ministers closes, having confirmed the principle of an unconditional surrender for Germany.

31. USSR: Soviet troops capture Chaplinka, cutting off the Crimea from German supply lines.→

31. Italy: The First Motorized Group is the first Italian unit to join the US Fifth Army as a "co-belligerent".→

Penicillin becomes a wonder drug for casualties of war

31 October
Despite, or perhaps because of, the increasingly sophisticated savagery of the war that now encircles the globe, medical treatments are being developed to halt diseases and infections of all kinds.

Countless lives are being saved by a new wonder drug known as penicillin. This is a type of mould, commonly found on old bread, which destroys a host of bacteria. It was discovered by accident by the Scottish scientist Alexander Fleming in 1928, but its crucial healing ingredient was only isolated in 1940. Now the drug is being given to war casualties by the thousand. One of its most valuable properties

Row upon row of the wonder drug.

is to combat blood poisoning from infected wounds. Inoculations are also being widely used to prevent the spread of disease.

In Germany there is a national institute working on ways of curbing infections such as typhus which reached epidemic proportions in the 1914-18 war. In Italy the use of the drug mepacrine against malaria has reduced mortality by as much as 70 per cent in some areas. Training for medical workers has also reduced the number of dead. While battle goes on around them, doctors crawl out to injured men to give them blood transfusions.

Rocket launch sites pinpointed by aerial photos

Britain, 28 October

An RAF Photographic Reconnaissance Unit (PRU) aircraft today brought back a photograph of a German V1 "flying bomb" launch site at Abbeville, in northern France. Although the British have reasonable knowledge of the V2 rocket, it is only in the last two months that they have become aware that the Germans have been working on the V1.

This photographic *sortie* was mounted as a result of a report by a local French agent and confirms that the Germans are constructing launch sites in northern France for a V1 offensive against England.

This illustrates only too clearly the value of photographic reconnaissance as an intelligence gathering asset. The RAF PRU itself was formed at Heston by Wing-Commander Sidney Cotton in April 1940. Cotton had been a civilian pilot before the war and worked for a company developing colour photography. Together with Group Captain Frederick Winterbotham of the Secret Intelligence Service he had pioneered covert PR over Germany in the months leading up to the outbreak of war.

The PRU is under the control of RAF Coastal Command, although it works for the admiralty, the war office and other agencies as well. It is equipped with specially-adapted Spitfires – the Mark IV-PR, powered by the 1,440hp Merlin 45 engine and carrying more fuel than the normal fighter versions. Its surfaces are also carefully polished to improve its aerodynamic performance. It has a range of over 1,700 miles (2,720 km) and, unarmed, relies on stealth to fulfil its mission. It uses a 20-inch lens camera.

The RAF Photographic Interpretation Unit at Wembley in West London then uses stereoscopic viewing instruments for significant intelligence breakthroughs (→5/12).

Red Army cuts off Germans in Crimea

Dejection and mistrust on the faces of Germans and Roumanians taken prisoner by Soviet forces in the Ukraine.

Moscow, 31 October

General Tolbukhin, the commander of the Fourth Ukrainian Front, has captured Chaplinka, 15 miles (24 km) north of Perekop, which guards the north-western entrance to the Crimea. With the main road cut and the railway under fire, this means that the Germans in the Crimea are virtually cut off by land from the rest of their forces in Russia. It is estimated that there are about 150,000 German and Roumanian troops occupying the Crimea, plus the bulk of the Seventeenth Army which has been withdrawn from Taman across the Kerch Straits.

They are all now in danger of being left behind as the Russians push forward along the Black Sea towards Kherson. The Germans enjoy one great advantage, however; their navy rules the Black Sea, with the Russians too fearful of Stuka attacks to risk their ships.

While this remains the case Hitler is unlikely to sanction an early evacuation on the grounds that the divisions still in the Crimea will tie down major Russian forces to guard against an attack in their rear. This reasoning does not please Field Marshal von Kleist, who would rather get his men, guns and tanks to safety (→6/11).

Autumn rains help Germans slow the Allied advance in Italy

Italy, 31 October

The Germans have lost their Italian allies; but they have the rain on their side, a steady remorseless deluge that turns the small fordable rivers of summer into fierce-flowing torrents and makes every mountain track a treacherous quagmire.

The infantry have the worst of it. Supplies are plentiful in the rear echelons, but for the men in the frontline of this campaign, life has become a matter of finding shelter in slit trench or gully and eating "nourishing" K-rations or bully beef cold from the tin. Hot meals are no more than a memory for thousands. And the Germans are fighting a skilled defensive battle with the aid of their new ally. Bridges are demolished, culverts are mined and booby traps are everywhere. Villages are flattened to deny shelter to the Allies.

The advance continues, however, but at a desperately slow speed. Earlier this month, the US Fifth Army managed to cross the Volturno river under an artillery barrage and a smoke screen. By 14 October, a four-mile-deep bridgehead had been established. In the east, General Montgomery paused to regroup the Eighth Army; as he did so, four German divisions moved up to oppose him (→2/11).

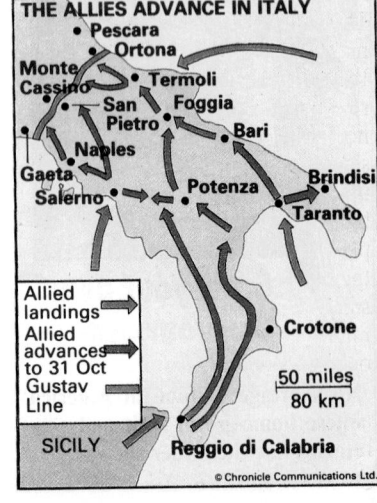

THE ALLIES ADVANCE IN ITALY

Pescara
Ortona
Monte Cassino
Termoli
San Pietro
Foggia
Naples
Bari
Gaeta
Salerno
Potenza
Brindisi
Taranto
Crotone
Reggio di Calabria

Allied landings
Allied advances to 31 Oct
Gustav Line
SICILY

50 miles
80 km

© Chronicle Communications Ltd.

"Death railway" to open in Thailand

Rangoon, Burma, 25 October
Japan has laid a railway from Bangkok to Burma. The single 300-mile (480-km) track, half across mountains and jungle, half along the river Kwai Noi valley, was built by 200,000 Asian and 69,000 Allied PoWs. "We will make you work in places no white man has worked before, and harder than any white has worked before," the Japanese said; and 100,000 Asian and 16,000 other PoWs died in the process.

British troops are forced from island

Kos, 26 October
After a week of living on locust beans and jam, British survivors of the ill-fated Kos invasion climbed aboard a *caique* tonight and made their way to the Turkish coast. They had fought hard, but constant attacks by Stukas, German artillery and 4,000 German infantrymen forced men of the 1st Battalion, the Durham Light Infantry, to disperse. The SS have shot 90 Italian officers for collaboration (→ 12/11).

Ecstatic homecoming for British PoWs

A home-coming serviceman is embraced, and applauded by a delighted crowd.

Italian partisans begin to fight Germans

Italians mourn villagers murdered in reprisal for the death of a German thief.

Leith, 25 October
Ship's sirens screamed, bagpipes skirled and the crowd of several thousand on the quayside gave a deep-throated cheer as 3,694 repatriated PoWs and civilian internees from Germany came ashore from the liners *Empress of Russia* and *Drottningholm* today. The men responded with a rousing rendering of *Roll Out the Barrel.* Cigarettes, chocolate and apples were handed out by Red Cross workers. All the men agreed that the Germans knew they were beaten. Sapper Richard Wray, of Leeds, said: "They expect defeat and needless to say we rubbed the idea in." The former PoWs later travelled to their homes all over Britain.

Italian bases put Vienna in bomber range

Brindisi, Italy, 24 October
Eleven days after Italy changed sides and declared war on Germany, Allied bombers have hit the *Reich* from Italian soil for the first time.

This raid, across the Alps, was against Austrian targets as far north as Vienna. Some 300 four-engined bombers with 200 fighters struck first in Styria, some 80 miles south-west of the Austrian capital. Top Nazi leaders were in the area today for a conference, and a crowd of 18,000 had gathered to watch a football match. Bad weather hampered the German anti-aircraft defences.

Rome, 31 October
The vindictive attitude of the Germans, now the occupiers, to the Italian population is fast creating a resistance movement which, in the north, is basing itself on the Yugoslav partisan army. Mass roundups of able-bodied men for forced labour in Germany are commonplace. Jews, never entirely sure of their future in Mussolini's Fascist state, are sharing the same fate as millions in the rest of Nazi-occupied Europe.

The partisans have few weapons, although many former soldiers have hidden their rifles and kept grenades. Home-made bombs have been used in the principal cities of Rome, Milan and Turin – although the Germans will automatically execute ten Italians for every German soldier killed.

In the industrial north, the strike weapon is applied regularly by the communist trade unions. Workers walk out daily in protest at being forced to work for the German war effort and the "theft" of materials.

German tanks have failed to force the workers back. The relatively few remaining Fascist blackshirts are reluctant to take on their countrymen. The latest move is the threat of the death penalty for industrial "sabotage".

Lord and Lady Wavell visit a Rotary Club kitchen in South Calcutta.

November

Su	Mo	Tu	We	Th	Fr	Sa
	1	2	3	4	5	6
7	8	9	10	11	12	13
14	15	16	17	18	19	20
21	22	23	24	25	26	27
28	29	30				

1. Solomon Islands: Fourteen hundred US troops land on Bougainville (→ 2).

2. Burma: Japan repels a series of Chinese attacks on the river Tarung (→ 28/12).

2. North Sea: The British blockade runner to Sweden, *Master Standfast*, is captured by the Germans.

2. Bougainville: US forces sink the Japanese destroyer *Hatsukaze* and the light cruiser *Sendai* in the Battle of Empress Augusta Bay, preventing Japan from landing reinforcements in the area.

2. New Britain: One hundred and sixty land-based aircraft attack the Japanese base at Rabaul.→

2. Italy: Allied patrols reach the river Garigliano, close to the German Gustav Line (→ 3).

2. Berlin: Goebbels writes that "we are in danger of slowly bleeding to death in the East".

3. Germany: Bernhard Lichtenberg, the Catholic priest imprisoned for saying public prayers for Jews, dies en route to Dachau.

3. Germany: Five hundred and thirty-nine B-17 bombers of the USAAF, using the H2X blind-bombing device, devastate Wilhelmshaven naval base (→ 8).

3. Italy: The US takes Sessa Aurunca from the 16th *Panzer* Division, which is transferred to the eastern front (→ 4).

3. Poland: Five SS factories in the Lublin area are closed and the Jewish workers shot: over 17,000 are machine-gunned into prepared graves. This is "Bloody Wednesday" and marks the end of Operation Harvest Festival in which 50,000 Jews have died (→ 11).

4. USA: A plutonium-manufacturing plant, codenamed "X-10", opens at Oak Ridge, Tennessee (→ 2/12).

4. Italy: The Eighth Army takes the Isernia road junction without opposition.→

6. North Atlantic: Captain F J Walker's 2nd Escort Group sinks two U-boats.

Russians recapture Kiev

Kiev, 6 November

Celebrations for tomorrow's anniversary of the 1917 Revolution started early today with the news that Kiev, the capital of the Ukraine, has been liberated after more than two years of German rule.

The battle to free the city was launched by General Vatutin three days ago. Vatutin first tricked von Manstein into thinking that he was going to attack out of the bridgehead across the Dnieper at Bukrin and then, when the Germans concentrated at Bukrin, made his assault out of the smaller lodgement at Lyutezh.

The Russians ripped a great hole in the German lines and swung west behind Kiev. It rapidly became obvious that the Germans would not be able to hold the city.

Von Manstein pulled out most of his men, leaving only the 88th Infantry Division behind as a rearguard. The 88th, outnumbered and outgunned, has been cut to pieces and its few survivors are straggling back to the German lines having lost all their heavy equipment.

The fall of Kiev marks not only a psychological victory for the Russians but also an end to a short series of successful German counterattacks.

They had virtually wiped out 7,000 paratroopers dropped across the Dnieper; they had foiled an early breakout from Bukrin and administered a severe check at Krivoi Rog, where they killed 10,000 Russians and captured 5,000. Now the Red Army is once again sweeping westwards (→ 7).

German troops on the retreat through Kiev after one more Russian victory.

Why the Red Army is now so successful

Moscow, 6 November

More men, more tanks, more guns, more aircraft – that is the secret of the Red Army's astonishing turnabout success against the most professional army in the world just when it seemed that the Soviet Union was about to collapse.

The inexhaustible supplies of men and materials emerging from the depths of Russia have ground down the Germans. The Red Army now fields 6.5 million men against 4.3 million Germans. The Russians

have 5,600 tanks against the Germans' 2,600. They have 90,000 guns against 54,000, and 8,800 aircraft against 3,000. But it is a matter of quality as well as quantity. Russian tanks and aircraft now match the once superior German equipment.

The Russians have also learnt how to fight a modern war. New commanders have emerged to use new tactics. But most important of all has been the fortitude and patriotism of the Russian soldier.

Peugeot boss helps to sabotage factory

France, 5 November

Industrial sabotage is being used with greater success than Allied bombing at the Peugeot plant which is producing war equipment on the Germans' orders. Following the RAF raid on 14 July, which proved to be as unsuccessful as it was bloody, Harry Ree, a member of Britain's clandestine Special Operations Executive, persuaded Armand Peugeot to sabotage the facilities of the plant with the help of his own engineers. The manufacturing of turrets for tanks has been interrupted indefinitely (→ 31/12).

German forces in Italy are regrouped

Italy, 6 November

German armour is being raced eastwards to counter a major threat to the Gustav Line by the Eighth Army which stormed Vasto yesterday, meeting fierce resistance from General Herr's tanks. British destroyers are giving supporting fire from the Adriatic as British and Canadian troops advance along the coast.

The 8th Indian Division has reached Palmoli and the US Fifth Army is reported to be ten miles (16 km) from Capua, a key point on the road to Rome, held up by torrential rain as well as the Germans.

World peace pact signed in Moscow

Moscow, 1 November

Britain, the US and the Soviet Union yesterday pledged themselves to work together for peace after the defeat of the Axis powers. A new United Nations organization will be created and national armaments will be controlled by agreement.

The three foreign ministers, Eden, Cordell Hull and Molotov, agreed to set up a three-power commission in London to consider European issues as the end of the war against Nazi Germany draws near. Austria's independence will be restored (→ 9).

New offensives launched in the Pacific by Allies

Taking the Japanese by surprise: US marines wade ashore on Bougainville.

US planes bomb Japanese shipping, the airstrip and Rabaul in New Britain.

Solomons: Americans extend beach-head

Torokina, Solomons, 5 November
Amid fierce but sporadic fighting, US marines have established a beach-head which is 6,000 yards long and three miles deep at Cape Torokina five days after seven battalions made an amphibious assault on the uninhabited western coast of Bougainville, the largest island in the Solomons. Engineers have now begun work on an airstrip intended for bombing Rabaul, in New Britain, Japan's HQ for the South-west Pacific. The US landings – Operation Cherryblossom – were coordinated with diversionary Allied attacks elsewhere in the Solomons. These took the Japanese commander, General Harukichi Hayakutake, by surprise. Most of his 40,000-strong Seventeenth Army is on Bougainville's south coast.

The first strategic Japanese response came 24 hours after the invasion as Admiral Omori's Eighth Fleet attempted to harass the US armada in Empress Augusta Bay. Omori quickly lost the light cruiser *Sendai* and the destroyer *Hatsukaze*, with three other warships damaged – a miscalculation that cost the admiral his command.

New Britain: US bombs Japanese base

New Britain, 5 November
For the first time since June last year US carriers have gone into action against a powerful Japanese base. Rear-Admiral Frederick C Sherman's task force TF38, with the carriers *Saratoga* and *Princeton*, was ordered to make a surprise attack on Rabaul today by Admiral Halsey. News had come through that a Japanese fleet of seven heavy cruisers, one light cruiser and four destroyers was on its way to Rabaul, preparatory to a major assault on US forces at Empress Augusta Bay. Halsey had to act quickly if he was to make any impression – and luck was with him today.

The carriers, shrouded in heavy cloud, were misidentified as cruisers by Japanese scout planes, and over Rabaul harbour itself the skies were clear for the US attack. Airborne Japanese fighters waited in vain for the tight formation to break up under anti-aircraft fire, and missed their chance to knock out leading bombers. The cruisers *Atago*, *Maya* and *Mogami* and three destroyers were damaged. All but ten US planes returned and the carriers withdrew unscathed (→ 7).

US strategy based on two advances

Washington, 2 November
Powerful US forces have been built up in the Pacific despite Washington's commitment to the "Hitler first" grand strategy. The Americans have decided on a double-pronged thrust. One, under Admiral Nimitz, will advance across the central Pacific and the other, under General MacArthur, from New Guinea to the Philippines. To avoid costly campaigns, large Japanese forces in South Pacific islands are not to be challenged in battle but isolated by air power (→ 5).

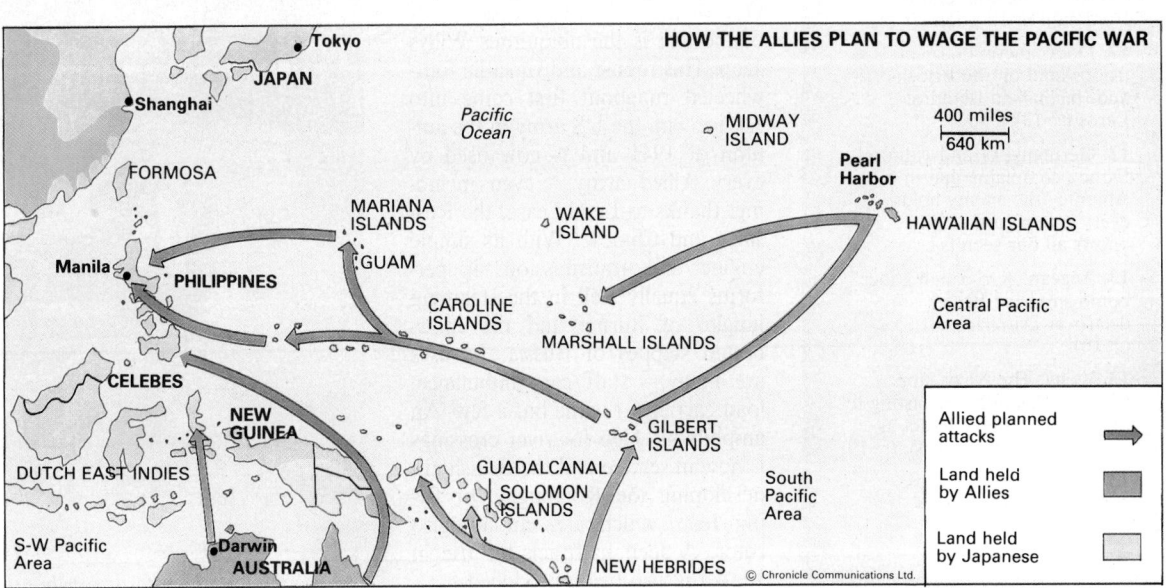

HOW THE ALLIES PLAN TO WAGE THE PACIFIC WAR

400 miles
640 km

Tokyo
JAPAN
Shanghai
FORMOSA
Pacific Ocean
MIDWAY ISLAND
Pearl Harbor
HAWAIIAN ISLANDS
MARIANA ISLANDS
WAKE ISLAND
Manila
PHILIPPINES
GUAM
CAROLINE ISLANDS
MARSHALL ISLANDS
Central Pacific Area
CELEBES
NEW GUINEA
DUTCH EAST INDIES
GILBERT ISLANDS
GUADALCANAL
SOLOMON ISLANDS
South Pacific Area
S-W Pacific Area
Darwin
AUSTRALIA
NEW HEBRIDES

Allied planned attacks

Land held by Allies

Land held by Japanese

© Chronicle Communications Ltd.

1943

November

Su	Mo	Tu	We	Th	Fr	Sa
	1	2	3	4	5	6
7	8	9	10	11	12	13
14	15	16	17	18	19	20
21	22	23	24	25	26	27
28	29	30				

7. USSR: The commander of the Forty-Fourth Soviet Army is captured when he drives accidentally into the German frontline at Nikopol (→ 13).

7. Solomon Islands: Japanese aircraft attack the US carriers *Saratoga* and *Princeton*, but inflict no damage (→ 11).

8. Italy: Eighth Army troops reach the Sangro river (→ 9).

9. Atlantic: U707 is sunk by the escort of convoy MKS-29A; Churchill announces that 60 U-boats have been sunk in the last three months.

9. Italy: The Allies take Castiglione (→ 10).

10. USSR: Two new military decorations are created: the Order of Victory – a large ruby star encrusted with 91 diamonds – for senior officers, and the Order of Glory for other ranks.

10. Italy: The Allied Control Commission is formed, to yoke the Italian economy into the overall Allied war effort (→ 15).

11. New Britain: In a US carrier strike on Rabaul, the Japanese lose about 35 aircraft, and a light cruiser and two destroyers are disabled.→

11. Mediterranean: German aircraft attack an Allied convoy off Oran, sinking four merchant ships.

11. Theresienstadt: 47,000 Jews are forced to stand outside in the cold and rain from 4am to 12 noon (→ 15).

12. Dodecanese: German troops land on the British-and-Italian-held island of Leros (→ 13).

12. Germany: Grand Admiral Dönitz complains that in the Atlantic "the enemy holds every trump card ... (he) knows all our secrets".

13. Aegean: A German glider bomb sinks the British destroyer *Dulverton* off Kos (→ 16).

13. Vichy: The Nazis stop Marshal Petain broadcasting to the nation. Unable to act as premier he goes on strike (→ 19).

13. USSR: Soviet troops complete the capture of Zhitomir (→ 24).

Third wave of US landings in Solomons

US Marine infantry in action in the swamp-filled jungles of Bougainville.

Torokina, Solomons, 13 November
US forces have consolidated their beach-head on Bougainville, the largest island in the Solomon group, after fending off a Japanese counter-attack and inflicting 400 casualties. Since the first landings 13 days ago US forces ashore under the Marine commander, Maj-Gen Hal Turnage, have swelled to 34,000 combat and service troops.

However, there is continuing Allied concern at the failure of Marine engineers to establish a fighter air-strip at Torokina. The knee-deep swamp conditions are to blame for the lack of progress and the snail's pace Allied advance.

It was these jungle swamps that first convinced the Japanese that an Allied attack on Bougainville's west coast was not feasible. Last week they tried to rectify this mistake by trying to destroy the Allied beach-head. But they only compounded their error by landing an under-strength task force that was quickly wiped out (→ 25).

Anti-French unrest spreads in Lebanon

Beirut, 11 November
All day Beirut's Moslem population has been rioting, following the arrest by Free French Senegalese troops of Lebanon's president (Bechara Khoury), prime minister (Riad Solh) and the entire cabinet. The arrests – and suspension of the constitution – follow the effective declaration of independence three days ago when Lebanon's parliament adopted Arabic as the sole official language, took control of foreign policy, and deleted from the constitution all references to "the prerogatives and powers of the mandatory state".

The Gaullists had offered Syria and Lebanon independence when the Anglo-Free French army invaded the French-mandated territories in 1941. "I come to put an end to the mandatory regime and to proclaim you free and independent," General Georges Catroux promised. But the Gaullist administration in Syria and Lebanon, fearing a reaction against it in metropolitan France – and British ambitions in the Middle East – resisted Anglo-US pressure to fulfil the promise. Catroux was replaced as delegate-general with a colonial hard-liner, Jean Helleu. Today's events will bring even more Anglo-US pressure to bear on the French.

The Jeep: versatile vehicle that covers all the terrains of war

7 November
One of the greatest success stories of the war is the ubiquitous Willys Jeep. This robust and versatile four-wheeled runabout first came into service with the US army in the autumn of 1941 and is now used by every Allied army – even including, thanks to Lend-Lease, the Russians and Chinese. With its simple engine and transmission, it performs equally well in the steaming jungles of Burma and the snow-bound steppes of Russia. Its uses are many – staff car, ambulance, load carrier, to name but a few. An amphibious Jeep for river crossings is now in service and the British are developing the Rotabuggy, or flying Jeep, which uses an autogiro rotor. A Jeep halftrack for use in Alaska is also being produced.

The amphibious Jeep fords a tributary of the Burso river in New Guinea.

"United Nations" will help refugees

A Russian and his grandson pick their way through their ruined home: now there is an organization to care for them.

Washington, 9 November
Forty-four nations today signed into being the first United Nations' organization – the Relief and Rehabilitation Administration, promising to bring immediate relief to the populations of liberated countries. The UNRRA may well become a model for future projects of the proposed "United Nations". Mr Roosevelt, who presided over the signing, emphasized that where relief had previously been a concern

of only Britain and the US, it was now shared by nations whose peoples constituted 80 per cent of the human race.

In a speech which followed the ceremony of signing, President Roosevelt declared: "It is hard for us to grasp the magnitude of the needs in occupied countries. [They] have been robbed of their foodstuffs and raw materials, and even of the agricultural and industrial machinery ... It will be for the UNRRA

first to assure a fair distribution of available supplies among all of the liberated peoples, and, second, to ward off death by starvation or exposure among these peoples. Tomorrow the UNRRA begins its first conference – and makes the first bold steps toward the practicable, workable realization of freedom from want. The forces of the United Nations march forward and the peoples of the United Nations march with them."

Hitler will avenge "terror bombing"

Munich, 8 November
Hitler visited Munich for his annual Beercellar speech and promised the German people that he would retaliate for the "terror bombing" of the *Reich* by Britain. "Even if for the present we cannot reach America," he said, "thank God that at least one country is near enough for us to tackle, and on that country we are going to concentrate. The hundreds of thousands of our bombed-out people will become the advance guard of revenge." He appealed to the German people not to lose their nerve and crack. He denounced "scoundrels" who wished for peace.

Hundreds seized in anti-Nazi protests

Grenoble, 11 November
Commemoration of the Armistice, banned by Marshal Petain, was turned into a patriotic demonstration by the Resistance here today. Police arrested 450 people who will be deported to Germany.

Grenoble is a major centre for the French Resistance, and the *Gestapo* is using every possible means to crush the growing opposition to the Nazi-dominated Vichy government. On the night of 13 November, a commando of the *Groupes Francs* blew up the *Werhmacht's* artillery depot. In retaliation, the Gestapo then assassinated all the leaders of the United Resistance Front (→ 13).

RAF group to wage electronic warfare

Britain, 8 November
The decision has been taken today to form the No 100 Group of the RAF. Its role, under Bomber Command, will be to wage the radio counter-measures war against the German air defences and so reduce bomber casualties. Under Air Vice-Marshal E B Addison's command, it will be located at airfields in northern Norfolk, its squadrons being mainly equipped with Halifaxes and Mosquitoes (→ 4/12).

De Gaulle becomes Free French president

Algiers, 9 November
Charles de Gaulle has emerged as the president of the French Committee of National Liberation (CFLN) in the place of General Henri Giraud, who resigned yesterday.

Gen Giraud will continue to function as commander-in-chief of French forces, but de Gaulle has won the political battle between the two men which has continued since Giraud's sensational escape from a prisoner-of-war camp last year. De Gaulle is now the undisputed

political leader of Free France, and he has broadened the membership of the CFLN to include men from the internal Resistance such as Emmanuel d'Astier de la Vigerie, the new home affairs commissioner, and former parliamentarians like Henri Queuille, one of three commissioners of state, and Andre le Trocquer, the commissioner for war and air. Foreign relations will be in the hands of the young but brilliant diplomat Rene Massigli, and finance goes to the advocate Pierre Mendes-France.

Stirring up fear of communism.

1943

November

Su	Mo	Tu	We	Th	Fr	Sa
	1	2	3	4	5	6
7	8	9	10	11	12	13
14	15	16	17	18	19	20
21	22	23	24	25	26	27
28	29	30				

14. Gilbert Islands: B-17 bombers raid Tarawa (→ 19).

14. Germany: U794, the German navy's first true submarine, goes into service at Kiel: it has a *Schnorkel* to provide the diesel engines with oxygen while it is submerged.

14. Off Bermuda: A live torpedo, fired in error by a US destroyer on exercise, narrowly misses the battleship *Iowa*, with Roosevelt on board.

15. Berlin: Himmler orders all gypsies to be sent to concentration camps (→ 16).

15. London: Air Chief Marshal Sir Trafford Leigh-Mallory is made C-in-C of the Allied Expeditionary Air Force.

15. USSR: A German counter-offensive launched yesterday retakes Zhitomir.

15-16. Europe: The British Special Operations Executive lands six agents in France and takes 12, including Francois Mitterrand, back to Britain.

16. Dodecanese: Germany captures Leros, and the Allies decide to evacuate all the islands except Castelrosso.

16. Europe: Two transports are taking over 2,000 Dutch Jews to Auschwitz-Birkenau camp (→ 6/12).

17. New Guinea: Australian tanks attack Sattelberg, the main centre of Japanese resistance (→ 29).

17. Atlantic: Grand Admiral Donitz takes personal charge of a U-boat assault on convoy SL-139/MKS-30, comprising 66 Allied merchant ships (→ 20).

19. Britain: Fido, a secret device to clear fog from runways [*see page 347*], is used for the first time to help bombers returning from the Ruhr to land.

19. Central Pacific: US carrier raids are made on Tarawa, Makin and Nauru.→

20. Atlantic: Donitz calls off his U-boats, as the convoy is protected by 19 warships and 24-hour air cover: three U-boats have been sunk.

20. USSR: Soviet troops cross the Dnieper near Cherkassy.

American troops land on Gilbert Islands

US marines wade through open sea after miscalculations with maps and tides.

Tarawa, 20 November
The crystal-clear waters of an equatorial paradise turned to blood today as hundreds of US marines were mown down by machine-gun fire as as they tried to wade ashore during a near-catastrophic amphibious assault on Tarawa atoll, in the Gilbert Islands.

By this evening the first wave of the 18,600-strong strike force had established a beach-head on Tarawa's Betio Island, the site of the Gilberts' only airfield, but is still being pinned down.

Another US task force has struck at the Japanese on Makin atoll, and a third is poised to attack in Apamama, both also in the Gilberts; the moves launch an "island-hopping" campaign through which the Allies will attempt to push back Japan in the central Pacific. Betio would give the Allies an airfield within striking distance of Japan's bases on the Marshall Islands.

Today's action on Tarawa began with an 18-ship shore bombardment of enemy defences. But marine casualties quickly started to mount as amphibious tanks and tracked personnel carriers ran aground on the coral reef, leaving their occupants to wade 800 yards through open sea because of miscalculations over tides (→ 21).

The corpses of US marines float in this battle-scarred Pacific lagoon.

Mosley is released on health grounds

London, 20 November
Just before 7am today, Sir Oswald Mosley was released through a back entrance of Holloway prison, where he has been detained under Regulation 18B since 1940. His release was on health grounds. He and Lady Mosley, who shared a flat in the prison, were reunited with their two sons, aged four and two, who were being cared for by friends. Protests at the Mosleys' release are being made by many Labour organizations, trade unions and factory deputations outside the Home Office. It has been stated by the government that Herbert Morrison, the home secretary, who ordered the release, still has wide powers to control Sir Oswald's movements (→ 1/12).

US attacks atomic target in Norway

Norway, 16 November
Some 155 bombers of the US Eighth Army Air Force today raided the heavy water plant at Vermork, west of Oslo, following up the successful commando attack last February. Although the plant was not damaged, the fact that the Allies can attack it from the air is worrying the Germans and should help to slow their atomic bomb programme down further. The Knaben molybdenum mines were also hit.

Labour controls are forecast by Bevin

Wigan, Lancs, 14 November
Ernest Bevin, the minister of labour, explained his plans for employment after the war here today. He foresaw that controls would be required for several years and a "human budget" would be needed every year to allocate labour. Rehousing alone would provide jobs for five million. "There is hardly a home in this country that is not short of domestic utensils. I want to compel the manufacture of goods of proper quality – no rubbish – to replenish our homes," said Mr Bevin (→ 2/12).

Guns fall silent in Italian stalemate

Italy, 15 November
The guns are silent along the entire Italian line. The invading armies are exhausted. The plight of the defenders is no better. Both the British and the Americans have given their all in the Fifth Army sector. On 5 November the British 56th Infantry Division attacked Monte Camino, a barren 3,000-foot mountain which the Germans had covered with mines and booby traps. At the half-way point, they faced a brutal series of counter-attacks by the 15 *Panzergrenadier* Division but held on. They were finally forced to retire through sheer exhaustion. The US VI Corps suffered days of attacking elusive German defenders. It was only then that General Mark Clark gave the order to withdraw.

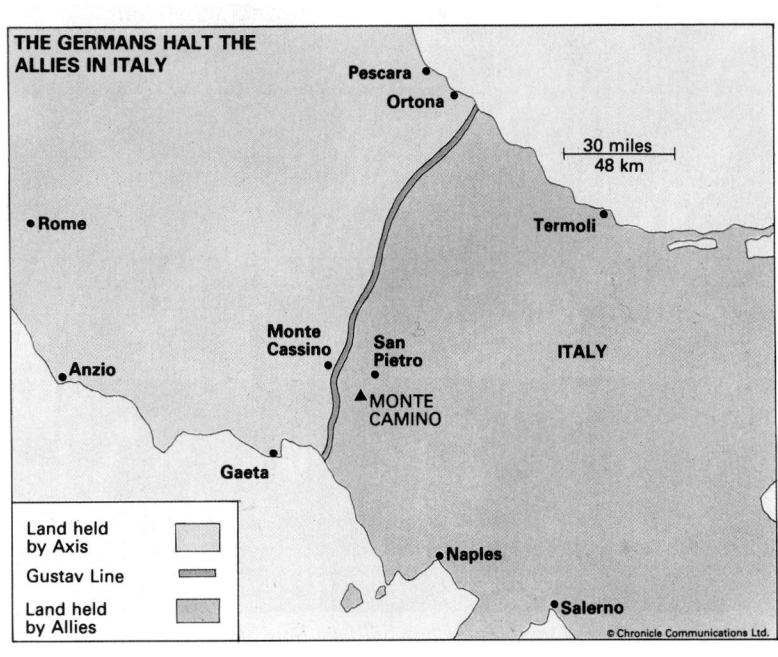

THE GERMANS HALT THE ALLIES IN ITALY

Pescara
Ortona

30 miles
48 km

Rome

Termoli

Anzio

Monte Cassino

San Pietro

ITALY

▲ MONTE CAMINO

Gaeta

Naples

Land held by Axis
Gustav Line
Land held by Allies

Salerno

© Chronicle Communications Ltd.

Germans take hostages in Milan in reprisal for sabotage

Milan, 15 November
SS men rounded up nearly 2,000 Italian workers in the industrial suburbs of Milan today and held them as hostages against further sabotage. Even so, explosions have continued to rock this northern city and other forms of sabotage have become widespread. Milan's population has already been fined £1 million ($4 million); more communal punishments have been threatened.

Frantic efforts are being made to remove thousands of British prisoners of war to Germany. Many took advantage of the confusion following the armistice and escaped. More have linked up with the fast-emerging communist-led partisan movement in the north. Former Italian soldiers are also swelling the guerrillas' ranks.

Resistance continues to grow against the German occupiers and Fascist collaborators. Six Fascists were killed in ambushes in the Florence district.

It was inevitable that Italy's Jewish population should bear the brunt of Nazi fury. At least 7,500 Jews are being rounded up in Rome and herded into trains bound for German death camps. Hundreds more are being sheltered from the *Gestapo* in Rome's labyrinth of catacombs where Christians once sheltered from persecution (→ 22).

A German tank outside Milan cathedral; the Nazis cannot stop the resistance.

Bomber Command begins its winter campaign on Berlin

Germany, 19 November
The Battle of Berlin has begun: 440 Lancasters and four Mosquitoes bombed the capital last night, dropping 2,300 tons of explosives in 30 minutes. Bad weather grounded *Luftwaffe* night fighters, and all but nine Lancasters returned. On the same night Mannheim was raided by 395 aircraft – making this Bomber Command's heaviest night of operations so far in the war.

In Berlin much of the fashionable *Wilhelmstrasse* was destroyed and 131 people died, but factories were undamaged. Sir Arthur Harris, the chief of Bomber Command, recently told Mr Churchill: "We can wreck Berlin from end to end ... It will cost between 400 and 500 aircraft. It will cost Germany the war." In the latest raid bombers followed Pathfinders over cloud cover all the way. Most did not see the target, releasing their loads (often one big bomb of 4,000 pounds or more) at an aiming point marked by a burning flare. Hopes that the USAAF would join the campaign against Berlin are unfulfilled. Americans like daylight raids and fighter escorts, but their Mustang fighters lack the range (→ 23).

Petain censored on Hitler's orders

Vichy, 14 November
Marshal Petain, having tried and failed to reintroduce a measure of legitimacy and thus free France and himself from the head of government, Pierre Laval, and his collaborationist clique, is now virtually a German prisoner.

Petain planned to say in a speech that he represented legitimate authority in France, and that on his death power would revert to the National Assembly. However, the contents of the speech were communicated to Hitler, who ordered Petain not to give it. Instead, the Germans plan to launch a campaign of repression and terror against the Resistance, exploiting what is left of Marshal Petain's reputation.

1943

November

Su	Mo	Tu	We	Th	Fr	Sa
	1	2	3	4	5	6
7	8	9	10	11	12	13
14	15	16	17	18	19	20
21	22	23	24	25	26	27
28	29	30				

21. Tarawa: The US marines make little progress against fierce opposition.→

22. Italy: The Eighth Army establishes a bridgehead of five battalions on the north bank of the Sangro river (→ 28).

22-23. Berlin: Seven hundred and sixty-four RAF bombers drop 2,000 tons of explosives on the city, killing 1,737 civilians (→ 24).

23-24. Berlin: RAF bombers return to Berlin, killing 1,315 people in a raid in which the Germans try to confuse the RAF by using a woman's voice to direct their fighters; the RAF respond by using a woman's voice to direct the bombers.→

24. USSR: The Germans force the Soviets back at Korosten.→

25. New Britain: US destroyers sink three Japanese destroyers in the Battle of Cape St George (→ 9/12).

25. Formosa: US aircraft destroy 42 Japanese planes in a raid on Shinchiku airfield.

25. France: The *Gestapo* rounds up students at Strasburg university.

25. Burma: Allied aircraft bomb Rangoon.

26. Insterburg, East Prussia: Hitler sees a demonstration of the prototype Me262 jet fighter, and orders it to be mass produced – as a *bomber*.

26. Mediterranean: An Hs293 glider bomb hits the British troopship *Rohna* off Bougie, in Algeria; 1,115 are killed.

28. Bogota: Colombia declares a "state of belligerency" with Germany after a U-boat sank a Colombian boat yesterday.

28. Italy: Montgomery declares that "the road to Rome is open" as the Eighth Army launches a heavy attack across the river Sangro (→ 30).

29. New Guinea: Australian forces capture the Japanese supply base at Bonga (→ 1/12).

30. Italy: The Eighth Army clears the area north of the Sangro; the Fifth Army mounts diversionary attacks to precede an assault on Monte Camino (→ 2/12).

Allies plan next moves in the Pacific war

Chiang Kai-shek, Roosevelt and Churchill take time off in the sunshine.

Cairo, 25 November
In a heavily-guarded, barbed-wire-protected compound in the shadow of the Pyramids outside Cairo, Churchill, Roosevelt and Chiang Kai-shek today ended a meeting to plan the next moves in the war against the Japanese empire. Called the "Sextant Conference", this has been the seventh wartime summit meeting between Churchill and Roosevelt, but the first involving China's Nationalist leader.

The first days of the conference were attended by Admiral Lord Louis Mountbatten, the supreme Allied commander in South-east Asia, and General "Vinegar Joe" Stilwell, the C-in-C of US Ground Forces in Burma, China and India.

Mme Chiang acted as interpreter for her husband. The conference compound has had to accommodate 320 delegates – 210 British, 90 American and 20 Chinese. Over 40 villas and a hotel were taken over and cleared of guests, and a specially installed telephone system connected the hotel conference rooms with delegates' villas. A tented camp was erected by US engineers for the 1,000 troops guarding the conference. Three Bedouin families on the site of the camp were persuaded by gifts to move. No official statement will be released until Chiang Kai-shek is back in China and Churchill and Roosevelt have left for another secret meeting [*see below*] (→ 28).

Churchill and Roosevelt fly to meet Stalin

Tehran, 28 November
Three renowned leaders, bound into the most powerful military alliance ever known, are gathering in the Iranian capital, Tehran, to set their strategy for final victory over Germany and Japan. But the three have different and sometimes conflicting aims and purposes.

Churchill seeks victory – victory at all costs, he said when he became prime minister – for Britain and its vast Empire. Roosevelt, too, wants victory, but he is looking to a post-war world fashioned in the American image, according to the ideals of

the Atlantic Charter and the "Four Freedoms". To this end he has decided that he needs the cooperation of Stalin and believes that he can charm the Soviet dictator as he does the politicians back home. He will let Stalin know that survival of the British Empire is no part of America's war aims.

As for Stalin, he has fought his war apart from the western Allies. There are no joint military staffs on the Anglo-American model, and no economic cooperation. Stalin is not saying what he will do with his victory when it comes (→ 4/12).

Red Army pushes north from Gomel

Gomel, 26 November
The Red Army has driven the Germans out of Gomel, north of the Pripet Marshes, and is chasing them along a 100-mile (160 km) front in White Russia. This powerful and well-timed blow has now cracked the *Wehrmacht's* winter line, and the Germans have been forced out of the deep belts of well-equipped dug-outs where they had intended to spend the winter in comparative comfort.

Now they are being hounded into the marshes and forests where the snow is already deep and the partisans lie in wait for the unwary. The German high command admits that the Russians are "trying to interfere with our disengaging movements" (→ 1/12).

Russia seeks to liberate its people.

Brazil to send task force to join Allies

Brazil, 22 November
A Brazilian expeditionary force is to be sent to Europe, the Brazilians announced today. At least 60,000 men will cross the Atlantic to assist the Allied fight on European soil. Brazil's air force, though heavily engaged in the defence of Brazil's extensive coastline, will also send a contingent to Europe. Brazil declared war on the Axis powers on 22 August last year, after a series of U-boat attacks on several merchant ships in Brazilian waters.

Air raids shatter Berlin

Britain, 27 November

RAF Lancaster bombers supported by Mosquitoes made their fourth big raid within a week against the city of Berlin last night. First German estimates are putting the number of dead from the raids at over 4,000, with 400,000 homeless.

Sir Arthur Harris, the chief of Bomber Command, says that the RAF will bomb the city until the heart of Nazi Germany stops beating. The capital is probably the most intensively blitzed city anywhere, hit this year by 12,000 tons of explosive, of which 5,000 have been dropped in the past few days.

Much of administrative Berlin has been hit, including the Air Ministry, Admiralty, Hitler's Chancellery and his train. The Fuhrer was not in town, but despatched fire engines to his capital from Brandenburg and Potsdam. Despite this, and the efforts of the army to create fire-breaks by blowing up buildings, fires spread rapidly.

Among several armaments factories hit was the Allkett tank factory. The greatest loss of life occurred when a bomber crashed onto a building, killing 92 people in the air-raid shelter. A Swede told journalists: "The Berlin we know has ceased to exist." The toll on the RAF is high, however, with 42 aircraft lost from the 450 planes involved in the raid, including 14 which crashed in Britain (→ 3/12).

Trying to put out the fires in Berlin.

Loading up incendiaries for Berlin.

US forces lose 1,000 in taking Gilberts

Tarawa, Gilbert Islands, 23 November

US troops have seized control of the Gilbert Islands, in the central Pacific, after three days of fighting and appalling casualties on both sides.

The fighting was heaviest at the island air base of Betio, on Tarawa, where 1,009 US marines died and 2,101 were wounded. Of Betio's 4,836-strong Japanese and Korean garrison only 146 have survived (all but 17 of them Koreans), with many of the dead having committed *hara-kiri*. Among the dead is Tarawa's last Japanese commander, Rear-Admiral Keiji Shibasaki. He was responsible for fortifying Betio, which measures only 3,800 yards long by 300 yards wide, with scores of concrete bunkers, 20 coastal defence guns and 25 artillery pieces. Before the attack he had exhorted his men to "make sure that a million men in a hundred years cannot take it".

The turning point came on day two after Major-General Julian Smith managed to get two more 8th Marines battalions ashore to rout a counter-attack and reinforce the costly attacks on Tarawa's 500 beach-head concrete and coconut-log pillboxes.

The US has also taken Japan's two other Gilbert Island bases. On Makin only one of the 800-strong Japanese garrison survived; US losses were 66 dead. At Apamama the garrison of 22 committed suicide rather than surrender (→ 4/12).

1943
December

Su	Mo	Tu	We	Th	Fr	Sa
			1	2	3	4
5	6	7	8	9	10	11
12	13	14	15	16	17	18
19	20	21	22	23	24	25
26	27	28	29	30	31	

1. USSR: Soviet troops cross the river Ingulets, and drive to within six miles of Znamenka (→ 3).

1. New Guinea: Australian troops capture Huanko, on the Huon Peninsula (→ 8).

1. USSR: Moscow claims that Byelorussian partisans have killed 282,000 German soldiers since war broke out (→ 3).

2. Italy: British troops spearhead an Anglo-US attack on Monte Camino (→ 3).

2. USA: Fifteen atomic scientists, including the Soviet spy Klaus Fuchs, arrive from Britain to join the US atomic research project.

3. Berlin: German defenders killed 228 Allied airmen last night, during a raid in which 36 Berliners died and 105 went "missing" (→ 25).

3. Pacific: The US submarine *Saltfish* sinks the Japanese carrier *Chuyo* off Honshu island.

3. Italy: Allied troops take the summit of Monte Camino (→ 5).

3. USSR: Soviet troops take Dovsk, south of Gomel; further south, they drive west of Cherkassy (→ 10).

3. Warsaw: In reprisal for an act of sabotage, the SS and *Gestapo* execute a hundred tram workers.

3. Berlin: Goering orders concentrated air attacks on British ports and industry "to avenge the terror attacks of the enemy".→

3-4. Germany: RAF raiders bomb Leipzig, killing or injuring over 1,000 citizens and causing extensive damage (→ 7).

4. La Paz: Bolivia declares war on Roumania and Hungary.

4. Kwajalein, Marshall Islands: Rear-Admirals Charles Pownall and Alfred Montgomery lead a US task force of six carriers and nine cruisers, which sinks six Japanese transports and damage two cruisers. Fifty-five Japanese aircraft are also shot down; the carrier *Lexington* is damaged by a torpedo (→ 8).

"Bevin Boys" face call-up to go down the mines for coal

Westminster, 2 December

Ernest Bevin, the minister of labour, announced in the House of Commons today that men are to be conscripted to serve in the coal mines in the same way as in the armed services. By next April 30,000 men of 25 or under will be chosen by ballot from those called up, and directed into the mines. A draw will be made of a figure between 0 and 9, and those whose national service registration number ended with that figure – one recruit in every ten – would be chosen.

After medical inspection, they would get four weeks' training, including underground training, and then would start work under supervision of experienced miners. They would not work at the coalface until they had been underground for four months.

Mr Bevin said he would not have resorted to compulsion but for reasons of "urgent national necessity": "I have delayed compulsion to the last possible moment because I don't like it any more than honourable members." Asked if he had power to do this without legislation, he replied, "Oh yes! I am entitled to direct anybody anywhere."

Coal production has fallen below 200 million tons this year and the number of miners at work has sunk to 700,000, despite the recall of many miners from the army.

He depends on you to get it!
COMMUNIST PARTY POSTER
MORE COAL FOR THE **SECOND FRONT**

The worker at the face is as vital to the war effort as the man at the front. ▷

Furore swells over release of Mosley

Poison gas is used in Japanese attack

Westminster, 1 December

The House of Commons today endorsed by a large majority the home secretary's decision to release the former fascist leader, Sir Oswald Mosley, from prison, where he has been held since May 1940. Labour speakers criticized Herbert Morrison, and an anti-Mosley demonstration outside Parliament was led away to Caxton Hall by Willie Gallagher, the Communist MP. One Labour MP compared Mosley's release to the freeing of Hitler by the Weimar government.

Mr Morrison, in a long and emotional speech, said that Mosley had been transferred from one kind of detention to another – "house arrest" in the country. He suffered from phlebitis, and outside doctors who had examined him, including Lord Dawson of Penn, believed that imprisonment would risk permanent damage to his health.

One MP objected that his condition was shared by thousands of charwomen with varicose veins. Mr Morrison said that he had been attacked and abused, particularly by his own party and in the news-

Workers gather to lobby their MPs in protest against the release of Mosley.

papers, and he did not like it. "I have had a very rough time. If anyone thinks I enjoyed putting my name to this order, they make a mistake. I had to make this decision and I made it, rightly or wrongly, knowing it would be unpopular. I would sooner go through all the misery I have gone through than

make a decision which was dishonest."

Arthur Greenwood, the acting leader of the Labour Party, said that if Sir Oswald Mosley saw that he had provoked such strength of feeling for a whole day in Parliament, it would be his most joyful day for a long time.

Changteh, 4 December

The handful of survivors of the Japanese invasion of the central Chinese city of Changteh surrendered today. As the Chinese capitulated, Japanese troops set fire to the city to flush out the few remaining defenders who have managed to survive despite a week of bombings which culminated in a poison-gas attack.

The survivors – 18 Chinese and two US radio operators who hid in a bank vault as they relayed target information to the US Fifteenth Army Air Force – are all that are left of the Chinese 57th Brigade which was ordered by Chiang Kai-shek to defend the city literally to the last man. Chiang today praised them, but threatened his surrendering commander with execution for disobeying orders.

The ancient city of Changte lies in China's vital rice-growing regions. Its loss may be a preliminary to a fourth battle for Changsha, the capital of Hunan province in central China, which the Japanese have often reached but never held (→ 9).

More airmen die in raid than Berliners

Berlin, 3 December

The capital of the *Reich* was the RAF's target again last night, in a raid notable because the number of casualties suffered by the RAF (230) was greater than those reported to have occurred on the ground (141 Berliners dead and missing). Because of the prevailing high winds it was a scattered raid; one pilot missed the target by 50 miles (80 km).

The RAF dead include two war correspondents, Captain Nordhal Grieg – a Norwegian related to the composer – of the *Daily Mail* and Norman Stockton of the *Sydney Sun*.

Tonight the city of Leipzig is being hit by 527 bombers on a blind-bombing mission led by two Lancasters fitted with a redesigned H2S radar, used in conjunction with Pathfinder "skymarking" of the city by flares. First reports indicate greatly improved accuracy.

Partisans elect a government for Yugoslavia with Tito as leader

Yugoslavia, 4 December

In a convent hall decorated with large pictures of Stalin, Churchill and Roosevelt, 54 delegates from Yugoslavia's partisan liberation committees today solemnly declared themselves to be the "anti-fascist council of national liberation of Yugoslavia".

Their leader, Josip Broz – the man known to the world as Tito – was elected general secretary and given the rank of marshal.

Tito's provisional government has settled for an unusually non-controversial programme which allows for individual rights, private property and free elections after the war. Tito, a dedicated communist, has been urged by Stalin to present a popular front. A non-communist, Ivan Ribar, is president. The question of what to do about King Peter, the exiled Yugoslav monarch, remains open.

The partisans now control at least one-sixth of Yugoslavia. With an army of more than 200,000, Tito

Tito (r) stands outside his secret headquarters with partisan commanders.

is now seen by the Allies as a vital force in the reconquest of Europe, tying down at least a dozen of Hitler's divisions. Partisan ranks have been swollen by former Italian

occupying troops, and Brigadier Fitzroy Maclean's British mission is now organizing the airlifting of weapons and military advisers into the country (→ 22).

Tehran summit commits Allies to second front in France by summer of next year

Tehran, 4 December

Making his first journey outside Russia since the Bolshevik Revolution of 1917, Stalin came to Tehran to hear Churchill and Roosevelt explain their plans for a cross-Channel invasion of France in the spring or summer of next year. A communique from the conference, which ended on 1 December, says that the three leaders "have concerted plans for the destruction of the German forces. We have reached complete agreement as to the scope and timing of the operations which will be undertaken from the east, west and south." This makes it clear that the Italian campaign will continue, though resources may be diverted to the French campaign. Stalin was not too pleased when Churchill said a landing in France depended upon Germany being prevented from bringing up substantial reinforcements during the first two months after the assault. The Soviet leader wondered aloud whether an invasion would ever happen.

Roosevelt was gratified to hear Stalin promise that "the moment Germany is defeated" the Soviet Union would join the war against Japan. This promise is judged to be so sensitive that the three leaders decided not to enter it in the record of the Tehran talks (→16).

Stalin, Roosevelt and Churchill with their aides at the Tehran summit.

German raid reveals Allied mustard gas

Bari, Italy, 2 December

Frantic attempts are being made to conceal the inclusion in an Allied ship's cargo of a consignment of mustard gas which is causing the deaths of dozens of troops and dockworkers after a surprise German air raid here today.

Eighty-eight German bombers roared in early today, hitting two ammunition ships which exploded, causing huge fires and extensive damage to the harbour as well as sinking 17 ships. Hundreds of survivors were picked out of the harbour and taken to hospital suffering from no more than shock, exposure and burns. Or so it seemed; but within a few hours these apparently only slightly hurt men began to die. They had succumbed to the effects of mustard gas, a weapon which caused thousands of casualties in the last war and which the Allies have in the past declared too horrific to be used by decent nations. One of the ships hit in the raid, the SS *John Harvey*, was carrying a top-secret US consignment of 2,000 deadly mustard-gas bombs; the Americans will spare no effort in covering the incident up.

Most of the dead and injured were stricken by gas escaping from the *John Harvey* as they swam through the water. Many more deaths from the effects of the gas are expected.

1943
December

Su	Mo	Tu	We	Th	Fr	Sa
			1	2	3	4
5	6	7	8	9	10	11
12	13	14	15	16	17	18
19	20	21	22	23	24	25
26	27	28	29	30	31	

5. India: The Japanese attack Calcutta port, killing 350 (→8).

5. Italy: The Indian 8th Division crosses the river Moro, pushing towards the supply port of Ortona (→7).

5. Britain: The US Eighth Army Air Force begins Operation Crossbow against German "Ski" rocket launch sites in northern France (→24).

6. Netherlands: Anton Mussert, the Dutch Nazi leader, says 150,000 Dutch Jews have been deported to eastern Europe (→21).

7. Italy: The US II and VI Corps launch a major attack in the Mignano Gap, attacking German positions at San Pietro and on Monte Sammucro (→8).

8. Marshall Islands: A US task force raids Kwajalein.

8. New Guinea: The Australians take Wareo and drive towards Wandokai and the Japanese stronghold of Sio (→15).

8. India: Eighteen Japanese bombers and 50 fighters attack the airfield at Tinsukia (→18).

8. Italy: French troops enter the front line for the first time (→9).

9. Italy: The British X Corps takes Rocca d'Evandro, completing the capture of Monte Camino (→10).

9. Solomon Islands: The Allied airstrip at Torokina, on Bougainville, 200 miles from Rabaul, in New Britain, becomes operational (→13).

10. Malta: Roosevelt visits the island, and pays tribute to its long-suffering populace.

10. Italy: Canadian troops join the attack on Ortona.→

10. USSR: Soviet forces retake Znamenka (→14).

11. New Delhi: USAAF and RAF units in South-east Asia Command are put under a single Eastern Air Command under Air Chief Marshal Sir Richard Peirse.

11. Germany: The USAAF raids the U-boat yard at Emden, losing 20 planes but claiming to have shot down 138 German fighters (→13).

Harris says bombs can beat Germany

London, 7 December

Air Chief Marshal Sir Arthur Harris, whose RAF bomber crews are fighting the brave but costly Battle of Berlin, has written to the air ministry to restate his belief that Germany can be bombed out of the war, and to claim that this can be done by Lancasters alone. He plans to have 40 squadrons of "Lancs" operational in the next three months. These, he says, will drop 13,850 tons of bombs a month and "produce in Germany a state of devastation in which surrender is inevitable". He predicts that this will happen by April 1944 (→11).

Rallying support for the bombers.

Thousands face war crimes court action

London, 7 December

Severe justice will be meted out to many thousands of war criminals. So Viscount Simon, Britain's Lord Chancellor, told parliament today. But he added: "There must be no mass executions of great numbers of nameless people. It must be justice administered to an individual." His comments come after Lord Vansittart, former head of the Foreign Office, had warned: "We shall not establish sanity in Germany without a considerable measure of sanitation. War criminals must be followed to the uttermost ends of the earth."

Film-makers go to war – and this time all the bullets and bloodshed are real

Italy, 11 December
As American soldiers battle to seize a small Italian town called San Pietro [*see report alongside*] their efforts are being filmed by a crew led by the Hollywood director Major John Huston. Both the US and Britain have sent their film-makers to war – with great popular success.

Desert Victory, the film of the Eighth Army's advance from El Alamein to Tripoli, is acknowledged as the outstanding documentary of the war. Since its release in March this year it has attracted huge audiences at home and abroad. It was filmed at the front by 26 cameramen of the Army Film and Photographic Unit, under Major David Macdonald, who once worked in Hollywood. Seven of his cameramen were killed or missing and four more taken prisoner. The awesome artillery barrage that begins El Alamein stuns audiences. Miles of film were edited by Captain Roy Boulting. Mr Churchill sent the film to President Roosevelt and Marshal Stalin, who ordered it to be shown to the Red Army.

The Crown Film Unit showed a documentary of a day and night in the life of a dockland fire station at the height of the Blitz, laconically titled *Fires Were Started*. All roles are taken by real firemen and the direction

Lilli Palmer and Barbara Waring in "The Gentle Sex".

by Humphrey Jennings is truthful and tragic. This year also saw two dramatized documentaries: *The Gentle Sex*, Leslie Howard's last film, about a mixed bag of girls joining the ATS, and a story of women directed to an aero engine factory, *Millions Like Us*, by Frank Launder and Sidney Gilliat.

The Hollywood director John Ford is shooting movies of the US Navy in action in the Pacific. He was wounded while filming *The Battle of Midway* (and awarded a Purple Heart). And Captain Clark Gable has been in England making a documentary which follows a bomber crew.

On film on the road from El Alamein to Tripoli in "Desert Victory".

Battle rages for hill village of San Pietro

San Pietro, Italy, 10 December
Hitler himself has reputedly selected this small Italian hill town on the slopes of Monte Sammucro to be the perfect example of a German position, dominating as it does the vital Liri Valley which forms their defensive Gustav Line.

For four days now the battle has raged as US forces struggle to push the Germans from their carefully-sited pill boxes. Troops of the 143rd Infantry Regiment managed to reach the barbed-wire defences – but they, were cut down by the machine-gun and mortar fire, and sustained over 300 casualties before they retired. Tanks are now being called up (→ 15).

Canadian troops search German prisoners taken on the Moro river.

Roosevelt postpones the draft for fathers

Washington, 10 December
After sailing close to, and perhaps over, the deadline for his action, President Roosevelt today signed a new draft bill which puts all men who were fathers before the US entered the war at the bottom of the list of men liable to be called up.

In so doing, he flouted his own chairman of the war manpower commission, Paul McNutt, who was in favour of calling up fathers. Maj-Gen Lewis Hershey looks likely to take over as the president's right-hand man for war manpower administration. He is the director of the selective service commission.

Previously, men were divided into four categories: single men, single men with dependants, married men with no children or with children born since Pearl Harbor, and other married men. From now on the president, reacting either to his own instincts or to his shrewd political reading of his countrymen's instincts, wants only two categories: fathers and non-fathers.

"Drop-tanks" give boost to fighters

London, 11 December
A remarkably simple piece of equipment, a "drop-tank" made out of corrugated paper, has started to arrive at US fighter bases in England and has already revolutionized the air war over Europe. Fighters fitted with these British-produced tanks, which carry 75 gallons of fuel, can now escort the American heavy bombers on their daylight missions far into Germany. It is no exaggeration to say that because of these tanks the US Eighth Army Air Force has seized the initiative from the *Luftwaffe*. The newly-introduced Mustang fighters equipped with two of these tanks each can fly 600 miles from their bases and still take on the German fighters at over 400mph.

Chinese forces take control of Changteh

Changteh, 9 December
After two weeks of some of the most intensive fighting seen on the Chinese mainland, Changteh, the central Chinese city twice occupied by the Japanese, has been recaptured by Chinese Nationalist troops after a massive cross-country supply operation by an army of coolies.

Changteh, a city of 160,000 south of the Yangtze and at the heart of a major rice-producing district, has been destroyed in the battle that saw bitter hand-to-hand fighting in the streets and the use of poison gas by the Japanese. The Chinese commander, General Hsueh Yueh, admitted that his losses had been heavier than Japan's, but said that it was felt that Changteh had to be retaken whatever the costs (→ 25).

1943

December

Su	Mo	Tu	We	Th	Fr	Sa
			1	2	3	4
5	6	7	8	9	10	11
12	13	14	15	16	17	18
19	20	21	22	23	24	25
26	27	28	29	30	31	

12. Rastenburg: Rommel is appointed C-in-C of Hitler's "Fortress Europe", under the overall command of Field Marshal Gerd von Rundstedt.

13. Germany: Seven hundred and ten USAAF bombers, escorted for the first time by new P-51D Mustang fighters, carry out raids on Bremen and Kiel (→ 17).

13. Goodenough Island, Pacific: The US Task Force 76 sails for New Guinea, whence it will carry out landings on New Britain (→ 26).

14. Greece: Three hundred Allied bombers raid Athens (→ 15).

14. USSR: The Red Army recaptures Cherkassy and launches a new offensive on the Nevel salient; but Radomyshl falls to the Germans.→

15. New Guinea: Australian troops take Lakona, 15 miles from Finschhafen (→ 19).

15. Italy: The Fifth Army attacks along the length of the Reinhard Line; Moroccan troops secure the San Michel Pass, but the Germans put up strong resistance (→ 16).

15. Europe: Allied bombers raid Piraeus harbour and Greek airfields, and attack Innsbruck and Bolzano, in the Tyrol.

16. Italy: US troops capture Monte Lungo, leaving San Pietro exposed; the Germans launch strong counter-attacks to mask their withdrawal.→

16-17. Germany: RAF aircraft bomb Berlin tonight, killing 717 people on the ground but meeting a stiff defence. Nearly 300 British and Canadian airmen die in the attack, including 148 lost when 29 Lancasters and a Stirling crash or are abandoned over Britain (→ 25).

18. New Delhi: General Joseph Stilwell is appointed to command all Chinese troops in India and north Burma.

18. China: Japanese aircraft raid Kunming, in Yunnan province, as part of a strategy to weaken the Allies prior to an attack on India (→ 25).

Russian army launches winter offensive

Soviet forces with T34 tanks push on across a snowy landscape west of Kiev.

Kiev, 14 December
The Red Army, pursuing its tactics of keeping the Germans on the wrong foot, has launched a major attack on Nevel, in Byelorussia. The Germans say they have abandoned some positions in the face of an assault by six divisions and two tank corps.

Meanwhile, south of Kiev, General Konev's men have stormed Cherkassy, the German stronghold on the west bank of the Dnieper, and are nearing Smyela, the vital junction 16 miles (26 km) southwest of Cherkassy. The Germans are in full retreat and are being harried from the air by Shturmoviks. One of the reasons for the defeat of the German Eighth Army at Cherkassy was the transfer of many of its tanks to von Manstein's attempt to retake Kiev. At first successful, this attempt inflicted many casualties on General Vatutin's First Ukrainian Front, but was halted by mud and Vatutin's artillery 25 miles from the Ukrainian capital.

General Hoth has been sacked for his failure to take Kiev. Now, both sides are gathering men and guns for the winter offensive which is bound to follow once the frost has hardened the ground (→ 16).

Germans urged to stay off the trains

Germany, 18 December
German citizens could face further curbs on rail travel and stiff fare rises this Christmas as the *Reichsbahn*, the state railway, is increasingly given over to military use. Already, in an attempt to prevent civilians from crowding the trains – especially long-distance ones – school summer holidays in the *Reich* begin on three different days, according to region, and travel at Easter, Whitsun, Christmas and New Year is restricted.

Czech-Soviet pact agrees mutual aid

Moscow, 12 December
Dr Benes, the Czechoslovak president, today shifted his country significantly closer to the Soviet Union when he signed a treaty of "amity, mutual aid and collaboration after the war". With Stalin looking on, he put his signature to the treaty during a Kremlin ceremony. Molotov signed for the Soviet Union. "The day of retribution for Germany will come," Benes said, "and our much-suffering people will have won a new, solid and lasting peace." Molotov replied: "Our army is fighting for all people under the German yoke."

Germans face Soviet justice in first trials for Nazi war crimes

Kharkov, 16 December
Retribution for German atrocities in former occupied areas of Russia has begun. The first war crimes tribunal was at Krasnodar in July, where eight Germans were shot for a horrific catalogue of crimes. Today three Germans and a Russian who worked for them are facing a military tribunal in a theatre in this war-ravaged city.

Captain Wilhelm Langheld, Corporal Reinhardt Retelav, Hans Ritz of the *Gestapo* and their driver, Mikhail Bulanov, allegedly took part in the killing of Soviet citizens by gassing in sealed vans, shooting, hanging and burning. The indictment says that 30,000 were killed in the Kharkov area during the occupation (→ 21).

Two of the thousands across Europe and Russia murdered by the Nazis.

1943
December

Su	Mo	Tu	We	Th	Fr	Sa
			1	2	3	4
5	6	7	8	9	10	11
12	13	14	15	16	17	18
19	20	21	22	23	24	25
26	27	28	29	30	31	

US sets Chinese immigration quota

Washington, 17 December
President Franklin Roosevelt today signed legislation permitting an annual quota for Chinese immigrants to the United States. This is, in effect, a repeal of the Chinese Exclusion Act of 1882 and of subsequent anti-Chinese legislation passed early in this century as a result of the "Yellow Peril" agitation against Chinese coolie labour. The president has pushed the state department, and now Congress, into reversing the Exclusion Acts because of his appreciation of the value of China as an ally in the war against Japan.

Churchill is taken ill with pneumonia

London, 16 December
For the second time this year Mr Churchill, now 69, is ill with pneumonia. He is still in the Middle East following the Tehran conference with President Roosevelt and Marshal Stalin. Tonight a medical bulletin said: "His general condition is as satisfactory as can be expected." Prayers for the prime minister's recovery are being said throughout the Empire and in other lands. Anxious MPs were assured that the new drug penicillin is available for treating him. His doctors will insist on a lengthy convalescence.

Germans withdraw from San Pietro

San Pietro, 17 December
It needed tanks, artillery, mortars, phosphorus grenades and outright guts to take San Pietro. Tonight, as the townsfolk emerge from their cellars to view their shattered town, the stiffening bodies of young American infantrymen are being placed in white cotton bags, with their identification discs tied to their combat boots. Their exhausted comrades look on. Some weep for fallen comrades; others stare vacantly ahead. No more than 100 *Panzergrenadiers* caused 1,500 American casualties here. There are hundreds more San Pietros to come (→ 21).

American troops land on New Britain

Sub-machine gun and grenade at the ready: US troops on New Britain.

New Britain, 18 December
The operation to capture New Britain has begun. Three days ago the US 112th Cavalry under Brigadier-General Julian Cunningham staged diversionary amphibious landings on the Arawe peninsula, on the south coast. Today, pre-invasion air attacks were intensified against Cape Gloucester, in the west.

The 112th, after embarking in New Guinea for Arawe on 14 December, followed a last-minute plan to establish four beach-heads. Three landings at the peninsula's tip were virtually unopposed. But a second wave in 15 rubber boats, trying to land halfway along the peninsula and take Arawe's grass airstrip, was spotted and lost 12 boats. The invasion is the start of the fifth and final phase of MacArthur's "Elkton" plan for Allied forces from New Guinea and the Solomons to converge and isolate the key base at Rabaul (→ 19).

The huge German "Gigant" Messerschmitt Me323: the largest land-based aircraft in the world. It is used for long-haul freight transport.

19. New Britain: US forces take the airstrip at Arawe, fending off strong Japanese counter-attacks (→ 20).

19. Moscow: The USSR adopts a new anthem to replace the *Internationale*.

20. New Britain: Japanese moving against the Arawe beach-head reach the Pulie river, east of Arawe (→ 25).

20-21. Germany: RAF bombers raid Frankfurt, dropping 2,000 tons of bombs; the USAAF raids Bremen.

21. Italy: Canadian troops launch an attack on Ortona and Monte Sammucro (→ 22).

21. USSR: The Russians destroy a German bridgehead across the Dnieper at Kherson (→ 24).

21. Auschwitz-Birkenau: Hersh Kurcwaig and Stanislaw Dorosiewicz escape from the camp after killing a guard (→ 22).

22. USSR: 14,284 Spanish soldiers are repatriated to Spain; 3,000 volunteer to continue fighting with the Nazis in the *Legion Azul* [Blue Legion].

22. Italy: Canadian troops enter Ortona (→ 28).

22. Warsaw: *Gestapo* police discover and execute 62 Jews hiding in a basement (→ 31).

23. Algiers: General Jean de Lattre de Tassigny arrives to take command of the French First Army.

24. USSR: The Soviet Army launches a major offensive in the Ukraine, intended to destroy the German salient on the Dnieper and open Galicia and Roumania (→ 25).

25. New Britain: Japanese forces attack the Arawe beachhead (→ 26).

25. India: Japanese bombers raid Chittagong.

25. USSR: Soviet troops cut the Vitebsk to Polotsk railroad, severing a major German supply route to the west. →

25. Arctic Sea: The battle-cruiser *Scharnhorst* sets sail to attack the Allied convoy JW-55B (→ 26).

Air war escalates in Chinese battle

Hunan Province, 25 December
The see-saw and bloody battle for northern Hunan province has swung in favour of the Chinese Nationalists, with *Kuomintang* troops today recapturing Kung-an. It was one of the first towns lost two months ago when 100,000 Japanese troops invaded the area in an attempt to stop Chinese troops moving from central China to southern Yunnan to support the new tripartite Allied plan to retake Burma.

The battle in Hunan has escalated the air war in China. At Changte, the epicentre of the campaign, the USAAF's effectiveness in dropping supplies and providing airborne artillery was met 14 days ago by a Japanese night attack on Allied airfields with the loss of 40 US and Chinese planes.

CHINA'S WAR IS OUR WAR

UNITED AID TO CHINA FUND

57 New Bond Street · London W1 · Tel. Mayfair 6911-5

Taking the Chinese cause to heart.

Christmas turkeys are in short supply

Britain, 25 December
Many families are without their Christmas bird today, but resourceful housewives will have concocted some kind of traditional pudding with dried fruit saved from their rations. Turkeys and geese have been allocated on a quota system: one suburban butcher with 800 customers received only 15 birds. Another estimated that one family in ten would enjoy a traditional fowl.

"Ike" to command European invasion

Roosevelt and Eisenhower, newly appointed to lead the invasion of France.

Washington, 24 December
In a Christmas Eve broadcast to the American people today, President Roosevelt announced that General Dwight ("Ike") Eisenhower has been appointed supreme commander of the Allied Expeditionary Force preparing for the cross-Channel invasion of France.

A decision on Eisenhower's deputy will be announced shortly, but General Sir Bernard Montgomery will command all Allied land forces until Eisenhower sets up his headquarters in France. Naval and air chiefs will be involved.

These appointments had been discussed at the recent Tehran conference with Stalin, when "every point concerning the impending east-west-south attack on Germany was decided". Roosevelt described as "brilliant" Eisenhower's performances in the campaigns in North Africa, Sicily and Italy.

Eisenhower's command in the Mediterranean is being taken over by General Sir Henry Maitland Wilson, who made his reputation in early North African campaigns before moving to the Middle East.

Roosevelt promised Wilson that America's forces "will stand by your side until every objective in the bitter Mediterranean theatre is attained" (→ 27).

Rocket launch sites bombed by USAAF

France, 24 December
Throughout the past three months the construction of V-weapon launch sites in northern France has been monitored by the RAF's Photographic Reconnaissance Unit. By 19 December no fewer than 54 sites had been established as being in an advanced state of construction. Operation Crossbow was launched on 4 December, and the USAAF carried out the first attack on the sites the next day. RAF attacks took place on 16-17 December. The RAF's involvement means diversions from the attacks on German cities, especially Berlin.

Allied forces press on in New Guinea

Wareo, New Guinea, 19 December
With only days to go before the main Allied invasion of New Britain, Australian 9th Division troops have captured the last Japanese coastal stronghold overlooking the crucial Vitiaz Straits that separate New Guinea from New Britain. Fighting in torrential conditions and in dense jungle, the 9th today routed the last Japanese defending the Mandang Wareo trail on the Huon Peninsula. Since taking Salamaua and Lae in September the 9th has inflicted heavy casualties, killing 3,099 Japanese (but only capturing 38). The 9th has lost 283 killed and 745 wounded (→ 2/1).

People of Berlin get an unwelcome Christmas present from RAF

Victims of RAF bombs are laid out for identification in a Berlin gymnasium.

Berlin, 25 December
The main weight of the RAF's Christmas raid on Berlin last night fell on the city's south-eastern suburbs, as well as on a ball-bearing factory at Erkner, 15 miles (24 km) away. The bombs killed 178 Berliners, compared with 104 aircrew killed and 16 taken prisoner. RAF PoWs were made to clear rubble after what was the month's second big raid. Nine days ago 438 Berliners and 279 slave workers (186 women, 65 men and 28 youths from eastern Europe) died during an attack on rail networks; so did 294 German airmen (→ 29).

Russia celebrates year of advances

Moscow, 25 December

The Red Army yesterday launched an offensive in the Ukraine along the Kiev-Zhitomir highway, aiming to prise open German ranks now defending Galicia and Roumania. In the Vitebsk sector Gorodok has been captured and German defensive positions are on the brink of collapse. The year thus ends, as it began, with Russia in the ascendant: a year which started with Stalingrad, ending the Russians' long retreat and humiliating the seemingly invincible Germans.

Since then the Russians have defeated the Germans at Kursk in the greatest tank battle yet fought, recaptured Kharkov for the second time, liberated Kiev, cut off the German Seventeenth Army in the Crimea, crossed the Dnieper and broken Hitler's "Eastern Wall".

This has, however, been not only a year of victories, but also a year in which the awesome reserves of the Soviet Union have been mobilized. Millions of men have been put under arms and those arms are of excellent quality.

The improved versions of the T34 and the heavy Stalin tanks with their 122mm guns have proved a match for the Germans, who scrambled desperately to get their Tigers and Panthers onto the battlefield to cope with the T34s pouring from Russian production lines.

It is the same story in the air, with the Russians producing excellent aircraft in great numbers – no fewer than 2,900 a month during 1943 of which 2,500 were combat planes. Added to them were 16,000 heavy or medium tanks, 3,500 light tanks, 4,000 mobile guns and 130,000 guns of all calibres during the year. As well as the Russians' own strength there was also the help sent from the west: mechanized divisions go into battle in American lorries; Soviet pilots fly Airacobras and Kittyhawks; generals scan intelligence decrypts.

All this strength is now being welded together into a formidable fighting machine. Stalin plans to clear the Ukraine, destroying the *Wehrmacht* in a series of "cauldrons" before marching on Poland, Roumania and Germany itself. The Germans are still fighting skilfully, but Russia now has the power (→ 26).

Soviets close in on a Focke-Wulf reconnaissance plane they have shot down.

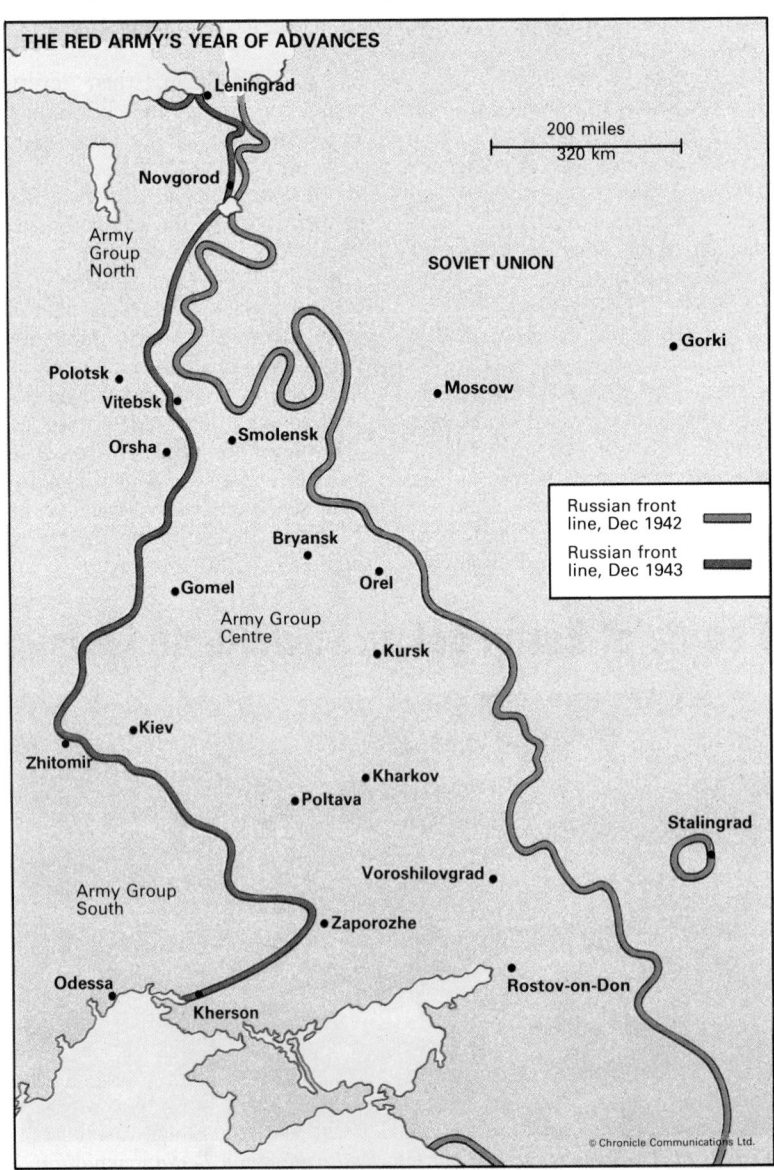

THE RED ARMY'S YEAR OF ADVANCES

200 miles
320 km

SOVIET UNION

Leningrad
Novgorod
Army Group North
Gorki
Polotsk
Vitebsk
Moscow
Orsha
Smolensk
Bryansk
Gomel
Orel
Army Group Centre
Kursk
Kiev
Zhitomir
Kharkov
Poltava
Stalingrad
Army Group South
Voroshilovgrad
Zaporozhe
Odessa
Rostov-on-Don
Kherson

Russian front line, Dec 1942
Russian front line, Dec 1943

© Chronicle Communications Ltd.

Solomons bombed in diversionary raid

Solomon Islands, 24 December

The Japanese received an unexpected Christmas present today when an American task force bombarded airfields and shore bases on the northern tip of Bougainville and the neighbouring island of Buka. The powerful force included cruisers and destroyers. The flagship fired the first salvo at 12.30am, unleashing a storm of shells onto air installations at Bonis, on Bougainville, and Buka, where they caused a huge fire – probably from a fuel or ammunition dump. Barge and patrol-boat bases in the islands and reefs off Buka were also hit. Japanese shore batteries could only offer a weak, and ineffective, response to the sea and air bombardment.

Public hanging for Nazi war criminals

Kharkov, 19 December

The three German war criminals, Langheld, Retelav and Ritz, and their Russian accomplice Bulanov, were hanged this cold grey morning in the market square of Kharkov, the war-scarred city where they had carried out massacres of Russian people with the utmost brutality. A crowd estimated at 50,000 watched as nooses were placed round their necks and the lorries on which they stood were driven away to leave them dangling from the scaffold of rough pine logs.

Tito sacks king who backed wrong side

Yugoslavia, 22 December

Marshal Tito, Yugoslavia's partisan leader, has told the country's exiled King Peter that his services will not be required after the war. The young king has angered the partisans by living in comfort in London – and by awarding a medal to a *Chetnik* commander who was living in Italian headquarters at the time. The Chetnik guerrillas, led by the royalist Drazha Mihailovich, are accused of switching sides since the Allies put their money on Tito as likely to cause Hitler most trouble.

1943

December

Su	Mo	Tu	We	Th	Fr	Sa
			1	2	3	4
5	6	7	8	9	10	11
12	13	14	15	16	17	18
19	20	21	22	23	24	25
26	27	28	29	30	31	

26. USSR: The Russians retake Radomyshl and over 150 other places in the Kiev salient (→ 29).

26. New Britain: The US 1st Marine Division lands at Cape Gloucester, following a heavy naval bombardment (→ 27).

27. New Britain: US forces advance three miles towards the airfield, hampered by swamps and torrential rain.→

27. London: Air Chief Marshal Sir Arthur Tedder is appointed deputy supreme commander of the Allied invasion forces, headed by General Eisenhower.

28. Burma: The Chinese 38th Division captures Japanese positions in the Tarung valley (→ 10/1).

28. Berlin: Himmler orders the death rate in the labour camps to be reduced, owing to a shortage of forced labourers for arms manufacture.

28. Italy: Ortona falls to the Allies.→

29. USSR: Soviet troops retake Korosten and Chernyakhov in a massive Ukrainian breakthrough (→ 30).

29. Italy: British 9 Commando raids the area near the mouth of the river Garigliano (→ 31).

29. Berlin: RAF aircraft killed 182 civilians in a bombing raid last night, for the loss of 81 crewmen (→ 3/1).

30. USSR: Soviet troops take Kazatin, south-west of Kiev (→ 31).

31. France: Resistants carry out a simultaneous bombing of rail depots and junctions.

31. USSR: The Russians recapture Zhitomir and lay siege to Vitebsk, now isolated (→ 4/1).

31. Karpiowka, Poland: The Germans burn 59 villagers to death for helping partisans.

31. Italy: Civilian casualties from Allied air raids in the last three months are 6,500 dead and 11,000 wounded (→ 3/1).

31. Britain: Civilian casualties from German air raids in the last three months are 247 killed and 561 wounded.

Royal Navy triumphs in sea battles

Some of the few survivors from the "Scharnhorst" on board the "Duke of York".

Arctic: "Scharnhorst" sunk in icy waters

Arctic Ocean, 26 December
One of Germany's two surviving battle cruisers, the 31,800-ton *Scharnhorst*, was sunk at 7.45pm today off the northern tip of Norway. She had left Altenfjord on Christmas Day in the hope of finding convoy JW-55B, which is carrying vital munitions to Russia.

The commander-in-chief of the British Home Fleet, Admiral Sir Bruce Fraser, had been hoping for just such an opportunity. He was himself in the area on the battleship *Duke of York*. The *Scharnhorst* was first spotted by the cruisers *Belfast*, *Norfolk* and *Sheffield* in the half-light of the Arctic dawn. They managed to inflict some damage, but the German ship then sped away leaving them far behind. Late this afternoon the *Duke of York* found her and holed her beneath the water line with her 14-inch guns.

Sir Bruce was then able to bring up two divisions of destroyers which fired no fewer than 55 torpedoes. Another cruiser, the *Jamaica*, scored the final hit which sank the mighty *Scharnhorst*.

Biscay: destroyers sunk by cruisers

Bay of Biscay, 28 December
A Royal Navy force of two cruisers sank three German destroyers in a two-and-a-half-hour running battle this afternoon with ten destroyers. Captain H Grant of the *Enterprise* described how shells were "whizzing all around the ship between the masts and skimming the bridge". However, the only damage to his ship was to the wireless aerial. The other cruiser, the *Glasgow*, suffered worse damage.

The victory over such superior numbers is the more surprising because five of the German force were of the new "Narvik" class. They are virtually mini-cruisers and their 5.9-inch guns have more hitting power than the six-inch guns on the much older *Enterprise*.

The German force had been sent out to protect a blockade-runner, the *Alsterufer,* bringing in valuable supplies. However, that ship was sunk yesterday by two Coastal Command Liberators and a Sunderland flying boat before the destroyers reached her.

The destroyers decided to take the shortest route back to harbour, but ran into a gale which slowed them down considerably and provided an opportunity for the cruisers to get in among them. Several other destroyers were badly damaged.

Jews fight back in Hitler's death camps

Europe, 31 December
With the opening of five new gas-chamber and crematorium complexes this year, the camp at Auschwitz-Birkenau has become the centre of the Nazi plan to exterminate the Jewish people. It has become the final destination for Jews from Poland, France, Greece, Italy, Russia, the Netherlands, Czechoslovakia and Germany.

Himmler's order this summer for all Polish and Russian ghettoes to be liquidated has mainly been carried out. The remnant of Polish Jews still alive are in hard labour camps, where few will survive. Yet this was also the year when the Jews started to fight back, assaulting guards, destroying camp buildings and property and setting up armed resistance to German troops in the ghettoes. Polish Jews have killed themselves in the transports, defying the Nazi death machine waiting at the end of the line.

Towards the end of this year, there has been a lull in the extermination process which has nevertheless killed at least one million people since 1 January. But resistance in the face of such a determined and well-armed enemy will always be crushed in the end.

We have just begun to fight!

PEARL HARBOR
BATAAN
CORAL SEA
MIDWAY
GUADALCANAL
NEW GUINEA
BISMARCK SEA
CASABLANCA
ALGIERS
TUNISIA

Rallying cry from a US poster.

Main invasion force lands on New Britain

US troops come ashore to send the Japanese packing from New Britain.

Cape Gloucester, 30 December
Three battalions of the 1st US Marine Division yesterday made a strategic breakthrough in the Southwest Pacific by taking an important airfield at Cape Gloucester, on the western coast of New Britain, four days after landing in force.

Early today Japanese Zeros began strafing the wrecked airfield which had been theirs only a few hours earlier. Once operational, the airfield will give the Allies air control of the important Dampier and Vitiaz Straits between New Guinea and New Britain. Possession of these are essential to any further advance by MacArthur's forces along New Guinea's north coast. At the same time control of the straits severs one of the main supply routes to Japan's increasingly isolated South-west Pacific HQ at Rabaul, in New Britain.

The Cape airfield was taken after a flanking action that began four days ago when the 1st Marines, Guadalcanal veterans who have been recharged by a year in Australia, waded through the surf on the Cape's south and north coasts. Japanese resistance was non-existent in the uncharted and treacherous waist-deep bogs behind the southern beach-head. Once on the airfield road the 1st encountered mortar, machine-gun and rifle fire from 12 bunkers at a place immediately christened Hell's Point as tanks obliterated the concrete and bamboo defences at point-blank range, killing 266 Japanese (→ 1/1).

THE ALLIED ATTACK ON NEW BRITAIN

100 miles
160 km

Rabaul
Cape Gloucester
NEW IRELAND
NEW BRITAIN
Arawe
BOUGAINVILLE
NEW GUINEA
Lae
Salamaua
SOLOMON ISLANDS
PAPUA
Buna
WOODLARK
Port Moresby

Land held by Japanese
Land held by Allies
Allied attacks

© Chronicle Communications Ltd.

A worldwide wartime production boom: how industries have gone into top gear

World, 31 December
An onlooker from another planet could be forgiven for describing the vicious conflict in which the people of earth are engaged as a mindless, endless cycle of production and destruction. The faster aircraft are shot out of the sky or ships are sent to the bottom of the oceans, the faster new planes and vessels are manufactured to replace them.

Production of military aircraft worldwide has soared since last year. The Russians have built 34,900 as compared with last year's figure of 25,436, while the US churned out a staggering total of 85,898, nearly doubling last year's figure of 47,836. Britain has made the smallest increase – from 23,672 to 26,263 – but the total production is still ahead of Germany's 24,807, itself a significant increase on last year's 15,409. The Japanese built 16,693 military aircraft this year, a huge leap from last year's 8,861.

The world's biggest wartime production boom is undoubtedly taking place in the US. Early last year it took 260 days to produce one "Liberty Ship" – now it takes a mere 40 days. Defence spending has risen during 1943 from just over $50bn to some $85bn.

In Britain the war has not stopped the workers demanding their rights: 1.8 million days were lost to strikes this year.

Putting the screws on the Axis: America's arms industry goes into top gear.

Allies' painfully slow progress to Ortona

Ortona, Italy, 28 December
Canadian troops fought their way through a wall of fire to oust a German division from this Adriatic seaport today. Flame-throwers have been rushed to the 200,000 Germans now estimated to be fighting to save Rome.

Like so many Italian towns in the wake of warring armies, Ortona is a ruin. But the shattered and burntout wreckage of buildings is ideal for the German defenders – in this case hardened Nazi *Waffen-SS* men who had to be winkled out one by one by infantrymen with tank support. However, Ortona finally fell late this afternoon. The remaining Germans have retreated to hill positions north-west of the town. The town has been a key objective in the Eighth Army's drive along the eastern coast of Italy. It is the eastern anchor of Field Marshal Kesselring's defensive Gustav Line.

But the Allied advance is slow. Each valley running from the Apennines to the sea has to be fought for. There are hundreds of valleys, and the few roads available have been heavily mined by the retreating Germans. Heavy rain and snowstorms are other problems (→ 29).

Big bands dominate the music scene in 1943

Cinema: war with an American accent

Hollywood is torn between making war films and offering pure escape from the war to the millions who flock to the cinema at least once, if not twice, a week. In Britain, from 25 to 30 million cinema seats are sold every week.

After his cynical neutrality in *Casablanca*, **Humphrey Bogart** is cast as a sergeant commanding a tank somewhere near El Alamein in **Zoltan Korda's** *Sahara*. The fact that his crew is mostly American, or Irish, may reflect the shortage of English accents available in Hollywood but has not helped its popularity in Britain. The Pacific War is now getting the Hollywood treatment in pictures like *Bataan*.

Stage Door Canteen showed the stars doing their bit, **Joan Crawford** by dancing with a GI, **Bette Davis** by jitterbugging. *Now, Voyager* brought us Miss Davis in more familiar vein of neurotic torment while **Ingrid Bergman** made her mark without make-up in *For Whom The Bell Tolls* and **Joan Fontaine** was *Jane Eyre* to **Orson Welles's** melodramatic Rochester. New female stars have risen. **Rene Clair** in *I Married a Witch* introduced the most ravishing of that species, the blonde siren **Veronica Lake**. The pin-up of every GI is **Betty Grable**, more appreciated for her legs and tight swimsuit than for her acting, but now top of the polls.

Glenn Miller and his orchestra before they were broken up by the draft board.

Music: Glenn Miller scores wartime mood

The American big band sound is sweeping Britain in the wake of the American troops, along with the craze of jitterbugging in the dance halls. The big names on the record labels are **Tommy Dorsey**, **Harry James**, **Artie Shaw** and **Woody Herman**, leading orchestras 30 strong or more. Top band by general consent is **Glenn Miller** and his Orchestra, whose string of hits goes back to "In the Mood" and "Moonlight Serenade" recorded in 1939. Their latest is "American Patrol". The band has been broken up by the war. Captain Miller volunteered for military service and is now modern-

izing military band music for the US Army Air Force, with swinging arrangements of numbers like "Blues in the Night".

Tommy Dorsey's former vocalist, **Frank Sinatra**, has ousted **Bing Crosby** from the top of the radio hit parade. Saved from the draft by a perforated eardrum, Sinatra is drawing ecstatic responses from female audiences with songs such as "You'll Never Know". Other hits of the year include "Brazil" and "My Heart and I". The one truly international war hit is "Lili Marlene", recorded in English by **Anne Shelton**.

Other arts: Proms are highbrow hit

It is not only popular music that is flourishing because of war. Classical music is being brought to more people than ever before. Week-long music festivals for the army, navy and RAF have been given this year. The **BBC Symphony Orchestra** broke the box office record at the Garrison Theatre, Aldershot, previously held by **Gracie Fields**.

ENSA began a series of symphony concerts for war workers in towns like Wigan where there are great concentrations of munitions factories. Ernest Bevin, the minister of labour, attended the first concert given in London at the People's Palace in Stepney. Where no hall is available, concerts are given in cathedrals. Chester Cathedral was crammed to the doors for **Pablo Casals** playing the Elgar cello concerto. All artists receive a standard fee of three guineas (£3.15/$12.70) a concert. The Proms drew audiences of 5,000 to the Albert Hall in London. **Sir Henry Wood** had a stroke on the podium during the season and his place has been taken by **Basil Cameron**.

In occupied France the leading intellectual **Jean-Paul Sartre** spelt out his existentialist philosophy of humanity's condition in *Being and Nothingness*, published by Gallimard with Nazi permission. Sartre also writes for the underground press and is in the Resistance.

The greatest romance of the war.

Sinatra: the man with "The Voice".

The singer Anne Shelton (centre).

The philosopher Jean-Paul Sartre.

"Headquarters Room" by Barnett Freedman.

January

Su	Mo	Tu	We	Th	Fr	Sa
						1
2	3	4	5	6	7	8
9	10	11	12	13	14	15
16	17	18	19	20	21	22
23	24	25	26	27	28	29
30	31					

1. Pacific: US naval aircraft attack a Japanese convoy off Kavieng, in New Ireland (→ 6).

1. London: General Sir Alan Brooke becomes a field marshal.

1. London: The US Strategic Air Forces in Europe Command – covering all US Army Air Forces in Britain – comes into effect; it is headed by General Carl Spaatz, who arrives today (→ 11).

2. London: Gen de Lattre de Tassigny is appointed C-in-C French Forces, North Africa (→ 1/2).

3. US: *Time* magazine declares the US chief of staff, Gen George Marshall, its Man of the Year for 1943.

3. Italy: The French Expeditionary Force starts fighting in the US Fifth Army.→

4. Rastenburg: Hitler refuses von Manstein's plea to pull troops out of the Dnieper Bend in order to free soldiers for the northern front (→ 4).

4. Europe: Allied aircraft start Operation Carpetbagger, regular supply missions to partisans in the Netherlands, Belgium, France and Italy (→ 7).

5. New Guinea: The Australians take Kelanoa, on the north coast of the Huon Peninsula (→ 15).

5. USSR: Soviet troops recapture Berdichev, south-west of Kiev.→

6. Britain: The RAF and USAAF announce their joint development of jet aircraft.

6. New Britain: US troops press southwards from Cape Gloucester to the Aogiri river (→ 8).

7. South-eastern France: Allied advisers parachute in to train Resistance fighters for guerrilla warfare after the invasion of Europe (→ 9).

8. Solomon Islands: US ships raid the Shortland Islands (→ 9).

8. USSR: The Red Army captures Kirovograd (→ 10).

8. London: General Sir Henry Maitland Wilson takes over as supreme Allied commander in the Mediterranean theatre.

Red Army enters Poland

German soldiers on the retreat through the mire of a battle-scarred land.

Kiev, 6 January
Thrusting west in a great salient from Kiev, General Vatutin's First Ukrainian Front has crossed the pre-war border of Poland and has chased the Germans to the gates of Sarny, an important junction on the railway from Kiev to Warsaw.

Vatutin is giving the Germans no chance to recover. He is pushing on in overwhelming strength, and in a special communique this morning the Soviet high command says that his men have killed more than 3,000 Germans and knocked out 83 tanks and 68 field guns. Many prisoners have been taken.

The Germans are making no attempt to hide the extent of their retreat in the Ukraine. A spokesman in Berlin said yesterday: "The German high command will make no effort to hold Russian territory purely for reasons of prestige."

"Should the German Army be compelled to retreat altogether from Russian soil, this would be only a secondary question compared with the importance of maintaining the front intact all along the line."

This announcement seems to presage a full-scale retreat by the Germans. The Russians have advanced 400 miles (640 km) since the opening of their campaign last July. If they achieve similar results this winter, then they will be in not only Poland but East Prussia, the heartland of German militarism (→ 8).

Tension grows over the future of Poland

London, 5 January
The Polish government in exile has tonight issued a statement on its attitude towards cooperating with the Soviet Union now that the Red Army has advanced in strength into Polish territory.

The declaration makes it clear that the Polish underground movement has been instructed to cooperate with the Red Army only in the event of a resumption of Polish-Soviet relations. It thus reflects the tension that exists between the Poles, who fear Moscow's intentions, and the Soviet Union, which has not yet recognized the Polish

London-based government in exile. Official circles in London gave the Polish declaration a cautious welcome, pointing out that without friendly relations between the two governments it would have been difficult for the Polish cabinet to instruct the underground movement to cooperate to the fullest degree.

The willingness of the Poles to re-establish good relations is noted with approval. The view is taken in Polish circles that their government has shown itself willing on many occasions to re-enter treaty relations with Russia, but no response has been made from Moscow (→ 11).

Air losses outweigh effectiveness of big RAF raids on Berlin

Berlin, 3 January
The RAF suffered heavily last night on its second 1,000-ton bombing raid in two nights on the German capital. Firemen stayed on the city's perimeter until the raid ended; in the past when they went into action during raids, fire and falling masonry destroyed many engines.

In fact, they need hardly have worried, because last night's raid added little to existing damage, described by a soldier on leave from the eastern front in the *Deutsche Allgemeine Zeitung*: "In the streets rubble is piled high and vast heaps of bricks tower in front of mutilated facades."

On the other hand, Bomber Command came off badly. In last night's raid, bombs were scattered over all parts of Berlin, with only 82 dwellings destroyed and 36 Berliners killed, while the RAF lost 27 Lancasters out of 383 aircraft and 168 aircrew were killed. In the previous raid 28 out of 421 bombers were lost; 168 aircrew were killed and 79 Berliners, 21 of whom died in a panic rush for a shelter.

The RAF losses last night represented seven per cent of the force dispatched, a rate which cannot for long be accepted. At a briefing for last night's raid, crews "gasped with horror or disbelief", according to an observer, when they saw Berlin was again the target (→ 21).

A Nazi medal is the reward for idle talk in wartime America.

Actor stars in real-life wartime drama

Britain, 7 January
Major James Stewart of the USAAF, better known as the star of *The Philadelphia Story*, brought his Liberators back intact today from a daylight mission on Ludwigshaven, despite being set upon by enemy fighters. Stewart, leading 48 bombers of 445th Group based at Tibenham, in Norfolk, had completed his mission when he saw that the 389th Group, the lead group of the raid's original 420 bombers, had taken a wrong bearing home, across German fighter airfields in France. Radio contact was lost, so he decided to follow and gave fire cover. Owing to Stewart's action, only eight of the strayed Liberators were lost.

Danish rebel killed

Copenhagen, 5 January
The bullet-riddled body of Denmark's leading poet and dramatist, Kaj Munk, was found in a Jutland wood this morning, several hours after he was abducted by a German-Danish Nazi gang known as the *Peter-Gruppe*. Munk, who was 45, regularly denounced the Nazis from his pulpit in the church at Vedersoe, in West Jutland, where he was priest (→ 19).

Allied forces go on the offensive in Italy

British troops in Italy stop their ears against the deafening noise of a mortar.

Southern Italy, 7 January
The British X Corps and the US II Corps have broken through the Germans' winter defensive line. The village of San Vittore fell yesterday and today, after a vicious battle, the Germans were driven off Monte Porchia. But the British 46th Division has been forced back after several attempts to get its tanks across the flooded river Peccia; no longer do the Allies talk of a "jolly romp to Rome".

Every yard of this mountainous terrain has to be fought for against a *Wehrmacht* which has recovered quickly from the loss of its Italian allies and shows no sign of retreating to a defensive line north of the Italian capital. However, a major Allied attack is imminent.

General Mark Clark is anxious to draw off the maximum number of German reserves before the seaborne landings at Anzio planned for 22 January. The Germans have meanwhile established defensive positions at the far end of the Liri valley – in the mountains overlooking Cassino (→ 9).

American troops land on New Guinea taking port and airfield

Saidor, 2 January
Troops of the US Sixth Army today made landings at Saidor, on New Guinea's north coast, cutting off Japanese rearguard forces from the main Japanese base, Madang, only 55 miles (88 km) away. US losses in Operation Dexterity were 55 killed; Japanese casualties were 1,275. The landings signal the long-awaited drive west by forces under General MacArthur to expel the Japanese from New Guinea.

The loss of Saidor, a Japanese supply depot, is a strategic disaster for the Japanese commander, General Adachi. The only escape route for his 20,000 men, now sandwiched between Australian and US units, is a 200-mile (320-km) inland retreat through dangerous, often impassable, jungle (→ 5).

US troops land at Saidor: now the Japanese are cut off from their main base.

Monty changes "Overlord" plan for the invasion

London, 6 January
The master plan for an Allied invasion of north-west Europe, which has been codenamed "Overlord", is being drastically revised after examination by General Montgomery, the ground force commander under General Eisenhower.

The plan was prepared by an Anglo-US team led by a Briton, Lieutenant General Frederick Morgan, the chief of staff to the supreme Allied commander (COSSAC). Because of the lack of landing craft, the assault force to be put ashore in Normandy was put at only three divisions. They would land north of Caen and, after consolidating the beach-head, swing north-west to capture the port of Cherbourg. Each flank of the landing force would be protected by an airborne division. Two seaborne divisions would follow as immediate reinforcements, leading to a build-up of 18 divisions.

In Churchill's view, an operation on such a limited scale could be mounted only if German forces in France were held down to 12 mobile divisions and enemy fighter strength was reduced.

On first seeing the COSSAC plan, Montgomery said that the Germans would have no difficulty in containing such a small landing area, and severe congestion would follow when reinforcements were brought in. He took his objections to Eisenhower, who agreed with him.

In three days this week at St Paul's school – his old school in West London – his 21st Army Group HQ, Montgomery hammered out a plan for five divisions to land on a 50-mile (80-km) front from the river Orne to the Cherbourg peninsula. A third airborne division will join the two already assigned to flank protection. The new plan calls for a greatly expanded force of landing craft, so D-Day will be delayed for a month, to the end of May (→ 16).

1944

January

Su	Mo	Tu	We	Th	Fr	Sa
						1
2	3	4	5	6	7	8
9	10	11	12	13	14	15
16	17	18	19	20	21	22
23	24	25	26	27	28	29
30	31					

9. New Britain: Australian forces secure the Aogiri Ridge in the face of a stubborn Japanese defence (→ 16).

9. Italy: US troops launch a final assault on the German winter line, striking at Cervaro and Monte Trocchio.→

9. Lyons: The shooting of two German soldiers is swiftly avenged by the execution of 22 Frenchmen (→ 11).

10. USSR: Soviet troops cut the Smela to Kristinovka rail link, and annihilate a Nazi pocket north of Kirovograd (→ 14).

11. Pacific: The British submarine *Tally Ho* sinks the Japanese cruiser *Kuma*.

11. Marshall Islands: US aircraft attack Japanese shipping and military bases on Kwajalein atoll [*see map, page 485*] as part of preparations for an operation to take the islands (→ 22).

11. Lyons: The *Milice* murders Victor Basch, the 84-year-old former president of the Human Rights League.

11. Germany: As part of the strategic bombing of the German aircraft industry, the USAAF raids Brunswick, Aschersleben and Halberstadt; 42 aircraft are lost and 125 damaged (→ 29).

12. Italy: After capturing Cervaro, US forces push forward towards Cassino (→ 17).

12. Loch Ewe, Scotland: The 20 ships of convoy JW-56 sail for Murmansk (→ 22).

13. Burma: Chinese forces destroy Japanese resistance at Yupgang Ga, pushing north across the river Tarung (→ 31).

14. USSR: The Red Army takes Mozyr and Kalinkovichi, near Gomel, and renews attacks around Novgorod to relieve Leningrad (→ 19).

14. Bulgaria: Sofia is to be evacuated after two heavy Allied air raids.

14. France: Saboteurs derail the Pau to Toulouse express train, killing 25 people.

15. New Guinea: Australian troops advance along the Huon Peninsula and take Sio (→ 16).

Allied troops push forward in Burma

A Gurkha soldier goes into action.

New Delhi, 10 January
Lt-Gen William Slim's British Fourteenth Army last night over-ran Maungdaw, the strategically important Burmese port on the Bay of Bengal. The victory was announced today in New Delhi by Mountbatten's recently-established Southeast Asia Command (SEAC).

Despatches from the front report that the Fourteenth Army has opened a limited offensive in the Arakan, and that the success of Maungdaw was the culmination of weeks of infiltration by British and Indian troops. Slim's objectives are to secure the mouth of the Naf river, Maungdaw and Buthidaung before moving southwards with the ultimate aim of capturing Akyab.

The seizure of Maungdaw was preceded by heavy night artillery bombardment, followed by a ground assault from British and Indian troops. The Japanese garrison was forced to withdraw after suffering heavy casualties.

SEAC had been planning Operation Buccaneer, a major amphibious campaign to seize the Andaman Islands. But the combined chiefs of staff decided that the allocation of the assault ships and landing craft needed would jeopardize plans for the invasion of Europe and American operations in the Pacific. Admiral Mountbatten thereupon postponed Buccaneer and released nearly half of his assault shipping for Europe (→ 13).

Roosevelt threatens to outlaw strikes

Washington, 11 January
President Roosevelt in his State of the Union message to Congress today announced some controversial new "win-the-war" proposals. He wants to introduce a national service law which will put every able-bodied man and woman at the service of the government. There are to be some exemptions, but no details of these are available yet.

The point of the law is not so much to increase the armed forces as to "prevent strikes" by giving the government new powers over workers at home. Trade union leaders described the law tonight as "quack medicine". They attacked the "evils inherent" in compulsory labour. And they said that the law would not be effective. They pointed out that strikes in Britain are increasing, despite legal controls over labour; Britain had more strikes in the first nine months of 1943 than in all of 1942.

Russia wants 1919 border with Poland

London, 11 January
The Soviet government has replied to the declaration by the Polish government in exile on relations between the two countries with a note suggesting that the Curzon Line, the frontier proposed by the Allies in 1919, could form the basis of a settlement. This would amount to the annexation of areas of eastern Poland by the Soviet Union (→ 15/2).

Operation Carpetbagger: Allies airlift supplies to resistance

London, 9 January
American and British bombers, seconded from their attacks on German cities, today begin the first full week of Operation Carpetbagger, an extensive campaign to arm the resistance movements of Europe in preparation for the forthcoming invasion. The bombers, their bomb-bays filled with canisters containing Sten guns, ammunition, explosives, mortars and wireless sets, have been parachuting their loads into dropping zones in France, Belgium, the Netherlands and Italy. It is estimated that enough weapons to arm 20,000 fighters have already been dropped to the Resistance. Special orders are sometimes supplied by fast Mosquito bombers a few hours after the request has been placed by radio.

Well-armed "Maquisards" attack a convoy of Axis vehicles in France.

Count Ciano executed by firing squad

Verona, Italy, 11 January
Count Galeazzo Ciano, Mussolini's son-in-law and the former foreign minister, was led in front of a firing squad in the prison here today and shot for treason. Four other Fascist ex-leaders were executed with him and 13 others were sentenced in their absence on 8 January.

Ciano's "crime" was to vote with his fellow-Fascists to oust Mussolini from office last July. Ciano and his wife, Edda, were lured to Bavaria last August by a report that their children were in danger. They had been promised safe conduct to Spain – only to be handed to Italy's new puppet Fascist government. Marshal Emilio de Bono, once one of the *Duce's* staunchest supporters, was also shot (→ 12).

Ciano and Hitler at the Berghof, the Fuhrer's Austrian retreat, in August 1939, when they saw eye to eye.

Churchill meets de Gaulle in Morocco

Marrakesh, 12 January
General de Gaulle flew into Morocco today to meet the British prime minister at the villa where he has been convalescing for a few weeks. Mr Churchill was in fine form, and when de Gaulle asked him if he still painted he replied: "I am too weak for that, but I am strong enough to wage war." The two imperious leaders made jokes at each other's expense but managed to agree on Franco-British co-operation for victory.

'Celanese' makes good use of Coupons

Everything is rationed now – even a little elegance for those all-too-short intimate reunions.

Dissident Japanese call for end to war

Yenan, 15 January
Japanese communists, dissidents and defecting PoWs are meeting here, the headquarters of the Chinese Communists, to form a Japanese People's Liberation League (JPLL). Draft proposals from Nosaka Sanzo, a leading Japanese communist, suggest a moderate democratic socialist line demanding a cessation of hostilities, the sacking of Japan's military elite, punishment of war criminals and free elections.

Britain turns island into navy "frigate"

Tristan da Cunha, 15 January
A new "frigate" was commissioned today, unsinkable and immovable: HMS *Atlantic Isle* is a volcanic island in the South Atlantic called Tristan da Cunha. Until the arrival of a Royal Naval landing party in 1942 to establish a wireless and meteorological station, its population of 200, descendants of British settlers forgotten generations ago, had never seen an aeroplane or a newspaper; their only contact with the 20th century was from the occasional passing whaler. They still amaze the seamen by speaking English like 18th-century sailors.

1944
January

Su	Mo	Tu	We	Th	Fr	Sa
						1
2	3	4	5	6	7	8
9	10	11	12	13	14	15
16	17	18	19	20	21	22
23	24	25	26	27	28	29
30	31					

16. New Guinea: Australian troops capture Finisterre (→ 23).

16. New Britain: Japan counter-attacks US forces in the Hill 660 sector (→ 17).

16. Britain: Eisenhower formally takes up the position of supreme C-in-C of the Allied invasion force (→ 17).

17. New Britain: Japanese resistance at Arawe ends (→ 24).

17. Melbourne: Meat rationing is introduced in Australia.

17. Italy: The British X Corps launches Operation Panther, an assault across the river Garigliano (→ 19).

17. London: Eisenhower appoints General Omar N Bradley to command the US Army in the field under him (→ 21).

19. Italy: British forces establish bridgeheads on the north side of the Garigliano.

19. Italy: Minturno falls to the US Fifth Army, which now attempts to cross the heavily-defended Rapido river.→

19. USSR: Soviet troops take Novgorod, and push on to Estonia.→

20. USSR: Soviet troops advancing south-west from Pulkovo and south-east from Oranienbaum join up, encircling the Germans around Leningrad and sealing off the corridor to Finland (→ 22).

20. English Channel: British coastal guns sink the German blockade-runner *Munsterland*.

21. London: Eisenhower holds a first meeting with his commanders to plan the Allied invasion of France (→ 1/2).

22. Pacific: The US invasion fleet ("Galvanic" Assault Force) sails for the Marshall Islands, opening Operation Flintlock, which aims at their capture (→ 31).

22. USSR: Soviet forces surround the Germans at Vitebsk (→ 24).

22. Rome: Allied aircraft drop millions of leaflets announcing that liberation is nigh.→

22. Loch Ewe, Scotland: Convoy JW-56B sails for Murmansk (→ 26).

"Bevin Boys" start training in the pits

Britain, 18 January
The first batch of 600 young recruits to the mines, known as "Bevin Boys" after the labour minister, Ernest Bevin, began training today. Their names were picked by ballot on 14 December and they are now under training by experienced miners. Those who have been taken down below said it was not as bad as they expected. They are being paid £2/10/6 (£2.52$^{1}/_{2}$p/$10.18) a week, but say that after deductions have been made for hostel lodgings, meals, laundry, insurance and transport to the pit, they are left with only 3/6 (17$^{1}/_{2}$p/71¢).

"Bevin Boys" getting fit for the pit.

Allies cross Italian river under gunfire

Italy, 19 January
Backed by naval gunfire, troops of the British X Corps led by General Richard McCreery have crossed the lower Garigliano river in landing craft and established vital bridgeheads on the northern bank. The town of Minturno also fell today, and further inland the 56th Division has succeeded in crossing the Rapido; however, fierce German fire has stopped a further assault by the 46th Division. The German commander, General von Vietinghoff, is transferring two armoured divisions to face this new threat (→ 22).

▷

Allied forces land at Anzio and set up beach-head

A handful of German prisoners awaits orders on a quiet sunny beach at Anzio.

A British Sherman tank comes ashore: it has not seen much action yet.

Anzio, 22 January
Midnight. In the inky blackness, British and American troops of VI Corps, taking part in Operation Shingle, boarded landing craft from a convoy of 243 ships that arrived off this small port on the Tyrrhenian Sea tonight. Heavy opposition was expected when the landing craft hit the beaches. The US commander, Major-General John Lucas, was gloomy about the whole affair. "I feel like a lamb being led to slaughter," he wrote 13 days ago after a meeting with the supreme commander, General Alexander.

Yet there was no slaughter when the Allied army came ashore.

Anzio is deserted, a ghost town; the inhabitants have been evacuated; there were no defenders. The German high command has been totally wrongfooted. As evening fell on Anzio tonight, nearly 50,000 men and 3,000 vehicles have landed with the loss of 13 men, mostly from mines. The road to Rome, 32 miles (51 km) to the north, is open. Intelligence reports that there are few, if any, German defenders on the route.

But with the memory of the near-debacle at Salerno still fresh in his mind, Lucas is determined to build up his beach-head defences before venturing forth. He had calculated

on a rugged defence, and has ordered his army to dig in to fight off counter-attacks.

Lucas's commander, General Mark Clark, arrived here this evening with General Alexander. The British commander is all for pushing forward with strong mobile forces. Clark has advised Lucas not to "stick his neck out". Winston Churchill, ever an enthusiast for this invasion, has cabled Alexander to say: "Am very glad you are pegging out claims rather than digging in." Lucas has established his headquarters in an underground wine cellar and shows no sign of pegging out claims (→ 23).

Australia signs pact with New Zealand

Canberra, 21 January
After a week of talks here the prime ministers of Australia and New Zealand have today signed the Australian-New Zealand pact. Australia's leader, Mr John Curtin, described the agreement as a landmark in international collaboration in the Pacific.

The text of the pact will not be published until it is formally ratified, but it covers the establishment of a regional defence zone in the South-west Pacific, cooperation in the war effort and agreement of armistice terms.

RAF stages heaviest raid yet on Berlin

Berlin, 21 January
In half an hour over Berlin, 769 Lancasters and Halifaxes last night dropped over 2,300 tons of bombs on the city. It was the heaviest blow yet directed at Hitler's capital, with bombs falling at 80 tons a minute. The city was covered by cloud and the effects of the raid are not yet clear; however, the main railway line to Hamburg was cut and a factory making radar for the *Luftwaffe* was destroyed. One plane dropped its bombs 30 miles (48 km) from the city, by chance wrecking a factory of the Todt Organization. The raid took place in the early evening. German radio stations went off the

air soon after six o'clock and came back some two hours later. But the RAF still lost 35 planes and 172 aircrew; 243 Berliners died.

In 11 major attacks on the city since the "Battle of Berlin" began on 18 November, the RAF has dropped 17,000 tons of bombs. Some 1,300 acres of buildings, equal to twice the area of Hyde Park and Kensington Gardens in London, have been destroyed. Despite the damage the results of this sustained onslaught are not as great as the RAF expected on either German morale or production – and its own losses are becoming unacceptably high (→ 9/2).

Germans arrest all Danish policemen

Copenhagen, 19 January
Early today, German military patrols swept through the deserted streets of Copenhagen, occupied all the city's police stations and disarmed and arrested the entire police force. The move, ordered by SS Lt-Gen Gunther Pancke, followed the capture by a German patrol vessel of a boatload of refugees fleeing to Sweden. The Germans believe that the Danish police have been aiding the escape of wanted Danes. Last week, the chief of the police passport department and his assistant fled to Sweden to escape arrest.

1944

January

Su	Mo	Tu	We	Th	Fr	Sa
						1
2	3	4	5	6	7	8
9	10	11	12	13	14	15
16	17	18	19	20	21	22
23	24	25	26	27	28	29
30	31					

Red Army breaches Leningrad siege line

A Russian photograph shows a Lenigrad square under enemy fire.

Leningrad, 19 January
After its stunning victories in the Ukraine the Red Army has turned its attention to the besieged city of Leningrad. In a coordinated offensive by the garrison troops and the armies of the Volkhov front, the Russians have torn a 25-mile (40-km) gap in the German siege lines.

In doing do they have smashed seven enemy divisions and captured 37 of the long-range guns which had been systematically bombarding the city in an attempt to fulfil Hitler's threat to destroy it when it was first besieged in September 1941. Tonight the Germans are reeling back from the beleaguered city. Columns of grim-faced Russian soldiers swing through its battered streets, heading south to Krasnoye Selo or out across the ice of Kronstadt Bay to Oranienbaum where a pocket of Russians has held out since the first days of the siege.

This pocket was reinforced in great secrecy before the battle opened a week ago. Men of the Second Shock Army were ferried in by boat at night. They hid by day, and when they came storming out they took the Germans by surprise (→ 20).

January 20. Air Chief Marshal Tedder watches a tank crew in action; he has been appointed deputy supreme commander to Eisenhower.

23. Anzio: 50,000 Allied troops have been landed on the beach-head; at dusk, a German air attack sinks the British destroyer *Janus* and damages her sister ship, the *Jervis* (→ 24).

24. New Britain: Over 200 US aircraft raid Rabaul, destroying 83 Japanese planes – one of many such raids which are being launched by the four carrier groups now at the disposal of the US Admiral Spruance (→ 15/2).

24. Anzio: *Luftwaffe* aircraft attack and sink the British hospital ship *St David*; Allied troops pause, giving Germany time to bring up reinforcements (→ 26).

24. USSR: The Red Army captures Pushkin and Pashovsk, and launches a major new offensive in the Ukraine (→ 25).

25. USSR: The Red Army captures the railway junction at Krasnogvardeysk, south-west of Leningrad. →

26. Off Iceland: Ten U-boats attack convoy JW-56A, sinking three merchant ships (→ 28/2).

26. Italy: Martial law is proclaimed in Rome (→ 30).

27. London: Churchill lays down two priorities for Bomber Command: first, to bomb targets on the continent, and second, to drop supplies to resistance fighters.

29. USSR: Soviet forces clear the important railway line between Moscow and Leningrad (→ 2).

29. Frankfurt: Seven hundred and sixty-three US bombers kill over 700 civilians; 29 planes are lost (→ 24/2).

29. Italy: A glider bomb sinks the cruiser HMS *Spartan*.

29. USSR: General Model replaces Field Marshal von Kuchler as commander of Germany's Army Group North.

30. Italy: USAAF aircraft attack *Luftwaffe* targets in the Po valley.→

31. Burma: Chinese forces capture Taro (→ 1).

Allies protest about Japanese atrocities

London, 28 January
Official statements concerning the sickening cruelty of the Japanese towards prisoners of war were made today in Britain and the United States. The British foreign secretary, Anthony Eden, said: "Let the Japanese government reflect in time to come that the record of their military authorities in this war will not be forgotten." The House of Commons and both houses of Congress heard blood-curdling accounts of the inhuman conditions the prisoners are kept in – without sufficient food, water or shelter – and barbarous tortures used by guards.

A Japanese guard poised to thrust his bayonet into a live Chinese PoW.

Argentina breaks ties with the Axis

Argentina, 26 January
The news that Argentina has severed relations with Germany and Japan brought cheering crowds out on to the streets of Buenos Aires today. President Ramirez signed the decree just after 8am, making his country the 21st American republic to turn against the Axis. This follows the uncovering of a vast enemy spy network in Argentina involving high-society figures. Many arrests have already been made. But diplomatic sources in neighbouring Chile see the move as no more than a practical expedient to avoid a break with the United States.

Red Army breaks siege of Leningrad

"Little Blitz" hits southern England as bombers return

Leningrad, 27 January
The siege of Leningrad has been broken after an ordeal by starvation, bombing and shelling which lasted for 872 days and took the lives of over a million people. The news was announced by General Govorov, the planner and commander of the onslaught which drove the Germans away from the beleaguered city. In an order of the day he announced: "The city of Leningrad has been completely freed from the enemy blockade and the barbaric artillery shelling."

Addressing his troops, sailors of the Baltic fleet and "workers of the city of Lenin", Govorov said that in 12 days' fighting the Red Army had liberated 700 places and driven back the Germans along the whole front for 40 to 60 miles (64-96 km).

Leningrad has suffered grievous damage. Many of its fine buildings have been destroyed by the Stukas and long-range guns. In the occupied southern suburbs the retreating Germans looted and set fire to buildings, and left the bodies of partisans hanging from the trees.

As the sound of gunfire faded from the city for the first time for nearly two and a half years, the people, gaunt and tired, emerged from their shelters to celebrate in the unusual safety of the streets.

A white advance for the Red Army as it nears the German defence zone.

They are the true victors of the siege. They withstood everything that the Germans threw at them. They watched their families die of starvation. They ate bread made of sawdust. Some even ate the dead. One million citizens died, mainly from hunger, along with 150,000 troops. But their city has become an example to the world that Hitler's military might could be defied.

Now, as they celebrate their release, their liberators are rushing on to the west in great strength, outnumbering Field Marshal von Kuchler's weakened Army Group North in men, arms and aircraft.

The Red Army is now approaching the German defence zone codenamed "Panther", which runs south from the Gulf of Finland, along the river Narva and the banks of Lakes Peipus and Pskovskoye, to the town of Ostrov. Hitler thinks the "Northern Wall" is impregnable: that remains to be seen (→ 29).

London, 31 January
London and south-east England have been hit by the *Luftwaffe* for the first time for months in a series of night raids, codenamed Operation *Steinbock* [Ibex], which began on 21-22 January. The usefulness of this "Little Blitz" to Germany's propaganda machine – as an antidote to constant RAF assaults on the *Reich* – is worth the cost; up to eight aircraft lost in a single raid. On the first raid 447 *sorties* were flown (the planes including He177 heavy bombers), during which only 32 tons of bombs were dropped for the loss of nine planes.

The total number of bombers involved is thus fewer than the 600 claimed by Germany (an RAF assessment is 200), but the raids seem to confirm intelligence reports that the Germans are still building aircraft at a rate which makes good their losses. If confirmed, such a situation would cast doubt on the belief of Sir Arthur Harris, the head of RAF Bomber Command, that strategic bombing alone will end the war. This claim is also under fire after the heavy losses which the RAF has suffered (as well as inflicted) in the raids on Berlin.

The face of the "Radio Doctor", Dr Charles Hill, who dispenses medical advice to the nation: his voice is known to millions from his regular slot with the BBC.

Australians clear Japanese from "Shaggy Ridge" in New Guinea

New Guinea, 26 January
In heavy fighting, veteran Australian troops have cleared the Japanese from strategic "Shaggy Ridge", in New Guinea's rugged Finisterre range. After the fall of Lae, the Australians – part of 18 Infantry Brigade of 7th Division – set out to clear the enemy from the Huon Gulf area as part of the campaign to crush Japanese resistance in the South-west Pacific.

The "diggers", patrolling in the foothills of the Finisterres, encountered Japanese entrenched in strong defensive positions. In late December the Australians assaulted the southern slopes of "Shaggy Ridge" and took the "Pimple". From 17 January, backed by heavy RAAF raids, the Australians advanced along the razor backs. Today the enemy finally broke (→ 10/2).

Australian troops start to dig in on the newly-captured "Shaggy Ridge".

Allied forces attack Marshall Islands

Pacific, 31 January
The American conquest of the central Pacific continued today when a powerful US amphibious force assaulted the Marshall Islands. The American force included 297 ships, 700 carrier-based and 475 land-based aircraft in support of 54,000 marines and soldiers.

Attacks by land-based aircraft from Tarawa and Makin, in the Gilbert Islands, had heavily damaged Japanese airfields, and most of the remaining aircraft were destroyed or put out of action by carrier raids earlier this month. Then, for three days before the landings, US battleships blasted the islands on each side of Kwajalein atoll.

Three assault groups struck today, and by 9.30am Majuro was secured without the loss of a single man. Tricky approaches through gaps in the coral reefs made the

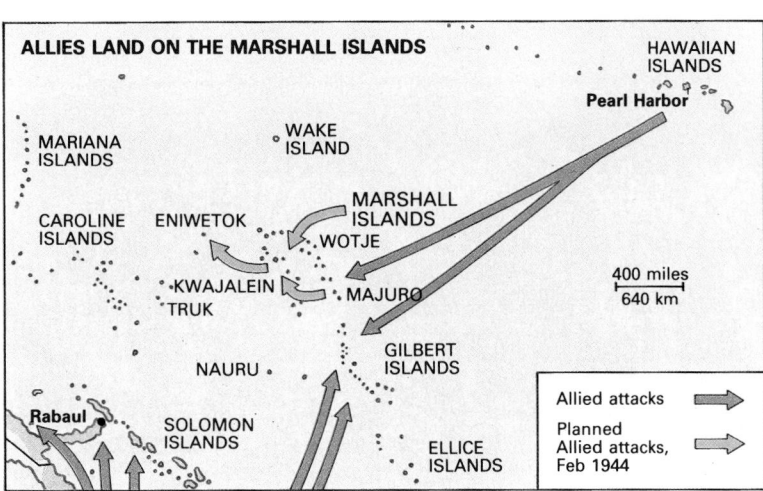

ALLIES LAND ON THE MARSHALL ISLANDS

landings more difficult at Roi and Namur Islands where the 4th Marine Division attacked. The Japanese combined fleet at Truk [*see map*], lacking carrier pilots, could only look on helplessly. On Kwajalein some 3,000 Japanese had survived the preliminary bombardment. They made attempts to push the invaders back into the ocean, but soon found themselves hopelessly outnumbered (→2/2).

"Superfortress" bombers to reinforce Allied air war in Pacific

Japanese shipping at Rabaul takes a hammering from Allied aircraft.

Pacific, 31 January
Despite the agreement between Britain and the US to give priority to the war against Hitler, a large proportion of the bombers, fighters and transport aircraft pouring from US factories is finding its way into combat squadrons assigned to the Pacific War, where Allied air power is now completely dominant.

A marked Japanese air weakness has developed, especially at sea as a result of the Japanese navy not only losing a large proportion of its fleet aircraft but also, and even more significantly, too many expertly-trained pilots. Japan's aircraft factories cannot match US production. The new American B-29 "Superfortress" bombers now flowing from the factories are to be assigned to the war against Japan.

German troops pin down Allies at the Anzio beach-head

Anzio, 31 January
Swift German reaction to the Anzio landing is threatening to turn the tables completely on the huge Allied army which landed here nine days ago. The element of surprise has gone. Instead of the dash to Rome, activity has been limited to cautious attacks with heavy Allied casualties. Field Marshal Kesselring has now pulled reserves from all over Italy to ring the beach-head.

US Rangers waded four miles (6.4 km) in darkness along a half-dry irrigation canal to attack the village of Cisterna, but were detected at the last moment and came under withering tank fire. Only six men survived. The British 24 Guards Brigade met stiff resistance on the night of 29-30 January at the small hamlet of Carroceto, where the 29th *Panzergrenadier* Regiment was dug in and waiting; and the Sherwood Foresters have suffered huge casualties in an assault on Campoleone (→1/2).

Taking cover from German snipers.

Russia blames Nazis for Katyn massacre

Moscow, 26 January
Russia today replied to German accusations that it was responsible for the murder of thousands of Polish officers in Katyn forest by charging the Germans with the massacre of the Poles. According to the findings of a special atrocity commission, the Poles were still alive when the Germans took over the area in July 1941. The German accusations led to the breakdown in relations between the Polish government based in London and the Soviet government, a situation which has become even more sensitive as the Red Army advances ever deeper into Poland.

German sentenced to death for espionage

London, 26 January
An Old Bailey jury today found 58-year-old Oswald Job guilty of espionage, and he was sentenced to death. Job was born in Stepney of German parents and moved to Paris in 1911. In 1940, as a British passport holder, he was interned by the Nazis. The German secret service recruited him from prison, and he returned to England posing as an escapee. From his room in Bayswater he wrote letters to PoWs, with invasion plans in invisible ink between the lines. The British authorities became aware of his activities thanks to the work of a double agent codenamed "Dragonfly".

1944

February

Su	Mo	Tu	We	Th	Fr	Sa
		1	2	3	4	5
6	7	8	9	10	11	12
13	14	15	16	17	18	19
20	21	22	23	24	25	26
27	28					

1. Burma: The Chinese 38th Division attacks Japanese positions at Taihapa Ga.→

1. Warsaw: Polish partisans assassinate the local *Gestapo* chief, SS Major-General Franz Kutschera (→ 2).

1. Anzio: US 3rd Division troops give up their assault on Cisterna (→ 3).

2. Marshall Islands: US forces complete the occupation of Roi and Namur Islands; Japanese casualties include 3,742 killed, against 190 US dead (→ 3).

2. Warsaw: In retaliation for yesterday's shooting of the *Gestapo* chief Franz Kutschera, the German authorities execute 100 Poles.

2. USSR: The Red Army advances across the Estonian border, capturing Vanakula.

2. Moscow: Stalin agrees to allow US aircraft to use six Soviet air bases for the shuttle bombing of Europe (→ 3).

3. Marshall Islands: US forces bombard Eniwetok Atoll and land on Burton Island.→

3. Italy: The New Zealand Corps, consisting of the 2nd New Zealand Division, and the 4th Indian Division under the command of Lt-Gen Sir Bernard Freyberg joins the US Fifth Army in the Cassino sector.→

3. USSR: The encirclement of 60,000 Germans troops in the Korsun pocket, south of Kiev, is announced and celebrated in Moscow.→

4. Pacific: The US Navy bombards Paramushiro, one of the Kurile Islands, in Japanese home waters.

5. USSR: The Red Army occupies Gdov, reaching Lake Peipus in the north.

5. USSR: Soviet forces occupy Rovno and Lutsk, in eastern Poland: they are now 50 miles from Brest-Litovsk (→ 7).

5. France: Michel Hollard, the British agent who has spied on the German V-bomb programme, is arrested by the *Gestapo*.

5. Italy: The Germans repel US attempts to capture Monte Cassino and Sant'Angelo (→ 12).

Germans begin to counter-attack in Italy

US troops on their way to reinforce the hard-pressed beach-head at Anzio.

Anzio, 3 February
Hitler has ordered that the Anzio beach-head "must be crushed in the blood of British soldiers". As dusk fell last night those soldiers were suffering a massive artillery barrage as the German Fourteenth Army prepared a full-scale counter-attack on the British salient.

Every German gun was trained on the "thumb" created by the British 1st Division on 30 January in an abortive attempt to reach Campoleone. "Anzio Annie", a 14-inch railway gun, was used to devastating effect. However, the Germans' latest secret weapon – "Goliath", a radio-controlled miniature tank packed with explosives – failed under small-arms fire.

By mid-morning the "thumb" was nearly severed. Over 1,400 men had been lost. The Germans suffered similar losses, but show no sign of letting up. Today the British VI Corps issued verbal orders to beach-head forces to prepare defensive positions (→ 5).

Resistance fighters plan a united front

France, 1 February
After months of political squabbling, French Resistance leaders have taken a major step towards creating a more efficient and unified organization to fight the German occupying forces. A newly-formed central committee, known as COMIDAC, will liaise between the French Forces of the Interior (FFI) and the National Resistance Committee (CNR) created by Jean Moulin in 1943. Two members of the new body represent all the factions within the Resistance.

COMIDAC's charter, which was approved today, defines its role as being a centralized command for all the armed forces of the Resistance – including communists, Gaullists and others who have been fighting independently of each other. This action committee is more appropriate for setting up clandestine operations on short notice than was the FFI command structure.

However, the move has not been welcomed by the Central Intelligence and Military Action Bureaux based in London, or by the Algiers-based General Intelligence Directorate. These groups see the decision as a new sign of the desire of the internal Resistance movements for more independence (→ 8).

Indian division comes under attack from Japanese in Burma

Arakan, Burma, 4 February
The British XV Corps' offensive in the Arakan has ground to a halt, with the veteran Japanese 55th Division making an attack on Taung Bazaar in the British rear. This evening the Japanese counter-attack (Operation *Ha-Go*) made its first contact with the British 7th Indian Division, led by Major-General Frank Messervy, in the Ngakyedauk Pass.

Since early December the British have been advancing down the Arakan towards Akyab, a vital airfield for any attack on Rangoon, but at the Maungdaw to Buthidaung road they were confronted by defences consisting of impenetrable tunnel systems. Now, with their rear threatened, the British risk a repeat of last year's defeat in the Arakan peninsula (→ 6).

A Japanese sentry guards a bridge blown up by retreating British forces.

American forces take Pacific staging post

The Stars and Stripes fly over a ruined Japanese HQ in the Marshall Islands.

Kwajalein, 4 February
After four days of fierce fighting against Japanese troops prepared to fight to the death rather than surrender, US forces have captured all the main atolls in the Marshall Islands, securing a strategic staging post for future Allied offensives in the central Pacific.

The Japanese-mandated islands, an important defensive link in Japan's Pacific perimeter [*see map, page 485*], are the first territory in the Japanese empire to fall to the Allies. Their loss was reported to the Japanese imperial *Diet* by the premier, General Tojo. He said: "The war situation is increasing in gravity day by day. For the first time, the enemy has really attacked Japanese soil."

The landings four days ago by 40,000 US infantry and marines on the three main islands of Kwajalein atoll – Kwajalein, Roi and Namur – were the largest operation yet staged by the Allies in the Pacific. Namur and Roi fell within two days. But mopping-up operations are still going on against a Japanese garrison holding out in a 400-yard stretch in the north-east of Kwajalein, where US troops of Major-General Charles Corlett's 7th Division now control 80 islands in the 60-mile (96-km)-long atoll.

Although outnumbered, the Japanese have fought to the death. On Namur and Roi 3,742 were killed and only 91 taken prisoner. US casualties were 737, including 190 dead. On Kwajalein 7,870 of the 8,000-strong garrison died; US losses were 372. Roi puts the Allies within bomber range of the Japanese naval base at Truk (→ 17).

Bogus army and false landings invented by Allied chiefs to confuse the Germans

London, 1 February
The Germans are eagerly monitoring the activities of the 1st US Army Group, stationed in Yorkshire and Norfolk. They have identified the training grounds, orders of battle and the invasion target – Calais, directly across the Channel.

There is just one problem. The 1st US Army Group does not exist. Like the Twelfth British Army, it is a phantom army created by the British and Americans to mislead the enemy as to where the landing in Europe will really be made.

Other bogus plans, passed on by a German agent who has been turned to work for the Allies, include Operation Fortitude North (an assault on Norway); Graffham (on Sweden); Zeppelin (on the Black Sea coast of Roumania). A tricky one for the enemy is Operation Royal Flush: the map that has fallen into their hands could be of the coastline of Sweden, Spain or Turkey. These elaborate deceptions have led the Germans to scatter their armies across Europe to cover the "threatened" invasion points.

A genuine intelligence success has left the Germans grinding their teeth with frustration. They monitored a Churchill and Roosevelt telephone conversation on some forthcoming military operation. It ended, with the Germans none the wiser about the subject, when Roosevelt said: "Well, we'll do our best. Now I'm going fishing" (→ 29).

The men responsible for the fake plans and for the real one: Allied supreme commanders line up for the camera, but Monty is anxious to get back to work.

Suit pockets and turn-ups are back

Britain, 1 February
After two years of suits without pockets and trousers without turn-ups, followers of fashion can go to the tailor today and order whatever fripperies their hearts desire. Mr Hillier, the secretary of the Bespoke Tailors' Guild, said today: "Popular opinion has killed the austerity suit. Nobody liked it." The limits on pleats and buttons on women's clothes are also removed.

German industry promised French labour

France, 2 February
The Vichy France leader, Pierre Laval, has agreed to extend the age limits of French workers liable for forced labour in Germany, it was reported today. Any male between 16 and 60 may find himself deported; and any childless female between 18 and 45 will also be liable.

Under the compulsory work service code which has been in effect since 1943, Laval is obliged to send one million men to the factories in the *Reich* by June. The new agreement has been signed with Fritz Sauckel, the *Reich* plenipotentiary for the allocation of labour. The development thwarts plans by Albert Speer, the Reich minister of armaments and war production, who wants to stop the recruitment of French workers and sees more profit in using French factories for the production of all consumer goods and weapons. Speer has forbidden the deportation of workers from factories in an order named *Speerbetriebe* (→ 1/3).

Moscow celebrates Red Army advances

Moscow, 3 February
Victory salvoes are crashing out in Moscow as the Russians celebrate victories all along the front. In a special order of the day Stalin has announced the trapping of ten German divisions in the Dnieper Bend in the biggest encirclement since Stalingrad. Meanwhile, in the north, General Govorov's troops have crossed the Estonian border in their great Leningrad offensive (→ 5).

1944

February

Su	Mo	Tu	We	Th	Fr	Sa
		1	2	3	4	5
6	7	8	9	10	11	12
13	14	15	16	17	18	19
20	21	22	23	24	25	26
27	28					

6. Burma: Major-General Orde Wingate leads a special force of Indian, British and US soldiers to engage the Japanese at Myitkyina (→ 10).

7. USSR: Hitler orders German troops trapped in the Korsun pocket to break out (→ 8).

8. USSR: The Third Ukrainian Front captures Nikopol, a vital centre of manganese production (→ 9).

9. France: Twelve Lancasters of 617 ("Dambusters") Squadron, led by Wing-Commander Leonard Cheshire, last night devastated the important Gnome and Rhone aero-engine factory at Limoges with 12,000-lb bombs, the heaviest of the war so far (→ 18).

9. Britain: The king and queen eat a 1/- (5p/20¢) lunch with Yorkshire miners and declare "It is a long time since we had a better meal."

9. USSR: Generals Malinovsky and Konev start to wipe out the German Eighth Army at Kirovograd.→

10. Caroline Islands: Japanese naval forces abandon Truk (→ 18).

10. Burma: Japanese troops take the Ngakyedauk Pass, cutting off the 7th Indian Division at Sinzweya (→ 18).

10. New Guinea: Australians from Sio link up with the Americans near Saidor (→ 29).

12. Indian Ocean: The Japanese submarine I-27 sinks the British troopship *Khedive Ismail*, killing nearly 2,000 people, and is herself sunk by the destroyers *Petard* and *Paladin*.

12. Anzio: The Allies have been forced back three miles, to their final defensive line.

12. Monte Cassino: Fierce opposition stops the US 34th Division less than 300 yards (270 metres) short of Cassino town.→

12. Rastenburg: Hitler merges the *Abwehr* [military intelligence] with Himmler's SD (*Sicherheitsdienst*) [Security Service] and *Gestapo*, after members are arrested for plotting against him.

Churchill angry over deadlock at Anzio

Anzio, 12 February

Back in London Churchill fumes: "We hurled a wildcat on the shores of Anzio – all we have is a stranded whale." The prime minister is livid that there are 18,000 vehicles in Anzio for 72,000 men – and yet no sign of the promised breakout.

Constant German attacks have put the beach-head on the defensive, and now the roles on two fronts are reversed. The Anzio landings were designed to break the deadlock at Cassino. Now attacks there are to be stepped up in an attempt to break through to Anzio.

Here on the beach-head, morale has reached its lowest ebb. General von Mackensen's Fourteenth Army is being reinforced almost daily, so that it will soon have ten divisions to confront the Allies' five. Although the main counter-offensive is yet to begin, German attacks on the beach-head have already pushed the Allies back towards the sea. The heavily-reinforced *Luftwaffe* is joining the attack on the beleaguered Allies.

War correspondents have been summoned to headquarters to be told that all news transmissions from the beach-head have been banned. One despatch happened to mention the possibility of evacuation, raising the unwelcome spectre of another Dunkirk.

No one can ban German leaflets that tell British soldiers: "The Yanks in England ... have loads of money and loads of time to chase after your women." The lurid pictures of naked women are becoming collectors' items, however (→ 15).

Caught in the crossfire: Italians with rags for shoes flee from Cassino.

Corruption charge by Bevan rejected

Aneurin Bevan makes his point.

Britain, 11 February

Anthony Eden, the foreign secretary, speaking as leader of the House of Commons, today denied allegations made yesterday by Aneurin Bevan, the fiery Welsh Labour MP, that the government is guilty of corruption in putting many MPs on the state payroll with jobs outside parliament. As a wartime measure the prime minister can exempt MPs from having to give up their Commons seats if they accept "offices of profit under the crown". Mr Bevan accused Mr Churchill of issuing such exemptions "like confetti" and thus buying parliamentary support. Many MPs have taken emergency jobs ranging from ambassadorships to posts on obscure public bodies. The government denied impropriety, but promised to review the system.

Guernsey arrest highlights plight of occupied Channel Islands

Channel Islands, 12 February

The weekly edition of G.U.N.S, Guernsey's underground newssheet, was running off the duplicating machine yesterday when *Gestapo* agents burst into a back room in the island's capital of St Peter Port. The paper's founder, Charles Machon, was arrested and will be tried before a German court which is likely to sentence him – and four others also held – to prison in France or Germany. Machon's arrest (and probable torture) highlights the dangers faced by people resisting Nazi rule in the Channel Islands – the only part of the United Kingdom subjected to German occupation.

Savage sentences are imposed on islanders found with radio sets, for instance. Stanley Green, a cinema projectionist, is in Buchenwald; a fellow Jerseyman, Harold Druillenec, in Belsen; and a rector who hid his radio in the organ loft is feared to be dying in a concentration camp at Spergau.

The islands are near to starvation, with the population living on a diet consisting mainly of turnips and other root vegetables. Yet relations between occupiers and occupied are mostly "correct", with the older islanders angered by liaisons between local girls and Germans.

Helsinki is bombed by Russian planes

Helsinki, 7 February
The Soviet air force raided the Finnish capital last night, inflicting the worst pounding Helsinki has suffered since 1941. The attacks, by 200 planes, were concentrated on the airfield at Malm, but incendiaries caused many fires in residential districts.

The attack is regarded here as the opening of a Russian bid to force Finland to sue for peace now that the siege of Leningrad has been lifted and the Red Army is advancing along the Baltic. But Tass, the Soviet news agency, denies that peace negotiations are already in progress between Russia and Finland (→ 16).

Britain signs an aid treaty with France

Algiers, 8 February
Two key agreements between the British government and the French Committee of National Liberation were signed at a villa on the outskirts of Algiers today. One provides for mutual assistance in the war effort, free of cost on both sides. The other establishes a common rate of exchange of 200 *francs* to the pound in all parts of the French empire. This will make it possible for something like normal trading to be resumed between the French territories (→ 11/3).

A Vichy-French poster accuses the Allies of dropping the first bombs.

Bishop protests against "immoral raids"

Westminster, 9 February
The bishop of Chichester, Dr George Bell, speaking in the House of Lords today, questioned the morality of the RAF's policy of area bombing. He said he was not forgetting Warsaw or Coventry; his concern was whether the government understood what area bombing was destroying now.

It was not only the vast material damage, much of it irreparable, but also the implications for the future relationships of the people of Europe, as well as morality. Speaking of Berlin, he added: "Men and women have been overwhelmed in a tornado of smoke and flames. It is said that 74,000 persons have been killed. The policy is obliter-

ation openly acknowledged. That is not a justifiable act of war."

He referred to Air Chief Marshal Sir Arthur Harris's threat to bomb Berlin until "the heart of Nazi Germany ceases to beat", and argued that "to justify methods inhumane in themselves by arguments of expediency smacks of the Nazi philosophy that might is right".

The bishop's qualms are doubtless shared by many but will carry little weight in the context of total war. In reply to Dr Bell, Viscount Cranborne, the secretary of state for the Dominions, denied that the RAF indulged in terror raids. He said Britain would continue bombing "with more crushing effect until final victory is secure".

Pursuing a policy of devastation: Bomber Command assesses the damage.

Doubts stir over whether bombing works

London, 9 February
The unease expressed by the bishop of Chichester about the RAF's policy of area bombing [*report above*] has raised questions about the effectiveness of the campaign as well as its morality. Air Chief Marshal Sir Arthur Harris's view that strategic bombing will bring about the downfall of Germany without the need for a costly invasion of Europe is well known. But is it correct?

Area bombing, such as the great firestorm of Hamburg last July, which killed 42,000 people, is known to have affected worker morale and industrial output seriously in the days immediately following the raids. But the Germans

are resilient people; they soon recover, and in the case of Hamburg only 50 working days were lost.

In fact, because of the efforts of Albert Speer, the armaments minister, production of weapons in Germany is steadily rising. Tank production had increased from 760 a month at the beginning of 1943 to 1,229 in December, while the production of aircraft rose from 15,288 in 1942 to 25,094 in 1943.

Perhaps the main achievement of Bomber Command's valiant effort has been the massive diversion of German resources to the air defence of the *Reich*, which has deprived the *Wehrmacht* in Russia and Italy of vital air support (→ 15).

Red Army advances on the Baltic front

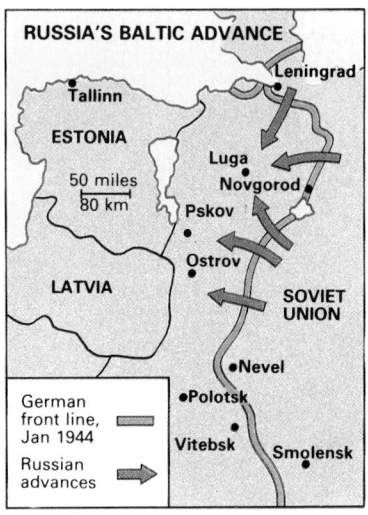

Leningrad, 12 February
The Red Army is maintaining its advance in the Baltic region despite stiffening resistance from the Germans. Hitler has sacked Field Marshal von Kuchler, replaced him with the tough tank expert General Model and rushed in reinforcements to hold the line.

Nevertheless, the Second Shock Army has stormed Kingisepp and reached Narva, on the Gulf of Finland. The town of Luga, 85 miles (136 km) south of Leningrad, was reached today and the Russians are heading for Pskov. If their advance continues they will soon be facing the Germans all along the "Panther" fortifications which bar their road to the Baltic states (→ 13).

Nazis wage war on "jazz perversion"

Germany, 12 February
Those swinging tunes from New Orleans that caused such uproar over 20 years ago when they first filled clubs across Europe are still incensing the German authorities. One National Socialist has written to Alfred Rosenberg, the head of the party's foreign affairs department, demanding that "war" be waged against jazz and other "un-German" influences. Nazi music critics are already waging a war of words, describing jazz as an "interminable knee-buckling perversion" and "an irreverence appealing to the lowest instincts of the masses".

1944

February

Su	Mo	Tu	We	Th	Fr	Sa
		1	2	3	4	5
6	7	8	9	10	11	12
13	14	15	16	17	18	19
20	21	22	23	24	25	26
27	28					

13. USSR: Soviet forces liberate Luga, Lyady and Polna, in the north (→ 14).

14. Malacca Straits: A German-crewed ex-Italian submarine, It-23, is sunk by the submarine HMS *Tally Ho*.

14. USSR: Soviet troops enter the Korsun pocket, meeting strong resistance from the Germans trapped inside (→ 16).

15. Solomon Islands: New Zealand and US forces land in the Green Islands, 117 miles east of Rabaul (→ 10/3).

15. London: The Polish government in exile rejects the Soviet proposal that the Curzon Line should be Poland's post-war eastern frontier (→ 15/4).

15. Argentina: Pro-Axis army officers attempt a *coup* (→ 27).

16. USSR: The III *Panzer Korps* leads German troops in an attempt to break out of the Korsun pocket.→

16. Stockholm: Finnish and Soviet diplomats meet to negotiate an armistice (→ 24).

16. Anzio: German forces launch Operation *Fischfang*, a major counter-attack to push the Allies into the sea (→ 17).

17. Marshall Islands: US forces overrun Eniwetok Atoll (→ 18).

17. Anzio: Allied aircraft drop over 1,000 tons of bombs to try to contain the German advance (→ 18).

17. London: The government announces plans for a free post-war health service (→ 8/3).

18. Moscow: Gen Ivan S Konev, the commander of the Second Ukrainian Front, is promoted to marshal of the USSR for driving the Germans out of Korsun. General Eisenhower is awarded the Order of Suvorov, First Class.

18. USSR: Soviet forces take Staraya-Russa and Shimsk (→ 22).

18. Anzio: The U-boat U410 sinks the light cruiser HMS *Penelope*.→

18. Marshall Islands: US forces land on Engebi Island (→ 22).

Historic monastery bombed by Allies

The monastery at Monte Cassino, now just a battered shell which is making a perfect hideout for the Germans.

Monte Cassino, 15 February
For 700 years the great monastery of St Benedict has dominated the Liri valley. Today it is a shattered ruin after a day and a night of blasting by 600 tons of bombs dropped by 142 B-17s, B-25s and B-26s.

The destruction of the historic monastery will be controversial. Yet there is no controversy among Allied troops fighting for every yard of ground in the valley below; they see it as a symbol of their frustration, and Allied commanders are anxious to break through to relieve the five divisions which are coming under renewed attack at Anzio [*see report below*].

It was Lt-Gen Sir Bernard Freyberg, whose newly-formed New Zealand Corps has the task of assaulting the heights, who asked for the monastery to be bombed on the grounds that it was being used as an observation post for German artillery. US generals were against bombing; and the decision was taken only when General Sir Henry Maitland Wilson, the supreme Allied commander in the Mediterranean, flew over the monastery and thought he saw radio aerials. He was wrong. The monastery was not occupied by Germans, though they had been there to help the monks remove books and manuscripts for safekeeping in the Vatican.

After the aerial bombardment the New Zealanders and the 4th Indian Division began their assault tonight – only to be repulsed by German paratroopers. Ironically, the Germans are now moving into the wrecked monastery, which makes a better defensive position (→ 16).

Anzio divisions check German offensive

Anzio, 19 February
After three days of desperate fighting the Allied divisions trapped on the Anzio beach-head today halted a major German offensive. The attack was launched on 16 February, with General von Mackensen's Fourteenth Army supported by the *Luftwaffe*. A sustained artillery barrage opened up a gap in the sector held by the US 45th Division, and for a time it appeared as though the Allies would be split in two. *Panzers* poured through the gap, but themselves came under attack as the Allies concentrated their own fire more effectively. Still, though, the Germans pushed the Allies back towards the beaches. But tonight determined fighting by the British 1st and US 45th Divisions, backed by air and naval bombardment, has checked the Germans at Carroceto Creek (→ 23).

Germans take over the French Riviera

Marseilles, 14 February
German officials have told the Vichy government that they are taking direct control of the Mediterranean coast which they say is threatened with invasion. Martial law will be declared tomorrow in the seven coastal departments between Italy and Spain; "non-essential" people have been urged to leave the coast.

Germans "wiped out", say Russians

Kiev, 17 February
The Red Army claims that it wiped out some 52,000 German soldiers last night when the 60,000-strong German force trapped in the Korsun pocket 75 miles (120 km) southeast of Kiev tried to break out. While the III *Panzer Korps* tried to batter its way into the pocket from the outside, the German commander in the pocket, General Wilhelm Stemmermann, plotted the breakout. As dawn broke the Germans neared Lysyanka, thinking they had escaped; then Russian tanks and Cossack cavalry loomed out of the icy mist. It was a massacre. Despite Russian claims, it is possible that as many as 30,000 got away; but there is no doubt that the *Wehrmacht* has suffered another costly defeat. The *Luftwaffe* has also lost 45 Ju52 transports (→ 18).

Russians smash fleeing Germans at the edge of a snow-covered pine forest.

"Jericho" bombing raid on Amiens jail to bring down walls

Amiens, 18 February
Fourteen RAF Mosquitoes flew out of winter snow at treetop height today to hurl 500-pound bombs against the walls of Amiens jail. The explosions blasted gaps in the western outer wall, which is 20 feet high and three feet thick, and sliced open the main prison block.

This was the top-secret Operation Jericho, to snatch Resistance leaders 24 hours before they were due to face a firing squad. Their message to rescuers led by the Australian Group-Captain Charles Pickard was "better blown up by British bombs than shot by Nazis".

The first three bombers missed the outer wall. The next two lowered their aim and scored as the next pair hit the guards' dining room. Finally, there was uproar as the main block was bombed in an effort to blast open cell doors without bloodshed.

But this ambitious operation has had one embarrassing result. Of 258 men freed, 179 are criminals. Some 56 *Resistants* died, many shot by guards as they ran for the gap. The most valuable man to get out was Louis Vivant, the *Maquis* leader in the Somme, but the 74 men left in the prison include another prominent patriot, Dr Mans. The RAF dead include Pickard himself, a veteran of many special operations, including the Bruneval raid, and a "star" in the 1941 film *Target for Tonight* (→ 6/3).

Japanese naval base devastated by US

South Pacific, 17 February
American military power is intensifying the pressure on Japan's Pacific empire. This week the focus of activity is the central Pacific, where forces under the command of Admiral Nimitz launched massive air raids on Truk, in the Caroline Islands, and today landed on Eniwetok Atoll, in the Marshall Islands [see map on page 485].

Bombers attacked Truk for two days and one night of continuous raids. The Americans destroyed 275 enemy planes – 220 of them on the ground – 15 warships and 25 merchant ships amounting to 200,000 tons of auxiliary shipping. Truk now seems unlikely to delay the American advance towards the Mariana Islands further north.

Further east, on Eniwetok, bitter fighting is under way after the US launched the final stage of its offensive in the Marshalls. This was to be expected, however, after the earlier bloodbath on Kwajalein atoll where 8,410 Japanese were killed; 332 Americans also died and 1,392 were wounded. But the sheer weight of numbers seems certain to give the US forces victory (→ 22).

Japanese defied by "admin" soldiers

Burma, 18 February
An unlikely array of Allied troops – clerks, cooks, pay corps orderlies and staff officers – have halted the Japanese offensive, Operation *Ha-Go*, launched earlier this month. Japanese troops cut the lines of the 7th Indian Division to attack the XV Indian Corps from the rear. But they have been stoutly resisted at XV Corps' forward administrative area at Sinzweya, now besieged in the "admin box" and being supplied entirely by air (→ 24).

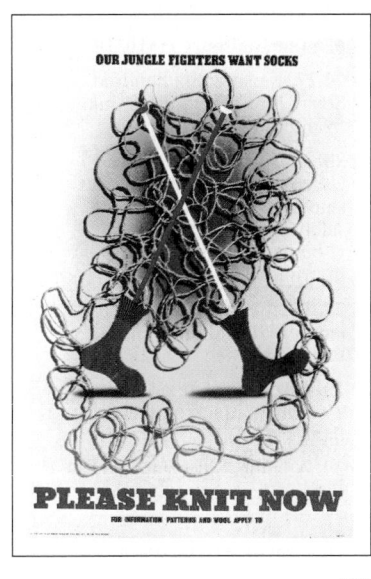

An aerial view of the Japanese naval base at Truk set ablaze by US bombers.

RAF sends bombers back to hit Berlin

Germany, 16 February
RAF Bomber Command last night resumed its onslaught on Berlin with a raid involving 891 aircraft. It was the first attack for over two weeks, as bad weather had halted the "Battle of Berlin" which the RAF launched last November. It may also be one of the last attacks for a while. Some 43 Allied planes are missing, and pressure is mounting on Bomber Command, to attack armament factories in less well-defended areas (→ 26).

February

Su	Mo	Tu	We	Th	Fr	Sa
		1	2	3	4	5
6	7	8	9	10	11	12
13	14	15	16	17	18	19
20	21	22	23	24	25	26
27	28					

20. Norway: SOE agents bomb and sink a ferry taking heavy water across Lake Tinnsjo *en route* to Germany for nuclear weapons research scientists.

20. Atlantic: The U-boat U413 sinks the destroyer HMS *Warwick* off Trevose.

21. China: The Eighth Route Army takes Taiku.

21. Dublin: The US requests that Dublin expel Axis diplomats (→ 10/3).

22. USSR: Soviet troops take the industrial centre of Krivoi Rog (→ 4/3).

22. Marshall Islands: The Allies complete their occupation of Eniwetok Atoll and land on Parry Island (→ 23).

23. Mariana Islands: US carriers attack Saipan, Tinian and Guam.→

23. Italy: Maj-Gen Lucien C Truscott takes over the command of the US VI Corps' assault at Anzio (→ 29).

24. Burma: The Allies clear the Japanese from the Ngakyedauk Pass, in the Arakan (→ 4/3).

24. Germany: USAAF bombers raid Schweinfurt; 11 out of 266 are lost.→

24. Helsinki: The prime minister says that Finland is prepared to make peace immediately with Russia, subject to conditions (→ 26).

25-26. Germany: Five hundred and ninety-four RAF bombers raid the aeroplane plant at Augsburg (→ 16/3).

26-27. Finland: Six hundred Soviet bombers raid Helsinki from 6pm to 6am.→

28. Murmansk: The Allied convoy JW-57 – 42 merchant ships and a tanker – arrives safely having sunk two U-boats but lost the British destroyer *Mahratta* (→ 10/3).

29. Pacific: US cavalrymen land on the Admiralty Islands, taking Los Negros airfield.→

29. Anzio: The Allies fend off a German attack on their right flank (→ 2/3).

29. Atlantic: Since January, 34 U-boats have been sunk here.

US launches "Big Week" of bomb raids

London, 26 February
US heavy bombers, escorted into the heart of Germany by long-range Mustang fighters, have won a great victory over the *Luftwaffe* in what has become known to the crews as "Big Week".

In six days, 1,000 bombers and 900 fighters have carried out 13 major attacks against the German aircraft industry in the campaign to destroy the Germans' strength in the air. In all, over 3,800 heavy bomber *sorties* were made. American losses were 226 aircraft, an acceptable rate of six per cent.

The bombers did not only inflict severe damage on the factories; they and the Mustangs shot down some 517 German fighters, killing 225 air crew and wounding 141, almost ten per cent of the skilled airmen in Germany. The *Luftwaffe* cannot sustain this rate of attrition.

The Mustang, with its American airframe and Rolls-Royce engine, has completely changed the pattern of aerial warfare over Europe. Now the bombers can be escorted all the way to their targets by a fighter superior in almost every respect to the Me109 and FW190.

The US bombers, who previously sought to evade the German fighters, are seeking them out, and the Germans, no longer able to wait until the escorting fighters turn back, are being forced to attack as soon as they cross the coast thus allowing shorter-range aircraft like the Spitfire to enter the battle. RAF Bomber Command has also taken part in "Big Week", with heavy raids on Leipzig and Stuttgart. It lost 78 bombers over Leipzig, but only ten over Stuttgart (→ 4/3).

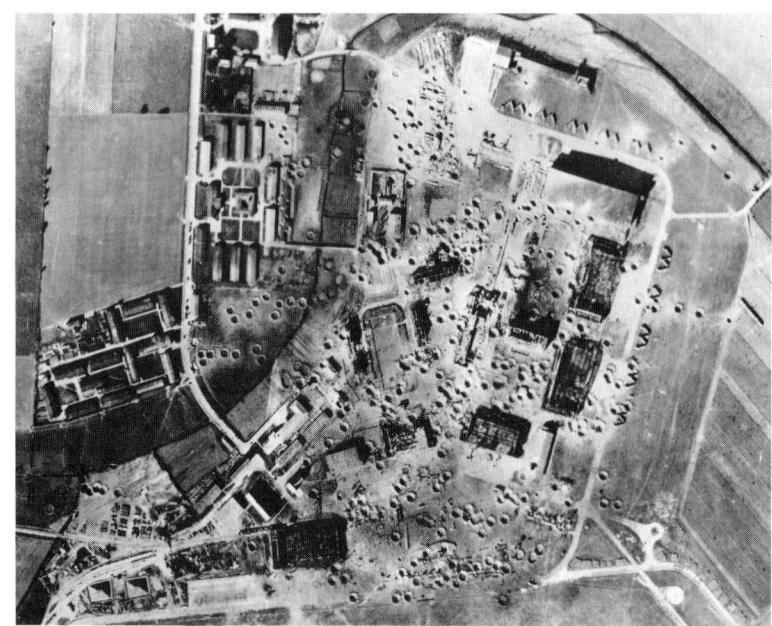
A German aircraft factory pockmarked with bomb craters after a raid.

Bomber Command raids German plant

Germany, 25 February
Allied air forces have rounded off their "Big Week" of bombings with a double blow on the Schweinfurt ball-bearing plant. Following last night's USAAF raid, RAF Bomber Command sent 662 more aircraft against this target tonight. But the raid was a failure: only 22 aircraft reached the target, and 33 were shot down.

Tojo takes over as army chief of staff

Cover general: a medal-bedecked Tojo on the front of a magazine.

Tokyo, 22 February
The Japanese premier, General Hideki Tojo, today sacked the heads of the Japanese army and navy following last week's catastrophic losses to the Allies at Truk, Japan's strategic outlying defence base in the South-west Pacific.

General Tojo, who takes over as chief of the army general staff, succeeding the disgraced General Sugiyama, is being accused of running a one-man cabinet. In addition to being premier, he is minister of war, controller of munitions, minister of commerce and industry, and minister of education. A protest has been issued by one of the emperor's brothers, Imperial Prince Chichibu, and dissident general staff officers have nicknamed Tojo "*Takauji*" – a reference to a 14th-century military upstart.

Soviet general ambushed by Ukrainians

Kiev, 29 February
General Nikolai Vatutin, commander of the First Ukrainian Front and one of the Red Army's most brilliant generals, was ambushed today by partisans fighting for an independent Ukraine. It is feared that his wounds may be fatal.

Vatutin, who had played a vital role in last year's battle at Kursk and in clearing the Ukraine, was fired on as he drove with his staff to visit front-line troops. His attackers are Ukrainian nationalists who went over to the Germans in the hope that they would establish a Ukrainian state. Now they fight both Germans and Russians.

Vatutin will be sorely missed by the Red Army. It was he who, with Konev, engineered the destruction of the German pocket at Korsun. Georgi Zhukov, the formidable defender of Leningrad and Moscow, has taken over command of the First Ukrainian Front (→ 1/3).

Finns debate Soviet terms for armistice

Helsinki, 29 February
The whole of Finland is waiting for the *Diet*, the Finnish parliament, to decide whether or not to agree to the Russian terms for the cessation of hostilities. These terms include territorial concessions similar to those laid down by the Russians after the "Winter War" of 1939-40, but they do not require unconditional surrender as a preliminary to peace talks. The sticking-point for the Finns is the Russians' insistence on resuming their occupation of the naval base of Hango, the key to the Gulf of Finland. Given the military situation, however, there is now little that the Finns can do but accept (→ 17/3).

Partisans ambush German troop train

Athens, 22 February
Four hundred German soldiers drowned when their train was blown into a flooded river here today by mines laid by Greek partisans. Hundreds more were injured. A general was amongst the dead. The ambush marks a new offensive in the Balkans, with British officers from the Special Operations Executive leading *Andarte* freedom fighters. Ten coaches plunged down a ravine on the main Athens to Salonika line. The surviving armoured coach was sprayed with machine-gun fire before the partisans disappeared into the countryside.

A heavily-armed Greek partisan.

Bismarcks barrier broken by US invasion

US troops come ashore in the Admiralty Islands during yesterday's offensive.

Pacific, 29 February
Today's invasion of the Admiralty Islands by the South-west Pacific Command is the final act in breaking the barrier of the Bismarcks. The isolation of the great enemy bastion of Rabaul has transformed it into a liability. With the sudden exodus of the combined fleet from Truk, Japan's outer defences are crumbling dramatically.

The Pacific War has gathered a new momentum, with MacArthur poised to thrust rapidly northwards to the Philippines and the enormously powerful US Pacific Fleet, backed by a fleet "train" and many divisions of marines and infantry, set to roll through the central Pacific (as it did this month in the attacks on the Marshall Islands).

American strategists are divided on which route should be taken to Japan. MacArthur insists that the Allies are morally obliged to liberate the Philippines on the way to Tokyo. Admiral King wants to bypass the archipelago and invade Formosa. The US joint chiefs have authorized a two-pronged drive and set the major objectives of invading Luzon, Formosa and the south China coast.

The joint chiefs believe that the central Pacific route is "strategically, logistically and tactically" better than the South-west Pacific route. However, they agree that by using both routes they will prevent the enemy from knowing where the next blow will fall. In 1942 the intention had been to take Rabaul. But in 1943 MacArthur was told to bypass it. Instead of being captured at a predictably high cost in lives, it was to be isolated and neutralized.

During 1943 the Allies had advanced ever closer to Rabaul. Bougainville was invaded in November, and in December the 1st Marine Division landed at Cape Gloucester in New Britain. Rabaul had also suffered devastating air attacks.

Rabaul is now neutralized. Most of the large enemy garrison will wait in vain to die for the emperor because the Allies have no intention of making a costly frontal attack. Bypassing enemy strongpoints has become one of the war's most momentous strategic concepts (→ 1/3).

Grimy with coral dust, a US soldier is hauled from the Pacific waters.

Plans for second front overshadow Italian campaign

Italy, 29 February
As the rain teems down on frustrated Allied troops before Cassino, a major question mark hangs over the whole of the Italian campaign. "Overlord", the invasion of Normandy, is due to take place in May. "Anvil", the diversionary landing in the south of France, is timed to coincide with the main thrust in the north.

In Italy, General Alexander's chief of staff, Lt-Gen John Harding, has produced a plan – Operation Diadem – which will bring the Eighth Army from the Adriatic front to join the US Fifth Army in a fullscale attack coordinated with a breakout from Anzio. The operation would be launched three weeks before the Normandy landings – and, it is hoped, draw off German divisions from France. "Anvil" would be abandoned under the British plan.

British chiefs of staff are enthusiastic. So, too, is Winston Churchill, desperate for what he sees as a "British" victory in Italy. The Americans are opposed. Apart from worries about losses in Italy and the slow pace of the campaign, they favour "Anvil" as more acceptable.

The British generals, Maitland Wilson – who has been made Allied supreme commander Mediterranean – and Alexander, insist that no troops should be withdrawn from Italy until the breakthrough has succeeded. They want the campaign there to go through to its decisive conclusion.

The American chiefs of staff, their attention distracted by events in the Far East, have nominated General Eisenhower, a firm supporter of "Anvil", as their representative. He has reluctantly agreed to postpone the operation until July. As preparations begin for the spring offensive in Italy, lengthy cables are being exchanged between Mr Churchill in London and President Roosevelt (→ 31/3).

1944

March

Su	Mo	Tu	We	Th	Fr	Sa
			1	2	3	4
5	6	7	8	9	10	11
12	13	14	15	16	17	18
19	20	21	22	23	24	25
26	27	28	29	30	31	

1. USSR: Marshal Zhukov takes over the command of the First Ukrainian Front from the injured General Vatutin; the German General Walter Model is promoted to field marshal (→14/4).

1. USSR: Soviet troops take Russaki, near Pskov (→4).

1. Admiralty Islands: US troops defending Los Negros drive off Japanese attacks on the perimeter (→3).

1. Berlin: Fritz Sauckel, the *Reich* plenipotentiary for the allocation of labour, says that there are five million slave workers in Germany.

2. Ankara: The Allies cut off lend-lease aid to Turkey because of its reluctance to help the Allied war effort.

2. Salerno: Over four hundred people who boarded a freight train in the absence of any other transport die of carbon monoxide poisoning when the train stops in a tunnel.

3. Admiralty Islands: US forces repel a major Japanese attack on Los Negros, inflicting severe casualties (→4).

3. Washington: Roosevelt says that the Italian fleet is to be distributed equally between Britain, the US and the USSR.

4. Admiralty Islands: US troops arrive to reinforce the Los Negros beach-head (→9).

4. Japan: All students are mobilized.

4. Burma: "Merrill's Marauders" go into action for the first time, erecting a roadblock at Walawbaum, in Hukawng Valley, as part of a move to take Myitkyina and reopen the Burma Road (→5).

4. Cracow: Governor Hans Frank reminds a Nazi meeting: "The Jews are a race which must be wiped out. Whenever we catch one, he will be exterminated" (→7).

4. USSR: The Red Army pushes German forces back across the river Bug, except for a pocket at Uman (→5).

4. Anzio: There is a lull in the fighting, giving the Germans time to rally their forces for defence (→15).

US aircraft join the bombing of Berlin

Germany, 4 March
US aircraft joined the Battle of Berlin for the first time today since the effort to destroy the German capital began on 18 November. Bombers escorted by P-38J Lightnings attacked the city, but many of the 249 B-17s dispatched hit other targets in Bonn, Dusseldorf, Cologne and Frankfurt because of bad weather and poor visibililty over much of the continent.

The inhibition on US operations against Berlin has always been the American faith in daylight operations. These require heavy fighter escort. Berlin has been beyond the range of such escorts until now. The Lightning and P-51D Mustang are expected to fill the gap. Today's 1,200-mile (1,920-km) round trip was made under heavy *flak*, but there was no sign of *Luftwaffe* interceptors. Even so, out of 502 bombers and 720 fighters, 39 were lost. The concentration of air defences around Berlin has already taken a heavy toll of RAF bombers. It seems unlikely that the frequency of attacks which characterized the winter raids will be resumed, at least in the short term (→6).

An American crew inspects the damage to its plane after returning from Berlin.

Italians strike in anti-Nazi protest

Zurich, 3 March
News has reached Switzerland that some six million workers are on strike today in a vast area of northern Italy, stretching from Tuscany and Emilia to the borders with France, Switzerland, Austria and Yugoslavia. Armaments factories of crucial importance to the *Wehrmacht* – Breda and Marelli, the Pirelli Italiana rubber and cable works and the Isotta Fraschini aero-engine manufacturers – have been brought to a standstill.

Notices posted by the strikers around the city of Milan demand an end to deportations of Italian forced labour to Germany, an improvement in living conditions in Italy and the repeal of the military service law. The underground communist newspaper *Unita Proletaria*, published in Rome, has recently exposed Fascist plans to deport one million more workers. Wages for these forced labourers are minimal, and the working conditions are so barbaric as to prove fatal for some.

Railway workers, too, have supported the stoppages. No trains have reached Switzerland from Milan since Wednesday night. In an attempt to terrorize the strikers into returning to work the Fascist press publishes accounts of punishments of anti-Fascists. Two partisans in Milan have been shot dead immediately on arrest (→8).

Rommel kept busy bolstering German anti-invasion defences

Rommel (r) with a fellow officer.

France, 1 March
Rommel has arrived in northern France to take command of the German forces awaiting the long-expected Allied invasion. The legendary "Desert Fox" has been dismayed to discover that the Fuhrer's vaunted "Atlantic Wall" is largely a figment of Hitler's imagination, and he is urgently throwing up fortifications along the Normandy coast.

Vital training programmes have had to be dropped because, unable to get labour and materials from the Todt Organization, he is having to use his troops as labourers to cut trees for stakes on the beaches. Fuel shortages have created transport problems, and he has been driven to depend on horses and carts. Field Marshal Rommel asked for 50 million mines to sow as the first line of defence on the beaches; he expects to receive about six million. He reckons that he needs 240 loads of cement daily for fortifications; he is receiving fewer than 50.

To compound Rommel's problems, he is in disagreement with Field Marshal von Rundstedt, the C-in-C West. Rommel considers that the Allied invasion will be mounted in Normandy; von Rundstedt is certain it will be in the Pas de Calais and is holding back an armoured reserve which Rommel argues is vital for hitting the enemy when he is weakest, at the moment of landing (→6/5).

German army calls off Anzio offensive

Bogged down in Italy: a British soldier struggles to dig out a 4.5 inch howitzer.

Anzio, 2 March
The rain stopped today, and bombers roamed the blue skies blasting the Germans who have attacked the Anzio garrison day and night since 28 February. Yesterday the Germans, hampered by driving rain, gave up the ground that they had won, and today the US 509th Parachute Infantry Battalion was relieved by the 30th Infantry Regiment of the 3rd Infantry Division. Despite Hitler's fury, Kesselring has called off the offensive (→ 4).

Forces pay row rocks British government

London, 2 March
The British government called the Home Guard to defend its parliamentary majority tonight. MPs rostered for duty in uniform as the city's last line of defence was summoned to bolster the vote on the touchy issue of service pay. During a debate promoted by the Independent MP for Grantham, Mr Kendall, a call for pay increases was defeated by only 23 votes, a dramatic fall from the usual majority of 580 enjoyed by a national coalition government. The war cabinet is to review service pay despite inflation.

A strange procession of US Thunderbolt planes down an English street.

1944
March

Su	Mo	Tu	We	Th	Fr	Sa
			1	2	3	4
5	6	7	8	9	10	11
12	13	14	15	16	17	18
19	20	21	22	23	24	25
26	27	28	29	30	31	

5. USSR: In a new Ukrainian offensive Soviet troops advance 31 miles and retake Izyaslav, Ostropol and Yampol (→ 10).

5. Burma: Chinese forces capture Maingkwan as three Chindit brigades land behind enemy lines at Indaw (→ 8).

6. Germany: By daylight, 658 US bombers drop 2,000 tons of bombs on Berlin; 69 planes are lost, the biggest loss in one day for the Eighth USAAF.

6. France: RAF bombers devastate Trappes railway yard as part of the plan to disable communications in the build-up to the invasion of Europe.

7. Auschwitz-Birkenau: In a routine gassing, 3,823 Czech Jews from the ghetto at Theresienstadt are killed (→ 10).

7-8. Burma: Lt-Gen Renya Mutaguchi launches Operation *U-Go* to capture the Imphal plain.→

8. Britain: A major post-war building programme for up to 200,000 houses a year is promised by the government.

8. Britain: Miners in Wales and Durham strike in support of a wage claim (→ 24).

9. Admiralty Islands: US aircraft begin operations from Momote airfield (→ 10).

10. New Britain: Talasea falls to US forces (→ 5).

10. USSR: Soviet troops take the German airbase at Uman.→

10. Mauthausen, Germany: Adolf Eichmann and his team meet to organize the deportation of Hungary's Jews to Auschwitz-Birkenau (→ 23).

10. Scotland: Convoy RA-57, returning from Russia, arrives safely in Loch Ewe having lost one ship, sunk three U-boats and damaged two others (→ 31).

11. Burma: As the 7th Indian Division takes Buthidaung, Japan advances to Witok.→

11. USSR: The Red Army captures Berislav, in the southern Ukraine (→ 13).

11. Algiers: The Free French government sentences Pierre Pucheu, the former Vichy minister of the interior, to death for treason (→ 20).

Crooners under fire for lowering morale

Westminster, 7 March
Female crooners on the BBC were attacked today in the House of Commons when Lord Winterton (Con) claimed: "They remind one of the caterwauling of an inebriated cockatoo. I cannot believe that all this wailing about lost babies can possibly have a good effect on troops who are about to endanger their lives." The parliamentary secretary to the minister of information, Mr Thurtle, said that the government would not interfere with the BBC. "I do not think a certain amount of crooning is likely to have a serious effect on the British Army," he said.

Vera Lynn: number one "crooner".

RAF pilots take off with faster Spitfire

Britain, 8 March
A new mark of Spitfire, the Mark XIV, is coming into RAF service. The Merlin engine of earlier marks has been replaced by the 2,050hp two-stage Griffon. This and the redesigned airframe enable the Mark XIV to reach speeds of almost 450mph (724kmph), as well as markedly improving the rate of climb. For some time now the Spitfire has been struggling against the Focke-Wulf Fw190. These improvements will enable it to match its rival on much better terms.

▷

Burmese battlefield springs to life as Allies attack

Merrill's Marauders - GIs and Kachins - on the march in the baking sun.

American troops serving with the Chindits clean their kit in the jungle.

"Merrill's Marauders" ease out Japanese

Northern Burma, 8 March
"Merrill's Marauders" have killed 800 Japanese in north Burma. The 3,000-strong unit is the US counterpart of the British Chindits, and was formed after the war department had appealed for recruits "for particularly hazardous and self-sacrificing operations". Commanded by Colonel Frank Merrill, it arrived in India last October.

Mountbatten assigned the unit to General Stilwell's Northern Combat Area Command. Stilwell was advancing towards Hukawng Valley with Kamaing, Mogaung and Myitkyina as objectives. By early February he was in the valley, and was reinforced by the Marauders and a Chinese tank unit. His aim was to encircle two Japanese regiments in Maingkwan. The Marauders were to make a wide eastward flanking movement, cutting in on the enemy rear at Walawbaum, while the Chinese 22nd Division attacked at Maingkwan.

The Japanese, anticipating Stilwell's tactics, concentrated for five days on the outnumbered Marauders who beat off repeated bayonet charges. One unit fought for 36 hours without food or water. By 7 March the Japanese were forced out of Walawbaum. Eight Marauders died and 37 were wounded (→ 9).

Chindits land again behind enemy lines

Indaw, Burma, 9 March
Operation Thursday, one of the most spectacular operations of the war in Burma, was launched when Brigadier Wingate's Chindits struck again some 200 miles (320 km) behind Japanese front lines [see map, page 500]. At dusk on 5 March, 9,000 members of two brigades began flying into an area known as "Broadway" in gliders. A third brigade is marching into enemy territory, but stores, mules and equipment have been flown in.

"Broadway" is 50 miles northeast of Indaw, and Wingate's task is to sever the arteries of supply to the enemy forces opposing General Stilwell's march towards Myitkyina from the north and the advance of Chinese troops from Yunnan.

The expedition was nearly cancelled when aerial photographs showed logs laid by the Japanese obstructing the ground at "Piccadilly" – 20 miles south of "Broadway" – where gliders crashed on landing, killing 31 crewmen. But landings at "Broadway" went ahead, and in 12 hours engineers had prepared an airstrip. The next night 55 DC-3 Dakota transports landed. The operation is to be supplied by air, and casualties are to be flown out by the No 1 Air Command of the USAAF (→ 11).

Japanese surprise Slim with pre-emptive strike towards Imphal

Burma, 11 March
Both sides in the battle for Burma are now trying to seize the initiative. In addition to two Allied offensives [reported above], Japan returned to the attack this week.

Last month saw the Japanese call off Operation *Ha-Go*, an attack on British positions in the Arakan peninsula. The Japanese 55th Division had slipped behind Allied lines at Taung Bazaar in an attempt to cut off supply lines both from the north and from the Ngakyedauk Pass, in the east. The Indian 5th and 7th Divisions were cut off in the "admin box" of Sinzweya. Supplied by air, they fended off repeated Japanese attacks until 25 February, when they were relieved from the east. The Allied capture of Buthidaung today removes the last major obstacle to an advance on Akyab.

Operation *U-Go*, launched by General Renya Mutaguchi's Fifteenth Army on the night of 7-8 March, is a pre-emptive strike to prevent an Allied offensive in northern Burma. Its main objective is the capture of the key communications and supply centre at Imphal, across the Indian border in Assam; today Japanese advance troops crossed the Manipur river, west of the Chindwin. Mutaguchi has ambitions ultimately to advance to Delhi and "liberate" the whole of India on behalf of the nationalist leader Subhas Chandra Bose.

U-Go took General Slim, the commander of the British Fourteenth Army, by surprise. He was expecting an attack next week, and is now rushing troops north from Buthidaung to Imphal (→ 13).

1944

March

Su	Mo	Tu	We	Th	Fr	Sa
			1	2	3	4
5	6	7	8	9	10	11
12	13	14	15	16	17	18
19	20	21	22	23	24	25
26	27	28	29	30	31	

Red Army breaks through in the Ukraine

Kiev, 10 March
The Red Army has made another breakthrough, the third in a week, in the Ukraine. On the whole 500-mile (800-km) front, from the approaches to the Dnieper estuary north to Tarnopol, von Manstein's Army Group South is in flight, desperately trying to avoid being encircled. The *Wehrmacht*, bogged down in the black Ukrainian mud, is abandoning arms and equipment in its flight. The Russians claim to have captured 200 Tiger and Panther tanks among the booty.

The new breakthrough was made by Konev's Second Ukrainian Front, which has torn a hole 110 miles (176 km) wide and 40 miles (64 km) deep in German lines. A *Pravda* report says that "it seems incredible that the army could advance one step in this flooded terrain, but it has reached that superlative point at which all obstacles are powerless to halt it" (→ 11).

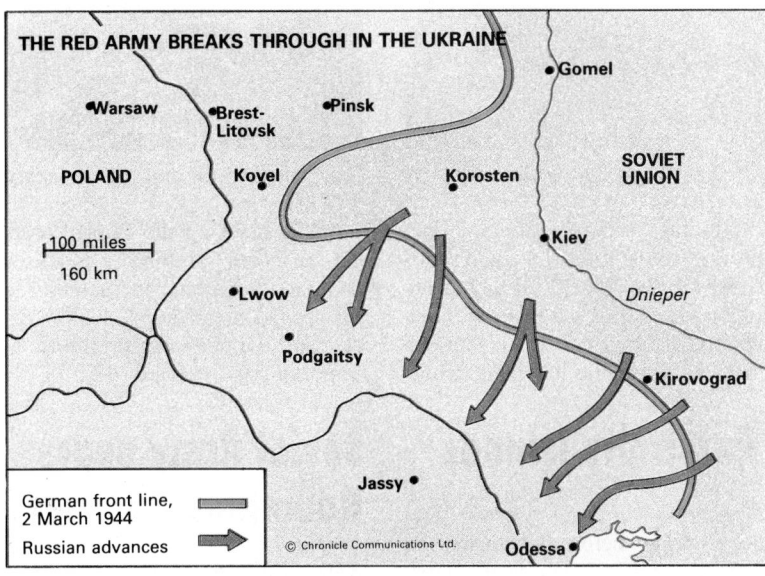

THE RED ARMY BREAKS THROUGH IN THE UKRAINE

Warsaw • Brest-Litovsk • Pinsk • Gomel

POLAND • Kovel • Korosten • SOVIET UNION

100 miles / 160 km

• Lwow • Kiev • Dnieper

• Podgaitsy • Kirovograd

Jassy •

German front line, 2 March 1944
Russian advances

Odessa •

© Chronicle Communications Ltd.

Eire refuses to oust diplomatic "spies"

Dublin, 10 March
Diplomatic "spies" in Eire endanger the lives of US troops awaiting orders to liberate Europe, the US told Dublin on 21 February; it urged the expulsion of Axis diplomats. Today Eire formally rejected the request, saying it would be "the first step to war". But the Irish say a radio transmitter at the German legation has been silenced (→ 12).

Germans use tanks as Italians strike

Milan, 8 March
More than a million Italian workers have marched out of the factories to strike against "German pillaging" in occupied northern Italy. German tanks and SS infantrymen are being used in an attempt to force the workers back. The Germans have also threatened to impose a quisling *Gauleiter* and martial law, with the death penalty for strike leaders.

German women conscripted for war effort

Germany, 7 March
A major propaganda campaign aimed primarily at women has been launched in an attempt to bolster Germany's depleted labour force. Though some three million women between the ages of 17 and 45 were registered for war work last year on the orders of Fritz Sauckel, the *Reich* plenipotentiary for the allocation of labour, more than two million have used family responsibilities and health reasons to avoid their allocated jobs. Members of the Nazi organization for women are going from house to house appealing to the women to work "in the service of the community".

---

12. London: The Czech government in exile broadcasts a "call to arms" to the civilian population.

13. USSR: The Red Army captures Kherson (→ 17).

13. Burma: Japan attacks the Chindit airstrip at "Broadway" (→ 16).

13. Moscow: The USSR and Italy re-establish diplomatic links.

13. Atlantic: The U-boat U575 is sunk by US ships and RAF aircraft.

14. China: The Communist Eighth Route Army captures Chinhsien, in Hupeh province (→ 8/4).

14. Peenemunde: Wernher von Braun and two assistants are arrested, accused of diverting resources from military rocket projects to peaceful ones, such as the movement of mail by rocket.

14. US: Wendell Willkie (Rep.) and Franklin D Roosevelt (Dem.) win their parties' New Hampshire primaries for presidential candidates (→ 5/4).

15. Monte Cassino: The third Allied offensive opens with a bombardment which destroys Cassino town, killing 140 civilians and 96 Allied soldiers.→

15. Europe: German forces mass on the Hungarian border (→ 18).

15-16. Germany: Stuttgart is raided by 863 RAF bombers.

16. New Guinea: US aircraft raid a Japanese convoy off Wewak (→ 19).

16. Burma: Allied troops take Mawlu, cutting the vital rail link from Mandalay to Myitkyina.→

17. USSR: The Red Army enters the Ukrainian road and rail junction of Dubno.→

17. Mediterranean: The U-boat U371 sinks the US troopship *Dempo*, killing 498 servicemen.

18. Salzburg: Hitler detains Hungary's regent, Admiral Miklos Horthy, in Salzburg and orders the German army to occupy Hungary (→ 19).

Allied planes bomb Cassino as soldiers prepare new attack

New Zealanders outside Cassino.

Cassino, 15 March
In four horrific hours today, 775 Allied bombers have flattened this pleasant valley town. The attack represented more than two aircraft for every one of the 350 German defenders – five tons of bombs for each soldier – such is the Allied determination to break the deadlock.

The Allies reckoned that no one could have survived the bombing – let alone the 195,969 shells that followed. Yet the New Zealand 6th Infantry Brigade came under intense defensive fire when it clambered over the debris into the town. A new assault is also being made on the Cassino monastery. Gurkhas have climbed to Point 435 on the army map, known as "Hangman's Hill", 440 yards from the monastery (→ 20).

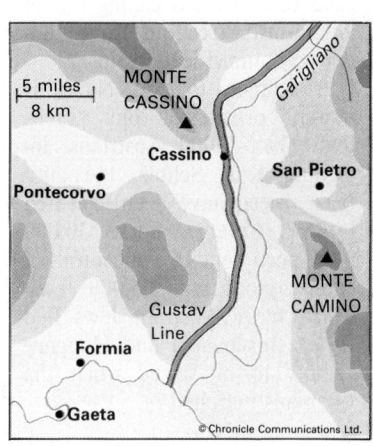

5 miles / 8 km

Garigliano

MONTE CASSINO ▲

Cassino

San Pietro

Pontecorvo

Gustav Line

MONTE CAMINO ▲

Formia

• Gaeta

© Chronicle Communications Ltd.

Vienna bombing puts Austrian role in the spotlight

Vienna, 17 March
American B-24s, escorted by P-47s and P-38s, today opened the Allied bombing assault on Austria with a raid by more than 200 planes on industrial targets in Vienna. The planes, of the US Fifteenth Army Air Force, flew from airfields in Italy. Some 100 B-17s aborted the raid because of bad weather.

Though many Austrians are serving in the German armed forces, the country has until now been largely untouched by war. The Allies appear to be in two minds about it; the Moscow declaration by Allied foreign ministers last November spoke of Austria as "the first country to fall victim to Nazi aggression", but then warned Austrians that they have "a responsibility for participation in the war at the side of Hitlerite Germany".

Some Austrians have become high-ranking Nazis: Arthur Seyss-Inquart, the *Reich* commissioner in the Netherlands, Ernst Kaltenbrunner, Himmler's deputy, and Otto Skorzeny, the commando leader. For Hitler Austria does not exist; it is simply another German *Land*. Most Austrians favoured the 1938 *Anschluss*, but Nazi attacks on the church have alienated the Catholic Christian Social party.

In Carinthia and Styria the minority Slovene peoples have forged links with Tito's partisans across the border in Yugoslavia and begun organized resistance. Moscow radio in broadcasts to Austria is calling for an anti-fascist "freedom front" under communist leadership.

Resistance to the Nazis is loosely organized, but persistent. Over 2,000 Austrians, including Karl Scholz, the anti-Nazi priest, have been executed by the *Gestapo*. Some 30,000 have been sent to concentration camps, along with 65,000 Jews. Many more Austrian Jews fled to Czechoslovakia and Hungary – only to be seized when the Germans marched in.

Allied troops rush to repel Japanese

Imphal, 18 March
As General Mutaguchi's men press forward towards the vital military base at Imphal, penetrating the Indian border on a massive front, General Slim is belatedly rushing troops north from the Arakan to try to repel them. The Japanese have caught him on the hop with their attack which came a week earlier than he had predicted.

To add to Slim's woes, Operation Thursday, the attack by glider-borne Chindits behind enemy lines near Indaw, has failed to make much impact. The plan was to cut off Japanese forces in northern Burma, reopening the route between Ledo and Kunming. Despite cutting the Mandalay to Myitkyina railway, Wingate's crack troops find themselves sidelined temporarily by the Imphal battle.

Slim's tactic is to pull his troops back to the Imphal plain and entice the Japanese to follow, thus length-

Japanese troops on the advance.

The Burma Road, now in US hands.

ening the enemy's supply lines through difficult territory and shortening his own. The 20th Indian Division, hard pressed by the Japanese 33rd Division, has withdrawn from Tamu to the hills and is now virtually blocking the Imphal road. To the north, Mutaguchi is poised to attack Sangshak, the gateway to his second main target: Kohima, a rail and supplies centre almost as important as Imphal (→ 22).

US steps up attacks on Admiralty Islands

Manus, 15 March
US troops of the 8th Cavalry of 2nd Brigade, 1st Cavalry Division, have attacked Manus island, in the Admiralty Islands, off the north coast of New Guinea. The force under Gen MacArthur's South-west Pacific Area Command landed after a heavy preliminary air and sea barrage. The first wave of attackers has so far managed to destroy land-mines, machine-gun nests and booby traps before advancing on Lorengau airfield, where the Japanese defenders are holding out.

Securing the Admiralties will safeguard the Allied rearguard, vital to MacArthur's plan to advance along New Guinea's north coast to the Vogelkop peninsula, the likely springboard for an eventual attack on the Philippines (→ 16).

Soviet Army nears Roumanian border

Kiev, 17 March
The swift advance of the Red Army in the Ukraine has brought it close to the Roumanian border. Dubno, the old fortress where the legendary Cossack warrior Taras Bulba fought, fell to Zhukov today and Konev crossed the river Dniester and wheeled north to encircle the First *Panzer* Army.

Tonight's communique says that the Red Army is fighting in the streets of the important railway junction of Mogilev-Podolski, only 40 miles (64 km) from the river Pruth where it forms the Roumanian border. The communique, describing the crossing of the Dniester, said: "The advance of the Soviet troops was so swift and stunning that in a number of places the Germans had no time to destroy the ferries and bridges. They suffered enormous losses." With the Lvov to Odessa railway line cut, the key supply route to the southern sector of von Manstein's Army Group has been broken, and as the Russians advance they threaten to split the German forces in Poland from those in southern Russia (→ 20).

Vital air cover in the Pacific war: a US Navy Hellcat prepares for take-off.

Irish travel banned as a security risk

Westminster, 12 March

With an invasion attempt on occupied Europe imminent the Allies have almost sealed off Eire from the rest of the world, following Dublin's refusal to expel Axis diplomats. For the time being 250,000 Irish citizens working in Britain cannot return home, nor can any of the 164,000 serving with British armed forces. Mr Churchill recognizes that the measure is "painful" in view of the contribution of so many Irishmen to the war effort. There were tears at Liverpool as some Irish girls were refused permission to sail home yesterday, but 1,000 others did leave (→ 9/5).

Finns reject Soviet peace overtures

Helsinki, 17 March

The Finns are procrastinating in their peace negotiations with the USSR despite being offered what seem reasonable terms to end their ill-fated alliance with Germany. The Finns' reply today is being described by the Russians as "negative". The sticking-point now seems to be not the proposed occupation of Hango base, but the fate of German forces in northern Finland. Commanded by General Dietl, they are 100,000 strong and well-equipped. Russia wants them interned, but Finland wants to repatriate them to Germany "with full military honours" (→ 22/4).

US poster: blue skies and bombs.

1944

March

Su	Mo	Tu	We	Th	Fr	Sa
			1	2	3	4
5	6	7	8	9	10	11
12	13	14	15	16	17	18
19	20	21	22	23	24	25
26	27	28	29	30	31	

19. New Guinea: The US shells the Japanese at Wewak for a second time (→ 20).

20. Algiers: Pierre Pucheu, the former Vichy interior minister found guilty of treason, is shot (→ 4/4).

20. USSR: The Red Army captures Mogilev-Podolski and Vinnitsa, key bases in the Ukraine (→ 23).

20. Bismarck Archipelago: US marines land on Emirau Island, meeting no opposition from Japan.→

22. Burma: Japanese troops cross the Indian border, penetrating into Manipur.→

22. Germany: Berlin announces the appointment of a new government for Hungary, led by Dome Sjotay.→

22. Ottawa: China and Canada sign a mutual aid pact.

22-23. Frankfurt: An RAF raid kills 948 people and makes 120,000 homeless.→

23. USSR: The Red Army surrounds the German military headquarters at Tarnopol (→ 26).

23. Greece: The Germans begin deporting Greek Jews to Auschwitz-Birkenau (→ 27).

23. Monte Cassino: The unsuccessful Allied assault, spearheaded by the New Zealand Corps, is called off (→ 15/4).

24. Rome: *Gestapo* police execute 336 civilians to avenge yesterday's partisan bombing of an SS parade.

24. Frankfurt: The city is hit by the third devastating Allied raid since 18 March (→ 25).

25. Admiralty Islands: Organized Japanese opposition to US forces on Manus island comes to an end (→ 29).

25. Germany: On the "Night of the Strong Winds" 72 out of 811 bombers raiding Berlin are lost and 50 are shot down by *flak* (→ 30).

25. London: Ignoring Churchill's request for aerial attacks on V-weapon bases in France, Eisenhower gives priority to the bombing of transport and communications centres.

Germans seize Hungary

Budapest, 19 March

With Stalin's armies now thrusting towards Germany's flank in southeastern Europe, Hitler has sent in troops to occupy Hungary and seize vital communications for the defence of the Danube plain – the highway into the *Reich*.

All civilian traffic has been ordered off the roads. Admiral Horthy, the regent of Hungary, was summoned to Klessheim Castle, Salzburg, where Hitler ordered him to appoint a pro-Nazi as premier, allow the German army to take over the Hungarian transport system, and give the SS a free hand in deporting Hungarian Jews. Horthy returned to Budapest to find a German guard of honour lined up to greet him. He retreated to his palace and has not been seen since.

Edmund Veesenmayer, the German ambassador plenipotentiary with "special powers" in Hungary, is mobilizing "all resources for final victory", and Hungary's 767,000 Jews, hitherto unharmed through four years of war, are to be sent on their way to Auschwitz.

Horthy joined forces with Hitler on 20 November 1940, but recently has shown signs of wanting to extricate himself from the increasingly perilous German alliance. He has informed the Allies that he will surrender unconditionally when Allied troops reached his borders (→ 22).

Hungarian forces: now they will have to continue fighting with the Nazis.

Germany reinforces occupied Roumania

Bucharest, 23 March

In the wake of their occupation of Hungary, the Germans today strengthened their position in Roumania, which was occupied in October 1940. The dictator, Marshal Ion Antonescu, a longtime admirer of Hitler, was told that 50,000 German troops were being sent in to safeguard communications and protect the oil wells for Germany.

With the Red Army on his borders, Antonescu was less than enthusiastic. Hitler was unmoved. Four *Panzer* and several infantry divisions have already moved in. Roumania's foreign policy has been largely determined by resentment at the territorial depredations of her neighbours. In June 1940 Roumania was forced to hand over Bessarabia and Northern Bukovina to Stalin. Roumanian troops retook them a year later, after they had joined Hitler in the German attack on the USSR.

In August 1940 the "Vienna Award" gave North Transylvania to Hungary. This week, when Germany occupied Hungary, two Roumanian divisions joined in. As Soviet troops advance into Bessarabia, the BBC today broadcast a warning to Roumanians: abandon the Nazis or face retribution from the Allies (→ 3/4).

Air crash kills Chindit leader Wingate

Imphal, India, 24 March

Orde Wingate has died in a plane crash. The weather was bad, with sudden rainstorms. The RAF had grounded its planes, but Wingate insisted on flying – dying, as he had lived, ignoring official advice. Some of his Chindits are grieving. Others are celebrating. In death as in life he produced mixed reactions.

An unstable crusader who had found a cause, Wingate had first achieved fame for his irregular skills, and notoriety for his brutality, in Ethiopia. His staff so hated him that when he failed to commit suicide with a razor in protest at the "betrayal of Ethiopia", Colonel Hugh Boustead said: "Bloody fool, why didn't you use a revolver?"

Yet after Wingate had put his ideas on long-range penetration into practice in Burma, Churchill wanted this "man of genius and audacity" in command.

Operation Thursday, launched three weeks ago, was designed to cut off the Japanese army in north-east Burma, and threaten its rear. Within ten days Brigadier Mike Calvert's 77th Brigade has captured Mawlu, cut all rail and road links with north-east Burma and established "strongholds" supplied by air. But Brigadier Bernard Fergusson's 16th Brigade, exhausted after a five-week march from Ledo, has failed to take the main Japanese supply base at Indaw.

Meanwhile, on the Imphal plain, Slim is mustering his forces to try to hold off against Mutaguchi's two divisions advancing on Imphal, Kohima and Dimapur. While the Japanese complain that they haven't seen one of their own aircraft for weeks, Slim has airlifted the 5th Indian Division over from the Arakan. More troops are pouring into the area from Manipur.

But the Chindits, their charismatic leader gone, are no longer sure of their objective. Having been told to cut off the Japanese facing China, Wingate appears to have decided, against orders, to shift his forces west and cut off the Japanese facing Imphal. He was well-known for never writing anything down or confiding in subordinates; his plans, whatever they were, are a mystery, scattered over the rain-soaked Imphal hillside (→ 29).

Major-General Orde Wingate who died as he had lived, ignoring official advice.

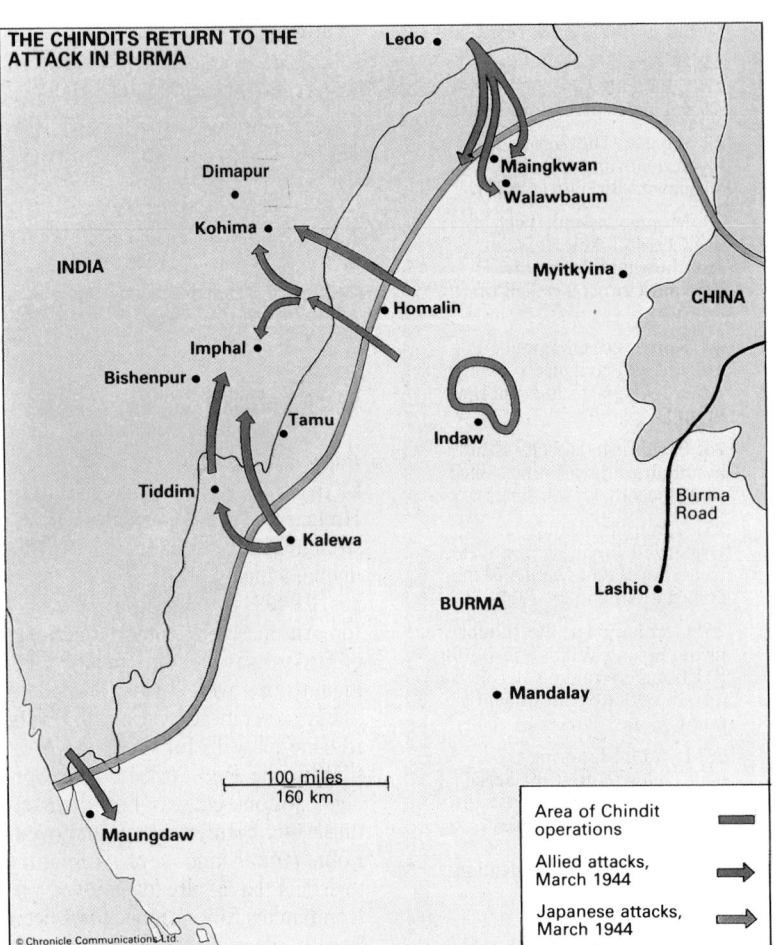

THE CHINDITS RETURN TO THE ATTACK IN BURMA

Ledo
Dimapur
Maingkwan
Walawbaum
Kohima
INDIA
Myitkyina
CHINA
Homalin
Imphal
Bishenpur
Tamu
Indaw
Tiddim
Burma Road
Kalewa
Lashio
BURMA
Mandalay

100 miles
160 km

Maungdaw

© Chronicle Communications Ltd

Area of Chindit operations

Allied attacks, March 1944

Japanese attacks, March 1944

"Maquis" attacked by German troops

France, 25 March

The full weight of the *Wehrmacht* with massive air support, has succeeded in defeating 465 Resistance fighters of the French *Maquis* on the plateau of Glieres. The widespread presence of the Maquis has become a continuing source of irritation and frustration to the Vichy and German authorities.

The first attack by the Vichy *Milice* was a failure; but today several battalions of Germans soldiers, backed by the Milice, are being used in the offensive. The majority of prisoners are reported to have been brutally tortured before being executed.

SS guns down 335 hostages in caves

Rome, 24 March

In a bloody and brutal night of savagery, the SS avenged the deaths of 33 of its men in a partisan bombing by killing 335 hostages – more than ten Italians for every German. The bomb exploded as a German unit was marching past.

The victims, drawn mostly from Rome's Jewish population, were taken by lorry to the Ardeatine caves outside the city. There, by torchlight, the shootings began. As the dead piled up, executioners and victims were forced to stand on bodies. Engineers sealed the caves.

Allies repel suicide attack by Japanese

Bougainville, 24 March

Three hundred Japanese died today as 2,000 enemy troops launched a suicidal attack against the Allied beach-head at Torokina, on Bougainville Island. The attack reflects Japan's increasingly desperate situation in the Solomons. Its main base for the area, at Rabaul, was bombed today for the 50th day in succession, with Allied planes dropping 150 tons of explosives on Rabaul's three airfields. The daytime offensive at Torokina was rebuffed, with US losses given as four dead and 47 wounded (→ 25).

Allied PoWs escape from prison camp

Non-stop air raids bombard Germany

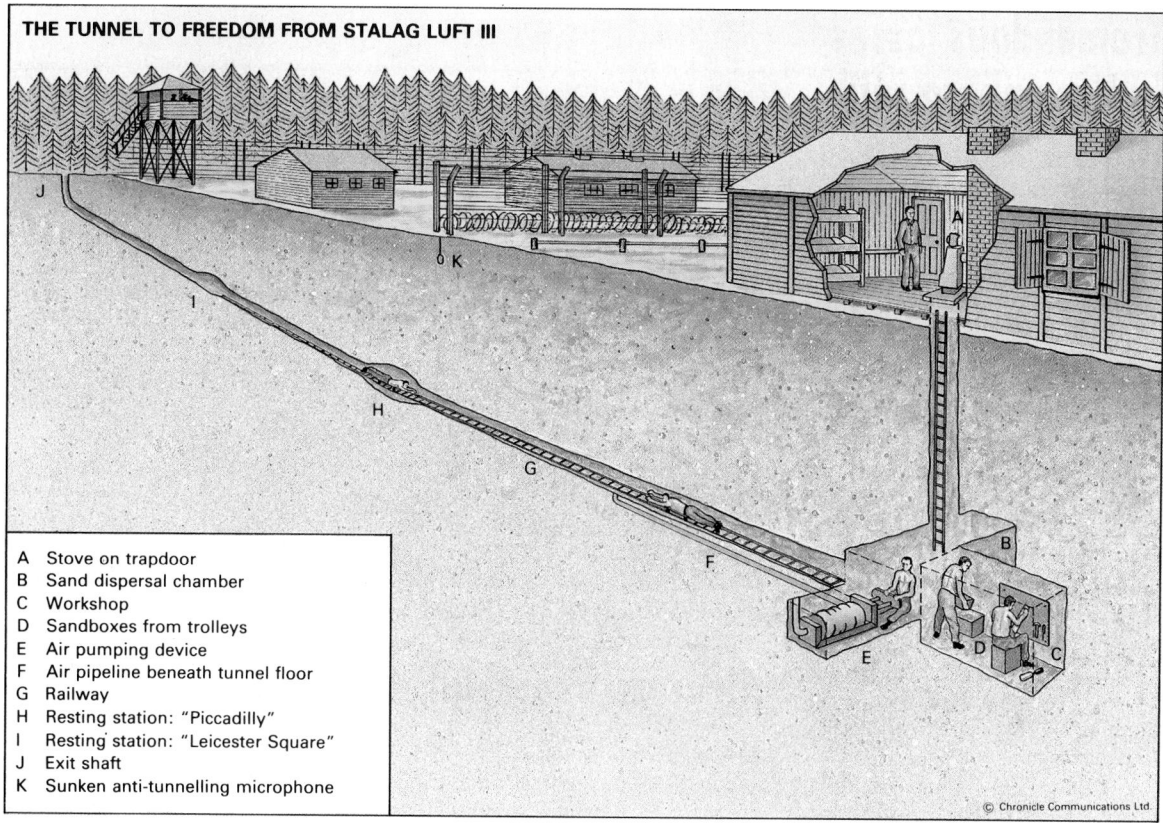

THE TUNNEL TO FREEDOM FROM STALAG LUFT III

A Stove on trapdoor
B Sand dispersal chamber
C Workshop
D Sandboxes from trolleys
E Air pumping device
F Air pipeline beneath tunnel floor
G Railway
H Resting station: "Piccadilly"
I Resting station: "Leicester Square"
J Exit shaft
K Sunken anti-tunnelling microphone

© Chronicle Communications Ltd.

Stalag Luft III, 24-25 March
They have been working on it for two years and now, just after dusk, the moment has arrived for the Allied airmen held in the German PoW camp at Sagan, 80 miles (128 km) south-east of Berlin. The last few feet of earth are removed and the first prisoners climb out into the wood beyond the barbed wire. The 365-foot tunnel, with air vents and

underground railway for moving debris, is the brain child of a Canadian mining engineer and Spitfire pilot, Wally Moody.

Two by two the men leave the tunnel and move off in different directions: south for Czechoslovakia, west for the attempt to pick up a train, and north for Baltic ports and Scandinavia. From time to time the ground beneath their feet shudders

under the impact of the 4,000-pound bombs that their RAF comrades are dropping on Germany. They move warily, for the camp guard is doubled during air raids.

As dawn begins to break, a guard, startled by movement close by, fires a shot that raises the alarm. Guards, some in night clothes, swarm through the camp; 76 PoWs have escaped.

Germany, 23 March
Every minute for 24 hours to noon today more than four tons of explosive were dropped by Allied airmen on Germany and occupied Europe. This new intensive onslaught dropped 3,000 tons of bombs on Frankfurt, in the most concentrated attack of the war, after diverting from Schweinfurt. Mines were laid off Kiel, leaflets dropped over France and minor diversionary raids made all over Germany. The variety of targets reflects a change of tactics, dispersing attacks to make defence more difficult. In daytime raids today the USAAF hit Brunswick and targets in France (→ 24).

British miners sign four-year pay deal

Britain, 24 March
Pit owners and miners' leaders today signed a new four-year deal to secure peace and higher output in Britain's coalfields. Under a government-sponsored plan, piece-rate wages will be more closely related to output and there will be job security until 1948. About one in 20 miners will also be graded as "skilled craftsmen" able to earn well over £5 ($20) a week. Union leaders appealed tonight for a return to work by 60,000 South Yorkshire miners in dispute over their home coal allowance.

New commander of the Canadian Corps

Cassino, 20 March
The new commander of the Canadian I Corps, Lt-Gen Eedson Burns – better known to his troops as "Smiling Sunray" because of his dour, unchanging manner – is a formidable intellectual and the complete antithesis of his predecessor, Lt-Gen Henry Crerar. The outgoing, dynamic Crerar has left for Britain where he will join General Montgomery in D-Day planning. Burns, who is inexperienced in tank warfare, commanded the 5th Canadian Armoured Division, part of Canadian I Corps (→ 23).

Allies count cost of battle for Cassino

Cassino, 25 March
After a week of bitter fighting around this bomb-shattered town in central Italy, the Allied offensive, aimed at dislodging the Germans from the monastery, has been called off. Last night the Gurkha, Essex and Rajput Regiments were evacuated from their position on Hangman's Hill. The losses sustained in this abortive attack have been severe. The 2nd New Zealand Division has lost 63 officers and over 800 men dead, wounded or missing, while the 4th Indian Division lost 1,000 men and 65 officers.

Far from home: the last resting place of men of the US 1st Cavalry Brigade, 1st Cavalry Division on Los Negros Island in the Admiralty Group.

March

Su	Mo	Tu	We	Th	Fr	Sa
			1	2	3	4
5	6	7	8	9	10	11
12	13	14	15	16	17	18
19	20	21	22	23	24	25
26	27	28	29	30	31	

26. Britain: Churchill broadcasts on the war situation, praising the efforts of Tito's partisans and solemnly declaring that "the hour of our greatest effort is approaching".

26. USSR: The Red Army breaks through to the river Prut on a 53-mile front (→ 27).

27. USSR: The Red Army takes Kamenets-Podolski, in the Ukraine.→

27. Roumania: German troops rush to reinforce the country as Soviet forces approach the border (→ 2/4).

27. Vichy France: The government authorizes Frenchmen to enrol in the SS.

27-28. Kovno, Lithuania: SS troops round up and shoot dead all Jewish children under thirteen years of age (→ 4/4).

28. Westminster: The government is defeated by a single vote when the House of Commons carries an amendment to introduce equal pay for women teachers.→

29. Pacific: US naval aircraft bomb Japanese ships anchored off the Palau Islands (→ 30).

29. Burma: Japanese forces cut the Imphal to Kohima road, and Chinese troops capture Shaduzup, at the entrance to the Mogaung valley (→ 6/4).

29. Washington: Congress authorizes $1,350 million to found the United Nations Relief and Rehabilitation Agency, to help the growing refugee problem in Europe.

30. Admiralty Islands: US forces occupy Pityilu Island, north of Manus (→ 1/4).

30. Germany: RAF bombers raid Nuremberg, losing 95 aircraft out of 795. Five hundred and forty-five British crewmen are killed, compared with 69 German civilians and 59 foreign slave labourers.→

31. Pacific: Admiral Mineichi Koga, the C-in-C of the Japanese combined fleet, is killed in a plane crash.

31. Britain: Two hundred and seventy-nine civilians were killed and 633 injured in air raids this month.

Allied bombing reaches new intensity

Tremendous losses in Nuremberg raid

Germany, 31 March
British forces last night suffered a disaster similar to the Light Brigade's destruction at Balaklava, when 545 aircrew of Bomber Command died in a single raid. The target was Nuremberg, a round trip of 1,500 miles (2,400 km) and eight hours for those who came back. The route was direct and predictably, in bright moonlight, onto the guns of *Luftwaffe* night fighters all the way from Aachen to the target. Some defenders dropped flares above the 795-strong air convoy to illuminate the bombers even more.

In all, 95 planes were lost. Twelve crashed as they landed, one a Halifax whose pilot, Cyril Barton, is to be recommended for a posthumous VC for sacrificing his life to avoid miners' cottages.

Another 59 aircraft suffered heavy damage. The percentage loss was 20.8 of men and 11.9 of machines. The Germans lost 19 airmen (a favourable ratio of one to 28) plus 69 civilians and 59 slave workers. Although 256 buildings were hit and thousands of people have been made homeless, photo-reconnaissance suggests that Germany's war industry is unaffected.

A pre-raid briefing for RAF and Canadian bomber crews.

Air crews' survival: the chance is 50-50

London, 31 March
Bomber Command is suffering losses which it cannot sustain. Germany is littered with the burnt-out carcasses of Lancasters shot down by German night fighters in the "Battle of Berlin", and there is no doubt that the *Luftwaffe* has won this battle. The last raid on Berlin was a week ago, when 72 out of 811 aircraft were lost, and no more are planned in the immediate future.

Since 18 November last year 1,117 bombers and their crews have been lost over Berlin and other targets. So terrible have the losses been that even the eager young men of the RAF's elite aircrews, many of them still under 20, have occasionally baulked. Many have been shot down on their first operation. The rest have just a 50-50 chance of completing their "tour" of 30 operations.

Allied air raids cause German concern about effects on morale

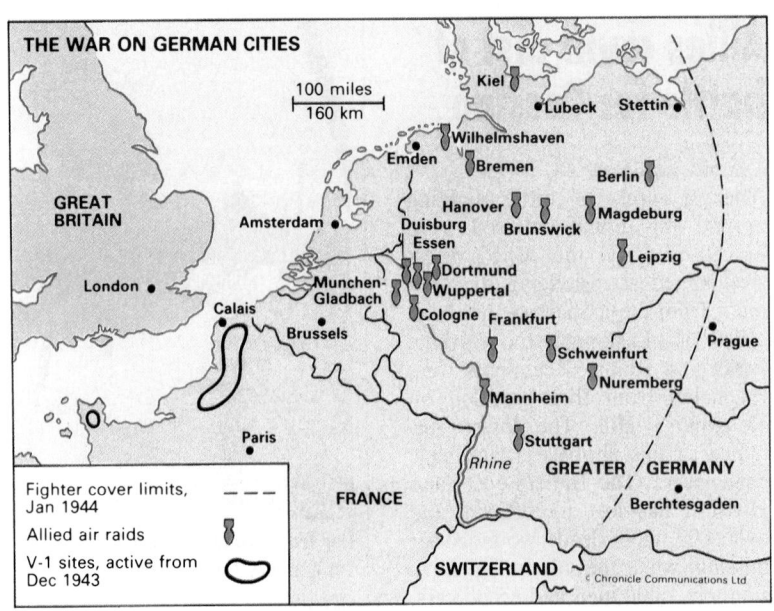

THE WAR ON GERMAN CITIES

100 miles / 160 km

Kiel
Lübeck   Stettin
Wilhelmshaven
Emden   Bremen
Berlin
GREAT BRITAIN
Hanover   Magdeburg
Amsterdam   Duisburg   Brunswick
Essen   Leipzig
London   Dortmund
Munchen-   Wuppertal
Gladbach   Cologne   Frankfurt
Calais   Prague
Brussels   Schweinfurt
Nuremberg
Mannheim
Paris
Stuttgart
Rhine   GREATER / GERMANY
FRANCE   Berchtesgaden
SWITZERLAND   © Chronicle Communications Ltd

Fighter cover limits, Jan 1944 — — —
Allied air raids
V-1 sites, active from Dec 1943

Germany, 31 March
Despite inflicting heavy losses on the RAF in last night's largely unsuccessful raid on Nuremberg – 95 out of 795 bombers failed to return – the Germans are increasingly concerned about the effect of Allied raids on the civil population.

A secret report on the domestic situation by the SD (Security Service of the SS) says that in Berlin, for example, people are living "in fear", especially of daylight raids. Berlin has been the target of 16 heavy raids in recent months – 11 this year alone – which have killed 6,166, and made 1.5 million homeless. The Nazis are putting greater pressure on parents to send their children to rural child evacuation camps from areas at risk (→ 15/4).

Invasion exercise ends in a muddle

Slapton Sands, Devon, 31 March
A full-scale investigation is to be launched next week in a bid to find out just what went wrong when the American VII Corps, under Major-General J Lawton Collins, staged an invasion exercise – Operation Beaver – at Slapton Sands, near Dartmouth, in Devon. The Sands, chosen because they are similar to a possible landing area in France, were to be captured by men coming ashore from landing craft after airborne troops had secured the flanks. Live ammunition was used, and a naval bombardment. But coordination between the units quickly broke down. "It was utter confusion," one man said (→ 5/4).

Churchill wins vote

Britain, 29 March
Mr Churchill forced MPs to eat humble pie today. Against government advice they had voted 117 to 116 last night for equal pay for women schoolteachers.

The prime minister immediately demanded and got a vote of confidence in his conduct of the war and, with it, reversal of the equal pay decision. "We had to show the government is in control. The German wireless was scoffing at us," he explained.

Russian advances provoke Hitler's fury

Von Manstein (l) and von Kleist: both accused of running away, and sacked.

Berlin, 30 March
Hitler, furious at the Russian victories in the Ukraine, has sacked two of his field marshals, von Manstein, commanding Army Group South, and von Kleist, in charge of Army Group A.

Von Manstein's dismissal is the culmination of a long series of quarrels in which he has refused Hitler's demand that the *Wehrmacht* should never retreat. Von Manstein, master of the defensive battle, won the last quarrel five days ago when Hitler summoned him to Berchtesgaden to demand that the army must stand on the line of the river Bug. Von Manstein replied that it was an impossible order, and that the First *Panzer* Army was in danger of being caught in a Stalingrad-type "cauldron".

Hitler backed down, but now he has had his revenge. He recognized that von Manstein was a master of manoeuvre, but said that what he wanted was someone who "would dash round the divisions and get the very utmost out of the troops". At the core of the quarrel is Hitler's belief that the army had run away in the Ukraine. In fact it was overwhelmed by the speed and weight of the Russian attack (→ 1/4).

Convoy JW-58 wins battle in Arctic Sea

Arctic Ocean, 31 March
Convoy JW-58 has triumphed in the face of one of the most powerful combined attacks of the war by German planes and submarines. The Allies were prepared for trouble and had provided the biggest-ever Arctic escort, comprising two aircraft carriers, five sloops, twenty destroyers, five corvettes and a cruiser. British aircraft shot down six German planes and sank one submarine. The navy sank another three U-boats, with the anti-submarine ace Captain F J "Johnnie" Walker leading the sloops from the bridge of HMS *Starling*. Not a single merchant ship was lost.

The work of the Royal Observer Corps observed

Britain, 31 March
One of the largely unsung groups involved in the air defence of Great Britain is the Royal Observer Corps. As its title suggests, the ROC, together with the Home Chain radar system, provides the eyes and ears of air defence.

Founded in the 1920s, the ROC is made up of civilian part-timers who man observation posts throughout the country 24 hours a day. Their task is primarily to track enemy aircraft once they have passed through the Home Chain screen. The posts are linked by telephone to the local RAF Fighter Command sector headquarters. The observers pass details of height, speed, number and type of aircraft to the sector HQ. This enables the controllers to scramble their fighters and direct them to the most advantageous position for tackling the enemy aircraft.

It was during the Battle of Britain that the Royal Observer Corps really won its spurs, especially during August 1940 when the *Luftwaffe* was hammering the Home Chain radar stations on the south coast. When the Blitz came, the observers also took on fire-watching duties – noting where incendiaries fell so that the fire services could deal with them before the fires they caused really took hold. After the *Baedeker* raids of spring 1942, life became somewhat quieter for the Corps. However, it has recently become busier again with the start of what is already being called the "Baby Blitz", the attacks on London and other cities by the Luftwaffe.

In the early days of the war the men of the ROC had no uniform and were lucky if they were even issued with steel helmets. They now wear smart blue battledress, although good hearing and eyesight, plus skills of aircraft recognition, are more important. Their watchword is constant alertness.

March 31. "Blitz babies", born during the German bombing of London, on a barrow at Euston station waiting for a train to the country.

April

Su	Mo	Tu	We	Th	Fr	Sa
						1
2	3	4	5	6	7	8
9	10	11	12	13	14	15
16	17	18	19	20	21	22
23	24	25	26	27	28	29
30						

1. USSR: The Russians surround 40,000 German troops at Skala, in the Ukraine (→ 5).

1. Switzerland: Twenty-six US bombers kill 50 Swiss civilians as they mistakenly bomb Schaffhausen.

1. Britain: A ten-mile-deep coastal belt from Land's End to the Wash is closed to the public.

2. USSR: The first Soviet troops cross the river Prut into Roumania east of Cernauti and occupy Gertza (→ 15).

2. Ascq, France: Members of the 12th SS *Panzer* Division *Hitler Jugend* slaughter 86 people after a resistance bomb derails their transport train.

3. New Guinea: US bombers attack Hollandia (→ 6).

3. Europe: RAF and USAAF bombers start to attack Budapest and other Hungarian targets, and Bucharest (→ 8/5).

4. Algiers: General de Gaulle takes control of Free French armed forces, squeezing General Giraud off the Committee of National Liberation.→

4. Poland: An Allied reconnaissance aircraft photographs part of the Auschwitz death camp.→

4. Egypt: The Greek Army Brigade mutinies (→ 22).

5. USSR: Soviet troops enter Tarnopol (→ 8).

5. USA: Wendell Willkie withdraws from the presidential race.

6. New Guinea: All but 25 Japanese aircraft at Hollandia have been destroyed (→ 12).

6. Britain: Pay-as-you-earn (PAYE) taxation starts today.

8. China: Japan bombs Honan province (→ 17).

8. Moscow: A 324-gun salute marks the First Ukrainian Front reaching Czechoslovakia and Roumania.→

8. USSR: Russia launches a major Crimean offensive (→ 10).

8. Germany: US aircraft bomb the Volkswagen plant at Fallersleben, near Hanover.

Soviets enter Roumania

German forces struggle to halt the Red Army advance into Roumania.

Moscow, 8 April
Mr Molotov, the Soviet foreign minister, announced today that the Red Army has crossed the river Prut into Roumania at several points and will pursue the Roumanian and German armies into Roumania until "their rout and complete capitulation". The first crossings were made on 2 April. The fact that the news was given by Molotov rather than by a general indicates the political implications of the advance. According to the official statement it is "the first step in the restoration of the frontier established by the Treaty of 1940 which Roumania broke by her treacherous attack in 1941 in the wake of Hitlerite Germany".

"At the same time," said Molotov, "the Soviet government declares that the entry into Roumania is dictated solely by military necessity, and is in no way aimed at the integrity of Roumanian territory or the existing social order." Meanwhile, the Red Army is advancing on Jassy, the Roumanian army's headquarters.

German battleship disabled by bombs

Norway, 3 April
Germany's one surviving battleship, the *Tirpitz*, has been disabled again by a daring naval attack. Repairs on the *Tirpitz* following the midget submarine attack last September had just been completed. The Royal Navy learnt from *Ultra* codebreaking that she was ready to sail and sent two carriers to Altenfjord. The *Victorious* and the *Furious* sailed as near as they dared and launched their 41 Fairey Barracuda bombers at 4.15 this morning, escorted by 41 fighters. They scored 14 hits on the *Tirpitz*. The bombs did not pierce the ship's heavy armour, but the *Tirpitz* will not sail again for months.

Telephone lines cut in build-up to the invasion of France

Britain, 5 April
As the cross-Channel invasion plans at last begin to unfold in an atmosphere of mounting tension, the British Isles are being sealed off from the outside world. All military leave has been stopped, and mail and telephone communications are allowed only under the strictest supervision.

There have been a few shocks. In Chicago a postal packet burst open in the main post office sorting department. It was found to contain top-secret papers about the invasion plans. It turned out that a sergeant in the US Army HQ in London had posted them to his sister by mistake, instead of putting them in the out-tray.

More seriously, a senior US officer, a West Point class-mate of Eisenhower, went to a reception at Claridge's hotel and boasted about the invasion date. He has been shipped back to the US and reduced in rank. General Patton, enjoying another party, believed he was in safe company and let drop an injudicious hint or two. He has survived.

In Germany, it is believed that the invasion is imminent. Press reports speak of massive daily bombardments of coastal defences by hundreds of Allied planes (→ 17).

April 3. The snow-capped peak of Mount Vesuvius erupts, putting on a display to rival the most intense bombing raids of the war so far.

Japan loses 150 planes in raid on Palaus

Japan halted in India

A Japanese freighter ablaze after the US attack in the western Carolines.

Imphal, India, 6 April
The Japanese "March on Delhi" has been stopped on the sun-baked plain of Imphal, 40 miles (64 km) inside India. The battle here, says the British commander, General Slim, will decide India's fate.

The invasion began three weeks ago when the 33rd Division of Lt-Gen Renya Mutaguchi's Fifteenth Army attacked the 17th Indian Division, aiming to draw off reserves at Imphal, the gateway to India. But Slim concentrated his three divisions in the plain, the 17th conducting a fighting withdrawal.

Today an airlift of reinforcements from the 7th Indian Division began from the Arakan front to Dimapur, north of Imphal. Two brigades are to join XXXIII Corps at Dimapur and a third is to join IV Corps at Imphal. Mutaguchi's men are now pressing in on Imphal from the south-west. Two more Japanese divisions have entered the battle: the 15th attacking Imphal from the south-east, with the 31st, attacking Imphal's line of communication with India at Kohima, 50 miles (80 km) north. The 5th Indian Division's 161 Brigade entered Kohima today, but other formations have been unable to break through.

The fighting has been ferocious: as many as half the men holding Nungshigum, a hill which dominates Imphal, were killed today. But time is on Slim's side. The Allies are supplied from the air; the 100,000 Japanese have only what they carry. If they do not capture supplies at Imphal, they will starve (→ 9).

South Pacific, 1 April
Three aircraft carrier groups of the US Navy have launched hundreds of aircraft in attacks on the Palaus and other isles of the Caroline Islands, sinking two destroyers, four escort vessels and 104,000 tons of merchant shipping, and destroying 150 Japanese aircraft.

The carriers despatched their planes at dawn on 30 March and again yesterday, losing 20 aircraft. The Japanese combined fleet had been forced out of Truk, and the concentration of its forward elements on the Palaus was seen as a potential threat to General MacArthur's advance along the north New Guinea coast. The Palau Islands are beyond the range of Allied heavy bombers based at Darwin, in Australia, so the US Navy was asked to send Task Force 58 – practically the whole of the US Fifth Fleet – to take out the base as it had taken out Truk.

A Japanese reconnaissance aircraft detected the approaching ships, and as a result the strike date was moved forward to 30 March while the Japanese flew in all the fighters they had from Peleliu and Yap to defend the new base. US aircraft mined passages to the main harbour, trapping many ships which then became prime targets.

Admiral Mineichi Koga, the Japanese navy chief, decided to move his headquarters from the battleship *Masashi* to Davao. He left the Palaus on 31 March for Davao, but his plane never arrived (→ 3).

Japanese troops in the jungle: they are desperate now to capture provisions.

De Gaulle triumphs over his army rival

Algiers, 4 April
General de Gaulle has finally triumphed over his rival, the First World War hero General Giraud. The French Committee of National Liberation, meeting here today, made de Gaulle head of the armed forces. He said tonight on Free French radio: "The efforts of all Frenchmen must depend on a single leadership." Giraud, C-in-C until today, has been offered the sop of being inspector-general.

Goebbels given absolute power in Berlin

Berlin, 7 April
In a desperate effort to rescue Berlin from the chaos created by Allied bombing, Hitler has suspended civil law and administration and installed Goebbels as *Stadtspresident* with unlimited powers. The city's military commanders, and the chiefs of police, fire brigades, medical, ambulance and rescue services, as well as food and relief organizations will be answerable to him alone. Shop assistants, office workers and commercial travellers are being drafted into labour units to clear bomb damage. Under the relentless air attacks, Berlin's firefighting services have broken down, relief organizations have failed to provide enough food and clothing for bombing victims, and widespread looting has been reported. There have been repeated outbreaks of disorder, with SS troops forced to intervene.

The destruction of police records has allowed what the authorities call "undesirable characters" to evade arrest and roam the city without identity papers.

Barbie to deport Jewish children

Izieu, Ain, 7 April
SS Lieutenant Klaus Barbie of the Lyons *Gestapo* today reported the destruction of the Jewish *Colonie des Enfants* [children's home] here in dutiful and businesslike words: "Captured – 41 children aged between three and ten years, and ten attendants. The transport will leave for Drancy tomorrow."

Drancy will be their only pause on the way to the gas chambers of Auschwitz-Birkenau (→ 15).

April

Su	Mo	Tu	We	Th	Fr	Sa
						1
2	3	4	5	6	7	8
9	10	11	12	13	14	15
16	17	18	19	20	21	22
23	24	25	26	27	28	29
30						

9. India: Japanese troops surround the British IV Corps at Kohima and Imphal.→

10. India: Slim orders his troops onto the offensive at Imphal and Kohima (→ 14).

10. USSR: Soviet troops recapture Odessa (→11).

11. USSR: The Russians take Kerch, in the Crimea, forcing a German retreat to Sevastopol (→12).

11. The Hague: RAF Mosquitoes precision-bomb a *Gestapo* building, destroying files on Dutch people earmarked for deportation.

12. Admiralty Islands: US troops clear Pak Island (→ 13).

12. USSR: Germany begins to evacuate the Crimea, despite Hitler's order to resist to the last man (→ 13).

12. Italy: King Victor Emmanuel announces his plan to retire when the Allies enter Rome, and appoints Crown Prince Umberto lieutenant of the realm (→ 17).

13. New Guinea: Australian troops retake Bogodjim (→18).

13. Stockholm: Britain and America demand that Sweden stop exporting ball bearings to Germany.

13. USSR: The Red Army captures Simferopol.→

14. Burma: Under pressure from the US, Ho Ying-chin, China's war minister, orders troops to cross the Salween river to attack the Japanese.→

14. Kiev: General Nikolai F Vatutin, injured on 29 February, dies of his wounds.

14. Bombay: The ammunition ship *Fort Stikine* explodes, killing 740 people, wrecking 27 ships and destroying 40,000 tons of food.

15. USSR: The Red Army captures Tarnopol.

15. Vilna: Forty Jewish prisoners, working as a "Blobel Commando" digging up and incinerating massacre victims buried at Ponar woods, try to escape; 25 are shot dead.→

15. Italy: The French take San Giorgio as the German Gustav Line starts to crumble (→ 5/5).

Air bombing switched to invasion targets

London, 15 April
The US Eighth Army Air Force and Bomber Command have switched their attentions from the cities and factories of Germany to the railways of France and Belgium to prepare for the Allied invasion.

It is not a move which pleases the commanders of the bomber forces. Sir Arthur "Bomber" Harris of the RAF still believes that he can bring Germany to its knees by area bombing, despite the terrible casualties inflicted on his aircrews during the Battle of Berlin. Remembering the slaughter in the trenches of the First World War, he has no confidence in the invasion. But it is his men who are being slaughtered

in this war. Lt-Gen Carl "Tooey" Spaatz, who commands the US Strategic Air Forces in Europe, agrees with Harris, but for different reasons. Spaatz believes that he can destroy the Germans ability to fight by destroying their oil plants. He also fears that supporting the army will compromise the air force's hard-won independence.

Their resistance forced General Eisenhower to go to his political bosses for a decision. He argued that if the "Transportation Plan" bombing campaign was not carried out, the invasion would fail. He won, and has assumed command of both British and US bombers for the period of the invasion (→19).

American bombers raid Ploesti oil field

Thick black smoke pours out of the oil storage tanks after the Allied raid.

Foggia, Italy, 15 April
A force of 448 Flying Fortresses and Liberators of the US Fifteenth Army Air Force escorted by 150 Mustangs fought its way to the Ploesti oilfields and the Roumanian capital, Bucharest, today against packs of German fighters to drop its bombs on railway targets.

The attacks were part of the Allied air assault on Nazi communications with the southern front, and brought the US bombers within 140 miles (224 km) of the Russian spearheads in eastern Roumania.

The Germans adopted new tactics by sending rocket-firing Do217 nightfighters against the Liberators attacking Bucharest. The *Luftwaffe*

lost 13 aircraft in the day's battles, while the Americans lost ten bombers and four fighters.

The raids were followed tonight by RAF Wellingtons which carried 4,000-pound bombs in their first raids on Roumania. Their target was Turnu Severin, a railway town on the north bank of the Danube, on the main line to Bucharest from Budapest and Belgrade.

The crews of the last wave of Wellingtons said that they could see the glow from fires 60 miles (96 km) away. They went in low, machine-gunning *flak* barges on the Danube and shooting up an airfield before dropping their bombs on the railway yards.

Gliders drop troops to back up Chindits

Indaw, North Burma, 9 April
Hundreds of gliderborne troops have been dropped into Burma to reinforce the Chindits, the long-range penetration force fighting behind Japanese lines. The first wave of Chindits was intended to cut the communications of the Japanese army facing Lt-Gen Stilwell's Chinese troops. This second wave has landed further west, joined up with one of the original Chindit columns, and aims to cut the lines of communication of the Japanese besieging Imphal (→ 10).

Midget submarine sinks Axis shipping

Norway, 10 April
The Royal Navy's X-craft, the midget four-man submarines which disabled the *Tirpitz* battleship last September, scored another devastating success today. And this time there was no loss of life. X24, commanded by Lieutenant M H Shean, managed to get in and out of the heavily-protected Bergen harbour without being detected.

Shean guided his midget submarine underneath the 7,500-ton merchant ship *Barenfels*, placed his charges and escaped, undetected, from the harbour before they went off. The explosion sank the *Barenfels* but did not harm a dock which was also targeted. The puzzled Germans have assumed that the attack was sabotage.

An X-craft running on the surface.

Red Army storms Crimean peninsula

Moscow, 14 April

The Red Army has reconquered the Crimea in a lightning campaign which lasted just six days. Only the southern tip around Sevastopol is holding out against Marshal Tolbukhin's Fourth Ukrainian Front. The attack was launched following the liberation of the Black Sea port of Odessa from which the Germans supplied General Jaenecke's Seventeenth Army in the Crimea.

Tolbukhin's men stormed across the Perekop peninsula in the north, outflanking defences by crossing the Sivash lagoon, thus unlocking the northern gate of the Crimea. General Eremenko then came in by the side door, attacking from his toehold at Kerch in the east.

Since then the Russians have rolled up the Germans who, under Hitler's orders, tried to hold a second line of defence south of Perekop instead of giving ground as Jaenecke wanted to do.

Now the Germans and their Roumanian allies have no choice. They have to fall back on the "Gneisenau Line" covering Sevastopol. Thousands of German and Roumanian non-combatant personnel and Russian auxiliaries are being evacuated from the Crimea to Constanta. Jaenecke wants to get his fighting man away before they are trapped, but Hitler has ordered that Sevastopol must be held at all costs.

That cost will be high. Moscow radio today broadcast this order: "Sailors and airmen. Don't allow them to escape! Destroy their ships! Shoot down their planes! Don't allow a single enemy to escape retribution!" (→ 16).

German military equipment abandoned in Odessa, now back in Soviet hands.

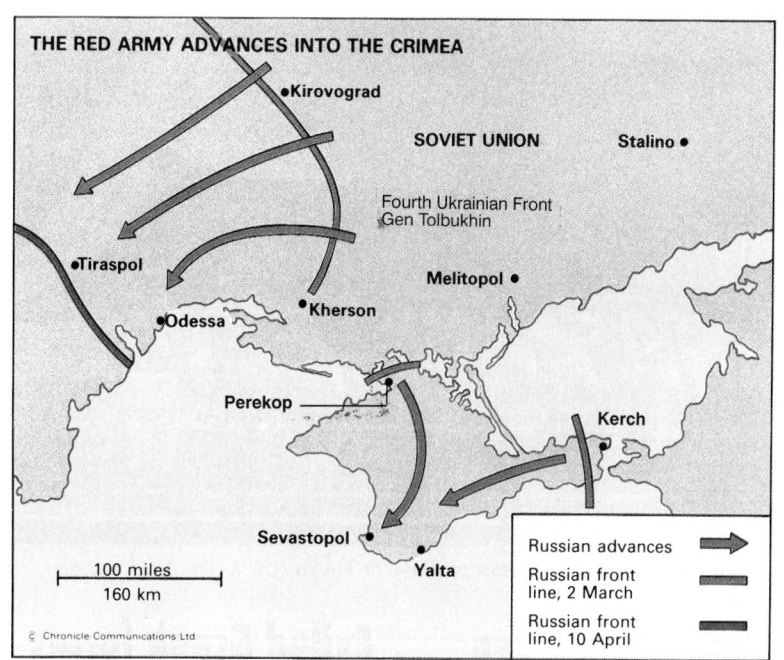

THE RED ARMY ADVANCES INTO THE CRIMEA

Kirovograd

SOVIET UNION   Stalino

Fourth Ukrainian Front
Gen Tolbukhin

Tiraspol

Melitopol

Odessa   Kherson

Perekop

Kerch

Sevastopol

Yalta

100 miles
160 km

© Chronicle Communications Ltd

Russian advances →
Russian front line, 2 March
Russian front line, 10 April

Allies race to beat Japanese offensive and the monsoons

Kohima, India, 12 April

Japanese forces, whose "March on Delhi" was halted last week on the Imphal plain by Lt-Gen Slim's troops, are fighting a bloody battle with the defenders of British India. Here at Kohima, 50 miles (80 km) north of Imphal, the Japanese 31st Division is locked in bitter combat with a scratch force of 3,500 Rajputs, Royal West Kents and Assamese, while Imphal is besieged by the Japanese Fifteenth Army and Subhas Chandra Bose's Indian National Army. For eight days Kohima has been under siege and the Imphal road has been cut, isolating the 100,000 Anglo-Indian troops fighting on the Imphal plain. Two Allied relief attempts have failed so far; one, by 161 Brigade of the 5th Indian Division, did get its leading elements to Kohima before itself being cut off at Jotsoma.

Today XXXIII Corps, responsible for the Kohima area, is being reinforced as rapidly as possible, with 23 Brigade of the 3rd Indian Division being ordered south to aid the British 2nd Division and cut Japanese communications.

Fighting also continues in Naga, a tiny village which clings to a mountain east of the Manipur road. Here the Allied troops are under mortar and artillery fire by day, and at night they are attacked by waves of hungry Japanese infantry without supplies. For both sides it is a fight for survival, and a race against time with the monsoon approaching next month (→ 20).

Nazis close the net on Hungary's 767,000 Jews

Hungary, 15 April

With today's round-up of Jews in the German-occupied areas of Ruthenia and Croatia, Hungary is no longer a safe refuge for Jewish people. The Hungarian government has hitherto stood up to German demands for the 767,000 Jews to be deported for "special treatment" in Poland. Miklos Kallay, who was premier until 22 March, refused to take any measures against the Jews, refusing German pressure to institute ghettoes and badges for them.

In April last year, Hitler reproached Hungary's regent, Admiral Miklos Horthy, for his liberal attitude. Horthy said he could not "beat the Jews to death"; the Fuhrer treated him to a lecture, saying that nations which did not rid themselves of Jews perished.

They met again last month. With the Red Army approaching the Hungarian border, Hitler was insistent. Horthy was to replace Kallay with Dome Sjotay, who boasted that he was a "true pioneer of anti-Semitism". It was agreed that a German plenipotentiary, Edmund Veesenmayer, and a security police force under SS Maj-Gen Otto Winkelmann were to supervise Hungary's internal affairs.

On 19 March German troops moved into Hungarian combat zones. At the same time Adolf Eichmann, the head of the *Gestapo* Jewish office, arrived in Budapest. His painstaking attention to detail has ensured the shipment of millions of European Jews to the extermination camps. He has brought a team of *Einsatzkommandos* with him to carry out the deportations with their customary brutality.

Meanwhile, at Auschwitz-Birkenau, the guards chuckle that "soon we'll be eating Hungarian salami". Engineers are checking and overhauling the gas chambers and crematoria. They are clearly expecting some big transports to arrive soon (→ 15/5).

1944

April

Su	Mo	Tu	We	Th	Fr	Sa
						1
2	3	4	5	6	7	8
9	10	11	12	13	14	15
16	17	18	19	20	21	22
23	24	25	26	27	28	29
30						

16. USSR: In the Ukraine, Marshal Rodion Malinovsky's troops cross the Dniester at Tiraspol.→

17. China: The Japanese launch Operation *Ichi-Go*, to crush Chinese resistance between the Yellow and Yangtze rivers and wipe out USAAF bases in Honan and Kwangsi provinces (→ 19).

18. USSR: Soviet troops retake Balaklava, in the Crimea (→ 6/5).

18. Britain: Incitement to strike is made a criminal act.→

18. Caroline Islands: US Liberators bomb Japanese military targets at Woleai (→ 19).

18-19. France: RAF bombers raid Rouen, Juvisy, Noisy-le-Sec and Tergnier, killing 1,383 French people.

19. Indian Ocean: Aircraft from the carriers HMS *Illustrious* and USS *Saratoga* attack Japanese airbases at Sabang, on Sumatra, as part of an operation to divert attention from the start of landings at Hollandia, in New Guinea (→ 21).

19. China: Japanese troops strike south along the Peking to Hankow railway, in Honan province (→ 22).

20. India: British forces reach the besieged Kohima garrison, but Japan still holds the surrounding land (→ 28).

20. Ankara: Turkey cuts off chrome exports to Germany.

20-21. Paris: An Allied air raid kills 641 people (→ 30).

21. New Guinea: US Task Force 58 attacks Japanese airbases at Sawar, Sarmi, Wakde Island and Hollandia to pave the way for tomorrow's landings.→

21 Naples: Marshal Pietro Badoglio forms a coalition goverment.

22. Marshall Islands: US forces take Ungelap, completing their occupation of the area.→

22. China: Japan captures Chengchow, in Honan province (→ 28).

Embattled Japanese plan attack in China

New Delhi, 22 April
The imperial Japanese army, already deeply emmeshed in a highly ambitious "March on Delhi" offensive from Burma, has now been committed to another equally ambitious offensive in China. Imperial headquarters has reinforced the China expeditionary force and ordered it to undertake an offensive to crush China.

On 17 April, the Japanese First and Twelfth Armies, supported by 200 aircraft, began a drive to open an overland supply route to the Southern Army in Thailand and Malaya and to occupy the new Allied airfields in south-east China which the Americans are using to attack shipping in Formosa Strait.

The offensive also aims to prevent long-range American bombers from using Chinese airfields to bomb the Japanese home islands. Another Japanese army is driving towards French Indochina. The Chinese high command in Chungking has announced the advance of Japanese columns in Honan where the Japanese claim to have routed 300,000 Chinese.

Three days before the Japanese attack, Chiang Kai-shek ordered divisions from Yunnan into Burma to help the hard-pressed General Stilwell. Until then, fearing a Japanese offensive, he had not only refused the help but had indicated that Chinese divisions already in Burma should "drag their feet". Chiang was persuaded to send his troops into the Burma theatre after President Roosevelt had cabled a stern request.

Japanese soldiers at a Shinto sanctuary in Tokyo bow to the dead warriors.

Lend-Lease given a new lease of life

Washington, 19 April
President Roosevelt has been given the go-ahead to make Lend-Lease contracts for a further year. The House of Representatives approved the move by a huge majority today. But behind the scenes intensive talks are going on about what to do about international payments now that the war is ending. Lend-Lease has provided the munitions, industrial materials and food for Britain to fight; now some Americans feel that the country is strong enough to start paying its way again.

Exiled Greek forces stage Egypt mutiny

Alexandria, 22 April
The Greek naval commander-in-chief, Vice-Admiral Petros Voulgaris, is preparing to board five warships whose refusal to obey orders sparked a virtual strike by 12 April of all Greek navy seamen in Egypt. The First Division of the Greek Army has also rebelled against its officers. Britain is keeping an eye on developments. The mutiny's causes are confused, but seem to stem from dissatisfaction with the Greek government in exile (→ 23).

Badoglio's cabinet quits office in Italy

Naples, 17 April
Italy's return to democracy is not coming easily. Nine months after Mussolini's downfall, the country is without a government. The dictator's successor, Marshal Pietro Badoglio, has announced the resignation of his entire cabinet.

Badoglio has been asked to form a new government with a broad base – and has approached the veteran communist leader Palmiro Togliatti as well as "Actionists", led by Prince Caracciolo, at the other end of the political spectrum.

From Zurich come reports that Mussolini, who has spent much of his time at his Lake Garda villa, has visited a Vienna cancer clinic, but has refused an operation (→ 21).

Finland breaks off Soviet peace talks

Moscow, 22 April
Peace negotiations between Russia and Finland have been broken off, it was announced tonight by the Soviet vice-premier and vice-commissar for foreign affairs, Andrei Vishinsky. This follows Finland's rejection of the armistice terms. These included the breaking of relations with Germany, the re-establishment of the 1940 Soviet-Finnish treaty and the payment of £150,000,000 reparations in goods within five years. The Allies have approved the Soviet reply.

A woman alights from a London "bus" bound for Liverpool Street.

508

MacArthur landings retake Hollandia

US invasion troops wade ashore.

The Hollandia expeditionary force brings a bulldozer to repair bomb damage.

Hollandia, 22 April

In a swift lightning strike that has wrongfooted the Japanese in northern New Guinea, a 52,000-strong Allied invasion force under General Douglas MacArthur today seized Hollandia, the administrative capital of Dutch New Guinea. The landings, made from 113 ships escorted by the US Fifth and Seventh Fleets, have cut off the escape route for Gen Adachi's main force, estimated to be 50,000 men, now surrounded at Wewak, where Adachi expected the attack. At the same time Australian troops have closed on nearby Madang. The amphibious Allied force swept ashore this morning at Hollandia, Aitape and Tanahmera Bay after US Navy aircraft from Pacific Fleet carriers had destroyed over 100 grounded Japanese planes at Hollandia and at support airstrips.

Hollandia was like a battered ghost town as the US advance guard, covered in red mud, entered. Everywhere there are signs of the panic as the 12,000-strong garrison of middle-aged reservists fled into the jungle following a dawn bombardment that seriously damaged all of Hollandia's buildings. In a bedroom a Japanese officer's polished boots still stand by his bed, a neatly-pressed uniform hangs on the door. In the school the day's lessons are still on the blackboard.

For MacArthur, who celebrated with a chocolate ice-cream soda as he toured the beach-heads, the victory is a consolation for his fading presidential hopes following his defeat in the Republican primary at Wisconsin three weeks ago (→ 24).

Red Army takes Yalta in push to clear Germans from Crimea

Moscow, 16 April

Yalta, the last port apart from Sevastopol through which the Germans could escape from the Crimea, has fallen to General Eremenko's Independent Maritime Army. Sevastopol's airfield at Kacha has also been captured and, as fighting rages across the old battlefields of Balaklava and Inkerman, the position of Germany's Seventeenth Army looks hopeless.

A terrible toll is being taken of the Germans as they try to escape. A German correspondent describes how "bombers, dive-bombers and fighters in endless procession are raining their bombs on our ships and riddling them with cannon fire". Sevastopol harbour is choked with sunken ships and the bodies of drowned men (→18).

Just one of the guns massacring the retreating Germans in the Crimea.

Plans set for D-Day
1: Diplomats face travel restrictions

London, 17 April

Under pressure from the military commanders for the "Overlord" invasion of Europe, the British war cabinet has clamped down on diplomatic privileges, held up diplomatic bags and put all foreign embassies under surveillance.

Even friendly embassies have been included, since it was reckoned that they could not be completely secure against spies, dupes or chumps. There has been only one protest about the restrictions – from officials of General de Gaulle's Free French.

The worrying gap in this security cordon is Eire, where de Valera's government remains at peace with Nazi Germany. German agents in Dublin move about freely. But the long, coiling border with Northern Ireland, where travellers pass to and fro freely in peacetime, is now under close guard (→ 27).

2: French railway targets are bombed

France, 19 April

Railway links and river crossings throughout northern and western France – vital for Germany's defence against an Allied invasion – are being attacked with unprecedented fury by RAF and USAAF bombers. In 36 hours some 7,000 tons of bombs have been dropped. Pilots are ordered to pick their targets with care to ensure that French casualties are kept to a minimum.

Last night, RAF Lancasters and Halifaxes struck at rail links outside Paris and at Rouen, dropping 4,000 tons of bombs. It was the biggest load carried in a single raid. In order to conceal the intended invasion area, for every ton of bombs dropped behind the invasion zone the Allies are dropping two tons elsewhere in France.

Aircraft losses are falling; 14 bombers were lost last night and five in the earlier raids. The Germans are believed to be restricting their use of fighters because of dwindling supplies of aviation fuel caused by Allied bombing of oil refineries.

1944

April

Su	Mo	Tu	We	Th	Fr	Sa
						1
2	3	4	5	6	7	8
9	10	11	12	13	14	15
16	17	18	19	20	21	22
23	24	25	26	27	28	29
30						

23. Alexandria: Greek officers board three striking warships, with the loss of 50 lives (→ 24).

24. New Guinea: Australian troops capture Madang (→ 25).

24. Britain: The actor and composer Ivor Novello is sentenced to two months' imprisonment for offences concerned with petrol rationing.

24. Alexandria: The remaining striking warships and the First Brigade of the Greek Army surrender, ending a three-week mutiny in the exiled Greek armed forces under the Allied High Command.

24. Washington: US military strategists agree that to defeat Japan it will be necessary to invade Japan itself.

25. New Guinea: Fresh waves of Allied troops land at Humboldt Bay (→ 26).

25. China: Japan attacks Loyang, in Honan province.

26. New Guinea: Australian troops capture Alexishafen, north of Madang.→

26. Arctic: Aircraft from HMS *Victorious* and HMS *Furious* and escort carriers sink three enemy ships, losing six planes.

26. Off Brittany: HMS *Black Prince* and four destroyers engage three German torpedo boats; one is sunk.

28. China: US aircraft bomb bridges on the Yellow River to hamper Japan's advance (→ 7/5).

28. Burma: Allied and Chinese soldiers push through the Mogaung valley towards Myitkyina (→ 5/5).

28. US: Frank Knox, the secretary of the navy, dies of a heart attack.

29. New Guinea: US forces take over the captured Japanese airfields at Hollandia.

30. Caroline Islands: Having destroyed the Japanese base at Truk and shot down 93 of Japan's 104 planes, nine US destroyers and eight cruisers shell the Sawatans (→ 1/5).

30. Britain: Civilian air raid casualties this month were 146 dead and 226 injured.

German commander on Crete snatched

Major Patrick Leigh-Fermor (2nd from r in front row) with Cretan partisans.

Crete, 26 April
General Heinrich Kreipe, the commander of the 22nd *Panzer-grenadier* Division in Crete, was being driven home this evening when his car was stopped by two men in German uniform waving a red light. The chauffeur was bundled out, the general forced into the back seat by Cretan *andartes* (guerrillas) holding a knife to his throat, and the car driven for 20 miles (32 km) by two British officers, one of them wearing the general's hat. German guards at 22 checkpoints stood aside and saluted when they recognised the general's pennants on the car.

The kidnappers – Major Patrick Leigh-Fermor and Captain Stanley Moss of British Combined Forces – abandoned the car near a beach on the north coast, hoping the Germans will assume they have been picked up by submarine. In reality, Leigh-Fermor and Moss spirited their captive into the mountains of central Crete. Accompanied by *andartes* they hope to reach the south coast of the island, there to be picked up by a British launch and taken to Cairo.

"Prefab" house is built in three days

London, 30 April
The first pre-fabricated or factory-made house has been erected in three days in London and is now on view. The single-storey house of 600 square feet (55 square metres) arrived in parts on Wednesday and was ready for occupation by Saturday afternoon. Mr Churchill has said that 500,000 will be erected for bombed-out families and demobilized servicemen after the war.

The "pre-fab", made of sheet steel lined with plywood, has two bedrooms, living-room, kitchen, bathroom, lavatory and bicycle shed. A single wall unit comprises a bath and wash-basin on one side and a cooker, sink and refrigerator on the other. It will cost £550 ($2,200).

Patton hits trouble

London, 25 April
The controversial Lt-Gen George S Patton has upset US congressmen by being reported today as telling a British audience that it was the destiny of Britain and the US to rule the world once they had won the war. One congressman described the speech as "barmy". A version of the speech published in Britain suggests that Patton included the USSR in the "destiny" remarks.

MacArthur to transform colonial town into largest Allied base

Hollandia, 26 April
Within days of its recapture from the Japanese this small quiet colonial Dutch town is being transformed into the largest Allied base yet built in the South-west Pacific.

Squads from the US Navy construction battalions, known as the "Seabees", have started work on extensive docks and airfields, while a city of huts is being erected on the edge of primaeval jungle. Some 140,000 men are to be based here for the next phase of MacArthur's Operation Cartwheel, intended to drive the Japanese from north-west New Guinea before attacking the Philippines. Meanwhile US flyers have bombed Wewak in pursuit of MacArthur's policy of "neutralizing" Gen Adachi's beleaguered garrison east of here (→ 29).

Australian troops establish themselves on an airstrip taken from the Japanese.

Invasion plans intensified in countdown to D-Day

Hundreds die in US practice landings

Slapton Sands, Devon, 29 April
At least 638 American soldiers and sailors were killed when an "Overlord" training exercise codenamed "Tiger" was attacked in the Channel by E-boats (German motor torpedo boats) in darkness. Some who took part in the exercise believe the death toll to be much higher because of a communications mix-up which also led to the men being shelled by their own warships on the beaches of Slapton Sands.

E-boats from Cherbourg slipped past patrolling British MTBs during the night of 27-28 April, sank LST (landing ship tank) 507 and LST 531, and torpedoed LST 289. Senior commanders were dismayed to learn that among the missing were ten men who had top-secret information about Overlord. All ten bodies have been recovered.

Some men involved in "Tiger" claim that some landing craft were not told of a one-hour postponement of the exercise and that men began going ashore while the naval bombardment continued (→ 6/5).

Allied servicemen assemble in Britain

Britain, 30 April
Southern England is a gigantic armed camp with vast tank, truck and artillery parks, and innumerable arms dumps, to equip an invasion force of over 3,500,000 men, over a million of them Americans.

The initial assault will be carried out by Americans, Britons – with Irish volunteers – and Canadians. But almost every occupied country in Europe will join in the assault on the Germans: the French have Gen Leclerc's 2nd Armoured Division from North Africa; the Poles an armoured division and nine air squadrons; the Belgians a brigade and two squadrons; the Dutch a brigade and two squadrons; the Norwegians four squadrons, and the Czechs three. The Australians and New Zealanders have five air squadrons each (→ 29).

Over northern France: a rail junction ablaze beneath a US A-20 Havoc.

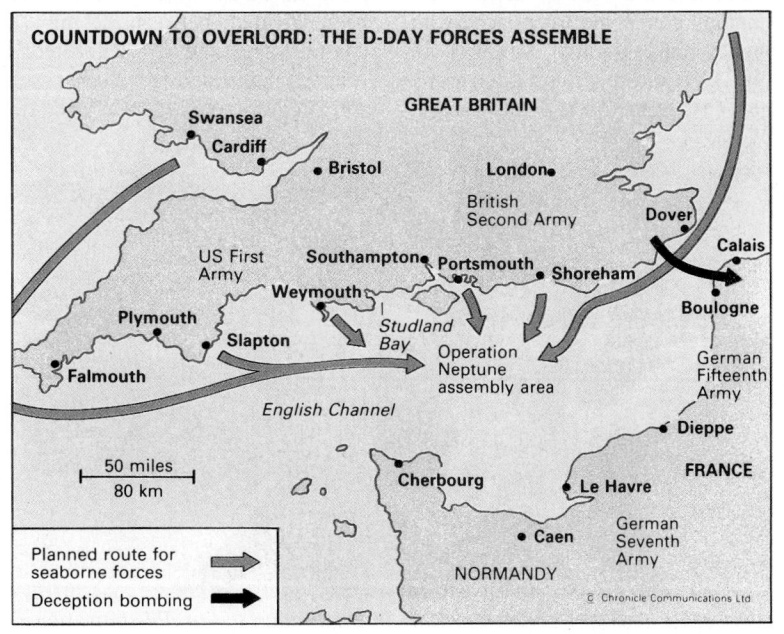

COUNTDOWN TO OVERLORD: THE D-DAY FORCES ASSEMBLE

GREAT BRITAIN
Swansea
Cardiff
Bristol
London
British Second Army
US First Army
Southampton Portsmouth Shoreham
Weymouth
Plymouth
Slapton
Studland Bay
Operation Neptune assembly area
Falmouth
English Channel
Dover
Calais
Boulogne
German Fifteenth Army
Dieppe
FRANCE
Cherbourg
Le Havre
Caen
German Seventh Army
NORMANDY

50 miles
80 km

Planned route for seaborne forces
Deception bombing

© Chronicle Communications Ltd.

Allies step up bomb campaign in Europe

Britain, 30 April
In an all-out aerial assault on enemy communications in northern Europe, goods trains, road and rail bridges, radar installations, wireless telegraphy stations and power station transformers within 150 miles (240 km) of the planned invasion zone are being pounded in day and night attacks. The bombing range, extending from Liege, in Belgium, to Orleans, in central France, is calculated to leave the Germans guessing as to the landing area.

About 1,000 locomotives have been knocked out in recent months; one squadron wrecked 34 on two nights under a "Bombers' moon". Trains seeking refuge in tunnels are sealed inside by bombs at each entrance. Some 18,000 labourers from the Todt Organization, allocated to Rommel after his urgent appeals for help in strengthening the coastal defences, have had to be put to work repairing railway tracks, some 75 per cent of which have become unusable in northern France (→ 7/5).

All foreign travel is banned indefinitely

Britain, 27 April
From midnight tonight all travel abroad from Britain will be banned. Exit permits granted to would-be travellers are no longer valid, unless they have been issued during the past week. Some visits to Ireland will be allowed after strict scrutiny.

Similar pre-invasion moves are being made by the enemy. Civilians are being removed from coastal areas, and German families evacuated from the Ruhr when the heavy bombing began are being sent back. Vichy France has cut communications with neutral countries in an effort to prevent military and political intelligence from reaching the Allies. In a hunt for Allied sympathizers, diplomatic bags for French military attaches in Madrid, Lisbon and Berne have been seized.

1944
May
Su	Mo	Tu	We	Th	Fr	Sa
	1	2	3	4	5	6
7	8	9	10	11	12	13
14	15	16	17	18	19	20
21	22	23	24	25	26	27
28	29	30	31			

1. Caroline Islands: The US Navy's Task Force 58 has destroyed about 120 Japanese planes, half on the ground, in a two-day attack on Truk (→4).

1. London: Commonwealth prime ministers meet to discuss the progress of the war.

1. London: A Yugoslav military mission from Tito arrives for consultations on closer cooperation with the Allies.→

3. Madrid: Spain agrees to cut wolfram (tungsten) exports to German in exchange for US oil supplies. →

3. Tokyo: Admiral Soemu Toyoda is appointed C-in-C of the Japanese combined fleet, replacing Admiral Mineichi Koga who died in a plane crash on 31 March (→14/6).

4. New Guinea: US reinforcements land at Aitape (→11).

4. US: Meat rationing ends, except for certain beef cuts.

5. Burma: Having taken the strategically vital Point 551, the Fourteenth Army counter-attacks at Imphal (→6).

5. Italy: General Alexander orders Allied units to break through the Gustav Line on 11 May (→13).

5. Germany: Intelligence services intercept a telephone conversation between Roosevelt and Churchill, but hear no secrets.

5. Italy: RAF Mustangs and RAAF and SAAF Warhawks attack the Torre Dam.

6. India: Mahatma Gandhi, imprisoned since August 1942, is released owing to ill health.

6. USSR: Soviet troops under General Fedor Tolbukhin launch an assault on Sevastopol with a heavy bombardment of *Katyusha* rockets (→8).

6. Burma: Chinese troops attack Japanese positions at Ritpong (→7).

6. Germany: Eighteen hundred slave labourers are requisitioned from France to work on the production of rocket bombs at Dora concentration camp.

Allies stage final invasion rehearsal

Slapton Sands, Devon, 6 May
A last effort to remedy the mistakes and muddles thrown up in the succession of invasion exercises held on the beaches of England has been made this week with Operation Fabius. This took place over five days and extended from Little-hampton in Sussex, through Hampshire and Dorset, to Slapton Sands, the scene of last month's disaster when 638 Americans were lost in a German E-boat attack during a previous D-Day exercise.

The American, British and Canadian forces were assigned to four separate beaches corresponding to the assault beaches in France. Two other exercises, involving naval forces, took place at the same time to familiarize the invasion fleet with the boarding, disembarkation and reinforcement plans. A third exercise, Operation Splint, handled the evacuation of wounded by landing craft.

Fabius has been judged satisfactory. Afterwards, though, Brigadier-General Norman Cota told his

In training for D-Day: British troops race up the shores of southern England.

headquarters staff of the US 29th Division that when the real thing came along "the little discrepancies that we tried to correct on Slapton Sands are going to be magnified and are going to give way to incidents that you might at first view as chaotic. The landing craft aren't going in on schedule and people are going to be landed in the wrong place ... The enemy will have some success in preventing our gaining lodgement. But we must improvise, carry on, not lose our heads" (→8).

Rommel builds steel ring around Europe

La Roche-Guyon, France, 6 May
At the German Army Group B's HQ in north-western France, Rommel has substantially reinforced the coastal defences from the Netherlands through the Pas-de-Calais to Normandy. Bunkers have been built, and the beaches bristle with innumerable angle irons laced with mined stakes slanted seawards. In the Cotentin pensinsula, covering the port of Cherbourg, a network of mined poles linked by wires stands as a defence against airborne landings. But the Germans are unable to agree on where the Allies will invade, so the six divisions of General Geyr von Schweppenburg's powerful *Panzer* Group West have been divided between Rommel's coastal forces and von Rundstedt's reserves near Paris.

Crossword writer's unwitting tip-offs

London, 2 May
The crossword in the *Daily Telegraph* has caused uproar among the D-Day planners today by apparently revealing two of the most closely guarded codewords of the invasion. The clue to 17 Across is "One of US" and that of 3 Down is "Red Indian on the Missouri". The answers – "Utah" and "Omaha" – are the names given to two of the American invasion beaches.

These clues were spotted with horror by senior officers who are among the devotees of the crossword. Their immediate reaction was that the invasion's secrets were being leaked to the Germans.

Their fears have been increased by the discovery that, in a puzzle prepared by the same compiler for publication a few days before D-Day, the answer to one clue is "Overlord", the codename for the whole invasion. MI5 is now investigating the compiler, Leonard Dawe, a 54-year-old teacher from Leatherhead, in Surrey.

Vast angle irons spike French beaches in preparation for an Allied invasion.

1944

May

Su	Mo	Tu	We	Th	Fr	Sa
	1	2	3	4	5	6
7	8	9	10	11	12	13
14	15	16	17	18	19	20
21	22	23	24	25	26	27
28	29	30	31			

Tito's partisans seize weapons in Zagreb

Yugoslavia, 5 May

Marshal Tito's partisan army, now numbering nearly 300,000 well-armed men and women, has fought its way into the Croatian capital of Zagreb, it was learned today. A huge cache of German weapons was captured, with lorryloads of prisoners, before the partisans "melted away" in typical fashion.

Tito's National Liberation Front now controls almost every town in mountainous Montenegro. It also took four German divisions to drive them from Slovenia; even so, few main roads or railways there are safe for troop transport. Twelve divisions of General Rendulic's Second *Panzerarmee* are being kept fully occupied by Tito's fiercely determined irregulars.

Although the Germans have retaken most of the Adriatic islands between Fiume and Split – captured by partisans when the Italian army collapsed last year – their garrisons are under constant harassment.

The head of the British military mission, Brigadier Fitzroy Maclean, has selected the outer island of Vis as a base for organizing British commando operations in Nazi-held Yugoslavia (→25).

Precision bombing hits Dutch capital

The Hague, Netherlands, 3 May

In the most successful example of precision bombing of the war – and probably the most accurate since the air weapon was invented – an RAF Mosquito today lobbed two bombs through the front door of the Air Ministry in the crowded centre of the Dutch capital. Two more bombs, delivered at the same time, penetrated windows on either side of the door. The building had to be struck at the first attempt from 50 feet (15 metres).

Fascist Spain leans towards the Allies

Madrid, 3 May

Pro-Nazi Spain bent under Allied pressure today and agreed to cut by a sixth its exports of wolfram – the steel hardening element – to Germany. General Franco, the Spanish dictator, has succumbed to British and US demands for the release of Italian ships held in Spanish ports, the withdrawal from the eastern front of his "Blue" division of 14,284 men and "Blue" air squadron, and the closure of the German "spy" consulate at Tangiers.

The White Cliffs of Dover: whole communities have taken refuge in caves in the cliffs from German shells which flash across from Calais.

7. China: Japanese forces link up at Suiping, on the Peking to Hankow railway (→13).

7. India: The Allies call off their attack in the Imphal area, having achieved little (→11).

7. Berlin: The US Eighth Army Air Force attacks the city for the second time in three days.→

8. Crimea: The second phase of the German evacuation begins.→

8. London: Eisenhower sets D-Day, the date for the Allied invasion of Europe, at 5 June (→9).

9. Berlin: Donitz says that he does not expect the Allies to invade in the near future (→15).

9. France: Allied bombers attack *Luftwaffe* bases in preparation for D-Day.→

10. Algiers: The Free French estimate that there are 175,000 Resistance fighters in France (→13).

10. Washington: James V Forrestal succeeds the late Colonel W Franklin Knox as secretary of the navy.

11. Japan: The Japanese navy launches Operation *A-Go*, the defence of the Mariana Islands, under Vice-Admiral Jisaburo Ozawa (→17).

11. Burma: About 40,000 Chinese troops cross the river Salween in a major offensive to retake northern Burma (→16).

12. London: The Allies call on the Axis satellites Hungary, Roumania and Bulgaria to withdraw from the war.

13. China: Chinese forces oust the Japanese from Suiping, regaining control of the Peking to Hankow railway.→

13. Crimea: The attempted German evacuation ends.

13. France: A Resistance attack halts production of self-propelled guns at the Lorraine-Dietrich Works at Bagneres de Bigorre (→15).

13. English Channel: Admiral Donitz loses his second son, Klaus, when the Free French destroyer *La Combattante* and British frigate *Stayning* sink the E-boat S147.

Eichmann to barter Jews for transport

Eichmann: holding Jews hostage.

Budapest, 8 May

Adolf Eichmann, the head of the Jewish office of the *Gestapo*, is holding the Jews of Hungary hostage. Joel Brand, a member of the Hungarian Jewish Assistance and Rescue Committee, is being sent to Turkey. To save the Jews, he must persuade Allied representatives there to provide Germany with 10,000 heavy trucks. But a first convoy of Hungarian Jews arrived at Auschwitz on 28 April; it is hard to imagine that it will be the last (→12).

Irish government is toppled from power

Dublin, 9 May

The government of Eire resigned tonight after defeat in the Irish assembly, the *Dail*, by one vote on the second reading of the Transport Bill. Defeat on this major issue is regarded as a no-confidence vote. The bill aimed to merge two big railway companies. An inquiry has begun into share dealings preceding publicity about the scheme.

Tonight's vote was the first since the election last June in which all the opposition parties – *Fine Gael*, Labour, Independent and Farmers – used their combined strength to defeat the minority *Fianna Fail* government of Eamon de Valera. The next general election will be held within four weeks of tonight's dissolution (→1/6).

Germany reels from attacks in both east and west

Siege lifted, ending Sevastopol's agony

Crimea, 9 May

Soviet troops today stormed the mighty fortress of Sevastopol, all but completing the liberation of the Crimea, the peninsula which the Germans called "our aircraft carrier in the Black Sea".

General Tolbukhin's soldiers fought their way into the ruined streets of the city after three days of bombardment by guns and dive-bombers. The dazed remnants of the German Seventeenth Army and its Roumanian allies caved in.

The Soviet Black Sea fleet, for so long unable to act for fear of the Stukas flying from the Crimea, has also played a large part in the freeing of its traditional base. Motor torpedo boats have been out at night causing havoc among the German ships trying to evacuate their troops. Now the fleet can return to Sevastopol; the port will need much repair work, but the ships will be able to use the natural harbour as a base for operations along the Roumanian coast.

A German spokesman admitted the crushing defeat in an astonishingly frank statement: "On the morning of the third day of the onslaught, when the Russians broke into the southern part of the city, the German Command decided to give up the struggle". About 20,000 Germans and Roumanians have been killed at Sevastopol and 24,361 taken prisoner (→ 13).

The war-torn Black Sea port of Sevastopol, now back in Russian hands.

Soviet marines keep the Germans in their sights in the liberation of the Crimea.

Germans abandon Crimean peninsula

Sevastopol, 13 May

The last remnants of the German Seventeenth Army routed at Sevastopol three days ago have been cleared from Cape Kherson, west of the fortress port. The whole peninsula has now been cleared of the Germans and their Roumanian allies.

The Russians claim to have killed 20,000 Axis troops and taken over 24,000 prisoner in Sevastopol. Among the prisoners are Generals Dehmut and Kruger, and the total of German casualties in the clearing of the Crimea amounts to 110,000 killed, wounded or taken prisoner. Those who tried to escape from Cape Kherson by sea were harried from the air, and from the sea where MTBs and submarines sank 191 vessels, including 69 heavily-laden transports; over 8,000 men died in the evacuation. The Germans were also attacked by marine commandos who raided behind their lines. A tremendous amount of booty fell into Russian hands, including 111 tanks and self-propelled guns, 2,304 guns and 49 aircraft; much more was destroyed.

It was a complete disaster for the Germans, and the swiftness of their collapse reflects the deep divisions in the German high command after Hitler had ordered his troops to fight to the last man, against the advice of his generals. The ordinary soldiers had the last word. They surrendered (→ 31).

Air raids intensify over France and Berlin

Germany, 8 May

US aircraft attacked Berlin and Brunswick, in north Germany, today. The *Luftwaffe* threw most of its resources into the resulting air battle. Brunswick was attacked by 287 Liberators and 49 Fortresses, and Berlin by 378 Liberators. More than 200 interceptors were reported over Brunswick and another 100 above Berlin. Allied pilots spoke of aircraft in combat from 23,000 feet (7,020 metres) down to ground level. In this aerial war of attrition, 119 German aircraft are said to

have been destroyed, 59 by US fighters and 60 by bomber gunners. Some German pilots are reported to have tried to bring down the heavy US bombers by ramming, a suicidal gesture. The Americans lost 36 bombers and 13 fighters.

The attack on Berlin was the second in two days. In other raids of the last 24 hours, the French and Belgian rail systems have been hit as part of the pre-invasion strategy. In another attack, aimed at cutting aviation fuel supplies, RAF planes bombed targets in Roumania (→ 9).

US bombers attack synthetic oil plants

London, 13 May

Lieutenant-General Carl Spaatz, the commander of the US bombing campaign on Germany, continued his attack on Germany's oil supplies yesterday with a massive raid by 621 Fortresses and 265 Liberators of the US Eighth Army Air Force. They seriously damaged synthetic oil plants at Zwickau, Brux, Merseburg, Luna, Lutzkendorf and Bohlen.

An armada of American and British fighters escorted the bombers and a tremendous air battle devel-

oped. The Americans lost 46 bombers, and 12 fighters failed to return. It is known that 21 German pilots were killed and 26 were wounded.

The German pilots fought skilfully, but "Tooey" Spaatz's plan to deprive them of fuel is evidently working, for fewer than 100 fighters came up to protect these most important targets. They failed, and "Ultra" intelligence reveals that there will be still less fuel for them after today's raids. The *Luftwaffe* will also find it increasingly difficult to replace the pilots lost (→ 15).

Germans resist new Allied moves in Italy

Italy, 13 May

Three major assaults have failed to dislodge the Germans from the Gustav Line at Cassino. But today, the biggest army yet – British, Polish, American, Canadian and French Colonials – is advancing on a narrow front and pushing northwards against stiff German opposition.

Today the French Moroccan soldiers of General Juin's *Corps Expeditionaire Francais* took Monte Faito – where the German 71st Division had obeyed orders to fight to the last man. On their right flank, the 8th Indian and 4th British Divisions launched assault boats into the fast-flowing Rapido river and established bridgeheads

under fierce German fire. The Polish II Corps is attacking Monte Cassino from the east and north. The US II Corps is pushing forward along the coastal plain.

Intensive planning has gone into this crucial offensive – timed to coincide with the coming invasion in France. The Eighth Army has been regrouped westwards under the cover of darkness and huge smokescreens. The Germans were fooled into moving two divisions in anticipation of a new seaborne landing north of Rome.

Two days ago, at 11pm, the silence of the Liri valley was broken by 1,600 heavy guns. At sunrise yesterday, the tanks began their attack, supported by 3,000 aircraft (→ 14).

US infantrymen move up in Italy: the Germans are putting up a hard fight.

Japan attacks B-29 bases in east China

Chungking, 11 May

Japan has hit airfields in China as part of its Operation *Ichi-Go*, which aims to prevent US B-29 bombers from using the bases for raids on Japan. Lieutenant-General Claire "Old Leatherface" Chennault, the commander of the US Fourteenth Army Air Force, fears that the raids could be successful and has appealed for help, but Japan's offensives in Burma have precluded extra supplies (→ 17).

Denmark's coast is closed by Germany

Copenhagen, 9 May

As western Europe prepares for the expected Allied invasion, all Denmark's North Sea coast has been closed to shipping. Any vessel sailing within ten miles (16 km) of the coastline will be fired on by shore batteries, General Haneken, who is responsible for the Danish sector of Germany's Atlantic Wall, said today. Danish islands are now isolated from the mainland, as are those of the Netherlands (→ 28/6).

1944

May

Su	Mo	Tu	We	Th	Fr	Sa
	1	2	3	4	5	6
7	8	9	10	11	12	13
14	15	16	17	18	19	20
21	22	23	24	25	26	27
28	29	30	31			

14. Italy: The British XIII Corps consolidates a bridgehead over the Rapido river, and advances into the Ausente valley (→ 15).

14. Britain: Intelligence officers decode a cipher message from Goering, uncovering a campaign to trick Allied bombers into raiding inactive airfields.

15. Budapest: The mass evacuation of Jews from Hungary to Auschwitz-Birkenau begins in earnest, at the rate of 4,000 a day (→ 25).

15. France: The Germans cancel all civilian trains because air attacks on the rail system are making military movement more difficult (→ 21).

15. Italy: The Free French take San Giorgio and Ausonia.→

16. Burma: Japanese resistance at Kohima is broken.→

16. Germany: Field Marshal Erhard Milch orders the long-range bombardment of England with FZG-76 (V1) missiles.

17. New Guinea: US forces land on Wakde Island.→

17. Java: Aircraft of the British Eastern Fleet sink ten Japanese ships in an attack on oil installations at Surabaya.→

17. China: On the Yunnan front a Chinese force takes the Huei-jen bridge area; forward elements penetrate Hongmoshu behind Japanese lines, but the village is recaptured by the Japanese (→ 25).

18. Ankara: The Turkish government declares martial law after a series of pro-Axis demonstrations (→ 2/8).

18. Norway: An RAF Catalina sinks the U-boat U241, two days after the sinking of U240 by an RAF Sunderland.

19. Italy: US troops occupy Gaeta and Monte Grande (→ 23).

20. Pacific: US carriers begin a two-day assault on Japanese positions on Marcus Island.

20. New Guinea: US forces break Japanese resistance on Wakde, killing 800 defenders (→ 29).

Allied prisoners are shot dead following their great escape

German guards at Stalag Luft III.

Stalag Luft III, 19 May

In one of the worst atrocities of the war involving PoWs, the *Gestapo* has shot 50 Allied airmen who were recaptured after escaping from a prison camp near Sagan, in Silesia, in March. The killings were without doubt carried out on Hitler's orders. Told of the escape of 79 PoWs, the Fuhrer screamed abuse at Himmler – the head of the Gestapo – and made him personally responsible for their recapture.

Only three of the PoWs – two Norwegians and a Dutchman – have reached England; they got to Stettin, on the river Oder, and got on a ship to Sweden. Others got as far as Saarbrucken, near the French border, before being retaken. All were handed over to the Gestapo instead of to the *Luftwaffe* as required by the Geneva Convention. The killings took place at Gorlitz prison, near Dresden.

Twenty men were sent back to *Stalag Luft* III, where they told fellow PoWs of the killings. The Germans have warned PoWs that all areas within several miles of camps are now "death zones"; anybody entering these areas without authority will be shot on sight.

One man still in the camp is the Canadian pilot Wally Moody, the mining engineer who applied his skills to design the escape tunnel; the alarm was sounded before his turn came to use the tunnel.

Road to Rome is opened as Cassino finally falls

Monte Cassino, 18 May

The Polish flag flutters today over the ruins of the ancient monastery which has become a symbol of German resistance and has repelled successive Allied attacks since the beginning of the year. In the valley below, troops of the British Eighth Army have at last occupied what is left of the town of Cassino itself. The Germans' Gustav Line of defence has finally been breached and American and Canadian troops are advancing in numbers along the Liri valley.

No one doubted that casualties would be high. In the two weeks before the attack, the Polish II Corps under General Wladyslaw Anders was under constant observation by the German defenders and losing as many as 30 men in a day as it prepared to attack.

When the moment came to storm the heights on 12 May, the Poles lost a fifth of their strength within the first 90 minutes of battle and were forced to withdraw when communications failed.

The British XIII Corps took heavy casualties when it crossed the Rapido river to find its way blocked by a mass of pillboxes, barbed wire and minefields. After three days the Eighth Army had still failed to break out into the Liri valley, its principal objective.

Near the coast, the US II Corps was failing to make progress when the Germans suddenly began to withdraw. The defenders had been taken by surprise in a brilliant action by the French 2nd Moroccan Division, which had crossed supposedly impassable mountainous ground at speed, outflanking the Germans. The German 71st Division was scattered in this battle, with 2,000 men taken prisoner and a huge toll in casualties.

With the French and British advancing in the valley below and on the hills opposite, it was for the undaunted Poles to take Monte Cassino. They attacked in waves yesterday, with 200 air *sorties* to support them, and continued to attack until late last night. The defending German paratroopers stood their ground and fought off the exhausted Poles until finally ordered to retreat under the cover of darkness (→ 19).

The shattered town of Cassino stands in the shadow of its ruined monastery: German defenders finally withdrew.

Bayonets at the ready, Allied troops prepare to flush out dogged German resistance inch by inch on Monte Cassino.

Japanese battle to hold Burmese base

Burma, 18 May

Allied troops today captured the railway station at Myitkyina, an important Japanese supply base on the Rangoon to Mandalay railway. Yesterday the 150th Regiment of the Chinese 50th Division took Myitkyina airstrip, which has the only hard-surface airstrip in northern Burma. But the 700 Japanese troops in Myitkyina threw back "Merrill's Marauders" – the US counterpart to the British Chindits. Brigadier-General Frank Merrill's 1,500 sick and exhausted men are now down to half strength after nearly three months of jungle war.

Since March they have made advances in parallel with the 38th Chinese Division south from Ledo, in north-east India. Despite taking Pamati yesterday, the Marauders must now wait for the 38th to arrive to attack Myitkyina again (→ 2/6).

Exiled governments plan for liberation

London, 16 May

With the liberation of their countries rapidly approaching, the exiled governments of Belgium, the Netherlands and Norway today agreed to give Allied military commanders a free hand in administering territories after the Germans have been expelled. Norway, a close neighbour of the Soviet Union, signed a separate pact with Moscow.

Agreements signed in London give the commanders "such measures of supreme responsibility and authority over the civil administration as may be required by the military situation". The arrangements are temporary, and the exiled governments will take over as soon as the military situation permits. Talks are now being held with General de Gaulle's Free French on the administration of liberated areas of France.

Overlord plan receives final VIP approval

"On your marks!" The cartoonist Philip Zec shows Churchill at the ready.

London, 15 May

A gigantic contoured map of the Normandy beaches was displayed on the stage of St Paul's school hall in London today. Set at a slope for the audience to view it clearly, it was big enough for officers explaining Operation Overlord to walk about on it and identify landmarks. In addition to the Overlord commanders, the audience included King George, Churchill and the South African prime minister, Field Marshal Smuts.

Gen Montgomery's presentation showed that he and Eisenhower had secured a vast increase in men and supplies over those originally said to be the limit. As a result, the Normandy landing area is extended to the Carentan estuary in the west and the river Orne in the east.

A massive bombardment of 72 selected targets, to knock out the enemy's communications, is going ahead despite criticism. Some commanders are sceptical, while Churchill has told Eisenhower of his fears for the "scores of thousands of French civilians, men, women and children, who will lose their lives or be injured" (→ 31).

Dominion prime ministers plan for peace

(L to r) Smuts, Mackenzie King, Churchill, Curtin and Fraser in London.

Britain, 17 May

The prime ministers of Britain, Canada, Australia, New Zealand and South Africa tonight endorsed not only war plans but also peace aims. At the end of a series of meetings in London, they declared: "We give thanks for deliverance from the worst perils and now we hold back nothing to end mankind's agony." The Empire leaders reaffirmed that after victory the British Commonwealth will join in setting up a world organization with necessary power to preserve peace.

They added: "We rejoice to proclaim our kinship to one another. We have stood together through two world wars and have been welded the stronger. This unity will do further service to mankind."

Admiralty Islands campaign triumphs

Pacific, 18 May

General MacArthur's intention of sealing off Japan's last supply routes to its South-west Pacific bases at Rabaul and Kavieng was finally realised today as US Army troops wiped out the last isolated pockets of Japanese resistance on the Admiralty Islands, off north-east New Guinea. US losses in the three-month campaign to take the islands and their airstrips are 326 dead, 1,189 wounded and four missing, compared with Japanese losses of 3,280 dead and 75 PoWs (→ 20).

Provisional French government likely

Algiers, 15 May

The French Committee of National Liberation will call itself the Provisional Government of the French Republic, if changes proposed by exiled leaders here today are agreed next month. The change of name will be voted on by the consultative assembly on 2 June and is expected to be approved, along with a vote expressing the confidence of the assembly that the government will reach new agreements with the Allies about the administration of French territory (→ 2/6).

1944

May

Su	Mo	Tu	We	Th	Fr	Sa
	1	2	3	4	5	6
7	8	9	10	11	12	13
14	15	16	17	18	19	20
21	22	23	24	25	26	27
28	29	30	31			

21. Europe: Allied air forces launch Operation Chattanooga, the systematic destruction by bombardment of enemy rail targets (→ 26).

23. Italy: The Allies start a drive from the Anzio beach-head toward the Alban hills (→ 24).

24. Italy: The Canadian I Corps takes Pontecorvo and the US 3rd Division reaches the key city of Cisterna; Hitler authorizes a withdrawal to the Adolf Hitler Line, west of Cassino.→

25. China: The Japanese capture Loyang (→ 1/6).

25. Budapest: 138,870 Hungarian Jews have been deported to Auschwitz-Birkenau, and at least half murdered immediately in the gas chambers(→ 29).

26. France: Allied aircraft bomb Lyons, Nice, St Etienne and Marseilles, killing 5,407 civilians (→ 28).

27. London: The Allies abandon plans to land paratroopers on the central Cotentin peninsula following "Ultra" intelligence of heavy German reinforcements in the area.

28. Germany: The USAAF attacks oil targets at Heide, Magdeburg, Rottensee, Leuna and Troglitz.→

29. Pacific: The first tank battle of the Pacific War is fought on Biak island.→

29. Poznan: Himmler promises Nazi officials that "before the end of the year the Jewish problem will be settled once and for all" (→ 31).

31. Moscow: Stalin and his staff complete the planning of Operation Bagration, a massive undertaking to liberate Byelorussia (→ 20/6).

31. Auschwitz-Birkenau: The SS reports that 80 pounds (40 kg) of gold have been recovered from the teeth of Hungarian Jews gassed since 17 May (→ 14/6).

31. At Sea: Only five Allied or neutral merchant ships were lost in May, at 27,000 tons the lowest monthly figure of the war so far.

French invasion targets are bombed

London, 31 May

The Allied air forces are hammering invasion targets all over Europe in a day and night onslaught. In daylight raids today attacks were made on the Seine bridges, four strategic railway yards in Germany and the oil refineries at Ploesti, in Roumania. Tonight, for the fifth successive night, Bomber Command is pounding the French coast between Calais and Boulogne, pouring hundreds of tons of bombs onto German batteries, beach defences and transportation targets. Other RAF aircraft crossed the east coast of England in strength at dusk heading towards Germany.

In the daylight raids, 1,000 heavy bombers, escorted by 1,200 fighters, ranged over France, Belgium and Germany. The *Luftwaffe* showed a remarkable reluctance to challenge them, and only one bomber and four fighters are missing.

The escorting fighters, thus relieved of their guard duties, shot up railway lines and airfields. Fighter-bombers took up the attack later in the day, swooping on two airfields in western Germany to set installations, fuel dumps and aircraft ablaze. One group shot down five Focke-Wulf FW190s.

These assaults, at the end of the Allies' greatest month yet in the air, followed raids on the previous night in which the RAF paid special attention to a single, secret target on the French coast. All the raiders returned safely from that night's work, which included a raid by 30 Mosquitoes on the chemical town of Leverkusen and extensive sea and river mining (→ 6/6).

A Havoc A-20 bomber drops its load over a strategic target in France.

"Any day now": Britain holds its breath on the eve of invasion

London, 31 May

More than 4,500 cooks are now on active service preparing meals for just one element of Overlord – the seaborne assault forces. All told, 54,000 men are employed on maintaining installations and getting 4,000 landing craft and barges ready for sailing with their crews.

The Americans, who will take off from Cornwall, Devon and Dorset, have supply and service networks that extend deep into the Midlands. The British and Canadians in Hampshire and Sussex have similar lengthy tails. For many men these last days are marked by services conducted by padres in open fields.

The commanders are spending much of their time visiting the troops. Lieutenant-General Omar Bradley squats on his haunches, chews a blade of grass and talks to his 12th Army Group troops as man to man. Monty approaches his troops, fixes the men with his steely gaze and then gives the order to break ranks before he makes a short speech. At other times he visits war factories, telling the workers that their efforts will make all the difference on D-Day. Eisenhower may lack Monty's swagger, but his relaxed confidence and the absence of an array of brass and medal ribbons have won approval from British and Americans alike. One colleague has said that the supreme commander's smile is worth 20 divisions (→ 1/6).

Life goes on in an English street as troops pour through en route to France.

US attackers lured into Japanese trap

Allies advance on Rome

Biak, New Guinea, 29 May
US forces spearheading General Douglas MacArthur's new thrust west in New Guinea appear to have been lured into a gigantic trap to-day by the Japanese force defending three airstrips in the heart of Biak island, off north-western New Guinea.

Men of the US 158th, 162nd and 186th Infantry Regiments were suddenly hit by withering crossfire, preventing any withdrawal as they made their first advance inland, 18 hours after making a virtually unopposed landing at Bosnik, on Biak, the largest island in the Schoutens group. The US force is trapped nine miles (14 km) west, at Mokmer.

Yesterday's advance to Mokmer, along a cliff wall that swings inland to create a deep valley, met only mortar and light machine-gun fire. This morning the easternmost air-strip was discovered empty with, surprisingly, all the buildings still intact. But as the US troops crossed the airstrip they were hit by salvoes from Japanese artillery hidden deep in cliffside caves where the Japanese commander, Colonel Naoyuki Kuzume, is believed to have garrisoned nearly all of his 11,000 men.

Dislodging them could take months, rather than the few weeks which MacArthur anticipated for this latest thrust, which puts him only 900 miles from the Philippines. He has ordered tanks into Mokmer and is getting bomber support from the USAAF. For the first time he is basing some Mitchells at Wakde, a coral islet just off the New Guinea coast 220 miles south-east of Biak. Wakde fell ten days ago after a three-day battle in which 809 Japanese and 43 Americans died (→ 7/6).

On the road to Rome, a lone Jeep threads its way across the Italian plain.

Unaware of the trouble ahead: US troops unload oil barrels on Biak island.

Allied pilots face lynch law in Germany

Germany, 30 May
Allied pilots who are shot down over Germany can no longer expect any mercy from the people. The *Reichsleiter* Martin Bormann has today issued a directive to all district and regional National Socialist leaders to the effect that lynch law is now approved by the government in Berlin.

This directive from Bormann, who is also Hitler's secretary, follows a newspaper article by the *Reich* propaganda minister, Josef Goebbels, which was published on 27 May. Under the headline "Comments on the Enemy Air Terror", Goebbels concluded that, in view of the "criminal combat methods" now employed by the Allied air forces, the authorities had no right to prevent the German people, in their "seething rage", from acting in their own defence and rewarding murder with murder. Bormann's directive has given the government seal of approval to Goebbels's incitement to mob justice.

Terracina, Italy, 25 May
Patrols of the US II and III Corps linked up on the Pontine Marshes near this coastal town, today bringing the four-month ordeal of the beach-head, to an end. The race to Rome is on, but the great political prize may prove harder to reach than the battle maps suggest. The German army is retreating systematically north-west to new defensive positions – the Caesar Line – after fierce resistance at Cisterna in which more than 950 men of the US 3rd Division were killed or injured.

The American commander, General Mark Clark, is anxious for the beach-head forces to head straight for Rome. However, the Allied supreme commander, General Alexander, has ordered a US attack on Valmontone which, he hopes, will trap the German Tenth Army in a pincer movement with the advance of the British Eighth Army in the south.

Clark has compromised. He has ordered the Anzio commander, Major-General Lucien Truscott, to split his forces and attack both along Highway 7 at Albano with the US VI Corps and at Valmontone to comply with Alexander's orders. The attack on Valmontone – a vital road junction on Highway 6 – began today, but was stopped almost immediately by German tanks and anti-tank guns (→ 4/6).

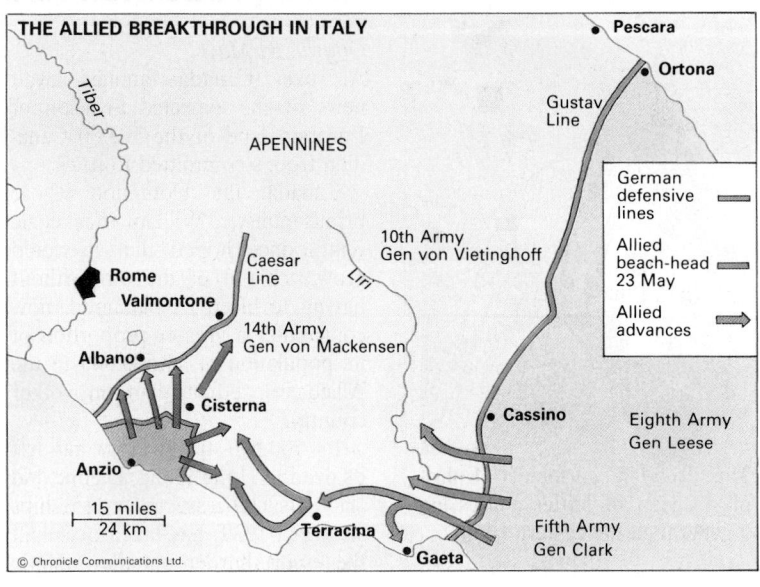

THE ALLIED BREAKTHROUGH IN ITALY

Tiber
Pescara
Ortona
Gustav Line
APENNINES
German defensive lines
Allied beach-head 23 May
Allied advances
10th Army Gen von Vietinghoff
Rome
Caesar Line
Valmontone
14th Army Gen von Mackensen
Albano
Cisterna
Cassino
Eighth Army Gen Leese
Anzio
15 miles
24 km
Terracina
Gaeta
Fifth Army Gen Clark
© Chronicle Communications Ltd.

1944

June

Su	Mo	Tu	We	Th	Fr	Sa
				1	2	3
4	5	6	7	8	9	10
11	12	13	14	15	16	17
18	19	20	21	22	23	24
25	26	27	28	29	30	

Tito and Churchill's son elude attackers

Drvar, Bosnia, 25 May

The partisan leader, Marshal Tito, and Winston Churchill's son, Major Randolph Churchill, narrowly escaped capture today when German parachutists and glider-borne troops surrounded partisan headquarters in this village. Major Churchill, who is serving with the British military mission here, had left the headquarters a few minutes before the attack. Tito was forced to leave one of his staff officers dying in agony from a head wound.

Two war correspondents, Stoyan Pribichevich of *Time-Life* and John Talbot of *Reuters*, were captured, although the *Time-Life* man managed to escape. The attack, known as Operation Knight's Move, is believed to have been masterminded by SS Major Otto Skorzeny, the man who rescued Mussolini. Other members of the British mission are understood to have left the headquarters several days earlier.

The strength of the operation, which was preceded by dive bombers and followed up by tanks and infantry, is a sure indication of the Germans' frustration at Tito's continual success. The partisan leader himself has escaped on horseback to a mountain hideout, and the Germans have taken out their frustration on the people of Drvar. Almost every villager – women and the smallest children included – was taken to the main square and shot.

Major Churchill weds Paula Digby in 1939: now he fights with Tito.

Principal areas of partisan activity

© Chronicle Communications Ltd.

The Russian cartoonist Kukriniksi's view of Hitler addressing a general on the eastern front.

Spaatz steps up oil war against Speer

Germany, 29 May

Flying Fortresses, their silvery skins sparkling in the high sun, with Mustangs speeding about them like swallows around eagles, flew to Germany again yesterday to bomb five of the synthetic oil plants they first attacked two weeks ago. Once more, their pattern bombing ripped the factories apart.

This oil battle is almost like a private war between the US bomber commander, Lt-Gen Carl "Tooey" Spaatz, and Albert Speer, the German armaments and war production minister. As fast as Speer rebuilds the plants, Spaatz knocks them down. Speer is brilliant, but the odds are on Spaatz (→ 31).

Post-war strategy to cut dole queues

Britain, 26 May

In post-war Britain there will be no more slumps, and general unemployment will be cured. So a government white paper said today. It explained that expansionist policies will mean plenty of jobs. There will be plans to spend more on public works in lean years and an economic "brains trust" to tell the government about world trade conditions. Subsidies will be used to maintain steady prices and prevent a rise in the cost of living.

Arms production hums in warlike Canada

Ottawa, 31 May

All over Canada families await news of the expected invasion of Europe – and of the 30,000 Canadian troops committed to it.

Canada, the Dominion whose prime minister, William Mackenzie King, once hoped that it would grow rich out of the war without having to bleed its manhood, now contributes a greater proportion of its population of 11,500,000 to the Allied war effort than any other country.

Its 500,000-strong army has left its dead in Hong Kong, Dieppe and Italy. Its 600-vessel navy (15 ships strong in 1939) has taken over half the escort burden on the Atlantic convoys. Its assembly lines are producing medium artillery (25-pounders) faster than Krupp's in Essen or the Soviet Magnitogorsk plant. Its slipways launch 20,000 tons of shipping a week. With new hydro-electric power from Lake St John, it is now the world's third largest producer of aluminium.

At Goose Bay, in the Newfoundland territory of Labrador, an airport has been built with concrete runways capable of taking planes heavy enough to cross the Atlantic. A similar airport has been built on the Pacific coast, on an island off British Columbia, to provide for the defence of the Aleutian Islands from Japanese invasion.

1. China: Japanese troops capture Pingchien and Changshouchie in a fourth attempt to take Changsha (→ 10).

1. London: The BBC transmits the first of two quotations from the poetry of Verlaine as a message to the French Resistance that invasion is imminent.

1. Britain: Operations Fortitude North and Fortitude South, to convince the Germans that the invasion force will strike at both Norway and the Pas-de-Calais, come to an end (→ 2).

2. Burma: Allied forces lay siege to the Japanese garrison in Myitkyina, as Indian troops force a slow Japanese withdrawal from Kohima (→ 16).

2. Algiers: The French Committee of National Liberation votes to call itself the provisional government of the French Republic (→ 6).

2. Europe: Operation Frantic, in which 130 Flying Fortresses shuttle from North Africa to Russia, bombing targets in Hungary and Roumania on the way, commences, as does Operation Cover, to convince the Germans that the invasion will take place at the Pas-de-Calais (→ 3).

3. Cherbourg: As bad weather in the Channel worsens, RAF bombers destroy the second of two major wireless intercept station at Ferme d'Urville (→ 4).

3-4. France: Two hundred and fifty-nine RAF aircraft bomb four gun positions, three in the Pas-de-Calais and one in Normandy, opening a wave of round-the-clock bombings.

4. Italy: US troops enter Rome.→

5. Portsmouth: Churchill and de Gaulle clash over plans for a military government for liberated France (→ 14/6).

5. France: Rommel leaves his HQ for Germany (→ 6).

5. France: As 1,136 RAF bombers bomb ten coastal batteries in Normandy, the first invasion troops, of the British 6th Airborne Division, land by glider at 11.55pm at Benouville, near Caen.→

US Fifth Army captures Rome intact

Rome, 4 June

Rome was still in darkness early today when the first American Jeeps made their cautious way across the Tiber and along the *Via di Conciliazione* to St Peter's Square. It was not until the square was bathed by the morning sun that the Americans could be sure that the Eternal City had been left unscathed by the Germans.

The first of the three major Axis capitals has thus fallen. Even as the US Fifth Army began to pour into Rome in huge numbers, the last Germans were fighting rearguard actions in the suburbs; but the great bulk of Kesselring's men are heading north to new defence lines, pursued by advance elements of the British Eighth Army.

It was not long before two million overjoyed Romans flooded into the streets, turning the arrival of the Americans into a glorious carnival. Every American vehicle was strewn with flowers, the passengers kissed and hugged and presented with bottles of *chianti*.

The wait had been agonizing. No one knew whether the Germans would wreak a savage revenge here as they had in Naples last October. The occupiers had declared Rome an open city, but no one, particularly the Allies, really believed them. Now the Germans are being pounded by continuous air attacks by 500 heavy bombers as they retreat towards Siena.

But this was Rome's day. Three huge flags – Italian, British and American – hang from the *Campidoglio* [town hall] where Lieutenant-General Mark Clark and his colleagues received frenzied acclamation from huge crowds. In St Peter's Square, the crowd was silent long enough to hear the pope say: "Yesterday Rome was trembling for her sons and daughters. Today she is able to look with renewed hope and faith to her salvation."

The Germans are likely to make the most of leaving Rome intact. Already Berlin radio is describing Hitler as "the saviour of the Eternal City", and claiming that Rome had no strategic value. The Allies have yet to be led to the Ardeatine caves near the city where the bodies of 335 hostages were left by their SS executioners (→ 7).

Joyful Italians welcome their liberators outside the unscathed Colosseum.

Allied troops race past a burnt-out tank in the streets of the Eternal City.

General Mark Clark and his men in victorious pose in St Peter's Square.

De Valera returned to power by voters

Dublin, 1 June

The Irish people today gave Eamon de Valera the vote of confidence denied him by the *Dail* and returned him to power with a majority of 14 over the combined opposition. His *Fianna Fail* party increased its representation from 67 deputies to 76. Political commentators think that one reason for the result is de Valera's strict neutrality policy, maintained to the point of defying Allied efforts to dislodge Axis missions from the Irish capital. The negative result of that policy is Eire's increasing economic isolation. This will be a priority for the new government; the poll followed a defeat over transport proposals.

Electronic decoding comes to Bletchley

Britain, 1 June

Crucial to the success of "Ultra", the operation at Bletchley Park, are the *Bombes*, the machines that do the deciphering of the German *Enigma* codes. Initially these were wholly mechanical, but early in 1943 an electro-magnetic version came into service. And today a new all-electronic model, codenamed Colossus, became operational. This has been developed at the Post Office Research Laboratory at Dollis Hill, in North London, and will radically speed up deciphering (→ 4).

Captured U-boat is intelligence coup

Sierra Leone, 4 June

Another success in the Battle of the Atlantic was signalled today by the capture of U505 by the US destroyer *Chatelain* off Cape Blanco, West Africa. Believing her to be about to sink, the U-boat's crew failed to carry out the proper scuttling drills in their haste to abandon ship. The boarding party seized *Enigma* codes and also identified *Zaunkonig* acoustic torpedoes. The plan was to tow the U-boat to Dakar, but this is thought to be full of spies and so she will be taken to Bermuda instead (→ 19).

Eisenhower gives invasion go-ahead

Portsmouth, 5 June

At 4pm today the die was cast and there can be no turning back. The day before, at Eisenhower's battle headquarters, Southwick House, Portsmouth, Montgomery had wanted to go ahead with the invasion, in spite of the rough weather. Many troops have been in cramped landing craft since the beginning of the month and are sick, tired and cold.

Eisenhower had overruled Montgomery then and postponed Overlord for 24 hours. Warships already at sea had to be recalled. When the commanders met again today they were told that the weather would improve for a brief period and then deteriorate. Everybody looked at Eisenhower. His deputy, Air Chief Marshal Tedder, wanted to postpone the operation: effective air cover needed good visibility. Montgomery and the naval commander, Admiral Ramsay, wanted to go.

Delay would push the operation to the end of the month. It needs a rising tide in daylight, as near to dawn as possible. For the night-time airborne drop a moon is desirable. These conditions set 5 and 6 June as good dates; after that the best is 19 June – but without a moon, and a million men and their supplies already loaded would have to be pulled back. Eisenhower's chief of staff, Lt-Gen Bedell Smith, was struck by the loneliness of his commander.

Eisenhower was writing: "Our landings in the Cherbourg-Le Havre area have failed to gain a satisfactory foothold and I have

General Eisenhower chats with US paratroopers at the ready for D-Day.

withdrawn the troops. My decision to attack at this time and place were based on the best information available. The troops, the air and navy did all that bravery and devotion to duty could do. If any blame or fault attaches to the attempt it is mine alone." He slipped the note in his pocket without telling the others of its contents.

"I'm quite positive we must give the order," he said slowly. "I don't like it, but there it is. I don't see how we can possibly do anything else." He paused and added: "OK, let's go" (→ 6).

German women control spotlights.

"Somewhere in England", tanks with the Allied white star ready for D-Day.

1944

June

Su	Mo	Tu	We	Th	Fr	Sa
				1	2	3
4	5	6	7	8	9	10
11	12	13	14	15	16	17
18	19	20	21	22	23	24
25	26	27	28	29	30	

12.16am. Caen Canal: Six British army gliders land to secure vital bridges.

1.30am. Normandy: The German army raises the invasion alert.

2.40am. France: As British paratroopers drop east of the Orne river, and US "floating headquarters" anchor off Utah and Omaha Beaches, von Rundstedt decides that the Allied landings are a feint to cover the real invasion force, about to land near Calais.

5.00am. Berchtesgaden: News of the Allied invasion reaches Hitler's headquarters, but no one wants to wake him from his drugged sleep.

5.30am Normandy: The British naval bombardment begins.

6.31am. Normandy: US infantry land on Utah Beach, a mile south of their target. Landings are also under way on Omaha beach.

7.25am. Normandy: British forces land on Sword and Gold Beaches.

7.35am. Normandy: Canadian infantry land on Juno beach, ten minutes late.

9.00am. Berchtesgaden: Hitler is woken and immediately calls a military conference.

12 noon. Klessheim, Germany: Hitler holds an ebullient situation conference.

4.00pm. La Roche Guyon: Rommel arrives back at his headquarters, having driven all the way from Germany since 6am.

4.55pm. Berchtesgaden: Hitler orders the Allied bridgehead "annihilated by the evening of 6 June".

6.50pm. Bletchley Park: British codebreakers discover that the Germans expect further landings but have no idea where they will be.

8.55pm. Normandy: Fighting dies down along the entire front.

11.00pm. Hitler holds his second situation conference of the day. He remains convinced that the landings are just a diversionary attack.

Massive infantry landings signal start of D-Day

Laden down with supplies to see them through the heaviest fighting, Royal Marines and amphibious Sherman tanks come ashore at Sword Beach.

Normandy

Suddenly, the men were up to their armpits in the chill water, weighed down by equipment, floundering, but holding their rifles high. Then they felt the grip of firm sand beneath their feet and they sloshed ashore, the dark sky above them filled with the roar of aircraft, the enemy strongpoints ahead vanishing in an inferno of shellfire from warships 12 miles (19 km) offshore.

The time is 6.31am. After 70 hours in ships, awaiting H-Hour of D-Day, the US 4th Infantry Division came ashore on the Cotentin Peninsula one minute late: 600 men in 20 landing craft of 30 men each. Utah Beach is established.

But they are not the first troops in Normandy; paras dropped overnight to seize key points on the flanks of the landing zone.

To the east of the 4th Infantry, for 50 miles (80 km), a similar drama is unfolding in four other sectors. Tidal variations call for different H-hours for Gold, Juno and Sword, where the landings are up to one hour and 25 minutes after Omaha and Utah.*

At Omaha, a stretch of sand enclosed by rocky outcrops, the US 1st Infantry was ordered to make a head-on assault against strongly defended positions while engineers cleared lanes through obstacles and minefields. But much of the vital

equipment was lost in heavy seas, as landing craft were pitched against sandbanks, throwing men into the sea. Unarmed, they then struggled ashore to be met by withering enemy fire. Only 100 tons of 2,400 tons needed have been put ashore.

For the British on Sword Beach it is a story of missed opportunities. The paras gained their objectives against heavy odds, but the British 3rd Infantry Division, spearheading the assault, dug in instead of pressing home its advantage. On Juno and Gold Beaches, the British and Canadians have had a mixed reception. Air and naval bombardments failed to silence the enemy guns. Landing craft and tanks were

hit, but the flail tanks drove paths through the minefields and the bobbin vehicles laid mattress tracks over rough ground.

All told, 75,215 British and Canadian and 57,500 American troops have landed by sea, and 7,900 British and Canadian and 15,500 US troops by air. The Allied death toll is 2,500 – 1,000 at Omaha. Total D-Day casualties – killed, wounded, missing or PoWs – are 6,603 Americans, 3,000 Britons, 946 Canadians and around 6,500 Germans. The Allies lost 114 aircraft.

Detailed reports on each of the beach-heads appear on the pages that follow, along with accounts of other aspects of the D-Day invasion.

▷

Paras begin the assault

Bloodiest battles are at Omaha Beach, as US forces face strong German resistance

The fields of Normandy are scattered with Allied gliders, now empty of men – the planes that towed them here wheel around to return to England.

Omaha Beach

Even before the men hit the beach Omaha was in trouble. At 3am the first of 34,000 men began to board the landing craft from ships anchored 12 miles (19 km) off-shore. Buffeted by a roaring south-westerly, ten craft foundered at once and 300 men were thrashing about in life-jackets. Amphibious tanks sank like stones; a third of the 96 tanks detailed to go in with the first 1,450 men were lost. Of 16 armoured bull-dozers sent in to clear obstacles, six arrived and three of these were lost.

The men who reached the beach were met by a storm of mortar, shell and machine-gun fire. Bombardments by warships and Liberators had left enemy strongpoints undamaged. Some men sought safety in the sea, some crawled towards the shelter of the sea wall, others lay paralysed on the sand amid the screams of the wounded and the wreckage of equipment.

For hours on end confusion prevailed. Yet many acts of heroism shone through the fog of war. A lieutenant attacked a strongpoint armed only with a few grenades. An engineeer probed for mines with a bowie knife. US Rangers clambered up precipitous cliffs to assault the German stronghold at Pointe du Hoc, only to find that much-

Wounded US assault troops rest.

feared gun batteries were not in place. Colonel George A Taylor came ashore and, picking himself up after being blown off his feet, told the men slumped all around him that soon the only men left on the beach would be the dead and those who were going to die. Hesitantly, and then with real effort, the men began to obey him.

Aboard the cruiser USS *Augusta*, Lt-Gen Omar Bradley had considered halting the operation. But the tide has turned: the Germans inflicted heavy losses but have no reserves, while Allied men and machines are pouring ashore (→ 7).

Normandy

Operation Overlord, the invasion of Europe, began in the first minutes of today with the landing by glider of men of the British 6th Airborne Division to seize the bridge over the canal at Benouville, north of Caen.

These few men, a small part of a force scattered by high winds, were the advance guard of a huge airborne army. No less than 23,400 men of Britain's "Red Berets" and the American 82nd and 101st Airborne Divisions have been landed behind Utah Beach, in the southern part of the Cotentin Peninsula, by parachute and by towed glider.

The high winds have caused chaos with the drop. Parachutists and gliders are spread over the Normandy countryside, and many of the men have been blown into trees.

Commanders are struggling to gather their units together, using any men they can find to attack

their vital initial objectives. However, the very disorganization of the drop is making it very difficult for the Germans to respond. To them it seems as if the whole of Normandy is swarming with aggressive troops, and they cannot see a pattern to the movements. Small groups of paratroopers are attacking the Germans wherever they come across them. One group from the 82nd has ambushed General Falley, the commander of the German 91st Division. His division is now paralysed and cannot respond to the landings on Utah Beach.

In one of the most courageous and bloody actions fought today, the British 9th Parachute Battalion, led by Lt-Col Otway, stormed the heavily-defended German battery at Merville, although Otway could muster only 150 men. So tonight the airborne warriors have secured both flanks of the invasion.

Pointe du Hoc after the hours of hell and confusion had paid off: with the Stars and Stripes draped on the cliff side, US troops round up their PoWs.

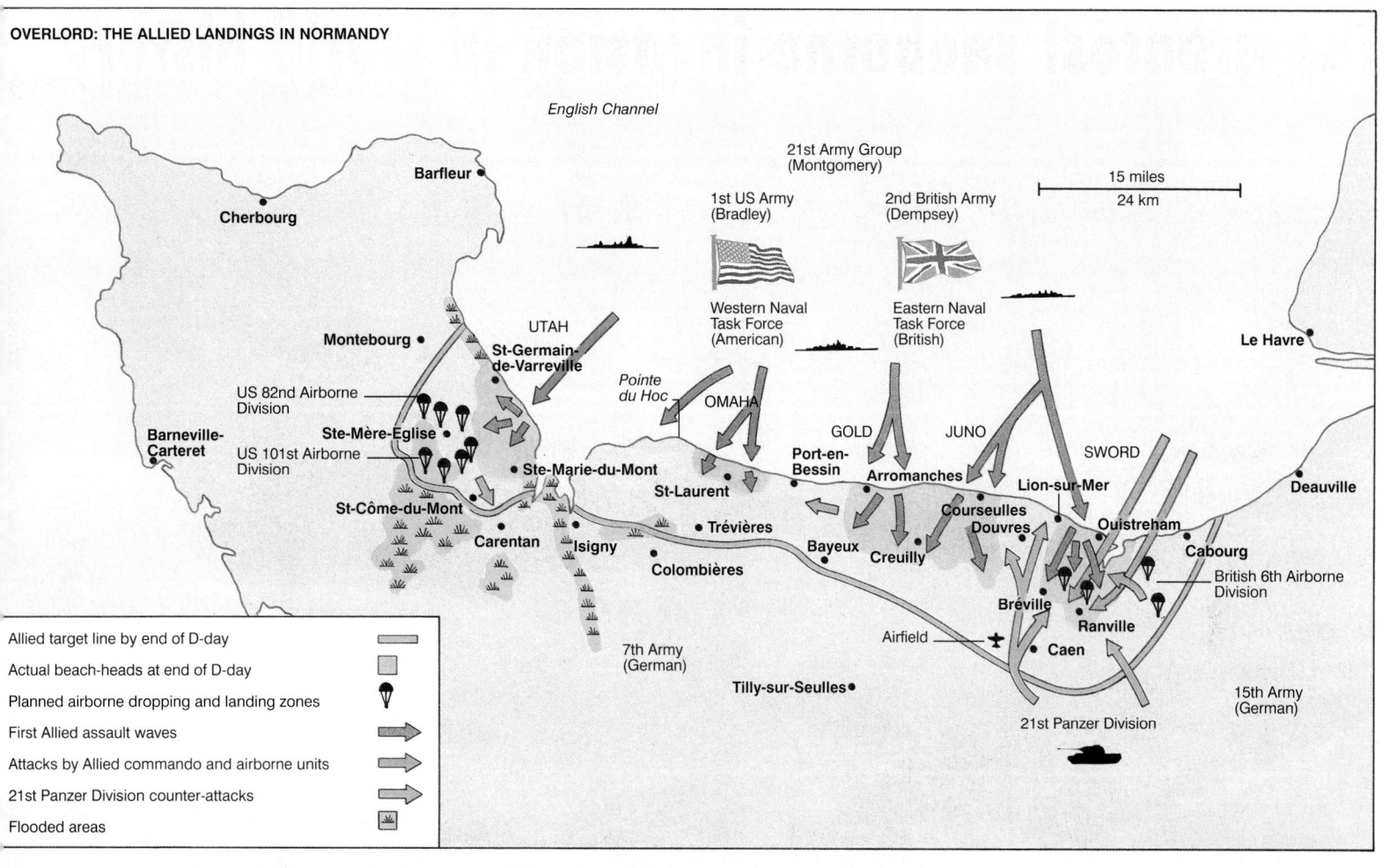

OVERLORD: THE ALLIED LANDINGS IN NORMANDY

Legend:
- Allied target line by end of D-day
- Actual beach-heads at end of D-day
- Planned airborne dropping and landing zones
- First Allied assault waves
- Attacks by Allied commando and airborne units
- 21st Panzer Division counter-attacks
- Flooded areas

How the invaders fared on the Normandy beaches

Utah: beach clears

Utah Beach

Two hours after landing, men of the US 4th Division are off the beach and driving towards the villages inland. By noon engineers have cleared the beach at a cost of six killed and 39 wounded. Enemy strongpoints are taken out by company-strength attacks. Most of the Germans surrender as soon as the Americans close in. At one point the defenders are found with only a few machine guns and mortars, a single 88mm gun and the turret of an old Renault tank set in the sands.

The worst that the Americans have to bear is the crossing of flooded fields behind the sand dunes, each man struggling with 68 pounds of equipment. At times the water is neck deep. But by nightfall, 23,000 men have landed with 1,700 tanks, guns and trucks, at a cost of just 197 casualties (→ 10).

Gold: cheers begin

Gold Beach

Major Dick Gosling, the commander of the artillery battery attached to the 1st Battalion, the Hampshire Regiment, is hit in the leg soon after coming ashore. He crawls down to a captured German pillbox to join other casualties. The Germans' breakfast of sausages and coffee is still warm. A letter from a French girl tells one of the Germans she will meet him this evening, 6 June.

There have been some nasty moments. Gold Beach is a mass of wrecked landing craft, tanks, blankets and equipment, and pulped bodies. But driving inland, the men are cheered by French civilians who throw flowers. By evening the 50th (Northumbrian) Infantry Division has reached the Bayeux to Caen road, and the 4th/7th Dragoon Guards have reported only light German resistance to their tank spearheads (→ 7).

Juno: Panzers wait

Juno Beach

The Canadians are late coming ashore, and on the rising tide they find themselves struggling with the submerged enemy mines and angle irons. Many of the first wave of landing craft are lost. When three craft are blown up, only two men are killed; the rest free themselves from the wreckage and race forward to attack.

Twelve lanes have been cleared by the Canadian 2nd Armoured Brigade before nightfall, and men are swarming inland after intense street fighting in Courseulles. Tank patrols, disregarding snipers, are at Brettonville.

Von Rundstedt has at last got Hitler's permission to move the powerful 12th SS *Panzer* Division. At midnight it reaches Evercy, nine miles (14.4 km) south-west of Caen. It lies in the path of the Allied thrust from Juno (→ 10).

Sword: roads jam

Sword Beach

Two hours after H-hour at 7.30am, a sense of order is emerging from the wreckage on Sword. Seven of eight planned exits inland are cleared. Free French commandos take Ouistreham, and by 1.30pm British commandos under Lord Lovat have seized Hermanville.

The King's Shropshire Light Infantry pushes on and at 4pm it is joined by the guns and armour of the Staffordshire Yeomanry. At Bieville, some three miles from Caen, 24 tanks of General Edgar Feuchtinger's 21st *Panzer* Division attack. After losing five tanks they pull back and swing west, probing the gap between Sword and Juno.

The Sword advance slows. In the rear, a massive traffic jam of armour has built up in the narrow roads, delaying supplies. Prudence becomes caution and Caen remains in enemy hands (→ 10).

The greatest seaborne invasion in world history

Just one part of the greatest invasion fleet in history disgorging vehicles, equipment and men by the thousand onto the sands of the Normandy beaches.

Portsmouth

Through a night of high winds and driving rain, the vast armada of over 6,000 ships – warships, merchantmen, landing craft and barges – sails down the marked channels cleared by flotillas of minesweepers. Fifty miles wide, and protected on the flanks by scores of fast-moving torpedo boats, the invasion fleet carries 185,000 men and 20,000 vehicles. Each man, each landing craft, each tank must arrive at a precisely-chosen place at a specific time.

Just ten days ago, Admiral Sir Bertram Ramsay, C-in-C naval forces for Overlord, arrived at his advance HQ in Southwick House,

Portsmouth. He carried a printed book, foolscap size, three inches thick; this is the Neptune plan, mapping every move of the 47 convoys for the launch of Overlord. Each ship bears a code that will take it to its destination and bring it back to a port in England where the guns will be cleaned and supplies loaded. Nearly 200,000 naval and merchant seamen are involved.

Some 200 miles (320 km) to the east, the RAF and Royal Navy are racing back and forth, creating – for enemy radar – the illusion of a sizeable fleet moving on Calais.

But Neptune is headed for a 50-mile line of beaches west of the Bay of Seine, and already the first

marker ships are on station, with Royal Marine MTBs ready to put out the smokescreen to shield the fleet from the big guns at Le Havre.

In all, 1,213 warships are taking part in Neptune. Well before dawn the big ships began the bombardment: seven battleships, including the *Warspite* and *Frobisher*, and 23 cruisers sent shells thundering into enemy positions, while 105 destroyers moved up for close-range firing. Frogmen and engineers were sent in to clear the shallows of mines and innumerable obstacles.

The 864 converted merchant ships and 4,126 landing craft begin manoeuvring for the assault. This is the most dangerous phase. The high

seas pose a greater threat than the enemy, sinking many landing craft.

The Eastern Task Force of the Royal Navy is supporting the British and Canadian landings on Sword, Juno and Gold Beaches with ships from six ports from Southampton to Shoreham. The Western Task Force of the US Navy, serving Utah and Omaha Beaches, is operating from six ports from Torbay to Poole. It is the greatest invasion fleet in history. As D-Day ends, Neptune has put 132,715 men ashore. But its task has only begun: now, 2,000,000 men must be shipped to France and supplied. Also on their way are two floating harbours (→ 12).

Ike's great gamble: how the weatherman helped to decide the timing of D-Day

Portsmouth

Jim Stagg, the softly-spoken Scottish group-captain who is Eisenhower's chief meteorologist, met the supreme commander twice a day to brief him on weather prospects for the beginning of June. As the meetings continued, Stagg says, "he could tell from my expression, even before I presented the forecast, what I was going to say".

At the end of May the Atlantic charts looked so black that "Ike" (as Eisenhower is known) ordered a 24-hour postponement of Overlord to 6 June. Beyond that, nothing could be done for a fortnight. "Mercifully, the almost unbelievable happened," Stagg says. "I told him on Sunday we could expect an interlude between two depressions. I convinced him the quieter period would arrive on Monday and continue into Tuesday."

After the Monday meeting had confirmed the forecast, Ike came out to his motor car and said to Kay Summersby, his English driver: "D-day's on. Nothing can stop it now."

The Germans have had weather stations on Iceland, Greenland, Spitzbergen and Jan Mayen Island, between Norway and Iceland. The Allies seized them, leaving the Germans to get their weather forecasts by looking out of the window. They decided invasion was off and Rommel went to Ulm for the birthday of his wife on 6 June.

How the Germans were taken by surprise

One unit of a giant landing force that caught the Germans unawares.

Team who planned Operation Overlord

The Allied supreme command in conference (l to r): Bradley, Ramsay, Tedder, Eisenhower, Montgomery, Leigh-Mallory and Bedell Smith.

London

General Dwight Eisenhower, a 54-year-old farm boy from Kansas, is touchy about his lack of battlefield experience. "I've had to do things that were so risky as to be almost crazy," he says. As supreme commander "Ike" has proved to be a leader who can persuade his senior officers to cooperate loyally.

His deputy, **Air Chief Marshal Sir Arthur Tedder**, flew bombing missions in the First World War. Ike speaks of him as "one of the few great military leaders of our time". **General Sir Bernard Montgomery**, the victor of Alamein, is acknowledged to be a brilliant soldier; he knows it and can be somewhat prickly to deal with. **Air Chief Marshal Sir Trafford Leigh-Mallory** has moved from a defensive role at Fighter Command to direct the air assault in France.

Lt-Gen Omar Bradley, after 30 years in uniform and coming up to the age of 50, first went into action in North Africa. **Lt-Gen Walter Bedell Smith** served in France in 1917. His grasp of detail is formidable, but he is abrupt and humourless.

Last, but by no means least, **Admiral Sir Bertram Ramsay** came out of retirement for the war. An expert in amphibious actions, he was knighted for his organization of the Dunkirk evacuation.

La Roche Guyon

General Edgar Feuchtinger, the commander of 21st *Panzer* Division, the most powerful striking force in Normandy, was missing on D-Day morning; his aides believe he was with his French mistress.

He was not the only senior German commander caught out. Rommel did not get back from his wife's birthday party until the afternoon. His chief of staff, General Hans Speidel, was having drinks yesterday evening with his fellow anti-Hitler plotters in the *chateau* on the Seine at La Roche Guyon, the HQ of Army Group B. General Friedrich Dollman, the Seventh Army commander, relaxed the standing alert for his men on the beach defences and went off with his senior officers for a map exercise in Rennes. In Paris, Gerd von Rundstedt, C-in-C West, was not interested when he was told that German radar stations between Cherbourg and Le Havre were being jammed and the BBC was transmitting many coded messages to the French Resistance. Von Rundstedt was sure that the Allies would strike at the Pas-de-Calais – and neither the airborne drops nor the beach landings changed his mind.

It was 9am before Hitler was awakened by the suddenly alarmed generals. At 4.55pm the Fuhrer issued his order to von Rundstedt: "The enemy beach-head must be cleaned up by not later than to-night." Yet already there was not one Allied beach-head but five.

Deception plans keep Germans guessing

France

A most encouraging feature of the Normandy landings, as far as the Allies are concerned, is that the Germans remain unconvinced that there will not be other landings on the north French coast, especially in the Pas-de-Calais. Allied deception measures are still working.

One of the most significant aspects has been the creation of a mythical army group apparently assembling in south-east England – Lt-Gen George Patton's 1st US Army Group. This has its own dummy camps and equipment, fake radio nets and mock newspapers. Captured German spies who have been "turned" under the Double Cross system also add to the myth. Last night RAF bombers enhanced the deception by dropping the "Window" foil or chaff in such a way as to make the Germans believe that invasion fleets were heading for Boulogne and Le Havre.

The immediate effects of all this have been a delay of the move of the German armour to the Normandy coast and a refusal to reinforce with elements of the Fifteenth Army, which is north of the Seine (→ 8).

Air power holds key to Allied success

French Resistance is "fifth column" of the Allied advance

Normandy

The Allied air forces have absolute superiority in the skies over the invasion beaches. They have put 13,743 aircraft into the air today, harrying the Germans, directing the warships' guns, towing gliders and dropping paratroopers.

Fighter-bombers come snarling down to rocket German strongpoints, while high overhead the fighters wait for the *Luftwaffe* to appear. Most of them will wait in vain. Luftwaffe air losses are such that it only has about 185 serviceable aircraft to put into the battle.

There can be no doubt that air power is the key to this new battle for France, just as it was in 1940. Then it was the Stukas and Bf109s that ruled the skies and made life unbearable for the men on the ground.

Today it is the Spitfires and Typhoons, the Thunderbolts and Mustangs, and of course the Lancasters, Flying Fortresses and Marauders which make sure that no German bomber can live in the Allied-ruled Normandy skies.

Air controllers are with every army unit, and their job is to call up help from the "cab-rank" circling overhead. Further forward, interdiction strikes are being made against railways, roads and German armour on the move. It is a clean sweep in the air today (→ 13).

An Allied B-26 Marauder keeps watch over the ships in the Channel below.

London

The BBC's French service yesterday broadcast a number of coded messages: "Mathurin likes spinach", "Acid makes litmus paper turn red" and "My wife has sharp eyesight". Among the listeners were an estimated 175,000 Resistance fighters all over France, who understood their special meaning: "Now is the time for action".

In the last few months, the Resistants have secretly been supplied with armaments and explosives. Each group has its special orders, and last night they carried them out with devastating results. About 950 out of their planned 1,050 sabotage missions of the railways were accomplished; Germans who took to the roads found them blocked. Meanwhile, French post office workers acted to cut off the enemy's military telephone network.

The Resistance has now "come of age" to become a fully integrated part of the Allied war plan. No fewer than 44 clandestine units are now operational behind enemy lines in occupied France. Each one is in radio contact with the Free French high command under General Pierre Koenig, which, in turn, acts under the direction of Eisenhower's headquarters in Portsmouth.

Allied heroes relive "longest day" of their lives

The paratrooper

Normandy

"It was five minutes to one when the light snapped off and a hole in the plane was opened. Under it we could see the coast of France below – and a garish sight it was, for *flak* from the coast defences was spouting flame everywhere ... And we were scared by it – until ... we were all madly shuffling down the hole and jumping into space ... As I stood up with my harness off ... I knew I was hopelessly lost ... Suddenly there was a rip and a tear in my flapping jumping-smock, and I flung myself to the ground as the machine guns rattled."

The naval officer

Normandy

"As flotilla officer I had charge of our landing craft ... The Germans had no 88mm guns firing off shore, but there was an eight-foot sea wall with mortar and machine-gun emplacements of concrete. The sea was even choppier than in the Sicilian landing, though there was no swell, and most of the troops had been seasick. But they were in the best of spirits ... German planes were nowhere to be seen, nor were the boasted secret 'weapons'. If they have anything up their sleeves it is curious that they did not bring it out to meet our landing ..."

The infantryman

Normandy

"As our line of craft approached the shore the navy's guns were blazing and smashing shells into fortifications guarding the strip of the beach we had to take ... 300 yards ahead of us was a concrete wall about 20 feet high ... the Jerries were lining the top and potting away at us, sweeping with their machine guns ... as we swept forward. Several of our lads fell, but we dashed forward and got under the base of the wall where the Jerries couldn't get at us ... Jerry was fighting hard, but soon the beach was swarming with our chaps ..."

The air navigator

Normandy

"It was wonderful. There they were, marching in to die, just as if they were going to a ball game ... The Germans had hidden themselves in cliffs facing the beach and were pouring deadly mortar fire down upon the advancing Americans ... They did not have any cover except bomb-made mounds, but they pushed forward, with men falling every way you could look. It was heart-breaking to hear their leader calling through his radio: 'For God's sake, get those mortars quick! Dig them out boys, they are right down our necks' ..."

Crabs and crocodiles conquer beaches

London

A British Army officer who was dismissed from the 7th Armoured Division because Wavell had no confidence in him has been responsible for devising ingenious contraptions for tackling German defences on the beaches. After leaving the army, Maj-Gen Percy Hobart, who is Monty's brother-in-law, joined the Home Guard and was about to be a humble lance-corporal when Churchill sent for him.

Hobart's armoured monsters have become known as "Funnies". The DD Duplex-Drive tank, with two propellers and a canvas screen, rides up to the beach under its own power; the screen then collapses and it becomes a conventional tank.

The "Crab", with chain-flail spinning at the front, can clear a ten-foot-wide path through a minefield. The "Bobbin" lays broad canvas matting over soft sand to provide a firm road. The Armoured Bulldozer's hefty blade sweeps aside most beach obstructions.

A Churchill tank fitted with a swivelling jib carries a bridge that can be dropped over a 30-foot gap in 30 seconds. The "Churchill Crocodile" is a flame gun with a range of 120 yards; it carries 400 gallons of fuel in a trailer.

Hobart insisted that each special vehicle must be able to operate as an assault weapon if necessary. He met

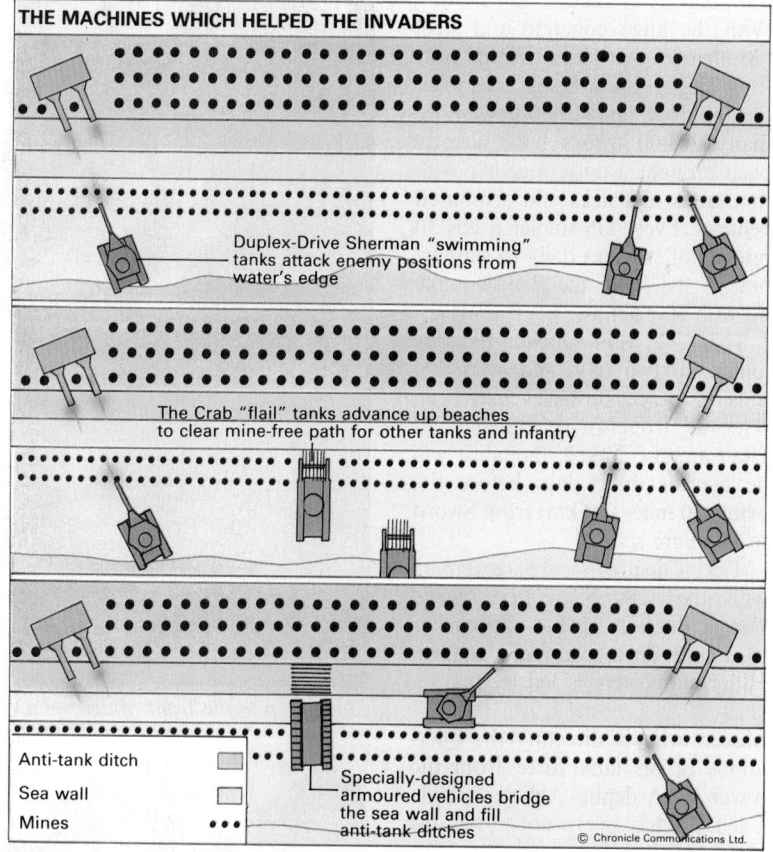

THE MACHINES WHICH HELPED THE INVADERS

Duplex-Drive Sherman "swimming" tanks attack enemy positions from water's edge

The Crab "flail" tanks advance up beaches to clear mine-free path for other tanks and infantry

Specially-designed armoured vehicles bridge the sea wall and fill anti-tank ditches

Anti-tank ditch
Sea wall
Mines

© Chronicle Communications Ltd.

resistance to his ideas from the military, and the Americans were sceptical. But Field Marshal Sir Alan Brooke, CIGS, organized these Funnies in a special tank formation, the 79th Armoured Division, to open gaps in beach defences before the infantry gets ashore. The men on Gold, Juno and Sword Beaches have been glad to have them. Had the Americans had the full range of Funnies, D-Day on Omaha could have been different. [*See also pages 698-99.*]

Allied leaders hail Normandy landings

London

Allied leaders spoke with quiet confidence today of the D-Day landings. Asked by a reporter: "How do you feel about the progress of the invasion?", President Roosevelt replied simply: "It's up to schedule." Then he smiled.

General de Gaulle broadcast to the French people: "The great battle has begun. After so much conflict, rage and grief the final clash ... is here. It is, of course, the battle of France." In London Churchill began his Commons address: "Many dangers and difficulties which this time last night appeared extremely formidable are behind us." Cheers resounded round the House.

A British commando is given a traditional welcome onto French soil.

Reporters – and censors – follow the troops ashore

Normandy

There was another army which invaded France today – no fewer than 558 journalists accredited by the Allies to cover the Overlord landings. Some had even been despatched to Scotland as part of the deception plans. But today it was for real: the BBC alone had 48 correspondents, and it was radio which brought the first eye-witness accounts of the landings.

And where there are reporters in this war there will also be censors. Today these could be found on the beaches, checking that reports did not contain "information which might be useful to the enemy". Ever since October 1939, when the first British reporters were permitted to visit Allied soldiers in France, there has been inevitable tension between reporters and censors.

Technically, censorship has been voluntary in Britain, with censors "consulted" about what might be "useful" to the enemy. But editors could be prosecuted and imprisoned for failing to follow such advice. In practice, in a war of national survival, few journalists have questioned the desirability of not giving aid or comfort to the enemy and many see themselves as part of the war effort. And also in practice, the services have sought to control information by exercising what the US services call "censorship at source" – denying access either totally or by limiting numbers through accreditation.

Nonetheless the arrival of American correspondents – and, indeed, US generals – improved access to service chiefs and to some extent loosened the stifling and petty censorship of the early days. Alan Moorehead, Ed Murrow, Drew Middleton, Richard Dimbleby and Ross Munro are among many journalists who have reported with courage and distinction, seeking to eliminate propaganda from communiques and risking their lives without ever being armed.

1944

June

Su	Mo	Tu	We	Th	Fr	Sa
				1	2	3
4	5	6	7	8	9	10
11	12	13	14	15	16	17
18	19	20	21	22	23	24
25	26	27	28	29	30	

7. New Guinea: US forces capture Mokmer airfield, on Biak (→ 8).

7. Italy: American troops capture Bracciano, Civitavecchia and Civita Castellana (→ 8).

7. Authie, Normandy: Members of the 12th SS *Hitler Jugend Panzer* division murder 34 Canadian prisoners.

7. Normandy: British commandos attack Port-en-Bessin, where the Omaha and Gold beach-heads meet (→ 10).

7. London: Increased air bombardment of German fuel installations is ordered, following the interception of messages revealing a serious shortage of aviation fuel.

8. New Guinea: US forces repel a Japanese fleet which attempts to supply the garrison on Biak island (→ 11).

8. Normandy: German troops capture a set of US operations plans; only now do they realize that the Normandy landings are the start of the planned invasion of France, not a diversionary attack (→ 9).

8. Italy: German forces withdraw along the Adriatic coast (→ 9).

9. Italy: Marshal Badoglio resigns as premier, and is succeeded by the pre-war politician Ivanoe Bonomi (→ 18).

9. Germany: Hitler's commanders remain convinced that the main thrust of the invasion is yet to come, and will be in Belgium or the Pas-de-Calais (→ 17).

9. Tulle, France: The 2nd SS *Das Reich Panzer* division kills 99 civilian men in reprisal for a local Resistance act of sabotage.→

10. China: Five Japanese divisions mass to attack Changsha (→ 12).

10. Normandy: As the Omaha and Utah Beaches link up, Allied forces cut road and rail links between Carentan and Cherbourg.

10. Normandy: Over 326,000 Allied soldiers and 54,000 vehicles have now been landed on the beaches.

Normandy beach-heads begin to link

Normandy, 10 June
With the huge concrete and steel "Mulberry" harbours floated out from England now being assembled on the Normandy beaches, more than 326,000 troops have already been brought ashore, together with thousands of trucks and armoured vehicles. Every US soldier needs 30 pounds of supplies daily to support him in the field; the British make do with 20 pounds.

The Gold and Omaha Beaches joined up two days ago after 900 tons of beach obstacles had been removed from Gold. Omaha and Utah are also linked, though it will be two or three days before the whole 50 miles (80 km) from Sword to Utah are secure.

The Canadians are grappling with the 12th SS *Hitler Jugend Panzer* division on the approaches to Caen. This group of fanatical Hitler supporters is led by the 33-year-old SS Colonel Kurt "Panzer" Meyer, who is directing the operations of his tank force from the tower of Ardenne Abbey, outside Caen. He has sworn not to halt his men until they have driven the Allies into the sea. At one point during a night attack, the Canadian command post was surrounded; but then Meyer lost six Panzers and broke off the action. The Canadians have been badly shaken, but they have defied Meyer's boasts.

Montgomery has come ashore to set up his tactical HQ in a *chateau* at Creully. He found the British troops grown weary after continuous contact with the enemy since D-Day. In part this is the reason for his refusal to make a frontal attack on Caen, despite its importance to the Germans as a communications centre. He has ordered the second Army to advance on Villers-Bocage and then Falaise, with the intention of enveloping Caen. A plan to drop the 1st Airborne Division behind Caen has been vetoed by Leigh-Mallory, who has little faith in parachute operations. After British Intelligence identified the HQ of Panzer Group West at La Caine, a bombing raid killed 17 German staff officers and wiped out all signalling equipment.

On the American beaches, enemy opposition has been patchy.

Moving up to the front: Allied vehicles pour through a street in Bayeux.

Relieved, or just puzzled? Some of the boys in Hitler's army - now PoWs.

Some supposedly German formations have turned out to be nothing of the kind. An American unit on the road linking Omaha with Gold was surrounded by armed men who proved to be Poles, Serbs and Russians, whose German officers and NCOs had taken off. The men claimed that a squadron of White Russians, also drafted into the *Wehrmacht,* was waiting to surrender. The toughest resistance to the Americans is coming from the Germans defending the approaches to Cherbourg. Thick hedgerows and flooded fields are hampering operations. The Americans still have not captured the Cotentin Peninsula. An impatient Bradley has ordered Maj-Gen J Lawton Collins of VII Corps to throw all he has at Carentan. "Take the city apart," Bradley ordered. "Then rush it and you'll get in" (→ 11).

Russia attacks Finland

Moscow, 10 June

The Red Army has opened an offensive in massive strength against the Finns entrenched on the Karelian isthmus, north of Leningrad. The Finns have been hit with a hurricane of shells and bombs. Even their long-established fortifications have proved no protection against the weight of the Soviet attack.

A murderous hail of steel mowed down barbed-wire entanglements, filled in trenches and dug-outs and shattered armoured bunkers. Nevertheless the Finns are still fighting with their customary stubborn courage, but as one Finn told his cap-tors: "You have such superiority that resistance is simply futile." The Finnish people have been shocked by the news. A Swedish correspondent in Helsinki reports: "Finnish arms have suffered a painful defeat at the very outset of operations."

There seems little doubt that the new offensive is designed to force the Finns to make peace rather than as a campaign of occupation. The Finnish government, dominated by the pro-German finance minister, Vaino Tanner, has procrastinated for too long; Stalin now intends to force its hand (→ 22).

GIs leave their stamp on British daily life

Britain, 7 June

Millions of men waited and trained for yesterday, turning Britain into an international barracks while the D-Day invasion force was prepared. The culture shock for many British communities was intense, and nowhere more so than where the American servicemen were based. New dances, new fashions, new words and new foods (if chewing gum can be so classed) have entered British life just as surely as many local girls will leave as "GI brides". Not everybody welcomed the brash newcomers, and one area of contention was the racial discrimination within the US forces. Attempts by the US authorities to confine black troops to certain bars or pubs, for instance, were resisted and led to clashes between Americans in which some were killed.

Black GIs: some died in race fights.

German massacre at Oradour-sur-Glane

London, 10 June

A new name has been added to the black list of Nazi atrocities, that of Oradour-sur-Glane, near Limoges, in central France, where 642 people, almost the whole population of villagers and refugees, were massacred by SS troops today.

The men were driven into barns and shot, the women and children herded into the church, which was set on fire. Those who escaped the fire and smoke were machine-gunned. Only seven or eight of the villagers escaped alive. A boy of eight ran away into the woods. A woman, Madame Rouffanche, hid behind the high altar of the church, where she found a ladder, and jumped from a ten-foot-high window.

The massacre was carried out by men of the 2nd SS *Das Reich Panzer* division, on its march north to join the battle in Normandy. Two days ago the same unit hanged 99 hostages in Tulle.

The Limoges region is largely under Resistance control, but there were no Resistance fighters present in Oradour (→ 28).

Su	Mo	Tu	We	Th	Fr	Sa
				1	2	3
4	5	6	7	8	9	10
11	12	13	14	15	16	17
18	19	20	21	22	23	24
25	26	27	28	29	30	

11. Marianas: US naval and air forces attack Guam, Saipan and Tinian, damaging about 200 Japanese aircraft.→

11. Normandy: The British 7th Armoured Division attacks Caen from the west, capturing Tilly-sur-Seulles (→ 12).

12. China: The Communist leader, Mao Tse-tung, announces that he supports Chiang Kai-shek, the Nationalist leader, in the war against Japan (→ 18).

12. Normandy: Montgomery tells reporters "we have won the battle of the beaches", as Allied forces take Carentan (→ 13).

13. Moscow: Stalin praises the D-Day landings extravagantly, saying: "In the whole history of war there has never been such an undertaking" (→ 14).

13. Sweden: An experimental A-4 [*V2*] rocket crashes, and the wreckage is recovered for study by the Swedish military.

13. England: Of the first ten German V1 rockets launched, four reach England and one kills six people in London.→

14. Japan: US aircraft raid Matsuwa, in the Kuriles.→

14. Normandy: The British assault on Caen fails after a determined defence by the 2nd *Panzer* Division.→

15. Normandy: Generals Montgomery and Bradley agree on Cherbourg as their next primary target (→ 16).

16. Burma: Chinese troops capture Kamaing (→ 22).

16. Normandy: A 16-inch shell from the British battleship *Rodney* lands twenty miles inland and kills the commander of the 12th SS *Hitler Jugend Panzer* division.

16. Normandy: King George visits the beach-heads, which are now five miles (8 km) from the front line (→ 18).

17. Mediterranean: Allied troops land on Elba from Corsica (→ 19).

17. Hungary: Over 340,000 Jews have been deported to slave labour and death camps since the German invasion (→ 27).

De Gaulle returns to liberated France

De Gaulle is welcomed to Bayeux.

Bayeux, 14 June

General de Gaulle paid his first visit to the liberated soil of France here today. On a platform decorated with the British, American and Canadian flags, he told his applauding audience: "What the country expects of you is to keep up the fight." De Gaulle also visited Isigny, so close to the front that dead bodies were still being dug out of the ruins. Bayeux has already greeted Winston Churchill, who was here two days ago with Field Marshal Smuts. Questions were asked in the House of Commons about why he had not asked de Gaulle to go with him (→ 6/7).

US B-29 bombers hit mainland Japan

Washington, 15 June

Forty-seven B-29 Superfortresses of the US Twentieth Army Air Force flew from China today to bomb the Japanese mainland, hitting an iron and steel works at Yahata, on Kyushu. Claims in the US Congress that the raiders hit targets in Tokyo and other cities were quickly denied by Tokyo radio, however. It is saying that little damage was done and six US planes were shot down (→ 8/7).

German resistance slows pace of Allied advance

Desert veterans fail in Caen attack

Villers-Bocage, 13 June
Montgomery's attempt to outflank Caen by seizing Villers-Bocage has collapsed in confusion with heavy losses. He sent in two of his most experienced formations from the Eighth Army, the 51st Highland and 7th Armoured Divisions.

The 7th, after a brush with the enemy at Livry, pushed on to Villers-Bocage without opposition. Lt-Col Lord Cranley sent A Troop of his 4th County of London Yeomanry, together with a motor company of the 1st Battalion, the Rifle Brigade, up to Point 213, high ground east of the town. There was no sign of the enemy.

Meanwhile Lieutenant Michael Wittman led a company of the 501st SS Heavy Tank Battalion out of the woods and along a sunken road into the village. There he destroyed four Cromwell tanks of the Yeomanry before backtracking to Point 213 where he attacked the British column. By mid-morning, Wittmann had killed or captured a hundred troops and destroyed 27 tanks; he then pulled back.

With German reinforcements continuing to arrive, the surviving British forces were pulled out, covered by an artillery bombardment. Another attempt, supported by fighter-bombers, failed to dislodge the Germans. The defeat is being blamed on the excessive caution exercised by the 7th Armoured Division, exhausted after continuous fighting since 1940 (→ 15).

US troops move up at the double through the ruins of a liberated French city.

Churchill visits the Normandy beaches in the company of Montgomery.

Hitler and generals clash over strategy

Soissons, France, 17 June
With the German forces being relentlessly ground down in Normandy, von Rundstedt, C-in-C West, and Rommel, commanding Army Group B, decided on a showdown with Hitler. They met today in the underground bunker built for the Fuhrer in 1940, when he talked of invading Britain.

Hitler was pale and haggard; hunched on a stool, he fiddled with his glasses as Rommel said that the struggle was hopeless against Allied superiority in the air, at sea and on land. At least, Rommel argued, they should pull back out of range of the Allies' devastating naval guns. The Fuhrer would have none of it. He blamed the two field marshals for the success of the Allied landings, and dismissed Rommel's complaints that fuel shortages and enemy fighter-bomber attacks ruled out a major German offensive.

They talked from 9am to 4pm, with a lunch of rice and vegetables, which Hitler wolfed down with an array of pills. The Fuhrer promised that the V1 flying bombs would devastate England and make the British sue for peace. There were "masses of jet fighters" on the way to drive the enemy out of the sky. At this point, Hitler was interrupted by Allied planes passing overhead. And then, shortly after von Rundstedt and Rommel departed, Hitler was shaken by a huge explosion. One of his own V1s had misfired and hit the bunker roof.

Euphoric Resistance to step up disruption

France, 13 June
There had been plenty of rumours, but few believed them. Now there is no longer any doubt: the Allies have landed, and one week after D-Day the euphoric Resistance is stepping up its attacks on the occupying army and its French supporters such as the *Milice*. News of the invasion has come as a terrible shock for collaborators. Speaking on Radio Paris, the announcer, Jean-Herold Paquis, said: "If

France is to live, England, like Carthage, must be destroyed."

Radio Vichy has broadcast a message from Marshal Petain in which he urges the French people to obey his government and not get involved in combat. But almost four years to the day after Paris fell, most Frenchmen see the hour of liberation at hand and plans are being laid for campaigns of disruption and strikes as well as military action by the Resistance (→ 28).

Channel ports bombed to protect supplies

London, 14 June
The brilliant bomber leader Wing-Commander Leonard Cheshire led a strong force of Lancasters in daylight today to attack the concrete pens at Le Havre which sheltered the German navy's last force of E-Boats (motor torpedo boats) in the approaches to the invasion beaches. The pens and the E-Boats were literally blown away. The raid, Bomber Command's first major daylight attack since May

1943, was ordered when "Ultra" intelligence revealed German plans to attack Allied ships shuttling across the Channel.

The fast, powerful German boats could have done tremendous damage with their torpedoes and guns among the thin-skinned transports. They showed their deadly potential by breaking into the Utah Beach anchorage on 12 June and sinking the US destroyer *Nelson*. That threat is now no more (→ 29/6).

Britain and Germany unveil their secret weapons

Like a vast, floating building: a concrete "bombardon" under construction.

A stretcher party struggles to pull out victims of a "doodlebug" in Clapham.

"Mulberry" harbour tames Channel gales

Normandy, 12 June
One of the more remarkable aspects of the whole Overlord operation came into use today off the Normandy coast. This is the "Mulberry" harbour, which is made up of a number of steel structures which are combined to make a floating dock. It will enable supply ships to unload off the landing beaches instead of having to wait until a proper port is in Allied hands.

It was the Dieppe raid of August 1942 which convinced the Allies that to base the Allied invasion of France on the immediate capture of a port was impracticable. Yet, if the armies were to be kept supplied once they were ashore, there had to be facilities available for ships to unload. The British had been thinking about the problem since early 1942 and quickly recognized the necessity of taming the often rough Channel seas. Various ideas for doing this were tried, including the use of streams of bubbles to cancel out the waves and vast floats, nicknamed "Lilos", made of welded rubber with concrete keels.

Eventually it was decided that a rigid breakwater was the best answer. Metal and concrete pontoons known as "Bombardons" were therefore designed and manufactured. After some modification, 15 of these were tested off Weymouth during the spring gales of April this year and passed with flying colours. Because they did not look like anything in particular, they were anchored in south-coast ports and German air reconnaissance never recognized their significance.

Bombardons enable ships to unload, but the supplies still have to be brought ashore. This is done on "Swiss Roll", a floating trackway strong enough for heavy lorries. Two Mulberries have been assembled at Arromanches and St Laurent to support the British and US Armies respectively (→ 19).

A "Swiss roll" with ambulances.

Flying bombs devastate London targets

London, 17 June
Germany's long-threatened pilotless planes or flying bombs are now falling thick and fast on London and south-east England. They first arrived four days ago, but a full-scale attack was only announced yesterday by Herbert Morrison, who claimed that damage was "relatively small". Not so: it is now becoming severe. According to figures issued at 6am today, 18 people have died and 166 have been injured in flying-bomb explosions since the first six casualties in Bethnal Green, in London, on 13 June. Yesterday 73 fell on Greater London, and today 24 people died in a single blast in a London pub.

The new weapon, today christened "V1" (V for *Vergeltungswaffe* – Reprisal Weapon) by Hitler, is a low-flying bomb launched from the Pas-de-Calais, fitted with stubby wings and a primitive pulse jet engine which is programmed to cut out over London. The V1 then nosedives silently to earth in 15 seconds with its warhead of nearly a ton of explosive. The damage can cover quarter of a mile in radius, mainly by blast. Windows are shattered, and debris lacerates anyone upright in the vicinity. Many are buried alive. The most demoralizing factor is the moment when the engine cuts out. People stare in silence and then fling themselves flat to wait for the explosion. The V1s are being called "doodlebugs" or "buzz bombs" for the drone of their engines (→ 18).

How the V1 robot plane reaches its target

Germany, 17 June
Germany's new weapon is, in essence, an all-metal monoplane powered by a ramjet engine, capable of up to 400mph. The most ingenious part of the system is its means of guidance. This is based on a gyroscopic autopilot, which detects variations in the missile's flight, such as rolling or altitude changes, and uses pneumatic servo units to adjust the rudder and elevators accordingly. This is combined with a compass, which is preset with a bearing, and a log to determine distance, activated by a propeller in the missile's nose. Once the missile has flown the required distance the elevators are fully deflected, causing the V1 to dive and the engine to cut out.

Because of the way in which the missile coasts down to earth, it explodes on or near the surface of the ground, causing a small crater but massive, and deadly, blast damage.

US forces storm Japanese-held Marianas

The first wave of men into Saipan keeps down while waiting for those behind.

Saipan, 17 June

After heavy preliminary bombardment by the US Navy yesterday, the US V Amphibious Corps (Marines) has stormed ashore on the Japanese-held island of Saipan in the Marianas. The Americans plan to seize Guam and Tinian also.

From the Mariana Islands, which are only 1,200 miles (1,920 km) from Tokyo, the Americans will be able to launch B-29 bomber raids on the Japanese home islands.

With an armada of 535 fighting ships and transports carrying 127,000 US soldiers and marines, the Marianas operation is the big-gest amphibious assault of the Pacific War. Coming within two weeks of the Normandy invasion, it highlights the enormous combat resources now available to the Allies.

The marines headed for the beaches of Saipan at 7am on 15 June. They went ashore in a four-mile (6.4-km)-long phalanx of 600 amphibious craft. Facing them were 32,000 Japanese troops, but by to-night the beach-head was secure and the US forces are consolidating their position. Japanese leaders realize that defeat here is inevitable, but pride compels them to carry on to the bitter end (→ 18).

Oil plants become Allies' prime target

London, 13 June

The destruction of Germany's vital synthetic oil plants has become one of the prime strategic objectives of Bomber Command and the US Eighth and Fifteenth Army Air Forces. "Ultra" intelligence has revealed the extent of the crisis caused by the raids in May, when the Eighth struck at the oil plants and the Fifteenth, flying from Italy, hit Germany's only source of natural oil at Ploesti, in Roumania. The Fifteenth has kept up the attack and the Eighth is returning to it after supporting the invasion in Normandy (→ 22).

Jews face one-way trip to Auschwitz

Greece, 14 June

All of Corfu's 1,795 Jews have arrived on the Greek mainland on their way to Auschwitz-Birkenau, where the great majority seem destined to perish in the gas chamber. Members of one of Europe's oldest Jewish communities, they were rounded up on 6 June – the day that the Allies invaded Europe. Since then they have had neither food nor water. The Germans showed no pity as they unloaded the Jews from launches onto trucks bound for Larissa railway station. There cattle trucks await them for the long journey to Poland (→ 17).

1944

June

Su	Mo	Tu	We	Th	Fr	Sa
				1	2	3
4	5	6	7	8	9	10
11	12	13	14	15	16	17
18	19	20	21	22	23	24
25	26	27	28	29	30	

18. Mariana Islands: US marines capture Aslito, on Saipan.→

18. Poland: The Germans launch a six-day sweep against partisans near Lublin (→ 22).

18. Italy: The Allies capture Assisi (→ 20).

18. France: US troops reach the west coast of the Cotentin Peninsula at Barneville (→ 24).

19. Bermuda: The U-boat U505, captured on 4 June by the US destroyer-escort *Chatelain*, yields her codebooks intact.

19. English Channel: The worst storm for 40 years destroys the artificial "Mulberry" harbour off Omaha Beach.

20. USSR: Soviet forces capture Viipuri.

20. Germany: Colonel Count Claus von Stauffenberg, a conspirator in a plot by high-ranking army officers to stage a *coup* against Hitler, is appointed chief of staff to General Friedrich Fromm, so gaining access to the Fuhrer's headquarters (→ 11/7).

20. USSR: The Red Army masses 166 divisions and 5,000 tanks in Byelorussia, poised for Operation Bagration.→

20. Italy: British troops take Perugia (→ 3/7).

21. New Guinea: US forces are unable to dislodge the Japanese from the caves of Biak (→ 23).

22. Chelm, Poland: The USSR sets up a puppet "Polish Committee for National Liberation" (→ 13/7).

22. Finland: Von Ribbentrop flies to Helsinki, promising arms and troops to try to keep Finland in the war (→ 28).

23. Lapland: General Eduard Dietl, the C-in-C of German troops on the Arctic front, is killed in a plane crash.

23. Mariana Islands: US and Japanese forces clash violently at "Death Valley", near Mount Tapotchau, on Saipan (→ 28).

24. France: Nearly 750,000 Allied troops have landed in Normandy.→

V1 robot kills 119 in Guards' Chapel

London, 18 June

A flying bomb fell on the Guards Chapel at Wellington Barracks, only yards from Buckingham Palace, during morning service today. The building was almost completely destroyed and 119 worshippers, half civilians, half servicemen, were killed. Another 102 were seriously injured. The V1s generally cause higher casualties than the usual aircraft bombing. Flying bombs come over from northern Europe in a steady stream, night and day, so no warnings can be given (→ 27).

A child is rescued: terrified but alive.

Japanese capture two Chinese cities

Changsha, 18 June

After two weeks of fierce fighting the 200,000-strong Japanese Eleventh Army has taken the central Chinese cities of Changsha and Chuchow. Its next target is Hengyang, 75 miles (120 km) away, an important railway junction on the Canton to Hankow line. The three-week-old Japanese offensive is intended first to capture key Chinese supply lines before advancing south and west to destroy Allied airfields in China. It is from these that the new long-range US B-29s bombed the Japanese mainland three days ago (→ 26).

Russia musters 1.2 million men to attack Germans

Soviet infantry troops push ahead in Byelorussia, as bombs explode all around them: many Germans are being bypassed in this Russian advance.

Moscow, 22 June

The Red Army has chosen today, the third anniversary of the German invasion, to launch a massive assault on the Nazi forces occupying Byelorussia. It is called Operation Bagration, after the Czarist general who was mortally wounded fighting Napoleon at Borodino in 1812, and its object is nothing less than to destroy Hitler's Army Group Centre.

Last night, partisans blew up railway lines, bridges and telephone cables in 10,500 separate places, effectively severing the Germans' supply and communications lines. Then the huge weight of the Red Army crashed into the German defences. The Russians have assembled nearly 1.2 million men in 124 divisions, 5,200 tanks and assault guns, and 6,000 aircraft to smash a German force of 400,000 men supported by just 900 tanks and heavy guns and 1,300 aircraft.

German intelligence reports had given General von Busch, the commander of Army Group Centre, clear warning of the Russian build-up, but Hitler, relying on his "intuition", has been deceived by a Russian *maskirova* (disinformation) operation into believing that the Red Army was planning a double thrust in the south to the Roumanian oilfields and Warsaw. He was so sure that he had out-guessed the Russians that he sent 48 infantry divisions and three *Panzer* divisions to Galicia, leaving von Busch's forces dangerously thin on the ground. The men and tanks he switched to the south have now been bypassed and are playing no part in the battle.

Hitler's mistake became apparent at 5 o'clock this morning when the Red Army opened up with its customary overwhelming barrage from guns which were virtually wheel to wheel along the front. When the barrage lifted, hordes of T34 tanks scurried towards the German defences, each followed by a tight group of infantry. Sturmoviks lurked overhead to pounce on strongpoints. The speed and punching power of the assault soon tore gaping holes in the attenuated German lines.

The Russians are racing west through these gaps, heading for Minsk. General Bagramyan's First Baltic Front has made a double breakthrough against Gen Reinhardt's 3rd Panzer Army to isolate Vitebsk, and some 30,000 Germans are in danger of being surrounded. As the hammer blows descend the whole German position in Byelorussia is under threat (→ 29).

French troops raise their flag over Elba

Elba, 19 June

Mountain fighters of the French Expeditionary Force have climbed to the highest point of the island of Napoleon's exile to raise the *Tricouleur*. Elba was taken by storm, the French troops landing by night and taking Porto Ferrario after a short and bloody battle. On the mainland, British troops are fighting for the road and rail junction of Perugia. Assisi fell earlier today. The British XIII Corps has reached the Albert Line which German troops have been ordered to defend "with tenacity" as their army withdraws to the Gothic Line.

US forces close on port of Cherbourg

Cotentin Peninsula, 24 June

After capturing Carentan, American troops have raced across to Barneville to seal off the Cotentin Peninsula, and now the battle has begun for the key port of Cherbourg. Two days ago, after a heavy air bombardment, Major-General J Lawton Collins launched his VII Corps into an attack on the Germans' outer defences – three ridges to the south of the port. These were soon reduced, the Germans surprising Collins by withdrawing almost at once to the inner forts. Hitler will not countenance the thought of giving up the port (→ 26).

Germany blasts US bombers in Russia

Poltava, 22 June

The *Luftwaffe* made a devastating attack on this Ukrainian airfield last night, killing 26 crewmen of the US Eighth Army Air Force, and destroying 47 and severely damaging 26 Flying Fortresses, which had landed here after attacking a German synthetic oil plant. They had flown on to Poltava, one of three airfields made available by the Russians. But they had been shadowed by a German plane, and later 75 He111s and Ju88s attacked. A fuel dump containing over two million litres of fuel exploded and the aircraft burst into flames.

June 10. David Niven on the cover of "Picturegoer", publicizing the new film "The Way Ahead".

Japan reels from Allied success at sea and on land

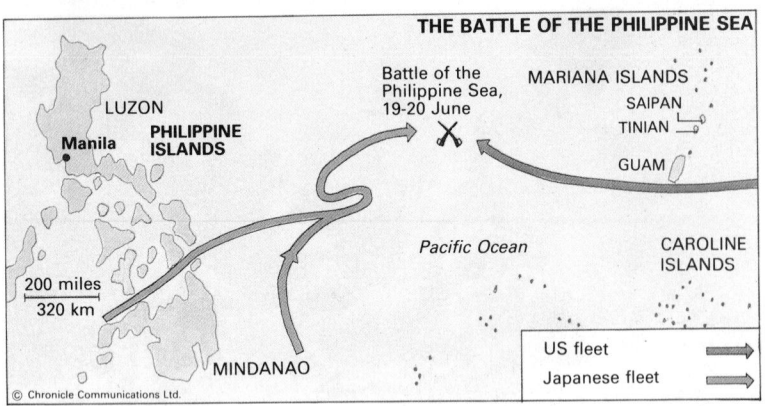

THE BATTLE OF THE PHILIPPINE SEA

"Turkey shoot" smashes Japanese navy

Pacific, 20 June
A US Navy victory in the Battle of the Philippine Sea over the last two days has decided the fate of the Marianas by giving command of the surrounding sea and air to the Americans. In the greatest aircraft-carrier battle of the war, the Japanese had so many aircraft shot down that the US pilots called it "the great Marianas turkey shoot".

The Japanese had hoped to use the US invasion of the Marianas as an opportunity to destroy the American carrier force. Planes based on the islands of Saipan, Tinian and Guam were to be reinforced by carrier-based aircraft of the Japanese fleet by Admiral Toyoda in Operation *A-Go*.

The Japanese fleet consisted of a main carrier force, a main battle force and a reserve carrier force. But the Americans had mustered the greatest naval force yet assembled in the Pacific – and its submarines spotted the Japanese fleet assembling. The US fleet to support the Saipan landings was formidable: five battleships, 11 cruisers and 12 escort carriers plus a carrier force under the command of Vice-Admiral Mitscher with no fewer than 15 carriers (and 956 aircraft). In reserve was Admiral Spruance's Fifth Fleet with seven battleships, 21 cruisers and 69 destroyers.

At 8.30am yesterday the Japanese launched their first strikes against the US carriers. But the attacks came only from their carriers, as the land-based aircraft had been wiped out by earlier US attacks. And the Americans saw the Japanese coming on their radar screens:

300 US fighters were dispatched to intercept them, shooting down 242 Japanese planes for the loss of only 29 American aircraft. To complete a bad day for Japan, two of their carriers, the *Shokaku* and the *Taiho*, were sunk by submarines, losing yet more planes.

Yet Admiral Ozawa, in charge of the carrier force, believed that many planes had landed on Guam and stayed in the area overnight. Today Mitscher sent 216 of his planes to attack the Japanese fleet, sinking one carrier, damaging several other warships and shooting down 65 aircraft; 20 US planes were lost in the battle, although 72 were lost returning home.

Tonight, as Ozawa withdraws towards Okinawa, Japan has lost 480 of its aircraft – three-quarters of the total with which the fleet set sail for what it proclaimed to be a "decisive battle" in the Pacific (→ 21).

A Japanese plane plunges seaward.

British and Indian troops on the Kohima to Imphal road, now in their hands.

Indian divisions break the siege of Imphal

Imphal, India, 22 June
The Allies have reopened the road between Imphal and Kohima. The Japanese Fifteenth Army which invaded India in March has been defeated; Operation *U-Go* has failed. Of the 100,000 Japanese who marched from Burma, 30,502 are dead and 23,003 wounded, at a total loss to the Allies of 2,700 killed and 10,000 wounded.

Imphal was under siege for three months. General Renya Mutaguchi sent three divisions of the Fifteenth Army against the Allies: the 33rd drove north from Tiddim, and the 15th and 31st attacked the Allied bases at Imphal and Kohima from the east. Against this the Allies mustered four Indian divisions under Lt-Gen Geoffrey Scoones. The 17th and 20th held the Imphal perimeter, and the 5th and 23rd hunted out the overstretched Japanese on the Imphal plain, hammering them against Imphal's anvil.

Allied control of the Imphal plain and the skies above it was backed by secure communications. Imphal has been supplied by air since April. Mutaguchi, however, refused to admit defeat at Imphal or Kohima, ignoring the realities of the field.

Lt-Gen Kotoku Sato withdrew his 31st Division from Kohima on 3 June when, with no prospect of supply, it ran out of ammunition

and food rations; he had refused Mutaguchi's demand to regroup and attack Imphal without even finding food. Sato's withdrawal freed two more Allied divisions for Imphal.

Mutaguchi has been ordering the 15th Division to mount ever more ambitious operations, simultaneously stripping its commander, Lt-Gen Masafumi Yamauchi, of manpower until today he commands a mere battalion and a half. No wonder Yamauchi has spent much of his time writing despairing *haiku* poetry.

The fighting has been close and bloody, with the besieging Japanese crawling over their dead to reach the trenches surrounding Imphal. Outside, the battle swayed to and fro, the highest casualties on both sides suffered on the Ukhrul road and the Shenam Saddle. Conditions are appalling: heavy rain, mist and thick jungle have made transport and observations difficult. The Imphal to Kohima road itself is a single track overlooked by high ridges from which the Japanese launched a series of deadly attacks and stubborn defences.

The turning-point in the battle came on 17 June, when the Japanese abandoned Mao Songsan ridge, the first time that they had given up a position without a fight in the entire campaign (→ 25).

1944

June

Su	Mo	Tu	We	Th	Fr	Sa
				1	2	3
4	5	6	7	8	9	10
11	12	13	14	15	16	17
18	19	20	21	22	23	24
25	26	27	28	29	30	

26. Cherbourg: The Germans start to destroy all port facilities.→

26. China: Japanese forces smash Chinese Tenth Army defences to capture Hengyang airfield from the US (→ 22/7).

26. Normandy: 5,287 Allied soldiers have been killed since D-Day.→

26. Obersalzberg: Hitler, forgetful and ill-looking, makes a confused and rambling speech to a group of leading industrialists (→ 29).

27. London: A V1 lands on Victoria station, killing 14 people (→ 30).

28. New Guinea: US forces clear the Japanese from the caves on Biak (→ 2/7).

28. Denmark: A general strike begins in Copenhagen (→ 1/7).

28. Washington: The US severs diplomatic relations with Finland.→

28. US: Thomas Dewey and John Bricker win the Republican nominations for president and vice-president (→ 11/7).

29. Germany: USAAF B-24 bombers raid 20 industrial targets, dropping incendiary bombs on the Volkswagen plant at Fallersleben.

29. Berchtesgaden: Von Rundstedt, Rommel, Sperrle and Kroncke attend a special "Fuhrer conference" at which Hitler does not allow them to tell him the true situation on the western front; instead, he promises more V-weapons and jet fighters (→ 6/7).

29. USSR: Soviet troops under Rokossovsky take Bobruisk.→

30. Auschwitz-Birkenau: The 1,795 Jews of Corfu arrive at the camp, having spent 27 days in sealed boxcars without food or water. Half have died on the way; the comatose remainder are gassed and cremated immediately (→ 8/7).

30. London: A V1 lands on Bush House in the Aldwych, killing 198 people (→ 3/7).

30. Britain: Civilian air raid casualties this month were 1,935 killed and 5,906 injured.

Red Army advance clears road to Minsk

The Russians forge ahead in Byelorussia: troops and guns ready for battle.

Moscow, 29 June
Bobruisk, the last German bastion at the southern end of the smashed "Fatherland Line" in Byelorussia, has been stormed by the Red Army. The road is now clear for a pincer movement to enfold the Byelorussian capital of Minsk.

Latest reports say that the Russians have already taken the railway junction of Osipovichi, only 60 miles (96 km) south-east of Minsk. These latest successes, following the crossing of the Dnieper on a 75-mile front and the wiping out of the German garrison of Vitebsk, are celebrated in an order of the day addressed to Gen Konstantin Rokossovsky. Arrested before the war on Stalin's orders, Rokossovsky is C-in-C of the First Byelorussian Front and planned this campaign, Operation Bagration. He has been rewarded today by promotion to marshal.

In an attempt to stop his advance Hitler has ordered that key towns such as Vitebsk, Mogilev and Polotsk be held as *Feste Platze* [firm positions] and defended to the last man and the last round. The result, as in Vitebsk, has been the sacrifice of units bypassed and then destroyed by the Russians (→ 3/7).

Germans form new jet fighter unit

Germany, 30 June
The Allies will shortly face the German Me262 jet fighter for the first time. A test unit, *Erprobungskommando* [Trials Detachment] 262, has been in existence since April, but now a new unit, I/KG51 (First Wing of No 51 *Kampfgeschwader* [Bomber Group]) has been formed. At Hitler's insistence the Me262 will serve as a fighter-bomber, although he has permitted development of the fighter version to continue. This has meant much modification to give the aircraft the structural strength to carry bombs. It is planned to deploy the new unit to France once it is fully operational.

Vichy minister slain

Paris, 28 June
Philippe Henriot, the Vichy secretary-general for information, was executed by the Resistance here today. Men disguised as police took over the ministry headquarters, and then went upstairs and shot Henriot in front of his wife.

Henriot, before the war an extreme right-wing deputy, was particularly hated for his propaganda broadcasts denouncing the Resistance as "criminal assassins" and its leaders as "cowards" (→ 7/7).

Weakened Chindits win month-long battle to trap Japanese

Mogaung, Burma, 27 June
The Chindit 77th Special Force Brigade under Brigadier Mike Calvert, supported by two battalions of the Chinese 114th Regiment, has taken Mogaung. The Japanese 18th Division, fighting Lt-Gen Joseph Stilwell's Chinese troops and the remnants of "Merrill's Marauders" at Myitkyina, is now isolated.

The Gurkha, Lancashire Fusilier, Staffordshire and Liverpool men have been fighting for Mogaung for a month. Casualties of battle wounds and ill-health have been so high that for today's assault across the key railway bridge Calvert had only 230 Gurkhas, 110 Fusiliers and men of the King's Regiment (Liverpool), and 180 Staffordshire men from battalions once 800 strong (→ 8/7).

The hardy men still in action in Burma: now they have taken Mogaung.

537

American soldiers capture Cherbourg

Cherbourg, 27 June
Organized resistance finally came to an end in Cherbourg today after the Germans had systematically sabotaged and wrecked port installations. It will be weeks before they are repaired and the Allies can start bringing in supplies. In the battle for the port the Americans lost 1,800 dead and 15,000 wounded; they took 45,000 prisoners.

Discipline among men of the US VII Corps broke down when they came across huge stores of champagne and brandy and proceeded to get drunk.

The German commander, General von Schlieben, wanted to surrender two days ago. "Among the troops defending the town," he reported to Rommel, "there are 2,000 wounded who cannot be treated. Is the sacrifice of the others still necessary?" Rommel answered: "In accordance with the Fuhrer's orders you are to hold out to the last round."

Yesterday, after a naval bombardment by three battleships, four cruisers and 11 destroyers, the Americans started firing straight in-

A vast column of German PoWs files past the town hall in Cherbourg.

to the tunnel defences. Fuhrer or no Fuhrer, von Schlieben had had enough; he walked out of the arsenal and gave himself up to the first American he met. This chanced to be Major-General Manton Eddy, commanding the 9th Division; he took the German general to lunch.

But von Schlieben, who brought 800 men with him, refused to order the rest of the garrison to surrender. It was another 24 hours before the Americans had cleared the port; now they face a ten-mile slog to attack Cap de la Hague, on the tip of the peninsula (→ 30).

British offensive fails in bid to outflank the Germans at Caen

Normandy, 30 June
Operation Epsom, an attempt by the British VIII Corps to break through German lines west of Caen, has been aborted. Lt-Gen Dempsey today withdrew the British 11th Armoured Division from Hill 112, overlooking the road to Caen. The ever-reliable "Ultra" intelligence intercepts showed that the Germans were about to launch a major attack on Hill 112 by two formations just arrived from the Soviet front: the 9th and 10th SS *Panzer* Divisions.

In the area as a whole Dempsey had 60,000 men and 600 tanks, supported by 700 guns; but he knew that he was still outranked by the Panzers. The offensive was abandoned; Caen will have to wait.

Since the 6 June landings, the Allies have lost 7,704 dead – 4,868 Americans, 2,443 Britons and 393 Canadians. Battle fatigue has also claimed 10,000 men in American units since D-Day – one-fifth of all casualties (→ 3/7).

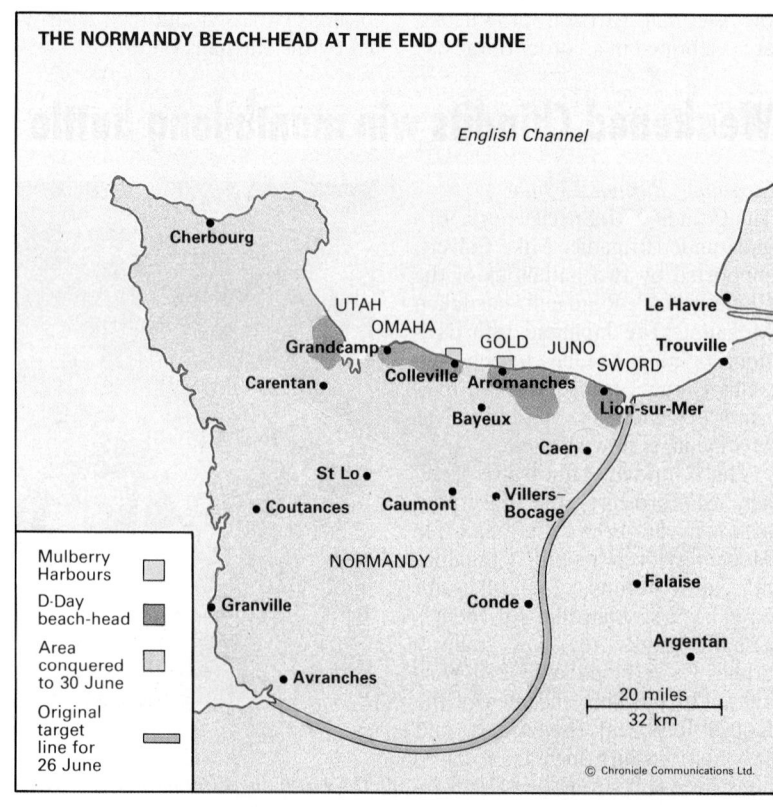

THE NORMANDY BEACH-HEAD AT THE END OF JUNE

English Channel

Cherbourg

UTAH
OMAHA
Grandcamp
Carentan
Colleville
Arromanches
Bayeux
St Lo
Coutances
Caumont
Villers–Bocage

GOLD JUNO
SWORD
Le Havre
Trouville
Lion-sur-Mer
Caen

NORMANDY

Granville
Conde
Falaise

Avranches
Argentan

Mulberry Harbours
D-Day beach-head
Area conquered to 30 June
Original target line for 26 June

20 miles
32 km

© Chronicle Communications Ltd.

Jews beg Allies to bomb camp railway

London, 27 June
Churchill was ploughing through his usual diet of documents today when he came across a telegram which upset him deeply. It came from the Jewish Agency in Switzerland, and contained a report of the gas chambers, allegedly based on the eye-witness account of some lucky escapees from Auschwitz-Birkenau. The report's authors, Chaim Weizmann and Moshe Shertok, beg the Allies to bomb the railway lines which bring trainloads of victims to the camp. Churchill is minded to agree (→ 30).

Pro-Nazi Finnish cabinet to fight on

Helsinki, 29 June
A pro-German clique, headed by President Risto Ryti, is planning to fight on against the Russians, in defiance of the wishes of the people and the majority of the democratic parliament. Six members of the government have resigned in protest, and Ryti is replacing them with men who will not oppose him despite the increasing hopelessness of Finland's military position. The latest blow to the Finns is a warning delivered by the US secretary of state, Cordell Hull, that America is considering breaking off diplomatic relations (→ 4/8).

Thousands injured by V1 flying bombs

London, 27 June
Herbert Morrison, the home secretary and minister of home security, today told the war cabinet that in less than two weeks, since V1 attacks began, 1,600 people have been killed and 4,500 seriously injured. The scale of the emergency is only being discussed behind closed doors. In a BBC broadcast yesterday the public heard that the "beastly, vicious things" were not upsetting southerners, who were "steadiness itself". The royal family are staying in London, though the king's tennis court was destroyed yesterday by a flying bomb (→ 30).

1944

July

Su	Mo	Tu	We	Th	Fr	Sa
						1
2	3	4	5	6	7	8
9	10	11	12	13	14	15
16	17	18	19	20	21	22
23	24	25	26	27	28	29
30	31					

1. Denmark: The German authorities proclaim a state of emergency because of the general strike.

1. US: Finance ministers meet at Bretton Woods for a conference to work out an international monetary system for after the war (→ 22).

2. New Guinea: US amphibious forces seize Noemfoor island (→ 4).

3. London: A V1 lands on a Chelsea block of flats, killing 74 people and injuring 50.→

3. Normandy: US forces launch a drive southwards towards St Lo, meeting stiff German opposition (→ 5).

3. Burma: The Allies capture Ukhrul from the Japanese after a brief struggle (→ 3/8).

4. New Guinea: US paratroopers take Kamiri airfield, with heavy losses.

4. Pacific: US Task Force 58 raids Japanese bases on Guam, Iwo Jima and Chichi Jima (→ 6).

4. USSR: The Red Army takes Polotsk, the gateway to Latvia, from the Germans (→ 6).

5. Normandy: US forces capture La Haye-du-Puits (→ 7).

6. Mariana Islands: The Japanese commanders, Admiral Chichi Nagumo and General Yoshitsugu Saito, commit suicide as American troops advance to complete the capture of Saipan (→ 7).

6. USSR: The Red Army captures Kovel (→ 7).

6. Washington: Roosevelt meets de Gaulle to discuss further aid for the Free French (→ 11).

7. Mariana Islands: Japanese forces attack the US garrison at Saipan, and are driven off with heavy losses.→

7. Lithuania: Soviet troops enter Vilna (→ 10).

7. Normandy: The British battleship *Rodney* shells German positions near Caen.→

7. France: The *Milice* murders the Jewish statesman Georges Mandel, who had been Reynaud's justice minister, as a "reprisal" for Philippe Henriot's execution last week.

Hungarian regent halts Jewish round-ups

Those they did not manage to save: Jews from Hungary arrive in Auschwitz.

Budapest, 8 July
At least 300,000 Hungarian Jews have been gassed or shot at Auschwitz-Birkenau in the last 46 days under Adolf Eichmann's carefully-thought-out plan to destroy the Jewish population of Hungary. But today Hungary's regent, Admiral Miklos Horthy, ordered a halt to Jewish deportations following concerted pressure from Allied governments, the Red Cross, the pope and the king of Sweden.

Hitler himself had to persuade Horthy, a natural defender of the Jews, to agree to the deportations in the first place. Now, with the Russians getting nearer every day, Horthy feels strong enough to stand up to him, sacking the veteran fascists Laszlo Baky and Vitez Endre who were helping to implement Nazi racial policies.

Although Eichmann remains determined to try to keep the trains running, he may have met his match in the form of Raoul Wallenberg, a Swedish diplomat. Wallenberg, on his way to Budapest clutching Swedish visas for 630 Hungarian Jews and British documents guaranteeing a further 700 entry to Palestine, is expected to arrive tomorrow. The king of Sweden has sent Wallenberg on a mission to save as many Jews as possible. His brief is simple: protect them while visas are prepared, then get them to a safe haven (→ 12).

British give Italians guns – and pride

Victorious partisans arrest Fascists.

Udine, Italy, 1 July
Despite a vicious crackdown by occupying Germans, thousands of Italian patriots, mainly communist-led, have taken to the hills in the north of Italy and are taking a major part in disrupting German communications. Meanwhile, the British Eighth Army is training and equipping Italian brigades – often composed of former enemies – who have been fighting alongside most Allied armies since the beginning of the year. "We had both sympathy and contempt for the Italians in the desert," said one commander. "Now we see them as real and dedicated fighters. We have given them pride again."

Brazil prepares to join Allies in Italy

Brazil, 2 July
The first contingent of the Brazilian Expeditionary Force has set sail from Rio de Janeiro heading for Naples to join the Allied forces in the desperate battle to liberate Italy. About 5,000 officers and men left aboard the American troop transport *General W A Mann*, escorted by three destroyers *Marcilio Dias*, *Mariz e Barros* and *Greenhalgh*. Brazil declared war on the Axis in August 1942 and its navy has participated in joint Allied action in the Atlantic. Last November it decided to send troops to join the fighting in Europe. The forces are to operate under the strategic command of the Americans.

US mounts further air raids on Japan

Washington, 8 July
American B-29 Superfortresses based in China have carried out a second attack on the Japanese mainland. Last night's raid by 20th Bomber Command was aimed at naval installations at Sasebo and the iron and steel works at Yahata, "Japan's Essen", first hit by B-29s three weeks ago. Sasebo, Omura and Tobata were also hit. General Arnold, the commander of the USAAF, set up the independent 20th to fly the huge bombers in any theatre of war. He has said that B-29s will only fly night raids until the shakedown stage is over (→ 18).

"The Ukraine is free!"

Suicides highlight Japanese attitude to surrendering

Saipan, 8 July

Victorious but stunned US troops on Saipan are still coming to terms with the mass suicide of 8,000 Japanese defenders and civilians in the final throes of the invasion. Ever since Tarawa, US veterans of the Pacific campaign have become used to the gruesome Japanese determination to fight to the death. On Saipan they were as ready as it is possible to be when the Japanese yesterday launched a last desperate lunge, quickly losing 1,500.

But this was as nothing compared with the shock when US troops broke through to Marpi and found thousands of bodies on the rocks and floating in the surf. Many were civilians, many of them children. According to survivors the terrified settlers hurled their children and themselves over the cliffs rather than be taken prisoner, heeding the warning by Saipan's commander General Saito that they would be tortured and killed if captured. Saito commited ritual suicide.

The survivors' stories bear out the results of a wider survey conducted among Japanese prisoners – many injured or unconscious when captured. Of the PoWs surveyed 84 per cent said they expected to be killed or tortured if taken prisoner. Fear of the consequences of surrender rather than any elevated sense of the *samurai* code of *bushido* motivated them to fight to the death.

Many are clearly affected by Japanese propaganda that never fails to call their American opponents subhuman "brutes" and "wild beasts", and depicts Roosevelt and Churchill as horned demons. One typical issue of a popular Japanese magazine portrays Americans as bestial degenerates, sex-obsessed, fiercely racist and capable of killing deformed children by bashing their heads against walls, a fear reinforced among Japanese by the recent US sinking of a hospital ship (→ 9).

Allies enter Caen after heavy bombing

British troops move up through La Deliverande on their way to Caen.

Caen, 8 July

After RAF bombers had dropped 2,276 tons of bombs on Caen overnight, and the battleship *Rodney* had delivered hundreds of 16-inch shells, British and Canadian troops attacked the next day, only to find SS Colonel Meyer's *Panzers* still firmly established outside Caen.

While the citizens of Caen huddled in cellars, the Germans stubbornly held out. Hitler has ordered that every square kilometre must be defended to the last man. But the Allies penetrated into the centre of the ruined city to the north bank of the river Orne. There they were held by Meyer's men. In a month of battles, every one of Meyer's battalion commanders has been killed and he has received no replacements. "Officers and men know the struggle is hopeless," Meyer wrote in his diary, "but they remain willing to do their duty to the bitter end" (→ 9).

Rundstedt sacked after D-Day defeat

Obersalzberg, 6 July

Von Rundstedt has been sacked as C-in-C West after he and Rommel told Hitler that the military situation was disastrous. This encounter was followed by a testy telephone conversation between von Rundstedt and Field Marshal Keitel, the chief of the OKW [Armed Forces High Command], who was told an allout attack by four SS *Panzer* divisions on the British had collapsed. "What shall we do now?" Keitel asked. "Make peace, you fools," von Rundstedt snapped. Von Kluge replaces him.

Field Marshal Gerd von Rundstedt.

Siena falls, then French conquerors prepare for a new invasion

In a flower-bedecked Jeep, French troops are given a joyous welcome to Siena.

Siena, 3 July

This beautiful Etruscan capital fell today to Algerian troops of the French Expeditionary Corps. There was little time for the victors to celebrate, however. Almost as soon as they had cleared the last German from the city, the 3rd Algerian Division was preparing to move south – to Naples and the planned invasion of the south of France. The Algerians have been replaced by the Moroccan 4th Mountain Division, which has wasted no time in heading for Florence and the Gothic Line. The US Fifth Army, which is also likely to lose much of its strength to the proposed invasion, today took the coastal town of Cecina and is close to encircling the port of Leghorn [*Livorno*] (→ 9).

German base at Minsk falls to Red Army

Moscow, 3 July

Minsk, the capital of Byelorussia and last great German-occupied base on Russian soil, fell to the Red Army today, ten days after the opening of *Operation Bagration*. This stronghold, the gateway to East Prussia, was first encircled and then stormed by General Cherniakhovsky's Third Byelorussian Front and Marshal Rokossovsky's First Byelorussian Front.

Not only have they taken 73,000 prisoners, including two generals – Michaelis and Konradi – they have also trapped a large force of Germans east of Minsk. The story is the same all along the line. In the north General Bagramyan's First Baltic Front has invested Polotsk and is pushing the Germans out of the city in hand-to-hand street fighting. When Polotsk falls Vilna, the capital of Lithuania, will come within striking distance. In the south, Marshal Zhukov has mounted an attack on Baranovichi, the key to the German right wing.

The Russians are, in the words of a congratulatory message to Stalin from Churchill, "pulverising the German armies". Hitler has sacked Field Marshal von Busch and replaced him by Model, but even that hardbitten warrior seems unable to stem the Russian tide (→ 4).

Left behind by the Germans: bodies of Russians shot in a concentration camp.

V1s bring second evacuation for London

London, 3 July

London is being evacuated again. Under the impact of the flying-bomb attack the government has announced a new scheme to move mothers of children under five and expectant mothers, as well as schoolchildren, to the country. Many others have made their own arrangements for evacuation. In the first two weeks of the attack over 1,700 people have been killed. The fact that V1s fall out of cloudy skies in daytime makes it harder to shelter.

In one of the worst incidents, on 30 June, a flying bomb glided low over the Thames and dropped beside Bush House in the Aldwych, which was crowded with lunch-hour office workers, killing 198 of them. Another which landed in

A flying bomb: the new Nazi terror.

Chelsea today killed 74. However, the anti-aircraft and balloon barrage now on the North Downs is bringing down more of the robot planes than before (→ 11).

1944
July

Su	Mo	Tu	We	Th	Fr	Sa
						1
2	3	4	5	6	7	8
9	10	11	12	13	14	15
16	17	18	19	20	21	22
23	24	25	26	27	28	29
30	31					

9. Italy: French forces drive towards Poggibonsi, and US troops capture Volterra.→

9. Britain: The band leader Glenn Miller gives the first concert of his British tour.

9. Mariana Islands: US forces finally overcome enemy resistance on Saipan, having killed 30,000 Japanese (→ 10).

10. New Guinea: Japanese troops attack US forces across the Wewak river (→ 14).

10. Normandy: Montgomery orders the British Second Army to attack east of Caen (Operation Goodwood) and the US First Army to secure St Lo (→ 12).

10. USSR: Hitler refuses to allow a strategic withdrawal of Army Group North behind the Dvina river.→

11. Berchtesgaden: Von Stauffenberg takes a bomb to a meeting with Hitler, but postpones the explosion because Himmler and Goering do not attend (→ 15).

11. London: Forty-one thousand mothers and children are evacuated (→ 18).

11. Washington: Roosevelt agrees to recognize de Gaulle's French provisional government as the legitimate administration of liberated France.

12. Auschwitz-Birkenau: The "family camp" of 12,500 Jews is closed down, and 4,000 of them are gassed (→ 18).

12. Normandy: US troops capture Hill 92, two miles (3.2 km) east of St Lo (→ 18).

13. Lithuania: The Red Army captures Vilna.→

13. Aegean Sea: The Allies take Symi island, north of Rhodes.

14. New Guinea: Allied naval forces start a long-term bombardment of Japanese positions near Aitape (→ 22).

14. USSR: Pinsk falls to the Red Army (→ 17).

15. Rastenburg: Von Stauffenberg's second attempt to assassinate Hitler is foiled when the Fuhrer leaves a conference unexpectedly early (→ 20).

Roosevelt runs for record fourth term

The veteran president, Roosevelt.

Washington, 11 July

President Roosevelt announced at his press conference today that he would run for an unprecedented fourth term in the White House. Ordering the doors of the Oval Office in the White House to be closed, to prevent a "mad rush" to the door, the president informed correspondents by reading out a letter he had written to Robert Hannegan, the chairman of the Democratic National Committee, accepting his invitation to run. Everyone in wartime, said the president, had a superior officer, and the commander-in-chief's superior officers were the American people (→ 20).

Lost German plane brings secrets haul

RAF Woodbridge, Suffolk, 13 July

A Ju88G nightfighter landed on the runway here today. It was based at Deelen, in Holland, but apparently the crew made a navigational error after a *sortie*. On board were three different radar sets, all designed to counter systems used by RAF bombers. The FuG 220 is impervious to "Window"; the FuG 227 *Flensburg* was found to be tuned to "Monica", used by bombers to warn of German fighters on their tails; and the FuG *Naxos* was tuned to H2S, which gives a downward radar scan. This will give British scientists food for thought.

▷

Monty under Allied fire

The bomb-shattered town of Caen: Monty is having trouble breaking out.

Caen, 9 July
Criticism of Montgomery's handling of operations in the Caen sector has been growing since the failure of repeated attempts to break out into open country. The Britons and Canadians of Dempsey's Second Army remain stalled at the river Orne inside Caen, with the Germans still holding Bourgebus Ridge to the south of the town. Another commanding height, Hill 112, has again been wrested from the enemy, only to be lost in a counter-attack. The high rate of infantry casualties

is causing anxiety. After almost four years of war, manpower is running low; this may help to explain Montgomery's caution.

Against this background, Montgomery's staff have produced a plan for exploiting the 21st Army Group's four-to-one superiority in tanks over the Germans. A mass attack by 750 tanks is to be mounted east of Caen with the aim of driving towards Falaise. "I have decided the time has come to have a real showdown on the eastern flank," Montgomery says (→ 10).

Troop losses could hit Italian advance

Italy, 14 July
It is eight weeks since the Allies struck along the Gustav Line from Cassino to the Tyrrhenian Sea, forcing the Germans from what seemed to be an impregnable position. Since then, they have taken Rome, forced the Germans back over 250 miles (400 km) over difficult terrain, almost destroyed ten German divisions, smashed two German armies and forced their way through two more defence lines. The Allies' relentless advance has been achieved by superior numbers and the concentration of forces, as at Cassino. But now, as the Allies face the Gothic Line, some American and French troops will be withdrawn for the coming invasion of southern France (→ 16).

Red Army captures Vilna in Lithuania

Lithuania, 13 July
Vilna [*Vilnius*] has fallen to the Red Army. Once part of Poland, the Lithuanian capital has been occupied by German troops since June 1941; now its garrison, prevented from surrendering by SS troops, has been annihilated. Among the casualties were paratroopers dropped into the city to "stand or die". Many were killed on the way down, others died as they landed on the city's roofs; the rest were wiped out in combat in the ancient streets. The way is now open for the Russians to cut off the Baltic states and advance into East Prussia. The indications are that the *Wehrmacht* is falling back to a new defence line on the Polish border just 55 miles (88 km) from Warsaw (→ 14).

Germany forced to withdraw in Ukraine

Moscow, 13 July
The Red Army, demonstrating that it is powerful enough to strike anywhere along the eastern front, has launched a two-edged drive from the Ukraine aimed at crossing the river Bug and capturing Lwow, one of the principal cities of pre-war Poland. The Russian forces, commanded by Marshal Konev, are advancing on the town of Brody where they aim to trap some 40,000

Germans in a "cauldron" where they could be systematically annihilated.

There is an important political aspect to this new Soviet advance, for the Bug marks the so-called Curzon Line which Stalin wants recognized as the western boundary of the Soviet Union. This would mean that Lwow, much-loved by the fiercely patriotic Poles, would fall under Soviet control (→ 14).

Humiliation for those who collaborated

French women accused of collaboration are paraded on 14 July, Bastille Day.

A US soldier in Saipan wheels a child through the sands: civilians are being taken to places of safety away from the fighting on the beaches.

1944

July

Su	Mo	Tu	We	Th	Fr	Sa
						1
2	3	4	5	6	7	8
9	10	11	12	13	14	15
16	17	18	19	20	21	22
23	24	25	26	27	28	29
30	31					

16. Italy: British troops take Arezzo, the key point of the German defensive line (→ 18).

17. Poland: Soldiers of the First Ukrainian Front trap 40,000 German troops at Brody (→ 21).

17. USSR: 57,600 German PoWs are paraded through the streets of Moscow (→ 20).

17. Norway: The British carriers *Furious, Formidable* and *Indefatigable* attack through a heavy German smokescreen, but fail to damage the last German battleship *Tirpitz*.

17. Poland: The Soviet Army crosses the river Bug on a 40-mile (64-km) front (→ 23).

17. France: US aircraft drop napalm for the first time, on a fuel depot at Coutances.

18. Aegean Sea: German troops round up the two thousand Jews of Rhodes and Kos for deportation, via Athens and Hungary, to Auschwitz-Birkenau (→ 24).

18. Italy: The Polish 2 Corps captures Ancona (→ 19).

19. Italy: US troops capture Leghorn [*Livorno*]; the Germans have demolished the port and laid 25,000 booby-trap bombs.→

19. England: To combat V1s, 1,596 anti-aircraft guns have been moved to the south coast.

20. US: Roosevelt is nominated as the Democratic presidential candidate.

21. Germany: Hitler replaces General Kurt Zeitzler, his chief of general staff, with General Heinz Guderian.

22. China: US official observers arrive to assess military cooperation between the US and China (→ 29).

22. Rastenburg: Hitler appoints Goebbels *Reich* plenipotentiary for total war, giving him powers second only to his own.

22. US: The Bretton Woods conference of international finance ministers ends, having set up the International Bank for Reconstruction and Development and the International Monetary Fund.

Allies step up Normandy offensives

British assault on Caen fails, but opens the way for Bradley

Caen, 20 July

Operation Goodwood, a bold attempt by Dempsey's Second Army to smash through the German defences south of Caen, has been called off after the British suffered 5,537 casualties and lost 400 tanks. The operation is widely seen by Allied leaders as a failure, despite claims by Montgomery that it was merely a diversionary exercise.

At dawn on 18 July, British and US bombers dropped 7,700 tons of bombs on German positions. The unceasing bombardment was such that some Germans committed suicide. Then, three armoured divisions of VIII Corps rolled forward east of Caen. Rapid progress was made, but by mid-morning the British were stuck in a long tailback behind the narrow bridgehead over the Orne river, hedged in by one of their own minefields and harried by the enemy.

The Germans were well prepared. The I SS *Panzer* Corps – 80 Panther and Tiger tanks commanded by the dashing SS General Josef "Sepp" Dietrich – rushed north to Bourgebus Ridge, south of Caen. By the end of the day the British

Allied troops take cover behind a hedge during Operation Goodwood.

and Canadian troops, already contained to the east, were halted at the ridge to the south. Over the last few days the Germans have held off repeated attacks on the ridge. Rather than risk more men and tanks in a bloody assault on superior forces, Montgomery today called off the attack. The Americans have accused him of being unadventurous, but Montgomery maintains that keeping up the pressure will wear down the enemy to the point when he will break. The British commander also argues that the attack has achieved the aim of obliging the Germans to rush troops to the east, thus making it easier for the Americans under Bradley to push out to Avranches in the west (→ 23).

Americans poised to win the battle of "bocage" country at St Lo

St Lo, 18 July

In one of the most bruising and brilliant actions of the Normandy campaign, the Americans today captured the heights of St Lo and are poised to break out of the difficult *bocage* country of hedgerows and narrow roads. The cost was heavy – 5,000 casualties – but the German 352nd Division has been smashed and General Meindel's crack Parachute Corps broken.

The Americans have been battling for the St Lo to Coutances road since the beginning of the month. After 12 days they had advanced seven miles (11 km) at a cost of 10,000 casualties. The bocage hedgerows shielding sunken lanes and bounding small fields has proved ideally suited to a defensive battle, providing ample cover for the Germans and making advance difficult (→ 20).

American troops with fixed bayonets move gingerly forward in St Lo.

German officers' conspiracy to murder Hitler fails

Fuhrer injured, but survives explosion

Rastenburg, E Prussia, 20 July
In the *Lagebaracke*, the conference barracks at Hitler's "Wolf's Lair" HQ, the Fuhrer was studying a map with a magnifying glass while he listened to a report on the calamitous situation on the Russian front. The time was 12.42pm. The briefing officer, General Adolf Heusinger, was stopped in mid-sentence by a powerful explosion that sent mangled bodies flying out of windows in a rush of smoke and flame.

A few hundred yards away, Colonel Count Claus von Stauffenberg, who had left the Fuhrer's presence only minutes before, was sure that Hitler must have been killed. He brushed past guards and hurried to the airfield to fly back to Berlin and join his fellow-conspirators.

The aristocratic von Stauffenberg, aged 37, had lost his right hand, two fingers of his left and his left eye in a minefield explosion in Tunisia in April 1943. For years the generals had talked half-heartedly about saving the honour of Germany by getting rid of Hitler. Von Stauffenberg – and the prospect of certain defeat in war – had at last produced a full-scale conspiracy.

After a three-hour flight, von Stauffenberg went to the War Min-

The two dictators view the destruction caused by the bomb intended for Hitler.

istry expecting to find the *coup* in full swing. But nothing had been done. The planned telephone call from a supporter at Rastenburg had come through, but the line had been poor and it was not certain that Hitler was dead.

It was soon clear that Hitler was alive, though injured. The briefcase in which von Stauffenberg had left the bomb had, by pure mischance, been moved by an officer seeking to get closer to the map that the Fuhrer was studying. Four officers died from injuries received in the

blast. Suspicion fell on von Stauffenberg when a sergeant recalled that "the one-eyed colonel" had left the room in a hurry. Staff officers then remembered that von Stauffenberg had placed the briefcase under the table. It was to be some hours before Hitler and his staff discovered the extent of the conspiracy. For the present, the Fuhrer, his eardrums punctured, his right arm temporarily paralysed and his legs burnt, had to turn his attention to receiving Mussolini, himself the victim of an Italian coup (→ 26).

How bomb plotters planned for peace

Berlin, 20 July
The circle of anti-Hitler conspirators was widened after von Stauffenberg became an active member. He rejected the safety-first conservative regime envisaged by the older generation of anti-Nazis, and insisted that socialists and trade unionists should be invited to join them.

Though it was accepted that military units in and around Berlin would have to be used for the seizure of power, it was agreed that the army must not dominate the new government. In order to end the war, the western Allies must be persuaded that German militarism was not being perpetuated.

These visionary plans now lie in ruins. Despite the failure to kill Hitler, von Stauffenberg insisted on going ahead with the *coup*. The task of surrounding government offices in the *Wilhelmstrasse* fell to a Major Otto Remer, who was also ordered to arrest Goebbels. When Remer arrived, the propaganda minister got Hitler on the phone and persuaded him to speak to Remer. A few hours later the dumbfounded conspirators heard a radio announcement that Hitler would be broadcasting to the people.

Atrocities turned colonel against Hitler

Berlin, 20 July
Von Stauffenberg spent months in hospital recovering from injuries sustained in Tunisia. One day, when he was visited by his wife, Countess Nina, he said: "I feel I must do something now to save Germany. We officers must accept our responsibility."

A Catholic and a monarchist, he had not, at first, been opposed to the Nazis. Posted to the Berlin War Academy in 1936, he became a general staff officer two years later. His doubts about the Fuhrer began to form during the anti-Jewish pogroms just before the war. His experience of SS atrocities in Russia finally convinced him of the evil of Nazism.

Von Stauffenberg (l): courageous mastermind of the attempted coup.

Who the new rulers would have been

Berlin, 20 July
The conspirators had planned to replace Hitler with General Ludwig Beck as head of state. Beck had resigned in 1938 as chief of the army general staff in protest at Hitler's war plans. Carl Goerdeler, a former lord mayor of Leipzig, was chosen as chancellor; he had broken with the Nazis in 1936. His vice-chancellor was to be Wilhelm Leuschner, the former trade union leader. Rommel had agreed to be C-in-C of the army. Ulrich von Hassell, a career diplomat and pre-war ambassador in Rome, was chosen as foreign minister. Of the 12 ministers named, only two, Beck and Rommel, were military men (→ 26).

General Ludwig Beck: he was to replace Hitler as head of state.

Troops pull out of Italian stalemate

Rome, 21 July
It was regrettable, but inevitable. The decision had been taken at the highest level, with Roosevelt and Stalin outvoting Churchill. The Allied command in Italy has lost 100,000 of its best troops to the forthcoming invasion of the South of France.

The whole of the US VI Corps and the French Expeditionary Corps are assembling in Naples – leaving fewer than 153,000 men, mostly British, Commonwealth and Polish, to face Germany's formidable Gothic Line. Churchill and his generals would have preferred to fight a Balkans campaign – cutting off German troops in Greece (→ 26).

V-bomb evacuation outstrips Blitz

Two children already asleep as London families settle down in a deep shelter.

London, 18 July
London is fast emptying under the flying-bomb attack. More than 500,000 mothers and children have been evacuated, and more are leaving daily. Another half a million people, including the elderly and the homeless, are leaving as "aided" evacuees, with rail warrants and billeting allowances. The evacuation is outstripping that of 1939-40. The eight deep shelters specially built after the Blitz, 100 feet underground, are being used for the first time. Each of them has bunks for 8,000 people. "Bomb Alley", the path that the flying bombs take across Kent and Sussex and the south-east suburbs of London such as Croydon, Lewisham, Bromley, Bexley and Orpington, is suffering particularly heavily. Some 200,000 houses have been destroyed or damaged.

Defences against the V1s have improved. Fast-flying fighters are patrolling the Channel 20 miles out to sea, shooting down V1s or tipping them over with their wingtips. Over 1,500 guns are massed along the coast, and on the Downs 1,750 balloons form a barrage. More than half of the incoming V1s are being destroyed (→ 19).

Tojo, chief of staff and premier, quits

Tokyo, 18 July
Japan's prime minister and chief of staff, General Hideki Tojo, and his cabinet have resigned after a behind-the-scenes *coup* by a cabal of ex-premiers convinced that Japan faces defeat unless drastic changes are made. The former leaders, who backed Tojo's appointment 33 months ago, have advised the emperor to summon General Kuniaki Koiso and Admiral Mitsumasa Yonai to form a new cabinet. The move marks a return to the traditional Japanese cabinet, with separate posts for the heads of the army and navy. Tojo tried to save his premiership by agreeing to step down as army chief, but this did not placate the ex-premiers.

Row over Poland

Moscow, 21 July
The simmering row between the Soviet Union and the London-based Polish government in exile flared into fury today with the announcement that the Russians intended to set up a committee of national liberation in those areas of Poland freed by the Red Army. The London Poles consider this committee to be a puppet organization controlled by the Russians and have denounced its members as a "band of usurpers" (→ 28).

Rommel injured by RAF fighter attack

Bernay, France, 17 July
Germany's most charismatic military leader, Field Marshal Erwin Rommel, suffered multiple skull fractures today on a lonely road in Normandy when an RAF fighter piloted by Squadron-Leader J J Le Roux from 602 Squadron strafed his staff car. Rommel, who now commands the forces fighting the Allied invasion force, was going to his HQ when the attack occurred. His driver saw the fighter coming and was trying to reach the cover of a tree-lined by-road when cannon shells tore through the vehicle. Tonight Rommel lies unconscious in hospital at Bernay.

Japan faces isolation from its "empire" as marines storm Guam

A US Pacific convoy under fire: but the Japanese are virtually cut off now.

Guam, 22 July
As US marines today established their second beach-head on Guam within 24 hours, the Allies' central Pacific strategy of cutting Japan off from its recently-acquired Pacific empire seems tantalizingly close to fruition. If Guam, the southernmost of the Marianas, falls, Japan's last lifeline to its bases to the east will have been severed. US bombers are hastening the process, today striking for the 37th successive day at Yap, in the western Carolines, 350 miles (560 km) to the south of Guam and Japan's nearest base to Guam. West of Yap, US forces also bombed the Japanese-held Palau Islands, a possible staging post for recapturing the Philippines (→ 24).

July

Su	Mo	Tu	We	Th	Fr	Sa
						1
2	3	4	5	6	7	8
9	10	11	12	13	14	15
16	17	18	19	20	21	22
23	24	25	26	27	28	29
30	31					

23. Poland: Red Army enters Lublin and Pskov (→ 27).

23. Rastenburg: Heinz Guderian, the new army chief of staff, swears an oath of loyalty to Hitler.

23. Normandy: The First Canadian Army, under General Henry Crerar, becomes operational (→ 26).

24. Europe: German armed forces adopt the Nazi salute, as a gesture of solidarity.

24. Mariana Islands: Two US divisions attack Tinian (→ 26).

25. Indian Ocean: The British Eastern Fleet attacks Japanese installations at Sabang.

26. Normandy: US forces capture Marigny (→ 28).

26. Rastenburg: Hitler orders the construction of an extra defensive line in Italy, at the foothills of the Alps.

26. Pacific: US carriers blast the Caroline Islands (→ 28).

27. USSR: The Russians take six key German strongholds, including Lwow and Bialystok.→

28. Normandy: US troops capture Coutances, the first objective of Operation Cobra.→

27. Lyon: Five prisoners of the *Gestapo* are shot dead after a Resistance bomb attack on a restaurant used by German officers.

28. Poland: The Red Army takes Brest-Litovsk.

28. Biak, New Guinea: US forces destroy Japanese defences at Ibdi (→ 30).

29. Manchukuo: US B-29s bomb the Showa steel works at Anshan, and Taku harbour.

29. Albania: Allied troops land south of Spilje.

30. New Guinea: US troops land on Middelburg and Amsterdam Islands.→

31. Rastenburg: Hitler orders a scorched-earth policy if retreat becomes necessary.

31. London: Admiral Sir Bruce Fraser succeeds Admiral Sir James Somerville as C-in-C of the Royal Navy's Eastern Fleet.

Red Army is 12 miles from Warsaw

Moscow, 31 July

The sound of the Red Army's guns was clearly heard in Warsaw today as Soviet tanks entered Wolomin, just 12 miles (19 km) east of the Polish capital. Radzynib to the north and Otwock to the south are expected to fall at any moment, leaving the way clear for Marshal, Rokossovsky's men to advance to the Vistula, the last German line of defence before the city. The Russians have, in fact, already crossed the Vistula at Sandomierz, 100 miles (160 km) to the south, and plan to swing up behind the capital.

These latest Russian successes are the culmination of a remarkable tank drive across the Polish plain following the liberation of Minsk. The last few days have brought the capture of Lublin and then Brest-Litovsk, the ancient fortress town captured by Hitler's *Panzers* in the first days of the invasion of Russia.

The Russians have covered 450 miles (720 km) in five weeks. They have destroyed Model's Army Group Centre, killing or capturing 31 of the group's 47 corps and divisional commanders. However, the very success of the drive has meant that the Red Army's lines of communication have become over-extended. At the same time, German resistance has stiffened, reinforcements have arrived, and the Germans have thrown back Rokos-

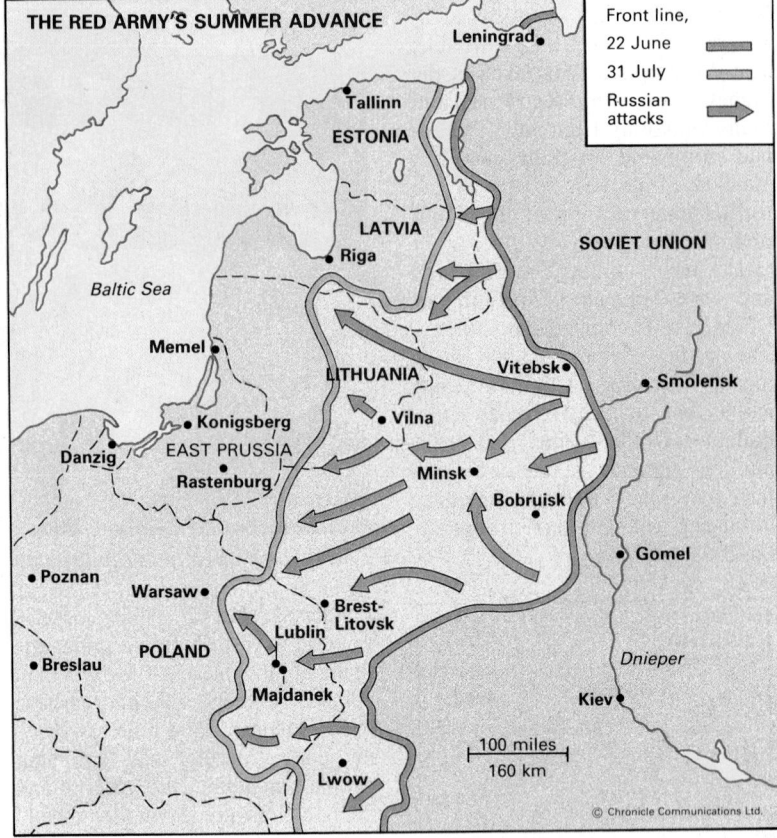

THE RED ARMY'S SUMMER ADVANCE

Front line, 22 June; 31 July; Russian attacks

Leningrad, Tallinn, ESTONIA, LATVIA, Riga, Baltic Sea, SOVIET UNION, Memel, LITHUANIA, Vitebsk, Smolensk, Konigsberg, Vilna, Danzig, EAST PRUSSIA, Rastenburg, Minsk, Bobruisk, Poznan, Warsaw, Brest-Litovsk, Gomel, Lublin, Breslau, POLAND, Majdanek, Dnieper, Kiev, Lwow

100 miles / 160 km

© Chronicle Communications Ltd.

sovsky's attempts to cross the Vistula close to Warsaw.

So, unable to seize the city "on the run", the Russians will have to call a halt to bring up supplies and reinforcements for a carefully-planned assault. This may take some time. Meanwhile the Polish Home Army in Warsaw is preparing to rise against the Germans; it is anxious to take the city to try to keep it out of Russian hands and provide a base for the government in exile in London (→ 1/8).

Majdanek charnel house horror revealed

Lublin, 24 July

Russian troops have discovered scenes of the utmost barbarity in the concentration camp of Majdanek on the outskirts of this Polish city. Hundreds of corpses hardly recognizable as those of human beings lie behind the barbed wire of the camp. The Russians also found seven sinister buildings in which people were gassed to death before being burnt in an incinerator. It seems that so great was the killing, the incinerator could not cope with all the bodies. Stories about the horrors of Hitler's death camps have been circulating in the west for some time, but this is the first time that one of the camps has been captured. The stories did not exaggerate.

The horrors of Majdanek revealed.

Manhunt begins for anti-Hitler plotters

Berlin, 26 July

Himmler has launched a nation-wide manhunt for anti-Hitler conspirators, and some 7,000 men and women are now in the *Gestapo*'s torture cells. The lucky ones are those who died on the night of 20 July. Beck tried unsuccessfully to shoot himself and was finished off by an army sergeant. Von Stauffenberg was taken into the courtyard of the War Ministry and shot. The Gestapo soon put a stop to that. Himmler wanted living plotters who could be tortured into betraying others. Some 5,000 of those now held face execution; the rest, mostly relatives of suspects, will be sent to concentration camps (→ 4/8).

US launches Normandy break-out

Avranches, 31 July
American armoured spearheads, plunging deep into the German lines, have entered Avranches after five days of "push and go" fighting, in the words of an infantry lieutenant. The whole western end of the enemy front has been ripped open and Bradley's First Army, now to be joined by Patton's Third, is preparing to break out westwards into the Brittany peninsula.

British and Canadian offensives south and east of Caen had convinced von Kluge, the C-in-C West, that the main Allied effort would remain in the Caen sector, and he had kept his best armoured units there. Opposed to 14 British and Canadian divisions are 14 German ones, six of them armoured. The Americans have 15 divisions opposed to 11 German ones, only two of which are armoured.

Bradley's offensive, known as Operation Cobra, started on 25 July with a heavy aerial bombardment. On two successive days US planes bombed their own men; 136 Americans were killed and 621 wounded, including the US 1st Army Group's commander, Lt-Gen Lesley McNair. After such a disaster, Lawton Collins's VII Corps moved off in a grim mood. Collins soon discovered that the *Panzers* could be outflanked.

He moved fast. Steel tusks welded to the front of Sherman tanks chewed through the thick Norman hedgerows in minutes. Overnight, the US tanks swept into open country against weakening German defences. The high-spirited Americans raced through villages, some of which greeted them warmly, others with complete indifference. Bloody fighting still lies ahead, but by today the enemy had given up hope of a successful counter-attack and was pulling back (→ 1/8).

Well-camouflaged Allied tanks on the move through a ravaged French town.

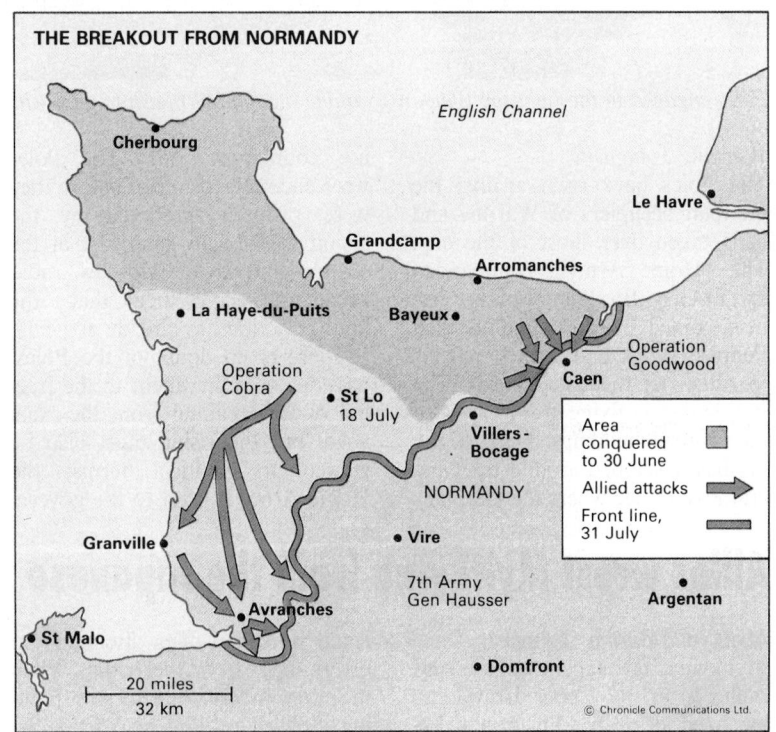
THE BREAKOUT FROM NORMANDY

English Channel

Cherbourg

Le Havre

Grandcamp

Arromanches

La Haye-du-Puits

Bayeux

Operation Goodwood

Operation Cobra

St Lo
18 July

Caen

Villers-Bocage

Area conquered to 30 June

Allied attacks

Front line, 31 July

NORMANDY

Granville

Vire

7th Army Gen Hausser

Argentan

Avranches

St Malo

Domfront

20 miles
32 km

© Chronicle Communications Ltd.

Germans send SS troops to crush Vercors uprising by "Maquis"

France, 23 July
The Germans have launched a ferocious attack on the Vercors, a mountainous area south-west of Grenoble controlled by the French Resistance. The "Republic of the Vercors" began life on 3 July, when the area was declared "liberated territory" and occupied by 3,000 *Maquisards*. Two days ago, however, the Germans responded by laying siege to the "republic" with 15,000 troops, including men from elite SS and alpine regiments, under General Karl Pflaum. The SS men took the Maquisards by surprise when they landed by glider on an airfield at Vassieux, ironically intended for Allied aircraft to bring assistance to the rebels. So far 650 Resistance fighters have fallen in heavy combat, and as a reprisal for their defiance the SS has shot the population of five villages.

Roosevelt backs MacArthur plan for Pacific War

Pearl Harbor, 31 July
After the fall of the Marianas this month and the occupation of northern New Guinea, the one great strategic issue in the Pacific War was where to strike next. American military strategists were sharply divided, but a decision could be delayed no longer. Would the next step on the road to Tokyo be the Philippines or Formosa?

General MacArthur had no doubts at all: he wanted to retake the Philippines. He believed that America was under "a moral obligation" to liberate the 17 million Filipinos before the assault on Japan. It would be militarily unsound, he claimed, to bypass the Philippines and attack directly across the Pacific Ocean.

Admiral King, the American navy chief, strongly advocated bypassing the Philippines in favour of Formosa. He saw avoidable heavy losses if the armed forces became entangled in costly jungle encounters in the larger Philippine islands.

Admiral Nimitz was wavering, but Admiral Halsey also had no doubts. He wanted to seize Okinawa, which would then become the springboard for the invasion of the Japanese home islands.

One area of certainty was that the China theatre would now have no major role in the final phases of the war. The long-range strategic bombing campaign against Japan, which had begun from China, would be transferred to the Marianas.

At a Pearl Harbor conference which began five days ago, the military chiefs argued their cases with the president. MacArthur felt that the Filipino people would not forgive a second betrayal, and that Luzon was too big to be bypassed. It was clear at the end of the session that MacArthur had won the argument. He later told officers the president had said "we will not bypass the Philippines" (→ 1/8).

1944

August

Su	Mo	Tu	We	Th	Fr	Sa
		1	2	3	4	5
6	7	8	9	10	11	12
13	14	15	16	17	18	19
20	21	22	23	24	25	26
27	28	29	30	31		

1. France: The US 12th Army Group, consisting of Patton's Third Army and Hodges' First Army, is formed under General Omar Bradley (→ 2).

1. Lithuania: Soviets take Kovno and isolate the Baltic states from East Prussia (→ 11).

2. Mariana Islands: US forces launch a further assault on Guam, capturing half the island (→ 3).

2. France: Patton's soldiers advance into Brittany, reaching Dinan and Rennes; Hitler orders that they be cut off (→ 3).

2. Ankara: Turkey cuts off diplomatic and commercial relations with Germany.

2. Italy: Germans deport 222 Jews from Verona to Auschwitz (→ 4).

3. Poland: Soviet forces cross the Vistula at Baranow (→ 4).

3. New Guinea: US forces push towards the Torricelli mountains.

3. Guam: US ships blast concentrations of Japanese troops on Mount Santa Rosa (→ 4).

3. English Channel: German mini-submarines attack invasion shipping, sinking the British destroyer *Quorn*.

3. France: US troops capture Mortain (→ 5).

4. Berlin: As 22 officers alleged to have had dealings with the 20 July plotters are given dishonourable discharges, Hitler tells Judge Roland Freisler, the president of the "People's Court" that he wants the conspirators "strung up like butchered cattle" (→ 8).

4. Italy: South African troops reach Florence's outskirts.→

4. Warsaw: The Polish Home Army asks for Allied aid (→ 11).

4. Helsinki: Marshal Carl Mannerheim becomes president of Finland, after the resignation of Risto Ryti (→ 2/9).

4-5. Pacific: US carriers shell Japanese positions on Chichi Jima and Iwo Jima, sinking an enemy destroyer (→ 8).

5. France: US troops capture Namur and Charleroi.→

Polish "Home Army" seizes Warsaw

Poles engaged in the fight for Warsaw examine a captured machine gun: will the Russians come to their aid in time?

Warsaw, 1 August
The Poles have risen against the German occupiers of Warsaw and have taken over most of the city. The "Home Army", commanded by Lt-Gen Bor-Komorowski, has been joined by the communist-led People's Army and armed civilians to drive out the hated Nazis. The Polish flag is flying from captured government buildings. Fierce fighting has developed around the General Post Office where the Germans are counter-attacking. The Poles were encouraged to rise before they were properly prepared by the sound of Russian guns east of the Vistula and by a Moscow radio broadcast telling them that "the hour of action has already arrived".

There is no doubt of the Poles' passionate commitment to the freeing of their capital from the Nazi yoke, but the rising must also be viewed in political terms; the Home Army is loyal to the government in exile in London, and it intends to be in control of Warsaw when the Russians arrive with their own Polish Committee of National Liberation. It is doubtful, however, if the poorly-armed Home Army can hold out for long against the Germans. Everything depends on the Russians, who are preparing their own assault on the city. Will they arrive in time? Or will Stalin wait until the Polish Home Army is defeated (→ 3)?

Allies wrest Myitkyina from the Japanese

Myitkyina, Burma, 3 August
Myitkyina, the Japanese base and railhead on the Upper Irrawaddy, has been taken by Chinese and US troops after a ten-week siege.

Yet for General "Vinegar Joe" Stilwell it has been a sour ten weeks. In the first failed assault two Chinese battalions got lost and started fighting each other, and the US forward commander, Brigadier Frank Merrill, had a heart attack. His men, "Merrill's Marauders", were in such bad shape that some cut away their trouser-seats – their numbers were so low that they could not allow their dysentery to divert them from the battle. When the "Marauders" had to stop fighting, Stilwell refused help from the British 36th Division and, speaking of the need "to keep an American flavour", brought in a battalion of US engineers from the Burma Road: untrained in combat, they were slaughtered almost to a man.

On 1 August, the day that Stilwell was promoted to four-star general, the 4,500 Japanese escaped the encircling forces, who entered the town today to find only a suicidal rearguard of 187 wounded (→ 14/9).

Education reforms win royal assent

Britain, 3 August
"We must make it a pleasure and a profit to be at school. Now we will develop the child's real bent." Thus R A Butler, the minister of education, hailed his far-reaching Education Act when it received the royal assent today. England and Wales will after the war have a national system of free secondary education for all children up to 15 and part-time tuition for pupils leaving school before 18, with teaching according to aptitude.

Retreating Nazis blow up Florence

Florence, 5 August
Although Marshal Kesselring solemnly declared this Medici capital an "open city", South African troops entered it today to find five of Florence's six bridges destroyed and mediaeval buildings flattened by demolition charges. Only the exquisite *Ponte Vecchio* with its goldsmiths' and jewellers' shops remains standing over the Arno river and, as in other places, many old houses have been destroyed and the approach roads mined to delay Allied access.

Now depleted by the removal of American and French troops for the planned invasion of southern France, the US Fifth and British Eighth Armies have advanced steadily on both sides of the Apennines. The British XIII Corps, augmented by South Africans, Indians and New Zealanders, took the important rail junction of Arezzo on 17 July, and pressed on towards Florence despite tough defensive fighting by German paratroopers and *Panzergrenadiers*.

Replacements on the Italian front include 25,000 men of the Brazilian Expeditionary Corps and the US 96th Division, consisting entirely of black troops. Neither unit has battle experience (→10).

US troops lead breakout from Normandy

US soldiers forging ahead in Normandy keep German prisoners under guard.

Brittany, 5 August
Men of Lt-Gen George S Patton's Third Army, newly arrived in France, are racing towards the ports of Brittany after a spectacular breakout from Normandy. Armoured units are moving so rapidly that they are out of radio contact with divisional HQ, and supplies are being delivered on the run since there has been no time to set up bases and dumps. In five days, advance units have reached Lorient after driving past Rennes, and with-

in 24 hours other units will be on the outskirts of Brest. All German forces in Brittany are withdrawing to the ports, which have been heavily fortified, and Hitler has ordered them to be held to the last man. For the first time in the Allied campaign French Resistance fighters are operating alongside regular Allied troops. Some 20,000 armed men and women are under the command of a French officer parachuted in from London, along with arms and ammunition (→6).

Japanese PoWs die in mass escape bid

Sydney, 5 August
Japanese prisoners of war wielding improvised weapons broke out of the Cowra prisoner-of-war camp early today. As they rushed the compound wire, Australian Army guards fired a machine gun at them until the Japanese knifed and clubbed them to death.

Of the 1,104 Japanese prisoners in the camp, 334 managed to get away, and 234 died and 108 were wounded in the attempt. Three of the camp's army guards were killed, and three wounded.

The Japanese had long planned to break out. This incident, the biggest prison escape of the war so far, is the first of its kind to take place in Australia.

Jets in first combat

Britain, 4 August
Aviation history was made today when Flying Officer Dean in a 616 Squadron RAF Gloster Meteor jet fighter engaged a V1, but his guns jammed. He overtook the missile, tipped it over by inserting his wingtip under its wing, and sent it out of control earthwards. This was the first time a jet had been in combat with another jet-propelled machine.

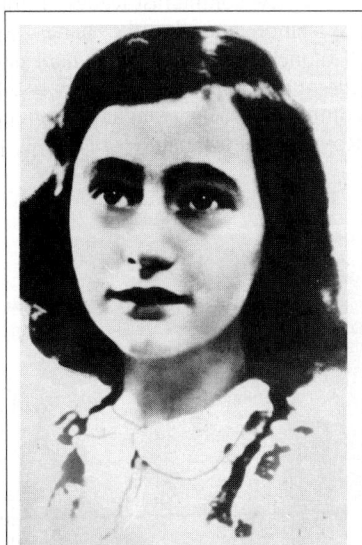
August 4. Anne Frank, a 14-year-old Jewish girl who has been living in hiding with her family in an Amsterdam attic since July 1942; today they were betrayed to the "Gestapo" (→14).

US troops take Pacific island with collapse of Japanese garrison

Tinian, 1 August
US forces have captured Tinian, the second of the three Allied island objectives in the Marianas, as Japanese resistance crumbled today on the island's southern cliffs after Marine reinforcements broke through.

In a crucial clifftop battle yesterday, more than 600 Japanese screamed the death-charge cry of *"Banzai"* as they launched a final, suicidal dawn assault to try to force a Marine unit off a toehold gained on the mile-wide escarpment. The remnants of Japan's 9,000-man defence force had retreated there after being fooled by a decoy landing that let 40,000 marines land almost unopposed on Tinian's north-west coast nine days ago. An estimated 9,000 Japanese have died in the battle. US losses are 394 dead and 1,961 wounded (→2).

US troops watch as a bombed Japanese ammunition dump on Tinian erupts.

1944

August

Su	Mo	Tu	We	Th	Fr	Sa
		1	2	3	4	5
6	7	8	9	10	11	12
13	14	15	16	17	18	19
20	21	22	23	24	25	26
27	28	29	30	31		

6. France: Von Kluge launches a counter-attack towards Avranches, as Allied forces cut off the Breton peninsula.

6. France: Montgomery issues an order for the destruction of the German army west of the Seine and north of the Loire (→ 7).

7. Britain: German V1s have killed over 5,000 people and destroyed 35,000 homes to date (→ 23).

7. France: The German counter-attack recaptures Mortain.

7. France: Eisenhower transfers his headquarters from London to Granville.→

8. Guam: US troops capture Mount Santa Rosa.→

8. China: Japanese forces occupy the strategic railway junction at Hengyang, after bitter fighting lasting nearly eight weeks (→ 25/9).

9. France: Rapidly-advancing Allied forces capture St Malo and Angers, but Canadian forces get bogged down north of Falaise (→ 11).

9. Algiers: The Free French declare the Vichy government null and void (→ 31).

10. Rastenburg: To combat the Allies' air superiority, Hitler orders all 2,000 of the *Luftwaffe*'s fighter aircraft to the western front.

10. Italy: Polish soldiers reach the Cesano river.→

10. Paris: Railway workers join the general strike.

11. France: Operation Totalize, the Canadian First Army offensive towards Falaise, has failed to break out and is called off.

11. Rastenburg: Hitler allows von Kluge's men to retreat from Mortain, recognizing the failure of his planned counter-attack (→ 12).

11. USSR: The Red Army begins a new offensive south of Lake Peipus.→

12. France: The US XV Corps occupies Alencon and halts the German offensive towards Avranches.→

Germans fail to stop Normandy advance

More hands than gum: a US soldiers opens his ration box in a French town.

North-west France, 12 August
With Brittany sealed off and its ports besieged, Patton has swung the bulk of his Third Army eastwards towards the Seine. Le Mans has fallen and Alencon, to the north, fell today.

The Allied plan is to put Patton's XV Corps in place at Argentan, opposite the Canadian First Army, now driving on Falaise, and trap the remnants of General Paul Hausser's II SS *Panzer* Corps, ten of whose divisions have disintegrated.

On Hitler's orders, Hausser has launched a counter-attack at Mortain, east of Avranches. In a bid to gain tactical surprise, the Panzers advanced without the usual artillery bombardment and overran two US infantry companies before pressing on to within nine miles (14.4 km) of Avranches.

"Ultra" intercepts, however, had alerted the Americans to the counter-attack. As the Panzers moved up they were hit by swarms of fighter-bombers and a strong infantry and artillery defence. The Germans collapsed in disorder. The massive forces deployed in the Fuhrer's directive for Operation *Luttich* did not exist. Of 1,400 Panzers assembled for the Normandy campaign, fewer than 150 remain, along with 30 self-propelled guns. Von Kluge's Army Group B's best move now would be to retreat to the Seine and save the bulk of its forces. This course Hitler has rejected (→ 13).

PLUTO to pump oil under the Channel

Normandy, 12 August
Now that the Allied armies have broken out of the Normandy beachhead they will be increasingly reliant on petrol to keep their armoured spearheads motoring as they fan out across France. In order to keep the fuel flowing across the Channel without interruption a pipeline has been laid from England to Cherbourg. Known as PLUTO (Pipe-Line Under The Ocean), it can deliver up to 700 tons of petrol per day. Trucks then ferry the petrol up the line to the forward troops.

RAF paves way for Operation Totalize

Normandy, 7 August
The RAF has been out in great strength, pounding German targets in preparation for Operation Totalize, a combined assault by Canadian infantry and Polish tanks on the SS armoured forces holding up the Allied advance on the Caen to Falaise road. Typhoons fired rockets at the *Panzers*, and 1,019 bombers dropped 3,462 tons of bombs on German positions. Ten Lancasters were lost. The USAAF was less accurate and bombed its allies, killing 65 servicemen (→ 9).

Paris strike-bound as freedom is near

Paris, 10 August
"Strike to push the *Boche* back." Obeying that order, the *cheminots* of Paris – the predominantly communist railway workers – went on strike today, paralysing the capital and disrupting the entire network.

The strike is seen as a flexing of muscles by the communist wing of the Resistance, both against the German garrison and to make sure that it is not ignored by the Allies when the future of a liberated France is decided. The stoppage of the railways was almost total, in spite of strict German decrees forbidding strikes. Some communist pickets turned doubters away from work at pistol point.

The strike is a bold move because the new German military commandant, General Dietrich von Choltitz, has the power of life and death over French civilians, and the strike threatens the German high command's reliance on the railways. Paris is the hub of the French rail network.

On 14 July, Bastille Day, posters appeared on the walls of Paris in the name of the communist *Front National*, calling Parisians to arms. The posters urged every man and woman to kill a German, a *Milicien* or a traitor.

The new communist leader in the Resistance goes by the name of "Colonel Rol". This is the *nom de guerre* of Henry Tanguy, a French communist who fought for the Republicans in Spain (→ 12).

The new Nazi commander in Paris: General Dietrich von Choltitz.

US troops retake Guam

US troops land on Guam: now it is to be an unsinkable aircraft carrier.

Guam, 10 August
The Allied conquest of the Marianas was completed today as US forces overran Pati Point on northeast Guam, the last outpost of Japanese resistance on the US protectorate which it has taken three weeks of fierce fighting to recapture.

With effective Japanese resistance now ended, US engineers are working to turn Guam, Tinian and Saipan – the first of the Mariana Islands invaded seven weeks ago – into "unsinkable aircraft carriers"

for B-29 Superfortresses capable of bombing Tokyo 1,600 miles away. Japanese losses on Guam are now thought to be a little over 10,000 dead out of an original force of 18,500, with 1,250 taken prisoner. US losses are 1,744 dead, and 5,970 wounded. These losses included marines fighting in northern Guam's dense jungle who were hit by their own artillery. The turning point came 15 days ago when two counter-offensives intended to break the US beach-head on the west coast failed (→17).

Anti-Hitler plotters strangled on hooks

Berlin, 8 August
Eight German officers, including Field Marshal Erwin von Witzleben, were hanged at the Ploetzenzee prison today for their part in the plot of 20 July to assassinate Hitler. They died by slow strangulation, hanging by piano wire from meat hooks, after having been dragged before the sadistic Roland Freisler, the president of the People's Court. Dressed in old clothes, without braces or belts for their trousers, they were given a humiliating show trial. The proceedings and the hangings were filmed on Hitler's orders, and the developed film has been dispatched to the Fuhrer for viewing in his private cinema (→18).

Italy campaign gets Churchillian boost

Naples, 11 August
The sight of a familiar figure wearing a homburg hat and a siren suit, and waving a big cigar, did much to cheer up British troops here today. Morale has not been good in the US Fifth and British Eighth Armies, particularly with the headlines at home dominated by events in Normandy and thousands of their comrades taken from the Italian front for the planned operation in the south of France. Churchill has flown here to meet Tito, with whose help he hopes to salvage earlier British plans for a Balkan campaign which the US rejected. He will also learn of a new plan by General Alexander to break through the Gothic Line (→13).

Pope begs Russians to aid Warsaw rebels

Rome, 11 August
The pope has allowed his concern for the fate of the Polish patriots fighting in Warsaw to be reflected tonight in the Vatican newspaper *Osservatore Romano*.

In a powerful commentary, the newspaper says: "The Russian advance is meeting no obstacles. When the news indicates there is a battle near some town, it is invariably followed by the entry into its suburbs and its occupation within a few hours. It is only at Warsaw that this does not happen.

"In Warsaw, Poles of the resistance movement have fought and are fighting. It is necessary to ask whether there is any connection between these two facts. Is this a division of the war effort?" The article goes on to ask why it was necessary

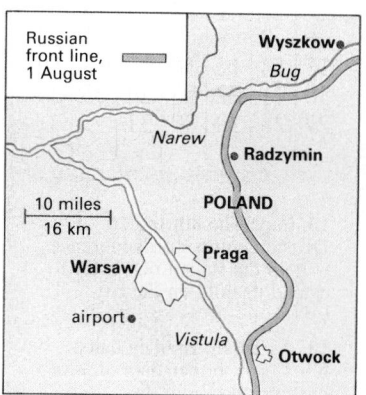

for the fighters to say "we ask for help from those who owe us help", and comments bitterly: "This help is not forthcoming ... Why for the past few days have the Russian bulletins ignored the fight in Warsaw?" (→13).

Red Army launches fresh Baltic offensive

Moscow, 11 August
The Soviet high command has announced the opening of a new offensive in the Baltic. It began at dawn yesterday with a heavy artillery barrage in the south-east corner of Estonia. The tanks and infantry of General Maslennikov's Third Baltic Front attacked as the barrage lifted, and quickly breached the German defences in the Pskov area. The Russians have advanced some

15 miles (24 km) and have captured the railway town of Pechory, sealing the fate of the 30 German divisions trapped in the Baltic states. These trapped divisions were "doomed to extermination owing to the strategy of the irresponsible Hitler", according to the captured German Generals von Kurowski and Lindemann who today called on the German people and military command to end the war (→18).

August 9. Lt-Gen Mark Clark and the secretary of the navy, James V Forrestal, inspect Japanese-American troops (from Hawaii) in Italy.

1944

August

Su	Mo	Tu	We	Th	Fr	Sa
		1	2	3	4	5
6	7	8	9	10	11	12
13	14	15	16	17	18	19
20	21	22	23	24	25	26
27	28	29	30	31		

13. Italy: The 8th Indian Division enters north Florence to help the Italian resistance to extend its hold on the city (→ 15).

13. Argentan: Bradley halts XV Corps, rather than order a push north to join the Canadians and thereby seal the "Falaise pocket" (→ 14).

14. Falaise: Canadian troops launch Operation Tractable, a renewed assault towards the town; 13 are killed and 53 injured when they light yellow flares to show their position, unaware that these are also Bomber Command target indicators.→

14. Paris: The police agree to go on strike and join the Resistance (→ 19).

15. Italy: Allied troops advance to the Gothic Line, between Pisa and Rimini (→ 25).

16. Moscow: The Soviet government describes the Warsaw rising as a "reckless, appalling adventure".→

16. Savoy, France: The Resistance launches a general rebellion to coincide with Allied landings in the south (→ 17).

16. Poland: Soviet troops reach Ossow, seven miles north-east of Warsaw.→

16. France: The German Me163 rocket-powered fighter sees action for the first time, against a formation of B-17s.

17. Normandy: Canadian forces capture Falaise.→

17. New Guinea: US paratroopers crush Japanese resistance on Noemfoor island (→ 20).

18. Philippines Sea: The US submarine *Rasher* sinks the Japanese carrier *Taiyo*.

18. USSR: The Red Army reaches the East Prussian border and takes Sandomierz, in southern Poland.→

18. Rastenburg: Hitler watches the film of the 20 July conspirators' execution (→ 30).

19. Rastenburg: Hitler orders von Choltitz, the military governor of Paris, to reduce the capital to a "field of ruins".→

Stalin refuses to support Warsaw rebels

Warsaw, 19 August
German forces have reduced General Bor-Komorowski's hold on the city to three isolated pockets, and the Polish Home Army and the attempt by communist partisans' (the "People's Guard") to regain control of Warsaw must now depend on substantial aid from the Russians, poised just on the other side of the river Vistula. But Stalin has refused to aid the valiant Poles.

In a message to the British government three days ago the Russians argued: "The Warsaw action is a reckless, appalling adventure which is costing the population heavy casualties. This would not have been the case if the Soviet command had been informed before the Warsaw action began, and if the Poles had maintained contact with it ... the Soviet command has come to the conclusion that it must dissociate itself from the Warsaw venture."

The Russians have three operational airfields a few minutes' flight from Warsaw, while the RAF and South African bombers attempting to drop supplies to the Poles must fly from Foggia across Europe under constant *Luftwaffe* attacks. Of ten bombers which set out for Warsaw from Italy three days ago, six failed to return. What makes the loss of these aircraft and crews especially sad is that Stalin will not allow the RAF supply planes to land on Russian-controlled airfields. The Poles seem doomed in the face of such intransigence (→ 28).

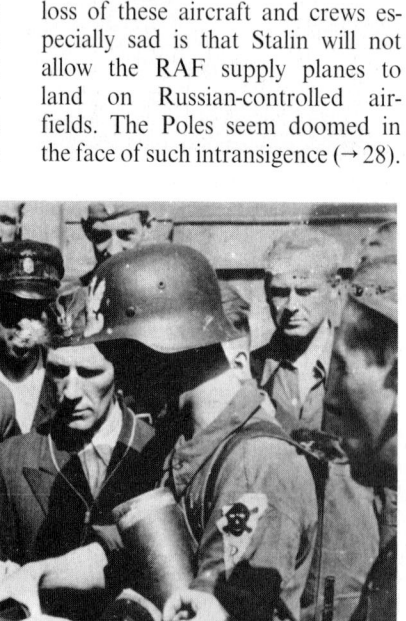

Polish fighters examine a Piat anti-tank weapon dropped by British planes.

German forces rally to counter Russia in the Baltic states

Riga, 19 August
In an attempt to save its Army Group North, cut off in Estonia by the advancing Red Army which had reached the Baltic at the Bay of Riga, the German high command has unleashed three *Panzer* divisions in the Autse area.

Striking at the over-extended left wing of General Bagramyan's First Baltic Front, the German tanks have crashed through the flank of the armoured column which had dashed to the coast. Despite desperate efforts by the Russians to seal the gap, the Germans have opened up a narrow corridor along the coast to restore land contact with General Schorner's divisions. The corridor is narrow, but it is being held with great determination and Schorner can now withdraw his men and their equipment from what threatened to become a "cauldron" in which they would have been cut up and destroyed.

This sudden blow by the Germans demonstrates that, despite their terrible defeats this summer, they can still muster strong reinforcements and defeat the Russians when not faced by overwhelming numbers of men and tanks. It also demonstrates the extent to which the Russians have stretched themselves since Operation Bagration. Their victories have been stupendous, but they have suffered great losses in men and material (→ 24).

SAS units spearhead guerrilla warfare behind German lines

Falaise, Normandy, 19 August
A fleet of RAF Dakotas today landed 60 SAS soldiers led by Captain Roy Farran on an airstrip behind enemy lines at Rennes. The force disappeared into a forest near Orleans to ambush German columns. This is the 32nd operation of its kind since D-Day.

From Brittany to Dijon, SAS soldiers are creating havoc by direct attacks on railways and telephone lines, by targetting RAF strikes on military headquarters and by stiffening the *Maquis* with weapons, supplies and fighting leadership. It might have been otherwise. The Army top brass wanted to insert the SAS, now a brigade of 2,500, immediately behind the coastal area between the German infantry and their supporting tanks: a recipe for disaster which led the SAS commander, Bill Stirling (brother of the founder, the captured David), to resign.

Hitler has developed a special distaste for these special forces. "Such men are dangerous" he affirms in an order for their execution as terrorists if captured. At Chambon 11 days ago Major Ian Fenwick deliberately drove into a German ambush with all guns firing from his Jeep and was killed. Near Auxerre, with two Jeeps and a few men, Captain Derrick Harrison stormed into a village square crowded with SS men, interrupting the execution of 20 hostages. His Vickers machine gun jammed; his driver dead, he escaped leaving 60 enemy bodies in the smouldering wreckage of their vehicles.

France comes under two-pronged Allied assault

Allied troops bring supplies ashore on the beaches of southern France.

A German ammunition dump north of Falaise goes up after an RAF raid.

Landings near Cannes open second front

Cannes, 15 August
The US Seventh Army stormed the beaches of the French Riviera at 8am today to open a second front in France. Three divisions of General Lucien Truscott's US VI Corps led the way, but they were backed by the French Army B under General Jean de Lattre de Tassigny, whooping for joy as they joined in Operation Dragoon, the Allied invasion of southern France.

The Germans were taken by surprise when six battleships and 21 cruisers began their barrage during the night. Five thousand tons of bombs fell on coastal gun emplacements before paratroops landed in dense fog. Three American infantry divisions were first ashore, securing a beach-head between Cannes and St Tropez with the help of French commandos and the Resistance. Allied casualties are very light: of the 400,000 men involved in the landings, just 320 are reported killed. The Free French forces are already fanning out, heading west for the ports of Marseilles and Toulon. De Tassigny has insisted on this task – promising to take both cities within a fortnight (→ 16).

Police rebel against Germans in Paris

Paris, 19 August
Paris has risen against its German garrison, led by the police. On 15 August, the 20,000 Paris police went on strike. Keeping their arms, they joined the Resistance. At 7am today 2,000 of them seized the Prefecture of Police, holding off a counter-attack and capturing 700 Germans. The police took the initiative from the communists whose leader, Colonel Rol, taken by surprise, turned up at the Prefecture on a bicycle and gave the orders for a general rising. Today the Germans cut the city gas supply (→ 20).

American captures hill single-handed

Southern France, 15 August
Lieutenant Audie Murphy, the 20-year-old son of a poor Texan sharecropper, captured a hill here today, single-handed. Murphy lost his temper after Germans – their hands raised in surrender – killed one of his men. He rushed the hill, hurling oaths and grenades, and captured a machine-gun post. Still mad, he grabbed the gun and wiped out the other Germans. He was recently criticized for punching a private. Said Murphy: "The regulations were too goddammed heavy to carry".

US forces reach Seine 40 miles from Paris

Mantes-Gassicourt, 19 August
During a night of pouring rain, units of Patton's Third Army crossed the Seine, 40 miles (64 km) from Paris. Some men walked across a dam, others went in assault craft at Mantes-Gassicourt, near La Roche Guyon, the German headquarters. While the heaviest fighting continues in the "Falaise pocket", near Argentan, where large *Panzer* forces are concentrated, Patton has sent three of his corps south and east to capture Orleans and Chartres, with advance units poised to take Fontainebleau.

The Germans retreating from the Falaise/Argentan pocket are being attacked from the air with devastating effect; but the confusion on the ground has on several occasions led to Allied troops being bombed by their own air forces. The British 51st Highland Division has reported 40 accidental air attacks in one day, causing 51 casualties.

Field Marshal von Kluge, sacked by Hitler as C-in-C Army Group B, committed suicide today by swallowing poison. Four days ago his car was shot up by Allied planes, his radio was wrecked and he was cut off from contact with Army HQ in Berlin. Hitler was convinced, mistakenly, that he was trying to make peace with the Allies. When communications were restored von Kluge refused to obey an order from Berlin to mount a counter-attack. His suicide note protested his devotion to the Fuhrer, but urged him to end the war: "The German people have borne such untold suffering that it is time to put an end to this frightfulness." Field Marshal Walter Model takes over (→ 20).

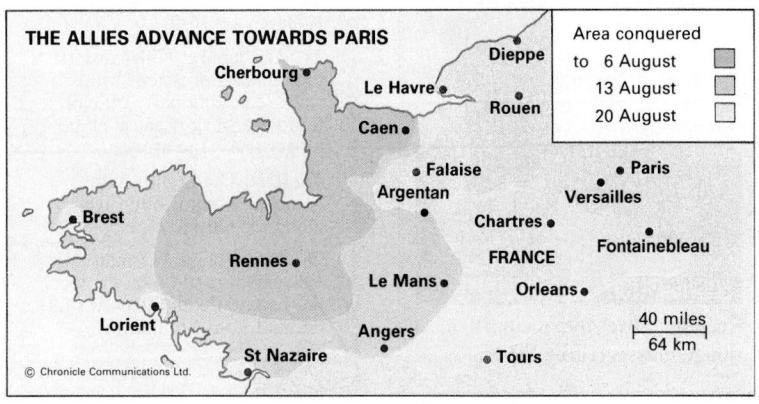

THE ALLIES ADVANCE TOWARDS PARIS

Area conquered
to 6 August
13 August
20 August

Dieppe
Cherbourg
Le Havre
Rouen
Caen
Falaise
Argentan
Paris
Versailles
Brest
Chartres
FRANCE
Fontainebleau
Rennes
Le Mans
Orleans
Lorient
Angers
St Nazaire
Tours

40 miles
64 km

© Chronicle Communications Ltd.

1944
August

Su	Mo	Tu	We	Th	Fr	Sa
		1	2	3	4	5
6	7	8	9	10	11	12
13	14	15	16	17	18	19
20	21	22	23	24	25	26
27	28	29	30	31		

Marshal Petain is arrested by the SS

Vichy, 19 August
German SS men today arrested Marshal Petain and ordered him to move to Belfort, where his prime minister, Pierre Laval, was sent two days ago. It is thought that both will be taken to Germany.

The troops broke down the door of the *Hotel du Parc*, where the head of the Vichy state has lived since 1940, and burst into the marshal's bedroom.

At first he refused German protection, but the Germans threatened to bomb the town of Vichy unless he agreed, and he was then arrested by the SS (→ 15/9).

Red Army uncovers horror of Majdanek

Majdanek, Poland, 14 August
Reports of the German death camp here, liberated on 24 July by the advancing Red Army, were published by London newspapers today. Britons are appalled by the description of the huge barracks, with the "world's biggest crematorium" in the centre.

Over half a million people from all over Europe, mainly Jews, were gassed and incinerated here. With macabre efficiency, the charred bones and ashes were mechanically pulverized and tinned, then shipped to Germany. The German people are fertilizing their fields with the corpses of their victims (→ 31).

Keeping alive the memory of a village massacred by the SS.

20. New Guinea: Fighting on Biak island ends. Japan has lost 4,700 dead to 2,550 US casualties (→ 16/9).

20. Paris: The Resistance leads an armed popular uprising against German rule.→

20. Falaise: Fighting is at its fiercest, as the German Seventh Army tries to break out of the "pocket" to join the SS 2nd *Panzer* Division at Mont Ormel (→ 21).

21. France: Model tells Hitler that the Seventh Army can no longer function as a fighting force.→

21. US: Representatives of the Allied nations meet at Dumbarton Oaks to make plans for world security after the war.

22. Norway: A British fleet attacks the German battleship *Tirpitz*, but misses because of smoke cover (→ 15/9).

22. Roumania: Soviet forces capture Jassy (→ 23).

22. France: The US 36th Infantry Division captures Grenoble without any opposition.→

23. Roumania: King Michael orders his armed forces to cease fire against the Allies, and dismisses the pro-Axis premier, Marshal Antonescu (→ 26).

23. Britain: A V1 bomb kills 211 civilians in East Barnet, in Hertfordshire, and a B-24 bomber crashes on an infants' school at Freckleton, in Lancashire, killing 57 people including 35 children (→ 28).

23-24. Sumatra: The British Eastern Fleet, under Adm Sir Bruce Fraser, attacks Padang.

24. USSR: Soviet troops take Kishinev (→ 16/9).

24. Rastenburg: Hitler orders the building of a new "west wall", charging party officials to do the work because he no longer trusts the army.

25. Italy: The Eighth Army launches a major offensive along the Gothic Line.→

26. Russelsheim, Germany: Villagers, urged on by the local SS, beat to death the crew of a crashed USAAF aircraft.

Allies take 50,000 prisoners at Falaise

Big smiles from Axis PoWs being transported through the ruins of Falaise.

Falaise, 21 August
The "Falaise pocket" was finally closed today two weeks after the Canadian First Army mounted Operation Totalize to cut off the otherwise encircled German forces. It has been a bloody battle, with Allied aircraft supporting the land forces with Typhoon and P47 rocket-firing fighter-bombers, and to the end the Germans fought with almost fanatical determination.

Some 30,000 Germans managed to escape across the Seine after Hitler yesterday allowed Field Marshal Walter Model, who replaced von Kluge four days ago, to withdraw. But 50,000 Germans have been captured, along with considerable stocks of equipment. An estimated 10,000 Germans were killed. The way is now open for a speedy advance towards Paris.

The town of Falaise had fallen by 17 August after determined resistance by the 12th SS *Panzer* Division. But remnants of the German 5th *Panzerarmee* and Seventh Army remained in the pocket, with a narrow gap between Falaise and Argentan allowing them to escape. Today Canadian, British and Polish forces pressing in from the north linked up with the US First Army driving from Argentan to the south, with Allied aircraft strafing the Germans as they retreated over wreckage-strewn roads (→ 22).

Japanese children called for war work

Tokyo, 22 August
Japanese schoolchildren are interrupting their studies to go into factories to support Japan's war effort, Tokyo radio reported today. Girls aged as young as 12 are working in munitions factories. The broadcast spoke of students "discharging their duties with high fervour in munitions factories amid the din of machinery". It quoted one boy as saying that he had decided "to work with all his might" after he heard the "tragic news" about the loss of Saipan.

Theatres give clue to wartime drama

London, 24 August
While the reopening of London theatres signals the defeat of the V1 flying-bomb offensive against the capital, the closure of theatres and amusements in Germany shows the desperate state the war has reached for the Nazis. Dr Goebbels announced today that all theatres, music halls and cabarets were to be closed from 1 September and all holidays suspended as part of total mobilization. Manpower released will be conscripted for war work. So will thousands of students.

Paris is liberated: French troops first to reach city

Paris, 25 August

Paris is free. At 2.30 this afternoon the German commander of the Paris area, General Dietrich von Choltitz, surrendered to Lieutenant Henri Karcher of the French 2nd Armoured Division, commanded by General Leclerc, the first Allied unit to enter Paris. German snipers are still active, but late this afternoon General Charles de Gaulle also entered the city.

The first of Leclerc's men drove their Sherman tanks into Paris last night to be greeted by cheering Parisians. Shortly after 7.00am today, Leclerc and the rest of his troops entered, with units of the US 4th Infantry Division. Karcher and his men stormed the German headquarters in the *Hotel Meurice*, shot up a picture of Hitler and overcame the garrison with a phosphorous grenade and a flame-thrower. Karcher found von Choltitz sitting behind a table. Karcher asked von Choltitz if he was ready to surrender. The German answered simply "*Ja*". "Then you are my prisoner," said Karcher.

The liberation of Paris has been won by not only the regular Allied forces but also the people of Paris itself who backed an uprising called by the Resistance on 18 August [*see report overleaf*]. Some 500 Resistance fighters and 127 other civilians have been killed. Many Germans also died – 50 were killed defending the French foreign office building. It has also been a time of summary justice for suspected collaborators. Tonight the retribution continues, along with a vast explosion of joy which will culminate tomorrow in parades. But behind the celebrations, a grim power struggle has been taking place.

De Gaulle had appealed to Eisenhower to take Paris without delay. Ike refused; he did not want to risk a bloody street-by-street battle, nor was he ready to take responsibility for feeding four million people. But de Gaulle argued that the uprising against the Germans in Paris and the denunciation of "collaborators" were being used by the communists as a cover for eliminating their opponents. He ordered Leclerc to detach his 2nd Armoured Division from the Allied command and head for Paris (→ 26).

Liberation: US troops march down the Champs Elysees in the symbolic shadow of the Arc de Triomphe.

The battle waged for control of Paris

A sniper scatters a crowd of Parisians gathered to celebrate liberation.

General de Gaulle begins his triumphal march through Paris.

A humiliated collaborator is threatened with summary justice.

The tables are turned: French Forces of the Interior round up Germans.

How the French helped to liberate their capital after four years of German rule

Paris, 25 August

The relative swiftness of the liberation of Paris is in large measure owing to the bravery of the French capital's own citizens. At least 3,000 were killed over the last week, along with 2,000 Germans.

On 18 August, the Resistance announced a general strike. The next day, French policemen occupied the Prefecture of Police and a general insurrection was declared by the Parisian Liberation Committee (CPL) and the National Council of the Resistance (CNR). On 20 August barricades went up, the *Hotel de Ville* [City Hall] was captured and German troops and installations were attacked. Soldiers were killed and military vehicles set alight. General von Choltitz, the German military commander of Paris, agreed to an offer from the Resistance of a ceasefire "until the German evacuation of Paris".

But SS units refused to cooperate, and on 22 August the Resistance leaders decided to break the truce. Hitler was also sending von Choltitz orders to crush the uprising. Paris, said the Fuhrer, must be held or "fall into the hands of the enemy only as a heap of rubble".

At nine o'clock last night, however, the church bells of Paris announced that the first units of Leclerc's 2nd Armoured Division had reached the Hotel de Ville. Von Choltitz ignored Hitler's orders. The Parisians had won (→ 26).

Notre Dame snipers fail to ruffle de Gaulle

Paris, 26 August

A violent burst of gunfire greeted General de Gaulle and the other leaders of the Free French as they walked up to the cathedral of *Notre Dame* today to celebrate the liberation with a *Te Deum*, following a triumphant victory march from the *Arc de Triomphe*.

In the taut atmosphere of the newly-liberated city, in which the official German capitulation had left numerous German and *Milice* snipers at liberty, a single shot set off a murderous fusillade in which several people were killed and 300 wounded near the cathedral. As the procession approached the cathedral Free French soldiers were firing at unseen targets among the pinnacles. General Leclerc tried to stop them, knocking down one man's rifle with his stick.

In the panic after a shot was heard in the cathedral, many Free French personalities took cover or threw themselves to the floor. General Koenig shouted: "Have you no pride? Stand up!" General de Gaulle was quite unruffled by the whole incident, and strode calmly up to the cathedral.

Collaborators pay as the reprisals begin

Paris, 26 August

The roar of heavy artillery still resounds in the suburbs, but Parisians are busy celebrating. The streets are not entirely safe yet [*see above*], but despite the dangers many Parisians are on the prowl, looking to vent their long bottled-up rage against those who collaborated with the Nazi occupation forces.

The people have not forgotten the 35 youths, aged between 17 and 25, who were massacred on 16 August at the *Bois de Boulogne* waterfall by French *Gestapists* working for the German secret police. They also remember the political prisoners at Romainville jail, shot dead by the German guards as they retreated before the approaching Allies a few days ago.

Their thirst for revenge is unlikely to be slaked. Most of the leading collaborators were able to flee Paris before the Allies entered the city, leaving behind only low-ranking militiamen and those women rather crudely termed "horizontal collaborators". The day before yesterday, a woman accused of having fraternized with Nazis was beaten and had her hair shaved off. She was then put on show at the police headquarters with a placard around the neck which proclaimed for all to see "She had her husband shot" (→ 27).

556

Allies advance on the Riviera front

Southern France, 25 August

Troops from the US 3rd Infantry Division entered Avignon today as the liberation of southern France gathers pace. Grenoble has also fallen, and though German forces still hold out in the ports of Marseilles and Toulon, elsewhere their compatriots are in retreat.

The Allied advance in southern France began on 15 August with the Operation Dragoon landings on the Riviera between Toulon and Cannes. From the outset the Allies encountered little German resistance; the Nineteenth Army under General Friedrich Wiese had only seven divisions to cover the entire coastline. Within three days nearly 100,000 troops from the US Seventh Army under Lt-Gen Alexander Patch, including the French Army B under General Jean de Lattre de Tassigny, were ashore. Inland the *Maquisard* [Resistance] fighters were also active, tying up German reserves (and being the first to enter Grenoble).

With the Nineteenth Army weakened by withdrawals to fight the Allies in Normandy, the Germans were in no position to defend on the southern flank, and for once Hitler recognized this. On 16 August the Fuhrer gave the order for the gradual withdrawal of German

A French tank rumbles through the streets of Avignon, liberated today.

forces in southern France to a line from Sens through Dijon to the Swiss border. The coded order, which in effect told the Allies that their progress would be largely unimpeded, was deciphered and conveyed to their land forces.

The Allied forces have advanced in two directions: by the mountains via Digne and Gap to Grenoble, and the coast towards Avignon from where the US Seventh Army

and French II Corps plan to head up the Rhone valley to Lyons. With Hitler's order, and the success of Operation Dragoon, the collapse of Vichy France has been swift. The Vichy premier, Pierre Laval, was compelled to leave Paris on 17 August, after refusing to leave in the hope of negotiating with the Allies; Marshal Petain was abducted from Vichy four days later. Both men are now being held at Belfort (→ 27).

Balkan states quit pact with Germany

Bucharest, 26 August

The German position in the Balkans is crumbling. The Roumanians, who fought alongside the Germans at Stalingrad and in the Crimea, declared war on Germany yesterday and seized their own capital after a sharp fight with the *Wehrmacht*. And the Bulgarians today announced their intention of withdrawing from the war, and began disarming German garrisons. Armistice talks are in their final stages.

Roumania's pro-German government collapsed four days ago when King Michael arrested Marshal Antonescu for refusing to make peace with the Allies and installed a new government which overcame German attempts to seize Bucharest (→ 30).

Eighth Army launches new assault in Italy

"This is the enemy": how the Italians are being told to regard the German Army which was once their ally.

Italy, 25 August

From an olive grove overlooking an Italian valley, Winston Churchill watched today as his Eighth Army began its advance towards the Gothic Line. "This was the nearest I got to the enemy and the time I heard most bullets in the Second World War," he recorded later.

The offensive has been planned by General Oliver Leese, the Eighth Army's commander. He has moved his forces from the west of Italy to attack on the eastern flank of the Apennines. The aim is to cross the Foglia river, break through the newly-completed defensive line near the Adriatic coast and clear the way for a mass tank breakout into the flood-plain of the Po valley. A tough fight is expected. Ten German infantry divisions face the Allies (→ 30).

Lack of fuel adds to Allied divisions over war tactics

France, 26 August

Yesterday's liberation of Paris is just the latest of a string of dazzling successes that the Allied armies in France have enjoyed during the past few weeks. The German armies in northern France have been decimated, and there seems to be little to stop the Allies from reaching the German border and penetrating the heart of Hitler's *Reich* well before winter sets in. Indeed, some are now saying that the war in Europe will be over by Christmas.

At present General Eisenhower is letting his two army group commanders in the north, Montgomery and Bradley, have their heads. Patton's US Third Army is now heading for the river Marne, well to the east of Paris, while Montgomery's forces secured a bridgehead over the Seine last night. His plan is to thrust parallel to the coast towards the Belgian border, secure Antwerp and then drive on to the Ruhr. Thus it would appear that the two army groups are beginning to move in divergent directions.

Montgomery still has operational control of the Allied armies in France, but Eisenhower is intending to take over the reins himself on 1 September. He wants to build on Patton's current success by thrusting into the Saarland while Montgomery secures Antwerp. Montgomery, on the other hand, does not like this splitting of the Allied forces. To take maximum advantage of the German disarray it is essential, in his eyes, to concentrate all available forces into a single lightning thrust.

The increasing problem of fuel shortages is likely to sharpen this broad versus narrow front debate. The Allies still rely on Cherbourg as their only port for supplies, especially fuel. Yet the deeper the Allies advance, the more stretched the supply lines, and the more difficult it will be to sustain momentum.

August

Su	Mo	Tu	We	Th	Fr	Sa
		1	2	3	4	5
6	7	8	9	10	11	12
13	14	15	16	17	18	19
20	21	22	23	24	25	26
27	28	29	30	31		

27. Germany: In Bomber Command's first major daylight raid on Germany since August 1941, 243 RAF bombers raid the synthetic oil refinery at Meerbeek, near Homberg.→

27. Provins, France: Retreating German soldiers massacre 22 villagers. Two days ago 126 civilians were murdered by the SS at Maille, Indre-et-Loire.

27. Paris: Eisenhower promises to supply de Gaulle with food, uniforms and military supplies.→

28. Hungary: General Lakatos forms a new, collaborationist government (→1/10).

28. France: Patton's leading troops cross the Marne at Chateau-Thierry; Rheims and Soissons also fall to the US advance (→30).

29. Rastenburg: Hitler orders extra fortifications on the North Sea coast between Denmark and the Netherlands (→9/9).

30. Lublin, Poland: The first war memorial of the conflict is unveiled, dedicated to the unknown Soviet soldier.

30. Germany: Following a failed suicide attempt, General Karl-Heinrich von Stulpnagel, the military governor of France implicated in the 20 July plot, is hanged (→14/10).

30. France: Canadian troops enter Rouen (→31).

31. Poland: Sixty-seven thousand Jews have been deported from the Lodz ghetto to the gas chambers at Auschwitz-Birkenau this month (→19/9).

31. Roumania: Soviet tanks receive a jubilant welcome as they roll into Bucharest (→9/9).

31. Algiers: The French provisional government moves to Paris.

31. France: As Allied and Resistance forces take control of all the bridges over the Somme, General Eberbach, the commander of the 5th *Panzer* Army, is taken prisoner in his pyjamas (→1/9).

31. Italy: British and Canadian troops break into the Gothic Line (→13).

French Mediterranean coast is liberated

The V sign from French troops in front of the old German HQ in Toulon.

Marseilles, 28 August
Last week General Schaeffer, the German commander in Marseilles, spurned a French proposal to surrender. Today he capitulated, as his counterpart in Toulon did yesterday; Free French forces under General de Lattre de Tassigny have captured the two great ports of southern France, and with their fall the entire French Mediterranean coast has now been liberated.

Marseilles surrendered after bloody, and often confused, fighting in which the regular French forces and the largely communist local Resistance fighters appeared at times to be waging a private war. Some 4,000 French casualties are feared, but German losses are heavier and about 37,000 prisoners have been taken. The port itself is a mass of twisted metal with 11 sunken ships blocking the main inlet.

The fight for Toulon, ringed by 30 forts, was no less fierce, often taking place in underground galleries built by the French but developed by the Germans. Today Adm Ruhfuss, the German commander, surrendered and agreed to hand over maps of his minefields (→28).

Roumanian oilwells taken by Red Army

Bucharest, 30 August
The Ploesti oilfields, a vital source of Germany's military fuel, have fallen to the Red Army. The Germans must now rely entirely on their much-bombed synthetic oil factories. Ploesti produces five million tons of crude oil a year, refined on the spot and sent to Germany by rail and by barges on the Danube. It has been the target for continual raids by the US Fifteenth Army Air Force flying from Italy. The bombers faced tough opposition, and many aircraft and their crews have been lost, but their attacks cut the refineries' output to two million tons, and RAF mining of the Danube prevented much of that from reaching Germany (→31).

Slovak rising starts

Prague, 29 August
Partisans fighting the Germans in Slovakia, the eastern part of prewar Czechoslovakia, issued a general call to arms today and declared the formation of a free Czechoslovak republic. The uprising is centred on the town of Banska Bystrica, in the centre of Slovakia, and the partisans have won control of large areas of the surrounding land. Hitler is reported to be furious and has ordered the *Wehrmacht* and the SS to crush the uprising (→24/9).

Allied air forces target synthetic oil plants for major attack

London, 27 August
Two hundred and sixteen Halifaxes, escorted by Mosquitoes and Lancasters, made a daylight attack on the Rheinpreussen synthetic oil refinery at Meerbeek in the Ruhr today. This is the RAF's first major daylight raid on Germany since 12 August 1941, and emphasizes the importance of these targets. Germany is running out of oil. The *Panzers*, whose Tiger tanks gobble fuel at two gallons a mile, are running dry, while the *Luftwaffe*, which needs 160,000 tons of high-octane fuel every month, is now getting only 10,000 tons a month. The factories are still making planes and tanks in record numbers, but they cannot move without fuel (→12/9).

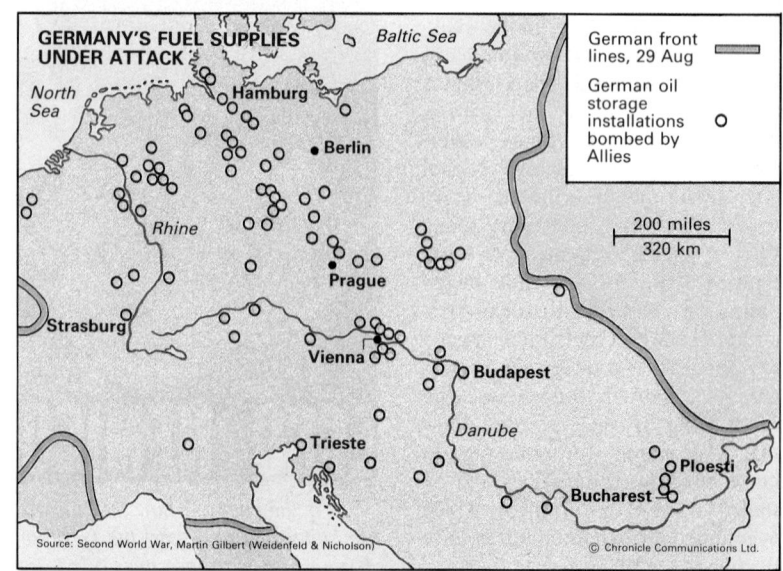

Strategy row threatens Allied unity

London, 31 August
Eisenhower called war correspondents to his London HQ today to praise Montgomery as his "great and personal friend ... and one of the great soldiers of this or any other war". The supreme commander also outlined the next stage of the Allied drive into Germany, which is flatly opposed to the plan Montgomery has been proposing.

Eisenhower told correspondents that the Allies will advance into Germany in three main columns. Montgomery's forces will strike at the Germans on the left, Bradley's Americans will drive forward in the centre, and the Mediterranean forces coming up from the south will move in on the right with Patton's Third Army. This is the "broad front" approach backed by Eisenhower and opposed by Montgomery, who favours a single concentrated thrust on the left, across northern France and Belgium.

Eisenhower has not got enough fuel to allow Montgomery in the north and Patton in the south to advance simultaneously. He dare not hold back Patton, who is immensely popular back home in the US; but he cannot be seen to be rebuffing Monty. So he will let Patton make his advance, and move the US First Army north to stand

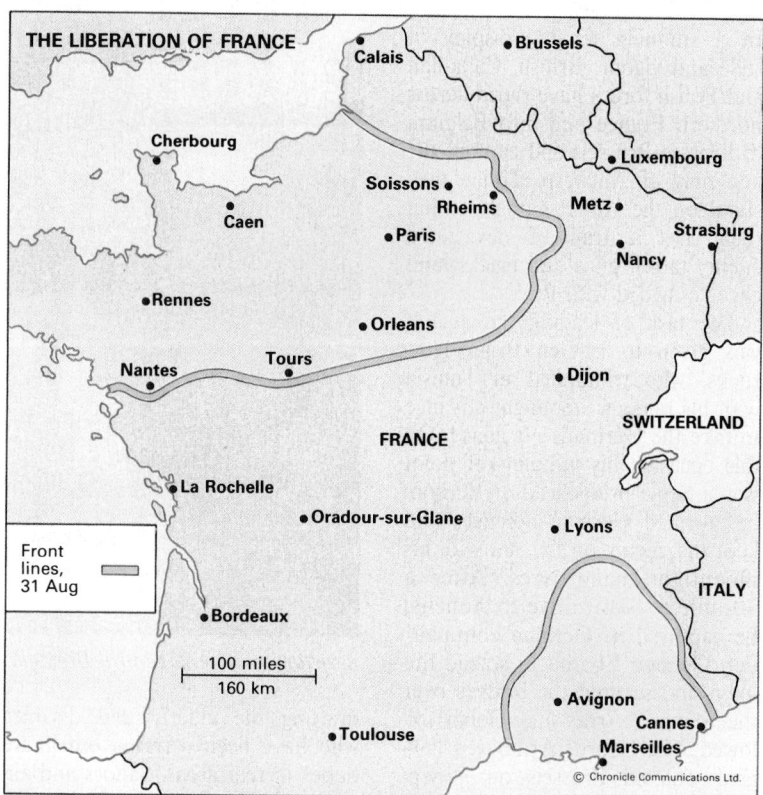

THE LIBERATION OF FRANCE

Front lines, 31 Aug

100 miles
160 km

© Chronicle Communications Ltd.

by Monty's 21st Army Group. Montgomery's immediate task, however, is not to attack the Ruhr, but to capture Antwerp. The Allies' nearest ports are in Normandy. Allied bombs have destroyed the railways. The US "Red Ball Route", a system of one-way military roads through France solely for the use of supply trucks shuttling between the Normandy beaches and the front, is badly overstretched. Antwerp must be taken if the Allies are to be kept supplied this winter (→ 1/9).

Britain beats off V-bomb challenge

London, 28 August
The V1 flying-bomb threat against England is being overcome. Of 94 V1s launched today, only four got through to London. The defence-in-depth tactics are now paying off. The missiles have first to face RAF fighter patrols over the Channel – and then a belt of anti-aircraft guns on the south coast. Behind this are further hungry fighters. Finally, as they begin their descent, they have to contend with a balloon barrage on the southern outskirts of the capital. Meanwhile, in France, the Allied armies continue to overrun launching sites (→ 8/9).

Paris handed over to the Free French

Paris, 30 August
The Free French General Pierre Koenig today took over from an American general as military governor of Paris at *Les Invalides*. The city had been under American military government since the US 4th Division entered the city along with General Leclerc's French troops on 25 August. General Koenig said he plans to put some of the French Forces of the Interior FFI Resistance fighters (FFI) into uniform. His priority, he added, is to restore law and order.

"Luftwaffe" drives Poles into sewers

Warsaw, 28 August
The Poles, fighting with their customary gallantry, continue to hold out in battered, starving Warsaw against the *Wehrmacht* while Stalin refuses to help and the Red Army waits on the far side of the Vistula. The *Luftwaffe* has been brought in to bomb the Poles, and heavy artillery is shelling the city to pieces. So fierce is the bombardment that the Home Army has been forced to abandon its positions in the Old Town and has gone literally underground – into the sewers, from whence its members emerge to attack the Germans. They are hungry, but what they really want are guns (→ 5/9).

Allies cross river to begin attack on "impregnable" Gothic Line

Italy, 30 August
Field Marshal Kesselring, a master of defensive strategy, has assured Hitler that the Gothic Line is impregnable. His boast is about to be put to the test: today the British V and Canadian I Corps, supported by air attacks on the minefields, crossed the Foglia river and, despite heavy casualties, began to attack the defensive position which the Germans believe to be equal to that of Cassino.

Houses have been razed, trees felled and vineyards bulldozed to create killing grounds for a great rash of concrete machine-gun nests, each carefully sited to protect its neighbour. Artillery posts have been blasted into the Apennine rock, and deep minefields planted from the Adriatic in the east to the distant Ligurian Sea (→ 31).

Allied tanks move up under cover of a smoke-screen to attack the Gothic Line.

1944

September

Su	Mo	Tu	We	Th	Fr	Sa
					1	2
3	4	5	6	7	8	9
10	11	12	13	14	15	16
17	18	19	20	21	22	23
24	25	26	27	28	29	30

1. Yugoslavia: Partisans join with the RAF and USAAF to launch Operation Ratweek, a seven-day attack on German communications (→ 6).

1. France: The 2nd Canadian Division captures Dieppe.

1. Europe: Eisenhower assumes direct command of Allied forces in Europe, and Montgomery is promoted to field marshal (→ 7).

1. France: Supreme Headquarters, Allied Expeditionary Force (SHAEF) starts operations at Granville.

2. Helsinki: Finland accepts the Soviet peace terms, breaks off diplomatic relations with Germany, and demands the withdrawal of German forces by 15 September.→

2. Rastenburg: Hitler orders the creation of 25 new *Panzer* divisions, to be split between the Seventh Army and the 5th and 6th Panzer Armies.

3. Belgium: German troops evacuate Brussels (→ 4).

4. Antwerp: The British 11th Armoured Division enters the port, and is ordered to halt because it is outstripping its 300-mile-long supply line (→ 8).

5. Moscow: The USSR declares war on Bulgaria (→ 28/10).

6. Caroline Islands: Sixteen carriers of Admiral Marc Mitscher's TF58 attack Palau.

6. Yugoslavia: Soviet forces cross the frontier from Roumania to link up with Tito's partisans (→ 27).

6. Britain: The Home Guard is partially stood down, and the blackout is relaxed.→

7. Europe: Allied forces capture Sedan and push forward to the Moselle river.→

8. Belgium: The US First Army captures Liege.→

8. Italy: The Eighth Army attacks German positions on the Germmano and Corriano ridges.

8. Greece: German forces begin to withdraw (→ 26).

9. Europe: US cavalrymen enter the Netherlands at Maastricht (→ 17).

Allies liberate Brussels

Belgium, 8 September
In a stunning ten-day display of style and vigour, British, Canadian and Polish forces have raced across northern France and into Belgium to liberate Brussels and capture the key port of Antwerp. Today they stand on the Albert Canal; behind them lies a trail of devastated enemy tanks, guns and trucks, and cages crowded with PoWs.

The task of leading the assault was given to Lt-Gen Brian Horrocks, who triumphed in Tunisia with his famous moonlight advance to take the Germans off guard. On this occasion his jumping-off point was a Seine bridgehead at Vernon; he stormed German defences and kept the enemy on the run with his moonlight manoeuvres. After a 40-mile (64-km) drive to Amiens, he captured its German commander, General Eberbach, seized the town and secured the bridges over the Somme. Arras and Douai followed. The Guards Armoured Division entered Brussels on 3 September; Antwerp fell to the 11th Armoured Division the next day.

The Canadians are besieging the Channel ports of Boulogne, Calais, and Dunkirk, where the Germans are clinging on in order to deny the Allies port facilities close to the front lines.

Hitler is desperately scrambling together new infantry divisions by

A victory parade in central Brussels.

drafting the elderly and disabled who have been carrying out guard duties in rear areas. Sailors and airmen are being turned into foot soldiers. The Fuhrer has recalled to active service the man he sacked only two months ago for failing to repel the Allied landing in Normandy. Field Marshal von Rundstedt returns as C-in-C West with orders to halt the Allies until winter arrives, with fog, night and snow, to give the Third *Reich* a respite (→ 10).

Fuel shortages put a brake on the Allies

Lorraine, 9 September
After a spectacular dash across central France, Patton's US Third Army has run out of petrol and is halted at the Moselle river, within striking distance of Germany. Only the capture of 37 carloads of German fuel has averted complete paralysis. While ammunition and food present no problems, fuel shortages are also holding up the US First Army within sight of Aachen, and Montgomery's 21st Army Group on the Albert Canal.

Some supplies are being airlifted by C47 transports, but the bulk must be carried by road on the chaotic "Red Ball Route" from the Allies' only working port, Cherbourg, more than 300 miles (480 km) to the rear (→ 11).

Montgomery: his army has ground to a halt on the Albert Canal.

Massive explosion as new V2 rocket hits London suburb

London, 8 September
The V2, a new type of German rocket, fell on a suburban road in Chiswick, West London, today at 6.40pm, killing three people and leaving a massive crater. It was fired, minutes before, from a mobile launcher in a suburban road of The Hague, in the Netherlands. The explosion, and a second in open country at Epping soon afterwards, could be heard over much of London. Each sounded like a double thunderclap followed by the rush of an express train. To avoid panic, and against the advice of scientists, no announcement of the new weapon was made. There are rumours that exploding gas mains were responsible. This morning, another rocket landed in the outskirts of Paris. By coincidence today Britons were told by Duncan Sandys, a junior minister, that the attack by V1 flying bombs was virtually over "except possibly for a few last shots". The launching sites near Calais have been captured, but a small number of V1s are still being air-launched by Heinkel bombers over the North Sea. In the 80 days since they began, 2,300 V1s got through to London, killing 5,475 people, injuring 16,000, and destroying 25,000 houses (→ 3/10).

Russian renegades will be sent home

London, 4 September
The cabinet decided today that all Russians captured by British forces will be sent back to the Soviet Union whether they want to go or not. There are something like 12,000 Soviet citizens being held in camps in Britain, and they are arriving at the rate of 2,000 a week from France.

Some of these prisoners are men who chose to fight with the Germans because of their hatred of Communism, but many were forcibly conscripted from prisoner-of-war camps and sent to build and man the invasion defences in France. Their presence has been the source of growing friction between Russia and Britain.

Red Army sweeps through Balkans

Bucharest, 9 September

The Red Army is pushing remorselessly into the Balkans as the Germans' control of the region falls apart. General Tolbukhin's Third Ukrainian Front met no resistance when it crossed into Bulgaria yesterday, and the Bulgarian government announced that it had declared war on Germany, adding that the Russians should be welcomed "as brothers".

The Russians are already here in Bucharest and the Roumanian army is fighting alongside them in the Carpathians, where they are forcing their way through the high mountain passes into Hungary.

As yet the Hungarian army remains loyal to the *Wehrmacht* and is fiercely resisting the Roumanians and the Russians, but Budapest is full of rumours that the Hungarian leader, Admiral Horthy, wants to change sides.

The situation is entirely different in Yugoslavia where Tito has liberated large areas in the south. The Russians crossed the border from Roumania three days ago and are expected to link up with the partisans in the next few days.

Agreement has already been reached between the two forces

Russian troops press on through the devastated towns of the Balkan states.

about the future conduct of operations. For the moment Tito's task is to cut the communications of the Germans retreating from Bulgaria and of General Alexander Lohr's Army Group E as it abandons its untenable situation in Greece.

The RAF and the USAAF have played a major role in the task with Operation Ratweek, cutting all the main German escape routes from Bulgaria and Greece to Vienna and

Budapest. Lohr and Field Marshal von Weichs of Army Group F in Yugoslavia will no doubt try to fight their way out to the north, but many men on the Greek islands stand no chance of escape. The question that is increasingly being asked by Allied leaders is: what form of government will be established in the Balkan countries in the wake of the Red Army's spectacular success (→13)?

Impassive Stalin ignores Allied pleas for fighting Warsaw

Warsaw, 5 September

Against all odds the Poles are still holding out in Warsaw despite the efforts of SS General Erich von dem Bach-Zelewski, the expert in crushing revolts. The Poles, girls and boys as young as ten among them, are defending every street, every house, every pile of rubble with enormous courage. The sewers have become their lines of communications, cellars their operating theatres.

Stalin still refuses to help, despite impassioned pleas from Churchill and from Roosevelt, who will not land American supply aircraft on Russian airstrips without Stalin's permission. The Soviet Army is in a difficult position across the Vistula, facing three strong *Panzer* divisions and with its own supply lines overstretched in the rear. But the Poles accuse Stalin of holding back for political reasons (→16/9).

A German patrol walks past a corpse in a devastated street in Warsaw.

Finns and Russians agree an armistice

Helsinki, 2 September

Finland has at last agreed to Russia's armistice terms, and its fruitless three-year-old second war with the Soviet Union ended today. The German legation in Helsinki is burning its papers, and General Rendulic, the commander of the German forces in northern Finland, is preparing to evacuate his men. The Russian terms stipulate that the Germans must be evacuated by 15 September or disarm and surrender. The Finns must also break off relations with Germany. All other questions are to be settled by negotiation in Moscow. Given the military situation, Marshal Mannerheim, the Finnish leader, had no option but to accept (→10).

Britain relaxes and brightens blackout

Britain, 6 September

The end of the blackout on 17 September was foreshadowed today. The blackout is to be replaced by a "dim-out" in which windows other than skylights can be curtained normally, except during air raids. Street lighting is to be stepped up and diffused car headlights allowed. The blackout will be abolished completely if circumstances permit. Fire-watching is to be abolished except at night in London and southeast England, and Civil Defence will become part-time only (→17).

US bombers launch raid on Manchukuo

Chungking, 8 September

Operating for the first time in daylight, a large force of China-based B-29 Superfortresses today bombed industrial targets at Anshan, in Japanese-controlled Manchukuo [*Manchuria*]. Its main target, attacked by 90 B-29s, was the Showa complex, the largest steel works in Manchukuo. Another 11 attacked rail targets at Anshan and nearby Sinsiang. Tokyo radio claimed that three B-29s had been shot down, but in fact the USAAF suffered no losses.

1944

September

Su	Mo	Tu	We	Th	Fr	Sa
					1	2
3	4	5	6	7	8	9
10	11	12	13	14	15	16
17	18	19	20	21	22	23
24	25	26	27	28	29	30

10. Moscow: The Russo-Finnish armistice is agreed (→ 19).

10. Berlin: Himmler orders the families of all deserters to be executed.

10. Belgium: Canadian forces enter Zeebrugge (→ 12).

10. Aachen: The first Allied vehicle, a US Jeep, crosses the border into Germany.→

11. Pacific: US submarines sink the Japanese transports *Rakuyo Maru* and *Kachidoki Maru*, killing 1,274 Allied PoWs en route from Singapore to Formosa.

11. Orleans: Nearly 20,000 Germans surrender to the 83rd US Infantry Division (→ 12).

11. Quebec: Churchill and Roosevelt meet for the "Octagon" conference (→ 16).

12. Belgium: German forces fall back behind the Escaut Canal (→ 9/10).

12. France: The French 2nd Armoured Division of the US Third Army links up with the French II Corps at Chatillon-sur-Seine, creating a solid Allied line between the Channel and the Swiss frontier. Twelve thousand Germans surrender at Le Havre (→ 16).

12-13. Frankfurt: Three hundred and eighty-six RAF bombers drop 400,000 incendiary devices (→ 14/10).

13. Washington: Enrico Fermi loads the first uranium slug into a plutonium-producing reactor (→ 19).

14. Burma: Japanese troops withdraw from the Manipur river Line (→ 2/10).

15. Paris: Francois de Menthon, the justice minister, orders the arrest of Petain and the Vichy cabinet on charges of collaboration.

15. Liverpool: Over a thousand British PoWs return from Germany on the liner *Arundel Castle*.

16. Beaugency, France: In the first capitulation on the western front, General Botho Elster surrenders to the US Ninth Army with 18,850 men of Group Elster of the XVI *Luftwaffe* Field Division (→ 20).

US First Army begins fight on German soil

Allied tanks pick out enemy observation posts in the advance on Aachen.

Trier, Germany, 11 September
American forces resuming their advance in the central sector today crossed the Germany/Luxemburg border north of Trier and began probing the Siegfried Line defences. In the north, other American forces crossed the Dutch border at Maastricht and are poised for a thrust on Aachen.

The British Second Army has broken out of its Albert Canal bridgehead, and advance units are moving into the Netherlands. A British spokesman said that during the operation more Germans were killed and more enemy equipment destroyed than in any one day since the Normandy landings began.

The roads into Germany are now packed with trucks, motor cars, and even bicycles, carrying soldiers and civilians fleeing the countries they have occupied for four years. These refugees are flooding into the Rhineland with atrocity stories, creating alarm and despondency among local people (→ 17).

Russians launch big new Baltic assault

Moscow, 16 September
The Red Army launched a new offensive on the Baltic front yesterday. Some 40 divisions with strong tank and air support are attacking the German positions on a 130-mile (208-km) front running from Valga on the Estonian border to Bauska, south of Riga, the Latvian capital. The Russians are trying to drive through the narrow German-held corridor on the Gulf of Riga in order to trap the much-battered Army Group North under General Schorner. They are also seeking to give themselves "elbow room" to build up their forces in preparation for their next campaign: the invasion of East Prussia (→ 22).

"Tirpitz" attacked

Norway, 15 September
Germany's only remaining super battleship, the *Tirpitz*, was disabled early today by Bomber Command. A few days ago two squadrons were sent to Yagodnik, in north Russia, which is within range of Altenfjord where the ship is berthed. Today 28 Lancasters flew in, 20 of them carrying 12,000-pound armour-piercing "Tallboy" bombs. One direct hit went straight through the forecastle and peeled back the deck like the lid of a sardine tin (→ 12/11).

Roumania signs pact with Allies in Moscow, ceding land to USSR

Moscow, 13 September
The armistice treaty between Roumania and the Allies signed here yesterday stipulates that the Roumanians must pay the Soviet Union £75 million for damage caused in Russian by the Roumanian army. Another key clause stipulates that the Soviet Union will keep Bessarabia and Northern Bukovina according to the terms of the 1940 treaty under which they were ceded to the Soviet Union. In recompense Roumania will get back that portion of Transylvania which Hitler gave to Hungary under the 1940 Vienna Award. The terms, signed by the newly-promoted Marshal Malinovsky, also commit Roumania to "wage war against Germany and Hungary".

Roumanian communists hold up their favourite Allied leader in Bucharest.

Stalin drops arms to besieged Poles

Warsaw, 16 September

Stalin has at last come to the aid of the Poles who have been fighting the German occupation for the last six weeks. The Red Army has halted at the gates of the city while Stalin has either refused, or been unable, to help the Poles whom he describes as "reactionary".

The Soviet leader has actively obstructed British and American efforts to drop supplies. More than 200 Polish, American, South African and British airmen have died in attempts to supply Warsaw. Flying from bases in Italy, they have been refused permission by Stalin to land on Russian airstrips.

In the last 48 hours, Stalin's forces have dropped two heavy machine guns, 50 pistols and a quantity of ammunition for the freedom fighters, a meagre offering made even more negligible by the Russian failure to use parachutes. With nothing to break their fall, most of the arms were damaged and made useless when they hit the ground.

Stalin's half-hearted aid has coincided with the opening of a Russian assault on Warsaw. The First Infantry Division of a Polish army raised in Russia has captured the suburb of Praga (→ 18).

War summit plans strategy against Japan

Roosevelt and Churchill in Quebec review Allied plans in Europe and Asia.

Quebec, 16 September

At the press conference concluding the Octagon Conference, the eighth summit of the war, President Roosevelt said that after Germany's surrender "the British Empire and the United States will work together" against Japan.

Much of the conference was taken up, however, with three different great questions: Anglo-US. cooperation on the "atom bomb"; the British prime minister's fear of Russian influence in central Europe

after the war; and the plans of the US treasury Secretary, Henry Morgenthau, for turning Germany into an "agrarian" country after the war. Sitting on the terrace of the citadel here known as "the deck", Mr Churchill called Japan an "evil and barbarous nation".

Mr Churchill has confided to Mr Roosevelt his fears of the "dangerous spread of Russian influence" in the Balkans, especially Greece and Yugoslavia, and FDR is beginning to agree.

Autumn rains come to aid the Germans

Italy, 13 September

For 24 hours it seemed that the Eighth Army was about to break through the Gothic Line at the Germmano and Coriano ridges and pour through on to the plains beyond. Then it came up against its old adversary: the weather. The rivers are flooding. Tanks of the 1st Armoured Division stand impotently in fields of mud at San Savino, while the British 4th Infantry Division has come under heavy artillery and mortar fire, delaying its move up to the start line. The delay has given the German chief, General von Vietinghoff, time to move his infantry into place, closing the gate to the Allies (→ 21).

Danish emergency

Copenhagen, 16 September

All Denmark stopped work today in protest at the shooting of 23 demonstrators by German soldiers in City Hall Square last night. The demonstrators were protesting at the removal of 190 Danes to concentration camps. Railways, trams and factories are still. The strike was called by the Danish Freedom Council, which coordinates the resistance with the discreet support of King Christian and the majority of his subjects (→ 19).

US forces launch twin offensive to win control of Pacific islands

Washington, 16 September

The two great American military drives across the Pacific Ocean converged yesterday when General MacArthur's forces, moving north from New Guinea, invaded Morotai, in the Dutch East Indies. At the same time Admiral Nimitz landed the US 1st Marine Division in an assault on five beach-heads on Peleliu Island, in the Palau group, 430 miles (688 km) north-east of Morotai. Both islands are within striking distance of the Philippines.

The landing at Morotai was virtually unopposed, but the situation was different on Peleliu, where the marines ran into fierce resistance, with heavy casualties on both sides. Ironically, while Morotai is considered strategically important, the seizure of Peleliu is now regarded by many senior officers as no longer necessary (→ 17).

Clusters of rockets scream towards land from US vessels off Peleliu.

Midget subs blast Norwegian harbour

Bergen, 14 September

One of Britain's most successful secret weapons – a midget submarine' able to penetrate the best-defended waterways – has struck again. This time the target was a big floating dock, blown up in Bergen harbour. Lt H P Westmacott skippered the four-man craft, X24, as it slipped through 30 miles (48 km) of islands offshore and a minefield and into a *fjord* to sail at periscope depth to the harbour. After diving to 35 feet to avoid collision with a merchant ship, Westmacott attached delayed-action charges to the target and escaped. It is the second such raid on Bergen by Westmacott in X24.

1944

September

Su	Mo	Tu	We	Th	Fr	Sa
					1	2
3	4	5	6	7	8	9
10	11	12	13	14	15	16
17	18	19	20	21	22	23
24	25	26	27	28	29	30

17. Britain: The blackout is replaced by the "dim-out", permitting a modified form of street lighting.

17. Netherlands: As the British Second Army nears the border, the government orders a general strike (→ 19).

18. Poland: After Stalin reluctantly gives his permission for the US to supply Bor-Komorowski's rebels, 107 Flying Fortresses drop food and arms over Warsaw: ninety per cent of the supplies land in German hands (→ 3/10).

19. Rastenburg: In an attempt to ensure that the army obeys the Nazi Party, Hitler orders all commanders to take advice from *Gauleiters*.

19. Helsinki: Finland signs an armistice with the USSR, paying a $300 million indemnity and ceding Petsamo and a small coastal strip to the Soviets (→ 2/10).

19. Denmark: A five-day strike begins in protest against German deportations (→ 21).

19. Netherlands: US airborne troops liberate Eindhoven.

19. Nijmegen, Netherlands: Civilians shave the heads of women who associated with Nazis during occupation (→ 21).

20. Cap Blanc-Nez, Normandy: 646 Allied bombers drop 5,600 high-explosive bombs in two hours on the German guns (→ 22).

21. Denmark: The Germans crush the general strike (→ 31/10).

21. Netherlands: British tanks cross the Waal at Nijmegen, and advance towards Arnhem where the Germans recapture the road bridge (→ 27).

21. Italy: The Allies capture Rimini.→

22. Estonia: Soviet forces take the capital, Tallinn.→

22. Boulogne: The German garrison surrenders to the Canadians.→

23. Caroline Islands: US forces on Ulithi atoll, abandoned by the Japanese last month, discover an immense lagoon, invaluable as a potential naval base (→ 24).

Red Army takes key German escape port

Moscow, 22 September
Marshal Govorov's tanks, slicing through the German defences along the Gulf of Finland, today captured the Estonian capital, Tallinn, thus depriving the German Army Group North of one of its last means of escape by sea. General Schorner will now have to retreat south and west in order to escape the complete destruction of his badly-mauled group.

The capture of Tallinn's first-rate port facilities will also give the Russians a valuable base for operations against the German Baltic fleet and the transports being used both to deliver supplies and to evacuate casualties. The Red Air Force sank three large transports in Tallinn harbour before it fell.

It seems that the sheer speed of Govorov's advance took the Germans by surprise. Covering 50 miles (80 km) in a day, the tanks left the infantry to mop up pockets of the German rearguard, giving Schorner's men no time to organize a proper line of defence. The depth of the Red Army's advance is demonstrated by the capture of the railway junction of Tapa and the town of Paide, 47 miles (75 km) south-east of Tallinn (→ 27).

SS removes traces of camp nightmare

Estonia, 19 September
As the Soviet Army advances, the Germans are desperately trying to destroy the evidence of the mass torture and murder that they have inflicted on occupied countries. With the Red Army on the brink of liberating the Klooga concentration camp, the SS today slaughtered all but 85 of the 3,000 forced labourers. Half of them were Jewish, the rest Estonian political prisoners and Soviet PoWs. Strangely enough, no captured Germans, or even local people, will own up to knowing anything about the camps in their midst (→ 26).

Atomic plan agreed by US and Britain

Hyde Park, New York, 19 September
The British prime minister, Winston Churchill, left President Roosevelt's family home here today after a three-day conference at which they reached an important agreement about atomic energy. They flatly rejected suggestions by the Danish physicist Niels Bohr that atomic secrets should be made public and the bomb put under international control. They agreed on "full collaboration" between Britain and the US on atomic energy after the war – and they decided that the bomb might be dropped on Japan after a warning.

US forces invade two more Pacific islands

Angaur, 17 September
The US 8th Infantry Division has captured the north-eastern third of Angaur, the southernmost of the Palau Islands. US forces on Angaur are finding resistance lighter than on Peleliu, six miles (9.6 km) to the north, which was invaded two days ago. There, 24,300 marines have been pinned down by 10,500 Japanese operating from a high ridge. Ironically, the Palaus are no longer essential to US plans. The islands, 800 miles (1,280 km) southwest of Guam, were intended as a staging area for an attack on Mindanao. However, two days ago General MacArthur told Washington that he now intends to attack the Philippines directly (→ 22).

US troops take control on Angaur.

Guy Gibson, hero of Dambusters, killed

Guy Gibson at his VC investiture.

Netherlands, 19-20 September
Wing-Commander Guy Gibson, awarded a Victoria Cross for leading the spectacular raid against three Ruhr dams last year, died when his Mosquito crashed near the village of Steenbergen. At his own request he had left a desk job to go on a raid against a German communications centre at Rheydt in the Ruhr. He acted as pathfinder and master bomber for a Lancaster force. It is thought that his aircraft either developed engine trouble or was shot down by *flak*, and it seems that he was flying too low for him or his navigator, Sqn-Ldr JB Warwick DFC, to parachute out.

Gibson had seemed untouchable – the only survivor out of 25 aircrew who enlisted at the same time. He had narrow escapes flying Blenheims before Dunkirk. After the Battle of Britain he flew night fighters on 99 missions in two months, destroying six enemy planes. He also crash-landed between trees with a wounded crewman. As a bomber pilot he was on the first 1,000-plane raid against Cologne before the "Dambuster" epic; after leading the attack, he stayed to protect others. Aged 25, he won a DSO and DFC as well as his VC.

Montgomery gambles to try to shorten the war

Arnhem, 17 September

Operation Market Garden was launched today with parachute and glider drops aimed at capturing bridges over the Dutch rivers near the German border. The plan is to bypass the fortified Siegfried Line and drive Allied forces into Germany by the lightly-defended back door. Montgomery says that the war could be over by Christmas.

American paratroopers have been assigned to seize a series of bridges across the Maas and the Waal while the British paras have been dropped at Arnhem, the far-thest target, to seize the two Lower Rhine bridges. The 1st Parachute Reconnaissance Squadron came down at 1.15pm without opposi-tion, eight miles (13 km) west of Arnhem. It was three-quarters of an hour in advance of the main force, the 1st Parachute and 1st Air Landing Brigade of the 1st Air-borne Division. Dutch civilians wel-comed the men, but their greetings delayed the paras' deployment.

By the time that the paras att-acked the railway bridge it was being blown up, while another group, attacking the northern app-roaches of the road bridge, found a strong German force in position at the southern end. There was worse to come. Not only had the British landed within two miles (3.2 km) of the HQ of Field Marshal Model but the 9th and 10th SS *Panzer* Divi-sions had recently arrived north of Arnhem for regrouping.

The British CO, Major-General Robert Urquhart, narrowly es-caped capture by hiding in a house. He ventured to the front when he lost contact with the landings. He has ended up trapped there, and still out of touch with his staff (→ 21).

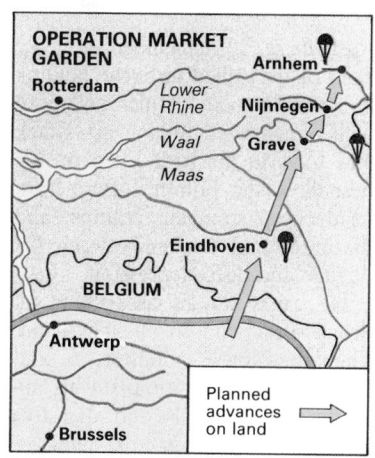

OPERATION MARKET GARDEN

Rotterdam
Lower Rhine
Waal
Maas
Arnhem
Nijmegen
Grave
Eindhoven
BELGIUM
Antwerp
Brussels

Planned advances on land

British paratroopers surrounded by enemy forces at Arnhem

Arnhem, 20 September

After four days and three sleepless nights, Allied paratroopers are hold-ing out in spite of heavy shelling and repeated attacks by infantry and *Panzers*. But the British are fighting in scattered units, with radio links disrupted, by trees and tall build-ings. Ground-to-air radio contact has also been disrupted and this has led to RAF resupply drops falling on zones still held by the enemy.

The command post in the Har-tenstein Hotel is out of contact with the 150 men holding the northern end of the road bridge. All attacks across the bridge by German arm-oured cars and half-tracks have been repelled, but food, water and ammunition are running low.

In an operation dogged by mis-fortune, the British battle plan has fallen into German hands; it was found in a crashed glider. So when Brigadier John Hackett's 4th Para-chute Brigade arrived, the enemy was waiting and picked off the men as they hung helplessly beneath their parachutes.

The planned link-up with the be-leaguered paratroopers has been mounted by the Guards Armoured Division, driving north from the Dutch border. American paras cap-tured the Maas bridges, but were unable to gain the next crossing over the Waal, which is the south branch of the Lower Rhine, until the Guards arrived to link up at Nij-megen. A concerted drive from there towards Arnhem has since encountered strong Panzer resis-tance (→ 21).

The V sign, thumbs up or whatever from optimistic troops before take-off.

In enemy territory, paratroopers who survived the drop advance cautiously.

Despite losses, the Germans fight back

Versailles, 23 September

With two million men now under his command, Eisenhower is moving his HQ forward to Ver-sailles. The US Seventh Army, which landed on the Riviera last month, has linked up with Patton's Third Army; the Allied front now runs in an unbroken line from the Swiss frontier to the Channel. Since D-Day, the Germans in the west have lost upwards of a million men, half of them prisoners.

Under pressure from Admiral Sir Bertram Ramsay, the naval C-in-C, Eisenhower is giving top priority to clearing the Scheldt es-tuary of enemy forces and bringing Antwerp's port into use. The task will be assigned to the Canadians.

As Allied forces begin pushing into Germany itself, resistance is stiffening, though there are signs of divisions between regular German forces and fanatical SS units. When US troops yesterday entered Stol-berg, a small town about 40 miles west of Cologne, the mayor offered to help the Americans in locating pockets of resistance. Two German officers appeared with a white flag and said they wished to surrender their platoon. SS units came up and put a stop to that. Deserters are a growing problem. The CO of the German 18th *Panzergrenadier* Divi-sion has issued an order which says that the families of "these bastards who have given away important military secrets" will have to atone for their treason (→ 29).

1944
September

Su	Mo	Tu	We	Th	Fr	Sa
					1	2
3	4	5	6	7	8	9
10	11	12	13	14	15	16
17	18	19	20	21	22	23
24	25	26	27	28	29	30

Drugged, insomniac Hitler loses his grip

Rastenburg, 17 September
Told of the Allied airborne landing at Arnhem today, Hitler collapsed with a suspected mild heart attack and took to his bed. Even on his best days, the Fuhrer suffers from headaches, stomach cramps and dizziness, and wavers between fits of rage and deep depression.

He exists on an assortment of drugs prescribed by his physician, Theodor Morell: Vitamins A and D and glucose to stimulate his appetite; anti-gas pills and digestive aids; Vitamultin-Ca to alleviate depression; caffeine and pervitin tablets to stimulate the brain; injections of heart and liver extracts; cocaine for headaches; sedatives for sleeping.

He harangues his generals about the new armies he will raise, the secret weapons that will appear, and the quarrels that will break out among the Allies; these factors will enable Germany to gain a victory that will endure for a hundred years, he says.

But anxiety over the looming defeat, the unhealthy existence in the underground bunker and Morell's drugs have made Hitler a physical and mental wreck. On the rare occasions when he leaves the bunker he sways and stumbles. Grey-faced, trembling, blinking his bloodshot eyes, he retreats into the *Wolfsschanze*.

London's West End prepares for the bright lights of peacetime: a pre-war globe is fitted to a lamp in Piccadilly Circus (→ 20/11).

Allies tighten their hold on Channel ports

The ruined wasteland of the harbour at Boulogne, now in Allied hands.

Brest, 21 September
US General Omar Bradley's controversial insistence on a drive west from Normandy to the outer rim of Finisterre reached its conclusion this week with the surrender two days ago of Brest after a 27-day siege. German prisoners total 35,000. The core garrison of 6,600 marched out in good order after tying up a third of Lt-Gen Patton's Third Army, when much more of the German force defending the road to the *Reich* might have been enveloped. As the 4th Armoured Division leader, Maj-Gen John Wood, said six weeks ago: "We're winning the war the wrong way: we ought to be going toward Paris."

Paris fell 25 days ago, and Brussels and Antwerp some two weeks before Brest. Bradley, doggedly loyal to the original Overlord plan, feared that a German counter-attack north, to the Channel coast, could cut Patton's tanks off from their logistical tail, with disastrous results. The Allies now control all ports in north Brittany. These are useful, but not war-winning, assets. On the Atlantic coast enemy garrisons at Lorient and St Nazaire refuse to give in; naval bombardment might be necessary (→ 23).

Eighth Army moves forward on Adriatic

Rimini, 21 September
After four weeks of bitter fighting, this ancient city fell to Canadian infantrymen and men of the Greek 3rd Mountain Brigade today, marking the end of one of the most critical battles of the Italian campaign. Other units of the British Eighth Army are fighting their way on to the Lombardy plains where, the generals believe, British armour will find the terrain smoother to fight its way to the foothills of the Alps and through to Austria. The eastern end of the Gothic Line has been broken; and, in the west, the US Fifth Army has begun an equally bloody attack (→ 3/10).

US makes first air raid on Philippines

Philippines, 22 September
US carrier-based flyers struck at Japanese airfields near Manila and elsewhere on Luzon today and yesterday, wrecking airfields and damaging installations in the first air raids on the Philippines since the fall of Corregidor. Planes from Admiral Halsey's Third Fleet, 145 miles east of Luzon, claimed 205 Japanese planes, 110 of them shot down and 95 destroyed on the ground at Nicholls and Clark Fields. Fifteen US planes were lost in the raids. Japanese shipping was hard hit, with 11 ships sunk and 92 damaged as the raiders struck Subic Bay and Cavite naval yard (→ 23).

24. Palau Islands: US infantry and marines come under a powerful Japanese attack on Peleliu (→ 26).

24. Czechoslovakia: The Red Army penetrates 20 miles over the Polish border (→ 6/10).

24. Washington: The US treasury plan for post-war Germany (the "Morgenthau Plan") is published; it proposes a Germany stripped of its industry and converted to an wholly agricultural economy.

25. China: Chiang Kai-shek demands that Stilwell be recalled from China (→ 6/10).

26. Palau Islands: US forces capture the vital area of Hill 120, creating several isolated pockets of Japanese (→ 5/10).

26. Auschwitz-Birkenau: Dr Josef Mengele presides over a "selection" of a thousand children, fixing a board to a post and sending all who fail to reach it straight to the gas chambers (→ 28).

26. Stresa, Italy: US advisers parachute down to set up an intelligence network for the Italian partisans (→ 29).

27. Pacific: A US submarine sinks the Japanese transport ship *Ural Maru*, and two thousand of the 2,350 passengers are drowned.

28. Auschwitz-Birkenau: Two hundred gypsies are gassed (→ 1/10).

29. Italy: Two SS regiments, under SS Major Walter Reder, start a reprisal operation against partisans in Bologna province.

29. Normandy: Canadian infantrymen capture the enormous German battery at Cap Griz-Nez (→ 30).

29. Washington: The Dumbarton Oaks conference of Allied foreign ministers agrees on a programme for post-war security, including the establishment of the United Nations Organization (→ 7/10).

30. Britain: This month 190 civilians have been killed and 360 wounded in air raids.

30. Atlantic: This month 19 U-boats have been sunk.

Beleaguered forces at Arnhem forced to surrender

A scene of utter desolation at Arnhem after the Allied defeat: less than a quarter of the British and Polish troops escaped captivity or death.

Arnhem, 27 September
The last British and Polish troops trapped at Arnhem surrendered to the Germans yesterday after holding the bridgehead against overwhelming odds for nine days. For the last three days many of the men were without water and survived on rations cut to one-sixth. During heavy rainstorms they gathered water in their capes. When at last the men were ready to leave, they stood with heads bowed while the padre said a prayer.

The order to abandon the operation was given by Montgomery on Monday, and the withdrawal south across the Rhine took place during the night of 25-26. Only 2,400 men out of more than 10,000 who took part in the operation got away in boats or by swimming across; 1,200 were killed and 6,642 have been taken prisoner. Allied HQ claims that 12,000 Germans were killed or wounded in the fighting.

Allied casualties could have been higher. Major Richard Lonsdale put together a rearguard force of men who had become separated from their units. With this force, he defended the bridgehead perimeter to allow others to escape. Then, despite his wounds, he swam across the mile-wide river to the safety of the south bank, where a battalion of the Dorsetshire Regiment had arrived, having overcome tenacious German resistance all the way from Nijmegen, ten miles distant.

Though the Allies failed to hold the Rhine crossing, Eisenhower reckons the operation was worthwhile; by securing the crossings of the Maas and the Waal it advanced the Allied front to Nijmegen and put the defence of Antwerp beyond doubt.

Horror and heroism: survivors tell their stories of Arnhem

Arnhem, 27 September
Every survivor has a tale to tell of terror by day and night under a hurricane of fire from the Germans, and the deeds of bravery and self-sacrifice are legion. "Give us a few tanks," they say, "and we'll go back and finish the job."

"The *Panzers* were causing us a lot of trouble," says Captain Bethune Taylor, from Cheltenham. "So a major went out with a Piat and took two on. Every time he put his head out the Panzers fired. But he set his Piat and bagged one." Lance-Corporal John Stilwell, of Hackney Wick, came under attack from flame-throwers. "They got a man next to me. He screamed in agony. We made our way to the river. One man did wonders, keeping three Vickers going to keep the escape channel open."

Allied soldiers held out at Arnhem for nine days despite a savage battering.

Hopes now fade for an early end to war

Allied HQ, France, 27 September
The failure at Arnhem puts paid to hopes of ending the war this year; it also means that Montgomery has lost his battle for a single concentrated all-out drive into Germany. Eisenhower is back to his "broad front" strategy which the Americans have favoured all along.

Too many corners were cut at Arnhem. To save aircraft, the paras made three separate drops over three days, and the Germans never felt the British 1st Airborne Division at full strength. Radio equipment was inadequate and communications failed. Intelligence reports of *Panzer* units at Arnhem were not believed. Then the paras landed too far from the bridges and some had an eight-mile march (→ 3/10).

Hitler to put "home guard" in front line

Berliners read of the "Volkssturm".

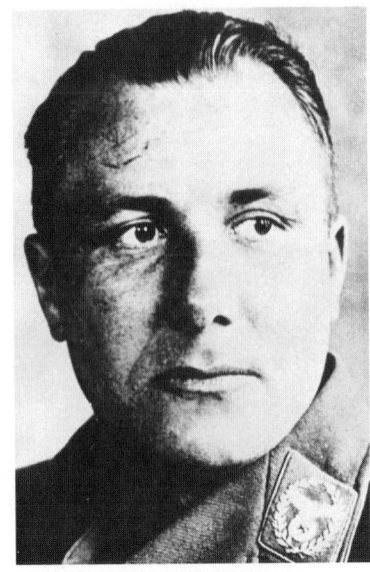

Bormann, who will run the force.

Berlin, 25 September
Allied Intelligence has a poor opinion of some of the new recruits appearing in the front line facing the Allies in the west – "policemen ... boys of 16 and men with duodenal ulcers have been taken prisoner recently". Hitler's new recruits are likely to be of yet poorer calibre. The formation of a new "home guard", the *Volkssturm*, was announced today. It will be organized by Nazi *Gauleiters* under the direction of Himmler and Bormann. Hitler's mistrust of his generals is such that he believes that the Nazi

Party, rather than the military, will mount the final defence of Germany. The Volkssturm will be operational next month.

On paper, the Fuhrer still has ten million men in his armed forces, seven and a half million of them in the army. Most are scattered across Europe, in the Baltic states, the Balkans, Scandinavia, the Netherlands and northern Italy, instead of coming to the defence of the *Reich*. Many of the regular formations assigned to home defence, and identified as divisions, are of no more than battalion strength (→ 5/10).

Germans retreating towards the Baltic

Moscow, 27 September
The Red Army is swiftly clearing Estonia of German troops as General Schorner conducts his skilful retreat through the Riga corridor to the comparative safety of Courland, the north-western part of Latvia where it bulges into the Baltic Sea. It remains to be seen how many men Schorner can get away as the Russians push through Latvia to seal off the corridor. With this manoeuvre the Russians are not only inflicting heavy casualties on the Germans but are also making sure that they will not be attacked from the rear when they open their inevitable assault on East Prussia (→ 5/10).

British troops cross the Italian Rubicon

Rimini, 26 September
Like Caesar's legions before it, the British Eighth Army crossed the Rubicon river today – this time in the opposite direction. The Allies are fighting hard on the flanks of the bridgehead opened on the Gothic Line, threatening to break out on the northern plains in full force along the eastern flank of the Apennines. General Sir Henry Maitland Wilson, the Allied Mediterranean C-in-C, has sent congratulations to the Allied armies. "I hope that the crossing of the Rubicon will lead, as with a famous commander in the past, to a decisive victory and the destruction of Kesselring's army," he wrote.

Allies join partisans on Adriatic islands

Yugoslavia's partisan leader Tito, at work with his secretary, Olga.

Dalmatia, 27 September
British troops have joined Yugoslav partisans on the Dalmatian islands and are poised to invade the Yugoslav mainland.

Royal Navy coastal forces based on Vis, the outermost of the islands, are dominating coastal traffic. British commandos are also using Vis as a base to establish artillery positions on the island of Brac from which to attack German supply lines and prevent German patrol boats from putting to sea.

Fierce battles are also taking place in Albania to the south where the German garrison has been ordered to protect the single railway line bringing escaping troops from Greece (→ 4/10).

September 27. Wounded US marines on Peleliu, Palau Islands. This key Japanese base in the central Pacific fell today after a 12-day fight.

Greek partisans agree deal to avert war

Caserta, Italy, 26 September
The threat of a civil war in Greece was staved off here today when the country's two extremist partisan leaders agreed to put their forces under a government which, in turn, will be backed by the British Army.

With German withdrawal from Greece seemingly imminent, the danger of a clash between the extreme left-wing ELAS party and the neo-fascist EDES appeared inevitable. ELAS is well-armed and disciplined, and the possibility that Greece might fall under the Soviet

mantle after the war is causing Churchill grave concern. The conference was called by General Sir Henry Maitland Wilson, supreme Allied commander Mediterranean. The ELAS commander General Safaris and General Zervas of EDES have agreed to serve under the exiled premier, George Papandreou, on his return.

It is a fragile truce, however. Both antagonists have laid claim to large areas of Greece, and they have had three years in which to prepare for civil war (→ 1/10).

Canadians push Germans out of Calais

Canadians patrol the streets of Calais after the German garrison surrendered.

Calais, 30 September
The prospect of a dour, bloody battle for Calais evaporated at midnight tonight with the sudden collapse of the last pockets of German resistance after two days' fighting. Yesterday opposing commanders met under flag of truce to arrange the evacuation of 25,000 civilians. By then the big guns of Cap Griz-Nez, which had shelled Dover, had been seized by the besieging Canadian 3rd Division. The Germans threatened to fight to the last man, but after some hours of shelling and air bombing they had had enough. White flags appeared, and 7,000 captives included the commander. Hitler's bunker mentality, his determination to hold the French coast, has cost 120,000 men.

Thus the month ends with the Allies in control of most of France. Huge swathes of the centre and south-west were liberated this month, but for the last three weeks there has been little progress be-

yond the Moselle along a line south of Aachen to Belfort. Patton's US Third Army has met strong resistance in Alsace-Lorraine, notably around Metz. Further north, limited forays have been made into Nazi territory, but there has been no breakthrough (→ 3/10).

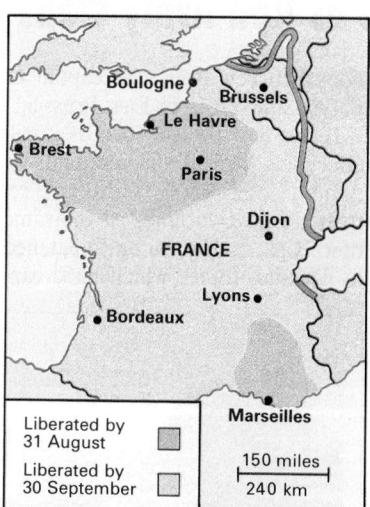

Boulogne · Brussels ·
· Le Havre
· Brest
Paris ·
Dijon ·
FRANCE
Lyons ·
· Bordeaux
Marseilles ·
Liberated by 31 August
Liberated by 30 September
150 miles
240 km

Food shortages worsen inside Germany

Germany, 30 September
Until last year the German people lived off the fat of the occupied lands, leaving the populations of Poland, France, Belgium, Greece and the Netherlands to starve as their food produce was diverted to the *Reich*. But with each new country liberated, the Nazi store cupboard becomes increasingly bare. Basic foodstuffs such as

bread, flour and fat are generally available, but people are beginning to feel the pinch of rationing. Daily consumption of fish and meat has fallen from the pre-war level of six ounces per person to just over three ounces, and of eggs from two-thirds to one-third of an ounce. People living in towns suffer most since railways are a prime target for Allied bombing.

1944
October

Su	Mo	Tu	We	Th	Fr	Sa
1	2	3	4	5	6	7
8	9	10	11	12	13	14
15	16	17	18	19	20	21
22	23	24	25	26	27	28
29	30	31				

1. Moscow: Hungarian officials arrive to negotiate a secret armistice (→ 10).

1. Greece: British commandos land on Poros, and Greek units land at Lemnos, Levita and Mitilini (→ 2).

1. Buchenwald: Seven homosexual prisoners are castrated in the name of medical research.→

1. Italy: Brazilian troops go on the offensive, launching an Allied drive towards Bologna.

2. Burma: Mountbatten orders an immediate offensive against Mandalay (→ 28).

2. Finland: The Red Army pushes into Lapland, pursuing the retreating Nazis (→ 23/11).

2. Greece: Allied troops land on Crete.→

3. Germany: US troops cross the river Wurm, and establish a bridgehead across the Siegfried Line (→ 4).

3. Dunkirk: The battling armies declare a truce to enable civilians to be evacuated (→ 1/11).

4. Yugoslavia: The Red Army captures Pancevo, on the east bank of the Danube (→ 12).

4. Aachen: *Panzers* stage an unsuccessful counter-attack to try to close the breach in the Siegfried Line (→ 8).

5. Peleliu, Palau Islands: The US 7th Marines, fighting in torrential rain, are relieved by the 5th Marines in the struggle to dislodge Japanese forces from the Mount Umurbrogol pocket (→ 9).

5. Germany: All hospitals are put under military control, and sixteen-year-olds are called up for military service (→ 18).

6. China: Roosevelt agrees to remove Stilwell from the post of chief of staff to Chiang Kai-shek. Stilwell retains command of Chinese troops in Burma and Yunnan province (→ 19).

6. Hungary: Soviets cross the border into Czechoslovakia over the Tisza river (→ 14/11).

7. Rastenburg: Hitler orders German forces to evacuate Greece (→ 10).

Allied plans dashed by dogged German resistance in Italy

Bologna, 3 October
Allied generals had every hope that their armour would move quickly across the flat country of the Romagna now that the Gothic Line has been pierced. It was not to be.

From the moment that the New Zealand Division – the Eighth Army's *Corps de Chasse* – was stopped by its old antagonists, the German 1st Parachute Division, after 27 separate attacks, it became clear that this would be no easy operation. The Marecchia river was six inches (15 cm) deep when the New Zealanders crossed a week ago. Today it is a roaring, 12-foot deep torrent.

Despite a shortage of infantry – General Mark Clark has reported losses of 550 men a day – the US Fifth Army is less than 20 miles (32 km) from Bologna (→ 26).

A few Germans give up the fight.

V2 menace returns

Britain, 3 October
Germany resumed its V2 bombardment of Britain today from new launch sites in the Netherlands. Some 35 V2 rockets were fired before 18 September when the Germans withdrew to sites further east; 44 V2s were then fired from Denmark at East Anglia, but only one caused any casualties. Now London is back in range (→ 10/11). ▷

569

Eisenhower warns of battle fatigue threat to victory

Europe, 4 October

There are signs that morale among the Allied armies in north-west Europe is not what it was a few weeks ago. A month ago it looked as though final victory was but a few weeks away. Since then there has been the failure at Arnhem, and desperate fighting continues around Aachen and Metz. The German armies have largely recovered from the disasters of the summer and have signalled their intention of fighting every inch of the Allied way forward.

The increased intensity of the fighting has caused a sharp rise in the number of battle fatigue casualties. In this context General Eisenhower has today issued to all combat units a report by the office of the US surgeon general on the subject. This stresses that battle fatigue, or shell shock, as it used to be called in the Great War, is caused by the fear of being killed or maimed, and affects every combat soldier. "Thus psychiatric casualties are as inevitable as gunshot or shrapnel wounds in warfare," says the report.

Battle fatigue can, however, be kept to a minimum through effective and caring leadership and regular rest from combat. Many of the best junior leaders have now become casualties, though, and some divisions have been in action since D-Day. This has happened because commanders are always tempted to use well-proven formations rather than fresh untried troops to tackle key objectives.

The British are more conscious than the Americans of the need to husband their fighting resources. Five years of war have created a manpower crisis, especially in the infantry, and Montgomery is being forced to disband some units in order to maintain others. The Americans, on the other hand, continue to send fresh divisions over to Europe and to keep units in the front line for much longer.

Poles lose the struggle for Warsaw

Warsaw, 3 October

Warsaw has fallen. The last shots were fired at 10pm yesterday after a struggle lasting 63 days against the full weight of the *Wehrmacht* and SS. Attacked by two *Panzer* divisions, General Bor-Komorowski, the commander of the Polish armed forces, had no ammunition, no food and no hope of Russian rescue. He had to surrender.

Surprisingly, the Germans, out of respect for the tremendous fight put up by the Poles, have agreed to treat them as prisoners of war rather than *franc-tireurs*. Some 15,000 Polish fighters died in the uprising along with an estimated 200,000 civilians, killed as the city was torn apart by bombs and shells. The Germans have lost 10,000 dead.

Announcing the surrender last night, Stanislaw Mikolajczyk, the Polish prime minister in exile, said: "The cessation of military operations took place after all supplies had been exhausted. The garrison and people were completely starv-

The beginning of their final journey: citizens of Warsaw are rounded up.

ed. Fighting ceased after vain attempts to fight their way out, after the successive fall of the Old Town, the suburbs of Mokotow, Zoliborz and finally, after all the hopes of relief from outside had vanished."

The surrendered fighters are being marched off to the prison camps, but as they go they sing their national anthem and are embraced by the civilian survivors. The spirit of Poland lives on (→ 24/11).

Germans fight for Riga as Red Army steps up Baltic offensive

Moscow, 5 October

The Red Army has launched a new offensive against the Germans in the Baltic in its carefully-staged build-up to the invasion of East Prussia. According to German reports, four tank corps and 14 rifle divisions have attacked their posi-

tions between Riga, the capital of Latvia, and Tilsit, in East Prussia.

If this new thrust succeeds it will effectively cut off the remnants of Army Group North which have retreated into Courland. At the same time Riga itself is being threatened by Russian forces which have cap-

tured the railway town of Ogre, 20 miles (32 km) to the south-east. There is no doubt that Germany intends to fight to retain control of Riga. Refugees escaping from the city report that the Germans are continuing to strengthen their defences (→ 10).

RAF bombs breach the Dutch sea wall

Netherlands, 3 October

Seven RAF Mosquitoes and 252 Lancaster bombers today breached the sea wall protecting the Dutch island of Walcheren, whose heavy guns threaten Allied shipping approaching Antwerp. Some of the attackers dropped 21-foot-long "Tallboy" bombs, each weighing 12,000 pounds. These penetrate hard targets, then trigger an explosion whose shock waves are as destructive as a direct hit. Over 100 islanders are feared to have died in the raid, either from the bombing itself or when the sea rushed through the breached wall (→ 25).

October 4. Blakenhall Crescent in East London, where a German V2 rocket exploded yesterday evening. Rescue teams go to work on the rubble and splintered wood, under which eight people are feared to have died.

Auschwitz workers attack camp guards

Auschwitz-Birkenau, 7 October
A violent revolt, yet more violently crushed, broke out at noon today during roll-call. Men of the "privileged" *Sonderkommando* [special commando], whose task is to empty the gas chambers of their dead fellow Jews, incinerate them and then scatter the ashes around the camp, attacked the SS guards with smuggled hammers and pickaxes.

The revolt spread as the Sonderkommandos set fire to their barracks and to Crematorium IV. SS reinforcements arrived immediately, wielding machine guns and hand-grenades against the prisoners' crowbars.

The blazing gas-chamber sparked off a mass breakout by Sonderkommandos loading the ovens in the next compound, Crematorium II. They killed three SS men and cut the wire, only to be machine-gunned dead or captured by patrolmen with dogs. The survivors can expect to be killed and burnt (→ 20).

British troops land on Greek mainland

Patras, Greece, 5 October
Peasants working their rockstrewn, barren fields watched as the multicoloured parachutes filled the clear blue sky before running to greet their liberators. The British Army has fulfilled the promise which it made three years ago – to return and liberate Greece.

The airborne forces dropped yesterday, a reconnaissance in force while the main force was still steaming towards the Peloponnese. Their first target was an airfield – which was found deserted and demolished, although the first Dakota was able to land within hours.

By the time the main force came ashore today, it was clear that the Germans are evacuating the Peloponnese. The British are hurrying eastwards along the Gulf of Corinth in the hope of trapping the 10,000-strong garrison in Athens.

The liberators are shocked by the level of starvation they see in every Greek face. Money is useless; food, cigarettes and quinine are the only acceptable currency (→ 7).

October

Su	Mo	Tu	We	Th	Fr	Sa
1	2	3	4	5	6	7
8	9	10	11	12	13	14
15	16	17	18	19	20	21
22	23	24	25	26	27	28
29	30	31				

8. Aachen: US troops start to move in on the city in a pincer operation (→ 10).

8. Britain: Two new ministries, of social insurance and civil aviation, are formed.

8. New York: Wendell Willkie, the Republican politician who acted as Roosevelt's special envoy, dies aged 52.

9. Belgium: Canadian troops land at Breskens, on the Scheldt estuary (→ 4/11).

9. Philippines: US forces enter the Lingayen Gulf (→ 12).

9. Pacific: A US task force bombards Marcus Island.

10. North Borneo: American B-24 bombers raid the oil refinery at Balikpapan, which produces 40 per cent of Japan's lubricating oils.

10. Latvia: Soviet and German troops join battle for the capital, Riga. →

10. Aachen: US troops warn that the city will be destroyed unless the garrison surrenders within 24 hours. →

10. Greece: British and Greek forces capture Corinth (→ 12).

12. East China Sea: Carriers of the US Third Fleet, under Admiral William Halsey, attack Formosa [*Taiwan*] (→ 14).

12. Yugoslavia: A joint force of Tito's partisans and Russian soldiers captures Subotica, cutting the Belgrade to Budapest railway line (→ 20).

12. Hungary: Soviet troops capture Oradea (→ 15).

12. Mediterranean: British commandos land on Corfu. →

13. Moscow: Stalin promises Churchill that the USSR will declare war on Japan once Germany has been defeated.

13. Antwerp: Two V2 rockets are fired on the city, killing 42 people.

14. Formosa: The US attack has destroyed 321 Japanese aircraft and 40 destroyers, for the loss of 71 US planes, two destroyers and a carrier (→ 18).

14. Germany: 1,013 RAF raiders drop 3,574 tons of bombs on Duisburg (→ 15).

American troops enter Aachen suburbs

American gunners during a lull in the fighting in Bismarckstrasse, Aachen.

Aachen, 13 October
American artillery and infantry today battered their way into the industrial suburbs of Aachen, Germany's most westerly city. Infantry preceded by fighter bombers acting as airborne artillery were opposed by 150 *Luftwaffe* fighters, of which a dozen were shot down, and by suicidal counter-attacks on the ground against a high ridge east of the city held by the Americans. At dusk, patrols probing into the debris found only fires, rubble and bodies until they came to the city centre, where fighting flared afresh.

Aachen saw the enthronement of 37 German emperors; now it occupies a key position on the Siegfried Line. Flames rising from it can be seen 40 miles away in Cologne. As the first major German centre to be invaded, it will not be surrendered without a bitter battle (→ 19).

Allies agree to set up "United Nations"

Washington, DC, 9 October
Details were announced here today of the conference held at Dumbarton Oaks, a mansion near Washington, to decide the structure of the post-war United Nations Organization. The conference broke up without fully resolving the deep divisions between the US, the USSR and Britain. Mr Roosevelt has succeeded in getting China counted as one of the four "great powers". (France will form a fifth when she has a legitimate government.) The USSR has successfully demanded a veto for each great power. It also wanted a vote for each of its 16 constituent republics, since several of the British Dominions have votes. A compromise was eventually reached by giving votes to three of the Soviet republics.

Delegates at the UN conference in Washington: deep divisions still exist.

Battles flare along 1,000-mile front

Baltic advance cuts off German soldiers

Moscow, 10 October
Soviet forces today reached the Baltic coast of Lithuania on the outskirts of Memel and at Palanga, cutting off German forces in the besieged Latvian capital of Riga and the Courland peninsula. Memel, the city which Hitler annexed in March 1939, is holding out against the Red Army's First Baltic Front under General Bagramyan. German reinforcements are being rushed northwards, but their aim is primarily defensive: to stop the Russians reaching East Prussia.

Tallinn, the Estonian capital, fell to the Russians on 22 September, just eight days after they opened their current offensive. With Riga apparently doomed and most of Lithuania now under Russian control, the Germans in Courland can escape only by sea. It is thought that as many as 33 divisions of the German Sixteen and Eighteenth Armies of Army Group North

Riga: blasted by retreating Nazis.

under General Schorner have retreated into Courland with much of their heavy equipment.

While the German navy still controls the Baltic with heavy ships like the *Admiral Hipper*, Schorner should be safe, but he is in danger of becoming irrelevant as the Russians sweep on to East Prussia (→ 19).

"Panzers" launch attack in Hungary

Budapest, 10 October
One of the fiercest tank battles yet seen in this war is raging on the Hungarian plain around the ancient city of Debrecen where two *Panzer* divisions of Germany's Army Group South, under the command of General Johannes Friessner, have cut off three of Marshal Rodion Malinovsky's tank corps advancing from the Ukraine.

German Tiger and Panther tanks are locked in combat with Russian T34s equipped with 85mm guns in a swirling melee. The Germans, supported by their Hungarian allies, are inflicting heavy casualties on the Russians who are supported by their new Roumanian allies.

Despite his initial success, which has given Hitler hope that his military fortunes have changed, Friessner knows that he will be unable to maintain his position once the full strength of Malinovsky's forces its brought to bear (→ 12).

Rommel, suspected of bomb plot, kills himself with poison

Rommel: linked to 20 July plot.

Ulm, 14 October
At his home on the Danube near Ulm, Rommel was visited today by two generals sent by Hitler. Soon afterwards he went upstairs to his wife. When he came down he said to his son Manfred: "I have just had to tell your mother that I shall be dead in a quarter of an hour." Germany's most popular general had been linked to the July plot against Hitler; the Fuhrer told him that if he took poison his family would not be arrested. Officially, he has died of wounds received when the enemy strafed his car. He will be given a state funeral (→ 15).

Churchill and Stalin on future of Europe

Moscow, 9 October
Churchill began his talks in Moscow today by asking Stalin about his intentions in eastern and southern Europe, where Soviet forces are driving out the Germans. Churchill said he was "not worrying very much about Roumania" – that country was very much a Russian affair. As for Yugoslavia, the British prime minister suggested a 50-50 division of influence. On Greece, Churchill was firm; he said that Britain, as the leading Mediterranean power, must have the major influence.

Allies, helped by Greek partisans, liberate Athens and Piraeus

Athens, 14 October
It was a sight that would have delighted Byron. Here, in the shadow of the Acropolis, was an English earl leading a small number of British troops and an ever-growing band of Greek partisans into the heart of this tortured city. Colonel Earl Jellicoe, a legend among Greek guerrillas, and his men have marched over 28 miles (45 km) of demolished roads from the airfield at Megara which they captured a few days ago.

The main British occupation force, Operation Manna, landed at Megara today. An enormous fleet of RN and Greek cruisers and destroyers, under the command of Rear-Admiral J M Mansfield, is disembarking two British brigades. First, they face the major task of feeding this city. Tins of bully beef, given readily by British soldiers, are being traded for gold in the black market. Electricity and water supplies were blown up by the Germans before they left, and a

Liberation – and a Union Jack for a solemn Greek boy outside Athens.

call has gone out for engineers to rebuild them.

The second task for the British is to maintain law and order in a country facing the threat of a civil war. Churchill fears that, in the absence of a properly-constituted government, communists will step into the

power vacuum left by the Germans. The communist "National Army of Liberation" (ELAS) and the nationalist EDES faction have been squaring up for a fight for years. Few walls in Athens are now without the red and blue propaganda of the opposing forces (→ 18).

572

1944

October

Su	Mo	Tu	We	Th	Fr	Sa
1	2	3	4	5	6	7
8	9	10	11	12	13	14
15	16	17	18	19	20	21
22	23	24	25	26	27	28
29	30	31				

15. Latvia: Riga falls to the Red Army.

15. Germany: Rommel's death, from "war wounds", is announced (→ 17).

16. Britain: Private Salter of the Pioneer Corps is the first British soldier to be demobilized, and given a regulation "demob suit".

16. Budapest: The Hungarian government is arrested and sent to Germany.→

17. Ulm: Rommel is given a state funeral, and von Rundstedt gives the oration in Hitler's name, calling him "a tireless fighter in the cause of the Fuhrer ... imbued with the National Socialist spirit".

18. Tokyo: The government orders Operation *Sho-go* [Victory], intended to remove the US threat to the Japanese home islands (→ 20).

18. Germany: Hitler orders the call-up of all able-bodied men between the ages of 16 and 60 for the *Volkssturm* [People's Front] home guard.

18. Athens: The premier, George Papandreou, and the Greek government, exiled since 1941, return to Greece (→ 1/11).

19. Germany: The Red Army pushes into East Prussia (→ 22).

19. Aachen: The German commander exhorts his men to fight to the last man.→

20. Hungary: Eichmann starts the rapid deportation of Jews to the death camps again.

20. Auschwitz-Birkenau: Huge bundles of camp documents are burnt in the crematorium to try to conceal the evidence of deaths, tortures and medical experiments (→ 25).

20. Marseilles: Pierre Laval is sentenced to death *in absentia* for collaborating with the Germans.

20-21. Philippines: US forces repel a night attack on Leyte, killing over 600 Japanese.→

21. Palau Islands: Japanese resistance on Angaur ends, leaving the other islands isolated and defenceless. For casualties of 264 dead and 1,355 injured, US troops have killed 1,300 Japanese (→ 22).

MacArthur keeps Philippines promise

Leyte, Philippines, 20 October

At noon today, two hours after the first US soldier had landed, General Douglas MacArthur, wearing a crisp new uniform specially donned for the occasion, stepped from the cruiser USS *Nashville* into the knee-deep surf on the east coast of Leyte island, in the central Philippines, to keep his promise made in 1942 of "I shall return".

Two hours later, with the Philippine president in exile, Sergio Osmena, by his side, MacArthur proclaimed in a voice trembling with emotion: "People of the Philippines, I have returned! ... Rally to me!" He said that the blow at Leyte would split the 225,000-man Japanese Philippines garrison in two, making its forces on Mindanao redundant.

The 600-ship invasion armada, the largest amphibious operation in the Pacific, had been accelerated by two months after reconnaissance had revealed surprising gaps in the defence forces. The landings began three days ago with the capture of three offshore islands. Tonight 100,000 US Sixth Army troops are dug in around Leyte's capital, Tacloban, and Dulag to the south.

The Leyte landings surprised the defenders, who put up little opposition after their beach pillboxes were captured. Most of Leyte's 21,500-strong garrison has now withdrawn inland. The Japanese Philippines C-in-C, Gen Yamashita, was expecting the main attack to be against Luzon, hit by US air raids again yesterday, and is hurriedly moving men to Leyte (→ 21).

The return: General MacArthur wades ashore on Leyte with fellow officers.

Heavily-laden US troops get down as enemy fire passes overhead.

Roosevelt to recall "Vinegar Joe" Stilwell

Washington, 19 October

Strong clashes between Allied leaders in China as the Japanese offensive progressed this autumn have persuaded President Roosevelt that the irascible General Joseph "Vinegar Joe" Stilwell, chief of staff to Chiang Kai-shek, had to go. It is surprising that he was not recalled sooner. Chiang had demanded his recall, claiming that Stilwell had no intention of co-operating with him. Roosevelt, finally convinced that the two were incompatible, informed Chiang yesterday that Stilwell was to be relieved and that he would supply another chief of staff.

It was Chiang's belief that Stilwell favoured the reconquest of Burma rather than the war in eastern China. Stilwell never hid his contempt for Chiang and referred to him both publicly and privately by his absurd codename "Peanut". Stilwell is to take up a desk job in the Pentagon. Mountbatten's deputy chief of staff, Lt-Gen A C Wedemeyer, replaces Stilwell as Chiang's adviser (→ 10/11).

Allies hit Duisburg to prove air power

Germany, 15 October

In a massive display of Allied air superiority, British and American bombers have this weekend battered the Ruhr. Last night the RAF attacked Duisburg in what the air ministry described as its biggest single night operation. The attacks yesterday and today involved 1,013 RAF Lancasters and Halifaxes plus 1,251 USAAF Flying Fortresses and Liberators. Cologne and the Sorpe dam were also hit (→ 30).

▷

Donitz gives new life to the U-boat battles in Atlantic

Berlin, 21 October
Once again Grand Admiral Donitz is showing himself to be a formidable opponent. The Royal Navy hoped that the war at sea would be virtually over as soon as the Allied forces captured the heavily-armoured French bases which have harboured the U-boats for most of the war.

Donitz was ahead of them. He moved the main U-boat fleet out to bases in Norway and has been rapidly refitting the fleet with a newer and more sophisticated *Schnorkel*. Yet despite the new device, the Allies managed to sink 19 U-boats last month.

The advantages of the Schnorkel were demonstrated by Count von Matuschka in U482. He did a round voyage from Norway of 2,729 miles (4,392 km), over 90 per cent of which was under water. He preyed undetected on the main sea route north of Ireland and sank the corvette *Hurst Castle* and four ships.

The Schnorkel is a long tube which extends up to the surface and enables air to be drawn into the submarine while it is submerged. It has a valve which closes if a large wave sweeps over the tube. The valve stops water getting in – but it also cuts off the air, brings the U-boat crew near to suffocation, and hurting their eardrums when the air rushes in again. The Germans first started to experiment with Schnorkel devices as early as 1940.

Donitz started to fit them in large numbers as soon as he realized that British aircraft were decimating the U-boats. The Schnorkel not only allows them to stay submerged but also enables them to pick up long-range wireless signals undetected by the British. It does tend to slow a U-boat by several knots. So far German successes have been small in number. But the presence of the Schnorkel boats is still tying up a large number of Royal Navy ships in escort duties for merchant ships.

Partisans and Russians free Belgrade

The partisans march in triumph.

Belgrade, 20 October
The First Proletarian Division, the elite formation of Tito's Army of National Liberation, helped to drive the Germans out of Belgrade today, freeing Yugoslavia's capital from the hated occupiers. Tito can now enter Belgrade in triumph.

It was, in fact, a combined operation between partisans led by two of Tito's most successful commanders, Dapcevich and Popovich, and troops of General Tolbukhin's Third Ukrainian Front. The strategy, if not the tactics, of the operation had been worked out with Stalin during Tito's clandestine visit to Moscow last month.

The liberation of Belgrade is a tremendous political victory for Tito, who has emerged as the clear winner in the struggle for power inside Yugoslavia with the royalist Draza Mihailovich. There seems little doubt now that he will impose a communist regime on Yugoslavia after the war.

The battle for Belgrade was a bloody affair, with the Germans fighting desperately to keep open their line of retreat from Greece and Albania. This retreat is under constant harassment from the RAF and USAAF, who are cooperating with the partisans.

The fall of the city will make tremendous difficulties for General Lohr's Army Group E on its fighting retreat to the north. Lohr is in grave personal danger. His occupation has been marked by cruelty. If he should fall into the partisans' hands, they would show him no mercy (→ 1/11).

Balkans collapse under weight of Red Army's non-stop drive

Belgrade, 20 October
The Balkan states are falling like dominoes to the Red Army. Roumania and Bulgaria collapsed swiftly and are now fighting against their erstwhile German allies. The Yugoslavs, who have conducted a brave guerrilla war against the Germans, have liberated their own capital and joined the Russians in harassing the retreating Germans.

Now it is Hungary's turn. The Hungarian army has been fighting with more conviction against the advancing Russians than it ever did as the *Wehrmacht's* ally on the eastern front, but there are signs that its resistance is coming to an end.

The First Hungarian Army which, with a stiffening of Germans, has been holding the Carpathian passes has thrown in its hand, and General Petrov's Fourth Ukrainian Front is pouring south through the mountain gorges which lead down into the valley of the upper Tisza.

At the same time Malinovsky, having defeated Friessner in the tank battle of Debrecen, is driving north towards Budapest. The Hungarian capital is in turmoil, with huge numbers of refugees passing through the city, and the government is appealing for discipline: "Panic-stricken flight must give way to calm and manliness." Another domino is about to fall (→ 29).

THE RED ARMY'S BALKAN OFFENSIVE

Warsaw
POLAND
Prague
Cracow
Lwow
Kiev
SOVIET UNION
Vienna
Budapest
Debrecen
HUNGARY
Odessa
Zagreb
ROUMANIA
Belgrade
Bucharest
Sarajevo
Sept: Bulgaria changed sides
YUGOSLAVIA
Sofia
Skoplje
BULGARIA
Tirana
Istanbul
100 miles
160 km
TURKEY
GREECE
Athens

Russian front line, 1 Sept
Russian front line, 20 Oct
Yugoslav partisan attacks

© Chronicle Communications Ltd.

German resistance at Aachen is broken

Civilian refugees pause to watch their defeated troops marching off as PoWs.

Aachen, 21 October
Aachen has fallen to the Allies after a ten-day siege and desperate efforts by elite German formations, including paratroopers, to relieve the city. The city was taken only after close-quarter battles fought from house to house. Five brave attempts to break the siege line were made last night, all broken by American fire power. This morning the garrison commander, Col Gerhardt Wilck, sent two US captives as messengers to negotiate surrender. With about 400 men he marched to the headquarters of Lt-Col John Cortez to insist upon proper treat-ment for his defeated soldiers. From the back of a US Jeep he told his men: "I believe further fighting is useless. I have acted against my orders, to fight to the last man. The American commander says I cannot give you 'Sieg Heil' or 'Heil Hitler', but we say it in our hearts."

The garrison, totalling 1,626 men, had run out of food, ammunition and water. Most of the town's ancient streets had become impassable because of debris. In the centre only the mediaeval cathedral was still basically intact. The civilian population demanded a surrender ten days ago (→ 16/11).

Horthy captured by "Mickey Mouse"

Budapest, 15 October
Admiral Horthy, the Hungarian regent, has been seized by the Germans a few hours after making a broadcast announcing that he was going to ask for an armistice.

Horthy's overthrow, which involved the kidnapping of his son, was carried out in Operation Mickey Mouse by the SS men Otto "Scarface" Skorzeny and Erich von dem Bach-Zelewski. It was Skorzeny who rescued Mussolini and Zelewski who destroyed Warsaw. The new premier is "acting regent" Major Ferenc Szalasi, the leader of the fascist Arrow Cross, who has pledged to "go on fighting alongside Germany and Japan" (→ 16).

Allies lay down law for occupied areas

Allied HQ, 18 October
Plans for an Allied military government of Germany were unveiled today at Eisenhower's HQ. The German government will be suspended; all state and Nazi Party property will be seized; armed resistance will be punishable by death; the courts of law will be purged of Nazi influence; newspapers will be shut down and new ones licensed.

English will be the official language of government. Fraternization between Allied personnel and German civilians will be forbidden. German laws involving discrimination on grounds of race, religion, or political opinion will be abrogated.

1944
October

Su	Mo	Tu	We	Th	Fr	Sa
1	2	3	4	5	6	7
8	9	10	11	12	13	14
15	16	17	18	19	20	21
22	23	24	25	26	27	28
29	30	31				

22. Pacific: Two Japanese squadrons sail from Brunei, one heading for the Mindoro Strait and the other for the Jolo Sea (→ 23).

22. East Prussia: Soviet forces stop short of Insterburg, 45 miles (72 km) from Hitler's Rastenburg headquarters (→ 1/11).

23. Leyte Gulf: The US submarines *Dace* and *Darter* sink the Japanese heavy cruisers *Atago* and *Maya* and hit the cruiser *Takao* (→ 24).

23. Paris: Treason trials open, with a journalist sentenced to death for collaborating with the Nazis.

23. London: The Allies recognise de Gaulle's cabinet as the provisional government of France.

24. Philippines: US troops land on Samar, a Japanese dive-bomber destroys the US carrier *Princeton*, and US aircraft sink the battleship *Musashi*, drowning over a thousand crewmen.→

25. Norway: Soviet forces seize the port of Kirkenes.

25. Netherlands: US troops attack the German pocket south of the Maas (→ 27).

25. Berlin: Himmler orders the *Reich* Anatomical Institute's collection of Jewish death camp victims' skeletons to be destroyed (→ 31).

26. Italy: Heavy rain halts the Allied advance (→ 31).

27. Netherlands: British troops capture Tilburg and Canadian troops take Bergen-op-Zoom.→

28. Burma: Chinese forces capture Myothit (→ 1/11).

28. Moscow: Bulgaria and the USSR sign an armistice under which Bulgarian armed forces come under Soviet control.

29. Moscow: Stalin orders the seizure of Budapest, regardless of cost (→ 1/11).

30. Leyte: US forces capture Dagami (→ 1/11).

31. Auschwitz-Birkenau: The gas chambers are closed down. The last transport, 1,700 Jews from Theresienstadt, was gassed yesterday (→ 1/11).

Air raid pinpoints "Gestapo" HQ

Aarhus, Jutland, 31 October
A young Danish pastor tortured to breaking point by the *Gestapo* at Aarhus university was set free by a pinpoint bombing raid today. The raid, led by the same Australian squadron that hit Amiens jail, destroyed archives that threatened the continued existence of Denmark's resistance network.

A total of 24 Mosquitoes flew over the North Sea at sea level in response to coded pleas from Danish patriots for help. Their bombs struck as Pastor Harald Sandbaek was about to tell what he knew. His torturers were killed. When compatriots dug him free, he begged them to kill him rather than risk his recapture. They smuggled him to Sweden instead.

More cities bombed

Germany, 30-31 October
Cologne was blitzed tonight by 493 RAF heavy bombers. The raid, in which 3,451 tons of bombs and 610 tons of incendiaries were dropped, killed 554 Germans.

Britain said that the destruction was necessary to ensure that Cologne was not used as an "advance base". In other raids aimed at oil refineries, 671 US bombers attacked eleven targets. A planned raid by 459 B-17s on the oil plant at Luena had to turn back because of bad weather (→ 1/11).

US crushes Japan in "greatest-ever sea battle"

Round One: Japan prepares its bait

Philippines, 24 October

The warships of the American and Japanese navies are today locked in what is potentially the greatest battle ever fought at sea, involving 282 warships around the Philippines.

Japan has thrown virtually its entire navy into the battle in an attempt to destroy the US Third and Seventh Fleets. The trigger for the Japanese operation (*Sho-1*) was the American plan to invade Leyte. Admiral Toyoda hoped to lure the US fleets away from Leyte to enable Vice-Admiral Kurita's First Striking Force heading from Brunei and Vice-Admiral Shima's Second Striking Force from Japan to attack the Leyte landing fleet. The bait was Admiral Ozawa's carrier force with Japan's four remaining aircraft carriers.

But in the early hours of yesterday two American submarines spotted Kurita's Task Force A – Kurita had split his fleet in order to attack Leyte from two directions. Later the same morning the US subs sank two cruisers and crippled another. Worse for the Japanese, the US admirals knew of their approach and were drawn to the strike force, not the decoy. Planes from US carriers of Admiral Halsey's Third Fleet joined the battle, as did Japanese planes from bases on Luzon and Ozawa's carriers.

Off the east coast of Luzon the US carrier, *Princeton*, was the first victim today: abandoned after being bombed by Japanese planes. A light cruiser and five destroyers were also damaged. Then, in the Sibuyan Sea, US planes descended on Kurita's naval force, sinking the battleship, *Musashi*. Kurita then headed west away from Leyte.

As news of this apparent withdrawal reached Halsey, US reconnaissance planes sighted Ozawa's carrier fleet further north off Cape Engano. Halsey tonight ordered his carriers to head north to attack Ozawa. The Japanese bait has been taken and Kurita has turned his strike force back towards Leyte and a US Seventh Fleet now lacking air cover (→ 26).

A suicidal Japanese pilot streaks across the Pacific sky towards a US ship.

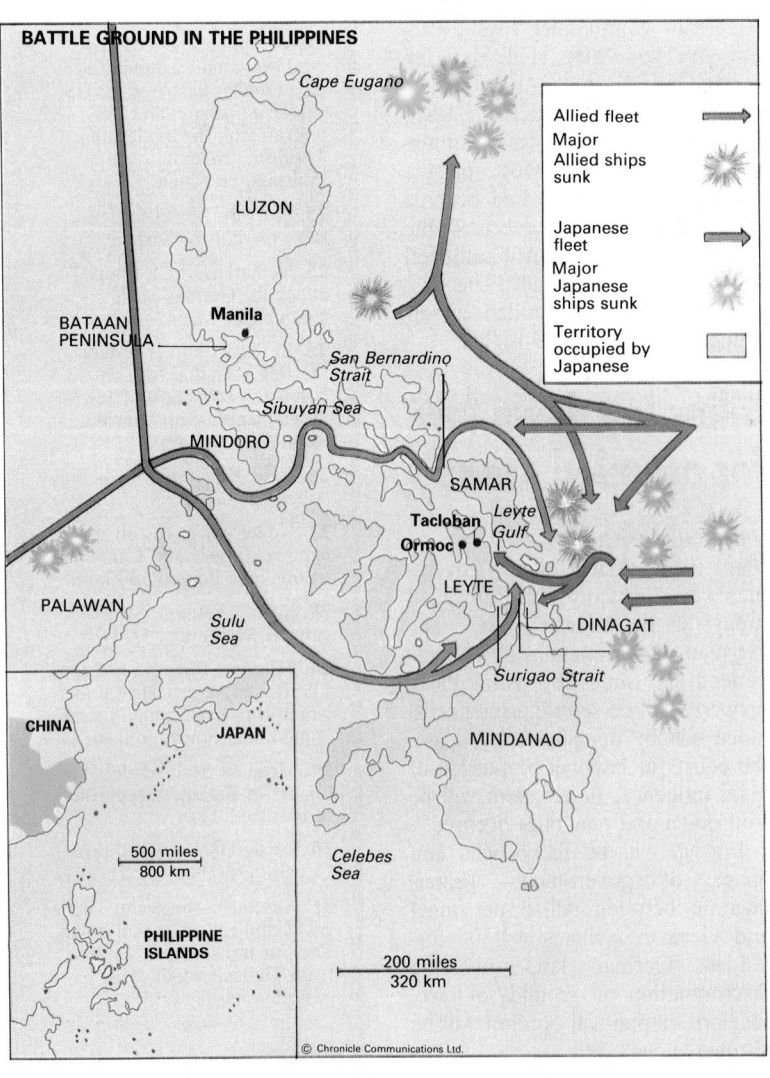

BATTLE GROUND IN THE PHILIPPINES

Cape Eugano

LUZON

| Allied fleet |
| Major Allied ships sunk |
| Japanese fleet |
| Major Japanese ships sunk |
| Territory occupied by Japanese |

BATAAN PENINSULA

Manila

San Bernardino Strait

Sibuyan Sea

MINDORO

SAMAR

Tacloban   Leyte Gulf

Ormoc

LEYTE

PALAWAN

Sulu Sea

DINAGAT

Surigao Strait

500 miles
800 km

CHINA   JAPAN   MINDANAO

Celebes Sea

PHILIPPINE ISLANDS

200 miles
320 km

© Chronicle Communications Ltd.

Round Two: the US wins by knock-out

Philippines, 26 October

Three days of sea warfare involving 282 ships – more than in any previous naval engagement – have ended with a crushing victory for the US Navy. Thirty-four warships have been sunk, of which no fewer than 28 were Japanese, including their last four aircraft carriers.

The fighting was focussed on the landlocked seas of Leyte Gulf in the Philippines, but in fact occurred in four separate areas: the Sibuyan Sea [*see report opposite*], the Surigao Strait, and off Samar Island and Cape Engano. On 24 October Admiral Halsey had despatched his carriers to meet Ozawa's carrier force off Cape Engano. As the US carriers sped north, a force under Admiral Nishimura entered the Surigao Strait to rendezvous with Kurita in Leyte Gulf. A US task force, under Rear-Admiral Oldendorf, attacked in one of the rare direct confrontations between rival battleships; Nishimura was the clear loser, going down in his own flagship, *Yamashiro*, one of the two Japanese battleships to be lost.

But while Oldendorf was tangling with Nishimura, Kurita's force had passed through the San Bernardino Strait unobserved and off Samar attacked Admiral T L Sprague's Seventh Fleet task force supporting the Leyte landings. Five US warships were sunk before Kurita surprisingly withdrew, fearing attack from carrier-based planes.

In fact, the US carriers were 300 miles (480 km) further north, engaging the Japanese carrier force. By this morning all four Japanese carriers had been sunk, along with two destroyers. Their loss capped a disastrous operation for Japan. US air and naval power has finished the Imperial Japanese Navy as a fighting force. Yet there was one worrying portent for the Americans. Yesterday, at the height of the battle, Japan unleashed suicidal *kamikaze* pilots who deliberately crashed their bomb-laden planes onto enemy targets. And they have claimed their first victim: the US escort carrier, *St Lo* (→ 25/11).

Allies set to open the battle for Antwerp

Netherlands, 31 October

The German Fifteenth Army is in full retreat from the southern Netherlands, with troops packing the ferries across the Maas and crowding the last two bridges at Moerdijk. Two German columns, a six-mile-long one approaching the bridges, and a second, 12 miles long, beyond the river, are being attacked from the air. The final battle to clear the approaches to Antwerp is about to start. Most of the Beveland isthmus has been cleared, but German positions on Walcheren, at the entrance to the Scheldt estuary, must be taken before the port can open.

The Americans, who captured Aachen ten days ago, today appointed a non-Nazi *burgomeister*; he cannot be named, because the Nazis have threatened death to the relatives of anyone who takes office under the Allies.

Further south, Patton's US Third Army is stalled for the time being on the Moselle. Aggrieved at being assigned lowest priority for supplies of fuel, he has sent his officers foraging among the dumps of the US First Army; they have returned with "quite a bit of gasoline". Though Patton is authorized only to carry out "continuous reconnaissance", he intends to head for the Saar.

The French First Army is pushing into the Vosges with the aim of seizing the Belfort Gap and striking north to Strasburg (→ 1/11).

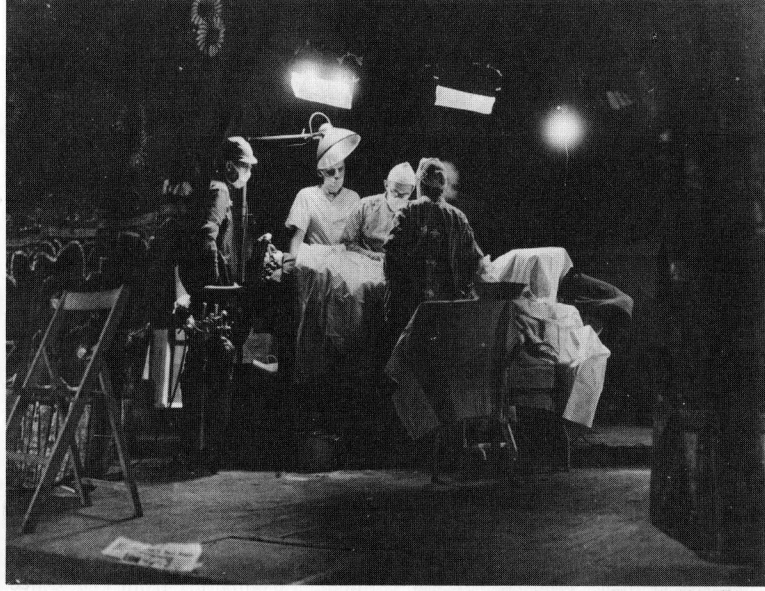

Offstage, the fighting; on this old stage doctors operate on a wounded man.

Italy's "D-Day Dodgers" face hard winter

Italy, 27 October

There is one song they do not – by order – play on the British Forces Broadcasting Service in Italy. The German *Lili Marlene* remains top of the Eighth Army hit parade, with Glenn Miller running a close second. The frowned-upon song (sung to the tune of *Lili Marlene*) is based on the alleged, and since denied, remark by a British MP, Lady (Nancy) Astor, and runs:

We are the D-Day dodgers,
out in Italy,
– always on the vino,
always on the spree;
Eighth Army scroungers
and their tanks,
We live in Rome among the Yanks.
We are the D-Day dodgers,
In Sunny Italy.

Sunny Italy it is not. Once again the Eighth Army is faced with a winter which has allied itself with the Germans, while west of the Apennines the US Fifth Army today called off its latest offensive. Despite huge casualty lists – more than 20,000 men have been killed, wounded or taken prisoner since Cassino – the Allied armies here have had little share in the world headlines since the Anzio landings, and are feeling forgotten (→ 1/11).

November

Su	Mo	Tu	We	Th	Fr	Sa
			1	2	3	4
5	6	7	8	9	10	11
12	13	14	15	16	17	18
19	20	21	22	23	24	25
26	27	28	29	30		

1. Tokyo: The Japanese army opens a bombing campaign against the US mainland, launching the first of 9,000 explosive balloons designed to float across the Pacific on the prevailing westerly wind.

1. Yugoslavia: Tito and the prime minister of the government-in-exile sign an agreement on a new constitution, in which King Peter II will continue to act as head of state (→ 2).

1. Greece: British forces take Salonika and the Germans evacuate Florina: relief measures are taken to alleviate famine in Athens.

1. Netherlands: British commandos destroy German field batteries on Walcheren island, and Canadian troops land on the island, only to be repelled by the Germans.→

2. Palau Islands: US forces renew their efforts to crush Japanese positions on Mount Umurbrogol, but meet strong resistance (→ 3).

2. Yugoslavia: Tito's partisans capture Zadar (→ 6).

2. Netherlands: Allied troops seize Flushing (→ 3).

3. Mariana Islands: Japanese planes raid USAAF airbases on Saipan and Tinian (→ 5).

3. China: Chinese troops retake Lungling, in Yunnan province and, in north Burma, reach the Irrawaddy river at Shegwu (→ 8).

3. Netherlands: The Germans end their resistance in the "Breskens pocket", and the Canadians capture 12,500 for the loss of 314 dead (→ 5).

4. Hungary: The Russians halt 40 miles from Budapest, held up by stiff resistance, rain and exhaustion (→ 15).

4. Germany: 1,160 USAAF bombers and 890 escorts raid oil and fuel installations at eight targets (→ 30).

4. Belgium: Allied minesweepers start clearing the Scheldt estuary (→ 16).

4. Washington: Field Marshal Sir John Dill, the head of the British Inter-Service Mission to Washington, dies.

Budapest set to be bitter battleground

Moscow, 1 November

Marshal Malinovsky's troops, advancing across Kecskemet Heath south-east of Budapest, are today within 37 miles (59 km) of the Hungarian capital. The town of Kecskemet, the key to the southern defences of the capital, has fallen after bitter house-to-house fighting. Moscow hopes that Malinovsky will celebrate the 27th anniversary of the Russian Revolution in a week's time with the capture of Budapest, but the Germans will not relinquish the capital without a struggle. Their position has been strengthened by the crushing of an uprising by Slovak nationalists (→ 4).

Hungarian Jews are under threat again

Budapest, 1 November

Now that the Nazis have installed a puppet government here, the reprieve for Hungary's Jews is over. Unlike Admiral Horthy (now under arrest) the regime of Ferenc Szalasi does not want to save them.

"Let no person of the Jewish race believe that ... he can circumvent the lawful measures of the Hungarian state," announced the interior minister on 18 October. Adolf Eichmann has returned to Budapest with a new plan to send the Jews to the death camps on foot, hoping that most will die on the way.

Szalasi's government will no longer recognize the passports issued to protect the Jews by the Swedish diplomat Raoul Wallenberg (→ 8/11).

I need you on the job *full time...*
DON'T GET HURT

Just an average day in the life of a global war

War at sea: fleet sails to Walcheren

Netherlands, 1 November
A naval force of 181 vessels and landing craft today carried out amphibious landings on Walcheren Island in the German-held Scheldt estuary, the gateway to Antwerp. Commandos and a British infantry brigade landed at Westkapelle and Flushing despite heavy fighting on land and at sea (→ 2).

Philippines: bitter fighting for Leyte

Philippines, 1 November
Savage fighting continues between American and Japanese forces for the island of Leyte. Offshore, *kamikaze* pilots make life difficult for US shipping. The US destroyer *Abner Read* was sunk today, three other destroyers were badly damaged, and two were hit by suicide and conventional bombers (→ 2).

Italy: advance in the north by British

Italy, 1 November
In the ongoing struggle for Italy the 10th Indian Division (V Corps) of the British Eighth Army advances to the Rabbi river at Collina, near Ravenna, building up its bridgehead across the Ronco river and taking the town of Meldola on the west bank. The 4th division is halted outside Forli airfield (→ 15).

Air war: round-the-clock Allied raids

Europe, 1 November
Daylight raids were made by the US Eighth Army Air Force against synthetic oil plants at Gelsenkirchen and railway targets in Hamm and Coblenz. All the bombers and all but one fighter returned. Last night RAF Halifaxes and Lancasters continued the offensive against the industrial centre of Cologne.

British troops with fixed bayonets comb the streets of Flushing for snipers.

Philippine guerrilla fighters welcome US invasion troops to Leyte island.

Red Army troops go into action during the Soviet advance on Budapest

Hungary: Soviet drive on Budapest

Hungary, 1 November
In a renewed thrust into Hungary, Red Army forces today took Kecskemet, Hungary's fourth-largest city, having seized 200 Hungarian towns and villages on their way. They are now just 50 miles (80 km) from Budapest and advancing along a 75-mile front between the Danube and Tisza rivers (→ 4).

Burma: British and Indians edge ahead

Burma, 1 November
Men of the British 36th Division, on the move again after a few days' rest at Mawpin, yesterday advanced two miles down the Myitkyina to Mandalay railway line, stopping one mile outside Mawlu. In the Chin Hills, troops of the 5th Indian Division wiped out a Japanese stronghold (→ 3).

East Prussia: Red Army closing in

East Prussia, 1 November
Red Army forces are closing in on East Prussia in a vast pincer movement. Pushing up from the south through Hungary and in from the west through Poland, they are now approaching the once free city of Danzig on a front along the Narew river. Waves of refugees are fleeing before the vengeful Russians (→ 20).

France: successful attack by US forces

France, 1 November
This afternoon the US 319th Infantry Regiment attacked enemy positions in the Adaucourt-Letricourt sector, on the Seille river near Nancy. Catching the Germans unawares, the Americans cleared both towns within an hour and a quarter, drove the enemy back across the river and took 162 PoWs (→ 9/11).

1944
November

Su	Mo	Tu	We	Th	Fr	Sa
			1	2	3	4
5	6	7	8	9	10	11
12	13	14	15	16	17	18
19	20	21	22	23	24	25
26	27	28	29	30		

5. Pacific: US B-29s bomb Singapore.→

5. Heusden, Netherlands: Retreating Germans herd 200 citizens into the Town Hall, and then blow it up (→6).

5. Cairo: Zionist Stern Gang terrorists assassinate Lord Moyne, the British minister resident in the Middle East.

5-6. Philippines: Admiral McCain's TF38 attacks Japanese targets in Luzon, destroying about 400 aircraft. *Kamikazes* damage the US carrier *Lexington* (→7).

6. Yugoslavia: Tito's forces take Monastir (→13).

6. Walcheren: Middelburg, the main town, falls to the Allies.→

7. Tokyo: Richard Sorge, the master Soviet spy, is executed.

7. Leyte: US troops wipe out Japanese resistance on Bloody Ridge (→13).

7. Moscow: Stalin refuses to renew diplomatic relations with Switzerland because of its ban on the Communist Party and its continuing arms trade with Germany.

8. Burma: Indian troops take Fort White, south of Tiddim (→18).

8. Hungary: Germany starts to deport 38,000 Jews to death camps in Germany (→10).

8. Germany: Major Walter Nowotny, a highly-decorated *Luftwaffe* hero with 258 "kills" under his belt, dies when his Me262 crashes.

10. China: Japanese forces capture the US airbases at Kweilin and Liuchow, in Kwangsi province (→25).

10. Auschwitz-Birkenau: The Red Cross makes a restricted visit to the camp, shielded from evidence of mass murder and atrocities (→25).

11. Tokyo: The aircraft carrier *Shinano*, with a steel and concrete construction supposedly capable of withstanding any bomb attack, joins the Japanese fleet.

11. Paris: Churchill attends the Armistice Day celebrations in Paris, and gets a wildly enthusiastic reception.

Patton's troops cross the Moselle river

Men of the Third Army cross the Moselle on a specially-built metal bridge.

Nancy, 9 November
Patton has thrown his Third Army across the Moselle on a broad front from Luneville in the south to Thionville in the north. Spearheads striking out north of Thionville have advanced to within two and a half miles of the German frontier.

Despatches from Field Marshal von Rundstedt's HQ say that Patton has deployed 1,000 tanks and 500,000 men. The Germans believe that Patton is delivering the first blow of the Allies' winter offensive.

The fortress city of Metz, which has held Patton up for the past two months, is being enveloped by pincers closing in from north and south. Allied chiefs called up Thunderbolt fighter-bombers to attack *Panzers* which have been de-laying the advance. Cheminot, south of Metz, was captured. On Patton's southern flank, tanks and infantry operating in cooperation with the Seventh Army captured Chateau-Salins, east of Nancy. In this area, Patton has driven seven miles in 72 hours, through rain and snow showers and over roads deep in mud and infested with mines.

The 1,500-foot Delme Ridge, commanding approaches to the Saar, and the last major obstacle before the German border, fell to Patton's men after a scary battle through vineyards and orchards sown with pepperpot mines hanging from tree branches. Guns and ammunition captured on the ridge were soon turned on their former owners, now in full retreat (→12).

Fall of Walcheren opens Antwerp to Allies

Walcheren, 8 November
Canadian and British commandos, joined by Dutch and French units, overran the last enemy defences on Walcheren island and opened the Scheldt estuary to Allied shipping sailing up to the port of Antwerp. Among the 8,000 prisoners taken was General Daser, commanding the German "Dyspeptic" Division, the 70th, largely manned by chronic invalids.

RAF bombers had blown a 400-yard (364-metre) gap in the West-kapelle dyke, and the whole of the centre of the island had been flooded. Backed by the guns of HMS *Warspite*, troops in amphibious craft landed on sanddunes and, waist-deep in water, advanced into Middelburg, the island capital, where Dutch families and German troops jammed the upper storey of houses. Fighting came to a halt as the Dutch welcomed the liberators. The Germans made no attempt to resist; they sat watching the cheering crowds before being taken prisoner and evacuated by boat. It will be two or three weeks before Antwerp can be opened. The 70-mile (110-km) Scheldt channel must be swept for mines and Antwerp's port installations repaired.

Chinese "Quisling" dies of pneumonia

Tokyo, 10 November
Wang Ching-wei, the leader and founder of China's Nanking-based collaborationist regime, the Reformed *Kuomintang*, died today of pneumonia in a Tokyo hospital. He was 62. Leadership of the regime passes to Ch'en Kungpo, acting head of state for the last eight months while Wang was ill. Wang will be buried in Nanking close to Sun Yat-sen, the founder of Nationalist China. Wang was considered his natural successor until ousted by Chiang Kai-shek in 1935. He set up the Reformed Kuomintang in 1938, believing that peace with Japan was the best way to preserve China's interests.

Wang Ching-wei, who died today.

Record set by US raid on Singapore

Singapore, 5 November
In the longest daylight mission ever, 53 B-29s of the US Twentieth Army Air Force based at Calcutta have bombed Singapore's dockyards and Sumatra's Pangkalan Brandon oil refinery, Japan's primary source of aviation fuel – a round trip of 3,700 miles (5,950 km). *Shonan* [Light of the South], as the Japanese call Singapore, is south-east Asia's biggest naval base. The main target was the former King George VI Graving Dock – the world's biggest dry dock (→7).

Fear of Reds and love of homeland inspire Germans

Europe, 5 November

In spite of Hitler's continued promises to the German people that the so-called miracle weapons will transform their fortunes it must be plain to them that nothing but defeat stares them in the face. Why then does the German soldier continue to resist so fiercely? It is certainly not because of faith in the counteroffensive which Hitler is now planning to launch against the western Allied armies. The secrecy surrounding it is so great that only the most senior commanders are privy to the plan, and have little confidence in it.

The *Waffen*-SS, as the military arm of National Socialism is known, is politically indoctrinated and does include fanatics in its ranks. Indeed, this trait was clearly displayed by the 12th SS *Hitler Jugend Panzer* Division in Normandy. The same is not true for the bulk of the German fighting forces, the *Wehrmacht*. The vast majority, from the C-in-C West, Field Marshal von Rundstedt, downwards, have little love for Hitler and want nothing better than for the war to end. What stops them, then, from wholesale surrender? The reasons are varied. There is, for instance, the traditional loyalty to the "Fatherland" which transcends what they might think of Hitler and his henchmen. The Allied demand for nothing but unconditional surrender is also a major factor. The German people interpret this as the wholesale destruction of the fabric of their country and hence consider that there is nothing to be gained by not continuing the fight.

Since the July bomb plot the regime has become doubly ruthless in eradicating all opposition, and fear of the consequences of disobeying orders plays its part. Above all, perhaps, is the fear of the enemy in the east. Many Germans sincerely believe that Stalin and his Communists are the true threat to Europe.

High-speed rockets smash Britain

Onlookers gather to watch firemen battle with a blaze caused by a V2.

An experimental version of the V2.

London, 10 November

Winston Churchill at last admitted today that Britain is under attack by the secret German long-range rocket, the V2. Nearly 100 have landed since the first hit Chiswick, in West London, on 8 September, but the British authorities have suppressed the information until today. As many as eight rockets a day have been launched from sites in the Netherlands – and their impact is far deadlier than that of the earlier V1, with hundreds of Londoners already killed.

This week German radio claimed that London was "devastated" by the new weapon. Mr Churchill today denied this. "The damage and casualties have not so far been heavy," he told parliament. But no single weapon has ever been more destructive than the V2 which rises to a height of 60-70 miles (96-112 km) and travels at 3,600mph, carrying a ton of explosive in its nose-cone. A single rocket killed 17 people in Southgate, in north London, and four rockets wrecked 2,000 houses in Croydon, in Surrey. Coming on top of the V1 attacks it means that Hitler's much-vaunted secret weapons have destroyed 25,000 houses and damaged a million others in five months. Antwerp, too, has been hit by the V2s.

What makes the V2 so alarming is that no public warning can be given; it is simply too fast. Nor is there much apparent defence; the rocket penetrates all but the deepest shelters. The first that anyone knows is the sound of the huge explosion followed by a whooshing sound, flashes and plumes of smoke. "A gasworks explosion" was the official explanation of the first blast at Chiswick, which was heard over much of West London. So often was this phrase trotted out that London would have been without gas had the explanations been true. "Another flying gas-main," one Londoner wrote sardonically in her diary during October.

It was in an effort to still the rumours of secret weapons and to counter Nazi propaganda that Mr Churchill lifted – at least partially – the official silence. "There is no need to exaggerate the danger. The scale and effect has not hitherto been significant," he claimed. Although there has been no panic, action against the V2s depends upon Allied forces destroying the rocket bases in the Netherlands.

The Germans were forced to withdraw their rocket launch sites eastwards in September. Attempts to use Denmark were not deemed successful because London remained beyond the 200-mile (320-km) range of the 46-foot-long rockets. Since 3 October, though, the battle has been resumed in earnest (→ 25).
* *How the V2 works: see Appendix Three, pages 708-9.*

Roosevelt wins fourth term as president

A sea of placards in support of the man who has led America through the war.

Washington, 8 November
Franklin Delano Roosevelt went to bed shortly after midnight this morning knowing that after rough campaigning by the Republican candidate, Thomas Dewey, he has been elected president for the fourth time. The aggressive Republican campaign included criticism of Roosevelt's family and even of his dog, Fala.

The president's victory was comfortable, though not a landslide. The latest results show President Roosevelt leading in 35 states with a total of 413 votes in the electoral college, against Mr Dewey's lead in 13 states with only 118 votes. In terms of the popular vote, Mr Roosevelt has so far won 23 million votes, and Mr Dewey has won 20 million.

Mr Roosevelt was resting today, but his press secretary issued a statement. "What is really important", it said, "is that we have again demonstrated that democracy is a living force."

The Democrats have gained 23 seats in the House of Representatives, and seven in the Senate. They have also kept control of Congress.

Yugoslavia: men of the 31st Light Anti-Aircraft Battery, the Royal Artillery, fire a mountain howitzer against an enemy base 1,200 yards away.

1944

November

Su	Mo	Tu	We	Th	Fr	Sa
			1	2	3	4
5	6	7	8	9	10	11
12	13	14	15	16	17	18
19	20	21	22	23	24	25
26	27	28	29	30		

12. Berlin: Hitler tells the German nation "my life does not matter" in a proclamation read out by Himmler.

12. France: US troops ford the Moselle river at Cattenom (→ 13).

13. Yugoslavia: German forces evacuate Skoplje, hitherto their headquarters in Macedonia.

13. France: US forces penetrate the heavy defences of Metz, but meet strong resistance as they press on to the Saar (→ 14).

13-14. Philippines: US aircraft attack Japanese shipping in Manila Bay, crippling the *Ushio* and four other destroyers and sinking the cruiser *Kiso*.→

14. France: Free French troops launch Operation Independence, to close the Belfort Gap (→ 18).

14. Prague: Andrei Vlasov, a renegade Russian general, is authorized by Hitler to set up an army to fight the USSR.

15. Italy: Workers in Turin stage a general strike in support of the Allies and partisans; at the same time more than 1,000 partisans elude a German operation in northern Italy (→ 20).

15. Hungary: The Red Army enters Jasbereny, 30 miles (48 km) east of Budapest (→ 29).

16. Belgium: Ten V-bombs kill 263 civilians in Antwerp (→ 18).

16. Germany: Allied aircraft raid enemy posts near Aachen.→

17. Yellow Sea: The US submarine *Spadefish* sinks the Japanese escort carrier *Shinyo*.

17. Albania: German resistance ends in the capital, Tirana (→ 19).

18. Brussels: At the request of the Allied armies, Belgian resistance fighters agree to lay down their arms and leave the battle to regular soldiers (→ 28).

18. France: The French First Army drives seven miles through the Belfort Gap (→ 21).

18. Paris: De Gaulle sets up a high court of five magistrates and 24 jurors to try Vichy leaders and collaborators.

RAF sinks the last German battleship in Norwegian fjord

Norway, 12 November
The *Tirpitz*, the sister ship of the *Bismarck*, was finally sunk today by some 30 Lancaster bombers from 9 and 617 Squadrons. They flew to Tromso Fjord from Lossiemouth, in Scotland, in near perfect visibility. They dropped their huge 12,000-pound "Tallboy" armour-piercing bombs from a height of 14,000 feet with deadly accuracy. At least two direct hits went right through the ship and caused the magazine to blow up with a massive explosion. The mighty ship capsized, trapping about half of the 1,900 crew in the upturned hull. Late tonight rescue teams could hear a few singing *Deutschland uber Alles*, but the chances of cutting through in time are remote.

The *Tirpitz* spent most of the war trapped in Norway's Altenfjord. Admiral Donitz did not want to risk her against the superior numbers of the Home Fleet. Because the fire-power of the German ship exceeded that of any single British ship, the navy had to keep several battleships and aircraft-carriers on hand in case she made a bid for the open sea. She caused the greatest convoy disaster (PQ-17) in July 1942 simply by leaving port: although she saw no action she drew off the big ships from the escort.

Royal Navy boosts Allies in the Pacific

Westminster, 15 November
British submarines have sunk 23 Japanese supply ships and one anti-submarine vessel, according to an admiralty statement tonight. This is in addition to the 45 sinkings announced by the admiralty on 11 November. It adds up to a score of 69 in five days, and shows that for the first time the Royal Navy is giving considerable help to the US Navy in the Pacific War.

Thanks to the successes in the North Atlantic more ships and submarines can be sent to the British Eastern Fleet in the Indian Ocean, leaving scope for major *sorties* into the Pacific (→ 24).

Invasion air chief dies in plane crash

London, 14 November
Air Chief Marshal Sir Trafford Leigh-Mallory and his wife Doris died today when the York transport carrying them to Ceylon crashed in atrocious weather on the *Cheminee du Diable* in the French Alps.

Sir Trafford was on his way to take up his new appointment as commander of the Allied air forces in South-east Asia. It would have been the culmination of a brilliant, if sometimes controversial, career.

He opposed Lord Dowding over his tactics in the Battle of Britain. Dowding won the battle, but lost the quarrel, and was bypassed while Leigh-Mallory went on to command the Allied Expeditionary Air Force for the invasion of Europe.

Air Chief Marshal Leigh-Mallory.

Allies ready for new drive into Germany

US Seventh Army troops advance through the peace of a misty French forest.

Europe, 18 November
Allied forces, now joined by a third US army, Lieutenant-General William H Simpson's Ninth, are poised for a three-pronged drive into Germany. The US First and Ninth Armies stand before the Aachen Gap, a 20-mile stretch of open country between Stolberg and Heinsberg. Here, the Roer river has almost certainly been incorporated into the Siegfried Line defences. Montgomery's 21st Army Group stands to the north.

To the south, Patton's Third Army still has to capture Metz and Thionville in order to secure a passage through Lorraine to the Saar. The Germans, occupying the Maginot Line, have turned its guns round to face west and hit Patton's men. Further south, the US-French Army Group, which includes General Jean de Lattre de Tassigny's First French Army, is poised to drive through the Belfort Gap between the Vosges and the Jura. There is a dangerous gap between Patton and the British and Americans to the north; only six US divisions hold the 70-mile (112-km) front in the Ardennes (→ 19).

German targets hit by Allied aircraft backing land forces

Germany, 16 November
Allied aircraft today launched major raids on enemy fortifications to support the land forces. The biggest contingent came from the US Eighth Army Air Force which deployed 1,208 B-17s and B-24s on targets such as railway lines and gun positions in Duren and Eschweiler near Aachen. RAF Bomber Command joined the attack on Duren, Julich and Heinsberg.

All three towns were seriously damaged, with 2,403 people killed in Duren. Around 9,400 tons of high-explosive bombs were dropped by the combined forces in an action to assist the US First and Ninth Armies as they prepare to attack across the Roer river. It reflects the increasing coordination between land and air forces.

Control of the air was an essential prerequisite for the success of the landings in Normandy, and the Allied air forces (including the Poles and Canadians) have continued to attack German airfields and supply lines. Launch sites for the V2 rocket and synthetic oil plants are prime targets, but Sir Arthur Harris, the head of Bomber Command, is now planning an outright assault on German cities, with Berlin as the prime target (→ 18).

Slim is the unsung hero as Allies put Japan on the defensive

Myitkyina, Burma, 18 November
All over Burma, along an 800-mile (1,280-km) front, the Japanese army is on the defensive. Chinese and US troops in the north, reinforced by the 36th Indian Division, are pushing south down the "railway corridor" towards Indaw, while further south in central Burma the Anglo-Indian Fourteenth Army is preparing to cross the Chindwin and the Irrawaddy.

The Allied offensive from the north – commanded by Lt-General Daniel Sultan since Stilwell's dismissal – began four weeks ago. It has advanced over 100 miles, along both the railway corridor and the upper Irrawaddy valley, where the 38th Chinese Division threatens Bhamo. Further east the New Chinese Sixth Army is marching along the Burma Road axis to meet them.

Confronting the force, General Masaki Honda's Thirty-Third Army has steadily retreated. He has no hope of reinforcements from Japan; indeed, one of his divisions has been taken away from him and sent to Indochina. He is faced with superior forces under Sultan, and also risks being cut off by Lt-Gen William Slim's Fourteenth Army, 175 miles (280 km) to the south.

There, Slim's army has been building roads and supply dumps for Operation Extended Capital, which Slim hopes will take his force across the Chindwin, destroy Lt-Gen Shihachi Katamura's Fifteenth Army on Shwebo plain, and carry on over the Irrawaddy. Slim is a largely unsung British hero. Of the original military commanders on the Burmese stage, Orde Wingate is dead, Stilwell in disgrace and Geoffrey Scoones (the victor of Imphal) in India; while on the Japanese side, the Burma Area Army commander, Masakazu Kawabe, the Fifteenth Army commander, Renya Mutaguchi, and nine other generals have been sacked since the Imphal debacle.

Only Slim remains, quietly exuding confidence and good nature. His brief now is to reopen the Burma Road, but he plans to go further and destroy the Japanese army in Burma. He has no illusions about the task, and calls the Japanese soldier "the most formidable fighting insect in history" (→ 19).

Mr Churchill with General de Gaulle in the liberated city of Paris, where they met for the Armistice Day celebrations.

1944

November

Su	Mo	Tu	We	Th	Fr	Sa
				1	2	3	4
5	6	7	8	9	10	11
12	13	14	15	16	17	18
19	20	21	22	23	24	25
26	27	28	29	30		

19. Burma: British troops launch Operation Extended Capital, aiming to sweep towards Rangoon and Meiktila on a wide front.

19. Albania: Partisan fighters led by Enver Hoxha liberate Tirana (→ 29).

19. Germany: Allied troops enter the Rhineland, and US tanks reach the Saar river (→ 20).

19. Washington: The cost to the US of fighting the war is estimated at $250 million a day.

20. London: Five years of darkness end as street lights are switched on in Piccadilly, the Strand and Fleet Street.

20. Germany: With the Red Army fast approaching Rastenburg, Hitler leaves his old headquarters and returns to Berlin (→ 28).

21. Off Formosa [*Taiwan*]: The US submarine *Sealion* sinks the Japanese battleship *Kongo*.

21. France: Free French soldiers capture Mulhouse.→

23. Finland: Finnish and Soviet troops drive the Germans out of Lapland.

23. Canada: Parliament votes to send conscripted men to Europe to join the hitherto voluntary Canadian Army.

24. London: Stanislaw Mikolajczyk, the Polish prime minister in exile, resigns in protest at Poland's proposed new eastern frontier and the Allies' lack of support for the Warsaw uprising.

25. Philippines: *Kamikaze* pilots attack US shipping, damaging four carriers.

25. Berlin: Hitler orders any military commander contemplating surrender to hand over command to the next most senior officer willing to carry on the fight, and fall in behind him.

25. Auschwitz-Birkenau: Demolition of the gas chambers and crematoria begins, with the dismantling of heavy plant for transport to other concentration camps further west (→ 26).

Red Army launches Baltic offensive

Soviet armour driving on a Baltic town; the Red Army aims to clear the region before heading for Prussia.

Riga, 20 November
German reports say that the Red Army has launched a great assault in Latvia. According to Berlin radio, the attack was launched along a 20-mile (32-km) front from the salient south-east of Liepaja, on the Baltic coast.

The broadcast spoke of a heavy artillery drumfire barrage preparing the way for the Russian troops and said "the Russians have thrown in an immense number of fighters, bombers, fighter-bombers and dive-bombers. They made full use of the frozen ground and sent in masses of tanks."

There is no confirmation of this report yet from Moscow, but the assault could be the opening of an attempt to wipe out the Germans trapped in Courland or the eradication of the bridgehead still held by the *Wehrmacht* around Memel.

The Russians are certainly making sure that their rear is clear before they open their attack on East Prussia. One Baltic operation which is just being successfully completed is the clearing of the islands of the Moonsund archipelago. This small but complicated operation started with seaborne landings on Muhu island on 29 September, and the Russians have worked their way along the archipelago until they have the remnants of the German garrison trapped on the tip of Saaremaa island.

Rocket bomb kills 160 in south London

London, 25 November
The most devastating V2 rocket so far scored a direct hit on the Woolworth's store in New Cross, in south-east London, at lunchtime today when it was crowded with Saturday shoppers. The Cooperative Stores alongside was also wrecked. No details have been made public, but 160 people were killed and 200 injured.

A young girl survivor described the scene after the explosion: "Things were still falling out of the sky, bits of things and bits of people. A horse's head was lying in the gutter. There was a pram hood all twisted and bent and there was a little baby's hand still in its woolly sleeve. Outside the pub there was a crumpled bus, still with rows of people sitting inside, all covered in dust and dead. Where Woolworth's had been, there was nothing. Just an enormous gap covered by clouds of dust. No building, just piles of rubble and bricks, and underneath it all, people screaming."

Nanning captured by Japanese forces

Nanning, 25 November
The Japanese authorities today claimed that their forces had taken Nanning, the former capital of Kwangsi province, 100 miles (160 km) from the Indochina border. Japanese forces have been driving south for the past week, and the capture of Nanning would effectively split China in two. Allied sources would not confirm the city's fall, but feared it was likely (→ 30).

1944
November

Su	Mo	Tu	We	Th	Fr	Sa
			1	2	3	4
5	6	7	8	9	10	11
12	13	14	15	16	17	18
19	20	21	22	23	24	25
26	27	28	29	30		

American bombers raid Tokyo by day

Saipan, 24 November

The USAAF raided Tokyo in daylight today for the first time, but the exercise was a dismal failure. Of the 111 B-29 Superfortresses that took off on the 3,000-mile (4,800-km) round trip from the new airbases at Saipan, in the Mariana Islands, 17 aborted due to engine failure and only 24 managed to drop their bombs in approximately the right area.

The main target, the Nakashima Aircraft Company's Musashi engine factory, was hardly touched. One B-29 was deliberately rammed by a Japanese fighter and destroyed. Another had to ditch when it ran out of fuel (→ 27).

Metz falls at last

Metz, 22 November

The last two pockets of German resistance succumbed to a sustained Allied attack today to end a bitter two-month battle for this ancient citadel in Alsace-Lorraine. Tonight a French general is military governor of the city after over four years of German occupation; but the military triumph is American. The 5th Infantry Division of Gen Patton's US Third Army pushed from the south as the 95th Infantry Division attacked from the north. Mulhouse has also fallen (→ 23).

Strasburg falls to Free French fighters

Flowers for the French from the women of Strasburg as PoWs march by.

Strasburg, 23 November

The first French troops entered Strasburg today after a two-pronged drive by Leclerc's 2nd Armoured Division and de Tassigny's First French Army. The Germans were apparently taken by surprise by the speed of the French advance, which was backed by units of Patch's US Seventh Army. Some 3,000 prisoners were taken. In the *Reich* Anatomical Institute, set up by Himmler after 1940, the Americans found scores of headless bodies.

An estimated 50,000 Germans remain in the "Colmar pocket" – an enemy salient projecting into the Allied lines below Strasburg as far south as Mulhouse. French artillery on the Rhine in Alsace, a few miles west of Basle, is bombarding German positions in Baden on the east bank. Shunting yards have been demolished and all rail traffic from the Swiss border halted. Fires have been started in the foothills of the Black Forest. With ferries on the Rhine either sunk or halted, some German units trapped on the west bank have fled into Switzerland.

When the capture of Strasburg was announced to the French Consultative Assembly in Paris, members cheered and stood up to sang the *Marseillaise*.

War reaches stalemate in Italy as both sides get bogged down

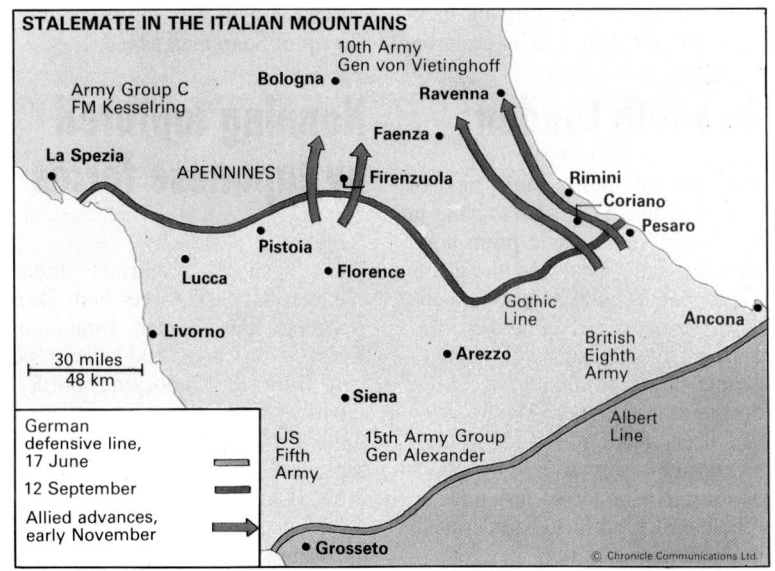

Northern Italy, 20 November

As the autumn rains turn to driving snow, General Alexander, the Allied commander-in-chief in Italy, has called a halt to the gruelling campaign and stood down his armies. British tanks have found the going almost impossible, particularly across hundreds of rivers in the marshy Po valley. The German defence in Italy has been outstanding – but costly. With the Germans equally exhausted, winter activity at the front lines seems likely to be confined to patrolling and occasional artillery duels. The Allies will devote much time to training, particularly in the skills of river crossing and the Alpine warfare yet to come (→ 26).

26. Auschwitz-Birkenau: The last 204 *Sonderkommandos*, privileged prisoners with the task of burying or cremating their gassed comrades, are murdered (→ 27).

26. London: General Sir Harold Alexander, the supreme Allied commander in Italy, is promoted to field marshal. The appointment is backdated to 4 June in order to make him senior to Field Marshal Montgomery.

27. Far East: US B-29 bombers raid Bangkok and Tokyo.

27. Palau Islands: Fighting comes to an end on Peleliu, with 13,600 Japanese soldiers killed and 400 captured for 1,792 US dead and eight thousand wounded.→

27. Auschwitz-Birkenau: Six hundred camp guards are awarded the Iron Cross for putting down the revolt on 7 October.

27. Off Norway: Aircraft of the British Fleet Air Arm sink a German prison ship; of the 2,248 Soviet PoWs on board, only 415 survive.

27. Washington: Edward Stettinius succeeds Cordell Hull, who has resigned, as secretary of state.

28. Germany: Patton's troops enter the Saar basin.

29. Kumano Sea: The supposedly unsinkable Japanese aircraft carrier *Shinano* is sunk by the US submarine *Archerfish*.

29. Albania: German forces evacuate Scutari, and start to retreat to the Drina river.

29. Hungary: Pecs and Mohacs fall to the advancing Russians and Yugoslavs.→

30. Chungking: Chiang Kai-shek recalls the Chinese 22nd and 38th Divisions from Burma to boost the effort to defend Kunming, now threatened by the Japanese advance.

30. Hungary: Soviet troops capture Eger.

30. Britain: Civilian air raid casualties this month are 716 dead and 1,511 wounded.

Reds cross Danube and enter Hungary

Budapest, 29 November
Marshal Tolbukhin, foiled by bad weather and ferocious German and Hungarian resistance in his attempt to take Budapest by storm, has swung west, forcing a crossing of the Danube and threatening to encircle the Hungarian capital.

The Russians made their crossing north of the Danube's junction with the Drava and are now swinging up towards Lake Balaton. They have already advanced 25 miles (40 km), capturing the provincial capital of Pecs and the Danube port of Mohacs. Berlin admitted last night that the German armies in southern Hungary face "a crisis" with the Red Army crossing the Danube "in considerable strength" (→ 30).

Arsenal explodes; 68 are feared dead

Burton-on-Trent, 27 November
Sixty-eight people were killed here today when an underground dump containing enough bombs for hundreds of major raids exploded. Two craters were formed, one 300 feet deep and half a mile across. Bombs were hurled into the air, causing devastation over a three-mile area. Buildings were destroyed and hundreds of animals were killed. The blast was heard 60 miles (96 km) away. In Coventry, 30 miles distant, doors were blown open and the windows rattled.

Nov 30. Britain's prime minister, Winston Churchill, is 70 today.

"Kamikaze" attacks take toll of shipping

A damaged Mitsubishi "Betty", one of the planes sent on suicide missions.

Pacific, 29 November
The suicide attacks of *kamikaze* pilots have continued without abatement into November and, together with conventional air attacks, have made the situation on Leyte hazardous for the Allies.

On 1 November a kamikaze crashed into the destroyer *Abner Read* which rolled over and sank within minutes.

After the landing at Leyte, three fast carrier groups of the US Third Fleet remained off shore providing continuous air support for the troops on Leyte, and the kamikaze pilots went after them. On 5 November, the carrier *Lexington* was attacked by three Zekes which were all shot down, but a fourth managed to crash into the starboard side, inflicting heavy casualties.

On 25 November, just before the carriers were to be released from supporting Leyte, the kamikaze attack was particularly threatening. No less than four carriers were damaged. Part of a disintegrated suicide plane hit the *Hancock's* flight deck and started a fire. The *Cabot*, *Intrepid* and *Essex* were also damaged. The battleships *Colorado* and *Maryland* were hit and heavily damaged.

American admirals and sailors alike are greatly concerned about the Kamikaze Corps. One in four kamikaze missions is finding a target and one in 33 is sinking a ship.

Antwerp becomes Allied supply port

Antwerp, 28 November
There was jubilation here tonight when the first British convoy arrived without loss. Guns, shells, transport and food can now be shipped in to within 60 miles (96 km) of the British troops fighting on the Maas. Minesweepers, which have been working for nearly a month to clear the Scheldt river, steamed ahead of the convoy clearing the last few mines. The escort was ready to fight off dive-bombers, but none appeared. The biggest danger for future convoys is V2 rockets.

British authorities reveal war secrets

London, 28 November
The secrecy surrounding Britain's war effort was lifted by the issuing tonight of a government white paper which shows that the output per head of the British population was greater than that of any other nation. The output of war weapons in the last five years included 102,600 warplanes, 25,000 tanks, 722 warships and 4,500,000 tons of new ships. One civilian has been killed for every three servicemen, and one in three British homes have been damaged or destroyed.

Allied air forces aim for different bombing targets

London, 30 November
The bombing of Germany is reaching a ferocious intensity. One thousand and forty US bombers, escorted by 849 fighters, made daylight raids yesterday on the Misburg oil refinery and railway yards at Hamm.

RAF Bomber Command is in full action. In the early hours of today Lancasters escorted by Spitfires and Mustangs bombed Dortmund. Today Mosquitoes struck at Duisburg in their first daylight raid on Germany since the spring of 1943; but most bombs missed the target.

These blows follow attacks by the RAF's heavy bombers on Essen and Neuss on 28-29 November. So many bombs are being dropped that the factories cannot keep up with the demand.

The bombers are having it all their own way. The *Luftwaffe* has faded away. Bombing techniques developed during the Normandy invasion should enable bombers to deliver their loads with greater accuracy.

It will be noticed, however, that while the USAAF is concentrating on the agreed primary targets of oil and communications, Sir Arthur Harris, the chief of RAF Bomber Command, has reverted to sending bombers to wipe out cities in "area attacks". He insists that it will shorten the war. It is a policy which is attracting increasing criticism on both practical and moral grounds. Bishop Bell has already voiced his misgivings in parliament and Sir Charles Portal, the Chief of Air Staff, has clashed with Harris because over half of his attacks are directed at cities.

Harris is unrepentant, and points to the alleged destruction of the Ruhr's industrial capacity as proof of the effectiveness of his policy. As for its morality, he says: "I do not regard the whole of the remaining cities of Germany as worth the bones of one British grenadier."

1944

December

Su	Mo	Tu	We	Th	Fr	Sa
					1	2
3	4	5	6	7	8	9
10	11	12	13	14	15	16
17	18	19	20	21	22	23
24	25	26	27	28	29	30
31						

1. Germany: The Third US Army, under General Patton, reaches the main German defensive line on the Saar river (→ 3).

2. Burma: The 11th East African Division reaches the Chindwin at Kalewa.

2. Moscow: De Gaulle meets Stalin for talks.

3. Germany: Patton's troops cross the Saar.→

3. Athens: Police fire on communist demonstrators (→ 5).

3. London: King George takes the salute from the Home Guard and orders it to stand down.→

4. Italy: Canadian troops capture Ravenna (→ 12).

5. Athens: British tanks open fire on left-wing protest marchers after several days of street fighting.→

6. London: Queen Elizabeth thanks women for their war work, saying that their efforts are one of the main factors in the Allied victory.

6-7. Germany: RAF bombers smash Merseburg-Leuna, one of the largest synthetic oil plants in Germany (→ 18).

7. Philippines: US forces begin landing operations at Ormoc Bay on Leyte, sinking several Japanese supply ships but coming under heavy attack from fighter and *kamikaze* aircraft (→ 11).

7. Hungary: The Red Army reaches Lake Balaton (→ 22).

7. France: French troops under de Tassigny attack German forces trapped in the "Colmar pocket" (→ 17).

7. Norway: Aircraft of the Fleet Air Arm carry out Operation Urbane, laying mines and attacking shipping off Stavanger.

8. Pacific: US ships and aircraft attack Japanese positions on Iwo Jima (→ 5/1).

8. Germany: US troops advance past Saarlautern to breach the Siegfried Line; Fort Driant, near Metz, falls (→ 12).

9. Hungary: Soviet troops reach the Danube north of Budapest.

British tanks embroiled in Greek civil war

Athens, 7 December
British tanks and troops have been ordered onto the streets of Athens today to crush an uprising by ELAS (the National Liberation Army), the military wing of KKE, the country's communist party, and EAM, a left-wing "front" organization. Dozens of people, some of them British troops, have died.

The trouble began on 1 December when George Papandreou, the Social Democratic premier of an Allied-installed coalition provisional government, went ahead with a decree to demobilize all guerrilla groups of both left and right which had fought against the Germans. EAM, which had left the coalition over the issue, called a general strike, and on 3 December bloody clashes between communists and police left 12 dead. On 5 December Churchill ordered the commander of British troops in Greece, Lt-Gen Ronald Scobie, to restore order whether or not Papandreou lent his authority. Scobie declared martial law in Athens as ELAS men moved to take over police stations and other key points. Before dawn today, ELAS moved into the city in strength, advancing on the government quarter where the outnumbered main force of British troops has put up barricades.

In Britain, Labour MPs have condemned Churchill's move against "popular movements which have vigorously assisted in the defeat of the enemy". But Churchill told MPs that no government could be secure if there were private armies "owing allegiance to a group, a party or an ideology instead of to the state or nation" (→ 15).

Moving farewell parade of Home Guard

The last parade of the valiant Home Guard passes the royal box in Hyde Park.

London, 3 December
Home Guard contingents from all over Britain held their last parade in the centre of London today. Their three-mile march through cheering crowds in the West End began in Hyde Park, where they marched past the king and gave their farewell salute. He was accompanied by the queen, the princesses and service ministers.

The march past was led by men of the London District and anti-aircraft gunners who defended London against the flying bombs. There were 29 sections, including the American Home Guard made up of US citizens in London.

In a broadcast tonight King George said: "I believe it is the voluntary spirit which has always made the Home Guard so powerful a comradeship ... You have found how men from all kinds of homes and occupations can work together in a great cause. I am very proud of what the Home Guard has done and I give my heartfelt thanks."

Olivier's "Henry V" kindles war spirit

Into the breach: Olivier as patriot.

London, 1 December
Shakespeare is stirring patriotic spirits – and attracting cinema queues – in London's West End, thanks to Laurence Olivier's rousing version of *Henry V* which has just opened. Olivier has produced and directed the film as well as starring in it; at £475,000 it is the costliest British picture yet.

"In overbright Technicolor and half an hour too long, at its worst it is vulgar and obscure," said the *News Chronicle*. The *People* called it the "most ambitious, difficult, annoying, boring, beautiful, exciting, baffling picture yet made." C A Lejeune told the *Observer's* readers that the French cavalry charge to William Walton's music is "the most exciting sequence I can remember". The parallel between Agincourt in 1415 and Europe in 1944 is not lost on audiences (→ 31).

Women called up

Germany, 5 December
The call went out today for all German women over 18 to volunteer for the army and air force. They are needed as auxiliaries by the *Wehrmacht* and *Luftwaffe* in order to free men for service at the front. Gertrud Scholtz-Klink, the *Reich's* women's leader, appealed to women to come forward because "the enemy's hatred is intent on annihilating the German people".

Patton crosses the Saar

Fort St Quentin's commander surrenders, handing over his gun to US officers.

Saarland, 5 December
The battle for the key industrial area of the Saar basin is moving towards a climax as Patton's US Third Army exploits the three bridge-heads established across the Saar river. Advances of up to nine miles (14.4 km) have been made, and in the central sector of the front the Americans are within five miles of the capital, Saarbrucken.

Fighting is taking place in Saarguemines, where the Germans are putting up stiff resistance. Saarlautern has been captured, and the first belt of the Siegfried Line defences is under attack. In the rear area, Fort St Quentin, one of the three remaining German-held forts around Metz, fell to a combined air and ground attack. Six hundred prisoners were taken.

Congresswoman Clare Booth Luce, the wife of the *Time* magazine publisher, arrived at the Third Army front today with other members of the House of Representatives. She was allowed to fire a 155mm howitzer at the German lines by pulling the lanyard (→8).

"Tokyo Rose" tells tales to US troops

Philippines, 7 December
American troops waging war against Japan in the Pacific have come to know one Japanese voice better than any other. It belongs to "Tokyo Rose", an American citizen of Japanese parentage featured in regular propaganda broadcasts to the Allied troops by the Japanese Broadcasting Company. Her message is not always very subtle; in a sexy, sultry voice she tells the GIs that the girls they left behind are being unfaithful. "Rose" – her real name is Iva Ikuko Toguri d'Aquino – will not have a victory to report tonight, however; today the US has successfully landed at Ormoc Bay, on Leyte (→11).

Heilbronn becomes latest bomb target

London, 5 December
RAF aircraft, carrying out "Bomber" Harris's threat to wreck Germany "from end to end", last night smashed Heilbronn, a city on a key north/south rail route. Virtually unopposed by the *Luftwaffe*, 282 Lancasters and ten Mosquitoes used their expertise to create the maximum devastation. The raid was controlled from the air by a Master Bomber who directed the dropping of markers and then sent in the Lancasters. High-explosive bombs opened up buildings as kindling for 2,000 tons of incendiaries. The city is in flames. Some 7,000 civilians are thought to have died; 12 Lancasters were lost (→6-7).

1944
December

Su	Mo	Tu	We	Th	Fr	Sa
					1	2
3	4	5	6	7	8	9
10	11	12	13	14	15	16
17	18	19	20	21	22	23
24	25	26	27	28	29	30
31						

10. Australia: The newly-formed British Pacific Fleet arrives at Sydney (→25/1).

10. China: Japanese troops from Operation *Ichi-Go* link up with compatriots from the French Indochina Garrison Army, gaining control of the vital Indochina to China rail link (→23).

10. Burma: Allied engineers complete a 1,154-foot-long Bailey bridge, the world's largest, across the Chindwin river (→15).

10. Moscow: France and the USSR sign a treaty of alliance and mutual assistance.

10. Germany: Hitler appoints Himmler to be C-in-C Army Group Rhine, and moves to his western front headquarters at Bad Nauheim (→11).

11. Leyte: US troops capture Ormoc.→

11. Bad Nauheim: Western front commanders note Hitler's uncontrollable trembling and pale, puffy appearance as he orders Operation Autumn Mist, a major offensive through the Ardennes towards Antwerp.→

12. Germany: German forces withdraw across the Roer river.→

12. Italy: British troops attack Faenza.

13. Sulu Sea: *Kamikaze* attacks damage the US cruiser *Nashville* and the destroyer *Haraden*.→

14. London: The Greater London Plan is published, advocating the creation of a "green belt" around the capital and the transfer of a million people to ten new towns.

15. Burma: Chinese troops capture Bhamo, but the Japanese garrison escapes (→20).

15. Czechoslovakia: Soviet troops cross the border at Sahy.

16. Tacloban, Philippines: MacArthur is promoted to a five-star general (→18).

16. Indian Ocean: British naval aircraft attack Japanese oil installations at Belawan-Deli, on Sumatra (→4/1).

Glenn Miller plane is reported missing

Paris, 16 December
There is no news here of the expected arrival of Major Glenn Miller, who took off from England yesterday in freezing rain in the plane of a US Army colonel. His band has been ordered to Paris by General Eisenhower. All other Channel flights were grounded. His band, due to give its first concert here on 21 December, still does not know that he is missing. In six months in England, his American Band of the Allied Expeditionary Force gave 71 concerts, mostly at US air bases, with Bing Crosby and Dinah Shore among guest artistes.

Glenn Miller: his plane is missing.

Gestapo chiefs are sentenced to death

Paris, 13 December
Nine French *Gestapo* members were sentenced to death in Paris today. They included Henri Lafont, aged 42, a former car salesman, who was in charge of the infamous Gestapo headquarters in the *Rue Lauriston*, and his associate, the former police inspector Pierre Bony, who won a reputation as a brilliant detective during the 1934 Stavisky affair. The trial had lasted for 12 days, and the court heard horrifying stories of torture, murder and extortion. There were originally 12 accused, but one died of diabetes during the trial and two were sentenced to life imprisonment (→27/1).

587

V2 rocket kills 567 in Antwerp cinema

Antwerp, 16 December
A V2 rocket hit the Rex Cinema in the *Avenue de Keyser* at 3.20pm today, killing 567 people, including 296 Allied servicemen. They were part of a capacity audience of 1,200 watching the popular *Buffalo Bill*. There was a flash, then the balcony and ceiling collapsed and the screen tumbled forward. The Germans have switched the main weight of the V2 attacks from London to Antwerp because of the Ardennes offensive. Three weeks ago a V2 killed 157 people. Today's rocket came from Enschede, in the Netherlands, just 130 miles (208 km) away (→ 24).

Battles follow day of peace in Greece

Athens, 15 December
As the sun set over the *Parthenon* tonight, Athens was once again wracked by artillery and machine-gun fire after a short and brittle pause in which British and Greek politicians strove for a solution to this bloody civil war. British para-troopers are besieged in the *Acropolis*, moving only at night to avoid snipers. British headquarters have come under fire from 75mm guns. As more British tanks move into the city, ELAS strongpoints have come under cannon fire from RAF Spitfires.

Future of Poland is dividing the Allies

London, 15 December
The disagreement between the Allies over the political future of Poland emerged strongly from Winston Churchill's speech in the House of Commons today. Official sources later emphasized the ur-gency of the prime minister's plea for a settlement. It is hoped that his speech, in which he deplored the lack of a clear American pronounce-ment on the Russo-Polish issue, may have an effect in Washington. It is felt that the danger of a rift between the Allies is too great to be left for attention at some time in the indefinite future.

Germans counter-attack in Ardennes

One of the "Panzer" mobile armouries which, with 13 infantry divisions, spearheaded the Ardennes attack.

Ardennes, 16 December
At 5.30am, as the GIs were rousing themselves for another uneventful day in the wooded snow-covered hills of the Ardennes, the stillness was shattered by the thundering roar of an artillery barrage. When the bombardment ended after an hour, the first of 20 German divi-sions emerged from the freezing fog to launch an attack which has stunned the Allies.

The offensive, under the overall command of Field Marshal von Rundstedt, is designed to hit the Americans in the lightly-defended Ardennes and recapture the strate-gically-vital port of Antwerp. The seven armoured divisions of Gen-eral Dietrich's 6th and General von Manteuffel's 5th *Panzer* Armies are leading the attack, but there are also four infantry divisions of General Brandenberger's Seventh Army. The immediate result has been confusion and panic in the American lines. This 60-mile sec-tor of the 500-mile front is held by just six US divisions, 83,000 men, with 420 tanks. Crashing down on them is a formidable enemy force of 250,000 men, with 950 tanks.

If Dietrich succeeds in his aim of seizing the Meuse bridges south of Liege and reaching Antwerp, he would cut off Montgomery's 21st Army Group from the bulk of the American armies.

Tonight, despite their early suc-cess [*see report below*], the Germans have been held up by the Ameri-cans in the north at Malmedy and in the south along the Luxemburg frontier. But the road to the key town of Bastogne lies open (→ 20).

Surprise, fog and bogus Yanks put US forces on the defensive

Ardennes, 16 December
The massive German attack launch-ed early today has certainly taken the American forces in the Ar-dennes by surprise. Much of this is attributable to the stringent se-curity measures which the Ger-mans have taken to conceal their intentions. Besides surprise, there are other factors in their favour.

Morale among the attacking troops is higher than for some time: during the first 12 days of December only four German sol-diers deserted to the Allies along the entire western front. Bad wea-ther, including persistent fog, also means that the Allies are unable to use their overwhelming air power, and the tactic of deeply-penetra-ting armoured spearheads is caus-ing confusion in the US lines. This is aggravated by SS Lieutenant-Col-onel Otto Skorzeny's men, who have infiltrated in US uniforms. Continuing success depends upon maintaining momentum.

The wet ground conditions and close terrain are already causing mobility problems, and German fuel stocks are limited. The Ger-mans must therefore rely on quickly capturing US fuel dumps. Above all, they must hope that the fog will continue; otherwise the Al-lied air forces will have a field day.

1944
December

Su	Mo	Tu	We	Th	Fr	Sa
					1	2
3	4	5	6	7	8	9
10	11	12	13	14	15	16
17	18	19	20	21	22	23
24	25	26	27	28	29	30
31						

US forces land on Mindoro in Philippines

Mindoro, 15 December

General MacArthur's forces spear-heading the second phase of the invasion of the Philippines have made rapid advances on Mindoro, in readiness for landings on the main island of Luzon, only a narrow strait of water away.

Since landing on Mindoro at 7.35am today, the US 24th Division has opened up a nine-mile-wide, 11-mile-deep front. With the Japanese garrison numbering only 100, resistance has been light. Objectives captured include the town of San Jose and four abandoned airstrips.

With the 24th is an RAAF airfield construction unit – the first Australian troops in the Philippine campaign. MacArthur plans more airstrips on Mindoro to extend US air cover as far north as Lingayen Gulf and Manila Bay, 150 miles (240 km) away, and make these areas untenable for Japanese shipping. To stop Japanese aircraft from Luzon attacking the Mindoro invasion force, Third Fleet carrier-based planes bombed airfields near

A hail of rocket shells for Mindoro.

Manila three days ago, damaging or destroying 242 enemy planes.

US losses have been greatest at sea. Ships supporting the landings after the 350-mile (560-km) voyage from Leyte were hit yesterday by fierce tropical storms with 75-foot waves that sank three destroyers, drowning 719 men (→16).

American fears grow over kamikaze kills

Leyte Gulf, 15 December

Allied war correspondents are being banned from reporting *kamikaze* suicide attempts by Japanese pilots who have so far crippled a carrier and two destroyers supporting the invasion of Mindoro. The news blackout has been ordered by General MacArthur and Admiral Nimitz. They fear that reports of the decks of US warships being dive-bombed will cause panic in the US. They justify the ban on the grounds that it prevents the Japanese from discovering how much damage their pilots inflict (→1/1).

December 11. Dancing with joy, French women are freed from a German prison in the Alsatian town of Hagenau during its liberation today.

17. France: The French First Army captures Keintzheim, in the "Colmar pocket" (→3/2).

18. Philippine Sea: A typhoon capsizes three destroyers of the US Third Fleet, drowning 757 out of 831 sailors and sweeping 150 aircraft off the decks of carriers (→25).

18. Germany: US aircraft attack German tactical and communications targets, including Cologne, Coblenz, Kaiserslautern, Bonn and Mainz.→

18. Off Gdynia, Poland: RAF bombers hit the German liner *Schleswig-Holstein*, which burns out, and sink eight other ships.

19. Versailles: Confined to his headquarters office by assassination threats, Eisenhower gives temporary command of the US First and Ninth Armies to Montgomery.→

19. Belgium: SS troops under Lieutenant-Colonel Joachim Peiper massacre 130 civilians who they claim were harbouring US soldiers.

20. Burma: The Indian 19th Division captures Kawlin.

20. Belgium: As German troops encircle the US 101st Airborne and 9th and 10th Armoured Divisions at Bastogne, the Allies impose a blackout on all news from the Ardennes fighting, which is now being called the "Battle of the Bulge" (→21).

20. France: Patton starts moving his 250,000-strong army from the Saar to the Ardennes (→25).

21. France: SS Lt-Col Otto Skorzeny leads the 150th *Panzer* Brigade in a pre-dawn attack on Malmedy.

22. Ardennes: The Allies evacuate St Vith.→

22. Hungary: A provisional Hungarian government, under Soviet protection, is formed at Debrecen (→29).

23. Ardennes: US troops at Bastogne are now completely surrounded. Montgomery writes: "Personally I am enjoying a very interesting battle, but we ought to be in tears at the tragedy of the whole thing" (→25).

RAF is besieged by Greek ELAS rebels

Athens, 20 December

British tanks and armoured cars today raced to the rescue of 350 RAF and army personnel holding out against the communist-backed ELAS rebels who captured the RAF rear headquarters at Kifissia, ten miles (16 km) from Athens. An army statement alleged that women and children had taken part in the assault backed by mortars and light artillery. The British were making their last stand in a dynamited hotel when the relief column arrived. In Athens, ELAS attacked and burnt a prison holding collaborators awaiting trial (→29).

ELAS gunmen aim for power.

"People's Army" is born in Indochina

Tonking, 23 December

Reports from French Indochina indicate that military units of the *Viet Minh* have been organized by Vo Nguyen Giap in areas close to the Chinese border. Giap, a former Hanoi schoolmaster, was earlier chosen to organize guerrilla bands and soon revealed outstanding ability, energy and audacity. Yesterday Giap formed a "People's Army" and, seeking an early success, plans to strike against French military posts in Indochina. Giap claims to have equipped his army with sub-machine guns, modern rifles and grenades (→19/1).

Fierce fighting rages in the "Battle of the Bulge"

Germans cut off US forces at Bastogne

Bastogne, 22 December
Trapped here in a network of road links are several thousand lightly-armed men of the 28th Infantry and 10th and 101st US Airborne Divisions. The Germans, with one infantry and two *Panzer* divisions around the town, this morning sent a courier with a message calling on the Americans to surrender. Brig-Gen Anthony C McAuliffe took the paper and scrawled: "To the German commander: NUTS! The American commander."

Despite McAuliffe's relaxed defiance the American position remains precarious, both here and elsewhere. A Panzer force passing north of Bastogne is headed for Ourtheville and Celle, within striking distance of Dinant and Namur. Further north the Americans, having lost 8,000 of some 22,000 men at St Vith, are pulling back.

Three days ago, in his headquarters at Versailles, Eisenhower met his field commanders, Bradley, Patton and Devers, of the US 6th Army Group in Lorraine. He told them he expected only cheerful faces – and then gave them the bad news. Part of Bradley's 12th Army Group, cut off north of the Ardennes bulge, is being transferred to Montgomery's command. Bradley took it badly, especially when told of Monty's swaggering into a US operational HQ and refusing a lunch invitation.

The tide of battle may be about to change, though. The German thrusts have repeatedly been stalled by fuel shortages and pockets of American resistance. Better still, the days of sleet and low cloud, which have protected the Germans from Allied air power, are about to end, according to the forecasters.

Meanwhile, Patton's Third Army is on the move. Eisenhower did not believe Patton when he promised that he would be at Bastogne by today; he had to disengage his men from battle on the Saar front, execute a 90-degree change of course and move over 130,000 vehicles 75 miles to the north. And he has done just that (→ 23).

The snow provides a good camouflage for an American Sherman tank.

The bodies of US PoWs gunned down by the SS lie in a Belgian field.

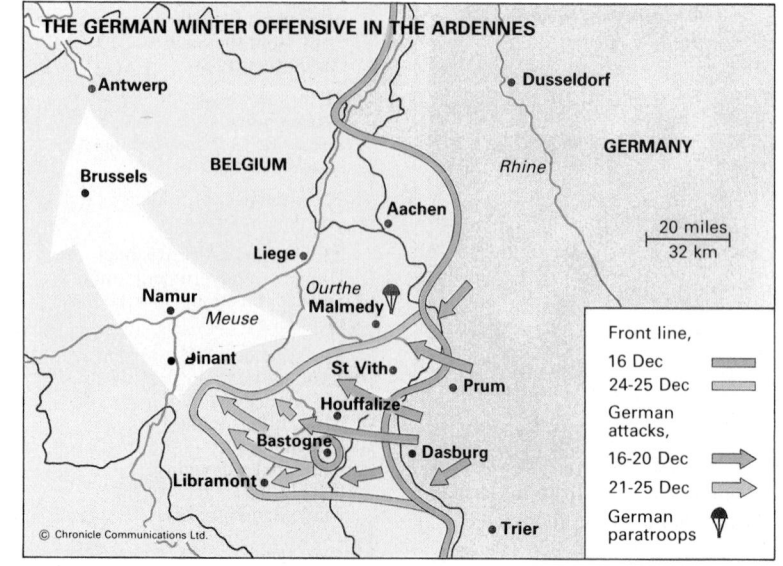
THE GERMAN WINTER OFFENSIVE IN THE ARDENNES

PoWs massacred by SS at Malmedy

Belgium, 17 December
A US field-artillery observation battery of 125 men found itself under enemy fire when its trucks came to a crossroads near Malmedy early this afternoon. *Panzers* of SS Lt-Col Jochen Peiper's Task Force rumbled into view and the Americans, who had no heavy weapons or tank support, surrendered.

They were taken into a nearby field under guard to await an escort to the rear. Half an hour later, SS troops moving up to the front were told of the American PoWs and went into the field. A pistol shot was heard, followed by a burst of machine-gun fire.

The SS men drove away, leaving at least 71 GIs dead. The rest feigned death, or lay unconscious, for several hours before gathering strength to limp into Malmedy after dark. Their story has already been passed on to GIs at the battle-front, stiffening their resolve to fight to the last (→ 21).

Impostor GIs cause havoc in US lines

Huy, 18 December
The American who turned up to guard the bridge over the Meuse at Huy, south-west of Liege, was unusually well-informed. American reinforcements moving up to the front were regaled with hair-raising stories of massive German *Panzer* forces wreaking havoc among the Allies.

It was some time before this talkative "American" was identified as an English-speaking German commando in GI uniform, driving a captured Jeep. Hitler had told SS Lt-Col Otto Skorzeny to train men to pose as GIs and infiltrate them behind the American lines, to spread panic and confusion and sabotage communications. The first wave succeeded, forcing the Americans to introduce time-consuming identity checks and trick questions about comics, the name of Roosevelt's dog or baseball scores (→ 31).

1944
December

Su	Mo	Tu	We	Th	Fr	Sa
					1	2
3	4	5	6	7	8	9
10	11	12	13	14	15	16
17	18	19	20	21	22	23
24	25	26	27	28	29	30
31						

Germany's bombed transport system is now near collapse

Germany, 23 December

Germany's bomb-shattered, overloaded transport system is in danger of grinding to a halt. The railway network is not only struggling to shift vast numbers of troops; it is also weighted down by refugees from the Russians in the east, and by the thousands of people being imported as forced labour, or deported to death camps.

During the early years of the war the Allies concentrated their bombing raids on transport networks in occupied France and Belgium. In September of this year they turned their attention to Germany, and systematically destroyed roads, bridges, waterways, railway junctions and airfields. Civilians are now required to have special authorization for train journeys, which can only be made for business or very pressing personal reasons.

Meanwhile in the cities frenetic commuters are travelling to work on tram running-boards, and bicycles that are used for anything other than war-related journeys are confiscated.

New unit is formed for secret weapon

Wendover, Utah, 17 December

A top-secret bombing team, the 509th Composite Group, assembled here today on the salt flats west of the Great Salt Lake. Its exact role is unknown to any of its members except for the commanding officer, Colonel Paul Tibbets, who had a distinguished flying record in Europe; but it is thought that the 509th is being trained to drop a new weapon, using atomic power, on Japan.

Wendover Air Force Base was chosen because it enjoys more than 300 days of sunshine a year. The 509th is equipped with B-29 bombers. It will practise daylight bombing with large dummy bombs from 20,000-30,000 feet, using a special diving technique to gain speed in order to outrun blast waves expected to be greater than those of any existing bombs (→ 30).

24. France: German troops murder all the men aged between 17 and 32 in the village of Bande, as revenge for a *Maquis* attack in September.

24. English Channel: The U-boat U486 sinks the US transport ship *Leopoldville* off Cherbourg, killing 819 US soldiers (→ 27).

24. Britain: Forty-five modified Heinkel He111s launch 31 V1 bombs aimed at Manchester; 17 reach the target area, killing 32 people and injuring 49 (→ 1/1).

25. Philippines: The cream of the Japanese troops on Luzon are transferred to Cebu and Mindanao, after Yamashita says that he can no longer guarantee getting supplies through to them (→ 26).

25. Ardennes: The Allies launch their counter-offensive.→

26. Philippines: A Japanese fleet bombards the US beachhead at Mindoro (→ 31).

26. Berlin: Guderian, convinced that the Ardennes offensive will end in failure, tries but fails to persuade Hitler to call it off.→

27. Atlantic: The Canadian ship *St Thomas*, escorting convoy HX-327, sinks the U-boat U877.

29. London: King George of the Hellenes appoints Archbishop Damaskinos to serve as regent on his behalf.→

29. Hungary: Soviet tanks roll into Budapest; German troops shoot dead two Russian envoys sent over to negotiate surrender terms.→

30. Los Alamos, New Mexico: Nuclear scientists working on the Manhattan Project estimate that the first atomic bomb will be ready by the end of July 1945 (→ 31/1).

31. Tokyo: Emperor Hirohito questions his cabinet about the deteriorating situation on Leyte and Luzon (→ 1/1).

31. Versailles: Eisenhower orders Montgomery to abandon the strategy of allowing the German army to exhaust itself and mount an attack on the north of the Ardennes front (→ 7/1).

Hungary declares war against Germany as Red Army fights in Budapest suburbs

The battle for the city of Budapest: Red Army soldiers on a house roof.

Budapest, 31 December

The Provisonal National Government of Hungary, set up under Russian control in the captured city of Debrecen, today declared war on Germany. The decision was adopted unanimously by its cabinet, which said that only the victory of the Allies could "strengthen the independence of Hungary".

Meanwhile the grim, bloody struggle for Budapest continues, with the Germans and their Hungarian allies holding out against the encircling Russians. The defenders know that they can expect no quarter after two Russian officers, carrying terms for surrender under the protection of the white flag, were shot down with cold deliberation. The Russians have already fought their way into the city limits and captured several blocks of streets. Budapest is enveloped in smoke, lit up by the glow of burning buildings and the sudden explosions of shells from the Red Army's massed guns. The defenders will not easily be overcome, however: they are well entrenched; the streets are mined; machine guns and mortars are set up in houses, snipers lurk on the roofs. They have orders to fight to the last man. After the murder of the Russian officers they will have no option.

An army of ambulances, made in Detroit, stands ready to go into battle.

Bastogne freed as Patton's troops counter-attack

US infantrymen move up through a wood on the outskirts of Bastogne.

It was a long, cold road to Bastogne: here US Shermans await orders.

Bastogne, 26 December

In the fast-gathering darkness a detachment of engineers manning the southern perimeter defences of Bastogne reported the approach of three armoured vehicles "believed friendly". They were Shermans from Patton's 4th Armoured Division, which had fought its way up through Luxemburg. Thus the German siege of the town, where five main roads meet, was lifted.

Lt-Gen Patton began his attack four days ago when he ordered the 4th Armoured: "Drive like hell." Favoured by the terrain, German parachute troops, fighting as infantry, stubbornly defended every village and patch of woodland, slowing the American armour. For the Americans inside Bastogne, it was touch-and-go whether they could hold out. Christmas Day began with a heavy overnight air bombardment; it was followed by an all-out *Panzer* attack directed at the western arc of the American defences. The battle lasted through the day, but the Panzers were badly mauled by the men of the US 101st Airborne and a hastily-gathered assortment of reinforcements. As night fell it was apparent that the German assault had been broken.

This is almost certainly the turning point in the Germans' Ardennes gamble. Von Manteuffel's Panzers, unable to take Bastogne, had swept westwards towards the Meuse, following the *Blitzkrieg* principle of keeping the armour moving. But 1940 is not to be replayed today.

For the past three days, since the cloud lifted, the Germans have been mercilessly pounded from the air, and Major-General "Lightning Joe" Collins's armour and infantry, joined by British armour, have smashed the German spearhead at Celles. Today the Panzer remnants have begun pulling back.

Von Manteuffel is bitter at Hitler's repeated failure to give him the reinforcements he needed. Only today was he told he could have the rest of the available reserves – and now they cannot be moved for lack of petrol. Yet had Peiper's *Kampfgruppe* pushed on through Stavelot ten days ago it could have taken a US fuel dump of over 2,500,000 gallons. Peiper, cut off and short of supplies, told his men on Christmas Eve to head for home; fewer than 800 of the original force of 4,000 have reached safety.

Hitler was told today that any idea of capturing Antwerp, as he had talked of doing, must now be ruled out. Even the Meuse is beyond the German grasp. Von Manteuffel telephoned Jodl at army HQ and said that the Allies were counter-attacking and he was pulling his men back from the Celles salient. Instantly, the order came down from the Fuhrer halting the withdrawal. Von Rundstedt, nominally the overall commander of the Ardennes offensive, but profoundly sceptical of the operation, has offered his verdict on Hitler's "No retreat" order: "This is Stalingrad Number Two." (→ 1/1)

German commandos are executed for impersonating US soldiers

Ardennes, 31 December

The Americans have produced a simple, ruthless solution to the problem of Skorzeny's phoney GIs operating behind the Allied front. Three of the Germans captured in American uniforms have been executed by firing squad, and 15 more await the same fate. The Americans have given warning that should any more turn up they, too, will be shot. Lt-Gen Omar Bradley is telling how he was stopped at a road block for an identity check and asked a trick question: Who is Betty Grable's husband?* He did not know, but the sentry still let him pass.

It was the trumpeter Harry James.

German soldiers discovered as "phoney GIs" face the firing squad.

Jet aircraft fly on first bombing raid

Germany, 24 December

An aviation first was scored today with the world's first jet bomber operation. Just before 11am German Arado 234B "Blitz" bombers, based at Munster-Handorf and led by Captain Dieter Lukesch, made a successful attack on a factory and marshalling yards at Liege, Belgium. All the jet bombers returned safely, although one damaged its undercarriage on landing. Later the jets returned to the same target, a vital supply centre for the fighting in the Ardennes, and enjoyed equal success (→ 1/1).

Arts: classical glories on stage, patriotic passions on screen

Britain, 31 December
Lovers of classical acting, who have enjoyed a wartime diet of **Donald Wolfit**'s Shakespeare and the Restoration comedies staged by **John Gielgud** and **Leslie Bank**, have had a season of theatrical treats. For many, the highlight was the revival of the Old Vic company, bombed out of its Waterloo home and re-constituted at the New Theatre under the leadership of **Ralph Richardson** and **Laurence Olivier** (both released from the Fleet Air Arm) and the director **John Burrell**.

On 31 August the company opened with Richardson in the name part of Ibsen's *Peer Gynt*, staged by **Tyrone Guthrie**. In the tiny part of the Button Moulder, whom Peer Gynt encounters at the end of his life's journey, Olivier made a memorably chilling appearance. Then followed Shaw's *Arms and the Man*, with Olivier as the ridiculous and fiery Sergius and Richardson as the unmilitary "chocolate soldier", Bluntschli.

Finally in Shakespeare's *Richard III* Olivier was hailed as the finest Richard of his generation and his performance compared by the critic **James Agate** to Henry Irving's "in the sardonic impudence, the sheer malignity and horror of it". It was also the year of John Gielgud's fourth *Hamlet*, of which Agate wrote: "I think there is no doubt that this is and is likely to remain the best Hamlet of our time."

Liberated Paris has been intrigued by a new play in which

Ralph Richardson (l) and Laurence Olivier (r) in "Arms and the Man".

three people, trapped eternally in each other's company, demonstrate that "hell is other people". The author of *Huis Clos* [Vicious Circle] is **Jean-Paul Sartre**, a philosopher and novelist, who played a part in the Resistance and advocates that writers be "engaged" in political debate. In the US a playwright from the South, **Tennessee Williams**, made his debut with *The Glass Menagerie*.

Apart from *Henry V* [*see page 586*] one notable war film has been *The Way Ahead*, showing the transformation of a bunch of raw army recruits into a fighting unit under their officer played by **David Niven**, directed by **Carol Reed**. The **Crown Film Unit** produced its ultimate

drama-documentary in praise of military teamwork: *Western Approaches* shows the tensions of men adrift in a lifeboat in the Atlantic for two weeks. It was shot in the Irish Sea in colour using merchant seamen reliving what was for them a real-life drama.

The 50th anniversary of the Proms was celebrated by a concert in the Albert Hall given by three orchestras, the BBC Symphony, the London Philharmonic and the London Symphony, conducted by **Sir Adrian Boult**, **Dr Malcolm Sargent** and **Basil Cameron**. **Sir Henry Wood**, who founded and conducted the Proms single-handed for so long, died on 19 August, having seen the audience double in wartime.

Real-life heroics in "Western Approaches" become a hit on the screen.

Sir Henry Wood: final Prom.

Churchill arrives in Athens for talks on government crisis

Athens, 28 December
A bizarre visit to Athens by the British prime minister, Winston Churchill, ended here today when the premier's aircraft took off on the return to Britain. Forgoing the Christmas celebrations, Mr Churchill and Anthony Eden, the foreign secretary, flew here after a spur-of-the-moment decision to resolve the political crisis which has led to civil war.

In his four days in Athens, the prime minister has had meetings, held by the light of hurricane lamps, with both British-approved Greek politicians and, despite their shellfire outside, representatives from the rebel ELAS movement. His ship, HMS *Ajax*, has been shelled – returning fire on the PM's orders – and a guest on the ship, Archbishop Damaskinos, the man favoured as the Greek regent, was mistaken for a member of the *Ajax*'s Christmas fancy-dress party.

During the talks in Athens, British Beaufighters were launching rocket attacks on ELAS a few streets away as the rebels, much to Churchill's delight, talked of Britain as "our great ally".

After machine-gun bursts hit the walls of the British embassy above him, a sniper's bullet narrowly missed the premier. "Cheek!" he said and walked on (→ 5).

Two governments for troubled Poland

London, 31 December
The Polish crisis was brought to a head last night when the Russian-sponsored Committee of National Liberation in Lublin declared itself to be the provisional government of Liberated Poland. This means that, theoretically, Poland now has two governments, the Lublin committee and that of Mr Arciszewski in London. The London Poles have made an "emphatic protest" against the action of the Lublin group, declaring that its unilateral assumption of the title of provisional government is illegal (→ 1/1).

"One of the Death Pits, Belsen" by Leslie Cole.

1945

January

Su	Mo	Tu	We	Th	Fr	Sa
	1	2	3	4	5	6
7	8	9	10	11	12	13
14	15	16	17	18	19	20
21	22	23	24	25	26	27
28	29	30	31			

1. Western Front: In Operation *Bodenplatte*, German fighters attack Allied bases, destroying 156 aircraft but losing 277 of their own.→

1. Alsace: Germany launches Operation North Wind, an attack along the river Saar.→

2. Copenhagen: Resistance fighters destroy a factory which manufactures parts for the V2 rocket (→ 17/2).

2. Atlantic: The Sikorski helicopter is used in convoy escort duties for first time.

3. Burma: A British artillery officer captures Akyab single-handed, the Japanese having pulled out 48 hours ago.→

3. Belgium: The Allies reveal the Nazi concentration camp at Breendonck (→ 18).

3. Canada: The first Canadian draftees to be sent to Europe sail from Halifax; many objectors drop their rifles into the sea as they walk up the gangplank.

3-4. Pacific: The US Third Fleet attacks Japanese targets on Formosa and in the Ryukyu Islands, destroying a hundred enemy aircraft (→ 6).

4. Philippines: A *kamikaze* aircraft sinks the US carrier *Ommaney Bay*, killing 93 crewmen (→ 6).

4. Indian Ocean: Carriers of the British Pacific Fleet attack oil refineries at Pankalan Brandan, in Sumatra (→ 24).

4. Burma: Allied troops complete the occupation of Akyab.→

5. France: German forces recross the Rhine and re-enter Alsace in the Gombsheim area.

5. Bonin Islands: US ships attack Iwo Jima, Haha Jima and Chichi Jima (→ 25).

5. Greenwich, London: Construction begins on Britain's first prefabricated houses (→ 20/3).

6. Japan: US bombers raid Tokyo (→ 10/2).

6. Philippines: Japan has only 35 aircraft left on Luzon, but continues to mount *kamikaze* attacks on US ships which kill over 150 crewmen today (→ 7).

Allied air and sea power hammer Japan

Japan, 1 January
The New Year is beginning with US air attacks bringing the war ever closer to the Japanese homeland. As the outer ramparts of Japan's Asiatic empire crumble in the face of the Allied advances, Japan is losing all control of the air and sea. Desperate for a reprieve from the slide to defeat, the Japanese are now resorting to bizarre methods of warfare, including *kamikaze* air attacks and suicide submarines.

The Japanese have strengthened the homeland by withdrawing aircraft and anti-aircraft weapons from outlying regions. Whole Japanese armies in the South-west Pacific have been abandoned by Japan after Allied forces bypassed them and left them to "wither on the vine" under Allied air attack and naval blockade.

In South-east Asia air mastery over the Japanese has long been established, and the Allied air forces maintain relentless pressure on the retreating enemy in Burma. The US Fourteenth Army Air Force is active in China, Indochina and Burma. In the East China Sea, fast carriers of the US Third Fleet are currently hammering enemy airfields on Formosa, the Pescadores, the Ryukyus and Luzon to frustrate

A "kamikaze", Japan's last bid.

the kamikaze planes waiting to pounce on MacArthur's invasion force approaching Lingayen Gulf.

The government in Tokyo was deeply shocked when the Americans invaded the Marianas last June, thus threatening a B-29 bombing campaign from only 1,500 miles (2,400 km). That threat became reality when the Americans based two wings of B-29s there. On 24 November, 111 B-29s took off to subject Tokyo to its first mass air raid. More will follow (→ 4).

Germans attack on 50-mile Saar front

Alsace, 1 January
German troops have launched an overnight offensive against Allied positions along a 50-mile front between Saarbrucken and Strasburg. The attack, known as Operation North Wind, was carried out by General Hans von Obstfelder's First Army with the aim of exploiting weaknesses in the US 6th Army Group caused by the withdrawal of forces to the Ardennes further north. Strasburg, which was only liberated last November, is the major city most at risk (→ 5).

Greek talks begin

Athens, 5 January
A peaceful solution to the civil war which has threatened to destroy Greece seemed likely today with the appearance of a moderate cabinet under a new prime minister, General Plastiras. The new premier has ignored demands from the left-wing ELAS organization for 50 per cent of the cabinet seats and has excluded all extremists. Plastiras urged "all who have been misled and have turned their arms against their country" to return to duty (→ 12).

Japanese retreat across Irrawaddy as British advance

Indian troops wade ashore at Akyab, on the west coast of the Arakan.

Burma, 5 January
Four weeks after crossing the river Chindwin the 19th Indian Division is poised to enter Shwebo. After advancing 90 miles (144 km) east to Indaw, where it linked up with the 36th Indian Division and Lt-Gen Daniel I Sultan's Chinese divisions on 15 December, the 19th marched south and is expected to take Shwebo tomorrow. The Allies have already captured Akyab on the coast this week.

Lt-Gen William Slim, the Fourteenth Army commander, had hoped to bring the main Japanese army in central Burma to battle on the Shwebo Plain, with its back to the Irrawaddy. Instead the Japanese are withdrawing east across the river. Now he is moving IV Corps 200 miles south in Operation Extended Capital, to take Japan's base at Meiktila and cut Japan's Fifteenth Army off from the rear (→ 7).

Air forces join the battle in the Ardennes

Ardennes, 5 January
The *Luftwaffe* opened the New Year with *Bodenplatte*, an attack by 1,035 fighters and bombers on 27 Allied airfields in Belgium and southern Holland. It knocked out 156 Allied aircraft, but cost 277 of its own planes, which were either shot down by the Allies or by its own *flak*. It could be the end of German air power in the west.

When Hitler was planning his Ardennes offensive, Goering promised a thousand aircraft. Hitler, recalling Goering's earlier inflated promises, cut the figure to 800. At best, though, the Germans could never have offered more than token resistance to the Allies, who can send up thousands of bombers to hit the German *Panzers*. Mist and low cloud were decisive in assisting the Germans in the first days of the offensive. Then, late on 22 December, six days after the first German attacks, a high wind built up, followed by heavy falls of snow. The skies cleared and the Allied aircraft came out in force, smashing up the Panzer columns at will. The C-47 transports, too, took off, lifting vital supplies to the besieged Americans in Bastogne.

By the middle of this week the weather had closed in again. Two armoured divisions backed by infantry, sent to attack Houffalize, were left struggling; visibility was so poor that not a single aircraft could support the attack (→11).

A wooden bridge is blown sky high by withdrawing American forces.

Dispute grows over Polish government

London, 1 January
The quarrel over the future of Poland deepened yesterday when Winston Churchill made it plain that, until a full discussion has taken place between Britain, the USSR and the United States, he will not switch his allegiance from the London-based government in exile to the Russian-sponsored Lublin Committee. With the Russians in control of the liberated areas of Poland, however, there seems little that Mr Churchill can do (→14).

Admiral Ramsay dies in air accident

Paris, 2 January
Admiral Sir Bertram Ramsay, the naval chief of the Allied Expeditionary Force, was killed today near here when the plane taking him to a conference in Brussels crashed just after take-off. Admiral Ramsay, aged 61, came back from retirement to take charge at Dover in 1939. He planned the evacuation from Dunkirk, the North African invasion and the invasion of Sicily. On D-Day he masterminded the naval operations.

1945
January

Su	Mo	Tu	We	Th	Fr	Sa
	1	2	3	4	5	6
7	8	9	10	11	12	13
14	15	16	17	18	19	20
21	22	23	24	25	26	27
28	29	30	31			

7. Luzon: Organized Japanese attacks on the US fleet come to an end, but individual *kamikaze* attacks continue.→

7. Moscow: Stalin agrees to Churchill's request that the USSR should mount an offensive to take the pressure off the Allies in the west.→

7. Danzig: Hitler authorizes German navy to evacuate soldiers and civilians cut off in the Courland peninsula and Memel (→24).

7. Hungary: German forces capture Esztergom, north-west of Budapest, in their drive to relieve the garrison in the capital (→11).

7. France: Montgomery enrages his American colleagues by giving a press conference in which he plays down US achievements in the Battle of the Bulge (→19).

8. Strasburg: Battle rages, with the US Seventh Army fending off a strong German attack at Rimling (→20).

9. Bad Nauheim: Hitler rejects Guderian's warning that the USSR is preparing for a massive offensive in the east.→

10. Germany: Hitler orders the death sentence for anyone found guilty of diverting supplies from the military (→16).

11. Ardennes: Troops of the US Third Army link up with the British XXX Corps at St Hubert.→

11. Versailles: Commanders of the Allied air forces in Europe agree to step up attacks on German fuel sources.

11. Budapest: Local *Nyilas* fascists torture, then murder, 92 patients and staff from the Jewish hospital (→20).

12. Berlin: Gertrud Seele, a 27-year-old nurse who said at a private party that she hated the Nazis, is executed for being an "enemy of the state".

13. Ankara: Turkey agrees to open its waters to Allied warships.

13. Ardennes: The Allies cut the St Vith to Houffalize road, as British and US divisions link up at the river Ourthe.→

Artillery announces start of Red Army's drive on Germany

Moscow, 12 January
The Red Army today unleashed its major winter offensive, hurling 163 divisions at the German positions in Poland and East Prussia, and is sweeping forward with massed tanks under a massive artillery bombardment and clouds of warplanes against 30 German divisions. The Germans are fighting from well-prepared defensive positions, but they are outnumbered by five tanks to one.

Hitler refused to believe intelligence reports of the massive Russian build-up, and rejected calls from General Guderian, now chief of the general staff, to transfer

"Freedom and life" – boys and old men are now fighting for Germany.

troops from the Ardennes offensive or call off attacks near Budapest. Yet today's attack by General Konev's First Ukrainian Front in southern Poland is only the first round of Russia's winter offensive.

From Memel, on the Baltic, to Warsaw, some 300 miles further south, the Red Army is poised to attack, with Warsaw the prime target for Marshal Zhukov's First Byelorussian Front when it joins the fray. The Russian commanders have their eyes on the industrial cities of Upper Silesia, but if they can cross the Vistula the German border will be less than 60 miles (96 km) away. Russia has stockpiled supplies to sustain a broad advance (→20).

597

Germans count the cost of the failed Ardennes offensive

Ardennes, 13 January

The Germans opened the Ardennes gamble with around 250,000 men; a month later, fighting a grim rearguard action, they have lost upwards of 120,000 killed, wounded and captured, and are facing a US force of 600,000. The Americans have lost 8,607 dead and 68,283 wounded or missing, and the British 1,400 dead.

For both the Germans and the Allies, the losses in weapons and equipment are considerable. The Germans lost about 600 tanks (compared with the Americans' 733) and 1,000 aircraft. For the Germans the losses are pretty well irreplaceable; yet the Allies will replace theirs within the next two weeks. The Germans fell far short of gaining their strategic objective, the port of Antwerp, though their V2 attacks on the city caused serious damage and loss of life. On 16 December, the day that the offensive opened, a V2 hit a cinema, killing 567 people, 296 of them British servicemen – the largest casualty toll yet from a single rocket.

The "Battle of the Bulge" tested the Allied capacity for delivering a fighting response in a crisis, but its only impact on the course of the war has been to delay the advance into Germany by a few weeks. Hitler has squandered men and equipment desperately needed to face the Russians, who opened their new offensive yesterday with 163 divisions; Hitler has only 30 (→ 15).

Two young German boys surrender.

US troops land 110 miles from Manila

Heavily-laden US invading forces ford a river en route to San Fabian: MacArthur bypassed Formosa to take Luzon.

Philippines, 9 January

Covered by the US Third Fleet and preceded by heavy beach-head bombardments, the US Sixth Army, commanded by Lt-Gen Walter Krueger, has landed at Lingayen Gulf, Luzon, 110 miles (176 km) north of Manila.

Japanese resistance was light, but en route to Lingayen, while sailing through the central Philippines and the South China Sea, the invasion force was subjected to frequent attack by *kamikaze* aircraft. The kamikaze terror sank or damaged 40 US vessels. One Allied cruiser, HMAS *Australia*, was hit no less than five times. Except for the loss of 44 sailors killed, the *Australia's* efficiency was unimpaired.

Before landing on Luzon, MacArthur's forces had, on 15 December, seized bases on Mindoro Island, south of Manila, from which US aircraft are now supporting the Luzon invasion. Soon after the landing the Sixth Army was in control of a beach-head 15 miles wide and up to three miles deep. By noon, San Fabian had been captured.

Admiral Ernest King, the US Navy chief of staff, had strongly advocated that Luzon be bypassed and that Formosa should be the next objective. MacArthur rejected Formosa, which might result in heavy casualties. He had long advocated the reconquest of the Philippines, and said after Leyte that Luzon should be invaded. The next landings are planned for Iwo Jima and Okinawa (→ 15).

Navy backs the Allied advance in Burma

Akyab, Burma, 7 January

Allied troops of the 81st and 82nd West African Divisions are advancing down the Burmese coast towards Myebon, buoyed by the capture of Akyab by XV Corps. British Army and Royal Marine commandos had landed there to try to cut off the Japanese retreat, but they were too late; the Japanese forces had been withdrawn towards Mandalay. Now more substantial landings are planned at Myebon and Ramree Island to support the land advance. These land operations have been supported by naval bombardment, notably last month when two Australian destroyers reinforced the light Allied naval force. But many small motor launches are playing an important role here, harrying enemy vessels in the maze of coastal inlets to disrupt supplies, and landing raiding parties (→ 14).

Greek rebels move closer to a truce

Athens, 12 January

Maj-Gen Ronald Scobie, the British GOC Greece, today faced four rebel leaders at a conference table and laid down his terms for a truce in the Greek civil war. And the indications are that the left-wing ELAS (National Liberation Army) will accept a form of armistice and agree to exchange prisoners (→ 5/2).

1945

January

Su	Mo	Tu	We	Th	Fr	Sa
	1	2	3	4	5	6
7	8	9	10	11	12	13
14	15	16	17	18	19	20
21	22	23	24	25	26	27
28	29	30	31			

14. Burma: Slim's crossing of the Irrawaddy starts in earnest, and Japanese attempts at defence are confused by numerous feints and patrol crossings (→ 15).

14. Poland: The Red Army cuts the railway line south of Cracow in its rapid advance towards Germany (→ 15).

15. Luzon: US troops cross the Agno river (→ 17).

15. Burma: Chinese troops take Namhkam, on the Ledo Road.→

15. Poland: The Red Army captures Kielce (→ 16).

15. France: US troops capture Houffalize (→ 27).

15. London: The boat-train service to the continent starts again after a five-year break.

16. Poland: Soviet troops capture Radom, and move to encircle Warsaw.→

16. Berlin: Hitler returns to the Chancellery, where Allied bombs drive him to shelter in a bunker 24 feet (7.2 metres) below ground level (→ 21).

17. Philippines: MacArthur urges more speed to capture Manila and Clark Field.→

18. Warsaw: The Soviet puppet government arrives from Lublin to take over the reins of government.→

18. Auschwitz-Birkenau: The Germans order the inmates to evacuate the camp immediately for transport – on foot or by train – to concentration camps in Germany (→ 27).

19. China: Japanese troops take Chingyuan, on the Canton to Hankow railway.

19. Versailles: Montgomery is furious as Eisenhower rejects his strategy for a push to the Rhine in favour of General Bradley's (→ 28).

20. Budapest: The provisional government agrees to pay $300 million reparations to the Allies and to join them in the fight against Germany (→ 13/2).

20. Washington: Roosevelt is inaugurated for a fourth term as president, and Harry S Truman is sworn in as vice-president.

US troops face massive force on Luzon

US soldiers take cover behind a hedge – a Sherman tank presses forward.

Philippines, 20 January
American forces of XIV Corps pushing inland from their beach-head at Lingayen Gulf on Luzon, the main Philippine island, are tonight on the outskirts of San Miguel, some 90 miles from Manila. The US troops had met no opposition on the beaches when they landed on 9 January, but the fighting has since been fierce, particularly at the Agno river.

General Yamashita, who commands an army of 260,000 in Luzon, the largest encountered in the Pacific campaign, saved his men from a beach-head mauling from American fire-power by withdrawing them from the shoreline. His plan was to let the Americans get ashore and then encircle them.

The US commander, General Douglas MacArthur, was certain that he would secure the Central Plain/Manila region in four to six weeks and he pressed his commanders to push on without delay. A key target for the Americans is Clark Field airbase, which is needed for the forthcoming invasions of Iwo Jima and Okinawa (→ 21).

City in panic after Germans hit back

Alsace, 20 January
The German counter-offensive in Alsace, Operation North Wind, has brought the enemy within eight miles (13 km) of Strasburg and caused near-panic in the city. The Germans have established a bridgehead over the Rhine and are poised to link up with another German force striking northward from the "Colmar pocket". Hitler launched North Wind on New Year's Day in the expectation that Blaskowitz's Army Group G would overwhelm the greatly over-extended American-French 6th Army Group, which holds a 120-mile (192-km) front that includes positions which Patton's men held before they moved up to the Ardennes (→ 23).

Churchill unity plea

Britain, 18 January
Winston Churchill today gave MPs his most confident and sparkling report of the whole war – now in its 65th month. He appealed for unity at home while the Allies use the overwhelming forces which are now poised to crush Nazi Germany. The prime minister warned the Germans that giving in now will be easier than enduring what the Allies have in store for them.

Burma Road to be reopened as two Chinese armies join forces

A Japanese train after an RAF attack: now Upper Burma has been cleared.

Mongyu, Burma, 15 January
Here at Mongyu, close by the Sino-Burmese border, two Chinese armies have met. From the northwest Lt-Gen Daniel Sultan's US-trained Chinese divisions have cleared the Japanese from Upper Burma and from the east a Chinese Nationalist army under General Wai Li-huang has made a ponderous march from Yunnan.

After three years – while Nationalist China was totally isolated from its Allies except for an airbridge from India – the Burma Road can now reopen. The US-built oil pipeline, laid along the Ledo Road, will be extended all the way to Yunnan. The last Japanese positions threatening the Burma Road, around Wanting and Namhkam, are now being mopped up (→ 21).

All-conquering Red Army powers through Poland

The First Polish Army, under overall Soviet command, fights for Warsaw.

Tanks lead the way as Rokossovsky's forces advance through Poland.

Devastated city of Warsaw finally falls

Warsaw, 17 January

Warsaw, the Polish capital, enslaved by Hitler for more than five years and devastated in the uprising of the Polish Home Army last August, fell to Marshal Zhukov's First Byelorussian Front today. Its fall came as the result of an operation by Zhukov which was both overwhelming in strength and brilliant in execution. Zhukov took infinite care with his preparations. Engineers built new roads, constructed bridges over the Vistula in the two bridgeheads held by Zhukov's front and cleared paths through the minefields. Huge quantitites of ammunition, supplies and fuel were gathered. Political preparations were also made with the acknowledgement by Moscow of the Lublin Committee as the government of Poland and the inclusion of General Rola-Zymierski's First Polish Army in Zhukov's forces.

The campaign opened on 12 January with Marshal Konev's First Ukrainian Front attacking out of its southerly bridgehead across the Vistula towards Cracow. Zhukov followed two days later, with his troops bursting out of their positions after a two-hour saturation shelling of the German defences. These defences were in two lines, two miles (3.2 km) apart. General Guderian had wanted the second line to be established much farther

back and to give up the front line when the Russians attacked, but Hitler would not agree. The result was that both lines were caught in the artillery storm.

Zhukov's infantry horde broke through the shattered lines and opened gaping breaches on both sides of Warsaw. Only then were the tanks unleashed, and they raced through the gaps to encircle the city and then push on to Sochaczew, 35 miles to the west of Warsaw. The Poles were given the honour of leading the assault on their capital, and by nightfall Warsaw was free. But it is a city of ruins, without people. The first of Europe's capitals to fall to the *Wehrmacht*, it has suffered the most appalling destruction under the Nazis (→18).

Russians advance 100 miles in a week

Moscow, 20 January

The Red Army is racing through Poland, covering over 100 miles (160 km) in a week as the great sweep west gathers pace. In the past the Russians had to pause to allow their infantrymen to rest; now, thanks to Lend-Lease, the infantry is motorized and able to keep up with the tanks.

The story is the same all along the line. In the north Gen Cherniakhovsky has torn a 40-mile (64-km) hole in the East Prussian defence zone and is 30 miles (48 km) inside Germany's "holy soil". Marshal Rokossovsky, driving through northern Poland, is on the East Prussian border 110 miles (180 km) south-east of Danzig and is threatening to cut off the whole of East

Prussia, the home of German militarism. Zhukov, having taken Warsaw, has now captured Lodz, the great textile and engineering city and an indispensable base for the advance on Berlin. At the southern tip of the line, Konev has taken Cracow, opening up the road from the north into Czechoslovakia. He has also taken Praszka and so reached the borders of German Silesia. The Russians seem unstoppable. Columns of tanks and lorries stretch for miles across the Polish plain. The Russian tactics are to advance with their fast mobile detachments moving ahead of their tank and combined-arms groups. When they run into resistance or it becomes necessary to wipe out bypassed German forces, separate units are assigned to deal with the problem while the main column crunches on.

Overhead, untidy groups of Soviet planes wheel like flocks of starlings ready to settle on German targets. Opposing them are men like the Stuka ace Hans-Ulrich Rudel who claims to have destroyed 500 Russian tanks and a battleship. But there is little that even Rudel can do to stop the Russians. There are just too many of them. Fear is spreading throughout eastern Germany as refugees flood back from the warzone. The vengeful Russians have many scores to settle (→24).

Soviet-backed Poles to round up rivals

Moscow, 19 January

The fears of the Polish government in London came true today when President Bierut, the leader of the Soviet-sponsored Lublin Committee, issued a decree announcing the round-up of "irresponsible members" of the Home Army and followers of the London government. The decree urged all armed forces in the liberated areas to outlaw the

"Home Army murderers who are provoking civil strife". Of General Bor-Komorowski, the leader of the Warsaw uprising, it says: "His provocative rising and later surrender of arms considerably aided the Germans." There seems little doubt now that the Lublin Committee intends to carry out a purge of all those who do not follow its communist line.

1945

January

Su	Mo	Tu	We	Th	Fr	Sa
	1	2	3	4	5	6
7	8	9	10	11	12	13
14	15	16	17	18	19	20
21	22	23	24	25	26	27
28	29	30	31			

21. Luzon: US forces capture Tarlac and advance on Clark Field (→ 31).

21. Burma: Indian troops land on Ramree Island and attack Kangaw (→ 22).

21. Berlin: Hitler orders all his commanders to report their decisions to him truthfully and quickly (→ 23).

22. Burma: The Indian 7th Division captures Tilin (→ 27).

23. Berlin: Hitler appoints Himmler, who has no experience of operational command, C-in-C Army Group Vistula.→

23. Berlin: Hitler belatedly agrees to a major new ship-building programme, and orders the extension of the slave-labour system in the northern dockyards (→ 30).

23. Berlin: Count Helmuth von Moltke, the leader of the "Kreisau circle" resistance movement, is executed.

24. Sumatra: RN aircraft attack oil targets at Palembang (→ 29).

24. Silesia: The Red Army captures Gleiwitz.→

24. Berlin: Guderian meets von Ribbentrop, the foreign minister, and tells him bluntly "the war is lost".→

25. Bonin Islands: Iwo Jima is heavily bombarded by US ships to prepare the way for landings next month (→ 17/2).

25. Indian Ocean: British carriers set sail for Australia, on their way to join the US Navy in the Pacific (→ 10/2).

25. East Prussia: German forces, almost cut off by the two-pronged Soviet advance, start evacuation (→ 31).

26. Washington: Lt Audie Murphy is awarded the Congressional Medal of Honor.

27. Burma: Chinese troops clear the Ledo Road of Japanese troops (→ 29).

27. Lyons: Charles Maurras, the leader of *Action Francais*, is sentenced to life imprisonment for collaborating with the Nazis.

27. France: German gains in the Ardennes are eliminated.

Russians free Auschwitz death camp

Soldiers shocked by "living skeletons"

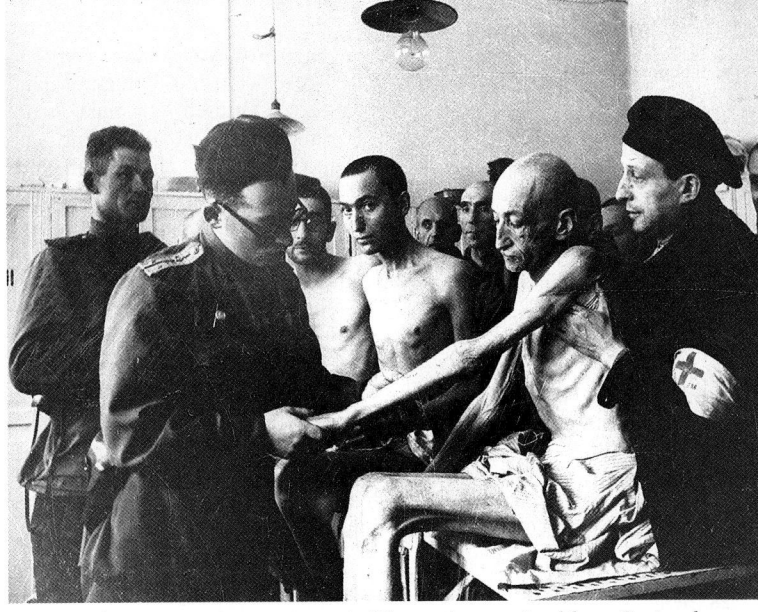

A man who was once an engineer in Vienna is examined by a Soviet doctor.

Auschwitz-Birkenau, 27 January
At midday, the four young Soviet cavalrymen, guns at the ready, came cautiously down the road that surrounded the camp. Looking through the barbed wire, they saw living skeletons moving slowly in a landscape of corpses sprawled in the snow, punctuated by broken-down and burnt huts. The Red Army had stumbled upon the Nazis' biggest extermination camp.

As the booming of Russian artillery came nearer, the Nazis attempted to conceal the traces of their hideous mass murder. They have burnt most of the camp's carefully-maintained records. Nine days ago they evacuated the twenty thousand prisoners with the most chance of survival. Those who were too weak to walk out of the camp were shot dead. The rest have been dispersed to other camps further west. Anyone falling behind on the long march to their new destination was shot and thrown into a ditch.

Meanwhile the SS blew up the crematoria and gas chambers, and set fire to the clothing stores, destroying 29 of the camp's 35 warehouses. In the remainder, the Russians have found huge piles of suits, dresses, children's clothing, shoes, carpets, shaving brushes, spectacles and false teeth. Enormous numbers of suitcases bear hotel labels from all over Europe; trade marks on clothing show that the victims come from countries as far apart as Hungary and the Netherlands.

The Germans left only a few hundred inmates behind in the camp's hospital block, most of them sick with diphtheria, scarlet fever or typhus. In the last few days they have led a twilight existence roaming the unguarded camp, a ragged, hollow-eyed, feverish horde, rifling the deserted and burnt huts for fuel and food. They have peered out through the fog at the *Wehrmacht* tanks and lorries retreating around them, and tentatively breached the wire to gather potatoes. Now, they regard the young Red Army troops with a jaundiced stare: can the nightmare really be over? Or is there more to come? (→ 6/2)

Faces of torment behind the wire.

Red Army is just 100 miles from Berlin

Moscow, 27 January
Marshal Konev has virtually severed the vital industrial area of Upper Silesia from the rest of the *Reich*. At the same time, according to German reports, Marshal Zhukov has outflanked Poznan and his forward patrols have reached Bentschen, only 100 miles (160 km) from Berlin. In the north Marshal Rokossovsky has burst through to the Baltic and cut off East Prussia. About two-thirds of the province has now been captured. Konigsberg, to the north, has been prac-

tically cut off and Danzig is threatened. Rokossovsky had to move fast today to beat off a desperate final German counter-attack to try to break out to the Vistula.

Meanwhile in Berlin the *Volkssturm*, consisting largely of old men and schoolboys, is to fight on. The streets are being cleared of refugees to make way for reinforcements. German radio is preparing the people for disaster: "This is our last chance. Victory or destruction is the slogan guiding the fate of the German people" (→ 28).

French Army halts German offensive

Strasburg, 23 January
The French First Army has halted the German offensive, North Wind, at the last bridge before Strasburg. General Eisenhower was willing to give up the city, liberated on 23 November, in order to allow the US Seventh Army to withdraw, but General de Gaulle threatened to remove his forces from the Allied command if Strasburg was sacrificed. Ike gave way, but said that the French must defend the city.

1945

January

Su	Mo	Tu	We	Th	Fr	Sa
	1	2	3	4	5	6
7	8	9	10	11	12	13
14	15	16	17	18	19	20
21	22	23	24	25	26	27
28	29	30	31			

28. China: The first supply convoy reaches China from Burma, via the reopened Ledo Road (→ 29).

28. Poland: The Red Army captures the Dabrowa coal mining area and the towns of Beuthen and Katowice.→

28. Lithuania: Memel is occupied by the Russians, completing their occupation of Lithuania.

28. Sofia: Prince Cyril of Bulgaria is sentenced to death for war crimes he committed when he was regent in 1943-44.

28. Berlin: Civilians are ordered to start digging anti-tank trenches around the city (→ 30).

28. Versailles: Eisenhower returns the command of the US Ninth Army, temporarily given to Montgomery, to Bradley (→ 8/2).

29. Burma: Japanese forces try but fail to drive the Chinese from their positions defending the "Stilwell Road" near Lashio.→

30. Malta: Churchill and Roosevelt meet in order to prepare for their imminent conference with Stalin in Yalta (→ 4/2).

30. Berlin: Speer writes a memo to Hitler, informing him that the state of German industry is so bad that food and electricity must now be given priority over arms production (→ 24/2).

30. Berlin: Hitler gives Goebbels the decorative title of Defender of Berlin, and makes a radio broadcast asking the German people to die in order to preserve Nazism.→

31. Philippines: The 11th US Airborne Division lands on the west coast of Luzon.→

31. Moscow: The first congress of the Russian Orthodox Church since the Revolution opens, with prayers for Stalin and victory.

31. East Prussia: Soviet troops surround Konigsberg.→

31. Hanford, Washington: The first weapon-grade plutonium is ready for shipment (→ 20/2).

Red Army crosses German frontier

Moscow, 31 January
Marshal Zhukov has crossed the German frontier, thrust 12 miles (19 km) deep into Pomerania and captured Driesen, 95 miles from Berlin. His men stand on the bank of the Oder river. The new advance has cut the railway line from Berlin to Danzig, and poses a threat to Frankfurt an der Oder, just 45 miles east of Berlin.

The imminence of danger to the capital of Germany has been admitted by Dr Ley, the Labour Front leader. Writing in *Der Angriff*, he pledges in a pale echo of Churchill's words: "We shall fight before Berlin, inside Berlin and behind Berlin." German hopes rest to some degree on the defence of the fortified towns which have been bypassed by the Red Army. Poznan, some miles behind the front on the Warsaw to Berlin road, is one of these towns and, with 60,000 troops behind its concrete defences, is resisting fiercely. The front-line troops are supported by the *Volkssturm* and cadets from an officers' training school who are used in defence while regular units mount counter-attacks, sometimes several battalions strong, with *Panzer* elements.

Elsewhere, the Red Army's advance continues. Marshal Rokossovsky has now cut off three German armies in East Prussia. When he captured Tannenburg, the scene of the crushing German victory over the *Czar's* army in the last war, he discovered that the Germans had removed the sarcophagus of the victor, von Hindenburg, and blown up the monument commemorating his victory. Von Hindenburg won his victory as czarist officers advancing into East Prussia were trying to decide which horses to ride into Berlin. It is doubtful if even he could have saved Berlin in this war (→ 5/2).

Troops of the Red Army: now fighting inside the war-shattered Third Reich.

THE RED ARMY ADVANCES INTO GERMANY

100 miles
160 km

Baltic Sea

Memel

Tilsit

Konigsberg

Danzig

POMERANIA

EAST PRUSSIA

Stettin

GERMANY

Berlin

Vistula

Frankfurt — an der Oder

Poznan

Bzura

Warsaw

Oder

Lodz

Lublin

POLAND

Dresden

Breslau

Katowice
Cracow

SILESIA

Front line,
11 Jan
2 Feb

© Chronicle Communications Ltd.

US forces capture key air base as they advance towards Manila

Luzon, 31 January
General MacArthur's US forces are closing fast from all sides on Manila since landing at Lingayen on Luzon three weeks ago. Clark Field, a key airbase 50 miles (80 km) north of the Philippines capital, was recaptured today by XIV Corps. South of the city US paratroops of the 11th Airborne Division landed at Nasagbu, taking the Japanese defence forces by surprise.

The fierce seven-day battle for Clark Field's cave and tunnel complex ended with survivors of the 30,000-man Kembu Group retreating further into the Zambales Mountains. General Yamashita, the Japanese Philippines C-in-C, is fighting similar delaying actions in the north-east with his 150,000man Shobu Group, hoping to prevent Luzon from becoming the launch-pad for an attack on Japan (→ 3/2).

Thousands die in torpedoed German liner

Danzig, 31 January
The German "Strength Through Joy" liner *Wilhelm Gustloff* was torpedoed by the Russian submarine S13 off the Hela peninsula last night. Crowded with refugees and wounded from East Prussia, the liner sank swiftly in the freezing seas and it is feared that some 7,000 people died, the greatest sea tragedy yet recorded. The refugees had struggled to get on board the doomed liner. As she cast off small boats appeared and women held up their children crying: "Take us with you. Save the children." The liner drifted while the ship's crew put out nets and the refugees scrambled aboard. Few survived.

The S13 is one of the Baltic submarines now active following the uncorking of the Baltic after Finland's departure from the war. Commanded by Captain Third Class Sasha Marinescu, she is based at the Finnish port of Turku. The tragic irony of this disaster is that Marinescu might not have been in position to intercept the *Wilhelm Gustloff* if he had not put to sea to escape the secret police after a heavy drinking bout.

Convoys open "Stilwell Road" in Burma

A truck bearing the Stars and Stripes sets out on the newly-opened road.

Myitkyina, Burma, 31 January
The Burma Road from India to China has re-opened, bringing supplies to Chiang Kai-shek's Nationalist armies. The road – which Chiang has named the "Stilwell Road" – runs via Ledo, Myitkyina and Bhamo. The first convoy, carrying 75mm and 105mm guns, has crossed the Chinese border and been greeted with fireworks. "During the years that China stood alone the Japanese militarists told their people that if the Burma Road were closed our courage would collapse," Chiang said. "Now comes this caravan, roaring into China over an area which they thought just yesterday to hold in everlasting peace" (→ 9/2).

Eddie Slovik, a US deserter, executed

France, 31 January
The US Army today shot dead Private Eddie Slovik for desertion. It was the first such execution since the American Civil War 80 years ago. Slovik, aged 24, a sub-literate petty criminal, failed to join his unit in Normandy and latched on to a Canadian corps instead. When he finally caught up with his own unit, he deserted for a second time.

Air raids damage Sumatran refineries

East Indian Ocean, 29 January
British carrier-based aircraft have inflicted massive damage on Japan's main source of aviation fuel with bombing raids on Japanese-controlled refineries in Sumatra, in the Dutch East Indies, over the last five days. The loss of the refineries means that crude oil will now have to be shipped to Japan for refining, doubling Japan's need for tankers.

1945

February →

Su	Mo	Tu	We	Th	Fr	Sa
				1	2	3
4	5	6	7	8	9	10
11	12	13	14	15	16	17
18	19	20	21	22	23	24
25	26	27	28			

1. Poland: The Red Army captures Torun.

2. Singapore: Eighty-eight US B-29s destroy the docks and Japanese naval base.

2. Ecuador: The government declares war on Germany.→

3. Philippines: Fighting gets fiercer north of Manila, and US reinforcements are landed on Tagaytay Ridge.→

3. Germany: US aircraft drop three thousand tons of explosives on Berlin.→

3. France: The German garrison at Colmar surrenders to the French First Army (→ 9).

4. Yalta, Crimea: Stalin, Roosevelt and Churchill meet (→ 8).

4. Wales: Rudolf Hess, under guard in an Abergavenny mental hospital, tries to commit suicide with a bread knife.

5. Germany: Troops of the Red Army start crossing the River Oder (→ 10).

5. Athens: Communist fighters lay down their arms, as the government it agrees an amnesty with EAM (→ 12).

6. Germany: Himmler's attempt, under the influence of his masseur Felix Kersten, to transfer some Jews from German camps to Switzerland is foiled when Hitler bans all evacuations (→ 19).

8. Yalta: Allied commanders take time off from the conference to visit the historic battlefield at Balaklava (→ 11).

8. Germany: Montgomery opens Operation Veritable, a British-Canadian offensive to clear the lower Rhineland.→

9. Burma: Indian troops complete the capture of Ramree Island (→ 15).

9. France: The "Colmar pocket" is cleared.

10. Australia: The British Pacific Fleet sails into Sydney harbour (→ 23).

10. Germany: The US advance is held up when the Germans open the Schwammenaul dam, making it impossible to bridge the Roer river. The Red Army reaches Elbing, on the Baltic, cutting off East Prussia.→

MacArthur leads US forces into Manila, but fight goes on

Manila, 6 February
General Douglas MacArthur tonight claimed that the recapture of Manila was imminent, as house-to-house fighting continued in the Philippine capital and US troops fought fires started deliberately by the trapped Japanese. MacArthur accused them of "general sabotage and destruction", saying that they had "wantonly set fire to the downtown business district".

Since the US 1st Cavalry took Manila's Santo Tomas prison camp three days ago, freeing 3,700 PoWs, US XIV Corps troops have fought for every street in their advance downtown. The Japanese commander, Admiral Iwabuchi, defying General Yamashita's orders to evacuate, believes that his 16,000 men can hold out for weeks from inside the walls of the old city (→ 13).

A young banana-seller in Manila.

PoWs from "death march" are rescued

Cabu, East Luzon, 2 February
In a dramatic raid 24 miles (38 km) behind enemy lines last night, US Rangers and Filipino guerrillas freed 510 haggard and emaciated PoWs held captive since Bataan fell in 1942. During the five-minute attack all 223 guards were killed, as elated prisoners shouted "the Yanks are coming". One PoW collapsed and died from excitement.

Zhukov grinds to a halt

Red Army troops advance through a village before the snow began to melt.

Moscow, 10 February
For ten days now, Marshal Zhukov has been halted on the Oder river after securing a small bridgehead at Kustrin, some 40 miles (64 km) short of Berlin. The halt has caused disappointment in Moscow, where it was hoped that the German capital would be captured this month.

There are, however, good reasons for Zhukov's reluctance to attack. He has suffered heavy casualties in his storming advance across Poland, has begun to outrun his supply lines and has had to divert strong forces to deal with the *Festung* [fortress] city of Poznan. At the same time "General Mud" has come to the aid of the Germans with a thaw turning the battlefield into a quagmire and melting the ice on the Oder. Zhukov therefore needs time to reorganize, resupply and prepare for a river crossing.

He is also conscious of the presence of strong German forces along his exposed northern flank in Pomerania. These forces, named Army Group Vistula, are commanded by SS *Reichsfuhrer* Heinrich Himmler, a man with no military training. His appointment reveals how little Hitler now trusts his generals.

Nevertheless, Himmler, the most feared man in Germany, is under orders to strike at Zhukov in five days time. The Russian high command, however, has already given Marshal Rokossovsky orders to strike into Pomerania to clear away the danger. This morning the Russians headed north (→ 15).

US delivers largest B-29 raid on Japan

Japan, 10 February
US B-29 bombers destroyed the Nakajima aircraft plant at Ota, near Tokyo, today in the largest daylight raid yet over the Japanese mainland. Out of the 84 B-29s that took off from US airbases on the Mariana Islands, 12 were lost over the target area as Japanese fighters put up heavy opposition, suffering 21 losses in the fight.

In a separate raid today, B-24s based on Guam bombed Iwo Jima and Okinawa (→ 16).

South Americans in rush to declare war

Paraguay, 9 February
The government here today declared war on Germany and Japan, boosting the growing tide of South American countries which are joining the Allies to secure an invitation to the "United Nations" conference. A Caracas newspaper today reports that Venezuela is considering declaring war on the Axis. Meanwhile Chile is denying rumours to the same effect. Ecuador declared war on Germany and Japan on 2 February (→ 22).

Allied bombers enjoy free run of Europe

Germany, 8-9 February
Allied bombing crews are being kept busy. Tonight RAF Bomber Command attacked strategic targets at Politz, Wanne-Eickel and Krefeld; last night Goch, Cleve and the Dortmund-Ems canal were hit. On 3 February the USAAF attacked Berlin with over 1,200 heavy bombers, escorted by 900 fighters. Five square miles of central Berlin were set on fire; Tempelhof airport was badly damaged. Among 1,000 casualties of the raid was Roland Freisler, the notorious president of the People's Court, who died when the court was bombed and he was hit by a falling beam.

Vienna has also been bombed by US Liberators, 29 of which were shot down, five during two minutes of intense *flak*. V2 rocket installations in the Netherlands were hit in daylight raids by RAF fighter-bombers. Other targets included E-boat shelters at Ijmuiden and – to assist the advance of XXX Corps across the German-Dutch border – troop concentrations near Goch, where there were also civilian casualties (→ 14).

A US Flying Fortress over Berlin.

Allied armies pour through Siegfried Line

Nijmegen, 9 February
After an overnight attack by heavy bombers and a 1,000-gun bombardment, linked to a second air strike, British and Canadian troops swept forward into the Siegfried Line. The front edge soon collapsed and the Canadians, crossing the flooded lowlands by amphibious trucks, reached the Rhine here today. Upstream, the US First Army is poised to seize the Roer dams, hoping to prevent the Germans from opening the floodgates. The enemy's front line is partly manned by men regarded as invalids, but behind them are the tough *Panzer* forces, which could yet trouble the Allies (→ 13).

An American tank finds a gap in the fortifications of the Siegfried Line.

1945

February

Su	Mo	Tu	We	Th	Fr	Sa
				1	2	3
4	5	6	7	8	9	10
11	12	13	14	15	16	17
18	19	20	21	22	23	24
25	26	27	28			

11. Brussels: Achille van Acker forms a government of national unity.

12. Berlin: German women between 16 and 60 are to be called up as auxiliaries to the *Volkssturm* [people's front] (→ 17).

13. Philippines: US forces capture the Cavite naval base and Nicholls Field airbase, near Manila.→

13. Berlin: General Walther Wenck, Guderian's chief of staff, is appointed to command the German offensive on Soviet positions east of Berlin (→ 17).

14. New York: William C Colepaugh and Erich Gimpel, German spies who landed by U-boat on 29 November, are sentenced to death.

15. Burma: Indian troops capture Pagan (→ 27).

15. Germany: Soviet forces under Konev encircle Breslau, where martial law is declared and the death sentence decreed for "undermining German resolution or striking power".

16. Caracas: Venezuela declares war on Germany and Japan.

16. Japan: US ships attack Tokyo and Yokohama (→ 17.)

17. Japan: The US Navy's Task Force 58 attacks Tokyo and Yokohama for the second time in two days, and launches the final wave of the bombardment of Iwo Jima before landings commence (→ 19).

17. Murmansk: The British corvette *Bluebell* is sunk by the U-boat U711. The escort HMS *Lark* sinks U425, but is then sunk.

17. Cairo: Churchill unwittingly drinks an aphrodisiac at a banquet for King ibn Saud of Saudi Arabia (→ 20).

17. London: The World Trades Union Conference opens.

17. Germany: General Wenck breaks his shoulder (→ 18).

17. Trieste: RAF bombers sink the Italian battleships *Conte di Cavour* and *Impero*, and a German destroyer.

Yalta reshapes Europe

Stalin, Roosevelt and Churchill in their palace conference quarters at Yalta.

Yalta, Crimea, 11 February
President Roosevelt, Marshal Stalin and the British prime minister Winston Churchill, the leaders of the "Big Three" Allied powers, today spelt out the decisions reached in a week's conference here. They have decided to divide Germany into four zones of occupation, one each for the Big Three and a fourth for France. A conference will be held in San Francisco in April to prepare the charter of a new United Nations organization.

Agreement was reached on new governments for Poland and Yugoslavia. The Soviet-backed Lublin government for Poland would include members from London, and the partisan leader, Marshal Tito, would join Ivan Subasich, the royalist prime minister, in the Yugoslav government. Other arrangements are being kept a little quieter: Stalin is to declare war on Japan within two months of the end of the war in Europe, and changes to the Polish borders will in effect move the country westwards, enabling the Russians to annex areas in the east. The conference was held in a former czarist palace overlooking the Black Sea, beautiful but plagued with bedbugs (→ 20).

US landings meet stiff opposition on Corregidor island

Philippines, 16 February
After a naval bombardment and an air strike, American paratroopers and a seaborne assault force have landed on the island fortress of Corregidor which dominates the entrance to Manila Bay. Corregidor is defended by some 5,200 Japanese sailors in superb condition and amply supplied with ammunition. The fort is the scene of the heroic last stand of the American and Filipino forces which were overwhelmed by the Japanese in 1942. The Japanese defenders, holed up in a mass of tunnels and caves, are putting up a fanatical resistance.

On 29 January an American force of 30,000 men landed uncontested north-west of Subic Bay in a move to seal off the Bataan peninsula. Two days later another force was landed south of Manila Bay at Nasugbu. The strategic Clark Field airbase fell to the Americans on 31 January, and by 3 February the 1st Cavalry Division had reached the outskirts of Manila.

Six weeks after the landing at Lingayen, Manila is practically surrounded, but MacArthur's expectation of a quick liberation of the "Pearl of the Orient" has not been realized. The Japanese army had ordered evacuation of the city, but a force of 16,000 Japanese sailors is fighting on to the bitter end (→ 21).

Budapest falls to the Red Army at the end of a 50-day siege

Budapest, 13 February
Budapest, the strongest of Hitler's "satellite" capitals, fell today to the Red Army after a bloody siege lasting 50 days. The German commander, General Pfeffer-Wildenbruch, was caught hiding in a sewer. According to Moscow, more than 49,000 German and Hungarian soldiers fell in the battle. Hitler made desperate efforts to hold on to the Hungarian capital, sending General Herbert Gilles's 4th SS *Panzer* Corps to its relief. Gilles got to within 12 miles (19 km) of the city, but was then stopped in his tracks. Now, says Moscow radio, "a major obstacle has been removed and the way to Vienna is open" (→ 7/3).

The Hammer and Sickle is placed on the parliament building in Budapest.

Allied bombs annihilate ancient city of Dresden

Over fifty thousand perish in firestorm

Germany, 14 February

Dresden, a city so rarely attacked that its citizens took no notice when air-raid warnings sounded, was devastated last night in the fiercest firestorm ever created by RAF Bomber Command. Over 50,000 people are believed dead in this city whose population of 700,000 had been swollen by as many as 500,000 refugees from the east. Conditions were perfect for Wing-Commander Maurice Smith and his 244 Lancasters. Most of Dresden's *flak* guns had been sent to the front, and the few available nightfighters did not arrive until too late.

The marker flares went down dead on target, then Smith ordered the destruction to start. High-explosive bombs opened up the buildings; then the incendiaries went down and soon the city was ablaze. "That's good bombing," said the controller. The bombers wheeled away and then came another wave of 529 Lancasters. In all, 1,478 tons of HE and 1,182 tons of incendiaries were dropped. Then the firestorm started. People were sucked into the inferno like leaves into an autumn bonfire. Many took shelter in cellars, only to die of suffocation.

Why has such devastation been visited on Dresden, a city of great architectural but little military value? The attack stems from plans for Operation Thunderclap designed to precipitate Germany's surrender by a series of heavy raids on the railway network. Dresden is a transit centre for part of the eastern front, but last night's attack was also explicitly aimed at hastening the end of the war by destroying German morale. There was opposition to this plan, especially from the Americans who called it "terroristic"; but it was ultimately endorsed on the grounds that it might help the Russians militarily, by attacking German communications, and politically, by being seen to support the Red Army. Thus, today the US also played its part in the terror: 311 USAAF B-17s dropped 771 tons of bombs on the smoking embers of the city (→ 21).

Miraculously, the figure of Justice still stands over the charred ruins of the city of Dresden: over 50,000 died.

Shell-shocked survivors of the Dresden firestorm begin the long task of identifying row upon row of dead bodies.

1945

February

Su	Mo	Tu	We	Th	Fr	Sa
				1	2	3
4	5	6	7	8	9	10
11	12	13	14	15	16	17
18	19	20	21	22	23	24
25	26	27	28			

Forest battles clear way ahead for Allies

Reichswald, 13 February
Troops from General Sir Henry Crerar's First Canadian Army have almost won a desperate hide-and-seek battle for the Reichswald, 50 square miles of close-growing evergreen firs on a hogsback between the Maas and Rhine rivers south of Nijmegen. The town of Cleve has been taken by the 43rd Division of Lt-Gen Sir Brian Horrocks's XXX Corps, after it broke free of a snarl-up of tanks and lorries churning around in rain-sodden roads.

Von Rundstedt brought up reserve *Panzers* too late to prevent the 43rd striking for Goch and Udem. Though held by no more than 10,000 poorly-trained troops, the Reichswald has offered limitless opportunities for the enemy's assault guns to fire down the rides – or avenues – and for snipers. General Meindl's First Parachute Army also provided more hardened opposition as the Allies pressed forward. Some strongpoints were taken only after bayonet charges.

The forest is the Germans' last strong defensive point in this area, and the Allies' Operation Veritable to clear the lower Rhine paid a high price to gain it from nine German divisions. But when the Americans attack further south, they will face a greatly weakened enemy (→ 22).

Shop dummies line the streets of Cleve as a British patrol walks through.

Greek partisans to give up their guns

Athens, 12 February
After all-night talks in a provincial schoolroom, a weary Harold Macmillan, the British minister resident in the Mediterranean, was able to report to London this morning that the civil war in Greece is over. The communist-backed ELAS rebels have agreed to hand in their arms to a newly-formed national guard. More than 40,000 rifles together with 108 heavy guns and 315 heavy machine guns are to be surrendered under the peace treaty. A former premier and revolutionary leader, General Gonatas, remains doubtful. "The treaty ... does not contain sufficient guarantees for the future," he said.

V2 site abandoned; women face call-up

Germany, 17 February
Two clear signs of German disarray in the face of the Russian onslaught have emerged this week. Five days ago a decree issued by Martin Bormann drafted women into service in the *Volkssturm*. As military difficulties increased, so have the numbers of women working to support the armed forces. Until 12 February, however, they had always been volunteers. The second sign of what the Allies will see as panic came today when the Soviet offensive forced the Germans to evacuate the rocket expert Wernher von Braun and other scientists from their top secret V-weapon station at Peenemunde (→8/3).

---

18. East Prussia: General Ivan Cherniakhovsky, the commander of the Third Byelorussian Front, dies of wounds; Marshal Alexander Vasilevsky succeeds him.

18. Germany: Wenck's offensive east of Berlin starts to falter (→ 27).

19. Bonin Islands: The US Fifth Fleet launches Operation Detachment, the invasion of Iwo Jima, landing 30,000 men against fierce resistance by Japanese forces (→ 21).

19. Germany: Himmler meets Count Folke Bernadotte, an official of the Red Cross, and makes overtures for peace talks with the west (→ 5/3).

19. US: The government imposes a midnight curfew on all places of entertainment.

20. Oak Ridge, Tennessee: the uranium plant K-25 has now produced enough weapon-grade uranium (U-235), to make an atomic bomb.

21. Philippines: Japanese resistance ends on Luzon, but battle continues on Corregidor and around Manila (→ 22).

21. Iwo Jima: *Kamikaze* aircraft sink the US carrier *Bismarck Sea* and damage the carrier *Saratoga*.→

22. Corregidor: An estimated 2,000 Japanese soldiers commit suicide by blowing up a vast ammunition dump (→ 27).

22. Burma: British troops land near Kangaw (→ 26).

22. Germany: US troops cross the Saar river.→

22. France: Eisenhower claims that 900,000 German prisoners are being held by the Allies.

22. Montevideo: Uruguay declares war on Germany and Japan.

23. Caroline Islands: The British Pacific Fleet, renamed Task Force 57, sails for Okinawa (→ 26/3).

23. Arctic: Ju88 dive-bombers sink the British merchant ship *Henry Bacon*.

24. Cairo: Egypt's premier, Ahmed Maher Pasha, is assassinated after reading out a royal decree declaring war on Germany and Japan (→ 26).

Indians break out at Nyaungu bridge

Nyaungu, Burma, 21 February
Seven days after crossing the Irrawaddy, Major General "Punch" Cowan's 17th Indian Division has broken out of the bridgehead and is racing to Meiktila, the main Japanese base in central Burma. The success of the crossing owes much to the British deception to persuade Lt-Gen Shihachi Katamura that the main crossing would be to the north of Mandalay. By striking south, Lt-Gen William Slim, the British Fourteenth Army commander, aims to cut off Katamura's Fifteenth Army and destroy it (→ 22).

Roer river crossed by US infantrymen

Roer River, 23 February
In a single day's fighting, Lt-Gen William Simpson's US Ninth Army has put 28 infantry battalions across the Roer. Seven tank-bearing bridges are almost complete. Bright moonlight made a smoke-screen necessary for the assault, Operation Grenade, at 3.30am. Simpson took the Germans off balance by attacking after they had sent some troops to the Reichswald. No serious counter-attack has yet been made, and Simpson will now head towards Dusseldorf.

Churchill weighs in for war with Japan

Cairo, 20 February
President Roosevelt and Winston Churchill, on their way back from the conference with Marshal Stalin in the Crimea, met for four hours here to plan the next phase of the war against Japan. Mr Churchill told the US president that his government was "determined to throw everything it had at the Japanese".

The prime minister and the president also conferred with King Farouk of Egypt, the emperor of Ethiopia, King ibn Saud of Saudi Arabia and other Arab leaders who were in Cairo for an Arab summit. King ibn Saud presented Mr Churchill with a gold-handled sword.

▷

607

Stars and Stripes raised on Iwo Jima

Transport links are battered by Allies

Germany, 21-22 February
Worms, a rail centre 12 miles (19 km) north of Mannheim, was one of 40 transport links hit in a major series of raids by the RAF and USAAF last night. Bomber Command's 349 aircraft dropped 1,116 tons of bombs on the town. The US Eighth Army Air Force sent 1,195 effective bombers, escorted by 650 fighters, to drop 400,000 incendiaries on Nuremberg. Recent targets in the same series included Dresden and Chemnitz and have raised some doubts about morality. After Dresden an AP correspondent wrote: "Allied air chiefs have adopted terror bombing of German populated centres ... to hasten Hitler's doom" (→ 27).

Poznan finally falls to Zhukov's troops

Moscow, 23 February
Poznan, the *Festung* (fortress) city in western Poland which has fought on for a month 100 miles (160 km) behind the front lines, fell yesterday to Marshal Zhukov. Assault troops scaled rope-ladders and climbed over the walls of the inner citadel while sappers dashed forward with dynamite to blast open the defences. The garrison finally surrendered after its commander shot himself. The capture of Poznan's railway network will make it much easier for Zhukov to build up his forces to attack Berlin (→ 28).

New U-boats make up for those sunk

Atlantic, 24 February
Three U-boats were sunk today by Allied action – two by air attacks and one by convoy escorts. This brings to 19 submarines which have been sunk already this month; naval action, aircraft attacks and mines have all claimed victims. But Germany is rapidly bringing new and more powerful U-boats into service – 30 were commissioned last month alone – and their *Schnorkel* equipment ensures that they remain a potent threat (→ 28).

US marines crawl forward across the black volcanic sands of Iwo Jima as the struggle to establish a beach-head begins.

Iwo Jima, 23 February
After four days of exceptionally fierce fighting that has cost 2,500 American lives, US marines today managed to raise the Stars and Stripes on top of Mount Suribachi, the vantage point summit controlling the southern end of Iwo Jima.

The event was greeted with shouts and whistles from below as the 30,000 men of the 4th and 5th Marine Divisions were able to raise their heads. They had been pinned down flat on their bellies by intense enemy artillery since landing on this barren volcanic rock of an is-land. The flag was raised at 10.20am today by a group from the 28th Regimental Combat team of the 5th Marines, using a discarded drainpipe for a flagpole. Shortly afterwards several Japanese soldiers emerged from hidden tunnels. They were killed by the marines, who had clawed and fought their way up the 550-foot summit.

But the fight for Iwo Jima, just four miles by two in size, is not over yet. Despite the American capture of one airfield on the first day, two more are still held by the Japanese. They are just as keenly aware as the Americans of Iwo's strategic value as a stepping stone for intensifying the B-29 bombings of Japan. Prior to Iwo's invasion, Japan's military chiefs in Tokyo – 650 miles (1,040 km) away – even contemplated how much explosive it would take to sink the island into the sea. Instead it opted for Iwo's 21,000 defenders to be dug into an elaborate 11-mile network of caves and tunnels that has already survived 75 days of aerial bombing and a three-day naval softening-up bombardment in which 40,000 shells were fired (→ 26).

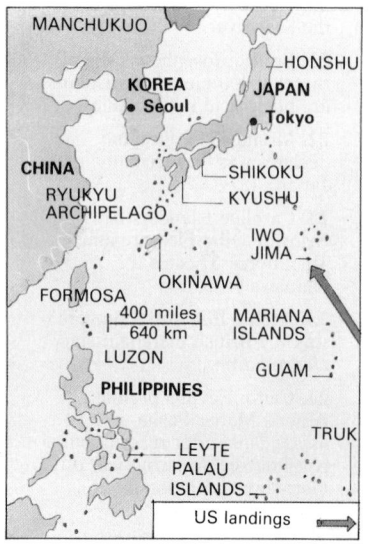

Image of victory: the Stars and Stripes goes up on Mount Suribachi.

1945

February

Su	Mo	Tu	We	Th	Fr	Sa
				1	2	3
4	5	6	7	8	9	10
11	12	13	14	15	16	17
18	19	20	21	22	23	24
25	26	27	28			

25. Japan: One hundred and seventy-two B-29s bomb Tokyo, dropping 450 tons of incendiaries and gutting 28,000 buildings (→ 10/3).

25. Germany: US troops capture Duren in the west, and the Red Army takes the fortress of Preussisch Friedland to the east. The German army stages a short-lived counter-attack from Stettin towards Pyritz.→

25. Germany: The American M26 Pershing tank sees its first combat action, crossing the Roer river with the 3rd Armoured Division.→

26. Burma: Thabuktong is captured in the drive for Meiktila, and Indian troops advance on Mandalay to distract attention from Slim's main thrust from Pagan.→

26. Damascus: The Syrian government declares war on Germany and Japan.→

26. Germany: The Canadian First Army launches Operation Blockbuster, a major offensive against Udem, Calcar and Xanten.→

27. Manila: An official ceremony formally re-establishes the Commonwealth of the Philippines.→

27. Beirut: Lebanon declares war on Germany and Japan.→

28. Germany: The US First Army crosses the river Erft, only just over six miles from Cologne, but meets strong resistance.→

28. Bucharest: The government resigns, and the USSR appoints a Soviet commissar to wield influence over Roumanian affairs (→ 2/3).

28. Westminster: A Commons motion expressing regret that the Yalta Conference did not allow the Poles to choose their own destiny is defeated by 396 votes to 25.

28. Scilly Isles: An RAF Lancaster bomber sinks the U-boat U327.

28. Britain: 307,201 members of the Empire's armed forces have been killed in action since war broke out; in the same period, 60,585 British civilians were killed by enemy bombs.

Two million Germans flee "red terror"

Danzig, 28 February
This great Baltic port is the scene of an amazing evacuation. Some two million people are being shipped to the west to escape the "red terror" being visited on the German people by the advancing Russians.

The Soviet soldiers are inflamed by the writings of the propagandist Ilya Ehrenburg, who tells them: "Break the racial pride of these Germanic women. Take them as your lawful booty. Kill. As you storm onwards, kill, you gallant soldiers of the Red Army."

The slogan "Blood for blood. Bread for bread" has been drummed into them, and as they roll through the villages of East Prussia they are exacting a terrible revenge. The men are shot, and for the women the order *"Frau komm"* means certain rape and probable death. Homes are looted of everything, with furniture being strapped onto tanks by drunken soldiers.

So the people are fleeing, stumbling across the icy fields, carrying what they can, prepared to leave everything behind to escape the rampaging Russians.

Those who reach the safety of the ports fight to get on board the evacuation ships. Babies are being thrown down to be used by another member of the family as a means to get aboard. At sea there is danger from mines, submarines and aircraft, but the ships are getting through and anything is better than facing the rampant terror of the Red Army (→ 1/3).

Red Army tanks rumble through a devastated town in East Prussia.

Indian troops encircle Meiktila in Burma

Burma, 28 February
After an 80-mile (128-km) advance from the Irrawaddy, "bumping" one Japanese roadblock after another, the 17th Indian Division and its accompanying 255th Indian Tank Brigade has enveloped Meiktila. The town, a landscape of temples reflected in lakes, is the bottleneck of all communications to the Japanese Thirty-third and Fifteenth Armies. If Major-General "Punch" Cowan's column can take the town, the bulk of the Japanese army in Burma will be "in the bag". To defend it Maj-Gen Kasuya has only 3,500 rear-echelon troops, but he is preparing a tenacious defence, even arming his walking wounded with bamboo spears (→ 4/3).

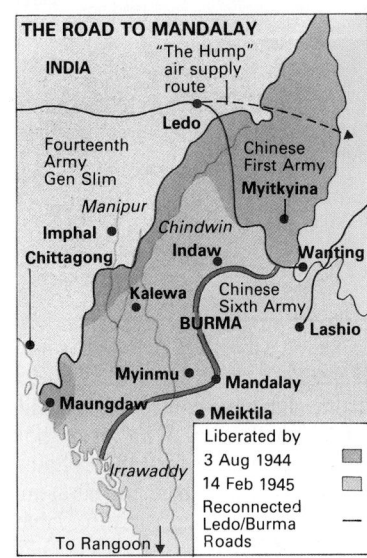

THE ROAD TO MANDALAY
INDIA
"The Hump" air supply route
Ledo
Fourteenth Army Gen Slim
Chinese First Army
Myitkyina
Manipur
Chindwin
Imphal
Indaw
Wanting
Chittagong
Kalewa
Chinese Sixth Army
BURMA
Lashio
Myinmu
Mandalay
Maungdaw
Meiktila
Liberated by
3 Aug 1944
14 Feb 1945
Reconnected Ledo/Burma Roads
Irrawaddy
To Rangoon

Allies push forward towards the Rhine

Rhineland, 28 February
Along a 150-mile (240-km) front from Trier in the south to Udem in the north, US, Canadian and British troops have launched Operations Lumberjack and Undertone to drive the Germans back to the Rhine. A British unit found four miles of the river at Calcar clear of the enemy. Units of the US Ninth Army have been moving forward so fast that a security blackout has been imposed on their positions. The Ninth was last reported two miles from Munchen-Gladbach, the gateway to Dusseldorf. Cologne, now just ten miles (16 km) from the front, is being shelled by American 155mm Long Toms (→ 7).

Berlin roasts under Allied fire-bombing

Berlin, 27 February
Another daylight USAAF raid, the biggest ever, in which 1,102 bombers rained fire-bombs on Berlin, set the city ablaze yesterday. And today 38 RAF Mosquitoes rekindled the fires which the suffering civilians had scarcely started to put out. The total quantity of high explosive dropped there represents one ton for every 60 inhabitants, a cumulative total of 60,000 tons. The aim is to create chaos (→ 2/3).

Saudi Arabia is late entrant to the war

Riyadh, 28 February
Saudi Arabia today became one of the last countries in the Middle East to declare war on Germany. Two days ago Syria joined the Allies, while Iraq and Iran declared a state of belligerence last year. The recent worldwide rush to join the Allies seems to have been caused by an announcement that only states which declare war before 1 March will be invited to a conference in San Francisco on the proposed post-war "United Nations" organization. However, only Iran, Egypt and Saudi Arabia of the Middle East nations have declared war on both Germany and Japan.

Americans take over airfield on Iwo Jima

Raising hell on Iwo Jima: two US marines turn flame-throwers on the enemy.

Iwo Jima, 26 February
The US Marines are predicting Allied control of Iwo Jima within days after seizing a second airstrip, Motoyami No 2, and Hill 382, a strategic artillery post, as fierce fighting continues. "We can expect to take this island in a few more days," said Maj-Gen Holland Smith, the commander of the Pacific Fleet Marine Force. The seizure of the central plateau airfield means that the Marines are no longer fighting uphill and can now fight on a broader front. Ahead to the north lie thick defences around Motoyami, behind which is a third airstrip, still under construction.

General Smith warned his men not to underestimate the task, even though the appallingly high daily US casualty rate is beginning to fall and there are signs that the enemy is short of water. "This fight is the toughest we've run across in 168 years," he said. The US needs Iwo's airfields to provide fighter cover for B-29 raids on Japan (→ 26/3).

US lands reinforcements in Philippines

Puerto Princesa, 28 February
US forces, swiftly following up the retaking of Manila and Corregidor during the last two days, this morning landed on Palawan, the fifth largest and westernmost island in the Philippines. The first wave of 41st Division troops, riding ashore in armed amphibious trucks, met no opposition; driving rapidly inland they took Puerto Princesa and two disused airstrips. Hopes of freeing 150 US PoWs thought to be on Palawan vanished, however, after five who had escaped said that the Japanese had burnt the rest alive in a dug-out in December.

MacArthur claimed that the lack of opposition was another indication of the enemy's failure to "diagnose our plans". Palawan is only 800 miles from China and 250 miles

from Japanese-controlled oilfields in North Borneo. With an anchorage deep enough for Liberty Ships, it will serve as a base for harassing enemy shipping en route to Japan from the Dutch East Indies (→ 3/2).

1945
March

Su	Mo	Tu	We	Th	Fr	Sa
				1	2	3
4	5	6	7	8	9	10
11	12	13	14	15	16	17
18	19	20	21	22	23	24
25	26	27	28	29	30	31

1. East Prussia: Soviet troops under Zhukov push on to Kolberg (→ 7).

1. Germany: US troops capture Munchen-Gladbach and Neuss.

2. Germany: In two raids, 858 RAF bombers raid Cologne, and the German army starts to retreat from the Rhine (→ 3).

3. Manila: The last pockets of Japanese resistance are cleared, over twenty thousand Japanese soldiers having died in the battle for the city.

3. Netherlands: RAF bombers kill over 500 civilians in the Hague when they miss their target, a V2 launch site (→ 6).

3-4. Britain: *Luftwaffe* fighters shoot down 20 British bombers as they return from bombing Kamen and the Dortmund-Ems canal.→

4. Helsinki: Finland formally declares war on Germany.

5. Hohenlychen, Germany: Felix Kersten, Himmler's masseur, tries to persuade his patient to free all Jews held in concentration camps (→ 12).

6. Netherlands: Resistance fighters ambush and attempt to execute SS General Hans Rauter, the arch-persecutor of the Dutch (→ 8).

7. Burma: Chinese forces capture Lashio (→ 17).

7. Poland: The Germans start to evacuate Danzig.→

8. Netherlands: The Nazi authorities kill 117 Dutchmen in reprisal for the attempted murder of General Rauter.

8. London: A V2 kills 110 people and injures 123 when it hits Smithfield market (→ 17).

9. Germany: US forces capture Bonn (→ 12).

10. Philippines: US troops land on Mindanao (→ 16).

10. Indochina: Japanese troops overwhelm the French and take over the administration (→ 23).

10. Berlin: Hitler retires von Rundstedt, who alienated him by correctly predicting disaster in the Ardennes, from his post of C-in-C West, replacing him with Field Marshal Albert Kesselring.

Key town falls to trap the Japanese

Meiktila, Burma, 4 March
Meiktila has fallen to the 17th Indian Division. The Japanese Fifteenth and Thirty-third armies are trapped at Mandalay. The first assault on 1 March, watched by the Fourteenth Army commander, Lt-Gen William Slim, brought the 255th Indian Tank Brigade onto the heights above the town. Later Slim watched his own Gurkhas push into the suburbs from the north. But the ferocious defence of Major-General Kasuya's scratch garrison, his deep tunnels, and the natural defences of the town's lakes, ensured that it was three days before the last sniper was killed. Today more than 2,000 Japanese bodies lie in the streets (→ 7).

Bucharest turmoil

Bucharest, 2 March
Andrei Vishinsky, the stony-faced Soviet deputy foreign commissar, is imposing Stalin's rule on Roumania with a ruthlessness reminiscent of his behaviour as prosecutor at the Moscow show trials. Spurning the Allies' protests, he has today ordered King Michael to dismiss the coalition Radescu government and appoint what amounts to a communist puppet regime.

Germany to enlist schoolboy soldiers

Germany, 5 March
Boys of 16 years old are now to be sent to the front to fight for Hitler's Germany. All male children born in 1929 are to be conscripted for military service and sent into battle against the advancing Allies.

Boys of 16 have been serving in the *Volkssturm* [people's front] since it was set up last September. Now they are to be sent to areas of combat across Europe. The Nazi propaganda machine is already busy showing newsreel of "Hitler's Boys" decorated with the Iron Cross for knocking out enemy tanks. Such pictures cannot disguise the fact that recruitment of boy soldiers is the last resort of a desperate nation (→ 17).

US Army crosses Rhine at Remagen

Americans take a break on the one bridge over the Rhine still standing.

THE ALLIES APPROACH THE RHINE

Wesel

Lippe

Venlo

Essen

Dortmund

Ruhr

Dusseldorf

Munchen-Gladbach

Rhine

GERMANY

Roer

Cologne

Aachen

Sieg

Bonn

Remagen

Coblenz

Bitburg

Front line, 8 Feb

20 miles
32 km

Allied attacks

Remagen, 7 March

Hitler gave orders that not a single Rhine bridge must fall intact into Allied hands. The US First Army under General Courtney Hodges reached the Rhine at Cologne today and found, as expected, that all bridges were down. Some 30 miles (48 km) to the south, however, Second Lieutenant Emmet J Burrows came out of the woods above Remagen to find disorganized German troops fleeing across the intact Ludendorff railway bridge.

Soon a platoon of US tanks was charging down to the bridge. As it approached, a German engineer detonated charges, which created a small crater. The Americans pushed on, shelling the Germans on the east bank. One shell knocked out the engineer responsible for firing the demolition charges. When he came to and turned the key, no-

thing happened. He tried again and still the detonators failed. An army sergeant raced onto the bridge and, amid a hail of American gunfire, ignited a fuse. A powerful explosion lifted the bridge up; it settled back and, incredibly, still stood. General Bradley (C-in-C of 12th Army Group) exclaimed to Hodges: "Hot dog, Courtney! This'll beat him wide open. Shove everything you can across it" (→ 17).

Germans shock the Allies by attacking port of Granville

Normandy, 8-9 March

German forces bypassed by D-Day landings 21 months ago made an impudent raid tonight from their Channel Islands base. They attacked Granville, 500 miles (800 km) behind the front line, with a commando force representing elements of Germany's three armed forces.

Thirty small craft, ranging from minesweepers to cutters, carried the 200-strong raiding party 25 miles (40 km) to the target. It should have been a disaster, since the raiders' plans were intercepted by British *Enigma* codebreakers while the fleet was spotted on radar. But the single US patrol craft, armed with a defective gun, sent to intercept was mauled.

The raiders landed unopposed at 1am and blew up port installations and four merchant ships. Fifteen American and eight British servicemen were killed, along with six French civilians. The raiders freed 79 German prisoners, nine of whom later arranged for their recapture. The raiders also took prisoner five American soldiers and eight Britons. The attackers lost three dead and one man captured. They left with some booty: a merchant ship and its cargo of coal.

Cathedral stands amid the bomb-shattered ruins of Cologne

Cologne, 6 March

Tanks and infantry of the US First Army drove into Cologne today to reach the Rhine in the cathedral district. A *Panzer* hit by an American shell was burning up in front of the cathedral, its ammunition exploding in erratic bursts. The infantry pushed into the southern suburbs, where remnants of the city's defenders are on the retreat to Bonn.

About three-quarters of the city has been destroyed by bombing and shell-fire. Remarkably, the 13th-century Gothic cathedral is hardly damaged; a priest and a Franciscan monk have continued to hold regular services in the vestry. Of the city's peacetime population of almost a million, fewer than 150,000 remain.→

An American tank is hit by a German shell in the streets near the cathedral.

Concern grows over Dresden bomb raid

London, 10 March

Unease appears to be growing in Britain and America about the air raids which devastated Dresden last month. Concern has been expressed in the House of Commons, while some US newspapers have echoed the German accusation that it was "terror bombing". In order to counter this criticism, the authorities here are arguing that the city was an important railway junction and as such was a key centre for organizing German resistance to the Red Army. Nevertheless there is a strong feeling, particularly among British church leaders, that at this stage of the war such destruction and the death of so many civilians cannot be justified (→ 12).

Germans counter-attack in Hungary

Budapest, 7 March
Hitler, in a desperate attempt to re-capture Budapest and the Hungarian oilfields, launched Operation Spring Awakening yesterday with two *Panzer* armies attempting an encircling movement around Lake Balaton. The southern arm has the extra task of disrupting the Russian advance on Vienna.

First reports from the battlefield tell of minor German gains as their tanks flounder in a sea of mud. It is also obvious that the Russians knew of the attack and prepared deep defensive positions. The Panzers would have been better employed on the Rhine and the Oder (→ 24).

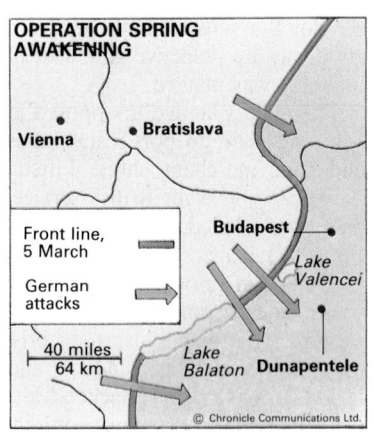

Red Army cuts off Stettin from Baltic

Moscow, 7 March
Marshal Zhukov, striking north to the Baltic, has smashed the 3rd *Panzer* Army and has cut off Stettin from the sea. According to German reports Zhukov is mounting heavy attacks along a 100-mile (160-km) stretch of the Oder running from the south-east of Berlin to the approaches to Stettin.

One of the points under attack is the fortress of Kustrin, 40 miles (64 km) due east of the German capital. A communique from the German high command says that the Russians intend to eliminate it before attacking Berlin.

Meanwhile, Marshal Rokossovsky continues to clear Pomerania. His men captured the German stronghold of Grudziadz, outside Danzig, yesterday (→ 12).

Tokyo raid kills over 80,000 people

An aerial view of Tokyo after the attack: only a handful of buildings is still standing on each block.

Tokyo, 10 March
In an awesome firebombing attack, US B-29 Superfortresses last night gutted 16 square miles of closely-packed industrial areas in Tokyo, killing at least 83,000 people. The death toll could even be as many as 130,000; certainly around one million are homeless, and 267,000 buildings have been destroyed in the most destructive and lethal air raid of the war so far, anywhere in the world. Two hundred and seventy-nine bombers attacked, led in over Tokyo by B-29 Pathfinders at 300 miles (480 km) per hour, dropping a total of 1,700 tons (1,727 tonnes) of fire bombs. Bright flashes lit up the sky as the incendiaries fell. Fanned by a stiffening breeze the fires which blossomed in the flimsy wood-and-plaster buildings spread quickly into a giant inferno.

In order to ensure bombing accuracy the B-29s had to fly at low altitudes where they were vulnerable to Japanese AA guns and night fighters. However, surprise and the inadequacy of Japan's defences resulted in only 14 B-29s being lost. The catastrophic raid has had a profound affect on Japanese morale. The dead are piled high on bridges and roads, and in canals.

Air force leaders see, in the enormous destruction thus wreaked, evidence that the Japanese could be forced to surrender without the need for an invasion of ground troops and the resulting carnage. It has confirmed the views of backers of strategic bombing (→ 11).

New tactics and island airfield put Japan at bombers' mercy

Japan, 10 March
The flying distance for B-29 bombers raiding strategic targets in Japan was halved in November 1944 when they began operations from the Mariana Islands. Using radar and flying at 30,000 feet in daylight, the bombers struck at the Japanese aircraft industry. They failed dismally. By January 1945 they had caused severe damage to only one of nine important factories listed. This month a change of tactics was introduced by General Curtis LeMay, who commands the USAAF in the Marianas. The bombers were to attack at low level at night, using incendiary bombs against highly inflammable urban industrial areas in Tokyo. At low level they would carry less fuel, and to increase the pay load further they were stripped of most of their defensive armament, although this made them more vulnerable. It was a gamble, but the Tokyo raid was the most destructive air raid ever.

1945

March

Su	Mo	Tu	We	Th	Fr	Sa
					1	2	3
4	5	6	7	8	9	10
11	12	13	14	15	16	17
18	19	20	21	22	23	24
25	26	27	28	29	30	31

11-12. Japan: Two hundred and eighty-five US B29s bombard Nagoya (→ 12).

11. Caroline Islands: A *kamikaze* attack on Ulithi atoll damages the US carrier *Randolph*.

12. Hohenlychen, Germany: Himmler signs an agreement promising to surrender the death camps to the Allies intact, with the prisoners still alive, and to order a halt to camp executions, contrary to Hitler's express orders (→ 16).

12. Germany: In a record raid, 1,108 RAF bombers drop 4,851 tons of bombs on Dortmund.→

12-13. Japan: Two hundred and seventy-four US aircraft bomb Osaka and wipe out 8.1 square miles of the city (→ 16).

14. Germany: Adolf Eichmann declares: "I shall go to my grave happy in the knowledge that I have helped to kill six million Jews" (→ 16).

15. Zossen, Germany: US bombers drop 25,000 incendiary and 6,000 HE bombs on the army general staff HQ (→ 18).

15. Bahamas: The Duke of Windsor resigns as Governor.

16. Philippines: US troops land on Basilan island (→ 18).

16. Germany: Rudolf Hoess, the former commandant of Auschwitz, declares that he gassed two million Jews on Himmler's orders between June 1941 and the end of 1943.

16. Hohenlychen: Himmler takes to his bed, feigning an attack of influenza (→ 21).

16-17. Japan: 307 US B-29 bombers set three square miles of Kobe alight, killing or injuring 15,000 people (→ 19).

17. Burma: The Chinese Sixth Army captures Hsipaw.

17. Europe: Eisenhower orders Patton not to advance towards Czechoslovakia, although there is nothing to stop him reaching Prague before the Russians.

17. Germany: The Remagen bridge, captured intact by the Allies on 7 March, collapses because of overloading – killing 28 US soldiers.

RAF drops biggest bomb yet on Germany

Britain, 14 March
The ace crews of RAF Bomber Command's 617 ("Dambuster") Squadron have today added another to their list of successes, this time with a new weapon. Their target was the Bielefeld viaduct; the means was the largest bomb so far used in the war, the 22,000-pound "Grand Slam".

To carry it some of 617's Lancasters have had to be specially adapted, with cutaway bomb bays, strengthened undercarriages and four 1,280hp Rolls Royce Merlin engines. To save weight two of the crew are dispensed with. Fourteen Lancasters took off from their base at Woodall Spa shortly after lunch. All but one, piloted by Sqn-Ldr Jock Calder DSO DFC, carried 12,000-pound "Tallboy" bombs. Calder had a "Grand Slam" and attacked the viaduct from just under 12,000 feet, scoring a direct hit. This destroyed over 200 feet of the viaduct. At the moment of release of the bomb, Calder's Lancaster shot up some 500 feet, giving the crew some knocks; but they soon forgot these in the realization that they had scored a bull's-eye (→ 15).

German V-rockets smash Britain again

The vast muddy crater blown open by a V2 rocket in West Hampstead.

London, 17 March
In spite of the efforts of the Allied forces to eradicate the V2 rocket launch sites, the Germans are still managing to strike targets in England and Belgium with them.

When the V2 offensive opened last September the launch sites were in the Netherlands, but were moved temporarily to Denmark during the Arnhem operation. At the beginning of October the rocket units returned to the Netherlands, and by the end of the year they were operating from a large wooded park, the *Haagsche Bosch*, outside The Hague. During January and February this was attacked repeatedly by RAF bombers and fighter-bombers. Eventually, at the beginning of this month, the Germans were forced to move, and this was the reason for the recent lull. Their new launch area is still near The Hague, this time on the *Duindicht* racecourse. There is, however, little cover here, and because of lack of time and the high water table, the Germans have been unable to follow their normal practice of constructing underground storage sites. Consequently RAF reconnaissance planes have identified the launch site and attacks on it are being mounted. This should drive the rockets further east into Germany, putting England beyond V2 range.

A further encouraging factor is that the Allied air offensive against German communications is making it increasingly difficult to maintain supplies of rockets and fuel (→ 27).

Red Army captures gateway to Berlin

Moscow, 12 March
The Red Army stormed the German fortress city of Kustrin, the gateway to Berlin, yesterday. It fell after a week of savage fighting which culminated in the street-by-street destruction of the citadel by dive-bombers, artillery and assault teams armed with mortars and flame-throwers. Kustrin was a vital roadblock in the German plan of defence for Berlin. Now Marshal Zhukov has a clear road and Berlin is only 40 miles (64 km) away.→

Japanese scholars to join war effort

Tokyo, 17 March
Japanese children from the age of seven are to give up school to work in factories to help the war effort, the cabinet ordered today. The drastic new measures will take effect from 1 April for a year. Only primary schools for children up to six will stay open. All other schools, colleges and universities will close, and students and teachers will work in food and munitions factories, air defence, research work and anything else that helps the war effort.

Tokyo radio said that this would mobilize students "as a powerful wing of national defence and a nucleus of production in strict consonance with the tense war situation".

General MacArthur, who took Manila, surveys the damage.

German refugees flee as Patton advances

Coblenz, 17 March

Patton's Third Army has jumped the east/west line of the Moselle and swept southwards to threaten from the rear the German forces holding the Siegfried Line in the Saar where Patch's US Seventh Army is attacking. Patton's columns, supported by American fighter-bombers, are roaming virtually at will, spreading havoc among the enemy. Roads are jammed with German troops and civilians fleeing eastwards to the Rhine, where the last three bridges remain open. Patton is now driving along the west bank from Coblenz to Mainz and beyond. The bag of prisoners taken by Patton and Patch is approaching 100,000 (→ 22).

What the Nazis leave behind them.

Allies smash vital Krupp arms plant

Germany, 11 March

The RAF has laid waste to the Krupp works at Essen, symbol of the German war machine. In a half-hour bombardment, 1,079 heavy bombers poured 4,661 tons of explosive onto a 2,000-acre site, killing 897 civilians. Later a British officer claimed: "Krupp's has been written off." Some Allied intelligence teams have concluded that the impact of strategic bombing on German war production has been less than decisive. American studies show that the Dresden raid hit the output of the German cigarette industry, but not much else (→ 12).

March 11. Belgian children are evacuated as fighting continues.

Girl's diary offers hope amid despair

Bergen-Belsen, 12 March

Disease is sweeping through the camp, killing the starved and weakened inmates with an efficiency that the Nazis might envy. Anne Frank, a fifteen-year-old German-Jewish girl, died of typhus today. She spent two years hiding with her family in Amsterdam before being betrayed to the *Gestapo* and deported to Auschwitz-Birkenau last August. Later she was moved on to Belsen. She hid her diary, to which she confided her deepest thoughts, in Amsterdam; it is a document of human dignity and hope in the face of relentless persecution (→ 14).

PoWs stage mass escape in Wales

Cardiff, 11 March

Sixty-six German prisoners of war broke out of a PoW camp at Bridgend, in Glamorgan, at four o'clock this morning, having tunnelled 45 feet under the barbed wire. The tunnel began inside a hut and ended in a ploughed field. Elaborate preparations had been made for weeks. By tonight, 43 of them had been recaptured as police, former Home Guards and Land Girls with pitchforks searched 100 square miles of lonely wooded country. Many were found hiding on farms.

1945
March

Su	Mo	Tu	We	Th	Fr	Sa
				1	2	3
4	5	6	7	8	9	10
11	12	13	14	15	16	17
18	19	20	21	22	23	24
25	26	27	28	29	30	31

18. East Prussia: The Polish First Army captures Kolberg, and the Soviet army closes in on the Baltic ports of Gdynia and Danzig.

18. Berlin: Albert Speer, the armaments minister, tells Hitler that the war is lost and economic collapse is nigh; Hitler insists that he retract these comments (→ 19).

18. Rome: Pope Pius XII attacks Nazi racial policies.

19. Berlin: Hitler issues the "Nero Command", ordering the destruction of all industry, transport links and agriculture.→

20. Berlin: At Guderian's suggestion, Hitler replaces Himmler as C-in-C Army Group Vistula with the experienced soldier Gotthard Heinrici (→ 21).

20. Paris: France signs an economic pact with the Benelux countries.

21. China: Japan launches a fresh offensive aimed at capturing the strategic US air bases at Laohokow and Ankong (→ 25).

21. Germany: Patton's US Third Army captures Mainz.→

21. Hohenlychen: Guderian fails to get Heinrich Himmler to go with him to Berlin to persuade Hitler to seek an armistice (→ 28).

22. Germany: Soviet troops under Konev bridge the Oder at Oppeln.→

22. Germany: Patton sends his troops across the Rhine at Nierstein, stealing the glory from Montgomery, who had long been planning a crossing on the next day.→

23. Paris: De Gaulle announces a limited form of self-government for Indochina, but insists that Vietnam, Laos and Cambodia remain French colonies or protectorates.

24. Burma: Lt-Gen Daniel I Sultan's Sino-American force links up with British troops at Kyaukme (→ 28).

24. Hungary: Szekesfehervar falls to the Red Army, as the German counter-attack fails with heavy losses (→ 29).

A "scorched-earth" policy is ordered

Germany, 19 March

Hitler today ordered a "scorched-earth" policy to be implemented. "If the war is lost, the nation will also perish," he declared, quashing Speer's objections. Military installations, rail and other transport links, industry and even food supplies are to be destroyed. In truth, much already lies in ruins. The scale, range and frequency of Allied air raids are now overwhelming German air defences, with the transport network a particular target for attack. Much of the railway system is virtually at a standstill – except where the Red Army has converted tracks to the Russian gauge (→ 20).

Guerrilla welcome for "invading" GIs

Panay, 18 March

Instead of bullets, surprised US troops landing on the island of Panay in the central Philippines today were met by a guard of honour laid on by Filipino guerrillas who had already taken control of the island. Further US landings are planned on this archipelago as part of MacArthur's scheme to liberate the Philippines completely. On Iwo Jima the US Marines are still battling after 26 days of fighting. US casualties there so far, including 4,189 killed, are 19,938 – more than half the number suffered in all previous Pacific campaigns (→ 1/4).

Houses are priority in post-war Britain

Britain, 20 March

Peace in Europe will signal a two-year period of national housing emergency in Britain. The coalition government announced today that the first aim is a separate home for every family wanting one. This will mean that 750,000 new dwellings will be needed. Pre-war slum clearance schemes will be revived and accelerated with plans for another 500,000 homes. The government is to give hundreds of thousands of building workers priority release from the forces after the war.

Hitler's "1,000-year Reich" attacked on all sides

Russian soldiers advance into the heart of Germany on a T34 tank.

US troops cross the Rhine at St Goer, legendary home of the "Lorelei".

Red Army is braced for battle of Berlin

Moscow, 24 March
The Red Army is preparing with great deliberation for its last campaign, the attack on Berlin, in its long march to the west from the very gates of its own capital. Marshal Zhukov, having taken the fortress of Kustrin, the last obstacle on the road to Berlin, is now enlarging his bridgehead across the Oder to set the scene for the drama which is about to unfold.

German reports say that in a new advance with six infantry divisions and two tank brigades he has reached the road junction of Golzow, just 33 miles (53 km) from greater Berlin. The advance is almost leisurely by Red Army standards, but it is

inexorable. In Hungary yesterday Marshal Tolbukhin finished off Hitler's ill-fated Operation Spring Awakening and is about to resume his march on Vienna.

In the north, Marshal Rokossovsky is tightening his grip on Danzig and Konigsberg as the Germans continue their feverish evacuation of East Prussia. It is the unfortunate General Schorner, rescued from command of the cut-off forces in Courland to take over Army Group A opposite Marshal Konev, who has felt the full weight of the Red Army in recent days. Konev has hit him hard near Oppeln in Silesia. Everything is now ready for Berlin (→ 28).

New offensive planned for Italian front

Italy, 24 March
A re-equipped and revitalized Allied army is braced for a major new offensive aimed at trapping the German army in the Po valley. Fears that Hitler is planning a fight to the death in a mountain redoubt have put pressure on Allied commanders to move quickly.

Field Marshal Alexander, supreme Allied commander, Mediterranean, is planning for the Eighth Army to attack westwards through the Argenta Gap, with the US Fifth Army attacking northwards, west of Bologna. Alexander hopes to achieve the critical element of sur-

prise by simulating preparations for seaborne landings north of the Po.

The Eighth Army's low morale of December has been improved by the arrival of new weapons, including flame-throwing tanks and 400 Fantails, tracked amphibious troop carriers, badly missed in the crossings of countless rivers in the previous advance.

The commanders have not been cheered by the loss of the Canadian Corps to north-west Europe; nor by the universal shortage of artillery ammunition which is restricting many batteries to five rounds daily for each gun (→ 5/4).

Allied armies cross the Rhine in force

Wesel, 24 March
Montgomery's crossing of the Rhine, meticulously prepared and impatiently awaited, is now under way, and in a message to his armies he says that they will soon be "chasing the enemy from pillar to post". Over 100 miles (160 km) to the south, Patton crossed the Rhine 24 hours ahead of Montgomery after boasting that he was not going to let the British field marshal "carry the ball". He went across at Nierstein against light opposition and swept down on Darmstadt.

While Patton has captured the headlines, Montgomery's operation, on a massive scale, has substantial strategic objectives; it is

aimed at taking Allied forces in a deep thrust across the north German plain, while the US Ninth Army seals off the Ruhr, the industrial heart of Hitler's *Reich*.

The assault force assembled behind a 20-mile-long smokescreen. With 1,250,000 Britons, Canadians and Americans under him, Montgomery has more than 5,500 artillery pieces, anti-tank guns and rockets. The British Second Army alone has 120,000 tons of ammunition, stores and other supplies above normal needs.

The British went across last night at Wesel; the town had been reduced to rubble by Allied bombing and shelling, but the Germans clung on for the best part of 24 hours. To the south, the US Ninth crossed against patchy opposition. "There was no real fight," a company commander said. "The artillery had done the job for us." There were 31 American casualties.

This morning, in Operation Varsity, over 21,000 airborne infantry were dropped north-east of Wesel. They quickly overcame enemy resistance and linked up with the main force. Only on the extreme left wing, near Emmerich, is resistance really tough. "The enemy", say the Canadians, "are fighting like madmen." There are now three bridgeheads between Wesel in the north and Mainz in the south: Montgomery's, Patton's, and the US First Army's at Remagen (→ 25).

A makeshift bridge carries heavy guns on their way to Frankfurt.

Japan surrenders Mandalay to the British

Mandalay, Burma, 20 March

Mandalay has fallen. The prime minister of Great Britain is happy: "Thank God we have got a place whose name we can pronounce."

The city was taken by the 19th Indian Division under Major-General Peter Rees, the five-foot "Pocket Napoleon". Three weeks ago the division, which had deliberately drawn the 15th and 53rd Japanese divisions on itself at its Irrawaddy bridgehead to facilitate the 17th Indian Division's attack on Meiktila, began its southward march down the road to Mandalay.

"Act boldly and go fast while the going is good," Rees briefed his commanders, "and take risks." "By 7 March they had reached Powa Taung, within sight of Mandalay Hill and its wreath of temples.

The division reached the suburbs on 9 March, the 4/4 Gurkhas and the Royal Berkshires taking the top of Mandalay Hill after ferocious fighting with swords, *kukris*, bayonets and grenades in the subterra-

Indian machine-gunners keep a look out on the road to Mandalay.

nean vaults of the Buddhist temples. In the ten days that followed every inch of street and historic wall was fought over. Finally, after crushing air attacks, the garrison slipped out yesterday (→24).

Thousands die as US bombs naval bases

Tokyo, 19 March

US Pacific Fleet carrier-based aircraft have bombed the Japanese mainland for the second day in a row. Tokyo estimates that approximately 1,400 planes took part in the raids on Kobe, Japan's main port, and Kure, its most important naval base. Thousands are feared

dead amid widespread damage. The Japanese responded today to the destruction wreaked on their country with *kamikaze* attacks on the carriers. The *Essex*, *Enterprise* and *Wolf* were hit, and on the *Franklin* 832 sailors were killed – the heaviest-ever casualty list from a kamikaze attack (→1/4).

RAF bombers hit school by mistake

Copenhagen, 21 March

Allied airmen broke open another *Gestapo* prison today, but at a terrible cost. In the basement of the Shell building, Danish resistance fighters were being tortured. On the top floor another 32 prisoners were held. RAF bombs had to destroy the remaining floors. They did. Around 100 Nazis died for the loss of six prisoners. Others escaped. But one of six aircraft that crashed set fire to a school. Other pilots bombed this, believing it to be the target. A total of 112 Danish civilians were killed, including 86 children and 17 teachers.

Churchill lands during a visit to Allied troops at the Rhine.

1945

March

Su	Mo	Tu	We	Th	Fr	Sa
				1	2	3
4	5	6	7	8	9	10
11	12	13	14	15	16	17
18	19	20	21	22	23	24
25	26	27	28	29	30	31

25. China: Retreating USAAF personnel blow up the Laohokow air base.

25. Germany: As British and US troops link up on the east bank of the Rhine, Montgomery forbids British troops to "fraternize" with the local population (→27).

26. Iwo Jima: The two hundred remaining Japanese troops (of an original garrison of 21,000) stage a final suicide attack on US positions.

27. Germany: A V2 bomb kills 131 people in a London block of flats; 2,745 civilians have been killed by the bombs, and 2,900 aircrewmen have died in the campaign against them (→29).

28. Burma: Members of the Burmese National Army fighting with the Japanese rise up and kill their commanding officers (→29).

28. Poland: The Red Army captures Gdynia.

28. Berlin: Hitler forces Guderian, his chief of the army general staff, to take six weeks' sick leave after a series of disagreements.

29. Burma: After the fall of Mandalay, and its failure to retake Meiktila, the Japanese army accepts defeat and orders a general withdrawal.

29. Germany: US forces, now marching almost unchecked into the centre of Germany, capture Frankfurt.

29. Hungary: The Red Army enters the former Czech province of Ruthenia.→

29. Sittingbourne, Kent: AA gunners shoot down what is thought to be the last V1 launched against Britain.

30. Poland: Soviet forces capture Danzig.

30. Germany: US aircraft bomb the three major ports of Bremen, Hamburg and Wilhelmshaven.→

31. Germany: Eisenhower broadcasts to the German armed forces, demanding their surrender.

31. Germany: De Tassigny's French First Army crosses the Rhine near Speyer.

Royal Navy boosts Allies in the Pacific

Far East, 26 March

Carrier aircraft of the British Pacific Fleet carried out attacks today on airfields on the Sakaishima Islands, between Okinawa and Formosa [*Taiwan*], to prevent their use by enemy aircraft. The role of the Royal Navy is to support the American invasion of Okinawa, the final step before the planned invasion of the Japanese home islands. A huge armada of 1,400 naval and merchant ships of many types carrying 182,000 assault troops is en route to Okinawa. The Japanese are expected to employ the full strength of their air forces against the armada; hence the "softening up" of their airfields (→6/4).

Nazi "werewolves" fight to last ditch

Germany, 26 March

The war-weary citizens of the Third *Reich* were today called upon by Martin Bormann, Hitler's deputy, to become "Werewolf" guerrillas in a last-ditch resistance against the Allies as they invade Germany. Bormann said: "The Werewolf has been born of National Socialism. It makes no allowances and knows no considerations as imposed on regular troops ... Hatred shall be our prayer and revenge our battle-cry ..." (→2/4)

Argentina declares war on Axis powers

Buenos Aires, 27 March

Today's declaration of war on Germany and Japan by Argentina is backed by a powerful groundswell of popular support. Though by no means traditional allies of the British, the Argentinian people have been showing their sympathy for the Allied cause with generous donations to PoWs through the Red Cross and other funds. It is also reported that the government in Buenos Aires is in the process of studying British laws with the intention of incorporating some elements in a reformed electoral system in its country (→13/4).

Ike lets Russians win race for Berlin

Allied HQ, 28 March

Eisenhower has ordered the Allied forces now thrusting deep into Germany not to advance beyond the Elbe river, thus giving Stalin the go-ahead to capture Berlin with his Red Army. As recently as last autumn Churchill and Roosevelt were contemplating a thrust to get to the city before the Russians. But western forces are still some 200 miles (320 km) short, while the

Russians are less than 50 miles away. Eisenhower says that he is not prepared to risk the lives of his men for the pursuit of political advantage over an ally.

The critics of the supreme commander's decision argue that the British, Canadians and Americans are meeting almost no resistance and could easily be first in Berlin, while the Russians are up against fanatical SS units ready to fight to

the last. Churchill, who has just returned from a visit to the Allied forces in Germany, is filled with foreboding. He believes that Stalin will exploit the political advantage to be gained by raising the Red Flag over the Fuhrer's capital. The British prime minister intends to appeal to Eisenhower to change his mind. "We should shake hands with the Russians as far to the east as possible," he says (→ 7/4).

Red Army crosses the Austrian border

Moscow, 30 March

Marshal Tolbukhin has crossed the Austrian border in strength about 50 miles (80 km) south of Vienna. At the same time Marshal Malinovsky, advancing on Tolbukhin's right on a 130-mile front, has broken through German lines to threaten Bratislava. It was Tolbukhin's Third Ukrainian Front which absorbed Hitler's Spring Awakening assault in Hungary and then, when the Germans faltered, did not counter-attack but simply resumed its march on Austria.

Tolbukhin's advance has been accompanied by a sudden loss of morale among the Germans, even among the *Waffen*-SS troops of the 6th SS *Panzer* Army. The *Wehrmacht* is crumbling away (→ 3/4).

Allies race through collapsed Germany

Allied HQ, 31 March

The Allies are poised for the final attack on Germany. Armies are moving round the Ruhr to link up between Munster and Paderborn; Montgomery's 21st Army Group is heading for Germany's Baltic ports; Patton is about to link up with US First Army at Kassel; the US Seventh Army is advancing on Heidelberg while the First French Army is swinging south to the Swiss border. Germany's defences have collapsed. Allied air supremacy is total; bombing raids have left roads, railways and canals in ruins, while sunken ships clog many harbours (→ 6/4).

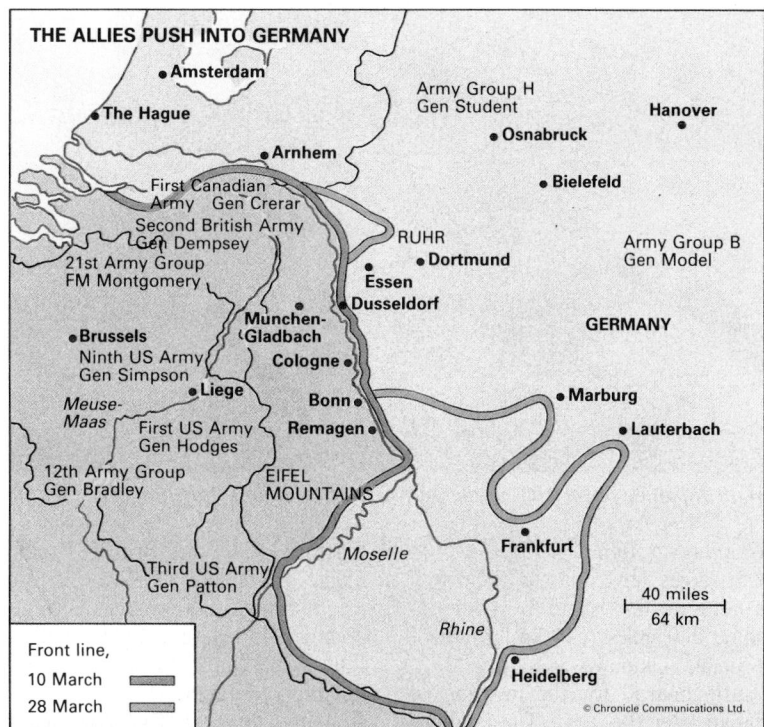

THE ALLIES PUSH INTO GERMANY

• Amsterdam
• The Hague
• Arnhem

Army Group H
Gen Student

• Osnabruck
Hanover •

First Canadian Army   Gen Crerar
Second British Army Gen Dempsey
21st Army Group FM Montgomery

• Bielefeld

RUHR
• Dortmund

Army Group B
Gen Model

• Essen
• Dusseldorf
Munchen-Gladbach

GERMANY

• Brussels
Ninth US Army Gen Simpson
Cologne •
• Liege

Bonn •
Remagen •

• Marburg
• Lauterbach

Meuse-Maas
First US Army Gen Hodges

12th Army Group Gen Bradley

EIFEL MOUNTAINS

Third US Army Gen Patton

Moselle

• Frankfurt

40 miles
64 km

Rhine

Front line,
10 March
28 March

• Heidelberg

© Chronicle Communications Ltd.

The Red Army marches into Austria and, symbolically, over the Nazi flag.

Miracle weapons arrive too late to save Germany

Germany, 31 March

With the western Allies now across the Rhine and the Russians preparing to thrust out of their bridgeheads on the Oder, the days of the Third *Reich* are strictly numbered. This makes Hitler's often-heard boasts of new miracle weapons which will dramatically change the outcome of the war seem very empty.

It was as early as November 1942 that Hitler first made mention of a new breed of secret weapon. He was alluding to the V-weapons. At that time they were still in a comparatively early stage of development, and it was to be almost 18 months before they were first used operationally. By then the Normandy landings had taken place and it could only be a matter of time before their launch sites were overrun or destroyed from the air. True, they caused considerable damage in England and Belgium, but they were too late to have any serious effect on the overall military balance of power in Europe.

The story is much the same with the German jet and rocket aircraft, the Me262, the Arado Ar234 "Blitz" bomber and the Me163. The dramatic effect that the Allied bombing has had on German communications and industry during the past few months has meant that there are too few with too little fuel to make any dent in the massive Allied air supremacy.

The story of too little and too late also applies to the new generation of U-boats, the Type XXI ocean-going and Type XXIII coastal Walther boats. Their high underwater speeds and ability to remain submerged for long periods could have caused the Allies very grave problems if they had been deployed in quantity before now. As it is, only three Type XXIIIs have set sail on operations, and then only in the past two months, and not a single Type XXI.

1945

April

Su	Mo	Tu	We	Th	Fr	Sa
1	2	3	4	5	6	7
8	9	10	11	12	13	14
15	16	17	18	19	20	21
22	23	24	25	26	27	28
29	30					

1. Philippines: US seaborne troops capture Legaspi, a vital airstrip on Luzon (→ 2).

1. East China Sea: A *kamikaze* attack kills 14 sailors on board the British carrier *Indefatigable* and damages the destroyer *Ulster*.→

1. Germany: The US First and Ninth Armies link up at Lippstadt to surround German forces in the Ruhr basin.→

1. Hungary: The Red Army captures Sopron, near the Austrian frontier south-east of Vienna (→ 3).

1. Paris: *Notre Dame* and the *Arc de Triomphe* are floodlit for the first time since war broke out (→ 14).

2. Philippines: US troops land on Tawi Tawi, on the Sulu archipelago (→ 10).

2. Berlin: Martin Bormann issues a proclamation calling for "victory or death".→

3. Austria: Soviet forces take Wiener Neustadt, near Vienna.→

3. Berlin: Albert Speer, the armaments minister, disobeys Hitler's "scorched-earth" policy, calling for the paralysis rather than the destruction of industrial plants (→ 23).

4. Slovakia: The Red Army occupies Bratislava (→ 18).

4. Germany: Gotha falls to the US and Osnabruck to British and Canadian troops, as US aircraft smash naval bases at Kiel and Hamburg.→

5. Moscow: Molotov, the Soviet foreign minister, tells the Japanese ambassador that he will not renew the 1941 non-aggression pact with Japan.→

5. Italy: US troops start an offensive to drive north from La Spezia (→ 10).

6. Eastern Front: The Red Army launches its attack on Konigsberg, East Prussia (→ 9).

6. Germany: The Germans move 15,000 Jewish prisoners out of Buchenwald camp (→ 12).

7. Moscow: Stalin cables Roosevelt, pointing out that German resistance in the east is much stronger than in the west.

US invasion force lands on Okinawa

With Japanese opposition nowhere in sight, US landing craft disgorge men and vehicles onto the beaches of Okinawa.

Okinawa, 6 April
US forces have blasted their way ashore at the island of Okinawa some 340 miles (544 km) south of Kyushu. Okinawa is to provide a "springboard" for the invasion of Japan later this year. The landings began on 1 April along a ten-mile (16-km) stretch of the south-west coast, with a mammoth invasion fleet in support. Within an hour 16,000 Americans were ashore, and by 10am the important Kadena and Yontan airfields were in US hands. The absence of any real opposition from the Japanese at the beachhead puzzled the Americans. It was like a peacetime army exercise.

The Okinawa invasion – Operation Iceberg – is the largest amphibious landing of the Pacific War. Expecting heavy opposition, the Americans assigned the Tenth Army, commanded by Lt-Gen Simon Buckner, comprising three Marine and five army divisions, to take Okinawa. The total force consists of 548,000 army, navy and Marine personnel with 320 combat and 1,140 auxiliary vessels. In support are task forces of the US Navy

together with the British Pacific Fleet. To isolate Okinawa before the landing, US carrier aircraft pounded Japanese airfields in Kyushu. B-29s interrupted their firebombing of Japanese cities to join in these attacks. The Americans plan to build air bases on the 60-mile (96-km)-long island for the aerial bombardment of Japan. The island also has room to provide bases to support the coming invasion of Japan itself.

The Japanese have some 120,000 troops on Okinawa. They avoided the crippling effects of US air and naval fire-power by stationing only token forces on the beaches and establishing strong defensive positions inland where they can meet the Americans in battle beyond the range of naval gunfire. But desperate measures are planned elsewhere. *Kamikaze* attacks are under way, and have already damaged the US battleship *West Virginia* and the British carrier *Indomitable*.

On Okinawa the US XXIV Corps, after cutting the island in two, turned south on 3 April in a drive towards the formidable Shuri

Line. At the same time III Amphibious Corps moved north, meeting ever-stiffer resistance. Today Japan made mass attacks on Allied naval forces, sinking six warships and heavily damaging the US fleet carrier *Hancock*. The Japanese used no fewer than 335 kamikazes, as well as a large number of other aircraft, in these attacks.→

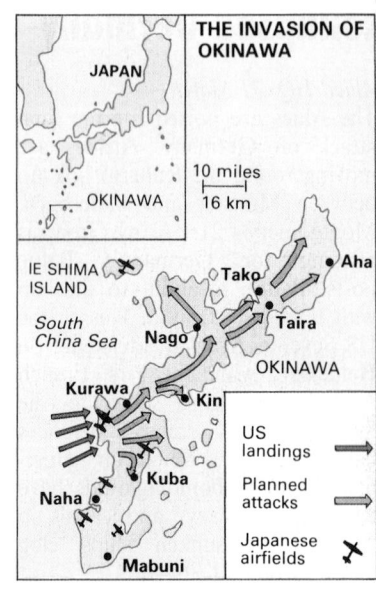

THE INVASION OF OKINAWA

JAPAN

OKINAWA

10 miles
16 km

IE SHIMA ISLAND

South China Sea

Tako
Aha
Nago
Taira

OKINAWA

Kurawa
Kin

Naha
Kuba

Mabuni

US landings →
Planned attacks ⇒
Japanese airfields ✈

German retreat becomes a rout as Allies advance

More than 100,000 surrender in Ruhr

Ruhr, 6 April
Two American armies with the Ruhr industrial heartland in their grip have been rounding up some 20,000 prisoners daily. With the figure already touching 100,000, they reckon the final total will be well over 300,000 when the last pockets of resistance from Field Marshal Walter Model's Army Group B have been eliminated.

Simpson's US Ninth Army came down from the north to join up with Hodges's First at Lippstadt, east of the Ruhr valley. In this area, Warburg was captured after German civilians, armed with bazookas, put up token resistance to the First Army. The Ninth is now clearing up Hamm, a railway centre and industrial town on the northern edge of the Ruhr and a regular RAF target over the years.

Some German units lodged in the many wooded areas in this region are apparently unaware of Allied movements. When fatigue parties came out to collect ammunition from a dump near Marburg they found Allied troops awaiting them.

Allied aircraft have dropped five million leaflets on the German forces trapped in the Ruhr, giving news of the British, American and Canadian advances deep into the heart of the Third *Reich* (→ 9).

Vienna burns: Russian soldiers press in on the defenders of Austria's capital.

Red Army blasts into suburbs of Vienna

Vienna, 6 April
In a dramatic broadcast tonight, Vienna radio announced that the Russians had broken into the suburbs of the city. The broadcast was interrupted by the noise of heavy gunfire as Marshal Tolbukhin's men penetrated to within a mile of the city centre.

"At this very moment," said the announcer, "shells are howling over our heads, over the ancient tower of St Stephen, the heavily-damaged *Burgtheater* and the castle of *Schonbrunn*. Our men are firing with all guns. Vienna *Volkssturm* formations have been deployed on a square. They are going into battle at any minute now to support the soldiers of the *Wehrmacht* fighting only a few kilometres away.

"We can see the bombs and shells crashing. The Russians are trying to enter the bulwark of the German south-east. The thunder of battle is enveloping the front-line city of Vienna." Then, after a short interlude of Viennese music, the announcer called for a "backs to the wall" defence of the city (→ 13).

"Collapse is near" admits Nazi paper

Germany, 5 April
The *Schwarze Korps*, Himmler's respected Nazi publication, has conceded that Germany is on the verge of "absolute collapse". In an unprecedented admission, the magazine today says that the German people are "being forced to acknowledge that it may be possible to defeat us militarily". The piece goes on to say, however, that they will never stop fighting and that "our belief in the rightness of our cause hasn't changed by a single letter".

Tank fuel runs out

Ruhr, 2 April
General Kurt Student was forced to postpone his planned counter-attack against the US Ninth Army in the Ruhr today because he has no fuel for his tanks. The shortage of fuel caused by Allied air attacks on synthetic fuel plants and the Red Army's occupation of the Roumanian and Hungarian oilfields has crippled Germany's forces. The occupation by Russian troops of Nagykanisza, the heart of the Hungarian oilfields, today shuts off the last tap (→ 3).

White flags greet Allies as they race across the German plain

North-west Germany, 7 April
The German army in the west is disintegrating under the impact of Allied columns racing for Bremen, Hamburg, Hanover, Magdeburg and the Elbe. The roads are filled with long columns of prisoners trudging westwards into the Allied prison camps.

The British are closing on Hanover on the *Autobahn* to Berlin, while another spearhead is driving for Bremen. In the south, the Americans have broken through to Wurzburg. The devastation of the Rhine battle zone has been left behind and the Allied forces are passing through towns apparently untouched by war, except for empty shelves in shops and white flags hanging outside houses (→ 8).

"Wehrmacht" soldiers surrender.

Royal Marine commandos advance in the damaged station at Osnabruck.

Russians plan to end pact with Japan

Moscow, 5 April
The Soviet Union plans to end its five-year neutrality pact with Japan, Moscow announced tonight, leading to speculation that Russia may enter the war against Japan. The pact still has a year to run. Moscow radio broadcast the contents of a diplomatic note delivered earlier by Mr Molotov, the commissar for foreign affairs, to the Japanese ambassador. It accused Japan of helping Germany in its war against the Soviet Union.

Allied leaders immediately welcomed the Soviet move. They believe that Russia must eventually enter the war against Japan, opening up a new front in Manchuria. Tokyo radio immediately warned the Japanese people that relations between the two nations could change swiftly. It said that the Japanese government is prepared to make the greatest possible efforts to maintain peace with Russia.

Explaining the Soviet decision the diplomatic note pointed out that the neutrality pact had been concluded in 1941, before Germany's attack on the Soviet Union and before the outbreak of hostilities between Japan, Britain and the US. "Since then the situation has radically changed," the note said.

"Germany attacked the Soviet Union, and Japan, the ally of Germany, is helping her in her war against the Soviet Union. In addition Japan is fighting against the United States and Great Britain who are allies of the Soviet Union. In such circumstances the pact of neutrality between Japan and the Soviet Union has lost its meaning and its extension is proving impossible."

Under the pact, if neither party had given notice of any change by next week, it would have been automatically extended for five years.→

US chiefs shake up Pacific commands

Washington, 3 April
General MacArthur has been appointed C-in-C of all US Pacific ground forces, and Admiral Nimitz will command all US naval units. The old geographic boundaries of "South-west Pacific" and "Pacific Ocean Areas" are to be discarded in favour of this new command structure in preparation for the coming invasion of Japan. The joint chiefs of staff in Washington have retained direct control of the US Twentieth Army Air Force and will exercise strategic command in the Pacific theatre (→ 14).

Japanese to have a new prime minister

Tokyo, 7 April
Japan's desperate elder statesmen today advised the emperor to summon 79-year-old Admiral Baron Kantaro Suzuki, a moderate, out of retirement to lead the new government following the resignation of General Kuniaki Koiso's cabinet on 5 April. The crisis of confidence in Koiso has been precipitated by the invasion of Okinawa and Russia's shock renunciation of its neutrality pact with Japan [*report above*]. The new premier has been told to end the war as soon as possible by court advisers, Baron Suzuki, a former grand chamberlain, led the peace faction opposed to escalating the war in China.

Still fighting: a Japanese soldier.

Americans sink Japan's giant battleship

Death throes: the world's largest battleship, the "Yamato", under attack.

East China Sea, 7 April
The 72,000-ton *Yamato*, the world's biggest and most powerful battleship, keeled over and went to the bottom today after a 90-minute onslaught by carrier-based US aircraft. Almost 2,500 men perished.

The *Yamato* was on a suicide mission. As she set sail, accompanied by the cruiser *Yahagi* and eight destroyers, her crew were told: "The fate of our empire truly rests on this one action." The *Yamato*'s last desperate mission was a reaction to the US invasion of Okinawa. Imperial general headquarters decided to commit every soldier, airman and ship to dislodge the enemy. The plan was for the *Yamato* to draw off American carrier planes, leaving Allied naval forces off Okinawa vulnerable to large-scale *kamikaze* attack. The *Yamato* had only sufficient fuel for a one-way passage. The battleship was then to blast her way through the US Navy and run ashore where her 2,000 crew members would join in the defence of Okinawa.

The US Task Force 58 (TF58) attacked the *Yamato* off Kyushu. Hit by five torpedoes and many bombs, the *Yamato* listed alarmingly and, with her rudder jammed, the doomed giant circled slowly. A huge column of smoke rose above her as she went down, taking her crew with her. TF58 also sank the *Yahagi* and four destroyers; ten US planes were lost (→ 11).

Allies to relaunch offensive in Italy

Cesena, Italy, 1 April
In a small cinema here four days ago, the commander of the Eighth Army, Lt-Gen Richard McCreery, summoned all officers over the rank of lieutenant-colonel. His intention, he told them, was to destroy the Germans south of the river Po in what could be the last great battle of the gruelling Italian campaign. Soon the Germans will face a massive assault from armies which include Americans (many of Japanese origin), Britons, Brazilians, Italians, New Zealanders, Poles, Indians, Gurkhas and a Jewish brigade. British commandos began their attack east of Lake Comacchio tonight (→ 5).

End of coalition is signalled by Bevin

Britain, 7 April
The impending break-up of Britain's coalition government was signalled by Ernest Bevin, the minister of labour, today. "We are at the parting of the ways," he said, and chided Mr Churchill for apparently favouring a post-war coalition which he hoped he could lead. Mr Bevin went on: "I have a profound admiration for the prime minister as a war leader – unfettered I gave him my loyalty in that position: I never gave it to him as leader of the Conservative Party." (→ 21/5)

1945

April

Su	Mo	Tu	We	Th	Fr	Sa
1	2	3	4	5	6	7
8	9	10	11	12	13	14
15	16	17	18	19	20	21
22	23	24	25	26	27	28
29	30					

8. Germany: Patton's troops discover art treasures and the entire *Reichsbank* gold reserves, hidden in a salt mine near Mulhausen (→ 11).

9. Germany: Admiral Wilhelm Canaris, the former head of the *Abwehr* [military intelligence], General Hans Oster, another ex-Abwehr officer, and Pastor Dietrich Bonhoeffer, a theologian, are hanged at Flossenburg for treason.

9. Essen: The US Ninth Army takes over the Krupp plant, the major source of German armaments (→ 13).

9. Kiel: RAF bombers damage the *Admiral Scheer*, one of Germany's two remaining pocket battleships, beyond repair, and seriously damage the heavy cruiser *Admiral Hipper*.

10. Philippines: US troops capture Jolo, in the Sulu archipelago, and reach Lamon Bay on Luzon (→ 16).

11. Okinawa: *Kamikaze* attacks on the US TF58 cripple the US carrier *Enterprise* and damage the battleship *Missouri* (→ 12).

11. Burma: British troops capture Pyawbe, opening the route to Rangoon (→ 16).

11. Germany: US troops find an intact V-weapon plant at Nordhausen, and remove as much material as possible to keep it from the Russians.→

12. Okinawa: US forces make little progress against the Japanese Shuri Line, and their destroyer *Mannert L Abele*, part of TF58, is sunk by a *baka* – a type of piloted bomb (→ 15).

13. Germany: Eisenhower turns down his third chance to capture Berlin, saying that it is just a political prize.→

13. Santiago: Chile declares war on Japan.

14. France: French forces attack the remaining German stronghold at Royan, in the Gironde estuary (→ 15).

14. Germany: Himmler orders that no prisoners at Dachau concentration camp "shall be allowed to fall into the hands of the enemy alive" (→ 17).

Americans mourn death of Roosevelt

Washington, 12 April
President Franklin Delano Roosevelt, the only American president ever elected four times, died suddenly in Warm Springs, Georgia, this afternoon while he was sitting for a portrait. He was 63. The whole country is mourning the Democratic president who offered the United States a "New Deal" of expansionist policies to end the economic crisis of the 1930s and then led it out of isolationism towards victory in a world war.

Although a decline in the president's health had been widely noticed in recent months, his death came as a shock to Washington. Around the world, some American soldiers and sailors refused to believe that he was dead.

His widow Eleanor said: "I am more sorry for the people of the country and of the world than I am for us." The words of his constant adversary, the Republican Senator Robert Taft, were typical of the response in Congress. Taft called the late president "the greatest figure of our time", removed "at the very climax of his career". "We were fortunate," said Harold Ickes, the secretary of the interior, "to have given to civilization the greatest leader in the history of our country."→

Roosevelt: some US servicemen have refused to believe that he is dead.

Harry Truman sworn in as new president

Washington, 12 April
Harry S Truman, the vice-president, was sworn in as the 33rd president of the United States at the White House this evening. "Boys," the new president told reporters, "if you ever pray, pray for me now." He said that he felt as if "the moon, the stars and all the planets had fallen on me". Minutes after the swearing-in, the secretary of war, Henry Stimson, told Mr Truman that the United States has developed a new explosive "of incredible power". Many here express worries about the former senator from Missouri's lack of experience. But the speaker, Sam Rayburn, said: "Truman will not make a great, flashy president like Roosevelt. But, by God, he'll make a good president, a sound president. He's got the stuff in him."→

Harry S Truman at the piano with Lauren Bacall on top: he won't have much time for making music now.

German delight at Roosevelt's death

Berlin, 13 April
Officially Germany reacted to the news of President Roosevelt's death with a correct silence. The Nazi leaders, however, greeted it as a ray of light in what is now a desperate situation for them. "My Fuhrer," Josef Goebbels told Hitler, "I congratulate you. Roosevelt is dead. It is written in the stars that the second half of April will be the turning point for us." The Nazis believe that Roosevelt's death will be the signal for the western allies and the Soviet Union to fall out. Some plan to hold out in redoubts in north and south Germany until this occurs. Other Germans fear that Roosevelt's death leaves them to the possibly less tender mercies of Churchill and Stalin.

▷

Major Italian offensive launched by Allies

Italy, 10 April
Few battles can have had such a devastating prelude. First came 234 US medium bombers, which dropped 24,000 20-pound incendiary bombs. Next, 740 fighter-bombers of the US Tactical Air Force swooped down on enemy gun and mortar sites. And then 825 heavies dropped 1,692 tons around Lugo.

No sooner had the dazed German defenders pulled themselves together than the artillery – 1,500 guns – opened up for 42 minutes. The Germans braced themselves for the infantry assault. But it did not come. Four more "false-alarm" barrages were to follow before the infantry, advancing behind flame-throwing tanks, crossed the Senio river. Four months of intensive training are paying a rich dividend. By dawn this morning the Allies

were crossing the river in strength over three Bailey bridges erected during the night by Royal Engineers. As bombers and artillery began a new barrage, Punjabis of the 8th Indian Division were preparing to cross the Santerno river. On the right flank, Fantails – tracked amphibious vehicles – of the 9th Armoured Brigade and 56th Infantry Division have been struggling through the shallow waters of Lake Comacchio to land behind the German lines and threaten Argenta and the Reno river.

The Allies are enjoying almost total domination of the air. Their navigators have a new card index of reconnaissance photographs to help to identify individual targets, and observers on the ground can call up fighter-bombers from a "cab-rank" above [*see pages 724-25*] (→ 17).

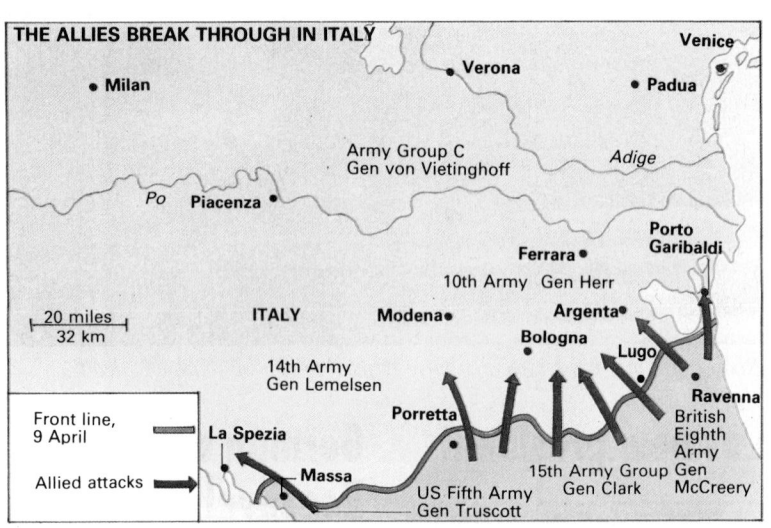

THE ALLIES BREAK THROUGH IN ITALY

Venice
Milan
Verona
Padua
Army Group C
Gen von Vietinghoff
Adige
Po Piacenza
Porto Garibaldi
Ferrara
10th Army Gen Herr
ITALY Modena
Argenta
Bologna
20 miles
32 km
Lugo
14th Army Gen Lemelsen
Ravenna
Front line, 9 April
Porretta
British Eighth Army Gen McCreery
La Spezia
Allied attacks
Massa
15th Army Group Gen Clark
US Fifth Army Gen Truscott

Allies smash Tokyo with fire-bomb raid

Tokyo, 14 April
Not a building is left standing in ten square miles of Tokyo after a four-hour fire-bomb raid last night by 327 USAAF B-29 Superfortresses. Where yesterday there were wooden homes, workshops and munitions factories, there is only smoking rubble in which thousands are feared to have died. The imperial palace was also damaged. The firestorm started as 2,139 tons of incendiaries filled with jellied petrol set buildings burning so fiercely that all air was consumed, creating strong winds that spread the fire further – until there was nothing left to burn (→ 5/5).

THAT'S THE SPOT TO HIT !

GIVE US THE STUFF AND WE'LL HIT IT!
Admiral Nimitz pinpoints the target.

Buchenwald camp freed

What the Third "Reich" leaves behind: a truckload of naked skeletal corpses.

Occupied Germany, 12 April
It was too much to take, even for America's three toughest generals. As they toured the Ohrdruf concentration camp today, Eisenhower and Bradley burst into tears. General Patton, the most battle-scarred of them all, was overcome by the sight and smell of the piled-up corpses: gagging at each fresh horror, in the end he simply bent down and vomited.

American troops are experiencing the same nausea. Yesterday morning they uncovered Buchenwald. One of Hitler's older camps, opened to house his opponents in 1938, it soon became another site for race murder. In 1941, 1,200 Jewish prisoners from Buchenwald were among the first to be gassed experimentally in the search for an efficient method to effect the "final solution" to the "Jewish question".

The GIs cannot believe their eyes. There are piles of unburied corpses, stacked higher than a man, at every turn. Inside the huts there are twenty thousand skeletal slave labourers lying in bare wooden pigeonholes that stretch from floor to ceiling. When a soldier opens the door, the prisoners, too weak to move, turn their heads feebly. Their eyes, peering out over hollow cheeks, look mournful, confused and resigned. There is no joy in survival.

These pathetic scraps of humanity are some of occupied Europe's

leading intellectuals and politicians. They come from Hungary, Russia, Poland, Austria, the Netherlands and Belgium; there are even French deputies who opposed the Vichy government and anti-Franco Spaniards.

As the Americans approached the camp, the Nazis hurriedly evacuated all the Jewish inmates, many of whom only arrived a few months ago from Auschwitz or other camps to the east. Most of them are now at Flossenburg. Himmler is keeping them alive as potential bargaining counters in what he still hopes will be peace negotiations with the Allies (→ 14).

Survivors look out of Buchenwald.

Allied forces scent victory as the "Reich" buckles

Konigsberg broken by 59-day siege

Moscow, 9 April
Konigsberg, the capital of East Prussia and stronghold of Germany's Baltic defences, fell to the Red Army today after a siege lasting 59 days. The fighting cost the Germans 42,000 men dead and 27,000 captured. A quarter of the city's population, 25,000 civilians, also died in the fighting because Hitler refused to allow their evacuation. General Otto Lasch, his situation hopeless, finally surrendered to prevent more bloodshed. Hitler is furious and has ordered him to be shot, but he is already a prisoner.

The shattered streets of Konigsberg, now under the control of the Red Army.

Vienna is liberated

Moscow, 13 April
Vienna, the first foreign capital occupied by Hitler, was liberated today by Marshal Tolbukhin, just seven years and one month after the *Wehrmacht* marched into Austria.

As agreed by the Allies in 1943, it appears that Austria will not be treated as a conquered nation. Moscow radio said tonight that because the people of Vienna and other parts of Austria had helped the Red Army fight the Germans they had "saved the honour of the Austrian nation" (→ 29).

British Churchill tanks rumble through the deserted streets of Arnhem.

Next target: Berlin

Moscow, 14 April
The scene is now set for the Red Army's assault on Berlin. The victorious marshals, Zhukov, Konev and Rokossovsky, are drawn up in overwhelming strength, ready to attack. Zhukov and Konev dislike one another, and there is keen rivalry between them for the honour of taking the German capital. Elsewhere, the Russians are slackening their advance. East Prussia is now harmless. Vienna has fallen. Graz is threatened. But it seems as if the Russians are holding their breath in readiness for the last 40-mile (64-km) march on Berlin. It will be a desperate affair (→ 18).

Looted by the Nazis: US soldiers examine Manet's "Winter Garden".

Russians close the gap with US Army

Central Germany, 14 April
With Patton's Third Army thrusting through the Thuringian Forest to Dresden and Leipzig, the gap between the Americans and the Red Army is closing rapidly and Germany is being sliced in two. There are fears that Hitler may attempt a last-ditch defence in the southern redoubt based on Berchtesgaden. French and American troops are closing on the Danube before crossing into Bavaria. In the north, the British are moving on Bremen, Hamburg and Wilhelmshaven to forestall any attempt to mount a defence of the ports (→ 19).

Bombing goes on

Germany, 14 April
Relentless Allied air attacks on Germany are wiping out the *Luftwaffe* on the tarmac and the pride of the *Kriegsmarine* in harbour. Figures compiled in the last 48 hours show that 1,738 enemy aircraft were destroyed in a week's attacks on 59 airfields. A total of 332 were shot down in air combat. Many German planes are limited by a lack of fuel. Another blow is the loss of the pocket battleship *Admiral Scheer*, which capsized after being bombed at Kiel five days ago.

PoWs on the march

Germany, 13 April
The Nazis have forced Allied PoWs to march up to 500 miles across Europe on starvation rations, according to reports published today in British newspapers. The reports allege that of 6,000 Russians, Britons and Americans who set out in January, only 553 are still alive. The Russians came from camps in Poland and the British and Americans from *Stalag* VIIIA, near Breslau. In January both groups marched to Gorlitz, in Silesia. In February they set out again. Most of them died of starvation, exhaustion or dysentery, and a few from the random cruelty of the guards.

April

Su	Mo	Tu	We	Th	Fr	Sa
1	2	3	4	5	6	7
8	9	10	11	12	13	14
15	16	17	18	19	20	21
22	23	24	25	26	27	28
29	30					

15. Okinawa: US marines on the Motobu peninsula suffer heavy casualties from Japanese artillery fire.→

15. Netherlands: British infantry capture Arnhem.

15. France: US bombers drop "napalm" bombs on German troops at Royan, in the Gironde estuary (→ 20).

16. Philippines: US forces invade Carabao after two days of intensive shelling, only to find that the Japanese are long gone (→ 22).

16. Germany: US troops take Colditz, freeing its PoWs.

16. Baltic: The RAF sinks the *Lutzow*, Germany's last pocket battleship.

16-17. Baltic: The Soviet submarine L-3 sinks the German liner *Goya*; 6,220 refugees drown.

17. Germany: Allied bombing destroys over a thousand *Luftwaffe* aircraft on the ground as US troops reach Magdeburg (→ 19).

17. Italy: The British V Corps captures Argenta (→ 19).

18. Heligoland: The RAF drops 5,000 tons of bombs on the island; German marines who arrange a peaceful hand-over of the island to British forces are shot by the SS as mutineers.→

18. Berlin: Goebbels burns his office files (→ 20).

18. Western Europe: Patton's US Third Army crosses the Czech frontier (→ 5/5).

19. Italy: The US Fifth Army breaks out of the Apennines onto the Po plateau.→

19. Germany: The US First Army captures Leipzig and the British Second Army reaches the Elbe.→

20. Berlin: At his 56th birthday party, Hitler is stooped and trembling, his uniform stained with food.→

20. Germany: The French First Army takes Stuttgart.

21. Wustrow, Germany: Himmler meets Norbert Masur of the World Jewish Congress, and refuses to free the Jews under his control (→ 29).

Allied troops take Bologna as it sleeps

A US tank in the outskirts of Bologna: the streets are strewn with rubble.

Bologna, 21 April
It was 5.50am when the last of the German garrison motored out of this university city. Bologna slept. Fifteen minutes later, advance units of the Polish II Corps drove in from the east and hoisted their national flag on the town hall, just a few minutes before American tanks rumbled in from the north, soon to be joined by Italian troops of the Eighth Army, their British steel helmets adorned with flowers and feathers.

Only then did Bologna awake to go noisily, crazily, mad with joy and relief. A stiff, street-by-street battle had been expected. The German commander had received the now almost rubber-stamped order to fight to the last man. Instead, it seems that he made a deal with the city's archbishop and the Fascist mayor. If partisans did not molest his retreating troops, he would not demolish Bologna's public services.

As the Poles advanced along the *Via Emilia*, a coded signal had to be sent to the partisans to rise up. Anticipating this, the Germans arrested and shot two of their leaders. Today, as Bologna went wild, the partisans shot two leading Fascists in revenge (→ 25).

Fierce fight for US troops on Okinawa

Okinawa, 20 April
A new US offensive on Okinawa has run into heavy resistance from General Ushijima's 80,000-man defence force concentrated on the southern end of the island. Despite intense bombardment, Lieutenant-General John Hodge's XXIV Corps, advancing on Machinato and Yonabaru airfields, has gained only 1,800 yards in two days, with the defenders operating from a vast network of tunnels and caves. US forces control the rest of Okinawa, and Ie Shima, an offshore island needed as an air base, has been taken after a six-day battle (→ 30).

Soviet moves over Poland worry West

London, 21 April
Churchill's fears about Stalin's post-war ambitions grew today with news of the signing of a mutual assistance pact between the USSR and its client Polish government based in Lublin. Meeting in Washington, the Big Three's foreign ministers, Eden, Stettinius and Molotov, have set out their positions, with Britain and America insisting on the widening of the government into one of National Unity.

Molotov refuses to budge, and Eden has written to Churchill: "No sign of progress. My impression is that the Soviet government is still cavalier in its attitude and will not accept the seriousness of the situation, unless it is brought up sharply against realities" (→ 5/5).

Burmese advances

Burma, 16 April
Allied advances are continuing in Burma, with the capital, Rangoon, now firmly in General Slim's sights. Today it was the turn of Taungup, in the Arakan peninsula, to fall to XV Corps, while inland IV Corps is chasing General Honda's Thirty-Third Japanese Army down the Sittang valley towards Pyinmanna. The Japanese forces are also in retreat along the Irrawaddy, where XXXIII Corps is driving south to oil-rich Yenangyaung (→ 23).

Ernie Pyle, creator of "GI Joe", killed

Ie Shima, Okinawa, 18 April
Ernie Pyle was killed today by a Japanese sniper. The war correspondent who, more than any other, brought the reality of war, the mud, the blood and the agony, into the American home, died among the ordinary GIs whose cause became his own personal battle; and it is those GIs who will mourn him most. For most of the war, Pyle had followed US servicemen in North Africa, Sicily, Italy and France, including the D-Day landing. He moved to the Pacific theatre after taking a rest in America. Ernest Taylor Pyle was 44.

April 15. An impressive funeral cortege for President Roosevelt: he will be buried at his home, Hyde Park, in New York.

The noose tightens around beleaguered Berlin

Russia opens drive for "Reich" capital

River Oder, 16 April
At 4am today, Marshal Zhukov looked towards Berlin from his bunker in the Kustrin bridgehead over the Oder and ordered: "Now, comrades! Now!" Three red flares floated above the lines and, instantly, the German positions were lit up with the blinding light of 143 searchlights and thousands of tank and lorry headlights. Three green flares soared into the sky. This was the signal for thousands of big guns, wheel to wheel, to open the heaviest barrage of the whole of the war in the east. Villages were blown away. Forests burst into flames, burning fiercely out of control.

The Russians have assembled 2,500,000 men, 6,250 tanks, 41,600 guns and mortars, 3,255 rocket launchers and 7,500 aircraft in three fronts under Zhukov, Konev and Rokossovsky for this final assault. It seemed this morning that nothing could stand against this awesome power. Much of that ground was empty, however, for General Heinrici, commanding Army Group Vistula with orders to save Berlin, had withdrawn his men to a second line of defence.

They are fighting now from well-entrenched positions on the Seelow Heights where *Flak* guns, moved from defending Berlin against Allied bombers, have taken a terrible toll of Zhukov's tanks. He is held up, but Konev's First Ukrainian Front to the south has made rapid progress after crossing the Neisse. And Rokossovsky to the north has yet to join the battle.→

Red Army troops on the move on the outskirts of bomb-shattered Berlin.

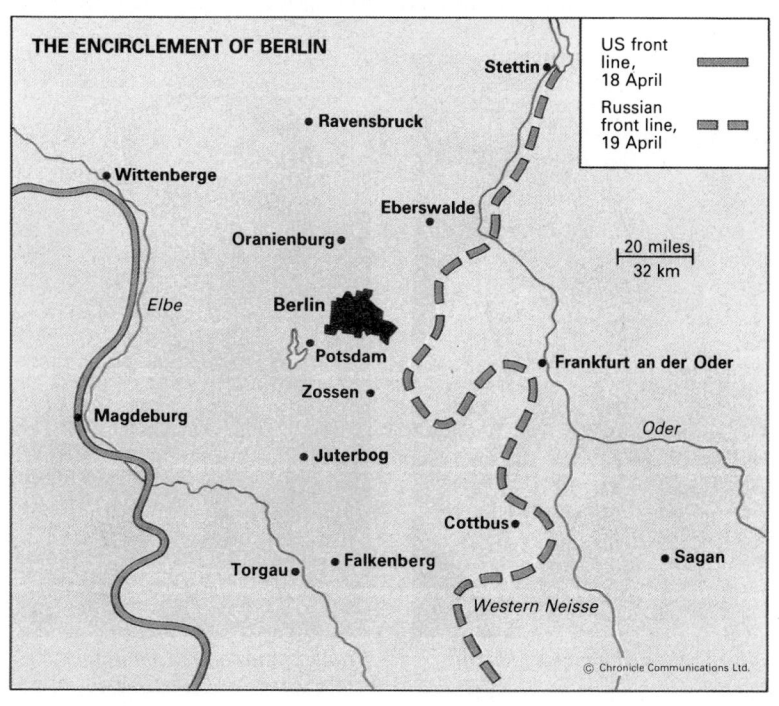
THE ENCIRCLEMENT OF BERLIN

US front line, 18 April
Russian front line, 19 April

Stettin
Ravensbruck
Wittenberge
Eberswalde
Oranienburg
Elbe
Berlin
Potsdam
Zossen
Magdeburg
Frankfurt an der Oder
Oder
Juterbog
20 miles / 32 km
Cottbus
Torgau
Falkenberg
Sagan
Western Neisse
© Chronicle Communications Ltd.

The Fuhrer retreats to his final bunker

Berlin, 16 April
Eva Braun has arrived in Berlin from Berchtesgaden to join Hitler in his bunker to share the last days of the Third *Reich* with him. When the Fuhrer told her that she should have stayed in Bavaria, she said that she had no desire to live in a Germany without him. "It would not be fit for a true German," she says. Eva, the secret mistress of the Nazi leader for more than 12 years, has spent the war in Hitler's mountain retreat, swimming and skiing, reading cheap love stories and watching romantic movies.

Albert Speer, Hitler's armaments minister, has been horrified by the directive from the Fuhrer that all military, transport and industrial installations must be destroyed in order to deny them to the enemy. He has protested vigorously, but Hitler remains adamant. If the war is lost, he told Speer, there will be no point in attempting to save the German people. Speer, however, is cooperating with army officers to frustrate the Fuhrer's directive.

Hitler sees betrayal everywhere. Today he sacked the *Reich* public health commissioner, Karl Brandt, after learning that Brandt had sent his wife and child to Thuringia so that they could surrender to the Americans. And as the Red Army opens its final assault on Berlin, Hitler, in his bunker beneath the ruins of his Chancellery, issued an order of the day to his broken army: "He who gives the order to retreat is to be shot on the spot" (→ 20).

Berliners struggle to stay alive for peace

Berlin, 18 April
The citizens of Berlin, like their Fuhrer, are taking refuge from impending disaster underground. As the Allied armies close in on their city they leave their cellars and dugouts only to fetch vital supplies of food and water. But the basic essentials are running short in Berlin and people often queue for hours – in the dead of night before the Russian bombardment begins at 5am – just in the hope of a loaf of bread. They are also taking refuge from their own people – from the SS which is reportedly shooting people on the spot on the accusation that they are "defeatists", or rounding them up to join the *Volkssturm* in the last desperate defence of the *Reich*. Many are now waiting only to surrender (→ 20).

Ruhr battle ends with 325,000 prisoners

Ruhr, 21 April
Three days ago the commander of German forces in the Ruhr, Field Marshal Walter Model, drove to the forest beyond Dusseldorf, left his car, drew his service pistol and shot himself. A few months ago, when he took over the western command, he issued a ringing call to battle: "None of us gives up a square foot of German soil while still alive ... Long live our Germany and our beloved Fuhrer! "

Now the Battle of the Ruhr has ended, with 325,000 prisoners in Allied hands; these include 30 generals and an admiral. Eisenhower, in an order of the day, says that "21 enemy divisions, including three *Panzer*, one *Panzergrenadier* and three Parachute divisions" have been smashed.

1945

April

Su	Mo	Tu	We	Th	Fr	Sa
1	2	3	4	5	6	7
8	9	10	11	12	13	14
15	16	17	18	19	20	21
22	23	24	25	26	27	28
29	30					

Horrors of Belsen stun British troops

Bergen-Belsen, 17 April

There is a pile of naked female corpses here, 80 yards long by 30 yards wide and four feet high. You can't see any faces; just bony elbows, knees and buttocks or twisted hands and feet. It looks like the overladen counter of an insane butcher's shop where flies dance on the mound of greying flesh.

It is two days since the British Army agreed a truce with the local German commander which enabled them to enter the camp peacefully. The Hungarian army guards, who stayed on duty "to prevent a mass breakout", have shot dead 83 prisoners for minor offences. Now the British are in full control, and a Jewish sergeant, Norman Turgel, has arrested Josef Kramer, the camp's commandant.

Kramer's men have been disarmed and put to work burying the estimated ten thousand dead lying around the camp. They have to be locked up to protect them from the vengeance of the prisoners. Yesterday seven *Kapos* [prisoner-guards] were savagely beaten to death.

About 30,000 victims, mainly Jews, gypsies and political prisoners, are still alive, but raging epidemics of typhus and dysentery threaten to finish off the deadly work that the Nazis started. British medical staff are now struggling to save lives and halt the spread of disease. Derrick Sington, the first British officer to enter the camp, told how a Hungarian-Jewish girl took him to a clearing: "Three hundred yards away was a mound of bodies, six feet high. A crosswind was blowing and carrying into our nostrils the stench of putrefying flesh" (→ 21).

Well-fed SS women pile emaciated bodies into a mass grave at Belsen.

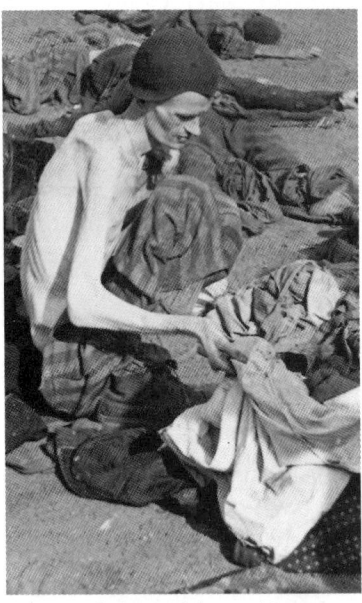
A living skeleton delouses his rags.

Kramer: murderer of thousands.

A bleak birthday for Hitler as Russia intensifies its offensive

Germany, 20 April

Hitler today celebrated his 56th birthday, although "celebrated" was scarcely the word as the sound of Soviet artillery rumbled ever closer to his capital city. The Second Byelorussian Front under Marshal Rokossovsky has now reinforced the offensives launched by Zhukov and Konev four days ago. Today Rokossovsky battled over marshy ground to cross the western branch of the Oder, effectively preventing the 3rd *Panzer* Army from reinforcing the defence of Berlin.

Further south Marshal Konev has crossed the river Spree, and today took Calau on the approach to Berlin from the south. Although the direct eastern attack by Marshal Zhukov's First Byelorussian Front has encountered strong resistance near Seelow, Germany's Ninth Army is being squeezed between the advancing armies of Zhukov and Konev. However, Hitler has resisted pleas that it should be allowed to withdraw. Some government departments are being moved to southern Germany and Schleswig-Holstein, but Hitler rejected suggestions that he should also leave. The Fuhrer emerged from his bunker just once today – to decorate members of the *Hitler Jugend* for bravery (→ 23).

22. Philippines: US forces gain control of Cebu island and overcome Japanese resistance on Jolo (→ 6/6).

22. Germany: Himmler meets the Swedish count Folke Bernadotte, and offers a German surrender to the British and Americans but not to the Russians (→ 27).

23. Burma: The First Division of the Indian National Army, fighting with the Japanese, surrenders *en masse* to the Allies (→ 29).

23. Berlin: Albert Speer bids Hitler farewell, confessing that he sabotaged the "scorched-earth" directive.

24. Berlin: Hitler orders Goering to be arrested after receiving a telegram from him offering to take over command of the *Reich* (→ 28).

24. Britain: The "dim-out" is abolished, except for a coastal belt five miles deep.

25. Germany: RAF bombers drop six-ton bombs on Hitler's home at Berchtesgaden (→ 27).

25. Milan: As Mantua, Verona and Parma fall to US forces just forty miles away, Mussolini flees to Como (→ 27).

27. Dongo, Italy: Partisans arrest Mussolini, who is hiding in the back of a lorry disguised as a *Luftwaffe* corporal.→

27. Germany: The Allies refuse Himmler's peace overtures, insisting on total, unconditional surrender (→ 28).

28. Berlin: On hearing a BBC report of Himmler's attempted peace negotiations, Hitler orders his immediate arrest and execution and has his liaison officer, Hermann Fegelein, shot dead.

29. Burma: British troops capture Allanmyo, in the Irrawaddy valley (→ 3/5).

29. Austria: The Red Army sets up a provisional government in Vienna (→ 15/5).

30. Okinawa: US and Japanese forces remain deadlocked along the Shuri Line (→ 4/5).

30. Germany: Soviet troops liberate Ravensbruck concentration camp (→ 14/5).

Axis forces crumble in the face of Allied armies

US-Soviet link-up on the river Elbe

Elbe, 27 April
A momentous announcement, revealing that Allied troops advancing from the west have linked up with the Russians on the river Elbe, was released simultaneously in London, Moscow and Washington this evening.

In a short broadcast, Churchill spoke of the "inflexible resolve" of the Allies "to fulfil our purpose and our duty". Stalin read his message on Moscow radio and paid tribute to "the valorous troops of our Allies". Truman said "this great triumph of Allied arms" was a tribute to the courage and determination of Franklin Roosevelt.

The official version of the meeting places it at Torgau yesterday afternoon, when news cameramen were present to show Americans and Russians shaking hands on a wrecked railway bridge, and the commander of the US 69th Infantry Division, General F E Reinhardt, clasping hands with an unidentified Russian general of the 58th Guards Division.

In fact the first meeting had occurred on 25 April, when a US patrol, led by Lt Albert Kotzebue of the US 69th, spotted a solitary

The official version of the meeting of the Americans and Russians at Torgau.

Soviet cavalryman near the village of Stehla. A few hours later, Lt William Robinson met other Soviet soldiers at Torgau. In a radio message to his command post, Kotzebue reported: "Mission accomplished. Making arrangements for meeting between commanding officers." The message ended with two significant words: "No casualties." – a reflection of western fears that a meeting with the Russians might lead to clashes.

With Hitler's *Reich* now sliced in two, the end must be fast approaching. Roads are filled with ex-PoWs,

German soldiers and civilians pushing handcarts, all trekking west to escape the Russians.

In the run-up to the Elbe, the American patrol passed through villages where white sheets hung from windows and faces hovered behind lace curtains. In Torgau they encountered wandering slave labourers, German nurses and a dozen or so men carrying piano accordions; others were wheeling carts loaded with tinned food. Further along, the Americans came to scores of Germans queueing up to loot a store.→

German forces sign surrender in Italy

Caserta, Italy, 29 April
After three weeks of tense negotiation, the German garrison in Italy surrendered unconditionally today. More than one million men – 22 German divisions and six Italian Fascist divisions in Italy and Austria – are preparing to lay down their arms and march into prison camps. A vast area of former Axis territory is now in Allied hands.

Negotiations began in great secrecy. The Germans had lost most of their heavy guns and tanks when they were trapped south of the Po. Fleeing survivors – including generals – had been forced to swim to safety as Allied tanks raced across the valley. Bologna had fallen and partisans had taken control of Milan and Turin. The German position was hopeless.

It was an SS general, Karl Wolff, who made the first overtures, using Cardinal Schuster of Milan as intermediary. The surrender document was signed at Allied headquarters here today. In a proclamation, General Heinrich von Vietinghoff, the German commander, told his soldiers: "Hitherto you have obeyed your Fuhrer. Today, you must obey your orders" (→2/5).

Revolted American troops execute 122 SS guards at Dachau

Dachau, 29 April
Enraged GIs who liberated Dachau death camp today killed any SS guards crossing their paths, including at least 122 who had surrendered. At Webling, about five miles (eight km) away, 43 SS men were killed, one an officer whose head was smashed open with an entrenching tool. The GIs, men of the 157th and 222nd Infantry Regiments, found mounds of bodies outside a crematorium, and lying inside and alongside rail cattle trucks. Local civilians were busy looting, accompanied by their children. An arrogant commander attempted a formal military handover. The GIs screamed "Kill 'em!" and opened fire. Eighty died before a colonel intervened (→30).

Still strong enough to experience joy: survivors of Dachau death camp.

Petain arrested at Swiss border post

Vallorbe, Switzerland, 26 April
With a soldier's bearing, Marshal Philippe Petain saluted the *aide-de-camp* of General Koenig, the Free French commander-in-chief. He then advanced towards Koenig with outstretched hand, which Koenig refused to shake. It took the aged marshal a moment to realize that he was under arrest.

He was transferred to a second-class train which will arrive in Paris early tomorrow. There the prosecutor in charge of his case, Andre Mornet, said that Petain's conduct deserved the death sentence "but he has reached an age where considerations of humanity should prevail" (→23/7).

Red Army wins nine-day battle for heart of Berlin

Day One: a ring of tanks tightens grip

22 April
Zhukov and Konev, having overcome the fanatical resistance of the defence zone before Berlin, are moving rapidly to put a ring of tanks round the capital. Zhukov's Forty-Seventh Army and Konev's Fourth Guards' Tank Army are both west of the city, and only 25 miles (40 km) separate them. Rokossovsky, after being held up crossing the Oder marshes, is preventing the 3rd *Panzer* Army from coming to Berlin's aid from the north.

Day Two: shelling

23 April
The Red Army has broken into Berlin from the north, east and south. Massed Russian artillery is shelling the central and western areas of the city. Buildings are collapsing piece by piece. *Shturmovik* aircraft dive over the rubble to silence German strongpoints. Latest reports say that Russian assault troops are smashing their way through the inner ring of SS resistance near the Stettiner railway station, one mile from the *Unter den Linden*.

Day Three: air raid

24 April
The RAF joined in the final battle of Berlin today with fighter-bombers of Bomber Command pouncing on General Wenck's Twelfth Army as it moves east after being switched from the western front to relieve Berlin. The pilots report that the entire eastern half of the city is on fire. On the ground Konev's men are crossing the heavily-defended Tetlow canal on bridges built by assault sappers under fire.

Day Four: encircled

25 April
Hitler's capital is now completely encircled by the Red Army. Zhukov's tanks, sweeping across the northern suburbs, have cut all the

The Red Army storms the shattered Reichstag by air, tanks and infantry.

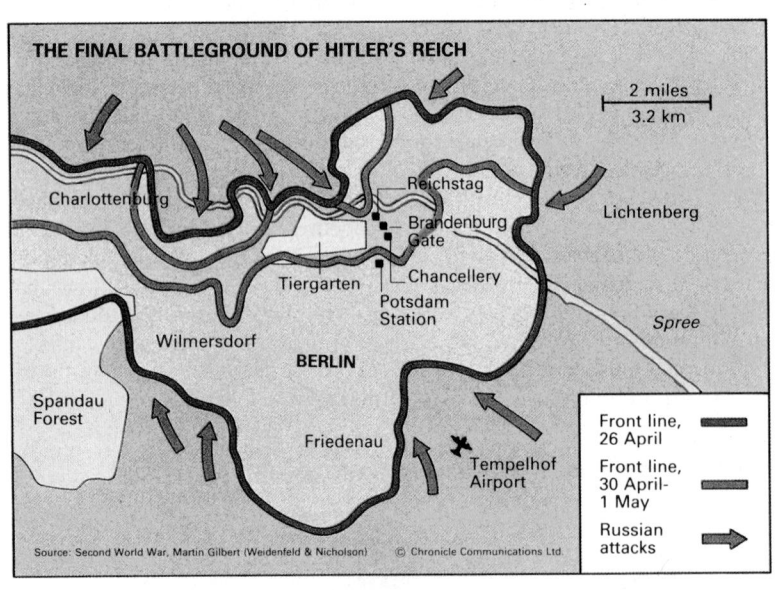

THE FINAL BATTLEGROUND OF HITLER'S REICH

2 miles
3.2 km

Charlottenburg
Reichstag
Brandenburg Gate
Lichtenberg
Tiergarten
Chancellery
Potsdam Station
Wilmersdorf
Spree
BERLIN
Spandau Forest
Friedenau
Tempelhof Airport

Front line, 26 April
Front line, 30 April–1 May
Russian attacks

Source: Second World War, Martin Gilbert (Weidenfeld & Nicholson)   © Chronicle Communications Ltd.

roads leading to the west and yesterday linked up with Konev's drive from the south at Ketzin. Inside the city, government buildings in the *Wilhelmstrasse* are under point-blank fire from field-guns.

Day Five: optimism

26 April
Russian tanks have crossed the Spree and reached the Jannowitz Bridge station within a few hundred yards of the Imperial Castle at the start of the *Unter den Linden*. There is, however, a surge of optimism in Hitler's bunker as General Wenck has launched his relief attack from the west and has made good progress towards the capital. On the Russian side, there is dismay at Konev's HQ because Stalin has divided Berlin between his armies and drawn the boundary so that Konev's rival, Zhukov, gets the plum prize, the *Reichstag*.

Day Six: closing in

27 April
Hitler's optimism evaporated today. Wenck has been stopped 15 miles short of Berlin and a breakout attempt by General Busse's trapped Ninth Army has been foiled while the Russians inexorably occupy Berlin, house by house, street by street, looting and raping as they go. Tonight the garrison is penned into a corridor three miles wide and ten miles long running east/west across the city. The SS rules there by way of instant execution.

Day Seven: hunger

28 April
The German garrison is running out of ammunition and food. General Weidling, the capital's commandant, estimates that the bullets will run out in another two days. The defence may not last that long as the Russians drive ever closer to the *Reichstag*. They are infiltrating through the subways and sewers, often storming the defences from below. Now not much more than the area round the *Tiergarten* remains in German hands.

Day Eight: doomed

29 April
There is little left now for the defenders of Berlin to die for. They are being split up into small groups which fall back to fight from the *Flak* towers and large air-raid shelters. Guns are set up in railway yards, squares and parks to hold off the advancing tanks. It appears that a last stand will be made in the *Tiergarten*, but more and more men, realizing that defeat is inevitable, are risking the SS execution squads and surrendering (→ 2/5).

Day Nine: all over

30 April
The *Reichstag* has fallen. The Russians turned their guns on the building at five o'clock this morning and pounded it until early this afternoon, when Zhukov's men poured through shell holes in the walls and fought their way, hand to hand, through the shattered corridors and rooms. The honour of raising the Red Flag over the building fell late tonight to two sergeants, M A Yegorov and M V Kontary. The final battle of Berlin is over.

Defeat brings death for warmongers of Europe

One of the last photographs of Hitler: inspecting decorated German boys.

Adolf and Eva in Berchtesgaden.

Benito Mussolini is killed by partisans

Milan, 28 April
The body of Benito Mussolini, Il Duce, dictator of Italy until his downfall in 1943, hangs upside-down over a garage forecourt in Milan. The body of his mistress, Clara Petacci, hangs next to it. Both bodies have been mutilated. Earlier today, a woman fired five revolver shots – "for my five dead sons" – into the Duce's body. Others spat at their former leader.

With his SS escort, Mussolini was heading towards the Alps where he believed that he could continue the war in the mountains with 3,000 fanatical Fascist followers. In fact, only 12 turned up at a rendez-vous. They then drove through dangerous, partisan-held territory.

The partisans caught up with Petacci and Mussolini, dressed in a German uniform, at Dongo, on Lake Como. After interrogation, a communist partisan, Walter Audisio, lined them up at the gate of the *Villa Belmonte* in Mezzegra. First, he shot Petacci, who clung to her lover. Then Mussolini opened his coat wide and asked to be shot in the chest. The machine gun rang out and the Duce slumped against the wall, breathing heavily. Audisio moved closer, and fired the final shot into his heart (→ 29).

Adolf Hitler and Eva Braun commit suicide in Berlin bunker

Berlin, 30 April
Eva Braun had no appetite for lunch today, so Hitler dined with his two secretaries and his cook. At 3.30pm, having finished the meal, he sent for Eva, his bride of 36 hours, and they retired to his quarters. In the passage, Goebbels and a few other faithful followers waited. A single shot rang out.

After some minutes they opened the door. The body of Adolf Hitler, dripping blood, was slumped on a couch. He had shot himself in the mouth. Beside him was Eva Braun. Two revolvers lay on the floor, but she had not used hers; she had taken poison. Hitler's valet, SS Major Heinz Linge, and a servant

carried Hitler's body, wrapped in an army blanket, up to the garden of the Chancellery. Martin Bormann brought Eva Braun's, then handed it to the Fuhrer's chauffeur Erich Kempka.

With Russian shells exploding all around, Linge and Kempka slid the bodies into a shell hole. The bodies were doused with petrol and set alight with a burning rag. Goebbels stood to attention and raised his right hand in the Nazi salute. The propaganda wizard had risen to the heights with Hitler; now he was preparing to follow him in death.

It was Himmler's "treachery" – the SS chief was trying to make a separate peace with the western Al-

lies – that persuaded Hitler that the end had come. But first his mistress's long-cherished desire must be fulfilled. In the early hours of Sunday, a city councillor called Wagner was tracked down fighting with the *Volkssturm* and brought to the bunker to marry the Fuhrer and Eva, who both swore that they were "of complete Aryan descent". In the space on the marriage form for the name of his father (Schickl-gruber) Hitler left a blank. The bride began to sign "Eva Braun", stopped, struck out the "B" and wrote "Eva Hitler". The next day a pistol shot put an end to the "Thousand Year *Reich*" that lasted for little more than twelve years.→

Hitler's last testament: the Jews are to blame for everything

Berlin, 29 April
In the last hours before his suicide, Hitler proclaimed his faith that the Nazi creed will arise again from the ashes of Germany's defeat. "I die with a happy heart," he says in his last testament, in the certainty that through the sacrifices of his soldiers and himself there "will spring up ... the seed of a radiant rebirth of the National Socialist movement and thus of a truly united nation".

The Fuhrer dictated his message to posterity during the night, soon after his wedding to Eva Braun. In it he says that "international Jewry" must bear "sole responsibility" for the war. Neither he nor "anybody else in Germany" wanted war, but "I left no one in doubt that this time not only would millions ... meet their death ... but this time the real culprits would have to pay for their guilt even though by more humane means [gas chambers for

Jews] than war."

He sees betrayal on all sides: in the army, the air force, even in the SS. And now Hermann Goering and Heinrich Himmler, two men who had been at his side since the early days of the party, had betrayed him by seeking to end the war.

He concludes by asking that his personal possessions be passed to his sister, Paula, "for maintaining a petty bourgeois standard of living" (→ 3/5).

The hated dictator and his mistress strung up, upside-down, in Milan.

Donitz named to be the new "fuhrer"

Flensburg, 30 April
The new German *"fuhrer"* is to be the commander of the German navy, Grand Admiral Karl Donitz. Appalled by Himmler's treachery and Goering's incompetence, Hitler appointed the former U-boat commander as president of the *Reich* because he was the only man left to trust. In a broadcast tomorrow, Donitz plans to say that the war will continue; but he must realize that all he can do is delay Germany's inevitable defeat.

The admiral created a deadly submarine fleet which has sunk 15 million tons of Allied shipping. He believed that having a strong enough fleet of U-boats would win the war, and that Germany lost the First World War because the U-boats were not used properly (→ 2/5).

The grand admiral, now "fuhrer".

Germans forced to face camp horrors

Bergen-Belsen, 27 April
Leaders of communities near concentration camps, including Belsen and Buchenwald, are being forced to see for themselves the horrors in their own backyard: the souvenirs of human skin; half-burnt and sometimes part-cannibalized corpses. At Belsen, where hundreds still die each week, town mayors protest that they knew nothing, in spite of continuous transport activities to this transit camp. At Buchenwald, 1,000 women marched in singing, but left in tears (→ 30).

May

Su	Mo	Tu	We	Th	Fr	Sa
		1	2	3	4	5
6	7	8	9	10	11	12
13	14	15	16	17	18	19
20	21	22	23	24	25	26
27	28	29	30	31		

1. Manila: The Mexican Expeditionary Air Force arrives to fight alongside the USAAF in the Philippines (→ 3).

1. Germany: Field Marshal Gerd von Rundstedt is captured by US troops.→

1. Yugoslavia: Tito's partisans capture the port of Trieste a few hours before Britain's Eighth Army (→ 14).

2. Berlin: German forces surrender to Marshal Zhukov, who immediately despatches troops to search for the bodies of Hitler and Goebbels.→

2. Germany: British troops capture the Baltic ports of Lubeck and Wismar, and Canadian forces take Oldenburg. RAF Mosquitos bomb Kiel (→ 3).

2. Italy: 490,000 German troops surrender, ending the war in Italy.→

3. Philippines: US forces clear Davao, on Mindanao, of Japanese resistance (→ 13).

3. Germany: Admiral Donitz moves his seat of government to Flensburg.→

3. Lisbon: Portugal observes a day of mourning for Hitler (→ 6).

4. Okinawa: The British carrier *Formidable* is damaged by a *kamikaze* attack off the Sakishima Islands.→

5. Okinawa: Japanese *kamikazes* sink 17 US ships; 131 Japanese aircraft are destroyed (→ 11).

5. Copenhagen: British paratroopers land after fighting breaks out between Danish civilians and Germans (→ 16).

5. USA: A Japanese "balloon bomb", floated across the Pacific, kills six civilians in Oregon (→ 8).

5. Austria: The French politicians Paul Reynaud and Edouard Daladier, with the French General Maurice Gamelin, the German pastor Martin Niemoller and the former Austrian chancellor Kurt von Schuschnigg, all imprisoned by the Nazis, are set free (→ 15).

5. Genoa: US forces seize the poet Ezra Pound, wanted on charges of treason (→ 29).

Allies capture Rangoon

Allied troops bring a 25-pounder ashore in newly-liberated Rangoon.

Rangoon, Burma, 3 May
The Burmese capital has fallen. By land, sea and air the Allies today took Rangoon without a fight, thus completing a highly successful campaign orchestrated by Lord Louis Mountbatten, the supreme commander in South-east Asia, and conducted by General Sir William Slim's Fourteenth Army.

A Gurkha parachute battalion which landed two days ago at nearby Elephant Point was reinforced yesterday by the 26th Indian Division landing by assault craft in Operation Dracula. Today they entered Rangoon to be welcomed by thousands of Burmese. News that the Japanese had evacuated came when an Allied pilot saw a message painted on the jail roof by PoWs: "Japs gone. Exdigitate."

Slim had sent XXXIII Corps and IV Corps driving down the Irrawaddy and Sittang river valleys in central Burma while XV Corps advanced down the Arakan peninsula. They were racing to beat the monsoons which burst in mid-May. The main Japanese armies had been broken, but General Slim feared that suicidal defences would hold up his army until the monsoons, giving Lt-Gen Masakazu Kawabe a four-month respite and delaying the attack on Malaya (→ 15).

Australians land on island off Borneo

Borneo, 1 May
The assault landing by Australian troops on Tarakan, off the coast of east Borneo, is the first move to free the Dutch East Indies from Japanese occupation. The 26th Infantry Brigade of the 9th Division stormed ashore today, thrusting aside a Japanese garrison of 2,100. The Australian government does not like to see its troops used in the Borneo campaign, which it regards as a mopping-up operation. It wants them to take part in the main offensive against Japan (→ 10/6).

Japanese tanks in Okinawa struggle

Okinawa, 4 May
Fighting rages across southern Okinawa as Gen Ushijima's Thirty-second Army launches a damaging attack using tanks. US positions were hit by a 13,000-shell bombardment followed by suicidal infantry attacks. Offshore, *kamikaze* boat and plane raids sank 17 US ships and damaged 11 others, with 682 US dead; but four daring sea raids by Japanese commandos behind US lines were all beaten back. Japanese losses are estimated at 5,000 dead; 131 aircraft have been lost (→ 5).

German forces in western Europe sign surrender

Luneburg Heath, 4 May
In a tent on the desolate Luneburg Heath, three generals and two admirals this evening put their signatures to the surrender of all German armed forces in north-west Germany, the Netherlands and Denmark. As Montgomery read out the capitulation terms, a nervous German general took out a cigarette; Monty, who disapproves of smoking, gave him a sharp

glance and the German hastily put it away. The German team was led by an admiral, Hans Georg von Friedeburg; he first appeared yesterday to ask Montgomery to accept the surrender of three *Panzer* armies which were retreating from the Russians, and to allow civilians fleeing from the Russians to pass through the British lines.

"No, certainly not," Montgomery said. He told von Friedeburg to

go back to Donitz and tell him that the armies fighting the Russians must surrender to them. As for the civilians, he would discuss that question after the surrender. He then produced a map of the battle situation. "That was a great shock to them," Montgomery says. He sent the Germans off to have lunch in a separate tent; throughout the meal, von Friedeburg was in tears. The surrender takes effect from

8am tomorrow. More than 500,000 troops are involved; these will join the 500,000 taken prisoner in the past 24 hours.

Tonight von Friedeburg and his fellow officers are sleeping at Montgomery's HQ; tomorrow they will be taken to Eisenhower's HQ at Rheims [*see page 634*] for more surrender talks. Montgomery, a teetotaller, this evening relaxed and drank a glass of champagne (→ 5).

The final days of a Reich that was supposed to last 1,000 years

Germany
May 1. Grand Admiral Donitz, Hitler's appointed successor, orders the German troops to fight to the end while Himmler, who has no authority, is attempting to negotiate favourable surrender terms with the Allies. British troops advance on Lubeck and Hamburg, and US forces are dug in on the west bank of the Elbe.

May 2. Soviet units in the north and south of Berlin link up on the *Charlottenburg Chaussee*. US and Soviet troops meet near Barow and Abbendorft. The defenders of Innsbruck begin to sue for peace. In Austria the French I Corps reaches Gotzis and Obersdorf. The British take Lubeck, and the Canadians take Oldenburg.

May 3. The Red Army makes contact with American troops on the Elbe, to the west of Berlin, and with British troops to the north. In the city itself it mops up the last pockets of resistance. US forces are advancing swiftly on Salzburg and Linz while British troops pursue the Germans up the Kiel Canal.

May 4. Units of the US Third Army complete the crossing of the river Inn, and Innsbruck finally sur-

Montgomery reads the surrender terms to sombre senior German officers.

renders. Salzburg too falls to US forces who then move on towards Berchtesgaden. Troops of the US First Army prepare to march into Czechoslovakia. German troops in Berlin try to reach the US and British lines, rather than be taken by the Russians.

May 5. Despite yesterday's armistice [*see story above*] resistance against the Russians continues.

Army Group Centre conducts a fighting withdrawal in Czechoslovakia with bitter fighting near Olmutz. At Haar, in Bavaria, Army Group G under General Hausser signs an unconditional surrender. On the Baltic coast Swinemunde and Peenemunde, the site of the rocket-weapon research centre that was supposed to win Hitler the war, are captured (→ 6).

Fighting goes on in Czechoslovakia

Prague, 5 May
Czech patriots rose against the Germans still occupying Prague today following several spontaneous revolts against the Nazis in other parts of the country. Street fighting is raging in the streets of the Czech capital. The situation tonight is that the patriots hold most of the city, but the Germans remain in control of several strongpoints while tanks and other *Wehrmacht* units move in from their bases outside.

Among the positions held by the Germans is one of the radio stations which is broadcasting repeated claims that "all important military positions are in the hands of the Wehrmacht". The patriots also control a radio station, and they have been broadcasting desperate appeals for the Allies to come to their rescue.

General Patton's US Third Army is now in Czechoslovakia, and could well make a dash for Prague, but the Russians insist that the Czech capital is their prize. The situation is complicated by the presence in Prague of General Vlasov's renegade Russian army (→ 6).

Goebbels is dead

Berlin, 1 May
First, the children had to be poisoned, all six of them: Helga, 12; Hilda, 11; Helmut, nine; Holde, seven; Hedda, five; and Heide, three. Having given them lethal injections, Josef Goebbels and his wife Magda left the bunker and asked an SS orderly to shoot them in the back of the head (→ 2).

RAF sinks ship full of camp survivors

Neustadt, Germany, 3 May
A tragic episode today claimed the lives of 8,000 people who had survived the living hell of the concentration-camp system. The victims, mainly Jews, were survivors from Neuengamme and Stutthof. The commandant, Max Pauly, had loaded them onto the liners *Cap Arcona*, *Thielbek* and *Deutschland* rather

than hand them over in their camps to the Red Cross or the Allies.

Their hopes ended this afternoon when three RAF Typhoon ground-attack fighters swooped low over Neustadt Bay and sank the ships in a rocket attack. Most drowned immediately. A few managed to jump overboard, only to run the gamut of Nazi machine-gun fire.

De Valera's sorrow

Dublin, 3 May
The prime minister of the Irish Free State, Eamon de Valera, was among several callers on the German minister here today tendering regrets on the death of Adolf Hitler. His action cannot but be seen as adding insult to the injury of continuing relations between Eire and Germany throughout the war (→ 18).

End of Third Reich that brought war to the world

Europe, 5 May
There are some who are too weak even to feel relief at the final downfall of Nazi Germany. Victory may have cut short their physical pain, but it will never erase their suffering. And there are cities in countries which have been battlegrounds that are too devastated to put on the faintest show of celebration. Yet celebration does go on, in a spirit of gratitude as much as triumph – snatched moments of joy and a sense of deliverance. Then the flag-wavers and merry-makers begin the long task of rebuilding their lives. From the ruins of Hitler's empire springs hope: the hope that the children of this war will grow up in peace.

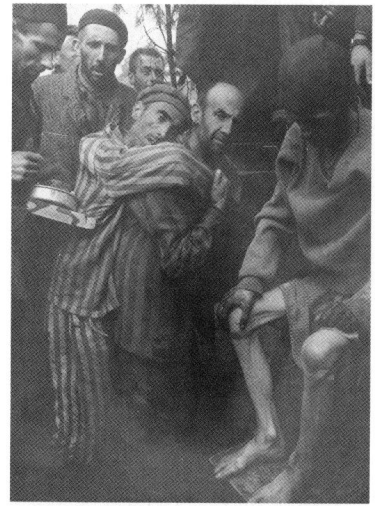
Camp survivors en route to hospital.

The face of defeat: former German officers line up at Esterwegen camp.

A fire still burns behind the Old Town Square in the centre of liberated Prague.

Danish citizens line their rubble-filled streets to cheer Allied soldiers.

Allied soldiers in the ruins of Hitler's home at Berchtesgaden, in Bavaria.

French children play with guns abandoned by retreating Germans troops.

SS man's role in German surrender

Italy, 2 May
A remarkable story of the dangerous intrigue that led up to the surrender of German forces in Italy began to emerge today. It was an SS man, Karl Wolff, who masterminded negotiations in Switzerland and north Italy with Allen Dulles, the representative of the US Office of Strategic Services (OSS), which was formed in 1942 to gather intelligence and aid resistance groups.

The first peace-feelers were put out in December by two SS men concerned with the possibility that Hitler's threat of a "scorched-earth" policy would destroy much of Italy's culture. Dulles took a cool view of Wolff's involvement, but agreed to talk when two Italian partisans were freed as a gesture of good faith.

Negotiations began seriously at Ascona, a resort on Lake Maggiore. Despite Russian objections, two Allied officers joined Dulles in total

Milan welcomes American troops.

secrecy. In grave danger, Wolff was recalled to Berlin but used his charm to escape Hitler's wrath. Even so, he and his co-conspirators faced death until the surrender was signed at Caserta (→ 14/7).

Russians arrest envoys of exiled Poles

San Francisco, 5 May
British and American delegates to the "United Nations" conference were horrified today when Molotov revealed that 16 Polish negotiators had been arrested by the Russians on charges of "diversionary activities against the Red Army". The western Allies consider that most of these men – General Okulicki, the successor to General Bor-Komorowski as chief of the Polish Home Army, and the leaders of the main political parties – should have been brought from Poland for consultation on the formation of the new Polish government. Mr Churchill is furious at what he describes as "the perfidy" by which the Poles were enticed into Russia (→ 7).

Liberation as seen by a Polish artist.

Air strikes signal end of the U-boat war

Germany, 5 May
Five German U-boats, including four of the powerful XXI types, were sunk today in an Allied air strike on the Kattegat, just 24 hours after Admiral Donitz had ordered the U-boats to cease hostilities and return to base. More air raids are planned to ram home the message that the six-year Battle of the At-

lantic is over; for the second time this century, Germany's attempt to defeat Britain by crippling its merchant fleet had failed. This time the U-boats sank more merchant ships, although their combined tonnage was less [*see table, page 668*]. Some 175 Allied warships, mostly British, were also lost; but so were 784 of Germany's 1,162 U-boats (→ 12).

1945
May

Su	Mo	Tu	We	Th	Fr	Sa
		1	2	3	4	5
6	7	8	9	10	11	12
13	14	15	16	17	18	19
20	21	22	23	24	25	26
27	28	29	30	31		

6. Prague: The US Third Army captures Pilsen, but is ordered to stay there to allow the Russians to occupy the rest of the country.→

6. Germany: Donitz sacks Himmler from all offices (→ 7).

6. Lisbon: Portugal severs diplomatic relations with Germany.

7. Oslo: Germany announces a cease-fire (→ 8).

7. Germany: The German garrison at Breslau surrenders to the Red Army, ending an 82-day long siege.→

7. Britain: U2336, a new type of German submarine, sinks the British coasters *Avondale Port* and *Sneland* off the Firth of Forth (→ 9).

7. Rheims: Admiral von Friedeburg and General Jodl sign the unconditional surrender of Germany's armed forces.→

8. Oslo: Eleven Allied officers arrive with Norwegian troops and Crown Prince Olav to liberate Norway (→ 10).

8. Fischhorn: US troops arrest Goering, who assumes that he will be taken to Eisenhower to negotiate a truce (→ 19).

8. Halifax, Nova Scotia: VE Day turns into a riot as Canadian sailors loot shops.→

8. Washington: President Truman warns the US that the war is only half won (→ 12).

9. Copenhagen: The cruiser *Prinz Eugen*, the only major German warship to survive the war, is surrendered.→

10. Norway: Resistance fighters arrest the Nazi puppet leader Vidkun Quisling, and the *Reichscommissioner* Josef Terboven commits suicide (→ 31).

11. Okinawa: US troops launch a fresh offensive aimed at the capital, Naha (→ 18).

11. Czechoslovakia: The last remnants of Army Group Centre surrender (→ 10/6).

11. Aegean Sea: German forces on the islands surrender.

12. Washington: The US suspends Lend-Lease shipments to the USSR.

Now the surrender is unconditional; it begins tomorrow

Rheims, 7 May
At 2.40 this morning, in an upstairs room of the Rheims *College Moderne de Garcons*, where French children played table tennis before the war, General Alfred Jodl, of the German high command, today signed the surrender of "all forces on land, sea and in the air who are at this date under German control". Jodl said that the German people and the German armed forces had "achieved and suffered more than perhaps any other people in the world. I can only express the hope that the victor will treat them with generosity."

The cease-fire covers the Soviet front as well as western Europe and comes into effect at 2301 hours tomorrow. It was witnessed by General Bedell Smith for Eisenhower's Allied command, General Suslaparov for the USSR and General Sevez for France.→

Australians launch New Guinea attack

New Guinea, 11 May
Australian troops of the veteran 6th Division today attacked Wewak, in New Guinea, where they seized the area occupied by the headquarters of the Japanese Eighteenth Army. The attack was a culmination of six months' arduous campaigning in steamy jungle country after the Australian Army had taken on responsibility for the continued neutralization of Japanese forces left stranded by MacArthur's leap-frogging advances.

The enemy garrisons, including those in New Britain and the Solomons, totalled in excess of 150,000, with the greatest concentration around Rabaul, in New Britain. American policy had been to allow bypassed Japanese to "wither on the vine", but the Australians set out to "destroy the enemy where it could be done with light casualties".

Even so the resulting loss of life among the Australians is now regarded by many as being too high a price to pay (→ 19).

The war is over! Dancing in the streets on VE Day

A mobile victory celebration makes its way round Parliament Square.

London is "a vast, happy village fete"

London, 8 May
"The German war is at an end. Advance Britannia! Long live the cause of freedom! God save the King!" The great crowds waiting all day in the streets of London fell totally silent to hear those words broadcast by Mr Churchill from 10 Downing Street at 3pm. The official announcement has been a long time coming, but they knew that the war was over. In this morning's *Daily Mirror* strip cartoon, the scantily-clad "Jane" has disrobed completely, as she had always promised to do for peace.

When at last the end was official, pent-up feelings broke loose.

Mr Churchill and George VI today.

People waved flags, blew whistles, climbed the lampposts, sang and danced in the streets. Above all they massed in front of Buckingham Palace, chanting "We want the king!" He soon appeared bareheaded on the balcony with his wife and daughters, a simple family group waving back to them as they sang "For he's a jolly good fellow and so say all of us". It was the first of eight appearances which the royal family made, up till midnight.

Meanwhile Mr Churchill had gone to read his statement to the House of Commons: "Finally almost the whole world was combined against the evil-doers who are now prostrate before us ... but let us not forget that Japan, with all her treachery and greed, remains unsubdued and her detestable cruelties call for justice and retribution."

Later Mr Churchill appeared on the Palace balcony with the king and queen and then on a balcony above the sea of faces in Whitehall. He waved his hat and joined in singing "Land of Hope and Glory". "This is your victory," he told them. "In all our long history we have never seen a greater day than this."

Tonight, floodlights and bonfires light up the capital and searchlight beams dance in the sky, to the sound of ships' sirens sounding the V sign.

Ticker tape and confetti fill the air as Wall Street celebrates victory.

New York, Paris and Moscow relish win

9 May
New York exploded into a huge party when the German unconditional surrender was announced as official by a US press agency on 7 May. On Wall Street enough makeshift confetti was thrown for a hundred weddings. Office workers left their desks by the thousand to celebrate in the streets and watch ticker tape, torn-up telephone directories and multicoloured paper being hurled from skyscrapers. All this in a city that had been exhorted to "keep calm". A young female lift attendant was found – still "going up" and "going down" – ecstatically shredding paper as she went.

The air was filled with songs and cries of joy, the din of aircraft circling overhead and the shrill whistles of ships in harbour. Traffic on many main roads came to a standstill. St Patrick's Cathedral, where Mass was held, was filled to overflowing with servicemen and working women who had covered their heads with handkerchiefs.

In **Paris**, six-inch headlines announced the surrender in the *Paris Soir*. The war-weary citizens stood cheering on their balconies to watch the Allied planes fly over. On VE Day they will have fireworks and an extra bottle of wine on ration for every adult.

In **Moscow** today the people spilled onto the streets in an enormous impromptu celebration; the cheering crowds hoisted Russian soldiers high above their heads. However, the officially-organized military parade to mark the victory over fascism and the end of the Great Patriotic War will have to wait until 24 June.

Prague is last capital to be liberated

Prague, 9 May
The last of Europe's capitals to be freed from the Nazi yoke, Prague, was liberated today after four days of bloody fighting between Czech patriots and the SS. It was the Red Army that put an end to the fighting. Advancing in their customary overwhelming strength, the men of three fronts surrounded the remnants of Schorner's Army Group Centre and raced into the city.

General Lelyushenko, who arrived with his Fourth Guards' Tank Army in the early hours of this morning, radioed to Konev: "Remaining fascist resistance destroyed. Many prisoners." One of the reasons for the speed of the Russians' advance was their fear that the Americans would get to Prague first, but Eisenhower has kept his agreement to stop at Pilsen and Lelyushenko is able to report: "There are no American forces."

The fierceness of the fighting between the Czechs and the *Waffen-SS* is evident from the debris of war which litters the streets. The bodies of 50 executed patriots still lie in the Masaryk railway station.

Sixty unarmed workers at Radio Prague died during a room-by-room struggle for the building which lasted for most of the first day and ended with ten SS men captured and 40 dead. From then

Photographers gather round as the "Swastika" goes up in flames in Prague.

on the patriots radioed their orders to the men on the barricades.

Last night, while the war ended in the rest of Europe, the guns continued to fire in Prague, and even after General Toussaint, the *Wehrmacht* C-in-C in Bohemia, surrendered at Prague's police headquarters, the SS men fought on. The Red Army dealt with them, and today T34 tanks line Prague's battered avenues while the Germans are heading for the safety of the American lines. Also heading for the American lines are General

Vlasov, the renegade Russian general, and his turncoat army of Russian prisoners of war who elected to fight against their former comrades.

They were caught in an impossible situation in Prague where the Czechs appealed to them as fellow-Slavs to help them in their uprising. Some did, despite Vlasov's orders to stay loyal to the Wehrmacht, but when the Germans moved in they fought alongside the SS. There is no doubt of their fate if they should ever fall into Stalin's hands (→ 11).

Germans hand over Channel Islands to end the occupation

Channel Islands, 9 May
Hundreds of illicit wireless sets were brought into the open today for the people of Jersey, Guernsey and Sark to learn from Winston Churchill that nearly five years of occupation were almost over. A German soldier climbed to the top of a crane in Jersey harbour to fly the Union Jack. In Guernsey, a British colonel's bald head was coated in *ersatz* lipstick; and on the destroyer HMS *Bulldog* the bailiff of Jersey, Alexander Coutanche, smoked real tobacco for the first time in years and washed his hands in real soap after signing the document of surrender.

The islanders – and the 10,000 occupying troops – were close to starvation. Many had been forced to eat food like rabbit skins and stewed cabbage for months. Nevertheless, even at the very end, the German commander, Vice-Admiral Huffmeier, remained fervently loyal to Hitler and threatened to fight on despite his country's collapse. A few weeks ago he drew up a list of potential hostages. Yesterday he ordered his men to give only the Nazi salute to British officers. Most were too drunk and relieved to obey him (→ 7/6).

Nazis kept waiting as Allies haggle over surrender signatures

Berlin, 8 May
Field Marshal Wilhelm Keitel and his navy and air force colleagues were kept waiting to surrender from afternoon until almost midnight while the Allies wrangled over who should sign the surrender document. Stalin's deputy foreign commissar, Andrei Vishinsky, arrived from Moscow and said that the French General de Lattre de Tassigny could sign, but not the American General Carl Spaatz, since the British Air Chief Marshal Tedder represented both the US and Britain. Spaatz said that if de Tassigny signed he would insist on signing. At last, after a call to Moscow, Vishinsky said that they could both sign, but lower down the page under a cut-off rule. The Germans were then sent for (→ 20).

General Jodl signs for Germany at the first surrender ceremony, in Rheims.

U-boats give up or scuttle themselves

Cape May, New Jersey, 12 May
U858 is steaming here under escort. Tomorrow she will come into port flying the black flag of surrender with most of her crew on deck. She will be the first U-boat to surrender since Admiral Donitz ordered his fleet to cease hostilities just over a week ago, on 4 May.

Donitz has agreed to the Allied demand that the U-boats should surrender rather than be scuttled in the German navy tradition. However, many of the commanders of the 377 U-boats still at sea bitterly resent his order. They are preparing to scuttle their boats or sail them to neutral countries to try to avoid the humiliation of surrendering to the enemy (→ 28).

"Kamikaze" pilots assail Allied navies

Pacific, 12 May
Hundreds of *kikusui* [floating chrysanthemums] airmen are committing suicide in a vain attempt to "annihilate" the American invasion of Okinawa. Up to yesterday no less than six major kikusui attacks, using a total of 1,092 suicide pilots as well as conventional air attack, had been mounted. Swarms of the body-crashing *kamikazes* have also assailed the Allied carrier task groups covering the Okinawa operation. During the sixth mass attack on 11-12 May the fleet carriers *Bunker Hill* and *Enterprise* were hit. The *Bunker Hill* suffered very heavy casualties, with 392 dead. Next day the battleship *New Mexico* was hit. The British Pacific Fleet again came in for its share of suicide attacks when it returned to the task of neutralizing the Sakishima Islands. On 4 May the *Formidable* and the *Indomitable* were hit and on 9 May the *Victorious* and the *Formidable* (again) were hit. The carriers suffered little damage, the kamikazes crumpling on their armoured decks (→ 14).

A "kamikaze" pilot flies his aircraft towards the US battleship "Missouri".

US bombers attack Japanese air bases

Guam, 8 May
All Japanese airbases on Kyushu, Japan's main base for its air attacks on the US invasion forces at Okinawa, have been wiped out, jubilant B-29 crews claimed as they returned from a raid today. They reported a total lack of fighter opposition and anti-aircraft fire as they bombed industrial targets in the 18th successive B-29 raid on the southern homeland island since 27 March. US fighter superiority over their Japanese counterparts was also shown when a flight of 65 Mustangs from Iwo Jima was able to bomb and strafe airfields and munitions in the Chiba and Kisarazu districts of Tokyo without meeting fighter opposition (→ 14).

Only Poland splits the UN conference

San Francisco, 7 May
The Big Four nations – the United States, the Soviet Union, Britain and China – reached agreement here today on all except the Polish and trusteeship questions. Tomorrow the smaller nations will try to finish the drafting of a charter for the new "United Nations". Two points of friction between the western Allies and the USSR were resolved today. The General Assembly will have the power to arbitrate in international disputes which threaten to erupt into war, and the UN will be given jurisdiction over future alliances. Settlement of the Polish question is being held up by the unexplained arrest of 16 Polish delegates in Moscow (→ 23/6).

1945

May

Su	Mo	Tu	We	Th	Fr	Sa
		1	2	3	4	5
6	7	8	9	10	11	12
13	14	15	16	17	18	19
20	21	22	23	24	25	26
27	28	29	30	31		

13. Philippines: US troops open up the Balete Pass on Luzon (→ 15).

14. Okinawa: US forces capture Yonabaru airfield.→

14. Japan: About 2,500 tons of incendiary bombs are dropped on Nagoya by 472 US B-29 bombers, and 20 Japanese fighters are shot down.→

14. Austria: The concentration camp at Ebensee, "more horrible than Buchenwald", is liberated (→ 18).

15. Philippines: US forces launch fresh attacks on Mindanao and Negros (→ 27).

15. Burma: Aung San, the Burmese Nationalist leader, joins the Allied drive against the Japanese (→ 26).

15. Yugoslavia: The last pocket of German resistance, at Slovenski Gradek, surrenders.→

15. Vienna: The republic of Austria is declared.

15-16. Indian Ocean: British destroyers sink the Japanese heavy cruiser *Haguro* in the Malacca Strait.→

16. Denmark: The German garrison on Bornholm Island surrenders.

18. Flensburg: Donitz issues an order of the day to the *Wehrmacht* in which he attempts to exonerate himself by expressing horror at the concentration camps and distancing the military from Nazi atrocities (→ 21).

18. Dublin: De Valera announces a £3 million ($12 million) food and clothing aid programme for Europe.

19. New Guinea: Australian forces capture Wewak, the last Japanese-held port on the mainland, after a bitter struggle.

19. Middle East: French troops arrive in Syria and Lebanon, sparking off nationalist demonstrations (→ 21).

19. Flensburg: Alfred Rosenberg, the Nazi Party's unofficial philosopher, responsible for formulating the party's race policies, is arrested (→ 21).

Japan pulls troops from Chinese ports

Foochow, 19 May
Japanese troops today abandoned the east coast treaty port of Foochow, seven months after capturing it. Two other east-coast ports, Amoy and Swatow, have also been abandoned, their forces retreating to Hong Kong, confirming reports that Tokyo has ordered a strategic withdrawal from south China. Since the US recapture of the Philippines these ports have come within US bomber range. In the event of an invasio these garrisons would be isolated, cut off from support from Japan or Formosa (→ 27).

Last Germans end fight in Yugoslavia

Belgrade, 15 May
The war is over in Yugoslavia, and now the counting begins. Out of a population of 15 million, 1.4 million civilians (including 55,000 murdered Jews) and 305,000 soldiers have perished. Few countries have suffered so much in terms of deaths per head of population. The Germans fought the partisans viciously, battling on for seven days after Zagreb was liberated. Tito is determined to keep his country united. He has accepted royalists in a provisional government, but has made it clear that Yugoslavia will be a communist state (→ 12/6).

A fiery death for the Nazi eagle.

Submarines play a key role in the Pacific campaign

Pacific, 15 May
US submarines operating from the Central Pacific and Australia have contributed enormously to Japan's desperate war situation by sinking 60 per cent of the merchant ships destroyed. Last year the US submariners reached the pinnacle of their success by sinking 2,387,780 tons of shipping. Japanese losses were then running at a rate exceeding 300,000 tons monthly.

Japan's war industries now face collapse as vital overseas supplies of oil and raw materials are sunk by submarine attack. The loss of imported food threatens the population with starvation. The main burden of the submarine offensive has been borne by the US Central Pacific force. In addition, US submarines have operated from Australian ports.

In September 1944 they were joined by the 8th Submarine Flotilla of the Royal Navy, which moved to Fremantle from Ceylon to join the Seventh Fleet. These and Dutch submarines concentrated their efforts in the waters around Singapore, Java, Indochina and the Philippines to which Japanese naval forces withdrew after leaving the Marshall Islands in February 1944.

As well as having made a major contribution to the destruction of Japan's merchant fleet, the US submarines have inflicted heavy losses on Japanese warships. Last year their battle successes included the sinking of the battleship *Kongo* off Formosa and of seven aircraft carriers, including the 59,000-ton supercarrier *Shinano*, then the largest and most powerful carrier afloat. The mammoth carrier had just been converted from a battleship and was on her way to Kure for final fitting-out when, on 29 November, she encountered the submarine *Archerfish* on lifeguard duty off Honshu to rescue B-29 crews. The *Archerfish* fired six torpedoes to sink the *Shinano*, which took 1,435 sailors with her.

US planes raid Japan's aircraft factories

A later photograph of Nagoya shows the devastation caused by fire-bombs.

Japan, 19 May
As 272 B-29s today hit Hamamatsu, it was revealed that a quarter of Nagoya, Japan's main aircraft-manufacturing city, has been flattened by two raids in the last week. The raids on the two cities are the start of attacks on Japan's secondary industrial centres with populations under 200,000.

Reconnaissance photos released today revealed the results of two fire-bomb raids by fleets of over 450 B-29s, the largest so far to strike at mainland Japan, which hit Nagoya three and five days ago, setting fire to 5.9 square miles of the city. Since incendiary attacks began, nearly 60 square miles of Japanese cities have been wiped out. Nagoya's Aichi aircraft works and two other key factories were destroyed, while Mitsubishi's aircraft plant, the world's largest, was damaged. Results of today's high-explosive raid on Hamamatsu, 120 miles (192 km) from Tokyo, are not known. Bombs were dropped through the clouds from medium altitude using precision instruments (→ 23).

Troubles not over, warns Churchill

London, 13 May
In his broadcast tonight to mark the victory in Europe, Churchill looked back over the five momentous years of his leadership, which had seen the British people recover from the brink of defeat and carry the war into Germany alongside the Americans and the Soviet Union. "I wish I could tell you tonight that all our toils and trouble were over," he said. "But we have to make sure that the simple and honourable purposes for which we entered the war are not brushed aside ... There would be little use in punishing the Hitlerites ... if totalitarian or police governments were to take their place."

Allies want Trieste

Trieste, 14 May
Britain and the United States are taking a firm line with Marshal Tito over the occupation of Trieste – a territory long in dispute between Yugoslavia and Italy. Marshal Tito has protested vigorously against the presence of Allied troops, claiming that his partisans captured the territory and that he would settle the matter with Italy in due course (→ 15).

Japanese inflict heavy casualties in bloody battle for Okinawa

Okinawa, 18 May
US marines yesterday launched an assault on Naha, the capital, in an advance that is turning into the modern equivalent of Flanders trench warfare – a slow, bitter, muddy and bloody confrontation costing thousands of lives.

In the past six weeks the US Tenth Army has averaged barely 133 yards a day and its casualties are close to 20,000 – in excess of those on Iwo Jima. The worst losses have come in the last five days with the assault on three positions near Naha. During the action the marines suffered 2,662 casualties, many from crossfire from nearby hillsides. Further east the US 77th Infantry Division made swift progress yesterday with a dawn raid bringing them close to Shuri, the heart of Japan's defensive line (→ 22).

US marines wait for an explosive to blow in a cave used by the Japanese.

1945

May

Su	Mo	Tu	We	Th	Fr	Sa
			1	2	3	4	5
6	7	8	9	10	11	12
13	14	15	16	17	18	19
20	21	22	23	24	25	26
27	28	29	30	31		

20. Berlin: The Soviet occupiers appoint Dr Arthur Werner as the city's *Oberburgermeister*.

21. Belsen: By order of the British, the last remaining hut of the concentration camp is burnt to the ground (→ 31).

21. Germany: Goering is transferred from Augsburg PoW camp to the Palace Hotel at Mondorf, where he joins other senior Nazis awaiting Allied interrogation.→

21. Blackpool: The Labour Party votes to withdraw its support from the coalition government.→

22. Okinawa: US troops capture Conical Hill and enter Yonabaru (→ 24).

22. Bremervorde, near Hamburg: A British patrol arrests Heinrich Himmler.→

23. Japan: US attacks bring shipping at Yokohama to a halt.→

23. St Johann, Germany: US troops dig up $4 million in mixed currencies, believed to be Himmler's personal *cache*.→

23. Britain: The Allies reveal PLUTO – the PipeLine Under The Ocean – which supplied them with fuel after the D-Day landings.

24. Okinawa: US aircraft attack airfields used by *kamikaze* pilots (→ 27).

24. New Guinea: Australian troops surround Wewak.

24. Germany: Field Marshal Ritter von Greim, appointed commander of the *Luftwaffe* in the last days of the Third *Reich*, commits suicide.

24. Paris: De Gaulle awards Montgomery the *Grande Croix* of the *Legion d'Honneur*.

25. London: Churchill asks all Allied commanders who had received information through "Ultra" to reveal neither the information nor its source.

26. Burma: Allied forces occupy Bassein, ninety miles west of Rangoon (→ 27).

26. Luneburg, Germany: Sergeants Ray Weston and Bill Ottery bury Himmler in an unmarked grave.

Nazi leaders arrested

Under arrest: Albert Speer, the armaments minister, and Admiral Donitz.

Flensburg, 23 May
Grand Admiral Karl Donitz, the so-called Flensburg *fuhrer*, was arrested this morning along with members of his "government". The German high command was also dissolved and the officers placed under arrest on the orders of General Eisenhower. Admiral Hans Georg von Friedeburg, who signed the surrender at Luneburg, was allowed to visit the lavatory after his arrest; there he took poison.

Outside the town, at *Schloss Glucksburg*, Albert Speer, the minister of armaments and war production, was in his bath when an Allied officer told him that he was under arrest. "A good thing too," he said. "It was just an opera anyway."

For some Germans, however, it is a different story. Wernher von Braun and other rocket scientists have been taken to France to be put on board a ship for the US. Reinhard Gehlen, a senior intelligence officer, brought with him the files on German agents in the Soviet Union. He too has been made welcome by the Americans (→ 5/6).

Himmler takes cyanide to cheat justice

Germany, 23 May
Heinrich Himmler, the chief architect of the Nazi terror and dedicated exterminator of the Jewish people, died tonight as he was being examined by a British doctor at Second Army HQ, Luneburg. He had been stripped and searched, but when the doctor put a finger in his mouth Himmler jerked his head back and crunched a tiny phial of cyanide. Stomach pumps and emet-

ics failed to save him. He was left in a heap on the floor until he had been seen by a Red Army liaison officer. Himmler, who was 44, went on the run after Germany's surrender. Stopped by a British patrol near Hamburg, he claimed to be a rural policeman called Heinrich Hitzinger, but under interrogation he removed the black eye patch he was wearing and put on the familiar full-moon glasses (→ 26).

Churchill resigns as prime minister, so elections will follow

Britain, 23 May
The general election – the first for ten years – will be on 5 July. The run-up to the contest to decide Britain's post-war future began today with Mr Churchill going to see the king.

He resigned as prime minister and thus automatically ended the wartime coalition government. The constitutional wheels had been well-oiled. Four hours later the king asked Mr Churchill to form a new government. He agreed. But would the king then graciously dissolve parliament next month to allow the July election?

The king assented. Mr Churchill at once started forming a caretaker team in which Labour leaders and most of the Liberals will refuse to serve. Earlier this week the prime minister asked Labour to stay in the coalition government at least until Japan is defeated. Under pressure from party activists Mr Attlee replied: "We will carry on only until October."

Mr Churchill said that this was unacceptable for it would herald a period of damaging uncertainty. There is a feeling at Westminster that Labour's vote-gathering organization is in a higher state of readiness than that of its rivals. This explains the tactical manoeuvring over the date (→ 4/6).

May 22. A direct hit on a Japanese train on a railway line in Burma; it was probably transporting oil to the Japanese armies.

1945

May

Su	Mo	Tu	We	Th	Fr	Sa
		1	2	3	4	5
6	7	8	9	10	11	12
13	14	15	16	17	18	19
20	21	22	23	24	25	26
27	28	29	30	31		

Japan battered by further bombing raids

Target Japan: today Tokyo's business district was wrecked by fire-bombs.

Japan, 26 May

Emperor Hirohito and the Japanese imperial family escaped with their lives today as flames started by B-29 fire-bomb attacks surrounded their main palace in Tokyo and destroyed the nearby business district of Marunouchi. Twenty-six Marianas-based B-29s were lost.

Later Tokyo radio confirmed US Army Air Force claims that parts of the imperial palace and Omiya palace had been damaged, but said that both the emperor and empress were safe and uninjured. The raid was the second in 48 hours, with 464 B-29 Superfortresses dropping 4,000 tons of incendiaries on the Marunouchi district just south of

the imperial palace. With scores of new buildings – many supposedly fire and earthquake proof – the area was, until today, the pride of modern Japan.

The Tokyo raid came as Japanese flyers, absent from combat in recent weeks, launched desperate mass *kamikaze* attacks on US ships off Okinawa plus bizarre suicide raids on the island's Yontan and Katena airfields. Planes deliberately crash-landed on the two airstrips before heavily-armed commandos jumped out with orders to cause maximum damage. All were killed immediately. Offshore, Japanese flyers damaged 11 US ships, sacrificing 111 aircraft in the attack (→ 29).

German PoWs start to rebuild Britain

London, 22 May

A gang of 25 German PoWs was put to work today in the suburbs of South-east London, to start re-building the country which their leader swore that he would defeat and destroy during the war. Equipped with picks and shovels, they began excavating an 18-foot sewage trench which will serve new houses, and were hard at it from 8.45am to 5.45pm. They were visited by Duncan Sandys, the minister of works, who spoke in German with some of the men. He said of them later: "We hope to get a lot of good work out of these chaps."

Syria and Lebanon demand freedom

Damascus, 21 May

Fresh violence in the Middle East seems likely in the wake of decisions today by Syria and Lebanon to break off negotiations with France. Arab nationalists are attempting to assert their claims for independence, but France has so far seemed determined to maintain its hold on the Levant through indirect rule. In 1941, when the Free French liberated Syria and Lebanon from Vichy, they offered independence. Since then limited self-government, with France controlling defence and external affairs, has been permitted, but attempts to attain full independence have been countered by French imperial troops (→ 29).

Rations cut again

Britain, 22 May

The cost of victory was emphasized again today with the announcement that rations of bacon, cooking fats and soap are to be cut. Supplies are now to be shared with the liberated European countries which were kept short of food by the Germans. The weekly ration of cooking fat is halved from two ounces to one ounce, that of bacon reduced from four to three ounces, and soap rations are cut by an eighth. Fish and fruit, though, are expected to become more plentiful. Rations for non-labouring PoWs are to be cut.

After evacuating the inmates, Allied troops raze Belsen death camp to the ground: a flame-thrower from a Bren-gun carrier ignites a verminous hut.

27. Okinawa: Japan launches a heavy air offensive against the US fleet; Japanese submarines make unsuccessful attacks on US convoy routes to Guam and Leyte.→

27. Philippines: On Luzon, US forces capture Santa Fe (→9/6).

27. Burma: An entire army is moved by air for the first time ever, when US aircraft fly the Chinese Sixth Army from Burma to China (→3/8).

28. Okinawa: US forces reportedly occupy two-thirds of Naha (→31).

28. London: The Royal Navy announces the abolition of convoys in the Atlantic, Indian and Arctic Oceans.

29. Japan: US Superfortress bombers drop incendiaries on Yokohama, burning 85 per cent of the port area.→

29. Japan: Admiral Jisaburo Ozawa replaces Admiral Soemu Toyoda as commander of the combined fleet.

29. Syria: French forces shell Hama and Damascus, and Syrian *gendarmes* attack French military posts.→

29. Norway: The Nobel-prize-winning author Knut Hamsun is arrested for allegedly collaborating with the Nazis.

29. Brussels: Belgian socialists call for the abdication of King Leopold, who agreed to surrender to the Germans in 1940 (→16/6).

30. Tehran: Iran asks Britain, the US and the USSR to withdraw their troops.

31. Okinawa: Japanese forces withdraw from Shuri (→4/6).

31. China: Song Ziwen (Dr T V Soong) succeeds Chiang Kai-shek as president of the Nationalist *Yuan*.

31. Norway: The government in exile returns to Oslo (→7/6).

31. Germany: Odilo Globocnik, a key figure in the organization of the Nazi death camps, commits suicide when arrested by a British patrol.

31. London: The last Underground shelter bunks are removed, from South Wimbledon station.

Chinese Nationalist army wins Nanning

Nanning, 27 May
Japan has suffered a major setback in southern China with the loss of Nanning. The southern gateway city only 78 miles (125 km) from the Indochina border has been a vital link in Japan's main overland supply lifeline to its armies in Burma, Thailand, Malaya and Indochina. Nationalist troops advancing from the north and west recaptured Nanning, Kwangsi province's capital. They also cut the north/south highway linking Indochina with the rail junction at Liuchow. The road, which has been recently improved, has served as the main route for moving Japanese troops and supplies (→6/6).

Ceasefire in Syria

Damascus, Syria, 31 May
For the second time in 18 months, Britain has intervened in Syria. Three days of fighting between Arab nationalists and French troops followed Syria's refusal to negotiate a quasi-independence treaty under duress. Now Anthony Eden, the British foreign secretary, has announced that Britain "can no longer stand aside", and arranged a cease-fire. With the US backing the Syrians, France's withdrawal from the Levant seems inevitable (→1/6).

Unexploded mines remain a danger

Great Yarmouth, Norfolk, 31 May
The first casualties of peace are the men responsible for clearing thousands of mines from the "invasion" beaches of East Anglia. Maps of the minefields have been lost; in some cases so have the minefields themselves, due to coastal erosion. Above the tideline the army has to clear the danger. Since 1943, 98 Royal Engineers have died and 26 have suffered serious wounds, some losing their sight, in this work. Below the tideline the Royal Navy has the job, often using divers to disarm the unexploded mines. The UXB teams on land also still have work to do, as unexploded bombs are unearthed in war-ravaged streets.

Propagandist "Lord Haw-Haw" captured

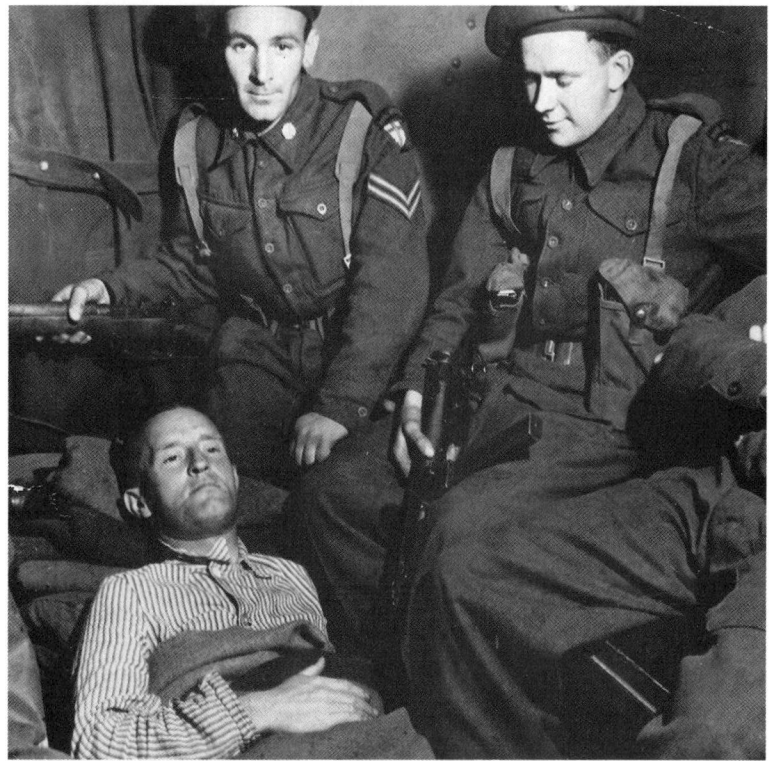

British soldiers surround their prisoner – an impassive William Joyce.

Hamburg, 28 May
William Joyce, nicknamed "Lord Haw-Haw" and well known for his propaganda broadcasts for the Nazis throughout the war, has been captured in a wood between here and the Danish frontier. His voice was his downfall. He boldly went up to two British officers collecting wood for a fire and started talking to them in German. Then he spoke English and they spotted the upper-class accent made famous by his "Jairmany calling" broadcasts.

When challenged Joyce moved his hand to his pocket, and one of the officers shot him in the thigh. He was later found to be unarmed and carrying a fake German passport in the name of Hansen (→25/6).

Okinawan capital is taken, claims US

Okinawa, 27 May
American marines today claimed to have crossed the Asato and captured part of the Okinawan capital of Naha as forces of the US Tenth Army battle to complete the conquest of this strategically vital island just 350 miles (560 km) south of mainland Japan. The north of the island has been under Allied control since 20 April, but heavy rains – and fierce resistance by General Ushijima's Thirty-Second Army – have slowed the US advance in the south. Infantry of the 7th Division is embroiled in a particularly tough fight for Shuri Castle, the key position on Japan's defensive line in the south (→28).

Air chiefs say that bombs can end war

Tokyo, 29 May
Will beleaguered Japan collapse under the intolerable pressure of aerial bombardment and surface blockade? Hundreds of square miles of heavily-populated urban industrial areas have been incinerated by B-29 fire-bomb attacks.

In the latest raids by B-29 Superfortresses, 16.8 square miles of Tokyo were gutted, making a total of some 50 square miles burnt out. Millions have fled to the countryside, abandoning blitzed war-production factories. Civilian morale has slumped profoundly.

The B-29s are also sowing mines in the Inland Sea and Shimonoseki Strait with startling results; they are sinking even more merchant tonnage than the US submarines and helping to cut Japan off totally from imported food and vital materials. In order to intensify the USAAF aerial onslaught to an intolerable level, yet more B-29s have been ordered to the Far East from India.

But Allied preparations for the invasion of Japan are under way. On past experience of Japanese military fanaticism this could result in much bloodshed. Yet air force chiefs believe that with enough bombs and aircraft, Japan could be forced into unconditional surrender without an invasion (→1/6).

The long journey home: former French PoWs and civilians liberated by the Red Army return to the sector of Germany controlled by US forces. Europe is teeming with people trekking through devastated countryside.

1945

June

Su	Mo	Tu	We	Th	Fr	Sa
					1	2
3	4	5	6	7	8	9
10	11	12	13	14	15	16
17	18	19	20	21	22	23
24	25	26	27	28	29	30

1. Japan: US aircraft drop over 3,000 tons of incendiary bombs on Osaka (→ 5).

1. Middle East: British troops occupy Syria and Lebanon (→ 5).

1. Berlin: Germans are warned not to provoke the Allies by making attacks on the occupying forces. →

2. Rome: The pope broadcasts his hopes that Germany will lay aside the spectre of Nazism and start a new life.

4. Okinawa: US troops land on the Oruku peninsula, launching an offensive to capture the heavily-defended Naha airfield (→ 5).

5. Japan: Four hundred and seventy-three B-29s bomb Kobe with 3,000 tons of incendiaries.→

5. Okinawa: A typhoon damages four battleships, eight aircraft carriers, seven cruisers and fourteen destroyers of the US Third Fleet, and *kamikaze* attacks cripple the battleship *Mississippi* and the heavy cruiser *Louisville*.→

5. London: Churchill rejects de Gaulle's accusation that the British incited civil war in Syria.

6. Luzon: US troops capture Bambang (→ 9).

6. Berlin: Soviet troops find a body, believed to be Hitler's, in the Chancellery gardens (→ 7).

6. London: It is announced that between D-Day and VE-Day the number of British and Canadian soldiers listed as dead, wounded or missing was 184,512.

7. Germany: All German citizens in the zone occupied by the western Allies are ordered to watch films of Belsen and Buchenwald (→ 16).

7. Norway: King Haakon returns, to a warm reception.

8. Java Sea: The British submarine *Trenchant* sinks the Japanese cruiser *Ashigara*.

9. Mindanao: US troops capture the last major defensive strongpoint on the island, at Mandog (→ 21).

9. Britain: The RAF reveals the Vampire, a new jet fighter which can fly at over 500mph.

Allied powers to divide Germany in four

Berlin, 5 June
The Four-Power Commission for the control of defeated Germany met today amidst the ruins of Berlin and issued its first proclamation. Germany is to be divided into four occupation zones and Berlin into four occupation sectors. The city will be administered by an inter-Allied governing authority whose decisions will have to be unanimous.

Eisenhower, Montgomery, Zhukov and de Lattre de Tassigny met in a riverside club which is the Soviet delegation's HQ. In a lengthy document containing 15 articles the four powers reaffirm the complete defeat of Germany, "which bears responsibility for the war", and assume authority over all aspects of life in the country.

Details of the exact zones to be occupied by the armies of the four powers have still to be worked out, but the general outline has been agreed. Russia takes the eastern zone, Britain the north-west, the US the south-west and France the western zone. Germany's frontiers are identified as those which existed on 31 December 1937 (→ 6).

Cossack collaborators sent back to USSR

White Russian Cossacks: repatriation means almost certain death for them.

Austria, 1 June
The British Army is beginning to hand over some 40,000 Cossacks, many of them accompanied by their families, to the Red Army. The Cossacks, led by General Timophey Domanoc, had served with the *Wehrmacht* and had surrendered to British forces.

In order to complete the handover without trouble British officers were told to continue the pretence that the Cossacks would be allowed to settle in the west. They were disarmed – with British troops under orders to shoot to kill if they resisted. The deception was maintained with the Cossack officers being summoned to a fake conference two days ago. When they realized that they were to be handed over to the Russians many resisted, but the British guards, swinging rifle butts and pick-handles and using bayonets, forced them into trucks.

There were even more distressing incidents when the main units were being forcibly loaded onto trains. Some Cossacks were shot, others, knowing what awaits them in Russia, committed suicide. The British soldiers have been told that the repatriations are being carried out under the terms of the Yalta agreement. Nevertheless, many of them feel that they have betrayed men whom they had grown to admire.

Churchill condemns Labour "Gestapo"

Britain, 4 June
In the first of a series of election political broadcasts, the Conservative leader Winston Churchill went to startling lengths tonight to warn against voting Labour. He said: "I declare this to you from the bottom of my heart. No socialist system can be established without a political police. They would have to fall back on some form of *Gestapo* – no doubt very humanely directed in the first place." Labour leaders accused him of "vile and vicious" tactics adopted in panic. However, Tory campaign managers remain confident of victory (→ 15).

Japanese routed by advancing Chinese

Liuchow, 6 June
Japan's front in southern China is collapsing in the face of a Chinese advance that has covered 150 miles in the last 11 days, and recaptured Liuchow and Mengshan, two key cities in Kwangsi province. Mengshan, a vital road junction, was taken without a fight as the Japanese abandoned their defences. The loss of Liuchow's airbase will expose Japanese garrisons in Hong Kong and Canton to fighter-supported US bombing attacks and menace Japanese attempts to reopen the overland corridor to Malaya. Last night Japanese forces were falling back on Kweilin, 90 miles (144 km) north of Liuchow (→ 14).

King George visits Channel Islands

Channel Islands, 7 June
Captured German howitzers welcomed King George and Queen Elizabeth with a 21-gun salute when they arrived on the liberated island of Guernsey today. Thousands lined the streets and lanes to wave red, white and blue bunting and flowers as the royal couple toured the holiday islands. The king told the States of Jersey (the island's parliament): "After long suffering, I hope the island will regain its former glory."

1945

Japanese raids end hopes of surrender

USAAF fire-bombs fall on Osaka.

Tokyo, 9 June
Japan has responded to the daylight pounding of three of its mainland cities and the imminent defeat of its forces on Okinawa by stepping up *kamikaze* raids on the US naval task force off Okinawa. In the last three days suicide pilots have sunk two US destroyers, killing 312 servicemen. Japan has lost 67 *kamikaze* flyers in the raids. The attacks have ended hopes that Japan is prepared to accept the Allied demand for an unconditional surrender. It is understood that even the premier, Mr Suzuki, a known moderate, is opposed to such a surrender, believing it to be a betrayal of Japanese forces still in the field.

In the latest raids on Japan – the first time that three cities have been hit on one day – a fleet of 110 unescorted B-29s dropped high-explosive bombs on aircraft factories at Nagoya, Narao and Akashi. At the same time US carrier-based fighters strafed bases on Kyushu used for kamikaze raids.

On Okinawa, Ushijima's defence force, confined to the island's southern tip, has been split in two after landings behind Japanese lines by US marines (→10).

June

Su	Mo	Tu	We	Th	Fr	Sa
					1	2
3	4	5	6	7	8	9
10	11	12	13	14	15	16
17	18	19	20	21	22	23
24	25	26	27	28	29	30

10. Okinawa: US forces reduce Japanese resistance on the Oruku peninsula to an area which is only 2,000 square yards (1,672 square metres) in size (→12).

10. Borneo: Australian troops land on the mainland at Brunei Bay and on the islands of Labuan and Muara.→

10. Frankfurt: Marshal Zhukov confers the Order of Victory – made of platinum encrusted with rubies and diamonds – on Eisenhower and Montgomery (→12).

11. Czechoslovakia: The Soviet authorities start the forcible expulsion of ethnic Germans from the Sudetenland to the west (→29).

12. Okinawa: The Japanese on Oruku, forced into a pocket of 1,093 square yards (914 sq m), start committing suicide to avoid surrender (→13).

12. Italy: Yugoslav forces withdraw from the disputed port of Trieste.

12. London: Eisenhower is awarded the Order of Merit and given the Freedom of the City of London.

13. Okinawa: Japanese resistance on Oruku ends (→16).

14. China: Chinese forces capture Ishan from the Japanese (→17).

15. Japan: US B-29 bombers drop 3,000 tons of bombs on Osaka (→16).

15. London: King George officially dissolves a parliament that has lasted for nine and a half years (→5/7).

15. Hamburg: British troops capture the former foreign minister, Joachim von Ribbentrop (→21/7).

16. Okinawa: US troops capture Mount Yuza (→17).

16. Dachau: Nearly 2,500 people have died, mainly of typhus, since the camp was liberated on 29 April.

16. Brussels: Achille van Acker, the Belgian premier, and his entire cabinet resign in protest against the contemplated return of King Leopold (→19).

Australian advance captures Brunei Bay

Australian troops wade ashore from US landing craft at Labaun island.

Borneo, 15 June
The Australian 9th Division met no opposition when it landed at Brunei Bay and on Labuan and Muara islands, after heavy air and naval bombardment, five days ago.

Brunei Bay is the best harbour on the north-west coast of Borneo, and the US chiefs of staff proposed it as an advance base for the British Pacific Fleet. The British argued that it was too far from the main theatre of operations and was in any case unlikely to be ready in time. Developing the naval base would be a waste of construction effort, they said, especially as it could not be made ready until the end of the year – and by then Singapore might have been recaptured. The operation has gone ahead nonetheless, using Australian troops supported by the US Seventh Fleet and the Royal Australian First Tactical Air Force.

A brigade of the 9th Division quickly occupied Labuan Island and secured the port on 10 June. By the end of the day it had also occupied the airport. Surviving Japanese withdrew into a pocket. Advancing against slight resistance, the Australians captured Brunei Town on 13 June and today reported the capture of the islands of Labuan and Muara (→20).

June 12. General Eisenhower is given the Freedom of the City of London.

1945

June

Su	Mo	Tu	We	Th	Fr	Sa
					1	2
3	4	5	6	7	8	9
10	11	12	13	14	15	16
17	18	19	20	21	22	23
24	25	26	27	28	29	30

Monty will "teach Germans a lesson"

Hamburg, 10 June

In a message broadcast by Hamburg radio this evening, Field Marshal Montgomery says that the German people must learn their lesson "once and for all", not only that they have been defeated, but that they were guilty of beginning the war, as they had been guilty in 1914. "If that is not made clear to you and your children," he says, "you may again allow yourselves to be deceived by your rulers and led into another war." Montgomery says that parents should read the message to their children and ensure that they understand it (→ 4/7).

Czech government faces Soviet threat

Prague, 10 June

The Czechs, so recently freed from Nazi rule, are becoming increasingly restive over what they see as Russian determination to impose "voluntary Sovietization" on them. The Russians have a stranglehold on the Czech economy and are using it to apply political pressure on the new Czech government. This is backed by the presence of three Russian divisions in the outskirts of the capital. "They are treating us", grumbled one Czech, "as if we were bad children in need of political education" (→ 11).

Royal Navy attacks Japan's air bases

New Guinea, 16 June

Seafires, Fireflies and Avengers from the aircraft carriers of the British Pacific Fleet have carried out a series of devastating attacks on Japanese bases in the Caroline Islands north of here over the last two days. To their surprise they met no Japanese aircraft, and only one plane was shot down from the ground. The raid started badly. One pilot radioed back: "Hell, the boss is in the Oggin." Translated from the Fleet Air Arm slang this meant that the flight commander's Avenger was in the sea, having crashed on take-off (→ 17).

17. Okinawa: Admiral Minoru Ota, the commander of the Japanese naval base, commits suicide (→ 18).

17. China: Japanese troops start withdrawing between the Yellow and Yangtze rivers (→ 18).

17-18. Japan: US bombers start a series of raids on civilians, targeting 58 secondary cities (→ 22).

18. China: Chinese forces recapture Wenchow port (→ 22).

18. Okinawa: Lieutenant-General Simon B Buckner, the C-in-C of the US Tenth Army, is killed by shrapnel.→

18. Moscow: Sixteen officers of the Polish Home Army are put on trial for fighting the Red Army.→

18. Britain: The armed services start demobilizing at the rate of 30,000 people a week.→

19. Belgium: King Leopold refuses to abdicate (→ 15/7).

19. San Francisco: Spain is banned from joining the United Nations as long as Franco is in power (→ 23).

20. Borneo: Australian troops capture the Seria oilfields, and reinforcements land at Lutong, in Sarawak (→ 22).

20. New York: Four million people cheer Eisenhower as he drives in a motorcade for 35 miles through the city.

21. Philippines: Aparri, the last Japanese port on Luzon, falls to the US (→ 23).

22. Japan: US B-29s bomb aircraft plants at Himeji, Akashi, Kagamigahara and Tamashima, and the naval arsenal at Kure (→ 26).

22. China: Japanese troops quit Liuchow, setting it on fire before the advancing Chinese (→ 26).

22. Borneo: Japanese resistance on Tarakan island comes to an end (→ 24).

23. Philippines: US troops link up with Filipino guerrilla forces on Luzon (→ 25).

23. San Francisco: The Big Four powers agree to admit Poland to the United Nations.→

Okinawa falls – at last

Dishonoured by surrender: three Japanese PoWs surrounded by their captors.

Okinawa, 21 June

The three-month-long battle for Okinawa, the bitterest campaign so far in the Pacific, is over. Admiral Chester Nimitz's HQ declared today that the stubborn Japanese defence force, reduced to 30,000 men in the last week, has finally disintegrated.

About 1,700 surrendered today and 1,000 yesterday. Hundreds of Japanese committed suicide by jumping from the cliffs into the sea, but most chose to follow their own code of honour and fight to the death. At least 9,000 Japanese have died in the last three days, since the final US push began with the arrival of reinforcements of the 8th Marine Regiment. One of the final victims was the US Tenth Army commander, Lt-Gen Buckner, killed by shrapnel as he inspected the ridgeline that the enemy had chosen for its final stand.

Okinawa now becomes the forward base for invading Japan, 400 miles away; B-29s bombing Japan from here will carry more bombs as they will need less fuel than is required for the 3,000-mile round-trip from the Marianas (→ 27).

US counts the cost of Okinawa victory

Okinawa, 21 June

The human price of the 82-day conquest of Okinawa dwarfs all other battles in the Pacific. US total casualties are 49,151, with 12,520 killed or missing and 36,631 wounded. American losses on Okinawa nearly exceed the total for the six Pacific campaigns that led to it. For the Japanese, Okinawa has been a struggle to the death with approximately 110,000 killed and only 7,400 taken prisoner. Civilian casualties are 80,000. US estimates fear that invading Japan will spark a worse death struggle, with 250,000 US dead.

Hirohito looks for diplomatic peace

Tokyo, 21 June

With US troops now only 400 miles from Japan, Emperor Hirohito yesterday urged senior ministers and service chiefs to find a way to end the war by diplomatic means. The emperor took the unusual initiative after a final farewell radio message from Okinawa indicating that collapse was imminent. It was sent by Generals Sho and Ushijima before they committed ritual suicide together by leaning on their sabres as they faced north to Tokyo. In a death-note General Sho wrote: "I depart without regret, shame or obligations" (→ 29).

1945

June

Su	Mo	Tu	We	Th	Fr	Sa
					1	2
3	4	5	6	7	8	9
10	11	12	13	14	15	16
17	18	19	20	21	22	23
24	25	26	27	28	29	30

London and Lublin Poles share power

Moscow, 23 June
Poland's immediate future has been settled after the two rival groups claiming the right to rule Poland came to an agreement today. American and British objections to the Soviet-sponsored regime of the Lublin Committee have been partly met by including three exiles from London. One of them is Stanislaw Mikolajczyk, the former premier, who is to be deputy premier.

Two non-Communists from within Poland are also included. Power will thus be shared between the Communists and their opponents more equitably than the western governments had thought possible. The deal, suggested to Stalin by President Truman's emissary, Harry Hopkins, should ease the tension between the Big Three (→ 28).

"Demob" to begin

Britain, 18 June
Mass demobilization begins today for servicemen in Britain's armed forces, even though the war continues in the Far East. Government officials predict that initially 30,000 men will return to "civvy street" each week, but this figure is expected to rise to around 60,000 a week by August. Some have already left, each kitted out in a "demob suit" and other civilian clothing on the day of release (→ 17/8).

A grand welcome awaits those who return home to "civvy street".

24. Borneo: British and US aircraft drop a thousand tons of bombs on Japanese positions (→ 25).

24. Thailand: British bombers destroy the bridge over the river Kwae, built by Allied PoWs with dreadful suffering.

25. Philippines: US troops capture Tuguegarao, Gattaran and Penablanca (→ 28).

25. Borneo: Australian forces occupy the Miri oilfield on Sarawak (→ 30).

25. London: William Joyce ("Lord Haw-Haw"), the Nazi propagandist from Berlin, is to be sent for trial on a charge of high treason.

26. Japan: US bombers attack war factories on Honshu (→ 28).

26. Ryukyu Islands: US marines land on Kume Island.

26. China: Chinese troops recapture Liuchow airfield (→ 1/7).

27. Okinawa: A *kamikaze* plane hits the US carrier *Bunker Hill*, killing 373 men (→ 12/8).

27. Washington: Edward Stettinius resigns as secretary of state to take up the post of ambassador to the United Nations (→ 30).

28. Philippines: MacArthur announces the end of operations on Luzon; the mopping up of 23,000 Japanese soldiers around the island will, however, have to continue (→ 4).

28. Japan: US aircraft drop fire-bombs on Moji, Nobeoka and Okayama (→ 2/7).

28. Warsaw: The Government of National Unity is formed; it includes several members of the old London-based Polish government in exile (→ 5/7).

29. Prague: Czechoslovakia cedes 4,781 square miles of Ruthenia to the USSR (→ 3/8).

30. China: Chungchin falls to Chinese forces, which advance into Indochina.

30. Borneo: US forces bombard Balikpapan (→ 3/7).

30. Washington: Truman appoints James F Byrnes to succeed Edward Stettinius as secretary of state.

Charter of United Nations is signed

Truman watches as Stettinius signs.

San Francisco, 26 June
With a bamboo brush the delegate from China was today the first of envoys from 50 countries to sign the charter of the new United Nations organization. No fewer than seven delegates signed for the USSR. The ceremony followed nine weeks of negotiations to fashion an organization charged with maintaining world peace. President Truman told the delegates that the charter is "a solid structure upon which we can build a better world".

He added: "It was the hope of such a charter that helped sustain the stricken peoples through the darkest days of the war. For it is a declaration of great faith by the nations of the earth – faith that war is not inevitable, faith that peace can be maintained. If we fail to use it, we shall betray all those who have died."

Truman approves plan to invade Japan

Washington, 29 June
Five million servicemen, most of them Americans, are expected to take part in the invasion of Japan. President Truman has approved a joint chiefs of staff directive calling for a landing on Kyushu (Operation Olympic) on 1 November and on the main island of Honshu (Operation Coronet) on 1 March 1946. The Honshu operation will rely heavily on troops no longer needed in Europe. General MacArthur has been given "prime responsibility" for the invasions and has issued a strategic outline plan for the assault on Kyushu, for which 13 divisions will be needed, and for Honshu, which will require 23 divisions, including the US First Army from Europe. The British will deploy a VLR (very-long-range) "Tiger" bomber force for the assault on Japan (→ 2/7).

Muscovites celebrate victory over fascism

Nazi standards in Russian hands.

Moscow, 24 June
The *Swastika* standard of the 1st SS *Panzer Adolf Hitler* division – once Hitler's personal bodyguard – was thrown to the ground before Lenin's tomb in Red Square today. The Soviet leaders watched from the top of the tomb as 200 captured flags were carried into the rain-soaked square by soldiers who threw them down to the rumble of hundreds of drums. Marshal Georgi Zhukov led the parade, riding a white horse, the traditional Russian mount for a conquering hero. Speaking later to the huge crowd, Zhukov said that the Red Army was the most powerful in the world, but Russia must not become "conceited or complacent".

1945

July

Su	Mo	Tu	We	Th	Fr	Sa
1	2	3	4	5	6	7
8	9	10	11	12	13	14
15	16	17	18	19	20	21
22	23	24	25	26	27	28
29	30	31				

1. China: Chinese forces liberate Liuchow (→6).

1. Germany: British troops withdraw from Magdeburg, which now becomes part of the Soviet occupation zone.→

2. Japan: Tokyo says that five million civilians have been killed or wounded by US fire-bombs (→9).

2. London: Mountbatten is ordered to launch Operation Zipper, the liberation of Malaya, in August (→26).

3. Borneo: Australian troops capture the major airfield at Sepinggang.→

4. Mindanao: US and Filipino guerrilla forces sweep Sarangani Bay, to try to clear a stubborn pocket of Japanese resistance (→12).

4. Manila: MacArthur announces the liberation of the Philippines (→12).

4. Berlin: Rumours that Hitler is still alive start to spread.→

5. Canberra: John Curtin, Australia's prime minister, dies at the age of 60 (→9).

5. Borneo: Australia lands reinforcements in Balikpapan Bay; they swiftly establish beach-heads and push on to the interior (→8).

5. Britain: Nationwide voting takes place in the general election, but the results will be delayed to allow servicemen's votes to be collected from abroad (→25).

5. Washington: General Carl "Tooey" Spaatz is appointed to command the US air offensive against Japan.

5. Washington: The US and Britain recognize Poland's Government of National Unity.→

6. Managua: Nicaragua is the first nation to ratify the United Nations Charter.

6. China: General Claire Chennault resigns his command of the Sino-US Fourteenth Army Air Force in protest at plans to disband it (→9).

6. Berlin: The Allied occupation forces hold a victory parade (→14/7).

British occupation forces arrive in Berlin

British troops parade by the Brandenburg Gate in the Russian zone of Berlin.

Berlin, 4 July
Watched by several thousand Berliners, the British occupation force arrived in the former capital of the Third *Reich* this afternoon. Women and children clambered over heaps of rubble to gain a better view as the 11th Hussars of the 7th Armoured Division appeared after a 14-hour, 120-mile (192-km) journey from the British occupation zone. They had been held up for three hours at Magdeburg waiting for the Russians to give them permission to enter their zone.

They passed lines of Russian infantry riding in horse-drawn carts. Beside the gleaming fresh paintwork of the Hussars' tanks, the Russians looked shabby and tattered. Berlin seems populated almost entirely by women, and thousands of them are employed by the occupation powers clearing the rubble, brick by brick. At first they worked 13 hours a day; that has now been reduced to seven. There are long food queues, fuel is scarce and most buildings lack glass (→6).

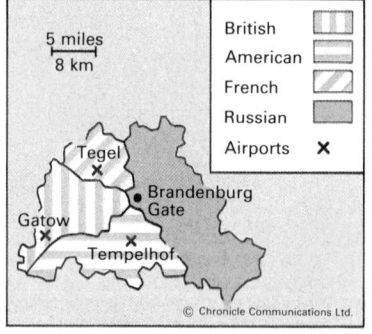

Allies to recognize new Polish cabinet

London, 5 July
The British and US governments today officially recognized the Polish Provisional Government of National Unity. A foreign office statement welcoming its establishment pointed out that under the Yalta agreement "free and unfettered elections" must be held as soon as possible on the basis of "universal suffrage and secret ballot". Ambassadors will be exchanged shortly. This means that Britain will now withdraw recognition from the Polish government in London (→16/8).

Australians assault Balikpapan oil port

Manila, 3 July
Two days after an assault landing at Balikpapan in the Dutch East Indies, the Australian 7th Division has seized control and is advancing inland and along the Borneo coast. The landing was preceded by a 15-day naval and air bombardment. Because of the massive fire support at his disposal the Australian commander chose to attack directly at the heart of the enemy's defences, relying on saturation bombardment to obliterate resistance. Earlier the Australian government told MacArthur that it did not want the 7th Division used. MacArthur insisted that another division could not be substituted in time (→5).

Scientists wanted

Washington, 6 July
The US chiefs of staff have today authorized a special operation, known as Overcast. Its purpose is to exploit "chosen, rare minds whose continuing intellectual productivity we wish to use" from among German scientists. The Allies have recognized that the Germans are ahead of them in many fields of science. One example is rocketry, and the V-weapon expert Wernher von Braun and his fellow-researchers have already been gathered together to prevent them from falling into Russian hands. This concern applies to other scientists as well.

Victory tea: young and old celebrate at a London summer street party.

1945

July

Su	Mo	Tu	We	Th	Fr	Sa
1	2	3	4	5	6	7
8	9	10	11	12	13	14
15	16	17	18	19	20	21
22	23	24	25	26	27	28
29	30	31				

8. Borneo: Australian troops land at Penajam (→ 10).

8. Utah, US: A soldier opens fire on German PoWs, killing eight and wounding 20.

9. Australia: Thirty thousand people line the streets of Perth for the funeral procession of John Curtin, Australia's late prime minister.

9. Japan: US bombers attack two airfields near Tokyo (→ 14).

9. Paris: De Gaulle proposes a national referendum to decide France's system of government.

10. Japan: The US Third Fleet joins the attack on Tokyo for the first time, sending 1,022 US fighter-bombers to raid 70 airfields and destroying 173 Japanese aircraft (→ 14).

10. Borneo: Australian progress east of Balikpapan is halted by Japanese barriers of flaming petrol (→ 12).

10. Argentina: The German U-boat U530, missing since the end of April, surfaces at Mar del Plata, sparking off speculation that it ferried high-ranking Nazis to sanctuary in South America.

11. Indian Ocean: British carrier aircraft bomb Japanese airfields on Sumatra.→

11. Berlin: The Russians hand over the western half of the city to British and US forces.→

11. Canada: William Mackenzie King wins the general election.

12. Borneo: Australian troops capture Maradi, in the north, and land near Andus.

12. Luzon: US forces drop "napalm" on Japanese pockets of resistance (→ 23/8).

12. Paris: Concentration camp survivors carry a huge cross through the city in memory of French victims of Nazism.

14. Japan: The US TF38 attacks Japanese shipping off the mainland (→ 15).

14. Konigsee: Eisenhower dissolves Supreme Headquarters, Allied Expeditionary Force (SHAEF).

14. Rome: Italy declares war on Japan.

China advances in southern Kwangsi

Nanning, 9 July
Chinese forces advancing rapidly east in southern Kwangsi have severed the last link between Japan's China Army and its garrison in Indochina. Since recapturing Nanning, a Chinese column has taken Nam Quan on the Indochina border. Two columns driving north are closing on the key rail junction of Kweilin, Japan's lifeline to south China. Its nearest major airbase at Tanchuk will be threatened if this rapid advance continues. With Nanning and Luichow recaptured, Chinese units now control the three US Fourteenth Army Air Force bases lost last year; these should be operational soon (→ 1/8).

Frauleins fair game for US soldiers only

Washington, DC, 14 July
GIs may "fraternize" with civilians in the American zone of Germany within carefully-defined limits under a scheme prepared by General Eisenhower, to be presented as part of an Allied plan for unified control of the country. Fraternization is forbidden in the British Army. However, the rumour among the troops is that if you offer a *Fraulein* a bar of chocolate you can get anything you like – and six eggs for change.

Japan asks Russia for help in peace move

A Japanese ferry hit in the continuing Allied barrage: will Japan surrender?

Moscow, 13 July
Japan may be ready to do a U-turn on its refusal to surrender. Diplomatic sources believe that today's hastily-arranged meeting between the Japanese ambassador in Moscow, Naotake Sato, and the Kremlin's commissar for foreign affairs, Mr Molotov, included a Japanese request to the Soviet Union to sound out Britain and the US about negotiations for surrender.

The move came three days ago, as 1,022 American planes bombed the Tokyo area, and Allied battleships ten miles (16 km) off the Japanese coast carried out a night bombardment of factories in the Hitachi area, 55 miles north-east of Tokyo. In Moscow, Sato said that he had been instructed that the emperor wants the war ended at once and wishes to send Prince Konoye, a former premier, to Moscow as a special envoy with power to discuss Soviet-Japanese relations, especially the Manchurian issue.

The Kremlin response to the request – the second in two months – is cool. It believes that further talks without an offer of unconditional surrender, an essential Allied precondition to peace talks, are pointless. Marshal Stalin, however, will raise the matter at the talks in Potsdam next week (→ 14).

Britain honours Soviet general with the Order of the Bath

Field Marshal Montgomery with the newly-decorated Russian generals.

Berlin, 12 July
Field Marshal Sir Bernard Montgomery, standing beneath the Brandenburg Gate in the heart of Berlin, today invested Marshal Georgi Zhukov with the Grand Cross of the Order of the Bath. Acting as the king's representative, Monty also invested Marshal Rokossovsky with the KCB and Generals Sokolovsky and Malinin with the KBE.

The King's Company of the Grenadier Guards formed the guard of honour, and tanks of the King's 8th Royal Irish Hussars were drawn up on either side. It was a proud occasion held in front of a banner proclaiming "Glory to the Soviet forces who planted the flag of victory over Berlin".

July

Su	Mo	Tu	We	Th	Fr	Sa
1	2	3	4	5	6	7
8	9	10	11	12	13	14
15	16	17	18	19	20	21
22	23	24	25	26	27	28
29	30	31				

15. Japan: The US battleships *South Dakota*, *Indiana* and *Massachusetts* bombard the Kamaishi steel works (→ 17).

15. Brussels: King Leopold repeats his refusal to abdicate (→ 20.)

15. London: The West End lights up again, ending over two thousand days of blackout and dim-out.

16. Berlin: Truman and Churchill arrive for the Potsdam Big Three conference of Britain, the US and the USSR (→ 20).

17. Pacific: The British Pacific Fleet, under Vice-Admiral Sir Bernard Rawlings, joins Halsey's US Third Fleet as Task Force 37 and raids Hitachi (→ 17-18).

17. Nottingham: Field Marshal Ernst Busch, the commander of Hitler's Army Group Centre in 1943-44, dies in a military hospital.

17-18. Tokyo: US and British carrier aircraft destroy the remnant of the Japanese navy, including its most powerful battleship, the *Nagato*, at Yokosuka naval base (→ 18).

18. Japan: The US Fleet drops two thousand tons of shells on Hitachi in fifty minutes.→

18. Canada: Fifteen people are killed when the naval arsenal at Halifax, Nova Scotia, explodes.

20. Potsdam: Truman says that the Allies are making no territorial claims, wanting only peace and prosperity and "man's greatest age" (→ 21).

20. Brussels: The premier, Achille Acker, tells King Leopold he should abdicate because of his "grave and unpardonable mistakes".

20. Washington: Congress ratifies the Bretton Woods monetary agreement.

21. Potsdam: Truman and Churchill agree to drop the atomic bomb on Japan if it fails to surrender unconditionally (→ 25).

21. Germany: The Allies select Nuremberg as the venue for the trial of the main Nazi war criminals (→ 8/8).

Americans test plutonium weapon

Alamogordo, New Mexico, 16 July
History was made here today in the New Mexico desert when the US tested a new kind of bomb, more powerful than any the world has yet known. In the instant of the explosion, Robert Oppenheimer, the director of the laboratory responsible for the "Manhattan Project", thought of some words from the *Bhagavad-Gita*: "If the radiance of a thousand suns were to burst into the sky, that would be like the splendour of the Mighty One." Now, he reflected, man could say like the god Krishna: "I am become death, destroyer of worlds."

Oppenheimer's awe was inspired by the successful explosion of the first atomic device. It worked by "imploding" segments of the element plutonium to form a critical mass in which neutrons would split the atomic nuclei, releasing enormous energy in a chain reaction. In this morning's test the explosion vaporized the steel tower to which the nuclear device was fixed. Exploding with a force equivalent to 19,685 tons (20,000 tonnes) of TNT, it fused sand into glass and sent a mushroom cloud 40,000 feet into the sky. Scientists who forgot to shield their eyes were momentarily blinded by the light, which was visible for 125 miles (→ 18).

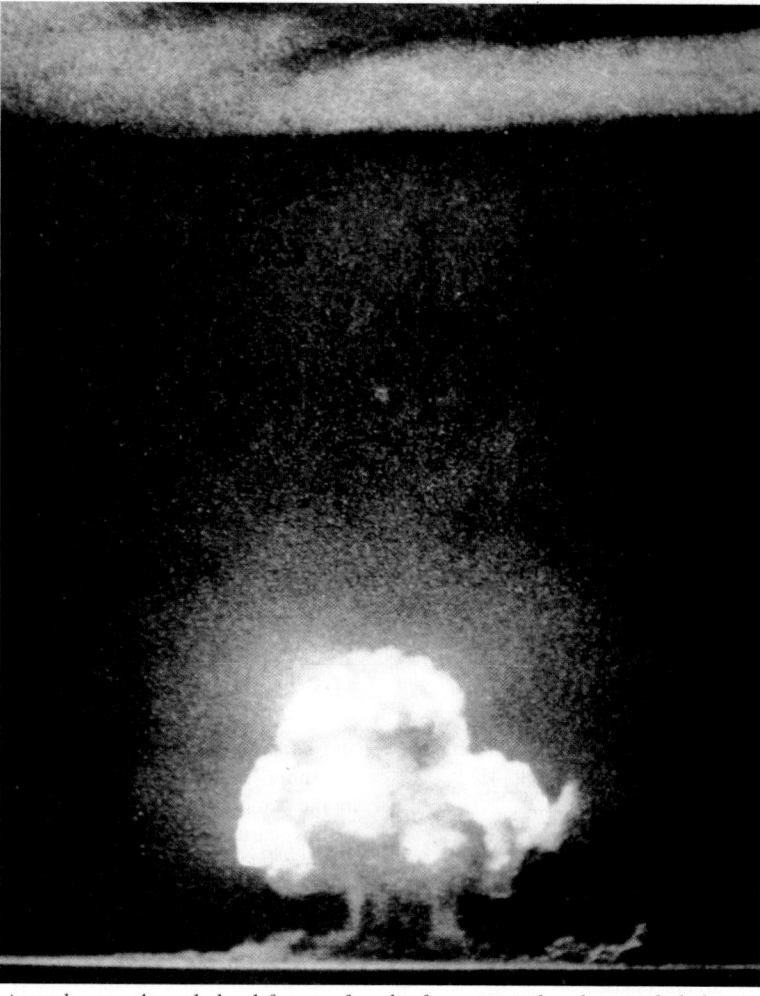

A mushroom-shaped cloud forms after the first atomic bomb is exploded.

Atomic explosion casts shadow over the peace talks at Potsdam

The three Allied leaders chat informally, with their interpreters at hand.

Potsdam, 18 July
The leaders of the conquering Allies met for their second plenary session in the *Cecilienhof*, a pretty 18th-century palace here, and their discussions were supposed to centre on the future peace of Europe and the future war against Japan.

For the Americans and the British the conference was dominated by the news that President Truman conveyed to the British prime minister in a cryptic note, "Babies satisfactorily born". He meant that the atomic bomb test in New Mexico had been successful.

Churchill thought that Stalin did not know about the test; others thought that his spies had told him. But it made the Americans far less keen to hold the Soviet Union to its promise to enter the war against Japan (→ 20).

1945

July

Su	Mo	Tu	We	Th	Fr	Sa
1	2	3	4	5	6	7
8	9	10	11	12	13	14
15	16	17	18	19	20	21
22	23	24	25	26	27	28
29	30	31				

22. Tokyo: Japan says that it is open to peace negotiations but not to threats.→

24. Japan: Over a thousand fighter-bombers attack the naval base at Kure and other targets along the coast from Osaka to Nagoya (→27).

24. Paris: Paul Reynaud and Edouard Daladier, both former premiers, and the former president Albert Lebrun testify against Marshal Petain (→17/8).

25. Potsdam: Truman orders the atomic bomb to be dropped on Japan as soon as possible after 3 August (→26).

25. Potsdam: Churchill, Eden and Attlee fly home for the election results.→

26. Tinian, Mariana Islands: The cruiser *Indianapolis* delivers the consignment of uranium-235 needed to assemble the atomic bomb. →

26. Malaya: British ships end a three-day bombardment of ports, railways and airfields.

26. Potsdam: Britain, China and the US issue the Potsdam Declaration, threatening "prompt and utter destruction" if Japan does not surrender unconditionally.→

27. Japan: US aircraft drop warning leaflets on 11 cities prior to targeting them for bombardment (→4/7).

27. London: The chiefs of staff have their last conference with Churchill.

28. Britain: Attlee, with Ernest Bevin, the new foreign secretary, flies out to rejoin the Potsdam conference (→2/8)

29. Europe: The British Eighth Army is disbanded (→25/8).

29-30. Pacific: The US cruiser *Indianapolis*, returning to the US after delivering nuclear material for the atomic bomb to Tinian airbase, is sunk by a Japanese submarine (→2/8).

30. Japan: US fighter-bombers have another day of intensive operations, including the bombing of Kobe, Kure and Honshu (→2/8).

31. Singapore: British frogmen sink the Japanese cruiser *Takao* with limpet mines.

Besieged Japan rejects surrender call

Tokyo, 28 July
The Japanese cabinet today rejected renewed Allied demands for an unconditional surrender as US bombers dropped thousands of leaflets on Japanese cities warning civilians to "flee or perish".

The premier, Mr Suzuki, said that the Potsdam Declaration two days ago by America, Britain and China, warning Japan to surrender or face "prompt and utter destruction", could only be ignored as it failed to answer several fundamental issues. The ultimatum had made no reference to the emperor or to the status of the throne after a surrender. Nor had Japan received any response to its request made to Moscow two weeks ago to mediate in peace negotiations and receive Prince Konoye as a special envoy. Hawks in the Japanese cabinet – identified as Korechika Anami, the war minister, Yoshijiro Umezu, the army chief of staff, and Soemu Toyoda, the navy chief of staff – argue that the deliberate absence of any reference to the emperor in the Potsdam Declaration is certain evidence of Allied determination to topple the throne.

With Allied invasion forces building up they want the *Ketsu-Go* plan implemented to defeat US landings. The plan calls for a force of 2.35 million troops, backed by four million reservists and a newly-recruited civilian militia of 28 million. The US leaflets listed 11 Japanese cities as targets and pictured B-29s dropping bombs. The leaflets promised that fire-bomb attacks would follow within the next few days: "Heed this warning and evacuate these cities immediately" (→30).

US B-29 Superfortresses fly past Mount Fujiyama en route to their targets.

Atomic bomb backed in US war strategy

Washington, 31 July
Today the US secretary of war, Henry Stimson, sent President Truman a memorandum on how to persuade Japan to surrender. As part of a package of measures which also includes conventional bombing, invasion and diplomacy, he took it for granted that the US would use the atomic bomb now under development. Policymakers are aware of the appalling effects of atomic bombs; but they are also concerned at possible Allied casualties in an invasion of Japan, estimated at 500,000. The formal decision was recommended by a US government committee on 31 May: "We could not give the Japanese any warning ... the most desirable target would be a vital war plant ... closely surrounded by workers' houses," it reported. Both Mr Stimson and Mr Churchill have made it plain that they consider the bomb a weapon of war like any other. There is little dissent among top officials or scientists, though some scientists long involved in the project have doubts about using it (→6/8).

Vichy leader Laval captured by Allies

The end of the road for Pierre Laval.

Linz, Austria, 31 July
Pierre Laval, the traitor prime minister of Vichy France, landed here this morning and is now in the hands of the Free French army at Baden-Baden, in Germany. After the Germans took him from France to Germany, he fled to Italy before taking refuge in General Franco's Spain. But after a "frank" talk between Franco and Sir Victor Mallet, the British ambassador in Madrid, Laval left Barcelona in the same Junkers Ju88 aircraft (a present from the Nazis) in which he had escaped from France. He was accompanied by his wife and a large quantity of luggage. He is expected to arrive soon in Paris, where he is second on the list, after Petain, of those charged with treason (→1/7).

Marshal Petain put on trial for treason

Paris, 23 July
The trial of Philippe Petain was twice suspended today in disorder. Paul Reynaud, the former president of the council of ministers, accused Petain of plotting to betray France in 1940. Petain, who is 89, was the hero of France in 1914-18, but collaborated with the Nazis as head of state from 1940-45. He denied the court's competence to try him and declared: "A marshal of France asks mercy of none" (→24).

▷

1945

August

Su	Mo	Tu	We	Th	Fr	Sa
			1	2	3	4
5	6	7	8	9	10	11
12	13	14	15	16	17	18
19	20	21	22	23	24	25
26	27	28	29	30	31	

UN organization combats Europe's refugee problem

Europe, 31 July

When the fighting finally stopped in Europe some 11,078,000 non-German men, women and children were homeless refugees. Some had fled before advancing armies, others had been forcibly deported by the Nazis, others still were ex-PoWs. About a quarter of the population of Germany was also destitute.

The Allied authorities were faced with a vast multi-lingual mass of destitute people – hungry, sick and often mentally disturbed. Many set off immediately on foot for their homelands, turning war-torn Europe into a huge web of chaotic migratory paths. Officials feared that the precarious post-war order would break down. It is thanks to the United Nations Relief and Rehabilitation Administration, in cooperation with organizations such as the Red Cross, that some 8,221,000 people have now been repatriated.

The displaced persons, as they are officially known, are first segregated according to nationality. Even this first step is complicated. Some survivors are so severely traumatized that they have no memory of their former lives. Others, many of them those whose homelands are now under Soviet domination, do not wish to return to their former homes. From camps divided by nationality the people are then transported by air, sea and land to reception camps in their native lands. Here they are given medical examinations, food, clothing, information about lost relatives, money, and transport to whatever may be left of their former homes. The current rate of repatriation across Europe is some 78,500 people per day. In northern Italy alone there are 40 reception camps; one at Treviso can take 20,000 people a day.

In China the problem is on a different scale. Here 43 million people fled from the Japanese, abandoning everything that they owned to save their lives.

Churchill ousted by poll

Britain, 26 July

Labour has won a sensational general election landslide victory. Tonight for the first time the party rules Britain with a secure parliamentary majority. It is a turning-point in the nation's history. The results of the 5 July polling announced today were Labour 393 seats, Tories and allies 213, Liberals 12, other parties 22.

Voters had cheered Winston Churchill wherever he went during the campaign. But millions had also decided long ago to punish the Tories for pre-war economic misery. They voted instead for a party apparently more earnestly dedicated to social reform. The forces overwhelmingly backed Labour.

Mr Churchill resigned this evening and the king sent for the Labour leader, Clement Attlee, to form the new government. With the help of Ernest Bevin, the trade union juggernaut, Mr Attlee had a few hours earlier survived a botched attempt by his deputy Herbert Morrison

Winning votes: a Labour poster.

and others to depose him. In his hour of defeat, the wartime prime minister accepted the verdict with grace: "I thank the British people for many kindnesses shown towards their servants."→

Clem Attlee: the new man at Number 10

Britain, 27 July

Clement Richard Attlee, now 62, got briskly down to business on his first full day as prime minister. He was probably as surprised as much of the nation was to find himself in the job, but he did not show it. Attlee is a calm, undemonstrative and taciturn man. He is probably the most self-effacing tenant 10 Downing Street has ever had. In contrast to Mr Churchill he will not be haranguing his cabinet, and he intends to run it like an active company chairman and not a dictator.

This quiet, pipe-smoking, cricket-loving premier knows his Whitehall onions. Apart from Mr Churchill himself he is the only politician to have served in the war cabinet from start to finish.

As deputy premier he presided over key cabinet committees and had a pivotal role throughout. At crucial moments he also often had an important restraining influence on Churchill. He managed that without raising his voice or ever saying anything more violent than "That's a bit thick, Winston". The two men have far greater mutual

Attlee: new tenant of No 10.

affection than their election campaign insult-swopping suggests, and Churchill does not pretend that he meant it when he quipped: "Attlee is a modest man and he has plenty to be modest about."

Labour's leader – one of the public-school, middle-class socialists – drifted into politics through doing good works in London's impoverished East End (→1/8).

1. Solomon Islands: Allied troops seal off Japanese forces at Buin, on the southern tip of Bougainville.

1. China: Allied mines, dropped by air, bring Japanese shipping on the Yangtze river to a halt (→ 5).

1. Paris: Pierre Laval is returned to the city, charged with treason and placed under armed guard to protect him from the French public (→ 15).

1. London: Labour MPs sing *The Red Flag* as the House of Commons meets to elect a new speaker (→ 3).

2. Japan: US B-29 bombers attack Nagasaki and virtually annihilate Toyama, claiming to have sunk 26 ships (→ 3).

2. Potsdam: The three-power conference comes to an end.→

2. Plymouth: Truman has lunch with King George on board the battleship *Renown* on his way back to the US.

3. Japan: US B-29s drop mines to seal off all of Japan's main ports, leaving the country totally blockaded (→ 4).

3. Burma: Organized Japanese resistance comes to an end as the Allies win the "Battle of the Breakthrough"; of 10,000 Japanese troops defending the Pegu Yoma range, 8,300 are dead (→ 25).

3. Czechoslovakia: All ethnic Germans and Hungarians are deprived of Czechoslovak citizenship.

3. France: The battle cruiser *Strasbourg*, scuttled in 1942, is refloated.

3. London: Attlee appoints 19 new ministers, including Aneurin Bevan as health minister (→ 17/8).

4. Japan: US aircraft drop leaflets warning of air attacks on 12 more cities (→ 5).

4. Java: US bombers raid Japanese positions at Surabaya.

4. Singapore: Japanese guards execute seven captured American airmen (→ 23).

4. Washington: General MacArthur's command is extended to the Ryukyu Islands, south of Kyushu.→

Potsdam deal dismembers Germany

Potsdam, 2 August
Germany will be disarmed, divided and deprived of the power to make war by the decisions announced today by the "Big Three" Allied powers. The conference's report was signed by President Truman, Marshal Stalin and Clement Attlee, who succeeded Winston Churchill as prime minister after the British general election results were announced during the conference.

A council of foreign ministers is to be established to continue three-power cooperation, though much in the deliberations and the atmosphere of the conference suggested that this will be difficult.

The Big Three propose that cartels, as well as war industries, in Germany are to be broken up. Going some way to accept the controversial proposal of the US treasury secretary, Henry Morgenthau Jr, the powers propose that the German economy should "give primary emphasis to agriculture" and "domestic industries".

There is a striking difference between the treatments proposed for Italy and Germany. Italy is to be offered a peace treaty. The Germans are to be convinced "that they cannot escape responsibility for what they have brought upon themselves". Allied reparations will be paid from German assets and major war criminals will be speedily brought to trial. Germany will lose territory to Poland and Russia.

Franco's Spain, "having been founded with the support of the Axis powers", will not be allowed to be a member of the United Nations. The signatories sent a message thanking Mr Churchill for his contribution not only to the earlier stages of the conference but also to the war itself (→ 13).

Attlee, Truman and Stalin sit for the photographers in the Potsdam sunshine.

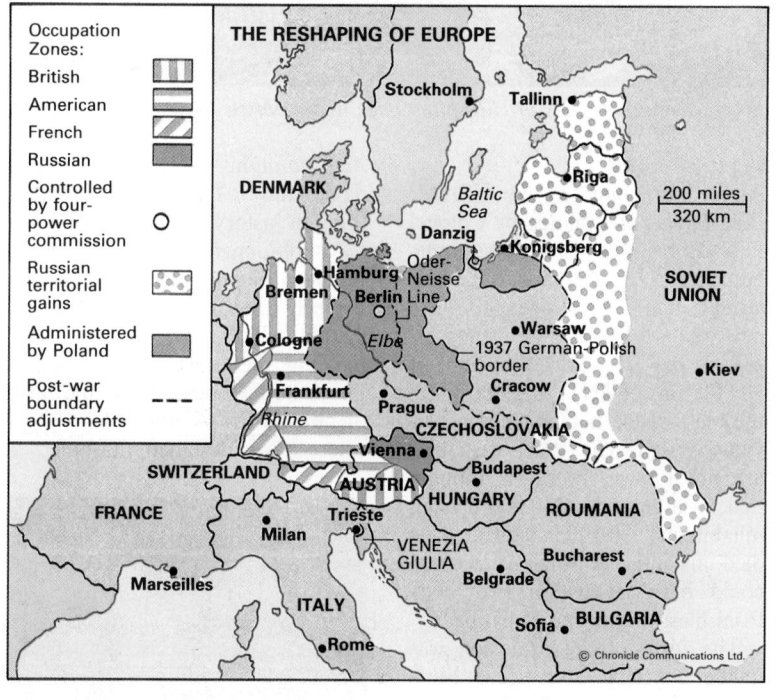

Occupation Zones:
British
American
French
Russian
Controlled by four-power commission
Russian territorial gains
Administered by Poland
Post-war boundary adjustments

THE RESHAPING OF EUROPE

Stockholm
Tallinn
Riga
DENMARK
Baltic Sea
Danzig
Königsberg
200 miles
320 km
SOVIET UNION
Hamburg
Oder-Neisse Line
Bremen
Berlin
Cologne
Elbe
Warsaw
1937 German-Polish border
Kiev
Frankfurt
Cracow
Rhine
Prague
CZECHOSLOVAKIA
Vienna
SWITZERLAND
AUSTRIA
Budapest
FRANCE
Trieste
HUNGARY
ROUMANIA
Milan
VENEZIA GIULIA
Bucharest
Marseilles
Belgrade
ITALY
Sofia
BULGARIA
Rome
© Chronicle Communications Ltd.

US sailors spend 48 hours adrift in sea

Philippines, 2 August
The 316 survivors of the crew of the US Navy's heavy cruiser *Indianapolis* have been telling harrowing tales of their sinking. She was torpedoed at midnight three days ago by the Japanese submarine I-58. She sank so quickly that many of the crew of 1,196 were trapped below decks and the radio officer could not send an SOS.

Luckily a patrol plane on a routine flight spotted some of the life-rafts. The chances of any of the missing 880 men being alive in the shark-infested Philippine Sea are remote. No further search for survivors will be made, because the *Indianapolis*'s mission – to carry nuclear material to Tinian airbase – remains top secret, and radio silence has been ordered. She was sunk on her way back to Leyte.

MacArthur gathers his invasion army

Manila, 4 August
General Douglas MacArthur is to lead the invasion force being assembled for the final conquest of Japan. He is to add 500,000 Allied troops in the Ryukyu Islands, which include Okinawa, to the 250,000 already under his command in the Philippines. In a statement today he said that from these resources "a mighty invasion force is being forged". The US plans to have 650,000 troops ready to invade Japan's southern island, Kyushu, by 1 November. A further million, including Australian, British, and Canadian troops, would land on Japan's main island, Honshu, next March (→ 5).

GI brides prepare for new life in the US

Britain, 1 August
Thousands of British girls are waiting for ships to take them to the US to marry the American servicemen who proposed during their tours of duty in Britain. Some 20,000 couples have already taken the plunge in Britain, and the total of "GI brides" is likely to reach 80,000. The American Red Cross is running "schools for brides". Although their pay and their standard of comfort caused jealousy amongst their allies, the GIs' popularity with the opposite sex never wavered in spite of the well-known taunt of being "overpaid, over-sexed and over here" and jokes about their effect on girls' knickers – "one Yank and they're off".

New US bombing unit joins raids on Japan

Mariana Islands, 1 August
While a select band of politicians and military chiefs wrestles with the problem of whether or not to drop the atomic bomb, another select group has been practising carrying out the task, if ordered to do so. Bombers from the specially-formed 509th Composite Group have been making practice raids on Japan since 20 July. An advance party from the group, which was formed in December last year, had arrived in the Marianas on 29 May and in June was reinforced by the B-29s of the USAAF's 393rd Squadron of very heavy bombers. The 509th is commanded by Col Paul Tibbets, who would lead any initial A-bomb attack (→ 6).

1945

August

Su	Mo	Tu	We	Th	Fr	Sa
				1	2	3	4
5	6	7	8	9	10	11
12	13	14	15	16	17	18
19	20	21	22	23	24	25
26	27	28	29	30	31	

5. Japan: B-29s drop leaflets over another 12 Japanese cities to warn of raids (→ 5-6).

5. China: Chinese troops capture Tanchuk and Hsinning from the Japanese (→ 9).

5-6. Mariana Islands: Seven US aircraft take off for Japan, including the *Enola Gay*, heading for Hiroshima armed with an atomic bomb.→

5-6. Japan: US bombers attack Imabari, Ube, Mayobashi, Saga, Nishinomiya and Mikage, fulfilling the threat made by leaflet drops.→

6. Guam: Admiral Fraser invests Admiral Nimitz with the Order of the Bath.

6. Japan: US aircraft raid Tarmuizu, Kagoshima and Miyakonoju.→

7. Japan: The Nakajima Kikka, a Japanese copy of the Messerschmitt Me262, makes its maiden flight.

7. Britain: The secret of radio direction finding (RDF), now called radar, is revealed.

8. Japan: Over two hundred B-29 bombers raid Yahata, Tokyo and Kukuyama (→ 9).

9. Japan: The premier, Mr Suzuki, says that the entry of the USSR into the war "makes the continuance of the war impossible" (→ 9-10).

9. Manchukuo [*Manchuria*]: Soviet forces under Marshal Aleksandr Vasilevsky push deep into Japanese-held territory.→

9-10. Japan: US carrier aircraft begin two days of concentrated strikes against airfields and other targets in Japan (→ 10).

10. Japan: US and British battleships bombard steel works at Kamaishi, while US aircraft attack strategic targets on Honshu.→

10. Manchukuo: Soviet forces have advanced 120 miles since declaring war on Japan (→ 12).

11. Manila: MacArthur, designated the Allies' supreme commander to accept Japan's formal capitulation, says that the atomic bomb was unnecessary since the Japanese would have surrendered anyway.→

Atomic bomb devastates Hiroshima

Where the thriving city of Hiroshima once was – only a few concrete buildings and burnt tree trunks still stand.

Japan, 6 August
At 8.15 this morning the USAAF B-29 *Enola Gay*, piloted by Colonel Paul Tibbets, devastated the Japanese city of Hiroshima with the first atomic bomb ever dropped. The new weapon has an astonishing explosive power: greater than that of 20,000 tons of TNT, or 2,000 times the blast of the heaviest bomb previously used. The exact casualties are not known, but it is thought that, in a city with 290,000 civilian inhabitants, 70-100,000 will have died instantly. A total of 200,000 could be dead within five years from blast, burns and radiation.

The force of the explosion was unlike anything ever seen. Birds burnt up in mid-air. People died in a myriad ways: their skin peeled off, their brains, eyes and intestines burst, or they burnt to cinders standing up.

A Jesuit priest reported: "In the Hakushima district, naked, burnt cadavers are particularly numerous. Frightfully injured forms beckon to us and then collapse." A history professor said: "I climbed Hikiyama Hill and looked down. Hiroshima had disappeared." President Truman, on board the cruiser *Augusta* on his way back from Potsdam, said: "This is the greatest thing in history."

Major-General Leslie Groves, the head of the military Manhattan Project, the code name for the $2,000 million effort that went into building the atomic bomb, called Dr Robert Oppenheimer, the head of the Los Alamos laboratory where it was designed and built.

"I'm very proud of you and all your people," he said. "It went all right?" Oppenheimer asked.

"Apparently it went with a tremendous bang."

Unlike the bomb exploded in the 16 July test in New Mexico, which used plutonium, the Hiroshima bomb was powered by a chain reaction in uranium-235 [*see report on opposite page*].

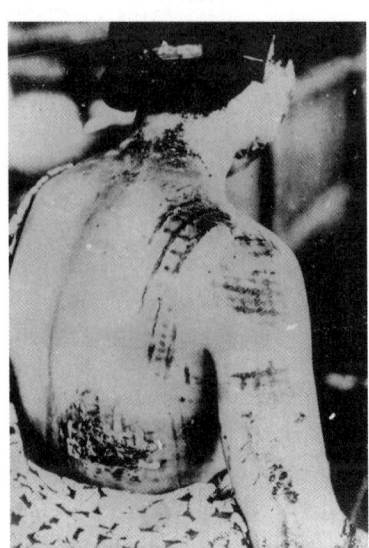

A victim of the blast: the pattern of her kimono was burnt onto her skin.

Colonel Paul Tibbets in the plane that wiped Hiroshima off the earth.

And its terrible power changes the world for ever

Nagasaki flattened by a second bomb

Nagasaki, 9 August
The Allies unleashed their atomic bomb on Japan again today. This time the target was Nagasaki, a major shipbuilding port of 250,000 people in western Kyushu. It is thought to have suffered the same level of devastation as Hiroshima where 60 per cent of the city was wiped out.

Aircrews near Nagasaki when the bomb exploded said that it went up in a roar of smoke and flame visible for 250 miles (400 km). A huge yellow and orange fireball shot 8,000 feet into the sky and then turned into a whirling ten-mile-high column of black smoke. It spread out until it blotted out targets which B-29s were bombing 50 miles away. Fires were still ablaze last night over a ten-square-mile area. The 10,000-pound bomb, which was nicknamed "Fat Man", was plutonium-charged. Nagasaki was only chosen after the pilot found his primary target, the military arsenal at Kokura, obscured by cloud. Tokyo radio condemned the act as an "atrocity", and commentators demanded peace talks.→

The awesome symbol of a new age? The mushroom cloud over Nagasaki.

How tiny particles lead to a big bang

Japan, 7 August
The atomic bomb dropped on Hiroshima wreaked its enormous damage by splitting the tiniest particles of matter: atoms. When hit by a neutron, the nucleus of an atom of uranium-235 splits and releases a lot of energy – and more neutrons – from within itself. These, in turn, bombard other nuclei, setting up a chain reaction which realizes such enormous amounts of energy, and with such speed, that a colossal explosion takes place. A specific amount of uranium-235, known as the "critical mass", is needed to trigger the reaction. Within the bomb the uranium is kept in two parts which are brought together to form the critical mass at the moment of detonation.→

Those who survived the bomb in Hiroshima queue for medical attention.

The race to get the nuclear superbomb

United States, 9 August
The race to develop the atomic bomb has been won. The result has been certain for some time, however. Before the outbreak of war scientists of many countries were pursuing the concept of nuclear energy. Many fled Nazi persecution and went to Britain and the USA. The Germans, though, stole a march when they took Norway in 1940, because at the time it had the only plant for manufacturing heavy water, vital for the nuclear process. But existing stocks of heavy water had been brought to England.

The British eventually realized that the resources needed to produce sufficent fissile material to create a bomb were beyond them and agreed to pool their expertise with the USA. The setting-up of the Manhattan Project in September 1942, which drew on heavy water from Canada, set the Allies on the path to success, and a special bombing team, the 509th Composite Group, was formed last year. The Germans fell behind, especially because of the repeated attacks on the Norwegian heavy-water plant.→

Did Truman have to drop the A-bomb?

Washington, 9 August
Official Washington's military and scientific communities are split over the decision to use the atomic bomb. Opponents, who include atomic scientists and Admiral Leahy, the US Navy Chief of Staff, argued that it was morally wrong and militarily unnecessary, given the success of conventional bombing and Japan's lack of oil. But the president's backers, led by General Marshall, the US Army Chief of Staff, claim that the A-bomb will force Japan to surrender, thereby avoiding possibly millions of US casualties inevitable in an invasion. A quick surrender now will also stop the Russians reaching Japan and allow the US to be the only power to occupy Japan (→ 11).

Soviet Union declares war on Japan

Moscow, 9 August
The Allies' steel ring around Japan snapped tight last night as Russia entered the Pacific War. Moscow announced its declaration of war on Japan at midnight. Ten minutes later and nearly 5,000 miles (8,000 km) away a vast Soviet army, assembled in secret over the last three months, invaded Manchukuo (as Japan renamed Manchuria), intent on dividing the province and surrounding the Kwantung Army. By this morning Russian columns had made rapid progress as Soviet aircraft bombed strategic points behind Japanese lines.

At Yalta, Stalin had promised Roosevelt that Russia would join in the attack on Japan three months after the end of the war in Europe. And he has kept his promise, perhaps helped by the US decision to drop the atomic bomb on the Japanese mainland.

In Moscow Mr Molotov, the Soviet foreign affairs commissar, said that the Soviet Union had declared war because Japan was the only great power preventing peace. He said that it was in the interests of shortening the war and bringing peace to the world that Moscow acceded to the Allied request made at Potsdam to join the war. He said that the Russians had been asked to mediate by Japan, but that proposal had lost all basis when Japan refused to surrender unconditionally.

The Soviet strike force is numerically superior and includes experienced troops from the European front. It has 1.2 million troops, backed by 3,900 aircraft, 5,500 tanks and 26,000 field guns. Japan's Kwantung Army has 780,000 troops, 1,000 aircraft, 1,155 tanks and 6,620 field guns (→ 10).

Soviet tanks and planes attack the rear of Japan's army in Manchukuo.

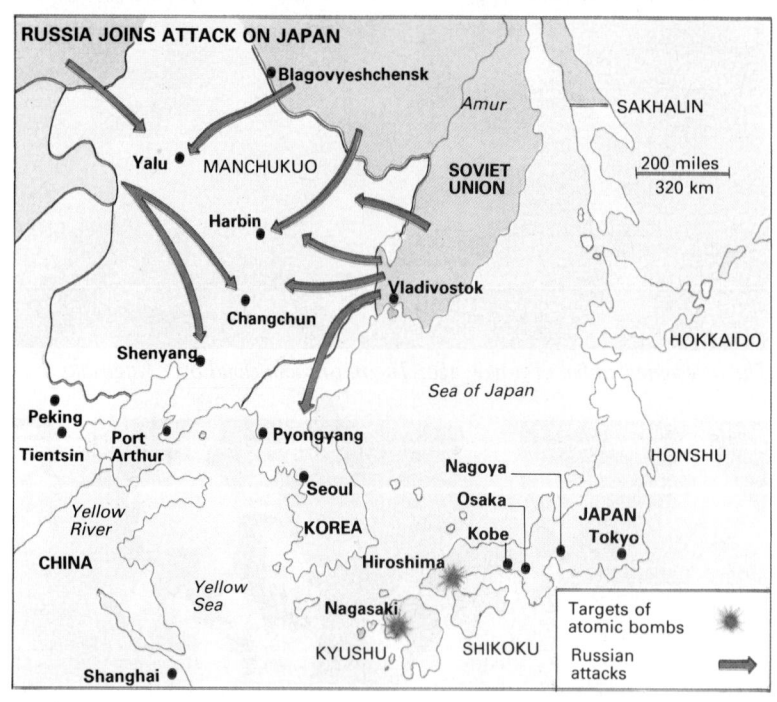

RUSSIA JOINS ATTACK ON JAPAN

Blagovyeshchensk · Amur · SAKHALIN · Yalu · MANCHUKUO · SOVIET UNION · 200 miles · 320 km · Harbin · Changchun · Vladivostok · HOKKAIDO · Shenyang · Sea of Japan · Peking · Port Arthur · Tientsin · Pyongyang · Nagoya · HONSHU · Seoul · Osaka · JAPAN · Yellow River · KOREA · Kobe · Tokyo · CHINA · Hiroshima · Yellow Sea · Nagasaki · Targets of atomic bombs · KYUSHU · SHIKOKU · Russian attacks · Shanghai

Hirohito backs the doves as ministers wrangle over peace

Tokyo, 11 August
The rapid moves towards peace in the last 24 hours have suddenly become deadlocked, with surrender negotiations between Japan and the Allies breaking down over the future role of Emperor Hirohito. The setback came today in a note from the US secretary of state, James Byrnes, to the Japanese cabinet. It rejected the Japanese offer of unconditional surrender because it was in fact still conditional, containing a demand that Emperor Hirohito's prerogative as sovereign ruler should not be compromised.

The Byrnes note refuses to offer any such guarantee. It says that the Allies envisage an unconditional surrender as one where the emperor will be "subject to" the supreme commander of the Allied powers and that, ultimately, Japan's form of government will be established "by the freely-expressed will of the Japanese people".

The US response has thrown the Japanese cabinet into disarray. It strongly hoped that it had found a way to end the war after an all-night session the previous night in a palace air-raid shelter at which hardliners had argued for many more conditions. These included no US occupation of Japan, self-demobilization by Japan and the trial of all war criminals by Japanese courts. The doves, led by the foreign minister, Shigenori Togo, wanted unconditional surrender provided that the emperor was protected. With the votes even, the emperor was asked for his view. He backed Togo, whose proposals were then adopted unanimously (→ 13).

War criminals face international tribunal

Nuremberg, 8 August
The trial of Nazi war criminals by a four-power military tribunal will open in Nuremberg, the traditional setting for the Nazi Party rallies and the city where the infamous decrees for the persecution of the Jews were promulgated. The top Nazis, now under arrest, are accused of planning to make war in violation of international treaties, violating accepted laws and customs of war, and murder, extermination, enslavement and deportation. Acting under orders will not be accepted as a defence.

Britain is represented by Lord Jowitt, the lord chancellor in the new Labour government; the United States, the Soviet Union and France are represented by supreme-court judges (→ 13).

A weapon for peace or world disaster?

London, 11 August
As the world struggles to understand the scale of the devastation wreaked on the Japanese cities, the Allied press is full of excited speculation about the industrial and commercial potential of the newly-harnessed energy of the atom.

A Tokyo radio station described the bomb as "a diabolical weapon", and the Allies as destroyers of "justice and mankind". President Truman, in a broadcast yesterday, spoke of guarding the secret of the bomb and ensuring that "its power be made an overwhelming influence towards world peace". He said: "We thank God that it has come to us, instead of to our enemies; and we pray that He may guide us to use it in His ways and for His purposes."

1945

August

Su	Mo	Tu	We	Th	Fr	Sa
				1	2	3	4
5	6	7	8	9	10	11
12	13	14	15	16	17	18
19	20	21	22	23	24	25
26	27	28	29	30	31	

12. Okinawa: A Japanese submarine sinks the US destroyer *Thomas F Nickel* and the landing craft *Oak Hill*.

12. Far East: Soviet forces advance towards northern Korea and land on Sakhalin Island (→ 13).

13. Japan: Tokyo radio says that Japan will surrender.→

13. USSR: Mongolia declares war on Japan.→

13. Berlin: French troops take up garrison duties in the British and US zones in the west of the city (→ 25).

13-14. Japan: Sixteen hundred US aircraft bomb Tokyo.→

14-15. Japan: B-29s strike Kumagaya and Isezaki, north-west of Tokyo, and the Akita-Aradi oil refinery.→

15. China: Chu Teh, the C-in-C of the Communist army, warns the Allies that the Communists expect a share in the Japanese surrender and post-war settlement (→ 18).

15. Paris: Marshal Petain is found guilty of treason and sentenced to death (→ 17).

15. US: The rationing of petrol and canned goods is abolished (→ 20).

16. Tokyo: As Emperor Hirohito orders all Japanese troops to lay down their arms, a new government is formed under Prince Naruhiko Higashikuni.→

16. Moscow: Poland and the USSR sign a treaty which fixes the new Russo-Polish frontier (→ 20).

16. London: In the House of Commons, Churchill speaks of an "iron curtain" descending across Europe.→.

17. Dutch East Indies: The former colony proclaims itself the independent republic of Indonesia.

17. Paris: The death sentence on Marshal Petain is commuted to life, on account of his advanced age.

17. London: The government announces a programme of social reform, with a national health service at its centre (→ 21).

World war ends as Japan surrenders

Tokyo, 14 August
Japan has surrendered unconditionally, bringing the world war to an end after nearly six years. The news was announced simultaneously in London, Washington and Moscow.

The US in its first response has ordered Japan to end fighting by all its forces on all fronts immediately. Japan has been told "to send emissaries at once to the supreme commander of the Allied powers with information of the disposition of the Japanese forces".

Allied armed forces have been ordered to suspend hostilities immediately. General Douglas MacArthur has been appointed supreme Allied commander to accept the Japanese surrender. Outside the imperial palace in Tokyo, where the imperial decision was read out, an emotional crowd gathered. Thousands of weeping people bowed to the ground wailing: "Forgive us, O Emperor, our efforts are not enough."

Inside Emperor Hirohito was recording a call to the people of Japan to respond loyally to his command to surrender. His broadcast tomorrow [*see below*] will be the first time that anyone outside court circles has heard the man believed by the Japanese to have been divinely appointed. The cabinet decision to surrender unconditionally came this morning after the US said that the imperial constitution will not be abolished. The emperor, asked for his opinion, ordered the cabinet to "endure the unendurable".→

Hirohito: endure the unendurable.

How Emperor Hirohito explained defeat

Tokyo, 15 August
Japan's Emperor Hirohito took the unprecedented step of making a radio broadcast to his people today to explain the country's surrender. In grief-stricken tones he told them: "Despite the best that has been done by everyone, the gallant fighting of the military and naval forces ... and the devoted service of our 100,000,000 people, the war situation has developed not necessarily to Japan's advantage ... Moreover the enemy has begun to employ a new and most cruel bomb, the power of which to do damage is indeed incalculable, taking toll of many innocent lives.

"Should we continue to fight, it would not only result in the ultimate collapse and obliteration of the Japanese nation but also it would lead to the total extinction of human civilization" (→ 16).

Palace attacked

Tokyo, 15 August
A desperate last-minute attempt by fanatical extremists to prevent Japan from surrendering has failed. Rebel officers who broke into the palace last night to persuade Emperor Hirohito to continue the war have given themselves up. Their leader, Major Kenji Hatanaka, who killed the commander of the imperial guard during the brief *coup*, has committed suicide.→

Word of surrender has yet to reach some outposts in Pacific

Red Army units push as deeply as they can into Japan, despite the surrender.

Guam, 18 August
Concern is growing among the Allies that it may be weeks, and possibly months or years, before all Japanese troops have surrendered. It is feared that long before Japan's surrender some soldiers in the outlying Pacific islands were ordered to go into hiding, harass the enemy and never give up. Without radios many will not have heard Emperor Hirohito's broadcast. Most will only accept their orders to fight on being countermanded by their own officers, many of whom are dead or missing. The issue has been highlighted by events in Manchukuo where the Japanese army fought until yesterday when it finally received Hirohito's order to surrender in writing – despite hearing it two days ago (→ 21).

Allied peoples all over the world celebrate VJ Day

The Union Jack and Old Glory are hung out in Battersea, in South London, as the residents line up for a photograph of their VJ Day celebrations.

15 August

After the announcement of Japan's unconditional surrender at midnight London time, Allied nations around the world plunged into heartfelt celebrations that the war was finally over.

In **Washington**, where the news broke at 7pm yesterday, the crowds outside the White House chanted "We want Truman". The president appeared on the portico, saying: "This is the day we've been waiting for since Pearl Harbor." A two-day holiday was proclaimed for all federal employees.

In **New York** Mayor La Guardia broadcast in a voice choked with emotion: "The day is not complete for he who brought it about is not with us. I know that 130 million

Americans are giving thanks tonight for Franklin Delano Roosevelt." Outside tons of ticker tape were scattered and crowds danced to the sound of taxi horns and ships' sirens. Outside St Patrick's Cathedral, hundreds knelt on the pavements.

In **Australia's** cities people had just got to work when the news was announced. They flooded out into the streets, and the dancing and fireworks continued all night.

In **London** the news was broadcast at midnight by Clement Attlee, the prime minister, but thousands of people who did not listen to the radio went to work today, only to leave again for a two-day holiday. The weather was wet, and the rain soaked the king and queen, driving

in an open carriage to the first state opening of Parliament since the war began. The queen sat smiling in a frail blue dress with her hat drooping. Every street was filled with milling crowds, and the Mall was a sea of people who fell silent for the king's broadcast at 9pm.

"The world has come to look for certain qualities from the peoples of the Commonwealth and Empire," he said. "We have our part to play in restoring the shattered fabric of civilization. It is to this great task that I call you now." The royal family made repeated appearances on the palace balcony. After dark the two princesses joined the rejoicing crowds in the streets outside. Earlier in the day Field Marshal Montgomery was wildly cheered in

the streets of Lambeth, where he was born, as he was driven to receive the freedom of the borough to cries of "Good old Monty!"

In **China**, Marshal Chiang Kai-shek broadcast to his people after the Japanese surrender had ended a conflict which began on 7 July 1937. "Our faith in justice through the black and hopeless days of eight long years of struggle has been rewarded," he said.

For the vanquished, of course, it was not a day of celebration. In **Tokyo**, as Emperor Hirohito made an unprecedented broadcast, a weeping crowd stood bowing to the ground before the imperial palace and a wireless commentator said: "Alas, in their shame, how can the people raise their heads?" (→ 19).

Rich and poor, young and old, they all celebrate the coming of peace at last

Members of London's Chinese community stage their own victory parade.

Britain's royal family waves from the balcony of Buckingham Palace.

Here's to peace: US servicemen get in a few beers to toast Allied victory.

Churchill fears "iron curtain" in Europe

London, 16 August

An "iron curtain" has come down across Europe, according to Winston Churchill. Now leader of the opposition, he told the House of Commons today of his fears that "tragedy on a prodigious scale is imposing itself behind the iron curtain which at present divides Europe in twain".

He was referring especially to the expulsion of millions of Germans from territory allotted to Poland in the west to compensate for that taken by Russia in the east. Many are unaccounted for. "Where have they gone? What is their fate?"

Going on to speak of what was happening in the newly communist-dominated countries, he said: "A family might be gathered around the fireside and enjoying the fruits of their toil when suddenly there is a knock at the door and heavily-armed policemen appear.

"It may be that a father or a son or a friend sitting in the cottage is called out and taken away into the dark and no one knows what is his fate. All they know is that they had better not inquire ...

"President Roosevelt laid down the Four Freedoms, and these are extant in the Atlantic Charter. Freedom from fear, but this has been interpreted as if it were only freedom from fear of invasion by a foreign country. That is the least of the fears of the common man. His patriotism arms him to withstand invasion. That is not the fear of the ordinary families in Europe tonight. Their fear is of the policeman knocking at the door" (→ 20).

Manchuria is to be returned to China

Moscow, 15 August

Manchuria, which Japan had called Manchukuo, is to be returned to Nationalist China within three months of the end of hostilities, following a treaty of friendship agreed between the Chungking government and the Soviet Union today. The treaty, which excludes China's Communists, is a tactical victory for Chiang Kai-shek's government over its Communist rivals. In exchange for returning Manchuria, the Soviet Union's interests are safeguarded with its former possession, Port Arthur, returned to be a joint naval base and Dairen a free port (→ 20).

Nazi tyrants enjoy luxurious "prison"

Luxemburg, 13 August

Hermann Goering is off drugs for the first time for years, but still takes breakfast in bed. Von Ribbentrop relaxes as his room-mate Frank, the "butcher" of Poland, reads aloud from the Bible. Like others of the top 24 Nazis held under guard at the Palace Hotel, Mondorf les Bains, Frank is a high suicide risk. He was admitted with multiple, self-inflicted knife wounds. Soon all will go on trial at Nuremberg, exchanging a sun terrace for the more forensic light of a war crimes tribunal. Hess pleads that he is a case of amnesia (→ 28).

Britain's plans for rapid demobilization

Westminster, 17 August

The long and the short and the tall may worry less about their "demob" dates – the day when British servicemen discard uniform and come home – as a result of a scheme to accelerate the release process. The official target increased today from 115,000 to 171,000 a month, to return a million men and 100,000 women by 31 December instead of 825,000. An additional million people will be released from munitions work within eight weeks, many of them to begin a belated retirement. Some service people will be disappointed when they study the small print of the Labour government's plan. An individual's release depends on his service trade and number. Men in trades where skills are scarce, such as Fleet Air Arm radar mechanics, will find themselves in uniform for months, perhaps years longer than simple truck drivers. The minister of fuel and power, Emmanuel Shinwell, has announced a drive to increase coal production by 18 million tons annually to avert fuel shortages.

1945

August

Su	Mo	Tu	We	Th	Fr	Sa
			1	2	3	4
5	6	7	8	9	10	11
12	13	14	15	16	17	18
19	20	21	22	23	24	25
26	27	28	29	30	31	

19. Formosa [*Taiwan*]: Subhas Chandra Bose, the Indian Nationalist leader, is killed in an air crash.

19. Britain: King George and Queen Elizabeth lead nation-wide thanksgiving services to mark Victory Sunday.

20. Manchuria: The Red Army occupies Mukden and Harbin.→

20. China: Communist and Nationalist troops clash in northern China.→

20. Poland: Anti-Semitic riots break out in Cracow.

20. Westminster: Ernest Bevin, the foreign secretary, condemns Soviet policy in eastern Europe as "one kind of totalitarianism replaced by another".→

20. Washington: The war production board lifts restrictions on the production of consumer goods.

21. Tokyo: Japan appeals to *kamikaze* pilots to cease operations (→27).

21. Westminster: The government announces its intention to nationalize the Bank of England.

22. Manchuria: The Japanese Kwantung Army surrenders to the Russians.→

22. Japan: The People's Volunteer Corps, the Japanese equivalent of the Home Guard, is disbanded.

22. London: Attlee says that the atomic bomb means a "naked choice between world cooperation and world destruction".→

23. Manila: MacArthur releases 5,000 Filipinos interned for security reasons.

23. Colombo: A British fleet sets sail to occupy Singapore.

23. London: Parliament ratifies the United Nations Charter.

25. China: Captain John Birch of the US Army is shot dead in a scuffle with Chinese Communist soldiers.→

25. Germany: British forces in Germany are redesignated the British Army of the Rhine (BAOR).

Japanese forces give up their arms

The people of Manchuria come forward to greet their Red Army liberators.

Manchuria: Soviet paras land in cities

Mukden, 21 August

Against fast-crumbling resistance Soviet forces have occupied nearly all of Manchuria, ending 14 years of Japanese occupation. Kwantung Army troops are surrendering at the rate of 100,000 a day.

Despite agreeing a surrender two days ago the Red Army is pressing forward to seize territory before the cease-fire. Yesterday Soviet advance paratroops landed in Manchuria's four main cities. Soviet forces estimate that they are a day away from regaining Port Arthur, seized by Japan from Russia in 1905. The 12-day campaign has been a triumph for Marshal Vasilevsky's use of three armies at separate points on the 1,500-mile front. Although outmanned and outgunned, the Japanese had the defensive advantage of mountains ringing the Manchurian basin. But they had reckoned without the fast Soviet armoured advance through the Hingan passes with tanks supplied by air with fuel and ammunition (→22).

Burma: military chiefs set to surrender

Rangoon, 25 August

The war in Burma effectively ended before Japan announced its intention of surrendering, but next week it becomes official. Lt-Gen Takazo Numata, the chief of staff to the ailing Field Marshal Count Terauchi, Japan's Southern Army commander, is to fly here from Saigon to surrender formally. Britain's Twelfth Army under Lt-Gen Montagu Stopford thwarted attempts by General Honda's Thirty-third Army to escape across the Sittang Bend towards Malaya three weeks ago; since then there has been only spasmodic fighting, with isolated Japanese units unaware of the emperor's call to "endure the unendurable" (→28).

Lt-Gen Takazo Numata surrenders.

China: Nationalists recapture Shanghai

Shanghai, 25 August

The liberation of China by its people has become a desperate race between the rival Nationalist and Communist forces. Generalissimo Chiang Kai-shek's *Kuomintang* troops today entered Shanghai and Nanking, the pre-war capital, as Communist forces were reported to be marching on both cities.

A Kuomintang dispatch claims that Nationalist troops had occupied western Shanghai. But Communists claim that 50,000 Chinese workers are occupying factories in Shanghai and putting up posters to welcome Communist forces.

At Nanking, where Chiang wants to re-establish his capital, Kuomintang troops have accepted the Japanese surrender with Communist troops three miles (five km) from the city. In the south the Communists claim to be advancing in Canton and near Hong Kong, and are close to Tientsin in the north.

At government level discussions between the two groups have reached stalemate. The Communist leader Mao Tse-tung refuses to answer Chiang's appeal to come to Chungking for discussions. Mao counters by offering Chou En-lai as his representative.

Manchukuo: "last emperor" arrested

Manchukuo, 22 August

The last emperor of China, 39-year-old Pu Yi, has been captured and interned by Russian forces in Manchukuo [*Manchuria*], where he had been head of the Japanese puppet state with the title Emperor Kang Teh. Pu Yi was emperor of China from the age of three to six when the Manchu dynasty abdicated. He was briefly reinstated in 1917. In 1924 he was finally evicted from the imperial palace in Peking, escaping to the Japanese legation and then to the Japanese concession in Tientsin. In 1932 Japan made him head of the new puppet state of Manchukuo, as Manchuria was renamed.

Truman scraps "Lend-Lease" lifeline

Britain, 25 August

The new British prime minister, Clement Attlee, is tonight preparing to warn the nation to brace itself for a long period of unprecedented peacetime austerity. Shortages of food and much else will be more acute than during the war.

Britain faces its gravest-ever financial crisis as a result of President Truman's sudden cancellation of US Lend-Lease four days ago. Under this mutual aid programme, begun by President Roosevelt in 1941, Britain has been getting food imports without cash payment.

It was stated grimly in Whitehall that on account of the American action there must be immediate reductions in imports of food, cotton, tobacco, petrol and many manufactured goods. Also, things produced in Britain for home consumption will increasingly be reserved for export. A high-level British delegation will leave for Washington next week in a bid for transitional arrangements to ease the situation.

US diplomats pointed out that the president was obliged by American law to end Lend-Lease as soon as the war was over. They also said that Britain can probably now get a massive new American loan. This buttered no parsnips in Whitehall.

Mr Churchill is known to share Mr Attlee's concern that the president acted without prior consultation. They see the crisis as a bitter legacy caused by having almost bankrupted the nation in the effort to win the war.

Quisling, Norway's arch-traitor, tried

Oslo, 20 August

Vidkun Quisling, Hitler's puppet ruler of Norway, sprang to attention in the Oslo courtroom today and proclaimed his innocence after listening to a 14-page indictment accusing him of high treason, murder and theft of royal property. The prosecution produced evidence, gleaned from Nazi files in Germany, that Quisling had been in regular and secret contact with Nazi leaders before the war. In 1939, according to one document, Quisling urged Hitler to occupy Norway because the people were almost all pro-British. He sat scowling in the dock as the evidence was given.

Corregidor hero is found in Manchuria

Mukden, 19 August

High-ranking Allied PoWs including Lt-Gen Jonathan Wainwright, who led the Americans' last stand on Corregidor in the Philippines in 1942, have been found safe and well today in a small PoW camp 100 miles from Mukden in Manchuria. They were rescued by a volunteer team of US doctors which parachuted into the area shortly before it fell under Russian control. Also among the 34 freed PoWs are Lt-Gen Arthur Percival, commander of the Singapore garrison at its surrender in 1942, and the governor-general of the Dutch East Indies, Mr van Starkenborch Stachouwer.

Concern grows over A-bomb death toll

The rubble left by the bomb: many are dying from its "uncanny" effects.

Tokyo, 22 August

The death toll from the two atomic bombs dropped on Hiroshima and Nagasaki has now reached 70,000 and is still rising. At least another 120,000 have been wounded and 290,000 made homeless by the bombs – a total of 480,000 people affected – Tokyo radio said today. An unknown number of bodies have still to be recovered from beneath the rubble.

The first Japanese scientist to inspect devastated Hiroshima said that he expected many more deaths. "Many of those who received burns cannot survive because of the uncanny effect the bomb produces on the human body," Suzeto Torii, a technician with Japan's air defence HQ, reported. "Even those who received minor burns looked quite healthy at first, only to weaken after a few days. Many have since died," he said.

Eye-witnesses told him that when the bomb exploded from a parachute 1,800 feet above Hiroshima there was a giant flash followed by smoke that turned into an atomic cloud. People on the ground saw "ripples of circular heat rays" that lasted for about two seconds. "Explosive pressure after the blast was felt for a considerable length of time. The relationship between the flash and the explosive pressure seems similar to that between lightning and thunder. Five to ten minutes after the bomb exploded, a black shower rained. It left black stains on white clothing."

The war is over, but problems of peace now begin

London, 25 August

The war may be over, but many problems are just beginning. That is the bleak view that the British government conveyed to the House of Commons this week. It sees a world where the difficulties go deeper than the inevitable detritus of warfare, refugees and devastated cities.

Ernest Bevin, the new British foreign secretary, said last Monday that economic reconstruction was the primary objective of foreign policy. Not just overseas, though: reports published in Britain this week stated that 700,000 houses in London alone needed repairs from bomb damage. And the next day economic problems came closer to home for Britain when President Truman abruptly cancelled the Lend-Lease programme which had sustained Britain during the war. "Very grave and disquieting," was the verdict of Winston Churchill, now the opposition leader, for the move implies severe shortages of food and prolonged rationing.

Britain's political leaders are also united in foreboding about the prospect of the USSR establishing subservient communist satellites in eastern Europe. Mr Bevin spoke of uncertainty over promises of free elections in Poland and "one kind of totalitarianism being replaced by another" in Bulgaria, Roumania and Hungary. Nor is the advance of communism confined to Europe. In China, with Japan defeated, there have been warnings this week from the Communists, led by Mao Tse-tung, to the Nationalists, led by Chiang Kai-shek, not to provoke a civil war.

Yet potentially dwarfing all this was a report on Wednesday from the Japanese News Agency that the numbers dying daily from burns caused by the atomic bombs is still increasing. It now seems that the bombs caused far more deaths through radiation than scientists had predicted.

1945

August

Su	Mo	Tu	We	Th	Fr	Sa
			1	2	3	4
5	6	7	8	9	10	11
12	13	14	15	16	17	18
19	20	21	22	23	24	25
26	27	28	29	30	31	

26. Britain: Sir Arthur Harris, the C-in-C of RAF Bomber Command, announces his resignation.

27. Japan: An enormous US naval force of 23 aircraft carriers, 12 battleships, 26 cruisers, 116 destroyers and escorts and 12 submarines sails into Tokyo Bay (→ 28).

28. Japan: The Allies set foot on Japanese soil for the first time, when US paratroopers land on the bomb-pocked runway of Atsugi airport, near Yokohama (→ 29).

28. Hanoi: Ho Chi Minh announces his provisional government for Vietnam, with all the main posts held by communists.

28. Burma: Japanese forces in Rangoon sign a formal surrender (→ 30).

29. Japan: The US battleship *Missouri* anchors in Tokyo Bay.→

29. China: Mao Tse-tung and Chiang Kai-shek meet at Chungking for talks to try to avert civil war betweeen the Communists and the Nationalists.

29. Hong Kong: The British fleet arrives to reclaim the colony for Britain.

29. Singapore: Japanese troops in South-east Asia surrender to Mountbatten.

30. Japan: MacArthur arrives to organise the US occupation, and sets up headquarters in Yokohama.→

30. Japan: The US cruiser *San Juan* starts to evacuate Allied PoWs.→

30. Burma: Japanese forces based at Abya surrender to the Allies.

31. Pacific: The Japanese garrison on Marcus Island surrenders to the US.

31. Manila: Japanese troops in the Philippines formally surrender.

31. Moscow: The USSR restores diplomatic relations with Finland.

31. Germany: Allied troops arrest Field Marshals von Brauchitsch and von Manstein.

Goering and Hess the first war criminals

Nuremberg, 28 August
The Nazi Party's "jovial brute", Hermann Goering, heads the first list of 24 German war criminals. Hess, once Hitler's deputy, who has been a prisoner in Britain since May 1941, is next in the list, followed by Martin Bormann, Hitler's last deputy, who vanished from the Berlin bunker and has not been seen since. The many civilians indicted include Baron Konstantin von Neurath, Hitler's first foreign minister; Gustav Krupp von Bohlen, the industrialist; Franz von Papen, Hitler's vice-chancellor in 1933-4, and Hjalmar Schacht, the financial wizard who fell out with Hitler after serving as a minister (→ 31).

Jovial brute: Hermann Goering.

Japanese medical experiments revealed

Tokyo, 31 August
Horrific details of atrocities carried out by Japanese doctors are emerging as Allied PoWs are released. Prisoners have been subjected to vivisection. Others have been used as human guinea-pigs and injected with acid, inoculated with fatal diseases or frozen at minus six degrees Fahrenheit (-20 C).

Eight US airmen shot down after B-29 raids in May died in vivisection experiments carried out by Professor Fukujiro at Kyushu university. One PoW's stomach was removed, and an artery cut to see how long it was before he died.

Many of the atrocities have been at Japan's top-secret bacteriological warfare Unit 731 at Harbin, in Manchuria. Prisoners were inoculated with anthrax, typhoid and cholera to test germ potency. Others have been boiled or dehydrated to death. Experiments included prolonged exposure to X-rays and prisoners subjected to a pressure chamber where the blood was forced out of their skin as they died in agony.

PoWs fear that 731's commander, Shiro Ishii, will escape prosecution in return for turning over germ warfare data to the US. Two released US doctors also revealed today how they were made to prepare lethal acid-based solutions for Japanese doctors to inject into US PoWs at a Tokyo hospital.→

Cruel pursuit of victory: kamikaze pilots make a bow.

Allies prepare for Japan's surrender

Yokohama, 31 August
General MacArthur today established supreme allied command at Yokohama, Tokyo's main port, as the first foreigner to take charge of Japan in 1,000 years.

MacArthur is working on Japan's formal surrender, which will be signed in two days' time aboard the USS *Missouri* in Tokyo Bay. He said: "The surrender plan has been going splendidly. There is every indication that the occupation will continue without bloodshed or friction." In Tokyo quiet has returned, although the corpses of 30 civilians who committed *hara-kiri* after the

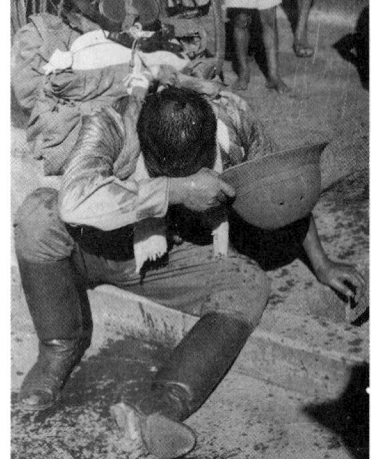
The face of defeat: a Japanese officer overcome by the shame of surrender.

initial surrender still lie outside the palace. Since the first wave of 7,500 US airborne troops landed three days ago, the US occupation has continued at a rate of 300 troop planes a day. Yokosuka, on Tokyo Bay, has become Pacific Fleet HQ after its surrender by two Japanese admirals to Admiral Halsey. The main landings at Yokohama and on the southern island of Kyushu will begin after the formal surrender.

MacArthur will accept Japan's surrender with the foreign minister, Mamoru Shigemitsu, and the army chief of staff, Yoshijiro Umezu, signing for Japan's new caretaker government. Representatives of each of the 12 Allied nations will sign the surrender. Britain will be represented by General Percival, the former commander of Singapore, who spent the war in captivity after its fall (→ 2/9).

Victims of war drift in a world suddenly at peace

A homeless family wanders the ruined streets of Berlin in search of shelter.

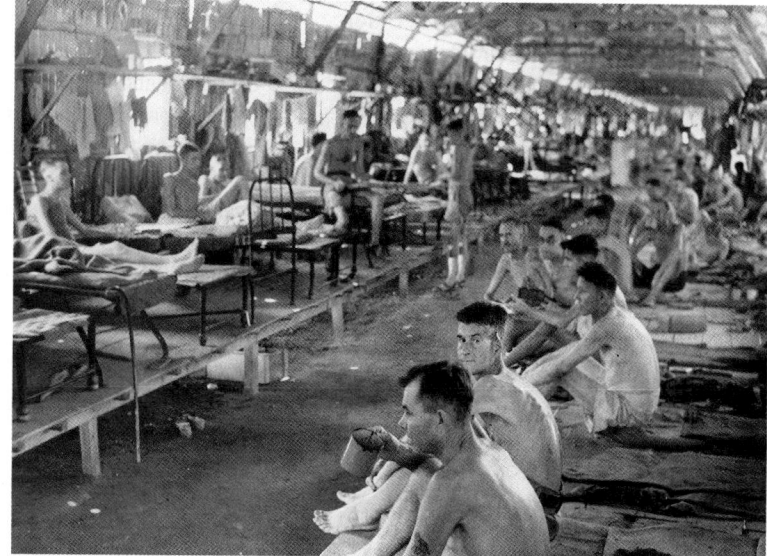

British PoWs who were lucky enough to survive captivity in Changi jail.

Millions of homeless refugees in Europe

Germany, 31 August
Europe is full of the flotsam of war, millions of people without food, homes or countries, migrating in search of safety. Some are trying to get back to villages from which they were transported thousands of miles. Others are fleeing from countries overrun by conquering armies.

There are Germans driven out of Poland and Silesia. There are five million Russian prisoners of war and forced labourers making their way home to an uncertain reception. There are eastern Europeans fleeing from the Red Army. There are Jews who, somehow, survived the death camps making their way to ports in the hope of reaching Palestine.

Germans who fled the bombing of their cities are going home to stake their claims in the rubble of their homes. One person in five in the western zone of Germany is a refugee. There are even leftovers from a previous conflict: 200,000 refugees from the Spanish Civil War living in southern France.

It is estimated that there are as many as 20 million people on the move in Europe. The care of these "displaced persons" has fallen primarily to the United Nations Relief and Rehabilitation Administration (UNRRA), first set up in 1943 to help refugees from the nations fighting the Axis powers. Financed in the main by the United States, it is

trying to bring order to the chaos left behind by the war [*see report, page 650*].

Some, mistrustful of all authority, are making their own way across Europe, begging in a ravaged countryside and risking violence as old scores are settled; retribution is rampant and often brutally indiscriminate. Others have settled into camp life, unwilling to forgo their tents and regular rations. Meagre as they are, these comforts are all-important in a world where a woman can be bought for a bar of soap.

A barefoot refugee with her child.

Prisoners of war expose horror of camps

Japan, 31 August
Harrowing tales of cruelty, filth and malnutrition are being told by Allied PoWs who have just been released from Japanese camps following the surrender. An official report on the main camp in the Tokyo Bay area states: "There has never been such a hell-hole."

Commodore Joel Boone, a doctor who has been involved in the evacuation of PoWs from the camp and the nearby Shinagawa hospital said: "Our prisoners were ill from having to eat rice and grass. Many of the men had dysentery as a result

of the filthy conditions in which they were housed."

Major Maurice Ditton told of his slave labour in Thailand where prisoners were forced to work building the Bangkok to Moulmein railway: "Many men died daily ... The survivors, working in the steaming jungle, became weak. Brutal Korean guards kept the sick working for 18 hours a day."

So far only 1,000 Allied PoWs have been evacuated to freedom. At least another 36,000 are believed to be awaiting liberation from camps across Japan.

Asia prepares for an uncertain future

Tokyo, 31 August
The greatest and most destructive conflict that the Pacific has known is now ended. Fanatical resistance by the Japanese military had not availed. Japan is to be occupied, disarmed and treated as a potentially dangerous enemy. The victors are making sure that there will be no repetition of the mistakes which in Germany after the First World War allowed the revival of militarism under Hitler. A great victory has been won, but suppressed antagonisms are now emerging among the Allies. China will succeed Japan as the dominant east Asian nation, and the struggle for control

is escalating with the USSR backing the Communist Chinese of Mao Tse-tung against Chiang Kai-shek's Nationalists. In Korea only the USSR and the US have troops available to disarm the Japanese. By agreement, the Russians will occupy the north and the Americans the south.

In the Dutch East Indies a revolutionary Indonesian nationalist movement is preparing for independence, and British troops could be caught up in the inevitable disorders. And in French Indochina the revolutionary leader Ho Chi Minh plans to declare independence.

Aftermath of War

World War II had two great victors: the United States and the Soviet Union. The realities of power meant that the key decisions shaping the postwar world would be taken in Washington and Moscow.

The general public expectation was that the victorious wartime alliance would continue into the postwar period. The United Nations Organization embodied this aspiration, which is why the five permanent members of the UN Security Council were the wartime allies — the United States, Britain, France, the Soviet Union, and China. But unfortunately, the central story of the postwar years is of the descent from wartime alliance into Cold War confrontation.

Germany divided

The locus for the initial breakdown in east-west relations was Europe, and above all Germany. The policy of unconditional surrender meant that there was no need to negotiate with the Germans; the country was occupied by the victors, who disposed of it as they wished. Germany was divided into four zones of occupation, American, British, French, and Soviet, under the overall administration of an Inter-Allied Control Commission. Although it lay deep within the Soviet sector, Berlin was also split between the four occupying armies, with a four-power military council, the Kommandatura, providing a joint administration for the city.

The Allies' agreed aim was to re-establish a united, demilitarized Germany after denazification was complete. The detachment of Austria from Germany was part of an approximate return to pre-Hitler borders in Europe. Czechoslovakia and Yugoslavia were restored as unified states, the latter under communist rule after the triumph of Tito's wartime partisan movement. The Yugoslav communists took the disputed region of Istria from Italy, although they were forced to withdraw from the city of Trieste, which they occupied at the end of the war. The largest change in borders was in Poland. The Soviet Union kept the area of eastern Poland that it had occupied in 1939, compensating the Poles with a comparable area of German territory in the west. In effect, Poland was

shifted westwards, to within 40 miles of Berlin. The Soviet Union also absorbed the Baltic states and took small pieces of territory from Finland, Czechoslovakia, and Romania.

The problem of German minorities in Poland and Czechoslovakia, which had played such a part in the build-up to the war, was solved brutally and definitively by the wholesale expulsion of ethnic Germans. About eight million became refugees, returning to their homeland or Austria. In the chaos of postwar Europe, many thousands of refugees, including Jewish survivors of the Holocaust, found their way out of Europe to build new lives in North America, Australia, or Palestine.

Nuremberg trials

The desire for justice, or simple revenge, against the Nazis and those who had collaborated with them found its highest-profile expression in the trial of leading Nazis before an International Tribunal at Nuremberg from November 1945 to August 1946. Ten were eventually executed, a fate Hermann Goering avoided by committing suicide. Prominent collaborators were also put on trial. Hundreds of thousands of less prominent figures in Germany and elsewhere were imprisoned, but many of the most guilty escaped justice. In communist-ruled areas the eradication of "class enemies" took place under the cloak of denazification. In the West,

former Fascist and Nazi sympathizers were soon being seen as useful allies against the threat of communism.

In the first two years after the war's end, there was no clear-cut political distinction between the area of Europe under Soviet occupation and western Europe. Communist and other left-wing parties enjoyed widespread support through most of mainland Europe. The communists were the most popular single party in both France and Italy, where they loyally participated in coalition governments.

Poland, however, was a bitter source of contention between east and west. Stalin assumed that Poland lay within his sphere of influence. He had no intention of allowing free elections, which would have returned anti-communist, anti-Soviet parties to power. The government-in-exile formed in London during the war was excluded from a share of power, and surviving members of the Polish resistance were mercilessly persecuted. The Western Allies could not ignore what was happening in Poland. After all, thousands of Poles had fought bravely for the Allied cause and Poland's freedom had been the issue that brought Britain and France into the war against Nazi Germany.

When former British prime minister Winston Churchill made a landmark speech at Fulton, Missouri, in March 1946, telling Americans that Europe had been divided by

Displaced Germans
Expelled from Poland, a German family finds its way into Berlin – passing a triumphant Soviet poster.

Berlin Airlift
British soldiers in charge of the
airfield and the distribution of cargo
at Wunstdorf Airfield, September 1948.

"an iron curtain", it was more of a prophecy than a statement of fact. But it was a view that played skillfully on American fears of communist expansion worldwide. Churchill and other anti-communist European politicians, including British foreign secretary Ernest Bevin, were acutely aware that they lacked the military forces to resist a Soviet invasion should Stalin attempt one. Their hope was that the United States could be induced to guarantee the security of western Europe and finance its economic recovery.

American opinion was not enthusiastic about adopting the role of a world power, but nor could the US administration reconcile itself to the apparently limitless expansion of communism. In 1947 Britain told the Americans that it could not afford to continue its military role in Greece, where it was backing a pro-Western government against communist partisans. At the same time, there was a perceived Soviet threat to the independence of Iran. In March 1947 President Truman announced that the United States would support the "free peoples" of the world against "attempted subjugation by armed minorities or by outside pressures".

Despite apparently interminable meetings of the foreign ministers of the four Allied powers, no agreement on progress towards a revival of German political or economic life had been forthcoming. In January 1947 the British and Americans took the first step towards a solution by merging their two zones of Germany into a single economic unit. The French joined them later – they were considerably more reluctant than Britain or the United States to see a German revival. At the same time, the denazification process was toned down in the zones under Western administration, allowing many German industrialists and civil servants compromised by their close links with the Hitler regime to return to public life.

In February 1948, at a meeting in London, the United States, Britain and France set in motion plans for the creation of a German government in their sectors. The Soviet Union responded by walking out of the Allied Control Commission. The split between the former Allies left Berlin in an incongruous position, surrounded by the Soviet-controlled zone and 120 miles from western Germany at the closest point. On 21 June 1948 the Western Allies introduced a new Deutschmark in the zones under their control. The Soviets saw this correctly as a step toward the creation of an independent capitalist West Germany. They responded three days later by blocking all land routes into Berlin from the west.

Soviet blockade

Neither side wanted to start World War III, so the Soviets did not attempt to block the air corridors into west Berlin from western Germany – this would have necessitated shooting down British and American aircraft. The Western Allies were thus able to attempt to keep their zones of Berlin supplied by air. Over the winter of 1948–49 the Berlin airlift saved west Berliners from starvation. It also effected a transformation in popular attitudes in Britain, the United States, and other Western countries: people accustomed themselves to the idea that the Germans had become the good guys and the Russians the villains. Admitting failure, the Soviets lifted the blockade in May 1949. In the same month, western Germany became a Federal Republic, and before the end of the year the Soviets had responded by declaring their own zone the German Democratic Republic under a communist government.

By this time the division of Europe in two was an established fact. The toughening American attitude towards communism seemed to have convinced Stalin that his control of eastern Europe needed tightening. In February 1948, non-communists were forced out of the Czechoslovak government and popular protests were suppressed. Single-party communist rule, feebly disguised by phony coalitions with other subservient political groupings, became the norm from Bulgaria in the south to Poland in the north. Alone among European communist states, Tito's Yugoslavia and, as a consequence, tiny Albania, remained outside of Stalin's control. Tito's independent line brought a torrent of invective from Moscow and expulsion from Cominform (the Communist International).

Eastern Europe diverged from the West not only politically, but economically. From 1948, under the Marshall Aid programme, the United States provided some $3.5 billion to refloat Europe's economies. Stalin refused to allow the countries under his control to participate in the programme.

The division of Europe was confirmed by the creation of the Nato alliance in 1949, tying the United States to the defence of western Europe. In 1955 the four Allied powers officially ended the occupation of Germany. West Germany became a member of Nato and East Germany joined the newly formed Warsaw Pact. Berlin remained an anomalous city, still occupied by the four powers.

From foe to friend

The transformation from enemy to friend was perhaps even more striking in the case of the Japanese, given the bitter hatred between Japan and the United States during the war and the savagery of the conflict. Japan was comprehensively demilitarized, with the disbandment both of the armed forces and the armaments industry. Large numbers of civil servants and businessmen identified with the wartime regime were "purged" from their jobs. But punitive action was limited to the trial of 25 wartime leaders, seven receiving the death penalty.

The post-war situation was simpler in Japan because the occupation was, in practice, exclusively an American affair. General Douglas MacArthur, the Supreme Commander for the Allied Powers, ruled with almost absolute authority. He endowed Japan with a democratic constitution of his own devising, heavily influenced by his personal admiration for the British parliamentary system. The Japanese proved willing pupils in the process of democratization.

From an American point of view, by 1948 the rehabilitation of Japan had become vital because China was slipping into the communist camp. During the war, Chiang Kai-shek's Kuomintang government and army had stagnated in southeast China, afflicted with mounting corruption and declining morale; meanwhile, in their strongholds in northeast China, Mao Tse-tung's Communist forces had increased in strength and in unity of purpose. When the war ended, it was the Communists who accepted the Japanese surrender through much of northern China. They quickly extended their influence into Manchuria, which was under Soviet occupation from the final days of the war through to 1946. The United States flew Kuomintang troops to Manchuria to secure the major cities from the Communists. Both the Americans and Soviets tried to persuade the opposing Chinese forces to compromise but by 1947 a full-scale civil war was under way.

It was a long-standing priority of American foreign policy to create a strong, united China under a friendly government. The United States had supported Chiang

Konrad Adenauer

The first Chancellor of the Federal Republic of Germany, from a painting by Graham Sutherland.

throughout World War II and it provided him with huge amounts of money and equipment to fight the civil war. But corruption and rampant inflation meant that the money evaporated. The Communists meanwhile followed a flexible strategy, occupying rural areas and cutting communications to isolate the Kuomintang forces in the cities.

Containing Communism

In January 1949 the Communists occupied Beijing, and by the following October they had control of the country as far south as Canton. Mao proclaimed the People's Republic of China, while Chiang and his remaining Kuomintang followers took refuge on the island of Formosa, now Taiwan. The Kuomintang government continued to claim to rule China, and was recognized as the sole legitimate Chinese government by the United States. But this unhelpful fiction could not disguise a massive defeat for the American policy of the containment of communism.

At the same time that the communists were marching to victory in China, the Soviet Union successfully tested its first atom bomb. A triumph both for Soviet scientists and Soviet espionage, the A-bomb test sent tremors of fear through the American psyche. Since 1947, the Un-American Activities Committee of the Republican-dominated House of Representatives had been mounting a witchhunt against alleged Communist subversion in the United States. In February 1950 Senator Joseph McCarthy lead the campaign to unmask covert communists in the government, the army, and other areas of American life.

The Korean War was the culmination of the earliest, most critical phase of the Cold War. At the end of World War II the Japanese colony of Korea had been divided into a Soviet occupation zone north of the 38th parallel and an American occupation zone in the south. Separate governments were set up in the two zones, communist in the north and pro-Western in the south, each claiming authority over the whole country. The occupation forces were withdrawn on both sides, but relations between North and South Korea remained tense. In June 1950 North Korean troops invaded the South. The Americans responded by obtaining a vote in the UN General Assembly in favour of

resisting aggression, and sent its forces into South Korea under the UN banner. Aided by a range of allied countries, including Britain, the Americans carried the fight into North Korea and advanced to the Chinese border. In the winter of 1950–51, Chinese Communist forces crossed the border en masse and drove the UN army back across the 38th parallel. Stalemate ensued. Eventually, in 1953, an armistice was signed that restored the situation that had existed before the North Korean invasion – the deaths of around two million people had achieved precisely nothing.

The Korean War, like the Berlin crisis before it, showed clearly how conflicts were going to be handled in the Cold War era. The commander of the UN forces, General MacArthur, wanted to respond to the Chinese intervention by attacks on targets inside China, but President Truman would not allow this expansion of the war and MacArthur was sacked for disagreeing. Also, although the United States had atomic bombs, it did not use them. Stalin, for his part, kept his army out of Korea. Both sides trod a careful line to prevent a local conflict opening out into a third world war.

Crumbling empires

This was just as well, because the potential for local conflicts was present worldwide as the empires of Britain, France, and other European powers, built up over three centuries, crumbled in as many decades. Nationalist movements in the European colonies were often communist-led or, at least, opposed to Western capitalism, leading to a crossover between colonial conflicts and the Cold War confrontation.

The era of European imperialism came to a close most rapidly in Asia, where the Japanese victories of 1941–42 had comprehensively undermined the myth of white superiority. The British Labour government was committed to granting independence to the Indian subcontinent; India, Pakistan, Burma, and Ceylon (Sri Lanka) duly became independent states in 1947–48. The Dutch were never able to re-establish control of Indonesia, which was granted formal independence in 1949. Britain did recover Malaysia and Singapore, and held on to them for long enough to defeat a communist uprising before handing over to a pro-Western independent government in 1957.

In French Indochina, Ho Chi Minh's communist-led Viet Minh nationalist movement declared Vietnam independent when the Japanese surrendered in 1945, but

Mao Tse-tung
This portrait appeared in Mao's famed Little Red Book, *copies of which were distributed worldwide in the 1960s.*

Churchill ended his last term as prime minister in 1955, and Eisenhower left the White House at the end of 1960. By then the shape of the postwar world was fixed, frozen by the Cold War. A nuclear arms race was well under way; both the United States and the Soviet Union were testing hydrogen bombs of awesome destructive power, while the development of intercontinental missiles made defence against nuclear attack impossible.

Europe divided by Iron Curtain

The division of Europe by the Iron Curtain was accepted as an unchallengeable fact of life. Neither the use of Soviet tanks to suppress an uprising in Hungary in 1956 nor the building of the Berlin Wall in 1961 provoked any military response from the West. Japan and West Germany had embarked on rapid economic growth as respectable liberal democracies. In the context of declining European power, the rivalry between European nation-states had lost its intensity, a fact reflected in the creation of the EEC in 1957 and a rapprochement between the French and the Germans. The United States

had taken on the role of global policeman, intervening to oppose the spread of communism and foster pro-Western regimes as decolonization spread across the world.

Reunification of Germany

Any further tying up of loose ends left over from World War II had to wait until the collapse of Soviet power in eastern Europe in the late 1980s. After the opening of the Berlin Wall in 1989, negotiations between the United States, Britain, France, and the Soviet Union produced a "Treaty of the Final Settlement with regard to Germany". Signed in Moscow on 12 September 1990, it sanctioned the reunification of Germany and provided for occupation troops to leave Berlin after 45 years. In effect, this was a belated official ending of World War II in Europe.

Yet, at the end of the millennium, the prosecution of war criminals and the search for compensation for victims of the Nazis and Japanese were still on the international agenda, while wide publicity was given to young hooligans in Germany who thought it clever to sport Nazi regalia and Nazi racist views. A surprising number of people were alarmed when Japanese soldiers participated in peacekeeping operations in Cambodia or German aircraft flew missions over Kosovo as part of Nato. World War II refused to disappear completely into the dustbin of history.

the British prevented them making good their claim to rule the south of the country, even rearming Japanese troops to defend Saigon. Indochina was handed back to the French, who drove Ho Chi Minh's forces out of Hanoi in 1946. But the French lacked the `will or resources to hold on for long against determined Viet Minh guerrilla fighters, and in 1954 military catastrophe at Dien Bien Phu persuaded France to pull out. A peace deal gave Ho Chi Minh's communists control of North Vietnam, but the United States took over the task of propping up an anti-communist government in the South.

Suez crisis

The decisive humiliation for Britain and France came in the Middle East. The Suez crisis of 1956 was an attempt by the two imperial powers, in collusion with Israel, to overthrow the assertively nationalist Egyptian government of Adul Gamal Nasser in order to retain control of the Suez Canal. The venture had to be abandoned because the United States was opposed to it. The European states had been shown up as paper tigers, with no real power to act independently. From that point the abandonment of empire was only a matter of time. By the late 1950s, leaders of wartime vintage were disappearing from the the political scene: Stalin died in 1953,

Korean War
A US Skyraider from the carrier USS Bonne Homme Richard *drops bombs over the Korean countryside.*

1939

WORLD WAR II IN EUROPE began with the German invasion of Poland on 1 September 1939. Britain and France reluctantly fulfiled their obligation to the Poles by declaring war on Germany two days later, although to no immediate practical effect. Soon invaded by the Soviet Union as well as Germany, Poland was quickly defeated and partitioned. There followed the period of the "phony war", as the two sides engaged in only relatively minor naval engagements. Meanwhile, a Soviet invasion of Finland in December met with unexpectedly stiff resistance.

Francisco Franco
In March 1939 General Franco triumphed in the Spanish Civil War: he could not have done this without the help of Hitler's Germany.

31 March
France and Britain agree to guarantee Poland against attack

| *January* | *February* | *March* | *April* | *May* | *June* |

22 May
Germany and Italy sign a 'Pact of Steel'

Last days of peace
Children of a school in Whitechapel, London, leave for their evacuation destinations on 1 September.

1 September
Germany invades
Poland

3–10 September
Australia, New Zealand,
India, South Africa and
Canada declare war on
Germany

4 September
British Expeditionary
Force starts moving
to France

Visiting Warsaw
*Adolf Hitler with a
group of officers in
the streets of Warsaw
during the German
invasion of Poland,
September 1939.*

17 September
USSR invades
Poland

27 September
Warsaw surrenders
to Germans

1 2 3 4 5 6 7 8 9 10 11 12 13 14 15 16 17 18 19 20 21 22 23 24 25 26 27 28 29 30

3 September
France and Britain
declare war on
Germany

July   *August*   *September*   *October*   *November*   *December*

23 August
Nazi-Soviet non-
aggression pact signed

4 November
US Neutrality
Act passed

14 October
British battleship
Royal Oak
torpedoed in
harbour at Scapa
Flow, Orkney
Islands

17 December
German pocket
battleship *Admiral
Graf Spee* is scuttled
in the river Plate,
South America,
after battle with
Royal Navy

30 November
USSR invades
Finland

Nazi-Soviet Pact
*Vyacheslav Molotov, Russian Foreign
Minister, signs the non-aggression
pact negotiated between Russia and
Germany, at the Kremlin. Behind him
are his German counterpart, Joachim
von Ribbentrop (left) and Joseph
Stalin (centre).*

1940

THE WAR IN EUROPE BEGAN in earnest in the spring of 1940. In a series of spectacular military offensives, Germany defeated France and drove British troops out of continental Europe. Italy belatedly joined in the war alongside Germany, spreading the conflict to the Mediterranean and North Africa. Hitler was forced to abandon plans for an invasion of Britain when his *Luftwaffe* failed to establish air superiority over the RAF in the Battle of Britain. Turning to night bombing, the Luftwaffe began the Blitz of London and other British cities.

Fallen Maginot line
In a communication tunnel under France's fortification, German officers order their new French prisoners to take them on tour.

9 April
Germany invades Denmark and Norway

10 June
Italy declares war on France and Britain

January	February	March	April	May	June

22 June
France and Germany sign armistice

1 2 3 4 5 6 7 8 9 10 11 12 13 14 15 16 17 18 19 20 21 22 23 24 25 26 27 28 29 30 31

15 May
Dutch army surrenders

28 May
Belgium army surrenders

12 May
Finnish-Soviet war ends

26 May–4 June
Dunkirk evacuation of British Expeditionary Force

10 May
Germany invades France, Belgium, and Netherlands. Churchill succeeds Chamberlain as British prime minister.

2 September
US and Britain
sign 'Destroyers
for Bases'
agreement

7 September
German Blitz
on London begins

12 September
Italian forces in
Libya invade Egypt

21–27 September
Germany, Italy, and Japan
sign Tripartite Pact

1 2 3 4 5 6 7 8 9 10 11 12 13 14 15 16 17 18 19 20 21 22 23 24 25 26 27 28 29 30

3 July
Royal Navy bombards
French fleet at Mers-el-
Kebir, Algeria

5 November
Roosevelt wins third
presidential term

July   *August*   *September*   *October*   *November*   *December*

July–October
Battle of Britain
between RAF
and *Luftwaffe*

Italian Retreat
Defeated at Sidi Barrani in Egypt,
vehicles of the Italian Army retreat
across the Egyptian desert.

11 December
Britain defeats
Italians at Sidi
Barrani in Egypt

20–24 November
Hungary, Romania, and
Slovakia join Tripartite Pact

11 November
Britain attacks Italian
fleet at Taranto

28 October
Italian forces in
Albania invade
Greece

1941

THIS WAS THE YEAR WHEN the war became a truly global conflict. The German invasion of the Soviet Union in June seemed at first likely to prove another swift and devastating victory, but Soviet resistance stiffened and Moscow did not fall. Meanwhile, the United States increasingly backed the British war effort, taking an active part in the desperate battle against U-boats in the Atlantic. On 7 December, the Japanese launched a surprise attack against the US naval base at Pearl Harbor. Germany and Italy then declared war on the United States.

6 January
Roosevelt delivers his 'Four Freedoms' speech

19 January–16 May
East African campaign: Britain completely defeats Italians in Somaliland and Abyssinia

12 February
Rommel arrives in Libya to head German *Afrika Corps*

6–8 April
Germans and Italians invade Yugoslavia and Greece

17 April
Yugoslavia surrenders

20 May–1 June
German invasion of Crete forces British evacuation

22 June
Germany invades USSR (Operation *Barbarossa*)

January   February   March   April   May   June

22 January
Australian troops capture Tobruk in Libya from Italians

10 May
Hitler's deputy, Rudolf Hess, flies to Scotland

27 May
German battleship *Bismarck* is sunk by Royal Navy

1 2 3 4 5 6 7 8 9 10 11 12 13 14 15 16 17 18 19 20 21 22 23 24 25 26 27 28 29 30 31

11 March
US Lend-Lease Bill is passed by Congress

25 March
Yugoslavia joins the Tripartite Pact

28 March
British naval success against Italians off Cape Matapan in Greece

27 March
After a coup d'etat Yugoslavia leaves the Tripartite Pact

Rommel in Africa
General Rommel stands alongside one of his aides while making a survey of the desert during the Nazi campaign in Libya.

10 December
Japanese sink British battleship *Prince of Wales* and battle cruiser *Repulse* off coast of Malaya. Japanese invade Philippines

8 December
Japanese invade Thailand and Malaya. Japanese successfully bomb Clark Field, main US air base in Philippines. US and Britain declare war on Japan

11 December
Germany and Italy declare war on US

24 December
Japanese capture Wake Island

15 December
Japanese invade Burma

17 December
Japanese invade British Borneo

25 December
Japanese capture Hong Kong

1 2 3 4 5 6 7 8 9 10 11 12 13 14 15 16 17 18 19 20 21 22 23 24 25 26 27 28 29 30 31

7 December
Japanese attack US fleet at Pearl Harbour, Hawaii

July   *August*   *September*   *October*   *November*   *December*

18 October
General Tojo becomes prime minister of Japan

27 November
German army almost in Moscow

Invasion of Russia
A German soldier in front of a burning farm building, during Germany's Operation Barbarossa, 1941.

German air superiority
Puffs of smoke issue from Soviet tanks hit by German Stukas during a tank battle in Russia, May 1941.

1942

This year was the turning-point of the war. German and Japanese conquests reached their greatest extent. Japan held all of southeast Asia, while German forces advanced east as far as the Volga. But in the second half of the year the United States scored victories over the Japanese at sea in the Battle of Midway and on land at Guadalcanal. In the autumn, a British victory at El Alamein and the invasion of North Africa guaranteed Allied success in the desert war. And, by the year's end, German forces were facing a bitter and humiliating defeat at Stalingrad.

15 February
Japanese capture
Singapore

9 April
US troops on the
Bataan peninsula
in the Philippines
surrender to
Japanese

4–8 May
In the Battle of the Coral Sea a
US carrier fleet deters a Japanese
carrier fleet from making an
amphibious landing at Port
Moresby in Papua

20 May
Last British
troops withdraw
from Burma

4–7 June
US carrier fleet defeats
Japanese carrier fleet in
the Battle of Midway,
western Pacific

January	February	March	April	May	June

11 March
General MacArthur
leaves Philippines,
saying *'I shall return'*

8 March
Japanese land
in New Guinea

18 April
Colonel Doolittle leads
a US bombing raid on
Japan, including Tokyo

6 May
Last US troops
in Philippines,
on Corregidor
Island, surrender
to Japanese

24 April
German bombers
start 'Baedeker' raids
on British cities

21 June
Rommel captures
Tobruk, Libya,
from the British

30 May
RAF mounts first
'1,000 bomber' raid
on Germany

Fall of Singapore
A Japanese soldier escorts a surrender party from the British authorities to Japanese headquarters in Singapore. The British party carries the white flag as well as the Union Jack.

Battle of Midway
The USS Yorktown *falls victim to the Japanese. Puffs of smoke in the air overhead are from exploding US anti-aircraft shells.*

8 November
North African campaign starts when US and British troops land in French Morocco and Algeria (Operation Torch)

19 August
Large-scale raid by Canadian and British forces on the German defences of Dieppe, in northern France

22 October
British male call up age is lowered to 18

27 November
The French fleet is scuttled at Toulon to prevent it falling into German hands

1–4 July
In First Battle of El Alamein, in western Egypt, British prevent Rommel breaking through towards Suez Canal

12 September
First German troops enter Stalingrad, on Volga river in Russia

| July | August | September | October | November | December |

4–7 July
British Arctic convoy PQ17, on way to Russia, is mistakenly ordered to scatter and suffers heavy losses

19–23 September
Russian armies encircle Germans in Stalingrad

11 November
Germany (and Italy) occupy previously unoccupied 'Vichy' France

7 August 1942–January 1943
In the Guadalcanal campaign in Solomon Islands, US land forces defeat Japanese

30 August–7 September
At Alam Halfa, near El Alamein in Egypt, Rommel's final attempt to break through British defences fails

23 October–4 November
In second battle of El Alamein, British under Montgomery force Rommel to retreat

1943

ALTHOUGH THE ALLIES HAD MOVED on to the offensive, the Germans and Japanese showed that they would fight to the finish. On the Soviet front, the Germans were forced back after the great tank battle of Kursk. Italy was invaded from North Africa and surrendered, but German troops still blocked the Allies' progress toward Rome. Allied bombers pummelled German cities and factories, although at heavy cost. To the relief of Britain, the German U-boat menace in the Atlantic was tamed. Meanwhile, in the Pacific, the United States began "island-hopping" toward Japan.

14–24 January
Churchill and Roosevelt meet at Casablanca in Morocco to discuss strategy

14–22 February
At the Battle of Kasserine Pass, Tunisia, German forces deliver a temporary reverse to the US advance to the coast

6 March
At the Battle of Medenine, Tunisia, Rommel's attack on Montgomery is beaten off with heavy losses

11–25 May
Churchill and Roosevelt meet in Washington to discuss strategy

24 May
Germany withdraws its surviving U-boats from the North Atlantic

| January | February | March | April | May | June |

2 February
Last German forces in Stalingrad surrender

2–3 March
In the Battle of the Bismarck Sea, north of New Guinea, US planes destroy a large Japanese troop-escorting convoy

19 April–16 May
In the First Warsaw Rising, Jews in the ghetto attack Germans trying to deport them

13 May
Last German troops in North Africa surrender

Kasserine Pass
Allied infantry and armour moving to positions in the front line during the battle of Kasserine Pass, February 1943.

US ships at Salerno
An American troop carrier and a host of other ships wait off the Italian coast before landing at Salerno, September 9th 1943.

20–23 November
US troops capture Tarawa, in the Gilbert Islands, from the Japanese. This marks start of US drive across central Pacific

3 September
British and US troops cross from Sicily to Italian mainland

7 October
Mountbatten becomes supreme commander of South East Asia Command

2 December
As part of development of atomic bomb, Enrico Fermi in Chicago successfully makes an 'atomic pile' 'go critical', producing energy and plutonium

4 July
General Sikorski, head of the Polish government-in-exile, is killed in a plane crash in Gibraltar

10 July
US and British troops invade Sicily

8 September
Italian surrender is announced

July	*August*	*September*	*October*	*November*	*December*

25 July
Mussolini is dismissed and arrested. Marshal Badoglio becomes Italian prime minister

9 September
US and British troops land at Salerno, near Naples, against German resistance

13 October
Italy declares war on Germany

26 December
German battle-cruiser *Scharnhorst* is sunk by the Royal Navy off Norway

17–24 August
Churchill and Roosevelt meet at Quebec: agreement on atomic bomb collaboration

5–12 July
The Russians defeat the Germans in a huge tank battle at Kursk

28 Nov–1 Dec
Roosevelt, Churchill, and Stalin meet in Tehran in Persia

Battle of Kursk
A German Tiger tank burns, while dead German soldiers lie in the foreground. At last the Red Army begins to gain the upper hand.

1944

The Allies hoped that this would be the year of victory in Europe. The successful D-Day landings in Normandy were followed by a breakout that liberated most of France and Belgium. Meanwhile the Red Army reached the outskirts of Warsaw. But, surviving an assassination attempt, Hitler refused to give in. He launched his V-weapons against Britain and, in December, threw German forces into a final desperate offensive in the West. In the Pacific, the United States established total air and sea superiority but there was no sign of Japanese resistance faltering.

22 January
Allies land at Anzio, on the west coast of Italy

1 February–18 May
Series of four fierce battles until Allies eventually capture Monte Cassino, south-east of Rome, from the Germans

6–20 February
In the 'Battle of the Admin Box' in Arkan, Burma, the British withstand a Japanese attack and then defeat it

5–20 April
In the battle of Kohima, in Assam in northern India, a small British force withstands a siege by vastly superior Japanese forces

Anzio landings
Hundreds of Sherman tanks and thousands of troops go ashore against German resistance in the Allied landings at Anzio.

January	February	March	April	May	June

30 Jan–23 Feb
US captures Marshall Islands, including Eniwetok, from Japanese

15 March
Japanese in Burma begin offensive towards Imphal in India

22 April–6 June
US captures Hollandia in Dutch New Guinea from Japanese

1 2 3 4 5 6 7 8 9 10 11 12 13 14 15 16 17 18 19 20 21 22 23 24 25 26 27 28 29 30

6 June: D-Day
US, British, and Canadian armies land in Normandy: Operation Overlord begins

15 June–9 July
US captures Saipan, in Mariana Islands, from Japan.

4 June
US troops enter Rome

13 June
Germans launch first V1s (flying bombs) against England

D-Day landings
US troops prepare to leave their landing craft and wade ashore in the Normandy landings, 6 June 1944.

1 Oct–8 Nov
Allies clear Germans from estuary of river Scheldt in Holland, so that port of Antwerp in Belgium can be used to supply Allied armies attacking Germany

7–18 October
Germans evacuate Greece

9–19 October
Churchill and Stalin confer in Moscow

20 October
Belgrade in Yugoslavia is captured from Germans by Russians and Yugoslav partisans

20 October
US troops begin invasion of Philippines by landing on Leyte Island. General MacArthur wades ashore on Leyte, saying '*I have returned*'

24–25 October
In battle of Leyte Gulf, US fleet defeats Japanese fleet

1 2 3 4 5 6 7 8 9 10 11 12 13 14 15 16 17 18 19 20 21 22 23 24 25 26 27 28 29 30 31

18 July
General Tojo resigns as Japanese prime minister

25 August
Germans in Paris surrender

6 November
Roosevelt wins fourth presidential term

July   *August*   *September*   *October*   *November*   *December*

20 July
An attempt by high-ranking German officers to kill Hitler fails; the bomb only wounds him

18 July
The Japanese offensive against Imphal in India is called off. The Japanese withdrawal becomes a disastrous retreat

1 August–2 October
In second Warsaw rising, the Polish Army tries, unsuccessfully, to expel Germans. Up to 250,000 Polish civilians are killed

15 August
US British and French troops invade the south of France, near Cannes

8 September
Germans launch first V2 rockets against England

11–16 September
Roosevelt and Churchill confer in Quebec

17–25 September
Unsuccessful attempt by British and US airborne troops to capture bridges across the Rhine at Arnhem in Holland

16 Dec–16 Jan
Germans counter-attack in the Ardennes in southern Belgium ('Battle of the Bulge') but are driven back by US forces

The Ardennes
US 82nd Airborne Division in the Battle of the Bulge.

1945

Victory in Europe came in May 1945, after the Red Army had fought its way into Berlin. Germany was divided into occupation zones as agreed by the Western allies and the Soviet Union at Yalta in February. The war in the Pacific was generally expected to last into the following year, although American bombers were devastating Japanese cities at will. In August, however, atomic bombs were dropped on the cities of Hiroshima and Nagasaki. At the same time, Soviet troops invaded Manchuria. These events sufficed to induce the Japanese to surrender.

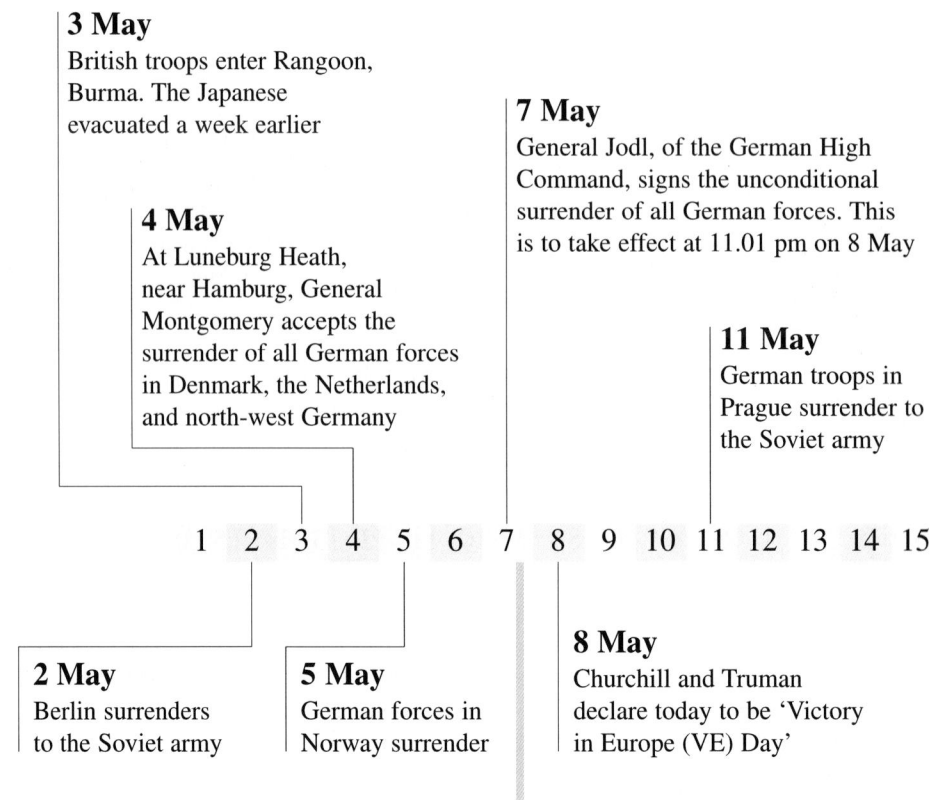

3 May
British troops enter Rangoon, Burma. The Japanese evacuated a week earlier

4 May
At Luneburg Heath, near Hamburg, General Montgomery accepts the surrender of all German forces in Denmark, the Netherlands, and north-west Germany

7 May
General Jodl, of the German High Command, signs the unconditional surrender of all German forces. This is to take effect at 11.01 pm on 8 May

11 May
German troops in Prague surrender to the Soviet army

1 2 3 4 5 6 7 8 9 10 11 12 13 14 15

2 May
Berlin surrenders to the Soviet army

5 May
German forces in Norway surrender

8 May
Churchill and Truman declare today to be 'Victory in Europe (VE) Day'

January *February* *March* *April* *May* *June*

17 January
The Soviet army captures Warsaw from the Germans

4–11 February
Churchill, Roosevelt, and Stalin meet at Yalta in the Crimea

20 March
British forces capture Mandalay in Burma from the Japanese

1 2 3 4 5 6 7 8 9 10 11 12 13 14 15 16 17 18 19 20 21 22 23 24 25 26 27 28 29 30

1 April–22 June
In a bitterly contested operation US troops eventually capture Okinawa, a vital air base for the planned invasion of mainland Japan

18 April
A German army group trapped in the 'Ruhr pocket' in Germany surrenders: 325,000 prisoners are taken

25 April
At Torgau, a village on the River Elbe, the first contact is made between US and German troops. Germany is effectively cut in two

30 April
In Berlin Hitler appoints Grand Admiral Donitz as his successor, then kills himself

12 April
Roosevelt dies, and the vice-president, Harry Truman, becomes US president

16 April
Soviet forces cross the River Oder, to the east of Berlin

25 April–26 June
The San Francisco conference, the inaugural meeting of the United Nations, is held

29 April
German forces in Italy surrender unconditionally

28 April
Mussolini is captured and shot by Italian partisans

Nazi Surrender
Montgomery reads surrender papers, 4 May 1945

8 August
The Soviet Union declares war on Japan with effect from 9 August

14 August
Emperor Hirohito announces the unconditional surrender of all Japanese forces

6 August
An American bomber drops an atomic bomb – the first ever to be used operationally – on Hiroshima. A large area of the city is destroyed, killing thousands

9 August
An American bomber drops the second operational atomic bomb on Nagasaki

15 August
Today is celebrated as 'Victory over Japan (VJ) Day'

1 2 3 4 5 6 7 8 9 10 11 12 13 14 15 16 17 18 19 20 21 22 23 24 25 26 27 28 29 30

16 July
The first atomic bomb is successfully tested at Alamogordo in New Mexico

28 August
Japanese forces in Burma formally surrender

| *July* | *August* | *September* | *October* | *November* | *December* |

26 July
When the general election result is declared Churchill resigns and is replaced as British prime minister by Attlee

12 September
Japanese forces in Singapore formally surrender

17 July–2 August
Truman, Stalin, and Churchill (replaced by Clement Attlee on 28 July, after the British general election) meet at Potsdam in Germany to discuss peace terms and the war against Japan

2 September
The surrender of Japan is officially signed on board the American battleship *Missouri* in Tokyo Bay

Victory and peace
Rejoicing crowds in Piccadilly Circus, London, during mass victory celebrations, 8 May 1945.

Who's Who

Alexander, Field Marshal Sir Harold *(1891–1969)*

He commanded the British army in France in May–June 1940 during the Dunkirk evacuation. In May 1942, although unable to stem the Japanese advance in Burma, he organized the retreat into India. Becoming C-in-C of Middle East Command in August 1942 he laid down the framework within which Montgomery could beat Rommel at the second battle of El Alamein and pursue him to defeat in Tunisia. From January to May 1943, as Eisenhower's deputy and commander of Allied ground forces in North Africa, he was responsible for the campaign leading to the Axis surrender. He was C-in-C of the 15th Army Group, which invaded Sicily in July 1943, and then C-in-C of the Allied forces during the subsequent campaign. From November 1944 he was Allied Supreme Commander in the Mediterranean.

Auchinleck, General Sir Claude *(1884–1981)*

As C-in-C in India from November 1940, he successfully and swiftly suppressed the April 1941 revolt in Iraq; this led Churchill to make him C-in-C of the Middle East two months later. His November 1941 offensive to push Rommel westwards was initially successful, but the tide turned, and the Eighth Army was eventually thrown back into Egypt. Although he succeeded in halting Rommel at the first battle of El Alamein in July 1942, he had lost the confidence of Churchill, who replaced him with Alexander. In June 1943 he again became C-in-C in India, with the critical task of organising India's resources for the campaign to expel the Japanese from Burma.

Bradley, General Omar N. *(1893–1981)*

In February 1943 he took up a role on Eisenhower's staff in North Africa, then became deputy commander of the 2nd US Corps before succeeding Patton as commander in April 1943. With his corps he distinguished himself during the campaign in Sicily that started in July 1943. June 1944 saw him commanding the First US Army attacking Omaha and Utah beaches during the Normandy landings, and in August 1944 he took over the Twelfth US Army Group. Among his major successes at this time was his contribution to the

closing of the 'Falaise pocket' and the consequent destruction of the German Seventh Army. During the Ardennes campaign of December 1944/January 1945 (the 'Battle of the Bulge') he made the crucial decision that Bastogne should be held at all costs, followed by the equally important decision to despatch Patton's Third US Army to relieve the town.

Chamberlain, Neville *(1869–1940)*

British Conservative Prime Minister from May 1937, in common with many others he believed that the right way to deal with Hitler was to 'appease' him, that is to agree to each of Hitler's demands, or acquiesce in each of his acts of aggression, in the hope that it would be his last. At the same time Chamberlain built up the British armed forces as an insurance policy. The high point of appeasement came in September 1938, when Chamberlain agreed in Munich that Germany could occupy the German-speaking frontier areas of Czechoslovakia. The next year brought increasing disillusionment with German intentions, Chamberlain agreed to guarantee Poland against attack, and in September 1939 he declared war on Germany when Hitler refused to withdraw from Poland. In May 1940, in a debate in the House of Commons on the fiasco of British attempts to expel German forces from Norway, it was clear that Chamberlain had lost the confidence of the House. He resigned, and Churchill took over as Prime Minister in a coalition government.

Chiang Kai-shek, Generalissimo *(1887–1975)*

As President of China and C-in-C of the Chinese armed forces he spent much of the 1930s compromising with the constantly probing and encroaching Japanese — who had occupied Chinese Manchuria in 1931 — while preparing to fight them. That day came, rather earlier than Chiang would have liked, in July 1937, and for the next four years China was Japan's only adversary. When war broke out in December 1941 between Japan and Britain and America, Chiang was appointed Supreme Commander of Allied Forces in the China theatre, and the American General Stilwell became his chief of staff. Although Chinese troops gave a good account of themselves against

the Japanese in Burma in late 1943, Chiang's main concern was always with China itself. His widening rift with his erstwhile Communist allies led him to reserve his best-equipped troops for fighting them rather than the Japanese. When the war ended, and the Japanese, undefeated in China, at last left the country, the stage was set for the showdown between Chiang and the Communists, which ended with his withdrawal to Taiwan in 1949.

Churchill, Winston Spencer *(1874–1965)*

During the 1920s he constantly warned about the dangers of a rearmed Germany, and during the period of appeasement in the 1930s he rallied the forces of those who were convinced that it would end in tears. In September 1939 a reluctant Chamberlain made him First Lord of the Admiralty, a job which he threw himself into with gusto. When the abject failure of British intervention in Norway (to a great extent actually of Churchill's making) led Chamberlain to resign, Churchill, as the only Tory acceptable to the Labour Party, became prime minister in a coalition government. Within six weeks France had fallen and Britain and the Empire had no allies. Churchill's personality and oratory maintained morale at home, and he devoted enormous effort to persuading the US to provide more help than neutrality should have allowed; Lend-Lease was the triumphant culmination of his efforts. He had always hoped that the US would enter the war, and when the Japanese attack in December 1941 brought it about he was sure that victory was certain. His experience of the problems of alliance politics in the First World War made him determined that the Grand Alliance should be a

living reality. Although at first he was able to dominate the Alliance because of his strategic vision developed when Britain was fighting alone, he accepted with reasonably good grace increasing American claims to seniority. Despite alarm at Roosevelt's tendency to think his relationship with Stalin could moderate Soviet plans to dominate postwar eastern Europe, he never let such differences develop into an Anglo-American rupture. His energy and strategic inventiveness continued almost unabated throughout the war, and it came as a severe shock to him to find himself rejected in the July 1945 general election, so that in the middle of the Potsdam meeting with Truman and Stalin he was replaced by Attlee.

Clark, General Mark *(1896–1984)*

In June 1942 he took command of the 2nd US Corps in England, and in November 1942 became Deputy Supreme Commander — under Eisenhower — for the North African landings. (Shortly before the landings he had been put ashore to hold discussions with pro-Allied French officers.) He was then appointed commander of the Fifth US Army for the Italian campaign. In September 1943 he commanded the landings at Salerno, during which he led a crucial defence against German tanks. Although his forces managed to capture Naples in October 1943, they were unable to break through German lines and reach Rome. Clark's landings in January 1944 at Anzio, behind the German lines, formed part of his efforts to escape from the impasse. In May 1944 the Allies embarked on a drive to reach Rome, and Clark was later criticized for what appeared to be an obsession with capturing the city ahead of the British, even though that meant disobeying his orders to encircle the Tenth German Army. He succeeded Alexander as Army Group commander in Italy in December 1944, and in May 1945 he received the surrender of German forces in Italy.

Crerar, General Henry *(1888–1965)*

Between the wars he was heavily involved in building up the Canadian army. In 1941 he became Chief of the Canadian General Staff, but later resigned in order to take command of the 1st Canadian Corps in the

Italian campaign of 1943. In the Normandy campaign starting in June 1944 he was C-in-C of the First Canadian Army and, despite disagreements with Montgomery, led his forces throughout much of the heavy fighting that culminated in German defeat in May 1945.

Cunningham, Admiral Sir Andrew *(1883–1963)*

When war broke out Cunningham was C-in-C of the British Mediterranean fleet. In July 1940, after the fall of France, when there was a danger that the French fleet in Algeria might pass into German hands, a Royal Navy force bombarded and disabled that fleet with heavy loss of French lives, although Cunningham persuaded another French fleet at Alexandria to disarm without bloodshed. In November 1940 he ordered a successful air attack on the Italian fleet in its home harbour at Taranto, and in March 1941 he was present at the night action off Cape Matapan in Greece when a powerful Italian naval force was surprised and destroyed. Thereafter Mussolini preferred to keep his vessels in port. Cunningham was responsible for evacuating British troops from Crete in May 1941 and for helping to supply Malta between June 1940 and May 1943. In October 1943 he became First Sea Lord — head of the British Admiralty — and was intimately involved in the vital naval arrangements for the D-Day landings of June 1944.

de Gaulle, Brigadier-General Charles *(1890–1970)*

After fighting in the campaign of May–June 1940 to stem the German invasion of France, de Gaulle was flown to Britain and made an appeal to the French people to reject the armistice with the Germans negotiated by Petain. Soon afterwards he was, with some hesitation and misgivings, recognized by the British government as "the leader of all free Frenchmen". Despite an initial failure of all but a handful to rally to his cause, and despite his complete — and distasteful — dependence on Britain (and later the US), he gradually made his organization into the accepted government-in-waiting of France. His regular forces played a significant, if junior, part in the 1944 Liberation of France, by which time the internal Resistance was also for the most part loyal to him. His long campaign, often monomaniac in its intensity, ensured that post-war France was treated as a victor and

that, despite the humiliations of defeat and the compromises of collaboration, she possessed the self-confidence and stability to again play a leading role in world affairs. Although he formed a provisional government in September 1944 he resigned in January 1946, possibly expecting an appeal to return which never — at least not until 1958 — materialized.

Doenitz, Grand Admiral Karl *(1891–1980)*

In 1935, when the post-First-World-War ban on Germany's building of submarines was lifted, Hitler appointed Doenitz C-in-C of U-boats. Although by the time war broke out he only had 22 U-boats capable of operating in the Atlantic, eventually over 1,000 were built. His concept of using the submarines as "wolf packs", and his close coordination and control of attacks, led to merchant shipping losses that caused grave Allied concern. In January 1943, while remaining in charge of U-boats, he replaced Raeder as C-in-C of the German Navy. Nominated as his successor by Hitler before his suicide on 30 April 1945, Doenitz was head of state and C-in-C of the armed forces until his arrest by the Allies on 22 May 1945. He received a ten-year sentence at the Nuremberg trials.

Doolittle, Colonel James *(1896–1993)*

Roosevelt was keen to retaliate against Japan for Pearl Harbor. The only possible platform for bombers was an aircraft carrier, but Japanese patrols meant that a carrier could not approach close enough to Japan to use normal carrier aircraft. It was decided to ship heavier, longer-range, B25 bombers instead, and for the planes

to fly on to China after their mission since they were incapable of landing on a carrier. Volunteers led by Doolittle trained by taking off from an airstrip marked to the size of the carrier flight deck, but they had no opportunity to practice from an actual carrier. In April 1942 USS *Hornet*, with 16 B25s on her deck (they were too big to go below), sailed on her mission. When it was realized that a Japanese patrol had reported the force's presence, the planes were launched to make the attack by day instead of by night. Several targets, including Tokyo, were successfully bombed, and all the planes flew on to their Chinese rendezvous. Of the 80 crew members, 71, including Doolittle, survived. He went on to command US bomber forces targeting North Africa in 1942, Italy in 1943, and Germany in 1944.

Dowding, Air Chief Marshal Sir Hugh *(1882–1970)*

He became C-in-C of the RAF's new Fighter Command in 1936, and spent the next four years improving Britain's air defences, including the building of a chain of radar stations round the south coast of England, the development of tactics to meet an air attack, and the construction of an efficient system of communications linking radar stations, command centres, airfields and planes. During the fighting in Norway and France in May–June 1940 he became unpopular with the government by resisting the move overseas of irreplaceable fighter squadrons. When in the summer of 1940 the *Luftwaffe* attempted to establish air superiority over southern England, Dowding's strategic handling of the 'Battle of Britain' allowed him to use to best effect his precarious resources of machines and pilots. Fighter Command's failure to intercept the devastating German raid on Coventry in November 1940 probably contributed to his being summarily replaced.

Eisenhower, General of the Army Dwight D. *(1890–1969)*

After filling several high staff posts in Washington he was sent to London in June 1942 as commanding general of the European Theater of Operations, US Army, the administrative headquarters for the build-up of US troops in Britain. He agreed with the British view that a cross-Channel invasion of France was out of the question for 1942. When, instead, it was decided to invade French North Africa, he became C-in-C of

the Allied Expeditionary Force, displaying his ability to make his American and British subordinates a unified team. After the successful conclusion of the North African campaign he was the Allied commander for campaigns in Sicily and Italy in 1943, and in January 1944 became Supreme Commander for the landings in Normandy. Against stiff opposition he insisted that in the period before D-Day in June 1944 a major air offensive should be directed against French railways: this is now seen as vital to the success of the invasion. Although his subordinate commanders — Montgomery, Bradley and Patton — were allowed great latitude, Eisenhower supplied the strategic overview. Once the Germans had begun to retreat he ordered a rapid pursuit, and during the invasion of Germany his "broad-front" strategy prevailed over Montgomery's preference for a quick dash to Berlin. Although taken by surprise by the counter-attack in the Ardennes in December 1944, he used the crisis as a welcome opportunity to smash the Germans' last reserves.

Freyberg, Lieutenant-General Sir Bernard *(1889–1963)*

As commander of the New Zealand Division in Greece he conducted a skillful withdrawal to Crete in the face of the overwhelming German invasion of April 1941. The next month, commanding all Allied forces in Crete, although unsuccessful in his defence of the island he did manage to have over half his 30,000 troops evacuated to Egypt. The forces that he then led in the Western Desert campaign fought with distinction, admired by their German opponents for their toughness and effectiveness.

Goebbels, Josef *(1897–1945)*

He introduced the use of the greeting, "Heil Hitler!" and the use of the term "Fuhrer" as applied compulsorily to Hitler. In March 1933, he became Minister of Information and Propaganda, and in this position was able to purge from creative life all Jews and anyone not prepared to support the Nazi line. As early as May 1933 he orchestrated the public burning of books by suspect authors. There was a consequent dramatic increase in emigration among creative people. He used his talents as a speaker to spread the Nazi message by radio, and during the war directed radio propaganda at all of Germany's enemies. Later he organized relief to areas devastated by Allied bombing in an effort to boost morale. He demonstrated his loyalty to Hitler in July 1944 when, after the explosion of the bomb intended to kill the Fuhrer, he assumed military command of Berlin to frustrate the designs of the conspirators. As a reward he was made Plenipotentiary for Total War, enabling him further to indoctrinate the German people. Although he was named Chancellor in Hitler's political testament, the day after Hitler's suicide in April 1945 he supervised the poisoning of his six children and had himself and his wife shot.

Goering, Reichsmarschall Hermann *(1893–1946)*

In 1933, when Hitler came to power, Goering was appointed Prussian Minister of the Interior, then President of Prussia. He used these positions to develop means of repression that were to become depressingly familiar, not least concentration camps and the Gestapo, the "state secret police". He also became Minister of Aviation and started the build-up of the *Luftwaffe*, in contravention of the Treaty of Versailles. In March 1935 he became C-in-C of the *Luftwaffe*, which by 1939 had become the most powerful air force in the world and performed spectacularly in Poland in September 1939, Norway in April–May 1940, and France and the Low Countries in May–June 1940. Thereafter its record was patchy. Although it still bombed British cities, it failed to destroy the RAF in the "Battle of Britain" in August–September 1940, it could not supply the German army besieged in Stalingrad in November 1942 to February 1943, and it became increasingly ineffectual against the Allied Strategic Air Offensive on Germany. In April 1945, with Hitler trapped in Berlin and Goering in south Germany, Goering's suggestion that power be transferred to himself resulted in his arrest by the SS. He escaped and gave himself up to the Americans. At the Nuremberg trials he was sentenced to death, chiefly for having signed the decree authorizing the "final solution" to the "Jewish problem". He committed suicide with cyanide a few hours before his intended execution.

Gort, Field Marshal Lord *(1886–1946)*

Chief of the Imperial General Staff since 1937, when the war started he became C-in-C of the British Expeditionary Force to France.

In May 1940, realizing that the BEF was in danger of becoming trapped, he fortunately disobeyed orders and maintained contact with the Channel coast, thus making the Dunkirk evacuation possible. Churchill ordered him to return to England from Dunkirk, which he reluctantly did, passing the command to Alexander. In April 1941 he became C-in-C in Gibraltar, and in May 1942 moved as C-in-C to Malta, where for the next two years he organized the island's defences effectively in the face of relentless Axis air attack.

Groves, General Leslie *(1896–1970)*

When the US government decided in August 1942 that it would go ahead with the development of a bomb depending on nuclear fission — an atomic bomb — it was clear that the programme, code-named the "Manhattan Project", would require a huge industrial and administrative effort in addition to the necessary physics research. The decision was also taken to have the military run it. Groves, an army engineer by training, was chosen to lead the project, and it was in no small part due to his energy, and to his administrative skills in managing a team 125,000 strong, that a practicable bomb was eventually successfully tested in July 1945 and was ready for use against Japan the following month.

Guderian, General Heinz *(1888–1954)*

In the 1930s he developed the theory that tanks could be used as the main method of mobile warfare. From 1935 onwards he was instrumental in building up the panzer divisions that were to embody his successful blitzkrieg tactics. He commanded a panzer corps in the Polish campaign of September 1939 and in France in May–June 1940, on both of which occasions blitzkrieg worked superbly. Although in the Russian campaign of Summer 1941 he and his 2nd Panzer Group initially swept all before them with panache and considerable success, disagreements with Hitler led to his being dismissed in December 1941. Only in March 1943 was he given another appointment, as Inspector-General of Armoured Troops. He refused to join — but did not betray — the July 1944 plot to kill Hitler. Becoming chief of the Army General Staff he again disagreed violently with Hitler, and in March 1945 he was sent on indefinite sick leave.

Halsey, Admiral William ("Bull") *(1882–1959)*

When the Japanese attacked Pearl Harbor in December 1941 Halsey was the most senior Pacific carrier admiral, and his carriers were fortunately at sea. During the next few months he led raids against various Japanese-held Pacific islands. He became Commander of Carriers, Pacific Fleet, and in April 1942 he commanded the task force from which Colonel Doolittle launched his raid on Tokyo. In October 1942 he took command of the South Pacific Force, and his ships played a key part in the successful Guadalcanal campaign. From early 1943 until early 1944 he directed the campaign in the Solomons, which culminated in the neutralization of Rabaul as a Japanese base. In October 1944, as commander of Third Fleet covering the landings on Leyte, he allowed his fleet to be lured away by a Japanese feint, and the subsequent decisive defeat of the Japanese in the battle of Leyte Gulf was due to luck, Japanese errors, and the prompt actions of his colleagues rather than to his own strategic acumen.

Harris, Air Chief Marshal Sir Arthur *(1892–1984)*

When he became C-in-C of RAF Bomber Command in February 1942 he had become convinced, by observing German attacks on London, that incendiaries were more effective than high explosive in the destruction of cities. He had also read the report, commissioned by the British war cabinet, that showed how ludicrously inaccurate, and therefore ineffective, RAF night bombing raids had been. In May 1942 he demonstrated the effectiveness of his 'area bombing' methods by mounting a huge '1,000 bomber' raid that devastated Cologne. He continued in his belief that area

bombing on its own could win the war despite mounting evidence that German morale was unaffected, despite increases in accuracy brought about by improved direction-finding techniques and the development of the Pathfinder force, and despite official Allied policy that bombing should concentrate on specified industrial targets.

Hess, Rudolf *(1894–1987)*

Sharing a cell with Hitler after the failure of their Munich putsch of 1923, Hess not only transcribed the bulk of Mein Kampf from Hitler's dictation, but contributed to the book the concept of Lebensraum — space for the expansion eastwards of the German people. Although he was nominally second (after Goering) to Hitler, in reality he steadily lost influence after Hitler's assumption of power in January 1933. Almost certainly without Hitler's knowledge, on 10 May 1941 he parachuted into Scotland to put forward a plan whereby Britain and Germany should enter into alliance against Russia. Churchill quickly decided to have no truck with the plan, nor did he allow mention of the plan to become public. Hitler denounced Hess as a madman, and he was detained in Britain under psychiatric supervision for the rest of the war. At the Nuremberg trials he was sentenced to life imprisonment, and by the time of his suicide in 1987 he had long been the last Nazi prisoner in Spandau prison, his release blocked by seeming Soviet vindictiveness.

Himmler, Heinrich *(1900–1945)*

Becoming head of the SS in 1929, he spent the next ten years increasing its numbers and developing it into a ubiquitous state security organization whose function was to disseminate

Nazi ideas and ensure the elimination of dissidents. After the German victory in Poland in September 1939, he and the SS were given complete control of the annexed parts of the country, and displaced a million and a half Poles eastwards to make way for German-speaking groups. When in August 1943 he was made Minister of the Interior he became responsible for administering the system of forced labour and the extermination programme against the Jews. During the final months of the war, seeing how things must end and believing that the Allies would see him as the German leader in place of Hitler, he scaled back the "Final Solution" and put out tentative peace feelers. After the German surrender he was captured while attempting to escape in disguise and took poison.

Hirohito, Emperor (1901–1989)

Although treated as a divine figure by most Japanese, Hirohito, who became Emperor in 1926, was, by established convention and his own inclinations, a constitutional monarch whose "Imperial Will" automatically coincided with the government's policy. Despite his private, behind-the-scenes attempts to avoid war, his sense of constitutional propriety made him acquiesce in the government's preparations. During the war itself he played no part in developing Japanese strategy. He did, however, recognize from 1942 onwards that the tide of war was likely to flow ever more strongly against Japan, and privately urged on General Tojo, the Prime Minister, the need for a settlement. Only in August 1945, after the destruction of Hiroshima and Nagasaki, and with the military still refusing to surrender, did the Prime Minister, Suzuki, a sympathiser with the Emperor's views, ask Hirohito to decide. On 14 August he broadcast his Imperial Will that the nation should "endure the unendurable" and accept defeat. During the postwar occupation he remained on the throne, although he renounced his divinity and had his powers more democratically circumscribed than before.

Hitler, Adolf (1889–1945)

Hitler was eventually, despite early derision and rejection, able to capitalize on the widespread bewilderment and resentment in Germany stemming from the perceived injustice of the Versailles settlement after the First World War. His National Socialist — Nazi — programme seemed to promise

national regeneration and self-respect. Although he became Chancellor in January 1933 by constitutional means, he soon set about dismantling the constitution so that within a few years he held all the reins of power as unchallengeable dictator. From 1935 onwards he outfaced the victors of Versailles in a series of bloodless victories: rearming Germany, occupying the demilitarized Rhineland, and taking over Austria and parts of Czechoslovakia. Only when he invaded Poland in September 1939 in pursuit of Danzig and access to East Prussia did he unexpectedly find that he had pushed Britain and France beyond the limits of acceptable appeasement. In the ensuing war he was at first extremely successful, particularly against France in May–June 1940, when he championed Manstein's plan in the teeth of opposition from his own high command. From the time of his surprise attack on the Soviet Union in June 1941 it was clear that his supreme confidence in his own military genius was in danger of losing the war. His insistence on personally making all important military decisions, combined with a refusal to countenance withdrawal whatever the circumstances, negated the undoubted prowess of German arms. The same faults again proved fatal in the Normandy campaign starting in June 1944. Not until April 1945 did he finally recognize that not even the huge self-sacrificial effort which he had induced his country to make could stave off utter defeat. He committed suicide, bitterly reproaching Germany for failing to be worthy of his leadership.

Jodl, General Alfred (1890–1946)

As a leading member — and latterly as chief — of the Operations staff of the German High Command throughout the war, he was one of Hitler's closest military advisers, and his advice was highly regarded by the Fuhrer. On 7 May 1945, at Reims, he signed on behalf of the German government the unconditional surrender of all German forces. At the Nuremberg trials he was found guilty on all four counts, sentenced to death, and hanged.

Kesselring, Field Marshal Albert (1885–1960)

In June 1936 he became the Luftwaffe's Chief of Staff, during the Polish campaign of September 1939 he commanded the First Air Fleet, and

in the French campaign of May 1940 the Second Air Fleet. His decision to use bombers against British airfields in the Battle of Britain in August–September 1940 could conceivably have led to victory if a decision had not been taken at a higher level to divert the attack to London. After a time in Russia and as C-in-C of Axis forces in the Mediterranean, he became C-in-C in Italy. He swiftly reinforced Sicily in response to the Allied landings of July 1943, then managed to extricate his forces across the strait of Messina to the mainland in an operation that was as creditable to him as it was shameful to the wrong-footed Allies. When Italy surrendered in July 1943 he moved with speed and efficiency to disarm Italian troops and occupy central and southern Italy. Becoming C-in-C of Army Group C in November 1943, he organized an extremely effective campaign that forced the Allies to fight bitterly for every mile. Injury in a road accident in October 1944 removed him from active service until he replaced the dismissed von Rundstedt in western Germany in March 1945. In May 1947 a British military court sentenced him to death for ordering the execution of Italian hostages, but following an appeal for clemency by Churchill, the former British Prime Minister, the sentence was commuted to life imprisonment.

Laval, Pierre (1883–1945)

French prime minister at various times in the 1930s, he finally resigned in 1936 when the Hoare-Laval Pact was repudiated by the British government. After the German defeat of France in June 1940 he became vice-premier in Petain's government. When Petain became head of state in the Vichy regime administering unoccupied France, Laval became his deputy. He instituted a policy of collaboration with the Germans, hoping thereby to extract German concessions. Lack of such concessions led to his resignation in December 1940, he was wounded in an assassination attempt in August 1941, and in April 1942 he became head of government. His renewed policy of collaboration continued to bear little fruit, so that he was unable to prevent the Germans from occupying Vichy France in November 1942, and his willingness to send French workers to Germany, and to hand over foreign Jews living in France, led to his being held in increasing contempt. In July 1945, having fallen into the hands of the new French authorities, he was

sentenced to death after a trial that lacked the usual legal decencies. Although he took cyanide minutes before his execution he survived for long enough to be brought before the firing squad.

Leahy, Admiral William D. (1875–1959)

A friend of Roosevelt from the time of the First World War, he was Chief of Naval Operations from 1937–1939. In 1941 he became US ambassador to Vichy France, where he tried to ensure that the government did not cooperate too wholeheartedly with Germany. When, in July 1942, he was appointed Roosevelt's Chief of Staff and chairman of the US Joint Chiefs of Staff, he became one of the president's closest advisers, accompanying him to all the Allied conferences. Although retained by Truman after Roosevelt's death, he had less influence.

LeMay, Major-General Curtis E. (1906–1990)

In October 1942 he was commanding a bomber group in England. During the course of the USAAF's strategic air offensive against Germany, in an effort to counteract the proven inaccuracy of daytime bombing he developed the tactic of "pattern bombing", in which an entire formation of bombers dropped its bomb load simultaneously. In August 1944 he took over Twentieth USAAF's 20th Bomber Command, which flew supplies from India to China and also bombed Japan using Superfortresses based in India but flying their missions from China. When in January 1945 he took command of Twentieth USAAF's 21st Bomber Command, which bombed Japan from the Marianas, he ordered a change in tactics from high-level, high-explosive, precision raids to low-level incendiary raids. One such raid in March 1945 destroyed a quarter of Tokyo in a firestorm. In July 1945 he was given command of Twentieth USAAF, and the next month became Chief of Staff to General Spaatz, commander of the USAAF's Strategic Air Forces in the Pacific.

MacArthur, General Douglas (1880–1964)

After serving as US army Chief of Staff in the 1930s he became military adviser to the Philippines government before retiring in 1937. In July 1941, recalled to active service, he was appointed Commander of US Forces in the Far East. Immediately after the Japanese attack on Pearl Harbor in December 1941, not only did he inexplicably fail to bomb Japanese airbases in Formosa, but he allowed his aircraft to be caught and destroyed on the ground when the Japanese — flying from Formosa — bombed US airfields in the Philippines. His defence of the Philippines against the subsequent invasion was unsuccessful, and when it was clear that the end was nigh Roosevelt ordered him to escape to Australia. "I shall return," he said. Based in Australia, in April 1942 he took command of Allied forces, at first chiefly Australian, in the South-West Pacific Area. Despite his claim to have originated "island-hopping" (that is, bypassing strong Japanese garrisons wherever possible and leaving them to be dealt with when they could no longer affect the Allied advance), he did not initially favour the technique, although later he used it to good effect. In October 1944 he fulfiled his promise to return to the Philippines by landing at Leyte Gulf. In April 1945, taking command of all US Army forces in the Pacific, he became Ground Commander for the projected invasion of Japan, and when the dropping of two atomic bombs made an invasion unnecessary he accepted the Japanese surrender in Tokyo Bay in August 1945. For some years thereafter he ruled occupied Japan as an enlightened despot.

Manstein, Field Marshal Erich von (1887–1973)

After serving as chief of staff to Rundstedt in the Polish campaign of September–October 1939, he managed, against bitter official resistance but with Hitler's backing, in altering the strategy for defeating France. His plan succeeded brilliantly in the short, decisive campaign of May–June 1940. He proved his competence in the field by leading a corps in the French campaign and in Russia in June 1941. Now given an army, he led it to further success in southern Russia. Commanding Army Group Don from November 1942, he was unable to relieve the German army in Stalingrad, which surrendered in February 1943. From now on, despite some brilliantly conducted counter-offensives, he became part of the general story of the German forces in Russia — dogged resistance but inexorable retreat. In March 1944 he was dismissed by Hitler. In 1949 a British military court found him guilty of war crimes in Russia. He served only four years of his eighteen-year sentence.

Marshall, General of the Army George C. (1880–1959)

Becoming US Army Chief of Staff in 1939 he pursued the task — often difficult and unrewarding in view of his country's neutrality and sentiment — of increasing the army's numerical strength and fighting potential. He persuaded Congress to introduce conscription, and by the time of Pearl Harbor in December 1941 he had ensured that the army was in a position where it could contemplate fighting. He remained convinced that the defeat of Germany must be given priority over that of Japan, and he consequently felt let down by British unwillingness to invade France in 1942. He was strongly opposed to the 1942 North Africa landings, considering that they would not contribute directly to Germany's defeat. Although he was the obvious choice to command the Normandy landings of June 1944, Roosevelt left the decision to him, he passed it back to the President, and the President decided to retain him in the post in which he was giving such valuable service. Soon after the war against Japan he retired, but from 1947 to 1949 he was US Secretary of State. During this period he instituted the Marshall Plan of large-scale economic aid to reinvigorate the exhausted economies of western Europe.

Molotov, Vyacheslav (1890–1986)

On 3 May 1939 Stalin replaced the Soviet People's Commissar for Foreign Affairs, Litvinov, with Molotov. This was a clear signal — at least to Hitler — of the abandonment of Litvinov's pursuit of a policy of "collective security" in collaboration with Britain and France, and of the beginning of moves to seek an

accommodation with Germany. On 23 August 1939 these moves reached fruition with the signature in Moscow of the Nazi-Soviet Pact by Molotov and Ribbentrop, the German foreign minister. The Pact enabled Hitler to invade Poland on 1 September 1939 free from the fear of a hostile Soviet reaction. When in due course, on 22 June 1941, the Germans invaded the Soviet Union, Molotov was as taken aback as Stalin, but remained cooler. He remained in his Foreign Affairs post throughout the war — and after — conducting negotiations with his new-found Western allies.

Montgomery, Field Marshal Sir Bernard (1887–1976)

Experience during the First World War made him determined that battles should be won with minimum casualties, which entailed detailed planning, endless training, and maximum support for his troops in the field. His conduct with the British Expeditionary Force in France in May–June 1940 was noticed by his corps commander, Brooke, which stood him in good stead when the latter became Chief of the Imperial General Staff. In August 1942, becoming Commander of the dispirited Eighth Army in North Africa, he reinvigorated his troops, and his meticulous planning led to victory over Rommel in the second battle of El Alamein in October 1942. This marked a turning point, and the Germans were, despite Allied setbacks along the way (some of them Montgomery's fault), eventually eliminated from North Africa. Although he commanded armies in Sicily and Italy the unalloyed success of El Alamein was not repeated. As Allied Land Commander (under Eisenhower) for the Normandy landings in June 1944 he contributed hugely to the planning, and then, after the breakout from the beaches, to the pursuit of the Germans across France and the Low Countries into Germany. Despite errors, notably the ill-advised attempt to capture the Rhine bridges at Arnhem, he eventually personally accepted the surrender, at Luneburg Heath in May 1945, of all German forces in north-west Germany, Denmark, and the Netherlands.

Morshead, Lieutenant-General Sir Leslie (1889–1959)

When the war began in 1939 he was commander of the Australian 18th Brigade. From April to October 1941 he and the 9th Australian Division caught the imagination of the Allied

public with their courageous defence of the port of Tobruk in Libya against determined German efforts to retake it. When two British offensives were unsuccessful in raising the siege, the Australian government insisted that Australian troops should be replaced with other nationalities, with the result that they were not in Tobruk when Rommel finally (though temporarily) captured it in June 1942. Morshead and his division played an important part in the second battle of El Alamein, which turned the tide in the Western Desert. They later fought against the Japanese in New Guinea. Commanding 1st Australian Corps from May 1945 he took part in amphibious operations in Borneo.

Mussolini, Benito (1883–1945)

He founded his Fascist party in 1919 as a militant anti-socialist and nationalist movement. By 1922 he was able to lead it in a march to Rome to demand power, and by 1925 he was dictator of Italy. Although he had grandiose ideas of establishing Italy as one of the great powers, he never planned for a major war, preferring smaller adventures like the occupation of Abyssinia in 1935–1936, help to Franco's Nationalists in the Spanish Civil War between 1936 and 1939, and the annexation of Albania in 1939. His signature of the Pact of Steel with Hitler in May 1939 never led to coordinated military planning, and when Britain and France went to war with Germany in September 1939 he declared Italy's "non-belligerence". Only in June 1940, with Germany clearly about to conquer France and with the British army chased back across the Channel at Dunkirk, did he feel the time ripe for him to enter the war on the side of the obvious winner. This was the beginning of the end for his dreams of Italian greatness. He lost his African colonies to the British; a large part of his Mediterranean fleet was sunk; only German intervention saved his armies in the Western desert from annihilation, and that annihilation was only postponed; and a similar dispiriting drama was played out with his invasion of Greece. In July 1943, in the aftermath of major industrial strikes in Milan and Turin in February and with the Allies consolidating their landings in Sicily, he was deposed by the Fascist Grand Council and arrested. After the Italian armistice of September 1943 the Germans set him free and installed him as head of a puppet regime, but in April 1945 he was captured and shot by communist partisans.

1945, and Okinawa in April–June 1945. In August 1945 he signed the Japanese surrender document on behalf of the US government.

Nimitz, Fleet Admiral Chester W. (1885–1966)

After the Japanese attack on Pearl Harbor in December 1941 the C-in-C of the US Pacific Fleet was retired in disgrace. Succeeding him, Nimitz immediately ordered carrier raids on Japanese-held islands and the Doolittle raid on Tokyo. He set about salvaging the ships sunk in Pearl Harbor and building new ships to an astonishingly fast schedule. In April 1942 he became C-in-C of the Pacific Ocean Areas. His conduct of the battle of Midway in June 1942 resulted in a stinging defeat for the Japanese; he followed it up with the successful Guadalcanal campaign of August 1942 to February 1943. While his submarines sank the bulk of Japanese merchant shipping, his amphibious operations gradually cleared the Central Pacific of Japanese garrisons. His forces were involved, together with MacArthur's, in the landings on Leyte in October 1944 and in the battle of Leyte Gulf, from which the Japanese navy never recovered. He ran the operations to capture Iwo Jima in February–March

Patton, General George S. (1885–1945)

In the North African landings of November 1942 he commanded the Western Task Force that landed at Casablanca. Taking command of the 2nd US Corps after their defeat in Tunisia in March 1943 he succeeded in restoring the Corps' shattered morale. Although his leadership of the Seventh US Army during the Sicilian campaign of July–August 1943 was aggressive and inspired, he narrowly avoided dismissal for his attitude toward soldiers suffering from combat exhaustion and for his at least moral complicity in two incidents involving the shooting of German and Italian prisoners of war. After training the 3rd US Army in England he led it from August 1944 in the Normandy campaign. By the end of that month his forces had crossed the Seine and reached the Meuse. No sooner had he captured Metz in December 1944 than the Germans launched their Ardennes counter-offensive. This was Patton's finest hour: by instantaneously changing his army's direction and moving with unprecedented speed he managed to relieve Bastogne and disrupt the German advance. By March 1945 he had crossed the Rhine, and by the end of the war he had reached Czechoslovakia and Austria. As military governor of Bavaria, in September 1945 he recommended that Nazis should hold administrative posts. He was thereupon relieved of his command, and in December 1945 he died following a road accident.

Petain, Marshal Philippe (1856–1951)

As the hero commanding the French army that had withstood the German onslaught at Verdun in 1916, Petain was brought out of retirement and appointed vice-premier in June 1940. On becoming premier a few days later his only policy was to seek an armistice. Under its terms the Germans occupied three-fifths of France, including Paris, and Petain's government settled in Vichy to administer the remainder. Although as head of the new state he attempted to portray himself as being removed from the collaborationist policies of governments under Laval and others, he cannot escape responsibility for the results of these policies. For example, the paramilitary Milice, notorious for

their brutality in hunting down Jews or members of the resistance, swore a personal oath of loyalty to Petain. In July 1945, having voluntarily returned to France from Switzerland, he was tried and condemned to death but had his sentence commuted to life imprisonment, from which only his death in 1951 released him.

Raeder, Grand Admiral Erich (1876–1960)

He became C-in-C of the German navy in 1928, and set about increasing its strength. The Anglo-German Naval Agreement of June 1935 accelerated the build-up, and the grand plan was to have a world-class fleet by 1944. But when war came, he realized that his plans would never be fulfiled. No further surface vessels were laid down; efforts were devoted to U-boats. In the early part of the war his auxiliary cruisers were successful against British merchant vessels, and the increasing number of U-boats in the Atlantic caused mounting Allied losses. But the sinking of the Bismarck in May 1941 led Hitler to withdraw his remaining large surface vessels from the Atlantic to Norwegian waters. In December 1942 the failure of the pocket battleship Lutzow and the cruiser Admiral Hipper to destroy a British Arctic convoy induced him to go further and effectively decommission the surface navy. This was too much for Raeder, who resigned. At Nuremberg he was sentenced to life imprisonment but was released in 1956.

Ramsay, Admiral Sir Bertram (1883–1945)

He organized the naval operation to pluck the British Expeditionary Force from the beaches at Dunkirk in May–June 1940, was deputy naval C-in-C for the North African landings of November 1942, and commanded one of the task forces for the Sicilian landings in July 1943. From December 1943 he was in charge of planning Operation Neptune, the assault phase of Overlord, the Normandy landings that eventually went ahead in June 1944. Neptune's success is a tribute to the brilliance of his planning. In January 1945 he was killed in an air crash.

Rommel, Field Marshal Erwin (1891–1944)

After distinguishing himself in the French campaign of May–June 1940 he took command of the newly-formed *Afrika Korps* in North Africa

in February 1941. Despite being under orders to act defensively, he launched an attack that drove the British a considerable distance back. Although in November 1941 he had to give ground, his January–July 1942 offensive captured Tobruk and, with the British preparing to evacuate Cairo, got as far as El Alamein in Egypt. At the second battle of El Alamein in November 1942 he was defeated by Montgomery and forced to start the retreat that eventually ended with his return to Germany in March 1943 and the surrender of all Axis forces in North Africa in May. In August 1943 his plans for occupying northern Italy were implemented, but when his views on the conduct of the campaign were not accepted he was put in charge of improving French coastal defences against the expected invasion. In January 1944 he became C-in-C of Army Group B, whose function was to repel any such invasion. He was badly wounded in an air attack on his car in July 1944, and after the failure later that month of the plot to kill Hitler one of the conspirators implicated him. Given the choice of trial or suicide he took poison on the understanding that his family would come to no harm.

Roosevelt, Franklin Delano (1882–1945)

With his country unwilling to get involved in a European war, Roosevelt, who began the first of his four presidential terms in 1933, felt he had no option but to go along with the national mood, while nevertheless striving to change it. Hitler's growing success in 1939 and 1940, and the realization that only Britain's defiance prevented Germany from controlling the Atlantic, enabled him to persuade Congress and the public to allow him to channel increasing quantities of vital aid to Britain; the Lend-Lease Agreement of March 1941 set the seal on America's becoming the "arsenal of democracy". When Japan attacked Pearl Harbor in December 1941, Germany immediately declared war on the US, although the escalating number of maritime incidents would in any case inevitably have led to war in a matter of months. Despite intense domestic pressure to direct the main effort at defeating Japan, he remained steadily in favour of "Germany first", although a considerable effort was put into the Pacific war. As American armed strength grew, his strategic vision played an increasingly important part in the conduct of the war. However warm and fruitful his personal relationship with Churchill, he always remained suspicious that Britain might be pursuing its own global agenda. Having met Stalin at Tehran in November 1943 he concluded that he could do business with him as one reasonable man with another, and the next seventeen months did not completely free him from this delusion, although he did not share with Stalin information about the secret project to develop an atomic bomb. In April 1945, three weeks before Germany surrendered, he suddenly died, to be succeeded by Vice-President Truman.

Rundstedt, Field Marshal Gerd von *(1875–1953)*

His adherence to the Prussian military code, involving both unquestioning loyalty and unwillingness to get involved in politics, made him admired by his fellow officers and therefore led to his being cultivated by Hitler as a means of securing the loyalty of the entire officer corps. He helped to plan the Polish campaign of September–October 1939, and led Army Group South. In May–June 1940, with equal success, he commanded Army Group A in the French campaign. He took command of the ground forces for the projected invasion of Britain, then, in June 1941, led Army Group South when Germany invaded the USSR. In December 1941 Hitler dismissed him for making a withdrawal contrary to orders but later forgave him when he realized the military necessity of Rundstedt's action. In March 1942 he became C-in-C West, organizing the occupation of Vichy France in November of that year. When Rommel served under him from late 1943 they differed over methods of defeating a likely invasion, but when it occurred in June 1944 they were as one in arguing against Hitler's refusal to allow any withdrawal. This led to Rundstedt's dismissal in July 1944, but later the same month he was ordered to preside over the "Court of Honour", which expelled the officers involved in the failed plot against Hitler so that they could face the "People's Court". Again becoming C-in-C West in September 1944 he conducted the inexorable retreat with considerable skill. (He disagreed with, and was not involved in, the Ardennes counter-offensive.) He was blamed by Hitler for allowing the Rhine bridge at Remagen to fall into American hands in March 1945, and yet again dismissed. The British charged him with war crimes, but his poor health led to the charges being dropped, and he was released in 1949.

Spaatz, General Carl A. ("Tooey") *(1891–1974)*

As an official US observer in England in 1940 he was responsible for reports that convinced Roosevelt that Britain could survive German air attack and thus was worth helping. In July 1942 he took command of Eighth USAAF in England, in November 1942 he became Allied Air Forces Commander in North Africa, in February 1943 Deputy (to Tedder) Allied Air Commander in the Mediterranean, and in December 1943 C-in-C of US Strategic Air Forces in Europe. The Combined Bomber Offensive had been suffering unacceptably heavy losses, but from February 1944 the losses were hugely diminished by Spaatz's tactics for the newly introduced long-range fighters. No longer did the fighter escort simply respond to enemy attack, but it went ahead of the bombers and actively sought out German fighters. Although Spaatz had to defer to Eisenhower's orders to divert bombers to attack French communications before and during the Normandy landings of June 1944, even his reduced attacks on German oil targets had a significant effect on Germany's ability to continue fighting. With Germany defeated, Spaatz formed and led US Strategic Air Forces in the Pacific, overseeing the strategic bombing, and eventually, in August 1945, the atomic bombing, of Japan.

Spruance, Admiral Raymond A. *(1886–1969)*

He commanded the cruiser screen for Halsey's carrier force during the raids on Japanese-held islands in January–February 1942, then imaginatively and deftly commanded one of the carrier groups in the decisive victory over the Japanese at the Battle of

Midway in June 1942. For over a year he was Chief of Staff to the C-in-C of the Pacific Fleet, Nimitz, before becoming Commander of the Central Pacific Force. His plans resulted in the capture of Tarawa and the Marshals, and he contributed to the capture of the Marianas (including Saipan), Iwo Jima, and Okinawa.

Stalin, Joseph *(1879–1953)*

During the period in the 1930s when Hitler was building up Germany's armed strength, Stalin was reasonably confident that any major war would involve only capitalist countries. On the other hand he felt it could do no harm to explore the options for collective security. British and French hesitancy in entering an agreement led him to produce his bombshell, the Nazi-Soviet pact of August 1939, which cleared the way for Hitler to attack Poland and for Stalin to seize eastern Poland and the Baltic countries. In the purges of the 1930s Stalin had exterminated almost all of the Soviet officer corps; this, together with a reliance on outmoded, non-motorized tactics, had an adverse effect on Soviet military efficiency during the war with Finland from November 1939 to March 1940. By the time Germany invaded the Soviet Union in June 1941 these deficiencies were beginning to be remedied, but the attack caught Stalin completely off guard. For some days he remained in a state of deep shock. At length he belatedly, but with demonic energy, set about organizing resistance. Entire factories were transported east of the Urals, there to begin the output of weaponry that was eventually to help push the Germans back. In the meantime Stalin's tactics were to prove costly in Soviet lives, and it was only when he began to leave the

fighting to some of his more talented generals that the German advance was stemmed at Stalingrad in February 1943 and turned into a relentless, two-year retreat. With his realization that Hitler was almost definitely going to be defeated, and that Soviet armies would reach Germany itself, he prepared to reap the rewards in terms of imposing communist regimes on most of eastern Europe, and even on half of Germany. It was a remarkable triumph for one nearly overwhelmed only four years earlier.

Stilwell, General Joseph W. *(1883–1946)*

In February 1942 Stilwell, a fluent Chinese speaker, became head of the US military mission in China and Allied Chief of Staff to Chiang Kai-shek, the Chinese Generalissimo. Leading two Chinese armies in Burma, he was caught up in the general retreat before the inexorable Japanese advance. Despite lack of high-level clarity about his terms of reference he laboured with a considerable degree of success to increase the fighting efficiency of his Chinese troops, and in August 1944 his efforts were rewarded by the capture of Myitkyina in northern Burma, which opened up a shorter air route for supplies to China than previously. About this time the Japanese began a major offensive in China. When Roosevelt suggested that Stilwell should take command of the Chinese forces, Chiang Kai-shek not only disagreed but ensured that Stilwell was removed from his post.

Tedder, Air Chief Marshal Sir Arthur *(1890–1967)*

In May 1941 he became C-in-C of the Middle East Air Forces and did a great deal to improve cooperation between the army and the air force, for example using bombers to clear a path for ground troops through enemy defences ("Tedder's carpet"). He was later appointed Vice Chief of Air Staff and in February 1943 Allied Air Commander in the Mediterranean. From December 1943, as Deputy Supreme Commander, Allied Expeditionary Force (that is, second in command to Eisenhower) he was in charge of planning the air aspects of the Normandy landings of June 1944. So complete an air superiority did he achieve that the *Luftwaffe* was almost completely unable to affect the landings, while the Allied air forces were able, virtually unmolested from the air, to intervene against any German counter moves.

Timoshenko, Marshal Semyon *(1895–1970)*

After commanding the Soviet forces that, unopposed, occupied eastern Poland in September 1939 under the terms of the Nazi-Soviet Pact, he led the assault on Finland in November 1939. This proved to be far from a walkover, and it was not until March 1940, after huge Soviet losses, that his campaign of attrition forced the Finns to the negotiating table. Now created People's Commissar for Defence, he set about making good, as best he could in Soviet circumstances, the grievous military deficiencies so painfully exposed by the Finns. In July 1941, soon after the German invasion of Russia, he took command of the Soviet armies in the Smolensk area and used them to delay the German advance on Moscow, but only at the expense of huge losses of men. In November 1941, in the eastern Ukraine, he contrived to force a German retreat which, although not sustainable, was a psychological boost to the Russians. In April–July 1942, in an abortive preemptive strike towards Kharkov and in the subsequent German counter-attack, he lost vast numbers of men and was recalled to Moscow to preserve the propaganda value of his reputation for competence. From October 1942 until his armies made contact with US forces in Austria in May 1945 he was responsible for coordinating operations in various parts of the immensely long German-Soviet front.

Tito (Josip Broz) *(1892–1980)*

Born in Croatia, he became a communist in the 1920s, and in the 1930s spent long periods in Moscow, where he was eventually chosen to lead the Yugoslav Communist Party. When Germany invaded Yugoslavia in April 1941 the existence of the Nazi-Soviet Pact meant that he was under Soviet instructions not to resist, but two months later, when the USSR was in turn attacked, he and his "partisans" (so called in homage to Soviet irregular formations) launched guerrilla war on the Germans and at the same time attempted to start a communist revolution in the country. Over the next few years his fortunes fluctuated. For much of the time he put as much energy into fighting the Cetnik guerrillas led by General Mihailovic — who were loyal to the Yugoslav government in exile in London — as into attacking Germans or Italians. In late 1943 the British decided to ignore his revolutionary proclivities and to channel military support to him as the more effective

anti-German leader. Soviet support followed later, and it was a joint Soviet-partisan army that liberated Belgrade. Despite half-hearted British attempts to ensure that non-communist elements were included in the postwar Yugoslav government, it was inevitable that Tito and the communists should soon squeeze out the last trace of opposition.

Tojo Hideki, General *(1885–1948)*

As chief of staff of the Kwantung Army that virtually ran Japanese-occupied Manchuria, he played an important part in the events that led to the outbreak of war between Japan and China in July 1937. From May 1938 until January 1939 he was Army Vice-Minister, and from July 1940 Army Minister, in the Japanese cabinet, representing the army position and opposing any compromise with the Chinese government. He was instrumental in Japan's signing the Tripartite Pact with Germany and Italy in September 1940. In October 1941 he was asked by the Emperor to become prime minister while remaining army minister and a general on the active list; two months later he launched the Japanese attack on Pearl Harbor. Despite Japan's initial string of stunning successes against the western powers, problems began to mount. Her maritime trade, and thus her ability to import vital raw materials, was progressively strangled by US submarine activity. The trend of military operations in the Pacific, whether land warfare or naval, was also clearly in the Allies' favour. In February 1944 Tojo appointed himself Army Chief of Staff so that he could direct campaigns personally, but the natural effect was that when such

campaigns failed — as at Saipan in June 1944 — he was personally blamed. Unable to withstand the tide of criticism he resigned in July 1944. After the Japanese surrender he made a botched attempt to shoot himself, was found guilty of war crimes, and was hanged in December 1948.

Truman, Harry S. *(1884–1972)*

Vice-President Truman suddenly found himself president when Roosevelt unexpectedly died on 12 April 1945, less than a month before Germany's surrender. At his conference with Churchill and Stalin at Potsdam in July–August 1945 he became convinced that post-war cooperation with Russia, valuable as it might be, could only be achieved on the basis of American toughness. When the first atomic bomb test proved successful (he had known nothing about its development until he became president) he decided to use the bomb against Japan, primarily because it would save the American casualties involved in an invasion, but undoubtedly also for its demonstration to Russia of the power of this weapon which only America possessed.

Wavell, Field Marshal Sir Archibald *(1883–1950)*

He was C-in-C of the Middle East Command from just before the war, and in 1940 and 1941 successfully put the Italians to flight in the western desert. Initially, in August 1940, unsuccessful in British Somaliland, he oversaw a campaign which resulted in total Italian defeat in East Africa by May 1941. Having had to divert many troops to meet the German invasion of Greece in April 1941, he was forced by Rommel to retreat in the western desert. Churchill thereupon, in July 1941, replaced him with Auchinleck and moved him as C-in-C to India. In January 1942 he moved to Java as head of ABDA (American/British/Dutch/Australian) Command, to try and repel the Japanese invasion of south-east Asia. When this proved impossible the command was dissolved and Wavell again became C-in-C in India; he now supervized the British withdrawal from Burma. In October 1943 he was appointed Viceroy of India, and his political skills — for example, persuading Gandhi not to actively oppose the war and attempting to reconcile the differences between Hindus and Muslims — ensured that he held the post until 1947, shortly before Indian independence.

Yamamoto Isoroku, Admiral *(1884–1943)*

When he was a vice admiral and vice minister for the navy in the 1930s his vehement opposition to war with the western powers led militaristic extremists to plot his assassination. He was convinced that should such a war break out Japanese success would be short-lived. When it became clear that his government was determined on war he concluded that Japan's best hope lay in destroying the bulk of the US fleet by a surprise attack on Pearl Harbor. Only after a long campaign of persuasion did his colleagues agree to what they saw as an appallingly high-risk venture, but Yamamoto's meticulously constructed plan was successfully carried out in December 1941. His next ploy, to lure the surviving US fleet to certain defeat at Midway Island in June 1942, turned into a severe Japanese defeat, partly thanks to American ability to read Japanese cyphers. In April 1943 a deciphered message revealed to American forces that he was about to make a flight in the Solomons. High-level permission was given to intercept his plane and shoot it down.

Zhukov, Marshal Georgi *(1896–1974)*

Stalin made him chief of the Soviet general staff in January 1941. Although his outspokenness led to his dismissal from the general staff six months later, he remained on the Stavka, the committee responsible for strategic planning. In September 1941, put in charge of the army group defending Leningrad, he appeared to have success in saving the city, although Hitler's orders were to besiege it but not enter it. Similarly, in October–December 1941, his defence of the western approaches to Moscow was greatly aided by the weather, first rain and mud, then a freeze. When, in August 1942, the German advance towards the Caucasus threatened to be unstoppable, Stalin gave Zhukov, together with another future marshal, Vasilevsky, carte blanche. Their plans resulted in the crushing German defeat at Stalingrad in February 1943, the lifting of the threat to the Caucasus, and the wiping out of the German gains of that summer. The Zhukov-Vasilevsky collaboration continued in 1943 — including the Soviet victory in the battle of Kursk in July–August — and 1944, when, in June–July, they destroyed German Army Group Centre around Minsk. Zhukov later led the drive towards Berlin, and it was his forces that captured the city in May 1945.

This index should be used in conjunction with the cross-references that have been added to many stories and chronologies to enable readers to follow events in particular areas more easily. Cross-references are either an arrow and a date, or just an arrow. The arrows point only forward in time, and the dates that follow may refer to stories or chronologies. If the next entry is in the same month, only a day will be given: for example, (→7). If the next entry is in a later month, the day and month are given: for example, (→3/8). If the next entry is in the following year, again the day and month only are given. Arrows on their own indicate that a story on the same topic follows, *in the same week*. To avoid confusion, only one cross-reference ever appears at the end of an entry. The index should be used to find earlier entries on a subject. The index itself includes "see" and "see also" cross-references. In addition, please note:

1. When one country invades another, subsequent events are shown under the name of the invaded country. So German and/or Japanese policy towards occupied countries after invasion is not listed under Germany and/or Japan (foreign affairs) but under Poland, China etc as appropriate.
2. Most capital cities have separate entries, rather than being included in the entries for their countries.
3. Page numbers in Roman type refer to main reports; those in italics refer to entries in the weekly chronology summaries.
4. The dates of entries in the index are those of the datelines of the reports, and not necessarily the dates of the events recorded in the reports.

A

A Nightingale Sang in Berkeley Square (song) 147
A-Go (operation) *513, 536*
A4 rockets *306, 338,* 402
– see also V-weapons
AA
– (see Anti-aircraft guns)
Aabo 58
Aachen 22, 560, *562, 569, 571, 575, 581*
Aalborg 73
Aalesund 236
Aaron Ward (destroyer) 397
Abadan 218
Abbendorft 632
Abbeville 94, 358
ABC1 *158, 159, 173*
ABDACOM *262, 276*
Abdul Ilah 176
Abercorn, Duke of 268
Abetz, Otto *144, 174*
Abner Read (destroyer) 578
Abwehr
– (see Espionage)
Abya *660*
Abyssinia 13
Acasta (destroyer) 91
Achates (destroyer) 364
Achilles (cruiser) 45, 47
Achse (operation) 443
Ack-ack
– (see Anti-aircraft guns)
Acker, Achille van *605, 648*
Aconit (corvette) *389*
Active (destroyer) *338*
Ad Tecesan 176
Adachi, Hatazo 479, 509
Adak 431
Addis Ababa *174,* 177, 185
Abbu Atoll *270,* 288
Aden 97, *103*
Admiral Graf Spee (pocket battleship) 26, 45, 47, 65
Admiral Hipper (cruiser) 73, *145, 161,* 166, 315, 364, *572, 621*
Admiral Scheer (pocket battleship) 26, 135, *273,* 315, *621*
Admiralty Islands 288, *492, 493, 494, 495, 498, 499, 506,* 517
Adolf Hitler Line *518*
Adriatic Sea *123, 141, 144, 530,* 559
Aegean Sea 182, *203, 444, 450, 455, 460, 541, 543, 634*
Afmadu 161
Afridi (destroyer) *78*
Afriker Korps 160, *161, 172,* 175, *210,* 230, 253, 264, 303, 311, 313, 329, 337, 348, 357, *383,* 407, 453
– see also Desert War; North Africa; Panzerarmee Afrika; Rommel, Erwin
Aftonbladet (newspaper) 454
Agate, James *593*
Agedabia *174*
Agira *428*

Agno river *599*
Agordat 159
Agreement (operation) 334
Aibrac, Raymond 268
Aichi D3A Val carrier-bombers 397
Ainsworth, Walden 373
Air Transport Auxiliary (see ATA)
Air-raid precautions (see ARP)
Air-to-surface-vessel (see ASV)
Airacobra fighters 472
Airacomet jet aircraft *338*
Airedale (destroyer) 309
Aisne river *94*
Aitape 509, *512, 541*
Ajax (cruiser) 45, 47, 65, 127, 172, *593*
Akagi (aircraft carrier) 248, 305
Akashi *643, 644*
Aksai river 361
Akyab 286, 297, 361, *420,* 480, 486, *596*
Alakamisy *344*
Alam el Halfa 329
Alamein
– (see El Alamein)
Alaska *344*
Albacore torpedo-bombers *280*
Alban Hills *518*
Albania
– Italian troops prepare to attack Greece 10/9/40 *118*
– Italian troops cross into Greece 28/10/40 133
– Greeks surround Koritsa 3/11/40 *134*
– Greeks take Koritsa from Italians 21/11/40 139
– Greeks advance 4/12/40 *141*
– Greeks bombard Klisura 20/12/40 *144*
– Greeks continue advance 23/12/40 *145*
– Greeks push towards Valona as Luftwaffe units arrive 4/1/41 *150*
– Soddu relieved of command as Greeks advance 13/1/41 *154*
– RAF raids Valona 20/1/41 *156*
– Italian counter-attack at Klisura fails 26/1/41 *158*
– Greeks hold out against Italian offensive 9/3/41 *168*
– Greek army cut off 14/4/41 *179*
– Declares war on USSR 28/6/41 *200*
– Freedom fighters kill Italian soldiers in Tirana 28/12/42 *363*
– Allied troops land 29/7/44 *546*
– Resistance ends in capital 17/11/44 *581*
– Partisan fighters liberate Tirana 19/11/44 *583*
Albert Canal 560
Alderney 101
Alencon 550
Alethangyaw *361*
Aleutian Islands

– US sends forces as Japanese prepare attack 20/5/42 *300*
– Japanese raid Dutch Harbor 3/6/42 306
– USAAF attacks Japanese positions on Kiska and Attu 15/6/42 *308*
– US Navy bombards Japanese on Kiska 7/8/42 *321*
– Japanese withdraw from Attu 16/9/42 *333*
– US troops land on Amchitka 12/1/43 *372*
– US Navy bombards Attu 19/1/43 *372*
– Japanese attempt to reinforce Kiska stopped 26/3/43 392
– US plans May invasion of Attu 31/3/43 *394*
– US invasion force sets out for Attu 24/4/43 *400*
– US forces land on Attu 11/5/43 *406*
– US retakes Attu 30/5/43 413
– Japanese to abandon Kiska 8/6/43 *415*
– US bombs Japanese on Kiska 27/6/43 *420*
– US bombards Kiska 22/7/43 *427*
– Japanese secretly evacuate Kiska 30/7/43 431
– US bombards Kiska 5/8/43 *432*
– US and Canadian forces take Kiska 15/8/43 437
Alexander, A V 86, *138*
Alexander, Harold
– Takes command of remaining troops at Dunkirk 31/5/40 *89*
– Last Allied soldier to leave Dunkirk 4/6/40 92
– Takes command of Allied forces in Burma 4/3/42 *278*
– Appointed C-in-C Middle East 6/8/42 *321*
– Orders no withdrawal at Kasserine Pass 20/2/43 383
– Reports success in Desert War to Churchill 13/5/43 407
– Worries about feud between Montgomery and Patton 17/7/43 426
– Arrives in Anzio 22/1/44 482
– Insists no withdrawals from Italy 29/2/44 493
– Orders troops to break Gustav Line 5/5/44 *512*
– Orders US attack on Valmontone 25/5/44 519
– Plans to break through Gothic Line 11/8/44 551
– Stands down armies in Italy 20/11/44 584
– Promoted to field marshal 26/11/44 584
– Plans Eighth Army attack in Italy 24/3/45 615
– Biography 680

Alexandria *103, 107, 187, 253,* 309, 313, *412*
Alexishafen *510*

Alfonso XIII, King of Spain *161*
Alfrey, C W *383*
Algeria
– see also Desert War
– Demilitarized zone to be established 24/6/40 100
– Allied Torch landings resisted 10/11/42 350
– RAF uses Blida as base for "shuttle" raids 24/6/43 419
Algiers 350, 357, *470, 489, 495, 517, 550, 558*
Ali Furughi 217
Ali Mansur 218
Aliens' Tribunals 84
All Hands (film) 62
Allanmyo *626*
Allen, Chesney 51
Allied Control Commission *663*
Allied Military Government of Occupied Territories
– (see AMGOT)
Allied Supreme War Council 21, 24, *38,* 61, 71, *87*
Allied Tactical Air Force *417*
Allies
– (see individual countries)
Alor Star 250
Alphand, Herve 226
Alsace-Lorraine 98, *105, 134, 327, 584*
Alsterufer (blockade-runner) 473
Altavilla 444
Altenfjord 315, 442
Altmark (supply ship) 62, 64, 353
Aluminium *103*
Amagiri (destroyer) *432*
Amba Alagi *184,* 187
Amboina 268, 275
Ambrosio, Vittorio 376
Amchitka *372*
Amery, Leo 83
AMGOT *425*
Amiens *87,* 91, 94, *325,* 491
Amoy *637*
Amsterdam 80, 81, *163, 164,* 166
Amsterdam Island *546*
Anamba Islands 272
Anami, Korechika 649
Anastasyevsk *394*
Anatolia 49
Anch'u *432*
Ancona *543*
Andalsnes *75, 76,* 78
Andaman Islands *276, 280, 286,* 480
Andarte 493
Anders, Wladyslaw *212,* 516
Anderson shelters 106, *153*
Anderson, John 84, 105, 447
Anderson, Kenneth 350, 383
Anding 65
Andrews, George 191
Andrews, John 268
Anemone (corvette) *151*
Angaur *543, 573*
Angers 27, *550*
Anglo-US Combined Chiefs of

Staff Committee 268, *270,* 286
Angriff, Der (newspaper) 602
Anielewicz, Mordechai 375
Ankara *515*
Ankong *614*
Anshan *546, 561*
Anson (battleship) *450*
Anson reconnaissance aircraft
– (see Avro Anson)
Antelope (destroyer) 60, *134*
Anthony (destroyer) 298
Anti-Aircraft Command 45
Anti-aircraft guns 117, 189
Anti-Comintern Pact (1938) 13, 15
Anton (operation) 351
Antonescu, Ion 118, 127, *138, 156,* 162, 232, 369, *422, 499, 554*
Antwerp 81, *84,* 397, 408, 557, 560, *571,* 577, 579, *581,* 585, *587,* 588, 598
Anvil (operation) 493
Anzac
– Troops arrive in Egypt 12/2/40 *62*
– Troops arrive in Britain and Palestine 30/6/40 100
– Troops in Greece 9/4/41 *177, 327, 584*
– Troops in Crete 22/5/41 191
– Losses in Crete 1/6/41 195
– Naval Squadron in Battle of Coral Sea 9/5/42 *296*
Anzio 482, *486, 488, 490, 492, 495, 518*
Aogiri *478, 480*
Aosta, Duke of 187
Apamama 465
Aparri 247
Apollonia *231, 239*
Apulia *161*
Aquila (liner) 216
Arabia *103*
Arado jet bombers *417, 592,* 617
Arakan *336,* 361, 380, *390,* 480, 486, *492,* 631
Arandora Star (liner) 102
Arawe *470, 481*
Arcadia conference 259
Archangel 221, 224, 231, 302, 336
Archerfish (submarine) *584,* 638
Arctic 74, *216,* 296, 298, 302, *312,* 315, *360, 450, 470, 473, 503, 510*
Ardennes 64, 81, 82, 85, *587, 591,* 598, 601
Arethusa (cruiser) 353
Arezzo *543, 549*
Argenta 615, 622, *624*
Argentan 550
Argentia Bay *206*
Argentina
– Pro-Nazi plot uncovered 10/8/41 *214*
– To remain neutral 6/7/42 *314*
– Pro-Allied military coup 5/6/43 415

– Breaks with Germany and Japan 26/1/44 483
– Coup attempt 15/2/44 *490*
– Declares war on Axis powers 27/3/45 616
– German U-boat surfaces 10/7/45 *647*
Argonaut (cruiser) 357
Argus (aircraft carrier) 214, 224, *239,* 300, 309
Argyrocastro *142*
Arita 75
Arizona (battleship) 248
Ark Royal (aircraft carrier) 21, 26, 37, *43,* 123, 161, *181,* 191, *192, 195,* 226, 239
Armavir 369, *372*
Armoured bulldozer 529
Arms and the Man (play) *593*
Army Catering Corps 235
Arnhem 565, 567, *624*
Arnim, Jurgen von 393, 407
Arno river *549*
Arnold, Henry H "Hap" *198,* 539
ARP 124
Arras 85, *87,* 560
Arromanches 533
Arsenic and Old Lace (play) 364, *409*
Artois *87*
Arts and Entertainment
– see also Broadcasting; ENSA
– The Lion has Wings (film) 30/10/39 *34,* 51
– Vaughan Williams composes music for wartime hymn 20/12/39 *47*
– Goodbye Mr Chips (film) 12/39 51
– Wuthering Heights (film) 12/39 51
– Stagecoach (film) 12/39 51
– The Wizard of Oz (film) 12/39 51
– Run, Rabbit, Run (song) 12/39 51
– We're gonna hang out the washing ... (song) 12/39 51
– Film censorship 22/1/40 59
– All Hands (film) 6/2/40 62
– Death of John Buchan 11/2/40 *62*
– Gone With The Wind (film) 2/40 66, 76, 414
– Pinocchio (film) 2/40 61, *69,* 147
– Lights out in Europe (film) 14/4/40 *75*
– Myra Hess's National Gallery concerts 20/4/40 75, 128
– Mrs Patrick Campbell (Beatrice Tanner) dies 9/4/40 75
– Writers in SS "black book" 6/7/40 103
– Spare a Copper (film) 8/40 112
– Der ewige Jude (film) 28/11/40 *140*
– The Great Dictator (film) 14/12/40 *142*

– Faithful for ever (song) 12/40 147
– We'll Meet Again (song) 12/40 147
– A Nightingale Sang in Berkeley Square (song) 12/40 147
– The Wizard of Oz (film) 12/40 147
– Rebecca (film) 12/40 147
– Ohm Kruger (film) 4/4/41 *174*
– Al Bowlly killed in air raid 16-17/4/41 *179*
– Target for Tonight (film) 26/7/41 209
– Citizen Kane (film) 12/41 259
– Dumbo (film) 12/41 259
– Fantasia (film) 12/41 259
– Pimpernel Smith (film) 12/41 259, 414
– 49th Parallel (film) 12/41 259
– Sincerely Yours (song) 12/41 259
– Promenade concerts 12/41 259
– Scum of the Earth (book) 12/41 259
– Walton's violin concerto 12/41 259
– Death of Virginia Woolf 12/41 259
– In Which We Serve (film) 12/42 364
– The First of the Few (film) 12/42 364
– The Goose Steps Out (film) 12/42 36
– Mrs Miniver (film) 12/42 364
– Went The Day Well? (film) 12/42 364
– The Maltese Falcon (film) 12/42 364
– Flare Path (play) 12/42 364
– Arsenic and Old Lace (play) 12/42 364, 409
– White Cliffs of Dover, The (song) 12/42 364
– Shostakovich's seventh (Leningrad) symphony 12/42 364
– Casablanca (film) 8/2/43 382
– This Happy Breed (play) 1/5/43 405
– Death of Leslie Howard 3/6/43 414
– The First of the Few (film) 3/6/43 414
– Pygmalion (film) 3/6/43 414
– Life and Death of Colonel Blimp (film) 11/6/43 415
– In Which We Serve (film) 25/8/43 43
– Roll out the Barrel (song) 25/10/43 457
– Filming of battle for San Pietro 11/12/43 468
– Desert Victory (film) 11/12/43 468
– Fires were Started (film) 11/12/43 468
– The Gentle Sex (film) 11/12/43 468
– Millions Like Us (film) 11/12/43 468
– The Battle of Midway (film) 11/12/43 468
– Casablanca (film) 12/43 475
– Sahara (film) 12/43 475
– Bataan (film) 12/43 475
– Stage Door Canteen (film) 12/43 475
– Now, Voyager (film) 12/43 475
– For Whom the Bell Tolls (film) 12/43 475
– Jane Eyre (film) 12/43 475
– I Married a Witch (film) 12/43 475
– In the Mood (song) 12/43 475
– Moonlight Serenade (song) 12/43 475
– American Patrol (song) 12/3 475
– Blues in the Night (song) 12/43 475
– You'll Never Know (song) 12/43 475
– Brazil (song) 12/43 475
– My Heart and I (song) 12/43 475
– Lili Marlene (song) 12/43 475
– BBC Symphony Orchestra 12/43 475
– Being and Nothingness (book) 12/43 475
– The Philadelphia Story (film) 7/1/44 479
– Nazis to wage war on jazz 12/2/44 489
– Target for Tonight (film) 18/2/44 491
– Peer criticizes female "crooners" 7/3/44 495
– Glenn Miller begins a British tour 9/7/44 *541*
– Theatres reopened in London 24/8/44 554
– We are the D-Day Dodgers (song) 27/10/44 577
– Laurence Olivier's film of Henry V 1/12/44 586
– Glenn Miller's plane goes missing 16/12/44 587
– Peer Gynt (play) 12/44 593
– Arms and the Man (play) 12/44 593
– Richard III (play) 12/44 593
– Hamlet (play) 12/44 593
– Huis Clos (play) 12/44 593
– The Glass Menagerie (play) 12/44 593
– The Way Ahead (film) 12/44 593
– Western Approaches (film) 12/44 593
Aruba *65*, *79*, *273*
Arundel Castle (liner) *562*
Arundel Island *440*
Arzeu 350
"Asian Co-Prosperity Sphere" 6
Assamu Maru *59*, *65*
Aschersleben *480*
Ascianghi (submarine) *427*
Ascona 634
Ascq *504*
ASDIC 34, 203, 341, 403
Ashigara (cruiser) *642*
Askey, Arthur 51
Aslagh *301*
Aslito *534*
Asmara *164*, 176
Assab *196*
Assam 496
Assiniboine (destroyer) *321*
Assisi *534*
Assoro 428
Astier de la Vigerie, Henri 362
Astor, Lady (Nancy) 360
Astor, Lord 183
Astoria (cruiser) 321
ASV *138*, 244
ASV II 390
ASV III 390, 403
ATA 38, 55, 106, 151
Atago (cruiser) 459, *575*
Atebrine 455
Athabaskan (destroyer) *438*
Athenia (liner) 18
Athens 164, 182, *469*, *577*, *586*, 593, *603*
Atlantic
– see also Atlantic, Battle of the; Convoys; U-boats
– U-boats sink liner Athenia 4/9/39 18
– U-boat crew captured after attack on Ark Royal 14/9/39 *21*
– First convoy sails from Canada to Britain 15/9/39 22
– U-boat activity stepped up 24/9/39 *26*
– Germans capture US cargo ship City of Flint 9/10/39 30
– RN takes up U-boat challenge 31/10/39 34
– Scharnhorst and Gneisenau sink HMS Rawalpindi 23/11/39 *40*
– German liner scuttled 19/12/39 *47*
– U-boats sink HMS Exmouth 21/1/40 *59*
– HMS Antelope sinks U-boat 5/2/40 *60*
– RN captures German merchant vessels 21/2/40 *64*
– U-boat sunk off Scottish coast 25/2/40 *65*
–"Queen Elizabeth" completes dramatic maiden voyage 7/3/40 67
– Over a million tons of Allied shipping lost 31/3/40 *71*
– U-boats sink Gladiolus, Arandora Star 2/7/40 *102*
– U-boat sinks British merchant cruiser 10/8/40 *109*
– U-boat sinks sloop 27/8/40 *114*
– U-boat torpedoes refugee ship 17/9/40 *120*
– Convoy HX-72 attacked 22/9/40 *123*
– U-boat threat grows 22/9/40 125
– U-boat "wolfpacks" attack convoys SC-7 and HX-79 19/10/40 129
–"Empress of Britain" damaged by bombs 26/10/40 *130*
– Severe Allied losses 29/10/40 133
– HMS Antelope sinks U-boat 2/11/40 *134*
– British submarine sunk 16/11/40 *136*
– British corvette sinks U-boat 21/11/40 *138*
– Armed merchant cruiser sinks U-boat 2/12/40 *141*
–"Admiral Hipper" damaged 25/12/40 *145*
– German battle cruisers reach ocean 3/2/41 *160*
– German raider sinks Egyptian liner 17/4/41 *179*
– U-boat sinks US merchant ship 19/10/41 *233*
– German armed merchantman captured 6/11/41 *237*
Atlantic, Battle of the
– Allied losses growing as U-boat numbers increase 22/2/41 163
– Churchill: "Battle has begun" 6/3/41 *166*
– Attack on convoy FS-429a repelled 9/3/41 *168*
– Scharnhorst and Gneisenau sink 22 ships in one cruise 22/3/41 *170*
– RN captures Kretschmer; Prien and Schepke drowned 17/3/41 171
– US convoy loses ten ships; Thor sinks Voltaire 4/4/41 *174*
– Churchill forms strategy committee as casualties mount 9/5/41 184
– Royal Navy sinks Bismarck 27/5/41 192
– Extended Allied air cover still excludes "Black Gap" 31/5/41 194
– U-boat wolfpack hits convoy HX-133 29/6/41 203
– Allies extend escort system 31/7/41 211
– U-boat sinks HMCS Picotee 12/8/41 *214*
– U-boat sinks SS Aquilla 19/8/41 *216*
– US Navy starts convoy protection 1/9/41 *220*
– U-boat attacks on US ships 4/9/42 22
– US escorts convoy HX-150 16/9/41 *223*
– USS Kearny lost aiding convoy SC-38 17/10/41 231
– HMS Cossack torpedoed 27/10/41 *235*
– USS Somers and Omaha capture the Odenwald 6/11/41 *237*
– HMS Devonshire sinks the Atlantis 22/11/41 *241*
– HMS Dunedin sunk by U124 24/11/41 *243*
– HMAS Nestor sinks U127 15/12/41 *253*
– Hannover sunk in convoy battle 21/12/41 *256*
– Convoy HG-76 sinks U-boats 23/12/41 257
– Type IX U-boats start second "happy time" off US coast 13/1/42 *264*
– U-boats' Triton code creates problems for Allies 1/2/42 270
– U-boat wolfpack hits US convoy 25/2/42 277
– Allied losses increase as Donitz steps up U-boats 1/4/42 287
– First US kill as USS Roper sinks U85 14/4/42 *289*
– German mines sink shipping off US coast 15/6/42 *308*
– King to adopt convoys as Allied losses grow in US waters 1/7/42 313
– British introduce Huff Duff 31/7/42 *319*
– HMCS Assiniboine sinks U-boat 6/8/42 *321*
– Convoy ON-127 suffers huge losses in wolfpack attack 14/9/42 *333*
– Convoy SC-104 survives battle with wolfpack 16/10/42 341
– RAF sinks U-boats 24/10/42 *342*
– Convoy SL-125 losses 31/10/42 *344*
– Churchill chairs Anti-U-Boat Committee 4/11/42 *347*
– Horton takes over as C-in-C Western Approaches 19/11/42 *351*
– One survivor from U515's sinking of SS Ceramic 7/12/42 *357*
– HMSS Hesperus and Vanessa sink U-boat 26/12/42 *361*
– Convoy ONS-15's escort sinks U356 27/12/42 *363*
– HMS Scylla sinks Rhakotis and Viminale 1/1/43 *368*
– U-boats attack convoy SC-118 4/2/43 *378*
– Winter nights help U-boats 9/2/43 382
– U-boats use Falke in attack on convoy UC-1 23/2/43 *384*
– U-boats attack convoy SC-121 6/3/43 *386*
– Allies reorganize defence zones as losses mount 1/3/43 387
– Harvester sunk in attack on convoy HX-228 11/3/43 *389*
– Italian submarine sinks Canadian liner 15/3/43 *390*
– Donitz concentrates attacks in "Black Gap" 21/3/43 393
– HMSS Black Swan and Stonecrop sink U-124 2/4/43 *396*
– HMSS Biter and Pathfinder sink U203 25/4/43 *401*
– New technology helps to close "Black Gap" 30/4/43 403
– U-boat losses in attack on convoy HX-237 13/5/43 *406*
– Donitz's son killed in attack on convoy SC-130 19/5/43 *409*
– Donitz recalls U-boats as German losses increase 24/5/43 413
– HMS Starling and an RAF Liberator both sink U-boats 1/6/43 *414*
– Allies increase attacks on U-boats in Biscay 1/7/43 422
– U-boat losses 24/7/43 *427*
– Battle of Convoys ONS-18 and ON-202 23/9/43 *446*
– 60 U-boats sunk in recent months 9/11/43 *460*
– Donitz commands unsuccessful attack on convoy 17/11/43 *462*
– RN cruisers sink German destroyers in Bay of Biscay 28/12/43 473
– U-boats sinks HMS Warwick 20/2/44 *492*
– US Navy joins RAF to sink U-boat 13/3/44 *497*
– US destroyer captures U505 and her secrets 4/6/44 521
– 19 U-boats sunk this month 30/9/44 *566*
– Schnorkel device improves U-boat capability 21/10/44 574
– Canadian escort sinks U877 27/12/44 *591*
– 5 U-boats sunk off Denmark 5/5/45 634
– RN abolishes convoy system 28/5/45 *640*
Atlantic Charter 9, 215, 262
Atlantic Convoy Conference 387
Atlantic Isle 481
Atlantic Wall *289*, 410
Atlantis (surface raider) *71*, *179*, *241*
Atomic bomb
– Roosevelt orders feasibility study 11/10/39 30
– British government receives proposals 21/3/40 70
– Discovery of plutonium announced 28/3/41 *172*
– British government receives Maud Committee report 30/6/41 203
– Speer reports to Hitler on German research 23/6/42 *310*
– Groves appointed to manage US programme 17/9/42 *333*
– Allies attack German heavy water plant at Vermork 19/11/42 *351*
– Los Alamos chosen as US bomb test site 25/11/42 354
– Roosevelt orders secrets not to be shared with British 28/12/42 *363*
– Second attack on Vermork plant 17/2/43 *383*
– Roosevelt orders research to be shared with British 20/7/43 *427*
– Anglo-US cooperation terms agreed 20/8/43 437
– Plutonium plant opens in Tennessee 4/11/43 *458*
– USAAF bombs heavy water plant at Vermork 16/11/43 462
– Scientists arrive in US to join research project 2/12/43 *465*
– Heavy water ferry sunk in Norway 20/2/44 *492*
– First uranium slug loaded into reactor 13/9/44 *562*
– Anglo-US discussion at Octagon Conference 16/9/44 563
– Churchill and Roosevelt agree on full collaboration 19/9/44 564
– Top-secret bombing team formed 17/12/44 591
– First weapon-grade plutonium ready for shipment 31/1/45 *602*
– Plant for weapon-grade uranium opens 20/2/45 *607*
– Tested in New Mexico 16/7/45 648
– Truman orders its use 25/7/45 *649*
– Preparations for the drop 1/8/45 651
– Enola Gay takes off 5-6/8/45 *652*
– Dropped on Hiroshima 6/8/45 652
– Nagasaki hit by second bomb 9/8/45 653
– Attlee speaks on implications 22/8/45 *658*
– Death toll continues to rise 22/8/45 659
ATS 38, 135, 164, 194, *289*, *406*, 431
Atsugi *660*
Attila (operation) *142*
Attlee, Clement
– Says Labour will join coalition under Churchill only 10/5/40 83
– Lord privy seal and deputy prime minister 14/5/40 86
– Urges nation to keep calm under Emergency Powers Act 22/5/40 88
– Backs Churchill over appeasement 30/5/40 90
– Broadcasts Atlantic Charter terms 14/8/41 215
– Deputy prime minister in reshuffled cabinet 19/2/42 273
– Chairs cabinet meetings in Churchill's absence 18/6/42 308
– Pays tribute to Stalin on Red Army Day 21/2/43 385
– Becomes lord president of the council 25/9/43 447
– Puts limit on Labour cooperation in coalition 23/5/45 639
– Flies home for election results 25/7/45 *649*
– Appoints new ministers 3/8/45 *650*
– Broadcasts news of VJ Day 15/8/45 656
– Speaks on the atomic bomb 22/8/45 *658*
– Warns the nation of coming austerity 25/8/45 659
Attu *306*, *333*, *394*, *400*, *406*, *409*, 413
Aubretia (corvette) 185, 185
Auchinleck, Claude 94, *176*, 198, *203*, 230, 241, 257, 271, 308, 311, 313, 316, *318*, 322, 323, 417, *434*, 680
Audacity (aircraft carrier) *237*, 257
Audisio, Walter 630
Augsburg 291
Augusta *425*
Augusta (cruiser) 215, 524, 652
Aurora (cruiser) *239*, 253, 357
Auschwitz *76*, *94*, 168, 221, *284*, *304*, *310*, *314*, 316, *337*, *353*, 385, 392, 395, *412*, 415, *444*, *448*, *452*, 454, 455, *455*, *462*, *470*, 473, *495*, *504*, 505, 507, 513, *515*, *518*, 534, *537*, 538, 539, *543*, *458*, *558*, *566*, 571, *573*, *575*, *579*, *583*, *584*, *599*, 601, *613*
Ausente valley *515*
Ausonia *515*
Australia (cruiser) 598
Australia (defence)
– see also Anzac; Australian Army; RAAF; Royal Australian Navy
– Conscription introduced 20/10/39 *32*
– Armed services in European war 26/12/39 50
– Menzies moves against Churchill 14/4/41 *179*
– Concern over threat from Japan 9/8/41 212
– Army leave cancelled as Japanese threat grows 5/12/41 245
– Preparations as war comes closer 31/12/41 257
– Japan warns against resisting 22/1/42 *266*
– Japan invades New Britain and New Ireland 24/1/42 267
– To be represented in British war cabinet 27/1/42 *268*
– Japanese attack Darwin 20/2/42 275
– Curtin refuses to send 7th Division to Burma 22/2/42 *276*
–"Australia First" members arrested 25/4/42 292
– Japanese midget subs attack Sydney harbour 1/6/42 *304*
– Fears of Japanese invasion grow 1/6/42 306
– Lend-Lease 3/9/42 *330*
– Japanese bomb Darwin 2/5/43 *404*
– Curtin says invasion danger over 18/6/43 *417*
– Japanese PoWs stage mass escape bid 5/8/44 549
Australia (economics and industry)

– Tax increase to fund defence spending 21/11/40 *138*
– Austerity measures in war effort 4/9/42 330
Australia (foreign affairs)
– Declares war on Germany 3/9/39 20
– Signs pact with New Zealand 21/1/44 482
Australia (home affairs)
– Menzies forms coalition cabinet 14/3/40 *68*
– Menzies re-elected 11/10/40 *127*
– Move to oust Menzies 21/4/41 *181*
– Menzies resigns; Fadden is new PM 28/8/41 *217*
– Curtin leads new government 3/10/41 228
– Austerity measures in war effort 4/9/42 330
– General election called 24/6/43 419
– Labor Party wins general election; Curtin PM again 21/8/43 *436*
– Meat rationing introduced 17/1/44 *481*
– Curtin dies 5/7/45 *646*
– VJ Day celebrations 15/8/45 656
Australia First Movement 292
Australian Air Force
– (see Royal Australian Air Force)
Australian Army
– Anzac troops arrive in Britain 30/6/40 100
– 6th Division at Bardia 17/12/40 144
– 16th Infantry brigade at Tobruk 7/1/41 153
– Fall of Tobruk 22/1/41 157
– At fall of Benghazi 7/2/41 160
– Troops arrive in Singapore 18/2/41 163
– Troops to go to Greece 27/2/41 *164*
– 9th Division besieged by Rommel at Tobruk 10/4/41 *176*
– 6th and 7th Divisions in Syria 13/6/41 197
– Troops take Damur 10/7/41 205
– "Rats" garrisoning Tobruk 18/8/41 217
– Forces fighting with Eighth Army 5/10/41 230
– Tobruk garrison to be relieved 12/10/41 *231*
– I Corps to join 8th Division in defence of Malaya 5/1/42 263
– 8th Division attacked by Japanese at Singapore 9/2/42 273
– Bennett leaves 8th Division for Sumatra 28/2/42 276
– 9th Division arrives in North Africa 4/7/42 *312*
– 7th Division starts landings at Port Moresby 19/8/42 *325*
– 7th and 18th Brigades defeat Japanese at Milne Bay 7/9/42 332
– Blamey takes command of land forces in New Guinea 23/9/42 *336*
– 9th Division at Second Battle of El Alamein 24/10/42 343
– Losses at Gona 10/12/42 358
– Losses at Buna 2/1/43 368
– Troops in Eighth Army 30/3/43 394
– Troops in Operation Cartwheel 30/6/43 421
– 9th Division attempts to take Lae 4/9/43 441
– Advances in New Guinea 19/9/43 *446*
– Special Forces group blows up Japanese ships 30/9/43 448
– Progress on New Britain 9/1/44 *480*
– Troops clear Japanese from Shaggy Ridge 26/1/44 484
– Troops launch attack on New Guinea 11/5/45 634
– Troops land in Borneo 10/6/45 *643*
Australian Navy
– (see Royal Australian Navy)
Australian and New Zealand Army Corps
– (see Anzac)
Austria
– Taken over by Germany 12/3/38 13
– Baldur von Schirach becomes Gauleiter of Vienna 10/8/40 *109*
– Germans begin to deport Jews to Poland 15/1/41 *161*
– Fuel rationing in Vienna factories 1/1/42 *262*
– Allies bomb Wiener Neustadt in first raid 13/8/43 *434*
– Allies in two minds about bombing 17/3/44 498
– French politicians and dissenters set free 5/5/45 *631*
– Declared a republic 15/5/45 *637*
– Allied forces withdraw (1955) 662
Autse 552
Autumn Mist (operation) *587*
Auxiliary Fire Service *54*, 140, 174, 178, 189
– see also National Fire Service
Auxiliary Military Pioneer Corps
– (see Pioneer Corps)
Auxiliary Territorial Service
– (see ATS)
Avalanche (operation) 443
Avellino 448
Avenger (carrier) 334
Avenger torpedo-bombers 426, 644
Avignon 557
Avondale Port (coaster) *634*
Avranches 543, 547
Avro Anson reconnaissance aircraft 99
Avro[co]
– see Avro Anson reconnaissance; Lancaster and Manchester bombers
Awatea (troop ship) 239
Axis
– (see individual countries)
Axmann, Artur *109*, *120*, 193, 270
Axum (submarine) 324
Azad Hind *453*
Azores 413, *436*, 452
Azov *381*
Azov, Sea of *228*, *230*, *233*, *378*, *442*
Azul Division 371, 399, *470*, 513

B

B-17 "Flying Fortress" bombers
– (see Flying Fortress bombers)
B-24 "Liberator" bombers
– (see Liberator bombers)
B-25 "Mitchell" bombers
– (see Mitchell bombers)
B-26 bombers 490
B-29 "Superfortress" bombers
– (see Superfortress bombers)
Ba Maw 432
Bach-Zelewski, Erich von dem 561, 575
Bad Nauheim *587*
Baden 584
Baden-Baden 649
Bader, Douglas 72
Badoglio, Pietro *141*, 429, 434, 440, *448*, 453, *508*, *530*
Baedeker raids *286*, 293, 294, 297
Baghdad *184*
Bagramyan, Ivan 535, 541, 552, 572
Bagration (operation) *518*, *534*, 537, 541
Bahamas *102*, *613*
Bahrein 129
Baker Island *440*
Baker, Josephine 46
Bakhmach 442
Baku 234, 312
Baky, Laszlo 539
Balaklava 509
Balakleya 300
Balcon, Michael 62
Balete Pass *637*
Bali 275
Balikpapan *266*, *571*, *645*
Balkan States 493, 557, 560, 561, 574, *425*
Ballale 405
Balloon bomb *631*
Baltic Sea *26*, *28*, *72*, 400, *401*
Baltic States
– see also Estonia; Latvia; Lithuania
– German-Soviet boundary and friendship treaty: effects 29/9/39 27
– Plebiscites show support for USSR union 15/7/40 *105*
– Ethnic Germans resettled in Reich 25/3/41 173
– German Army Group North moving through to Leningrad 30/6/41 202
– Jews to wear yellow badge 8/7/41 *205*
– 230,000 Jews killed by SS since June 1/12/41 *245*
– 229,052 Jews reported killed by SS Einsatzgruppe 31/1/42 *268*
– Germans confiscate all Jews' property 13/10/42 *340*
– Isolated from East Prussia by Red Army 1/8/44 *548*
– 30 German divisions trapped by Red Army 11/8/44 551
– German counter-offensive 19/8/44 552
– Russians launch major assault on Germans 16/9/44 562
– Red Army launches new offensive 5/10/44 570
Bambang *642*
Bamber Bridge 418
Ban Pong 310
Band Waggon (radio comedy) 34, 51
Bande *591*
Bangkok *340*, *353*, *584*
Banks, Leslie 593
Banska Bystrica 558
Bantry Bay *308*
Baraka river 159
Baranovichi 541
Baranow *548*
Baranowicze *278*
Barbara Line *452*, *455*
Barbarossa (operation) 8, *140*, 144, *158*, *166*, 173, 180, 200
Barbie, Klaus 505
Barce 175
Bardia *110*, *142*, 144, *150*, *151*, *262*, *349*
Barenfels (merchant ship) 506
Barents Sea *294*
Barents Sea, Battle of the 364
Barentu 159
Barham (battleship) *49*, 123, *150*, 172, *192*, 244
Bari *138*, *444*, 450, 467
Barlow, Thomas 278
Barmantsak, Lake 352
Barneville *534*
Barrow 632
Barrage balloons 45, 189
Barre, Louis *349*, 353
Bartholomew, Harry Guy 282
Bartley Ridge *428*
Bartolomeo Colleoni (cruiser) *105*
Barton, Cyril J (VC) 502
Basabua *325*
Basch, Victor *480*
Basilan Island *613*
Basra *179*, *184*
Bassein *639*
Bastia 451
Bastogne 588, *589*
Bataan 258
Bataisk *319*
Batavia *276*
Bath 293
Batory *97*
Battipaglia 443, *444*
Battle light bombers
– (see Fairey Battle light bombers)
Battle of Britain
– Under way 10/7/40 *103*
– RAF counters Luftwaffe attack at "Hellfire Corner" 29/7/40 107
– Luftwaffe offensive postponed by weather 5/8/40 *109*
– RAF Fighter Command counters increased Luftwaffe attack 8/8/40 109
– RAF and Luftwaffe losses after Adlertag 15/8/40 *110*
– RAF counters Luftwaffe attacks all round coast 17/8/40 111
– RAF heroism 16/8/40 112
– Luftwaffe wrecks RAF planes on airfields 18/8/40 *112*
– Biggin Hill among RAF airfields hit by Luftwaffe 31/8/40 *114*
– RAF fighter losses as Luftwaffe starts Blitz on cities 7/9/40 117
– RAF and Luftwaffe losses 9/9/40 *118*
– Luftwaffe tactics change gives RAF respite 14/9/40 118
– RAF success against Luftwaffe 15/9/40 7, *120*
Battle of Midway 9
Battleaxe (operation) *198*
Battles
– (see under name, except for Battle of Britain)
Batu Pahat 267
Batumi 312
Baudouin, Paul 102, *150*
Bauska 562
Bavaria 623
Bayeux 531
Baytown (operation) 440
BBC
– (see Broadcasting)
Beaufighter fighters 136, 171, 304, 386
Beaufort bombers *174*, *196*
Beaugency *562*
Beaver (operation) 503
Beaverbrook, Lord 86, *103*, 109, 186, *200*, 228, 273, 290, 447
Beaverburn (freighter) 61
Beck, Ludwig 544, 546
Beda Fomm *160*
Beeson 439
BEF
– Prepares to leave for France 3/9/39 17
– Strength in France 11/9/39 21
– Strength in France 11/10/39 *30*
– Condition 28/10/39 *34*
– Leave cancelled 1/4/40 *57*
– Concentrated at Dunkirk 25/5/40 87
– Resisting Germans while evacuation from Dunkirk starts 27/5/40 89
– Evacuation from Dunkirk completed 4/6/40 92
– Losses at Dunkirk 4/6/40 93
– Troops on Lancastria lost 17/6/40 99
Being and Nothingness (book) 475
Beirut *196*, 206, 207, 460
Belev, Alexander 390
Belfast *179*, *184*, 301, *330*
Belfast (cruiser) *40*, 473
Belfort Gap 577, *581*
Belfrage, Bruce 147
Belgian Congo *140*
Belgium
– Belligerents' troops to be interned 3/9/39 20
– Neutrality to be respected by Germany 11/11/39 *36*
– German invasion threat 5/11/39 37
– Allies agree line of defence 14/11/39 *38*
– On state of alert for German invasion 13/1/40 *55*
– Troops' leave cancelled 14/1/40 *57*
– Warned by Vatican of imminent German attack 30/4/40 77
– State of emergency declared 9/5/40 *79*
– Germany invades 10/5/40 80
– Allies plan defensive line 11/5/40 81
– Forces pull back behind Meuse 11/5/40 82
– Brussels falls 17/5/40 *84*
– King Leopold sets up HQ at Bruges 18/5/40 85
– German forces reach Channel 20/5/40 *87*
– Surrenders on King Leopold's orders 28/5/40 90
– Troops rescued at Dunkirk 4/6/40 92
– Government in exile moves to London from France 19/6/40 *97*
– Germans annex towns 29/7/40 *107*
– La Libre Belgique begins 15/8/40 *110*
– Government established in London 22/10/40 131
– Degrelle wants more collaboration with Germany 1/1/41 *150*
– Independent Front resistance formed 15/3/41 *168*
– Colonial troops seize Gambelo in Ethiopia 22/3/41 *170*
– Free Belgian troops accept Italian surrender in Ethiopia 4/7/41 205
– Anti-Bolshevik campaign 7/7/41 *205*
– Degrelle leads Walloon Legion to fight USSR with Germans 8/8/41 *212*
– Red Orchestra spy network broken by Germans 20/6/42 308
– Government in exile asks US to warn on Axis atrocities 31/7/42 319
– First trainload of Jews sent to Auschwitz 4/8/42 *321*
– 5,000 Jews deported to Auschwitz 30/9/42 *337*
– Rexists asked to spy for Germany 2/12/42 *356*
– Civilians killed in USAAF raid on Antwerp 5/4/43 397
– Colonial troops fighting with Allies 4/43 402
– RAF and USAAF raids 14/5/43 408
– Resistance workers publish fake Nazi newspaper 2/11/43 *458*
– Hitler Jugend slaughters 86 people 2/4/44 *504*
– Exiled government gives Allies free hand 16/5/44 517
– German army evacuates Brussels 3/9/44 *560*
– US First Army takes Liege 8/9/44 *560*
– Canadian forces enter Zeebrugge 10/9/44 *562*
– Canadian troops land at Breskens 9/10/44 *571*
– Resistance fighters agree to lay down arms 18/11/44 *581*
– Germans counter-attack in the Ardennes 16/12/44 588
– Battle of the Bulge: US troops cut off at Bastogne 22/12/44 590
– Air forces join battle in the Ardennes 5/1/45 597
– Government of national unity formed 11/2/45 *605*
– Socialists call for king's abdication 29/5/45 *640*
– Premier and cabinet resign 16/6/45 *643*
– King refuses to abdicate 19/6/45 *644*
Belgrade *168*, 177, 574
Belhamed 245
Bell[co]
– (see Airacomet jet aircraft; Airacobra fighters)
Bell, George 301, 489
Bellicose (operation) 419
Belostrov *220*
Belsen 488, 614, 626, *639*, *642*
Belzec *280*, *296*, *337*, *344*, *353*, 420
Ben Gardane 382
Benes, Eduard 14, *38*, 105, 469
Benevento *450*
Bengal (minesweeper) *349*
Bengal, Bay of 381, 480
Benghazi *120*, *138*, *154*, 160, *163*, *174*, *181*, *195*, 257, 335, 399
Benina *138*
Bennett, Donald 329
Bennett, Gordon 257, 274, 276
Benouville *520*
Bentschen 601
Berbera 114
Berchtesgaden *522*, *537*, *541*, *626*, 632
Berdichev *478*
Berdyansk *230*
Beresina river 206
Bergen *73*, 74, *353*, 506, 563
Bergen-op-Zoom *575*
Berggrav, Bishop *288*
Bergman, Ingrid 382, 475
Berislav *495*
Berka *138*
Berle, Adolf 170
Berlin
– see also Berlin, Battle of
– Leaflet raid by RAF 2/10/39 *28*
– First air raid 7/6/40 *91*
– RAF bombs 26/8/40 *114*
– RAF bombing 24/9/40 *123*
– RAF raid 25/10/40 *130*
– RAF raid 12/5/41 187
– Russian raid 8/8/41 213
– Remaining Jews to be transported 18/8/41 *216*
– Heavy damage in RAF raid 8/9/41 *221*
– RAF raid 7-8/11/41 *237*
– Jews attack anti-Soviet exhibition 18/5/42 300
– Bombed by Red Air Force 29/8/42 328
– Opera House reopens after British bombing 12/12/42 *357*
– RAF attack includes 8,000-lb bombs 16/1/43 370
– Heaviest raid so far by RAF 2/3/43 387
– Continuing RAF raids expected 17/3/43 391
– RAF raid on Hitler's birthday 21/4/43 400
– "Free of Jews", says Goebbels 19/5/43 *409*
– Goebbels says non-vital citizens to be evacuated 1/8/43 432
– One million evacuated 3/9/43 *440*
– Goebbels given absolute power over city 7/4/44 505
– Hitler returns to Chancellery 16/1/45 *599*
– Red Army approaches 27/1/45 601
– USAAF drops incendiaries 27/2/45 609
– Red Army prepares to attack 24/3/45 615
– Russians ready to attack 14/4/45 623
– Civilians struggle to stay alive 18/4/45 625
– Russians attack 16/4/45 625
– German troops surrender to Zhukov 2/5/45 *631*
– Nazis kept waiting while Allies argue over surrender 8/5/45 636
– Lord mayor warns against attacks on occupying forces 1/6/45 *642*
– British occupation forces arrive 4/7/45 646
– Russians hand over western half of city 11/7/45 *647*
– French troops take up garrison duties 13/8/45 *655*
– Russians blockade from west

24/6/48 663
– After creation of NATO (1949) 664
– The Wall 665
Berlin, Battle of 463, 467, *469*, 471, *473*, 478, 482, 491, 494, *495*, *499*, 502, *513*
Bermuda *176*
Bernadotte, Folke *607*, *626*
Berwick (cruiser) *66*, *140*, *145*
Bessarabia *100*, 202, 499, 562
Best, S Payne 37
Bethlehem 145
Bethnal Green 533
Betio 465
Beuthen *602*
Bevan, Aneurin 158, 488, *650*
Beveridge, William 283, 356
Bevin Boys 465, 481
Bevin, Ernest 86, 88, 91, *125*, 167, 169, 181, 205, 273, *319*, 404, 412, 431, 441, 447, 449, 462, 465, 481, 620, 650, *658*
Bf109 fighters
– (see Messerschmitt Bf109 fighters)
Bhamo *587*
Biak Island *518*, 519, *530*, *534*, *537*, *546*, *554*
Bialystok *22*, *200*, 206, *347*, 385, *436*, *546*
Biancavilla 432
Bielefeld 613
Bielgorod *381*, *386*, *390*, *432*
Bieville 525
Big Dora (gun) 308
Big Week 492
Biggin Hill *114*
Bihac *347*
Bilboa 341
Bilin river *273*
Billancourt 278
Billotte, Gaston 81, 85
Bir Hakeim 303, *304*, *306*
Bir el-Gubi *243*
Birch, John *658*
Bird, Kenneth (Fougasse) 62
Birdsong (operation) 315
Birkenau
– (see Auschwitz)
Birkenhead 169, 185
Birkett, Norman 67
Birmingham *62*, *138*, *141*, *142*, 169, *176*, 178, 181
Biscani *425*
Biscay, Bay of 390, 422, *438*, 473
Bismarck (battleship) *190*
Bismarck Islands 321, 493, *499*
Bismarck Sea 397
Bismarck Sea (aircraft carrier) *607*
Bismarck Sea, Battle of the 386
Bison (destroyer) *78*
Biter (escort carrier) *401*
Bizerta *195*, *360*, 396, 404
Black (operation) 408, 412
Black Gap 382, 393, 403, 422
Black Prince (cruiser) *510*
Black Sea 49, 113, *378*, *442*
Black Swan *396*
Blackburn Skua dive-bombers *73*, 77
Blackout 20, *21*, 25, *30*, 34, *35*, *40*, 41, *49*, *54*, 55, 57, 68, *71*, *192*, *330*, *560*, *564*, *626*, *648*
Blade Force *353*, 356
Blaha, Franz 441
Blamey, Thomas *336*
Blaskowitz, Johannes von 599
Blenheim bombers 26, 58, *68*, *151*, 204, 214, 257, 264, *278*, 288, 304, 564
Bletchley Park 65, *75*, 87, 121, 185, 244, 270, *304*, 346, 360, 411, *515*, 521, *522*
– see also Enigma; Ultra intelligence
Blida 419
Blissful (operation) *455*
Blithe Spirit (play) 204
Blitz 117, *123*, 124, 126, *127*, *128*, 130, 131, *132*, 133, 135, *140*, *142*, *145*, *151*, *154*, 161, *164*, *166*, *168*, *170*, *172*, *174*, *176*, 178, *179*, 183, *184*, 186, *210*
Blitzkrieg 19, 80, 85, 90, 180, 376, 383
Blobel, Paul *417*
Blockbuster (operation) *609*
Blomberg, Werner von 14
Bloody Ridge *331*, *579*
Bloody Wednesday *458*
Blucher (cruiser) 74
Blue Division/Legion
– (see Azul Division)
Bluebell (corvette) *605*
Blum, Leon 273
BOAC 168
Boat Race *66*
Bobbin tank
– (see Tanks)
Bobruisk 283, *537*
Boca de Felso 396
Bochum 408
Bock, Fedor von 202, *253*, 300, 312, 313, *316*
Bodenplatte (operation) *596*
Boeing[co]
– see Flying Fortress, Liberator, Mitchell, Superfortress bombers
Bofors guns 291
Bogart, Humphrey 382, 475
Bogodjim *506*
Boguchar 317
Bohlen 514
Bohlen, Gustav Krupp von *428*, 660
Bohr, Niels 449, 564
Bokpyin *256*
Bolivia
– Declares war on Axis 7/4/43 *396*
– Declares war on Roumania and Hungary 4/12/43 *465*
Bolkhov *427*
Bologna *566*, *624*
Bolzano *469*
Bomb disposal 120
Bombardons 533
Bombay *506*
Bombe
– (see Enigma)
Bomber Command
– (see RAF)
Bonaventure (cruiser) *145*, *172*
Bone 350, *356*
Bongyaung 387
Bonhoeffer, Dietrich *132*, 301, *396*, *621*
Bonin Islands *596*, *601*, *607*
Bonis 472
Bonn 494, *589*, *610*
Bonnard, Abel 378
Bonnet, Georges 17, 21
Bonnier de la Chapelle, Fernand 362
Bono, Emilio de 481
Bonomi, Ivanoe *530*
Bony, Pierre 587
Books
– (see Arts and Entertainment)
Boomerang fighter-bombers *301*
Boone, Joel 661
Bootle 185
Bor-Komorowski, Tadeusz 548, 552, 570
Boram 437
Bordeaux 96, *233*, *336*, 359
Borghese, Prince Giunio 224
Boris III, King of Bulgaria 155, *394*, 438, 390
Borisov 315, *414*
Borizza 396
Borkum *42*, *68*
Bormann, Martin *397*, 519, 568, 607, 616, *618*, 630, 660
Borneo
– Indian troops sabotage Sarawak and Brunei oilfields 13/12/41 *247*
– Japanese land in Sarawak 23/12/41 *256*
– Japanese take Jesselton 8/1/42 263
– US bombers raid Balikpapan oil refinery 10/10/44 *571*
– Australian troops land on Tarakan 1/5/45 631
– Further landings by Australians 10/6/45 *643*
– Australians take Seria oilfields 20/6/45 *644*
– Japanese positions are heavily bombed 24/6/45 *645*
– Australians land at Penajam 8/7/45 *647*
Bornholm *438*, *637*
Bose, Subhas Chandra *401*, *417*, *418*, 432, *453*, 496, *658*
Bosnia 297, 416
Bosnik 519
Boston bombers 314, 352, 386
Bottai, Giuseppe 427
Bottomley, Norman 214
Bou Arada *372*
Bougainville *288*, 401, *420*, 426, 451, *453*, 472, 500, *650*
Bougie 350
Boulogne *87*, *100*, 560, *564*
Boult, Adrian 593
Boulting, Roy 468
Bouncing bombs 410
Bourgebus Ridge 542
Bourke White, Margaret
– (see White, Margaret Bourke)
Boustead, Hugh 500
Bovington 183
Bowlly, Al *179*
Brabazon, Lord 186
Brac Island 568
Bracciano *530*
Bracken, Brendan 207, 236
Bradley, Omar *481*, 518, 524, 527, 530, *531*, 543, 547, *548*, *552*, 559, 566, 590, 592, *599*, 611, 622, 680
Brains Trust (radio programme) *150*, 259
Braithewaite, Lilian 364
Bramble (minesweeper) 364
Brand, Joel 513
Brandt, Karl 625
Brandt, Willi 662
Bratislava 617, *618*
Brauchitsch, Walter von 16, *26*, *105*, *216*, *660*
Braun, Eva 625, 630
Braun, Wernher von 338, *497*, 607, 639, 646
Brava *163*, 165
Brazil 26
– Breaks off relations with Axis powers 28/1/42 *268*
– Axis property seized after merchant shipping sunk 11/3/42 *280*
– Signs defence pact with US 23/5/42 301
– Declares war on Germany and Italy 22/8/42 325
– Italy declares war 7/9/42 *331*
– US troops start using Natal port 26/9/43 *448*
– Task force to Italy to fight with Allies 22/11/43 464
– Expeditionary Force sets sail for Italy 2/7/44 539
– Expeditionary Force in Italy 5/8/44 549
– Troops go on the offensive in Italy 1/10/44 *569*
Breconshire (supply ship) 253, 284
Breendonck *596*
Breker, Arno 100
Bremen *150*, 187, 205, 310, *469*, *470*, *616*, 619, 623
Bremerhaven *45*
Bren guns 191
Brennero 70
Breskens *571*, *577*
Breslau *605*, *634*
Brest *97*, 166, *172*, *174*, *195*, *203*, 270, 272, 393, *397*, 566
Brest-Litovsk *22*, 24, 202, *208*, *486*, *546*
Bretton Woods *539*, *543*, *648*
Brettonville 525
Brevity (operation) *187*
Briare 96
Bricker, John *537*
Brindisi *442*, *446*
Brisbane Star (motor vessel) 324
Bristol *141*, *154*, 171, *174*, 178, *327*
Bristol Channel *103*
Bristol[co]
– (See Beaufighter, Beaufort, Blenheim, Bulldog fighters/bombers)
Britain (defence)
– see also British Army; Royal Navy; RAF
– Armed forces mobilized 3/9/39 17
– Auxiliary Military Pioneer Corps formed 26/10/39 *34*
– German merchant shipping to be seized 21/11/39 *40*
– Seizure of German exports at sea ordered 28/11/39 *42*
– House of Commons' secret session on arms supplies 13/12/39 47
– Losses at sea 31/12/39 50
– Conscription increased 1/1/40 54
– Merchant shipping to be armed 14/2/40 *62*
– Northern Scotland to be restricted area 26/2/40 *65*
– Proposed defence union between Eire and Northern Ireland 1/5/40 78
– Anderson air-raid shelters 16/7/40 106
– SOE set up 22/7/40 107
– US to swap destroyers for British bases 16/8/40 112
– Invasion alert 6/9/40 *116*
– Blitz under way 14/9/40 119
– Arms deal with US 26/10/40 131
– Purchases from US 19/12/40 144
– Twenty Committee meets 2/1/41 *150*
– Fire-watching made compulsory 20/1/41 156
– ABC1 meetings with US 27/1/41 159
– Expenditure on war 4/2/41 160
– National Service Bill 26/3/41 174
– N Ireland conscription halted after protests from Eire 27/5/41 194
– Conscription extended 4/12/41 245
– Anglo-American talks agree on war priorities 31/12/41 259
– Conscription extended 5/3/42 *278*
– US and Britain agree on war responsibilities 30/3/42 285
– Cripps backs second front call 17/5/42 301
– Allies plan Operation Torch to invade North Africa 25/7/42 *318*
– Servicewomen want equal injury compensation 6/1/43 368
– "Wings for Victory" National Savings campaign 7/3/43 390
– Morgan appointed to Anglo-US European command (COSSAC) 23/4/43 *400*
– German rocket offensive feared 30/4/43 402
– Anglo-US agreement on "Ultra" intelligence exchange 17/5/43 *409*
– Signposts to be replaced and blockades removed 30/6/43 420
– Anglo-US atomic weapons agreement 20/8/43 *427*
– Corona device for confusing German bombers 23/10/43 455
– Civilian casualties 31/3/44 *502*
– Royal Observer Corps 31/3/44 503
– South coast closed to public 1/4/44 *504*
– Communications cut in preparation for D-Day 5/4/44 504
– Inventions for tackling German defences on D-Day 6/6/44 529
– Designing of Mulberry harbours and Swiss Roll 12/6/44 533
– RAF captures German plane with three radar sets 13/7/44 541
– Casualties 30/9/44 *566*
– Civilian casualties 30/11/44 *584*
– Last parade of Home Guard 3/12/44 *586*
– Numbers killed since war broke out 28/2/45 *609*
– Difficult task of disarming coastal mines 31/5/45 641
Britain (economics and industry)
– Taxes raised 27/9/39 26
– Food profiteering 9/10/39 *30*
– Cost of living 4/11/39 36
– Cost of living 16/11/39 *38*
– National savings scheme launched 22/11/39 *40*
– Unemployment figures 9/1/40 57
– Government to control railways 13/2/40 57
– National campaign to save waste and scrap 30/1/40 59
– Food availability 2/2/40 61
– Women taking over men's work 6/2/40 62
– Army wives' allowances 12/2/40 63
– Recruiting and training drive for skilled labourers 24/2/40 64
– Success of National Savings scheme 3/3/40 *66*
– Meat rationing starts 11/3/40 68
– Notts miners forgo holidays 17/3/40 *69*
– Government to keep food prices down 1/4/40 *72*
– Taxes raised 23/4/40 77
– Petrol prices raised 22/5/40 *87*
– Emergency Powers Act broadens government control 22/5/40 88
– Strict controls on all working practices; strikes banned 5/6/40 91
– Aluminium for war effort campaign 11/7/40 *103*
– Buying and selling of new cars banned 20/7/40 *105*
– Emergency budget 23/7/40 108
– "Dig for victory" campaign 31/7/40 108
– Food prices rise and purchase tax starts 21/10/40 *130*
– Orange imports delayed 20/11/40 139
– Fruit and vegetable imports cut 26/11/40 141
– New merchant ships ordered from US 3/12/40 *141*
– Food prices controls 14/1/41 155
– Expenditure on war 4/2/41 160
– Essential Work Orders 7/3/41 167
– Employment of women 9/3/41 169
– Income tax raised 7/4/41 178
– Women sign up for work under Employment Order 19/4/41 181
– Post-war building plan outlined 26/2/42 *276*
– Utility clothes introduced 4/3/42 278
– Jowitt in charge of planning for post-war reconstruction 4/3/42 279
– War expenditure 10/3/42 *280*
– "National bread" to replace white bread 11/3/42 281
– Budget includes purchase tax increases 14/4/42 290
– Clothing material economies 15/4/42 291
– Government to run coal-mines 3/6/42 *304*
– Harriman and Lyttleton form combined war industry board 29/7/42 *319*
– Utility furniture 31/8/42 327
– Unemployment at all-time low 23/1/43 373
– Annual consumption reduced 1/3/43 388
– "Wings for Victory" National Savings campaign 7/3/43 390
– Keynes Plan published 7/4/43 397
– Tax increases 12/4/43 399
– Compulsory war work for women 8/5/43 404
– War materials provided by clothes rationing 17/5/43 411
– Bevin warns that coal production is too low 24/5/43 412
– War production at highest and industrial welfare better 30/6/43 421
– Manpower shortage sends women into factories not forces 29/7/43 431
– Britain is most mobilized country 1/9/43 441
– Pay-as-you-earn tax plan announced 23/9/43 446
– Manpower crisis 24/9/43 447
– Unofficial strikes hamper war effort 30/9/43 449
– Thames dockers strike 29/10/43 *455*
– Bevin's post-war employment plans 14/11/43 462
– "Bevin boys" to go down coal mines 2/12/43 465
– Increase in aircraft production 31/12/43 474
– Strikes 11/1/44 480
– Miners strike in support of wage claim 8/3/44 *495*
– Miners sign deal 24/3/44 501
– PAYE tax starts 6/4/44 *504*
– Incitement to strike is made a criminal act 18/4/44 *508*
– Post-war plans to cure unemployment 26/5/44 520
– Government reveals Britain is most productive nation 28/11/44 585
– Bank of England to be nationalized 21/8/45 *658*
– Problems of peacetime begin 25/8/45 659
– Results of war 662
Britain (foreign affairs)
– Response to Hitler's invasion of Austria 12/3/38 14
– Sends military mission to USSR 8/39 15
– Secret talks with anti-Hitler emissaries 1/9/39 16
– Declares war on Germany 3/9/39 17
– Rejects Hitler's "spurious" peace offer 20/9/39 24
– German peace proposals dismissed 3/10/39 *28*
– Dismisses Hitler's peace proposals 6/10/39 30
– Signs pact with Turkey 19/10/39 *32*
– White Paper exposes concentration camp system 30/10/39 *34*
– Aid to Finland 9/12/39 44
– Anglo-French troops to be sent to help Finns 5/2/40 61
– Volunteers to join Finnish Foreign Legion 14/2/40 *62*
– Norway asked to intern Altmark 18/2/40 *64*
– Troops and planes promised for Finland 9/3/40 *66*
– German coal exports to Italy seized 5/3/40 67
– Secret meeting with Turkey 21/3/40 *69*
– Fleet sails for Norway 7/4/40 *73*
– Troops land in Iceland 10/5/40 79
– Troops land in Dutch West Indies 11/5/40 *79*
– Response to German invasion of Low Countries 10/5/40 80
– Details of union plan which France has rejected 22/6/40 99
– Recognizes de Gaulle as

leader in exile of France 28/6/40 100
– Closes Burma Road temporarily 18/7/40 105
– To pull out of Shanghai and northern China 9/8/40 *109*
– Promises aid to Greece 22/8/40 *112*
– To reopen Burma Road after Japan joins Axis 29/9/40 124
– Eden, Smuts, Wavell & Haile Selassie meet in Khartoum 28/10/40 *132*
– Agreement with Turkey 27/2/41 165
– Breaks off diplomatic relations with Bulgaria 5/3/41 167
– Lets US grain ships through to Vichy France 22/3/41 *170*
– Troops to go to Iraq 10/4/41 *176*
– Intelligence learns date of German attack on USSR 6/6/41 *195*
– Anglo-Soviet mutual aid agreement 24/6/41 *200*
– Freezes Japanese assets 26/7/41 208
– Will aid Turkey if attacked 10/8/41 *214*
– Agrees "Atlantic Charter" with USA 14/8/41 215
– Invades Iran with USSR 25/8/41 *217*
– Aid for USSR 29/9/41 227
– Declares war on Finland, Hungary and Roumania 6/12/41 247
– Declares war on Japan 8/12/41 251
– Treaty with Iran 29/1/42 268
– 20-year pact with USSR 26/5/42 *301*
– Renounces Munich agreement 6/8/42 *321*
– Promises help to Turkey if it is forced into war 30/1/43 *376*
– Red Army Day celebrated 21/2/43 385
– Recognizes French Committee of National Liberation 26/8/43 *438*
– Promises aid to USSR 19/10/43 *453*
– Protests against Japanese atrocities 28/1/44 483
– Signs agreement with France 8/2/44 489
– Demands that Sweden stop vital exports to Germany 13/4/44 *506*
– Clamps down on foreign diplomats before D-Day 17/4/44 509
– Newspapers publish descriptions of Majdanek 14/8/44 554
– Cabinet decides to send all Russians home 4/9/44 560
– Intervention in Greek civil war 7/12/44 586
– Intervention in Syrian crisis 31/5/45 641
– Troops occupy Syria and Lebanon 1/6/45 *642*
– Army repatriates Cossacks 1/6/45 642
– Recognizes new Polish government 5/7/45 *646*
– Bevin condemns Soviet foreign policy 20/8/45 *658*
– Ratifies UN Charter 23/8/45 *658*
– Opposes Ho Chi-minh in Vietnam (1945) 665
– Commits to Indian sub-continent independence (1947-8) 665
– Plans German government 2/48 663
– Suez Crisis (1956) 664

Britain (home affairs)
– Evacuation 3/9/39 17
– Blackout rules inquiry opens 12/9/39 *21*
– Rationing to be introduced with other war measures 15/9/39 22
– Petrol rationing begins 22/9/39 *22*
– National census 29/9/39 *26*
– "Spy fever" 16/11/39 39
– Rationing begins 8/1/40 56
– Poor train services 10/1/40 57
– Evacuation scheme fails 31/1/40 59
– Film censorship 22/1/40 59
– New guidelines for BBC war reporting 6/2/40 61
– Careless talk campaign 6/2/40 62
– Paper rationing starts 12/2/40 *62*
– Meat rationing starts 11/3/40 68
– New pound and 10-shilling notes 28/3/40 *71*
– Chamberlain falls over Norwegian campaign 8/5/40 83
– Internment policy 12/5/40 84
– Emergency Powers Act broadens government control 22/5/40 88
– Signposts removed 31/5/40 *89*
– National Day of Prayer 26/5/40 90
– Overseas evacuation plan 5/6/40 91
– Preparations for invasion 30/6/40 101
– Preparations for invasion 8-10/7/40 104
– Compensation for air-raid damage 3/9/40 *116*
– Blitz under way 14/9/40 119
– Blitz casualties 30/9/40 *123*
– Blitz deaths 17/10/40 *128*
– Evacuation from London 18/10/40 130
– Civilian deaths 31/10/40 *132*
– London bomb damage repair plans 31/10/40 133
– Craigavon, Northern Ireland PM, dies 24/11/40 140
– Civilian deaths 30/11/40 *140*
– Civilian casualties 31/12/40 *145*
– Morrison closes Daily Worker 28/1/41 158
– Civilian deaths 28/2/41 *164*
– Rationing increased 17/3/41 *170*
– Civilian casualties 31/3/41 *172*
– Sunday opening of theatres rejected 1/4/41 *174*
– Ministry of wartime communications created 1/5/41 186
– Plans for those made homeless as Blitz casualties grow 13/5/41 189
– Clothes rationing 1/6/41 196
– Beaverbrook becomes minister of supply 29/6/41 *200*
– Ex-miners recalled from forces as coal is rationed 4/7/41 205
– Tighter controls on news and propaganda under Bracken 20/7/41 207
– Civilian Blitz casualties 31/7/41 *210*
– National Fire Service set up 18/8/41 216
– Eating of more vegetables urged as rationing extended 17/9/41 224
– Growing use of American foodstuffs 16/9/41 225
– Education affected by evacuation 1/10/41 229
– Civilian casualties in air raids 31/10/41 *235*
– British Restaurants popular 6/1/42 263
– Soap rationing 9/2/42 271
– Churchill reorganizes cabinet 19/2/42 273
– Black marketeering penalties increased 11/3/42 *280*
– Ban on Daily Mirror threatened 19/3/42 282
– Fuel rationing 17/3/42 283
– Government loses Grantham by-election 25/3/42 *284*
– Civilian casualties 30/4/42 *294*
– Clothes rationing affects stockings 14/5/42 299
– Government loses Maldon by-election to Independent 26/6/42 *310*
– Fuel economies 30/6/42 310
– Sweet rationing 26/7/42 319
– Bevin announces state pension scheme 29/7/42 *319*
– Daily Worker ban lifted 26/8/42 327
– Utility furniture 31/8/42 327
– Milk and sugar rationing increased 25/10/42 346
– Morrison promoted in cabinet reshuffle 22/11/42 353
– Beveridge outlines "welfare state" proposals 1/12/42 356
– VD epidemic 15/12/42 360
– Parliament backs "welfare state" principle 18/2/43 383
– Red Army Day celebrated 21/2/43 385
– Annual consumption reduced 1/3/43 388
– Civilian casualties in air raids since January 31/3/43 *394*
– Church bells ban lifted 20/4/43 400
– Road deaths increase 30/4/43 401
– Effects of clothes rationing 17/5/43 411
– Concern over moral decline 1/6/43 415
– Signposts to be replaced and blockades removed 30/6/43 420
– Education reform planned as birth rate rises 16/7/43 426
– Cabinet reshuffle 25/9/43 447
– Landscape altered by "Dig for Victory" campaign 30/9/43 448
– Christmas turkeys in short supply 25/12/43 471
– Civilian air raid casualties 31/12/43 *473*
– End of the "austerity" suit 1/2/44 487
– Bevan charges government with corruption 11/2/44 488
– Bishop protests against area bombing 9/2/44 489
– Plans announced for free health service 17/2/44 *490*
– Forces pay issue rocks government 2/3/44 495
– Government promises post-war building programme 8/3/44 *495*
– Conservative peer criticizes "crooners" 7/3/44 495
– Government defeated over equal pay bill 28/3/44 *502*
– Incitement to strike is made a criminal act 18/4/44 *508*
– Demonstration "pre-fab" built 30/4/44 510
– Foreign travel banned before D-Day 27/4/44 511
– Influence of GIs 7/6/44 531
– V1s begin to devastate London 17/6/44 533
– Education Act 3/8/44 548
– Home Guard partially stood down 6/9/44 *560*
– Over 1,000 PoWs return from Germany 15/9/44 *562*
– Blackout replaced by dim-out 17/9/44 *564*
– Two new ministries formed 8/10/44 *571*
– First soldier demobilized 16/10/44 *573*
– Construction of first "prefabs" begins 5/1/45 *596*
– Commons motion on Yalta defeated 28/2/45 *609*
– Housing to be post-war priority 20/3/45 614
– Bevin signals end of coalition 7/4/45 620
– Labour Party votes to withdraw from coalition 21/5/45 *639*
– German PoWs begin rebuilding work 22/5/45 640
– Conservative election campaigning 4/6/45 642
– King George dissolves parliament 15/6/45 *643*
– Mass demobilization begins 18/6/45 *644*
– General election is held 5/7/45 *646*
– Churchill ousted by general election 26/7/45 650
– New ministers appointed 3/8/45 *650*
– Programme of social reform announced 17/8/45 *655*
– Plans to speed up demobilization 17/8/45 657
– Faces severe austerity after Lend-Lease is cut 25/8/45 659

British Army
– see also BEF; Commandos; Desert War; theatres of war eg Burma
– Mobilized 3/9/39 17
– Intelligence officers kidnapped by Gestapo 9/11/39 37
– First death on Western Front 9/12/39 *43*
– Dill replaces Ironside as CIGS 27/5/40 *89*
– Allied evacuation of Cherbourg begins 15/6/40 *94*
– Brooke replaces Ironside as C-in-C Home Forces 19/7/40 *105*
– Evacuates Somaliland 19/8/40 114
– Invasion alert 7/9/40 116
– Troops land on Crete 31/10/40 *132*
– Brooke-Popham C-in-C Allied Forces Far East 14/11/40 *136*
– Western Desert force opens Operation Compass 9/12/40 *142*
– Eritrea offensive opened 19/1/41 *156*
– Fall of Tobruk 22/1/41 157
– King's African Rifles in Kenya 24/1/41 157
– King's African Rifles in Somaliland 14/2/41 161
– 2nd Armoured Division replaces 7th in Libya 14/2/41 162
– To aid Greece as soon as possible 19/2/41 *163*
– Defeating Italy in Somaliland 25/2/41 165
– Highlanders in Battle of Keren 27/3/41 174
– Freyberg takes command in Crete 30/4/41 *181*
– Tank regiments reorganized 22/4/41 183
– Freyberg orders evacuation of Crete 27/5/41 *192*
– "Habforce", including Arab Legion troops, takes Baghdad 30/5/41 193
– Losses in Crete 1/6/41 195
– Allied troops, including Arab Legion, in Syria 13/6/41 197
– "Habforce" returns to Iraq from Syria 21/6/41 *198*
– Auchinleck is C-in-C Middle East; Wavell C-in-C India 1/7/41 *203*
– Cunningham to take charge of Eighth Army 5/10/41 230
– Army Catering Corps formed 31/10/41 235
– Brooke becomes CIGS 18/11/41 242
– Neil takes over Eighth Army command from Cunningham 26/11/41 *243*
– Hong Kong garrison besieged 13/12/41 250
– 18th Division moved from Middle to Far East 5/1/42 263
– Auchinleck takes over Eighth Army from Ritchie 30/6/42 311
– Alexander C-in-C Middle East; Gott commands Eighth Army 6/8/42 *321*
– Dieppe raid 19/8/42 326
– Equipped with American M4 Sherman tanks in Desert War 31/10/42 344
– Victories 10/42 and 11/42 9
– Losses at Battle of the Kasserine Pass 25/2/43 385
– Regulars query value of Chindits 26/3/43 392
– Scots, Welsh, English and Irish in Eighth Army 30/3/43 394
– Eighth Army lands in Sicily 10/7/43 424
– British Eighth Army lands in Italy 3/9/43 440
– Allied landings near Salerno 9/9/43 443
– Eighth Army links up with US Fifth Army near Salerno 16/9/43 445
– Mutiny after Salerno landings revealed 23/9/43 446
– Laycock appointed chief of Combined Operations 21/10/43 *453*
– Bogus Twelfth British Army 1/2/44 487
– Troops under Wingate in Burma 6/2/44 *488*
– D-Day landings 6/6/44 *522*
– To back Greek government 26/9/44 568
– Mountbatten orders attack on Mandalay 2/10/44 *569*
– Fulfils promise by returning to liberate Greece 5/10/44 571
– Alexander promoted to field marshal 26/11/44 *584*
– Troops under Montgomery cross the Rhine 24/3/45 615
– Troops liberate Belsen 17/4/45 626
– Eighth Army is disbanded 29/7/45 *649*
– Forces in Germany redesignated British Army of Rhine 25/8/45 *658*

British Broadcasting Corporation
– (see Broadcasting)

British Empire
– (see individual countries)

British Expeditionary Force
– (see BEF)

British Overseas Airways Corporation
– (see BOAC)

British Somaliland
– (see Somaliland)

British Union of Fascists and National Socialists 88, 105

British War Relief Society 178

Brittany 400, 547, 549

Britten, Benjamin 174

Broadcasting
– see also individuals eg Churchill, Joyce, Roosevelt
– BBC creates "Home Service" and suspends TV service 3/9/39 20
– BBC's ITMA: first wartime episode 19/9/39 *22*
– Jews' wireless sets confiscated in Germany 23/9/39 *22*
– BBC departments evacuated 30/9/39 28
– Popular programmes 24/10/39 34
– BBC's "Shadow of the Swastika" begins 8/11/39 *36*
– Popular BBC programmes 12/39 51
– New guidelines for BBC war reporting 6/2/40 61
– BBC Forces' Programme to have dance music on Sundays 15/2/40 63
– Audiences for Lord Haw-Haw as BBC "Onlooker" talks start 1/3/40 67
– Churchill makes his first broadcast as prime minister 19/5/40 *87*
– Priestley starts talks on BBC 5/6/40 91
– Radio Caledonia from Germany starts 18/7/40 *105*
– Waters sisters' comedy 11/40 138
– Popularity of BBC programmes at home and abroad 12/40 147
– BBC starts Brains Trust 1/1/41 *150*
– GS1 begins 23/5/41 *190*
– P G Wodehouse starts talks from Berlin 26/6/41 203
– BBC launches V for Victory campaign on overseas service 20/7/41 207
– More propaganda on BBC's overseas services 20/7/41 207
– British propaganda blamed for resistance in Norway 1/8/41 212
– BBC news used to print "Tobruk Truth" 18/8/41 217
– BBC starts Desert Island Discs 29/1/42 *268*
– Chiang Kai-shek urges Indians to fight Japan 21/2/42 *273*
– Part played in counter-intelligence 21/3/42 283
– French Resistance attacks German stations 9/5/42 298
– Harris speaks to Germans as Bomber Command attacks 31/7/42 319
– Germany executes youth for listening to foreign news 27/10/42 *344*
– Popular songs 12/42 364
– Italian PoWs in Britain start Radio Risorgi 16/2/43 *383*
– German television starts in Paris 7/5/43 *404*
– Milano-Liberta calls for Sicilians to revolt 13/5/43 407
– Germans confiscate wireless sets in Netherlands 16/5/43 *409*
– BBC appeal for French holiday pictures 25/5/43 412
– BBC warns workers in occupied Europe to leave factories 17/6/43 *417*
– "Music While You Work" raises production 30/6/43 421
– Vatican radio reports pope's appeal not to bomb Rome 24/7/43 428
– BBC warns Roumanians to abandon Nazis 23/3/44 499
– BBC transmits messages to the Resistance 1/6/44 *520*
– BBC correspondents in Normandy on D-Day 6/6/44 529
– Anti-Allied propaganda on Radio Vichy and Radio Paris 13/6/44 532
– BBC minimizes damage done by V1 rockets 27/6/44 538
– Moscow radio encourages Warsaw uprising 1/8/44 548
– Tokyo Rose on Japanese Broadcasting Company 7/12/44 587
– Eisenhower demands German surrender 31/3/45 *616*
– Czech patriots broadcast to Allies 5/5/45 632
– Montgomery broadcasts to German people 10/6/45 644
– Hirohito broadcasts to his people 15/8/45 655

Broadway 496

Brody 542, *543*

Broke (destroyer) 350

Bronte *434*

Brooke, Alan
– Says "nothing but a miracle can save BEF" 25/5/40 87
– Taken off beach at Dunkirk 30/5/40 *89*
– Becomes C-in-C Home Forces 19/7/40 *105*
– Becomes CIGS 18/11/41 242
– Replaces Pound as chairman of Chiefs of Staff Committee 4/3/42 *278*
– Complains to Churchill about handling of Dieppe raid 29/8/42 *327*
– Promises to help Turkey if it is forced into war 30/1/43 *376*
– Becomes a field marshal 1/1/44 *478*

– Organizes 79th Armoured Division 6/6/44 529
Brooke-Popham, Robert *136*, 247, *256*
Broome 279
Brossolette, Pierre *392*
Brown, Ernest 62, 360
Broz, Josip
– (see Tito, Josip)
Bruges 85
Brunel *247*, *575*
Bruneval 277
Brunswick *480*, 501, 514
Brussels 80, *84*, *560*
Brux 514
Bryansk *226*, *230*, 268, 315, *440*, 444
Buccaneer (operation) 480
Buchan, John (Lord Tweedsmuir) *62*
Bucharest 506, *558*
Buchenwald 36, *164*, 441, 488, *569*, *618*, 622, *642*
Buckner, Simon B 618, *644*
Budapest *330*, 513, *515*, 575, *575*, *586*, *591*, *597*, 605
Buenos Aires *47*
Buerat *370*
Buffalo Bill (film) 588
Bug river 24, 43, *494*, 503, 542, *543*
Buin *650*
Buin-Faisi 426
Buitenzorg 280
Buka 472
Bukovina (Northern) *100*, 499, 562
Bukrin 458
Bulanov, Mikhail 469
Bulgaria
– Claims on Roumanian territory 28/6/40 101
– PM meets Hitler 27/7/40 *107*
– To gain Roumanian territory 21/8/40 113
– Refuses to join Axis 25/11/40 *140*
– Germans to move through to invade Greece 13/12/40 143
– Laws against Jews and Freemasons 20/12/40 *144*
– Ethnic Germans to be resettled in Reich 31/12/40 147
– Pressed to join Axis 13/1/41 155
– Terms of military cooperation with Germany agreed 23/1/41 *156*
– Agrees to German troops entering country 8/2/41 *160*
– To allow German troops in 12/2/41 162
– German troops arrive 22/2/41 *163*
– Signs treaty with Turkey 17/2/41 164
– Joins Axis 1/3/41 *166*
– German troops move on Greek border 2/3/41 167
– Luftwaffe bases 27/3/41 *172*
– RAF bombs Sofia 7/4/41 *176*
– US declares war 5/6/42 *304*
– Anti-Nazi protests in Sofia 13/1/43 *370*
– 11,000 Jews from Thrace and Macedonia to be deported 22/2/43 *384*
– Public outcry saves 50,000 Jews from deportation 10/3/43 390
– King Boris has consultations with Hitler 31/3/43 *394*
– Two-day curfew in Sofia 5/5/43 404
– Anti-Axis protests 23/7/43 427
– Anti-Nazi riots after death of king 28/8/43 438
– Sofia evacuated 14/1/44 *480*
– Allies call for withdrawal from the war 12/5/44 *513*
– Announces withdrawal from war 26/8/44 557
– Red Army meets no resistance 9/9/44 561
– Signs armistice with USSR 28/10/44 *575*
– Prince Cyril sentenced to death for war crimes 28/1/45 *602*
– Bevin expresses anxiety about the country's future 28/5/45 659
Bulge, Battle of the *589*, 592, *597*
Bulldog (destroyer) 185
Bulldog fighters 44
Bullitt, William 96
Buna *330*, 349, *351*, *360*, *363*, 368
Bund 22, *26*, *42*, *57*
Bunker Hill (aircraft carrier) 637, *645*
Buq Buq 144, *181*
Burchill, Leonard *286*
Burcorps
– (see Burma Corps)
Burma
– Britain will not promise independence 14/11/41 *239*
– Japanese troops infiltrate from Thailand 12/12/41 *247*
– Japan invades with first aim of taking Rangoon 15/12/41 255
– British drive Japanese at Bokpyin back into Thailand 29/12/41 *256*
– U Maung Saw arrested in Palestine by British 18/1/42 266
– Japanese begin drive on Moulmein after taking Tavoy 21/1/42 *266*
– Rangoon threatened as Moulmein falls 31/1/42 269
– Rangoon evacuated as Japanese cross Bilin river 18/2/42 *273*
– Allied losses at Sittang Bridge 23/2/42 276
– Alexander takes command of Allied forces 4/3/42 *278*
– Rangoon falls to Japanese 8/3/42 280
– Slim takes command of Burma Corps 19/3/42 282
– Allies abandon Magwe to Japanese 22/3/42 *284*
– Japanese take Akyab as Burma Corps abandons Prome 2/4/42 *286*
– Japanese attack British while moving on Migyaungye 11/4/42 *288*
– Burma Corps destroys Yenangyaung oilfields 16/4/42 289
– Chinese forces aid Burcorps troops 19/4/42 *292*
– Stilwell to withdraw to India 30/4/42 *294*
– Burma Corps begins retreat as Chinese lose Burma Road 30/4/42 295
– Japanese take Mandalay 1/5/42 *296*
– Both sides held up by monsoon 12/5/42 *298*
– Chinese Fifth Army takes up positions at Myitkyina 18/5/42 *300*
– RAF bombs Japanese at Prome, Mandalay and Rangoon 11/9/42 *331*
– Allied counter-offensive in the Arakan 21/9/42 *336*
– Supplies disrupted by cyclone in Bengal 16/10/42 *340*
– British and Japanese clash in the Arakan 23/10/42 *342*
– Chiang Kai-shek gives Stilwell 15 Chinese divisions 3/11/42 *347*
– 14th Indian Division occupies Buthidaung 17/12/42 *360*
– Japanese resist Allies at Rathedaung and Donbaik 6/1/43 *368*
– British use tanks against Donbaik and Rathedaung 3/2/43 380
– Chindits begin operations 8/2/43 *381*
– 55th Indian Brigade attacks Japanese at Donbaik 17/2/43 *383*
– Operation Cannibal stopped by Japanese 4/3/43 *386*
– Chindits cut more railway bridges 6/3/43 387
– Renewed Japanese offensive in the Arakan 17/3/43 *390*
– Chindits ordered to withdraw 24/3/43 *392*
– Japanese overrun British HQ at Mayu 5/4/43 *396*
– Chindit survivors cross Chindwin into India 30/4/43 402
– British retreat after Japanese take Buthidaung 7/5/43 *404*
– Total failure of Allied offensive 14/5/43 406
– RAF bombs Akyab 28/6/43 *420*
– Allies attack Japanese at Maungdaw 9/7/43 422
– Declares war on Allies as Japan proclaims it independent 1/8/43 432
– Auchinleck proposes stopping all offensives 13/8/43 *434*
– South-east Asia Command (SEAC) set up under Mountbatten 23/8/43 439
– Slim takes command on Arakan front 6/10/43 *450*
– Japan lays railway from Bangkok 25/10/43 457
– Japan repels Chinese attacks 2/11/43 *458*
– Allies bomb Rangoon 25/11/43 *464*
– Chinese 38th Division takes Japanese positions 28/12/43 *473*
– Chinese destroy Japanese resistance at Yupgang Ga 13/1/44 *480*
– Chinese forces take Taro 31/1/44 *483*
– Chinese attack Japanese at Taihapa Ga 1/2/44 *486*
– Allied admin troops halt Japanese 18/2/44 491
– Allies clear Japanese from Ngakyedauk Pass 24/2/44 *492*
– Merrill's Marauders go into action 4/3/44 *494*
– Chinese forces take Maingkwan 5/3/44 *495*
– Japanese hit Chindit airstrip 13/3/44 *497*
– Japanese troops cross border into India 22/3/44 *499*
– Japanese cut Imphal to Kohima road 29/3/44 *502*
– Japanese surround British troops 9/4/44 *506*
– Allied troops counter-attack at Imphal 5/5/44 *512*
– Japanese resistance at Kohima broken 16/5/44 *515*
– Allies take Myitkyina 18/5/44 517
– Chinese troops take Kamaing 16/6/44 *531*
– Allies reopen Imphal to Kohima road 25/6/44 *537*
– Allies take Ukhrul 8/7/44 *539*
– Myitkyina falls to US and Chinese 3/8/44 548
– Japanese troops withdraw from Manipur river Line 14/9/44 *562*
– Mountbatten orders attack on Mandalay 2/10/44 *569*
– Chinese forces take Myothit 28/10/44 *575*
– British push on after few days' rest 1/11/44 578
– Indian troops take Fort White 8/11/44 *579*
– Japanese army on the defensive on 800-mile front 18/11/44 582
– East African troops reach Chindwin 2/12/44 *586*
– World's largest bridge built across Chindwin river 10/12/44 *587*
– Indian troops take Kawlin 20/12/44 *589*
– West African troops advance 7/1/45 598
– Indian troops' advance continues 14/2/45 *605*
– Allied drive on Meiktila continues 26/2/45 *609*
– Meiktila falls to Allies 7/3/45 *610*
– Sino-American and British forces link up 24/3/45 *614*
– Mandalay falls to Allies 20/3/45 616
– Native troops rise up against Japanese commanders 28/3/45 *616*
– British troops open the road to Rangoon 11/4/45 *621*
– Allied advances continue 16/4/45 624
– Indians fighting with Japanese surrender 23/4/45 *626*
– Rangoon falls to the Allies 3/5/45 631
– Nationalist leader joins Allies 15/5/45 *637*
– Organized Japanese resistance comes to an end 3/8/45 *650*
– Military chiefs to surrender 25/8/45 658
– Formal surrender signed 28/8/45 *660*
Burma Corps 282, 292, 299
Burma Road *100*, 105, 124, 129, 208, *239*, 269, 292, 295, *296*, 388, 454, *494*, 582, 599
Burmese National Army *616*
Burns, Eedson 501
Burrell, John 593
Burrows, Emmet 611
Burton Island *486*
Burton-on-Trent 585
Burye 166
Busch, Ernst von 535, 541, *648*
Bush, Vannevar 337
Busse, Theodor 628
Bustard (operation) *296*
Buthidaung *360*, *390*, *404*, 480, *495*
Butler, Richard 548
Butterfly bombs *417*
Buxian *294*
Buzz bombs
– (see V-weapons)
Bydgoszcz *16*, 19, 31
Byelorus 8
Byelorussia *35*, 202, *518*, 535, 541
Byrnes, James *645*, 654
Bzura River, Battle of the *16*, 23

C

C-47 transports 560, 597
C38M enciphering machines 411
Cabot (aircraft carrier) 585
Cactus Air Force 380
Caen 479, *522*, 530, *531*, *539*
Caesar Line 519
Cagliari *394*, *420*
Cairo *130*, 464, *579*, 607
Cairo (cruiser) 309, 324
Calabria 440
Calais 87, *89*, 560, 569
Calau 626
Calcar *609*
Calcutta *360*, *455*, *467*
Calcutta (anti-aircraft cruiser) *195*
Calder, Jock 613
California (battleship) 249
Caltanisetta *427*
Calvert, Mike 391, 500, 537
Cambodia 165, 211, *614*
Cambrai *84*
Cameron, Basil 475, 593
Camm, Sidney 111
Campbell, A B 259
Campbell, Mrs Patrick (Beatrice Tanner) 75
Campbell, Ronald 99
Campbeltown (destroyer) 285
Campoleone 485, 486
Camranh Bay 211
Canada (defence)
– see also Canadian Army; RCAF; Royal Canadian Navy
– Military HQ set up in London 13/11/39 *38*
– Troops in Britain 25/2/40 66
– Air training scheme for Empire 29/4/40 78
– Joint board established with US 18/8/40 *112*
– More called up 15/9/40 *120*
– Shipbuilding agreement with US 19/3/41 170
– Collaboration with US to help Britain 21/4/41 183
– King asks US to support Britain against "barbarians" 4/9/41 220
– Conscription to be introduced 19/2/42 *273*
– Japanese Canadians interned 25/2/42 277
– Country split on conscription 28/4/42 295
– U-boat torpedoes ship in St Lawrence Seaway 11/5/42 *298*
– Japanese shell Vancouver Island 20/6/42 *308*
– Joint Canadian-US chiefs of staff committee formed 3/7/42 *312*
– Conscription for overseas service 29/7/42 319
– Additional money for war effort 7/5/43 *404*
– Airports built 31/5/44 520
Canada (economics and industry)
– Production of armaments 31/5/44 520
Canada (foreign affairs)
– Declares war on Germany 10/9/39 *21*
– Role in war defined 14/9/39 22
– Volunteers to fight for Finland 5/3/40 *66*
– Breaks off relations with Vichy France 9/11/42 349
– Recognizes French Committee of National Liberation 26/8/43 *438*
– Signs mutual aid pact with China 22/3/44 *499*
Canada (home affairs)
– Parliament dissolved over war preparations 25/1/40 *59*
– Mackenzie King wins general election 29/3/40 71
– Anti-conscription candidates defeated in by-elections 9/2/42 *271*
– Meat rationing 26/5/43 *412*
– Parliament votes to send conscripts to Europe 23/11/44 *583*
– First draftees sail from Halifax 3/1/45 *596*
– Mackenzie King wins elections 11/7/45 *647*
– 15 die in naval arsenal explosion 18/7/45 *648*
Canadian Army
– First troops arrive in Britain 17/12/39 48
– Allied evacuation of Cherbourg begins 15/6/40 *94*
– Canadian corps to be formed in Britain 24/12/40 145
– Troops reinforce Hong Kong garrison 15/11/41 239
– Losses in Dieppe raid 19/8/42 326
– Forces in Sicilian campaign 18/7/43 *427*
– Troops use Wolfe ruse to take Assoro 22/7/43 428
– Forces with US take Kiska 15/8/43 437
– Troops fighting with British Eighth Army in Italy 3/9/43 440
– Troops join the attack on Ortona 10/12/43 *467*
– New commander of Canadian Corps at Cassino 20/3/44 501
– Contribution to war around the world 31/5/44 520
– Landings on Juno Beach on D-Day 6/6/44 525
– PoWs murdered by Germans 7/6/44 *530*
– Fighting Hitler Jugend Panzer division outside Caen 10/6/44 530
– First Canadian Army becomes operational 23/7/44 *546*
– Troops killed by Bomber Command in France 14/8/44 *552*
– Troops enter Rouen 30/8/44 *558*
– Troops land at Breskens, Belgium 9/10/44 *571*
– Conscripts to go to Europe 23/11/44 *583*
– Forces take Ravenna 4/12/44 *586*
– Wins battle for Reichswald 13/2/45 607
– Troops under Montgomery cross the Rhine 24/3/45 615
– Forces take Oldenburg 2/5/45 *631*
Canadian Women's Auxiliary Air Force *203*
Canaris, Wilhelm 375, *621*
Canberra (cruiser) 321
Canea 191
Cannes 553
Cannibal (operation) *386*
Canoes 359
Cantelupo *455*
Canterbury 347
Canton, 258, *344*, 658
Cap Arcona (liner) 632
Cap Blanc-Nez *564*
Cap Griz-Nez *566*
Cap Serrat *394*
Cap de la Hague 538
Cape Bon 181, *247*, *400*
Cape Engano 576
Cape Esperance *370*, *378*
Cape Finisterre *368*
Cape Gloucester 470, *473*, *478*
Cape Inubo *361*
Cape Matapan 172
Cape Spada *105*
Cape Sportivo, Battle of *140*
Cape St George, Battle of *464*
Cape Town *43*
Capetown (cruiser) *176*
Capri *444*
Capua *450*, 458
Carabao *624*
Caracciolo, Prince 508
Cardiff 113, 150, 169
Careless talk campaign 62
Carentan 517, 530, *531*
Caribbean 313, *327*
Carinthia 498
Carmineo, Nicolangelo 174, 176
Carnaby 347
Carol, King of Roumania *38*, *97*, 103, *114*, 118
Caroline Islands *488*, 491, 505, 505, *508*, *510*, *512*, 545, *546*, *560*, *564*, 644
Carpetbagger (operation) *478*, 480
Carroceto 485, 490
Carsonia *217*
Carton de Wiart, Adrian 76, 79, 440
Cartwheel (operation) 421, 451, 510
Casabianca (submarine) 447
Casablanca 350
Casablanca (film) 382
Casablanca Summit 370
Casals, Pablo 475
Caserta *450*
Casey, Richard 419
Cassino 479, *480*, *488*, *497*, 501, 516
– see also Monte Cassino
Castellana *530*
Castellano, Giuseppe *436*, 440
Castelrosso *164*, *442*, *462*
Castiglione *460*
Castillo, Ramon 415
Castore (torpedo boat) *414*
Catalina flying boats 225, 264, 403, 452, *515*
Catania *154*, 432
Catapult (operation) 102
Catona *440*
Catroux, Georges *243*, 414, 460

Cattenom *581*
Caucasus 234, *237*, 312, *325*, *340*, *344*, *361*, *363*, *370*, *372*, *376*, *401*, 426
Cavalier tanks
– (see Tanks)
Cavallero, Ugo *141*, *154*, *376*, *442*
Cavalry 19, 85, 197
Cavite *247*, *262*, *605*
Cebu *288*, *591*, *626*
Cecina 540
Celebes *264*
Celles 590, 592
Censorship 39, 55, *59*, 158, *179*, 205, 207, 254, 282, *296*, 529
Centaur (hospital ship) 406
Central Intelligence and Military Action Bureau 486
Cephalonia *138*
Ceramic (liner) *357*
Cerberus (operation) 272
Cernavoda 165
Cervaro *480*
Cesano river *550*
Cesaro *434*
Ceylon
– British fleet disperses as Japanese fleet approaches 4/4/42 *286*
Ch'en Kungpo 579
Chad *114*
Chahar *212*
Chamberlain, Neville
– Response to German take-over of Austria and Sudetenland (1938) 14
– Signs Munich agreement 9/38 14
– Promises Britain and France will support Poland 30/3/39 15
– Secret talks with anti-Hitler emissaries 1/9/39 16
– Announces war with Germany; recalls Churchill and Eden 3/9/39 17
– Policy on Poland criticized 20/9/39 24
– Dismisses German "peace offensive" 29/9/39 28
– First wartime broadcast 26/11/39 *42*
– Visits Western Front 15/12/39 *45*
– Meets Sumner Welles 11/3/40 *68*
– Joint declaration with Reynaud 28/3/40 71
– "Hitler has missed the bus" speech 5/4/40 72
– Invites Labour to form coalition 9/5/40 *79*
– Resigns after vote of no confidence over Norway 8/5/40 7, 83
– Opposes Churchill over Italy's mediation offer 30/5/40 90
– Resigns from government 3/10/40 *125*
– Dies 9/11/40 134
– Biography 680
Chanel, Coco 46
Chang-kang-ling 167
Changi jail 275, 329, *357*
Changsha *226*, 258, 405, 417, *520*, 534
Changsha, First Battle of *28*
Changsha, Second Battle of *221*, *230*
Changshouchie *520*
Changteh 466
Channel Islands
– Germany bombs Jersey and Guernsey 28/6/40 *100*
– Germans occupy Guernsey 30/6/40 101
– Commando raid on lighthouse 3/9/42 *330*
– Commando raid on Sark 3-4/10/42 *338*
– Resistance workers arrested 12/2/44 488
– Germans end the occupation 9/5/45 636
– King George visits 7/6/45 642
Chantiers de Jeunesse *107*, 153
Chaplin, Charles *142*, 221
Chaplinka *455*
Chariots *368*
Charleroi *548*
Charlotte, Grand Duchess of Luxemburg 80
Chartres 553
Charybdis (cruiser) 309, *453*
Chasseurs Alpins 76
Chateau-Thierry *558*
Chatelain (destroyer) 521, *534*
Chatfield, Lord 24, *72*
Chatillon-sur-Seine *562*
Chattanooga (operation) *518*
Chavasse, Bishop 415
Chekiang 301, 328
Chelm *43*
Chelmno *247*, *264*, *276*, *278*, 304, *353*
Cheminot 579
Chen Tan-chi *448*
Chengchow *508*
Chengtu *68*
Chennault, Claire L *212*, *389*, 515, *646*
Cherbourg *94*, *97*, *125*, *127*, 205, *370*, *397*, 479, 530, 535, 557, 560
Cherkassy *469*
Cherniakovsky, Ivan 541, 600, *607*
Chernigov *221*, *446*
Chernovsky *205*
Chernyakhovsk *473*, *368*
Cherryblossom (operation) 459
Cheshire, Leonard (VC) *488*, 532
Chetniks 235, 297, 399, 412, 419, 447, 472
Chevalier, Maurice 46
Chiang Kai-shek
– Leads first successful Nationalist attack on Japanese 6/10/39 29
– Nationalists lose Nanning to Japanese 24/11/39 41
– United front with Mao Tse-tung crumbling 1/40 58
– Talks with Japanese break down 30/11/40 140
– Breaks off relations with Axis over Reformed Kuomintang 1/7/41 203
– Makes Flying Tigers members of Chinese armed forces 1/8/41 212
– Calls for western democracies to act against Japan 17/11/41 *241*
– Becomes C-in-C of Allied forces in China 3/1/42 *262*
– Urges Indian nationalists to join fight against Japan 9/2/42 *271*
– Troops attack Nanking 5/5/42 *296*
– Says collapse of Japan is near 7/7/42 316
– Reincorporates Sinkiang into China and asks USSR to go 5/10/42 *338*
– Meets Wendell Wilkie 4/10/42 339
– Warns of dangers of factional fighting 22/10/41 343
– Gives Stilwell divisions for Burma campaign 3/11/42 *347*
– Presses Britain and US to give up rights in China 17/1/43 372
– Agrees to exchange manpower in Burma for US aid 7/2/43 *381*
– Encourages troops at Shih-pai 14/6/43 417
– Becomes acting president of National Government 2/8/43 *432*
– Asked by Stilwell to join Communists 6/9/43 *442*
– Elected president of National Govt of China 13/9/43 *444*
– Executes leading Communists 27/9/43 *448*
– Persuaded not to sack Joseph Stilwell 19/10/43 454
– Meets Churchill and Roosevelt in Cairo 25/11/43 464
– Threatens surrendering commander with execution 4/12/43 466
– Persuaded to send his troops into Burma 22/4/44 508
– Mao Tse-tung announces his support 12/6/44 *531*
– Demands Stilwell's recall 25/9/44 *566*
– Recalls troops from Burma 30/11/44 *584*
– Succeeded as president of Nationalist Yuan 31/5/45 *640*
– Broadcasts to his people on VJ Day 15/8/45 656
– His troops enter Shanghai and Nanking 25/8/45 658
– Meets Mao Tse-tung for talks 29/8/45 *660*
– His part in Asia's uncertain future 31/8/45 661
– Takes refuge on Formosa (1949) 664
– Biography 680
Chiang Kai-shek, Madame *383*, 464
Chicago (cruiser) 306, 321
Chicago Tribune (newspaper) *306*
Chichagof *409*
Chichi Jima *539*, *548*, *596*
Chichibu, Prince 492
Children's Overseas Reception Board 91
Chile
– Pro-Nazi plot discovered 10/8/41 *214*
– Comments on Argentinian declaration of war 26/1/44 483
– Denies it will declare war on Axis 9/2/45 604
– Declares war on Japan 13/4/45 *621*
Chilga *239*
China (defence)
– Nanking occupied by Japan 12/37 13
– Nationalists defeat Japan at First Battle of Changsha 6/10/39 29
– Nationalist offensive against Japan ordered 19/11/39 *40*
– Nationalists lose Nanning to Japan 24/11/39 41
– Japanese claim 25,000 Chinese killed in battle 8/1/40 *55*
– Communists retake Anding from Japanese 28/2/40 *65*
– Japan shoots down Chinese planes over Chengtu 14/3/40 *68*
– Nationalists recapture Wuyuan from Japanese 2/4/40 72
– Japanese advance towards Yangtze river 1/5/40 *78*
– Japanese seize Tsaoyang 8/5/40 *79*
– Japan launches bombing campaign against south-east 31/5/40 *89*
– Hsiangyang falls to Japanese 1/6/40 *91*
– Japanese attack Ichang 10/6/40 *94*
– Burma Road temporarily closed by British 18/7/40 105
– Communists attack Japanese in Shansi 20/8/40 114
– Communist Hundred Regiments Offensive against Japan 20/9/40 *120*
– Japanese lose Nanning 29/10/40 133
– Communist 100 Regiment campaign disrupts Japanese 5/12/40 142
– Kuomintang to disband Communist New Fourth Army 15/1/41 155
– Japanese occupy Tamshin 3/2/41 *160*
– Chinese crush Japanese offensive and retake Sinyang 7/2/41 160
– Japan launches offensive in Hupeh 6/3/41 167
– Nationalists repulse Japanese in Hupeh 13/3/41 168
– Japanese take Fengxin 15/3/41 *168*
– Battle of Shanggao ends 2/4/41 *174*
– Japanese occupy Fuzhou after taking Ningbo 22/4/41 *181*
– Japanese attack Shansi 7/5/41 *184*
– Nationalists defeat Japanese at Chungtiao Shan 25/5/41 194
– Pro-Japanese troops attack New Fourth Army at Kiangsu 18/7/41 *206*
– Japan bombs Chungking and hits US gunboat 30/7/41 211
– American "Flying Tiger" volunteers help Nationalists 1/8/41 212
– Japan launches "Three All" attack on Communists 1/8/41 *212*
– Chungking devastated by Japanese bombing 13/8/41 *214*
– Foochow recaptured from Japanese 3/9/41 *220*
– Second Battle of Changsha starts 7/9/41 *221*
– Second Battle of Changsha ends 8/10/41 *230*
– Flying Tigers shoot down ten Japanese bombers 20/12/41 *253*
– Japanese threaten Changsha 24/12/41 258
– Chiang Kai-shek becomes C-in-C Allied Forces 3/1/42 *262*
– Stilwell becomes C-in-C 2/2/42 *270*
– Stilwell appointed US C-in-C 11/3/42 281
– Supplies airlifted from India 8/4/42 *288*
– Japanese besiege Nationalists at Buxian 29/4/42 *294*
– Japan enters Yunnan as Nationalists attack Nanking 5/5/42 *296*
– Japanese reprisals for Doolittle raid 15/5/42 *298*
– Japanese advance in Chekiang 29/5/42 301
– Japanese attack Taihang 11/6/42 *306*
– Japanese defeated in Shansi 30/6/42 *310*
– Japanese plan to control guerrillas on Lower Yangtze 1/7/42 312
– Japanese occupy Futou Island 11/7/42 *314*
– Japanese launch new attacks as factions fight 12/8/42 324
– Japanese withdraw eastwards after destroying airfields 28/8/42 328
– Stilwell plans for more forces for Burma 19/10/42 *342*
– USAAF raids Canton 26/10/42 *344*
– Japanese troops cross Yangtze river 8/3/43 *389*
– US Fourteenth Army Air Force under Chennault created 10/3/43 *389*
– Japanese launch offensive near Changsha 5/5/43 405
– Chinese halt Japanese advance on Chungking 29/5/43 *412*
– US and Chinese airmen hit Japanese at Ichang 1/6/43 414
– Japanese seize shipping on Upper Yangtze 3/6/43 *414*
– Nationalists defeat Japanese in Hupeh 14/6/43 417
– Nationalists attacked by Communists and Japanese 12/8/43 435
– Japanese bomb Chungking 23/8/43 *438*
– Stilwell asks Nationalists to join Communists 6/9/43 *442*
– Supplies to be flown in over Himalayas 19/10/43 454
– Changteh capitulates to Japanese 4/12/43 466
– Japanese aircraft raid Kunming 18/12/43 *469*
– Battle for Hunan province 25/12/43 471
– Eighth Route Army take Taiku 21/2/44 *492*
– South coast to be invaded by US 29/2/44 493
– Communist army takes Chinhsien 14/3/44 *497*
– Japan bombs Honan province 8/4/44 *504*
– Troops ordered to attack Japanese 14/4/44 *506*
– Japanese launch Operation Ichi-Go 17/4/44 *508*
– Japanese attack Loyang 25/4/44 *510*
– Japanese forces link up at Suiping 7/5/44 *513*
– Japan hits US airfields 11/5/44 515
– Japanese take Loyang 25/5/44 *518*
– Japanese divisions mass to attack Changsha 10/6/44 *530*
– Japanese take Changsha and Chuchow 18/6/44 534
– US observers arrive to observe military cooperation 22/7/44 *543*
– Japanese forces take Hengyang 8/8/44 *550*
– Chiang Kai-shek asks for Stilwell to be withdrawn 25/9/44 *566*
– Japanese forces take US airbases 10/11/44 *579*
– Japan claims to have taken Nanning 25/11/44 583
– Troops from Burma called in as reinforcements 30/11/44 *584*
– Japanese troops gain control of vital rail link 10/12/44 *587*
– Japan launches new offensive 21/3/45 *614*
– Japanese pull out of ports 19/5/45 637
– Chinese Sixth Army flown from Burma 27/5/45 *640*
– Japanese forces lose Nanning 27/5/45 641
– Japanese front collapsing 6/6/45 642
– Chinese forces take Ishan from the Japanese 14/6/45 *643*
– Chinese troops continue their advance 26/6/45 *645*
– Chinese advance in the south continues 9/7/45 647
– Chinese troops continue to push back Japanese 5/8/45 *652*
– Nationalist and Communist forces race to liberate 25/8/45 658
China (foreign affairs)
– Japan recognizes Wang Chingwei's regime 30/11/40 140
– Wang Chingwei recognized by Axis 1/7/41 *203*
– Nationalists endorse Atlantic Charter 17/8/41 *216*
– Nationalists ask Britain for air cover for Burma Road 12/11/41 *239*
– Chiang Kai-shek calls for western action against Japan 17/11/41 *241*
– Nationalists declare war on Axis powers 9/12/41 *247*
– Chiang Kai-shek asks India to help against Japan 21/2/42 *273*
– Lend-lease aid from US 2/6/42 *304*
– Kuomintang needs more aid to continue to stop Japanese 7/7/42 316
– Reincorporates Sinkiang and demands that USSR withdraws 5/10/42 *338*
– Pro-Japan Reformed Kuomintang declares war on Allies 9/1/43 368
– Britain and US give up territorial rights 17/1/43 372
– To provide manpower for Burma in exchange for US aid 7/2/43 *381*
– US trains Chinese infantrymen 31/3/43 *394*
– Excluded from Allied conferences 18/8/43 *436*
– Recognizes French Committee of National Liberation 27/8/43 *438*
– USA introduces annual quota of Chinese immigrants 17/12/43 470
– Signs mutual aid pact with Canada 22/3/44 *499*
– To be included in UN 9/10/44 571
– Manchuria to be returned 15/8/45 657
– Army engages American troops in North Korea (1950-1) 664
China (home affairs)
– Nationalists and Communists clash at Ningxian 14/12/39 *45*
– Wang Chingwei sets up rival Nationalist government 30/12/39 50
– Reformed Kuomintang government set up in Nanking 30/3/40 71
– Supplies threatened by Japanese cut-off 7/40 8
– Chungking becomes Nationalist capital 6/9/40 *116*
– Nationalists attack Communists at Taixing 1/10/40 *125*
– Nationalists attack Communists at Maolin 5/1/41 *151*
– Floods 31/1/41 *158*
– Communists in army rise against Nationalists 3/8/42 322
– Chiang Kai-shek warns of danger of internal divisions 22/10/42 343
– Wang Chingwei meets Hsin-min-hui leaders 27/10/42 346
– Sun Tien-ying defects to Japanese 25/4/43 *401*
– Famine in Hunan 31/7/43 *428*
– Chiang Kai-shek acting president of National Government 2/8/43 *432*
– Chiang Kai-shek elected chairman of National Government 13/9/43 *444*
– Mao Tse-tung says he supports Nationalists 12/6/44 *531*
– T V Soong is new president of Nationalist Yuan 31/5/45 *640*
– 43 million refugees 31/7/45 650
– Communists want a share in Japanese surrender deal 15/8/45 *655*
– Chiang Kai-shek broadcasts on VJ Day 15/8/45 656
– Communist and Nationalist troops clash 20/8/45 *658*
– Chiang Kai-shek and Mao Tse-tung meet for talks 29/8/45 *660*
– Civil War (1947) 664
Chindits *381*, *383*, 387, 391, *392*, 402, 434, *495*, *497*, 500, 506, 537
Chindwin river 402, 496, 582, *586*, *587*, 596
Chingmen *91*
Chingyuan *599*
Chittagong *470*
Chivenor 390
Choiseul *455*
Cholera *455*
Choltitz, Dietrich von *552*, 555
Chou En-lai 658
Christensen, Ingolf *75*
Christian X, King of Denmark 73, 75, *349*, 439, 563
Chronometer (operation) *196*
Chu Shih-ming 316
Chu Teh *655*
Chu-chi 301
Chuchow *304*, 328, 534

Chuhsien *432*
Chuikov, Vasili *331*, 352
Chungchin *645*
Chungking *89*, 94, *116*, *118*, 140, 167, *214*, *412*, *438*
Chungtiao mountains *184*
Church bells *89*, 106, 116, 352, 400
Churchill, Clementine 385, 434
Churchill, Mary 434
Churchill, Randolph 520
Churchill, Winston
– Recalled to be first lord of the admiralty 3/9/39 17
– Says Britain is winning U-boat war 26/9/39 *26*
– First wartime broadcast 1/10/39 *28*
– Speech on Royal Navy 8/11/39 37
– Dismisses peace appeal by Wilhelmina and Leopold 12/11/39 39
– Proposes mining Rhine 19/11/39 *40*
– Attacks German methods of sea warfare 5/12/39 44
– Condemns Russian invasion of Finland 20/1/40 *57*
– Says Britain has no quarrel with USSR 30/3/40 *71*
– Visits France 4/4/40 *72*
– Plan for mining Norwegian waters 3/4/40 72
– Admiration for Dill 18/4/40 76
– Becomes prime minister 10/5/40 7, 83
– Asks Roosevelt for aid 14/5/40 *84*
– "Blood, toil, tears and sweat" speech 13/5/40 86
– First broadcast as PM 19/5/40 *87*
– Urges BEF to fight on but orders RN to assemble ships 25/5/40 87
– Dunkirk "a miracle of deliverance" 4/6/40 92
– "We shall fight on the beaches" speech 4/6/40 93
– Tells French "We shall fight on forever" 11/6/40 96
– "Finest hour" speech 17/6/40 97
– Attitude to France 22/6/40 99
– Approves Shelley as broadcasting stand-in 30/6/40 101
– Orders destruction of French fleet at Oran 3/7/40 102
– Burma Road not to be closed permanently 18/7/40 105
– Bastille Day message to Free French 14/7/40 106
– Impressed by RAF gallantry in Battle of Britain 17/8/40 111
– Negotiates destroyers/bases swap with US 16/8/40 112
– "Never in the field of human conflict" speech 20/8/40 113
– Expects invasion soon 11/9/40 *118*
– Replaces Chamberlain as Tory leader 9/10/40 127
– Broadcast call to French to help against Hitler 21/10/40 *130*
– Supports Greece 21/11/40 139
– Enjoys "The Great Dictator" 14/2/40 *142*
– Sees bomb damage at Harrow 18/12/40 *144*
– Tells Menzies Australia more important than Med 23/12/40 *145*
– Assistance for Greece promised 6/1/41 152
– Need for US defence materials 17/1/41 155
– "Give us the tools" broadcast 9/2/41 162
– "Battle of the Atlantic has begun" 6/3/41 *166*
– "We shall give it to them back" 22/3/41 171
– Warns USSR of impending German attack 3/4/41 *174*
– Shipping losses not to be published 14/4/41 *179*
– Insists Crete must be held after evacuation of Greece 16/4/41 181
– Insists Egypt must be held 27/4/41 *181*
– Ends reinforcement of Singapore and Malaya 28/4/41 *181*
– Prepares Cyprus for possible German invasion 2/6/41 195
– Defends record in debate on Crete 10/6/41 197
– Decides to replace Wavell by Auchinleck 20/6/41 198
– Promises aid to USSR 22/6/41 *200*
– Launches V for Victory campaign 20/7/41 207
– Meetings with Roosevelt produce Atlantic Charter 14/8/41 215
– "Merciless butchery" of Nazis broadcast 25/8/41 217
– Condemns German reprisal killings 25/10/41 *233*
– Writes to Jewish Chronicle about Jews under Hitler 14/11/41 *239*
– Says Britain will back US if Japan makes war on it 10/11/41 241
– "Hard time ahead" in Far East 11/12/41 251
– Visits US for talks with Roosevelt 22/12/41 *256*
– Addresses US Congress 26/12/41 259
– Orders Singapore to be "defended t the death" 20/1/42 *266*
– Government wins vote of confidence 29/1/42 269
– Broadcasts on fall of Singapore 16/2/42 274
– Concern over health 27/2/42 *276*
– Plans to take Diego Suarez on Madagascar 1/3/42 278
– Opposes Indian independence 21/3/42 283
– Views on second front 18/4/42 290
– Warns Germany against use of poison gas 10/5/45 *298*
– Nominates Eden as successor if he dies 16/6/42 *308*
– Visits Roosevelt to discuss latest plans 18/6/42 308
– Survives vote of censure 2/7/42 312
– Tells Stalin there will be no more Arctic convoys 17/7/42 *316*
– Visits North Africa and decides to replace Auchinleck 4/8/42 322
– Refers to Stalin as a peasant 12/8/42 *322*
– Meets Stalin and explains Anglo-US campaign plans 15/8/42 323
– At Westminster Abbey for National Day of Prayer 3/9/42 330
– Announces measure against Indian Congress Party 10/9/42 *331*
– Promises Stalin second front "as quickly as possible" 8/9/42 333
– Message to Jewish victims 29/10/42 346
– Chairs first meeting of Anti U-boat Committee 4/11/42 *347*
– "End of the beginning" speech 10/11/42 350
– Demotes Cripps and promotes Morrison 22/11/42 353
– Meets Roosevelt at Casablanca to plan next moves 14/1/43 370
– Promises help to Turkey if it is forced into war 30/1/43 *376*
– Visits troops at Tripoli on Middle East tour 4/2/43 380
– Watches Casablanca 8/2/43 382
– Ideas for Britain after war 21/3/43 *392*
– Announces lifting of ban on church bells 20/4/43 400
– Holds "Trident" talks with Roosevelt on next steps 11/5/43 *406*
– Attitude to Bletchley Park 17/5/43 411
– Addresses Congress on Alliance strategy 19/5/43 411
– Arrives in Tunisia with Marshall to plan for Italy 27/5/43 412
– Visits troops in North Africa 1/6/43 415
– Wishes to ban "Colonel Blimp" 11/6/43 415
– "Shunts aside" Wavell and Auchinleck 18/6/43 417
– Orders British military mission to join Tito 23/6/43 419
– Privately questions bombing of Germany 25/6/43 419
– "Sword of justice" and "Unconditional Surrender" speech 30/6/43 *420*
– Wants to "strike at the knee" in Italian campaign 13/7/43 *425*
– Plans to use icebergs as floating air bases 19/7/43 *427*
– Italy will be "scarred" if it does not surrender 27/7/43 *428*
– Allied leaders meet in Quebec 13/8/43 434
– Suggests common citizenship between UK and US 9/9/43 444
– At Sextant Conference in Cairo 25/11/43 464
– At Teheran Conference 28/11/43 9
– Ill with pneumonia 16/12/43 470
– Views on Overlord invasion plan 6/1/44 479
– Meeting with de Gaulle 12/1/44 481
– Lays down priorities for Bomber Command 27/1/44 *483*
– Conversation with Roosevelt monitored 1/2/44 487
– Angry about Anzio landings 12/2/44 488
– Desperate for British victory in Italy 29/2/44 493
– Broadcasts on war situation 26/3/44 *502*
– Gets vote of confidence in conduct of war 29/3/44 503
– Attends Overlord briefing 15/5/44 517
– Clashes with de Gaulle 5/6/44 *520*
– Visits liberated France 14/6/44 531
– Reads description of Auschwitz gas chambers 27/6/44 538
– Visits troops in Italy 11/8/44 551
– Watches Eighth Army approach Gothic Line 25/8/44 557
– Attends Octagon Conference in Quebec 11/9/44 *562*
– Agrees collaboration on atomic bomb with Roosevelt 19/9/44 564
– Talks with Stalin about post-war Europe 9/10/44 572
– Attends armistice celebrations in Paris 11/11/44 *579*
– Admits London is under attack by V2s 10/11/44 580
– 70th birthday 30/11/44 585
– Criticized for armed intervention in Greece 7/12/44 586
– Visits Athens during government crisis 28/12/44 593
– Stands his ground on Poland 1/1/45 597
– Appeals for unity at home 18/1/45 599
– Meets Roosevelt in Malta 30/1/45 *602*
– Drinks an aphrodisiac 17/2/45 *605*
– Holds talks in Cairo 20/2/45 607
– Worried about Russians arriving first in Berlin 28/3/45 617
– Announces Allied link-up on Elbe 27/4/45 627
– Furious at Russian arrest of Polish negotiators 5/5/45 634
– Broadcasts to the nation on VE Day 8/5/45 635
– Says our troubles are not over 13/5/45 638
– Resigns as prime minister 23/5/45 639
– Says Labour would stoop to Gestapo tactics 4/6/45 642
– Arrives for Potsdam conference 16/7/45 *648*
– Flies home from Potsdam for election results 24/7/45 *649*
– Loses election 26/7/45 650
– Speaks of iron curtain in Europe 16/8/45 *655*
– Makes speech in Fulton, Missouri 3/46 663
– Biography 681
Chuyo (aircraft carrier) *465*
Ciano, Galeazzo *45*, *65*, 69, 70, *71*, 95, 125, *158*, 365, 380, 427, 481
Cisterna 485, *486*, *518*
Citadel (operation) 411, 420, 423, 425
Citizen Kane (film) 259
City of Benares (liner) *120*
City of Flint (cargo ship) 30, *34*, *35*, 37, *59*
Civil Defence 22, 174
Civita *530*
Civitavecchia *530*
Clacton *76*
Clair, Rene 475
Clairvaux *154*
Clark Field *599*, *601*, 602
Clark, Kenneth 62
Clark, Mark *342*, 349, 440, 443, 445, 463, 479, 482, 519, 521, 551, 569, 681
Clauberg, Karl 316, 391, 415
Clermont-Ferrand *414*
Cleve 604
Clevesy Pass *409*
Clyde Estuary *392*
Clyde, Firth of *62*
Clydesdale *168*
CNR 486
Coal-mining *69*, 151, 242, 242, *294*, *304*, 412, *414*, *414*, 449, 465, *495*, 501, 657
Coastal Command
– (see RAF)
Coblenz 578, *589*, 614
Cobra (operation) *546*, 547
Cocanada *288*
Codes
– (see Bletchley Park; Ultra intelligence; individual names eg Enigma)
Cohen, Jack *415*
Colchester *322*
Colditz
– (see PoWs)
Cold War
– Americans alarmed by Churchill's Fulton speech 3/46 663
– USSR blockade Berlin and 'Stalinism' emerges (1948-9) 663
– Wars in Korea and Vietnam 664, 665
Colepaugh, William *605*
Collina 578
Collins, J Lawton 503, 530, 535, 547, 592
Colmar 584, *586*, *589*, *603*, *603*
Cologne *198*, *205*, 214, *237*, 270, 302, *420*, *422*, 494, 573, 575, 578, *589*, 609, *610*, 611
Colombia
– Declares state of belligerency with Germany 28/11/43 *464*
Colombo *286*
Colorado (battleship) 585
Columbus (liner) *45*, *47*
Comacchio, Lake 620, 622
Combined Chiefs of Staffs Committee
– (see Anglo-US Combined Chiefs of Staff Committee)
Combined Operations 235, 285, 290, 326, 439
COMIDAC 486
Comintern 13, 408
Commandos *100*, 106, 166, 193, *239*, 257, 285, *304*, *330*, *331*, *338*, 343, 349, *401*, *422*, 443
Commonwealth
– (see individual countries)
Commonwealth Ca12 "Boomerang" fighter-bombers
– (see Boomerang fighter-bombers)
Communist Manifesto *32*
Communist Party (British) 28, 158, 290
Communist Party (French) *26*
Compass (operation) *142*
Compiegne 98, 285
Comps, Andre *448*
Conant, James 356
Concentration camps
– see also Germany (racial policies); PoWs; individual camps by name
– Details revealed in Britain 2/11/39 36
– Scope expanded 1/5/45 184
– Role in final solution 31/7/41 210
– New gas chambers and incinerators 2/4/42 286
– Medical experiments at Auschwitz and Dachau 7/7/42 316
– Kaltenbrunner becomes head of RSHA 29/1/43 *376*
– Precautions to avoid mass breakouts during air raids 8/2/43 *381*
– Situation 28/2/43 385
– Himmler orders evidence of mass murders to be destroyed 31/7/43 431
– Uprising at Treblinka 2/8/43 433
– Medical experiments on human guinea-pigs 2/9/43 441
– Photographs published in French underground paper 30/9/43 *448*
– Himmler orders all gypsies to be interned 15/11/43 *462*
– Allied reconnaissance aircraft photographs Auschwitz 4/4/44 *504*
– Jews beg Allies to bomb railways to camps 27/6/44 538
– Russian troops capture Majdanek 24/7/44 546
– Breendonck revealed by Allies 3/1/45 *596*
– Russian soldiers discover Auschwitz 27/1/45 601
– Evacuation attempt by Himmler foiled by Hitler 6/2/45 *603*
– Himmler promises to surrender them intact 12/3/45 *613*
– 15,000 Jews moved out of Buchenwald 6/4/45 *618*
– US generals and troops horrified 12/4/45 622
– Liberation of camps continues 29/4/45 627
– German people forced to visit 27/4/45 631
– Donitz tries to distance military from atrocities 18/5/45 *637*
– Globocnik commits suicide 31/5/45 *640*
– Germans ordered to watch films 7/6/45 *642*
– Survivors carry cross through Paris 12/7/45 *647*
Conical Hill *639*
Coningham, Arthur 398
Conscientious objectors 174, 286
Conscription *32*, 36, *43*, *54*, 64, *120*, 122, *128*, 174, 194, *203*, 216, *220*, 245, 251, 254, *271*, *278*, 292, 295, 319, 330, 434, 480
Conservative Party 83, 86, 127
Constance, Lake 419
Constanta 507
Conte di Cavour (battleship) *605*
Conti, Leonardo 238
Convoys
– see also Arctic; Atlantic; Atlantic, Battle of the; Mediterranean; U-boats
– First Atlantic convoy leaves Canada for Britain 15/9/39 22
– Germany to torpedo without warning 16/10/39 *32*
– Churchill claims system is a success 5/12/39 44
– Germany steps up attacks on merchant shipping 15/2/40 63
– Neutral convoy attacked in North Sea 20/3/40 *69*
– Raided in British home waters 10/7/40 *103*
– Attacked off Dover 10/7/40 104
– Dodge cross-channel guns 22/8/40 114
– HX-72 suffers heavy losses 22/9/40 *123*
– RN worried by growing German threat 22/9/40 125
– British ships sink German convoy 13/10/40 *128*
– U-boat "wolfpacks" unleashed 19/10/40 129
– Italy attacks British convoy in Red Sea 21/10/40 *130*
– "Admiral Scheer" attacks HX-84 5/11/40 135
– Italian attack at Cape Sportivo 27/11/40 *140*
– Force H escorts Malta convoy 6/1/41 *151*
– Face stronger German attacks 22/2/41 163
– Vichy France to defend food convoys against British 10/3/41 170
– RN sinks German supply ships 16/4/41 181
– Operation Tiger 7/5/41 *184*
– "Substance" leaves for Malta 21/7/41 *208*
– First Arctic convoy 21/8/41 *216*
– "Halberd" reaches Malta 28/9/41 226
– First Arctic convoy, PQ-1, docks at Archangel 11/10/41 231
– U-boats attack PQ-8 17/1/42 *264*
– Maltese convoy attacked 15/2/42 *273*
– Benghazi attacked to protect Maltese convoy 20/3/42 *282*
– Convoy reaches Malta 24/3/42 284
– US adopts convoy system as PQ-13 reaches Murmansk 1/4/42 287
– QP-11 attacked; Russian gold sunk 2/5/42 297
– Luftwaffe smashes PQ-16 30/5/42 302
– Harpoon and Vigorous head for Malta 11/6/42 *306*
– Harpoon and Vigorous attacked 16/6/42 309
– PQ-17 sails 27/6/42 *310*
– PQ-17 sighted by Germans 1/7/42 *312*
– Allied shipping losses reach new peak 1/7/42 313
– PQ-17 shattered 7/7/42 315
– U-boats on the US east coast admit defeat 19/7/42 *318*
– Huff Duff boosts British convoy defences 31/7/42 *319*
– Pedestal escort HMS Eagle sunk 11/8/42 *322*
– Operation Pedestal gets through to Malta 15/8/42 324
– PQ-18 reaches USSR 18/9/42 334
– Operation Stone Age breaks siege of Malta 20/11/42 353

– RN sinks German military convoy 2/12/42 357
– JW-51A reopens Arctic supply route 15/12/42 *360*
– JW-51B wins Battle of Barents Sea 31/12/42 364
– Suspension of Arctic route infuriates Stalin 30/3/43 *394*
– British ships reach Alexandria without loss 26/5/43 *412*
– British-Greek force attacks Italian convoy 2/6/43 *414*
– Battle of Convoys ONS-18 and ON-202 23/9/43 *446*
– Donitz takes charge of attack on SL-139 17/11/43 *462*
– Scharnhorst to attack JW-55B 25/12/43 *470*
– JW-55B escorts sink Scharnhorst 26/12/43 473
– JW-56 sails for Murmansk 12/1/44 *480*
– JW-56B sails for Murmansk *481*
– JW-56A attacked 26/1/44 *483*
– RA-57 returns to Scotland 10/3/44 *495*
– JW-58 weathers heavy attack without loss 31/3/44 503
– Convoy system abolished 28/5/45 *640*
Copenhagen 73, 381, 449, 482, *537*, *596*, 616, *631*
Coral Sea, Battle of the *296*
Corap, Andre 85
Corfu *138*, *448*, *571*
Corinth *571*
Corinth Canal *181*
Corinth, Gulf of 571
Corlett, Charles 487
Cornwall (cruiser) *184*, 288
Cornwallis, Kinahan 184
Corona 455
Coronet (operation) 644
Corps Franc d'Afrique
– (see Free French)
Corregidor *282*, 289, *294*, *296*, 605, *607*
Corriano *560*
Corsica *442*, 447, 451
Cortez, John 575
Cos *444*, *450*, 457
COSSAC *400*
Cossack (destroyer) 64, *235*
Cossacks 24, 318, 642
Cota, Norman 512
Cotentin Peninsula *518*, 523, 530, *534*
Cottbus (operation) *414*, 414
Cotton, Billy 60
Cotton, Sidney 456
Coulommiers 82
Counter-intelligence 283
– see also Double agents; Twenty Committee
Courageous (aircraft carrier) 25
Courland 568, 583, *597*
Courseulles 525
Coutances *543*, *546*
Coventry 136, 178, 352
Coventry (cruiser) 334
Cover (operation) *520*
Cowan, David 607, 609
Coward, Noel 103, 204, 364, 405
Crab 529
Cracow *30*, 361, 431, *494*, *599*, *658*
Craigavon, Viscount 140
Craigie, Robert 109
Cranborne, Viscount 489
Cranley, Lord 532
Crawford, Joan 475
Crazy Gang 51
Crerar, Henry *38*, 501, *546*, 607, 681
Crete *105*, *132*, *172*, *179*, *181*, *187*, *190*, *378*, *422*, *452*, 510, *569*
Crimea *214*, *237*, *253*, *280*, *296*, *314*, 438, *455*, *504*, *506*, 509, *513*
Cripps, Stafford *174*, 206, 273, 283, 301, 353, 385
Croatia *176*, *190*, *223*, 317, 399
Cromwell tanks
– (see Tanks)
Crosby, Bing 475, 587
Crossbow (operation) *467*, 471
Crowborough *444*
Crown Film Unit 209
Cruiser-type tanks
– (see Tanks)
Crusader (operation) 230, *241*, 247
Crusader tanks
– (see Tanks)
Cruwell, Ludwig *210*, 243, 392
Cruz Point *347*, *351*
Csaky, Istvan 139
Cuba
– Pro-Nazi plot discovered 10/8/41 *214*
Cumberland (cruiser) 47
Cunningham, Alan 157, 161, *163*, 165, *170*, 178, 230
Cunningham, Andrew *103*, 152, *154*, 172, 244, *286*, *404*, 444, 451, *453*, 681
Cunningham, John *453*
Cunningham, Julian 470
Cup Final 186
Curacao *79*, *273*
Curacao (cruiser) *338*
Curlew (cruiser) *89*
Currie, Laughlin 168
Curtin, John 228, 245, *256*, 269, *276*, 292, 306, 336, *417*, *436*, 482, 517, *646*
Curzon Line 480, 542
Cvetkovich, Dragisa *161*, 173
Cyprus *55*, 195
Cyrenaica *158*
Cyril, Prince of Bulgaria *602*
Czechoslovakia
– see also Free Czechs
– Sudetenland demanded by Germany 9/38 14
– Czech National Army in exile formed in France 2/10/39 *28*
– German brutality in Prague 28/10/39 35
– Benes sets up Czech National Committee in Paris 17/11/39 *38*
– Nazi arrests and executions 19/11/39 *40*
– Nazis make more arrests in Prague 2/1/40 *54*
– Jewish businesses closed by Germans 10/2/40 61
– Provisional govt under Benes set up in London 23/7/40 107
– Government in exile signs treaty with USSR 18/7/41 *206*
– Slovak troops fighting with Germany against USSR 9/9/41 222
– Heydrich becomes deputy protector of Bohemia & Moravia 29/9/41 227
– 1,000 Jews deported to Poland from Theresienstadt 27/4/42 *294*
– Attack on Heydrich in Prague 27/5/42 303
– Lidice razed as reprisal for Heydrich killing 10/6/42 307
– Heydrich's assassins kill themselves after gun battle 18/6/42 308
– Government in exile asks US to warn on Axis atrocities 31/7/42 319
– 6,000 Theresienstadt Jews killed at Maly Trostenets 30/9/42 *337*
– Government in exile gives Jews promise for future 29/10/42 346
– RAF raids 14/5/43 408
– Signs pact with USSR 12/12/43 469
– Government in exile broadcasts call to arms 12/3/44 *497*
– Partisans declare free republic 29/8/44 558
– Red Army forces enter 24/9/44 *566*
– Soviet troops enter 15/12/44 *587*
– Eisenhower orders US Army not to advance 17/3/45 *613*
– US Third Army crosses the frontier 18/4/45 *624*
– US First Army troops prepare to march in 4/5/45 632
– Patriots rise against the Germans 5/5/45 632
– Last remnants of German army surrender 11/5/45 *634*
– Prague is liberated 9/5/45 636
– Russians begin to impose their rule 10/6/45 644
– Cedes territory to USSR 29/6/45 *645*
– Germans and Hungarians deprived of citizenship 3/8/45 *650*, 662
– Non-communists repressed 2/48 663
Czerniakow, Adam 141, 318
Czestochowa *418*

D

D'Aquino, Iva Ikuko Toguri
– (see Tokyo Rose)
D'Argenlieu, Thierry 226
D-Day
– See also France (Allied land attacks)
– Montgomery changes plan for Overlord 6/1/44 479
– Invasion exercise 31/3/44 503
– Training exercise goes disastrously wrong 29/4/44 511
– Allied servicemen assemble in Britain 30/4/44 511
– Final training exercise 6/5/44 512
– Eisenhower sets date 8/5/44 *513*
– Europe bombed in preparation for landings 21/5/44 *518*
– Eisenhower gives go-ahead 5/6/44 522
– Allied landings in Normandy 6/6/44 523
– Omaha Beach 6/6/44 524
– Parachutists and gliders begin the assault 6/6/44 524
– Gold Beach 6/6/44 525
– Juno Beach 6/6/44 525
– Sword Beach 6/6/44 525
– Utah Beach 6/6/44 525
– The invasion fleet 6/6/44 526
– Influence of the weather 6/6/44 527
– The men who planned Overlord 6/6/44 527
– How the Germans were taken by surprise 6/6/44 527
– The deception plans 6/6/44 527
– Allied air supremacy 6/6/44 528
– The part of the French Resistance 6/6/44 528
– Eyewitness accounts by servicemen 6/6/44 528
– Ingenious inventions to tackle German defences 6/6/44 529
– Reporters 6/6/44 529
– Numbers killed since invasion 26/6/44 *537*
"D-Day Dodgers" 577
Dabrowa *602*
Dace (submarine) *575*
Dachau 36, *136*, *187*, 210, 316, *381*, 441, *458*, *621*, 627, *643*
Dagabur *168*
Dagami *575*
Dahlerus, Birger 15, 16, 28
Daily Herald (newspaper) 279
Daily Mirror (newspaper) 279, 282
Daily Telegraph (newspaper) *310*, 512
Daily Worker (newspaper) 158, 282, 327
Dainty (destroyer) *164*
Dairen 657
Dakar *103*, 123, *192*, *353*, 521
Dakota transports 417, 444, 496, 552, 571
Daladier, Edouard 14, 17, 21, 24, 28, 30, 32, *43*, *66*, 69, *79*, 81, 86, *91*, *231*, 273, *631*, *649*
Dalai Lama 65
Dalton, Hugh 86, *105*, 108, *208*, *276*, 283
Damascus 189, *198*
Damaskinos, Archbishop *591*
Dambuster raid 410, *488*, 613
Damur 205
Dannecker, Theodor 285, 390
Danube river 162, 165, 167, 506, *569*, 578, 584, *586*, 623
Danzig 16, *22*, *35*, 314, 328, 398, 578, *597*, 601, 609, *610*, *614*, *616*
Dapcevich 574
Dardenelles *166*
Daring (destroyer) *64*
Darlan, Jean 24, 102, 145, *160*, 162, *164*, 170, 187, 233, 289, *342*, 352, *356*, *360*, 362
Darmstadt 615
Darnand, Joseph *376*
Darter (submarine) *575*
Darwin *275*, *404*
Dasher (escort carrier) *392*
Dauntless dive-bombers 405, 426
Dautry, Raoul 21, 24
Davao 505, *631*
Davis, Bette 475
Dawe, Leonard 512
Dayan, Moshe *196*
DC-3 Dakota transports
– (see Dakota transports)
DD Duplex-Drive tank
– (see Tanks)
De Gaulle, Charles
– Views on French defence 21/3/40 69
– Worried about French army command 11/5/40 82
– Joins government 5/6/40 *91*
– Advocates military tactics like Guderian's 5/6/40 94
– Broadcasts from London calling for continued resistance 18/6/40 *97*
– Forms French national committee in London 23/6/40 *100*
– Recognized by Britain as leader in exile of France 28/6/40 100
– Sentenced in absentia to imprisonment 6/7/40 102
– Bastille Day celebrations in London 14/7/40 106
– Sentenced to death in absentia 2/8/40 *109*
– Invasion of Dakar fails 25/9/40 123
– In French Equatorial Africa 27/10/40 132
– To end French mandate in Syria and Lebanon 15/7/41 207
– Forms national committee 23/9/41 226
– Asks Resistance to stop killings because of executions 23/10/41 *233*
– Wants Resistance united with Free French 26/1/42 262
– Sends Free French to take Madagascar from British 14/5/42 *298*
– Backs Russian call for second front 24/5/42 *301*
– Reaction to Giraud's appointment 26/12/42 362
– Meets Giraud at Casablanca summit 14/1/43 370
– Asks Giraud to declare Free French republic in N Africa 23/2/43 *384*
– Begins talks with Giraud on provisional government 31/5/43 *412*
– Calls for fourth republic 6/6/43 416
– To lead Fighting French in all areas but North Africa 22/6/43 *418*
– President of National Defence Committee 1/8/43 *432*
– Becomes president of CFLN 9/11/43 461
– Flies to Morocco to meet Churchill 12/1/44 481
– Takes control of Free French forces 4/4/44 *504*
– Complains about British restrictions before D-Day 17/4/44 509
– Clashes with Churchill 5/6/44 *520*
– Broadcasts on D-Day 6/6/44 529
– Returns to liberated France 14/6/44 531
– Meets Roosevelt 6/7/44 *539*
– Enters liberated Paris 25/8/44 555
– Allies recognize his provisional government 23/10/44 *575*
– Meets Stalin for talks 2/12/44 *586*
– Refuses to sacrifice Strasburg 23/1/45 601
– Announces limited self-government for Indochina 23/3/45 *614*
– Decorates Montgomery 24/5/45 *639*
– Proposes referendum on French system of government 9/7/45 *647*
– Biography 682
De Guary, Gerald 197
De Havilland[co]
– (see Mosquito bombers; Mosquito fighters)
De Jongh, Andree 355
De Lattre de Tassigny, Jean
– See De Tassigny, Jean de Lattre
De Ruyter (cruiser) 276
De Tassigny, Jean de Lattre *453*, *470*, *478*, 553, 557, 582, 584, *586*, *616*, 636, 642
De Valera, Eamon
– Wants emergency powers for crackdown on IRA 6/1/40 55
– Seeks to maintain Eire's neutrality 1/5/40 78
– Mobilizes armed forces 16/6/40 *97*
– Refuses to allow Britain use of Irish naval bases 7/11/40 134
– Protests to Germany about air raids 3/1/41 *150*
– Sways Churchill against conscription in Ulster 27/5/41 194
– Says Eire needs more troops to defend neutrality 3/2/42 271
– Fails to gain overall majority in general election 25/6/43 418
– Calls general election after Dail defeat 9/5/44 513
– Returned to power 1/6/44 521
– Regrets death of Hitler 3/5/45 632
De Wiart, Adrian Carton
– (see Carton de Wiart, Adrian)
De Witt, John 275
De la Chapelle, Fernand Bonnier 362
De la Vigerie, Henri Astier 362
Deakin, F W 412
Dean, Basil 60
Deat, Marcel 161, 218
Death Valley *534*
Death camps
– (see Concentration camps)
Debrecen 572, 591
Defense de la France (newspaper) *448*
Defiant aircraft 113
Degaussing 48
Degrelle, Leon *150*, *212*
Dehmut, General 514
Deir el-Zor *203*
Dejean, Maurice 226
Dekanozov, Vladimir 200
Delme Ridge 579
Delmer, Sefton 283
Delvino *142*
Demobilization *573*, *644*, 657
Demon (operation) 182
Dempo (troopship) *497*
Dempsey, Miles 538
Demyansk 264, *271*, 277, *292*, *386*
Denmark
– Declares neutrality 3/9/39 20
– Declares neutrality in Russo-Finnish war 7/12/39 *43*
– Protests at German sinking of ships 15/2/40 63
– Reaffirms neutrality 25/2/40 *65*
– Invasion ordered by Hitler 1/3/40 *66*
– Iceland severs links 10/4/40 *73*
– Germany invades 9/4/40 73
– Boycotting Germans 14/4/40 75
– RAF continues to bomb German airfields 3/5/40 *78*
– Withdraws from League of Nations 19/7/40 *105*
– Volunteers in RAF Reserve 21/9/40 122
– Kauffman signs Greenland bases agreement with US 12/4/41 178
– Volunteers to fight USSR with Germany 24/6/41 *200*
– Riots as government signs anti-Comintern pact 27/11/41 *243*
– Attacks on Danes fighting with Germans 3/10/42 339
– Christian forced to appoint Scavenius prime minister 9/11/42 *349*
– RAF raids on U-boat engine works at Copenhagen 13/2/43 381
– Anti-Nazi coalition wins election 23/3/43 *392*
– Scavenius refuses to send saboteurs for trial in Germany 9/8/43 *434*
– Martial law as resistance to Nazis grows 29/8/43 *438*
– Jews smuggled out 30/9/43 449
– Anti-Nazi priest murdered 5/1/44 479
– Germans arrest all policemen 19/1/44 482
– Coast closed by Germany 9/5/44 515
– General strike in Copenhagen 28/6/44 *537*
– Hitler orders fortifications on North Sea coast 29/8/44 *558*
– General strike 16/9/44 563
– Gestapo building precision-bombed 31/10/44 *575*
– Fighting breaks out between Germans and civilians 5/5/45 *631*
– Germans on Bornholm Island surrender 16/5/45 *637*
Depth charges *55*
Der Sturmer (newspaper) *28*
Derna *142*, *158*, *176*, *195*, 253, 311
Derousseaux, Olivier 85, 90
Desert Island Discs (radio programme) *268*
Desert Rats 217, 394, 426
– see also Desert War
Desert War
– see also North Africa
– Benghazi falls as British defeat Italians at Beda Fomm 7/2/41 *160*
– British retreat as Italians retake Keren 12/2/41 *161*
– British and German troops clash at El Agheila 20/2/41 *163*
– Siege of Tobruk begins 4/5/41 *184*
– Operation Brevity starts 15/11/41 *187*
– RAF bombs Benghazi and Derna 7/6/41 *195*
– Operation Battleaxe 15/6/41 *198*
– German and Italian air forces bomb Tobruk 23/6/41 *200*
– Axis bombards Tobruk 9/7/41 205
– Axis forces reorganized 31/7/41 *210*
– "Rats" garrisoning Tobruk 18/8/41 217
– Heavy fighting at Sidi Rezegh 22/11/41 241
– Eighth Army starts Operation Crusader 18/11/41 *241*
– Allies capture General von Ravenstein 28/11/41 *243*

– Guderian's renewed attack halted by weather 28/10/41 *235*
– Halder plans final assault 12/11/41 *239*
– Germans blame defeat on weather 13/12/41 247
– German losses 15/1/42 *264*
– Celebrations that Germans are trapped in Korsun pocket 3/2/44 *486*
– German PoWs paraded through the streets 17/7/44 *543*
– First congress of Russian church since Revolution 31/1/45 *602*
– VE Day celebrations 9/5/45 635
– Victory over fascism celebrated 24/6/45 645
Moselle river *560*, 560, 577, 579, *581*
Mosley, Diana 105
Mosley, Oswald 88, 105, 462
Mosquito bombers *140*, *301*, 363, 378, 381, 387, *394*, 441, 461, 463, 480, 491, *506*, 513, 518, 558, 564, 570, *575*, 585, 587, *631*
Mosquito photo-reconnaissance aircraft 402
Mosquito target-markers 408
Moss, Stanley 510
Mosul *195*
Moszhaisk *231*
Motobu peninsula *624*
Mottistone, Lord 420
Moulin, Jean *136*, 268, 418, 422, 486
Moulmein *266*
Mount Austen *360*, 361, *368*, 373
Mount Chiunzi 443
Mount Durmitor 372
Mount Etna 424, 426, 428, 432
Mount Olympus 177, *179*
Mount Parnassus 182
Mount Santa Rosa *548*, *550*
Mount Suribachi 608
Mount Umurbrogol *569*, *577*
Mount Vesuvius 504
Mountbatten, Lord Louis 191, 235, 285, 290, 326, 402, 439, *452*, 454, 464, 480, *569*, 631, *646*, *660*
Moyale 110
Moyne, Lord 207, *579*
Mozdok *368*
Mozhaisk 262, *266*
Mozyr *480*
Mrocza 19
Mrs Miniver (film) 364
Msus *176*, *268*
MTBs 334, *340*
Mtsensk *427*
Mu river *386*
Muar 267
Muar river 265
Muara Island *643*
Mufti of Jerusalem
– (see Haj Amin al-Husseini)
Muhu island 583
Mukden *658*
Mulberry harbours *450*, *452*, 526, 530, 533, *534*
Mulheim 419
Mulhouse *583*
Munaji, Hurada 280
Munassib Depression 337
Munchen (weather ship) *184*
Munchen-Gladbach 214, 609, *610*
Munda *353*, *368*, *386*, 405, *406*, *414*, 421, *428*, 433, 439
Munich 37, *134*, *336*, 384, 461
Munich (operation) 283
Munk, Kaj 479
Munro, Ross 529
Munster 416, 617
Munsterland (blockade-runner) *481*
Murdoch, Richard 51
Murmansk *34*, 42, *200*, 287, 297, 302, *394*, *480*, *481*, *492*
Murphy, Audie 553, *601*
Murphy, Robert 363
Murrow, Ed 529
Musashi (battleship) *575*
Muselier 102, 106, 226
Music
– (see Arts and Entertainment)
Music While You Work (radio programme) 147, 421
Mussert, Anton 270, *360*, *467*
Mussolino, Benito
– Pre-war political ideals 6
– Invades Abyssinia 10/35 13
– Gives aid to Franco's Nationalists (1930s) 13
– Invades Albania (1939) 15
– Does not support German invasion of Poland 31/8/39 15
– Territorial ambitions in Europe 9/9/39 20
– Meets Sumner Welles 26/2/40 *65*
– Meets Hitler at Brennero 18/3/40 70
–Tells king Italy must eventually enter war 31/3/40 *71*
– Says Germany cannot be defeated in Europe 1/5/40 *78*
– Tells Hitler Italy will enter war next week 30/5/40 *89*
– Declares war on Allies 10/6/40 95
– Invades Greece 6/40 7
– Meets Hitler to discuss French armistice terms 18/6/40 97
– Calls Punta Stilo a victory 9/7/40 105
– Doubts Hitler's claim to have won war 4/10/40 125
– Orders invasion of Greece against Hitler's wish 15/10/40 *128*
– Greek invasion essential 18/11/40 *138*
– Asks Hitler for military aid 19/1/41 157
– Says victory is assured 23/2/41 *164*
– Leads forces in Albania 9/3/41 *168*
– Meets Hitler to hear war plans 2/6/41 195
– Meets Hitler at Rastenburg and visits Italian troops 25/8/41 *217*
– Urges Japan to fight Britain 8/10/41 *230*
– Predicts destruction of Allies 28/10/41 *235*
– Arrives in Tripoli expecting victory for Axis 29/6/42 *310*
– Returns to Rome 20/7/42 *318*
– Vetos Rommel's proposal to withdraw from North Africa 24/11/42 354
– Sacks Ciano as morale in Italy worsens 5/2/43 380
– Withdraws troops from eastern front 2/3/43 *386*
– Refuses Rommel's evacuation plea & offers more troops 10/3/43 389
– Meets Hitler at Salzburg 11/4/43 396
– Calls for reinforcements in Sardinia after Mincemeat 13/5/43 407
– Rejects Roumania's suggestion of leaving war 1/7/43 *422*
– Morale low at meeting with Hitler while Rome is bombed 19/7/43 427
– Stripped of office by king and arrested 25/7/43 429
– Imprisoned on Maddalena Island 8/8/43 *434*
– Forms rival government to Badoglio administration 15/9/43 *444*
– Snatched to freedom by German paratroopers 12/9/43 445
– Son-in-law executed for plotting to overthrow him 11/1/44 481
– Visits Vienna cancer clinic 17/4/44 508
– Flees advancing Allied forces 25/4/45 *626*
– Killed by partisans 28/4/45 630
– Biography 685
Mustang fighters 463, 468, *469*, 492, 494, 494, 506, *512*, 520, 528, 585, 637
Mutaguchi, Renya *495*, 498, 500, 536, 582
Myebon 598
Myitkyina 297, *300*, *383*, 388, *488*, *494*, 496, *497*, *510*, 517, 537
Myothit *575*
Myshkova river 361, *361*
Myslenice 31

N

NAAFI 331
Nadzab *442*
Naf river 480
Naga 507
Nagasaki *650*, 653
Nagato (battleship) *648*
Nagoya *613*, *637*, 638, 643
Nagumo, Chuichi 248, 286, 305, *539*
Nagykanisza 619
Naha *634*, *640*
Naiad (cruiser) *280*
Nakajima Kikka fighters *652*
Nalchik *344*, *368*
Namhkam *599*
Namsos *75*, 77, 79
Namur 80, 81, 82, *84*, 485, *548*, 590
Nancy 82, 96
Nanhsien *404*, *414*
Nanking 29, 71, 140, *296*, 579, 658
Nanning 41, 133, 583, 641
Nanomea *438*
Nantes *446*
Napalm *543*, *624*, *647*
Napopo *360*, *363*
Naples 356, *412*, *417*, *432*, *446*, *448*, 450, *452*, *508*
Narao 643
Narew river 578
Narew-Vistula-San River Line 24
Narva 489
Narva river 484
Narvik 61, *69*, 70, 71, *72*, *73*, 73, 74, *75*, 77, *78*, *84*, *89*, *94*
Narwhal (submarine) *65*
Nasagbu 602
Nashville (cruiser) 573, *587*
Nasi, Guglielmo *243*
Nasser, Abdul Gamal 665
National Committee for a Free Germany *425*, *427*
National Gallery concerts 75, 128
National Liberation Front (Greece)
– (see EAM)
National Resistance Committee
– (see CNR)
National Savings 390
National Socialist Party
– (see Nazi Party)
National bread 281
Natunga 394
National disasters
– Earthquake in Turkey 27/12/39 *49*
– Earthquake in Roumania 8/11/40 *134*
– Floods in China 31/1/41 *158*
– Earthquake in Greece 1/3/41 *166*
– Cyclone in India 16/10/42 *340*
– Famine in China 31/7/43 *428*
– Typhoon sinks US ships in Philippines Sea 18/12/44 *589*
– Typhoon damages battleships off Okinawa 5/6/45 *642*
NATO 664
Nauplia *181*
Naura Island *462*, *145*, *400*, 435
Nautsi 46
Navicerts *40*, 108
Nazi Party
– see also Germany (racial policies), Germany (home affairs)
– Emergence (1930s) 12
– Attacks Jews (Kristallnacht) 11/38 14
– Foreign investments alleged 21/9/39 *22*
– Der Sturmer publishes "hymn of hate" against England 5/10/39 *28*
– Treatment of Jews and dissidents exposed in Britain 30/10/39 *34*
– Brutalities in concentration camps 2/11/39 36
– Confiscates Thyssen's assets 24/11/39 41
– Opposed to employment of women 13/1/40 56
– Opposed to compulsory employment of women 27/4/40 78
– Plans for conquered Britain 6/7/40 103
– French art treasures seized 17/9/30 *120*
– Frank's speech on Jewish policy 22/1/41 *156*
– Policy on women relaxed 9/3/41 169
– Policy on Christianity 30/4/41 183
– History of anti-Semitism 31/7/41 210
– Bishop Graf condemns policy of killing old and ill 3/8/41 212
– Allies warn of war crimes trials 13/1/42 265
– Offers reward for information on Heydrich killing 10/6/42 307
– Members arrested in New York 11/7/42 314
– Shock at Stalingrad defeat 6/2/43 379
– Koch says Germans are "master race" 5/3/43 *386*
– Der Sturmer says extermination of Jews in progress 25/3/43 *392*
– Nazis to wage war on jazz 12/2/44 489
– Army, navy and air force adopt Nazi salute 24/7/44 *546*
– Hitler orders members to build new "west wall" 24/8/44 *554*
– Hitler orders commanders to consult Gauleiters 19/9/44 *564*
– Gauleiters to organize Volkssturm 25/9/44 568
– Pope speaks out against Nazism 18/3/45 *614*
Nazi-Soviet non-aggression pact
– (see German-Soviet non-aggression pact)
Neave, Airey 264, 341
Nebelwerfer rocket-launchers 383
Neberjaisk *404*
Nedich, Milan *217*
Nehring, Walther 329, 356
Nehru, Pandit *289*
Nelson 34
Nelson (battleship) *118*, *226*, 324, *448*
Nelson (destroyer) 532
Neptune (cruiser) *253*
Neptune (plan) 526
Nero Command *614*
Nestor (destroyer) *253*, 309
Netherlands
– see also Dutch East Indies
– Partial state of siege proclaimed 1/11/39 *35*
– Defensive flooding zone widened 8/11/39 *36*
– German invasion threat 5/11/39 37
– Outrage at mining of liner 20/11/39 39
– On state of alert for German invasion 13/1/40 *55*
– Troops' leave cancelled 14/1/40 *57*
– C-in-C resigns 5/2/40 *60*
– Border garrisons alerted 2/4/40 *72*
– Warned by Vatican of imminent German attack 30/4/40 77
– Crackdown on anti-government elements 4/5/40 *78*
– Allies demolish ports 10/5/40 *79*
– Germany invades 10/5/40 80
– Germans advance but fail to capture Queen Wilhelmina 11/5/40 81
– Government in exile in London after surrender 14/5/40 84
– Seyss-Inquart appointed Reich commissioner 20/4/40 *87*
– Troops rescued at Dunkirk 4/6/40 92
– Germans arrest Winkelman 3/7/40 *102*
– RAF bombs German airstrips 11/7/40 *103*
– Navy escapes to Britain 20/12/40 144
– Jews ordered to register 10/1/40 *151*
– SS arrests Jews in Amsterdam 22/2/41 *163*
– SS quells protests over treatment of Jews 25/2/41 *164*
– Volunteers fighting with Germans against USSR 9/9/41 222
– Council of Churches protests at Nazi treatment of Jews 5/1/42 263
– Japan declares war 12/1/42 *264*
– Germans execute resistance leaders 4/5/42 297
– Jews to wear yellow Star of David 1/6/42 304
– 2,000 Jews from Amsterdam deported to Auschwitz 15/7/42 *316*
– Government in exile asks US to warn on Axis atrocities 31/7/42 319
– 987 Jews deported to Auschwitz 7/8/42 *321*
– 6,000 Jews deported to Auschwitz 30/9/42 *337*
– RAF bombs Eindhoven 6/12/42 *357*
– Hitler appoints Anton Mussert as leader 13/12/42 *360*
– RAF bombs Philips factory at Eindhoven 30/3/43 *394*
– Germans proclaim martial law 9/5/43 406
– Germans confiscate wireless sets 16/5/43 *409*
– RAF precision-bombs Gestapo building in The Hague 11/4/44 *506*
– Coastal defences reinforced 6/5/44 512
– RAF precision-bombs Dutch air ministry 3/5/44 513
– Exiled government gives Allies free hand 16/5/44 517
– Hitler orders fortifications on North Sea coast 29/8/44 *558*
– US cavalrymen enter at Maastricht 9/9/44 *560*
– Advance British units move in 11/9/44 562
– General strike as British troops approach 17/9/44 *564*
– RAF bombers breach Walcheren island sea wall 3/10/44 570
– Allies attack German pocket south of Maas 25/10/44 *575*
– British troops land on Walcheren island 1/11/44 *577*
– Resistance fighters try to execute SS general 6/3/45 *610*
– British troops take Arnhem 15/4/45 *624*
– Loses Indonesia (1949) 665
Neuengamme 632
Neuer Vorwarts (newspaper) *79*
Neurath, Konstantin von 660
Neuss 585, *610*
Neutrality 375
Neva river 221, 222, 371
New Britain 267, *273*, *338*, *351*, *361*, *381*, 397, 421, 433, *458*, *469*, *478*, *481*, *495*
New Caledonia *120*, *280*, *292*
New Georgia *353*, *368*, *406*, *414*, *418*, *428*, 439
New Guinea
– see also Papua, New Guinea
– Japan invades New Britain and New Ireland 24/1/42 267
– Japanese land at Lae and Salamaua 8/3/42 *280*
– Japanese forces land at Hollandia and Sorong 1/4/42 *286*
– Japanese land at Basabua 18/8/42 *325*
– Japanese withdraw from Napopo to Giruwa 27/12/42 *363*
– Japanese reinforcements land at Lae 7/1/43 *368*
– Eichelberger commands Allied operations 13/1/43 *370*
– Australians repel Japanese near Wau 1/2/43 *378*
– US troops poised for fresh offensive on Kumusi river 10/2/43 *381*
– Operation Elkton starts 12/2/43 *381*
– Battle of the Bismarck Sea 5/3/43 386
– Japanese bomb Wau 9/3/43 *389*
– Allies force Japanese into slow retreat 14/3/43 *390*
– US troops under Mackechnie land at Waria river mouth 31/3/43 *394*
– US Sixth Army sets up HQ at Milne Bay 20/6/43 *418*
– Allies approach Rabaul in Operation Cartwheel 30/6/43 421
– USAAF destroys Japanese air strength at Wewak 18/8/43 437
– Allied air attacks on Japanese at Lae 1/9/43 *440*
– Australians take Kaiapit 19/9/43 *446*
– Australians take Finschhafen 2/10/43 *450*
– Australians reinforce Finschhafen 20/10/43 *453*
– Australians hit main centre of Japanese resistance 17/11/43 *462*
– Australians take Huanko 1/12/43 *465*
– Australians take Lakona 15/12/43 *469*
– Last Japanese stronghold taken 19/12/43 471
– Australians take Kelanoa 5/1/44 *478*
– Australians take Finisterre 16/1/44 *481*
– Australians link up with Americans near Saidor 10/2/44 *488*
– US aircraft raid Japanese convoy 16/3/44 *497*
– US bombers hit Hollandia 3/4/44 *504*
– Australians retake Bogodjim 13/4/44 *506*
– Diversionary attack planned 19/4/44 *508*
– US reinforcements land at Aitape 4/5/44 *512*
– US forces land on Wakde Island 17/5/44 *515*
– US troops in trouble on Biak Island 29/5/44 519
– US forces take airfield on Biak Island 7/6/44 530
– Japanese troops hold out in Biak caves 21/6/44 *534*
– Japanese attack across the Wewak river 10/7/44 *541*
– US forces destroy enemy defences at Ibdi 28/7/44 *546*
– US forces push towards Torricelli mountains 3/8/44 *548*
– Japanese resistance on Noemfoor Island crushed 17/8/44 *552*
– Australians launch attack 11/5/45 634
– Australians reach Wewak 19/5/45 *637*

– Australians surround Wewak 24/5/45 *639*
New Hebrides *322*
New Ireland 267, *478*
New Jersey (battleship) *357*
New Mexico (battleship) 637
New Zealand
– see also New Zealand Army, Royal New Zealand Navy
– Declares war on Germany 3/9/39 20
– Michael Savage dies 26/3/40 *71*
– US marines arrive 14/6/42 *308*
– Lend-Lease 3/9/42 *330*
– Mass breakout by Japanese PoWs 25/2/43 *384*
– Butter rationing introduced 28/10/43 *455*
– Signs pact with Australia 21/1/44 482
New Zealand Army
– see also Anzac
– Forces fighting with Eighth Army 5/10/41 230
– Forces from Egypt capture Fort Capuzzo in Libya 21/11/41 *241*
– Forces link up with Tobruk garrison 27/11/41 *243*
– Troops defeat Italians at Alam Nayil 3/7/42 *312*
– LRDG patrol hunted by Luftwaffe after Barce raid 14/9/42 335
– Troops take Miteiriya Ridge 24/10/42 343
– Troops and tanks in Mareth Line manoeuvres 20/3/43 390
– Troops break through at Mareth Line 27/3/43 393
– Troops in Eighth Army include Maoris 30/3/43 394
– Freyberg's New Zealand Corps joins US Army in Cassino 3/2/44 *486*
– Troops land on the Green Islands 15/2/44 *490*
– Freyberg's troops assault Monte Cassino 15/2/44 490
– Troops with British XIII Corps in Italy 5/8/44 549
Newall, Cyril 125
Newcastle (cruiser) *208*
Newcastle, NSW 307
Newcastle-upon-Tyne 178
Newfoundland *298*
Newfoundland (cruiser) *427*
News Chronicle (newspaper) 279, 586
Newspapers and periodicals
– see also Censorship
– Der Sturmer attacks England as "curse of world" 5/10/39 *28*
– German Social Democrat paper closes after staff flees 5/5/40 *79*
– La Gerbe starts in Paris 11/7/40 *103*
– The Times personal column 10/7/40 104
– Picture Post publisher sets up Osterley Park 8/7/40 104
– La Libre Belgique starts 15/8/40 *110*
– Daily Worker closed down 28/1/41 158
– Attempted assassination of L'Oeuvre editor Deat 27/8/41 218
– Fri Ragbevegelse calls on Norwegians to resist 10/9/41 223
– Success of Picture Post 18/10/41 233
– Suddeutsche Volksstimme objects to war payments 31/10/41 236
– Volkischer Beobachter supports clothing appeal 20/12/41 254
– Post-war reconstruction of Britain discussed 4/3/42 279
– Morrison threatens to ban Daily Mirror 19/3/42 282
– Censorship problems 19/3/42 282
– MacArthur's censorship powers 6/5/42 *296*
– Liberty Barricade reports killings of Polish Jews 1/6/42 304
– Kolnische Zeitung announces evacuation 4/6/42 304
– Chicago Tribune report endangers codebreaking 7/6/42 *306*
– Daily Telegraph reports Nazi killings of Jews in Europe 30/6/42 *310*
– Daily Worker reappears on British streets 26/8/42 327
– Affected by shortage of newsprint 1/3/43 388
– Der Sturmer says extermination of Jews in progress 25/3/43 *392*
– The Times carries Major William Martin's death notice 30/4/43 402
– Regime Fascista reveals discontent in country 13/5/43 407
– German press celebrates Mussolini's 60th birthday 29/7/43 *428*
– Daily Telegraph reports German massacres of Poles 27/7/43 431
– Times bogus report on sabotage for Twenty Committee 18/8/43 437
– Red Star reports fighting in Ukraine 9/9/43 442
– Defense de la France prints concentration camp pictures 30/9/43 448
– Swedish newspaper reports German "catastrophe" 22/10/43 454
– Resistance workers publish fake issue of Le Soir 2/11/43 *458*
– Deutsche Allgemeine Zeitung reports air raids on Berlin 3/1/44 478
– Editor of GUNS arrested in Guernsey 12/2/44 488
– Unita Proletaria exposes deportation plans 3/3/44 494
– Pravda reports breakthrough in Ukraine 10/3/44 497
– Security scare about Daily Telegraph crosswords 2/5/44 512
– Osservatore Romano reports pope's concern for Warsaw 11/8/44 551
– British film critics review "Henry V" 1/12/44 586
– Der Angriff on German determination to defend Berlin 31/1/45 602
– Schwarze Korps says collapse is near 5/4/45 619
Ngakyedauk Pass 486, *488*
Nibeiwa 143
Niblack (destroyer) *176*
Nicaragua
– Ratifies UN charter 6/7/45 *646*
Nice 518
Nicholls Field *605*
Nicholson, James 112
Nicosia *428*
Niemoller, Martin *631*
Nierstein 615
Nieuport 89
Nigeria (cruiser) 302, 324
Night of the Strong Winds *499*
Nikolayev *216*
Nikopol *460*
Nile Delta 138, 313
Nimitz, Chester W *253*, 296, 358, 459, 491, 547, 563, 589, 620, *652*, 685
Ningbo *181*
Ningxian *45*
Nishinomiya *652*
Nishumura, Shoji 576
Niven, David 535, 593
Nizhne Chirskaye 361, 359
NKVD 95
Nobel peace prize *42*
Nobeoka *645*
Noble, Percy *351*
Noemfoor Island *539*, *552*
Nomaru, Kochisaburo *163*
Norfolk (cruiser) 302, 473
Normandie (liner) 189, *271*
North Africa
– see also Western Desert; Desert War; individual placenames
– British troops capture Italians on Egypt-Libya border 12/6/40 *94*
– British tanks to be sent 10/8/40 *109*
– Italian offensive at Sollum 13/9/40 *118*
– Italian forces dig in 18/9/40 *120*
– British withdraw as Italians reach Sidi Barrani 16/9/40 122
– British advance as Italians fortify Sidi Barrani 15/11/40 138
– RAF raids Benghazi, Benina and Berka 21/11/40 *138*
– O'Connor prepares to take Bardia 17/12/40 144
– Italian losses at Bardia 4/1/41 150
– Allies advancing on Tobruk 7/1/41 153
– Tobruk falls 22/1/41 157
– Italians counter-attack at Derna 30/1/41 158
– Rommel arrives in Libya 12/2/41 *161*
– British and Germans clash at El Agheila 20/2/41 *163*
– British naval losses off Derna and Tobruk 24/2/41 *164*
– Allies take Jarabub 21/3/41 170
– Afrika Korps reoccupies El Agheila 24/3/41 *172*
– British tanks break down in retreat from El Agheila 1/4/41 *174*
– O'Connor and troops captured by Afrika Korps at Derna 7/4/41 *176*
– Rommel rebuffed at Tobruk but expecting reinforcements 14/4/41 179
– Supply convoy broken by RN 16/4/41 181
– Afrika Korps attacks at Halfaya Pass 25/4/41 *181*
– Rommel's troops enter Egypt while Tobruk holds out 26/4/41 183
North Borneo *453*, 610
North Sea 39, *42*, *55*, *57*, *60*, *62*, *64*, *68*, *69*, *71*, *73*, 79, 91, *107*, *109*, *114*, *128*, *458*
North Weald 113
North Wind (operation) *596*
Northampton (cruiser) 357
Norway
– Declares neutrality 3/9/39 *16*
– Interns German prize crew of City of Flint 4/11/39 *35*
– Declares neutrality in Russo-Finnish war 7/12/39 *43*
– German invasion planned 14/12/39 *45*
– Protests at German sinking of ships 15/2/40 63
– Altmark incident 16/2/40 64
– Reaffirms neutrality 25/2/40 *65*
– Invasion ordered by Hitler 1/3/40 *66*
– Allied plan to mine territorial waters 28/3/40 71
– Churchill's plan for Allied mining adopted 3/4/40 72
– Germany invades 9/4/40 73
– Quisling heads Nazi regime 9/4/40 *73*
– Government moves to Hamar before fall of Oslo 9/4/40 74
– Becomes Reichskommissariat under Terboven 19/4/40 *75*
– Germany declares war 27/4/40 *76*
– Government moves to Tromso 30/4/40 *76*
– British troops start to leave Andalsnes 30/4/40 *76*
– Troops surrender to Germans 1/5/40 *78*
– British landing plans criticized 7/5/40 *79*
– Allied troops advance on Narvik 13/5/40 *84*
– All Allied troops to be withdrawn 24/5/40 *87*
– Allied forces occupy Narvik 28/5/40 *89*
– Importance of iron ore to Germany 31/5/40 90
– Allied forces evacuated from Harstad 4/6/40 *91*
– Haakon and government evacuated with last Allied troops 8/6/40 *91*
– Narvik reoccupied by Germans; army surrenders 9/6/40 *94*
– German troops get transit rights through Finland 12/9/40 *118*
– Volunteers in RAF Reserve 21/9/40 122
– Terboven nominates Quisling to replace king 28/9/40 *123*
– Chief justice resigns in anti-Nazi protest 21/12/41 *144*
– British raiding party attacks Hammerfest 12/4/41 *176*
– Royal Navy attacks Germans at Kirkenes 30/7/41 *210*
– Germans declare state of emergency 1/8/41 212
– Anglo-Canadian-Norwegian sabotage team on Spitzbergen 19/8/41 *216*
– Volunteers fighting with Germans against USSR 9/9/41 222
– Germans declare martial law in Oslo 10/9/41 223
– Nazis tell people to cooperate as unrest grows 4/10/41 *228*
– RAF bombs German ships at Aalesund 30/10/41 236
– Combined forces raid Vaagso 27/12/41 257
– Quisling becomes leader again on Hitler's orders 1/2/42 270
– British Albacores attack Tirpitz 9/3/42 *280*
– Quisling govt shaken by clerical anti-Nazi resignations 7/4/42 286
– SS executes 258 Jews 28/5/42 *301*
– Government in exile asks US to warn on Axis atrocities 31/7/42 319
– Quisling reintroduces death penalty 17/9/42 *333*
– Martial law declared at Trondheim 6/10/42 *338*
– Operation Freshman attack on Vermork fails 19/11/42 *351*
– Germans deport Jews from Bergen to Auschwitz 25/11/42 *353*
– Air force squadrons in Allied raids on Europe 6/12/42 358
– Clergy attack persecution of Jews 26/12/42 *361*
– Commandos land to attack Vermork heavy water plant 17/2/43 *383*
– Eskdale sunk in English Channel by Germans 13-14/4/43 *397*
– British commandos caught mining German ships 29/4/43 *401*
– U-boat sunk off Trondheim 24/7/43 *427*
– Sweden cancels German transit rights 5/8/43 433
– State of siege as defiance of Germans spreads 20/8/43 437
– Ferry carrying heavy water bombed 20/2/44 *492*
– Makes pact with USSR 16/5/44 517
– Russians seize the port of Kirkenes 25/10/44 *575*
– British planes lay mines and bomb ships 7/12/44 *586*
– Germany announces ceasefire 7/5/45 *634*
– Government in exile returns to Oslo 31/5/45 *640*
– King Haakon returns 7/6/45 *642*
– Quisling goes on trial 20/8/45 659
Norwich 294
Noumea *280*
Nova Scotia *634*
Novello, Ivor *510*
Novgorod *214*, 219, 286, *480*, *481*
Novi Sad *266*
Novikov, Aleksandr 218
Novocherkassk *318*, *381*
Novorossiisk *330*, *378*, *394*, *442*
Nowotny, Walter *579*
Noyelles *87*
Nubian (destroyer) *192*, 417
Nuclear bomb
– (see Atomic bomb)
Numata, Takazo 658
Nungshigum 505
Nuremberg *231*, *384*, *434*, *502*, 608
Nuremberg Laws
– (see Germany (racial policies))
Nuremberg trials *648*, 654, 660

O

O'Connor, Richard 143, 144, 153, 160, *176*
Oak Hill (landing craft) *655*
Obedient (destroyer) 364
Oberg, Karl *296*, *318*, 374
Obersalzberg *537*
Obersdorf 632
Oboe 363, 369, 387, 408
Observer (newspaper) 586
Observer Corps 121
Obstfelder, Hans von 596
Oceania *164*
Octagon Conference *562*
October Revolution (battleship) 222
Odense 439
Odenwald (armed merchantman) *237*
Oder river 515, 602, *603*, *614*
Odessa 211, *228*, 232, *506*
Odette
– (see Hallowes, Odette M C (VC))
Office of Strategic Services 317
Ogre 570
Ohio (tanker) 324
Ohm Kruger (film) *174*
Ohrdruf 622
Oil 108, 234, 237, 242, *247*, 265, 272, 272, *273*, *289*, 307, 312, 313, *321*, *322*, 347, *376*, 433, 506, 509, *512*, 514, *515*, *518*, 520, 534, 535, 550, 557, *558*, 558, *571*, 578, 579, 585, *586*, *587*, *596*, 603, 610, 612, 619, *645*, *655*
Oise river 96
Oivi *347*
Okayama *645*
Okimura 604
Okinawa
– Halsey wants to invade 31/7/44 547
– Landings planned 9/1/45 598
– Huge armada en route to 26/3/45 616
– US invasion force lands 6/4/45 618
– US marines suffer heavy casualties 15/4/45 *624*
– Fresh offensive aimed at capital 11/5/45 *634*
– Japanese suicide pilots try to dislodge Americans 12/5/45 637
– US troops advance 22/5/45 *639*
– US marines claim to have taken capital 27/5/45 641
– Fresh US landings 4/6/45 *642*
– Falls after three-month battle 21/6/45 644
– US destroyer sunk by Japanese submarine 12/8/45 *655*
Olav, Crown Prince of Norway *634*
Olbrich 179
Oldenburg *631*
Oldendorff, Jesse 576
Olivier, Laurence 147, 385, 586, 593
Olmutz 632
Olympic (operation) 644
Omaha (cruiser) *237*
Omaha Beach
– (see D-Day)
Ommaney Bay (aircraft carrier) *596*
Omori, Sentaro 459
Omura 539
Ondina (tanker) *349*
Onega, Lake *228*
Onslow (destroyer) 364
Operations
– (see individual names, eg Barbarossa, Dynamo)
Opolchenye 222
Oppenheimer, J Robert 354, 648, 652
Oradea *571*
Oradour-sur-Glane 531
Oran *97*, 102, 350, *360*, *378*
Oranienbaum *481*
Oranienburg *319*
Ordhonikidze 347
Ordu *49*
Oregon *631*
Orel *226*, *228*, 382, *425*, 431
Orete Cove *440*
Orion (cruiser) 172
Orion (merchant raider) *187*, *216*
Orleans 553, *562*
Ormoc Bay *586*
Orne river 517, *522*, 540, 543
Oro Bay *452*
Orpheus (submarine) *97*
Ortona 474
Oruku peninsula *642*
Orzel (submarine) *73*
Osaka *613*, *642*, *643*
Osipovichi 537
Osiris (submarine) *123*
Oslo *35*, 74, *634*
Osmena, Sergio 573
Osnabruck *618*
Osservatore Romano (newspaper) 551
Ossow *552*
Ostend 85, *89*, 90
Oster, Hans *396*, *621*
Osterley Park 104
Ostropol *495*
Ostrov *205*, 484
Ostwall 70
Ota 604
Ota, Minoru *644*
Ottowa (destroyer) 203
Otto (operation) *125*
Otwock 546
Oudna *353*
Oued Zarga 353
Oum el-Araneb *368*
Ourthe river *597*
Ourtheville 590
Ouvry, J G D 40
Overcast (operation) 646
Overlord (operation)
– see also D-Day
– Cross-Channel landings planned 21/5/43 *409*
– Churchill and Roosevelt agree on plan 25/5/43 412
– Becomes top priority in second front 23/8/43 439
– Plan being drastically revised 6/1/44 479
– Eisenhower is C-in-C of invasion force 17/1/44 *481*
– Italy overshadowed by 29/2/44 493
– Travel restrictions in run-up to 17/4/44 509
– Final invasion rehearsal 6/5/44 512
– Presentation of plan to VIPs 15/5/44 517
– Preparation of troops 31/5/44 518
– Paras begin the assault 6/6/44 524
– Background to the planning of

6/6/44 527
Owen Stanley Mountains *316*, 332, 336, 349, 352
Ozawa, Jisaburo 272, *513*, 536, 576, *640*

P

P-38 Lightning fighters
– (see Lightning fighters)
P-40 fighters *68*, 212
P-47 Thunderbolt fighters
– (see Thunderbolt fighters)
P-47 fighters
– (see Thunderbolt fighters)
P-51D Mustang fighters
– (see Mustang fighters)
Paasikivi, Juho 66
Pacific War
– see also specific places eg Aleutian Is; New Guinea; Solomon Is
– German ship bombards Australian protectorate of Nauru, 27/12/40 *145*
– US unprepared for Pearl Harbor attack 9/12/41 250
– USAAF hit by Japan in Philippines despite warnings 13/12/41 252
– Nimitz succeeds Kimmel as admiral of Pacific Fleet 17/12/41 *253*
– Japan halted at Wake Island 20/12/41 255
– Curtin warns Churchill and Roosevelt of importance 26/12/41 *256*
– Japanese paratroopers land on Sumatra 28/12/41 *256*
– British troops leave Borneo as Japan continues advance 31/12/41 258
– Wavell becomes supreme commander ABDACOM 3/1/42 *262*
– US marines land on Samoa 24/1/42 *266*
– Pacific War Council formed 27/1/42 *268*
– US attacks Japanese on Gilbert and Marshall Islands 1/2/42 *270*
– ABDACOM abolished 25/2/42 *276*
– MacArthur leaves Philippines for Australia 11/3/42 280
– MacArthur and Nimitz to be supreme commanders 30/3/42 285
– Japanese land on Admiralties and Solomons 6/4/42 *288*
– US troops land on New Caledonia 25/4/42 *292*
– Japanese carriers sail to attack Port Moresby 30/4/42 *294*
– Battle of the Coral Sea begins 4/5/42 *296*
– US troops sent to Midway and Aleutians 20/5/42 *300*
– Battle of Midway 6/6/42 305
– US bombs Japanese on Wake Island 27/6/42 *310*
– US starts to build base in New Hebrides 12/8/42 *322*
– Japanese reinforcements land on Java 28/9/42 *337*
– US marines set up base on Funafuti Atoll 2/10/42 *338*
– Halsey succeeds Ghormley as commander 18/10/42 *342*
– Battle of Santa Cruz 27/10/42 346
– Situation 31/12/42 365
– First US land victory as Japanese leave Guadalcanal 4/2/42 380
– Operation Elkton starts 12/2/43 *381*
– Japanese bomb Russell Islands 6/3/43 *386*
– Battle of the Bismarck Sea 5/3/43 386
– US stops Japanese convoy to Kiska 26/3/43 392
– Japanese raid Russell Islands 31/3/43 *394*
– Allied advance limited by available resources 28/3/43 395
– Japanese navy completes Operation I 14/4/43 *397*
– USAAF bombs Japanese on Nauru 20/4/43 *400*
– US troops land on Trobriand Islands 23/6/43 *418*
– Allies approach Rabaul in Operation Cartwheel 30/6/43 421
– Britain approves US plans for next stage 23/8/43 434
– US forces land on Nanomea, in Ellice Islands 28/8/43 *438*
– US task force prepares for Gilbert Islands campaign 1/9/43 *440*
– Liberators raid Tarawa 17/9/43 *444*
– US Task Force 14 shells Wake Island 5-6/10/43 *450*
– Build-up to invasion of Bougainville 27/10/43 *455*
– Two-pronged US thrust planned 2/11/43 459
– Battle for Gilbert Islands continues 21/11/43 *464*
– US task force sails for New Guinea 13/12/43 *469*
– US marines land on New Britain 26/12/43 *473*
– Beginning of US operation to take Marshall Islands 22/1/44 *481*
– US force attacks Marshall Islands 31/1/44 485
– Roi and Namur Islands taken by US 2/2/44 *486*
– Japanese forces abandon Truk 10/2/44 *488*
– US intensifies pressure on Japanese empire 17/2/44 491
– Gathers new momentum 29/2/44 493
– US steps up attack on Admiralty Islands 15/3/44 498
– British Eastern Fleet attacks Sabang island 19/4/44 *508*
– First tank battle fought on Biak Island 29/5/44 *518*
– US aims to cut Japan off from its empire 22/7/44 545
– Liberation of Philippines next on US list 31/7/44 547
– British Eastern Fleet attacks Padang 23-24/8/44 *554*
– US carriers hit Palau 6/9/44 *560*
– Forces under MacArthur and Nimitz converge 16/9/44 563
– US forces enter Lingayen Gulf in the Philippines 9/10/44 *571*
– US forces land on the Philippines 20/10/44 573
– Battle of Leyte Gulf 24/10/44 576
– US ships and planes hit Japanese on Iwo Jima 8/12/44 *586*
– War approaches Japanese homeland 1/1/45 596
– Preparations for Allied invasion of Okinawa 26/3/45 616
– Remnant of Japanese navy destroyed 17-18/7/45 *648*
– Russia enters 9/8/45 654
– News of surrender may take months to reach troops 18/8/45 655
– Japan surrenders 14/8/45 655
– End of war brings uncertain future 31/8/45 661
Pacific War Council *268, 271,* 284
Pacifism *30*
Pact of Steel 15
Padang *554*
Paderborn 617
Pagan *605, 609*
Paget, Bernard *76*
Pahlevi, Mohammed Reza, Sha of Iran 223
Paide 564
Pak Island *506*
Paladin (destroyer) *488*
Palanga 572
Palau Islands *502*, 505, 545, *560, 566, 569, 573, 577, 584*
Palawan 610
Palembang 272, *601*
Palermo 221, *389, 420*, 428
Palestine
– At war with Germany 9/9/39 20
– Australian troops in country 26/12/39 50
– Anzac troops in country 30/6/40 100
– Italians bomb Haifa 16/7/40 *105*
– Italians bomb Jerusalem 24/7/40 *107*
– Italians bomb Tel Aviv 9/9/40 *118*
– Jewish refugees blow up ship at Haifa 25/11/40 *140*
– Bethlehem blacked out 25/12/40 145
– Troops fighting with Allies in Desert War 6/6/42 *304*
– Axis air raids on Haifa 1/7/42 *312*
– Palestine Regiment created 7/8/42 *321*
– Troops in Eighth Army 30/3/43 394
Palmoli 458
Palmyra 189, *203*
Pamati 517
Pampas (freighter) 284
Panama Canal *452*
Panay *289*, 614
Pancevo *569*
Pancke, Gunther 482
Pangsan Pass 388
Pantelleria *151, 406, 414, 415*
Panther (operation) *481*
Panther line 489
Panther tanks
– (see Panzers; Tanks)
Panzer (2nd) Army *221*
Panzer (3rd) Army *221*
Panzer Group 2 *206*, 211, 213
Panzer Group 3 213
Panzerarmee Afrika *210, 266, 360*, 382, 383
– see also Afrika Korps
Panzerkampfwagen V tanks
– (see tanks)
Panzers
– see also Desert War; Eastern Front; German army, Italy (Allied land attacks); North Africa
– In invasion of Poland 1/9/39 16
– Battle of the Bzura river 9/9/39 19
– Hitler considers Ardennes plan 24/2/40 64
– In invasion of Low Countries 10/5/40 80
– Guderian's troops in Ardennes 11/5/40 81
– Strength at invasion of France 11/5/40 82
– Divisions under Guderian, Rommel and Reinhardt at Sedan 13/5/40 *84*
– Success of Guderian's technique as Germans cross Meuse 14/5/40 85
– Hitler orders halt outside Dunkirk 25/5/40 87
– XV Corps breaks through Somme defences near Amiens 6/6/40 *91*
– 7th Division under Rommel reaches Rouen 8/6/40 94
– At fall of Paris 14/6/40 96
– Hitler orders 16th Division into Balkans 13/12/40 143
– Moving into Bulgaria 23/2/41 165
– Division in Afrika Korps's successful Libyan offensive 5/4/41 175
– Reach Salonika in invasion of Greece 9/4/41 177
– Tanks hit by British gunners at Tobruk 14/4/41 179
– In fall of Athens 27/4/41 182
– Tanks superior to British armour 26/4/41 183
– British Battleaxe offensive in Western Desert defeated 17/6/41 198
– Troops under Guderian and Hoth in invasion of USSR 30/6/41 202
– Troops take Minsk and prepare Smolensk attack 10/7/41 206
– 2nd Group moves south on eastern front 19/7/41 *206*
– Attack on Leningrad delayed by shell shortage 31/7/41 211
– 2nd and 3rd Groups destroy Red Army at Smolensk 5/8/41 213
– Bad treatment of PoWs 16/8/41 215
– Fierce fighting as von Leeb's troops approach Leningrad 22/8/41 216
– Guderian's 2nd Group sent to attack south, not Moscow 23/8/41 *216*
– Weather delays von Leeb's troops at Leningrad 31/8/41 219
– 1st Division under von Leeb reaches Leningrad 8/9/41 222
– 1st and 2nd Armies continue advances on eastern front 30/9/41 *226*
– New Russian T34s superior to German tanks 30/9/41 227
– Troops under Hopner and Hoth attack in Vyazma area 4/10/41 *228*
– Von Leeb's forces from Leningrad to attack Moscow 2/10/41 229
– 4th Division takes Mozhaisk 18/10/41 *231*
– 2nd, 3rd and 4th Groups in attack on Moscow 15/11/41 240
– 21st Division clashes with Allies at Sidi Rezegh 22/11/41 *241*
– Troops under von Kleist take Rostov-on-Don 21/11/41 242
– Von Ravenstein captured in Libya 28/11/41 *243*
– Modern warfare techniques in Desert War 1/12/41 245
– Rommel retreats in Libya after loss of Derna 19/12/41 253
– Russians split forces at retaking of Medya 14/1/42 *264*
– Massive counter-attack forces British retreat in desert 21/1/42 266
– 22nd Division destroyed by Russians at Sevastopol 20/3/42 *282*
– Troops annihilate Russians at Battle of Kerch 18/5/42 *300*
– 1st Army in struggle for Kharkov 22/5/42 300
– Troops in desert reach Sidi Rezegh 15/6/42 *308*
– Rommel leads tank force at fall of Tobruk 21/6/42 311
– 4th Army advances into Ukraine 28/6/42 312
– First Battle of El Alamein 3/7/42 313
– 4th Army moved as Hitler changes Stalingrad priorities 17/7/42 *316*
– Motorized square tactic in struggle for Voronezh 17/7/42 317
– 4th Army crosses Don 3/8/42 *321*
– Abandoned tanks in desert retreat disabled by British 3/9/42 330
– Divisions in Stalingrad assault 14/10/42 341
– Heavy losses at Second Battle of El Alamein 31/10/42 344
– Von Kleist's 1st Army troops stopped by lack of oil 31/10/42 347
– Forces retreat from El Alamein 3/11/42 348
– Hoth's 4th Army troops trapped at Stalingrad 26/11/42 355
– Remainder of 4th Army launches relief attempt 12/12/42 359
– Russians plan to trap Hausser's troops at Kursk 8/2/43 382
– Panzerarmee Afrika wins Battle of the Kasserine Pass 20/2/43 382
– Troops attack Krasnograd on eastern front 7/3/43 *389*
– Counter-attack near Mareth Line smashed by RAF 22/3/43 *392*
– 15th Division to cover retreat from Mareth Line 27/3/43 393
– Troops counter-attack as retreat in Tunisia continues 6/4/43 396
– 10th Division in battle at Sebkret el Kourzia 22/4/43 401
– 5th Army surrenders in Tunisia 13/5/43 407
– Panther and Tiger tanks inferior to USSR's T34s at Kursk 9/7/43 423
– Hermann Goering division uses Tigers on Sicily 10/7/43 424
– Losses at Battle of Kursk 26/7/43 431
– 4th Army cut off at Kharkov 14/8/43 435
– Troops in Italy evacuate Reggio di Calabria 3/9/43 440
– Three divisions and Panzergrenadiers defend Salerno 9/9/43 443
– Von Vietinghoff orders withdrawal from Salerno 16/9/43 445
– 16th Division transferred from Italy to eastern front 3/11/43 *458*
– III Corps leads efforts to break out of Korsun pocket 16/2/44 *490*
– Troops in attack on Allied positions at Anzio 19/2/44 490
– 1st Army encircled by Russians near Roumanian border 17/3/44 498
– Von Manstein dismissed after refusing Hitler's orders 30/3/44 503
– Group West under von Schweppenburg in defence of France 6/5/44 512
– 12th SS Division in path of Canadians from Juno Beach 6/6/44 525
– Meyer leads 12th Division against Canadians at Caen 10/6/44 530
– 2nd SS Das Reich Division kills civilians at Tulle 9/6/44 *530*
– 3rd Army under Reinhardt pushed back in Byelorussia 22/6/44 535
– 9th and 10th SS Divisions reinforce Germans at Caen 30/6/44 538
– Troops under Meyer hold Caen 8/7/44 540
– SS Corps holds Bourguebus Ridge with Tigers & Panthers 20/7/44 543
– Outflanked in Allies' Operation Cobra 31/7/44 547
– Allies plan trap at Falaise 12/8/44 550
– Falaise pocket sealed on 5th Panzerarmee and 7th Army 21/8/44 554
– Eberbach taken prisoner 31/8/44 *558*
– 25 new divisions created 2/9/44 *560*
– Troops attack Allied forces at Arnhem 20/9/44 565
– Troops counter-attack at Aachen on Siegfried Line 4/10/44 *569*
– Tigers & Panthers used against USSR's T34s at Debrecen 10/10/44 572
– Troops delay Allied advance at Metz 9/11/44 579
– Troops from 5th, 6th and 7th Armies attack in Ardennes 16/12/44 588
– Battle of the Bulge 22/12/44 590
– Assault fails as Bastogne relieved 26/12/44 592
– Troops opposing Russian advance on Berlin at Poznan 31/1/45 602
Papagos, Alexander 135, 181
Papandreou, George 568, *573*, 586
Papen, Franz von 660
Papua, New Guinea
– see also New Guinea
– Japanese bomb Port Moresby 3/2/42 *270*
– Australians cross Owen Stanley Mts to defend Kokoda 12/7/42 *316*
– Horii's troops take Gona and push along Kokoda Trail 21/7/42 318
– Japanese take Kokoda 29/7/42 319
– Papuans fighting with Australians in Maroubra Force 8/8/42 *321*
– Australian troops land at Port Moresby 19/8/42 *325*
– Japanese land at Milne Bay 26/8/42 328
– Japanese reinforce Buna garrison 3/9/42 *330*
– Australians defeat Japanese at Milne Bay 7/9/42 332
– Japanese reach Imita Ridge on approach to Port Moresby 14/9/42 *333*
– Blamey's troops push Japanese back from Port Moresby 26/9/42 336
– US troops join assault on Wairopi 28/9/42 *337*
– Heavy fighting at Eora Creek 17/10/42 *340*
– Australians land on Goodenough Island 22/10/42 *342*
– Australians retake Kokoda 2/11/42 *347*
– Australians attack Japanese at Oivi 5/11/42 349
– Japanese land at Buna, Gona and Sanananda 17/11/42 *351*
– Japanese retreat as Australians advance 17/11/42 352
– MacArthur orders Eichelberger to take Buna 30/11/42 354
– Australians take Gona 9/12/42 *357*
– Allies attack Buna again 15/12/42 *360*
– Buna falls to US and Australian troops 2/1/43 368
– Allied forces end campaign by occupying Sananda 21/1/43 *372*
– Japanese navy attacks Milne Bay at end of Operation I 14/4/43 *397*
Paquis, Jean-Herold 532
Parachute troops 74, 80, 81, *97*, 104, *161*, 177, *181*, 191, 241, *256, 264, 266*, 272, 277, 315, *325*, 350, 424
Paraguay
– Declares war on the Axis powers 9/2/45 604
Paramushiro *486*
Paris
– Notre-Dame stained glass removed 13/9/39 *21*
– Luftwaffe reconnaissance planes driven away 26/2/40 *65*
– Air raid 3/6/40 *91*
– Germans approach 7/6/40 94
– Declared open city 11/6/40 *94*
– Falls to Germans 14/6/40 96
– Hitler visits 23/6/40 100
– Collaborationist newspaper La Gerbe begins 11/7/40 *103*
– Germans break up student demo 11/11/40 *136*

– First execution by Nazis 23/12/40 *145*
– Art treasures taken by Nazis 15/3/41 169
– German officer cadet shot 22/8/41 217
– German NCO shot 3/9/41 *220*
– Jewish leaders arrested as hostages 8/9/41 *221*
– Curfew 20/9/41 *223*
– State of siege declared 23/9/41 *226*
– Terrorism against Germans continues 5/12/41 245
– Peri and 100 hostages executed 15/12/41 *253*
– Foreign-born Jews rounded up for Auschwitz 16/7/42 317
– Oberg threatens reprisals on Resistants' families 19/7/42 *318*
– Reprisal executions 18/9/42 *333*
– German television starts 7/5/43 *404*
– Allied air raid kills 641 20-21/4/44 *508*
– General strike 10/8/44 *550*
– Police join the Resistance in general strike 14/8/44 *552*
– US forces just 40 miles away 19/8/44 553
– Police, Resistants seize Prefecture 19/8/44 553
– Resistance leads armed popular uprising 20/8/44 *554*
– Is liberated 25/8/44 555
– De Gaulle faces sniper at Notre Dame 26/8/44 556
– Eisenhower promises de Gaulle arms and food 27/8/44 *558*
– Treason trials open for collaborators 23/10/44 *575*
– Churchill attends armistice celebrations 11/11/44 *579*
– High court set up to try collaborators 18/11/44 *581*
– Floodlit for first time since war broke out 1/4/45 *618*
– VE day celebrations 9/5/45 635
– Concentration camp survivors' march 12/7/45 *647*
– Pierre Laval brought back for trial 1/8/45 *650*

Paris Protocols *192*
Park, Keith 111, 113, 121, 139
Parker, Cecil 204
Parma *626*
Parry Island *492*
Partisans
– Eastern front: detachments link up with Red Army 24/1/42 267
– Eastern front: Germans launch Operation Munich 19/3/42 283
– France: Francs-tireurs et Partisans created 28/3/42 *284*
– Yugoslavia: army fights its way north 9/5/42 297
– France: blow up radio mast 9/5/42 298
– Czechoslovakia: kill Heydrich 27/5/42 303
– Eastern front: Germans launch major operation against 5/6/42 *304*
– Eastern front: 100,000 fighting Germans 30/6/42 *310*
– Yugoslavia: Germans launch an attack 3/7/42 *312*
– Eastern front: Germans launch Operation Swamp Flower 6/7/42 *314*
– Yugoslavia: Tito's forces push back the Nazis 16/7/42 317
– Germany: Hitler orders greater efforts against 18/8/42 *325*
– Eastern front: Germans launch offensive in Mogilev 2/9/42 *330*
– Eastern front: destroy German supply station 24/9/42 *336*
– Eastern front: Germans launch Operation Regatta 3/10/42 339
– Poland: Jews join resistance movements 22/12/42 361
– Yugoslavia; Germans launch biggest offensive yet 15/1/43 372
– Eastern front: made Heroes of the Soviet Union 28/2/43 386
– Greece: Jews join up 15/3/43 391
– Eastern front: Khatyn village massacred as a deterrent 22/3/43 392
– Yugoslavia: Allies parachute in to join them 15/4/43 399
– Yugoslavia: Axis forces launch fifth offensive 15/5/43 408
– Eastern front: Germans launch Operation Gypsy Baron 16/5/43 *409*
– Yugoslavia: British support arrives 28/5/43 412
– Eastern front: Germans launch Operation Cottbus 3/6/43 *414*
– Eastern front: Luftwaffe efforts against 5/6/43 414
– Yugoslavia: Churchill orders military mission to aid 23/6/43 419
– Eastern front: "rail war" against Germans planned 20/7/43 427
– Italy: movement grows in north 31/10/43 457
– Italy: industrial sabotage in Milan 15/11/43 463
– Eastern front: Byelorussians claim German casualties 1/12/43 *465*
– Occupied Europe: Allies to airlift supplies 4/1/44 *478*
– Austria: activities 17/3/44 498
– Poland: Germans launch six-day sweep 18/6/44 *534*
– Eastern front: Byelorussians assist Operation Bagration 22/6/44 535
– Italy: helped by US advisers 26/9/44 *566*
– Yugoslavia: join British invasion troops 27/9/44 568
– Italy: strike in north 15/11/44 *581*
– Albania: liberate Tirana 19/11/44 *583*

Partridge (destroyer) *360*
Pas-de-Calais *120*
Pasha, Ahmed Masha *607*
Pashovsk *483*
Pastorius (operation) *308*
Patani 250
Patch, Alexander C *357,* 361, 557, 614
Paterno 432
Pathfinder (destroyer) *401*
Pathfinders
– (see RAF)
Pati Point 551
Patras *132*
Patroclus (armed merchant cruiser) *134*
Patterson (destroyer) 321
Patton, George S
– Commands US forces at Operation Torch landings 10/11/42 350
– Appointed to command US II Corps 6/3/43 *386*
– II Corps takes Gafsa and advances on El Guettar 18/3/43 *390*
– Unhappy about role of Fifth Army in Sicily invasion 10/7/43 424
– Relationship with Montgomery in Sicilian campaign 17/7/43 426
– Seventh Army takes Palermo 23/7/43 427
– Slaps soldiers in hospital 10/8/43 435
– Upsets congressmen with controversial speech 25/4/44 510
– Bogus First US Army Group under his control 6/6/44 527
– His troops advance into Brittany 2/8/44 *548*
– Swings forces east towards the Seine 12/8/44 550
– Troops cross the Seine 19/8/44 553
– Troops head for river Marne 26/8/44 557
– Role of troops in drive on Germany 31/8/44 559
– Third Army runs out of petrol at Moselle river 9/9/44 560
– Third Army's battle at Brest 21/9/44 566
– Third Army stalled at Moselle 31/10/44 577
– Third Army has crossed the Moselle 9/11/44 579
– Third Army still to take Metz 18/11/44 582
– Troops enter Saar basin 28/11/44 *584*
– Begins to move army from Saar to the Ardennes 20/12/44 *589*
– Troops free Bastogne 26/12/44 592
– Ordered not to advance on Czechoslovakia 17/3/45 *613*
– Third Army threatens Siegfried Line 17/3/45 614
– Third Army takes Mainz 21/3/45 *614*
– About to link up with US First Army 31/3/45 617
– Shocked by Ohrdruf PoW/concentration camp 12/4/45 622
– Third Army is in Prague 5/5/45 632
– Biography 685

Paul, Prince of Yugoslavia 167, 171, 173
Paulus, Friedrich 323, 330, 351, 355, 359, 369, 373, *376*
Pauly, Max 632
Pavelich, Ante *176,* 297, 317, 372
Pavlograd *383*
Pavlov, Dmitri *163, 200*
Payne, Jack 60
Pearl Harbor 6, 9, 237, 248, *356*
Peccia river 479
Pechory 551
Pecs *584*
Pedestal (operation) *322,* 324
Peenemunde 229, *306, 308,* 338, 361, 402, *436, 497,* 607, 632
Peer Gynt (play) 593
Pegu Yoma *650*
Peierls, Rudolf 70
Peiper, Joachim 590
Peirse, Richard 125, *467*
Peking 29, *513*
Peleliu Island 505, 563, *566, 569*
Peloponnese *181, 406,* 571
Pembroke 50
Pembroke Dock *112*
Penablanca *645*
Penang *253*
Penelope (cruiser) *239,* 253, 294, *450, 490*
Penicillin 455
Pennsylvania (battleship) 248
People, The (newspaper) 586
Perak 255, 258
Percival, Arthur 265, 274, 659, 660
Perekop 230
Perekop peninsula 507
Peri, Gabriel *190, 253*
Periwinkle (escort) *195*
Perla (submarine) *314*
Pernot, Georges 21
Perpetual (operation) *239*
Perseus (submarine) *245*
Perth (cruiser) 154, 172
Peru
– Ambassador to Japan warns of Japanese attack 27/1/41 *158*
– Declares war on Ecuador 6/7/41 *205*
– Truce with Ecuador 26/7/41 *208*

Perugia *534*
Pescadores 596
Petacci, Clara 630
Petain, Philippe
– Vice-premier 18/5/40 86
– Prepares armistice appeal 11/6/40 96
– Sets up Vichy government 7/40 7
– Head of state and prime minister 10/7/40 103
– Says France must abandon traditional allies and foes 11/10/40 *127*
– Agrees terms of cooperation with Hitler 26/10/40 *130*
– Dismisses Laval 13/12/40 143
– Imposes fascist rule 12/8/41 214
– Believes collaboration only hope 1/2/42 270
– Ceremonial position as Laval is made head of government 16/4/42 *289*
– Congratulates Germans after Dieppe raid 21/8/42 *325*
– Goes on strike 13/11/43 *460*
– Urges people not to join the fighting 13/6/44 532
– Arrested by the SS 19/8/44 554
– His arrest ordered by French justice minister 15/9/44 *562*
– Arrested on Swiss border 26/4/45 627
– His trial begins 23/7/45 649
– Sentenced to death 15/8/45 *655*
– Biography 685

Petard (destroyer) 353, *488*
Peter Hendricks (destroyer) *206*
Peter II, King of Yugoslavia 173, 180, 466, 472, *577*
Peter's Corner *400*
Peter-Gruppen 479
Petrov, General 574
Petrozadovsk *228*
Petsamo 42, 46, 61, 65, *210, 564*
Petworth 337
Peugeot [co] 458
Pfeffer-Wildenbruch, K 605
Pflaum, Karl 547
Phalconera *156*
Philip, Andre 414
Philip, Prince of Greece *150*
Philippines
– Armed forces incorporated into US Army 26/7/41 *208*
– Threat from Japan in Indochina 25/7/41 208
– Japan plans attack 3/11/41 237
– Japanese forces leave Palau 6/12/41 *245*
– Japan destroys Clark Field air base before invading 8/12/41 *247*
– US resistance as Japanese advance 20/12/41 255
– MacArthur declares Manila open and withdraws to Bataan 23/12/41 *256*
– Japanese call for US surrender during Bataan fighting 10/1/42 *262*
– Japan sets up puppet government 23/1/42 *266*
– US counter-attacks as Japanese reinforcements arrive 6/2/42 *270*
– US rejects request for immediate independence 8/2/42 *271*
– Roosevelt orders MacArthur to leave 11/3/42 280
– US forces retreat to Corregidor 21/3/42 *282*
– Hukbalahaps formed 29/3/42 *284*
– Remaining US forces in Bataan hit by illness 1/4/42 *286*
– Japanese defeat US 21st Division at Mount Samat 5/4/42 *288*
– US PoWs face long march after surrender at Bataan 9/4/42 289
– Japan reinforces Mindanao task force 26/4/42 *294*
– US and Filipino casualties on death march 28/4/42 294
– Japan launches major attack on US on Corregidor 4/5/42 *296*
– To join UN 14/6/42 *308*
– Japanese grant independence 21/10/43 *453*
– As part of a two-pronged US thrust 2/11/43 459
– MacArthur poised to attack 29/2/44 493
– US forces within striking distance 16/9/44 563
– MacArthur plans attack 17/9/44 564
– First US air raids on Luzon and Manila 22/9/44 566
– US forces enter Lingayen Gulf 9/10/44 *571*
– US forces land on Leyte 20/10/44 573
– Battle of Leyte Gulf 24-26/10/44 576
– Bitter fighting continues 1/11/44 578
– TF 38 attacks Japanese targets on Luzon 5-6/11/44 *579*
– US aircraft hit Japanese shipping in Manila Bay 13-14/11/44 *581*
– US forces begin landing at Ormoc Bay 7/12/44 *586*
– Second phase of US invasion begins 15/12/44 589
– Yamashita withdraws troops from Luzon 25/12/44 *591*
– US forces land at Lingayen Gulf 9/1/45 598
– US troops cross Agno river on Luzon 15/1/45 *599*
– 11th US Airborne Division lands on Luzon 31/1/45 *602*
– Fierce fighting north of Manila 3/2/45 *603*
– Japanese resistance on Luzon ceases 21/2/45 *607*
– Formally re-established as a commonwealth 27/2/45 *609*
– US troops land on Mindanao 10/3/45 *610*
– US forces take vital airstrip on Luzon 1/4/45 *618*
– Further US progress 10/4/45 *621*
– US Army advance continues 22/4/45 *626*
– US advances continue 13/5/45 *637*
– US forces take Santa Fe 27/5/45 *640*
– US troops capture Bambang 6/6/45, Mandog 9/6/45 *642*
– Last Japanese port on Luzon falls 21/6/45 *644*
– MacArthur announces liberation 4/7/45 *646*
– Napalm dropped on pockets of Japanese resistance 12/7/45 *647*
– Japanese troops formally surrender 31/8/45 *660*

Philippine Sea *552*
Philippine Sea, Battle of the 536
Philips [co] 358, *394*
Phillips, Frank 147
Phillips, Thomas 252
Phillips, William *78*
Phoney War 33, 46, 81
Piccadilly 496
Pickard, Charles 491
Picture Post (magazine) 104, 233, 279
Pieczerski, Aleksandr 452
Pierlot, Hubert 131
Pigeons 101, *325*
Pilica 26
Pilsudksi, Joseph 15
Pimpernel Smith (film) 259, 414
Pingchien *520*
Pinguin (merchant raider) *184*
Pinocchio (film) 61, *69,* 147
Pinsk *344, 541*
Pioneer Corps *34,* 133
Piotrkow *16, 342*
Pipe Line Under The Ocean
– (see PLUTO)
Piraeus *128, 166, 176, 469*
Pisa 161, *552*
Pitomnik airfield *370*
Pityilu Island *502*
Pius XII, Pope *34,* 49, *59, 414,* 428, 450, 551, *614, 642*
Placentia Bay 215
Plan Dog 159
Plans (German)
– (see Fall eg Fall Weiss)
Plate, River, Battle of the 45, *47*
Platon, Admiral 378
Platt, William *156, 368*
Plays
– (see Arts and Entertainment)
Ploesti 307, 433, 518, 534, 558
Plomley, Roy *268*
Plum Pudding Island 435
PLUTO 550, *639*
Plutonium *172*
– see also Atomic bomb
Plymouth *154,* 171, 183
Plzen *132*
Po plateau *624*
Po river *483,* 620
Po valley 557, 584, 615
PoWs
– Russians shoot Polish officer PoWs in Katyn forest 5/4/40 *72*
– SS massacres Royal Norfolk PoWs at Le Paradis 27/5/40 90
– Australians take 45,000 Italians in Bardia 4/1/41 150
– Red Cross reports on camp conditions in Germany 1/2/41 160
– First escapee from German camp 31/3/41 *172*
– First escapee from Colditz 11/4/41 *176*
– British taken in Greece 27/4/41 182
– Vichy collaboration buys freedom for 100,000 19/5/41 *190*
– 12,000 Allied troops to be left in Crete 1/6/41 195
– Germans make no provision for those taken in USSR 30/6/41 201
– Germans estimate 150,000 Russians taken 30/6/41 202
– 300,000 Russians taken by Germans 9/7/41 *205*
– Polish army to be formed from Poles held in Russia 30/7/41 211
– Germans take 38,000 Russians at Kazaki 8/8/41 *212*
– Russians treated savagely by Germans 16/8/41 215
– Broadcast by Lord Haw-Haw prevents exchange 6/10/41 231
– USSR protests against barbaric treatment by Germans 25/11/41 243
– Axis troops transported through Tobruk 10/12/41 247
– Thousands of Russians frozen to death 21/12/41 *256*
– British escapees from Colditz 15/1/42 264
– Concern grows over Allies in Japanese hands 16/2/42 275
– Death march in Philippines 28/4/42 294
– French exchanged for workers 11/8/42 324
– Hitler orders release of 800 French 27/8/42 *327*
– Treatment of Allies by Japanese and Germans 31/8/42 329
– U-boat sinks Laconia with 1,500 Italians on board 12/9/42 331
– Japanese leave 840 Britons and Canadians to drown 1/10/42 338
– In chains in Germany and Britain 8/10/42 339
– Escape lines set up across France 17/10/42 341
– Belgian woman organizes escape route 30/11/42 355
– Build Shinto shrine in Changi jail 7/12/42 *357*
– Russians in Poland die of starvation 31/12/42 *363*

– Spain a regular part of escape route 23/1/43 375
– Germans taken by Russians at Stalingrad 6/2/43 379
– Italians in Britain begin anti-fascist radio 16/2/43 *383*
– Japanese stage mass breakout in New Sealand 25/2/43 *384*
– Roosevelt condemns Japanese execution of Americans 21/4/43 *400*
– "Comet" escape line in Europe is betrayed 7/6/43 *415*
– Hitler wants Russians put to work, not shot 8/7/43 *422*
– Germans in USSR form National Cttee for Free Germany 12/7/43 *425*
– Germans taken in Italy 17/7/43 426
– Allies claim 40,000 taken on Sicily 21/7/43 *427*
– Hedley Verity dies in Italian camp 31/7/43 *428*
– Eisenhower offers to free Italians 30/7/43 429
– Indian National Army formed from Indians in Burma 1/8/43 432
– British escape from Stalag 383 in disguise 26/8/43 439
– Exchange of British and German prisoners 19/10/43 453
– Ecstatic homecoming for freed British prisoners 25/10/43 457
– Allies protest about Japanese atrocities 28/1/44 483
– Allied prisoners in "Great Escape" 24-5/3/44 501
– Gestapo shoots 50 airmen involved in "Great Escape" 19/5/45 515
– Canadians murdered by SS division at Authie, in Normandy 7/6/44 *530*
– Germans paraded through Moscow 17/7/44 *543*
– Mass escape attempt by Japanese in Australia 5/8/44 549
– Allies take 50,000 prisoners at Falaise 21/8/44 554
– Germans captured as Allies liberate Belgium 8/9/44 560
– Over 1,000 British return from Europe 15/9/44 *562*
– Russians die when Allies bomb prison ship 27/11/44 *584*
– US soldiers massacred at Malmedy 17/12/44 590
– Survivors of "Death March" rescued in Philippines 2/2/45 603
– Eisenhower claims 900,000 Germans are prisoners 22/2/45 *607*
– Germans stage mass escape attempt in Wales 11/3/45 614
– Nazis force Allied prisoners to march 500 miles 13/4/45 623, *624*
– Colditz is liberated by US troops 16/4/45 *624*
– Japanese gone, prisoners' sign tells Allies in Rangoon 3/5/45 631
– German prisoners put to work in Britain 22/5/45 640
– Bridge over river Kwae destroyed by bombers 24/6/45 *645*
– US soldier opens fire on German prisoners 8/7/45 *647*
– Corregidor hero found alive in Manchurian camp 19/8/45 659
– US cruiser begins evacuation of prisoners from Japan 30/8/45 *660*
– Horror of Japanese medical experiments revealed 31/8/45 660

Poggibonsi *541*
Pogradec *142*
Pogradets *145*
Poha river *347*
Pointblank (offensive) 416, 436, 455
Pointe de Grave 359
Pointe du Hoe 524
Poison gas
– (see Gas (poison); Concentration camps)
Poland
– See also Free Poles; Warsaw; Warsaw Ghetto
– Germany invades 1/9/39 15
– Strength of armed forces as Germans invade 1/9/39 16
– Germans massacred at Bydgoszcz 3/9/39 *16*
– Appealing for military aid 7/9/39 18
– Massacres of Jews by SS Einsatzgruppen begin 9/9/39 19
– Army recaptures Lowicz from Germans 12/9/39 *21*
– Russian and German armies join up at Brest-Litovsk 19/9/39 *22*
– Battle of the Bzura river 9-18/9/39 23
– Germany and USSR disagree over division 22/9/39 24
– Oppression by Gestapo and SS 22/9/39 26
– Government in exile in France 30/9/39 27
– Final surrender at Hel 1/10/39 *28*
– Deaths during invasion 6/30/39 29
– Government in exile recognized by USA 7/10/39 30
– Frank appointed head of "General Government" 12/10/39 *30*
– Gestapo campaign of terror against Jews 13/10/39 31
– Jewish ghetto established at Lublin 19/10/39 *32*
– Gold reserves arrive in Paris 24/10/39 *34*
– Enigma cryptologists in France 31/10/39 34
– German treatment of Poles 26/10/39 35
– Germany formally annexes western Poland 1/11/39 *35*
– Warsaw Ghetto established 2/11/39 36
– Frank orders Judenrats in ghettoes 28/11/39 *42*
– SS kills inmates of mental asylums 6/12/39 *43*
– Jews in General Government area to do forced labour 11/12/39 *45*
– German revenge executions 27/12/39 *49*
– SS kills mental patients 9/1/40 *55*
– Warsaw Ghetto death rate 14/1/40 *57*
– German atrocities 16/1/40 58
– 18,000 prominent Poles have been killed by Nazis 29/1/40 *59*
– Air force reconstituted in France 18/2/40 *64*
– RAF leaflet raids 7/3/40 *66*
– Government in exile reveals German plan to invade USSR 14/3/40 *68*
– Jewish ghetto established in Lodz 30/4/40 78
– Auschwitz officially opened 14/6/40 *94*
– Government in exile moves to London from France 19/6/40 *97*
– Germany starts Operation Otto 1/10/40 *125*
– Frank's speech on Jewish policy 22/1/41 *156*
– Germans shoot civilians 10/3/41 *168*
– Germany begins building extermination camps (1941) 8
– Government in exile signs treaty with USSR 30/7/41 211
– Forces fighting with Eighth Army 5/10/41 230
– SS massacres 17,000 Jews at Rovno 7/10/41 *230*
– Jews killed by exhaust fumes at Kalisz 27/10/41 *235*
– Government in exile signs pact with USSR 4/12/41 *245*
– 700 Jews deported from Kolo to Chelmno for killing 7/12/41 *247*
– 700 Jews deported from Lodz to Chelmno 13/1/42 *264*
– 10,000 Jews from Lodz gassed at Chelmno 28/2/42 *276*
– 3,200 Jews from Zychlin gassed at Chelmno 3/3/42 *278*
– Second Jewish death camp opens at Belzec 13/3/42 *280*
– Sobibor death camp opened 15/4/42 291
– US lend-lease for government in exile 1/7/42 *312*
– Total cleansing of Jews from Gen Govt area ordered 19/7/42 *318*
– Government in exile asks US to warn on Axis atrocities 31/7/42 319
– Germans kill 500 Jewish families in Zagrodski 15/5/42 *322*
– 75,000 Jews deported from Lwow to Belzec 22/8/42 *325*
– 2,000 Jews killed at Dzialosyce and remainder deported 2/9/42 *330*
– 20,000 Jews killed at Belzec 30/9/42 *337*
– 20,000 Jews sent to Treblinka from Piotrkow 21/10/42 *342*
– 64,000 Jews and gypsies killed at Belzec and Treblinka 31/10/42 *344*
– Government in exile gives Jews promise for future 29/10/42 346
– 4,000 Jews from Lublin arrive at new Majdanek camp 9/11/42 *349*
– Deportations of Jews to death camps almost complete 30/11/42 *353*
– Air force squadrons in Allied raids on Europe 6/12/42 358
– Zionist resistance campaign in Cracow 22/12/42 361
– Germans liquidating ghettoes 28/2/43 385
– Russians intend to keep eastern part 1/3/43 *386*
– Cracow ghetto dismantled and Jews dispersed by SS 13/3/43 *389*
– Government in exile asks Red Cross to investigate Katyn 16/4/43 *397*
– Government in exile withdraws Red Cross Katyn request 30/4/43 *401*
– Squadrons with RAF bomb Munster 12/6/43 416
– Sikorski killed in air crash 4/7/43 422
– German massacres in Lublin, Cracow and Radom areas 27/7/43 431
– Enigma codebreakers reach England 3/8/43 *432*
– Deportations from Bialystok ghetto start 16/8/43 *436*
– 50,000 Jews killed in Operation Harvest Festival 3/11/43 *458*
– Gestapo massacres 100 tram workers in Warsaw 3/12/43 *465*
– Germans burn villagers to death 31/12/43 *473*
– Tension grows as Red Army marches in 5/1/44 478
– Russia suggests Curzon Line as border 11/1/44 480
– Katyn massacre controversy 26/1/44 485
– Red Army occupies towns in the east 5/2/44 *486*
– Government in exile rejects Soviet border proposals 15/2/44 *490*
– Red Army takes Tarnopol 15/4/44 *506*
– Germans launch sweep against partisans 18/6/44 *534*
– Committee for National Liberation set up 22/6/44 *534*
– 40,000 Germans trapped at Brody 17/7/44 *543*
– Row erupts between Poles and Russians 21/7/44 545
– Russian troops cross the Vistula 3/8/44 *548*
– Uprising in Warsaw 1/8/44 548
– Mikolajczyk resigns 24/11/44 *583*
– Allies divided over country's future 15/12/44 588
– Has two governments 31/12/44 593
– Dispute over government deepens 1/1/45 597
– Rapid advance by the Red Army 14/1/45 *599*
– Red Army advance continues 1/2/45 *603*
– New government agreed at Yalta 11/2/45 605
– USSR tightens links with Lublin government 21/4/45 624
– Polish negotiators arrested in USSR 5/5/45 634
– Members of Home Army put on trial in Moscow 18/6/45 *644*
– Rival groups agree government 23/6/45 645
– Government of National Unity formed 28/6/45 *645*
– Signs treaty fixing border with USSR 16/8/45 *655*, 662
– Anti-Semitic riots break out 20/8/45 *658*
– Bevin doubtful about elections 25/8/45 659
– Post-war Soviet domination 663
Polikarpov I-15 fighters 202
Polikarpov P-2 biplanes 333
Polish Corridor 14, *35*
Politz 604
Politzer, Georges *273*
Polna *490*
Polotsk 537, 541
Poltava *446*, 535
Pomerania 602
Ponar *206, 221, 228, 396*
Poniatowa *363*
Pontarlier *97*
Pontecorvo *518*
Pontine Marshes 519
Pope
– (see Pius XII)
Pope (destroyer) 278
Popov, Markian 446
Popovich 574
Popski's Private Army 349
Poros *569*
Porpoise (submarine) *75*
Port Arthur 657
Port Moresby *270*, 280, 296, 318, *325*, 332, *333, 336*, 352
Port Swettenham 255, *264*
Port T *270*
Port-en-Bessin *331*
Portal, Charles 72, 125, 194, 254, 358, 585
Porto Rafti 182
Portsmouth *103*, 113, *151, 168*
Portugal
– Lisbon is refugees' haven 15/3/41 168
– Maintains neutrality while used for espionage 23/1/43 375
– SOE scuttles ships at Goa 10/3/43 389
– Britain to use military bases in Azores 17/8/43 *436*
– Lends Azores to Allies 12/10/43 452
– Observes a day of mourning for Hitler 3/5/45 *631*
– Severs diplomatic relations with Germany 6/5/45 *634*
Posen *35*
Postscripts (radio news programme) 147
Potatoes 221, 224, 388, 395
Potsdam (Allied conference) 648, *648, 649, 650*
Pound, Dudley 315, *453*
Pound, Ezra *631*
Powa Taung 616
Power Jets Ltd [co] 176, 387
Pownall, Charles *465*
Pownall, Henry 81, *256*
Poznan 58, *518*, 601, 608
Pozzallo *425*
Praga 563
Prague 35, *38, 54, 57*, 61, 303, *581*, 632, 636
Prasca, Visconti 133, 135
Praszka 600
Pravda (newspaper) 497
Premeti *141*
Preussisch Friedland *609*
Pribichevich, Stoyan 520
Prien, Gunther 31, 129, *166*, 171
Priestley, J B 91, 103, 147
Prince of Wales (battleship) 190, 215, 226, *233, 245*
Princeton (aircraft carrier) 459, *575*
Prinz Eugen (cruiser) *190, 195, 203*, 272, *273, 300, 634*
Prioux, Rene 80, 81
Prisoner-of-war camps
– (see PoWs)
Prisoners of war
–(see PoWs)
Probst, Christoph *384*
Prokhorova 425
Proletarska *319*
Prome *286, 331*
Promenade concerts 259, 475, 493
Propaganda 31, 47, 55, 61, 67, *100*, 104, 105, *112*, 134, 135, 158, *174, 190*, 206, 207, 212, 215, 216, 217, 221, 229, 230, 236, 254, 298, 301, 304, 327, 397, 432, *444*, 488
Provins *558*
Prut river 498, *502, 504*
Pskov *205*, 489, *546*, 551
PT-109 *432*
Pu Yi *100*, 658
Pucheu, Pierre *434, 495*
Puerto Princesa 610
Pulie river *470*
Pulkovo *481*
Punjabi (destroyer) *296*
Punta Stila 105
Purple code *123*, 401, 411
Pushkin *483*
Pyatigorsk *325, 370*
Pygmalion (film) 414
Pyinmanna 624
Pyle, Ernie 624

Q

Qattara Depression 316, 343
Quadrant conference 434, 439
Quebec *562*
Queen Elizabeth (battleship) 253
Queen Elizabeth (liner) 67
Queen Mary (liner) 67, *69, 338*
Quentin (destroyer) 357
Quezon, Manuel *271*, 275
Quiberon (destroyer) 357
Quincy (cruiser) 321
Quisling, Vidkun *45, 47, 73, 75, 123*, 270, *333, 634*, 659
Quorn (destroyer) *548*

R

RAAF
– No 10 Squadron arrives in Britain 26/12/39 50
– Empire air training scheme 29/4/40 78
– Sunderland flying boat sinks U26 in Atlantic 1/7/40 *102*
– Japan attacks Broome airfield 3/3/42 279
– Participating in Empire Training Scheme 19/5/42 300
– Boomerang fighter-bomber makes first flight 29/5/42 *301*
– Successes at Battle of the Bismarck Sea 5/3/43 386
– Bombs Munster 12/6/43 416, 589
Rabat *342*
Rabaul 267, *273*, 321, *338, 351, 361*, 397, 421, *428*, 433, 441, *452, 453, 458, 460, 483*, 493, 500, 517
Rabbi river 578
Radar 111, 321, *376*, 405, 408, 419
– see also RDF
Rademacher, Franz 103
Radio Counter-measures Organisation 136
Radio Direction Finding
– (see RDF)
Radio Resurge *383*
Radio guidance systems *87*, 99, *134, 138*, 172, 189, 198, 214, 272, 277, 281, *284*, 293, 294, *296, 319*, 363, 369, *376*, 390, 403, 455, 461
– see also RDF; Radar
Radio-location
– (see RDF; Radio guidance systems)
Radom 431, *599*
Radomyshl *469*
Radun *298*
Radzynib 546
Raeder, Erich 104, 115, *161*, 186, 315, *368*, 622, 685
RAF
– see also Atlantic, Battle of the; Battle of Britain; Berlin, Battle of; types of aircraft eg Spitfire
– Thirteen squadrons in France 9/9/39 *16*
– Propaganda drops over Germany 3-9/9/39 18
– Clashes with Luftwaffe over Aachen 20/9/39 *22*
– Heligoland raids 29/9/39 26
– Leaflet raid on Berlin 2/10/39 *28*
– First German aircraft shot down over British Isles 28/10/39 34
– Attacks Luftwaffe mine-laying seaplanes at Borkum 28/11/39 *42*
– Bombs German shipping 3/12/39 43
– Heligoland battle with Luftwaffe 18/12/39 48
– Leaflet raids on Prague and Vienna 17/1/40 *57*
– Leaflet raids on western Poland 7/3/40 *66*
– Leaflet raid on Warsaw 15/3/40 *68*
– Bombs Sylt 19/3/40 70
– Spitfire shot down by Heinkel over Yorkshire coast 3/4/40 *72*
– Portal appointed C-in-C Bomber command 3/4/40 72
– Lays mines in Danish waters 13/4/40 *73*
– Bombs Nazi airfields in Norway 23/4/40 *76*
– Empire air training scheme 29/4/40 78
– Bombers shot down over Belgium 12/5/40 *84*
– Resisting Luftwaffe at Dunkirk 25/5/40 87
– Fighter Command losses at Dunkirk 4/6/40 92
– Bombs Milan and Genoa 12/6/40 *94*
– Airmen on Lancastria lost 17/6/40 99
– Blind Flying Development Unit 22/6/40 99
– Free Polish fighter squadron formed 13/7/40 *103*
– Battle of Britain: counters Luftwaffe attack on convoy 10/7/40 104
– Bombs Germany and Netherlands 16/8/40 *110*
– Types of planes used in Battle of Britain 17/8/40 111
– Bombs German targets 20/8/40 *112*
– Coastal Command sets up air base in Iceland 27/8/40 *114*

– Bombs Lorient base 3/9/40 *116*
– Organization during Battle of Britain 17/9/40 121
– Bombs Berlin and Channel coast 25/9/40 *123*
– Bombs German targets 3/10/40 *125*
– Portal and Peirse promoted 4/10/40 125
– Bombs German targets 9/10/40 *127*
– US volunteers join Eagle Squadron 9/10/40 128
– Bombs Kiel 17/10/40 *128*
– Raids Berlin and Hamburg 25/10/40 *130*
– Bombs Plzen 27/10/40 *132*
– Squadron arrives in Greece 2/11/40 *134*
– Bombs Ruhr 7/11/40 134
– German raids 10/11/40 138
– Bombs Italian bases in North Africa 21/11/40 *138*
– Dowding retired from Fighter Command and Park replaced 17/11/40 139
– Harris becomes deputy Chief of Air Staff 25/11/40 *140*
– Bombs Dusseldorf and Turin 4-5/12/40 *141*
– Health care for pilots includes McIndoe's Burns Unit 1/12/40 142
– Bombs Italian bases at Derna and Bardia 13/12/40 *142*
– Bombs Mannheim 16/12/40 *144*
– Bombs Bremen 1/1/41 *150*
– Strength in Mediterranean 1/1/41 *150*
– Further squadrons in Greece 9/1/41 *151*
– Bombs Italians in Ethiopia 9/1/41 152
– Bombs Benghazi 14/1/41 *154*
– Raids Valona 20/1/41 *156*
– Stirling bomber in Rotterdam raid 11/2/41 *161*
– Bombs Asmara 28/2/41 *164*
– New Manchester bombers raid Brest 24-5/2/41 166
– Raid on Le Havre includes Halifax bombers 11/3/41 *168*
– Eagle Squadron operational 28/3/41 *172*
– Torpedoes Gneisenau at Brest 5/4/41 *174*
– 9 and 149 Squadrons drop 4,000-lb bombs on Emden 1/4/41 175
– Bombs Sofia 7/4/41 *176*
– Bombs Hamburg, Bremen, Berlin, Emden & Rotterdam 12/5/41 187
– Bombs Luftwaffe on ground in Vichy-French Syria 15/5/41 189
– Fighters leave Crete for Egypt 19/5/41 *190*
– Losses in Crete 1/6/41 195
– Tedder becomes C-in-C Middle East 1/6/41 *195*
– Begins raids on Ruhr and Rhineland 11/6/41 *196*
– Bombs Cologne, Duisburg and Dusseldorf 17-18/6/41 *198*
– Bombs Prinz Eugen at Brest 2/7/41 *203*
– Eagle Squadron fatalities in French raid 2/7/41 204
– Bombs Cologne 7-8/7/41 *205*
– To attack transport and break German morale 9/7/41 205
– Bombs Scharnhorst at La Pallice 24/7/41 *208*
– Aircrew star in "Target for Tonight" 26/7/41 209
– Two squadrons leave for USSR 12/8/41 *214*
– First use of Gee in Munchen-Gladbach raid 12/8/41 214
– Bomber command accuracy queried by Butt 31/8/41 218
– Heavy raid on Berlin 8/9/41 *221*
– Bombs Italy from bases in Britain and North Africa 12/9/41 221
– Bombs Hamburg 16/9/41 *223*
– Squadrons 81 and 134 in USSR 14/9/41 224
– No 15 Group Coastal Command in Battle of the Atlantic 16/9/41 225
– Raids Stettin and Hamburg 29-30/9/41 *226*
– Bombs Nuremberg 12-13/10/41 *231*
– Bombs Hamburg 26-27/10/41 *235*
– Bombs German ships in Norway 30/10/41 236
– Attacks Sicily 3/11/41 *237*
– Coastal Command sinks first U-boat 30/11/41 244
– Evacuates remaining Singapore planes to Sumatra 16/1/42 *264*
– Bomber Command uses Luftwaffe tactics in German raids 1/2/42 270
– Bomber Command directed to hit civilian targets 14/2/42 272
– Harris becomes C-in-C of Bomber command 22/2/42 276
– First use of Lancaster bombers 3/3/42 *278*
– Bombs Renault works in France 4/3/42 278
– First large scale use of Gee in Essen raid 9/3/42 281
– Fights off Luftwaffe at Malta 26/3/42 *284*
– Bombs Lubeck using Gee in area bombing offensive 29/3/42 284
– 8,000-lb bomb dropped on Essen 11/4/42 *288*
– 44 and 97 Squadrons bomb Augsburg 17/4/42 291
– Bombs Rostock to hit Heinkel factory 25/4/42 293
– Radio jamming on Luftwaffe's Baedeker raids 5/5/42 *296*
– Repels Axis air attack on Malta 9/5/42 298
– Shoots down German transport planes off North Africa 12/5/42 *298*
– Air training scheme in Canada, Australia and Rhodesia 19/5/42 300
– Singleton recommends Harris's intensive bombing plan 20/5/42 *300*
– Attacks Axis transport in Desert War 31/5/42 *301*
– 1,000-bomber raid on Cologne 31/5/42 302
– Coastal and Bomber Commands combine for Bremen raid 26/6/42 310
– Bombs Wilhelmshaven 9/7/42 *314*
– Kammhuber Line deters bombers 16/7/42 317
– Bombs Hamburg 27/7/42 *319*
– Harris broadcasts to Germany as Bomber Command attacks 31/7/42 319
– Pathfinder force to be set up for bombers as Gee jammed 11/8/42 *322*
– In Dieppe raid 19/8/42 326
– Bombs Dusseldorf 10-11/9/42 *331*
– Bombs Munich and Saarbrucken 20/9/42 *336*
– Coastal Command's Liberators make first "kill" 12/10/42 *340*
– Lancasters bomb Schneider works at Le Creusot 17/10/42 340
– Establishing air superiority at El Alamein 20/10/42 *342*
– Bombs Milan and Genoa 24/10/42 342
– To install Fido to help bombers against fog 4/11/42 347
– Raids Turin 20/11/42 *351*
– Uses 8,000-lb bomb on Turin 29/11/42 353
– Daylight raid on Eindhoven 6/12/42 *357*
– Future role of Bomber Command under discussion 6/12/42 358
– Bomber Command installs Oboe for bombing raids 31/12/42 363
– Uses Oboe in raid on Essen 9/1/43 369
– Begins attacks on U-boat bases in France 14/1/43 *370*
– Recommences Berlin air raids with 8,000-lb bombs 16/1/43 370
– Raids Hamburg using H2S radar 30/1/43 *376*
– Mosquitoes bomb Berlin twice 30/1/43 378
– Bomber Command's new directive includes U-boat industry 4/2/43 380
– Starts campaign of night raids on Wilhelmshaven 11/2/43 *381*
– Bombs Lorient as part of U-boat destruction campaign 13/2/43 381
– Bombs Milan 14/2/43 *383*
– Hits Nuremberg in round-the-clock bombing with USAAF 25/2/43 *384*
– Bombs Krupp works, at Essen, in Battle of the Ruhr 6/3/43 387
– 172 Squadron fitted with ASV III 20/3/43 390
– Bombs Philips factory at Eindhoven 30/3/43 *394*
– Role in battle for Mareth Line 30/3/43 394
– Bombs Kiel 4/4/43 *396*
– Mass air raids with USAAF on Mediterranean targets 5/4/43 396
– Pilot kills spectators during firing demonstration 13/4/43 *397*
– Allied air forces in Mediterranean reorganized 15/4/43 398
– Bombs Berlin, Rostock and Stettin on Hitler's birthday 21/4/43 400
– Bombs Duisburg 26-27/4/43 *401*
– Bomber command mines Baltic Sea 29/4/43 401
– Highest civilian fatalities yet in Dortmund raid 4/5/43 *404*
– Air attack as Allies take Tunis 7/5/43 404
– Intensifies raids on continent 14/5/43 408
– 617 Squadron uses "bouncing bombs" in "Dambuster" raid 17/5/43 410
– Bombs Sicily and Sardinia 20/5/43 411
– Dortmund raid brings bomb tally to 100,000 tons 23-24/5/43 *412*
– Bombs Dusseldorf 11-12/6/43 *415*
– Harris disagrees with Eaker's "Pointblank" plan 10/6/43 416
– Bombs Naples after Allied Tactical Air Force created 17/6/43 *417*
– Flying ambulance service 19/6/43 417
– Starts "shuttle" raids on Germany and Italy 20/6/43 *418*
– Bombs Wuppertal in Battle of the Ruhr 25/6/43 *418*
– Bombs Cologne 28/6/43 *420*
– Bombs Turin 12/7/43 *425*
– Bombers use "Window" in Operation Gomorrah on Hamburg 24/7/43 428
– Huge raid on Nuremberg 10/8/43 *434*
– Drops incendiaries on Milan 12/8/43 *434*
– Bombs Peenemunde research centre 18/8/43 436
– Bombs Berlin despite previous heavy losses 4/9/43 441
– Corona used as raids on Germany increase 23/10/43 455
– Photo-reconnaissance of V1 launch site 28/10/43 456
– No 100 Group formed 8/11/43 461
– Leigh-Mallory made C-in-C of Expeditionary Air Force 15/11/43 *462*
– Fido used to clear fog from runways 19/11/43 *462*
– Begins Battle of Berlin 19/11/43 463
– Bombs Leipzig 3-4/12/43 *465*
– Pathfinder skymarking of bomb targets with flares 3/12/43 466
– Units in SEAC put under Air Chief Marshal Peirse 11/12/43 *467*
– Attacks V-weapon launch sites 24/12/43 471
– Possible doubt cast on strategic bombing 31/1/44 484
– Dambusters drop heaviest bombs of war so far 9/2/44 *488*
– Bishop protests at area bombing 9/2/44 489
– Raids Augsburg 25-26/2/44 *492*
– Bombs French railway yard in preparation for invasion 6/3/44 *495*
– New mark of Spitfire coming into service 8/3/44 495
– Raids Stuttgart 15-16/3/44 *497*
– Kills 948 people in raid on Frankfurt 22-23/3/44 *499*
– Raids Nuremberg 30/3/44 *502*
– Raids begin on Budapest and Bucharest 3/4/44 *504*
– Precision-bombs Gestapo building in The Hague 11/4/44 *506*
– Switches attention to railways of France 15/4/44 506
– Bombs French targets 18-19/4/44 *508*
– Heavy attacks on French railways 19/4/44 509
– Precision-bombs Dutch air ministry 3/5/44 513
– Bombs targets in Roumania 8/5/44 514
– Bombs French coast and Germany 31/5/44 518
– Destroys two wireless intercept stations in France 3/6/44 *520*
– Increased bombardment of German fuel targets ordered 7/6/44 *530*
– Daylight raid on German navy at Le Havre 14/6/44 532
– German synthetic oil plants become a primary target 13/6/44 534
– Bombers fly from Italy to Warsaw 19/8/44 552
– Raids synthetic oil plant near Homberg 27/8/44 *558*
– Attacks German communications in Yugoslavia 1/9/44 *560*
– Drops incendiary bombs on Frankfurt 12-13/9/44 *562*
– Drops 3,574 tons of bombs on Duisburg 14/10/44 *571*
– Bombs the Ruhr 15/10/44 573
– Harassing retreating Germans in the Balkans 20/10/44 574
– Bombs Cologne 30-31/10/44 *575*
– Launches major raids to support land forces in Germany 16/11/44 582
– Resumes area bombing on Germany 30/11/44 585
– Raids Merseberg-Luena synthetic oil plant 6-7/12/44 *586*
– Drops incendiaries on Heilbronn 5/12/44 587
– Sinks German liner off Poland 18/12/44 *589*
– Bombs strategic targets in Europe 8-9/2/45 604
– Drops incendiaries on Dresden 14/2/45 606
– Hits transport centres in Germany 21-22/2/45 608
– Kills 500 civilians in The Hague 3/3/45 609
– Bombs Dortmund 12/3/45 *613*
– Drops biggest bomb yet on Germany 14/3/45 613
– Hits school in Copenhagen by mistake 21/3/45 616
– Bombers damage German battleship 9/4/45 *621*
– Sinks the Lutzow, Germany's last pocket battleship 16/4/45 *624*
– Bombs Heligoland 18/4/45 *624*
– Bombs Berchtesgaden 25/4/45 *626*
– Joins in the final battle for Berlin 24/4/45 628
– Reveals new Vampire jet fighter 9/6/45 *642*
– Harris resigns 26/8/45 *660*

RAF Balloon Command 45
RAF Volunteer Reserve 122
Ragusa *425*
Rakuyo Maru (transport) *562*
Ramillies (battleship) 303
Ramree Island 598, *601*
Ramsay, A M 88
Ramsay, Bertram 89, 522, 526, 527, 565, 597, 685
Ramsgate 106, 113, 115
RAN
– (see Royal Australian Navy)
Randolph (aircraft carrier) *613*
Ranger (aircraft carrier) *450*
Rangoon 255, 269, *273, 278, 331, 464*, 486, 517, *583, 621*, 631
Rapido river 453, *481*, 515
Rasch, Otto 227
Rascher, Sigismund *187, 192, 381*, 441
Rasher (submarine) 552
Rashid Ali 176, 193, *262*
Rastenburg *198*
Rathbone, Basil 147
Rathedaung *361, 368*, 380, *390*
Rationing 22, *26*, 29, *38, 40*, 43, *45*, 50, *54, 55*, 56, 61, *62*, 65, 67, 68, *69, 89, 102*, 141, *141*, 147, *150, 163*, 170, *170*, 196, *200*, 205, 224, *262, 270*, 271, *273*, 299, 319, 346, *356*, 388, 411, *412*, 413, 420, *455*, 471, 481, *481*, 487, *510, 512*, 569, 640, *655*
Rattigan, Terence 364
Ratweek (operation) *560*, 561
Rauter, Hans *610*
Ravenna *586*
Ravensbruck 36, 441, *626*
Rawalpindi (armed merchant cruiser) *40*
Rawson, Arturo 415
Rayak 189
Rayburn, Sam 239, 251, 621
RCAF
– First battle squadron arrives in Britain 25/2/40 66
– Empire air training scheme 29/4/40 78
– First Battle of Britain success 15/8/40 *110*
– Air training scheme for Empire expanded 19/5/42 300
– Squadrons in Allied raids on Europe 6/12/42 358
– Catalinas support convoy ONS-5 30/4/43 403
– Bombs Munster 12/6/43 416
RDF *47*, 104, 109, 111, 117, 121, 136, 158, 189, 198, 244, 277, 288, *314*, 341, 357, *652*
– see also Radar
Reading, Marchioness of 38, *103*
Rebecca (film) 147
Recklingshausen *55*
Red Air Force
– Strength at German invasion 23/6/41 200
– Huge losses as fields and craft shattered by Luftwaffe 30/6/41 202
– Bombs Berlin 8/8/41 213
– Escorts Churchill to summit with Stalin 15/8/42 323
– Bombs Berlin, Konigsberg, Danzig and Stettin 29/8/42 328
– Bombs Warsaw 2/9/42 *330*
– Supports Red Army in "Uranus" at Stalingrad 20/11/42 352
– Bombs Danzig and Konigsberg 15/4/43 398
– Bombs Tilsit 21/4/43 400
– Bombs Helsinki 7/2/44 489
– Raids Helsinki 26-27/2/44 *492*
– Sinks three large transports in Tallinn harbour 22/9/44 564
– Covering Red Army advance into Poland 20/1/45 600
– Bombs Kustrin in advance on Berlin 12/3/45 613
– Final assault on Berlin 16/4/45 625
Red Army
– Joins up with German army at Brest-Litovsk 19/9/39 *22*
– Clashes with German army in Poland 22/9/39 24
– Condition at invasion of Finland 30/11/39 42
– Stopped by Finns 16/12/39 46
– Pushed back over Russian border by Finns 31/12/39 51
– Timoshenko to take over in Finland 5/1/40 54
– Defeated by Finland at Suomussalmi 8/1/40 56
– 54th Division at Kuhmo 28/1/40 *59*
– Losses in Finland 1/2/40 *60*
– Enters Lithuania 15/6/40 95
– Strength at German invasion 23/6/41 200
– T34 tanks effective against Germans 29/6/41 201
– Retreats before Germans 30/6/41 202
– Counter-offensive 15/7/41 *206*
– Casualties 31/7/41 211
– 16th, 20th and 28th Armies defeated at Smolensk 5/8/41 213
– Losses at Battle of Kerch 18/5/42 *300*
– Defections to Germans 25/7/42 318
– Stalin downgrades political commissars 9/10/42 *338*
– 62nd Army divisions wiped out at Stalingrad 14/10/42 341
– South-west, Don and Stalingrad Fronts attack Germans 20/11/42 352
– Secret of turn around against Germany 6/11/43 458
– Two new military decorations created 10/11/43 *460*
– Konev promoted to marshal of USSR 18/2/44 *490*
– Changes in command following Ukrainian defeats 30/3/44 503
– Attacks Finland 10/6/44 531
– Poised to clear Byelorussia of Germans 20/6/44 *534*
– Enters Czechoslovakia 24/9/44 *566*
– Launches winter sweep of Baltic 20/11/44 583
– Begins major winter offensive 12/1/45 597
– Soldiers discover Auschwitz 27/1/45 601
– 100 miles from Berlin 27/1/45 601
– Crosses the German frontier 31/1/45 602
– Storms gateway to Berlin 12/3/45 613
– Takes Berlin 3/45 10
– Sets up provisional government in Vienna 29/4/45 *626*
– Enters Japanese territory in Manchukuo 9/8/45 *652*
– Advances towards north Korea 12/8/45 *655*

Red Cross 160, *397, 579, 607*, 650
Red Sea *130, 176*, 196
Red Star (newspaper) 442

Reed, Carol 593
Rees, Peter 616
Refugees 156, 168, *502*, 650, 661
Regatta (operation) 339
Regensburg 436
Regensburg (blockade-runner) *394*
Reggio di Calabria *314, 440*
Regulus (submarine) *141*
Rehe 29
Reichenau, Walther von 230, *245*, 264
Reichssicherheitshauptamt *26*, 125, 210, *376*
Reinhard Line *469*
Reinhardt, F E 627
Reinhardt, Georg-Hans *84*, 535
Reith, John 55
Rejewski, Marian *432*
Remagen 611
Remarque, Erich 12
Remer, Otto 544
Renault [co] 278
Rendel, George 167
Rendova 421, 422, *425*
Rendulic, Lothar 513, 561
Rennell Island 378
Rennes *548*, 549, 552
Reno river 622
Renown (battlecruiser) *43, 73*, 161
Renown (battleship) *650*
Repatriation 650
Republic [co]
– (see Thunderbolt fighters)
Repulse (battlecruiser) *245*
Resistance (French) *190*, 197, *217*, 218, *221*, 268, 272, *280*, *284*, *289*, *292*, 298, 341, 355, *376*, *392*, *414*, 418, 422, 461, 463, *473*, *478*, 480, 486, 491, 500, *513*, *520*, 527, 528, *530*, 531, 532, 537, 547, 549, 550, *552*, 553, 557, 558, 559, *591*
Retelav, Reinhardt 469
Rethymnon 191
Retribution (operation) *404*
Reuben James (destroyer) 235
Reunion 354
Reuters 520
Revenge (battleship) *118*
Rexist Party *356*
Reykjavik *310*
Reynaud, Paul 69, *71*, *76*, *79*, 86, 88, 92, 96, *231*, *631*, *649*
Rhakotis (blockade-runner) *368*
Rheims *94*, *558*
Rheinpreussen 558
Rhine river 80, 565, 584, *596*, 607, *610*, 611
Rhineland 12, *196*, 419, *583*
Rhodes *140*, *282*, *452*
Rhodesia
– Empire air training scheme 29/4/40 78
– Air force participating in Empire Training Scheme 19/5/42 300
– Airmen arrive in Britain 6/8/40 110
Rhododendron (corvette) *138*
Rhone valley 557
Ribar, Ivan 466
Ribbentrop, Joachim von 27, 70, 98, 173, 177, *534*, *601*, *643*, 657
Ribbentrop-Molotov Pact 15
Riccardi, Arturo *161*
Rice anchorage 422
Richard III (play) 593
Richardson, Ralph 385, 593
Richelieu (battleship) *103*, 123
Richthofen, Wolfram von 219, 328, 414
Ridgeway, Matthew B 445
Riga *203*, 562, 570, *573*
Right Club 88
Rimini *552*, *564*
Rimling *597*
Rio de Janeiro (troopship) *73*
Riordan, Robert 378
Ritchie, Neil *243*, 266, 271, 308, 311
Ritpong *512*
Ritz, Hans 469
River Plate, Battle of the (see Plate, River)
Riverdale, Lord 78
RN
– (see Royal Navy)
RNZAF
– Squadrons in Allied raids on Europe 6/12/42 358
Robert C Tuttle (destroyer) *308*
Robert, Georges *420*
Robin Moor (merchant ship) *190*
Robinson
– (see Enigma)
Robinson, William 627
Roc fighters 77
Rocket-propelled weapons *306*, *308*, 338, 392, 402, *428*, 436
– see also V-weapons
Rockets
– (see Rocket-propelled weapons; V-weapons)
Rodney (battleship) *73*, *118*, 192, 226, 324, *531*, *539*
Roer river 582, *587*, 604, 607
Rohna (troopship) *464*
Roi 485
Rokossovsky, Konstantin
– Emerges as leader in fight against German invaders 31/7/41 211
– Commands Don Front in plan to trap Germans 20/11/42 *351*
– Offers honourable surrender to Germans at Stalingrad 9/1/43 369
– Begins to annihilate Germans in Stalingrad pocket 16/1/43 371
– Accepts Paulus's surrender at Stalingrad 31/1/43 376
– Ordered to attack with only half forces available 25/2/43 *384*
– Troops under his command take Bobruisk 29/6/44 *537*
– Part in Operation Bagration 3/7/44 541
– Troops poised for advance to Vistula 31/7/44 546
– Forces on East Prussian border 20/1/45 /600
– East Prussia cut off 27/1/45 601
– Ordered to strike into Pomerania 10/2/45 604
– Continues to clear Pomerania 7/3/45 612
– Tightens grip on Danzig 24/3/45 615
– Prepares for attack on Berlin 14/4/45 623
– Keeps 3rd Panzer Army back from Berlin 22/4/45 628
– Decorated by Montgomery 12/7/45 647
Rolls-Royce [co] 387, 449
Roma (battleship) 444
Roman Catholic Church
– (see Vatican; Pius XII)
Rome
– USAAF raids 19/7/43 *427*
– Allies bomb railyards 13/8/43 *434*
– Declared "open city" by Badoglio 14/8/43 434
– German forces occupy the city 10/6/43 443
– German troops loot art works 6/10/43 450
– 1,000 Jews rounded up by SS 16/10/43 *452*
– Germans fighting to save the city 28/12/43 474
– Allies drop leaflets about liberation 22/1/44 *481*
– Martial law proclaimed 26/1/44 *483*
– Gestapo police execute civilians 24/3/44 *499*
– Allied advance on 25/5/44 519
– US troops enter 4/6/44 *520*
Rome-Berlin Axis 13
Romford 113
Rommel, Erwin
– Commanding Panzer division at Sedan 13/5/40 *84*
– Troops surround Arras 20/5/40 *87*
– Tactics cut French Tenth Army in two 8/6/40 94
– Ease of advance into France 22/6/40 98
– Commands Afrika Korps 6/2/41 *160*
– Arrives in Libya 12/2/41 *161*
– Troops retake Agedabia and Zuetania 2/4/41 *174*
– Rapid advance in North Africa 5/4/41 175
– Tobruk attack continues while other forces enter Egypt 26/4/41 183
– Ordered to attack Sollum and leave Tobruk 16/5/41 187
– Commands Panzerarmee Afrika 31/7/41 *210*
– Commando attempt at start of Operation Crusader fails 18/11/41 241
– "Dash for the wire" at Tobruk 24/11/41 *243*
– Afrika Korps and Italian troops retreat into Cyrenaica 19/12/41 253
– Successful attack at Agedabia despite Hitler's orders 21/1/42 266
– Reputation amongst British grows as Benghazi falls 29/1/42 269
– Pulls forces back to "Cauldron" 30/5/42 *301*
– Takes charge personally at Bir Hakeim 13/6/42 307
– Promoted to field marshal 22/6/42 *310*
– Troops repelled by Eighth Army at El Alamein 9/9/42 316
– Ill with jaundice while troops attacked at Alam Halfa 31/8/42 329
– Flies home for medical treatment 23/9/42 *336*
– Recalled after Stumme's death 24/10/42 *342*
– Orders retreat from El Alamein despite Hitler's orders 3/11/42 348
– Retreating Afrika Korps resists at Mersa Brega 12/12/42 357
– Appointed to command Army Group Africa 24/2/43 *384*
– On sick leave after Hitler refuses evacuation appeal 10/3/43 389
– Ordered to assemble forces in Italy 30/7/43 429
– Meets Italian general to discuss Rome being "open city" 14/8/43 434
– Appointed C-in-C of Fortress Europe 12/12/43 *469*
– Arrives to take charge in northern France 1/3/44 494
– Reinforces Europe's defences 6/5/44 512
– Leaves HQ for Germany 5/6/44 *520*
– Arrives back at French HQ 6/6/44 *522*
– Showdown with Hitler 17/6/44 532
– Attends special Fuhrer conference 29/6/44 *537*
– Orders no surrender in Cherbourg 27/6/44 538
– To command army after coup 20/7/44 544
– Injured in car crash 17/7/44 545
– Commits suicide 14/10/44 572
– Biography 685
Ronco river 578
Roosevelt, Eleanor 299, 338
Roosevelt, Franklin D
– Tries to revise Neutrality Law to benefit Allies 9/9/39 20
– Urges repeal of Neutrality Act 21/9/39 25
– Atomic bomb study ordered 11/10/39 30
– Signs new Neutrality Act 4/11/39 35
– Wants to increase defence spending 5/12/39 *43*
– Defence budget requirements 4/1/40 *54*
– Asks Mussolini to help bring peace 29/4/40 *76*
– Urges Mussolini to stay out of war 1/5/40 *78*
– Believes US is vulnerable to German attack 11/5/40 82
– Asks Congress to increase military spending 16/5/40 *84*
– Asks Congress for more money for defence 31/5/40 *89*
– "Five freedoms" speech 5/7/40 103
– Asks Congress for more defence spending 10/7/40 *103*
– Wins Democratic nomination 17/7/40 *105*
– US to swap destroyers for British bases 16/8/40 112
– Rejects appeasement 12/10/40 *127*
– Reluctant to lead US into war 30/10/40 133
– Wins third presidential term 5/11/40 134
– Outlines Lend-Lease scheme 17/12/40 *144*
– Arranges British purchases of defence materials 19/12/40 144
– Broadcast call to US to become arsenal of democracy 30/12/40 147
– Sends Hopkins to London 3/1/41 151
– "Four freedoms" speech 6/1/41 152
– Provides arms to Britain 3/41 7
– Aid for democracies promised 15/3/41 170
– Agrees US/Canada joint aid for Britain 21/4/41 183
– Says US arming for self-defence against Nazi menace 27/5/41 193
– Calls Nazis outlaws 20/6/41 *198*
– Urges Americans to defend freedom 4/7/41 *203*
– Recalls MacArthur 26/7/41 *208*
– Meetings with Churchill produce Atlantic Charter 14/8/41 215
– Announces navy's "shoot-first" policy in broadcast 11/9/41 223
– Wants US merchant ships in Atlantic armed 9/10/41 *230*
– Cancels holiday because of Japanese threat 30/11/41 244
– Sends personal letter to Hirohito 6/12/41 247
– Describes Pearl Harbor attack as "infamy" 8/12/41 248
– Given war powers by Congress 19/12/41 254
– Advocates India's independence 21/3/42 283
– Broadcasts as nation is put on war footing 28/4/42 295
– Holds talks with Churchill in Washington 18/6/42 308
– Accepts invasion of Europe not yet possible 22/7/42 *318*
– Broadcasts warning of "toughest war" 8/9/42 *331*
– Nationwide tour of war industries 17/9/42 *333*
– Takes charge of arms supply to hold Guadalcanal 24/10/42 342
– Defends Eisenhower's agreement with Darlan 17/11/42 352
– Says offensive is under way on Pearl Harbor anniversary 7/12/42 358
– Atomic secrets not to be shared with British 28/12/42 *363*
– Meets Churchill at Casablanca to plan next moves 14/1/43 370
– Promises post-war trials for Japanese over PoW killings 21/4/43 *400*
– Holds "Trident" talks with Churchill on next steps 11/5/43 *406*
– Urges Italians to overthrow Mussolini 11/6/43 *415*
– With Churchill, urges Italians to depose Mussolini 16/7/43 *425*
– Atomic bomb research to be shared with British 20/7/43 *427*
– Allied leaders meet in Quebec 13/8/43 434
– Warns Germans of war crimes trials to come 29/8/43 *438*
– Says Fortress Europe can be broken 17/9/43 *444*
– Speech at signing of UNRRA charter 9/11/43 461
– On board ship nearly hit by US torpedo 14/11/43 *462*
– At Sextant conference in Cairo 25/11/43 464
– At Teheran conference 28/11/43 9
– Puts fathers at bottom of draft list 10/12/43 468
– Christmas Eve broadcast 24/12/43 471
– Wants to introduce new law to curb strikes 11/1/44 480
– Conversation with Churchill monitored 1/2/44 487
– Says Italian fleet is to be shared out 3/3/44 *494*
– Wins New Hampshire primary for presidential election 14/3/44 *497*
– Requests Chinese Nationalist aid in Burma 22/4/44 508
– On D-Day 6/6/44 529
– Meets de Gaulle 6/7/44 *539*
– To run for fourth term as president 11/7/44 541
– Attends Octagon Conference in Quebec 11/9/44 *562*
– Agrees collaboration on atomic bomb with Churchill 19/9/44 564
– Persuaded to recall Stilwell from China 19/10/44 573
– Wins fourth term as president 8/11/44 581
– Inaugurated for fourth term 20/1/45 *599*
– Meets Churchill in Malta 30/1/45 *602*
– Holds talks in Cairo 20/2/45 607
– Dies 12/4/45 10, 621
– Biography 686
Roper (destroyer) *289*
Rosenberg, Alfred *168*, 169, *170*, *206*, 489, *637*
Roslavl 213, 315, 446
Rosselsprung (operation) 315
Rossosh *314*
Rostock 293, 400
Rostov-on-Don *237*, *241*, *314*, *316*, *318*, 369, 379, *383*
Rotmistrov, Pavel 425
Rottensee *518*
Rotterdam 80, 81, *84*, *125*, 187, 205
Rouen 94, *94*, 96, 293, 325, 339, *558*
Roumania
– Calinescu assassinated 22/9/39 25
– Polish leaders interned 24/9/39 *26*
– King Carol's mediation offer rejected by both sides 16/11/39 *38*
– Signs trade convention with Germany 22/12/39 *47*
– Iron Guard members swear allegiance to King Carol 15/3/40 *68*
– King Carol heads National Party 21/6/40 *97*
– USSR demands Bessarabia and Northern Bukovina 26/6/40 *100*
– King Carol orders general mobilization 28/6/40 101
– New government turns away from Allies towards Axis 5/7/40 *102*
– Withdraws from League of Nations 11/7/40 *103*
– British oil interests seized 24/7/40 *107*
– Anti-Semitic legislation passed 10/8/40 *109*
– To cede territory to Bulgaria 21/8/40 113
– King Carol survives assassination attempt 3/9/40 *114*
– Antonescu forces Carol to abdicate in favour of Michael 6/9/40 118
– Axis powers take over 7/10/40 127
– Earthquake damages oilfields 8/11/40 *134*
– Joins Tripartite Pact 23/11/40 *138*
– Massacre by Iron Guards 27/11/40 *140*
– Army quells unrest 4/12/40 *141*
– German forces to be built up for Greek invasion 13/12/40 143
– Ethnic Germans to be resettled in Reich 31/12/40 147
– Urged by Germany to enter war 14/1/41 *154*
– Iron Guards massacre Jews 21/1/41 156
– Iron Guard revolt quashed 24/1/41 *156*
– Relations with Britain broken as German troops move in 10/2/41 162
– Luftwaffe bases 27/3/41 *172*
– Jews massacred at and deported from Jassy 29/6/41 *200*
– At war with USSR 27/6/41 201
– Troops occupy Chernovsky 6/7/41 *205*
– Jews to register for forced labour 12/8/41 *214*
– Troops advancing on Odessa 9/9/41 222
– Britain declares war 6/12/41 247
– US declares war 5/6/42 *304*
– Ploesti oilfields attacked by USAAF 12/6/42 307
– Troops overwhelmed at Stalingrad 20/11/42 352
– Iron Guard attempts coup in Bucharest 6/1/43 369
– Antonescu's suggestion of leaving war rejected by Italy 1/7/43 *422*
– Anti-Axis protests 23/7/43 427
– USAAF hits Ploesti oilfields 2/8/43 433
– Red Army plans entry 24/12/43 *470*
– Red Army close to border 17/3/44 498
– Germans strengthen their position 23/3/44 499
– Soviet troops enter the country 2/4/44 *504*
– Allies call for withdrawal from the war 12/5/44 *513*
– Hit by RAF raids 8/5/44 514
– Bombed by Flying Fortresses 2/6/44 *520*
– Soviet forces take Jassy 22/8/44 *554*
– Declares war on Germany 26/8/44 557
– Soviet tanks roll into Bucharest 31/8/44 *558*
– Army fighting alongside Russians on the way to Hungary 9/9/44 561
– Terms of armistice with Allies 13/9/44 562
– Troops now fighting with Red Army 10/10/44 572
– Soviet commissar appointed 28/2/45 *609*
– Russians order king to dismiss government 2/3/45 610
– Bevin expresses anxiety 25/8/45 659
Roux, J J Le 545
Rovno *230*, *486*

Royal Air Force
– (see RAF)
Royal Australian Air Force
– (see RAAF)
Royal Australian Navy
– see also Pacific War
– Ships under British orders 26/12/39 50
– Action off Cape Spada, Crete 19/7/40 105
– German armed raider Kormoran sinks HMAS Sydney 19/11/41 242
– Canberra lost off Savo Island 8/8/42 321
– Voyager sunk while supplying "Sparrow Force" on Timor 23/9/42 *336*
– Special Forces group blows up Japanese ships 30/9/43 448
Royal Auxiliary Air Force 45
Royal Canadian Air Force
–(see RCAF)
Royal Canadian Navy
– see also Atlantic; Atlantic, Battle of the
– Providing convoy cover in Battle of the Atlantic 9/5/41 184
– Escort areas in Atlantic redefined 1/3/43 387
Royal Engineers 120
Royal Flush (operation) 487
Royal Marines 295, 298, 359, 402
Royal Navy
– see also Atlantic, Battle of the; Fleet Air Arm; theatres of war
– War stations 3/9/39 17
– Convoys begun 2/9/39 22
– Hunts Graf Spee and Deutschland 31/10/39 *34*
– Steps up offensive against U-boats 31/10/39 34
– Losses 8/11/39 37
– First destroyer loss of war 13/11/39 *38*
– Lays mine barrier 26/12/39 *49*
– To attack German shipping in Pan-American neutral zone 23/1/40 *59*
– German merchant vessels interception operation 12/2/40 *62*
– Rescues prisoners from Altmark 16/2/40 64
– Intercepts more German merchant shipping 21/2/40 *64*
– King George V (new battleship class) launched 28/2/40 *65*
– Intercepted German merchant ships scuttle themselves 2-3/3/40 *66*
– Scapa Flow base raided 16/3/40 69
– Intercepts and sinks German merchant ship 24/3/40 *71*
– Home Fleet sails for Norway 7/4/40 *73*
– First Battle of Narvik 10/4/40 *73*
– Second Battle of Narvik 13/4/40 *73*
– Fleet Air Arm's role in Norway 30/4/40 77
– Churchill orders assembling of small ships 25/5/40 87
– Operation Dynamo begins 27/5/40 89
– Losses at Dunkirk 29/5/40 *89*
– Operation Dynamo completed 4/6/40 92
– Losses at Dunkirk 4/6/40 93
– Mediterranean war begins 16/6/40 *97*
– Seizes French ships in British ports 3/7/40 *102*
– Destroys French navy at Oran 3/7/40 102
– Force H clashes with Italian navy off Calabria 9/7/40 105
– Action off Cape Spada, Crete 19/7/40 *105*
– German blockade extended 30/7/40 108
– Mediterranean Fleet bombards Italian positions in Libya 17/8/40 *110*
– De Gaulle's invasion of Dakar fails 25/9/40 123
– Concern over U-boat menace in Atlantic 22/9/40 125
– Bombards Cherbourg 10/10/40 *127*
– Ajax sinks Italian destroyers 11/10/40 127
– Bombards Dunkirk and Tromso 16/10/40 *128*
– Sinks Italian subs off Gibraltar 20/10/40 *130*
– Attacks in Dodecanese 29/10/40 *132*
– Fleet Air Arm hits Italian fleet at Taranto 11/11/40 138
– Fleet Air Arm raids Tripoli and Rhodes 26/11/40 *140*
– Fleet Air Arm attacks Italian targets on Rhodes 26/11/40 *140*
– Mediterranean Fleet shells Sollum 11/12/40 *142*
– Bombards Bardia 2/1/41 *150*
– New types of RDF 31/1/41 158
– Command HQ for Western Approaches moves to Liverpool 7/2/41 *160*
– Bombs Genoa, Leghorn and Pisa 9/2/41 161
– Defeats Italians at Cape Matapan 29/3/41 172
– Italian attack at Suda Bay 26/3/41 *172*
– Breaks German convoy to North Africa 16/4/41 181
– Evacuates Allied troops from Greece to Crete 30/4/41 182
– Hood lost 24/5/41 190
– Sinks Bismarck 27/5/41 192
– Evacuates troops from Crete 28/5/41 193
– Losses in Crete 1/6/41 195
– Sinks Vichy ship off Syria 16/6/41 *198*
– Patrol ship sunk by German destroyer off Wash 19/7/41 *206*
– Bombards Dieppe 26/7/41 *208*
– Attacks Kirkenes and Petsamo 30/7/41 *210*
– Captures U-boat with Enigma gear intact 27/8/41 *217*
– Western Approaches HQ's role in Battle of the Atlantic 16/9/41 225
– Loss of Ark Royal leaves Med Fleet without a carrier 14/11/41 239
– Barham sunk off Crete by U-boat 25/11/41 244
– Prince of Wales and Repulse sunk by Japanese 10/12/41 252
– Severe losses in Mediterranean 19/12/41 253
– Combined Ops raid on St Nazaire 28/3/42 285
– Indian Ocean loses 9/4/42 288
– Mediterranean Fleet losses in siege of Malta 28/4/42 294
– Loss of Edinburgh 2/5/42 *296*
– FAA attacks Prinz Eugen 18/5/42 *300*
– Convoy PQ-17 destroyed 7/7/42 315
– Eagle sunk by U-boat 11/8/42 *322*
– In Dieppe raid 19/8/42 326
– PQ-18 re-starts convoys to USSR 18/9/42 334
– Horton replaces Noble as C-in-C Western Approaches 19/11/42 *351*
– Operation Stone Age convoy reaches Malta 20/11/42 353
– Sinks Axis convoy in Mediterranean 2/12/42 357
– Escort areas in Atlantic redefined 1/3/43 387
– Launches first X-craft (midget submarine) 15/3/43 *390*
– Murmansk convoys suspended 30/3/43 *394*
– Operation Mincemeat 30/4/43 402
– Fraser replaces Tovey as C-in-C Home Fleet 8/5/43 *404*
– Takes PoWs off Tunisia at end of Desert War 13/5/43 407
– Bombardment of Pantelleria 11/6/43 416
– Special Boat Squadron lands on Cos 15/9/43 444
– Midget subs sink Tirpitz 22/9/43 447
– Andrew Cunningham appointed chief of naval staff 4/10/43 451
– New appointments in top ranks 21/10/43 *453*
– Sinks three German destroyers in Bay of Biscay 28/12/43 473
– Fraser becomes C-in-C of Eastern Fleet 31/7/44 *546*
– Forces based on Vis 27/9/44 568
– Boosting US Navy in the Pacific 15/11/44 581
– Ships arrive in Sydney 10/12/44 *587*
– Carriers set sail to join US Navy in Pacific 25/1/45 *601*
– British Pacific Fleet arrives in Sydney 10/2/45 *603*
– British Pacific Fleet sails for Okinawa 23/2/45 *607*
– Announces abolition of convoys 28/5/45 *640*
– Attacks Japan's naval bases 16/6/45 644
– Pacific Fleet joins US Third Fleet 17/7/45 *648*
– Fleet sets sail to occupy Singapore 23/8/45 *658*
Royal New Zealand Navy *187*
Royal Oak (battleship) 31
Royan *621*
RSHA
– (see Reichssicherheitshauptamt)
Rubber 264, *418*
Rubicon river 568
Rudel, Hans-Ulrich 600
Rudnya 449
Ruge, Otto 74, 79, 94
Ruhr 84, 134, *196*, 238, 304, 317, 319, 391
– see also Ruhr, Battle of the (air and land)
Ruhr river *603, 609*
Ruhr, Battle of the (air) 387, 398, 408, 410, 413, 419, 573, 585
Ruhr, Battle of the (land) 557, *618*
Run, Rabbit, Run (song) 51
Rundstedt, Gerd von
– Commands siege of Warsaw 16/3/39 23
– Suggests halt outside Dunkirk pocket 25/5/40 87
– Promoted to field marshal 19/7/40 *105*
– Commands Army Group South in USSR 30/6/41 202
– Kharkov and Crimea operation delays attack on Moscow 30/9/41 227
– Sacked by Hitler for abandoning Rostov-on-Don 30/11/41 *243*
– Appointed C-in-C Atlantic Wall defences 16/4/42 *289*
– In charge of German invasion of unoccupied France 11/11/42 351
– Fortress Europe under his overall command 12/12/43 *469*
– Disagrees with Rommel over Allied landings 1/3/44 494
– Decides Allied landings are feint 6/6/44 *522*
– Obtains Hitler's permission for Panzer reinforcements 6/6/44 525
– In Paris in run-up to D-day 6/6/44 527
– Showdown with Hitler 17/6/44 532
– Attends Fuhrer conference 29/6/44 *537*
– Sacked as C-in-C West 6/7/44 540
– Returns as C-in-C West 8/9/44 560
– Speaks at Rommel's funeral 17/10/44 *573*
– Commands German attack in the Ardennes 16/12/44 588
– Sceptical of German Ardennes offensive 26/12/44 592
– Brings up Panzers too late in Reichswald 13/2/45 607
– Retired by Hitler 10/3/45 *610*
– Captured by US troops 1/5/45 *631*
– Biography 686
Russaki *494*
Russell Islands *386, 394*
Russell, Bertrand 103
Russelsheim *554*
Russia
– (see USSR)
Ruthenia *616*
Rutherford, Margaret 204
Ruweisat Ridge *318*
Ryabchichi *336*
Ryder, Lisle 90
Ryezh *228*
Ryti, Rysto 66, 68, *144*, 538, *548*
Ryukyu Islands 596, *645, 650*
Rzhev 268, *327*, 379, *386*

S

Saar river 577, 579, *581*, 582, *583*, *586*, *596*, *607*, 614
Saarbrucken *336*, 596
Saaremaa island 583
Saarguemines 587
Saarland 21, 33, 557
Saarlautern *586*
Sabang Island *508, 546*
Sabotage *306, 312, 321, 322, 336, 351, 353*, 355, *418*, 422, *434*, 437, 439, 463
Sachsenhausen 36, 184, 243
Saga *652*
Sahara 399
Sahy *587*
Saidor 479, *488*
Saigon 211
St David (hospital ship) *483*
St Etienne *518*
St Hubert *597*
St Jean-de-Luz *97*
St Laurent 533
St Lawrence Seaway *298*
St Lo *539, 541*, 543
St Lo (escort carrier) 576
St Malo *97, 397, 550*
St Nazaire 99, 285, 381, 566
St Paul's Cathedral 120
St Peter Port 488
St Pierre 257
St Quentin *84*
St Thomas (convoy escort) *591*
St Vith *589*
Saipan *492, 531, 534, 539, 541, 577*, 584
Saito, Yoshitsugu *539*
Sakai, Takaishi 255
Sakhalin Island *655*
Sakishima Islands 616, *631*, 637
Salamaua *280*
Salazar, Antonio 452
Salerno 440, *494*
Salinas (supply ship) *235*
Salla *57*
Salo *444*
Salonika *134*, 167, 177, 391, *415, 577*
Salsk *321, 372*
Salt Lake City (cruiser) 392
Saltfish (submarine) *465*
Salween river *506, 513*
Salzburg *492*, 632
Samar island *575*
Samoa *266*
Samos *138, 444*
Samothrace *181*, 391
Samsun *49*
Samuel, Viscount 360
San Bernardino Strait 576
San Fabian 598
San Giorgio *506, 515*
San Jose 589
San Juan (cruiser) *660*
San Michel Pass *469*
San Miguel *599*
San Pietro 468, 470
San Vittore 479
San, Aung *637*
Sananada *351, 360, 372*
Sandakan *264*
Sandbaek, Harald *575*
Sandomierz 546, *552*
Sandys, Duncan 402, 560
Sangro river *460, 464*
Sangshak 498
Sansom, Odette M C (GC)
– (see Hallowes, Odette M C (GC))
Sant'Agata *434*, 435
Sant'Angelo, *455*
Santa Cruz, Battle of 346
Santa Fe *640*
Santerno river 622
Santi Quaranta *141*
Sanzo, Nosaka 481
Sarajevo *179*, 180
Sarajoglu 165
Sarande *141*
Sarangani Bay *646*
Saratoga (aircraft carrier) 459, *508, 607, 327*
Sarawak *247, 256, 645*
Sardinia *394, 396*, 402, *406*, 407, *409, 417, 420*, 424, *442*
Sargent, Malcolm 593
Sark 101, 106, *338*
Sarmi *508*
Sarny 478
Sartre, Jean-Paul 475, 593
SAS 241, 335, 349, 552
Sasebo 539
Sato, Kotoku 536
Sato, Naotake 647
Sattelberg *462*
Saturn (operation) 361
Sauckel, Fritz 283, *292*, 293, *301*, 324, *327, 386*, 487, *494*, 497
Saud, ibn, King of Saudi Arabia *605*, 607
Saudi Arabia
– Declares war on the Axis powers 28/2/45 609
Saundby, Robert 218
Savage, Michael *71*
Savo Island, Battle of 321
Sawar *508*
Sawatan Islands *510*
Saydam 165
Sbeitla *383*
Sbiba *384*
Scampton 410
Scandinavia
– see also Denmark; Norway; Sweden
– German invasion plans 16/1/40 *57*
– Foreign ministers meet 24/2/40 *64*
Scapa Flow 17, 31, *32*, 69, *72*
Scarpanto *192*
Scavenius, Erik *349, 434*
Schacht, Hjalmar 660
Schaffhausen *504*
Scharnhorst (battle cruiser) *40, 73*, 91, *160*, 163, *170, 172, 208, 264*, 270, 272, 442, *470*, 473
Scheldt river 80, 85, 565, *571*, 577, 578, 585
Schellenberg, Walther 37
Schepke, Joachim 171
Schillinger, Josef 454
Schirach, Baldur von *109*
Schlabrendorff, Fabian von 389
Schleswig-Holstein 99, 626
Schleswig-Holstein (liner) *589*
Schlieben, Karl von 538
Schlusselburg 222, 371, 374
Schneider [co] 340
Schnorkel (device) 202, 396, 608
Schoenfeld, Hans 301
Scholl, Hans 384
Scholl, Sophie 384
Scholtz-Klink, Gertrud 586
Scholz, Karl 498
Schorner, Ferdinand 552, 562, 564, 568, 572, 615, 636
Schraege Musik cannon 436
Schuschnigg, Kurt von 14, *631*
Schuster, cardinal 627
Schutzstaffel
– (see SS)
Schwarze Korps (newspaper) 619
Schweinfurt 436, 452, *492*, 501
Schweppenburg, Geyr von 512
Scobie, Ronald 586, 598
Scoones, Geoffrey 392, 536
Scorza, Carlo 427
Scott, Norman 340
Scrap metal
– (see Waste and scrap)
Scum of the Earth (book) 259
Scutari *584*
Scylla (cruiser) *368*
SEAC 480
Seafire fighters 644
Seal (submarine) *79*
Sealion (operation) *103, 105*, 115, 116, 121, *271*
Sealion (submarine) *583*
Seattle *358*
Sebkret el Kourzia 401
Sedan *84*, 85, *560*
Seele, Gertrud *597*
Seelow Heights 625
Segi Point *418, 420*
Seille river 578
Seine river 96, 518, *550*, 557
Seine, Bay of 526
Sele river 443
Sendai (cruiser) *458*
Senegal
– De Gaulle abandons attack 25/9/40 123
– Joins Allies 23/11/42 *353*
Senio river 622
Sens 557
Sepinggang *646*
Serafimovich 352
Seraph (submarine) 349, 402
Serbia 204, *217, 223*, 297, 412
Seria *253*
Service National du Travail *333*
Service Obligatoire du Travail *383*
Sessa Aurunca *458*
Sevastopol 232, *235*, 242, *280, 304, 306*, 314, *506*, 509, *512*, 514
Severn (destroyer) *212*
Sextant Conference 464
Seyss-Inquart, Arthur *87*, 405, 498
Sfax 356, *396*
Shadow of the Swastika (radio drama-documentary) *36*
Shaduzup *502*
SHAEF *560, 647*
Shaggy Ridge 484
Shanggao *168, 174*
Shanghai 29, *100, 114, 247*, 298, 658
Shansi 114, *184, 212*
Shantung *294*, 322, 324, *432*, 435
Shaposhnikov, Boris *210*
Shark (submarine) *102*
Shark code 360
Shaw, Artie 475
Shaw, Bernard 103
Shean, M H 506
Sheffield *142*
Sheffield (cruiser) 473
Shegwu *577*
Shelley, Norman 101
Shelton, Anne 475
Shenam Saddle 536
Sherbrooke, Robert St V (VC) 364
Sherman tanks
– (see Tanks)
Sherman, Frederick C 459
Shertok, Moshe 538
Shetland Islands 39, *73*
Shibasaki, Keiji 465
Shigemitsu, Mamoru *400*, 660
Shigure (destroyer) 433
Shih-pai 417
Shikari (destroyer) *91*
Shimonoseki Strait 641
Shimsk *490*

an 626
, 342, *351*, 353,
270

lks with USSR
27/12/39 *49*
ergency after
der incident

ing with Britain

with Bulgaria

with Britain 27/2/41

oin Axis 4/3/41 *166*
with Germany
USSR will aid if
8/8/41 *214*
orts to Germany
30/9/41 *226*
treaty with
/10/41 *230*
Hitler orders war to increase
oth sides 23/1/43
nises help if forced
20/4/43 *508*
declared 18/5/44
ns with Germany

1 460
mond 421
rin 506
orts to Germany
r, Lord (see
ohn)
mittee 240, 437
1
peration) 228
hters 221, 331, 528,
632

U

aw 239, 266, 280
ation) *495*, 536

lantic, Battle of the;
Mediterranean
rpedoed in Atlantic

s sunk by U29 off
7/9/39 25
eamer and British
sunk in Atlantic

47, sinks Royal Oak
Flow 14/10/39 31
s sunk 18/10/39 *32*
ays one in three
k attack 31/10/39 34
redicts win after that
acked 31/10/39 34
ing claims 8/11/39 37
s civilian shipping in
20/11/39 39
hghtly damaged by
4/12/39 *49*
sunk in Atlantic

by Antelope in south-
oproaches 5/2/40 *60*
ses to be played
BBC 6/2/40 61
by Gleaner in Firth of
2/40 *64*
rs unlimited war,
eutrals 15/2/40 63
by Gurkha in
3/2/40 *64*

— Enigma rotors taken from
scuttled U33 28/2/40 65
— U31 sunk in North Sea by
Blenheim bomber 11/3/40 68
— Fortune sinks U44 off Narvik
20/3/40 69
— Allied shipping losses 31/3/40
71
— U50 sunk off Shetlands by
Hero; U4 sinks Thistle 10/4/40
73
— Fearless sinks U49 off Norway
15/4/40 75
— U26 sunk in Atlantic 1/7/40 102
— Attacks on convoy HX-72
22/9/40 123
— RN concerned about growing
menace 22/9/40 125
— Dönitz orders "wolfpacks" as
Prien attacks in Atlantic
19/10/40 129
— Allied shipping losses 29/10/40
133
— Allied losses grow as numbers
increase 29/10/40 134
— Hitler orders war to increase
24/2/41 165
— US Navy to shoot first after
attack on Creer 11/9/41 223
— First one enters Mediterranean
24/9/41 226
— Lehigh torpedoed off West
Africa 19/10/41 233
— Ark Royal sunk by U81 and
U205 off Gibraltar 14/11/41 239
— Barham torpedoed by U331 in
Ionian Seas 25/11/41 244
— Type IXs begin second "happy
time" off US 13/1/42 264
— Brazilian shipping sunk 11/3/42
280
— Shipping menaced worldwide
as Dönitz orders more attacks
1/4/42 287
— Edinburgh torpedoed in Barents
Sea 30/4/42 294
— Transport ship torpedoed in St
Lawrence Seaway 11/5/42 298
— Attack on convoy PQ-16 in
Arctic 30/5/42 302
— Allied losses as offensive
spreads to US waters 1/7/42
313
— Success of British Leigh Light
device 5/7/42 314
— Attack on convoy PQ-17 in
Arctic 7/7/42 315
— Withdrawn from east coast of
US 19/7/42 318
— U94 sunk in Caribbean 28/8/42
327
— Controversy after Laconia
sinking in South Atlantic
12/9/42 331
— Active sinks U179 off Cape
Town 7/10/42 338
— Allies set up Anti-U-Boat
Committee 4/11/42 347
— Allied shipping hit in Indian
Ocean 5/12/42 357
— Convoy JW-51B wins Battle of
Barents Sea 31/12/42 364
— RAF attacks bases at
Cherbourg and Lorient 14/1/43
370
— Harris says industry is RAF
target 4/2/43 380
— RAF attacks Lorient 13/2/43
381
— Hitler gives tanks and aircraft
more priority 11/4/43 397
— Five merchant ships sunk off
West Africa 29/4/43 401
— RAF mines Baltic Sea 29/4/43
401
— Recalled in anticipation of Allied
invasion of Europe 29/6/43 420
— U792, prototype Walter boat,
launched 28/9/43 448
— Churchill says 60 have been
sunk in last three months
9/11/43 460
— U794 goes into service with a
Schnorkel 11/12/43 467
— Emden raided by USAAF
11/12/43 467

— Convoy JW-56A attacked off
Iceland 26/1/44 483
— Penelope sunk by U410 at
Anzio 18/2/44 490
— Convoy JW-57 sinks two in
Arctic 18/2/44 490
— Convoy RA-57 sinks three and
damages two 10/3/44 495
— Attack on convoy JW-58 in
Arctic fails 31/3/44 503
— Allied flying boats sink two off
Norway 18/5/44 515
— Chatelain seizes Enigma
material from U505 4/6/44 521
— War effort aided by Schnorkel
21/10/44 574
— U486 sinks Leopoldville in
English Channel 24/12/44 591
— U711 sinks Bluebell; U425 sunk
by Lark 17/2/45 605
— Newer, more powerful, ships
commissioned 24/2/45 608
— U327 sunk by Lancaster
bomber in Scilly Isles 28/2/45
609
— Types XXI and XXIII (Walter
boats) arrive too late 31/3/45
617
— Five sunk in Kattegat as
hostilities cease 5/5/45 634
— Some scuttle themselves
though Dönitz orders surrender
12/5/45 636
— U530 surfaces off Argentina
10/7/45 647

Ube 652
Uckermark
— (see Altmark)
Udem 609
Udet, Ernst 176, *241*
Udine 429, 539
Uganda (battleship) 445
Ukhrul 536, *539*
Ukraine 8, 35, 60, 202, 216, *217*,
378, 438, 470, 472, 483, 492,
495, 497, 499, 508, 542
Ulithi atoll 564, 613
Ulster (destroyer) 618
"Ultra" intelligence 409, 514,
518, 521, 532, 534, 538, 550,
639
— see also Enigma
Uman 494, 495
Umberto, Crown Prince of Italy
407, 506
Umezu, Yoshijiro 649, 660
Umpire (patrol ship) 206
UN
— (see United Nations)
**Un-American Activities
Committee** 664
Unbeaten (submarine) 282
Underground
— (see PoWs; Resistance
(French))
Underground railway 120, 126,
128, 159, 388
Undertone (operation) 609
Ungelap 508
Union of German Socialists
170
**Union of Soviet Socialist
Republics**
— (see USSR)
Unita Proletaria (newspaper)
494
United Nations 262, 409, 458,
566, 571, 605, 609, 634, 637,
644, 645, 646, 650, 658
**United Nations Relief and
Rehabilitation Administration**
— (see UNRRA)
United Services Organization
160
United States Army Air Force
— (see USAAF)
United States of America
— (see USA)
UNRRA 461, *502*, 650, 661
Unshaken (submarine) 401
Upholder (submarine) 190, 223,
262, 289
Upper Silesia 597
Upright (submarine) 164
Ur 192
Ural Maru (transport ship) 566

Urbane (operation) *586*
Urge (submarine) 286
Urquhart, Robert 565
Ursula (submarine) 70
Uruguay
— Wrecked Admiral Graf Spee
sold for scrap 29/2/40 65
— Recognises French National
Liberation Committee 11/6/43
415
— Declares war on Axis powers
22/2/45 607
US Army
— see also theatres of war eg
Pacific War; D-Day
— Extra money provided by
Congress 13/6/40 94
— MacArthur to command in Far
East 26/7/41 208
— Strength 13/12/41 251
— First troops arrive in British
Isles 26/1/42 268
— New Caledonia Task Force
reaches Noumea via Australia
12/3/42 280
— Troops arrive in Northern
Ireland 18/5/42 301
— Eisenhower to command in
Europe 25/6/42 310
— Dieppe raid 19/8/42 326
— 32nd Infantry Division joins
attack on Wairopi 28/9/42 337
— First unit arrives at Guadalcanal
13/10/42 340
— Troops sail for North Africa as
part of Torch 23/10/42 342
— Patch takes over from
Vandegrift in Solomons 9/12/42
357
— Losses on Guadalcanal 4/2/43
380
— Losses in Battle of the
Kasserine Pass 25/2/43 385
— Patton appointed to command
II Corps 6/3/43 386
— Engineers build new Burma
Road 1/3/43 388
— Seventh Army and Rangers in
Sicily landings 10/7/43 424
— Fifth Army to land at Salerno
3/9/43 440
— Launches major attack at San
Pietro 7/12/43 467

US China Air Task Force
— (see Flying Tigers)
US Navy
— Naval Supply Act provides $
1,000m 11/6/40 94
— Roosevelt's "two-ocean" navy
plan approved by Congress
19/7/40 105
— Opens Bermuda base 7/4/41
176
— Planes start patrolling North
Atlantic 17/4/41 203
— Convoy protection in Atlantic
1/9/41 220
— Roosevelt orders "shoot-first
policy" 11/9/41 223
— Escorts British convoy HX-150
16/9/41 223
— First loss in Atlantic 31/10/41
233
— Japanese destroy yard at
Cavite 13/12/41 247
— Pacific Fleet losses at Pearl
Harbor 8/12/41 248
— Volunteers join up after Pearl
Harbor 13/12/41 251
— King becomes C-in-C 20/12/41
253
— King accepts British view on
convoys 1/4/42 287
— King demands more warships
15/5/42 298
— Victory at Midway Island 6/6/42
305
— King agrees that convoy
method is best against U-boats
1/7/42 313
— Task force defeats Japanese
flotilla off Guadalcanal 12/10/42
340
— Halsey succeeds Ghormley in
South Pacific 18/10/42 342
— Carriers sail for North Africa as
part of Torch 25/10/42 344
— Urges night radar after Battle of
Guadalcanal 15/11/42 351
— Report on Pearl Harbor 5/12/42
356
— Launches USS New Jersey
7/12/42 357
— Launches 15 new ships on
Pearl Harbor anniversary
7/12/42 358
— Confident of success in Pacific
31/12/42 365
— Losses at Guadalcanal 4/2/43
380
— Escort areas in Atlantic
redefined 1/3/43 387
— US torpedo nearly hits ship with
Roosevelt on board 14/11/43
462
— Penetrates Japanese home
waters 4/2/44 486
— Secretary of the navy dies
28/4/44 510
— New secretary of the navy
appointed 10/5/44 513
— Submarines sink Japanese
transports killing PoWs 11/9/44
562
— Key role of submarines in
Pacific War 15/5/45 638
— Attacked by Japanese air force
off Okinawa 27/5/45 640
— Survivors of Indianapolis
disaster tell their tale 2/8/45
651
— Vast force enters Tokyo Bay
27/8/45 660

USA (defence)
— see also US Army; US Navy;
USAAF
— Naval Supply Act passed
11/6/40 94
— GIs in Britain 13/6/44 531
— 12th Army Group formed in
France 1/8/44 548
— Plagued by phoney GIs
18/12/44 590
— Executes deserter 31/1/45 603
— Losses taking Iwo Jima and
Okinawa 2/5/45 10
— Troops under Montgomery
cross the Rhine 24/3/45 615
— Patton's troops discover
German gold reserves 8/4/45
621
— Senate approves conscription
16/9/40 122
— No change to policy when
Japan joins Axis 27/9/40 124
— Draft registrations 15/10/40 128
— 1942 budget 8/1/41 151
— Peru warns of impending
Japanese attack on Pearl
Harbor 27/1/41 158
— ABC-1 meetings with British
27/1/41 159
— Lend-Lease Bill becomes law
11/3/41 168
— Shipbuilding agreement with
Canada 17/3/41 170
— Axis ships impounded 30/3/41
174
— First military encounter with
Germany 10/4/41 176
— Greenland bases to have
established 12/4/41 178

— Enforces new Atlantic security
zone 25/4/41 181
— Collaboration with Canada to
help Britain 21/4/41 183
— U-boat sinks merchant ship
inside security zone 21/5/41
190
— First experimental blackout
26/5/41 192
— 1942 budget 5/6/41 195
— Troops to replace British
garrison in Iceland 11/6/41
196
— Draft registration for over-21s
1/7/41 203
— Army and navy appropriations
11/7/41 205
— Volunteer "Flying Tiger" pilots
aid Chinese Nationalists 1/8/41
212
— Military strength 22/8/41 216
— Axis shipping in US waters to
be sunk 26/9/41 226
— Merchant ships in Asian waters
to go to friendly ports 17/10/41
231
— Japan destroys fleet at Pearl
Harbor 7/12/41 247
— Rush of volunteers to forces
13/12/41 251
— Anglo-American talks agree on
war priorities 31/12/41 259
— Roosevelt promises US troops
and more aid for Britain 6/1/42
262
— U-boats extend Battle of the
Atlantic to US coast 13/1/42
264
— Japanese Americans to be
interned 18/2/42 275
— Japanese bombard Santa
Barbara oil refinery 23/2/42 276
— Forces to be built up in Britain
to attack Germany 14/3/42 280
— US and Britain agree on war
responsibilities 30/3/42 285
— Country placed on war footing
28/4/42 295
— Signs pact with Brazil 23/5/42
301
— U-boat lands saboteurs on
Long Island 16/6/42 306
— Agrees with second front while
sending USSR more aid
11/6/42 307
— Japanese shell Fort Stevens,
Oregon 21/6/42 310
— Joint Canadian-US chiefs of
staff committee formed 3/7/42
312
— Office of strategic services set
up 13/7/42 317
— Allies plan Operation Torch to
invade North Africa 25/7/42 318
— Four million in military service
28/7/42 319
— Kaiser put in charge of mass-
production of weapons 30/7/42
320
— Servicemen in Britain not
subject to national law 4/8/42
322
— Japanese sea-plane attacks
Oregon 28/8/42 327
— Joint board established with
Canada 18/8/40 112
— Groves appointed to manage
atomic weapons research
17/9/42 333
— Italian-Americans taken off
"enemy aliens" list 12/10/42
340
— Los Alamos chosen for atomic
bomb research 25/11/42 354
— Atomic secrets not to be shared
with British 28/12/42 363
— High command restructured
6/2/43 378
— Morgan appointed to Anglo-US
European command
(COSSAC) 23/4/43 400
— Expenditure 30/4/43 402
— Anglo-US atomic weapons
agreement 20/8/43 427
— Draft revised 14/8/43 434
— Draft bill reaches fathers at
bottom of list 10/12/43 468
— Japan begins bombing

Shinano (supercarrier) 579,
584, 638
Shinchiku 464
Shingle (operation) 482
Shinwell, Emmanuel 657
Shinyo (escort carrier) 581
Sho-I (operation) 576
Sho-go (operation) 573
Shoho (aircraft carrier) 294,
296
Shokaku (aircraft carrier) 248,
294, 296, 346, 536
Shore, Dinah 587
Short [co]
— (see Stirling bombers;
Sunderland flying boats)
Shortland Islands 327, *478*
Shostakovich, Dmitri 278, 364
Shropshire (cruiser) 163
Shuri 640
Shuri Line 618, *621*, 626, 638
Shwebo 582, 596
Sibuyan Sea 576
Sicilian Narrows 404
Sicily
— RAF strafes Catania 154
— Royal Navy landing party
demolishes rail bridge 28/8/81
217
— British "chariots" sink Italian
cruiser at Palermo 3/1/43 368
— British submarines sink Axis
transports off coast 5/2/43 380
— Allies bomb Palermo 18/4/43
389
— Ports hit by mass Allied
Mediterranean raids 5/4/43 396
— USAAF bombs Catania,
Palermo and Syracuse 17/4/43
397
— Operation Mincemeat to divert
attention to Sardinia 30/4/43
402
— Cunningham starts Operation
Retribution in Narrows 8/5/43
404
— Hitler downgrades defence,
giving priority to Sardinia
12/5/43 406
— Allied bombing 22/5/43 409
— Lampedusa Island surrenders
to Cohen 12/6/43 415
— Pantellaria surrenders 11/6/43
416
— Heavy bombardment as
Narrows closed to Axis
shipping 16/6/43 417
— USAAF bombs Messina
28/6/43 420
— Allied landings 10/7/43 424
— AMGOT set up 17/7/43 425
— Allies claim to hold half 21/7/43
427
— German forces trapped 30/7/43
428
— Allies take Catania and Paterno
5/8/43 432
— Losses in campaign as Allies
take Messina 17/8/43 437
— Allies cross Straits of Messina
to mainland 3/9/43 440
Sidamo 205
Sidi Barrani 120, 122, 138, 143
Sidi Bou Zid 383
Sidi Rezegh 241, 245, 308
Sidon 198
Sidra 301
Siegfried Line 18, 21, 33, 36, 51,
70, 562, 565, 569, 586, 604
Siemrap 250
Siena 521, 540
Sikh (destroyer) 247
Sikorski, Wladyslaw 27, 38,
211, 245, 265, 346, 405, 422
Sikorsky helicopters 596
Silverman, Sidney 356, 360
Sima, Horia 369
Simeni Creek 368
Simmons, F K 274
Simon Bolivar (liner) 39
Simon, John 26, 77, 360
Simovich, Dusan 173, 180
Simpson, William 582, 607, 619
Sims (destroyer) 296
Sinatra, Frank 475

Sincerely Yours (song) 259
Sinclair, Archibald 86, 268
Singapore
— Churchill asks Roosevelt for
help in defence 4/10/40 125
— Menzies shocked at state of
defences 29/1/41 158
— Waters mined by Britain
16/2/41 163
— Garrison strengthened 18/2/41
163
— US will not send ships 24/2/41
166
— Churchill ends reinforcement
28/4/41 181
— Threat from Japan in Indochina
25/7/41 208
— Repulse and Prince of Wales
arrive 2/12/41 245
— Reinforcements requested as
Japan advances in Malaya
20/12/41 255
— Fortification of north coast as
Japan advances in Malaya
9/1/42 263
— Churchill orders defence "to the
death" 20/1/42 266
— Air raids as Japan nears Johore
causeway 20/1/42 267
— British rearguard joins garrison
as Japanese approach 31/1/42
269
— Japan demands surrender
4/2/42 270
— Japanese hospital atrocities
14/2/42 271
— 30,000 Japanese troops land
and attack Australians 9/2/42
273
— Surrenders to Japanese
15/2/42 274
— Australian troops blow up
Japanese shipping 30/9/43
448
— Bombed by Flying Fortresses
5/11/44 579
— US bombers raid Japanese
naval base 2/2/45 603
— British fleet sets sail to occupy
23/8/45 658
— Mountbatten accepts Japanese
surrender 29/8/45 660
Singora 250
Sington, Derrick 626
Sini 444
Sinkiang 338
Sino-Japanese War 7, 13
Sinsiang 561
Sinyang 160
Sinzweya 488, 491
Sio 467, 480
Sirius (cruiser) 357, 450
Sirte 160, 253, 361
Sittang Bend 658
Sittang river 273, 631
Sivash lagoon 507
Six, Franz 123
Sjotay, Dome 499, 507
Skagerrak 73, 75
Skaggerak 455
Skala 504
Skoplje 581
Skorzeny, Otto 445, 498, 520,
575, 588, 589
Skua dive-bombers
— (see Blackburn Skua dive-
bombers)
Slang 70
Slapstick (operation) 443
Slapton Sands 503, 511, 512
Sledgehammer (operation) 318
Slim, William
— Leads attack at Gallabat
6/11/40 134
— Wounded at Keru 27/1/41 159
— Leads force in Iranian invasion
25/8/41 218
— Takes command of Burma
Corps 19/3/42 282
— In charge of British retreat from
Burma 30/4/42 295
— Burma Corps arrives at Imphal
behind refugees 15/5/42 299
— Reports on situation on front in
Burma 14/5/43 406

— Made C-in-C Eastern
Command 6/10/43 450
— Fourteenth Army overruns
Maungdaw 10/1/44 480
— Surprised by Operation U-Go
11/3/44 496
— Rushes troops to Imphal
18/3/44 498
— Holds off Japanese at Imphal
24/3/44 500
— Continues fighting on Imphal
plain 6/4/44 505
— Launches Operation Extended
Capital 18/11/44 582
— Japanese retreat as Extended
Capital troops advance 5/1/45
596
— Crossing of the Irrawaddy starts
14/1/45 599
— Watches Gurkhas at taking of
Meiktila 4/3/45 610
— Troops take Rangoon 3/5/45
631
Slovakia 34, 140, 222, 618
Slovenia 438, 513
Slovik, Eddie 603
Smela 480
Smetana, Bedrich 20, 95
Smigly-Rydz, Edward 16, 26, 27
Smith, Holland 465
Smith, Julian 465
Smith, Maurice 606
Smith, Walter Bedell 440, 522,
527, 634
Smolensk 206, 210, 213, 283,
363, 384, 389, 444, 446
Smuts, Jan Christian 16, 20, 35,
59, 126, 132, 190, 280, 342,
422, 517, 531
Smyela 469
Sneland (coaster) 634
Sobibor 286, 291, 301, 353, 385,
452
Sochaczew 600
Society of Friends 178
Soddu 190
Soddu, Ubaldo 136
SOE 105, 194, 208, 312, 317,
349, 355, 389, 458, 462, 492,
493, 528
Sofia 370, 404, 427, 480
Soissons 94, 558
Sokolovsky, Vasiliy 647
Solh, Riad 460
Sollum 118, 142, 187, 264
Solomon 128
Solomon Islands
— Japanese land at Bougainville
6/4/42 288
— Japanese land on Tulagi 3/5/42
296
— US submarine sinks Japanese
minelayer 11/5/42 298
— US bombs Japanese airfields
on Guadalcanal and Tulagi
31/7/42 319
— Savo Island Battle follows US
taking of Guadalcanal 8/8/42
321
— US planes land at Henderson
Field, on Guadalcanal 20/8/42
325
— Japan loses more than US in
Battle of Eastern Solomons
25/8/42 327
— Battle of Bloody Ridge 14/9/42
333
— Wasp torpedoed off
Guadalcanal 15/9/42 335
— US marines attack Japanese
from Henderson Field 9/10/42
338
— US task force defeats
Japanese off Guadalcanal
12/10/42 340
— US marines repel Japanese at
Matanikau river 24/10/42 342
— Japanese troops land at Koli
Point 3/11/42 347
— USAAF bombs Japanese
battleship 13/11/42 349
— Battle of Guadalcanal 15/11/42
351
— Japanese prepare to build
airfield at Munda point 4/11/42
353

— Battle of Tassafaronga 1/12/42
357
— Patch takes over command
from Vandegrift at Guadalcanal
9/12/42 357
— Japanese resist US at Mount
Austen 18/12/42 360
— British troops take Hargeisa
20/3/41 170
— Japan to pull back from
Guadalcanal to New Georgia
31/12/42 363
— Japanese resist US troops on
Mount Austen on Guadalcanal
2/1/43 368
— US offensive on Guadalcanal
begins 10/1/43 370
— US demands Japanese
surrender at Gifu 17/1/43 372
— US TF18 hit by Japanese off
Rennell Island 30/1/43 378
— First US land victory as
Japanese leave Guadalcanal
4/2/42 380
— Battle of the Bismarck Sea
5/3/43 388
— Japanese aircraft sink Allied
ships in Ironbottom Sound
7/4/43 397
— Yamamoto killed 18/4/43 401
— US air attack on Japanese
8/5/43 405
— Halsey launches Operation
Toenails to take Munda 3/6/43
414
— US forces repel major assault
on Guadalcanal 16/6/43 417
— US troops take Segi Point, in
New Georgia 21/6/43 418
— US shells Bougainville and
Kolombangara 29/6/43 420
— Battle of Kula Gulf 6/7/43 422
— Battle of Kolombangara 13/7/43
425
— USAAF hits Japanese at Buin-
Faisi 17/7/43 426
— US reconnaissance party lands
in Vella Lavella 22/7/43 427
— US forces attack Horseshoe
Hill, New Georgia 27/7/43 428
— Fighting Italians in Ethiopia
20/6/40 99
— Air force bombs Somaliland
29/8/40 114
— Battle of Vella Gulf after US
forces take Munda 7/8/43 433
— Halsey orders occupation of
Vella Lavella 11/8/43 434
— Japanese losses as Allies take
New Georgia 25/8/43 439
— US infantry reach Orete Cove
1/9/43 440
— Japanese abandon fight
21/9/43 446
— US landings at Kolombangara
6/10/43 450
— US invasion of northern islands
ordered 15/10/43 452
— US bombs Japanese air base
on Bougainville 18/10/43 453
— US landings on Bougainville
1/11/43 458
— New Allied airstrip becomes
operational 9/12/43 467
— Bombed in diversionary raid
24/12/43 472
— US ships raid Shortland Islands
8/1/44 478
— New Zealand and US forces
land on Green Islands 15/2/44
490
— Suicidal Japanese attack on
beach-head 22/4/44 509
— Allies seal off Japanese at Buin
1/8/45 650

— Cunningham's troops advance
from Kenya 24/1/41 157
— Italians retreat 14/2/41 161
— South African troops advance
16/2/41 163
— Mogadishu falls 25/2/41 165
— British troops take Hargeisa
20/3/41 170
— Vichy French troops join Free
French 28/11/42 354
— Free French troops take Jibuti
to Addis Ababa railway
26/12/42 361
Somers (destroyer) 237
Somervell, Donald 322
Somerville, James 102, *286*,
508, 546
Somme 91
Somme river 558
Song Ziwen
— (see Soong, T V)
Songs
— (see Arts and Entertainment)
Songsan, Mao 536
Soong, T V 436, 640
Sopron 618
Sorge, Richard 187, 231, 337,
579
Sorong 286
Sorpe dam 410, 573
Soryu (aircraft carrier) 248, 305
Souk el Arba 351
Sousse 336, 397
South Africa
— Declares war on Germany
6/9/39 16
— Smuts promises to defend
British colonies in Africa 3/11/39
35
— Blackshirt plot to sabotage vital
industry 9/11/39 36
— Call for separate peace with
Germans in USSR 11/1/43 371
— War Measures Bill passed
1/4/40 72
— Air force bombs Italian aircraft
and depots in Libya 12/6/40 95
— PT-109 under Kennedy sunk
1/8/43 432
— Troops fighting Italians in Kenya
24/1/41 157
— Troops fighting in Somaliland
14/2/41 161
— Troops fighting in Ethiopia
18/2/41 163
— 1st Brigade in capture of Addis
Ababa 6/4/41 178
— Navy and RN intercept Vichy
convoy off Cape Town 4/11/41
237
— Troops fighting at Sidi Rezegh
22/11/41 241
— Air force in attack on Gondar
27/11/41 244
— Gold mines sabotaged 28/1/42
268
— Breaks off diplomatic relations
with Vichy France 23/4/42 292
— 7th Brigade fighting on
Madagascar 10/9/42 332
— US ships raid Shortland Islands
24/10/42 342
— Troops take Miteiriya Ridge
24/10/42 343
— Troops lost when transport ship
sunk in Indian Ocean 5/12/42
357
— Troops in Eighth Army 30/3/43
394
— Smuts wins general election
7/7/43 422
— Endorses Commonwealth
peace plans 17/5/44 517
— Smuts visits Normandy with
Churchill 14/6/44 531
South America
— see also individual countries
— Latin America to unite against
Axis 15/1/42 265
South China Sea 252
South Dakota (battleship) 648
South Seas 100
South Shields 113
South-east Asia Command
— See SEAC
Southampton 138

Southampton (cruiser) 151
Southdown (destroyer) 168
Southern Rhodesia
— (see Rhodesia)
Sovětsky 355
Soviet Union
— (see USSR)
Spaak, Paul-Henri 131
Spaatz, Carl 325, 398, 478, 506,
514, 520, 536, 646, 686
Spadefish (submarine) 581
Spahis 197
Spain
— Franco appeals for war to be
limited to Poland 3/9/39 20
— Friendship pact with Germany
ratified 29/11/39 42
— Rail links with France reopened
1/1/40 54
— Bans Freemasonry 24/1/40 59
— Troops occupy Tangiers
14/6/40 94
— German troops reach Franco-
Spanish border 27/6/40 100
— Franco refuses to join Axis
23/10/40 130
— Signs pact with Britain 2/12/40
141
— Franco refuses to allow
German invasion of Gibraltar
12/12/40 142
— Signs secret treaty with
Germany 10/2/41 161
— Gives Germany Morocco's
residence in Tangiers 17/3/41
170
— Volunteers to fight USSR with
Germany 24/6/41 200
— Franco sacks Falangists 3/9/42
330
— Azul "volunteers" fighting with
Germans in USSR 11/1/43 371
— Maintains neutrality while used
as Allied escape route 13/1/43
375
— Soldiers repatriated 2/2/43
470
— Agrees to cut wolfram exports
to Germany 3/5/44 512
— Banned from UN while Franco
is in power 19/6/45 644
Spanish Civil War 13, 15, 19
Spare a Copper (film) 112
Sparrow Force 336
Spartan (cruiser) 483
Spearfish (submarine) 73, 109
Special Air Service
— (see SAS)
Special Boat Section 349
Special Operations Executive
— (see SOE)
Speer, Albert 100, 271, 310,
338, 410, 412, 440, 444, 489,
520, 602, 614, 614, 618, 622,
625, 626, 634
Speidel, Hans 527
Spergau 488
Sperrle, Hugo 537
Sphakia 192
Sphinx (minesweeper) 60
Spiders 41
Spies
— (see Espionage)
Spilje 546
Spitfire fighters 32, 72, 104,
107, 109, 111, 113, 121, 141,
272, 278, 291, 292, 298, 300,
306, 318, 324, 344, 394, 397,
456, 492, 495, 528, 585, 588
Spitzbergen 216, 442
Splendid (submarine) 360
Splint (operation) 512
Sprague, Thomas 576
Spree river 626, 628
Spring Awakening (operation)
612, 615
Spruance, Raymond 483, 536,
686
Sri Lanka
— (see Ceylon)
SS
— In Poland 9/9/39 19
— Polish oppression 22/9/39 26
— Heydrich's "final solution" plan
26/10/39 35
— Kills inmates of Polish mental

asylums 6/12/39 43
– Mental patients killed in Poland 9/1/40 55
– New regiment including Danes and Norwegians to be made 20/4/40 75
– Jewish ghetto established in Lodz 30/4/40 78
– Totenkopf division near Arras 18/5/40 85
– Massacres Royal Norfolk soldiers at Le Paradis 27/5/40 90
– "Black Book" of dangerous Britons 6/7/40 103
– Reports on conditions in Reich 11/1/41 151
– Quells protests at treatment of Jews in Netherlands 25/2/41 164
– Reports on conditions in Reich 3/41 172
– Reports on conditions in Reich 17/4/41 180
– Einsatzgruppen massacring Jews in USSR 30/6/41 201
– Atrocities in Lithuania 10/7/41 205
– Einsatzgruppen receive orders for USSR work 17/7/41 207
– Kills Jews and White Russians at Minsk 21/7/41 208
– Einsatzgruppen massacre Jews in USSR 31/7/41 210
– Einsatzkommandos massacre Jews in Latvia 3/8/41 212
– Special action massacre of Hungarian Jews in Ukraine 29/8/41 217
– Einsatzkommando murders Jews at Ponary 12/9/41 221
– Adolf Hitler division captures Soviet Ninth Army 6/10/41 230
– Massacres 17,000 Jews at Rovno 7/10/41 230
– Massacres in eastern Europe shock Wehrmacht officers 15/10/41 233
– 230,000 Jews killed since June in Baltic States 1/12/41 245
– Security Service reports on German atrocities 19/1/42 267
– 229,052 Jews killed in Baltic States by Einsatzgruppe 31/1/42 268
– Executes 258 Jews in Norway 28/5/42 301
– Hunts Heydrich's killers in Prague 4/6/42 304
– Murders 93 gypsies at Cracow 3/7/42 312
– Begins deportations from Treblinka from Warsaw Ghetto 22/7/42 318
– Himmler orders brothels for Waffen-SS in France 17/11/43 374
– Stroop in charge of liquidating Warsaw Ghetto 21/1/43 375
– Kaltenbrunner becomes head of RSHA 29/1/43 376
– Panzer Korps ordered to defend Kharkov to the death 6/2/43 379
– Russians plan to trap Panzer Korps at Kharkov 8/2/43 382
– Crack divisions in Panzer Korps 19/2/43 384
– Dismantles Cracow ghetto 13/3/43 389
– Waffen-SS forces retake Kharkov 15/3/43 391
– Khatyn massacre 22/3/43 392
– Massacres 4,000 Jews at Ponar 5/4/43 396
– Troops under Stroop driven out of Warsaw Ghetto 19/4/43 400
– Mengele appointed to Auschwitz 24/5/43 412
– Reports on state of Reich 31/5/43 413
– Lwow ghetto destroyed after fierce resistance 27/6/43 420
– Massacres in eastern Poland 27/7/43 431
– Team to destroy evidence of murder of Jews in camps 31/7/43 431
– Guards killed in Treblinka uprising 2/8/43 433
– Bialystok ghetto liquidated 27/8/43 438
– Himmler speaks about Jews 4/10/43 451
– Rounds up Jews in Rome for deportation 16/10/43 452
– Auschwitz women attack guards 23/10/43 454
– Factories closed and Jewish workers shot 3/11/43 45
– Rounds up hostages in Milan 15/11/43 463
– Given free hand to deport Hungarian Jews 19/3/44 499
– Shoots Jewish children under 13 in Kovno 27/3/44 502
– Hitler Jugend division slaughters 86 Belgians 2/4/44 504
– Rounding up Jews in Hungary 15/4/44 507
– Massacres 642 at Oradour-sur-Glane 10/6/44 531
– Commander of 12th Hitler Jugend division killed 16/6/44 531
– Defending Caen 13/6/44 532
– Prevents Vilna garrison from surrendering 13/7/44 542
– Attacks Resistance in Vercors 23/7/44 547
– Arrests Petain 19/8/44 554
– Units refuse to agree ceasefire in Paris 25/8/44 556
– Massacres French civilians 27/8/44 558
– Tries to destroy evidence at Klooga camp 19/9/44 564
– Prevents regular soldiers from surrendering 23/9/44 565
– Starts reprisal operations against Italian partisans 29/9/44 566
– Auschwitz guards attacked by prisoners 7/10/44 571
– Arrests Admiral Horthy 15/10/44 575
– Fanaticism 5/11/44 580
– Massacres Belgian civilians 19/12/44 589
– Murders US PoWs at Malmedy 17/12/44 590
– Attempts to destroy evidence of murder at Auschwitz 27/1/45 601
– Disbands Comintern to patch up rift caused by Katyn 15/5/43 408
– Shoots surrendering Germans 18/4/45 624
– Shooting defeatists in Berlin 18/4/45 625
– Men killed by GIs liberating Dachau 24/4/45 627
– Rules by instant execution in Berlin 27/4/45 628
– Karl Wolff's role in Italian surrender negotiations 2/5/45 634
– Fights to the last in Prague 9/5/45 636
– Biography 686

Stalingrad
– German attack planned 28/6/42 312
– Timoshenko takes charge of defence 17/7/42 316
– Russians pull back as Germans advance 27/7/42 320
– Russian 62nd Army holding German sixth Army at Don 13/8/42 323
– German paratroopers massacred 22/8/42 325
– Attacked by Luftwaffe as defences crumble 23/8/42 327
– State of siege declared 25/8/42 328
– Russian counter-attack ordered as Germans enter suburbs 3/9/42 330
– Von Kleist takes over German attack from List 9/9/42 331
– German attacks repelled as Russian marines hold silo 18/9/42 333
– Hand-to-hand fighting breaks out as Germans take silo 22/9/42 336
– Tractor factory overrun but Red October works hold out 14/10/42 340
– First snows fall 22/10/42 342
– Germans advance towards Volga 27/10/42 344
– Paulus's Kampfgruppen take factory in new attack 13/11/42 351
– Russian counter-offensive "Uranus" 20/11/42 352
– Russians trap German Sixth Army and Panzers in city 26/11/42 355
– Hitler refuses to allow German sixth Army to pull out 11/12/42 357
– Von Manstein launches Winter Storm rescue operation 12/12/42 359
– Luftwaffe flies in supplies to Sixth Army 14/12/42 360
– 4th Panzer Army tries to relieve Sixth Army in city 16/12/42 361
– Russian victory as Sixth Army troops die 31/12/42 365
– Paulus refuses Russian surrender terms for Sixth Army 9/1/43 369
– Russians begin major offensive 10/1/43 370
– Gumrak falls as Hitler tells Paulus "no surrender" 21/1/43 372
– Paulus becomes field marshal on eve of German surrender 30/1/43 376
– Last Germans surrender 2/2/43 378
Stalino 233, 440
Stalinogorsk 247
Stampalia 132, 444
Stanley, Oliver 63
Stanley (sloop) 479
Stauffenberg, Claus von 534, 541, 544, 546
Stavanger 73, 74, 75
Staraya Russa 286, 490
Stayning (frigate) 513
Stehla 627
Steinbock (operation) 484
Stellbrink, Karl Friedrich 288
Stemmermann, Wilhelm 491
Stephen Hopkins (Liberty Ship) 337
Sterlet (submarine) 75
Stern Gang 579
Stettin 226, 328, 400, 515, 609
Stettinius, Edward 584, 624, 645
Stevens, Richard 37
Stewart, James 479
Stier (raider) 337
Stilwell Road 660
Stilwell, John 567
Stilwell, Joseph 270, 281, 292, 300, 342, 347, 388, 442, 444, 454, 464, 469, 496, 506, 548, 566, 573, 686
Stimson, Henry L 290, 337, 621, 649
Stirling bombers 161, 221, 284, 353, 381, 387, 390, 398, 408, 469
Stirling, Bill 552
Stirling, David 241, 335, 349
Stockholm 490
Stolberg 565, 582
Stone Age (operation) 353
Stonecrop 396
Stopford, Montagu 658
Stralsund 43
Strasbourg (battle cruiser) 102, 650
Strasburg 464, 577, 584, 596, 597, 599, 601
Stresa 566
Stringbags
– (see Swordfish aircraft)
Stronghold (destroyer) 278
Stroop, Jurgen 375, 400, 402, 405, 409
Stuart tanks
– (see Tanks)
Student, Kurt 193, 619
Stuka dive-bombers 16, 23, 74, 85, 88, 107, 109, 110, 152, 180, 191, 192, 202, 222, 224, 235, 279, 298, 302, 303, 309, 312, 314, 328, 383, 414, 431, 514, 528
Stulpnagel, Karl-Heinrich von 134, 233, 558
Stumme, Georg 336, 342
Sturmovik assault planes 246, 262, 469, 628
Sturmovik bombers 352
Sturmovik fighters 423, 431
Stuttgart 398, 442, 492, 497, 624
Stutthof 632
Styria 146
Subasich, Ivan 605
Subic Bay 566, 605
Submarines
– see also Atlantic, Battle of the; Convoys; Mediterranean; Pacific war; U-boats; individual navies
– British submarines scuttled 7/1/40 55
– HMS Tarpon sunk 14/4/40 75
– Italians sink two British submarines 16/6/40 97
– HMS Shark sunk 6/7/40 102
– German navy to attack Soviet submarines 11/5/41 198
– Italian mini-subs attack Gibraltar 20/9/41 224
– Japanese minelayer I124 sunk by Edsall 21/1/42 266
– Role of RN in supplying Malta 16/4/42 291
– US ship sinks Japanese minelayer in Solomons 11/5/42 298
– Japanese midgets raid Sydney harbour 1/6/42 306
– Italian ship captured by Hyacinth 9/7/42 314
– Italian ship sinks Thunderbolt in Mediterranean 14/3/43 390
– Japanese ship sinks Australian hospital ship Centaur 15/5/43 406
– Truculent sinks U308 off Faeroes 4/6/43 414
– British midgets blow up Tirpitz 22/9/43 447
– Saltfish sinks Japanese carrier in Pacific 3/12/43 465
– Tally Ho sinks Japanese cruiser in Pacific 11/1/44 480
– Tally Ho sinks It-23 in Malacca Straits 14/2/44 490
– Rasher sinks Japanese carrier in Philippine Sea 18/8/44 552
– Dace and Darter sink Japanese cruisers in Leyte Gulf 23/10/44 575
– Spadefish sinks Japanese carrier in Yellow Sea 17/11/44 581
– Sealion sinks Japanese battleship off Formosa 21/11/44 583
– Archerfish sinks Japanese carrier in Kumano Sea 29/11/44 584
– Japanese use suicide ships in Pacific 1/1/45 596
– Tally Ho sinks Japanese cruiser in Malacca Straits 11/1/45 597
– Japanese merchant shipping losses in US attacks 15/5/45 638
– Trenchant sinks Japanese cruiser in Java Sea 8/6/45 642
Subotica 571
Substance (operation) 208
Suda Bay 172, 191
Sudan 99, 102, 110, 139, 141, 156, 159, 174
Sudetenland 14, 643
Suddeutsche Volksstimme (underground newspaper) 236
Suez 139, 307
Suez Canal 166, 221
Suez Crisis 664
Suffolk (cruiser) 75, 231
Sugiyama, Hajime 492
Suho Island 342
Suiping 513
Sullivan, Francis L 259
Sultan, Daniel I 582, 596, 614
Sulu Sea 587
Sulu archipelago 618, 621
Sumatra 256, 272, 360, 508, 554, 579, 587, 596, 601, 603, 647
Summa 57, 61, 62
Summersby, Kay 527
Summerskill, Edith 360
Sun Li-jen 292
Sun Tien-ying 401
Sunderland flying boats 50, 59, 102, 138, 328, 515
Suomussalmi 43, 45, 46, 48, 49, 51, 56
Supercharge (operation) 348
Superfortress bombers 336, 383, 485, 515, 531, 534, 534, 539, 546, 551, 561, 579, 584, 584, 591, 603, 604, 609, 610, 612, 613, 618, 622, 637, 638, 640, 640, 641, 642, 643, 643, 644, 644, 649, 650, 652, 655
Supermarine [co]
– (see Spitfire fighters)
Supreme Headquarters, Allied Expeditionary Force
– (see SHAEF)
Surabaya 270, 276, 280, 515, 650
Surcouf (submarine) 273
Surigao Strait 576
Suzuki, Kantaro 620, 643, 649, 652
Swamp Flower (operation) 314
Swansea 103, 113, 154
Swatow 637
Sweden
– Declares neutrality 3/9/39 20
– Offers to mediate between USSR and Finland 4/12/39 43
– Aid to Finland 9/12/39 44
– Allies try to send aid through to Finland 27/12/39 49
– Finland's request for assistance rejected 17/2/40 62
– Protests at German sinking of ships 15/2/40 63
– Reaffirms neutrality 25/2/40 65
– Iron ore exports to Germany 21/3/40 70
– Asks Germany to return crown jewels and gold reserves 3/5/40 79
– Allows German troops to use rail link with Norway 5/7/40 102
– BOAC starts secret flights 2/3/41 168
– Norwegian ships break out for England 1/4/42 286
– Maintains neutrality by trading with both sides 23/1/43 375
– Protests at German mining of territorial waters 28/4/43 401

– Cancels German transit rights to Norway 5/8/43 433
– Germany blocks the Skaggerak 27/10/43 455
– Britain and USA demand end of vital exports to Germany 13/4/44 506
– Swedish military recover a crashed V2 rocket 13/6/44 531
Swinemunde 632
Swiss Roll 533
Switzerland
– Declares neutrality 1/9/39 16
– Bans exports to belligerents 3/9/39 20
– Invasion contingency plans 1/11/39 35
– Country on military alert 10/5/40 79
– Pro-Nazi movement banned 19/11/40 138
– Severs relations with USSR 21/12/40 144
– Policy on Jews and gypsies questioned 29/8/42 329
– Acts as protecting power for British and Germans PoWs 8/10/42 339
– Maintains neutrality while used for Allied espionage 23/1/43 375
– US bombers mistakenly raid Schaffhausen 1/4/44 504
– USSR refuses to renew relations 7/11/44 579
– Trapped German units seek safety 23/11/44 584
Sword Beach
– (see D-Day)
Swordfish (submarine) 136
Swordfish aircraft 112, 138, 142, 161, 172, 192, 266, 272
Sydney 304, 307
Sydney (cruiser) 105, 242
Sykes, R S 310
Sylt 70
Symi Island 541
Syracuse 424
Syria
– Calls on France to continue to fight 25/6/40 100
– Paris Protocols give Germany access to military bases 27/5/41 192
– Free French forces enter 8/6/41 196
– Free French and Vichy French fight 13/6/41 197
– Allies take Palmyra and Deir el-Zor 3/7/41 203
– Armistice between British and French 12/7/41 206
– To be independent after war 15/7/41 207
– Free French forces agree to guarantee independence 16/9/41 223
– Declares war on Axis powers 26/2/45 609
– Nationalist demonstrations against French troops 9/5/45 637
– Asserts claim for independence 21/5/45 640
– French forces battle with gendarmes 29/5/45 640
– British troops go in 1/6/45 642
Szalasi, Ferenc 575, 574
Szekesfehervar 614

T

T34 tanks
– (see Tanks)
Tabarka 351
Tabriz 218
Tacloban 573
Taft, Robert 621
Taganrog 233, 312, 379, 438
Tagaytay Ridge 603
Taihang 306
Taihapa Ga 486
Taiho (aircraft carrier) 536
Taihu 357
Taiku 492
Taipale 48
Taivu 331
Taiwan
– (see Formosa)
Taixing 125
Taiyo (aircraft carrier) 552
Takao (cruiser) 575, 649
Takrouna 400
Taku 546
Talabot (freighter) 284
Talasea 495
Talisman (submarine) 239
Tallboy bombs 562, 570, 581, 613
Tallinn 211, 564
Tally Ho (submarine) 480, 490
Tamashima 644
Tamatave 334
Tamshin 160
Tamu 498
Tanahmera Bay 509
Tananarive 332
Tanchuk 647, 652
Tangiers 94, 170, 264
Tanguy, Henry 550
Tani, Masayuki 99, 337
Tanks
– see also Panzers
– In German attack on Poland 1/9/39 16
– Guderian's new tactics 9/9/39 19
– French and German deployments as Germans attack 11/5/40 82
– British regiments sent to North Africa 10/8/40 109
– US to supply 4,000 to Britain 11/8/40 110
– 4th Armoured Brigade pushes Italians back to Mechili 24/1/41 156
– British and Australian forces take Benghazi 7/2/41 160
– British armour breaks down on retreat from El Agheila 1/4/41 174
– British armour inferior to German 5/4/41 175
– German armour forced back from Tobruk 14/4/41 179
– Wavell complains about quality of British armour 26/4/41 183
– Matilda, Crusader, Cavalier and Cromwell Cruiser-types 22/4/41 183
– Huge British losses in "Battleaxe" 17/6/41 198
– German strength at German invasion 23/6/41 200
– Russians introduce T34s as German Panzers break down 31/7/41 211
– T34s go into action on Moscow front 11/10/41 232
– American M3 Stuart has trials in Operation Crusader 18/11/41 241
– New techniques by Allies and Axis at Tobruk 1/12/41 245
– Fierce battle at Kharkov 12/5/42 299
– American Grant M3 becomes operational with Eighth Army 27/5/42 301
– British disable abandoned Axis armour in Western Desert 3/9/42 330
– Grants and Shermans at First Battle of El Alamein 24/10/42 343
– Allied and Axis losses at El Alamein 3/11/42 348
– T34s in Russian counter-attack at Stalingrad 20/11/42 352
– Valentine is first tank to enter Tripoli 23/1/43 373
– British armour in unsuccessful attacks in Burma 3/2/43 380
– Allied armour at Battle of the Kasserine Pass 20/2/43 383
– Allied and Axis losses at Kasserine Pass 25/2/43 385
– Allied armour superior to Medenine 6/3/43 388
– Allied armour outfights Axis in Tunisia 22/4/43 401
– T34s superior to Tigers and Panthers at Kursk 9/7/43 423
– T34s continue success against Tigers and Panthers 25/12/43 472
– Tigers and Panthers captured by Russians in Ukraine 10/3/44 497
– "Funnies" in D-Day landings 6/6/44 529
– T34s in Operation Bagration assault on Germans 22/6/44 535
– British armour lost to Tigers and Panthers at Caen 20/7/44 543
– Modified Shermans spearhead breakthrough in Normandy 31/7/44 547
– Shermans of French 2nd Armoured Div liberate Paris 25/8/44 555
– T34s in combat with Panzers and Tigers 10/10/44 572
– US Shermans in relief of Bastogne 26/12/44 592
– US Third Armoured Division uses M26 Pershings in Ruhr 25/2/45 609
– T34s in liberation of Prague 9/5/45 636
Tannenberg 602
Tanner, Vaino 531
Tapa 564
Tarakan 264, 631, 644
Taranto 138, 443, 450
Tarawa 444, 462
Taro 483
Tarpon (submarine) 75, 453
Tarung river 458, 480
Tarung valley 473
Tassafaronga 351
Tassafaronga, Battle of 357
Taung Bazar 486
Taunggyi 292
Taungup 624
Tavoy 266
Tawi Tawi 618
Taxes 26, 77, 77, 108, 130, 178, 290, 388, 399, 446
Taylor, Bethune 567
Taylor, George 524
Tebaga 393, 394
Tebourba, Battle of 353
Tedder, Arthur 172, 195, 398, 473, 483, 522, 527, 636, 686
Teheran 9, 217, 464
Tel Aviv 118
Tel el Eisa 314, 344
Telecommunications Research Establishment 214
Teleki, Paul 71, 175
Tempeleni 170
Tempest fighters 330
Temple, William 279, 346
Tenaro 381
Tenaru river 325, 342
Tenedos (destroyer) 288
Ter Poorten, Hein 278, 280
Terauchi, Hisaichi 658
Terboven, Josef 75, 123, 223, 339, 634
Terek river 340
Terijoki 43
Termoli 450
Terracina 510
Territorial Army 17
Terror (monitor) 164
Tetlow Canal 628
Tetis code 270
The Makham 310
Thailand
– Signs treaty with Japan 6/12/40 141
– Gains parts of Laos and Cambodia from Indochina 28/2/41 165
– Government surrenders as Japan invades to attack Malaya 8/7/41 247
– Declares war on Britain and US 25/1/42 268
– Allied PoWs to extend Singapore to Bangkok railway 24/6/42 310
– US submarines mine approaches to Bangkok 16/10/42 340
– USAAF attacks Bangkok oil refinery 26/11/42 353
– Japanese try to open supply route to troops 22/4/44 508
– British bombers destroy bridge over river Kwae 24/6/45 645
Thala 384
Thames 117
Thames Estuary 38, 40, 49, 128, 136
Thasos 181
The Hague 80, 81, 84, 506, 513, 610
Thebes 182
Theresienstadt 294, 337, 444, 450, 460, 495, 575
Thermopylae 182
Thielbek (liner) 632
Thionville 579, 582
This Happy Breed (play) 405
Thistle (submarine) 73
Thoma, Wilhelm von 347, 392
Thomas F Nickel (destroyer) 655
Thomas, Cecil 282
Thomas, Shenton 247
Thor (merchant raider) 174, 353
Thrace 384
Thummel, Paul 36, 284
Thunderbolt (previously Thetis) (submarine) 73
Thunderbolt fighter-bombers 452, 495, 498, 528, 579
Thunderbolt fighters 356, 387
Thunderclap (operation) 606
Thuringian Forest 623
Thursday (operation) 496, 498, 579
Thyssen, Fritz 41, 49
Tianjin 29, 247
Tibbets, Paul 591, 651, 652
Tiber river 521
Tibet 65
Tiddim 536
Tientsin 658
Tiger (operation) 184, 187, 511
Tiger tanks
– (see Panzers; Tanks)
Tigre 187
Tigris (submarine) 389
Tikhvin 237, 242, 246, 279
Tilburg 81, 575
Tilin 601
Tilly-sur-Seulles 531
Tilsit 400, 570
Time (magazine) 478, 520
Times, The (newspaper) 104, 437
Timor 275, 336
Timoshenko, Semyon 42, 54, 61, 63, 66, 79, 203, 213, 220, 233, 268, 298, 316, 320, 686
Tinian 492, 531, 546, 549, 577, 649
Tinsukia 467
Tippett, Michael 174
Tirana 363, 581, 583
Tiraspol 508
Tirpitz (battleship) 127, 264, 280, 287, 315, 442, 447, 543, 554, 562, 581
Tiso, Joseph 34
Tisza river 569, 574, 578
Tito, Josip
– Raises partisans to fight Axis occupiers 5/7/41 204
– Fails to agree strategy with Mihailovich 19/9/41 223
– Partisans fighting Ustachi and Axis without Allied aid 9/5/42 297
– Partisans liberate Croatia and execute Ustachi 16/7/42 317
– Request for aid refused as Axis offensive begins 15/11/43 372
– Allied liaison officers reach partisans 15/4/44 399
– Evades capture by Axis forces 11/6/43 416
– British military mission to join partisans 23/6/43 419
– British brigadier joins him as adviser 19/9/43 447
– Sets up provisional government 4/12/43 466
– Tells king his services are not needed 22/12/43 472
– Sends military mission to London 1/5/44 512
– Narrowly escapes capture 25/5/44 520
– To meet Churchill 11/8/44 551
– Soviet forces link up with his troops 6/9/44 560
– At work with his secretary 27/9/44 568
– To join royalist prime minister in government 11/2/45 605
– In dispute with Britain and US over Trieste 14/5/45 638
– Remains independent of Soviets after the war 663
– Biography 687
Tizard, Henry 110
Tobata 539
Tobruk 151, 156, 176, 179, 183, 184, 198, 200, 205, 217, 230, 231, 243, 247, 303, 308, 311, 334, 350
Todt, Fritz 69, 90, 270
Toenails (operation) 414
Togliatti, Palmiro 508
Togo, Shigenori 330, 654
Tojo, Hideki 203, 232, 242, 274, 330, 417, 487, 492, 545, 687
Tokat 49
Tokyo
– US bombers make unexpected raid 18/4/42 290
– US Congress claims targets bombed 15/6/44 531
– Soviet spy executed 7/11/44 579
Tokyo Express 335, 344, 357, 380
Tokyo Rose 587
Tolbukhin, Fedor 438, 456, 507, 512, 514, 561, 575, 585, 615, 617, 623
Tolstoy, Alexei 234
Tolvarjarvi 51
Tomislav I, King of Croatia 190
Tondern 73
Torbay (submarine) 203, 231, 239
Torch (operation) 318, 340, 342, 344, 350, 365
Torgau 627
Torii, Suzeto 659
Torokina 459, 500
Torquay 412
Torre dam 212
Torun 35, 603
Totalize (operation) 550, 554
Toulon 349, 351, 354, 553, 557, 558
Toungoo 284
Tours 94, 96
Tovey, John 404
Toyama 650
Toyoda, Soemu 512, 536, 576, 640, 649
Toyoda, Teijiro 208
Tractable (operation) 552
Train, Jack 51
Traitors
– (see individuals eg Joyce,

campaign against US mainland 1/11/44 *577*

USA (economics and industry)
– Merchant ship building plan 3/1/41 151
– Government take-over threat as coal-miners strike 20/11/41 242
– Sales of new cars and trucks banned to save steel 1/1/42 *262*
– Enemy-owned patents seized 21/4/42 *292*
– Roosevelt places economy on full war footing 27/4/42 *294*
– Harriman and Lyttleton form combined war industry board 29/7/42 *319*
– Women join war effort in industry 30/9/42 338
– Longer working week in labour shortage areas 9/2/43 381
– Office of mobilization established 28/5/43 *412*
– Miners' strike 1/6/43 *414*
– Increase in aircraft production 31/12/43 474
– Roosevelt proposes new law on national service 11/1/44 480
– War is costing $ 250 million a day 19/11/44 *583*
– Position after the war (1945) 662

USA (foreign affairs)
– see also Pacific War
– Neutrality becomes official 5/9/39 *16*
– Roosevelt tries to revise Neutrality Law for Allies 9/9/39 20
– Isolationist campaign growing 15/9/39 22
– Recognizes Polish government in exile 7/10/39 30
– Isolationism weakened by stories of Nazi atrocities 4/11/39 35
– Americans advised to leave Netherlands 10/11/39 *36*
– Protests at British blockade of Germany 8/12/39 *43*
– Loan to Finland 10/12/39 *45*
– Bans technical data exports to belligerents 20/12/39 *47*
– Protests at British detention of ships 20/1/40 *57*
– Supports Finland against USSR 10/2/40 *60*
– Moral embargo on USSR 18/2/40 *64*
– Lifts arms embargo for Allies to buy planes 11/3/40 *68*
– Refuses to recognize Japanese regime in Nanking 30/3/40 *71*
– Concerned about Pacific 17/4/40 *75*
– Roosevelt asks Mussolini to help bring peace 29/4/40 *76*
– Establishes Greenland consulate 1/5/40 *78*
– Reaction to Italy's declaration of war 12/6/40 95
– Technical exports to Japan banned 5/7/40 *102*
– Britain permitted to buy aircraft 23/7/40 *107*
– Embargo on export of aviation fuel 31/7/40 108
– 4,000 tanks for Britain 11/8/40 *110*
– Bans iron & steel exports other than to Britain 26/9/40 *123*
– Warns citizens to leave Far East 8/10/40 *127*
– Arms deal with Britain 26/10/40 131
– Leahy becomes ambassador to Vichy France 23/11/40 *138*
– Export licence system extended 10/12/40 *142*
– Lend-Lease bill considered 10/1/41 153
– Refuses Vichy request to take Jewish refugees 24/1/41 156
– Will not send ships to Singapore 24/2/41 166
– Lend-Lease Bill becomes law 11/3/41 7, 168
– To repair British warships 4/4/41 *174*
– Supplies flour to Vichy France 5/5/41 *184*
– To seize foreign shipping in US ports 15/5/41 189
– To train RAF pilots on American planes 29/5/41 *192*
– Axis assets frozen 14/6/41 197
– German consulates closed 17/6/41 199
– Air base in Newfoundland 15/7/41 *206*
– Freezes Japanese assets 26/7/41 208
– Aid for Soviet war effort discussions 30/7/41 *210*
– Aviation fuel export ban 1/8/41 *212*
– Agrees "Atlantic Charter" with Britain 14/8/41 215
– Aid for USSR 29/9/41 227
– Imposes trade embargo against Japan 9/41 9
– Grew warns Roosevelt of possible Japanese attack 1/11/41 *237*
– Neutrality Act revised 13/11/41 239
– Rejects Japan's proposals 21/11/41 242
– Troops occupy Dutch Guiana to guard bauxite mines 23/11/41 *243*
– Tension over Pacific situation 30/11/41 244
– Roosevelt sends personal letter to Hirohito 6/12/41 247
– Declares war on Germany and Italy 11/12/41 *247*
– Declares war on Japan 8/12/41 251
– Signs pact with Brazil 23/5/42 301
– Declares war on Bulgaria, Hungary and Roumania 5/6/42 *304*
– Breaks off relations with Vichy France 8/11/42 349
– Recognizes French Committee of National Liberation 26/8/43 *438*
– Averell Harriman appointed ambassador to USSR 1/9/43 *440*
– Promises aid to USSR 19/10/43 *453*
– Protests against Japanese atrocities 28/1/44 483
– Gives money to found UNRRA 29/3/44 *502*
– Demands that Sweden stop vital exports to Germany 13/4/44 *506*
– Another year of Lend-Lease contracts to be made 19/4/44 508
– Breaks off diplomatic relations with Finland 28/6/44 *537*
– Morgenthau Plan for post-war Germany published 24/9/44 *566*
– Puts further military pressure on Japan (1945) 10
– Truman approves plans for invasion of Japan 29/6/45 644
– Recognizes new Polish government 5/7/45 *646*
– Wants top German scientists 6/7/45 646
– Drops atomic bombs on Japan 8/45 11
– Plans renewed German government and airlifts to Berlin (1948) 663
– Provides Marshall Aid to Europe (1948) 663

USA (home affairs)
– Anti-war sentiments (1930s) 13
– Roosevelt wins Democratic nomination 17/7/40 *105*
– Special powers for president as country on war footing 19/12/41 254
– Country placed on war footing 28/4/42 295
– Petrol rationing 15/5/42 299
– Nationwide petrol rationing 1/12/42 *356*
– Annual quota of Chinese immigrants introduced 17/12/43 470
– Roosevelt proposes new national service law 11/1/44 480
– Run-up to presidential elections 14/3/44 *497*
– Wilkie withdraws from presidential race 5/4/44 *504*
– Meat rationing ends 4/5/44 *512*
– Dewey and Brickey win Republican nominations 28/6/44 *537*
– Roosevelt to run for fourth term 11/7/44 541
– Roosevelt wins presidential election 8/11/44 581
– New secretary of state 27/11/44 *584*
– Roosevelt inaugurated for fourth term 20/1/45 *599*
– Roosevelt dies, Truman sworn in 12/4/45 621
– Byrnes beomes secretary of state 27/6/45 *645*
– Restrictions on production of consumer goods lifted 20/8/45 *658*
– Fears communist expansion (1946) 663
– Attitudes to Japan changing as communism grows (1944-8) 664

USAAF
– Arnold becomes C-in-C 20/6/41 *198*
– Japan destroys half Far East force in Philippines 13/12/41 252
– First European HQ formed in Britain 22/2/42 *276*
– Bombs Japanese fleet in Andaman Islands 2/4/42 *286*
– Doolittle leads raid on Japan 18/4/42 290
– B-24 Liberators from Suez Zone attack Ploesti oilfields 12/6/42 307
– Joins RAF in daylight raid on Netherlands airfields 4/7/42 314
– First attacks in Desert War 16/8/42 *325*
– Flying Fortresses make first raid in Rouen attack 17/8/42 325
– RAF Eagle Squadrons transferred 16/9/42 *333*
– Eighth air force hits Lille in new daylight campaign 9/10/42 339
– Bombs Bangkok oil refinery 26/11/42 *353*
– First raid on Italian mainland hits Naples 4/12/42 356
– Bombs Lille and Abbeville 6/12/42 358
– Gives Christmas party for London children 12/42 363
– Bombs Wilhelmshaven 27/1/43 378
– Losses at Guadalcanal 4/2/43 380
– Hits Nuremberg in round-the-clock bombing with RAF 25/2/43 *384*
– Fifth air force successes at Battle of the Bismarck Sea 5/3/43 386
– Air bridge temporarily replaces Burma Road 1/3/43 388
– Fourteenth air force created under Chennault in China 10/3/43 *389*
– Bombs Vegesack 18/3/43 *390*
– Bombs Cagliari, in Sardinia 31/3/43 *394*
– Lady be Good lost over Western Desert 5/4/43 *396*
– Mass air raids with RAF on Mediterranean targets 5/4/43 396
– Antwerp raid kills civilians after Luftwaffe attack 5/4/43 397
– Eaker proposes combined bombing offensive with RAF 17/4/43 398
– Bombs Japanese on Nauru 20/4/43 *400*
– Bombs Sicily and Sardinia 20/5/43 411
– Bombs Naples 31/5/43 *412*
– Forces in China hit Japanese at Ichang 1/6/43 414
– Eaker's bombing plan modified and adopted as Pointblank 10/6/43 416
– Losses to Luftwaffe in Kiel raid 13/6/43 *417*
– Bombs synthetic rubber plant at Huls 22/6/43 *418*
– Eighth air force men riot after English pub brawl 25/6/43 418
– Destroys 45 Japanese planes over Rendova 15/7/43 *425*
– Hits Japanese at Buin-Faisi in Solomons 17/7/43 426
– Bombs Rome 19/7/43 *427*
– Joins RAF in Operation Gomorrah on Hamburg 31/7/43 430
– Bombs Naples 4/8/43 *432*
– Loses 56 out of 177 Liberators in Ploesti oilfields raid 2/8/43 433
– Losses to Luftwaffe on Schweinfurt and Regensburg raids 18/8/43 436
– Destroys Japanese air strength at Wewak, in New Guinea 18/8/43 437
– Bombs Nantes 23/9/43 *446*
– US ninth air force formed 16/10/43 *452*
– Bombs Japanese base at Buin, on Bougainville 18/10/43 *453*
– Fifteenth air force to strike from Italy 23/10/43 455
– Uses H2X blind-bombing device 3/11/43 *458*
– Bombs heavy water plant at Vermork 16/11/43 462
– Eighth air force attacks rocket launch sites in France 5/12/43 *467*
– Units in SEAC put under Peirse 11/12/43 *467*
– Daylight raids boosted by "drop tanks" 11/12/43 468
– Bombers escorted by Mustang fighters 13/12/43 *469*
– Attacks on V-weapon launch sites 24/12/43 471
– US Strategic Air Forces in Europe Command 1/1/44 *478*
– Raids German aircraft industry targets 11/1/44 *480*
– Raids Japanese airfield at Rabaul 24/1/44 *483*
– Raids Schweinfurt 24/2/44 *492*
– US aircraft join Battle of Berlin 4/3/44 *495*
– Biggest one day loss in raid on Berlin 6/3/44 *495*
– Fifteenth air force raids Vienna 17/3/44 498
– Daytime raid on Brunswick 23/3/44 501
– Bombers begin to raid Budapest and Bucharest 3/4/44 *504*
– Switches attention to railways of France 15/4/44 506
– Raids Ploesti oilfields 15/4/44 506
– Japan aims to wipe out bases in China 17/4/44 *508*
– Heavy attacks on French railways 19/4/44 509
– Bombs Yellow River bridges to hamper Japanese advance 28/4/44 *510*
– Attacks Berlin 7/5/44 *513*
– Hits oil targets in Germany 28/5/44 *518*
– Bombs Japanese mainland from China 15/6/44 531
– German synthetic oil plants become a primary target 13/6/44 534
– Badly hit at Poltava airfield 22/6/44 535
– Raids German industrial targets 29/6/44 *537*
– Drops napalm on fuel depot in France 17/7/44 *543*
– Kills 65 Allied servicemen in Normandy 7/8/44 550
– Crew of crashed aircraft beaten to death in Germany 26/8/44 *554*
– Attacks German communications in Yugoslavia 1/9/44 *560*
– Bombs the Ruhr 15/10/44 573
– Harasses retreating Germans in the Balkans 20/10/44 574
– Bombs oil and fuel targets in Germany 4/11/44 *577*
– Raids synthetic oil and rail targets in Germany 1/11/44 578
– Bombs Singapore 5/11/44 *579*
– Launches major raids to support land forces in Germany 16/11/44 582
– Raids Tokyo by day 24/11/44 584
– Raids German tactical and communications targets 18/12/44 *589*
– Activities in South-east Asia 1/1/45 596
– Drops 3,000 tons of explosives on Berlin 3/2/45 *603*
– Bombs Vienna 8-9/2/45 604
– Hits transport centres in Germany 21-22/2/45 608
– Drops incendiaries on Berlin 27/2/45 609
– New tactics in the Pacific 10/3/45 612
– Blows up Laohokow air base in China 25/3/45 *616*
– Makes four-hour fire-bomb raid on Tokyo 14/4/45 622
– Drops fire-bombs on Tokyo 26/5/45 640
– Japan collapsing under pressure of aerial bombardment 29/5/45 641
– Drops incendiaries on Osaka 1/6/45 *642*
– Begins raiding civilian targets in Japan 17-18/6/45 *644*
– Bombs war factories on Honsu 26/6/45 *645*
– Plan to disband Sino-US fourteenth air force 6/7/45 *646*
– Bombs airfields near Tokyo 9/7/45 *647*
– Over a thousand fighter-bombers hit Japanese base 24/7/45 *649*
– Bombs Japanese positions in Java 4/8/45 *650*
– Drops leaflets to warn Japanese of raids 5/8/45 *652*
– Drops atomic bomb on Hiroshima 6/8/45 652
– Drops atomic bomb on Nagasaki 9/8/45 653
– Continues to bombard Japan 13-14/8/45 *655*

Ushant *136*

Ushijima, Mitsuru 624, 631, 641, 644

Ushio (destroyer) *581*

USSR (defence)
– see also Eastern Front; Red Air Force; Red Army
– Timoshenko appointed commissar for defence 8/5/40 *79*
– Zhukov chief of general staff & deputy defence commissar 12/2/41 *161*
– Army intelligence chief says Germany will not attack 20/3/41 *170*
– Churchill warns of impending German attack 3/4/41 *174*
– Army units transferred westwards 11/6/41 *196*
– Stalin goes on holiday despite fresh invasion warning 18/6/41 *198*
– Strength of armed forces as Germany invades 22-3/6/41 200
– Committee of Defence under Stalin takes control 29/6/41 *200*
– Timoshenko becomes western front commander 2/7/41 *203*
– Stalin calls for scorched-earth policy 3/7/41 204
– US promises military aid 4/8/41 *212*
– Conscription 3/9/41 *220*
– Ethnic Germans in Volga area exiled to Siberia 8/9/41 *221*
– Eden and Stalin agree policy for conduct of war 22/12/41 259
– Asks Churchill to open second front 16/3/42 *282*
– Molotov visits London to demand second front 18/4/42 290
– Zhukov promoted to marshal of Soviet Union 18/1/43 *372*
– Zhukov receives Order of Suvorov 31/7/43 *428*
– Moscow's claims about Byelorussian partisans 1/12/43 *465*
– Konev promoted to marshal of the Soviet Union 18/2/44 *490*
– Ukrainian partisans ambush Vatutin 29/2/44 492
– Agrees to Churchill's request for new offensive 7/1/45 *597*

USSR (economics and industry)
– Signs agreement with Estonia 28/9/39 *26*
– Trade agreement to be signed with Germany 10/2/40 *60*
– Factories put on seven-day working week 27/6/40 *100*
– Signs agreement with Germany 10/1/41 151
– War loan subscription opened 14/4/42 *289*
– Increase in aircraft production 31/12/43 474
– Industrial centre of Krivoi Rog falls to Red Army 22/2/44 *492*

USSR (foreign affairs)
– Effect of communism on western Europe (1930s) 13
– Nazi-Soviet non-aggression pact signed 23/8/39 15
– Armistice with Japan 15/9/39 *21*
– Promises to respect neutrality of Finland 17/9/39 *22*
– Invades Poland 17/9/39 23
– Signs agreement with Estonia 29/9/39 *26*
– Signs boundary and friendship treaty with Germany 29/9/39 27
– Khrushchev announces communization of eastern Poland 3/10/39 *28*
– Signs treaty with Latvia 5/10/39 29
– Signs treaty with Lithuania 10/10/39 *30*
– Fresh talks with Finland 22/10/39 *34*
– Finland refuses to give military base 3/11/39 *35*
– Prepares for war with Finland 13/11/39 *38*
– Renounces 1932 Russo-Finnish non-aggression pact 28/11/39 *42*
– Invades Finland 30/11/39 42
– Sets up puppet Finnish government 1/12/39 *43*
– Rejects League of Nations' call for peace with Finland 12/12/39 *45*
– Expelled by League of Nations 14/12/39 47
– Ambassador to Italy recalled 1/1/40 *54*
– Defeated by Finland at Suomussalmi 8/1/40 56
– Welles to negotiate peace settlement 9/2/40 *60*

– Turkish border incident 23/2/40 *64*
– Final peace terms offered to Finland 23/2/40 65
– Finland defeated 9/3/40 66
– Peace treaty with Finland 12/3/40 *68*
– Opposed to alliance of Scandinavian countries 20/3/40 *69*
– To stay neutral in European war 29/3/40 *71*
– Shoots Polish officers at Katyn 5/4/40 *72*
– Invades Lithuania 15/6/40 7, 95
– Troops sent to Latvia and Estonia 17/6/40 *97*
– Demands Bessarabia and Northern Bukovina from Roumania 26/6/40 *100*
– Occupies Bessarabia and Northern Bukovina 28/6/40 101
– Baltic states join Soviet Union 21/7/40 107
– Signs trade agreement with Germany 10/1/41 151
– Warns Bulgaria over joining Axis 3/3/41 *166*
– Treaty with Yugoslavia 5/4/41 *174*
– Signs neutrality (non-aggression) pact with Japan 13/4/41 9, 180
– Britain warns of impending German attack 6/5/41 *184*
– Sorge warns of German June invasion 15/5/41 *187*
– Invaded by Germany 22/6/41 8
– Bombs Helsinki 25/6/41 *200*
– Signs treaty with Czech government in exile 18/7/41 *206*
– Signs treaty with Polish government in exile 30/7/41 211
– Will aid Turkey if attacked 10/8/41 *214*
– Stalin signs pact with Polish government in exile 4/12/41 *245*
– Treaty with Iran 29/1/42 268
– 20-year pact with Britain 26/5/42 *301*
– Intends to keep eastern Poland 1/3/43 *386*
– Diplomatic relations with Poles broken off over Katyn 30/4/43 401
– War crimes trial at Krasnodar 14/7/43 426
– Recognizes French Committee of National Liberation 27/8/43 *438*
– Aid pledged by UK and USA 19/10/43 *453*
– Signs pact with Czechoslovakia 12/12/43 469
– Charges Germany with Katyn massacre 26/1/44 485
– Negotiations with Finns for armistice 16/2/44 *490*
– Re-established links with Italy 13/3/44 *497*
– Stalin says Warsaw uprising is reckless 16/8/44 *552*
– Declares war on Bulgaria 5/9/44 *560*
– Britain agrees to send Soviet deserters home 4/9/44 560
– Signs armistice with Finland 10/9/44 *562*
– Gains from armistice with Roumania 13/9/44 562
– Stalin promises to declare war on Japan 13/10/44 *571*
– Armistice with Bulgaria 28/10/44 *575*
– Stalin refuses to renew relations with Switzerland 7/11/44 *579*
– Signs treaty of mutual assistance with France 10/12/44 *587*
– Will not renew non-aggression pact with Japan 5/4/45 *618*
– Tightens links with Polish government in Lublin 21/4/45 624
– Arrests Polish negotiators 5/5/45 634
– Declares war on Japan 9/8/45 654
– Invades Manchuria (1945) 11
– Hands Manchuria back to China 15/8/45 657
– Signs treaty fixing border with Poland 16/8/45 *655*
– Restores relations with Finland 31/8/45 *660*
– Absorbs Baltic states after the war 662
– Blockades Berlin (1948-9) 663
– Represses Hungarian uprising (1956) 665
Ustachi 297, 317, 372, 399, 408
Utah Beach
– (see D-Day)
Utility production 278, 327, 388, 399, 411
Uzice *237*

V

V for Victory campaign 207
V-weapons 396, 402, *438*, *448*, 456, 471, *486*, *497*, *499*, *515*, *531*, *531*, 532, 534, *537*, *537*, *543*, 545, 549, *550*, *554*, 554, 559, 560, 569, *571*, 580, *581*, 583, 585, 588, *591*, *596*, 598, 604, 607, *610*, 613, *616*, *616*, *621*, 646
Vaagso 257
Vaivara *432*
Valentine (destroyer) *84*
Valetta 291, 353
Valga 562
Valguanerna *427*
Valiant (battleship) *116*, *150*, 172, 253, *440*
Vallat, Xavier *172*, *174*
Valona *150*, *156*
Vampire (destroyer) 288
Vampire jet fighters *642*
Vanakula *486*
Vandegrift, Alexander *357*
Vanessa (destroyer) *361*
Vannes 194
Vanoc (destroyer) 171
Vargas, Getulio 281, 325
Varsity (operation) 615
Vasilevsky, Alexander *607*, *652*, 658
Vasto 458
Vatican
– Pope condemns racism, dictators and treaty violations 27/10/39 *34*
– Pope's peace appeal 24/12/39 49
– Pope condemns Nazi rule in Poland 21/1/40 *59*
– Rationing starts 14/2/40 *62*
– Warns Belgium and France of imminent German attack 30/4/40 77
– Worldwide day of prayer for Poland 8/10/42 *338*
– Neutral but acting as anti-Nazi contact point 23/1/43 375
– Pope asks Allies not to bomb Rome 24/7/43 428
– Ringed by Nazi paratroopers 6/10/43 450
Vatutin, Nikolai *351*, 435, 458, 469, 478, 492, *494*, *506*
Vaughan Williams, Ralph *47*
VE Day 635
Veesenmayer, Edmund 499, 507
Vegesack *390*
Vella Gulf, Battle of 433
Vella Lavella *434*, *436*, 439, *440*, *446*
Venereal disease 360, 454
Venetia *444*
Venetia (destroyer) *128*
Venev 242
Venezuela
– U-boats shell oil refineries 16/2/42 *273*
– Considering declaring war on Axis powers 9/2/45 604
– Declares war on Axis powers 16/2/45 *605*
Vercors 547
Verdun *94*
Veritable (operation) *603*
Verity, Hedley *428*
Vermion mountains 177
Vermork *351*, *383*, 385, 462
Vernon 560
Verona *626*
Versailles 565
Versailles Treaty 12, 14
Vian, Philip 79, 231, *253*, 284
Vichy *102*
Vichy France
– Third Republic replaced by Etat Francais at Vichy 10/7/40 7, 103
– Naturalized Jews deprived of French citizenship 16/7/40 *105*
– Death penalty for French servicemen in foreign armies 31/7/40 *107*
– Laval offers help to Germany in Battle of Britain 10/8/40 *109*
– Breaks off relations with govts in exile 28/8/40 *114*
– To pay for army of occupation 14/9/40 118
– Jews to carry special identity cards 27/9/40 *123*
– Bombs Gibraltar 24/9/40 123
– Bans Jews from state posts and army 3/10/40 *125*
– Algerian Jews deprived of citizenship 7/10/40 *127*
– Married women banned from state jobs 14/10/40 *128*
– Jews banned from positions of authority 18/10/40 *128*
– Petain agrees collaboration with Hitler 26/10/40 *130*
– Laval becomes foreign minister 28/10/40 *132*
– Jean Moulin sacked 11/11/40 *136*
– Petain dismisses Laval 13/12/40 143
– Darlan gains more power 17/12/40 145
– Baudouin resigns 3/1/41 *150*
– Compulsory service in Chantiers de Jeunesse 9/1/41 153
– Request to US to take Jewish refugees refused 24/1/41 156
– Oath of allegiance to Petain 27/1/41 *158*
– Darlan succeeds Flandin as foreign minister 8/2/41 *160*
– Darlan becomes vice-premier and Petain's successor 14/2/41 162
– Darlan becomes head of government 24/2/41 *164*
– Accepts Japan's ultimatum over Indochinese/Thai dispute 28/2/41 165
– Darlan warns RN over convoy seizures 10/3/41 170
– Britain lets US grain ships through 22/3/41 *170*
– Vallat becomes commissioner for Jewish questions 29/3/41 *172*
– Jewish emigration to be speeded up 3/4/41 *174*
– Permits Germans troops to go through Syria to Iraq 6/5/41 *184*
– Darlan tells Petain he will collaborate with Hitler 14/5/41 *187*
– Germany releases PoWs in return for more collaboration 19/5/41 *190*
– Allows Germany use of overseas naval & military bases 25/5/41 *192*
– Allows Axis to use Bizerta 2/6/41 *195*
– Troops in Syria fight Allies and Free French 13/6/41 197
– Signs armistice with Allies and Free French in Syria 12/7/41 206
– Deports British subjects 25/7/41 208
– Gives Japan control in Indochina if attacked 29/7/41 *210*
– Petain imposes fascist rule 12/8/41 214
– Anti-terrorist laws aimed at Resistance 24/8/41 *217*
– Compulsory single trade union 4/10/41 *228*
– Petain orders arrest of pre-fall French leaders 16/10/41 *231*
– Reprisals for killing of Holz in Nantes 21/10/41 233
– Convoy from Indochina stopped by Allies off S Africa 4/11/41 237
– Huntziger killed in plane crash 12/11/41 239
– German pressure leads to dismissal of Weygand 20/11/41 *241*
– Daladier, Blum and Gamalin tried at Riom 19/2/42 273
– Laval warns Petain of need for more collaboration 26/3/42 *284*
– Laval to be head of government and Petain head of state 16/4/42 *289*
– Laval calls for more cooperation with Germany 20/4/42 *292*
– Jewish deportations urged by Himmler 11/6/42 *306*
– 5,000 Jews to be deported to Auschwitz 15/8/42 *322*
– Forced labourers sent to Germany in exchange for PoWs 11/8/42 324
– 7,000 Jews rounded up for Auschwitz 28/8/42 *327*
– Service National du Travail 13/9/42 *333*
– Nazis to execute hostages in reprisal for sabotage 22/9/42 *336*
– Laval calls for more French workers for Germany 20/10/42 342
– Severs relations with US 8/11/42 *349*
– German occupation 11/11/42 351
– Fleet scuttles itself at Toulon 27/11/42 354
– Darlan claims leadership of France from Algiers 1/12/42 *356*
– Laval says he wants Germany's victory 13/12/42 *360*
– Darnand forms Milice 30/1/43 *376*
– Service Obligatoire du Travail introduced 16/2/43 *383*
– Sauckel demands 100,000 forced workers 5/3/43 *386*
– Giraud to abolish anti-Semitic legislation 18/3/43 390
– Channel ports to be evacuated 16/4/43 *397*
– Laval refuses German demand for deportation of all Jews 14/8/43 *434*
– Petain forbidden to broadcast to the nation 13/11/43 *460*
– Patriotic demonstration in Grenoble 11/11/43 461
– Allied advisers parachute in to train Resistance 7/1/44 *478*
– 22 Frenchmen executed 9/1/44 *480*
– Saboteurs derail train 14/1/44 *480*
– Labour promised to Germany 2/2/44 487
– Germans take control of Mediterranean coast 14/2/44 490
– Former minister sentenced to death by Free French 11/3/44 *495*
– 465 Resistance fighters defeated by Germans 25/3/44 500
– Frenchmen authorized to join SS 27/3/44 *502*
– Cuts communications with neutral countries 27/4/44 511
– Resistance executes minister 28/6/44 537
– SS arrests Petain 19/8/44 554
– Swift collapse 25/8/44 557
Vickers Armstrong [co] 449
Victor Emmanuel III, King of Italy 69, *71*, 429, *506*
Victorious (aircraft carrier) *210*, *280*, 324, *510*, 637
Vienna *57*, 604, 612, 615, 619, 623, *626*
Viet Minh 589
Vietinghoff, Heinrich von 443, 445, 481, 563, 627
Vietnam
– Viet Minh formed 15/6/41 199
– To remain as French protectorate 23/3/45 *614*
– Ho Chi-minh announces provisional government 28/8/45 *660*
– Ho Chi-minh's forces defeat French (1954) 665
Vigan *247*
Vigorous (operation) *306*
Viipuri 58, 65, *66*, 68, *210*, 219, *534*
Vijose river *168*
Vila 373, *386*, *406*, 451
Villers-Bocage 530, 532
Vilna 209, *220*, *432*, 446, *506*, 541, *541*
Vincennes 81
Vincennes (cruiser) 321
Vinnitsa *226*, *331*, *340*, *499*
Viru Harbour *420*
Vis island 568
Viscount (destroyer) 341
Vishinsky, Andrei 508, 610, 636
Vistula river 546, *548*, 552, 597, 601
Vitebsk *205*, *444*, 472, *473*, *481*, 535, 537
Vittorio Veneto (battleship) 172
Vivant, Louis 491
Vizagatapam *288*
Vizzini 426
VJ Day 656
Vlasov, Andrei 268, 318, *363*, *581*, 632, 636
Vo Nguyen Giap 589
Vogelkop 498
Volga river *330*, *344*, 351
Volkhov river *214*, 268
Volkischer Beobachter (Nazi Party newspaper) 254
Volkssturm 568, *573*, 601, *605*, 619, 625
Volkswagen [co] *504*, *537*
Volokolamsk *253*
Volos *166*
Volterra *541*
Volturno river 450
Voronezh 312, *370*
Voroshilov, Klimenti *216*
Voroshilovgrad 316, *383*
Voroshilovsk *321*, *372*
Vosges *100*, 577, 582
Voyager (destroyer) *336*
Vyazma *228*, *230*, *266*, 268, 283, *288*, *327*

W

WAACS 338
WAAF 38, 135, 164, 431
Waal river *564*, 565
Wadi Akarit 394, *396*
Wadi Zigzaou 390
Waffen-SS
– (see SS)
Wagner, Adolf 183
Wai Li-Huang 599
Wainwright, Jonathan 280, 289, 297, 659
Wairopi *337*
Wakde Island *508*, *515*
Wake Island *247*, 255, *310*, *450*
Walawbaum *494*
Walcheren *84*, 570, 577, *577*, 579
Walker (destroyer) 171
Walker, F J 503
Wallace, Henry A 134, 251
Wallasey 169, 185
Wallenberg, Raoul 539, 577
Wallis, Barnes 410
Walney (sloop) 350
Walter boats *448*, 617
Walton, William 259
Wanderer (escort) *195*
Wandokai *467*
Wang Chingwei 50, 71, 140, 346, 368, 579
Wanne-Eickel 604
Wanting 599
War crimes 265, *338*, 340, 426, *438*, 453, 467, 469, 654, 660
– see also Nuremberg trials
Warburg 619
Warburton-Lee, Bernard (VC) 74, 91
Wareo *467*
Warhawk fighters *512*
Waria river *394*
Warner, Jack 138
Warsaw
– see also Warsaw Ghetto
– Bombed 1/9/39 16
– German army in suburbs 9/9/39 19
– Jewish quarter bombed 16/9/39 *21*
– Besieged by German army 16/9/39 23
– Division between Germany and USSR re-arranged 22/9/39 24
– Surrenders after three-day bombardment 27/9/39 27
– German-Soviet boundary and friendship treaty 29/9/39 27
– Hitler tours city 5/10/39 *28*
– Civilian deaths during siege 6/10/39 29
– Ghetto established 4/11/39 36
– Ghetto edict withdrawn 7/11/39 *36*
– Gestapo shoots Jews 18/1/40 *57*
– RAF leaflet raid 15/3/40 *68*
– Bombed by Red Air Force 2/9/42 *330*
– Germans execute Poles for sheltering Jews 29/6/43 *420*
– 100 tram workers executed by SS and Gestapo 3/12/43 *465*
– 62 Jews in hiding discovered and executed 22/12/43 *470*
– Partisans assassinate Gestapo chief 1/2/44 *486*
– Polish Home Army prepares to rise up 31/7/44 546
– Poles control most of the city 1/8/44 548
– Polish control falters; no help from USSR 19/8/44 *552*
– Poles take to sewers but continue to fight 28/8/44 559
– Stalin drops some arms to Poles 16/9/44 563
– Falls to Russians 3/10/44 570
– Prime target of Zhukov's forces 12/1/45 597
– Soviet troops move to surround 16/1/45 *599*
– Falls to Soviet troops 17/1/45 600
Warsaw Ghetto *40*, *57*, *125*, *128*, *136*, *138*, 141, 159, *163*, 233, *276*, *294*, 302, 318, 332, *338*, 375, *400*, 409
Warspite (battleship) *150*, 152, 172, *440*, 445, 526, 579
Warwick (destroyer) *492*
Wash *206*
Wasp (aircraft carrier) 191, *292*, 298, 335
Waste and scrap 59, 88, 215, 254, 338
Waterhouse, John 341
Waters, Elsie and Doris 138, 147
Watson-Watt, Robert 111, 198
Watt, Harry 209
Wau *368*, *378*, *389*

campaign against US mainland 1/11/44 *577*

USA (economics and industry)
- Merchant ship building plan 3/1/41 151
- Government take-over threat as coal-miners strike 20/11/41 242
- Sales of new cars and trucks banned to save steel 1/1/42 *262*
- Enemy-owned patents seized 21/4/42 *292*
- Roosevelt places economy on full war footing 27/4/42 *294*
- Harriman and Lyttleton form combined war industry board 29/7/42 *319*
- Women join war effort in industry 30/9/42 338
- Longer working week in labour shortage areas 9/2/43 381
- Office of mobilization established 28/5/43 *412*
- Miners' strike 1/6/43 *414*
- Increase in aircraft production 31/12/43 474
- Roosevelt proposes new law on national service 11/1/44 480
- War is costing $ 250 million a day 19/11/44 *583*
- Position after the war (1945) 662

USA (foreign affairs)
- see also Pacific War
- Neutrality becomes official 5/9/39 *16*
- Roosevelt tries to revise Neutrality Law for Allies 9/9/39 20
- Isolationist campaign growing 15/9/39 22
- Recognizes Polish government in exile 7/10/39 30
- Isolationism weakened by stories of Nazi atrocities 4/11/39 35
- Americans advised to leave Netherlands 10/11/39 *36*
- Protests at British blockade of Germany 8/12/39 *43*
- Loan to Finland 10/12/39 *45*
- Bans technical data exports to belligerents 20/12/39 *47*
- Protests at British detention of ships 20/1/40 *57*
- Supports Finland against USSR 10/2/40 *60*
- Moral embargo on USSR 18/2/40 *64*
- Lifts arms embargo for Allies to buy planes 11/3/40 *68*
- Refuses to recognize Japanese regime in Nanking 30/3/40 *71*
- Concerned about Pacific 17/4/40 *75*
- Roosevelt asks Mussolini to help bring peace 29/4/40 *76*
- Establishes Greenland consulate 1/5/40 *78*
- Reaction to Italy's declaration of war 12/6/40 95
- Technical exports to Japan banned 5/7/40 *102*
- Britain permitted to buy aircraft 23/7/40 *107*
- Embargo on export of aviation fuel 31/7/40 108
- 4,000 tanks for Britain 11/8/40 *110*
- Bans iron & steel exports other than to Britain 26/9/40 *123*
- Warns citizens to leave Far East 8/10/40 *127*
- Arms deal with Britain 26/10/40 131
- Leahy becomes ambassador to Vichy France 23/11/40 *138*
- Export licence system extended 10/12/40 *142*
- Lend-Lease bill considered 10/1/41 153
- Refuses Vichy request to take Jewish refugees 24/1/41 156
- Will not send ships to Singapore 24/2/41 166
- Lend-Lease Bill becomes law 11/3/41 7, 168
- To repair British warships 4/4/41 *174*
- Supplies flour to Vichy France 5/5/41 *184*
- To seize foreign shipping in US ports 15/5/41 189
- To train RAF pilots on American planes 29/5/41 *192*
- Axis assets frozen 14/6/41 197
- German consulates closed 17/6/41 199
- Air base in Newfoundland 15/7/41 *206*
- Freezes Japanese assets 26/7/41 208
- Aid for Soviet war effort discussions 30/7/41 *210*
- Aviation fuel export ban 1/8/41 *212*
- Agrees "Atlantic Charter" with Britain 14/8/41 215
- Aid for USSR 29/9/41 227
- Imposes trade embargo against Japan 9/41 9
- Grew warns Roosevelt of possible Japanese attack 1/11/41 *237*
- Neutrality Act revised 13/11/41 239
- Rejects Japan's proposals 21/11/41 242
- Troops occupy Dutch Guiana to guard bauxite mines 23/11/41 *243*
- Tension over Pacific situation 30/11/41 244
- Roosevelt sends personal letter to Hirohito 6/12/41 247
- Declares war on Germany and Italy 11/12/41 *247*
- Declares war on Japan 8/12/41 251
- Signs pact with Brazil 23/5/42 301
- Declares war on Bulgaria, Hungary and Roumania 5/6/42 *304*
- Breaks off relations with Vichy France 8/11/42 349
- Recognizes French Committee of National Liberation 26/8/43 *438*
- Averell Harriman appointed ambassador to USSR 1/9/43 *440*
- Promises aid to USSR 19/10/43 *453*
- Protests against Japanese atrocities 28/1/44 483
- Gives money to found UNRRA 29/3/44 *502*
- Demands that Sweden stop vital exports to Germany 13/4/44 *506*
- Another year of Lend-Lease contracts to be made 19/4/44 508
- Breaks off diplomatic relations with Finland 28/6/44 *537*
- Morgenthau Plan for post-war Germany published 24/9/44 *566*
- Puts further military pressure on Japan (1945) 10
- Truman approves plans for invasion of Japan 29/6/45 644
- Recognizes new Polish government 5/7/45 *646*
- Wants top German scientists 6/7/45 646
- Drops atomic bombs on Japan 8/45 11
- Plans renewed German government and airlifts to Berlin (1948) 663
- Provides Marshall Aid to Europe (1948) 663

USA (home affairs)
- Anti-war sentiments (1930s) 13
- Roosevelt wins Democratic nomination 17/7/40 *105*
- Special powers for president as country on war footing 19/12/41 254
- Country placed on war footing 28/4/42 295
- Petrol rationing 15/5/42 299
- Nationwide petrol rationing 1/12/42 *356*
- Annual quota of Chinese immigrants introduced 17/12/43 470
- Roosevelt proposes new national service law 11/1/44 480
- Run-up to presidential elections 14/3/44 *497*
- Wilkie withdraws from presidential race 5/4/44 *504*
- Meat rationing ends 4/5/44 *512*
- Dewey and Brickey win Republican nominations 28/6/44 *537*
- Roosevelt to run for fourth term 11/7/44 541
- Roosevelt wins presidential election 8/11/44 581
- New secretary of state 27/11/44 *584*
- Roosevelt inaugurated for fourth term 20/1/45 *599*
- Roosevelt dies, Truman sworn in 12/4/45 621
- Byrnes beomes secretary of state 27/6/45 *645*
- Restrictions on production of consumer goods lifted 20/8/45 *658*
- Fears communist expansion (1946) 663
- Attitudes to Japan changing as communism grows (1944-8) 664

USAAF
- Arnold becomes C-in-C 20/6/41 *198*
- Japan destroys half Far East force in Philippines 13/12/41 252
- First European HQ formed in Britain 22/2/42 *276*
- Bombs Japanese fleet in Andaman Islands 2/4/42 *286*
- Doolittle leads raid on Japan 18/4/42 290
- B-24 Liberators from Suez Zone attack Ploesti oilfields 12/6/42 307
- Joins RAF in daylight raid on Netherlands airfields 4/7/42 314
- First attacks in Desert War 16/8/42 *325*
- Flying Fortresses make first raid in Rouen attack 17/8/42 325
- RAF Eagle Squadrons transferred 16/9/42 *333*
- Eighth air force hits Lille in new daylight campaign 9/10/42 339
- Bombs Bangkok oil refinery 26/11/42 *353*
- First raid on Italian mainland hits Naples 4/12/42 356
- Bombs Lille and Abbeville 6/12/42 358
- Gives Christmas party for London children 12/42 363
- Bombs Wilhelmshaven 27/1/43 378
- Losses at Guadalcanal 4/2/43 380
- Hits Nuremberg in round-the-clock bombing with RAF 25/2/43 *384*
- Fifth air force successes at Battle of the Bismarck Sea 5/3/43 386
- Air bridge temporarily replaces Burma Road 1/3/43 388
- Fourteenth air force created under Chennault in China 10/3/43 *389*
- Bombs Vegesack 18/3/43 *390*
- Bombs Cagliari, in Sardinia 31/3/43 *394*
- Lady be Good lost over Western Desert 5/4/43 *396*
- Mass air raids with RAF on Mediterranean targets 5/4/43 396
- Antwerp raid kills civilians after Luftwaffe attack 5/4/43 397
- Eaker proposes combined bombing offensive with RAF 17/4/43 398
- Bombs Japanese on Nauru 20/4/43 *400*
- Bombs Sicily and Sardinia 20/5/43 411
- Bombs Naples 31/5/43 *412*
- Forces in China hit Japanese at Ichang 1/6/43 414
- Eaker's bombing plan modified and adopted as Pointblank 10/6/43 416
- Losses to Luftwaffe in Kiel raid 13/6/43 *417*
- Bombs synthetic rubber plant at Huls 22/6/43 *418*
- Eighth air force men riot after English pub brawl 25/6/43 418
- Destroys 45 Japanese planes over Rendova 15/7/43 *425*
- Hits Japanese at Buin-Faisi in Solomons 17/7/43 426
- Bombs Rome 19/7/43 *427*
- Joins RAF in Operation Gomorrah on Hamburg 31/7/43 430
- Bombs Naples 4/8/43 *432*
- Loses 56 out of 177 Liberators in Ploesti oilfields raid 2/8/43 433
- Losses to Luftwaffe on Schweinfurt and Regensburg raids 18/8/43 436
- Destroys Japanese air strength at Wewak, in New Guinea 18/8/43 437
- Bombs Nantes 23/9/43 *446*
- US ninth air force formed 16/10/43 *452*
- Bombs Japanese base at Buin, on Bougainville 18/10/43 *453*
- Fifteenth air force to strike from Italy 23/10/43 455
- Uses H2X blind-bombing device 3/11/43 *458*
- Bombs heavy water plant at Vermork 16/11/43 462
- Eighth air force attacks rocket launch sites in France 5/12/43 *467*
- Units in SEAC put under Peirse 11/12/43 *467*
- Daylight raids boosted by "drop tanks" 11/12/43 468
- Bombers escorted by Mustang fighters 13/12/43 *469*
- Attacks on V-weapon launch sites 24/12/43 471
- US Strategic Air Forces in Europe Command 1/1/44 *478*
- Raids German aircraft industry targets 11/1/44 *480*
- Raids Japanese airfield at Rabaul 24/1/44 *483*
- Raids Schweinfurt 24/2/44 *492*
- US aircraft join Battle of Berlin 4/3/44 *495*
- Biggest one day loss in raid on Berlin 6/3/44 *495*
- Fifteenth air force raids Vienna 17/3/44 498
- Daytime raid on Brunswick 23/3/44 501
- Bombers begin to raid Budapest and Bucharest 3/4/44 *504*
- Switches attention to railways of France 15/4/44 506
- Raids Ploesti oilfields 15/4/44 506
- Japan aims to wipe out bases in China 17/4/44 *508*
- Heavy attacks on French railways 19/4/44 509
- Bombs Yellow River bridges to hamper Japanese advance 28/4/44 *510*
- Attacks Berlin 7/5/44 *513*
- Hits oil targets in Germany 28/5/44 *518*
- Bombs Japanese mainland from China 15/6/44 531
- German synthetic oil plants become a primary target 13/6/44 534
- Badly hit at Poltava airfield 22/6/44 535
- Raids German industrial targets 29/6/44 *537*
- Drops napalm on fuel depot in France 17/7/44 *543*
- Kills 65 Allied servicemen in Normandy 7/8/44 550
- Crew of crashed aircraft beaten to death in Germany 26/8/44 *554*
- Attacks German communications in Yugoslavia 1/9/44 *560*
- Bombs the Ruhr 15/10/44 573
- Harasses retreating Germans in the Balkans 20/10/44 574
- Bombs oil and fuel targets in Germany 4/11/44 *577*
- Raids synthetic oil and rail targets in Germany 1/11/44 578
- Bombs Singapore 5/11/44 *579*
- Launches major raids to support land forces in Germany 16/11/44 582
- Raids Tokyo by day 24/11/44 584
- Raids German tactical and communications targets 18/12/44 *589*
- Activities in South-east Asia 1/1/45 596
- Drops 3,000 tons of explosives on Berlin 3/2/45 *603*
- Bombs Vienna 8-9/2/45 604
- Hits transport centres in Germany 21-22/2/45 608
- Drops incendiaries on Berlin 27/2/45 609
- New tactics in the Pacific 10/3/45 612
- Blows up Laohokow air base in China 25/3/45 *616*
- Makes four-hour fire-bomb raid on Tokyo 14/4/45 622
- Drops fire-bombs on Tokyo 26/5/45 640
- Japan collapsing under pressure of aerial bombardment 29/5/45 641
- Drops incendiaries on Osaka 1/6/45 *642*
- Begins raiding civilian targets in Japan 17-18/6/45 *644*
- Bombs war factories on Honsu 26/6/45 *645*
- Plan to disband Sino-US fourteenth air force 6/7/45 *646*
- Bombs airfields near Tokyo 9/7/45 *647*
- Over a thousand fighter-bombers hit Japanese base 24/7/45 *649*
- Bombs Japanese positions in Java 4/8/45 *650*
- Drops leaflets to warn Japanese of raids 5/8/45 *652*
- Drops atomic bomb on Hiroshima 6/8/45 652
- Drops atomic bomb on Nagasaki 9/8/45 653
- Continues to bombard Japan 13-14/8/45 *655*

Ushant *136*

Ushijima, Mitsuru 624, 631, 641, 644

Ushio (destroyer) *581*

USSR (defence)
- see also Eastern Front; Red Air Force; Red Army
- Timoshenko appointed commissar for defence 8/5/40 *79*
- Zhukov chief of general staff & deputy defence commissar 12/2/41 *161*
- Army intelligence chief says Germany will not attack 20/3/41 *170*
- Churchill warns of impending German attack 3/4/41 *174*
- Army units transferred westwards 11/6/41 *196*
- Stalin goes on holiday despite fresh invasion warning 18/6/41 *198*
- Strength of armed forces as Germany invades 22-3/6/41 200
- Committee of Defence under Stalin takes control 29/6/41 *200*
- Timoshenko becomes western front commander 2/7/41 *203*
- Stalin calls for scorched-earth policy 3/7/41 204
- US promises military aid 4/8/41 *212*
- Conscription 3/9/41 *220*
- Ethnic Germans in Volga area exiled to Siberia 8/9/41 *221*
- Eden and Stalin agree policy for conduct of war 22/12/41 259
- Asks Churchill to open second front 16/3/42 *282*
- Molotov visits London to demand second front 18/4/42 290
- Zhukov promoted to marshal of Soviet Union 18/1/43 *372*
- Zhukov receives Order of Suvorov 31/7/43 *428*
- Moscow's claims about Byelorussian partisans 1/12/43 *465*
- Konev promoted to marshal of the Soviet Union 18/2/44 *490*
- Ukrainian partisans ambush Vatutin 29/2/44 492
- Agrees to Churchill's request for new offensive 7/1/45 *597*

USSR (economics and industry)
- Signs agreement with Estonia 28/9/39 *26*
- Trade agreement to be signed with Germany 10/2/40 *60*
- Factories put on seven-day working week 27/6/40 *100*
- Signs agreement with Germany 10/1/41 151
- War loan subscription opened 14/4/42 *289*
- Increase in aircraft production 31/12/43 474
- Industrial centre of Krivoi Rog falls to Red Army 22/2/44 *492*

USSR (foreign affairs)
- Effect of communism on western Europe (1930s) 13
- Nazi-Soviet non-aggression pact signed 23/8/39 15
- Armistice with Japan 15/9/39 *21*
- Promises to respect neutrality of Finland 17/9/39 *22*
- Invades Poland 17/9/39 23
- Signs agreement with Estonia 29/9/39 *26*
- Signs boundary and friendship treaty with Germany 29/9/39 27
- Khrushchev announces communization of eastern Poland 3/10/39 *28*
- Signs treaty with Latvia 5/10/39 29
- Signs treaty with Lithuania 10/10/39 *30*
- Fresh talks with Finland 22/10/39 *34*
- Finland refuses to give military base 3/11/39 *35*
- Prepares for war with Finland 13/11/39 *38*
- Renounces 1932 Russo-Finnish non-aggression pact 28/11/39 *42*
- Invades Finland 30/11/39 42
- Sets up puppet Finnish government 1/12/39 *43*
- Rejects League of Nations' call for peace with Finland 12/12/39 *45*
- Expelled by League of Nations 14/12/39 47
- Ambassador to Italy recalled 1/1/40 *54*
- Defeated by Finland at Suomussalmi 8/1/40 56
- Welles to negotiate peace settlement 9/2/40 *60*

– Turkish border incident 23/2/40 *64*
– Final peace terms offered to Finland 23/2/40 65
– Finland defeated 9/3/40 66
– Peace treaty with Finland 12/3/40 *68*
– Opposed to alliance of Scandinavian countries 20/3/40 *69*
– To stay neutral in European war 29/3/40 *71*
– Shoots Polish officers at Katyn 5/4/40 *72*
– Invades Lithuania 15/6/40 7, 95
– Troops sent to Latvia and Estonia 17/6/40 *97*
– Demands Bessarabia and Northern Bukovina from Roumania 26/6/40 *100*
– Occupies Bessarabia and Northern Bukovina 28/6/40 101
– Baltic states join Soviet Union 21/7/40 107
– Signs trade agreement with Germany 10/1/41 151
– Warns Bulgaria over joining Axis 3/3/41 *166*
– Treaty with Yugoslavia 5/4/41 *174*
– Signs neutrality (non-aggression) pact with Japan 13/4/41 9, 180
– Britain warns of impending German attack 6/5/41 *184*
– Sorge warns of German June invasion 15/5/41 *187*
– Invaded by Germany 22/6/41 8
– Bombs Helsinki 25/6/41 *200*
– Signs treaty with Czech government in exile 18/7/41 *206*
– Signs treaty with Polish government in exile 30/7/41 211
– Will aid Turkey if attacked 10/8/41 *214*
– Stalin signs pact with Polish government in exile 4/12/41 *245*
– Treaty with Iran 29/1/42 268
– 20-year pact with Britain 26/5/42 *301*
– Intends to keep eastern Poland 1/3/43 *386*
– Diplomatic relations with Poles broken off over Katyn 30/4/43 401
– War crimes trial at Krasnodar 14/7/43 426
– Recognizes French Committee of National Liberation 27/8/43 *438*
– Aid pledged by UK and USA 19/10/43 *453*
– Signs pact with Czechoslovakia 12/12/43 469
– Charges Germany with Katyn massacre 26/1/44 485
– Negotiations with Finns for armistice 16/2/44 *490*
– Re-established links with Italy 13/3/44 *497*
– Stalin says Warsaw uprising is reckless 16/8/44 *552*
– Declares war on Bulgaria 5/9/44 *560*
– Britain agrees to send Soviet deserters home 4/9/44 560
– Signs armistice with Finland 10/9/44 *562*
– Gains from armistice with Roumania 13/9/44 562
– Stalin promises to declare war on Japan 13/10/44 *571*
– Armistice with Bulgaria 28/10/44 *575*
– Stalin refuses to renew relations with Switzerland 7/11/44 *579*
– Signs treaty of mutual assistance with France 10/12/44 *587*
– Will not renew non-aggression pact with Japan 5/4/45 *618*
– Tightens links with Polish government in Lublin 21/4/45 624
– Arrests Polish negotiators 5/5/45 634
– Declares war on Japan 9/8/45 654
– Invades Manchuria (1945) 11
– Hands Manchuria back to China 15/8/45 657
– Signs treaty fixing border with Poland 16/8/45 *655*
– Restores relations with Finland 31/8/45 *660*
– Absorbs Baltic states after the war 662
– Blockades Berlin (1948-9) 663
– Represses Hungarian uprising (1956) 665
Ustachi 297, 317, 372, 399, 408
Utah Beach
– (see D-Day)
Utility production 278, 327, 388, 399, 411
Uzice *237*

V

V for Victory campaign 207
V-weapons 396, 402, *438*, *448*, 456, 471, *486*, *497*, *499*, *515*, *531*, *531*, 532, 534, *537*, *537*, *543*, 545, 549, *550*, *554*, 554, 559, 560, 569, *571*, 580, *581*, 583, 585, 588, *591*, *596*, 598, 604, 607, *610*, 613, *616*, *616*, *621*, 646
Vaagso 257
Vaivara *432*
Valentine (destroyer) *84*
Valetta 291, 353
Valga 562
Valguanerna *427*
Valiant (battleship) *116*, *150*, 172, 253, *440*
Vallat, Xavier *172*, *174*
Valona *150*, *156*
Vampire (destroyer) 288
Vampire jet fighters *642*
Vanakula *486*
Vandegrift, Alexander *357*
Vanessa (destroyer) *361*
Vannes 194
Vanoc (destroyer) 171
Vargas, Getulio 281, 325
Varsity (operation) 615
Vasilevsky, Alexander *607*, *652*, 658
Vasto 458
Vatican
– Pope condemns racism, dictators and treaty violations 27/10/39 *34*
– Pope's peace appeal 24/12/39 49
– Pope condemns Nazi rule in Poland 21/1/40 *59*
– Rationing starts 14/2/40 *62*
– Warns Belgium and France of imminent German attack 30/4/40 77
– Worldwide day of prayer for Poland 8/10/42 *338*
– Neutral but acting as anti-Nazi contact point 23/1/43 375
– Pope asks Allies not to bomb Rome 24/7/43 428
– Ringed by Nazi paratroopers 6/10/43 450
Vatutin, Nikolai *351*, 435, 458, 469, 478, 492, *494*, *506*
Vaughan Williams, Ralph *47*
VE Day 635
Veesenmayer, Edmund 499, 507
Vegesack *390*
Vella Gulf, Battle of 433
Vella Lavella *434*, *436*, 439, *440*, *446*
Venereal disease 360, 454
Venetia *444*
Venetia (destroyer) *128*
Venev 242
Venezuela
– U-boats shell oil refineries 16/2/42 *273*
– Considering declaring war on Axis powers 9/2/45 604
– Declares war on Axis powers 16/2/45 *605*
Vercors 547
Verdun *94*
Veritable (operation) *603*
Verity, Hedley *428*
Vermion mountains 177
Vermork *351*, *383*, 385, 462
Vernon 560
Verona *626*
Versailles 565
Versailles Treaty 12, 14
Vian, Philip 79, 231, *253*, 284
Vichy *102*
Vichy France
– Third Republic replaced by Etat Francais at Vichy 10/7/40 7, 103
– Naturalized Jews deprived of French citizenship 16/7/40 *105*
– Death penalty for French servicemen in foreign armies 31/7/40 *107*
– Laval offers help to Germany in Battle of Britain 10/8/40 *109*
– Breaks off relations with govts in exile 28/8/40 *114*
– To pay for army of occupation 14/9/40 118
– Jews to carry special identity cards 27/9/40 *123*
– Bombs Gibraltar 24/9/40 123
– Bans Jews from state posts and army 3/10/40 *125*
– Algerian Jews deprived of citizenship 7/10/40 *127*
– Married women banned from state jobs 14/10/40 *128*
– Jews banned from positions of authority 18/10/40 *128*
– Petain agrees collaboration with Hitler 26/10/40 *130*
– Laval becomes foreign minister 28/10/40 *132*
– Jean Moulin sacked 11/11/40 *136*
– Petain dismisses Laval 13/12/40 143
– Darlan gains more power 17/12/40 145
– Baudouin resigns 3/1/41 *150*
– Compulsory service in Chantiers de Jeunesse 9/1/41 153
– Request to US to take Jewish refugees refused 24/1/41 156
– Oath of allegiance to Petain 27/1/41 *158*
– Darlan succeeds Flandin as foreign minister 8/2/41 *160*
– Darlan becomes vice-premier and Petain's successor 14/2/41 162
– Darlan becomes head of government 24/2/41 *164*
– Accepts Japan's ultimatum over Indochinese/Thai dispute 28/2/41 165
– Darlan warns RN over convoy seizures 10/3/41 170
– Britain lets US grain ships through 22/3/41 *170*
– Vallat becomes commissioner for Jewish questions 29/3/41 *172*
– Jewish emigration to be speeded up 3/4/41 *174*
– Permits Germans troops to go through Syria to Iraq 6/5/41 *184*
– Darlan tells Petain he will collaborate with Hitler 14/5/41 *187*
– Germany releases PoWs in return for more collaboration 19/5/41 *190*
– Allows Germany use of overseas naval & military bases 25/5/41 *192*
– Allows Axis to use Bizerta 2/6/41 *195*
– Troops in Syria fight Allies and Free French 13/6/41 197
– Signs armistice with Allies and Free French in Syria 12/7/41 206
– Deports British subjects 25/7/41 208
– Gives Japan control in Indochina if attacked 29/7/41 *210*
– Petain imposes fascist rule 12/8/41 214
– Anti-terrorist laws aimed at Resistance 24/8/41 *217*
– Compulsory single trade union 4/10/41 *228*
– Petain orders arrest of pre-fall French leaders 16/10/41 *231*
– Reprisals for killing of Holz in Nantes 21/10/41 233
– Convoy from Indochina stopped by Allies off S Africa 4/11/41 237
– Huntziger killed in plane crash 12/11/41 239
– German pressure leads to dismissal of Weygand 20/11/41 *241*
– Daladier, Blum and Gamalin tried at Riom 19/2/42 273
– Laval warns Petain of need for more collaboration 26/3/42 *284*
– Laval to be head of government and Petain head of state 16/4/42 *289*
– Laval calls for more cooperation with Germany 20/4/42 *292*
– Jewish deportations urged by Himmler 11/6/42 *306*
– 5,000 Jews to be deported to Auschwitz 15/8/42 *322*
– Forced labourers sent to Germany in exchange for PoWs 11/8/42 324
– 7,000 Jews rounded up for Auschwitz 28/8/42 *327*
– Service National du Travail 13/9/42 *333*
– Nazis to execute hostages in reprisal for sabotage 22/9/42 *336*
– Laval calls for more French workers for Germany 20/10/42 342
– Severs relations with US 8/11/42 *349*
– German occupation 11/11/42 351
– Fleet scuttles itself at Toulon 27/11/42 354
– Darlan claims leadership of France from Algiers 1/12/42 *356*
– Laval says he wants Germany's victory 13/12/42 *360*
– Darnand forms Milice 30/1/43 *376*
– Service Obligatoire du Travail introduced 16/2/43 *383*
– Sauckel demands 100,000 forced workers 5/3/43 *386*
– Giraud to abolish anti-Semitic legislation 18/3/43 390
– Channel ports to be evacuated 16/4/43 *397*
– Laval refuses German demand for deportation of all Jews 14/8/43 *434*
– Petain forbidden to broadcast to the nation 13/11/43 *460*
– Patriotic demonstration in Grenoble 11/11/43 461
– Allied advisers parachute in to train Resistance 7/1/44 *478*
– 22 Frenchmen executed 9/1/44 *480*
– Saboteurs derail train 14/1/44 *480*
– Labour promised to Germany 2/2/44 487
– Germans take control of Mediterranean coast 14/2/44 490
– Former minister sentenced to death by Free French 11/3/44 *495*
– 465 Resistance fighters defeated by Germans 25/3/44 500
– Frenchmen authorized to join SS 27/3/44 *502*
– Cuts communications with neutral countries 27/4/44 511
– Resistance executes minister 28/6/44 537
– SS arrests Petain 19/8/44 554
– Swift collapse 25/8/44 557
Vickers Armstrong [co] 449
Victor Emmanuel III, King of Italy 69, *71*, 429, *506*
Victorious (aircraft carrier) *210*, *280*, 324, *510*, 637
Vienna *57*, 604, 612, 615, 619, 623, *626*
Viet Minh 589
Vietinghoff, Heinrich von 443, 445, 481, 563, 627
Vietnam
– Viet Minh formed 15/6/41 199
– To remain as French protectorate 23/3/45 *614*
– Ho Chi-minh announces provisional government 28/8/45 *660*
– Ho Chi-minh's forces defeat French (1954) 665
Vigan *247*
Vigorous (operation) *306*
Viipuri 58, 65, *66*, 68, *210*, 219, *534*
Vijose river *168*
Vila 373, *386*, *406*, 451
Villers-Bocage 530, 532
Vilna 209, *220*, *432*, 446, *506*, 541, *541*
Vincennes 81
Vincennes (cruiser) 321
Vinnitsa *226*, *331*, *340*, *499*
Viru Harbour *420*
Vis island 568
Viscount (destroyer) 341
Vishinsky, Andrei 508, 610, 636
Vistula river 546, *548*, 552, 597, 601
Vitebsk *205*, *444*, 472, *473*, *481*, 535, 537
Vittorio Veneto (battleship) 172
Vivant, Louis 491
Vizagatapam *288*
Vizzini 426
VJ Day 656
Vlasov, Andrei 268, 318, *363*, *581*, 632, 636
Vo Nguyen Giap 589
Vogelkop 498
Volga river *330*, *344*, 351
Volkhov river *214*, 268
Volkischer Beobachter (Nazi Party newspaper) 254
Volkssturm 568, *573*, 601, *605*, 619, 625
Volkswagen [co] *504*, *537*
Volokolamsk *253*
Volos *166*
Volterra *541*
Volturno river 450
Voronezh 312, *370*
Voroshilov, Klimenti *216*
Voroshilovgrad *316*, *383*
Voroshilovsk *321*, *372*
Vosges *100*, 577, 582
Voyager (destroyer) *336*
Vyazma *228*, *230*, *266*, 268, 283, *288*, *327*

W

WAACS 338
WAAF 38, 135, 164, 431
Waal river *564*, 565
Wadi Akarit 394, *396*
Wadi Zigzaou 390
Waffen-SS
– (see SS)
Wagner, Adolf 183
Wai Li-Huang 599
Wainwright, Jonathan 280, 289, 297, 659
Wairopi *337*
Wakde Island *508*, *515*
Wake Island *247*, 255, *310*, *450*
Walawbaum *494*
Walcheren *84*, 570, 577, *577*, 579
Walker (destroyer) 171
Walker, F J 503
Wallace, Henry A 134, 251
Wallasey 169, 185
Wallenberg, Raoul 539, 577
Wallis, Barnes 410
Walney (sloop) 350
Walter boats *448*, 617
Walton, William 259
Wanderer (escort) *195*
Wandokai *467*
Wang Chingwei 50, 71, 140, 346, 368, 579
Wanne-Eickel 604
Wanting 599
War crimes 265, *338*, 340, 426, *438*, 453, 467, 469, 654, 660
– see also Nuremberg trials
Warburg 619
Warburton-Lee, Bernard (VC) 74, 91
Wareo *467*
Warhawk fighters *512*
Waria river *394*
Warner, Jack 138
Warsaw
– see also Warsaw Ghetto
– Bombed 1/9/39 16
– German army in suburbs 9/9/39 19
– Jewish quarter bombed 16/9/39 *21*
– Besieged by German army 16/9/39 23
– Division between Germany and USSR re-arranged 22/9/39 24
– Surrenders after three-day bombardment 27/9/39 27
– German-Soviet boundary and friendship treaty 29/9/39 27
– Hitler tours city 5/10/39 *28*
– Civilian deaths during siege 6/10/39 29
– Ghetto established 4/11/39 36
– Ghetto edict withdrawn 7/11/39 *36*
– Gestapo shoots Jews 18/1/40 *57*
– RAF leaflet raid 15/3/40 *68*
– Bombed by Red Air Force 2/9/42 *330*
– Germans execute Poles for sheltering Jews 29/6/43 *420*
– 100 tram workers executed by SS and Gestapo 3/12/43 *465*
– 62 Jews in hiding discovered and executed 22/12/43 *470*
– Partisans assassinate Gestapo chief 1/2/44 *486*
– Polish Home Army prepares to rise up 31/7/44 546
– Poles control most of the city 1/8/44 548
– Polish control falters; no help from USSR 19/8/44 *552*
– Poles take to sewers but continue to fight 28/8/44 559
– Stalin drops some arms to Poles 16/9/44 563
– Falls to Russians 3/10/44 570
– Prime target of Zhukov's forces 12/1/45 597
– Soviet troops move to surround 16/1/45 *599*
– Falls to Soviet troops 17/1/45 600
Warsaw Ghetto *40*, *57*, *125*, *128*, *136*, *138*, 141, 159, *163*, 233, *276*, *294*, 302, 318, 332, *338*, 375, *400*, 409
Warspite (battleship) *150*, 152, 172, *440*, 445, 526, 579
Warwick (destroyer) *492*
Wash *206*
Wasp (aircraft carrier) 191, *292*, 298, 335
Waste and scrap 59, 88, 215, 254, 338
Waterhouse, John 341
Waters, Elsie and Doris 138, 147
Watson-Watt, Robert 111, 198
Watt, Harry 209
Wau *368*, *378*, *389*

Shinano (supercarrier) *579, 584,* 638
Shinchiku *464*
Shingle (operation) 482
Shinwell, Emmanuel 657
Shinyo (escort carrier) *581*
Sho-I (operation) 576
Sho-go (operation) *573*
Shoho (aircraft carrier) *294,* 296
Shokaku (aircraft carrier) 248, *294,* 296, 346, 536
Shore, Dinah 587
Short [co]
– (see Stirling bombers; Sunderland flying boats)
Shortland Islands 327, *478*
Shostakovich, Dmitri *278,* 364
Shropshire (cruiser) *163*
Shuri *640*
Shuri Line 618, *621, 626,* 638
Shwebo 582, 596
Sibuyan Sea 576
Sicilian Narrows *404*
Sicily
– RAF strafes Catania *154*
– Royal Navy landing party demolishes rail bridge 28/8/81 *217*
– British "chariots" sink Italian cruiser at Palermo 3/1/43 *368*
– British submarines sink Axis transports off coast 5/2/43 380
– Allies bomb Palermo 10/3/43 *389*
– Ports hit by mass Allied Mediterranean raids 5/4/43 396
– USAAF bombs Catania, Palermo and Syracuse 17/4/43 *397*
– Operation Mincemeat to divert attention to Sardinia 30/4/43 402
– Cunningham starts Operation Retribution in Narrows 8/5/43 *404*
– Hitler downgrades defence, giving priority to Sardinia 12/5/43 *406*
– Allied bombing 22/5/43 *409*
– Lampedusa Island surrenders to Cohen 12/6/43 *415*
– Pantelleria surrenders 11/6/43 416
– Heavy bombardment as Narrows closed to Axis shipping 16/6/43 417
– USAAF bombs Messina 28/6/43 *420*
– Allied landings 10/7/43 424
– AMGOT set up 17/7/43 *425*
– Allies claim to hold half 21/7/43 *427*
– German forces trapped 30/7/43 *428*
– Allies take Catania and Paterno 5/8/43 432
– Losses in campaign as Allies take Messina 17/8/43 437
– Allies cross Straits of Messina to mainland 3/9/43 440
Sidamo 205
Sidi Barrani *120,* 122, 138, 143
Sidi Bou Zid *383*
Sidi Rezegh *241, 245, 308*
Sidon *198*
Sidra *301*
Siegfried Line 18, 21, 33, *36,* 51, 70, 562, 565, *569, 586,* 604
Siemrap 250
Siena 521, 540
Sikh (destroyer) *247*
Sikorski, Wladyslaw 27, *38,* 211, *245,* 265, 346, 405, 422
Sikorsky helicopters *596*
Silverman, Sidney *356,* 360
Sima, Horia 369
Simeni Creek 368
Simferopol *237, 253, 506*
Simmons, F K 274
Simon Bolivar (liner) 39
Simon, John 26, 77, 360
Simovich, Dusan 173, 180
Simpson, William 582, 607, 619
Sims (destroyer) 296
Sinatra, Frank 475
Sincerely Yours (song) 259
Sinclair, Archibald 86, 268
Singapore
– Churchill asks Roosevelt for help in defence 4/10/40 125
– Menzies shocked at state of defences 29/1/41 *158*
– Waters mined by Britain 16/2/41 *163*
– Garrison strengthened 18/2/41 163
– US will not send ships 24/2/41 166
– Churchill ends reinforcement 28/4/41 *181*
– Threat from Japan in Indochina 25/7/41 208
– Repulse and Prince of Wales arrive 2/12/41 *245*
– Reinforcements requested as Japan advances in Malaya 20/12/41 255
– Fortification of north coast as Japan advances in Malaya 9/1/42 263
– Churchill orders defence "to the death" 20/1/42 *266*
– Air raids as Japan nears Johore causeway 20/1/42 267
– British rearguard joins garrison as Japanese approach 31/1/42 269
– Japan demands surrender 4/2/42 *270*
– Japanese hospital atrocities 14/2/42 *271*
– 30,000 Japanese troops land and attack Australians 9/2/42 273
– Surrenders to Japanese 15/2/42 274
– Australian troops blow up Japanese shipping 30/9/43 448
– Bombed by Flying Fortresses 5/11/44 *579*
– US bombers raid Japanese naval base 2/2/45 *603*
– British fleet sets sail to occupy 23/8/45 *658*
– Mountbatten accepts Japanese surrender 29/8/45 *660*
Singora 250
Sington, Derrick 626
Sini *444*
Sinkiang *338*
Sino-Japanese War 7, 13
Sinsiang 561
Sinyang 160
Sinzweya *488,* 491
Sio *467, 480*
Sirius (cruiser) 357, *450*
Sirte 160, *253, 361*
Sittang Bend 658
Sittang river *273,* 631
Sivash lagoon 507
Six, Franz *123*
Sjotay, Dome *499,* 507
Skagerrak *73, 75*
Skaggerak *455*
Skala *504*
Skoplje *581*
Skorzeny, Otto 445, 498, 520, 575, 588, *589*
Skua dive-bombers
– (see Blackburn Skua dive-bombers)
Slang 70
Slapstick (operation) 443
Slapton Sands 503, 511, 512
Sledgehammer (operation) *318*
Slim river 258
Slim, William
– Leads attack at Gallabat 6/11/40 *134*
– Wounded at Keru 27/1/41 159
– Leads force in Iranian invasion 25/8/41 218
– Takes command of Burma Corps 19/3/42 282
– In charge of British retreat from Burma 30/4/42 295
– Burma Corps arrives at Imphal behind refugees 15/5/42 299
– Reports on situation on front in Burma 14/5/43 406
– Made C-in-C Eastern Command 6/10/43 *450*
– Fourteenth Army overruns Maungdaw 10/1/44 480
– Surprised by Operation U-Go 11/3/44 496
– Rushes troops to Imphal 18/3/44 498
– Holds off Japanese at Imphal 24/3/44 500
– Continues fighting on Imphal plain 6/4/44 505
– Launches Operation Extended Capital 18/11/44 582
– Japanese retreat as Extended Capital troops advance 5/1/45 596
– Crossing of the Irrawaddy starts 14/1/45 *599*
– Watches Gurkhas at taking of Meiktila 4/3/45 610
– Troops take Rangoon 3/5/45 631
Slovakia *34, 140,* 222, *618*
Slovenia *438,* 513
Slovik, Eddie 603
Smela *480*
Smetona, Bedrich 20, 95
Smigly-Rydz, Edward 16, *26,* 27
Smith, Holland 610
Smith, Julian 465
Smith, Maurice 606
Smith, Walter Bedell 440, 522, 527, 634
Smolensk 206, *210,* 213, 283, *363,* 384, 389, 444, *446*
Smuts, Jan Christian *16,* 20, *35,* 59, 126, *132,* 190, *280,* 342, *422,* 517, 531
Smyela 469
Sneland (coaster) *634*
Sobibor 286, 291, *301, 353,* 385, 452
Sochaczew 600
Society of Friends 178
Soddu *190*
Soddu, Ubaldo *136*
SOE *105,* 194, *208, 312,* 317, 349, 355, 389, 458, *462, 492,* 493, 528
Sofia *370,* 404, 427, *480*
Soissons *94, 558*
Sokolovksy, Vasiliy 647
Solh, Riad 460
Sollum *118, 142,* 187, 264
Solomon 128
Solomon Islands
– Japanese land at Bougainville 6/4/42 *288*
– Japanese land on Tulagi 3/5/42 *296*
– US submarine sinks Japanese minelayer 11/5/42 *298*
– US bombs Japanese airfields on Guadalcanal and Tulagi 31/7/42 *319*
– Savo Island Battle follows US taking of Guadalcanal 8/8/42 321
– US planes land at Henderson Field, on Guadalcanal 20/8/42 *325*
– Japan loses more than US in Battle of Eastern Solomons 25/8/42 327
– Battle of Bloody Ridge 14/9/42 *333*
– Wasp torpedoed off Guadalcanal 15/9/42 335
– US marines attack Japanese from Henderson Field 9/10/42 *338*
– US task force defeats Japanese off Guadalcanal 12/10/42 340
– US marines repel Japanese at Matanikau river 24/10/42 *342*
– Japanese troops land at Koli Point 3/11/42 *347*
– USAAF bombs Japanese battleship 13/11/42 *349*
– Battle of Guadalcanal 15/11/42 *351*
– Japanese prepare to build airfield at Munda point 4/11/42 *353*
– Battle of Tassafaronga 1/12/42 357
– Patch takes over command from Vandegrift at Guadalcanal 9/12/42 *357*
– Japanese resist US at Mount Austen 18/12/42 *360*
– Japan to pull back from Guadalcanal to New Georgia 31/12/42 *363*
– Japanese resist US troops on Mount Austen on Guadalcanal 2/1/43 *368*
– US offensive on Guadalcanal begins 10/1/43 *370*
– US demands Japanese surrender at Gifu 17/1/43 *372*
– US TF18 hit by Japanese off Rennell Island 30/1/43 378
– First US land victory as Japanese leave Guadalcanal 4/2/42 380
– Battle of the Bismarck Sea 5/3/43 386
– Japanese aircraft sink Allied ships in Ironbottom Sound 7/4/43 397
– Yamamoto killed 18/4/43 401
– US air attack on Japanese 8/5/43 405
– Halsey launches Operation Toenails to take Munda 3/6/43 *414*
– US forces repel major assault on Guadalcanal 16/6/43 *417*
– US troops take Segi Point, in New Georgia 21/6/43 *418*
– US shells Bougainville and Kolombangara 29/6/43 *420*
– Battle of Kula Gulf 6/7/43 *422*
– Battle of Kolombangara 13/7/43 *425*
– USAAF hits Japanese at Buin-Faisi 17/7/43 426
– US reconnaissance party lands in Vella Lavella 22/7/43 *427*
– US forces attack Horseshoe Hill, New Georgia 27/7/43 *428*
– PT-109 under Kennedy sunk 1/8/43 *432*
– Battle of Vella Gulf after US forces take Munda 7/8/43 433
– Halsey orders occupation of Vella Lavella 11/8/43 *434*
– Japanese losses as Allies take New Georgia 25/8/43 439
– US infantry reach Orete Cove 1/9/43 *440*
– Japanese abandon fight 21/9/43 *446*
– US landings at Kolombangara 6/10/43 *450*
– US invasion of northern islands ordered 15/10/43 *452*
– US bombs Japanese air base on Bougainville 18/10/43 *453*
– US landings on Bougainville 1/11/43 *458*
– New Allied airstrip becomes operational 9/12/43 *467*
– Bombed in diversionary raid 24/12/43 472
– US ships raid Shortland Islands 8/1/44 *478*
– New Zealand and US forces land on Green Islands 15/2/44 *490*
– Suicidal Japanese attack on beach-head 24/3/44 500
– Allies seal off Japanese at Buin 1/8/45 *650*
Somali (destroyer) *184*
Somaliland
– Troops from British Somaliland fighting with Britain 20/6/40 99
– Demilitarized French Somaliland zone to be established 24/6/40 100
– Italy invades British Somaliland and takes Hargeisa 5/8/40 110
– Somali Camel Corps remains as British evacuate 19/8/40 114
– Italian bases bombed by SAAF 29/8/40 *114*
– HMS Dorsetshire bombards Zante 18/11/40 *138*
– Cunningham's troops advance from Kenya 24/1/41 157
– Italians retreat 14/2/41 161
– South African troops advance 16/2/41 *163*
– Mogadishu falls 25/2/41 165
– British troops take Hargeisa 20/3/41 *170*
– Vichy French troops join Free French 28/11/42 354
– Free French troops take Jibuti to Addis Ababa railway 26/12/42 *361*
Somers (destroyer) *237*
Somervell, Donald 322
Somerville, James 102, *286, 508, 546*
Somme *91*
Somme river *558*
Song Ziwen
– (see Soong, T V)
Songs
– (see Arts and Entertainment)
Songsan, Mao 536
Soong, T V *436, 640*
Sopron *618*
Sorge, Richard *187,* 231, *337, 579*
Sorong *286*
Sorpe dam 410, 573
Soryu (aircraft carrier) 248, 305
Souk el Arba *351*
Sousse 356, *397*
South Africa
– Declares war on Germany 6/9/39 *16*
– Smuts promises to defend British colonies in Africa 3/11/39 *35*
– Blackshirt plot to sabotage vital industry 9/11/39 *36*
– Call for separate peace with Hitler rejected 27/1/40 59
– War Measures Bill passed 1/4/40 *72*
– Air force bombs Italian aircraft and depots in Libya 12/6/40 95
– Fighting Italians in Ethiopia 20/6/40 99
– Air force bombs Italians in Somaliland 29/8/40 *114*
– Troops fighting Italians in Kenya 24/1/41 157
– Troops fighting in Somaliland 14/2/41 161
– Troops fighting in Ethiopia 18/2/41 *163*
– 1st Brigade in capture of Addis Ababa 6/4/41 178
– Navy and RN intercept Vichy convoy off Cape Town 4/11/41 237
– Troops fighting at Sidi Rezegh 22/11/41 *241*
– Air force in attack on Gondar 27/11/41 244
– Gold mines sabotaged 28/1/42 *268*
– Breaks off diplomatic relations with Vichy France 23/4/42 *292*
– 7th Brigade fighting on Madagascar 10/9/42 332
– Troops take Miteiriya Ridge 24/10/42 343
– Troops lost when transports sunk in Indian Ocean 5/12/42 357
– Troops in Eighth Army 30/3/43 394
– Smuts wins general election 7/7/43 *422*
– Endorses Commonwealth peace plans 17/5/44 517
– Smuts visits Normandy with Churchill 14/6/44 531
South America
– see also individual countries
– Latin America to unite against Axis 15/1/42 265
South China Sea 252
South Dakota (battleship) *648*
South Seas *100*
South Shields 113
South-east Asia Command
– See SEAC
Southampton *138*
Southampton (cruiser) *151*
Southdown (destroyer) *168*
Southern Rhodesia
– (see Rhodesia)
Sovetsky 355
Soviet Union
– (see USSR)
Spaak, Paul-Henri 131
Spaatz, Carl 325, 398, *478,* 506, 514, 520, 636, *646,* 686
Spadefish (submarine) *581*
Spahis 197
Spain
– Franco appeals for war to be limited to Poland 3/9/39 20
– Friendship pact with Germany ratified 29/11/39 *42*
– Rail links with France reopened 1/1/40 *54*
– Bans Freemasonry 24/1/40 *59*
– Troops occupy Tangiers 14/6/40 *94*
– German troops reach Franco-Spanish border 27/6/40 *100*
– Franco refuses to join Axis 23/10/40 *130*
– Signs pact with Britain 2/12/40 141
– Franco refuses to allow German invasion of Gibraltar 12/12/40 *142*
– Signs secret treaty with Germany 10/2/41 *161*
– Gives Germany Morocco's residence in Tangiers 17/3/41 *170*
– Volunteers to fight USSR with Germany 24/6/41 *200*
– Franco sacks Falangists 3/9/42 330
– Azul "volunteers" fighting with Germans in USSR 11/1/43 371
– Maintains neutrality while used as Allied escape route 13/1/43 375
– Soldiers repatriated 22/12/43 *470*
– Agrees to cut wolfram exports to Germany 3/5/44 *512*
– Banned from UN while Franco is in power 19/6/45 *644*
Spanish Civil War 13, 15, 19
Spare a Copper (film) 112
Sparrow Force *336*
Spartan (cruiser) *483*
Spearfish (submarine) *73, 109*
Special Air Service
– (see SAS)
Special Boat Section 349
Special Operations Executive
– (see SOE)
Speer, Albert 100, 271, *310,* 338, 410, *412, 440, 444,* 489, 520, *602, 614,* 614, *618,* 622, 625, *626,* 639
Speidel, Hans 527
Spergau 488
Sperrle, Hugo *537*
Sphakia *192*
Sphinx (minesweeper) *60*
Spiders 43
Spies
– (see Espionage)
Spilje *546*
Spitfire fighters 32, 72, 104, 107, 109, 111, 113, 121, 141, 272, *278,* 291, *292,* 298, *300, 306, 318,* 324, *344,* 394, 397, 456, 492, 495, 528, 585, 588
Spitzbergen *216, 442*
Splendid (submarine) *360*
Splint (operation) 512
Sprague, Thomas 576
Spree river 626, 628
Spring Awakening (operation) 612, 615
Spruance, Raymond *483,* 536, 686
Sri Lanka
– (see Ceylon)
SS
– In Poland 9/9/39 19
– Polish oppression 22/9/39 26
– Heydrich's "final solution" plan 26/10/39 35
– Kills inmates of Polish mental

asylums 6/12/39 *43*
– Mental patients killed in Poland 9/1/40 *55*
– New regiment including Danes and Norwegians to be made 20/4/40 *75*
– Jewish ghetto established in Lodz 30/4/40 *78*
– Totenkopf division near Arras 18/5/40 *85*
– Massacres Royal Norfolk soldiers at Le Paradis 27/5/40 *90*
– "Black Book" of dangerous Britons 6/7/40 *103*
– Reports on conditions in Reich 11/1/41 *151*
– Quells protests at treatment of Jews in Netherlands 25/2/41 *164*
– Reports on conditions in Reich 3/41 *172*
– Reports on conditions in Reich 17/4/41 *180*
– Einsatzgruppen massacring Jews in USSR 30/6/41 *201*
– Atrocities in Lithuania 10/7/41 *205*
– Einsatzgruppen receive orders for USSR work 17/7/41 *207*
– Kills Jews and White Russians at Minsk 21/7/41 *208*
– Einsatzgruppen massacre Jews in USSR 31/7/41 *210*
– Einsatzkommandos massacre Jews in Latvia 3/8/41 *212*
– Special action massacre of Hungarian Jews in Ukraine 29/8/41 *217*
– Einsatzkommando murders Jews at Ponary 12/9/41 *221*
– Adolf Hitler division captures Soviet Ninth Army 6/10/41 *230*
– Massacres 17,000 Jews at Rovno 7/10/41 *230*
– Massacres in eastern Europe shock Wehrmacht officers 15/10/41 *233*
– 230,000 Jews killed since June in Baltic States 1/12/41 *245*
– Security Service reports on German workers 19/1/42 *267*
– 229,052 Jews killed in Baltic States by Einsatzgruppe 31/1/42 *268*
– Executes 258 Jews in Norway 28/5/42 *301*
– Hunts Heydrich's killers in Prague 4/6/42 *304*
– Murders 93 gypsies at Cracow 3/7/42 *312*
– Begins deportations to Treblinka from Warsaw Ghetto 22/7/42 *318*
– Himmler orders brothels for Waffen-SS in France 17/1/43 *374*
– Stroop in charge of liquidating Warsaw Ghetto 21/1/43 *375*
– Kaltenbrunner becomes head of RSHA 29/1/43 *376*
– Panzer Korps ordered to defend Kharkov to the death 6/2/43 *379*
– Russians plan to trap Panzer Korps at Kharkov 8/2/43 *382*
– Crack divisions in Panzer Korps 19/2/43 *384*
– Dismantles Cracow ghetto 13/3/43 *389*
– Waffen-SS troops retake Kharkov 15/3/43 *391*
– Khatyn massacre 22/3/43 *392*
– Massacres 4,000 Jews at Ponar 5/4/43 *396*
– Troops under Stroop driven out of Warsaw Ghetto 19/4/43 *400*
– Mengele appointed to Auschwitz 24/5/43 *412*
– Reports on state of Reich 31/5/43 *413*
– Lwow ghetto destroyed after fierce resistance 27/6/43 *420*
– Massacres in eastern Poland 27/7/43 *431*
– Team to destroy evidence of

murder of Jews in camps 31/7/43 *431*
– Guards killed in Treblinka uprising 2/8/43 *433*
– Bialystok ghetto liquidated 27/8/43 *438*
– Himmler speaks about Jews 4/10/43 *451*
– Rounds up Jews in Rome for deportation 16/10/43 *452*
– Auschwitz women attack guards 23/10/43 *454*
– Factories closed and Jewish workers shot 3/11/43 *45*
– Rounds up hostages in Milan 15/11/43 *463*
– Given free hand to deport Hungarian Jews 19/3/44 *499*
– Shoots Jewish children under 13 in Kovno 27/3/44 *502*
– Hitler Jugend division slaughters 86 Belgians 2/4/44 *504*
– Rounding up Jews in Hungary 15/4/44 *507*
– Massacres 642 at Oradour-sur-Glane 10/6/44 *531*
– Commander of 12th Hitler Jugend division killed 16/6/44 *531*
– Defending Caen 13/6/44 *532*
– Prevents Vilna garrison from surrendering 13/7/44 *542*
– Attacks Resistance in Vercors 23/7/44 *547*
– Arrests Petain 19/8/44 *554*
– Units refuse to agree ceasefire in Paris 25/8/44 *556*
– Massacres French civilians 27/8/44 *558*
– Tries to destroy evidence at Klooga camp 19/9/44 *564*
– Prevents regular soldiers from surrendering 23/9/44 *565*
– Starts reprisal operations against Italian partisans 29/9/44 *566*
– Auschwitz guards attacked by prisoners 7/10/44 *571*
– Arrests Admiral Horthy 15/10/44 *575*
– Fanaticism 5/11/44 *580*
– Massacres Belgian civilians 19/12/44 *589*
– Murders US PoWs at Malmedy 17/12/44 *590*
– Attempts to destroy evidence of murder at Auschwitz 27/1/45 *601*
– Shoots surrendering Germans 18/4/45 *624*
– Shooting defeatists in Berlin 18/4/45 *625*
– Men killed by GIs liberating Dachau 29/4/45 *627*
– Rules by instant execution in Berlin 27/4/45 *628*
– Karl Wolff's role in Italian surrender negotiations 2/5/45 *634*
– Fights to the last in Prague 9/5/45 *636*
Stagecoach (film) 51
Stagg, Jim 527
Stalin Line 70, *203*, 219
Stalin, Joseph
– Alliance with Hitler (1939) and post-war extension of Soviet rule 6
– Destruction of Polish resistance 8
– Allies with Germany 23/8/39 15
– Disagrees with Hitler over division of Poland 22/9/39 24
– Puts pressure on Baltic states 5/10/39 29
– Attitude to Hitler 21/12/39 49
– Refuses to meet Hitler to discuss Polish border 26/3/40 *71*
– Worried by German invasion of Balkans 12/4/41 177
– Chairman of council of people's commissars 6/5/41 *184*
– Orders Pavlov and staff to be executed 30/6/41 *200*

– Broadcasts call for scorched-earth policy 3/7/41 204
– Son captured by Germans 16/7/41 *206*
– Becomes commissar of defence 20/7/41 208
– Replaces Zhukov with Shaposhnikov 29/7/41 *210*
– Appoints himself army C-in-C 7/8/41 *212*
– Asks for British troops 15/9/41 *223*
– Remains in Moscow and declares state of siege 20/10/41 234
– Speech calling for second front 7/11/41 238
– Holds talks with Eden on conduct of war 22/12/41 259
– Orders general offensive along eastern front 5/1/42 *262*
– Says has no territorial ambitions abroad 1/5/42 *296*
– Ignores German plans found in crashed plane 28/6/42 312
– Orders Red Army to stop retreat before Stalingrad 31/7/42 *320*
– Hears Anglo-US campaign plans from Churchill at summit 15/8/42 323
– Blames German successes on lack of second front 6/11/42 347
– Plans to cut German supplies to Stalingrad 12/12/42 *357*
– Reminds Casablanca meeting of need for second front 14/1/43 370
– Orders Rokossovsky to attack towards Gomel and Smolensk 25/2/43 384
– Thanks British for "Red Army Day" 21/2/43 385
– Orders partisan warfare to spread 28/2/43 386
– Becomes marshal of the Soviet Union 6/3/43 *386*
– Says Churchill and Roosevelt traitors over second front 16/3/43 390
– Suspects political motive for suspension of convoys 30/3/43 *394*
– Pleased with damage to German industry 12/4/43 *397*
– Renews links with Poles after split over Katyn 5/5/43 405
– Disbands Comintern to patch up rift caused by Katyn 15/5/43 408
– Promises award to soldiers crossing the Dnieper 25/9/43 446
– Meets Roosevelt and Churchill in Tehran 28/11/43 9, 464
– Allows US aircraft to use Soviet air bases 2/2/44 486
– Completes plan to liberate Byelorussia 31/5/44 518
– Praises D-Day landings 13/6/44 *531*
– Refuses aid to Poles 19/8/44 552
– Still refusing to help Warsaw uprising 5/9/44 561
– Finally provides some aid for Warsaw uprising 16/9/44 563
– Promises to declare war on Japan 13/10/44 *571*
– Talks with Churchill about post-war Europe 9/10/44 572
– Meets de Gaulle for talks 2/12/44 586
– Meets Roosevelt and Churchill at Yalta 4/2/45 *603*
– Sends cable to Roosevelt 7/4/45 *618*
– Announces Allied link-up on Elbe 27/4/45 627
– To raise question of Japanese surrender 17/7/45 647
– Expels Yugoslavia from Comitern and blockades Berlin (1948-9) 663
– Role in Korean War 665

– Biography 686
Stalingrad
– German attack planned 28/6/42 312
– Timoshenko takes charge of defence 17/7/42 *316*
– Russians pull back as Germans advance 27/7/42 320
– Russian 62nd Army holding German sixth Army at Don 13/8/42 323
– German paratroopers massacred 22/8/42 *325*
– Attacked by Luftwaffe as defences crumble 23/8/42 *327*
– State of siege declared 25/8/42 328
– Russian counter-attack ordered as Germans enter suburbs 3/9/42 *330*
– Von Kleist takes over German attack from List 9/9/42 *331*
– German attacks repelled as Russian marines hold silo 18/9/42 333
– Hand-to-hand fighting breaks out as Germans take silo 22/9/42 *336*
– Tractor factory overrun but Red October works hold out 14/10/42 340
– First snows fall 22/10/42 *342*
– Germans advance towards Volga 27/10/42 *344*
– Paulus's Kampfgruppen take factory in new attack 13/11/42 351
– Russian counter-offensive "Uranus" 20/11/42 352
– Russians trap German Sixth Army and Panzers in city 26/11/42 355
– Hitler refuses to allow German sixth Army to pull out 11/12/42 *357*
– Von Manstein launches Winter Storm rescue operation 12/12/42 359
– Luftwaffe flies in supplies to Sixth Army 14/12/42 360
– 4th Panzer Army tries to relieve Sixth Army in city 16/12/42 361
– Russian victory as Sixth Army troops die 31/12/42 365
– Paulus refuses Russian surrender terms for Sixth Army 9/1/43 369
– Russians begin major offensive 10/1/43 370
– Gumrak falls as Hitler tells Paulus "no surrender" 21/1/43 *372*
– Paulus becomes field marshal on eve of German surrender 30/1/43 376
– Last Germans surrender 2/2/43 *376*
Stalino 233, 440
Stalinogorsk 247
Stampalia 132, 444
Stanley, Oliver 63
Staraya Russa 286, *490*
Starling (sloop) 414
Stauffenberg, Claus von 534, 541, 544, 546
Stavanger 73, 74, *75*
Stayning (frigate) 513
Stehla 512
Steinbock (operation) 484
Stellbrink, Karl Friedrich 288
Stemmermann, Wilhelm 491
Stephen Hopkins (Liberty Ship) 337
Sterlet (submarine) 75
Stern Gang 579
Stettin 226, 328, 400, 515, *609*
Stettinius, Edward *584*, 624, 645
Stevens, Richard 37
Stewart, James 479
Stier (raider) *337*
Stilwell Road 602
Stilwell, John 567
Stilwell, Joseph 270, 281, *292*, 300, 342, 347, 388, *442, 444*, 454, 464, *469*, 496, 506, 548,

566, 573, 686
Stimson, Henry L 290, 337, 621, 649
Stirling bombers *161*, 221, 284, 353, 381, 387, 390, 398, 408, 469
Stirling, Bill 552
Stirling, David 241, 335, 349
Stockholm 490
Stolberg 565, 582
Stone Age (operation) 353
Stonecrop 396
Stopford, Montagu 658
Stralsund 43
Strasbourg (battle cruiser) 102, *650*
Strasburg *464*, 577, 584, 596, *597*, 599, 601
Stresa 566
Stringbags
– (see Swordfish aircraft)
Stronghold (destroyer) 278
Stroop, Jurgen 375, *400*, 402, 405, 409
Stuart tanks
– (see Tanks)
Student, Kurt 193, 619
Stuka dive-bombers 16, 23, 74, 85, 88, 107, 109, *110*, 152, 180, 191, *192*, 202, 222, 224, *235*, 279, 298, 302, 303, 309, 312, 314, 328, 383, 414, 431, 514, 528
Stulpnagel, Karl-Heinrich von *134*, 233, *558*
Stumme, Georg 336, *342*
Sturmovik assault planes 246, 262, 469, 628
Sturmovik bombers 352
Sturmovik fighters 423, 431
Stuttgart 398, *442*, 492, *497*, *624*
Stutthof 632
Styria 498
Subasich, Ivan 605
Subic Bay 566, 605
Submarines
– see also Atlantic, Battle of the; Convoys; Mediterranean; Pacific war; U-boats; individual navies
– British submarines scuttled 7/1/40 *55*
– HMS Tarpon sunk 14/4/40 *75*
– Italians sink two British submarines 16/6/40 *97*
– HMS Shark sunk 6/7/40 *102*
– German navy to attack Soviet submarines 15/6/41 *198*
– Italian mini-subs attack Gibraltar 20/9/41 224
– Japanese minelayer Il124 sunk by Edsall 21/1/42 *266*
– Italian ship captured by Hyacinth 9/7/42 *314*
– Italian ship sinks Thunderbolt in Mediterranean 14/3/43 *390*
– Japanese ship sinks Australian hospital ship Centaur 15/5/43 406
– Japanese midgets raid Sydney harbour 1/6/42 306
– Truculent sinks U308 off Faeroes 4/6/43 *414*
– British midgets blow up Tirpitz 22/9/43 447
– Saltfish sinks Japanese carrier in Pacific 3/12/43 *465*
– Tally Ho sinks Japanese cruiser in Pacific 11/1/44 490
– Tally Ho sinks It-23 in Malacca Straits 14/2/44 *490*
– Rasher sinks Japanese carrier in Philippine Sea 18/8/44 552
– Dace and Darter sink Japanese cruisers in Leyte Gulf 23/10/44 575
– Spadefish sinks Japanese carrier in Yellow Sea 17/11/44 *581*
– Sealion sinks Japanese

battleship off Formosa 21/11/44 *583*
– Archerfish sinks Japanese carrier in Kumano Sea 29/11/44 *584*
– Japanese use suicide ships in Pacific 1/1/45 596
– Tally Ho sinks Japanese cruiser in Malacca Straits 11/1/45 *597*
– Japanese merchant shipping losses in US attacks 15/5/45 638
– Trenchant sinks Japanese cruiser in Java Sea 8/6/45 *642*
Subotica 571
Substance (operation) 208
Suda Bay *172*, 191
Sudan 99, *102*, 110, 139, *141*, 156, 159, 174
Suddeutsche Volksstimme (underground newspaper) 236
Sudetenland 14, *643*
Suez 139, 307
Suez Canal *166*, 221
Suez Crisis 664
Suffolk (cruiser) *75*, 231
Sugiyama, Hajime 492
Suho Island *342*
Suiping 513
Sullivan, Francis L 259
Sultan, Daniel I *582*, 596, *614*
Sulu Sea 587
Sulu archipelago 618, 621
Sumatra 256, 272, *360*, 508, 554, 579, *587, 596,* 601, 603, 647
Summa 57, 61, *62*
Summersby, Kay 527
Summerskill, Edith 360
Sun Li-jen 292
Sun Tien-ying *401*
Sunderland flying boats 50, *59*, *102, 138*, 328, 515
Suomussalmi *43, 45, 46, 48, 49,* 51, 56
Supercharge (operation) 348
Superfortress bombers *336*, 383, 485, 515, 531, 534, 534, 539, *546*, 551, 561, *579*, 584, *584*, 591, *603*, 604, *609*, 610, 612, *613*, 618, 622, 637, *637*, 638, 640, *640*, 641, *642*, 643, *643, 644*, 644, 649, *650*, 652, 655
Supermarine [co]
– (see Spitfire fighters)
Supreme Headquarters, Allied Expeditionary Force
– (see SHAEF)
Surabaya 270, 276, *280*, 515, *650*
Surcouf (submarine) 273
Surigao Strait 576
Suzuki, Kantaro 620, 643, 649, 652
Swamp Flower (operation) 314
Swansea 103, 113, *154*
Swatow 637
Sweden
– Declares neutrality 3/9/39 20
– Offers to mediate between USSR and Finland 4/12/39 *43*
– Aid to Finland 9/12/39 44
– Allies try to obtain aid through to Finland 27/12/39 49
– Finland's request for assistance rejected 17/2/40 62
– Protests at German sinking of ships 15/2/40 63
– Reaffirms neutrality 25/2/40 *65*
– Iron ore exports to Germany 21/3/40 70
– Asks Germany to return crown jewels and gold reserves 3/5/40 79
– Allows German troops to use rail link with Norway 5/7/40 *102*
– BOAC starts secret flights 2/3/41 168
– Norwegian ships break out for England 1/4/42 *286*
– Maintains neutrality by trading with both sides 23/1/43 375
– Protests at German mining of territorial waters 28/4/43 *401*

– Cancels German transit rights to Norway 5/8/43 433
– Germany blocks the Skaggerak 27/10/43 *455*
– Britain and USA demand end of vital exports to Germany 13/4/44 *506*
– Swedish military recover a crashed V2 rocket 13/6/44 *531*
Swinemunde 632
Swiss Roll 533
Switzerland
– Declares neutrality 1/9/39 *16*
– Bans exports to belligerents 3/9/39 20
– Invasion contingency plans 1/11/39 *35*
– Country on military alert 10/5/40 *79*
– Pro-Nazi movement banned 19/11/40 *138*
– Severs relations with USSR 21/12/40 *144*
– Policy on Jews and gypsies questioned 29/8/42 329
– Acts as protecting power for British and Germans PoWs 8/10/42 339
– Maintains neutrality while used for Allied espionage 23/1/43 375
– US bombers mistakenly raid Schaffhausen 1/4/44 *504*
– USSR refuses to renew relations 7/11/44 *579*
– Trapped German units seek safety 23/11/44 584
Sword Beach
– (see D-Day)
Swordfish (submarine) *136*
Swordfish aircraft *112*, 138, *142*, 161, 172, *192*, *266*, 272
Sydney *304*, 307
Sydney (cruiser) *105*, 242
Sykes, R S 310
Sylt 70
Symi Island *541*
Syracuse 424
Syria
– Calls on France to continue to fight 25/6/40 100
– Paris Protocols give Germany access to military bases 27/5/41 *192*
– Free French forces enter 8/6/41 *196*
– Free French and Vichy French fight 13/6/41 197
– Allies take Palmyra and Deir el-Zor 3/7/41 *203*
– Armistice between British and French 12/7/41 206
– To be independent after war 15/7/41 207
– Free French forces agree to guarantee independence 16/9/41 *223*
– Declares war on Axis powers 26/2/45 *609*
– Nationalist demonstrations against French troops 19/5/45 *637*
– Asserts claim for independence 21/5/45 640
– French forces battle with gendarmes 29/5/45 *640*
– British troops go in 1/6/45 *642*
Szalasi, Ferenc 575, 577
Szekesfehervar *614*

T

T34 tanks
– (see Tanks)
Tabarka *351*
Tabriz 218
Tacloban 573
Taft, Robert 621
Taganrog *233*, 312, 379, *438*
Tagaytay Ridge *603*
Taihang *306*
Taihapa Ga *486*
Taiho (aircraft carrier) 536
Taihu *357*
Taiku *492*
Taipale 48
Taivu *331*
Taiwan
– (see Formosa)
Taixing *125*
Taiyo (aircraft carrier) *552*
Takao (cruiser) *575*, *649*
Takrouna *400*
Taku *546*
Talabot (freighter) 284
Talasea *495*
Talisman (submarine) *239*
Tallboy bombs 562, 570, 581, 613
Tallinn 211, 564
Tally Ho (submarine) *480*, *490*
Tamashima *644*
Tamatave 334
Tamshin *160*
Tamu 498
Tanahmera Bay 509
Tananarive 332
Tanchuk 647, *652*
Tangiers *94*, *170*, *264*
Tanguy, Henry 550
Tani, Masayuki 99, *337*
Tanks
– see also Panzers
– In German attack on Poland 1/9/39 16
– Guderian's new tactics 9/9/39 19
– French and German deployments as Germans attack 11/5/40 82
– British regiments sent to North Africa 10/8/40 *109*
– US to supply 4,000 to Britain 11/8/40 *110*
– 4th Armoured Brigade pushes Italians back to Mechili 24/1/41 *156*
– British and Australian forces take Benghazi 7/2/41 160
– British armour breaks down on retreat from El Agheila 1/4/41 *174*
– British armour inferior to German 5/4/41 175
– German armour forced back from Tobruk 14/4/41 179
– Wavell complains about quality of British armour 26/4/41 183
– Matilda, Crusader, Cavalier and Cromwell Cruiser-types 22/4/41 183
– Huge British losses in "Battleaxe" 17/6/41 198
– Russian strength at German invasion 23/6/41 200
– Russians introduce T34s as German Panzers break down 31/7/41 211
– T34s go into action on Moscow front 11/10/41 *230*
– American M3 Stuart has trials in Operation Crusader 18/11/41 *241*
– New techniques by Allies and Axis at Tobruk 1/12/41 245
– Fierce battle at Kharkov 12/5/42 299
– American Grant M3 becomes operational with Eighth Army 27/5/42 *301*
– British disable abandoned Axis armour in Western Desert 3/9/42 330
– Grants and Shermans at First Battle of El Alamein 24/10/42 343
– Allied and Axis losses at El Alamein 3/11/42 348
– T34s in Russian counter-attack at Stalingrad 20/11/42 352
– Valentine is first tank to enter Tripoli 23/1/43 373
– British armour in unsuccessful attacks in Burma 3/2/43 380
– Allied armour at Battle of the Kasserine Pass 20/2/43 383
– Allied and Axis losses at Kasserine Pass 25/2/43 385
– Allied armour superior at Medenine 6/3/43 388
– Allied armour outfights Axis in Tunisia 22/4/43 401
– T34s superior to Tigers and Panthers at Kursk 9/7/43 423
– T34s continue success against Tigers and Panthers 25/12/43 472
– Tigers and Panthers captured by Russians in Ukraine 10/3/44 497
–"Funnies" in D-Day landings 6/6/44 529
– T34s in Operation Bagration assault on Germans 22/6/44 535
– British armour lost to Tigers and Panthers at Caen 20/7/44 543
– Modified Shermans spearhead breakthrough in Normandy 31/7/44 547
– Shermans of French 2nd Armoured Div liberate Paris 25/8/44 555
– T34s in combat with Panzers and Tigers 10/10/44 572
– US Shermans in relief of Bastogne 26/12/44 592
– US Third Armored Division uses M26 Pershings in Ruhr 25/2/45 *609*
– T34s in liberation of Prague 9/5/45 636
Tannenburg 602
Tanner, Vaino 531
Tapa 564
Tarakan *264*, 631, *644*
Taranto 138, 443, 450
Tarawa *444*, *462*
Target for Tonight (film) 209, 491
Tarlac *601*
Tarmuizu *652*
Tarnopol 497, *499*, *504*
Tarnow *94*
Taro *483*
Tarpon (submarine) *75*, *453*
Tarung river *458*, *480*
Tarung valley *473*
Tassafaronga *351*
Tassafaronga, Battle of 357
Taung Bazar 486
Taunggyi *292*
Taungup 624
Tavoy *266*
Tawi Tawi *618*
Taxes 26, 77, 77, 108, *130*, 178, 290, 388, 399, 446
Taylor, Bethune 567
Taylor, George 524
Tebaga 393, 394
Tebourba, Battle of *353*
Tedder, Arthur *172*, *195*, 398, *473*, 483, 522, 527, 636, 686
Teheran 9, *217*, 464
Tel Aviv *118*
Tel el Eisa *314*, 344
Telecommunications Research Establishment 214
Teleki, Paul *71*, 175
Tempeleni 170
Tempest fighters *330*
Temple, William 279, 346
Tenaro *381*
Tenaru river 325, 342
Tenedos (destroyer) 288
Ter Poorten, Hein 278, 280
Terauchi, Hisaichi 658
Terboven, Josef *75*, *123*, 223, 339, *634*
Terek river *340*
Terijoki *43*
Termoli *450*
Terracina 519
Territorial Army 17
Terror (monitor) *164*
Tetis code 270
Tetlow Canal 628
The Makham 310
Thailand
– Signs treaty with Japan 6/12/40 *141*
– Gains parts of Laos and Cambodia from Indochina 28/2/41 165
– Government surrenders as Japan invades to attack Malaya 8/7/41 *247*
– Declares war on Britain and US 25/1/42 *268*
– Allied PoWs to extend Singapore to Bangkok railway 24/6/42 310
– US submarines mine approaches to Bangkok 16/10/42 *340*
– USAAF attacks Bangkok oil refinery 26/11/42 *353*
– Japanese try to open supply route to troops 22/4/44 508
– British bombers destroy bridge over river Kwae 24/6/45 *645*
Thala *384*
Thames 117
Thames Estuary *38*, 40, *49*, *128*, *136*
Thasos *181*
The Hague 80, 81, 84, *506*, 513, *610*
Thebes 182
Theresienstadt *294*, *337*, *444*, *450*, *460*, *495*, *575*
Thermopylae 182
Thielbek (liner) 632
Thionville 579, 582
This Happy Breed (play) 405
Thistle (submarine) *73*
Thoma, Wilhelm von *347*, 392
Thomas F Nickel (destroyer) *655*
Thomas, Cecil 282
Thomas, Shenton 247
Thor (merchant raider) *174*, *353*
Thrace *384*
Thummel, Paul *36*, *284*
Thunderbolt (previously Thetis) (submarine) *390*
Thunderbolt fighter-bombers 452, 495, 498, 528, 579
Thunderbolt fighters *356*, 387
Thunderclap (operation) 606
Thuringian Forest 623
Thursday (operation) 496, 498
Thyssen, Fritz 41, *49*
Tianjin 29, *247*
Tibbets, Paul 591, 651, 652
Tiber river 521
Tibet 65
Tiddim 536
Tientsin 658
Tiger (operation) *184*, *187*, 511
Tiger tanks
– (see Panzers; Tanks)
Tigre 187
Tigris (submarine) *389*
Tikhvin *237*, 242, 246, 279
Tilburg 81, *575*
Tilin *601*
Tilly-sur-Seulles *531*
Tilsit 400, 570
Time (magazine) *478*, 520
Times, The (newspaper) 104, 437
Timor 275, *336*
Timoshenko, Semyon 42, 54, 61, 63, 66, *79*, *203*, 213, *220*, *233*, 268, *298*, *316*, 320, 686
Tine river 401
Tinian *492*, *531*, *546*, 549, *577*, *649*
Tinsukia *467*
Tippett, Michael 174
Tirana *363*, *581*, *583*
Tiraspol *508*
Tirpitz (battleship) *127*, *264*, *280*, 287, 315, 442, 447, *543*, *554*, 562, 581
Tiso, Joseph *34*
Tisza river *569*, 574, 578
Tito, Josip
– Raises partisans to fight Axis occupiers 5/7/41 204
– Fails to agree strategy with Mihailovich 19/9/41 *223*
– Partisans fighting Ustachi and Axis without Allied aid 9/5/42 297
– Partisans liberate Croatia and execute Ustachi 16/7/42 317
– Request for aid refused as Axis offensive begins 15/1/43 372
– Allied liaison officers reach partisans 15/4/43 399
– Evades capture by Axis forces 11/6/43 416
– British military mission to join partisans 23/6/43 419
– British brigadier joins him as adviser 19/9/43 447
– Sets up provisional government 4/12/43 466
– Tells king his services are not needed 22/12/43 472
– Sends military mission to London 1/5/44 *512*
– Narrowly escapes capture 25/5/44 520
– To meet Churchill 11/8/44 551
– Soviet forces link up with his troops 6/9/44 *560*
– At work with his secretary 27/9/44 568
– To join royalist prime minister in government 11/2/45 605
– In dispute with Britain and US over Trieste 14/5/45 638
– Remains independent of Soviets after the war 663
– Biography 687
Tizard, Henry *110*
Tobata 539
Tobruk *151*, *156*, *176*, 179, 183, *184*, *198*, *200*, 205, 217, 230, *231*, *243*, 247, 303, *308*, 311, 334, 350
Todt, Fritz *69*, 90, *270*
Toenails (operation) *414*
Togliatti, Palmiro 508
Togo, Shigenori *330*, 654
Tojo, Hideki 203, 232, 242, 274, *330*, *417*, 487, 492, 545, 687
Tokat 49
Tokyo
– US bombers make unexpected raid 18/4/42 290
– US Congress claims targets bombed 15/6/44 531
– Soviet spy executed 7/11/44 *579*
– Leader of China's collaborationist regime dies 10/11/44 579
– Raided by US bombers 27/11/44 *584*
– First mass air raid 1/1/45 596
– US ships attack 16/2/45 *605*
– Incendiary raid 25/2/45 *609*
– 16 square miles gutted in incendiary attack 10/3/45 612
– Four-hour incendiary raid 14/4/45 622
– US Third Fleet joins attack 10/7/45 *647*
– Raided by US bombers 8/8/45 *652*
– Raided by 1,600 US bombers 13-14/8/45 *655*
Tokyo Express 335, *344*, 357, 380
Tokyo Rose 587
Tolbukhin, Fedor 438, 456, 507, *512*, 514, 561, 574, 585, 615, 617, 623
Tolstoy, Alexei 234
Tolvarjarvi 51
Tomislav I, King of Croatia *190*
Tondern 73
Torbay (submarine) *203*, *231*, *239*
Torch (operation) *318*, *340*, *342*, *344*, 350, 365
Torgau 627
Torii, Suzeto 659
Torokina 459, 500
Torquay *412*
Torre dam *512*
Torun 35, *603*
Totalize (operation) 550, 554
Toulon *349*, 351, 354, 553, 557, 558
Toungoo 284
Tours *94*, 96
Tovey, John *404*
Toyama *650*
Toyoda, Soemu *512*, 536, 576, *640*, 649
Toyoda, Teijiro *208*
Tractable (operation) *552*
Train, Jack 51
Traitors
– (see individuals eg Joyce, William; Treachery Act 1940)
Transdniestria *231*
Transylvania 101, 113, *114*, 499, 562
Transylvania (armed merchant cruiser) *71*, *109*
Trappes *495*
Treachery Act 1940 88, 205
Treasury Islands *455*
Treblinka 286, 318, 332, *342*, *344*, *353*, *384*, 385, 402, 433, *436*, 438
Trenchant (submarine) *642*
Trenchard, Lord 72
Trento (cruiser) 309
Trials for war crimes
– (see War crimes)
Trident (talks) *406*
Trieste 429, 638, *643*
Trieste (cruiser) *396*
Trigno river *453*
Trincomalee 288
Trinder, Tommy 101
Trinidad (cruiser) 287, *298*
Tripoli *140*, *142*, *145*, *181*, *310*, *370*
Tristan da Cunha 481
Triton (submarine) *144*
Triton code 270
Trobriand Islands *418*
Troglitz *518*
Tromso *76*, *79*, *91*, *128*
Trondheim 74, *75*, *76*, 77, 91, 315, *338*, *427*
Troodos Mountains 195
Trotobas, Michael *418*
Trotsky, Leon *34*, *87*, 113, *397*
Truant (submarine) *73*
Truculent (submarine) *414*
Truk 325, 485, 487, *488*, 491, *510*, *512*
Truman, Harry S
– Sworn in as vice-president 20/1/45 *599*
– Sworn in as 33rd US president 12/4/45 621
– Announces Allied link-up on Elbe 27/4/45 627
– Warns that war is only half won 8/5/45 *634*
– Speaks at signing of UN Charter 26/6/45 645
– Arrives for Potsdam conference 16/7/45 *648*
– Orders atomic bomb to be dropped on Japan 25/7/45 *649*
– Lunch with King George 2/8/45 *650*
– Comments on dropping of atomic bomb 6/8/45 652
– In Washington on VJ Day 15/8/45 656
– Formulates "doctrine" on communism 3/47 663
– Sacks MacArthur for disagreement over Korean War (1951) 665
– Biography 687
Truman Doctrine 663
Truscott, Lucien C *492*, 519, 553
Tsaoyang *91*
Tsarskoe Selo *228*
Tsimlyansky *321*, *368*
Tube Alloys
– (see Atomic bomb)
Tug Argan *110*, *110*
Tuguegarao 255, *645*
Tula *231*, 240, 246
Tulagi *296*, *319*, 321
Tulearon *337*
Tulle *530*
Tungting Lake 405, 414
Tunis *192*, 353, 356, 396, 404, *406*
Tunisia
– see also Desert War
– Demilitarized zone to be established 24/6/40 100
– German reinforcements land 12/11/42 *349*
– Allies approach from Algeria 14/11/42 350
– Giraud deposes bey of Tunis for collaboration 15/5/43 *406*
Tupolev SB-2 bombers 202

Turgel, Norman 626
Turin *141*, 221, 342, *351*, 353, *425*, *581*
Turing, Alan 270
Turkey
– Breaks off talks with USSR 17/10/39 *32*
– Earthquake 27/12/39 *49*
– State of emergency after Russian border incident 23/2/40 *64*
– Secret meeting with Britain 21/3/40 *69*
– Signs treaty with Bulgaria 17/2/41 164
– Agreement with Britain 27/2/41 165
– Refuses to join Axis 4/3/41 *166*
– Signs treaty with Germany 18/6/41 *198*
– Britain and USSR will aid if attacked 10/8/41 *214*
– Chrome exports to Germany embargoed 30/9/41 *226*
– Signs trade treaty with Germany 9/10/41 *230*
– Maintains neutrality and is spy centre for both sides 23/1/43 375
– Britain promises help if forced into war 30/1/43 *376*
– Confirms neutrality and friendship with USSR & Germany 15/6/43 *417*
– Allies cut off lend-lease 2/3/44 *494*
– Cuts off chrome exports to Germany 20/4/44 *508*
– Martial law declared 18/5/44 *515*
– Cuts relations with Germany 2/8/44 *548*
Turnage, Hal 460
Turner, Richmond 421
Turnu Severin 506
Tutuila (gunboat) 211
Tweedsmuir, Lord (see Buchan, John)
Twenty Committee 240, 437
Twingon 292
Tyneside 111
Typhoon (operation) *228*
Typhoon fighters *221*, *331*, 528, 550, 554, 632
Tyre *196*
Tyrol, South *444*
Tyrrhenian Sea 542

U

U Maung Saw *239*, 266, 280
U-Go (operation) *495*, 536
U-boats
– see also Atlantic, Battle of the; Convoys; Mediterranean
– Athenia torpedoed in Atlantic 4/9/39 18
– Courageous sunk by U29 off Hebrides 17/9/39 25
– Swedish steamer and British cargo ship sunk in Atlantic 24/9/39 *26*
– Prien, in U47, sinks Royal Oak in Scapa Flow 14/10/39 31
– Churchill says one in three have been sunk 18/10/39 *32*
– RN increases offensive after Nelson attacked 31/10/39 34
– Churchill predicts win after Ark Royal sinking claims 8/11/39 37
– Mines sink civilian shipping in North Sea 20/11/39 39
– Barham slightly damaged by torpedo 28/12/39 *49*
– Exmouth sunk in Atlantic 21/1/40 *59*
– One sunk by Antelope in south-western approaches 5/2/40 *60*
– British losses to be played down on BBC 6/2/40 61
– One sunk by Gleaner in Firth of Clyde 12/2/40 *62*
– Hitler orders unlimited war, including neutrals 15/2/40 63
– One sunk by Gurkha off Faeroes 23/2/40 *64*
– Enigma rotors taken from scuttled U33 28/2/40 65
– U31 sunk in North Sea by Blenheim bomber 11/3/40 *68*
– Fortune sinks U44 off Narvik 20/3/40 *69*
– Allied shipping losses 31/3/40 *71*
– U50 sunk off Shetlands by Hero; U4 sinks Thistle 10/4/40 *73*
– Fearless sinks U49 off Norway 15/4/40 *75*
– U26 sunk in Atlantic 1/7/40 *102*
– Attacks on convoy HX-72 22/9/40 *123*
– RN concerned about growing menace 22/9/40 125
– Donitz orders "wolfpacks" as Prien attacks in Atlantic 19/10/40 129
– Allied shipping losses 29/10/40 133
– Allied losses grow as numbers increase 29/10/40 *134*
– Hitler orders war to increase 24/2/41 165
– US Navy to shoot first after attack on Creer 11/9/41 223
– First one enters Mediterranean 24/9/41 *226*
– Lehigh torpedoed off West Africa 19/10/41 *233*
– Ark Royal sunk by U81 and U205 off Gibraltar 14/11/41 239
– Barham torpedoed by U331 in Ionian Sea 25/11/41 244
– Type IXs begin second "happy time" off US 13/1/42 *264*
– Brazilian shipping sunk 11/3/42 *280*
– Shipping menaced worldwide as Donitz orders more attacks 1/4/42 287
– Edinburgh torpedoed in Barents Sea 30/4/42 *294*
– Transport ship torpedoed in St Lawrence Seaway 11/5/42 *298*
– Attack on convoy PQ-16 in Arctic 30/5/42 302
– Allied losses as offensive spreads to US waters 1/7/42 313
– Success of British Leigh Light device 5/7/42 *314*
– Attack on convoy PQ-17 in Arctic 7/7/42 315
– Withdrawn from east coast of US 19/7/42 *318*
– U94 sunk in Caribbean 28/8/42 *327*
– Controversy after Laconia sinking in South Atlantic 12/9/42 331
– Active sinks U179 off Cape Town 7/10/42 *338*
– Allies set up Anti-U-Boat Committee 4/11/42 *347*
– Allied shipping hit in Indian Ocean 5/12/42 357
– Convoy JW-51B wins Battle of Barents Sea 31/12/42 364
– RAF attacks bases at Cherbourg and Lorient 14/1/43 *370*
– Harris says industry is RAF target 4/2/43 380
– RAF attacks Lorient 13/2/43 381
– Hitler gives tanks and aircraft more priority 11/4/43 *397*
– Five merchant ships sunk off West Africa 29/4/43 *401*
– RAF mines Baltic Sea 29/4/43 401
– Recalled in anticipation of Allied invasion of Europe 29/6/43 *420*
– U792, prototype Walter boat, launched 28/9/43 *448*
– Churchill says 60 have been sunk in last three months 9/11/43 *460*
– U794 goes into service with a Schnorkel 14/11/43 *462*
– Emden raided by USAAF 11/12/43 *467*
– Convoy JW-56A attacked off Iceland 26/1/44 *483*
– Penelope sunk by U410 at Anzio 18/2/44 *490*
– Convoy JW-57 sinks two in Arctic 28/1/44 *492*
– Convoy RA-57 sinks three and damages two 10/3/44 *495*
– Attack on convoy JW-58 in Arctic fails 31/3/44 503
– Allied flying boats sink two off Norway 18/5/44 *515*
– Chatelain seizes Enigma material from U505 4/6/44 521
– War effort aided by Schnorkel 21/10/44 574
– U486 sinks Leopoldville in English Channel 24/12/44 *591*
– U711 sinks Bluebell; U425 sunk by Lark 17/2/45 *605*
– Newer, more powerful, ships commissioned 24/2/45 608
– U327 sunk by Lancaster bomber in Scilly Isles 28/2/45 *609*
– Types XXI and XXIII (Walter boats) arrive too late 31/3/45 617
– Five sunk in Kattegat as hostilities cease 5/5/45 634
– Some scuttle themselves though Donitz orders surrender 12/5/45 636
– U530 surfaces off Argentina 10/7/45 *647*
Ube *652*
Uckermark
– (see Altmark)
Udem *609*
Udet, Ernst 176, *241*
Udine 429, 539
Uganda (battleship) 445
Ukhrul 536, *539*
Ukraine 8, *35*, 60, 202, 216, *217*, *378*, 438, *470*, 472, *483*, 492, *495*, *497*, *499*, *508*, 542
Ulithi atoll *564*, *613*
Ulster (destroyer) *618*
"Ultra" intelligence *409*, 514, *518*, 521, 532, 534, 538, 550, *639*
– see also Enigma
Uman *494*, *495*
Umberto, Crown Prince of Italy 407, *506*
Umezu, Yoshijiro 649, 660
Umpire (patrol ship) *206*
UN
– (see United Nations)
Un-American Activities Committee 664
Unbeaten (submarine) *282*
Underground
– (see PoWs; Resistance (French))
Underground railway *120*, 126, *128*, 159, 388
Undertone (operation) 609
Ungelap *508*
Union of German Socialists *170*
Union of Soviet Socialist Republics
– (see USSR)
Unita Proletaria (newspaper) 494
United Nations 262, *409*, 458, *566*, 571, 605, 609, 634, 637, *644*, 645, *646*, 650, *658*
United Nations Relief and Rehabilitation Administration
– (see UNRRA)
United Services Organization *160*
United States Army Air Force
– (see USAAF)
United States of America
– (see USA)
UNRRA 461, *502*, 650, 661
Unshaken (submarine) *401*
Upholder (submarine) *190*, *223*, *262*, *289*
Upper Silesia 597
Upright (submarine) *164*
Ur *192*
Ural Maru (transport ship) *566*
Urbane (operation) *586*
Urge (submarine) *286*
Urquhart, Robert 565
Ursula (submarine) 70
Uruguay
– Wrecked Admiral Graf Spee sold for scrap 29/2/40 *65*
– Recognises French National Liberation Committee 11/6/43 *415*
– Declares war on Axis powers 22/2/45 *607*
US Army
– see also theatres of war eg Pacific War; D-Day
– Extra money provided by Congress 13/6/40 *94*
– MacArthur to command in Far East 26/7/41 *208*
– Strength 13/12/41 251
– First troops arrive in British Isles 26/1/42 268
– New Caledonia Task Force reaches Noumea via Australia 12/3/42 *280*
– Troops arrive in Northern Ireland 18/5/42 301
– Eisenhower to command in Europe 25/6/42 310
– Dieppe raid 19/8/42 326
– 32nd Infantry Division joins attack on Wairopi 28/9/42 *337*
– First unit arrives at Guadalcanal 13/10/42 *340*
– Troops sail for North Africa as part of Torch 23/10/42 *342*
– Patch takes over from Vandegrift in Solomons 9/12/42 *357*
– Losses on Guadalcanal 4/2/43 380
– Losses at Battle of the Kasserine Pass 25/2/43 385
– Patton appointed to command II Corps 6/3/43 *386*
– Engineers build new Burma Road 1/3/43 388
– Seventh Army and Rangers in Sicily landings 10/7/43 424
– Fifth Army to land at Salerno 3/9/43 440
– Launches major attack at San Pietro 7/12/43 *467*
– Bogus 1st US Army Group 1/2/44 487
– Troops under Wingate in Burma 6/2/44 *488*
– Troops land on the Green Islands 15/2/44 *490*
– Strategists agree that Japan must be invaded 24/4/44 *510*
– D-Day landings 6/6/44 *522*
– GIs in Britain 7/6/44 531
– 12th Army Group formed in France 1/8/44 *548*
– Plagued by phoney GIs 18/12/44 590
– Executes deserter 31/1/45 603
– Losses taking Iwo Jima and Okinawa 2/45 10
– Troops under Montgomery cross the Rhine 24/3/45 615
– Patton's troops discover German gold reserves 8/4/45 *621*
US China Air Task Force
– (see Flying Tigers)
US Navy
– Naval Supply Act provides $ 1,000m 11/6/40 *94*
– Roosevelt's "two-ocean" navy plan approved by Congress 19/7/40 105
– Opens Bermuda base 7/4/41 *176*
– Planes start patrolling North Atlantic 1/7/41 *203*
– Convoy protection in Atlantic 1/9/41 *220*
– Roosevelt orders "shoot-first policy" 11/9/41 223
– Escorts British convoy HX-150 16/9/41 *223*
– First loss in Atlantic 31/10/41 235
– Japanese destroy yard at Cavite 13/12/41 *247*
– Pacific Fleet losses at Pearl Harbor 8/12/41 248
– Volunteers join up after Pearl Harbor 13/12/41 251
– King becomes C-in-C 20/12/41 *253*
– King accepts British view on convoys 1/4/42 287
– King demands more warships 15/5/42 *298*
– Victory at Midway Island 6/6/42 305
– King agrees that convoy method is best against U-boats 1/7/42 313
– Task force defeats Japanese flotilla off Guadalcanal 12/10/42 340
– Halsey succeeds Ghormley in South Pacific 18/10/42 *342*
– Carriers sail for North Africa as part of Torch 25/10/42 *344*
– Urges night radar after Battle of Guadalcanal 15/11/42 351
– Report on Pearl Harbor 5/12/42 *356*
– Launches USS New Jersey 7/12/42 *357*
– Launches 15 new ships on Pearl Harbor anniversary 7/12/42 358
– Confident of success in Pacific 31/12/42 365
– Losses at Guadalcanal 4/2/43 380
– Escort areas in Atlantic redefined 1/3/43 387
– US torpedo nearly hits ship with Roosevelt on board 14/11/43 *462*
– Penetrates Japanese home waters 4/2/44 *486*
– Secretary of the navy dies 28/4/44 *510*
– New secretary of the navy appointed 10/5/44 *513*
– Submarines sink Japanese transports killing PoWs 11/9/44 *562*
– Key role of submarines in Pacific War 15/5/45 638
– Attacked by Japanese air force off Okinawa 27/5/45 *640*
– Survivors of Indianapolis disaster tell their tale 2/8/45 651
– Vast force enters Tokyo Bay 27/8/45 *660*
USA (defence)
– see also US Army; US Navy; USAAF
– Naval Supply Act passed 11/6/40 *94*
– Congress votes extra money for army 13/6/40 *94*
– Roosevelt's "two-ocean" navy plan approved by Congress 19/7/40 105
– Hull calls for arms build-up 6/8/40 *109*
– To swap destroyers for British bases 16/8/40 112
– Joint board established with Canada 18/8/40 *112*
– Senate approves conscription 16/9/40 122
– No change to policy when Japan joins Axis 27/9/40 124
– Draft registrations 15/10/40 *128*
– 1942 budget 8/1/41 *151*
– Peru warns of impending Japanese attack on Pearl Harbor 27/1/41 *158*
– ABC1 meetings with British 27/1/41 159
– Lend-Lease Bill becomes law 11/3/41 168
– Shipbuilding agreement with Canada 19/3/41 170
– Axis ships impounded 30/3/41 174
– First military encounter with Germany 10/4/41 *176*
– Greenland bases to be established 12/4/41 178
– Enforces new Atlantic security zone 25/4/41 *181*
– Collaboration with Canada to help Britain 21/4/41 183
– U-boat sinks merchant ship inside security zone 21/5/41 *190*
– First experimental blackout 26/5/41 *192*
– 1942 budget 5/6/41 *195*
– Troops to replace British garrison in Iceland 11/6/41 *196*
– Draft registration for over-21s 1/7/41 *203*
– Army and navy appropriations 11/7/41 205
– Volunteer "Flying Tiger" pilots aid Chinese Nationalists 1/8/41 212
– Military strength 22/8/41 216
– Axis shipping in US waters to be sunk 26/9/41 *226*
– Merchant ships in Asian waters to go to friendly ports 17/10/41 *231*
– Japan destroys fleet at Pearl Harbor 7/12/41 *247*
– Rush of volunteers to forces 13/12/41 251
– Anglo-American talks agree on war priorities 31/12/41 259
– Roosevelt promises US troops and more aid for Britain 6/1/42 262
– U-boats extend Battle of the Atlantic to US coast 13/1/42 *264*
– Japanese Americans to be interned 18/2/42 275
– Japanese bombard Santa Barbara oil refinery 23/2/42 *276*
– Forces to be built up in Britain to attack Germany 14/3/42 *280*
– US and Britain agree on war responsibilities 30/3/42 285
– Country placed on war footing 28/4/42 295
– Signs pact with Brazil 23/5/42 301
– U-boat lands saboteurs on Long Island 13/6/42 *306*
– Agrees with second front while sending USSR more aid 11/6/42 307
– Japanese shell Fort Stevens, Oregon 21/6/42 *310*
– Joint Canadian-US chiefs of staff committee formed 3/7/42 *312*
– Office of strategic services set up 13/7/42 317
– Allies plan Operation Torch to invade North Africa 25/7/42 *318*
– Four million in military service 28/7/42 *319*
– Kaiser put in charge of mass-production of weapons 30/7/42 320
– Servicemen in Britain not subject to national law 4/8/42 322
– Japanese sea-plane attacks Oregon 28/8/42 *327*
– Groves appointed to manage atomic weapons research 17/9/42 *333*
– Italian-Americans taken off "enemy aliens" list 12/10/42 *340*
– Los Alamos chosen for atomic bomb research 25/11/42 354
– Atomic secrets not to be shared with British 28/12/42 *363*
– High command restructured 6/2/43 *378*
– Morgan appointed to Anglo-US European command (COSSAC) 23/4/43 *400*
– Expenditure 30/6/43 *420*
– Anglo-US atomic weapons agreement 20/8/43 *427*
– Draft revised 14/8/43 434
– Draft bill keeps fathers at bottom of list 10/12/43 468
– Japan begins bombing

Wavell, Archibald
– Signs pact with Turkey 19/10/39 *32*
– As C-in-C Middle East faces Italian threat 15/1/40 57
– Meeting with Eden, Smuts and Haile Selassie 28/10/40 *132*
– Personality 17/12/40 144
– Can offer only small force in reply to Greek request 13/1/41 *154*
– Agrees that Greece should have all possible help 19/2/41 *163*
– Complains about quality of Allied tanks 26/4/41 183
– Launches Operation Brevity 15/5/41 *187*
– Sends troops to Syria 13/6/41 197
– Reports failure of Operation Battleaxe 17/6/41 198
– Appointed C-in-C India 1/7/41 *203*
– Supreme commander ABDACOM 3/1/42 *262*
– Advises that Singapore cannot be defended for long 31/1/42 269
– In Singapore to try to stave off fall 15/2/42 274
– Returns to India after ABDACOM abolished 25/2/42 *276*
– Plans attack on Akyab 19/12/42 361
– To be viceroy of India instead of C-in-C 18/6/43 417
– In India to take up post of viceroy 20/10/43 *453*
– Biography 687
WAVES 338
Wavre 81
Wawer *49*
Way Ahead, The (film) 593
We'll Meet Again (song) 147
We're gonna hang out the washing … (song) 51
Weather *57*, 58, 60, *62*, 151, *205*, *230*, 234, *239*, *245*, 247, 254, 269, *342*, 456, 527, *575*, 584
Webb, Beatrice 103
Wedemeyer, A C 573
Wehrmacht
– (see German army)
Weichs, Maximilian von *316*, 561
Weihaiwei *125*
Weizmann, Chaim 538
Welles, Orson 259, 475
Welles, Sumner *60*, *65*, *66*, *68*, 69, 265
Wellesley 255
Wellington bombers 43, 48, *55*, 84, 138, 175, 179, *205*, 214, *214*, 270, 272, 284, *314*, 353, 381, 387, 396, *420*, 452, 506
Wells, H G 103, 131
Welshman (minelayer) 291, *378*
Wenchow *644*
Wenck, Walther *605*, *607*, 628
Wendover 591
Went The Day Well? (film) 364
Werner, Arthur *639*
Weserubung *45*, *72*
West Indies
– British land on Curacao and Aruba 11/5/40 *79*
West Virginia (battleship) 618
Western Approaches
– (see Atlantic, Battle of the)
Western Approaches (film) 593
Western Desert 162, 187, 198
– see also Desert War; North Africa
Western Front
– see also Belgium; France; France, Battle of
– British and French deployment 11/9/39 21
– French attacks on German border 24/9/39 *26*
– German Tenth Army prepares arrival 3/10/39 *28*
– German army pushes French back to Maginot Line 16/10/39 *32*
–"Phoney War" 21/10/39 33
– Germany reinforces Siegfried Line 10/11/39 *36*
– First British death 9/12/39 *43*
– King George visits Allied troops 9/12/39 44
– Increase in German reconnaissance flights 17/12/39 *47*
– First Indian troops arrive 28/12/39 *49*
– Cypriot troops arrive 9/1/40 *55*
– Germans advance 18/5/40 *84*
– Allies fall back on Dunkirk after loss of Boulogne 25/5/40 *87*
– Weygand replaces Gamelin as Allied C-in-C 20/5/40 88
– Evacuation of Dunkirk begins 26/5/40 *89*
– German army winning on Somme front 8/6/40 94
Western White Russia *35*
Westkapelle 578
Westmacott, H P 563
Wewak 437, *448*, *497*, 634
Wewak river *541*
Wexford 114
Weygand, Maxime *32*, 88, 92, *94*, 96, 98, *241*
Whitby *60*
White Cliffs of Dover, The (song) 364
White Rose 384
White Russia *35*, 530
White Sea 334
Whitley bombers 18, *57*, 70, 179, 244, 302
Whitshed (destroyer) *59*
Whittle, Frank 176, 187, 387
Whitworth, 74
Wiart, Adrian Carton de
– (see Carton de Wiart, Adrian)
Wiese, Friedrich 557
Wilck, Gerhardt 575
Wild Sow tactic *422*
Wild Swan (sloop) *308*
Wildebeest biplanes 264
Wilhelm Gustloff (liner) 603
Wilhelm II, ex-Kaiser of Germany 81, *195*
Wilhelmina, Queen of the Netherlands 28, 37, *38*, 39, *79*, 81, *84*
Wilhelmshaven *127*, *314*, 378, *381*, *384*, *458*, *616*, 623
Wilkie, Wendell 133, 134, *154*, *160*, 339, *497*, *504*, *571*
Wilkinson, Norman 62
Williams, Ralph Vaughan
– (see Vaughan Williams, Ralph)
Williams, Tennessee 593
Wilson, Henry Maitland 122, *166*, 177, *417*, 471, *478*, 490, 493, 568
Winant, John Gilbert *160*
Window 428, 430
Windsor Castle (troop ship) *392*
Windsor, Duke of *21*, 25, *102*, 109, *613*
Wingate, Orde 185, 205, 381, 387, 391, *392*, 402, 434, 439, *488*, 496, 500
Wings for Victory campaign 390
Winkelman, Henri 84, *102*
Winkelmann, Otto 507
Winter Storm (operation) 359
Winter War
– (see Finland)
Winterbotham, Frederick 456
Winterton, Lord 495
Wintringham, Tom 104
Wirraway fighters 267
Wismar *631*
Witok *495*
Wittman, Michael 532
Witzleben, Erwin von 551
Wizard of Oz, The (film) 51, 147
Woburn Abbey 283
Wodehouse, P G 203, 206
Wohlhynien 60
Woleai *508*
Wolf (carrier) 616
Wolff, Karl 627, 634
Wolfit, Donald 593
Wolfpacks
– (see Atlantic, Battle of the; U-boats; Submarines; Convoys)
Wolomin 546
Wolverine (destroyer) *166*
Women Accepted for Volunteer Emergency Service
– (see WAVES)
Women's Auxiliary Air Corps
– (see WAACS)
Women's Auxiliary Air Force
– (see WAAF)
Women's Land Army
– (see Land Girls)
Women's Royal Naval Service
– (see WRNS)
Women's Voluntary Service for Civil Defence
– (see WVS)
Women's war work 38, 55, 62, 78, 106, 135, 164, 169, 181, 186, *237*, 245, 286, 292, 293, 307, 331, 338, 368, 373, 381, 385, 404, 421, 431, 441, 447, 497, *586*, 586, *605*
Wood, Henry 475, 593
Wood, John 566
Wood, Kingsley 108, *125*, 160, 273, 399, 447
Woodbridge 347
Woodlark Island 421
Woolf, Virginia 103, 259
Woolton, Lord *72*, 155, 281, 319
Worcester (destroyer) *168*
Worden (destroyer) 372
World Bank *543*
Worms 608
Worthing (hospital ship) 93
Wrens
– (see WRNS)
WRNS 38, 135, 164, 431
Wryneck (destroyer) 182
Wuhan 50, 160
Wuppertal 413, *418*
Wurm river *569*
Wurm, Theophil *425*
Wurzburg 277, 619
Wurzburg radar 419
Wustrow *624*
Wuthering Heights (film) 51
Wuyang 160
Wuyuan 72
WVS 38, 43, *103*, 178

X

X-Gerat 189
X-craft
– (see Midget submarines)
Xanten *609*
Xinyang *78*
XP-59 Airacomet jet aircraft
– (see Airacomet jet aircraft)

Y

Yagodnik 562
Yahagi (cruiser) 620
Yahata 531, 539, *652*
Yakovlev fighters 352
Yalta 10, *237*, 509, *602*
Yamamoto, Isoroku 237, 305, 397, 401, 687
Yamamuchi, Masafumi 536
Yamashiro (battleship) 576
Yamashita, Tomoyuki 250, 273, 274, 573, *591*, 599, 602
Yamato (battleship) 620
Yampol *495*
Yamschchikova, Olga *336*
Yangtze river *78*, *94*, 167, 312, *389*, 405, *414*, *508*, *644*
Yap 505, 545
Yaroslavl *415*
Yarra (sloop) *278*
Yefremov, Mikhail *288*
Yeisk *378*
Yelets 246
Yellow River 194, *508*, *644*
Yellow Sea *581*
Yelna *220*, *438*
Yenangyaung 289, 624
Yessentui *325*
Yi-meng Shan 435
Yichang 228
Yochow 414
Yokohama *605*, *639*, *640*, *660*, 660
Yonabaru 624, *639*
Yonai, Mitsumasa 58, *105*, 545
Yong Peng *266*, 267
Yontan 618
York 294
York (cruiser) *66*, 127, *172*, *190*
York transports 582
Yorktown (aircraft carrier) *270*, 296, *301*, 305, *440*
Young, Mark 255
Ypres 88, *89*, 90
Yu Hsueh-chung 322, 324
Yuezhou *230*
Yugoslavia
– Volunteers in RAF Reserve 21/9/40 122
– Signs friendship pact with Hungary 12/12/40 *142*
– Hitler urges Cvetkovich to join Pact 14/2/41 *161*
– Regent agrees to join Axis despite national feeling 4/3/41 167
– Cabinet crisis over joining Axis 21/3/41 171
– Anti-Nazi demonstrations 23/3/41 *172*
– Cvetkovich signs pact with Axis 25/3/41 173
– Treaty with USSR 5/4/41 *174*
– Croatia becomes Axis state under Pavelich 12/4/41 *176*
– Luftwaffe destroys Belgrade as German 12th Army invades 6/4/41 177
– German forces cut off Greeks through Monastir Gap 14/4/41 *179*
– Surrenders to Germany 17/4/41 180
– Tito calls for resistance against Germans 5/7/41 204
– Germany and Italy plan partition 8/7/41 *205*
– Nedich heads Nazi puppet government in Serbia 30/8/41 *217*
– Martial law; Tito & Mihailovich meet Hudson 17/9/41 *223*
– Serbs massacred at Kragujevac after partisan attacks 21/10/41 *233*
– Partisans and Chetniks fighting Germans 26/10/41 235
– Partisans and Chetniks clash at Uzice 2/11/41 *237*
– Hungarian soldiers massacre Jews and Serbs at Novi Sad 23/1/42 *266*
– Tito's partisans challenge Ustachi 9/5/42 297
– Germans launch attack on partisans 3/7/42 *312*
– 700 killed in reprisals at Zagreb 14/7/42 *316*
– Tito's partisans liberate Croatia 16/7/42 317
– Government in exile asks US to warn on Axis atrocities 31/7/42 319
– Partisans take Bihac 3/11/42 *347*
– Axis offensive against Tito's partisans 15/1/43 372
– Tito's partisans fight major Axis offensive in Croatia 15/4/43 399
– Axis launches Operation Black against partisans 15/5/43 408
– Britain to aid Tito as partisans face Operation Black 28/5/43 412
– Britain to aid Tito and continue supplying Mihailovich 23/6/43 419
– Germans and Croatians attack Italians at Ljubljana 27/8/43 *438*
– Partisans take Split 11/9/43 *442*
– British military adviser joins Tito 19/9/43 447
– Partisans sabotage Krupp factories 13/10/43 453
– Provisional government headed by Tito 4/12/43 466
– Tito sacks King Peter 22/12/43 472
– Military mission in London for talks 1/5/44 *512*
– Tito evades capture 25/5/44 520
– Partisans join with RAF and USAAF in Operation Ratweek 1/9/44 *560*
– Russians due to link up with partisans 9/9/44 561
– Partisans and British forces poised to invade 27/9/44 568
– Red Army takes Pancevo 4/10/44 *569*
– Churchill suggests 50-50 share of influence with USSR 9/10/44 572
– Tito's army drives Germans out of Belgrade 20/10/44 574
– New constitution is agreed 1/11/44 *577*
– New government agreed at Yalta 11/2/45 605
– Tito's partisans take Trieste 1/5/45 *631*
– Tito disputes control of Trieste with Allies 14/5/45 *637*
– Troops withdraw from Trieste 12/6/45 *643*
– Communist forces win control (1946) 662
– Tito remains independent of Soviets after the war 663
Yunnan 41, *296*, 388, *515*, 599
Yupgang Ga *480*
Yuyangkwan *412*
Yuza, Mount *643*

Z

Zadar *577*
Zagare *228*
Zagreb *223*, *316*, 513, 637
Zaluchie *386*
Zanana *422*
Zante *138*
Zaporoje 216
Zaporozhe 449
Zaunkonig (acoustic torpedo) 521
Zec, Philip 517
Zeebrugge *562*
Zeitzler, Kurt *543*
Zeneca 453
Zengo, Yoshida 159
Zeppelin (operaation) 487
Zero fighters *118*, 248, 263, 279, 380, 386, 426, 474
Zhdanov, Andrei 219
Zhidra *436*
Zhitomir *210*, 233, *460*, *462*, *473*
Zhukov, Georgi
– Chief of general staff and commissar for defence 12/2/41 *161*
– Sacked by Stalin for advising surrender at Kiev 29/7/41 *210*
– In charge of defence of Leningrad 30/9/41 227
– Called back to Moscow to take charge of defences 10/10/41 230
– Takes over northern sector of command system 23/10/41 *233*
– Directs counter-attack before Moscow 6/12/41 246
– Counter-offensive against German winter line 10/1/42 262
– Troops head for Bryansk and Vyazma 31/1/42 268
– Appointed to take charge of Stalingrad defence 27/8/42 *327*
– Conscripts civilians to help in attack on Germans 5/9/42 330
– Launches "Uranus" counter-attack at Stalingrad 20/11/42 352
– Launches Operation Saturn on Italians at Stalingrad 16/12/42 361
– Ordered back to Leningrad by Stalin to break siege 31/12/42 365
– Launches Operation Iskra against Germans 11/1/43 371
– Promoted to marshal of the Soviet Union 18/1/43 *372*
– Decorated with Order of Suvorov 31/7/43 *428*
– Takes command of First Ukrainian Front 29/2/44 492
– Troops take Dubno 17/3/44 498
– Troops mount fresh attack on German right wing in USSR 3/7/44 541
– Warsaw to be prime target 12/1/45 597
– Forward patrols 100 miles from Berlin 27/1/45 601
– Troops grind to a halt on Oder river 10/2/45 604
– Poznan falls to troops 23/2/45 608
– Troops push on to Kolberg 1/3/45 *610*
– Troops prepare to attack Berlin 24/3/45 615
– Troops ready to attack Berlin 14/4/45 623
– Orders the attack on Berlin to begin 16/4/45 625
– 47th Army is west of Berlin 22/4/45 628
– Sends men to search for Hitler and Goebbels 2/5/45 *631*
– Meets Allied military leaders in Berlin 5/6/45 642
– Decorates Eisenhower and Montgomery 10/6/45 *643*
– Leads victory parade in Moscow 24/6/45 645
– Decorated by Montgomery 12/7/45 647
– Biography 687
Zipper (operation) *646*
Zmiev *436*
Znamenka *465*, *467*
Zossen *613*
Zuetania *174*
Zuiho (aircraft carrier) 346
Zuikaku (aircraft carrier) 248, *294*, 296, 346
Zwickau 514
Zychlin *278*
Zydowska Organizacja Bojowa 375
Zygalski, Henryk *432*
Zygielboim, Szmul 408

Photo Credit Index

The positions of the pictures are indicated by the following letters: B: Bottom, T: Top, M: Middle, L: Left, R: Right, X: Middle Left, Y: Middle Right. When several smaller pictures are used together, the positions of the pictures are completed by a number (eg BR1, BR2, BR3). FP indicates that the picture fills the entire page.

Agencies

Some agency names have been abbreviated in this index.
The list below provides full names of the picture agencies:

AP: Associated Press
C.A.H.A.: Christopher Ailsby Historical Archive
Chronicle UK: Chronicle UK New
IWM: Imperial War Museum
Mary Evans: Mary Evans Picture Library
M.A.R.S.: Military Archive and Research Service
Newark: Peter Newark's Pictures
P.C.: Private Collection
Popper: Popperfoto
R. Hunt: Robert Hunt
Topham: Topham Picturepoint

Paintings

The paintings used as year dividers are:

52/53: *Battle of Britain* by Paul Nash (IWM)
148/149: Detail from *Devastation 1941: An East End Street* by Graham Sutherland (Tate Gallery)
260/261: *The Battle of Egypt 1942 – Bombing up* by Anthony Gross (IWM)
366/367: Detail from *Shipbuilding on the Clyde – Riveters* by Sir Stanley Spencer (IWM)
476/477: *Headquarters Room* by Barnett Freedman (IWM)
594/595: *One of the Death Pits, Belsen* by Leslie Cole (IWM)

TR: Popper
163 - BM: Popper - **TM:** R. Hunt Library
164 - BY: Robert Opie - **TL:** Topham
165 - ML: Chronicle UK - **TR:** Topham/AP
166 - BL, ML, TL: D.I.T.E. - **MR:** Newark
167 - BM: Barnaby's Picture Library - **TM:** Hulton-Deutsch
168 - BL: Robert Opie - **TY:** US National Archive/M.A.R.S.
169 - BY: Glasgow Herald/Evening Times - **TM:** Hulton-Deutsch - **BL:** Topham
170 - MR: Camera Press - **TL:** R. Hunt Library
171 - TM: Popper - **MX:** R. Hunt Library - **MY:** Topham
172 - MR: Chronicle UK - **TR:** National Maritime Museum/M.A.R.S.
173 - MR: Illustrated London News - **BR:** Topham
174 - BL: Popper - TL:R. Hunt Library
175 - MR: Chronicle UK - **BX:** Popper - **BL:** Robert Opie - **TR:** Topham/AP
176 - TL: Popper - **MY:** Topham/AP
177 - MM: Chronicle UK - **TM:** Newark
178 - TL: Camera Press - **BM:** Hulton-Deutsch - **MR:** Popper
179 - MR: Newark - **BX:** Popper - **TL:** R. Hunt Library
180 - TL: Camera Press - **MR:** David King Collection
181 Both pictures - Popper
182 - TM: E T Archive - **BM:** Topham
183 - BR: Camera Press - **TM:** Hulton-Deutsch
184 - TR: Topham
185 - BM: Camera Press - **TM:** Liverpool Museum
186 - TY: Hulton-Deutsch - **TX:** Popper - **BL, MR:** Topham
187 - TM: Camera Press - **BL:** Newark
188 Both pictures - Popper
189 - MX: Hulton-Deutsch - **TR:** Newark - **BR:** Popper
190 - BR: Camera Press - **TM:** M.A.R.S.
191 - BM: Camera Press - **TL:** Topham/AP
192 - MR: Chronicle UK - **BY:** Newark - **BR, TR:** Topham
193 - TM: Camera Press - **BM:** R. Hunt Library
194 - BL: IWM - **TM:** Topham - **BR:** Topham/AP
195 - MR: Chronicle UK - **TR:** Hulton-Deutsch
196 - BL: Popper - **TL, MR:** R. Hunt Library
197 - TY: Chronicle UK - **MR:** Newark - **TL:** Popper
198 - MM: Chronicle UK - **BR, BX:** Popper
199 - TR: Camera Press - **BM:** Hulton-Deutsch - **TL:** R. Hunt Library
200 - TR: Camera Press
201 - TR: Camera Press - **BR:** Novosti - **MR:** Topham
202 - BM: Chronicle UK - **TM:** M.A.R.S.
203 - BR: Popper - **TR:** Topham
204 - MR: Newark - **BM:** Popper - **TL, TM:** Topham
205 - BL: Mary Evans - **TR:** Topham/AP
206 Both pictures - Camera Press
207 - MR: Robert Opie - **MX:** Topham - **TM:** Topham/AP
208 - MM: Popper - **TR:** R. Hunt Library
209 - TL: Camera Press - **BY:** E T Archive - **TR:** IWM
210 - TX: Popper - **MM:** R. Hunt Library
211 Both pictures - Topham
212 - BR: Popper - **TM:** Topham
213 - TM: R. Hunt Library - **BM:** Tass
214 - MR: Mary Evans - **MM:** Topham
215 - TM: Camera Press - **BM:** Topham
216 - MM: Tass - **TR:** Topham
217 - TR: Newark - **TL:** R. Hunt Library - **BR:** Robert Opie
218 - MM: Chronicle UK - **TM:** IWM
219 - BM: Chronicle UK - **TM:** Tass
220 - BR: Hulton-Deutsch - **TM:** National Archives, Canada
221 - BX: Novosti - **ML:** Popper
222 - TR: Chronicle UK - **TL:** Tass
223 - BL: Mary Evans - **TR:** Popper - **TX:** Topham
224 - BM: Popper - **TM:** Topham/AP
225 - TX: Camera Press - **BL:** Chronicle UK - **TR:** Topham/AP
226 - TM: IWM - **BM:** Topham/AP
227 - BR: Camera Press - **BL:** IWM - **TM:** Topham/AP
228 - BM: E T Archive - **MR:** Popper - **TM:** Topham/AP
229 - ML: Camera Press - **BR:** E T Archive - **TR:** R. Hunt Library
230 - BY: Newark - **TM:** Topham/AP
231 - ML: IWM - **BX:** Robert Opie
232 - TM: Tass - **BR:** Topham
233 - TX: Camera Press - **BX:** Hulton-Deutsch - **BR:** IWM
234 - TR: Chronicle UK - **TL:** Topham/AP
235 - MM: Hulton-Deutsch - **TR:** R. Hunt Library
236 All - E T Archive
237 - TY: D.I.T.E. - **BR:** IWM/M.A.R.S.
238 - BR: IWM - **TM:** Tass
239 - BM: Popper - **TR:** Topham
240 - BM: Tallandier
241 - MR: Chronicle UK - **MR:** Popper - **BL:** Robert Opie
242 - BR: Mary Evans - **BX:** Topham - **TY:** Topham/AP
243 - TM: Chronicle UK - **BR, BR:** IWM
244 - BL: IWM - **MR:** R. Hunt Library - **TL:** Topham
245 - MR: Camera Press - **BX:** Robert Opie
246 - TL, TR: Camera Press - **BR:** Chronicle UK
247 - TX: Popper
248 - TM: US Navy/P.C.
249 - BM: Chronicle UK - **TL:** Hulton-Deutsch - **TR:** Topham
250 - TM: R. Hunt Library - **BR:** US Navy/P.C.
251 - BM: D.I.T.E. - **TM:** Topham
252 - TL: National Archives/PC - **TR:** Topham - **BM:** Topham/AP
253 - BR: Popper - **MM:** R. Hunt Library
254 - TY: Barnaby's Picture Library - **BR, BX, TX:** Popper
255 - BM: P.C. - **TM:** R. Hunt Library
256 - TM: Camera Press
257 - BX: Camera Press - **BM:** Popper - **TM:** R. Hunt Library
258 - BM: Fuji Fotos/M.A.R.S. - **TM:** R. Hunt Library
259 - TR: Hulton-Deutsch - **TX:** Popper - **BR:** Ronald Grant Archive
262 - BR: Popper - **MM:** Topham/AP
263 - BL: R. Hunt Library - **TM, BR:** Robert Opie
264 - MY: Newark - **BX:** Popper - **TM:** Topham/AP
265 - BX: Chronicle UK - **MR, TM:** R. Hunt Library
266 Both pictures - Popper
267 - BR: Camera Press - **ML:** Chronicle UK - **TM:** R. Hunt Library
268 - MM: Illustrated London News - **BR:** R. Hunt Library
269 - BM, TM: R. Hunt Library
270 - BR: Bundesarchiv/P.C. - **TX:** P.C.
271 - ML: Chronicle UK - **MR:** Hulton-Deutsch - **BL:** Popper
272 - BM: Chronicle UK - **TM:** IWM/PC
273 - MR: Popper - **BL, TL:** R. Hunt Library
274 - TL: Topham
275 - BL: Popper - **TX:** R. Hunt Library - **TR:** Topham/AP
276 - MM: Chronicle UK - **TR:** Newark
277 -TR: Camera Press - **BR:** E T Archive - **ML:** Topham
278 - BY: Robert Opie - **TM:** Topham/AP
279 - TR: Camera Press - **ML:** IWM - **BR:** Newark
280 - BL: Topham/AP - **TR:** United Press International/P.C.
281 - BX, MR: Newark - **TX:** R. Hunt Library
282 - MR: IWM - **TM:** Syndication International
283 - MM: Newark - **TY:** Popper
284 - TM: IWM - **BR:** Popper
285 Both pictures - Popper
286 - MR: E T Archive - **TM:** R. Hunt Library
287 - BR: Camera Press - **TR:** Chronicle UK - **ML:** Popper
288 - TR: R. Hunt Library - **BR:** Robert Opie
289 - BL: Chronicle UK - **TL:** P.C. - **TR:** Topham
290 - MM: US Air Force/P.C. - **TM:** US Navy/P.C.
291 - MM, TM: Camera Press - **BM:** Chronicle UK
292 - TY: R. Hunt Library - **BR:** Topham
293 - BL: Chronicle UK - **TM:** Popper
294 - BR: Bundesarchiv/P.C. - **TM:** Popper
295 - BR: Newark - **TM:** Popper - **BX:** R. Hunt Library
296 - TR: Popper - **BR:** R. Hunt Library
297 - MY: Chronicle UK - **ML:** R. Hunt Library - **TY:** US Marine Corps/P.C.
298 - TL: IWM - **BM:** R. Hunt Library
299 - BL, BR: Hulton-Deutsch - **TM:** Novosti
300 - MM: Chronicle UK - **BY:** E T Archive
301 - BR: Kharbine-Tapabor - **TL:** Popper
302 - TM: R. Hunt Library
303 - MR: Camera Press - **TL, TR:** Newark
304 - BR: Newark - **TM:** Popper
305 - BR: Chronicle UK - **TM:** Topham
306 - MM: National Archives/P.C.
307 - MM, TY: Camera Press - **BL:** Popper
308 - MY: Popper - **TX:** R. Hunt Library
309 - BM: Chronicle UK - **TL, TR:** IWM
310 - TM: Camera Press - **BY:** IWM
311 - BL: Chronicle UK - **BR:** IWM - **MM:** Topham - **TM:** Topham/AP
312 - BL: Chronicle UK - **BR:** E T Archive
313 - MM, TM: IWM - **BR:** Newark
314 - TL: Camera Press - **BX:** Newark - **TR:** Popper
315 - TR: Camera Press - **BL:** Chronicle UK - **BL:** R. Hunt Library
316 - MY: Popper - **TL:** R. Hunt Library - **BL:** Topham/AP
317 - MR: IWM - **BL:** Newark - **TM:** R. Hunt Library
318 - MR: Camera Press - **TM:** Popper
319 - BM: Newark - **TM:** R. Hunt Library
320 - BR: E T Archive - **TL:** Topham
321 - BR: Chronicle UK - **TR:** Popper
322 - ML: IWM - **TM:** R. Hunt Library
323 - BR: E T Archive - **ML:** IWM - **BX, TR:** Popper
324 - TR: Camera Press - **BY:** Popper - **BR:** Topham/AP
325 - TM: Bundesarchiv/P.C.
326 - BM, TL: Popper - **TR:** Topham/AP
327 - BR: "Utility Furniture" booklet - **TM:** US Navy/P.C.
328 - TL: Camera Press - **BX:** Popper - **MY:** R. Hunt Library
329 - TR: Popper - **BR:** Topham - **TR:** US Army/P.C.
330 - BL: Popper - **TM:** Topham/AP
331 - TL: Hulton-Deutsch - **BR:** National Archives, Canada - **BX:** Order of St. John
332 - TL: Popper - **BM, MR:** R. Hunt Library aa333 - BR: Chronicle UK - **ML:** Newark
334 Both pictures - Imperial War Museum
335 - TR: Chronicle UK - **BL, TL:** R. Hunt Library
336 - TM: Australian War Memorial/P.C. - **BM:** Chronicle UK - **MR:** Popper
337 - BL: Newark - **TX:** R. Hunt Library
338 - BX: Hulton-Deutsch - **TL:** Popper - **BR:** Robert Opie
339 - TM: D.I.T.E. - **ML:** Popper - **TM:** Topham
340 - BM: Chronicle UK - **TM:** R. Hunt Library
341 - MM: Camera Press - **TL:** R. Hunt Library
342 - BR: Popper - **TM:** R. Hunt Library
343 - TL: Camera Press - **BM:** Chronicle UK
344 - TR: Chronicle UK - **BR:** Topham
345 - BR: Camera Press - **TS:** Popper - **BL:** Topham
346 - MM: Chronicle UK - **BR:** Popper - **TM:** R. Hunt Library
347 - MR: Camera Press - **BL:** Robert Opie
348 - MR: Popper - **ML, TR:** R. Hunt Library
349 - ML: Camera Press - **BR:** Robert Opie
350 - MM: R. Hunt Library
351 - BR: E T Archive - **TL:** R. Hunt Library
352 - BM: Camera Press - **TL:** David King Collection
353 - BL: Chronicle UK - **TL:** IWM - **TR:** Popper
354 - BR: R. Hunt Library - **TL:** Tallandier
355 - TM: Camera Press - **MM:** Chronicle UK
356 - MR: Newark - **TM:** TRH Pictures
357 - MR, TL: Newark - **BL:** R. Hunt Library
358 - BL: Newark - **BR:** R. Hunt Library - **TM:** Topham
359 - TL: Camera Press - **MR:** Chronicle UK - **BL:** Kharbine-Tapabor - **BR:** Topham
360 - BR: Newark - **MM:** R. Hunt Library
361 - BX: Chronicle UK - **TL:** Popper
362 - TR: David King Collection - **BL, BR:** Popper - **TL:** Topham/AP
363 - TM: Chronicle UK - **BR:** Topham/AP
364 - BR: Chronicle UK - **TL:** Popper - **BL:** Ronald Grant Archive - **TR:** Topham/AP
365 All - Newark
368 - TR: Australian War Memorial/P.C. - **MR:** Topham/AP
369 - TM: Popper - **BM:** US Marine Corps/P.C.
370 - TM: D.I.T.E. - **BR:** Popper
371 - TS: Camera Press - **BL:** Chronicle UK - **BR:** Popper
372 - TX: R. Hunt Library - **BL:** US Army/P.C.
373 - BR: Camera Press - **MM:** Chronicle UK - **BX:** D.I.T.E. - **TM:** R. Hunt Library
374 - TL: Novosti - **BM:** Popper - **MR:** Popper
375 - TL: R. Hunt Library - **BY:** Tallandier
376 - BM: Chronicle UK - **TM:** Novosti
377 - BL: Camera Press - **BM, BR, TM:** Popper
378 - TL: R. Hunt Library
379 - TM: Kharbine-Tapabor - **BM:** Popper
380 - BR: E T Archive - **BL:** Popper - **TM:** R. Hunt Library
381 - BR: Hulton-Deutsch - **TM:** R. Hunt Library
382 - MM: Chronicle UK - **BR, TM:** Popper
383 - TR: Chronicle UK - **BR:** Popper - **TM:** R. Hunt Library
384 Both pictures - Newark
385 - BM: Popper - **TM:** R. Hunt Library
386 - BL: Camera Press - **BR:** Newark - **TX:** R. Hunt Library
387 - TM: Hulton-Deutsch - **BR:** Popper
388 - BR: Popper - **TM:** R. Hunt Library
389 - TM: R. Hunt Library - **BM:** Topham/AP
390 - BL: Illustrated London News - **TR:** R. Hunt Library
391 - MM: Chronicle UK - **TM:** R. Hunt Library
392 - TM: Chronicle UK - **BR:** R. Hunt Library
393 - MM: Chronicle UK - **TM:** D.I.T.E. - **BR:** Popper
394 - BX: Chronicle UK - **BR:** Popper - **TM:** R. Hunt Library
395 - ML: Camera Press - **TR:** D.I.T.E. - **BR:** Popper
396 - TM: R. Hunt Library - **BR:** Topham/AP
397 - BL: National Archives/P.C. - **MR:** R. Hunt Library
398 - BM: Popper - **ML:** R. Hunt Library - **TM:** Topham/AP
399 - BR: Camera Press - **TM:** R. Hunt Library
400 - TM: Popper - **TR:** R. Hunt Library - **BX:** Robert Opie
401 - TX: Newark - **BL:** Popper
402 - BR: D.I.T.E. - **TM:** Newark
403 - BM: Chronicle UK - **MM:** D.I.T.E. - **TM:** Popper
404 - MR: Chronicle UK - **TR:** R. Hunt Library
405 - TM: Camera Press - **BM:** Chronicle UK - **MR:** Illustrated London News
406 - BY: Chronicle UK - **MR:** E T Archive - **TM:** Keystone/P.C.
407 - BM: Camera Press - **TM:** D.I.T.E.
408 - BL: Bridgeman Art Library - **BR:** R. Hunt Library - **TM:** Topham/AP
409 - BR: Popper - **TR:** R. Hunt Library
410 - MM: Camera Press - **MR, TR:** R. Hunt Library
411 - BM: Popper - **TM:** Topham/AP
412 - TR: Hulton-Deutsch - **MM:** R. Hunt Library
413 - TX, TY: E T Archive - **BR:** US Navy/P.C.
414 - MR, TM: Topham/AP
415 - TX: E T Archive - **BL:** Popper - **BR:** Ronald Grant Archive

416 - BL: Popper - MR, TM: R. Hunt Library
417 - BR: E T Archive - TX: Popper
418 - BR: E T Archive - TM: Popper
419 - MY: Camera Press - TM: Popper
420 - BR, BR: Camera Press - TR: R. Hunt Library
421 - BM: Chronicle UK - TL: US Marine Corps/P.C.
422 - BR: Newark - TY: R. Hunt Library - MR: Topham/AP
423 - BL, BR: Chronicle UK - TS: Topham
424 - TL: Popper - BM: R. Hunt Library
425 - BL, TR: Camera Press - MR: Magnum
426 - TM: Camera Press - MM: R. Hunt Library
427 - BR: E T Archive - TR: Topham/AP
428 - BM: Chronicle UK - TM: R. Hunt Library
429 - MY: Hulton-Deutsch - TL: P.C. - TR: R. Hunt Library
430 Both pictures - R. Hunt Library
431 - BM: Popper - TY: R. Hunt Library
432 - TM: Kharbine-Tapabor - BR: Popper - BX: R. Hunt Library
433 - TM: Newark - MM: US Air Force/P.C.
434 - TY, BR: Topham/AP
435 - MR: Hulton-Deutsch - BR: Popper - TR: Topham
436 - TR: US Air Force/P.C.
437 - BR, TM: Popper - ML: R. Hunt Library
438 - TY: Chronicle UK - MY: Topham/AP
439 - ML: National Archives, Canada - TR: R. Hunt Library
440 - MR, TR: Camera Press - BR: R. Hunt Library
441 - TM: Australian War Memorial/P.C. - BM: R. Hunt Library
442 - MR: Chronicle UK - BM: R. Hunt Library
443 - TR: Chronicle UK - BM: Popper - TL: US Army/P.C.
444 - TR: E T Archive - BM: R. Hunt Library
445 - BM, TR: R. Hunt Library - TL: Topham
446 - TY: Chronicle UK - TM: Topham
447 - MR: Popper - BL, TM: Topham/AP
448 - BM: Chronicle UK - BR: E T Archive - MM: R. Hunt Library
449 - TR: IWM - BR, ML: Newark
450 - TR: Camera Press
451 - TR: D.I.T.E. - BL: IWM - BY: Popper
452 - BR: E T Archive - TM: Topham
453 - ML: Camera Press - BR: Topham/AP
454 - BX, MR: R. Hunt Library - TL: Topham/AP
455 - TX: E T Archive - BL: IWM - MR: Topham/AP
456 - BR: Chronicle UK - TR: Popper
457 - BR: Hulton-Deutsch - ML, TR: Topham/AP
458 - MM: Popper

459 - BR: Chronicle UK - TL, TR: R. Hunt Library
460 - BR: Popper - TM: Topham
461 - TL: Camera Press - BR: Newark
462 Both pictures - R. Hunt Library
463 - TM: Chronicle UK - BM: Topham/AP
464 - MR: E T Archive-TM: Topham/AP
465 - MM: IWM - MX: R. Hunt Library - TY: Topham/AP
466 - TM: Popper - MR: R. Hunt Library
467 - MR: IWM - ML: R. Hunt Library
468 - BL: British Film Institute/IWM - TR: National Archives, Canada - TX: Ronald Grant Archive
469 - BL: Novosti/P.C. - TM: Topham
470 - TM: R. Hunt Library - BM: Topham/AP
471 - ML: IWM - TM: Popper - BM: Ronald Grant Archive
472 - BR: Chronicle UK - TM: R. Hunt Library
473 - BL: E T Archive - TM: R. Hunt Library
474 - TL: Australian War Memorial/P.C. - BL: Chronicle UK - MR: Newark
475 - BR: Hulton-Deutsch - BY, TM: Popper - BL, BX: Ronald Grant Archive
478 - BR: Newark - TM: Popper
479 - BM: Australian War Memorial/P.C. - TM: R. Hunt Library
480 - BR: Kharbine-Tapabor - TX: R. Hunt Library
481 - MR: Hulton-Deutsch - BL: Mary Evans - TX: R. Hunt Library
482 - TL: Camera Press - MR: Chronicle UK - TR: R. Hunt Library
483 - MR: Camera Press - TL: David King Collection - BL: Topham
484 - BR: Australian War Memorial/P.C. - TM: D.I.T.E. - BL: Hulton-Deutsch
485 - ML: Camera Press - TM: Chronicle UK - MR: Popper
486 - TM: Camera Press - BR: Keystone/P.C.
487 - TL: D.I.T.E. - MR: Topham/AP
488 - TR: Hulton-Deutsch - MM: US Army/P.C.
489 - TR: Chronicle UK - MM: Popper - BL: Topham
490 - TR: R. Hunt Library
491 - BL: D.I.T.E. - BR: E T Archive-TM: Novosti
492 - TR: Newark - MM: R. Hunt Library
493 - BL, BY: D.I.T.E. - TM: US Army/P.C.
494 - MM: P.C.-BX: R. Hunt Library
495 - MR: Hulton-Deutsch - TL: R. Hunt Library - BL: US Air Force/P.C.
496 - TR: D.I.T.E. - BR: Newark - TL: US Army/P.C.
497 - BR, ML: Chronicle UK - TR: R. Hunt Library

498 - BM, TR: D.I.T.E. - TY: R. Hunt Library
499 - BL: Newark - MR: R. Hunt Library
500 - BM: Chronicle UK - TM: Topham
501 - TL: Chronicle UK - BM: US Army/P.C.
502 - BL: Chronicle UK - TR: Popper
503 - BL: Popper - TX, TY: R. Hunt Library
504 - TM: R. Hunt Library - BR: US Navy/P.C.
505 - TL: D.I.T.E. - MR: R. Hunt Library
506 - MM: IWM/P.C. - BR: Popper
507 - TM: Chronicle UK - TM: Novosti
508 - MM: Newark - BR: Topham/AP
509 - BM: Kharbine-Tapabor - TL, TM: US Army/P.C.
510 - BR: Australian War Memorial/P.C. - TM: R. Hunt Library
511 - BM: Chronicle UK - TM: R. Hunt Library
512 - BM, TR: Topham
513 - TR: Popper - BL: Topham/AP
514 - MM: Kharbine-Tapabor - TM: Novosti
515 - TR: Camera Press - ML: US Army/P.C.
516 Both pictures - Camera Press
517 - ML: Popper - TR: Topham
518 - MR: D.I.T.E. - TR: Topham
519 - TR: Camera Press - BR: Chronicle UK - ML: National Archives/P.C.
520 - MX: Chronicle UK - BL: Newark-TX: Popper
521 - BM: Camera Press - MM, TM: D.I.T.E.
522 - TM: D.I.T.E. - BL: Popper - BM: Topham/AP
523 - TS: Camera Press
524 - TL: Newark - BR, TR: Topham
525 - TS: Chronicle UK
526 - FP: Camera Press
527 - TR: Camera Press - ML: Popper
528 - TM: Topham
529 - BL: Camera Press - TM: Chronicle UK
530 - TR: Popper - MR: R. Hunt Library
531 - TR: Camera Press - MX: R. Hunt Library
532 - MM: Popper - TM: R. Hunt Library
533 All - Popper
534 - MR: Popper - TL: R. Hunt Library
535 - TM: Camera Press - BR: Newark
536 - TL: Chronicle UK - TR: R. Hunt Library - BM: US Navy/P.C.
537 - BR, TM: R. Hunt Library
538 - BM: Chronicle UK - TM: Topham/AP
539 - BX: D.I.T.E. - BR: Kharbine-Tapabor - TM: Weimar Archive
540 - MR: Camera Press - BM: D.I.T.E. - TM: Popper
541 - MX: Camera Press - ML: Novosti - TR: Popper
542 - BL: D.I.T.E. - BR, TL: Popper
543 Both pictures - R. Hunt Library

544 - BR: Popper - BX, TM: R. Hunt Library
545 - ML: Chronicle UK - TM: Popper - BR: R. Hunt Library
546 - TR: Chronicle UK - BY: Novosti
547 - MM: Chronicle UK - TM: R. Hunt Library
548 - TR: R. Hunt Library
549 - BR, TM: D.I.T.E. - BL: Popper
550 - TM: D.I.T.E. - BR: Hulton-Deutsch
551 - TR: Chronicle UK - BR: D.I.T.E. - BR: R. Hunt Library
552 - MM: R. Hunt Library
553 - BR: Chronicle UK - TL, TR: D.I.T.E.
554 - BL: Kharbine-Tapabor - TR: Popper
555 - TR: Topham/AP
556 - BL, MX: D.I.T.E. - TL: Topham - ML: Topham/AP
557 - BY: E T Archive - TM: Topham
558 - BR: Chronicle UK - TM: D.I.T.E.
559 - TM: Chronicle UK - BM: D.I.T.E.
560 - MY: Popper - TY: Topham/AP
561 - TM: D.I.T.E. - BM: Popper
562 Both pictures - D.I.T.E.
563 - BM: Newark - TM: R. Hunt Library
564 - BY: D.I.T.E. - TM: Popper
565 - BM, MM: Camera Press - TR: Chronicle UK
566 - TM: Topham - BL: Topham/AP
567 - TT: Camera Press - BM: D.I.T.E.
568 - BL: D.I.T.E. - TX: Newark - MX: Topham/AP - TL: Ullstein Bilderdienst
569 - MX: Chronicle UK - MR: D.I.T.E. - TL: Topham/AP
570 - TM: D.I.T.E. - BR: Popper
571 - BR: D.I.T.E. - TR: Popper
572 - MM: D.I.T.E. - TX: Novosti - TR: Topham
573 Both pictures - R. Hunt Library
574 - BR: Chronicle UK - TX: R. Hunt Library
575 - BR, BR: Robert Opie - TR: Topham/AP
576 - TM: Chronicle UK - TM: R. Hunt Library
577 - ML: D.I.T.E. - BR: Newark
578 - MM: D.I.T.E. - BM: R. Hunt Library - TM: Topham/AP
579 - TM: D.I.T.E. - TM: Topham
580 Both pictures - Popper
581 - TM: Newark - BL: R. Hunt Library
582 - TM: D.I.T.E. - BR, ML: Popper
583 - TM: David King Collection
584 - BL: Chronicle UK - TM: D.I.T.E.
585 - BM: Newark - TM: Popper
586 - TR: Ronald Grant Archive - MM: Topham/AP
587 - TL: D.I.T.E. - MR: Popper
588 - TR: D.I.T.E.
589 - BL, MR: D.I.T.E. - TX: R. Hunt Library

590 - TM: Camera Press - BM: Chronicle UK - MM: D.I.T.E.
591 - TL: Camera Press - BR: Newark - TR: R. Hunt Library - TR: Topham
592 - BM: Camera Press
593 - BL: Crown Film Unit/C.O.I - TY: Hulton-Deutsch - TM: John Vickers
596 - TY: Hulton-Deutsch - BM: R. Hunt Library
597 - ML: D.I.T.E. - MR: E T Archive
598 - BL: Chronicle UK - TR: Topham
599 - BM: Popper - TM: R. Hunt Library
600 - TL: Popper - TR: Tass
601 Both pictures - Novosti
602 - TR: Camera Press - MR: Chronicle UK
603 - ML: R. Hunt Library - MR: Topham
604 - TL: Camera Press - TR: Popper-BR: Tallandier
605 - BR: Camera Press - TM: P.C.
606 - BR, TR: Popper
607 - ML: Topham
608 - BX: Chronicle UK - BR, TR: Topham/AP
609 - BY: Chronicle UK - MM: Tass
610 - BX: Chronicle UK - TL: US Marine Corps/P.C.
611 - TY: Chronicle UK - BM: Popper - TL: R. Hunt Library
612 - ML: Chronicle UK - TR: US Air Force/P.C.
613 - BR: Newark - MM: Popper
614 - TX: Camera Press - BL: National Archives, Canada
615 - TR: Camera Press - TL: P.C. - BY: Topham/AP
616 - TX: Popper - BL: R. Hunt Library
617 - MM: Chronicle UK - BM: David King Collection
618 - BR: Chronicle UK - TR: R. Hunt Library
619 - TM: Camera Press - BR: Popper - BL: R. Hunt Library
620 - MM: Newark - BL: P.C.
621 - BY: Popper - TR: Topham/AP
622 - BR: Camera Press - ML: Chronicle UK - TR: Tallandier - BX: US National Archive/P.C.
623 - TM: Camera Press - BM: R. Hunt Library - MM: Topham/AP
624 - TM: Newark - BR: R. Hunt Library
625 - MM: Chronicle UK - TM: Newark
626 - MX, MY: Camera Press - TM: Popper
627 - BM: D.I.T.E. - TM: Topham
628 - MM: Chronicle UK - TM: Tass
629 - FP: Novosti
630 - BR: Hulton-Deutsch - TY: Popper - TL: R. Hunt Library
631 - ML: Newark - TR: Popper
632 - MM: Popper
633 - BL, ML: Camera Press - TR: Popper - BR, MR: R. Hunt Library - TX: US Army/P.C.
634 - MX: E T Archive - TX:

Hulton-Deutsch
635 - BL: Newark - TL: Popper - TR: Topham
636 - TM: Camera Press - BM: Tallandier
637 - ML: R. Hunt Library - BR: Tallandier
638 - BR: R. Hunt Library - TM: US Air Force/P.C.
639 Both pictures - Popper
640 - TL: IWM - BM: Popper
641 - TM: Camera Press - BR: Tass
642 - MM: Camera Press
643 - BR, TR: Popper - TL: US Air Force/P.C.
644 - TR: R. Hunt Library
645 - BY: Camera Press - BL: Robert Opie - TY: US National Archive/P.C.
646 - MY: Chronicle UK - BR, TM: Popper
647 - BM: Tallandier - TR: US National Archive/P.C.
648 - TR: Newark - BM: Popper
649 - TR: Associated Press/ P.C. - MM: R. Hunt Library
650 - TY: Labour Party - MY: Popper
651 - TM: Camera Press - MM: Chronicle UK
652 - BY, TR: Popper - BR: R. Hunt Library
653 - BM: Popper - TM: R. Hunt Library
654 - MM: Chronicle UK - TM: Novosti
655 - BL: Novosti - TR: R. Hunt Library
656 - TM: Popper
657 - ML: Popper - BL, TL: P.C.
658 - TM: Novosti - BY: Topham/AP
659 - MM: Hulton-Deutsch
660 - TY: Associated Press/P.C. - MR: Camera Press - BM: R. Hunt Library
661 - TR: Popper - BX, TL: Topham/AP
662 - BR: Corbis/Hulton-Deutsch
663 - TR: Hulton Getty/Bert Hardy
664 - BL: Mary Evans
665 - TL: DK Picture Library - BR: Hulton Getty
666 - TM: Hulton Getty - B: Popper
667 - BL: Hulton Getty - TM: Popper
668 - TR: Corbis
669 - BL: Hulton Getty
670 - BL: Hulton Getty
671 - BR: Hulton Getty - BL: Newark
672 - BL: Hulton Getty
673 - TL: Corbis/Bettmann
674 - BL: Corbis/Bettmann
675 - BY: Newark
676 - MY: Corbis - BR: Popper
677 - BR: Hulton Getty
679 - TR: Popper - BR: Topham
680 - TY: Hulton Getty
681 - BX: Newark
682 - TR: Topham - TY: TRH Pictures/US National Archives
684 - TX: Newark
685 - TL: Topham
686 Both pictures - Topham
687 - TX: Corbis/Bettmann
Back endpaper Searching for loved ones, Ukraine 1942 - David King Collection

728